NOVELS IN ENGLISH
BY WOMEN, 1891–1920

GARLAND REFERENCE LIBRARY
OF THE HUMANITIES
(VOL. 202)

NOVELS IN ENGLISH
BY WOMEN, 1891–1920
A Preliminary Checklist

Janet Grimes
Diva Daims

with the editorial assistance of
Doris Robinson

GARLAND PUBLISHING, INC. • NEW YORK & LONDON
1981

The preparation of this volume was made possible (in part) by a grant from the Program for Research Tools and Reference Works of the National Endowment for the Humanities, an independent federal agency, Russell Sage College, and the State University of New York at Albany.

Library of Congress Cataloging in Publication Data

Grimes, Janet.
    Novels in English by women, 1891–1920.

    (Garland reference library of the humanities ; v. 202)
    Includes index.
    1. English fiction—Women authors—Bibliography.
2. American fiction—Women authors—Bibliography.
I. Daims, Diva, joint author. II. Robinson, Doris.
III. Title.
Z2013.5.W6G75   [PR1286]   016.823′912   79-7911
ISBN 0-8240-9522-7

Printed on acid-free, 250-year-life paper
Manufactured in the United States of America

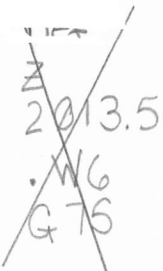

CONTENTS

PREFACE

AIM

The purpose of the bibliography is to provide a near complete list of English-language novels by women from 1891 to 1920. We are revising and completing this bibliography as we compile the entries for the period 1781–1890 and would be grateful for additions, corrections and any other relevant information which could be included in revision.

SCOPE

The bibliography lists 5,267 authors and the titles of 15,174 novels published in England and the United States. These include translations and 306 anonymous novels. Where information was available, the fullest form of the author's name, nationality and birth and death dates are provided. Second publishers are included when a novel was published in both the United States and England. Seventy-five percent of the novels are annotated. The annotations—working notes not originally intended for publication— are both eclectic and informal.

The bibliography does not systematically include English-language publications of countries other than England and the United States. It does not include juvenile fiction unless it was classified as adult fiction by our sources; frequently what we today would define as young adult or juvenile was not distinguished as such during the time period. Works from other genres such as autobiographies, short stories and travel books may be included occasionally when our sources, either by classification or review, describe them as novels. Novels by joint authors have been excluded when one of the authors is male.

METHODOLOGY

To compile as complete a listing of novels as possible, we searched for all male pseudonyms used by women authors during the period. Then we searched through all issues of *Publishers' Weekly* and *Bookseller* (the two journals of record for book publishing during the period) and selected all novels which might have been written by women. This file was then carefully checked against the *British Museum General Catalog of Printed Books*, the *National Union Catalog, Pre–1956 Imprints* and Robert Glenn Wright's *Author Bibliography of English Language Fiction in the Library of Congress through 1950* to verify the bibliographic accuracy of the entry and to establish the names of the authors. Those novels by authors whose names were not definitely female were further checked in a number of biographical sources. Nationality and birth and death dates were added from the above works as well as from Wright's *American Fiction, 1876–1900*. To determine the contents of the novels, a systematic search was made through the major review sources. We also used various other review sources.

ARRANGEMENT

The bibliography consists of three series, numbered sequentially, each arranged alphabetically by authors' names, then by titles of novels. The first series is a list of entries that have been verified. The second series, also verified, is a list of novels by anonymous or pseudonymous authors or by authors whose names conceal sex (such as initials in place of first names and names like Evelyn) and whose sex we have been unable to identify. The third series lists novels discovered in *Publishers' Weekly*, *Bookseller* or the review sources, but which we were unable to verify. An inclusive title index follows the three series.

INFORMATION GIVEN
IN THE ENTRIES

Author's names; we have provided the fullest form of the author's name, a procedure that necessitated an extensive number of cross-references. In alphabetizing the names, we have adhered to the following rules. Hyphenated names are alphabetized by the second part of the name; surnames preceded by a preposition or article are alphabetized by the preposition or article. Novels by more than two authors are entered under the author heading "Multiple Authors." No titles of rank, office or nobility are included except where such titles are parts of pen names or where the title helps represent the fullest form of the name provided by the catalogs, such as Mrs. E. Young or Lady X. In these cases "Mrs." or "Lady" is considered part of the name and alphabetized accordingly. Where an initial is given in place of a first name but where the second name is clearly that of a woman (S. Emily Clark), such a name is assumed to be a woman's. Names beginning with initials which our sources have identified as belonging to women are entered in the first series. Initial only names (A.F.D.) are considered pseudonyms, but where the author's name is represented by words like the epithets "A Lady" or "Borderer," such works are considered anonymous and are entered under the author heading "Anonymous Author—Not Identified." Anonymous novels are entered in the second series under the author heading "Anonymous Author—Not Identified."

Biographical information; where the information was available, nationality and birth and death dates are provided. The designation "Nationality Unknown" follows our use of the *Author Bibliography of English Language Fiction in the Library of Congress through 1950* and indicates those authors whose nationality Wright was unable to determine in the sources he used.

Titles and title notes; brief miscellaneous information in parentheses may follow the catalog location.

Pen names; where the information was available and when the name used by the author on the title page differs from the fullest form of the name under which her works are entered, the pen name follows the title, and a "see" reference is provided.

Publishing information; copyright dates are given only when imprint dates are not available. If the novel was published in England and the United States, both publishers are included.

Catalog locations; locations are given for each title in the first two series. In the third series the source of the citation is given.

Annotations; the kind and amount of annotation vary because the methodology for note taking changed during the five-year period of research. The notes represent information about the novels gathered in the search for novels with feminist characters and/or themes, and fuller notes are likely to be provided for these novels. Often the original phrasing of the reviews is presented, but most of the notes are summaries. The spelling is both British and U.S.-American—and frequently turn of the century. Words used frequently have been abbreviated.

USE OF COMPUTER

The computer helped to make this bibliography possible and enabled us to prepare the material for all kinds of retrievals. In order to alphabetize correctly, it was necessary to standardize the spelling of all names beginning with Mc and M' to Mac, St. to Saint and Ste. to Sainte. Abbreviations are alphabetized as spelled. The cost of fully editing a computer file of this size proved to exceed the limits of our budget, and we were compelled to allow some errors in the annotations to remain uncorrected.

ACKNOWLEDGMENTS

In a seminar held on publishing in 1974 by David L. Mitchell, Asst. Professor, Library and Information Science, State University of New York at Albany, a search for feminist novels published in 1913 proved to be the pilot project for an annotated bibliography of feminist novels from 1891 to 1920. During that spring and summer Mitchell provided us with guidance concerning sources and methods as well as the sympathy and enthusiasm necessary to launch the project. During that same year Ann Prentice, then Asst. Professor, Library and Information Science, SUNYA, advised us on the design of our research. The importance of their help in establishing a basically sound research design proved to be particularly important as the scope of our research widened to include the present bibliography and the earlier time period, 1781–1890. We remember their companionship in sharing our early excitement.

We did our research at the New York State Library, developing our method by identifying male pseudonyms used by women writers, determining those periodicals whose reviews would give us the best information on the novels, and compiling the file of all novels written by women during the thirty-year period. We have spent several years working in the New York State Library, and we are most grateful to the staff for their efforts to provide us with the working space and materials needed. The Cataloging Department provided an area for use and access to their copies of the National Union Catalog and the British Museum Catalog during those months the library closed for moving, and we enjoyed the quiet of the stack area and direct access to the books in the library's new location. Eric Daims greatly facilitated the compilation of entries by his careful and accurate recording of thousands of titles.

In 1976 we realized that the work would take years to complete without funding. It was then we applied to the National Endowment for the Humanities under the generous sponsorship of Russell Sage College. Christopher Reaske, Provost, Russell Sage College, gave us full encouragement by his wholehearted support of our grant proposal, a support which he has continued to give the project. When the National Endowment for the Humanities funded one year of full-time research, 1977–78, Gerald Tyson of NEH gave us very special assistance through all stages of the work during and after the grant period. In addition we had the generous help and counsel of Melissa E. Fountain, Director of Sponsored Programs, Russell Sage College.

In the fall of 1977 Michael Dolence, then head of Reproduction Services, Junior College of Albany, introduced us to the possibilities of using the computer. This led to a series of discussions with Academic Services of the Computing Center at SUNYA and subsequently, through the efforts of John Gerber, Chair, English Department, SUNYA, and John T. Shumaker, Dean, College of Humanities and Fine Arts, SUNYA, we were given computer funding. At the SUNYA Computing Center we had excellent help and advisement from John E. Tuecke, Associate Director; Steve Greenstein, Program Analyst; Robert Burgess, Manager, User Services; and David Kass.

We have spent the past two years revising the material for publication. The drudgery of this phase of the project was lightened by Cheryl Reeves, Library Intern; Isabel Nirenberg, editing consultant; and Jim Myers, Denise McCarthy and Kathryn Schabert, editors. During this phase of the project our work was based at the Albany Campus Library of Russell Sage College. We are indebted to the library staff, in particular to Connie Kilroy and Denise McCarthy for their careful typing and Deborah Priest for processing numerous inter-library loan requests and for their support in a variety of ways. We particularly thank Don Ryan, Director of Libraries, for his encouragement and support, which has included not only the provision of work space but also funding when it was needed.

Finally, we are especially indebted to Florence Boos and William Grimes for their unique contributions.

Diva Daims
Janet Grimes
Doris Robinson

ABBREVIATIONS

ACAD	Academy and Literature
ATH	Athenaeum
BKM	Bookman (New York)
BM	Book Monthly
BMC	British Museum Catalog
BRD	Book Review Digest
BS	Bookseller
CR	Critic
IND	Independent
LBKM	Bookman (London)
LC	Wright, Robert Glenn. Author Bibliography . . .
LIT	Literature
LW	Literary World
NUC	National Union Catalog
NYT	New York Times Book Review
PW	Publishers' Weekly
SP	Spectator
SR	Saturday Review
TLS	Times Literary Supplement
W	Wright, Lyle Henry. American Fiction . . .

SOURCES

MAJOR REVIEW SOURCES

Academy and Literature. London, Oct. 9, 1869–Sept. 1916. (Title varies.)

Athenaeum: a Journal of Literature, Science, the Fine Arts, Music and the Drama. London, Jan. 2, 1828–Feb. 11, 1921. (Subtitle varies.)

Baker, Ernest Albert. A Descriptive Guide to the Best Fiction, British and American, Including Translations from Foreign Languages. London: S. Sonnenschein, 1903.

————. A Guide to the Best Fiction, English and American, Including Translations from Foreign Languages, rev. ed. London: G. Routledge, 1913.

————. A Guide to the Best Fiction, English and American, Including Translations from Foreign Languages, rev. ed. London: G. Routledge, 1932.

Bookman. London, Oct. 1891–Dec. 1934.

Bookman; a Review of Books and Life. New York, Feb. 1895–Mar. 1933.

Critic; an Illustrated Monthly Review of Literature, Art, and Life. New York, Jan. 15, 1881–Sept. 1906.

Literary World. Boston, June 1870–1904.

New York Times Book Review. New York, Oct. 10, 1896– .

Publishers' Weekly. New York, 1872– .

Saturday Review. London, 1855–July 16, 1938.

Spectator. London, July 5, 1828– .

Times Literary Supplement. London, 1902– .

OTHER SOURCES

Arena. Boston, etc., Dec. 1889–Aug. 1909.

Book Monthly. London, Oct. 1903–June 1920.

Book News Monthly. Philadelphia, Sept. 1882–Aug. 1918.

Book Review Digest. New York: Wilson, 1905– .

Dial. Chicago; New York, May 1880–July 1929.

Franklin, Margaret Ladd. The Case for Woman Suffrage; a Bibliography. New York: National College Equal Suffrage League, 1913.

Godey's Magazine. Philadelphia, July 1830–Aug. 1898.

Harper's Magazine. New York, June 1850– .

Independent. New York; Boston, Dec. 7, 1848–Oct. 13, 1928.

Johnson, Reginald Brimley. The Women Novelists. London: W. Collins, 1918.

Literature. London, v. 1–10, Oct. 23, 1897–Jan. 11, 1902.

Literature. [American ed.] New York, Oct. 23, 1897–Nov. 24, 1899.

Nation. New York, 1865– .

Overton, Grant. The Women Who Make Our Novels, rev. ed. New York: Dodd, Mead, 1928.

Review of Reviews. London, 1890–Feb. 1936.

Wellington, Amy. Women Have Told; Studies in the Feminist Tradition. Boston: Little, Brown, 1930.

Woman's Journal. (National American Woman Suffrage Association). Boston, Chicago, 1870–May 26, 1917.

BIBLIOGRAPHIC SOURCES

Bookseller. London, 1858– .

British Museum. Department of Printed Books. General Catalog of Printed Books. Photolithographic edition to 1955. London: Trustees, 1959–66.

National Union Catalog. Pre–1956 Imprints. [London]: Mansell, 1968– .

Publishers' Weekly. New York, 1872– .

Wright, Lyle Henry. American Fiction, 1876–1900; a Contribution toward a Bibliography. San Marino, Calif.: Huntington Library, 1966.

Wright, Robert Glenn. Author Bibliography of English Language Fiction in the Library of Congress through 1950. Boston: G.K. Hall, 1973.

BIOGRAPHICAL SOURCES

Adams, Oscar Fay. A Dictionary of American Authors, 5th ed. Detroit: Gale Research Company, 1969.

American Women: the Standard Biographical Dictionary of Notable Women. Teaneck, N.J.: Zephyrus Press, 1974.

Browning, David Clayton. Everyman's Dictionary of Literary Biography English and American, rev. ed. London: Dent; New York: Dutton, 1962.

Burke, W.J., and Will D. Howe. American Authors and Books 1640 to the Present Day, Augmented and Revised by Irving R. Weiss. New York: Crown Publishers, 1962.

Contemporary Authors. Detroit: Gale Research Company, 1962.

The Dictionary of National Biography. Edited by Sir Leslie Stephen and Sir Sidney Lee. London: Oxford University Press, 1921–22.

Halkett, Samuel, and John Laing. Dictionary of Anonymous and Pseudonymous English Literature, new and enlarged edition, 7 volumes. Edinburgh and London: Oliver and Boyd, 1926.

Havlice, Patricia P. Index to Literary Biography. Metuchen, N.J.: Scarecrow Press, 1975.

Kunitz, Stanley J., and Howard Haycraft. Twentieth Century Authors: a Biographical Dictionary of Modern Literature. New York: Wilson, 1942.

Lawrence, Alberta, ed. Who's Who among Living Authors of Older Nations. Los Angeles: Golden Syndicate Publishing Company, 1931–32.

———. Who's Who among North American Authors, v. 3. Los Angeles: Golden Syndicate Publishing Company, 1927–28.

New York Times Obituaries Index, 1858–1968. New York: New York Times, 1970.

Sharp, Harold S. Handbook of Pseudonyms and Personal Nicknames. Metuchen, N.J.: Scarecrow, 1972. Supplement, 1975.

Wallace, William Stewart. Dictionary of North American Authors Deceased before 1950. Toronto: The Ryerson Press, 1951.

Who Was Who in America; a Companion Biographical Reference Work to Who's Who in America. 1897– . Chicago: Marquis, 1942.

Who Was Who in Literature, 1906–1934, 2 volumes. Detroit: Gale Research Company, 1979.

ADDED AUTHOR INFORMATION

SECOND SERIES

AINSLIE, NOEL: Pseudonym of Edith Lister.—Stonehill, Charles A. Anonyma and Pseudonyma, 2nd ed. New York: Milford House, 1969.

B., H.N., pseud.: Pseudonym of Hannah Newton Baker. Australia.—Miller, E. Morris. Australian Literature: a Bibliography to 1938 Extended to 1950, rev. ed. Sydney: Angus and Robertson, 1956.

CHATTERJI, BANKIM CHANDRA: Male.—Gowen, Herbert. A History of Indian Literature from Vedic Times to the Present Day. New York: D. Appleton, 1931.

DEE, R.K.: Pseudonym of John James O'Hara Wood.—Miller.

FIGGIS, DARRELL: Male.—Boylan, Henry. A Dictionary of Irish Biography. New York: Barnes and Noble, 1978.—Brown, Stephen G. Ireland in Fiction. Shannon: Irish University Press, 1969.

HARRIS, S.M.: Miss. Fourth daughter of William Harris. United Kingdom.—Brown.

HENNESSEY, J. DAVID: John David Hennessey.—Miller.

KNOWLES, R.B. SHERIDAN: Son of R.B. Knowles.—Brown.

LOCKE, SUMNER: Sumner Locke Elliott (Mrs. H.L. Elliott).—Miller.

LUMSDEN, D. FRASER: Daniel Fraser Lumsden.—Miller.

MEE, HUAN, pseud.: Composite pseudonym of the brothers Mansfield. Dawson, Lawrence Hawkins. Nicknames and Pseudonyms. . . . Detroit: Gale Research Co., 1974.

MORRIS, E. O'CONNOR: Daughter of Judge O'Connor Morris. 1861–1917. United Kingdom.—Brown.

NELSON, H. ARNOLD: Harriet Arnold Nelson. Australia.—Miller.

SCOTT, G. FIRTH: George Firth Scott.—Miller.

SMITH, JOHN, pseud.: Pseudonym of Horace Hutchinson.—Stonehill.

SUNDOWNER, pseud.: Pseudonym of Henry Tichborne.—Miller.

WILSON, RATHMELL: Son of Katherine and Rathmell George Wilson.—Lawrence, Alberta. Who's Who among Living Authors of Older Nations. Detroit: Gale Research Co., 1966.

THIRD SERIES

CRAWFORD, R.: Pseudonym of George Rankin.—Miller.

M., A.: Pseudonym of James Murdoch.—Miller.

D.R.
December 1980

FIRST SERIES

ABBOT, CAROLINE LUXBURG.

000001   THE WANDERER; OR, LEAVES FROM THE LIFE
STORY OF A PHYSICIAN. London: J. Clarke, [1905] BMC
NUC.

ABBOTT, AVERY. See ABBOTT, MABEL AVERY (RUNDELL).

ABBOTT, ELEANOR HALLOWELL. See COBURN, ELEANOR HALLOWELL
(ABBOTT).

ABBOTT, HELEN RAYMOND. See BEALS, HELEN RAYMOND (ABBOTT).

ABBOTT, JANE LUDLOW (DRAKE). B. 1881. United States.

000002   HAPPY HOUSE. Philadelphia and London:
J.B. Lippincott, 1920 BMC NUC.

ATH Influence (broadening) of college girl on
household in Vermont. Anne Leavitt also changes
village bringing much needed reforms over the summer.
NYT June 27, 1920, p. 17. "goody-goody" story.
"bedtime story." Two college friends change places,
the one with the "jolly careless disposition" visiting
the relatives, leaving the other free to go to Siberia
as a teacher.

ABBOTT, LAURA HUNSAKER.

000003   DAN, THE TRAMP: A STORY OF TO-DAY.
Chicago: C H. Kerr, 1897 NUC.

ABBOTT, LUCY HESTER (THURSTON). B. 1883. United States.

000004   NAOMI OF THE ISLAND. Boston: L. C. Page,
1912 NUC.

PW-Young woman earns her way thru school and
college-then what?

ABBOTT, MABEL AVERY (RUNDELL). United States.

000005   CAPTAIN MARTHA MARY. BY AVERY ABBOTT. New
York: Century, 1912 BMC NUC.

11 year old girl, head of family of five, tries to
keep family together. Taken to juvenile court.

A BECKETT, URSULA. United Kingdom.

000006   IN EXTENUATION OF SYBELLA. London: S.
Paul, [c1910] NUC BMC.

TLS-silly tattle.

ACKERMAN, A. W. United States.

000007   THE PRICE OF PEACE: A STORY OF THE TIMES
OF AHAB, KING OF ISRAEL. Chicago: A. C. McClurg, 1894
NUC.

ACKERMAN, LURA M.

000008   BEING LED; A STORY OF TRUTH. Newark,
N.J.: Mutual, [c1917] NUC.

Religious theme. NYT

ACLAND, EMILY ANNA.

000009   THE LOST KEY; AN INTERNATIONAL EPISODE.
BY THE HON. LADY ACLAND. London: J. Macqueen, 1901 BMC
NUC. (Malta-fic)

000010   LOVE IN A LIFE; A NOVEL. London: K. Paul,
1893 BMC.

Should be called "two lovers and a split life." A thin
plot, some modern politics and foreign affairs. SR 75,
381.
Young man jilted by fast girl. He goes on to a career
in diplomacy and a marriage to a "plainer" woman, but
a good wife. She-the fast girl-Hilda Lestrange makes a
bad marriage, flirts, gambles "more or less redeemed
at the end." Dies of cholera. ACAD 43:347.

ACLAND, HON. LADY. See ACLAND, EMILY ANNA.

ACTON, JEANIE HERING.

000011   ROSEBUD. London: Routledge, 1891 BMC.

ADAIR, CECIL, pseud. See GREEN, EVELYN EVERETT.

ADAMS, ELLINOR DAVENPORT.

000012   A GIRL OF TO-DAY, ETC. London: Blackie &
Son, 1899 BMC. New York: A. L. Burt, 1901 PW.

000013   MISS SECRETARY ETHEL: A STORY FOR GIRLS
OF TODAY. London: Hurst and Blackett, 1898 BMC.

For girls? She's learned in science, history,
politics. She's a reporter, a brilliant orator and an
ideal private secretary to her chief Sir Edgar
Allesley. Long struggle to win his heart (in fatherly
way) as she's won his wife's in a motherly way. ATH
110:818

ADAMS, EVELYN. Australia.

000014   IS MARRIAGE A LOTTERY? 16547. New York:
E. Adams, 1891 NUC.

ADAMS, JANE.

000015   THE TEST. London: J. Long, 1910 BMC.

TLS NY Literary and matrimonial life.
ATH Male publisher's reader steals plot of woman's
novel. She later falls for him marries him. Book is a
chronicle of their unhappy marriage. final
reconciliation.

ADAMS, MARY, pseud. See WARD, ELIZABETH STUART (PHELPS).

ADAMS, MRS. LEITH. See LAFFAN, BERTHA JANE (GRUNDY) LEITH
ADAMS.

ADDISON, JULIA DE WOLF (GIBBS). B. 1866. United States.

000016   FLORESTANE THE TROUBADOUR; A MEDIAEVAL
ROMANCE OF SOUTHERN FRANCE. Boston: D. Estes, [1903]
NUC.

Courtly love, witches' caves of Middle Ages.. PW
10-3-03

000017   MRS. JOHN VERNON; A STUDY OF A SOCIAL
SITUATION. Boston: R. G. Badger, 1909 NUC.

Rich widow. BKM
"A story of social life in Boston, the scenes being
laid chiefly among the artistic and musical people of
that city. The principal character is a rich widow."
BKM v 28 1908-9.
PW-marries after birth of her daughter; scandal forces
her out of society and on to the stage.

ADELAIDE, SISTER MAGDALENE. See SHEPHERD, MARGARET LISLE.

ADELINA.

000018   MUST YIELD TO WIN. London: H. J. Drane,
[1901] BMC.

ADOLPH, ANNA. United States.

000019   ARQTIQ: A STUDY OF THE MARVELS AT THE
NORTH POLE [ANONYMOUS]. [Hanford, Calif.]: The Author,
1899 NUC. (Wright attributes pub. to Carruth and
Carruth, Oakland, Calif.)

AGNEW, ALEXANDRA GEORGETTE.

000020   THE BREAD UPON THE WATERS. BY GEORGETTE
AGNEW. London: W. Heinemann, 1911 BMC.

TLS:Iris Hawthorne, actress and Kitty O'Kelly,
artist's model.
SP: Iris raises herself to good position through own
character and excellence; but her past prevents her
happiness.
ATH: Leaves the man she loves for her father's sake
because father was good to her in her studio days.

000021   THE NIGHT THAT BRINGS OUT STARS. BY
GEORGETTE AGNEW. London: W. Heinemann, 1908 BMC.

TLS-Unhappy wife leaves husband and struggles in
London to make a living
SR-Meets a stranger, is unaware that the novels she
sends to a publisher are acted on by him. Then what?
ATH-She is unconventional, impulsive, full of
imagination. She probably marries publisher but
becomes successful artist first.

AGNEW, GEORGETTE. See AGNEW, ALEXANDRA GEORGETTE.

AGNEW, MARY.

000022   THE PESTILENCE THAT WALKETH IN DARKNESS.
AN ANTIRITUALISTIC NOVEL. London: Sonnenschein, 1900
BMC.

AGRESTI, OLIVIA ROSSETTI AND HELENE ROSSETTI ANGELI.

000023   A GIRL AMONG THE ANARCHISTS. BY ISABEL
MEREDITH. London: Duckworth, 1903 BMC.

Experience of a young woman who drifted into anarchist
circles in London and edited an anarchist journal.
Anarchists, their ideals and their doings presented
sympathetically BKM 17 (1903) 545

AHLBORN, LUISE (JAEGER).

000024   WIFE AND WOMAN. BY L. HAIDHEIM. New York:
R. Bonner, 1891 NUC. (Tr. Mary J. Safford)

Couple estranged because the wife is constantly
reminded by the husband that she's inferior to wife
#1. PW 7-25-01.

AHRENS, LILLIAN SINCERE. United States.

000025   THE BLOOD STAINED ROSE; A ROMANCE. New
York: The Author, [c1917] NUC.

000026   A CHILD OF SORROW. New York: Broadway,
[c1913] NUC.

AIDA, pseud. See BAKER, FRANCES DAVIS.

AIKEN, EDNAH (ROBINSON). B. 1872. United States.

000027   THE RIVER. Indianapolis: Bobbs-Merrill,
[c1914] BMC NUC.

PW 86 10/31/14:1402 "Here the great Colorado River
decides the fate of towns and individuals. Story
begins as K C Rickard arrives in Tuscon to succeed
Hardin as head engineer for the railroad. This is
especially humiliating to Hardin, because years before
the woman he married had jilted Rickard for him. His
foolish wife now undertakes to flirt with Rickard.
Innes Hardin stands by her brother, who by his own
reading is "a man of no luck." When the river
threatens the levee, Hardin is not at his newly
appointed place. Innes goes and directs the work. In
the end, from cooly observant enemies, Rickard and
Innes come to understand each other's worth."

AILENROC, M. R., pseud. See MURRELL, CORNELIA RANDOLPH.

AKINS, ZOE. 1886-1958. United States.

000028   CAKE UPON THE WATERS. New York: Century,
1919 BMC NUC.

Humorous-involves millions of dollars and a robbery.
NYT
Light reading; a widow Kitty Davenant, lavish with
gifts, extravagant, gains and almost loses a fortune,
learns not to be so extravagant. NYT 468, 9-14-19

AKUNIAN, ILSE (LEVIEN). 1852-1908.

000029   HEAVY LADEN AND OLD-FASHIONED FOLK. BY
ILSE FRAPAN. London: T. F. Unwin, 1892 BMC NUC. (Tr.
Helen A. Macdonell)

SP 68:564. Heavy Laden is story of male murderer who
has killed out of jealousy and is filled with remorse.
Old fashioned folk is story of some young
people-romance.

ALAN, MIRIAM.

000030   WEDNESDAY'S CHILD. London: S. Low, 1891
BMC.

Purpose: to denounce and expose "the practice of
publicly and shamefully whipping girls" a practice
rampant in Irish R. C. convent schools. Autobiography
of Hester Steele-her gruesome experiences. A
depressing story. ATH 98, 92

ALBANESI, E. MARIA. See ALBANESI, EFFIE ADELAIDE MARIA.

ALBANESI, EFFIE ADELAIDE MARIA. 1866-1936. United Kingdom.

000031   ABOVE ALL THINGS. BY EFFIE ADELAIDE
ROWLANDS. London: G. Newnes, [1915] BMC.

000032   AFTER MANY DAYS. BY EFFIE ADELAIDE

ROWLANDS. London: G. Newnes, [1907] BMC.

000033   AT A GREAT COST: A NOVEL. BY EFFIE
ADELAIDE ROWLANDS. Longmans, 1891 BS. New York: R.
Bonner, 1895 NUC.

Barbara Vereker has a secret past. Meets Lady
Bridgewater who's jealous of Barb and who believes
Barb is about to come between herself and her lover.
Therefore Lady Bridgewater plots vs. Barb. PW
7-27-95:142.

000034   BARBARA'S LOVE STORY. BY EFFIE ADELAIDE
ROWLANDS. London: Hodder and Stoughton, [1911] BMC.

000035   THE BELOVED ENEMY. BY E. MARIA ALBANESI.
London: Methuen, 1913 BMC NUC.

The early 60's Elizabeth Thornton is intensely human.
Makes a loveless marriage. Husband conveniently dies.
Remarries for love.

000036   BENEATH A SPELL. BY EFFIF ADELAIDE
ROWLANDS. New York: Street & Smith, [1900] NUC.
London: S. Paul, [1910] BMC.

000037   BETH MASON. BY EFFIE ADELAIDE ROWLANDS.
London: Hodder and Stoughton, [1913] BMC.

000038   THE BLUNDER OF AN INNOCENT. London:
Hutchinson, 1899 BMC.

A variety of English types. The villain:
Bettine-without heart or principles, a monster but
real; clever, beautiful. Makes one family unhappy,
jilts, ruins and makes fools of men. LBKM 16:83
Anne Baillie innocent heroine commits the
blunder--refuses a man, then discovers she loves him.
The man is then entrapped by the villain. Bettine
Sylvester--brilliant heartless, jealous of Anne. SP
82:759

000039   THE BROWN EYES OF MARY. London: Methuen,
1905 BMC.

Nymph-like heroine unselfish, loyal-so much so the
reviewer finds her irritating ATH 607 , 05

000040   THE CAP OF YOUTH. London: Hutchinson,
1914 BMC.

LBKM-Heroine, because of a trivial unconventional act,
finds herself in deep disgrace and at 16 runs away.
Her aunt cuts her off. The man who unintentionally was
the cause of her troubles offers her marriage, and
finds she has escaped one difficulty for another.
Mother-in-law problem. How does it end?
TLS Essentially a romance

000041   CAPRICIOUS CAROLINE. BY E. MARIA
ALBANESI. London: Methuen, 1904 NUC BMC.

LBKM-Character study of an unconventional heroine
ATH-Hero is in the "pattern of priggish perfection"

000042   CARLTON'S WIFE. BY EFFIE ADELAIDE
ROWLANDS. London: Ward, Lock, 1911 BMC.

A man takes upon self the guilt of his brother's sin
ATH

000043   A CHARITY GIRL. New York: Street & Smith,
[1900] NUC. London: S. Paul, [1911] BMC.

000044   CONTRARY MARY. BY EFFIE ADELAIDE
ROWLANDS. London: Hodder & Stoughton, [1910] BMC.

000045   A DANGEROUS WOMAN. BY EFFIE ADELAIDE
ROWLANDS. London: Ward, Lock, 1910 BMC.

TLS Tangle of compromising secrets.

000046   DARE AND DO. BY EFFIE ADELAIDE ROWLANDS.
London: S. Paul, [1911] BMC.

000047   DIANA FALLS IN LOVE. London: Ward, Lock,
1919 BMC.

She gives up being a nursery governess to become a
secretary. Her employer is a woman "a level-headed
controller of an important business" on one side and
on the other an "infatuated wife of a young husband
who had married her for her money."TLS
Diana prefers independence to living on charity; can
enjoy life even in shabby clothes. Marlie Carrew
bachelor girl in London. Strong affection for Diana.

000048   "DRUSILLA'S POINT OF VIEW," A STORY OF
LOVE. London: Hurst & Blackett, 1908 BMC. Leipzig: B.
Tauchnitz, 1908 NUC.

TLS-love story

000049   ELSIE BRANT'S ROMANCE. BY EFFIE ADELAIDE
ROWLANDS. London: Cassell, 1913 BMC.

000050   THE END CROWNS ALL. BY EFFIE ADELAIDE
ROWLANDS. London: G. Newnes, [1910] BMC.

000051   ENVIOUS ELIZA. London: E. Nash, 1909 BMC.

TLS: Lady Eliza writes "serial shockers"; has "mild"
envy for women who have children; envies "great"
writers because she's a popular writer.
LBK: Real heroine is Patricia Etchington. We learn
about her sufferings. "not sentimental."

000052   A FAITHFUL TRAITOR. BY EFFIE ADELAIDE
ROWLANDS. W. Stevens, 1896 BS. Philadelphia: J. B.
Lippincott, 1896 NUC.

LW 27:329. Villain, Richard Saville. Avaricious
grandmother of Elizabeth, who is patient and amirable,
finally marries happily.

000053   FALSE FAITH. BY EFFIE ADELAIDE ROWLANDS.
London: "Daily Mail", [1911] BMC.

000054   THE FAULT OF ONE. BY EFFIE ADELAIDE
ROWLANDS. London: K. Paul, 1897 BMC. Philadelphia: J.
B. Lippincott, 1897 NUC.

Young man wins a fortune and title. Makes a bad
marriage. Zillah elopes and dies-she's wife #1.
Marries again-a woman whose heart melts when she
learns he has a blind son. LBKM 12:130.
Wife no 2 is Sheila Thurso. Wife # 1 has "inborn
vulgarity" (quote from novel) Zillah dies in
mid-channel on her way to her lover in Paris.

000055   FOR EVER AND A DAY. BY EFFIE ADELAIDE
ROWLANDS. London: "Daily Mail", [1911] BMC.

000056   FOR EVER TRUE. BY EFFIE ADELAIDE
ROWLANDS. London: Hodder & Stoughton, [1910] BMC.

000057   FOR LOVE OF SPERANZA. BY EFFIE ADELAIDE
ROWLANDS. London: Hodder & Stoughton, [1910] BMC.

000058   THE FORBIDDEN ROAD. BY MARIA ALBANESI.
New York: Empire Book, [c1907] NUC.

PW-Widow who gambles and forges check
BKM- But the heroine is the governess of her children
and there is a hero

000059   THE GAME OF LIFE. BY EFFIE ADELAIDE
ROWLANDS. London: Ward, Lock, 1910 BMC.

BM Insight into sweetness of human life.
TLS Insight into sweetness of human life. villains,
heroes, mystery LBKM

000060   A GIRL WITH A HEART. BY EFFIE ADELAIDE
ROWLANDS. London: Ward, Lock, 1911 BMC.

Beautiful waif removed from happy convent life to act
as hired companion to her mother ATH

000061   THE GLAD HEART. BY E. MARIA ALBANESI.
London: Methuen, 1910 NUC BMC.

BM-"quiet happy, admirable young people"
TLS-"quiet happy, admirable young people"

000062   A GOLDEN DAWN. BY EFFIE ADELAIDE
ROWLANDS. London: Hodder & Stoughton, [1912] BMC.

000063   THE HAND OF FATE. BY EFFIE ADELAIDE
ROWLANDS. London: Hodder & Stoughton, [1914] BMC.

000064   HEARTS AND SWEETHEARTS. London:
Hutchinson, 1916 BMC.

ATH- Inheritance, vulgar girl picture of present day
London.

000065   HEARTS AT WAR. BY EFFIE ADELAIDE
ROWLANDS. London: Hurst and Blackett, 1913 BMC.

000066   A HEART'S TRIUMPH. BY EFFIE ADELAIDE
ROWLANDS. London: Hodder & Stoughton, [1912] BMC.

000067   HER HEART'S LONGING; OR, MY LADY OF
DREADWOOD. BY EFFIE ADELAIDE ROWLANDS. London:
Skeffington, [1918] BMC.

000068   HER HUSBAND. A NOVEL. BY EFFIE ADELAIDE
ROWLANDS. London: Chatto & Windus, 1914 BMC.

ATH Heroine rebels, sins, has to bear the
consequences.
TLS "highly moral" Heroine impersonates her dead
friend.

000069   HER KINGDOM. BY EFFIE ADELAIDE ROWLANDS.
London: "Daily Mail", [1910] BMC.

000070   HER MISTAKE. BY EFFIE ADELAIDE ROWLANDS.
London: "Daily Mail", [1911] BMC.

000071   HESTER TREFUSIS. BY EFFIE ADELAIDE
ROWLANDS. London: Hurst & Blackett, 1912 BMC.

000072   THE HOUSE OF SUNSHINE. BY EFFIE ADELADIE
ROWLANDS. London: S. Paul, [1912] BMC.

000073   I KNOW A MAIDEN. London: Methuen, 1906
BMC.

ACAD heroine does something about a will and a
marriage contract.
ATH-Stepmother does daughter out of her inheritance
for sake of her two natural children, then knows no
peace after that. Stepdaughter becomes the sole
support and comfort of miserable woman.
Lady Atterburne, a widow, inherits wealth when second
husband dies,lavishes it on her children. She knows of
a later will but she keeps it secret. She falls in
love in time. "Sureness of touch about the women
characters." SR

000074   IN LOVE'S LAND. BY EFFIE ADELAIDE
ROWLANDS. London: Ward, Lock, 1912 BMC.

ATH-Typical romance

000075   THE INVINCIBLE AMELIA; OR, THE POLITE
ADVENTURESS. BY E. MARIA ALBANESI. London: Methuen,
[1909] NUC BMC.

"unscrupulous little adventuress;" numerous and
audacious escapades; " doesn't deserve to come to a
good end" TLS

000076   AN IRISH LOVER. BY EFFIE ADELAIDE
ROWLANDS. London: Hodder & Stoughton, [1914] BMC NUC.

000077   JOHN GALBRAITH'S WIFE. BY EFFIE ADELAIDE
ROWLANDS. London: Hodder & Stoughton, [1910] BMC.

000078   JOHN HELSBY'S WIFE. A NOVEL. BY EFFIE
ADELAIDE ROWLANDS. London: Hurst & Blackett, [1920]
BMC. [1921] NUC.

TLS- Fay is shallow and selfish

000079   THE JOY OF LIFE. BY EFFIE ADELAIDE
ROWLANDS. London: Cassell, 1913 BMC.

000080   A KING AND A COWARD. BY EFFIE ADELAIDE
ROWLANDS. New York: Street & Smith, [c1899] NUC.
London: Hodder & Stoughton, [1912] BMC.

000081   THE KINGDOM OF A HEART. BY EFFIE ADELAIDE
ROWLANDS. London: G. Routledge, [1899] BMC.

ACAD 58:14. Romance. Two sisters.
LIT 6:172. Heroine married three times before 21. All
wrong men, killed.
SP 84:144. Young widow.
ATH 115:9. Marries on the condition that husband leave
her absolutely alone for one year. An officer of the
Guards he is shot to avenge a girl he had betrayed and
deserted.

000082   LADY PATRICIA'S FAITH. BY EFFIE ADELAIDE
ROWLANDS. London: Hodder and Stoughton, [1913] BMC.

000083   THE LAUGHTER OF LIFE. BY MARIA ALBANESI.
New York: Cupples & Leon, [c1908] NUC.

000084   LEILA VANE'S BURDEN. BY EFFIE ADELAIDE
ROWLANDS. London: The Daily Mail, [1911] BMC.

000085   A LIFE'S LOVE. BY EFFIE ADELAIDE
ROWLANDS. London: Hodder & Stoughton, [1911] BMC.

000086   A LITTLE BROWN MOUSE. BY MADAME ALBANESI.
London: Hodder & Stoughton, [1909] BMC NUC.

ACAD- Children's

000087   LITTLE LADY CHARLES. BY EFFIE ADELAIDE
ROWLANDS. New York: Street & Smith, [1899] NUC.
London: S. Paul, [1910] BMC.

000088   LOVE AND LOUISA: A NOVEL. BY E. MARIA
ALBANESI. Philadelphia: J. B. Lippincott, 1902 NUC.
London: Sands, 1902 BMC.

NYT 12-27-02

000089   LOVE FOR LOVE. BY EFFIE ADELAIDE
ROWLANDS. London: Hodder & Stoughton, [1910] BMC.

000090   A LOVE MATCH. BY EFFIE ADELAIDE ROWLANDS.
London: "Daily Mail", [1912] BMC.

000091   THE LOVE OF HIS LIFE. BY EFFIE ADELAIDE
ROWLANDS. London: S. Paul, [1912] BMC.

000092   LOVE-IN-A-MIST. London: Hodder &
Stoughton, 1907 BMC.

SR: "Typical traditional love story"
TLS: "Pretty love tale"

000093   LOVE'S HARVEST. BY EFFIE ADELAIDE
ROWLANDS. London: "Daily Mail", [1911] BMC.

000094   LOVE'S MASK. BY EFFIE ADELAIDE ROWLANDS.
London: S. Paul, [1913] BMC.

000095   LOVE'S SHADOW. BY EFFIE ADELAIDE
ROWLANDS. London: G. Newnes, [1920] BMC.

000096   THE MADNESS OF LOVE. BY EFFIE ADELAIDE
ROWLANDS. London: Hodder & Stoughton, [1911] BMC.

000097   THE MAN AT THE GATE. BY EFFIE ADELAIDE
ROWLANDS. London: "Daily Mail", [1911] BMC.

000098   THE MAN SHE LOVED. BY EFFIE ADELAIDE
ROWLANDS. New York: Street & Smith, [1900] NUC.
London: Ward, Lock, 1911 BMC.

Elderly rich baronet; young wife their
misunderstandings TLS
Kit Marlove a kind of Cinderella, her two loves,
nothing new LBKM

000099   THE MAN SHE MARRIED. BY EFFIE ADELAIDE
ROWLANDS. London: S. Paul, [1910] BMC.

000100   THE MAN WITH THE MONEY. BY EFFIE ADELAIDE
ROWLANDS. London: Hurst & Blackett, 1912 BMC.

Man "unused to wealth" inherits large sum; several
immoral persons try to get hold of same ATH TLS

000101   MARGARET DENT. BY EFFIE ADELAIDE
ROWLANDS. London: Cassell, 1913 BMC.

000102   MARIAN SAX; A NOVEL. BY E. MARIA
ALBANESI. London: Hurst and Blackett, 1905 BMC NUC.

Story of intrigue and a thousand coincidences ACAD
545.05 LBKM 27-28.102

000103   THE MARRIAGE OF MARGARET. London: C.A.
Pearson, 1909 BMC.

Innocent lovely foolish heroine ATH

000104   THE MASTER OF LYNCH TOMERS. BY EFFIE
ADELAIDE ROWLANDS. London: Hodder & Stoughton, [1910]
BMC.

000105   THE MISTRESS OF THE FARM. BY EFFIE
ADELAIDE ROWLANDS. London: S. Paul, [1910] BMC.

000106   MONEY OR WIFE? BY EFFIE ADELAIDE
ROWLANDS. London: Ward, Lock, 1914 BMC.

ATH Male hero renounces financial future when female
employer objects to his marriage. The second time the
opportunity is offered, his wife leaves him and goes
to work. Finally reunited.

000107   "MY PRETTY JANE". BY EFFIE ADELAIDE
ROWLANDS. London: W. Stevens, [1894] BMC.
Philadelphia: J. B. Lippincott, 1894 NUC.

CR 25:329. Jane's father marries when she is seventeen
a heartless worldy young woman of 19, interested only
in his fortune. She had a lover whom she abandoned and
who subsequently comes into a fortune. He meets Jane
and falls for her. Stepmother is jealous of Jane.
London, love story between "respectable people." Much
action. BOOK NEWS '97-8, 638.

000108   OLIVIA MARY. BY E. MARIA ALBANESI.
London: Methuen, [1912] NUC BMC.

ATH-0
TLS- Two women who are pregnant and single,
sensational domestic.
SP- Pleasant tale
LBKM-Chafes at her son's protection but when he
rejects her because of secret in past is quick to
realize her only happiness is to be with him.

000109   ON THE HIGH ROAD. BY EFFIE ADELAIDE
ROWLANDS. London: Hurst and Blackett, 1914 BMC.

TLS Inheritance and romance two penniless sisters.

000110   ONE MAN'S EVIL. BY EFFIE ADELAIDE
ROWLANDS. New York: Street & Smith, [1900] NUC.
London: G. Newnes, [1910] BMC.

000111   ONE OF THE CROWD. A NOVEL. London:
Chapman and Hall, 1913 BMC.

Actor's daughter left by father in her aunt's care.
Becomes a drudge until stepmother rescues her. Later
becomes an actress-musical comedy and famous in
serious drama, marries in the end. ATH
BKM-Celia, an orphan is partly raised by drug-addicted
step mother and a school in France. Decides to make
acting her career. Bohemian friends, love, success.

000112   THE ONE WOMAN. BY EFFIE ADELAIDE
ROWLANDS. London: Hodder & Stoughton, [1911] BMC.

000113   PATRICIA AND LIFE. BY E. MARIA ALBANESI.
London and Melbourne: Ward, Lock, 1920 BMC NUC.

TLS Sunny, healthy. Patricia an accurate model of
emancipated energetic girlhood today. Took destiny in
her own hands and found a more suitable husband than
scoundrel she was doomed to wed.

000114   PETER, A PARASITE. A NOVEL. London:
Sands, 1901 BMC.

Blackguard forsakes heroine when poverty comes upon
her ATH 12-21-01

000115   POPPIES IN THE CORN. London: Hutchinson,
1912 BMC.

Leila Arundale has no heart (Poppy) Katherine is the
good one TLS
Ends in submission to a strong man ATH

000116   THE POWER OF LOVE. BY EFFIE ADELAIDE
ROWLANDS. London: "Daily Mail", [1911] BMC.

000117   PRETTY PENELOPE. BY EFFIE ADELAIDE
ROWLANDS. London: Cassell, 1907 BMC.

Fresh engaging TLS

000118   THE PRICE PAID. BY EFFIE ADELAIDE
ROWLANDS. London: Chatto & Windus, 1914 BS. London:
People's Friend Library, [1921] BMC.

ATH-Trapped into a mock marriage, eventually meets the
man she really loves. Happy ending

000119   PRUDENCE LANGFORD'S ORDEAL. BY EFFIE
ADELAIDE ROWLANDS. London: Pearson, 1914 BS. London:
R. Hale, [1937] BMC.

000120   A QUESTION OF QUALITY. London: Hurst &
Blackett, 1909 BMC.

Girl makes restitution for her wronged family TLS

000121   THE ROSE OF LIFE. BY EFFIE ADELAIDE
ROWLANDS. London: Ward, Lock, 1912 BMC.

ATH sens

000122   RUTH'S ROMANCE. BY EFFIE ADELAIDE
ROWLANDS. London: Hodder and Stoughton, [1913] BMC.

000123   A SHADOWED HAPPINESS. BY EFFIE ADELAIDE
ROWLANDS. London: G. Newnes, [1915] BMC.

000124   SISTER ANNE. London: Hodder & Stoughton,
1908 BMC.

ATH- Her sacrifice proves to be her life's happiness
TLS-Atones for her bad half sister by a marriage.

000125   THE SPELL OF URSULA. BY EFFIE ADELAIDE
ROWLANDS. Philadelphia: J. B. Lippincott, 1894 NUC.

A cruel passionate young woman can't win her married
lover; therefore makes his and his wife's lives
miserable. Parallel story of sweet love between
Catherine and Chestermere. LW 26:7
PW-Beautiful, mixed character, her spell works havoc
in many hearts and wrecks the lives of several men.
English, Born and reared in India, after father's
death comes to England to care for aunt.

000126   SPLENDID LOVE. BY EFFIE ADELAIDE
ROWLANDS. London: "Daily Mail", [1911] BMC.

000127   A STRANGE LOVE STORY. BY EFFIE ADELAIDE
ROWLANDS. London: Hurst & Blackett, [1919] BMC.

Not strange-commonplace love story TLS

000128   STRANGER THAN TRUTH. BY EFFIE ADELAIDE
ROWLANDS. London: Hodder and Stoughton, [1913] BMC.

000129   THE STRONGEST OF ALL THINGS: A NOVEL.
London: Hurst and Blackett, 1907 BMC.

Elizabeth has heart of child. Repressed, taught to
obey mother, but learns the truth about who her mother
is, learns to love, bu she fears what the shame of her
past will mean to her husband. kills self? LBKM 7-07,
143
Many good female characters TLS
Elizabeth is wonderful "adorable a true natural
lovable woman" SR

000130   THE SUNLIT HILLS. BY E. MARIA ALBANESI.
London: Hutchinson, 1915 NUC BMC.

Young man marries rich woman TLS

000131   SUNSET AND DAWN. BY EFFIE ADELAIDE
ROWLANDS. London: Ward, Lock, 1915 BMC.

Traditional love stuff TLS

000132   THE SUREST BOND. BY EFFIE ADELAIDE
ROWLANDS. London: Cassell, 1913 BMC.

Fortunes of a young woman who resolves to avenge her
father's death. Her scheme is to marry the moneylender
who led her father to suicide and to squander his
money ATH

000133   SUSANNAH AND ONE ELDER. London: Methuen,
1903 BMC.

000134   SUSANNAH AND ONE OTHER. BY E. MARIA
ALBANESI. London: Methuen, 1903 BMC NUC. New York:
McClure, Phillips, 1904 NUC. (BMC: Another ed. of
Susannah and One Elder.)

PW- innocent and good heroine with gambler mother and
flirt of a sister
"A novel which has already appeared in London under
the title "Susannah and One Elder." There seems to be
a diversity of opinion about the book itself. BKM v.
19, 1904
NYT-Kind of girl who becomes conv matron
ACAD 65,84 Short desc
To save her sister's reputation, pretends to be
engaged to a man she's just met? ACAD 65, 150

000135   TEMPTATION. BY EFFIE ADELAIDE ROWLANDS.
London: G. Newnes, [1912] BMC.

000136   THEY LAUGH THAT WIN. BY EFFIE ADELAIDE
ROWLANDS. London: G. Routledge, [1899] BMC NUC.

Constance Featherstone loses her memory because of a
railway accident. Only a few weeks are blotted
out--the time she heard of her brother's death. Only
he could testify that the secret marriage she made to
a Baronet who was killed in the accident was no
marriage--since they were wed that morning. SP 83:353

000137   THROUGH WEAL AND THROUGH WOE. BY EFFIE
ADELAIDE ROWLANDS. London: Ward, Lock, 1913 BMC.

Marriage of convenience develops eventually into one
of love. ATH

000138   TO LOVE AND TO CHERISH. BY EFFIE ADELAIDE
ROWLANDS. London: Everett, [1912] BMC.

000139   TONY'S WIFE. London: Holden & Hardingham,
1919 BMC.

Trad romantic TLS

000140   TRUANT HAPPINESS. London: Ward, Lock,
1918 BMC.

000141   TWO WAIFS. BY EFFIE ADELAIDE ROWLANDS.
London: Hodder & Stoughton, [1914] BMC.

000142   WHEN MICHAEL CAME TO TOWN. London:
Hutchinson, 1917 BMC.

conventional story TLS

000143   WHITE ABBEY. BY EFFIE ADELAIDE ROWLANDS.
London: S. Paul, [1911] BMC.

000144   A WILD ROSE. BY EFFIE ADELAIDE ROWLANDS.
London: "Daily Mail", [1911] BMC.

000145   THE WILES OF A SIREN; OR, MARY'S GREAT
MISTAKE. BY EFFIE ADELAIDE ROWLANDS. New York: Street
and Smith, [c1906] NUC.

000146   A WOMAN WORTH WINNING. BY EFFIE ADELAIDE
ROWLANDS. London: "Daily Mail", [1911] BMC.

000147   THE WOMAN'S FAULT. BY EFFIE ADELAIDE
ROWLANDS. London: Hurst & Blackett, 1915 BMC.

Unhappily married, leaves, becomes successful opera
singer, returns to husband. TLS

000148   A WOMAN'S HEART. BY EFFIE ADELAIDE
ROWLANDS. London: Hodder & Stoughton, [1911] BMC.

000149   THE WOOING OF ROSE. BY EFFIE ADELAIDE
ROWLANDS. London: Lloyds, [1919] BMC.

000150   A YOUNG MAN FROM THE COUNTRY. London:
Hurst & Blackett, 1906 BMC.

ACAD-Settles down in country village with three
children and no explanations. There are two willful
young sisters.
TLS Unhappy marriage-unattractive wife (most
interesting character in book)

ALBANESI, MADAME. See ALBANESI, EFFIE ADELAIDE MARIA.

ALBANESI, MARIA. See ALBANESI, EFFIE ADELAIDE MARIA.

ALBERT, AGNES ELNOR. United States.

000151   ALICE REYDEN; OR WEIGHED IN THE BALANCE.
New York: Broadway, [c1910] NUC.

ALBERT, MARY.

000152   BROOKE FINCHLEY'S DAUGHTER. London:
Chatto and Windus, 1891 BMC.

Plot turns around the disappearance of Finchley and
his return. ACAD
Sensational novel. ATH 98, 189
During his absence his wife remarried and widowed
again. She thought he was dead. This Mrs. Finchley is
a hard woman who is miserable to her old aunt. Judith
works for the old aunt-treated like a servant though
she is niece. Finchley absent because he's a burglar.
Wife tried to wipe him out of her memory. Judith is
his daughter, gains fortune. Finchley's return-he's
now a changed man. Wife accepts him-a second
honeymoon. Wife even loves the aunt now and Judith
weds. SR 9-19-91, 339

000153   THE DIAMOND SHOE BUCKLES. London:
Roxburghe Press, [1897] BMC.

000154   THE LUCKIEST MAN IN THE WORLD: A NOVEL.
London: Simpkin and Marshall, [1896] BMC.

000155   THE SHELLING OF THE PEAS. London: Hurst
and Blackett, 1892 BMC.

ATH 99:338. Parson's daughter heroine. Romance.
SP. Silly heroine.

ACAD. She marries, husband dies on wedding day. She
becomes victim of vicious plot of drunken village
family whereby she loses her new title, her new
estate, and the parents she had always believed hers.
In the course of time all these are restored to her as
well as the man she truly loved.

ALCOCK, D. See ALCOCK, DEBORAH.

ALCOCK, DEBORAH. 1835-1913. United Kingdom.

000156   NOT FOR CROWN OR SCEPTRE. BY D. ALCOCK.
London: Hodder and Stoughton, 1902 BMC. New York:
American Tract Soc., [1903?] NUC.

Gustavus, Prince of Sweden 1568-1607

000157   ROBERT MUSGRAVE'S ADVENTURE. A STORY OF
OLD GENEVA. London: S. W. Partridge, [1909] BMC.

000158   UNDER CALVIN'S SPELL; A TALE OF THE
HEROIC TIMES IN OLD GENEVA. London: R.T.S., [c1902]
BMC. New York: F. H. Revell, [1910] NUC.

Calvin, Jean-Fiction.
Geneva-Hist-Fiction.
Historical.

ALDEN, CYNTHIA MAY (WESTOVER). B. 1862.

000159   BUSHY; A ROMANCE FOUNDED ON FACT. BY
CYNTHIA M. WESTOVER. New York: Morse, 1896 NUC.

PW 10-17-96. Story of Becky and her following her
father on his geological trips from 4 to 16.
Escapes drowning and scalping, kills buffalo, and
Indians, choked rattle snakes. Catches horse
thieves-has all the experiences of a
pioneer-trapper-cowboy. CR 26, 30:57 JUV?

000160   BUSHY; OR, THE ADVENTURES OF A GIRL.
London: Chapman and Hall, 1897 BMC.

ALDEN, ISABELLA (MACDONALD). 1841-1930. United States.

000161   AS IN A MIRROR. BY MRS. G. R. ALDEN
(PANSY). Boston: Lothrop, [c1897] NUC. London: C. H.
Kelly, 1898 BMC.

PW-Hero adopts life of tramp to test certain truths.

000162   THE BROWNS AT MT. HERMAN. BY PANSY.
Boston: Lothrop, Lee & Shepard, [1908] NUC.

PW-Mistaken identity.

000163   DAVID RANSOM'S WATCH. BY PANSY (MRS. G.
R. ALDEN). Boston: Lothrop, [1905] NUC.

Story of an inheritance (small) pleasing commonplace
sent. NYT, 447, 05

000164   FOUR MOTHERS AT CHAUTAUQUA. BY PANSY.
Boston: Lothrop, Lee & Shepard, [1913] NUC.

"The four girls of "Four girls of Chautauqua" return
after twenty-five years to Chautauqua, bringing with
them their husbands and children, and the book tells
of what happened on that occasion and how important a
part the place played in the lives of the second
generation." PW 84:422

000165   THE LONG WAY HOME. BY PANSY. Boston:
Lothrop, Lee & Shepard, [1912] NUC.

PW-story of a young marriage.

000166   LOST ON THE TRAIL. BY PANSY. Boston:
Lothrop, Lee & Shepard, [1911] NUC.

morality about a girl forced to live without rel. for
10 years. PW 4-15-11
girl lived 10 years of her young life on an isolated
mt top in Far West under the sole charge of mother &
brother who were fugitives; up to age 16, ignorant of
rel. Then gets on the trail of civilization where she
is lost in all its contradictions. NYT

000167   MAKING FATE. BY PANSY. (MRS. G. R.
ALDEN). Boston: Lothrop, [1896] NUC.

LW 27:365. Margaret loves Ralph who proves unworthy.
She is strengthened by "faith which is to be her
support in after life."

000168   MARA. BY PANSY. (MRS. G. R. ALDEN).
Boston: Lothrop, [1903].

PW: Fortunes in love of 4 schoolmates.
One's fiance marries another woman. One's husband dies
on wedding day; a third throws over her fiance who is
cheating on her. The 4th finds she is wed to a Mormon
who already has 6 wives. The first 3, now single, are
teachers and nurse. They come to #4's rescue. At the
end a train runs over the Mormon husband. NYT 03, 672

000169   MISSENT: THE STORY OF A LETTER. BY PANSY
(MRS. G. R. ALDEN). Boston: Lothrop, 1900 NUC.

PW-romance and Christmas season.

000170   OUT IN THE WORLD: THE STORY OF CLAIRE
BENEDICT. BY PANSY. London: T. Nelson, 1901 BMC.

000171   OVERRULED. Boston: Lothrop, 1897. London:
C. H. Kelly, 1897 BMC.

Sequel to "Making Fate." In this novel Ralph Brainlett
"conquers fate". PW 51:916.

000172   PAULINE. BY PANSY. (MRS. G. R. ALDEN).
Boston: Lothrop, [c1900] NUC. London: C. H. Kelly,
1901 BMC.

"The flight of a high-spirited young wife from her
husband." ends in peace and reunion. BOOK NEWS 6-01.
A happy ending certain. NYT

000173   RUTH ERSKINE'S SON. BY PANSY. Boston:
Lothrop, Lee & Shepard, [1907] NUC.

widow with son. strong woman. PW 10-5-07
devotes her life to her son. BKM.

000174   TWENTY MINUTES LATE. BY PANSY. Boston: D.
Lothrop, 1893 NUC. London: C. H. Kelly, 1893 BMC.

Caroline Bryant's whole life changed by missing a
train. Gets on wrong train; ends up in Philadelphia.
Is quarantined in a house where there's scarlet fever.
A doctor befriends her. Learns stenography and typing.
PW 5-20-93

000175   UNTO THE END. BY PANSY (MRS G. R. ALDEN).
Boston: Lothrop, [1902] NUC. London: C. H. Kelly, 1902
BMC.

000176   "WANTED." BY MRS. G. R. ALDEN (PANSY).
Boston: Lothrop, [c1894] NUC. London: C. H. Kelly,
1894 BMC.

LW 25:266. Rebecca, long a comrade of her widowed
father, rebels when he marries. She takes a job,
involving the care of a child whose mother is an opium
eater. Eventually grows to love her stepmother and to
become one herself.

ALDEN, ISABELLA (MACDONALD) AND MARCIA MACDONALD
LIVINGSTONE.

000177   BY WAY OF THE WILDERNESS. BY PANSY (MRS.
G. R. ALDEN) AND MRS. C. M. LIVINGSTONE. Boston:
Lothrop, 1899 NUC. London: C. H. Kelly, 1900 BMC.

PW-hero leaves home because of stepmother impulsively.
His impulsiveness brings him much trouble in many
crises, including a love affair.

000178   JOHN REMINGTON, MARTYR. BY PANSY (MRS. G.
R. ALDEN) AND MRS. C. M. LIVINGSTON. Boston: D.
Lothrop, [c1892] NUC.

ALDEN, MRS. G. R. See ALDEN, ISABELLA (MACDONALD), Also
ALDEN, ISABELLA (MACDONALD) AND MARCIA (MACDONALD)
LIVINSTONE.

ALDINGTON, MAY. Nationality Unknown.

000179   THE KING CALLED LOVE. London: Heath,
Cranton and Ouseley, [1913] BMC.

TLS-Lynda Gray yielded prematurely to her own and her
lover's passion, with usual consequences. She ends as
wife of lover, now widower after 20 years of married
life; her career a feeble and nerveless story.

000180   LOVE LETTERS THAT CAUSED A DIVORCE. BY
MRS. A. E. ALDINGTON. New York: G. W. Dillingham,
[c1906] NUC. London: Sisley's, 1906 BMC.

PW-Unhappy woman enters into Platonic friendship with
friend's husband.

000181   LOVE LETTERS TO A SOLDIER. London: T. W.
Laurie, [1915] NUC BMC.

"Wounded are you, my soldier man? Well come home to me
and let me nurse you well and send you back again."
And so on. TLS
European War 1914

000182   A MAN OF KENT. London: A. M. Garner,
[1913] BMC.

000183   "MEG OF THE SALT-PANS". London: Everett,
1909 BMC.

The trouble she gets into that casts a shadow on her
marriage. TLS
Theme of "marriage of a pregnant girl to a man who
believes in her chastity." ATH

000184   SONGS OF LIFE AND LOVE. London: D. Nutt,
1907 BMC.

ALDINGTON, MRS. A. E. See ALDINGTON, MAY.

ALDIS, MARY (REYNOLDS). 1872-1949. United States.

000185   DRIFT. New York: Duffield, 1918 NUC.

PW-Restless & dissatisfied. Eileen drifts thru life &
marriage, destroys herself, (Husband loves someone
else & she loses Robert who had loved her).
NYT June 9, 1918, p. 267. Eileen Picardy is a
"complex, carefully studied character, a woman weak
and restless, possessed of many gifts, yet absolutely
futile. She is minutely analyzed, and she is
consistent throughout, down to the final demonstration
of her inability to make a resolve and go through with
it, which ends the book." Partly because of a terrible
shock she suffered while residing in a settlement
house at 19, when she faces an "especial fact of life
in its ugliest form."

ALDON, ADAIR, pseud. See MEIGS, CORNELIA LYNDE.

ALDRICH, ANNE REEVE. 1866-1892. United States.

000186   GABRIEL LUSK. New York: G. W. Dillingham,
1894 NUC.

ALDRICH, CLARA CHAPLINE (THOMAS).

000187   ENCHANTED HEARTS. BY DARRAGH ALDRICH.
Garden City, N.Y.: Doubleday, Page, 1917 NUC. London:
Jarrolds, [1919] BMC.

"A story which is as wholesome for grown-ups as it is
enchanting to younger readers. Little Comfort, the
heroine, sleeping or waking, inhabits her castle of
dreams where she is Fairy-godmother. "That," she says,
"Is what I truly am; but of course my business is
peeling potatoes and things and washing dishes. I wait
on tables, too, mostly-when I am not making beds." In
the boarding house where she wields alternately her
fairy wand and the paring knife is her Princess who
writes stories. Fairy-godmother observes that when the
fat envelope comes back, gloom prevails. Her work is
to hunt up a Prince who can save the Princess." BRD
1917

ALDRICH, DARRAGH, pseud. See ALDRICH, CLARA CHAPLINE
(THOMAS).

ALDRICH, DR. (MRS.) F. L. S. See ALDRICH, FLORA L.
(SOUTHARD).

ALDRICH, FLORA L. (SOUTHARD). 1859-1921. United States.

000188   THE ONE MAN. BY DR. (MRS.) F. L. S.
ALDRICH. Boston: Roxburgh, [c1910] NUC.

Protege of old Knickerbocker family marries rich old
lumberman for mercenary reasons-rather than man she
loves. Finds herself at last, realizes love and honor
far outweigh power of gold. PW

ALERAMO, SIBILLA, pseud. See FACCIO, RINA (COTTINO).

ALEXANDER, ARABEL WILBUR. Nationality Unknown.

000189   LIGHT THROUGH DARKENED WINDOWS; A
"SHUT-IN" STORY. Cincinnati: Jennings and Pye, [1901]
NUC.

PW 3-73-01.

ALEXANDER, ELEANOR JANE.

000190   LADY ANNE'S WALK. London: E. Arnold, 1903
BMC NUC. New York: Longmans, Green, 1903 PW.

"Womanly chat about personal surroundings and
experiences" ACAD 65, 507
Cataloged as history, subject: "Beresford, Lady Anne.
2. Armage,Ireland.

000191   THE LADY OF THE WELL. New York: Longmans,
1906 NUC. London: Edward Arnold, 1906 NUC BMC.

PW-Historical romance of a troubador
NYT romance of a troubador
ACAD romance of a troubador

000192   THE RAMBLING RECTOR. London: E. Arnold,
1904 BMC NUC.

NYT-old fashioned
ATH
Clericall life sympatheticaly drawn. BAKER 13-161

ALEXANDER, EVELYN.

000193   THE ESSENCE OF LIFE. London: J. Long,
1911 BMC.

Crowded moments of social life ending in marriage. TLS

000194   THE HEART OF A MONK. London: J. Long,
1910 BMC.

TLS-governess finds romance in Irish castle.

ALEXANDER, GRACE. United States.

000195   JUDITH; A STORY OF THE CANDLE-LIT
FIFTIES. Indianapolis: Bobbs-merrill, [1906] BMC NUC.

PW-Makes a tragic marriage
NYT--husband conveniently dies

ALEXANDER, MIRIAM. United Kingdom.

000196   BEYOND THE LAW. New York & London: G. P.
Putnam's Sons, 1912 NUC.

PW-Historical
BKM-Historical

000197   THE HOUSE OF LISRONAN. London: A.
Melrose, 1912 BMC NUC.

TLS-grim, stark. Ireland under William III male hero
Irish problem
SP-new form of pain
ACAD-Catholics forced out of home, mother becomes
paralyzed etc.
BAKER 32-7

000198   MISS O'CORRA, M.F.H. London: A. Melrose,
1915 BMC.

Noreen inherits Irish estate, gets made MFH right
away. Passion for horses hunting experiences. TLS

000199   THE PORT OF DREAMS. New York: G. P.
Putnam's Sons, 1912 NUC. London: A. Melrose, 1912 NUC
BMC.

PW-"By the author of the prize story "Beyond the Law,"
Tale is concerned with the Jacobite cause and its
Irish supporters. John Clavering had served the
Stewarts for thirty years with courage and ability,
only to fail on three critical occasions, overcome by
cowardice. There had been cowards before in his
family, but he had always held fear at bay, and his
overwhelming shame, the influence of his failures on
the cause and his friends amid stirring adventures
make an interesting story."
Young Irish girl in Jacobite times; she's "deficient
in some of the finest attributes of her sex." Her mind
is dominated by a single obsession. "Her unbalanced
mind might, in the present day, have rendered her
responsible for window smashing and pillarbox
outrages." She doesn't appreciate what nature demands
of women for her political zeal. Her hero worship
results in a young lover's death. ACAD. 3-1-13.
Kathleen Desmond -- NYT
ATH-hero is a coward.
TLS-historical romance

000200   THE RIPPLE. New York & London: G. P.
Putnam's Sons, 1913 NUC. London: A. Melrose, 1913 BMC.

"Tale of love and adventure, the scene of which begins
in Ireland and ends in northern Germany. Time is last
half of the seventeenth century, when the Jacobites
were in a constant turmoil, and when to be Irish was
anathema. Heroine is Deidre, an Irish girl, whose
father has curried favor with King William, and who
has been brought up to hate her fellow-countrymen. She
goes to Germany, falls in love with Maurice of Saxe,
and to save her from him her cousin marries her. There
is love on his side, but none on hers, but at last,
after adventures and peril, they win through to peace
and happiness." PW 84:1285.
Young woman-Diedre; a spitfire, aflame, pursues hated
kinsman across Europe with many a busy adventure. TLS

ALEXANDER, MRS., pseud. See HECTOR, ANNIE (FRENCH).

ALEXANDER, MRS. THOMAS.

000201   IERNE: A ROMANCE OF ST. PATRICK'S WELL,
TRINITY COLLEGE. Dublin: E. Ponsonby, 1895 BMC.

ALFORD, ELIZABETH MARY.

000202   DOROTHY, THE COOMBEHURST NIGHTINGALE.
London: S. W. Partridge, 1899 BMC. (Another ed. of the
Romance of Coombehurst.)

000203   STANHURST. London: S. B. Barrett, 1893
BMC.

ALIEN, pseud. See BAKER, LOUISA ALICE, Also HUMPHREYS,
ELIZA MARGARET J. (GOLLAN) AND LOUISA ALICE BAKER.

ALLAN, ELLAM FENWICKE, pseud. See ANNE, EDITH CHARLTON.

ALLATINI, R. See SCOTT, ROSE LAURE (ALLATINI).

ALLCOCK, FLORENCE B.

000204   A MODERN CINDERELLA. London: Drane,
[1915] BMC.

000205   MY FACSIMILE; OR ISA'S STORY. London: H.
J. Drane, 1912 BMC.

ALLEMAN, JULIA SUESSEROTT. United States.

000206   POSTMARKED "COLIMA". Philadelphia:
Lutheran Pub. Soc., [c1900] NUC.

LW 31:268. A lost letter with a proposal delays
marriage for 25 years.

ALLEN, ANNE STORY. Nationality Unknown.

000207   MERRY HEARTS; THE ADVENTURES OF TWO
BACHELOR MAIDS. New York: H. Holt, 1903 NUC.

"Two bachelor maids" Very brief description BKM (1903)
18,447

ALLEN, EMMA SARAH (GAGE). B. 1859. United States.

000208   AFTERWARDS. New York: E. J. Clode,
[c1914] NUC.

story of love, intrigue, etc. PW 1-16-15
NYT--male hero with amnesia

000209   THE AWAKENING OF THE HARTWELLS; A TALE OF
THE SAN FRANCISCO EARTHQUAKE. New York: Am. Tract
Soc., [c1913] NUC.

"Carol Thurman goes to San Francisco to visit her
wealthy aunt and finds her two girl cousins worldly
and selfish, while Percy, the son, is dissipated and
reckless. Through her influence, Percy begins to see
that there is something better than the life he has
been leading and then comes the earthquake and fire,
which sweeps away the Hartwell fortune and forces them
to begin over at the bottom of the ladder. Carol and
her family are of the greatest help, and through them
the Hartwells win a prosperity and happiness they have
never known." PW

000210   THE FURNACE FOR GOLD. New York: American
Tract Society, [c1919] NUC.

the divine evil PW

000211   THE HIGH ROAD. New York: Meridian Press,
[c1917] NUC.

story of prohibition NYT

000212   THE HOUSE OF GLADNESS. Philadelphia: G.
W. Jacobs, [1915] NUC. London: R. T. S., [1921] BMC.

"Superficially a love story. In reality a plea for the
education of girls along useful lines." BKM 1915-16
Because she received the most adequate kind of
education--Virginia Tyrell is able to support herself
when the times comes; "much moralizing." NYT

ALLEN, FRANCES NEWTON (SYMMES). B. 1865. United States.

000213   HER WINGS. Boston: Houghton Mifflin, 1914
NUC.

PW 86 10/3/14:116 "Georgia Frame's mother had taught
her to be a man-hater. She grows up intellectually
strong, but emotionally unresponsive. After Mrs.
Frame's death, Georgia is softened somewhat by
association with a widowed college chum and her family
of children. Georgia had thought herself a new woman,
but Dr. Craig, a young doctor, teaches her to be a
diferent kind of feminist."
NYT-She is absorbed in her work as a suffragist and
philanthropist.

000214   THE INVADERS. Boston: Houghton Mifflin,
1913 NUC.

Slavs and Celts invade New England town: suspicion
changes to warmer friendliness. NYT
The young men and women of the town are not interested
in each other but in "our foreign importations."
Theme: racial intermixture improves the species. BKM

000215   THE PLAIN PATH. Boston: Houghton Mifflin,
1912 NUC.

PW-Storm of religious doubt from which she emerges
with a belief in God.
Get other reviews. BKM 35 (1912) 192-3
NYT-300 pages of Nietzsche and religion.
NYT-Story of a brilliant girl. Child of a German
agnostic, her development under the spell of German
iconoclastic thought.

ALLEN, LINDA MARGUERITE SANGREE. United States.

000216   FLORINE; OR, THE INNER LIFE OF ONE OF THE
"FOUR HUNDRED." BY THE AUTHOR OF "MIGNONNETTE," "THE
DEVIL AND I," ETC. [ANONYMOUS]. New York: G. W.
Dillingham, 1891 NUC.

She's a gambler's daughter. Keeps journal for her own
daughter to read someday. Covers her life from 9 to 30
years old. PW

ALLEN, MARY.

000217   ON THE CARDS; OR THE RETURN OF THE
PRINCESS: A NOVEL. London: Jarrold, 1895 BMC.

Helen Harwood works at a draper's shop. A gypsy tells
her she will be loved by royalty. Next day an Egyptian
prince calls and proposes. As it is "on the cards" she
can't refuse him. and she lives very unhappily ever
after till he dies. ACAD 47:354.
She repents "at leisure in his harem." ATH 105:438
SP 76:455. "Unknown Author Series." Moral: think twice
before marrying male Egyptian, Jap, Mandarin or
half-caste Indian.

ALLEN, MARY HOUSTOUN ANDERSON.

000218   THE LOVE LETTERS OF A LIAR. BY MRS.
WILLIAM ALLEN. New York: Ess Ess, 1901 NUC.

ALLEN, MRS. WILLIAM. See ALLEN, MARY HOUSTOUN ANDERSON.

ALLEN, PHOEBE.

000219   COLD BLOW CORNER. London: S.P.C.K.,
[1906] BMC.

000220   THE FIRST DROP AND THE LAST. London: E.
Stock, [1909] BMC.

000221   THE FORBIDDEN ROOM: OR, "MINE ANSWER WAS
MY DEED". London: W. Gardner, [1901] BMC.

000222   GRANFER GARLAND. London: S.P.C.K., [1906]
BMC.

000223   HER SILVER WEDDING DAY. London: S.P.C.K.,
[1897] BMC.

000224   THE LIPS OF A FOOL. A STORY FOR MOTHERS'
MEETINGS. London: S.P.C.K., [1899] BMC.

000225   MEG: A CHATTEL. A TRUE STORY. London: S.
P. C. K., [1902] BMC.

000226   THE MYSTERY OF COXFOLLY. London: W.
Gardner, 1908 BMC.

000227   THE 'OLD ORDER CHANGETH' ETC. London:
Masters, 1908 BMC.

TLS--domestic novel promoting the observance of
Sunday.

000228   A PENNYWORTH OF KINDNESS. London:
S.P.C.K., [1900] BMC.

000229   THE PICK OF THE BASKET, ETC. London:
S.P.C.K., 1902 BMC. New York: E. & J. B. Young, 1902
PW.

ALLIOTT, MRS. JAMES BINGHAM.

000230   THE DOWAGER LADY TREMAINE. London: Elliot
Stock, 1895 BMC.

ACAD 49:218. Spiritualism

000231   A LIFE-BOY'S DIARY. London: Elliot Stock,
1910 BMC.

000232   "THOU SHALT NOT SURELY DIE." A ROMANCE.
London: Simpkin, Marshall, [1900] BMC.

000233   A WOMAN WITH A HISTORY IN HER FACE.
London: Simpkin, Marshall, 1894 BMC.

ALLONBY, EDITH.

000234   THE FULFILLMENT. London: Greening, 1905
BMC.

ATH--heroine is schoolmistress and novelist. Reviewer
feels novel is product of disordered mind: "Miss
Allonby died in order that her book might be issued
exactly as she wrote it... in the circumstances it was
a pity to publish the book at all." Allonby killed
herself.

000235   JEWEL SOWERS; A NOVEL [ANONYMOUS].
London: Greening, 1903 BMC NUC.

000236   MARIGOLD. A STORY. BY THE AUTHOR OF
"JEWEL SOWERS" [ANONYMOUS]. London: Greening, 1905
BMC.

ALLPORT, ELLEN.

000237   THE DESIRE OF THE MOTH. BY CAPEL VANE.
London: R. Bentley, 1895 BMC.

LW 27:60. Passionate Italian woman in loveless
marriage abandons husband and child for lawless love.
History repeats itself with deserted daughter. Moral
tone.

ALLSTON, MARGARET, pseud. See BERGENGREN, ANNA (FARQUHAR).

ALLYN, EUNICE GIBBS. United States.

000238   ONE THOUSAND SMILES. [Dubuque]: [M. S.
Hardie], [c1898] NUC.

ALMIRALL, N. See ALMIRALL, NINA LOUISE.

ALMIRALL, NINA LOUISE. B. 1877. United States.

000239   THE MASTER-FEELING: THE STORY OF AGATHA
PEYNTON. BY N. ALMIRALL. Boston: R. G. Badger, 1903
NUC.

Woman of dominant disposition but she gives in in the
end to her guardian "changes her opinion about the
strength of women's wills." 12-5-03 PW

ALMY, CHARLOTTE WALES.

000240   MARRAQUITTA: A ROMANCE OF MONTE CARLO.
London: H.J. Drane, [1905] BMC.

Bachelor and trusting Italian girl "crudish" tale TLS
203,05

ALSOP, GULIELMA FELL. B. 1881.

000241   MY CHINESE DAYS. Boston: Little, Brown,
1918 BMC NUC. London: Hutchinson, [1920] BMC.

SP Am. woman Dr. in China, Adventures in flood and
fire, etc.
China--Soc. life & cust.
Missions--China DS721

ALTIERI, OLGA CANTACUZENE. B. 1843.

000242   MY INDIAN SUMMER. BY PRINCESS OLGA
CANTACUZENE ALTIERI. London: A. anc C. Black, 1894 NUC
BMC. (Tr. Agnes Euan-Smith.)

Estate of Ventaglia, Flo. Father and daughter. Father
too interested in people to care for business. The
estate begins to fail. Daughter becomes very attached
to woman who lives in nearby estate. She's a woman who
does not love her husband, but loves instead a young
officer that the younger woman (the daughter) also
loves. The older woman talks the officer into marrying
Palma (the daughter). He dies, Palma's left with a
daughter. She writes her life story to a cousin whose
appearance brings "the real tragedy." CR 24:231

AMBER, MILES, pseud. See SICKERT, ELLEN MELICENT (COBDEN).

AMES, ELEANOR MARIA (EASTERBROOK). 1831-1908. United
States.

000243   LIBRA: AN ASTROLOGICAL ROMANCE. BY
ELEANOR KIRK. Brooklyn: Eleanor Kirk, [1896] NUC.

PW 8-8-96. The influence of the planets on the
characters in the story. Elizabeth is a Libra; hero is
a Capricorn. She sighs for freedom; he would control.
"The story ends with the girl's refusal to promise to
"obey" the man she is going to wed.

AMINOFF, CONSTANCE LEONIE CAROLINE (BORGSTROM). B. 1870.

000244   THE BROAD WALK. BY LEONIE AMINOFF.
London: Constable, 1912 BMC.

ATH-love in a placid backwater of Russia.
TLS-told by daughter wooed by Englishman.

AMINOFF, LEONIE. See AMINOFF, CONSTANCE LEONIE CAROLINE
(BORGSTROM).

AMORY, ESMERIE.

000245   THE EPISTOLARY FLIRT. IN FOUR EXPOSURES.
Chicago: Way and Williams, 1896 NUC BMC.

BKM 4:374. Subtle, witty. Two poets, male and female
begin exchange of aesthetic, impersonal, flattering
letters, another poet looks on. Then they meet.
CR 29:383. Two versifiers, she a flirt, and a poet.

ANDERSON, ADA (WOODRUFF). B. 1860. United States.

000246   THE HEART OF THE RED FIRS; A STORY OF THE
PACIFIC NORTHWEST. Boston: Little, Brown, 1908 NUC.

NYT--quote from book on Alice - "strong in executive
ability, clear-headed."
PW-Northwest
BKM Alice Hunter and sister brought up by a judge in
Puget Sound Country. She becomes a teacher and thinks
she will marry the judge out of gratitude, but she
marries the man she loves. She fights a forest fire,
rescues her husband and finds his lost claim. POV?

000247   THE RIM OF THE DESERT. Boston: Little,
Brown, 1915 BMC NUC.

about a widow PW 4-17-15
Alaskan mining expert's love for his dead male friend,
hatred for the widow who he feels deserves punishment
for her treatment of the dead man. Forces her to
finish her husband's great project.
This Mrs. Weatherbee, so selfish at the beginning
finds her true character at the end. NYT

000248   THE STRAIN OF WHITE. Boston: Little,
Brown, 1909 NUC. Toronto: Musson Book, [1909] NUC.

"heroine the daughter of an American soldier and a
Yakima Indian Maid." R OF R June 1909
educated "half breed" woman and her nobility PW

ANDERSON, AGNES.

000249   "JOHNNIE" OF QUEEN MARY'S ARMY AUXILIARY
CORPS [ANONYMOUS]. London: Heath, Cranton, [1920] BMC

NUC. (BMC: Elizabeth S. Johnston. Biog?)

ANDERSON, CELIA. United States.

000250   JULE MAGHEE'S ANARCHY. Mobile, Ala.: 1892
NUC.

ANDERSON, MARY.

000251   IN THE PROMISED LAND. London: Downey,
1898 BMC.

ATH 111:626. Biblical romance. Jericho. Heroine
notorious figure from the Bible. Contemporary with
Joshua. Who?
SR 85:825. Story of Rahab, the prostitute. She falls
for one of Joshua's spies, failing to win his
affection, she plots his murder, fails in this.
Repentance follows, and at Joshua's suggestion she
starts a rescue society.

000252   OTHELLO'S OCCUPATION: A NOVEL. London:
Chatto and Windus, 1895 BMC.

story of Othello before he meets Desdemona---all his
advents. before he settles down. A Morocco maiden
Marisa shares his fortunes.
ACAD 48:144

000253   A SON OF NOAH. London: Digby, Long,
[1893] BMC.

Story of Shem, Noah's son in the English of James I
Bible. He's gentle in love, terrible in war. Plenty of
fighting, the heroine becomes his wife. Ends with the
Deluge. SR 75, 519.

000254   TALES OF THE ROCK. London: Downey, 1897
BMC.

ANDERSON, MRS. FINLEY. United States.

000255   A WOMAN WITH A RECORD: A NOVEL. New York:
G. W. Dillingham, 1896 NUC.

PW 12-5-96. First person account of the life of an
adventuress. Lenoir lives in New York, is witty,
cynical, enjoys gambling, dinners, theatres etc. One
of the lovers is stabbed by a jealous friend.

ANDERSON, STELLA (BENSON). 1892-1933. United Kingdom.

000256   I POSE. BY STELLA BENSON. London:
Macmillan, 1915 NUC BMC. New York: Macmillan, 1916
NUC.

Gardener and Suffragette. he becomes a lover, she goes
on with her work PW 1/22/16: 295
NYT witty epigrammatic
BKM " Whimsical fooling carried out with refined
grotesquery and delicate touch" The Gardener and a
Suffragette carrying "a mustard colored bag of
sinister implication" travel together, go to the
Trinity Islands, meet many people, have adventures.
She has an overmastering obsession to do something
with the contents of the bag. (she is symbol of
English violent suffrage.)
Heroine, a militant suffragette. "Should probably be
called a suffrage novel" TLS
"descr of slums and its inhabitants" ATH
"expresses the sentiments of a clever and untamed
young generation" The author "writes in the pen of an
impudent and assertive young woman." ACAD
"She not only lets us know what she thinks of her
character but constantly intervenes with comments and
asides and nods and nudges and even recitals of her
own experiences." Confesses that she loves her
heroine, the militant suffragette, a great deal. Male
principal character an insufferable egoist yet can
show her attracted to an unworthy young man whom she
shakes off SPEC

000257   LIVING ALONE. BY STELLA BENSON. London:
Macmillan, 1919 BMC NUC.

intrusion of what is more real into the real world: "A
witch rides a broomstick in an air raid; breaks into
community meetings; sets respectable ladies doing the
oddest things; complicates life terribly for grocers
and policemen and people of that sort" "effect of a
little truth to self upon truth made up of codes and
conventions" the novel is "out of proportion
destructive." TLS
Angela, a witch, caretaker of small general shop, part
convent, monastery, nursing home, college for those
who wish to be alone. She's poor, clever always

radiant. ATH
A fantasy. The scene alternately the London streets
and a magic boarding house on an island in the Thames;
"Satire of a civilization that engages illogically in
war is mingled with uproarious farce, as when during
an air raid, the dead come out of their graves
thinking it is the last day" BAKER 32, p. 50
SR-fantasy about the witch who visits a committee and
brings to the surface their discontent. They visit her
at the house of Living Alone

000258   THIS IS THE END. BY STELLA BENSON.
London: Macmillan, 1917 BMC NUC.

War background; people's daydreams TLS
Jay is a bus conductor, and idealist. Not a heroine
(author says she's never met one) Jay takes nothing
for granted; to everything, asks why. LBKM
She escapes from high society to be a bus driver. ATH
She and brother are wards to robust and self centered
feminist novelist who is very domestic in real life.
This Mrs. Gustus turns her whole life into material
for novels. Jay is a rebel vs conventions domestic and
other. Proves her independence and almost "embraces
one of the modern extra-marital arrangements" She and
brother leave their guardian; contacts with people in
slums. Jay has high ideals, holds on to these until
war shatters her secret dream world. Brother dies in
war. She gives up. "Slumps into" marriage and
respectabity. BKM

ANDERTON, DAISY. United States.

000259   COUSIN SADIE. Boston: Stratford, 1920
NUC.

ANDREWS, ANNULET. See OHL, MAUDE ANNULET (ANDREWS).

ANDREWS, KATHERINE.

000260   STEPHEN KYRLE. AN AUSTRALIAN STORY.
London: T. F. Unwin, 1901 BMC.

Passionate woman destined to prove his evil genius.
ATH 11-30-01
BAKER 13-162

ANDREWS, MARIAN.

000261   AS WE SOW. A WEST COUNTRY DRAMA. BY
CHRISTOPHER HARE. London: Osgood, 1897 BMC.

000262   BROKEN ARCS: A WEST COUNTRY CHRONICLE. BY
CHRISTOPHER HARE. London and New York: Harper, 1898
BMC.

Rustic love story. Wicked squire wants son to clear
his debts by marriage. The vicar's daughter claims the
son. She has trouble when he's off in the Crimean war
and she keeps her promise to conceal their marriage.
LIT 1:84

000263   FELICITA: A ROMANCE OF OLD SIENA. BY
CHRISTOPHER HARE. London and New York: Harper, 1904
BMC. New York: F. A. Stokes, [1909] NUC.

Historical romance of 14 c Siena-traditional.

000264   HOW CYNTHIA WENT A-MAYING. A ROMANCE OF
LONG AGO WHEREIN THE SIEGE OF WARDOUR CASTLE IS TRULY
CHRONICLED. BY CHRISTOPHER HARE. London: Isbister,
1901 BMC.

000265   IN THE STRAITS OF TIME: A ROMANCE OF OLD
FRANCE. BY CHRISTOPHER HARE. London: Cassell, 1904
BMC.

A story of the Huguenots 1684.

ANDREWS, MARY RAYMOND (SHIPMAN). 1865?-1936. United
States.

000266   BETTER TREASURE. Indianapolis: Bobbs,
Merrill, 1902 NUC.

Career of a man NYT

000267   BOB AND THE GUIDES. New York: C.
Scribner's Sons, 1906 NUC.

000268   THE COUNSEL ASSIGNED. London and New
York: Bickers, 1912 BMC. New York: C. Scribner's Sons,
1912 NUC.

Abe Lincoln-Fic

000269   THE COURAGE OF THE COMMONPLACE. New York:
C. Scribner's Sons, 1911 NUC.

Centers on a young man and his scholarly work. PW
10-7-11

000270   A GOOD SAMARITAN. New York: McClure,
Phillips, 1906 NUC.

000271   HER COUNTRY. New York: C. Scribner's
Sons, 1918 NuC.

WWI

000272   A KIDNAPPED COLONY. New York and London:
Harper, 1903 BMC NUC.

Whimsical tale of the capture of an administrative
official in Bermuda. 12-5-03 PW

000273   THE LIFTED BANDAGE. New York: C.
Scribner's Sons, 1910 NUC.

000274   THE MARSHAL. Indianapolis: Bobbs-Merrill,
[c1912] BMC NUC.

BKM-tr. male hero.
France-Hist-Fic.

000275   THE PERFECT TRIBUTE. New York: Scribner,
1906 BMC NUC.

PW-Lincoln & dying soldiers. Story dealing with
Lincoln's Gettysburg speech.

000276   THE THREE THINGS; THE FORGE IN WHICH THE
SOUL OF A MAN WAS TESTED. Boston: Little, Brown, 1915
NUC BMC.

NYT-Male hero, inspirational; rel.

000277   VIVE L'EMPEREUR. New York: C. Scribner's
Sons., 1902 NUC.

historical, focus on a woman.

ANGELI, HELENE ROSSETTI, jt. au. See AGRESTI, OLIVIA
ROSSETTI AND HELENE ROSSETTI ANGELI.

ANGELL, BRYAN MARY (DOYLE). B. 1877.

000278   THE EPISODES OF MARGE: MEMOIRS OF A
HUMBLE ADVENTURESS. BY H. RIPLEY CROMARSH. 1903 BMC.

000279   THE SECRET OF THE MOOR COTTAGE. BY H.
RIPLEY CROMARSH. Boston: Small, Maynard, 1906 NUC.
London: 1907 BMC.

"A story written by the sister of A. Conan Doyle. The
plot holds a mystery which involves a beautiful young
woman who had wedded and later killed a villainous
Russian count. An unprofessional sleuth is on the
track of the tangle, and works out the puzzle only to
satisfy a very justifiable curiosity." BRD

ANGELLOTTI, MARION POLK. United States.

000280   THE BURGUNDIAN; A TALE OF OLD FRANCE. New
York: Century, 1912 BMC NUC.

PW--Hist. Heroine disguised as man becomes best
swordsman in Provence. Goes to Paris as woman, plays
for high stakes--love not ambition is worthwhile
NYT her name is Rosemonde of Provence, "wild slip of a
girl" Schemes with craftiest of princes, fights with
mightiest of warriors BKM

000281   THE FIREFLY OF FRANCE. New York: Century,
1918 BMC NUC.

PW--love, spies, male hero

000282   HARLETTE. New York: Century, 1913 NUC.

"Robert of Normandy, called "the Devil" falls in love
with Harlette, a peasant woman of steadfast heart, the
only being who does not fear him. Robert has had his
brother poisoned and suffers tortures of remorse.
Harlette consults a sooth-sayer, who counsels Robert
to make a pilgrimage to Jerusalem seeking forgiveness
at the Holy Sepulchre. Before going he proclaims
Harlette's son, afterwards, William the Conqueror, his
heir. He finds peace, but dies on his way home and
Harlette goes back to her obscurity." PW 83 6/28/13
p.2202

000283   SIR JOHN HAWKWOOD; A TALE OF THE WHITE
COMPANY IN ITALY. New York: R. F. Fenno, [c1911] NUC.

ANGELO, FLORENCE.

000284   THE GREATNESS OF JOHN. London: J. Long,
1914 BMC.

TLS- Anglo-Indian society, extra-marital love affairs.

ANICHKOVA, ANNA MITROFANOVNA (AVINOVA).

000285   THE SHADOW OF THE HOUSE. BY IVAN
STRANNIK. New York: McClure, Phillips, 1906 BMC NUC.
(Tr. Emma A. Clinton)

NYT--young woman, ardent, unconventional marries a
blackguard as a result of her uneducated state,
typical of European families. Falls for another man,
asks for divorce, husband will take child, she refuses
to give up child and so must resign herself to life of
misery.

ANNA CATHARINA, pseud. See REBEK, LILLIE.

ANNE, EDITH CHARLTON.

000286   ONE SUMMER HOLIDAY: A FAIRY STORY.
London: J. Macqueen, [1898] BMC.

000287   TWO WOMEN AND A MAN: A SOCIETY SKETCH OF
TO-DAY. BY ELLAM FENWICKE ALLAN. London: W. Scott,
[1897] BMC.

000288   A WOMAN OF MOODS: A SOCIAL
CINEMATOGRAPHE. London: Burns and Oates, 1897 BMC.

"novel of half a dozen purposes" RC sm. falconry are
two, Main one: vs marr. for those with an hereditary
illness. Valeria Villiers English mother wed to Ital.
marquis, raised in convent, became a companion, won
(amicably) her dearest friend's lover. Ideal marr.
Then Valeria learns her father died mad. Shuts herself
off, studies the subject. Then one night, kissed
husband goodbye, cut mother's throat, delivered a
still born, threw herself in the river but not before
writing to her two elder children not to marry. Also
designed a new order for these women who won't marry.
ACAD 52 Fic Sup 61.
LIT 2:451. A very good and beautiful woman, hereditary
insanity brings her to tragic end. Her children,
according to her wish, take vows of celibacy. Veronica
founds a new order, based on the theory that "as there
are more women than can marry, only the healthiest in
mind and body should undertake the responsibility of
continuing the race."

ANNESLEY, MAUDE. United Kingdom.

000289   ALL AWRY. London: Mills and Boon, 1911
BMC.

TLS: "Clo" Mayne hates being a girl; hates being
"ladyish", hates being courted. Goes to sea disguised
as a man. Is assistant purser aboard a ship that is
shipwrecked. Her rescuer wins her.

000290   BLIND UNDERSTANDING. London: Duckworth,
1915 BMC. New York: Duffield, 1916 NUC.

diary form--diary of a man TLS

000291   THE DOOR OF DARKNESS. London, New York:
J.°Lane, 1908 BMC NUC.

PW--Monte Carlo, occultism, romance
TLS o
ACAD--Paoli who has drunk the elixer of life has a
horror of marrying Berthe who will die while he goes
on living thru the ages

000292   SHADOW-SHAPES. New York: John Lane, 1911
NUC. London: Methuen, [1911] BMC.

Man dying of incurable disease gets dr. (whom he
suspects loves his wife) to care for him for he claims
he's hypnotized his wife to die when he does. Story of
battle of the two over her.? PW 7-1-11
BKM 33 (1911) 649-50

000293   THE SPHINX IN THE LABYRINTH. New York:
Duffield, 1913 NUC. London: Mills and Boon, 1913 BMC.

After wife dies, other woman won't marry him because
she refuses to hurt the dead woman's soul ATH
"Story of the perplexing question a man faces who is

13

actually in love with, and loved by, two women. One's sympathy is aroused by the self-sacrifice and generosity of the one, and the noble character of the other." PW 84:1525
Man realizes the possibility of loving and being loved by 2 women--his invalid wife and a "girlfriend who stays with them; his wife realizes the possibility also." TLS

000294   THIS DAY'S MADNESS. London: Methuen, [1909] BMC NUC.

Pamela Carmichael wed to dull Scot loves a weak musician and later another stronger man. The Scot is killed in an accident. TLS
"machine-like" heroine but she refuses to marry when husband dies, convinced to do so at end ATH

000295   WIND ALONG THE WASTE. New York: J. Lane, 1910 NUC. London: Methuen, 1910 BMC.

Clandestine passion of an American Parisian woman (artist and woman of fashion) for a ruffian. He takes her out on his thugging jaunts at night. When the guillotine claims him, she has another lover immediately-the son of that ruffian. Replete with horrors. NYT
BM--Gondo in Paris mixed up with an Apache.
TLS-She is an artist, leads a double life as his companion, has pitiable end. Lurid.
ACAD-dissatisfied with her painting, she meets one of a group of Apaches, Faux-Col, and tries to trifle with him; he will have none of it and knocks her down. She then disguises herself in blue spectacles and becomes honored in Apache circles as Verre Bleu. Downfall at end.
LBKM-Gonda in one escapade escapes daringly from prison. Faux-Col is executed and Gonda pays dearly for her escapades, author is relentless moralist.

000296   THE WINE OF LIFE. London and New York: J. Lane, 1908 NUC BMC.

divorce, her feelings toward other men are "unpleasant" PW 12-14-07
revolts against the injustice of the charges of divorce (innocent) launches on a voyage of amorous advent. TLS
ACAD--Interesting fem with "ideas about love"

ANSTRUTHER, E. H., pseud. See SQUIRE, EILEEN HARRIET ANSTRUTHER (WILKINSON).

ANSTRUTHER, EVA ISABELLA HENRIETTA. 1869-1935.

000297   THE INFLUENCE OF MARS. London: G. Richards, 1900 BMC.

LBKM 18:189. Dedicated to "all those on whom war's shadow has rested." 12 war stories.
SP 85:181. War as a purifier is what she wishes to demonstrate.

000298   A LADY IN WAITING: BEING CERTAIN LITTLE SCENES OF MIRTHFUL TRAGEDY AND OF TRAGICAL MIRTH THAT AN ACTOR OF SMALL ACCOUNT IN THE HUMAN COMEDY HAD LEISURE TO OBSERVE. London: Smith, Elder, 1904 BMC.

ATH-a semi-independent woman who stays with her married friends, analysis and observations of them.
ACAD-chronicle of modern manners delicate humor
Unselfsih woman, the hard life of women, the lady "finds her affinity" in the end? LBKM 27-8,273.

ANTHONY, GERALDINE. D. 1912. United States.

000299   FOUR-IN-HAND: A STORY OF SMART LIFE IN NEW YORK AND AT A COUNTRYCLUB. New York: D. Appleton, 1903 BMC NUC.

PW: Effie is impulsive, undisciplined. Begins by disliking the man she eventually marries. At one point she punches him with her fist.

000300   A VICTIM OF CIRCUMSTANCES. New York & London: Harper, 1901 BMC NUC.

CR: "An indomitable old lady governs her family with an iron hand.
DIAL "Its substance is frothy."
NYT: Madame Trevor-The "old lady" is a strong character. The younger heroine is married to the wrong man.

ANTONA, ANNETTA HALLIDAY. United States.

000301   CAPTIVES OF CUPID: A STORY OF OLD DETROIT. Detroit: J F. Eby, 1896 NUC.

ANTONY, C. M. See WOODCOCK, CATHERINE MARY ANTONY.

ANTROBUS, C. L. See ANTROBUS, CLARA LOUISA.

ANTROBUS, CLARA LOUISA. United Kingdom.

000302   QUALITY CORNER. A STUDY OF REMORSE. BY C. L. ANTROBUS. London: Chatto & Windus, 1901 BMC. New York: G. P. Putnam's Sons, [1902] NUC.

domestic novel.
BAKER-male hero 13-164.

000303   THE STONE EZEL. London: Chatto & Windus, 1910 BMC.

TLS-love story?

000304   WILDERSMOOR. A NOVEL. BY C. L. ANTROBUS. London: R. Bentley, 1895 BMC NUC. New York: G.P. Putnam's Sons, 1901 NUC BMC.

murder story NYT
"mild, innocuous" tragedy: "mystery plot, love tale, sociological criticism and rustic humor combined." BAKER 03,68
SR-Murder in which hero lets another take the blame.

ANTROBUS, SUZANNE. See ROBINSON, SUZANNE (ANTROBUS).

APLINGTON, KATE ADELE (SMITH). United States.

000305   PILGRIMS OF THE PLAINS. A ROMANCE OF THE SANTA FE TRAIL. Chicago: F. G. Browne, 1913 BMC NUC.

"Tells of the trail across the prairies in Kit Carson's day. Delia Randall with her brother, who is not strong, go with a trading caravan. They have adventures in plenty, all of which are told in Delia's diary, which also records her love story." PW

APPLETON, AMELIA, pseud. See HAWES, AMELIA APPLETON (PRENDERGAST).

APTED, EVELYN.

000306   CHARLES QUANTRILL. London: Methuen, 1915 BMC.

ARDAGH, W. M. See ARDAGH, WINIFRED MARY.

ARDAGH, WINIFRED MARY. United Kingdom.

000307   THE KNIGHTLY YEARS. BY W. M. ARDAGH. London and New York: J. Lane, 1912 BMC NUC.

PW-historical romance.
TLS
ACAD

000308   THE MAGADA. BY W. M. ARDAGH. London, New York: J. Lane, 1910 NUC BMC.

Historical romance. PW
TLS-
ACAD

ARDEN, JOAN.

000309   A CHILDHOOD. Cambridge: Bowes and Bowes, 1913 BMC NUC.

Sensations & experiences of her childhood at boarding school in London. ATH

ARMFIELD, ANNE CONSTANCE (SMEDLEY). 1881-1941. United Kingdom.

000310   AN APRIL PRINCESS. BY CONSTANCE SMEDLEY. New York: Dodd, Mead, 1903 NUC. London: Cassell, 1903 BMC.

Her sparkIng audacity, (makes Daisy Miller look like a prude) daring adventure, more than unconventional yet completely, innocently wayward "in real life she would shake to its centre the most tolerant society" "only bolts and bars could protect her reputation." NYT 03, 653.
impatience with domesticity, her adventures with several men. ACAD 64, 366.
refers to men as pals ACAD 64, 414.
to escape from convention, for new sensation, to fall in & out of love as often as possible; outrages

everyone. TLS, 129, 03

her own. ATH

000311   THE BOUDOIR CRITIC. London: Harper, 1903
BMC.

000312   COMMONERS' RIGHTS; A NOVEL. BY CONSTANCE
SMEDLEY (MRS. MAXWELL ARMFIELD). London: Chatto &
Windus, 1912 BMC NUC.

TLS-purpose is to encourage a "love of righteousness",
deals with people's rights & common lands & relations
between husband & wife from different walks of life.
SR-aesthetic radicalism is her creed, people's rights.
Cause of the female suffragist is touched upon
lightly, in a moderate manner.
LBKM-Family life in its relation to the individual and
to the community.
ATH--O

000313   CONFLICT. BY CONSTANCE SMEDLEY. London:
A. Constable, 1907 BMC. New York: Moffat, Yard, 1907
NUC.

"The heroine of this novel is a business woman who
rejoices in her economic independence. Her love of
work & contempt for "beauty culture" are a constant
source of amazement to her friends, & the discussions
that arise are amusing & effective. There are some
serious defects in the management of the plot, but
some of the situations are telling." FRANKLIN
Conflict of feminist ideas in mod soc by a woman who
uses her sensuality to get a man and a woman who wants
to develop her ind., energy, LBKM 4-07, 31
Mary a born fighter, a conscience, much common sense,
craving for work. ACAD TLS
Mary Von Heyton does get brain fever. Must rest, meets
"unpleasant Bohemians" BKM 25 (1907) 392
Stenographer so good her boss leaves her the business.
a non-conforming actress-Rosalys "an attack on the
false ideals of womanhood." Woman needs love & work
NYT

000314   THE DAUGHTER; A LOVE STORY. BY CONSTANCE
SMEDLEY. New York: Moffat, Yard, 1908 NUC. London: A.
Constable, 1908 BMC.

Delia Willett young woman involved in women's
emancipation, socialism. Author's POV? Tabor seems
convinced that heroine abandons her feminism.--BKM 27
1908.
ACAD Marries a man she has never seen for 10,000
pounds to be donated to the Neo-Suffragist Soc. Then
what?
SR-"Final tableau shows us Delia, the ideal wife,
reading fairy stories to her 3 babies in the afternoon
& addressing mass meetings at night."
ATH-converts her husband. Portraits of various types
of feminists-1 into scientific housewifery 1 a
repellent study of the earlier "women's rights" woman
Marriage proposal: for 10,000 pounds if she will marry
& keep house for a laborer for 1 year-he masquerades
as the laborer."... besides having a suffrage worker
for its heroine, gives a vivid picture of the conflict
in feminine ideals between the older & younger
generation. The characters on both sides are drawn
with humor, & while the writer plainly shares the
views of her independent young people, she makes it
clear that they themsleves are no better than their
elders-that it is simply the changed spirit of the
times that enables them to be more useful & happy."
FRANKLIN

000315   THE EMOTIONS OF MARTHA. London: Religious
Tract Society, 1911 BMC.

Girl restless in her home life yearns for independence
in London. TLSHer emotions concern ambitions in art.
SP. "breakdown of her aspirations under the ordeal of
artistic training"

000316   FOR HEART-O'-GOLD. A ROMANTIC NOVEL.
London & New York: Harper, 1904 BMC.

ATH-Allegory
ACAD-fairy tale for children.a romance of Princes &
princesses. LBKM p. 43, 29-30

000317   THE JUNE PRINCESS. London: Chatto &
Windus, 1909 BMC.

The Princess organizes an International society to
bring women together from different countries. Much
sprightly dialogue on subject of women. TLS
Frank, fascinating up to date young person; she's bent
on career as only way of life worth having. Accepts a
position which brings her individuality & a flat of

000318   THE LARGER GROWTH (MOTHERS AND FATHERS).
New York: E. P. Dutton, [c1911] NUC.

Isolated family in small town. 4 children raised in a
secluded home life but they all feel the urgings of
the new freedoms. Each finds place & work in the
world. Thesis "The family ought to be the training
ground in all that makes for the health & happiness
and unity of the whole human family" TLS
Mr. & Mrs. Maddox try hard to be companions to their
children, but ruin their relationship with other
people. Review leaves unclear whether parents' or
children's relationships with others are ruined. SP
Agnostics, educate children this way. Their over
concern drives the family apart. ATH

000319   MOTHERS AND FATHERS. A NOVEL. BY MRS.
MAXWELL ARMFIELD (CONSTANCE SMEDLEY). London: Chatto &
Windus, 1911 BMC NUC.

000320   NEW WINE AND OLD BOTTLES. London,
Leipsic: T. F. Unwin, 1913 BMC.

Penelope Valentine, after a stay in Italy, returns to
Scroose. Sets out to become popular with the
townspeople, organizes a pageant. Love comes. The real
story is the undercurrents of life in Scroose. ACAD.

000321   ON THE FIGHTING LINE. BY CONSTANCE
SMEDLEY. London & New York: G. P. Putnam's Sons., 1915
BMC NUC.

"European social conditions & tendencies" BKM 41 1915
independent woman, publishes her father's poetry,
writes a journal about her work in London-PW 2-20-15
Battle of woman to earn her daily bread; Minnie Blunt
orphan expert stenographer. She works for Alliance
Trust & believes in it, in the womanly woman, success,
the whole bit. Her disillusionment is the plot. Meets
a radical who radicalizes her on women's problems. NYT
"interesting commentary on woman in business." draws
25 shillings a week, banks 3 every Saturday proud to
be part of the Empire. Meets suffragist, talks to lots
of people about the war. End: "finds happiness with
the poet" TLS

000322   REDWING: A NOVEL. BY CONSTANCE SMEDLEY.
London: G. Allen & Unwin, 1916 BMC NUC.

TLS-Story of Mimsy, who left home at 17 "for some sort
of place, odd indeed with odd sort of people." She was
nearly caught by an explorer with fascinating manners,
but finally finds her right mate. There is a good deal
about a women's club & many feminine arts &
subtleties. dress becomes a weapon & the whole book
typifies the modern revolt of women. Redwing is boy
she has to look after.

000323   RUTH'S MARRIAGE. London: R. T. S., 1912
BMC.

ATH-influence of trade and prestige
TLS-dutiful & high-minded Ruth Spence "happiness is
won by simple life & devotion to duty"

000324   SERVICE. A DOMESTIC NOVEL. London: Chatto
& Windus, 1910 BMC.

TLS-Phebe, the maid, too good to be true, does in the
socially prejudiced self mother love in middle class
family, even, by implication, the whole idea of the
family. "daring, almost malicious book"
LBKM in Him service is perfect freedom, they also
serve who only stand & wait? She was offered a poultry
farm of her own when her mother died, turned it down &
became a servant.
SP reviewer is indignant over Phebe's hours of work (5
am-midnight) over which the author, Phebe, & Sturge
family seem very complacent.

000325   UNA AND THE LIONS. A NOVEL. London:
Chatto & Windus, 1914 BMC.

LBKM-young woman teacher full of dreams about travel
wins prize in limerick contest, a month's tour of
northern Italy, story of her adventures.
TLS-"simple prattling diary of a school-mistress."
Adventure mostly among women...but there is the man at
the end." "Other schoolmistresses will enjoy it best."

000326   THE WAYS OF HER HOUSEHOLD. London:
Headley, [1914] BMC.

000327   WOMAN: A FEW SHRIEKS! SETTING FORTH THE

NECESSITY OF SHRIEKING TILL THE SHRIEKS BE HEARD. BY X. [Letchworth, Herts]: [Garden City Press], [1907] BMC NUC. (Attributed to Anne C. S. Armfield in NUC.)

Appendix by Mrs. Philip Snowden

ARMFIELD, MRS. MAXWELL. See ARMFIELD, ANNE CONSTANCE (SMEDLEY).

ARMOUR, FRANCES J. Nationality Unknown.

000328   THE BROTHERHOOD OF WISDOM. New York: J. Lane, 1908 NUC. London: Brown, Langham, 1908 BMC.

PW-astral bodies, etc.
TLS-ditto

ARMOUR, MARGARET.

000329   AGNES OF EDINBURGH. London: A. Melrose, 1911 NUC.

cheery reading about little Agnes. TLS

ARMSTRONG, ANNE AUDUBON (WETZELL). 1872-1958. United States.

000330   THE SEAS OF GOD; A NOVEL. New York: Hearst's International Library, [c1915] NUC. London: Mills & Boon, 1916 BMC.

TLS-Lydia, beautiful and alluring, varies her economic struggle in various capacities by decoying married men from their wives.
young Virginian woman finds it necessary to leave her sheltered home & make her own way. "sympathetic realism" "much char study" "remarkable novel" NYT
Lydia is a "distinctly unlovely child" except for her devotion to her father. When he dies, she alienates herself from all in that small town. Friends would support her in her home; she makes her own arrangements for a wider, freer life (1) travels for a publishing co. & appoints agents to sell books. But her youth & beauty get in the way. (2) tries to make a marriage (3) at last, meets a young married man "without hesitation or conjunction, her fall promptly follows" (4) for a brief period lives a respectable life; but the story "is that of one of the hetairai-and it is told simply, plainly, with a realism and a power that are almost appalling." "There is nothing of the white slavery theory here. Choosing a freer life put her in the way of prostitution. The initiative always came from her." "A liaison is with her purely a commerical matter" no sent. illusions "With open eyes she pays the price for a luxurious life" Love for child redeems her. "masculine nature makes a bad showing in the story."
"The problem of a southern girl of refinement left alone to earn her living" BKM 41 1915
deserted with a child "takes the line of least resistance till she learns about her mother ; the whole battle of char vs. heredity PW 4-24-15

ARMSTRONG, ANNIE E.

000331   MARIAN; OR THE ABBEY GRANGE. London: Blackie, 1892 BMC.

000332   MONA ST. CLAIRE. London & New York: F. Warne, 1897 BMC.

The troubles and social truimphs of a family of girls whose father though arist, must live in genteel poverty. Mona has a poor nervous system tends to sleep walk. She's good-helps her brother. She also inherits money from her grandfather and can at last do the philanthropic work she wants-establish a convalescent home. Other sisters are more worldly; Irene, Daphne and Hilda. SP 79:566.

000333   MY LADIES THREE. London and New York: F. Warne, 1898 BMC.

000334   THREE BRIGHT GIRLS: A STORY OF CHANCE AND MISCHANCE. London: Blackie, 1892 BMC NUC.

000335   VIOLET VEREKER'S VANITY. London: Blackie, 1897 BMC.

A study of snobbishness. Violet and her woman friend are aloof to new members of the community, people who are connected with soap-boiling. But Violet soon changes her mind. SP 78:27.

ARMSTRONG, ELISA. See BENGOUGH, ELISA (ARMSTRONG).

ARMSTRONG, ESTELLE AUBREY. United States.

000336   THE INDIAN SPECIAL. New York: H. Lechner, [c1912] NUC.

PW-Young woman works on Indian Reservation.

ARMSTRONG, FRANCES CHARLOTTE.

000337   CHANGED LOTS; OR, NOBODY CARES. London: Griffith, Farran, [1891] BMC.

Two children one aristocrat one poor change frocks, and the change in the two girls remains undetected for several years. Gipsy girl (the poor one) turns out to be twin sister of the other. SP 67:893

000338   A FAIR CLAIMANT: A STORY FOR GIRLS. London: Blackie, 1894 BMC.

000339   OLD CALEB'S WILL; OR THE FORTUNES OF THE CARDEW FAMILY. London: Jarrold, [1893] BMC.

SR 72:412 Temperance novel.

ARMSTRONG, ISABEL JULIEN.

000340   PASSPORTS. London: T. F. Unwin, 1897 BMC.

000341   TWO ROVING ENGLISHWOMEN IN GREECE. London: S. Low, Marston, 1893 NUC BMC.

ARNOLD, ADELAIDE VICTORIA (ENGLAND). United Kingdom.

000342   THE FIDDLER. BY MRS. J. O. ARNOLD. London: A. Rivers, 1911 BMC NUC.

Sheila Delacourt marries a young dr. "beneath her" but learns to love him when fame and then misfortune fall upon him. TLS
Lady Weybourne disapproves of son's marriage, takes the child from daughter-in-law whom she considers belongs to the family, would raise the girl in such a way as to crush out her mother's characteristics. But the girl doesn't allow it. LBKM
The girl Sheila thinks her mother is dead, is very attached to her memory. Also the mother told that her child was dead. Later mother returns rich and the two meet. SP

000343   FIRE I' THE FLINT. London: A. Rivers, 1911 BMC.

LBKM-Morris dancers. Ezra's daughter becomes an artiste in this respect in London & Paris. Cecil is not a fit mate for this fine woman. Happy ending. Esther Smith becomes a fashinable dancer in London: her mental development, her 2 loves TLS
Fr. village dancer to finished artist. ATH

000344   HONOURS EASY. London: Methuen, 1912 BMC.

ATH-pleasant, amusing, love-interest.
TLS-ditto
SP-ditto

000345   MEGAN OF THE DARK ISLE. BY MRS. J. O. ARNOLD. London: A. Rivers, 1914 BMC NUC.

LBKM-David is bequeathed a house he refuses to live at because of possibility of other claimant. Megan, the ill-used wife of a disreputable poacher comes to work for him as secretary-"in his blindness"? Sinister influence provided by Mother Glynn, a reputed witch, and her evil daughter Sionel, who urges the quiet pace on to tragedy.
TLS 13:262 Megan is a "love-child"

000346   REQUITAL. BY MRS. J. O. ARNOLD. London: Methuen, [1913] NUC BMC.

TLS: subplot concerns two women authors: Mrs. Wylde and Jane Buchanan. Focus on Beatrice who marries rich old Sir Henry Dacre.
SP. The sacrifice entailed by her ambition and her loveless marriage.

ARNOLD, BIRCH, pseud. See BARTLETT, ALICE ELINOR (BOWEN).

ARNOLD, ETHEL M. Nationality Unknown.

000347   PLATONICS. A STUDY. London: Osgood, McIlvaine, 1894 NUC BMC.

SP 72:112, Supp. Three characters Ronald, Susan and Kit. Ronald loves Susan, a widow, but her "theories of

16

life" forbid marriage. Her best friend Kit comes on
the scene, weds Ronald. Susan and Kit part on this,
but later are friends again.
SP 72:511. Just as Susan is not completely able to
give up her love for Ronald, so Kit cannot give up her
friendship for Susan and the "spoilt happiness of the
one who resigns least and enjoys most is also very
vividly and subtly delineated."
ATH 103:110
PW Story of friendship of two cultured women.
Triangle: Susan Dormer keeps her reserve toward man
she loves and toward the other woman. Dies of natural
causes. SR 76:654

ARNOLD, LILIAN S. United Kingdom.

000348   ALSO JOAN. London: John Long, 1911 BMC.

a teacher; careers of two sisters. A man comes near to
wrecking ne's life. ATH

000349   THE ENCHANTING DISTANCE. London: J. Long,
1915 NUC BMC.

Patricia Case leaves her home with her aunt to earn
her living; finds the life she left best for her TLS
LBKM

000350   LIEGE LADY. A NOVEL. London: Jarrold &
Sons, 1903 BMC.

000351   THE STORM-DOG; A ROMANCE OF CORNWALL.
London: J. Long, [1912] BMC NUC.

ATH-two generations of unfortunate heroines in Cornish
family-gloomy, thankless theme.
TLS- theme of anti-religion-bleak

ARNOLD, MAUD.

000352   BLOOD ROYAL. London: Greening, 1908 BMC.

TLS-sent & morbid story of a typewriter whose
confession of a past which includes a dead baby
shocked Francis & in turn caused her flight &
insanity.
ACAD-from which she recovers & then dies

000353   A PITIFUL PART. London: Digby, Long, 1903
BMC.

LBKM -unconventional love story of a stage loving girl
& unconventional clergyman.

ARNOLD, MRS. J. O. See ARNOLD, ADELAIDE VICTORIA (ENGLAND).

ARTHUR, FRANCES BROWNE.

000354   THE AWAKENING OF BENJAMIN HAY. BY RAY
CUNNINGHAM. Stirling: Drummond's Tract Depot, [1898]
BMC.

000355   FOR GILBERT'S SAKE. BY RAY CUNNINGHAM.
Stirling: Drummond's Tract Depot, [1899] BMC.

ARTHUR, MARY LUCY. United Kingdom.

000356   THE BATON SINISTER: A STUDY OF A
TEMPERAMENT AND A TIME. BY GEORGE DAVID GILBERT.
London: J. Long, 1903 BMC.

000357   IN THE SHADOW OF THE PURPLE: A ROYAL
ROMANCE. BY GEORGE DAVID GILBERT. London: J. Long,
1902 BMC.

000358   TO MY KING EVER FAITHFUL. THE LOVE STORY
OF MRS. FITZHERBERT 1782-1837. BY GEOPGE DAVID
GILBERT. London: The Author, 1909 BMC. London: E.
Nash, 1909 NUC.

ASH, GEORGINA M. I.

000359   A BAD THREE WEEKS. BY RAYMOND JACBERNS.
London: W. Gardner, parton, 1907 BMC.

000360   BECKY COMPTON, EX-DUX. BY RAYMOND
JACBERNS. London and Edinburgh: W. and R. Chambers,
1909 BMC.

000361   AN EVERY-DAY ROMANCE. BY RAYMOND
JACBERNS. London: W. Gardner, 1910 BMC.

000362   A FAMILY GRIEVANCE. BY RAYMOND JACBERNS.
London: W. Gardner, 1904 BMC.

000363   A HARD BIT OF ROAD. BY RAYMOND JACBERNS.

London: W. Gardner, 1908 BMC.

000364   HOME FETTERS. BY RAYMOND JACBERNS.
London: Christian Knowledge Soc., [1904] BMC.

000365   HOW THINGS WENT WRONG. BY RAYMOND
JACBERNS. London: W. Gardner, 1905 BMC.

000366   ROBIN. BY RAYMOND JACBERNS. London:
Christian Knowledge Society, [1901] BMC.

000367   RULER-IN-CHIEF. BY RAYMOND JACBERNS.
London: W. Gardner, 1906 BMC.

000368   WITCH DEMONIA. BY RAYMOND JACBERNS.
London: S. Sonnenschein, 1895 BMC.

ASHFORD, DAISY. See ASHFORD, MARGARET MARY.

ASHFORD, MARGARET MARY. United Kingdom.

000369   THE YOUNG VISITERS; OR MR. SALTEENA'S
PLAN. BY DAISY ASHFORD. New York: G.H. Doran, [c1919]
NUC. London: Chatto and Windus, 1919 BMC.

Story of a man of 42 written "by a little girl of
nine" PW Much tir about authenticity of author's age.
Miss Ethel Monticue "finds a chaperone quite
superfluous when she accepts invitations to visit our
hero." PW Book Review
Mr. Salteena plans to become a real gentleman and
marry haughty Miss Monticue. "amusing, high-falutin
pictures of society" "obligations to "Ouida," BAKER
32, p. 16.
"The unaided effort in fiction of an authoress of nine
years" (Preface)

ASHTON, AIMEE.

000370   HER PRICE FOR SEEING LIFE. London:
Pearson, 1920 BS. London: Pearson's Big Three Pennies,
1936 BMC.

ASHTON, HELEN ROSALINE. 1891-1958. United Kingdom.

000371   ALMAIN. London: I. Pitman, 1914 BMC.

TLS-Bohemian art students. Male hero and "doormat"
devotion of Linny.

000372   MARSHDIKES. London: T.F. Unwin, 1917 BMC.
New York: Brentano's, 1917 NUC.

Opens with an admirable piece of conversational
fencing between men and women. Letty later wants to
marry the man, but finds another and "engages in the
political conflict" "modern, emotional" TLS
A young couple try to get a friend (male) married off
but things get complicated when the bachelor falls in
love with someone other than the woman they chose and
the woman does the same. NYT 137 4-15-17

000373   PIERROT IN TOWN. London: I. Pitman, 1913
BMC.

Anatole (Pierrot) a young Englishman calls the
conventional Londoners to work, love, youth (gospel of
youth) a kind of Peter Pan SP
Interlaced tragedies of a scientist wearied of his
work, his embittered wife Gillian (20 years his
junior) Morley Page who is Gillian's tame cat, and
Lola brilliant Jewess with her young admirer. Pierrot
youth, call of wild, Satyr-like; at one point or an
ther each character is about to prove their
independence but fate intervenes; they all end up as
they began except each is wiser and more
disillusioned. TLS

ASHTON, WINIFRED. United Kingdom.

000374   FIRST THE BLADE; A COMEDY OF GROWTH. BY
CLEMENCE DANE. London: W. Heinemann, 1918 BMC. New
York: Macmillan, 1918 NUC.

TLS-Justin Cloud has exaggeratedly (by author) male
shortcomings.
LBKM-Rev suspects that Laura, his childhood playmate,
cared more for his mother than for Justin.
SR-Development of character is followed in pair till
at last the woman finds that her love demands that the
man shall know what love is before she marries, & the
story ceases on an unresolved discord.
NYT May 19, 1918 p. 237. "The sense of a
half-pathetic, half-ironic comedy of human
relationships is admirably sustained all through the
book." Justin looks on her as a convenient person to

have around, but is "very human...blundering kindness
and absolute lack of perception."

000375   LEGEND. BY CLEMENCE DANE. London: W.
Heinemann, 1919 BMC NUC. New York: Macmillan, 1920
NUC.

chief character never appears, character develops by
converstions about her. Madala Grey dies one year
after leaving her literary set to marry. The group
gets the news; talk of her. All that is sweet in her
the group dislikes; all that is simple they can't
understand. Each mirror distorts her. Two only
understand & they are silent. One who tells the tale
is learning of her for the first time. She/we watch
the character growing out of the talk. Madala's vision
appears to the 2 silent ones in the end. we know no
one will ever now see the author except thru the eyes
of those who don't know her. TLS, 649
one of the members Anita Serle is a critic now about
to write autobiog. How could she have thrown up her
art for a mere man? group wonders. Madala -the
complete genius (author's view) wrote about
prostitution strong sex scenes Throws her blazing gift
away by falling in love ATH
LBKM-Jenny, narrator has never met Madala, heroine who
has died on night of marriage & is a novelist. Anita
her cousin & closest friend, a Boswell, really
understands nothing, Jenny does. An attack on all
hagiology; does even Jenny understand?
SR-Group cannot understand why she chose love &
marriage in stead of further lit success. Ghouls
making a fine feast of her life & manners. Malevolent
group.
BKM-Anita Searle, intimate friend, can now write
successful biography. Group is discussing Madala when
a man who loved her brings news of her death. "Dead at
26" "died in childbirth" finished Anita, and her voice
made it an unclean & shameful end. Reviewer Margaret
Emerson Bailey, says that unlike male heroes or genius
whose genius sweeps them outside the law & causes them
to fail to perceive the beauty of human relationships,
Madala's genius does not exclude a practical nature &
temperate sanity. Dane writes with an almost personal
vindictiveness against one of her sex.
NYT Jan 25 '20 p. 50. Group succeeds in creating myth
about woman, which, it is evident, her biographer will
perpetuate. A myth which undercuts her as a woman and
as a writer.

000376   REGIMENT OF WOMEN. BY CLEMENCE DANE.
London: W. Heinemann, [1917] BMC NUC. New York:
Macmillan, 1917 NUC.

"abnormal psychological manifestation-the crush." A
"vampire" woman who can produce a crush upon herself
when she wishes to feed her vanity. "Her girl devotees
are ready to lie for her, live for her, die for her"
NYT
2 teachers in a girls' school, Clare Hartill tries to
dominate Alwynne and even to point of influencing her
against a lover, but A. marries. PW 91:352 2/3/17
author shows preference for co-ed schools. Clare is
cruel, tyrant over fellow teachers & pupils. Her love
of adoration & power drove Louise Denny to suicide,
"she devoured people's souls" But author never allows
us to forget "the beauty & the attractiveness of her"
she's real "there is no touch of spite in the
portrait" TLS
"women's rule in a girls' school, of the old-fashioned
kind, contrasted with an ultra modern example of
co-ed" vs the "inquisitorial & repressive methods."
Clare-the absolutist-"but her individual interest
overwhelms the scholastic thesis. She is a human
vampire, fascinating, ruthless, feeding her cold heart
on the devotion of pet after pet." One kills self.
Psycho-analysis used to cure another girl of like
obsessions. BAKER 32, p. 128
"daily round of girls' school" mistress: Clare Hartill
who wants power over the girls. One of 13 commits
suicide because Clare alternately pets & bullies her.
Her assistant must choose between Clare & a man she
loves. Louise, well-read, yet naive. Author yet makes
us sympathize with Clare.

ASKWITH, ELLEN GRAHAM.

000377   THE DISINHERITED OF THE EARTH. BY MRS.
HENRY GRAHAM. London: A. Rivers, 1908 BMC.

TLS-Lady Verrier has system of bringing up her
children which proves disastrous. Daughter sentenced
for murdering her child. Earnest and gloomy.
ATH 0

000378   THE TOWER OF SILOAM. BY MRS. HENRY

GRAHAM. London: A. Rivers, 1905 BMC.

Two women marry two fickle, vicious, selfish men. Both
husbands and one wife are unfaithful. For this one the
lover proves just as false. The other's husband dies,
makes a 2nd loveless marriage. Nina is presented
sympathetically. ACAD 1264,05
ATH 5,719
LBKM - society novel.

ASLACHSEN, EDITH (HENDERSON) SHIELDS.

000379   A HUMAN SPIDER: A NOVEL. London: Digby
and Long, [1891] BMC.

The spider is a mesmerist with several victims. SR
8-8-91, 170

ASLING, STELLA EUGENIE. See RIIS, STELLA EUGENIE (ASLING).

ATHERTON, GERTRUDE FRANKLIN (HORN). 1857-1948. United
  States.

000380   AMERICAN WIVES AND ENGLISH HUSBANDS; A
NOVEL. New York: Dodd, Mead, 1898 NUC. London: Service
& Paton, 1898 BMC NUC.

SP 80;450. "A welcome change from the lurid
sensationalism of Patience Sparhawk." Lee marries
Cecil, an Englishman. He is involved in politics. She
is bored and is contemplating a long visit back to San
Francisco with an admirer when her father-in-law blows
his brains out. He has discovered that his American
wife (Chicago) has been supporting herself and him
with her lover's fortune. Lee decides to remain with
Cecil, dismisses her admirer.
ACAD 53:309, 394.
ATH 111:597 "...by creating a living woman, who is
human and not a mere bag of views, she makes
intelligible the point which Sarah Grand and others
wish to make, and goes far towards proving it. She
brings her heroine from America, where the women are,
as a rule, far better educated than in England, and
where they have far more independence of thought and
initiative; she makes her deeply in love with her
English husband, who, in his stolid, somewhat limited
way, is a fine honest gentleman, and, in spite of
their real love and respect for one another, she shows
how the woman's individuality is being gradually
crushed out by the husband's obtuseness in not seeing
that, while loving him, she may have interests of her
own in addition to her interest in his ambitions."
SR 85:501.
CR 32:329. She "married a big, strong Englishman, who
quietly assumed that he was the master, and made of
her an admirable woman ...the author needs an
editor--a firm, unflinching literary master."
BKM 7:251.

000381   ANCESTORS: A NOVEL. New York & London:
Harper, 1907 NUC. London: J. Murray, 1907 BMC.

BKM: Isobel Otis, disillusioned with men, won't take
dangerous step of depending on a man. At 25 feels
women need her as a leader. Runs a chicken farm-her
own. Travels unchaperoned in Europe. Avoids love
because she must be self reliant, resolves to be a
leader of women. She says to her suitor. "I want
nothing that your sex has left to offer."
BKM 26:528 LBKM 148: In rubber boots, on her chicken
farm, avoids love, won't marry man, marr. is bondage
to her; other relations are degrading. Turns to
concerns of the intellect.

000382   THE ARISTOCRATS; BEING THE IMPRESSIONS OF
THE LADY HELEN POLE DURING HER SOJOURN IN THE GREAT
NORTH WOODS AS SPONTANEOUSLY RECORDED IN HER LETTERS
TO HER FRIEND IN NORTH BRITAIN, THE COUNTESS OF EDGE
AND ROSS [ANONYMOUS]. London & New York: J. Lane, 1901
NUC BMC.

BAKER 32-17 Lady Helen strong intellect finds the men
of her circle have "water in the blood," wants
something stronger. Exposes women types too, even
women writers.BOOK NEWS 6-01 doesn't add much
Capital character sketching; love interest minor. BOOK
BUYER 01
Bloodless men and women (Amers.) described and
satirized NYT 01
Satire against women; men treated more kindly. ATH
6-22-01

000383   THE AVALANCHE; A MYSTERY STORY. London:
J. Murray, 1919 BMC. New York: F. A. Stokes, [c1919]
NUC.

a society "of idle & tediously wicked people" and a mystery TLS
Deals more with marriage and idle young wife but "it scarcely goes deep enough to meet the demands of the problem-novel reader." San Francisco society a child wife, a husband absorbed in business & a conspiracy about a ruby. Hovering about this world of high society are the working people, gamblers, adventurers, the kinds of people who parented this high society & show how thin the social crust is. NYT

000384   THE CALIFORNIANS. London and New York: J. Lane, 1898 BMC NUC.

SP 81:445. Magdalena, daughter of Spanish hidalgo and New England woman. A disappointment to her father because she is not beautiful. She illustrates the incrongruous and even tragic results of the union. She loves a weary viveur, a middle-aged prodigal.
LIT 3:328.
ACAD 54:295. She and a friend Helena, dressed as a boy, escape from house one night to watch a fire. She tells her father because she regrets episode; he beats her. Helena is not sorry, tells no one, and is taken to Europe.
ACAD 55:31. "The varying relations of one man with two girls." "He falls in and out of love with each of them in turn." On one occasion Magdelena thinks of killing Helena (Helena has told her that she has thrown the man over because she has found he has an impure past. Magdelena knows this; it is one of the reasons she loves him.)
SR 86:648. Helena is a mixture of half southern Cal, half Nor. She tells Magdalena that she is not mixed; she is just "hooked together."
NYT 1898:686. Story of Magdalena, her repressed childhood, love for an older man after believing she could never have marriage. Life crisis.

000385   THE CONQUEROR; BEING THE TRUE AND ROMANTIC STORY OF ALEXANDER HAMILTON. New York, London: Macmillan, 1902 NUC BMC.

historical romance based on Hamilton papers. BAKER 32, 17.

000386   A DAUGHTER OF THE VINE. London & New York: J. Lane, 1899 NUC. London: Service & Paton, 1899 BMC.

Part of California series. California in the 60s. Theme: degradation and horror of dipsomania. The Randolphs are a hospitable happy family, but there's something strange behind the gaiety: Nina drinks. And this passion grows and the mood of the book changes to one of desolation and remorse. LIT 4:374
Gradual degradation of a beautiful and gifted woman. Terrible end. LBKM 16:83
Nina Randolph. Idea of heredity. Her mother drank. Falls in love with Thorpe. His silence and distance lead her to marry a disreputable doctor. After he dies, she returns to her mother whom she hates, yields to drinking. She dies in the end. Repulsive, sordid. SP 82:419
Love affair with Thorpe, illegitimate child. ACAD 56:359
Barmaid mother secretly feeds Nina alcoholic drink in infancy. SR 87:729
Does this because husband leaves her. He goes to California (was of good family.) She, the mother, remained in England. CR 35:698

000387   THE DOOMSWOMAN. New York: Tait, Sons, [c1893] NUC. London: Hutchinson, [1895] BMC.

California in old Spanish days. She is Chonita, beautiful proud, hungry for knowledge. Her mind wars with superstitions of her family. Falls for a man who is the enemy of her family. Ends unhappily. LW 93, 193.
She's called Doomswoman because of her supposed power to curse/heal humanity. PW 6-3-93.
Based on superstition that a woman who is a twin is doomed. This man has a great power over her; therefore, she knows she can't marry him. Confesses she loves him upon leaving him forever. CR 20, 23:86

000388   THE GORGEOUS ISLE, A ROMANCE; SCENE: NEVIS, B. W. I., 1842. New York: Doubleday, Page, 1908 NUC. London: J. Murray, 1908 BMC.

BKM v28 1908-9 alcoholic poet. Woman demands he stop if she marries him (killing himself with it)-has she right to dry up his "well of creativity"?
ATH-0
NYT-0

BAKER 32-17
portrayal of a West Indian isle problems of artist who needs drink to create & wife's dilemma-to deny him drink & deny his genius? BKM
Fictional account of Algernon Charles Swinburne.

000389   HEART OF HYACINTH. New York: Harper, 1903 NUC.

000390   HIS FORTUNATE GRACE. New york: D. Appleton, 1897 NUC. London: Sands, 1897 BMC.

Duke of Bosworth comes to New York to find a rich wife. Wins Augusta Forbes, rich, plain, intell. Father opposes the marriage. Mother approves, carries couple off to England, announces engage. Father gives in-makes settlement of millions on the couple. PW 51:776.
SP 81:253 Heroine, a socialist. Her father, an American millionaire is opposed to her marrying an English duke; her mother is for it.
ACAD 53:347. Duke is decrepit, in search of money to improve his impoverished acres. She falls for him. Mother is socially ambitious. Father furious at the idea of selling his daughter for a title. Mother leaves and takes daughter to England, sure that husband's love will send him after her. It doesn't, but her pregnancy does. Daughter gets Duke, but apparently relationship between mother & father has suffered a loss.

000391   JULIA FRANCE AND HER TIMES; A NOVEL. New York: Macmillan, 1912 NUC. London: J. Murray, 1912 BMC.

Intellectual & political evolution of modern woman, progress during recent years of suffrage movement. "presents the obstacles before the feminist, the suffering, inhumanity & martyrdom awaiting the suffrage leader." BKM
NYT 1915--"all the social & legal wrongs under which English women labor. "politics, gets into suffrage movement, friendships with women, goes to jail, wives in business independently.
LBKM is victim of mother's pride & man's selfishness (makes a bad marriage & lives with him only with a pistol in reach). Becomes involved in fem. movement. Happier life at end, probably marriage.
"The story of a woman who makes a worldly marriage & later becomes a suffrage leader in London" PW
"heroine...is supposed to be the most brilliant figure among the English suffragettes, and a large part of the book is devoted to an account of her militant activities..." But heroine marries "the slangiest of Americans" because of an astrological prediction. She embraces suffrage for the same reason.
FRANKLIN BIB.--Caustic evaluation.

000392   MRS. BALFAME; A NOVEL. New York: F. A. Stokes, [1916] NUC. London: J. Murray, 1916 BMC.

"Mrs. Balfame shrank from divorce so she decided to poison her husband. Husband shot, innocent Mrs. B. held for the murder. Interest is divided between solving the mystery & studying the satire on the members of a quasi-fasionable suburb under this strain on the conventions." PW 89:3/11/16:930
NYT there is also boyish Sarah Austin, a reporter.
LBKM-Mrs. B. points to carnage of the Great War as palliative for her murder.
ATH-She didn't do it, she just had made up her mind to.
SP. She got poison from fem MD who is her friend. The women's club supports her even though they believe she is guilty & constitute a body guard of "sob sisters" in court.

000393   PATIENCE SPARHAWK AND HER TIMES: A NOVEL. London and New York: J. Lane, 1897 BMC NUC.

Latimore Burr, intell. anarchist, about to marry Patience's sister-in-law starts flirting with the newly wed Patience. Tries to kiss her. Husband eavesdrops. The two men argue. Later meets another anarchist. Does not love her husband. Very sarcastic review. SR 84:203.
"A defiant portrait of a defiant woman." "her strong belief in the sanitary influence of brains". Experiences among WCTU women. Condemned to electric chair. LBKM 12:48.
Her life from her early days on western ranch to the moment she's rescued from the electric chair. "dwells on the passionate and animal side of love with a startling frankness." She is put on trial for poisoning her husband in New York. Attacks rottenness of sensational journalism. SP 78:597.

Father dead; mother drinks. Patience tries to kill her
mother. Leaves rural home for the city. Later becomes
a news woman. ACAD 51: 472.
Her mother is a beast; her husband a fiend. Episodes
in her life. "The men are beasts and brutes." She's "a
very much emancipated young woman." Her friend Rosita
is a variety actress. NYT 5-15-97.

000394   PERCH OF THE DEVIL. New York: F.A.
Stokes, [1914] NUC. London: J. Murray, 1914 BMC.

"Gregory Compton is a creative dreamer; a miner whose
greatest passion is for his mine; a money-maker for
whom money is second to the adventure of making it.
While still in the School of Mines Compton marries
Ida, an ignorant, ambitious girl. He sees his mistake
almost at once, but resolves that she shall be fitted
outwardly, at least, for her future position. Ora
Blake, a woman of cultivation and charm, helps him in
this. Ida develops into a woman of character and fire,
with a deep new love for her husband. It becomes a
situation of one man and two women-out of which Ida,
the one of most understanding and power, evolves a
true happiness for herself and her husband." PW 86
8/29/14:594
ATH 144:306-Rev. calls whichever woman had been in
Europe an adulteress at heart.
TLS-Ida travels in Europe; "travel and training
changed her in a year or two from a vulgar little
nobody into a woman of style and power, but through
all she remained a woman of Butte at heart." "She
reeks, if we may put it so, of Butte."
BKM-Theme is superiority of wife to husband, her
unlimited adaptability contrasted with his
self-centeredness. Ida is an elemental, untutored
young woman from Butte, Montana. He soon wearies of
her and half scornfully offers to pay for lessons to
fit her for position she will someday fill as he
advances. She takes him at his word and takes lessons
from older woman who is destined to be her rival. Ch.
development under this tutelage, conflict between
women.
NYT-Ida is more controlled, ambitious; Ora is
supercivilized combined with a reckless passion. Ida
wins conflict over her husband but shows a generous
nature toward her rival.
author has given us "one of the strongest, most
consistent, most carefully developed woman characters
of which the last half century can boast."BKM

000395   A QUESTION OF TIME. New York: U. S. Book,
[c1891] NUC. London: Gay and Bird, [1892] BMC.

Boradil Trevor beautiful widow of 46, a fine painter,
a good musician. Meets young genius male of 22. They
marry. Author approves of such marriages. LW
Four-in-hand are four lovers, four men who propose to
the same widow on the same morning. PW

000396   REZANOV: A NOVEL. New York and London:
The Authors and Newspapers Association, 1906 NUC BMC.

ACAD-Male hero but Concha is much more successful
character
BKM 0
Story of the experience of young Russian nobleman in
Spanish California

000397   REZANOV AND DONA CONCHA. 1906-07 [] NUC.

000398   RULERS OF KINGS; A NOVEL. New York and
London: Harper & Brothers, 1904 NUC. London:
Macmillan, 1904 BMC.

NYT-Politics of power
ATH-0
BAKER 32-17
PW male hero
BKM 19 1904

000399   SENATOR NORTH. New York and London: J.
Lane, 1900 BMC NUC.

NYT 1900:371. Political novel. Betty Madison, rich and
independent, wishes to establish a political salon in
Washington. The Madisons have a high position in
society and her mother does not like the idea of
politicians being admitted to her home. Betty studies
Congressional Record, etc. Betty has certain qualities
which no decent man would like to find in a woman.
BKM 11:589. Betty is 29. She comes to love Senator
North, a 60 year old married man, in an exalted pure
way; he feels the same toward her. Harriet, an
illegitimate child of mixed blood, and tragedy.
SP 85:308. She marries North after his wife dies.
Harriet is an ooctaron, her half-sister, whom she

befriends and educates, keeping her secret. When
Harriet's husband discovers, he suicides, Harriet
follows.
ATH 116:307. "The Negro question is here roundly
asserted to be insoluble and racial antagonism
impossible to assuage." North is encouraged to
persevere in Republican conservation and resistance as
far as may be possible against the growing evils of
democracy

000400   TOWER OF IVORY; A NOVEL. New York:
Macmillan, 1910 NUC. London: John Murray, 1910 BMC.

attracts man married to a beautiful wealthy American
woman PW
BKM v.31 1910
NYT Hero is shown to be what he is. Women ch's are
deceived by his intelligence.
LBKM-wife dies
ATH Ordham is brutal to young American woman, she is
foolish spoilt child. great prima donna succeeds in
controlling situation between Ordham and herself until
he is married-then what?
SR-he killed both wife and child. Why do all the women
find him so attractive? Why is the mature opera singer
so fond of him?
BKM. Singer kills herself over him. Why are all the
women so immersed in the fantasy of his brilliance,
sacrificing for a common place person? POV?

000401   TRANSPLANTED. A NOVEL. New York: Dodd,
Mead, 1919 NUC.

000402   THE TRAVELLING THIRDS. London and New
York: Harper, 1905 NUC BMC.

BKM 22:368
NYT 1905: 645 Account of travels in Spain.
BKM (1905) 22, 368-9-
Catalina Shore-outrages conventional fellow travellers
PW 10-21-05
Catalina not really mod., more "a heroine of romance"
a fun book, not her serious stuff NYT 671,05
Critical of different types of women especially
American. Catalina utterly contemptuous of conventions
by a curious athletic feat overcomes a brigand in
single combat ATH 93.05

000403   THE VALIANT RUNAWAYS. New York: Dodd,
Mead, 1898 NUC BMC. London: J. NIsbet, 1899.

000404   A WHIRL ASUNDER. New York and London: F.
A. Stokes, [c1895] NUC BMC.

BOOK NEWS 11-02
Wild primitive red wood forest of California. The
battle between a young California woman of passionate
nature and an Englishman of the gentlemanly type. "She
with a word dismisses her lover." He is more bound,
loving her more. ACAD 48:360
Helena Belmont. ATH 106:351
SR 81:82. Naughtiness. Manly hero.
SP 77:121. Helena , a California heiress, "takes her
will between her teeth." Attempts to woo Clive an
Englishman from girl he is engaged to.
PW-There is a final tragedy after Helena's and Clive's
confession of mutual love.

000405   THE WHITE MORNING: A NOVEL OF THE POWER
OF GERMAN WOMEN IN WARTIME. New York: F. A. Stokes,
[c1918] NUC.

PW-Gisela, freed from her father by his death,
abandoned her title and went to U.S. as a governess.
Fell for a German who would not marry her because of
her supposed low status. Returned to Germany a thinker
and a writer-war-became a Red Cross nurse. Then
disillusionment with Germany. Stifling her passion for
her lover she killed him and then became the leader of
German women in a revolt which led to abdication of
emperor. Establishment of universal peace through
holocaust of their rebellion

ATHERTON, MAIMIE.

000406   GREY SAND. London: Everett, [1915] BMC.

Man with political ambitions tries to cover up his
seduction of a young woman by a mock marriage. He
comes to a bad end. TLS

ATKINSON, BLANCHE.

000407   A COMMONPLACE GIRL. London: A. and C.
Black, 1895 BMC.

Motto is Browning's: the world's for us no blot or blank. It means intensely and means good. ATH 106:831 SR wholesome English heroine and curate who gives her up to man she loves.
ACAD 49:43. Also sketch of girl who thinks she is an artist but has no talent.
SP 76:138.

ATKINSON, ELEANOR (STACKHOUSE). 1863-1942. United States.

000408   HEARTS UNDAUNTED; A ROMANCE OF FOUR FRONTIERS. New york and London: Harper, [1917] NUC.

Kidnapped by Indians, many advents. PW
She learns woodcraft as a girl, learns all about Indian lore, because she's raised by Indians. Returned to colony she becomes a frontier wife-all the hardships for women described, goes through War of 1812. Escapes dangers wonderful courage demanded of her. NYT

000409   JOHNNY APPLESEED; THE ROMANCE OF THE SOWER. New York and London: Harper, 1915 BMC NUC.

Story of Johnny and his dedication to apples PW 4-3-15

000410   MAMZELLE FIFINE; A ROMANCE OF THE GIRLHOOD OF THE EMPRESS JOSEPHINE ON THE ISLAND OF MARTINIQUE. New York: D. Appleton,

history. PW
child's historical romance. NYT 03, 796

000411   "POILU", A DOG OF ROUBAIX. New York and London: Harper, [1918] BMC NUC.

NYT Dec. 29 '18 p 582. French family during the war. German atrocities. WWI

ATKINSON, SYBIL H. W.

000412   THE GREAT VENDETTA. London: Murray and Evenden, [1920] BMC.

AUDOUX, MARGUERITE. 1863-1937. France.

000413   MARIE CLAIRE. New York: Doran, 1911 NUC. London: Chapman & Hall, 1911 NUC BMC. (Tr. J. N. Raphael)

BKM: Naturalistic picture of farmlife.
Autobiographical account of orphan after 10 years, moved to farm. Her work as shepardess and domestestic. Escapes back to orphanage, then to Paris. "Author shrinks from none of the harsh and repellant details of the ugly passions" or of physical coarseness. BKM NYT: "Unfinished record of a forsaken orphan's life, breaking off abruptly at its crucial moment." Becomes a seamstress; compared to Colette huge success.

000414   MARIE CLAIRE'S WORKSHOP. New York: T. Seltzer, 1920 NUC. London: Chapman & Hall, 1920 NUC BMC. (Tr. F. S. Flint)

TLS sequel. Staged in dressmaker's work room where she is employed.
PW - Small Parisian workshop. Realistic portrait of lives of women workers, sordid, ugly, grim, remorseless toil. NYT 11-21-20 P. 20

AUSTIN, JANE (GOODWIN). 1831-1894. United States.

000415   BETTY ALDEN, THE FIRST-BORN DAUGHTER OF THE PILGRIMS. Boston and New York: Houghton, Mifflin, 1891 NUC.

Historical romance. Plymouth colony: NATION 11-19-91, 395.
Miles Standish is hero in this series of which this novel is the second book. PW 11-7-91.

AUSTIN, MARTHA WADDILL. United States.

000416   TRISTRAM AND ISOULT. Boston: Poet Lore Co., 1905 NUC.

000417   VERONICA. New York: Doubleday, 1903 NUC. London: Isbister, 1904 BMC.

ACAD-"girly" creation
love story of Louisiana 3-14-3 PW

AUSTIN, MARY (HUNTER). 1868-1934. United States.

000418   THE FLOCK. Boston: Houghton Mifflin, 1906 NUC. London: A. Constable, 1906 BMC.

ACAD: Shepherds on trail in California-San Joaquin Valley.

000419   THE FORD. Boston: Houghton Mifflin, 1917 NUC.

Life and social conditions in California PW 91:1274 4/21/17
Focus on male hero; four women characters represent types "rattle headed Virginia", for example, would live the rights of women and reform the world BKM
Anne-cool "able to cope with men; business men, at least, on their own ground" BKM
Concerns a group of people who compete for water rights, small and big farmers, oil, etc. T. Richmond successful irresistable man is central but other characters too. Little to do with romance. Broad, inclusive story. NYT 4-22-17

000420   THE GREEN BOUGH; A TALE OF THE RESURRECTION. Garden City, N.Y.: Doubleday, Page, 1913 NUC.

Jesus Christ

000421   ISIDRO. Boston: Houghton', 1905 NUC. London: A. Constable, 1905 BMC.

PW: about a "shepherd," a noble aiming for priesthood. NYT: a picaresque story of a young man.

000422   THE LOVELY LADY. Garden City, New York: Doubleday, Page, 1913 NUC.

PW: How Peter is guided by his vision of the lovely lady and how he finds her.

000423   NO. 26 JAYNE STREET. Boston: Houghton Mifflin, 1920 NUC.

PW-Girl leaves luxury home for little apartment in N Y

000424   OUTLAND. BY GORDON STAIRS. London: J. Murray, 1910 BMC NUC. New York: Boni & Liveright, 1919 NUC.

TLS-fantasy country, war between outliers and far folk over buried treasure. Narrated by House-folk woman.
LBKM-does it have a purpose?
BAKER 32-21
PW-Christmas romance. West.
NYT Jan 18 20, p.22 Outliers, fairy folk, visited by Mona and Herman.

000425   SANTA LUCIA, A COMMON STORY. New York and London: Harper, 1908 BMC NUC.

PW-Mismated couples
TLS-0
ATH-0 3 couples
BKM 0-a few isolated lives in a small town.

000426   A WOMAN OF GENIUS. Garden City, N.Y.: Doubleday, Page, 1912 NUC.

PW Olivia.
NYT-Purports to be the autobiography of an actress of tragedy. Portrays her struggle with conventional demands vs demands of her art. Struggle is deepest between obligations of marriage and that part of her which refuses to be submerged. Her genius held its own against every outside influence-husband, family, friends.

AUSTIN, MAUDE MASON. United States.

000427   'CENSION: A SKETCH FROM PASO DEL NORTE. New York: Harper, 1896 NUC.

Ranch life: Mexicans and railroad building. 'Cension is a young woman (daughter of wealthy rancher.) loves a bold handsome man of 38. She's Mexican, pure and trusting. He's a cad from whom her brother saves her. PW 12-14-95:1141

AYRES, DAISY (FITZHUGH). Nationality Unknown.

000428   THE CONQUEST. New York: Neale, 1907 NUC.

Psych study of love-logic: woman tries to dicover why husband attracted to another woman PW 4-6-07
Goes to Washington (her husband a senator) under assumed name becomes popular! Character study of her dissecting her motives and her love for husband. BKM (1907) 25, 323

Very modern and daring- makes self popular in official
society, catches an Italian count. a "fearless tale".
NYT

AYRES, RUBY MILDRED. B. 1883. United Kingdom.

000429   A BACHELOR HUSBAND. New York: W. J. Watt,
[c1920] NUC. London: Hodder and Stoughton, [1920] BMC.

TLS- truly feminine wife

000430   THE BEGGAR MAN. London: Hodder and
Stoughton, [1920] BMC.

000431   THE BLACK SHEEP. London: Hodder and
Stoughton, [1917] BMC.

000432   CASTLES IN SPAIN. THE CHRONICLES OF AN
APRIL MONTH. London: Cassell, 1912 BMC.

TLS- bachelor with his widowed sister-sent?

000433   THE DANCING MASTER. London: Hodder and
Stoughton, [1920] BMC.

000434   FOR LOVE. London: Hodder and Stoughton,
[1918] BMC.

000435   THE GIRL NEXT DOOR. London: Hodder and
Stoughton, 1919 BMC.

Sweet Joy Lambert becomes engaged but discovers she
loves another, innocent type TLS

000436   "INVALIDED OUT". London: Hodder and
Stoughton, [1918] BMC.

TLS- love and war

000437   THE LONG LANE TO HAPPINESS: A NEW RICHARD
CHATTERTON NOVEL. London: Hodder and Stoughton, 1915
BMC.

000438   THE MAKING OF A MAN. London: Newnes'
Sixpenny Copyright Novels, [1915] BMC.

000439   A MAN OF HIS WORD. London: Hodder &
Stoughton, 1916 BMC.

TLS-Jean constantly argues with guardian
ATH - she loses money at cards, she had planned a
clandestine marriage and meets guardian instead.

000440   THE MARRIAGE OF BARRY WICKLOW. London:
Hodder and Stoughton, [1920] BMC. New York: W.J. Watt,
[c1921] NUC.

000441   THE MASTER MAN. London: Hodder and
Stoughton, [1920] BMC.

000442   THE ONE WHO FORGOT. London: Hodder and
Stoughton, [1919] BMC.

Story of soldier who loses memory TLS

000443   PAPER ROSES. London: Hodder & Stoughton,
1916 BMC.

TLS-hackneyed romance
ATH-ditto

000444   THE PHANTOM LOVER. London: Hodder and
Stoughton, [1919] BMC. New York: W.J. Watt, [c1921]
NUC.

Esther Shepstone engaged to man who doesn't love her
but who pretends to. Fits her story together by a
series of quite unlikely coincidences. TLS

000445   THE REMEMBERED KISS. London: Hodder and
Stoughton, [1918] BMC.

TLS- Love and romance and inheritance

000446   RICHARD CHATTERTON, V.C. London: Hodder
and Stoughton, 1915 BMC. New York: W.J. Watt, [c1919]
NUC.

PW-Romance of a wealthy girl and a poor man,
war-invalided hero etc.
NYT 1920:237. Love story, traditional ending. He is
reported killed in war but returns.

000447   THE ROAD THAT BENDS. London and New York:
Cassell, [1916] NUC BMC.

TLS: Mother ran away from brutal husband, lived with a
man, bore Millicent-a love-child. Millicent leads a
life of ignominy and neglect, marries a cruel and
sullen husband. Meets a man she loves. Will her story
repeat her mother's ?

000448   THE SCAR. London: Hodder and Stoughton,
[1920] BMC. New York: W.J. Watt, [c1921] NUC.

TLS- Sent. romance male hero

000449   THE WINDS OF THE WORLD. London: Hodder
and Stoughton, [1918] BMC. New York: Grosset & Dunlap,
[c1921] NUC.

000450   THE WOMAN HATER. London: Hodder and
Stoughton, [1920] BMC.

TLS- Two men in love with adventuress

000451   THE YEAR AFTER. London: Newnes, [1916]
BMC.

B., E. V., pseud. See BOYLE, ELEANOR VERE (GORDON).

B., H., pseud. See BOURCHIER, HELEN.

B., M. A., pseud. See BROTHERHOOD, MAY A.

BABCOCK, BERNIE (SMADE). B. 1868. United States.

000452   AT THE MERCY OF THE STATE. Chicago: The
New Voice Press, 1902 NUC.

000453   THE DAUGHTER OF A REPUBLICAN. Chicago:
New Voice Press, 1900 NUC.

PW-temperance.

000454   JUSTICE TO THE WOMAN. Chicago: A.C.
McClurg, 1901 NUC.

"Cruel injustice of...men towards women." Unwed
mother's plight; rejects the villain, faces poverty
with her child, saved from suicide. saved by
physician; they later marry. WOMAN'S JOURNAL 9-28-01
"Discovery of the betrayer's villainy by the women of
the community and the resolve of the women's clubs to
defeat his election as U.S. Senator." So he offers
marriage which she rejects; moral "women suffrage will
bar the political success of seducers..." WOMAN'S
JOURNAL 11-21-03

000455   THE MARTYR: A STORY OF THE GREAT REFORM.
Chicago: New Voice Press, 1900 NUC.

000456   THE SOUL OF ANN RUTLEDGE; ABRAHAM
LINCOLN'S ROMANCE. Philadelphia and London: J.B.
Lippincott, 1919 NUC.

Novel based upon Lincoln's love-<seems to focus on
him> for Ann Rutledge PW
NYT 5-11-19 270

BABCOCK, WINNIFRED (EATON). B. 1879. United States.

000457   DAUGHTERS OF NIJO: A ROMANCE OF JAPAN. BY
ONOTO WATANNA. New York: Macmillan, 1904 BMC NUC.
London: Macmillan, 1904 NUC.

NYT love stories of two sisters.
BKM-

000458   THE DIARY OF DELIA; BEING A VERACIOUS
CHRONICLE OF THE KITCHEN, WITH SOME SIDE-LIGHTS ON THE
PARLOUR. BY ONOTO WATANNA. London, New York:
Doubleday, Page, 1907 BMC NUC.

Diary of Irish servant; she tells of family
weaknesses. PW 6-1-07

000459   THE HEART OF HYACINTH. BY ONOTO WATANNA.
New York and London: Harper, 1903 BMC NUC.

American girl born in Japan and an English/Japanese
young male friend later her lover. PW 9-19-03

000460   THE HONORABLE MISS MOONLIGHT. BY ONOTO
WATANNA. New York and London: Harper, 1912 BMC NUC.

PW-? doesn't sound promising.
NYT-it seems a husband left his wife (defied
tradition) to marry a geisha. She had alternative of
divorce or suicide. Last chapter is happiest one.

000461   A JAPANESE BLOSSOM. BY ONOTO WATANNA. New

York and London: Harper, 1906 BMC NUC.

PW-mixed marriage

000462   A JAPANESE NIGHTINGALE. BY ONTONO
WATANNA. London and New York: Harper, 1901 BMC NUC.

Half caste Geisha girl and American man.
ATH- sentimental.
CR

000463   THE LOVE OF AZALEA. BY ONOTO WATANNA. New
York: Dodd, Mead, 1904 NUC. London: B. F. Stevens &
Brown, 1904 BMC.

PW-marriage between Japanese girl and American
minister.
NYT-

000464   ME: A BOOK OF REMEMBRANCE [ANONYMOUS].
New York: Century, 1915 NUC. London: T. F. Unwin, 1915
BMC.

"Said to be the autobiographical work of a well-known
woman novelist, covering a period of about one year.
The narrator at 17 leaves her home to make her way in
the business world." BKM 42 1915-16
Girl's life from 17 to her coming to NY as a writer
pushes her way into business world, daringly goes into
other "field": daughter of a wandering tight-rope
dancer (woman.) PW 8-21-15
Nora Ascough one of 16 children. At 17 goes off into
the world on her own confident in her talent as a
writer. Does newspaper work in Jamaica. One year of
her life engaged to three men at same time, but really
loves a 4th. NYT
The solution for her life is to write. TLS
LBKM-autobiography of novelist, a year when she was 17
and had left home with $10 to conquer life.

000465   TAMA. BY ONOTO WATANNA. New York and
London: Harper, 1910 BMC NUC.

A mysterious fox woman, a blind girl shunned and
detested as a witch, condemned to an awful isolation.
All this in contemporary Japan with its lingering
superstitions. NYT
BM prettily sentimental story.
PW
NYT

000466   THE WOOING OF WISTARIA. BY ONOTO WATANNA.
New York and London: Harper, 1902 BMC NUC.

Japanese love story-woman turns traitor to her lover
because of father's command. BKM 502,16
ATH 12-20-02--hist.

BABCOCK, WINNIFRED (EATON) AND SARA BOSSE. B. 1879. United
States.

000467   MARION; THE STORY OF AN ARTIST'S MODEL.
BY HERSELF AND THE AUTHOR OF "ME" [ANONYMOUS]. New
York: W. J. Watt, [c1916] NUC.

Realistic story of a New York artist (a woman) BKM
The plot made possible by a "peculiar" divorce law.
TLS 03,33
She's engaged to a law student but that doesn't stop
her from earning her living in Bohemia as actress and
model or "any unconventional and hazardous thing that
comes to hand." She passes through many compromising
situations (once she's ready to live with a man
without marriage); thrilling adventures and
hair-breadth escapes "from want and infamy." NYT
4-1-17,115

BACK, BLANCHE EATON. United Kingdom.

000468   ESTRANGED; OR LOVE UNQUENCHABLE. BY DEREK
VANE. London: Aldine, [1894] BMC.

000469   THE FERRYBRIDGE MYSTERY. BY DEREK VANE.
New York: Moffat, Yard, 1920 NUC.

"A suburb of London is the scene of Derek Vane's
story. Basil Monck, a member of the London stock
exchange, whose antecedents are unknown to his most
intimate acquaintances, is found shot dead in his
home. There is not the slightest clue to the identity
of the murderer, but there are many people who might
logically be suspected of the crime. Monck had more
enemies than friends; he was generally known to have
used his fascinating personality unscrupulously in his
dealings with women, and more than one man blamed him
for the loss of a fortune. Motives for the murder are

plentiful and every man or woman who had cause to hate
Monck falls naturally under suspicion." NYT

000470   LADY VARLEY. BY DEREK VANE. London:
Stanley Paul, 1914 BMC.

000471   THE MYSTERY OF THE MOAT HOUSE. BY DEREK
VANE. Bristol: Cosmopolitan Printing, [1901] BMC.

000472   THE PARADISE OF FOOLS. BY DEREK VANE.
London: Everett, [1913] BMC.

husband and wife quarrel, he falls and hits his head;
she thinks he's dead, great mystery about his death
that effects his wife and secretary. TLS

000473   THE SECRET DOOR. BY DEREK VANE. London:
Everett, 1907 BMC.

000474   THE SIN AND THE WOMAN: A STUDY FROM LIFE.
BY DEREK VANE. London and Sydney: Remington, 1893 BMC.

The woman commits the sin "conveying" to get money to
publish hr novel which makes her famous. ACAD 44:545.
Eleanor Monroe. Made to confess by unscrupulous
admirer. Conscience makes a coward of her. Dies? ATH
102:804.

000475   THE SOUL OF A MAN. BY DEREK VANE. London:
Holden and Hardingham, [1913] BMC.

neglected wife leaves husband, divorces, remarries,
learns she prefers #1; "author is obliged to kill off
the second to provide a happy ending." ATH

000476   THE SPELL OF DELILAH. BY DEREK VANE.
London: Aldine, [1895] BMC.

000477   THE THREE DAUGHTERS OF NIGHT. BY DEREK
VANE. London: Hutchinson, 1897 BMC.

Study of a strong man: John MacGregor. His temptations
at the end. "Why does a writer drag in these rather
unpleasant things?" at the end. SP 79:627.
Irma Fawcett has a past; weds an artist. But Irma is
portrayed as "perfectly unsoiled." Their friend
MacGregor who adds to the little money paid the
husband whose failing sight affects his painting.

000478   VERNER GALBRAITH'S WIFE. BY DEREK VANE.
London: Aldine, [1895] BMC.

BACKUS, EMMA HENRIETTE (SCHERMEYER). B. 1876. United
States.

000479   THE CAREER OF DR. WEAVER. BY MRS. HENRY
BACKUS. Boston: L. C. Page, 1913 NUC.

000480   A PLACE IN THE SUN; A STORY OF THE MAKING
OF AN AMERICAN. BY MRS. HENRY BACKUS. Boston: Page,
[1917] NUC.

000481   THE ROSE OF ROSES. BY MRS. HENRY BACKUS.
Boston: Page, 1914 NUC BMC.

Toni, singer in Germany wants career in America.
Questenberg offers voyage to NY in return for "trial
engagement." PW 856/13/14:1933

BACKUS, MRS. HENRY. See BACKUS, EMMA HENRIETTE
(SCHERMEYER).

BACON, DOLORES, pseud. See BACON, MARY SCHELL (HOKE).

BACON, DOLORES MARBOURG, pseud. See BACON, MARY SCHELL
(HOKE).

BACON, EDWARD, pseud. See BACON, MARY D.

BACON, EUGENIA (JONES). B. 1840. United States.

000482   LYDDY: A TALE OF THE OLD SOUTH. New York:
Continental, 1898 NUC BMC.

Civil War-desolation of 50 homes and old plantation
life. LW 30:54.

000483   THE RED MOON. New York: Neale, 1910 NUC.

Story of woman's brave endurance. PW

BACON, JOSEPHINE DODGE (DASKAM). 1876-1961. United States.

000484   THE BIOGRAPHY OF A BOY. New York and
London: Harper, 1910 BMC NUC.

BKM-silly nonsense.

000485   THE DOMESTIC ADVENTURERS. New York:
Charles Scribner's Sons, 1907 NUC.

BKM 26 (1907) 278-9. Three bachelor girls in NY, one
is 40. One housekeeps, one teacher, one is editor. And
their wild adventures. Give up city apartment for
suburban life.

000486   AN IDYLL OF ALL FOOLS' DAY. New York:
Dodd, Mead, 1908 NUC.

PW-love story, comedy.

000487   THE IMP AND THE ANGEL. New York: C.
Scribner's Sons, 1901 NUC.

000488   IN THE BORDER COUNTRY. New York and
London: Doubleday, Page, 1909 NUC BMC.

000489   THE INHERITANCE. New York and London: D.
Appleton, 1912 NUC BMC.

Biographical story of man's medical career and his
learning; and of the old nurse who raised him. TLS
PW-male and money.
ACAD-factory conditions. Workers blamed for putting up
with and supporting them.

000490   THE LUCK O' LADY JOAN; A FAIRY TALE FOR
WOMEN. Chicago: F. G. Browne, 1913 BMC NUC.

Allegory of Christmas. NYT

000491   MARGARITA'S SOUL; THE ROMANTIC
RECOLLECTIONS OF A MAN OF FIFTY. BY INGRAHAM LOVELL.
New York and London: J. Lane, 1909 BMC NUC.

Heroine kept on island comes to live in society. PW
10-16-09
ACAD-innocent fantasy.
ATH-man after man succumbs to her savage charm; she
suddenly blossoms into a prima donna then question of
art vs. love. She was married in a state of incredible
ignorance, hence her unconventional behavior.
NYT-Bacon is anti-suffrage, this, her 1st novel, is an
expression of it.

000492   THE MEMOIRS OF A BABY. BY JOSEPHINE
DASKAM. New York and London: Harper, 1904 BMC NUC.

PW-maiden aunt is a meddler.
NYT

000493   OPEN MARKET. New York and London: D.
Appleton, 1915 BMC NUC.

Wealthy woman left penniless; proposes marriage to a
cripple who has never seen a woman before (!).
Happiness comes to this extraordinary couple. PW
5-12-15
Evelyn Jaffrey. Hero confined to wheelchair. Evelyn
cares for aunt for years, but aunt leaves her nothing
in her will. Evelyn uses her small savings to buy some
good clothes. Immediately gets invited to Adirondacks:
marries a backwoods man crippled who has never seen a
woman. She proposes. She will show him the world.
Realizing she's entering upon a new kind of slavery.
In Bermuda she educates him. Soon becomes erudite A
Pygmalion in reverse. NYT
He's cured and all ends well. BKM

000494   TABLES FOR THE FAIR. BY JOSEPHINE DODGE
DASKAM. New York: C. Scribner's Sons, 1901 NUC.

000495   TEN TO SEVENTEEN; A BOARDING SCHOOL
DIARY. New York and London: D. Appleton, 1908 NUC BMC.

000496   TO-DAY'S DAUGHTER. New York and London:
D. Appleton, 1914 BMC NUC.

PW 86 9/19/14:772 "Lucia Stanchon, a modern young
woman of good family, with every advantage of New York
life, is eager for economic independence. To please
her father, she agrees to "try out" marriage with one
of his professional friends. The "try out" comes near
to ending in disaster, but Lucia's attitude toward
life changes and from "To-day's daughter the mother of
To-morrow had been born."
NYT-Lucia is nationally known for her work in prison
reform. At 30 her father objects to her taking her
work seriously and working regular hours just like a
man compelled to earn a living. She ought to be
content house-keeping for him or another man. She
loves him and ends up marrying a broad-minded surgeon

she does not love enough to marry, but is still
completely absorbed in her work. There are other
women--artist, interior decorator, manager of a large
farm. POV?
"A novel dealing with the problems that confront the
woman of today who wishes to have an independent
career and with the question of how far she has the
right to live her own life." NYT 7-11-15
Lucia Stanchon, antagonized by father's aggressive
conservatism, hurried into marriage, surrounded by
older women with advanced ideas who have careers,
wakes up in time to be a real woman! BKM"Author forces
no conclusions on reader, puts no limits on modern
woman except to show she can't be a dozen different
women with success in all repects."? LW

000497   WHILE CAROLINE WAS GROWING. New York and
London: Macmillan, 1911 BMC NUC.

Natural sincere bewitching girl from 10th year to
maidenhood. PW 3-11-11

BACON, MARY D. B. 1866. United States.

000498   THE LAST HURDLE. BY EDWARD BACON. New
York: Knickerbocker Press, 1909 NUC.

BACON, MARY SCHELL (HOKE). 1870-1934. United States.

000499   CRUMBS AND HIS TIMES. BY DOLORES BACON.
New York and London: Doubleday, Page, 1906 NUC BMC.

000500   THE DIARY OF A MUSICIAN. BY DOLORES
MARBOURG BACON. New York: H. Holt, 1904 BMC NUC.

000501   IN HIGH PLACES. BY DOLORES BACON. London
& New York: Doubleday, Page, 1907 BMC. New York:
Doubleday, Page, 1907 NUC.

Race for wealth. Jean up-to-date stenographer helper
to overworked business man. Wife jealous; he fires
her. Still she looks after his business, saves him
financially. PW 10-19-07
Miss Jean Meredith makes $10,000. Wife gets jealous,
betrays business secrets, almost ruins him. NYT

000502   A KING'S DIVINITY. BY DOLORES BACON. New
York: H. Holt, 1906 NUC BMC.

PW romance.
NYT-

BACON, SUSIE LEE. United States.

000503   A SIREN'S SON. Chicago: C. H. Kerr, 1895
NUC.

Famous singer separates from husband after child born.
Child raised by father. When father dies Paul
Lemotherin returns to ma, love affair with Margaret.
Shows havoc women like his mother bring in men's
lives. PW 2-9-95:296.

BAGNOLD, ENID. See JONES, ENID (BAGNOLD).

BAGNOLL, NORAH.

000504   MAUDE ORMOND. A NOVEL. London: J.
Macqueen, 1901 BMC.

About the actress.

BAILEY, ALICE (WARD). B. 1857. United States.

000505   MARK HEFFRON: A NOVEL. New York: Harper,
1896 NUC.

BKM 3:557. A little hynotism, Christian Science, the
World's Fair, and the extortions of a Chicago
boardinghouse proprietor keep hero and heroine amused
for 350 pages.
LW 27:329. Anti-Christian Science, or, at least,
mind-cure.
PW 5-16-96. The position of the women, Eloise and
Margeurite, a former pupil of Heffron's, mental
science, Buddhism, and other metaphysical questions,
are more interesting than the love interest.

000506   THE SAGE BRUSH PARSON. BY A. B. WARD.
Boston: Little, Brown, 1906 NUC.

PW-finds himself in Nevada mining town, falls in love
with wealthy widow and is later convicted of murder of
his wife and child who have followed him from England.
Happy conclusion.
NYT-wife jumps off cliff with son. Parson has never

bothered to mention he was married.

BAILEY, EDITH LAWRENCE (BLACK).   United States.

000507   CRECY. BY EDITH LAWRENCE. New York: F. M.
Buckles, [1904] NUC.

NYT hist romance.

BAILEY, IRENE TEMPLE. D. 1953. United States.

000508   CONTRARY MARY. BY TEMPLE BAILEY.
Philadelphia: Penn, 1914 NUC. London: Duckworth,
[1916] BMC.

Passion for work and independence and real love. PW
2-20-15 wants to be economically independent. "Boyish
manner" "free independent ways, modern ideas of love;
love story is big and splendid--she helps a man face
the world. The Book Review, PW
"Prefers work in a government office to marriage for
the sake of support or a home which would mean
economic dependence." NYT
Contrary because she will not marry, prefers to
support self rather than being cared for. Does marry
in the end.

000509   GLORY OF YOUTH. BY TEMPLE BAILEY.
Philadelphia: Penn, 1913 NUC. London: J. Richmond,
1917 BMC.

Mistaken pairing of a man to gentle little Bettina who
"passes over" to young airman. The first man gets real
love from Diana. TLS
PW 84 11/29/13:272 "Should an engagement bind two
people who have discovered that they do not love each
other? Here is the theme of this love story in which
four lives are tangled. Two women there are who do not
know their own hearts until too late--two men who know
where their happiness lies and are bound by their code
of honor not to seek it. The comedy runs perilously
near to tragedy before a puff of wind clears away the
clouds, and in bringing tears brings happiness and
content."

000510   MISTRESS ANNE. BY TEMPLE BAILEY.
Philadelphia: Penn, 1917 NUC.

Of good family but must work. Teaches. Then makes
right choice between dr. and writer. PW
Ann Warfield. NYT 250 7-1-17

000511   THE TIN SOLDIER. BY TEMPLE BAILEY.
Philadelphia: Penn, 1918 NUC. London: Skeffington and
Son, [1919] BMC.

Hero takes on all the abuse and credit of staying out
of war to care for his father, a general, who drinks?
TLS
Woman shares his humiliation and helps him win out.
She's fluffy but charming. PW
NYT: he falls in love with his doctor's daughter, a
beautiful patriotic young woman, Jean, but problems
between them come through Hilda Merritt, a trained
nurse, who schemes to get jewels belonging to the
young man's family. All turns out well.
WWI-fic.

000512   THE TRUMPETER SWAN. BY TEMPLE BAILEY.
Philadelphia: Penn, [c1920] NUC. London: Hurst and
Blackett, [1921] BMC.

PW-love story, love, gallantry, roses, candlelight,
courtesy etc.

BAILEY, MAY HELEN MARION (EDGINTON). B. 1883. United
Kingdom.

000513   THE ADVENTURES OF NAPOLEON PRINCE. BY MAY
EDGINTON. New York and London: Cassell, 1912 BMC NUC.

PW-invalid criminal
ATH-hero of romantical fraud
TLS-hero of romantical fraud

000514   BRASS. London: Everett, 1910 BMC.

TLS-male hero looking for a wife

000515   THE MAN WHO BROKE THE RULE. London:
Cassell, [1919] BMC.

rich elderly widow falls desperately in love with a
young man in his 20's, proposes to him, marries him.
Her love and jealousy, his trying to do his duty by
her even when he loves another woman; her death. TLS

000516   MARRIED LIFE; OR, THE TRUE ROMANCE. BY
MAY EDGINTON. London, New York: Cassell, [1917] BMC
NUC.

Woes of married life in a small flat when wife does
all the housework. Wife's views shown sympathetically.
More money helps solve some of their problems though
the discomforts are more convincing than the
relatively bettered conditions at the end. TLS
Couple devoted to each other; begin married life with
rosiest hopes. Neither realizes restraints necessary.
Husband becomes selfish, inconsiderate and finally
welcomes the chance to go to America on business. Wife
left with kids. Returns to find her views very
different. ATH
Liked her freedom so well refuses to take him back,
but then does a turnabout. We leave her on another
course of domesticity. SP
PW-story of marriage.
NYT-realistic account of man and woman, both of whom
are working, who marry, and their first year of bliss
and subsequent six years when his income must be
stretched to meet needs of five and she is worn out
with housework and child-bearing. He is selfish,
morose, she tired irritable. Author solves all
problems and returns them to state of happiness by
their suddenly having enough money.

000517   A MODERN EVE. BY MAY EDGINTON. New York:
F. A. Stokes, [1913] NUC.

"Ellen leaves college eager to reform the world, her
chosen cause being woman. Two men struggle against
each other to wake her and win her away from the
cause." PW 84:1137. "with...depth of feeling a modern
young woman espouses suffrage, while two strong men
battle with each other and with her for her love."

000518   OH! JAMES! (THE STORY OF A MAN WHO TRIED
TO PROVE THE GOODNESS OF THE WORLD). BY H. M.
EDGINTON. London: E. Nash, 1914 BMC. Boston: Little,
Brown, 1914 NUC.

PW 86 8-15-14:480-"James Bright makes money fast, and
his wife won't spend it. It is his belief that money
should circulate. So the great Idea comes to him. In
five different cities, he determines to support a
home, and within it some deserving woman in luxury.
Five young women are thus established, with James in a
harmless, paternal attitude behind them. When he takes
a trip to India, five young men are hired to watch
over the young women. Now it is time for Mrs. James
Bright to have her Idea, and it saves the situation,
and some of the money for her own use."
NYT-does not say what she does.

000519   THE SIN OF EVE. BY MAY EDGINTON. London,
New York: Hodder and Stoughton, [1913] BMC NUC.

The heroine is determined never to marry until the
wrongs against women are righted and the vote is won.
She works ardently for the W.S.P.U. She has two
lovers. ATH
Ellen Flamartin, brave, adventurous. A millionaire
newpaperowner and an actor-manager playwright woo her.
Ardent organizer for WSPU. LBKM
A militant suffragist-TLS

000520   THE STREET OF GOLD. London: Cassell, 1918
BMC.

TLS-Nance is lovely, selfish, engaged to millionaire.
Goes to Canada, falls for poor man, needs money even
more. Gets shipwrecked on way home.

000521   THE WEIGHT CARRIERS. London: Everett,
[1909] BMC.

wife married to man she despises, married for money.
Her husband is a weakling. Denise is a "callous,
unprincipled unfaithful wife." There is "another". TLS

BAILEY, TEMPLE. See BAILEY, IRENE TEMPLE.

BAIN, CHARLOTTE.

000522   ACE O' HEARTS. London: Hurst and
Blackett, 1898 BMC.

SP 81:253. Treatment of love. Heart on book's cover is
black.
ATH 111:83. Four families. Crimean days.

000523   HER BEAU-IDEAL. London: Digby, Long,
[1895] BMC.

BAINES, MINNIE WILLIS. See MILLER, MINNIE (WILLIS) BAINES.

BAIRD, JEAN KATHERINE. 1872-1918. United States.

000524 THE BOY NEXT DOOR. New York: American Tract Society, [1910] NUC.

000525 THE HEIR OF BARACHAH. Cincinnati: Monfort, 1911 NUC.

BAKER, AMELIA LOVISA (SVENSON). B. 1864.

000526 A MODERN VALKYRIE. BY EMILY SVENSON. New York: Cochrane, 1909 NUC.

Conversations with a diary." Pt-1)an act of self-defense 2)the extracts from a working woman's diary 3)servants 4)a sure cure for despotic rule 5)a true life drama 6)second discussion 7)third discussion; an appeal to every woman. BKM v30 1909-10 HQ 1426 1)servants 2)woman-social and moral questions

BAKER, AMY J. See CRAWFORD, AMY JOSEPHINE (BAKER).

BAKER, EMILY.

000527 PEGGY GAINSBOROUGH; THE GREAT PAINTER'S DAUGHTER. London: F. Griffiths, 1909 BMC.

A family circle. TLS

BAKER, EMMA EUGENE HALL. United States.

000528 VERNAL DUNE, IN WHICH IS SHOWN THE END OF AN ERA. BY EUGENE HALL. New York: Neale, 1913 NUC.

BAKER, ESTELLE. Nationality Unknown.

000529 THE ROSE DOOR. Chicago: C. H. Kerr, 1911 NUC.

BAKER, ETTA IVA (ANTHONY). United States.

000530 MISS MYSTERY; A NOVEL. Boston: Little, Brown, 1913 NUC.

PW 83 3/15/13 p.982. "A young girl who has evidently met with an accident, depriving her of all memory, is found lying on a bed in a house where she is unknown. Her plight awakens the sympathy of her hostess, and as all clues to her identity fail, she gradually falls into the position of daughter in the household, endearing herself to the family and their friends by the charm of her personality and the beauty of her character. The solving of her identity and the straightening of the tangles which she all unwittingly causes, form the basis of a romantic story."

BAKER, FRANCES DAVIS. United States.

000531 UPLANDS: A NOVEL. BY AIDA. Buffalo, N.Y.: G. M. Hausauer, 1898 NUC.

BAKER, JOSEPHINE R. United States.

000532 GEE'S TRAP; OR THE LAMBS AND FIELD STREET. Boston: Congregational Sunday-school and Pub. Society, [c1895] NUC.

Field St. is a dingy neighborhood at edge of Lamb estate. Contrast of Aster lamb and 'Lize Clossen and effect each had on other.PW 3-30-95:512

BAKER, JOSEPHINE (TURCK). D. 1942. United States.

000533 THE BURDEN OF THE STRONG. Evanston, Ill.: Correct English Pub. Co., [c1915] NUC.

Julia has indulged in the pleasures of society life. At first wants a divorce but later decides to remain with her husband for the sake of the child. PW 90:684 9/2/16.

BAKER, LOUISA ALICE. B. 1858. United States.

000534 ANOTHER WOMAN'S TERRITORY. BY ALIEN. New York: F. T. Neely, 1894 NUC. Westminster: A. Constable, 1901 BMC.

Husband and wife estranged, the other woman and wife become friends, honest with one another. BOOK BUYER '01

000535 A DAUGHTER OF THE KING. BY "ALIEN". London: Hutchinson, 1894 BMC. Chicago: F. T. Neely,

1894 NUC.

ACAD 46:420. "She has studied the Story of an African Farm neither wisely nor well. Daughter of musician, an orphan, is taken in by Mrs. Arnold. Florence marries the wrong man and keeps her daughter from her unloved husband by accusing herself of immorality. PW-faces the woman problem with great seriousness. Florence marries the wrong one of her two adopted brothers (both love her) to please her adopted mother. A fair presentation of what marriage without love means to a strong character. Florence is a violinist.

000536 THE DEVIL'S HALF-ACRE. BY ALIEN. London: T.F. Unwin, 1900 BMC.

SP 85:532. New Zealand. Requires and rewards close reading.
ATH 116:374. The ethics of murder and murderous sentiments. Sombre & serious study.
ACAD 59:262. John is in gold fields attempting to expiate a crime (unsuspected murder) by saving other's lives.
LIT 7:326. By saving souls. Rose is the gay note in his life. Her trials and love.

000537 A DOUBLE BLINDNESS. BY ALIEN. London: Digby, Long, 1910 BMC.

TLS-love story. Two sisters and a man.
ACAD-0
LBKM-0

000538 HIS NEIGHBOURS' LANDMARK. BY "ALIEN". London: Digby, Long, 1907 BMC.

New Zealand. ACAD
Woman becomes famous opera singer. TLS

000539 IN GOLDEN SHACKLES. BY ALIEN. London: Hutchinson, 1896 BMC. New York: Dodd, Mead, 1896 NUC.

Ed. cultured man brutalized by drink and lust for gold. He apparently marries the fair Bell. The old man dies at the end still obsessed with gold. Bell has a new lover. There's a murder too.
SR 83:230.
A minor char. Ralph sacrifices much for Bell-goes to prison in place of her father. ACAD 51:46
ATH 108:902. New Zealand. Father with two children, takes daughter to mining camp, she chooses the less likely of two uncouth men because of sacrifice he has made for her father.

000540 A MAID OF METTLE. BY "ALIEN" (MRS. L. "ALIEN" BAKER). Philadelphia: G. W. Jacobs, [1902] NUC. London: Digby, Long, 1913 BMC.

000541 THE MAJESTY OF MAN; A NOVEL. BY "ALIEN". London: Hutchinson, 1895 BMC. New York: Dodd, Mead, 1896 NUC.

Weighs spiritual against natural life. Two women; Sister Lillian gives up personal and sexual life and serves others. Dora, the natural woman. Between them Brit Montgomery who married and lost one and now offers friendship to Lillian. Years past, wife shows up. Struggle in the man between the two. ACAD 47:294 The hero divided between power and the sacrifice of power. He gets both insofar as he becomes organizer and lecturer in slums of Melbourne. ATH 105:373 ambitious young man has his hopes dashed by an accident; he gives 10 years of his life to reform work; settles down to family life in SO. mining country. LW 28:43
PW 10-24-96. Young man from New Zealand, driven by artistic needs, seeks city life. He marries, jealousy prompts him to commit a crime, he disappears. 10 years later he and his wife meet and they discuss various ways of saving sinners.
Difficulties between man and woman in love. Psychological study. Set in New Zealand and Australia . BOOK NEWS: 97-8:138.

000542 NOT IN FELLOWSHIP: A NOVEL. BY "ALIEN," AUTHOR OF "THE UNTOLD HALF". London: Digby, Long, 1902 BMC.

Heroine marries "to sacrifice herself in honour of her uncle's good qualities;" uncle dies; she divorces, marries another in the end. Heroine beauty and virtue personified and she dogmatizes all the time. ATH 121,173

000543 OVER THE BARRIERS. BY 'ALIEN'. London: Isbister, 1903 BMC.

ATH 122,790

000544 THE PERFECT UNION. BY "ALIEN". London: Digby, Long, 1908 BMC.

TLS-themes of heredity, temperament, theories of marriage.
ATH-old-fashioned fairy tale.

000545 A SLUM HEROINE. BY ´ALIEN´. London: Digby, Long, 1904 BMC.

A kitchen-maid.

000546 AN UNREAD LETTER. BY "ALIEN". London: Digby, Long, 1909 BMC.

Widow living with two step daughters and a mystery. TLS

000547 THE UNTOLD HALF. BY ALIEN. London: Hutchinson, 1899 BMC. New York and London: G. P. Putnam´s Sons, 1899 NUC.

New Zealand: the wild scenery and primitive conditions. The cross purposes of 4 characters. Cordelia, Marvel, Max, and the artist Wynn Winter. LIT 5:186
One of the women is an educated self-possessed ascetic Quakeress, the other a wild child of the mountains. The untold half is that part of the story left to the readers´ imagination. PW 56:116
Romance of passion in wild New Zealand mountains. BAKER 03,247

000548 WHEAT IN THE EAR. BY ALIEN. London and New York: Hutchinson, 1898 BMC NUC.

ACAD 53:309. New Zealand. "Rough course of true love of a professor and a farmer for Joan." Joan baptized by a deaf parson as John and told to fight, was carried from the Church yelling that she wouldn´t. Tragic ending for professor.
PW-Joan "received her education from a Girton woman, who carefully develops her intellectual gifts while teaching her to stifle all feelings and emotions. The results...illustrated in Joan´s tragical mistakes when old enough to marry."

BAKER, LOUIE, jt. au. See HUMPHREYS, ELIZA MARGARET J. (GOLLAN) AND LOUISA ALICE BAKER.

BAKER, MRS. HEBRON. United States.

000549 THE WYNASTONS. New York: Broadway, [c1911] NUC.

NYT-Romance

BAKER, MRS. L. "ALIEN". See BAKER, LOUISA ALICE.

BALBACH, JULIA ANNA NENNINGER. B. 1852. United States.

000550 CUPID INTELLIGENT. New York: [Press of J. J. Little and Ives], 1910 NUC.

About a group of intelligent people actuated by social conscience. Author´s idea of equal education for the sexes comes through PW

BALCH, ALLIE SHARPE.

000551 SUNSHINE, RAIN AND ROSES. New York and London: G. P. Putnam´s Sons, 1911 BMC NUC.

BALDWIN, MARY.

000552 THE COTTAGE IN THE WOOD. London: S.P.C.K., [1920] BMC.

BALDWIN, MARY RUTH. United States.

000553 ALONG THE ANATAW. THE RECORD OF A CAMPAIGN. New York: Hunt and Eaton, 1891 BMC NUC.

Temperance cause. Jessie Ward strong loveable self sacrificing. IND
Town of Masson cursed by love for drink; Deacon and wife campai gn virorously against it. PW

BALDWIN, MRS. ALFRED. See BALDWIN, MRS. L.

BALDWIN, MRS. L.

000554 RICHARD DARE. BY MRS. ALFRED BALDWIN.

London: Smith, Elder, 1894 BMC NUC.

SP 73:4115. Runs away from home, becomes a great surgeon. Does a dangerous operation on his mother who doesn´t recognize him. His father was a drunken blacksmith, who when cured of alcohol was possessed of "spirits not less unclean."

000555 WHERE TOWN AND COUNTRY MEET. BY MRS ALFRED BALDWIN. London: Longmans, 1891 BMC NUC.

Alternates between squalid town and open country. Farmer loves dressmaker-both had been previously jilted. ATH 98 759
Sturminster the town. Mary Gravenall cares for blind sister, marries Farmer Applegarth. PW 12-26-91, 728.
ACAD 41:35. Romance of simple country people, a breath of fresh air.

BALDWIN, OLIVIA ARTEMISIA. 1858-1931. United States.

000556 SITA; A STORY OF CHILD-MARRIAGE FETTERS. New York: F. H. Revell, [1911] BMC NUC.

BALDY, ALICE MONTGOMERY. Nationality Unknown.

000557 THE ROMANCE OF A SPANISH NUN. Philadelphia: J. B. Lippincott, 1891 NUC.

Two lovers separated first by fate, then by church. Both suffer. LW
Magdelena de Laheria is a sculptor´s model. Falls in love with the sculptor. Before they are to marry, he goes away. She gets religious and enters nunnery. That´s the crisis. PW 2-14-91.

BALFOUR, ETHEL.

000558 IN TIME´S STOREROOMS. London: J. Ouseley, [1912] BMC.

ATH-popular rom.

000559 A WINNING LOSER; A NOVEL. London: J. Ouseley, 1908 BMC.

TLS-persecution of Royalists in Scotland.

BALFOUR, M. C. See BALFOUR, MARIE CLOTHILDE.

BALFOUR, MARIE CLOTHILDE. United States.

000560 THE FALL OF THE SPARROW. BY M. C. BALFOUR. New York: Putnam, 1897 NUC. London: Methuen, 1897 BMC.

3 or 4 principal chars are studies in weakness: Nathaniel Forster, a dreamy person of indecision. Walter Borthwick, a zealot, happy only when praised. One woman weak-burns with passion for the priest Walter. Feels a sense of duty to poor but does nothing. Phillipa strong shrewd, original, firm willed, sym. "quick to see the issue of events, bold to grasp an opportunity." ACAD 52 Fic Sup:115.
Boy and two girls in rectory in Lincoln-shire. Boy devotes himself to literature; one girl marries; one devotes herself to church work. Scene shifts to London and main char. who struggles for his salvation. He´s a preacher. PW 52:670.
Gertrude engaged to Nathaniel loves walter; Phillippa loves Nathaniel but marries Dr. Dale. LIT 1:85.
ATH 111:114. Dreamy young hero and his relations with two girl cousins.
LBKM 14:133 Rise, fall and regeneratidn of Borthwick, the overwrought preacher in the East End.

000561 MARIS STELLA. Boston: Roberts, 1896 NUC. London: J. Lane, 1896 BMC.

ATH 108:713. Keynote Series. "Lacks the unpleasant flavor of decadent morbidity" of some of its predecessors. Subject is the ill-starred marriage of Laumec LeBraz and ´Poldine. Two obstinate people, devoted to each other. Conflict results in ´Poldine´s madness. Setting is French seaport. Tragic close. Dedicated to Joseph Jacobs and Alfred Nutt.
BKM 4:375. He has an illeg. child whose mother dies. ´Poldine can forgive what he has done but shrinks with "uncontrollable horror" from all contact with the child. Husband "forgets his remorse in defiant anger as the sympathy and help he needs so desperately are withheld."
PW 10-31-96. "After losing her husband by her hardness she devotes her life to the care of his illegitimate child, whom she has rendered imbecile by striking him in anger."

Sad tragic story of a Breton fisherman and his
bourgeois wife: his strong temperament. "The narrow
conventional type of girl"- Poldine. SP 79:627.
Low class French seaport life. Poldine weds a sailor
who loves her "clean superiorty." But their marriage
fails because he conceives of her as a shining goddess
too far above. One day in an argument she defies him.
He leaves. Neither will yeild to the other. The rest
of the story is a study of her going insane. LBKM
11:124
Tragedy, remorse, madness CR 26,30:76

000562   WHITE SAND. THE STORY OF A DREAMER AND
HIS DREAM. BY M. C. BALFOUR. London: T.F. Unwin, 1896
BMC. New York: Merriam, [c1896] NUC.

ATH 107:14 "Fin de siecle." Mrs. Carpenter "and other
invertebrate animals." Jack Borlase is "attractive."
Author shows a laborious determination to be flippant
and emancipated.
ACAD 49:281. Sylvia is "as unstable and shiftless as
white sand." Runs away with a man, then back to her
husband who feels "this pretty, weak, pleasure-loving
little woman needs his protection." Claire marries a
man incapable of fidelity "so that she may, in some
measure, protect him from himself. "Largeness and
wholesomeness of this book."
PW 12-12-96. Principal character devoid of moral
responsibility whose life is made gay and brilliant by
her elderly husband who married her because he had
loved and lost her mother.
Sylvia, selfish flirt "without heart or principle,"
marries a noble man, deserts him. Husband follows her
to Paris, tries to lure her from lover by promising
all the money she can spend and freedom to go wherever
she wishes. Contrast between self sacrificing husband
and selfish lover. LW 28:59.
Man loves a "bad" woman and a good one at the same
time. Expects the good one to understand. BKM 5:353

BALL, HYLDA (RHODES).

000563   OF FINER CLAY. London: J. Long, 1920 BMC.

TLS love st
ATH 3 or four love affairs, only one ends happily.
LBKM
SR

000564   THE SECRET BOND. London: J. Long, [1917]
BMC.

Lenore Mortimer "betrayed", fought vs poverty, came
under influence of hypnotist, went on stage, joins the
ranks of "the companion age" as a means of earning
money? TLS
Only when she finds a man who has also "sinned" does
she find peace and happiness. Before this, lonely,
endeavors to atone for her past; her lost self haunts
her. Her past haunts her. LBKM
Detrimental hypnotic influence which demands the
utmost power of resistance of which the heroine is
capable. ATH. Includes a picture of a communist
village.

000565   A STAR ASTRAY. London: Holden and
Hardingham, [1916] BMC.

Traditional love story. TLS
Heroine, out of sympathy with her family, falls in
love with married man, but "finds relief from her
sorrows" in music. ATH

000566   THE UNHALLOWED VOW. London: J. Long,
[1918] BMC.

TLS--Occult. Woman utilizes powers of darkness in
carrying out her vow of vengeance against a man with
whom she lived, would not marry her and is now a
widower.

000567   A VASE OF CLAY. London: Holden and
Hardingham, [1914] BMC.

Yorkshire village--heroine enticed to London by French
chauffeur. Eventually marries a farm laborer ATH

000568   WHAT SNOW CONCEALS. London: J. Long, 1919
BMC.

young woman forced to marry a man twice her age--by
wicked uncle bent on revenge for having been jilted by
her mother. A bomb takes care of the husband and
leaves the young woman rich and free to marry the man
of her choice. TLS
Mrs. Lestrange an actress LBKM

Wicked uncle chose a broken-down man about town for
her husband. The uncle pays this man's debts, has a
detective spy on the couple leaves property to the man
on condition that they never separate or divorce. SR

BALL, OONA HOWARD (BUTLIN). B. 1867.

000569   BARBARA GOES TO OXFORD. BY BARBARA BURKE.
London: Methuen, [1907] NUC BMC.

Two women visit Oxford, describes their experiences in
letters. TLS

000570   A QUIET HOLIDAY. London: Cassell, 1912
BMC NUC.

TLS-She is commissioned to write a country book and
retires to village in search of rural matter.
ATH Lack of inspiration but jots everything down.

000571   THEIR OXFORD YEAR. London: Methuen,
[1909] NUC BMC.

BALLARD, EVA C. United States.

000572   SHE WANTED TO VOTE; OR HOME INFLUENCES.
Crawfordsville, Ind.: Brower Bros., 1901 NUC.

BALLOU, CLARA E. Nationality Unknown.

000573   PLAYED ON HEARTS. New York: J. S.
Ogilvie, 1902 NUC.

BAMFORD, MARY ELLEN. B. 1857. United States.

000574   ELEANOR AND I: A TALE OF THE DAYS OF KING
RICHARD II. Boston: Congregational Sunday-school and
Pub. Society, [c1891] NUC.

Eleanor learns to read the Bible for herself. Brother
(I) tries to cure her with a relic but she dies. PW
10-3-91

000575   JANET AND HER FATHER. Boston:
Congregational Sunday-School and Pub. Society, [c1891]
NUC.

Semi-rel novel, hist. persecution of the Covenanters.
LW
Janet's father escapes persecution in time of James II
of Scotland. PW 10-3-91.

000576   JESSIE'S THREE RESOLUTIONS. Philadelphia:
American Baptist Publication Society, [c1894] NUC.

LW 25:267. Young woman interested in missionary work
accomplishes much even though kept at home by
"duties." Propaganda.

000577   MISS MILLIE'S TRYING. New York: Hunt and
Eaton, 1893 NUC.

PW-Millie; through writing articles for the press,
provides for herself and her sister the meager
necessities of life. An unexpected bargain with a real
estate agent ends her struggles.

BANCROFT, LADY. See BANCROFT, MARIE EFFIE (WILSON).

BANCROFT, MARIE EFFIE (WILSON). 1839-1921.

000578   THE SHADOW OF NEEME. BY LADY BANCROFT.
London: J. Murray, 1912 BMC NUC.

TLS-Heroine belongs to all ages, secondary character
is very modern.
ATH 0

BANFIELD, AGNES HOUGHTON.

000579   UNDER BLUE SKIES, AND OTHER STORIES.
Philadelphia: International Printing, [c1900] W. (Also
Contains: Jason and Matilda-Moonlight.)

BANG, ELIZABETH. Nationality Unknown.

000580   STELLA'S ROOMERS: THE ASTONISHING STORY
OF A NEW YORK ROOMING HOUSE. BY STELLA CARR. New York:
Brandu's, [c1911] NUC.

Humor about getting rid of unwelcomed guests and the
like. PW 9-2-11
13 sketches. NYT

BANGS, CHARLOTTE REBECCA (WOGLOM).

000581   WRONGS TO RIGHT. BY CHARLOTTE R. VAN
WOGLOM. New York: H. B. Lounsbury, 1892 NUC.

BANGS, ELLA MATTHEWS. United States.

    000582   THE KING'S MARK; A STORY OF EARLY
    PORTLAND. Boston: C. M. Clark, 1908 NUC.

    PW—Hist romance.

BANGS, MARY ROGERS. United States.

    000583   HIGH BRADFORD. Boston: Houghton Mifflin,
    1912 NUC.

    PW—Romance—women stay at home.
    NYT Romance

BANKS, ELIZABETH L. 1870-1938. United States.

    000584   THE AUTOBIOGRAPHY OF A "NEWSPAPER GIRL".
    London: Methuen, 1902 BMC. New York: Dodd, Mead, 1902
    NUC.

    PN 4874 Journalism.

    000585   CAMPAIGNS OF CURIOSITY. JOURNALISTIC
    ADVENTURES OF AN AMERICAN GIRL IN LONDON. London:
    Cassell, 1894 BMC. Chicago: F. T. Neely, 1894 BMC NUC.

    An American young woman astonishes the British press
    by a series of campaigns in which she impersonates
    various people; a servant, in order to learn what the
    re. to master is like; an heiress to learn about
    arist. society; laundry girls & also "offers various
    examples of women's emancipation." PW 1-19-95,52.

    000586   THE MYSTERY OF FRANCES FARRINGTON.
    London: Hutchinson, 1909 BMC. New York: 1909 NUC.

    A writer who has two identities; as Margaret Allison
    she writes light comedy; as Frances Farrington,
    serious stories. Farce includes a trial of Margaret
    for the murder of Frances. TLS
    She can't succeed as serious writer because of her
    reputation as popular writer; Must kill off that
    identity. ATH
    Attacks Amer. judicial insts. SP.

BANKS, ISABELLA (VARLEY). 1821-1897. United Kingdom.

    000587   BOND SLAVES: THE STORY OF A STRUGGLE. BY
    MRS. G. LINNAEUS BANKS. London: Griffith, Farran, 1893
    NUC BMC.

    The Luddite agitation in the North and Midland
    counties. BAKER 03, 69.
    Full of information concerning the industrial life in
    Yorkshire at the beginning of nineteenth century and
    love story. ATH 102:189.
    SP 72:377. Luddite riots. Walter, hard-working tailor
    and the troubles and misfortunes that befell him after
    he took the Luddite vow.

    000588   GLORY: A WILTSHIRE STORY. London:
    Griffith, Farran, [1892] BMC.

    000589   A ROUGH ROAD; OR HOW A BOY MADE A MAN OF
    HIMSELF. London: Blackie, [1892] BMC.

    000590   THE SLOWLY GRINDING MILLS. London:
    Griffith, Farran, 1893 BMC.

    Out-of-date conventionalities of old-fashioned
    melodramatic fiction. SP 71:147.
    A villian who remarries his first wife after he kills
    the second. The wife poisons him. And the love
    interest of Miss Octavia is not a bit modern. SR
    76:102.

BANKS, MRS. G. LINNAEUS. See BANKS, ISABELLA (VARLEY).

BANKS, NANCY HUSTON. C. 1850. United States.

    000591   THE LITTLE HILLS. New York and London:
    Macmillan, 1905 BMC NUC.

    Sent 7-1-05 PW
    Loveable little heroine and step mother who is a
    terror. NYT 478,05.

    000592   OLDFIELD, A KENTUCKY TALE OF THE LAST
    CENTURY. New York and London: Macmillan, 1902 NUC BMC.

    ATH 8-9-02
    DIAL 8-02 Spinster? Drawn with loving care?

NYT 6-21-02 "Sweetest, demurest, most innocent,
angelic" characters. Vegetate. "Men are not
interesting."

    000593   ROUND ANVIL ROCK; A ROMANCE. London and
    New York: Macmillan, 1903 NUC BMC.

    BAKER 32-32
    Sweet pure simple love story NYT 468 03
    Also BKM 17,518
    also, LBKM 10-03,54
    also ATH 122, 342

BANNING, MARGARET (CULKIN). B. 1891. United States.

    000594   THIS MARRYING. London: Hodder and
    Stoughton, [1920] BMC. New York: G. H. Doran, [c1920]
    NUC.

    TLS Sent. Journalistic world, diverse problems of mrg.
    and claims of men upon women and vice versa.
    PW--modern girl falls in love with editor of
    struggling paper she is working for.
    NYT 6/27/20 p. 17. Horatia is a dedicated journalist,
    prefers career to taking care of children (which she
    is very capable at too). "Story ends the way most
    readers desire."

BARBARA, pseud. See WRIGHT, MABEL (OSGOOD).

BARBER, MARGARET FAIRLESS. 1869-1901.. United Kingdom.

    000595   THE GATHERING OF BROTHER HILARIUS. BY
    MICHAEL FAIRLESS. London: J. Murray, 1901 BMC NUC. New
    York: E. P. Dutton, 1913 NUC.

    Story of Black Death

BARBOUR, A. M. See BARBOUR, ANNA MAY.

BARBOUR, A. MAYNARD. See BARBOUR, ANNA MAY.

BARBOUR, ANNA MAY. D. 1941. United States.

    000596   AT THE TIME APPOINTED. BY A. MAYNARD
    BARBOUR. Philadelphia and London: J. B. Lippincott,
    1903 NUC BMC.

    000597   THE AWARD OF JUSTICE; OR, TOLD IN THE
    ROCKIES. A PEN PICTURE OF THE WEST. BY A. M. BARBOUR.
    Chicago: Rand, McNally, [c1901] NUC.

    1st pub. 1897 "Told in the Rockies"

    000598   BREAKERS AHEAD. BY A. MAYNARD BARBOUR.
    philadelphia and London: J. P. Lippincott, 1906 BMC
    NUC.

    PW—male hero, trifler.
    NY-strong wife.

    000599   THAT MAINWARING AFFAIR. BY A. MAYNARD
    BARBOUR. Philadelphia and London: J. B. Lippincott,
    1901 NUC BMC.

    PW-Murder mystery of rich old New York stockbroker.
    Detective work.
    detective story BKM 1901

    000600   TOLD IN THE ROCKIES: A PEN PICTURE OF THE
    WEST. BY A. MAYNARD BARBOUR. Chicago and New York:
    Rand, McNally, [c1897] NUC.

    LW 29:102. Young husband investigates fraudulent
    mining co. Two love episodes. "Clean."

BARCLAY, EDITH NOEL (DANIELL). B. 1872. United Kingdom.

    000601   A DREAM OF BLUE ROSES. BY MRS. HUBERT
    BARCLAY. London and New York: Hodder and Stoughton,
    1912 BMC NUC.

    PW 83 3/1/13:763 "Barbara Claudia Vincent grows up
    knowing nothing about her parents or family. At seven
    she was given over to the care of a fine old French
    couple, a sufficient sum for her maintenance being
    sent each year. When Pere Joseph dies, Barbara and the
    Petite Mere find themselves in very straightened
    circumstances, and the girl, now of age, goes to
    London, to the lawyer, whose name was given to her
    guardians to claim the fortune she believes is hers.
    Disappointment is the only result of her visit and she
    is obliged to find work. How she does this, the
    people, some of them quaint, some of them merry, whom
    she meets, and her love for a fine man finish the
    story."

Old fashioned, uncomplicated, simple quiet tale. NYT
ATH "Prettily told" French girl is a companion in Eng.
country village.
TLS-Pleasing, loveable girl happy ending.

000602   EAST OF THE SHADOWS. BY MRS. HUBERT
BARCLAY. London and New York: Hodder & Stoughton,
[c1913] BMC NUC.

PW 3-14-14 964 "A man worshipped a woman, then he met
with an accident and the woman did not care enough to
stand by him. From that point on life stood still for
him in every sense. In appearance he grew no older.
His mind lived in memories of the past. And then came
the niece of his false love, the same in name, the
same in face but very different in heart. Her
unselfishness and devotion restore his health and his
romance, but spell heartache for her."
Man loves memory; wife remarries. 22 years later he
sees his niece and believes her to be his old love.
TLS

000603   THE TASTE OF BRINE. BY MRS. HUBERT
BARCLAY. London and New York: Hodder and Stoughton,
[1914] NUC BMC.

ATH young man feels he has lost his self respect after
6 months in jail.
ATH 144:533 Heroine reassures him, a "womanly woman."

000604   TREVOR LORDSHIP. BY MRS. HUBERT BARCLAY.
New York: Macmillan, 1911 NUC. London: Macmillan, 1911
BMC.

an estate and a dutiful wife. 3-11-11 PW
Marriage that begins cool but where love grows. TLS
Two couples. SR
BKM 33 (1911) 318 BKM

BARCLAY, FLORENCE LOUISA (CHARLESWORTH). 1862-1921. United
Kingdom.

000605   THE BROKEN HALO. London and New York: G.
P. Putnam's Sons, 1913 BMC NUC.

Man 28 marries woman of 60? Male hero. PW 84 10.
4/4/13, p. 435
Review NYT BR 1913,600
Dick Cameron, young dr. presses older wealthy woman to
marry him. There has been a terrible tragedy in her
past life. ACAD
"Feeble sentimentality." SP
She's twice a widow. He later turns his attentions to
a younger widow. LBKM

000606   THE FOLLOWING OF THE STAR; A ROMANCE.
London and New York: G. P. Putnam's Sons, 1911 BMC
NUC.

Young clergyman inspires wealthy woman. She can't give
money to him unless he's her husband. They go through
the service--he goes off with his work, she devotes
her life to humanity. PW 10-14-11
BKM 34 (1911) 311-12
Diana Rivers must marry to keep her fortune.
"Emotionally rel. romance that might be better in
verse." TLS
Diana vs marr. but proposes to the young minister who
needs money for missionary work. They fall in love,
happily ever after. LBKM
"Heroine is a modern of moderns, who doesn't believe
in marriage and spurns the whole world of men unless
they will consent to be just good fellows and good
friends." NYT

000607   THE MISTRESS OF SHENSTONE. New York and
London: G.P. Putnam's Sons, [c1910] NUC BMC.

Lady Ingleby is widowed after 10 years of marriage
without affection, falls in love, there are
complications but finally a satisfactory ending. PW
TLS--sent. love story.

000608   MY HEART'S RIGHT THERE. London and New
York: G. P. Putnam's Sons, 1914 BMC NUC.

Sent and patriotic little war story. NYT
Sentiment overdrawn.
Story of soldier's wife. LBKM

000609   RETURNED EMPTY. London and New York: G.
P. Putnam's Sons, 1920 BMC NUC.

LBKM--Spiritualism.
PW--A man dies young in a tragic way--leaving a woman
alone with her memory of a great love. Written first

and foremost to women mourning a promising young life
cut off by sudden death.

000610   THE ROSARY. New York and London: G. P.
Putnam's Sons, 1909 NUC BMC.

Jane Champion plain 30 awakens love of friend of 27.
Refuses to marry because he's a boy and painter,
afraid he'll regret it. She travels. PW 12-4-09.
Story ends in bliss. TLS
Artist finds his ideal in a "plain" girl. NYT
NYT--love story.

000611   THROUGH THE POSTERN GATE; A ROMANCE OF
SEVEN DAYS. New York and London: G. P. Putnam's Sons,
1911 BMC NUC. London: Putnam, 1912 BMC.

PW--Charming love story.

000612   THE UPAS TREE; A CHRISTMAS STORY FOR ALL
THE YEAR. London and New York: G. P. Putnam's Sons,
1912 BMC NUC.

Male novelist goes to Africa for material for his
novels. Wife has a child but husband never gets the
news because of an evil cousin. When he returns there
are problems between husband and wife and all ends
happily. Husband is mad for a while. SP

000613   THE WALL OF PARTITION. London and New
York: G. P. Putnam's Sons, 1914 BMC NUC.

LBKM--male author hero, love interest, plenty of moral
teaching
NYT 1914:448.
"Ten years before Rodney Steele's fiancee, Madge, had
forsaken him, when confronted with love letters in his
hand, addressed to a nurse. On his return to London,
Steele finds his signed novels best-sellers, but his
"Great Divide" written under a nom de plume and
chronicling his blasted romance, is a sensational
success. Steele still loves Madge as fervently as
ever, although he believes her married to another. At
length a "kind voice," which greets Steele daily over
the telephone, is the means of removing the wall of
partition between two faithful hearts." PW 86
10/10/14:1200
"A romance of a widow and her former fiance." WOMAN'S
EDU. ASSOC. April 1915 No. 31

000614   THE WHEELS OF TIME. New York: T.Y.
Crowell, [1908] NUC. Toronto: McClelland and
Goodchild, 1912 NUC.

000615   THE WHITE LADIES OF WORCESTER; A ROMANCE
OF THE TWELFTH CENTURY. London and New York: G. P.
Putnam, 1917 BMC NUC.

Mora enters a convent because she believes she's lost
her lover. He returns but can't convince her to leave
convent until Bishop helps. PW

BARCLAY, HARRIET MARIA.

000616   LIGHT FROM ASIA. London: Heath, Cranton
and Ouseley, [1914] BMC.

ATH Male hero renounces fiance for Bhuddism, changes
his mind and returns to Christ and engaged.

BARCLAY, MRS. HUBERT. See BARCLAY, EDITH NOEL (DANIELL).

BARCYNSKA, COUNTESS, pseud. See EVANS, MARGUERITE FLORENCE
HELENE (JERVIS).

BARCYNSKA, COUNTESS HELENE, pseud. See EVANS, MARGUERITE
FLORENCE HELENE (JERVIS).

BARKER, AMELIA M.

000617   TOM-ALL-ALONE. London: J. Macqueen, 1899
BMC.

London waif. Becomes very wealthy as a man. Looks for
his family; is chased by a young adventuress, finally
marries happily. ACAD 56:560

BARKER, ELLEN (BLACKMAR) MAXWELL. 1853?-1938. United
States.

000618   THE BISHOP'S CONVERSION. BY ELLEN
BLACKMAR MAXWELL. New York: Cranston and Curts, 1892
NUC.

000619   THREE OLD MAIDS IN HAWAII. BY ELLEN
BLACKMAR MAXWELL. New York: Curts and Jennings, 1896

NUC. New York: Eaton & Mains, 1896 BMC.

PW 8-29-96. Three women take a trip td Hawaii-what they saw. Native customs, superstitions, scenes of native life.

000620   THE WAY OF FIRE. BY ELLEN BLACKMAR MAXWELL. New York: Dodd, Mead, 1897 NUC.

Eurasian woman married to English doctor who comes into money and high society after the marriage and regrets his marriage until a young English woman Helen Sunderland schools the Eurasian wife so she "rises to her husband's level." PW 52:639.
When the wife realizes she's her husband's "intellectual inferior," she goes away to England, gets schooling. "Domestic cares, child-bearing, natural limitations-many causes conspire to prevent her overtaking her freer and stronger mate in the race of life." BKM 6:259.

BARKER, ELSA. 1869-1954. United States.

000621   LAST LETTERS FROM A LIVING DEAD MAN. London: W. Rider, 1914 BMC. New York: M. Kennerley, 1919 NUC.

PW 85 5/9/14 1552 "By author of "The Son of Mary Bethel," etc. Book is made up of letters which Miss Barker says in her introduction, came to her from a friend who had died. She was one day strongly impelled to take up a pencil and write. Yielding to the impulse, her hand was seized as if from the outside, and a message of a personal nature came, followed by the signature "X". Later she learned that "was a nickname for an old friend in America, of whose death she did not learn until after writing the letters." BF 1301 Spiritualism.

000622   THE SON OF MARY BETHEL. London: Chatto & Windus, 1909 BMC. New York: Duffield, 1909 NUC.

Story of Christ in Modern environment.

BARKER, HELEN MANCHESTER (GATES) GRANVILLE. D. 1950. United States.

000623   AN APPRENTICE TO TRUTH. BY HELEN HUNTINGTON. New York and London: G.P. Putnam, 1910 BMC NUC.

Opening in a small New England town, the scene shifts to NY, and the story deals with some of the phases of social life in the metropolis. BKM 31,1910.
Marah Langdon (father poor Vt. Dr.) becomes companion to woman in NYC. The woman, her cousin, is "vain, shallow, and vindictive with a disgraceful secret." Also a hopeless social climber. PW
TLS-suitable for girl reader.
SR-worn down by cruelty Marah betrays her confidence which brings her nothing but guilt. Depressing end.
NYT-Psychological study of relationship between Marah and her cousin, who grow to hate each other.

000624   EASTERN RED. BY HELEN HUNTINGTON. New York and London: Putnam, 1918 BMC NUC.

PW-two unhappily married women. Mr. Harcourt wants a divorce. Rose Durand, a singer, suicides.
TLS-a good deal is heard of the suffrage movement; main interest is feminine.
NYT-a study of the modern woman who has outgrown dependence and is not yet ready for freedom. Rose is not able to hurt her husband by leaving him so kills herself, Elsie is not able to face publicity of divorce.

000625   MARSH LIGHTS. BY HELEN HUNTINGTON. New York: C. Scr'sibner Sons, 1913 NUC.

PW 84 9/20/13 p. 767 "Young army officer marries a beautiful girl, gives up the army for her sake, and is drawn by her into a life of business and society which gradually wears out their love. Another man helps her to get money in Wall Street and makes love to her; the husband gets interested in a woman who likes solitude and pretty fancies better than society, falls in love with her, and is just about to elope with her when she suddenly dies."

000626   THE MOON LADY. BY HELEN HUNTINGTON. New York: C. Scribner's Sons, 1911 NUC.

Son tries to save mother from drink. PW 11-4-11

000627   THE SOVEREIGN GOOD. BY HELEN HUNTINGTON.

New York and London: G. P. Putnam, 1908 BMC NUC.

PW-friendship between rich American young woman and poor European young man.
BKM 28,1908-9-- A story which deals with the social gaieties of the New York smart set.
NYT-woman is 12 years older than he, he marries a young bride. St. of her char.

BARKLEY, CHRISTINA A.

000628   THE SHACK ON CEDAR CREEK. Greenock: J. McKelvie, 1917 BMC.

BARKSDALE, EMILY WOODSON. Nationality Unknown.

000629   STELLA HOPE. New York: Neale, 1907 NUC.

BKM-15 yr old suppressed by her aunt goes to convent to learn and becomes what she has longed for a "beautiful young lady."
Girls are actors. Stella "Intense love for the beautiful." 7-6-07 PW

BARLOW, HILARE EDITH.

000630   THE MYSTERY OF JEANNE MARIE. London: Lynwood, 1913 BMC.

Secret marriage between a disguised nobleman and a peasant young woman whose daughter finds herself an heiress later in life. ATH

000631   THE SENTENCE OF THE JUDGE. London: Lynwood, 1912 BMC.

BARLOW, JANE. 1860-1917. United Kingdom.

000632   FLAWS; A NOVEL. London: Hutchinson, 1911 BMC NUC.

Irish story with many, many characters and their doings. TLS
Amusing, cheerful ATH
BAKER 32-35

000633   THE FOUNDING OF FORTUNES. London: Methuen, 1902 BMC. New York: Dodd, Mead, 1902 NUC.

ATH 10-18-02 Story of male millionaire
Lively pictures of Irish life of all degrees. LBKM 1-03,169
BAKER 32:34

000634   FROM THE LAND OF THE SHAMROCK. New York: Dodd, Mead, 1900 NUC. London: Methuen, 1901 BMC.

000635   IN MIO'S YOUTH; A NOVEL. London: Hutchinson, 1917 BMC NUC.

Irish 1860-1917.
Irish soc, orphan taken in, becomes engaged. TLS
"A decaying landed family with a medley of sons and daughters and a sensitive and imaginative adopted child." BAKER 32, p.35

000636   KERRIGAN'S QUALITY. London: Hodder and Stoughton, 1894 BMC. New York: Dodd, Mead, 1894 NUC.

LBKM 7:55. Story of Irish peasantry. Martin Kerrigan returns to Ireland from Australia, settles in a little village Glenore, buys the "Big house" and lets it to people of quality, the O'Connors, who have been staying at his farmhouse as a result of an accident. Merle is a cousin of Sir Benjamin O'Connor, and influences Martin to use his fortune to make the lot of the landed gentry and landless peasants more equal. ATH 104:601. Irish peasant life, tragic catastrophe. Series of vignettes of Irish life held loosely by a narrative. ACAD 47:9

000637   MAC'S ADVENTURES. London: Hutchinson, 1911 BMC NUC.

Story of a boy TLS

BARLOW, MADGE.

000638   THE CAIRN OF THE BADGER. New York: Cassell, 1908 PW. London: Cassell, 1908 BMC.

PW-Conflict of two willful men; feminine intrigue holds the issue?
TLS Conv. rom.
ATH

BARMBY, BEATRICE HELEN. D. 1904. United States.

000639   BETTY MARCHAND. New York: G. H. Doran,
[c1918] BMC NUC.

PW--Left alone at 17 and preferring independence to
life with rich relations, enters business world and
begins hard and bitter struggle.
NYT--Nov. 8, 1918 p 471. Story of Betty's life from 6
to 35. Begins as stenographer, becomes a successful
business woman, is sent to work in New York by London
firm.
TLS--concentrates on the courage of the young woman
who works and strives and "makes good" in the busy
American world.

000640   THE GODS ARE JUST. London: Duckworth,
1904 BMC NUC.

TLS--Analysis of the two men rather than the woman
they love.

000641   SUNRISE FROM THE HILLTOP. New York: G. H.
Doran, [c1919] BMC NUC.

Young English woman marries Amer. man but must give up
her beloved English home to live in NY apartment. PW
Marries a young American instead of a great landowner.
Her experiences and final sacrifice are recounted. NYT
787, 12-28-19.
TLS Girl coming from quiet Eng. home to NY and finding
herself.

BARNBY, ADELINE.

000642   A TROPICAL ROMANCE. London: Murray &
Evenden, 1920 BMC.

TLS Nellie goes to India to join her fiance, Max. Hero
is Rajah of Bisnohor. Nellie in circle of intrigue.

BARNES, ANNIE MARIA. B. 1857. United States.

000643   AN AMERICAN GIRL IN KOREA. Philadelphia:
Penn, 1905 NUC.

Korea-desc. and travel.

BARNES, DJUNA (CHAPPELL). B. 1892. United States.

000644   THE BOOK OF REPULSIVE WOMEN; 8 RHYTHMS
AND FIVE DRAWINGS. New York: Bruno Chap Books, 1915
NUC.

v. 1 Alicat Bookshop Press, 1948 (reprint) series
note-outcast Chapbook, 14

BARNETT, ADA.

000645   FOR THE LIFE OF OTHERS: A NOVEL. BY G.
CARDELLA. London: Sonnenschein, 1897 BMC.

Devonshire. The fortunes of the Garnsworthies and the
Hannafords, farmers. ACAD 52 Fic Sup. 97.
A girl should not marry if there's an hereditary
disease in the family. Theme ATH 110:714.
LIT 2:148. Saintly heroine, from a family cursed with
hereditary insanity, gives her life to preaching that
persons in her position should avoid mrge. for others'
sakes.
SR 85:501. She establishes a hospital and a
settlement.

000646   A KING'S DAUGHTER. A NOVEL. BY G.
CARDELLA. London: S. Sonnenschein, 1892 BMC.

SP 68:469. Wholesome, pretty heroine, reviewer
compares parts of it to Little Lord Fauntleroy.
two heroines, one full of high aspiration, the other a
beauty who wants wealth. plus two heroes. Everyone
gets what they want in this optimistic novel. ATH 98
859

000647   THE PERFECT WAY OF HONOUR. BY G.
CARDELLA. London: S. Sonnenschein, 1894 BMC.

SP 72:906. Mary Carruthers discovers her husband has
an illegitimate son older than their own. She forces
him to acknowledge this claim, catching small-pox and
dying in performing a mother's duty to the nameless
waif.
ATH 103:609. She treats her husband's defect of will
in the grand style of the modern young woman destined
to regenerate the world.

BARNETT, ANNIE.

000648   DRIFTING THISTLEDOWN. BY MRS. P. A.
BARNETT AND ANOTHER. London, New York: Longmans,
Green, 1910 BMC NUC.

SP-incorrigible flirt, sense of humor, but
shrewd-believes that when all professions are open to
women marriage will have to compete and therefore be
made more attractive. Professional woman-has advantage
of financial independence--and not all old married
women are happy.
NYT 0

BARNETT, EDITH A. United Kingdom.

000649   A CHAMPION IN THE SEVENTIES: BEING THE
TRUE RECORD OF SOME PASSAGES IN A CONFLICT OF SOCIAL
FAITHS. Chicago: H.S. Stone, 1898 NUC. London: W.
Heinemann, 1898 BMC.

LIT 2:648. Heinemann. London. Tabby leaves her home
and goes to London to work to avoid the idleness
imposed on women in her home. Almost starves, but she
cannot go home unless she renounces her ideals.
ACAD 53:469. She is a champion of women's
independence.
ACAD 54:126. "Not a tract from the Pioneer Club but a
study in reality."
SR 85:785. The "state of things" in the 70's is gone;
"this might make women contented with what they have
now."
NYT 1898:422. Author: Her Tabitha life and her death
proved as to woman's strength of body nothing except
that this woman never had a fair chance. They proved a
good deal to some of us as to one woman's strength of
mind, and she will be the first to say that her life
and her work were not wasted, if they gained for women
less strong than herself the right to try in an easier
way.
PW-she works for the social betterment of women and
edits the Woman's Patriot.

000650   DR. AND MRS. GOLD: AN EPISODE IN THE LIFE
OF A CAUSE. London: Sonnenschein, 1891 BMC.

Clara David is an earnest anarchist, a revolutionary
inspired by the cause of social anarchism. Gives her
entire devotion to it. She's strong, noble. "Poor
Clara's doom might easily have been even more terrible
than it was". ATH 98 683
Becomes mistress of a male revolutionary who has none
of her passion for the cause. ACAD
SP. Inner life of a Nihilist or anarchist community,
focussed on the conflict in a woman's mind whether she
should give herself to the cause or to the "worthless
person who typifies it to her." Review infers she
chose the man.
SR 73:45. Clara David. She marries Dr. Gold. He
already has a wife whom he deserted.

000651   THE FETICH OF THE FAMILY. A RECORD OF
HUMAN SACRIFICE. London: W. Heinemann, 1902 BMC NUC.

One sister is weak and clever; the other strong in
body but mentally unfit. An over painful book. ACAD
64, 106
Two cousins marry late have an idiot child; three
years later, a normal one. But mother sacrifices
second daughter to insane resolve that no difference
will be made between the two. Young girl feels idiot
sister her cross. Mother's character fully drawn. ACAD
64, 276
Couple have a half witted daughter and a "sound" one.
The first is given her own way--all else sacrificed.
Out of sisterly duty, the other feels she must devote
her life to her sister. The sound one consequently
leads a shut-away life. LBKM 3-03, 248

000652   A GARDEN OF EDEN: KEMPTON PARK ONCE UPON
A TIME. London: A. Constable, 1905 BMC NUC.

A pretty piece, misleading title. LBKM 27-8, 139

000653   SUNNINGHAM AND THE CURATE. London:
Chapman and Hall, 1899 BMC.

Another novel in Cranford mode. LIT 4:502.
Semi-suburban neighborhood in the 60s. SP 82:616
Fine portrait--Rev. Hilary Davies. Painful reading in
parts. SR 87:792

000654   A WILDERNESS WINNER. London: Methuen,
1907 BMC.

Phoebe's crushing disillusionment with emigration to
the Amer. West. TLS

Visit of Englishwoman who's used to all the comforts. Shows the gloom of it all. ATH
Realistic life of a woman in Amer. West "not a very pleasing picture." SP

BARNETT, EVELYN SCOTT (SNEAD). D. 1921. United States.

000655   THE DRAGNET. New York: B. Huebsch, 1909 NUC.

Trad-mystery PW 11-20-09
Detective. NYT

000656   MRS. DELIRE'S EUCHRE PARTY, AND OTHER TALES. Franklin, Ohio: Editor Pub. Co., [c1895] NUC.

BARNETT, MRS. P. A. See BARNETT, ANNIE.

BARNUM, FRANCES COURTENAY (BAYLOR). 1848-1920. United States.

000657   CLAUDIA. A NOVEL. BY FRANCES COURTENAY BAYLOR. London: Osgood, McIlvaine, 1894 BMC.

000658   CLAUDIA HYDE: A NOVEL. BY FRANCES COURTENAY BAYLOR. Boston and New York: Houghton, Mifflin, 1894 NUC.

SP 72:796. Romance of young man who emigrates to Virginia. She reads poetry but also manages father's house.
LW 25:218. Womanly. Daily life of impoverished but cultivated Southern family; the father is a scholar. Gerald Midmay, financially ruined and jilted leaves England in answer to an ad to learn farming in Virginia. After paying, comes to Virginia, finds it's a fraud. But meets Southern Claudia and her family--in them all the South--the hospitality, etc. now existing in genteel poverty. CR 23:27

000659   THE LADDER OF FORTUNE. BY FRANCES COURTENEY BAYLOR. Boston and New York: Houghton, Mifflin, 1899 NUC. London: A. P. Watts, [1899] BMC.

The moral is money brings misery if it's used only for selfish purposes. A couple struggle hard to gain money, social position. They succeed. One daughter marries a French noble who spends all her money and abuses her. The other refuses to marry to satisfy mother's ambition, weds an artist. They are the only two nice people in a good study of unadmirable folk. CR 35:844
A good unspoiled daughter, a foolish one who buys a title, with her father's millions. The first gets a chivalrous virginian. NYT 7-22-99,484
Lizzie Thompson is a milliner with ambitions to be a society leader, marries a businessman. Story of that family. Moral; mothers--don't marry your daughters to foreigners, especially French who abuse their wives once the ceremony is over. NYT 5-28-99,335

000660   MISS NINA BARROW. BY FRANCES COURTENAY BAYLOR. New York: Century, 1897 BMC.

BARONTI, GERVE, pseud. See DANNER, MRS. PAUL.

BARR, AMELIA EDITH (HUDDLESTON). 1831-1919. United States.

000661   THE BEADS OF TASMER. New York: R. Bonner's Sons, [c1891] NUC.

The beads form a rosary-a family heirloom-that helps smooth the way for a marriage between Roberta of the Free Kirk and a Catholic man. It helps bring understanding of greater spiritual religion. PW 10-16-91.
Story of true love. Scottish Clan. LW 23:43.

000662   THE BELLE OF BOWLING GREEN. New York: Dodd, Mead, 1904 NUC. London: B. F. Stevens and Brown, 1904 BMC.

PW--love story of 1812.
NyT--womanly.

000663   BERNICIA. New York: Dodd, Mead, 1895 NUC. London: B. F. Stevens, 1895 BMC.

It is the ancient name for Northumberland, where Bernicia lived until her father lost his life in the cause of the Stuarts. Then she went to London. Historical novel PW 11-2-95:741
ATH 107:776. Historical romance. 18th century. Northumbria Jacobite family. Lively and petulant heroine.
SP 77:51. Historical romance. George II. Lovable

coquette.
BKM 3:167. Her romance.

000664   THE BLACK SHILLING: A TALE OF BOSTON TOWNS. New York: Dodd, Mead, 1903 NUC. London: T.F. Unwin, 1904 BMC.

Witchcraft trials 10-10-03 PW
Cotton Mather drawn as a savage? 11-03 NYT 796
LBKM--witchcraft in 18th c Am.
ATH--witchcraft in 18th c Am.

000665   CECILIA'S LOVERS. New York: Dodd, Mead, 1905 NUC. London: T.F. Unwin, [1905] BMC.

Young woman on her own. Aims to become a great cook and earn a lot of money; becomes a secretary to an artist. Many "lovers". Makes an intelligent choice of one at the end. PW 10-7-05.

000666   CHRISTINE, A FIFE FISHER GIRL. New York and London: D. Appleton, 1917 BMC NUC.

Christine Ruleson, fisherman's daughter, unselfish, chooses a fisherman husband over a lord of a nearby manor. Happily married, becomes a well-known novelist. PW
Her Scottish parents are ambitious for their son Neil because he's the brightest. But it was Christine who tutored Neil. Parents want him to be minister, but he chooses law. Christine has many suitors. Discovers she can write, has stories and poems published. She's a strong, generous person. NYT

000667   THE FLOWER OF GALA WATER: A NOVEL. New York: R. Bonner's Sons, 1895 NUC. London: S. Low, 1895 BMC.

A Scott lassie, a fortune, a disagreeable step Father, a sweet mother and two lovers. CR 23:48
Katherine Janfarie: guardian betrothes her to his nephew; she c hooses her own partner. PW 1/19/95:52
SP 77:56. Love story of Katherine and her two suitors. Some shorter stories appended.

000668   GIRLS OF A FEATHER: A NOVEL. New York: R. Bonner's Sons, 1893 NUC.

New York City two cousins prominent in society are much alike. PW 12-16-93.

000669   THE HANDS OF COMPULSION. New York: Dodd, Mead, 1909 NUC. London: Cassell, 1910 BMC.

Love and murder. PW

000670   THE HEART OF JESSY LAURIE. New York: Dodd, Mead, 1907 NUC. London: C. Brown, 1907 BMC.

PW 10-19-07

000671   THE HOUSE ON CHERRY STREET. New York: Dodd, Mead, 1909 NUC. London: B.F. Stevens and Brown, 1909 BMC.

Hist. PW
Colonial N.Y. NYT
Progressive daughter.

000672   I, THOU, AND THE OTHER ONE: A LOVE STORY. New York: Dodd, Mead, 1898 NUC. London: T. F. Unwin, 1899 BMC.

Love story. Period of the Reform Bill. LIT 5:25.
Scotland. Kate Atheling wants to be mistress of Exham Hall. Her father istroubled by the reform mvt. in his dis trict in which his son has part. Kate is loved by a duke's son but parents oppose the match. A coquette appears on the scene. She dies in the end. SR 88:176
Semi-historical. Annabel Vyner is the coquette. BKM 9:281

000673   JOAN; A ROMANCE OF AN ENGLISH MINING VILLAGE. New York and London: D. Appleton, 1917 BMC NUC.

When trouble develops in the mines, Joan organizes the women to fight for the welfare of their children. PW
Middle-class English woman and the Yorkshire coal mines. BKM
In Yorkshire dialect--most of it. Study of the miners and their home life. NYT

000674   THE KING'S HIGHWAY. New York: Dodd, Mead, 1897 NUC.

Moralistic tone-her doctrines of love and marriage, kindness to animals, use of money. Socialism. LW 28:464
BKM 6:561. International mrge, father wants the title, daughter loves humble Am. But Jessie who loves and marries a Bohemian against her judgment who turns out an heir to a million is more interesting than Alice the faultless.

000675   A KNIGHT OF THE NETS. New York: Dodd, Mead, 1896 NUC. Toronto: W. Briggs, [1896] BMC.

BKM 4:258. Scotch fisher-folk and their loves. Andrew is the hero, gives all to love.

000676   THE LION'S WHELP: A STORY OF CROMWELL'S TIME. New York: Dodd, Mead, 1901 NUC. London: T.F. Unwin, 1902 BMC.

000677   THE LONE HOUSE. New York: Dodd, Mead, [c1893] NUC. London: Hodder and Stoughton, 1894 BMC.

ACAD 46:349. Character study of uncompromisingly moral Scotsman who endures many trials.
PW-Romance of daughter-Western Scotland.

000678   LOVE FOR AN HOUR IS LOVE FOREVER. New York: Dodd, Mead, [c1891] NUC. London: Hutchinson, [1892] BMC.

Yorkshire a generation ago. The Loom-lord is murderd. His murduress lives in a house with ghosts as her companions. ATH 100-444.
Love story, unsmooth, of the son of a cotton spinner. Cotton famine of 1861-65. PW

000679   LOVE WILL VENTURE IN. London: Chatto and Windus, 1907 BMC. (Another ed. of The Man Between.)

Review dwells on grammar faults. ACAD
International romance. TLS

000680   THE MAID OF MAIDEN LANE. A SEQUEL TO "THE BOW OF ORANGE RIBBON": A LOVE STORY. New York: Dodd, Mead, 1900 NUC. London: T.F. Unwin, 1901 BMC.

NYT 1900:700. Wholesome historical romance. Elevating for young reader.

000681   A MAID OF OLD NEW YORK; A ROMANCE OF PETER STUYVESANT'S TIME. New York: Dodd, Mead, 1911 NUC. London: B.F. Stevens and Brown, 1911 BMC.

Hist rom. PW

000682   THE MAN BETWEEN; AN INTERNATIONAL ROMANCE. New York and London: Authors and Newspapers Association, 1906 NUC. Toronto: McLeod & Allen, [1906] BMC.

000683   THE MEASURE OF A MAN. New York and London: D. Appleton, 1915 BMC NUC.

Mother of one determines not to have more children. Learns better? PW
Refuses to have more children because there are so many other things she wants to do. "Every home needs children." NYT

000684   MICHAEL AND THEODORA: A RUSSIAN STORY. Boston: Bradley and Woodruff, [1892] BMC NUC.

000685   AN ORKNEY MAID. New York and London: D. Appleton, 1918 BMC NUC.

Call of Crimean war breaks up life of families. Trad. stuff.
PW--Love and war.
NYT--One of the two heroines, goes to the front as a nurse to take care of her lover. Crimean War. Founding of Red Cross.

000686   THE PAPER CAP; A STORY OF LOVE AND LABOR. New York and London: D. Appleton, 1918 BMC NUC.

Industrial life in England about 1800. Cap symbolizes English workman, focuses on a man. TLS
PW--Laboring classes a century ago.
NYT--October 13, 1918 p 446. English village. Weavers who set their own hours of work, etc., replaced by machine looms. Turmoil over the Reform Bill and Squire Annis and his family. Squire a farsighted and broadminded man.

000687   PLAYING WITH FIRE. New York and London:

D. Appleton, 1914 BMC NUC.

"Picture of a man's struggle with his conscience, battle between faith and doubt. Ian Macrea, a stern Calvinist preacher, has built up an enormous congregation through his strong religious convictions. He becomes interested, however, in a number of books on free thought, and modern German philosophy, and gradually his faith becomes undermined. His estrangement from his family, his withdrawal from his sacred duties, his ten years' effort to find the God he has lost and his ultimate restoration to faith, make up the novel." PW 85 5-2-14 p.1442.
ATH--Struggles of conscience of Glasgow minister.

000688   THE PREACHER'S DAUGHTER: A DOMESTIC ROMANCE. Boston: Bradley and Woodruff, [c1892] NUC. London: S. Low, 1893 BMC.

PW-Salome, a Wesleyan Minister's-daughter, marries a wealthy mill owner and finds herself as unhappy in her luxurious home as she was in the rectory. Love for a scape grace brother leads her to temptations-husband's patient love wins through.

000689   PRISONERS OF CONSCIENCE. New York: Century, 1897 NUC. London: T. F. Unwin, 1897 BMC.

Serious novel: Early 19th, set in Lerwick Shetland Islands. ACAD 52 Fic Sup 70
The influence of Calvinism, the strange ancestral curse. The son throws off these influences, but Nanna won't marry him for fear her children won't be numbered among the Elect. ATH 110:416
Nanna has already lost a child unbaptized. BKM 5:345

000690   PROFIT AND LOSS. New York and London: D. Appleton, 1916 BMC NUC.

Jan sees people as having only a money value to him. Learns through love that the whole world not worth loss of a man's soul. PW 90:1118 9-30-16.
NYT--Addressed to young men.

000691   A RECONSTRUCTED MARRIAGE. New York: Dodd, Mead, 1910 NUC. London: T. F. Unwin, 1911 BMC.

Theodora's troublesome marriage, her flight to California, reconciliation. TLS
Mother rules with an iron hand her two "faded 30 year old daughters." The son casts aside the maternal authority, marries a rich wife; the couple returns to live with the family. The two sisters back up the Mother in her spite for the new bride. The clash of these 5 temperaments. Final scene, Mother calls upon God to curse her son. "Masterpiece of gloom and loathing." ACAD
A marriage that promises to fail because of family prejudice is "reconstructed through efforts of a brave moral wife. Husband woos her a second time; they make a new life in a new land." PW

000692   A ROSE OF A HUNDRED LEAVES: A LOVE-STORY. New York: Dodd, Mead, 1891 NUC. London: J. Clarke, 1892 BMC.

Aspatria Anneys becomes the wife of Lord Fenwick. Discovers she lacks the culture and refinement s uitable for her new life. The story describes her efforts to improve herself. PW 12-12-91.
Romance: "Innocent affection and Stalwart men." LW 23:14.
"Dainty little love story" CR 17: 100.

000693   SHE LOVED A SAILOR. New York: Dodd, Mead, [c1891] NUC. London: J. Clarke, [1892] BMC.

Historical novel financial crisis in New York in Jackson's time. LW
Also realistic depiction of Abolition days and a love story of Virginia Mason. PW
Pre Civil war. Two couples. Virginia and Captain Bradford; Jane Ketelton and Nigel Forfar. Latter affair unpleasant and tragic. SP 68:754

000694   SHEILA VEDDER. New York: Dodd, Mead, 1911 NUC. London: T.F. Unwin, 1912 BMC.

Simple, homey, folksy. PW
How a man woos and wins a wife. NYT

000695   A SINGER FROM THE SEA. New York: Dodd, Mead, [c1893] NUC. New York and London: B. F. Stevens, [1893] BMC.

Simple Cornish fisher-folk-Joan and John Penelles. The

story is of their daughter lured away from the simple
life by a man who promises her a career in singing.
Her child dies, she wanders around for a while and
then returns to her parents. She had married the man.
(He thought he'd live off Dena's voice.) SP 71:841.
She supported him all the while she was singing. He
dies. LW 93:210.

000696   A SISTER TO ESAU. New York: Dodd, Mead,
[c1891] NUC. London and Rahway, N. J.: B. F. Stevens,
[1891] BMC.

Historical romance. Establishment of Free Church in
Scotland; contrasts two sisters. Minister's fears of
his fiancee's liberal religious views. LW
Two sisters, one good, one bad, inheritance romance.
CR 17:35.

000697   A SONG OF A SINGLE NOTE; A LOVE STORY.
New York: Dodd, Mead, 1902 NUC. London: B.F. Stevens
and Brown, 1902 BMC.

Maria's tyrannical father forces her to marry--at the
altar, she says no. ATH

000698   SOULS OF PASSAGE. New York: Dodd, Mead,
1901 NUC. London: T.F. Unwin, 1901 BMC.

ATH--reincarnation. 8-31-01.

000699   THE STRAWBERRY HANDKERCHIEF; A ROMANCE OF
THE STAMP ACT. New York: Dodd, Mead, 1908 NUC.

000700   THYRA VARRICK; A LOVE STORY. New York:
J.F. Taylor, 1903 BMC NUC. London: T.F. Unwin, 1904
BMC.

LBKM--hist. love story.

000701   TRINITY BELLS: A TALE OF OLD NEW YORK.
New York: J. F. Taylor, 1899 NUC. London and
Cambridge, Mass.: B. F. Stevens, 1899 BMC.

Historical romance: the bells symbolize hope in story
of father captured by pirates. Efforts to ransom him,
sacrifices of mother and daughter--Catherine Van
Cliffe. PW 56:1262
Tranquil picture of life in NY 100 years ago.
Narration of family life. Father captured by pirates.
BAKER 03,70
SR 90:728. Family in New York 100 years ago. Charming.

000702   WAS IT RIGHT TO FORGIVE? A DOMESTIC
ROMANCE. Chicago and New York: H. S. Stone, 1899 NUC
BMC. London: T. F. Unwin, 1900 BMC.

"Theorizes very fully on the separate standard of
morality required of men and women." NYC suburbs: a
mother, a self-absorbed father, their son and daughter
and those of a Dutch Calvinist builder. PW 56:1220
CR 36:375. Domestic romance. Two married women
contrasted, one strong, the other weak, with a love
for wine.
SP 84:454. Contrast between immaculate virtue and vice
of New York society.
ATH 115:331. It was right to forgive her frivolous and
unfaithful husband.
Adriana forgives her frivolous husband; "it is equally
clear that Antony...having a vain wife...should also
forgive" though she drags his name through the
mud...she drinks. ATH 115:331

000703   THE WINNING OF LUCIA; A LOVE STORY. New
York and London: D. Appleton, 1915 BMC NUC.

Lucia wavers between two lovers PW
Sweet love story, wholesome, old fashioned. NYT
Her 65th novel, written at age 84.

BARRATT, FRANCES LAYLAND.

000704   BEATRIX CADELL: AN EPISODE IN THE LIFE OF
A MAN OF THE WORLD. London: Simpkin and Marshall, 1892
BMC.

BARRETT, LILLIAN (FOSTER). B. 1884. United States.

000705   THE SINISTER REVEL. New York: A. A.
Knopf, 1919 NUC.

Focus on a millionaire and his debauchery TLS
Good woman who reforms him. ATH
Weak man and his dissipations PW
Drinks a lot NYT 11-2-19,623
BKM--Drunken rich hero marries nice Constance. He is a
philanderer, (his 1st mistress died in squalid

circumstances). She redeems him.

BARRINGTON, EMILIE ISABEL (WILSON). D. 1933. United
Kingdom.

000706   HELEN'S ORDEAL. London: Osgood,
McIlvaine, 1894 BMC.

SP 73:305. Helen marries artist whom she discovers is
incapable of love and not worthy of her. Is miserable.
Loses her baby. Goes to church, I think gets religion.
ATH-cheerful ending.

000707   LENA'S PICTURE. A STORY OF LOVE.
Edinburgh: D. Douglas, 1892 NUC. London: Osgood,
McIlvaine, 1893 BMC.

SP 69:926. Both Lena's mother and sister are insane.
Novel is a character study of Lena, her love and
compassion for her sister, her recognition that she
cannot marry, her repugnance at the idea that she
could be happy in a love affair while her sister is
suffering alone. She arrives at a state of peace and
serenity and strength from a non-defined spiritual
source, a mysterious light.
SR 74:773. Her decision not to marry was difficult to
arrive at. She dies shortly thereafter.
brother and sister, Lena-reject family because mother
and sister are both in lunatic asylums. A Great Lady
takes Lena off to forget. Lena meets "her fate,"
refuses him. Lena dies of consumption. ATH 101, 49

BARROW, E. N. See BARROW, ELIZABETH N.

BARROW, ELIZABETH N. B. 1869. United States.

000708   THE FORTUNE OF WAR: BEING PORTIONS OF
MANY LETTERS AND JOURNALS WRITTEN DURING...THE TIME OF
THE STRUGGLE FOR THE INDEPENDENCE OF THE COLONIES. New
York: H. Holt, 1900 NUC.

NYT 1900:185. New York. American Revolution.
Katherine, daughter of an English officer loves an
American officer, enters into a plot to free him from
capture, is captured herself by the Americans. Marries
him. New York under British occupation.

000709   THE KING'S RIVALS. BY E. N. BARROW. New
York, London, and Bombay: Longmans, Green, 1898 NUC.

BARSTOW, EMMA MAGDALENA ROSALIA MARIA JOSEFA BARBARA ORCZY.
1865-1947. United Kingdom.

000710   BEAU BROCADE: A ROMANCE. BY BARONESS
ORCZY. Philadelphia: J.B. Lippincott, 1907 BMC NUC.
London: Greening, 1908 BMC.

TLS--male hero romance.

000711   THE BELOVED OF THE GODS; A ROMANCE. BY
THE BARONESS ORCZY. New York: Knickerbocker Press,
1905 NUC.

000712   A BRIDE OF THE PLAINS. BY BARONESS ORCZY.
London: Hutchinson, 1915 BMC. New York: G.H. Doran,
[c1915] NUC.

Elsa marries thinking the man she loves is dead; he's
gone 3 yrs in military-reported dead; on first day of
wedding ceremony (it lasts days) her lover returns. PW

000713   THE BRONZE EAGLE; A STORY OF THE HUNDRED
DAYS. BY BARONESS ORCZY. London: Hodder and Stoughton,
1915 BMC. New York: G.H. Doran, [c1915] NUC.

Traditional historical romance. PW

000714   BY THE GODS BELOVED. A ROMANCE. BY
BARONESS ORCZY. London: Greening, 1905 BMC. New York:
Dodd, Mead, 1921 NUC.

Adventure in Egypt LBKM v 29-30:39
ATH 05:539
Romance of ancient Egypt, pass. love, weird
adventures. LBKM

000715   THE CASE OF MISS ELLIOTT. BY BARONESS
ORCZY. London: T.F. Unwin, 1905 BMC NUC.

000716   ELDORADO; AN ADVENTURE OF THE SCARLET
PIMPERNEL. BY BARONESS ORCZY. New York: Hodder and
Stoughton, [c1913] NUC. London: Hodder and Stoughton,
[1913] BMC NUC.

"In this book the Scarlet Pimpernel is engaged in
rescuing the little Dauphin from the Temple Prison .

His success is only won through his own capture, and
then we have this daring rescuer of fallen royalists
attacking the hard problem of freeing himself,
protecting rash, young Armand St. Just, and rescuing
his own wife from the Committee of Safety." PW 83:220

000717   THE ELUSIVE PIMPERNEL. BY BARONESS ORCZY.
New York: Dodd, Mead, 1908 NUC. London: Hutchinson,
1908 BMC NUC.

000718   THE EMPEROR'S CANDLESTICKS. BY THE
BARONESS EMMUSKA ORCZY. London: C.A. Pearson, 1899
BMC. New York: C.H. Doscher, [c1908] NUC.

A Czar, a Cardinal, an Emperor, many Nihilists and a
Russian spy--a woman of high rank. SP 83:961

000719   FIRE IN STUBBLE. BY BARONESS ORCZY.
London: Methuen, [1912] BMC NUC.

TLS--Hist rom. male hero.
ATH--Hist rom. male hero.
ACAD--Hist rom. male hero.

000720   THE FIRST SIR PERCY. AN ADVENTURE OF THE
LAUGHING CAVALIER. BY BARONESS ORCZY. London: Hodder
and Stoughton, [1920] NUC BMC. New York: G.H. Doran,
[c1921] NUC.

TLS--hist.

000721   FLOWER O' THE LILY. A ROMANCE OF OLD
CAMBRAY. BY BARONESS ORCZY. London: Hodder and
Stoughton, [1918] BMC NUC.

TLS--Historical romance.
Medieval romance of chivalry--a gallant gentleman
serves his king and lady. PW

000722   THE GATES OF KAMT. BY BARONESS ORCZY. New
York: Dodd, Mead, 1907 NUC.

Adventure about a found city and a beautiful woman. PW
6-29-07.

000723   THE HEART OF A WOMAN. BY BARONESS ORCZY.
New York: Hodder and Stoughton, [c1911] NUC.

murder & intrigue. PW 9-9-11.

000724   HIS MAJESTY'S WELL-BELOVED: AN EPISODE IN
THE LIFE OF MR. THOMAS BETTERTON AS TOLD BY HIS FRIEND
JOHN HONEYWOOD. BY BARONESS ORCZY. New York: G.H.
Doran, [c1919] NUC. London: Hodder and Stoughton,
[1919] BMC NUC.

LBKM--Male letter writer adventure.
NYT--Adventure Thomas Betterton.

000725   I WILL REPAY: A ROMANCE. BY THE BARONESS
ORCZY. Philadelphia: J. B. Lippincott, 1906 NUC.
London: Greening, 1906 BMC.

PW--Story of Fr. Rev.
TLS--Scarlet Pimpernel.

000726   IN MARY'S REIGN. BY BARONESS ORCZY. New
York: Cupples and Leon, [c1907] NUC.

PW--Hist. romance.

000727   LADY MOLLY OF SCOTLAND YARD. BY THE
BARONESS ORCZY. London, New York: Cassell, 1910 BMC
NUC.

LBKM--Has a female Watson. In last story she clears
her husband of murder charge and retires from
detective work.

000728   THE LAUGHING CAVALIER; THE STORY OF THE
ANCESTOR OF THE SCARLET PIMPERNEL. BY BARONESS ORCZY.
New York: G.H. Doran, [c1914] NUC. London: Hodder and
Stoughton, 1914 BMC NUC.

Villain, helpless maid, hero who saves her over and
over--traditional historical romance. BKM
"So it seems that the Scarlet Pimpernel had a daring
and romantic ancestor, who has had a place of his own
in art, and now takes another in fiction. He was the
original of the famous Hals portrait. His story tells
how he served the Lord of Stoulenberg; how he held my
lord's destiny and that of many others in his power;
but how, when it came to his own fate, that lay in the
hands of the beautiful Gilda of Haarlem." PW 86:967
9-26-14.
LBKM--a Dutch philosopher, Diogenes gallant, genial,

adventure.

000729   THE LEAGUE OF THE SCARLET PIMPERNEL. BY
BARONESS ORCZY. New York: G.H. Doran, [c1919] NUC.
London: Cassell, [1919] BMC.

Rescues of women children and men from clutches of
friends. 8 episodes or short stories of such rescues.
NYT

000730   LEATHERFACE: A TALE OF OLD FLANDERS. BY
BARONESS ORCZY. New York: G.H. Doran, [c1916] NUC.
London: Hodder and Stoughton, 1916 BMC NUC.

Historical novel. Girl forced to marry father's
choice. PW 90:1170 10-7-16.

000731   LORD TONY'S WIFE; AN ADVENTURE OF THE
SCARLET PIMPERNEL. BY BARONESS ORCZY. London: Hodder
and Stoughton, [1917] BMC. New York: G.H. Doran,
[c1917] NUC.

A rescue, crime, revolts, etc. Scarlet Pimpernel rides
again. TLS

000732   THE MAN IN GRAY; BEING EPISODES OF THE
CHOUAN CONSPIRACIES IN NORMANDY DURING THE FIRST
EMPIRE. BY BARONESS ORCZY. London: Cassell, 1918 BMC
NUC.

NYT Sept. 29,1918, p.410--He is a secret agent who
deals with crimes baffling to local police. "Brave and
resourceful little gentleman."

000733   MEADOWSWEET. BY BARONESS ORCZY. London:
Hutchinson, 1912 BMC. New York: Hodder and Stoughton,
[c1912] NUC.

ATH--Sweet.
SP--sweet.
BKM--Sweet.

000734   THE NEST OF THE SPARROWHAWK: A ROMANCE OF
THE 17TH CENTURY. BY THE BARONESS ORCZY. New York:
F.A. Stokes, [1909] NUC. London: Greening, 1909 BMC
NUC.

PW--Hist. rom.

000735   THE NOBLE ROGUE; A CAVALIER'S ROMANCE. BY
BARONESS ORCZY. New York: Hodder and Stoughton,
[c1912] NUC.

Published in England under title "Fire in Stubble".
PW--hist. rom.
NYT--hist. rom.

000736   THE OLD MAN IN THE CORNER. BY BARONESS
ORCZY. London: Hodder and Stoughton, [1909] NUC BMC.

Criminal mystery. TLS

000737   PETTICOAT GOVERNMENT. BY BARONESS ORCZY.
New York: Doran, [1910] PW. London: Hutchinson, 1910
NUC BMC.

Hist. rom. PW
TLS--Hist. rom.

000738   PETTICOAT RULE. BY BARONESS ORCZY. New
York: Hodder and Stoughton, [c1910] NUC.

000739   THE SCARLET PIMPERNEL. BY BARONESS ORCZY.
New York and London: G. P. Putnam's Sons, 1905 NUC.
London: Greening, 1905 BMC.

French heroine as brave and enthusiastic as the Eng.
hero. PW 10-7-05
Romantic adventure. NYT 05:671.

000740   A SHEAF OF BLUEBELLS. BY BARONESS ORCZY.
New York: G.H. Doran, [c1917] NUC. London: Hutchinson,
1917 BMC NUC.

Traditional historical romance. PW
Traditional historical romance. TLS
Exciting story of Royalist plotting. NYT

000741   A SON OF THE PEOPLE: A ROMANCE OF THE
HUNGARIAN PLAINS. BY THE BARONESS ORCZY. New York:
G.P. Putnam's Sons, 1906 NUC. London: Greening, 1906
BMC.

PW--Male adventure story.
NYT--Story of a mrg. between young man and woman given
by her father. She despises him because she has been a

payment, love conquers all.

000742   THE TANGLED SKEIN. BY THE BARONESS ORCZY.
London: Greening, 1907 BMC NUC.

"For young readers." Romance, Ursula promised as child
to a man, father's will: must marry him or enter
convent. LBKM 7-07,143. ACAD, SR.

000743   A TRUE WOMAN. BY BARONESS ORCZY. London:
Hutchinson, 1911 BMC NUC. Leipzig: B. Tauchnitz, 1912
NUC.

Louise Harris a true woman-commonplace well-to-do
Englishwoman.
TLS Murder story. SP

000744   UNTO CAESAR. BY BARONESS ORCZY. London:
Hodder and Stoughton, 1914 BMC. New York: G.H. Doran,
[c1914] NUC.

"Setting is Rome in the days of the mad Emperor
Caligula. Taurus Antinor, praefect and great soldier
has riches and honors heaped upon him by Caesar, and
when a conspiracy against the ruler becomes open and
successful rebellion, he is the man chosen to succeed
to the imperial throne. Taurus had seen and heard
Jesus seven years before and had become a Christian.
He refuses to accept the crown because of his oath of
loyalty to Caligula, is the means of restoring the
emperor to power, even though it means renouncing Dea
Flavia Augusta, the woman he loves. Dea Flavia also
becomes a Christian, follows her lover into exile and
when she finds him, goes with him to teach their faith
to the heathen." PW 85:1447 5-2-14

BARTELS, MRS. HUGO.

000745   A MARRIAGE IN JEST; A NOVEL. London: J.
Ouseley, 1909 BMC.

Intrigue to get control of a woman's money by allowing
her to think a mock marriage is real. TLS

BARTLETT, ALICE ELINOR (BOWEN). 1848-1920. United States.

000746   A NEW ARISTOCRACY. BY BIRCH ARNOLD. New
York: Bartlett, 1891 NUC.

Two daughters and one son of a rector of a small
Western parish must fend for themselves when he dies.
They sell his books, rent a place and begin kitchen
farming. One daughter becomes a cook for a rich
family. The other starts a society of Universal
Brotherhood and gives lectures on the "New Aristocracy
of heart and brain." PW
LW 29:11. "Story of a young woman dependent on her own
resources," working "in the midst of a socialistic
movement among the workers of a great city." She is of
the "new aristocracy" wherein "moral worth and purpose
count first, with brain and healthy digestion a good
second." Idealistic

BARTLETT, LUCY RE.

000747   TRANSITION. A PSYCHOLOGICAL ROMANCE. BY
LUCY RE. London: Longmans, Green, 1914 NUC BMC.

LBKM-unfolds the psychology of the women's movement
with commanding sincerity.
ATH-Author presents people with mystical powers,
contrasting "their special views, special feelings,
special tensity and rapidity of psychological
development," with the "stolid restiveness of the
ordinary type."
TLS-Novel is a defense of militant feminism. Maimie is
"morbid and neurotic girl." Militancy is in rev's
opinion, "an orgy of emotion...to the neglect of the
convenience of the rest of the world."
Maimie Elder's lover has followed double standard of
morality. She prefers to earn her living rather than
marry. Hugh accepts new feminism. PW 85 6/20/14:1980

BARTLETT, VANDA WATHEN.

000748   THE GAP IN THE GARDEN. London and New
York: J. Lane, 1903 BMC.

Julian, testy, beaut, semi invalid always wrangling
with her maiden aunt murdered by an old mad woman NYT
03 339
Short desc ACAD 64, 366
Heroine under influence of occult forces; one man
believes she is the creation of his will; Hate is a
mad Scotchwoman who destroys the heroine, an
allegory--ACAD 64,413.

One sister wholesome, the other beautiful, passionate
but maimed and irritable. ATH 121, 751
Drama of two sisters, quiet at first, tragic in the
end. TLS 115,03

000749   HEART'S DESIRE. London: J. Lane, 1899
BMC.

Mrs. Glannock is unsatisfied with her husband and her
life. Meets and is attracted to Mrs. Beauvigne. Their
meetings and discussions that hide their true passion
are the story. But in the end she chooses to remain
with her husband Norman. LBKM 16:168
Temptation resisted, Vail Glannock--very clever,
dreamy, moody. SP 83:57
CR 36:183. Clever capricious woman who would rather be
lonely than bored. Married to man fond of country
life, another man lends interest to her life. "An
instance of what a woman writer is capable of when she
conscientiously analyzes the feelings of a woman."
LW 31:93. "Boldly faced the truth that a woman whose
heart is not satisfied by her husband's affections can
love another acknowledging it to herself, but not
finally succumbing to its power."

BARTLEY, NALBRO ISADORAH.   B. 1888.   United States.

000750   THE BARGAIN TRUE. Boston: Small, Maynard,
[c1918] NUC 1919 BMC.

"problem of whether fundamental married happiness is
found only in the response of youth to youth" PW
Dale Aldes is illegal daughter of a dancer and a lord.
Educated in convent, now parents are dead, lives on
the estate, falls for a truck farmer before her
guardian, a South African diamond king, arrives. Her
guardian falls for her and tries without success to
win her from her humble lover. NYT
NYT young woman's marriage problem, Dale Aldes,
illegal daughter of Farmer, dancer, chooses a farmer
(over an explorer) as husband. NYT

000751   THE GORGEOUS GIRL. Garden City, N.Y.:
Doubleday, Page, 1920 NUC.

PW-Life among idle rich. Gorgeous girl shows hero how
to spend money; plain girl shows him how to be happy.

000752   THE GRAY ANGELS. Boston: Small, Maynard,
[c1920] NUC BMC.

TLS-
ATH-war.

000753   PARADISE AUCTION. Boston: Small, Maynard,
[1917] BMC NUC.

Darly Heath gave up the stage after her divorce for
the sake of her son. She watches him grow to marry the
wrong woman and to degenerate. Asks herself whether
her sacrifice was worth it. She's remarkable and
admirable. NYT 222, 6-10-17

000754   A WOMAN'S WOMAN. Boston: Small, Maynard,
[c1919] NUC BMC. London: Hodder and Stoughton, [1920]
BMC.

"development of a family...during last half century"
PW
Densie 37 thought old fashioned by daughter, dreary by
husband. Only son believed her perfect. Densie revolts
vs it all "rose to heights that left the others; all
come together effusively at end vowing that home life
is only thing to live for."

BARTNETT, HARRIET.   United States.

000755   ANGELO, THE MUSICIAN. New York: G. A. S.
Wieners, 1903 NUC.

About a boy and his development. PW 5-09-03
Musical fiction.

BARTON, C. JOSEPHINE.   See BARTON, CATHERINE JOSEPHINE
(WIGGINTON).

BARTON, CATHERINE JOSEPHINE (WIGGINTON).   United States.

000756   EVANGEL AHVALLAH; OR, THE WHITE SPECTRUM.
A NOVEL WHOSE INCIDENTS ARE LINKED TOGETHER BY A CHAIN
OF METAPHYSICAL DEDUCTIONS. BY C. JOSEPHINE BARTON.
Kansas City, Mo.: 1895 NUC. (Illustrated and Published
By Author)

BARTON, HESTER.

000757   THE BARON OF ILL-FAME; A ROMANCE OF
FLORENCE IN THE TIME OF DANTE. London: S. Paul, [1911]
BMC.

Hist romance of Dante's Florence. TLS

BARTON, MARION T. (DAVIS). Nationality Unknown.

000758   AN EXPERIMENT IN PERFECTION. London and
New York: Doubleday, Page, 1907 BMC NUC.

The experiment is the marriage between two who have
been "engaged" since childhood. He prepares for
ministry, she for nursing. The marriage lasts six
months. Husband dies from overwork. Heroine has a very
close woman friend with whom she discusses everthing.
PW 4-6-07

BASCOM, LEE. United States.

000759   A GOD OF GOTHAM: A ROMANCE FROM THE LIFE
OF A WELL-KNOWN ACTRESS. New York: G. W. Dillingham,
1891 NUC.

Takes place in New York. Donita Lorraine is a
celebrated actress. Her romance with a society man. PW

BASELEY, MRS.

000760   THE DOWAGER'S SECRET; LEAVES FROM FRANK
CAPEL'S DIARY. BY MIGNON. London: Simpkin, Marshall,
1897 BMC.

BASH, BERTHA (RUNKLE). United States.

000761   THE HELMET OF NAVARRE. BY BERTHA RUNKLE.
New York: Century, 1901 NUC. London: Macmillan, 1901
BMC.

PW 5-4-01 ATH 6-15-01 Historical romance.

000762   THE SCARLET RIDER. BY BERTHA RUNKLE. New
York: Century, 1913 BMC NUC.

PW 83 5/31/13:1962 "Story of a peer by birth, a
highwayman by profession, who took to the road in a
spirit of bravado and stayed there to rehabilitate his
fortunes. No one knows he is the Scarlet Rider, least
of all his charming daughter Lettice, who has secretly
given shelter to a fugitive and disguises him as a
footman, her home on the Isle of Wight.
Then come King George's troopers and there are
exciting scenes and many dangers out of which Letty
successfully leads her footman, but during which her
father is killed."

000763   STRAIGHT DOWN THE CROOKED LANE. BY BERTHA
RUNKLE. New York: Century, 1915 NUC BMC. London: E.
Nash, 1916 BMC.

Traditional detective mystery. PW 9-25-15

000764   THE TRUTH ABOUT TOLNA. BY BERTHA RUNKLE.
New York: Century, 1906 BMC NUC.

PW-two men in conflict over girl, comedy.
NYT-opera singers.

BASHKIRTSEVA, MARIIA KONSTANTINOVNA. 1860-1884.

000765   LETTERS OF MARIE BASHKIRTSEFF. New York:
Cassell, 1891 BMC NUC. London: (Tr. Mary J. Serrano.
Not fiction.)

Audacious letters with same qualities as her journal.
PW 7-11-91.

BASKERVILLE, BEATRICE C. United Kingdom.

000766   BALDWIN'S KINGDOM. A STORY OF RUSSIAN
LIFE. London: Hurst & Blackett, 1917 BMC.

Russia. Love story and murder TLS
His exceedingly egotistical love affair ATH

000767   LOVE AND SACRIFICE. London: Hurst &
Blackett, 1918 BMC NUC.

TLS-Polish family and destruction of war
ATH Husband condemned to be shot as a spy

000768   PASSOVER. A NOVEL. London: T.
Butterworth, [1920] BMC NUC.

Action takes place in Poland and deals with marriage
of a wealthy Christian to a Jewess

000769   THE PLAYGROUND OF SATAN. New York: W. J.
Watt, [c1918] NUC.

"courage, the faith, the sufferings of the Polish"
during the war. PW
Love story intertwined, no promise BKM
NYT 3-30-19, 167 centers on noble family whose ancient
homestead is in the path of war. Begins in peace time;
war comes, brothers are on opposite sides. When city
evacuated, the family won't leave but they hear
Germans plan to kill them, so they escape. They see
their home destroyed. The trials of their escape, help
from Princess Ostrov who runs a hospital.

000770   THEIR YESTERDAY. A CHRONICLE OF MISTAKES.
London: Everett, 1909 BMC.

struggle of artist's wife (whose past rose up against
her) to control her "baser instincts." Trouble with an
old lover, husband leaves her. Ends sadly. TLS

000771   WHEN SUMMER COMES AGAIN. London: Simpkin,
Marshall, 1915 BMC.

Young Irish girl left in poverty upon father's
suicide, becomes companion to Jewish family in Vienna
. Gets involved in espionage, suffers from the
rascality of a German husband who dies and a German
secret service agent, escapes to Russia ATH
Sympathy for her fall from indep. to marry TLS

BASSETT, MARY E. (STONE). 1857-1924. United States.

000772   JUDITH'S GARDEN. Boston, Mass.: Lothrop,
[1902] NUC.

"Is there something in a garden that leads to colossal
egoism?"

000773   THE LITTLE GREEN DOOR; A NOVEL. Boston:
Lothrop, [1905]. London: Kegan Paul, 1905 BMC.

Hist. rom. 9-2-05 PW
Hist. rom. NYT 557,05.
Louis XIII, king of France.

000774   A MIDSUMMER WOOING. Boston: Lothrop, Lee
& Shepard, [1913] NUC.

PW 83 5/3/13:1563 "The real heroine is the woman who
tells the story. She finds true happiness in her
luxuriant garden, and successfully deals with the
whims of quaint natures until she brings about a happy
wedding, by means of her summer-house just large
enough for two."

000775   A RIDDLE OF LUCK. BY MARY E. STONE.
Philadelphia: J. B. Lippincott, 1893 NUC.

Man allows ghost to inhabit his body for six months of
each year in exchange for the ghost's dictation of
super novels that the publishers fight over. LW
93:147.
He's an unsuccessful writer. The point of the story is
to criticize too prolific authorship. PW 5 -13-93.
CR 21:145. Hero sells his body to a spirit for six
months of the year. Caused hero marital problems.

BASSETT, SARA WARE. B. 1872. United States.

000776   THE HARBOR ROAD. Philadelphia: Penn, 1919
NUC.

N E; Tressie is beautiful and good. TLS
Cape Cod family take summer boarders. PW

000777   THE TAMING OF ZENAS HENRY. New York: G.
H. Doran, [c1915] NUC. London: Hodder and Stoughton,
1916 BMC.

"By the influence of a capable woman...the hero and
three old sea captains are transformed into normal
useful men" She adopts a child.--PW 5-29-15.
Cape Cod rom. WOMAN'S EDUC. ASSOC Nov 1915 No. 32

000778   THE WALL BETWEEN. Boston: Little, Brown,
1920 BMC NUC.

PW-Tale of New Hampshire Village.

000779   THE WAYFARERS AT THE ANGEL'S. New York:
G. H. Doran, [1917] NUC.

Three lonely fishermen learn it's nice to have a woman
around. One marries her. PW

The Angel's is their shack NYT

BATEMAN, MAY GERALDINE FRANCES.

000780   THE ALTAR OF LIFE. London: Duckworth,
1898 BMC. Philadelphia: Lippincott, 1899 NUC.

SP 81:656. A woman's jealousy and vengeance, in a
measure overcome by the splendid trustfulness of her
innocent rival. Anglo-Indian.
LIT 3:401. Adventuress socially and professionally
ruins Captain Trench. A sympathetic study of his
character.
ACAD 55:333.
Heroine gives up wealth, social position for her
lover's sake. He in turn is inspired to be self
sacrificing by her model. PW:288.

000781   FARQUAHARSON OF GLUNE. London: Chapman &
Hall, 1908 BMC.

TLS-About politics and women in politics, but for or
against?
ACAD ?

000782   THE GLOWWORM. London: W. Heinemann, 1901
BMC NUC.

Development of a woman's character from childhood to
death-at hands of old lover. Career as successful
novelist, unsuccessful marriage. Aseneth is loveable
eager passionate creative; marries a blackguard ACAD
01
"Like Story of an African Farm" Aseneth a rebel
already at age 5; at 17 leaves home takes to writing
novels. becomes famous, agnostic. 11-9-01 ATH

BATES, EMILY KATHARINE. Nationality Unknown.

000783   THE BOOMERANG. A NOVEL. London: Holden
and Hardingham, [1914] BMC.

The Occult. ATH.
Reincarnation-theme LBKM

000784   CHILDREN OF THE DAWN. London: K. Paul,
Trench, Trubner, 1920 NUC BMC. New York: E. P. Dutton,
1920 BMC.

On psychical research.

000785   THE COPING STONE. London: Greening, 1912
BMC.

<On mental science.>

BATES, FANNY D. United States.

000786   TATTERS: A NOVEL. BY BEULAH. Boston: Lee
and Shepard, 1892 NUC.

CR 17:314. Child of the tenements rises to success,
inference that dukes and princes do for her what she
could have done for herself.

BATES, HARRIET TRUE. United States.

000787   TWO MEN OF THE WORLD: A NOVEL. New York:
G. W. Dillingham, 1891 NUC.

Heroine has two suitors, crisis comes when she must
decide between them. PW

BATES, LAURA BRACE. B. 1851. United States.

000788   BACHELOR BIGOTRIES; COMP. BY AN OLD MAID
AND APPROVED BY A YOUNG BACHELOR. ILLUSTRATED BY AN
EX-BACHELOR. PUBLISHED BY A YOUNG MARRIED MAN
[ANONYMOUS]. San Francisco: P. Elder, [1903] NUC.

PN 6161 "Am. wit and humor 2. Birthday books.

BATES, MARGRET HOLMES (ERNSPERGER). 1844-1927. United
States.

000789   IN THE FIRST DEGREE. New York: R.G.
Cooke, 1907 NUC.

BKM-young man becomes prosecuting attorney against his
mother's will who does not believe in capital
punishment but in accord with his wife's wishes then
trial of a woman who is a former friend of his--she is
saved at the last moment.
capital punishment. PW 12-7-07.

000790   JASPER FAIRFAX. BY MARGARET HOLMES. New

York: R. F. Fenno, [c1897] NUC.

Civil War, freeing of slaves-its many complications.
Jasper told by aunt that he should not marry his
fiance because she has Negro blood. PW 52:789.

000791   PAYING THE PIPER. New York: Broadway,
1910 NUC.

000792   THE PRICE OF THE RING. BY MARGRET HOLMES.
Chicago: F. J. Schulte, [1892] NUC.

PW-Direct plea for social purity and one code of
morals for both husband and wife. Involves infidelity
on both sides.

000793   SHYLOCK'S DAUGHTER: A NOVEL. Chicago: C
H. Kerr, 1894 NUC.

PW-dedicated to the People's Party. John Longwood, a
People's Party legislator, represents miners and
farmers. Shylock, a senator, encourages his daughter
to influence Longwood to vote in a way that will
benefit her large mining interests.

000794   SILAS KIRKENDOWN'S SONS. Boston: C.M.
Clark, 1908 NUC.

BATES, MARTHA E. (CRAM) AND MRS. M. K. BUCK.

000795   ALONG TRAVERSE SHORES. BY MRS. M. E. C.
BATES AND MRS. M. K. BUCK. Traverse City, Michigan:
[F. Herald Office], 1891 NUC.

BATES, MARY I.

000796   PAUL FLEMING. London: Murray and Evenden,
[1912] BMC.

Title refers to hero's maternal grandfather, a weaver.
Hero raised without knowledge that his father's side
of family is aristocratic. Love story follows. ACAD
TLS-secret marriage of squire's son and weaver's
daughter.

BATES, MRS. M. E. C. See BATES, MARTHA E. (CRAM) AND MRS.
M. K. BUCK.

BATES, SYLVIA CHATFIELD. United States.

000797   THE GERANIUM LADY. New York: Duffield,
1916 NUC.

PW--island romance with happy ending.
NYT-

000798   THE VINTAGE. New York: Duffield, 1916
NUC.

Civil war incident and the writing of The Battle Hymn.
BKM

BATSON, HENRIETTA M. United Kingdom.

000799   ADAM, THE GARDENER. London: Hurst and
Blackett, 1894 BMC.

SR 78:414. Adam, son of baronet, lives with peasants
to study them. When it is assumed by them that he is
going with a girl he is merely studying closely, he
marries. Subsequent problems, her death.
SP 73:566. Wife is a shrew and jealous. Wealthy
American widow abducts Adam on her yacht. Wessex.

000800   DARK: A TALE OF THE DOWN COUNTRY
[ANONYMOUS]. London: Smith, Elder, 1892 BMC. Leipzig:
B. Tauchnitz, 1893 NUC.

realistic pictures of peasant life. Young man gets
young woman "into trouble." He is the vicar's son. And
there's a "faithful swain who always loved the heroine
and tells her to holler when she wants him back." SR
1-28-93, 100
Dark is her name; Jem Simmons is the swain. ATH 101,
214.

000801   THE EARTH CHILDREN. London: Hutchinson,
[1897] BMC.

Rustic love making, betrayal, trag. end. Lil Goodeve,
Dick Jennings love each other from childhood. Lil is
red haired. A commercial traveler Clement Drury
pretends to marry Lil, when Dick is in prison. ACAD
6-26-97, 24 Fict. Sup.
Like Tess by Hardy. Wessex. Lil flies from husband
wanders thru Wessex looking for work. Returns to

faithful Dick, murders the wicked Drury. LBKM 12:42.

000802   THE GAY PARADISES. London: S. Paul, 1909
BMC.

Lady Paradine conceals birth of daughter Nan because
she fears her wicked family. TLS
Nan raised as pauper; later identifed. Nan married to
gross farmer, in love with a different man, is saved
from being "sold to any amorous bidder". ATH

000803   A SPLENDID HERITAGE. London: S. Paul,
[1910] BMC.

TLS- romance
ACAD male hero

000804   SUCH A LORD IS LOVE: A WOMAN'S HEART
TRAGEDY. London: A.D. Innes, 1893 BMC.

SP 72:270. Adria deserts the husband she loves. Her
marriage is a "grim comedy."
ACAD 103:47. Marriage a dismal failure. Three Miss
Temples and five men. The fourth married and had 10
babies. Lady Waldron marries a man she doesn't love;
Elizabeth jilted her fiance almost at altar; Adria ran
away from her husband. SR 76:545.
Three sisters; a widow who married for money and
suffered but not for long; one woman a taste for
literature. Adria's husband loves another woman. She
leaves him, then returns. Widow ends up marrying a
preacher who demands obedience from wife. The writer
marries a priggish Oxford don. But she writes. Such a
lord is love. These are the situations love leads to.
LBK 5:56.

BAUDER, EMMA POW (SMITH). B. 1848. United States.

000805   CHRYSOLYTE; OR, THE JOURNEY TO LIGHT. BY
MRS. EMMA POW SMITH. San Francisco: Brunt, 1891 NUC.

000806   RUTH AND MARIE: A FASCINATING STORY OF
THE NINETEENTH CENTURY. Chicago, Philadelphia,
Stockton: American Bible House, [c1895] NUC.

BAXENDALE, FLORENCE.

000807   THE DISENCHANTMENT OF NURSE DOROTHY: A
STORY OF HOSPITAL LIFE. London: Skeffington, 1900 BMC.

SP 84:604. Disenchanted in life but ends in matrimony.
ACAD 58:274. From book: "a worm eats at the root of
the common hospital system, and causes suffering to
patients and nurses alike...the microbe of over-work."
Rev. thinks she suffers more from a housesurgeon's
love.
LIT 6:445. Some very unpleasant hospital experiences,
motive to expose faults in the hospital system.

BAXTER, LUCY E. (BARNES). 1837-1902.

000808   THE CASTLE OF VINCIGLIATA. BY LEADER
SCOTT. Florence: G. Barbara, 1897 BMC NUC.

000809   THE RENUNCIATION OF HELEN. BY LEADER
SCOTT. London: Hutchinson, 1898 BMC.

LIT 3:160. Her self-sacrifice. Concerns inheritance.
ACAD 53:547. Dorset. Dialect. Story of quiet
middle-class life.
ATH 111:786. When she discovers her lover's
inheritance is actually hers, she gives it all up, or
at least tries to.

BAYLISS, HELEN.

000810   AN ACT OF IMPULSE; A STORY. London:
Greening, 1904 BMC.

TLS- a burned will

000811   SLAVES OF PASSION. London: J. Long, 1904
BMC.

TLS- theatrical and sent treatment of modern society

000812   A WOMAN AT BAY. London: J. Long, 1904
BMC.

000813   A WOMAN IN THE CITY: A NOVEL. London: J.
Long, 1903 BMC.

A woman of strong passions and impulses, without any
standard of moral action; her main desire-to be
luxuriously free-shown in various moods, under various
influences LBKM 6-03,115.

BAYLOR, FRANCES COURTENAY. See BARNUM, FRANCES COURTENAY
(BAYLOR).

BAYLY, ADA ELLEN. 1857-1903. United Kingdom.

000814   THE AUTOBIOGRAPHY OF A TRUTH. BY EDNA
LYALL. New York: Longmans, Green, 1896 NUC. London:
Longmans, 1896 BMC.

LW 27:349. Profits of book donated to relief fund for
Armenia. Armenian hero.

000815   DOREEN: THE STORY OF A SINGER. BY EDNA
LYALL. London: Longmans, 1894 BMC. New York: Longmans,
Green, 1894 NUC.

LW 25:164. She loses her voice because of an illness
brought on by her imprisonment. An Irish patriot by
heredity and by conviction.
CR 25:328. Her father imprisoned as a Fenian and dies
soon after his release. She is a popular singer,
becomes an active member of the Ladies Land League and
is imprisoned. Book closes with her marriage to an
Englishman, who also was in same prison. She retires
from the stage.
PW-after father's release from prison, family
emigrates to U.S. with death of parents, she, at 18,
is responsible for family
Advocates cause of Irish evicted tenants; vs
landlords. Brave, merry, unselfish devoted alike to
her lover, country, and her career as a professional
singer. Always true to herself. Gives strenuous
support to those who resist English legislation. SP
74:234
Contrasted with kinsfolk in Bloomsbury, becomes a
great singer. ATH 105:115
Helps the cause of Home rule <in Ireland> by her
singing. BAKER 13,132

000816   THE HINDERERS; A STORY OF THE PRESENT
TIME. BY EDNA LYALL. New York: Longmans, Green, 1902
NUC. London: Longmans, 1902 BMC.

ATH 6-2-02 a critique of war.
DIAL 8-02 rev. not helpful. Does have a heroine.

000817   HOPE THE HERMIT; A NOVEL. BY EDNA LYALL.
London: Longmans, 1898 BMC. New York: Longmans, Green,
1898 NUC.

SP 81:566. Cumberland. 17th c romance. Magnanimous
hero.
LIT 3:401. Wholesome, old-fashioned.
NYT 1898:684. Last half of 17th century, reign of
William and Mary. Highlands of Scotland. Hero does not
know his parentage, must discover it before he can
declare his love to heroine. Their love story;
eventually all is well.

000818   IN SPITE OF ALL. A NOVEL. BY EDNA LYALL.
New York: Longmans, Green, 1901 NUC. London: Hurst &
Blackett, 1901 BMC NUC.

Historical romance. Eng. Fic. Civil War 1642-49.
11-23-01 ATH

000819   MAX HEREFORD'S DREAM. BY EDNA LYALL. New
York: United States Book, [c1891] NUC. London: Simpkin
& Marshall, 1891 BMC.

000820   TO RIGHT THE WRONG; A NOVEL. BY EDNA
LYALL. London: Hurst and Blackett, 1894 BMC. New York:
Harper, 1894 NUC.

000821   WAYFARING MEN; A NOVEL. BY EDNA LYALL.
New York: Longmans, 1897 NUC. London: Longmans, 1897
BMC.

Concerns actresses and actors. Gives a rosey picture
of the seamy side of life. SP 79:692
Confers her benediction on this profession and "urges
the iniquity of Eng. divorce laws" Christine Greville
engaged to one actor makes a marriage for money and
cannot get a divorce when her husband proves
unfaithful. ATH 110:704
SR 85:502. Deals with the actor and actress. "Entirely
harmless and obviously well-intentioned."

BAYLY, ELISABETH BOYD.

000822   FORESTWYK; OR, TEN YEARS AFTER. London:
Jarrold, 1896 BMC.

ATH 108:899. Temperance tract.

000823   HONOR GREENLEAF, OR ENJOYING POOR HEALTH.
London: Jarrold, 1900 BMC.

000824   UNDER THE SHE-OAKS. Philadelphia: Union
Press, 1905 PW. London: R.T.S., [1903] BMC.

    Pioneering in Australia. PW 6-3-05.

000825   ZACHARY BROUGH'S VENTURE. London:
Jarrold, 1894 BMC.

    ACAD 46:553. Painful. Brough's attempt to rescue
    artist from drink, aided by two children. Elevating.
    Temperance. He's a business man. SP 74:827.

BAYNTON, BARBARA. Australia.

000826   COBBERS. London: Duckworth, 1917 BMC.

000827   HUMAN TOLL. London: Duckworth, 1907 NUC
BMC.

    "Degenerate, uncivilized people in Australian bush
    life--repugnant." ACAD
    Study of childhood-infancy to dawning womanhood.
    Ursula sinister, grim truthful, tragic. Australian.
    ATH

BAZAN, EMILIA PARDO. 1852-1921. Spain.

000828   THE ANGULAR STONE. New York: Cassell,
[c1892] NUC. (Tr. Mary J. Serrano)

    CR 17:225. Man "a product of discipline in all its
    forms" (army, priesthood, teacher etc.) becomes
    garroter. But he eventually kills himself rather than
    execute a young woman tried for murder.

000829   A CHRISTIAN WOMAN. New York: Cassell,
[c1891] BMC NUC. (Tr. Mary Springer)

    Carmen won't stay in father's house because he keeps a
    mistress and her staying would sanction it. So she
    marries an old man she doesn't love. Question: Is she
    Christian? or like "prostitute she condemns?" Anti RC
    and anti priests PW 4-18-91.
    She finds marriage harder than she thought, but
    remains loyal though sorely tempted by her love for
    Salustio. Realistic portrait of life in Madrid.
    Salustio depends on uncle-old man who weds Carmen.
    Salustio lives with them, falls in love with her, CR.
    Salustio tells the story. "How much more virtuous was
    she than the girl who does not exact the wedding ring
    as a prelude to her diamonds and her brougham?" LW
    5-9-91
    Incoherent and pointless DIAL 6-91

000830   MIDSUMMER MADNESS. Boston, Mass.: C. M.
Clark, 1907 NUC. (Tr. from Spanish by Amparo Loring)

    unconventioal love story in Spain. author is "an
    ardent upholder of equal rights..ed. social &
    political." Her theories are exploited by the hero
    throughout the novel. PW 3-23-07
    R OF R v. 35 1907 intense love affair

000831   MORRINA (HOMESICKNESS). New York:
Cassell, [c1891] BMC NUC. (Tr. Mary J. Serrano)

    She's a servant in Dona Autora's household, in Madrid,
    she's friendless, homesick (that's what her name
    means). Finds a home in that house, is seduced by Dona
    Autora's spoiled son Rogello. Mother takes him away.
    Morrina suffers terrible melancholy. LW 26 Sept 1891.
    Kills herself.

000832   THE MYSTERY OF THE LOST DAUPHIN (LOUIS
XVII). New York and London: Funk & Wagnalls, 1906 BMC
NUC. London: (Tr. A. H. Seeger)

    PW-Hist
    NYT-0

000833   THE SON OF THE BONDWOMAN. London: J.
Lane, 1908 BMC NUC. New York: J. Lane, 1908 BMC NUC.
(Tr. Ethel Harriet Hearn)

    @ a priest in Galacia PW 12-7-07
    ACAD

000834   THE SWAN OF VILAMORTA. New York: Cassell,
[c1891] NUC. (Tr. Mary J. Serrano)

    The Swan is a young poet who allows a school teacher
    mother of a cripple to support him until she ruins
    herself and ignores her child. Middle-aged woman-young

selfish Galician artist. PW 11-14-91.
He goes off to South America; Leocadia kills herself.
She loves his poetry. Hers is an intellectual love.
Another woman Madrilena had a quick passion for him
and forgets him. Her old husband dies because he knows
of her affair. LW 19 Dec 1891,497

000835   A WEDDING TRIP. New York: Cassell,
[c1891] NUC. (Tr. Mary J. Serrano)

    Pilar-fine portrait of "modern hysterical girl" Lucia
    was sold by father for rank and social position to an
    old selfish worn-out rake who marries her to get a
    large income. Accident separates the newlyweds. Lucia
    alone without money thinks husband deserted her, falls
    in love with young Artegui. Old husband makes her life
    miserable with his jealousy. LW 8-1-91 255

BEACH, GERTRUDE.

000836   HER GUARDIAN EVER: BEING THE STORY OF A
YOUNG GIRL'S LIFE. London: Roxburghe Press, [1897]
BMC.

BEACH, MRS. WILLIAM HICKS. See BEACH, SUSAN EMILY
(CHRISTIAN) HICKS.

BEACH, SUSAN EMILY (CHRISTIAN) HICKS. United Kingdom.

000837   ARDINA DORAN. London: Smith, Elden, 1903
BMC.

    Short desc. ACAD 64,634.
    Ardina marries an arson goes insane? ACAD, 65 14
    Marries a cave-man type? LBKM 8-03,188
    At 18 shows up in her father's social life. Heroine
    remains aloof to it all; author allows her to touch
    all the chords of romance only to tear them away. ends
    in anti-climax TLS 225,03

000838   AN INLAND FERRY. London: Smith, Elder,
1902 BMC.

    ACAD. character study of female.
    ATH 6-21-02 not helpful

000839   A POT OF HONEY. London: T. F. Unwin, 1897
BMC.

000840   SHUTTERED DOORS. BY MRS. WILLIAM HICKS
BEACH. London and New York: J. Lane, 1919 NUC BMC.

    TLS Relationship of Duller Place to various members of
    family who own it.
    SP. three generations. Heroine is Aletta (rev says not
    too many readers will like her).
    SR-Aletta is a fine woman and an unexpected fortune
    makes her marry well and suitably, while her life runs
    on to its close and the house remains.
    NYT 8-8-20 Aletta is "an exceedingly dull English lady
    of highly respectable connections and habits".

BEAL, MARY LOUISE (BARNES). B. 1844. United States.

000841   A MISUNDERSTOOD HERO. Boston: Pilgrim
Press, [1905] NUC.

BEALE, ANNE. United Kingdom.

000842   CHARLIE IS MY DARLING. London: Hurst and
Blackett, 1891 BMC.

    Charlie is really maudlin, the opposite of a darling.
    Goes to Canada to claim an inheritance, fails, dies
    there. ATH 98 448.
    Answers "next of kin" ad. His sister left at home to
    slave to maintain the family. She yearns for her
    brother. The true heir who turned up in Canada comes
    to England and marries a daughter of the family. ACAD

000843   CONCEALMENT. London: W. Scott, 1906 BMC.

BEALE, MARIA (TAYLOR). B. 1849. United States.

000844   JACK O'DOON: A NOVEL. New York: H. Holt,
1894 NUC.

    Mercy Blessing, sea captain's daughter and her two
    suitors, one a noble sailor Jack O'Doon, the other an
    artist. CR 23:439

BEALS, CHRISTINE. United States.

000845   THE WINEPRESS. New York: The Bookery,
[c1912] NUC.

BEALS, HELEN RAYMOND (ABBOTT). B. 1888. United States.

000846   THE MERRY HEART. BY HELEN RAYMOND ABBOTT.
New York: Century, 1918 NUC BMC.

PW-oldest sister on New England farm, selfish family
and how she made her fight and won.
NYT-story of three sisters on NE farm.

BEAN, FANNIE. United States.

000847   COL. JUDSON OF ALABAMA; OR, A
SOUTHERNER'S EXPERIENCE AT THE NORTH. New York: United
States Book, [c1892] NUC.

000848   PUDNEY AND WALP. New York: J. W. Lovell,
[c1891] NUC.

000849   RUTH MARSH: A STORY OF THE AROOSTOOK. New
York: United States Book, [c1892] NUC.

BEARNE, CATHERINE MARY (CHARLTON).

000850   THE CROSS OF PEARLS; OR, THE STORY OF A
FRENCH FAMILY IN THE FOURTEENTH CENTURY. London: E.
Stock, 1903 BMC.

000851   IN PERILOUS DAYS. A TALE OF THE FRENCH
REVOLUTION. London: S.P.C.K., [1920] BMC.

000852   MAX AND HIS BROTHERS. London: Catholic
Truth Society, 1906 BMC 1908 NUC.

BEAUMONT, DONNA BROOKS. United States.

000853   SHE OF THE HOLY LIGHT. BY JOHN G. CAXTON.
New York: Western Authors' Assoc., 1893 NUC.

BEAUMONT, MARY. United Kingdom.

000854   JOAN SEATON: A STORY OF PERCIVAL-DION IN
THE YORKSHIRE DALES. London: J.M. Dent, 1896 NUC. New
York: F. A. Stokes, [c1897] NUC.

ATH 108:900. Yorkshire at time of Indian Mutiny.
Shocking crime in quiet place.
"Her pluck and loyalty and unerring perception of the
right." Can meet all emergencies. A fine type. A
mortgage on the family seat had to be paid off before
Joan's marr. A love story. BKM 6:75
Heroine "firm and sweet and spirited." Her
parents-well drawn. Rural setting of life in the
Yorkshire dales-details of that life. NYT 8-21-97,3

BECKER, ELAINE.

000855   A SOUL'S REDEMPTION; A PSYCHOLOGICAL
ROMANCE. London: G. Redway, 1899 BMC.

"Soul of a dissipated violinist takes possession of a
young lady. "Author uses the incident for discussion
of the woman question.SP 83:352

BECKETT, CECIL (GRIFFITH).

000856   CORINTHIA MARAZION. BY CECIL GRIFFITH
(MRS. S. BECKETT). London: Chatto and Windus, 1892
BMC. Philadelphia: J. B. Lippincott, [1892] NUC.

LW 23:166. Out of pity, Corinthia "big-brained and
big-hearted" marries, after an 8 year engagement to
her cousin (broken by him), a minister. He struggles
for 8 months between loving his wife and loving his
soul and then dies. Three years later she makes a good
marriage. She is not a Christian.
ATH 99:176. She is an agnostic and is forced to marry
a clergyman whom she doesn't love because she was
compromised by having to spend a night with him on an
island.
PW-She was the literary associate of her adopted
father, a scientist.
SR 73:218.

000857   THE UTTERMOST FARTHING. BY CECIL
GRIFFITH. [n.d.] BMC.

BECKETT, MRS. S. See BECKETT, CECIL (GRIFFITH).

BECKLEY, ZOE. United States.

000858   A CHANCE TO LIVE. New York: MacMillan,
1918 NUC.

Poor family; father dies; at 14 Annie Hargan must

undertake role of provider. $2.00 a week as a cash
girl to $10.00 as factory worker. Factory burns; she's
safe but no job. Then office work at $6.00; becomes
head stenographer at $12. BOOK, meets the man,
marries, hard time.
PW-Annie, from slums, is 1st in factory, then a switch
board operator then typist. Love later. Struggle to
make enough money to live on.

BECKMAN, MRS. WILLIAM. See BECKMAN, NELLIE SIMS.

BECKMAN, NELLIE SIMS. United States.

000859   UNCLEAN AND SPOTTED FROM THE WORLD. BY
MRS. WILLIAM BECKMAN. San Francisco.: Whitaker and
Ray, 1906 NUC.

BECKWITH, CARMELITA, jt. au. See SHAW, ADELE MARIE AND
CARMELITA BECKWITH.

BEDDOW, ELIZABETH RUSSELL. B. 1860. United States.

000860   THE ORACLE OF MOCCASIN BEND; A STORY OF
LOOKOUT MOUNTAIN. BY MRS. CHARLES P. BEDDOW. New York:
Neale, 1903 NUC.

BEDDOW, MRS. CHARLES P. See BEDDOW, ELIZABETH RUSSELL.

BEDFORD, H. LOUISA.

000861   DANIEL'S FALLEN DAGON. London: R.T.S.,
[1900] BMC.

000862   THE DEERHURST GIRLS; OR, A TRIPLE
ALLIANCE. London: T. Nelson, 1907 BMC.

000863   DRUSILLA THE SECOND. London: S.P.C.K.,
[1910] BMC.

000864   FIGHTING HIS WAY; OR, CAREW OF BURCOMBE.
London: R.T.S., [1904] BMC.

000865   HER ONLY SON ISAAC. London: S.P.C.K.,
[1901] BMC.

000866   HIS WILL AND HER WAY. London: S. Paul,
1911 BMC.

Jennie King inherts a mill from her father; her
dealings with her manager, her factory girls, her
worthless brother inherits only an annuity. TLS

000867   A HOME IN THE BUSH. London: S.P.C.K.,
[1913] BMC.

000868   I WILL BE A SAILOR. London: R.T.S.,
[1899] BMC.

000869   JACK, THE ENGLISHMAN. London: S.P.C.K.,
[1914] BMC.

000870   LOVE AND A WILL O' THE WISP. London:
R.T.S., [1908] BMC.

000871   A MAID WHOM THERE WERE NONE TO PRAISE.
London: R.T.S., [1901] BMC.

000872   MAIDS IN MANY MOODS. London: S. Paul,
1912 BMC.

TLS-wedding bells and no sex problem.
ATH-wedding bells and no sex problem.

000873   MISS CHILCOTT'S LEGACY. London: S.P.C.K.,
[1891] BMC.

000874   PRUE THE POETESS. London: Skeffington,
1897 BMC.

Her chief struggle is to overcome jealousy. Tragic
end. SP 79:903

000875   RALPH RODNEY'S MOTHER. London: S.P.C.K.,
[1898] BMC.

000876   ROBIN THE REBEL. London: S.W. Partridge,
[1903] BMC.

000877   THE SIEGE OF MR. JOHNSON. London:
S.P.C.K., [1915] BMC.

000878   TO DO AND DARE. London: R.T.S., [1907]
BMC.

000879   UNDER ONE STANDARD; OR, THE TOUCH THAT
MAKES US KIN. London: S.P.C.K., [1906] BMC.

000880   THE VENTURES OF HOPE. London: R. T. S.,
1914 BMC.

ATH-ups and downs of family guided by older sister.

000881   THE VILLAGE BY THE RIVER. London:
S.P.C.K., [1900] BMC.

BEDFORD, H. LOUISA AND EVELYN EVERETT GREEN.

000882   ENID'S UGLY DUCKLING. London: R.T.S.,
[1896] BMC.

BEDFORD, H. LOUISA, jt. au. See GREEN, EVELYN EVERETT AND
H. LOUISA BEDFORD.

BEDFORD, JESSIE. United Kingdom.

000883   THE BRIDAL OF ANSTACE. BY ELIZABETH
GODFREY. London and New York: J. Lane, 1906 BMC NUC.

PW-bride is deserted; mystery finally solved.
NYT-reappearance of earlier wife believed dead.
ACAD-white haired bride is a Griselda
TLS
ATH o

000884   CORNISH DIAMONDS. BY ELIZABETH GODFREY.
London: Bentley, 1895 NUC BMC.

Hero loses interest in heroine for a slight reason,
flirts with a married woman; when this woman's husband
dies, he becomes engaged to her. The widow though,
throws him over when she meets an old flame. Then the
hero returns to heroine, but she no longer loves him.
Loves the Violin, holds out for a long time for music,
but marries in the end. SR 79:518
Tangled love affairs of Jenifer Lyon, Cornish girl and
her sailor Alick Studland.

000885   THE CRADLE OF A POET. BY ELIZABETH
GODFREY. New York and London: John Lane, 1910 BMC NUC.

Therese impulsive marries an architect who goes down
hill; she takes up Greek dancing to support them. She
finally marries someone else-an old lover. PW
SR. Male poet is central figure, but it includes "an
advanced young woman remorselessly portrayed". POV?

000886   THE HARP OF LIFE. BY ELIZABETH GODFREY.
G. Richards, 1900 BS. New York: H. Holt, 1900 NUC.

NYT 1900:359. Wife married to musician. Unhappy, she
leaves home, finds that her craving for liberty does
not bring happiness. She has cast aside "a good man's
love." Almost loses him to a womanly woman who comes
into his life in her absence.

000887   POOR HUMAN NATURE; A MUSICAL NOVEL. BY
ELIZABETH GODFREY. London: G. Richards, 1898 BMC. New
York: Holt, 1898 NUC.

SP 81:873. Hero marries wrong woman. After he has lost
her and his voice he finds happiness with other woman,
an English prima donna.
ACAD 55:291. German schoolmaster and American prima
donna sing together in opera, fall. But his sense of
duty requires him to marry someone else. Miserable
years follow until wife dies.
ATH 112:710. Simple love story.
Opera people in Germany. Much about wagnerian opera
and differences between English society and German.
LIT 4:346
Dahlman's voice lacks passion-it comes at the price of
pain. LW 17:5
Basically the story of a man wed to a woman he
discovers is selfish who finds true love of a noble
woman. BKM 8:588

000888   A STOLEN IDEA: A NOVEL. BY ELIZABETH
GODFREY. London: Jarrold, 1899 BMC.

A young woman happens upon an idea in a manuscript and
writes a novel about it. It's a success. Author of
idea finds what he considers to be his work a success,
but himself unknown. They get together and all is
well. LIT 4:558
Delicia Walson, aspiring author, steals a plot. SP
83:386.

000889   'TWIXT WOOD AND SEA. London: Chapman and
Hall, 1892 BMC.

Story of Eleanor Baxendale told by herself. All the
other characters are drawn as they stand in relation

to her, seen and understood only as she saw and
understood them. Self contemplative. Melancholy. SR
1-14-93,45
Widow-her first and second marriages. ACAD 43,218
Heroine's description of her childhood and girlhood.
Theme of marry in haste and repent in leisure. ATH
101,118

000890   THE WINDING ROAD. BY ELIZABETH GODFREY.
New York: Henry Holt, 1902 NUC. London and New York:
J. Lane, 1903 BMC.

BOOK NEWS 02- woman joins gypsy on road, tragedy at
end
CR-when she has her baby, mother in her asserts
itself, she stays, he goes-tragedy. "her heart breaks
for road and man."
Becomes pregnant, goes into hospital in France, he
goes to Tibet, she finds refuge with her family in
England, he returns eventually but she is dead NYT
5-10-02
ATH 10-11-02

BEDFORD, RUTH, jt. au. See MACKELLAR, ISOBEL MARION
DOROTHEA AND RUTH BEDFORD.

BEE, DORA.

000891   THE BATTLE BY THE LAKE. London: R.T.S.,
[1913] BMC.

000892   THE MAN WITH THE MESSAGE. London: R.T.S.,
1911 BMC.

Rel. ATH

000893   OUR MARATHON RACE. London: R.T.S., [1910]
BMC.

BEEBE, JESSIE HOLLIS. United States.

000894   RED SKY'S ANNIE; A STORY OF THE BAD
LANDS. Boston: Roxburgh, [c1911] NUC.

BEECHER, CAROLYN. United States.

000895   MAID AND WIFE. New York: Britton, [c1919]
BMC NUC.

"girl brought up in luxury...forced to seek her living
in New York" PW
Father dies; family penniless becomes sales girl in
large dept. store. Repulses the floor-walker who has
her fired on the charge that she stole. Marries but
finds marriage too dull-goes back to New York to take
up her business career. In the end goes back home. NYT

000896   ONE WOMAN'S STORY; A NOVEL. New York:
Britton, [c1919] BMC NUC.

Art of getting along in the world PW
Margaret Drayton raised in well-to-do family marries
but knows nothing about housework. Husband expects her
to cook, to put up with his wining and dining women
clients (he's a lawyer). She tries to devote herself
to music. He'll have none of it. And so on until at
the very end, a tragedy draws them together. NYT 701
11-30-19

BEECHER, MAY HOWELL. 1854-1923. United States.

000897   THE EIGHTH HUSBAND. Boston: Sherman,
French, 1913 NUC.

"Story of a girl who was cursed by an old Indian
woman. Seven times the girl married and each time the
bridegroom was killed within a few hours of the
ceremony. Finally
PW 11/8/12 1526 another man was brave enough to risk
the curse and through another squaw the doom was
lifted"

000898   JACQUEMINOT, THE ROMANCE OF A ROSE. New
York and London: F.T. Neely, [1901] NUC.

BEEKMAN, HELEN. Nationality Unknown.

000899   DAINTY DEVILS; A NOVEL [ANONYMOUS]. New
York: W.H. Young, 1903 NUC.

Young bride in NYC meets fashionable set who drink,
flirt, scheme to get her divorced. PW 5-9-03
Very brief description. BKM 17 (1903) 542
Depraved types in NY. Arist. The servant question. A
woman on drugs. A woman tired of her husband who loves
a boy. Woman in large family who neglects them all.

All looked upon with scorn it seems. NYT 405,03

BEGBIE, JANET.

000900   MORNING MIST. London: Mills & Boon,
[1916] NUC.

BEHENNA, KATHLEEN.

000901   SIDARTHA: A STORY OF MYSTERY. London:
Digby, Long, [1896] BMC.

It's a snake that kills off most of the characters,
but likes the heroine who befriends an old woman who
leaves her a fortune. "wild nonsense" SR 83:128

BEHRENS, BERTHA. 1850-1912.

000902   BEETZEN MANOR. A ROMANCE. BY W. HEIMBURG.
New York and London: International News, [c1895] NUC.
(Tr. Elise Lathrop)

Sophie von Kronen lives a lonely gloomy existence in
German household where death of young heir brings
great grief. Because she's lonely she marries the
first man she meets. Story of the consequenses. PW
10-26-92:705.

000903   THE CHAPLAIN'S DAUGHTER. MISUNDERSTOOD
AND JASCHA. BY W. HEIMBURG. Chicago: E. A. Weeks,
[c1894] NUC. (Tr. Kate Dykers)

PW-her husband, a Bohemian at heart, fled with another
woman on the eve of their marriage. Repents years
later.

000904   DEFIANT HEARTS. BY W. HEIMBURG. New York:
R.F. Fenno, [c1897] NUC. (Tr. Annie W. Ayer and H.T.
Slate)

Rural Germany young lt. gives up his love to marry
money. She tries to marry but finds her love for him
is too strong.Goes to Dresden and becomes a singer.
After many years they get together. PW 52:1136

000905   ELSIE. BY W. HEIMBURG. Chicago: Rand,
McNally, 1891 NUC. (Tr. Hettie E. Miller   Same
story as A Penniless Girl PW 10-10-91)

Same story as "A Penniless Girl" PW 10-10-91.
Published in 1884. Charming little German love story.
IND

000906   FOR ANOTHER'S WRONG. A NOVEL. BY W.
HEIMBURG. New York: R. Bonner, 1895 NUC. (Tr. A. W.
Ayer and H. T. Slate   Pub. also as: For Another's
Fault.)

Young Annaliese suffers much sorrow because of her
mother's second marriage. PW 2-9-95:296
German setting: efforts of son to clear father's good
name. PW 4-27-95:680

000907   HORTENSE. BY W. HEIMBURG. Chicago: Rand,
McNally, 1891 NUC. (Tr. Mary E. Almy)

000908   AN INSIGNIFICANT WOMAN: A STORY OF ARTIST
LIFE. BY W. HEIMBURG. New York: R. Bonner's Sons,
[1891] NUC. (Tr. Mary Stuart Smith)

A patient Griselda. An artist uses her money to
surround self with luxury, takes a mistress. She puts
up with it all until he's tired of it and reforms. PW
7-25-91.
German sentimental novel: young artist dislikes wife,
wastes money. Adversity sets him straight.
LW.

000909   A MAIDEN'S CHOICE. BY W. HEIMBURG. New
York: Worthington, 1891 NUC. (Tr. Elise L. Lathrop
Same story as Lottie of the Hill 1882. PW10-10-91)

Same as "Lottie of the Mill" published 1882. PW
10-10-91.
Caste conquered by love in spite of obstinate
relatives. LW

000910   MARTHA THE PARSON'S DAUGHTER AND UNDER
THE MUSES' BAN. BY W. HEIMBURG. New York: Street and
Smith, 1891 NUC.

Leaves home, becomes an actress, after a short career
meets a sad fate. Second story: tale of an old house.
PW

000911   MISJUDGED. BY W. HEIMBURG. Chicago: Rand,

McNally, 1891 NUC. (Tr. Mary E. Almy   Same story as
An Insignificant Woman PW 8-8-91)

Same as An Insignificant Woman PW 8-8-91

000912   MISS GOOD-FOR-NOTHING. BY W. HEIMBURG.
Chicago: E.A. Weeks, [c1893] NUC. (Tr. Hettie E.
Miller)

000913   MISS MISCHIEF: A NOVEL. BY W. HEIMBURG.
New York: R. Bonner's Sons, 1893 NUC. (Tr. Mary Stuart
Smith)

Young Italian was brought to Germany, a country
strange and unsuitable for her. Those who raise her
misunderstand her. But she becomes a noble
self-sacrificing, etc. woman and repays them well. PW
4-29-93.

000914   A POOR GIRL. BY W. HEIMBURG. New York:
Worthington, 1892 NUC. (Tr. Elise L. Lathrop)

000915   WAS SHE HIS WIFE? BY W. HEIMBURG. London:
Eden, 1891 BMC. (Tr. Helen Wolff)

Sacrifices of mother and sister for the sake of their
son/brother. ACAD
Lore and Kathe van Tollen, poor, proud, superior
high-born sisters. Both love and desert the one man (a
non-arist) that they accept. He's a schoolmaster. SP
66, 388

BEHYMER, IDA HOLMES. United States.

000916   THE SEAL OF DESTINY. New York: F.T.
Neely, [1901] NUC.

BELDEN, JESSIE PERRY (VAN ZILE). 1857-1910. United States.

000917   ANTONIA. London: J. Murray, 1901 BMC.
Boston: L.C. Page, 1901 NUC.

ATH 2-15-02. . Conv. Historical novel

000918   FATE AT THE DOOR. Philadelphia: J. B.
Lippincott, 1895 NUC.

Society life. Woman and man attempt a platonic
relation. Most of the novel relates their
conversations and meetings. But in the end she sends
him off "banished to the other side of the world"
because she is convinced that a platonic relation
between a man and a woman is impossible. She's
married. LW 26:253
Mrs. Courtlandt PW 8-10-95:200 Establishes the
relation because she thinks her husband is falling out
of love with her.

BELL, ALICE. United States.

000919   TANGERINES. Jacksonville, Fla.:
Vance-Garrett Press, 1894 NUC.

BELL, CLARA INGRAHAM. United States.

000920   DEBORAH GRAY. BY FRANCES C. INGRAHAM. New
York: Neale, 1903 NUC.

Quiet story of 3 generations. PW 12-19-03

BELL, EVA MARY (HAMILTON). B. 1878. United Kingdom.

000921   IN THE WORLD OF BEWILDERMENT. A NOVEL. BY
JOHN TRAVERS. London: Duckworth, 1912 BMC.

TLS-struggle of a man between simple homely brave wife
and soulless siren.
ATH-he decides to go straight, tells other woman; she
tells him calmly that she loves another man. Touches
on women's suffrage. POV?

000922   SAHIB-LOG; AN ANGLO-INDIAN TALE. BY JOHN
TRAVERS. London: Duckworth, 1910 BMC. London:
Duckworth, [1913] NUC.

000923   SECOND NATURE: A STUDY IN CONTRASTS. BY
JOHN TRAVERS. London: Duckworth, 1914 BMC.

ATH-hero, to inherit his fortune, must marry a woman
who has been sentenced to a term in prison. He does
so, but since Society is shocked by his wife's
manners, he takes her to a lonely station on the
Indian frontier.

BELL, FLORENCE EVELEEN ELEANORE (OLLIFFE). 1851-1930.

000924 THE ARBITER. London: E. Arnold, 1901 BMC.

000925 THE GOOD SHIP BROMPTON CASTLE, A NOVEL. BY LADY BELL. London: Mills & Boon, [1915] NUC BMC.

takes the trad love talk and reverses the normal roles: presents the boy as Hildred and "the pretty woman as, yes reader, a naval officer" without restraint chases Ralph-Knew his club, walked up and down outside till she met him. Boards his ship in pursuit, leads him to the altar aboard ship . To emphasize the audacity of Hildred, the author creates Antona who also loves Ralph but she's so passive, reticent lady-like TLS

000926 MISS TOD AND THE PROPHETS. A SKETCH. London: R. Bentley, 1898 BMC.

SP 80:796. Miss Tod took a prediction of the end of the world in one year seriously. A retired governess, she spent her capital of 1,300 pounds as income, only to have the fatal day pass and herself penniless. "Touching denouement."

000927 THE STORY OF URSULA. BY MRS. HUGH BELL. London: Hutchinson, 1895 BMC NUC.

Ursula Vane, English, but French by ed. is governess at age 22. Mother of house finds her son kissing Ursula. Out she goes. Takes another governess position. Is persuaded by her aged employer to wed him. Marriage is a success for a while. Then Ursula gets depressed, leaves, and goes to join a married friend-Leila Witherell. When Leila doesn't show up, Ursula spends a night with a old love she chanced to meet. Leila shows up and delivers Ursula home. She has a child which is not her husband's but doesn't tell him for 12 years. He forgives her and that's that. "So nauseous an ending." ACAD 47:333.
She's as "egotistical, conscienceless and heartless as any New Woman" but preserves some characteristics of traditional woman-clings, cries. ATH 105:501
The intercepted loves letter. Sudden fall of Ursula and "her fellow sinner Dick Mariner." "The incident at the Dover hotel is nauseating" She was pure. SP 74:723.

BELL, GERTRUDE.

000928 TRUE TO THE PRINCE: A TALE OF THE SIXTEENTH CENTURY 1567-1575. London: Digby, Long, 1892 BMC.

ATH 100:189. Catherine Van Baardhoven dressed as a page carries messages to the Prince of Orange through crowded streets of Antwerp. From this goes on to further adventures. Historical romance.

BELL, GERTRUDE A.

000929 SARABANDE. London: Greening, [1914] BMC.

Combines a travel book with a kidnapping. TLS

BELL, IDA.

000930 COUNTRY CLASH; THE SAYINGS AND DOINGS OF MEGGY BOWMAN. London: Hodder and Stoughton, 1914 BMC.

TLS-gossip of Scottish village of Inchrossie; Scottish vernacular.

BELL, KATHERINE VIRGINIA. United States.

000931 STELLA RUSSELL. New York: Neale, 1907 NUC.

BELL, LADY. See BELL, FLORENCE EVELEEN ELEANORE (OLLIFFE).

BELL, LILIAN. See BOGUE, LILIAN LIDA (BELL).

BELL, LILIAN LIDA. See BOGUE, LILIAN LIDA (BELL).

BELL, MARIA.

000932 THE COUNTRY MINISTER'S LOVE STORY. London: Hodder and Stoughton, 1895 BMC. New York: A.D.F. Randolph, 1895 NUC.

Scot. Oxford man becomes minister of small village; feels out of place with simple shopkeepers-except with Jane Frederick who is a kindred soul to Henry Millie. They marry after some hesitation on her part, due to another suitor. SP 75:117
He dies prematurely; because of that other suitor; he never recovers from the blow, ACAD 47:461

BELL, MRS. HUGH. See BELL, FLORENCE EVELEEN ELEANORE (OLLIFFE).

BELL, MRS. W. F. IRVINE.

000933 THE FORRESTER'S GIRL. London: W. and R. Chambers, 1919 BMC.

Simple love story. TLS
Anita Lalonne marries forester in California. He's jealous of a man from her past. Tragedy comes with forest fire, husband sacrifices his life for hers. ATH

BELL, NANCY R. E. (MEUGENS). D. 1933.

000934 PIERRE: A TALE OF NORMANDY. London: J. M. Dent, 1904 BMC.

BELL, PEARL DOLES. United States.

000935 GLORIA GRAY, LOVE PIRATE. Chicago: Roberts, [c1914] NUC.

"Gloria Gray longs to enter business life, and fresh from a business college at seventeen begins her career. She has love affairs with two men who employ her before she learns that she has been playing with fire, and at last finds her real place in life and happiness with the man who has known and loved her always." PW

000936 HER ELEPHANT MAN, A STORY OF THE SAWDUST RING. New York: R. M. McBride, 1919 NUC. London: J. Bale, [1921] BMC.

Circus story. Wistful and appealing. PW

000937 HIS HARVEST. New York and London: J. Lane, 1915 NUC.

Conflict of love vs career as singer. PW 10-30-15

BELLINGER, MARTHA IDELL (FLETCHER). B. 1870. United States.

000938 THE STOLEN SINGER. Indianapolis: Bobbs-Merrill, [c1911] NUC.

Love and adventure. 12-16-11 PW
Agatha Redmond is kidnapped in NY with an admirer hot on the trail. She was mistaken for a Princess. NYT

BELSER, SUSAN M. United States.

000939 THE WILL AND THE WAY. Philadelphia: Lutheran Pub. Soc., [c1900] NUC.

PW 4-27-01

BENEDIALL, B. Y. See BENEDIALL, BRIDGET YVA.

BENEDIALL, BRIDGET YVA. United Kingdom.

000940 BLIND SIGHT. BY B. Y. BENEDIALL. London: Mills and Boon, 1915 BMC. New York: Dodd, Mead, 1915 NUC.

Hero loves a blind girl. TLS
Detective story. Clerk/detective falls in love with blind daughter of the house. An accident reveals her true feeling; recognizes value of true love. PW 89 1/8/16 p. 116.

000941 THE CHILD-LOVER. BY B. Y. BENEDIALL. London: Mills and Boon, [1916] BMC NUC.

TLS-bachelor who loves children, loves a highly intelligent woman who won't marry him because she is afraid of childbearing, marries an intellectual nurse. Rev thinks tries too hard to be clever.

000942 JEREMY'S LOVE STORY. BY B. Y. BENEDIALL. London: Mills and Boon, [1916] BMC.

TLS male hero.

BENEDICT, CLARE. United States.

000943 THE LOVE SAINT. A STORY IN FIVE PARTS. Edinburgh: A. Elliot, 1913 BMC. New York: E. S. Gorham, 1914.

BENGOUGH, ELISA (ARMSTRONG). United States.

000944 THE TEACUP CLUB. BY ELIZA ARMSTRONG.

Chicago: Way and Williams, 1897 NUC.

Young woman quarrels with her lover, proposes organization of a women's club for the advancement of women. They discuss women in politics, men's real attitudes toward women's progress, the new woman, etc. Gentle satire. PW 52:736.

000945   THE VERY YOUNG MAN AND THE ANGEL CHILD. BY ELISA ARMSTRONG. New York: Dodge, [c1900] NUC.

PW-two young women in a flat, objects of curiosity to the janitor and their neighbors, who annoy them. Two of the most annoying are mentioned in the title.

BENGOUGH, M. A. See BENGOUGH, MARION AGNES.

BENGOUGH, MARION AGNES. Nationality Unknown.

000946   IN A PROMISED LAND; A NOVEL. BY M. A. BENGOUGH. London: Bentley, 1893 BMC. New York: Harper, 1893 NUC.

In South Africa. Both men love their wives, neither of wives loves husband at first. One comes to love her as she "elevates her character." In the other the husband godlike is brought down to his wife's level. This couple Mattie and Jesse. "Jesse's loathing for Mattie's infidelity is conquered by his animal passion for her person." ATH 101:343
Sarah Bowman and Mattie Williams have been raised in the sheltered life of a sect called the Primitive Gospellers. Suddenly learn they are to marry two laborers and go to South Africa. Story studies their marriages. Also a strong characterization of Runciman, a man who is part black. SP 70, 549.
Sarah Arkwright is one of the heroines. LW 93, 178.
Sarah finds her husband is a Philistine; she's high minded, only slowly comes to love him. Mattie weds a man with Kaffir blood-passionate explosive nature beneath the facade of civility. SR 76:44 3.

000947   SO NEAR AKIN, A NOVEL. London: R. Bentley, 1891 NUC BMC.

Chief character is Anne Paton-completely sym portrayal of a lively young woman who runs away from home to join an Uncle Will. Many experiences closed to respectable young women. ACAD
Anne is daughter of respectable, religious family. As a very young girl ran away to live with black sheep of family, a strolling player. She's brought back, but runs off again to escape her fiance. Ends up marrying a cousin who's worried about her reputation. ATH 98 187
Anne Paton joins the players. Later engaged to Sir Henry Stephens, but runs off and ends up with cousin who writes plays. SR 9-1-91, 142

BENNETT, ALICE HORLOCK. B. 1866. United States.

000948   THE OTHER MRS. SCARLETTE. London: K. Paul, [1917] BMC.

TLS-she is newly appointed secretary of Ladies Helpers Assoc. at seaside town. Sly and sarcastic portrayal of the advanced ladies who form the association's committee.

BENNETT, ETTA BUCHANAN.

000949   THE LEAVEN OF THE PHARISEES. London: H.J. Drane, [1907] BMC.

The heroine is most militant. ACAD

000950   A SCOTTISH BLUEBELL. A NOVEL. London: Jarrold, [1904] BMC.

000951   ZELIA. A NOVEL. London: Jarrold, [1905] BMC.

BENNETT, JENNIE (FREEMAN). B. 1855. United States.

000952   A LIGHT IN THE WINDOW; A STORY OF THE WANDERINGS AND SUFFERINGS OF A WAYWARD BOY. Chicago: W.B. Conkey, [1913] NUC.

BENNETT, MAISIE, pseud. See NIXSON, EDITH MAY MAYER.

BENNETT, MARY E. B. 1841?. United States.

000953   JEFFERSON WILDRIDER. BY ELIZABETH GLOVER. New York: Baker and Taylor, [c1898] NUC.

PW-History of a New England family. Jefferson breaks

one woman's heart by marrying the other; his wife's brain gives way from strain of slaving for support of his children.

BENNETT, MRS. ROLF.

000954   FELICITY. BY KATHERINE HARRINGTON. London: G. Alden & Unwin, 1919 BMC.

SR- Daughter of hard father and weak mother. Works for a scholarship.
Brutal puritan father keeps young woman from being a school teacher. She goes into service, then marries a literary man; some harsh scenes but conv. end. ATH

BENNETT, SUSAN EMILY.

000955   BEWITCHED. A LOVE STORY. London: R. Bentley, 1895 BMC.

Young man falls in love with a pretty face on train. He's bewitched. Tracks her down. There's a mystery and much sensationalism.
ACAD 48:202
Auto of a 40 yeax old man. Marwell Tute "a girl's hero" acts like a woman, and Suzanne Wildwood. ATH 106:124
Maxwell Tute, artist looking for a scene, falls in love with woman on train. Tracks her down where she lives with grumpy father. Suzanne Wildwood. mystery surrounds her, even a ghost is involved. SP 75:275

BENNING, HOWE, pseud. See HENRY, MARY H.

BENSON, M. E. See BENSON, MARY ELEANOR.

BENSON, MARY ELEANOR. 1863-1890.

000956   AT SUNDRY TIMES AND IN DIVERS MANNERS. London: K. Paul, 1891 NUC BMC.

Wholesome, very real description of habits and lives of the very poor. ACAD

000957   STREETS AND LANES OF THE CITY. BY M. E. BENSON. London: Privately Printed, [1891] BMC NUC.

BENSON, STELLA. See ANDERSON, STELLA (BENSON).

BENTLEY, EMMA.

000958   SILVIO BARTHOLI, PAINTER. A STORY OF SIENA. London: T.F. Unwin, 1896 BMC.

SR-Travel, useless characters, confused plot.
ATH 107:742. Italy
ACAD 49:424. Siena. Simple love story, young painter, Luigi, his wife Margherita, and heroic Vera, Silvio's daughter.
SP 77:344. Luigi is adopted son of Silvio, goes to Rome to widen his knowledge of art and forgets his betrothed. Happy ending.

BENTON, KATE A. D. 1899. United States.

000959   GEBER: A TALE OF THE REIGN OF HARUN AL RASCHID, KHALIF OF BAGDAD. New York: F. A. Stokes, [c1900] NUC. London: G. Richards, 1900 BMC.

NYT 1900:149. Posthumous; 1st book. Mysterious East 1,000 years ago. Story of intrigue and bloodshed. Relieved by romance of pure young love and the power of Christianity. Geber, a philosopher, his scheme for vengeance and remorse before dying. Oriental characters.

BENTZON, TH., pseud. See BLANC, MARIE THERESE (DE SOLMS).

BERESFORD, MAX, pseud. See HAMILTON, ANNIE E. (HOLDSWORTH) LEE.

BERGENGREN, ANNA (FARQUHAR). B. 1865. United States.

000960   THE DEVIL'S PLOUGH: THE ROMANTIC HISTORY OF A SOUL CONFLICT. BY ANNA FARQUHAR. London: J. Macqueen, 1901 BMC. Boston: L. C. Page, 1901 NUC.

PW 3-9-01
ATH 6-8-01

000961   AN EVANS OF SUFFOLK. BY ANNA FARQUHAR. Boston: L. C. Page, 1904 NUC.

Woman, daughter of criminal and former waitress, lives lie, married to young society scion. Love triumphs. ARENA 1904

000962   HER BOSTON EXPERIENCES: A PICTURE OF
MODERN BOSTON SOCIETY AND PEOPLE. BY MARGARET ALLSTON.
Boston: L. C. Page, 1900 NUC.

PW Margaret tells story. Clever love story.

000963   HER WASHINGTON EXPERIENCES AS RELATED BY
A CABINET MINISTER'S WIFE IN A SERIES OF LETTERS TO
HER SISTER. BY ANNA FARQUHAR. Boston: L. C. Page, 1902
NUC.

000964   THE PROFESSOR'S DAUGHTER. BY ANNA
FARQUHAR. New York: Doubleday and McClure, 1899 NUC.

Her eyes suffer for the help she gives in her father's
research. Their trip to Rhode Island coast brings her
to good health and to love. PW 55:672
Louise marries doctor who orders rest for her eyes. LW
30:182

000965   A SINGER'S HEART. BY ANNA FARQUHAR.
Boston: Roberts, 1897 NUC.

Education and love affairs of an American opera
singer. LW 28:227.
Eleanora Dean of N.E. Goes to Eng. to get better
instruction from a master. Career vs love. First loves
a German musician who's married and who almost "wins"
her. That happened in U.S. In London her next love
affair ends tragically. PW 51:709.
This second love dies. To this woman singer
everything, even love, is subordinate to her artistic
genius. BKM 5:353.

BERINGER, AIMEE (DANIELL). B. 1856.

000966   THE NEW VIRTUE. London: W. Heinemann,
1896 BMC.

SR-nasty.
ATH 107:542. Morbid, dismal. "The women still clamor
for mercy and justice both and demand more than the
old sale and barter. How tired readers are of this
new, or rather old, cry in fiction!"
ACAD 49:525. Margaret faints during a thunderstorm.
While she is unconscious, Teddy, her companion, is
tempted and rapes her. He is immediately struck by
lightning and killed. Soon after Margaret is wooed by
Henry Bethune and they marry. One month later he
discovers she is about to become a mother. Having seen
his wife as a symbol of purity, in despair he consults
a friend, a doctor, who succeeds in reestablishing his
faith. The tragedy of Lady Arbuthnot's life is a
background.
LW 27:121

BERMAN, HANNAH.   United Kingdom.

000967   MELUTOVNA; A NOVEL. London: Chapman and
Hall, 1913 NUC BMC.

Describes Jewish life in Russia a half century
earlier--the miserable conditions. ACAD
peasant family in Mekitovna. ATH

BERNARD, MARGUERITE AND EDITH SERRELL.

000968   DEER GODCHILD. New York: M. E. Demetre,
1918 NUC BMC. London: T. W. Laurie, [1919] BMC.

Published for the Fatherless Children of France.
WWI-fic.
Letters from little American boy to French boy orphan
about war. ATH

BERNARD, MARY N.   United States.

000969   WHERE THE WORLD KNEELS: A NOVEL. BY
CHRISTIE STEELE. Culler, N.C.: W. C. Phillips, 1893
NUC.

BERNHARD, MARIE. B. 1852. Germany.

000970   THE HOUSEHOLD IDOL. New York:
Worthington, 1892 NUC. (Tr. Elsie L. Lathrop.)

LW 23:182. Heroine is a selfish beauty who almost
wrecks hero's life.
PW Romance. Rome, Germany.

000971   "THE PEARL"; A ROMANCE FROM THE GERMAN.
London: International News, [1894] BMC. New York:
International News, [c1894] NUC. (Tr. Mary Stuart
Smith)

PW-Old fashioned love story.

000972   THE RECTOR OF ST. LUKE'S: A NOVEL. New
York: Worthington, 1891 NUC. (Tr. Elise L. Lathrop)

Annie Gerold meets a rector, his cousin and a famous
artist at a dinner party. All love her; she loves
artist. Rector learns secret about artist, wonders how
to use it. Focus on him. PW
Preacher ponders whether to tell a young woman that
her fiance murdered a man in his youth. Heroine is
sweet and submissive. LW
Military town in Germany. Godey's 123,90.

BERNSTEIN, HENNY.

000973   ONE FOR MANY: CONFESSIONS OF A YOUNG
GIRL. BY VERA. New York: J. S. Ogilvie, [c1903] NUC.
(Trans. H. Britoff.)

Very brief description. BKM 17:539

BERRY, GRACE ISABEL.

000974   ISCAH: A TALE FOR THE TIMES. London: R.
Banks, 1898 BMC. (Bookseller Shows Full Title: Past,
Present and Future, Historical, Religious and
Political)

BERRY, MARY LEE.   United States.

000975   PHILIP HARUM, THE NIHILIST STUDENT. BY
GERALD STEWART. New York: I. H. Brown, 1892 NUC.

BESKOW, ELISABETH MARIA. 1870-1928.

000976   VOICES. BY RUNA. Rock Island, Ill.:
Augustana Book Concern, [c1912] NUC.

BETH. See DAWSON, LISABETH.

BETHUNE, ANNE FLORENCE LOUISE MAY PATTON.

000977   BACHELOR TO THE RESCUE. London:
Remington, 1894 BMC.

SR 78:185. Lena, bold and bad, with strain of dark
blood, attempts to take soldier away from English girl
by foul means.
ACAD 46:100. Smokes cigarettes and drinks brandy and
soda. Murders inconvenient husbands, stabs a
half-hearted lover. Goes mad and is killed by
Bachelor, a dog, while attempting to murder her rival.
ATH-old-fashioned villainess.

000978   DEBONNAIR DICK. London and Sydney: Eden,
1892 BMC.

BETTS, LILLIAN WILLIAMS.   Nationality Unknown.

000979   THE STORY OF AN EAST-SIDE FAMILY. New
York: Dodd, Mead, 1903 NUC.

wife becomes a leader & acknowledged power in her
neighborhood. PW 4-25-03.
Mary daughter of alcoholic mother becomes important in
her neighborhood "a person to be reckoned with in
times of elections." her children grown she ceases to
be a power in her home. One by one her children fail
her. - 289, NYT 03.

BETTS, NANNIE DEADERICK.   Nationality Unknown.

000980   THE FLOWER OF THE SEASON. New York:
Broadway, 1912 NUC.

BETTY, pseud. See GARITY, MARY E.

BEULAH, pseud. See BATES, FANNY D.

BEVANS, NEILE, pseud. See VAN SLINGERLAND, NELLIE BINGHAM.

BEWICKE, A. E. N. See LITTLE, ALICIA HELEN NEVA (BEWICKE).

BEWSHER, MRS. M. E.

000981   MISCHIEF-MAKERS; OR THE STORY OF
ZIPPORAH. London: [1891] BMC. Sydney: Griffith,
Farran, Okeden and Welsh, [1891] NUC.

BIANCHI, MARTHA GILBERT (DICKINSON). D. 1943. United
States.

000982   A COSSACK LOVER. London: Everett, [1913]
BMC.

American heiress loves a Cossack. Her guardian objects to the marriage, but after a year's suspense, they marry. ATH TLS

000983   THE CUCKOO'S NEST. New York: Duffield, 1909 NUC.

Smart Americans in Paris. PW 6-19-09.
Criss-cross loves. BKM
3 travellers and wide-roving thoughts on sundry subjects. NYT BKM v.30, 1909-10,

000984   THE KISS OF APOLLO. New York: Duffield, 1915 NUC.

"Career of a modern Am. girl" BKM 41:1915
Brilliant unusual Judith-her marriage is no marriage. her work in philanthrophy. Julian is her comrade. PW 5-15-15
As a girl Judith liked to play act stories from mythology but never would do "the kiss of Apollo." That kiss becomes her dread. "She was intensely, fiercely virginal, shrinking with an unnamed horror from the sex in man." She hates her boyfriend; after he steals the kiss, she says, "I am going to give my whole life to helping girls not to love men...women are happy & good until some man kisses them... It is just the way Apollo drove poor Cassandra mad..." In order to work at her plan, she gets married in name only. (Marriage will make her freer to move about.) In the end throws over all the ideas. "The closing chapter is strange reading for these days of feminism." NYT

000985   A MODERN PROMETHEUS. New York: Duffield, 1908 NUC.

PW Unhappy marriage, husband is murdered, shall she go into a convent or marry another?
NYT question still not answered at end of book. Clare probably unable to decide.

000986   THE POINT OF VIEW. New York: Duffield, 1918 NUC.

PW- hero discovers how much he loves Sapphira when war breaks out and she throws herself into war work. She changes her point of view (away from unconv) with bishop's influence.
NYT Jul 14,1918, p.314. In the style of Henry James.

000987   THE SIN OF ANGELS. New York: Duffield, 1912 NUC.

PW-American marriage.
NYT-to Austrian girl. American women and men are clumsy in act of love, therefore problems.

BIANCO, MARGERY (WILLIAMS). 1880-1944. United States.

000988   THE LATE RETURNING. BY MARGERY WILLIAMS. New York, London: Macmillan, 1902 NUC. London: W. Heinemann, 1902 BMC.

ATH 7-19-02 rev. not too helpful. On last page heroine dressed as boy is shot as rebel.
DIAL 8-02 rev. not helpful
NYT-Vanda becomes mistress of President, deserts him for the people during an uprising to return to an earlier love, disguised as a man, the 2 are captured & shot.

000989   THE PRICE OF YOUTH. BY MARGERY WILLIAMS. New York, London: Macmillan, 1904 NUC. London: Duckworth, 1904 BMC.

BKM 19 1904 "not altogether innocent" (?) girl suffers "doubts & questions" from man she loves concerning her past. POV? what is the Phemy Martin episode? true, but shouldn't have been said.
NYT--0
LBKM --0

000990   SPENDTHRIFT SUMMER. London: Heinemann, 1903 BMC.

Marital complications ACAD. 65, 170.
Bohemian atmosphere: wife resents the affection between her husband & his brother-a quiet tragedy results. Subtle study of these 3 LBKM, 10-03, 56.

000991   THE THING IN THE WOODS. BY MARGERY WILLIAMS. London: Duckworth, 1913 BMC NUC.

eerie, in Pennsylvania horror, mystery. ATH

doctor investigates strange deaths. TLS

BIBBINS, RUTHELLA BERNARD (MORY). 1865-1942. United States.

000992   MAMMY 'MONGST THE WILD NATIONS OF EUROPE. New York: F.A. Stokes, 1904 NUC. London: G. Richards, 1904 BMC.

PW- Colored nurse of "golden-haired" charge travels with family.

BIDDER, MARY. See PORTER, MARY (BIDDER).

BIDDLE, S. M. See BIDDLE, SARA MELISSA.

BIDDLE, SARA MELISSA. B. 1851. United States.

000993   THE NEW DOCTOR; OR HEALTH AND HAPPINESS; A STORY. BY S. M. BIDDLE. Chicago: F.E. Ormsby, 1900 NUC.

BIDDLE, SARAH.

000994   SOME LETTERS OF AN AMERICAN WOMAN CONCERNING LOVE AND OTHER THINGS. Philadelphia: International Printing, 1902 NUC.

PS 3503

BIDDULPH, MRS. WRIGHT.

000995   CRESSIDA. A NOVEL. London: Greening, 1906 BMC.

TLS-could turn herself into a snake.

000996   PIRATES OF SOCIETY. London: Heath, Cranton, [1919] BMC.

Arist. marriage mongers, swindlers, black-mailers, SP

BIGELOW, EDITH EVELYN (JAFFRAY). 1861-1932. United States.

000997   DIPLOMATIC DISENCHANTMENTS: A NOVEL. New York: Harper, 1895 NUC. London: Osgood, McIlvaine, 1895 BMC.

Professor in small N.E. college becomes ambassador in Germany. Comments on customs, life, etc. Happy to return to his quiet home. PW 6-29-95:998 N.E. University professor appointed as minister to Germany. We hear much about Berlin. Takes wife, daughter, niece. Love story included concerns a Hungarian artist, selfish, only his art matters yet women fall at his feet. BKM 2:57

000998   THE MIDDLE COURSE. BY MRS. POULTNEY BIGELOW. New York: Smart Set, 1903 NUC.

married woman involved with artist, has brutal husband. PW 9-5-03
Title refers to a bond between the sexes somewhere between friendship & love-& the rude shattering of that belief. American woman, English husband, she's dissatisfied after 8 years of marriage the artist won't take the middle course. They're about to break up, husband sees them together, goes off to get divorced. NYT 672, 03.

000999   WHILE CHARLEY WAS AWAY. BY MRS. POULTNEY BIGELOW. New York: D. Appleton, 1901 NUC. London: W. Heinemann, 1901 BMC.

woman's hunger for love feverish craving for excitement, constant demands of vanity. BOOK NEWS 12'01.

BIGELOW, MARGUERITE OGDEN. See WILKINSON, MARGUERITE OGDEN (BIGELOW).

BIGELOW, MRS. POULTNEY. See BIGELOW, EDITH EVELYN (JAFFRAY).

BIGG, LOUISA.

001000   IN QUEST OF KIN. London: K. Paul, 1920 BMC.

TLS-family.

BIGGER, GLADYS SINGERS.

001001   BLUE EARTH. London: Heath, Cranton & Ouseley, [1914] BMC.

BIGOT, MARIE (HEALY). B. 1843.

001002   AN ARTIST. BY MADAME JEANNE MAIRET. New
York: Cassell, [c1891] NUC. (Tr. Anna D. Page)

Woman loves her husband and her art; he's selfishly
jealous of her profession. She refuses to give it up.
They make peace, decide to make the best of each
other. LW
Diane Verrot was student of Bernard Ozanne, French
artist. He taught her that love and art don't mix-for
women. He loves her, she won't marry because she won't
give up art. Then they do marry.
PW J4

BILBRO, MATHILDE. United States.

001003   THE MIDDLE PASTURE. Boston: Small,
Maynard, [c1917] NUC BMC.

Traditional romance. PW 91:628 2/24/17
A harum-scarum tom-boy. BKM
Beatrice Crawford, spirited chronicler, concerns a
farm. BKM
Pleasant little story of a contested piece of land-the
pasture and two brothers who fought over it. Their
children play on it. Beatrice is one of them who tells
the tale of the local romances, the arrival of Dr. St.
John, etc. NYT 99 3-18-17

BILLINGS, EDITH S. United States.

001004   CLEOMENES. THE NEW QUO VADIS. BY MARIS
WARRINGTON BILLINGS. New York, London: J. Lane, 1917
NUC. London: Jarrolds, [1920] BMC.

Romance in Greek mythological terms. PW
Rome-historical fiction.
TLS-foolish, male hero.

001005   AN EGYPTIAN LOVE SPELL. BY MARIS
HERRINGTON BILLINGS. New York: Central Publishing,
[1914] NUC.

BILLINGS, MARIS HERRINGTON, pseud. See BILLINGS, EDITH S.

BILLINGS, MARIS WARRINGTON, pseud. See BILLINGS, EDITH S.

BILSBOROUGH, MRS.

001006   HIS PLACE IN THE WORLD! London: Ward,
Lock, 1915 BMC.

Man loses his memory. TLS
Dr. loses his memory. ATH

BINSTEAD, MARY (OPENSHAW). United Kingdom.

001007   AFTERTHOUGHTS. BY MARY OPENSHAW. London:
Simpkin, Marshall, [1915] NUC BMC.

LBKM-Hist. rom.
Ravishing beauty; her successful marriage TLS
Visits England; causes havoc among Quakers. ATH

001008   THE CROSS OF HONOUR. BY MARY OPENSHAW.
London: T.W. Laurie, 1910 BMC. Boston: [1911] NUC.

Hist. rom. 7-1-11 PW
ACAD-Hist. rom. male hero

001009   GLORY EVERLASTING; A STORY OF THE TIMES.
BY MARY OPENSHAW. London: Simpkin, Marshall, [1917]
NUC BMC.

How a family converted from money making to endowing a
hospital TLS

001010   LAUGHTER STREET, LONDON. London &
Glasgow: Collins' Clear-Type Press, [1920] BMC.

TLS Elderly love story
ATH pretty. Concerns Laffert Street, a neighborhood of
tiny gardens, houses not of a soul-destroying
uniformity, and people more adept at living than
making money. Mostly painters & writers.

001011   LITTLE GREY GIRL. BY MARY OPENSHAW.
London: J. Ouseley, 1913 BMC. New York: Dillingham,
[c1913] NUC.

PW 6-7-13:2007 "Story of England and France at the
time of the siege of Paris and the Franco-Prussian
War. Silence Strangeways, a little Quaker girl, goes
to live in an English village with her old Quaker
cousins, while her father is in Paris. There he falls

in love with the lovely Comtesse de Castelle, and
Silence manages to get mixed up in it in a most
surprising manner. There is a villain and arch plotter
who almost secures the Comtesse and her fortune, but
is defeated by Silence and her father, both of whom
marry and live happy ever after."
Born in quiet English village but longs to see the
world. gets to Paris at beginning of France-Germ war.
meets the Empress. ACAD

001012   THE LOSER PAYS: A STORY OF THE FRENCH
REVOLUTION. BY MARY OPENSHAW. London: T. W. Laurie,
[1908] BMC. Boston: Small, Maynard, [c1911] NUC.

TLS-male heroes
ATH
Hist. rom. PW 10-14-11

001013   SUNSHINE. THE STORY OF A PURE HEART. BY
MARY OPENSHAW. London: Heath, Cranton & Ouseley,
[1914] BMC NUC.

SR 147:477. Sylvia, pretty, fragile, lovable.
Conventional story of mrg to older man, eventually a
widow, then happiness.

BIRCHENOUGH, MABEL CHARLOTTE (BRADLEY). 1860-1936. United
Kingdom.

001014   DISTURBING ELEMENTS. London: Smith,
Elder, 1896 BMC.

001015   POTSHERDS. London: Cassell, 1898 BMC.
Leipzig: B. Tauchnitz, 1899 NUC.

SP 81:530. William, northern Englishman, loves
Philippa, cultured and artistic. Helena, also from
north, loves William, is self-sacrificing, finally
dies shielding him from an assassin.
ACAD 55:30. Staffordshire potteries.
ATH 112:524.
A murder, an injust accusation, a compromising letter,
art students in Latin Quarter. LIT 4:239
Old man does the murdering then commits suicide. SR
87:57

BIRD, MARY PAGE.

001016   WEDDED TO A GENIUS. BY NEIL CHRISTISON.
London: R. Bentley, 1894 BMC.

SR 78:363. She married him because Phelan had gone
away for a year and hadn't come back after two. He
made her do all sorts of things she disliked,
scientifically observing her. When the doctor runs
across Phelan, he has a greater scope for his
interests. Eventually he is remorseful.
Sp 73:409. Harrowing mental torture which in an urbane
way he makes appear perfectly reasonable, sometimes
even to the victim herself. Turned his child into an
idiot and separated him from his mother.
ACAD 46:229. Wife (Judith) finally rebels.
ATH 104:218. "His superior way of treating her and
speaking to her is naturally a little galling, but she
makes it more galling than it need have been by
keeping her mind constantly fixed upon it. She does
not give him instinctive love, or submission, or
accommodation, but is always asking herself, 'Why this
chasm between me and this strange man? How is it that
he does not think more with me and of me?' Domestic
bliss does not flow in that channel. The husband is
undoubtedly a trying person, but the author has not
made him bad enough to earn our full sympathy for the
wife. It is true that Dr. Courtney pins her down to a
rather harrowing and perilous situation in order to
test and study her, as he might study a moth on a
cork. Yet the reader may see reason to conclude that
she pinned herself down, and insisted on part of her
torture."

BIRDSALL, ANNA HUNTINGTON.

001017   A CONFLICT OF SEX: A NOVEL. London and
New York: F. T. Neely, [1898] NUC.

PW-Katherine, poor, marries millionaire. At the end
she is Lady Superior of a convent in Ireland.

BIRKHEAD, ALICE. United Kingdom.

001018   DESTINY'S DAUGHTER. London, New York: J.
Lane, 1915 NUC.

private secretary becomes successful actress PW
2-20-15
Gabrielle about to be married gives him over to her

49

sister. NYT

001019   THE MASTER-KNOT. London, New York: J.
Lane, 1908 BMC.

TLS-O
PW-2 women brilliantly educated & talented- "learn to
appreciate faithful love offered them in place of
their visionary ideals & self deceptions."
ACAD-heroine Damaris is a combination of Cyrano &
Roxanne.
ATH-one is driven by the slanderous tongue of a
jealous employer to exchange her occupation as a
governess for marriage with an Irish country doctor &
after sundry alarms and one excursion; settles down,
more or less, to domesticity. The other-a
distinguished novelist by day & a distinguished
actress by nite loses her sight, breaks her heart & in
this shattered state falls back on the devotion of a
suitor previously contemned.

001020   SHIFTING SANDS. London: J. Lane, 1914
BMC.

ATH 144:329 Heroine is a "Bluestocking and an altruist
who allows her sisters to supplant her." First a
secretary, then an actress. Brilliant and attractive,
fails to fulfill her aspirations.
TLS-She is at the end an apparently successful actress
(unmarried). Reviewer does not like her. "She never
learned to conquer herself or her emotions. She could
not face the discipline of life or 'the horrible
monotony of working in an office.'"

BIRRELL, OLIVE M.

001021   THE AMBITION OF JUDITH. London: Smith,
Elder, 1898 BMC.

ACAD 53:681. She is a red-haired beauty with whom most
men fall in love. "There is a rich aunt, a hocussed
will, and a pale artist, and a lady Social Democrat.
And the Social Democrat wins. Judith settles in Paris.
Her home is the street; her family, those who are in
sickness or distress."
ATH 111:61. Unscrupulous Jewess who wants to be rich
contrasted with another woman.
LBKM 14:140. Judith wants money, lies and cheats for
it, and finds it a curse when she gets it.

001022   ANTHONY LANGSYDE. A MODERN LOVE STORY.
London: Osgood, McIlvaine, 1894 BMC.

SR 78:543. He is a barrister, editor, playwright,
philanderer. He is turned down by beautiful Celia,
marries a plain girl who suffers but they are truly
wedded at last. There is Violet, a wicked and
cigarette-smoking modern girl.

001023   BEHIND THE MAGIC MIRROR. London: Osgood,
McIlvaine, 1896 BMC.

SR-Young girl encouraged to display and increase her
"spiritual" powers; tracing of corresponding growth of
insincerity. "The tangle of troubling confusion brings
her to the verge of madness."
ATH 107:742. "Filled out into the form of a novel the
framework supplied by the poem "Mr. Sludge."
(Browning). "The assignment to two separate persons of
the parts of conscious and unconscious imposter which
Browning's hero combines in one person".

001024   LOVE IN A MIST. London: Smith, Elder,
1900 BMC.

LBKM 19:90. About socialism, but author takes no
stand. Poor heroine marries rich man but vows not to
wear jewels.
SP 85:717. Father is high-minded Socialist whose
family has gone neglected and half-starved. Sybilla is
rebellious, but at death of father her eyes are opened
to the nobility of his character.
ACAD 59:517. She later lives in a flat with 2 other
women.

001025   NICHOLAS HOLBROOK. London: Smith, Elder,
1902 BMC.

ATH 5-3-02

BISHOP, CONSTANCE E. United Kingdom.

001026   FLAME OF THE FOREST; A NOVEL. New York:
Benziger, 1920 NUC.

001027   THE MOON SLAVE. London: Cranton, [1920]

BMC.

TLS--R.C.

001028   A VISION SPLENDID. London: Heath,
Cranton, [1917] BMC.

Two Eurasian women. Clyte becomes a doctor the other
Jinny completely renunicates self. Each provided with
a love story TLS

BISHOP, MRS. GEORGE.

001029   TWO MEN AND A WOMAN. A NOVEL. London:
Ward & Downey, 1893 BMC.

Muriel Lascelles, pure-minded, is unhappy with her
profligate, untrue husband. He's a brute SR 75,489.
"Mrs Bishop should know that, as the law stands,
simple adultery, unaccompanied by physical cruelty or
lengthened desertion, does not enable a wife to get a
divorce." ACAD 43:501
Author's long discourse on the text "men were
deceivers ever." Muriel made very symp. ATH 101,533.

BISLAND, ELIZABETH. See BROUGHTON, RHODA AND ELIZABETH
(BISLAND) WETMORE, Also WETMORE, ELIZABETH (BISLAND).

BLACK, CLEMENTINA. United States.

001030   AN AGITATOR. London: Bliss, Sands, 1894
BMC.

ACAD 46:529. Character study of idealistic and honest
male labor agitator.
Career of a young Fabian man who at 23 becomes a labor
leader then stands for Parliament. Is accused of
"abstracting ballots," tried, convicted, then
pardoned. CR 23:159
Christopher Brand LW 26:41
PW-Kit Brand is a dedicated man working entirely to
help his fellow workmen. Suspicion falls on him
wrongly, and he is imprisoned and prosecuted.
Political movements in the career of a socialist. He
is a strike leader in London, goes to prison on false
charge. BAKER 03,77

001031   CAROLINE. London: J. Murray, 1908 BMC.

TLS- tr. hist. rom. SR, ATH
BAKER 13-182

001032   THE PRINCESS DESIREE. London: Longmans,
1896 BMC.

An arranged marriage for a German princess. She's
beautiful, of strong principle and refuses to have
anything to do with the proposed marriage. Asserts
herself but comes out of it "Grand Duchess and
triumphant." LBKM 11:125

001033   THE PURSUIT OF CAMILLA. London: C.A.
Pearson, 1899 BMC. Philadelphia: Lippincott, 1900 NUC.

Very clever and independent Camilla--plot to win her
love. Historical romance. A Pole, not an Englishman,
wins her. LBK:17:90
Camilla Veneroni is abducted by a Marquis who wants to
marry her. He happens to be a lady-killer, so Camilla
is attracted to him. Meantime her Polish lovers and
others are in pursuit of the kidnapped heroine.
Escapes, weds the Pole. SP 83:613
Anglo-Italian girl, abducted by a scoundrel, pursued
by two other men. BAKER 03 77
LW 31:172. Daughter of Italian father and English
mother in Italy. She is always disappearing.
PW-she is pursued by one man for her money, by another
in an attempt to rescue her from her enemies. Her
father is an Italian political refugee.

BLACK, DOROTHY.

001034   HER LONELY SOLDIER. London: Hodder and
Stoughton, 1916 BMC.

TLS- wartime romance.
LBKM-wartime romance.

001035   THE MAN WITH A SQUARE FACE. London:
Hutchinson, 1916 BMC.

TLS-love story
LBKM-o

BLACK, EDITH FERGUSON. B. 1857. Canada.

50

001036   A BEAUTIFUL POSSIBILITY. Philadelphia:
Union Press, 1904 NUC. London: R.T.S., [1907] BMC.

001037   A PRINCESS IN CALICO. London: R.T.S.,
[1903] BMC.

Pauline too good to be true. NYT 282,05

BLACK, MARGARET HORTON (POTTER). 1881-1911. United States.

001038   THE CASTLE OF TWILIGHT. BY MARGARET
HORTON POTTER. Chicago: A. C. McClurg, 1903 NUC.
London: C.F. Cazenove, 1903 BMC.

3 brave & beautiful women in feudal times; loneliness
of isolated castles-10-31-03 PW
a moving story the chill melancholy of these women's
lives while the men off warring & hawking.

001039   THE FIRE OF SPRING. BY MARGARET POTTER.
New York: D. Appleton, 1905 BMC NUC.

unhealthy story "an intrigue carried on under a
husband's roof" with the servants' help. "By an even
more unhealthy shaping of circumstances" the pair
makes peace. PW 2-18-05
unwisdom of mothers who urge their daughters to marry
wealth. young Virginia marries elderly millionaire.
She enjoys the marriage preparations. Mother later
tortured with misgivings for arranging the whole
thing. Virginia is disgusted by her old husband;
inexperienced bored neglected, she takes a lover.
Author treats the women sympathetically-NYT 173, 05

001040   THE FLAME-GATHERERS. BY MARGARET HORTON
POTTER. New York, London: Macmillan, 1904 BMC NUC.

PW historical novel
NYT-"vague, mystic"

001041   THE GENIUS. BY MARGARET POTTER. London &
New York: Harper, 1906 BMC NUC.

PW-based on life of Russian composer (male)
NYT-0

001042   THE GOLDEN LADDER; A NOVEL. BY MARGARET
POTTER. New York & London: Harper, 1908 BMC NUC.

BKM 27 1908-actress, "downfall"?
PW-?
TLS sympathetic portrait of businessman's wife,
unmarried mother
ATH-0
SP-Kitty Clephane, at first mistress of John Kildare,
refuses to marry him because of his poverty & goes on
the stage. He eventually becomes a success. "aims &
objectives of the American middle class world" Potter
calls her book "an American comedy of gold."
unpleasant reading.
BKM-Kitty becomes pregnant "pretty face"is her one
asset-refuses his offer of reparation "varied
fortunes, before the footlights, final desperation
that tempts her to blackmail"

001043   THE HOUSE OF DE MAILLY; A ROMANCE. BY
MARGARET HORTON POTTER. New York & London: Harper,
1901 BMC NUC.

PW 6-1-01
ATH 8-3-01
American countess knows all about poisons-her
knowledge put to use historical romance. DIAL 7-01
Historical romance NYT

001044   ISTER OF BABYLON, A PHANTASY. BY MARGARET
HORTON POTTER. New York & London: Harper, 1902 BMC
NUC.

CR female goddess who expresses many modern
sentiments.
ATH 11-1-02

001045   THE PRINCESS. BY MARGARET POTTER. London
& New York: Harper, 1907 BMC NUC.

unhappy wife; husband unfaithful PW 3-16-07
Russian imperial families. "revolting story"
"unutterable horrors." women here are long suffering.
The 3 women find it impossible to "make alliances" and
end their days together. The prince is victim of conv.
which makes royal marriage a political matter. She
suffers but makes the best of it finding some meaning
in her son. NYT

001046   A SOCIAL LION. BY ROBERT DOLLY WILLIAMS.

Chicago: R. R. Donnelley, 1899 NUC.

001047   UNCANONIZED: A ROMANCE OF ENGLISH
MONARCHISM. BY MARGARET HORTON POTTER. Chicago: A. C.
McClurg, 1900 NUC.

NYT 1900:700. A brief for King John, based on the
thesis that he was villified by the monks. Hero is
Antony, illegitimate son of Archbishop Walter.

BLACK, MARGARET MOYES.

001048   DISINHERITED. Edinburgh & London:
Oliphant, 1891 BMC.

Story of old lady Hernhurst near 90 who for 50 years
of widowhood has hated her husband's family and the
grandchildren. Though in every other way she's kind
and charitable. ACAD 9-12-91:214.

001049   THE GHOST OF GAIRN. A TALE OF "THE FORTY
FIVE". Edinburgh and London: Oliphant, 1894 BMC.

001050   THE HOUSE OF CARGILL: A TALE OF THE
SMUGGLING DAYS. Edinburgh and London: Oliphant, 1895
BMC.

001051   A MOST PROVOKING GIRL: A TALE OF THE EAST
COAST. Edinburgh and London: Oliphant, [1896] BMC.

ATH 107:33. Scotch. Dialect. Mischievous but innocent
and gentle Nannie.
ACAD 50:29. M. B. belongs to school of Annie Swan.
Nance is for a short time an actress. The man she
loves dies of cholera; she marries another.

001052   A WOMAN AND PITIFUL: A DEESIDE STORY.
Edinburgh and London: Oliphant, 1893 BMC.

This woman has a mysterious and chequered past: Effie
Reid, Scot, easily impressed but is too carefully
raised and watched to go astray. ACAD 44:290.

BLACK, MARGARET (SHAFER). United States.

001053   HADASSAH; OR, ESTHER, QUEEN TO AHASUERUS.
BY MRS. T. F. BLACK. Chicago: Laird and Lee, [c1895]
NUC.

BLACK, MRS. T. F. See BLACK, MARGARET (SHAFER).

BLACKALL, EMILY (LUCAS). 1836-1900. United States.

001054   WON AND NOT ONE. Philadelphia: J. B.
Lippincott, 1891 NUC.

IND 44:413. "Two lives rubbed out with the friction of
opposing religions."

BLACKBURN, ELIZABETH VERNON.

001055   THE DUCHESS ILSA. A PAGE FROM THE SECRET
MEMOIRS OF THE COURT OF HOHENAU-SESSELSTADT. London:
R. & T. Washbourne, 1914 BMC.

TLS-historical romance. South Germany, 19th c.

BLACKBURN, MARGARET ELIZABETH. 1847-1902. United States.

001056   KATHARINE CONWAY. Buffalo: C. W. Moulton,
1899 NUC.

BLACKFAN, JOSEPHINE H. United States.

001057   BETWEEN TWO WORLDS. New York: F. T.
Neely, [c1899] NUC.

BLACKMAN, FRANCES.

001058   LOVE IN A LIFE. London: Drane's, [1913]
BMC.

poor child becomes a nurse, marries a man she's known
all her life. ATH

BLACKWOOD, MRS. HANS.

001059   IN A NEW WORLD. London: Hurst and
Blackett, 1894 BMC.

ACAD 46:276. Daisy and her loves.

BLADEN, ELIZABETH SIMPSON.

001060   CURIOUS COURTSHIP: A SKETCH OF SOCIETY IN
PHILADELPHIA AND CAPE MAY. Philadelphia: 1900 NUC.

001061   ROMADA: A TALE OF LOVE IN A BALLOON.
[Philadelphia]: Spangler, [n.d.] NUC.

001062   AN UNPREMEDITATED HEROINE. Philadelphia:
[n.d.] W.

BLAIKLEY, EDITHA L.

001063   ALONE IN A CROWD. London: Heath, Cranton,
1913 BMC.

Simple, healthy story of suburban life. ATH 779
Dolce, pretty well to do coquette is bypassed by
suitors who prefer Ursula. The quiet, solitary
governess. TLS

001064   DOROTHY GAYLE. London: J. Ouseley, [1912]
BMC.

TLS- love story.

001065   THE ENCHANTED PEN. A ROMANCE. London:
Methuen, 1919 BMC.

Literally the make believe story of princesses and the
pen. TLS

BLAIR, ELIZA (NELSON). 1859-1907. United States.

001066   LISBETH WILSON, A DAUGHTER OF NEW
HAMPSHIRE HILLS. Boston: Lee and Shepard, [c1895] NUC.

She's a faithful, obedient daughter who must choose
between her bigoted father and her lover, between
Orthodox Methodism of father and new sect of Methodism
of lover. LW 26:170
N.E. a generation earlier. PW 4-20-95:653.
N.E. - religious and social differences; very like
Pembroke; autobiog. BKM 4:416

BLAKE, CECELIA M.

001067   AMONG THE WATER LILIES. London: Simpkin,
Marshall, [1895] BMC.

BLAKE, EMILY (CALVIN). B. 1882. United States.

001068   MARCIA OF THE LITTLE HOME. New York and
London: D. Appleton, 1911 BMC NUC.

001069   SUZANNA STIRS THE FIRE. London: C.F.
Cazenove, 1915 BMC. Chicago: A.C. McClure, 1915 NUC
BMC.

TLS-too sweet family.

BLAKE, KATHARINE EVANS. B. 1859. United States.

001070   HEARTS' HAVEN. Indianapolis: Bobbs-
Merrill, [c1905] BMC NUC. (Harmony society-fic.)

community of celibates-New Harmony-strange system of
raising adopted children PW 10-14-05
ideal socialism; leader believes family ties divert
the mind from God; children should be protected from
parents by common nursery where they would be raised
as foundlings. Husbands & wives torn apart for the
spiritual welfare of the community. Celibacy promoted.
Son of one couple raised this way until love comes to
him. Seems to end with a rejection of the scheme NYT

001071   THE STUFF OF A MAN. Indianapolis:
Bobbs-Merrill, 1908 NUC.

PW-Male hero with racial prejudices

BLAKE, M. M. See BLAKE, MATILDA MARIA.

BLAKE, MABEL P. United Kingdom.

001072   THE COURTS OF LOVE. BY FARREN LE BRETON.
London: J. Long, 1915 BMC.

001073   FRUITS OF PLEASURE. BY FARREN LE BRETON.
London: Holden and Hardingham, [1914] BMC.

001074   HOYA. BY FARREN LE BRETON. London: Holden
and Hardingham, [1914] BMC.

ATH-Heroine leaves her husband who has ill-treated
her, takes up music as a profession, meets a young
governess who also has suffered from same man.
TLS Husband has car accident, leaving heroine free to
marry. "conventional" "familiar"

001075   INSPIRATION. BY FARREN LE BRETON. London:
J. Long, 1918 BMC.

001076   STAIRS OF SAND. BY FARREN LE BRETON.
London: J. Long, [1919] BMC NUC.

Lois Baily, typist and Julian Le Marchland. She is the
selfish unawakened partner Julian the faithful
long-suffering love who forgives all to his erring
wife. TLS
She marries for money, has an affair, neglects husband
when his eyesight & money go but again becomes a
loving wife about the time her husband's fortune
improves. ATH
Picked up from dreary "cold mutton life" for luxury in
Paris "Julian De Marchland offers her everything for
nothing." She takes all, gives nothing to husband. Her
affair with a man. "But the husband deserves most of
his tribulation" LBKM
disgusted with marriage husband becomes blind,
reconciliation ? LBKM

BLAKE, MARGARET, pseud. See SCHEM, LIDA CLARA.

BLAKE, MATILDA MARIA.

001077   THE BLUES AND THE BRIGANDS. BEING THE
RECOLLECTIONS OF ETIENNE-MARIE CARRAUD, NANTAIS,
1789-94. London: Jarrold, 1898 BMC.

SP 80:251. French revolution. Written for boys and
girls. Male narrator.

001078   COURTSHIP BY COMMAND: A STORY OF NAPOLEON
AT PLAY. BY M. M. BLAKE. London: Hutchinson, 1895 BMC.
New York: D. Appleton, 1895 NUC.

001079   THE GLORY AND SORROW OF NORWICH TOLD IN
PEN AND PENCIL. BY M. M. BLAKE. London: Jarrold,
[1899] BMC. Boston: L. C. Page, 1900 NUC.

BLAKELY, ELIZABETH SEAL. United States.

001080   UNTO THE FOURTH GENERATION: ONE SOLUTION
TO THE NEGRO PROBLEM. Cincinatti, Ohio: H. H. Bevis,
1894 NUC.

Heredity-said to occur in black-white marriages even
when one partner has 1/16 "colored blood." Author
suggests emigration as solution to black" problem." PW
5-4-95:704

BLANC, MARIE THERESE (DE SOLMS). 1840-1907.

001081   JACQUELINE. BY TH. BENTZON. New York:
Boussod, Valadon, 1893 NUC. (Tr. Elizabeth W. Latimer)

Young woman upon leaving convent where she has been
educated is married to a man she doesn't know or love.
Becomes a model love, feels affection towards another
man. CR 24:178.

001082   TCHELOVEK. BY TH. BENTZON. Paris: Calmann
Levy, [1900] NUC.

BLANCHARD, AMY ELLA. 1856-1926. United States.

001083   BECAUSE OF CONSCIENCE; BEING A NOVEL
RELATING TO THE ADVENTURES OF CERTAIN HUGUENOTS IN OLD
NEW YORK. Philadelphia & London: J. B. Lippincott,
1901 NUC.

domestic & social life of Huguenots PW 11-2-01

001084   BONNY LESLEY OF THE BORDER. Boston: W. A.
Wilde, [1904] NUC.

PW-goes west with her grandfather, Juv?

001085   A FRONTIER KNIGHT: A STORY OF EARLY TEXAN
BORDER-LIFE. Boston: W. A. Wilde, [c1905] NUC.

new "Pioneer series " story man & 2 sisters emigrate
from Kentucky to Texas shortly before Mexican war.
Portrays border life-Mexican peasant, rancher & the
Texas Ranger all have part. BRD

001086   GIRLS TOGETHER. Philadelphia: J.B.
Lippincott, 1896 BMC NUC.

One studies art, the other music-in New York. They
live quite independent "Bohemian" lives. The brother
of one-a law student- plays hero. PW 11-2-95:741

001087   THE GLAD LADY. Boston: D. Estes, [c1910]
NUC.

Patty American lives in Spain with married sister. She tries her sister sorely with flirtations til Mr. Right comes along. PW

001088   TAKING A STAND. Philadelphia: G.W. Jacobs, 1896 BMC NUC.

PW 8-29-96. "Robina and Allen Brainerd, recognizing the necessity of immediate action if they wish to retrieve the fallen fortunes of the family, take the management of home affairs into their own hands. Story tells their plans, why Allen went to Ky., how he spent his college days there."

001089   TALBOT'S ANGLES. Boston: D. Estes, [c1911] NUC.

old estate in legal trouble, heroine must leave to earn her own living. PW 9-9-11 NYT

001090   TWO GIRLS. Philadelphia: J.B Lippincott, 1894 NUC. London: G. Newnes, 1895 BMC.

001091   TWO MARYLAND GIRLS. Philadelphia: G. W. Jacobs, [1903] NUC.

great sisterly love PW 10-17-03

001092   WIT'S END. Boston: D. Estes, [1909] NUC.

open race between 2 women for a man; one a fearless frank aggressive woman NYT

BLAND, EDITH (NESBIT). 1858-1924. United Kingdom.

001093   DAPHNE IN FITZROY STREET. BY E. NESBIT. London: G. Allen, 1909 BMC NUC. New York: Doubleday, Page, 1909 NUC.

mischevious girl, her awakening nature, experiences in black artist's colony PW 10-16-09
Daphne & sister run away from uncongenial aunt & uncle; take a flat, plunge into artist's life & love? TLS
marries "pleasant little story" ATH
for children SP
BKM-She & her younger sister run away from home, live in London falls in love with art student.

001094   DORMANT. BY E. NESBIT. London: Methuen, [1911] BMC NUC.

Bohemian life and a man searching for the elixir of life & experiments on corpse of beautiful woman. Brings her to life after a sleep of 50 years TLS
Eugenia put to sleep in 1861 with idea of conferring on her eternal youth. Kept there till he can finish the job. The nephew of the alchemist who put her to sleep discovers her "rather dusty but otherwise quite beautiful" ; farce like events follow SR

001095   THE HOUSE WITH NO ADDRESS. BY E. NESBIT. New York: Doubleday, Page, 1909 NUC. London: G. Newnes, [1914] BMC.

BKM v29 1909-professional dancer in a secret house in London-problem with ex husband. Hides away from lovers & ex husband. She does a Salome dance in which ex-husband's head is used; she doesn't realize this till the dance is over.

001096   THE INCOMPLETE AMORIST. A NOVEL. BY E. NESBIT. New York: Doubleday, Page, 1906 NUC. London: A. Constable, 1906 BMC.

PW-girl alone in Paris.
NYT-hero a self proclaimed expert in Ovidian art, characters tell lies. Interesting women-Miss Julia Desmond.
ACAD-too light a handling of difficult problems.

001097   THE INCREDIBLE HONEYMOON. BY E. NESBIT. New York & London: Harper, [1916] NUC. London: Hutchinson, [1921] BMC.

a happy summer spent wandering through England. BKM Young woman "longing for freedom without being in the least capable of vice" meets a young man who has recently inherited money. There's a mock marriage that keeps them at arm's length for a time. Then the discovery that it was no mock marriage. BKM 508 "pleasant little story" of the fairy tale type, with a princess, prince-the works. The pair travel through England and their romance "grew and flourished" as they traveled. NYT 41, 2-4-17

young woman from conventional family "hates houses and bric-a-brac and will not marry the middle aged lover her father chose for her. She takes off with the hero after a mock marriage that "shall leave them free when they wish to travel different ways." PW

001098   THE MAGIC CITY. London: Macmillan, 1910 BMC.

London

001099   THE MAGIC WORLD. BY E. NESBIT. London: Macmillan, 1912 BMC NUC.

001100   MAN AND MAID. London: T. F. Unwin, 1906 BMC NUC.

001101   THE RED HOUSE: A NOVEL. BY E. NESBIT. New York & London: Harper, 1902 NUC. London: Methuen, 1902 BMC.

NYT 11-22-02 Story of newly married owners of a 29 room house-they shared domestic jobs "one gathers that his heart lay in the dishpan, and that he was happiest when washing up the tea things."
Story of a marriage of 6 months, arguments-conclusion is a baby ? ACAD 64, 136
narrated by husband; reviewer insists Nesbit should have used a woman narrator; that she makes this husband effeminate. ACAD 64, 226
young marrieds in a big home early married life of Len & Chloe in the Red House, book opens with a quarrel, ends with a cradle? LBKM 3-03, 253
writer of novels, & illustrator (wife) inherits a mansion, but with little money to keep it up. ATH 121, 269

001102   ROSE ROYAL. BY E. NESBIT. New York: Dodd, Mead, 1912 NUC.

001103   SALOME AND THE HEAD: A MODERN MELODRAMA. London: A. Rivers, 1909 BMC.

Starts with Sylvia's girlhood. Dances Salome dance & one night actually has a real human head in her hands! TLS
Sylvia kills the man, uses head on the stage; the man is her husband-all in detail. Another man confesses to the murder to save Sylvia & he's freed from the charge ACAD.
Sylvia a dancer by force of genius. LBKM

001104   THE SECRET OF KYRIELS. BY E. NESBIT. London: R. Tuck, [1896] NUC. London: Hurst and Blackett, 1899 BMC.

LW 31:71. Secret is an insane wife, Jane Eyre school. SP 81:873. Sensational melodrama. Esther is the heroine. Her father is keeping a woman a secret prisoner. Her cousin is attempting to marry her so that he becomes her father's heir. She finally escapes.

001105   THIRTEEN WAYS HOME. BY E. NESBIT. London: A. Treherne, 1901 BMC.

BLENEAU, ADELE. United States.

001106   THE NURSE'S STORY, IN WHICH REALITY MEETS ROMANCE. Indianapolis: Bobbs-Merrill, [1915] BMC NUC.

She narrates; anti-war goes to France as Red cross nurse; works n field hospital. Here she saves the life of an English officer; both captured by Germans but she continues to serve as a nurse. Forced to act as spy for Germans. The two end up happily together. NYT

BLINN, EDITH. United States.

001107   THE ASHES OF MY HEART. New York: Mark-well Pub. Co., 1916 BMC NUC.

Rhoda soon after her marriage is overcome with the passion for drugs & gambling. When she seems past help, a surgeon restores her through science & mind control. He turns out to be her husband-(they didn't recognize each other through the cure!)
PW An =unpleasant tale". Rhoda's father was a professional gambler, his wife a slave to opium. He refuses to rear child and asks neighbor to dispose of it. She hangs it on the arm of a gentle austere convent teacher who accepts. Rhoda becomes a dual personality. When her husband discovers her in a robbery, he leaves her. She sinks lower and lower, becoming the "Lady of Smoke" in an opium den.--NYT.

001108   THE EDGE OF THE WORLD. New York: Britton,
[c1919] NUC. London: H. Jenkins, 1921 BMC.

elderly woman runs a restaurant for woodchoppers and
trappers. She's mother Lee and she cares for everyone
& preaches all the time. NYT 359, 7-6-19

BLISS, ELLA THEODORA (CROSBY). B. 1864.

001109   WITH SOUTH SEA FOLK: A MISSIONARY STORY.
BY E. THEODORA CROSBY. Boston: Pilgrim Press, [c1898]
NUC.

Missionary life on island in Pacific below equator.
BOOK NEWS 98-9, 309

BLISSETT, NELLIE K. United Kingdom.

001110   BEGGARS' LUCK. London: Chapman and Hall,
1905 BMC.

001111   THE BINDWEED; A ROMANTIC NOVEL CONCERNING
THE LATE QUEEN OF SERVIA. London, New York: M. Vynne,
1904 NUC. Westminster: Constable, 1904 BMC.

LBKM-woman marries man she does not love, runs away
with another, husband kills himself, king is attracted
to her & lover persuades her to become a queen.
Tragedy at end.

001112   BRASS: A NOVEL. London: Hutchinson, 1899
BMC.

Young woman marries nephew of English priest made
Pope. But she runs off with an Austrian archduke, goes
on the Variety stage, and is rescued by a painter. SP
82:420
Uberto is an English Cardinal-the villain. ACAD 56:360

001113   THE CONCERT-DIRECTOR. London: Macmillan,
1898 NUC BMC.

SP 80:766. The story of Princess Tarasca, an opera
singer who married and was left a widow in 3 weeks.
Viennese impressario Spada pays Scaramanga to persuade
her to go back to her career. Scaramanga abandons his
woman and child to marry P. Tarasca. She eventually
loves a man who has adopted Scaramanga's son. The son
shoots Scaramanga, without regrets.
LIT 3:230.
ACAD 54:35. Scaramanga is a Jew; he becomes the
concert director. Roubetain is the piano player.

001114   FROM THE UNSOUNDED SEA; A ROMANCE. New
York: D. Appleton, 1901 NUC.

PW 6-22-01
NYT story of devils, mystery

001115   THE MOST FAMOUS LOBA; A ROMANCE.
Edinburgh: W. Blackwood, 1901 BMC. New York: D.
Appleton, 1901 NUC.

BAKER 13-184 historical romance

001116   THE SEA HATH ITS PEARLS; A PHANTASY.
London: Hutchinson, 1901 BMC.

heroine cruel and beautiful.

001117   THE SILVER KEY. A ROMANCE OF FRANCE AND
ENGLAND, 1669-70. London: Chapman and Hall, 1905 BMC
NUC. New York: Smart Set, 1906 NUC.

001118   THE WISDOM OF THE SIMPLE. London: A.D.
Innes, 1896 BMC.

SR-Story of a Puritanical woman married to a "blatant
would-be genius with 'advanced' views." She writes the
book of the season. "She was a pathetic person while
colorless and crushed."
ATH 108:899. She is quiet, plain, neglected by every
one; tells no one but the hunchback French poet of her
authorship.
"Cant of innocence": Mme. Valerie Mayer attacks all
modern movements. ACAD 51:76.

BLITZ, MRS. A.

001119   AN AUSTRALIAN MILLIONAIRE. London, New
York: Ward, Lock and Bowden, 1894 NUC BMC.

Near relations live closely together without realizing
they are related until some letters become known. Some
bewildering complications follow; a man and father
rival for same woman not knowing they are father and

son and a woman became engaged to her brother. SP 70
824.
All ends well in this comedy of errors. ATH 102,126

BLIVEN, MARY ANN (LILLIBRIDGE). B. 1834. United States.

001120   THE WEB OF DESTINY. New York: Broadway,
[c1907] NUC.

BLODGETT, MABEL LOUISE (FULLER). 1869-1959. United States.

001121   AT THE QUEEN'S MERCY. Boston, New York,
and London: Lamson, Wolffe, 1897 NUC.

Two men in the wilds of Africa are given the secret of
the palace of Queen of Tab, by a dying priest. The
advents., perils and escapes of the quest. LW 28:244.
Supernatural horrors. Lah has her reluctant lover
"devoured alive by the Mad Man of the moon." Lah is
the Queen. BKM 6:76.
CR 32,216 Hero, Mr. Dering, narrator. Eery and
gruesome adventures. "His feats are a series of
superhuman efforts," among blood-thirsty savages,
living visages, squirming pythons, snarling tigers and
ladies who display this "cold fury" one moment and
'irresistable tenderness" the next. He does not win a
woman after successfully performing all these brave
deeds, remains a bachelor.

BLOEDE, GERTRUDE. 1845-1905. United States.

001122   THE STORY OF TWO LIVES. BY STUART STERNE.
New York: Cassell, [c1891] NUC.

Journal of woman of 30; describes her home life and
her study of sculpture with a man she comes to love.
Later they meet on a steamer. Both are artists by
then. Learns of his past unhappy marriage, divorce,
affair, illegitimate child but forgives him. Her name
is Maud; his is Malcolm. BOOK NEWS. 107:479.

BLOOR, N. A.

001123   NOTHING; OR, THE DREAM OF MY LIFE.
Indianapolis: Carlon-Hollenbeck, 1892 NUC.

BLOUNT, MELESINA MARY. United Kingdom.

001124   DELPHINE CARFREY. BY MRS. GEORGE NORMAN.
London: Methuen, [1911] BMC NUC.

all about wooing. TLS
Modern study of life of a woman with a great passion
for the hero, one that "will not easily be
comprehended by the reader" SP

001125   JUST OURSELVES. BY MRS. GEORGE NORMAN.
London: Chapman & Hall, 1916 BMC.

001126   LADY FANNY. BY MRS. GEORGE NORMAN.
London: Methuen, 1911 BMC.

She goes to Switzerland by herself, "thrown into
dangerous companionship with a prince. Rebirth of love
in husband who took her for granted. TLS
after 7 years of happy married life, finds husband
unworthy, leaves home, travels abroad alone, meets the
man she should have married, but renounces him to
return to husband. ACAD
"only slightly consoled by the renewed devotion of her
negligent husband" Dr. orders her to go abroad and "by
way of a mental tonic" take up mild flirtations.
Whole: =impression of futility" ATH

001127   THE SILVER DRESS. BY MRS. GEORGE NORMAN.
London: Methuen, [1912] BMC NUC. New York: Duffield,
1913 NUC.

ATH has no friends but women until she is 35-then
meets husband-complications-happy ending.
Eve Martindale had reached the age of thirty-five
without having met any men, living her quiet life in
Chelsea with an old aunt, going to and giving
luncheons and teas, to which came women as detached
from the world as herself. Then suddenly she enters
society, meets a man younger than herself, who proves
to her that at thirty-five a woman is not necessarily
old and undesirable. Eve's learning of this lesson
makes the story.

001128   THE SUMMER LADY. BY MRS. GEORGE NORMAN.
London: Methuen, [1913] BMC NUC.

too many artifices keep the hero and heroine apart.
ATH
Lady Golden falls for a man of lower class; after much

misunderstanding, become engaged. TLS

001129   SYLVIA IN SOCIETY. BY MRS. GEORGE NORMAN. London: T. F. Unwin, 1908 BMC.

TLS-young American woman (little girl) in Parisian society.

001130   THE WONDERFUL ADVENTURE. BY MRS. GEORGE NORMAN. London: Chapman & Hall, 1914 BMC.

ATH-Young adventurous woman journeys to Lucerne. Set free from restraint, meets her "fate" there.
TLS 13:449 Rev. is ambiguous about Rosemary. She is not a flirt, not an adventuress, yet "is really far more shameless than the author would have us believe." Romantic affairs.

BLUE, KATE LILLY. United States.

001131   THE HAND OF FATE: A ROMANCE OF THE NAVY. Chicago: C. H. Kerr, 1895 NUC.

A group of Southerners spend time in California while the Atlantic is stationed there after the Civil War. PW 10-19-95:671

BLUNDELL, AGNES. United Kingdom.

001132   PENSION KRAUS. London: Herbert & Daniel, [1912] BMC NUC.

TLS-humorous tale of young English widow in Germ. pension
SP romance of elderly Lili Broun is prettily told. German boarding house.

BLUNDELL, MARY E. (SWEETMAN). D. 1930. United Kingdom.

001133   BECK OF BECKFORD. BY M. E. FRANCIS. London: G. Allen and Unwin, 1920 NUC.

TLS--Male hero and family.

001134   CHRISTIAN THAL; A NOVEL. BY M. E. FRANCIS (MRS. FRANCIS BLUNDELL). London, New York: Longmans, Green, 1903 BMC NUC.

She serves as inspiration to musician. PW
She lost her voice, works for him to achieve what she couldn't. NYT 03:735
Two women, one older, one younger--Annola gets him first, dies, Juliet the older one gets him. NYT 03:834
German hero--musician; capricious moods, Juliet is strong in self-surrendor and self repression. Annola lost her voice, a volcanic nature, passionate soul. ACAD 65

001135   DARK ROSALEEN, A STORY OF IRELAND TODAY. BY M. E. FRANCIS (MRS. FRANCIS BLUNDELL). New York: P. J. Kenedy, 1917 NUC. London: Cassell, 1915 BMC.

Religious differences--marriage problems. PW 91:1016
Story of contemporary Jewish life. NYT
Two families in Ireland; one Protestant, one Catholic. The children grow up together but parents fear the influence of one on the other, so they drift apart. Years later there is a romance between son of one family, daughter of other. A child is born. Tragedy closes the tale. (No clear description of plot.) NYT 4-29-17:167
RC--Protestant mixed marriage in Ireland. TLS
Religion looms large. ATH
Problems of mixed marriage. SP

001136   A DAUGHTER OF THE SOIL. A NOVEL. BY M. E. FRANCIS. London: Osgood, McIlvaine, 1895 BMC. New York: Harper, 1895 NUC.

Man marries farmer's daugher; his wife turns up "her face painted in streaks," the virtuous swain, etc. SR 79:765
S.W. Lanchashire-its manner of life, the land itself, speech. SP 75:217
Hero returns to England after 20 years; falls in love with wealthy farmer's daughter. After they are married Ruth learns her husband has a wife whom he pays to quiet her. Ruth leaves. He's furious about this, so that when wife #1 dies and Ruth is prepared to return, he says he loves her no longer and marries another woman out of spite. CR 23:458
Ruth has the education of a lady-had been to convent. ATH 105:702
"The saving power of love is set forth with the grace of Catholic piety." LW 26:185
The man with a past marries her. Loves her. Then his

wife shows up; the daughter of the soil returns to her father. BKM 4:420

001137   THE DUENNA OF A GENIUS. BY M. E. FRANCIS. London: Harper, 1898 BMC. Boston: Little, Brown, 1898 NUC.

SP 81:493. Story of two sisters, Hungarians, musicians in London. Their love stories. Margot, the duenna is very proper. Valerie serenades her lover in the woods on her violin. Both marry.
ACAD 55:31. The hero, a rich aristocrat woos Margot, but she refuses, believing it her duty to stay with her sister. Once Valerie is betrothed, then she accepts hero.

001138   FLANDER'S WIDOW; A NOVEL. BY M. E. FRANCIS (MRS. FRANCIS BLUNDELL). New York, London: Longmans, Green, 1901 BMC NUC.

Widow rejects many suitors, does her own proposing but all the while her fiance plots for her to marry his nephew, a more suitable match. The widow is "awakened" by nephew after the proposal. BOOK NEWS
Rosalie's youth asserts itself, ends with no heartbreak. Crit 01
Heroine 18 homeless, "familyless" marries a man of 58. He dies; she gets a farm. She has many marriage offers, accepts none. She proposes to an old man who really plots to bring his nephew and her together. Happily ever after ending. NYB

001139   FRIEZE AND FUSTIAN: A NOVEL. BY M. E. FRANCIS. London: Osgood, McIlvaine, [1896] NUC BMC.

SP 76:881. Frieze is Irish; Fustian English. Sh. stories.

001140   GALATEA OF THE WHEATFIELD. London: Methuen, [1909] NUC BMC.

Sweet Dorsetshire romance. TLS
Beautiful rustic loves above her station; lover turns snob; marries a farmer. ATH
Charming idyll. SP

001141   GENTLEMAN ROGER. BY M. E. FRANCIS (MRS. FRANCIS BLUNDELL). London and Edinburgh: Sands, 1911 BMC NUC.

Pastoral romance. ATH

001142   HARDY-ON-THE-HILL. BY M. E. FRANCIS (MRS. FRANCIS BLUNDELL). London: Methuen, [1908] BMC NUC.

ATH--Triangle.
TLS--O.

001143   HONESTY. BY M. E. FRANCIS. London: Hodder and Stoughton, [1912?] BMC NUC.

TLS--Marriage of 40 and 20 in a travelling van.
SP--Peddlars, misunderstanding between them.
LBKM--sell crockery.

001144   IN A NORTH COUNTRY VILLAGE. BY M. E. FRANCIS. Boston: Little, Brown, 1893 NUC. London: Osgood, 1896 BMC.

Thornleigh is a small English village close to a great manufacturing city, but a place untouched by change in several hundred years. Study of types and characters in the town. PW 12-16-93.

001145   LYCHGATE HALL, A ROMANCE. BY M. E. FRANCIS (MRS. FRANCIS BLUNDELL). London, New York: Longmans, Green, 1904 NUC.

NYT--Gothic romance.
ATH--0
TLS--0

001146   A MAID O' DORSET. BY M. E. FRANCIS. London: Cassell, [1917] BMC NUC.

Traditional. TLS
Bright light story LBKM

001147   MAIME O' TH' CORNER: A NOVEL. BY M. E. FRANCIS. New York: Burr, 1897 NUC. London and New York: Harper, 1898 BMC.

The poor of Thornleigh. Maime is taken from workhouse, raised by Mrs. Prescott. Maime then meets Joe who works for a farmer. They finally marry after Maime has been jilted by Mrs. Prescott's son. But poverty stays

with them till the bitter end when they have a bit of
luck. Very modest happiness allowed. SP 79:805.
Is near starvation with her husband but there's no
agency to help.-Just the workhouse. Life of grinding
poverty. No happy end. LIT 1:53.
ACAD 53:4 Lowly life in a Lancashire village. Sad,
Pathetic.

001148   THE MANOR FARM; A NOVEL. BY M. E. FRANCIS
(MRS. FRANCIS BLUNDELL). New York, London: Longmans,
Green, 1902 BMC NUC.

ATH 12-6-02--Quiet country story.
Dial 11-16-02

001149   MARGERY O' THE MILL. BY M. E. FRANCIS.
London: Methuen, [1907] BMC NUC.

Light romance. TLS

001150   MATTHEW STRONG, THE STORY OF A MAN WITH A
PURPOSE. BY MRS. FRANCIS. Philadelphia: J. B.
Lippincott, 1908 NUC. London: S. Low, Marston, 1908
BMC.

001151   MISS ERIN: A NOVEL. BY M. E. FRANCIS. New
York: Benziger, 1898 NUC. London: Methuen, 1898 BMC.

LIT 2:648. Irish. Spirited orphan heroine who has
taken Ireland for her mother, burns to become the
Irish Joan of Arc.
ACAD 53:469. Finally is called Irish Joan of Arc, "on
rather slender grounds, preliminary to settling down
in life." Also writes patriotic poetry.
ATH 111:689. Ireland from nationalist point of view.

001152   MOLLY'S TORTURES. BY M. E. FRANCIS.
London: Sands, [1913] BMC. St. Louis: Herder, 1914.

Love story for girls. TLS

001153   NOBLESSE OBLIGE. BY M. E. FRANCIS.
London: J. Long, 1909 BMC.

Charming. TLS
Dainty love tale. LBKM

001154   OUR ALTY. BY M. E. FRANCIS (MRS. FRANCIS
BLUNDELL). London: J. Long, [1912?] BMC NUC.

ATH--Love story.
TLS--Love story.
Rural Lancashire Alty--"one of the most favorable
examples of modern feminism." SP
Two men court her, one educated the other a farmer.
Alty's awakening. LBKM

001155   PENTON'S CAPTAIN. BY M. E. FRANCIS.
London: Chapman and Hall, 1916 BMC.

TLS--War and Love.
ATH--War and Love.
War--love story heroine a loveable domestic drudge.
LBKM

001156   ROSANNA DEW. BY M. E. FRANCIS. London:
Odhams, [1920] BMC.

001157   SIMPLE ANNALS. BY M. E. FRANCIS (MRS.
FRANCIS BLUNDELL). London, New York and Bombay:
Longmans, Green, 1906 NUC.

"These Dorset stories are studies of working women.
They make no pretensions at analysing conditions or
grappling with problems. Their main purpose is to
picture some of the joys and sorrows of a large and
varied class. There are fourteen stories in all. Some
of the titles are: The Breadwinner, Patchwork, Mrs.
Angel, A Widow Indeed, The Transplanting of a Daisy,
etc." BKM v.24, 1906-7.
ACAD--Symp. port. of Mrs. Angel, midwife. "Optimistic
and light."

001158   THE STORY OF DAN. BY M. E. FRANCIS.
London: Osgood, McIlvaine, 1894 BMC. Boston: Houghton
Mifflin, 1894 NUC.

SR 78:543. Tragic story of Dawn's misfortunes in hands
of Irish "slut" with imbecile brother.
PW-peasant class.

001159   THE STORY OF MARY DUNNE. BY M. E. FRANCIS
(MRS. FRANCIS BLUNDELL). London: J. Murray, 1913 BMC
NUC. New York: Longmans, Green, 1913 NUC.

Girl kidnapped for white slave traffic. SP

BKM--Irish peasant girl whose friend had gone to U.S.
to earn money so they can marry. She decides to take
servant's job so she can save too, but falls into
hands of white slavery, tries to kill her self under
wheels of auto. He returns, kills the man responsible,
but refuses to go near her until she lays her soul
bare on the witness stand trying to defend him.
Concerns white slavery. Irish girl captured in
Liverpool. ATH
Irish girl imprisoned in house in Liverpool. Her lover
kills man responsible for her downfall. PW

001160   THE THINGS OF A CHILD. BY M. E. FRANCIS.
London: W. Collins Sons, [c1918] NUC.

001161   WHITHER? A NOVEL. BY M. E. FRANCIS.
London: Griffith, Farran, 1892 BMC.

LBKM 3:61. Melodrama set in Catholic community in
Northwest England.
ACAD 42:454. Heroine is accused of uncle's murder and
is tried. Is barely let off, becomes a governess and
attempts to escape her past. She dies before
everything gets straightened out
a village idyll sandwiched between two melodramas with
a sad end. time of reformation: Rural S.W. Lancashire
is loyal to the crown. Here Virginia Wentworth under
an assumed name is school teacher. Story centers on
her. SP 70 131

001162   THE WILD HEART. BY M. E. FRANCIS (MRS.
FRANCIS BLUNDELL). London: Smith, Elder, 1910 BMC NUC.

TLS--Village life.
LBKM--Marries a murderer; (he has been guilty of
manslaughter in a poaching fray.
ATH--Also has a study of a "rustic Delilah" gypsy
spirit.
SR--His "wild heart" brings him to an untimely end.
But this sadness is not unduly depressing.

001163   WILD WHEAT; A DORSET ROMANCE. BY M. E.
FRANCIS (MRS. FRANCIS BLUNDELL). New York: Longmans,
1905. London and Bombay: Longmans, Green, 1905 NUC.

About a strange will and its effects on a Dorset
family; story seems to center upon one of the sons .
NYT 05:923
Centers on a man and his two loves. ACAD 05:1132

001164   YEOMAN FLEETWOOD. BY M. E. FRANCIS.
London and New York: Longmans, Green, 1900 NUC BMC.

CR 37:86. Love story of a squire. Pretty.
LW31:156. Has education of a gentleman. Lancashire and
Brighton.
SP 84:143. He's a farmer's son, romance with squire's
daughter.

BLUNDELL, MRS. FRANCIS. See BLUNDELL, MARY E. (SWEETMAN).

BLUNT, ELIZABETH (LEE). B. 1839. Nationality Unknown.

001165   WHEN FOLKS WAS FOLKS. New York: Cochrane,
1910 NUC.

BOCHKAREVA, MARIIA LEONTIEVNA (FROLKOVA). B. 1889.

001166   YASHKA, MY LIFE AS PEASANT, OFFICER AND
EXILE. BY MARIA BOTCHKAREVA, COMMANDER OF THE RUSSIAN
WOMEN'S BATTALION OF DEATH, AS SET DOWN BY ISAAC DON
LEVINE. New York: F. A. Stokes, [c1919] NUC BMC.
London: Constable, [1919] NUC BMC. (BMC: By M.
Botchkareva in title line.)

Seduced at 15, feigns illness to keep father from
punishing her; marries, runs off, later tries to kill
husband with ax; freed of marriage wrecks a "house of
shame." Remarries, husband convicted of helping
escaped criminals. She joins him in Siberia. Violated
by a governor. attempts suicide; new husband hangs her
but he repents in time to cut her down. War--walks 130
miles living on bread and water. Enlists, joins a
regiment hand to hand combat with Germans. Never
squeamish. Organized Women's Battalion of
Death--object to kill Germans. Won't form committee on
Kerensky's order and so on. ATH. Suspected by
Bolsheviks, escapes to U.S.

BODDINGTON, HELEN.

001167   THE AWAKENING. London: Hurst and
Blackett, 1902 BMC.

001168   A VOICE FROM THE VOID. London: Hurst and
Blackett, 1904 BMC.

TLS--young girl novelist--pretty love story.

BODRUTHAN, ALGA.

001169   WEIRD: AN OWER TRUE TALE. London: Digby,
Long, [1893] BMC.

BOEGLI, LINA.

001170   FORWARD; LETTERS WRITTEN ON A TRIP AROUND
THE WORLD. Philadelphia and London: J. B. Lippincott,
1904 BMC.

PW--Young woman without money decides to work her way
around the world. Spends 10 years. True?

BOEHME, MARGARETE. B. 1869.

001171   THE DEPARTMENT STORE; A NOVEL OF TO-DAY.
New York and London: D. Appleton, 1912 NUC BMC. (Tr.
Ethel C. Mayne)

PW--heroine orphan salesgirl marries proprietor's son.
BKM--Portrayal of juggernaut role of store over
crushed and broken lives. Bird's eye view of manners
and customs. Life history of a dozen families.
BKM 35 (1912) 411-12. Little Karen N. who works her
way up from shop girl to head of art department.
ATH--O
SP--O

001172   THE DIARY OF A LOST ONE. London:
Sisley's, [1908] BMC. New York: Hudson Press, [c1908]
NUC.

BOETTGER, CLEMENTINE.

001173   THE GOVERNESS; OR, THE BARONESS IN
DISGUISE. BY S. MELNEC. London: Eden, Remington, 1891
BMC. (Tr. H.A.M.H.)

BOGART, CLARA LORING. United States.

001174   EMILY: A TALE OF THE EMPIRE STATE.
Ithaca, N.Y.: [Andrus & Church], 1894 NUC.

BOGGS, MARTHA FRYE. United States.

001175   JACK CREWS. New York: G. W. Dillingham,
1899 NUC.

Railroad life in Rockies. He's a railroad worker who
brings several criminals to justice. PW 56:1263

001176   A ROMANCE OF THE NEW VIRGINIA. Boston:
Arena, 1896 NUC. (Also published as: Margaret Steyne:
a Romance of the New   Virginia. New york: G. W.
Dillingham Co., 1899.)

BOOK NEWS Historical romance, lofty idealism.

BOGGS, SARA ELISABETH (SIEGRIST). B. 1843. United States.

001177   SANDPEEP. Boston: Little, Brown, 1906 BMC
NUC.

PW-Fisher girl of Maine becomes governess. Gets
involved in mystery
NYT-sent girl's story

BOGGS, WINIFRED. B. 1882. United States.

001178   BACHELORS' BUTTONS; THE CANDID
CONFESSIONS OF A SHY BACHELOR. BY EDWARD BURKE.
London: H. Jenkins, 1912 BMC NUC. New York: Moffat,
Yard, 1912 NUC.

001179   THE BEWILDERED BENEDICT. THE STORY OF A
SUPERFLUOUS UNCLE. BY EDWARD BURKE. London: H.
Jenkins, 1914 BMC. Toronto: Bell, n.d. NUC.

001180   ETHEL PILCHER. London: Ward, Lock, 1907
BMC.

001181   MY WIFE. BY EDWARD BURKE. London: H.
Jenkins, 1917 NUC BMC. New York: E. P. Dutton, [1917]
NUC.

001182   THE RETURN OF RICHARD CARR. London:
Hutchinson, 1907 BMC.

Man gone for 7 years, returns to find wife has been
faithful, assumes disguise to court her anew rather
than call on her sense of duty. LBKM 5-07:69

001183   THE SALE OF LADY DAVENTRY [ANONYMOUS].
London: H. Jenkins, 1913 BMC NUC. New York:
Brentano's, 1914 NUC.

Marriage of the daughter of a vicar with an old noble;
(He's in his 70s) asks her if she will be true to him.
They have a child (but we learn it's not really his).
Ends in her suicide. Sensation novel. ATH

001184   SALLY ON THE ROCKS. London: H. Jenkins,
1915 BMC. New York: Brentano's, 1915 NUC.

Sally has her hair color changed by X-ray? Spends 6
years in Paris trying to make it as an artist, returns
to her home town tries to get a husband. Her
competition with a young widow for a rich banker. Wit,
sarcasm. NYT

001185   VAGABOND CITY. New York and London: G. P.
Putnam's Sons, 1911 NUC BMC.

A male novelist, his conventional wife, a
woman-artist-genius, the man's true mate a triangle
and tragedy. PW
Woman artist dies? ACAD
Elf (woman) is a great artist. ATH
After three days of marriage couple "feel the galling
of their chains." He's a wanderer. Then comes the Elf.
No explanation of the ending. NYT

001186   YESTERDAY: BEING THE CONFESSIONS OF
BARBARA. London: H. Jenkins, 1919 BMC NUC.

TLS--Writer of dozen or so novels. Killed a man in her
teens.
Girl of old family raised under terrible grandfather's
tutelage. He dies, she settles in London "various
adventures with publishers"; "in search of material
for copy." ATH

BOGUE, LILIAN LIDA (BELL). 1867-1929. United States.

001187   ABOUT MISS MATTIE MORNINGGLORY. BY LILIAN
BELL. Chicago: Rand McNally, [c1916] NUC BMC.

Mattie married to a much younger man is so shocked to
learn he's worthless that she ends up in the hospital.
But all turns out rosy. PW
NYT

001188   ABROAD WITH THE JIMMIES. BY LILIAN BELL.
Boston: L. C. Page, 1902 NUC. London: Ward, Lock,
[1902] BMC.

Europe-Descr & trav.

001189   ANGELA'S QUEST. BY LILIAN BELL. New York:
Duffield, 1910 NUC.

Two wicked men kidnap girl, hide her in convent, story
of escape, search for parents, etc. NYT
Girl raised in convent escapes, searches and finds her
parents. PW

001190   AT HOME WITH THE JARDINES. BY LILIAN
BELL. Boston: L. C. Page, 1904 NUC.

PW amusing account of young marriage.
NYT Marriage true key to happiness, making a home in
busy New York City

001191   CAROLINA LEE. BY LILIAN BELL. Boston: L.
C. Page, 1906 BMC NUC.

PW Christian Science

001192   THE CONCENTRATIONS OF BEE. BY LILIAN
BELL. Boston: L. C. Page, 1909 NUC.

001193   THE DOWAGER COUNTESS AND THE AMERICAN
GIRL. BY LILIAN BELL. New York and London: Harper,
1903 BMC NUC.

Witty; gentle duel between the two women. PW 6-27-03
Sequel to "Sir John and the American Girl"

001194   THE EXPATRIATES; A NOVEL. BY LILIAN BELL.
New York and London: Harper, 1900 NUC. London:
Hutchinson, 1902 BMC.

ATH 5-3-02
BKM 12:301. Author is now Mrs. Arthur Hoyt Bogue. Rose
Hollanden, spectacular heroine, her sister Maria
physically grotesque. Hollenden family in France,
Maria marries Frenchman who can't stand her, she
suicides. Hollendens are finally glad to go back to

American ways.
NYT 1900:700. An invective against the French
aristocracy. Americans fleeced; Maria married for her
money by Raoul, lets her drown. The hero, part cowboy,
shoots off 2 of his fingers.

001195   HOPE LORING. BY LILIAN BELL. London:
Ward, Lock, 1902 BMC. New York: American News, [1902]
NUC.

Finds conventions irksome -PW
NYT 12-6-02 Rev not helpful
TLS girl of strong character who saves her father from
ruin
ACAD-wholly conventional, healthy and sentimental, for
girls.

001196   THE INTERFERENCE OF PATRICIA. BY LILIAN
BELL. Boston: L. C. Page, 1903 BMC NUC.

Rides like Buffalo Bill and talks like a cowboy. Love
story full of surprises; she assaults Denver society
with much daring. PW 7-18-03

001197   A LITTLE SISTER TO THE WILDERNESS. BY
LILIAN LIDA BELL. Chicago: Stone and Kimball, 1895
NUC. London: S. Low, 1895 BMC.

Beautiful young woman with a mind, in dull environment
in W. Tenn. where there's no culture. Meets a Lady
Revivalist Preacher who reads to her, Matrimony. SR
79:703
Sense of the life of sm. Tenn. hamlet. ATH 105:769.
The young woman comes to know a life of "love and
service." LW 26:170
Poor whites in malarial bottom-lands of W. Tenn. PW
5-4-95:704 Mag's relatives and friends. But Mag is
atypical-misunderstood, superior and the preacher with
a secret sin. Dialect humor. BKM 4:260.

001198   THE LOVE AFFAIRS OF AN OLD MAID. BY
LILIAN BELL. New York: Harper, [1893] NUC. London: S.
Low, 1895 BMC.

Very brief desc. BKM 17 (1903) 345
Her love affairs "are those of other people
delightfully told and full of noble thoughts for the
married and unmarried." "tommorrow I shall be an old
maid," she writes on the eve of her 30th birthday. PW
6-10-93.
Gives lots of good advice. CR 20, 23:395.
She's 30, critical, observant "enjoys her love affairs
by proxy. Discusses the love affairs of Peg
Winterbotham and others. SR 80:119.

001199   SIR JOHN AND THE AMERICAN GIRL. BY LILIAN
BELL. New York and London: Harper, 1901 BMC NUC.

001200   THE UNDER SIDE OF THINGS: A NOVEL. BY
LILIAN LIDA BELL. New York: Harper, 1896 NUC. London:
S. Low, 1896 BMC.

BKM 3:550. Kate Vandervoort, a "frivolous" belle, is a
strong, admirable young woman. She is contrasted with
Alice, a "Maiden never bold" and completely subdued to
parental authority. Alice is married to Gordon, at
West Point, faces choice between his interests and her
mother's. Kate helps her. Author does not like
"Flossie-girls" or "Lucy-girls."
LW 27:285.

BOHAN, ELIZABETH BAKER. 1849-c.1942. United States.

001201   THE DRAG-NET, A PRISON STORY OF THE
PRESENT DAY. Boston: C.M. Clark, 1909 NUC.

NYT--Prison abuse and reform also love story. Editor
of paper calling for penal reform, he also loves a
woman he rescues from jail.

001202   UN AMERICANO: A STORY OF THE MISSION DAYS
OF CALIFORNIA. Los Angeles, Cal.: Los Angeles Printing
Co., 1895 W.

BOHANNON, HATTIE DONOVAN. United States.

001203   THE LIGHT OF STARS. New York: R. F.
Fenno, [c1909] NUC.

unconventional love story PW 5-1-09
focuses upon a man BKM

BOILEAU, ETHEL MARY (YOUNG). 1882?-1942. United Kingdom.

001204   THE FIRE OF SPRING; OR, THE GARDEN OF
DREAMS. London: E. Nash, 1914 BMC.

ATH-"Society," unhappy marriage & a lover.
TLS Gushing, sometimes sensuous emotion.

BOLDREWOOD, ROSE, pseud. See BROWNE, ROSE.

BOLTON, HENRIETTA IRVING. D. 1930.

001205   THE MADONNA OF ST. LUKE: THE STORY OF A
PORTRAIT. New York, London: Putnam, 1895 NUC.

BONAPARTE, LAURA ELIZABETH.

001206   THE GREEK E: A NOVEL. London: H.S.
Nichols, 1896 BMC.

SR-Widow vows revenge on man who has insulted husband
by anonymous letter. He uses the Greek E; so does her
husband. Violence and confusion follow.
ACAD 50:219. Her lover is dying by the time it's
straightened out. At conclusion she is married to a
man she doesn't care for; her mad brother, locked up
and guarded, is living with them.
Frances Harrold's husband dies. Then she gets a letter
expressing delight that the man is dead. The letter
writing shows an unusual "e". SP 78:846

BOND, AIMEE. United Kingdom.

001207   AN AIRMAN'S WIFE [ANONYMOUS]. London: H.
Jenkins, 1918 BMC NUC.

WWI - Fiction

001208   MONA-LISA-NOBODY. London: H. Jenkins,
1920 BMC NUC.

Young woman develops into extremely feminine type;
left alone upon death of grandfather. TLS
Struggle of woman trying to earn her living by
journalism in New Orleans. SP
Marries a journalist in the end. ATH

001209   MY AIRMAN OVER THERE. BY HIS WIFE
[ANONYMOUS]. New York: Moffat, Yard, 1918 NUC.

001210   A PAIR OF VAGABONDS. London: H. Jenkins,
1919 BMC NUC.

2 Englishwomen operate a canteen in France near the
front line. SP

BONE, FLORENCE. United Kingdom.

001211   ALISON'S QUEST; OR, THE MYSTERIOUS
TREASURE. London: S. W. Partridge, [1910] BMC.

001212   A BURDEN OF ROSES. London: R.T.S., 1913
BMC.

A foundling goes to London to seek her fortune, fails
bravely finds love and happiness. ATH

001213   DOCTOR OGILVIE'S GUEST. London: R.T.S.,
[1918] BMC.

001214   THE FURROW ON THE HILL. London: R.T.S.,
[1912] BMC.

001215   THE HEART OF SILVIA. London: S.P.C.K.,
[1907] BMC.

001216   THE HIDDEN HIGHWAY. London: R. T. S.,
[1911] BMC.

Scotsman battles with faith TLS
novel with a purpose picture of social work in
Edinburgh ATH

001217   THE IRON SACRIFICE. A TALE OF THE GREAT
WAR. London: C. H. Kelly, [1917] BMC.

001218   THE LAMP IN THE WINDOW. London: S. W.
Partridge, [1908] BMC.

001219   THE LAVENDER HEDGE. London: C. H. Kelly,
1915 BMC.

SP unconv. matter

001220   A MAID OF QUALITY. London: Epworth Press,
1920 BMC.

TLS romance

001221   MARGOT'S SECRET OR THE FOURTH FORM AT

VICTORIA COLLEGE. London: S. W. Partridge, [1910] BMC.

001222   THE MORNING OF TO-DAY. New York: Eaton & Mains, [c1907] NUC.

hist 11-2-07 PW

001223   THE PRICE OF A TREASURE. London: R. T. S., 1920 BMC.

TLS tale of rectory hall & factory

001224   A ROSE OF YORK. London: R.T.S., [1910] BMC.

001225   THE SAIL OF THE SILVER BARGE. London: R.T.S., 1912 BMC.

001226   THE SAPPHIRE BUTTON. A ROMANCE OF THE ROAD IN STUART DAYS. London: Morgan & Scott, [1920] BMC.

TLS historical romance

001227   THE SPLENDID STARS. London: S. W. Partridge, [1913] BMC.

001228   THE VALLEY OF DELIGHT. London: R.T.S., 1913 BMC.

001229   THE WEB OF THE LOOM. London: R.T.S., [1915] BMC.

001230   THE WONDERFUL GATE. London: R.T.S., 1911 BMC.

BONE, GERTRUDE HELENA (DODD). B. 1876. United Kingdom.

001231   THE BROW OF COURAGE. London: Duckworth, 1916 BMC NUC.

001232   CHILDREN'S CHILDREN. London: Duckworth, 1908 BMC NUC.

Concerns old man. BAKER 32,64.

001233   WOMEN OF THE COUNTRY. London: Duckworth, [1913] BMC NUC.

Character studies of hard working and poor English women--"always from a woman's point of view." Chief character Anne Hilton. Neighbors think she's peculiar--can blaze with anger yet be tolerant of blackguards. Feels responsible for the actions of others --like the young woman she knows who goes off to live with a man and is deserted and dies in childbirth in workhouse. Anne adopts the child. Describes a woman's ward in the workhouse. SP, where the deserted young woman goes after her husband deserts her. The rooms are full of old and young women with babies. Shows us the misery but still the quality of human nature that endures it. TLS

BONNER, GERALDINE. 1870-1930. United States.

001234   THE BLACK EAGLE MYSTERY. New York, London: D. Appleton, 1916 NUC BMC.

"Harland found dead on the sidewalk. Lawyer and detectives strike a clue that leads to a young and beautiful woman. But they are all proved wrong by Molly Babbitts, the lively telephone operator". PW 89: 2-26-16 p.689.
NYT--Molly Morgenthau Babbitts, formerly "The Girl at Central" had given up business after her marriage but the Whitney offices asked for her help in solving the case.

001235   THE BOOK OF EVELYN. Indianapolis: Bobbs-Merrill, [c1913] NUC BMC.

Friendship, loyalty. 33 year old widow in NYC has male friend Roger, a writer. She expresses feminist ideas. Begins a diary that ends up being story of beautiful woman who wants to be great opera star. Evelyn lives in apartment house (Bohemian setting.) Is from a proper family. Friends with Lizzie who is mistress to man who would make her a diva. Her debut a failure. He leaves her. She ill from his leaving. No remorse about sleeping with him. Roger falls for Lizzie. Evelyn's dilemma--shouldshe tell him all? Never does. Suffering gives Lizzie the voice, the feeling. She's a great success in Europe. Evelyn marries Roger. Lizzie the heroine. (Book)
"A widow...drawn into the lives of her Bohemian fellow-lodgers" including Lizzie whose morals are

different from hers." After a short and unhappy married life, Evelyn Drake, a young widow, returns to New York. An old friend, Roger Clements of Gramercy Park appears. Everything is going well when a certain Miss Harris, a singer, handsome and magnetic, captures the man's heart. Though Evelyn knows her secret, she cannot tell her old friend he is mistaken in the woman he fancies he loves, and very nearly pays for her loyalty with her happiness." PW 8-30-13

001236   THE CASTLECOURT DIAMOND CASE; BEING A COMPILATION OF THE STATEMENTS MADE BY THE VARIOUS PARTICIPANTS IN THIS CURIOUS CASE, NOW, FOR THE FIRST TIME, GIVEN TO THE PUBLIC. New York and London: Funk and Wagnalls, 1906 NUC.

BRD--detective story.

001237   THE EMIGRANT TRAIL. New York: Duffield, 1910 NUC. London: Hutchinson, 1910 BMC.

Phip and his daughter travel from Rochester to California. She's vital, full of determination. She faces cholera, Indians, and love problems. PW NYT--heroine a particularly good piece of work. The slow wearing down of travel on the Overland Trail. Slow pace and settling back of man and woman to unlovely elemental bases.

001238   THE GIRL AT CENTRAL. New York and London: D. Appleton, 1915 NUC BMC.

"A detective story solved by a clue obtained by a day operator." BKM
A telephone operator gathers up clues that lead to a solution of the mystery and incidentally to a romance. NYT

001239   HARD-PAN: A STORY OF BONANZA FORTUNES. New York: Century, 1900 NUC BMC.

NYT 1900:743. Romance. Father has lost his fortunes. Letitia, high spirited, chooses in love.
PW-father borrows money from her rich lover. When she discovers this, she insists on paying it back, selling their house, and moving to another city.
Letitia: prosperous, high-souled. What a woman really is (?). CR'01.

001240   MISS MAITLAND, PRIVATE SECRETARY. New York, London: D. Appleton, 1919 BMC NUC.

Detective story dealing with theft of her employer Mrs. Janney's jewels. There's a "young woman detective". TLS
"Molly Babbitts clears up the double mystery of a big jewel theft and a kidnapping." PW
Molly has pluck, perseverance, quick wit. NYT

001241   THE PIONEER, A TALE OF TWO STATES. Indianapolis: Bobbs-Merrill, [1905] NUC BMC.

Heroine's mind literally controlled. ARENA

001242   RICH MAN'S CHILDREN. Indianapolis: Bobbs-Merrill, [1906] BMC NUC.

Berny schemes to marry a man she doesn't love but who will serve as a stepping stone to higher social circles. Delia Ryan (moth er of the man) was a cook in a mining camp, now a social power in San Francisco dislikes Berny. Berny, unloved wife who learns her husband is unfaithful. The other woman is Rose Cannon. Rose's father would "buy off" Berny but Berny won't divorce. Ends melodramatically? BKM

001243   TOMORROW'S TANGLE. Indianapolis: Bobbs-Merrill, [1903] NUC BMC. London: Cassell, 1904 BMC.

BKM--Mormon, on way West, exchanges his 1st wife, a delicate 19 yr. old and her 3 wk. old baby for a fresh team of horses lea ving her in a mining camp. Then what? 25 years later he dies, baby is a young woman earning a pittance as a music teacher. Refu ses to claim her inheritance because of the cruelty of father to mother. Then what? ATH.
ACAD--Includes a self-reliant alert female journalist. She courts a young MD her father has wronged so that he will inherit money (she has one year to live) honorably. Mormom with 2 wives, sells one (sells a daughter too). Years later as a wealthy man hears of her wonderful voice, offers to get her training. PW 10-10-03

001244   TREASURE AND TROUBLE THEREWITH. A TALE OF

CALIFORNIA. New York, London: D. Appleton, 1917 NUC
BMC.

Concerns a treasure and San Francisco earthquake. PW
There is a hold-up, highwaymen steal and bury it;
tramp digs it up--lives high on it. Pancha Lopez star
of San Francisco operetta doesn't know her father is
the bandit. She, the young lawyer, the tramp--all
threads come together at time of San Francisco
earthquake. NYT

BOOLE, MARY (EVEREST).

001245   THE FORGING OF PASSION INTO POWER.
London: C. W. Daniel, 1910 BMC. New York: Kennerley,
1911 NUC.

BOOTH, EMMA (SCARR). B. 1835. United States.

001246   A WILFUL HEIRESS. Buffalo: C. W. Moulton,
1892 NUC.

BOOTH, MAUD BALLINGTON (CHARLESWORTH). B. 1865.

001247   THE RELENTLESS CURRENT. BY M. E.
CHARLESWORTH. New York: G. P. Putnam's Sons, 1912 BMC
NUC.

PW-man convicted and electrocuted for murder of which
he is innocent. Young woman marries him in prison and
spends rest of her life helping falsely accused men.
TLS-she found another husband.
ATH-0
NYT-She watches her uncle's operations until she is
able to enlighten world famous MD's on details of
their cases.

BOOTH, VENUS G. United States.

001248   AS THE FATES DECREE. New York: Fifth Ave.
Pub. Co., [c1916] NUC.

001249   THE MYSTERY OF RACHEL. Boston: Stratford,
[c1920] NUC.

PW a prophecy covering 6,000 years

001250   THE WIVES OF THE DEACON. New York: Fifth
Ave. Pub. Co., 1917 NUC.

BOREL, MARGUERITE (APPELL). B. 1883.

001251   THE MAN WHO SURVIVED. BY CAMILLE MARBO.
New York & London: Harper, [1918] NUC. (Tr. Frank
Hunter Potter)

PW-Man with dual personality
NYT June 9, 1918, p. 266. Two friends shot on
battlefield; personality of one survives in body of
the other. War

BORRADAILE, KATHLEEN.

001252   THE RECURRING TRACK. London: E. Stock,
1915 BMC.

ATH-return of the spirit of a great musician in the
body of an inarticulate girl.

BOSANQUET, THEODORA, jt. au. See SMITH, CLARA AND THEODORA
BOSANQUET.

BOSCH, MRS. HERMANN. Nationality Unknown.

001253   BRIDGET. New York: B. W. Dodge, 1908 NUC.

PW-Irish servant, humor

BOSHER, KATE LEE (LANGLEY). 1865-1932. United States.

001254   "BOBBIE". BY KATE CAIRNS. Richmond,
Virginia: B. F. Johnson, 1899 NUC.

001255   HIS FRIEND, MISS MCFARLANE; A NOVEL. New
York and London: Harper, [1919] NUC BMC.

mountain boy struggles to get ed. with girl's help PW
he gets himself put in a State reform school so he'll
get to school. Meets a beautiful benefactress We get
her romance and details of the State institution. NYT
5-25-19 P.295

001256   THE HOUSE OF HAPPINESS. New York and
London: Harper, 1913 BMC NUC.

BKM-doom in a sanitarium

"Taska Laird and Rives Colburn are both inmates in a
tuberculosis sanitarium. The boy Cricket, who learned
at eight that "you can't whistle and whine at the same
time" and who has been whistling ever since, is
Taska's friend and crony. Together they take Rives
Colburn in hand and lead him to the "house of
happiness," and when Rives and Taska enter in, the
cheerful Cricket is still remembered and finds with
them the home and family he never knew before." PW
1-8-13 1526
hero and heroine threatened with TB.. set in
sanitarium NYT

001257   HOW IT HAPPENED. New York and London:
Harper, 1914 BMC NUC.

"Carmencita is a slum child who gets her pleasures
second-hand, listening to the tales of her father, a
blind harper. At Christmas time she scrapes a
curb-stone acquaintance with Mr. Van Landing, a rich
and bored bachelor. She chatters of an adored
settlement worker who turns out to be the woman Van
Landing has loved and lost. Carmencita brings them
together and at last has some first-hand pleasures."
PW 86 9/26/14:965
TLS Sugary and thin
NYT 1914:448

001258   KITTY CANARY: A NOVEL. New York and
London: Harper, [1918] BMC NUC.

PW- Young woman invades small Va. town, her suitors,
she brings happiness to many people.
TLS-Sent gushings of American ingenue describing a
summer holiday
NYT-Romance of 16 year old

001259   THE MAN IN LONELY LAND. New York and
London: Harper, 1912 NUC BMC.

Bachelor has everything but is lonely, falls for a
southern woman; they marry. BKM 516
PW- love
TLS- lush sent

001260   MARY CARY: "FREQUENTLY MARTHA". New York
and London: Harper, 1910 BMC NUC.

girls book TLS
girls book NYT

001261   MISS GIBBIE GAULT. A STORY. New York and
London: Harper, 1911 NUC BMC.

works to improve mills and schools in Va. 5-13-11 PW
"the very independent elderly Miss Gibbie" TLS

001262   PEOPLE LIKE THAT: A NOVEL. New York and
London: Harper, [1916] BMC NUC.

Danbridge believes she's "her sisters' keeper";
therefore goes to live in slums. In part she's trying
to teach the man she loves to care for the
unfortunates of the world. Both are upper class, and
he's shocked at her move to the slums. She cares for a
deserted mother and child and discovers the father is
her lover's brother? PW
NYT Ernest is sincere, a young educated and cultured
woman wishes to get close to those who suffer social
injury especially women and children. She comes to the
final conclusion that women themselves are responsible
for a large measure of the world's sin and vice.
BKM-In other words until more fortunate women
recognize less fortunate women as their sisters and
human beings and look after them, there can be no hope
of improvement.

001263   WHEN LOVE IS LOVE: A NOVEL. New York:
Neale, 1904 NUC.

BOSSE, SARA, jt. au. See BABCOCK, WINNIFRED (EATON) AND
SARA BOSSE.

BOTCHKAREVA, MARIA. See BOCHKAREVA, MARIIA LEONTIEVNA
(FROLKOVA).

BOTELER, MATTIE M. United States.

001264   THE CONVERSION OF BRIAN O'DILLON.
Cincinnati, Ohio: Standard, [c1896] NUC.

BOTSFORD, EVA BELL. United States.

001265   LUCKY: A TALE OF THE WESTERN PRAIRIE.
Buffalo: Peter Paul Book Co., 1895 NUC.

BOTTOME, PHYLLIS. 1884-1963. United Kingdom.

001266   "BROKEN MUSIC". London: Hutchinson, 1914
NUC BMC. Boston: Houghton Mifflin, 1914 NUC.

LBKM-vivid realism, male in Paris
ATH-male hero, suffers under spell of 2 sirens.
Trad. romance PW 85 6/20/14:1975

001267   THE CAPTIVE. London: Chapman & Hall, 1915
BMC NUC.

good study of young Rosamund Beaumont a painter who
never really throws off the chains of conventionalism
forged by upbringing and tradition though she moves in
the Bohemian world of Rome. The 2 share quarters in
Rome; Maisie, in contrast, is a struggling happy art
student. Rosamund marries but her marriage is a
fiasco. "careful study of mental qualities" TLS
Neither of their lives is right or happy at the end SP

001268   A CERTAIN STAR. London: Hodder &
Stoughton, 1917 BMC NUC.

a suppressed artist who wears curious robes, story of
a man wrecked by war, a broken engagement and growth
of another affection. TLS

001269   THE COMMON CHORD. London: M. Secker, 1913
BMC. Boston: Houghton Mifflin, 1914 NUC. (Same as
"Broken Music")

"Broken Music" (same work pub. under a different
title) Judith St. Calvert secretary lives by herself
in London. Another woman character is Sonja, a great
dancer, very convincing portrait of a genius. SP
Judith owns a studio in Hammersmith SR

001270   THE DARK TOWER. New York: Century, 1916
NUC.

Man marries wrong woman later meets the right one.
Claire does not know he is married. PW 90:1282 1
0/14/16
NYT romance

001271   HELE I OF TROY AND ROSE. New York:
Century, 1918 NUC.

001272   THE IMPERFECT GIFT. London: J. Murray,
1907 BMC NUC. New York: Dutton, 1907 PW.

Widow and two daughters who study music; one refuses a
morganatic marr. PW 7-13-07
Two sisters contrasted. Marjory goes on stage, becomes
a leading lady. She marries an actor-manager who has
had previous affairs-The imperfect gift. LBKM. 8-07
180
The other sister marries a drinking boor; fair &
perfectly featured elder sister; dark and strange
younger, plain. ACAD
Lives of the two sisters developed before our eyes
"considerable analytical ability with studious
sincerity" ATH
Marjory Delamaine goes on stage, marries actor-mgr.
"great artistic success." SP

001273   LIFE, THE INTERPRETER. New York:
Longmans, Green, 1902 BMC NUC.

ATH 11-15-02 Experiences of an independent woman,
self-absorbed experiences at the "club," forrook
society for the slums, women are "vulgar"

001274   THE MASTER HOPE. London: Hurst &
Blackett, 1904 BMC NUC.

LBKM Triangle, wholesome, happy ending, high life.
ATH-0 tragedy, matrimonial failure

001275   THE SECOND FIDDLE. New York: Century,
1917 NUC.

Marian refuses to marry Julian about to go off to war
or to marry him when he returns crippled. PW
Marian's friend, Stella Waring does her own thinking
and working. She's modern because she never absorbed
the old ideas. She is Julian's secretary. Focus of
book: unfolding of Stella's personality. She's the
main support of her family. PW
When Marian refuses him, Stella falls in love with
him; They wed and live happily. NYT

001276   SECRETLY ARMED. London: Chapman & Hall,
1916 NUC BMC. (American ed. title: The Dark Tower.)

focus on a hero, his loves. LBKM
TLS-love story of soldier.
ATH-love story of soldier.

001277   A SERVANT OF REALITY. London: Hodder &
Stoughton, 1919 BMC. New York: Century, 1919 NUC.

Heroine "fallen," falls in love. dies of cancer. TLS
Psych. condition of ex German prisoner of war SP
Focus on him. LBKM
"No record of War's physical or material devastation
could be more appalling than this account of spiritual
working of the casting away of a life like Kitty's".
"Stoops to a dissolute life...because her love has
been reported missing in battle." Father taught her
her only obligation is to fascinate. Sells herself
repeatedly. BKM Nov-Dec '19 389
Capt. Anthony Arden, prisoner of war in Germany,
returns, shattered; feels people at home have no idea
of what war means. We learn of the tortures he
suffered. A love story-Kitty, "butterfly broken on the
wheel of life." "enemy of society" is a source of
goodness. NYT 10-12-19, 534

BOUCICAULT, RUTH (HOLT). United States.

001278   THE ROSE OF JERICHO. New York and London:
G. P. Putnam's, 1920 NUC BMC.

TLS--Stage, sent. loves and liaisons of young actress.
ATH--Sheelah, with her young son Michael whom she
loves has more than 1 adventure in love. Poverty and
relations which end in bigamy or separation are among
the themes.
TLS--Americans.
NYT 1920:170. She is an actress, finally famous. Story
of her life from time of her marriage until she is 40.

001279   THE SUBSTANCE OF HIS HOUSE. Boston:
Little, Brown, 1914 NUC. Toronto: Copp, Clark, 1914
BMC.

BKM--Mary marries an older man, falls for a younger
man whom she marries when husband dies. They go to
California. A woman from the past appears on the
scene.
PW--"In London, Lady Mary Stanhope falls in love with
Philip Carmichael, a young and brilliant M. P., and
though she refuses the divorce her husband offers her,
the way is made clear for her marriage with the other
man. They start life anew in California, and then
comes the aftermath, in which the woman's greater love
and the man's selfishness are revealed. A great crisis
shows Philip his life in a startling light and
develops his soul through his and Mary's great and
triumphant love."
Mary Lord married to an M. P. and then to another. TLS
ATH--vague.

001280   THE WOMAN HERSELF [ANONYMOUS]. New York:
Stuyvesant Press, 1909 NUC.

BOULGER, THEODORA (HAVERS). D. 1889. United Kingdom.

001281   THE CASE OF A MAN WITH HIS WIFE. BY THEO
GIFT. London: A. Treherne, 1901 BMC.

001282   AN ISLAND PRINCESS. A STORY OF SIX
WEEKS-AND AFTERWARDS. BY THEO GIFT. London: Lawrence
and Bullen, 1893 BMC. New York: G. P. Putnam's Sons,
1895 NUC.

Young man ruthlessly jilts a young woman, Jean
Coniston of the title. She was too good for him any
way. Island is a thousand miles away in mid-Atlantic.
It's called Las Malvinas and it's a sad place where
people must choose between meloncholia or D.T.; most
choose D.T. (No explanation) Heroine rises above these
surroundings. DT must mean alcohol. "Depressing
realism of...English settlement in mid-ocean." She
dies in the end. ATH 102:621.

001283   WRECKED AT THE OUTSET. BY THEO. GIFT.
London: Jarrold, 1894 BMC.

SR 78:628. Inexpressibly sad. Lives of a nursery
governess, a neglected wife of a well-to-do doctor,
and a law copyist.
3 stories-in two women wrecked through the deliberate
vice or callow selfishness of the monster man. ACAD
47:10

BOULNOIS, HELEN MARY.

001284   SOME SOLDIERS AND LITTLE MAMMA. London:
J. Lane, 1919 NUC BMC. New York: J. Lane, 1919 NUC

BMC.

"Letters of a young woman who entertained soldiers in France." PW

BOULTON, HELEN M.

001285   BATS AT TWILIGHT. London: W. Heinemann,
1904 BMC.

BKM--Unhappy marriage between young woman who is deaf
and nasty old man. What happens?
TLS--Portrayal of the life and world of a young deaf
girl, her childhood, her half-perceptions of the
world, its misinterpretations and animosities, her
marriage finally to a ne'er do well twice her age.

001286   BESS. London: Osgood, McIlvaine, 1896
BMC.

001287   JOSEPHINE CREWE: A NOVEL. London:
Longmans, 1895 BMC NUC.

Vice and squalor. her wretched childhood in London
slums. Drunken mother dies; she goes to live with
uncle. Loves a cousin and is loved by him, learns he
too is an alcoholic. Tries to save him but cannot.
ACAD 48:432
Morbid realism, dreary. ATH 106:514
She's illeg.; first pers narrator. PW 10-12-95:629.
LW 27:76 She started out amongst the rough and
vicious, ended up wife of English gentleman. "Only
God's mercy saved her from making a total wreck of her
life, and we leave her bitterly regretting that she
was saved."

BOURCHIER, HELEN.

001288   THE CROWN OF ASPHODELS. WRITTEN DOWN BY
H. B. London: Theosophical Pub. Co., 1904 BMC.

001289   DARRY'S AWAKENING. London & New York:
Warne, 1907 BMC.

Darry's relation. to her father-they never get to know
each other, from this lack of confidence comes her
awakening. PW 6-1-07
for girls Darry, learns meaning of love TLS

001290   A GREAT RENUNCIATION. London: Hutchinson,
1907 BMC.

adventure & mystery TLS

001291   THE RANEE'S RUBIES. London: A. Treherne,
[1901] BMC.

ATH 7-12-02

001292   THE WHITE LADY OF THE ZENANA. London: H.
J. Drane, [1904] BMC.

ATH--Anglo-Indian marriage. She is very unhappy, a
slave girl loses her life in helping her escape, a
deed which is made successful thru efforts of an Eng.
Champion.

BOURGOIN, SAIDEE. Nationality Unknown.

001293   SARAH MARTHA IN PARIS: A NOVEL. New York:
Merriam, [c1895] NUC.

Am. girl studies singing in Paris. The fact that her
chaperone drinks and leaves her "to her own devices
results in some very questionable episodes." PW
10-12-95:629

BOURKE, FLORENCE BLANCHE MADELINE.

001294   FAITHFULNESS IN HIGH PLACES. A
FASHIONABLE ROMANCE IN HISTORICAL TIMES. Dublin:
Hodges, Figgis, 1912 NUC BMC.

A Duchess almost lets herself "fall" for a young MP
while husband is at the Boer war. Saves herself in
time. TLS

001295   HOW SARAH JANE. Crawley: A. E. Willett,
1907 BMC.

BOURKE, MRS. HUBERT.

001296   A POLITICAL WIFE. London: Eden,
Remington, 1891 BMC.

Margaret Broughton has strong conservative political

views and does a great deal of canvassing for the
candidate of her choice. Loves a man whose views are
radical, but she won't budge an inch. He's the one
who changes his views completely to suit her. Story
ends inconclusively but it looks like a wedding ahead.
ACAD Also ATH 98 36
Irish politics SR 7-4-91, 22

BOUSTEAD, LEILA.

001297   THE BLUE DIAMONDS. London: F.V. White,
1898 BMC.

ACAD 53:149. Woman marries her lover's twin brother by
mistake. Finds out when he dies and other twin shows
up.

BOUVE, PAULINE CARRINGTON (RUST). United States.

001298   THEIR SHADOWS BEFORE: A STORY OF THE
SOUTHAMPTON INSURRECTION. Boston: Small, Maynard, 1899
NUC BMC.

LW 31:157. Nat Turner rebellion narrated by little
girl. Her sympathy makes her a friend of Nat's and
when the other whites are massacred he carries her
away to safety.

BOUVET, MARGUERITE. See BOUVET, MARIE MARGUERITE.

BOUVET, MARIE MARGUERITE. 1865-1915. United States.

001299   CLOTILDE. BY MARGUERITE BOUVET. Chicago:
A. C. McClurg, 1908 NUC.

PW-Mother & daughter-selfish cold mother gets her
come-uppance.

001300   MY LADY: A STORY OF LONG AGO. BY
MARGUERITE BOUVET. Chicago: A. C. McClurg, 1894 NUC.

CR 25:428. Love story of 1st part of century.

001301   PIERRETTE. BY MARGUERITE BOUVET. Chicago:
A. C. McClurg, 1896 NUC.

PW-Daughter of lacemaker in Paris, eking out a
livelihood. On her way delivering lace she meets M. Le
Page, who wishes to adopt her.

001302   THE SMILE OF THE SPHINX. BY MARGUERITE
BOUVET. Chicago: A. C. McClurg, 1911 NUC.

tutor in girls' school makes intimate friendship with
another woman; both love one man; one marries him,
dies, the other marries him ? PW 11-4-11
old fashioned love story. NYT

BOUVIER, CLARA. United States.

001303   THE LILY HE PLUCKED: A ROMANCE. New York,
St. Louis: I. H. Brown, 1891 NUC.

BOWDEN, MRS.

001304   NELLA OF PRETORIA. London: Digby, Long,
1907 BMC.

love story. Boer war TLS

001305   THE WHITE FLAG. London: Digby, Long, 1905
BMC.

BOWEN, GRACE GREENWOOD.

001306   ROSALYS HARPER; OR, THE TURN OF THE WHEEL
OF FORTUNE. [n.d.] W.

BOWEN, HELEN M. United States.

001307   A DAUGHTER OF CUBA. New York: Merriam,
[c1896] NUC BMC.

PW 7-25-96. Lithgow Hamilton goes to Cuba partly in
the commercial interests of Jersden and Lester, New
York, and he is also commissioned by a lawyer to find
a missing heir. Having done this, he joins the forces
of the insurgents and becomes the hero in an episode
of love and war, in which a Cuban girl is the heroine.

BOWEN, M. See LONG, GABRIELLE MARGARET VERE (CAMPBELL)
COSTANZO.

BOWEN, MARJORIE, pseud. See LONG, GABRIELLE MARGARET VERE
(CAMPBELL) COSTANZO.

BOWER, B. M., pseud. See SINCLAIR, BERTHA (MUZZY).

BOWER, MARIAN. United States.

001308   THE GUESTS OF MINE HOST. London: Cassell,
1899 BMC.

Amusing account of life in a big mountain hotel. SP
83:961
Young woman very unhappy in her marriage and two men
interested in her. A cosmopolitan crowd at the Beau
Rivage Hotel at La Severie. ACAD 57:574
LBKM 17:155. Hero is a V.C. His chivalrous actions
when heroine is surrounded by tourists in hotel in
embarrassing situation

001309   THE LOVE STORY OF GUILLAUME-MARC. London:
Hutchinson, 1917 BMC.

A pretty romance-trad hist. TLS
rescue, etc. LBKM

001310   MARIE-EVE. London: Cassell, 1903 BMC.

Raised on the continent, goes to live with English
aunt when father remarries. ACAD 65, 14
fantasia of female treachery. ACAD 65, 60
2 sided nature, modern love story. LBKM
ATH-wrong marriage-then what

001311   PAYNTON JACKS, GENTLEMAN. London: T. F.
Unwin, [1893] BMC. Philadelphia: 1893 NUC.

Josiah Jacks makes a fortune by dealing in cat's meat.
Wants his son to be a gentleman. The way he works out
this plan. PW 12-16-93.
Son determined to marry a lady. ACAD 43:478.
Father married a governess to get educated, makes a
fortune. Son gets in politics. Father lives to see him
triumph. Gleam of humor. CR

001312   THE PUPPET SHOW. London: A. Constable,
1900 BMC.

LW 31:269. Published as John Thisselton in U.S.
SP 85:567. Modern novel of society. Tangled loves and
marriages.
SR 89:179. Wife deserted by her husband assumes her
maiden name. Hero falls for her and resents her
concealment of 1st marriage. Then 1st husband dies and
all ends well.
LIT 7:396. Some of the characters are depressing,
dying girl and her dying lover, Babette's parents.
PW-John's family has insanity; he vows never to marry,
wanders. Four love stories, curtain rises on each, as
in a puppet show.

001313   SAMSON'S YOUNGEST: A NOVEL. London: T.F.
Unwin, 1895 BMC.

matrimonial designs of Martha, also Millicent and her
unhappy marriage. SR 80:640.
In dialect; arist man marries "vulgar" woman, then
proceeds to mistreat her and to drink. ATH 106:678

001314   SKIPPER ANNE, A TALE OF NAPOLEON'S SECRET
SERVICE. London, New York: Hodder & Stoughton, [1913]
BMC NUC.

French nobleman enters Napoleon's secret service; sent
to relatives to spy upon enemies of the republic. ATH

001315   THE STORY OF MOLLIE. London: W. Andrews,
[1897] BMC. Boston: Roberts, 1897 NUC.

Story of a misunderstood child-sent. LW 28:243

001316   THE WRESTLERS. London: Ward, Lock, 1907
BMC.

Horrid people with no manners. Does the wife leave?
ACAD

BOWLES, EMILY. United Kingdom.

001317   AURIEL SELWODE. St. Louis: Herder, 1908
PW. Edinburgh, London: Sands, 1908 NUC BMC.

TLS-- historical male hero.
"Jacobite Court at St. Germain & the Court of Queen
Anne at St.James-the Queen and other notables
appearing"-BAKER

BOWLES, EVELYN MAY (CLOWES) WIEHE. 1877-1942. United
Kingdom.

001318   BELLAMY. BY ELINOR MORDAUNT. London:
Methuen, [1914] BMC NUC. New York: J. Lane, 1914 NUC.

LBKM-0 "Bellamy is an ambitious youth who through
personality and will power scaled the social ladder.
He was a boy in a silk mill, and after he got into
trouble with the firm, he went to London. Here all the
roles he assumed met with complete success. He became
rich, and was engaged to a society girl, not for love,
but because of her position. Then, at the moment of
achievement, he saw the futility of it all. he longed
for the freedom of his childhood, for Jane in the silk
mill, and he left London and went back to them." PW 86
9/27/14: 967.
TLS 13:143--Jane Irwin most attractive and surely
drawn, more than merely a pathological study.

001319   THE COST OF IT. BY ELEANOR MORDAUNT. New
York: Sturgis & Walton, 1912 NUC. London: W.
Heinemann, 1912 BMC NUC.

TLS-male hero who casts off his father to join Creole
mother. Marries an English girl, book closes on tragic
anxiety over issue of their marriage.
ATH--0
LBKM-Claire's terror over birth of child-deals with a
woman in childbirth.
NYT "a novel which no white American can read without
wishing to throw it into the fire. Such a book is
hopelessly immoral-the more so because it is
well-written."

001320   THE FAMILY. BY ELINOR MORDAUNT. New York:
John Lane, 1915 NUC. London: Methuen, [1915] BMC NUC.

study of a family focusing on one of daughters and one
of sons TLS
11 children; the parents are of the old ways, can't
help children adjust to the new TLS
Trag. of family is that only two of 11 children show
any sympathy for each other ACAD
"barren failure of the family". Mother lives only in
the family life. "The writer's thoughts are much
concerned with the problems of how, if at all, sexual
questions should be presented to children" SP
quote from book: "If you had loved me desperately, you
would not have been content with waiting. I believe
that's it. I need some one who loves me desperately. I
don't want patience, or affection, or even goodness. I
want something different. I don't know what; but
something that will sweep me off my feet... I don't
want life to be made easier. I don't think I would
mind if it was made terrible--only it must be life."
But (R. B. JOHNSON)"having missed her ideal, she found
happiness in self-sacrifice."

001321   THE GARDEN OF CONTENTMENT. BY ELENOR
MORDAUNT. London: W. Heinemann, 1902 BMC NUC.

ATH 8-30-02.

001322   THE LITTLE SOUL. A NOVEL. BY ELINOR
MORDAUNT. London: Hutchinson, [1920] BMC NUC. New
York: J.A. McCann, [c1921] NUC.

SP-Psych study of completely self-absorbed male.
ATH-illegitimate.
LBKM-Charles Hoyland is utterly selfish man of the
world, horrible career, is full of nausea as tho not
digesting life. Becomes tutor of weak minded lad and
meets tranquil Diana who attracts him by her
indifference. He cunningly tries to win her without
success. He dies almost as though rent by a devil.
Powerful, lacking in sunshine.

001323   LU OF THE RANGES. BY ELENOR MORDAUNT.
London: W. Heinemann, 1913 NUC BMC. New York: Sturgis
& Walton, 1913 NUC.

"Lu, as a child is left to fend for herself and her
two younger brothers in a hut in the Australian bush.
the forlorn and starving family is rescued by a
vagabond author, and the girl finds employment on a
neighboring farm for its support. She is betrayed and
deceived by the one man she has learned to trust; but
still undaunted in courage, she begins life anew, amid
the temptations and dangers of the town, and achieves
a brilliant career as a popular and successful dancer,
finally to return again to the bush." PW:84
10/18/13:1289
she's a "common girl," an immense wealth of
affection-wastes it on Julien Arde who deserts her.
There is "a glimpse of the species of ugliness in
life" which most decent authors avoid(?). Last
chapters "disgust." ACAD
left, a small girl, to look after brother and a baby.

We see her as a "slavey", then in a maternity
hospital, brilliant career as dancer, returns to
pastoral work. ATH
"The young girl who is the central figure in this
story of Australia is one of the pathetic victims of
an adverse fate, but by sheer strength of will and of
character she lifts herself above the need for pity
and enacts in its stead admiration. Even after her
abandonment by the light-minded, characterless
Englishman, who first rescues her from a life of
degradation and hardship, then amuses himself with her
for an hour and deserts her, she is so much bigger and
better than he, that it is he who appears as the
pitiable figure. the conclusion is a little vague, but
one can, if one wishes, see in it the promise of a
happier future for Lu." BRD
"all the bitterness of the feminine revolt against
sensual man". ATH

001324   THE PARK WALL. BY ELINOR MORDAUNT.
London: Cassell, 1916 BMC.

TLS-Alice Ingpen marries a man who is a total cad.
They sail to West Indies for honeymoon he sends her
back on same ship with friend, divorces her
immediately. Her family shut their doors to her. She
is pregnant finds factory work, etc.
revolt of a married woman who leaves her husband,
insisting "that her small son was illegitimate, simply
to satisfy her passionate determination that he should
grow up her own, hers only, knowing nothing...of his
father" R. B. JOHNSON

001325   THE PENDULUM. BY ELINOR MORDAUNT. London
and New York: Cassell, [1918] BMC NUC.

ATH-powerful, ch study. Modern
LBKM-male hero

001326   THE PROCESSIONALS. BY ELENOR MORDAUNT.
London: Cassell, 1918 BMC.

TLS-family of "caterpillars" who proceed according to
their code aimlessly. To rebel is to form another
procession. But some of the d'Eath's are left on verge
of a fresh procession.

001327   THE ROSE OF YOUTH. BY ELINOR MORDAUNT.
New York: John Lane, 1915 NUC. London: Cassell, [1915]
NUC BMC.

girl of high society and boy of lower class meet,
love, bring great reform to a business establishment.
PW 10-23-15
Story focuses on a man NYT
Celia Fielding, heiress, love, advent stuff TLS
Hero's love of freedom, gets away from girl he
seduced. LBKM

001328   ROSEMARY: THAT'S FOR REMEMBERANCE. BY
ELEANOR MORDAUNT. Melbourne: T.C. Lothian, 1909 BMC.
London: W. Scott, 1909 BMC.

001329   A SHIP OF SOLACE. BY ELEANOR MORDAUNT.
New York: Sturgis & Walton, 1911 NUC. London: W.
Heinemann, 1911 BMC NUC. (Elenor sp. N. Y. ed.)

two young women on sailing voyage to Australia,
vivacious, full of humor. The rude comforts and
discomforts PW 9-30-11
"two pretty love tales woven in" LBKM

001330   SIMPSON. BY ELINOR MORDAUNT. Boston:
Houghton Mifflin, 1913 NUC BMC.

LBKM-male hero establishes males only country club
where members must pay a heavy fine if they leave for
matrimonial purposes. Most of them do.
ATH-Story involves the storming and capitulation of
their citadel.
Several love stories in one Simpson's a bachelor.
"Simpson, a retired business man in the prime of life,
organizes a bachelor's club of congenial spirits and
leases a fine old English country estate. Here they
are to be secure from feminine wiles and live
contented and happy for the rest of their days. First
one, then another deserts for sentimental reasons,
until only Simpson is left, and his final surrender
finishes the tale." PW 10-18-13 1287
He's a retired business man; leases an old estate to
live in "dolce far niente" untroubled by feminism of
any form." NYT

001331   WHILE THERE'S LIFE. BY ELINOR MORDAUNT.
New York: H. Holt, 1919 NUC.

man having short time to live comes to new wisdom of
life. PW
wealthy Englishman learns he has only a few months to
live. NYT He's a widower, bored by his many children
and also ruled by them. He gets away, finds real love.
NYT 5-25-19 295

BOWLES, JANET BYFIELD (PAYNE).

001332   GOSSAMER TO STEEL. New York: Dunstan,
[c1917] NUC.

PW-Tragedy presenting the story of a girl's soul and
dealing with the psychical disturbances & reactions of
life.

BOWLES, MAMIE. Nationality Unknown.

001333   THE AMAZING LADY. London: W. Heinemann,
1899 BMC.

A neurotic young woman visits her brother's country
vicarage for a change, embroiders altar cloths and
complicates the lives of two young men. LIT 4:479
Miss Magda Stacpoole--engaged and ultimately rescued
from her decadent fiance. SP 82:312
A modern woman with leanings towards decadence. Her
relations with two lovers. ACAD 56:327
Delicacy of body and decadence of mind. ATH 113:334.

001334   GILLETTE'S MARRIAGE. London: W.
Heinemann, 1901 BMC.

Unsuccessful marriage, unhappy wife excellently drawn.
A vegetarian. George loathes her, marries her for her
money. ACAD

001335   SEVEN LADIES AND AN OFFER OF MARRIAGE; A
COMEDY OF THE CRINOLINE PERIOD. London: Duckworth,
1902 NUC BMC.

ATH--7 Women play joke on minister by writing a
proposal, the author of which is to be identified by
manner of dress. All 7 wear same costume.

001336   THE SUPREME SACRIFICE; OR GILLETTE'S
MARRIAGE. New York: G. W. Dillingham, 1901 NUC.

Hy of a unsuccessful marr. Separation--divorce. BOOK
NEWS

BOWYER, EDITH M. (NICHOLL). United States.

001337   BY THEIR FRUITS. BY EDITH M. NICHOLL
(MRS. BOWYER). New York: Abbey Press, [c1901] NUC.

001338   GABRIEL THE ACADIAN. Philadelphia:
American Baptist Society, [1902] NUC. (Bound with The
Angel of His Presence by Grace Livingston Hill
[Lutz]./)

001339   THE HUMAN TOUCH, A TALE OF THE GREAT
SOUTHWEST. BY EDITH M. NICHOLL. London: K. Paul, 1905
BMC. Boston: Lothrop, [1905] NUC.

Wealthy cattle king remarries after wife dies--but she
returns. Second wife takes up her abode in the west
because her own people discard her. PW 4-22-05.
Mismates, wife travels a lot, husband attracted to
another woman wife reported dead, the husband marries
the woman. The first wife returns. Story of
heartbreak, selfishness of wife #1; Sylvia (#2)
gallops along the trail bullets whizzing past her,
sporting a six shooter, rescues the man and they are
reunited. NYT
A wife "addicted to nerves." Gets a quick divorce
because she's tired of her husband (not because he
remarried.) All made to seem natural, satisfactory by
the author. ATH 05:467.

001340   TALES OF MOUNTAIN AND MESA. BY EDITH M.
NICHOLL. Cincinnati: Editor Pub. Co., 1899 NUC.

BOYCE, NEITH. See HAPGOOD, NEITH BOYCE.

BOYD, DREDA.

001341   MAUD IRVING. BY AUDREY DEHAVEN. Glasgow
and Edinburgh: W. Hodge, [1905] BMC.

001342   THE SCARLET CLOAK. BY AUDREY DEHAVEN.
Edinburgh and London: W. Blackwood, 1907 BMC.

Hist romance ACAD

BOYD, L. See BOYD, LUCINDA JOAN (ROGERS).

BOYD, LOUISA REID.

001343   THE QUEST FOR JOY. London: A. Melrose,
1912 BMC.

ATH-Boy's upbringing
TLS-Boy's upbringing

BOYD, LUCINDA JOAN (ROGERS).

001344   THE SORROWS OF NANCY. BY L. BOYD.
Richmond, Va.: O. E. Flanhart Printing, 1899 NUC.

BOYD, MARY STUART.

001345   BACKWATERS: A MYSTERY. London: Chapman
and Hall, 1906 BMC.

TLS--Mystery of a young woman, pleasant.
BKM--Lively characters, sensational.

001346   THE FIRST STONE. London: Hodder and
Stoughton, 1909 BMC.

Wife leaves her unfaithful husband, lives alone in
farmhouse for most of book. Meets him again at the
end? TLS
Leaves him because he's a minister who won't confess
"a sensual fault." Falls in love yet returns to
husband who is physically repulsive to her in order to
"appease an appetite which threatens to lead him to
further wrong doing." "A memorable portrait.= ATH.

001347   THE GLEN; A NOVEL OF THE WEST HIGHLANDS.
London: Mills and Boon, 1910 BMC.

TLS--Love story.

001348   HER BESETTING VIRTUE. London: Hodder and
Stoughton, 1908 BMC.

TLS--Romance.
BKM--Romance.

001349   THE MAN IN THE WOOD; A NOVEL. London:
Chapman and Hall, 1904 BMC.

BKM--pleasant love story.
ATH--Pleasant love story.

001350   THE MISSES MAKE-BELIEVE. New York: H.
Holt, 1906 NUC. London: Chapman and Hall, 1906 BMC.

PW--Silly romance.
NYT--Silly romance.
ACAD--Silly romance.

001351   THE MYSTERY OF THE CASTLE. London: J.
Nisbet, 1911 BMC.

Lonely life of young woman in Scottish castle; she's
"spirited, sharp-witted, impulsive". What happens? SP

001352   WITH CLIPPED WINGS. London: Hutchinson,
1902 BMC.

BOYDEN, EMMA. United States.

001353   BOTH WERE MISTAKEN: A NOVEL. BY ARLINE
DARE. New York: G. W. Dillingham, 1892 NUC.

Sensational story of a high society man who falls in
love with a young woman who has no heart. They ruin
each other's lives. Ends in tragedy in Mexico. PW
1-21-93

BOYLAN, GRACE (DUFFIE). 1862-1935. United States.

001354   THE KISS OF GLORY. London, New York: T.
F. Unwin, 1902 BMC. New York: G. W. Dillingham, [1902]
NUC.

Biblical story

001355   THE STEPS TO NOWHERE. New York: Baker and
Taylor, 1910 NUC.

Story of little boy PW

001356   THE SUPPLANTER. Boston: Lothrop, Lee &
Shepard, [1913] BMC NUC.

"Janet Allen, nurse, takes into her heart a baby whose
mother is insane from his birth. She brings him up and
loves him as her own. Gossip about her and the father

forces her to decide she will give the boy up. The
wife sets the house on fire, and is rescued by Janet.
The shock restores her reason; her husband takes her
abroad with the boy but she, missing her baby, does
not get fond of the big son, and at last he is sent
back to the nurse he looks on as his real mother." PW
84:766.
"a human impulse never before expressed in print" New
feminist books for sale at the headquarters of the
Women's Political Union. (Women's Political World)

BOYLE, C. NINA. See BOYLE, CONSTANCE ANTONINA.

BOYLE, CONSTANCE ANTONINA. B. 1865. United Kingdom.

001357   OUT OF THE FRYING PAN. BY C. NINA BOYLE.
London: G. Allen and Unwin, 1920 BMC. New York: T.
Seltzer, 1923 NUC.

TLS--A mess of criminals, card sharks, adventuresses.
SR--Maisie Pleydele, hotel clerk, is brought under
care of her mother whom she hasn't seen in years.
Finds herself in a circle of gamblers. When mother
dies, she looks up Pa who is a worse crook. Now
private secretary to politician she gets goods on him,
is arrested herself first. Ends with marriage and some
measure of justice.

BOYLE, ELEANOR VERE (GORDON). 1825-1916.

001358   SYLVANA'S LETTERS TO AN UNKNOWN FRIEND.
BY E. V. B. London: Macmillan, 1900 BMC NUC.

about gardens

BOYLE, VIRGINIA (FRAZER). 1863-1938. United States.

001359   BROKENBURNE: A SOUTHERN AUNTIE'S WAR
TALE. New York: E. R. Herrick, 1897 NUC.

Plantation life, anti bellum Mississippi "strained
relationships, broken happiness, and sundered loves"
with happy end. Transfor-mation of happy Brockenburne
to place of war. It's a mansion. Virginia
Balfour-fascinating heroine, her strained love is
broken by her devotion to family and principle. All
seen thru Aunt Bene's eyes. BKM 6:348.
NYT 1898:416. Family quarrels, happy ending. South.

001360   LOVE SONGS AND BUGLE CALLS. New York: A.
S. Barnes, 1906 NUC.

001361   SERENA; A NOVEL. New York: A. S. Barnes,
1905 NUC BMC.

Takes place of her twin brother--when he deserts--and
leads his men of Confederate Army to victory. NYT

BOYLE, ZOLA M. United States.

001362   A MASTER OF LIFE. New York: G. W.
Dillingham, 1900 NUC.

NYT 1900:519. Romance. Marjorie, penniless, with dying
brother, received help in form of money and cure for
brother from a Dr. Seaton. Cures him with a word.
Marjorie becomes successful actress, believes it's his
influence. Years later she meets a Herbert Selwyn whom
she believes to be Seaton. She then falls in love and
when lover cools, thinks it is Seaton's influence. But
Selwyn marries and her lover proposes.

BOYNTON, HELEN (MASON). B. 1841. United States.

001363   THE SONG OF A HEART: CHRISTMAS
MILESTONES. BY HELENE HALL. Cincinnati: R. Clarke,
1901 NUC.

BRABY, MAUD (CHURTON). United Kingdom.

001364   DOWNWARD: "A SLICE OF LIFE". London: T.W.
Laurie, [1910] NUC BMC. New York: W. Rickey, 1912 NUC.

LBKM--Unusually frank and outspoken.
ATH--Unfortunate in birth and more unfortunate in her
inherited qualifications, the principal character has
an illegitimate cild. Author tries to make a brighter
horizon with a happy ending. Chain of misery.
PW--Nursing vs. stage, one wrong step.

001365   THE HONEY OF ROMANCE: BEING THE TRAGIC
LOVE-STORY OF A PUBLISHER'S WIFE. [London]: T. W.
Laurie, [1915] BMC NUC.

Marriage--unhappiness--another man--divorce court. TLS

001366   THE LOVE-SEEKER, A GUIDE TO MARRIAGE. New York: Sturgis, 1913 PW. London: H. Jenkins, 1913 NUC BMC.

"There is wit and frankness in this book of advice and suggestion to those in or out of love, married or single. The American girl will disagree with some of it, as it is written by an English woman, from observations of English girls and men, but there is much wholesome truth in it as well as entertainment." PW

BRADDON, M. E. See MAXWELL, MARY ELIZABETH (BRADDON).

BRADDON, MISS M. E. See MAXWELL, MARY ELIZABETH (BRADDON).

BRADLEY, MARY LINDA.

001367   FROM THE FOOTHILLS. Portland, Me.: Mosher Press, 1914 NUC.

BRADLEY, MARY WILHELMINA (HASTINGS). United States.

001368   THE FAVOR OF KINGS. New York and London: D. Appleton, 1912 BMC NUC.

PW--Ann Boleyn historical fiction..

001369   THE FORTIETH DOOR. New York and London: D. Appleton, 1920 NUC BMC.

TLS--Adv., male hero, harem.
BKM--Sensational, he rescues heroine.
NYT--0

001370   THE PALACE OF DARKENED WINDOWS. New York, London: D. Appleton, 1914 NUC BMC.

American girl abducted by Turkish officer in Cairo, rescued, marries rescuer. ATH
"An American girl in Egypt with friends, accustomed to the freedom of her own environment, fails to realize the difference between her position and the women of Egypt. Misinterpreting her attitude, a young Turkish officer falls in love with her and determines to secure her at any cost, and judging his standards by her own, she agrees to visit his sister in an old Turkish palace. Too late she finds herself trapped. An American engineer rescues her. They have a terrifying escape through the desert to the safety of their own flag." PW 86 9-5-14:626.

001371   THE SPLENDID CHANCE. New York, London: D. Appleton, 1915 NUC BMC.

Katherine King refuses marriage, goes to Paris to study art; has two men after her, war comes, one goes blind; she's a musician. PW
Strong anti-war novel--effect of war on individual people. NYT

001372   THE WINE OF ASTONISHMENT. New York and London: D. Appleton, 1919 NUC BMC.

High-spirited Evelyn Day after her engagement to one man is broken, marries another-- a marriage in name only. She finds him a sad contrast to man she loves. "Chafes at her intolerable compact." Husband dies, but she can't marry the lover for she won't face poverty and he won't live on money she inherited from husband. Story seems to focus on the lover who finds someone else in the end. LBKM
Chicago society "manifold tribulations" of the couple; meet in college, but she's married off by socially ambitious mother to a man who dies. Evelyn and that young man go off (unknown to each other) to find independence in US service in France. NYT

BRADSHAW, ANNIE. United Kingdom.

001373   ASHES TELL NO TALES. A DRAMATIC STORY. London: Greening, 1899 BMC.

SR 90:123. "Medley of grotesque and incongruous sensationalism."
ATH 115:110. Julie, villainous and good with poisons. wrecks all her friends' domestic peace, locks up her husband in insane asylum, is betrayed by her maid and pretty much forgiven by the author and her gentlemen friends.

001374   THE CABINET RECITER. London: A. Treherne, 1902 BMC.

001375   FALSE GODS. London: Henry, 1897 BMC.

SR 83:553-Long review of grammar and punctuation faults.
About a woman who loves money and clothes above all else. Married and has child but upon learning she inherits money if she's single, gives them up without a word. Then her husband shows up in the household she's part of. Then he dies. She ends up very well-married to a fine gentleman who loves her for herself, knowing all about her. LBKM 12:129.
Flavia Thornton. ACAD 52 Fic Sup. 46 "We feel that poetic justice has hardly been done."

001376   THE GATES OF TEMPTATION. A NATURAL NOVEL. London and Amsterdam: L. Greening, 1898 BMC.

ACAD 55:480. Passionate love. Mrs. A.S. Bradshaw. Orphan heroine supports family by singing on the stage. She becomes engaged to an English merchant then falls in love with a French artist. Conflict between love and duty leads to suicide. SP 83:94

001377   THE RAGS OF MORALITY. London: Digby, Long, 1911 BMC.

001378   THE STAR RECITER. London: Greening, 1906 BMC.

BRADSHAW, MARGARET. Nationality Unknown.

001379   MY HEART REMEMBERS HOW. Boston: James H. Earle, [c1897] NUC.

BRADY, ADELINE, jt. au. See BRUGIERE, SARA (VAN BUREN) AND ADELINE BRADY.

BRAINE, SHEILA E.

001380   THE TURKISH AUTOMATON. A TALE OF THE TIMES OF CATHARINE THE GREAT OF RUSSIA. London: Blackie, 1899 BMC NUC.

It's a figure of a Turk sitting on a large box with a chessboard in front of him. The figure plays excellent chess. The box contains a certain young Pole trying to get out of Russia. Then Catherine the Great heard of the automaton and commanded that it be brought to her. LIT 4:121

BRAINERD, ELEANOR (HOYT). 1868-1942. United States.

001381   BETTINA. London: Doubleday, Page, 1907 BMC. New York: Doubleday, Page, 1907 NUC.

A comic case of misunderstanding PW 1-26-07
Beauty is the chief end of woman. NYT

001382   CONCERNING BELINDA. London, New York: Doubleday, Page, 1905 BMC NUC.

Teacher in girls finishing school & the typical boarding school types PW 10-7-05

001383   HOW COULD YOU, JEAN? Garden City, New York: Doubleday, Page, 1917 NUC. London: T. Nelson, [1920] BMC.

Raised in luxury, now penniless can only cook. Gets job, meets handy man who turns out to be of rich family PW

001384   IN VANITY FAIR: A TALE OF FROCKS AND FEMININITY. New York: Moffat, Yard, 1906 NUC. London: T. F. Unwin, 1907 BMC.

sketches of the Parisienne

001385   THE MISDEMEANORS OF NANCY. BY ELEANOR HOYT. New York: Doubleday, Page, 1902 NUC. London: G. Richards, 1902 BMC.

BKM 1901-"Looked upon from the old-fashioned chaperones & minuet manners, she is unquestionably a most improper young person but then she is not a vulgar self-conscious little female cad like the...English Elizabeth."

001386   THE PERSONAL CONDUCT OF BELINDA. New York: Doubleday, Page, 1910 NUC. London: Hodder & Stoughton, 1910 BMC.

"Belinda Carewe the youngest teacher in a select boarding-school for girls, had planned to assist her associate, Miss Barnes, in conducting a small party on a tour thru Europe. At the last moment Miss Barnes finds herself unable to make the trip and Belinda is persuaded to take her place...Belinda starts out with

all the rules and regulations obtainable from
guide-books, etc; which, however, prove wholly
inadequate for the unforeseen emergencies, such as
"personal engagements", and at the end of the tour
Belinda is forced to admit that her personal
conducting has been bad enough, but that her personal
conduct has been a scandal." BKM, v. 31, 1910.
LBKM. She is safely married at end but book is
concerned with her adventures before marriage.
Teacher of literature takes party of young women to
Europe, sent.? PW
LBKM--silly.

BRAINERD, THOMAS H., pseud. See JARBOE, MARY HALSEY
(THOMAS).

BRAKE, JOSEPHINE WINFIELD. United States.

001387   AS IT HAPPENED: BEING A STORY IN THREE
BOOKS AND SEVERAL MANNERS. Washington: Neale, 1899
NUC. (Also published as: How It Happened: Being a
Story in Three Books. New York: The American News
Company [cop. 1900].)

BRAMSTON, MARY. B. 1841. United Kingdom.

001388   ABBY'S DISCOVERIES. London: National
Society's Depository, [1891] BMC 1892 NUC.

Abigail Hall tells of the feelings and experiences of
her child hood, the people like nurse, stepmother,
etc. SP 67 892

001389   THE ADVENTURES OF DENIS. London: National
Society's Depository, [1892] BMC.

SP 69:625. 1845, Highland chief, Jacobites.

001390   LOTTIE LEVISON: A STORY OF SOUTH LONDON.
London: National Society's Depository, [1892] BMC.

SP 69:625. Lottie has a desire to rise above her
surroundings, but at some point she gives up this
desire to return to her sick mother. Marries finally.

001391   NEAL RUSSELL: THE STORY OF A BRAVE MAN.
London: S. Sonnenschein, 1891 BMC.

He turns to evil ways when he's jilted by girl he
loves, but saved in time. Then he must "pay" for his
sins. Goes to prison for a crime he didn't commit.
(Prison life of innocent man depicted very strongly.)
Released, goes to Canada, meets another woman, falls
in love. SP 67, 789

001392   SHAVEN CROWN; A STORY OF THE CONVERSION
OF THE SURREY BORDER. London: S.P.C.K., [1895] BMC.

001393   THE STORY OF A CAT AND A CAKE DURING THE
THIRTY YEARS' WAR. London: National Society's
Depository, [1896] BMC.

001394   THEIR FATHER'S WRONG. London: National
Society's Depository, [1895] BMC.

001395   TOLD BY TWO. London: National Society's
Depository, [1898] BMC.

001396   TOO FAIR A DAWN. London: Hurst and
Blackett, 1896 BMC.

ACAD 49:32. Crystal, portrait of weak, vain,
worshipped woman who sinks to dishonour after mrge.
while husband rises to heights of nobility.
SP 76: 137. She steals a diamond necklace; he has a
passion for gambling but rises.
Fall of a woman, "an angel." Becomes a part of her
father-in-law's gambling set-that her husband has been
trying to free himself from since he met her. A
tragedy SR 80:808.
Crystal Rowhurst so impresses her lover with her
purity that he mends his ways. But she in the meantime
takes up the ways he gave up . Story of her
deterioration. ATH 106:602

001397   A VILLAGE GENIUS; A TRUE STORY OF
OBERAMMERGAU. London: National Society's Depository,
[1891] BMC.

A musical genius living in the years 1779-1822. Author
uses his life as basis for her story. SP 67 892

001398   WINNING HIS FREEDOM. London: National
Society's Depository, [1893] BMC.

BRANCH, MARY LYDIA (BOLLES). 1840-1922. United States.

001399   THE KANTER GIRLS. New York: C. Scribner,
1895 NUC. London: Downey, 1896 BMC.

BRANDON, BEATRIX.

001400   LADY MAUD. London: Digby, Long, [1895]
BMC.

weak husband, bad wife, unscrupulous paramour. The
wicked Lady Maud gets rid of drunken "half-idiotic
husband by having him burned" and weds the
paramour.-Dr. Morgan. Their child is an idiot who
looks like the late husband. ACAD 47:442

BRANDON, D. See BRANDON, DOROTHY.

BRANDON, DOROTHY.

001401   BEAU REGARD. A DREAM OF THE DARK AGES.
London: A. Melrose, 1920 BMC.

TLS Eleanor of Aquitaine.
ATH Male hero & romantic love

001402   THE DAVOSERS. BY D. BRANDON. London: J.
Long, 1911 BMC. New York: G. H. Doran, [1912] NUC.

centers on friendship between two men. TLS

BRAY, BLANCHE ALICE. B. 1873. United States.

001403   HIS WARD. New York: Cosmdpolitan Press,
1911 NUC.

PW-Male brings up a little girl, marries her.

BRAZELTON, ETHEL MAUDE (COLSON). United States.

001404   THE STORY OF A DREAM. BY ETHEL MAUDE
COLSON. Chicago: C. H. Kerr, 1896 NUC.

BREDON, JULIET. United States.

001405   SIR ROBERT HART, THE ROMANCE OF A GREAT
CAREER. TOLD BY HIS NIECE. New York: Dutton, [1909]
NUC. London: Hutchinson, 1909 BMC NUC.

BREITENBACH, LOUISE M. See CLANCY, LOUISE MARKS
(BREITENBACH).

BRENAN, FLORENCE MACCARTHY. B. 1854. United States.

001406   MARGARET; OR, WAS IT MAGNETISM? BY
GILBERT GUEST. Omaha: Burkley, 1920 NUC.

001407   MEG. THE STORY OF AN IGNORANT LITTLE
FISHER GIRL. BY GILBERT GUEST. Omaha: Western
Chronicle, 1896 NUC.

001408   SNAPSHOTS BY THE WAY. BY GILBERT GUEST.
Omaha: Burkley, 1920 NUC.

BRENDA, pseud. See SMITH, MRS. G. CASTLE.

BREWER, ANNETTE (FITCH).

001409   THE STORY OF A MOTHER-LOVE. Akron, O.:
New Werner, [c1913] NUC.

Narrative of a divorced woman's fight for the
possession of her son.

BREWER, ESTELLE HEMPSTEAD MANNING. B. 1882.

001410   TREASON OF THE BLOOD. Cedar Rapids, Iowa:
Torch Press, 1912 NUC.

NYT-Problem of African color taint. Heroine unaware of
this problem in hero's family, as is hero. There is a
murder, a body tossed down a well, and an execution
conducted with much pomp by heroine.

BRICE, SHIRLEY.

001411   THE MIGHT OF A WRONGDOER. London: J.
Long, 1906 BMC.

ATH-male hero, mystery, crime.

BRIDGES, MRS. COLONEL. United Kingdom.

001412   DEAREST. BY MRS. FORRESTER. London: Hurst
& Blackett, 1893 BMC. New York: Tait, [c1893] NUC.

English country family: a worldly selfish mother. Twin

daughters, "ugly" younger daughter, step son and
brother, head of house-all come under influence of
Dearest. PW 5-13-93
"It pays to be deceitful and scheming." She a
governess wants social advancement and money-thru
marriage to her pupil's wealthy brother. She tells
lies, feigns love, "accomplishes her end, makes
everybody devotedly grateful" and ends loving the man
she weds. Only once she comes near confessing a lie
but checks the impulse. LW 26:154
Eva Huntingtower employs Rachel le Breton. ACAD 43:501
Ends up as squire's wife. ATH 101, 405.

001413   THE LIGHT OF OTHER DAYS. BY MRS.
FORRESTER. London: Hurst and Blackett, 1894 BMC.
Philadelphia: J.B. Lippincott, 1894 NUC.

ATH 104:90. Comparison of modern with Victorian women,
favoring the latter.
PW-author does not believe in women's rights or
emancipation.

001414   OF THE WORLD WORLDLY. BY MRS. FORRESTER.
London: Hurst and Blackett, 1892 BMC. New York:
Lovell, Coryell, [c1892] NUC.

ATH 99:788. Society siren jilts young man because of
his poverty; he finally recovers and comes to
appreciate charming young girl.
LW 23:295. Career of a beauty, a married woman with
many admirers.
ACAD 41:88 "the society siren-that worthless creature
who finds no happiness in her home, who reads French
novels by day and haunts heated ballrooms by night."

001415   TOO LATE REPENTED. BY MRS. FORRESTER.
London: Hurst and Blackett, 1895 BMC.

A couple agree to part because they are hopelessly
alienated. They loved each other, and once parted seek
each other out. But they "miss" each other. He dies at
sea. She meets a man she'll be happier with. ACAD
48:202
They miss each other when he sails to America and he's
not on the ship she thinks he's booked for. PW
7-20-95:105
SP 76:116. Ethel's husband thinks that "she takes too
much upon herself;" she thinks he has married her for
her money. She is brought to repent these bitter
thoughts.

BRIDGES, PHILIPPA BEATRICE.

001416   THE GREEN WAVE OF DESTINY. Edinburgh and
London: W. Blackwood, 1911 NUC BMC.

2 men adventure in desert. TLS SP

BRIGGS, OLIVE MARY. B. 1873. United States.

001417   THE BACHELOR DINNER. New York: C.
Scribner's Sons, 1912 NUC.

001418   THE BLACK CROSS. New York: Moffat, Yard,
1909 NUC.

Russian woman involved in plot with gbvernment PW
2-20-09
escapes in disguise of a boy gypsy; she can sing
marvelously. "The death of the Grand Duke Stepan is
decreed by a band of Nihilists belonging to a society
known as "The Black Cross." It falls to the lot of the
Countess Kaya to perform the deed of assassination.
She meets the Grand Duke at a ball and shoots at him,
killing him instantly, as she believes. She flees to
Velasco, a famous violinist, whose aid she had already
solicited. In order that she may travel as his wife
and thus cross the frontier in safety, she requests
that he marry her at once, promising to give him up as
soon as she is out of danger. Together they make their
escape from Russia by disguising themselves as gypsies
and travelling in gypsy fashion. True to her promise,
the Countess Kaya leaves the musician despite his
protests. His efforts to find her prove futile until
one night in a theatre in Germany, where he is
conducting the orchestra, he is surprised to find on
the stage in the character of Brunnhilde the object of
his long search. They recognise each other at once,
but she still refuses to claim him, as she believes
herself to be a murderess and under the curse of the
"Black Cross." All her scruples disappear, however,
when Velasco assures her that her shot has not proved
fatal and that the Grand Duke Stepan is alive and in
fact in the audience." BKM 29 1909.

001419   THE COURTING OF MISS PARKINA. New York:

Winthrop Press, 1914 NUC.

001420   THE FIR AND THE PALM. New York: C.
Scribner's Sons, 1910 NUC.

Fascinating brilliant woman a lion tamer; she's part
of a traveling show, has many adventures. Tumultuous
love relations with a great physician? PW
BKM-marries him and leaves him when she gets a letter
filled with scorn from his sister.
NYT-laughs to scorn his appeals that she leave the
circus and get an education.

BRIGHAM, HARRIET CONWAY. United States.

001421   THE NEW SAINT CECILIA [ANONYMOUS].
Detroit, Mich.: Farrand and Votey, 1895 NUC.

BRIGHT, ANNIE.

001422   A SOUL'S PILGRIMAGE. London: Simpkin,
Marshall; 1907 BS. Melbourne: 1907 NUC.

Advanced view of psychic phenomena. TLS
Spiritualism.

BRIGHT, FLORENCE.

001423   A GIRL CAPITALIST. London: Chatto &
Windus, 1902 BMC.

001424   ONE PRETTY PILGRIM'S PROGRESS. London: E.
Nash, 1903 BMC.

BRIGHT, MARY CHAVELITA (DUNNE) MELVILLE CLAIRMONTE GOLDING.
1860-1945. Australia.

001425   THE AFRICANDER: A PLAIN TALE OF COLONIAL
LIFE. London: 1896 NUC.

001426   DISCORDS. BY GEORGE EGERTON. London: J.
Lane, 1894 BMC. Boston: Roberts, 1894 NUC.

Three studies: two of women alcoholics. "Gone Under,"
a woman's fall "Virgin soul," revulsion of feeling of
a girl of 17 who marries in ignorance. Reviewer
objects that author gets too angry in this story.
"Psychological Moment" young woman who reads at
British museum goes to bed with a man because he has
proof that will get someone in trouble. "The
Regeneration of Two". She starts a foundling
establishment. Lives with a man freely. Gives "a new
influence, an idealized man". SR 79:416
"Dismal threnodies over everything that is pure and
hopeful in life" "very nauseous" her "ferment of
rebellion" SP 74:541

001427   FLIES IN AMBER. BY GEORGE EGERTON.
London: Hutchinson, 1905 BMC.

001428   KEYNOTES. BY GEORGE EGERTON. London: E.
Mathews and J. Lane, 1893 BMC. Boston: Roberts, 1893
NUC.

CR 21:405. Studies, not stories of sexuality. She says
nothing new about woman's sexuality, but the work does
have a "tingling sense of indecency" which is
powerful.
"Stories of the femme incomprise, introspective
studies of woman's impulses which are acknowledged
without false shame." BAKER 03,104
Six short stories "To many of us that little volume
came with a fine air of discovery; we felt we had at
last a woman writer rising out of the multitude of
women writers; an almost masculine strength of
conception..." SR 79:416

001429   ROSA AMOROSA. THE LOVE-LETTERS OF A
WOMAN. BY GEORGE EGERTON. London: G. Richards, 1901
BMC. New York: Brentano's, 1901 NUC.

001430   SYMPHONIES. BY GEORGE EGERTON. London: J.
Lane, 1897 BMC. London and New York: 1897 NUC.

"Studies of the feminine temperament and of erotics"
BAKER 03,104
Only one story is like her earlier ones: "At the Heart
of the Apple." The theme is "to depict the race of
women and they are many, to whom the child is first,
the man always second." LBKM 12:100
Six short stories. "Nobody loves well enough to marry
or to be faithful, the lovers love and ride away, the
loveresses commit suicide or console themselves with
maternity-or other lovers-" LW 28:211

001431   THE WHEEL OF GOD. BY GEORGE EGERTON.

London: G. Richards, 1898 BMC. New York: Putnam's
Sons, 1898 NUC.

LIT 2:729. "If only the 'obsession' of her one subject
would pass away from her! If only feminism would raise
the siege." Story of Mary, her two marriages, is, at
last, left a widow. Second marriage to irresponsible
young man.
ACAD 53:625. "Psychological study of a sensitive,
emotional girl among unsympathetic people."
SR 86:352. Author is egotist. No plot. Book falls into
three parts; childhood, independent life in New York
and London, and marriage to second husband, a
worthless doctor.
LBKM 14:168. She drifts through life to middle-age,
when she has a "fund of love and tenderness for other
women into whose struggles and dreary lives she has
gained great insight."
Three short stories. Shop girl in cheap New York
boarding house-frail, helpless (bound to God's wheel).
From girlhood to womanhood, weds an elderly man
because she doesn't know what else to do. He dies,
marries a second who dies leaving her to look for a
third-still not made happy. She concludes: "The men we
women today need, or who need us, are not of our
time-it lies in the mothers to rear them for the women
who follow us." BKM 9:280.
Faces much adversity. CR 34:470
Three stages of her life: (1) a poetic child (2) the
shattering of her ideals (3) a disillusioned woman.
"Author reasons that all women's efforts for equality
with man are useless; that only unadulterated
femininity is a deadly weapon if wisely directed
against the male." PW 55:49.

BRINTON, SYBIL G.

001432   OLD FRIENDS AND NEW FANCIES; AN IMAGINARY
SEQUEL TO THE NOVELS OF JANE AUSTEN. London: Holden &
Hardingham, 1913 NUC BMC.

About 40 of Austen's characters brought into the
story. Attempts to amplify their after-adventures.
Austen's style preserved. ACAD

BRISCOE, MARGARET SUTTON. See HOPKINS, MARGARET SUTTON
(BRISCOE).

BROAKER, JULIA FREDERIKA (LUTH). United States.

001433   THE YOUNGER MRS. COURTNEY. A NOVEL. BY
MRS. FRANK BROAKER. New York: Alwood, 1903 BMC NUC.

"A novel of broken marriage vows, with a number of
sensational climaxes." BKM, v. 19, 1904
NYT-Degenerate husband and virtuous wife who faints a
lot.
PW-Divorce novel, but pro or con?

BROAKER, MRS. FRANK. See BROAKER, JULIA FREDERIKA (LUTH).

BRODERICK, THERESE. B. 1870. United States.

001434   THE BRAND, A TALE OF THE FLATHEAD
RESERVATION. BY THERESE BRODERICK (TIN SCHREINER).
Seattle, Wash.: Alice Harriman, 1909 NUC.

NYT-story of the Flathead Reservation. Heroine goes
west from NY,has a half Indian (wealthy tho) suitor.
What then?
Love story-American girl-"half breed." PW
"A story of the flathead reservation in Montana whose
characters and settings have been studied first hand
by the author who lives on the shore of Flathead
lake. man from New York who goes to the Flathead
region with her brother and there meets a number of
people characteristic of the West." BRD 1910

BRODHEAD, EVA WILDER (MACGLASSON). 1870-1915. United
States.

001435   BOUND IN SHALLOWS: A NOVEL. New York:
Harper, 1897 NUC.

Strong woman makes every effort to redeem a decadent
young man but fails. LW 28:227
Theme: to raise one up, another is bound to be
sacrificed. This woman gave up. PW 51:368.
Two women and a scamp. Lumbering town in Ky. called
Streamlet. Lucy Morrow, sweet well bred, Alexa Bohun,
wild unmannered and Dillon who is dishonest (a
swindler) but Lucy forgives. He's dishonest again, she
gives up and he turns to Alexa who has always wanted
him but had almost married to spite him. Then her
fiance dies. Story focuses on the attraction women
like Lucy feel for a sinner. NYT 3-13-97.

001436   DIANA'S LIVERY. BY EVA WILDER MCGLASSON.
New York: Harper, 1891 NUC BMC.

Everyday life of Shakers. The community breaks down.
Young Quakeress free to give her love to young man of
the world. Clandestine relationship between young
Shaker woman and Elder exposed.Ends sadly. LW
Laban violated his vow of celibacy and took an earthly
bride-Naamah. Both suffer. Community at Pleasant Hill
breaks up. Naamah goes to live in the world, finds
another man. CR

001437   AN EARTHLY PARAGON: A NOVEL. BY EVA
WILDER MCGLASSON. New York: Harper, 1892 NUC.

PW-Sylvia accompanies her brother to the wilds of
Kentucky. She is beloved by all who see her. How she
uses this gift is the story.
NATION 145:396. Kentucky. Sylvia thinks of herself as
a "thin and insufficient person." She is tired of
having to form the literary taste of every man she
meets, and says to a man she has rejected "people are
happy in marriage in proportion as they are too stupid
to find each other out or clever enough to keep up
prenuptial illusions." She lives in a hotel; her
"adventures are interesting."
LW 23:496. Reviewer can't stand Sylvia.
Village of Chamouni, Kentucky. Sylvia not a native,
moved there when parents died to live with uncle.
Expects much of the town life but is disappointed. But
she's a person "interesting in herself." not beauty.
"She seems, without any intention of so doing to leave
a blight wherever she moves." Marries, goes away
leaving "the surviving wrecks of all the unhappiness
she has created" behind. CR 14, 21:19

001438   MINISTERS OF GRACE: A NOVELETTE. BY EVA
WILDER MCGLASSON. New York: Harper, 1894 NUC.

001439   ONE OF THE VISCONTI: A NOVELETTE. New
York: C. Scribner's Sons, 1896 NUC.

BKM 4:373. Naples. Piccarda is engaged to unscrupulous
Italian whose cruelty caused death of his American
wife. Young American falls for her; his mother tells
her the truth about her fiance. She breaks her
engagement and marries the American. Another American
couple, the wife selfish in her desire to live in
Europe, is brought together by death of child.
PW 10-3-96.
Fortunes of 3 couples thru an Italian writer: the
daughter of the house of Visconti and her fiance, a
Ky. lawyer, the Fannings. Mrs. Fanning is a study of a
woman who believes in European culture "for the sake
of the children" but also becomes disillusioned in it.
CR 26,30:218

BRODRICK, EMILY HESTER.

001440   ANANIAS. London: Methuen, 1898 BMC.

SP 81:446. Wealthy and eccentric testator and his
heirs.
ATH 112:524. Alicia manages to marry Richard. He is
persuaded by family's need for money; he brings her
position. He is an artist, falls for Hetty, another
artist. She spurns him when she discovers his
marriage.
LBKM 15:59. Richard marries the woman he loathes and
deceives the woman he loves, then writes a novel about
it.

001441   THE CREED OF PHILIP GLYN. London: Ward
and Downey, 1896 BMC.

SR-principal character is an artist, Keith, whose wife
is distasteful to the author because she has a loud
voice and a partiality for brandy. Tries to kill
herself. He loves someone else and leaves her to die.
Philip hushes up story of this "virtual murder" and
helps Keith marry other woman.
ATH-Wife is "afflicted with a craving for drink."
ACAD 49:343. Philip's creed is the gospel of love.

BRODSKY, ANNA (SKADOVSKY). Russia.

001442   NATASHA; THE STORY OF A RUSSIAN WOMAN.
London: J. M. Dent, 1910 NUC BMC.

TLS-Russian unhappy marriage to happiness at last.
BAKER 32-72

BROOKE, ALISON, pseud. See MASON, CAROLINE (ATWATER).

BROOKE, E. F. See BROOKE, EMMA FRANCES.

BROOKE, EMMA FRANCES.   United Kingdom.

001443   THE CONFESSION OF STEPHEN WHAPSHARE. New
York and London: G. Putnam, 1898 NUC. London:
Hutchinson, 1898 BMC.

SP 80:174. Stephen marries the wrong woman, gives her
an overdose of a narcotic. She is so self-sacrificing
that she writes a suicide note before she loses
consciousness. The woman he wants to marry refuses
him.
LIT 2:260. First person narrative. His wife is a
Puritanically devout invalid, so interested in the
salvation of her soul that she is unaware of temporal
sufferings. Stephen is a prig.
BKM 7:168. His "soul has been crushed out of him" at
end of book then some fantastic mystic religion of the
author's creation. Stephen and his wife were both
dedicated Christians; he has always wanted to do
large, heroic deeds, she has an inward piety. He feels
trapped by his illness, loathes himself; he has never
had the courage to act for himself.
LW 29:187. "His sacrifice is as pitiful as her
soulless course is exasperating."

001444   THE ENGRAFTED ROSE; A NOVEL. London:
Hutchinson, 1899 BMC. Chicago: H. S. Stone, 1900 NUC.

LBKM 18:62. Development of Rosamunda's character, a
strong nature. Second in importance is Mrs. Thorsbye,
R's supposed mother, fresh and unique. The supreme
moment of Rosamunda's life is her awakening to love.
ACAD 58:273. She was changed at birth. Learns who she
is at 20, member of aristocratic family. She has been
living with a mill- owning family. Her gypsy like
adventures not believable to rev.
LIT 6:336. Artistic temperament, obsessed with playing
the violin.
PW-rural England,1847-1867. "When originality in women
still startled their associates." Conventionally
reared, at 17 her original, artistic nature breaks
out.

001445   THE HOUSE OF ROBERSHAYE. London: Smith,
Elder, 1912 BMC. New York: Duffield, 1912 NUC.

PW-struggle between two men.
TLS-one a musician with ideas of social reform. Other
a businessman; struggle for idealistic heroine.
ATH--heroine only a profile.

001446   LIFE THE ACCUSER, A NOVEL IN TWO PARTS.
BY E. F. BROOKE. London: Heinemann, 1896 NUC. New
York: E. Arnold, 1896 NUC.

SR-states view that sensual passivity in women is a
fallacy, tragic in its effect when treated as fact.
The wife tells husband her passion for him, not her
purity, has kept her faithful to him. He is horrified.
Issue of heredity, also.
ACAD 50:489. "Original and striking scene" between
Norman and Constantia Dayntrie, after his infidelity
and her accidental discovery of it. Touches "rather
closely on facts of sex which it is more usual to wrap
up in silences and conventions. We by no means say
that such subjects should never be treated, even in a
novel; but we do say that, seeing how much in them
there is to disturb and disquiet, they should not be
handled lightly, but left to those who can wield them
with confidence and discretion."
PW-12-19-96. Heroine states at 17 that the only law
she knows is need and nature.
3 women contrasted. Rosalie Trelyon "is one of the
emancipated who confuse license with liberty." Eliza
respectable but always doing the wrong thing.
Constantia whose husband is unfaithful. CR 28,31 46.
A husband's unfaithful; wife tries to understand-a
"vain piteous striving." LW 28:58.
Grey, Melancholy. A triangle; analysis of the 3, a
couple and the other woman. BKM 4:468.

001447   THE POET'S CHILD. London: Methuen, 1903
BMC.

Married woman has child outside of marriage, the
poet's. ACAD 250,v64
Hero's mother's life a tissue of complex incredible
lies. LBKM 5-03,74 ATH 121,590

001448   SIR ELYOT OF THE WOODS. A NOVEL. London:
W. Heinemann, 1907 BMC. New York: Duffield, 1907 NUC.

Young woman without a conscience, but story focuses on
Elyot who would be free of debt. PW 4-27-07
The book gives little attention to the wife. ACAD TLS

Heroine impossible disagreeable. SP
Loses all in the end--the man and the fortune she
plotted to get. BKM
Punishment comes to those who desired too much?
Unhappiness of mother whose daughter's life is so much
like her own NYT

001449   THE STORY OF HAUKSGARTH FARM. A NOVEL.
London: Smith, Elder, 1909 BMC.

Icelanders & their homestead. Nanna's misdeeds
gradually unfold. She's one of three principal
characters, portrayal unsympathet ic. TLS
Silence Whinnery a fine type. About farm people. LBKM.
charming, soothing. SP

001450   A SUPERFLUOUS WOMAN. A NOVEL [ANONYMOUS].
London: W. Heinemann, 1894 BMC NUC. New York: Cassell,
[c1894] NUC.

SR 77:394. Jessamine is dying in first chapter, saved
by doctor. After her recovery she yearns for simple
life and serviceable work. However, she weds a
coronetted ghoul, her children are idiots, she suffers
acute mental torture.
SP 72:270. Reviewer says the term superfluous woman
means a woman who has not found either her mate or her
work, an odd woman as Gissing would put it. Jessamine
does not fit this definition. After her recovery she
found refuge in a Scotch village, fell passionately in
love with a farmer. He mistakes her confession of
"unconditional surrender" as terror and says he has no
intentions of violating her honor; she in turn
mistakes this as a rejection of her love, and flees
back to London, humiliated. Hence her marriage to Lord
Heriot and subsequent suffering.
ACAD 45:286. Died in labour with 3rd child, also an
idiot.
ATH 103:144. "Last volume is full of lurid lights and
coal black shadows in which realities have little to
do." Problem of heredity in a vicious and effete
aristocrat, outworn physically and morally.

001451   SUSAN WOOED AND SUSAN WON. London: W.
Heinemann, 1905 BMC NUC.

Story of nonconformists, murder. LBKM 38, 29-30
Really about crime and temperament. Striking and
unconventional book but Susan is colourless. ATH
05,466

001452   TRANSITION, A NOVEL. BY THE AUTHOR OF A
SUPERFLUOUS WOMAN [ANONYMOUS]. Philadelphia: J. B.
Lippincott, 1895 NUC. London: W. Heinemann, 1895 BMC.

concerns Socialism. "Honora Kemball, the Girton
first-class" shares many social ideas with Leslie
Lyttleton before the two come together. Honora's
friend becomes disillusioned with a "comrade" in
socialism who believes in free love although he's
married. This friend of Honora's dies. SP 75:89
"A political tract" showing difference between
socialism and anarchism. Honora, "fresh from brilliant
career at Cambridge" returns home ready to improve her
father's rectory and continue her studies. But father
gives up his titles to the church. She takes work-in
charge of girls' school in London. Her growth toward
society, her suitors, one of whom is a socialist.
Author believes in "constructive socialism" CR 23:433

001453   THE TWINS OF SKIRLAUGH HALL. A MYSTERY.
London: Hurst and Blackett, 1903 BMC.

Twin sisters antagonists from birth reenact tragedy of
love and madness of their ancestors. ACAD 65,415

BROOKE, MAGDALEN, pseud. See CAPES, HARRIET MAY (MOTHER
MARY REGINALD).

BROOKES, MABEL BALCOMBE.

001454   BROKEN IDOLS. London: A. Melrose, 1918
NUC BMC.

Egypt seen through eyes of Aust. soldier & his wife.
SP
Moral lapses, due to separation because of war
reconciliation. ATH
Woman discovers her solid husband is involved with
German secret agent (a woman). At this time, her love
cools, and an ex-love appears. Husband killed in
action? SR
TLS-war and marital infidelity.

BROOKFIELD, FRANCES MARY (GROGAN). United Kingdom.

001455   THE DIARY OF A YEAR; PASSAGES IN THE LIFE
OF A WOMAN OF THE WORLD. EDITED BY MRS. CHARLES
BROOKFIELD. Boston: L. C. Page, 1903 NUC. London: E.
Nash, 1903 BMC.

Married woman, husband unfaithful, wife almost so;
heart sorrows and disagreements of the pair-ATH 121,
716.
"Books of this sort are getting so numerous as to be
irritating."

001456   A FRIAR OBSERVANT. St. Louis, Mo.:
Herder, 1909 NUC. London: I. Pitman, 1909 BMC.

Married woman travelling alone describes her
"entanglement" with another man. Discussion of
divorce. 8-29-03 PW
Traditional historical romance male hero-ATH. Friar
witnesses dissolution of the monasteries in 1539 in
Germany during the reign of Charles V, comes in
contact with Luther, of whom an unflattering portrait
is drawn.

001457   MY LORD OF ESSEX, THE ROMANTIC EPISODE OF
CADIZ. London: I. Pitman, 1907 BMC.

historical romance TLS

BROOKFIELD, MRS. CHARLES. See BROOKFIELD, FRANCES MARY
(GROGAN).

BROOKS, AMY. United States.

001458   AT THE SIGN OF THE THREE BIRCHES. Boston:
Lothrop, Lee & Shepard, 1916 NUC.

"Sylvia must spend a certain time at a mansion once a
tavern to meet terms of her eccentric godmother's
will. Struggle against a masterful suitor. She has
pluck and follows her best impulses to an unexpected
ending." PW 90:767 9/9/16

BROOKS, HILDEGARD. B. 1875. United States.

001459   THE DAUGHTERS OF DESPERATION. New York:
McClure, Phillips, 1904 NUC. Edinburgh and London: W.
Blackwood, 1904 BMC.

"These desperate daughters are rather charming young
women who become amateur anarchists. The plot is
lively, and the humour is abundant." BKM, V. 19. 1904
LBKM--0

001460   THE MASTER OF CAXTON. New York: C.
Scribner's Sons, 1902 NUC.

NYT 6-14-02--not encouraging, philanthropy, etc.
Light satire of various people in small Southern
community.

001461   WITHOUT A WARRANT. New York: C.
Scribner's Sons, 1901 NUC.

Young woman kidnapped, kept in men's clothes. "She not
hero captures and subdues the villain single handed"
BOOK NEWS May '01
Kate-"another recruit to the ever-growing ranks of
heroines in boy's clothes" brave, high-spirited girl
full of wit and resource, a spitfire. NYT '01

BROOKS, MARY WALLACE. United States.

001462   A PRODIGAL. Boston: R. G. Badger, 1907
NUC.

Woman redeems alcoholic. 11-9-07 PW

BROSTER, D. K. See BROSTER, DOROTHY KATHLEEN. Also BROSTER,
DOROTHY KATHLEEN AND GERTRUDE WINIFRED TAYLOR.

BROSTER, DOROTHY KATHLEEN. United Kingdom.

001463   SIR ISUMBRAS AT THE FORD. BY D. K.
BROSTER. London: J. Murray, 1918 BMC NUC.

TLS Male hero.
NYT Dec 1 '18 p 530. French Revolution. Fighting.

001464   THE YELLOW POPPY. BY D. K. BROSTER.
London: Duckworth, [1920] NUC BMC. New York: R. M.
McBride, 1922 NUC.

TLS historical, trag. of late summer love.
ATH-Heroine returns to a mansion as caretaker which
she had once been mistress of. Becomes involved in
intrigue over Royalist jewels.

BROSTER, DOROTHY KATHLEEN AND GERTRUDE WINIFRED TAYLOR.

001465   CHANTEMERLE: A ROMANCE OF THE VENDEAN
WAR. BY D. K. BROSTER AND G. W. TAYLOR. London: J.
Murray, 1911 NUC BMC. New York: Brentano's, 1911 NUC.

Historical romance-France- Revolution

001466   THE VISION SPLENDID. BY D. K. BROSTER AND
G. W. TAYLOR. London: J. Murray, 1913 NUC BMC. New
York: Brentano's, 1914 NUC.

Daughter of rector marries a French nobleman. They
live in France. There's an English hero who comes
under the influence of the tractarian movement. ATH SR
Concerns religious polemics--Oxford movement. TLS
LBKM-Turn of 19th century, Horatia Grenville, parson's
daughter marries a French count and leads an unhappy
life in Paris.

BROTHERHOOD, MAY A.

001467   CAVERTON MANOR; OR FORESHADOWED. London:
W. H. Allen, 1893 BMC.

"Diana Ashton-who, like her ancient namesake-was fond
of the chase." ACAD 43:171.

001468   THREE MIDSUMMER DAYS. BY M. A. B.
Westminster: Printed For Private Circulation, 1891
BMC.

BROUGHTON, IDA MAY (LINKINS). B. 1863. United States.

001469   A MODERN BECKY SHARP. BY MAY LINCOLN.
Boston: R. G. Badger, [c1916] NUC.

Young woman's adventure in Japan. BKM

BROUGHTON, RHODA. 1840-1920. United Kingdom.

001470   A BEGINNER; A NOVEL. New York: D.
Appleton, 1894 NUC. London: R. Bentley, 1894 BMC.

SR 77:477. Emma Jocelyn writes a novel treating the
interaction of the passions. When published, has an
adverse effect on her family. Then the reviewers kill
it. She enters an innocent flirtation with the first
literary man she has ever met, Edgar Hatcheson. Her
novel, finally, is recalled.
ATH 103:574. Lesbia is a fiol to Emma's staidness. She
is a frisky matron.
LW 25:139. She becomes a wife instead of a novelist.
PW-seldom entertains literary people.

001471   BETWEEN TWO STOOLS. Leipzig: B.
Tauchnitz, 1912 NUC. London: S. Paul, [1912] NUC BMC.

TLS- invalid husband, wife bound to his couch and
intimate friend. daughter discovers?
ATH-mild wife bullied by invalid husband, her lover
proposes to someone else on day her husband dies
daughter an unpleasant child.
SP-nothing much here. They both suffer from guilt
endlessly.
LBKM-The compassionate portrait of patient wife who
has been worn down by harshness of husband, watched by
a precocious daughter and fearful of being betrayed by
her, finds herself drifting into love with friend of
husband whom she had formerly disliked until husband
compelled her to tolerate him. They just acknowledge
their love for each other, she almost drives him to a
charming woman, but all ends well.

001472   CONCERNING A VOW. London: S. Paul, 1914
BMC NUC. Leipzig: B. Tauchnitz, 1914 NUC.

ACAD 87:263. Sally vowed to her dying sister she would
never have anything to do with Edward, who had jilted
them both. She finally broke it, made her husband's
life miserable, and committed suicide.
TLS 13:370 She doesn't really break it, she lives with
him without marriage.

001473   DEAR FAUSTINA; A NOVEL. New York: D.
Appleton, 1897 NUC. London: R. Bentley, 1897 BMC.

The present tense, wit, farcical trag. William and
Clare; the society girl 6 ft tall who wants to do
social work. SR 84:46.
She's the adventuress "up to date", energetic, of
quick intellect. Althea follows her to the slums, but
finds Faustina is not the woman she believed in. LBKM
12:74.
Faustina Bateson seeks personal glory through

71

exploiting "gospel of humanity" She revolted vs domesticity "joined the extreme left wing of the emancipation mvt. and by virtue of her vulgar tongue and facile pen, her tireless energy and indomitable self-assertion, has won for herslf a prominent position in the ranks of professional philanthropists." Recruits young society women like Althea Vane who though she becomes disillusioned with Faustina's methods, her insincerity and lies, does meet women in like work who are the best models and she herself becomes one. SP ;78:771.

001474   THE DEVIL AND THE DEEP BLUE SEA. London:
Macmillan, 1910 BMC NUC. Leipzig: Tauchnitz, 1910 NUC.

SR.-man and woman meet at hotel, he was crippled. Fall
for each other, but he is identified as an ex-footman
and he flees. Comes back and she discovers he is a
blackguard. He asks to marry her-whether she does
(since each was friendless) is left unanswered.
TLS--O.
LBKM--O

001475   FOES IN LAW. London: Macmillan, 1900 BMC.
New York: Macmillan, 1900 NUC.

SP 85:891. Letitia refuses suit of curate believing
her brother needs her. He marries, she acccepts curate
who falls in love with brother's wife. Eventually her
eyes are opened.
ATH 116:819. Their home invaded by in-laws, trying but
happy-go-lucky.

001476   A FOOL IN HER FOLLY. London: Odhams
Press, [1920] BMC NUC.

Heroine sets out to write novel that shall reveal for
the first time what it is to love without knowing
anything herself.
SP From the 90's onward RB's stories are studies in
disillusionment. Autobiographic, premature efforts at
authorship, then attempt to translate theories into
fact, is deceived and disillusioned, resigns literary
ambtions and marries commonplace husband, then returns
home with her youth shattered.
ATH-Seems to spend next 60 years repenting-for what?
Victorian

001477   THE GAME AND THE CANDLE. London:
Macmillan, 1899 NUC. New York: D. Appleton, 1899 NUC.

No happy ending. Young woman and man seemingly ready
to marry and live happily, argue when she discovers
him kissing another woman. LIT 4:556
Jane Etheredge weds an exacting, highly educated rich
man when she leaves school. He's 30 years older. It's
a loveless marriage. And when he dies tries to get her
to promise not to wed Miles, a man she was earlier
attracted to. She refuses; he leaves his money to his
sister. She spends much time hoping Miles will come
back to her life and when he does, discovers he's just
a flirt unworthy of her. The novel ends there SP
82:560
Jane barely 17 marries an old rich famous scientist
though she loves John Miles. On his death she must
promise not to marry John or her husband will leave
her penniless. (Married 8 years.) She refuses. Then a
year later, John returns from travels. She scrutinizes
him and her idol is shattered. Realizes his physical
beauty was all. Left inconclusive. "You may work out
your own conclusions as you please." NYT 8-12-99, 535
"A somewhat cynical story of a woman's passion and
disillusionment...characters drawn with candor and
effervescent satire." BAKER 03,82

001478   LAVINIA. London and New York: Macmillan,
1902 NUC BMC.

ATH 11-22-02 "son's sympathy and tact in dealing with
his troublesome father are in consonance with his
feminine character, which is perhaps the most original
in the book"

001479   MAMMA. London: Macmillan, 1908 NUC BMC.
Leipzig: B. Tauchnitz, 1909 NUC.

ATH-"Granny is our God and Aunt Lucia is the burnt
sacrifice we offer her everyday" Niece attempts to
rescue her from Mamma.

001480   MRS. BLIGH; A NOVEL. London: R. Bentley,
1892 NUC. New York: D. Appleton, 1892 NUC.

ATH 100:660. She is a widow of 29, "self conscious,
cleverish and, though shrewish, not distinctly
uncivil.

SP 69:857. Angular and plain with "great capacity for
enjoying life" and "talent for saying and doing the
right thing in the wrong way or at the wrong time."
SR 74:571. Pamela Capel-Smith worships her, part of
the story describes the rise and fall of this youthful
infatuation; Mrs. Bligh becomes at times "furiously
and obviously jealous" of Pamela who is strong in
qualities lacking in herself. They visit an old school
friend of Mrs. Bligh, who is now married to a
celebrity, a wit. His family are slaves to him, to the
wonderment of Mrs. Bligh and Pamela.

001481   SCYLLA OR CHARYBDIS? London: R. Bentley,
1895 NUC. New York: D. Appleton, 1895 NUC.

Honor Lisle is engaged to Harry Clarence. She's very
unconventional. Then he learns that for generations
insanity in his family has been transmitted from
father to son. Won't marry Honor, but then learns
something "almost more hideous"-that he was illeg. His
pure and saintly mother to whom he was devoted had
been unfaithful. SR 75:771
SR-81:81. Timid and saintly widow and her son. He
falls in love is told by friend of his father's
homicidal Mania (Scylla); is told by nurse he is not
father's son, but is deprived of his mom's reputation
(charybdis). He marries; they are happy.

001482   A THORN IN THE FLESH. London: S. Paul,
[1917] BMC NUC.

A beautiful woman who cannot fall in love; young
soldier despairs of her cold aloofness. Hearing he's
missing does it. At this moment in bicycle accident,
face disfigured. What happens? LBKM
Two young men; two old women, two young women-TLS.
their conversations, rudenesses to each other.

001483   A WAIF'S PROGRESS. London: Macmillan,
1905 NUC BMC. New York: Macmillan, 1905 NUC.

heredity of drink, immorality, mother dies of drink at
34. She' well educated in the demi-monde of Paris,
wants to make a place for herself in the right English
society. Innocent in her familiarity with evil; an
actress NYT 759, 05
charming, impulsive, indiscreet, says and does daring
things-treated sympathetically. Disreputable mother,
brought up among outcasts, knows everything, lies
about everything-ACAD 1335, 05
girl, 17, orphan "up" in the ways of the world, wise,
amoral mantra in the end-to old widower. ATH 05, 504.
created havoc in the "straight-laced family"

BROUGHTON, RHODA AND ELIZABETH (BISLAND) WETMORE.

001484   A WIDOWER INDEED. BY RHODA BROUGHTON AND
ELIZABETH BISLAND. New York: D. Appleton, 1891 NUC.
London: J. R. Osgood, McIlvaine, 1891 NUC BMC.

Dull and dreary. Widower Edward Lygon is very
helpless, fretful-an unattractive person. Georgia
Wrenn is lively. ATH 98 798.
Oxford is the scene. Bursar loses young wife; he's
left with children. Georgia's efforts to console him
end drastically. PW
CR 17:182. He is desolate at wife's death, falls
victim to scheming mother and is married to daughter
within the year, with disastrous results.
LW 23:58. He is college bursar at Oxford is persecuted
by gossips and other women wishing to marry him. He is
tricked into a marriage against his will, "dies raving
mad three days later."
ACAD 41:10. Harrowing and unnatural conclusion.

BROWER, LORRAINE CATLIN. United States.

001485   THE VALE OF ILLUSION. Chicago: Reilly and
Britton, [1915] NUC.

Eleanor rejects one man to marry Paul; after 3 years
the woman he wronged turns up; the couple separates:
Eleanor falls in love with someone else; Fate brings
husband and wife together when he's fighting a drug
habit. PW 4-17-15
equal std. of morality between sexes. Woman refuses
first man because he had previous lover. Takes another
thinking he's pure; woman from his past with his
childshows up. They separate, she travels, falls in
love with another man. They come together, live for
months as friends. April the Book Rev. PW
NYT age old problem of double standard of morals and
how 1 woman solved it without prejudice to either sex.

BROWN, ALICE. 1857-1948. United States.

72

001486   THE BLACK DROP. New York: Macmillan, 1919
NUC.

story of a scheming man the one "bad" member of an
otherwise "normal" family. PW
BKM-melodrama German spy.

001487   BROMLEY NEIGHBORHOOD. New York:
Macmillan, 1917 BMC NUC.

Ellen Brock shrinks from lovemaking but marries;
learns later her childhood friend really loves her and
that she loves him. She leaves her husband and gives
herself to war relief work. PW
Mary Neale-another strong woman BKM
Mother of grown sons, she's dignified, handsome. Meant
to be a giving person, but "cramped and thrown back
into herself" by her narrow, cold husband. At times
she rebels but can't take action. NYT

001488   THE COURT OF LOVE. Boston: Houghton,
Mifflin, 1906 NUC.

"A wealthy woman adopts an unusual manner of spending
her money. Every one who comes to her home gets what
they most desire, if money can buy it. All are placed
on the same level and no questions are asked. This
arrangement gives the impression that it is an insane
asylum, and the name given to it by the neighbourhood
is "madhouse." A light plot runs through the story.
BKM v.24, 1906-7.

001489   THE DAY OF HIS YOUTH. Boston and New
York: Houghton, Mifflin, 1897 NUC.

Man stricken with grief at death of wife, raises his
son in isolated country setting, seeing no one for
years. The boy matures. A camping party comes "She" is
among them. The rest in form of letters between them.
He's a simple child of nature; she's the woman of the
world-Hard, disillusioned. CR 26,30:317 Reversal of
roles.
Young man raised in wilderness is "an absolutely
genuine" person. Meets a woman who is a cynic-who does
not believe his pronouncement of eternal love. He
follows after her. Ends in trag. for him. NYT
8-28-97,8.

001490   JOHN WINTERBOURNE'S FAMILY. Boston:
Houghton Mifflin, 1910 BMC NUC.

ACAD-story of a family. Adopted daughter cannot be
made into a "lady" takes command. One of the mothers
is a suffragist.
"well sugared" story of likeable people, one a
level-headed girl" who does things instead of talking"
PW
NYT

001491   JUDGMENT, A NOVEL. New York and London:
Harper, 1903 NUC BMC.

woman more delicate of thought loves husband but finds
him unbending, tyrannical; step-mother: visionary,
political step-daughter clearheaded, efficient. BKM 18
(1903) 302-3
second wife gets close to her husband's children;
makes him see he's a tyrant; she almost sacrifices her
life for one of the daughters. PW 10-3-03
mother of "wronged" daughter avenges her by telling
Rosamund of the affair. Rosamund is engaged to the man
who did the wrong. But Rosamund not bothered much by
the news; triumph of truth and love over everything.
NYT 03, 745.
Sympathetic picture of hyper-sensitive woman; story of
a wrong done by a man, some love letters a
black-mailing mother. the fiance learns of the
wrong-shocked that he "bruised the thing he should
have cherished" story ends on that note.

001492   KING'S END. Westminister: A. Constable,
1901 BMC. Boston: Houghton, Mifflin, 1901 NUC.

father steals his illegitimate baby from its
grandmother, his experiments in feeding & rasing the c
hild. WOMAN'S JOURNAL 3-23-01, 91
Julia is an interesting strong woman LBKM 8-01 $BKM 13
(1901) 287-8.
conflict between love and a "call" BOOK NEWS 4-01
NYT '01 Huldy is coy, provoking-once betrothed "she
thinks his thoughts and makes a god of him"
rejects her persistent lover to go off preaching with
a half-crazed evangelist PW 3-23-01.

001493   THE MANNERINGS. Boston: Houghton,
Mifflin, 1903 NUC. London: E. Nash, 1903 BMC.

unconventional country life 4-4-03 PW
wife about to leave her husband-ACAD 64, 578.
Strong, capable, childless wife yoked to a selfish
dullard who publishes anonymously a story written by
his wife-the story she meant for him alone explaining
the reasons for her attitude of revolt. ACAD 634.
set of young people, so hungry for sensation and
exper. and their foils, the old feeble characters. TLS
193, 03

001494   MARGART WARRENER. Boston: Houghton,
Mifflin, 1901 NUC.

Group of workers live together in Boston-artists
writers-modern intellectuals. Marg. loses husband's
love to another woman, sees his weaknesses, left a
widow. Laura-the Titaness, heartless, grim, vampire
with "the brain of a man," her virtue is her
fellowship, her "vice is absolute selfishness and love
of the game"; two singers, one actress, one journalist
who gambles. Husband loses his talent as wife gets
stronger in her art; he fails. A masterpiece NYT.

001495   THE MERRYLINKS. New York: McClure,
Phillips, 1903 NUC.

001496   MY LOVE AND I. BY MARTIN REDFIELD. New
York: Macmillan, 1912 NUC. London: Constable, 1912
BMC.

NYT-love story, male narrator.
BKM 40 1914-15 Martin discovers his wife's bankbook
contains an amount of money not possible on his
income.He wants to kill her, but forbears. His sober
second thoughts save his wife from open disgrace, his
son from a motherless childhood. Years later, as book
closes, he looks over the head of his happy son at the
pale, sad-faced, prematurely aged wife, and feels that
although she has thrown away his "man's love for a
woman," he should give her compassion. He muust try
harder. Adjustment in marriage; husband finds wife has
a big bank account (not his). All worked out so that
husband doesn't kill the man, woman not disgraced,
child not left motherless. BKM
PW--triangle.
SP--0

001497   PARADISE. Boston: Houghton, Mifflin, 1905
NUC. London: A. Constable, 1905 BMC.

Barbara an ex palmist in a circus PW 11-4-05
Husbands and wives imprisoned in marriage many odd
characters N YT 676, 05
tender, humorous story of a village. ACAD 1365, 05
ATH-village life,

001498   THE PRISONER. New York: Macmillan, 1916
BMC NUC.

wife repudiates reformed prisoner but step-sister
keeps him. PW
NYT-2 of them. He is hero of book
ATH-deals with social unrest, politics, self
sacrifice.
SP. His wife Esther lives with grand mother who has
friend (fem) who is a humorous harpy. His sister Lydia
is intensely human. I think harpy gets involved with
Addington's politics.
BKM. His wife has a harpy aunt, Mme. Beatrice who owns
a priceless necklace which Esther has stolen from her.
It can't be pawned or sold (gift from royalty) so Mme.
Beatrice blackmails husband who embezzles and is
caught. They all are prisoners of necklace.

001499   ROBIN HOOD'S BARN. New York: Macmillan,
1913 NUC.

PW 84 10-18-17 1285. "Alarie Stayson has just
completed a biography of Speed, a succeeful writer,
and while the work is good, there is something
missing. Then a girl comes to him to ask him to write
her father's life, he refuses, but through her
stumbles upon the key to his mystery, finds the
meaning of Speed's references in some letters to Robin
Hood's Barn, and is the means of the fulfilling of a
beautiful dream."

001500   ROSE MACLEOD. Boston and London:
Houghton, Mifflin, 1908 NUC BMC. London: A. Constable,
1908.

BKM 27 1908 "frisky old lady" (widow) with "absurd
lack of principles" (memoirs are a fake), novelist,
talented young woman. Electra is hopelessly normal.
ACAD-to marry Rose to Osmond is to spoil an otherwise

irreproachable novel.
SP-Grandmother is real focal point of story

001501   THE SECRET OF THE CLAN. New York:
Macmillan, 1912 NUC. London: Constable, 1913 BMC.

001502   THE STORY OF THYRZA. London: A.
Constable, 1909 BMC. Boston and London: Houghton
Mifflin, 1909 BMC NUC.

Single parent-the father of the child marries her
sister. Girl of emotion and imaginative nature BKM.
V29, 1909.
Her lover marries her sister, Thyrza has a child, sews
to educate him. when she meets a man she loves who
loves and wishes to marry her, she won't name father
of her child for her sister's sake. She remains single
rather than bring suspicion. BKM
"girl...with an ambitious thirst for knowledge" R OF R
June, 1909.
girl wants to play piano, take a lover, be part of
great world. She yields to Andy who marries her
sister, bears a child whose upbringing is her comfort
and pain. ACAD
unwed mother single parent gives child college
education. Sympathetic portrayal Angelica "an up to
date 20th century large hearted large minded woman"
WOMAN'S JOURNAL 5-8-09.

001503   THE WIND BETWEEN THE WORLDS. New York:
Macmillan, 1920 NUC BMC. London: E. Nash, 1921 BMC.

TLS Olympium-to communicate with departed spirits Gill
lies to help father.
PW-question of life after death & communication with
the dead.
NYT 1920:15 Novel is concerned with mourning after
death. Two families are involved, the Doves and the
Harveys; various members of both families represent
multiple points of view. Rev. (Louise Field) believes
author's own point of view is given to Mme. Brooke, a
woman of 80 "physically active and with a mind 'like a
sharp-edged sword,'" the "real heroine of the book."
She believes psychic research dangerous to the
individual. Her daughter becomes oblivious to rest of
family (including husband) in effort to communicate
with son killed in war. Andrea Dove's father, a
scientist, is experimenting with the substance
"Olympium," loses his mind finally.

BROWN, ANNA ROBESON. See BURR, ANNA ROBESON (BROWN).

BROWN, ANNIE G. United States.

001504   FIRESIDE BATTLES: A STORY. Chicago: Laird
and Lee, [1900] NUC.

PW Struggles of "thoughtless but lovable" mother and
daughter in overcoming poverty, ill-will, and
discouragement after death of father. South.

BROWN, CAROLINE, pseud. See KROUT, CAROLINE VIRGINIA.

BROWN, DEMETRA (VAKA). 1877-1946. United States.

001505   A CHILD OF THE ORIENT. BY DEMETRA VAKA
(MRS. KENNETH-BROWN). Boston: Houghton Mifflin, 1914
NUC.

001506   THE GRASP OF THE SULTAN. Boston: Houghton
Mifflin, 1916 NUC. London: Cassell, 1917 BMC.

young Englishman, teaches in harem in Turkey-guided by
rule that he shouldn't teach them too much.
Young woman hates the Sultan TLS
Beautiful harem Greek girl defies the Sultan who
strives to take her son away. She manages to recover
her child, falls in love with English tutor Sultan
employs plots & hair breath escape follow. PW
But tutor is hero. NyT

001507   HAREMLIK; SOME PAGES FROM THE LIFE OF
TURKISH WOMEN. BY DEMETRA VAKA (MRS. KENNETH-BROWN).
Boston: Houghton Mifflin, 1909 NUC. London: Constable,
1909 NUC. (British ed. omits Haremlik from title.)

How women of polygamous Turks live in the seclusion of
their harems. 10 typical episodes "based on fact". NYT

001508   IN THE SHADOW OF ISLAM. BY DEMETRA VAKA
(MRS. KENNETH-BROWN). London: Constable, 1911 BMC.
Boston: Houghton Mifflin, 1911 NUC.

American girl gets abducted in Turkey. TLS
American girl visits Turkey with the idea of uplifting
Turkish women and has many adventures. ATH

grad of Radcliffe. NYT
SP-Millicent Grey, an American girl goes to
Contantinople convinced woman must be brought out of
above shadow. She meets a Turk and finds, to her
wrath, that she can hardly resist him. Becomes friends
with young Greek woman and as story progresses comes
to realize that in spite of Turk's memory of wrongs
that the women of his race have suffered, he is unable
to share his rights as a male with women.
Radcliffe grad in Constantinople "study of cleavage of
races, part played by race in arousing and stifling
woman's love". PW 10-14-11.

BROWN, EDNA ADELAIDE. 1875-1944. United States.

001509   RAINBOW ISLAND. Boston: Lothrop, Lee &
Shepard, [1919] NUC.

Young people's story. PW

001510   THE SPANISH CHEST. Boston: Lothrop, Lee &
Shepard, [1917] NUC.

About a MS concerning a treasure. PW

001511   THAT AFFAIR AT ST. PETER'S. Boston:
Lothrop, Lee & Shepard, [c1920] NUC.

PW-mystery story in which silver disappears in church.

BROWN, HELEN DAWES. 1857-1941. United States.

001512   A CIVILIAN ATTACHE: A STORY OF A FRONTIER
ARMY POST. New York: C. Scribner's Sons, 1899 NUC.

Title refers to young woman from the east who spends a
summer with her friend whose husband is an army
officer. She finds love .Climax comes when her train
involved in Pullman Strike and her fiance is heroic.
PW 55:772

001513   HER SIXTEENTH YEAR. Boston: Houghton,
Mifflin, 1901 NUC.

"autobiography of a bright young girl" from age 7 till
she arrives at Harvard "cheerful, helpful, gracious,
personality" WOMAN'S JOURNAL, 11-16-01.

001514   HOW PHOEBE FOUND HERSELF. Boston:
Houghton Mifflin, 1912 NUC.

001515   MR. TUCKERMAN'S NIECES. London: A.
Constable, 1908 BMC. Boston: Houghton Mifflin, 1908
NUC BMC.

TLS-pleasing and sympathetic picture of American
girlhood.
NYT-3 orphans go to live with bachelor uncle.
pleasant, lovely girls
bachelor becomes ward to 3 girls PW 11-2-07

001516   ORPHANS. Boston: Houghton Mifflin, 1911
NUC.

effect of divorce on child.

001517   THE PETRIE ESTATE. Boston and New York:
Houghton, Mifflin, 1893 NUC.

SP: conscientious young woman comes into property
largely consisting of houses in New York, which it was
no credit to possess.
ACAD 45:54. She is "head assistant mistress of the
Mill Hill Seminary, and a girl of high aspiratons."
Minor characters include Mrs. Bisbee, an
"unconventional Shakespaere philosopher," and Miss
Devine, the "society elocutionist."
Heroine uses her wealth to improve New York slums. ATH
102:344
Turns on a lost will. Miss Coverdale enjoys the estate
for a while. She represents the highest ideal of
modern woman-the best of man and woman is contained in
her. "It is our unbiased opinion that no living woman
has yet reached Miss Coverdale's height, but we have
little doubt that if all women keep on shouting, some
one athletic woman will get there some day, then
immediately and gladly die."
She's a teacher, institutes many reforms on the
estate. PW 10-7-93

BROWN, JANET.

001518   AILLIE'S PRAYER. Edinburgh: Oliphant,
Anderson and Ferrier, [1892] BMC.

001519   ELEANOR'S DISCIPLINE. Edinburgh and

London: Oliphant, Anderson and Ferrier, 1892 BMC.

ACAD. Rural life in Scotland.

BROWN, KATE CLARK. United States.

001520   BEAUTY FOR ASHES. Boston: Arena, 1895
NUC.

Story of a marriage in which the theory of
reincarnation is worked out. PW 12-21-95:1177

BROWN, KATHARINE HOLLAND. D. 1931. United States.

001521   DAWN. New York: T. Y. Crowell, [c1907]
NUC.

BRD 1907 P. 54 "An overworked surgeon goes to the
northern wild to rest and to avert a nervous
breakdown. While there the miracle of restoration is
wrought thru a night of service to a woman whose life
he fought for and won."

001522   DIANE. A ROMANCE OF THE ICARIAN
SETTLEMENT OF THE MISSISSIPPI RIVER. New York and
London: Doubleday, Page, 1904 BMC NUC. London: W.
Heinemann, 1905 BMC NUC.

Story of a socialist commune, of issues of abolition
not much said about Diane. ACAD 128, 05
Diane a "taking little lady" winsome ATH 237, 05
PW Story of Fr. Communists
NYT Conv.

001523   THE HALLOWELL PARTNERSHIP. New York: C.
Scribner's Sons, 1912 NUC.

PW-brother and sister
"The story of a partnership between a brother and
sister. Marian Hallowell, a Wellesley girl obliged to
give up college work after a serious illness, is
persuaded much against her will to accompany her
brother to Illinois where he is sent as assistant
engineer on a big drainage contract. The girl is
spoiled and selfish and overfond of luxury, but when
she comes face to face with hardships she shows what
is in her, becomes in truth a partner to her brother,
and helps him to swing his big contract successfully."
BRD
"A pleasant story, with good local color but no love
interest." ALA BKL 9:208 Ja '13

001524   THE MESSENGER. New York: Scribner's Sons,
1910 NUC.

"A story of how one woman who had suffered became thru
her splendid faith the bearer of hope and comfort to
another." BKM v31, 1910
NYT young widow is comforted by Irishwoman who tells
how she was comforted during loss of her husband by
kind words of MD who turns out to be widow's husband.

001525   PHILLIPA AT HALCYON. New York: C.
Scribner's Sons, 1910 NUC.

"Wholesome view of college life for girls and its
benefits." The plans and ambitions of "natural,
healthy lovely girls" PW
NYT for girls, sane and wholesome feminine

001526   UNCERTAIN IRENE. New York: Duffield, 1911
NUC.

Couple, both in business are business enemies; parents
object to the match, send her abroad with woman
Professor Irene (brilliant) whose wooing by a lover of
her young days involves her knocking him down; ducking
him, having him arrested, shooting him. PW 11-11-11.
Diary, two women on a tour of the Mediterranian. Irene
Kemper Bradbury seeks to forget a love affair. Turns
to study archeology. Philura, Her companion tells the
story.

001527   WHITE ROSES. New York: Duffield, 1910
NUC.

Corinna Curtis "absolutely bewitching" has every man
within 60 miles in love with her PW
NYT gives some of the results of her studies of the
racial problem along the Mexican border.
An idyll. Corinna Curtis has no inclination to accept
any of her suitors, moves to railroad site with cousin
and his wife. Here she meets a rustic hero El Amigo
who sends her white roses periodically. Meantime she
gives up all others for her memory of him. All ends
well. BKM

Lovers galore, all rich ones NYT

BROWN, LILIAN KATE ROWLAND. 1863-1959. United Kingdom.

001528   THE CRAFTSMAN. BY ROWLAND GREY. London:
Ward and Lock, [1897] BMC.

All characters are writers or actors. Novel begins
with the failure of Markham Le Mesurier's play and
closes with a success and his happy marriage to Melita
Frayne. He is contrasted to a more frivolous
playwright-Hawtrey Sharron. ACAD 52. Fict Sup. 27.
SP 80:149. The failure of Hawtrey Sharron. The world
of the theatre.
LIT 2:325 Comparison a good man (failure) and worldly
man (success).

001529   GREEN CLIFFS: A SUMMER LOVE STORY. BY
ROWLAND GREY. London: Hutchinson, 1905 BMC.

001530   LA BELLE ALLIANCE. BY ROWLAND GREY.
London: Smith, Elder, 1915 BMC.

001531   MYSELF WHEN YOUNG. BY ROWLAND GREY.
London: Ward, Lock, [1902] BMC.

001532   THE POWER OF THE DOG. BY ROWLAND GREY.
New York: International News, 1896 NUC. London:
Jarrold, 1896 BMC.

SR-Story of a beautiful bored woman and artist who is
painting her but cares only for art.
ATH-Author typifies high principle, early Victorian
sentiment, and innocent romance. The affair is
prevented by interruption of a dog.
ACAD 50:29. He dies of hydrophobia.

001533   THE STORY OF CHRIS. BY ROWLAND GREY.
AUTHOR OF "IN SUNNY SWITZERLAND," "BY VIRTUE OF HIS
OFFICE," "LINDENBLUMEN," "JACOB'S LETTER". London:
Methuen, 1892 NUC BMC.

SP 69:966 "record of one episode in the life of a
really interesting woman"
ACAD 41:226 =The girl journalist, whose single romance
is robbed by fate of its ordinary fulfillment, is one
of the freshest and most charming of recent heroines;
and among many other things for which she deserves to
be thanked Rowland Grey deserves the gratitude of all
sensible readers for doing what in her lies to dispose
of the sentimental fiction that if a woman cannot
marry the man she loves, her life must either end or
be spoiled." (James Ashcroft Noble, Academy)

001534   SURRENDER. BY ROWLAND GREY. London:
Hutchinson, 1909 BMC.

001535   THE UNEXPECTED. BY ROWLAND GREY. London:
Ward, Lock, 1902 BMC.

BROWN, LOUISE.

001536   PAUL STRANGE. A NOVEL. London: Hodder &
Stoughton, 1917 BMC.

Career of a man with devoted mother, two women in his
life. TLS

BROWN, MARY JOSEPHINE. 1875-1912.

001537   THE GIRLHOOD OF OUR LADY. BY MARION J.
BRUNOWE. New York: Cathedral Lib., [c1903] NUC.

BROWN, MRS. KENNETH. See BROWN, DEMETRA (VAKA).

BROWN, NANCY KEEN.

001538   A BROKEN BONDAGE. Boston: Roxburgh,
[c1911] NUC.

So. rom. complete with villain. PW 9-9-11

BROWNE, ALICE (HARRIMAN). 1861-1925. United States.

001539   CHAPERONING ADRIENNE; A TALE OF THE
YELLOWSTONE NATIONAL PARK. Seattle: Metropolitan
Press, [c1907] NUC.

Nice little story about a widow and girl who take a
trip through Yellowstone. Both end up wedded. PW
10-5-07

001540   A MAN OF TWO COUNTRIES. BY ALICE
HARRIMAN. New York: A. Harriman, 1910 NUC.

Englishman in Montana. PW

001541   SONGS O´ THE OLYMPICS. Seattle: Alice
Harriman, 1909 NUC.

BROWNE, ALICE M.

001542   THE RECTOR OF AMESTY. BY A NOVEL. JOHN
RYCE. London: S. Lane, 1891 BMC. London: S. Low,
Marston, 1891 NUC.

BROWNE, ISABEL.

001543   THE LIFE STORY AND STRANGE ADVENTURES OF
MARAQUITA DE SOLIS. London: Drane´s, [1914] BMC.

ATH-Half Spanish heroine returns to mother´s family in
England after father dies. Becomes victim of plots and
intrigues, marries the son of a neighbor.

BROWNE, LIDA BRIGGS.

001544   WORDS THAT BURN: A ROMANCE. Utica, N.Y.:
Daniel B. Briggs, 1900 NUC.

LW 31:266. Author´s portrait on title page.
PW-story of home life, love and marriage. English girl
of noble birth marries American against father´s
wishes. Husband prospers, their "handsome home in
American suburban town."

BROWNE, MARY. 1807-1833.

001545   THE DIARY OF A GIRL IN FRANCE IN 1821.
London: J. Murray, 1905 BMC. New York: E. P. Dutton,
1905 NUC.

14 yr old English girl spent summer in France in
1821-France seen through child´s eyes.

BROWNE, MRS. W. P.

001546   TRAGEDY AND TRIFLE. London: B. Johnson
and Ince, 1905 BMC.

Hurried into marriage to a middle-aged vicar she
almost disliked to save her father´s life. An
apparition saves her! ACAD 544,05

BROWNE, ROSALIND DENIS.

001547   THE FIRE OF HEAVEN. London: Simpkin,
Marshall, [1913] BMC.

Diary of young woman engaged to curate, falls in love
with musician; "safe" for young readers. ATH

BROWNE, ROSE.

001548   THE COMPLICATIONS AT COLLAROI. BY ROSE
BOLDREWOOD. London: J. Ouseley, 1911 BMC NUC.

Fresh love tale. TLS ATH

BROWNE, T. M.   See BROWNE, TRYPHENA MATILDA (ARCHER).

BROWNE, TRYPHENA MATILDA (ARCHER). 1837-1933. United
States.

001549   CLAIR; OR A HUNDRED YEARS AGO. London: S.
W. Partridge, [1896] BMC.

001550   DAWSON´S MADGE; OR THE POACHER´S
DAUGHTER. London: S.W. partridge, [1892] BMC.

001551   GERALD THURLOW; OR, THE NEW MARSHAL; A
STORY OF CALIFORNIA. London: S. W. Partridge, [1896]
BMC.

SP 77:525. Life in California. Wholesome, not
sensational.

001552   JIM´S DISCOVERY; OR, ON THE EDGE OF A
DESERT. London: S. W. Partridge, [1895] BMC.

001553   UNDER THE LIVE OAKS. BY T. M. BROWNE. New
York: T. Whittaker, 1893 NUC. Edinburgh & London:
Oliphant, Anderson and Ferrier, 1894 BMC.

ACAD 45:532. California pure and moral without being
goody-goody. Showing the good which may be
accomplished in her own sphere by even one young girl.

BROWNELL, ANNA GERTRUDE (HALL). B. 1863. United States.

001554   APRIL´S SOWING. BY GERTRUDE HALL. London:
McClure, Phillips, 1900 BMC. New York: McClure,
Phillips, 1900 NUC.

not helpful. BKM 1901 (13) 616
Delightful flirt, pays for her fun by almost losing
her man, Nellie discovers the state of her heart in
time. (?)CR ´01
PW-study in the education of American girls. Spoiled
and petted heroine did not want her mid-west lover.
Later she went to Germany to study music, learning
much from a Dresden hausfrau. Woman painter brings
lovers together.

001555   AURORA THE MAGNIFICENT. BY GERTRUDE HALL.
New York: Century, 1917 BMC NUC.

"Plot revolves around Aurora´s identity...and the way
she is...more than a friend to Gerald Fane" PW 91:1018
3/24/17.
crude upbringing, impossible manners; bursts upon
Florentine high society. She´s a philistine, newly
rich, but she´s magnificent in heart. Mrs. Aurora
Hawthorne was married; it-her marriage-was unhappy.
Her daughters have dragged her name down (?) Finds a
Florentine-american painter to love. BK
Aurora and Estelle Madison go to Florence where they
want "everything"-house, servants, horses, etc. Aurora
is jovial generous very rich. NYT

001556   MISS INGALIS. BY GERTRUDE HALL. New York:
Century, 1918 BMC NUC. London: Skeffington, [1919]
BMC.

PW-Grace tries to earn living painting, meets artist.
Goes on cruise and becomes engaged to Clarence. Stays
with his family and when she decides to leave is held
prisoner. Artist helps her escape.
NYT Sept. 8, 18 p. 378. The Overcome family is
ruthless and rapacious, under their ordinarily good
dispositions and manners. Grace, who has come to stay
with family before her marriage to Clarence, with whom
she is very much in love, is prepared to love family.
But glimpses of the Overcome traits bring out in her a
strength of spirit, steel meeting steel.
Emotional woman smothered by family of her husband-the
Overcomes. She frees herself at last from them and her
husband and "we sympathize warmly with her escape."
TLS

001557   THE TRUTH ABOUT CAMILLA. BY GERTRUDE
HALL. New York: Century, 1913 NUC. London: W.
Heinemann, 1913 BMC.

8 years old to 50. Cold blooded self sufficient,
efficient-admirable. SP
"Story of a fascinating Italian adventuress, daughter
of a peasant woman and a nobleman, educated by her
unacknowledged father, then left to shift for herself.
She is by nature a consummate and dramatic actress and
fabricator, but with a power that brings all men and
most women under the spell of her gifts; and the days
which make her in turn paid companion to a famous
literary woman, a princess, the wife of an opera
singer, a lace-maker, and, finally, a deeply religious
marchioness, are crowded with color and adventure."
Italy as the setting. PW 84 10/18/13:1286.
"Makes up fantastic stories of her birth and
parentage, is, altho she never knows it, the daughter
of an Italian nobleman. Her father provides for her
education, then lets her drift. She is successively a
teacher of languages in a pension, the companion of an
elderly woman novelist, the wife of an opera singer,
proprietor of a lace shop, and finally, as the
Marchesa Filibeti, a grand lady in her own right." BRD
Her governing instinct: to create herself, to make
something of life. This intrepid child of the people
longs for adventure; she has dreams. She has
absolutely no respect for truth. "Phenomenal
concentration on her own interests" but likeable.
Competent, conscientious. fiery emotions. Latin
temperament LBKM
BKM-Daughter of waiting maid to countess. Rumored that
Count Marc is her parent. Priest and she argue with
count and get financial assist. for her education.
Teaches at pitifully small wage for a while, then
becomes companion of New England woman for 7 years.
Rewarded by legacy, she marries a Russian prince and
enjoys society. Past forty, love comes into her life
for 1st time.

001558   THE UNKNOWN QUANTITY. BY GERTRUDE HALL.
New York: Henry Holt, 1910 NUC.

BKM 31, 1910 widow of a husband who believed her
unfaithful involved in divorce suit (but charges
dropped) single parent finds happiness (marriage)
finally.

NYT She has an alcoholic lover with an eccentric mother. Misunderstanding about her past almost causes loss of her lover.

BROWNELL, ELIZABETH B.

001559   REALLY BABIES. Chicago: [c1908] NUC.

BRUCE, ANDASIA KIMBROUGH. B. 1868. United States.

001560   UNCLE TOM'S CABIN OF TODAY. BY MRS. WILLIAM LIDDELL BRUCE. New York: Neale, 1906 NUC.

BRUCE, CORINNA.

001561   ALL IN ALL. London: Hurst and Blackett, 1897 BMC.

"On the old lines of multiple marriage and heirs in the background." Melo. ATH:109:413.

001562   THROUGH HER. A NOVEL. London: H.J. Drane, [1913] BMC.

Beautiful, selfish woman learns father is in a lunatic asylum; mother dies, she moves to London, takes an Irish woman (a psalmist) to live with her. They love the same man. Disaster follows. ATH

BRUCE, MARY (GRANT).

001563   CAPTAIN JIM. London: Ward, Lock, 1919 BMC.

001564   DICK. London: Ward, Lock, 1918 BMC.

001565   DICK LESTER OF KURRAJONG. London and Melbourne: Ward, Lock, 1920 BMC.

001566   FROM BILLABONG TO LONDON. London: Ward, Lock, 1915 BMC.

001567   GLEN EYRE. London: Ward, Lock, 1912 BMC.

001568   GRAY'S HOLLOW. London: Ward, Lock, 1914 BMC.

001569   JIM AND WALLY. London: Ward, Lock, 1916 BMC NUC.

001570   A LITTLE BUSH MAID. London: Ward, Lock, 1910 BMC.

001571   NORAH OF BILLABONG. London: Ward, Lock, 1913 BMC.

001572   'POSSUM. London: Ward, Lock, 1917 BMC.

001573   TIMOTHY IN BUSHLAND. London: Ward, Lock, 1912 BMC.

BRUCE, MRS. WILLIAM LIDDELL. See BRUCE, ANDASIA KIMBROUGH.

BRUCE, TYDANCE, pseud. See NEILL, MAIDIE.

BRUERE, MARTHA S. (BENSLEY). B. 1879. United States.

001574   MILDRED CARVER, U.S.A. New York: Macmillan, 1919 NUC.

"Story of the future when young people will be required to give a year's service to their country." Young woman runs a tractor in Minn. with an East Side girl and a Greenwich village girl. PW
The Year is devoted to unskilled labor; young people in city go to work in country and vice versa. Harmony results in these working conditions. Mildred Carver is very rich, from New York family. She and fiance ordered to service. She goes to a flour mill in Minnesota, falls in love, does tractor work. Goes back to society after her year is up; finds life dull. Goes to work in factory-then in steel mill. NYT

BRUGIERE, SARA (VAN BUREN) AND ADELINE BRADY. United States.

001575   THE MAJOR'S NIECE. New York: Abbey Press, [1903] NUC.

BRUNKHURST, HARRIET. United States.

001576   THE WINDOW IN THE FENCE. New York: G. H. Doran, [1916] NUC. London: Hodder & Stoughton, 1916 BMC.

Wife is artist; husband writer, married 15 years.

Their lives are bland-no hope for fame, love has dimmed; then they discover the window in the fence! PW
TLS She is 35
ATH Sent and pathos pleasantly balanced

BRUNNER, ETHEL (HOUSTON). 1877-1926. Nationality Unknown.

001577   CELIA AND HER FRIENDS. London: A. L. Humphreys, 1917 BMC. New York: Macmillan, 1920 PW.

Guests state what they think of each other, Celia told she is too attractive and flirtatious. TLS
PW-Wealthy young woman-advs., whims, conversations, friends.
NYT 3/28/20 p. 2 "Small talk," her male friend is the narrator.

001578   CELIA ONCE AGAIN. London: A. L. Humphreys, 1918 BMC 1919 NUC. New York: Macmillan, 1920 PW.

NYT Frothy account of young wife's activities in London social set.

001579   THE ELOPEMENT; OR CELIA INTERVENES; A COMEDY. London: A. L. Humphreys, 1917 BMC NUC.

BRUNOWE, MARION J., pseud. See BROWN, MARY JOSEPHINE.

BRYAN, ELLA HOWARD.

001580   BEHIND THE VEIL [ANONYMOUS]. Boston: Little, Brown, 1899 W.

Virginia artist marries daughter of poor artist in NYC. Poverty drives him to labor-work. Freezes in street; is unconscious.
Has vision of after-life. PW 56:1152

BRYAN, EMMA LYON. United States.

001581   1860-1865: A ROMANCE OF THE VALLEY OF VIRGINIA. [Harrisonburg, Va.]: [J. Taliaffer], [c1892] NUC.

BRYANT, ANNA (BURNHAM).

001582   THE CHRISTMAS CAT. Boston: Pilgrim Press, [1902] NUC.

BRYANT, EMILY M.

001583   OVER STONY WAYS; A ROMANCE OF TENNYSON-LAND. London: Jarrold, 1904 BMC NUC.

ACAD Five children; one girl becomes a singer, another a minister.

BRYANT, MARGUERITE. See MUNN, MARGUERITE (BRYANT).

BRYANT, ROSE CULLEN. United States.

001584   RUTH ANNE. Philadelphia and London: J. B. Lippincott, 1913 NUC.

PW 84 10/11/13:1141 "Romance of Ruth Anne, sweet and womanly, and Dr. Hollander, a big, magnetic physician. Unconsciously they are drawn together by the similarity of their ideals. Ruth Anne, seeing the glorious possibilities in a life of service, at first takes up nursing as a career and later goes in for settlement work. In all of the scenes and incidents picturing her experiences the author brings us in close touch with a real and varied humanity, but it is the effect which some of the sordid realities of life have upon Ruth Anne that is of interest as we follow the gradual unfolding of her character. Her problems throughout are those which concern the men and women of today."

BRYCE, MRS. CHARLES. Nationality Unknown.

001585   THE ASHIEL MYSTERY. A DETECTIVE STORY. London: J. Lane, 1915 NUC BMC. New York: J. Lane, 1915 NUC BMC.

traditional detective-10-23-15 PW

001586   THE LONG SPOON. London, New York: J. Lane, 1917 NUC BMC.

Lady Averill discovers soon after her marriage that her husband has fits of insanity. After having had many narrow escapes from death at his hands, she comes upon a witch with a cure. Thru the mysteries of necromancy her husband disappears and finally dies. PW

"he meets with a fate that he richly deserves" The
heroine has some startling adventures but ultimately
finds happiness ATH
She visits a witch who can get rid of undesirable
husbands. Thirza is married to a brutish German who
terrorizes her. Two men want to help her. NYT 9-16-17,
349.

001587   MRS. VANDERSTEIN'S JEWELS. New York: J.
Lane, 1914 NUC. London: J. Lane, 1914 BMC.

LBKM. detective story. Widow and her companion
disappear.
ACAD 86:795. Mrs Vanderstein and Miss Turner are
captured and detained. An old lady is buried in a
flower box by a French manicurist. Madame Querterot
impersonates the murdered woman.
ATH-Mrs. V. is murder victim. She is a kindly soul.
"Plot hinges on the mysterious disappearance from
London of Mrs. Vanderstein who wears priceless jewels
and is accompanied by her ward Barbara Turner. The
latter has a fondness for the race track and a lover,
Joe Sidney, in debt and disfavor with his aunt, Mrs.
Vanderstein. A designing French masseuse, her
daughter's suitor who believes wealth is criminal, and
a rejected claimant for Mrs. Vanderstein's hand
complicate the situation."PW

BRYHER, W., pseud. See ELLERMAN, ANNIE WINIFRED.

BUCHAN, ANNA. D. 1948. United Kingdom.

001588   OLIVIA IN INDIA. THE ADVENTURES OF A
CHOTA MISS SAHIB. BY O. DOUGLAS. London, New York:
Hodder and Stoughton, [1913] BMC NUC.

Olivia-knack for making friends, good friends with her
brother. She goes to India to see him, passion for
climbing mountains, Matterhorn. She's very well read,
candid, very appreciative of her own sex. form of
letters to France. She goes away to test her
attachment to him. We see her on the liner, in
Calcutta, in jungle, camping. SP
Real everyday social life in India.

001589   PENNY PLAIN. BY O. DOUGLAS. New York: G.
H. Doran, [c1920] NUC. London: Hodder and Stoughton,
[1920] BMC.

SP-Cranford like village in Scotland. All nice people.
Mrs Hope makes age seem lovely and desirable.
ATH-Heroine Jean Jardine who inherits fortune from
shabby stranger who had been her guest.

001590   THE SETONS. BY O. DOUGLAS. London: Hodder
& Stoughton, [1917] BMC.

family chronicle-happy minister. Son and daughter who
keeps house. TLS

BUCHANAN, EMILY HANDASYDE. B. 1872. United Kingdom.

001591   FOR THE WEEK END. BY HANDASYDE. London:
J. Lane, 1907 BMC NUC.

Three weekends during which Blanche & Mortimer meet.
Blanche is married to easy-going husband. Tragedy
comes (What?) ACAD

001592   A GIRL'S LIFE IN A HUNTING COUNTRY. BY
HANDASYDE. London: J. Lane, 1903 BMC NUC.

Short desc ACAD 69, 366 says little.

001593   THE HEART OF MARLEYBONE. BY HANDASYDE.
London: Hutchinson, 1910 BMC NUC.

TLS-love love love
ATH-love love love

001594   OTHER THINGS THAN LOVE. BY HANDASYDE.
London: Hutchinson, 1909 BMC.

Man whose wife of a year lies dead goes over the dream
and reality of her "with a reeling brain." This is the
prologue. Story involves his later life-politics, his
horses, different women in his life. End not described
by reviewer TLS
ATH The second woman seems to be important in the
story, what is she like?
"Not wholely to our liking" SP

BUCHANAN, MERIEL. See KNOWLING, MERIEL (BUCHANAN).

BUCK, MRS. M. K., jt. au. See BATES, MARTHA E. (CRAM) AND
MRS. M. K. BUCK.

BUCKLEY, EDITH E. United States.

001595   THE SNARE OF CIRCUMSTANCES. Boston:
Little, Brown, 1910 NUC.

Mystery, detective PW
BKM Myst males
NYT myst

BUCKLEY, HARRIET.

001596   LA LECSINKA. London: Digby, Long, [1895]
BMC.

BUCKROSE, J. E., pseud. See JAMESON, ANNIE EDITH (FOSTER).

BUDGETT, FRANCES ELIZABETH JANES. 1873-1928. United
States.

001597   THE FAR TRIUMPH. BY ELIZABETH DEJEANS.
Philadelphia and London: J. B. Lippincott, 1911 BMC
NUC.

Rich man injured in auto accident on wedding day. Told
his lover died. She has a child, tries to see him and
can't; after 3 years they meet. PW 10-21-11

001598   THE HEART OF DESIRE. BY ELIZABETH
DEJEANS. Philadelphia and London: J. B. Lippincott,
1910 BMC NUC.

BKM v. 31 1910-Hildegard Hawthorne very favorable but
does not give plot.
NYT-Kate has had an unhappy 1st marriage then decides
to marry her old friend, fate decides otherwise.
Modern. Her expectations are numerous and
disappointments no less.

001599   THE HOUSE OF THANE. BY ELIZABETH DEJEANS.
Philadelphia and London: J. B. Lippincott, 1913 BMC
NUC.

PW 6-7-13:1004 "Story of a man who married a woman for
whom he felt passion rather than love, while she
married him for what his money could bring of social
position and luxurious living. He helps Mary Kelly, a
lovely young girl, a child of the streets, and in her
finds the affection lacking in his home. Through her
he is saved from his desire to ruin those who stood in
the way of his ambition."
violation of the 7th commandment. ATH
The hero "was very much in need of knowledge of
femininity..." The author "has to deal him some pretty
hard blows before he finally learns anything-about
women..." a self centered, ruthless business man,
dominant in whatever he touches-carries these traits
to his private life (John Thane) His attempts to build
a "house" for sons to come who will inherit his
masterfulness fail. NYT 1913:562.

001600   THE LIFE-BUILDERS. A NOVEL. BY ELIZABETH
DEJEANS. New York and London: Harper, 1915 BMC NUC.

"discussion of which is the more conservative in
marriage, the man or the woman." BKM 4/1915.
woman craves a different kind of life, finds her
husband conv.; leaves him, falls for a married man;
they are entitled to seek happiness together. PW
4-24-15
title refers to ideal relationship between husband and
wife "comradship, mutual understanding and respect,
equal participation in the duties of marriage."
Heroine looks forward to such a marriage, very
disillusioned. Her husband has no patience with her
ideals. But another man does. Story concerns the
working out of this problem. "much psychological study
of motives, purposes and temperaments." modern idea of
marriage is auther's theme; sym. heroine. NYT

001601   THE MORETON MYSTERY. BY ELIZABETH
DEJEANS. Indianapolis: Bobbs-Merrill, [c1920] NUC BMC.

PW-suspicion rests on unconventional adopted daughter
of murdered millionaire
NYT Sept 19, 1920 p. 19 Realistic, U. S. in 1918, but
"nationalism" in a mystery is propaganda out of place.

001602   NOBODY'S CHILD. BY ELIZABETH DEJEANS.
Indianapolis: Bobbs-Merrill, [c1918] BMC NUC.

PW-Ann Pennington's mother died at her birth, her
father abandoned her. She lives in South next door to
Westmores with whom her family has been feuding for
generations, she doesn't know why. Her father hates
her and so does Judith Westmore because Ann attracts

her admirers. After a series of tragedies, it is discovered she is Mr. Westmore's illegitimate. Love story.

001603   THE TIGER'S COAT. BY ELIZABETH DEJEANS. Indianapolis: Bobbs-Merrill, [c1917] NUC. London: T. Butterworh, 1923 BMC.

Mystery of Marie's origin. PW 91:881 3/10/17. She's a refugee from Belgium. Setting is mid-west. She's an actress "with the grace of a tigress and the primitive tastes of a savage." She's mysterious and worldly-This golden woman. NYT. She's a dancer; becomes a successful movie star.

001604   THE WINNING CHANCE. BY ELIZABETH DEJEANS. Philadelphia and London: J. B. Lippincott, 1909 NUC. London: J. Milne, 1909 BMC.

"Mrs. Dejeans novel...has for its theme the big problem of the American girl who enters upon a business career" BKM v. 29 1909.
"The problem of an American girl who enters into a business career" Ad, ARENA 1909.
Janet supports blind mother and lame brother; stenographer; for money becomes mistress of her boss. When he wants to marry her, she turns him down-has fallen for a friend of the past. Character development-true artistry. PW.

BUEL, ELIZABETH CYNTHIA (BARNEY). 1868-1943.

001605   THE TALE OF THE SPINNING WHEEL. Litchfield, Conn.: 1903 NUC.

BUELL, MARY E. United States.

001606   THE SIXTH SENSE; OR, ELECTRICITY. A STORY FOR THE MASSES. Boston: Colby and Rich, 1891 NUC.

BUERSTENBINDER, ELISABETH. 1838-1918. Germany.

001607   THE ALPINE FAY; A ROMANCE FROM THE GERMAN OF E. WERNER. Philadelphia: J. B. Lippincott, 1897 NUC. (Tr. Mrs. A. L. Wister)

001608   BEACON-FIRES. A NOVEL. BY E. WERNER. London: R. Bentley, 1891 BMC NUC. New York: G. Munro, 1899 NUC. (Translation of Flammenzeichen Munro Ed. Tr. by Mary S. Smith and Gessner H. Smith)

Young man disowned by father, takes mother's name-parents divorced. He becomes a poet-is like his mother by nature. Father a military man. SP 67, 762
Relation of father and son. Father highly disciplined wants son the same. But Hartmut is also his mother's son. She's Roumanian. She's divorced, gets him to leave military school, to defy father. For 10 years a poet; then proves himself in war, reconciled to father. SR 10-3-91, 392.
Relation of father and son. Father highly disciplined wants son the same. But Hartmut is also his mother's son. She gets him to leave military school, to defy father. For 10 years he's a poet, then proves himself in war. Reconciled to father. SR 10-3-91 392
Young man disowned by father, takes mother's name--parents divorced. He becomes a poet-is like his mother by nature. Father a military man. SP 67,762

001609   "CLEAR THE TRACK" (FREIE BACN). A STORY OF TO-DAY. BY E. WERNER. London, New York: International News, [1893] BMC NUC. (Tr. Mary Stuart Smith)

001610   THE MASTER OF ETTERSBERG. BY E. WERNER. New York: Street and Smith, 1891 NUC.

The Count of Ettersberg discovers he's not the true heir to the estate. Story centers on his decision concerning what to do. PW A1

001611   THE NORTHERN LIGHT. BY E. WERNER. New York: R. Bonner, 1891 NUC. (Tr. from the German of E. Werner by Mrs. D. M. Lowrey)

001612   THE PRICE HE PAID. BY E. WERNER. New York: Street & Smith, [1891] NUC.

A love between Gabrielle and a young man very much affected by a feud between her guardian (governor of the province) and a doctor. PW 9-5-91.
German life in official circles. The governor Baron Von Raven, his tragic end.
Two plots--one sweet, one tragic. Merge in Washington. Big Tom W's career and love story. NYT 12-2-99,811
Neighbors in Hamlin County. Fallen factory girl.

Wonderful old maid. Diplomacy and political intrigue involve claim that would reinstate Tom in his birthright. Same, p. 846.
BKM 10:599. Tom de Willoughby is too soft to be doctor his father wanted, too clumsy in society, so patrician hot-headed father throws him out. He goes to little village in N. Carolina, is postmaster. He adopts Margery's illegitimate daughter when she dies. She grows up to have idyllic love. Latimer, Margery's brother, a clergyman, discovers his clergyman friend was Margery's betrayer.
LBKM 17:119. Tom makes good family claim for sake of his young nephew who is marrying his adopted daughter

001613   THE QUILL-DRIVER. BY E. WERNER. Chicago: E. A. Weeks, [1895] NUC. (Tr. from the German of E. Werner by Hettie E. Miller)

001614   SHE FELL IN LOVE WITH HER HUSBAND. BY E. WERNER. Chicago: Rand, McNally, [c1892] NUC.

PW-Originally translated and published under title: Good Luck, in 1874.

001615   THE STOLEN VAIL. BY E. WERNER. New York: R. Bonner's Sons, 1892 NUC. (Tr. Mary J. Safford. Bound with The Unsigned Will by E. Von HoltZ.)

BUGG, LELIA HARDIN. United States.

001616   ORCHIDS: A NOVEL. St. Louis, Mo.: B. Herder, 1894 NUC.

PW-American heroine, at end of her school days visits French home, is introduced to a convent. While visiting she meets Lord Parkhurst. Then a pathetic renunciation.

001617   THE PEOPLE OF OUR PARISH: BEING CHRONICLE AND COMMENT OF KATHARINE FITZGERALD, PEW-HOLDER IN THE CHURCH OF ST. PAUL THE APOSTLE. EDITED BY LELIA HARDIN BUGG. Boston: Marlier, Callanan, 1900 NUC.

BUHLER, BEULAH. B. 1890.

001618   REVERIES OF A BACHELOR GIRL. BY HERSELF [ANONYMOUS]. New York: A.L. Chatterton, [c1911] NUC.

BUKLAND, ANNE WALBANK.

001619   MARGARET MOORE, SPINSTER: HER LOVE STORY. London: Ward and Downey, 1897 BMC. (Bookseller adds the following to the title: Found in an Old Escritoirie and Transcribed)

Domestic life in England at end of 18th. Margaret tells her story of how Capt. Leslie, a real scoundrel, jilted her for her sister and how the Reverend remained loyal to her. Covers many years and much trag. SP 78:447.
Old fashioned novel. ATH 109:309.

BULL, KATHARINE THOMAS (JARBOE).

001620   AILA. BY KATE THOMAS. San Francisco: [c1896] NUC.

BULLOCK, HARRIET OSGOOD (NOWLIN).

001621   ON SHIFTING SANDS: A SKETCH FROM REAL LIFE. Chicago: Donohue, Henneberry, [c1895] W.

BUNKER, JANE. United States.

001622   DIAMOND CUT DIAMOND. Indianapolis: Bobbs-Merrill, [c1913] BMC NUC.

PW 9/27/13 949. "When a staid, middle-aged woman intent on writing a book of travel is made the unwilling chaperone of a charming young girl, bound for Paris and New York, she anticipates merely annoyance. But instead, she is plunged into plots, intrigues, and thrills, involving an international gang of gem thieves. Story tells how this came about and what was the outcome. Author is said to be well-known writer who wishes to conceal her identity." She is a well known writer of mystery stories; uses a pseudonym. Doesn't wish to be known for these works but for her literary work. NYT
"A story of many mysteries in which a spinster entirely devoid of romantic notions has a role that would severely strain the nerves of a man accustomed to mysteries, guns and sensations of all sorts, but she moves calmly along, working during the few quiet intervals of her ten days of melodrama, on her new book, 'Belgian byways.' All the time she has concealed

in her stocking--and she never put anything extraneous
there before--or somewhere in her flat, a million
dollars worth of blood-red diamonds." She doesn't know
whose diamonds they are but she enters into the spirit
of the game valiantly, resolved to save them at any
cost. BRD

BURDICK, ANNIE MABELLE. B. 1868. United States.

001623   FURNISHED ROOM HOUSES: A TALE OF NEW YORK
CITY. BY SILAS WRIGHT'S WIDOW. (ANNIE M. BURDICK). New
York: F. T. Neely, [1902] NUC.

Cover-title: Furnished rooms to let.

BURGESS, L. A. See TRUDGIAN, MRS. T. D.

BURGESS, M. L. See BURGESS, MARIE LOUISE.

BURGESS, MARIE LOUISE. United States.

001624   AVE MARIA. A TALE. BY M. L. BURGESS.
Boston: Press Of Monthly Review, 1895 NUC.

BURHANS, VIOLA. United States.

001625   THE CAVE-WOMAN; A NOVEL OF TODAY. New
York: H. Holt, 1910 NUC.

This women is literally in a dark cave. The hero is
her companion but he keeps her identity and self
hidden. Another woman-one involved in a jewel
robbery-is also in the cave. ? PW
BKM v. 31 1910 Kleptomania reporter meets her in her
cave, loves her madly but doesn't know what she looks
like. Finds her in a thunderstorm.
NYT-She has the counter-mania for returning things.

001626   THE CONFLICT. New York: Broadway, [c1907]
NUC.

BURKE, BARBARA, pseud. See BALL, OONA HOWARD (BUTLIN).

BURKE, EDWARD, pseud. See BOGGS, WINIFRED.

BURKE, KATHLEEN. B. 1887.

001627   THE WHITE ROAD TO VERDUN. London and New
York: Hodder and Stoughton, 1916 BMC NUC.

Relief work in Fr narrated. PW
WWI-Pers. narr.

BURMEISTER, KATE. United States.

001628   "THE INDIAN MAIDEN'S DREAM": A NOVEL.
Kansas City, Mo.: Published By Author, 1895 NUC.

BURMESTER, FRANCES G.

001629   A BAVARIAN VILLAGE PLAYER. London:
Greening, 1911 BMC.

Mysticism TLS

001630   CLEMENCY SHAFTO. London: Smith, Elder,
1906 BMC.

ACAD-woman of 40 has daughter who loves half brother
unwittingly because of mother's earlier indiscretion.
Lots of sentiment no strength.

001631   DAVINA. London: Smith, Elder, 1909 BMC.

"half school girl-half woman" "queer" made attractive.
TLS
Deaf girl married to man who doesn't love her but who
feels responsible for her deafness. All ends well. ATH

001632   THE DOGS OF WAR. London: W. Heinemann,
1916 BMC.

Action centers on war's effect on English woman,
Germans. TLS

001633   JOHN LOTT'S ALICE. London: G. Richards,
1902 BMC.

ATH 4-12-02 Alice "is a remarkable character" "we are
haunted by the scenes in which her child dies, and in
which she makes her statement at the revivalist
meeting."

001634   A NOVEMBER CRY. London: Smith, Elder,
1904 BMC.

LBKM - "Fresh, serious, strong"
ATH Essex lady farmer who is also an aspiring
novelist.
TLS-falls for a man who is a publisher's reader; he
has rejected her MS but does not admit his guilt until
he dies before they are wed.
ACAD-actually 2 women living together farming.
Rebecca's lover is shadowy

BURN, IRENE.

001635   THE BORDER LINE. London: Chapman & Hall,
1916 BMC.

TLS-Dangers of race mixture, Eurasian Dr. and English
girl.

001636   GENEROUS GODS. Leek: W. H. Eaton, 1908
BMC. London: Simpkin, Marshall, 1908 BMC.

TLS-study of a woman's temperament, Cassandra
Fallowfield B.A. Greek is her chief interest.
"apparently sexless," husband has deserted her
marriage of comradeship to find love but "after his
death the joy of life is in store for her as she waits
for a lover"

001637   THE UNFORGIVING MINUTE. A NOVEL. London:
T. F. Unwin, 1913 BMC.

gossip, teas, dances, matchmaking in British India.
ATH

001638   THE UNKNOWN STEERSMAN. London: T. F.
Unwin, 1912 BMC. New York: Brentano's, 1912 NUC.

ATH-didactic novel of skillful writing, problems of
education of women and "white man's burden". condition
of Indian women.
SP-not pleasant

BURNESIDE, MARGARET.

001639   THE DELUSION OF DIANA. London: E. Arnold,
1898 BMC.

SP 81:607. Marian, a musical composer of great talent
and her friend Diana, love Le Pallier, a weak,
selfish, but fascinating musician. Diane is not aware
of Marian's love or of Le Pallier's treachery and
becomes engaged. Marian reveals her secret and her
misery in a delerium. Both women are disillusioned but
still affected by him. Diane is unforgiving of Marion.
ATH 112:710. In the style of Charlotte Yonge. safe and
dull.
Witty, daring and beautiful, and her dear woman
friend, the Saintly Marion. Diana spoils Marion's life
and the life of a man she thought she loved. SR 87:90.

BURNETT, FRANCES HODGSON. See TOWNESEND, FRANCES ELIZA
(HODGSON) BURNETT.

BURNETT, IVY COMPTON. 1892-1969. United Kingdom.

001640   DOLORES. Edinburgh and London: W.
Blackwood, 1911 NUC BMC.

Women's college part of background. Dolores devotes
self to father TLS

BURNETT, YELVA.

001641   WINGS OF WAR. London: Methuen, 1915 BMC.

trad melodrama TLS
Woman with idealistic principles marries a drunkard to
reform him but fails. ATH

BURNHAM, CLARA LOUISE (ROOT). 1854-1927. United States.

001642   CLEVER BETSY, A NOVEL. Boston: Houghton
Mifflin, 1910 BMC NUC. Constable, 1910.

A house servant for 26 years. She manages everyone,
including lovers. PW

001643   DR. LATIMER: A STORY OF CASCO BAY. Boston
and New York: Houghton, Mifflin, 1893 NUC.

Summer reading. He's a philanthropist, hero of
Josephine Ivison. Other assorted lovers, happy end. LW
93, 210.
Three orphaned young women begin a kindergarten in a
little flat on the outskirts of Boston. "An
encouraging book for women bread-winners." PW 5-6-93

001644   FLUTTERFLY. Boston: Houghton Mifflin,
1910 BMC.

001645   THE GOLDEN DOG. Boston: Houghton Mifflin,
1913 NUC. London: Gay and Hancock, 1913 BMC.

001646   A GREAT LOVE. Boston and New York:
Houghton, Mifflin, 1898 NUC.

PW-love affairs of two heroines, one a Colorado girl
studying music in Boston (slangy and amusing) and a
beautiful society girl with a unique voice who wants
to make music her profession.

001647   HEART'S HAVEN; A NOVEL. Boston: Houghton
Mifflin, 1918 NUC. London: Constable, 1919 BMC.

NYT Nov. 24, 1918 p. 505. Romantic love story.
SR. Christian Science and saccharine. Love
NYT Jan 18, 1920 p.33. Fairy tale.

001648   IN APPLE-BLOSSOM TIME; A FAIRY-TALE TO
DATE. Boston: Houghton Mifflin, 1919 NUC.

Modern fairy tale-love story PW

001649   THE INNER FLAME. A NOVEL. Boston:
Houghton Mifflin, 1912 NUC. London: A. Constable, 1912
BMC.

PW- male hero
ATH- Christian Science

001650   INSTEAD OF THE THORN; A NOVEL. Boston:
Houghton Mifflin, 1916 NUC.

Linda rich daughter of Chicago man who loses fortune:
Linda broods about it, blames her father's young
associate-whom she eventually weds.

001651   JEWEL; A CHAPTER IN HER LIFE. Boston:
Houghton Mifflin, 1903 NUC. Westminister: A.
Constable, 1904 BMC.

Child of 8 with Christian Science upbringing
reconciles parted relatives--PW 10-3-03
a child's book. NYT 657, 03

001652   JEWEL'S STORY BOOK. Boston: Houghton,
Mifflin, 1904 NUC. London: Gay and Bird, 1905 BMC.

001653   KATE'S WISE WOMAN; A NOVEL. London: Gay
and Bird, 1896 BMC.

SR-
ATH 107:744. Loves and flirtations of young people,
guided and advised by "benevolent elderly spinster."

001654   THE LEAVEN OF LOVE; A NOVEL. Boston:
Houghton Mifflin, 1908 NUC. London: A. Constable, 1908
BMC.

PW-triangle happy ending
TLS-unknown mrg., religious strand
Matrimonial misunderstanding heroine; Sibyl. SP

001655   MISS ARCHER ARCHER: A NOVEL. Boston and
New York: Houghton, Mifflin, 1897 NUC.

Ill assorted lovers, and rose-tinted misery till they
are properly assorted. Happy, optimistic summer
reading. CR 28, 31:73.
Scene: partly coast of Maine, partly va. PW 51:736.
Sweet Va. girl. Two heroines and 2 gallant gentlemen,
in Southern accent. NYT 7-17-97,3.

001656   MISS BAGG'S SECRETARY: A WEST POINT
ROMANCE. Boston and New York: Houghton, Mifflin, 1892
BMC NUC.

LW 23:88. For girls. "Bright and pretty romance."
CR 17:224. He is a West Point cadet; she follows his
advice in everything. He marries her protogee. Sweet.

001657   MISS PRITCHARD'S WEDDING TRIP; A NOVEL.
Boston: Houghton Mifflin, 1901 NUC.

4-27-01 PW

001658   THE OPENED SHUTTERS, A NOVEL. Boston:
Houghton Mifflin, 1906 NUC BMC. London: A. Constable,
[1909] BMC.

2 were engaged, a difficulty set them apart, they meet
years later & realize it was for the best that they
didn't marry. They remain friends. A mutual relative

Sylvia works her way into their lives; she's
"fascinatingly honest". Promising LBKM
PW-totally undisciplined young orphan girl.

001659   THE QUEST FLOWER. London: A. F. Bird,
[1908] BMC. Boston: Houghton Mifflin, 1908 NUC.

001660   THE RIGHT PRINCESS. Boston: Houghton,
Mifflin, 1902 NUC. London: A. P. Watt, 1902 BMC.

Christian Sci.-woman "awakes" prince

001661   THE RIGHT TRACK. London: Constable, 1914
BMC. Boston: Houghton Mifflin, 1914 NUC.

"A Widower, James Barnes, with a son and daughter,
becomes infatuated with a young girl, who marries him
because of the opportunities his fortune will give
her. Diverse personalities and the young wife's
neglect of her duties create an uncomfortable
situation upon which comes a little hunchback woman, a
former schoolmate of Mr. Barnes. She has acquired a
new and spiritual outlook on life which has raised her
above her unhappiness. Gradually the strength of her
belief reconciles the conflicting elements, and all
win back their happiness." PW 86:772 9-19-01

001662   SWEET CLOVER: A ROMANCE OF THE WHITE
CITY. Boston and New York: Houghton, Mifflin, 1894
NUC.

LW 25:371. Pleasant romance-among the glories of the
White City. Religious sentiment.
PW-Columbia Exposition, which she and sister visit
shortly after she's widowed and rich; new love
stories.
Novel or guide book. A love story runs through scenes
of the Fair. CR 23:458

001663   THE WISE WOMAN: A NOVEL. Boston and New
York: Houghton, Mifflin, 1895 NUC.

She's an elderly aunt. Theme is the absurdity of class
distinction in U.S. Helps bring a change in the life
of the milliner Marguerite and the workman. LW 26:428
She's an older woman who influences young woman. "That
there is no true foundation for the generally received
conventionalities of society." PW 10-5-95:581

BURNHAM, S. M. See BURNHAM, SARAH MARIA.

BURNHAM, SARAH MARIA. 1818-1901. United States.

001664   A CHOICE IN THE GATHERING; OR, SOWING AND
WAITING. BY S. M. BURNHAM. Boston: A. I. Bradley,
[c1901] NUC.

PW 9-21-01

BURR, AMELIA JOSEPHINE. B. 1878. United States.

001665   A DEALER IN EMPIRE; A ROMANCE. New York
and London: Harper, 1915 NUC BMC.

Traditional historical romance NYT

BURR, ANNA ROBESON (BROWN). 1873-1941. United States.

001666   THE BLACK LAMB. BY ANNA ROBESON BROWN.
Philadelphia: J. B. Lippincott, 1896 NUC.

PW 1-18-96. Noel, self-sacrificing hero, mystical,
Bhuddist, and the black lamb, an English adventurer.
Melodramatic plot.

001667   A COSMOPOLITAN COMEDY. BY ANNA ROBESON
BROWN. New York: D. Appleton, 1899 NUC.

Comedy about a pearl and its supposed theft; Widow of
Russian Prince, Princess Sarrazine returns to her
family's home in US and uses her wealth to restore the
old place. She has a fondness for jewels and by
intrigue gets hold of a valuable pearl owned by a
Cuban patriot. PW 55:998
A Russian artiste disguised as a boy. LW 30:250

001668   THE IMMORTAL GARLAND: A STORY OF AMERICAN
LIFE. BY ANNA ROBESON BROWN. New York: D. Appleton,
1900 NUC.

PW-three young persons, aspiring to be poet, actor,
portrait painter. Treating personal, social, artistic
evolution.

001669   THE JESSOP BEQUEST. Bostdn: Houghton
Mifflin, 1907 NUC.

NYT-Female sculptor and male philosopher who are
idealists and inspire each other. His patronage of
Diane is offensive. Analysis of mental processes,
story makes an appeal to intellect rather than
emotions.
Criticism of Society 11-16-07 PW
young woman with artistic talent. NYT

001670   THE MILLIONAIRE'S SON. BY ANNA ROBESON
BROWN. Boston: D. Estes, [1903] NUC.

about a young man, intellect vs money 8-29-03 NYT 03,
604

001671   SIR MARK: A TALE OF THE FIRST CAPITAL. BY
ANNA ROBESON BROWN. New York: D. Appleton, 1896 NUC.

CR 29:117. First part narrated by Sir Mark, takes
place in England and involves the recovery of family
property from another member of the family who is a
scoundrel. Second half is narrated by a flour-merchant
in Philadelphia, sedate, prosperous, with young
daughter. Mark comes to him with letters from friends
in Holland.

001672   TRUTH AND A WOMAN. BY ANNA ROBESON BROWN.
Chicago: H. S. Stone, 1903 NUC.

001673   THE WINE-PRESS. BY ANNA ROBESON BROWN.
New York: D. Appleton, 1905 NUC BMC.

woman's college: older girl almost sacrifices her life
to the younger who is an emotional artist. BKM 22
(1905) 38.
prejudice against men harsh judgement of them-PW
5-13-05
history of Giovanna, American mother, Italian father;
father deserted mother. Giovanna bitter goes to a
woman's college; man hater especially since men at the
adjoining college won't give women university
privileges. Meets half sister, daughter of her father
and woman he took up with. Serious studying, cares for
her sister, share apartment, one teaches. the other is
in music. NYT 362, 05.

BURR, JANE, pseud. See WINSLOW, ROSE GUGGENHEIM.

BURT, KATHARINE (NEWLIN). B. 1882. United States.

001674   THE BRANDING IRON. Boston: Houghton
Mifflin, 1919 NUC. London: Constable, 1919 BMC.

Joan Landis "a woman of the mountains;" her husband, a
cowboy and a city man influence her. PW
Wyoming and NY. Joan at beginning of story is married,
18, intelligent, beautiful voice, ignorant of world
(father raised her isolated from everything for fear
she'd turn bad as her mother did, he had killed her
mother). Meets a preacher who lends her books. After a
jealous rage on the part of her husband, she leaves
thinking him dead. Becomes a famous actress in New
York. NYT
SR-moral is that women like to be mastered. Husband
brands her in drunken rage, rescued by a city man,
stays with him a while before he goes back to city.
Then what?

001675   HIDDEN CREEK. Boston: Houghton-Mifflin,
1920 NUC. London: Constable, 1921 BMC.

PW-Romance in the west, orphaned heroine adopted by
westerner becomes good angel to the frequenters of the
hotel's barroom and his drunken son. Adventures-hotel
burns, she flees to wilderness.

001676   THE RED LADY. London: Constable, 1920
BMC. Boston: Houghton Mifflin, 1920 NUC.

ATH-a shocker, original theme
PW-Young housekeeper in lonely amd mysterious country
house in North Carolina.
NYT June 27, 1920, p. 27 janice, the housekeeper is
heroine in Gothic mystery.
ATH-American.
In this Gothic mystery set in a lonely country house
in North Carolina, the young housekeeper Janice
courageously solves the mystery surrounding the Red
Lady--the famous detective hired for the purpose
suspects Janice. The Red Lady turns out to be Janice's
mother--a brilliant international criminal whose
crimes have always been attributed to the less
ingenious men with whom she has worked. The Red Lady
admires Janice's courage and intelligence in a
penultimate scene in which she is preparing, with some
regret, to kill her. In the final chapter Janice

forgives the detective his suspicions and marries him.

BURTON, ALMA HOLMAN. United States.

001677   MASSASOIT: A ROMANTIC STORY OF THE
INDIANS OF NEW ENGLAND. New York: Morse, 1896 NUC.

He's an Indian hero, upright and brave. Story tells of
tribe-their home life. For young people? NYT 2-7-97.
Story of disappearance of Indians from Northeast.
Massasoit is the chief of Wampanoags. Study of these
Indians. PW 51:337

BURTON, MINA E. Nationality Unknown.

001678   RULING THE PLANETS; A NOVEL. London: R.
Bentley, 1891 BMC. New York: Harper, 1892 NUC.

Story of impersonation by a male doctor for the
purpose of defeating the conditions of a will. Dr. who
wants to "rule the planets" finds a look-a-like of the
heir who dies a few hours before his uncle, the
consequence of which is the money would go to
charities. ATH 98 349.
Money would go to hospitals. If doctor's plot succeeds
money goes to wife of uncle (Mrs. Fanshawe), her
daughters and son. SR 9-19-91, 337
PW-Man on the street consents to impersonate a man who
has just died, his double, for a few days in order to
secure money for his family. complications.
IND 44:881. Sensational, mystery, suffering, sorrow.

BUSH, BERTHA EVANGELINE. B. 1866.

001679   A PRAIRIE ROSE. Boston: Little, Brown,
1910 NUC 1925 BMC.

Girls PW

BUSHNELL, BELLE (JOHNSTON). B. 1859. United States.

001680   JOHN ARROWSMITH-PLANTER. Cedar Rapids,
Ia.: Torch Press, 1910 NUC.

Love & conflict. Sounds like straight hist rom. PW
12-4-09

BUSSELL, DOROTHEA.

001681   THE NEW WOOD NYMPH. London: S. Paul,
[1912] BMC.

TLS-Eve waldron, a young discontented enthusiast,
seeks light and consolation in the woods around her
home. A curious adventure, in which she loses her
self-control, leads to consequences which at the end
leave the reader unsatisfied.
ATH-also becomes a college student and an audacious
flirt.

BUTLER, ELIZABETH SOUTHERDEN (THOMPSON).

001682   LETTERS FROM THE HOLY LAND. London: A. &
C. Black, 1903 BMC NUC. New York: Macmillan, 1903 PW.

BUTLER, MARY.

001683   THE RING OF DAY. London: Hutchinson, 1906
BMC NUC.

TLS-Nationalistic novel of Ireland
"A romance, the interest f which centres in the
aspirations of the Irish Ireland movemen t." NUC

BUTLER, MAUDE MARY. United Kingdom.

001684   A SOLDIER'S SON. Boston: Davis & Bond,
[c1912] NUC.

Christian science.

001685   VIOLETTE; A STORY OF SEEKING AND FINDING.
Boston: Davis & Bond, [c1917] NUC.

BUTT, BEATRICE MAY. United Kingdom.

001686   ANN: A BRIEF TRAGEDY, AND A FREE PASS. BY
THE AUTHOR OF "MISS MOLLY" [ANONYMOUS]. London: John
Ouseley, [1907] BMC.

BKM-Two stories. Rare psych studies.

001687   DAN RIACH, SOCIALIST. BY THE AUTHOR OF
"MISS MOLLY" [ANONYMOUS]. London: Smith, Elder, 1908
BMC.

TLS-male hero
ACAD male hero
ATH-Lived with D. R´s niece without marrying her and
separated from her when the commoness of her mind grew
distateful. Also lost faith in Socialism.

001688   A FRIEND. BY THE AUTHOR OF "MISS MOLLY"
[ANONYMOUS]. London: Griffith, Farran, [1891] BMC.

001689   THE GREAT RECONCILER. BY THE AUTHOR OF
"MISS MOLLY" [ANONYMOUS]. London: Methuen, 1903 BMC.

LBKM-Two women, characterization
Married to drunken husband. ACAD 65, 443
Two women, two alcoholic husbands-one husband dies
straight off, the other a little later. ATH 122, 610

001690   INGELHEIM. BY THE AUTHOR OF "MISS MOLLY"
[ANONYMOUS]. Edinburgh: W. Blackwood, 1892 BMC NUC.

ATH 100:126. Miniature German court, complex persons,
male and female.
SP 69:650. Three heroines, one is trained as a singer.
ACAD 42:127. "Human nature in the drawing room."
SR 74:109. Virginia Shore, an intellectual heroine who
fences verbally with another character. Author´s real
interest is Virginia, with her "slight mocking smile."
Delores is a singer, is in Ingleheim for voice
training.

001691   KEITH DERAMORE. BY THE AUTHOR OF "MISS
MOLLY" [ANONYMOUS]. New York: Longmans, Green, 1892
NUC. London: Longmans, Green, 1893 BMC.

A prince charming. All the women love him. Marries,
goes to Egypt. He´s a "fascinating dog." NATION 56,
297.
He´s a gambler. Falls in love with Armine Curtis and
she with him. SR 75, 325
Armine is married. Leaves her for Francoise Martin.
ACAD 43:346
Englishman traveling in France goes in search of a
famous piece of statuary. Hears the history of it. On
second visit, finds a young girl there. Looks at what
he thinks are her sketches and believes her a genius.
Will devote life to her career. But the girl has lied;
the sketches are her brother´s. On this lie the plot
revolves. CR 14,2Q:253
The girl´s name is Francoise Martin. Armine´s husband
dies, Keith marries her after rejecting Francoise.
ACAD 43:346
PW-British office with a weakness for flirting
develops a better character with support of mother
and a good woman.

001692   THE LAWS OF LEFLO. BY THE AUTHOR OF "MISS
MOLLY" [ANONYMOUS]. London: J. Ouseley, 1911 BMC.

Little community shut away from world in heart of
Africa. Socialist--all citizens may have what is
necessary; story of the exceptional man and woman who
conflict with laws that do not allow for exceptions.
SR.

BYNG, EVELYN (MORETON) BYNG. 1870-1949.

001693   ANNE OF THE MARSHLAND. BY THE LADY BYNG
OF VIMY. London: Holden and Hardingham, [1914] BMC.
Toronto: McClelland and Steward, [c1921] NUC.

Unhappy marriage-Anne vs. rural life of husband
deserts him (a village squire) for a vivacious
journalist (who conceals the fact that he´s married).
ATH
LBKM-dramatic matrimonial problems. Anne is selfish,
shallow, but loveable becase of her human failings.
The reader will feel a mixture of contempt and
admiration for husband who suffers her infidelity with
such fortitude (author of Barriers).
SR-0

001694   BARRIERS. BY THE HONORABLE MRS. JULIAN
ByNG. London: Holden and Hardingham, [1912] BMC NUC.
Toronto: McClelland and Stewart, [c1921] NUC.

TLS-Implausible that calm and masterful Clover goes
down before a man mediocre in everything but his
passions. Women may, for all we know, be subject to
such crises of physical emotion, but we should doubt
that such crises come so disastrously to women so well
equipped for life.
SR-Becomes pregnant, father is a soldier and killed.
In a moment of self-abasement reveals her secret to
crippled ex-soldier who offers to marry her (not
mentioning he loves her). She ultimately consents.
Child dies and finally Clover tells husband she loves

him, happy ending.

BYNG, MRS. JULIAN. See BYNG, EVELYN (MORETON) BYNG.

BYNG OF VIMY, LADY. See BYNG, EVELYN (MORETON) BYNG.

BYRD, EVIE SARTOR. United States.

001695   A MODERN EVIL. New York: Broadway, 1907
NUC.

tangled fates of several young people all mismatched
in marriage. Some choose divorce, others stick it out:
"waiting for the compassionate hand of death." Author
supports the divorce solution.

BYRDE, MARGARETTA.

001696   THE INTERPRETERS. A STORY OF
CROSS-PURPOSES. London: T. F. Unwin, 1905 BMC.

ACAD complex plot.

001697   THE SEARCHERS. A STORY IN FOUR BOOKS.
London: T. F. Unwin, 1902 BMC.

BYRNE, EMMA BEAVER. United States.

001698   THE SONG BENEATH THE KEYS. Boston:
Roxburgh, [c1916] NUC.

Triangle story of Katheryne who does not love her
husband and of Philip, the husband´s friend, who loves
K. PW 90:767 9/9/16

BYRON, GERTRUDE.

001699   "POOR ANGELA". London: A. Melrose, [1920]
BMC.

TLS-Charlotte Bronte style. Angela is an invalid and
darling of intellectuals.
LBKM-brilliant daughter victim of accident.
SP Study of an egoist who goes to great lengths to
maintain her central position in circle of friends.
ATH-Prefers to remain an invalid in appearance after
she has ceased to be one in reality.
LBKM-Bitter moment when secret has to be revealed.
Novel closes with her engagement to man who had been
1st admirer of her early promise.

C., M. L., pseud. See CRAWFORD, MINNIE LEOLA.

CABALLERO, FERNAN, pseud. See DE FABER, CECILIA BOHL.

CABELL, ISA (CARRINGTON). United States.

001700   SEEN FROM THE SADDLE. New York: Harper,
1893 NUC.

CABLE, JEROME, pseud. See TIPPETTS, KATHERINE (BELL).

CABOT, ELISABETH LYMAN. United States.

001701   IN PLAIN AIR. New York: H. Holt, 1897
NUC.

N. E. Marion glimpsed the outside world and found
Brookfield´s standards too narrow. (It´s a town.) She
befriends several young men whom the society frowns
upon. She sends one off to Europe to be cultured.
Comes to love Gould Whitmore, but suspects he´s
unfaithful CR 26,30:424.
She´s travelled widely; her values are different from
those of the provincial towns-people. Her ways
immediately lead to scandal. PW 51: 777.
Has the pluck to alone befriend 3 young men that the
town dislikes. In every way Marion is different from
her relatives and her neighbors. BKM 5:521.

CADELL, JESSIE. 1844-1884.

001702   WORTHY: A STUDY OF FRIENDSHIP. London:
Remington, 1895 BMC.

Historical romance. Franco-Prussian War. Helen is the
heroine. SR 80:247

CAFFYN, KATHLEEN MANNINGTON (HUNT). D. 1926. United
Kingdom.

001703   ANNE MAULEVERER. BY IOTA. London:
Methuen, 1899 BMC. Philadelphia: J. B. Lippincott,
1899 NUC.

She´s an artist. Half Irish. She works and studies in

Italy. Here she takes a great interest in the horses
of the Royal stables for she knows all about horses.
LIT 4:527.
She's a sculptor. She's Irish upper class,
emancipated, motherly, indulgent to men, wise, a great
artist, friend to every man she meets. "She can stem a
revolution as easily as you can call a cab." She's
commissioned by King of Italy to go to Ireland to buy
horses for him and take charge of grooms and horses on
the way. LBKM 16:82
She's "half Madonna, half Amazon." Was jilted for a
lady but nursed her former lover in his last illness
and adopted his child. SP 82:616
In love at start of book. He dies at end of Chapter 1.
Her achievements run from "sculpture to diagnosis of
curb wholly undiscovered by stud-groom or vet." SR
87:728
Her daring riding, her eccentric ways. She adopts the
young son of a man she once loved who married and was
miserable and died. The boy is always with her. Never
finds the right man. Story leaves her "celibate from
choice." Quote from novel. PW 56:352

001704   AT A REST HOUSE OF THE FOOT-HILLS
[ANONYMOUS]. London: "Daily Mail", [1904] BMC.

001705   CHILDREN OF CIRCUMSTANCE: A NOVEL. BY
"IOTA". London: Hutchinson, 1894 BMC. New York: D.
Appleton, 1894 NUC.

SP 73:851. She gives the women dinners with music,
gets to know them this way. Iota doesn't believe in
preaching..."studies of emotion in the fantastic and
distorted shapes which it assumes in neurotically
diseased females."
ACAD 46:396. Dignified pathos. "Analysis of emotions
and actions conducted with an appreciative humor."
(John Barrow Allen)
ATH-wife seeks out girl her husband has fallen for; he
then arrives.
SR 78:440. 20 year old Margaret Dering works in East
London rescuing fallen women. Caroline Brett or Davis
is one of them. "No man could endure to see his
girl-sister or girl-cousin in such a place, though he
might be less sensitive with regard to his aunt." says
rev.
LBKM 7:55. Geoffery marries his cousin and then makes
love to Margaret. They meet, discuss the mess, there
is an abortive elopement and then all three act nobly.
He devotes himself to his political career. His wife,
constitutionally unable to convince him of her
devotion, hides her ill health, encourages him in his
career and makes friends with Margaret whom she
assumes will succeed her after her death. Margaret
organizes supper parties and amusements for social
outcasts. Thesis of the book: "by a cultivation of the
natural affections and graces, women will do much more
for the regeneration of the world than by taking up
missions, or by improving their intellects." Book is
full of preachy characters, rampant dissatisfactions
and strenuous defiances of all the codes of propriety
and morality. Respectable people made hateful;
religious people, absurd. Heroine creature of senses.
Other heroine arranges things so that her husband and
rival can get together when she takes off. She's the
victim of 3 ancestral diseases. LW 26:6

001706   A COMEDY IN SPASMS. BY IOTA. New York: F.
A. Stokes, [1895] NUC. London: Hutchinson, [1895] BMC.

Australian young woman marries wrong man for the good
of her family. When the right man comes, he persuades
her to stand by her mistake. CR. 24:156
Then they find "the original obstacles to their
marriage vanish" but another takes its place. CR
24:406
Elizabeth Marrable quick witted, clever talker, easy
to fall in love, can abandon herself completely or
renunciate herself wholely. ATH 106:255
Australian heroine has "bouts of deep discontent,"
though on the whole she is level-headed. Admires
physical force and beauty. Marries (to help out family
financial problems) a physically weak but very
intelligent man. Then she meets a Hercules-Adonis and
is about to break free of her marriage bond but he
stops her. BKM 2:231
Elizabeth, Australian. Her father's death, her return
to England, great love and necessary renunciation,
marriage and unhappiness. LW 27:7. Introspective study
of Elizabeth, thoughtful, high-strung, goes to England
from Australia after father's death. Her loves and
eventual loveless marriage.

001707   DORINDA AND HER DAUGHTER. London: Hurst
and Blackett, 1910 BMC.

Passion in middle life of heroine Lady Dorinda for
youthful lover. TLS

001708   THE FIRE-SEEKER. BY IOTA (KATHLEEN
CAFFYN). London: E. Nash, 1911 BMC NUC.

Mrs. Tom Pemberton is a "vampire" who sucks the
strength out of her husband. TLS
Daughter flees from mother's influence. Flouts
convention with a soldier and "wins through." ATH

001709   HAPPENINGS OF JILL. BY IOTA. London:
Hutchinson, 1901 BMC.

Brilliant girl with a temper, strong unconventional.
Powerful intellect, unconquerable spirit,
misunderstood. Suffers in her marriage and out of it.
Proves the supremacy of the human soul over all mere
events. Fine fire of her nature shrivels up the
meanness in others. Noble woman. ACAD

001710   HE FOR GOD ONLY. London: Hurst and
Blackett, 1903 BMC.

Misunderstood wife. ATH
Husband so involved in his parish work; wife wants
love. He calls upon her to sacrifice her health (and
turn out her child) for his parish. She finally
acknowledges to self and others that he has neglected
his duty to her. TLS

001711   MAGIC OF MAY. BY IOTA. London: Nash, 1908
BMC.

TLS--"Is Iota aware how complete her surrender is?"
"The woman...so far from living her own life is not
alive at all except in and for this husband."
She is "studied to the depths". ACAD

001712   MARY MIRRILIES. London: Hurst and
Blackett, 1916 BMC.

TLS--Couple separate and reunite. She an intellectual
prig.
ATH--She is married to an army man in India and has
vague aspirations for something more than children.
Has 1. Things get straightened, but OK in end.

001713   THE MINX. BY MRS. MANNINGTON CAFFYN. New
York: F. A. Stokes, [1899] NUC. London: Hutchinson,
1900 BMC.

SP 84:637. "Quite free from the excesses of the
emancipation novel." Normal characters. Represents a
transitional phase. Heroine and two suitors, becomes
engaged to the wrong one, marries the right one.
Country society.
ATH 115:560. Joyce was a passionate humanitarian and
very beautiful. Jock, a fox-hunter, she eventually
marries, rather than James, the chemical expert, or
perhaps its the reverse. She addresses the field on
the wrongness of fox hunting.
LIT 6:408. She loves Jock.

001714   MISS MILNE AND I. BY THE AUTHOR OF "A
YELLOW STAR" [ANONYMOUS]. New York: G. Munro, [1895]
NUC.

001715   PATRICIA: A MOTHER. BY "IOTA". London:
Hutchinson, 1905 BMC. New York: D. Appleton, 1905 NUC.

"Graphic characterization" study of mother love; widow
and son. PW 10-7-05.
Husband was slimy. She magnificent. He leaves a will
that is a slur on the widow; leaves her little,
everyone else, everything. The slur could easily be
explained for the wife had turned for help when her
husband's cast off mistress and child showed up. Wife
supports this woman and child. Struggle between Pat
and mother-in-law over the son. (Pat can swim, hunt
and fish.) Two widows. Older one a saint with a lust
for benevolent dominion. Younger a rebellious red
head, reckless. The tussle between them over what the
younger's husband was really like and over Tom, the
son whom Pat buys out of trouble. Pat comes out best:
courage, dash, honest, strong. ACAD 1905:398.

001716   POOR MAX. BY IOTA. Philadelphia:
Lippincott, 1898 NUC. London: Hutchinson, 1898 BMC.

LIT 2:509. He responds to life as aesthetic sensation,
shrinks from pain. "Harsh and ugly" ending.
ACAD 53:201. He is married to Judith, Irish, "frank
and impulsive and a passionate fighter for the truth."
They drift apart, Judith becomes engrossed with
another man. Max dies because of "too nobly caring for

a sick friend."
ATH 111:370. "As might be expected, his character only
interests the author as far as it affects the woman
whom he marries." Story is "made to turn on the
financial straits to which Judith is reduced by her
husband's indiscriminate generosity. The consequence
is that Judith becomes frozen up by her need of making
money, and she adopts a pitying, half-tolerant
attitude to her husband...like Sarah Grand and others,
Iota seems to imagine that no woman has any real
dignity who does not adopt this attitude of crushed,
and yet tolerant, martyr to the inferior sex."
LW 29:263. Her trials with self-indulgent artistic
type. His character "suggests the Jew of the Egoist."
Her moral and intellectual development. She does not
marry Sandy, the other man.
PW-a 2nd marriage ends the story. They go into debt;
Judith becomes Max's nurse and protector.

001717   SMOKE IN THE FLAME. BY IOTA. London:
Hutchinson, 1906 BMC.

TLS--Conventional.
ATH
BKM

001718   TWO WAYS OF LOVE. BY MRS. MANNINGTON
CAFFYN "IOTA". London: Hurst and Blackett, 1913 BMC
NUC.

Heroine is uncertain of husband's loyalty. ATH

001719   "WHOSO BREAKETH AN HEDGE". BY MRS.
MANNINGTON CAFFYN ("IOTA"). London: Hurst and
Blackett, 1909 NUC BMC.

Audrey "petulant audacious" appallingly voluble "her
Pagan heart" fighting duty to husband against love for
another man. Author's "untiring flow of admiration for
her." TLS
Evolution of the soul of a young woman married to a
"mild mathematician "but harbouring a former love."
Audrey is exasperating and vulgar. ATH

001720   A YELLOW ASTER: A NOVEL. BY IOTA. New
York: D. Appleton, 1894 NUC. London: Hutchinson, 1894
BMC.

ACAD 45:245. On the subject of maternal love. Gwen's
parents devote themselves to writing philosophical
treatises; after her children are grown, Mrs. Waring
realizes she has missed one of the supreme pleasures
of life, that of being a mother.
SR 77:231. Gwen marries, cannot respond to her
husband's love, they part. She has a child whom she
cannot love until he almost dies. Then she is able to
love-everyone. Becomes a "new Madonna, before whom the
whole world must kneel and rise up to call her
blessed." Rev. doesn't like Gwen with her hot brain
and cold heart.
SP 72:407. Gwen's parents are educated agnostics. Her
mother, dying, is remorseful that she did not allow
herself to show her love or love Gwen more, its being
the cause of Gwen's inability to love. It is through
this exchange that Gwen's awakening takes place. Gwen
is educated, very intelligent.
LBKM 6:24. The newest, most fashionable heroine is
"beautiful of course, in a large and haughty way. She
is icily pure, and rather like Crimhilde in her
dislike of the marriage bond. She despises the world
and men, and herself, and is superbly unhappy. In
spite of her purity she is not very wholesome; she
generally has a mission to solve the problems of
existence. In the end Gwen turns into a domestic,
sweet-smelling flower, by a process which is a little
dark to us."

CAFFYN, MRS. MANNINGTON. See CAFFYN, KATHLEEN MANNINGTON
(HUNT).

CAIRD, MONA (ALISON). United Kingdom.

001721   THE DAUGHTERS OF DANAUS. London: Bliss,
Sands, 1894 BMC NUC.

SR 78:665. Hadria is "grossly insulted by all the
habits of life of women." She does not dislike her
husband personally; she dislikes marriage. Her
children are "the tribute exacted of my womanhood. It
is through them I am to be subdued and humbled." She
wants to start a revolution. She left her husband for
a while to study in Paris, but returned because it was
breaking her mother's heart.
ACAD-"Mona Caird is associated with a controversy
which assumed some prominence in the holiday season
five or six years ago." Duties and privileges of woman

in the married state.
Strongly anti-marriage. Hadria, a musician, brooding,
introspective, bent on personal freedom; but pressed
by the man and her friends, she marries young. She's
in full rebellion against institutions of which she
disapproves. Home, family lose all sanctity to her-to
her sister Algitha. Domestic life is intolerable;
motherhood a reproach. Her attitude toward children,
her own two sons, is one of indifference because they
are products of the tyrannous system of marriage,
because they are boys (members of the domineering
sex.) Deserts children and husband without a pang,
goes to live in Paris to study music. Can't see that
it matters who raises the children; best she can do is
not be there to mother them. Ends with Hadria still
rebellious

001722   THE PATHWAY OF THE GODS: A NOVEL. London:
Skeffington, 1898 BMC.

SP 81:446. Love affairs of an artist.
LIT 3:423. Rev. is perplexed.
ATH 112:450. Julian is induced to forego the Vampire,
with blank Atheism and an unhappy temper, for a
Platonic attachment to the Queen of the Beautiful Past
and the Prophetess of the Beautiful Future. "Beauty is
Truth, it is Love, and it is Life, and those who
follow it shall someday tread the Pathway of the
Gods." Julian is rescued from Vampire by able women
who believe the above.
SR 86:680. "Sketch...of the exacting, attractive,
strenuous, exhausting, intelligent, quite intolerable
young neurotic woman, who is still a type of the day,
though its fiction has exploited her ad nauseum. We
pity Anna, she has a capacity for passion bigger than
her lover's but every mortal man would have fled from
her vampire-like ardour to the friendship of..."
LBKM 15:58. Serious literature. Study of Anna, strong
intellect, artistic temperament. Her fiance did not
have an easy time.

001723   A ROMANCE OF THE MOORS. Bristol: [1891]
BMC. New York: H. Holt, 1891 NUC.

Two women are loved by young Yorkshire farmer. Engaged
to simple farm girl, attracted to artist from London
who comes to sketch the moors. The novel covers a
week. At the end, both women leave him to his newly
found interest in art and retire to comfort each
other. LW
The farmer attracted to Shelley. The widow artist
feels pity for her rival when the farmer confesses
he's engaged to the farm girl. SR 9-19-91, 340.

001724   THE STONES OF SACRIFICE. London: Simpkin,
Marshall, 1915 BMC.

A Novel of ideas; small group of people in Scotland.
Much talk of advanced young men and women about
society and feminism; changing ideas of family life.
TLS

CAIRNS, KATE, pseud. See BOSHER, KATE LEE (LANGLEY).

CALDWELL, WILLIE WALKER. B. 1860. United States.

001725   THE TIE THAT BINDS: A STORY OF THE NORTH
AND THE SOUTH. Franklin, Ohio: Editor Publishing Co.,
1895 NUC.

CALHOUN, ALICE J. United States.

001726   WHEN YELLOW JASMINE BLOOMS; A STORY OF
THE SOUTHLAND. New York: Neale, 1904 NUC.

Trad. heroine.

CALLAGHAN, STELLA. United Kingdom.

001727   JACYNTH. London: Constable, 1914 NUC BMC.

ATH-romance. Pretty and foolish heroine.

001728   THE LITTLE GREEN GATE. London: Constable,
1911 BMC NUC. New York and London: G. P. Putnam's
Sons, 1911 NUC.

Love complications. PW 11-18-11
SP-gardening heroine pleasant etc.

001729   VISION. London: Constable, 1913 BMC.

A male poet who is most blessed when he loses all
worldly possessions. Anthony Watt has a vision. SP

CALLAHAN, DORIS EGERTON (JONES). Australia.

001730   THE COCOANUT PLANTER. BY D. EGERTON JONES. London and New York: Cassell, [1916] NUC BMC. New York: (NUC: Coconut)

TLS-Cynthia Shale after losing her husband leaves Sidney for Papua to run plantation. Meets Nevil on boat, they have love affair, then Terry, husband shows up, book closes with both of them leaving for battle (war).

001731   GREEN EYES. London: Hodder & Stoughton, 1915 BMC.

First person narrative of woman teacher and her love and marr. in Australia TLS

001732   PETER PIPER. London: Cassell, 1913 BMC. Philadelphia: G. W. Jacobs, [191-?] NUC.

She's a girl in boy's clothing living alone in Western Australian bush, the inevitable lover appears, loves and takes off. Gives up her boy's clothes, becomes engaged to another, tells of her past, is jilted. Ends up in original lover's arms. TLS
"peter Piper was a girl brought up in the Australian bush. Her strange, morose father dresses and treats her like a boy, and never tells her anything of her mother. Then a man, a young lawyer, comes to East Magnet, wins Peter's heart, brings castastrophe upon her and rides away. Peter's father sends her to Adelaide and she makes her debut in her diary and the reader learns of her social success, her engagement to a pleasant fellow who leaves her when he hears her story; of the clearing up of the mystery surrounding her mother and the reappearance of her lawyer-lover. What she does in this crisis ends the tale." PW 85 4/11/14 . 1263

001733   TIME O' DAY. BY D. EGERTON JONES. London and New York: Cassell, [1915] BMC NUC. New York:

"a love story from woman's pov." BKM 41 1915
Vivacious diary about romance, life, people and things PW 5-29-1
Written by Thyme O'Dea for her great grand children NYT

001734   THE YEAR BETWEEN. London: Cassell, 1918 BMC. Philadelphia: G. W. Jacobs, [c1919] NUC.

TLS Romance-Jan was a 17 yr old child-widow of drunken mineworker and rev says most normal person in story is a woman lawyer.
January Ellice, 17, "believes herself the wife of a dissolute young engineer of West Australia" Story shows how real love comes to her. PW

CALVERT, ELIZABETH HENDERSON (MACROBIE). United States.

001735   THE TWO HOUSES. Boston: Roxburgh, [c1918] NUC.

PW-love story of Northwest.

CAMBRIDGE, ADA. See CROSS, ADA (CAMBRIDGE).

CAMERON, CHARLOTTE (WALES-ALMY). D. 1946.

001736   A DURBAR BRIDE. London: S. Paul, [1912] BMC NUC.

001737   A PASSION IN MOROCCO: A NOVEL. London: Stanley Paul, [1911] BMC.

A Prince wins an English girl. ATH
Author speaks of wisdom of the Moslem as being more honest than the English in dealing with women yet does not let the women survive very long. SR

001738   ZENIA: SPY IN TOGOLAND. London: T. W. Laurie, [c1916] BMC NUC.

She's used as tool by cousin to do spy work. LBKM
TLS-She is rescued by man.

CAMERON, E. LOVETT. See CAMERON, EMILY (SHARP).

CAMERON, EMILY (SHARP). United Kingdom.

001739   A BACHELOR'S BRIDAL. BY MRS. H. LOVETT CAMERON. London: F. V. White, 1894 BMC. Philadelphia: J. B. Lippincott, 1897 NUC.

ACAD 46:116. Young woman flees ward to solicitor's

chambers in London late at night. He feels bound in honor to marry her and does so, but immediately after ceremony he sends her to a solitary mansion in the country, " a proceeding utterly inexplicable to the doting bride." Tragic end.
Pleasant till 10 pages from the end--then catastrophic. LW 28:165.
Solicitor of 40, determined not to marry, gets involved in the settlement of a young heiress. She seeks him for protection against the cruelty of her guardian. He marries her to preserve her good name. Sad marriage follows. PW 51:425

001740   A BAD LOT. A NOVEL. BY MRS. LOVETT CAMERON. Philadelphia: J. B. Lippincott, 1894 NUC. London: F. V. White, 1895 BMC.

ACAD 46:552. Three daughters of a near bankrupt wheeler-dealer father. The oldest bet on the races, the 2nd played billiards, tennis, smoked cigarettes in public and a pipe in private, the 3rd was pure and innocent but was jilted by a barrister when he heard talk about her. She makes a good marriage, however.
ATH 104:824. Dottie and Millie are hoidens, Nell is a womanly woman.
LW 25:372. Book takes one into bad company; tone is low and unclean.
PW-none of them is a bad lot except father, although mother elopd with her coachman when her youngest was 1 year old. Story of various careers of daughters. Nell Forrester is raised in Bohemian family but the story is conventional. She spends some time with a man of unsavory reputation. A gossip observes this and later the information breaks up her engagement to one man. But she marries another. SP 74:270.

001741   BITTER FRUIT. New York: Brentano's, 1901 NUC. London: J. Long, [1914] BMC.

Anne looked upon with prudish horror? ATH 7-13-01.

001742   THE CRAZE OF CHRISTINA. London: J. Long, 1899 BMC.

"Wronged and dispossessed" young woman. LIT 5:375
Middleshire. The heroine "is merely horrid," tricky and calculating. Hero Mark Clifford inherits lots of money with lots of provisos attached. LBKM 17:31
The provisos are impossible. The young Australian woman tries to help him overcome these conditions of the will. They end up marrying. SP 83:129
Farcical, broadly funny. SR 88:240
PW-journalist inherits, but will lose most of fortune if he marries within a certain time. He has a restless and impatient disposition.

001743   A DAUGHTER'S HEART: A NOVEL. BY. MRS. H. LOVETT CAMERON. London: F. V. White, 1892 BMC. Philadelphia: J. B. Lippincott, 1892 NUC.

LW 23:262. Cinderella story.

001744   DEVIL'S APPLES. London: F. V. White, 1898 BMC.

ACAD 53:93. Jenny Maxwell. Four parts; Renunciation, temptation, degradation, expiation.
ACAD 53:371. Blanche becomes a homicidal maniac.
ATH 111:211. She is rich, proposes to him. He is a treacherous and cruel husband. He abandons the girl whom he has made a mother without marriage.
SR 86:279. Old theme of man's selfishness and woman's weakness.

001745   A DIFFICULT MATTER. London: J. Long, 1898 BMC. New York: Street and Smith, [c1899] NUC.

ACAD 53:495. Sensational.
ATH 111:657. Brother makes useless sacrifice for sister.

001746   A FAIR FRAUD. BY MRS. EMILY LOVELL [SIC] CAMERON. London: J. Long, 1899 BMC. New York: Street & Street, [c1899] NUC.

She's not such a fraud though her father is a convict and her mother has an alias. Her father gets himself mistaken for her lover. Makes a good marriage in the end. LIT 4:528
Marian. Her mother is unscrupulous in getting her married well. ACAD 56:360
She renounces her lover because of her father's crimes and in shielding father brings suspicion on herself. Happy end. PW 56:813

001747   A HARD LESSON. BY E. LOVETT CAMERON. New

York: J. A. Taylor, [c1891] NUC.

Helen tells one lie and we learn its effects. LW.
Helen Dacre, encouraged by old school-mistress,
becomes engaged to old school master. Suddenly she
gets an inheritance, goes off to England and forgets
about the old man. PW 12-12-91.

001748   AN ILL WIND. BY MRS. H. LOVETT CAMERON.
London: J. Long, 1901 BMC. New York: A. L. Burt,
[1902] NUC.

11-2-01 ATH

001749   LITTLE LADY LEE. London: F. V. White,
1896 BMC.

ATH 107:212. Young bride of man 3 times older than
herself, vicious and cruel, Has other enemies, and one
good friend.
ACAD 49:238. When she does not give him an heir he is
brutal to her, moves his mistress on to the estate, he
eventually dies and she marries the one good friend,
the heir of the baronet.

001750   A LOYAL LOVER. BY E. LOVETT CAMERON. New
York: J. A. Taylor, [c1892] NUC. London: C. A.
Pearson, 1900 BMC.

PW-romance

001751   A MAN'S UNDOING. BY MRS. H. LOVETT
CAMERON. London: F. V. White, 1897 BMC. New York and
London: F. M. Buckles, 1899 NUC.

She's rich; he's poor. He marries the nearest
adventuress, who dies so they can wed. SR 84:475.
He marries a girl socially "beneath" him. She drinks.
Duped him into marrying her tho he loves another
woman. They are miserable. She maims her child, "dooms
him to an early death," kills self. Next a young girl
in love with him has to drown so he can marry the
woman he always loved. ATH 110:416.
Capt. Guy Ripley must resign from army because of ill
health. Returns to England, gets well, Makes a
miserable marriage, recomes an editor of London paper
and a war correspondent. Two other women influence his
life. PW 56:253
Hero proposes to two women he doesn't love-out of
duty. His wife meets a bad end, shipwreck removes the
woman he feels pledged to. He's united with his true
love. LW 30:279

001752   A MIDSUMMER MADNESS. A NOVEL. BY MRS. H.
LOVETT CAMERON. London: J. Long, [1902] BMC. New York:
A. L. Burt, [1903] NUC.

001753   A PASSING FANCY. BY MRS. LOVETT CAMERON.
London: J. Long, 1899 BMC NUC.

Widow of 40 refuses to marry a man she loves--refuses
15 times. Then he weds a younger woman who threw
herself at him. LIT 5:570
When that wife dies, he returns to the widow. SP
83:844. Ambrosia
LBKM 17:153. 40 year old widow, her 30 year old lover,
her unworthy son and his fiancee are principal
characters. Lover marries son's fiance after vainly
proposing to widow for 20 years, is unhappy. The
generous practical widow loves him. All works out.

001754   PROVED UNWORTHY. BY MRS. EMILY LOVETT
CAMERON. London: W. Stevens, [1891] BMC. New York:
Street and Smith, [1900] NUC.

001755   REMEMBRANCE. London: J. Long, 1904 BMC.

ACAD-tr. love story
ATH-love story

001756   ROSAMOND GRANT. London: J. Long, 1905
BMC.

001757   A SISTER'S SIN. A NOVEL. BY MRS. LOVETT
CAMERON. London: F. V. White, 1893 BMC. Philadelphia:
J. B. Lippincott, 1893 NUC.

Lil is betrayed. sister must raise child. CR 14,
20:95.
Lilian Garnier is of lower class than Eric; marriage
out. Sister Daphne ACAD 43.32.
ATH 100:736. Crimes, curses, malice and murder.
SR 74:744. Lil is seduced. She is helped by a "little
bottle" stolen from a doctor. Her siser Daphne swore
to be revenged.
Lil, half invalid, motherless, spends most of her time
on couch, only knowledge of life is novels. Attracts
and loves Eric Denison. But he's persuaded to marry a
woman his mother chooses; Lil commits suicide. Daphne
her sister gives up her lover, a better man than Eric,
to seek Eric and avenge her sister. SP 70 131

001758   A SOUL ASTRAY: A NOVEL. London: F. V.
White, 1895 BMC NUC.

Yeoman Steven Hardy sacrifices self for his family's
and foster-sister Zillah the Gipsy's honor. She's been
"compromised" by a rake. Zillah is pregnant. Steven
loves Mary Clover but weds Zillah, leaves her at
church door and goes to Africa as a soldier. Is
wounded, meets the rake who seduced Zillah, and Zillah
now dead, Steven can marry Mary. ACAD 48:243
ATH 107:245 Stock characters, minor adventure.

001759   A TRAGIC BLUNDER: A NOVEL. BY MRS. LOVETT
CAMERON. London: F. V. White, [1893] BMC.
Philadelphia: J. B. Lippincott, 1894 NUC.

Highwaymen knock the wrong man on the head and steal
the wrong stuff. Leave the man with amnesia. He
marries the wrong woman. ATH 102:767.
SR 77:179. "The butchering of the hero's wife and the
heroine's fiance to make a marriage for the two
strikes us as both feeble and immoral."
PW-Hero is beaten, suffers loss of memory.

001760   TWO COUSINS AND A CASTLE; A NOVEL. BY
MRS. H. LOVETT CAMERON. London: F. V. White, 1896 BMC.
New York: F. M. Buckles, 1901 NUC.

Tom Spinks commits suicide-in contrast to the farcical
mode-Mab's love story and Dorothy Duke playing up to
Tom's millionaire father. ATH 109:146

001761   A VAIN SACRIFICE. BY MRS. LOVETT CAMERON.
London: C. A. Pearson, 1895 BMC. New York: Brentano's,
1900 NUC. (Published as A Loyal Lover in 1900)

SP 84:604.
ACAD 58:274. Good sister and bad sister. Good one
marries a man to protect bad one from scandal, a vain
sacrifice.
LIT 6:372. Happy ending.

001762   THE WAYS OF A WIDOW. London: F. V. White,
1898 BMC.

ACAD 44:193. 2 sisters, 1 a widow; and 2 lovers, 1 a
baronet. Which weds which?

001763   WEAK WOMAN. A NOVEL. London: F. V. White,
1892 BMC NUC.

ATH 99:176. Involves a 10 year contract during which
time Gerald could marry no one but Dora. He was not
good to her.
SP 68:470. He is a coward; the contract was made with
a widow, they no longer love each other, but still he
is afraid to release himself, there are no weak women.
ACAD 41:178. Heroine is Helen, a school teacher who
inherits a large sum of money. She is engaged to the
principal's son but loves someone else, Gilbert
Nugent. He goes abroad. She marries her guardian to
escape persecutions of Warne, her former fiance. He
dies eventually and she marries Gilbert.

001764   A WOMAN'S NO. BY MRS. H. LOVETT CAMERON.
London: J. Long, 1902 BMC. New York: F. M. Buckles,
1902 NUC.

equivalent to her yes.
NYT 8-9-02

CAMERON, MARGARET. See KILVERT, MARGARET (CAMERON).

CAMERON, MRS. EMILY LOVETT. See CAMERON, EMILY (SHARP).

CAMERON, MRS. H. LOVETT. See CAMERON, EMILY (SHARP).

CAMERON, MRS. LOVETT. See CAMERON, EMILY (SHARP).

CAMERON, NELLIE.

001765   IN THE MERRY MONTH OF MAY. London: Digby,
Long, 1910 BMC.

CAMPBELL, DAISY RHODES. B. 1845. United States.

001766   THE FIDDLING GIRL: THE STORY OF VIRGINIA
HAMMOND. Boston: Page, 1914 NUC.

"Story opens a short time previous to the second

marriage of Virginia Hammond's father. Of course,
Virginia looks forward to the coming of her new mother
with considerable fear and doubt, but the stepmother
proves to be one of "the other kind" and Virginia
grows to love her dearly. Through the new mother's
interest, Virginia is sent away to a city school and
meets with many novel experiences. Finally, she is
able to realize her ambitions to become a violinist."
PW 85 4-11-14:1261

001767   THE PROVING OF VIRGINIA. Boston: Page,
1915 NUC.

3 years of her college life, sets out to work to earn
money to study music in Paris. PW

001768   THE VIOLIN LADY. Boston: Page, 1916 NUC.

Makes a success as violinist. 2 girls study in Paris,
absorbed in music "romance claims them". PW

CAMPBELL, FRANCES.

001769   DEARLOVE: THE HISTORY OF HER SUMMER'S
MAKEBELIEVE. London: Hodder and Stoughton, 1906 BMC.
New York: E. P. Dutton, [1906] NUC.

001770   FOR THREE MOONS. London: Digby, Long,
1900 BMC.

SP 84:638. Sea voyage from Queensland to England.
Characters on board, for 3 months, their love-making,
anecdotes, quarrels, troubles with an alcoholic. Some
of the characters appeared in an earlier novel.

001771   LOVE, THE ATONEMENT. A ROMANCE. London:
Digby, Long, 1901 BMC.

Heroine promising. ATH 8-24-01

001772   THE MEASURE OF LIFE. London: Chapman &
Hall, 1906 BMC. New York: E. P. Dutton, [1906] NUC.

001773   A PILLAR OF DUST. London: J. W.
Arrowsmith, 1905 BMC.

Innocent man convicted of forgery. ACAD 1265, 05
LBKM v29-30, 90

001774   A SHEPHERD OF THE STARS. London: Hodder
and Stoughton, 1907 BMC. New York: E. P. Dutton,
[1907] NUC.

Pretty love story in Morocco. LBKM 5-07,69

001775   TWO QUEENSLANDERS AND THEIR FRIENDS.
London: A. Moring, 1904 BMC NUC.

CAMPBELL, HARRIETTE (RUSSELL).   B. 1883. United States.

001776   IS IT ENOUGH? A ROMANCE OF MUSICAL LIFE.
New York and London: Harper, 1913 BMC NUC.

"Has learned that the woman is not merely a servant to
minister to his wants." PW
"The author is an erratic musical genius who marries a
young country girl, takes her to the city, and
neglects her while he devotes himself to his art. She
is a secondary matter to him; that she should cook for
him and keep him comfortable is all he asks of her.
Gradually, however, he learns that he cannot treat her
thus cavalierly; he finds that he is dependent on her
for spiritual as well as for material sustenance; he
finds that even as an artist he is helpless without
her." "Whether H.R.C. intends a glorification of
musical genius or a satire on it we cannot determine."
BRD.
Hild has ambition to be great singer--music means
everything to her. Mother pushes her to marry a
musical genius, Jean, a German. It's really her love
of music that makes her marry him. The moment they're
married, she's unhappy. He wants a competent
wife--she's not that. In their music they are
comrades; she sings, dances, plays piano, and she's
very good. As husband and wife they're strangers.
Discussion of degradation of wife asking for money, of
her aversion to him. She leaves for a weekend against
his wishes. She takes a Nora pose. He shuts her out.
Friends urge her to divorce him. Friends mixed up with
socialism, anarchism; when he's down and out and
disappears, she goes to look for him. She finds him
somewhat changed. He's accused of a bombing, goes on
trial, is released. Writes a great opera--once she's
back. She plays a part in it. They are famous at the
end and it is enough to be his wife.

CAMPBELL, HELEN (STUART). 1839-1918. United States.

001777   BALLANTYNE; A NOVEL. Boston: Little,
Brown, 1901 NUC BMC.

Young woman in Boston becomes disheartened with
American soc. and pols. decides to make London her
home. Many modern theories. Socialism. ARENA
She meets Ballantyne who loves Amer. "Between the
two...there rages a conflict for the mastery" she's
subdued at the end(?) BOOK NEWS 6-01.
Ed. and refined woman passing as a man and for years
deceiving intimate housemates. Inner hy of communal
life. Both characters fight for a principle.

001778   SOME PASSAGES IN THE PRACTICE OF DR.
MARTHA SCARBOROUGH. Boston: Roberts, 1893 NUC.

Temperance novel. She is motherless child of village
doctor, educated by her father. Father builds a
sanitorium. Vs. unsanitary modes of living and
unhygienic cooking. LW 93, 147.
She's 10. Gets to help her father. CR 14, 20:363.
Children's

CAMPBELL, JOSEPHINE ELISABETH.

001779   FERRIBY. BY MRS. VERE CAMPBELL. London:
Methuen, [1907] NUC BMC.

Tragic and strong passions in a family. About a murder
and the tangle of motives and effects TLS

001780   FOR NO MAN KNOWETH. THE SKETCH OF A
ROMANCE. London: Greening, 1910 BMC.

TLS-artist's life.

001781   THE MASTER SCHEMER. London: Greening,
1909 BMC.

Mystery about a title. TLS

001782   OF THIS DEATH. London: Ward and Downey,
1891 BMC.

History of Phyllis Eden. ACAD
"A girl's distorted soul and body shown in painful
precision and uncompromising detail." ATH 98 481
SR 73:246. Phyllis runs away with an opera singer;
demonic Ralph Nickleby brings their intrigue to a
close, a double tragedy.

001783   THE PROBLEM OF PREJUDICE. BY MRS. VERE
CAMPBELL. London: T. F. Unwin, 1896 BMC NUC.

LBKM 10:120. Margaret Marey is irrevocably unhappy
with husband. Opportunity for release comes in a
dignified and moral form. Work and liberty are
available to her. She chooses to remain with her
husband. "It is the very depth of brutality in her
husband, his bestiality, which has left him helpless
and alone, which appeals to her."

001784   RENDER UNTO CAESAR. London: Mills and
Boon, [1909] BMC.

Lots of cross-love making among artist types TLS
ATH

001785   THE SHIBBOLETH. London: Ward and Downey,
[1894] BMC.

SR-disagreeable situations.
ACAD 45:346. Novel is "the outcome of a high state of
mental exaltation." A combination of realism and
idealism. To be understood only " by those who have
dived deep into the dark waters of spiritual
experience." Ghoulish experiment...of creating his
counterpart in a woman in whom he hopes to fulfill his
duality. "Sometimes one suspects Mrs. Campbell of
being in alliance with the neurotic writers of the
hour: the women we all pity, in that a malady, half
mental, half physical, has afflicted them with what
may fitly be called a dry-rot of the passions, so that
they mistake impotence for purity." James Stanly
Little.
ATH 103:242. Lunatic heroine. Unpleasant suggestions.
Darkly incomprehensible.
LBKM 6:25. Temperature of 105 degrees throughout.
Browning is lucid in comparison.

CAMPBELL, MRS. VERE. See CAMPBELL, JOSEPHINE ELISABETH.

CAMPBELL, PHYLLIS.

001786   LINED WITH RAGS. A NOVEL. London: Mills and Boon, [1920] BMC.

001787   THE WHITE HEN. London: Mills & Boon, [1920] BMC NUC.

TLS-sugary romance.

CANDEE, HELEN (CHURCHILL) HUNGERFORD. 1858 (?) 1861-1949. United States.

001788   AN OKLAHOMA ROMANCE. New York: Century, 1901 NUC.

Heroine contests lover's claim to land. PW 10-26-01

CANFIELD, DOROTHY. See FISHER, DOROTHEA FRANCES (CANFIELD).

CANNING, ETHEL.

001789   THE SKY-LINE. London: Digby, Long, 1913 BMC.

Story of a man who was disinherited because he would not be come a lawyer. Loses faith but believes again through his sweet sister and her clergyman husband. TLS

001790   SYBELLA. London: S. H. Stockwell, [1910] BMC.

TLS visit to Japan.

CANUCK, JANEY, pseud. See MURPHY, EMILY (FERGUSON).

CAPES, HARRIET MAY (MOTHER MARY REGINALD). B. 1849. Nationality Unknown.

001791   THE STORY OF ELEANOR LAMBERT. BY MAGDALEN BROOKE. London: T. F. Unwin, 1891 NUC BMC. New York: Cassell, [1891] NUC.

"The moral must be that in woman's world men are of no importance." ATH 97 215
Felicia Gray and Eleanor are bosom friends. Felicia is engaged to a man who in spite of self loves Eleanor and she him. Felicia begs her to give him up and she does. They wed and don't meet for 10 years till dying husband wants to see Eleanor. CR
English setting. IND
ATH 97 215

CARD, SUSAN.

001792   AGNES'S DILEMMA. London: Drane's, 1913 BMC.

Dangers that beset young unprotected women in London. ATH

CARDELLA, G., pseud. See BARNETT, ADA.

CAREW, S. MOORE, pseud. See FIFIELD, SALOME (HOCKING).

CAREY, ALICE V.

001793   LOUISA AVONDALE; OR, TWO SOUTHERN GIRLS. New York: Irving, [c1894] NUC.

001794   PARADISE WOLD. New York: G.W. Dillingham, 1896 NUC.

PW 3-21-96. Virginia, hated by her half-sister who attempts to drown her, flees from her home in Ky. Goes to Washington, then Los Angeles where she has obtained a situation. On route attacked by robbers, she is carried off by captain, many other adventures.

CAREY, MARY ELIZABETH. United States.

001795   ALICE O'CONNOR'S SURRENDER. Boston: Angel Guardian Press, 1897 NUC.

CAREY, ROSA NOUCHETTE. 1840-1909. United Kingdom.

001796   THE ANGEL OF FORGIVENESS. Philadelphia and London: J. B. Lippincott, 1907 NUC. London: Macmillan, 1907 BMC.

BKM- strange. Githa, a young woman whose close relations with her father are described learns on her 17th birthday that the cousin she has visited each year is really her mother. Gets everyone together. Sent story of girl who unites her parents. PW 10-19-07

001797   AT THE MOORINGS. London: Macmillan, 1904 BMC. Philadelphia and London: J. B. Lippincott, 1904 NUC.

Homespun romance. LBKM 27-8, 31
NYT-conventional love story.
ATH-Old fashioned.

001798   BUT MEN MUST WORK. London: Bentley, 1892 BMC. Philadelphia: J. B. Lippincott, 1893 NUC.

ACAD:Heroine is narrator.
ATH 100:317. Romance with a mystery. Governess stumbles on a family secret, the discovery of which aids the happiness of the two sisters of the family. Miss Osborne, mid-aged governess tells the story of her backward pupil and of the mystery in the Hillyard family that keeps her pupil and her sister from the men they love. Takes place in village outside London PW 3-18-93
"trashy, silly, sentimental" CR, 14, 20:404

001799   BY THE ORDER OF THE BROTHERHOOD: A STORY OF RUSSIAN INTRIGUE. BY LE VOLEUR. London: Jarrold, 1895 BMC.

Duchesse de Poma has many startling adventures before she marries her co-conspirator Count Paul. "A terrible indictment" of Czarist Russia and the Czar's spies. ACAD 47:462

001800   THE CHAMPINGTON MYSTERY. BY LE VOLEUR. London: Digby, Long, 1900 BMC.

001801   COUSIN MONA: A STORY FOR GIRLS. London: R. T. S., [1897] BMC. Philadelphia: J. B. Lippincott, 1896 NUC.

001802   DOCTOR LUTTRELL'S FIRST PATIENT. London: Hutchinson, 1897 BMC. Philadelphia: J. B. Lippincott, 1897 NUC.

The doctor, his young wife. Their struggle till the practice brings in patients. For girls? LW 28:279. He's practicing among the poor, aspires to a lucrative practice, gets his chance when a very wealthy man slips on orange peel and he's called in to help. NYT 9-11-97,3.

001803   FOR LOVE OF A BEDOUIN MAID. BY LE VOLEUR. London: Hutchinson, 1897 BMC. Chicago and New York: R. McNally, [c1897] NUC. (Napoleon I - Fic)

Paris 1797 just before Waterloo. Sensational hist rom. ACAD 52 Fic Sup 101.
SP 80:125. St. Just. an officer of Napoleon, saves his life and accompanies him to Egypt. Here he falls for Halima, a Bedouin, who turns him against Napoleon, she thirsts for revenge. He finally reverts to his original loyalty to Napoleon.

001804   HERB OF GRACE. London: Macmillan, 1901 BMC. philadelphia: J. B. Lippincott, 1901 NUC.

001805   THE HIGHWAY OF FATE. Philadelphia: J. B. Lippincott, 1902 NUC. London: Macmillan, 1902 BMC.

ATH 10-11-02 Not helpful.

001806   THE HOUSEHOLD OF PETER; A NOVEL. Philadelphia & London: J. B. Lippincott, 1905 NUC. London: Macmillan, 1905 BMC.

3 maiden aunts devoted to nephew-doctor. 10-7-05 PW
ATH 539,05

001807   IN THE TSAR'S DOMINIONS. BY LE VOLEUR. London: Hutchinson, 1899 BMC.

A Russian noble saves the Czar's life; is given permission to make an unconventional marriage to Anne, daughter of land steward. She's kidnapped by a rival and the noble rescues her. SP 82

001808   THE KEY OF THE UNKNOWN. London: Macmillan, 1909 BMC NUC. Philadelphia: J. B. Lippincott, 1909 NUC.

Couple's love runs counter to family wishes but all ends happily. PW 10-9-09
Pleasant domestic tale. ATH

001809   LIFE'S TRIVIAL ROUND. London: Hutchinson, 1900 BMC. Philadelphia: J. B. Lippincott, 1900 NUC.

NYT 1900:420. Family story, comfortable and pleasant.

001810   THE MISTRESS OF BRAE FARM: A NOVEL.
London: R. Bentley, 1896 BMC. New York: A. L. Burt,
1896 NUC.

PW 10-17-96. young womanly woman and her cousin, a
widower, quietly drifting into love with her. Then
another cousin, a widow, arrives to stay for awhile.
Complications ensue.
Miss Lee a spinster; Mrs Herbert, a widow. Miss Lee
gives up the Col. when she believes he has become
interested in Mrs. Herbert. Mrs. Herbert gets the
Col.; Miss Lee has her virtue. CR 28,31:34.
Too many plots: story of Ellison Lee and Lorraine
Herbert coworkers; love-troubles of Ruth; plot
involving Mr. Yolland and Sam Brattle; another about
Rev. Eric Vincent. SP 78:896
LW 27:456. Wholesome, for girls. Old Welsh lady.

001811   MOLLIE'S PRINCE: A NOVEL. Philadelphia:
J. B. Lippincott, 1899 NUC.

Molly is old fashioned cloistered type. She has a
friend who ends up developing into a prince in
disguise. They live happily. LIT 4:239
She's lame. LW 30:23
ACAD 54:326. Domestic love story.
ATH 112:604. Old fashioned, for girls, a survival.

001812   MRS. ROMNEY. A NOVEL. London: R. Bentley,
1894 BMC.

LW 27:202. Truthful Elsie, and her sister-in-law who
has a secret which Elsie must reveal to husband.

001813   MY LADY FRIVOL. London: Hutchinson, 1899
BMC. Philadelphia: J. B. Lippincott, [c1899] NUC.

LIT 6:23. Romance of governess--heroine. Minus
passionate note of Jane Eyre.

001814   NO FRIEND LIKE A SISTER. London:
Macmillan, 1906 BMC. Philadelphia: J. B. Lippincott,
1906 NUC.

PW?
TLS-Well-bred domesticity.
ATH-well bred domesticity.

001815   OTHER PEOPLE'S LIVES. Philadelphia: J. B.
Lippincott, 1898 NUC. London: Hodder & Stoughton, 1897
BMC.

001816   OUR BESSIE. London: R. T. S., [1891] BMC.
Philadelphia: Lippincott, [1891] NUC.

001817   A PASSAGE PERILOUS. Philadelphia: J. B.
Lippincott, 1903 NUC. London: Macmillan, 1903 BMC.

Heroine dependent upon uncongenial relatives agrees to
marry. They grow together. PW 10-3-03
NYT 03,75
Marriage in name only of a ne'er do well and young
woman who agrees to help him gain independence. Uncle
insists he marry or face disinheritance. They end up
and all ends up happily tied together. A dangerous
young woman. ACAD 15,292
Wife whose husband forced to leave her on wedding day
comes to love him. LBKM 11-03,106
ATH 122,513

001818   RUE WITH A DIFFERENCE. London: Macmillan,
1900 BMC. Philadelphia: J. B. Lippincott, 1901 NUC.

LW 31:268. Pleasant story, cathedral town.
ATH 116:680. Relationship between Pansy and her
step-mother.
LIT 7:350. "Wholesome women and girls and rather more
unreal men."

001819   SIR GODFREY'S GRANDDAUGHTERS: A NOVEL.
London: R. Bentley, 1892 BMC. Philadelphia: J. B.
Lippincott, 1892 NUC.

ATH 100:626. Domestic romance of pretty young woman.
CR 18:249. English village.
PW-Grand daughter Gerda often clashes with his old
fashioned and arbitrary commands. "author always
brings out the possibilites and duties of family
life."
familiar domestic situations. "Stupid, pig-headed" Sir
Godfrey insists on making matches for his daughters
and when they don't go well, acts like a lunatic. SP
70 131

001820   THE SUNNY SIDE OF THE HILL. Philadelphia:
J. B. Lippincott, 1908 NUC. London: Macmillan, 1908

BMC.

"A story of English country life. Maureen Brydon
leaves her home, where she is the youngest daughter of
a large family, and goes to live with a rich maiden
aunt. Contrary to her expectations, Maureen finds Aunt
Margaret a delightful comrade and she leads a very
happy life in her new surroundings." BKM v.28 1908-9
TLS-love for both.
ACAD Innocuous story for girls.
Wholesome, charming. NYT

CARLETON, KATHARINE.

001821   DOROTHY, THE MOTOR GIRL. New York:
Century, 1911 BMC NUC.

Girl wins a car and has many adventures and
misadventures. Good girls' book. PW 9-30-11 p 27

CARLETON, S., pseud. See JONES, SUSAN CARLETON.

CARLETON-MILECETE. See JONES, SUSAN CARLETON AND HELEN
MILECETE.

CARLYLE, ANTHONY, pseud. See MILTON, GLADYS ALEXANDRA.

CARNIE, ETHEL. United Kingdom.

001822   MISS NOBODY. London: Methuen, [1913] NUC
BMC.

Part 1, the drab life of workers, weddings, funerals,
prejudices of the poor. In part 2 heroine left a
fortune. Carrie, a Manchester girl marries a man she
hardly knows, leaves him, returns. Caroline Evelyn
Brown sells oysters and delights in penny novelettes.
Lives in grimy surroundings, she's tough, determined.
Thrown on her own resources moves to Manchester, works
in factory (vivid picture of such life.) Marries,
separates, reconciled. We leave her with almost grown
children. TLS

CARO, MADAME E. See CARO, PAULINE (CASSIN).

CARO, PAULINE (CASSIN). 1835-1901.

001823   A YOUNG GIRL'S LOVE. BY MADAME E. CARO.
Chicago: Donohue, Henneberry, 1892 NUC. (Tr. Alexina
Lorangier)

PW-Lise Daunay's love and disappointment.

CAROLIN, EMILY OLIVIA.

001824   THE VERGE OF TWILIGHT. London: Hurst &
Blackett, 1911 BMC.

Hotel-keeper's daughter Elsie-sombre passionate wants
love. Irene "a vulgar hussy" a "sordid" story,
"miserable" end. TLS
Aunt and niece in slum setting; Aunt's sour, secret
longing for love, rages at her own plainness, hatred
of niece's beauty. Elsie Grey goes on the street out
of despair. ATH.

CAROTHERS, ROSE. United States.

001825   MOTHER'S WALTER AND WALTER'S MOTHER; A
STORY FROM INCIDENTS OF REAL LIFE. Toledo, O.: Studio
Press, c1906 NUC.

CARPENTER, EDITH. United States.

001826   MODERN ROSALIND: A STORY. Chicago: 1894
NUC.

001827   YOUR MONEY OR YOUR LIFE: A STORY. New
York: C. Scribner's Sons, 1896 NUC. London and New
York: S. Low, 1896 BMC.

SR Termination of murder trial in U.S. in a wedding.
humorous. Janet gives her backward lover an object
lesson in courting. Far-fetched, funny.
ATH 108:253. Bored with the monotony of their
engagement, she impels Tom to cast off his job in a
commercial treadmill and go west.
SP 77:313. High-spirited. Geraldine and Tom Nelson,
the head of the gang of train robbers, for whom Tom
Norrie is mistaken, are married in trial.
BKM 3:455. Double wedding "guarded by the levelled
revolvers of some score or so of Masked outlaws." Book
is a protest against "sacrifice of the things worth
living for to mere money making." Janet and Tom
abandon money-making to go to Europe to enjoy art,
etc. Tom the robber abandons trains to assist the

Cuban patriots.

CARR, ALICE VANSITTART (STRETTEL). B. 1850. United
Kingdom.

001828   THE ARM OF THE LORD. London: Duckworth,
1899 BMC.

Tragedy of humble life--stubborn, unforgiving
Methodist yeoman and his wayward grandchild that he
wants to save from damnation. BAKER 03,88
Nonconformist tragedy. A tyrannical Wesleyan farmer,
his wayward granddaughter, a rakish squire. LIT 5:26
Nancy is defiant. Her Methodist grandfather tries to
tame her; but she mocks the rel. He arranges a
marriage for her. She refuses it. He casts her out.
Still at the end he refuses to admit her dead body
into his house. LBKM 16:141
Jesse Macadams' cruel tyrannical grandfather (a
Wesleyan farmer) ruins high-spirited joyful young
Nancy through his revolting and fanatical religious
views. SR 88:23

001829   BY WAYS THAT THEY KNEW NOT. BY MRS.
COMYNS CARR. London: Chapman & Hall, 1910 BMC NUC.

BM-Tangled love and tangled marriage-"East Lynne with
a difference."
TLS-Lawyer becomes engaged believing his wife dead.
She is not, and she and fiancee become friends when
they meet.
SR- In tradition of inconvenient wives whose health is
extremely precarious.

001830   COTTAGE FOLK. London: Heinemann, 1897
BMC.

Reviewer gives a column to discussion of dialect,
especially the word certain. SR 84:631. Short story.

001831   JOHN FLETCHER'S MADONNA. London: A.
Constable, 1905 BMC.

Complications between English man and Italian wife.
TLS 83, 05

CARR, MILDRED EMILY. B. 1877. United Kingdom.

001832   GEORGE GORING'S DAUGTERS. London: Smith,
Elder, 1903 BMC.

Two girls and the early influences on them ACAD 64,
438
Two girls in lovely moorland home, at 20 and 22 go to
school for first time-thrown among ordinary women.
ACAD 64, 486
Their romantic ideas from books, glimpses of real
world through father (mother's fate becomes an
engrossing theme) and a lawyer. They go forth to be
educated; sisters are close; come to love same man. He
loves Lucy who refuses to marry him because of his
previous relation with another woman. Ann Goring (the
mother) tells the tale. ATH 122, 184
Two girls in the moor country, saturated with its
influences, father visits. Their discovery of his
cruelty to their mother TLS, 177, 03

001833   A KNIGHT OF POLAND. London: Smith &
Elder, 1910 BMC.

BM Male Hero-historical romance
TLS Male Hero

001834   LOVE AND HONOUR. London: Smith & Elder,
1901 BMC. New York: G.P. Putnam's Sons, 1901 NUC.

ATH 3-30-01--Historical novel emphasis on hero; women
traditional types.

001835   THE POISON OF TONGUES. London: Smith,
Elder, 1906 BMC.

ACAD-Male hero wrongfully accused of forgery.
ATH-male hero wrongfully accused of frogery
BKM-Male hero wrongfully accused of forgery

CARR, MRS. COMYNS. See CARR, ALICE VANSITTART (STRETTEL).

CARR, SARAH (PRATT). B. 1850. United States.

001836   THE IRON WAY, A TALE OF THE BUILDERS OF
THE WEST. Chicago: A. C. McClurg, 1907 NUC.

Story of railroad PW 3-16-07

CARR, STELLA, pseud. See BANG, ELIZABETH.

CARRIER, ELSE HAYDON.

001837   A SOUL IN SHADOW. London: J. Long, 1913
BMC.

Hero makes an unsuitable marriage; it almost wrecks
his life; he stoops to crime, but manages to
rehabilitate himself. ATH

CARRINGTON, EDITH.

001838   A NARROW, NARROW WORLD. London:
Sonnenschein, 1894 BMC.

001839   NOBODY'S BUSINESS. London: Griffith,
Farran, [1891] BMC.

CARRUTH, FRANCES WESTON. See PRINDLE, FRANCES WESTON
(CARRUTH).

CARRUTH, RUTH TAMAR.

001840   SCILLIA OF THE SCILLIES. London: Heath,
Cranton, [1917] BMC.

CARRUTHERS, ANNIE.

001841   A LEFT-HANDED MURDER. London: Gale and
Polden, [1892] BMC.

CARRUTHERS, CLAIRE.

001842   A GIRL IN LOVE: BEING THE LETTERS OF
CLAIRE CARRUTHERS TO HER FRIEND BETTY BROOKE. London:
H. J. Drane, [1903] BMC.

CARRY, MABEL D. Nationality Unknown.

001843   BETTY MOORE'S JOURNAL. Chicago: Rand,
McNally, 1912 NUC.

PW-unhappy marriage, works out
NYT--The situation is mainly a hatrack on which to
hang such questions as "what is the job of the
middle-class married woman." Considers issues of
salaries for housework, women's management of
government.
Book--Pro suffrage and women in government; pro
family.

CARSON, NORMA (BRIGHT). B. 1883. United States.

001844   ROSEMARY-FOR REMEMBRANCE. London: Hodder
and Stoughton, [1913] BMC. New York: G. H. Doran,
[c1914] NUC.

"Love letters from a woman to her husband in South
Africa. She is dying, but she bravely hides all traces
of her suffering. She wants him to have his chance at
his work unhampered." PW 86 10/24/14:1339

001845   TRUEHEART MARGERY. New York: G. H. Doran,
[c1917] NUC.

Father resents daughter because mother died at her
birth. When she refuses to marry man he chooses,
disinherits her. Her marriage doesn't go well,
husband leaves, supports self and child, dies. Father
reconciled with her daughter PW

CARSON, SHIRLEY. United States.

001846   THE MOTTO OF MRS. MCLANE; THE STORY OF AN
AMERICAN FARM. London: E. Arnold, 1911 NUC BMC. New
York: Doran, [1913] NUC.

"To give the helping hand to whatever comes along was
Mrs. McLane's motto. Therefore, though she had five
children and very little money, she cheerfully offered
a home to the orphan daughter of her half sister.
Though the girl, Eva, has lived a very different life
in California, she adapts herself to the hardships of
the Wisconsin farm, and endears herself to the simple
neighbors, till good fortune once more smiles upon
her." PW
Wholesome little tale. NY T

CARSWELL, CATHERINE ROXBURGH (MACFARLANE). B. 1879. United
Kingdom.

001847   OPEN THE DOOR! New York: Harcourt, Brace
& Howe, 1920 NUC. London: A. Melrose, [1920] NUC BMC.

TLS-character analysis. Development of Joanna
SP-20 years in life of mother and daughter with a

particularity which is embarrassing. "Eminently a
Feminist novel. for the women are much stronger
characters than the men." Joanna's emotional odyssey
from one love to another.
ATH--Quote from bk. "at eighteen, a little weary of
friutless emotion, a little dream-sick, the conviction
had begun to force itself on Joanna that she was
without attraction. For the past ten years she had
lavished unreciprocated passion on individuals of both
sexes."
PW--daughter of a Glasgow family, brought up in severe
piety moves to unconventional freedom.
NYT 7/11/20 p23. Sexual history from age 7.

CARTER, ADA. United Kingdom.

    001848   CHILDREN OF THE RESURRECTION. BY A.
CHANNEL. London: A. F. Bird, [1909] BMC.

    001849   PRIEST AND LAYMAN. London: T. W. Laurie,
[1910] BMC. New York: Wessels & Bissell, 1911 NUC.

    man (Christian Scientist) rehabilitates another man.
5-20-11 PW
A lady named Gabriel Grand (?) TLS

    001850   THE SEAMLESS ROBE. A TWENTIETH CENTURY
IMPRINT OF THE IDEAL. London: T. W. Laurie, [1907]
BMC. New York: A. Wessels, 1909 NUC.

    Christian Science. NYT

CARTER, BELLA.

    001851   DERRYMOUNT. Edinburgh: W. P. Nimmo, 1900
BMC NUC.

    ATH 90:790. Scotland. Sweet and beautiful heroine's
romance.

CARTER, LAURA ARMISTEAD. D. 1935.

    001852   WIND AND BLUE WATER. Boston, Mass.:
Cornhill, [c1920] NUC BMC.

    Verses-BMC
    PS3505

CARTER, MARGARET. Canada.

    001853   THE STOWAWAY'S INHERITANCE. New York: The
Bookery, 1912 NUC.

    Lad has run away from home in England, wretched aboard
ship, tossed overboard by wicked first mate, marries a
young woman who saw him go through all this. NYT

CARTER, SARAH NELSON. United States.

    001854   FOR PITY'S SAKE: A STORY FOR THE TIMES.
BEING REMINISCENCES OF A GUEST AT A COUNTRY INN.
Boston, Mass.: De Wolfe, Fiske, [c1897] NUC.

CARTER, WINIFRED. United Kingdom.

    001855   ASHES OF EDEN. London: Simpkin, Marshall,
1915 BMC.

    Perils facing ind. young woman; Katherine ends up in
poultry farm that minister sets up to save girls.? TLS

CARTWRIGHT, MRS. EDWARD.

    001856   JENNY: A TALE. London: Gardner, Darton,
1897 BMC.

    001857   A SLIGHT INDISCRETION. London: T. F.
Unwin, 1896 BMC.

CARVALHO, C. N. See CARVALHO, CLARA N.

CARVALHO, CLARA N.

    001858   OTTERBURN CHASE. London: S. P. C. K.,
[1898] BMC.

    PW Two sons of paper mill owners reduced to poverty by
extravagance of older son. The youngest goes to work
at the mill as a clerk; the oldest lives off his
friends.

CARYL, VALENTINE, pseud. See HAWTREY, VALENTINA.

CASE, FRANCES POWELL. United States.

    001859   THE BY-WAYS OF BRAITHE. BY FRANCES

POWELL. New York: C. Scribner, 1904 NUC. London:
Harper, 1904 BMC.

    NYT-Gothic
    LBKM -
    ATH-0

    001860   THE HOUSE ON THE HUDSON. BY FRANCES
POWELL. New York: C. Scribner, 1903 NUC. London:
Harper, 1903 BMC.

    Naive heroine, a bit of a pagan, orphaned, becomes
housekeeper and companion and is drawn into a mesh of
horrors. LBKM 7-03:152
    ATH 121:779

    001861   AN OLD MAID'S VENGEANCE. BY FRANCES
POWELL. New York: C. Scribner, 1911 NUC.

    Vengeance vs a man who made love to her because of her
money and then jilted her. PW 3-25-11

    001862   OLD MR. DAVENANT'S MONEY. BY FRANCES
POWELL. New York: C. Scribner, 1908 NUC.

    PW-inheritance, romance.
    NYT-inheritance, romance.

    001863   THE PRISONER OF ORNITH FARM. BY FRANCES
POWELL. New York: C. Scribner, 1906 NUC.

    PW-young woman abducted by mysterious man.

CASEY, SADIE KATHERINE. See MAYNARD, SARA KATHERINE
(CASEY).

CASH, MRS. M. I. United States.

    001864   NAAMAN, THE LEPER, AND PRINCESS SARAH,
THE CAPTIVE MAID. Cincinnati: Editor Pub. Co., 1899
NUC.

CASSAVETTI, CECILE.

    001865   ANTHEA: A TRUE STORY OF THE GREEK WAR OF
INDEPENDENCE. London: Cassell, [1892] BMC.

    ATH 100:813. Story of "the ruin of a Yanina family by
Ali Pasha, and of the flight of the heroine with her
three little children to the coast." "painfully
graphic"
    Realistic narrative of advents, during Greek war of
independence of Anthea after her escape from the
"sensualist and murderer" Ali Pasha who killed her
husband. ACAD 43:57

CASSIDY, JAMES, pseud. See STORY, EDITH MARY (STEANE).

CASTELAR, ISABELLA, pseud. See WINTER, ELIZABETH
(CAMPBELL).

CASTELLO, ALMEDA MERCHANT. B. 1856. United States.

    001866   FOUR IN HAND. BY MRS. A. M. CASTELLO.
Boston: Pilgrim Press, [c1901] NUC.

    PW 10-12-01

CASTELLO, MRS. A. M. See CASTELLO, ALMEDA MERCHANT.

CASTLE, AGNES (SWEETMAN). D. 1922. United Kingdom.

    001867   MY LITTLE LADY ANNE. BY MRS. EGERTON
CASTLE. London: J. Lane, 1896 BMC. Philadelphia: H.
Altemus, 1896 NUC.

    LBKM 10:87. Anne, daughter of ambitious, unloving
mother is duped into a financially advantageous mrge
with a dissipated cousin. Final tragedy.
    ATH 108:417. Narrated by her nurse. Anne is a half
wit, the marriage drives away the remainder of her
reason. They separate, the mother brings them back
together. She is introduced to a drunken orgy of his
friends during which he is killed. She becomes
completely demented and soon dies.

CASTLE, MRS. EGERTON. See CASTLE, AGNES (SWEETMAN).

CASTLEMAN, VIRGINIA CARTER. B. 1864. United States.

    001868   A CHILD OF THE COVENANT. Milwaukee, Wis.:
The Young Churchman, 1894 NUC.

    001869   ROGER OF FAIRFIELD. New York: Neale, 1906
NUC.

CATHARINA, ANNA, pseud. See REBEK, LILLIE.

CATHER, WILLA SIBERT. 1873-1947. United States.

001870   ALEXANDER'S BRIDGE. London: Constable,
1912 BMC. Boston: Houghton Mifflin, 1912 BMC NUC.

PW-Triangle.
ATH-Love story. Alex, wife, 1st love actress who still
holds him, he dies.

001871   MY ANTONIA. Boston: Houghton Mifflin,
1906 NUC. London: W. Heinemann, 1919 NUC BMC.

Western prairie life, pioneer farm. Jim Burden,
narrator. Bohemian Antonia. Lena Lingard.

001872   O PIONEERS! Boston: Houghton Mifflin,
1913 NUC. London: W. Heinemann, 1913 NUC BMC.

"Story of Scandinavian and Bohemian pioneers of
Nebraska. Alexandra Bergson at eighteen has to take
care of her mother and three brothers. She has
business ability, her farm prospers and she becomes
the richest and most influential citizen of her
country, but success is embittered by the jealousy of
her less intelligent brothers. The second heroine is
Marie Tovesky, a Bohemian, full of gayety, life,
youth, but whose story is tragic. It is an interesting
tale with a new setting." PW
At middle-age feels terribly lonely, a freak. Swedes,
Bohemians Nebraskan uplands their struggles. No hero,
interest centers upon two women, friends "some might
call it a feminist novel, for the two heroines are
stronger, cleverer, and better balanced than their
husbands and brothers-but we are sure that Miss Cather
has nothing so inartistic in mind." NYT.
"A New Woman" "who succeeds on the western plains
where her father had failed."

001873   THE SONG OF THE LARK. Boston: Houghton
Mifflin, 1915 NUC BMC. London: J. Murray, 1916 NUC.

ATH-Character analysis of singer
"German girl in Colorado...becomes an opera singer."
Spends all her money for voice lessons, career as
opera star, struggle between the human and the
artistic in her nature. PW 10-2-15
WOMAN'S EDUCATION ASSOC. Nov 1915, no 32, Resists
pressures that would make her a powder puff, Thea
Kronberg, beautiful on stage; off, haggard, worn, her
life empty.

CATHERWOOD, MARY (HARTWELL). 1847-1902. United States.

001874   THE DAYS OF JEANNE D'ARC. New York:
Century, 1897 NUC. London: Gay and Bird, 1898 BMC.

001875   THE LADY OF FORT ST. JOHN. Boston and New
York: Houghton, Mifflin, 1891 NUC. London: S. Low,
[1893] BMC.

Historical romance. Story of French in America. The
fort garrisoned by Charles de la Tour. LW
Seventeenth century. His wife represents "the highest
feminine ideal of her day." She's named Marie. PW
ATH 99:789. "Heroic life and tragic end of Marie de la
tour" wife of Acadian chief, Historical romance of
Nova Scotia.
NATION 1:45 153. There is a female creature who flies
about on a swan.

001876   LAZARRE. London: B. F. Stevens and Brown,
[1901] BMC. Indianapolis: Bowen-Merrill, [c1901] NUC.

Williams, Eleazer 1787-1858-Fic

001877   OLD KASKASKIA. Boston and New York:
Houghton, Mifflin, 1893 NUC BMC.

Dr. Dunlap kills a man. Local color-Illinois. LW 93,
178
Early 1800s: Old French woman of nearly 100 years-a
tyrannical bed-ridden aristorcrat, six young women,
two priests, several other men are the characters. PW
5-20-93.
About a town (title). Jean Lozier, a young man, dreams
of making his home there. Can't until grandfather
dies. Then it's too late. The town drowned by the sea.
CR 20-23:87.

001878   THE QUEEN OF THE SWAMP, AND OTHER PLAIN
AMERICANS. Boston and New York: Houghton, Mifflin,
1899 NUC.

001879   SPANISH PEGGY: A STORY OF YOUNG ILLINOIS.

Chicago and New York: H. S. Stone, 1899 NUC.

LW 31:75. Indian adopts Spanish girl. Attempts were
made to steal her to gain her money; Abraham Lincoln
among others interfered.

001880   THE SPIRIT OF AN ILLINOIS TOWN, AND THE
LITTLE RENAULT: TWO STORIES OF ILLINOIS AT DIFFERENT
PERIODS. Boston and New York: Houghton, Mifflin, 1897
NUC.

(1) Cont. Trail City, Ill.-"the squalor, the rush, the
intensity, the intoxication of life in a growing
western town." Seth Adams comes from Europe where his
wife spent all his money and left him. Here he meets
Kate Keene who lives a brief life. (2) Pathetic tale
of Ill. in 1680. CR 26,30:247.

001881   THE WHITE ISLANDER. New York: Century,
1893 NUC. London: T. F. Unwin, 1893 BMC.

Early French colony in US. Young Indian woman saves
Englishman from massacre. A French Canadian woman,
being raised to be chief's wife, hides him and
protects him. He's saved from the fire by a Jesuit
priest. Marries the French Canadian woman. LW 93, 367.
Tied to the stake, the flames licking at his feet, the
hero calls on the priest to marry him to the white
Islander, the French Canadian woman. Nation 57, 452.
Fur trading.

CATREVAS, CHRISTINA.

001882   THAT FRESHMAN. New York and London: D.
Appleton, 1910 NUC BMC.

Girls

CAULFEILD, KATHLEEN MARY (EDGE).

001883   THE AFTER COST. London: E. Nash, 1904
BMC.

ATH 0

001884   AHANA. BY K. M. EDGE. London: Chapman &
Hall, 1902 BMC NUC.

ATH 7-12-02

001885   THE SHUTTLES OF THE LOOM. London: J.
Murray, 1909 BMC.

Forest life in India. TLS
Involves two women that inspire "deep interest"; one
is Beatrice. TLS
Focuses on the hero. ACAD

001886   THROUGH THE CLOUDY PORCH. London: J.
Murray, 1912 BMC.

So. Africa; charm of veld. African politics charming
heroine but "her relations to Bertram are exceedingly
unattractive." SP
Naomi is flawless-patient, saintly, courageous. LBKM
ATH-Story of women's self-sacrifice
TLS Story of women's self-sacfifice-worn as lightly as
a flower.

CAUSTON, SELINA MARY.

001887   TWIXT TWO ETERNITIES. London: Routledge,
1893 BMC.

Between the past and future. Oliver de Winton is a
malcontent, too limp to do anything about his
complaints. Lady Katherine, brilliant, high-bred,
loves him. Her rival is a humble clergyman's daughter.
Lady Katherine is devoted to good works, turns her
living room over to lectures, visits slums. SP 71,
215.

CAVENDISH, E. CECILLE. United States.

001888   POPULAR OPINION. Meriden, Conn.: Journal
Pub. Co., 1898 NUC.

CAVENDISH, PAULINE BRADFORD (MACKIE) HOPKINS. B. 1873.
United States.

001889   A GEORGIAN ACTRESS. BY PAULINE BRADFORD
MACKIE (MRS. HERBERT MUEELLER HOPKINS). Boston: L. C.
Page, 1900 NUC.

PW-romance, reign of George III, England & U.S. Life
and adventures of a talented young actress.

001890   THE GIRL AND THE KAISER. BY PAULINE
BRADFORD MACKIE. Indianapolis: Bobbs-Merrill, [1904]
BMC NUC.

     PW juv.?

001891   MADEMOISELLE DE BERNY: A STORY OF VALLEY
FORGE. BY PAULINE BRADFORD MACKIE. Boston and London:
Lamson, Wolffe, 1897 NUC BMC.

     CR 32:165. Story of Valley Forge. Hero is a blind boy
     who in his desire to be a man and a soldier betrays
     washington's plans to the British.
     BKM 7:166.
     LW 29:27. Heroine, boy's sister, is detained at Valley
     Forge when she comes inquiring after him. "Atmosphere
     of refinement and thorough breeding."
     1778. She has a blind brother, their guardian, a spy
     for George Washington. Pretty love tale, Hist. rom. PW
     52:1159.

001892   THE STORY OF KATE, A TALE OF CALIFORNIA
LIFE FOR GIRLS. BY PAULINE BRADFORD MACKIE (MRS.
HERBERT MUELLER HOPKINS). Boston: L. C. Page, 1903
NUC.

     BOOK NEWS 12.02 "work and life of a school teacher in
     Southern California.

001893   THE VOICE IN THE DESERT. BY PAULINE
BRADFORD MACKIE (MRS. HERBERT MUELLER HOPKINS). New
York and London: McCllure, Philips, 1903 BMC NUC.

     Attractions and repulsions between men and women; deep
     temperamental conflicts in Arizona desert; couple and
     two children 4-18-03 PW
     NYT 306 02

001894   THE WASHINGTONIANS. BY PAULINE BRADFORD
MACKIE (MRS. HERBERT MUELLER HOPKINS). Boston: L. C.
Page, 1902 BMC NUC. London: G. Bell, 1903 BMC.

     career of woman powerful in official circles BOOK NEWS
     12 '01
     Works to get her father the Presidency, failure? Women
     in politics. Washington life and politics at time of
     Civil War BKM 13 1901 433
     ATH
     Portia gets into politics wants to push husband to be
     president. LBKM note 9-03, 226

001895   YE LYTTLE SALEM MAIDE: A STORY OF
WITCHCRAFT. BY PAULINE BRADFORD MACKIE. Boston, and
London: Lamson, Wolffe, 1898 NUC.

     BKM 8:165. Salem witchcraft. A thorough study.

CAWTHORNE, ELSIE M.   United States.

001896   CONFESSIONS OF THAT LITTLE ENGLISH GIRL;
OR, SO INEXPERIENCED. Chicago: Fagan, [c1896] NUC.

001897   A YEAR WITHOUT A CHAPERONE. London: J.
Long, [1912] NUC BMC.

     ATH-Autobiography of an English girl in New York.

CAXTON, JOHN G. pseud. See BEAUMONT, DONNA BROOKS.

CHALLACOMBE, JESSIE.

001898   DAVID'S DIACONATE, OR GATHERING UP THE
FRAGMENTS. London: S.P.C.K., [1912] BMC.

001899   FAITHFUL POLLIE. London: S.P.C.K., [1901]
BMC.

001900   GILT AND GOLD. London: R.T.S., [1910]
BMC.

001901   HOW THE FIRE SPREAD. London: S.P.C.K.,
[1902] BMC.

001902   JANE STIGGINS. London: S.P.C.K., [1910]
BMC.

001903   NELL GARTON. London: S.P.C.K., [1904]
BMC.

001904   A POOR MAN'S PALACE REBUILT. London:
S.P.C.K., [1902] BMC.

001905   "TOPS". THE STORY OF A POOR WAIF. London:
S. W. Partridge, [1913] BMC.

001906   WAIT AND WIN. London: S. P. C. K., [1912]
BMC.

CHALLIS, MIMA.

001907   EASTWOOD OLD HALL: A TALE OF DERBYSHIRE
LIFE IN THE SIXTEENTH CENTURY. Chesterfield: W.
Edmunds, [1896] BMC.

CHALMERS, MARGARET REBECCA (PIPER). B. 1879. United
States.

001908   SYLVIA'S EXPERIMENT; THE STORY OF AN
UNRELATED FAMILY. BY MARGARET R. PIPER. Boston: Page,
1914 NUC.

     PW 86 10/3/14:1122 "Sylvia was an orphan, and besides
     lots of money, she owned a big house. Even when she
     was at school, because she had no family, she was
     lonely. It made her want to be kind to other lonely
     people. So she planned a Christmas house-party for
     those she knew. They all came, and someone else, too,
     who was the beginning of Sylvia's romance."

CHAMBERLAIN, ESTHER AND LUCIA CHAMBERLAIN.

001909   THE COAST OF CHANCE. Indianapolis:
Bobbs-Merrill, [1908] NUC.

     PW-Mystery and love story.
     BKM mystery and love story-

001910   MRS. ESSINGTON; THE ROMANCE OF A
HOUSE-PARTY. New York: Century, 1905 NUC BMC.

     widow and younger composer-lets him go-problem of
     difference in age; she's 10 years older PW 5-20-05
     Brief description. BKM 21 (1905) 547
     Widow, older, brainy competes with young athletic
     woman (rides, golf) for young composer. The widow
     straightens out the tangle, gives up own happiness NYT
     365,05

CHAMBERLAIN, LUCIA. Nationality Unknown.

001911   THE OTHER SIDE OF THE DOOR. Indianapolis:
Bobbs-Merrill, [1909] NUC.

     Murder story-PW 5-8-09
     And love story. BKM
     NYT

001912   SON OF THE WIND. Indianapolis:
Bobbs-Merrill, [c1910] NUC.

     Story of a man and a woman who feel opposite ways
     about a wild horse; he would tame it; she would free
     it. They quarrel, part when he gets his way. The horse
     dies in the breaking of it. End? PW
     Title refers to a horse, a wild one. Blanche Rader
     loves horses; she alone knows where the wild one
     feeds. "He is hers because he's free." Blanche falls
     in love with a rancher who secretly wants the horse.
     The horse breaks its back trying to throw the rancher.
     NYT

CHAMBERLAIN, LUCIA, jt. au. See CHAMBERLAIN, ESTHER AND
LUCIA CHAMBERLAIN.

CHAMBERLAIN, MARIE CECELIA. United States.

001913   IN THE GLOAMING. Chicago: Scroll, 1900
NUC.

CHAMBERLAYNE, EFFIE.

001914   BEFORE THE CURTAIN. London: J. Long, 1916
BMC.

001915   A KING OF NO-MAN'S LAND. London: Century
Press, 1911 BMC.

     Hist. romance TLS

CHAMBERS, ROSA. B. 1886. United States.

001916   THE HIPPODROME; A NOVEL. BY RACHEL
HAYWARD. London: W. Heinemann, 1913 BMC NUC. New York:
G.H. Doran, [c1913] NUC.

     Romance of anarchy and love; equestrienne ATH
     "Story of Fatalite, a present-day Carmen-a girl, half
     Irish, half Austrian, who comes to Barcelona to ride
     in The Hippodrome. the leader of the Spanish
     Terrorists uses her as a go between. The adventure
     fascinates Fatalite, and she enters upon a life and

association where the amenities of life and the difference of sex are ignored. Then she finds that she is a woman who loves and makes the supreme sacrifice of her life for the man." PW
She has a contradictory nature: boy-like and self confident but womanly too. Becomes a revolutionary; different view of anarchists-The brotherhood. The cause, devotion and liberty. Irish-Jewish heroine-rides beautifully, then when family loses fortune, becomes a circus rider, meets an anarchist who immediatley sees how he can use her. Comradeship grows between them; she loves another. BKM
"The heroine of Rachel Hayward's vivid story is Arethelli of the Hippodrome in Barcelona. Half Irish and half Austrian by birth, she is by nature a many-sided creature whose unusual and contradictory character is well conceived and portrayed in clear, rapid, convincing strokes...She falls among the Terrorists on her arrival in Barcelona, and one of their leaders seeing in her the material they want, gradually enmeshes her in the cause and she becomes one of a band of conspirators who sing of liberty and deal in death. There is a good picture of these people, their meetings and plans." BRD

001917   LETTERS FROM LA-BAS. BY RACHEL HAYWARD. Boston: J. W. Luce, 1914 NUC. London: W. Heinemann, [1914] BMC.

"By author of "The hippodrome." "La-Bas" is Paris slang for the "Lower regions." Book is made up of letters from a young Englishwoman, by descent one fourth Russian, but by temperament pleased to consider herself much more Russian than English. She lives with her disagreeable old grandfather, an archaeologist. At first he potters around Lyons, then goes to northern France, near Lille, the "La-Bas." Letters are written to heroine's rather smug, young English fiance, and are entertaining revelations of a complex personality." PW 3-21-14 1021
SR Letters express opinions on love, marriage and feminism.
From a large hearted woman to a cold hearted man ATH 143: 227. O
TLS She abandons him finally for a Russian.
LBKM- Her last letter announces her departure for Paris with a lover.

CHAMBLIN, JEAN. Nationality Unknown.

001918   LADY BOBS, HER BROTHER, AND I. A ROMANCE OF THE AZORES. New York and London: G. P. Putnam's Sons, 1905 BMC NUC.

Actress's letters about Azores. PW 11-18-05
Actress tired of things in general goes to Azores for a rest, romantic. --NYT 825,05

CHAMPION, JESSIE. United Kingdom.

001919   THE FOOLISHNESS OF LILIAN. London: J. Lane, 1918 NUC BMC. New York: J. Lane, 1918 NUC BMC.

PW-A slum beauty, goes from factory to stage to literature to war nursing, falls in love with literary collaborator.
TLS- Actually, she is of superior birth-her father had fallen because of carrying another man's guilt. She is interested in philosophy. Sounds light, popular. ATH O
LBKM-Becomes a cultured actress. Then she devotes herself to the interests of a widow, a friend who had been kind to her.
NYT May 5, 1918, p 213. Eventually chose the right man and lived happily everafter.

001920   JIMMY'S WIFE. London: J. Lane, 1917 NUC BMC. New York: J. Lane, 1917 NUC BMC.

Story of a successful matchmaking PW
Man and wife-both unconventional SP
Vicar's wife tells of fascinating young actress and rich tobacconist who are new to the community. After complications, a match is made and a happy everafter end. NYT 4-15-17 155
TLS- Told by Vicar's wife

001921   THE RAMSHACKLE ADVENTURE. London: Hodder & Stoughton, [1920] BMC.

LBKM-Man and his car.

001922   SUNSHINE IN UNDERWOOD. London and New York: J. Lane, 1919 NUC BMC.

CHAMPNEY, ELIZABETH (WILLIAMS). 1850-1922. United States.

001923   A DAUGHTER OF THE HUGUENOTS. New York: Dodd, Mead, 1901 NUC.

10-26-01 PW Hist rom.

001924   MARGARITA; A LEGEND OF THE FIGHT FOR THE GREAT RIVER. New York: Dodd, Mead, 1902 NUC.

NYT 10-18-02 hist.
Louisiana-Hist-Col. Period.

001925   ROMANCE OF THE BOURBON CHATEAUX. New York and London: G. P. Putnam's Sons, 1903 BMC NUC.

hist rom. PW 10-10-03
France-Hist-Bourbons

CHAMPNEY, MRS. EBEN FREEMONT. United States.

001926   LOVE'S DREAM; OR, DID HE MEAN TO WRONG HER? New York: J. S. Ogilvie, [c1900] NUC.

CHAMPNEYS, ADELAIDE MARY. United Kingdom.

001927   BRIDE ELECT. London: E. Arnold, 1913 BMC.

Psychological study: a mutinous orphan devoted to mother's memory. Aunt packs her off to 2nd rate girls' school. Audrey keeps a diary which teacher attempts to take from her. Her guardian three times her age, now widowed, offers her marriage. (she's 17.)She accepts out of gratitude. But on eve of marriage, she learns of his infatuation with Eve, a great actress. Engagement broken; he dies; she ends up in a convent. She's angel-like throughout. ATH

001928   THE RECOILING FORCE. London: E. Arnold, 1914 BMC.

ATH-male hero, wealthy S. African. Spoiled his life by marrying for position.
TLS 13:506. This rev. says Madeline is the heroine, a 17 year old whose aunt is arranging an advantageous marriage for her. When she is repelled by his driving off after running over a child, she marries Ralph Helyer. He is a rotten husband and does not repay her love. She rebels. "Dulcie--good hearted, common, sensible, womanly--is our refuge; but even Dulcie is a practising feminist, and rest from feminism is the one temporary mercy we owe to perfidious Prussia."

CHANCELLOR, LOUISE ISABEL (BEECHER). 1871-1908. United States.

001929   THE PLAYERS O' LONDON. A TALE OF AN ELIZABETHIAN [SIC] SMART SET. New York: B. W. Dodge, [1909] NUC BMC.

Phyllis, twin of boy player in Lord Leicester's Co., takes part of Juliet, wins Shakespeare's Love (!) NYT

CHANCELLOR, OLIVE.

001930   THE LADY GARDENER. A ROMANCE OF SIX MONTHS. London: Drane's, [1914] BMC.

ATH Wealthy bachelor advertises for lady gardener. She's fantastic, romance.

CHANDLER, IZORA CECILIA. D. 1906. United States.

001931   A DOG OF CONSTANTINOPLE. New York: Dodd, Mead, 1896 NUC.

001932   ELVIRA HOPKINS OF TOMPKIN'S CORNER. New York: Wilbur B. Ketcham, [c1899] NUC.

CHANNEL, A., pseud. See CARTER, ADA.

CHANNING, BLANCHE MARY. 1863-1902.

001933   THE BALASTER BOYS, A STORY. Boston: W. A. Wilde, [1902] NUC.

001934   WINIFRED WEST. A STORY. Boston: W. A. Wilde, 1901 NUC.

Heroine studies violin. 10-5-01 PW

CHANNON, E. M. See CHANNON, ETHEL MARY.

CHANNON, ETHEL MARY. B. 1875. United Kingdom.

001935   THE AUTHORESS. London: Hutchinson, 1909 BMC.

Vivia Mortlake wrongly gains authorship of a book -
"pathetic story" TLS

001936   THE BOY NEXT DOOR. London: R.T.S., [1920]
BMC.

001937   CATO'S DAUGHTER. London: Mills and Boon,
1913 BMC.

Doris Cato and school chum Esther; Valencia Hermoine
Shelmerdine, millionaire's daughter-vain, selfish with
a shocking temper. Two lose wealth, learn what life's
all about TLS

001938   THE GRAND MISS GABRIELLE. London: R.T.S.,
[1917] BMC.

001939   THE KEEPER OF THE SECRET. London: Mills &
Boon, 1912 BMC.

TLS-Male hero, love

001940   MISS KING'S PROFESSION. London: Mills and
Boon, 1913 BMC.

woman "mistakes literary work for talent, sacrifices
her family in the process"; "justly punished in the
end by marrying a priggish clergyman." SP.
Satire on young women who take up novel writing
(second rate stuff) rather than doing something use
ful. Gives up career for love.

001941   THE REAL MRS. HOLYER. BY E. M. CHANNON
(MRS. FRANCIS CHANNON). London: Hutchinson, 1911 BMC.
Garden City, N.Y.: Doubleday, Page, 1912 NUC.

NYT-Her husband is missing at sea. She makes no
inquiries for five years because he wished their
marriage a secret. She suffers especially of being an
unmarried mother.
Margaret Lennard- Sympathetically drawn-suffers as
governess and waits years for husband who went to
Jamaica and disappeared. ?TLS
Remarries-SP

001942   STONELADIES. London: Hutchinson, 1912
BMC.

ATH- Two girls entrusted to care of miserly cousin.

001943   A STREET ANGEL. London: Hutchinson, 1910
BMC.

TLS- "nice" story of village life and handsome curate-

001944   THE STRENGTH OF WEAKNESS. London: Mills &
Boon, 1915 BMC.

Little girl learns father wanted a son "contrives that
her upbringing shall be that of a boy." The man she
loves is not attracted by her lack of feminine
weaknesses, marries a "true woman" and is miserable.
The two get together in the end. ATH

CHANNON, MRS. FRANCIS. See CHANNON, ETHEL MARY.

CHANT, LAURA ORMISTON (DIBBIN). 1848-1923.

001945   SELLCUTS' MANAGER. BY MRS. ORMISTON
CHANT. London: G. Richards, 1899 BMC NUC.

Concerns theatrical life. Hero is a theatre manager.
LIT 5:349.
Sellcut is a music hall. Author known for her views on
proper control of such places. ACAD 57:336
Author portrays her ideal music hall with all sorts of
attractions like nurseries, wash-houses, oratorios, to
make up for absence of alcohol. SR 88:559

CHANT, MRS. ORMISTON. See CHANT, LAURA ORMISTON (DIBBIN).

CHANTER, GRATIANA, pseud. See KNOCKER, GRATIANA LONGWORTH.

CHAN TOON, MABEL MARY AGNES.

001946   HELEN WYVERNE'S MARRIAGE. London: Digby,
Long, 1912 BMC.

001947   LEPER AND MILLIONAIRE. A NOVEL. London:
Greening, 1910 BMC.

TLS-male millionaire leper
SR male millionaire leper

001948   A MARRIAGE IN BURMAH. A NOVEL. London:

Greening, 1905 BMC.

English woman married to a Burmese-a violent, lying,
immoral drunk. Wife suffers in the extreme.
Is author bent on showing danger of mixed marr? a true
psych study? LBKM 27-8, 211

001949   A SHADOW OF BURMAH. London: Digby, Long,
1914 BMC.

TLS-Mystery about Miss Hoy who had been in Burma and
lived on remote Scottish island.

CHAPEAU, ELLEN CHAZAL. B. 1844. United States.

001950   UNDER THE DARKNESS OF THE NIGHT:
HISTORICAL ROMANCE. Washington, D. C.: Neale, 1901
NUC.

CHAPIN, ANNA ALICE. 1880-1920. United States.

001951   DISCORDS. New York: Pelham Press, 1902
NUC.

001952   THE EAGLE'S MATE. New York: W. J. Watt,
[c1914] NUC. London: R. Hayes, [1920] BMC.

"For twenty-five years Mrs. Breckenridge has lived the
life of a southern lady, after her husband's death,
centering all her affection on his young cousin,
Anemone, when the Mornes, her mountain kinsmen, raid
the valley and make a jail delivery. A Morne must
always succor a Morne, so Mrs. Breckenridge has to
shelter them when they demand it. The result is that
Anemone is kidnapped and carried away to their
mountain home, where she is married to lancer Morne,
the leader. There are numerous fights, captures, and
escapes, in which Anemone plays a surprising part,
learning at last that her only happiness is in these
mountains." PW

001953   JANE. New York and London: G. P. Putnam's
Sons, 1920 BMC NUC.

TLS Love story.
PW-Irish girl turned out by her father joins acting
troupe and becomes successful actress.

001954   MOUNTAIN MADNESS. New York: W. J. Watt,
[c1917] NUC.

Romance PW 91:629 2/24/17

001955   THE UNDER TRAIL. Boston: Little, Brown,
1912 NUC. London: I. Pitman, 1912 BMC.

PW Wild adventures in Virginia mountains of nurse.
TLS love story.
NYT-Melodrama. Narration of love of an educated woman
for a primitive man. Hair-raising adventures in the
mountains.

CHAPMAN, KATHARINE (HOPKINS). 1872-1930.

001956   THE FUSING FORCE; AN IDAHO IDYL. Chicago:
A. C. McClurg, 1911 NUC.

NYT-romance.
Western mining town setting of love story. 9-23-11 PW

CHAPPELL, JENNIE.

001957   A LADY OF HIGH DEGREE. London: S.W.
Partridge, [1899] BMC.

Heroine born deformed in a family famous for beauty.
Her mother dies, she's given over to poor family to
raise. She's a twin. Eventually reunited with family
and operation makes her beautiful. SP 83:613

CHARLES, FRANCES ASA. B. 1872. United States.

001958   THE AWAKENING OF THE DUCHESS. Boston:
Little, Brown, 1903 NUC. London: Ward, Lock, 1904 BMC.

Mother's love for daughter; mother's interested in
missions, charitable. PW 10-31-03

001959   IN THE COUNTRY GOD FORGOT. A STORY OF
TODAY. Boston: Little, Brown, 1902 BMC NUC.

Ariz. NYT 6-14-02

001960   PARDNER OF BLOSSOM RANGE. Boston: Little,
Brown, 1906 NUC.

PW-?

001961   THE SIEGE OF YOUTH. Boston: Little,
Brown, 1903 BMC NUC.

CHARLESWORTH, M. E., pseud. See BOOTH, MAUD BALLINGTON
(CHARLESWORTH).

CHARNWOOD, DOROTHEA MARY ROBY (THORPE) BENSON. 1876-1942.
United Kingdom.

001962   THE DEAN. BY LADY CHARNWOOD. London:
Constable, 1919 NUC.

Focus on a high ecclesiastical circle. TLS, SP,
LBKM

001963.   THE FULL PRICE. BY LADY CHARNWOOD.
London: Smith, Elder, 1915 NUC.

Lord Shelford 60ish tries to win a girl in her teens.
Story traces their feelings about each other. TLS
Says very little LBKM
"Old fashioned novel" ATH

CHARNWOOD, LADY. See CHARNWOOD, DOROTHEA MARY ROBY (THORPE)
BENSON.

CHARTRES, A. VIVANTI. See CHARTRES, ANITA (VIVANTI).

CHARTRES, ANITA (VIVANTI). 1868-1942. United Kingdom.

001964   THE DEVOURERS. BY A. VIVANTI CHARTRES.
New York: G. P. Putnam's Sons, 1910 NUC. London: W.
Heinneman, 1910 BMC NUC.

A very talented and intellectual woman whose
intellectual aspirations are curtailed by her interest
in a child left to her care . This child also grows to
womanhood and is on the way to fulfilling her artistic
mission and is faced with the same duty. Both are
geniuses. PW
TLS--The mother and whole family make sacrifices for
child genius (poet). Then she marries and does no more
with her talent but has genius child (violin player)
and like her mother is also devoured by the needs of
genius. Character study. Last line: "In the shadowy
cradle the baby opened its eyes and said, "I am
hungry."

001965   THE OUTRAGE New York: A. A. Knopf, 1918
NUC.

PW-2 young women and child have Germans quartered 1
night. Child becomes deaf and dumb.
WWI-fiction

001966   VAE VICTIS. London: E. Arnold, 1917 BMC.

Germans in Belgium come upon a child, a young girl and
a young married woman. The grinding misery which is to
follow only begins after they go to England and then
return to Belgium. The child is deaf and dumb because
of the horror; the girl and woman raped and left
pregnant. English surgeons abort; one child does live:
symbol of hope. TLS

001967   WINNING HIM BACK. New York: Smart Set,
1904 NUC.

NYT--Marital comedy.

CHASE, AMANDA (MATHEWS). B. 1866. United States.

001968   THE HEART OF AN ORPHAN. BY AMANDA
MATHEWS. New York: D. Fitzgerald, [c1912] NUC.

NYT-pathetic and amusing child.

CHASE, BEATRICE, pseud. See PARR, OLIVE KATHARINE.

CHASE, JESSIE (ANDERSON). B. 1865. United States.

001969   CHAN'S WIFE, A STORY. Boston: M. Jones,
1919 NUC.

Boston male artist and Chicago woman find many
complications in marriage before they adjust. PW

001970   THREE FRESHMEN: RUTH, FRAN AND NATHALIE.
Chicago: A. C. McClurg, 1898 NUC.

One from Chicago, one from Boston, one from the South
at Smith, merry studious and happy BOOK NEWS 98-9,308.

CHATTERTON, G. G. United Kingdom.

001971   THE ANGEL OF CHANCE. London: J. Long,
1900 BMC.

LIT 6:481. Old-fashioned romance.

001972   THE COURT OF DESTINY. London: J. Long,
1902 BMC.

001973   A DARN ON A BLUE-STOCKING: A STORY OF
TODAY. London: Bellairs, 1896 BMC.

001974   THE DICTIONARY OF FOOLS. London: J. Long,
1907 BMC.

001975   FATALITY. London: J. Long, 1908 BMC.

heroine, love starved in her marriage of convenience,
suspected of poisoning husband till nurse confesses,
heroine "really loveable" TLS

001976   THE GATE OF NEVER. London: J. Long, 1903
BMC.

001977   THE GIRL WITH THE ODDS AGAINST HER.
London: J. Long, 1910 BMC.

001978   HOBSON'S CHOICE. London: J. Long, 1913
BMC.

001979   THE HUMAN STARLING. A STUDY OF A WOMAN'S
NATURE. London: J. Long, [1918] BMC.

TLS-struggle of Barbara for independence, different
jobs and love affairs marries in end wrong man. "I
can't get out" caged starling

001980   THE SPORT OF CIRCUMSTANCE. London: J.
Long, 1899 BMC.

001981   STRAIGHT SHOES. London: J. Long, 1900
BMC.

CHAUNDLER, CHRISTINE.

001982   JUST GERRY. London: Nisbet, [1920] BMC.

001983   THE REPUTATION OF THE UPPER FOURTH.
London: Nisbet, [1919] BMC.

CHEATHAM, CARRIE VANDIVER. Nationality Unknown.

001984   BEATRICE SUMPTER. Boston: C. M. Clark,
1908 NUC.

CHEEVER, HARRIET ANNA. Fl. 1890-1911. United States.

001985   DOCTOR ROBIN. Boston: D. Estes, [1902]
NUC.

001986   ELMCOVE. New York: American Tract
Society, [1902] NUC.

001987   GIPSY JANE. Boston: D. Estes, [1903] NUC.

young gypsy girl wonderful dancer and musician goes on
stage 10-17-03 PW

001988   JOSIE BEAN: FLAT STREET. Boston: D.
Estes, [c1905] NUC.

ambitious, uned.-first milliner's assistant. Young
woman rises from poverty to become a prominent artist.
At 18 faces happy future. PW

001989   LOU. Boston: D. Estes, [1904] NUC.

001990   MADAME ANGORA. Boston: D. Estes, [1901]
NUC.

CHELLIS, MARY DWINELL. United States.

001991   OLD BENCHES WITH NEW PROPS. New York:
National Temperance Society, 1891 NUC.

CHENERY, SUSAN, pseud. See GORE, SUSAN FRANCES (RICHARDS).

CHENEY, ELIZABETH. United States.

001992   THE HOUSE OF LOVE. New York: Abingdon
Press, [c1914] NUC.

PW 86 10/3/14:1117 "Doris built for herself a house
where she could be free from the outside sufferings of
her life. As a child, circumstances placed her as a
servant for ignorant, hard farmers. But circumstances

can change, and her house of love became a house of joy as well."
NYT-O

001993   THE KING'S GOLD: A STORY. New York: Eaton and Mains, [c1900] NUC.

001994   THE LAPIDARIES, AND AUNT DEBORAH HEARS "THE MESSIAH". New York: Eaton and Mains, [c1900] NUC.

CHER, MARIE, pseud. See SCHERR, MARIE.

CHERBONNEL, ALICE. B. 1854.

001995   FATE'S LETTERS. BY JEAN DE LA BRETE. London: Digby, Long, [1897] BMC. (Tr. Mrs. F. Hoper-Dixon)

001996   MY UNCLE AND MY CURE. BY JEAN DE LA BRETE. New York: Dodd, Mead, 1892 NUC. (Tr. Ernest Redwood)

LW 23:391. Autobiography of Mademoiselle De Lavalle

001997   THE STORY OF REINE; OR MY UNCLE AND MY CURE. BY JEAN DE LA BRETE. Boston: Roberts, 1891 NUC. (Tr. Mrs. J. W. Davis)

001998   UNCLE. BY JEAN DE LA BRETE. London: Dean, 1892 BMC. (Tr. J. Berwick)

SP. Reine is heroine. Her education is superintended by her uncle who is "delighted and terrified by her ingenuity in acquiring contraband knowledge," Story has a "sweet simplicity."

CHERRY, AUNT, pseud. See ROWLAND, JANE.

CHESSON, NORA (HOPPER). 1871-1906. United Kingdom.

001999   THE BELL AND THE ARROW: AN ENGLISH LOVE STORY. London: T. W. Laurie, 1905 NUC BMC.

Margaret is fascinating and fickle ACAD 420, 05
TLS 129, 05
Two pairs of lovers. Stresses the value of maternity; young woman about to be a mother adopts a child out of "mere desperate maternal feelings of an animal." ATH 05, 459
BAKER 32-102

002000   FATHER FELIX'S CHRONICLES. London: T. F. Unwin, 1907 NUC BMC.

Told by monk in days of Henry IV-vivid pictures of 15th century. Nothing about female characters SP.

CHESTER, ELIZA, pseud. See PAINE, HARRIET ELIZA.

CHESTER, EVELYN. United States.

002001   MISS DERRICK: A BOSTON SOCIETY GIRL'S DIARY. New York: G. W. Dillingham, 1894 NUC.

PW-diary form. Describing follies of flirtations verging on indecency, skirt-dancing, cigarette smoking, champagne drinking carried to excess by women as well as men; her elopement with a married man.

CHESTER, NORLEY, pseud. See UNDERDOWN, EMILY.

CHESTERTON, ADA ELIZABETH (JONES).

002002   AN EYE FOR AN EYE. BY JOHN KEITH PROTHERO. London: Mascot Novels, [1917] BMC.

002003   MOTLEY AND TINSEL. A STORY OF THE STAGE. BY JOHN KEITH PROTHERO. London: S. Swift, 1911 BMC.

CHETWYND, HON. MRS. HENRY. See CHETWYND, JULIA BOSVILLE (DAVIDSON).

CHETWYND, JULIA BOSVILLE (DAVIDSON). D. 1901.

002004   A BRILLIANT WOMAN. BY THE HON. MRS. HENRY CHETWYND. London: Hutchinson, 1892 BMC NUC.

ATH 100:736. Estrangement and reconciliation of Mr. & Mrs. Burlington. "Decorous," "amiable."
SR 74:538. Development of her realization that her husband is her superior in every way.

002005   THE MEMBER'S WIFE, A NOVEL. London: C. A. Pearson, 1898 BMC.

SP 81:873. Placid amiable story of good baronet and

his romance, loved by good woman and bad cousin. Happy ending.
Dreary story of misunderstanding of lovers. They part; he weds the woman who came between and when she dies, lovers unite. SR 88:369.

CHILDS, CARRIE GOLDSMITH. United States.

002006   AND THE SWORD FELL. Floral Park, N.Y.: Mayflower, 1895 NUC.

PW1-11-96. A wife's study of her married life told through her journal; a few years of happiness are followed by suspicion and estrangement.

002007   LOST LINEAGE. Floral Park, N.Y.: Mayflower, 1897 NUC.

Young farmer's daughter marries secretly. She's about to have a baby; father calls doctor to remote farmhouse, wants the doctor to kill the child because he's angry with his daughter. PW 51:808.

CHILDS, ELEANOR STUART (PATTERSON). B. 1876. United States.

002008   AVERAGES: A STORY OF NEW YORK. BY ELEANOR STUART. New York: D. Appleton, 1899 NUC BMC.

Modern New York. Two women--both have unhappy marriages. One is a novelist, the other is editor of the Day Star, organ of the Early Bird Circle of World's workers. CR 35:1152.
BKM 10:502. No plot. Cornelia, married to "poor little man" with money. She flirts mildly, tells foolish lies, absolutely colorless. New York
LW 31:71. She tolerates husband. She has written a book published in England. Jane Dupuis, a woman who works helping working women, reads it, admires it, and writes to her. Cornelia keeps up the correspondence under her nom de plume. Actually Jane is her nearest neighbor and friend. When she is found out she incurs the anger of the doctor and the loss of a friend. Dr. is Jane's husband.

002009   THE POSTSCRIPT. BY ELEANOR STUART. New York: McClure, 1908 NUC.

PW-widow, orphan, romance, intrigue.

002010   THE ROMANCE OF ALI. BY ELEANOR STUART. New York and London: Harper, 1913 BMC NUC.

Focuses upon an Arab boy raised in a harem who at 14 is turned over to an English tutor. Then to England and Germany to complete his education. Complex and interesting personality. NYT TLS

002011   STONEPASTURES. BY ELEANOR STUART. New York: D. Appleton, 1895 NUC BMC.

LW 27:76. Life in a mining community.
PW 2-1-96. Stuart is a pseudonym. Soot City, Penn. Swede loves a young woman who is a barber. On their wedding day a rival lets him get near a blast without warning, he is a physical wreck. Story is of their life from this point on.

CHILDS, JESSIE DOW (HOPKINS).

002012   THE SEA OF MATRIMONY. A NOVEL. New York: Broadway, [c1909] NUC.

CHILES, ROSA PENDLETON.

002013   DOWN AMONG THE CRACKERS. Cincinnati: Editor Pub. Co., 1900 NUC.

CHIPPERFIELD, ROBERT ORR, pseud. See OSTRANDER, ISABEL EGENTON.

CHISHOLM, BELLE V. United States.

002014   STEPHEN LYLE, GENTLEMAN AND PHILANTHROPIST. Cincinnati: Cranston and Stowe, 1891 NUC.

CHOLMONDELEY, ALICE, pseud. See RUSSELL, MARY ANNETTE (BEAUCHAMP) ARNIM RUSSELL.

CHOLMONDELEY, MARY. 1859-1925. United Kingdom.

002015   AFTER ALL. New York: D. Appleton, 1913 NUC.

BKM-Annette, after an unhappy love affair, is rescued

from jumping into the Seine by Dick, who takes her to
Fontainebleau for a week, buying her a wedding ring
for appearance. He is stricken with paralysis the next
day, Annette, before his family arrives, goes to
English aunts. His relatives are from same village,
and his cousin Roger falls in love with her, but can't
bring himself to marry her until she offers to
sacrifice her good name by making public that she
witnessed a will in which Dick left all his money to
Roger.
"By author of "Red pottage" Annette Georges is on the
verge of drowning herself in the Seine when she
happens to meet an eccentric young Englishman, who
owns race horse. He suggests that she go with him for
a week to Fontainebleau. Desperate and half dazed, she
consents. The young man becomes dangerously ill. In a
lucid interval he makes a will, Annette being one of
the witnesses, and shortly afterwards develops
paralysis. Annette goes to England to make her home
with some aunts, and later develops a love affair with
the cousin of the young racing man. The latter dies
and his will comes to light, and then Annette finds
herself in a decidedly embarrassing situation." PW
"A young girl, in hopeless despair after her first
revelation of life's ugliness, is about to drown
herself. She is rescued by a light, adventurous young
Englishman who persuades her to run away with him.
Fate takes him out of her life as suddenly as he
entered it. The girl is left untouched and unchanged,
but the shadow of the episode hangs over her, and for
a time seems perilously near to blotting out the sun
of happiness that dawns for her." BRD

002016   A DEVOTEE: AN EPISODE IN THE LIFE OF A
BUTTERFLY. London: E. Arnold, 1897 BMC NUC.

Fashionable young men and women. Mr. Loftus' first
wife ran away from him. ATH 109:413.
She's selfish, "a self-worshipper." She proposes.
After her marriage moves from being content to
wretchedness. Rev. is confused about the aim of this
part of the novel. BKM 6:76.

002017   DIANA TEMPEST. London: R. Bentley, 1893
BMC. New York: D. Appleton, 1893 NUC.

A novel "which George Eliot would never have dared to
publish". Diana is loved by John the owner of
Overleigh. She's his first cousin. The novel turns on
his paternity. Turns out the man he thought his father
was not. Gives up his inheritance because he thinks
he's illegitimate. Diana comes from bad stock. She
gets the inheritance he gave up and transfers it back
to him by marrying him. SR 76 653
Social novel. Also sensational and detective story
like. Attempts on hero's life. BKM 5:87
Mystery involving hired assassins. Diane's love story:
"women who know something about life--of the great
demands of marriage of the absolute sacrifice of the
individual that it involves, "when the great passion
comes, "some...give all, counting not the cost--a very
few--count the cost and then give all. Di was one of
these." SP 72:560
She is a "chaste, high-spirited girl, unspotted by the
world and superior to the ambitions of fashionable
life, rejecting wealth rather than honor." BAKER
'03:89
Di "thinks for herself" and remains "sweetly womanly."
ACAD 44:564

002018   THE HAND ON THE LATCH. New York: Dodd,
Mead, 1909 NUC.

"Containing four short stories, in each of which the
woman suffers through love and self-sacrifice. "The
Hand on the Latch" is the first story and is concerned
with the cruel fate which befell a trusting woman.
Left alone at night, miles from any civilization, to
guard a large sum of money which her husband had
collected as taxes and hidden under the floor of the
kitchen for safe keeping, while he was away on a trip
which he assured his wife he was obliged to make, the
woman is greatly frightened when some one, claiming to
be a wounded soldier, begs admittance. Despite the
promise to her husband that she would open the door to
no one, she is unable to turn the sufferer away. Later
in the night she is alarmed again by a strange noise.
She calls to her assistance the wounded man , and the
two arm themselves and stand waiting for the burglar
to enter. The woman fires the shot that kills, and
upon removing the mask from the man's face she looks
upon her own husband. To save the honour of the man
she had loved and trusted, she lies to her companion,
in response to his inquiry as to whether she knew the
man, saying, "He is a stranger to me." BRD

002019   NOTWITHSTANDING. London: J. Murray, 1913
NUC BMC.

We first meet Annette the heroine meditating suicide
in the Seine; she's a fugitive from her father's
house-where her honour is not safe. Saved by a man she
goes off with, but she's "saved" from him because he
immediately falls ill. She witnesses a will upon which
the plot turns when she later marries this man's
cousin. Raised by 3 aunts who are a popular novelist, one
a Christian Scientist, one "practical". At 21 goes to
live with father, leaves him because he tries "to sell
her" to a musician and then to a gentleman. Then about
to throw self in Seine. LBKM

002020   PRISONERS; FAST BOUND IN MISERY AND IRON.
New York: Dodd, Mead, 1906 NUC. London: Hutchinson,
1906 BMC NUC.

BKMN 24 1906-7 study of a miserably weak woman.
PW-woman has affair with cousin who confesses to a
murder he has not done to save her reputation. He
remains in jail even after her husband's death because
she does not clear his name.
TLS She is a prisoner of her conscience and finally
clears his name. Study in development of character.
Author is never "unkind" to her weak heroine.
NYT

002021   RED POTTAGE. London: E. Arnold, 1899 BMC.
New York and London: Harper, 1899 NUC.

Opens with Lord Newhaven and Hugh Scarlett drawing
lots for death, unknown to Lady Newham and Rachel
West. Another woman character Hester Gresley is
contrasted to Rachel. LIT 5:495
Lady Newhaven is Hugh's lover and her husband has
discovered the fact. Hugh loses the wager and must
kill himself. Then Hugh falls for Rachel West, the
heroine, so he doesn't kill self. Then Lord Newhaven
kills himself leaving his wife a note telling all so
she'll be sure to ruin Hugh's happiness. Lady N
exposes him, he kills self. Hester is an
"intellectually emancipated modern woman." SP 83:612
Male novelist whose books come slowly and his
relationship to two friends--women, Hester is a
novelist. The women are really his best friends. ACAD
57:485
Considered a masterpiece. ACAD 57:575.
Searching analysis of motive and conduct. Serious
criticism of modern life. BAKER 03,90

CHOPIN, KATE (O'FLAHERTY). 1851-1904. United States.

002022   THE AWAKENING. Chicago and New York: H.
S. Stone, 1899 NUC.

Kentucky girl marries Creole against parents' wishes
because he's Catholic. He takes her to New Orleans.
Opens--she's 28 with two sons spending summer at Grand
Isle. Contrast with Adele. This summer she realizes
her life doesn't satisfy her.
"Two men stir her emotional nature for a short time.
There is a tragical end." PW 55:772
"Particularly poignant is the woman's awakening...you
feel pity for the most unfortunate of her sex." NYT
6-24-99 408

CHRISTIANSON, BARBARA. United States.

002023   A TRUIMPHANT DEFEAT. New York and London:
F. T. Neely, [1901] NUC.

CHRISTIE, AGATHA. See MALLOWAN, AGATHA MARY CLARISSA
(MILLER) CHRISTIE.

CHRISTISON, NEIL, pseud. See BIRD, MARY PAGE.

CHURCH, VIRGINIA WOODSON (FRAME). B. 1880. United States.

002024   COMMENCEMENT DAYS; A NOVEL. Boston: L.C.
Page, 1910 NUC.

Young women at college to their graduation day when
one popular girl is suspected of theft. PW

CHURCHILL, LIDA ABBIE. United States.

002025   A GRAIN OF MADNESS: A ROMANCE. New York,
London: The Abbey Press, [1902] NUC.

NYT woman painter, illegitimate child of priest is
pupil of a male painter on condition she not marry for
10 years and then only a greater artist than herself.
He falls in love with her but she is a better painter.
Then what?

CLANCY, LOUISE MARKS (BREITENBACH). United States.

002026   CHRISTINE OF THE YOUNG HEART; A NOVEL.
Boston: Small, Maynard, [c1920] NUC.

NYT9-26-20, p 23. Sent, Pollyana misunderstood
debutante.

002027   ELEANOR OF THE HOUSEBOAT. BY LOUISE M.
BREITENBACH. Boston: Page, 1916 NUC.

soupy story about good Eleanor PW
PZ7

CLAPPERTON, MRS. FRANK.

002028   THE OTHER RICHARD GRAHAM. London: E.
Stock, 1911 BMC.

Murder story TLS

CLARE, AUSTIN, pseud. See JAMES, WILHELMINA MARTHA.

CLARE, CORA ESTELLA BENNETT (STEPHENSON). B. 1872. United
States.

002029   THE HAND OF GOD. BY CORA BENNETT
STEPHENSON. Boston: Ball Pub. Co., 1909 NUC.

Love story PW 5-1-09

CLARE, FRANCES. United Kingdom.

002030   WILD JUSTICE. London: A. Melrose, 1912
BMC. New York: Duffield, 1913 PW.

"However strong may be a woman's temptation to defy
conventional morality at the call of true love, she
can only secure her permanent happiness by putting it
resolutely away from her." PW
"Marriage martyrdom," endeavor to hold fast to a bad
marriage NYT "Two tumultuous but steadfast
temperaments...<in> the long tale of marriage
martydoms..." The characters remain married only
because "it is their ideal of the way in which
obligations already assumed must be met." NYT 1913, p.
66.
TLS—Tame chronicle of the relations between two men
and two women.

CLARE, KATHLEEN, pseud. See MACCHESNEY, DORA GREENWELL.

CLAREMONT, NITA.

002031   THEIR MONTH. London: J. Long, [1914] BMC.

CLARK, FANNY BECKWITH. United States.

002032   A MODERN EXPERIENCE. Cleveland: [The
Imperial Press], 1897 NUC NUC.

CLARK, FELICIA (BUTTZ). 1862-1931. United States.

002033   THE CITY OF MYSTERY. London: C. H. Kelly,
1914 BMC.

ATH Modern politics in Rome.

002034   THE CRIPPLE OF NUREMBERG. Cincinnati:
Jennings & Pye, [1900] NUC. London: C. H. Kelly, 1901
BMC.

PW Germany, 16th c. Charles and his efforts to
reestablish Roman Catholicism, pitting family members
against each other in his vain attempt.

002035   DAVID GOLDING. Cincinnati: Jenmings &
Pye, [1903] NUC.

Noble heroism 10-31-03 PW

002036   GUIDO THE CHOIR-BOY. London: C. H. Kelly,
[1906] BMC.

002037   THE JESUIT. New York: Eaton & Mains,
[c1908] NUC.

PW—Catholicism from Protestant pov

002038   LAUGHING WATER. London: C. H. Kelly, 1915
BMC.

Englishman gone astray keeps daughter in seclusion in
Far West. ATH.

002039   SCHWESTER ANNA: A TALE OF GERMAN HOME
LIFE. New York: Eaton and Mains, [c1898] NUC.

PW 1898:705

002040   THE SWORD OF GARIBALDI. New York: Eaton &
Mains, [1903] NUC.

Hist. novel PW 10-31-03

002041   THE TREASURE OF REIFENSTEIN. London: C.
H. Kelly, [1906] BMC.

CLARK, GEORGINA BINNIE.

002042   A SUMMER ON THE CANADIAN PRAIRIE. New
York: Longman's, Green, 1910 NUC. London: E. Arnold,
1910 BMC.

Two women and brother develop a free grant of land in
northwest. PW

CLARK, HATTIE ARNOLD. United States.

002043   FATHER JEROME. A STORY OF THE SPANISH
INQUISITION. New York: Amer. Tract Soc., 1899 NUC.

16th c. Spain. reformation and inquisition. PW 56:697

CLARK, IMOGEN. D. 1936. United States.

002044   A CHARMING HUMBUG. New York: G. P.
Dutton, 1909 NUC. London: Methuen, 1911 BMC.

002045   THE DOMINE'S GARDEN. A STORY OF OLD NEW
YORK. London: J. Murray, 1901 BMC.

002046   GOD'S PUPPETS; A STORY OF OLD NEW YORK.
Toronto: W. J. Gage, 1901 BMC. New York: C. Scribner's
sons, 1901 NUC.

Peggy a madcap, a jockey CR 6/01 v38:566

002047   THE HERESY OF PARSON MEDLICOTT. New York:
T. Y. Crowell, [c1900] NUC.

002048   THE LAS' DAY. New York: A. D. F.
Randolph, [c1892] NUC.

002049   THE VICTORY OF EZRY GARDNER. New York,
Boston: T. Y. Crowell, [c1896] NUC.

LW 27:266. Nantucket. Character study of old man who
neighbors have always believed was a hero during the
war but actually he was afraid. Can scarely hold up
his head, then rescues someone from drowning and
confesses his former cowardice

CLARK, JANET MACDONALD.

002050   THE BOURGEOIS QUEEN OF PARIS. London:
Greening, 1910 BMC.

Amita Nitouche "wins immense power" in this hist rom.
"by wit, beauty and personality." ? TLS

CLARK, KATE (UPSON). 1851-1935. United States.

002051   UP THE WITCH BROOK ROAD. A SUMMER IDYL.
New York: J. F. Taylor, 1902 NUC BMC.

Told years later by older woman: experiences of a
young precocious girl about her two aunts, points out
differences between modern young women and the type of
50 years ago. NYT 03, 264
DIAL 4-18-02-semi rural idyl.

CLARK, MRS. HUGH.

002052   IN THE HEYDAY OF YOUTH. London: J. Long,
1916 BMC.

Love story on trad. lines. ATH

CLARK, MRS. S. R. GRAHAM. See CLARK, SUSANNA REBECCA
(GRAHAM).

CLARK, MURIEL.

002053   SISTER JEFFERIES. London: J. Nisbet, 1914
BMC.

ATH—Woman journalist gives up prospects and lover on
joining the Salvation Army.

CLARK, S. C. See CLARK, SUSIE CHAMPNEY.

CLARK, SUSANNA REBECCA (GRAHAM). B. 1848. United States.

002054   ADAM ARGHAM. London: S. W. Partridge,
[1908] BMC.

TLS-religious novel.

002055   THE CRY OF THE TWO-THIRDS. BY MRS. S. R.
GRAHAM CLARK. Boston: J. H. Earle, 1901 NUC.

002056   GAIL WESTON. BY MRS. S. R. GRAHAM CLARK.
Philadelphia: Griffith & Rowland Press, [1907] NUC.

religious story 11-2-07 PW

002057   JANET VARDOFF. BY MRS. S. R. GRAHAM
CLARK. Philadelphia: Griffith & Rowland Press, [1910]
NUC.

girls' story PW

002058   PHYLLIS BURTON; A TALE OF NEW ENGLAND. BY
MRS. S. R. GRAHAM CLARK. Philadelphia: Griffith &
Rowland Press, 1905 NUC.

CLARK, SUSIE CHAMPNEY. B. 1856. United States.

002059   ALL THAT MAN SHOULD BE UNTO WOMAN; A
PSYCHIC STORY. Boston: C. M. Clark, 1910 NUC.

002060   LORITA, AN ALASKAN MAIDEN. Boston: Lee
and Shepard, 1892 NUC.

CR 17:19. Brought up in Alaska, falls in love with
Indian. Is adopted by American meets Russian father
and Indian lover in Venice.
impressions of spiritualism and faith cure. Slim plot
threaded thru travel guide of Alaska, Calif. She was
born in Alaska, daughter of Russian. Ma died when she
was born. Grows up and marries. Father thought she was
dead. He returns to Alaska a noble. LW

002061   THE OPEN DOOR OF THE SOUL. BY DEBORAH
MORRISON. Boston: C. M. Clark, 1908 NUC.

002062   PILATE'S QUERY. BY S. C. CLARK. Boston:
Arena, 1895 NUC.

the "soul history" of a young man married to an
Episcopalian. He's a doubter-tries theosophy, etc.
Ends in spiritualism. PW 6-29-95:999.

CLARKE, AGNES SPENCER.

002063   SEVEN GIRLS. London: Simpkin, Marshall,
1899 BMC.

CLARKE, AMY (KEY).

002064   IN JACOBITE DAYS. BEING A PLAIN NARRATIVE
OF CERTAIN EVENTS CONNECTED WITH THE LANDING OF KING
WILLIAM AT TORBAY, AND WITH THE BURNING OF TEIGNMOUTH
BY THE FRENCH. WRITTEN BY THE REV. GILBERT LANE, D.D.,
RECTOR OF WITHYCOMBE. London: T. Nelson, [1903] BMC.

Hist 12-5-03 PW
"An advent LBKM 1903 Christmas Sup. 20

002065   JENNIFER'S FORTUNE. New York: E. & J. B.
Young, 1893 PW. London: Christian Knowledge Society,
[1893] BMC.

Jennifer Carah goes to live with her aunt. Thought
she'd inherit from her aunt, but her aunt favors a
young man of no relation until he displeases her.
Novel tells of final disposition of her wealth. PW
12-2-93

002066   REUBEN THORNE'S TEMPTATION. London:
Christian Knowledge Society, [1898] BMC.

PW-uprising of the Kaffirs in the Transvaal. He
misleads searchers who are looking for his cousin
after a raid. Story ends in England.

002067   THE ROSKERRY TREASURE. A TALE OF WYATT'S
REBELLION. BY MRS. HENRY CLARKE. London: Nelson,
[1906] NUC BMC.

002068   A TRUSTY REBEL; OR, A FOLLOWER OF
WARBECK. BY MRS. HENRY CLARKE. London: Nelson, [1904]
NUC.

CLARKE, CLARA SAVILE.

002069   THE POET'S AUDIENCE; AND DELILAH. London:
Cassell, 1891 BMC NUC.

Pure young woman attracted to literary charlatan, cad,
liar. Surroundings sordid. In "Delilah" young
politician attracted to vicious woman who murders his
wife. Repulsive stories ATH 98 798
ACAD 41:85. Greek tragedy. The Poet's...woman treats a
wealthy and generous husband with studied coldness and
discourtesy. Delilah-Husband deserts wife for another
woman.
SR 73:18. Poet resides in a London lodging house; has
a dedicated audience for his readings which includes a
young woman and a journalist. The poet moves on; she
is in love with him but marries the journalist.
"Painful process of her disillusion."

002070   THE WORLD'S PLEASURES. London: Bliss,
Sands and Foster, 1893 BMC.

CLARKE, I. See CLARKE, ISABEL CONSTANCE.

CLARKE, IDA CLYDE (GALLAGHER). B. 1878. United States.

002071   RECORD NO. 33. New York and London: D.
Appleton, 1915 NUC.

Romantic adventure involving a record, a girl and a
Fr. Professor. PW 9-4-15
Pretty, naive, slim story of a girl who falls in love
with a Fr. Professor on a record. NYT

CLARKE, ISABEL CONSTANCE. D. 1951. United Kingdom.

002072   BY THE BLUE RIVER. A NOVEL. BY I. CLARKE.
New York: Benziger, 1913 NUC. London: Hutchinson, 1913
BMC.

PW 11/15/13 1585-"Aubrey Amory, living in luxury in
London with his wife and child, is arrested for
embezzlement and then skips his bail. Frances, his
wife, goes to northern Africa to live and wait for him
and after some years he sends word he is going to risk
re-arrest and join her. In the meantime a fine man has
fallen in love with Frances and she with him. Aubrey
is drowned on his way to join his wife and after a
while she is happy with the other man."
Author writes with some skill of the Algerian Colony.
Heroine has a son, adventures with Arabs. ATH
Heroine made noble and dignified TLS

002073   CHILDREN OF EVE. New York: Benziger, 1918
NUC. London: Hutchinson, 1918 BMC.

PW-Catholicism.
TLS Catholicism.
NYT 1918:582 Struggle between Rina and Protestant
family for hero's soul. R. C. wins.

002074   THE DEEP HEART. A NOVEL. London:
Hutchinson, 1917 BMC. New York: Benziger, 1919 NUC.

Love triangle with an RC tone TLS
Story of Italy PW

002075   THE ELSTONES. A NOVEL. London:
Hutchinson, [1919] BMC. New York: Benziger, 1919 NUC.

Story of conversions to RCsm TLS

002076   THE EPISODE OF ALETHEA: A FAMILY RECORD.
London: A. D. Innes, 1897 BMC.

Artist goes blind. A woman who marries the man she
doesn't love because there are legal reasons vs her
marrying the man she does love. LBKM 12:44.
Blind artist has an insane wife but loves Althea and
vice versa. She's responsible for herself. She gives
up the artist to marry an uninteresting man. Althea
does it for her sister to whom she devotes her life.
ACAD 51:425.
Morna, Althea's consumptive sister; there's a suicide.
ATH 109:537.

002077   EUNICE: A NOVEL. New York: Benziger, 1919
NUC.

Catholic story PW

002078   FINE CLAY. A NOVEL. London: Hutchinson,
1914 BMC. New York: Benziger, 1914 NUC.

TLS-Romance and RC
PW 86 10/10/14:1202--"Beautiful, high-minded Yolande
Pascoe makes a secret marriage with Gifford Lumbeigh,
a younger son. She had been strictly reared in her

mother's faith, the Roman Catholic, which her husband
does not follow. Their child, Ambrose, is brought up
in surroundings hostile to this religion, but his
mother's faith has taken a deep hold upon him. He
becomes heir to his English grandfather's title and
estates, but learning that the Roman faith would bar
his inheritance, he renounces his claim to become a
priest."
ATH no, he becomes a priest.

002079   JULIAN: A NOVEL. London: Hutchinson,
[1920] BMC.

C, Conversion TLS

002080   LADY TRENT'S DAUGHTER; A NOVEL. New York:
Benziger, 1920 NUC. London: Hutchinson, [1920] BMC.

TLS-Study of relations between mother and daughter who
have been made to love the same man. Mother's
evolution from heartless woman of the world into
devoted mother. Combat of wills. He and daughter
become RC.
LBKM. Real beings with capacity for intense suffering
and joy.

002081   THE LAMP OF DESTINY. A NOVEL. London:
Hutchinson, 1916 BMC. New York: Benziger, 1927 NUC.

ATH-Author has created, sympathetically, a mulishly
obstinate heroine. She is adopted from a shipwreck and
hated by her adopting mother

002082   ONLY ANNE. A NOVEL. London: Hutchinson,
1914 BMC. New York: Benziger, 1916 NUC.

Love intrigues of Myrtle Ellington PW
ATH-Helps her friend marry man they both love.

002083   THE POTTER'S HOUSE. London: Hutchinson,
1916 BMC. New York: Benziger, 1921 NUC.

TLS- Anti-divorce.
ATH-opening days of war and heroine's awakening.

002084   PRISONERS' YEARS. BY I. CLARKE. London:
Methuen, 1912 BMC. New York: Benziger, 1912 NUC.

TLS- R. C.
ATH R. C.

002085   THE REST HOUSE. New York: Benziger, 1917
NUC.

Peggy met RC PW. Of wealthy family attempt to marry
her off.

002086   THE SECRET CITADEL. London: Hutchinson,
1913 BMC. New York: Benziger, 1914 NUC.

Melanie Ettrington takes 200 pages to decide to make a
Prot-R C marriage. But marriage changes the man; he
drives his wife to the "gates of death," but we're
left to assume love will conquer him. ACAD
Her patience and near escape from death bring
conversion of husband to RCsm. TLS
PW85 4/4/14 p. 1157--Catholic wife-Protestant husband.
He's finally brought into her church.

002087   URSULA FINCH. A NOVEL. New York:
Benziger, 1920 NUC. London: Hutchinson, [1921] BMC.

PW-Family drudge who finds happiness

002088   WHOSE NAME IS LEGION. London: Hutchinson,
1915 BMC. New York: Benziger, 1919 NUC.

Religion, crime and occult TLS
"Conflict between Catholicity and spiritualism" PW

002089   YOUNG CYMBELINE. A NOVEL. London:
Hutchinson, 1917 BMC.

A family of pacifists, one turns hero TLS, ATH

CLARKE, MRS. HENRY. See CLARKE, AMY (KEY).

CLARKE, QUEENIE.

002090   ACROSS THE BORDER. THE ADVENTURES OF
MALCOLM JEANIE AND DON. A GEOGRAPHY STORY. London: I.
Pitman, [1914] BMC.

CLARKE, REBECCA SOPHIA. 1833-1906. United States.

002091   THE CAMPION DIAMONDS. BY SOPHIE MAY.

Boston: Lee and Shepard, 1897 NUC.

Who stole the diamonds is the story. PW 52:567.

002092   HER FRIEND'S LOVER. BY SOPHIE MAY.
Boston: Lee and Shepard, 1893 W.

002093   IN OLD QUINNEBASSET. BY SOPHIE MAY.
Boston: Lothrop, Lee and Shepard, [c1891] NUC.

Diary 1788. Advents of Eliz. Gilman 17, 2 suitors. One
a strict and powerful minister.

CLARKE, VIOLET. D. 1907?.

002094   LEAVES. London: W. Heinemann, 1909 BMC
NUC.

Stories TLS

CLAVERING, VERE.

002095   A HARVEST OF TARES. London: Hurst and
Blackett, 1891 BMC NUC.

Traditional stuff: house with secret passages,
pictures of ancestress, good old uncle, crooked
solicitor. Heroic young woman exposes all the
wickedness, burning of the wicked woman by upset lamp.
ATH 97 35.
Brother and sister reduced from wealth to poverty. He
goes to work in a library; he's a Eton-Oxford man. SR.
7-4-91, 22

002096   HUGH DEYNE OF PLAS-IDRYS. London: Hurst &
Blackett, 1893 BMC.

Hugh has wealth, everything. Nearly marries his
sister's friend Eva Canning in order to complete his
life. But fate intervenes in the form of a gang of
poachers who beat him so he can't walk for a while.
"The violence...a blessing in disguise" kept him from
Eva. Maude Verrinker left orphaned becomes his ward.
Grows into a beauty. She ends up married to him in
volume 2. In the meantime we get Eva Canning's career.
She's a shrewd woman who knows how to handle men and
gets what she wants. Continues doing so even after
marriage. Ends up dying of burns. SR 75:352.

002097   SIN FOR A SEASON. London: Hurst and
Blackett, 1897 BMC.

ACAD 50:490. Story of two lives, Herbert Meredyth and
Blanche Cheriton, ruined by a "youthful liaison."

CLAY, BEATRICE ELIZABETH.

002098   THE ADVENTURES OF DUKE HUON OF BORDEAUX.
London: H. Marshall, 1903 BMC.

CLAY, BEATRICE ELIZABETH AND CLARIBEL SPURLING.

002099   A HOLIDAY ENGAGEMENT. London: Hodder and
Stoughton, [1913] BMC.

Cheerful amusing stories of two young women and a
guide who tour Norway-ends in romance. ATH TLS

CLAY, JOSEPHINE RUSSELL. United States.

002100   FRANK LOGAN: A NOVEL. BY MRS. JOHN M.
CLAY. New York: Abbey Press, [1901] NUC.

002101   SOME LITTLE OF THE ANGEL STILL LEFT: A
NOVEL. BY MRS. JOHN M. CLAY. Cincinnati: R. Clarke,
1893 NUC.

Racing horses, stables, etc. described fully. Captain
Neville doesn't often show he's a bit of an angel.
There's a beautiful widowed marquise. Time of Crimean
War. 4-22-93 PW.

002102   UNCLE PHIL: A NOVEL. BY MRS. JOHN M.
CLAY. New York: F. T. Neely, [c1899] NUC.

CLAY, MRS. JOHN M. See CLAY, JOSEPHINE RUSSELL.

CLEARY, KATE (MACPHELIM). United States.

002103   LIKE A GALLANT LADY. Chicago: Way and
Williams, 1897 NUC.

Goes to wild Nebraska to find her brother and inquire
about the circumstances of her lover's death. The
dissipated life of men who go west for fortune. The
drought and the misery of farmers. Chinese opium

eaters. A hero.--perhaps her old lover really alive. PW
52:737.

CLEEVE, LUCAS, pseud. See KINGSCOTE, ADELINE GEORGINA
ISABELLA (WOLFF).

CLEGHORN, SARAH NORCLIFFE. 1876-1959. United States.

002104   THE SPINSTER; A NOVEL WHEREIN A
NINETEENTH CENTURY GIRL FINDS HER PLACE IN THE
TWENTIETH. New York: H. Holt, 1916 NUC.

Ellen Graham grows up in 90's in Vermont. She has a
passion forpoetry. She goes to Radcliffe where her
literary interests take 2nd place to her passion for
justice. She joins many progressive movements, has a
love affair that ends unhappily, but she's not left
bitter. At the end she devotes her pen to the cause of
justice. PW
NYT-Happy as a spinster conscientious study of her
evolution from sentimental schoolgirl to contented
spinster. There is a love story in her life, but more
important is the growth of her sense of social
justice. she inherits some money, the companies in
which it is invested are the corporations she believes
criminal.
BKM-S. Cleghorn is a socialist and anti-vivisectionist
and Radcliffe alumna as is the heroine.

002105   A TURNPIKE LADY, BEARTOWN, VERMONT
1768-1796. New York: Holt, 1907 NUC.

Historical idyll. NYT
Sentimental story of a young woman in colonial America
who almost became a spinster but didn't. (Book)

CLEGHORN, SARAH NORCLIFFE AND DOROTHEA FRANCES (CANFIELD)
FISHER.

002106   FELLOW CAPTAINS. BY SARAH N. CLEGHORN AND
DOROTHY CANFIELD FISHER. New York: H. Holt, 1916 NUC.

The subconscious forces. Five neither young nor old
American women representing as many types meet for
twice-a-week conversations. Begins with one telling
how she became the captain of her soul. About half the
book is poems to be repeated in various emergencies.

CLELAND, MARY.

002107   THE SILVER WHISTLE. London: Heath,
Cranton, [c1920] BMC.

TLS-love.

CLEMENT, ELLIS (MEREDITH). B. 1865. United States.

002108   HEART OF MY HEART. BY ELLIS MEREDITH. New
York: McClure, phillips, 1904 NUC. London: Methuen,
1905 BMC.

"A romance of married life which portrays an intimate
study of maternity. The author is a Denver newspaper
woman who has made quite a name for herself as a
political reporter." BKM. v. 19, 1904.
Diary of experiences, plans, etc. of woman expecting
first child. Treatment is frank and free. ATH 141,05.

002109   THE MASTER-KNOT OF HUMAN FATE. BY ELLIS
MEREDITH. Boston: Little, Brown, 1901 BMC NUC.

"A sort of glorified, idealized, feminized...Robinson
Crusoe." Heroine: divorced devotes life to charity and
philanthropies; successful opera singer is comrades
with a lawyer (male) on a island alone; live together
for a year. fall in love. They question whether to
start the human race over again. decision left to
woman ending unsettled. New Adam & Eve. CR '01
WOMAN'S JOURNAL, 4-20-01,123

002110   UNDER THE HARROW. BY ELLIS MEREDITH.
Boston: Little, Brown, 1907 NUC.

3 ind. girls in New York. Ms's and illustrations are
returned and their money low. The disappointments and
blasted hopes of the three PW 4-13-07
Chances of success of woman earning her living by her
brains in New York City. NYT

CLEMENTIA, pseud. See FEEHAN, MARY EDWARD.

CLENNELL, EMILY M. H.

002111   TIMOTHY'S LEGACY. London: Digby, Long,
[1895] BMC.

He must marry in four months. Refused by woman he
loves, he marries someone else, but is destined for
the one he loves. ACAD. 48:360
SP 76:901. Male bequeathed a fortune provided he
marries in the year the testator dies. All works out
well.

CLERKE, ELLEN MARY.

002112   FLOWERS OF FIRE; A NOVEL. London:
Hutchinson, 1902 BMC.

CLEVELAND, JESSIE.

002113   VALENTINE FFRENCH; OR, THE GIRL WHO WOULD
WED A SOLDIER. London: Digby, Long, [1893] BMC.

CLIFFORD, ELIZABETH LYDIA ROSABELLE (BONHAM) DE LA PASTURE.
1866-1945. United Kingdom.

002114   ADAM GRIGSON. BY MRS. HENRY DE LA
PASTURE. London: Smith, Elder, 1899 BMC. New York:
Harper, 1900 NUC.

He's a self-made man who makes a marriage with the
only ignoble member of an aristocratic family now
struggling with poverty. LIT 5:570
History of three generations of an English
family--from old fashioned Lady Mary to her modern
granddaughter, Elizabeth. From aristocratic poverty to
affluence through wealthy marriages. The center of
interest is Lady Mary who loves her children,
especially her son--who grows up to marry a low-bred
flirt and this breaks Mary's heart. Then she revives
an old love--finishes a book he started. LBKM 17:62
Disappointed in her own marriage (to a Squire Western
type) and in her children, plots a good marriage for
her grandchild. Lady Mary is at center. She's a bit of
a snob. SP 83:573

002115   CATHERINE OF CALAIS. BY MRS. HENRY DE LA
PASTURE. London: Smith, Elder, 1901 BMC NUC. New York:
Dutton, 1906 NUC.

history romance PW 4-13-07

002116   CATHERINE'S CHILD. BY MRS. HENRY DE LA
PASTURE. New York: E.P.Dutton, 1908 NUC. London:
Smith, Elder, 1908 BMC NUC.

Mother daughter PW 1-30-09
Catherine, a hopelessly depressed mother, her child
age 16, melodramatic NYT
ATH-Sacrificing mother.

002117   CORNELIUS. BY MRS. HENRY DE LA PASTURE.
London: Smith, Elder, 1903 BMC 1904 NUC.

Story of inheritance, two sisters ACAD. 64, 318
ACAD 64, 413
ATH 121, 493
TLS 113,03

002118   DEBORAH OF TOD'S. BY MRS. HENRY DE LA
PASTURE. London: Smith, Elder, 1897 BMC. New York: E.
P. Dutton, 1907 NUC.

Orphan of gentle birth on father's side, lived her 21
years on a farm. She's attracted to an old General who
had commanded her father's regiment. But he's old
enough to be her grand father, but they wed and he
introduces this rustic girl to his smart set. He's a
senile philanderer she soon finds out. But she wins
over her step-children and an earl who eventually
becomes her second husband. SP 79:939.
She speaks in Devonshire accent. When he dies she
returns to farm. ACAD 52:Fic Sup 130.
LIT 3:54. Devonshire. Deborah is young mistress of
farm; marries an elderly officer and languishes in
London in smart society.
She longs for Devonshire. SR 85:435.
NYT-young farm woman marries miserable old husband and
moves to London, becomes a widow and returns to farm.

002119   ERICA. BY MRS. HENRY DE LA PASTURE (LADY
CLIFFORD). London: Smith, Elder, 1912 BMC NUC.

ATH "psych st of a thoughtless woman"
TLS-arranges her own marriage, uses trousseau given
her by another man, her character is tested.
SP-Auth is obviously fond of her heroine. Sequel to
Master Christopher.
SR-greedy, amoral, woman as she is not supposed to be.
Lacks all the so-called feminine qualities, devoid of
spiritual inspiration, does not feel the impulse of
the flesh. Delicacy is so far from her she can

scarcely conceive it. She does not seem to find her
husband objectionable. We cannot be convinced of her
interest in her baby. A tribute to her creator that we
detest her.
She's cold, self-centered, marries, problems follow.
Becomes a mother but is still cold and selfish except
for protective feeling toward her son ACAD

002120   THE GREY KNIGHT. AN AUTUMN LOVE-STORY. BY
MRS. HENRY DE LA PASTURE. New York: E.P. Dutton, 1908
NUC. London: Smith, Elder, 1908 BMC.

PW- Widow nurses great lord who falls for her.
TLS- a Patient Griselda.
ACAD 0
BKM 27 1908

002121   THE HONORABLE MRS. HARRY. BY MRS. HENRY
DE LA PASTURE. New York: E.P. Dutton, [c1912] NUC.

NYT o

002122   THE LONELY LADY OF GROSVENOR SQUARE. BY
MRS. HENRY DE LA PASTURE. New York: E.P. Dutton, 1906
NUC. London: J. Murray, 1907 BMC.

Poor country girl inherits large estate in London,
marries PW 2-9-07
Heroine is winsome, innocent, fragile, makes little
mistakes LBM3-07, 275
Jeanne's social blunders and successes as mistress of
the house of her brother ACAD
Heroine's lonely life in London, review says little
else about her SP
Jeanne feels as one "moving in worlds not realized"
She's lonesome in her marriage SR
Woman's devotion to brother who then married; she
takes wife to her heart, dainty wholesome story NYT

002123   THE MAN FROM AMERICA. A SENTIMENTAL
COMEDY. BY MRS. HENRY DE LA PASTURE. London: Smith,
Elder, 1905 NUC BMC. New York: E.P. Dutton, 1906 NUC.

all is summer ACAD 1201, 05
NYT -sentimental love story.

002124   MASTER CHRISTOPHER. BY MRS. HENRY DE LA
PASTURE (LADY CLIFFORD). London: Smith, Elder, 1911
BMC NUC. Leipzig: B. Tauchnitz, 1911 NUC.

Erica Clow brings Christopher and other men to her
feet. Her relations to her mother are the best part of
the book TLS Bullies her mother mercilessly tries to
trap every man who comes along LBKM
Erica is "perfectly unscrupulous and utterly selfish"
yet made attractive ?SP
Review discusses only Christopher SR
Focuses on Christopher. NYT

002125   MICHAEL FERRYS. BY MRS. HENRY DE LA
PASTURE (LADY CLIFFORD). London: Smith, Elder, 1913
BMC. New York: E.P. Dutton, [c1913] NUC. (Am. ed.
Title: MICHAEL)

Winifred-very rel. falls in love with wealthy atheist.
Michael must convert to marry her but finds he can't
believe in RCsm. Then she dies and he calls on God to
make her reappear-she does; he becomes a believer.
ACAD
Wife is RC. Michael (husband to be) does all he can to
comply with her demands and the church's. Even to
going on a retreat, but can't believe. Wants to marry
her anyway; returns to find her drowned. That vision
was really Winifred's sister. Sequel-He meets mod.
ind. Edith Roath in every respect his superior. She's
agnostic. Willing to give him up knowing he needs a
faith. encourages him to love Winifred's sister ends
with his conversion SP
He inherits vast fortune in So African mines. Engaged
to Catholic woman; Michael is agnostic. He is wealthy.
But he can't believe; then a miracle occurs. BKM

002126   PETER'S MOTHER. BY MRS. HENRY DE LA
PASTURE. New York: E.P. Dutton, 1905 NUC. London:
Smith, Elder, 1905 BMC NUC.

Conflict between mother and daughter (young widow) for
love of a man PW 8-5-05
Dense masc. selfishness. The squire who makes life
unbearably dull for the wife he snatched from young
girlhood. Their son, like father, who goes off to war,
loses an arm returns to make his mother miserable (Now
the father is dead). This woman is all giving. She
puts the son in shape. Two gross, selfish men; eternal
trag of motherhood. NYT 510,05
Our sympathy directed toward the mother ACAD 149, 05

At the end she leaves for the world outside TLS 05,65
Repressed by husband and his family for 20 yrs; her
gaiety and beauty have paled; old at 35. Love comes to
her but son can't possibly understand ATH 303,05

002127   A TOY TRAGEDY: A STORY OF CHILDREN. BY
MRS. HENRY DE LA PASTURE. London: Cassell, 1894 BMC.
New York: E. P. Dutton, [1906] NUC.

002128   THE TYRANT. BY MRS. HENRY DE LA PASTURE.
London: Methuen, [1909] BMC NUC. New York: E.P.
Dutton, 1910 NUC.

LBKM-family: father a tyrant is defeated by the other
NyT-Portrayal of a family victimized by father,
particularly the wife who is made to suffer most
keenly thru her motherhood as he uses his children as
a safety valve. She is blamed by him for her inner
revolt (altho she is absolutely self sacrificing) and
by her children for her lack of courage and by the
world for her subservience.
Rough welch squire neglects his wife and kids.
Children's contempt of him; wife goes on loving him.
TLS
Daughter Annie marries vs. his will, contributes her
diary to the story. ATH

002129   THE UNLUCKY FAMILY. A BOOK FOR CHILDREN.
BY MRS. HENRY DE LA PASTURE. London: Smith, Elder,
1907 BMC. New York: E.P. Dutton, 1908 NUC.

NYT-Comedy-11 children

CLIFFORD, ETHEL. See DILKE, ETHEL (CLIFFORD).

CLIFFORD, JOSEPHINE. See MACCRACKIN, JOSEPHINE (WOEMPNER)
CLIFFORD.

CLIFFORD, LADY. See CLIFFORD, ELIZABETH LYDIA ROSABELLE
(BONHAM) DE LA PASTURE.

CLIFFORD, LUCY (LANE). D. 1929. United Kingdom.

002130   AUNT ANNE. BY MRS. W. K. CLIFFORD.
London: R. Bentley, 1892 BMC. New York: Harper, 1892
NUC.

ATH 100:252. "Old and spare and withered," Aunt Ann is
sympathetically portrayed as an older woman needing
love and companionship. She accepts a marriage
proposal from a young fortune seeker. See this review
for lengthy quotation from novel on her reasons for
doing this.
CR 18:164. An "inconsequent career with a pitiful
conclusion." One never loses sympathy for her
DIAL 13:310. "An old lady of amiable character, who is
hopelessly unpractical in the conduct of life and
whose vagaries suggest a mind that has nearly, if not
quite, lost the balance it may once have had." "Her
infatuation for and marriage to a young adventurer."
LW 23:273. Character study of an "apparently
contradictory, inconsistent old lady." Mrs. North is a
divorced woman who at end of story is about to live
happily with her lover.
SP 69:195. "She is ...a curious, delicate, real being"
"perfectly independent" "never for a moment ridiculous
even when she makes us laugh." 60 years old, an
uncontrollable wink in her left eye. "An old woman is
not generally considered an attractive object. Neither
in life nor in fiction is common opinion very
favorable to her." She has a maddening habit of buying
presents for people with an utter disregard for paying
her bills.

002131   A FLASH OF SUMMER: THE STORY OF A SIMPLE
WOMAN'S LIFE. BY MRS. W. K. CLIFFORD. New York: D.
Appleton, 1894 NUC. London: Methuen, 1895 BMC.

Cruel tragedy. Katherine has money but why would
anyone marry such a woman as Katherine is, asks the
reviewer. Leaves husband; she's not 20 yet-conceals
the fact that she's married. She then meets and loves
Jim Alford, but he dies and she kills herself by
throwing herself before a train. The book ends there.
SP 75:937
A virtuous heroine and hero and an ogre of a villain.
She's forced to marry the villain. Struggles to free
herself, leaves him, posing as unmarried, meets hero.
Hero forgives her deception. Ogre recaptures her in
the end. CR 23:202
After she reveals her marriage to the man she loves,
he and his mother convince her to return to her
husband. But at this very time the man she loves dies,
so she kills herself. First part has to do with her
unusual childhood-solitary, her dreary walks to the
little school. A dull terror haunts her life. ATH

106:639
LW 25:385. "delicate" character study. Brought up in
lonely household, forced to marry a hard brutal man by
her equally hard and brutal uncle. After a year of
mental and physical abuse she leaves her husband and
travels with friends who are unaware of her marriage.
Their son falls for her; they persuade her it is her
duty to return to husband. Returns to him, but more
for love of the son, Alford, than duty.

002132   THE GETTING WELL OF DOROTHY. BY MRS. W.
K. CLIFFORD. London: Methuen, Leipzig: B. Tauchnitz,
1907 NUC.

002133   THE HOUSE IN MARYLEBONE; A CHRONICLE.
London: Duckworth, 1917 BMC NUC.

All the tenants are working women. Descriptions of
parties, private struggles in gaining independence
many different characters. TLS
A girls' lodging house series of studies of various
working women making careers but most end up married.
SP

002134   LOVE-LETTERS OF A WORLDLY WOMAN. BY MRS.
W. K. CLIFFORD. London: E. Arnold, [1891] BMC. New
York: Harper, 1892 NUC.

ATH 99:145: 3 women 1) A modern correspondence-she is
a "visionary, impulsive, ill-regulated femme
incomprise of the latter end of the century." She
doesn't marry the "old-fashioned, healthy-minded
Englishman." 2) She is thrown over by man she loves,
marries an aging baronet. She finds happiness in this
mrge, not in love but companionship, does not want
children, looks forward to the power her salon will
eventually have. 3)"On the Wane"-"In her advanced state
Gwen has certain affinities with the heroine of "A
modern correspondence" though she is less aggressive."
She is first in love with someone who throws her over
and then wants to marry her, but she can't because her
views of life have changed.
LW 23:165. Marie Bashkirtseff type of women. "The
contrast between the visionary, idealizing love of an
unconventional young girl, and the practical point of
view of the average beefy Englishman-who is looking
for a wife-has never been better brought out."
SP-Not love letters in the ordinary sense of the word.
ACAD 41:131. "Very modern" women.
CR 7-2-92 p5. Three sets of letters written by women
who loved the world.

002135   MARGARET VINCENT; A NOVEL. BY MRS. W. K.
CLIFFORD. New York and London: Harper, 1902 NUC.

NYT 5-10-02 not helpful.

002136   MARIE MAY; OR CHANGED AIMS. London and
New York: F. Warne, 1893 NUC.

002137   MISS FINGAL. BY MRS. W. K. CLIFFORD.
Edinburgh and London: W. Blackwood, 1919 NUC BMC. New
York: C. Scribner's Sons, 1919 NUC.

Alice Fingal orphan at 21, only enough money to afford
a small flat, lives a solitary life for 8
years-speaking to no one but her charwoman. Reads
novels, spends hours on her balcony watching people.
Never occurs to her to make a profession or meet
people. Then her whole life changes. She inherits
money, can't get used to new fancy house. Enjoys the
little country cottage most. She becomes obsessed with
the story surrounding the cottage-a young couple whose
marriage came to grief. She goes to stay near the
forsaken woman to meet her. They're drawn to each
other Linda Alliston is dying of a mysterious disease.
Her husband unfaithful: they divorce. Alice so
indentifies with Linda that when Linda dies Alice
herself falls unconscious. Awakens completely changed.
She has taken on Linda's personality completely-her
one object to get the children. TLS
Adopts children, the husband dies in war. SP

002138   PROPOSALS TO KATHLEEN. New York: A. S.
Barnes, 1908 NUC.

"Kathleen, at 8 and 20 is perfectly reconciled to
marrying a man with whom she is not in love, but whom
she says is "clever, well-off...well connected,
well-placed, and on the whole will suit me precisely."
On the eve of her wedding she takes a farewell to
maidnhood, going thru many letters each containing a
proposal, criticising each suitor in turn and
destroying their letters." BKM v27, 1908.
NYT-lectures on man in general and on suitors in
particular-is on her way to becoming a worldly woman.

002139   SIR GEORGE'S OBJECTION. BY MRS. W. K.
CLIFFORD. London, New York: T. Nelson, [1910] BMC NUC.

TLS-love story
ATH-love story
ACAD-love story.
English girl raised in Italy by ma curious about
England and her father 1-28-11 PW
The girl "with one taint" is objected to by Sir George
a strong believer in heredity and father of young man
the girl is engaged to. NYT

002140   A WILD PROXY. A TRAGIC COMEDY OF TO-DAY.
BY MRS. W. K. CLIFFORD. London: Hutchinson, 1893 BMC.
New York: Cassell, [c1893] NUC.

Wild eccentric hero Frank Merreday-a bad influence in
the lives of several women. PW 4-8-93.
A man leaves preparations for his wedding to his
friend. After ceremony, he's delayed by accident. The
friend takes off with the bride-to France and Italy.
All a practical joke. CR 14, 20:400.
Returns her. ATH 101:501.

002141   A WOMAN ALONE. THREE STORIES. BY MRS. W.
K. CLIFFORD. New York, London: Macmillan, 1898 NUC.
London: Methuen, 1901 BMC.

Three stories, theme of isolation in marriage. "her
needs are too many for her to be satisfied;" her
husband a brute, "a modern monster". LBKM 9 '01.
another story-man falls in love, uxoricide. ACAD 01
Ambitious intelligent wife revels in politics eager to
have her husband distinguish himself. He disagrees,
and leaves her to entertain the notables. They argue,
he leaves for they agree to separate. She repents, but
too late because he dies. NYT '01

002142   WOODSIDE FARM. BY MRS. W. K. CLIFFORD.
London: Duckworth, 1902 NUC BMC. Leipzig: B.
Tauchnitz, 1902 NUC.

ATH 5-10-02 a widow.

CLIFFORD, MOLLIE LEE.

    002143   POLLY; THE AUTOBIOGRAPHY OF A PARROT.
    Boston: H. M. Caldwell, [c1906] NUC.

    002144   YOPPY. THE AUTOBIOGRAPHY OF A MONKEY.
    Boston: H. M. Caldwell, [c1905] NUC. London: Gay and
    Bird, 1906 BMC.

CLIFFORD, MRS. W. K.   United States.

    002145   GEORGE WENDERN GAVE A PARTY. BY JOHN
    INGLIS. New York: C. Scribner's Sons, 1912 NUC.

    PW

CLIFFORD, MRS. W. K.   See Also CLIFFORD, LUCY (LANE).

CLINGHAN, CLARICE IRENE.

    002146   THAT GIRL FROM BOGOTA: A NOVEL. New York:
    Home Pub. Co., [c1896] NUC. London: Routledge, 1896
    BMC.

    PW 5-16-96. Virginia Lamar, leaving a school in South
    America on account of an epidemic among the pupils,
    comes to Cragskill on the Hudson to visit the
    Maxwells, who are relatives. Unfortunately they are
    travelling. Virginia and her Inca maid force an
    entrance to the house, where they live uncomfortably
    until Assunda the maid seeks help from the rector.
    There is a murder and other sensational incidents.

CLOSE, EVELYNE. B. 1874.   United Kingdom.

    002147   CHERRY ISLE. Philadelphia: C. W. Jacobs,
    [c1920] NUC. London: G. Richards, 1920 BMC NUC.

    PW-Career of a woman singer.
    TLS-Religious regeneration of cold singer.

    002148   THE HARVEST. London: Lynwood, [1911] BMC.

    Helen Wood has a child by one man, marries another?
    ACAD
    "Only one so sternly conscientious as Helen would
    sacrifice husband, friends and motherhood." ATH

    002149   THE ROLL OF HONOUR. London: A. Melrose,
    [1915] BMC.

sounds like an anti-war story of German atrocities.
Tragedy of soldier married just before he went to
front, loses but recovers capacity for love. TLS

CLOUSTON, ADELLA OCTAVIA. B. 1864. United States.

002150   A TITLE-REJECTED: A NOVEL. BY OCTAVIA
CLOUSTON. New York: G. W. Dillingham, 1894 NUC.

Criticism of American weakness for titles--no matter
who holds them. Also secret doors, identities, etc. PW
1-19-95:53

002151   WHAT WOULD THE WORLD THINK? A NOVEL. BY
OCTAVIA CLOUSTON. New York: Dodworth House, [c1897]
NUC.

Mother and father of an illegitimate girl die when
she's 9; the mother leaves her a letter so that her
daughter can trace her mother's husband-the man she
ran away from. The daughter finds him, He's wealthy,
makes a place for her in high society. PW 51: 297.

CLOUSTON, OCTAVIA. See CLOUSTON, ADELLA OCTAVIA.

CLOWES, ALICE ADA.

002152   MABEL PERCIVAL'S MARRIAGE. London: G.
Routledge, 1912 BMC.

002153   MONA: A NOVEL. London: S. Sonnenschein,
1899 BMC NUC.

Beautiful Irish girl marries and comes to England to
live. She learns he gambles, so she leaves expecting a
child--to make her own living. Gets help from a former
servant now a laundress. At the end meets and forgives
husband though he's lost his business and house so
prospects look bad. SP 83:57.
Forgives for the children's sake. ACAD 57:16

002154   MRS. FREDERICK GRAHAM, A NOVEL. London:
S. Sonnenschein, 1900 BMC.

SR 90:654. Without hero, heroine or plot.
ATH 116:545. Marriage projects of young ladies.

002155   SENEX: A NOVEL. London: S. Sonnenschein,
1898 BMC.

SP 81:874. Story of Sybil's marriage to 60 year old
general. Apparently happy.
ATH 112:892. She has an unhappy love affair; story
goes on after her marriage.

002156   STRANDED. A TALE. London: Sonnenschein,
1902 BMC.

CLUETT, ISABEL MAUD (PEACOCKE). B. 1881. New Zealand.

002157   CINDERELLA'S SUITORS: A NOVEL. BY ISABEL
MAUD PEACOCKE. London: Ward, Lock, 1918 BMC.

SR-Traditional romance.

002158   THE GUARDIAN, A NOVEL. BY ISABEL MAUD
PEACOCKE. London: Ward, Lock, 1920 BMC.

TLS-Love story

002159   MY FRIEND PHIL. BY ISABEL MAUD PEACOCKE.
New York: Rand, McNally, [c1915] NUC. London: Ward,
Lock, 1915 BMC.

About a little chap. PW

002160   PATRICIA-PAT. BY ISABEL MAUD PEACOCKE.
London: Ward, Lock, 1917 BMC.

CLYDE, CONSTANCE.

002161   A PAGAN'S LOVE. London: T. Unwin, 1905
BMC.

Love, social conditions, maternity-in modern
Australia. LBKM 71, v28-9
Slums, boarding houses, social helpers Dorothea and
her close friend a woman journalist. TLS 99 05

CLYDE, IRENE.

002162   BEATRICE THE SIXTEENTH. London: G. Bell,
1909 BMC.

science fiction type of story: narrator finds herself
in an Eastern country where people know nothing about

our world. They are "unaware of the difference between
the sexes." Most of the people are called "she". Once
in a while there's a "he". There is a weekly service
of babies from a neighboring country of 'barbarians'
which keeps up the populations." TLS

CLYDE, MARGARET HORNER. B. 1877. United States.

002163   THE THREAD THAT IS SPUN. Boston: Sherman,
French, 1915 NUC.

NYT- story of Scotch-Irish and Pennsylvania Germans
and Presb. ministers.
Scotch Irish & Penn German types. PW 11-27-15.
Simple charm of community life. NYT

COALE, MRS. JAMES CAREY. United States.

002164   THE COTTAGE BY THE SEA. Baltimore: J.
Murphy, 1896 NUC.

PW 10-24-96. "Career of a bright New England girl from
her simple home life on the coast of Maine-through the
temptations, joys, and griefs in the French capitol
and back again to the quiet scenes of her happy
childhood."

COATES, ANNE.

002165   RIE'S DIARY. London: Chatto and Windus,
1897 BMC.

COBB, MARGARET SMITH. United States.

002166   BLAXINE, HALFBREED GIRL. New York: Neale,
1910 NUC.

Beautiful young woman--a tragedy. PW
NYT-white man of foreign birth has half a dozen Indian
wives with intention of making himself a king in the
area. Book opens when male school teacher arrives
after most of wives are dead & children almost grown.
Tragedy and retribution.

COBDEN, ELLEN MELICENT. See SICKERT, ELLEN MELICENT
(COBDEN).

COBURN, ELEANOR HALLOWELL (ABBOTT). B. 1872. United
States.

002167   THE INDISCREET LETTER. BY ELEANOR
HALLOWELL ABBOTT. New York: Century, 1915 BMC NUC.

sent NYT

002168   LITTLE EVE EDGARTON. BY ELEANOR HALLOWELL
ABBOTT. New York: Century, 1914 BMC NUC. London:
Hodder and Stoughton, [1917] BMC.

"Eve could dance like an angel, read Sanskrit as well
as her dad, ride a horse, and discuss paleontology.
The secret passion of her life was for a home. Her
father's idea of marrying her to a middleaged
scientist on an outlandish island in the tropics did
not appeal to Eve. A rather conventional young man
survives the shocks administered by Eve's unusual
conduct, and comes to the conclusion that life without
her would be very uninteresting." PW 86 9/19/14:772.
NYT-She was 30, badly dressed and worse mannered.
Small in size but physically very strong.
heroine dances, reads sanskrit, refuses to marry,
works out her own salvation and somebody else's PW

002169   LOVE AND MRS. KENDRUE. London: W.
Heinemann, 1919 BMC.

rich shrewd widow, crippled for life makes the most of
her life "by making huge purchases and sending to
various recipients presents of dubious suitability"(?)
strong love interest too. TLS

002170   MOLLY MAKE-BELIEVE. BY ELEANOR HALLOWELL
ABBOTT. New York: Century, 1910 BMC NUC. London: W.
Heinemann, 1911 BMC.

002171   THE NE'ER-DO-MUCH. BY ELEANOR HALLOWELL
ABBOTT. New York: Dodd, Mead, 1918 NUC. London: Hodder
and Stoughton, [1919] BMC.

PW-at a dinner party two men and two women tell the
tragedy of their lives, keeping identity secret. Two
were fiction, two were true.
wealthy man invites 500 people he'd like to know to
dinner. Story focuses on a table of them, their
confessions, etc. TLS

002172　　OLD-DAD. BY ELEANOR HALLOWELL ABBOTT. New York: E. P. Dutton, [c1919] NUC.

a female college professor, Miss Claudis Merrimayne expels Daphne Bretton whom she caught in a "compromising position" in the middle of the night. Scandal follows, but most of story involves Daphne and the eventual revelation of that past experience. Girl expelled from college makes friends with father PW

002173　　PEACE ON EARTH, GOOD-WILL TO DOGS. BY ELEANOR HALLOWELL ABBOTT. New York: E. P. Dutton, [c1920] NUC.

Dogs-legends and stories, Christmas stories.

002174　　THE STINGY RECEIVER. BY ELEANOR HALLOWELL ABBOTT. New York: Century, 1917 BMC NUC.

Eccentric Mrs. Tom Gallien is a wealthy bed-ridden woman. A poor young doctor, "sweet little story" Norway girl Solvei Kyilland comes to U.S. to learn about Montessori method. Her romance with Dr. Sam. NYT 3-18-17 99

002175　　THE WHITE LINEN NURSE. BY ELEANOR HALLOWELL ABBOTT. New York: Century, 1913 BMC NUC. London: Hodder and Stoughton, [1914] BMC.

PW 9/27/13:949 She undertakes general heart work for the crusty senior surgeon.
TLS-On eve of graduation as trained nurse, has hysterics and becomes involved in adventures with the Senior Surgeon.

COCAYNE, EDITH K. United States.

002176　　SUE MCFARLAND, SCHOOLMARM. Baltimore, Md.: Saulsbury, [1918] NUC.

girl leaves home to teach out west PW

COCHRAN, KATHERINE MADISON.

002177　　POSIE; OR, FROM REVEILLE TO RETREAT. AN ARMY STORY. BY MRS. M. A. COCHRAN. Cincinnati: R. Clarke, 1896 NUC.

PW 8-8-96. Northern captain and Southern wife. Stationed at Western military outpost Fort Harney, Oregon while the Bannock or Piute prisoners were held there.

COCHRAN, MRS. M. A. See COCHRAN, KATHERINE MADISON.

COCKE, SARAH JOHNSON. B. 1865. United States.

002178　　THE MASTER OF THE HILLS; A TALE OF THE GEORGIA MOUNTAINS. New York: E. P. Dutton, [c1917] NUC.

Part I-Minnie Mason, hill girl marries wealthy man. He dies and his family can't find her. II: 25 years later a young man shows up: the family educates him. He's the son of Minnie. NYT 287 8-5-17
Georgia hills; story of two generations. How these mountain people intermarry with others. PW

CODMAN, ANNA KNEELAND (CRAFTS). B. 1869. Nationality Unknown.

002179　　AN ARDENT AMERICAN. BY MRS. RUSSELL CODMAN. New York: Century, 1911 BMC NUC.

American girl rejects marriage to foreigner, comes back to the States a declasse pilgrim and to happiness. 5-20-11 PW. Diary.

CODMAN, MRS. RUSSELL. See CODMAN, ANNA KNEELAND (CRAFTS).

COFFIN, JULIA (HASKELL).

002180　　THE VENDOR OF DREAMS. New York: Dodd, Mead, 1917 NUC.

Philosophic story of the East. NYT

COGHLAN, LIDA LAVINIA. B. 1860. United States.

002181　　THE WATERS OF LETHE. Baltimore, Md.: J. Murphy, [1904] NUC.

PW-"for Catholic readers."

COHEN, ROSE (GALLUP). B. 1880.

002182　　OUT OF THE SHADOW. New York: G. H. Doran, [c1918] NUC BMC.

PW-Russian immigrant tells her own story and how she comes to understand real meaning of America.
NYT Dec 1, '18 p. 530, Russian Jewish immigrant to U.S. at 12, life of hardship and suffering for family (mother and children fell ill from starvation in 1893), lightened through the work of Miss Brewster and Miss Wald on Henry Street. First meets Americans after years in New York in hospital, for the first time out of the immigrant neighborhood.
autobiographical CT 275

COHN, CLARA (VIEBIG). B. 1860. Germany.

002183　　ABSOLUTION. BY CLARA VIEBIG. London, New York: J. Lane, 1908 NUC BMC. (Tr. H. Raahauge)

PW- murder
TLS-Poland-Young woman given to a coarse elderly peasant whom she loathes and tries to kill. Finallly he kills himself. She is only calm one at his grave. She loves another man. Author seems to sympathize with her.
SR-"really repulsive feature of the book is the close study of the emotional religious hysteria of a very young girl" I think this is the maid.

002184　　OUR DAILY BREAD. BY CLARA VIEBIG. New York: J. Lane, 1909 BMC. London: J. Lane, 1909 BMC NUC. (Tr. Margaret L. Clarke)

PW-unhappy forced marriage of servant.
TLS-lower classes in Berlin, realism.
ATH-story of 2 girls who go to Berlin and enter domestic service. Realistic view of the painful aspects of life .

002185　　THE SON OF HIS MOTHER. BY CLARA VIEBIG. New York: J. Lane, 1913 NUC. London: J. Lane, 1913 BMC NUC. (Tr. H. Raahauge)

"Paul Schlieben and his wife, while devoted to each other, realize that their happiness is incomplete because they have no child. They adopt a boy of peasant origin, but as he grows up they find their joy in him largely mingled with despair, because of his hereditary tendencies, with which they feel incompetent to cope. They are forced to acknowledge that while he is the son of their adoption , still he must always be the son of his mother." PW
Dual theme; force of heredity; women's desire for children. As study of heredity-poor; no allowance for environment. Good study of devoted motherhood. ACAD.
Peasant child adopted by people of wealth. NYT
For the woman wanting a child is an obsession that disorders her whole nervous system. Needs doctors' care, visits to spas. On one such trip sees the child, raises question of adoption to husband (they had never discussed their disappointment). He agrees. Boy grows to be like his real mother-base coarse vicious; physically weak-gets sick. "Death a release for the couple." BKM

COLBURN, FRONA EUNICE WAIT (SMITH). 1859-1946. United States.

002186　　YERMAH THE DORADO. BY FRONA EUNICE WAIT. San Francisco: William Doxey, 1897 NUC BMC.

Yermah is an idealized man of the time of the golden Age of Atlantis. Author has studied the age. Her ideas of theosophy are revealed. LW 28:479.
BKM 7:168. History and tradition of Calif. settled by the Atlantians, led by Yermah, Description of their cities. Some love interest between celibate priest and priestess.

COLCOCK, ANNIE T. United States.

002187　　HER AMERICAN DAUGHTER. New York: Neale, 1905 NUC.

"This story turns on a wager made by three Spaniards, in Madrid, to the effect that one of them might, without an introduction, induce Raven Woodward, an American girl, to sup with him unchaperoned at midnight in a fashionable cafe. Whether he succeeds or fails is the story itself." BKM v23 1906

COLDICOTT, FRANCES A.

002188　　HOLLINHURST. London: Chapman and Hall, 1898 BMC.

SP 81:656. Daughter of a poor rector secretly marries heir to an earldom.
ACAD 55:75. For romantic girls.

COLE, PATIENCE (BEVIER). B. 1883. United States.

002189   DAVE'S DAUGHTER; A NOVEL. New York: F. A. Stokes, [c1913] BMC NUC.

"Two little old maid twins rushed into the love affairs of the billion dollar girl, where people more worldly would not have dared to step. Miss Mattie and Miss Matie lived in a little gray house in a Long Island village--a homey place for Christabel to run away to from New York gaiety, in her automobile. She told the quaint pair about the West, about copper mines--and about Dave. Dave was her father, and he had died before the story begins. A poor, proud young man won't marry Christabel because of her wealth until the little old ladies make him see his error." PW 9-27-13,950

COLE, SOPHIE. B. 1862. United Kingdom.

002190   ARROWS FROM THE DARK. London: Mills and Boon, [1909] NUC BMC.

Eugenia widow publishes love letters her husband received without naming the woman involved. Story involved the sensation this causes and the complications. TLS
She does it for money. author paints her as admirable. ACAD

002191   BLUE GREY MAGIC. London: Mills and Boon, 1910 BMC.

TLS-romance between angelic domestic and MD
ATH-romance between angelic domestic and MD

002192   THE CYPRESS TREE. London: Mills and Boon, [1920] BMC NUC.

ATH-romance

002193   THE DEVIL'S CHAPEL. London: Mills and Boon, 1919 BMC.

orphan twins Mark and Mollie Quain-she's "a new soul-, tip-toe for adventure" She's the main character her experience studied closely. He is the visionary, she is the realist. Study of her gradual loss of assurance and hardness, her heartless treatment of husband, elopes with another man, later realizes she loves husband. TLS
End purgational; she repents and is forgiven. SR

002194   THE GATE OF OPPORTUNITY. London: Mills and Boon, [1918] BMC.

TLS-Gabrielle asks friend to finish her father's play.
SP-difficult to believe in hero but heroine is presentment of educated girl working for her living.

002195   THE HOUSE IN WATCHMAN'S ALLEY. London: Mills and Boon, 1915 BMC.

TLS-family in creaking house and effect of war.
W.W.I--fiction

002196   IN SEARCH OF EACH OTHER. London: Mills and Boon, 1913 BMC.

Father and daughter are separated in a crowd; he loses his memory. ATH
Marcelli lives among Bohemians in Soho, among them a woman journalist. She -Marcelli-falls in love with a dentist; the journalist, with Marcelli's father. LBKM

002197   THE LOITERING HIGHWAY. London: Mills and Boon, 1916 BMC.

TLS-Story of three children, one of them Valeria Vesper, a nameless (illegitimate) child who becomes an actor.

002198   A LONDON POSY. London: Mills and Boon, [1917] NUC BMC.

Setting is London; Johnson's house a kind of dream house. Iris loves George, her husband comes in and out of the story. But Iris and George are made for a happy end. TLS
Idyllic and pretty story. ATH
Hero is boy and "other pretty characters to match" BAKER 32, p. 107

002199   PATIENCE TABERNACLE. London: Mills and Boon, 1914 BMC.

ATH 144:96 her life story
TLS-13:346 love story.

002200   PENELOPE'S DOORS. London: Mills and Boon, 1913 BMC.

Her brave outlook saves her from disaster. ATH
She loses her money, starts a shop, fails in business, falls in love with a good man. TLS

002201   A PLAIN WOMAN'S PORTRAIT. London: Mills and Boon, [1912] BMC NUC.

TLS-Came to London as an office worker, at 37 is established novelist about to marry a man who "was quick to appreciate her but slow to realize his opportunity."
LBKM-Writes a book and gains success only to find that there is something greater and more to be admired.

002202   RACHEL CHALFONT. London: Duckworth, 1908 BMC.

TLS-"hereditary tendency toward relations non-matrimonial" women are much better than the men.
ATH-"interesting and sympathetic heroine."

002203   SKIRTS OF STRAW. London: Mills and Boon, 1915 BMC NUC.

Rhoda (work-house bred, maid-of-all-work). Artist interested in her sketches. Loses a little son upon whom her life centered at end still unwed. Sympathetic heroine. TLS

002204   THE THORN-BUSH NEAR THE DOOR. London: Mills and Boon, 1912 BMC.

TLS-dev. of girl thru self-sacrifice.
SP-She is married to weak artist. Seems to have only the slightest prospect of happiness at close of story.
ACAD-She developed strength of character, she was a bore.

002205   A WARDOUR STREET IDYLL. London: Mills and Boon, 1910 BMC.

TLS-antique dealer and his capable secretary fall in love. There is a wife and another man but all ends well.

COLEBROOKE, HELEN.

002206   FETTERS OF THE PAST. London: J. Murray, 1914 BMC.

Heroine frees self from the fetters. ATH
ATH-young man discovers marvelous drug.
TLS-her husband a convict, she, secretary to another man, does not tell him she is married. Misunderstanding etc.

002207   WINGED DREAMS. London: W. Blackwood, 1908 BMC.

TLS-there is a cousin who is a suffragist. Diana is wooed but not successfully.
ACAD-Suffragist is only horrible vulgar character.

COLEMAN, KATHARINE E.

002208   THE WOOING OF PHYLLIS. London: Gay and Bird, 1896 BMC.

SR-Pleasant romance, toy passions.
ATH 108:91. Heroine with two lovers.

COLERIDGE, CHRISTABEL ROSE. 1843-1921. United Kingdom.

002209   AMETHYST: THE STORY OF A BEAUTY. London: A. D. Innes, 1891 BMC. New York: D. Appleton, 1892 NUC.

Social novel; she's daughter of a man who has squandered fortune; family now in genteel poverty. Struggles of her own and sister Una. Her four proposals; Una's two love affairs. ACAD
Study of her character (Her mother is amoral). She struggles between principle and instinct-a Lily Bart type. Much of story is painful. Una Haredale. She has passed exams at Cambridge with distinction. But aunt won't let her teach, sends her back to social life of

mother. "In a couple of years she has been battered into something very like a professional beauty." The descent and the struggle out of it. ATH 98:758. Amethyst-beauty is all but fatal. Taken young from mother's influence, raised by aunt, well educated.

002210   A BAG OF FARTHINGS. London: National Society's Depository, [1893] BMC. New York: Whittaker, [1893] BMC.

002211   BESSIE'S ENGAGEMENT. London: Wells, Gardner, [1892] BMC.

002212   A COLT FROM THE HEATHER. London: S. P. C. K., [1896] BMC.

002213   FIFTY POUNDS: A SEQUEL TO "THE GREEN GIRLS OF GREY THORPE". London: National Society's Depository, [1891] BMC. New York: T. Whittaker, [1891] BMC.

Linda Inglewood is restless in her grandfather's house. She is dissatisfied with common duties and wants a successful career in literature. Writes novels about high born heroes and heroines and their uncommon adventures. SP 67 854

002214   GERTRUDE'S LOVER: A STORY OF AN UNHEROIC HERO. London: S. P. C. K., [1895] BMC.

002215   THE MAIN CHANCE. London: Hurst and Blackett, 1899 BMC NUC.

Basic plot is that a man sacrifices own interests for truth and is better, though poorer for it. "Pretty little imbecile Kitty." LBKM 15:155
SP 81:781. Feeling of fear possessed by heir is removed by the love of a good woman.
LIT 3:603. Moral is that young ladies should behave like ladies and with circumspection. Theology and psychical research as well.

002216   MISS LUCY; A CHARACTER STUDY. London: Hurst & Blackett, 1908 BMC. London: 1908 NUC.

TLS-Lucy marries gamekeeper, virtuous fellow-happy ending.
SR-Rev calls it a misalliance.
BKM o
ATH-character study.

002217   THE PROPHET'S MANTLE. London: Isbister, 1897 BMC NUC.

SP 80:604. An aunt persuades two people to marry who don't love each other. Story is of his trying to win her love.

002218   ROUGH CAST. London: S. P. C. K., [1898] BMC.

SR 86:763. Moral is the happiness of fulfilling one's duty, Grace happily goes back to keep house of her farm family when her mother dies. Love story also.

002219   THE TENDER MERCIES OF THE GOOD. London: Isbister, 1895 BMC NUC.

ATH 107:246. "An eloquent indictment of the dangers of domestic repression."
SR- Fairford family. Hilda at 38 had never thought of independent action until she at last realizes that her position as "one of the girls" is intolerable.

002220   THE THOUGHT-ROPE. London: Hurst and Blackett, 1898 BMC NUC.

SP 81:313. Love story of a hereditary clairvoyant.

002221   TRICKS AND TRIALS; OR, SIX MONTHS IN WESTERFORD. London: Hurst and Blackett, 1899 BMC NUC.

A country town. A school master inherits a large draper establishment in town. SP 83:614

002222   WAYNFLETE. London: A. D. Innes, 1893 BMC NUC.

Family ghost-supernatural mystery. SR 76:19.
"How the Waynflete estate was redeemed thru the energy of a female member." Curse on a man exorcized by love of good wife. ACAD 44:108.

002223   THE WINDS OF CATHRIGG. London: Isbister, 1901 BMC.

COLERIDGE, CHRISTABEL ROSE AND HELEN SHIPTON.

002224   RAVENSTONE. London: A. D. Innes, 1896 BMC.

LBKM 11:51. Brother and sister, come into money, marry.
SR Pleasant, wholesome.
SP 77:822. Young man loves and leaves her while she is farm girl; when she comes into a title, they are married.

COLERIDGE, CHRISTABEL ROSE, jt. au. See YONGE, CHARLOTTE MARY AND CHRISTABEL ROSE COLERIDGE.

COLERIDGE, M. E. See COLERIDGE, MARY ELIZABETH.

COLERIDGE, MARY ELIZABETH. 1861-1907. United Kingdom.

002225   THE FIERY DAWN. BY M. E. COLERIDGE. London: E. Arnold, 1901 BMC. New York: Longmans, Green, 1901 NUC.

BAKER 13-110 historical romance.
ATH-12-7-01

002226   THE KING WITH TWO FACES. BY M. E. COLERIDGE. London: E. Arnold, 1897 BMC. New York: J. Lane, 1898 NUC.

Hist rom: Gustavus III of Sweden. with focus upon Adolph Count Ribbing "exiled for avowed complicity in the assassination of the king." SP 79:776. Includes Count Ribbing's contact with Madame de Stael-her salon and conversations well drawn. LIT 1:113.
Hist romance, Mme. de Stael introduced. BAKER 03,92.
BKM 6:474. Romance of Adolph and Tala in the midst of Mme de Stael's circle. Adventure, thrilling escapes.

002227   THE LADY ON THE DRAWINGROOM FLOOR. BY M. E. COLERIDGE. New York: Longmans, Green, 1906 NUC. London: E. Arnold, 1906 BMC NUC.

PW-
TLS-romance

002228   THE SEVEN SLEEPERS OF EPHESUS. London: Chatto and Windus, 1893 BMC NUC.

Title concerns a brotherhood of that name. Its members cause much commotion. ACAD 43:302.
A triangular marriage complication; a play about it by one of the three, a secret society, a theatre in flames, an escape from the law; a small revolution in a small German state, one of the revolutionaries takes the throne. ATH 101:406.

002229   THE SHADOW ON THE WALL. A ROMANCE. London: E. Arnold, 1904 BMC NUC.

LBKM-two young women heroines.
ATH-man kills his friend rather than allow him to become involved in an affair.
TLS-O

COLLIN, GRACE LATHROP. Nationality Unknown.

002230   PUTNAM PLACE. New York and London: Harper, 1903 BMC NUC.

Story of a town, an argument that gets heated (between two women), history of a woman who never married--many details of a New York town. Seems like sentimental pictures of older women. NYT 03,186

COLLINGS, MARY ADAMS.

002231   LIFE'S PHASES. A DOMESTIC STORY. London: E. Stock, 1904 BMC.

COLLINGS, MAYSIE.

002232   THE ROMANCE OF HUGO, LORD AVONDALE. London: J. Blackwood, [1903] BMC.

COLLINS, E. BURKE, pseud. See SHARKEY, EMMA AUGUSTA (BROWN).

COLLINS, FLORENCE.

002233   THE LUDDINGTONS. London: W. Heinemann, 1906 BMC.

TLS- mother is dying of cancer, daughter captures MD famous for his treatment.
ATH-Cancer is concealed from fiance so that he will not reject daughter who has hereditary tendency.
Father leaves money to his son-in-law.

COLLINS, JANE S.

002234   FREE AT LAST. Pittsburgh: Murdoch, Kerr, 1896 NUC.

PW 2-8-96. Missionary work amongst freedmen in South, crusade against drink and proselytizing efforts of the Roman Catholic Church.

COLLINS, MABEL. See COOK, MABEL (COLLINS), Also DESPARD, CHARLOTTE AND MABEL (COLLINS) COOK.

COLMORE, G., pseud. See WEAVER, BAILLE GERTRUDE RENTON (COLMORE).

COLSON, ETHEL MAUDE. See BRAZELTON, ETHEL MAUDE (COLSON).

COLTER, ALICE MARGUERITE. B. 1891. United States.

002235   TUMBLEWEED. Indianapolis: Bobbs-Merrill, [c1916] BMC NUC. London: Hodder and Stoughton, [1917] BMC.

An open air child, extracting from her career the last drop of fascination. Girls? TLS
Tumbleweed, an imaginative little girl who loves nature and the wind. As she grows up, struggles to overcome her desire to be different from other people. Happy in end partly through help of her Prince Charming. PW 90:9/2/16 p685

COLTER, HATTIE E. United States.

002236   A GENTLE BENEFACTRESS. BY MRS. J. J. COLTER. Boston: D. Lothrop, [c1892] NUC BMC.

PW Angela, an orphan who has much money, spends life helping people with it. Story concludes with her happy marriage.

COLTER, MRS. J. J. See COLTER, HATTIE E.

COLTHARP, JEANNETTE DOWNES. United States.

002237   BURRILL COLEMAN, COLORED: A TALE OF THE COTTON FIELDS. Franklin, Ohio: Editor Pub. Co., 1896 NUC.

COLVILL, HELEN HESTER.

002238   THE INCUBUS. London: Chatto and Windus, 1910 BMC.

TLS-two sisters, 1 voluptuously evil.
ACAD-

002239   LADY JULIA'S EMERALD. New York: J. Lane, 1908 BMC. London: J. Lane, 1908 BMC NUC.

PW-loses it, finally gets it back.
TLS-intricate narrative of the career of a heroine of independent character and artistic gifts. Not to be taken for the ordinary missing jewels story. Also wrote novel of merit, "The Stepping Stone."
ACAD O
ATH O
NYT-artist-love story.

002240   OUR WILLS AND FATES. BY KATHARINE WYLDE. London: Osgood, McIlvaine, 1897 BMC.

A man's chosen wife turns out to be daughter of his worst enemy. They part. SR 84:206.
Second plot of intrigue, murder and judicial blundering. ATH 110 92.

002241   THE PRINCESS ROYAL. A NOVEL. BY KATHARINE WYLDE. London: R. Bentley, 1894 BMC NUC.

SP 73:734. Wooing of a patrician by a plebian who turns out to be her cousin and the head of the family. She was Lilith Turold-an heiress, falls in love with adopted son of a nouveau riche family who moved into neighborhood. Father and a cousin try to keep them apart but in the end the adopted son turned out to be an heir. They wed. SR 79:230

002242   THE STEPPING STONE. London: A. Constable, 1905 BMC.

Anna, a singer; the stepping stone for a man she rescues from crime. He almost marries another but turns to Anna. A gossip tells Anna he doesn't love her--off she goes and disappears, dies. We're made to love Anna. ACAD 367,05

COLVIN, MARY KROH. United States.

002243   IRONICA; A ROMANCE OF THE ROCKIES. New York: H. Lechner, [c1911] NUC.

NYT-romance in the Rockies.

COMBE, MRS. KENNETH. See COMBE, THEODORA (WILLIAMSON).

COMBE, T., pseud. See HUGUENIN, ADELE.

COMBE, THEODORA (WILLIAMSON). United Kingdom.

002244   CECILIA KIRKHAM'S SON. BY MRS. KENNETH COMBE. Edinburgh and London: W. Blackwood, 1909 BMC.

Sentimental story of self sacrificing mother and son who makes up to her when she's poor. TLS

002245   CHIEF OF THE STAFF. BY MRS. KENNETH COMBE. Edinburgh and London: W. Blackwood, 1914 NUC BMC.

ATH-Story of a great European war.

002246   IN FULL PAYMENT. BY MRS. KENNETH COMBE. London: Skeffington, [1920] BMC.

TLS-blackmail and inheritance

002247   SEEKERS ALL. BY MRS. KENNETH COMBE. Edinburgh and London: W. Blackwood, 1910 BMC. New York: Hodder and Stoughton, 1911 NUC.

LBKM-love story.
rich girl and 2 love affairs ? PW 4-8-11

002248   THE UPWARD FLIGHT. BY MRS. KENNETH COMBE. London: Skeffington, [c1919] BMC.

Philippa Ferrington-pure self sacrificing-refuses to divorce (is separated) so that husband can remarry. Believes in the insolubility of marriage even tho she loves another man. Rel. makes her that way. Author suggests she's the product of propaganda-believes that "until women help to make the laws there is no progress." TLS

COMER, CORNELIA ATWOOD (PRATT). D. 1929. United States.

002249   THE DAUGHTER OF A STOIC. BY CORNELIA ATWOOD PRATT. New York and London: Macmillan, 1896 NUC.

BKM 4:74. Imitation of John Oliver Hobbes. Heroine who is mentally awake but still emotionally asleep. Her development thru a "high-souled pagan gentleman."

COMFORT, BESSIE (MARCHANT). 1862-1941. United Kingdom.

002250   THE ADVENTURES OF PHYLLIS; A STORY OF THE ARGENTINE. New York: Funk & Wagnall, 1914 PW. London: Cassell, [1910] BMC.

"To arrive in a strange country, be met and taken to a remote hut in which is a dreadful old Chilian woman and a seriously injured man is what happens to Phyllis Talbot when she answers an advertisement for a nursery governess. Who the man is, how he was wounded and came to the hut, are the mysteries which Phyllis unravels through a series of exciting adventures". PW 85 1-31-14:375.

002251   THE ADVENTUROUS SEVEN. THEIR HAZARDOUS UNDERTAKING. London: Blackie, [1914] BMC.

002252   AMONG HOSTILE HORDES. A STORY OF THE TAI-PING REBELLION. London: Gall and Inglis, [1901] BMC.

002253   AMONG THE TORCHES OF THE ANDES. Edinburgh: W. P. Nimmo, 1898 BMC.

002254   THE APPLE LADY. London and Glasgow: Collins' Clear-Type Press, [1908] BMC.

002255   ATHABASCA BILL: A TALE OF THE FAR WEST. BY BESSIE MARCHANT (MRS.J. A. COMFORT). London: Christian Knowledge Society, [1906] BMC. London: Sheldon Press, 1906 [?] NUC.

002256   THE BERTRAMS OF LADYWELL. London: W.
Gardner, 1902 BMC.

002257   THE BLACK COCKATOO; A STORY OF WESTERN
AUSTRALIA. London: R.T.S., [1910] BMC.

002258   THE BONDED THREE. London: Blackie, 1899
BMC.

002259   A BRAVE LITTLE COUSIN. London: Christian
Knowledge Society, [1902] BMC.

002260   A CANADIAN FARM MYSTERY; OR PAM THE
PIONEER. BY BESSIE MARCHANT. London: Blackie, 1917 BMC
[1932] NUC.

002261   THE CAPTIVES OF THE KAID. London:
Collins' Clear-Type Press, [1904] BMC.

002262   CASPAR'S FIND. London: R. Culley, 1905
BMC.

002263   CICELY FROME, THE CAPTAIN'S DAUGHTER.
Edinburgh: W. P. Nimmo, [1900] BMC.

002264   A COUNTESS FROM CANADA. A STORY OF LIFE
IN THE BACKWOODS. London: Blackie, 1911 BMC.

002265   A COURAGEOUS GIRL: A STORY OF URUGUAY.
London: Blackie, 1909 BMC.

002266   CYNTHIA WINS: A TALE OF THE ROCKY
MOUNTAINS. London: Blackie, [1918] BMC.

002267   A DANGEROUS MISSION: A TALE OF RUSSIA IN
REVOLUTION. London: Blackie, [1918] BMC.

002268   DARLING OF SANDY POINT. London: Christian
Knowledge Society, [1907] BMC.

002269   A DAUGHTER OF THE RANGES: A STORY OF
WESTERN CANADA. London: Blackie, 1906 BMC.

002270   DAUGHTERS OF THE DOMINION: A STORY OF THE
CANADIAN FRONTIER. London: Blackie, 1909 BMC.

ACAD--A story for girls but one with such an
independent and adventurous young woman that boys
would be interested in it as well.

002271   THE DEBT OF THE DAMERALS. London: J.
Clarke, [1905] BMC.

002272   DENVER WILSON'S DOUBLE: A STORY OF NEW
MEXICO. London: Blackie, [1915] BMC.

002273   THE DEPUTY BOSS. A TALE OF BRITISH
HONDURAS. London: Christian Knowledge Society, [1910]
BMC.

002274   THE FERRY HOUSE GIRLS. AN AUSTRALIAN
STORY. London: Blackie, 1912 BMC.

002275   FLECKIE: A STORY OF THE DESERT. London:
Blackie, [1902] BMC.

002276   FROM THE SCOURGE OF THE TONGUE. London:
A. Melrose, [1901] BMC.

Orphan sisters reorder their lives successfully run a
farm. BKM
ATH 116:819. Wildly improbable. "Sketch of girl
farmers, their work, their workers, their neighbors."
Belinda's husband a ruffia

002277   THE GHOST OF ROCK GRANGE. London:
Christian Knowledge Society, [1900] BMC.

002278   A GIRL AND A CARAVAN: THE STORY OF IRMA'S
QUEST IN PERSIA. London: Blackie, [1915] BMC.

002279   THE GIRL CAPTIVES. A STORY OF THE INDIAN
FRONTIER. London: Blackie, 1900 BMC.

002280   A GIRL MUNITION WORKER. London: Blackie,
[1916] BMC.

002281   A GIRL OF DISTINCTION. A TALE OF THE
KARROO. London: Blackie, 1912 BMC.

002282   A GIRL OF THE FORTUNATE ISLES. BY BESSIE
MARCHANT. London: Blackie, [1907] BMC NUC.

Family works to pay back money one stole. PW

002283   THE GOLD MARKED CHARM: THE STORY OF A
MYSTERY IN THE BLUE NILE COUNTRY. London: Blackie,
1918 BMC.

002284   GRETA'S DOMAIN. A TALE OF CHILOE. London:
W. Rainey, 1911 BMC.

002285   HELD AT RANSOM. A STORY OF COLONIAL LIFE.
London: Blackie, 1901 BMC.

002286   HELEN OF THE BLACK MOUNTAIN: A STORY OF
MONTENEGRO. London: Blackie, [1914] BMC.

002287   THE HEROINE OF THE RANCH. A STORY OF
TIERRA DEL FUEGO. London: Blackie, 1914 BMC.

002288   HEROINE OF THE SEA. London: Blackie, 1904
BMC.

002289   HIS GREAT SURRENDER. London: Christian
Knowledge Society, [1912] BMC.

002290   HOPE'S TRYST: A STORY OF THE SIBERIAN
FRONTIER. London: Blackie, 1905 BMC.

002291   THE HOUSE AT BRAMBLING MINSTER. London:
Christian Knowledge Society, [1902] BMC.

002292   THE HUMBLING OF MARK LESTER. London:
Simpkin, Marshall, [1899] BMC.

Melodrama. Story of misunderstandings in married life.
ACAD 57:160

002293   IN PERILOUS TIMES: A TALE OF OLD
CANTERBURY. BY BESSIE MARCHANT. London: Gall and
Inglis, [1902] NUC BMC.

002294   IN THE CRADLE OF THE NORTH WIND.
Edinburgh: W. P. Nimmo, 1896 BMC.

002295   IN THE TOILS OF THE TRIBESMEN. A STORY OF
THE INDIAN FRONTIER. London: Gall and Inglis, [1900]
BMC.

002296   AN ISLAND HEROINE. London: Collins'
Clear-Type Press, [1909] BMC.

002297   JENNY'S ADVENTURE; OR, ON THE TRAIL FOR
KLONDYKE. London: J. W. Butcher, [1909] BMC.

002298   JOYCE HARRINGTON'S TRUST: AN ARGENTINE
MYSTERY. London: Blackie, 1916 BMC.

002299   JULIETTE, THE MAIL CARRIER. London:
Collins' Clear-Type Press, [1907] BMC.

002300   KENEALY'S RIDE: A TALE OF THE PAMPAS.
London: Gall and Inglis, [1906] BMC.

002301   LEONARD'S TEMPTATION: A STORY OF
GAMBLING. London: R. Culley, 1902 BMC.

002302   LOIS IN CHARGE: OR, A GIRL OF GRIT: THE
STORY OF A PLANTATION IN BRAZIL. London: Blackie,
[1918] BMC.

002303   LOST ON THE SAGUENAY. London and Glasgow:
W. Collins, Sons, [1903] BMC.

002304   THE LOYALTY OF HESTER HOPE. A STORY OF
BRITISH COLUMBIA. London: Blackie, [1914] BMC.

002305   MAISIE'S DISCOVERY. London and Glasgow:
Collins' Clear-Type Press, [1906] BMC.

002306   MOLLY ANGEL'S ADVENTURES: A STORY OF
BELGIUM UNDER GERMAN OCCUPATION. London: Blackie,
[1915] BMC.

002307   MOLLY OF ONE TREE BEND. A STORY OF A
GIRL'S HEROISM ON THE VELDT. London: J. W. Butcher,
[1910] BMC.

002308   A MYSTERIOUS INHERITANCE; A STORY OF
ADVENTURE IN BRITISH COLUMBIA. BY BESSIE MARCHANT.
London: Blackie, 1915 BMC NUC.

002309   THE MYSTERY OF THE SILVER RUN. London:
Wells Gardner, Darton, 1907 BMC.

002310   NO ORDINARY GIRL: A STORY OF CENTRAL
AMERICA. London: Blackie, 1908 BMC.

002311   NORAH TO THE RESCUE: A STORY OF THE
PHILIPPINES. London: Blackie, [1919] BMC.

002312   THE OLD HOUSE BY THE WATER. London: Religious Tract Society, [1894] BMC.

002313   THE OWNER OF RUSHCOTE. London: R. Culley, 1903 BMC.

002314   A PRINCESS OF SERVIA. A STORY OF TO-DAY. London: Blackie, [1912] BMC.

002315   QUEEN OF SHINDY FLAT. London: W. Gardner, 1905 BMC.

002316   THE RAJAH'S DAUGHTER; OR, THE HALF-MOON GIRL. London: S. W. Partridge, 1899 BMC.

002317   REDWOOD RANCH. London: Christian Knowledge Society, [1911] BMC.

002318   ROLF THE REBEL. London: Christian Knowledge Society, [1908] BMC.

002319   SALLY MAKES GOOD. A STORY OF TASMANIA. London: Blackie, [1920] BMC.

002320   THE SECRET OF THE EVERGLADES; A STORY OF ADVENTURE IN FLORIDA. BY BESSIE MARCHANT. London: Blackie, [1902?] NUC BMC. New York: Mershon, [1915] NUC.

002321   THE SIBYL OF ST. PIERRE. A TALE OF MARTINIQUE. London: W. Gardner, 1912 BMC.

002322   SISTERS OF SILVER CREEK: A STORY OF WESTERN CANADA. London: Blackie, 1908 BMC.

002323   TELL-TALE-TIT. London: R. Culley, [1899] BMC.

002324   THAT DREADFUL BOY! London: R. Culley, [1901] BMC.

002325   THREE GIRLS IN MEXICO: A TALE OF LIFE IN THE INTERIOR. London: Blackie, 1910 BMC.

002326   THREE GIRLS ON A RANCH. A STORY OF NEW MEXICO. London: Blackie, [1901] BMC.

002327   A TRANSPORT GIRL IN FRANCE. London: Blackie, [1919] BMC.

002328   UNCLE GREG'S MAN HUNT. A STORY OF TEXAN HORSETHIEVES. London: R. Culley, [1906] BMC.

002329   THE UNKNOWN ISLAND: A TALE OF ADVENTURE IN THE SEYCHELLES. London: Blackie, [1916] BMC.

002330   THE WESTERN SCOUT. BY BESSIE MARCHANT. London: Christian Knowledge Society, [1912] BMC. Toronto: Musson, n.d. NUC.

002331   THE YOUNGEST SISTER: A TALE OF MANITOBA. BY BESSIE MARCHANT. London: Blackie and Son, 1913 BMC NUC.

002332   YUPPIE (THE LAND BEYOND THE FLOOD). London: R. Culley, [1898] BMC.

COMFORT, MRS. J. A. See COMFORT, BESSIE (MARCHANT).

COMMANDER, LYDIA KINGSMILL.

002333   MARRED IN THE MAKING. New York: P. Eckler, [c1902] NUC.

Concerns a lust-begotten child...strong problem story. ARENA 1902

COMMELIN, ANNA OLCOTT. United States.

002334   NOT IN IT. New York: Fowler & Wells, [c1897] NUC. London: L. N. Fowler, [1897] BMC.

COMRIE, MARGARET SIMPSON. B. 1851. Nationality Unknown.

002335   A LOYAL HUGUENOT MAID. Philadelphia: G. W. Jacobs, [1902] NUC.

002336   MAID MERLE. London: R.T.S., [1920] BMC.

TLS--hist.

002337   THE SECRET OF LAKE KABA. London: R. T. S., [1911] BMC.

COMSTOCK, ANNA (BOTSFORD). 1854-1930. United States.

002338   CONFESSIONS TO A HEATHEN IDOL. BY MARIAN LEE. London: Doubleday, Page, 1906 BMC. New York: Doubleday, Page, 1906 NUC.

"secret hopes and fears of a brave hearted woman of 40, left a widow at 24. There is an old lover in the background. who was a friend of her husband and thinks of her as Paul's widow. Doesn't marry in the end. Confesses to a statue. BKM
"An unusual story in which a woman of forty tells the story of her loves to a small teak-wood idol on her desk." BKM v.24 1906-7
NyT--Has a "very feminine heart."
PW--"Pretty love story."

COMSTOCK, HARRIET THERESA (SMITH). B. 1860. United States.

002339   GLEN OF THE MOUNTAINS, OR UNBROKEN LINES. New York: Grosset and Dunlap, [c1919] NUC.

002340   JANET OF THE DUNES. Boston: Little, Brown, 1908 NUC. London: T. Nelson, 1920 BMC.

Life on the south shore of Long Island. Janet is "careless of conventions" and lingers on the dunes talking to a strange artist and poses for him and alone in his shack but she comes out "unscathed by the trials and temptations which beset her." BKM v.27 1908.

002341   JOYCE OF THE NORTH WOODS. London: Hodder and Stoughton, 1911 BMC. Garden City, N. Y.: Doubleday, Page, 1911 NUC.

At her father's command, Joyce married to a drunkard; awakens to real womanhood when she falls in love with a stranger; goes to his cabin one night, scandalous, but he treats her like a sister. PW
After rushing to his cabin, she stays there. Deeply moving study. NYT

002342   MAM'SELLE JO. Garden City, N. Y.: Doubleday, Page, 1918 NUC. London: Hodder and Stoughton, 1924 BMC.

PW--St. Lawrence country.
Jo Morey, at 40, is finally able to pay off her father's debts and has turned the run-down property into a modestly prosperous farm. She adopts a child, Donelle, from the local orphanage. There is a mystery about her birth, and the town believes that Donelle is Jo's illegitimate daughter. When Donelle is old enough to hear and understand this gossip, she believes it also, and her loyalty to Jo causes her to turn down an opportunity to become trained as a musician and to marry rashly. The end of the story is happy for both women. They are very different but both strong and independent and each sympathetic and supportive to the other throughout. (Book)

002343   THE MAN THOU GAVEST. Garden City, N. Y.: Doubleday, Page, 1917 NUC. London: Hodder and Stoughton, [1924] BMC.

Nella Rose girl from the hills. Lydia Kendall a woman who summoned him back to civilization. City man goes to mountains for his health. Meets and loves mountain maid. She's left pregnant, but no problem--gets to marry her lover who understands all. He goes back to modern young woman who has solved the problem of economic independence and intends to marry on equal partner basis. Unusual marriage arrangement: live apart. When Lydia wants a child, adopts the mountain woman's child. She just happens along at this time. BKM

002344   THE PLACE BEYOND THE WINDS. Garden City, N.Y.: Doubleday, Page, 1914 NUC. London: C. Brown, 1914 BMC.

Priscilla Glenn craves for life, repressed by fanatical narrow-minded pa, finds relief in dancing a kind of natural pagan dance; finds her way to NY," becomes a trained nurse, transgresses all the ethics of her profession" by revealing true condition of a patient to a girl about to marry that male patient. Eugenics, votes for women, anti saloon are the subjects of this purpose novel. BKM
"Presents the question of eugenics and the ethics of silence on certain matters affecting marriage." OVERTON
"Nathaniel Glenn didn't believe in book knowledge for girls, but his daughter Priscilla's thirst would not be denied. So began a disastrous friendship with Jerry-Jo through the medium of a book. Later on she

meets Richard Travers, the boy from the Far Hills
Place, in her quest for knowledge. Priscilla holds
steadily to her ideals through many trials to find,
finally, the boy grown up and no longer far away." PW
86 10-3-14:1117.
NYT--Canadian community. Her father is a bigot and a
tyrant, in spite of him she gets an education. Becomes
a nurse. Then comes a problem in medical ethics, "the
right of the child not to be born." Her decision means
the renunciation of her profession and the "inflicting
of a life-long anguish upon her dearest friend."Not
unhappy ending. NYT 1914:463.

002345   THE QUEEN'S HOSTAGE. Boston: Little,
Brown, 1906 NUC.

PW--Historical romance.
NYT--Historical romance.

002346   A SON OF THE HILLS. Garden City, N. Y.:
Doubleday, Page, 1913 NUC.

"Story of a Virginia mountain lad's spiritual growth.
When Sandy Morley with his pitiful little treasure of
$30, the savings of long years of chores, set out down
the mountain side, traditions were smashed into a
thousand bits. Many Morleys had felt the call, but
none had ever put his foot seriously, determinedly on
the path as Sandy did. Sandy's parting with his father
had moved them both deeply. But he left some one
else--Cynthia the child of the big house, who had
taught him what he knew. What Sandy did out in the
world, and what he did when he returned to Lost
Mountain make the tale." PW 84:1585
"Poor whites...Marcia Howe, the little woman doctor
from Mass...fighting a brave battle for the Hill
people...her appeal to Mart in Morley is an
illuminating epitome of much of the feminist
movement." NYT 1913:768

002347   THEN MARCHED THE BRAVE. Philadelphia: H.
Altemus, [1904] NUC.

The story of a boy in the Revolutionary War who was
crippled and yet served his country. Juvenile. (Book)

002348   UNBROKEN LINES. New York: Doubleday, 1919
NUC.

Girl marries wrong man. PW
Gwenn raised by father in unsophisticated way weds
wrong man. He wishes to make her over. Her other lover
would keep her as she is; with this lover she had a
comradeship. The author explores the question of
whether Gwenn should stay married to a man she's
unsuited for. NYT

002349   THE VINDICATION. Garden City, N. Y.:
Doubleday, 1916 NUC BMC. London: C. Brown, 1916 BMC.

Story of a Doctor and heredity. PW

COMSTOCK, SARAH. D. 1960. United States.

002350   PIONEERS; THE STORY OF A SODDY. London:
Hodder & Stoughton, [1913] BMC.

002351   THE SODDY. Garden City, N.Y.: Doubleday,
Page, 1912 NUC.

BKM v. 36 1912-13 Pioneer story-strong wife who sticks
to farm when husband gives up and goes home-he comes
back later. She first is seen struggling by herself
(parents are dead) with care of a younger brother and
sister. Then marries a young man from the East with
very little capital. Record of failures, fire,
drought, winds. She refuses to go back East with him.
PW Jerry, heroine

002352   THE VALLEY OF VISION. Garden City, N.Y.:
Doubleday, Page, 1919 NUC BMC.

Young man and young woman rebel vs the narrowness of
the "best" people of a Puritan town. PW
Marcia Warren a misfit in Banbury and in her own
family. "Should have been a boy"-not a bit "girl"
like: tempestuous, energetic, no thought for clothes,
digs earthworms, Town and family looked upon her as
strange. Only one boy understood her. But he went off
to school She reads voraciously, isolated, unhappy,
21. Becomes a nurse in order to do welfare work. Works
as visiting nurse. Meets that boy who now is wed. They
plan to make the town and factory what it should be.
NYT 228, 4-20-19

COMYN, MARIAN.

002353   REDIVIVIA. London: Hurst and Blackett,
1896 BMC.

SR-hero is tempted by uncle's beautiful wife; refuses,
but there is a sense of regret.
ATH 107:709. Many had thought that the sensation novel
of thirty years ago had been killed by the problem
novel. This is a poor thing compared with thrillers of
Braddon and Wood. Nephew is accused of uncle's murder,
is saved by his widow.

CONANT, CHARA BROUGHTON. United States.

002354   NAOMI. New York: American Tract Society,
[1898] NUC.

PW-voluntary conversion of a Jewess to Christianity.
Americans in Paris.

CONKLIN, JENNIE MARIA (DRINKWATER). 1841-1900. United
States.

002355   LOOKING SEAWARD. BY JENNIE M. DRINKWATER.
Boston: A. I. Bradley, [c1893] NUC.

"Longing for work, Helen Kline decides to remain
single because 'a single middleaged woman has glorious
opportunities. I honor the wife and mother, but there
is much she cannot do for her girls'". PW 9-2-93.
Consequently she devotes her life to working for girls
and young women of all types.

002356   PAUL FRENCH'S WAY. BY JENNIE M.
DRINKWATER. Boston: A. I. Bradley, [c1896] NUC.

PW 2-29-96. Idealistic young hero gives up woman he
loves because he believes it is his mission to be
minister of country parish, she wouldn't conform.

002357   SECOND BEST. BY JENNIE M. DRINKWATER.
Boston: Bradley and Woodruff, [c1891] NUC.

Rachel Ennis' father goes blind, she must give up
luxury for life of privation in the country. N. E.
She's self sacrificing. PW

002358   THREE-AND-TWENTY. BY JENNIE M.
DRINKWATER. Boston: A. I. Bradley, 1895 NUC.

Leah Ritchie, N. E. young woman, her girlhood, her
life as a journalist in New York, proposal of marr. at
23. PW 3-9-95:420.

CONKLIN, JENNIE MARIA (DRINKWATER) AND ELLA A. DRINKWATER.

002359   SET FREE. BY JENNIE M. DRINKWATER AND
ELLA A. DRINKWATER. New York: Ward and Drummond,
[c1891] NUC.

Sentimental...hysterical didacticism: IND
Jane Nelson's exps. in farm house and Hospital PW
9:12-91

CONNEY, MRS.

002360   GOLD FOR DROSS. London: Hutchinson, 1893
BMC NUC.

SP 72:270. "Dull awkward, uninteresting, but loving
and devoted wife" gives her "coined and uncoined gold"
to husband and gets nothing but dross.
Rev. thinks story is about husband; Jean, his wife,
should have "tried harder to understand him."

002361   JUDY, A JILT: A NOVEL. London: Jarrold,
1897 BMC.

She's impossible, tempestuous. Daughter of a sharper
and a ballet dancer. Not suited for the drawing room.
At home in the hunting field. Becomes engaged to an
old colonel, but loves another whom she tries to trick
into marrying her. Tragedy. ACAD 51:304.
SR Doleful end.
ATH 108:871. Like the fiction of the 60's. Heroine
whose face is her fortune believes mrge. only reason
for existing. Havoc in the hearts of men, fear in
hearts of women. Drowns.

002362   A LINE OF HER OWN. London: Hurst &
Blackett, 1891 BMC.

Combines hunting story with love story; lively
descriptions of cross-country ruins, etc: ACAD
Other standard ingredients: lovers, scheming widow who
wants the man, villain who tries to help the widow and

to make hero lose the race, etc. SP 66, 312

002363   PEGGY'S PERVERSITY. London: Hurst and
Blackett, 1891 BMC.

She's really healthy, normal, also very active,
candid. Treats men as friends; not a proper lady of
old fashioned type as her brother and guardian wish
her to be. Jealous of her lover's attentions to
Blanche, her brother's wife. SP 67, 681
Blanche is an alcoholic and the two men try to keep
this secret. All turns out well. ACAD
Peggy Treherne angular and gawky transformed in six
months to a radiant belle. ATH 98 645
SR 73:246. Peggy is brought up as a tomboy in country
house, at 19 becomes lady of her brother's house.
Vacillates between two ways of life, unable to make up
her mind which she wants.

002364   A RUTHLESS AVENGER. London: Hutchinson,
1893 BMC. Philadelphia: J. B. Lippincott, 1896 NUC.

LW 27:153. Innocent man under suspicion of murder.
Robbery, wills, love story.
PW 2-8-96. Also under suspicion of illegitimacy.
Includes a romance, illegitimacy, theft, murder, an
inheritance, etc. Lady Helen Evelyn a well drawn
character-love interest. ACAD 44:128.
A kind of Bluebeard, excessively jealous. How his
first wife died is not clear. He knifed the second and
tried to knife the third, five minutes after he killed
a man with whom she had flirted. But wife #3 is saved.
Also a jewel robbery, another villain. SR 75:662.
Virtue and villainy, crimes, jewels, elopement. ATH
101:760.

CONNOLLY, JANE.

002365   OLD DAYS AND WAYS. London: E. Arnold,
1912 BMC NUC.

Personal recollections of life at Woolwick, England.
NUC

CONNOLLY, MRS. R. M.

002366   BERMADU; A TALE OF MODERN MALAYA. London:
Greening, 1911 BMC NUC.

White colony and their unpicturesque doings. TLS
Eng. woman married to a scoundrel who has a Malayan
paramour whose husband murders her. ATH

CONNOR, JEAN. United States.

002367   BOND AND FREE. New York: Benziger, 1913
NUC.

Hugh Trevelyn tortured by memory of a murder, but the
murdered man is alive and his sister comes to love
Trevelyn. ATH

002368   SO AS BY FIRE. New York: Benziger, 1909
NUC.

Barbara Graeme, poor, father in prison; impersonates
another girl to take advantage of new life; confesses;
returns to own life, marries happily. PW

CONQUEST, JOAN. United Kingdom.

002369   DESERT LOVE. London: T.W. Laurie, 1920
BMC NUC. New York: Macmillan, [c1920] NUC.

ATH Jill Carden seeks adventure, goes to Egypt,
marries an Arab and they live very happily in his
desert palace.
LBKM traditional romance.
PW
NYT 9-19-20 p. 23 Author approves of interracial mrg
with Arabs, but not with Hottentots.

CONSTANCE, E.

002370   ALONG THE ROAD. A NOVEL. London:
Hutchinson, 1899 BMC NUC.

Ella loves good and pretty things. And has a great
respect for herself. A governess-popular with
children, but prefers the company of adults. Frank
opinions about kids shock her friends. Has no
sentimentality about things. Even her marriage is a
faute de mieux. She regards it coldly and clearly.
She's ready to make the best of it--but she will never
call ugly things by pretty names. LBKM 16-169.
Wretched sea-side school. Ends with wedding, but

unconventional. She has wed a vulgar good-natured man;
she has doubts about the marriage. SP 82:793

CONSTANCE, LADY [pseud.].

002371   BECAUSE OF A KISS. BY LADY CONSTANCE.
London: S. Paul, [1911] BMC.

Romance-TLS

CONVERSE, FLORENCE. B. 1871. United States.

002372   THE BURDEN OF CHRISTOPHER. Boston:
Houghton, Mifflin, 1900 NUC.

NYT 1900:408. Hero attempts to run business on
Christian principles discovers that in modern
competition he can't succeed. In despair he
appropriates money to save business and in the end
suicides.
NYT 1900:417. Author is against modern philanthropy
and benevolence, for workers having an equal share of
money. Christopher attempts to run his business this
way, as contrasted with Peter Watson who puts his
profits into charities, skimping on wages.
BKM 11:494.
PW. English manufacturing town. The value of women's
labor is specially discussed.

002373   THE CHILDREN OF LIGHT. Boston:
Houghton-Mifflin, 1912 NUC. London: J.M. Dent, 1912
BMC.

PW-Female Socialist, deals with ideas.
NYT-Not a love story, idealistic, full of enthusiasm
and elan, student of Robert Owen.
"The story in autobiographical form of a child born to
socialism-to use the term in its broad, generalized
sense. We first meet her as a girl participator in a
communistic experiment. On becoming an heiress, she is
thrown into the companionship of two other idealists
who have taken St. Francis as their model. The efforts
made by the two boys and the girl to carry their
theories into practice presage with a fine pathos the
trials of their maturity. They start a Labour paper,
interest themselves in election work, take a leading
part in a strike which becomes 'general' and one of
the men finally achieves his greatest success in
defending with his life a renegade, and the other by
incurring a year's imprisonment." ATH
NYT 17:680 N 17 '12 350w "If the incidents are not
well built, they enable us to become acquainted with
the medley of generous enthusiasm, sordid aims and
lawless instinct, of loving-kindness and clamorous
self-interest, that make up the socialistic movement
as it really exists. This ought to be one of the most
widely read books of the season-particularly among the
college men and college women who can see in the
mystical intensity of Miss Converse's characters a
projection of the finest blend of their
aspirations-culture that shall enrich the individual
and an aggressive philanthropy that shall remove from
it all taint of self-indulgence."
ATH-girl born to Socialism, participates in a
communistic experience. She and two men start a Labour
paper, participate in a strike.
TLS Blend of Franciscan and Socialist ideals. One dies
in strike, other goes to prison. Young woman is
narrator.
Clara raised in a cooperative settlement, which proves
a failure. "How the children try to carry out their
socialistic and other principles." point of view? ACAD

002374   DIANA VICTRIX: A NOVEL. Boston and New
York: Houghton, Mifflin, 1897 NUC.

Two women from N.E. visit a Creole family in New
Orleans. One is a teacher of social science in Boston.
She's a self-sufficient person and has come to involve
her old school mate in a more active life. The eldest
son of the family falls in love with her. The action
of this self-sufficient woman is thereafter
interesting; she is last seen living contentedly in a
Boston tenement. PW 52:604.
NYT 1898:416. Considers a grave social problem. Diana
heroine is a teacher and a lecturer, too devoted to
her work to need any man's love. Two other women
illustrate other phases of contemporary American
femininity: a little French Creole maiden with old
fashioned ideas is a foil for all three.
LW 29:10. Impoverished but proud Southern family,
Dumaris. Sylvia and Enid two northern bachelor girls
come to board for a winter. "Their aversion to
marriage is as unnatural as their absorbing love for
each other. Of course the young Southerners fall in
love with them, but being what they are, the damsels

prefer each other, although Sylvia quite loses her
head as well as her heart. Northern coldness is well
contrasted with Southern fervor. The story has
pathetic episodes, tragic in poor Joanne's case, and
the end comes near being depressing, but turns out the
best for all concerned."

002375   LONG WILL; A ROMANCE. Boston: Houghton,
Mifflin, 1903 NUC. London: Longmans, Green, 1903 BMC.

Piers the Plowman, his wife and daughter-whose beauty
attracts all, goes on a pilgrimage, refuses wealth,
marries the right man. ACAD 65, 504
Piers, Chaucer-everyone shows up in this 14th cent
rom. 122, 680 ATH

CONWAY, ADALINE MAY. B. 1882.

002376   A SILENT PEAL FROM THE LIBERTY BELL.
Philadelphia: G. W. Jacobs, [c1914] NUC.

"The Liberty Bell itself tells the story of its
stirring career, how it was made in England for the
Philadelphia State House, cracked on its first
ringing, was recast, cracked again and was once more
recast, this time successfully, and for twenty-five
years before the signing of the Declaration was used
to summon people to the State House, and to announce
events of political importance. Book ends with the
cracking of the bell while tolling for Chief Justice
John Marshall the last of the signers, and a plea
against being carried about the country to
expositions." PW

CONWAY, EMMA ELLIS.

002377   TO PORTS BEYOND. Ridgewood, N. J.: Editor
Pub. Co., 1910 NUC.

CONWAY, KATHARINE SAINT JOHN. See GLASIER, KATHARINE SAINT
JOHN (CONWAY) BRUCE.

CONWAY, KATHERINE ELEANOR. 1853-1927. United States.

002378   LALOR'S MAPLES. Boston: Pilot Pub. Co.,
1901 NUC.

Story of Catholic home life.

002379   THE WAY OF THE WORLD AND OTHER WAYS: A
STORY OF OUR SET. Boston: Pilot Pub. Co., 1900 NUC.

CONYERS, DOROTHEA (SMYTH). B. 1873. United Kingdom.

002380   THE ARRIVAL OF ANTONY. London:
Hutchinson, 1912 BMC NUC. New York: E. P. Dutton,
[1912?] NUC.

TLS-Hunt and horse
ATH-Hunt and horse
SP-hunt and horse

002381   AUNT JANE AND UNCLE JAMES. London:
Hutchinson, 1908 BMC.

TLS-typical Conyers

002382   B. E. N. London: Methuen, 1919 BMC.

Foxhunting: Irish stories with Ben (young woman) a
thread between them. orphan, poor, hard exist, self
reliant; tries various war jobs with little success,
becomes a second whip (?) to the West Cara Hounds but
falls ill from the work. TLS
"Episodes of the hunting-field linked together by Ben,
orphan girl making her own way as a whip." BAKER 32,
p. 113

002383   THE BLIGHTING OF BARTRAM. London:
Methuen, 1918 BMC.

TLS-Ireland and horses.

002384   BLOOM OR BLIGHT. London: Hurst and
Blackett, 1901 BMC.

002385   THE BOY, SOME HORSES AND A GIRL, A TALE
OF AN IRISH TRIP. London: E. Arnold, 1905 BMC NUC.

Rollicking Irish hunting tale. ACAD 65, 508

002386   CLOTH VERSUS SILK. London: Hutchinson,
1905 BMC NUC.

002387   THE EXPERIMENTS OF GANYMEDE BUNN. London:
Hutchinson, 1917 BMC [1918?] NUC.

002388   THE FINANCING OF FIONA. London: G. Allen
and Unwin, 1916 BMC.

pretty story about Fiona's horse and no money to run
it and love. LBKM
TLS--Love story.
pretty story @ Fiona's horse and no money to run it
and love. LBKM
TLS-love story.

002389   FOR HENRI AND NAVARRE. London:
Hutchinson, 1911 BMC NUC.

historical romance, male hero. TLS

002390   IRISH STEW. London: Skeffington, 1920
BMC.

002391   LADY ELVERTON'S EMERALDS. London:
Hutchinson, 1909 NUC BMC.

love and crime TLS

002392   MEAVE: A NOVEL. London: Hutchinson, 1915
BMC NUC.

shabby wild girl from Ireland (Meane) a splendid
mount. TLS
She's "a young Irish Amazon accompanied by several
dogs, a talking magpie and Irish handyman." Invades an
English bachelor establishment-had to come to live
with uncle; father summoned to Australia. Meane is out
of place in this extremely well-regulated household.
She's ill-dressed, unconventional, unpunctual. Always
gets the best of her bellowing uncle, humanizes him.
At end wedding bells aren't far off? SP.

002393   A MIXED PACK. London: Methuen, 1915 BMC.

002394   OLD ANDY. London: Methuen, 1914 BMC.

SR 118:117. Ireland. Kind-hearted farmer hero.

002395   PETER'S PEDIGREE. London: E. Arnold, 1904
BMC 1907 NUC.

002396   SALLY: A NOVEL. London: Methuen, [1912]
BMC NUC.

ATH-Irish romance.
TLS-Irish romance.
LBKM- Irish romance.

002397   SANDY MARRIED. London: Methuen, 1913 BMC.

About hunting and racing and Sandy the hero; life-like
picture of horse sales. SP
And a fantastic will-ATH

002398   THE SCRATCH PACK. London: Hutchinson,
1916 BMC.

TLS-hunting in Ireland.

002399   SOME HAPPENINGS OF GLENDALYNE. London:
Hutchinson, 1911 BMC NUC.

Melodrama mystery-TLS

002400   THE STRAYINGS OF SANDY. London:
Hutchinson, 1906 BMC NUC.

TLS-Male hero Ireland.
BAKER 13-211

002401   THE THORN BIT. London: Hutchinson, 1900
BMC.

SP 85:85. Romance of conventional wild Irish girl.
ATH 115:812. Runs away from her husband in an hour of
marriage. Pleasant and light. "Thorn bit of marriage
to a colt."

002402   THREE GIRLS AND A HERMIT. London:
Hutchinson, 1908 BMC. New York: E. P. Dutton, 1908
NUC.

TLS-three girls paired off with good husbands.

002403   TIRANOGUE. London: Methuen, 1919 BMC.

her father leaves his fortune to her not to the mother
who never loved him. Irish setting, horses. end? TLS

002404   TWO IMPOSTERS AND TINKER. London:

Hutchinson, 1910 NUC BMC. New York: E. P. Dutton, 1911
NUC.

brother and sister; "girl has spirit for both" "she
dresses as a young man and conquers the country" PW
3-18-11
adds little except that love makes a happy ending to
the tale. NYT
TLS-Irish hunting
ACAD-Irish hunting.

002405   UNCLE PIERCE'S LEGACY. London: Methuen,
1920 BMC.

TLS-5000 pounds to elderly Honor and Evelyn Nutting
providing they kept the hounds and hunted.

CONYNGHAM, DANE, pseud. See CURRAN, MRS. L. P. M.

COOK, GRACE LOUISE. Nationality Unknown.

002406   WELLESLEY STORIES. Boston: R.G. Badger,
1901 NUC.

7 stories Friendships between women; intell
involvement in studies NYT O1

COOK, MABEL (COLLINS). 1851-1927. United Kingdom.

002407   A DEBT OF HONOUR. BY MABEL COLLINS. New
York: J. W. Lovell, [c1891] NUC. London: Eden,
Remington, 1892 BMC.

LW 27:349. Romance of innkeeper's daughter and young
squire. He marries an heiress; she suicides.

002408   JULIET'S LOVERS. BY MABEL COLLINS.
London: Ward and Downey, 1893 BMC.

SP-"Exceeding unpleasant" men are "profligate scamps."
"moral sensibilities of the heroine less acute than
(the author) imagines them."
ACAD 45:9. A protest against bringing up women in
ignorance of "the ways of life." Juliet is abandoned
by her father (her mother is dead) who gives her his
illegitimate daughter as a companion. She becomes a
successful actress, marries an actor and on day of
wedding confronts another woman claiming his name.
Plot: Lover number 1 shoots at Juliet; #2 shoots lover
#3; #3 marries Juliet; #1 shoots #3; #2 marries
Juliet. Much agony and passion. SR 76 711
All characters but two are shockingly evil or
shockingly victimized by evil people. Juliet's father
has a wife and mistress. So has her husband. One woman
director is a wicked woman who wears a live snake as a
bracelet. Sensational, about theatrical life. ATH
102:694.

002409   MORIAL THE MAHATMA. BY MABEL COLLINS. New
York: Lovell, Gestefeld, [1892] NUC.

LW 23:310. "Utterly confused plot"
CR 18:275. Powerful Tibetan mystic whose capacity for
evil is destroyed by woman calling on the spirit of
truth, etc.

002410   THE STAR SAPPHIRE. BY MABEL COLLINS.
London: Downey, 1896 BMC. Boston: Roberts, 1896 NUC.

ATH 108:753. "Drunkeness in an educated woman is as
horrible as it fortunately is rare. Even a great
master could not make the subject anything but
offensive; but when, as here, it is treated as a mere
theme for the most commonplace of society novels, it
becomes positively bothersome." Private hospital.
PW 10-31-96. Young and talented woman leading an
aimless social life, while visiting discovers secret
of man-about-town's marriage. Strong, and helpful, he
associates her with a star sapphire which in certain
light achieves great brilliancy. Problem of hereditary
inebriety is dealt with.
Beautiful with vicious habit of drink kills the love
of her husband. Laurence Monkwell is the sapphire, the
hospital nurse. ACAD 51:328
Best part Laurence's experience as a hospital nurse.
LW 28:145
ATH 3-29-02 heroine loves married man.

002411   SUGGESTION. BY MABEL COLLINS. New York:
Lovell and Gestefeld, [c1892] NUC BMC.

PW-Margery, the squire's-daughter, is happily engaged
to Rex. Oliver, Rex's brother mesmerizes Margery and
fills her with doubts and fears. His power over her is
finally exorcised.

COOK, MABEL (COLLINS), jt. au. See DESPARD, CHARLOTTE AND
MABEL (COLLINS) COOK.

COOKE, ALICE M. PEPPARD.

002412   HIS LAUREL CROWN. A PLAYER'S ROMANCE.
London: Downey, 1900 BMC.

ATH 116:52 Life on the English stage.
LIT 7:142 Irish peasants.

COOKE, FRANCES. Nationality Unknown.

002413   HER JOURNEY'S END. New York: Benziger,
[c1911] NUC.

Raised among anarchists, escapes, much adventure PW
4-15-11

002414   "MY LADY BEATRICE". New York: Benziger,
1908 NUC.

PW-Catholic story, wholesome country life.

002415   THE SECRET OF THE GREEN VASE. New York:
Benziger, 1907 NUC.

Advent-mystery. PW 12-14-07

002416   THE UNBIDDEN GUEST. New York: Benziger,
1909 NUC.

Mystery with rel theme. PW 12-4-09

COOKE, GRACE (MACGOWAN). B. 1863. United States.

002417   THE GRAPPLE; A STORY OF THE ILLINOIS COAL
REGION. Boston: L. C. Page, 1905 NUC.

Story of a strike in mining town. PW 9-16-05

002418   THE JOY BRINGER; A TALE OF THE PAINTED
DESERT. Garden City, N.Y.: Doubleday, Page, 1913 NUC.

"Young man comes home from Arizona and elopes with a
lovely Kentucky girl who had meant to run away with
his brother. Because she has married the wrong man she
is disinherited. Her newly wedded husband has no money
so they have to go back to Arizona, where he has a
ranch and a store. Even if she does maintain that she
does not love her inadvertently acquired husband, the
bride has considerable anxiety as to whether or not he
will have an Indian wife. Did this big-hearted
westerner really marry the wrong woman? That is a
problem worked out in an interesting way." PW

002419   THE POWER AND THE GLORY. New York:
Doubleday, Page, 1910 NUC.

NYT-Heroine is Johnnie, a mill-worker. She loves
machinery, has invented an improvement to the looms,
drives a mad chase in auto down mountain after half
hour of driving. She is desperately ambitious-for the
sake of the younger children in family who are also in
the mill.
Love Story.-- BM

002420   THEIR FIRST FORMAL CALL. New York and
London: Harper, 1906 NUC.

COOKE, GRACE (MACGOWAN) AND ALICE MACGOWAN.

002421   AUNT HULDAH; PROPRIETOR OF THE WAGON-TIRE
HOUSE AND GENIAL PHILOSOPHER OF THE CATTLE COUNTRY.
London: Hodder and Stoughton, 1904 BMC. Indianapolis:
Bobbs-Merrill, [1904] NUC. (English ed. Title: Huldah,
. . .)

LBKM —widow with orphans who runs a coffee house in
the west.
NYT-Runs a hotel, adopts orphans, kind to all.

002422   THE STRAIGHT ROAD [ANONYMOUS]. New York:
G. H. Doran, [c1917] NUC.

PW 91:1278-9 4/21/17 "Callie left her husband, and
taking her little boy, started into the world to make a
living. The narrative is a true story of a pretty
woman's fight against predatory men. Includes
recognizable incidents, such as the white-slave trade
and the riot in the hop fields of California."

002423   WILD APPLES, A CALIFORNIA STORY. BY THE
AUTHOR OF "THE STRAIGHT ROAD" [ANONYMOUS]. New York:
G. H. Doran, [1918] NUC.

PW-Male hero love
NYT-Julian, 19, has an affair with a 17 year old
factory girl, Lynnie. She refuses to marry him, his
family buys her family off, not wishing to see him
tied for life to an ignorant girl. He runs away, all
works out in end.

COOKE, GRACE (MACGOWAN) AND ANNE MACQUEEN.

002424   THE GIRLS OF SILVER SPUR RANCH. Chicago:
M.A. Donohue, [c1913] NUC.

COOKE, GRACE (MACGOWAN) AND ANNIE BOOTH MACKINNEY.

002425   MISTRESS JOY; A TALE OF NATCHEZ IN 1798.
New York: Century, 1901 NUC.

Joyce intends to become a preacher, almost marries,
spends month thinking about what direction she'll
take. She becomes a social belle; doesn't tell ending.
NYT

COOKE, GRACE (MACGOWAN) AND CAROLINE WOOD MORISON.   America
LC.

002426   WILLIAM AND BILL. New York: Century, 1914
NUC.

COOKE, GRACE (MACGOWAN), jt. au.   See MACGOWAN, ALICE AND
GRACE (MACGOWAN) COOKE.

COOKE, JANE GROSVENOR.   Nationality Unknown.

002427   THE ANCIENT MIRACLE. New York: A. S.
Barnes, 1906 BMC NUC.

PW-Romance of Canadian wilderness
NYT-Willful heroine but is probably trad.

002428   AN INTERRUPTED HONEYMOON. New York: A. S.
Barnes, 1907 NUC.

Woman leaves husband on wedding night, for four years
neither explains why. PW 11-9-07
After four years the couple learn the meaning of life
and love NYT
BKM-"A Story of conflict between a man and a woman who
become acquainted with each other and with the
realities of life and love four years after they were
married."
NYT years and experience teach Sall the real meaning
of life and love etc.
Brief desc. BKM 26 (1908)558

COOKE, MARJORIE BENTON.   1876-1920.   United States.

002429   BAMBI. Garden City, N. Y.: Doubleday,
Page, 1914 NUC. London: Jarrold's, 1915 NUC.

PW 86 9/19/14:773-"Charming whimsical Bambi marries
impractical play-writing Jarvis off-hand to take care
of him. He tries unsuccessfully to sell his play in
New York and then suddenly realizing his indebtedness
to Bambi, he remains there, reduced even to
cab-driving to make a living. Meanwhile, Bambi puts
herself into a novel and induces Frohman to allow
Jarvis to dramatize it. He quite falls in love with
the unknown author during their correspondence. The
disclosure is a shock to Jarvis, but all ends
happily."
She writes popular novel, publishes it, in her spare
moments, all the while helping her husband in his
efforts to become a dramatist. Light. (Book)
Irresponsible young daughter of a professor and
married to a playwright braves theatrical managers
wins success for husband. TLS
Thinks and acts for two men <pa and husband> and in
between writes a successful book that "springs into
fame" Husband contacts the author of that novel, falls
in love with her (own wife) LBKM

002430   CINDERELLA JANE. Garden City, N. Y.:
Doubleday, Page, 1917 BMC NUC. [London]: Jarrolds,
[1917] BMC.

attempts writing returns to cooking for Greenwich
village geniuses. Marries one, tries again to write,
baby comes, solved happily-PW
"difficulties which arise from marriage being
considerd as a social contract terminable by
inclination" SP
"Takes 2 publishing houses by storm and then the
public." BKM
Sure of herself from the start: already recognized in
her home town as a writer, comes to New York. Writes
for 5 years till she's sure she's good; earns her

bread and butter as a drudge to artists. Accepts
marriage with one-because wifehood and motherhood will
be useful for her purpose-of writing. She's determined
to be a modern wife. Feels her work is none of his
business, keeps her work room and goes there to write
leaving him to mind the baby. She is a
genius-unrecognized, even by husband. Then she acts
Salome on stage, writes a remarkable novel. Her woman
friend is a successful sculptor. Argues successfully
with husband, completely worsting him. Tells him she
married for the good the experience of marriage and
maternity would do her writing. She converts him to
accept a brilliant famous woman as wife. "best part of
book..remarks regarding women's careers and economic
positions." NYT 4-29-17
ATH-New York society questions, deep. Author gives
prominence to women's view of them, but their
seriousness is not felt to be the least oppressive.
LBKM-Amusing, but Jerry has to learn how to accept
being husband of a famous writer. Jane strong,
independent, talented. writes a great book, is famous.
A notable critic falls for her.She takes her child off
to decide between him and her husband. Chooses to
remain married to her husband.

002431   THE CLUTCH OF CIRCUMSTANCE. New York: G.
H. Doran, [c1918] NUC. London: Skeffington, [1919]
BMC.

PW-Mystery, international plots.
NYT Nov 10 '18 p. 484. Lady Roberta Trask, brought up
in U.S., has the opinion that it "grabs and orates."
After war breaks out she becomes an agent for the
Germans; she and an Irish officer are tried by
court-martial, she confesses. "Forthwith the people
who had unmasked her wept and humbly apologized for
interfering with her. She forgave them nobly,....and
expired in an odor of sanctity. The author seems to
admire her immensely. The book is dull, and more than
a little pro-German in tendency."
American wife (part German) becomes German secret
service agent.Lady Trask condemned to death? loving
last days of husband and wife. TLS

002432   THE CRICKET. London: Jarrolds, 1919 BMC.
Garden City, N.Y.: Doubleday, Page, 1919 NUC.

Isabelle Bryce is the cricket, energetic organized
American a problem to her parents-mother named Max-but
she marries. TLS
Dismally fails on the stage, then marries. ATH
Elopes "uninvited with an adored hero" Finally finds
her true romance when she wrecks a great play and is
sent away to Bermuda. PW
A bad little precocious girl is straightened out in
the end by love. NYT 6-8-19 321

002433   DR. DAVID. Chicago: A. C. McClurg, 1911
NUC.

Married woman blind after child birth, falls in love
with her eye doctor. Another woman helps husband and
wife get thru these difficulties. PW 9-23-11
Nanette Brandon married to a man wrapped up in
business. Is bored with her society life. Falls for
the doctor. Childbirth ends in blindness for her-she
blames and hates the child. Loves the doctor madly. He
loves her but won't show it. Husband knows all and
waits. All turns out well-Nanette loves baby and
husband. The doctor marries another. NYT

002434   THE DUAL ALLIANCE. Garden City, New York:
Doubleday, Page, 1915 NUC.

"A short story of the love of an Irish actress and how
she turned politician." BKM 42 1915-16
Bob an actress PW 10-16-15
Barbara Garratry first supports self and ill father at
15 then writer, interior decorator. A famous actress
and a successful male lawyer marry but by previous
agreement they live separate lives. The climax comes
when she makes "a big and sensational political speech
in New York which helps to land the lawyer in the
Governor's chair." At 24 popular actress and noted
playwright. NYT

002435   THE GIRL WHO LIVED IN THE WOODS. Chicago:
A.C. McClurg, 1910 NUC. [London]: Jarrolds, 1917 BMC.

artist, carpenter, gardener and she does for herself
all alone in a cabin in the woods. NYT
arranged marriage is unhappy. Anna Harmon brought
closer to husband at time of financial problems. Their
child makes friends with girl in the woods, an artist
recluse. The child wins her back to society. PW
Cecilia Carni, Thoreau-like independent individual

full of eager socialist theories. Her first experience
of a society, secret of her parentage, the fight of
trusts and industrial revolutionaries. TLS

002436   THE REDEMPTION OF ANTHONY. Indianapolis:
Bobbs-Merrill, [1911] NUC.

002437   THE THRESHOLD. A STORY. Garden City, New
York: Doubleday, Page, 1918 NUC. [London]: Jarrolds,
[1918] BMC.

Saccharine type of fiction.
PW-Joan worked way thru college and becomes tutor and
social housekeeper to mill owner. Loves him but
sympathy lies with mill workers. She becomes arbiter
between the 2 factions in strife and all ends
well.-American author
TLS-She came herself from factory class. Fought for
her education, is fighting now for factory workers.
NYT p. 142 Mar 31, 1918 300 w-Results of her efforts
included a strike and the building of a model village
and factory.

COOKE, MATILDA VANCE. United States.

002438   THE ZIG-ZAG PATHS OF LIFE: A NOVEL.
Chicago: C. H. Kerr, 1895 NUC.

Methodist minister ruined one young woman. At opening
of story marries a woman who, upon hearing of his
past, leaves him. Minister is finally murdered by the
brother of his 3rd victim. PW 5-4-95:704.

COOKSON, SYBIL IRENE ELEANOR (TAYLOR). B. 1890. United
Kingdom.

002439   THE AUCTION MART. BY SYDNEY TREMAYNE.
London: J. Lane, 1915 BMC. New York: J. Lane, 1915
NUC.

woman resents her father's ideas, leaves, becomes a
private secretary, then a famous dancer, his illness
brings her home. PW 6-19-15
Father convinced all women are vampires raises his
illegitimate daughter to be a blood-sucker. "Be very
expensive, Jacqueline." But out in the world, keeps
straight, even waits for father to die before
marrying. TLS
Man trains illegitimate adopted girl to find
satisfaction in shallow desires--all he feels women
are capable of. ATH

002440   ECHO. BY SYDNEY TREMAYNE. London, New
York: J. Lane, 1919 BMC NUC.

ATH-Mother is unfaithful and divorced. She lives with
aunts and escapes to Paris. She is a Bohemian, marries
unfortunately and deserted by husband.
NYT 1920:273 Relationship between mother and daughter,
the former appearing respectable and reformed, but she
"has one or two escapades" and marries South American.
Author refers to him as a "dago", calls Negroes
"niggers."
Slow revelation of her character "Echo was the
future-change, rebellion, but life, energy, realities,
and freedom." Rebels vs. being chaperoned in park,
visits men in their rooms, kisses on first meeting but
fundamentally conventional. TLS

COOLEY, ELLEN HODGES. Nationality Unknown.

002441   THE BOOM OF A WESTERN CITY. Boston: Lee
and Shepard, 1897 NUC.

Fargo, Dakota. A Vt. family comes to town. Their
experiences. PW 52:567.
LW 29:456. Vermont farm family go West to get ahead;
return to N. Eng. gratefully.

COOLEY, WINNIFRED (HARPER).

002442   THE NEW WOMANHOOD. New York: Broadway,
1904 NUC.

HQ1426 woman-Soc & moral

COOLIDGE, ASENATH CARVER. United States.

002443   BETWEEN TWO REBELLIONS. Watertown, N.Y.:
[Hungerford-Holbrook], 1909 NUC.

002444   CHERRY FEASTS FOR BARBAROUS FOURTHS.
Watertown, N.Y.: [Hungerford-Holbrook], 1909 NUC.

002445   CHRISTMAS VS. FOURTH OF JULY. Watertown,
N. Y.: [Hungerford-Holbrook], 1908 NUC.

002446   HUMAN BEINGS VS. THINGS. Watertown, N.
Y.: Hungerford-Holbrook, 1910 NUC.

Heroine awakens to knowledge that women spend too much
time with things, too little with down and out people.
Arraigns vs. men who make instruments of war and
on-rushing commercialism of the day. PW

002447   THE INDEPENDENCE DAY HORROR AT KILLSBURY.
Watertown, N. Y.: Hungerford-Holbrook, 1905 NUC.

002448   THE MODERN BLESSING FIRE. New York,
London: Abbey Press, [1902] NUC.

WOMANS JOURNAL 12/6/1902. "Strong-minded women";
suffrage sentiment and equality expressed by both men
and women.

002449   ON THE WATCHTOWER. Boston: 1912 NUC.

002450   OUR NATION'S ALTAR. Watertown, N. Y.:
[Hungerford-Holbrook], 1910 NUC.

Written in ironic humorous style. Anti-war, and
anti-patriotic traditions that train boys to kill. (47
pages). --Book

002451   PROPHET OF PEACE. Watertown, N. Y.:
Hungerford-Holbrook, 1907 NUC.

"equal rights, clothing reform. WOMAN'S JOURNAL
3/28/1908
PW-woman dedicated to peace, member of Society of
Friends, emmigrates to U.S.

002452   RECIPROCITY; A STORY OF LOVE AND MINING.
Watertown, N. Y.: Hungerford-Holbrook, 1911 NUC.

COOLIDGE, EMMA DOWNING. B. 1884. United States.

002453   AT THE KING'S PLEASURE. Boston: C. M.
Clark, [c1911] NUC.

Hist romance. NYT

002454   THE DREAMER. Boston: Pilgrim Press,
[c1915] NUC.

COOLIDGE, SUSAN, pseud. See WOOLSEY, SARAH CHAUNCEY.

COOPER, ELIZABETH. 1877-1945. United States.

002455   DRUSILLA WITH A MILLION. New York: F. A.
Stokes, [1916] NUC.

Drusilla "almost old" the drudge of an Old Ladies Home
left money. Decides to share her money with people who
needed it. Began with babies and young people who
needed opportunities to develop their talents. PW
89:2/5/16:390
NYT-Drusilla, dear, old, quaint, inherits a million at
70. A baby is dropped on her doorstep. when she
decides to keep it, 12 more arrive. charming, sent,
etc.

002456   THE HEART OF O SONO SAN. New York: F. A.
Stokes, [c1917] NUC. London: G. G. Harrap, [1920] NUC.

raised in obedience code. Her lover goes away, father
arranges a wealthy alliance, she submits. Involves
self in son: he dies, once again submits to fate. PW
TLS-Part of Japanese womanhood, showing how culture
makes ideal women.

002457   LIVING UP TO BILLY. New York: F. A.
Stokes, [c1915] NUC.

dancer cares for nephew Billy. PW 9-11-15
NY dancing girls. Girlish letters to sister imprisoned
for theft. She raises her sister's baby. Letters tell
of her career in East side dance halls and Broadway
shows. A sweet pure girl. NYT 10/31/15

002458   MY LADY OF THE CHINESE COURTYARD. New
York: F.A. Stokes, [1914] NUC.

BKM-author has saturated herself with the pov of the
high-caste Chinese woman. 1st part of book about young
wife, 2nd about her middle age.
DS 725 women in China
PW-"Life story of a high class Chinese woman, as told
by herself. Her life as a young wife is described in
human, intimate terms-her subjection to her
mother-in-law, her many duties in the patriarchal
family, her great and almost pathetic joy over the

birth of a son. Later we see her as the honored mother of children, but encompassed by the change and turmoil of new China. The place of Christianity in her life is interestingly shown. Book brings home how near akin are the wives and mothers of East and West. Author lived for many years in Shanghai."

COOPER, LOUISE BATTLES. United States.

002459   BEHIND A MASK: A NOVEL. Chicago: Laird and Lee, 1891 NUC.

Heroine assumes name of Mrs. Brown (her mask) wins all hearts at Mass. summer resort. Mrs. Thearle comes and an old feud starts up again between them. PW 3-14-91.

002460   IS THIS TRUE? San Francisco: Published By Author, 1893 NUC.

COOPER, MARJORIE.

002461   AILEEN, A TALE OF DEEDS AND MISDEEDS. London: Lynwood, [1912] BMC.

Simple love story, fine portrait study of heroine her high spirit, keen sense of humor, her many suitors. ACAD
A winsome tale. ATH
A flirt, her entanglements to happy end. TLS

CORBALLIS, CONSTANTIA LUCRETIA.

002462   GLEN INSCH. London: Roxburghe Press, [1898] BMC.

002463   RAOUL DE BERIGNAN. London: Burns and Oates, [1893] BMC.

CORBETT, ELIZABETH BURGOYNE. B. 1846.

002464   DEB O'MALLY'S. London: Hurst and Blackett, 1895 BMC.

She leaves Lancashire to work in factory. Dissatisfied, determines to educate herself so she can meet her father and denounce him on equal terms. Writes books, becomes a great successful author. "How her father, by a graceful conceit of the author, proposes to marry her;" she marries a bigamist. SR 80:514
Deborah Pendlebury, illeg daughter of military man. She has blue blood becomes a social success in smart London society, gets a proposal from own father who doesn't know her. SP 75:405
Has her portrait painted and leaps into fame at Royal Academy. ATH 106:316

002465   THE MARRIAGE MARKET: A SERIES OF CONFESSIONALS COMPILED FROM THE DIARY A SOCIETY OF GO-BETWEEN. London: R. A. Everett, 1905 BMC.

Lady needs money acts as go between. Not a wholesome story, not humorous. LBKM 27-8, 215

002466   A MERE MASQUERADE. London: C. A. Pearson, 1895 BMC.

002467   MRS. GRUNDY'S VICTIMS. London: Tower, 1893 BMC.

002468   WHEN THE SEA GIVES UP ITS DEAD: A THRILLING DETECTIVE STORY. London: Tower, 1894 BMC NUC.

Annie Cory and her father are detectives.

002469   A YOUNG STOWAWAY: HIS SURPRISING ADVENTURES AND HAIRBREADTH ESCAPES. London: J. Nisbet, [1896] BMC.

CORBETT, ELIZABETH FRANCES. B. 1887. United States.

002470   CECILY AND THE WIDE WORLD; A NOVEL OF AMERICAN LIFE TODAY. New York: H. Holt, 1916 NUC. London: Hurst and Blackett, 1918 BMC.

TLS-Avery and Cecily part are reunited in end. She is typically American in her independence. He is a MD.
ATH-She leaves him and her children and carves out a career for herself.
SR-A serious study of problems that arise when husband and wife develop interests in different directions. Reader feels first critical, then sympathetic and finally admiring of Cecily.
Cecily gave up her comfortable home and established social position to work for her own and children's

living in a distant city. Divorce followed and Cecily came near to marrying another lover. Marries again but to 1st husband. PW 90:798 9/16/16
NYT-Dr. Fairchild, disgusted with society and his society wife (Cecily), follows Lois Butler, a splendid new woman into apprenticeship in "Health Ed.", leaving Cecily and two children without support. She develops from a society doll into an efficient business woman, running a tea shop. They are eventually back together but in the meantime there is a divorce and other liaisons, all of which experience seems to help them develop as people.

002471   PURITAN AND PAGAN. New York: H. Holt, 1920 NUC.

PW-Studio and theatrical life in New York, conflicting wills of two women. Hero is enmeshed in toils of Pagan, an actress, marries Puritan, a painter. "Damn women with careers!" he is quoted as saying. New York background, women are interesting.
NYT 12-26-20 "both women are independent in spirit," sympathetically portrayed.

002472   THE VANISHED HELGA. New York: G. H. Doran, [c1918] NUC BMC.

PW-wealthy woman whose heart had never been touched and her final surrender.
NYT Nov 3 '18 p. 470. Helga is a yacht. Terribly beautiful Zoe invites friends for cruise (Helga is hers) including John Whittaker who woos and finally wins her.

CORELLI, MARIE, pseud. See MACKAY, MARY.

CORFIELD, CLARA.

002473   PRINCESS LOUISE; A TALE OF THE STUARTS. BY CRONA TEMPLE. London: T. Nelson, 1895 BMC NUC.

Fr. 1697. Princess was young daughter of James second of England. Her story and that of her friend Mary Plowden. PW 9-7-95:294.

CORKEY, ETHEL.

002474   THE WAY OF THE HUNDRED STARS. London: R.T.S., 1918 BMC.

TLS Love of a girl (who becomes a famous artist) is threatened by a danger from heredity, but ends happily.

CORKRAN, HENRIETTE. D. 1911.

002475   LUCIE AND I. London: T. F. Unwin, 1905 BMC.

Confidential style of love story LBKM 27-8, 106

002476   ROUND OUR SQUARE. London: Hurst & Blackett, 1906 BMC.

ACAD-Female artist tells story of Bohemian life.
TLS-Gives no offense
Series of char. sketches SR

CORNELIUS, JOHN, pseud. See SHOOK, MARTHA CAROLINE (DIAL).

CORNELIUS, MARY ANN (MANN). 1827-1918. United States.

002477   UNCLE NATHAN'S FARM: A NOVEL. Chicago: Laird and Lee, 1898 NUC.

002478   THE WHITE FLAME. AN OCCULT STORY. Chicago: Stockham, [c1900] NUC.

PW-story of a chair purchased by one of the family, which has a spirit sitting in it talking of spirit world, etc. White flames come out of chair when he leaves.

CORNELIUS, OLIVIA SMITH. B. 1882. United States.

002479   THE EYES AT THE WINDOW. New York: Broadway, [c1911] NUC.

About two bachelors, love & idleness PW 9-9-11

002480   THE PERSIAN TASSEL. New York: Neale, 1914 NUC.

CORNELL, LILLIAN. United States.

002481   A COUNTRY GIRL. New York: Irving, [c1896]

NUC.

CORNER, CAROLINE.

002482   CROWN, CORONET AND CLOVER. London:
Greening, 1911 BMC.

Prince falls in love with peasant girl, marries her
morganatically. He leaves her, marries a princess,
wants to come back when this marriage goes bad, Sadie
rejects him. Wants to take her child, make him hers.
Sadie won't part with the child. Sadie, of course,
turns out to be a princess herself. ACAD

CORSON, GEOFFREY, pseud. See SHOLL, ANNA MACCLURE.

CORWIN, MINNIE LAHR. United States.

002483   ETHEL WRIGHT, OR ONLY A MUSIC TEACHER.
New York: Cochrane, 1909 NUC.

CORY, MATILDA WINIFRED MURIEL (GRAHAM).

002484   ANGELS, AND DEVILS, AND MAN. BY WINIFRED
GRAHAM CORY. London, New York: Cassell, 1904 BMC NUC.

ATH-psychic phenomena and the smart set. heartless and
worldly widow.

002485   THE BEAUTIFUL MRS. LEACH. London: Ward,
Lock, 1900 BMC.

SP 84:929. Virtuous scientific baronet hero foils
scheme of gang of criminals, and Australian widow one
of them, a decoy and fiancee of his father.

002486   CAN A MAN BE TRUE? BY WINIFRED GRAHAM.
London and New York: M. Kennerley, 1915 NUC.

intrigue and romance.

002487   A CHILD AT THE HELM. London: G. Newnes,
1902 BMC.

002488   CHRISTIAN MURDERERS. London: Everett,
1908 BMC.

TLS-anti Christian.

002489   CROSSROADS. London: Mascot Novels, [1916]
BMC.

002490   EMMA HAMILTON'S MINIATURE. London: F. V.
White, 1906 BMC.

002491   THE ENEMY OF WOMAN. BY WINIFRED GRAHAM.
London: Mills and Boon, [1910] BMC NUC. New York: M.
Kennerley, 1914 NUC.

PW 86 11/7/14:1448. "Famous as an opponent of the
suffrage movement in England, Lionel Marsh, instead of
denouncing it in his waited-for parlimentary speech,
pleads eloquently for it. The simple explanation of
this is that Meg Marsh, his twin sister, has spoken in
his place in disguise. She is a militant leader and
willing even to die for the cause. The results of this
are farther reaching than the separation of the
brother and sister, and contrast the methods of the
militant with those of women who "use silent infuence
in politics," In the end Meg merges her own career in
her brother's, and agrees with him that she has been
her own worst enemy. Though set up in 1910, the book
is just placed on the general market."
NYT 1914:517. Results are: after she leaves, Lionel
falls into the clutches of Mrs. Bruce, a wily widow.
She sent him to an employment office on an errand,
while there, he disovered her "dreadful reputation"
and, panic stricken, induced Meg to return. Mrs.
Bruce, thus scorned, joined the militant suffragettes
declared that "a man must die," hurled a bomb at
Lionel, and was removed to an insane asylum."
TLS-anti suffrage.

002492   EZRA THE MORMON. BY WINIFRED GRAHAM.
London: Everett, 1908 BMC NUC.

Mormonism presented as criminal religion. TLS

002493   FALLING WATERS. BY WINIFRED GRAHAM.
London: Hutchinson, [1919] BMC NUC.

name of a house, love complications-TLS

002494   THE GODS OF THE DEAD. BY WINIFRED GRAHAM.
London: W. Rider, [1912] BMC NUC.

Cosmo Turnus owns a mummy that he feels brings him bad
luck. Decides to destroy it at moment daughter Camilla
is born. Its spirits affect her. Eerie mystery.

002495   THE GREAT HOUSE OF CASTLETON, AND
PATRICIA. London: C. A. Pearson, 1898 BMC.

002496   HER HUSBAND'S SECRET. London: C. A.
Pearson, 1912 BMC.

002497   THE IMPERIAL MALEFACTOR. London: T. W.
Laurie, 1915 BMC.

English heroine loved by German count who turns evil.
American saves her. TLS

002498   JUDAS OF SALT LAKE. London: E. Nash, 1916
BMC.

TLS-anti Mormon crusade
ATH-Mormon preacher lures two girls to utah.
Incredible description of life led by this man.
ATH-Cory (Mrs. Winifred, Nee Graham)

002499   THE LOVE STORY OF A MORMON. BY WINIFRED
GRAHAM. London: Mills and Boon, [1911] BMC NUC.

Mormon agent tries to abduct an English girl-TLS
written frankly to warn young women against Mormons.

002500   MARY. BY WINIFRED GRAHAM. London: Mills
and Boon, 1909 BMC. New York: M. Kennerley, 1910 NUC.

lady gardener madonna like exerts her beneficient
influence over all. TLS
She is a reincarnation of Christ's mother who argues
vs. the cult of the madonna (a Prot. view). Virgin was
"just woman." Mary as a gardener has miraculous power
over things like flowers and over the souls of men.
NYT

002501   MAYFAIR. London: F. V. White, 1904 BMC.

002502   MERESIA. London: Hurst and Blackett, 1898
BMC.

ACAD 53:309. Begins with friendship of hero, Jose, and
Bertie, Eton schoolboys. Then Meresia and her lovers.
ATH 111:498. Meresia murders her husband a Spanish
judge who supervised the torture of Anarchist
prisoners. The reader invited to sympathize with her.

002503   A MIRACLE OF THE TURF. London: F. V.
White, 1906 BMC.

TLS-is the male jockey actually a female?

002504   THE NEEDLEWOMAN. London: Mills and Boon,
1911 BMC.

The title refers to queen of Egypt returned to earth
as Mrs. Romme. TLS

002505   ON THE DOWN GRADE. London: Chapman, 1896
BMC.

ACAD 50:346. Purportedly for cyclists, but no one
rides or even mentions a bicycle. Mr. Gisbourne and
his "career."

002506   THE PIT OF CORRUPTION. London: S. Paul,
[1913] BMC NUC.

Adventures of the dis-embodied soul of the heroine.
ATH
She was killed in an auto accident awaits her lover
who joins her in the end. TLS

002507   THE SIN OF UTAH. London: Everett, [1912]
BMC.

002508   A SOCIAL PRETENDER. London: J. Long, 1901
BMC.

002509   SONS OF STATE. London: Mills and Boon,
1912 BMC.

TLS-sens.

002510   THE STAR CHILD. London: Hurst and
Blackett, 1898 BMC.

SP 81:694. Villainous uncle keeps his nephew, a
musical prodigy, locked up and palms off his
compositions as his own. The boy escapes and has his
own concert.

ATH 112:524.

002511   A STRANGE SOLUTION. London: Chapman and
Hall, 1896 BMC.

ATH 108:899. Strange. Two people marry before
husband's funeral.
She buries her brutish vulgar husband marries another
man the next day. SR 83:153

002512   THE VISION AT THE SAVOY. BY WINIFRED
GRAHAM. New York: F. H. Revell, [c1905] NUC. London:
F. V. White, 1905 BMC.

PW-soul-saving of the rich.
NYT-male hero
About a vision and temple-TLS 319,05

002513   WHEN THE BIRDS BEGIN TO SING: A NOVEL. BY
WINIFRED GRAHAM. London: Pearson, [1897] BMC.

002514   WICKEDNESS IN HIGH PLACES: A NOVEL.
London: F. V. White, 1905 BMC.

widow engages her lover to sister-in-law to be near
him. TLS 108 05

002515   WORLD WITHOUT END. BY WINIFRED GRAHAM
CORY. London: A. Rivers, 1907 BMC NUC.

002516   THE ZIONISTS. BY WINIFRED GRAHAM CORY.
London: Hutchinson, 1902 BMC BMC.

ATH 6-14-02

CORY, VIVIAN. United Kingdom.

002517   ANNA LOMBARD. BY VICTORIA CROSS. London:
J. Long, [1901] BMC NUC. New York: Kensington Press,
[190-?] NUC.

Imagines herself a man. Heroine is "hysterically
sexual" pleads with her fiance to be allowed to
continue with her "amour" with an Asiatic for a little
while after their marriage. After the fiance sees the
Asiatic, he agrees. ACAD.
Anna is horrible; her ill-regulated sensuality is
disgusting. But author wants us to admire her. ATH

002518   THE ETERNAL FIRES. BY VICTORIA CROSS. New
York: Kennerley, [c1910] NUC. London: T. W. Laurie,
[c1910] NUC BMC.

School teacher in love with god Apollo, travels with
him through the Milky Way; after this she can no
longer love mortals. Later "called" again to join the
Gods. PW Book--She bears Apollo's son on Earth,
remains unwed, supports herself by writing and as an
artist's model.

002519   FIVE NIGHTS. BY VICTORIA CROSS. New York:
M. Kennerley, [c1908] NUC. London: J. Long, 1908 BMC.

002520   A GIRL OF THE KLONDIKE. BY VICTORIA
CROSS. London: W. Scott, [1899] BMC.

She is daughter of a Polish saloon keeper. She drinks
and gambles. A young man educated as a missionary
tries to reform her. They marry, but the monotony of
matrimony is more than she can bear. She returns to
the saloon and the reforming has to begin all over
again. Ends in a shoot out at the saloon. LIT 4:239
Her name is Katrine. ACAD 56:192

002521   THE GREATER LAW. BY VICTORIA CROSS.
London: J. Long, [1914] NUC BMC.

SR 118:422. "A trashy book." Quotes from book: "mind
and body together in her were like some splendid
musical instrument, ready to vibrate in glorious
melody the moment the hand of its owner called it
forth." This of a woman floating with a man on Lake
Como, enjoying expensive dinners at a 1st class hotel
at the height of the season. Author's sympathy for
conventional people. "Suffering and agonized, like
poor helpless slaves driven chained to the
market-place, they go the altar." These books sell in
"thousands." Typical of Cross.

002522   HILDA AGAINST THE WORLD. New York:
Macaulay, 1914 NUC.

002523   LIFE OF MY HEART. BY VICTORIA CROSS.
London: W. Scott, 1905 NUC BMC. New York: Macaulay,
1915 NUC.

002524   THE LIFE SENTENCE. BY VICTORIA CROSS. New
York: Macaulay, [1914] NUC. London: J. Long, 1912 BMC.

ATH--Anti divorce laws as "surveyed from the plane of
unbridled passion."

002525   LIFE'S SHOP WINDOW. BY VICTORIA CROSS.
London: T. W. Laurie, 1907 BMC. New York: M.
Kennerley, [1907] NUC.

Finds husband dull, goes off with lover, when he gets
curt she nearly leaves him. Life in this book means
love-making means passion of the carnal kind. TLS
Passions and emotions in the life of a young girl are
drawn in detail in the manner of Zola. NYT

002526   THE NIGHT OF TEMPTATION. BY VICTORIA
CROSS. London: T.W. Laurie, [1912] BMC. New York:
Macaulay, 1914 NUC.

Rich, beautiful, perfect, passionate men and women.
ATH.
TLS--foolish and unwholesome.

002527   PAULA: A SKETCH FROM LIFE. BY VICTORIA
CROSS. London: W. Scott, [1897] BMC. New York: G.
Munro, [1898] NUC.

ATH 108:522. A "brat who takes herself and her
exaggerated emotions too seriously." "An exponent of
the new selfishness and new self-consciousness" She
reads novels and writes plays while her brother makes
tea and keeps the room in order. She smokes. She goes
from lover to husband and back again. Beats a record
at walking and has her blood transfused into veins of
anemic lover. Dies.
ACAD 50:490. Consents to marry manager to get her play
produced; then runs away with man she loves. Husband
writes her he will remove play from production if she
doesn't return. POV?

002528   THE RELIGION OF EVELYN HASTINGS. BY
VICTORIA CROSS. London: W. Scott, 1905 BMC NUC. New
York: Kennerley, 190- []NUC.

NYT--rel. experience.
About a woman who believes in prayer and will not
accept her husband's death "repulsive realism." ATH
237,05

002529   SELF AND THE OTHER. BY VICTORIA CROSS.
New York: [Press of W. G. Hewitt], 1911 NUC. London:
T. W. Laurie, [1911] BMC.

Male college student sacrifices career for Indian
girl-nurse. TLS

002530   SIX CHAPTERS OF A MAN'S LIFE. BY VICTORIA
CROSS. London and New York: W. Scott, 1903 NUC BMC.

Neurotic story. ACAD
Extravagant sensuous. Fervid story of illicit passion.
ATH.

002531   SIX WOMEN. BY VICTORIA CROSS. New York:
M. Kennerley, [1906] NUC. London: T. W. Laurie, 1906
BMC.

TLS--6 tales of passion, mostly oriental, cloying
animalism.

002532   TO-MORROW? BY VICTORIA CROSS. London: W.
Scott, 1904 BMC NUC.

NYT--Male artist as hero.
ATH--Male artist as hero.
The narrator is a novelist who is engaged to his
cousin, an artist. His father disapproves of their
marriage and refuses to give it his financial support
unless his son gets a job or succeeds in publishing
one of his novels (which he doesn't think possible).
He does eventually publish a novel in France (his
writing is too daring for the English taste), but when
he returns triumphant to his cousin, he finds that she
has burned herself out in her work. Within the year
she is dead. She was too passionate to wait for him
indefinitely and too single-minded to turn to someone
else. (Book)

002533   THE WOMAN WHO DID NOT. BY VICTORIA CROSS.
London: J. Lane, 1895 NUC. Boston: Roberts, 1895 NUC.
(Also "The Woman Who Didn't")

describes with "luxuriant imagination" the feelings
and private behavior of a man who loves a married
woman. She loves him but "doesn't"-out of duty. Man

"coarse and tawdry" In the end "declares for the
angels" SR 80:387
refuses to commit adultery with a cad. "The back slums
of social life" "positively reeks of whiskeys and
sodas and of physical passion." ATH 106:351
They meet aboard ship. She's married. They fall in
love but she won't sleep with him. Her "laughing
indifference" to their separation and to the life she
returns to. LW 16:332
SP: offends propriety
CR 29:56. Married woman and her relationship with
another man. Unclear from review what happens.

CORY, WINIFRED GRAHAM. See CORY, MATILDA WINIFRED MURIEL
(GRAHAM).

CORYELL, ELEANOR HOOPER.

002534   OUT OF THE PAST. New York: Street and
Smith, [c1899] NUC. London: J. Henderson, [1899] BMC.

High society, Paris and US. BOOK NEWS 355

COSBY, ELISABETH.

002535   A SERVANT OF THE STATE. London: Cassell,
1911 BMC.

Man in diplomatic service TLS

COSENS, MONICA, jt. au. See GIRVIN, BRENDA AND MONICA
COSENS.

COSGROVE, MABEL.

002536   WHAT WAS THE VERDICT? London: Simpkin,
Marshall, Hamilton, Kent, 1892 BMC.

COSTANTINI, ANNA MILLER. B. 1880. Europe.

002537   THE GULF BETWEEN; A NOVEL. Philadelphia:
J. C. Winston, 1912 NUC.

PW-Unhappy marriage.
NYT-American girl married to Italian count-gulf is
almost too wide to be spanned by love.

002538   RAGNA, A NOVEL. New York: Sturgis &
Walton, 1910 NUC. London: Greening, 1910 BMC.

BKM-At the point of leaving her Italian husband she
decides to remain for the sake of the children.
BKM 31, 1910-young woman develops into a passionate
woman, gets pregnant, marries another man (brute) she
does not love who almost beats both her children to
death.
TLS-pure Norwegian girl, 1st seduced by a prince, then
marries a brute. What are her relations with the
count? Document of ill treatment.
Swedish girl "of orginality" lacks self control; her
story is "serious and frank and fearless." PW
NYT-She starts out in a love affair with a titled
personage of such rank that marriage seems out of the
question.

002539   YESTERDAY; A NOVEL. London: Greening,
1912 NUC BMC.

TLS-Italian & American wife-development of character
to final compromise.
ATH-inevitable reconciliation

COSTELLO, FANNY KEMBLE (JOHNSON). United States.

002540   THE BELOVED SON. BY FANNY KEMBLE JOHNSON.
Boston: Small, Maynard, [c1916] NUC.

Dave struggles against drink. PW
NYT-David, a writer, whiskey and his father.

COTES, EVERARD. See COTES, SARA JEANNETTE (DUNCAN).

COTES, MRS. EVERARD. See COTES, SARA JEANNETTE (DUNCAN).

COTES, SARA JEANNETTE (DUNCAN). 1862?-1922. Canada.

002541   AN AMERICAN GIRL IN LONDON. BY SARA
JEANNETTE DUNCAN. London: Chatto and Windus, 1891 BMC.
New York: D. Appleton, 1891 NUC.

Compares English conventionality to American freedom:
BAKER 03, 243
She's ind., smart, ignorant of conventions. Mamie Wick
of Chicago. LW
She goes alone to London. Finds relatives cold, makes
friends with an English woman of title. An Englishman

considers her his betrothed she's shocked to learn,
panics and returns to US: NATION 4-30-91, 369
Mamie travels around the world. She's American. Starts
out alone (father busy with politics; mother invalid).
On steamer escapes one woman's efforts to curb her
freedom. Her travels in England. People she meets like
the thoroughly English Miss Peter Corke,
unconventional. CR
Mamie Wick goes off to London, gives her impressions
of "the servile adherence of the women to
conventionality" among other things. Critical of
English society. PW 3-28-91.

002542   THE BURNT OFFERING. BY MRS. EVERARD COTES
(SARA JEANNETTE DUNCAN). London: Methuen, 1909 BMC.
New York: John Lane, 1910 NUC.

Joan Mills and father, socialists, go to India, incite
natives to rebel; Joan falls in love with a native but
he dies in a bombing; she returns to England. PW Ends
abruptly, we are not allowed to see Joan's feelings
when he is killed. SR
NYT--She represents modern womanhood, advanced thought
in every direction. She comes to India, ready to give
herself to its wrongs and in the end finds India does
not want her. Denouement is as unexpected as it is
dramatic. Impassable barrier.
A woman earnest in her sympathy for people in India
stirs the hearts of English official and Indian
revolutionary. TLS
Joan Mills is the burnt offering, saved from an
unwanted marriage to native agitator because he's
killed. SP

002543   A CANADIAN GIRL IN LONDON. BY MRS.
EVERARD COTES (SARA JEANNETTE DUNCAN). New York:
Macmillan, 1908 NUC.

002544   THE CONSORT. BY MRS. EVERARD COTES (SARA
JEANNETTE DUNCAN). London: S. Paul, [189-?] NUC BMC.

TLS--Mary Pargeter, head of a great banking house, is
married to a man who is the consort of title. He is
lovable weak and brilliant--unhappy marriage. She dies
from heart attack.
ATH--Psych st. of her, self-sacrificing.

002545   COUSIN CINDERELLA. BY EVERARD COTES (SARA
JEANNETTE DUNCAN). New York: Macmillan, 1908 NUC.
London: Methuen, 1908 BMC.

PW--Not much, comments on Eng.
BKM--Satire on English life.

002546   THE CROW'S NEST. BY MRS. EVERARD COTES
(SARA JEANNETTE DUNCAN). New York: Dodd, Mead, 1901
NUC.

Invalid woman, loneliness. BOOK BUYER

002547   A DAUGHTER OF TO-DAY: A NOVEL. BY MRS.
EVERARD COTES (SARA JEANNETTE DUNCAN). London: Chatto
& Windus, 1894 BMC. New York: D. Appleton, 1894 NUC.

SR 77:668. First she is an artist, then a journalist.
Marries, finally suicide. Elfrida Bell.
SP 73:120. Epitaph on her tombstone (at her request):
Pas-femme-artiste.
ACAD 46:132. She is unable to reconcile her theories
with experience, therefore suicide.
AT"H 103:705. Her creator touches her with an almost
malignant hand, illuminating her egotism, her
affectation, her heartlessnessthe ill-breeding of her
gospel of art and life, in letters of flame. She is
cleverly contrasted with another girl of greater
intellectual power, a truer artist, and also a truer
woman." Unique amongst Cotes' novels in that it is
serious.
LBKM 6:88. Satire, not successful as such. She has a
hunger and thirst for success, magnificent conceit,
admirable understanding of art, pluck, good nature,
idealism, and loyalty to art. Successive blows come,
the last an attack on her novel in manuscript by a
literary adviser to a publisher. She dies.
LW 25:179. Moral is that opposition to "customs and
institutions by the restraints of which civilization
painfully protects itself from the beast can cause
disaster." POV?

002548   HILDA: A STORY OF CALCUTTA. BY SARAH
JEANETTE DUNCAN (MRS. EVERARD COTES). New York: F. A.
Stokes, 1898 [c] NUC. (Same as the Path of a Star.)

She's an actress, a leading lady in Calcutta. Gets a
priest in her spell. When he won't break his vows for
her, she becomes a Sister on probation. Holds him in

her arms when he dies. Laura Filbert in Salvation
Army. BKM 9:282
Comedy, light satire of group of characters in
Calcutta, a beautiful young Salvationist, a brilliant
actress, a society lady all fall in love with wrong
persons. BAKER 03,243
The difficulties described throughout the book are not
resolved but evaded by an assassin's dagger and a
woman's change of mind. Calcutta. One heroine is a
Salvation Army worker; the other an actress. LIT 5:303
Heroine an actress; a genius with a future, a lonely
young woman Salvation Army Captain, a society woman, a
priest and a Calcutta business man. Actress loves
priest; Salvation Army woman loves business man. The
Salvationist finds someone she likes more; jilts the
businessman. The actress has no hope of response from
the priest, joins in order to be close to him. But the
author "has to kill the priest to save Hilda for her
art." Hilda "most modern in mind, brilliant
unconventional, an honest devotee to her profession."
LBKM 17:30
She wants money, fame, expects big things from
herself. So taken by the priest, gives up stage for a
while for nursing sisterhood. SP 83:323. Anglo-Indian
life. Captain Laura Filbert of Salvation Army.

002549   HIS HONOR AND A LADY. BY MRS. EVERARD
COTES (SARA JEANNETTE DUNCAN). London: Macmillan, 1896
BMC. New York: D. Appleton, 1896 NUC.

LBKM 10:58. Anglo-Indian story. Dull hero with a sense
of duty, church, Ancram, a complex character, rejected
by two "remarkable" women who had fallen in love with
their idea of him.
SR-dissection of Ancram, with humor.
ATH 107:742
ACAD 50:28. One of the women is married to a dull
English colonial.
LW 28:43 Bengal.

002550   HIS ROYAL HAPPINESS. BY MRS. EVERARD
COTES. New York: D. Appleton, 1914 NUC. London: Hodder
and Stoughton, 1915 BMC.

Involves Queen of England--fanciful. TLS LBKM
NYT--Eng. prince and American daughter of president,
romance.

002551   THE IMPERIALIST. BY MRS. EVERARD COTES
(SARA JEANNETTE DUNCAN). New York: D. Appleton, 1904
NUC. Westminster: A. Constable, 1904 BMC.

Domestic life in Canada. PW

002552   ON THE OTHER SIDE OF THE LATCH. BY SARA
JEANNETTE DUNCAN (MRS. EVERARD COTES). London:
Methuen, 1901 BMC NUC.

002553   THE PATH OF A STAR. London: Methuen, 1899
BMC. (See Hilda, a Story of Calcutta.)

002554   SET IN AUTHORITY. BY MRS. EVERARD COTES
(SARAH JEANNETTE DUNCAN). New York: Doubleday, Page,
1906 NUC. London: T. Nelson, [1910] BMC.

Racial antagonism. BKM 24, 1906-7.
PW--Viceroy in India.
NYT--Much atmosphere, little plot.
ACAD--Not just politics but story of men and women,
mature, philosophic.
TLS--philosophical, concerning social equality.

002555   THE SIMPLE ADVENTURES OF A MEMSAHIB. BY
SARA JEANNETTE DUNCAN. London: Chatto and Windus, 1893
BMC. New York: D. Appleton, 1893 NUC.

Young English woman marries and makes her home in
India. (Memahib means married lady). Her simple
adventures with the native ideas concerning
housekeeping, all the unusual customs. PW 6-10-93.

002556   THE STORY OF SONNY SAHIB. BY MRS. EVERARD
COTES (SARA JEANNETTE DUNCAN). London: Macmillan, 1894
BMC. New York: D. Appleton, 1895 NUC.

He is restored to his father who thought him lost.
India, late 18th. ACAD 47:10.
His ma died of exposure during Indian mutiny. Father
did not hear of his birth for several years. PW
4-27-95:681.

002557   THOSE DELIGHTFUL AMERICANS. BY MRS.
EVERARD COTES (SARA JEANNETTE DUNCAN). New York:
Appleton, 1902 NUC. London: Methuen, 1902 BMC.

002558   VERNON'S AUNT: BEING THE ORIENTAL

EXPERIENCES OF MISS LAVINIA MOFFAT. BY MRS. EVERARD
COTES (SARA JEANNETTE DUNCAN). New York: D. Appleton,
1895 NUC.

Miss Lavinia Moffat after years of quiet existence in
small rural English parish goes off to Orient to visit
a brother. She's "a spinster." Met by elephant she
must mount. All her fascinating experiences. CR
23:203.
Goes uninvited. PW 2-2-95:264
LBKM 7:91. Spinster, "equally greedy of experiences
and respectful to the proprieties," travels to India,
"some grotesque situations."

002559   A VOYAGE OF CONSOLATION (BEING IN THE
NATURE OF A SEQUEL TO THE EXPERIENCES OF "AN AMERICAN
GIRL IN LONDON"). BY SARA JEANNETTE DUNCAN (MRS.
EVERARD COTES). London: Methuen, 1898 BMC. New York:
D. Appleton, 1898 NUC.

SP 80:451. Mamie, on her return to U.S. quarrels with
her betrothed Yale professor over her Anglomania and
his accent. She sweeps her parents off to Europe and
with others they travel, a feminine Tramp Abroad.
Satire, wit. Reconciliation at end.
ACAD 53:395. 1st person narration, Mamie.

COTTERELL, CONSTANCE. United Kingdom.

002560   THE HONEST TRESPASS. London: E. Nash,
1911 BMC.

Young wife (husband in institution for mad people)
yields to her love for an earlier though unworthy
suitor. Author makes Lesbi a strongly appealing to the
reader. TLS
Full of individuality. ATH

002561   AN IMPOSSIBLE PERSON. London: T. F. Unwin
[Autonym Library], 1896 BMC NUC.

SR "Brilliant sketch of an 'intense' and gushing
school-girl, married to an elderly gourmand whom she
idealizes and adores, neglecting his dinners in her
worship of the great soul she insists on ascribing to
him.

002562   LOVE IS NOT SO LIGHT. London: T.F. Unwin,
1898 BMC.

Penelope is an inarticulate young woman. She can't put
two sentences together in speech. Becomes engaged to
wrong man. He cuts her ear to mark her as his. Then
she meets the right man. LBKM 15:120
Hero is a giant Quaker. SP 83:59.
Lady Sallien and Bridget with her innocent longing to
be wicked. ATH 113:239
LIT 3:603. "Witty at times, full of natural and
entertaining people."
ACAD 55:547. Story of Anthony, a Quaker, living with
his sister Anna and his cousin Phoebe. He is involved
with Lady Sallien, a "bad woman."

002563   THE PERPETUAL CHOICE. London: Methuen,
1915 BMC.

Orphaned girl, problems of love and poverty. Morgan Le
Fee--tries writing too. Happiness in love. TLS
3 lovers to choose from. ATH.
Ambitious girl, budding novelist sets up housekeeping
with a woman composer. ATH. A radiant future for the
heroine?

002564   TEMPE: A NOVEL. London: R. Bentley, 1893
BMC. New York: Harper, 1894 NUC.

Heroine expounds her views on love, marriage, duty of
opposing public opinion, the absurdity of religious
belief. She analyses herself and others. SP 71, 947.
SR 77:96. Tempe is innocent, does what the reviewer
finds outrageously flirtatious, but author claims is
"frank, simple, unafraid." She is a novelist. Romance.
She dislikes the embraces of an uncle, which she
describes as "too passionate" and having a "wild
tenderness". Reviewer finds this "distinctly
disagreeable."
ACAD 45:78. "Vivid and sympathetic understanding of
the partially veiled or hidden springs of action with
maiden fancy free and fancy bound."
ATH 103:241. "Elaborate study of the type recently
labelled as the 'revolting dauther.'"
LW 25:139. She is a genius, rebellious against
conventions, with an "impetuous heart loyal to noble
ideals."
PW-"her literary work."

002565   THE VIRGIN AND THE SCALES. London: Methuen, 1905 BMC.

ATH--Good development of heroine's character.

COTTRELL, MARIE, pseud. See HARLAN, MRS. M. R.

COTTRELL, MINNYE CREIGHTON. United States.

002566   NORTON HARDIN; OR, THE KNIGHT OF THE XX CENTURY. Boston: Mayhew, 1907 NUC.

COUCH, L. QUILLER. See COUCH, LILIAN M. QUILLER.

COUCH, LILIAN M. QUILLER. United Kingdom.

002567   THE MARBLE KING: A MYSTERY. Bristol: J. W. Arrowsmith, [1899] BMC.

Two boys come upon a beautiful town in the Adriatic. The town of the Marble King and never again can the heroes find it. ACAD 56:328
A gruesome tale. We're left to wonder if the horror happened or if it was a dream. ATH 113:463

002568   A SPANISH MAID. BY L. QUILLER-COUCH. London: Service and Paton, 1898 BMC. New York: Dodd, Mead, 1898 NUC.

BKM 6:564. Spanish gypsy maid saved on the Cornish coast and treated kindly by the villagers of Landecarrack.

COUCH, MABEL QUILLER.

002569   THE CARROLL GIRLS; OR HOW THE SISTERS HELPED. London: Hodder and Stoughton, [1906] BMC. New York: E.P. Dutton, 1907 NUC.

002570   TROUBLESOME URSULA. Philadelphia: J. B. Lippincott, 1907 NUC. London and Edinburgh: W. & R. Chambers, 1907 BMC.

Ursula goes to live with grandmother--many problems follow. PW 11-23-07.

COUCH, STATA B.

002571   IN THE SHADOW OF THE PEAKS. A NOVEL...THE SCENES OF WHICH ARE LAID IN THE VALLEY OF CUERNAVACA, MEXICO. London: Greening, 1909 BMC.

Story of abduction in Mexico. TLS

COURTNEY, ETTA.

002572   CHECKMATE. London: E. Arnold, 1904 BMC.

002573   RIVER MISTS. London: Marshall, Russell, [1898] BMC.

LIT 3:500. Short stories.

COURTNEY, MARY KING. Nationality Unknown.

002574   THE PICTURES OF POLLY. New York and London: Harper, 1912 BMC NUC.

PW-love story.
TLS love story

COUVREUR, JESSIE CATHERINE (HUYBERS). 1848-1897. Australia.

002575   A FIERY ORDEAL. BY TASMA. London: R. Bentley, 1897 BMC. New York: Appleton, 1898 NUC.

Ruth Fenton of Aust. orphan of Fr. pol. refugee. First is a teacher, then escapes that drudgery by early marriage to a squatter and gambler, he loses everything then starts afresh as horse-trainer, but by the time Ruth is 21, her child is dead and her husband is a bankrupt drunkard. Then they get financial help from a wealthy man who falls in love with Ruth. Ruth leaves her husband. Husband goes mad and nearly burns up the whole place. All escape but husband. SP 79:939.
NYT 1898 p 167. Australia. Ruth an orphan is married to Jem, a drunk, a gambler, and a brute. He sends his wife to Brewer, who holds their mortgage and is about to foreclose. She meets en route, Brewer's son, they are attracted to each other, he assumes mortgage. Then Jem wants to use her to inveigle money out of him. She tells young Brewer how awful husband is. Jem goes mad, sets Brewer house on fire, is killed; Ruth marries young Brewer.

002576   A KNIGHT OF THE WHITE FEATHER. BY TASMA. London: W. Heinemann, 1891 BMC. Leipzig: Heinemann and Balestier, 1893 NUC.

ATH 120:736. An Australian girl trained in Positivism by French professor, settles in Melbourne. Has 3 male admirers. Doesn't sound like a romance.
SP 69:685. Apparently she did not fully love any of them but married the one she came closest to loving although he had some weakness, which he eventually overcame in response to his wife's scorn. After his death she feels remorse that she cannot grieve for him as though she had fully loved him, but knows this is unreasonable as she has damaged her own life as well. SR. He was a coward.

002577   NOT COUNTING THE COST. BY TASMA. AUTHOR OF "UNCLE PIPER OF PIPER'S HILL" "IN HER EARLIEST YOUTH" "A KNIGHT OF THE WHITE FEATHER" ETC. London: R. Bentley, 1895 BMC NUC. New York: Appleton, 1895 NUC.

Tasmanian family move to London; they live "gaily on no income at all," "their metaphysical discussions."
SR 80:624
Eila Croft of this family unhappily married since girlhood to a man now in asylum.--"a hopeless lunatic." A man offers to help out family if Eila will live with him and she seriously considers he offer. Eila now Mrs Frost is "emancipated," not repulsed by the offer from this deformed man. SP 75:405.
The Clare family comes to London. Then Paris to search for rich cousin to help them. The rich cousin tries to exact his price. He's the one who wants Elia but she's saved. When little more than a child Elia was married, but she has forgotten the young man. ACAD 48:314. A beautyshow in Paris.

002578   THE PENANCE OF PORTIA JAMES. BY TASMA. London: W. Heinemann, 1891 BMC NUC. New York: J. W. Lovell, 1891 NUC.

Powerful novel. Heroine and strong-minded friend in Paris. ATH 98 758.
She's betrothed to a man she doesn't love, almost from childhood. Won't shake herself free of him, won't admit she loves someone else. On wedding day learns her husband unfaithful. Well-written. SP 1-21-93, 87.
Born in Australia, bush, but novel set in London. On wedding day learns husband betrayed a poor man's daughter. "Leaves the impatient bridegroom...and departs secretly on a wedding tour all her own." Her penance (it's not clear what her sin is) is to return to him after the betrayed girl dies. CR 20, 23:70
LW 23:127. Loveless wife tries to decide what her duties are: chooses "submission to social customs and laws."
SR 73:156.
CR 17:253. Portia marries an artist and leaves him at once because of gossip which she later discovers is unfounded, spends rest of her life doing penance.
PW-Portia on her wedding day learns of husband's unfaithfulness. Leaves him, supports herself as a model, does penance by caring for his child, sacrificing her own happiness.

002579   THE WHITE FEATHER. BY TASMA. New York: Lovell, Coryell, [c1892] NUC.

See a Knight of the White Feather.

COVENTRY, EVA.

002580   CATHERINE; OR AN UNFORTUNATE DECISION. London: H. J. Drane, [1910] BMC.

COVEY, ELIZABETH (ROCKFORD). B. 1873. Canada.

002581   COMRADES TWO. BY ELIZABETH FREMANTLE. London: Heinemann, 1907 BMC. Toronto: Musson Book, [n.d.] NUC.

A diary-written within the despised daily round of housekeeping has a mind above the occupations of a housewife a desire to achieve. She's a writer, a pianist. ACAD

002582   THE ONE, AND I. BY ELIZABETH FREMANTLE. Philadelphia: George W. Jacobs, [1908] NUC.

"The scenes of this love story are laid in the wilds of the great Canadian northwest. The story is told in the form of a diary." BKM 28 1908-9
NYT-
Diary form, she is English in Canadian Northwest. She yearns for occupations other than the lot of housekeeping which falls to the women in this country,

but her closing entry states that the diary shall be kept as a "monument of folly whereon is written a Tale of Vanity," that the prairies of Canada are "the sweetest spot on earth," and "the making of books, poems, pictures... may possibly delight and suffice some people; but they are not to be mentioned in the same breath with such things as housecleaning, bread-making..." (Book)

COWEN, HELENE E. A. (GINGOLD).

002583   THE CHILLINGFIELD CHRONICLES. BY HELENE GINGOLD. London: T. F. Unwin, [1899] BMC.

ATH 115:9. Mid century record of English country family. Two sisters.

COWPER, EDITH ELISE.

002584   ENTER PATRICIA; BEING AN ACCOUNT OF HER STRANGE ADVENTURES ON A VISIT TO THE CORNISH COAST. London: Cassell, [1913] BMC. New York: Funk & Wagnall, PW.

"Patricia Foster goes down to Cornwall to stay with the Belleroche family. Some of the young people decide she will be a dreadful bore and make her anything but welcome, but when they have an adventure with a convict who hides in their house, they see a side of Patricia's character of which they never dreamed and they change their opinion of her." PW

002585   THE INVADERS OF FAIRFORD. London: S.P.C.K., [1907] NUC.

Hist. Charles I 1625-49

COX, ANNE.

002586   A CHILD OF ART. BY ANNABEL GRAY. London: Simpkin, Marshall, 1901 BMC.

002587   COMRADES. BY ANNABEL GRAY. London: Drane, [1896] BMC.

ACAD 49:195. Crowded with characters, a murderer, Eldred Aulstyne M. P., Jowskys, Blavintskys, gin-drinking Socialist family. Slums, below stairs and vulgar society.

002588   FORBIDDEN BANNS. BY ANNABEL GRAY. London: F. V. White, 1899 BMC.

The agonies and agitations of a mother-an innocent bigamist who dies on learning her error—and her daughter who seeks solace in a convent. ATH 113:686 Bigamy, murder, the art passion, avarice, and priestism. SR 87:761

002589   JEROME: A NOVEL. BY ANNABEL GRAY. London: S. Sonnenschein, 1891 BMC NUC.

Young male artist loves Parisian opera star twice his age who once was his father's mistress. "Processes of analysis and dissection carried to such an alarming extent." ACAD
SP 67:78 Also ATH 47:677
Focus on Jerome who moves from one passion to another with great speed. The prima donna is Iris- she has a hy compounded of the adventures of three of the leading actresses and singers of our time. SR 5-30-91, 657

002590   THE MYSTIC NUMBER SEVEN. BY ANNABEL GRAY. London: Simpkin, Marshall, [1900] BMC.

ACAD 59:74. Melodrama. Glen, wealthy actress, independent, shuddered as she thought of ordinary life.

002591   THROUGH RIFTED CLOUDS: A NOVEL. BY ANNABEL GRAY. London: Eden, Remington, 1891 BMC NUC.

ATH 99:113. Heroine in love with worthless man.
ACAD 41:84. She is seduced and abandoned; in mid-suicide she is saved by former admirer. On her supposed death bed she is visited by the scoundrel responsible, tortured with remorse.
SR 73:128. She marries admirer, they have psychic powers.

COX, CHARLOTTE CRISMAN. United States.

002592   IONE: A SEQUEL TO "VASHTI". Boston: Eastern, 1900 NUC.

Argument for the setting aside of the word obedient in marriage service. PW

COX, EMILY. United States.

002593   COURTSHIP AND CHEMICALS. London: Ward, Lock, [1898] BMC.

ACAD 54:325. Love story laid in Newnham College and its chemical laboratory. Heroines are Lois, reserved and studious, and Francesca, merry and bold.
LBKM 15:57. Pleasant, light.

COX, MARIAN (METCALF). B. 1882. United States.

002594   THE CROWDS AND THE VEILED WOMAN. New York and London: Funk & Wagnalls, 1910 BMC NUC.

Really a treatise, ostensibly a novel, on psych of love and speculation of future of humanity. Pessimistic. PW

COXE, VIRGINIA ROSALIE. United States.

002595   THE EMBASSY BALL. New York: F. T. Neely, [c1897] NUC.

PW NY smart set. Hero is back in New York after a European tour. Two kinds of women are portrayed, the young but blase married woman and the ingenue.

COXON, ETHEL. United Kingdom.

002596   WITHIN BOUNDS. London: A. Constable, 1898 BMC.

LIT 3:606. Olive a lively girl in a quiet place marries a placid, dull man.
ATH 112:485. "She settles to what she recognizes as uncongenial with such apathy as to exclude our sympathies."

COXON, MRS. SIDNEY. See COXON, MURIEL (HINE).

COXON, MURIEL (HINE). United Kingdom.

002597   APRIL PANHASARD. BY MURIEL HINE (MRS. SIDNEY COXON). London: J. Lane, 1913 BMC. New York: J. Lane, 1913 NUC.

Heroine divorces her faithless husband, hides her identity...seeks a quiet village in which to live out her life...meets an American gentleman; her divorced husband shows up again. NYT
Injustice to women of English divorce laws. NYT 1913:413 361.
"Lady Essendine is reluctantly compelled to divorce her unfaithful, dissipated husband. To escape the scandal she goes to a quiet village under the name of April Panhasard. Here she meets an American and his sister, and is greatly drawn to him. Her husband turns up before the six months necessary to make the divorce absolute has elapsed, and places her in a compromising situation. She is freed through a strange accident and at last marries her American." PW

002598   AUTUMN. BY MURIEL HINE (MRS. SIDNEY COXON). New York: J. Lane, 1917 NUC. London: J. Lane, 1917 BMC NUC.

Diedre Carodoc married. Husband's bad temper drives her to her country cottage. Love comes to her in the autumn of her life but it's shortlived. PW
Her autumn friendship with a country squire. Neglected by gad about husband; has no child; she's conventional; meekly accepts her misery; inherits house of her own and income. She then leaves husband and thinks now of herself as a rebel. Meets Rollo, a sort of waster, a man with nice ideas about women. They fall in love, just as Rollo's daughter falls in love with married man. All believe in sanctity of love, have no rel. scruples. Cop out end--Rollo dies-drowns. Hyacinth promises to be good. TLS
Nearly 40--very attractive character. SP
2 unsatisfactory marriages. NYT

002599   THE BEST IN LIFE. BY MURIEL HINE (MRS. SIDNEY COXON). London: J. Lane, 1918 BMC NUC. New York: J. Lane, 1918 NUC.

PW--Love story of dressmaker's model who inherits money.
TLS--Adventuress?
ATH--Independent but not faultless girl who has experiences in London and abroad.
LBKM-- travels to Venice, embroiders her circumstances

to V. C. and mannish Jane who like her anyway. Title probably refers to love.
SP a fairly innocent adventuress.
NYT--Traditional happy ending.

002600   THE BREATHLESS MOMENT. BY MURIEL HINE. London: J. Lane, 1920 BMC NUC. New York: J. Lane, 1920 NUC.

TLS--Sabine works as housekeeper for fanatic pacifist woman who prevented her nephew from going to war until she died. Sabine seduces him before he leaves. POV?
ATH--Title refers to war wedding in which ceremony is omitted. Nephew is already married and although superfluous lady finally removes herself, complications have arisen which cannot wholly be smoothed away.
LBKM--Moment lasts a month. She's pregnant. Says Pa is Australian soldier who dies. Mark comes home from war with no memory for past 2 years. Happiness at last obtains.
NYT 8-1-20,p.26. Author's point of view is tolerant and broad-minded, without being lax.

002601   EARTH. BY MURIEL HINE (MRS. SIDNEY COXON). New York: J. Lane, 1912 BMC NUC. London: J. Lane, 1912 NUC.

"Breaks loose of conventions, carves out a career. A man teaches her the need of a healthy body too." PW 12-2-11
Love, disillusionment, distrust and love again. TLS
"Displays a curious mingling of shrewd insight into male character and lack of comprehension of the possible effects of modern movements on many of the other sex." ATH.
ACAD--Diana wants to keep sex out of her life but the painter Ericson apparently persuades her there is nothing on earth to equal passion and she marries the major.
LBKM--Live, lively Diana, half a boy, noble and sane. Falls in love with the major, the old philanderer. Why is not clear. Ericson buoyant, big hearted, was more likeable.

002602   HALF IN EARNEST. BY MURIEL HINE. London: J. Lane, 1910 BMC. New York: J. Lane, 1910 NUC.

Unsavory set of fashionable people neglected wife led astray by naughty lover--half in earnest--and redeemed by another who is the soul of altruism. ATH
A wife's intrigue with her politician husband's secretary. This secretary also gets a girl into trouble. Outcome is a surprise? PW
TLS--He makes love to 2 women. Candida wants to be true to herself. Dislikes husband, eventually throws over Derrick. Then what?SR--Derrick gets a woman in trouble and does not see her through. He has an intense desire for personal freedom. Candida does not blame him.

002603   THE HIDDEN VALLEY. BY MURIEL HINE. London: J. Lane, 1919 NUC BMC. New York: J. Lane, 1919 NUC BMC.

Sheila's 3 loves--seeks a certain kind of man unconventional artist is the one whom she loves. TLS
Sheila Travers--her fortunes modern in her views, advocate of votes for women. Sp
She works for suffrage. 4 lovers and a husband who was no lover. LBKM
Disillusioned with 1st suitor, breaks off marriage. 2nd man she marries, he dies in war. 3rd--the right one, a painter. LBKM
At 19 sheltered, rich, ignorant of the world. She's athletic, swims, rows, rides, longs to be a man, attractive heroine. NYT

002604   THE INDIVIDUAL. BY MURIEL HINE (MRS. SIDNEY COXON). London: J. Lane, 1916 BMC NUC. New York: J. Lane, 1916 BMC NUC.

Surgeon devoted to Eugenics, marries a woman after careful study of family yet discovers later there's insanity in the family. He refuses to have children. Wife rebels--won't be a wife if she can't be a ma. Has child, sneaks it away (husband was away, didn't know) all ends happily. Threat to their child removed. TLS
Orde Tavernet, a brilliant surgeon, must choose between his own ideas and his wife's happiness. Solution of their conflict comes from unexpected death-bed confession. PW 89:2-26-16:689.
NYT--Eugenics--heredity.
SP--Elizma is a fine violinist and a poet. Book is concerned with their marriage. He is, in opinion of reviewer, dogmatic, and lacking in consideration for

his wife. Problem of hereditary insanity.

002605   THE MAN WITH THE DOUBLE HEART. BY MURIEL HINE (MRS. SIDNEY COXON). London: J. Lane, 1914 NUC BMC. New York: J. Lane, 1914 NUC.

NYT--Peter believes he has 2 hearts, tries to love 2 women unsuccessfully, inherits. Finds his only heart beats for 1 woman.
ATH--"The space devoted to castigating the militant suffrage movement seems now but a mistaken effort to galvanize back to life a dead controversy."
"McTaggart consults a doctor who credits him with a double heart. This quality of existence pursues him morally as well as physically. He is concerned with a Parisian adventuress and Cydonia the beautiful daughter of a nouveau riche. These episodes come to a logical end. He marries a charming English girl, and surprises her with an Italian estate and a title, which he has inherited from his mother's family." PW
Jill's mother, a widow, neglects her home and children in her devotion to the cause of suffrage; she goes to prison and refuses to eat. The author is critical of the divisiveness of the movement and of the mother's inability to respect the rights of her daughter. The author approves of Jill's college education, intelligent questioning attitude, and independence. (Book)

CRADDOCK, CHARLES EGBERT, pseud. See MURFREE, MARY NOAILLES.

CRADDOCK, FLORENCE NIGHTINGALE. Nationality Unknown.

002606   EDGAR FAIRFAX: A STORY OF WEST POINT. New York: G.W. Dillingham, 1896 NUC.

PW 8-22-96. Hero marries the wrong woman, a German actress, gets a divorce. Meets the right woman who thinks divorce is wrong. The first marriage was secret so he keeps the divorce secret and marries. A jealous woman reveals the story and trouble follows.

CRAIG, COLA AMANDA BARR. B. 1861. United States.

002607   WAS SHE? A NOVEL. BY MRS. BENJAMIN H. CRAIG. New York: Neale, 1906 NUC.

CRAIG, KATHERINE LEE. B. 1862. United States.

002608   JUDGE GREYBURN AND KATHLENE LEE. New York and London: Abbey Press, [1902] NUC.

CRAIG, MRS. BENJAMIN H. See CRAIG, COLA AMANDA BARR.

CRAIGIE, PEARL MARY TERESA (RICHARDS). 1867-1906. United Kingdom.

002609   THE AMBASSADOR: A COMEDY IN FOUR ACTS. BY JOHN OLIVER HOBBES. London: T. F. Unwin, 1898 BMC NUC. New York: F. A. Stokes, [1898] NUC.

CR 33:518. This is a drama.

002610   THE ARTIST'S LIFE. BY JOHN OLIVER HOBBES . London: T.W. Laurie, 1904 BMC NUC. New York: M. Kennerley, 1907 NUC.

002611   A BUNDLE OF LIFE. BY JOHN OLIVER HOBBES. London: T. F. Unwin, 1893 BMC NUC. New York: J. S. Tait, 1894 NUC.

002612   DOWRIES. BY JOHN OLIVER HOBBES . London: Daily Mail, [1904] BMC.

002613   THE DREAM AND THE BUSINESS. BY JOHN OLIVER HOBBES. London: T.F. Unwin, 1906 BMC NUC. New York: D. Appleton, 1906 NUC.

Mismatched lovers--Tessa Marlesford. Sophy Fermalden--writes books, intelligent, writes art criticism, studies Greek from 6-8 in morning, reads French, German, Italian literature, plays piano. Poised in London's highest society. Survives everything, practical. The ordeal of life. Tessa dies young, crushed by burden of life.
PW-?
ACAD-unhappy marriage. Reviewer feels women are too fully realized intellectually.
TLS-good portrayal of three women.
BKM-final message is religious. Anti divorce.
BAKER 32-119

002614   THE FLUTE OF PAN. A ROMANCE. BY JOHN OLIVER HOBBES. New York: D. Appleton, 1905 NUC. London: T.F. Unwin, 1905 BMC NUC.

A submissive princess makes her man govern her
kingdom. PW 10-28-05
Light, witty. NYT 469,05
ACAD 615,05
All about a misunderstanding. LBKM 172,27-8
"The plot hinges on a slight misunderstanding between
a young English earl who has gone to Venice to paint
and lead the simple life, and the Princess of Siguria
who comes to ask him to be her prince consort; other
aristocratic characters enter into and complicate the
story." BRD 1905-06.

002615   THE GODS, SOME MORTALS AND LORD
WICKENHAM. BY JOHN OLIVER HOBBES. New York: D.
Appleton, 1895 NUC. London: Henry, 1895 BMC NUC.

Women speaking back, anger. School of scold,
references to Heavenly Twins, "the unwomanliness" of
the author, etc. CR 24:55
Study of a man strong in intellect, weak in emotions.
And a "corrupt hysterical wanton young woman, Anne.
Absolutely no moral sense." ACAD 48:67
The degradation of Anne is the central note. Simon
Warre proposes to her after seeing her three times:
"the excessive filthiness of her mind is not rendered
credible enough to make its loathsomeness tolerable.
Good characterization of a weak sensualist of crude
vulgarity." ATH 105:638
Anne Passer Deleware destroys life of young doctor.
She demands he marry her: he does though he loves a
"sweet thing." On wedding he learns she had affair. He
doesn't consumate marriage. She leaves him. He goes
off to tropics and works self to death.
"A good man's marriage to a woman with a past. Lord
Wichenham, confident of the husband and commentator on
the events, expounds the moral that a man should marry
the goddess that he loves, and not from weakness stoop
to earth. Severe on the shams of high life." BAKER
03,96

002616   THE HERB-MOON: A FANTASIA. BY JOHN OLIVER
HOBBES. London: T. F. Unwin, 1896 BMC NUC. New York
and London: F. A. Stokes, [1896] NUC.

LBKM 11:95. Old-fashioned love story of woman whose
husband is insane but eventually dies, leaving her
free, etc.
ATH 108:752. Rose.
Fantasy: Herb moon means long courtship for a farmer's
wife in the novel. Long sad courtship of young woman
whose huband is in asylum for insane by a young clerk
in the mill office. CR 26, 30:426
NYT Oct 24, 1896 p4. London during time of Sepoy
Rebellion. Romance between man and woman with insane
husband.
Faded heroine married to insane man who dies in end;
she remarries.

002617   LOVE AND THE SOUL HUNTERS. BY JOHN OLIVER
HOBBES. New York: Funk & Wagnalls, 1902 NUC. London:
T.F. Unwin, 1902 BMC NUC.

Wife deserts husband and becomes successful actress,
rears idealistic daughters. ARENA 1902
ATH 10-11-02. Not helpful.
DIAL 11-16-02. Seems to describe a different book.
BAKER-Morganatic marriage. 13-111

002618   ROBERT ORANGE. BEING A CONTINUATION OF
THE HISTORY OF ROBERT ORANGE, M.P., AND A SEQUEL TO
"THE SCHOOL FOR SAINTS". BY JOHN OLIVER HOBBES.
London: T. F. Unwin, 1900 BMC NUC. New York: F. A.
Stokes, [c1900] NUC.

BKM 12:28.
SP 85:53. Tragic consequences of his marriage to Mrs.
Parflete. Immediately after marriage, news that Mr.
Parflete is alive. Robert becomes a priest; she an
actress. Then Parflete dies. She does not tell Robert
as she refuses to blunt his resolve. She stays in her
profession.

002619   THE SCHOOL FOR SAINTS. BY JOHN OLIVER
HOBBES. New York: Century, 1896 BMC. London: T. F.
Unwin, 1897 BMC NUC.

Yr. 1869 time of Disraeli and the Irish Church Bill.
Heroine is a Cath. living apart from husband. Divorce
and marr. fearlessly discussed. PW 52:1096.
A panoramic history, hero is complex mixes with most
brilliant soc. Enters political life under Disraeli's
care. His conversion to Catholicism, the Carlist
Rebellion. SP 79:938
Robert Orange is hero. ATH 110:817.
He falls in love with Henrietta Duboc, Parisian music

hall singer, mistress later morganatic wife of
Archduke of Alberia; their child is next love interest
of Orange. LIT 1:242
NYT 1898 p 41. Political life in 1860's. Hero becomes
member of parliament.
Bridgit is an actress. High minded heroine goes to
Spain to join cause of Carlists, active in cause, but
story centers on Robert and his career. Bridget
marries twice, claims throne of Alberia, causes two
duels, international scandal. At end rejects Robert
for stage. They do marry (Robert and Bridget) but he
learns of a first husband. Their marriage not
consumated, they part.
Intellectual characters, lofty in ideals, thoroughly
modern. Focuses on Robert Orange. BAKER 03 97.

002620   THE SERIOUS WOOING: A HEART'S HISTORY. BY
JOHN OLIVER HOBBES. London: Methuen, 1901 BMC NUC. New
York: F.A. Stokes, [1901] NUC.

Married at early age; separated from insane husband.
Falls in love with a man of advanced democratic views
who urges her to live openly with him. She does so not
knowing that her husband had died (relatives kept the
information from her for fear she'd go off with that
man.) Her lover a Socialist goes off on a mission.
Relatives intercept their letters. She thinks he's
forgotten her. Marries. When her lover returns, she
leaves this husband. Bold, utter defiance of
conventions. NYT 01
Violent love.

002621   THE SINNER'S COMEDY. BY JOHN OLIVER
HOBBES. London: T. F. Unwin, 1892 BMC NUC. New York:
Cassell, [c1892] NUC.

CR 7-16-92. Dying nobleman and death requests to his
three children: eldest son to be loyal to feudalism,
2nd son to stop smoking, daughter to consider love
vanity.
PW-Heroine is a Bohemian and an artist married to
dissolute husband is attracted to English peer. Rude
awakening.
Woman married to worthless husband can't divorce (is
R. C.) is jilted by one lover (who marries for money)
She falls for a clergyman, but dies. the clergyman
loves the man who jilted the woman. Love treated with
chilly detachment. Selfish shallow chars survive;
sensitive ones destroyed.

002622   SOME EMOTIONS AND A MORAL. BY JOHN OLIVER
HOBBES. London: T. F. Unwin, 1891 BMC NUC. New York:
Cassell, [c1891] NUC.

Several finely drawn characters. An unhappy couple-man
who is unfaithful realizes his wife is too- when she
hears of his best friend's (her lover's) suicide.
Cynthia Heathcote's love goes poorly. Theme: condemns
unsuitable marriages. ACAD
SR 73:246. Cynthia wants success and notoriety in
marriage ; succeeds only in being unhappy with wealth
and mediocrity.

002623   SOME GOOD INTENTIONS AND A BLUNDER. BY
JOHN OLIVER HOBBES. New York: Merriam, [c1895] NUC.

Lady Boyd Hopjay--matchmaker--tries to bring heiress
and a decadent (the Egg) together. PW 5-11-95:745

002624   A STUDY IN TEMPTATIONS. BY JOHN OLIVER
HOBBES. London: T. F. Unwin, 1893 BMC NUC. New York:
Cassell, [c1893] NUC.

SR 77:70. Comedy
ACAD-Woman of 30 and her love affair.
ATH-"not one man in the book is anything but a poor
creature."
LBKM-Satire of Lady Mallinger
LW 25:57 Verbal pyrotechnics.
PW-Unromantic love story. Teresa, a plain heiress, and
Lady Mallinger are rivals for Sidney Wicke.
Sophia Jeyn's mother died at her birth; father killed
himself. She's raised by his artist friend. Becomes an
actress. "Impulsive, wayward." Marries the artist but
marriage kept secret for the sake of her career. PW
4-15-93.
CR 21:181. Intellectual fads.

002625   THE VINEYARD. BY JOHN OLIVER HOBBES.
London: T.F. Unwin, 1903 BMC NUC. New York: D.
Appleton, 1904 NUC.

NYT-very careful study of emotions.
BKM-egoist with artistic temperament marries and then
regrets, is unfaithful to wife, then what?
ATH-Jennie is a modern woman.

TLS-Author's pov is cold, scientific analysis; she
shows contempt for all the characters.
Jennie Sussex, refined, intelligent bookish learns
painfully to subdue her ego in a good but unromantic
marriage. Rachel Tredegar all ego, half mad, sexually
frustrated, bored. picture of middle class mediocrity.
See BAKER 13,111. Modern affectation of culture.

CRAIK, GEORGIANA M. See MAY, GEORGIANA MARION (CRAIK).

CRAM, MILDRED. B. 1889. United States.

002626   LOTUS SALAD. New York: Dodd, Mead, 1920
NUC.

PW-story of a young American's adventure in Magella.
NYT-7/25/20 p. 28. Male hero and his enjoyable
adventures.

CRAMPTON, GERTRUDE M. (HAYWARD).

002627   NO PLACE OF REPENTANCE. BY GERTRUDE M.
HAYWARD. London: Hurst and Blackwood, 1892 BMC.

SP-Story of Margery, her experiences at a pensionnat,
her experiences friendless and penniless in London.
Richard a Court befriends her there in a way that
seriously compromises her, an offense which apparently
the writer and the heroine consider unpardonable.
ATH 99:820. Ultra traditional romance.

002628   THE OTHER ONE. BY GERTRUDE M. HAYWARD.
London: C. A. Pearson, 1901 BMC.

CRANE, LILLIE.

002629   THE DIAMOND BANGLE. London: Digby, Long,
[1897] BMC.

002630   MY LADY DIMPLE. London and Sydney:
Remington, 1894 BMC.

ACAD 46:189. Story of Nanette, a young French woman
brought up in convent on Riviera and then is set free
in England. She enslaves two men.
LBKM 6:184. A "winning little sinner;" reviewer wishes
however she had died in the accident, for while she at
last chooses the steady lover, "while she lives there
will be danger to her husband's household peace." The
secret of Nanette's parentage makes a disagreeable
plot.

CRANFORD, HOPE.

002631   IDA LLYMOND AND HER HOUR OF VISION.
London: Skeffington, 1905 BMC.

CRANSTON, RUTH. United States.

002632   ASHES OF INCENSE, A NOVEL. BY THE AUTHOR
OF "MASTERING FLAME" [ANONYMOUS]. London: Mills and
Boon, 1912 BMC. New York: M. Kennerley, 1912 NUC.

A woman without a conscience turns the people about
her into puppets unwittingly subservient to her will.
NYT 1913:66.
ATH--her wifely existence is made tolerable by her
spirit of mischief which feeds on itself until she has
ended her mad career by compassing her own murder.
Awakens to fact her life has been one long outrage?

002633   THE BEST PEOPLE. BY ANNE WARWICK. New
York: J. Lane, [c1918] NUC.

PW--Widow, travel and love.
NYT--She travelled when her husband died because she
was bored with small midwestern town. There is a man
back home who loves her. Light reading.
Japanese travel. Nancy, young widow, looking for
independent meaningful life. Relationship with older
worldly sensible woman. Contemplates marriage of
convenience for sake of life with artists, etc,
freedom, but decides freedom would not be possible in
this marriage. Tries & fails in an acting career.
Realizes value of works of service & old male friend
who is labor reformer and whom she marries at close of
book. Believes this marriage will provide greatest
opportunity to develop freely as herself.

002634   THE CHALK LINE. BY ANNE WARWICK. New
York: J. Lane, 1915 NUC.

Woman, lover, husband, former lover all quarantined
together: woman sees them all in various lights, can't
decide what she really wants. PW
Hilary Comer, concert singer, leaves staid husband for

the passion of her life. Goes to his bungalow, but
their lips hardly meet before old friend who used to
preach mutual freedom of sexes now tries to get Hilary
to go home. Husband then comes and quarantine set.
Hilary, husband, former lover new lover in a few
rooms. BKM

002635   COMPENSATION. BY ANNE WARWICK. New York:
John Lane, 1911 BMC NUC.

A triangle worked out in a very unusual way. PW
After the wife's death, the husband realizes his love
for her and her influence on him. NYT

002636   MASTERING FLAME [ANONYMOUS]. London:
Mills and Boon, [c1911] BMC.

002637   THE UNKNOWN WOMAN. BY ANNE WARWICK. New
York: J. Lane, 1912 BMC NUC.

TLS--beautiful passionless egoist Sandra.
PW--Artist.
BKM--author has been playing ducks and drakes with
ethics and morality. Sandra has killed her love for
every member, has loved no one for 10 years. Awakens
to new suffering when family comes to NY. Also, Kent
tells Maury he slept with Sandra before their
marriage; when Kent wishes to marry their daughter
Muffet, Maury forces Sandra to tell her. Topsy turvy
moral reactions.
NYT--Sandra is still unfailingly alluring at
thirty-nine!

002638   VICTORY LAW. BY ANNE WARWICK. New York:
J. Lane, 1914 BMC NUC. Toronto: Bell and Cockburn,
1914 BMC.

BKM--"need not detain us long. It is simply one more
variant upon a theme which has become a sort of
obsession with all the women writers of today who
happen to be interested in the feministic movement. It
once again raises the familiar battlecry of woman's
inalienable rights to self-expression; if a husband
interferes with a career, let her cut out the husband.
She marries son of old family who believes theatre is
corrupt. He in turn believes she is as bad as the
worst of her associates and takes her away from it.
She endures for a couple of years, rebels and returns
to acting."
BKM--actress marries, leaves husband, returns to
stage.
PW--"Victory Law is a beautiful actress, whose passion
for the stage is quite as human as her love for the
aggressive young lawyer whom she finally decides to
marry. The story is concerned not only with the
inevitable after-marriage adjustment of the man and
the woman and the actress. A picturesque figure in the
shape of a former leading man, complicates matters by
his secret and remarkable influence over Victory as an
artist; but in the end he is brought to use this
influence to aid in a most happy denouement."

CRAVEN, HELEN EMILY.

002639   KATHARINE CROMER. London: A.D. Innes,
1897 BMC.

Lady Craven pursued by English Lord and Italian opera
singer. ACAD 52 Fic Sup 92.
Extremely up to date. Lady Craven and the smart set.
She's noisy, slangy, self willed and self-advertising.
The friend who tells the story is a little less
forward, but there is no rest in Kitty. She likes a
singer and brainless Lord Tabby. Marries singer
against parents' objections. ATH 110:668
SP 81:448. Smart people. Narrated by woman friend,
tells story of Katharine's marriage to opera singer.
LIT 2:452. She is not in love but in sympathy with
him. Marries against father. Ends not happily ever
after but with conclusion that the marriage is an
experiment.

002640   THE OUTCAST EMPEROR. London: Hutchinson,
1900 BMC.

ATH 116:819. Adventure involving emperor of Cathay.
Slight love interest. Author "attempts to write like a
man."
ACAD 59:518. Narrated by wealthy man with too much
time and money, who has taken some friends on a yacht
to the far East.

CRAVEN, PRISCILLA, pseud. See SHORE, FLORENCE TEIGNMOUTH.

CRAWFORD, A. MARIA. See CRAWFORD, ANNIE MARIA.

128

CRAWFORD, AMY JOSEPHINE (BAKER). B. 1895. United Kingdom.

002641   DEAR YESTERDAY. London: J. Long, 1917
BMC.

S. African veld, soc. life before war; Boer and Briton
join peaceably to defeat the Huns. TLS
War story nothing unusual. ATH

002642   I TOO HAVE KNOWN. London: J. Long, 1911
BMC.

n Two teachers in up-country in So. Africa. TLS

002643   THE IMPENITENT PRAYER. London: J. Long,
1913 BMC.

Eliz. Baring falls in love through seeing a portrait.
When they meet, it's love at first sight. But she
won't marry right away. Is unsophisticated, from a
convent school. She 25, he's nearly 50, wealthy,
worldly. Another impediment is Eva Sheldon who has
been living in the man's house for 12 years. Marriage
postponed till the 2 get ill. All works out when Eva
falls for a much younger man. ACAD
She's engaged in scientific work. Good S. African
bkgd. ATH

002644   THE KING'S PASSION. London: J. Long, 1920
BMC.

TLS -- Traditional historical romance.

002645   MOONFLOWER. London: J. Long, 1916 BMC.

TLS--Her courageous fight with circumstances in the
veld and in Johannesburg.
LBKM--She spends some time working for a beauty
doctor.

002646   THE SNAKE GARDEN; A TALE OF SOUTH AFRICA.
London: J. Long, 1915 BMC.

Theo Hambridge, independent young woman runs her own
estate and has had a very unconventional love
experience. TLS

002647   TYRIAN PURPLE; A ROMANCE OF THE ANCIENT
WORLD. BY AMY J. BAKER (MRS. MAYNARD CRAWFORD).
London: J. Long, 1918 NUC BMC.

Based upon Biblical characters. TLS

CRAWFORD, ANNIE MARIA. B. 1884.

002648   ROSES AND RUE. BY A. MARIA CRAWFORD.
Boston: R. G. Badger, 1910 NUC.

CRAWFORD, MARY S.

002649   HAZEL GRAFTON. London: J. Long, 1911 BMC.

"Crudely written tale of little interest." TLS

CRAWFORD, MINNIE LEOLA.

002650   SEVEN WEEKS IN HAWAII. BY AN AMERICAN
GIRL <M.L.C.>. Chicago, 1913 NUC.

Vivacious letters, exceedingly graphic show her
enjoyment of and appreciation of the Island. NYT

CRAWFORD, MRS. E.

002651   JO OF AUCHENDORASS: A NOVEL. London:
Hutchinson, 1896 BMC NUC.

SR Three lovable heroines, sisters, of the "Beatrice
Whitby" type. Wholesome.
ATH Romance, Scottish manse.
ACAD 50:280. Jo, a Scotch girl, goes to London,
captures many hearts. Meets a Socialist, their
romance.

002652   THE PROBLEM OF JANUS. London: A.
Treherne, 1902 BMC.

LBKM 5-02. History of unusual humanity.
ATH 4-26-02. Story of a freak.

002653   SORRELTOP. London: H. J.Drane, [1905]
BMC.

CRAWFORD, MRS. MAYNARD. See CRAWFORD, AMY JOSEPHINE
(BAKER).

CREED, MRS. J. PERCY. See LEYLAND, MARIE LOUISE (MACK)
CREED.

CREED, SIBYL. United Kingdom.

002654   THE FIGHT: A NOVEL. Edinburgh and London:
W. Blackwood, 1904 BMC.

ATH -tale of a girl's rise after fighting against
squalid circumstances and sordid men to a position of
ease and happiness.
TLS-a novel of serious workmanship.

002655   THE VICAR OF ST. LUKE'S. New York:
Longmans, Green, 1901 NUC. London: Longmans, Green,
1901 BMC.

PW 6-15-01
ATH 6-29-01. Male religious hero.

CREEVEY, CAROLINE ALATHEA (STICKNEY). 1843-1920.

002656   AT RANDOM. New York and London: G. P.
Putnam's Sons, 1920 NUC.

002657   A DAUGHTER OF THE PURITANS, AN
AUTOBIOGRAPHY. New York and London: G. P. Putnam's
Sons, 1916 NUC.

Ordinary life of New England woman in mid 19th. PW

CRESSWELL, CLARICE M. United Kingdom.

002658   THE MAKING AND BREAKING OF ALMANSUR.
London: Chatto and Windus, 1915 BMC NUC. New York:
Dodd, Mead, 1915 NUC.

Traditional historical romance. TLS
NYT-historical, male heroes.

002659   PILATE GAVE SENTENCE. London: Methuen,
[1919] NUC BMC.

TLS-heroine is Pilate's wife. She becomes convinced of
truth and would be a disciple of Christ but sight of
her husband, haunted by guilt and dread, reminds her
of abandoned Jesus and she remains with him, he
clinging to her strength as his last support.

CREVELING, CLARA BRADWAY.

002660   INTERLUDES. Philadelphia: J. C. Winston,
1913 NUC.

CREWDSON, LULA (COX). B. 1869. Nationality Unknown.

002661   AN AMERICAN BABY ABROAD, HOW HE PLAYED
CUPID TO A KENTUCKY BEAUTY. BY MRS. CHARLES N.
CREWDSON. Boston: Little, Brown, 1910 NUC.

Two women travel and study in Europe. One marries has
a child. Her husband goes off to Egypt; she leaves
child with her friend to join him. This friend "meets
Cupid at close range"? PW
BKM-Friend and colored nurse travel with baby in a
leisurely way to Egypt.

CREWDSON, MRS. CHARLES N. See CREWDSON, LULA (COX).

CRICHTON, FRANCES ELIZABETH (SINCLAIR). 1877-1918. United
States.

002662   THE BLIND SIDE OF THE HEART. London and
Dublin.: Maunsel, 1915 BMC.

ATH-male hero visits Ireland. Returns home to marry
English girl.

002663   THE SOUNDLESS TIDE. London: E. Arnold,
1911 BMC NUC.

Irish married woman awakens to love of man young
enough to be her son--who loves her niece. Had made a
loveless marriage. PW 9-16-11
Gillian Ward bright wayward mind unusual with
difficult subtleties. She comes face to face with
herself. Touching study of an anguished soul. TLS
The man lives in the same house. Her husband dies, she
learns the young man is about to leave, confesses her
love. A humiliating rejection follows. What happens?
Mrs. Ward, fastidious, witty, unhappy. SP

002664   TINKER'S HOLLOW. London: E. Arnold, 1912
BMC NUC.

TLS-love story.

CRICHTON, MADELINE.

002665   LIKE A SISTER. London: Digby, Long,
[1893] BMC.

    Kathleen Tredennick and her sister's romances. Begins
    with Kathleen jumping into the harbour at Hong Kong to
    save her sister and finding when she surfaces that her
    sister and the boat are gone. SR 76:103.
    Sister Amy-she's heedless, passionate for pleasure,
    lured into a marriage with a bad theatre man, suffers
    till he dies. Kathleen drifts into a misunderstanding
    with her lover, suffers too. She's reserved,
    high-principled. ACAD 44:317.

CRIM, MARTHA JANE. United States.

002666   ADVENTURES OF A FAIR REBEL. BY MATT CRIM.
New York: C. L. Webster, 1891 NUC. London: Chatto &
Windus, 1892 NUC BMC.

    Rachel is from Georgia. Time is Civil War. She's a
    staunch rebel who aids the confederate army, travels
    through the south for their cause, has many
    experiences. Falls for Union Soldier. PW 11-14-91.
    CR 17:69. Romance between young Southern woman and
    Union soldier during Civil War. She is with an amateur
    theatrical troupe. ATH 99:306

002667   ELIZABETH, CHRISTIAN SCIENTIST. BY MATT
CRIM. New York: C. L. Webster, 1893 NUC.

    She cures a bad case of sprained ankle, lameness,
    drunkenness and various other ills. LW 93, 194.
    There's a love story too. NATION 56, 408
    She's a school teacher with strong inspiration to help
    people. PW 4-15-93.
    She falls ill, but eventually weds man with sprained
    ankle. CR 14, 20:400.

CRIM, MATT. See CRIM, MARTHA JANE.

CRISPE, WINIFRED.

002668   CORRY THORNDIKE. London: Hurst and
Blackett, 1908 BMC.

    TLS--Male Hero.
    ACAD--Male hero.
    ATH--male hero.

002669   GOLDEN APHRODITE. London: S. Paul, [1909]
BMC.

    She's a caged plaything; subdues two men with her
    charms. TLS

002670   SNARES: A NOVEL. London: Hutchinson, 1904
BMC.

    BKM--woman of 30.
    ATH--diary of a woman, plain with strong sexual
    feelings and a somewhat morbid longing to attract a
    man. "The topic dealt with pertains to real life, but
    so do many others that by no means lend themselves
    gracefully to the hand of the writer of fiction, least
    of all to the lady writer of fiction." ATH. 10-1-04,
    p.441

CROAL, FRANCES A.

002671   THE FLY IN THE OINTMENT. BY FRANCES
HAMMOND. London: Chapman and Hall, 1912 BMC.

    TLS-story of lovely girl who is slightly deformed.
    ATH-scheming woman gets lover to kiss her in front of
    girl, etc.
    LBKM-Hunchback Theodora goes thru much suffering in
    her longing for love and treacheries of enemies and a
    weak lover. Emerges at last, "Purified..comes into
    spirual inheritance saved from warping of character
    threatened by a life of bitterness."

002672   LET THEM SAY! BY FRANCES HAMMOND. London:
Chapman and Hall, 1913 BMC.

    Heroine, unconventional, not sure she wants to marry,
    takes in a child who happens to look like her. The
    community assumes she's the real mother; they cut her
    out. ATH
    "Wins through to a marriage." TLS

002673   THE MAGIC FIRE. BY FRANCES HAMMOND.
London: Chapman and Hall, 1913 BMC.

an unmarried mother-the heroine. SP
Man whose wife is hopelessly insane loves Norma
Dundas, who doesn't at first know he's married. After
much suffering, a happy solution. TLS

CROFTON, HELEN ROSE ANNE (MILMAN). B. 1857.

002674   THE LITTLE LADIES. BY HELEN MILMAN.
London: Griffith, [1891] BMC. Philadelphia: J. B.
Lippincott, 1892 NUC.

    They're twins. Sweet old fashioned. IND.

CROKER, B. M. See CROKER, BITHIA MARY (SHEPPARD).

CROKER, BITHIA MARY (SHEPPARD). D. 1920. United Kingdom.

002675   ANGEL: A SKETCH IN INDIAN INK. BY B. M.
CROKER. New York: Dodd, Mead, 1901 NUC. London:
Methuen, 1901 BMC.

    escapes a hated marriage flies to India. PW 11-2-01
    Clever impulsive masterful with man's power of self
    control, shrewd, rash, unscrupulous sense of honor
    11-2-01 ATH

002676   BABES IN THE WOOD. A ROMANCE OF THE
JUNGLES. BY B. M. CROKER. London: Methuen, [1910] BMC
NUC. New York: Brentano's, 1911 NUC.

    BM Set in India
    TLS officer and his sister
    ACAD 0
    SR Male hero

002677   BEYOND THE PALE: A NOVEL. BY B. M.
CROKER. [New York]: [P. F. Collier], [1896] NUC.
London: Chatto and Windus, 1897 BMC.

    Anglo Irish man returns to Ireland after making a
    fortune in Liverpool. Anthony Money rents a hugh
    estate now in the hands of a poor heiress Geraldine
    O'Beirne who is a horse-breaker. Wins Anthony and his
    reluctant mother. SP 78:309.
    She is "Galloping Jerry" the first lady in the county,
    descendent of Kings. Anthony helps her regain her
    status. ATH 109:504. Light, amusing, millionaire's
    son, poor girl "whom misfortunes have put beyond the
    pale" but she's really an heiress. BAKER 03 235.
    LW 29:204. Wealthy Eng. family take a house in
    Ireland. The "emotional step daughter of an
    unprincipled horse dealer" is heroine.

002678   BLUE CHINA. BY B. M. CROKER. London:
Hutchinson, 1919 BMC. New York: Brentano's, [1919]
NUC.

    "Widow smashes a priceless collection of china as
    revenge for having been jilted by the collector" Widow
    not sym. portrayal either; all women here shown as
    conniving SP
    "The character of the crafty and intriguing niece of
    the enthusiast in old China is interesting." BAKER,
    32, p125
    BKM-Man has a passion for collecting blue china and
    out of jealousy for his collection jilts widow he
    planned to marry. She smashes his collection with a
    sledge hammer.
    NYT Jan 4 '20 p5. There is a niece (a skeleton in the
    closet) of questionable birth who knows a lot about
    blue china.

002679   BRIDGET. London: Hutchinson, 1918 BMC.

    TLS-typical Irish romance.

002680   THE CAT'S PAW. BY B. M. CROKER.
Philadelphia: J. B. Lippincott, 1902 NUC. London:
Chatto and Windus, 1902 BMC.

    Lured to India on false pretenses refuses to marry
    imposter; becomes nurse, companion etc. finally
    marries.

002681   THE CHAPERONE. London: Cassell, [1920]
BMC.

    TLS Reminiscesnces of divorcee

002682   THE COMPANY'S SERVANT, A ROMANCE OF
SOUTHERN INDIA. London: Hurst & Blackett, 1907 BMC.
London: 1907 NUC.

002683   FAME. London: Mills & Boon, 1910 BMC.
London: 1910 NUC.

TLS-Novelist in attempt to gain attention of the
literary women's world is reduced to meannesses to
recover her position-claims as her own a great novel
written by her cousin.
SR. O POV ?

002684   A FAMILY LIKENESS: A SKETCH IN THE
HIMALAYAS. BY B. M. CROKER. London: Chatto and Windus,
1892 BMC. Philadelphia: J. B. Lippincott, 1893 NUC.

ATH 100:850. Heroine is Juliet Carwithen an
Anglo-Indian whom her father (rich, English, and
remarried) had deserted as a baby. Someone meets her
and sees a family resemblance.
SP 69:857. Happy ending. Anglo-Indian society.
Juliet Carwithen never stirs till she's 19 from school
on the Northern slopes of the Himalayas but speaks
French and German and plays piano. Goes from school to
dreary months as a lodger, inevitable lover is a young
soldier. SR 1-7-93,17
She has a bore of a father-a social pretender, who
knows all about the upper classes, what they do, etc.
Also cheats at horse race. Humorous. CR 14, 20:95

002685   GIVEN IN MARRIAGE. London: Hutchinson,
1916 BMC.

TLS loathing turned to love

002686   THE HAPPY VALLEY. BY B. M. CROKER.
London: Methuen, [1904] BMC NUC. Leipig: B. Tauchnitz,
1905 NUC.

ATH-sent sunny book about a picnic.

002687   HER OWN PEOPLE. London: Hurst and
Blackett, 1903 BMC NUC.

002688   IN OLD MADRAS. BY B. M. CROKER. London:
Hutchinson, 1913 BMC NUC.

Young man in India searching for missing uncle.
Conventional happy end after many adventures. SP
A modern quixote much dramatic action LBKM

002689   INFATUATION; OR, MARIA'S MISFORTUNES. BY
B. M. CROKER. London: Chatto and Windus, 1899 BMC.
Philadelphia: J. B. Lippincott, 1899 NUC.

Maria Talbot is companion to her tyrannical aunt. She
loves Captain Borrodaile whose love for her has
cooled. Maria remains true to him though he's
unworthy, and she's a slave to her aunt. Another woman
character American Miss Fontaine makes friends with
Maria who ends up with a faithful suitor--John
Harland. LIT 4:153
She's a drudge to her aunt for 12 years. The Capt.
despairs of shaking her free. Then Maimie Virginia
Fontaine comes along and makes things right--restores
Maria's self confidence. SP 82:93

002690   INTERFERENCE: A NOVEL. London: F. V.
White, 1891 BMC. Philadelphia: J. B. Lippincott, 1906
NUC.

Betty, Heroine is a splendid, fearless rider (horse).
She's sacrificed by bad aunt who cares only for her
own daughter. LW
Aunt intercepts letter to Betty (proposal of
marriage), sends own daughter to India to marry the
man. He marries her (Isabel Redmond) but she comes to
a bad end when she discovers her husband never loved
her. He felt he had to marry her, give up Betty. ACAD
Set in Ireland and then India. Isabel is ignorant of
mother's interference. On her death bed, Mrs. Redmond
confesses the deed. She had written to George that
Betty was engaged. Isabel's (Belle's) voyage,
reception, tantrums, signs of approaching madness,
death subtly described. SR 10-24-91, 480

002691   JOHANNA. BY B. M. CROKER. London:
Methuen, 1903 BMC. Philadelphia: J. B. Lippincott,
1903 NUC.

trials that keep a couple separate and unhappy LBKM 9
-03 225 BAKER 32-125

002692   KATHERINE THE ARROGANT. London: 1902 NUC.
London: Methuen, 1909 BMC.

born of good family, orphaned, becomes a maid
companion. Story gives full picture of her boarding
house life. Then life in fashionable society. Gets
love and prosperity in the end. TLS ATH
"the woman who has to conquer the world for herself"
SP

002693   LISMOYLE; AN EXPERIMENT IN IRELAND. BY B.
M. CROKER. London: Hutchinson, 1914 BMC NUC. New York:
Brentano's, 1914 NUC.

LBKM
SR 147:710. Ireland romance.
TLS 13:202

002694   MARRIED OR SINGLE? BY B. M. CROKER.
London: Chatto and Windus, 1895 BMC NUC. [New York]:
[P. F. Collier], 1895 c NUC.

Madeline West is a teacher in a fashionable boarding
school who marries a young barrister. Patient in her
marriage, he gets sick, she has a child. Then her
father becomes a millionaire but threatens to give her
no money if she marries a poor man. (He's been
reported dead and shows up) She takes off her wedding
ring and resumes her maiden name." One suspects the
author of thinking it a pardonable and even amiable
weakness in a pretty young woman to prefer diamonds
and flattery to the company of a kind husband and a
delicate child." SP 75 937.
Treated sym. She deserts husband and child. The child
dies, but husband and wife are eventually reunited.
ATH 106:830
LBKM 10:163. Madeline's father is missing. She marries
a poor man; they are happy. Father returns with
millions. She keeps marriage a secret, living life of
unmarried heiress. Baby dies. At last father is told;
accepts husband, every one happy.
SR- Before father's return husband becomes ill, he is
out of work, all is in pawn, she is heroic in poverty.
She takes money from father to send husband to country
to convalesce and she plays part of unmarried
daughter. But time goes on and she doesn't tell
father-actually dreads a return to poverty.

002695   MISS BALMAINE'S PAST. BY B. M. CROKER.
London: Chatto and Windus, 1898 BMC. Philadelphia: J.
B. Lippincott, 1898 NUC.

SP 80:175. Rosamond secretly marries a civil engineer
on the eve of his departure for New Zealand. He is
shipwrecked for 3 years. She is deceived into
believing that he has betrayed her; she also thinks
her child died at birth. He finally returns and
eventually misunderstandings are cleared away and they
are reunited, along with the child.
LIT 2:325.

002696   MR. JERVIS. BY B. M. CROKER. London:
Chatto and Windus, 1894 BMC. Philadelphia: J. B.
Lippincott, 1895 NUC.

SR 78:688. Matchmaking schemes of two aunts and two
nieces in Anglo-Indian society.
SP 73:851. Wife tempted to go off with former lover,
elects to stay with perfectly good husband.
Anglo-Indian. Two rival match-makers. Mrs. Langrishe
and Mrs. Brande both bring nieces to the station.
Jervis, a millionaire also comes--but he changes
identities with a friend. The flirtatious niece--Lalla
gets the imposter; the good niece Honor gets Jervis.
ACAD 47:78.

002697   A NINE DAY'S WONDER. London: Methuen,
[1905] BMC NUC. Leipzig: B. Tauchnitz, 1906 NUC.

Country girl BAKER 32, 125

002698   THE PAGODA TREE. BY B. M. CROKER. London:
Cassell, [1919] NUC BMC.

A tree and its golden fruit and plantations. TLS
Father causes problems for daughter SP

002699   PEGGY OF THE BARTONS. London: Methuen,
1898 BMC. New York and London: R. F. Fenno, 1898 NUC.

SP 81:283. Peggy married the wrong man. Eventually he
is bitten by a monkey and dies. Happy ending.

002700   QUICKSANDS. London: Cassell, 1915 BMC
NUC.

Eva Lingard tells her story, orphaned. She and brother
sent to India. TLS

002701   A RASH EXPERIMENT. London: Hutchinson,
[1917] BMC.

002702   THE REAL LADY HILDA: A SKETCH. BY B. M.
CROKER. London: Chatto and Windus, 1896 BMC NUC. New
York: F. M. Buckles, 1899 NUC.

SR. Mrs Hayes nurses and cares for Lady Hilda in
India. Back in England she seeks her out with open
arms, only to be allowed to die, with pneumonia,
uncared for, at Lady Hilda's gates.
ACAD 49:466. Gwen is the heroine, story is about her,
made penniless by her father's death while he was in
India.
SP 77:218. Told in 1st person. Happy ending.
Mrs Hayes is left poor when her doctor husband dies.
They are in India and he had lived in the rajah's
court. Mrs. Hayes must now struggle to support herself
and step-daughter. Now that she's poor, Lady Hilda
snubs her. PW 55:726

002703   THE ROAD TO MANDALAY; A TALE OF BURMA. BY
B. M. CROKER. London: Cassell, 1917 BMC NUC.

Man in Burma wife's addiction to drugs. LBKM

002704   A ROLLING STONE. BY B. M. CROKER. London:
F.V. White, 1911 BMC. New York: Brentano's, 1912 NUC.

Uncle and his heir and inheritance TLS

002705   THE SERPENT'S TOOTH. BY B. M. CROKER.
London: Hutchinson, 1912 NUC BMC. Leipzig: B.
Tauchnitz, 1912 NUC.

TLS unhappy mrg, lover, divorce. When daughter grows
up leaves mother for rich father.
SP an orphan makes disagreeable marriage under
compulsion from disagreeable aunt. POV?

002706   THE SPANISH NECKLACE. BY B. M. CROKER.
London: Chatto and Windus, 1907 BMC NUC.

002707   TERENCE. BY B. M. CROKER. London: Chatto
and Windus, 1899 BMC NUC. New York: F. M. Buckles,
[c1899] NUC.

London fashion set on holiday in County Kerry,
Ireland. The love adventures and misunderstandings of
Maureen D'Arcy and Terence. LIT 5:448
Irish officer of good family takes job driving a
tourist coach, meets an Australian heiress. He wins
her hand and her millions. SP 83:499
The Australian heiress is masquerading as a poor
relative. SR 88:773
Rich Australian girl, poor man--once aristocratic.
BAKER 03,235
PW-romance between coach driver and Australian
heiress, aided by discovery of his superior birth.

002708   A THIRD PERSON: A NOVEL. BY B. M. CROKER.
London: F. V. White, 1893 BMC NUC. Philadelphia: J. B.
Lippincott, 1899 NUC.

Lady of 60, younger than her daughter, rides, flirts,
smokes, owns to a chestnut toupee-Mrs. Baggett. ACAD
44:564.
Captain Hope returns from India learns to love
granddaughter of a retired officer; unexpected
developments. PW 11-4-93.
Amusing scenes. Cousin Clara finds herself grandmother
to man she had schemed to wed. SR 76:711

002709   WHAT SHE OVERHEARD. BY B. M. CROKER.
London: Hutchinson, [1917] NUC.

002710   THE YOUNGEST MISS MOWBRAY. BY B. M.
CROKER. London: Hurst & Blackett, 1906 BMC NUC.

ACAD-retelling of Cinderella for girls?
TLS- Retelling of cinderella for girls.
ATH--Retelling of Cinderella for girls.

CROMARSH, H. RIPLEY, pseud. See ANGELL, BRYAN MARY (DOYLE).

CROMARTIE, COUNTESS OF. See MACKENZIE, SIBELL LILIAN
(BLUNT).

CROMARTY, DEAS, pseud. See WATSON, ELIZABETH SOPHIA
(FLETCHER).

CROMMELIN, MARIA HENRIETTA DE LA CHEROIS. D. 1934. United
Kingdom.

002711   BAY RONALD. London: Hurst and Blackett,
1893 BMC NUC.

Historical romance: Napoleonic Wars. Bay is a horse.
Hero a boy of eight. SP 71, 611.
He wins the race, the property and the wife. His
masters and mistresses kidnapped, escape, dispossessed
and restored, fall in and out of love. SR 76:389.

S W. Kent ATH 102:351

002712   BETTINA. London: J. Long, 1900 BMC.

SP 84:779. Gaddi keeps kidnapping her, she is, she
discovers, a Russian princess.

002713   CRIMSON LILIES. London: J. Long, 1903
BMC.

Mystery of heroine's parentage; we first find her as a
boy acrobat in a travelling fair, leave her a great
lady, granddaughter and heiress. LBKM 3-03,249
ATH 121 300

002714   A DAUGHTER OF ENGLAND. BY MAY CROMMELIN.
London: J. Long, 1902 BMC.

ATH 2-1-02

002715   "DIVIL-MAY-CARE" ALIAS RICHARD BURKE,
SOMETIMES ADJUTANT OF THE BLACK NORTHERNERS. London:
F.V. White, 1899 BMC.

Black Northerners of Ireland. Its adjutant and his
loves and adventures. Patsy Bragin's awful end at the
hands of his comrades in the secret society. Aileen
and her wild sister Loo. ATH 113:81
ACAD 55:516. Irish. Hero is adjutant of Black
Northerners, his narration.

002716   DUST BEFORE THE WIND: A NOVEL. London:
Bliss, Sands and Foster, 1894 BMC NUC.

SP a "nightmare." Story of a thoroughly depraved woman
who uses a man who loves her and ruins his life. He in
turn ruins the life of her daughter.
ACAD 45:392. Stella, married to a man twice her age,
did not endure nobly, is chided by rev. She elopes with
her daughter whom she idolizes; she returns home to
die of a broken heart. Author's pov?

002717   FOR THE SAKE OF THE FAMILY. BY MAY
CROMMELIN. New York: J. W. Lovell, [c1891] BMC NUC.
London and Sydney: Eden, Remington, 1892 BMC.

ATH 100: 814. Heroine takes on a crime for family's
sake.
CR 18:164. She goes to S. Africa as a companion, is
shipwrecked, decides she must marry "worthless fellow"
for his money, but he is murdered and she is
implicated.

002718   THE GOLDEN BOW. London: Holden &
Hardingham, 1912 BMC.

002719   HALF AROUND THE WORLD FOR A HUSBAND: A
COMEDY OF ERRORS. BY MAY CROMMELIN. London: T. F.
Unwin, 1896 BMC. Chicago and New York: Globe Library,
1898 NUC.

A proxy marr. with the wrong bride and "a supposed
aged bridegroom who turns out to be the young prince"
Quaint Anne, the bride. For girls? SR 83:100
Ann & Anita very alike. Planned marr. in Chili for
Anita. She sends Ann in her place. West Indian and So.
American life. Ann Montague a fine heroine. ATH 109:81
PW-Chilean girl is promised to Spanish don by parents
when a child. She loves a Scotsman, persuades a friend
to personate her to avoid mrge. Her friend Ann's
experiences and adventures.

002720   HER FAITHFUL KNIGHT; A NOVEL. BY MAY
CROMMELIN. New York: A. L. Burt, [1902] NUC.

002721   THE HOUSE OF HOWE. London: J. Long, 1907
BMC.

Mainly an account of a tour in Palestine of a spinster
and her guardian TLS

002722   "I LITTLE KNEW!" London: J. Milne, [1908]
BMC.

TLS-story of an elderly spinster who travels around
the world. Sounds sentimental.

002723   KINSAH: A DAUGHTER OF TANGIER. London: J.
Long, 1899 BMC.

British legation "and their womenfolk." Christian and
Mohammdean life in Tangier. ACAD 57:574.
Story of harem life in Morocco. Also by Jebli, the
leper. The chequered experiences of Kinisah and her
gallant Ahmed. ATH 114
SR 89:179. Heroine is native of Tangiers, her story

from childhood to entrance of harem.

002724   LOVERS ON THE GREEN. London: Hutchinson, 1910 BMC.

TLS-a nice story of various society types.
ATH-

002725   THE LUCK OF A LOWLAND LADDIE. BY MAY CROMMELIN. London: J. Long, 1900 BMC. New York: F. M. Buckles, [c1900] NUC.

LBKM 19:91 A 7th son of a 7th son.
LIT 7:465. Inheritance. Chile.

002726   MADAM MYSTERY: A ROMANCE IN TOURAINE. BY MAY CROMMELIN. London: Hutchinson, 1910 BMC. Boston: D. Estes, [1912] NUC.

Unpleasant situations, unclean, more Spanish like than English.
PW 9-2-11
BM History and romance.
TLS-history and romance.

002727   MR. AND MRS. HERRIES: A NOVEL IN ONE VOLUME. London: Hutchinson, 1892 BMC.

They marry, she's 16 and an heiress. Then they lose that money, move to a cottage and through her affection and good sense overcome difficulties and achieve wealth and happiness. PW 1-7-93, 5

002728   ONE PRETTY MAID AND OTHERS. London: J. Long, 1904 BMC.

ATH-housemaid's story.

002729   PARTNERS THREE. London: J. Long, 1903 BMC.

Orphan inherits a fortune, wants to help the poor.
LBKM 10-03,56
ATH 122,410

002730   PHOEBE OF THE WHITE FARM. London: J. Long, 1906 BMC.

ACAD-a few adventures for a young girl and then marriage.
TLS-a few adventures for a young girl and then marriage.

002731   PINK LOTUS; A COMEDY IN KASHMIR. London: Hurst and Blackett, 1914 BMC.

ATH 144:649. Romantic comedy.

002732   SUNSHINE ON THE NILE. A NOVEL. London: Jarrolds, 1920 BMC.

TLS-romance. Male hero.

002733   THE WHITE LADY. London: J. Long, 1905 BMC.

Scientist marries a governess. He's pedantic, pompous and she idealizes him. He begins to go mad? ACAD 881,05
He plans his wife's funeral. After his suicide, she can finally marry the one she should have married in the first place. ATH 268,05
Sympathetic treatment? Focus on the woman?

002734   A WOMAN-DERELICT. London: J. Long, [1901] BMC.

Woman with amnesia. ATH-6-22-01,

CROMMELIN, MAY, pseud. See CROMMELIN, MARIA HENRIETTA DE LA CHEROIS.

CROPPER, ELEANOR.

002735   IN THE STRAITS OF HOPE. London: J. Murray, 1904 BMC.

ATH-Bohemian life wayward, unconventional heroine
TLS-o

CROSBIE, MARY. United Kingdom.

002736   BRIDGET CONSIDINE. London: G. Bell, 1914 BMC NUC.

West of Ireland, not ordinary woman even as child, we see her pagan-like, building an altar to forgotten gods in her garden. Poor childhood, reared by pa., spends days in street. "Absolutely fearless and bound by no convention." Comes under influence of a smug young man "who spared her no enlightenment" and would have her share his jaundiced view of life but she remains an idealist and epicurean. Later loved by man bound by strict conventions. SR
TLS 13: 346 - She is a bit of a poet and unlucky in her circumstances and love.

002737   DISCIPLES. London: Methuen, 1907 BMC.

Denise, unconventional "detached, egoistic, cold"; Maev's dreams, child like mind ACAD
Denise-determined to seek "the nakedness of things," regrets Dr's love for her "heroic faiths" Maev-simple, writes poetry. TLS

002738   ESCAPADE. London: E. Arnold, 1917 BMC NUC.

Daphne Carey, weary of comfort, is on island off Cornish coast with Justina, a would-be vagabond, Henry a vagabond longing for civilized living and Jill a real vagabond. Daphne plays at the simple life (with a bank roll on reserve) Jill treated most seriously ? TLS
A wealthy American woman buys (or thinks she has bought) an island-to escape convention only to find that the simple life is much too complicated for her and convention is best LBKM

002739   KINSMEN'S CLAY. London: Methuen, [1910] BMC.

TLS, about two women, in the tradition of George Eliot.
ATH-Menage a trois, one of the women is crippled.
BAKER 32-125

CROSBY, E. THEODORA. See BLISS, ELLA THEODORA (CROSBY).

CROSFIELD, T. H. See CROSFIELD, TRUDA H.

CROSFIELD, TRUDA H.

002740   A LOVE IN ANCIENT DAYS. BY T. H. CROSFIELD. London: E. Mathews, 1908 BMC NUC.

SR-Eng. in 519 with an "up to date sporting girl debutante heroine."
BKM-not too promising but obscure.

CROSS, ADA (CAMBRIDGE). 1844-1926. Australia.

002741   THE DEVASTATORS. BY ADA CAMBRIDGE. London: Methuen, 1901 BMC NUC. New York: D. Appleton, 1901 NUC.

husbands and wives who devastate marriage tragedy of ill-assorted marriages. ACAD 01

002742   THE ETERNAL FEMININE. BY ADA CAMBRIDGE. London: Hurst and Blackett, 1907 NUC BMC.

Aunt Carrie-gushing, meddlesome. TLS

002743   FIDELIS. BY ADA CAMBRIDGE. London: Hutchinson, 1895 BMC NUC. New York: D. Appleton, 1895 NUC.

Sympathetic view of a child Little Adam and history of Richard Delavel and his wife (or wives) SR 79:766
Young couple who persist in misunderstanding each other-long alienation of Fidelia and Adam Drewe, and Sarah French "worth two or three Fidelias" SP 74:723
I: hero's troubled youth. ATH 105:469
He has a frog's mouth (?) and goggle eyes. Thinks no woman can endure his ugliness. Marries the heroine when she's half blind, gives her back her sight, finds she loves him still. LW 26:170

002744   A HAPPY MARRIAGE. BY ADA CAMBRIDGE. London: Hurst & Blackett, 1906 BMC. London and Bombay: G. Bell, nd [] NUC.

ACAD-Author's pov there is probably no such thing, however through time and tribulations her couple make it to middle age.
TLS Domestic

002745   A HUMBLE ENTERPRISE. BY ADA CAMBRIDGE. London: Ward, Lock and Bowden, 1896 BMC NUC.

SR Plucky young heroine a wholesome ideal for girls.

Romance.
ATH 108:188. Until wealthy suitor comes along, she
supports herself, her mother and sister by running a
tea shop.
BKM 4:164 Author views mrge. as an unfortunate
necessity.

002746   A LITTLE MINX: A SKETCH. BY ADA
CAMBRIDGE. London: Heinemann, 1893 BMC. New York: D.
Appleton, 1893 NUC.

Set in Australia, but she's English. She's married to
the curate but all the men are attracted to her. Nancy
gets two husbands in the story and nearly a third.
She's utterly irresistible to men, completely avoids
close friendships with women. "Two has hitherto been
the allotted limit." Nation 56:475.
Not intelligent, just charming. Pleasant life-she had
in two marriages. Then in second half her true
awakening: learns to love, not just to be loved. She
finds a true love after being twice widowed. She's
swept overboard in a storm travelling to her sailor
lover. Completely sympathetic portrayal of woman "that
brings the whole world to her feet." CR 20, 23:70
Author "unsparing critic of her sex"-except for the
heroine who is most attractive. ATH 101:534.

002747   THE MAKING OF RACHEL ROWE. BY ADA
CAMBRIDGE. London and New York: Cassell, 1914 BMC NUC.

ATH-Australian heroine visits relatives in Yorkshire,
makes a disastrous union with man who is wanted for
bigamy.
TLS-She has illegal son, her character develops under
tribulations, Australian doctor who has loved her
finds her and takes her home to happiness.

002748   A MARRIAGE CEREMONY. BY ADA CAMBRIDGE.
London: Hutchinson, 1894 BMC. New York: D. Appleton,
1894 NUC.

SR 78:277. Rutherford and Betty marry because they
must in order to collect fortune. Rutherford falls in
love with her. But Hilda, a poet with a birth mark
covering half her face, loved him and married a bank
clerk because she wanted to suicide. Then she really
does and things work out for the others.
ATH 103:275. Setting in Australia.
CR 25:38. Characters without ideals.
LW 25:91.

002749   MATERFAMILIAS. BY ADA CAMBRIDGE. London
and New York: Ward, Lock, [1898] BMC. New York: D.
Appleton, 1898 NUC.

SP 81:313. Autobiography of middle-aged matron;
impressionable, indiscreet, jealous but affectionate
mother and wife.
LIT 3:87. Australia. Experiences as daughter, wife,
mother, grandmother.
ATH 111:816. "Happy domestic life varied by slight
misunderstandings and unimportant quarrels."
BKM 8:164.
LW 29:219. Her "rare examples of virtue cannot blind
the reader to the hatefulness of such a woman." "An
hysterical bundle of inconsistencies." Rev is
surprised a woman author would choose type so
frequently satirized by male writers, a puppet rather
than a person, etc.

002750   NOT ALL IN VAIN. BY ADA CAMBRIDGE.
London: Heinemann, 1892 BMC. New York: D. Appleton,
1892 NUC.

ATH 99:338. Heroine, three suitors, Australia
CR 17:168. Hero serves 18 year term for murder of man
who annoyed heroine. She works. At the moment before
their marriage they discover they are not in love and
depart from each other to the ones they love.
LW 23:75. Katherine follows man who has killed while
protecting her from violence to Melbourne where he is
serving 20 yrs term. She opens a hospital and together
with surgeon friend makes it a success. She inherits a
lot of money just before he is released. However, he
has changed, and falls for a younger woman. Katherine
releases him, Ends happily for her.
SP 68:499. She turns to a man who has been her friend
for years.
ACAD 41:298. marries the surgeon. "offensive and
abnormal" scenes should have been omitted-specifically
scenes on board the Huntingdonshire, "described with
realistic but repulsive power."

002751   PATH AND GOAL. BY ADA CAMBRIDGE. London:
Methuen, 1900 BMC NUC. New York: D. Appleton, 1900
NUC.

LBKM 19:29. Hero's adventures. Shipwreck.
SP 85:343. Minute description of life in cathedral
town. Shipwreck ends book.
SR 90:432. Hero is a country MD. There is an original
and interesting woman.
ATH 116:307. Constantly bringing the physiological
aspect of sexual relations and other matters unduly to
the front. Hero is high-minded and conscientious, has
failed with 3 women and is united with 4th on doomed
ship.
LIT 7:419. Four single young women in Wakeminster,
more or less in waiting. Enter Dr. Adrian Black. He
believed in eugenics, thinks one after the other of
the 4 is perfect mate.

002752   A PLATONIC FRIENDSHIP. London: Hurst and
Blackett, 1905 BMC.

002753   SISTERS. A NOVEL. London: Hutchinson,
1904 BMC.

LBKM 0
ATH 0

002754   THE THREE MISS KINGS: AN AUSTRALIAN
STORY. BY ADA CAMBRIDGE. London: Heinemann, 1891 BMC.
New York: D. Appleton, 1891 NUC.

Women's lives; they're Australian; "full of dainty
details of household life." Men's lives-full of time
to adore women. LW
Elizabeth weds a mid-aged preacher; Patty, a newsman;
Eleanor (not beautiful) also marries. ACAD.
Sisterly love. ATH 98, 36
Left orphans. Go to Melbourne to make their own way.
All are pianists. Then on tour "their graceful and
athletic forms had never worn stays" because of their
isolated life. They read a lot, all played piano
beautifully-one a genius. All unsophisticated. Off to
Melbourne. They later inherit a great deal of money.
SR 7-25-91, 114

CROSS, MARGARET BESSIE.

002755   BLIND BATS. London: Hurst and Blackett,
1897 BMC.

An irate aunt, a stubborn male guardian, a spoiled
child. All works out well. LBKM 11:153.
Robert Ward leaves the guardianship of his daughter
not to wife's family with whom he has differences, but
to a friend. This friend and Barbara Plowden, the
wife's half sister have much conflict. SP 79:285.
The friend. Tom Westropp and Barb end up marrying.
Barbara-"a little soured" because she's not so young
any more. Cares for sister's child "as compensation."
Sister is dead. Then learns the child is to go to a
friend of the husband's. ATH 109:207.

002756   LOVE AND OLIVIA. London: Hurst and
Blackett, 1899 BMC. (Bookseller adds: Being the
Sentimental Troubles of a Clever Woman to the title)

She is a lecturer on the classics and a very modern
young woman. One man fears her superiority and turns
to an old-fashioned feminine woman. Another sees the
woman behind the lecturer and loves Olivia. LIT:
4:316.
She almost made a secret marriage to the first after
winning honors at Cambridge. Then they are separated
for 7 years when he returns he's a bit uncomfortable
with this intelligent woman. She marries a rival
lecturer of classical archeology. SP 82:206
Olivia Wynworth. Blue stocking. Does her research on
Persephone. ACAD 56:192
The world of cultivated professional single women. She
has attained distinction and fame. ATH 113:239
A modern talented woman; wins literary fame; an old
lover shows up--he's not a literary person; troubles
arise because of this situation; both relieved to find
more suitable mates. BAKER 03,07
The world of the cultivated professional single woman.
ATH 113:239.

002757   NEWLY FASHIONED. London: Hurst and
Blackett, 1895 BMC.

Heroine is a young woman tried and accused of
stealing. And she is guilty. The young man who falls
in love with her in court waits for her to be
released. In the end we leave them struggling for
their lives in the ocean-one with a broken leg and one
with a wounded head. SR 79:765
Beatrice Hayes stole a purse from the woman she worked
for as companion. Jim Fyffe meets her in court,

believes she's innocent and his "ideal," proposes. In fact she's guilty, but is acquitted. She marries him and does grow into that ideal. Then one day she tells him the truth. SP 74:723
A cousin is a murse very much involved in parish poitics. The fate of hero and heroine left very doubtful. ATH 105:566

002758   OPPORTUNITY. London: Chatto & Windus, 1910 NUC.

TLS-widow and two daughters, both have love story, well contrasted.
ATH-widow is jovial, good-hearted but absolutely unscrupulous about money. Matrimonial tactics for her daughters.
SR-she believes it the business of men to provide and women to be provided for; men to give and women to take--all they can get. Level-headed, also picks up other people's purses.

002759   A QUESTION OF MEANS. London and Edinburgh: Thomas Nelson & Sons, [1917] BMC.

Rose Marvell and Oliphant (young man). But story seems to focus on his career? TLS
Marry by 6th chapter. Couple faces financial problems with each child that comes; conflict between the parents--each presented very sympathetically. ATH
ACAD:Rose Oliphant is the heroine, struggles with her many babies, with many financial difficulties. Must have husband ask for money from her old lover.

002760   RICHARD'S AFFAIR; A NOVEL. London: Ward, Lock, [1904] BMC.

002761   THE SAFFRON ROBE. London: Hurst and Blackett, 1893 BMC.

Young couple, friends from childhood, argue all the time. Their's is a fencing match with love. Both oppose the sentimental type of relationship. Diana looks at marriage with a common-sense eye-she expects their relationship to be a comradeship. She's wise, quick-witted. Story focuses on her. SP 70:824.
Dick and Diana. "We are told a great deal more than we want to know about Diana's thoughts and feelings." SR 75:662.
She's "magnificent" ACAD 44:107. Diana Moore.

002762   STOLEN HONEY. London: Hurst and Blackett, 1892 BMC.

ATH 99:401 - Romance of two sisters, vicar's daughters
SP. Bigamy
ACAD. Major Blake marries Susie without telling her he already has a wife, then confesses to her and expects forgiveness. Her "descent into rebellious womanhood." "painful." major Blake is "essentially good."
SR 73:423. She learns that she is not really married when intoxicated wife dies; she is pregnant. They marry, but from this point on she refuses to be his wife in anything but name. She takes a lover. Reviewer loses all sympathy for her.

002763   UP TO PERRIN'S. London: Chatto & Windus, 1912 BMC NUC.

TLS-story of English authoress.
ATH-fishing village. Tragic end.

CROSS, MARY.

002764   AS GOLD IN THE FURNACE. London: E. Stock, 1895 BMC.

old-fashioned novel. Philip Beresford leaves bad father, becomes great author. Then later in life he meets brother but Philip hides his identity. Tries to save brother from dissipation. Man's love of a good woman Elsie. ACAD 48:127

002765   FALSE WITNESS. London: Oliphant, Anderson and Ferrier, 1891 BMC.

CROSS, VICTORIA, pseud. See CORY, VIVIAN.

CROTTIE, JULIA M. B. 1853. United Kingdom.

002766   THE LOST LAND. A TALE OF A CROMWELLIAN-IRISH TOWN, BEING THE AUTOBIOGRAPHY OF MISS ANNITA LOMBARD, 1780-1797. London: T. F. Unwin, 1901 BMC NUC.

ATH 3-16-01
BAKER 32-1901

CROUCH, FRANCES. Nationality Unknown.

002767   FEMININE FINANCE. New York: B.W. Dodge, 1907 NUC.

three women try to get farmer to pay a note. Two help a third woman out of difficulty. PW 11-16-07.
Bachelor woman tries to collect on a promisory note. The farmer refuses to pay; she "pelts him with stones." NyT
BKM-"a bachelor farmer is visited by two women on two separate days in an endeavor to collect money due a third, on a note." Amusing story told of what resulted. Brief description. BKM 26 (1908) 559.

CROW, LOUISA.

002768   MOLLIE'S MAIDENS. London: Cassell, 1894 BMC.

CROW, MARTHA (FOOTE). 1854-1924.

002769   THE WORLD ABOVE; A DUOLOGUE. Chicago: Blue Sky Press, [c1905] NUC.

A duologue between Jean, a young workman in the Darker Realm, and Angelica, a daughter of another workman. BKM

CROWELL, BERTHA. United States.

002770   WINGS OF THE CARDINAL. New York: G. H. Doran, [c1917] NUC.

To help her poor family, Ferol sells herself to wealthy man to whom she never gave her love. When love comes faced the dilemma but stayed with husband till his death, PW
Finally rescued by the sacrifices of the one who loved her NYT 326,9-2-17

CROWELL, KATHARINE RONEY. B. 1854.

002771   THE CALL OF THE WATERS; A STUDY OF THE FRONTIER. New York: F.H. Revell, [c1908] NUC.

CROWLEY, MARY CATHERINE. D. 1920. United States.

002772   A DAUGHTER OF NEW FRANCE, WITH SOME ACCOUNT OF THE GALLANT SIEUR CADILLAC AND HIS COLONY ON THE DETROIT. Boston: Little, Brown, 1901 NUC BMC.

historical. NYT

002773   THE HEROINE OF THE STRAIT: A ROMANCE OF DETROIT IN THE TIME OF PONTIAC. Boston: Little, Brown, 1902 BMC NUC.

002774   IN TREATY WITH HONOR; A ROMANCE OF OLD QUEBEC. Boston: Little, Brown, 1906 NUC.

PW-male hero. Historical.
NYT-hero, historical.
Perils, adventures. NYT

002775   LOVE THRIVES IN WAR: A ROMANCE OF THE FRONTIER IN 1812. Boston: Little, Brown, 1903 BMC NUC.

Historical romance. PW 6-6-03

CROWNFIELD, GERTRUDE. 1867-1945. United States.

002776   PRINCESS WHITE FLAME. New York: E. P. Dutton, [c1920] NUC. London and Toronto: J. M. Dent, 1923 BMC.

CROWNINSHIELD, MARY (BRADFORD). 1854-1913. United States.

002777   THE ARCHBISHOP AND THE LADY. BY MRS. SCHUYLER CROWNINSHIELD. London: McClure, Phillips, 1900 BMC. New York: McClure, Phillips, 1900 NUC.

Gartha an amusing and shockingly precocious child of the type belonging only to fiction. ATH 6-22-01
NYT 1900:830. House party at French estate. Heroine has "inexplicable marriages" and a "peculiar attitude toward life."
PW. Saved by American hero.

002778   LATITUDE 19 DEGREES: A ROMANCE OF THE WEST INDIES IN THE YEAR OFOUR LORD EIGHTEEN HUNDRED AND TWENTY. BEING A FAITHFUL ACCOUNT AND TRUE OF THE PAINFUL ADVENTURES OF THE SKIPPER, THE BO'S'N, THE SMITH, THE MATE, AND CYNTHIA. BY MRS. SCHUYLER CROWNINSHIELD. New York: D. Appleton, 1898 NUC BMC.

CR 33;527. Haiti in 1820. Party of American males,
their adventures with the Blacks.
Historical romance. Haiti. Cynthia Archer, Captain's
niece. Adventures on schooner captained by pirates.
Witnesses voodo rites and human sacrifice. Includes
love story. NYT 1-21-99,36

002779   SAN ISIDRO. BY MRS. SCHUYLER
CROWNINSHIELD. Chicago and New York: H. S. Stone, 1900
NUC BMC.

BKM 10:599. West Indies. Aqueda is Don Beltran's
housekeeper; they are in love. Then he tires of her,
makes love to his cousin Felicia. A flood, Aqueda
gives up her place in boat so other two may be saved.
As she goes down at the last moment he calls to her,
but it is too late.
CR 36:90. Aqueda is a native woman, other 2 are not.
LW 31:68. Mexico.
On coast of Mexico, a place of storms and floods
relations of masters and servants, love relations of
several native couples. Manners and customs of the
country. Tragic. PW 56:1222.
Colonial Spanish setting (Cuba maybe). Aqueda falls in
love with man who promises her marriage, but he's
lured away by an American woman who wants his money.
Aqueda later sacrifices her life for the pair. NYT
11-18-99 773

002780   VALENCIA'S GARDEN. BY MRS. SCHUYLER
CROWNINSHIELD. London & New York: McClure, Phillips,
1901 NUC BMC.

Girl-wife frank fresh natural impulsive; aged
bridegroom. BOOK NEWS 7-01
Painfully ingenuous heroine: uneven teeth and a cast
in her eye, her bursts of expansiveness towards him.
Villain a woman. Hero enslaved to two women.
The Countess constantly gaining in grace as her
character is tested. Not too helpful NYT 01

CROWNINSHIELD, MRS. SCHUYLER. See CROWNINSHIELD, MARY
(BRADFORD).

CRUGER, JULIE GRINNELL (STORROW). D. 1920. United States.

002781   COUNTESS OBERNAU. BY JULIEN GORDON. New
York: R. Bonner, 1894 NUC.

PW-young widow living in Dresden. Believing herself to
be in love with a baron, becomes engaged and wins love
of two others, resulting in sensational complications.

002782   EAT NOT THY HEART. BY JULIEN GORDON.
Chicago and London: H. S. Stone, 1897 BMC NUC.

Elizabeth Bush, farmer's wife, reads the Sunday papers
and follows the life of a socialite-Mrs. Marston,
tries to copy that woman's life. She's "unwilling to
concede that wealth makes a difference", is
"determined to assert full equality" as an Amer.
citizen. At the end, loses her mind in knowing how
ridiculous she is, sets fire to her employer's house.
LW 28:479.
Author protests against "love and always love " as the
subject of poetry and fiction. Crude Amer girl weds
farmer. NYT 11-20-97, 5.
No love theme. Young woman marries farmer in small
village but the life of society is her chief interest.
Her husband gets a position on a magnificent L. I.
estate belonging to the Marstons. Heroine has followed
the life of Mrs. Marston. She expects to be invited to
tea with the Marstons; slowly her envy of this woman
"rises into an insanity of destructive rage." NYT
11-20-97,5.

002783   HIS LETTERS. BY JULIEN GORDON. New York
and London: Cassell, [1892] NUC BMC.

114 love letters by a successful "world-worn" man to
an artist whose painting he has seen. The first 38 are
written before he saw her; the remaining, after one
glimpse of her. LW '93, 193
She's a very successful artist. The man is first
attracted to the genius he sees.
To his lady. Ideal love, 115 letters "violent
protestations pitched in a high key" LW 28:297

002784   MARIONETTES. BY JULIEN GORDON. New York:
Cassell, [c1892] NUC. London: Gay and Bird, 1893 BMC.

DIAL 13:102. "world of a very narrow and hothouse
sort" "its ethical tone all that could be expected
under the conditions."
PW-Marquise, 30 year old widow of Frenchman, returns

to New York. Father was separated from mother and she
now gets to know him for the first time.
heroine, American married to French noble, left a
widow. Bertha le Moyne then falls in love with a
handsome dilettante. Other women characters
"intolerably vulgar" "the authoress is merciless
towards her own sex." SP 70 491
No plot, "the conflicting emotions and analysis of
purposes" married woman and mid-aged bachelor
"establish an intimacy." A fascinating woman gains his
affection. But when she learns of the "avowal of
affection" involving the other woman, she bids the
bachelor to leave her forever. ACAD 43:151

002785   MODERN DAUGHTER. New york: Ess Pub. Co.,
1900 NUC.

002786   MRS. CLYDE: THE STORY OF A SOCIAL CAREER.
BY JULIEN GORDON. New York: D. Appleton, 1901 BMC NUC.
London: Methuen, 1902 BMC.

Social power of a young woman's long and successful
social career. An attractive heroine. Study her from
youth to old age. BOOK NEWS 3-01
Her "selfhood panted for expansion" little country
girl triumphs-BOOK BUYER'S
Love motif minor-study of whole woman "to arrive" is
her great ambition and to keep "her high place in the
world" Not a bad woman, impulses are generous, never a
snob, but her life coarsens her value. End is
tragic-it's all so worthless. mother-daughter social
climber-negative picture NYT

002787   POPPAEA. BY JULIEN GORDON. Philadelphia
and London: J. B. Lippincott, 1895 BMC NUC.

LW. Marital misery
PW-Married a man twice her age for his money. Then
meets a brilliant journalist a few years later. Sudden
and tragic ending.
Three good male characters-like her husband-the man of
"ready made beliefs"; her young cousin and her lover.
"A modern American counterpart of the Empress of old
Rome. SR 80:322
"a very modern woman" longs for all the world offers
in pleasure. Marries an older man for his money. Gets
all she wanted, is content till love comes. About to
leave him, the crash comes, won't desert. Husband dies
but Poppaea doesn't wed the other. Here her story
begins. She does all sorts of things-that show she's
mad, says the reviewer. CR 23:440.
She is much more noble than her lover. Her
"half-insane recklessness" at the end. ATH 106:351

002788   A PURITAN PAGAN: A NOVEL. BY JULIEN
GORDON. New York: D. Appleton, 1891 NUC. London: S. S.
McSure, 1891 BMC.

The husband is half Puritan and half Pagan. As pagan
is untrue to his wife; as Puritan, confesses to her.
PW
She regards him with loathing upon his confession.
DIAL 12-91
Proud, sensitive, she leaves him. Once he's gone, he
loves her most. Expresses all in letters that are
returned unopened. She becomes a social success.
Reconciled in the end. CR

002789   A SUCCESSFUL MAN. BY JULIEN GORDON.
Philadelphia: J. B. Lippincott, 1891 W.

Daniel Lawton, candidate for Governor, enters world of
fashionably idle. LW.
He's married, but woman of fashion Constance Gresham
takes his career in hand and he succeeds. Wife
realizes she had not attended to his career as she
should have; CR. Also ATH 97 470
"illicit love is the main feature." IND

002790   VAMPIRES. MADEMOISELLE RESEDA. BY JULIEN
GORDON. Philadelphia: J. B. Lippincott, 1891 NUC.
London: Ward, Lock, Bowden, 1891 BMC.

Two women, daughter and mother exhaust vitality of a
man. LW
The man is a boarder in a second class boarding house.
Sympathetic portrayal of him. Two women rivals for a
man. M. Reseda is a governess. PW
Vamp-CR 17:153. Male hero who marries and serves wife
and her mother (two vampire types) for rest of his
life.
SP: Mlle. Reseda; concerns two divorces.

002791   THE WAGE OF CHARACTER; A SOCIAL STUDY. BY
JULIEN GORDON. New York: D. Appleton, 1901 BMC NUC.

PW 10-19-01. The adventure with Lady Eglinton is
repulsive. A broken marriage; strikes her husband
"A social study" -NYT

CRUGER, MARY. 1834-1908. United States.

002792   BROTHERHOOD. Boston: D. Lothrop, [c1891]
NUC.

CRUIKSHANK, JULIA.

002793   WHIRLPOOL HEIGHTS. THE DREAM-HOUSE ON THE
NIAGARA RIVER. London: G. Allen and Unwin, [1915] BMC
NUC.

Woman writes a diary of her every day life as wife in
house on Niagara River. TLS

CRUTTWELL, MAUDE. Nationality Unknown.

002794   FIRE AND FROST. New York: J. Lane, 1913
NUC. London: J. Lane, 1913 BMC NUC.

Out of pity and self-sacrifice an Englishwoman marries
an Egyptian prince; she forsakes her career in art and
letters to do so. The result is mutual unhappiness,
ending in divorce. She is then free to resume her
literary pursuits. ATH

CUBITT, MRS. NEVILLE.

002795   UNFAIR PLAY. A NOVEL. London: J. Ouseley,
1909 BMC.

Pleasant love story. TLS

CUDLIP, ANNIE HALL (THOMAS). 1838-1918. United Kingdom.

002796   THE CLEEVERS OF CLEEVER. London: A.
Treherne, 1902 BMC.

002797   COMRADES TRUE. BY ANNIE THOMAS (MRS.
PENDER CUDLIP). London: Chatto and Windus, 1900 BMC.
New York: F. M. Buckles, 1900 NUC.

CR 37:467. Young man falls into title and fortune.
ATH 115:682. A singer and Stella are heroines.

002798   DICK RIVERS: A NOVEL. London: F. V.
White, 1898 BMC.

ACAD 53:149. Disinherited hero loses fiancee but
eventually wins nicer girl and his inheritance.
ATH 111:245. Wholesome.

002799   THE DIVA. London: John Long, [1901] BMC.

002800   ESSENTIALLY HUMAN. A NOVEL. London: F. V.
White, 1897 BMC.

Helen Charmouth, first met at a presentation tea.
Father has one husband in mind for her; but she loves
a playwright. When father learns the playwright is
from wealthy trades people stock, he packs Helen off
to Aunt's. But in the end love overcomes.
ACAD 51:497.

002801   FALSE PRETENCES. London: Digby, Long,
1895 BMC.

Trixy Baron "with the heart of a woman and the mind of
a man" is the modern type, worrisome to her mother who
is bent on marrying her off. Then there's Madame
Josephs, the bigamist. ATH 105:342.

002802   FOUR WOMEN IN THE CASE. A NOVEL. London:
F. V. White, 1896 BMC.

ATH 108:383. Two young women cousins, two older women
separated from their husbands. Male characters are
cads. Jenny Wyvern, honest wholesome, loves Donald
Cleve before she knows he's married. He "is released
from his burden" and the two are happy. SP 78:570.

002803   A GIRL'S FOLLY: A NOVEL. London: F. V.
White, 1895 BMC.

Sylvia penniless and pretty marries a wealthy old man
who is poisoned. Now she's ready to marry the poor man
she loved-Dick-but he's got money now and pursued by
several young woman; one who confesses to the
poisoning, one killed herself-any way the coast was
clear finally for Sylvia to wed Dick SR 79:196 ACAD
47:166 Belle Warrener is one of the other young women ACAD
47:166

002804   THE HONOURABLE JANE. A NOVEL. BY ANNIE
THOMAS. New York: J. W. Lovell, [c1891] NUC. London:
F. V. White, 1892 BMC.

ATH 100:515. The only decent character is Jane; a
"sordid company." "The expedient (that of confessing
an imaginary act of shame) by which <Dolly Abbott>
forces the wretched Capt. Abbott to marry her is about
the vilest thing we have seen suggested in fiction."
SP 69:600. She tells her guardian of a seduction which
never took place; he puts pressure on the man to marry
her. The heroine invites a man into her home, where
she lives alone, and reads sentimental poetry to him,
"which acts as a provocation to nauseating embraces."
ACAD 42:358. Jane's "acts of self-abnegation are
foolish rather than heroic"
SR 74:481. "not a bad specimen of the trashy society
novel." A wife who has run away from her husband and
begs a bachelor to run with her, is returned to
husband, thanks to bachelor's ability to control his
passions.

002805   A LOVER OF THE DAY. A NOVEL. London:
Digby, Long, [1895] BMC.

Sholto Graham is "a profligate and selfish vulgarian."
Worms his way into a young woman's affections, jilts
her, marries an older woman for money, kills her by
his neglect and deserts his child. The young woman is
Patrice. There is also an adventuress along the way of
Sholto's experiences-ATH 106:866.
SR-faithless husband, suffering wife
ACAD 49:114. Sholto and Patrice.

002806   NO HERO, BUT A MAN. A NOVEL. BY ANNIE
THOMAS (MRS. PENDER-CUDLIP). London: F. V. White, 1894
BMC NUC.

SP 73:409. Impersonation of an heir who dies in
railway car; impersonator turns out to be real heir
after all.
ACAD 46:46. There is also a well-developed lady of
middle age, who gets up private theatricals in order
to pose as a statue of Venus in a love-sick poet's
chamber.

002807   OLD DACRES' DARLING; A NOVEL. BY ANNIE
THOMAS (MRS. PENDER-CUDLIP). London: F. V. White, 1892
BMC. Philadelphia: J. B. Lippincott, 1892 NUC.

ATH 100:220. "unsavoury" "Maundering kisses, hot and
clammy embraces." Mrs Dacres has a "sinuous" form,
"writhes" down the stairs. The young baronet sobs
easily, the squire "slobbers."
SP. Traps a man into an engagement, marries the friend
who tries to save him, and as a widow makes fools out
of the men in her husband's family.
PW-"After breaking almost all of the commandments,
ends career as a suicide."
ACAD 41:610. "a very bad young woman" "Her first
impulse, when anything or anyone is inconvenient to
her-cat, dog, uncle, or lover-seems to be to poison it
or to leave it to drown, or something of that kind.
This is not right, and Miss Thomas very properly
punishes her for it."

002808   A PRETENDER. London: Digby, Long, 1905
BMC.

ATH--an adventuress, presented with unpleasant vigour.
"If this sort of girl is going to be the future
heroine of many novels, what is to become of one's
ideal of true girlhood?"

002809   THE ROLL OF HONOR. BY ANNIE THOMAS. New
York: United States Book, [c1891] NUC.

Officer who had been on roll of honor has his career
ruined for a small breach of discipline. Also a love
story. Mystery surrounds the young woman. Her name
nearly ruined. PW
Summer reading. LW

002810   THE SIREN'S WEB; A ROMANCE OF LONDON
SOCIETY. London: Chatto & Windus, 1900 BMC.

Young man struggles between a good love and
infatuation. SP 83:920.

002811   SOCIAL GHOSTS, A NOVEL. London: F. V.
White, 1903 BMC.

Woman of "low birth" with a pretty face revealed to
hero in the end as "foolish and uncultivated." ACAD
65, 268

002812   THAT AFFAIR. London: F. V. White, 1891
BMC.

"Luscious sentimentality" ACAD
Military story of an Irish Lord an Adonis in
appearance about whom there's a scandal that separates
him from his friend. The adventurer Mrs. Carelton has
much to do with it, but the Irish Lord is innocent.
ATH 97 307

002813   UTTERLY MISTAKEN. BY ANNIE THOMAS (MRS.
PENDER CUDLIP). London: F. V. White, 1893 BMC. New
York: Cassell, 1893 NUC.

The wrong persons invariably fall in love... "Women
having two husbands." A puzzle, imbroglio, mix up. BK
News 130:463.
Guy St. Austle has seen a lot of war as a
correspondent. He's well known. His love affair and
that of his cousin. Mrs. Jones is a vulgar character
in her tight dresses. SP 71:496
Ella, Guy, Sir Walter, Ted, May Meredith fall in and
out of love with each other. SR 76:215.
Two brothers: one marries for money; falls in love
with another woman as soon as wife dies, demands this
second woman forego duties and love of parents in
order to marry him. She refuses; he marries another.
The second man resolves to remodel the woman he weds,
fails, revenges his failure, makes her miserable. All
the women characters "worship man." LW 93, 257.
CR 21:145. False ideals.

CUDLIP, MRS. PENDER. See CUDLIP, ANNIE HALL (THOMAS).

CULTER, MARY NANTZ (MACCRAE). B. 1858. United States.

002814   FOUR ROADS TO HAPPINESS: A STORY OF
HOOSIER LIFE. Philadelphia: Union Press, [c1900] NUC.

002815   THE GIRL WHO KEPT UP. Boston: Lee and
Shepard, 1903 NUC.

two young people close friends thru high school (boy
and girl) and keen rivals (the girl winning often) Boy
goes to college, girl helps at home. She's determined
and does keep up with her friend in securing an
education. PW

002816   A JOLLY HALF DOZEN. Cincinnati: Jennings
and Graham, [c1910] NUC.

002817   A PRODIGAL DAUGHTER. Cincinnati: Monfort,
1908 NUC.

Finds love and happiness through religion.

CUMINGS, HILDA P. See PRICE, HILDA P. (CUMINGS).

CUMMINGS, LETTIE M. United States.

002818   PROFESSOR HUSKINS. Boston: R. G. Badger,
[c1916] NUC.

Focuses upon a psychology professor. PW

CUMMINGS, MAY. United States.

002819   THE THRESHOLD OF NIRVANA. Baltimore, Md.:
McLean, [c1916] NUC.

002820   TRANSPLANTED. Baltimore: Saulsbury, 1918
NUC.

CUMMINS, G. D. See CUMMINS, GERALDINE DOROTHY.

CUMMINS, GERALDINE DOROTHY. B. 1890. United Kingdom.

002821   THE LAND THEY LOVED. BY G. D. CUMMINS.
London: Macmillan, 1919 BMC NUC. New York: Macmillan,
1919 NUC.

Record of the progress of an Irish servant into the
arms of the obviously predestined young man. TLS
Kate Carmody returns to Ireland after five years of
domestic service in the states. Works on brother's
farm. Would have married her suitor but he's not the
"whole" man she needs. Goes to Dublin-domestic
servant. Tough, individual, self reliant with a
scarifying tongue refuses to be treated as a drudge or
slave. Feels the tug of the land. SP
Story line seems to be that she works in U.S. as a
domestic, returns to Ireland, almost marries but
becomes disillusioned with the man; goes off to work
again: at the end comes back to the land. NYT

CUNINGHAME, CAROLINE MADELINA FAIRLIE.

002822   THE LITTLE SAINT OF GOD. A HEROINE OF THE
RED TERROR. London: Hurst & Blackett, 1901 BMC.

002823   A SIN OF THE SOUL. London: H. Cox, 1895
BMC.

"a gay dog," loses money, mistreats wife and another
social beauty. Mother-in-law throws him overboard. SR
80:514
Stephen Beauclerk. Mother-in-law causes his death.
"Richly deserves his fate." ACAD 48:314.

002824   THE SLAVE OF HIS WILL: A NOVEL. London:
S. Blackett, 1891 BMC.

Iris Winton falls under the spell of a Russian man
with dangerous psychic powers—the spell persists even
after her marriage. Finally he's convinced to break
his hold. ACAD
She's hypnotized-forced to try poison on husband. ATH
97 470
Iris tall, languid, victim of anemia but absolutely
lovely and rich. Ivan Zellanoff is the villain . Iris
hypnotized chases after him. When he's away, she
marries Jack. When Ivan returns she tries to join him,
husband stops her, she poisons him. Husband knocks
Ivan out but saves him. Ivan touched, goes off willing
that Iris forget all. SR 3-21-91, 358

002825   A WANDERING STAR. London: Ward and
Downey, 1892 NUC BMC.

SP 58:751. Vega, whose father has lost a fortune
gambling, is induced to marry an elderly alcoholic
parvenu. She subsequently elopes with a former lover
and, I think, is saved from the divorce court by her
husband's death. "feverish unwholesomeness."
ATH 99:562. Father was caught cheating.
SR. 73:603. Elopement is only considered. She "mopes
to death."

CUNNINGHAM, FRANCES BERKELEY. Nationality Unknown.

002826   PRIEST OR PRETENDER; A NOVEL. Boston: C.
M. Clark, 1908 NUC.

Story of a priest. PW 4-3-09

CUNNINGHAM, RAY, pseud. See ARTHUR, FRANCES BROWNE.

CUNNINGHAME, ALICE.

002827   DOROTHEA OF ROMNEY MARSH. A ROMANCE OF
THE COMMONWEALTH. London: Heath, Cranton and Ouseley.,
[1914] BMC.

TLS historical romance.

002828   THE LOVE STORY OF GIRALDUS: A ROMANCE OF
THE TWELFTH CENTURY. London: F. Griffith, 1907 BMC
NUC.

ACAD-male hero, a romance.
ATH-Eleanor of Poitou, wife of Henry II is the central
character.

CURLEWIS, ETHEL SYBIL TURNER. 1872-1958. Australia.

002829   THE STORY OF A BABY. London: Ward, Lock
and Bowden, 1895 BMC.

LW 27:47. Young marrieds and their baby. Focus on
their relationship, he inclines to the tyrant, she
only plays at being grown up.

CURRAN, MRS. L. P. M. United States.

002830   EUNICE QUINCE: A NEW ENGLAND ROMANCE. BY
DANE CONYNGHAM. New York: Lovell, Coryell, [c1895]
NUC.

CURTIN, MARTHE TROLY. United Kingdom.

002831   PHRYNETTE. Philadelphia and London: J. B.
Lippincott, 1911 NUC.

002832   PHRYNETTE AND LONDON. London: G.
Richards, [1911] BMC NUC.

French girl comments on English life. 6-3-11 PW

002833   PHRYNETTE MARRIED. London: G. Richards,
1912 BMC.

TLS-pure femininity

CURTIS, ALICE (TURNER). United States.

002834   A CHALLENGE TO ADVENTURE. BY MRS. IRVING
CURTIS. Boston: M. Jones, 1919 NUC.

Young woman left alone in the world "joins forces"
with man seeking a patent on airplane equipment and
"helps thwart a gun spy plot"-PW

CURTIS, FELICIA.

002835   IN THE LEAN YEARS. London and Edinburgh:
Sands, 1913 BMC. Edinburgh:

Persecution of RCs under George II. Heroine loves a
Jacobite, gets him out of Newgate. They marry. ATH

002836   A MORE EXCELLENT WAY. London and
Edinburgh: Sands, 1916 BMC.

TLS religious, pro Catholic, anti Protestant.

002837   UNDER THE ROSE. Edinburgh, London: Sands,
[1911] BMC NUC.

Traditional hist rom. TLS.
Persecutions of the Roman Catholics in the court of
Elizabeth.

CURTIS, ISABEL (GORDON). 1863-1915. United States.

002838   THE CONGRESSWOMAN. Chicago: Browne and
Howell, 1914 NUC BMC.

PW 3-24-14 1111 "Author of "Lapse of Enoch Wentworth"
and "The Woman from Wolverton" has chosen Oklahoma as
scene. After devoting nearly twenty years of married
life to an unresponsive husband in an arid,
desert-country, he dies leaving her with a son and
some land in "Lone Squaw Strip," ten miles of flat
desert. Oil is discovered. The widow becomes a
millionaire and is successfully run for Congress by
the women voters of her state. Her ways of gaining the
election, her thoughts on universal suffrage,
woman-suffrage, women's character and ideals, her
plans for educating her son, etc., are worked into a
plot to prove that woman will be an irresistible force
for public good when she has cultivated her highest
possibilities as a home maker."

002839   THE LAPSE OF ENOCH WENTWORTH. Chicago: F.
G. Browne, 1913 BMC NUC.

"Inspired by the confidence of Dorcas Wentworth,
Andrew Merry, a comic actor, pulls himself together
and writes a play. By reason of an old bond won at
gambling, Enoch Wentworth, the brother of Dorcas,
claims the play and produces it as his own. Zilla
Paget an actress, learns the truth and blackmails
Enoch. Who after being nearly killed by a falling
curtain, recovers and makes restitution." PW By author
of "The Woman from Wolverton."

002840   THE MAKING OF A HOUSEWIFE. New York: F.
A. Stokes, [1906] NUC.

PW-Young bride's instruction.
TX295 Domestic economy.

002841   THE WOMAN FROM WOLVERTON; A STORY OF
WASHINGTON LIFE. New York: Century, 1912 BMC NUC.

PW--Politician's wife.
NYT-By wife of Washington newspaper man. Simple,
sincere, homespun.
NYT-Old fashioned wife and mother.

CURTIS, MARGUERITE.

002842   THE BIAS. Edinburgh and London: W.
Blackwood, 1908 NUC BMC.

Cynthia Jerome has two guardians, one gives her "every
possible occasion for falling into temptation, so as
to prove the bias of woman's nature is naturally bad."
SP
TLS Experiment on an unconscious orphan girl to show
that the natural bias of women is toward evil by a
psychiatrist, and a physician who thinks the opposite.
"Experiment is pleasantly narrated.
ATH--Tragic finish is too lightly handled.

002843   THE DIVIDING LINE. London: C. H. Kelly,
1913 BMC.

Fortune left to woman on condition she marry an R. C.
by age 30. Story follows the trials of the heroine.
ATH

002844   MARCIA: A TRANSCRIPT FROM LIFE. Edinburgh
and London: W. Blackwood, 1909 BMC.

Serious psychological study of Marcia thru girlhood.
Marcia has a dual personality: one evil-one good. Very
sympathetically written, "insightful"-TLS
She begins to feel accursed, evil rather than ill.
LBKM
"Heart gripping" mentally unstable, "liable to
automatic actions on the part of her subconscious self
abhorrent to her normal will" "brave and
loveable"-ATH

002845   OH! FOR AN ANGEL. Edinburgh and London:
W. Blackwood, 1911 BMC.

centers on minister-TLS
involved a love affair-LBKM

CURTIS, MARION. United States.

002846   THE SHADOW OF THE SCARLET SIN; A NOVEL OF
"REAL LIFE". New York: Broadway, [c1910] NUC.

CURTIS, MRS. IRVING. See CURTIS, ALICE (TURNER).

CURTISS, ALICE EDDY. United States.

002847   NEIGHBORS IN BARTON SQUARE. Boston:
Congregational Sunday School & Pub. Soc., [c1892] NUC.

PW-story of lovable, hard-working, self-sacrificing
dressmaker.

002848   THE SILVER CROSS, A STORY OF THE KING'S
DAUGHTERS; AND, MISS MARIGOLD'S TITHES. Boston:
Congregational Sunday School & Pub. Soc., [c1891] NUC.

1)Mary, poor almost invalid, works wonders on Conner
St., a rough neighborhood.
2)Sunny old maid does kindly acts. PW 10-3-91

CURTOIS, M. A. See CURTOIS, MARGARET ANNE.

CURTOIS, MARGARET ANNE. United Kingdom.

002849   THE STORY OF A CIRCLE. BY M. A. CURTOIS.
London: Methuen, [1914] BMC NUC.

ATH-foolish wife starts circle for psychical
experiments, which meets only once. Unconventional and
tragic ending.
TLS 13:214. A study of character. Several mediums
involved.

002850   A SUMMER IN CORNWALL. London: Digby,
Long, 1913 BMC.

ACAD 86:15. young and delicate couple take up
residence. Set of bad people rent house in
neighborhood, bring tragedy. Sordid, without beauty or
dignity.
A woman-promoter of several dishonorable schemes tries
to separate a honeymoon couple. ATH

CUST, ALBINIA LUCY. See WHERRY, ALBINIA LUCY (CUST).

CUTHELL, EDITH E.

002851   A BAIREUTH PILGRIMAGE. London: S. Low,
Marston, 1894 BMC.

SR 78:75. Music mad heroine, guide book.

002852   BY A HIMALAYAN LAKE. BY AN IDLE EXILE,
AUTHOR OF "INDIAN IDYLLS" [ANONYMOUS]. New York:
Cassell, [c1892] NUC. London: Ward & Downey, 1893 BMC.

Much flirting, polo ponies. Heroine is a sensuous
child of nature. She's buried alive in the end. Story
concerns her romances. SR 75:691.
Anglo-Indian. Both hero and heroine Mrs. Helda
Crauston and Alan Adayre die painfully sudden deaths .
But mostly light stuff. ACAD 44:10.
LW 23:181. Romance of Hetty Mainwaring who goes to
India to marry Jim but for a while hesitates between
Jim and Jack.

002853   CAUGHT BY A COOK. London: H. Cox, 1895
BMC.

002854   HER HEART WAS TRUE: A STORY OF THE
PENINSULAR WAR FOUNDED ON FACT, BY AN IDLE EXILE
[ANONYMOUS]. New York: Cassell, 1893 [c] NUC.

Set in Egland coastal quarries, then Spain and
Waterloo. Bessie Sweetapple is true to Robin Norcott
who gets in trouble with smugglers and follows Duke of
Wellington for two years. PW 2-25-93
while he's away, he marries and brings his wife back
when peace comes. Bessie becomes the woman's friend
and even nurses her when she's ill. The woman dies. CR
14, 20:254

002855   IN TENT AND BUNGALOW. BY AN IDLE EXILE
[ANONYMOUS]. New york: Cassell, 1892 [c] NUC. London:
Methuen, 1892 BMC.

002856   ONLY A GUARD-ROOM DOG. London: Methuen,
1892 BMC. New York: Cassell, 1893 NUC.

002857   SWEET IRISH EYES: A NOVEL. London:
Skeffington, 1897 BMC NUC.

Sweet old-fashioned love story. Rich uncle wants
nephew to marry one woman, but he loves another who is
accused of stealing a diamond brooch. SP 79:465.
Eila Ravensheuch and her two lovers, one a cowboy, the
other a wicked barrister. They are cousins, would-be
heirs of the same fortune. All comes out well. ATH
109:573.

002858   THE WEE WIDOW'S CRUISE IN QUIET WATERS.
BY AN IDLE EXILE. London: Ward and Downey, [1895] BMC.
New York: Cassell, [c1892] NUC. (Published anonymously
in the U. S.)

A widow and young woman named Dickie go on a cruise in
the "SPk," their "crew consisting of one 'John'" They
visit lots of places. In the end both marry men. ACAD
47:312
love and yachting combined, living aboard the yacht.
ATH 105:406

CUTTING, CERES.

002859   THE PRAYING GIRL. London: Duckworth, 1912
BMC.

Series of thoughts on many subjects by a "sane,
reasonable" girl. "When in doubt she consults her
lover." Subjects: Anger, Wives, Husbands. ACAD
ATH-Such prayers should not be published.

CUTTING, MARY STEWART (DOUBLEDAY). 1851-1924. United
States.

002860   THE BLOSSOMING ROD. Garden City, New
York: Doubleday, Page, 1914 NUC.

PW 86 11/7/14:1447 "Langshaw had set his heart on
buying himself a Christmas present of a trout rod with
an unexpected ten dollar bill, but one child after
another needed financial support until father's bill
had quite disappeared. Yet Langshaw's Christmas was
not the cut and dried affair of other years after
all."
NYT 1914:585. Christmas family story.

002861   HEART OF LYNN. Philadelphia and London:
J. B. Lippincott, 1904 BMC NUC.

PW attempts to support her family, "a pretty love
story."
NYT-suitable for a young person.

002862   THE LOVERS OF SANNA; A NOVEL. New York:
McBride, Nast, 1912 NUC. London: G. P. Putnam, 1912
BMC.

PW-love story.
ATH love story.

002863   THE UNFORSEEN. Garden City, New York:
Doubleday, Page, 1910 NUC. London: Hodder & Stoughton,
1910 BMC.

Evelyn Gaynor becomes editor of New York magazine. She
has a disheartening struggle, almost decides to go
home when two men come into her life. PW
TLS Love breaks in on the weariness. POV?
Young woman comes to New York to earn a living;
rescued from poverty by marriage. NYT

002864   THE WAYFARERS. New York: McClure, 1908
NUC.

PW-Male husband hero
BKM male husband hero

D., R. K., pseud. See DUNLAP, ROBERTA K.

DABNEY, JULIA PARKER. B. 1850. United States.

002865   LITTLE DAUGHTER OF THE SUN. Boston:
Roberts, 1896 NUC BMC.

PW 10-31-96. Romance and mystery of birth.

DAFFAN, KATIE. United States.

002866   THE WOMAN ON THE PINE SPRINGS ROAD. New
York: Neale, 1910 NUC.

Conversations between young girl and elderly woman
"filled with loving kindness and clearsighted
charity." PW 1-7-11

DAGGETT, MABEL ANNA (POTTER). 1871-1927.

002867   WOMEN WANTED; THE STORY WRITTEN IN BLOOD
RED LETTERS ON THE HOR HE HORIZON OF THE GREAT WORLD
WAR. London and New York: Hodder and Stoughton, 1918
BMC NUC. New York: G. H. Doran, [c1918] NUC. (Fiction
?)

D639 WWI-Women's work; Women-Employment

DAGGETT, MARY (STEWART). 1856-1922. United States.

002868   THE HIGHER COURT. Boston: R. G. Badger,
[c1911] NUC.

Priest marries-PW 12-9-11
NYT-Priest hero marries, thrown out by bishop,
remorse.

002869   MARIPOSILLA: A NOVEL. BY MRS. CHARLES
STEWART DAGGETT. Chicago and New York: Rand, McNally,
1895 NUC.

LW 27:220. Southern Cal. Spanish heroine who loves
U.S. hero and dies when he moves on. Narrated by a
woman from New York staying in San Gabriel.

002870   THE YELLOW ANGEL. Chicago: Browne &
Howell, 1914 BMC NUC.

PW 85 5/9/14 1553 "Most of book is taken up with
series of sketches in which Sue Chang, a Chinese cook,
is the principal character. Effect upon him, first of
the Boxer outbreak, then of the establishment of the
Chinese Republic, is described with considerable
detail. There are also, in the book, three short
stories of Los Angeles's Chinatown."

DAGGETT, MRS. CHARLES STEWART. See DAGGETT, MARY (STEWART).

DAHLGREN, SARAH MADELEINE (VINTON) GODDARD. 1825-1898.
United States.

002871   CHIM, HIS WASHINGTON WINTER. New York: C.
L. Webster, 1892 NUC.

002872   THE SECRET DIRECTORY: A ROMANCE OF HIDDEN
HISTORY. Philadelphia: H. L. Kilner, [c1896] NUC.

PW 12-19-96. The secret directory consist of heads of
Carbonari. Soc. Mazzini is one, he is represented as a
robber. Setting is Washington in 1860. There is a
romance, also a gypsy woman with hypnotic powers.

DAINTREY, LAURA. United States.

002873   ACTAEON. New York: Empire City Pub. Co.,
[c1892] NUC. London and New York: S. Low, Marston,
Searle and Rivington, 1892 BMC.

PW-N.Y. City life amongst the 400. Abuses of modern
society.

002874   THE ARROWS OF LOVE. New York: G. W.
Dillingham, 1893 NUC.

002875   GOLD: A NOVEL. New York: G. W.
Dillingham, 1893 NUC.

Satricial view of New York social woman in this murder
story. head of colossal dry goods establishment
murdered. How the suspect is cleared points out the
different kinds of love two women have for him. PW
7-15-93.

002876   THE KING OF ALBERIA: A ROMANCE OF THE
BALKANS. London: Methuen, 1895 BMC NUC.

   SR-Mysticism, on lines of a fairy tale

DAKE, LAURA M.   United States.

   002877   THE FLIGHT OF THE SHADOW. Cincinnati, O.:
   Editor, 1899 NUC.

DALE, ALICE MARY.

   002878   DUNCAN FALCONER'S REVENGE. London: G.
   Routledge, 1909 BMC.

   Lady Monckton adopts a girl-baby to bring up with her
   own so no one will know which is the true heiress.
   adventurers. TLS

   002879   MARCUS WARWICK, ATHEIST. London: K. Paul,
   Trench, Trubner, 1898 BMC NUC.

   LIT 2:451. He is converted in last chapter, conversion
   accomplished in a "terrible manner."

   002880   THE PERIL OF A LIE: A NOVEL. London: G.
   Routledge, 1898 BMC NUC.

   ACAD 53:602. Bad baronet, good son.
   ATH 111:816. Young woman personates her sister when
   she dies in childbirth and comes to England as a
   widow. Her adventures.
   PW. She marries but lie brings sad experience.

   002881   WITH FEET OF CLAY. London: Swan
   Sonnenschein, 1895 BMC.

   The hero-scoundrel is Julian, then Lord Erlingford.
   Evelyn Conway, beautiful and vindictive, "almost" Lady
   Erlingford. Julian shows his true colors to his wife
   Bertha when he tries to be rid of her. ACAD 47:442
   Later Julian is reformed and he and wife are reunited.
   ATH 105:606
   The peerage. Bertha interrupts Lord Erlingford's
   wedding. She's his wife. SR 79:453

DALE, DARLEY, pseud.   See STEELE, FRANCESCA MARIA.

DALE, ESTER.

   002882   MADAME MARIE, SINGER. London: Leadenhall
   Press, [1901] BMC.

DALE, LUCY AND GERTRUDE MINNIE FAULDING.   Nationality
Unknown.

   002883   MERELY PLAYERS. BY LUCY DALE AND G. M.
   FAULDING. London: T. F. Unwin, [1917] BMC NUC.

   TLS-Close psychological study of Judith, calm and self
   repressed and Madeleine, impulsive and light hearted.
   Dennis marries Madeleine, but finds happiness with
   Judith.
   ATH-Madeleine is a playwright and too wrapped up in
   her productions to give much time to husband.

   002884   TIME'S WALLET. BY LUCY DALE AND G. M.
   FAULDING. London: Sidgwick and Jackson, 1913 BMC NUC.

   Several people correspond; concerns Nan Bosanquet's
   engagement to Everard Shaw, but he's the wrong man.
   Finds Mr. Right, a man she's known all her life and
   Shaw finds someone else. Amusing comments on modern
   life and literary criticism. ACAD
   Two women well educated, independent write to each
   other. Miss Nan Bosanquet and Miss Helen Daventry
   (single, older, close friends, free to travel, read,
   work) write to each other. The letters..."a pleasant
   presentment of modern educated femininity..independent
   and sane." TLS

DALE, MARIANNE.

   002885   CROWNED WITH THE IMMORTALS. London: H. S.
   Nichols, 1896 BMC.

   SR-Hist rom. central figure is Camille Desmoulins.

DALE, MARY.   See DAWSON, MARJORIE.

DALEY, MYRA.   Nationality Unknown.

   002886   JERD CLESS. New York: Cochrane, 1909 NUC.

DALIN, TALMAGE, pseud.   See VILLARI, LINDA (WHITE) MAZINI.

DALLAS, MARY (KYLE).   1830-1897.   United States.

   002887   BILLTRY. New York: Merriam, [c1895] NUC
   BMC.

   Parody on "Trilby," reversing the characters of that
   novel. The three artists are young professional women
   of Gotham, their model is masculine, not feminine.
   Farcical, racey, humorous. PW 2-16-95':321.

DALLYN, VIOLA (MEYNELL).   1886-1956.   United Kingdom.

   002888   COLUMBINE. BY VIOLA MEYNELL. London: M.
   Secker, [1915] BMC NUC. London: G.P. Putnam's Sons,
   1915 NUC.

   Man and two women in his life, one serious the other
   childlike. He chooses the weak one PW 12-27-15
   Lily Peak is a dancer and would-be actress artifical
   in appearance, a drifting mind, first part concerns
   her marr to Dixon. Second part concerns Jennifer Watts
   business like efficient conscientious, Hard working;
   novel studies her complex relationship with Dixon NYT
   hero is a serious critic, first falls for Lily then
   for Jennifer, a secretary who dies and hero goes back
   to Lily. TLS Lily-"appealing to us as a woman to be
   loved" "really beautiful image of this vulgar chorus
   girl, small in mind and heart, tedious in utterance."
   SR-Very high praise for this char study.

   002889   CROSS-IN-HAND FARM. BY VIOLA MEYNELL.
   London: Herbert & Daniel, [1911] NUC BMC.

   LBKM-Dorcas Liliot experimented with her emotions,
   with the cooperation of Evan Davidson, her lover.
   Sounds good. Eng Village life. TLS
   Pleasant enough ATH

   002890   LOT BARROW. BY VIOLA MEYNELL. London: M.
   Secker, 1913 BMC. Boston: R. G. Badger, [1913] NUC.

   She's a servant-a tragedy behind her-her development.
   ATH
   Her first adventure terminates disastrously. Mrs.
   Child another clever portrait-keeps a brave face for
   husband and lodgers, otherwise she's waspish and
   nagging. Lot Barrow with her splendid physique, her
   Atalanta-like power of running. The three men in her
   life. LBKM

   002891   MARTHA VINE, A LOVE STORY OF SIMPLE LIFE
   [ANONYMOUS]. London: Herbert and Daniel, 1910 BMC.

   "slow revelation of her character", 18, moves with
   family from London to the country. Falls in love but
   her love is not returned.
   She's drawn vs her will" to a coarse laborer. ? LBKM.
   ATH
   LBKM--Mar. 1912 p.302.

   002892   MODERN LOVERS. BY VIOLA MEYNELL. Boston:
   R. G. Badger, [c1914] NUC. London: M. Secker, [1914]
   BMC NUC.

   PW 85 4/4/14 p.1160 "Chronicle of the Rutherglen
   family, father, mother and two daughters, Effie and
   Millie. None of them have any real affection for each
   other, each of the girls is only seeking her own ease
   and comfort, things hard to attain in the house of
   their coarse selfish father and shallow mother: Milly
   marries a rich neighbor while Effie carries on love
   affairs with two men, her ingrained insincerity and
   lack of truth making it impossible for her to break
   with the one she no longer cares for. An accident
   clears her path and we leave her happy with the man
   she prefers."
   SR 147:87. Father is a tyrant. Both Millie and Effie
   eventually find husbands.
   ATH 143:59. Intimate character study.
   TLS Study of a liar, "a girl brought up to petty
   deceits by a mother who uses trivial falsehoods as a
   defense from a harsh husband. Effie is "still
   attractive and loveable."
   LBKM-Sisters return home to live with parents; both
   fall in love with vain selfish Clive Maxwell, Sisters
   are human and delightfully feminine. He must "love
   universally" but Millie tires of this and leaves him
   to Effie who has to ask him "very kindly" to press her
   hand.

   002893   NARCISSUS. BY VIOLA MEYNELL. New York: G.
   P. Putnam's sons, 1916 NUC. London: M. Secker, [1916]
   BMC NUC.

   Two brothers, their mother and their friends. PW
   NYT 0

TLS Victor and his various young women.

002894　　　SECOND MARRIAGE. BY VIOLA MEYNELL.
London: M. Secker, [1918] BMC NUC. New York: G. H.
Doran, [1919] NUC.

TLS-Concerns three daughters of country family.
LBKM-O there is a male hero Arnold.
Generations of an Eng. Family--PW.
They own a large farm at the edge of Skirth Fen. Three
daughters, Ismay marries rich. Rose "has nothing
within her" is completely imitative, marries and is a
devoted wife. Ismay's husband dies and she returns.
She's beautiful but not very intelligent, didn't love
her husband but is now passionately in love with
younger man. She gives this man money for a project-to
drain the fen. ? NYT 6-1-19 307

D'ALPENS, MARQUESA, pseud.　See WILLIAMSON, ALICE MURIEL
(LIVINGSTON).

DALRYMPLE, LEONA.　See WILSON, LEONA (DALRYMPLE).

DALTON, EDITH LEVERETT.　United States.

002895　　　A SLIGHT ROMANCE. Boston: Damrell and
Upham, 1896 NUC.

SP 81:123. Study of first love.

DALTON, LILIAN HOWARD.

002896　　　WHICH HERITAGE? London: Constable, 1913
BMC.

Huguenots in France in late 18th century; conflict
between religion and worldly interests. TLS

DALZIEL, L. BEITH, pseud.　See DILL, BESSIE.

DAMPIER, ELEANOR MARY SMITH.

002897　　　CORDELIA. London: A. Melrose, [1916] BMC.

002898　　　INEFFECTUAL FIRES. London: A. Melrose,
1913 BMC.

Ineffectual genius-a man with "painter's blood in his
veins" but no skill, frustration of being inspired but
not being able to paint-days of Sir Joshua Reynolds.
He's a failure. Sabina Blanchflower, harsh, provincial
compels admiration. (What does she do?) ACAD.
Sabina self-sacrificing for him.

002899　　　OIL OF SPIKENARD. A ROMANCE. London: A.
Melrose, 1911 BMC.

Hist romance but Corinna 17, learned daughter of an
Oxford scholar, "very very superior" to her
commonplace aunt and cousins. She aimed to be the
perfect woman. Succumbs to men and "was a prig no
more"? TLS

DANA, OLIVE E.　United States.

002900　　　UNDER FRIENDLY EAVES. Augusta, Maine:
Burleigh and Flynt, 1894 NUC.

DANBY, FRANK, pseud.　See FRANKAU, JULIA (DAVIS).

DANE, CLEMENCE, pseud.　See ASHTON, WINIFRED.

DANE, JOAN.

002901　　　PRINCE MADOG, DISCOVERER OF AMERICA; A
LEGENDARY STORY. London: E. Stock, [1909] BMC. Boston:
Everett, [1916?] NUC.

Trad hist rom. TLS

D'ANETHAN, ELEANORA MARY (HAGGARD).　B. 1860.　United
Kingdom.

002902　　　HER MOTHER'S BLOOD. London: Skeffington,
[1918] BMC.

TLS--wholesome

002903　　　HIS CHIEF'S WIFE. London: Chapman and
Hall, 1897 BMC.

LIT 2:178. Pretty love story in the world of
diplomacy. Brazil.

002904　　　IT HAPPENED IN JAPAN. London: Brown,
Langham, 1906 BMC.

ACAD-- heroine divorces unbearable husband, is victim
of slander, leaves England and comes to Tokyo hoping
for peace. 3 years pass and an old lover appears,
complications which end in her death. POV?
TLS old lover shows up with new wife
ATH--woman wears the martyr's halo also, straining to
the breaking point a strong man's reason after
renunciation of a life long desire

002905　　　THE TWIN-SOUL OF O'TAKE SAN. London: S.
Paul, 1914 BMC.

LBKM The Garlestons quarrel, he goes to Japan, meets
--"ending is obviously happy." O'Take San. Then war
with Russia, to which he goes, returns to wife finding
her nursing baby of dead O'Take-San

002906　　　TWO WOMEN. London: T.F. Unwin, 1909 BMC.

Lady Beaumont and daughter Ruby--their diaries.
Mother's diary reveals that her daughter's father was
not her husband. Lady B. leaves her offensive husband.
Ruby marries not for love, but money TLS
"conspicuous for modernity" ATH

DANIEL, ELOISE MATILDA.　United States.

002907　　　THE TRUTH ABOUT IT, AND OTHER SKETCHES.
St. Paul, Minn.: Dispatch Job Printing, 1897 NUC.

DANIELS, CORA LINN (MORRISON).　B. 1852.　United States.

002908　　　AS IT IS TO BE. Franklin, Mass.:
Published By Cora Linn Daniels, [c1892] NUC. Boston:
Little, Brown, 1900 BMC.

002909　　　THE BRONZE BUDDHA: A MYSTERY. Boston:
Little, Brown, 1899 NUC. London: Gay and Bird, 1899
BMC.

Psychological romance, miracles, Eastern flavor. SP
83:961. An idol from an Eastern temple is lost. The
search which takes the action to New York and a
western town is the story. CR 3 5:1154
LW 31:71. A missing Buddha. Love story. A lot of
Brahminism and Buddhism. Manhatten and Colorado.

002910　　　SARDIA: A STORY OF LOVE. Boston: Lee and
Shepard, 1891 NUC.

Two heirs must marry in order to inherit fortune. They
do, establishing a comrade relation. But wife does
love husband. PW
Wife willing to give him up to another woman who loves
him until she learns the woman was a thief. The
marriage is saved by an Indian mystic. CR

DANIELS, GERTRUDE POTTER.　United States.

002911　　　ESHEK, THE OPPRESSOR. Chicago: Rand,
McNally, [1902] NUC.

About the oil business. NYT 9-03,602.

002912　　　HALAMAR. Chicago, New York: G. M. Hill,
1900 NUC.

PW-love story, NY, apartment of a noted actress.

002913　　　THE WARNERS; AN AMERICAN STORY OF TODAY.
Chicago: Jamieson-Higgins, 1901 NUC.

Typewritest anarchist a woman? socialist themes. BKM
13 (1901) 503
Futile tale of true love, honest toil, loud-mouthed
anarchism, dynamite... NATION
Women don't seem to be involved in politics. NYT

DANILEVESKAYA, LAPPO.　See DANILEVSKAIA, NADEZHDA
ALEKSANDROVNA (LIUTKEVICH) LAPPO.

DANILEVSKAIA, NADEZHDA ALEKSANDROVNA (LIUTKEVICH) LAPPO.　B.
1876.　Europe.

002914　　　MICHAIL GOURAKIN; THE HEART OF A RUSSIAN.
BY LAPPO-DANILEVESKAYA. New York: R. M. McBride, 1917
NUC. (Pub. in Eng. under title: Michail; or, The Heart
of a Russian.)

002915　　　MICHAIL; OR, THE HEART OF A RUSSIAN. A
NOVEL IN FOUR PARTS. BY A RUSSIAN LADY [ANONYMOUS].
London: W. Heinemann, [1917] NUC.

World of the highest circles-a "society where the
mistakes of legal marriage are ignored and its members

live in monagamy, polygamy, promiscuity or polyandry without any more considerations." All described with a simple unconsciousness of outside judgement. SR

DANNER, MRS. PAUL. United Kingdom.

002916   THE RED LAUGH. BY GERVE BARONTI. Boston: Cornhill, [c1918] NUC.

DANVERS, CLARICE.

002917   ADRIAN BURNABY: THIEF. London: C. Danvers, 1902 BMC.

002918   A STOLEN OPERA. London: C. A. Pearson, 1901 BMC.

DANVIN, CATHERINE RADZIWILL KOLB.

002919   BECAUSE IT WAS WRITTEN. London: Cassell, 1916 BMC.

TLS-Horrors of the great war.
ATH Gr war fulfills a prophecy

002920   THE DISILLUSIONS OF A CROWN PRINCESS; BEING THE STORY OF THE COURTSHIP AND MARRIED LIFE OF CECILE, EX-CROWN PRINCESS OF GERMANY. New York and London: J. Lane, 1920 BMC.

PW-Account of unhappy marriage told by intimate friend.

D'APERY, HELEN (BURRELL). 1842-1915. United States.

002921   THE SOCIABLE GHOST. BEING THE ADVENTURES OF A REPORTER. WRITTEN DOWN BY OLIVE HARPER AND ANOTHER. New York: J. S. Ogilvie, [c1903] NUC.

Fantasy about a male reporter. PW 8-1-03

002922   WHAT DO YOU THINK? A NOVEL. BY OLIVE HARPER. New York: G.W. Dillingham, 1895 NUC.

Vices and follies of society people attacked.
6-8-95:911 PW

DARCHE, MURIEL.

002923   COQUETTE. London: J. Long, 1909 BMC.

Matrimonial and other experiences of woman who becomes Lady Walford. TLS

002924   THE PORTERS OF WOODTHORPE. London: J. Long, 1908 BMC.

TLS-families in a small town, pleasing, simple, will not harrow or depress.

D'ARCY, ELLA. 1851-1939. United Kingdom.

002925   THE BISHOP'S DILEMMA. London and New York: J. Lane, 1898 BMC.

LIT 3:209. Story of upper-class Romanism in England, study of bishop.
ACAD 53:417. Worldly bishop has problem of conscientious young priest, Father Taylor. Mary Deane involved.
ACAD 53:603. After she is fired as Lady Wilford's companion, he takes to drink and must be moved to another sphere. Story does not mention what happens to Mary.
BKM 8:164. Lady Wilford central character, only one with any vitality.

DARDAY, OLGA.

002926   CRAB APPLES; HUNGARIAN SOCIETY SKETCHES. London: M. Goschen, 1914 BMC.

ACAD 87:155. Middle-class, discontented wives. A "suffrage pamphlet" of Hungarian origin. Sketches and stories-wives-theme.

DARE, ARLINE, pseud. See BOYDEN, EMMA.

DARING, HOPE, pseud. See JOHNSON, ANNA.

DARMESTETER, MADAME JAMES. See DUCLAUX, AGNES MARY FRANCES (ROBINSON) DARMESTETER.

DARR, LIZZIE (TOWNSEND).

002927   THROUGH TROUBLED WATERS: A STORY FOUNDED

ON FACT. FROM THE FRENCH. BY MRS. FRANCIS J. A. DARR. New York: Town Topics, 1895 NUC.

PW-Sir Charles Dilke's divorce proceedings. Young and pretty unprincipled woman has no difficulty in influencing a jury and ruining a public man.

DARR, MRS. FRANCIS J. A. See DARR, LIZZIE (TOWNSEND).

DARRELL, GRATIANA.

002928   THE HAUNTED LOOKING GLASS. London: Digby, Long, [1897] BMC.

DART, EDITH C. M. United Kingdom.

002929   LIKENESS. London: Mills & Boon, 1911 BMC.

A close resemblance between two women enables a poor Typewriter to impersonate the other at a fashionable ball. ATH

002930   THE LOOM OF LIFE. London: Mills & Boon, 1916 BMC.

TLS-love story.

002931   MIRIAM. London: E. Arnold, 1908 BMC.

TLS-Story of a girl of the tenant class placed, as "general factotum" in a manor in a doubtful social position.
ATH O

002932   REBECCA DREW. London: Mills & Boon, 1910 BMC.

BM-simple rural idyll-refreshing
TLS.-simple rural idyll-refreshing
BAKER 32-129

002933   SAREEL. London: P. Allan, 1920 BMC. New York: Boni and Liveright, [c1922] NUC.

TLS Conv. lines, story of work house girl and her love.
SP-becomes farm servant, development of her character.
LBKM-Careful workmanship, like D. Richardson.

DASHWOOD, EDMEE ELIZABETH MONICA (DE LA PASTURE). 1890-1943. United Kingdom.

002934   CONSEQUENCES. BY E. M. DELAFIELD. London and New York: Hodder & Stoughton, [1919] BMC NUC.

Alex Clare might have been "happy & useful" "if she had met with more sympathy" She's too self conscious, too irresolute, can't say or do the right thing at the right time, clumsy, lacks perspective. Nothing went right for her. Branded black sheep of her arist. family, makes herself more alienated by breaking engag. to man she found too stupid to tolerate. Sought from God what had been denied her by man-that effort failed.-joined order in convent. Demanded and got released after 10 yrs. returned to world as a real outcast. There's no place for her. Further estranged friends and relations by act of embezzlement (She's penniless at that point) Every thread that bound her to life being cut off, drowns self. Suffered the aimlessness of a Vict. ed., felt a failure in parents' eyes because she did not attract men, suffered spiritual loneliness of convent. No place for her in "This world's economy." TLS, SP

002935   THE PELICANS. BY E. M. DELAFIELD. London: W. Heinemann, [1919] BMC NUC. New York: A.A. Knopf, 1919 NUC.

TLS- Mrs Tregaskis, guardian of Hazel who marries happily but against her wishes, Frances who dies in a convent, Rosamund who on last page gives her hand to a man.
LBKM- All 3 eventually defy overbearing mothering and determine their own lives.
SP-Excellent description of the inhuman world of the convent. There is a Nina Severing, older woman whose life is a succession of poses and is objectionable.
SR. Nina and Bertha are intimate enemies.
PW: "When Bertha misunderstands her unfortunate protegees, she is like an elephant trampling down their souls with joyful trumpetings."
Bertie Tregaskis is a bore and nuisance first to her children, then to self. Piteous. Author makes her sympathetic. BKM 6-19,457
Frances Grantham 18 dies in a convent to which her sister was denied admittance. Two sisters Frances and

Rosemund go to live with cousin Bertha, a jovial woman
who has a daughter of her own but raises the three
well. Frances decides to be a nun, enters convent.
Story describes the suffering this causes her sister
who loves her. NYT

002936   TENSION. BY E. M. DELAFIELD. London:
Hutchinson, [1920] BMC. New York: Macmillan, 1920 NUC.

TLS- Pauline breaks off engagement to returning
soldier who is disabled. She is willing to live with
man whose wife is institutionalized for alchohol, but
he is concerned about soc. status. She is
superintendent of commercial college. Lady Rossiter
makes trouble for her (nothing violent)
LBKM- Lady Rossiter's test of conversation "Is it
kind, is it wise, is it true?"
PW-Humorous novel concerning the defenses put up by
two fine and sensitive spirits against a society of
vulgarians.
NYT 10-17-20 p. 12

002937   THE WAR-WORKERS. BY E. M. DELAFIELD. New
York: A.A. Knopp, 1918 NUC. London: Heinemann, [1918]
NUC BMC.

PW-Satire on woman war worker who finds war the
opportunity for her ego.
TLS-o
LBKM-Miss Vivian often needlessly overworks herself
and others because she is actuated not by a passionate
patriotism but by a love of exercising authority,
being admired, feeling indispensable. Of her staff,
only Miss Jones sees thru her. Two men play minor
parts, otherwise all women. Kindness and tolerance
beneath the satire.
NYT Nov 3, '18 p. 466-0

002938   ZELLA SEES HERSELF. BY E. M. DELAFIELD.
New York: A.A. Knopf, 1917 NUC. London: W. Heinemann,
[1917] NUC BMC.

Thru childhood tries to make self charming by agreeing
with every body until she develops an unreal self,
acting a part. Almost ready to marry a man like
herself, gets a true perspective of herself thru the
aid of her cousin. PW
From 7-19 French father dead, Eng. mother. She's
imaginative and introspective "sees herself always
posing," depends on opinions of others exclusively.
Her life in a convent, able to see self in true
perspective for the 1st time. Refuses to marry-story
ends there. TLS
Mother dies; when she is 14 hypersensitive,
over-anxious to please "drawn with sympathetic
understanding" SR
"Zella is a self-centered person who is always trying
to be what she thinks the world will admire" made
likeable.
BAKER, 32, p. 135 , NYT 381, 10-7-17

DASKAM, JOSEPHINE. See BACON, JOSEPHINE DODGE (DASKAM).

DASKAM, JOSEPHINE DODGE. See BACON, JOSEPHINE DODGE
(DASKAM).

DASKEIN, MRS. See DASKEIN, TARELLA (QUIN).

DASKEIN, TARELLA (QUIN). Australia.

002939   A DESERT ROSE. BY MRS. DASKEIN. London:
W. Heinemann, 1912 BMC NUC. New York: E. P. Dutton,
1913 NUC.

TLS Australian bush, Betty; a squatter's daughter who
plays her part in the drama of one woman and two men.

002940   FRECKLES. London: A. Moring, 1910 BMC
NUC.

002941   KERNO. A STONE. London: W. Heinemann,
1914 BMC.

LBKM-Judith Acton, fleeing from a brutal husband,
seeks rest and peace at Kerno, Wynne Holland's remote
but prosperous sheep farm, from which he draws his
income but resides in Melbourne. He is an elegant
lawyer. Judith draws him back to Kerno, they have a
child, Margaret. City proves too strong for him, but
he escape Kerno only to die.
ATH 144:96
TLS 13:358

DAULTON, AGNES WARNER (MACCLELLAND). B. 1867.

002942   THE GENTLE INTERFERENCE OF BAB. New York

and London: D. Appleton, 1912 BMC NUC.

PW-not clear.
PZ 7

002943   THE MAROONING OF PEGGY. New York and
London: D. Appleton, 1915 BMC NUC.

DAVID, MARIE (DE SAFFRON). 1831-1885.

002944   CAPTAIN POSCOFF: A STORY OF THE FRENCH
REVOLUTION. BY RAOUL DE NAVERY. New York: P. J.
Kenedy, 1899 NUC. (Tr. from French by P. P. S.)

002945   THE GALLEY SLAVE. AN INCIDENT IN THE LIFE
OF ST. VINCENT OF PAUL. FROM THE FRENCH OF RAOUL DE
NAVERY. London: St. Anselm's Society, 1893 NUC.

DAVIDGE, FRANCES. Nationality Unknown.

002946   THE GAME AND THE CANDLE. New York: D.
Appleton, 1905 BMC NUC.

Wife wants a divorce. PW 10-28-05

002947   THE MISFIT CROWN. New York: D. Appleton,
1904 BMC NUC.

PW-unhappy mrg.
NYT-0

DAVIDSON, LILLIAS CAMPBELL. United Kingdom.

002948   THE CONFESSIONS OF A MATCHMAKING MOTHER.
New York: J. F. Taylor, 1902 NUC. London: T. F. Unwin,
1901 BMC.

002949   FALSE GOLD. London: Digby, Long, 1909
BMC.

Brilliant Gabrielle Strangeways steals diamonds, lets
another girl suffer for it. TLS

002950   A GIRL'S BATTLE. London: S. W. Partridge,
[1904] BMC 1913 [] NUC.

002951   THE GREEN POWDER. London: Aldine, [1914]
BMC.

002952   HOUSES OF CLAY. London: S. W. Partridge,
[1912] BMC.

ATH-sentimental, of stolen invention, Male, etc.

002953   THE LOST MILLIONAIRE. London: Cassell,
1908 BMC.

PW-woman doctor involved.
TLS-inheritance plot.
ATH-inheritance plot.

002954   PURPLE AND FINE LINEN. London: Ward,
Lock, 1916 BMC.

TLS-another inheritance.
ATH

002955   A SWORD IN AMBUSH. London: Cassell, 1909
BMC.

Margaret Wyldbeck's strange action when alone with her
uncle before his death and the fortune he left her.
TLS

002956   THE THEFT OF A HEART. London: C. A.
Pearson, 1902 BMC.

ATH 3-22-02 Travels-not helpful.

DAVIDSON, MARIE AGNES. Nationality Unknown.

002957   THE TWO RENWICKS. New York and London: F.
T. Neely, 1899 NUC.

High spirited girl loves an argument well ed. but when
she meets her match argues most about rel. NYT

DAVIDSON, MARY M.

002958   EDWARD THE EXILE. A ROMANCE OF HISTORY.
London: Hodder & Stoughton, 1901 BMC.

DAVIDSON, MRS. DAN M. United States.

002959   ALICE MOON; OR, A BROTHER'S CRIME.
Detroit: Speaker Printing Co., 1898 NUC.

DAVIDSON, O. M. See DAVIDSON, OLIVIA MAITLAND.

DAVIDSON, OLIVIA MAITLAND.

002960   THE LETTERS OF EVE. BY O. M. DAVIDSON,
EVE OF THE TATLER. London: Constable, 1918 BMC.

Soupy letters in fashionable babyisms. SR

DAVIES, HELEN. See TAINTER, HELEN (DAVIES).

DAVIESS, MARIA (THOMPSON). 1872-1924. United States.

002961   ANDREW THE GLAD. Indianapolis:
Bobbs-Merrill, [c1913] BMC NUC.

"Caroline Darrah Brown, daughter of a splendid
southern mother and a despicable "carpetbagger" father
who has wronged her mother's dearest friends, comes to
Major Buchanan's home after her father's death. Andrew
Sevier falls in love with her against his will, but
believes marriage with her to be impossible, as her
father ruined old Andrew Sevier. The straightening out
of this complicated situation makes the story. David
Kildau and his uncertain Phoebe make a lively strain
in the tale." PW
"A southern story in which two heroines share the
honors. One is Phoebe Donelson, daughter of an old
southern house, a plucky young woman who insists on
earning her own living when the family fortune fails;
the other is Caroline Darrah Brown whose mother had
married a despised "carpetbagger," and who comes back
from the north to give, anonymously, a monument to her
mother's native town in honor of the women of the
confederacy. There are two heroes in the tale, too,
and in addition to these there is a devoted pair of
middle-aged lovers, "The Major" and "Mrs. Matilda,"
who lend a guiding hand in the affairs of the young
people."BRD.

002962   BLUE-GRASS AND BROADWAY. New York:
Century, 1919 BMC NUC.

"Small town Kentucky girl...plunged into theatrical
work" in NYC PW

002963   THE DAREDEVIL. Chicago: Reilly and
Britton, [c1916] NUC BMC.

Modern young heroine disguises self as a man. Marquise
de Grez comes to America to get her rich uncle to help
her and her lame brother. In disguise becomes her
uncle's secretary and "has a most adventurous career
in that capacity and her man's attire." PW
NYT proves her right to nickname of title by her
various exploits. Mrg at end.

002964   THE ELECTED MOTHER; A STORY OF WOMAN'S
EQUAL RIGHTS. Indianapolis: Bobbs-Merrill, [c1912] BMC
NUC.

This little story of the young mother who was elected
mayor of Wahoo city is reprinted from a book of short
stories by the author.

002965   THE GOLDEN BIRD. New York: Century, 1918
NUC.

PW-Ann leaves Mathew and his wealth to return home and
restore family fortunes by raising chickens.
Counselled by Adam, she was financially successful.
NYT Sept 22 '18 p 408. 0

002966   THE HEART'S KINGDOM. Chicago: Reilly &
Britton, [c1917] BMC NUC.

Charlotte Powers, agnostic, resents the Reverend but
ends up marrying him after her spiritual awakening. PW
Because he's won over everyone in her town including
her friends in her absence. NYT

002967   THE MATRIX. New York: Century, 1920 BMC
NUC.

PW-Nancy Hanks' courtship and marriage.
NYT 4/4/20 Nancy was "probably the first woman in
Kentucky to enter trade and secure her own financial
independence" (Author). was a weaver and dyer
(business woman).
Lincoln, Nancy Hanks 1784-1818-Fic.

002968   THE MELTING OF MOLLY. Indianapolis:
Bobbs-Merrill, [c1912] NUC.

PW obesity in a widow

002969   MISS SELINA LUE AND THE SOAP-BOX BABIES.
Indianapolis: Bobbs-Merrill, [1909] NUC.

Village storekeeper, widow. NYT
A super mom figure who comes to everyone's rescue with
her comfort, help. NYT

002970   OUT OF A CLEAR SKY. A NOVEL. New York and
London: Harper, [1917] BMC NUC.

Fairy tale (mod) princess from one country, prince
from another wicked uncle, a chase, a rescue by hero.
PW
Modern version of fairly tale-American hero rescues
Belgium princess lost in forest NYT
Delightful fairy tale for grownups. NYT 6-3-17, 218

002971   OVER PARADISE RIDGE; A ROMANCE. New York
and London: Harper and London, [1915] NUC.

A love story of to-day BKM 42 1915-16
BKM 42 1915-16
Must choose between poet and farmer. PW 11-6-15
Given much freedom by parents but all her affectionate
demonstrations are innocent. "breezy readable" NYT

002972   PHYLLIS. New York: Century, 1914 BMC NUC.

PW 86 9/26/14:966 "Phyllis grew to be almot sixteen
with only a multi-millionaire father, an invalid
mother and no friends until she came to Byrdsville.
Then because she was plucky and honest as well as
awkwardly loving she captured the hearts of young and
old in the aristocratic little town and became one of
its leading citizens." Girls book

002973   THE ROAD TO PROVIDENCE. Indianapolis:
Bobbs Merrill, [c1910] NUC.

Tenn. country folk; mother Mayberry with her great
heart, good sense, finds solutions to all problems BKM
adds 0 NYT
BKM v32 1910-11 But there is a singer
Doctor loves woman a famous singer but sounds sent. PW

002974   ROSE OF OLD HARPETH. Indianapolis:
Bobbs-Merrill, [c1911] NUC. London: Religious Tract
Society, [1914] BMC.

Happy love story about Rose and engineer. 9-30-11 PW

002975   SUE JANE. New York: Century, 1912 BMC
NUC.

002976   THE TINDER-BOX. New York: Century, 1913
BMC NUC.

PW 84 11/8/13:1527 "Tale of how a southern belle who
has become imbued with woman's rights goes back to her
Tennessee home to put into practice her convictions.
Chief of these convictions is the right of a woman to
propose to the man she loves. What happens when these
new ideas are introduced makes a merry, whimsical
little story.
"What happened to a So. beauty who decided to break
the deadlock of sex inequality by proposing to the man
of her choice-and induced the girls of Tenn. to follow
her example." comes to Harpeth Valley...and does more
for its women in a few months than they have been able
to do for themselves in thrice as many years. NYT 606
(1913) 1913 NYT 550
BKM-Evelina, after several yrs of art study in Paris,
returns to Harpeth Valley with very advanced ideas.
Jane Mathers, a New England millionaire new woman; is
a firebrand in the community, the comm. of Glendale
grows to like the women's movement.

002977   THE TREASURE BABIES. Indianapolis: Bobbs
Merrill, [c1911] NUC.

DAVIS, ARLINE E. United States.

002978   THE ROMANCE OF GUARDAMONTE. New York: J.
S. Tait, 1896 [c] NUC.

LW 27:330. Two American girls in Italy and their
romances.

DAVIS, EDITH (SMITH). 1859-1917. United States.

002979   WHETHER WHITE OR BLACK, A MAN. Chicago,
New york, Toronto: F. H. Revell, 1898 NUC. London:
S.W. partridge, 1898 BMC. (Eng. ed. title: Major
Brown; or Whether White or Black, a Man!)

DAVIS, ELIZABETH S.

002980   ROPES OF SAND. New York: Guarantee Pub.
Co., [1906] NUC.

PW-Girl from Kentucky with beautiful voice is made
pregnant by visiting preacher. They meet years later.

DAVIS, ELLEN LOUISA.

002981   ERRINGTON HALL, OR MARGARET'S ADVENTURE.
London: R.T.S., [1895] BMC.

Sir Reginald is shy and reserved: is brusque with
women, a bachelor trying to keep his distance from
women. Margaret Willmore gradually wins him. SP 75:801

DAVIS, ETHEL. United States.

002982   WHEN LOVE IS DONE: A NOVEL. Boston: Estes
& Lauriat, 1895 NUC.

"The title stands for a problem that looms up large in
some women's lives." Set near Boston, a modern and
very personal story of Mary Eldredge's quiet
tragedy-which is "women's tragedy." LW 26:331.

DAVIS, HARRIET RIDDLE. United States.

002983   IN SIGHT OF THE GODDESS: A TALE OF
WASHINGTON LIFE. Philadelphia: J. B. Lippincott, 1896
NUC BMC.

LIT 27:235. Love story, unsmooth.
PW 6-20-96. Alternate narration by hero and heroine.
Washington social life.

DAVIS, HELEN.

002984   ANGUS MURRAY. London: Sonnenschein, 1897
BMC.

Account of a man of sterling char. who struggles vs. a
terrible weakness. The young woman who might have
saved him doesn't. Descriptions of Aust. home life.
LBKM 12:45

002985   A DANGEROUS INTIMACY. London: Simpkin,
Marshall, Hamilton, Kent, [1899] BMC.

DAVIS, JESSIE AINSWORTH.

002986   A FORSAKEN GARDEN. London: J. Long, 1909
BMC.

Story of self-sacrifice of woman for father. TLS
Self-renunciation. ACAD

002987   WHEN HALF-GODS GO. Edinburgh and London:
W. Blackwood, 1907 BMC.

Mary's moment of compromising passion. How this
related to husband and lover. A fine study. Looks
good. LBKM 4-07,31 Mary wooed by one man, an
unfortunate incident mars her happiness, marries
another? TLS
Mary's mother and brother die; father remarries; she
goes off with Beaton who puts off the marriage.
Assured he'll marry her to save her reputation. But
she runs off before the wedding, lives in terror
someone will discover her sin. Later marries a man who
thinks her fear ridiculous. SP

DAVIS, KATE. United States.

002988   A PERILOUS PATH; OR, APPLES OF SODOM. New
York: Abbey Press, [c1901] NUC.

DAVIS, LEELA B. United States.

002989   A MODERN ARGONAUT. San Francisco:
Whitaker and Ray, [c1896] NUC.

LW 29:252. Kate Merrill is the argonaut and the helper
and saver of her family. Barbara Merrill falls for
Reginald who engages himself to someone else. In a fit
of pique she marries an elderly suitor.

DAVIS, M. E. M. See DAVIS, MARY EVELYN (MOORE).

DAVIS, MARTHA CAROLY. United States.

002990   THE REFINER'S FIRE. New York: J. Pott,
1896 NUC.

PW 4-4-96. Her husband died a drunkard. Her other

suitor, now a rich successful lawyer, is a
disinterested friend in her adversity. Must struggle
to educate Phillip and Dolly.

DAVIS, MARY DIUGUID. United States.

002991   SHE WAITED PATIENTLY. Lynchburg, Va.: J.
P. Bell, 1900 NUC.

DAVIS, MARY EVELYN (MOORE). 1852-1909. United States.

002992   THE LITTLE CHEVALIER. BY M. E. M. DAVIS.
Boston: Houghton, Mifflin, 1903 NUC.

Adventure and love. 11-21-03 PW, NYT 03,860

002993   THE PRICE OF SILENCE. BY M. E. M. DAVIS.
London: A. Constable, 1907 BMC. Boston: Houghton,
Mifflin, 1907 NUC BMC.

Romance of an aristocratic woman with "taint of Negro
blood." 4-13-07 PW
Civil war story. LBKM 8-07, 178
TLS-very crude. Sensation novel.

002994   THE QUEEN'S GARDEN. BY M. E. M. DAVIS.
Boston and New York: Houghton, Mifflin, 1900 NUC.

NYT 1900:406. Yellow fever in New Orleans. Romance of
strangely met lovers in Creole garden.
PW-Noel, an orphan, arrives to visit her aunt to find
she is sick and house is quarantined. Male neighbor
next door. Pretty love story.

002995   UNDER THE MAN-FIG. BY M. E. M. DAVIS.
Boston and New York: Houghton, Mifflin, 1895 NUC BMC.

Wholesome love story set in the So. Named after an
immense tree in Texas where political campaigns are
planned. LW 26:154

002996   THE WIRE CUTTERS. BY M. E. M. DAVIS.
Boston and New York: Houghton, Mifflin, 1899 NUC.
London: A.P. Watt, [1899] BMC.

Texas settlers fence their land; wire-cutters let in
the cattle to get at water. Hero resembles his
mother's ex-husband, now divorced from his mother. His
mother and father hate him. His brother is the
villain. PW 55:369
Mother had no children by first marriage. Hero is son
of her second husband. The kid is banished at age 4
because of the resemblance. Ex husband adopts him.
Then his own life on ranch in west. LW 30:92
W. Texas. Purchasers of public lands put up fences
regardless of rights of way to water. The cattle hurt
on fences getting to water and wire cutters cut the
fences. Two brothers one resembles mother's divorced
first husband so much he repels both parents. Is
adopted by chance by his father. Two brothers are very
different. Their meeting. NYT 4-1-99, 219

DAVIS, NORAH. B. 1878. United States.

002997   THE NORTHERNER. New York: Century, 1905
BMC NUC.

Story of a capitalist in the So. 10-14-05. PW

002998   THE OTHER WOMAN. New York: Century, 1920
BMC NUC.

PW-man's struggle with a dual personality and
resulting crisis in his married life.
NYT 1920:321. Rev. calls this a "source novel", the
kind of novel which starts a new fashion in fiction
and which will have an inevitable wake of imitators. A
man disappears after kissing his wife and son goodbye
to go to work, and has been missing for 7 years.

002999   WALLACE RHODES; A NOVEL. New York and
London: Harper, 1909 NUC BMC.

Unconventional plot: father and son love Veronica. PW
4-10-09

003000   THE WORLD'S WARRANT. Boston:
Houghton-Mifflin, 1907 BMC NUC.

A highly sophisticated society girl advertises for a
husband for native girl "ignorant, tarnished" both end
up loving the man who replies. 5-11-07 PW
Alabama girl's love story. NYT
Getting a wife by advertising. Story of illiterate
girl who has fallen and the efforts of two women, one
unmarried, to get her wed by answering an ad for her.

DAVIS, PEARL ULILLA. United States.

003001　　　　IGNORANCE UNVEILED. New York, London: Broadway, [1904] NUC.

DAVIS, REBECCA (HARDING). 1831-1910. United States.

003002　　　　DOCTOR WARRICK'S DAUGHTERS: A NOVEL. New York: Harper, 1896 NUC.

LW 77:154. The dr. is a dreary inventor, his wife a saint who died from bearing his burdens. Penn. contrasted with the South. Love of money misleads one daughter, love of simplicity keeps the other true and happy.
PW 2-22-1896. Their romances and marriages. Older sister marries for money, is unhappy. Ann marries unselfish young man, is happy. Mildred-selfish, fond of money, has two suitors, one from South she loves, the other wealthy from Penn. She chooses the latter. Then learns the other had wealth too. The Doctor is a fussy tyrant capable of sacrificing the family's necessities to his selfish whims. The daughters, one tall, other short, are inconsistent characters. The tall one begins with an inherent irresistible charm, but becomes repelling--without explanation. The other starts out sly, becomes soulful, reverts to slyness--again without explanation. Review goes on to discuss two male characters--not plot.
BKM 3:166. Anti-Southern bias. Novel is a shapeless mass.

003003　　　　FRANCES WALDEAUX: A NOVEL. New York: Harper, 1897 NUC. London: Osgood,McIlvaine, 1897 BMC.

Self-sacrificing mother lives completely thru her son. She's shocked when he falls in love with a woman he first thought vulgar. "The after-effects of the son's marriage upon the mother's char open up for the latter depths of emotion and actualities of evil in her own soul which she had never faintly suspected..."
Powerful story of her later life. Our sympathy is with her. CR 26, 30:251.
Makes a living writing a daily column "of Rabelasian fun." Son marries without her (his mother's) knowledge. Almost murders the new wife who is an unscrupulous woman. Melod. BKM 5:167.
PW 12-19-96. She travels with spoiled son; he meets and marries an adventuress, then separation and estrangement of mother and son. Her hurt and dislike of mrge lead to her disordered mind, tragedy.

DAVIS, VARINA ANNE JEFFERSON. 1864-1898. United States.

003004　　　　A ROMANCE OF SUMMER SEAS: A NOVEL. New York and London: Harper & Brothers, 1898 NUC.

CR 33;104. Motley group of people on board a steamer. Slander is the keynote. Woman slanders one of her own sex.
NYT 1898:485. Male narrator, a traveller, a kind of bore called the Globe Trotter, in the smoking room of a Bar Harbour summer house. A group of strangers on a steamer near Singapore includes a young Englishman travelling in charge of a young woman, Minerva Primrose. A spinster, a disciple and missionary of Eastern religions starts a story reflecting on her reputation. This leads to misunderstandings among men, a duel. When all is worked through, Minerva and Englishman marry.
LW 29:279."Nothing pleasant or innocent, malodorous. Let our women novelists leave themes and characters like these to the daily papers, and let them devote their gifts to the delineation of things that are pure and lovely and of good report...we will give Miss V.A.J.D. one more chance..."(Veiled Doctor was cancerous, disgusting too.)

003005　　　　THE VEILED DOCTOR: A NOVEL. New York: Harper & Brothers, 1895 NUC.

Old decaying town and arist. Hopelessly behind the times. "The utilzation of a disfiguring disease "concealed by a veil or mask". The sacrificing love of a repentant woman." Focus on the Dr. and his wife. CR 24:103
has cancer of the face, hides behind black crepe. Heroine is a fool and a liar; hero, a prig BKM 2:54
Young wife had been restless, before the tragedy hits her husband. Then realizes she threw hers and husband's happiness away. Illness described in minute detail. BOOK NEWS:157:27

DAVY, E. M. See DAVY, MRS. E. M., Also LEE, SUSAN RICHMOND

AND MRS. E. M. DAVY.

DAVY, MRS. E. M.

003006　　　　CALUMNIES. BY E. M. DAVY. London: C. A. Pearson, 1899 BMC.

They are of the common variety and true love triumphs in the end. LIT 4:555.
How a young man mismanaged his relations with his wife. ACAD 56:486

003007　　　　SEVEN OF THEM. BY E. M. DAVY. London: W. Scott, 1903 BMC.

DAVY, MRS. E. M., jt. au. See LEE, SUSAN RICHMOND AND MRS. E. M. DAVY.

DAWE, GWENDOLINE L.

003008　　　　THE WAY OF THE TRANSGRESSOR. London: Ward, Lock, 1909 BMC.

DAWN, MARIE.

003009　　　　JOIE DE VIE. A ROMANCE. London: H. J. Drane, [1913] BMC.

Story retold from a girl's diary by her sister concerns family life and love of a man. ATH

DAWS, MAUD. United States.

003010　　　　CRANKADOM. Lincoln, Neb.: Jacob North, 1895 NUC.

DAWSON, AGNES.

003011　　　　THE VIRGIN AND THE SCALES. Bristol: J. W. Arrowsmith, 1901 BMC.

DAWSON, LISABETH. Nationality Unknown.

003012　　　　A MISJUDGED HERO. BY BETH. New York: Neely, [c1900] NUC.

DAWSON, MARJORIE. United States.

003013　　　　BOTTLED SUNSHINE. BY MARY DALE. New York: Bookery, [c1912] NUC.

003014　　　　DOLL-LAND. New York: [c1914] NUC.

003015　　　　MISS EAGLE, THE SUFFRAGETTE. BY MARY DALE. New York City: Aberdeen, 1909 NUC.

The matter of woman suffrage discussed by birds. Miss Eagle is the leading suffragette and the Magpie, the Raven, Mrs. Barnyard , the Owl, and the rest join the discussion. NYT

DAWSON, MRS. FREDERICK.

003016　　　　THE UPPER HAND. London: G. Richards, 1909 BMC.

Fricka Stickland drives a smart motor car. (Lady Mabel is her bosom friend), but she cheats at cards, levied toll on her rich relatives to pay her debts. She's not worthy of her suitor. TLS

DAY, F. E.

003017　　　　THE DREAM OF PILATE'S WIFE. BY MRS. HAROLD DAY. Westminster: Roxburghe Press, [1897] BMC.

Ancient Rome. hero the reincarnation of Cain. The Heroine Nerina refuses to wed him since in primeval "time she was Cain's sister-wife." (?) marries Pilate. SP 83:449.

DAY, MAIE DOVE. United States.

003018　　　　VIRGINIA, PREHISTORIC AND ANTEBELLUM [ANONYMOUS]. [Danville, Va.]: [Dance Bros.], [1899] NUC.

DAY, MRS. HAROLD. See DAY, F. E.

DEAKIN, DOROTHEA. United Kingdom.

003019　　　　"GEORGIE". New York: Century, 1906 BMC NUC. London: Gay and Bird, 1907 BMC.

PW-comedy, male hero
NYT-silly hero

A dear boy-TLS

003020   THE GODDESS GIRL. London, New York:
Cassell, 1910 BMC NUC.

    TLS-
    LBKM-

003021   THE POET AND THE PIERROT. London: Chatto
and Windus, 1905 BMC.

    Older sister supports a "not nice" younger sister,
    happy ending for all. Heroine shocks conventional
    village one of the sisters writes serial stories for a
    living. Pierette honestly admits to her suitors that
    there's no lasting quality to her love. LBKM 27-8, 139

003022   THE PRINCESS AND THE KITCHEN-MAID.
London: Chatto and Windus, 1905 BMC.

    Fairy tale with the moral that housework is fun. 1081,
    05 ACAD
    Angelic kitchen maid, ATH 05, 642

003023   THE SMILE OF MELINDA. New York and
London: Harper, 1903 BMC.

    African homestead, a woman "trifles with the maternal
    instinct" She has changed from the sweet 18 year old
    Melinda. She practically deserts her child but to her
    husband she's still loveable and he still daydreams of
    what she was. ACAD 65, 622

003024   TORMENTILLA, OR THE ROAD TO GRETNA
GREENE. London: Smith, Elder, 1908 BMC.

    TLS-? "boyish charm" "good sport".
    ACAD-young woman decides to play chess with people in
    the country, filled with women.
    ATH-matchmaker,

003025   THE YOUNG COLUMBINE. London: Methuen,
1908 BMC.

    TLS-young actress disgusted with her profession seeks
    her fortune elsewhere, pleasant.
    ATH-sad, augmented by the stamp of truth, heroine
    (milk, roses and gold beauty) cannot succeed elsewhere
    because of her past as an actress.

DEAMER, DULCIE.

003026   THE SUTTEE OF SAFA; A HINDOO ROMANCE. New
York: G. W. Dillingham, [1913] BMC.

    Hindu romance of the triumph of mother love. King
    loves Safa but her son is one of his prisoners. Coil
    of intrigue treachery battle death. NYT
    "Akbar, ruler of a kingdom of India, has a beautiful
    daughter, Dil-Khusha, who has been carefully brought
    up in the Zenana. As the Bride's Choice she is
    expected, against her will, to cast the symbolical
    wreath upon the shoulders of Kama... Adhiraj, defies
    the wrath of Akbar and, aided by the Yogi powers of
    Safa, escapes with Dil-Khusha Safa, who should have
    burned suttee-wise upon the pyre of her royal husband
    some years before, remains in the court of Akbar to
    protect Kama, who is in reality her own child, not by
    her husband, but by Asaf, one of the captains of
    Akbar's army." PW

DEAN, MRS. ANDREW, pseud. See SIDGWICK, CECILY (ULLMANN).

DEAN, S. ELLA WOOD. Nationality Unknown.

003027   LOVE'S PURPLE. Chicago: Forbes, 1911 NUC.

    Marries wealth, is miserable till husband dies;
    marries suitor of her youth. PW 11-18-11
    Her high ideals, lofty ambitions and quest for ideal
    love and soulmate. ATH

DEAN, SARA. B. 1870. United States.

003028   A DISCIPLE OF CHANCE; AN 18TH CENTURY
LOVE STORY. New York: F. A. Stokes, [1910] NUC.

    NYT-historical romance.
    PW-historical romance. Male hero.

003029   TRAVERS; A STORY OF THE SAN FRANCISCO
EARTHQUAKE. New York: F. A. Stokes, [1908] NUC.

    PW-
    BKM-mental and moral revolution effected in men and
    women when faced with a cataclysmic force of nature.

Male hero regenerated by a woman.
NYT-

DEAN, TERESA H. United States.

003030   REVERIES OF A WIDOW. New York: Town
Topics, 1899 NUC. London: G. Routledge, [1899] BMC.

    Heroine's first husband dies; she divorces the second.
    PW 55:369

DEANE, ETHEL. Nationality Unknown.

003031   "NONE SO BLIND". Boston: Reid, 1910 BMC
NUC.

    Christian science.

DEANE, HYLDA.

003032   APPLES OF SODOM. London: A. H. Stockwell,
1919 BMC.

DEANE, MARY BATHURST.

003033   EVE'S APPLE. London: R. Bentley, 1894
BMC.

    SR 77:499. French Revolution. Story of Vivienne who
    writes a political satire, is arrested, tried, and
    sentenced to deportation.
    SP 72:591. She has a complex nature--not a single
    conventional touch in her portrait. She is part of the
    old aristocracy afterafter the revolution, a survivor
    of an old society and a pioneer in a new one.

003034   KINSFOLK. London: Hurst & Blackett, 1891
BMC.

    A very intricate, complex plot. Time end of 18th
    beginning of 19th, Bonaparte's usurpation, as well as
    English life. Not one hero or heroine but more than a
    dozen including Napoleon, Josephine, a siren
    Parthenope, Anaple; gentle but strong, Germaine too.
    ACAD
    Exceptionally good book tho "complexing". Sp 67, 76.
    Also ATH 97, 533

003035   THE LITTLE NEIGHBOUR. London: J. Murray,
1905 BMC. .

    Suicide. Loneliness, poverty, fragile physique,
    wayward, weird. ATH 05,74

003036   MR. ZINZAN OF BATH; OR, SEEN IN AN OLD
MIRROR: A NOVEL. London: A. D. Innes, 1891 BMC. New
York: E. P. Dutton, 1891 NUC.

    Story of Bath in the days of George II when Beau Nash
    was king of Bath. PW
    Dolly Chesney fights valiantly for her lover against a
    heartless young woman. SR 10-24-91, 480. NATION
    54:115. Heroine's first season.

003037   THE OTHER PAWN. London: Methuen, 1907
BMC.

    Nice book for family reading. ACAD
    "Babbling," harmless sentimental.ACAD
    Good studies of feminine characters, the two pawns. SP

003038   THE ROSE SPINNER. London: J. Murray, 1904
BMC NUC.

    LBKM-historical, traditional.
    ATH-
    ACAD-untraditional-wonderful and fascinating group of
    sisters.

003039   TREASURE AND HEART. London: J. Murray,
1903 BMC.

    Story of an antiquario. ACAD 65,328, LBKM 11-03, 105,
    ATH 122, 611.
    Heroine is rel., merry. TLS, 280,03

DEARBORN, LAURA, pseud. See PICTON, NINA.

DEARMER, JESSIE MABEL (WHITE). 1872-1915. United Kingdom.

003040   THE ALIEN SISTERS. London: Smith, Elder,
1908 BMC.

    TLS-no deep insight, story of legitimate and
    illegitimate sisters, inheritance.
    TLS-earnest work, comedy, realism.

ACAD-Scoundrel falls for illegitimate sister, wrongs, degrades her and engages himself to the legitimate one. Then what?
SR-Gives a view of illegal prisons into which women drift. "The real purpose of the book is to attack the conditions which allow women to starve upon wages of 5 shillings or 7 shillings and sixpence a week at honest work and so force them to "pick up" what they can in the streets."

003041   BROWNJOHN'S. London: Smith, Elder, 1906 BMC.

003042   THE DIFFICULT WAY. London: Smith, Elder, 1905 BMC NUC.

Nan, a pagan spirit, leaves art and studio to marry, gradually domesticated. ACAD 1264, 05
Two naturally antagonistic temperaments frankly pagan wife. Nan's permanent exaltation after her husband's death. Two men love her. 641, 05. ATH

003043   GERVASE. London: Macmillan, 1909 BMC.

Centers on man, his boyhood, at Eton, marries a woman he discovers is pregnant by his best friend; she dies, baby dies, etc. TLS
Contrast between two sisters, one clever, famous artist, other coarse half-educated. ACAD

003044   THE NOISY YEARS. London: Smith, Elder, 1902 BMC.

003045   THE ORANGERY; A COMEDY OF TEARS. London: Smith, Elder, 1904 BMC.

LBKM-0
ATH-willful young woman willing to cut off her nose to spite her face.
ACAD-love story
BAKER 32-132

003046   THE SISTERS. BY MRS. PERCY DEARMER. New York: McClure, 1908 NUC.

A story dealing with the lives of two daughters of an English nobleman and the consequences entailed upon them through the misdeeds of their father. BKM V 27 1908

DEARMER, MRS. PERCY. See DEARMER, JESSIE MABEL (WHITE).

DEASE, ALICE.

003047   THE LADY OF MYSTERY. Dublin: J. Duffy, 1913 BMC. New York: Benziger, 1913.

003048   REFINING FIRES; A NOVEL. New York: P. J. Kenedy & Sons, [c1916] NUC.

Contrasts two French families connected by marriage. Lucienne's fortune was embezzled by father's clerk. She spent much of her time among poor. PW 90:1610 11/11/16

DE BATHE, EMILIE CHARLOTTE (LANGTRY).

003049   ALL AT SEA. BY LILLIE LANGTRY. London: Hutchinson, 1909 BMC.

Light comedy aboard ship. TLS

DEBBY, AUNT, pseud. See OSBORN, MRS. PETER E.

DEBENHAM, MARY H.

003050   A FLOOD TIDE. London: E. Arnold, 1905 BMC.

The righting of a wrong--a pretty story. ATH 05,890

003051   FOR KING AND HOME. London: National Society's Depository, [1891] BMC.

The rising of La Vendee. The unselfish devotion of Etiennette SP 67 854

003052   KEEPERS OF ENGLAND: A STORY OF A THOUSAND YEARS AGO. London: National Society's Depository, [1900] NUC BMC. New York: T. Whittaker, [1900] NUC. (A Tale of King Alfred's Reign. Anglo-Saxon Historical Fiction)

003053   THE LAIRD'S LEGACY. London: National Society's Depository, [1896] BMC. New York: T. Whittaker, [1896] BMC.

PW 12-5-96. Scotch lord, loyal to James I, exiled in France. Hist Rom.

003054   ONE RED ROSE. New York: T. Whittaker, [1896] BMC. London: National Society's Depository, [1898] BMC.

Title refers to fee paid by the Brents each year for the manor. Alicia Brent time of Geo. III is last ruler except for Rosamund. Story opens with the two coming to the manor. Alicia is formal; the other not. SP 79 802

003055   THE RULER OF THIS HOUSE. London and New York: Warne, [1898] BMC.

003056   THE WATERLOO LASS. London: National Society's Depository, [1901] BMC. New York: T. Whittaker, [1901] BMC.

DE BOINVILLE, NANCY MILLICENT CHASTEL.

003057   MARGOT. London: A. & C. Black, 1918 BMC.

Easter rebellion woman used as tool by a family she visits. ATH

003058   O'REILLY OF THE GLEN. London: Hutchinson, 1918 BMC.

Easter rebellion woman used as tool on a family she visits. ATH

003059   SONS OF THE SETTLERS. London: Hurst & Blackett, 1920 BMC.

TLS-couple without scruples a moral tale.

DE BOURG, PRINCESS [pseud.].

003060   THE AMERICAN HEIRESS. BY THE PRINCESS DE BOURG. London: Digby, Long, [1896] BMC. New York: G.W. Dillingham, 1896 NUC.

DE BREMONT, ANNA (DUNPHY).

003061   THE BLACK OPAL, A FANTASTIC ROMANCE. London: Jarrolds, [1918] BMC.

PW-Girl who has committed a crime and her search for happiness.
TLS-German spies and airraids.
LBKM-She is used as tool by Germans.

003062   DAUGHTERS OF PLEASURE: BEING THE HISTORY OF NEARA, A MUSICIAN, ATHENE, AN ACTRESS, AND HERA, A SINGER. London: Greening, 1900 BMC.

ACAD 58:534. Three heroines, their loves, theatrical life. Marriages at end and success.
LIT 7:87. Hera, Atene and Neaera, not related. All have "unclassed themselves," they relate their histories.

003063   THE GENTLEMAN DIGGER; A STUDY OF JOHANNESBURG LIFE. London: S. Low, Marston, 1891 NUC BMC.

Johannesburg, South Africa during gold fever-effect of gold on the people, dehumanizing. Also effects of introducing liquor to blacks. Author attacks these evils. ACAD
The mingled sordidness and luxury of a boom city. ATH 95 93

003064   LADY LILIAN'S LUCK. A ROMANCE OF OSTEND. London: Greening, 1907 BMC.

She gambles to make money to marry as she likes. TLS

003065   THE LIONESS OF MAYFAIR. London: Everett, 1909 BMC.

woman is a sculptor who abandons for marriage her devoted model, a princess "an orgie of hectic emotion" TLS

003066   MRS. EVELYN'S HUSBANDS. A PROBLEM IN MARRIAGE. London: Greening, 1903 BMC.

003067   A SON OF AFRICA: A ROMANCE. London: Greening, [1899] BMC.

LIT 6:23. Story of a half-breed, son of a bishop who "passed a few years of almost ideal happiness" living

with daughter of Indian chief. Passages reminiscent of
Haggard and others of Schreiner.

DE BURY, F. BLAZE. Nationality Unknown.

003068   THE NYMPH. London: F. V. White, 1906 NUC
BMC.

ACAD-woman passionately in love with artist husband
who is killed in a duel amongst decadent friends. The
"nymph" who is unfettered by ordinary standards holds
out the hand of friendship to his murderers but
refuses to bow to the tyranny of the family that has
wronged her.
TLS-O striking picture of the dowager.
ATH-nymph is "intellectually emancipated."

003069   PHANTOM FIGURES. London: F. V. White,
1907 BMC.

ATH-widow, daughter
Love outside of marriage and divorce. TLS

003070   STEPHEN ORMOND. A MAN'S LIFE. London: J.
Long, 1913 BMC.

The ghost of his past comes back to overcome him and
those dear to him. ATH
He goes West to make fortune, leaves wife behind;
falls in love, marries the young woman after they have
a daughter. Then he returns to a prosperous happy
domestic life in England until daughter of his first
marriage shows up. TLS

003071   THE STORM OF LONDON: A SOCIAL RHAPSODY.
London: J. Long, 1904 BMC NUC. Boston: Turner, 1905
NUC.

Dream in which London made void of all material goods
'a typical modern woman is one of chief speakers." PW
7-22-05
LBKM-after a storm all of London is naked and they
gradually grow accustomed to it.
ATH-Marriage becomes obsolete, class distinctions
vanish, music hall artist (male) undertakes to teach
fashionable folk to recognize one another without
their trappings.
ACAD O

DE CARRET, ALICE. United States.

003072   FLAMES AND ASHES. New York: G. W.
Dillingham, 1898 NUC.

PW-New England governess marries Cuban and goes with
him to Cuba. Suffers all kinds of indignities loves
another but they decide they must try to forget each
other. By the time she is a widow he has succeeded.

DECCAN, HILARY.

003073   LIGHT IN THE OFFING. London: Hurst and
Blackett, 1892 BMC NUC.

SP 68:750. Rev. refers to author as woman. Irish
story, pleasant, old-fashioned characters.

DE CHAVANNE, LOVEAU. United States.

003074   OUIRDA; OR AMERICAN GOLD REGILDING THE
CORONETS OF EUROPE. BY THE COUNTESS LOVEAU DE
CHAVANNE. Philadelphia, London: D. Biddle, 1900 NUC.

NYC 1900:518. Ouirda is American heiress educated in
France. Is tricked into marrying roue. Childhood
friend fights duel and kills him. She returns
broken-hearted to U.S. He follows and marries her.
NYT 1900:408. Autobiographical. She married the count
who left her a widow in 1893, after running through
her fortune.

DE COU, MAY ALLIS. United States.

003075   DESTINY: A TALE OF THE MISSISSIPPI.
Cincinnati: Editor Pub. Co., 1898 W.

DE COULEVAIN, HELENE FAVRE. 1871-1913.

003076   AMERICAN NOBILITY. BY PIERRE DE
COULEVAIN. New York: Scribner, 1897 NUC. London and
Cambridge, Mass.: Sampson Low, Marston, 1898 BMC.

LIT 3:472. French aristocrat marries American woman,
then has affair with French woman. Nobility and
straight-thinking of wife change him. Several chapters
on the status of women in U.S.

Written in 90's, translated then; American heiress
marries French nobleman, learns husband is unfaithful
to her, forgives him. International marriage--problems
of Annie Villars has 12 million but is unworldly.
She's an idealist, never expected husband to be
unfaithful. Can't understand distinction between
passion and love. NYT
International marriage; its good and bad sides.
Clearly outlined difference between the mental, moral,
and physical makeup of the American woman and her
French sister. No male characters. CR 28:31:247

003077   EVE TRIUMPHANT. BY PIERRE DE COULEVAIN.
New York and London: G. P. Putnam's Sons, 1902 NUC.
(Tr-Alys Hallard, pseud.)

BOOK NEWS 02- 2 American women in Paris.
CR--Character study of two American women.
"Admires American men but finds them vastly inferior
to American women" NYT 03-08-02

003078   THE HEART OF LIFE. BY PIERRE DE
COULEVAIN. New York: E. P. Dutton, [1912] NUC. (Tr.
Alys Hallard, pseud.)

Maia without the least idea of marriage-marries. She's
very intelligent, super-nervous. Soon after honeymoon
they separate and then divorce. Narrator lets us hear
from both sides. Each has learned to love the other
after the separation. Author "prepares us for the
reconciliation". NYT
BKM-by Hildegarde Hawthorne. Slight story of Maia, a
divorced French young woman who eventually returns to
her husband.
TLS-Largely autob. but a story runs thru about Maia
who divorced her husband and becomes engaged to him
after.
LBKM-Young pair, hastily divorced, travel together and
slowly understand each other.
BKM 35 (1912) 202-3
NYT--Most of the book, however, is the author's
self-analysis and a rather copious journal of her day
to day existence. She obviously thinks of herself as a
person of superior charm and intelligence; this may be
annoying.

003079   ON THE BRANCH. BY PIERRE DE COULEVAIN.
New york: Knickerbocker Press, 1903 NUC. London: E.
Nash, 1909 NUC. (Tr. Alys Hallard, pseud.)

BKM v31 1910 57 yr. old widow of faithless husband
novelist.

003080   THE UNKNOWN ISLE. BY PIERRE DE COULEVAIN.
New York: Cassell, 1911 NUC. London: Cassell, 1911
NUC. (Tr. Alys Hallard, pseud.)

describes country and people of the isle, no plot,
blend of fiction and fact? 6-10-11 PW
BKM 34 (1911) 81-85
The isle is England, the deficiencies of the Eng.
desc. of Eng in form. of letters ATH NYT

003081   THE WONDERFUL ROMANCE. BY PIERRE DE
COULEVAIN. New York: Dodd, Mead, 1914 NUC. (Tr. Alys
Hallard, pseud.)

NYT 1914:504. Philosophical, with small stories of
human interest woven in. Most personal of her novels.
Sense of Providence underlying all.

DE COULEVAIN, PIERRE, pseud. See DE COULEVAIN, HELENE
FAVRE.

DE CRESPIGNY, ROSE CHAMPION.

003082   THE COMING OF AURORA. London: E. Nash,
1909 BMC.

Aurora descends out of a snowed-up motor car upon a
monastery. She's a regular hurricane. The monks are
victims of her practical jokes. One falls in love with
her, leaves the monastery. Later there's a dainty
romance between them. TLS
She contrives to get herself snowbound at monastery?
ATH

003083   THE FIVE OF SPADES. London: Mills & Boon,
1912 BMC.

ATH-devotion of a wife to husband who has falsely been
accused of cheating at cards. A professor makes
studies of women by their skulls.
TLS

003084   FROM BEHIND THE ARRAS. London: T. F.

Unwin, 1902 BMC.

Historical novel with a murder told by Alaine raised
in a convent-a most unexpected end to her love life.
LBKM 1-03,169
ATH 10-25-02 Historical novel-heroine plays heroic
part "singularly emancipated"-wedding bells at last.

003085   THE GREY DOMINO. London: E. Nash, 1906
BMC.

ACAD - tr. historical romance.
ATH

003086   HESTER AND I. London: Mills & Boon,
[1915] BMC.

Hester & I go to live in a French village where I
paints. War comes to Paris. TLS

003087   MALLORY'S TRYST. London: Mills and Boon,
1914 BMC.

LBKM-focus on author who has had great success under a
pseud and strikes up correspondence with young woman
ATH-male novelist-finally meets correspondent in
Dartmoor.

003088   THE MARK. London: Mills and Boon, 1912
BMC.

TLS-on her wrist, and psychic influence. Puritanical
husband.
ATH-0

003089   THE MISCHIEF OF A GLOVE. London: T. F.
Unwin, 1903 BMC.

Historical romance. ACAD 64,578 ATH 121,810

003090   THE ROSE BROCADE. London: E. Nash, 1905
BMC.

Historical romance. Plucky romance. LBKM 27,8,136

003091   THE SPANISH PRISONER. London: E. Nash,
1907 BMC.

Spanish tale. TLS
ACAD-love and adventure.

003092   THE VALLEY OF ACHOR. London: Mills &
Boon, 1910 BMC.

DE FABER, CECILIA BOHL. 1796-1877.

003093   HOLY NIGHT. BY FERNAN CABALLERO. [1904?]
NUC. (Tr. Katherine Lee Bates)

DE FOREST, JEAN LOUISE. United States.

003094   THE LOVE AFFAIR OF A HOMELY GIRL. New
York: Sully & Kleinteich, 1914 NUC.

PW:85 1/31/14:374 "When a girl is homely and has been
used to regarding herself as most unattractive there
is a wall built between her and the world in general
that is difficult to surmount. Becky Vanderpool was
such a girl and her friend, Maud Haverhill determined
that the wall should be utterly destroyed. To this end
she persuaded Becky's mother to allow Martin Lewis,
who suddenly became blind, to stay with them and told
Becky and she informed him that she was a beauty. Of
course Becky and Martin fall in love, and then Martin
regains his sight, what happens then makes a
satisfactory climax."

003095   MOLLY. New York: Sully & Kleinteich, 1915
BMC NUC.

Girl takes in animals, a baby. PW 3-6-15
Spends a night out in the fields with her
boyfriend--innocently, but she eventually needs to
make it public. PW the Book Review.
A teen's book. NYT

DEHAN, RICHARD, pseud. See GRAVES, CLOTILDE INEZ MARY.

DEHAVEN, AUDREY, pseud. See BOYD, DREDA.

DE JAN, MRS. HENRY. See DE JAN, WINIFRED LEWELLIN JAMES.

DE JAN, WINIFRED LEWELLIN JAMES.

003096   BACHELOR BETTY. BY WINIFRED JAMES.
London: A. Constable, 1907 BMC. New York: Dutton, 1907

NUC.

Seeks fame as novelist. Furnishes a flat. PW 7-13-07
Plenty of shrewd comment on modern women. Promising.
LBKM 8-07, 177
Betty: vivacious Australian girl, comes to England to
be a journalist. Independent but comes at last into
the safe haven of matrimony. SR
BKM v.27 1908 p. 18. Young woman journalist struggling
for independence" ends in complete surrender to the
man against whom the heroine has been trying steadily
to still her heart." Author's pov? A toy elephant
plays an important part.

003097   LETTERS OF A SPINSTER. BY WINIFRED JAMES.
London: Chapman & Hall, 1911 BMC. London: G. Bell,
1911 NUC.

Chatty letters to a man from France, Corsica, etc. TLS
Sympathetic and delightful woman. LBKM

003098   THE MULBERRY TREE. BY WINIFRED JAMES. New
York: Dodd, Mead, 1913 PW. London: Chapman and Hall,
1913 BMC NUC.

PW 84 10/11/13:245 "Book of travel, full of
interesting and entertaining comment on men and things
not necessarily closely connected with the places
visited, but not the less charming for that. The West
Indies and Central America, Panama, particularly, were
the ports of call of this English woman, author of
'Letters to my son,' etc., who travelled with her eyes
open, and her sense of humor ever present."

003099   PATRICIA BARING. BY WINIFRED JAMES.
London: A. Constable, 1908 BMC.

TLS-diary of an Australian girl feminine book for
feminine readers.
ATH-feminine.
Heroine is a child at start, grows up. SP

003100   SATURDAY'S CHILDREN: A STORY OF TO-DAY.
BY WINIFRED JAMES. London: Blackie, 1910 BMC NUC.

003101   A WOMAN IN THE WILDERNESS. BY WINIFRED
JAMES (MRS. HENRY DE JAN). New York: Doran, [1916]
NUC. London: Chapman & Hall, 1915 BMC NUC.

Intimate letters by English woman of pluck and humor
married to an American in Panama. She describes her
emotions and the tropics. PW

DE JANVILLE, SYBILLE GABRIELLE MARIE ANTOINETTE (DE RIQUETTI
DE MIRABEAU) MARTEL. 1849-1932.

003102   BIJOU. BY GYP. London: Hutchinson, 1897
BMC. (Tr. A. Hallard)

A young girl is a chronic flirt but passes for a saint
even with her victims. SR 84:475.
SP 80:486. Story of a heartless coquette who finally
marries a middle aged lover simply because her friend
is betrothed to him and is jealous.

003103   BIJOU'S COURTSHIPS, A STUDY IN PINK. BY
GYP. New York: F. T. Neely, 1896 NUC. (Tr. Katherine
Berry Di Zerega)

PW 10-10-96. Told through conversations. She has many
admirers, marries a man very much her senior.
Feminine selfishness and heartlessness of a loveable
young woman who hurts everyone and is responsible for
a domestic tragedy. BKM 4:572

003104   CHIFFON'S MARRIAGE. BY GYP. Chicago: E.
A. Weeks, [c1895] NUC. London: Hutchinson, Zeit-geist
Library, 1895 BMC. (Am. ed.: Tr. Nora Teller; Eng.
ed.: Tr. Mrs. Patchett Martin.)

Author's ideal french girl-"slangy, impulsive tom-boy,
half child, half woman" says what she thinks. CR.
24:102
Innocent self-willed. ACAD 47:480
She's but a child when mother is determined to marry
her to an old Duke. But Chiffon knows what marriage is
and refuses the old man though every one presses hard
for the match. Chooses her own love in the end. LW
26:253
SP 76:814. Chiffon is very truthful, unsettling for
those about her, mother, pastor, suitors.

003105   CLOCLO. London: Chatto and Windus, 1905
BMC. (Tr. Nora M. Statham.)

Pretty idyl. LBKM 210:27-8.

003106   A DEGENERATE. BY GYP. New York: A. E. Cluett, 1896. (Tr. Arthur Hornblow)

003107   GINETTE'S HAPPINESS. BY "GYP". London: T. F. Unwin, 1896 BMC. New York: R. F. Fenno, [c1896] NUC. (Tr. Ralph Derechef)

ACAD 49:444. O
PW 7-18-96. Paris, James Chavoy acts as electioneering agent for Marquess de Thiele. Marquess' mrge. has been one of convenience; for 15 years she has managed his stud farm and campaigns but their political views are no longer harmonious and she refuses to be involved. Chavoy "taught the clever woman that she possessed a heart."

003108   AN INFATUATION. BY GYP. New York: R.F. Fenno, [1895] NUC. (Tr. Elise Paul)

She, the heroine, is unhappily married. Bored with her numerous lovers. "Has a strong desire to do some loving on her own account." Especially because her husband is unfaithful. "Forms her own code of morals," goes after a man. Apparently not successfully. Review suggests it ends in "morphine suicide in white velvet lunch gown." LW 26:332

003109   LITTLE BOB. BY GYP. London: Heinemann, Pioneer Series, 1900 BMC. (Tr. Alys Hallard)

LIT 6:463. He is l'enfant terrible, his correspondence with parents, etc.

003110   A LITTLE LOVE AFFAIR. BY GYP. London: Tower Pub. Co., 1895 BMC NUC. (Tr. by Mrs. Patchett Martin)

003111   THOSE GOOD NORMANS. BY GYP. Chicago: Rand, McNally, 1896 NUC. (Tr. Marie Jussen)

PW 5-9-96. the Dutrac family, with a new fortune, buy a chalet in Normandy and attempt to win over society and launch M. Dutrac on a political career.

DEJEANS, ELIZABETH, pseud. See BUDGETT, FRANCES ELIZABETH JANES.

DE JOUVENAL, SIDONIE GABRIELLE (COLETTE) GAUTHER-VILLARS. 1873-1954. France.

003112   BARKS AND PURRS. BY COLETTE WILLY. New York: D. Fitzgerald,, [c1913] NUC.

Dialogue between French domestic pets bulldog and angora cat-reflects nature and idiosyncracies of master and mistress. NYT

DE KOVEN, ANNA (FARWELL). 1860-1953. United States.

003113   BY THE WATERS OF BABYLON. Chicago: H. S. Stone, 1901 NUC.

6-1-01 PW
Historical romance. NYT

003114   A CLOUD OF WITNESSES. BY ANNA DE KOVEN (MRS. REGINALD DE KOVEN). New York: E. P. Dutton, [c1920] NUC.

NYT 1920:230. Narrator is Mrs. de Koven's sister, who is dead, Mrs. Vernon. Mrs. de Koven is psychic. Also other members of the family speak.

003115   A SAWDUST DOLL. BY MRS. REGINALD DE KOVEN. Chicago: Stone and Kimball, 1895 NUC. London: G. Routledge, 1895 BMC.

beautiful woman married to old man. Falls for a young man. They confess their love and part. Rich Americans. SR 80:55
Helen Rivington rejects him, ATH 106:156
She's lonely, loves the artist but lies to him in letting him go; the lie makes Philip Arytown, the artist, a bitter wreck. LW 26:137.
She was 20 when she married; husband was 50. PW 4-20-95:653
Social novel-the humdrum social life, but respectable BKM 4:266

DE KOVEN, MRS. REGINALD. See DE KOVEN, ANNA (FARWELL).

DE LA BRETE, JEAN, pseud. See CHERBONNEL, ALICE.

DELAFIELD, E. M., pseud. See DASHWOOD, EDMEE ELIZABETH MONICA (DE LA PASTURE).

DELAMARE, HENRIETTE EUGENIE. 1858-1937. United States.

003116   THE ADVENTURES OF FOUR YOUNG AMERICANS. Philadelphia: H. L. Kilner, [c1912] NUC.

003117   HER HEART'S DESIRE. Philadelphia: H. L. Kilner, [c1915] NUC.

003118   THE LITTLE APOSTLE ON CRUTCHES. New York: Benziger, 1912 NUC.

003119   NELLIE KELLY; OR, THE LITTLE MOTHER OF FIVE. Philadelphia: H. L. Kilner, [c1912] NUC.

003120   RONALD'S MISSION. Philadelphia: H. L. Kilner, [c1913] NUC.

DELAND, ELLEN DOUGLAS. 1860-1923. United States.

003121   CLYDE CORNERS. New York and London: D. Appleton, 1918 NUC BMC.

PW- woman comes to C.C. as governess and is believed a spy.

003122   COUNTRY COUSINS. New York and London: D. Appleton, 1913 NUC BMC.

"Story of Harriet Posdick, who when her parents go abroad for a year, is sent to some country cousins at Marshfield, instead of going back to a fashionable school. She learns not to be selfish and narrow-minded, and has some exciting times when the place is threatened by a bursting dam." PW 10/11/13,1243

003123   CYNTRA. New York and London: D. Appleton, 1915 BMC NUC.

Story of woman who adjusts to America and step mother. PW 11-6-15
Cyntra Waring raised by Eng. Grandmother when mother died. Harmless book for girls. NYT

003124   THE FORTUNES OF PHOEBE. New York and London: D. Appleton, 1912 BMC NUC.

003125   THE GIRLS OF DUDLEY SCHOOL. New York and London: D. Appleton, 1911 BMC NUC.

003126   JOSEPHINE. New York and London: Harper, 1904 BMC.

PW-two girls on a visit to their uncle.
NYT-for girls.

003127   KATRINA. Boston: W. A. Wilde, [c1898] NUC.

PW Brought up by aunt in remote vermont village. Development of her ch. thru visit to friends in New York. Girl's book?

003128   THREE GIRLS OF HAZELMERE, A STORY. Boston: W. A. Wilde, [1903] NUC.

Trip abroad, each has particular line of study. PW 10-31-03

003129   THE WARING GIRLS. New York and London: D. Appleton, 1917 NUC BMC.

Amer. family; 2 sisters and effect of war on their romances PW

DELAND, MARGARET WADE (CAMPBELL). 1857-1945. United States.

003130   THE AWAKENING OF HELENA RICHIE. New York and London: Harper, 1906 BMC NUC.

Extra-marital relationship single parent. BKM v.24, 1906.

003131   AN ENCORE. New York and London: Harper, 1907 BMC NUC.

Frustrated elopement of a pair that meet 25 years later. Indian summer romance complicated by their respective children. PW 10-12-07
Letty Norris meets old lover after 48 years. Both widowed with grown children. "reawakening of love in old people's minds" and efforts to overcome their respective children's objections. TLS

003132   GOOD FOR THE SOUL. New York and London:
Harper, 1899 NUC.

003133   THE HANDS OF ESAU. New York and London:
Harper, 1914 BMC NUC.

PW 86 9-19-14:773-"Lucky Tom Vail was brought up not
knowing that his father was a criminal. Nina accepts
him although she has learned his antecedents. A man
whom Vail senior has injured blurts out the story to
young Tom and Nina knows that he knows. But Tom does
not tell, and the fact changes Nina's whole life."

003134   THE IRON WOMAN. New York and London:
Harper, 1911 BMC NUC.

"woman who ran an iron mill..." Mrs. Martland, her
"unsatisfied son." TLS

003135   AN OLD CHESTER SECRET. New York and
London: Harper, [c1920] NUC BMC.

PW-Miss Lydia, the "little wet hen," raises Johnny,
the child the Smiths wouldn't claim. He finally grown,
judges the parents who deserted him.
NYT-Lydia is a "timid, gallant little old maid." But
she had refused to marry a man she didn't respect and
she refused to try to conceal her poverty, was
indifferent to her shabbiness. She hears gossip
created by her adoption of child.

003136   PARTNERS. New York and London: Harper,
1913 BMC NUC.

PW "For twenty years a widow and her spinster daughter
had conduted the post-office at Pennysville in a
leisurely fashion. Then a new postmaster was appointed
and connived with the daughter to keep the news from
her mother as long as possible, as she feared the
effect it would have on the old lady's health. At last
a way was found to keep the position in the family."
84:1243.
"Mother and daughter; their harmless, peaceful lives,
which they found so interesting" (daughter is an old
maid) "the strong inarticulate love between them."
"Feeling themselves...persons of dignity and
importance." "their pride of office." NYT 1913, 579
"The partners of the story are mother and daughter,
joint postmistresses in a small Vermont village. Both
have made sacrifices in the civil war-a husband and a
father, and a young boy lover were given to the
cause-and both women feel a superior sense of dignity
in the thought that they too are serving the
government. Old orders change, however, and the most
peaceful of careers may be affected thereby; Cleveland
is elected and a new postmaster appointed for Purham,
Vermont. It is then that William Sprague, the new
executive devises a scheme whereby Amanda can avert
the blow to her mother's pride. The partnership is
enlarged to include three." "Mrs. Deland's picture of
her women is consistent; the contrast between the
great emotional value and the impoverished
intellectual worth of their lives gives a kind of
poetical interest to the little story." BRD

003137   PHILIP AND HIS WIFE. Boston and New York:
Houghton, Mifflin, 1894 NUC BMC. London: Longmans and
Green, 1894 BMC.

ATH 104:854. Cecilla's unconventional, rev. likes her
a lot, says title should have been Cecilla and her
Husband. Their return to Old Chester. Character study.
CR 25:325. He is a prig with a hypersensitive nature,
wants himself and others to live up to certain ideals.
She is complicated. Her sister, Alicia, is guilty of
"immoral unselfishness...characteristic of many
women...abnegation of their comforts, their rights,
their necessities even" (Deland) in relationship with
her selfish invalid mother.
LW 25:445. Only way out of a happy marriage is through
it, because lives cannot be put back to where they
were before.
PW-Mrs. Deland fails to solve the problem. He is an
artist, ascetic, severe.
Motto of novel: marriage is not a result but a
process. Laden with discussions of marriage and
divorce. So. Pennsylvania village. The Shores are
unhappily married because Philip married a beautiful
body not a beautiful soul. After three years asks Is
not marriage without love as spiritually illegal as
love without marriage is civilly illegal? SR 79:55.
Alicia. Philip is perfectly impossible, a prig of the
worst kind. Philip's wife Cecilla is very human. ACAD
47:122.
He would bend her will; she wants freedom. Joins
Pushahead Women's Club. Thought women would support

women here, but finds they judge each other harshly
and they're cyclists, they separate. He learns he
never allowed her to express her individuality. LW
26:282.

003138   THE PROMISES OF ALICE: THE ROMANCE OF A
NEW ENGLAND PARSONAGE. New York and London: Harper,
[1919] NUC.

"Girl brought up as missionary" Alice Alden fights vs.
temptation to marry because she vowed to be a
missionary. The author has dared to create "an
uninteresting heroine" lives a secluded, determined,
unadventurous life. PW
Vermont, clergyman's family and Alice, whose mother
dies but who has been pledged to be a missionary that
is, mother made a vow to God. Alice feels she must do
this though she's scared. Powerful portrait of effect
of dead on the living. NYT 8-31-19

003139   THE RISING TIDE. London: J. Murray, 1916
BMC. New York and London: Harper, [1916] NUC.

BKM-Freddy smokes and swears-is a monster in her
mother's eyes. Tide-force of feminist ideas. Frederick
works in office, advocates suffrage and birth control.
Proposes to Howard. He refuses her.
PW: 90:665 9/2/16. Conflict between young woman who
wants liberty and the restraining, conventional older
generation. Feminists and anti-feminists alike find it
alternately trying and gratifying
NYT-When Howard turns down her proposal, she goes thru
shame and wounded pride. Thinks over all the advice
the older women had been giving her and realized its
truth. Marries a man 20 years her senior whom she
doesn't love.
TLS-Her brother is an imbecile because of father's VD.
Her most poignant disillusionment was when arrested in
suffrage riot she discovered Howard was more worried
about her than the cause.

003140   THE STORY OF A CHILD. Boston and New
York: Houghton, Mifflin, 1892 NUC BMC. London:
Longmans, Green, 1892 BMC.

LW 23:497. Not really a novel. Probably
autobiographical.
Remarkable story of child Ellen Dale who can withdraw
at will into her deeper self and whose pagan instincts
are like those of Marie Bashkirtseff. Runs away from
strict grandma and quiet Old Chester, Pa. Other
characters of the town: Mrs. Dale leading a dead life
with her brilliant weak old doctor husband. And two
children besides Ellen-Effie who teaches Ellen to be
discontent with her surroundings and her grandma's
system of education. They agree to run away together,
but only Ellen has the courage to do it. In the end
she returns. Author shows effect of heredity,
environment on Ellen, but also her unique image. A
beautiful study of the workings of her lively mind. SP
70,328
Constantly planning her own martyrdom to punish cruel
grownups very real. NATION Jan. 5, 93, 16
Effie is "a precocious shallow little worlding." She
doesn't take Ellen seriously. When Ellen runs away she
worries about what will be done with her things. So
she makes a will. SR 75,211

003141   THE VOICE. New York and London: Harper,
1912 NUC BMC.

NYT-Dr Lavender and a new heroine.

003142   THE WAY TO PEACE. New York and London:
Harper, 1910 NUC BMC.

Athalia, lovely but moody, daughter of actress
pampered by husband. Villagers don't approve of her
especially when she goes to live with Shakers. Then
husband becomes a Shaker but they part. He stays in
Shaker world; she returns to the world. They only meet
once more when Athalia is dying. PW
NYT-when she becomes a Shaker, he goes to live nearby
the community so he can take care of her affairs and
be ready to receive her when she leaves which he knows
she will do when her emotional attachment is worn out.
She stays longer and he becomes a Shaker in the
meantime, entering the community on the day she
leaves.

003143   WHERE THE LABORERS ARE FEW. New York and
London: Harper, 1909 BMC NUC.

three women harbor acrobat in their barn. One
encourages him to ministry but he's advised to go back
to where the laborers are few. PW 10-23-09

Three "old maids" near poverty, conceal their
circumstances with the pride of gentlefolk. NYT

DELANO, EDITH (BARNARD). D. 1946. United States.

003144   THE COLONEL'S EXPERIMENT. New York and
London: D. Appleton, 1913 NUC BMC.

003145   THE LAND OF CONTENT. New York and London:
D. Appleton, 1913 BMC NUC.

"Rosamund Randall, young woman of wealth and social
prominence, goes, mainly because of a whim, to live in
a little mountain community in Virginia. There she
meets Dr. Ogilvie, a brilliant young physican, who is
devoting his time and talent to the service of the
mountaineers. The story deals principally with
Rosamund's efforts to make a place for herself in the
community, the growth of affection between herself and
Dr. Ogilvie, and her struggle out of selfishness and
dissatisfaction into usefulness and "the land of
content." PW 3-1-13 769
Rosamund's gradual development from spoiled,
self-centered beauty into a fine strong woman who
learns the joys of service. NYT

003146   RAGS. New York and London: D. Appleton,
1915 BMC NUC.

Rags grows up to find happiness in love PW 9-4-15
Little spitfire from mining town; wears rags; father a
drunken criminal; lives in mt. shanty, runs wild first
16 yrs. pet goat NYT

003147   TO-MORROW MORNING; CHRONICLE OF THE NEW
EVE AND THE SAME OLD ADAM. Boston: Houghton Mifflin,
1917 NUC.

Martha Ramsay 30ish competent, bright, on several
committees, active in suffrage- thoroughly modern. But
she finds husband attracted to girl who becomes part
of household-"like old Adam, making a fool of himself
over a pretty face." This is one incident in capable
Martha's busy life. "Women," she says "are learning to
keep step with men,"..ready for them as we never were
before." NYT 11-11-17 469
Married couple in their late 30s Martha & Bert Ramsey.
Young coquette comes to visit but Martha's strategies
hold Bert in place PW

003148   WHEN CAREY CAME TO TOWN. New York: Dodd,
Mead, 1916 NUC.

Carey, unsophisticated, from Virginia, comes to the
big city; shocked at poverty she sees in the mill
town; brings a new ideal into the rich operators'
lives. Interwoven love plot. PW
NYT-Brainless, she arrives in clothes of the 50's
(they think she's on her way to a masquerade). Decides
to travel after her Aun dies-chooses biggest house in
town to stay at.

003149   ZEBEDEE V. Boston: Small, Maynard,
[c1912] BMC NUC.

A promoter turns a country village upside down with
his schemes:marries a third wife he meets by way of a
news ad. NYT
PW Male, sounds like sent comedy.

DELANOY, M. FRANCES HANFORD. See DELANOY, MARY FRANCES
HANFORD.

DELANOY, MARY FRANCES HANFORD. United States.

003150   COALS OF FIRE. BY M. FRANCES HANFORD
DELANOY. New York and London: Abbey Press, [c1902]
NUC.

DE LA PASTURE, MRS. HENRY. See CLIFFORD, ELIZABETH LYDIA
ROSABELLE (BONHAM) DE LA PASTURE.

DE LA RAMEE, MARIE LOUISE. 1840-1908. United Kingdom.

003151   AN ALTRUIST. BY OUIDA. London: T.F.
Unwin, 1897 BMC. London and New York: F. T. Neely,
[1897] NUC.

Satiric study of a young son of a peer who is into all
kinds of movements-collectivism, Tolstoism, etc-but
really doesn't understand them. He's a bit thick. LBKM
12:157.
He runs a socialist paper. Is left a fortune, declines
it. Decides to marry daughter of a washerwoman. Then
there's the smashing disillusionment-the young woman
prefers one of her own class; he's robbed; his orator

becomes a drunkard,-all idealism goes sour. SP 79:283
Wilfred Bertram.

003152   HELIANTHUS; A NOVEL. BY OUIDA. New York:
Macmillan, 1908 NUC. London: Macmillan, 1908 BMC NUC.

PW-political and diplomatic novel.
TLS-anti war and governmental power.

003153   LE SELVE. BY OUIDA. London: T. F. Unwin,
1896 BMC NUC.

SP 77:944. Story of Russian Socialist's attempt to
help Italian peasants. They are brutal, cruel, and his
life is spared at their hands by a niece of the
assailants, who pays with her own life.
Russ. guardsman condemned to Siberia for nihilism;
escapes to Italy where he dreams of his lost love.
Tries to convert the Ital. peasants to Tolstoi ideals
not very successfully. Rescued from death by Muriella.
Also receives a letter from his "lost love"- Marie. SR
83:254
Title refers to estates inhabited by beasts in the
guise of men. Muriella dies for helping save him. LBKM
11:124
LeSelve is a part of Italy-where the lowest
half-starved humanity reside. Muriella protects the
man who comes full of Tolstoi's idealism to help these
people. PW 52:143

003154   THE MASSARENES. A NOVEL. BY OUIDA.
London: S. Low, Marsten, 1897 BMC NUC.

Lashes at the sins and follies of very high
society-even kings and Dukes. The lady villain lives
in corrupt London world with her disreputable noble
husband. Makes money by presenting the new rich to
society. Takes the Massarenes in hand. They're from
Kerosene City, N.D. But their daughter is not easy to
or eager to break into society. LBKM 12:43.
This duchess is ill bred, a liar, a spendthrift
(Duchess of Otterbourne). Massarenes are in England to
enjoy their wealth. He is coarse, illiterate. The
duchess launches him and bleeds him, becomes his
mistress. She escapes scandal because he's shot. His
daughter (truly noble) a foil and contrast to the
Duchess. ATH 109:536.
"Ouida no longer revels in the delineation of high
life." She's no longer an Ovid but a Juvenal. Mayfair
is shown as vulgar. The heroine is the pearl in the
dunghill. Ital. Life. SP 78:596.
Duchess of Otterbourne steals a diamond, becomes
mistress of Wm. Massarene, ex-boss of western city
where he made a fortune in disreputable ways. He's
back in England, respectable church goer, MP, owner of
several estates. Lady kenilworth is a "hyena" and"a
tiger"-greedy, guilty of every crime save murder.
completely, negative picture of Eng. high society.
"Also the baser side of life." NYT 6-19-97.

003155   THE SILVER CHRIST AND A LEMON TREE. BY
OUIDA. London and New York: Macmillan, 1894 NUC.
London: T.F. Unwin, 1894 BMC.

ACAD 46:230. Animalistic love and savage superstition.
In both stories the heroine's love is ignoble; one is
a singer.

003156   THE TOWER OF TADDEO. BY OUIDA. London: W.
Heinemann, 1892 BMC NUC. New York: Hovendon, [1892]
NUC.

ATH 100:881. Story of a bibliophile and his daughter.
Modern Italy. Denunciation of destruction of ancient
architecture and monuments and its replacement with
ugly and dirty factories.
LW 23:497
PW She is rescued from poverty by an old lover.
Misfortunes of an old bibliophile-bookseller who
stores his treasures in an ancient Florentine tower.
More a sketch than a novel, thin. SP 70 130.
He's proprietor of the tower, man of 65 with daughter.
CR 14, 20:216.
This bibliophile sacrifices all he has, including
daughter, for a rare Dante Ms. ACAD 43:101

003157   TOXIN: A STORY OF VENICE. BY OUIDA.
London: Century, 1895 BMC. New York and London: F. A.
Stokes, [c1895] NUC.

Venice. Countess Veronica Zananegra drops her necklace
into the Lido; Prince Adrianis finds it. She's a rich
beauty. Both Prince and his physcian love her.
Comparison of the two men. Dr. injects the prince with
a toxin, kills him, marries her SR80:662
ACAD 49:53. Repulsive. A villainous doctor kills

Veronica's loved one and then marries her through his magnetic power over her will.

003158   TWO OFFENDERS. BY OUIDA. Philadelphia: J. B. Lippincott, 1894 NUC. London: Chatto and Windus, 1894 BMC.

ACAD 45:207. Short stories.

003159   THE WATERS OF EDERA. BY OUIDA. New York: R. F. Fenno, 1899 NUC. London: T.F. Unwin, 1900 BMC.

NYT 1900:302. A valley in Italy. pro peasants; labor struggle.
LW 31:99. Community unites to fight the elimination of the river in the interest of an electric railway and an acetelyne factory, being brought to valley by syndicate.

DE LASZOWSKA, JANE EMILY (GERARD). 1849-1905.

003160   THE EXTERMINATION OF LOVE. A FRAGMENTARY STUDY IN EROTICS. BY EMILY GERARD. Edinburgh: W. Blackwood, 1901 NUC.

BAKER '13:246.
ACAD '01: too fantastic
Frank-ATH 6-22-01

003161   A FOREIGNER: AN ANGLO-GERMAN STUDY. BY E. GERARD (MADAME DE LASZOWSKA). Edinburgh and London: W. Blackwood, 1896 BMC NUC.

ATH 107:578. Anglo-German marriage. Euphemia, Scotch girl, her trials, rebellion, and repentance. Nothing which could arouse the most patriotic German.

003162   THE HERON'S TOWER; A ROMANCE. London: Methuen, [1904] BMC.

TLS-picturesque romance.

003163   HONOUR'S GLASSY BUBBLE. BY EMILY GERARD. Edinburgh: W. Blackwood, 1906 BMC NUC.

ACAD-purpose novel against duels.

003164   A SECRET MISSION [ANONYMOUS]. Edinburgh and London: W. Blackwood, 1891 BMC. New York: Harper, 1891 NUC.

Roman Starwolski a Pole in German army. Sent as spy to his home land for information. Love between him and brother. There are two simple rustic sisters and a powerful character-Biruta Massalowska who changes one of brother's lives. ACAD
Well written; contrast between two brothers. ATH 97 245
Roman is a spy for the Berlin War office. Falls victim to Countess Biruta who hoodwinks the Russian general to steal the dispatches. Not clear whose side she's on. SR 2-28-91, 272

003165   THE TRAGEDY OF A NOSE. BY E. GERRARD. London: Digby, Long, 1898 BMC.

SP 80:864. Hero has incredibly beautiful nose. Insulted by a snub nosed Bohemian in the presence of his loved one. Duel follows, both noses sliced off. Loved one marries Bohemian; their children all have snub noses.

003166   THE VOICE OF A FLOWER. BY E. GERRARD. London: A. D. Innes, 1893 BMC. New York: D. Appleton, 1893 NUC.

The flower is the only heirloom of a now poor aristocratic family of Livia's. SR 76:130.
The very exceptional carnation is owned by an Italian family. There's a legend attached to it. It becomes the daughter's dowry. The flower helps save this woman from marrying the slayer of her earlier and truer love. LW 93, 178.

DE LASZOWSKA, JANE EMILY (GERARD) AND DOROTHEA (GERARD) LONGARD DE LONGGARDE.

003167   A SENSITIVE PLANT. BY E. AND D. GERARD. London: K. Paul, 1891 BMC. New York: D. Appleton, 1891 NUC.

The plot turns upon misunderstandings. Janet Sinclair thinks her fiance is a murderer while he thinks she doesn't love him. SP 66, 596
Life of a girl from childhood: an extremely shy girl. BAKER 03, 111.

She's frightened, painfully shy. Spends much of young years alone in garden watching flowers grow. Mother dies. Grows up. Struggles to support self in Venice. CR.
She's not a beauty, but loved by man who has his pick of women. ACAD
Her inconceivable timidity, overpowering nervousness. SR 2-7-91, 173

DE LASZOWSKA, MADAME.   See DE LASZOWSKA, JANE EMILY (GERARD).

DE LA VAL, JEANNETTE.

003168   THE HUMAN OCTOPUS. London: Murray and Evenden, [1915] BMC.

Concerns white slave traffic. ATH

003169   SCARLET BY FATE. London: Murray and Evenden, 1913 BMC.

2 divorce suits. ATH

DELEDDA, GRAZIA. See MADESANI, GRAZIA COSIMA (DELEDDA).

DELL, ETHEL MAY. 1881-1939. United Kingdom.

003170   THE BARS OF IRON. New York and London: G. P. Putnam's Sons, 1916 NUC. London: Hutchinson, 1916 BMC.

Man marries a woman whose husband he shot years before. This is unknown to either. But they learn of it as story traces their adjustment. PW
NYT-male squire with devilish temper is hero.

003171   THE DESIRE OF HIS LIFE. London: Holden and Hardingham, [1914] BMC. New York: A.L. Burt, [1928] NUC. (1914 ed. with "Her Compensation".)

003172   THE ELEVENTH HOUR. New York and London: G. P. Putnam's Sons, 1915 NUC.

003173   GREATHEART. London: T.F. Unwin, 1918 BMC NUC. New York and London: G.P. Putnam's Sons, 1918 NUC.

PW-love story
TLS-Dinah is overwhelmed by mother's hate and Sir Eustace's savage love (cruelty and brutality). The weak undersized brother gets Dinah in end.

003174   HER COMPENSATION. London: Holden and Hardingham, [1918] BMC. (originally published with "The Desire of his Life")

003175   THE HUNDREDTH CHANCE. New York and London: G.P. Putnam's Sons, 1917 NUC. London: Hutchinson, 1917 BMC.

Maud Brian (artist) marries a race-horse trainer but her affections go to Lord Saltash. Husband's love saves her. PW
Story concerns the first few years of their stormy marriage. Had to marry-"upon terms."(?) They're unsuited to each other but happy end. TLS
Early in story: physical punishment of a woman of 25 by her stepfather, whom she speaks of as "a loathsome coward" and "bully". LBKM
Insufferable conditions for herself Maud Brian and crippled brother. NYT 5-20-17

003176   THE KEEPER OF THE DOOR. London: T.F. Unwin, 1915 NUC BMC. New York and London: G.P. Putnam's Sons, 1915 NUC.

Heroine tries to kill someone? euthanasia? PW 4-17-15 about euthaniasia: the hero is a burly type NYT Olga: father a doctor crisis of book: death of her friend Violet who had "homicidal mania in her blood and to whom at the last Olga gave out of pure pity a dose which saved her from the horrors of life." Olga's brain doesn't retain the memory learns at the end. TLS
Much melodrama? ATH
But story seems to focus primarily upon whether Olga will marry the doctor. BKM
Not analysis, melodramatic for enjoyment. SP

003177   THE KNAVE OF DIAMONDS. London and New York: G. P. Putnam's Sons, 1912 NUC. London: T. F. Unwin, 1913 BMC.

PW 5-3-13:1564-"By author of "The way of an eagle." Story deals with the moral development of a man whose volcanic temperament is the outcome of a mixed blood,

American and Indian. Nap Errol knows but one
restraint, his love for his invalid half-brother, and
his wild nature makes him an object of dislike in the
English country place they come to live in. He falls
in love with Lady Carfax, whose drunken husband is
lord of the manor. At first his passion is absolutely
uncontrolled, but in a hard school he learns
self-sacrifice and emerges worthy of the happiness he
wins."
Descendant of white father, Indian mother. Hero: an
Indian "halfbreed." Action is violent. He wants the
woman to run away with him, willing to shoot the
husband. ATH

003178   THE LAMP IN THE DESERT. London:
Hutchinson, [1919] NUC BMC. New York and London: G.P.
Putnam's Sons, 1919 NUC.

"a little harmless bigamy" love vs honour. ATH
Man willing to sacrifice all for woman he loves. PW
love-"tropic in its intensity", unhappy heroine
discovers husband already married. The hero forces the
husband to leave, fake suicide. Hero marries heroine
only to learn that wife of husband # 1 died a few days
before his own marriage. Everything gets hectic but
all the unconvenient people including the illegitimate
baby "depart this life conveniently."

003179   THE LUCKY NUMBER. New York and London: G.
P. Putnam's Sons, 1920 NUC.

003180   THE PRINCESS'S GAME. London: Henry
Hardingham, [1920] BMC.

003181   THE ROCKS OF VALPRE. New York and London:
G.P. Putnam's sons, 1913 NUC. London: T.F. Unwin, 1914
BMC.

SR-Chris, forced to marry for money. Remains married
and is reconciled to husband in spite of appearance of
man she loves, who dies.
"Tale of the "eternal triangle." A woman consents to
wed the man who dominates her, before she fairly
realizes that he is a stranger within her gates. And
then the "preux chevalier" of her girlhood strays into
her life, and she is brought to a realization of the
fact that this companion of her summer idyll
challenges with her husband the permanent possession
of her heart." PW

003182   THE ROSE OF DAWN. New York and London:
G.P. Putnam's sons, 1917 NUC.

003183   THE SACRIFICE. New York and London: G.P.
Putnam's Sons, 1919 NUC.

003184   THE TOP OF THE WORLD. London, New York:
Cassell, [1920] BMC NUC.

TLS-melodrama, male hero
PW-love story of a girl torn between two lovers.

003185   THE WAY OF AN EAGLE. New York and London:
G. P. Putnam's Sons, 1911 NUC. London: T.F. Unwin,
1912 BMC.

TLS-male with heart of gold rescues lady love on
Indian frontier.

DE LONGGARDE, DOROTHEA (GERARD) LONGARD. 1855-1915. United
Kingdom.

003186   ANGELA'S LOVER. Westminster: A.
Constable, 1895 BMC.

"Short married life of fair Angela and her
hunch-backed musician...and the clumsy fate that snaps
their thread of happiness at the hands of the
unwitting country boor, who sees only that the lady of
his adoration is unhappy" ATH 109:649

003187   AN ARRANGED MARRIAGE. BY DOROTHEA GERARD.
London: Longmans, 1895 BMC. New York: D. Appleton,
1895 NUC.

Man dies of head disease just before he is to duel;
there's a virtuous heroine and a wicked rival. SR
79:839
Two sets of parents. Luigi's mother is a proud arist
now poor, a woman of swift insight. Brand, Annie's
father, is a self made millionaire, rough, wild,
uncouth. Luigi has title; Annie has money-this is what
concerns the two parents. Brand would force the
marriage; the principessa would plot to get the two
together. She almost succeeds but thru a cleverer
woman the young couple learn of the plot. They do end

up together. SP 75:898.
And the match turns out to be a ideal one. ATH
105:702.

003188   THE BLOOD-TAX. A MILITARY ROMANCE. BY
DOROTHEA GERARD. London: Hutchinson, 1902 BMC NUC. New
York: Dodd, Mead, 1902 NUC.

BOOK NEWS suggests unconventional women.
ATH 7-12-02-anti-military; does not mention women.
DIAL 11-16-02

003189   THE BRIDGE OF LIFE. A NOVEL WITHOUT A
PURPOSE. London: Methuen, 1904 BMC. Leipzig: B.
Tauchnitz, 1904 NUC.

Story of heredity and mercy killing. LBKM
ATH--Male M.D.
ACAD--Male M.D.

003190   THE CITY OF ENTICEMENT. London: S. Paul,
[1911] BMC. Leipzig: B. Tauchnitz, 1912 NUC.

Venice and its delights. TLS

003191   THE COMPROMISE. BY DOROTHEA GERARD
(MADAME LONGARD DE LONGGARDE). London: Hutchinson,
1906 BMC NUC. Leipzig: B. Tauchnitz, 1906 NUC.

TLS-male minister-weak women.
LBKM--ditto

003192   THE CONQUEST OF LONDON. BY DOROTHEA
GERARD (MADAME LONGARDE DE LONGGARDE). London:
Methuen, 1900 BMC. New York: F. M. Buckles, 1900 NUC.

LBKM 19:28. Four impoverished orphan sisters decide to
take London. They are not successful, but just as they
have run out of money, they are rescued by a
millionaire.
SP 85:379. Husband hunting excursion.

003193   ETELKA'S VOW: A NOVEL. BY DOROTHEA
GERARD. London: Eden, Remington, 1892 BMC. New York:
D. Appleton, 1892 NUC.

ATH 100:586. A story of revenge. "the struggle of the
simple, passionate girl-wife with forces too strong
for her.
LW 23:291. When Etelka discovers that she has married
the man responsible for his death, she dies of brain
fever.
CR 9-17-92, p 148. As result of duel, a man pledges to
suicide by a certain date. Falls for Etelka, asks for
release from pledge, but is refused because other one
loves her too. He releases him too late, he has
already killed himself. Etelka vows to find his
murderer.

003194   THE ETERNAL WOMAN. BY DOROTHEA GERARD
(MADAME LONGARD DE LONGGARDE). New York: Brentano's,
1903 NUC. London: hutchinson, 1903 BMC.

Disgusted with job of governess (men won't leave her
alone) becomes a nurse. PW
Rejects chance to be a new woman, works as governess
for a while then sets her cap for an artist. NYT
1903:370.
Has the right to win for herself a husband by
deliberate use of the eternal feminine in her? Under
compulsion of poverty goes forth to do so. Study of
woman question.Clara in circus: rejects chance for
education to live by her wits. ACAD 64:414.

003195   EXOTIC MARTHA. BY DOROTHEA GERARD (MADAME
LONGARD DE LONGGARDE). London: S. Paul, 1912 BMC NUC.
Leipzig: B. Tauchnitz, 1913 NUC.

TLS- English bride in Batavia faithless bridegroom,
unexpected fortune and a murder trial before she
settles down to English domestic life.
NYT-is it Java? Self reliant capable heroine, happy
ending.

003196   A FORGOTTEN SIN. BY DOROTHEA GERARD
(MADAME LONGARD DE LONGGARDE). Edinburgh & London: W.
Blackwood, 1898 BMC. New York: D. Appleton, 1898 NUC.

ACAD 53:173. Story of a mercenary marriage which after
all involves no sacrifice of personal happiness.
ATH 111:244.
SR 85:401. I don't understand this rev.
LBKM 14:190. Father is on brink of financial ruin,
sees salvation in his daughter's marriage to a wealthy
man. But the man is being distracted by a dancer. The
father goes to her to appeal to her and discovers that

she is his illegitimate daughter. Vengeance is hers.
NYT 1898:268. La Belveda, his daughter, relents and
Esme's marriage takes place, but shock is too great
for Morell and he suicides. He was a professional
beauty, married at 30 when his hair started to thin
and then spent all his wife's money.
LW 29:187. Signora Belveda "wins reader's sympathy and
admiration."

003197   A GLORIOUS LIE. London: J. Long, 1912
BMC. Leipzig: B. Tauchnitz, 1912 NUC.

TLS-wife says she is soldier's mistress to save his
life because he was also married to another. Goes on
to describe her career as a public singer in Vienna.
ATH-he married other on her deathbed to give her
relief-she lives-brother pursues 1st wife with
threats.
Concerns a moral coward-Letenski (male) and his
relation to Daria and to an aristocratic Prussian
woman. SR

003198   THE GRASS WIDOW. London: J. Long, 1910
BMC. Leipzig: B. Tauchnitz, 1910 NUC.

TLS-male hero sensational romance.
ATH-meets a man in 1st chapter, marries him in the 2nd
and is immediately deserted.

003199   HOLY MATRIMONY. London: Methuen, 1902
BMC. Leipzig: B. Tauchnitz, 1902 NUC.

ACAD 7-1902--Theme that loveless marriages can never
be happy. Regardless of money.
Elder daughter-irresponsible, tough. ATH.

003200   THE HOUSE OF RIDDLES. BY DOROTHEA GERARD
(MADAME LONGARD DE LONGGARDE). London: Hutchinson,
1906 NUC BMC.

003201   THE IMPEDIMENT. Edinburgh and London: W.
Blackwood, 1898 BMC. New York: D. Appleton, 1898 NUC.

SP 81:494. Jessie marries the wrong man, a baronet. He
eventually blows his brains out and she marries the
man she really loves.
ATH 112:861. Although at first his suicide is the
impediment to her remarriage.
Title refers to husband of heroine who killed himself
because his wife loved someone else more. Though his
wife was faithful. But the death keeps the lovers
apart for a long time until another woman helps unite
them. LBKM 15:155

003202   THE IMPROBABLE IDYLL. London: Methuen,
[1905] BMC NUC. Leipzig: B. Tauchnitz, 1905 NUC.

003203   THE INEVITABLE MARRIAGE. BY DOROTHEA
GERARD (MADAME LONGARD DE LONGGARDE). London: J. Long,
[1911] BMC NUC. Leipzig: B. Tauchnitz, 1911 NUC.

Winnie Mowbray in India tries to support self, gets
ill, poor, marries for convenience. She comes to love
him. TLS

003204   ITINERANT DAUGHTERS. BY DOROTHEA GERARD
(MADAME LONGARD DE LONGGARDE). London: J. Long, [1907]
BMC NUC. Leipzig: B. Tauchnitz, 1907 NUC.

How 4 girls tried the experiment of filling each
other's places in their respective homes. SP.

003205   LOT 13. BY DOROTHEA GERARD. London: A. D.
Innes, 1894 BMC. New York: D. Appleton, 1894 NUC.

SR 78:717. West Indian setting. Virtuous Marian and a
girl of startling beauty, but less virtuous. Marian's
father inherits Lot 13, a sugar plantation. Bernard
owns more valuable portion of original estate. Marian
loves him but he loves someone else who jilts him when
he loses his estate to Marian's father through
discovery of unwitting bigamous marriage of his
father. He gets Marian.

003206   MADE OF MONEY. London: Methuen, 1904 BMC.
Leipzig: B. Tauchnitz, 1904 NUC.

TLS-troubles and tragedy of a millionaire.

003207   THE MILLION. BY DOROTHEA GERARD (MADAME
LONGARD DE LONGGARDE). New York: Dodd, Mead, 1901 NUC.
London: Methuen, 1901 BMC.

Story of intrigue, heroine in love with engineer
betrothed to a count. Father switches letters she
writes to each showing her preference for the

engineer. She never hears from him, marries Count,
years later discovers father's trick, elopes with a
3rd man, about to take poison but doesn't. NYT

003208   MISS PROVIDENCE: A NOVEL. BY DOROTHEA
GERARD. London: Jarrold, 1897 BMC. New York: D.
Appleton, 1897 NUC.

She breaks her engagement when she learns her lover
once wooed a governess. At the end, the couple is
reconciled. ACAD 52 Fic sup 83.
Florence Crossly likes to settle her friends' lives
(thus, the title.). She bids him marry the governess.
He does, discovers the governess has a husband and
that she is an adventuress. PW 52:1097.

003209   ONE YEAR. BY DOROTHEA GERARD. Edinburgh
and London: W. Blackwood, 1899 BMC. New York: Dodd,
Mead, 1900 NUC.

East Galacia: life and manners. A wayward
unconventional heroine and an English governess are
contrasted. SP 82:920
English governess works for a year for a Polish family
in East Galacia. ACAD 57:632.
Jadwiga-"the mental and nervous fibres of the Polish
girl who commits suicide at 20." Raised in a hothouse
atmosphere. Her rival loves. Of wealthy family. ATH
114:755
Tragic romance-love of man for girl whose father
cheated his father at cards. Polish character. BAKER
03,110
BKM 11:190. English governess tells story of her year
with Polish family in East Galacia. Daughter's unhappy
marriage, happy ending for governess
LIT 6:264. She is "governessy."

003210   PASSION AND FAITH. BY DOROTHEA GERARD
(MADAME LONGARD DE LONGGARDE). London: S. Paul, [1915]
NUC BMC.

Marian Scott married meets "the" man. They live
together until she gets urge to join RC Church;
problem of struggle between passion and faith. TLS
Conversion to Roman Catholicism. SP

003211   POMP AND CIRCUMSTANCE. BY DOROTHEA GERARD
(MADAME LONGARD DE LONGGARDE). New York: B. W. Dodge,
1908 NUC. London: J. Long, 1909 BMC.

PW international--hero and heroine.
Focuses on a man. Course of true love and all that.
TLS ACAD
Modern Antigone saves father from suicide. SP

003212   A QUEEN OF CURDS AND CREAM. BY DOROTHEA
GERARD. London: Eden, Remington, 1892 BMC. New York:
D. Appleton, 1892 NUC.

ATH 100:126. Heroine is a countess without a fortune
who lives by running a dairy farm in Austria. Then she
comes into a large income in England and goes to
London.
LW 23:229.
PW Ulrica
ACAD: a strong character a dairy farmer by choice, she
can also handle London society.
CR 8-27-92 p 107. "An untrained savage, her
rudimentary virtues of honesty, courage and fidelity"
remain "unsoftened" by the graces of gentleness and
love." She is daughter of a count and a peasant
mother, father's death leaves her nothing but title
and huge debt. Works to pay it off, defends her honor
on the job with her fists.

003213   THE RED-HOT CROWN; A SEMI-HISTORICAL
ROMANCE. London: J. Long, 1909 BMC.

Hist rom. politics and murder. TLS

003214   RESTITUTION. London: J. Long, 1908 BMC
NUC. Leipzig: B. Tauchnitz, 1908 NUC.

TLS--trad. romance.

003215   THE RICH MISS RIDDELL. BY DOROTHEA
GERARD. Edinburgh: W. Blackwood, 1894 BMC. New York:
D. Appleton, 1894 NUC.

SR 78:46. Rich and ugly woman afraid of being married
for her money and a poor man who loves her who would
rather die than live on his wife's money.
ATH She has a Viennese governess protege.

003216   SAWDUST: A ROMANCE OF THE TIMBERLANDS. BY
DOROTHEA GERARD (MADAME LONGARD DE LONGGARDE). London:

W. Heinemann, 1901 BMC NUC. Philadelphia: J. C.
Winston, 1905 NUC.

High spirited woman. PW
Heroine, daughter of woman of easy morals? poor Jews
are crafty and piteous. Review says little about the
heroine. NYT

003217   A SPOTLESS REPUTATION. BY DOROTHEA GERARD
(MADAME LONGARD DE LONGGARDE). Edinburgh: W.
Blackwood, 1897 BMC. New York: D. Appleton, 1897 NUC.

A young woman of a cold sexual nature but of great
beauty wins many admirers in London and Vienna. "She
lures them to their doom while she stands safe in her
spotless reputation." Comes to a sad but awful end.
LBKM 12:19.
She was raised in complete isolation till 17 by
eccentric father. Then married to first man she had
ever known, after a very brief courtship, then carried
into high soc. by the fact of her husband's
prof-diplomacy. "Absolutely beautiful and absolutely
passionless" sheer vanity makes her seek conquest
after conquest. "Since society would adore, she was
beginning to understand that it is not entirely
unpleasant to be adored" sets out to win a woman's
husband solely because he loves his wife. ATH 109:773.
A man marries an extremely beautiful young woman
against the warning of his friends. She hits London
soc and Vienna society like a thunderstorm. Dazzling
every man, breaking hearts, causing suicide. But all
the while she is pure, even shocked when men make
passes because she's empty, a puppet without emotion.
A child rather than a mature person. Helen Lambert is
her foil. SP 78:597.
Geraldine Nolebrook, unconscious of the power of her
phenomenal beauty, cold, then she gets into soc. and
lures 6 men to ruin. She takes arsenic at the end
after her face gets burned accidently. ACAD 51:377.
Takes arsenic from a quack doctoress to regain her
complexion. Took an overdose. NYT 10-30-97,5.

003218   THE SUPREME CRIME. BY DOROTHEA GERARD
(MADAME LONGARD DE LONGGARDE). London: Methuen, 1901
BMC. New York: T.Y. Crowell, 1901 NUC.

Murdering her sister-the supreme crime? BOOK NEWS
Zenobia jilted by the seminarist in favour of her more
beautiful younger sister.The sister is poisoned on her
wedding day and Zenobia calmly marries the seminarist
defying public opinion and taking an oath that she's
not the murderer. ACAD
Hero Father Gregor but our sympathy is with his
unfortunate wife. Devoted wife unjustly suspected of
murder. Nation

003219   THE THREE ESSENTIALS. BY DOROTHEA GERARD
(MADAME LONGARD DE LONGGARDE). London: Hutchinson,
1905 BMC NUC. Leipzig: B. Tauchnitz, 1905 NUC.

Satirizes the cool matrimonial bargaining of man and
woman in fashionable society. TLS ATH

003220   THE UNWORTHY PACT. London: S. Paul,
[1913] BMC. New York: Benziger, 1913 NUC.

RC-point of view concerns question of conscience. SP
A will with an awkward condition. Then a later will
shows up. ATH
Condition of will is that he give up RC sm. TLS

003221   THE WATERS OF LETHE. London: S. Paul,
1914 BMC. Leipzig: B. Tauchnitz, 1914 NUC.

LBKM-story of two brothers.
ACAD 86:178-machine made plot
TLS-13:77.

003222   THE WRONG MAN. BY DOROTHEA GERARD.
Edinburgh and London: W. Blackwood, 1895 BMC. New
York: D. Appleton, 1896 NUC.

LBKM 10:162. Stepan Milnovics is wounded in a foolish
duel and is forced to give up his military career and
return to his peasant family, taking the position of
schoolmaster. He falls in love with the lady of the
manor, and she might have returned his love if it had
not been for the chance that his opponent of the duel
came on the scene and won her. He struggles to acquire
the stoic fatalism of his peasant kindred. When the
other feels remorse and offers reparation, his family
say, "It may amuse you to call yourself the cause of
his misfortune, say but you are really nothing at
all...an inert mass..."
ATH 107:48. Austrian Poland. There is a Socialistic
heroine who works for village reform.

ACAD 49:218. Antonina, one of the three principal
characters, develops from a girl to a woman.
SP 76:244. Depressingly sombre. Even Antonina, "with
her active brain, warm heart, and energetic will" and
desire to be guardian angel to village, fate has
decreed to "play her part in darkening the shadow in
which poor Stepan lives his life."

DE LONGGARDE, DOROTHEA (GERARD) LONGARD, jt. au. See DE
LASZOWSKA, JANE EMILY (GERARD) AND DOROTHEA (GERARD)
LONGARD DE LONGGARDE.

DE LONGGARDE, MADAME LONGARD. See DE LONGGARDE, DOROTHEA
(GERARD) LONGARD.

DEMAREST, VIRGINIA. Nationality Unknown.

    003223   THE FRUIT OF DESIRE; A NOVEL. New York
    and London: Harper, 1910 NUC BMC.

    John Kenton though innocent went to prison to save
    brother, meets heroine also an unfortunate. They
    travel to New York, are taken for man and wife. She
    has "strong convictions agains marriage." The story
    tells of her "working out her scheme of existence." PW
    BKM v 32 1910

    003224   NOBODY'S; A NOVEL. New York and London:
    Harper, 1911 NUC BMC.

    About a beautiful woman in south with negro blood in
    her, sounds racist. PW 7-29-11
    Relations between whites and blacks in Tennessee. A
    white man in danger of lynching for his interest in
    that woman. ATH
    Celeste endowed with many gifts that make her akin to
    genius. But mother a former slave though almost white.
    Celeste proven at the end to be in truth pure white!
    NYT

DE MATTOS, MRS. Nationality Unknown.

    003225   THROUGH THE RED LITTEN WINDOWS, AND THE
    OLD RIVER HOUSE. BY THEODOR HERTZ-GARTEN. London: T.
    F. Unwin, 1892 BMC. New York: Cassell, [c1892] NUC.

    LW 23:89. First story is a psychological study, weird
    like Poe.
    ACAD. 2nd story is of "life in one of its quietest, if
    also in one of its saddest, aspects."

DE MEISSNER, SOPHIE (RADFORD). B. 1854. United States.

    003226   A TCHERKESSE PRINCE. Boston: De Wolfe,
    Fiske, [c1892] NUC.

    PW-romance-heroine and two admirers; St. Petersburg
    social life.

DEMENS, INNA. United States.

    003227   HE WHO BREAKS. New York: Dodd, Mead, 1918
    NUC.

    PW-Elsa, musician, lives in country with artist
    Theodore. His art calls him and she realizes limits of
    his love. Period of trial and in end she refuses to
    marry him and is happy living with her child.

DE MEYER, MAHRAH (CARACCIOLO). B. 1875. United States.

    003228   NADINE NARSKA. New York: Wilmarth, 1916
    NUC.

    Nadine's girlhood "darkened by her mother's irregular
    mode of life". Nadine left her husband who obtained a
    divorce. PW 91:630 "Strong friendship between women"
    (reviewer says no more) she's gifted, reared in the
    worst possible fashion, unhappily married and unhappy
    in her romantic relations. NYT 5-20-17,202

DE MONE, MILLICENT PEPPARD.

    003229   THE LITTLE WORLD; A HOSPITAL ROMANCE.
    Kansas City, Mo.: Burton, [c1920] NUC.

DEMPSTER, CHARLOTTE LOUISA HAWKINS. 1835-1913. United
Kingdom.

    003230   THE DANCE OF THE HOURS. BY THE AUTHOR OF
    "VERA" [ANONYMOUS]. [London]: Methuen, 1893 BMC NUC.

    Hero after suffering ill health and a bad marriage
    dies while performing violin part of Dance of the
    Hours. Many topical illusions and naming of real
    people. SR 75:519. Vincent Bartholomew. ACAD 43:282

DE NAVERY, RAOUL, pseud. See DAVID, MARIE (DE SAFFRON).

DENDRON, BERTRAM, pseud. See TOMPKINS, FLORENCE.

DENDY, MARY.

003231   ONLY A BUSINESS MAN. A STORY. London:
Sherratt & Hughes, 1910 BMC.

TLS-male hero

DENISON, MARY (ANDREWS). 1826-1911. United States.

003232   CAPTAIN MOLLY: A LOVE STORY. Boston: Lee
and Shepard, 1897 NUC.

Rich, spoiled young woman, gives it all up, joins
Salvation Army; her lover follows, works as a printer
and wins her. They marry and she gives up her work. LW
28:195.

003233   IF SHE WILL SHE WILL. Boston: Lee and
Shepard, 1891 NUC.

A sweet girl; two lovers; a servant woman who is not
what she seems and who makes a mistake that almost
ruins several lives. LW
Two cousins one Australian, the other US-born, look
alike but don't know about each other. Both named
Andrew Temple. One made to pay for other's sins. PW
Margy and Andrew Temple, the senator-GODEY'S 1891, 548

003234   THE YELLOW VIOLIN. Akron O.: Saalfield,
1902 NUC.

DENNEN, G. A. See DENNEN, GRACE ATHERTON.

DENNEN, GRACE ATHERTON. 1874-1927. United States.

003235   THE DAWN MEADOW. BY G. A. DENNEN. Boston:
R. G. Badger, 1911 NUC.

Love in an earthquake. 6-3-11 PW

DENNY, MARY PUTNAM. United States.

003236   THE CHIMES OF FREEDOM. Boston: R. G.
Badger, [c1913] NUC.

003237   THE PROPHET OF FLORENCE. Boston: R. G.
Badger, [c1911] NUC.

NYT-historical lives. Savonarola, Girolamo Maria
1452-98
Historical romance. PW 12-16-11

DE PINETON, CLARA LONGWORTH.

003238   BREAKING THE KING ROW; OR, THE ACTIVITIES
OF MR. FRESHLEIGH, MAN-AMERICAN. London: Simpkin,
Marshall, [1916] BMC.

003239   PIECES OF THE GAME, A MODERN INSTANCE.
New York and London: G. P. Putnam's Sons, 1915 BMC.

Young matron takes revenge, feels no responsibility
for the tragedy that followed. PW 6-12-15
About Washington society; intrigue. NYT

DEPPEN, ANNA CHASE. Nationality Unknown.

003240   OUR RIGHT TO LOVE. New York: J. S.
Ogilvie, [c1905] NUC.

DE PRATZ, CLAIRE. D. 1934. United Kingdom.

003241   THE EDUCATION OF JACQUELINE. New York:
Duffield, 1910 NUC. London: Mills & Boon, [1910] BMC
NUC.

Comes to understanding of real value of life through
her education. Clear contrast between status of
older/younger women in France and French/American
ideals and traditions concerning women. Author is
interested in feminist movement in France. PW
BKM v.31 1910-0
TLS-of the feminist type.
SP-has an experience which no mother would wish a
young girl t to go through.
NYT-young widow raises her daughter to be an
independent thinker, well-educated, etc. Does not want
her to be like her own generation of women which did
not know itself and lived only to serve others.
Mother-daughter relationship.

003242   ELIZABETH DAVENAY. London: Mills & Boon,
[1909] NUC BMC. New York: M. Kennerley, 19--? [] NUC.

NYT-she is a professor of English at Lycee George Sand
until she leaves to join staff of La Revolte, a paper
started and managed by women alone. Gives English
lessons to a cocotte for the purpose of learning her
view of life. Full of discussion of feminism,
intelligent etc.
A feminist living in Paris, teaches at Lycee George
Sand but she finds no pleasure in humdrum regular
work. She discourses largely on feminism, resists
marrying because her intellectuality would merge with
the man's. Woman of advanced ideas-no thought of love
or home or children, devotes self to career as English
professor; becomes editor of feminist newspaper. Then
comes love and clash of her ideals with the reality
shocks her into a state bordering on despair. Gives
him up to work for her sisters in England. Fine
character study. La Revolte feminist newspaper part of
story. SP

003243   EVE NORRIS. London: W. Heinemann, 1907
BMC.

Eve has a voice, her family (Phillistines) have no
understanding of her gift. She's very different from
all her relatives. Escapes to Paris, most of novel
relates her life as voice student. Violently feminist
in her principles. Development through sorrow of a
fine character. Drifts into a liaison out of desire to
live. Positive portrayal: noble; our sympathy.
Description of girl-student life in Paris.

003244   POMM'S DAUGHTER. London: Hutchinson, 1914
NUC BMC.

ACAD 86:463. Pleasant romance of young woman adopted
by retired naval officer and her sculptor suitor.

DE SAVALLO, DONA TERESA. See WILLIAMSON, ALICE MURIEL
(LIVINGSTON).

DE SELINCOURT, ANNE DOUGLAS (SEDGWICK). 1873-1935. United
Kingdom.

003245   AMABEL CHANNICE. BY ANNE DOUGLAS
SEDGWICK. New York: Century, 1908 NUC. London: E.
Arnold, 1908 BMC.

"Dealing with English society life. Lady Channice is a
young woman who has married early in life and
discovers that her husband is not a man that she can
love. A young artist comes into her lonely life and
her mad infatuation for him paves the way for the
years of sorrow which follow." BKM v. 28 1908-9
TLS--she conceives his child, lives by herself, son
discovers his parentage. Raises child by herself.
ATH. Husband consents to regard her son as his own
because he needs her money, thereby earning her
worship. Her growing disillusionment and anxiety over
how the boy will take the secret of his birth is the
subject of the book.

003246   THE CONFOUNDING OF CAMELIA. BY ANNE
DOUGLAS SEDGWICK. London: Heinemann, 1899 BMC. New
York: C. Scribner's Sons, 1899 NUC.

"Evolution of a girl's character from flagrant egoism
to sincerity and humility, very frank in its analysis
of feminine foibles and containing some strong
emotional situations." BAKER 03,174
Liar. "Can laugh at the deepest defect in herself
recognize it, analyze it and stick to it." Her taste
inclines violently toward the less conventional.
Shifty, irresponsible. But slowly her latent nobility
shows through. Character novel. NYT 6-10-99,375.
A very precocious young woman-clever, beautiful
arrogant. Preys on her cousin to whom she is superior
in all ways. The cousin dies and her death converts
Camelia. LBKM 16:57.
She has all kinds of suitors, but engages with
unconscious cruelty in an unequal conflict with her
unattractive cousin for a man once her mentor. She
then realizes what she has done--her cruelty--and
tries to make up to her cousin for it. Mary finally
forgives her and helps bring Camelia and the man
together at her own death. SP 82:459.
She's a bright, beautiful carefree young woman. Had
two suitors but loves one. Gets the other to propose
so she can turn him down only to find she's lost the
one she loves. Life is a game. Cabinet ministers at
her feet. ACAD 56:484
Brilliant, beautiful, unconscious of rights of others.
Tells lies, is deceitful. But she is always attractive
to the reader. CR 35:647

003247   THE DULL MISS ARCHINARD. BY ANNE DOUGLAS
SEDGWICK. London: Heinemann, 1898 BMC. New York: C.
Scribner, 1898 NUC.

SP 80:864. Widower Peter Odd and his love affairs with
2 sisters, Hilda & Katherine. Happy ending.
LIT 3:135. Hilda is a painter and makes some sacrifice
to support life-style of family. Peter, after 10 year
period, finds her dull and asks Katherine to marry
him. He ends up with Hilda.
PW-she spends mornings working in her studio, her
afternoons teaching art. Money used for clothes for
her sister, luxuries for her invalid mother, home for
her father. She is considered dull because she is too
tired to go out in society.

003248   THE ENCOUNTER. BY ANNE DOUGLAS SEDGWICK
(MRS. BASIL DE SELINCOURT). London: E. Arnold, 1914
BMC. New York: Century, 1914 NUC.

TLS 13:462 Persis "a chill and shallow moon" around
which the three men revolve. An "intellectual
neophyte." Rev. respects her, doesn't like her, "her
sex is the very key of her infelicity."
NYT 1914:446. The men are: a German philosopher,
Nietszchean, and his two German disciples. Persis
becomes his student and follower. Disillusion follows,
gives her affection to crippled disciple, then the
3rd. But she is really not in love with any of them
and returns to her cool self.
PW 86 10/10/14:1207. "Eleanora, an impoverished
Italian woman of quality; three German philosophers of
intense temperaments; Mrs. Fennamy, a self-exiled
American, and Persis, her daughter, are the actors in
this emotional tangle. Each of the men loves the cool,
quiet Persis, and each has his attraction for her.
Persis is very young. She plays the men against each
other, and loses heavily. What she gains is an insight
into values of nobleness and pride, which she may be
wise enough to consult at "future encounters.""
ATH 144;392. Persis is a "contemporary product of
transitory feministic ideas, attracted temporarily to
the policy of force, but quick to repent and revert to
those ideals which have kept womanhood essentially
sane and healthy."
Nietzsche's ideas; 3 philosophers woo Persis, who
proves impossible for the 3. LW
Nietzsche in a fictionalized setting LR

003249   A FOUNTAIN SEALED. BY ANNE DOUGLAS
SEDGWICK (MRS. BASIL DE SELINCOURT). New York:
Houghton Mifflin, [c1907] BMC NUC. New York: Century,
1907 BMC.

Mother-daughter: daughter's disapproval, patronizing,
jealous. The working out of their relation. Daughter
Imogen NYT
Brief desc. BKM 26 '07 449
Wife tires of her priggish husband separates from him;
husband dies, she has renewed love for her child.
Relation between mother and daughter explored.
Daughter struggles as a reformer. PW 10 12 07

003250   FRANKLIN KANE. BY ANNE DOUGLAS SEDGWICK
(MRS. BASIL DE SELINCOURT). London: E. Arnold, 1910
BMC NUC. New York: Century, 1910 NUC.

TLS-Ch st, comparison of two English with two
Americans in favor of latter. Helen is hard,
self-centered but fascinating & best character of the
4.
SP-Althea is American cosmopolitan spinster takes a
fancy to Helen (English girl) and buys an English
country estate. F.K. is American who loves Althea. She
becomes engaged to Helen's cousin who is interested in
her money. Helen loves him. F. K. ends up with Althea
BKM. No-finally he ends up with Althea.
NYT-Althea & Helen are 33. Althea is well educated
with a feeling for charm. Helen & her cousin have
charm.
Tangled love affairs of 4 char. 2 poor, 2 wealthy. PW

003251   PATHS OF JUDGMENT. New York: Century,
1904 NUC. London: A. Constable, 1904 BMC.

PW character study
NYT character study of four people.
Book-An in depth analysis of the relationships between
a young woman, her father, two men and another woman.
ACAD- Subject of strength (fem) to weakness (m)

003252   THE RESCUE. BY ANNE DOUGLAS SEDGWICK. New
York: Century Co., 1902 NUC. London: J. Murray, 1902
BMC.

BKM 7-1902
CR-honest portrayal of relationship between mother,
daughter, and man.
WOMAN'S JOURNAL 5-24-1902--Young man falls in love
with picture of older (47) widow with beautiful young
daughter. Chooses mother, helps save daughter from
foolish elopement. Older woman-younger man,
mother-daughter.
ATH 5-10-02

003253   THE SHADOW OF LIFE. BY ANNE DOUGLAS
SEDGWICK. New York: Century, 1906 NUC. London: A.
Constable, 1906 BMC.

PW-friendship between two men, story of their lives.
NYT young man weary of life-childhood friend, young
woman filled with life-meet again.
ACAD-0
TLS- she attempts to win him but finally is baffled by
his belief that to marry her would be to ruin her.
Finely wrought, difficult, grasp of character.

003254   TANTE. BY ANNE DOUGLAS SEDGWICK (MRS.
BASIL DE SELINCOURT). New York: Century, 1911 NUC.
London: E. Arnold, 1911 BMC NUC.

PW-Psych study of relationship between strong woman,
her ward and her ward's husband
ACAD- in style of Henry James
SR.- Egotistical pianist who likes to play mother
occasionally struggles with barrister husband for
Karen, former illeg ward of pianist
NYT Char. study of Mme. Okraska; a concert pianist of
world-wide fame. Egoist, pianist, 46 yrs old.
BKM (1912) 34, 655-7
Mercedes Okraska vs. Karen Woodruff her overmastering
jealousy of Karen. Characters studied with care are
women; author "is a little hard on her sex" but
Mercedes a monster with "a due allowance of charm."?
TLS
Madame Okraska is a great pianist. Crisis comes when
Karen (who idolized Tante) is engaged to man who
doesn't bow down to Tante. ATH

003255   THE THIRD WINDOW. BY ANNE DOUGLAS
SEDGWICK (MRS. BASIL DE SELINCOURT). London: M.
Secker, 1920 BMC. Boston: Houghton Mifflin, 1920 NUC.

TLS- Bevis and Antonia (Tony) are kept from marriage
by spidery spinster's insinuations that her dead
husband's ghost was "walking."
ATH. She is sister of Tony's husband who died in the
war. Finally, acting as a medium she convinces Antonia
that her husband's spirit exists; Antonia cannot
decide about Bevis in face of sister's influence that
she should be true to husband, so she kills herself.
Miss Latimer is left with Bevis, a one legged veteran.
NYT 1920:292.

003256   VALERIE UPTON. BY ANNE DOUGLAS SEDGWICK.
London: Constable, 1908 BMC NUC.

Valerie's daughter Imogen, complacent superiority,
egoist, calm acceptance of homage, wants to strengthen
everyone she meets. (Those who don't wish to be
strengthened she deems unworthy). Valerie-human, real
culture, stifled in atmosphere of husband and
daughter. Goes to live in England while father and
daughter live their superior lives in America. Father
dies, Valerie returns-then the relationship between
mother and daughter explored-the pain of the mother,
the discomfiture of the daughter. Imogen's vicious
selfishness comes thru. She lures and entices her
mother's old lover who had planned to marry the
mother.
SR. ch st.--Mother and daughter relation. Daughter is
arrogant, heartless, mother is unselfish and
unappreciated by daughter who, after her father dies,
wishes to raise her to her own "moral altitude." Her
fiance comes to appreciate mother more than she.

DE SELINCOURT, IRENE RUTHERFORD (MACLEOD). B. 1891.

003257   GRADUATION: A NOVEL. BY IRENE RUTHERFORD
MCLEOD. London: Chatto & Windus, 1918 BMC NUC.

TLS- Frieda is into art study, social work and
suffrage. Has three love affairs. Rev. thinks too
intimate an accounting.
A woman's progress and methods in love. An ardent
suffragette and social reformer fascinated with
handsome artist. Then of men of different types.
Account of her settlement work ATH

DE SELINCOURT, MRS. BASIL. See DE SELINCOURT, ANNE DOUGLAS
(SEDGWICK).

DESMOND, CLIVE, pseud. See DUNCAN, C. E.

DESMOND, FRANK, pseud. See SMITH, MRS. H. SCOTT.

DE SOUCANTON, ALEXANDRA.

003258   TOWARD THE HEIGHTS. London: Heath,
Cranton, [1920] BMC.

ATH-0

DESPARD, CHARLOTTE AND MABEL (COLLINS) COOK.

003259   OUTLAWED. A NOVEL ON THE WOMAN SUFFRAGE
QUESTION. BY CHARLOTTE D London: H. J. Drane, [1908]
BMC.

DE SULMALLA, COUNTESS.

003260   UNDER THE SWORD. London: Digby, Long,
1901 BMC.

ATH 1-18-02

DE VANE, I. C. See DE VANE, ISABELLA CORNELIA.

DE VANE, ISABELLA CORNELIA. United States.

003261   DOCTOR CARRINGTON. BY I. C. DE VANE. New
York: Abbey Press, [1901] NUC.

PW 10-5-01

DEVEREUX, M. See WATSON, MARY DEVEREUX.

DEVEREUX, MARY. See WATSON, MARY DEVEREUX.

DEVI, SRIMATI SVARNA KUMARI. See GHOSAL, SRIMATI SVARNA
KUMARI DEVI.

DE VILLENEUVE, LOUIS, pseud. See GIBBONS, LOUISE ELISE.

DEVOORE, ANN. B. 1872. United States.

003262   OLIVER IVERSON: HIS ADVENTURES DURING
FOUR DAYS AND NIGHTS IN THE CITY OF NEW YORK IN APRIL
OF THE YEAR 1890. Chicago and New York: H. S. Stone,
1899 NUC.

Mystery, surprise, excitement concerning a mansion on
Second Ave in NYC, a philanthropist and a young poet.
PW 30:234
Love and crime. LW 30:234

DEWETT, MARY.

003263   THE SEVEN WATCHMEN. London: Century
Press, 1907 BMC.

Story of impersonation: a change of babies in infancy.

DEWEY, KATHARINE FAY.

003264   STAR PEOPLE. Boston: Houghton-Mifflin,
1910 NUC. London: Longmans, Green, 1910 BMC.

Sailors and advents with Star people PW
PZ8

DEWING, E. B. See KAUP, ELIZABETH BARTOL (DEWING).

DE WITT, JULIA A. WOODHULL. D. 1906. United States.

003265   LIFE'S BATTLE WON. New York: Hunt and
Eaton, 1893 NUC.

Power of Christian influence in life's battles is the
theme. Civil War time. Introduces Lincoln and Grant.
PW 9-2-93.

DIBDIN, EMILY, jt. au. See MARSHALL, EMMA (MARTIN) AND
EMILY DIBDIN.

DI BRAZZA, COUNTESS. See SAVORGNAN, CORA A. (SLOCOMB)
BRAZZA.

DI CADHILAC, MARGARET ISABELLA (COLLIER) GALLETTI.

003266   THE SCHOOL OF ART. BY ISABEL SNOW.
London: T. F. Unwin, 1891 BMC NUC.

Emmeline Harris is "plain" intensely practical
artistic genius. The signs of her genius first attract
the man she marries. ACAD
Gross injustice done to her in art school-it was
suggested that the work she exhibited was not her own.
ATH 97 436
Ends up marrying a Royal Academician who visits the
school and declares her work shows genius. SR 4-11-91,
446

DICKENS, MARY ANGELA (EVANS). 1838-1896. United Kingdom.

003267   AGAINST THE TIDE. London: Hutchinson,
1898 BMC.

ACAD 53:173. Homicidal maniac marries older sister of
twins. Hilary and Darrent.
ACAD 53:523. Hilary overhears a conversation between
the bridegroom and his best man on the eve of her
sister's wedding. She knows she should tell what she
has heard, but she is jealous of her older sister,
Darrent preferring her to Hilary, and knows she will
be happier with her sister gone. Eight years later,
her sister and husband return from abroad and she is
plunged into trouble which as child she could have
averted.
ATH 111:400. Tessa's torment, Hilary's remorse.

003268   CROSS CURRENTS: A NOVEL. London: Chapman
and Hall, 1891 BMC NUC. New York: D. Appleton, 1892
NUC.

Selma Malet is on her way to brilliant success when
love distracts her. She's a born actress and has the
courage to match her genius. She gives up love, is a
great success on stage. ATH 98 546.
Ends with questions: conflicting claims of love vs
art; strong psychological study.
CR 18:275. Selma, who has "considerable dramatic
talent," finally decides on acting career rather than
a mrge she has been considering. She is successful and
then follow disappointments.
LW 23:303. There are no disappointments. She devotes
herself to her art, and it does not fail her. "She
refuses every offer of marriage and we leave her a
sweetly grave woman who finds her pure satisfactions
in high dedication to her art." Mary Dickens, reviewer
states, is grand daughter of Charles Dickens.

003269   THE DEBTOR. London: Hutchinson, 1912 BMC.

TLS-R. C.
ATH R. C.

003270   THE LOVE THAT WINS. Chicago and New York:
Rand, McNally, [1897] NUC.

PW Hilary's concealment "reacts on the twin-brother
for whom Hilary sacrificed both herself and her
sister." Also her "pathetic wooing."

003271   A MERE CYPHER: A NOVEL. London and New
York: Macmillan, 1893 BMC NUC.

Mrs. Custance is a silent, withdrawn woman. She saves
Norman Strange who comes to live in the house (her
husband is a doctor) and in a great moment of strength
defends him before her villain husband. SP 70:528
Leila Custance, her passion concealed even from
herself, unique study, novel of social reform. LW
93,89.
She's "overwhelmed by the tyranny of her marriage."
BAKER 03,99.
Hero comes to live in her house. He's an alcoholic
under the husband's (a doctor) cure. But she's the one
who cures him. Later he becomes a rich man and the
doctor tries to extort money from him by falsely
accusing him of a crime. Mrs. Custance commits murder
for him. PW 3-11-93.
She is "unattractive." SR 75,270.
Sp 72:380. A man, a habit, a "feeble creature" who
helps him control it. A "needless horror" of passion
and crime at end, spoiling Mrs. Custance.
CR 21: 181. Her husband tries to frame the hero for
murder; she kills her husband, dies in prison.
She's utterly colourless, unattractive, tame,
featureless with the fidelity of a "faithful
half-witted slave." At climax revealed as strong. Her
crime-kills husband and self. But this changed person
she becomes at climax was always there under the
surface. ACAD 43:322

003272   ON THE EDGE OF A PRECIPICE. London:
Hutchinson, 1899 BMC NUC.

Loss of memory by a blow on the head; restoration of
memory by a second blow. LIT 4:479
Heroine thrown from bike, loses memory, comes under
spell of villainous cousin and his unscrupulous
sister--Violet Cochrane. ATH 113:591

003273   PRISONERS OF SILENCE. London: Osgood,
McIlvaine, 1895 BMC.

LBKM 10:161. Branston renounced all that meant
anything to him, found sweetness in the desert he
shared with the woman who had cursed his life. "Two
lovers who really touch the borderland of the
prohibited degrees of kindred."
SR-Discovers that the woman he loves is the widow of
his father and the stern harsh older sister who has
brought him up is actually his mother. He grows
depressed and goes to India.
SP 76:244. Is the last third of the novel a "study of
the stealthy approach of insanity"? /

003274   A VALIANT IGNORANCE: A NOVEL. London and
New York: Macmillan, 1894 BMC NUC.

SP 72:863. Mrs. Romayne's husband, she discovers after
his suicide, was a swindler and a profligate. Fearing
that her son will inherit all this, altho outwardly
she appears a social butterfly, she devotes herself to
preventing it. It happens anyway. Gloomy. ACAD 46:7
LW 25:171. Mother dies.

003275   THE WASTREL. London: Hutchinson, 1900
BMC.

ATH 1-26-01

DICKER, CONSTANCE (MACEWEN).

003276   MR. HORATIO MANDEVILLE'S EXPERIENCES; OR
THE BACHELOR. BY CONSTANCE MACEWEN. London: Eden,
Remington, 1892 BMC.

003277   THREE WOMEN IN ONE BOAT: A RIVER SKETCH.
BY CONSTANCE MACEWEN. London: F. V. White, 1891 BMC.

DICKINSON, EVELYN ELIZABETH. Australia.

003278   HEARTS IMPORTUNATE. London: Heinemann,
1899 BMC. New York: Dodd, Mead, 1900 NUC.

BKM 11:285. Australia. "Heroine is distant, unlovable,
detached from her surroundings, and morbidly conscious
of a past which is in truth dead." A man who knows
about this past steadfastly loves her and she finally
yields to him. Quote from book: "Hazell knew, as all
men know, that woman has fair cause of complaint
against man and against society. He knew that it was
required of her to be an exquisite kind of
paradox--good and pure, steadfast in her constancy,
and yet abundant in a piquant sauce of coquetry and
wiles; and should the one part predominate, she is
heavy, unattractive; and should the other, she is
light, unworthy. To be fascinating, the reason of her
being-she must maintain unstable equilibrium. Man,
were he asked to do this, would refuse the endless
effort."
SP 84:45. "Author is sympathetically disposed toward
the highly educated amazon of today."
ATH 115:264. Heroine is Avis.
ACAD 58:506. Avis wished there were no men and women,
only slightly materialized angels. World had "pointed
its finger" at her. She had a hatred of sex.

003279   ONE MAN'S WAY. London: D. Allen, 1914
BMC.

ATH-Male hero, MD, & his relations with various women,
including his wife who dies half way thru book.
ATH 143:823
TLS He has a "wild intrigue of erotic abandonment
until...his moral sanity reasserts itself."

003280   A VICAR'S WIFE. London: Methuen, 1892 BMC
NUC.

ATH 99:370. He is a monster. Has a 17 year old
daughter. She dislikes him openly. Book concludes with
his horsewhipping of her and he "soon after expires
(with unpleasant detail) in his own gore."
SP "The history of a madman."
SR 73:423. His wife leaves him. Author shows a "fury
of resentment" "against the hypocrisies of society"
"The author pursues him (the vicar) with whips of
scorpions and leaves no spot unlashed."

DICKINSON, MARY (LOWE). 1839-1914. United States.

003281   FROM HOLLOW TO HILLTOP? Philadelphia:
American Baptist Society, 1896 NUC.

LW 27:365. Mrs. Burke returns to village where she

once taught school.

003282   SPRING BLOSSOMS: AN EASTER STORY.
Philadelphia: C. H. Banes, [c1895] NUC.

003283   THE TEMPTATION OF KATHARINE GRAY.
Philadelphia: A. J. Rowland, 1895 NUC.

Katharine Gray marries for wealth and social position.
After her child is born she realizes her husband is a
no good drinker. When starvation for herself and
daughter is imminent she's entrusted with the care of
a child who has inherited a small fortune. PW
12-7-95:1075

DICKSON, MISS S. O'H. See DICKSON, SALLIE O'HEAR.

DICKSON, SALLIE O'HEAR. D. 1916. United States.

003284   RALPH FABIAN'S MISTAKES. BY MISS S. O'H.
DICKSON. New York: Broadway, [c1908] NUC.

PW-family life.

DIEHL, ALICE (MANGOLD). 1844-1912. United Kingdom.

003285   AN ACTOR'S LOVE STORY. London: Hurst and
Blackett, 1908 BMC.

TLS--naive girl who wants to be a nun--tragic results
of love story.
ACAD--marries a man already married. Rev. thinks she's
shallow, sent.
ATH--Rev. thinks she's priggish.

003286   A BORN GENIUS. London: Digby, Long, 1909
BMC.

TLS--centers on a man.

003287   BREAD UPON THE WATERS. A NOVEL. London:
Hurst and Blackett, 1905 BMC.

Loveable Hester, a kindly story. TLS

003288   THE CONFESSIONS OF PERPETUA. London:
Stanley Paul, [1912] BMC.

ATH--unhappy mrg, divorce and new mrg. prospect.
Sentimental.

003289   THE DESBOROUGH MYSTERY. London: Digby,
Long, 1903 BMC.

003290   DR. PAULL'S THEORY: A ROMANCE. BY MRS. A.
M. DIEHL. Bristol: J. W. Arrowsmith, [1893] BMC. New
York: D. Appleton, 1893 NUC.

His theory has to do with education of his daughter
Lilia. She's kept prisoner in country home away from
all contacts. Becomes sensitive, introspective,
delicate. Attaches herself completely to a person-has
no self. Disastrous effect of this education. After
she marries she hangs on her husband, "Killing with
her weight." She dies shortly after their marriage. CR
20, 23:6
Romance of the occult: visions, reincarnations, etc.
LW 93:163.
Friendship between doctor and patient, big businessman
and womanhater. Doctor married to woman who is
fiercely jealous, makes him promise at her death that
he'll kill himself. He's saved for a happy love. His
theory involves souls and their power here and beyond.
PW 3-18-93.

003291   ELSIE'S ART LIFE: A NOVEL. BY MRS. A. M.
DIEHL. London: R. Bentley, 1893 BMC NUC.

Elsie is a pianist of great ability. She's much loved
by Frank Clare who is unhappily wed to a fast woman.
SR 75, 574.
Elsie Gerhard is discovered by Frank. He "loses
happiness in his endeavor to present her genius to the
world." But we lose sympathy with him when he makes
this born artist sacrifice her art in order that she
fill a void in his life. ACAD 43:501.

003292   THE END OF A PASSION. London: J. Long,
1907 BMC.

Madge "an emotional prig". TLS

003293   ENTRAPPED. London: J. Long, 1904 NUC BMC.

LBKM--murd. myst.

003294   FROM PILLAR TO POST. London: J. Long,
1914 BMC.

   LBKM--Betty and her mother live in a state of
   apathetic melancholy after death of her father until
   motor-car accident brings young man into their home.
   She falls wildly and passionately in love, he
   reciprocates, but then tells her he is married to a
   woman he has never loved and then leaves her to a
   world of darkness and despair.
   TLS--Betty and her mother visit aristocratic relatives
   in France, she marries one and goes back home to Col.
   Austin.

003295   THE GARDEN OF EDEN. London: Digby, Long,
1907 BMC.

   Has a voice; becomes famous. Course of her love and
   her career run side by side to a dramatic close. POV?
   TLS
   Althea and Clifford. SR

003296   HER LADYSHIP OF THE SEASON. London: J.
Long, 1908 BMC.

   TLS--Beatrice and 4 other ladies start a home--lovers
   "redeem the situation."

003297   IN HUMAN SHAPE. London: Railway and
General Automatic Library, [1892] BMC.

003298   INCOMPARABLE JOAN, A NOVEL. London: J.
Long, 1912 BMC.

   Concerns an assumption of another identity--by a male.
   A wedding interrupted by an arrest of the bridegroom
   "a far-fetched" story. Joan is truly incomparable (but
   review doesn't say why). ACAD
   A heroine who insists upon the hero's committing a
   bigamous alliance. ATH

003299   ISOLA. London: J. Long, 1911 BMC.

   She's suspected of murder, ends up marrying clergyman.
   TLS

003300   A LAST THROW. London: Digby, Long, [1897]
BMC.

   Contains a thorough villain-M. Diaz de Sorrente. SP
   79:654.
   Sens. chars. are wicked, live in gorgeous palace of
   gambling. ATH 109:647.

003301   A LONELY FIGHT. London: Hurst and
Blackett, 1905 BMC.

   BKM--migration of heroine from poverty through
   companionship with tartaress to married happiness and
   conquering of the Tartaress.

003302   LOVE AND LIARS. London: J. Long, 1904
BMC.

   BKM--heir
   ATH--heir

003303   THE LOVE OF HER LIFE. London: Ward, Lock,
1905 BMC.

003304   A LOVELY LITTLE RADICAL. London: J. Long,
1907 BMC.

   Heroine wants levelling of classes, loves the gardener
   of her mansion, teaches him Italian, he becomes a
   singer who takes Italy by storm, marries. Engagingly
   modern. TLS

003305   LOVE'S CROSSWAYS. London: Digby, Long,
1901 BMC.

003306   LOVE--WITH VARIATIONS. A NOVEL. London:
J. Long, 1906 BMC.

   TLS--2 M.D.'s
   ATH--One is a child killer.

003307   A MAN IN LOVE. London: Digby, Long, 1903
BMC.

003308   THE MARRIAGE OF LENORE. A NOVEL. London:
S. Paul, 1911 BMC.

   Man gives up call for monastic life to marry. ATH

003309   MISS STRANGEWAYS. London: J Long,, [1909]

BMC NUC.

   Unhappy couple: husband was a criminal; wife comes
   close to poisoning him in the end. TLS

003310   A MODERN HELEN. London: Hurst and
Blackett, 1896 BMC.

   ATH 108:481. O
   ACAD 50:305. In bad taste and without purpose. Lady
   Helen is an impossible type.

003311   A MYSTERIOUS BOHEMIAN. London: Digby,
Long, 1908 BMC.

   TLS--male hero.

003312   A MYSTERIOUS LOVER. A NOVEL. London: S.
Paul, [1911] BMC.

   About an aviator. ATH

003313   THE SECRET OF SIR GEORGE HARTLEY. London:
Digby, Long, 1910 BMC.

   TLS--trivial rom.

003314   THE TEMPTATION OF ANTHONY. London: J.
Long, 1905 BMC.

   Eve tempts Anthony because she has unbearable
   problems, but Eve has a husband and Anthony was a
   celibate. LBKM 27-8:263.

003315   THEIR WEDDED LIFE. A NOVEL. London: S.
Paul, [1912] BMC.

   ATH--Silly.

003316   A WOMAN MARTYR. London: Ward, Lock, 1904
BMC.

003317   A WOMAN'S CROSS. London: Digby, Long,
[1896] BMC.

   Joan Burney bears a thousand crosses. "An incessant
   torrent of emotion" and painful tragedies. ACAD 51:146

003318   A WOMAN'S WHIM: A NOVEL. London:
Hutchinson, 1894 BMC.

   SR 78:300. Tesera's whim is to become an operatic
   singer. Her friend Les Burns attempts to keep her from
   this; she dismisses him and goes into training. She
   falls for a sinister Italian singer; he is murdered,
   and she continues her career.
   SP 23:56. She believes in being a worker, gives up
   home, rank, and fortune to do so.

DIEHL, MRS. A. M. See DIEHL, ALICE (MANGOLD).

DIEUDONNE, FLORENCE LUCINDA (CARPENTER). B. 1850. United
States.

   003319   KATHERINE: A NOVEL. Washington, D.C.: W.
   J. Brewer, [c1898] NUC.

   003320   XARTELLA. Washington: Gedney and Roberts,
   [c1891] NUC.

DILKE, ETHEL (CLIFFORD).

   003321   LOVE'S JOURNEY. BY ETHEL CLIFFORD. London
   and New York: J. Lane, 1905 BMC NUC.

   Poems-BMC NUC

DILL, BESSIE.

   003322   THE FINAL GOAL. London: Hutchinson, 1899
   BMC.

   A Scottish Laird has defrauded his wife and children.
   This and other wrongs are righted amid wedding bells.
   ACAD 57:456
   LW 31:119. Cheerful Scotch story.
   SP 84:248. Father stubbornly refuses to marry his
   son's mother, although they have lived happily
   together. He is a lord. All ends well.
   PW-story is about the son. He distinguishes himself in
   Africa as a soldier.

   003323   THE LORDS OF LIFE. London: J. Long, 1901
   BMC.

   story for girls.

003324   MY LADY NAN. London: Hurst and Blackett,
1907 BMC.

Simple little romance. ACAD

003325   THE SILVER GLEN. A STORY OF THE REBELLION
OF 1715. London: Digby, Long, 1909 BMC.

Hist romance. TLS

003326   THE STORY OF BELL. BY L. BEITH DALZIEL.
London: Ward and Downey, 1896 BMC.

A mild touch of fin-de-siecle freedom. The heroine
keeps up an unlawful attachment with her cousin's
husband after her marriage. Suicide. ATH 109:81

003327   SWEET WATER AND BITTER; A TALE OF TEN
YEARS AGO. London: Digby, Long, 1910 BMC.

TLS-sent rom.

DILLINGHAM, LUCY. United States.

003328   THE MISSING CHORD: A NOVEL. New York: G.
W. Dillingham, 1894 NUC.

PW-Juliet is daughter of woman devoted to social
pleasure. She decides to study music in Berlin for a
year before making her debut. Love changes her
artistic bent; she marries an American professor
devoted to the improvement of his fellow men. After a
short year of marriage her life is once more wholly
changed.
Young English girl goes to Berlin to study music,
meets an American and a German musician; both love
her. Then the German musician comes to U.S., plays a
composition for which the woman supplies the one
missing chord. CR 23:459.

DILLON, MARY C. (JOHNSON). D. 1923. United States.

003329   THE AMERICAN. New York: Century, 1919 BMC
NUC.

young social worker in a settlement house in a city
slum. She's from well-off family must choose between
new lover and one of old life. PW
Settlement worker, head resident of Sunshine House in
her early 20's. Liked and successful. Helen Seymour.
Helps everyone, breaks up a gang. Two men love her
"sentimental and sugary." They become buddies in the
war. One dies saving the other. NYT 19:250.

003330   COMRADES. New York: Century, 1918 NUC
BMC.

PW--War and love.
NYT--group of students in German pension all good
friends. War breaks out. Male narrator, English, is in
love with American, Beatrice. He enlists, she goes to
front to drive motor ambulance. They marry, reuniting
group at wedding, including German who is now a POW in
England.

003331   THE FARMER OF ROARING RUN. New York:
Century, 1920 NUC BMC.

PW--Story of a wealthy young Philadelphia farmer and
his plantation in Virginia.

003332   IN OLD BELLAIRE. New York: Century, 1906
NUC BMC.

PW--love story of female school teacher.
NYT--or is she a governess in a college president's
house during Civil War.

003333   THE LEADER. New York and London:
Doubleday, Page, 1906 NUC BMC.

PW--story of William Jennings Bryan.

003334   MISS LIVINGSTON'S COMPANION. A LOVE STORY
OF OLD NEW YORK. New York: Century, 1911 NUC BMC.

003335   THE PATIENCE OF JOHN MORLAND. London and
New York: Doubleday, Page, 1909 BMC NUC.

Historical novel--days of Jackson. LBKM NYT

003336   THE ROSE OF OLD ST. LOUIS. New York:
Century, 1904 NUC.

NYT--hist novel.

PW--historical novel.

DILLON, MRS. G. F. See TURNBULL, DORA AMY DILLON.

DITMAR, VIRGINIA.

003337   LOVE'S QUICKSANDS. New York: F. T. Neely,
[1901?] NUC.

DITSON, LINA BARTLETT. United States.

003338   THE SOUL AND THE HAMMER: A TALE OF PARIS.
New York: G. A. S. Wieners, 1900 NUC.

Narrated by a Dutch-American painter, who was rescued
from suicide by heroine, a famous writer and singer
who lives with her mother in Paris. Later he helps her
care for a blind husband and little child. PW.

DIVER, KATHERINE HELEN MAUD (MARSHALL). 1867-1945. United
Kingdom.

003339   AWAKENING; A STUDY IN POSSIBILITIES. BY
MAUD DIVER. New York: J. Lane, 1911 NUC.

Eng. man: Hindu girl. Tragedy of mixed marriage. Eng.
title: Lilaman: sympathy for the woman.
BKM 34 (1911) 310-11. She shrinks from Western manners.
Then husband comes to realize he might have a "dark"
child. She almost commits suicide because of knowing
his feelings but awakening (?) comes in time.

003340   CANDLES IN THE WIND. BY MAUD DIVER. New
York: J. Lane, 1909 NUC. Edinburgh: W. Blackwood, 1909
BMC.

Life and work on Indian Frontier. Wife married to man
who didn't tell her he has "Eastern blood in his
veins." She loves a man more like herself. Lyndsay is
a poet, an artist; author never tires of praising her.
TLS
Lyndsay Vereker married to Eurasian dr. Story of her
disillusionment with life in India, race conflict. Her
husband dies; she meets her true love. ACAD
Too much "space is occupied with the lady's emotions
and difficulties and female friends." ATH

003341   CAPTAIN DESMOND, V.C. BY MAUD DIVER.
Edinburgh: W. Blackwood, 1907 BMC. New York: Lane,
1908 NUC.

Captain marries "Ladybird." TLS
PW--military man extra-marital relation
PW 86 8/8/14:439 "Story of love and heroism on the
Indian frontier. In the background are hill tribes,
the station and camp. In the foreground is a man,
devoted, valiant; a girl, fragile as a flower and as
incapable, whom the man marries; and her chum."

003342   DESMOND'S DAUGHTER. BY MAUD DIVER.
Edinburgh and London: W. Blackwood, 1916 BMC NUC. New
York and London: G. P. Putnam's, 1916 NUC.

Anglo-Indian novel-Tirah campaign. Thea soldier's
daughter. PW 90:7/29/16:385. Vincent's love for Thea
holds him to ideal of service-given chance--becomes "a
soldier" through and through. NYT
LBKM TLS

003343   THE GREAT AMULET. BY MAUD DIVER. New
York: J. Lane, 1908 NUC. Edinburgh and London: W.
Blackwood, 1909 NUC BMC.

PW-more military life in India.
TLS-story of a marriage, she an artist, he a dope
fiend, all ends well.
BKM 0
ATH 0
NYT-she also a flirt.

003344   THE HERO OF HERAT. A FRONTIER BIOGRAPHY
IN ROMANTIC FORM. BY MAUD DIVER. London: Constable,
1912 BMC. New York and London: G. P. Putnam's Sons,
1913 NUC.

"Captain Desmond, V. C. and other Anglo-Indian tales
have shown the author's familiarity with life in
India. In this book the central figure is Eldred
Pottinger, an historic personage whose life, full of
adventure, had all the charm of romance. Setting of
the story is Afghanistan and the first Afghan war,
with its many blunders and disasters. Author promises
in another book, "Retribution," to tell of Pottinger's
return to Afghanistan, of the Kabul disasters, the
imprisonment and final vengeance." PW

003345 THE JUDGMENT OF THE SWORD. THE TALE OF
THE KABUL TRAGEDY AND OF THE PART PLAYED THEREIN BY
MAJOR ELDRED POTTINGER, THE HERO OF HERAT. BY MAUD
DIVER. London: Constable, [c1913] NUC BMC. New York
and London: G. P. Putnam's Sons, 1913 NUC.

1)Pottinger, Eldred 1811-43 2)Afghan Wars-fiction.

003346 LILAMANI: A STUDY IN POSSIBILITIES. BY
MAUD DIVER. London: Hutchinson, 1911 BMC NUC. (Am. ed.
title: Awakening.)

Young Hindu woman comes West to study medicine; falls
in love with artist who paints her. They marry (mixed
marriage problems). "The difficulty she has in
adapting herself to the role of an English wife shows
how impossible would have been the plan of her
studying medicine." SP
Author sympathetic. ATH

003347 LONELY FURROW. BY MAUD DIVER. Boston:
Houghton Mifflin, 1913 NUC. London: J. Murray, 1923
BMC.

India-

003348 STRANGE ROADS. BY MAUD DIVER. London:
Constable, [1918] NUC BMC.

Seems to focus on hero. Wife Lois killed off "just in
time." LBKM
TLS-male hero.

003349 THE STRONG HOURS. BY MAUD DIVER. London:
Constable, 1919 NUC BMC. Boston: Houghton Mifflin,
1919 NUC.

Purely conventional war story. TLS
Patriotic. ATH
Focuses on Derek Blount; Gabrielle de Vigne heroine;
bad German who tried to get control of English
businesses. Not a war novel, no battles, but testing
of character of Derek, in social work, learns to
understand workers' point of view. NYT 671,11-23-19
Fortunes of an English family during the European War,
at the Western front and in various parts of the
British Empire completes story of Blounts of Avonleigh
begun in Strange Roads.
BKM-war-brave male hero who marries girl unworthy of
him.

003350 UNCONQUERED; A ROMANCE. BY MAUD DIVER.
New York and London: G. P. Putnam's, 1917 NUC. London:
J. Murray, 1917 BMC.

Bel Alison "shallow but fascinating" opposes her
fiance going to war; vs. marriage when he returns
semi-paralyzed. Her friend Sheila ends up wooing him.
PW
Bel is a pacifist; book filled with "old platitudes
for and against the militant suffragists, pacifism."
Critic warns her to stay off that old stuff. TLS
An indictment of democratic government. ATH
Sheila is patriotic? SP
Two different views of war. Bel, shallow, adventurous
captures Sir Mark-uses her power to keep him out of
war. Sheila "more reasonable and patriotic." Sir Mark
comes home paralyzed. Bel gives him up. Sheila takes
him. NYT
"Author refrains from saying Bel is bound to marry a
maimed man. It all depends on the woman's character
and temperament." "Bel is not made abnormal or
vicious." SP
Subtle characterization. SR

DIVER, MAUD. See DIVER, KATHERINE HELEN MAUD (MARSHALL).

DIX, BEULAH MARIE. B. 1876. United States.

003351 THE BATTLE MONTHS OF GEORGE DAURELLA. New
York: Duffield, 1916 NUC.

War and rescue. PW
NYT--From pacifist pov. Heroine is a Red Cross nurse
working in military hospital.

003352 THE FAIR MAID OF GRAYSTONES. New York:
Macmillan, 1905 NUC BMC. London: Macmillan, 1905 NUC.

003353 THE FIGHTING BLADE. New York: H. Holt,
1912 NUC. London: Hodder and Stoughton, 1913 BMC.

PW hist.
NYT--madcap heroine.
Days of Cromwell, hero a dangerous swordsman, his love
is a great heiress betrothed to another man. ATH TLS

003354 THE GATE OF HORN. New York: Duffield,
1912 NUC. London: Methuen, [1913] BMC.

PW--dreams?
NYT--dreams of former lives, love story.
Through dreams, the heroine pieces together her life
in a previous incarnation. ATH
Girl's life from childhood to college life. Dreams
play a big part in her thoughts. Sidney Considine. TLS

003355 HANDS OFF! New York: Macmillan, 1919 NUC.
London: E. Nash, 1920 BMC.

Advent story of man in Mexico. PW
TLS--west rom.

003356 HUGH GWYETH: A ROUNDHEAD CAVALIER. New
York and London: Macmillan, 1899 BMC NUC.

The great Rebellion-sympathy with the Royalists.
Historical romance. SP 82:793

003357 KAY DANFORTH'S CAMP. New York: Duffield,
1917 NUC.

003358 THE LIFE, TREASON, AND DEATH OF JAMES
BLOUNT OF BRECKENHOW. New York, London: Macmillan,
1903 NUC BMC. (Compiled from the Rowlestone papers.)

soldiers and military duty; exchange of letters
between two families in Civil War. ACAD

003359 A LITTLE CAPTIVE LAD. New York:
Macmillan, 1902 BMC NUC. London: Macmillan, 1902 NUC.

003360 LITTLE FAITHFUL. London: Mills and Boon,
1914 BMC.

ATH--Betty's struggle between love and success as
author and playwright. Discovers that without love
life is barren.
TLS--essentially a traditional romance. Betty is a
wealthy novelist and playwright.

003361 THE LITTLE GOD EBISU. New York: Duffield,
1914 NUC.

"Of course, it was more play than belief that the
little god of luck could change her fortunes. Still,
Oru put ginger by his image for him to eat, while she
was working all day. And things did happen, rather
adventures, and ended happily enough to make the
little god smile." PW 86 10-10-14:1202.
NYT--old fashioned love story, young woman who hated
teaching.

003362 MAID MILICENT. New York: Hearst's
International Library, 1914 BMC NUC.

NYT--slight, romance, heroine is a "girl of spirit and
wit and cleverness with a reckless courage that is
ready for any adventure." At 17 she is sent to England
to marry the son of her father's old friend; they have
been betrothed since childhood. He resents this and
runs away to join a group of Irish fighters.
Eventually they meet.

003363 THE MAKING OF CHRISTOPHER FERRINGHAM. New
York: Macmillan, 1901 NUC BMC. London: Macmillan, 1901
NUC.

003364 MERRYLIPS. New York: Macmillan, 1906 NUC
BMC. London: Macmillan, 1906 NUC.

003365 MOTHER'S SON; A NOVEL. New York: Holt,
1913 NUC.

BKM--Hugo Mehring, a delicate small German man ends up
somehow in America. New England authoress Betty
Willard learns to take him seriously as he proves how
much of a person he is.
"Hugo Von Mehring, good looking and generally humorous
even in adversity, but a spendthrift and a toy
soldier, is disowned by his family and exiled to
America. He strikes bottom physically but not
morally--and then becomes a man. The heroine, Betty
Willard, successful playwright, but all woman in her
indecision, headlong generosity and self-surrender,
has most to do with helping Hugo, the mother's son.
The scene is Boston and vicinity and New York, and
Hugo's return from the wreck of the Titanic brings a
thrill with the happy ending." PW 84:1527
Hugo is so good looking that everyone spoils him,
especially his mother. Even Betty doesn't take him
seriously until she learns more about him. Hugo on

165

Titanic at the end; that event from Betty's point of view. BKM

003366   SOLDIER RIGDALE: HOW HE SAILED IN THE "MAYFLOWER" AND HOW HE SERVED MILES STANDISH. New York and London: Macmillan, 1899 BMC NUC.

SP 84:637. Hero a little boy. Mayflower settlers.
ATH 115:143

DIX, BEULAH MARIE AND CARRIE ANNA HARPER.

003367   THE BEAU'S COMEDY. New York and London: Harper, 1902 BMC NUC.

ATH 6-14-02

DIX, DOROTHY, pseud. See GILMER, ELIZABETH (MERIWETHER).

DIX, GERTRUDE. United States.

003368   THE GIRL FROM THE FARM. Boston: Roberts, 1895 NUC. London: J. Lane, 1895 BMC NUC.

daughter leaves father (blind); goes to do rescue work. She's "more unloveable than even the average New Daughter." SR 80:55
"This is one of those wearisome books that deal with the modern daughter of emancipated views." She's a dean's daughter. Struggle in her mind between duty to parents and philanthropic work, girl from farm seduced. ATH 106:156. Graduate with honors-Newnhan.
"The compatibility of higher ed and true womanhood" PW 48:160

003369   THE IMAGE BREAKERS. New York: F. A. Stokes, [c1900] NUC. London: W. Heinemann, 1900 BMC.

LBKM 19:27. =Lent a peculiar pathos and dignity to that generally unpopular kind of woman who outrages public opinion in the name of Duty." Rosalind's discovery that life has died out of her early vision of the Cause causes reader regret. Conflict of ideals vs craving for personal comforts. Tragic, but 1 of the heroines ends comfortably. London.
SR 90:524. Socialism. "Chapters...are taken up describing the efforts of an ordinary, nice minded man to persuade the girl, who is his wife in everything but name, to marry him."
ATH 116:438. Rosalind is the wife of a wealthy manufacturer. Leslie is a friend, an artist. Both turn Socialist and decide to run away together. Rosalind goes to a House of Charity, Leslie gets job as governess. Eventually they get to London. Socialism is a background rather than an atmosphere for their love stories.
NYT 1900:774. "The 2 women...show how miserable are the lives of 2 well-meaning women, infected with what is a mental disease."
PW-two women's lives are devoted to the work of raising women and giving them ideals and help. Both women fail by reason of the weakness of their own character. Shows up the shams of reform in merciless manner.
LIT 7:372. "Viewed as an essay in the direction of social reform and the probable failure of reformers." Socialism is passe, belonged to the 90's, reviewer says. Girl from the farm, Keynote Series.

DIXIE, FLORENCE CAROLINE (DOUGLAS). 1857-1905.

003370   IZRA; A CHILD OF SOLITUDE. London: J. Long, [1906] BMC.

TLS--Manifesto--love of animals, hatred of sport and gambling, social tyrannies, religion, championship of women.

003371   LITTLE CHERIE; OR, THE TRAINER'S DAUGHTER, A RACING AND SOCIAL NOVEL. London: A. Treherne, 1901 BMC.

003372   THE STORY OF IJAIN; OR, THE EVOLUTION OF A MIND. London: Leadenhall Press, [1903] BMC.

Child tells her story. TLS

DIXON, ELLA HEPWORTH. B. 1832. United Kingdom.

003373   MY FLIRTATIONS. BY MARGARET WYNMAN. London: Chatto & Windus, 1892 BMC. Philadelphia: J. B. Lippincott, 1893 NUC.

Her flirtations with a dozen or so suitors and crisp obervations on society. CR 14, 20:128.
ATH 100:586. Sketches of heroine's admirers, satire on

various types of men.
PW 13. All short lived, none tragic.
SR. 74:419. Portraits of "latter-day Lotharios." Very funny.

003374   THE STORY OF A MODERN WOMAN. London: W. Heinemann, 1894 BMC. New York: Cassell, [1894] NUC.

SR 77:668. Heroine is a journalist, remains single. "Miss Dixon has a poor opinion of the relations between the sexes."
ATH 103:770. "Mary Erle is a gentle and essentially feminine creature, who only took to journalism and a solitary life in London lodgings owing to the stress of outward circumstances." She knew no inner call to forsake home ties and duties in order to lead a higher life and to get her own way. Makes what money she can by writing in a second rate way."Loses her lover through his weakness."
LBKM 6:88. Mary had a precocious and unconventional childhood, but in contrast is particularly submissive and unaspiring in her career. After being jilted by Vincent, a high-powered egotistical intellectual, she takes to indifferent work and gets tired out. He comes back; she refuses him and lives to struggle on in London.
LW 25:202. "An earnest, patient woman who accepts her life and makes one of the great army of working women, unnoticed in their heroism and endurance."
Mary undertakes to order her own life. She's the orphaned daughter of Professor Erle. Tries art but fails at it. Tries writing and is more successful. When her lover returns from India she discovers he loves someone else and marries her. Years later he comes to beg her to elope with him. She refuses and continues her ind. life. LW 26:282.

DIXON, LILIAS H.

003375   THE MASTER OF HELMESMERE. A NOVEL CONCERNING MATTERS OF NO VITAL IMPORTANCE. A SIMPLE RECORD OF HOME AND SOCIAL LIFE. London: F. Griffiths, 1912 BMC.

ATH Love and marriage.

DOBBIN, GERTRUDE (PAGE). D. 1922. United Kingdom.

003376   THE EDGE O' BEYOND. BY GERTRUDE PAGE. London: Hurst and Blackett, 1908 BMC. London: G. Bell, 1908 NUC.

TLS--wife runs off with another man and lives five dear years with him. Sent
SP--Book is dedicated to all the women in the Colonies of the British Empire who are roughing it for the sake of husband, fathers, etc.

003377   FAR FROM THE LIMELIGHT. BY GERTRUDE PAGE. London, New York: Cassell, [1918] NUC BMC.

003378   FOLLOW AFTER! BY GERTRUDE PAGE. London: Hurst and Blackett, [1915] BMC NUC.

Two men, excitement, war. TLS
Intense loyalty to the Empire. ATH
Simple minded optimism. SP

003379   THE GREAT SPLENDOUR. BY GERTRUDE PAGE. London: Hurst and Blackett, 1912 BMC NUC.

TLS--romance of boyish girl love, is the splendour.

003380   JILL'S RHODESIAN PHILOSOPHY; OR THE DAM FARM. BY GERTRUDE PAGE. London: Hurst and Blackett, [1910] BMC NUC.

003381   LOVE IN THE WILDERNESS: THE STORY OF ANOTHER AFRICAN FARM. BY GERTRUDE PAGE. London: Hurst and Blackett, 1907 BMC. London: Bell, [1907?] NUC.

003382   THE MYSTERIOUS STRANGERS. [Ottawa]: Warwick and Rutter, 1902 BMC.

003383   PADDY-THE-NEXT-BEST-THING. BY GERTRUDE PAGE. London: Hurst and Blackett, 1908 BMC. New York: F. A. Stokes, [c1916] NUC.

TLS--to a boy. Mother of a hero, which is also the next-best-thing.
NYT--Romance, spirited, dominating heroine who was disappointment to father who wanted a son.

003384   THE PATHWAY. BY GERTRUDE PAGE. London: Ward, Lock, 1914 BMC NUC.

LBKM--Sympathy for the lot of the woman pioneer.
ATH--Rhodesia. Shows how essential is the help of
self-sacrificing, broad-minded women in the work of
empire building.
ATH--Romance. tribute to women of Rhodesia.

003385   THE RHODESIAN. BY GERTRUDE PAGE. London:
Hurst and Blackett, 1912 BMC NUC.

TLS--Male imperialistic hero.

003386   THE SILENT RANCHER. London: Hurst and
Blackett, 1909 BMC.

Tragedy of a man in Rhodesia. TLS

003387   SOME THERE ARE--. BY GERTRUDE PAGE.
London: Hurst and Blackett, 1916 NUC BMC.

TLS--romance.
LBKM--Alastair is visited by Doris Strangeways who was
sacrificed to marriage early, has since husband died
been travelling the world and Doreen, waiting for her
dream lover. Doreen proves to be a real heroine in
submarine episode. She discovers a base on the coast
and rushes from northern Scotland to South England to
report it to authorities, narrowly escaping death.
Alastair is a misogynist.

003388   THE SUPREME DESIRE. London: Ward, Lock,
1916 BMC.

TLS--tr. romance.
LBKM--Love story. Three suitors.

003389   TWO LOVERS AND A LIGHTHOUSE. London:
Hurst and Blackett, 1910 BMC.

An irregular alliance between a Cabinet Minister and a
lady who escapes an unhappy marriage. SP
BM--Charming.
TLS--A Cabinet Minister and his love (his wife is in a
home for inebriates) settle on the Cornish Coast. She
narrates, is of noble birth although he rescues her
from the streets.

003390   THE VELDT TRAIL. BY GERTRUDE PAGE.
London: Cassell, 1919 BMC. London and New York:
Cassell, [1921] NUC.

Bride separates from husband when she learns he
cheated during their engagement. Insists he go
abroad--he's mauled to death by leopard. She takes up
with his partner but he's repulsed by her and takes
off? TLS

003391   WHERE THE STRANGE ROADS GO DOWN. BY
GERTRUDE PAGE. London: Hurst and Blackett, 1913 BMC
NUC.

Rhodesia, local color. A young Englishwoman, immature
and inexperienced comes to the comparative wilds of
Rhodesia. Story describes the pitfalls which open
before her. ACAD
Focuses on a Rhodesian Don Juan, Joe the heroine, wife
of Rhodesian settler, another wife who comes under Don
Juan's spell-she's altogether disillusioned with
Rhodesian life. Her life and Joe's described--a double
thread. Theme: life of overstrained woman in a new
country. TLS

003392   WINDING PATHS. BY GERTRUDE PAGE. London:
Hurst and Blackett, 1911 NUC BMC. New York: D.
Appleton, 1911 NUC.

Hal Pritchard is strong throughout her life,
contrasted to weaker people wins her own way and reaps
her reward. PW 6-22-11.
Young woman who practices freely the habit of being
pals with men. Much to say about female independence.
Hal is a journalist and Lorraine an actress. Author
has deep admiration for Hal. TLS
Lorraine Vivian, one of London's leading actresses.
ACAD
NYT--Hal is a journalist, a jolly girl. Author intends
to illustrate the present status of the working woman
in London, a little disquisition on the suffrage
question.

DOBELL, NORA.

003393   TWO WOMEN OF KENT. London: H. J. Drane,
1905 BMC.

DODD, ANNA BOWMAN (BLAKE). 1855-1929. United States.

003394   THE AMERICAN HUSBAND IN PARIS. Boston:
Little, Brown, [1901] BMC NUC.

Very questionable. BOOK BUYER '01
Wife underestimates her husband; in Paris learns he's
a great man and feels proud of him. Yet the author
shows a pair who do not really understand each other.
NYT '01
Wife comes to see her husband as a great man after
she's had the experiences of traveling in Paris and he
visits for the first time but is a hit.

003395   IN AND OUT OF A FRENCH COUNTRY HOUSE. New
York: Dodd, Mead, 1910 NUC.

PW More a travel book.

003396   ON THE BROADS. London and New York:
Macmillan, 1896 BMC NUC.

Cruise on the Broads and a love story. The skipper, a
practical old lady. A hero-artist, hist. facts about
Norwich. SP 79:153

003397   ON THE KNEES OF THE GODS. New York: Dodd,
Mead, 1908 NUC. London: B. F. Stevens and Brown, 1908
BMC.

PW-hist. rom.
BKM hist rom.

003398   STRUTHERS, AND THE COMEDY OF THE MASKED
MUSICIAN. New York: Lovell, Coryell, 1894 [c] NUC.

CR 25:186. Struthers: story of a married couple moving
up in society because of increasing income. They give
up society and go to Europe. Comedy: woman procures
money for education of two street musicians in Italy,
man and wife, the man the disinherited son of the
nobleman she has asked for money.

DODD, CATHERINE ISABEL. 1860-1932. United Kingdom.

003399   A VAGRANT ENGLISHWOMAN. London: Smith,
Elder, 1905 BMC NUC.

Conversations of handful of university people in
Germany. Theme: emancipation of German women,
Englishwoman among them. ACAD 05:617.
No love story, pension life in a German University
town. LBKM
She's conscious that her sisters have much to put up
with, that men are unsatisfactory creatures. ATH
05:589.

DODDS, MINNIE MILBANK. United States.

003400   IN THIS WORLD OF OURS. New York:
Shakespeare Press, 1912 NUC.

PW-Love story.

DODGE, JANET.

003401   AN INN UPON THE ROAD. London: Sidgwick
and Jackson, 1913 BMC.

Natalie Herbert, extremely sensitive, utterly
unawakened; problem of sex frightened her to such an
extent that she declines to marry two days before the
wedding, the man who awakened her and thus lost her.
Author displays all of Natalie's "analytical
indecency." Love is just an Inn, a momentary place for
women. It's a threshhold, not the whole end. The
masculine Helen influences Natalie to separate from
her lovers. In the end Natalie can't assimilate the
idea of self sacrifice to true love. Helen smokes a
pipe. LBKM

003402   TONY UNREGENERATE. London: Duckworth,
1912 BMC.

TLS--reveals her (Tony) determination in holding her
own ideas, one of them being the unnecessary fetters
of the marriage tie.
ATH--She lives with married musician for a time.
SP--Has his baby, he is a weakling who gets his
inspiration from women and falling in love. She tells
him off; he is either struck by a car or kills
himself. She is not sorry she has known him.

DODGE, MARY THURSTON, pseud. See LE FEUVRE, AMY.

DOISSY, LOUISE. Nationality Unknown.

003403   A BUSINESS VENTURE IN LOS ANGELES; OR, A

167

CHRISTIAN OPTIMIST. BY Z. Z. Cincinnati: R. Clarke, 1899 NUC.

DOLING, ANNA (MOONEY). B. 1875. United States.

003404   BRILLA. New York: Neale, 1913 NUC.

DOLMAN, MARIA, pseud. See DUDMAN, ADA.

DON, ISABEL.

003405   ONLY CLARCHEN: A NOVEL. London: Eden, Remington, 1891 BMC.

English living in Germany and Hungary: ACAD
She's half English half German; her love story. SP 67 233
Clare Melville travels among worldly relatives to Hungary. Austin, one relative, bewitched by the Countess Souvarrow but then comes to appreciate and love Clare. ATH 98:58
(Clare) Cinderella in modern dress wins her wealthy prince though he is attracted to Augusta Folliot and to the Countess. SR 7-4-91, 22

003406   A STRONG NECESSITY: A NOVEL. London: Jarrold, 1897 BMC.

Lochton, Scot. The heroine, the silent antagonism between her parents. ATH 110:597.

DON CARLOS, COOKE. See DON CARLOS, LOUISA COOKE.

DON CARLOS, LOUISA COOKE. B. 1874. United States.

003407   A BOTTLE IN THE SMOKE. BY COOKE DON-CARLOS. Boston: Mayhew, 1907 NUC.

PW-historical novel.

003408   VIRGINIA'S INHERITANCE. BY COOKE DON-CARLOS. Boston: Davis & Bond, [c1915] NUC.

DONELSON, KATHARINE. United States.

003409   RODGER LATIMER'S MISTAKE: A NOVEL. Chicago: Laird and Lee, [c1891] NUC.

PW-Scenes partly in Chicago, party Europe.
LW-Novel with a purpose to show "blessing of home life and true affection and folly of social ambitions." Male hero, heroine proves "inscrutable extent of a woman's forgiveness."

DONNELL, ANNIE (HAMILTON). B. 1862. United States.

003410   MISS THEODOSIA'S HEARTSTRINGS. Boston: Little, Brown, 1916 BMC NUC.

NYT-rom and sugary

003411   REBECCA MARY. New York: Harper, 1905 NUC. London: Hodder & Stoughton, 1906 BMC.

TLS pretty, sentimental-young girl and stern aunt. ATH 0
About a child-sent PW 10-7-05

DONNELLY, ELEANOR CECILIA. 1838-1917. United States.

003412   THE FATAL DIAMONDS. New York: Benziger Brothers, 1897 NUC.

Dr. Kendrick used money meant for charity to buy jewels for his wife. How she lost them, other episodes in her life that show "The beauty of humility". PW 51:841.

003413   STORM-BOUND: A ROMANCE OF SHELL BEACH. Philadelphia: H. L. Kilner, [c1898] NUC BMC.

DONWORTH, GRACE. Nationality unknown.

003414   DOWN HOME WITH JENNIE ALLEN. Boston: Small, Maynard, [c1910] NUC.

Quaint letters of a good wife PW
NYT quaint letters of a good wife.

003415   THE LETTERS OF JENNIE ALLEN TO HER FRIEND, MISS MUSGROVE. Boston: Small, Maynard, 1908 NUC.

"These are the letters of a generous and kind-hearted woman. She is poor and works hard for the little she has, but all this fails to deaden her sense of humour or cause her to overlook the needs of others. Her letters are full of quaint humour and common sense." BKM V. 28 1908-9
NYT- Sugar coated moralities.

DOONAN, GRACE (WALLACE). B. 1873. United States.

003416   JUST HAPPY: THE STORY OF A DOG--AND SOME HUMANS. BY GRACE KEON. New York: Devin-Adair, [c1920] NUC.

003417   "NOT A JUDGEMENT-". BY GRACE KEON. New York: Benziger, [1906] NUC.

PW-a good good girl born in NY's East Side.

003418   THE RUBY CROSS; A NOVEL. BY MARY WALLACE. New York: Benziger, 1917 NUC.

Anne Holloway is deserted because husband discovers she's poor Another man tries to help her gain wealth through stocks. He even tries to steal the ruby cross. PW

003419   "WHEN LOVE IS STRONG". BY GRACE KEON. New York: Benziger, 1907 NUC.

Mystery story. PW 6-1-07

DORMAN, C. T. See DORMAN, CAROLINE TROTTI.

DORMAN, CAROLINE TROTTI. B. 1853. Nationality Unknown.

003420   UNDER THE MAGNOLIAS. BY C. T. DORMAN. New York: Abbey Press, [1902] NUC.

DORR, JULIA CAROLINE (RIPLEY). 1825-1913. United States.

003421   IN KINGS' HOUSES: A ROMANCE OF THE DAYS OF QUEEN ANNE. Boston: L. C. Page, 1898. London: Duckworth, 1899 BMC.

BKM 7:523. Historical romance of Queen Anne, both weak and soft-hearted.
NYT 1898:422. Story of a page in Queen Anne's court who discovers he is an heir to a fortune and a title.
LIT 5:304. Historical romantic time of Queen Anne who is a character. Not a traditional type of study. Anne is unheroic and sympathetic.

DORR, LOUISE SNOW. Nationality Unknown.

003422   THE MILLS OF THE GODS. New York: A. S. Barnes, 1900 NUC.

DORRANCE, ETHEL ARNOLD (SMITH). B. 1880. United States.

003423   A MAID AND A MAN. New York: Moffat, Yard, 1909 NUC.

Series of dialogues between them-an intellectual flirtation NYT

DORSET, MARIA. Nationality Unknown.

003424   BOUGHT OR WON? A STORY. Boston: J. H. Earle, 1896 NUC.

DOSTOEVSKAIA, LIUBOV FEDOROVNA. B. 1869.

003425   THE EMIGRANT. BY L. F. DOSTOIEFFSKAYA. London: Constable, 1915 BMC NUC. New York: Brentano's, 1916 NUC. (Tr. Vera Margolies)

TLS--Author pov? Rev. finds Irene ridiculous, unpleasant with a perverted and sterilized mind but says reader is not compelled to dislike her because of author's sympathy. She leaves Russia for home after Russo-Japanese war, disgusted with her country. Saw no hope after war for their attempts for reform. Is persuaded to become an RC nun. Meets a man, leaves faith and convent to marry but ends with suicide. Rev. blames Irene for her dreamy idealism lacking energy and unable to deal with disorder.
ATH--gloomy but powerful.

DOSTOIEFFSKAYA, L. F. See DOSTOEVSKAIA, LIUBOV FEDOROVNA.

DOUBLEDAY, ROMAN, pseud. See LONG, LILY AUGUSTA.

DOUDNEY, SARAH. 1843-1926. United Kingdom.

003426   BITTER AND SWEET. London: J. Nisbet, 1896 BMC.

003427   A CHILD OF THE PRECINCT. London:

Hutchinson, [1892] BMC. New York: 1892 NUC.

ATH 100:814. For girls. Heroine left alone in the world, "suffers many things before she wins happiness."

003428   GODIVA DURLEIGH. A NOVEL FOR GIRLS. London: S. Low, 1891 BMC NUC. New York: Randolph, 1893 NUC.

Her father, ed. and owner of a radical journal and a man of unconv. ideas, dies leaving her poor. She goes to live with cousins. A love affair. Eng. home life. PW 1-7-93
Modern: young woman ups and downs of love. Two old-lady aunts. Wholesome, sent. the good are very good, the bad very bad. ACAD. For all ages.
She's irritating; forgives her cousin's cruelties over and over but cruel to her lover when he's once attracted to another woman. SP 67 926
Earnest plea for Christian humility and long suffering and charity. ATH 98 858

003429   KATHERINE'S KEYS: A TALE. London: J. Nisbet, 1896 BMC.

PW 11-7-96. Katherine's loves. Her father moves from London to country, move to country is good for her character and she is loved there by a man "worthy of all her respect."

003430   LADY DYE'S REPARATION. London: Religious Tract Society, [1901] BMC. London: "Leisure Hour" Library Office, [1907] NUC.

003431   LOUIE'S MARRIED LIFE. London: Partridge, [1894] BMC.

003432   THE LOVE-DREAM OF GATTY FENNING. London: Hutchinson, [1892] BMC.

003433   ONE OF THE FEW. London: Hutchinson, 1904 BMC.

TLS-Old love renewed in after years.

003434   PILGRIMS OF THE NIGHT: A NOVEL. London: W. H. Addison, 1897 BMC.

Lelia Wooledge backs off from eloping with Bennet Daughton (married to a "low-born" woman he seduced). Then there's Dulcie Daughton, a good study. She writes short stories, and that her husband should appreciate his wife's accomplishment indicates how he has been converted by her love. ATH 109:746.

003435   A ROMANCE OF LINCOLN'S INN. London: Hutchinson, 1893 BMC NUC.

ATH Rev-Heroine is a foundling, believed to have a gypsy mother. Two suitors, she chooses one; I believe he goes mad.
A man idealizes a young woman, realizes strength from the experience. Writes a novel. "Writes in tradition of Miss Yonge" a "harmless, necessary" novelist. SR 79:54.
Young woman jilts poor man to marry a peer. The young man gets ill but recovers. The peer turns out to be insane. Tries to kill wife, succeeds in killing self. Lady Wynburn then tries to take up with the poor ex lover but he'll have none of it. She's Nellie Stanley, with gypsy blood, a governess. ACAD 44:545.

003436   SHADOW AND SHINE. London: Hodder & Stoughton, 1906 BMC. Cincinnati: Jennings & Graham, [1908] PW.

TLS-For young ladies not too advanced.
PW-Story of three women's lives.
LBKM trad rom.

003437   THROUGH PAIN TO PEACE: A NOVEL. London: Hutchinson, 1892 BMC. New York: J. A. Taylor, [1892] NUC.

ATH 100:443. Tracy rejects a "worldly-wise" baronet, becomes religiously devout and engaged to an ascetic churchman.
SP 69:599. "A very womanly writer" at a time of "so much feminine masculinity"
PW-Breaks with baronet, devotes herself to art, falls for a clergyman. Then a new break in her life and she turns to a life of service for others and finds peace. SR 74:395. Dies very soon, reviewer suggests "worried to death" as more fitting title.

003438   A VANISHED HAND. London: J. Nisbet, 1896 BMC. Boston: A. I. Bradley, [189-?] NUC.

PW 8-22-96. Elsie, feeling that she is guided by the spirit of a dead writer, and feeling her life to be purposeless otherwise, finds a posthumous manuscript and searches for the child it describes. Elsie's adventures and love-story follow.
BOOK NEWS Elsie is 28, living alone on $750 a year.

003439   VIOLETS FOR FAITHFULNESS. London, New York: M. Ward, [1893] NUC BMC.

DOUGALL, L. See DOUGALL, LILY.

DOUGALL, LILY. 1858-1923. Canada.

003440   BEGGARS ALL; A NOVEL. BY L. DOUGALL. New York, London and Bombay: Longmans, Green, 1891 BMC 1903 NUC.

Esther Thompson answers a marriage ad because her invalid mother and crippled sister need help. The man is a good sort, sympathetic with her mother and sister. Esther learns he's not just a journalist but a burglar who steals only from people who get their money dishonestly; uses no arms. At the end he goes off to America to honest work. ACAD
Ends in hope that he'll be reclaimed. LW. Also ATH 98 415
keen, sustained psychological analysis. He's Hubert Kent-his crude kind roughness; her grace and sweetness. SR 10-3-91, 391
NATION:145:263. Hubert Kent is the product of an orphanage; author shows relation of his treatment there to his belief in his right to a share of power, even thru a criminal act.
DIAL 13:310. "A tale of serious human interest" young woman who responds to matrimony ad. Hero is a professional burglar.
CR 17:69. Can't make enough money as shop girl; can't support mother and young sister. Therefore marries. He takes good care of them. "Beggars all for human sympathy."

003441   THE EARTHLY PURGATORY. London: Hutchinson, 1904 BMC.

LBKM--2 sisters, murder mystery, "one of the two might have been provided with a husband" psychological study.
ATH--Almost entire lack of love interest.
TLS--Fine book.
ACAD--Sufferings of 2 sisters, sordid character. Good book. Love interest is not missed in recital of suffering and suspicions of two sisters.

003442   THE MERMAID: A LOVE TALE. BY L. DOUGALL. London: R. Bentley, 1895 BMC. New York: D. Appleton, 1895 NUC.

Pr. Edward Is. Girl impersonates a mermaid. Young doctor is unconsciously in search of a woman to love. The mermaid is also a woman; whose husband is odious. Then there's O'Shea who murders Josephine Le Maitre's husband. SP 74:540
Josephine Le Maitre disguises as a mermaid wins Caius' love. Then he later must go to Cloud Island where there's a plague; she bids him go; he's a doctor. ACAD 47:354
She actually wears a costume-life preserving garment made to resemble fish skin and supported by bladders. She marries him in the end. LW 26:137.
He is a young doctor who as a child saw a mother-deranged by her husband's cruelty-throw her child into the sea. PW 3-23-95:484.

003443   THE MORMAN PROPHET. London: A. and C. Black, 1899 BMC NUC. New York: D. Appleton, 1899 NUC.

A half historical, half imaginative account of Joseph Smith founder of Mormonism. LIT 4:375.
He's presented as very human-sometimes only half sure of his revelations--like that of polygamy. Susannah is a high spirited heroine who supports the cause of Mormonism. Marries a Mormon, Halsey, buries him and her child at Harin's Hill after the battle there. And Joseph Smith convinces her to be his "spiritual or supplementary" bride. LBKM 16:17 Susannah moved by the persecution of the Mormons throws in her lot with them, but she remains a skeptic though fascinated by Smith. She refuses his offer to be part of his harem. Her child and husband are killed by anti-Mormons in her sight. Susannah Halsey. SP 82:386
Her love of justice makes her support the Mormons. BKM 9:374

Career of Joseph Smith and picture of Mormons. BAKER
03,244

003444   PATHS OF THE RIGHTEOUS. BY L. DOUGALL.
London: Macmillan, 1908 BMC NUC.

TLS--Serious and careful study of blend of religion
and unconscious worldliness in the mind of the wife of
the vicar, issue of nonconformity.
BKM--mostly male.

003445   A QUESTION OF FAITH. BY L. DOUGALL.
London: Hutchinson, 1895 BMC. Boston: Houghton,
Mifflin, 1895 NuC.

ATH 107:13. Heroine loves a mystery and to test the
faith of her suitor.
ACAD 49:10. Ending is uncertain. Does the squire
reconcile Alice to orthodoxy? Does she marry him?
SP 77:465. Alice is independent.
BKM 2:436. Novel is ruined by author's
preachiness-about what?

003446   THE SPANISH DOWRY: A ROMANCE. London:
Hutchinson, 1906 BMC. Toronto: Copp, Clark, [1906?]
NUC.

ATH--Male boy hero.

003447   THE SUMMIT HOUSE MYSTERY; OR THE EARTHLY
PURGATORY. BY L. DOUGALL. New York and London: Funk
and Wagnalls, 1905 NUC.

Strong willed, long suffering rel. woman; mystery amd
cri me. NYT 05:102.

003448   WHAT NECESSITY KNOWS. BY L. DOUGALL.
London: Longmans, 1893 BMC. New York: Longmans, 1893
NUC.

SR 77:150. Two brothers, one a butcher and one a
rector, in same town. A young woman escapes "her
isolated life and importunate lover" by taking her
father's place in a coffin and finding a position as a
servant.
CR-Two brothers love same woman.
The Reverend Robert Tremholme must learn to live with
the fact that his father was a butcher. Canadian
story. Sissy Cameron must overcome hardness; and
Sophie Rexford, pride. Each is purged of the fault
that weighs them down. SP 71, 688.
Sissie Cambridge revolts. She's independent but
finally submits. Robert trained at Oxford. Later he
and brother who goes into business move to Canada. LW
93, 379.
Elisa Cameron is the mysterious interesting dear-who
remains a puzzle to the end. ATH 102:658.

003449   THE ZEIT-GEIST. BY L. DOUGALL. New York:
Longmans, Green, 1893 NUC. London: Hutchinson, 1895
BMC.

SP 76:814. Male hero, who, having saved himself, helps
others.
Long and painful climb of a soul from a lower to
higher place. ACAD 47:502
Canadian romance about rel. problems. Also a love
story. ATH 105:605.
Bartholomew Toyner a profligate and Ann Markham, a
murderer's daughter, Toyner's conversion and how he
won Ann. LW 26:232.

DOUGHERTY, JEANNETTE M. B. 1861. Nationality Unknown.

003450   THE SECRET NAME. Cincinnati: Jennings &
Pye, [1903] NUC.

DOUGLAS, AMANDA MINNIE. 1837-1916. United States.

003451   BETHIA WRAY'S NEW NAME. Boston: Lee and
Shepard, 1893 NUC.

003452   THE HEIR OF SHERBURNE. New York: Dodd,
Mead, [c1899] NUC.

Gertrude Maurice is a secretary to a wealthy woman.
"Much space is devoted to her career and character"
Also her sisters' lives.PW 56:648

003453   THE HEIRS OF BRADLEY HOUSE. Boston: Lee
and Shepard, 1892 NUC.

Fortune of Mrs. Halford, her daughters and three
gentlemen. Winterburne and his sister in social reform
work among mill hands. Also story of what happens to
old homestead. PW.

003454   HELEN GRANT AT ALFRED HOUSE. Boston:
Lothrop, Lee and Shepard, [1905] NUC.

Heroine, not romantic but ambitious ready for college
must choose between career and lovers. PW
Brief description. BKM

003455   HELEN GRANT, GRADUATE. Boston: Lothrop,
Lee and Shepard, [1908] NUC.

003456   HELEN GRANT IN COLLEGE. Boston: Lothrop,
Lee and Shepard, [1906] NUC.

PW--series.

003457   HELEN GRANT, SENIOR. Boston: Lothrop, Lee
and Shepard, [c1907] NUC.

003458   HELEN GRANT, TEACHER. Boston: Lothrop,
Lee and Shepard, [1909] NUC.

Teacher rules big boys through love. Earnest capable
teacher. PW

003459   HELEN GRANT'S DECISION. Boston: Lothrop,
Lee and Shepard, [c1910] NUC.

2nd year as high school teacher gets offer from a
college but stays where she is. She also makes another
decision? PW

003460   HELEN GRANT'S FRIENDS. Boston: Lothrop,
Lee and Shepard, 1904 NUC.

003461   HELEN GRANT'S HARVEST YEAR. Boston:
Lothrop, Lee and Shepard, [1911] NUC.

Teacher travels abroad; intellectual woman hates to
give up her work for domestic sphere, but does in the
end. PW

003462   HELEN GRANT'S SCHOOLDAYS. Boston: Lee and
Shepard, 1903 NUC. London and Glasgow: Collins
Clear-type Press, [1910] BMC.

Dependent but always wanted a good education, a
wealthy woman gets her to a good school. PW

003463   HER PLACE IN THE WORLD. Boston: Lee and
Shepard, [c1897] NUC.

Two young women, one a butterfly type, the other a
mature, sensible woman. The first marries the man who
becomes friends with the second. She becomes his
adviser, inspiring him to success. She also finds "her
sphere." PW 52:604.
LW 29:102. "A gentle and perfectly ladylike assault on
the chains of convention which have barred a woman's
horizon across her domestic hearth." Can be read with
"perfect safety."

003464   HONOR SHERBURNE. New York: Dodd, Mead,
[1904] NUC.

Young couple, lawyer and wife, in Washington politics.
The wife comes under influence of another woman. Wife
buys stock that almost ruins husband's reputation. But
she's haughty, cold about itall. Her pride purged by
an illness; sister's love affair in marriage, a
spinster poet: many other characters. NYT
PW--Series book about a conventional heroine.

003465   IN THE KING'S COUNTRY. Boston: Lee and
Shepard, 1894 NUC.

CR 21:374. One of three young women attempts to
persuade others to do God's work amongst humanity with
her.
PW-the scheme involved an old house. Sabrina and Pearl
work together; also romance for Sabrina.

003466   IN THE SHERBURNE LINE. New York: Dodd,
Mead, 1907 NUC.

Woman flees from fiance to spare him a mother in law
who's an addict. When mother dies at end, all happily
resolved. PW 10-19-07.

003467   IN WILD ROSE TIME. Boston: Lee and
Shepard, 1895 NUC.

Dilsey Quinn cares for her helpless sister Bessie.
Pictures life among the poor. PW 1-19-95:53

003468   THE MISTRESS OF SHERBURNE. New York:

Dodd, Mead, 1896 NUC.

Dell Sherburne travels to Pacific coast, returns and becomes Dell Carew, The events of her married life BOOK NEWS 96-7:139.

003469   A QUESTION OF SILENCE. New York: Dodd, Mead, 1901 NUC.

PW 3-9-01. Woman insane, strange treatment by the doctor.

003470   SHERBURNE HOUSE. London: B. F. Stevens, [1892] BMC. New York: Dodd, Mead, [1892] NUC.

PW-Aristocratic Virginia family. Heir marries an English dancing girl, their daughter returns to Virginia and is firebrand to pecae and decorum.

003471   A SHERBURNE INHERITANCE. New York: Dodd, Mead, 1901 NUC.

PW--sequel to the Heir of Sherburne.

003472   A SHERBURNE QUEST. New York: Dodd, Mead, [c1902] NUC.

NYT--juv?

DOUGLAS, GEORGE, pseud. See FERME, MRS. GEORGE.

DOUGLAS, JULIA, pseud. See EVERETT, MRS. H. D.

DOUGLAS, KATHARINE WALDO. See FEDDEN, KATHARINE WALDO DOUGLAS.

DOUGLAS, MAUD ISIDORE.

003473   FOR MRS. GRUNDY'S SAKE: A NOVEL. London: Digby, Long, [1893] BMC.

DOUGLAS, O., pseud. See BUCHAN, ANNA.

DOUGLAS, THEO, pseud. See EVERETT, MRS. H. D.

DOUGLASS, MRS. AKEN.

003474   BERYL; OR THE SILENT PROMPTER. A NOVEL. Chicago, Ill.: Scroll Publishing and Literary Syndicate, 1900 NUC.

DOUIE, MARJORIE. United Kingdom.

003475   THE POINTING MAN: A BURMESE MYSTERY. London: Hutchinson, 1917 BMC. New York: E. P. Dutton, [c1920] NUC.

Traditional detective. TLS ATH
PW-crime of a white man.

DOW, JOY WHEELER. United States.

003476   MISS POLLY FAIRFAX [ANONYMOUS]. New York: P. F. Mcbreen, 1898 NUC BMC.

DOW, MRS. J. C., SR. United States.

003477   THE BLUE AND THE GREY; OR, AFTER MANY DAYS. Chicago: M. A. Donohue, [1904] NUC.

DOWDALL, HON. MRS. See DOWDALL, MARY FRANCES HARRIET (BORTHWICK).

DOWDALL, MARY FRANCES HARRIET (BORTHWICK). 1876-1939. United Kingdom.

003478   THE BOOK OF MARTHA. BY THE HON. MRS DOWDALL. London: Duckworth, [1913] BMC NUC.

She wrestles with servant problem, with the cook, housemaid, butler, charwoman and their gradual reformation, she's shrewd; gets her way. ATH

003479   JOKING APART. London: Duckworth, 1914 BMC NUC.

Martha says a lot of witty things. Reviewer says little. LBKM
"ridiculous" "exasperating" "hardly worth reading-not funny sketches of provincial society" SP

003480   THE KALEIDOSCOPE: A NOVEL. London: Duckworth, 1915 BMC.

Gladys Burbecu marries George the plumber who becomes a baronet story jerks from episode to episode deadly

portrait of women. TLS

003481   SUSIE, YESTERDAY, TO-DAY, AND FOREVER. London: Duckworth, 1919 BMC.

Brainless, faithless, alluring, vain, her loves. SR Great mission is motherhood, expects father to perform his function and fall into the background. Love is really irrelevant. Artist musician wildly in love with her. Her marriage is successful even tho she continues relationship with artist and sees herself as a madonna while husband sees her as tabby. Portrayed with loving hatred. She is an anachronism (rev).
SP-Susie fell victim to the most brutal of her admirers? Secret of her success was genius for adaptation. "without the least understanding of what was going on in other people's minds"--author. There are three types of unselfish womanhood, her cousin Lucy, Mrs Jamison and musician's sister Anne. Susie's portrait "is offered with the kindest intentions to the future fathers of the race."
LBKM-quote from author: "Susie went out very little and had no occupation at home. Her mind was a riot of femininity. She had been educated by elderly ladies in whose ideas men figured as professional rivals, or interesting friends, or dangers to the community, or pupils' fathers...Finding nothing in her education to explain the mysteries they suggested she thought about them... all day. Their admiration became a thing to work for like points scored in a game, and she played her cards to that end." Preface-"Do you know Susie? You may even have loved her. She is as old as her sex and has many disguises." Rev-Clever but somewhat cruel study of character.

DOWIE, MENIE MURIEL. See FITZGERALD, MENIE MURIEL (DOWIE) NORMAN.

DOWNES, MARION GRACE.

003482   SWAYED BY THE STORM; A STORY OF AUSTRALIA TODAY. London: H. J. Drane, [1909] BMC. Melbourne: T. C. Lothian, 1911 NUC.

DOWNS, MRS. GEORGE SHELDON. See DOWNS, SARAH ELIZABETH (FORBUSH).

DOWNS, MRS. GEORGIE SHELDON. See DOWNS, SARAH ELIZABETH (FORBUSH).

DOWNS, SARAH ELIZABETH (FORBUSH). B. 1843. United States.

003483   THE CHURCHYARD BETROTHAL; OR COALS OF FIRE. BY MRS. GEORGIE SHELDON. New York: Street & Smith, [1907] NUC.

003484   DOROTHY'S JEWELS. BY MRS. GEORGIE SHELDON. F. Henderson, 1894 BS. New York: Street & Smith, [1900] NUC.

003485   EDRIE'S LEGACY. BY MRS. GEORGIE SHELDON. New York: Street & Smith, 1892 NUC.

003486   FAITHFUL SHIRLEY; OR, A ROYAL QUEEN OF HEARTS. BY MRS. GEORGIE SHELDON. London: J. Henderson, 1892 BMC. New York: Street & Smith, [1899] NUC.

003487   GERTRUDE ELLIOTT'S CRUCIBLE. BY MRS. GEORGE SHELDON DOWNS. New York: G.W. Dillingham, [1908] NUC.

PW-Young woman robbed of inheritance, forgives, works as a housekeeper, fortune restored, marries happily. BKM-"Wonderfully patient"

003488   GRAZIA'S MISTAKE. BY MRS. GEORGIE SHELDON. New York: Street & Smith, 1899 [] NUC.

003489   HER HEART'S VICTORY; A SEQUEL TO MAX, A CRADLE MYSTERY. BY MRS. GEORGIE SHELDON. New York: A. L. Burt, [1892] NUC.

003490   A HERITAGE OF LOVE, A SEQUEL TO THE GOLDEN KEY. BY MRS. GEORGIE SHELDON. New York: A.L. Burt, [1905] NUC.

003491   KATHERINE'S SHEAVES. BY MRS. GEORGIE SHELDON (MRS. GEORGE SHELDON DOWNS). New York: Federal Book, [c1904] NUC. London: Shurmer Sibthorp, [1904] BMC.

PW Christian Sci.

003492   LOVE'S CONQUEST; A SEQUEL TO HELEN'S VICTORY. BY MRS. GEORGIE SHELDON. New York: A. L. Burt, [1900] NUC.

003493   THE MASKED BRIDAL. BY MRS. GEORGIE
SHELDON. New York: Street & Smith, [c1900] NUC.

003494   MAX. A CRADLE MYSTERY. BY MRS. GEORGIE
SHELDON. New york: Street & Smith, [1892] NUC.

003495   NORA; OR, THE MISSING HEIR OF CALLONBY.
BY MRS. GEORGIE SHELDON. New York: Street and Smith,
[c1904] NUC.

003496   REDEEMED. BY MRS. GEORGIE SHELDON DOWNS.
New York: G.W. Dillingham, [c1911] NUC.

Begins with divorce; man remarries a prima donna who
soon tires of him; meets his ex wife, realizes his
mistakes. She helps him out but refuses to remarry
him. PW 9-16-11

003497   RISING TO HONOUR. BY MRS. GEORGIE
SHELDON. London: J. Henderson, 1892 BMC.

003498   RUBY'S REWARD. BY MRS. GEORGIE SHELDON.
New York: Street and Smith, [1892] NUC. London: Ward,
Lock & Bowden, 1896 BMC.

003499   THE SHADOW OF A CRIME. BY MRS. GEORGIE
SHELDON. London: Aldine, [1897] BMC.

003500   SISTER ANGELA. BY MRS. GEORGIE SHELDON.
London: J. Henderson, 1894 BMC.

ACAD 46:553. Wife rescues husband twice from death at
hands of matrimonial schemers. Sensational.

003501   STEP BY STEP; A STORY OF HIGH IDEALS. BY
MRS. GEORGE SHELDON DOWNS. London: T.F. Unwin, 1906
BMC. New York: G.W. Dillingham, [1906] NUC.

003502   THREADS GATHERED UP. BY MRS. GEORGIE
SHELDON. New York: A. L. Burt, [c1891] NUC. (Sequel to
Virgie's Inheritance)

003503   THRICE WEDDED, BUT ONLY ONCE A WIFE. BY
MRS. GEORGIE SHELDON. New York: Street and Smith, 1891
NUC.

003504   TINA, THE LITTLE LACE-MAKER. BY MRS.
GEORGIE SHELDON. New York: Street and Smith, [1892]
NUC.

003505   TWO KEYS; OR, MARGARET HOUGHTON'S
HEROISM. BY MRS. GEORGIE SHELDON. New York: Street and
Smith, [1891] NUC. London: Ward, Lock and Bowden, 1896
BMC.

003506   WEDDED BY FATE; OR, SISTER ANGELA. BY
MRS. GEORGIE SHELDON. New York: Dodd, Mead, [c1892]
NUC. London: B. F. Stevens, 1892 BMC.

Man is asphyxiated in Boston hotel. Can live only by
blood transfusion. A nurse volunteers. The two marry,
but his family can't accept her for many reasons
besides that she is of lower class. These reasons are
the story. CR 14,21:44

003507   THE WELFLEET MYSTERY. BY MRS. GEORGIE
SHELDON. London: J. Henderson, [1901] BMC.

003508   WITCH HAZEL. BY MRS. GEORGIE SHELDON. New
York: Street and Smith, [1892] NUC. London: Ward, Lock
and Bowden, [1896] BMC.

DOWSON, MARY EMILY. B. 1848.

003509   FROM THE FOREST. BY WILLIAM SCOTT PALMER.
London: Duckworth, 1912 BMC NUC.

Essays, Eng.

003510   PILGRIM MAN. BY WILLIAM SCOTT PALMER.
London: Duckworth, 1911 BMC.

003511   WINTER AND SPRING. BY WILLIAM SCOTT
PALMER. London: Duckworth, 1912 BMC NUC.

DOWSON, ROSINA (FILIPPI). B. 1866.

003512   BERNARDINE. London: Duckworth, 1912 BMC.

TLS--Light fantasy.

003513   THE HEART OF MONICA. London: Cassell,
1914 BMC.

ATH--Published anonymously 5 years ago, is now

revised.
TLS--Letters to a male friend revealing tragedy of her
life, union to a hopeless drunkard. Withdrawn from
sale first time published.

DOYLE, MARTHA CLAIRE (MACGOWAN). B. 1868 or 69?. United
States.

003514   MINT JULIP. BY MARTHA JAMES. New York: W.
D. Lane, 1909 NUC.

Good husband and wife team. 12-4-09 PW

DRAGOUMIS, JULIA D. United Kingdom.

003515   A MAN OF ATHENS. Boston: Houghton
Mifflin, 1916 BMC NUC.

Life in high society of modern Athens. BKM
Theodora Douka is of Byzantine royal blood. Marries a
professor of peasant origin. Story is set in
present-day Greece. PW
NYT-quiet domestic.

DRAKE, JANET. United States.

003516   WEDDING BELLS OUT OF TUNE, AND THE
DEVIL'S WIFE (AN ALLEGORY). New York: Republic Press,
1898 NUC.

DRAKE, JEANIE. United States.

003517   IN OLD ST. STEPHEN'S: A NOVEL. New York:
D. Appleton, 1892 NUC.

CR 18:275. "trashy little story," a supposed diary of
old Southern gentleman, Civil war.
NATION 145:436. Virginia, historical

003518   THE METROPOLITANS. New York: Century,
1896 NUC BMC.

BKM 4:372. Satire of New York society. Typical hero
and heroine of romance. Spurned, he goes to Arctic, is
rescued by young gypsy woman who sacrifices her life.
I don't think they're part of the satire.
PW 10-10-96. His character is improved by his stay in
Alaska.

DRAKE, MARY TYRWHITT.

003519   THE LIGHT BEARERS. BY M. A. SYLVESTRE.
London: J. Long, 1912 BMC.

ATH-prostitution.
TLS-melodrama-rather than realism.

003520   VALENCIA VARELST. BY M. A. SYLVESTRE.
London: S. C. Brown, Langham, 1903 BMC.

DREW, ANNA ATWOOD. United States.

003521   THE KARLS OF KARLTONVILLE AND THEIR NEW
THOUGHT; OR THE LIFE BEAUTIFUL. Boston: J. H. Earle,
1905 NUC.

DREW, SARA.

003522   THE GIRL BEHIND: A STORY BASED UPON THE
LIFE OF A SHOP-GIRL. London: J. Ouseley, 1908 BMC.

003523   THE HARLOT IN HEAVEN. London: J. Ouseley,
[1910] BMC.

Orphaned girl given good education by relatives,
turned adrift in London for a month. Falls in hands of
a dissolute artist and a scoundrel who makes her a
"decoy of men." She falls for one such man but he must
rescue her from the man who wishes to keep her for
business purposes. ACAD

DRINKWATER, ELLA A., jt. au. See CONKLIN, JENNIE MARIA
(DRINKWATER) AND ELLA A. DRINKWATER.

DRINKWATER, JENNIE M. See CONKLIN, JENNIE MARIA
(DRINKWATER).

DRISCOLL, CLARA. 1881-1945. United States.

003524   THE GIRL OF LA GLORIA. New York and
London: G. P. Putnam's Sons, 1905 BMC NUC.

Texas adventure of revenge. PW 2-25-05. dyllic
romance, h roine dies. NYT 160,05
ACAD-495,05
ATH- 556,05

003525 IN THE SHADOW OF THE ALAMO. New York and London: G. P. Putnam's Sons, 1906 BMC NUC.

NYT-historical romance.

DRISCOLL, KATHERINE ELIZABETH. B. 1867.

003526 A STORY FROM THE PHILLIPINES. New York and London: Abbey Press, [1902] NUC.

Amer. soldier tells of Phillipine adventures. PW 3-28-03

DROMGOOLE, WILL ALLEN. See DROMGOOLE, WILLIAM ALLEN.

DROMGOOLE, WILLIAM ALLEN. 1860-1934. United States.

003527 THE FARRIER'S DOG AND HIS FELLOW. BY WILL ALLEN DROMGOOLE. Boston: L. C. Page, 1897 NUC.

003528 THE FORTUNES OF THE FELLOW; A COMPANION BOOK TO THE FARRIER'S DOG AND HIS FELLOW. BY WILL ALLEN DROMGOOLE. Boston: L. C. Page, 1898 NUC.

003529 THE ISLAND OF BEAUTIFUL THINGS: A ROMANCE OF THE SOUTH. BY WILL ALLEN DROMGOOLE. Boston, Mass.: L. C. Page, 1912 NUC BMC. London: D. Putnam, 1912 BS.

TLS-sickly sentimental matrimony.

003530 A MOONSHINER'S SON. BY WILL ALLEN DROMGOOLE. Philadelphia: Penn, 1898 NUC.

PW-Tennessee. Development of his character and successful career in large city.
Shy heroine, Tennessee mountain girl. Loved by mid-aged doctor. There's a rival. The doctor's defiance of formal religion comes to them. She dies. NYT 6-24-99,407.

003531 THE VALLEY PATH. BY WILL ALLEN DROMGOOLE. Boston: Estes and Lauriat, 1898 NUC.

NYT 1898:308. Alicia Reams, rural Tennessee. Heroine loved by self-sacrificing and egocentric doctor and by a local man. She has potential for training, education, etc., which doctor sees but feels his rival has prior claim. She dies before marrying either.
PW-Tennessee. Love story, but motive of book seems to be to contrast a practicing religion with perfunctory or conventional religion.

DROWER, ETHEL STEFANA (STEVENS). B. 1879. United Kingdom.

003532 ALLWARD. A STORY OF GYPSY LIFE. BY E. S. STEVENS. New York: Dodd, Mead, [c1915] NUC. London: Mills and Boon, 1915 BMC.

"Living the life of the broad highway, he finds happiness and adventure and in time a fit mate, in Mary, the gypsy girl" PW 89 18/16 p.121
NYT-Male hero and romance- Mary is very very sweet. Story of a man newly freed from marriage who lives it up-joins gypsies. TLS

003533 AND WHAT HAPPENED; BEING AN ACCOUNT OF SOME ROMANTIC MEALS. BY E. S. STEVENS. London: Mills and Boon, [c1916] BMC NUC.

LKBM, Letty comes to London to Cradock School of Journalism. Her life with group of literary young women and men (Bohemian). What then? Pov? (Reviewer says her tragedy is not lasting and she is happy on last page.)
ATH pleasant and amusing.

003534 THE LONG ENGAGEMENT. BY E. S. STEVENS. London: Mills and Boon, 1912 BMC NUC. New York: Hodder and Stoughton, G.H. Doran, [c1912] NUC.

ATH-about devastating effect on girl's life.
TLS country story of people of upper middle class.
SR-He lethargically and stoically waits for years because of lack of money; she rebels-comes into the danger of exchanging bad for worse. 2nd engagement. Onslaught against the tyranny of custom.
"Love versus caution is the theme. Is it better to marry when love calls or wait for a bank account? Dominick Ellaby, engaged to Melody Waller, still thought at the end of four years that the latter was the right course. His three sisters were dependent upon him and he had no prospects. In despair Melody decides to marry a rich man, but at the eleventh hour literally, cannot do it, runs away to Dominick in her wedding gown, and they take the step they should have

four years before. Besides their story there is the love affair of altogether delightful Joan Ellaby, making a large part of the book's interest."PW

003535 THE LURE. BY E. S. STEVENS. London: Mills and Boon, 1912 BMC NUC. New York: J. Lane, 1912 NUC.

PW--marries and leaves career?
TLS--female journalist gets entangled with editor of a society journal, who is a villain. Woman journalist.
ATH--describes 2 events in career of Huntley Goss, adventurer. 1st he is managing a journal by the aristocracy for the aristocracy. 2 years later he is in Sudan with a fraudulent crocodile farm and now a full fledged scoundrel. Escapes from justice but we are glad.
ACAD--2 fine character studies of Anna and Huntley whom one can't help liking. Anna marries another man, a stock character.
SR--Anna is pursued by Huntley even after marriage. Meets him on a trip on the Nile.
BKM--he is slowly poisoning his faded middle aged wife and making plans for doing away with his half witted son.

003536 MAGDALENE: A STUDY IN MEDHODS. BY E. S. STEVENS. London: Cassell, [1919] BMC NUC.

Kathleen daughter of cleric had fallen when only in her teens. Now 40 and married. She interests herself in rescue work. The novel's purpose is to show that Rescue Homes are bad--that Victims of social evil need help rather than reprobation and should not be confined to a joyless repressed life. TLS
Attacks old fashioned penitential methods of conducting rescue homes for fallen women. Rigid patroness vs trustee with ultra modern views. SP

003537 THE MOUNTAIN OF GOD. BY E. S. STEVENS. London: Mills and Boon, [1911] BMC NUC.

Passion of western woman for a Moslem. They part at the end. TLS
English man and woman visit Moslem world. Schmidt Pasha (German and Moslem) has his own religion's ideas of women. He's a powerful savage that the English woman is attracted to. His Turkish woman will not discard her veil? SR.

003538 THE SAFETY CANDLE. BY E. S. STEVENS. London: Cassell, [1917] BMC NUC.

Agnes Tempest was a safety candle--her beauty gave light but didn't burn. Young man and older woman love each other. TLS
Widow marries a man considerably her junior. The result is not ideal happiness. Complications of a much younger woman.? ATH

003539 SARAH EDEN. BY E. S. STEVENS. London: Mills and Boon, [1914] NUC. New York: Dodd, Mead, 1914 NUC.

LBKM--contains a description of the foundation of Sarah's community in the sacred city and of its daily life.
NYT--Growth and birth of a fanatic sect. Celibate community whose principles are to live spotlessly, hold all wealth in common, do good works and keep themselves in readiness for the second coming which Sarah has seen in visions.
TLS--inference that community modifies its stand on celibacy.
"Sarah Eden, a Devonshire girl, makes a loveless marriage with her cousin John. She is a highly religious temperament, with a personality which attracts and dominates. In the charitable work into which she throws herself she becomes associated with Charters as collaborator, she goes to Jerusalem as chief of a community who wait there the second coming of the Lord. Helena, Sarah's daughter, in deference to the community's views, renounces her lover, but the mother in Sarah makes the sacrifice unnecessary." PW 86 9-12-14:745.

003540 THE VEIL; A ROMANCE OF TUNISIA. BY ETHEL STEFANA STEPHENS. London: Mills and Boon, 1909 BMC. New York: F.A. Stokes, [c1909] NUC.

BKM 30, 1909-10 African dancer, spy, etc.
Mabrouka Arab girl introduced to European life rebels against her confinement, escape with French officer whom when she learns he has no intention of setting her free, she robs and murders, mysterious career as dancer and political spy. PW 9-18-09
As a child has a glimpse of freedom of women in

western life. Now as part of harem yearns for freedom.
Officer helps her escape, but makes advances, she
stabs him. Her life moves on from there to various
adventures. LBKM
"She's a spy in the destiny of nations" BKM
ever-present fear of Mafia SP

DRUM, BLOSSOM. See OLIPHANT, BLOSSOM DRUM.

DRUMMOND, ANNIE.

003541   THE BROKEN BOND. London: R. Culley, 1910
BMC.

DRUMMOND, FLORENCE. Nationality Unknown.

003542   AN AMERICAN WOOING. London: G. Richards,
1912 BMC. Boston: Houghton Mifflin, 1912 NUC.

PW-love story.
TLS
ATH
NYT

003543   THE CASTLE OF FORTUNE. London: G.
Richards, 1914 BMC.

ATH-male hero, London clerk, visits castle which
should be his but is in hands of another man.

DU BOIS, CONSTANCE GODDARD. United States.

003544   COLUMBUS AND BEATRIZ: A NOVEL. Chicago:
A. C. McClurg, 1892 NUC BMC.

IND 44:776.
CR 8-27-42. Historical romance, Columbus and his wife,
long suffering

003545   A MODERN PAGAN: A NOVEL. New York:
Merriam, [c1895] NUC.

He is Gerald Maynard, marries a rich woman to further
his career, tires of her, returns to woman he loves,
but needs the money. Attempts suicide. wife learns of
his dilemma, goes off to Europe for three years while
he enjoys his opera career and "an intimate Platonic
affection" for his love. He also gets into "good
works." LW:26:202.
A saintly wife helps restore her free thinking
irresponsible artist husband BKM 4:415

003546   THE SHIELD OF THE FLEUR DE LIS: A NOVEL.
New York: Merriam, [c1895] NUC.

In 1431 Jeanne Darc was burned at the stake. Three
years later a stranger comes to the place of her birth
and learns all the details of her life. PW
12-28-95:1209

003547   A SOUL IN BRONZE: A NOVEL OF SOUTHERN
CALIFORNIA. Chicago and New York: H. S. Stone, 1900
NUC.

CR 37:468. story of a noble Indian, Antonio La Chusa.

DUBOIS, LOUISE. United States.

003548   HILTON HALL; OR, A THORN IN THE FLESH. A
NOVEL. Salt Lake City, Utah: G. Q. Cannon, 1898 NUC.

DUBOIS, MARY CONSTANCE. B. 1879.

003549   COMRADE ROSALIE. New York: Century, 1919
BMC NUC.

Northern France in time of war. NYT

003550   THE LEAGUE OF THE SIGNET RING. New York:
Century, 1910 BMC NUC.

Girls PW

DUCHESS, THE, pseud. See HUNGERFORD, MARGARET WOLFE
(HAMILTON).

DUCLAUX, AGNES MARY FRANCES (ROBINSON) DARMESTETER.
1857-1944. United Kingdom.

003551   A MEDIAEVAL GARLAND. BY MADAME JAMES
DARMESTETER. London: Lawrence and Bullen, 1898 BMC
NUC. (Tr. May Tomlinson)

DUDENEY, ALICE (WHITTIER). 1866-1945. United Kingdom.

003552   THE BATTLE OF THE WEAK, OR GOSSIPS GREEN.

BY MRS. HENRY DUDENEY. New York: G. W. Dillingham,
[1906] NUC.

"A loveless marriage and its results are here vividly
portrayed. The hero is a wild, untamed youth. He loves
and is loved by the wife of the country physician. The
bitterness through which all pass before happiness
finally comes supplies the story." BKM v.24 1906-7.

003553   CANDLELIGHT. BY MRS. HENRY DUDENEY.
London: Hurst and Blackett, [1918] BMC NUC.

ATH--Psych. study Edith has a passion for admiration
that causes her to be unfaithful. Results on 5 lives.
LBKM--Billy is Edith and Wilfrid's son, but George is
his father. George is engaged to Ann, Wilfrid's
sister. Mrs. Brewberry the charwoman is far removed
from the comic relief

003554   A COUNTRY BUNCH. London: Hurst and
Blackett, 1905 BMC.

003555   FOLLY CORNER. BY MRS. H. DUDENEY. London:
W. Heinemann, 1899 BMC. New York: H. Holt, 1899 NUC.

BKM 11:342. Character study of Pamela Crisp, an
up-to-date independent young woman of London. She
loved sheltered life, protection, ease, lack of
responsibility, all that was simple and good. Jethro
offered all that. Edred however has aroused her
passions-he was the 1st man she kissed. When he is
released from prison, she marries him; he beats her,
asks her to leave. Finally goes when she finds he has
a 1st wife, returns to Jethro. However, never loses
feelings of passion for Edred even though she despises
him.
CR 36:550. Author knows the effect of a garden on
feminine nerves. Garden was also important to Harriot
Wicken. (Cornelia Pratt)ACAD 58:126

003556   GOSSIPS GREEN. London: Cassell, 1906 BMC.

ACAD--husband goes off, then what? Woman and lover
cannot be confined by Puritanical conventions.
TLS--brutish husband who finally shares p.o.v. of
lovers.
ATH--There is a piquancy about Mrs. Dudeney's
persistent diatribes against the modern woman.

003557   HAGAR OF HOMERTON. London: C. A. Pearson,
1898 BMC NUC.

LIT 3:231. Temporary adoption of girl from East End by
widow. Study of vulgar people.
ACAD 53:575. She adopts Hagar for diversion, being
bored.
SR 86:119. Hagar is a suspected thief, a shop girl.
She does not adapt to Cheltenham Terrace. She likes
the pretty frocks and leisure time, but she continues
her ties with family and friends, marrying one of the
young men.

003558   THE HEAD OF THE FAMILY. BY MRS. HENRY
DUDENEY. London: Methuen, [1917] BMC NUC.

Beausire Fillery with her infinite capacity for a
grand passion evoked by William and in rebellion vs
the lifelong dependence which her late aunt had
revelled in. William is married to Phoebe. Primitive
passions--unrequited desire of Beausire for Wm. , her
snatching at crumbs woos him directly, glories in her
shame. Finally discovers her idol to be of clay and
marries the Head of the Family. LBKM

003559   HOLLY CORNER. New York: H. Holt, c1900
NUC.

003560   A LARGE ROOM. BY MRS. HENRY DUDENEY.
London: W. Heinemann, 1910 BMC NUC. New York:
Brentano, 1911 NUC.

BM-Heroine is educated.
SR--lives with a man in bogus marriage, leaves him;
lives with another casually, marries a 3rd-
BAKER--says this is a collection of 4 novels.
An innocent friendless poetic girl and her trials with
stepmother is betrayed by a mock marriage with a
stupid and fleshy husband. Amaza Meeks is precocious
as child, apart from other children. ACAD

003561   MAID'S MONEY. BY MRS. HENRY DUDENEY.
London: W. Heinemann, 1911 BMC NUC. New York:
Duffield, 1912 NUC.

NYT--In order to keep money they must live together
and remain unmarried. They don't like each other.

PW--interesting: two 40 year old maids inherit money
with unusual conditions.
SP--Sarah Peacock longs for Amy's death. Believes she
has actually murdered her. Sordid and unpleasant.
SR.--Sarah, life-hungry, and Amy, placid, are both
overjoyed to find money has brought suitors. These
turn out to be merely adventurers and rev. infers both
women recover quickly. Women are finely
portrayed--Sarah has been a companion in suburbs, Amy
a governess in best houses.
LBKM--Brilliantly written, shrewd touches of sarcasm
and grim humor. Laban (the inventor) does love Sarah
in his way but also sees she is old, even older than
he.
Two heroine cousins are 40, come into riches on
understanding they'll live together and never marry;
the differences in their temperament. Their daily life
makes up the tale. TLS
Tale of thwarted womanhood. All characters over 40.
Interesting and arresting. ATH

003562   A MAN WITH A MAID. BY MRS. HENRY DUDENEY.
London: Heinemann, 1898 BMC NUC.

LIT 2:325. Pioneer Series, 19th v. profoundly sad.
Didactic.
ACAD 53:121. "Tom's way with Tabbie turns out sad,
mad, and bad; Tabbie's way out of her trouble is mad
and sad too."
ACAD 53:202. She is a milliner's assistant; he is a
gentleman. She is simple and fond of him, stays with
him in his rooms for 3 weeks. He is to marry money;
she is to marry butcher's son. Just as Tom is married,
"Tabbie's sin finds her out."
LBKM 14:191. Tom's marriage drives Tabbie to despair
and death.

003563   MANHOOD END. BY MRS. HENRY DUDENEY.
London: Hurst and Blackett, [1920] NUC BMC.

TLS--Story of Rainbird and Sophy. He calls himself a
priest but is married. She goes off with someone,
returns, but is changed. Goes off again after death of
child. After that they are shadows, even with the sad
intensity of her final return. Both are near death.
ATH--She can't help being bored. When baby dies, she
runs anywhere. They die soon after her return while
planning another honeymoon.

003564   THE MATERNITY OF HARRIOTT WICKEN. BY MRS.
HENRY DUDENEY. London: W. Heinemann, 1899 BMC NUC. New
York and London: Macmillan, 1899 NUC.

Subject of heredity. The Wicken family, it seems,
carries evil and disease in their blood. Harriott
marries Dandie Darnell. All goes on its conjugal way
till her child "an idiot of the most hopeless kind" is
born. She does everything to conceal this from her
husband. A good novel "in spite of much quite
unnecessary vilification of the suburbs and
housewifely qualities." LIT 4:477
She farms out her idiot child, procures an orphan and
passes it off as hers (her husband was away.) A
succession of tragedies follows ending in her suicide.
SP 82:616
Moves from hatred of to love of the child. Good
psychological study. SR 87:632

003565   MEN OF MARLOWE'S. BY MRS. HENRY DUDENEY.
London: J. Long, 1900 BMC. New York: H. Holt, 1900
NUC.

LBKM 19:60. Life of a mean and trivial class, not
amusing.

003566   THE ORCHARD THIEF. London: W. Heinemann,
1907 BMC.

Innkeeper, pastoral poet and Julia; sounds rather
old-fashioned.TLS
Julia Wing is pretty and brainless--her Puritan
training and non intellectual nature make her fall for
good-looking artist. The primitive woman in her
despises the landlord with his intellectual nature.
Sounds like a negative study of Julia. SR

003567   RACHEL LORIAN. BY MRS. HENRY DUDENEY. New
York: Duffield, 1909 NUC. London: W. Heinemann, 1909
NUC BMC.

BKM--crippled husband, but then what?
She is awakened by a lover but remains loyal to her
embittered crippled husband till he dies. PW 3-20-09.
Husband maimed on wedding day. Rachel then loves
Patrick Rivers with a white heat kind of love. But she
stays loyal till husband dies. On eve of marriage to

her new love, finds him with mistress--a widow with a
child. Rachel is revolted but she adopts the child
with whom we leave her happy. TLS
At end, the most joyful woman in the whole world.
Married at 18, husband mangled and disfigured in
accident on honeymoon. Nurses him 15 years. She rebels
but pity keeps her there. Falls in love. She and lover
frank about their feelings but she's loyal to husband.
Husband dies but she still refuses to marry at once.
Wants to wait a year. When she learns he was untrue in
that year, she scorns him; he marries another. Tragic
intensity. LBKM

003568   ROBIN BRILLIANT. BY MRS. HENRY DUDENEY.
London: Hodder and Stoughton, [1902] BMC. New York:
Dodd, Mead, 1903 NUC.

Loten the male, does nothing till woman pulls him
after her. Robin tries hard to be wicked--the heir of
suicide and remorse--she's not heroine but hero, male
like. BKM 12-02.
She is Robin. PW 3-21-02.
A woman's dual nature; she sacrifices self and lover.
Loyal, fearless, high bred, unflinching; the other
woman is the opposite to whom she sacrifices her
lover. Lives out her life alone. NYT
Sensuous pleasure in prolonging the courtship. Feels
it will end with marriage. BKM 16,534.

003569   A RUNAWAY RING. BY MRS. HENRY DUDENEY.
New York: Duffield, 1913 PW. London: W. Heinemann,
1913 NUC BMC.

PW--"There is a suggestion of mystery from the first
when Aunt Frussannah and her niece Fanny are
introduced searching for a house in the country where
they may live on their small income. As the mystery
unfolds it shows Frusannah addicted to drink, and
moreover, to be Fanny's mother, her father being an
Austrian Duke--facts which the girl only learns after
her marriage and from her husband. Her marriage with
Ninian Baigent, which she regards as a way of escape
from poverty, turns out very different from her
expectations, when she lives with her husband's
stodgily virtuous British family." 84:423.
Family hounds youngest daughter into a fatal operation
for fear of her living on to shame them by being an
old maid? Abortion? SP
Unwed mother conceived of with tenderness. ATH
Frusannah, dies drunk in railway station, had an
illegitimate child, Fanny. That young woman marries
son of Mrs. Baigent. Is ill at ease with that family
because she has lived on the edge of ugliness. She
rebels against the order, the pressure to have
children. Author shows the vulgarity of domesticity.
Frusannah is a vital woman, clear ly defined. TLS
Strange, complex woman. "Typically British in the
subservience of the woman to the masculine members of
the family" NYT 13:488.
"The author's methods are merciless. On the one side
she shows us romance as represented by Frusannah, the
elderly, disreputable sister of an ecclesiastical
dignitary, and on the other there is stability as
represented by old Mrs. Baigent and her numerous
offspring, the children of one whom society must have
chosen for honour in any show of British matrons,...in
a simple summary the story of Frusannah is sordid, and
Mrs. Dudeney does nothing to varnish it in all her
chapters, yet the light of romance is left shining
over the woman who could not even redeem life by
death. It is rather like the illumination given by
tapers to an ugly corpse. Fanny married young Mr.
Baigent...the spirit of Frusannah, which was romantic
and ill regulated did battle with the Baigents, who
were all stable and well regulated, and their
contention was for the body and soul of Fanny." SR

003570   THE SECRET SON. BY MRS. HENRY DUDENEY.
London: Methuen, [1915] NUC BMC.

Story of 3 generations. Man betrays laundrymaid Nancy
Pinyoun, his betrothed is Enid. He loves Nancy but
won't marry her because he worships respectability,
sets things up so another man will marry Nancy; she
fiercely rebels, but hounded and tempted by money,
marries but husband drowns self. Enid marries the
first man in the meantime. Has 7 kids. Nancy's son
weaker type. TLS
A weak man's passion and all that follows because he
avoids the responsibility. Nancy mother of secret son.
Self reliant, indomitable, contrast to weak man. This
son's wife unfaithful he learns at end of his own
origin. LBKM
SR--The husband thrust upon her by the squire who has
betrayed her can bear life no longer when he finds he
loves his wife. The son learns of his mother's secret

shame, his real parentage and the unfaithfulness of
his wife all at once. Thru suffering and heartbreak
his mother has cared for him, only to have him turn
away forever. She is strong, vital; enduring; all
other characters seem weak and feeble.

003571   SET TO PARTNERS: A NOVEL. BY MRS. HENRY
DUDENEY. London: Heinemann, 1913 NUC BMC. New York:
Duffield, 1914 NUC.

Angelina Peachey, curious mixture of staunchness and
waywardness. By the end she supports her two lovers,
with both of whom she has lived--though her standards
would not permit her to marry either. One is
paralyzed, the other blind. She keeps a second-hand
furniture shop and attends auctions. ACAD
A young woman's sincerity keeps her from marriage to a
man who cares for her, keeps her from giving herself
wholely to a man she loves, turns her from rel.,
convention, even friendship. SP
At age 10, precocious "love affairs" with boys. Falls
in love but won't marry, will only live with him. For
7 years all goes well. Then she falls for his friend,
goes away with him. Later he becomes paralyzed, her
first lover blind. At the end, she runs a curio shop,
supports both men. They are wholly dependent upon her.
LBKM SR TLS
PW--"There is a medley such as one would expect from
the old-fashioned dance phrase that gives title to
this story of England in the 80's. Angelina Peachey,
beautiful beyond her place in life, her wonderful and
wicked old grandmother, her adoptive mother, Lady
Johns, are among the chief characters. How Angelina
loves two men, but is the lawful wife of neither, and
in the end devotes her life to both of them, make the
tale." PW 85:1553.

003572   THE SHOULDER-KNOT. BY MRS. HENRY DUDENEY.
London: Cassell,, 1909 NUC BMC.

BKM--male hero.
NYT--Mad poet married to young wife (there is a
child.) He sporadically has periods when he sees the
world as devilish--and then he writes about it. His
great fear is that in one of these times his wife will
take on the devil's mask. Imagine what it's like for
her.
Ordinary standards of morality are insisted upon. ATH

003573   SPADE WORK. BY MRS. HENRY DUDENEY.
London: Hurst and Blackett, 1919 NUC BMC.

Development of a girl to a woman capable of self
sacrifice. Mother and daughter go from life of hard
work and poverty to luxury. Daughter's love story ends
tragically. SP
Social aspirations of Caroline Paybody-Beech and
Mother clash. ATH
Caroline works at leather work and beads. Wealth comes
to them. She develops into a strong, competent, aloof
wife but doesn't do anything except bring lovers
together. Physically restless. LBKM

003574   SPINDLE AND PLOUGH. BY MRS. HENRY
DUDENEY. New York: Dodd, Mead, 1901 NUC. London: W.
Heinemann, 1901 NUC BMC.

BKM--June 1902.
Shalisha--landscape gardener. Refuses to marry the man
she loves and who loves her because she wanted to
preserve life she has. Does she marry finally?
Physically active. Woman a landscape gardener, sworn
to celibacy but becomes a grouchy resentful old maid
till she marries and lives happily ever after. BKM
An advanced woman. Equality with man in play, passion,
love and intellectual pursuits and muscularity and
physical effort. Shalisha an old maid by temperament
"with a constitutional shrinking from men and
matrimony" still with maternal feelings. Father sees
she's against conventional marriage, gives her
practical training in landscaping. Gets a job as
landscaper. Magnificent physical strength but not a
beauty. Her vigorous boyish impulses, lusty health and
bodily purity. BOOK NEWS 5-02
Modern story of home life and love affairs. Red-headed
Shalisha. ACAD

003575   THE STORY OF SUSAN. BY MRS. HENRY
DUDENEY. London: W. Heinemann, 1903 NUC BMC. New York:
Dodd, Mead, 1904 NUC.

Poor clinging tearful Susan, pretty, winsome estranged
from first love because of his harsh Methodism,
marries another who dies , ends up with the first.
ACAD 65:504.
Susan publicly rebukes those who judge her? ATH

122:750.
Uneducated lady's maid, believes she's marked for
destruction. Has much to do with rel. TLS 05:313.

003576   THE THIRD FLOOR. BY MRS. HENRY DUDENEY.
London: Methuen, 1901 NUC BMC.

Mother divorces husband, takes child and becomes a
platform woman, remarries. ATH
Valencia thrills when her husband calls her the missus
ACAD

003577   THIS WAY OUT. BY MRS. HENRY DUDENEY.
London: Methuen, [1917] BMC NUC.

Murder story. Two men vie for a woman, compete over an
invention, one kills the other. Story goes on to study
the later generations. One character, Jane Vaguener,
is a writer of popular fiction. writes a play of
inventive genius but never knows how good it was. TLS
Her brother could have told her her play was great,
lets her believe she's finished as a writer. TLS
Jane: vulgar, industrious, her loud laugh, breezy
vanity who makes a more than comfortable living
writing cheap serials. Her brother believes self to be
a literary artist, sponges on Jane though he despises
her work. Bizarre tragedy of Jane's death half way
through the novel? LBKM

003578   TRESPASS. BY MRS. HENRY DUDENEY. Boston:
Small, Maynard, [1909] NUC.

Woman loves two men, does mischief to both. PW

003579   WHAT A WOMAN WANTS. BY MRS. HENRY
DUDENEY. London: W. Heinemann, [1914] NUC BMC.

The woman is pathetically faithful to a worthless man.
Women must have men to love. Chrismas Hamlyn initiated
to sex by sailor who takes off. She waits till middle
age for him. When they meet (he's been married and had
a child) they marry. "I want you. There's nothing else
for women." SR
ATH--Tragedy of woman who, finally free of family goes
to London with small inheritance, of which she is
robbed. Marrying at last, she is left with a brutal
husband. Also delineation of revolt of womanhood, the
stirrings of which have out-distanced the feet of the
agitator.
TLS 13:494--Chrismas Hamlyn, child of a Sussex farm,
uneducated, never forgot the sailor who took her to
tea when she was a young girl, yearned all her life
for dependence and love.

003580   THE WISE WOODS. BY MRS. HENRY DUDENEY.
London: Heinemann, 1905 NUC BMC.

Sordid tragedy. Vashti driven to violent acts of folly
in order to escape; hideous things happen, abnormal
characters. When she marries, the wreck of it is a
foregone conclusion. ACAD
Heroine capable of anything at any moment.
Unsatisfactory husband. LBKM 27,28:136.
Tumult of elemental passions and humdrum life at
Tooting. Vashti is half gypsy, half priest. Rebels vs
Christian traditions. TLS
Her extraordinary mode of action. Suburban life to
woods where gypsy engages in free fights with men of
her own tribe. ATH

DUDENEY, MRS. H. See DUDENEY, ALICE (WHITTIER).

DUDENEY, MRS. HENRY. See DUDENEY, ALICE (WHITTIER).

DUDEVANT, AMANTINE LUCILE AURORE (DUPIN). 1804-1876.

003581   THE MASTER MOSAIC WORKERS. BY GEORGE
SAND. Boston: Little, Brown, 1895 NUC. J. M. Dent,
1895 BMC. (Tran. Charlotte C. Johnston)

History novel. Life in Venice when Titian, Tintoretto
and Georgine were in their Zenith. The quarrels
between the brothers and their rivals make the story.
Study of brotherly love. LW 26:624

DUDLEY, ROSETTA.

003582   THE EMERALD CROSS. London: H. J. Drane,
[1908] BMC.

DUDMAN, ADA. United States.

003583   THE PEGSTICKS. BY MARIA DOLMAN. New York:
H. Lechner, [c1911] NUC.

Mid-class country life in Canada. NYT; Title: widow of

man with wooden leg.

DUER, CAROLINE KING. 1865-1956. United States.

003584   UNCONSCIOUS COMEDIANS. New York: Dodd,
Mead, 1901 NUC.

DUER, ELIZABETH. Nationality Unknown.

003585   THE PRINCE GOES FISHING. New York: D.
Appleton, 1906 NUC.

PW-romantic comedy.
NYT-romantic comedy.

DUERING, STELLA M. United Kingdom.

003586   BETWEEN THE DEVIL AND THE DEEP SEA.
London: A. D. Innes, 1898 BMC.

ACAD 55:248. Society story melodrama.
ATH 112:747. "Carefully thought-out romance." Two
women exchange places, one has a child whom the other
makes her heir.
"Impossible deeds of two shameless and intriguing
women." SR 87:90

003587   DISINHERITED. Philadelphia: J.
Lippincott, 1907 BMC NUC. London: J. Milne, 1908 BMC.

Marriage of ancient baronet, birth of his child. PW
6-8-07
TLS-girl brought up as boy to get inheritance, turns
into a girl for love of true heir who marries someone
else.

003588   THE END OF THE RAINBOW. London: Chapman
and Hall, 1909 BMC NUC. Philadelphia: J. B.
Lippincott, 1910 NUC.

Lilith "always misunderstood, always involved in the
mesh of compromising circumstances," from her "initial
imprudent act." NYT
Lower middle class girl educated "above her station"
but expected to be contented with no occupation for
her mind, meets resists temptation. "Wins happiness at
the end"? PW
TLS-striving for a fuller life.
ATH-painstaking characterization. Lilith's struggles
to distract herself
SR-young artist lures her into his studio, gives her
tea, a kiss, and makes a sketch of her head. She is
expelled from school (school mistress feels the artist
ought to marry her). Later, the artist uses the sketch
in a photo with nude figures and the man about town
jumps to conclusions similar to school mistress.
Lillith is 16 at beginning of book, 17 when it ends.

003589   LOVE'S PRIVILEGE. Philadelphia: J.B.
Lippincott, 1909 NUC. London: Cassell, 1911 BMC.

Traditional detective. PW 5-22-09
murder-TLS
two sisters Nora and Ailie Richmond. Nora kissed by a
rival lover at her wedding. Husband kills the man?
LBKM

003590   MALICIOUS FORTUNE. London: G. Allen, 1901
BMC.

moral cowardice of the man-ATH 7-20-01

003591   THE TEMPTATION OF CARLTON EARLE. London:
Ward, Lock, 1920 BMC.

TLS-murder.
ATH-murder.

DUFF, LILY GRANT.

003592   PERIWINKLE. London: J. Murray, 1906 BMC.

ACAD---Excels Pam because she is vital, strong, etc.
TLS-freely sexual young woman possessing a
joi-de-vivre, is intimate with men with whom she is
not in love.
ATH-irresistibly winning, pov?
BKM-finds husband's care of her and respectability an
interference with her freedom.

003593   VACATION. London: J. Murray, 1910 BMC.

TLS-conflict of work and love.
ATH-the natural calls to maternity and paternity are
not ignored but at the close of the narrative there is
not even the promise of fulfillment.

SR-two sisters-one becomes Anglican nun, the other
with physical disability becomes a successful painter.

DUFF, MARY E. United States.

003594   STAR; OR, HER CROSS AND HER CROWN.
Franklin, Ohio: Editor Pub. Co., 1895 W.

DUFFIN, HELEN.

003595   OVER HERE. London: Methuen, [1918] NUC
BMC.

TLS-wholesome Irish story.

DUGANNE, PHYLLIS. United States.

003596   PROLOGUE. New York: Harcourt, Brace and
Howe, 1920 NUC.

PW-young woman at start of career in NY at beginning
of war.

DUGGAN, JANIE PRICHARD. United States.

003597   AN ISLE OF EDEN; A STORY OF PORTO RICO.
Philadelphia: Griffith and Rowland Press, 1912 NUC.

PW-love-Puerto Rico

003598   A MEXICAN RANCH: OR BEAUTY FOR ASHES: A
PRIZE STORY. Philadelphia: American Baptist Society,
1894 NUC.

PW Adventures of Mary Summers, a Baptist Missionary
working as nurse, teacher, and proselytizer in Mexico.

DUMILLO, ALICE.

003599   ON THE GOGMAGOGS. London: T. F. Unwin,
1897 BMC.

DUMOND, ANNIE (HAMILTON) NELLES. B. 1837. United States.

003600   CHRISTLIKE-SAVE THE FALLEN. St. Louis:
Published By Author, 1896 NUC.

003601   THE HARD TIMES: THE CAUSE AND THE REMEDY.
St. Louis: Published By Author, [c1895] NUC.

DUNBAR, RUTH. United States.

003602   THE SWALLOW; A NOVEL BASED UPON THE
ACTUAL EXPERIENCES OF ONE OF THE SURVIVORS OF THE
FAMOUS LAFAYETTE ESCADRILLE. New York: Boni and
Liveright, 1919 NUC.

Male American in foreign legion. TLS
Wartime romance of aviator. PW
WWI-fic. Man determined to go to war--all his effort,
heroism, etc. NYT 6-1-19,307

DUNBAR, VIRGINIA LYNDALL. United States.

003603   A CUBAN AMAZON. Cincinnati, Ohio: Editor
Pub. Co., 1897 NUC BMC.

DUNCAN, BEATRICE.

003604   VIRGINIA'S VENETIAN. London: Drane's,
[1913] BMC.

She prefers him to the homely English doctor and
marries him. ATH

DUNCAN, C. E. United Kingdom.

003605   DEREK GASCOYNE. BY CLIVE DESMOND. London:
Hodder and Stoughton, [1920] BMC.

003606   INTRIGUE. BY CLIVE DESMOND. London:
Hodder & Stoughton, [1919] BMC NUC. New York: Hodder
and Stoughton, [1919] NUC.

DUNCAN, FRANCES. See MANNING, FRANCES DUNCAN.

DUNCAN, GEORGIA ELIZABETH. United States.

003607   SAMANTHY BILLINS OF HANGIN'-DOG. Atlanta,
Ga.: Mutual, 1905 NUC.

DUNCAN, SARA JEANNETTE. See COTES, SARA JEANNETTE (DUNCAN).

DUNCAN, SARAH JEANNETTE. See COTES, SARA JEANNETTE
(DUNCAN).

DUNFORD, EMILIE.

003608   FROM MORN TILL EVE. London: Digby, [1893]
BMC.

"Evangelical treatise". Fred Morgan seduces a young
woman. ACAD 44:270.

DUNHAM, ANNA (CROSS). B. 1846. United States.

003609   THE CORDUROY ROAD; A TALE OF PIONEER LIFE
IN THE MIDDLE WEST. Akron, O.: Werner, [c1909] NUC.

Tales of pioneer lives 1840's.

DUNHAM, EMILY J.

003610   A WOMAN'S LOVE LESSON. London: Hurst and
Blackett, 1895 BMC NUC.

SR 78:717. Anna Broughton is the heroine. Barbara is a
"modern young woman." Lesson is that forgiving love is
a stronger power for good than fulfillment of laws.
ACAD 46:529. "after bitter separation and shame "Anna
and her husand find "mutual help" happier than "mutual
idolizing."
Many prigs of both sexes. Rev. John Broughton father
of young woman who gets the love lesson, is a prig and
a domineering tyrant SP 74:433

DUNIWAY, ABIGAIL SCOTT. 1834-195. United States.

003611   FROM THE WEST TO THE WEST; ACROSS THE
PLAINS TO OREGON. Chicago: A. C. McClurg, 1905 NUC.

Pioneer life of 1850. Account of a trip by wagon from
Illinois to Oregon. Brief desc. BKM 21 (05) 442
WOMAN'S JOURNAL 9-9-05

DUNLAP, ROBERTA K. United States.

003612   MABEL GORDON. A NOVEL. BY R. K. D. New
York: J. S. Ogilvie, 1901 NUC.

DUNLOP, MONA.

003613   THE GUARDED TRUST. London: Ward, Lock,
1915 BMC.

Trad. murder story. TLS
Mystery-traditional. ATH

DUNN, ELLA HEUSTIS. B. 1851. United States.

003614   THE CASTLE OF MANY MIRRORS AND THEIR
SEQUEL. Chicago: M. A. Donohue, [c1906] NUC.

DUNN, MARTHA (BAKER). 1848-1915. United States.

003615   'LIAS'S WIFE; AN ISLAND STORY. Boston: L.
C. Page, 1901 NUC.

003616   MEMORY STREET. A STORY OF LIFE. Boston:
L. C. Page, 1900 NUC. London: Jarrold, 1901 BMC.

NYT 420. Autobiographical style life of young woman
who was a child in American Revolution, her romance.

DUNTZE, HARRIET ELIZABETH ISABELLA.

003617   INFELIX: A SOCIETY STORY. London: Ward
and Downey, 1892 BMC. London: 1899 NUC.

SR 64:653. Story of a poor girl, Jeth, who marries a
rich man without love. She has a daughter, loves her
husband's friend. Her daughter dies; she several times
thinks of running off with the friend, but a lack of
money keeps her from leaving. She will not be
unfaithful to husband while living with him. Finally
affair grows cold.
ACAD. She poisons herself.

DURAND, ALICE MARIE CELESTE (FLEURY). 1842-1902.

003618   AURETTE. BY HENRY GREVILLE. Chicago:
Morrill, Higgins, [1893] NUC.

003619   AURETTE'S HUSBAND. Chicago: 1892 NUC.
(Tr. Max Maury)

PW-Aurette at 30 is content to devote her life to her
young nephew. Then she meets his physics professor.

003620   THE BEAURAND MYSTERY. BY HENRY GREVILLE.
New York: Mershon, [1900] NUC. (Tr. from the French by
Anna Dyer Page)

003621   FORBIDDEN; OR, NIKANOR. BY HENRY
GREVILLE. Chicago and New York: Rand, McNally, [1898]
NUC. (Tr. E. E. Chase)

003622   THE HEIRESS. BY HENRI GREVILLE. New York:
Worthington, 1892 NUC. (Tr. Emma C. Hewitt and Julian
Colmar)

PW-Marcelline warned by her father in his will not to
marry a sailor, falls for one. A close rereading of
the will justifies hergoing ahead.

DURANT, M.

003623   FIRST-FRUITS. London: J. Long, [1915]
BMC.

TLS-amateurish story (daughters changed at birth etc),
theme is of early unhappiness in marriage. later
happiness.

003624   RAINBOW RANCH: A CANADIAN ROMANCE.
London: Mills and Boon, 1918 BMC.

TLS-Discerning studies of character. Mary on ranch in
Br. Col.

003625   A RAISED SIEGE. London: W. White, 1909
BMC.

Dorothea assumes another identity. TLS

003626   REPENTANCE. London: Mills and Boon, 1917
BMC.

Problem novel-divorce; divorced man and Miss Marsh.
TLS
reviewer doesn't know whether the novel is for or
against divorce though ending suggests the latter.
Couple have an argument, she goes off to lover but
very shortly, and before anything happens, writes to
explain. He divorces his innocent wife, wife makes no
defense. "The wife is twice divorced without proper
cause" TLS

003627   WHITE HARVEST. London: Mills and Boon,
[1919] BMC.

Mrs. Vavasour's two daughters were not a comfort to
her or vice-versa. Eldest took off with chauffeur to
escape elderly fiance. Younger, the heroine jilts
lover when he loses his money, but as soon as he
marries someone else, takes off with him to Canada.
TLS
Mother seems to have set up the marriage. concluding
triangle of madness and murder. ATH
characters; detestable; and; gruesome. Mother:
mercenary widow.Lois, eldest daughter throws over old
baronet runs off with chauffeur and mother's rolls
royce. Writes to say she'll keep the car as wedding
gift. Younger sister Claude. Life in Canada, boredom.
poverty. Claude and David punished review doesn't say
how. SR

DURHAM, JULIAN, pseud. See HENSHAW, JULIA WILMOTTE
(HENDERSON).

DURLEY, ELLA HAMILTON. United States.

003628   MY SOLDIER LADY. Boston: C. M. Clark,
1908 NUC.

Letters-newsy, gossippy. NYT

DURYEA, NINA LARREY (SMITH). 1874-1951. United States.

003629   THE HOUSE OF THE SEVEN GABBLERS. New York
and London: D. Appleton, 1911 NUC BMC.

medley of busy people disrupt a countess' life. Joyous
tale of Margaret Chanler artist who goes to Paris to
paint; six other people of various ages and
nationalities. TLS

003630   A SENTIMENTAL DRAGON. New York: G.H.
Doran, [c1916] NUC.

Mrs. Bradish wants European culture for self and
beautiful daughter. They get to Europe. Story traces
their social success there. PW
NYT-her wealth is from a fortune she (mother) has made
from an invention. She wants and does marry daughter
to European artist.

003631   THE VOICE UNHEARD; A STORY OF DINARD.

London: Simpkin, Marshall, [1913] NUC BMC.

English couple in a French seaside resort Lady Mayne,
her worthless husband and her unknown "correspondent,"
side by side with a happy love story. TLS

DU TERTRE, FANNY. United States.

003632   THE LYNN'S COURT MYSTERY. BY DENZIL VANE.
London: S. Low, [1892] BMC.

Unscrupulous man with hypnotic powers influences
excitable young woman and is finally "baffled." ACAD
43:33

003633   A POLISH CONSPIRACY; OR, A WANDERING
STAR. London: Low, 1893 BMC.

Etelka Serezny's brother is a rebel for free Poland.
He and his group are terrorists for the cause . To get
money Jan induces his sister to give him the family
sapphire. The travels of the sapphire. The ironing out
of domestic differences between Etelka and her Count
(husband) SR 75:490.

003634   THE STORY OF A STAR. BY MISS DU TERTRE.
New York: P. F. Collier, 1892 NUC.

DU TERTRE, MISS. See DU TERTRE, FANNY.

DUTTON, ANNIE VICTORIA. Nationality Unknown.

003635   A CLOUD OF DAWN. London: Chapman and
Hall, 1898 BMC.

ATH 112:786. Socialist and capitalist struggle. Una,
heroine has Utopian scheme, an experiment which costs
her love, health, fortune, and even life.
Socialism--arguments for and against. There's the
apostle and the heroine who dies as a victim to his
ideals. She is Pauline Maurice. LIT 4:21.
Depressing. SP 83:93.
She's converted to his cause. Apparently he's
presented as a rabid socialist. SR 87:217

003636   LOVE WITHOUT WINGS: A STORY. London:
Hurst and Blackett, 1907 BMC.

003637   WISDOM'S FOLLY: A STUDY IN FEMININE
DEVELOPMENT. London: R. Bentley, 1896 BMC. New York:
H. Holt, 1896 NUC.

ATH 107:839. Eleanor, after her engagement to Cedric,
lapses from "strong, loyal, pure-hearted womanhood"
into "vulgar and slightly coarse flirtation with her
husband's friend." Catastrophe follows.
ACAD 50:238. She has a desire for experience. Rapid
changes take place in Eleanor while her lover remains
under the influence of one idea-the wish to make her
his own-despite all.
LW 29:253 "deep underlying womanliness."
Sp 77:249. Has a complication which is unpleasant.

DUTTON, LOUISE ELIZABETH. United States.

003638   THE GODDESS GIRL. New York: Moffat, Yard,
1915 NUC.

Conv girl who meets with man whose courtship is along
unconventional lines. PW 10-30-15.
Rose Saxon small town wholesome young woman, leaves
the town when her father becomes poorer to seek better
fortunes for self in New York. Joins Bohemians and
"throws all conventions 'over the windmills.'"
Encourages a lover who declares he can't marry her by
insisting she can take care of herself. (but doesn't
go all the way). NYT

003639   THE WISHING MOON. Garden City, N.Y.:
Doubleday, Page, 1916 NUC.

Love story set in New England. BKM
Judith and Neil steal away to escape the fate that
parents and social inequalities have hung about their
necks. PW

DUXBURY, MRS. C. RICHMOND.

003640   NEW ENGLAND FOLK. New York: Abbey Press,
[1901] NUC.

DWYER, VERA G.

003641   CONQUERING HAL. London: Ward, Lock, 1916
BMC.

003642   MONA'S MYSTERY MAN. London: Ward, Lock,
1914 BMC.

003643   A WAR OF GIRLS. London: Ward, Lock, 1915
BMC.

003644   WITH BEATING WINGS. AN AUSTRALIAN STORY.
London: Ward, Lock, 1913 BMC.

DYAN, MEG.

003645   ALL IN A MAN'S KEEPING. London: W. A.
Allen, 1894 BMC.

SR 78:185. Passionate physical love binds Dick
Urquhart and a modern woman to each other despite
passage of time and matrimony on both sides. He is a
soldier. Reviewer finds them disgusting and
indifferent to their honor barely being saved.
ACAD 46:99. Urquhart treats Rose and his Afghan wife
badly, the latter dying from a broken heart and his
betrayal.

DYAR, MURIEL CAMPBELL. B. 1876. United States.

003646   DAVIE AND ELISABETH, WONDERFUL
ADVENTURES. New York and London: Harper, 1908 NUC.

"Davie and Elizabeth are an elderly couple who live on
a New England farm. While not blessed with an
overabundance of this world's goods, they find
happiness and contentment in each other's love and in
the little things which go to make up their every-day
life." BKM v 28 1908-9
NYT-nothing here.

DYE, EVA (EMERY). B. 1855. United States.

003647   THE CONQUEST: THE TRUE STORY OF LEWIS AND
CLARK. London: C. F. Cazenove, 1902 BMC. Chicago: A.
C. McClurg, 1902 NUC.

ATH-historical epic.

003648   MCDONALD OF OREGON; A TALE OF TWO SHORES.
London: C. F. Cazenove, 1906 BMC. Chicago: A. C.
McClurg, 1906 BMC NUC.

McDonald, Ranald, 1824-94 Fiction

003649   MCLOUGHLIN AND OLD OREGON: A CHRONICLE.
Chicago: A. C. McClurg, 1900 NUC BMC.

DYER, ANNIE RUSSELL. United States.

003650   THE TOUCH OF A VANISHED HAND. Providence,
R.I.: American Book Exchange, 1897 W.

Tries to prove that communication after death is
possible. Old Rector, dying, promises his daughter
he'll return from death if he can. His daughter's
experiences described. PW 52:788.

DYKES, MARY.

003651   RAINBOW WINGS. Manchester: Lawlors,
[1916] BMC.

Sketches

E., A. L. O., pseud. See TUCKER, CHARLOTTE MARIA.

EAGAN, M. B., pseud. See SMITH, MARY PAULINE.

EARLE, MARY TRACY. B. 1864. United States.

003652   THE FLAG ON THE HILLTOP. Boston:
Houghton, Mifflin, 1902 NUC.

Boy during Civil War-PW

003653   THE WONDERFUL WHEEL. New York: Century,
1896 NUC.

CR 29:260. Port on the Gulf of Mexico.
Father-daughter, and niece who cares for them when he
is accidentally disabled. He is suspected by neighbors
of voodoo; finally ends well.
PW 10-10-96. He owns a "luminous wheel," he believes
it has brought "Voodoo" down on them; his efforts to
live it down. Creoles of Louisiana.

EARLE, VICTORIA. See MATTHEWS, VICTORIA (EARLE).

EASTMAN, CHARLOTTE WHITNEY. United States.

003654   THE EVOLUTION OF DODD'S SISTER: A TRAGEDY
OF EVERYDAY LIFE. Chicago and New York: Rand, McNally,
1897 NUC.

"Teaches that womanhood must be the aim of women's
education; motherhood, strong and capable must be the
focal point of her development." Dodd's sister has the
wrong kind of upbringing. PW 52:170.

EASTMAN, REBECCA LANE (HOOPER).

003655   THE BIG LITTLE PERSON; A ROMANCE. New
York and London: Harper, [1917] NUC.

Arathea loses her hearing and her lover because of it.
Writes for hearing aid; correspondence develops
between her and inventor of aid; they end up marrying.
PW

EASTON, MRS. C. F. United States.

003656   "CONSIDERATIONS". New York: J. B. Alden,
1894 NUC.

EASTWICK, F. E. See MAXWELL, BEATRICE ETHEL HERON AND
FLORENCE E. EASTWICK.

EASTWICK, FLORENCE E., jt. au. See MAXWELL, BEATRICE ETHEL
HERON AND FLORENCE E. EASTWICK.

EASTWICK, MRS. EGERTON.

003657   "BEYOND THESE VOICES". A NOVEL. London:
Burns and Oates, 1901 BMC.

Heroine works havoc on her uncle's old fashioned ways;
personally ambitious, ready to perpetuate any crime.
Founds an institution to perpetuate her views? ATH
8-10-01

003658   THE RESIDENT-COUNCILLOR. Singapore:
"Straits Times" Press, 1898 BMC.

Mrs. Mainwaring-a blameless adventuress. SR 87:437.

003659   THE RUBIES OF RAJMAR; OR, MR.
CHARLECOTE'S DAUGHTERS: A ROMANCE. BY MRS. EGERTON
EASTWICK (PLEYDELL NORTH). London: G. Newnes, 1895
BMC.

Intricate puzzle of events. Amy Charlecote wants
revenge. ACAD 48:47
Marriage of a country vicar's daughter to an Indian
prince. The vicar is well-learned in Eastern languages
and ideas. Mystery concerning an oriental family; plot
hinges on a set of historic jewels. ATH 106:93

003660   THE TRIAL OF MARGARET BRERETON. BY
PLEYDELL NORTH. London: [J. Stanley], 1891 NUC.

EATON, ELIZABETH.

003661   WHEN THE SHADOWS FALL. London: Wells
Gardner, 1912 BMC.

TLS-Pretty and harmless diary of invalided young
woman.

EATON, FRANCES U. United States.

003662   A FEARLESS INVESTIGATOR [ANONYMOUS].
Chicago: A. C. McClurg, 1896 NUC.

PW 10-31-96 Young man, recovering from typhoid, visits
in country with friends interested in such new
theories and speculations as spiritualism, telepathy,
materializing etc. He has a relapse "and his fearless
investigations are so told as to leave the reader in
doubt whether they are the ravings of fever or real
occurrences.
Speaker John Hardy visits friends' house-meets all
kinds of reformers, faddists. Author shows these as
ludicrous. LW 28:164

EATON, IMOGENE CAMMETT. United States.

003663   GWENDOLENE HOPE: A TALE OF GLOUCESTER.
Fall River, Mass.: J. H. Franklin, 1897 NUC.

EATON, ISABEL GRAHAM. United States.

003664   BY THE SHORES OF ARCADY. New York:
Outing, 1908 NUC.

Pretty romantic story

ECCLES, CAROLINE A.

003665   THE HOME COMING. AN IDYLL. London: S.
Sonnenschein, 1910 BMC.

TLS-sent love story.

ECCLES, CHARLOTTE O'CONOR.

003666   ALIENS OF THE WEST. BY THE AUTHOR OF "THE
REJUVENATION OF MISS SEMAPHORE" [ANONYMOUS]. London:
Cassell, 1904 BMC.

003667   THE MATRIMONIAL LOTTERY. London: E. Nash,
1906 BMC.

Fantasy about a marriage lottery with a man as a
"Prize". LBKM 192,07 Jan
ACAD-prize is a husband

003668   THE REJUVENATION OF MISS SEMAPHORE; A
FARCICAL NOVEL. BY HAL GODFREY. London: Jarrold, 1897
BMC. Boston: L.C. Page, 1899 NUC.

Funny. Agatha and Prudence are "old maids" of 50 and
35 living in a boarding house. They read an ad about
Water of youth. Spend $1,000.00 for it. Oldest takes
it first, but as it is spilled, licks it all up. Next
day her sister finds a baby in her sister's bed. And
all the complications that follow. BKM 8:589

EDEN, FANNIE.

003669   MARK STRATHMORE'S RENUNCIATION. London:
Hodder & Stoughton, 1901 BMC.

EDGE, K. M. See CAULFEILD, KATHLEEN MARY (EDGE).

EDGINTON, H. M. See BAILEY, MAY HELEN MARION (EDGINTON).

EDMONDS, ELIZABETH MAYHEW (WALLER).

003670   AMYGDALA: A TALE OF THE GREEK REVOLUTION.
BY MRS. EDMONDS. London and New York: G. Bell, 1894
NUC. London: Bell, 1894 BMC.

ACAD 46:945. Daintily printed and prettily bound
romance.
Young man devotes life to Hellenism. Disguised as
shepherd; falls in love, but result very unexpected.
CR 23:48
Means almond tree-to send a twig means I love you.
Love, heroism and suffering in Greek Revolution of
1825. English artist loves Irene who dies for her
country. He lives to devote himself to his sister. LW
26:25.

003671   JABEZ NUTYARD, WORKMAN AND DREAMER: A
NOVEL. London: Jarrold, 1898 BMC.

ACAD 53:601. Old fashioned story, male hero,
Socialistic teaching between the lines.
LBKM 14:40. Tame and aimless.

EDMONDS, MRS. See EDMONDS, ELIZABETH MAYHEW (WALLER).

EDWARDS, ANNIE. D. 1896. United Kingdom.

003672   THE ADVENTURESS. London: R. Bentley, 1894
BMC NUC.

SP 73:701. Adventuress with a heart is heroine.
Richard has a past-should not have been cast as a
hero.
ACAD 46:326. Rose Hathaway looking for security at
Riviera finds a husband worldy, dangerous but not
worthless.
ATH 104:348. Very naughty but womanly little American.

003673   A PLASTER SAINT. London: Chatto and
Windus, 1899 BMC NUC.

Heroine tells of her earlier love for a rake who loved
and left and who almost ruined her life. He went on to
a miserable marriage and then to take holy orders. LIT
5:520
Reverend Gervase, philanders for material for his
sermons. SP 83:536 Polly Erne abandoned by the Rev. is
almost finished but finds peace in religion. ATH
114:487

EDWARDS, EDITH M.

003674   MARION HARLING'S AWAKENING. London:
Sunday School Union, [1897] BMC.

Returns home educated, full of plans for doing good,
comtemptuous of duties close at hand. Taught to see
life "more truly." SP 79:627

EDWARDS, JEANNETTE LLEWELLYN. United States.

003675   A GIRL AND THE DEVIL; A NOVEL. New York:
Broadway, [1903] NUC.

EDWARDS, LOUISE BETTS. D. 1928. United States.

003676   THE TU-TZE'S TOWER; A NOVEL.
Philadelphia: H. T. Coates, 1903 NUC.

Heroine in revolt vs civilzation; survives her husband
and writes his book. Her adventures are unusual. PW
5-16-03
the widow ends up in the Tu Tze's arms after he shut
her up in his tower having chosen her to be his wife.
NYT---03 488

EDWARDS, M. BETHAM. See EDWARDS, MATILDA BARBARA BETHAM.

EDWARDS, MATILDA BARBARA BETHAM. 1836-1919. United
Kingdom.

003677   THE CURB OF HONOUR. BY M. BETHAM-EDWARDS.
London: A. and C. Black, 1893 BMC. New York:
Anglo-American, [c1893] NUC.

Rolo Rugden attractive, well loved, lonely, marries
Lamenta "queer old maid" in order to end the hope in
the woman he does love and who loves him that they
will ever marry. He has decided not to have children
because of a physical weakness they would inherit. But
Lamenta loves him and they are really very well
matched in their wit and temperaments. SP 71:773.
He has a misshapen body. BKM 5:89.
Lamenta or Lavinia Tart. ACAD 44:527.

003678   THE DREAM CHARLOTTE: A STORY OF ECHOES.
BY M. BETHAM-EDWARDS. London: A. and C. Black, 1896
BMC. New York: Macmillan, 1896 NUC.

LBKM 10:175. Two friends leave convent together. The
peasant girl is much influenced by the rich girl
Charlotte, and lives her life as a missionary.
Pleading and defending liberty and tolerance, feeling
all the while she is imitating her friend. Charlotte
(Corday) reappears years later on her way to Paris to
avenge the wrongs of France by the death of Marat.
SP 77:119. Airelle is "offered up on the altar of
family interest, and the expansion is so complete as
to annihilate all possibilities for the expansion of
her individuality. Passing resignation is the keynote
of her character...Miss B prepares us for a new Joan
of Arc." Substitution of devotion to the domestic
ideal for mystical enthusiasm, dreary and
disappointing.

003679   THE LORD OF THE HARVEST. BY M.
BETHAM-EDWARDS. London: Hurst & Blackett, 1899 BMC
NUC.

Suffolk in first years of 19th. Romance of Aimee,
governess and young farmer at center of careful
studies of old customs and types of country lore. LBKM
17:61
Local customs and modes of life of Suffolk before
repeal of Corn Laws. BAKER 03,104

003680   A NORTH-COUNTRY COMEDY. BY M.
BETHAM-EDWARDS. London: Henry, [1891] BMC.
Philadelphia: J. B. Lippincott, 1892 NUC.

Two "old maids" on a quest: ATH 99:370
Division of relics of a country estate: CR 17:140
LW 23:42. Humorous without "villainy or coarseness."
Healthy Heroine and her lovers. Miss Sabrina is
"humourously sententious."
PW-"Two maiden ladies no longer young," one gets
married both have financial fortune.

003681   REMINISCENCES. BY M. BETHAM-EDWARDS.
London: G. Redway, 1898 NUC BMC.

LBKM 14:72. Autobiography.

003682   THE ROMANCE OF A FRENCH PARSONAGE. BY M.
BETHAM-EDWARDS. New York: J. W. Lovell, 1891 [c] NUC.
London: Chapman and Hall, 1892 BMC.

An apostate priest takes charge of a fishing village
of Huguenots. A young nun who loves him, escapes from
convent and unknowingly takes refuge in his home.
Eventually they marry but she lives only one year. LW

93, 26
SP: French priest becomes Protestant minister. Two
women. Bertrande escapes from a convent and stays with
him. "It may give serious offense." Deals with
problems in a fair and serious way.
ACAD 41:60. Assigned to a quiet country parish by the
sea. When Bertrande flees the convent, they are
married. One year of happiness before she dies, and he
is alone again.
SR 73:18. Before Bertrande appeared, he planned to
marry the middle-aged widow who was his neighbor, not
a love relationship but friendship.
PW-Brilliant Lutheran pastor in small parish on coast
of France, influence of Carmelite convent,
relationship with rich generous noble widow.
Mild domestic romance that begins with a Carmelite nun
who escapes the nunnery to join her lover, one of two
priests who leave the church. Author is Miss Betham
Edwards. ATH 98-829.

003683   A ROMANCE OF DIJON. London: A. and C.
Black, 1894 BMC. New York: Macmillan, 1894 NUC.

LBKM 7:90. Old-fashioned historical romance, French
Revolution and the taking of the Bastille.
Pernelle Nesmond, young tradeswoman at outbreak of
Revolution. Wants to marry a young man solely because
he'll be useful in the business. She's super
intelligent, business-like, self-contained and
beautiful. But he loves a peasant girl who marries
another peasant and gives up the young man Pernelle
wants (Laurent). In the meantime she has loved and
lost her real love-Velours. CR 23:258.

003684   A STORM-RENT SKY: SCENES OF LOVE AND
REVOLUTION. London: Hurst and Blackett, 1898 BMC NUC.

ACAD 53:201. French Revolution's effect on humble
village life in the Champagne district.
ATH 111:400. There is "a maiden of heroic mould who
prefers patriotism to love and the common destiny of
womankind." A grande dame adopts various disguises and
is a central character.

003685   A SUFFOLK COURTSHIP. London: Hurst and
Blackett, 1900 BMC. Leipzig: B. Tauchnitz, 1900 NUC.

SP 85:975. East Anglia 50 years ago. Fortunes of four
orphan daughters of farmer.

003686   TWO AUNTS AND A NEPHEW. London: H. Henry,
The Victorian Library For Gentlewomen, [1892] BMC NUC.

SP 69:42. Xenia is an unusual heroine.
ACAD 41:610. Story is of two aunts who take their
nephew to Paris for a vacation, they meet three
American girls and Russian singer Xenia

EDWARDS, MRS. HENRY SUTHERLAND.

003687   THE SECRET OF THE PRINCESS: A TALE
OF...LIFE IN RUSSIA. London: Chapman and Hall, 1891
BMC.

Russian court life. Princess Volhousky and three
children. ACAD
She's a widow with two daughters and a son. Son
killed; daughter loves a Pole who is banished to
Siberia: SP 66, 354

EDWARDS, NAOMI.

003688   A SELF-WORSHIPPER: A STORY FOR WOMEN.
Bristol: J. W. Arrowsmith, [1897] BMC.

EDWOOD, MAY.

003689   THE AUTOBIOGRAPHY OF A SPIN: A STORY OF
ANGLO-INDIAN LIFE. Calcutta & London: Thacker, Spink,
1893 BMC.

Anglo-Indian life. Title appears to mean spinster.
She's 29 and ready to wed at the end. Juanita
Desmond-a selfish heartless flirt of the ordinary
type. SP 71:773.
A spin is a worn-out flirt who is "on the shelf". ACAD
44:460.
"The brutally frank analysis of the thoughts, motives
and feelings...of a thoughtless, heartlss flirt. She
pretends that her heart was soured and hardened by the
conduct of a man who was simply amusing himself with
her and that she has avenged herself on the sex by
amusing herself with subsequent admirers." ATH
102:551.

003690   ELSIE ELLERTON: A NOVELETTE OF

ANGLO-INDIAN LIFE. Calcutta: S. Thacker, 1892 NUC.

EGERTON, BEATRICE.

003691   LIPPA: A NOVEL. London: Eden, Remington,
1891 BMC.

Young woman accepts proposal of marriage but gives it
up when she hears her mother has gone mad. When she
learns it's not hereditary, marries the man. ATH 98
252
Phillipa Seton of fashionable London life. SR 9-19-11,
390

EGERTON, GEORGE, pseud. See BRIGHT, MARY CHAVELITA (DUNNE)
MELVILLE CLAIRMONTE GOLDING.

EGLANTINE [pseud.].

003692   GLADYS WOODLEY; OR, THE BRIDE OF AMIEL.
BY EGLANTINE. London: Elliot Stock, 1895 BMC.

ELIOT, ANNIE, pseud. See TRUMBULL, ANNIE ELIOT.

ELISCU, EUGENIE R. United States.

003693   SATAN'S HOOF AND THE TWO WITCHES. Boston:
Banner Of Light, 1899 NUC.

ELLA, pseud. See HURLBUT, ELLA CHILDS.

ELLER, pseud. See ELLERMAN, ANNE ELIZABETH.

ELLERMAN, ANNE ELIZABETH.

003694   THE PRIME MINISTER OF WURTEMBURG. BY
ELLER. London: W. Andrews, [1897] BMC.

ELLERMAN, ANNIE WINIFRED. B. 1894. United Kingdom.

003695   DEVELOPMENT; A NOVEL. BY W. BRYHER.
London: Constable, 1920 BMC NUC. New York: Macmillan,
1920 NUC.

TLS-an autobiography, a note book. Nancy at four
desires to be a boy, go to sea. She travels. Insists
on studying paleontolgy at twelve. She also wants to
be an artist. At 18 she publishes a book of poetry.
The end. Review says she's a prig.
SP-"Adventure" will be the sequel.
ATH-wishes to keep her art free from the taint of
school, which was a prison. We are told she possesses
"the intellect, the hopes, the ambitions of a man,
unsoftened by any female attribute." Laments that she
is not a boy and is of necessity sheathed in
convention.
LBKM

ELLIOT, ANNE. Nationality Unknown.

003696   EVELYN'S CAREER: A NOVEL. BY THE AUTHOR
OF "MY WIFE'S NIECE," "DR. EDITH ROMNEY." "AN OLD
MAN'S FAVOR," ETC. [ANONYMOUS]. London: R. Bentley,
1891 BMC.

Lady Cunningham adopts her dead son's daughter, raises
her to be a great heiress. But Evelyn at 20 feels a
call to the cause of working women. Goes to London to
work with the poor. Brings about many reforms. PW
11-14-91.
Well-written, realistic portrayal of poor. Evelyn uses
fortune to help poor. Has discouraging experience at
first, marries, then sees how she can be more
effective, returns and succeeds. LW
She's an agnostic with deep faith in people. Gives
lectures to rich about the poor. ATH: says Evelyn
failed in her work "whether author thinks so or not."
98,187
Starts a haven of rest in the country for poor people.
Many young women join in the project. SR 9 -26-91, 365

003697   LORD HARBOROUGH. London: Hurst &
Blackett, 1896 BMC NUC.

Boy raised as a "joiner" becomes an earl. Sketches of
lower classes. LBKM 11:182
SR Male with carpentry antecedents turns out to be
aristocrat.
ATH 108:219, Raised to be a socialist.
ACAD 50:218, But he does not remain a Socialist once
he has money.
SP 77:274. he remains a generous friend to the working
classes.

003698   MANSELL'S MILLIONS. London: Hurst and
Blackett, 1903 BMC.

ATH
True "hero" is the millionaire's secretary. TLS 03,
139

003699   A MARTIAL MAID. London: Hurst and
Blackett, 1900 BMC.

SP 84:604. Clare goes to England with child of
shipwrecked mother to reclaim its birthrights, is
considered an adventuress, fights till success.

003700   THE MEMOIRS OF MIMOSA. BY HERSELF. EDITED
BY ANNE ELLIOT. New York: Moffat, Yard, [1912] NUC.
London: S. Paul, [1912] BMC.

brilliant, undisciplined woman resolves to "live every
moment of her life" NYT

003701   MICHAEL DAUNT: A NOVEL. BY THE AUTHOR OF
"DR. EDITH ROMNEY" [ANONYMOUS]. London: Hurst and
Blackett, 1895 BMC.

He marries Agnes Raymond. He's an artist impractical;
she cares nothing for art, thinks only of paying the
bills. Sympathy for both sides, but the sense of it is
that Daunt should face up to his marriage and domestic
responsibilities more than he does. SP 75:115.
Their marriage reaches a crisis when the artist is
attracted to another woman. ACAD 48:107
She stresses order, responsibility. ATH 106:93

003702   WHERE THE REEDS WAVE. A STORY. London: R.
Bentley, 1897 BMC.

SP 81:474. Tragedy of a man who has sinned in his
youth, watches same happen with his child and is
powerless to help. East Anglia.
SR 85:502. Mother dares not interfere with her child's
ruin because of sin in her own past.
Life in E. Anglican village. Hy. of a fisherman's
family. An artist in middle life returns to the scene
where he seduced a woman, finds he's the father of the
heroine. ATH 110:486

003703   WINNING OF MAY. BY THE AUTHOR OF "DR.
EDITH ROMNEY" [ANONYMOUS]. London: Hurst and Blackett,
1893 BMC.

Arthur Beresford is a supreme egoist but a grand one.
He's accused of murder. May Leslie, who loves him,
gives evidence to prove he's innocent but in doing so
ruins her reputation. They are engaged but he doesn't
love her, only feels obligated. Then she learns the
truth. SP 71, 147.
May Leslie is a novelist making her own way after her
parents die. Takes dingy lodgings in Fulham Rd. She
meets Arthur a deformed man and both she and her
friend Ernestine fall for him. SR 76:76.
"Brilliantly written." When she learns the truth,
leaves town but they marry in the end. ACAD 44: 148.
Beresford torments heroine right up to the end or near
end. She finds it difficult to assert herself against
him. ATH 102:450.

003704   A WOMAN AT THE HELM. BY THE AUTHOR OF
"DR. EDITH ROMNEY" [ANONYMOUS]. London: Hurst and
Blackett, 1892 BMC.

SP 69:42. Clare is manager of Thurston and Co., but is
no longer toward end of story. Reviewer is not sure of
author's intention, but suspects that it is "not well
that a woman should be at the helm...apt to have her
attention...distracted" by romance.
SR 73:603. Her dying father leaves business to her
rather than her brother. She is "capable, sensible,
clear-headed and shrewd." She guides the business out
of financial troubles into prosperity; is subsequently
ousted by a man. romance with touchy, easily offended
hero who lacks "Clare's finer manliness."

ELLIOTT, DELIA BUFORD. Nationality Unknown.

003705   ADELE HAMILTON. New York: Neale, 1907
NUC.

Bravery of a southern woman who at her husband's death
finds herself penniless, and takes her five children
to California hoping that in a new country...she may
fight her financial battle and win.

ELLIOTT, EMILIA, pseud. See JACOBS, CAROLINE EMILIA.

ELLIOTT, L. ELWYN. See JOYCE, LILIAN ELWYN (ELLIOTT).

ELLIOTT, MAUD (HOWE). 1854-1948. United States.

003706   HONOR: A NOVEL. BY MAUD HOWE. St. Paul:
Price-McGill, [c1893] NUC.

Young woman seduced, abandoned when her father loses
his money. The man of the world who catches her on the
rebound, the fresh young lover who weds her in the
end. Reviewer finds the illustrations in direct
contradiction to the text. "The fair pampered beings
of the story are depicted as the scrub woman type." LW
93, 291.

003707   PHILLIDA. BY MAUD HOWE. New York: United
States Book, [c1891] NUC.

She's an American who becomes involved with an English
man. For a long time she doesn't know he's married.
What happens when she meets the "cold proud" Lady
Lawton is the story. PW 9-26-91.
American heroine in London society. Author wants to
show crudeness of American society by contrast. LW
Phillida Langdon loves and is loved by Sir John, but
he's married. That breaks up and she makes a wiser
choice of lovers. Author is critical of British arist.
which she says is doomed. NATION 12-17-91, 471
CR 17:35. Love; possibility of extramarital affair
considered and rejected.

ELLIOTT, SARAH BARNWELL. 1848-1928. United States.

003708   THE DURKET SPERRET: A NOVEL. New York: H.
Holt, 1898 NUC. (Also contains: An Idle Man.)

BKM 8:69. Hannah was employed by a professor and his
family as a waitress. She is ruined, at least the
reverend thinks she is, but is not sure just how it
happened. She was dismissed from the family. Tennessee
mountains.
LW 29:286. Hanna is a "beautiful, strong character,
womanly and genuine." "Charming" story.

003709   JERRY: A NOVEL. New York: H. Holt, 1891
NUC. London: Osgood, McIlvaine, 1891 BMC.

Mining life in West; feverish life of boomtown; the
misery. ATH 98 384
Hero a waif, raised by miner. His development as a
moral and personal force in the town. CR
Brutal father; mother tortured by fear of him, hero's
wanderings. Joe makes a gentleman of him, but he gets
gold fever. LW.
Runs away in search of mother. PW
No love, no important female characters. SR 7-11-91,
53

003710   JOHN PAGET: A NOVEL. New York: H. Holt,
1893 NUC.

Two brothers are separated as boys after Civil War.
One becomes a fashionable man; the other a clergyman.
They later meet. John wants to help the poor.
Fashionable churches are criticized in the novel. PW
5-6-93.
Claude raised in lap of luxury from boyhood as son of
a man who believes only in money. John grows up in
Texas and leads a hard rough life full of hardships.
CR 20,23:98
Several woman characters. Claudia worldly-marries an
aged cynic; Elizabeth Marsden whose father is a bandit
is saved from going bad by John. A beautiful, Mexican
woman. Beatrice-"type of blind abiding faith." BOOK
NEWS 130:460

003711   THE MAKING OF JANE; A NOVEL. New York:
Scribner's Sons., 1901 NUC.

Study in individualism: sacrifices luxury to have her
own way: schoolteacher, milliner, mgr of a large
department store. Marries a millionaire. NATION '01
The true sphere of women? PW 11-2-01
Finds self she's lost thru voluntary return to poverty
and self-dependence unusual intell. yet falls for a
worthless man. NYT

ELLIS, BETH. See ELLIS, ELIZABETH.

ELLIS, EDITH MARY OLDHAM (LEES). 1861-1916. United
Kingdom.

003712   ATTAINMENT. BY MRS. HAVELOCK ELLIS.
London: A. Rivers, 1909 NUC BMC.

Rachel Merton wants a wider life, settles in London
flat, works for poor, helps form Brotherhood of the
Perfect Life. Learns love is all that matters-comes
home and marries. TLS

Lives in a kind of commune which, says the reviewer,
the members decide to disband for no apparent reason.
LBKM
Brotherhood of the Perfect Life-experiment in living
equally with different classes. Ann; servant class,
done with a little humor concerning problems of
communal living of group of individualistic people. SP

003713   THE IMPERISHABLE WING. BY MRS. HAVELOCK
ELLIS. London: S. Paul, [1911] NUC BMC.

003714   KIT'S WOMAN; A CORNISH IDYLL. BY MRS.
HAVELOCK ELLIS. London: A. Rivers, 1907 BMC NUC.
(Revised edition of: Seaweed.)

"morbid realism" "modern craving for moral dissection"
Kit crippled by an accident after two years of
marriage; the story "will shock the sensibilities of
many readers" Kit's "lapse from virtue" but shown as a
fine woman. SR
ATH-"question of a man allowing his wife to take a
lover for sake of posterity-wife prefers her own
husband."

003715   LOVE-ACRE: AN IDYL IN TWO WORLDS. BY MRS.
HAVELOCK ELLIS. New York: M. Kennerley, 1914 BMC NUC.
London: G. Richards, 1915 BMC NUC.

PW 86 12-12-14: 1978-"Tobias Trewidden is a young
idealist who, misunderstood, lives with Nature and his
dreams in the midst of a family of stepbrothers and
sisters. "Love-Acre" is the garden spot he pictures as
the home of his mother, who died shortly after he was
born. Here he meets and woos Loveday, a village girl.
But another sister of Loveday's puts Tobias in a wrong
light, and his sweetheart casts him off. Tobias
becomes an outcast and a pilgrim, yet his life is not
in vain."
NYT 1914:556. -Her fate is more dire by far.

003716   STEVE'S WOMAN. BY MRS. HAVELOCK ELLIS.
New York: J. McBride, 1909 NUC.

ELLIS, ELIZABETH. United States.

003717   BARBARA WINSLOW, REBEL. BY BETH ELLIS.
Edinburgh and London: W. Blackwood, 1903 BMC. New
York: Dodd, Mead, 1906 NUC.

Barbara's involved in the Monmouth rebellion-LBKM
Barbara is no tame dove holds her own-and a rapier
besides-with any man. ATH
NYT-defies king and is pursued by his armies across
England.

003718   BLIND MOUTHS. BY BETH ELLIS. Edinburgh:
W. Blackwood, 1907 BMC.

Struggle of labor vs capital. A woman organizes a mvt.
vs social vices and luxury. Love interludes.

003719   "THE FAIR MOON OF BATH". BY BETH ELLIS.
New York: Dodd, Mead, 1908 NUC.

PW-romance.
BKM-romance.

003720   THE GIRL WHO WON. BY BETH ELLIS. New
York: Dodd, Mead, 1910 NUC.

Historical adventure. PW
Gt. Britain-William and Mary

003721   A KING OF VAGABONDS. BY BETH ELLIS.
Edinburgh and London: W. Blackwood, 1911 NUC BMC.

historical novel-TLS

003722   THE KING'S BLUE RIBAND. BY BETH ELLIS.
London, New York: Hodder & Stoughton, [c1912] NUC BMC.

PW 83 3/22/13 p.1099 "England in Jacobite days is the
scene. Sir Anthony Claverton, ruined, seeks an heiress
in marriage and also to save her from a villain. He
falls in love with Sylvia as soon as he sees her, but
she rejects him as a fortune hunter and declares she
will marry the other man. Anthony goes to France to
get, for a wager, the Cordon-bleu order always worn by
King Louis. Excitement and adventures follow thick and
fast, involving Jacobites, Sylvia, Anthony and many
others, but in the end love triumphs and all is well."

003723   THE KING'S SPY. BY BETH ELLIS. Edinburgh
& London: W. Blackwood, 1910 NUC.

Jacobite conspiracy during time of Wm. III of England.

003724   MADAME, WILL YOU WALK? BY BETH ELLIS.
Edinburgh: W. Blackwood, 1905 BMC.

Graceful old-time comedy-LBKM

003725   THE MOON OF BATH. BY BETH ELLIS.
Edinburgh: W. Blackwood, 1907 BMC.

charming, delightful, etc-LBKM
historical novel. TLS

ELLIS, MRS. HAVELOCK. See ELLIS, EDITH MARY OLDHAM (LEES).

ELLISON, EDITH NICHOLL (BRADLEY). United States.

003726   THE BLOSSOMING OF THE WASTE. New York:
Calkins, 1908 NUC.

PW-Male lawyer hero

003727   THE BURNT-OFFERING. New York: Broadway,
[c1908] NUC.

Story of woman with TB and love nothing new BKM

003728   THE UPWARD TRAIL. New York: Rowland &
Ives, [c1918] NUC.

ELLISON, NINA E. United States.

003729   NADINE: A ROMANCE OF TWO LIVES.
Nashville, Tenn.: Gospel Advocate Pub. Co., 1897 NUC.

ELLSWORTH, LOUISE C. United States.

003730   FURONO AMATI: A ROMANCE. New York: United
States Book, [c1892] NUC.

Hero begins as a boot-black in NYC. A German gives him
a violin and because he can't play it, the boy smashes
it-just as he later destroys the woman he marries
because she loves his music and not him. PW 2-4-93
Becomes a great artist but "with his fiery Italian
nature perfectly untamed." Marries a woman of high
birth from New York. CR 14,20:216

ELMORE, MAUD (JOHNSON).

003731   THE REVOLT OF SUNDARAMMA. New York: F. H.
Revell, [c1911] NUC BMC.

Hindu woman studied from time of 8 year old child.
-married!-author "interprets the life of the women of
India for their sisters in America." Sundaramma
revolts vs the marriage. But fate and law and priests
force her to submit. Later she learns of a different
religion and a different philosophy of woman's life
and the "possibility opens for her and her little girl
to enter a new way of life." NYT

ELMSLIE, THEODORA C.

003732   GLADDIE'S SWEETHEART: A TRUE STORY.
London: Ward and Downey, 1894 BMC.

ACAD 46:252. Love story (happy) of an orphan.

003733   HIS LIFE'S MAGNET: A NOVEL. London: F.
Warne, 1892 BMC. New York: D. Appleton, 1892 NUC.

ATH 100:700. Male hero, handsome, passionate,
adventurous, etc. "dashing prodigal" rescuing lives of
others at risk of his own.

003734   THE LITTLE LADY OF LAVENDER. London: Ward
& Downey, [1896] BMC. Philadelphia: American
Sunday-school Union, 1899 NUC.

003735   THE PILGRIM CHILD. London: Ward & Downey,
[1896] BMC. Philadelphia: American Sunday-School
Union, [c1896] NUC.

EMERY, FLORENCE (FARR). D. 1917.

003736   THE DANCING FAUN. BY FLORENCE FARR.
London: E. Mathews and J. Lane, 1894 BMC. Boston:
Roberts, 1894 NUC.

SR 78:305. Lady Geraldine offers married card sharp
half her income if he will live with her. He explains
he can do better financially by sticking with his wife
a promising actress. Lady Geraldine shoots her. Murder
goes unpunished.
LW 25:233. Her conduct after the murder is

"unnatural."
ACAD 46:148. Keynotes Series. Lady Geraldine leads an
after life of remorse.
ATH 104:187. Lady Geraldine shoots him.
LBKM 6:120. Yes, she shoots him not wife, "goes back
and lives happy she has done so. Verdict being
suicide, there are no inconvenient consequences.
PW-He is utterly unprincipled. Title page designed by
Aubrey Beardsley

003737   THE SOLEMNIZATION OF JACKLIN. SOME
ADVENTURES ON THE SEARCH FOR REALITY. BY FLORENCE
FARR. London: A. C. Fifield, 1912 NUC BMC.

TLS-"making the mind clear by experience" for Jacklin
is divorcing her husband, marrying another and going
back to first. All the women are "rakes or prigs."

EMERY, SARAH ANNA. 1821-1907. United States.

003738   MY GENERATION. Newburyport [Mass.]: Moses
H. Sargent, 1893 NUC.

Customs, manners and beliefs of early 19th. LW 26:106.

ENGLAND, FRANCES.

003739   SMALL CONCERNS. London: Digby, Long,
[1897] BMC.

ENGLISH, MARIA.

003740   AS THE SHADOW OF A GREAT ROCK. London:
Digby, Long, 1896 BMC.

SR-Earnest, naive story of two brothers, 1 good and 1
bad.
ACAD-goody-goody hero.

ENSELL, MRS. E. J.

003741   ANGEL. A CORNISH ROMANCE. London: Digby,
Long, 1898 BMC.

SP 81:837. Bridegroom disappears on wedding-day.
Mystery eventually cleared up, happy ending.

ERSKINE, ANGELA SELINA BLANCHE (FORBES) SAINT CLAIR. B.
1876.

003742   THE BROKEN COMMANDMENT. BY LADY ANGELA
FORBES. London: E. Nash, 1910 BMC NUC.

BM Circulating Libraries censored this.
TLS-defends adultery on the grounds of personality
development.

003743   THE OTHER WOMAN'S SHADOW. London: E.
Nash, 1912 NUC BMC.

TLS-commonplace.

003744   PENELOPE'S PROGRESS. London: E. Nash,
1911 BMC.

She has an unconventional education, wins success on
stage, breaks off engagement when she tells her lover
she's illegitimate. Ends happily (?) ATH

ERSKINE, BEATRICE CAROLINE (STRONG). United Kingdom.

003745   THE MAGIC PLUMES. London: Methuen, 1907
BMC.

Carlotta, a great opera singer-TLS

003746   THE RING OF NECESSITY. London: A. Rivers,
1913 NUC BMC.

Mrs. Derrimere beautiful heroine in a "fashionable"
divorce case and a desolate old woman swindled by
callous relatives. ATH
"some chapters on matrimonial matters and the divorce
court." SR
pathos of decayed gentlewoman now poor but she keeps a
cheerful, buoyant spirit. TLS

ERSKINE, EMMA (PAYNE). 1854-1924. United States.

003747   THE EYE OF DREAD. BY PAYNE ERSKINE.
Toronto: McClelland & Goodchild, 1913 BMC. Boston:
Little Brown, 1913 NUC.

003748   A GIRL OF THE BLUE RIDGE. BY PAYNE
ERSKINE. Boston: Little, Brown, 1915 NUC BMC.

"Little Lury Bab, daughter of a distiller of illicit whiskey, is the heroine of this story of the southern mountains. She grows up amidst the most sordid surroundings, but has in her something fine that responds to everything beautiful and noble that comes within her limited reach. Outside influences come to the mountain settlement, first in the form of the automobile road which the northern engineers are building over the mountains, next in the school established by two northern women." BRD 1915

003749   THE HARPER AND THE KING'S HORSE; A TALE. BY PAYNE ERSKINE. Chicago: Blue Sky Press, [c1905] NUC.

003750   JOYFUL HEATHERBY. BY PAYNE ERSKINE. Boston: Little, Brown, 1913 NUC BMC.

"Joyful Heatherby is the sweet, romance-scented name of the heroine. She is a country girl as the name suggests, a girl of the New England coast who lives with an old seafaring grandfather. To their little village comes Mark Thorn, a discouraged artist who has grown weary of the attempt to hold to his ideals in the face of commercialism and the false values of society." BRD 1913

003751   THE MOUNTAIN GIRL. BY PAYNE ERSKINE. Boston: Little, Brown, 1912 NUC. London: S. Low, [1912] BMC.

Mountaineers-Fic
"A love story of the North Carolina mountains..Dr Thrying, an Ennglishman of aristocratic family, comes into the mountains in search of health. He finds it, and finds more-happiness and usefulness among the simple, primitive people; and in Cassandra Merlin, daughter of the mountains, is embodied his ideal of womanhood. The happiness of their married life is broken when he is called to England. Absorbed back into his old life, he seems for a time to forget her, but when he hears that she has come to join him and then, fearing to make her self known lest she shame him before his people, has returned, he follows her back to the mountains." BRD

003752   WHEN THE GATES LIFT UP THEIR HEADS; A STORY OF THE SEVENTIES. BY PAYNE ERSKINE. Boston: Little, Brown, 1901 NUC BMC.

Advocates interracial marriage. "The heroine declares that "The great Caucasian race must stoop to these (Indians, Chinese, and Negroes) before it can rise higher. They have reached the boundary line past which they cannot move toward God's likeness until they have learned to place God's estimate of value upon a human soul of whatever race or condition. ...the heroine with a theory showing that it is really her duty to marry some one not of her own race is Miss Erskine's own discovery... Prophecy is dangerous, but it would not be surprising if the story marked a turning point in the subject of American fiction." NYT 6-22-01, 488.

ERSKINE, PAYNE, pseud. See ERSKINE, EMMA (PAYNE).

ERVIN, MABEL CLARE. United States.

003753   AS TOLD BY THE TYPEWRITER GIRL. New York: E. R. Herrick, [c1898] NUC.

NYT 1898:826. Incidents in life of a type girl, humorous. Series of stories.
Series of stories about the intrigues of the profession of the typewriter girl. A girl bachelor of the present day. NYT 6-24-99,408.

ESCHENBACH, MARIE VON EBNER. 1830-1916.

003754   BEYOND ATONEMENT. New York: Worthington, 1892 NUC. (Tr. Mary A. Robinson.)

CR 14.20:144. Morbid emotion. Feverish intensity. PW-Irma is unfaithful to her husband, then comes to love him. He dies, she lives on with lover's child, friends are willing to forgive her but she feels she is beyond atonement and expiates her sin in solitude.

003755   THE CHILD OF THE PARISH. A NOVEL. New York: R. Bonner, 1893 NUC. (Tr. from the German by Mary A. Robinson)

Mother sent to penitentiary, father hanged for murder, Pavel becomes the charge of the parish. Grows to be a respectable person. PW 4-8-93

003756   THE TWO COUNTESSES. London: T. F. Unwin,

1893 NUC BMC. New York: Cassell, [1893] NUC. (Tr. Mrs. Waugh)

Two German women-very different from each other with different home environments relate their experiences. One writes letters to a friend; the other keeps a journal. "In both cases the heroines have revolted against marriage made for them by their parents regardless of their personal feelings." PW 6-17-93: Two stories: in one a young man brought into home; purpose, marriage. But he falls in love with one of the guests. In the second, countess hates her betrothed. Takes great effort on her part and on the part of her married sister to get parents to let her marry the man she loves. CR 20, 23:1 00.

ESCOMBE, EDITH.

003757   LOVE'S GHOST AND "LE GLAIVE". London: Duckworth, 1903 BMC.

The elemental passions "too strong for civilized limitations" ACAD 65, 14.
two stories

003758   PHASES OF MARRIAGE. London: E. Mathews, 1907 NUC BMC.

003759   STUCCO AND SPECULATION. London: Remington, 1894 BMC.

SR 78:628. Stucco: a new woman of the very newest type. She and her husband both believe in friendships outside marriage and support each other in this. Her friend, Gresham the painter, also takes care of her child while she and her husband are away. Speculation: hero and heroine enter into five-year marriage contract, their parents are consenting parties.

003760   A TALE THAT IS TOLD. London: Eden, Remington, 1893 BMC.

Helen Denham, exceedingly morbid, self-analytical. Marries, is miserable. The story ends there "because that is the only way in which we can end stories truly," says the author. ACAD 43:282.
Hettie married unhappily amuses herself with husband's friends. "A delicate and purposely inconclusive story of the temptations to which some of the most attractive women are subject." ATH 101:374.

ESLER, E. RENTOUL. See ESLER, ERMINDA (RENTOUL).

ESLER, ERMINDA (RENTOUL). United Kingdom.

003761   THE AWAKENING OF HELENA THORPE. London: S. W. Partridge, [1902] BMC.

003762   A MAID OF MANSE. London: S. Low and Marston, 1895 BMC.

003763   'MID GREEN PASTURES. BY E. RENTOUL ESLER. New York: J. Pott, 1895 NUC. London: S. Low, 1895 BMC.

SR Village tales
SP 76:881. Grimpat. Another Cranford

003764   THE TRACKLESS WAY; THE STORY OF A MAN'S QUEST FOR GOD. London: R. B. Johnson, 1903 BMC.

ATH-married to an intelligent woman who leaves him out of boredom and jealousy, publishes a book without author's permission, conceited.

003765   THE WARDLAWS. London: Smith, Elder, 1896 BMC.

LBKM 10:175. Decay of an Irish family after generations of extravagance. Fortunes rebuilt in England by John Wardlow, only to fall into hands of his extravagant sons. He takes a way out (suicide), tragic. Youngest son and daughter then do something good and his partner improves. Also story of friendship of his half-sister Margery and her niece. ATH 107:742. Novel divided into 2 parts, one concerns John, the other his half-sister who, when he went to England, remained in Ireland to operate a grocery shop.

003766   YOUTH AT THE PROW. London: J. Long, 1898 BMC.

LIT 2:536. Short stories.

ESTABROOK, ALMA MARTIN. Nationality Unknown.

003767   THE RULE OF THREE; A STORY OF PIKE'S
PEAK. Boston: Small, Maynard, [c1909] NUC.

Nice story of young man and maiden aunt 5-1-09 PW
love's complications BKM

EUBANK, LULU KATHERINE. United States.

003768   OLD GLORY; A ROMANCE OF BALTIMORE. New
York: Abbey, [c1901] NUC.

9-7-01 PW

EUFAULA, AULA, pseud. See MOORE, AULA.

EUSTIS, EDITH LIVINGSTON (MORTON). B. 1874. Nationality
Unknown.

003769   MARION MANNING, A NOVEL. New York:
Harper, 1902 NUC.

BKM, Jul 1902
ATH 6-14-02

EVANS, ELIZABETH EDSON (GIBSON). 1832-1911. United States.

003770   CONFESSION: A NOVEL. London: S.
Sonnenschein, 1895 BMC NUC.

A new minister comes to Bloomfield, Vt. He's very
popular but then the town learns he has a past. It is
also learned that two young members of congregation
have the same. "Shocking episode of Lucy Allen's
School days." ATH 106:640
ACAD 49:260. David Stearns, Vermont clergyman,
proposes to Lucy, who confesses to him a misfortune.
He has had similar, but does not tell his. Years
later, her secret is revealed by a trouble-maker; the
shock kills her. Rev. Stearns buries her. Lucy's
protege, suspected of killing an illegitimate baby,
throws herself into the river.

003771   FERDINAND LASSALLE AND HELENE VON
DONNIGES. London: S. Sonnenschein, 1897 BMC NUC.

003772   TRANSPLANTED MANNERS: A NOVEL. London: S.
Sonnenschein, 1895 BMC NUC.

Chronicles of the Pension Irgendwo by an elderly
American "Maiden" lady whose main business is watching
people in the German boarding house.-a hotbed of love
affairs, intrigues, jealousies, a foolishly kind
American mother and her wicked daughter. SR 79:488

EVANS, FLORENCE (WILKINSON). United States.

003773   THE LADY OF THE FLAG-FLOWERS. BY FLORENCE
WILKINSON. Chicago: H. S. Stone, 1899 NUC.

A mythical lady of Indian folklore-the myth plays an
important part in the tragedy of a Huron Indian woman.
PW 55:946

003774   THE SILENT DOOR. BY FLORENCE WILKINSON.
New York: McClure, Phillips, 1907 NUC.

"Subtle study of childhood." BKM

003775   THE STRENGTH OF THE HILLS. A NOVEL. BY
FLORENCE WILKINSON. New York and London: Harper, 1901
BMC NUC.

Allison: woman of the world, lofty in soul, high in
courage, untrammeled by convention. There is a
marriage. Modern rural fiction: set in North country.
NYT

EVANS, MARGUERITE FLORENCE HELENE (JERVIS). B. 1894.
United Kingdom.

003776   CHICANE. BY OLIVER SANDYS. London: J.
Long, 1912 BMC.

TLS-heroine becomes partner of Lady Webride in
business of cheating at bridge, stealing jewelry, and
general swindling.

003777   THE HONEY POT; A STORY OF THE STAGE. BY
THE COUNTESS BARCYNSKA. London: Hurst and Blackett,
1916 BMC. New York: E. P. Dutton, 1916 NUC.

Two girls struggling on comic opera stage help each
other through temptation. One succumbed and both found
happiness in the end. PW 89 2-26-16:688.
NYT-Alexandra is an aristocratic prig; Maggie the real
heroine. Review says there is an awful lot of the

author's moralizing.

003778   IF WISHES WERE HORSES. BY THE COUNTESS
BARCYNSKA. New York: E. P. Dutton, [c1917] NUC.
London: Hurst and Blackett, 1917 BMC.

Career of a man. TLS
Rose Liffley-the immortal woman who conquers by
sweetness; her "mental limitations are nothing in view
of her tenacity of character" A woman whom life can't
defeat. BKM
Focus is on Martin, self made ambitious ruthless. His
career, the adoration of his sweet wife who stands by
though Martin abuses their children. NYT 4-15-17:155.

003779   THE LITTLE MOTHER WHO SITS AT HOME.
EDITED BY THE COUNTESS BARCYNSKA. New York: E. P.
Dutton, [c1915] NUC. London: T. C. and E. C. Jack,
[1915] BMC.

Letters of mother to son in his 5th to 25th years.
Simple letters, "tug the reader's heart." She exists
only for her son. Will sacrifice everything for him.
NYT

003780   LOVE MAGGY. BY COUNTESS HELENE BARCYNSKA.
London: Hurst and Blackett, 1918 BMC.

TLS-sequel to Honey Pot. Misunderstandings arising out
of her past, fight with husband, returns to stage,
stardom, nothing upsetting.

003781   LOVE'S LAST REWARD. BY COUNTESS HELENE
BARCYNSKA. London: Hurst and Blackett, [1920] BMC.

003782   PRETTY DEAR; A ROMANCE. BY THE COUNTESS
BARCYNSKA. London: Hurst and Blackett, 1920 BMC NUC.

TLS-From shopgirl to peeress, soaked in honey, pretty
and dear.

003783   ROSE O' THE SEA, A ROMANCE. BY THE
COUNTESS BARCYNSKA. Boston: Houghton Mifflin, 1920
NUC.

PW-Romance of a waif flower-vendor.
NYT 10-24-20. Rose had "marvelous beauty and charm,"
had been cast up by the sea as a baby and cared for by
an old man. Then he died, she went to London, became a
flower girl, then position in floral department of
store. Then she repels the dishonorable advances of
Denis, therby winning his heart with whom she falls
in love but agrees, for love of him, to marry his son
who soon strays. She inherits a fortune in a necklace,
loses it, but "in a month or so" becomes a movie star.

003784   SANITY JANE. BY THE COUNTESS BARCYNSKA.
London: Hurst and Blackett, [1919] NUC BMC.

Love mixups, divorce-TLS

003785   THE WOMAN IN THE FIRELIGHT. BY OLIVER
SANDYS. London: J. Long, 1911 BMC.

EVANS, MARY RUTH. United States.

003786   THE STORY OF EDAH. New York: Broadway,
1914 NUC.

EVANS, MAY.

003787   THE COMPACT; A STUDY IN PSYCHOLOGY.
London: W. Scott, 1904 BMC.

Faustian theme

EVELYN, CONSTANCE.

003788   ALISON WALSH: A STUDY OF TO-DAY. New
York: T. Nelson, 1891 PW. London: T. Nelson, 1891 BMC.

She loses faith in Christianity and then thru much
effort regains it. PW 11-14-91.

EVERARD, FLORENCE. Nationality Unknown.

003789   A NOBLE FOOL. New York: Stitt, 1906 NUC.
Bristol: J. W. Arrowsmith, 1907 BMC.

PW-Tangled passions
NYT Creature of the wild set down in London, an
egotist, runs away with another man-then?
Dying "woman curses everybody heartily and
indiscriminately and dies" Her daughter is a worthy
descendant of this woman. Dorothy, fascinating but
non-moral ACAD

EVEREST, KATE.

003790   THE SHADOW ON THE PURPLE. RECOLLECTIONS
OF AN EX-ATTACHE. RECORDED BY A PEERESS [ANONYMOUS].
London: Lynwood, 1911 BMC.

Story of Princes, ladies of "inferior birth" violence,
etc. ACAD
Morganatic marriage. TLS

EVERETT, MRS. H. D.   United States.

003791   BEHIND A MASK. BY THEO DOUGLAS. London
and New York: Harper, 1898 BMC.

ACAD 53:600. "Curious blend of quietude and
sensationalism." Domestic drama; love, scandal,
madness, fire at a ball, etc.
ATH 112:93. Country life. Part of the narration is a
woman's diary. "We hear too much of disasters to
women."

003792   A BRIDE ELECT. BY THEO DOUGLAS. London:
Macmillan, 1896 BMC.

LBKM 10:89. Sensational. A mad occultist and scientist
hypnotizes and spirits away bride on eve of her
wedding. Kills her and preserves her body with a
secret formula. Someone else is accused of doing away
with her. Mystery is eventually cleared up when he is
killed in one of his experiments.

003793   CARR OF DIMSCAUR. BY THEO DOUGLAS.
London, New York: Harper, 1899 BMC.

Sens. novel of a man whose one obsession is to stay
alive to a certain day in order to disinherit his
widowed daughter who displeased him. LIT 4:479
He has to live to a certain year to get inheritance;
if he doesn't, his daughter gets it. He holds on to
life, forcing his daughter, who was married and is
deserted, to be nurse to him. This daughter is Agatha.
Another daughter keeps appearing, but it's really her
ghost. SP 82:242

003794   COUSIN HUGH. London: Methuen, 1910 BMC.

TLS-love and sens.
ATH-love and sens.

003795   DEERHURST; OR THE RIFT IN THE CLOUD. BY
JULIA DOUGLAS. Boston: A. I. Bradley, 1893 NUC.

Nurse steals child who finds a home in Deerhurst on
the Hudson. At the end restored to parents. PW
10-14-93.

003796   A GOLDEN TRUST. BY THEO DOUGLAS. London:
Smith, Elder, 1905 NUC BMC.

Storming of the Tuileries and the massacre of the
prisoners in Sept, 1792.
Historical romance. ACAD 1362, 05

003797   THE GREY COUNTESS. London: Cassell, 1913
BMC.

LBKM-Involves the memoirs of a Russian countess and a
house of mystery and Lucas Adair. Dangerous Russian
with a complicated past has a secret. ATH
Saddie Dobreski the heroine; murder, ghosts, hypnosis.
TLS

003798   HADOW OF 'SHAWS. London: Methuen, 1913
BMC.

Late 18th; concerns devices adopted by young woman to
avoid becoming a wife to the man she married. Camilla
Hadow finally falls madly in love with him(?) SP
Tries to escape obligations of her marriage by a
feigned death. So dismayed at return from India of a
husband she was forced to marry four years earlier
that she arranges a mock death and funeral of herself.
ATH

003799   IRAS: A MYSTERY. BY THEO DOUGLAS.
Edinburgh and London: Blackwood, 1896 BMC. New York:
Harper, 1896 NUC.

ATH 108:793. Supernatural. Ancient Egyptians in
London. Hero is a scholar and an ardent Egyptologist.
PW 10-17-96. He marries Iras who has been in a
hypnotic trance for three years and awakes at his
touch. They are henceforth pursued by the astrological
body of Savak, a priest who loved her in her former

existence.
Beautiful young woman, hypnotized at time of 20th
Dynasty, awakens to life in modern times. LW 28:91
Lavenham, an Egyptologist sends for a mummy, but the
case held a beautiful Eng. speaking woman. She's a few
thousand years old Her decay comes about by the
"gradual robbing of the pendants of her necklace by a
ghostly hostile hand." He marries her. Then she
disappears; he loses memory. LBKM 11:125

003800   A LEGACY OF HATE. BY THEO DOUGLAS.
London: C. A. Pearson, 1899 BMC.

Detective: sens. melodrama. LIT 5:520

003801   A LOST SUMMER. BY THEO DOUGLAS. London:
Cassell, 1907 BMC.

Story of a man who had amnesia and married during the
time he had no memory. LBKM

003802   MALEVOLA. London: Heath, Cranton and
Ouseley, [1914] BMC.

ATH-Malign influence of older woman on younger.
ATH 144:425 She is a vampire and a violinist, draws
beauty and vitality from her victims.
TLS-She does it through massage. She is a pianist.

003803   MISS CAROLINE; A NOVEL. BY THEO DOUGLAS.
London: E. Arnold, 1904 BMC.

ATH-honey-sweet heroine
BAKER 13:227.

003804   MISS MAYBIRD: MARRIAGE-MAKER. BY THEO
DOUGLAS. London: P. Allan, 1920 BMC.

003805   NEMO. BY THEO DOUGLAS. London: Smith,
Elder, 1900 BMC.

LBKM 18:28. Heroine is victim of a conjuring father,
she animates a lifeless image giving it voice, motion,
even part of her soul till it possesses her.
SP 84:354. Modern variation on Frankenstein. She
becomes weaker as time passes, her lover and an
American guess what is happening and try to rescue her
by smashing the automaton, but unfortunately they
choose a time when she is animating it.

003806   ONE OR TWO: A ROMANCE. BY THEO DOUGLAS.
London: Brown, Lanham, 1907 BMC NUC.

Mrs. Bethune reincarnates her former self, husband
falls in love with that woman, disowns the older one
who dies. ACAD
A stout lady makes herself thin by spiritualistic
means? TLS
The wife "having deteriorated morally and becoming
very stout" reduces thru mysticism but the person who
appears (materializes) is herself at 17. "This is very
disagreeable to the dominant personality." SR

003807   WHITE WEBS. A ROMANCE OF SUSSEX. London:
M. Secker, 1912 BMC.

TLS-Historical novel 1746
ATH-"threads of loyalty which sustained the cause of
the White Rose were being woven at White Webs and
elsewhere, largely by women's hands."

003808   A WHITE WITCH. BY THEO DOUGLAS. London:
Hurst and Blackett, 1908 BMC.

BAKER 13:227--historical romance, witchcraft.

003809   WINDY GAP. BY THEO DOUGLAS. Bristol: J.
W. Arrowsmith, [1898] BMC.

SR 86:248. Heroine is alone in the world, while upset
goes into a meeting house of a "quaint, primitive
sect," hears the call for a sister to work in the
West. She feels it was meant for her and goes,
although part of the call involves marriage to an
elderly brother working there. When she arrives, she
finds he has died of old age.

EVERETT, RUTH. United States.

003810   THAT MAN FROM WALL STREET; A STORY OF THE
STUDIOS. New York: G. T. Long, [1908] BMC NUC.

PW Three women artists with low moral standards.

EVESON, MARIE LOUISE.

003811   SWEET LILAC: A NOVEL. London: Roxburghe
Press, [1896] BMC.

EWELL, A. M. See EWELL, ALICE MAUDE.

EWELL, ALICE MAUDE. 1860-1946. United States.

003812   A WHITE GUARD TO SATAN: BEING AN ACCOUNT
OF MINE OWN ADVENTURES AND OBSERVATION IN THAT TIME OF
THE TROUBLE IN VIRGINIA NOW CALLED BACON'S REBELLION,
WHICH SAME DID TAKE PLACE IN 1676, BY MISTRESS
ELIZABETH GODSTOWE. RECOVERED BY A. M. EWELL. Boston
and New York: Houghton, Mifflin, 1900 NUC.

PW narrated by heroine, an account of an incident
during Bacon's Rebellion when women and children were
put in front line of attacking force.

EWENS, EDITHA.

003813   THE STARS IN THEIR COURSES: A MODERN
ROMANCE OF THE HIMALAYAS. London: Ward and Downey,
1898 BMC.

ATH-111:114. Anglo-Indian. A woman's temptation, fall,
sudden death. Passionate woman.

EWING, JULIANA HORATIA (GATTY). 1841-1885.

003814   MADAM LIBERALITY. Boston: L. C. Page,
1901 NUC.

EYLES, MARGARET LEONORA (PITCAIRN). 1890-1960. United
Kingdom.

003815   MARGARET PROTESTS. London: E. Macdonald,
1919 BMC.

Her marriage and early poverty stricken widowhood; her
unwanted child and her extra ordinary career until she
retires to a peaceful simple rural life-"all a
continuous and passionate protest on the subject of
maternity." "Dissectingly frank" Margaret's violent
rebellion when plunged into a world "demoralized by
sex and by business" "the tragedies of sex among the
poor" TLS
begins "in a state of white-hot indignation vs. men"
pictures the monotonous lives of very many married
women, selfishness of husbands: women's economic
problems "the only way a woman can get money is by
selling herself to a man -either getting married, or
the other thing." At the end heroine leads a simple
life in the country with a compatible man. Ends on
fairly hopeful note but sombre on the whole. ATH

EYRE, KATE.

003816   A STEP IN THE DARK. London: Cassell, 1894
BMC.

EYSTER, NELLIE BLESSING. See EYSTER, PENELOPE ANNA
MARGARETTA (BLESSING).

EYSTER, PENELOPE ANNA MARGARETTA (BLESSING). 1831?-1922.
United States.

003817   A CHINESE QUAKER; AN UNFICTITIOUS NOVEL.
BY NELLIE BLESSING-EYSTER. New York: F. H. Revell,
[c1902] NUC.

Chinese in Calif.

F., A. C., pseud. See FRASER, C. A.

F., L. pseud. See HAWKER, MORWENNA PAULINE.

F., M., pseud. See FISHER, MARY.

FABER, CHRISTINE, pseud. See SMITH, MARY E.

FABREGUE, AIMEE.

003818   CRUCIFIX. London: Tower Publishing,
[1896] BMC. (Tr. D. H. Fisher)

ACAD 49:10. Diary form. Story of "sentimental and
candid" young woman whose mother has leprosy and who
expects to be a leper herself.

FACCIO, RINA (COTTINO). B. 1876. Italy.

003819   A WOMAN AT BAY (UNA DONNA). BY SIBILLA
ALERAMO. New York and London: G.P. Putnam's Sons, 1908
NUC BMC. (Tr. Maria H. Lansdale)

New woman (Rina) with some of the eternal feminine.

Eager for life and full of talent enters her father's
business, is entrapped by an employee when she is only
15. Leaves husband; longs for Beatrice and Dante
relation. Does not want to be touched. Il Passaggio is
sequel.
BKM 28 1908-9--Woman married to faithless drunk,
unfairness of Italian divorce laws.
BAKER 32-7
"picture of the dawn of the feminist movement in
contemporary Italy. FRANKLIN

FAHNESTOCK, HARRIETTE ZEPHINE (HUMPHREY). B. 1874. United
States.

003820   GRAIL FIRE. BY ZEPHINE HUMPHREY. New
York: E.P. Dutton, [c1917] NUC.

Struggle in a man between call of rel and love. The
author advocates the Episcopalian over the Catholic
church NYT 4-8-17 126

003821   THE HOMESTEAD. BY ZEPHINE HUMPHREY. New
York: E.P. Dutton, [c1919] NUC.

"imaginative woman brought up in the monotonous
environment of a New England farm" PW
The development of this woman, Barbara Marshall
inherits the love of travel along with the need for
roots in her homestead. Love story's incidental. It is
the struggle between a woman's temperament and
environment. NYT 7-20-19 374

003822   OVER AGAINST GREEN PEAK. BY ZEPHINE
HUMPHREY. New York: H. Holt, 1908 NUC.

PW- Woman makes home in New England village.

003823   RECOLLECTIONS OF MY MOTHER. BY ZEPHINE
HUMPHREY. New York: F. H. Revell, [c1912] NUC.

003824   THE SWORD OF THE SPIRIT. BY ZEPHINE
HUMPHREY. New York: E.P. Dutton, [1920] NUC.

PW-Dangers of emotional mysticism. Relations of a
temperamental woman, her commonplace husband, and a
young Episcopalian priest.
NYT 7-18-20- Near break-up of their marriage, he
becomes more spiritual, she more material and down to
earth.

003825   UNCLE CHARLEY. BY ZEPHINE HUMPHREY.
Boston: Houghton Mifflin, 1902 NUC.

FAHY, MINA.

003826   ST. CLEMENTS. A STORY OF SCHOOL LIFE.
London: G. Allen, 1910 BMC.

FAIRBRIDGE, DOROTHEA. 1862?-1931.

003827   PIET OF ITALY. London: Mills and Boon,
[1913] BMC NUC.

Piet is a foundling, outcast bred in S. Africa who
became Pietro of Italy. TLS

003828   THAT WHICH HATH BEEN. Capetown: Cape
Times, 1910 NUC BMC. London: Sampson Low, 1913 BMC.

Dutch rule on the Cape. The governor and his
administration. TLS

003829   THE TORCH BEARER. London: Mills & Boon,
1915 BMC. Capetown: J. C. Juta, [1915] NUC.

Agatha Lumsden spinster goes to S. Africa to begin her
work with women. Teaches them to cook. It turns out
they cook better than she. Always putting her foot in
her mouth. For the sake of the Empire. TLS

FAIRFAX, DINAH.

003830   SPARKS AND MONGRELS: A NOVEL. London:
Heath, Cranton, [1920] BMC.

Man believes women marry for money, makes a wager,
does get the woman to marry him; she learns of wager.
All ends well. ATH

FAIRFAX, MILDRED. Nationality Unknown.

003831   AT MOUNT DESERT: A SUMMER'S SOWING.
Boston: Congregational Sunday School and Pub.
Society., [c1893] Nuc.

Story of romantic interests centering on Basil

Wilmerding who accompanies his sister to Mount Desert, then sets out to reconcile self with grandfather in order to get an inheritance. PW 8-26-93.

003832   IN THE VULTURE'S NEST; OR THE HUGUENOTS AT THE COURT OF FRANCE IN 1572. Boston: Congregational Sunday-School and Pub. Society., [c1892] BMC NUC.

PW Hist rom. Heroine brought up in Catherine d' Medici's influence is so good and innocent that she learns Catherine's true character only by the St. Bartholemew massacre.

FAIRFIELD, CICILY ISABEL ANDREWS. B. 1892. United Kingdom.

003833   THE RETURN OF THE SOLDIER. BY REBECCA WEST. New York: Century, 1918 NUC. London: Nisbet, 1918 BMC.

PW_ Chris is shell-shocked and lapses back 15 years. His wife, exquisite, and his country estate mean nothing to him; he is only interested in Margaret, an uncouth country maid he had loved then. A psychologist says perhaps he has reverted in an effort to rid himself of the past 15 years. His wife can hardly stand watching him wander about the place with Margaret. Jenny, his cousin is desperately unhappy for him. Story centers on Margaret-she brings him back to himself and his wife.
TLS-O
Kathy Baldry a parasitic creature "all clothes with a wiped out face"- "made more contemptible by contrast was a women whose life is love & service." Wellington

FAIRLESS, MICHAEL, pseud. See BARBER, MARGARET FAIRLESS.

FAIRWEATHER, MARY. United States.

003834   THE PASSION STROKE; A TALE OF ANCIENT MASONRY. Boston: R. G. Badger, 1906 NUC.

PW-mystical love story of ancient Greece.

FALCONER, LANOE, pseud. See HAWKER, MORWENNA PAULINE.

FALL, ANNA CHRISTY. B. 1855. United States.

003835   THE TRAGEDY OF A WIDOW'S THIRD. Boston: I. P. Fox, 1898 NUC.

"A story illustrating the injustice of Massachusetts law regarding a widow's rights in her husband's estate. Written by a member of the Boston bar." Publishers Weekly.

FALLS, ROSE C. United States.

003836   CHENIERE CAMINADA; OR, THE WIND OF DEATH. THE STORY OF THE STORM IN LOUISIANA. New Orleans: Hopkins Print Office, 1893 NUC.

FANE, FRANCES GORDON. B. 1867. United States.

003837   RICHARD WYNDHAM; A NOVEL. New York: G. W. Dillingham, [1902] NUC.

003838   THE WAY OF A MAN WITH A MAID. New York: G. W. Dillingham, 1901 NUC.

An artist and an unhappy marriage. PW 4-20-01

FARISS, AMY CAMERON. United States.

003839   THE SIN OF SAINT DESMOND. Boston: R. G. Badger, 1905 NUC.

NYT-infatuation for another's wife. Faints?
"The scenes of this novel are laid in California. The heroine, to please her mother and to be relieved from want, marries a man whom she does not love. She becomes infatuated with Vandell, a scoundrel, and is on the point of eloping with him when the plans are interfered with by Saint Desmond, a minister of splendid qualities. She becomes very ill and Saint Desmond takes her under his care. In order to quiet her ravings, he impersonates Vandell, for whom she constantly calls. This leads to his really caring for her. The rest of the tale tells how the heroine is freed from her husband, the stand Saint Desmond takes, and her ultimate fate. A gold mine plays a prominent part in the story." v. 25 1906-7 BKM

FARJEON, ELEANOR. 1881-1965. United Kingdom.

003840   GYPSY AND GINGER. London: J.M. Dent, 1920 BMC. New York: E.P. Dutton, [c1920] NUC.

ATH- Whimsical. When Gypsy and Ginger marry, Gypsy proposes they live in one room house with two doors. In fair weather she would go out her door and he would do cooking, etc., in foul weather the reverse. Book tells how the plan worked out.

FARLEY, AGNES.

003841   ASHDOD. London: Chapman and Hall, 1907 BMC.

Trad romance TLS
Young orphan given home by relatives-a couple who haven't exchanged a word in 40 years. Her views clash vs those of French relatives. Fights vs idea of "putting the family before the individual." Fanlls for a older artist; their elopement is interrupted. In the end Thomasine de Pommeral "finds a way of reconciling the claims of family and the individual" and does so voluntarily. She had refused her family's "arrangement" for her. SR

003842   THE BELMONT BOOK. BY VADOS. New York: E. P. Dutton, [1911] NUC.

fiction? about a town, its sport, scenery-etc. TLS. Normandy

FARLEY, J. ELIZABETH. See FARLEY, JUDITH ELIZABETH.

FARLEY, JUDITH ELIZABETH. B. 1844. United States.

003843   DON LOPEZ DE VERE: A ROMANCE. BY J. ELIZABETH FARLEY. Melvern, Kas.: A. and W. P. Ball Pub. Co., [c1895] NUC.

FARMER, LYDIA HOYT. See PAINTER, LYDIA (HOYT) FARMER.

FARNINGHAM, MARIANNE, pseud. See HEARN, MARY ANN.

FARQUHAR, ANNA. See BERGENGREN, ANNA (FARQUHAR).

FARQUHARSON, A. C. See FARQUHARSON, AGNES C.

FARQUHARSON, AGNES C. Nationality Unknown.

003844   A CRUCIAL EXPERIMENT. BY A. C. FARQUHARSON. London: E. Arnold, 1909 BMC.

Wealthy musician marries a promising girl student Gabriel Arden. The marriage fails. She is appealing "inscrutable". Book closes after her death. TLS

003845   ST. NAZARIUS. BY A. C. FARQUHARSON. New York: Macmillan, 1901 NUC. London: Macmillan, 1901 BMC NUC.

12-28-01 ATH

FARR, FLORENCE. See EMERY, FLORENCE (FARR).

FARR, JULIA. United States.

003846   VENNA HASTINGS: STORY OF AN EASTERN MORMON CONVERT. Independence, Mo.: Zion's Ptg. & Pub. Co., 1919 NUC.

"To arouse interest in the Mormon faith." PW

FARRAR, GERALDINE. 1882-1967.

003847   GERALDINE FARRAR: THE STORY OF AN AMERICAN SINGER. BY HERSELF. New York and Boston: Houghton Mifflin, 1916 BMC NUC.

Prima donna's career--years of struggle. Crowned with success. PW
Autobiog? In 1938 wrote the Autobiography of...

FARRAR, MRS. F. A.

003848   RUTH FIELDING: A DOUBLE LOVE STORY. London: E. Stock, 1905 BMC.

Joyce and Ruth contrasting types LBKM 175 v27-8
Well suited for girls TLS 196,05

FARRELL, AGNES.

003849   LADY LOVAN: A NOVEL. London: Hutchinson, 1895 BMC.

"a jumble of lawless passions, free thinking ideas and advanced views." "The apotheosis of free love." Evelyn Burnie-is independent but gets "caught" by libertine

Lord Lovan. They marry but Evelyn only believes in
marriage "with freedom of divorce for incompatibility,
and the same application for women as for men." (her
words) He runs around and then comes back to her with
plea that he never "loved" anyone else. She throws him
out. She takes a lover. Another woman in the book
stays with her faithless husband solely for money and
security. ACAD 48:243
ATH 107:83. "triple obsession of the sex question,
marriage laws, and socialism." "A somewhat violent
contribution to the fiction of revolt" "Rank, fashion
and social respectability are throughout the book
synonymous with vice, dissipation, and animalism."
"Miss Farrell's pictures of ´gentlemen and ladies´-the
especial detestation of her hero and heroine-are just
as extravagant as those of the early Ouida, though
their points of view are poles apart."
sub plot of tragedy of marital disillusionment of
Lilian Bain and her husband. Her thesis-the
author's-is that cultivated wealthy class is removed
from life, is contemptible, repulsive. Lord Lovan is
cultured but contemptible marries a sincere woman,
daughter of a writer. Foil to Lord Lovan is also a
writer. SR 80:624

FAULDING, G. M. See DALE, LUCY AND GERTRUDE MINNIE
FAULDING.

FAULDING, GERTRUDE MINNIE, jt. au. See DALE, LUCY AND
GERTRUDE MINNIE FAULDING.

FAUSSETT, MABEL GODFREY.

003850   THE DUAL HERITAGE. London: Richards, 1908
BMC.

TLS-2 sisters, love, religion.
SR-2 sisters, love, religion. $ATH

FAVERSHAM, JULIE (OPP). 1873-1921. United States.

003851   THE SQUAW MAN; A NOVEL. New York and
London: Harper, 1906 BMC NUC.

From the play by male author. (Edward Milton Royle).
BMC

FEARING, LILIAN BLANCHE. 1863-1901. United States.

003852   ASLEEP AND AWAKE. BY RAYMOND RUSSELL.
Chicago: C. H. Kerr, 1893 NUC.

003853   ROBERTA: A NOVEL. Chicago: C. H. Kerr,
1895 NUC.

Chicago. Roberta Green's father dies. She is led after
this "by force of sheer ignorance of moral laws into
transgressing them. The effects of her acts are traced
for an evident moral purpose." PW 6-29-95:999

FEARN, MAGGIE.

003854   VALENCIA. London: Religious Tract
Society, [1891] BMC.

SP-- Rom and religion.

FEDDEN, KATHARINE WALDO DOUGLAS. D. 1939. United States.

003855   THE ROCK. London: Mills & Boon, 1915 BMC.

tracing of relations between members of a community in
small N Y S town. TLS
Published in US Shifting Sands

003856   SHIFTING SANDS. BY MRS. ROMILLY FEDDEN
(KATHARINE WALDO DOUGLAS). Boston: Houghton Mifflin,
1914 NUC.

Young woman's relation with man who adopted her--PW
2-20-15
Combines mystery of father's death with story of
development of orphan from childhood to womanhood;
aside from her "practically doing the proposing,"
nothing here BKM
NYT-Young woman first glories in fleeting conquests,
then tires of them and returns home.
NYT 1914:557. Jean, mostly Puritan with a strain of
Spanish blood, from 12 to 18. Upper New York State
village. Mrs. Fedden is American, married an
Englishman and resides in England.

003857   THE SIGN. BY MRS. ROMILLY FEDDEN
(KATHARINE WALDO DOUGLAS). London: Macmillan, 1912 BMC
NUC. New York: Dodd, Mead, 1912 NUC.

TLS-three male artists in Breton
ATH-Three male artists in Briton
SP- The sign is Monik a mystic who goes to the people
to tell them of her vision of the Virgin. Sturd alone
of the three comprehends and sympathizes with her. Her
sacrifice (tragedy) convinces him that art is not for
him but the passion of service is and he returns to
humanity in the slums of London.
ACAD-Plot is secondary to atmosphere. Book is Greek in
conception and execution.
BKM-0
NYT-Monik believes herself called to suffer for her
people and be punished for their sins.

003858   THE SPARE ROOM. AN EXTRAVAGANZA. BY MRS.
ROMILLY FEDDEN. Boston: Houghton Mifflin, 1913 NUC.
London: Duckworth, 1913 BMC.

PW:85 1/31/14:374-"The Cardens for their honeymoon,
take a villa in Capri. Only a few of the rooms are
furnished, but there is one spare room which is a
source of such pride to them, that every time they
write to a relative or friend they invite him or her
to occupy that room. On the same day, seven people
avail themselves of the invitation and the Cardens
have an awful time stowing them away, pacifying their
cook, and trying to appear hospitable. The guests only
remain twenty-four hours, but those hours are full
enough for a week and sufficient to form the climax of
two romances."

FEDDEN, MRS. ROMILLY. See FEDDEN, KATHARINE WALDO DOUGLAS.

FEE, MARY HELEN. B. 1864. United States.

003859   THE LOCUSTS' YEARS. Chicago: A. C.
McClurg, 1912 NUC.

NYT- unhappy marriage between an American pearl fisher
in the Phillipines and a weary New England nurse.

FEEHAN, MARY EDWARD. B. 1878.

003860   THE QUEST OF MARY SELWYN. BY CLEMENTIA.
New York: Benziger, 1917 NUC.

003861   UNCLE FRANK'S MARY; THE FIRST OF A
SERIES. BY CLEMENTIA. Chicago: M. A. Donohue, 1916
NUC.

FEILD, ELSIE, pseud. See STREATFEILD, LILIAN CECIL.

FELDSMITH, MATTIE DOHERTY. United States.

003862   THE HOME ON THE MOUNTAIN. Milwaukee:
Evening Wisconsin Co., 1897 NUC.

FELKIN, ELLEN THORNEYCROFT (FOWLER). 1860-1929. United
Kingdom.

003863   BEAUTY AND BANDS. BY ELLEN THORNEYCROFT
FOWLER (HON. MRS. ALFRED FELKIN). London: Constable,
1920 BMC NUC.

TLS-theme love
SP Viola runs away from boring husband, but ends up
with him again due to amnesia.

003864   CONCERNING ISABEL CARNABY. BY ELLEN
THORNEYCROFT FOWLER. London: Hodder and Stoughton,
1898 BMC. New York: D. Appleton, 1899 NUC.

SP 80:831. Isabel is brilliant and spoiled. Writes an
anonymous novel which achieves a scandalous success,
she is eventually united with man she loves, regrets
authorship of novel.
LIT 3:65. Isabel is "lovable in spite of her moral
cowardice."
ACAD 53:661. Conversations are amusing.
PW-Isabel is wealthy and a member of an old family.
After spending 4 years in India she returns to England
and is a brilliant figure in society. Her relationship
to Paul Seaton, a tutor, and son of a nonconformist
minister, becomes a successful novelist.
A bright story of Isabel-witty, clever, quick-and her
love Paul Seaton, level headed genius of the soldier
type. Many interesting minor characters. BKM 8:491.

003865   CUPID'S GARDEN. BY ELLEN THORNEYCROFT
FOWLER. London: Cassell, 1897 BMC. New York: D.
Appleton, 1900 NUC.

LIT 3:18 Studies of passion.

003866   A DOUBLE THREAD. BY ELLEN THORNEYCROFT
FOWLER. London: Hutchinson, 1899 BMC. New York: D.

Appleton, 1899 NUC.

The heroine is two women-Ethel and Elfrida, we learn
2/3 through the novel. The two are very different. She
believes Mr. Cartwright will propose but he doesn't.
Hero is Jack Le Mesurier. LIT 4:373
Miss Harland. LBKM 16:51
New: a heroine that leads a double life. Elfrida a
twin, adopted, cut off from her family. But visits her
mother in the person of her twin sister who is dead.
As Ethel, poor governess, falls for a captain.
Confesses to him. At first he breaks off engagement,
then they are reconciled. Disguise was prompted by
idea that since she was adopted by very rich noble,
she wants someone to love her for herself. SP 82:459
Soldier loves two women, one rich, one poor who prove
to be the same person. BAKER 03 108

003867   THE FARRINGDONS. BY ELLEN THORNEYCROFT
FOWLER. London: Hutchinson, 1900 BMC. New York: D.
Appleton, 1900 NUC.

NYT 1900:romance of wealthy heiress and poor lover.
Elizabeth is strong, alert, will appeal to women. He
has a doglike devotion to her.
NYT 1900:408. Heroine retired in mining town in hotbed
of Methodism, goes to London where broader views and
more liberal tastes are more congenial.
LIT 6:300. Story of a woman. Much wit in book.

003868   FUEL OF FIRE. BY ELLEN THORNEYCROFT
FOWLER. New York: Dodd, Mead, 1902 NUC. London: Hodder
and Stoughton, 1902 BMC NUC.

Nancy is witty, sophisticated, but essentially a
heroine of the traditional romance. (From book).

003869   HER LADYSHIP'S CONSCIENCE. BY ELLEN
THORNEYCROFT FOWLER (THE HONBLE. MRS. ALFRED FELKIN).
New York and London: Hodder and Stoughton, [c1913] BMC
NUC.

Her uncomfortable conscience causes her to do much
harm-refuses a man because he's younger. Many
"reflections on the feminist point of view" related to
equality of sexes-that older women and younger men
should as freely couple as old men young women. SP
"Tells of Lord Westerham's love for Lady Esther Wyvern
and her refusing to marry him because she is forty and
he twelve years younger. She invites her beautiful,
selfish cousin to stay with her and throws her in
Westerham's way with the result that he falls in love
with Beryl and marries her, only to discover her
shallow selfishness does not fill his life as Esther's
sweetness and goodness could have. There is abundance
of witty dialogue in the story's telling and a happy
ending, which comes, as it should, just when things
seem most impossible for the hero and heroine." PW
85:1158.

003870   IN SUBJECTION. BY ELLEN THORNEYCROFT
FOWLER (MRS. ALFRED LAURENCE FELKIN). London:
Hutchinson, 1906 BMC 1907 NUC.

TLS-a brief for husbands- whatever their faults-and
the subjection of their wives.

003871   MISS FALLOWFIELD'S FORTUNE. BY ELLEN
THORNEYCROFT FOWLER (THE HON. MRS. ALFRED FELKIN). New
York: Dodd, Mead, 1908 NUC. London: Cassell, 1908 BMC.

Contrast of two love affairs: Miss F's at age 40 and
that of her young niece; Miss F. receives a fortune
before she marries; She's lost at sea soon after
marriage. BKM
More concerned with the fortune after her death BKM
"Depicting life in a small English town. Two love
affairs are contrasted: that of Miss Fallowfield, who
meets a man after her own heart when she has reached
the age of forty, and the romantic affair of her young
niece. There are many complications in regard to the
fortune which came to Miss Fallowfield before she
married. Shortly after the marriage she is lost at sea
and her husband is believed to have perished with her.
He, however, returns just as matters are about to be
adjusted among his wife's heirs." 28 1908-9 BKM
TLS-Fowler has had a change of view toward women,
"wishes them no Parliamentary vote, but has wise
things to say of a development in their relations to
men."
SR-
ATH-

003872   PLACE AND POWER. BY ELLEN THORNEYCROFT
FOWLER (MRS. ALFRED LAURENCE FELKIN). New York: D.
Appleton, 1903 NUC. London: Hutchinson, 1903 BMC NUC.

patient Griselda, story has a religious
moral-God/Godlessness NYT 03.652
Focus on hero's struggle between money and faith PW
9-12-03.
focus on an ambitious man ACAD 65, 212
Review LBKM 10-03, 43-Griselda a conv. type, story
centers on guilt, rel. of her husband.
ATH 122, 409
Review TLS 03, 255, story focuses on hero

003873   THE SUBJECTION OF ISABEL CARNABY. BY
ELLEN THORNEYCROFT FOWLER (MRS. ALFRED LAURENCE
FELKIN). New York: Dodd, Mead, 1906 NUC. (Eng ed: In
Subjection)

"A sequel to "Concerning Isabel Carnaby." The new book
depicts Isabel happily married, her "subjection" being
simply her graceful acceptance of the yoke of
matrimony. English society and English politics and a
beautiful East Indian girl enter into the story." BKM
v. 24 1906-07
NYT

003874   TEN DEGREES BACKWARD. BY ELLEN
THORNEYCROFT FOWLER (THE HONBLE. MRS. ALFRED FELKIN).
London and New York: Hodder & Stoughton, [1915] NUC
BMC.

Twin disrupts her brother's marr 10-23-15 PW
Reams of theological dissertation; marr of older man,
younger woman all turns out ok NYT SP
Devout Christian of 42 marries Fay 18. She's jealous
of his sister whom he confides in regularly. Takes off
for Australia and the stage, but she's chaperoned by
brother. TLS LBKM
Narrator the baronet of 42; all made right by their
rel. ATH

003875   THE WISDOM OF FOLLY. BY ELLEN
THORNEYCROFT FOWLER (MRS. FELKINS). Boston: School of
Printing, 1907 NUC. London: Hodder & Stoughton, 1910
BMC.

TLS two sisters in remote village.
ATH-One murders her husband to save her baby. He is a
murdering maniac. Three live together. The unmarried
one dies. The other remarries but is adopted by a
kindly couple first.
SR. He roasted his child alive. Tragic death of
sister. Daughter becomes rival of mother in regard to
lover, she is pursued by justice but escapes with "an
exchange of personalities."

FELKIN, HON. MRS. ALFRED. See FELKIN, ELLEN THORNEYCROFT
(FOWLER).

FELKIN, MRS. ALFRED LAURENCE. See FELKIN, ELLEN
THORNEYCROFT (FOWLER).

FELKINS, MRS. See FELKIN, ELLEN THORNEYCROFT (FOWLER).

FELLOWS, FEDORA. United States.

    003876   DELLADINE: A STORY OF A HEART OF PRIDE.
    AN EARLY SCENE IN THE SCIOTO VALLEY. Los Angeles: W.
    A. Vandercook, 1891 W.

FENNELL, CHARLOTTE. Nationality Unknown.

    003877   THE CALICO PRINTER: A NOVEL. London:
    Hutchinson, [1895] BMC NUC.

    history of Leonora Challis, has vulgar mother. She
    takes after her father who is more refined. She's
    divinely tall and a perfect lady. She's passionate
    about music. Is sent to live with cousins; two young
    women relatives make things hard for her, but she
    meets the calico printer, an arist laying low. He
    loves music too. They wed. ACAD 48:336
    No. Country people in manufacturing town ATH 106:528
    SR-Satire of attractive heroine with aristocratic
    father and impossible mother. She admires her father's
    family and aristocracy in general, looks down on
    mother and her family. Mother "best-drawn character."

FENOLLOSA, MARY (MACNEIL). D. 1954. United States.

    003878   ARIADNE OF ALLAN WATER. BY SIDNEY MCCALL.
    Boston: Little, Brown, 1914 NUC BMC. London: A.
    Melrose, [1915] BMC.

    BKM-Ariadne bound by promise to dying father is stuck
    with stepmother who immediately marries European
    adventurer who soon tires of her and pursues Ariadne
    who is saved by sweetheart Randy.

Melodramatic episodes TLS
rescued from step parents by her lover ATH
"Story opens in Virginia, later scenes shift to The
Hague and London. Ariadne finds herself as a result of
her father's unwise will and her stepmother's
subsequent marriage to an adventurer in a most
difficult situation. If she leaves her stepmother the
latter will be penniless, so the husband gets money
from Ariadne whenever he wants it and she is dragged
about Europe wherever they wish to go. Seven tragic
years go by in this way, but at last the girl is free
and may take the happiness she has refused so long."
PW 85 4/4/14 p.1158

003879   THE BREATH OF THE GODS. BY SIDNEY MCCALL.
London: Hutchinson, 1905 NUC BMC. Boston: Little,
Brown, 1905 NUC.

romantic story, political troubles. Ambassador and
daughter PW 5-20-05
Yuki-ko marries a man she does not love for the good
of country (she's of samarai blood) is then resp for
loss of valuable papers when she hides Pierre (the man
she loves) in her home. She's innoc. but kills
herself.? NYT 364,05
Yuki had an American ed., but she goes back to her
family-the utter subordination of indiv. Her
patriotism shown. ATH 05, 575 cheerful sacrifice of
ind. to the system

003880   CHRISTOPHER LAIRD. BY SIDNEY MCCALL. New
York: Dodd, Mead, 1919 NUC.

Romance of a nature lover in Carolina mts. PW
Native boy becomes a famous naturalist. He loves Miss
Mary who though she marries another, is soon widowed
and available. NYT 10-19-19 584

003881   THE DRAGON PAINTER. BY SIDNEY MCCALL.
Boston: Little, Brown, 1906 NUC. London: S. Paul,
[1910] BMC.

TLS conflict between art and passion
BKM 24 1906-7

003882   RED HORSE HILL. BY SIDNEY MCCALL. Boston:
Little, Brown, 1909 NUC.

Married to brutal husband, leaves him, thinking him
and her child dead, marries another. Comes to live in
Milltown. Rediscovers her daughter when she learns of
child whose arm was crushed. PW 5-22-09
See BKM v 29 1909.
Child labor in So. mills. Maria Alden, the heroine,
impulsive, passionate, courageous. Through no fault of
hers her life was "blackened and outraged." Loves
husband. But has a secret. Ruth cool, balanced, "a
modern of moderns". College bred, scientifically
inclined. Suffering children of the mills "the agony
of squalor and brutality." BKM
Direct appeal for mill children and mill women. Ruth's
sister-in-law university prof of Sociology. NYT

003883   THE STIRRUP LATCH. BY SIDNEY MCCALL.
Boston: Little, Brown, 1915 BMC NUC.

compares Victorian type of women to ultra mod. PW
10-30-15
Cicely Dering married very young left widow with two
daughters. Her cousin and Julia dear friend is also a
widow, with a son. Cicely and Julia meet as the story
opens after long separation when Julia was in England.
Cicely now a household drudge, a slave to her
daughters who ignore and despise her. Julia instead is
youthful, companion to her son who adores her. She's
intell, charming alive. Sets out to rescue Cicely. NYT

003884   THE STRANGE WOMAN. BY SIDNEY MCCALL. New
York: Dodd, Mead, 1914 NUC.

NYT mid-westerner brings home from Paris a new woman
with strange ideas.
French widow (had divorced husb. now dead) Inez
pierrfond whose own exper. taught her that marriage is
"accursed, wicked, wrong", falls in love with an
American; together they write a novel about Inez's
opinions on matrimony. End up marrying. Vows never to
marry "believes in full emancipation of women, in
their right to live their own lives, regardless of
conventional morality." NYT
She convinces the young American man of her point of
view, though he loves her and wants to marry. Then
story moves from Paris to American western town with
its conventional narrowness. She's rejected by town
that she openly accuses of hypocrisy. Does marry at
the very end. BKM

Adapted from Wm. J. Hurlbut's play of the same name.
"After some years abroad as a student, the town's most
promising young man comes back. He brings with him his
future wife, young beautiful, witty, but who, from the
point of view of the townspeople, is a mystery. There
are inevitable misunderstandings which lead to
suspicions and grow dislikes. When it is known that
she is a New Woman in the fullest, most modern
meaning, there is a climax which threatens the peace
of the town and of the young man and woman. The
solution comes through the influence of the man's
mother, who loves both him and the strange woman." PW
86 11/28/14:1836
BKM 40 divorcee

003885   SUNSHINE BEGGARS. BY SIDNEY MCCALL.
Boston: Little, Brown, 1918 NUC.

PW--an Italian fam.
NYT-Sentimental story of families as neighbors.

003886   TRUTH DEXTER. BY SIDNEY MCCALL. London:
C.A. Pearson, [1902] BMC. Boston: Little, Brown, 1901
BMC NUC.

Mrs. Orchid: intellectually keen as a rapier's edge a
scintillating conversationalist; covets all knowledge,
as a plaything for personal conquest BOOK BUYER 01
Orchid tries to trap the newly married husband into
indescretions.
NYT " a pretty story" 01
Real love of a modern eve PW 3-23-01

FENWICK, FRANCES DE WOLFE. United States.

003887   THE ARCH-SATIRIST. Boston: Lothrop, Lee &
Shepard, [1910] NUC.

devotion of woman to her brother, a genius without
morals. Her life is forever "dulled and shadowed" even
after she's free of him. PW
BKM promise to her mother
NYT-"Justice had been done and time, the
arch-satirist, had had his joke out" Hardy. Her life
almost ruined.

FERBER, EDNA. 1887-1968. United States.

003888   DAWN O'HARA, THE GIRL WHO LAUGHED. New
York: F. A. Stokes, [1911] NUC. London: Methuen, 1925
BMC.

BKM 33 (1911) 534.newspaper woman; marries man who
makes her miserable; he goes insane; she supports self
and husband; has a breakdown; returns to work; rom.
adventures. 10 yrs strain of work and hospital bills
breaks her; sister and brother in law pick her up and
take her to their home for peace and quiet; can't
think marriage; but meets loveable doctor who cures
her. Then husband cured comes to Milwaukee to claim
her. wants to be a bustling old maid but attracted to
women's roles.

003889   EMMA MCCHESNEY AND CO. New York: F. A.
Stokes, [1915] NUC BMC.

reviewed in Forerunner by C.P. Gilman.
"tired business woman" combines womanly virtue with
successful career; travelling sales woman, now
married, her amusing advents. business-a dictator of
women's fashions, a matchmaker and a philosopher
reaches top as bus woman, good mother, housewife. PW
10-2-15.

003890   FANNY HERSELF. New York: F.A. Stokes,
[1917] BMC NUC. London: Methuen, 1923 BMC.

Fanny Brandeis, Jewish, works out her own destiny.
Helps mother in store in western town; after mother's
death, important position in mail order house in
Chicago. But there's longing in her. Finds relief in
sketching. At length responds to love. PW
second part of novel; Fannie's career-she's also a
brilliant cartoonist. first half: her mother's story;
incompetent husband; she runs a general store after
husband died. The store prospers in her hands. Her
buying trips; relation between her and Fannie. Fannie
wants to live life differently from mother's. Denies
her Jewishness. NYT

003891   PERSONALITY PLUS; SOME EXPERIENCES OF
EMMA MCCHESNEY AND HER SON, JOCK. New York: F.A.
Stokes, 1914 BMC NUC.

"For many years Emma McChesney traveled on the road
for the Featherloom Petticoat Co., all for the sake of

Jock, her son. Jock emerged safely from the cub stage,
not without causing his mother some anxiety. But
although Jock was "snappy" and cocksure to a high
degree, he had traces of his mother's grit and common
sense, which saved him. Her advice at critical
moments, if it wasn't rejected, saved him, too. Jock
captures a splendid advertising job, and Mother Emma
has time for a little romance." PW 86 9/19/14:
NYT—Mrs McChesney's experiences as modern business
woman make her a better mother in helping and
understanding her son. She encounters problems in her
career when a younger person challenges her methods as
being old-fashioned.

003892   ROAST BEEF MEDIUM; THE BUSINESS
ADVENTURES OF EMMA MCCHESNEY. New York: F.A. Stokes,
[1913] NUC BMC. London: Methuen, 1920 BMC.

"author tells the career of Emma McChesney from the
beginning. She is a business woman-a traveling saleswoman for petticoats. She can sell a bill of goods to
a hard customer as well as she can bake a cake in a
balky oven. She is the kind that takes hold and does
things. Yet she steps out of the sleeper at Bay City,
Michigan, at 5 a.m., looking as fresh and trim as if
she had just come from the witchcraft of a French
maid. And she likes a little pink satin bow in the
lining of her hats. Appeared serially in the American
Magazine." PW.
"Emma knows how to take care of herself and rely on
herself." Emma has been a wife and is a mother, she
has a boy of 17. "there is a love story...(one that)
doesn't leave any one in any one's arms in the last
paragraph." NYT, 1913, 232
TLS— travelling saleswoman, Emma McChesney, becomes
secretary of the firm.
LBKM She has divorced her husband and is devoted to
her son. 36 yrs old; fun, frankly sent.

FERGUSON, EMILY. See MURPHY, EMILY (FERGUSON).

FERGUSON, EMMA (HENRY). 1840-1905. United States.

003893   COURAGE AND LOYALTY: A NOVEL. Cincinnati:
Editor Pub. Co., 1898 NUC.

FERME, MRS. GEORGE.

003894   TIB. BY GEORGE DOUGLAS. Edinburgh:
Oliphant, Anderson and Ferrier, 1892 BMC.

FERRIS, LYNN.

003895   JOHN HEATHLYN OF THE OTWAY. London:
Heath, Cranton, 1916 BMC NUC.

TLS—male missionary.

FERRIS, MARY C. Nationality Unknown.

003896   AS A MAN LIVES. Cincinnati, Ohio: Editor
Pub. Co., 1898 NUC.

PW—Janet's father came to U.S. to flee from creditors
in England. Settled in rough mining camp and killed in
a gambling row. After some disagreeable episodes in
her life Janet returns to England.

FERRUGGIA, GEMMA. 1868-1930.

003897   CATERINA SOAVE. New York: G. W.
Dillingham, 1896 NUC. (Tr. from the Italian)

PW 1-18-96. Italian story of crime and tropical love.

003898   WOMAN'S FOLLY. London: Heinemann, 1895
BMC. (Tr. E. Zimmern)

Introduction by Gosse:"leaves George Egerton and Sarah
Grand panting far behind." "Characters are sadly
lacking in imaginative justice towards man." ACAD
:49:75.

FESSENDEN, LAURA CANFIELD SPENCER (DAYTON). D. 1924.
United States.

003899   BONNIE MACKIRBY: AN INTERNATIONAL
EPISODE. Chicago: Rand, McNally, [c1898] NUC.

PW—she at mother's request has married an impecunious
Englishman. Realizes how bad marriage is after birth
of children, but endures husband's brutality for their
sake. He is addicted to arsenic and overdoses on it.
She is accused of his murder and sentenced to life
imprisonment.

003900   A COLONIAL DAME: A PEN-PICTURE OF
COLONIAL DAYS AND WAYS. Chicago and New York: Rand,
McNally, [c1897] NUC.

FESTING, GABRIELLE.

003901   FROM THE LAND OF PRINCES. London: Smith,
Elder, 1904 BMC.

003902   HONOUR AMONG THIEVES. Edinburgh: W.
Blackwood, 1917 BMC NUC.

Traditional historical romance.TLS

FEVEZ, CORALIE.

003903   IRA LORRAINE. London: Greening, 1901 BMC.

FIASTRI, VIRGINIA GUICCIARDI. B. 1864. Italy.

003904   FROM OPPOSITE SHORES. London: M. Goschen,
1914 BMC NUC. (Tr. Helene Antonelli.)

SR 147:743. Dorinda, a widow washer-woman, torn
between love of her little daughter and God.
Sacrifices her to convent, but agony of the sacrifice
kills her.
ATH 143:754 Socialism and the church in conflict.
Italy.
TLS 13:298. First she rejects lover because he is a
socialist, changes her mind and waits four years for
his return to discover he is now married. Then,
educating her daughter at the convent, loses her to
the church. Gradual realization that she has been
tricked by the priests and nuns.

FIELD, CHRISTINE, pseud. See LAURENCE, FRANCES ELSIE (FRY).

FIELD, ISOBEL (OSBOURNE). B. 1858. United States.

003905   THE GIRL FROM HOME: A STORY OF HONOLULU.
BY ISOBEL STRONG. New York: McClure, Philips, 1905
NUC.

South sea island romance. PW 4-29-05.
All about Hawaii. NYT 1905:342

FIELD, LOUISE FRANCES (STORY). B. 1856. United Kingdom.

003906   BID ME TO LOVE. London: W. Gardner and
Darton, 1891 BMC.

003907   DENIS: A STUDY IN BLACK AND WHITE.
London: Macmillan, 1896 BMC.

LBKM 11:20. Ireland before and during Black '47.
Futility and waste of it all.
SR non-partisan
ACAD "Genuine humour which pervades almost very page."
SP 77:50. Despite humor, depicts suffering, famine,
failure. Shows religion in form of superstition,
patriotism as a passion that causes men to give their
money to political causes when it takes food out of
mouths of their children. Mervyn is a philanthropic
landlord who earnestly struggles to improve his
tenants' lot. But he does something terrible to Mary
without remorse for her "after-fate." Denis is the
hero, a young man of the lower class, destroyed by
Mervyn's guilt

FIELD, LOUISE MAUNSELL. United States.

003908   KATHERINE TREVALYAN. New York: McClure,
1908 NUC.

PW--Orphan in wicked NY.

003909   THE LITTLE GODS LAUGH; A NOVEL. Boston:
Little, Brown, 1917 BMC NUC.

To Nita Wynne, life is one long period of
disillusionment; discovers the real character of man
she idealized. Comes up against realities of NY
society and world of business. Falls in love with
married man, but they wait till he gets divorced. PW

003910   A WOMAN OF FEELING. New York: Dodd, Mead,
1916 NUC.

NYT--Psychological study of bored rich married woman
who cares for nothing but her own pleasure and a poor
relative, Sylvia Farnham who is shallow, vain, eager
for pleasure and luxury. Mrs. Dareth has affair with
young artist. POV of author?
Mrs. Vida Dareth in the midst of an affair of the
heart with Maurice, an artist. Husband offers divorce

but no alimony. She refuses, Maurice being too poor to support her in luxury. PW 89:2-19-16:605.

FIELD, MARY HANNAH (BACON). 1833-1912. United States.

003911 KATE THURSTON'S CHAUTAUQUA CIRCLES. Meadville, Penn.: Flood and Vincent, 1893 NUC.

FIFIELD, SALOME (HOCKING).

003912 BELINDA THE BACKWARD: A ROMANCE OF MODERN IDEALISM. BY SALOME HOCKING. London: A.C. Fifield, 1905 BMC NUC.

Belinda leaves home to join a settlement of "the simple life" TLS 05,59

003913 A CONQUERED SELF. BY S. MOORE CAREW. London: F. Warne, 1894 BMC.

Character studies of middle-class English life. Bernice Yorke, daughter of Lidford bookseller, gets engaged but learns he has money motives. Her action is both surprising and self-sacrificing. PW 7-29-93.

FINDLATER, JANE HELEN. 1866-1946. United Kingdom.

003914 A DAUGHTER OF STRIFE. London: Methuen, 1897 BMC. New York: Dodd, Mead, 1897 NUC.

London and So. of Eng. A joyous romance at the same time, a grim tragedy. Caroline and Philip love each other but Philip's father is his enemy. Philip's father is murdered and dies believing his own son killed him. LBKM 13:105.
first part concerns Annie Champion and the trick of a mock marriage which she discovers. Leaves her "husband." Her old lover returns and almost kills the guy. Annie's son and the old lover's daughter: (Philip and Caroline) make up the second part. The son Philip is tried convicted for the murder. He escapes execution by agreeing to have his hand amputated by the old lover--Sebastian. But he's innocent. Real murderer turns up after he loses his hand. ACAD 52:Fic Sup 118.
Friend of her betrothed tells her her fiance has been false, gets her to marry him--mock marr. PW 52:1041.
SP 81:448. Surgeon's friend through deceit gets girl in a bogus mrge. She dies. Remorse. Then surgeon's daughter comes to be loved by bastard son of friend. BKM 6:563. Joyous romance of Philip and Caroline.

003915 THE GREEN GRAVES OF BALGOWRIE. London: Methuen, 1896 BMC. New York: Dodd, Mead, 1896 NUC.

ATH 107:712. Two sisters, brought up by insane mother, isolated, are very close. One is an intellectual; the other is betrayed by a lover. Both die. Scotland
SP 76:487. They are the pupils of Dr. Cornelius, local pastor. Henrietta becomes engaged to him. He has an alcohol problem.
BKM 4:161. Henrietta dies on the eve of her mrge. difficult to believe the mother could be so near insanity and yet sane. J. F.'s writing is not conventional, there is a "mark of genius."
Unkind mother goes mad; her daughter then raised by a minister. BAKER 03 207.

003916 THE LADDER TO THE STARS. London: Methuen, 1906 BMC. New York: D. Appleton, 1906 NUC.

PW--dissatisfied young woman, writes about friends and relations for newspaper. "Finally love teaches her the secret for climbing the ladder to the stars."
NYT--is not beautiful, climbs from servant class to journalism, then what?
ACAD--Grave, sane outlook lends her a gracious dignity and saves her from disaster.
TLS--finally leave her on the road to a happy marriage.
ATH--her nature does not expand with her new life.

003917 RACHEL. London: Methuen, 1899 BMC. New York: Doubleday & McClure, 1899 NUC.

Rachel loves Michael, son of a gypsy woman who leaves her husband for a man of her own people. Michael reads fortunes, has a second sight, becomes a great hit in London as head of a mystic religion--foreseers. But he marries Ellen Morrison and Rachel is hurt, but not undone. He dies in the end.
LIT 4:476. Michael Fletcher. Retells life of Edward Irving's career and the woman who became Jane Carlyle but very imaginatively. LBKM 16:20
She is completely sympathetic in spite of her rudeness, her sharp tongue, her love of freedom, her

Bohemian aspirations. Celebrates the release of Michael, the mystic, in death. SP 82:492

003918 THE STORY OF A MOTHER. London: J. Nisbet, 1902 BMC NUC.

ATH 5-3-02-- Wife of a severe minister, vital, brave.

FINDLATER, JANE HELEN, jt. au. See FINDLATER, MARY AND JANE HELEN FINDLATER.

FINDLATER, MARY. 1865-1946. United Kingdom.

003919 BETTY MUSGRAVE. London: Methuen, 1899 BMC. New York: E. P. Dutton, 1913 NUC.

Bloomsbury boarding house. Study of dipsomania. Heroine who is rather helpless. LIT 4:557.
Betty's mother is the alcoholic, a very sympathetic portrayal. Betty marries Oliver Lacy. LBKM 16:21
Mrs. Musgrave begs, borrows or steals to maintain her habit. The family's resources go. Mother and daughter move to London. The daughter's care of her mother. SP 82:311
Domestic story. Noble woman in squalid surroundings. Delicate character study. BAKER 03,207.
Bread and butter heroine, not fascinating type. Theme: alcoholic mother. Mrs. Lacy NYT

003920 A BLIND BIRD'S NEST. London: Methuen, 1907 NUC BMC.

"Heroine wins her way...into a haven of prosperity and happiness." Agnes Sorel, father in prison when she's a child (shot man who dishonored her sister Clare, an unworthy sort of "sponger, a woman of mental and moral slackness." Mother is a stoic, noble character. Agnes as girl knows nothing of this background. Almost marries later but shame of her father prevents her. Becomes a spinster's companion, later goes off to nurse her ill father . Strong in characterization.

003921 A NARROW WAY. London: Methuen, 1901 BMC NUC. New York: E. P. Dutton, [n.d.] NUC.

Fascinating study of a new feminine type "impatient of calf love," in control of her sentiment, sane. ATH
Kitty Cameron--a bread and butter Miss. NYT

003922 OVER THE HILLS. London: Methuen, 1897 BMC. New York: Dodd, Mead, 1897 NUC.

Six well contrasted women chars. Annie Fraser is "an incorrigible flirt, absolutely without scruples." Two men rival for her. She jilts her fiance for the rival, then lets her fiance go to prison for forgery she committed. Jane Anne--Admirable portrait of a "gentle old-maid;" Dinah Jemington strong and self reliant elopes in an emigrant ship. SP 79:776.
"A very unconv. story of Scottish villagers... mostly feminine." One is non-moral; another "simpler, nobler." BAKER 03,207.

003923 THE ROSE OF JOY. New York: McClure, Phillips, 1903 NUC. London: Methuen, 1903 BMC.

Susan marries selfish shallow man whose first wife appears. He leaves the country, she devotes herself to art. PW 11-3-03.
Man loves, loses a woman; 20 yrs. later meets her when she's a widow. ACAD 65:212.
Susan not pretty, doesn't dress well but attractive artistic temperament, love of beauty. Her unsatisfactory marriage comes to an end, a man she doesn't love proposes to her, she prefers the single life. Hers was an unhappy marriage of convenience, neither are suited to the domestic life. Gives up her life to painting. In the end, her marriage a failure, she gives herself to art. LBKM 10-05,55.
Mother "excellent study of ineffectual womanhood." ATH 122:409.
Heroine makes an unpromising marriage, prospects get dimmer, child dies in infancy; heroine leaves, is free, devotes self to art and is happy. TLS

003924 TALES THAT ARE TOLD. London: Methuen, 1901 BMC.

003925 TENTS OF A NIGHT. London: Smith, Elder, 1914 BMC. New York: E. P. Dutton, [1914] NUC.

NYT--self-centered young woman with two lovers is miserable, has all she needs to be happy in a quiet way and doesn't want it. At close she has lost lovers and is happy anyway--because of an accident in quicksand after which she realized life is a good

thing.
LBKM--Anne is discontented and critical of life, well
described dreariness of her Brittany tour. Her
awakening is a result of falling out of love (she has
found falling in love disappointing) and world takes
on a new interest. Barbara is a flapper, born 10 yrs
after Anne, the perfect embodiment of a new spirit,
free swift movements, brusque way of speaking to
elders, air of being able to take care of herself.

FINDLATER, MARY AND JANE HELEN FINDLATER.

003926   CONTENT WITH FLIES. New York: E. P.
Dutton, 1906 NUC. London: Smith, Elder, 1916 BMC.

003927   CROSSRIGGS. London: Smith, Elder, 1908
NUC BMC. New York: E. P. Dutton, 1913 NUC.

Heroine is "a dear" TLS
ACAD o
ATH o

003928   PENNY MONYPENNY. London: Smith, Elder,
1911 NUC BMC. New York: E. P. Dutton, 1913 NUC.

LBKM-Penny is wooed by her physician; weak 1st cousin
loves him, family oppose, he turns to a vulgar Creole
married woman, Pen's eyes are rudely opened, she meets
a very different man.
Life of Scotch gentlefolk TLS
Penny is a fine creature; Lorin is "perverse." SP
"It is curious that when a woman describes
domesticity, she nearly always paints it much less
attractively than does a man. "All the Scots homes are
gloomy, domestic existence is dispiriting and
pervasive. Only the young escape because they are
foolish and ignore what they see. SR

FINDLAY, JESSIE PATRICK. Nationality Unknown.

003929   MICHAEL LAMONT, SCHOOLMASTER. London:
Hodder & Stoughton, 1893 BMC.

Pitiful story of a man with "a veneer of popular ed.
overlying a commonplace and facile nature." Severe
lessons in self-knowledge. "Phyllis Winter, the
minister's daughter, with her keenness of perception
and her pathetic longing for a career withheld from
her by the narrow surroundings of her home and the
more insuperable obstacle of her bodily weaknesses, is
a more complex and more interesting study." ATH
102:910
SR. Two brothers. Michael a snob, Will a botanist. Two
sisters, one died of consumption, the other wrote her
father's sermons.

003930   NORMAN REID, M.A. New York: Hunt and
Eaton, [1891] NUC. Edinburgh: Oliphant, Anderson and
Ferrier, [1898] BMC.

Hero is a clergyman; heroine an artist. She rejects
him because she loves her work. Story deals with the
troubles each has in her/his own work. Eventually they
marry. PW 3-28-91.

FINLEY, MARTHA (FARQUHARSON). 1828-1909. United States.

003931   THE TRAGEDY OF WILD RIVER VALLEY. New
York: Dodd, Mead, [c1893] NUC. London: B. F. Stevens,
[1893] BMC.

"Two lynchings, several murders, a burglary and other
crimes." American rural life. BOOK NEWS 130:4 63.

FINNEMORE, EMILY PEARSON.

003932   THE BONDAGE OF GOD. London: Digby, Long,
1905 BMC.

Woman of high principle and intense family pride
allows one man to remain in jail knowing that the man
she's engaged to really killed her father TLS 05:315.

003933   A BRUMMAGEM BUTTON. London: D. Nutt, 1907
BMC.

Girl marries wrong man under pressure of step-mother.
ACAD
Happy end. TLS

003934   FATE'S HANDICAPS. London: Digby, Long,
1904 BMC.

ATH--Heroine through early training in cricket has
lost the merely feminine attributes of vanity and self
love. Becomes a professional carrier.

003935   JOHN DOBBY'S BETTER NATURE. London:
Christian Knowledge Society, [1900] BMC.

003936   A KING OF SHREDS AND PATCHES. A NOVEL.
London: Lawrence and Bullen, 1898 BMC NUC.

SP 81:914. Life history of son of mechanic who rises.
He is George, a plumber with good blood. He loves a
woman of his own class and a lady above him in class.
Heard the lady was engaged, married woman. Then he was
sorry for he learned the lady was free and loved him.
Then a chimney fell and killed off his wife. LIT.
4:20.
The lady then woos him though now he's blind. Story of
his long, long struggle for this ideal woman and the
worlds that separated them. LBKM 15:120.

003937   A MAN'S MIRROR. London: Cassell, 1903
BMC.

Woman marries for money but learns to love her husband
once he's blind. ACAD

003938   THE MARRYING OF SARAH GARLAND. London:
Hurst and Blackett, 1904 BMC.

Stern love problem. He's imprisoned.

003939   MARY LOUISA QUAYNE; OR, A BELATED LOVE
AFFAIR. London: Christian Knowledge Society, [1904]
BMC.

003940   MEG'S FORTUNE. London: Christian
Knowledge Society, [1909] BMC.

003941   MRS. GROOM'S LEGACY. London: Christian
Knowledge Society, [1903] BMC. New York: E. and J. B.
Young, [1903] BMC.

003942   THE POSTWOMAN. London: Christian
Knowledge Society, [1898] BMC.

003943   TALLY. London: Hurst and Blackett, 1904
BMC.

ATH--Tragedy of a woman
TLS--two individuals trapped in loveless marriages,
man accidentally kills her husband, she lets him go to
the gallows rather than see other woman keep him, very
tragic.

003944   UNCLE ISAAC'S MONEY. London: Christian
Knowledge Society, [1898] BMC.

FINNEMORE, HILDA.

003945   THE MOUNTAIN-SIDES OF DREAMS. London and
Toronto: J. M. Dent, 1914 NUC BMC.

TLS-male child, recollected by him.

FINNY, VIOLET GERALDINE.

003946   A DAUGHTER OF ERIN. London: Blackie, 1898
BMC 1908? [] NUC.

LIT 2:261. Irish heroine, English cousin, their love
story. They are slow to realize they love each other.

FIRESTONE, MAY ELIZABETH (COSTELLO). 1869-1909. United
States.

003947   THE CRUCIAL TEST. Chicago: A. L.
Firestone, [c1899] NUC.

FIRMAN, ALICE FREEMAN.

003948   A WOMAN'S HOPE. New York: Pilgrim Press,
[c1913] NUC.

PW 84 12/6/13:1960 "describes the gradual growth of
hope in her saddened soul after a period of despairing
grief and gloom, and the means by which this hope was
fostered and gloom gave way to joy."

FIRTH, ELIZABETH BOTTOMLEY.

003949   A QUAKER MAID. London: T. F. Unwin, 1898
BMC.

ACAD 55:292. Mrs. J.F.B. Firth. Author is a Quaker.
Comparison of "old unbending" Quakerism and
"larger-minded type now more commonly met with."
Shows two kinds of Quakerism--the narrow unbending
type and the modern philanthropic. Priscilla develops

into a gentle person in spite of restrictions of
parents. But her sister Naomi of different
temperament, is driven to deceit and disaster by the
restraints. LIT 4:122.

FISH, ANNE HARRIET.

003950   THE FIRST BOOK OF EVE. DRAWN BY FISH.
WRITTEN AND DESIGNED BY FOWL. London: [1916] BMC. New
York: Brentano's, 1916 NUC.

Reproduced from "The Tatler."

003951   THE NEW EVE. DRAWINGS BY FISH. WRITTEN
AND DESIGNED BY FOWL. London: J. Lane, 1917 BMC NUC.

Reproduced from "The Tatler."

003952   THE THIRD EVE BOOK. DRAWINGS BY FISH.
WRITTEN AND DESIGNED BY FOWL. London, New York: J.
Lane, 1919 BMC NUC.

Reproduced from "The Tatler."

FISHER, BERTHA MARY.

003953   THE PLAYER. London: H. J. Drane, [1912]
BMC.

ATH-boy's school story.

003954   AN UNPOPULAR SCHOOLGIRL. London: S. W.
Partridge, [1913] BMC.

FISHER, CAROLINE.

003955   ONE LONDON SEASON. Edinburgh: W.
Blackwood, 1904 BMC.

ACAD-young woman of 25 behaves like a child, silly,
trifling.

FISHER, DOROTHEA FRANCES (CANFIELD). 1879-1958. United
States.

003956   THE BENT TWIG. BY DOROTHY CANFIELD. New
York: H. Holt, 1915 NUC. London: Constable, 1916 BMC.

Girl brought up in stern scholastic Puritanism...at
last finds her real self. Contrast between two
sisters. WOMAN'S EDU. ASSOC. , Nov. 1915.
Girl realizes her home considered shabby by fellow
students, doesn't get invited to college fraternity,
spurns youth for sensuous love making. Sylvia: in
purpose she's marble, in action fire. Judith likes to
battle public opinion. PW 10-15 Review.
She is "bent" by environment particularly influence of
mother. Early scenes in university where father is a
teacher. NYT
First half: Sylvia's youth in univ. town. Second half:
Inherits money, it almost changes her personality but
early influence wins out. NYT
TLS--Story of Sylvia Marshall, brought up in college
professor's household where poverty is combined with
simple life. Then she goes to live with rich
aunt--temptations--then?
BKM--She and her brother have been brought up to be
responsible for making their own decisions. Wealth,
luxury and social functions least impressive things in
life compared with truth, duty and a sense of beauty.
What then?

003957   GUNHILD; A NORWEGIAN-AMERICAN EPISODE. BY
DOROTHY CANFIELD. New York: H. Holt, 1907 BMC NUC.

A rich American loves a Norwegian girl who spent youth
in Kansas. BKM

003958   THE SQUIRREL-CAGE. BY DOROTHY CANFIELD.
New York: H. Holt, 1912 BMC NUC.

PW--young woman a Minotaur of social convention,
wholesome.
BKM--she is forced by family to marry a man she is
unhappy with. He is a businessman, she hates her empty
life. But she does not bring it to an end; she is left
a widow through an accident, she is sickly and expects
a child, tries to make plans for a liberal education
for her children and protection of them from her
conventional family clan.
TLS--Restless struggle for riches and social position
ruining family life and imprisoning the wife.

003959   UNDERSTOOD BETSY. BY DOROTHY CANFIELD.
New York: Holt, 1917 NUC. London: Constable, 1922 BMC.

Betsy pampered by aunt never thought things out for
herself as a child. Moves to Putney Farm where she's
expected to work for self and think for herself.
Undercurrent of suggestions about child rearing makes
it an adult book too. PW

FISHER, DOROTHEA FRANCES (CANFIELD), jt. au. See CLEGHORN,
SARAH NORCLIFFE AND DOROTHEA FRANCES (CANFIELD) FISHER.

FISHER, DOROTHY CANFIELD. See CLEGHORN, SARAH NORCLIFFE AND
DOROTHEA FRANCES (CANFIELD) FISHER.

FISHER, JACOB, pseud. See WOOD, SABINE W.

FISHER, MARY. B. 1858. United States.

003960   GERTRUDE DORRANCE. A STORY. Chicago: A.
C. McClurg, 1902 NUC.

003961   THE JOURNAL OF A RECLUSE, TR. FROM THE
ORIGINAL FRENCH [ANONYMOUS]. New York: T. Y. Crowell,
[c1909] NUC. London: Gay & Hancock, 1910 BS.

"Translator's preface signed: M.F." NUC
TLS-Male

003962   KIRSTIE. BY M. F. New York: T. Y.
Crowell, [1912] NUC.

BKM -nurse in love with M.D. whose wife she has been
engaged to care for; nurse sickens and dies.
PW Heroine is nurse.

003963   THE TRELOARS. New York: T. Y. Crowell,
[c1917] NUC.

A family's complicated life. PW
One of the daughters, Catherine, "has brains enough
only for the hard and selfish part of the modern
feminist practice." She's hardly touched upon in a
story of conventional love BKM
Much commentary on modern life; long conversations on
every conceivable topic. NYT 7-15-17 268

FISHER, MARY ANN. B. 1839. United States.

003964   AMONG THE IMMORTALS, IN THE LAND OF
DESIRE; A GLIMPSE OF THE BEYOND. New York: Shakespeare
Press, [c1916] NUC.

003965   LOUISA FORRESTER. New York: [Printed by
J. J. Little], 1905 NUC.

Minister pledged to celibacy becomes engaged to woman
with broad religious views. He dies because of her
failings to see religion as he does. PW 12-23-05

003966   YOUNG DOCTOR HAMILTON. New York:
Cochrane, 1908 NUC.

003967   YOUNG MRS. MORTON; A NOVEL. New York:
Cochrane, 1911 NUC.

FISHER, SOPHIE. United Kingdom.

003968   THE IMPRUDENCE OF PRUE. Indianapolis:
Bobbs-Merrill, [c1911] NUC. London: Everett, [1912]
BMC.

Historical romance. 3-18-11 PW

FISLER, MAY (LEWIS). B. 1866. United States.

003969   "SYLPH," A NATION'S HONOR IN A WOMAN'S
HANDS; THE ROMANCE AND INTRIGUE OF A GREAT POLITICAL
RING. BY MAY JUNEAU. Chicago, Ill.: W. R. Vansant,
[c1911] NUC.

FITCH, A. H. See FITCH, ABIGAIL HETZEL.

FITCH, ABIGAIL HETZEL. United States.

003970   THE BREATH OF THE DRAGON. BY A. H. FITCH.
New York and London: G. P. Putnam's Sons, 1916 BMC
NUC.

Legation life in Peking. Betty, daughter of the
Minister to China befriends Follingbee who is
distrusted by all her associates.
PW 90:1121 9/30/16
NYT-Thrilling adventure. Chinese heroine named
A-lu-te.

FITZCLARENCE, WILHELMINA.

003971   A SCOTCH EARL. London: Hurst and

Blackett, 1891 BMC.

Author's contempt for society of rank and wealth. SP
67 297
Story really concerns matrimonial problems of Spanish
woman and her rake of a husband rather than the earl.
She is an acrobat, then becomes Lady Deville. She's
proud and ambitious and only slowly adapts to life
with her invalid husband much her senior whom she
married for position and wealth. ATH 9 8 187
The Scotch Earl-Lord Invergordon is a drunkard, dies
at end of Vol. I. Heroine Mrs. Grandison- she has an
inordinate fear that every little sin has its price.
SR 8-8-91

FITZGERALD, EILEEN. Fl. 1908-1937. United Kingdom.

003972   ELEANOR'S HUSBAND. London: J. Long, 1918
BMC.

ATH--Love temptation, war in background, full
recovery.

003973   A FETISH OF TRUTH. London: Hutchinson,
1909 BMC.

Misunderstanding in marriage easily cleared up. TLS

003974   THE HEART OF A BUTTERFLY. London:
Hutchinson, 1908 BMC.

TLS--romance.
ATH--Romance.

003975   JANE HOBBS. London: J. Long, 1919 BMC
NUC.

TLS--Level attitude towards 2 social problems.
ATH--A butler's daughter, she marries into employer's
family, most of whom look down on her. Hoping to gain
status in her children's eyes, she takes lessons and
one day electrifies her children by her playing.
Henceforth she plays new role in family which book
describes.

003976   THISTLEDOWN. London: J. Long, 1918 BMC.

Daughter of Cornish squire gets engaged, tragedy,
engagement broken. ATH
Manslaughter, divorce, near bigamy. SR

003977   A WAYFARING WOMAN. London: J. Long,
[1917] BMC.

Dolores Carr's daughter sent off to be raised by
mother's sister. The daughter's engagement brings them
together. TLS Dolores lives a life by no means beyond
reproach. Her ruling idea is to promote the future
well-being of her daughter, whom at all costs she's
determined to shield from a life like her own. ATH

FITZGERALD, ENA.

003978   AND THE STARS FOUGHT; A ROMANCE. London:
Greening, 1912 BMC.

ACAD--Murderer leaves his wife and daughter to join
the priesthood. Mother and daughter are devoted, the
latter a successful sculptor. Then mother meets
father, sees that he has not expiated his sin and she
loses faith in church. At same time daughter loses her
talent, apparently because of the symbiotic
relationship of mother, daughter.
ATH--O

003979   PATCOLA: A TALE OF A DEAD CITY. London:
Greening, 1908 BMC.

TLS--Historical romance.
ATH--ditto

003980   THE WITCH QUEEN OF KHEM. A TALE OF A
WRONG MADE RIGHT. London: Greening, 1909 BMC.

Historical tale of Ancient Greece; imaginative. TLS

FITZGERALD, KATE M.

003981   SISTER CONSTANCE. Edinburgh and London:
Oliphant, Anderson & Ferrier, 1893 BMC.

FITZGERALD, MENIE MURIEL (DOWIE) NORMAN. 1866-1945. United
Kingdom.

003982   THE CROOK OF THE BOUGH. BY MENIE MURIEL
DOWIE. London: Methuen, 1898 BMC. New York: Scribner,

1898 NUC.

SP 80:766. Islay Netherdale, was a dowdily dressed
typewriter until she went on a holiday trip with her
brother to the near East and fell in love with finery
and the concept of herself as an ornament. Capt.
Hassan falls for her because he believes she is
intelligent and useful but when he finally meets her
she is in her ornamental phase and he abandons his
suit. Contrast with Grahame "whose body was but an
engine; to Islay hers had become the airy shining
temple of her hopes." POV?
LIT 2:756. Ineffective satire on the stupidity of the
modern woman.
ATH 111:688.
SR 86:23. Signed review by Frank Danby. She says that
impropriety of behaviour is out of fashion in novels,
this was the vein Dowie wrote in formerly. Islay's
change was a result of her 1st meeting with Capt.
Hassan.
NYT 1898:334. "More wholesome and edifying than
Gallia." Very modern heroine, her adventures in
Vienna, Sofia and Constantinople. Title refers to the
easy comfortable place the monkey rested in before he
took up responsibilities of being a man; refers
directly to irresponsibility of unemancipated woman.

003983   GALLIA. BY MENIE MURIEL DOWIE. London:
Methuen, 1895 BMC. Philadelphia: J. B. Lippincott,
1895 NUC.

She's unconventional. What's more, she has reasons for
all that she does. She has lived much by herself,
thought on her own, has come to strong ideals. Story
shows how she lives them. ATH 105:470.
Author "has gone further in sheer audacity of
treatment of the sexual relations and sexual feelings
of men and women than any woman before." Heroine is a
modern type weighted down with knowledge of all kinds.
Her father works at the Colonial Office; her Mother is
a "nonentity." Gallia has had every
advantage--finishing up at Oxford. A prodigious
reader, thoroughly independent, knows and lives social
ethics. Completely outspoken. "Femininity," we are
informed, "reached her late, was resented fiercely,
and fought and subdued promptly." Hero: Oxford fellow,
literary man about town, a decadent. "The feelings of
the girl as she unconsciously falls in love and
afterwards gnaws her heart as she realizes that she
has been played with and tossed aside, are analyzed
with extraordinary keenness and penetration into the
secrets of the female heart." Even so, she declares
her love for him openly but he's too much the cynic to
appreciate her sincerity. Her love passages are
extraordinary. Tells him she'll marry a man she
doesn't love in order to have a child. To her friends
Miss Essex and Miss Janion she's even more open--such
as having a woman other than a wife supply a child, a
kind of baby farm. Marries Mark Gurdon in order to
have a father for her children. Love and marriage are
separate in her mind. SR 79:384
A social novel of the fast type which touches rather
freely on the Bohemian life of artistic Paris and on
sex problems. BAKER 03100.

003984   A GIRL IN THE KARPATHIANS. BY MENIE
MURIEL DOWIE. New York: Cassell, [1891] NUC. London:
G. Philip, 1891 BMC.

Young Scottish woman of about 24 narrates her story.
She speaks French and German, rides, swims, shoots
like a man, drinks beer and smokes and dresses like a
man to travel more comfortably-in E. Galacia, Russia,
Poland, Hungary and Austria. Travels alone. Studies
the people. Keen observations. PW 9-5-91.

003985   LOVE AND HIS MASK. BY MENIE MURIEL DOWIE.
London: W. Heinemann, 1901 NUC BMC.

Widows' freindship with a man to whom she writes
letters pouring out her whole mind. He remains the
friend of her spirit; she marries someone else. LBKM,
9-01
Leslie, the heroine-her emotional life at 27 wants
everything. ACAD 01
Modern, pretty, clever, complex rich widow, writes
straightforward letters to the general.
ATH 8-17-01.

003986   SOME WHIMS OF FATE. BY MENIE MURIEL
DOWIE. London and New York: J. Lane, 1896 NUC BMC.

ACAD 50:560. Short stories, compressed style.

003987   THINGS ABOUT OUR NEIGHBORHOOD. BY MENIE
MURIEL DOWIE. London: G. Richards, 1903 BMC NUC.

FITZPATRICK, CATHERINE. United States.

003988   LIZBETH. New York: Broadway, [c1906] NUC.

FITZPATRICK, KATHLEEN. United Kingdom.

003989   THE WEANS AT ROWALLAN. London: Methuen,
1905 BMC. New York: Coward-McCann, 1937 NUC. (NUC: The
Weans of Rowallan.)

Thoughts and pranks of a family. TLS, 05 31
ATH 05,204

FITZROY, ISOBEL.

003990   A QUIXOTIC WOMAN. London: J. Murray, 1905
BMC.

Submits to marriage as way of paying a debt but is
quite capable of looking after herself later on. ACAD
545,05

003991   WAS HE THE OTHER? Philadelphia:
Lippincott, 1893 NUC. London: T. F. Unwin, 1893 BMC.

Told in first person, unsophisticated young woman
meets a man on a train who insults her; meets the same
man in rich society. Mystery explained. PW 4-15-93.
Dual nature makes man seem like two personalities.
Heroine likes the rough one who kisses her on the
train. Then realizes she has received two proposals
from same man. CR 20, 23:70.
Like Gyp's naughty novels. She's Geraldine Fraser.
ACAD 43:458.

FLANDRAU, GRACE C. (HODGSON). United States.

003992   COUSIN JULIA. New York and London: D.
Appleton, 1917 BMC NUC.

Julia wife of rising businessman believed social
success the most important thing in life. Story
concerns her plans to marry off her two daughters, one
adopted. PW
Virginia Bradford the daughter. The mother is Cousin
Julia. Mother so dominates her that at the end
Virginia thinks she's doing her own thing when it's
really her mother's plan. NYT

FLANIGAN, MARY LEEDY.

003993   A SUMMER IDYL. New York: Cosmopolitan
Press, 1911 NUC.

FLATAU, DOROTA. United Kingdom.

003994   BAIT; A NOVEL. BY DOROTHEA FLATAU.
London: Hutchinson, [1919] BMC NUC.

Novel of social life, making money nothing here TLS
Cinema life SP

003995   SEVEN JOURNEYS. BY DOROTHEA FLATAU.
London: Hutchinson, [1920] BMC NUC.

003996   YELLOW ENGLISH. BY DOROTHEA FLATAU.
London: Hutchinson, 1918 BMC NUC.

PW Intrigues of a rich German in English society.
TLS A yellow Englishman is a naturalized alien.

003997   YELLOW SOULS. BY DOROTHEA FLATAU. New
York: G. H. Doran, [1918] NUC.

FLATAU, DOROTHEA. See FLATAU, DOROTA.

FLATT, ANNIE MACCALLUM. United States.

003998   THE DAWN OF A NEW ERA. Boston: R. G.
Badger, [c1920] NUC.

FLEHARTY, CLARA VIOLA. United States.

003999   THE RADIANCE OF THE MORNING CLUB. Boston:
R. G. Badger, [c1911] NUC.

004000   A STUDY IN LIFE TINTS. Chicago, Ill.: M.
A. Long Book and Pub. House, 1907 NUC.

004001   A WILD ROSE. Boston: R. G. Badger,
[c1911] NUC.

Two families, one conv. one freer. Madge from conv.
family makes a poor marriage. Katherine from freer
family, a better one PW 7-29-11

FLEMING, ALICE MACDONALD (KIPLING). B. 1868. United
Kingdom.

004002   A PINCH-BECK GODDESS. BY MRS. J. M.
FLEMING. London: Heinemann, 1897 BMC. New York: D.
Appleton, 1897 NUC.

Madeline Norton is unattractive, dull, neglected in
India where she visits a match making matron. Then
there's a dashing, elegant wigged widow. They are the
same woman. The deception conceived "as a sort of
revenge for former neglect."SR 84:147.
There's a Lilian Miles who loves and is loved by her
husband but is miserably unhappy. Does not say the
goddess and Madeline are one char. ACAD 51:353.
Was sent to India to be married, rebels, returns to
Eng. goes back as widow to amuse herself and
compensate for past suffering. Astonishes Simla with
her audacious manners. (Before she was penniless and
got no attention) Now she has a fortune so the men
flock around. She has her revenge on several. But
falls in love with one. A comedy. CR 26,30:248. BKM
5:438.

FLEMING, GEORGE, pseud. See FLETCHER, JULIA CONSTANCE.

FLEMING, MAY AGNES (EARLY). 1840-1880. Canada.

004003   EDITH PERCIVAL: A NOVEL. New York: G. W.
Dillingham, 1893 NUC.

004004   THE SISTERS OF TORWOOD: A NOVEL. New
York: G. W. Dillingham, 1898 NUC.

004005   WEDDED FOR PIQUE: A NOVEL. New York: G.
W. Dillingham, 1897 NUC.

FLEMING, MRS. J. M. See FLEMING, ALICE MACDONALD (KIPLING).

FLEMING, SARAH LEE BROWN. United States.

004006   CLOUDS AND SUNSHINE. Boston: Cornhill,
[1920] NUC.

004007   HOPE'S HIGHWAY, A NOVEL. New York: Neale,
1918 NUC.

PW--Amer. Negro story by black woman.

FLEMMING, HARFORD, pseud. See MACCLELLAN, HARRIET (HARE).

FLETCHER, JULIA CONSTANCE. 1858-1938. United States.

004008   FOR PLAIN WOMEN ONLY. BY GEORGE FLEMING.
New York: J. Lane, 1896 NUC BMC.

LBKM-Aunt Lavinia discourses with much wit and common
sense to Theodore and Fanny on follies of women's
dress, etc.
BKM
PW 2-8-96. Starts with the assertion that "No woman
under 40 has the moral right to look irrecoverably
plain."

FLETCHER, MARGARET.

004009   THE FUGITIVES. London and New York:
Longmans, Green, 1912 BMC NUC.

PW--Paris artist life--English girl looking for
freedom. Three women art students.
TLS--author's pov very serious on temperaments of
young women.
ATH--tragedy of one on the brink of success pulled by
her family back into domestic servitude.

004010   THE SCHOOL OF THE HEART. London:
Longmans, Green, 1904 BMC NUC.

FLEWELLYN, JULIA (COLLITON). B. 1850. Canada.

004011   HILL-CREST. Boston: Arena, 1895 NUC.

Family of Irish Amer farmers in country town in
US-farmer, 4 daughters, old maid sister-in-law. A
fashionable cousin. A young clergyman. PW
12-14-95:1143

FLINT, ANNIE AUSTIN. B. 1866. United States.

004012   THE BREAKING POINT. New York: Broadway,
1915 NUC.

Rosa Kreppel "big limbed, fresh faced wholesome
creature of a woman" married to a man who's not the

man she married. (Husband is a split personality). The
person she wed is non existent now. It is her tragedy;
sympathetic depiction. NYT

004013   A GIRL OF IDEAS. London: Ward, Lock, 1903
BMC. New York: C. Scribner's Sons, 1903 NUC.

Business career, writer opens office for selling ideas
to established writers, successful. PW 4-4-03
college graduate in business of selling ideas to
authors. Has office on Broadway, devoted woman friend,
all her adventures with different kinds of authors.
Satire of literary life. A heroine full of surprises
right up to her triumphant exit, always true to
herself, intelligent noble. NYT 03, 224

FLOYD, ANNA.

004014   THE ROUGH ROAD TO THE STARS. London: T.
W. Laurie, [1920] BMC.

TLS-Barbara is driven to the streets to support her
illegitimate child. She hates the life and the men,
then meets hero, falls for him, then happiness,
sacrifice, more happiness, death.

004015   THE WOMAN'S HARVEST. London: T. W.
Laurice, [1915] BMC.

FOAKES, GERTRUDE M. FOXE.

004016   THE POOL OF GOLD. London: G. Allen and
Unwin, 1915 BMC.

Vera Forwood half Russian, tired of living with
widowed mother and sister near Moscow. A bachelor
offers to train her voice and make her
famous...marries him, runs off with an English
composer to England. Returns to Russia to husband to
fame. He forgives all. TLS

004017   THE RUSSIAN WIFE. London: G. Allen, 1911
BMC.

Poet loves married Russian countess who refuses to fly
off with him. He's resolved to await the return of the
Count (to kill him?). She strikes him down with an
axe, hides his body in cellar. Rest of story has to do
with the poet's son. ACAD
Common infidelity of Russian husband. ATH

FOLEY, KATHLEEN P. (EMMETT).

004018   A GIRL SOLDIER. London: F. V. White, 1903
BMC.

Bert fought in Boer war, keeps her unconventionality
in London society. TLS 155, 03

004019   THE SILVER ZONE: A HINDU NOVEL. London:
J. Murray, 1908 BMC.

TLS-Hindu married life, pleasant.
SR-"alive to the ugly spasmodic cruelty towards women
and animals" but in the main a series of quiet
domestic scenes.
ATH-"One sees how the marriage laws and customs and
superstitious traditions decide the destinies of the
women, weigh on their characters and imagination, and
determine their love of or indifference to their
children."

FOLKARD, MARY H.

004020   A CRUEL DILEMMA. BY MARY H. TENNYSON.
London: F. Warne, 1894 BMC.

SR 78:304. Melodrama. Wealthy old man falls into hands
of scheming couple, his daughter finds herself
impoverished. Scoundrels are finally discovered and
all ends well.
SP-four villains.
English baronet of 60 travels alone to Folkstone,
meets and marries an adventuress who first drives his
daughter out of his home, then tries to poison him
slowly. Daughter's lover discovers daughter in London
just before she starves to death. PW 8-31-95:270

004021   THE FOOL OF FATE. BY MARY H. TENNYSON.
London: Ward, Lock, 1893 BMC.

SR 77:395. Husband George good man in every way except
inability to keep from lying, blowing up the routine
of his life to numberless adventures. Wife does not
realize this for 18 months. Tragic outcome; he fills
house with flowers to get her back; she refuses, her

faith irretrievably shattered.
SP 72:867. "He invents romantic situations of which he
is the hero." He "sincerely loves his wife."

004022   A SINLESS SINNER: A NOVEL. BY MARY H.
TENNYSON. London: J. Macqueen, 1897 BMC.

Wretched parents argue about sending one of their
children to Dover to prolong its life. One sister
poisons the other. ACAD 52 Fic Sup 102.
A child murderer tortured in a reformatory. She killed
for brother's sake. ATH 110:744.
SR 85:119. An unselfish and kind child murderess; her
dreary life in the Reformatory.

FONDA, MARY ALICE (IVES) SEYMOUR. Fl. 1857-1892. United
States.

004023   IMPERIA: A STORY FROM THE COURT OF
AUSTRIA. BY OCTAVIA HENSEL. Buffalo: C. Wells Moulton,
1892 NUC.

FOOTE, MARY (HALLOCK). 1847-1938. United States.

004024   THE CHOSEN VALLEY. Boston: Houghton,
Mifflin, 1892 NUC. London: Osgood, McIlvaine, 1892
BMC.

PW-Western locale. Hero, who has spent his life in
Europe with his mother, returns and gets to know his
father who is feuding with a neighbor who has a
daughter.
American Western. Robert Dunsmuir, an engineer,
struggles against capitalists' effort to make quick
money through irrigation rather than to concern
themselves with long range effects on the environment.
LW 93,11
Contrast between Norrison the American engineer, who
didn't care how the canal was built and Dunsmuir, the
Scot, who was concerned about how the job was done not
profit. NATION 56, 201.
Scots engineer wants to use irrigation to fertilize.
Defeated. CR. 14,20:379

004025   COEUR D'ALENE. Boston: Houghton, Mifflin,
1894 NUC BMC.

CR 25:327. Bloody description. Foote seems to be
anti-strikers.
LW 25:372. Heroine seeking shelter from storm in
mining camp. Union tries to kill hero. Happy ending.
PW-manager of mine lacks principal. Hero has been sent
from London by directors to investigate manager, who
is heroine's father.

004026   THE DESERT AND THE SOWN. Boston:
Houghton-Mifflin, 1902 NUC.

ATH-not helpful

004027   EDITH BONHAM. Boston: Houghton Mifflin,
1917 NUC.

She and Nanny Aylesford friends at art school. Edith
travels with artist father; Nanny marries. Strong bond
between them. Edith goes to her friend to help her
with children; finds her dead; raises the kids, finds
'middle-aced' love. PW
Edith tells the story; ends up learning she loves the
widower. They marry. BKM

004028   THE GROUND-SWELL. Boston: Houghton
Mifflin, 1919 NUC.

Mother tells story of a family of a retired army
officer. PW
NYT-thoroughly modern Katherine plans to marry
Spanish-American hero(!) with parental approval but
she dies of grippe in France on war duty just as Tony
has spent his fortune on a home for her. Effect of war
(ground swell?)

004029   A PICKED COMPANY; A NOVEL. Boston:
Houghton Mifflin, 1912 NUC.

004030   THE PRODIGAL. Boston: Houghton, Mifflin,
1900 NUC.

PW-hero, Clunie, repeatedly wastes his father's money,
is finally saved by schoolmistress.

004031   THE ROYAL AMERICANS. Boston: Houghton
Mifflin, 1910 NUC. London: Houghton Mifflin, 1910 BMC.

Colonial romance-PW
ACAD-colonial romance.

SR-as study of American womanhood at the end of the
Colonial period it has value.

004032   THE VALLEY ROAD. Boston: Houghton
Mifflin, 1915 NUC.

Wealthy family life PW

FORBES, ANNABELLA (KEITH). D. 1922. United Kingdom.

004033   HELENA; A NOVEL. BY MRS. H. O. FORBES.
Edinburgh and London: W. Blackwood, 1905 BMC NUC.

Heroine a half caste Maori TLS 295, 05

FORBES, ETHEL M.

004034   A DAUGHTER OF THE DEMOCRACY. London:
Cassell, 1911 BMC.

Betty, orphaned soc-reformer's daughter, goes to work
in the slums after being a governess. She's joined by
Aileen. They and their friends live poorly but are
idealistic. Betty "deserves a better close to her
touching love story"? TLS
"Deals with present unrest in the minds of the modern
woman and the desire to break from the old
conventional life." ATH

004035   A HEART'S HARMONY. London: A. Melrose,
[1905] BMC.

ACAD-Sunny heroine, scanty material

004036   THE LOVE-TALE OF A MISANTHROPE. London:
E. Stock, 1909 BMC.

Daisy perfect-captivates everyone. TLS

FORBES, EVELINE LOUISA MITCHELL (FARWELL). 1866-1924.
United Kingdom.

004037   BLIGHT. London: Osgood, McIlvaine, 1897
BMC.

Makes people uncomfortable if they stand in her way.
Becomes a companion and then Lady Easton. She drives
her husband and his daughter to their graves, makes
her own children miserable, who are finally rescued
from her by an aunt. She is a blight. SR 84:398.
She's unlovely, intensely and incurably selfish. Study
of a woman who wants to love but has no way of
inspiring it; doesn't know how. Author writes with
"wide sympathies" ACAD 52 Fic Sup 85.
SP 80:177. Portrait of a selfish narrow-minded woman.
Blow dealt her daughter-in-law also struck her own
child.

004038   DUMB. London: Chatto and Windus, 1901
BMC.

004039   A GENTLEMAN. London: J. Murray, 1900 BMC.

LBKM 19:90. Dressmaker struggles so son shall live as
gentleman. He is unaware of her occupation, thinks she
writes. Lives oblivious to her travail. Focus is on
his travels, etc. Not much in book about her.
ATH 116:721. Succeeds in sending him out on 2,000
pounds a year.

004040   HIS ALIEN ENEMY. London: J. Murray, 1918
BMC.

TLS-war, wife in Germany

004041   LEROUX. London: Greening, 1908 BMC.

TLS-romance of French Rev.
ACAD-Leroux claims Gabrielle, a prisoner, as his
bride, thus transforming her from a condemned
aristocrat to the wife of a good "citizen." Then what.
ATH-Then she chooses to remain his wife. He has, in
the meantime, become a general.

004042   NAMELESS; A NOVEL. London: J. Murray,
1909 BMC.

SR-two young women, one at least, a genius. A tragic
marriage is one part of the story.
Cecil Grey, famous authoress-intense wisdom. TLS

004043   UNOFFICIAL. A TWO DAYS' DRAMA.
Westminister: A. Constable, 1902 BMC. New York: D.
Appleton, 1903 NUC.

ATH 11-29-02-light romance, but strong older woman.

Clever villian outdone by a cleverer woman and her
triumphant tactics. NYT 03, 168.

004044   VANE ROYAL. London: J. Long, 1908 BMC.

TLS-marriage problem
ACAD-a sweet gentle woman married to an impossibly
selfish husband, she runs away with another man but
only tragedy results and she dies.
SR-she jumps off the yacht the a.m. after, husband
arrives in time to murmur forgiveness.

FORBES, HELEN EMILY (CRAVEN). B. 1874.

004045   THE BOUNTY OF THE GODS; A STUDY IN POINTS
OF VIEW. London: Duckworth, 1910 BMC NUC.

TLS-male heroes
ACAD male heroes

004046   HIS EMINENCE; A STORY OF THE LAST
CENTURY. London: E. Nash, 1904 BMC.

ATH Hist, struggle for power between cardinal and
duchess widow.
ACAD-

004047   IT'S A WAY THEY HAVE IN THE ARMY. London:
Duckworth, 1905 BMC.

004048   LADY MARION AND THE PLUTOCRAT. London: J.
Long, 1906 BMC.

TLS---
ATH -Ultra meek and mild prim heroine.

004049   THE POLAR STAR. London: Duckworth, 1911
BMC.

Marr/separation/reconciliation TLS

004050   THE PROVINCIALS. London: J. Long, 1905
BMC.

A Hunting story ATH 141, 05

FORBES, HILDA.

004051   DIABELLA. London: Digby, Long, 1907 BMC
NUC.

Mystery TLS

FORBES, JESSIE A. NORQUAY.

004052   JOHN GENTLEMAN, TRAMP. Edinburgh:
Oliphant, 1892 BMC.

Glasgow waif reaches manhood and discovers his father
and secret of his birth. Becomes a good man thru love
of a good woman.
ACAD 43:11

FORBES, LADY ANGELA. See ERSKINE, ANGELA SELINA BLANCHE
(FORBES) SAINT CLAIR.

FORBES, MRS. H. O. See FORBES, ANNABELLA (KEITH).

FORD, ISABELLA O.

004053   ON THE THRESHHOLD. London: Arnold, 1895
NUC.

SR Two modern young women living together and "setting
wrong right." Anti-climax of "prettier one's"
marriage. The entrance to womanhood of Kitty and
Lucretia, "their apprehension of the unknown sorrows
and degredation of existence, especially of the
obscure lives of wandering Londoners." ATH 106:788.

FORD, MARY HANFORD (FINNEY). B. 1856. United States.

004054   OTTO'S INSPIRATION. Chicago: S. C.
Griggs, 1895 NUC BMC.

PW-Tramp with fiddle goes to Germany to study
classical music. Later, he and his wife devote their
lives to the helpless.

004055   WHICH WINS? A STORY OF SOCIAL CONDITIONS.
Boston: Lee & Shephard, 1891 BMC NUC.

Miseries of poor; professes establishment of peoples'
party to give wives a partnership in husband's
property & control of their own vs monopolies; vs all
capitalists. NATION 10-1-91,264.

Story of two American men. One believes in equality of
wealth and labor; the other, gain and wealth and
power. The second gains all-even woman the first man
loved. The first dies in poverty. PW 3-16-91
Labor reform. the degradation of labor and power of
capital. Book dedicated to "Farmers Alliance, a third
party. Godey's 123,90.

FORD, MAY.

004056   THE REVOKE OF JEAN RAYMOND. London: S.
Swift, 1911 BMC.

LBKM-Jean leaves her husband Bernard Gretton because
she is bored to death by his passion for Wordsworth
and vivisection. Mary Margetson, a bachelor friend of
Jean's. with "socialist tendencies and excellencies
sufficient to wreck the peace of any home."
Theme: justification of marriage separation: Jean
leaves husband because he talks too much and because
he's a bore. Decides she has grounds for separation.
She's very independent, takes child with her. The
author claims all our sympathy for Jean. TLS
promulgates the ideals of society. Married at 32,
independent agnostic husband worries her into illness
with his endless talk of religion. She leaves, goes to
live with a woman friend, finds happines. There is a
kind of reconcilliation at her husband's deathbed.
"Jean is left in the care of a rather jolly former
lover" who's been waiting around all the while.
"Splendidly drawn woman of determination." ACAD

FORD, MRS. GERARD.

004057   I, TOO: A NOVEL IN TWO BOOKS. London:
Simpkin and Marshall, 1892 BMC.

ATH 100:575. Diary of Ursula, "unfolding of her
character, and her brother and her brother's friend."

FORD, PENELOPE.

004058   A PAGE IN A MAN'S HISTORY. London: J.
Long, 1913 BMC.

That page concerns wayward, selfish, charming rich
young woman; treats the man who loves her as badly as
man she loves treats her. A very "interesting woman."
ATH
He will not marry her though they love each other
because it will interfere with his career. She commits
suicide. She was first a tomboy, then a brilliant
wayward society girl with a genius for dancing. Her
states of mind are depicted with insight.

FORD, SARAH LOUISE.

004059   INTERWOVEN; LETTERS FROM A SON TO HIS
MOTHER [ANONYMOUS]. Boston: G. H. Ellis, 1905 NUC.

Foreword signed: S.L.F. Letters were written through a
medium

FORDE, GERTRUDE. Nationality Unknown.

004060   LADY LANARK'S PAYING GUEST. London:
Chapman and Hall, 1898 BMC.

An aristocratic woman now poor and her son. And an
American heiress chaperoned by the woman for a
consideration. LIT 4 :502
Heiress was a paying guest in a boarding house,
pleased an old gentleman who left her money. LBKM
15:187
Miranda Higgs. The American. SP 83:207.
Poses as an heiress, gets to court, becomes engaged to
a Marquis. By this time her $15,000 is spent.
Ultimately marries her truelove. ATH 113:239.

004061   RUPERT ALISON; OR BROKEN LIGHTS. Londdon:
Hurst and Blackett, 1891 BMC.

He's lame from football accident. Later "ensnared" by
a young woman, but escapes. Later rescues a child in
Naples, but in so doing hurts his leg and is lamer.
Meets Marietta whom he loves platonically, but her
jealous lover won't be convinced and tries to kill him
several times. Gets mixed up with a man who tries to
kill his wife and ends up killing self. Shot at by
brigands, earthquake in Naples, rescues two children,
a young woman and her bedridden mother and almost
saves the jealous man who tried to murder him earlier.
Saves a woman drowning in Thames. Marries Marietta now
in London giving singing lessons. SR 3-14-91, 329

FORDYCE, ELLA.

004062   HAD I BUT KNOWN. London: Sonnenschein,
1892 BMC.

ATH 100:317. Romance involving a foreign lover, a
gypsy fortune-teller, and a suppressed letter which
causes complications.

004063   SPINDRIFT OF THE SALT SEA WAVES: A
ROMANCE OF THE SEA. London: S. Sonnenschein, 1904 BMC.

ACAD-Ordinary love story

FORGAN, DORA.

004064   JOAN AVENEL. London: T. F. Unwin, [1917]
BMC.

Triangle; Joan, husband, billeted soldier vague review
TLS
Awakening of a wife by a soldier. ATH.

FORGET-ME-NOT, pseud. See KELLEY, EMMA DUNHAM.

FORRESTER, IZOLA LOUISE. B. 1878. United States.

004065   THE DANGEROUS INHERITANCE; OR THE MYSTERY
OF THE TITTANI RUBIES. Boston: Houghton Mifflin, 1920
NUC.

PW International intrigue surrounding valuable jewels
willed to girl.

004066   KIT OF GREENACRE FARM. Philadelphia: G.
W. Jacobs, [1919] NUC.

"Girl goes to a western college town and proceeds to
wake up everyone" she meets; girls? PW

004067   THOSE PRESTON TWINS. Boston: W. A. Wilde,
[1910] NUC.

004068   "US FELLERS". Philadelphia: G. W. Jacobs,
[1907] BMC NUC.

FORRESTER, MRS., pseud. See BRIDGES, MRS. COLONEL.

FORRESTER, MRS. JOHN.

004069   MYRTLE: A NOVEL. Melbourne: G. Robertson,
1891 NUC.

FORSSLUND, LOUISE, pseud. See FOSTER, MARY LOUISE.

FORSSLUND, M. LOUISE., pseud. See FOSTER, MARY LOUISE.

FORSYTH, JEAN, pseud. See MACILWRAITH, JEAN NEWTON.

FORSYTH, MAY.

004070   PETER OF GUNNEROY. London: J. Long, 1911
BMC.

Australian life ATH

FORTESCUE, WILL, pseud. See MACCHESNEY, DORA GREENWELL.

FOSDICK, GERTRUDE CHRISTIAN. United States.

004071   OUT OF BOHEMIA: A STORY OF PARIS STUDENT
LIFE. New York: G. H. Richmond, 1894 NUC.

LW 25:352. Heroine studies art in Paris, has
adventures, but comes out unscathed.

FOSTER, BERTHA CLEMENTIA.

004072   THE HOUSE ON THE MINE. London: H. J.
Drane, [1903] BMC.

a vixen type, when financial problems come, she
becomes an immensely successful novelist. TLS

004073   "SAINT BASIL," A NOVEL. London: H. J.
Drane, [1904] BMC.

FOSTER, CATHERINE AND FLORENCE FOSTER.

004074   "THE GOBLIN." A NOVEL. London: Gardner,
Darton, 1900 BMC NUC. (NUC: Catherine Foster only.)

ATH 90:754. Wholesome story of family and children.
Old fashioned heroine.

FOSTER, EDITH FRANCIS.

004075   MARY 'N MARY. Boston: D. Estes, [c1905]
NUC.

FOSTER, EDNA ABIGAIL.

    004076   CORDELIA'S PATHWAY OUT. Boston: Lee &
    Shepard, [1905] NUC.

    004077   HORTENSE-A DIFFICULT CHILD. Boston: Lee &
    Shepard, 1902 NUC.

FOSTER, EMILY.

    004078   HONOURED BY THE WORLD. London: Digby and
    Long, [1891] BMC.

FOSTER, FLORENCE, jt. au. See FOSTER, CATHERINE AND
FLORENCE FOSTER.

FOSTER, FRANCES G. KNOWLES.

    004079   JEHANNE OF THE GOLDEN LIPS. New York: J.
    Lane, 1910 NUC. London: Mills & Boon, 1910 BMC.

        Queen Jehanne is beauiful, wise, a genius in
        government in this historical romance. NYT
        ACAD- Historical novel.
        PW historical novel.

    004080   THE WRITTEN LAW. London: Mills & Boon,
    [1912] BMC NUC.

        TLS- Burmese story of mixed marriage.
        ATH-Heroine has infirmity of purpose.

FOSTER, M. LOUISE, pseud. See FOSTER, MARY LOUISE.

FOSTER, MABEL G. United States.

    004081   THE HEART OF THE DOCTOR; A STORY OF THE
    ITALIAN QUARTER. Boston: Houghton Mifflin, 1902 NUC.

        Love story NYT 10-18-02

FOSTER, MARY FARRINGTON. Europe.

    004082   DOTY DONTCARE: A STORY OF THE GARDEN OF
    THE ANTILLES. Boston: Estes and Lauriat, 1895 NUC BMC.

FOSTER, MARY LOUISE. 1873-1910. United States.

    004083   OLD LADY NUMBER 31. BY LOUISE FORSSLUND.
    New York: Century, 1909 BMC NUC. London: Gay and
    Hancock, 1909 BMC.

        Humor, pathos: old couple PW 4-3-09
        Sentimental TLS
        Thirty women in old age home adopt an old man rather
        than see him go off to old man's home. BKM

    004084   THE SHIP OF DREAMS; A NOVEL. BY LOUISE
    FORSSLUND. New York and London: Harper, 1902 NUC BMC.

        DIAL 11-16-02--Story of degenerate descendants sin of
        an ancestor-terrible consequences in the life of a
        young girl.
        BKM 10-02 -Love story, sentimental.

    004085   THE STORY OF SARAH. BY M. LOUISE
    FORSSLUND (M. LOUISE FOSTER). London: G. Richards,
    1901 BMC. New York: Brentano's, 1901 NUC.

        "The heroine behaves so preposterously that we wish
        the villain would carry her off but he doesn't."
        NATION '01
        Sarah-fine char. connected with members of the life
        saving station PW 3-23-01
        BKM 13 (1901) 457-458
        11-30-01 ATH

FOSTER, MILDRED.

    004086   A ROSE AMIDST SCOTCH THISTLES. London: J.
    Ouseley, [1912] BMC.

        TLS-Experience of young nurse.

FOSTER, NANCY KIER. B. 1865. Nationality Unknown.

    004087   NOT OF HER RACE. Boston: R.G. Badger,
    1911 NUC.

        Woman comes to love Mexican employed by man she's
        engaged to. PW
        So. Calif. Boston girl takes invalid sister to
        California where her fiance is in business. She grows

tired of his taking her for granted. Finds his Mexican
employee more to her liking. NYT

FOSTER, THEODOSIA MARIA (TOLL). B. 1838. United States.

    004088   THE BOYNTON NEIGHBORHOOD. BY FAYE
    HUNTINGTON. Boston: Congregational Sunday School &
    Pub. Society, [1895] NUC.

        Samuel Boynton after returning to home town and
        finding morals lax starts home bible classes. PW
        10-5-95:583

    004089   HIS FIRST CHARGE. BY FAYE HUNTINGTON.
    Boston: Lothrop, 1897 [c] NUC.

        Young minister's first parish is smack in the center
        of hop county-hops used to make beer. And he's for
        temperance. Works out the problem of what is his duty.
        PW 52:568
        LW 29:219. Temperance. Slight story.

FOTHERGILL, CAROLINE. United Kingdom.

    004090   THE COMEDY OF CECILIA; OR, AN HONOURABLE
    MAN. London: A. and C. Black, 1895 BMC NUC.

        She detests idea of marriage to Philip but he
        persists. Also her brother insists and she must marry
        with his permission or lose her fortune. Finally
        Philip "bores her into marriage only to find now that
        her fortune is secure she intends to go her way and
        leave him to go his." SR 79:797
        She has original views "determined to enjoy
        emancipation," runs away intending on a new career in
        London, this before she marries. ACAD 48:28
        BKM 3:171. Modern, intelligent heroine coerced into
        marriage with a mecieval dullard to secure her
        independent fortune. Flies to a friend who supports
        her at first but then falls for brother. Marries at
        last, but informs groom on wedding day that having
        secured her fortune, she means to lead an independent
        life and have a good time at it.
        LW. 27:75. If he says anything, she will leave him.
        Witty, "the novel of the new woman with a vengeance."

    004091   A MATTER OF TEMPERAMENT. London: A. and
    C. Black, 1897 BMC.

        Amusing story of a man who flirts when his love is
        away but who loves her all the more when she returns
        and forgives. SR 83:453
        Henrietta leaves the dr. on his own to go to Egypt to
        tend to an invalid sister. ACAD 51:400 Henrietta
        Farrington.

    004092   A POINT OF VIEW. Bristol: J. W.
    Arrowsmith, [1898] BMC.

        LIT 2:649. Philippa and her two suitors, Simon and
        Matthew.
        ACAD 53:394. A number of people and their sorting out
        into married couples.
        ATH 112:154.
        SR 85:726. Although a formula plot, there is novelty
        and interest in the "self-tormenting" Philippa and her
        relations with her three suitors.

    004093   A QUESTION OF DEGREE. London: A. and C.
    Black, 1896 BMC NUC.

        SR-Humorous heroine. Breaks engagement rather than
        live with doting mother-in-law.
        ATH 107:578. Dialogue style.
        ACAD 49:506. Epigrammatic.
        SP 77' 273. Theodora has painful interviews with
        jealous mother. she is "willful, high-spirited,
        generous." David ends up marrying someone else in six
        months. Theodora returns to London.

FOTHERGILL, JESSIE. 1851-1891. United Kingdom.

    004094   ORIOLES' DAUGHTER. New York: Tait, 1892
    [c] NUC. London: W. Heinemann, 1893 BMC.

        Fulvia Dietrich's character studied. first she seems
        weak and dependent on her father. But it's only an
        outer crust of weakness and she is not the prey of her
        heartless mother and vulgar husband but a strong
        rebel. SP 70:528.
        Minna Hastings, 28 yr. old widow, studies art in Rome,
        goes to live in Casa Dietrich where Signor Orioles is
        a waiter (was rich). Fulvia, landlady's daughter and
        Minna become friends and after Fulvia is unhappily
        married and leaves her husband, ends her days in
        Sicily as Oriole's daughter. PW 5-13-93.

Fulvia is forced to marry by mother. A dreadful
husband, repulsive. SR 75:489.
Author attacks the social custom of "marrying young
girls for money." Heroine illegitimate daughter of
Italian Signor Oriole. Returns to him in the end. CR
20, 23:184.
Endured husband for 5 years. ACAD 43:434.

FOWKES, ELLEN M.

004095   SECOND LOVE. London: T. Unwin, 1920 BMC.

TLS Guardian and ward marry. But strong conflict of
wills.

FOWL, pseud. See FISH, ANNE HARRIET.

FOWLER, ADA DAYRELL.

004096   BIRD-CHAT. BY DAYRELL TRELAWNEY. London:
Church Newspaper, 1898 BMC.

004097   THE BISHOP'S WIFE: A SKETCH. BY DAYRELL
TRELAWNEY. London: R. Bentley, 1893 BMC.

She seems to have a mystery about her but an act of
heroism at time of a fire clears the air. She was
really too anxious about her new duties and homesick.
ACAD 44:228.

004098   THE KING'S FRIEND. BY DAYRELL TRELAWNEY.
[London]: Church Newspaper, 1899 BMC.

004099   A MAN OF NO ACCOUNT. BY DAYRELL
TRELAWNEY. London: Church Newspaper, 1899 BMC. (#2 of
Records of Craysmore Village)

ACAD 54:296. Pathos of some poor people. "No. 2 of the
Records of Craysmere Village."

004100   RECORDS OF CRAYSMORE VILLAGE. BY DAYRELL
TRELAWNEY. London: Church Newspaper, 1899 BMC. (3
Numbers)

004101   THE UNBELIEVER. BY DAYRELL TRELAWNEY.
London: Church Newspaper, 1899 BMC. (#3 of Records of
Craysmore Village)

004102   WAITING FOR THE SPRING. BY DAYRELL
TRELAWNEY. London: Church Newspaper Co., [1898] NUC.
(Records of Craysmere Village, No. 1.)

FOWLER, EDITH HENRIETTA. See HAMILTON, EDITH HENRIETTA
(FOWLER).

FOWLER, ELLEN THORNEYCROFT. See FELKIN, ELLEN THORNEYCROFT
(FOWLER).

FOWLER, MABEL E.

004103   CHARITY. London: Christian Knowledge
Society, [1895] BMC.

004104   CHELVEY COURT. Bristol: Arrowsmith,
[1893] BMC.

A ghost of the old fashioned sort, an ancestral ghost.
Short novel. SR 76:497.

004105   FAITH. London: Christian Knowledge
Society, [1894] BMC.

004106   IN FAIR FLORENCE: A ROMANCE. Clevedon: A.
H. Ransford, [1896] BMC.

004107   THE STORY OF PRISCILLA. London: Christian
Knowledge Society, [1899] BMC.

FOX, ALICE THEODORA (RAIKES) WILSON. B. 1863. United
Kingdom.

004108   HEARTS AND CORONETS; A STORY FOR YOUNG
PEOPLE. New York: Macmillan, 1910 BMC NUC.

BM- "sweet novel"
PW-"sweet novel"
ACAD -

004109   LOVE IN THE BALANCE. A NOVEL. London:
F.V. White, 1911 BMC.

more for girls TLS

004110   A REGULAR MADAM. London: Macmillan, 1912
BMC NUC.

Lady Barbara is "a little too mannish." When her
father marries again, she won't be civil, is sent to
young ladies' seminary, shoots a highwayman with his
own pistol, runs off to Canada to search for her
brother, finds him and lover. Many adventures among
the Indians. Time, close of 18th c. ACAD
TLS--book for girls.

004111   TOO NEAR THE THRONE; AN HISTORICAL
ROMANCE. London: S.P.C.K., [1918] BMC.

FOX, DAVID, pseud. See OSTRANDER, ISABEL EGENTON.

FOX, FRANCES BARTON. B. 1887. United States.

004112   THE HEART OF ARETHUSA. Boston: Small,
Maynard, [c1918] NUC.

PW-love story.

FOX, MARION INEZ DOUGLAS (WARD). B. 1885. United Kingdom.

004113   APE'S FACE. London and New York: J. Lane,
1914 BMC NUC.

"Following the tradition of their house, that one
member of the family had always slain another every
hundred years at Christmastide, the Delane-Mortons on
Christmas Eve find themselves in the grasp of the
monster Hatred. Ordinarily an amicable household,
brother now rises against brother in a quarrel over a
woman, and the master of the house awakes from sleep
to find himself in the clutches of a bat-like creature
that almost murders him. The intuition and courage of
a girl, the only daughter of the house, prevents
tragedy, restores peace and goodwill, and breaks the
power of the curse. Incidentally, the strange night's
work has a romantic ending for the girl, Ape's-face,
so nicknamed by her brothers." PW 11/7/14:1447
TLS 13:427 There is a man named Armstrong visiting.
Ape's-face, whose face is like a monkey's and who has
a half-soft, half-rasping voice, convinces him of the
reality of the curse.
NYT 1914:517 50 yr. old Armstrong is terrified.

004114   THE BOUNTIFUL HOUR. London and New York:
J. Lane, 1912 BMC NUC.

Charlotte's development, meets a young man, has run
away from home several times since her mother died; is
independent of father. "Miss Fox maintains the
atmosphere of the 18th century so successfully that we
really feel Charlotte to be a rapturously
unconventional person. Fancy a woman taking the
liberty of thinking for herself and justifying
sentiments she ought not even to harbor!" SR
PW hist
ATH

004115   THE HAND OF THE NORTH. London: J. Lane,
1910 NUC. New York: J. Lane, 1911 NUC BMC.

hist. romance PW, SR
ACAD--Male hero.

004116   THE MYSTERY KEEPERS. London and New York:
J. Lane, 1919 BMC NUC.

mystery-family in which eldest son is found dead in
each generation NYT 8-24-28 434

004117   THE SEVEN NIGHTS: A JOURNEY. London: E.
Stock, [1910] BMC NUC.

TLS hist rom. peasant revolt of 14th c.
ATH--ditto

FRANCIS, M. E., pseud. See BLUNDELL, MARY E. (SWEETMAN).

FRANCIS, MARIAN.

004118   WHERE HONOUR LEADS. London: Hutchinson,
[1902] BMC.

FRANCIS, MARY CORNELIA. United States.

004119   DALRYMPLE. New York: J. Pott, 1904 NUC.

NYT Hist. rom.

FRANCIS, MRS. See BLUNDELL, MARY E. (SWEETMAN).

FRANKAU, JULIA (DAVIS). 1864-1916. United Kingdom.

004120   BACCARAT. A NOVEL. BY FRANK DANBY.
London: W. Heinemann, 1904 BMC. Philadelphia & London:

J.B. Lippincott, 1904 NUC.

an erring wife and a husband who forgives her out of
love and duty. The last event removes the child that
might have hindered a perfect reconciliation. LBKM
27-28, p. 222.
BKM 20 1904 convent bred woman seized with madness for
gambling-falls into hands of croupier roue-forsakes
husband and children-found-rest too horrible for
reviewer to tell
NYT--Author too good to heroine
ATH author believes sexual passion most powerful force
in men and women

004121   CONCERT PITCH. BY FRANK DANBY. London:
Hutchinson, 1913 BMC NUC. New York: Macmillan, 1913
NUC.

heroine Manuella Wagner, holds our sympathy throughout
in her dealings with stepmother and lunatic husband.
Stepmother urges her to marry to be rid of her; goaded
into eloping with man she cares nothing for NYT
"This is a story of the artistic temperament. Manuella
Wagner, the daughter of a man of newly acquired
millions, after breaking two engagements that are
arranged for her by a socially ambitious step-mother,
elopes with Harston Migotti, a musical genius.
Manuella is eighteen and she learns on the day of her
wedding that in the duet of their married life she is
always to play the bass; that they two are to be one
but that he is the one they must be. To the end of her
husband's career Manuella plays the part assigned her,
but thru all her bitter experience she remains at
heart a child." BRD
composer of an English opera, deserts his wife for the
soprano who is to create the leading role in his
opera. He does so to insure her devotion to his work.
The soprano's husband shoots to kill her on stage.
Kills the composer. NYT

004122   FULL SWING. BY FRANK DANBY. Philadelphia:
J. B. Lippincott, 1914 NUC. London: Cassell, 1914 BMC.

"Hero is wild Irish lordling, the apple of his
mother's eye and the scapegrace lover of his loyal
little cousin Eunice. Out to the war in South Africa
he goes, smuggled into the service, the unsatisfactory
pupil of a brilliant army coach, the secret husband of
Gabrielle, red haired and eke a convict's widow; back
he is brought by Eunice's strong, silent love. Now, he
is "No Surrender Grindelay," the hero of a desperate
fight, freed from his siren spouse, ready to forgive
and be forgiven by his odd, generous mother, and to
marry his fair haired cousin-but no!-there are still a
hundred pages to be covered before the novel is
complete."
PW 85 5/30/14;1774
BKM-Agatha, his mother, has led empty life, unable to
bring herself to marry man who loves her and briefly
married to a drunken Irish brute. In attempting to
control her son and niece's lives for their sakes, she
brings on near-disaster after disaster, culminating in
attempt to kill son's baby by a questionalbe mrg.
SR 147:443. Agatha had too much conscience, always
chose the difficult path.

004123   THE HEART OF A CHILD. BEING PASSAGES FROM
THE EARLY LIFE OF SALLY SNAPE, LADY KIDDERMINSTER. BY
FRANK DANBY. London: Hutchinson, 1908 NUC BMC. New
York: Macmillan, [c1908] NUC.

BKM 27 1908-author's thesis is that a woman can go on
the stage and remain pure.
PW-Young impoverished woman becomes successful dancer
with the "honor of a man and heart of a child"TLS
SR-Not as the title suggests but "sexlessness and
stupidity" "for Sally in fact owed her safety to the
combination of her sexlessness and her stupidity, one
of which is so often closely related to the other, and
her virtue is a much more negative and uninteresting
affair than the author would lead us to imagine."

004124   AN INCOMPLETE ETONIAN. BY FRANK DANBY.
London: W. Heinemann, 1909 NUC BMC.

TLS focuses on a man
Vanessa Randall is a successful novelist, ill matched
to husband, much older. She never loved him, jealous
that he and her son share so much. She loves her son
passionately, is ambitious for him. He disappoints her
by leaving school to join father in his business. LBKM
Vanessa, "modern type" whose head dominates her heart
though she's wrapped up in her son. She neglects her
husband who is "consciously mediocre." SP
both son and mother awakened to reality. PW 4-24-09
Vanessa, mother, is central figure; a famous author of

fiction. She's proud of her fame; "it is the slow
devel of Vanessa, thru the bitter trials, her pride
and love, her son's choice of career and his marr.
keen study of one sort of maternal feeling NYT

004125   JOSEPH IN JEOPARDY. BY FRANK DANBY. New
York: Macmillan, 1912 NUC. London: Methuen, 1912 BMC.

PW Husb tempted by another woman, happy ending.
TLS dumb wife, dutiful and good; triumphs.
ATH-Mabel grows to fill place a woman should take in
her husband's life; Diana, the Potiphar's wife,
defeated her own ends.
BKM-Danby is anti-suffrage in this work
idea of emancipation from housework, study of unhappy
marriage. BKM 35 (1912) 294-5.
ATH
LBKM. Joseph finds happiness in fidelity to his
wedding vow even tho he loves and is loved elsewhere.
Danby is ably defending fidelity in mrg. Mabel his
wife is colourless, vulgar and disagreeably
unattractive at beginning of book-turns into a capable
delightful woman suddenly.

004126   LET THE ROOF FALL IN. BY FRANK DANBY. New
York: D. Appleton, 1910 NUC. London: Hutchinson, 1910
BMC.

Rosaleen O'Daly, young Irish girl, seduced by young
Lord who is killed. To his cousin falls the "burden of
shouldering Ranmore's sin against the girl" NYT

004127   PIGS IN CLOVER. BY FRANK DANBY. London:
W. Heinemann, 1903 BMC. Philadelphia: J. B.
Lippincott, 1903 NUC.

ATH 121, 715
BKM 17 (1903)509-13
Joan, "a clear, virile brain" lives estranged from the
husband who won't sell his farm to Louis who wants it
for gold. She will inherit farm. Louis conquers her.
One of the boldest novels in depicting sex; He's very
attracted to her wildness. She's a novelist. Then she
finds out. Their affair begins to wear out but he
wants the farm. She denies him-always level headed in
business. Later in London destitute with her child.
Louis' brother makes up for it all by marrying her in
name only. ACAD 64 509

004128   SEBASTIAN. BY FRANK DANBY. New York:
Macmillan, 1909 NUC.

See "An Incomplete Etonian"

004129   THE SPHINX'S LAWYER. BY FRANK DANBY. New
York: F. A. Stokes, [1906] NUC. London: W. Heinemann,
1906 BMC.

BKM 23 1906?
NYT unspeakable
ACAD unspeakable, stated purpose of book is to awaken
sympathy for man of genius.
ATH homosexuality- Oscar Wilde
LBKM-Sphinx is his wife

004130   THE STORY BEHIND THE VERDICT. BY FRANK
DANBY. London: Cassell, [1915] BMC. New York: Dodd,
Mead, 1915 NUC.

"Keightley Wilbur, a young man of many interests, is
called on to testify before a coroner's jury. His
testimony, cleverly contrived to conceal the truth,
achieves its end and the verdict brought in has no
relation to the facts. This incident leads him to
wonder about the stories behind other verdicts and he
sets out to investigate them. His adventures are told
in the eight chapters that follow." BRD 1915

004131   TWILIGHT. BY FRANK DANBY. New York: Dodd,
Mead, 1916 NUC. London: Hutchinson, 1916 BMC.

NYT-Woman novelist retires to house in London, ill
with neuritis. Study 1st of her illness, then of her
morphia dreams in which she learns story of previous
occupant, a woman novelist. Dr. who is attending her
continues to give her morphia because he loved dead
woman, is insane and wants to hear more about her thru
this woman's dreams. She becomes aware of his intent
as he begins to confuse her with dead woman.
Woman writer, ill and under the influence of drugs
learns her physician, Dr. Kennedy, had administered a
deadly drug to Margaret whom he loved to end her
suffering. Writer becomes involved in this story. PW
89:2/19/16:605

FRAPAN, ILSE, pseud. See AKUNIAN, ILSE (LEVIEN).

FRASER, AGNES. 1859-1944. United Kingdom.

004132   RELICS. BY FRANCES MACNAB. London: W.
Heinemann, 1893 BMC. New York: D. Appleton, 1893 NUC.

Old lovers brought together after 20 years. PW
11-4-93.
ACAD 45:166. Reminiscenses of an elderly spinster who
marries late in life. "Genial fancy"
ATH 103:11. A couple of violent incidents, Gentle
personality yet shrewd
LBKM 6:153. Her long lost lover returns at end of
story.

FRASER, AUGUSTA ZELIA (WEBB). D. 1925.

004133   LUCILLA: AN EXPERIMENT. BY ALICE SPINNER.
London: K. Paul, Trench, Trubner, 1895 BMC NUC.

She is a governess who weds a Quadroon in W. Indies
and experiences all the evils of prejudice English
society can give. All the clergy pretended to be ill
when they wanted to marry. SR 79:488
Lucilla St. John goes from England to San Jose to
teach black girls in Grove Hill College music. College
run by Colonial Govt. She's not happy in her work. At
ball meets fairly wealthy half-breed who wants to
"contract a white-alliance." Her dismal marriage. "The
intensity of W. Indian race antipathy" the social
penalties that fall on a woman reckless enough to make
such a marriage. SP 74:585
She finds out shortly what a "sensual villain he is."
The reverse situation is shown in Capt. Despard's
"capture" of a wealthy Creole young woman Liris
Morales, cultured and refined. Saved from him by
another Creole woman. This reviewer believes the
author is against mixed marriages. ACAD 47:376.
Novel emphasizes the prejudice against dark skinned
people. ATH 105:605
SR-"Social wrongs inflicted on the mixed race in the
West Indies by the whites." She is an Englishwoman of
weak brain and no principle, who makes a failure of
teaching native girls, and recklessly gives it up to
marry a "rather dark" young man, with a smooth manner
and beautiful eyes. "Contemptible though Lucilla may
be, in every way, the author yet manages to enlist our
sympathies for her when the risky experiment works out
to its tragic end."
ATH 108:155."Weary aloofness and utter social
excommunication that follow these ill-assorted unions"
"West Indians regard mixed marriages with feelings of
contempt and horror." Miss Gale, another character, is
principal of woemn's college.
SP 77:273. "If such people as Madame de Souza and
Liris Morales really exist, there is hope for the
Negro in spite of himself and of such rash
experimenters as Lucilla."

004134   A RELUCTANT EVANGELIST, AND OTHER
STORIES. BY ALICE SPINNER. London: E. Arnold, 1896 NUC
BMC.

PW 10-3-96
NYT 10-31-1896, p4. West Indies. Lives of blacks and
whites. White boy brought up by blacks becomes a fiery
politician for their rights.

004135   A STUDY IN COLOUR. BY ALICE SPINNER.
London: T. F. Unwin, 1894 NUC BMC.

SR 77:313 "...has no plot worth speaking of; it is a
description of life among the coloured inhabitants of
the West Indies, and more especially the coloured
women. What romance there is in it--if, indeed,
romance it can be called--consists in the overweening
desire by black women to have white or yellow, or, at
the very least, yellowish-brown babies, be the costs
or circumstances what they may. He would be a grave
man who could read the book from end to end without a
smile. Although it does not profess to be violently
funny. If any remarks of ours should lead ladies to
read this little book, they had better be prepared to
find the manners and morals of niggers somewhat
different from their own."
SP 72:799. Author has been living among coloured
people. "Theycare nothing about the 7th and 8th
commandments and would rather have an illegitimate
yellow baby than a legitimate black baby."
ATH 103:441.

FRASER, C. A. Canada.

004136   ATMA: A ROMANCE. BY A. C. F. Montreal: J.
Lovell, 1891 [c] NUC.

FRASER, GEORGIA. United States.

004137   CROW-STEP. New York: Witter & Kintner,
[1910] BMC NUC.

Revolutionaray War, rom PW

FRASER, JULIA AGNES.

004138   SHILRICK THE DRUMMER; OR, LOYAL AND TRUE:
A ROMANCE OF THE IRISH REBELLION OF 1798. London:
Remington, 1894 BMC NUC.

1044 pages, historical romance of Bush Rebellion of
1798. ACAD 47:78.

FRASER, MARY (CRAWFORD). 1851-1922. United Kingdom.

004139   A CHAPTER OF ACCIDENTS. London:
Macmillan, 1898 BMC.

SP 80:175. Comedy, satire, country house. Widow
pursues middle -aged male who foolishly hopes to win a
17 year old. The latter eventually manages to abandon
them together on an island for a day.
ACAD 53:93. Happy ending for the widow.

004140   A DIPLOMATIST'S WIFE IN JAPAN: LETTERS
FROM HOME TO HOME. BY MRS. HUGH FRASER. London:
Hutchinson, 1899 BMC. New York: Dodd, Mead, 1910 NUC.

Reminiscences LIT 5:81

004141   DORA MURRAY'S IDEAL AND HOW IT CAME TO
HER. London: Religious Tract Society, [1896] BMC.

004142   GIANNELLA. BY MRS. HUGH FRASER. London:
Methuen, 1909 BMC. St. Louis, Mo.: B. Herder, 1909
NUC.

hist romance involving an orphan girl TLS

004143   THE HEART OF A GEISHA. BY MRS. HUGH
FRASER. New York and London: G. P. Putnam's Sons,
[c1908] BMC NUC.

interesting account of geisha life. BKM

004144   IN THE SHADOW OF THE LORD. A ROMANCE OF
THE WASHINGTONS. By MRS. HUGH FRASER. London: Methuen,
1906 BMC NUC. New York: H. Holt, 1906 NUC.

PW novel about the G. Washington family
NYT

004145   A LITTLE GREY SHEEP; A NOVEL.
Philadelphia: J. B. Lippincott, 1901 NUC. London:
Hutchinson, 1901 BMC.

Nina, two stupid men, virtue is made narrow and
conventional; Nina-sacrifices her work for her friend
NYT 01
"almost violently modern" "loves and emotions of a
partly fashionable, partly artistic group rusticating
on the banks of the river of pleasure." ATH 3-30-08

004146   THE LOOMS OF TIME. BY MRS. HUGH FRASER.
London: Isbister, 1898 BMC. New York: D. Appleton,
1898 NUC.

SP 80:798. Charming and picturesque. Gilda travels to
Chile to see brother she hasn't seen since childhood.
Is met by an imposter. Is rescued, I think, by Captain
Reggie McCalmont, whom she met on boat.
NYT 1898:485. Gilda, wealthy, beautiful, self-reliant,
and aristocratic meets Reginald on boat bound for S.
America. Romance on boat, but when shore is reached,
turns to melodrama with cursed abandoned gold mine
part of the story.
LW 29:339. Modern life on a ranch in Chile.
PW-Gilda has come to Chile to find out what is wrong
with her property. McCalmont helps her defend her
rights.

004147   A MAID OF JAPAN. BY MRS. HUGH FRASER. New
York: H. Holt, 1905 NUC.

Idyllic Madame Butterfly situation PW 6-17-05
a human flower NYT 446,05

004148   MARNA'S MUTINY. BY MRS. HUGH FRASER.
London: Hutchinson, 1901 BMC. New York: Dodd, Mead,
1901 NUC.

Marna, wilful daughter of Scand. Consul in Japan,
mutinies vs her father's 2nd marr.; Betty is an

unconventional woman having a sordid affair LBKM 9-01
BKM review 13 (1901) 306-7

004149   PALLADIA. BY MRS. HUGH FRASER. London:
1896 BMC. New York and London: Macmillan, 1896 NUC
BMC.

ACAD 50:560. Book is full of characters, many of them
die (there are two dynamite explosions, among other
misfortunes. Palladia is heroine, illegitimate
daughter of a gypsy. Her father arranges her mrge. to
a duke; she eventually is wife of Johnny (after Duke's
death).
SP 77:943
Tragic lives in time of white tsar. A princess and
grand duke forced to marry and are wretched. BKM 5:352

004150   THE SPLENDID PORSENNA. BY MRS. HUGH
FRASER. London: Hutchinson, 1899 BMC. Philadelphia: J.
B. Lippincott, 1900 NUC.

Modern Roman society. Porsenna is a wicked count who
marries an English woman and bullies her. LIT 5:519
"To read the horrible end of the marriage between the
maniac scion of the house and the beautiful English
girl is to feel shocked." LBKM 17:89.
He's shot in a duel; wife weds an old friend. SP
83:754
CR 36:182. English and American girls shouldn't marry
Italians. Porsenna tries "daggers, poison, pistols,
and finally drops her into the vault..."

004151   THE STOLEN EMPEROR, A TALE OF OLD JAPAN.
BY MRS. HUGH FRASER. London: J. Long, 1903 BMC NUC.
New York: Dodd, Mead, 1904 NUC.

Hist Japanese novel, the Empress mother a noble woman
ACAD 65, 414
PW- story of old Japan, baby is kidnapped is restored
through efforts of mother who is "a striking figure"

FRASER, MRS. ALEXANDER.   Nationality Unknown.

004152   A MAYFAIR TRAGEDY. London: F. V. White,
1894 BMC.

004153   A MODERN BRIDEGROOM. London: F. V. White,
1893 BMC 1895 NUC.

An English social novel in which Aileen Ferrer jilts
her betrothed, and believing she loves Sittart,
marries him. Soon after, he's unfaithful. Tragic and
sensational consequences follow. PW 1-7-93.

FRASER, MRS. ALICK.

004154   THE MINISTER'S MARRIAGE. London: J.
Ouseley, [1912] BMC.

ATH-male hero.

FRASER, MRS. HUGH.   See FRASER, MARY (CRAWFORD).

FRAZIER, ESTHER YATES.   United States.

004155   PEARL: AN OCEAN WAIF. Denver, Col.: The
Reed Pub. Co., 1903 NUC.

FREEMAN, MARY ELEANOR (WILKINS).   1852-1930.   United States.

004156   THE BUTTERFLY HOUSE. New York: Dodd,
Mead, 1912 NUC.

PW-bored woman in suburban community tries to do
something worthwhile.
NYT-Cranford like-, part of town in commuting distance
of New York, very few men. Adolesc. young woman is
secretly writing successful novels.

004157   BY THE LIGHT OF THE SOUL; A NOVEL. New
York and London: Harper, 1906 BMC NUC.

intimate story of a young girl's heart devotion to
impetuous selfish sister PW 1-26-07
Middle-class American girl's relationship to father,
stepma and half-sister. Part I: Faithful to mother's
memory. Part II: faithful to self TLS
girl's devel; childhood-?womanhood, ma dies, pa
remarries, hurried into a boy-girl marriage, love for
her half-sister. TLS
Tragic effect on woman's life of a concealed marriage
which is no real marriage. Maria Edgham (15 or 16)
learns her half-sister whom she loves is lost. Sets
out to find her with two friends, one male. Because
they must be away overnight Maria's convinced to marry
the boy to preserve their reputations. Maria becomes a

teacher BKM
both under twenty NYT

004158   THE DEBTOR; A NOVEL. London and New York:
Harper, 1905 BMC NUC.

story of a family PW
The chief debtor's efforts to earn money. ACAD 1177,05

004159   "DOC" GORDON. New York and London:
Authors and Newspapers Association, 1906 NUC. Toronto:
McLeod and Allen, [c1906] BMC NUC.

love in a tangle of horror and mystery LBKM 9-07 212
ACAD
Dr Gordon passes off his wife as a sister 95-119 SR

004160   EVELINA'S GARDEN. BY MARY E. WILKINS. New
York and London: Harper, 1899 NUC.

004161   THE GREEN DOOR. New York: Moffat, Yard,
1910 NUC. London: Gay and Hancock, 1912 BMC.

girl steps thru green door to life in the past-lives
as grandma had, learns to appreciate her life. NYT
girls' book NYT

004162   THE HEART'S HIGHWAY; A ROMANCE OF
VIRGINIA IN THE SEVENTEENTH CENTURY. BY MARY E.
WILKINS. London: J. Murray, 1900 BMC. New York:
Doubleday, Page, 1900 NUC.

NYT 1900:405. Virginia, 17th c. Romance. First
historical romance by author. Mary Cavendish is
heroine.
NYT 1900: 418. Similar to To Have and To Hold. Hero is
a convict.
CR 37:276. She sits beside him in the stocks.

004163   IN COLONIAL TIMES; THE ADVENTURES OF ANN,
THE BOUND GIRL OF SAMUEL WALES, OF BRAINTREE, IN THE
PROVINCE OF MASSACHUSETTS BAY. BY MARY E. WILKINS.
Boston: Lothrop, 1899 [c] NUC.

004164   THE JAMESONS. BY MARY E. WILKINS. New
York and London: Doubleday, McClure, 1899 BMC NUC.

N.E. "an emancipated New Yorker, the maitresse femme
of a meek and unsuccessful merchant." The two descend
on a small N.E. village and transform it with their
modern ideas of hygiene, dress, literature, etc. The
strong-minded woman has a weak stomach--carries on a
crusade against cake. Introduces Ibsen to the
community. Love story of Mrs. Jameson's daughter. SP
83:535
A caricature: Mrs. Jameson, nervous, dyspeptic--wants
to elevate rustic Linnville. Does ridiculous things
like put socks on chickens. CR 35:746
Humorous. Narrative. Plain and rural New England
widow. Set in Linnville. The Jamesons come to live
where they can save money. She practices all her
reforms. Minor character is Mrs. Lucy Beers Wright, a
famous author, who comes to read from her works but
Mrs. Jameson takes up the time. Her reform
efforts--bringing Ibsen into sewing circle, for
instance, made humorous. NYT 5-27-99,355

004165   JANE FIELD: A NOVEL. BY MARY E. WILKINS.
London: Osgood & McIlvaine, 1892 BMC. New York:
Harper, 1893 NUC.

SR 74:774. Three or four old women, among them Jane
impersonated her sister for an inheritance for her
sick daughter. Women are "rough, uneducated and
unattractive," each with a strong personality.
PW-story of middle-aged NE widow struggling to provide
for her daughter who is fading under poor fare and
hard work. Temptation comes to which she yields for
sake of child.
Widow with daughter lives in NE. Mother is anxious
about Lois' health-walks too far in the sun to teach
school. Letter arrives for Jane Field's now dead
sister concerning an inheritance. Jane decides to
impersonate her sister Esther. When Lois learns the
deceit, is as cruel as youth can be. When the money
comes, Jane refuses to take that which she denied her
identity to get. She and daughter are half starved on
what they earn. And then Jane confesses endlessly to
people on the street till she regains her balance. Her
daughter gains her health and romance. LW 1893:3.
They live on the wealth. Then Jane becomes deranged
from her guilt. CR 14, 20:126.

004166   JEROME, A POOR MAN: A NOVEL. BY MARY E.
WILKINS. New York and London: Harper, 1897 NUC 1898
BMC.

Covers many years. Good study of half a dozen chars.
Focus on farmer's son-farmer disappears and this boy
of 12 must support family. His struggle to free mother
from debt, his love for Lucinda. SP 79:604.
N. E. His mother is crippled, sister Elmira is
younger, struggles to pay mortgage. The unfolding of
his char-his pride, honesty . ACAD 52 Fic Sup 99.
He would die rather than go back on his word. won't
keep an inheritance that is not rightfully his though
it means he can have all the good things if he does.
His haunting fear of not being able to pay the
mortgage. Grasping local doctor and grocer. His love
for Lucinda that he is so slow in admitting to her.
Ascetic, Grim N. E. Life. NYT 9-4-97,3.

004167   MADELON: A NOVEL. BY MARY E. WILKINS. New
York: Harper, 1896 NUC. London: Osgood, 1896 BMC.

LRKM 10:85. Passionate Madelon loves Fickle Burr, is
loved by him and Lot. In a burst of anger at a dance
she stabs Burr but gets Lot by mistake. Burr is
accused of the crime, no one believing Madelon's
self-accusations. Lot recovers and saves Burr by
stating that he stabbed himself, in exchange for
Madelon's consenting to marry him. He releases her on
the eve of their mrge; she goes back to Burr, but the
crime still pursues them and Lot finally kills himself
to free them.
SR 82:16. Wildly beautiful talented half-breed.
BKM 3:360. Subtle, unlike any of author's previous
work.

004168   PEMBROKE; A NOVEL. BY MARY E. WILKINS
London: Osgood, McIlvaine, 1894 BMC. New York: Harper,
[c1894] NUC.

SR 77:667. Charlotte and Barney kept apart by quarrel
between Barney and her father. Deborah, sternly
religious woman kills her child after MD's warning not
to rod him. Her daughter's fall, who for years after
her marriage lives in memory of her shame.
SP 72:858. Characters with an incapacity for willing
themselves to do what they want to do.
ATH 103:739. An indictment of obstinancy.
LW 25:147. Deborah is a monster, Barney an ass,
Charlotte to be pitied.

004169   THE PORTION OF LABOR. BY MARY E. WILKINS.
New York and London: Harper, 1901 BMC NUC.

intell; drawn beyond circle of home; she's her lover's
uncompromising judge; factory workers Ellen-indep char
PW 11-16-01
Leader of a strike, ideal of womanhood finding its
highest recompense in work study of her growth from
childhood

004170   THE SHOULDERS OF ATLAS; A NOVEL. New York
and London: Harper, 1908 BMC NUC.

TLS-Lucy Ayres' "primitive instincts amount to a
disease"
ATH-Also a strong middle-aged woman
BKM-Older couple inherit a fortune but are too habit
bound to enjoy it. Lucy attempts to poison two women
she is jealous of
NYT-"More than one young person whose symptoms are
abnormal." Study of a conscience of a plain New
England woman.
"Elderly couple, Sylvia Whitman and her husband, who
come into possession of a large fortune, but who have
lived their narrow and hardworking life so long that
they are unable to enjoy the newly acquired treasure.
Horace Allen, the principal of the village school,
falls in love with Rose Fletcher, a young girl living
with the Whitmans, and whom Sylvia Whitman believes to
be the rightful heir to the fortune. She does not
confess her belief, however, until the eve of the
girl's wedding. Then it is discovered that she has
been mistaken. Another interesting character is Lucy
Ayres, who becomes infatuated with Horace Allen, and
jealousy leads her to attempt by poisoning the death
of two women whom she believes to be her rivals." BKM
v. 27 1908

004171   SOME OF OUR NEIGHBORS. BY MARY E.
WILKINS. London: J. M. Dent, 1898 NUC BMC.

Short stories.

004172   THE YATES PRIDE. A ROMANCE. New York and
London: Harper, 1912 BMC NUC.

PW sounds a little sentimental.
NYT sounds a little sentimental.

FREEMAN, MARY ELEANOR (WILKINS) AND FLORENCE (MORSE)
KINGSLEY.

004173   AN ALABASTER BOX. New York and London:
Appleton, 1917 BMC NUC.

Young woman's atonement for her father's crime;
father's a banker who ruins his clients and is sent to
jail. Lydia Orr wants to pay back the debts her father
owed, but she's met with such resentment toward her
father that she can hardly carry out her plan. She
must hide her identity and bring wealth to the town by
establishing water works, other reforms that bring
money. When her two suitors learn of all this, one
proves himself worthy; the other, not. NYT 4-1-17:115

FREMANTLE, ELIZABETH, pseud. See COVEY, ELIZABETH
(ROCKFORD).

FRENCH, ALICE. 1850-1934. United States.

004174   AND THE CAPTAIN ANSWERED. BY OCTAVE
THANET. Indianapolis: Bobbs-Merrill, [1917] BMC NUC.

War-hating mother tries to keep son from taking
federal oath butshe's won over. PW
There is a psychological struggle in her but when her
son goes it is expected that the patriotic sentiment
will triumph. NYT

004175   BY INHERITANCE. BY OCTAVE THANET.
Indianapolis: Bobbs-Merrill, [c1910] NUC.

Woman in South comes up against discrimination vs
blacks, sponsos mulatto through Harvard. The two have
great plans for his race, but bitter experience leads
to disillusionment. PW
BKM--she comes to believe higher education is not an
immediate need of the Negro.
NYT?--There is a fallen woman who retains her
innocence. Complex.

004176   THE CAPTURED DREAM, AND OTHER STORIES. BY
OCTAVE THANET. New York and London: Harper, 1899 NUC.

004177   THE LION'S SHARE. BY OCTAVE THANET.
Indianapolis: Bobbs-Merrill, [1907] NUC.

Love and revenge. PW
Adventure. BKM

004178   THE MAN OF THE HOUR. BY OCTAVE THANET.
Indianapolis: Bobbs-Merrill, [c1905] NUC BMC.

Woman-anarchist. Mother of main character is the
socialist. Lesson of novel-socialism is bad. Mother:
passionate Russian socialist; marr to American fails,
they separate. Story seems to focus on son who's torn
between the parents. PW 8-12-05.
Plowmaker marries Russian princess. She marries to get
out of Russia. The two are utterly irreconcilable: a
child makes things worse, they compete for its
affection. She leaves for Switzerland. Story goes on
to focus on son, grown up, who seems to choose the
father's way, not socialism. NYT 05:590.

004179   A STEP ON THE STAIR. BY OCTAVE THANET.
Indianapolis: Bobbs-Merrill, [c1913] NUC BMC.

"Dr. Roger Hamilton lay dying and nought could save
him, not even the thought of the unfinished work on
his great discovery for the relief of human suffering.
His spirit left his body and his mother came to him
and took him out beyond space and told him something
of the mysteries, as much as one just come could
grasp. Then she told him he might choose to stay or go
back, take up his burden of pain and years again and
complete his work. He chooses the latter for the sake
of suffering fellowman." PW 83:1192

004180   WE ALL. BY OCTAVE THANET. New York:
Appleton, 1891 NUC. (Southern States - Stories)

Arkansas life: local color-IND

FRENCH, ANNE RICHMOND (WARNER). 1869-1913. United States.

004181   AS QUEENS ARE WED. London: Gay and
Hancock, 1908 BMC.

TLS--love story.

004182   THE GAY AND FESTIVE CLAVERHOUSE. AN
EXTRAVAGANZA. BY ANNE WARNER. Boston: Little, Brown,
1914 BMC NUC.

NYT--a man who is about to die attempts to kill love
of a girl for him.
"If one is only two points from a title, and the world
calls one wicked and extravagant, when it is really
amused by one's pranks, it doesn't matter, you know.
That would express Claverhouse's philosophy. But when
he got ill, he became rather serious, and decided if
he had only six months to live he must kill every bit
of love Madeleine Wythe had for him. He succeeded,
only to regret his success. Then there was nothing to
do but forget the time limit, and begin all over
again." PW: 86 10-3-14:1119.

004183   HIS STORY, THEIR LETTERS [ANONYMOUS].
Chicago: F.J. Drake, [1902] NUC.

004184   HOW LESLIE LOVED. BY ANNE WARNER. Boston:
Little, Brown, 1911 NUC. New York: A. L. Burt, [1913]
NUC.

Fascinating and most open minded of American widows, a
traveler. Knows a lot of nice men, no one man can
possibly crush the life of a woman who knows a lot of
other men, she says. But ends up with one. NYT

004185   IN A MYSTERIOUS WAY. BY ANNE WARNER.
Boston: Little, Brown, 1909 NUC.

Heroine's self sacrifice; disfigured man? Loquacious
village postmistress? PW
Postmistress, storekeeper, dressmaker-has a voice in
affairs of the town. BKM

004186   JUST BETWEEN THEMSELVES. A BOOK ABOUT
DICHTENBERG. BY ANNE WARNER. Boston: Little, Brown,
1910 NUC. London: T. F. Unwin, 1910 BMC.

Six adults and small boy at German inn express
opinions freely to point of straining friendships. PW
ATH
BKM-Americans in Germany.

004187   LESLIE'S LOVERS. BY ANNE WARNER. London:
T. F. Unwin, 1911 BMC.

Amusing adventures of a merry widow from the other
side of the Atlantic. SP

004188   THE PANTHER. A TALE OF TEMPTATION. BY
ANNE WARNER. Boston: Small, Maynard, 1908 NUC.

Two souls struggle against their love for each other,
only in death does the struggle cease. BKM
"The sub-title describes this book as a Tale of
Temptation. It tells the story of two souls in their
struggle against their love for each other. The
temptation, which is as a tiny spark at first, grows
and grows until it gets almost beyond them, is
symbolised by the panther, which appears first as a
very small, soft creature, but increases in size and
power, remaining constantly by the woman. She resists
to the end, and only in death, at the hands of the
panther, does the struggle cease." BKM 28 1908-9.

004189   THE REJUVENATION OF AUNT MARY. BY ANNE
WARNER. Boston: Little, Brown, 1905 NUC. London: Gay &
Bird, 1907 BMC.

Deaf, eccentric maiden lady, guardian of several
children. Wild fun. PW

004190   SEEING ENGLAND WITH UNCLE JOHN. BY ANNE
WARNER. New York: Century, 1908 BMC NUC. London: Gay
and Hancock, 1908 BMC NUC.

PW--amusing travels.
BKM

004191   SEEING FRANCE WITH UNCLE JOHN. BY ANNE
WARNER. New York: Century, 1906 BMC NUC. London: Gay
and Bird, 1906 BMC NUC.

Pw--two girls travelling with uncle.
PZ3

004192   SUNSHINE JANE. THE STORY OF A GIRL WITH A
NOVEL MISSION. BY ANNE WARNER. Boston: Little, Brown,
1914 NUC. London: R. T. S., 1914 BMC.

"Sunshine Jane was a nurse whose mission was not to
care for sick bodies but to heal sick souls. She
belonged to a band of sunshine nurses whose religion
was New Thought. Jane believed that whatever one
wanted and had faith to be assured, that one would
have. When she came to care for her invalid aunt, who

promptly discarded the invalidism, and expounded her
beliefs to the villagers in general, the place found
itself quite upset, and as various neighbors became
converts, astonishing results ensued." PW

004193   SUSAN CLEGG AND A MAN IN THE HOUSE. BY
ANNE WARNER. Boston: Little, Brown, 1907 NUC.

Her visit to a woman's convention and views on
Republican and Democratic parties. Her boarder has
novel views about conduct of the press. BKM
Susan is a positive joy. Series of stories about her.
Her contempt for the mere male and the matrimonial
chains with which he endeavors to bind to himself the
other sex. Susan visits a woman's convention. Makes
caustic evaluation of political parties. NYT

004194   SUSAN CLEGG AND HER FRIEND MRS. LATHROP.
BY ANNE WARNER. London: Dean, [1904] BMC. Boston:
Little, Brown, 1904 NUC.

Love of scandal, a gossip of humorous commentary. LBKM
NYT

004195   SUSAN CLEGG AND HER LOVE AFFAIRS. BY ANNE
WARNER. Boston: Little, Brown, 1916 NUC BMC.

Soupy stuff PW

004196   SUSAN CLEGG AND HER NEIGHBORS' AFFAIRS.
BY ANNE WARNER. Boston: Little, Brown, 1906 NUC BMC.
London: Gay and Bird, 1906 BMC.

004197   SUSAN CLEGG, HER FRIEND AND HER
NEIGHBORS. BY ANNE WARNER. Boston: Little, Brown, 1910
NUC.

004198   THE TAMING OF AMORETTE; A COMEDY OF
MANNERS. BY ANNE WARNER. Boston: Little, Brown, 1915
NUC.

Thorough flirt who makes her husband promise to let
her go on flirting. PW
Husband enjoys taming his irresponsible wife who has a
new flirtation every week. He urges her to be generous
with kisses. She loses the desire to stray especially
when he expects her to regard his same actions with
casual regard. Tame at the end.NYT

004199   THE TIGRESS. BY ANNE WARNER. New York: W.
J. Watt, [c1916] NUC.

Beautiful "cruelly selfish" Nina Daring left India
after the "supposed suicide of husband. But she
reconsiders her ways and takes Andrew's love
seriously. PW

004200   WHEN WOMAN PROPOSES. BY ANNE WARNER.
Boston: Little, Brown, 1911 NUC.

Natalie falls in love at first sight, determines to
marry him, takes extraordinary measures to get him,
remarkable ending. Pw 9-23-11.
Satiric: decides on the man that must marry her: to
bring it about spends millions: stops an army in its
tracks when it's ordered out to stop a strike; gets
laws passed to revolutionize conditions of labor and
soldiers' salaries. Woman shown as resourceful and of
great energy, ready to cope with any and all
situations. Nathalie Arundel, young widow, at
reception spies this stranger, takes off her wedding
ring and announces "I don't want it any more because I
am going to marry that man down there." He won't marry
because salary is low. He won't marry a rich woman; so
she gives it all up. NYT

004201   A WOMAN'S WILL. BY ANNE WARNER. Boston:
Little, Brown, 1904 NUC.

PW--widow asserts she will never marry again, is
persuaded otherwise.
NYT--widow is willful, not strongwilled; light
reading.

FRENCH, LILLIE HAMILTON. 1854-1939. United States.

004202   HEZEKIAH'S WIVES. Boston: Houghton
Mifflin, 1902 NUC.

004203   MRS. VAN TWILLER'S SALON. New York: J.
Pott, 1905 NUC.

A collection of typical moderns discuss various
subjects in a modern salon. NYT 765,05

004204   MY OLD MAID'S CORNER. New York: Century,

208

1903 BMC NUC.

FRENCH, MINNIE REID. United States.

004205   A LITTLE COURT OF YESTERDAY. New York,
London, Montreal: Abbey Press, [c1900] NUC.

FRESHFIELD, FRANCES HEATH.

004206   AT ALL HAZARDS; A STORY OF THE ENGLISH
REVOLUTION. London: G. Allen, 1910 BMC.

TLS-Hist rom-
SR-Heroine with brains and spirit whose love story is
worth telling
BAKER 13-243

004207   THE WROTHAMS OF WROTHAM COURT. London:
Cassell, 1897 BMC.

LBKM 14:162. Two brothers, period of the Restoration.
One a young dramatist in London, the other a Quaker
who emigrates to New World.

FRIEDERICHS, HULDA.

004208   THE ROMANCE OF THE SALVATION ARMY. New
York and London: Cassell, 1907 NUC.

FRIVOL, LADY.

004209   THE ICE MAIDEN; A NOVEL. BY "LADY
FRIVOL". London: Greening, 1903 BMC.

FROOKS, DOROTHY. B. 1899. United States.

004210   THE AMERICAN HEART. Kansas City, Mo.:
Burton Pub. Co., [c1919] NUC.

Letters "between a patriotic American girl and a boy
of German parentage...in the German army" PW

FROTHINGHAM, EUGENIA BROOKS. B. 1874. United States.

004211   THE EVASION. Boston: Houghton Mifflin,
1906 BMC NUC.

PW--Male hero unjustly accused of cheating at poker.
NYT--Heroine who frankly shirks the higher issues.
Villain triumphs?
ACAD--Numerous evasions including author's pov.
TLS--Quiet, thoughtful tale.

004212   THE FINDING OF NORAH. Boston: Houghton
Mifflin, 1918 NUC.

PW--2 young people engaged in Boston at beginning of
war. He interpreted her aversion to war and opposition
to joining allies a s pro-Germanism. At last they
decided they could never be happy together.
NYT--He was stupid; she was not. It annoyed her to be
called pacifist or pro-German simply because she
admired the newly elected president.

004213   HER ROMAN LOVER. Boston: Houghton
Mifflin, 1911 BMC NUC.

International marriage theme. He doesn't trust her;
separation. PW
American girl marries a Roman who is jealous of
her--can't understand her harmless coquetry, her frank
comradeship of another American especially since the
American man shows he loves her. One day she wears a
ribbon her friend chose for her. Roman husband is
furious, leaves her. BKM
TLS--Love story.

004214   THE TURN OF THE ROAD. Boston: Houghton
Mifflin, 1901 NUC.

Gives up love for ambition as a singer. Rejects her
suitor year after year when he comes to her school in
Paris. When tragedy befalls him, she realizes she
cares for him. Ambitious self reliant girl. BOOK NEWS
Art is not enough to satisfy a woman. Winifred awakens
through the blindness of her lover. CR
Renounces her ambition? Devoted to her art. Conflict
of art and affection. Opera singer. Walks unscathed
through a thousand dangers. Receives respect.

004215   THE WAY OF THE WIND. Boston: Houghton
Mifflin, 1917 NUC. London: Constable, 1917 BMC.

Janet Eversly spending summer with middle aged friend
Fanny Chilworth whose half-brother of dissolute habits
is a trial to Janet's precise and competent nature;

they become engaged. She meets her fiance's
ex-mistress. He goes off to life of abstinence to
return cleansed and acceptable. TLS
Heroine attempts to reform her lover eight years
younger than self. SP
She's past 30, single, attractive; he's 23 and she
loves him, very sympathetic study of her. NYT
4-15-17,139.

FRY, E. N. LEIGH, pseud. See LEFROY, ELLA NAPIER.

FRY, SHEILA KAYE (SMITH). 1887-1956.. United Kingdom.

004216   THE CHALLENGE TO SIRIUS. BY SHEILA KAYE
SMITH. London: Nisbet, [1917] BMCNUC. New York: E. P.
Dutton, [1918] NUC.

TLS-he travels and returns middle-aged to wed his
widowed boyhood sweetheart.
SR-As a young man he goes to London for a literary
career, meets a novelist Rita and lives with her a few
years. Returns to Sussex Gorse to find Maggie married
and with large family. Makes love to her in her
"husband's kitchen" (rev), goes to U S, becomes
engaged to southern girl who is murdered by Negros
(Civil War). Is shipwrecked off Yucatan where he is in
employ of immoral priest for 11 years. Then back to
Maggie.
Man's life from little Sussex Village thru American
Civil War to forest of Yucatan, back to Sussex. PW
"He knows enough to leave his London mistress (surely
a very modern young woman for the Victorian 50's) when
the news of his country sweetheart's marriage reveals
to him his real passion. dogs her but she has no
notion to leave husband." Goes to America returns to
find her a widow, marries. BKM
Hero from 12 to 60 raised on farm; at 22 goes to
London to write. Meets a woman novelist Rita
Simons-she's quite successful. He returns to farm and
to an earlier sweetheart who is now married. He goes
to US, fights for South in Civil War. Murders and love
stories follow. NYT
Story of a man's incredible battles with fate. All the
stereotypes of women here. TLS
"A long novel handling characters and love-motives in
the author's usual way"? BAKER

004217   THE FOUR ROADS. BY SHEILA KAYE SMITH. New
York: G. H. Doran, [1919] NUC.

English village in war time. PW
Small farmers the Beatups, simple people, hardworking,
growing patriotism in the family two sharply
contrasted daughters BKM
Ivy and Nell, minor characters: Thyrza Honey, a widow,
keeps a shop. Little plot-- changes in people because
of war. NYT 9-21-19:479.

004218   GREEN APPLE HARVEST. BY SHEILA KAYE
SMITH. London and New York: Cassell, [1920] NUC.

TLS- Robert pursues sex, gets rel. becomes a preacher,
falls again, comes out of jail and is going to drown
himself, stops. What else?
SP-a psychological study.
LBKM-portrayal of an earthy man who is immoderate in
both physical and spiritual desires. Looked on by
author only with compassion for another human being-no
glamorization, no contempt. His brother's wife
remarks, "He never had any sense. He wouldn't be dead
now if he had any sense." Seems to have died in a pond
while drugged. Sussex setting no love interest.

004219   ISLE OF THORNS. BY SHEILA KAYE SMITH.
London: Constable, 1913 BMC NUC. New York: E.P.
Dutton, [1924] NUC.

Sally Adiarne a very modern heroine with no idea of
conventional morality. Attempts murder-but cannot be
called immoral. She gives the staid hero many a shock.
The story concerns life on the road-for as she
announces in the first chapter she's a gentleman
tramp. SP
Treated sympathetically. Sally Adiarne unsuccessful
novelist and gypsy has paseed through some ugly
experiences, has stabbed her lover. Takes up with show
people on the open road. TLS

004220   LITTLE ENGLAND. BY SHEILA KAYE SMITH.
London: Nisbet, [1918] BMC NUC.

TLS-non-conformity in Sussex people under influence of
war. Family of two daughters, two sons. Ivy becomes a
tram conductress. Nell, a pupil-teacher, is unable to
bring her convictions to a practical test.
War story. TLS

004221   SPELL LAND. THE STORY OF A SUSSEX FARM.
BY SHEILA KAYE SMITH. London: G. Bell, 1910 BMC NUC.
New York: E. P. Dutton, [1926] NUC.

BM-story of a Sussex Farm.
ATH-unhappy love affair. Reminiscent of Jude the
Obscure. Title refers to a farm, Claude is the central
figure. As a boy meets Emily (of a different class.)
She marries and eventually leaves her unfaithful
husband. Then meets Claude again. Here the critic
can't go on; he's so upset. Claude and Emily become
sordid. Author "turns King's evidence on her own sex?"

004222   STARBRACE. BY SHEILA KAYE SMITH. New
York: Macmillan, 1909 PW. London: G. Bell, 1909 BMC
NUC.

Historical romance. Study of a gentleman and his love
for Miss Straight-ways. TLS
Focuses on him. ATH

004223   SUSSEX GORSE: THE STORY OF A FIGHT. BY
SHEILA KAYE SMITH. New York: A.A. Knopf, 1916 NUC.
London: Nisbet, [1916] BMC NUC.

Adventure story of a man's life. PW
ATH-ambition to increase his farm and possessions.
Married a woman in order that she might bear him male
children and slowly murdered her. His children rebel
against his thralldom, son becomes a criminal and
daughter a prostitute.

004224   TAMARISK TOWN. BY SHEILA KAYE SMITH.
London, New York: Cassell, [1919] NUC BMC.

Concentrates on a male hero. TLS
Conflict of love of town and a woman. ATH
He won't give her up for town; she kills herself.
BAKER
NYT-Edward Monepenny, a visionary who dreams of
building small fishing town into a select resort. He
loves Morgan but chooses dream of city rather than
love of her. She suicides. Although he eventually
marries he belongs to Morgan completely and ends up
attempting to undo what he has built in a city he has
grown to hate. Senselessly killed by a mob of drunken
vacationers. His son and Morgan's daughter love each
other with a wraith like passion. 1920:273.
PW-governess and Moneypenny. She asks to dance with
him. He's a successful resort builder.

004225   THREE AGAINST THE WORLD. BY SHEILA KAYE
SMITH. London: Chapman & Hall, 1914 BMC NUC.

LBKM-leading love stories go hopelessly wrong. Sister
and brother realize love is sweeter in dreams than in
life.
TLS-Len dies of illness. Janey's poet lover marries
the young woman Nigel adored. A grim story. Each
brother playing in turn Orestes to Electra.
"A closely united family, two men and a girl, struggle
against circumstances. Nigel Furlonger, a musician, is
a noble charact er, but Janet is the great appeal of
the story. She is another Tess of the D'Urbervilles,
keeping her brothers straight by her love for them;
and making her great sacrifice for a man unable to
appreciate her. After the younger brother's death,
Janet and Nigel go up to London to begin life anew in
ambition for Nigel's musical career. Published in
England under title Three against the world." PW 86
9-19-14.
NYT-Furlongers are English farmers in Sussex, work
together and stick together even after return of Nigel
from prison where he has served time for doubtful
financial dealings.

004226   THE THREE FURLONGERS. BY SHEILA KAYE
SMITH. Philadelphia and London: J. B. Lippincott, 1914
NUC.

004227   THE TRAMPING METHODIST. BY SHEILA KAYE
SMITH. New York: Macmillan, 1908 PW. London: G. Bell,
1908 BMC NUC.

PW-description of Methodist village life.
TLS-male preacher hero.
ATH-his romance leads him to be arrested for murder,
ends with he and his love setting off to tramp the
roads together.
Story of crimes and dark secrets, not conventional.
LBKM

FRY, SUSANNA MARGARET DAVIDSON. 1841-1920. United States.

004228   A PARADISE VALLEY GIRL. Chicago: Woman's

Temperance Publishing Assoc., 1899 NUC.

FULCHER, CICELY.

004229   BEHIND THE WAINSCOT. London: A. Treherne,
1901 BMC.

FULLER, ANNA. 1853-1916. United States.

004230   KATHERINE DAY. New York and London: G. P.
Putnam's Sons, 1901 NUC.

Review in CR.
Katherine is a good girl, likes her parents' ideas,
grows to be a fine woman but is a dull character. NYT
01

004231   A LITERARY COURTSHIP UNDER THE AUSPICES
OF PIKE'S PEAK. New York, London: G. P. Putnam's Sons,
1893 NUC BMC.

Fortunes of a nom de guerre which ends in love. LW 93,
210.
Colorado and Pike's Peak. NATION 56 475.
One evening at a men's club, several men discuss why
women use pseudonyms. All but one agree that it's
because of double standard in criticism. John Blunt,
the exception tries to prove them wrong. Issues his
next novel under Lilian Leslie Lamb. Another Lilian
Leslie Lamb opens a correspondence with him. Amusing
incidents follow. PW 5-13-93

004232   ONE OF THE PILGRIMS: A BANK STORY. New
York and London: G. P. Putnam's Sons, 1898 NUC BMC.

About a clerk in Pilgrim Savings Bank-a man. Love,
business and adventure. ATH 113:303.
He meets a nice girl, Ruth Ware. CR 34:166.
SP 81:782 Genial, restful love story of a bank clerk
and a philanthropist.

004233   A VENETIAN JUNE. New York, London: G. P.
Putnam's Sons, 1896 NUC BMC.

BKM 4:76. Two American girls in Venice, their
romances, but mainly Venice from the tourist's eye.

FULLER, CAROLINE MACOMBER. B. 1873. United States.

004234   ACROSS THE CAMPUS: A STORY OF COLLEGE
LIFE. New York: C. Scribner's Sons, 1899 NUC.

004235   THE BRAMBLE BUSH. New York and London: D.
Appleton, 1911 BMC NUC.

Woman is greater artist than hero; but story focuses
upon hero and young girl he loves-hates PW 4-1-11
Amusing American love story. ATH
Conversations of several "arty" people who are after
all human like all of us. NYT

004236   BRUNHILDE'S PAYING GUEST. A STORY OF THE
SOUTH TODAY. New York: Century, 1907 BMC NUC.

"over 30...still unawakened, owing to her peculiar
circumstances." "conquered...by fire." PW 9-7-07
Paying guest is a New Yorker. 8 yrs younger than
landlady. He falls in love with her and wins her. BKM
Three young women take on N. Yorker as boarder;
hostess and he quarrel continually. He falls for "this
modern Brunhilde". NYT

FULTON, MARY. United Kingdom.

004237   BLIGHT. London: Duckworth, 1919 BMC.

Illustrates the blight of passion without love; career
of a typewriting heroine. TLS
Many central figures: the strong, the weak, the pagan
woman. ATH
Influence of Stanley Baird on Irene Redfern to whom he
was engaged; on Elsie Redfern whom he married and
Grace Manners with whom he had an affair. No happy
end. SR

004238   THE PLOUGH. London: Duckworth, [1919] NUC
BMC.

Young woman marries, he goes to war, she's widowed
with a child,"goes to the land and finds herself." TLS
Finds happiness with her child. ATH
SP--Patricia (heroine) urged by parents to marry
aristocrat roue refuses, is aided by his cousin Sally,
dope addict, who loves him. Sally commits suicide,
Pat's husband is killed in war, remainder of book best
part, story of her and other woman working on the

land.

FURMAN, LUCY S. 1870-1958. United States.

    004239   MOTHERING ON PERILOUS. New York:
    Macmillan, 1913 NUC BMC.

    PW 84 10/18/13:1286 "Experinces of a young woman who,
    to escape from grief and loneliness, goes to work in a
    settlement school in the Kentucky mountains. There she
    instantaneously "acquires a family" of a dozen small
    boys and henceforth finds her life " crammed with
    human interest." The ludicrously funny and sometimes
    pathetic doings of the little, untamed feudists,
    moonshiners, and hero worshippers, form the subject
    matter of the tale. Story centers about one fo the
    boys who has an "active war" in his family, and whose
    martial adventures with those of his grown-up brother
    furnish an exciting climax."
    "A young woman who, to escape from grief and
    loneliness goes to work in a settlement school in...
    Kentucky..." NYT 1913 548
    "What she found <there> and how full and rich her life
    became...pupils enough to fill heart as well as
    hands." NYT 1913, 646

    004240   SIGHT TO THE BLIND; A STORY. New York:
    Macmillan, 1914 NUC 1915 BMC.

    An account of the rural social settlement and school
    at Hindman, Ky. NUC

FURSDON, F. R. M.

    004241   THE STORY OF AMANDA. London: Simpkin and
    Marshall, 1914 BMC.

    ATH-Heroine rises from slums to wife of English
    statesman.
    TLS Lot of talk about politics inc. Suffrage.
    Manifesto for national service.

FUTRELLE, MAY (PEEL). B. 1876. United States.

    004242   LIEUTENANT WHAT'S-HIS-NAME, ELABORATED
    FROM JACQUES FUTRELLE'S THE SIMPLE CASE OF SUSAN.
    Indianapolis: Bobbs-Merrill, [c1915] NUC. London: G.
    Newnes, [1916] BMC.

    Love comedy 3-13-15 PW

    004243   SECRETARY OF FRIVOLOUS AFFAIRS.
    Indianapolis: Bobbs-Merrill, [c1911] NUC.

    Woman gets job as a kind of soc. secretary PW 8-5-11
    BKM 34 (1911)99
    Two young women deprived of wealth, one becomes social
    secretary BKM
    TLS-Becomes soc. sec. to rich family; ends in son's
    arms.

FYFE, ETHEL DUFF.

    004244   THE NINE POINTS. London: J. Long, 1908
    BMC.

    TLS-male hero's inheritance.

    004245   THE RELENTLESS GODS. London: J. Long,
    1910 BMC.

    TLS-story of a half Bengali, half Persian simple maid.

    004246   WRITTEN ON OUR FOREHEADS. London: Chapman
    and Hall, 1913 BMC.

    3 parts: I-child wife (9 years old) in Bengali; the
    Bengali homes of her father and husband. II-girl-widow
    living in English home of the Deputy Marshall of an
    Indian station: this man's wife is jealous of her.
    III-her life in a mission convent; marriage to a
    European.

FYTCHE, M. AMELIA. Canada.

    004247   KERCHIEFS TO HUNT SOULS. New York: F.T.
    Neely, 1897 NUC.

    Doris Pembroke from Canada, after teaching school for
    5 years, goes to Europe to study. A young widower
    offers her marriage on the basis of his friendship and
    respect. She wants love. Is loved in Paris by an
    artist who almost breaks her heart. PW 51:961

GALE, MARIE JOSEPHINE. Nationality Unknown.

    004248   ALICE BRENTON, A TALE OF OLD NEWPORT IN
    REVOLUTIONARY DAYS. Boston: C. M. Clark, 1909 NUC.

    Trad hist. PW 6-12-09

GALE, SARAH HELEN.

    004249   THE GRAIL BROTHERS; OR WAS IT AN
    ACCIDENT? London and New York: F.T. Neely, [1899] NUC.

    2 brothers, their sister and her fiance are yachting
    in Graftonville. One of the brothers is drowned. Then
    Natalie the sister marries. Story points to theories
    of spiritual influences. PW 55:727

GALE, ZONA. 1874-1938. United States.

    004250   BIRTH. New York: Macmillan, 1918 BMC NUC.

    PW-
    NYT Nov 17 '18, p. 490. Focus on an unlikely male
    hero, Marshall Pitt, a little freckled, awkward,
    ineffectual but kind and loving man. He marries
    Barbara, in the small village of Burage, they have a
    child, another man comes on the scene and Barbara
    leaves Pitt- and the story. Remaining half of book
    focuses on their son, a smaller Pitt, and his
    relationship to his father.
    Full-blooded young woman with a heart starving for
    "she knows not what" marries an awkared inarticulate
    man. the union ends in disaster there's a son. TLS
    Social life of small town; its simple pleasures and
    crass ignorance, snobbishness and ambition newly weds.
    Woman conscious of her good looks craves finery and
    ostentation. Man pathetic, gauche, marriage, ends in
    catastrophe the tragedy renewed in their son.
    SR
    BKM

    004251   CHRISTMAS. A STORY. New York: Macmillan,
    1912 BMC NUC.

    Old trail town experiences a depression because the
    factory is shut down and the people can't pay their
    Christmas bills. TheCommunity votes that the coming
    year there will not be Christmas gifts. A spinster of
    the community learns her sister has died & she's to
    receive the child of her dead sister. NYT

    004252   A DAUGHTER OF THE MORNING. Indianapolis:
    Bobbs-Merrill, [c1917] NUC BMC.

    Cosma wakely's devel. fr. illiterate country girl to a
    woman of "charm and usefulness." Leaves farm. Later
    the same courage helps her break away from life of
    luxury to devote self to poor. Meets man who earlier
    helped inspire her to better herself, finds he now
    loves her. He understands the revolt of modern
    women-"the drudgery which love sometimes makes so
    sweet." She tells the story from incoherent
    stammerings; she did see the tyranny around her and
    wouldn't let even love stop her from her plan to
    improve self. distinctly mod book but ends with a
    tragic marr. PW
    breaks with country lover; takes wife, child of a
    drunken brute with her when she goes to seek
    employment in the city. She's sent to school,
    improved-a lady. Becomes secretary to man who first
    inspired her to better herself. Marries but refuses to
    be absorbed in housework; tells him she's no
    mother-woman, wants to make the whole world right for
    all children. wins him over. NYT

    004253   FRIENDSHIP VILLAGE. New York: Macmillan,
    1908 BMC NUC.

    BKM 28 1908-9 not helpful
    PW-Mid-western Cranford Much of Cranford here. Miss
    Postmaster Sykes and many other Cranford-like women
    BKM "an American Cranford" SP

    004254   HEART'S KINDRED. New York: Macmillan,
    1915 NUC BMC.

    BKM 42 1915-16
    Runs away on day she's to marry, takes up with a rough
    man, softens him PW 10-16-15
    One of the big scenes takes place at the Women's Peace
    Congress, and "in the course of the action there are
    introduced bits of the speeches delivered at its
    recent session." Dedicated to those who obey "thou
    shall not kill." "the nations must cease to interrupt"
    the world's work. women from warring and neutral
    countries meet in washington "to demand that war be
    abolished." Lory Moor travels to Chicago where she and
    male friend attend a mass meeting of patriots. Lory

cries out "They're voting to kill folks." "author
believes war is organized murder." NYT

004255   THE LOVES OF PELLEAS AND ETARRE. New
York: Macmillan, 1907 BMC NUC. London: Macmillan, 1907
NUC.

Loving old couple of do-gooders. 11-2-07 PW

004256   MISS LULU BETT. New York and London: D.
Appleton, 1920 BMC NUC.

TLS- mrg. trag.
PW Mar. 1920:991-Lulu, 30-ish, lives with younger
married sister is family beast of burden. Household
cook, she eats her meals alone, does not share family
outings. Sister's highest ambition is to make herself
the mental and moral jellyfish that is her husband's
ideal of a wife. He is pompous and arrogant. When his
widely-travelled brother Ninian arrives and actually
talks to Lulu, she sees him as the only opportunity
she has ever had. Tragedy follows.
BKM-O
NYT Mar 28 '20 ;1. Ninian, Lulu discovers on her
honeymoon, already has a wife.

004257   MOTHERS TO MEN. New York: Macmillan, 1911
BMC NUC.

Mother love the great theme. NYT
Young woman adopts an orphan, causes breaking of her
engagement, later marries Professor devoted to social
work. PW 10-28-11
Reviewed in Forerunner by Gilman.

004258   NEIGHBORHOOD STORIES. New York:
Macmillan, 1914 BMC NUC.

elderly woman, prophet, creator of new utopia. In the
community animated by her ideals, social problems are
no more.
Communal life of Friendship Village. vs charity.
"Shows greatest intensity of feeling on viewing a
women's parade and the impulse that leads her to join
them" ATH

004259   ROMANCE ISLAND. Indianapolis:
Bobbs-Merrill, [1906] BMC NUC.

PW-editor transformed to rich man, sails to island.

004260   WHEN I WAS A LITTLE GIRL. New York:
Macmillan, 1913 BMC NUC.

Elusive spirit of childhood. not autobiography, nor a
continuous narrative but detached scenes in child's
life, its feelings and fantasies, illustrated by
allegories NYT

GALTON, GWENDOLEN DOUGLAS. See GASCOIGNE, GWENDOLEN
(GALTON) TRENCH.

GAMBIER, KENYON, pseud. See LATHROP, LORIN ANDREWS.

GANT, ANNA MARIA ELIZABETH. B. 1877.

004261   THE PSYCHIC CRISIS: THE PERSONAL HISTORY
AND EXPERIENCE OF ELIZABETH LEGAUNT. BY JEAN THORNTON.
Valparaiso, Ind.: Press of Wade & Wise, [c1916] NUC.

GANZ, MARIE.

004262   REBELS, INTO ANARCHY-AND OUT AGAIN. New
York: Dodd, Mead, 1920 NUC.

NYT-NY lower east side, heroine is daughter of
pushcart peddlar.
Anarchism -U. S.

GARDENER, HELEN HAMILTON (CHENOWETH). 1853-1925. United
States.

004263   PRAY YOU, SIR, WHOSE DAUGHTER? Boston,
Mass.: Arena, 1892 NUC.

ATH 100:882. Also published Pulpit, Pew, and Cradle, a
pamphlet on the ill treatment of women in Biblical
doctrines. Author introduces her novel by stating that
marriage and maternity are incidental to woman's
existence. ATH lists Brentano as publisher.
PW-"an arraignment of the injustice of men who pass
laws affecting women without allowing them
representation. A girl college graduate who has held
her own with the men with whom she has associated for
four years, fights against holding a position of
dependence in her father's household to which her

mother has become resigned.

004264   AN UNOFFICIAL PATRIOT. Boston: Arena,
1894 NUC.

GARDINER, LINDA.

004265   MRS. WYLDE: A NOVEL. London: Jarrold,
1897 BMC.

SP 81:474. Lalage is companion to her. Mrs. Wylde
turns out to be an adventuress.

004266   THE SOUND OF A VOICE. London: Hurst and
Blackett, 1897 BMC.

Heroine as a child recognizes the voice of a man and
years later identifies him as murderer of her
guardian. Sens. ATH 109:504.

GARDINER, MRS. STANLEY.

004267   WE TWO AND SHAMUS. London: Duckworth,
1913 NUC BMC.

Caravan in West Ireland; Shamus is a horse. TLS
Ireland-Desc.

GARDINER, RUTH (KIMBALL). 1872-1924. United States.

004268   THE HEART OF A GIRL. New York: A.S.
Barnes, 1905 NUC BMC.

Home is scarcely a value to Margaret, she's aloof from
her family, anxious to learn, free-thinking, utterly
secretive toward mother and sister not a "nice girl,"
The boys have a place in her life other than that
supposed by mother. Defied teachers, God, uses white
lies in meeting any difficulty. Never does author
censure her. Goodness has no appeal to her. She's
still noble, the reviewer must admit.
A young woman's friendships, disillusionments and self
realization. PW 9-16-05

004269   THE WORLD AND THE WOMAN. New York: A. S.
Barnes, 1907 NUC.

woman deserted tries to get a good match for daughter
who is "selfish, ind" and who ends up making a match
for herself. PW 11-16-07
NYT-wife deserted by husband, teaches for 20 years, he
returns but she sends him about his business and goes
to Washington with her daughter to make her way in
society.
She tries to make a good match for her independent
daughter, but the young woman makes her own match.

GARDNER, CELIA EMMELINE. B. 1844. United States.

004270   WON UNDER PROTEST: A ROMANCE. New York:
G. W. Dillingham, 1896 NUC.

PW 10-24-96. 1st person narrative. Disappointed in
love years before, heroine finds herself next door
neighbor to her fickle lover and his beloved wife.
"The writer carefully explains the various phases of
her feelings, before, when circumstances had changed,
she was 'won under protest.'"

GARDNER, ETTA M.

004271   THE OLD GRAHAM PLACE. New York, London,
Montreal: Abbey Press, [c1900] NUC.

GARDNER, MRS. S. M. H. See GARDNER, SARAH M. H.

GARDNER, SARAH M. H.

004272   THE FORTUNES OF MARGARET WELD. BY MRS. S.
M. H. GARDNER. Boston: Arena, 1894 NUC.

PW-artist at 28 loses the fortune left her by her
father and attempts to earn her living, never
hesitating to express her doubts of religion, to
demand the same moral law for men and women,
recognizing the soul in some fellow beings she meets,
but denying the existence of soul in herself. She is
finally redeemed through love. A whole souled Roman
Catholic priest and a lovely Quakeress and her son
teach Margaret many lessons. POV?
PW-in annotation for Quaker Idyls by same author: 8
studies of quaker life, one a series of purported
letters, one of which gives a striking picture of
Lucretia Mott, sitting beside a Negro slave on trial
in the Quaker City.

GARITY, MARY E.

    004273   REAL LETTERS OF A REAL GIRL. BY BETTY.
Boston, Mass.: C. M. Clark, 1909 NUC.

GARNER, MILDRED. United Kingdom.

    004274   HARMONY. London: Duckworth, [1916] NUC
BMC.

    TLS-Types of feminine perfection.
    ATH

GARNETT, MARTHA (ROSCOE). B. 1869. United Kingdom.

    004275   AMOR VINCIT. A ROMANCE OF THE
STAFFORDSHIRE MOORLANDS. BY MRS. R. S. GARNETT.
London: Duckworth, 1912 NUC BMC.

    TLS-?
    SP-Traditional story of a man who loved a vain woman,
    who dies soon in the story.
    ACAD Feud between him and man who loved his wife.

    004276   THE INFAMOUS JOHN FRIEND. BY MRS. R. S.
GARNETT. New York: H. Holt, 1909 NUC. London:
Duckworth, 1909 BMC.

    BKM v. 30, 1909-10 Discontented wife "unfortunate
frankness."
    7-31-09 PW TLS Innocent,
    simplistic heroine. ACAD
    Chastened, disciplined wife. LBKM

GARNETT, MRS. R. S. See GARNETT, MARTHA (ROSCOE).

GARNETT, OLIVIA RAYNE.

    004277   IN RUSSIA'S NIGHT. London: W. Collins,
[1918] BMC.

    TLS-Story of orphaned English girl who marries
Russian. Unhappy, she drifts into revolutionary
circle, loves, rising of 1905-tragedy-return to
England.
    LBKM-Loves Muromsky, a radical who is slain. While
trying to care for his body, she is clubbed by a
soldier and dies too.

GARRATT, EVELYN R.

    004278   AGAINST THE WORLD. London: R. T. S.,
[1910] BMC.

    004279   BETTY OF RUSHMORE. London: A. Rivers,
1916 BMC.

    TLS Dom. tale-
    ATH Dom. tale-

    004280   THE CRY. Ipswich: Smiths, 1919 BMC.

    004281   A DIAMOND IN THE ROUGH. Ipswich: Smiths,
1913 BMC.

    "Orphan" discovers mother and sisters live close by.
She insists on knowing them, marries, invites them to
wedding, mother is a diamond in the Rough. ATH

    004282   MEG OF THE HEATHER. London: R.T.S.,
[1920] BMC.

    004283   THE OLD SQUARE PEW. Ipswich: Smiths, 1904
BMC.

GARRETT, EDWARD, pseud. See MAYO, ISABELLA (FYVIE).

GARRETT, LUDA BELL. United States.

    004284   VALDA; A NOVEL. St. Louis, Mo.: Becktold
Printing & Book Mfg., 1904 NUC.

    PW-"A story of love and war with scenes in the south
and in Cuba".

GARRISON, ADELE. United States.

    004285   REVELATIONS OF A WIFE; THE STORY OF A
HONEYMOON. New York: Universal Press, [c1917] NUC.

    Madge was a teacher; marries Dick an artist.
contrasting temperaments. Madge faces the fact that
marriage has not killed her husband's admiration for
other women. Dick jealous of her, leaves. Friends help
reunite them PW

GARTEN, THEODOR HERTZ, pseud. See DE MATTOS, MRS.

GARVEY, INA. Nationality Unknown.

    004286   A COMEDY OF MAMMON. Boston: D. Estes,
[c1908] NUC. London: G. Richards, 1908 BMC.

    PW diaries kept by three girls
    ACAD satire of social butterfly.
    NYT-O-

    004287   THE DROPPING OF AN H. BEING THE STORY OF
A FAMILY COMPLICATION. London: H. J. Drane, [1901]
BMC.

    004288   ROSAMOND'S STORY: A NOVEL. London: Ward
and Downey, 1893 BMC.

    Finds marriage with the clerk very incongenial goes on
to commit many crimes, but not of her own
making-remains sympathetic throughout. ATH 101, 149
    Beautiful artistic girl raised in depressing deadening
atmosphere of London suburbs. Marries a clerk, then
his illness makes their life destitute. To support him
and children she goes on stage. A noble tries to
seduce her, but she refuses him, though husband dies
of shock when he thinks she's unfaithful. She then
marries the noble. Story skips 20 years. She's a widow
and leader of society. Accidently learns her step-son
is about to seduce a young woman. She warns the young
woman who kills herself and who turns out to be
Stella, Rosamund's own daughter. SP 70 259.
Goes on stage as Miss Vernon. ACAD 43:219.

GARVIN, MARTHA JANE. Nationality Unknown.

    004289   A BALANCE OF DESTINY. Boston: C. M.
Clark, [c1911] NUC.

GARVOCK, BLANCHE A. L.

    004290   RAYMOND'S ANGEL: A STORY OF TWO LIVES
LAID DOWN. London: E. Stock, 1896 BMC.

GASCOIGNE, GWENDOLEN (GALTON) TRENCH.

    004291   LA FENTON: A NOVEL. BY GWENDOLEN DOUGLAS
GALTON. London: Eden, 1891 BMC.

    Philip Darrel villain poisons father's mind vs
(Philip's) brother, puts father away in insane asylum,
takes over estate, finally murdered by father who now
really is mad. La Fenton is the estate. Even tried to
get his niece to marry his son. But Stella
Darrel-first loved an artist, then finds a better
mate. Also ATH 97, 405 ACAD
    England and Palermo. Stella Darrel leaves Palermo for
England with guardian suspected of murder. But the
victim is in reality alive, drugged, prisoner in La
Fenton. Stella threatened if she doesn't marry man of
guardian's choice. Horrors of old castle. SR 4-25-91,
508

    004292   "A STEP ASIDE". BY GWENDOLYN DOUGLAS
GALTON. London: H. Cox, 1893 BMC NUC.

    SP 72:138. Villainous baronet with a mad wife in
Australia marries an English woman.
    Two US-American women oldest sister marries a
bigamist-bad bold baronet who has a mad wife in Aust.
Younger sister engaged to wicked noble. Sticks to him
though she detests him and loves another. Diptheria
takes care of the baronet, drowning, the noble. Better
days come for the two heroines. But the real heroines
are the two "old maid" sisters, one ill who dies. SR
76:680. Introduces a new type of man-a "miniature
painter who trims hats and arranges draperies on his
visits to country homes"

GASKELL, CATHERINE HENRIETTA (WALLOP) MILNES. United
Kingdom.

    004293   EPISODES IN THE LIVES OF A SHROPSHIRE
LASS AND LAD. London: Smith, Elder, 1908 BMC NUC.

    004294   A WOMAN'S SOUL. London: Hurst and
Blackett, [1919] NUC BMC.

    Stories about the war and war activities. TLS
    Women run military hospital (country house converted,
German cruelties, etc.) ATH

GASTON, ANNIE BUNN (GAY). B. 1869.

    004295   THE LEGEND OF LAI-CHOW. New York: F.H.
Revell, [c1916] NUC.

GATES, ELEANOR. 1875-1951. United States.

004296   APRON-STRINGS; A STORY FOR ALL MOTHERS
WHO HAVE DAUGHTERS AND FOR ALL DAUGHTERS WHO HAVE
MOTHERS. New York: Sully and Kleinteich, 1917 BMC NUC.

Sue MIlo a woman with much love sacrifices her life to
an exacting mother; finds some outlet in caring for
orphans. And ends up taking care of brother's
illegitimate child. PW
She's 45 author never considers economic freedom for
the daughters in the work-says reviewer. NYT

004297   THE BIOGRAPHY OF A PRAIRIE GIRL. New
York: Century, 1902 NUC. London: G. P. Putnam, 1904
BMC.

DIAL 11-16-02. Not too helpful; absence of love
interest.
NYT 11-22-02. "consumed with an anomalous craving for
a college education." Physically active-horseriding
cattle stampeding, etc.

004298   CUPID: THE COW-PUNCH. New York: McClure,
1907 NUC.

Cowboy love story PW 12-7-07

004299   GOOD NIGHT (BUENAS NOCHES). New York: T.
Y. Crowell, [c1907] NUC.

004300   PHOEBE. New York: G. Sully, [c1919] BMC
NUC.

NYT-Contemporary and the new problems facing American
students. Heroine is 14 called to make a sudden
journey by mother separated from father. The
loneliness of this girl; her view of the adult world.
All is OK at the end when she gets a new mother "a
very good substitute for the old one" not really a
girl's book.

004301   THE PLOW-WOMAN. New York: McClure,
Phillips, 1906 NUC. London: Methuen, 1907 BMC.

BKM 24 1906-07--young woman farmer who takes care of
her crippled father.
NYT-Dallas Lancaster-"immature story"
Dakota pioneer woman-TLS
Her love for her childish sister and tyrannical
imbecile father.ATH
Powerful story of life in Dakota. Dallas Lancaster,
the rude life of pioneering does a man's work at the
plow, her fear of losing the land, bearing the bad
temper of father who turns her lover from the door.
BKM

004302   THE POOR LITTLE RICH GIRL. New York:
Duffield, 1912 NUC. London: Hodder and Stoughton,
[1913] BMC.

Life of millionaire's daughter in New York, her
illness. SP
From child's point of view: she neglected by all,
passed from parent to servant; almost dies. Story made
from a current play. NYT

GATEWOOD, JULIA GREENLEAF (HOWARD).

004303   WEDDED UNWOOED: A NOVEL. New York: G. W.
Dillingham, 1892 NUC.

PW-Sensational. Mystery of Odessa and Carl's marriage.

GATTLE, CAROLINE A. B. 1871. United States.

004304   INSPIRATION; A STORY OF TO-DAY. BY CAROL
GORDON. New York: G. W. Dillingham, [c1914] NUC.

PW 86 8/8/14:440 "Olga marries for money and has to
bear the news of her husband's infidelity when she is
mourning for her dead child. A canoeing accident
involving "the other women" makes Olga a widow. In
Paris she meets once more a girlhood lover, an artist,
and discovers that she had been the inspiration of his
great Salon picture which gave him at one bound both
fame and wealth. What follows proves to them both that
"Love is best."
NYT She is in love with artist when she marries, gives
her husband nothing, returns to artist and "love"
after husband dies leaving her his money. "Pinchbeck"
fiction.

GAUNT, ELEANOR.

004305   A ROMANCE OF THE IMAGINATION. London:
Digby, Long, [1894] BMC.

GAUNT, MARY. See MILLER, MARY ELIZA BAKEWELL (GAUNT).

GAY, MARIE FRANCOISE SOPHIE (NICHAULT DE LAVALETTE).
1776-1852.

004306   MARIE DE MANCINI: A ROMANTIC EPISODE OF
THE EARLY DAYS OF LOUIS XIV. BY SOPHIE GAY. London:
Lawrence and Bullen, 1898 BMC NUC. (From the French.)

ACAD 55:120. Historical romance. Reign of Louis 14th.
Paris: Dumont 1839 Historical romance of Louis XIV.
Marie is the Cardinal's niece.
The Cardinal is ambitious so he encourages the
friendship between Marie and the King. But the
Queen-mother thwarts his plan. Excellent picture of
Court of Louis XIV. LIT 4:20
She almost became the Queen for Louis loved her.
Christina of Sweden is a bizarre, unconventional
woman. LBKM 15:155

GAY, MAUDE (CLARK). B. 1876. United States.

004307   THE KNITTING OF THE SOULS. A TALE OF 17TH
CENTURY BOSTON. Boston: Lee and Shepard, 1904 NUC.

PW-historical romance of Boston

004308   PATHS CROSSING; A ROMANCE OF THE PLAINS.
Boston: C. M. Clark, 1908 NUC.

PW-two women teachers in Indian school

GAY, SOPHIE. See GAY, MARIE FRANCOISE SOPHIE (NICHAULT DE
LAVALETTE).

GAZZAM, ANNA READING.

004309   A SKETCH IN THE IDEAL: A ROMANCE
[ANONYMOUS]. Philadelphia: J. B. Lippincott, 1891 NUC.

"Crude story of love in the Indian summer of life."
Theological views are out of place. "Sentiment is
inspired." IND

GELLIE, MARY E.

004310   RAFFAN'S FOLK: A STORY OF A HIGHLAND
PARISH. London: Innes, 1891 BMC [1892] NUC.

A Scot Highland setting. Several characters: young man
who takes up farming; croter's son who becomes a
minister. ACAD
Elsie Ogilvie who is loyal to him inspite of another
lover's efforts in using forged letters. ATH 98 415
Colin Fraser from farmboy to university graduate. SR
10-3-91, 392

GEORGE, HELEN.

004311   THE CLAY'S REVENGE. London: Stephen
Swift, 1912 BMC.

ATH-wife married to effete author
TLS-st of a completely non-moral wife, book divided
into three parts: The Husband, the Father (who is not
the husband), and the Lover (who is the same person as
the father but in a new role)
ACAD Bertha marries man who loves her with his
brain-after a time the clay in her asserts itself.
Relationship then to a mere brute, attraction for each
is purely physical. Symp. with the woman-neither of
the men.

GEPPERT, DORA (HIGBEE).

004312   "UN ZE STUDIO": AN IDYL OF THE HOUSETOPS.
BY D. HIGBEE. Atlanta, Ga.: Franklin Print. and Pub.
Co., 1895 NUC.

GERARD, D. See DE LASZOWSKA, JANE EMILY (GERARD) AND
DOROTHEA (GERARD) LONGARD DE LONGGARDE.

GERARD, DOROTHEA. See DE LONGGARDE, DOROTHEA (GERARD)
LONGARD.

GERARD, E. See DE LASZOWSKA, JANE EMILY (GERARD), Also DE
LASZOWSKA, JANE EMILY (GERARD) AND DOROTHEA (GERARD)
LONGARD DE LONGGARDE.

GERARD, EMILY. See DE LASZOWSKA, JANE EMILY (GERARD).

GERARD, LOUISE. B. 1878. United Kingdom.

004313　　　　DAYS OF PROBATION. London: Mills and
Boon, 1917 BMC NUC.

Life of a probationer in a hospital-its hard daily
routine, severe discipline, tyranny of sisters and
nurses, bad food, unattractive picture of inside life
of a large hospital with a love interest. TLS

004314　　　　FLOWER-OF-THE-MOON; A ROMANCE OF THE
FOREST. London: Mills and Boon, 1914 BMC.

004315　　　　THE GOLDEN CENTIPEDE. London: Methuen,
[1910] BMC NUC. New York: E. P. Dutton, 1910 NUC.

TLS-sens. romance
ATH-sens. romance

004316　　　　THE HYENA OF KALLU. London: Methuen, 1910
BMC.

TLS-Male hero; white vs. black.
ATH-Male hero; white vs. black.

004317　　　　LIFE'S SHADOW SHOW. London: Mills and
Boon, [1916] BMC NUC.

TLS-HIstory of Lorraine who married Bramley who
already had a wife. Discovering one, she runs away and
hides herself-but, she still sees him, has a baby
("she had done wrongly and the fruit was joy"-author).
First wife dies. Lorraine becomes a writer.

004318　　　　THE MYSTERY OF "GOLDEN LOTUS". London:
Mills and Boon, 1919 BMC.

detective, love conv-ATH

004319　　　　A SPANISH VENDETTA. London: Mills and
Boon, [1920] BMC NUC.

TLS-romance

004320　　　　THE SWIMMER. London: Mills and Boon,
[1912] BMC NUC.

The swimmer is a genius, a poet-Lisle Thornton who is
not financially successful. SP
ATH-Life study of a low-class girl and her struggle,
ultimate marriage.
TLS-goes to London and becomes an author and finds
true lover.

004321　　　　A TROPICAL TANGLE. London: Mills and
Boon, [1911] BMC NUC.

Nurse in LOndon then Ashanti West Africa. TLS
Misunderstood by a patient, she adopts a forbidding
attitude. He falls in love with her and "sees her made
a fool of by a polished murderer (?)". All ends
cheerfully. ATH

004322　　　　THE VIRGIN'S TREASURE; A ROMANCE OF THE
TROPICS. London: Mills and Boon, 1915 BMC.

004323　　　　THE WITCH-CHILD: A ROMANCE OF THE SWAMP.
London: Mills and Boon, [1916] BMC.

TLS-West Africa. Author believes regiment of women is
proper order of nature in Europe and Africa. Luliya is
stolen by slave of new breed of witches from a
murdered Sp. Marquis. She is sent to study medicine in
England, returns to Africa but when later learns
Blacks killed her family, she returns to England to
found a medical mission.

GERMAINE, LOTTIE.　Nationality Unknown.

004324　　　　THE WOMAN WITH GOOD INTENTIONS. BY MEG
MERRILIES. New York: G.W. Dillingham, 1896 NUC.

PW 3-21-96. Canadian girl marries New York stock
broker. Unfortunate speculations ruin him, and to help
him pay a large debt she sacrifices her honor to the
importunities of the creditor.

GERMAINE, QUINCY, pseud.　See WRIGHT, CAROLINE.

GEROULD, KATHARINE (FULLERTON).　1879-1944.　United States.

004325　　　　A CHANGE OF AIR. New York: C. Scribner's
Sons, 1917 NUC.

Miss Wheaton wealthy woman gives her money away so
that fifty people can follow their own bent. When
she's penniless only one of them comes to her rescue
PW

GERRARD, EDITH C.

004326　　　　LOVE OR LUCRE. London: F.V. White, 1910
BMC.

TLS-secret of birth, love, mystery.

GERRY, MARGARITA (SPALDING).　1870-1939.　United States.

004327　　　　AS CAESAR'S WIFE; A NOVEL. New York and
London: Harper, 1912 BMC NUC.

PW jealous husband.
TLS political life.
BKM

004328　　　　THE FLOWERS. New York and London: Harper,
1910 NUC.

BKM friendship between old man and little boy.

004329　　　　HEART AND CHART. New York and London:
Harper, 1911 BMC NUC.

Life of a nurse PW 10-18-11
TLS exp of American nurse related in 1st person
somewhat sent. at times but knowledge of human nature

004330　　　　THE MASKS OF LOVE; A NOVEL. New York and
London: Harper, 1914 BMC NUC.

"Marjorie Spofford, cultivated, intelligent and
attractive, wanted to go on the stage, not because she
expected to make a great success or thought she had
great talent, but because she wanted adventure and to
get away from her own social class. She gets an
engagement and arranges her life exactly as if she had
only her salary to live on and no social backing. The
life behind the scenes is depicted without the
coarseness and vulgarity so frequently attributed to
it. Marjorie's love affair with Newbold, the theater
manager draws her to a gradual realization that there
must be something of the primitive brute in the manly
man, while Newbold learns that a woman can be a real
comrade." PW.
TLS-Story of Marjorie's relations with manager.

004331　　　　THE SOUND OF WATER. New York and London:
Harper, 1914 NUC BMC.

"A country house, eight miles from a Maine town and
accessible only by a rowboat, is rented at a large
figure by an apparently rich couple. Their complete
isolation arouses the suspicions of the natives. The
wife disappears, and the husband is arrested. A
country officer finds a shoe buckle, a clue which
leads him across the ocean before the mystery is
cleared up." PW 86 10/10/14 1203.
TLS 1914:476, medical myst.

004332　　　　THE TOY SHOP; A ROMANTIC STORY OF LINCOLN
THE MAN. New York and London: Harper, 1908 NUC.

Lincoln, A.-fic

GERSTENBERG, ALICE.　United States.

004333　　　　THE CONSCIENCE OF SARAH PLATT. Chicago:
A. C. McClurg, 1915 NUC.

"a woman's movement novel dealing with the expression
of one's own individuality and the human being first
and women afterward ideas." BKM 41 1915
Teacher "moulded by the influence of a last love" The
man, married, returns. The result tragedy.
PW 4-10-15 "How far can a woman be herself,
untrammeled by the weight of her childhood's narrow
training?" PW
Sarah is mid-aged, unmarried, primary school teacher
in New York City "lonely, shy, out-of-touch." A man
she used to love years before comes back into her
life, but he's now married. He takes her about, opens
her eyes to modern life. They have a comradeship but
conscience asserts itself, ends in tragedy. "The
author's purpose is evidently to make a preachment in
favor of feminism of the right of a woman to the
expression of her own individuality, to a full, free
life."

004334　　　　UNQUENCHED FIRE; A NOVEL. Boston: Small,
Maynard, [c1912] NUC. London: J. Long, 1913 BMC.

Young woman gives up her good social position and life
to be free to make her living on the stage. Her stage
career and love career "are cleverly blended."

PW-actress, comrades in marriage until she becomes a
star.
NYT-daughter of a millionaire becomes increasingly
dissatisfied with social activities. She decides to go
on stage and second third of book is devoted to her
struggles. Final third deals with her success in her
profession, and failure in personal affairs.

GESTEFELD, URSULA NEWELL. 1845-1921. United States.

004335   THE LEPROSY OF MIRIAM. New York:
Gestefeld Library and Pub. Co., 1894 NUC.

PW-she was intellectual, ambitious for power and
influence; refused to marry a man if he made public
his illegitimate son.
Miriam of Exodus spoke against Moses and was stricken
with leprosy. "Even so," says the author, "it is with
women today...." Faiing to recognize that part of our
dual nature which is the true leader to higher things,
and because of her intellectual ambition (speaking
against Moses) she has been smitten with the leprosy
of scientific materialism; and thus she is as one
dead, because not alive to her own higher nature and
true office. LW 26:58.

004336   THE MASTER OF THE MAN. Chicago: Exodus,
1907 NUC.

004337   THE WOMAN WHO DARES. New York: Lovell,
Gestefeld, [1892] NUC BMC.

Woman true to her ideals in the face of bitterest
opposition triumphs in the end-leads her husband to her
ideals. NYT 1901.
PW-"The author is a 'woman who dares' as well as her
heroine. She writes with a purpose. She holds that
women are responsible for their bondage to man, and
especially points out to wives the duty of maintaining
their individuality and asserting the rights of their
womanhood in the marriage relation. She believes that
a wife can influence her husband to control his
physical as well as his moral passions, and bring them
all into subjection to the high purpose to make of his
life the very best his talents fit him for. Not
suitable for the general novel reader."
"the most baffling of social questions...the frequent
injustice of ordinary relations between husband and
wife." Wife Murva complains that she and husband were
only lovers. LW

GHOSAL, MRS. See GHOSAL, SRIMATI SVARNA KUMARI DEVI.

GHOSAL, SRIMATI SVARNA KUMARI DEVI. 1857-1932.

004338   THE FATAL GARLAND. BY MRS. GHOSAL
(SRIMATI SVARNA KUMARI DEVI). S. K. Lahiri, 18-- NUC.
Calcutta: Kuntaline Press, [1910] BMC NUC.

NYT-15th century romance badly written by Tagore's
sister...Heroine is forceful but dies for sake of her
lover and is replaced by ultrafeminine rival. Author
deplores inequality of men and women.
The garland means betrothal. Skabti considers self
married when prince throws the garland around her
neck, but he takes the act lightly. Marries another,
unhappy, sacrifices self. ATH

004339   TO WHOM? OR AN INDIAN LOVE-STORY. BY MRS.
GHOSAL (SRIMATI SVARNAKUMARI DEVI). Calcutta: S. K.
Lahiri, [1910] NUc [1913] BMC. (Tr. from the original
Bengalee by Sovona Devi)

004340   AN UNFINISHED SONG. BY MRS. GHOSAL
(SRIMATI SVARNA KUMARI DEVI). London: T. W. Laurie,
1913 BMC. New York: Macmillan, [1913] NUC.

PW "Moni, the narrator, tells first of her childhood
in a beautiful and cultured home in Bengal. When she
was nine years old, she fell in love with Chota, a
monitor in the school. Once she heard him sing a
snatch of a song that he did not finish. Several years
later, Moni heard the song again, and on account of
his singing, this new singer won her love. Their love
episode was very unhappy, and Moni fell ill. Her
father presented another bridegroom, and with delight,
Moni heard him sing the whole song as no one else
could." 86:588.
ATH-Mrs. Ghosal is a prominent member of the Reformed
Party of Bengal which has done much to break down the
purdah. Tagore's sister and India's first woman
novelist. Insight into psychological life of Hindu
girl, whose marriage is arranged by her father.
TLS-Mrs. Ghosal is a pioneer in the movement for
education and emancipation of Indian women.

GIBB, ELEANOR HUGHES.

004341   GILBERT RAY. London: Heath, Cranton and
Ouseley, [1914] BMC.

ACAD 86:495--An idealist. Takes an interest in
industrial questions, sees through Socialism, meets a
woman he loves who refuses to marry him unless he
becomes a Socialist. Gives up marriage, drifts through
life, helping ironworkers.

004342   HIS SISTER; A NOVEL. London: J. Ouseley,
1908 BMC.

TLS--divorced brother and his sister unconventional,
sounds promising.

004343   THE SOUL OF A VILLAIN. London: J. Long,
1905 BMC.

Study of motherhood, an undisciplined affection that
leads the mother to strange lengths. Sara the daughter
is bright, irresponsible. The mother is silent,
reserved, strong willed. The two love each other
enormously. For the mother, it's a master passion, a
jealous protective instinct that causes her "to throw
herself into the breach" at the first sign of danger
to her daughter. Minute study of the growth and
ultimate transformation of a certain form of mother
love. ACAD 05:809.
Commits a sin to save her daughter. ATH 05:331.

004344   THROUGH THE RAIN. London: J. Long, 1906
BMC.

ATH--Old fashioned love story.

GIBBON, M. MORGAN. See GIBBON, MURIEL MORGAN.

GIBBON, MURIEL MORGAN. United Kingdom.

004345   JAN: A NOVEL; BY M. MORGAN GIBBON.
London: Hutchinson, [1920] BMC. Garden City, New York:
Doubleday, Page, 1920 NUC.

Wales, school and college scenes, somewhat irritating
heroine.
LBKM--Jan and her only cousin John, a childhood
playmate, are alike in their craving for freedom,
hatred of rules. They are mysteries to the world,
understand only each other, are divided by
circumstances and later by temperament. relentless
realism of ch. drawing.
PW--She sets out to become a modern woman.
NYT--Led to safe haven at end. Wholesome.

GIBBONS, LOUISE ELISE.

004346   JANET; OR, THE CHRISTMAS STOCKINGS. New
York: Knickerbocker Press, 1899 NUC.

004347   TRUTH: A NOVEL. BY LOUIS DE VILLENEUVE.
New York: Published By Author, 1894 NUC.

CR 25:444. Truth, a Southern girl, marries one of her
admirers, has a son, divorces, and marries her
godfather, an aristocratic doctor. 1,000 people are
invited to the wedding reception from New York's
fashionable world, "a small exclusive set, much to the
chagrin of the larger number, who felt the slight."
(author) He gave her all the mulled cider she wanted,
published her books at his expense and abused her
critics. But when Truth discovered he abused his
washerwoman, she decked out the ballroom as a mortuary
chapel and died.
PW--introduces psychic phenomena and spiritual
manifestations.

GIBBS, EDITH A.

004348   A DAUGHTER IN JUDGEMENT. London: J. Long,
1910 BMC.

TLS-typical romance.
ATH- insight into women. Two wronged by the same man.
Influence a young woman. A friendship between two
women.

GIBERNE, AGNES. 1845-1939.

004349   THE ANDERSONS, BROTHER AND SISTER.
London: J. Nisbet, 1894 BMC.

PW-Brother loses sight of his sister in his desire to
succeed in life until a sad experience.

004350   ANTHONY CRAGG'S TENANT. London: R. T. S.,
[1901] BMC.

004351   THE DALRYMPLES. London: J. Nisbet, 1891
BMC.

Hermoine Fitzalan was to inherit much money from her
grand uncle who expected her to marry his grand
nephew. Uncle died before he could change his will to
allow for her after his nephew shows up married to
someone else. Story shows nephew's gradual releasing
of money due her. SP 67 540

004352   THE DOINGS OF DORIS. London: R. T. S.,
[1914] BMC.

ATH--Love affairs of rector's daughter.

004353   ENID'S SILVER BOND. London: J. Nisbet,
[1898] NUC.

004354   EVERYBODY'S BUSINESS. London: J. F. Shaw,
[1898] BMC.

SR 85:24. Wholesome girls' book.

004355   IDA'S SECRET; OR, THE TOWERS OF
ICKLEDALE. London: J. F. Shaw, 1892 NUC 1893 [] BMC.

004356   LIFE IN A NUTSHELL: A STORY. London: J.
F. Shaw, [1893] BMC.

004357   LIFE'S LITTLE STAGE. London: R. T. S.,
1913 BMC.

004358   LIFE-TANGLES: OR, THE JOURNAL OF RHODA
FRITH. London: J. F. Shaw, [1896] BMC.

004359   MILES MURCHISON. London: J. Nisbet, 1894
BMC.

004360   MISS DEVEREAU, SPINSTER: A STUDY IN
DEVELOPMENT. London: Longmans, 1893 BMC.

Theme of heredity. Women "pleasantly drawn;" men
"priggish and feminine." SR 5-30-91:657.
She's put in charge of her nephew who breaks away from
her influence. Sybella a well drawn character. ATH 97,
697.
SP 72:277. Character study of narrow-minded,
talkative, confused, authoritarian woman in late 40's.
Confrontation with her nephew/ward.

004361   MISS PRIMROSE. London: J. F. Shaw, [1896]
BMC.

004362   OLD COMRADES. London: J. F. Shaw, [1896]
BMC.

SP 77:903. Colonel Tracey is a boor par excellence. A
girl is his sole companion.

004363   THE PRIDE O' THE MORNING. London: S. C.
Brown, 1905 BMC.

Phyllys raised in atmosphere of repression but rebels
against the grey monotony of her days. She leaves her
home--whole world opens up to her. Marries one of her
2 lovers. ACAD

004364   THE RACK OF THIS TOUGH WORLD. London:
Hutchinson, 1902 BMC.

A gambler and his family--review says little. LBKM
Jan. 1903:168.
Innocent man goes to prison to shield brother in law
and to save his sister agony. But brings misery to
all. TLS 1903:25.

004365   ROWENA. London: T. W. Laurie, [1906] BMC.

TLS--Sounds like a traditional love story.

004366   ROY: A TALE IN THE DAYS OF SIR JOHN
MOORE. London: G. Routledge, 1904 NUC.

English travellers held prisoners by Napoleon during
the Napoleonic Wars.

GIBERNE, I. See SIEVEKING, ISABEL GIBERNE.

GIBSON, L. S. See GIBSON, LETTICE SUSAN.

GIBSON, LETTICE SUSAN. B. 1859. United Kingdom.

004367   BURNT SPICES. BY L. S. GIBSON. London:

Chatto and Windus, 1906 BMC.

ACAD--Occult.
TLS--Occult.

004368   THE FREEMASONS. BY L. S. GIBSON. London:
Chatto and Windus, 1905 BMC.

About a Master Mason, a doctor who gets too intimate
with a lady patient--both are unhappily married. He
saves them both. LBKM
Dr. marries lady his social superior but cold: he has
numerous affairs. Another man marries a sensitive
spiritual wife, can't understand her, neglects her.
Dr. gets together with this woman. To save her and him
he makes a freemason of this man--masonic vow will
keep him in tow. ATH 05:504.

004369   THE OAKUM PICKERS. BY L. S. GIBSON.
London: Methuen, [1912] BMC NUC.

ATH--Stories of two women, both unfold tragic
consequences of unsatisfactory divorce laws.
TLS--Elizabeth Ellison married to cold and barren
professor, Mrs. Arden to a brute who finally dies in
an asylum. Both fall in love elsewhere.

004370   SHIPS OF DESIRE. BY L. S. GIBSON. London:
Chatto and Windus, 1908 BMC NUC.

TLS--Character study of women, insight, judgment young
governess.
SR--strong but wholesome, 3 pure loves. Modern story
about long engagements. SP

GIELOW, MARTHA (SAWYER). 1854?-1933. United States.

004371   THE LIGHT ON THE HILL; A ROMANCE OF THE
SOUTHERN MOUNTAINS. New York: F.H. Revell, [c1915]
NUC.

Log cabin dwellers. Appalachian people-an appeal for
them; character studies. NYT

004372   MAMMY'S REMINISCENCES AND OTHER SKETCHES.
New York: A. S. Barnes, 1898 NUC.

Sketches of Negro life that author used in her public
readings. Best is "Blow, Lil Breezes Blow" which she
composed. LW 30:1899

004373   OLD ANDY, THE MOONSHINER. [Washington,
D.C.]: [W.F. Roberts], [c1910].

"Dedicated to the work of the Southern Industrial
Educational Assoc. of Washington, D.C."

004374   OLD PLANTATION DAYS. New York: R.H.
Russell, 1902 NUC.

004375   UNCLE SAM. New York: F.H. Revell, [c1913]
NUC.

GIFT, THEO, pseud. See BOULGER, THEODORA (HAVERS).

GILBERT, GEORGE DAVID, pseud. See ARTHUR, MARY LUCY.

GILBERT, LADY. See GILBERT, ROSA (MULHOLLAND).

GILBERT, ROSA (MULHOLLAND). 1841-1921. United Kingdom.

004376   AGATHA'S HARD SAYING. BY ROSA MULHOLLAND
(LADY GILBERT). New York: Benziger, 1912 NUC.

Woman fearing her children might inherit family
tendency to drink (all died from it) decides not to
marry but to devote herself to orphans of inebriates.
"Responsible Motherhood."

004377   COUSIN SARA. A STORY OF ARTS AND CRAFTS.
BY ROSA MULHOLLAND. London: Blackie, 1909 BMC NUC.

004378   THE CRANBERRY CLAIMANTS. BY ROSA
MULHOLLAND. New York: P. J. Kenedy, [1914] NUC.

004379   CYNTHIA'S BONNET SHOP. London: Blackie,
1901 BMC NUC. New York: Scribner, 1901 PW.

004380   THE DAUGHTER IN POSSESSION; THE STORY OF
A GREAT TEMPTATION. London: Blackie, 1915 BMC.

004381   FATHER TIM. BY ROSA MULHOLLAND (LADY
GILBERT). London: Sands, 1910 NUC.

004382   A GIRL'S IDEAL. BY ROSA MULHOLLAND (LADY
GILBERT). London: Blackie, 1905 BMC. New York:

Benziger, [1905] NUC.

004383   THE GIRLS OF BANSHEE CASTLE. New York:
Mershon, [1903] NUC. (Publishing information from PW.)

004384   NANNO: A DAUGHTER OF THE STATE. BY ROSA
MULHOLLAND (LADY GILBERT. London: G. Richards, 1899
BMC NUC.

Her struggle back to respectability. Pictures of
Dublin workhouse. Full of sympathy and pathos.
SP 81:745. Ireland. Workhouse girl betrayed and
deserted at 17, Nanno, filled with fierce resolve,
becomes a farm labourer. She breaks off with man who
loves her because she refuses to reveal her past. She
makes a home for her child, wins friendship and
respect of her neighbor, finds happiness in hard work.
ACAD 55:479. Returned to the poorhouse, where she was
born, and from which a year ago, she had been turned
into the world. "For the girls to come back burdened
as Nanno was burdened is only too common an
experience."
ATH 112:786. She leaves infant at the workhouse and
goes forth to win respectability for herself and him.
She cheats, forges, deceives, and lies, concealing her
past.

004385   NARCISSA'S RING. London: Blackie, 1916
BMC.

004386   NORAH OF WATERFORD. BY ROSA MULHOLLAND
(LADY GILBERT). New York: P.J. Kenedy, 1915 NUC.

004387   O'LOGHLIN OF CLARE. BY ROSA MULHOLLAND
(LADY GILBERT). London: Sands, 1916 BMC. New York:
P.J. Kenedy, 1916 NUC.

1746-Ireland. Hugh a Protestant helps Catholic family,
converts and flees country with Brona. PW
NYT ditto
TLS ditto

004388   ONORA. London: G. Richards, 1900 BMC NUC.

LBKM 17:191. Pleasant, rural.
SP 84:212. Begins with eviction, "ends with act of
extraordinary generosity," from a woman to another
woman. Ireland
ACAD 58:106. "Irish peasant girl who after many
privations finally comes to good fortune."

004389   THE O'SHAUGHNESSY GIRLS. New York:
Benziger, [1910] NUC. London: Blackie, 1911 BMC.

004390   OUR SISTER MAISIE. BY ROSA MULHOLLAND.
London: Blackie, 1907 BMC NUC.

004391   THE RETURN OF MARY O'MURROUGH. Edinburgh:
Sands, 1908 NUC BMC.

004392   THE SQUIRE'S GRAND-DAUGHTERS. BY ROSA
MULHOLLAND. London: Burns and Oates, 1903 BMC.
Baltimore: McCauley & Kilner, [1903?] NUC.

ATH review-all about style 122, 184

004393   THE STORY OF ELLEN. London: Burns and
Oates, 1907 BMC. New York: Benziger, [1907] BMC NUC.

    parentage story TLS

004394   TERRY, OR SHE OUGHT TO HAVE BEEN A BOY.
London: Blackie, [1900] BMC. London: Blackie, [1904?]
NUC.

004395   THE TRAGEDY OF CHRIS. London: Sands, 1903
BMC. St. Louis: B. Herder, 1904 PW.

Friendship of two girls; Sheila is in a workhouse,
sells flowers with Chris; Chris gets into bad company
and disappears. Sheila searches London for her. ACAD
65 586

004396   TWIN SISTERS. AN IRISH TALE. BY ROSA
MULHOLLAND. London: Blackie, 1913 BMC NUC.

GILBREATH, OLIVE. United States.

004397   MISS AMERIKANKA; A STORY. New York and
London: Harper, [1918] BMC NUC.

PW-travel and love.
NYT-Young American girl goes to Russia during first
months of the war.

004398   RUSSIA IN TRAVAIL. London: J. Murray,

1918 NUC.

GILCHRIST, ANNIE (SOMERS). 1884-1906. United States.

004399   KATHERINE SOMERVILLE; OR THE SOUTHLAND
BEFORE AND AFTER THE CIVIL WAR. Nashville, Tenn.:
Press of Marshall and Bruce, 1906 NUC.

GILCHRIST, BETH BRADFORD. 1879-1957.

004400   CINDERELLA'S GRANDDAUGHTER. New York:
Century, 1918 BMC NUC.

PW-trad. love

GILCHRIST, ROSETTA LUCE. United States.

004401   TIBBY, A NOVEL DEALING WITH PSYCHIC
FORCES AND TELEPATHY. Washington, D.C.: Neale, 1904
NUC.

GILDER, JEANNETTE LEONARD. 1849-1916. United States.

004402   THE AUTOBIOGRAPHY OF A TOMBOY. New York:
Doubleday, Page, 1900 NUC. London: G. P. Putnam,
[1905] BMC.

NYT 1900:764. Recollection of childhood pranks, etc.
until she first started working in an office to help
support family.

004403   THE TOMBOY AT WORK. New York: Doubleday,
Page, 1904 NUC. London: Doubleday, Page, 1904 BMC.

Fic. PS 1739

GILES, FAYETTE STRATTON. United States.

004404   SHADOWS BEFORE; OR A CENTURY ONWARD. New
York: Humboldt, [1894] BMC NUC.

PW-vision of world in 1993 expressing theories of
national and individual life. BMC- no. 57 of the
Twentieth Century Library.

GILES, MARIE FLORENCE. United States.

004405   THE END OF THE JOURNEY. New York: G. W.
Dillingham, 1897 NUC.

Vera Courteney's strength and devotion to duty result
from her great temptation and sorrow. PW 51:393

004406   THOUGH YOUR SINS BE AS SCARLET. London
and New York: F. T. Neely, 1898 NUC.

PW-position of the Catholic Church on divorce brought
out--pro or con? Two sisters. One marries rich old man
for his money. Other lives with a divorced man or one
who claims to be divorced. Conventional and
unconventional virtues of the two heroines contrasted.

GILKISON, ELIZABETH.

004407   THE STORY OF A STRUGGLE: A ROMANCE OF THE
GRAMPIANS. London: A. and C. Black, 1892 BMC NUC.

ATH 99:466. Scotch clergyman, his ambitions, Elsie's
vengeance. "James's purgation through the processes of
an unfortunate marriage.
ACAD 41:539. Pragmatic, priggish minister, unhappy
marriage. "Wife takes to alcohol and opium, husband
very nearly takes to murder." "Eventually they are
restored to a better frame of mind." It's not clear
whether Elsie is his wife or the gentle girl he didn't
marry.
SR 73:660. James asked Elsie whether he should marry
her or go to Aberdeen to read for Holy Orders. She had
been brought up to sacrifice herself and told him to
go. She died of a broken heart, and her mother brought
up her sisters in a different way. Mary his wife was
ill with periods of insanity "during one of which
James met an old woman whose 'wrinkles...revealed how
frightfully she must have suffered from distress,
compression and intimidation.'"

GILL, MARY (GILL). D. 1937. United States.

004408   A STRANGE RECORD. BY MOUNT HOUMAS. New
York: Neale, 1908 NUC.

PW-woman MD has two patients in one year. Disguises
herself as a male, changes her name on diploma, moves
to Barbados and has successful practice.
NYT-Suitor finds her in Barbados about 15 yrs later;
they are on a sinking ship when he discloses he knows

who she is—she is thrown against him but we will never
know if by the force of her emotions or the lurch of
the sinking ship.

GILLMORE, INEZ HAYNES. See IRWIN, INEZ (HAYNES).

GILMAN, CHARLOTTE (PERKINS) STETSON. 1860-1935. United
  States.

    004409   THE CRUX; A NOVEL. New York: Charlton,
    1911 NUC.

    004410   MOVING THE MOUNTAIN. New York: Charlton,
    1911 NUC.

    PW—story of a man in a world of women who are equal.
    NYT—Utopia created by women who won the vote and men
    who woke up and helped them.

    004411   WHAT DIANTHA DID; A NOVEL. New York:
    Charlton, 1910 NUC. London: T.F. Unwin, 1912 BMC.

    A servant becomes a public speaker not advocating
    domestic service but housework "a la Gilman." servant
    question.
    TLS—fictionalized version of CPG's household reform.
    SP-o

    004412   THE YELLOW WALL PAPER. BY CHARLOTTE
    PERKINS STETSON. Boston: Small, Maynard, 1899 NUC.

    "...a woman's gradual mental unbalancing; she goes
    with her husband to a quiet country place for rest and
    sleeps in a room papered with a hideous yellow paper;
    her mind dwells upon its ugliness, and she imagines
    things about it, till she becomes insane." PW 55:974

GILMAN, DOROTHY FOSTER. B. 1891. United States.

    004413   THE BLOOM OF YOUTH. Boston: Small,
    Maynard, [c1916] BMC NUC.

    Leslie at Radcliffe. comes to feel her lover Herbert
    is "old-fashioned" but decides after all he is man she
    wants. Influenced by young college radical and his
    English Socialist wife. PW 89:2-19-16 p.605.
    NYT—Heroine reverts to type in the end "being a
    cultured and winsome lady, none the worse for her
    Higher Education.
    BKM (Florence F. Kelly)—relation of Radcliffe,
    Harvard, and Bostr family is scandalized by her choice
    of Radcliffe and her friends are scandalized by
    friendship with a Socialist.

GILMAN, STELLA LUCILE.

    004414   THAT DAKOTA GIRL. New York: United States
    Book, [c1892] NUC.

    LW 23:295. Nitelle M'Jarrowe "with her unusual
    accomplishments may be true to life till the most
    important crisis comes. Then with unseemly haste, she
    throws over her lover, and so neutralizes the
    favorable impression she has made." ?
    PW—Ranch life, heroine has to choose between Eastern
    lover and Western lover.

GILMAN, WENONA, pseud. See SCHOEFFEL, FLORENCE BLACKBURN
  (WHITE).

GILMER, ELIZABETH (MERIWETHER). 1861-1951.

    004415   MIRANDY. BY DOROTHY DIX. New York:
    Hearst's Internat'l Lib., 1914 NUC BMC. London: S.
    Low, 1914 BMC.

    PW 85 5/9/14 p. 1553 "There is no subject in the whole
    range of human experience that this untiring, dusky
    philosopher of the wash tubs fears to tackle. From the
    feminist question to the revision of the ten
    commandments she reviews them all and Mirandy-isms are
    as amusing as they are wise."
    BKM 0

GILMORE, MINNIE L.

    004416   A SON OF ESAU. New York: Lovell, Coryell,
    [c1892] NUC. London: G. Routledge, 1895 BMC.

    LW 23:310. "Pure and saintly Althea" and "disreputable
    persons."

    004417   THE WOMAN WHO STOOD BETWEEN. New York:
    Lovell, Coryell, [c1892] NUC. London: G. Routledge,
    1895 BMC.

PW—Narrated by hero in his prison cell awaiting
capital punishment. He is an anarchist, had met a
woman who wanted to work with him but "cannot agree to
become his wife." "His tragic end spoils his
self-appointed scheme to right the wrongs of
humanity."
Criminal in cell just before he dies tells of his
crimes, etc. and the moral of his life CR 14,20:61

GINGOLD, HELENE. See COWEN, HELENE E. A. (GINGOLD).

GIRARDOT, MARION REID. United States.

    004418   STEVE OF THE BAR GEE RANCH; A THRILLING
    STORY OF LIFE ON THE PLAINS OF COLORADO. New York and
    London: Broadway, [c1914] NUC BMC.

    Western romance 4-24-15

GIRVIN, BRENDA.

    004419   CACKLING GEESE. London: J. Long, 1909
    BMC.

    The ladies of the little world of Fern Bank, "a funny
    lot" led by Mrs. Ramsey Smith another Cranford? TLS
    Satire on suburban life ATH

    004420   THE SCHOOLGIRL AUTHOR. London:
    Hutchinson, [1920] BMC.

GIRVIN, BRENDA AND MONICA COSENS.

    004421   THE DANCING CHILD. London: Chapman &
    Hall, 1913 BMC.

    Indictment vs those who exploit children on the stage,
    the heroine an Irish child dancer. ATH
    Ethel Paton exploits adopts the child and under the
    name of Berry Trail, 10 year old wins fame at West End
    Theatre. Treated with meanness, makes the child a
    willing slave. LBKM

GLASGOW, ELLEN ANDERSON GHOLSON. 1874-1945. United States.

    004422   THE ANCIENT LAW. New York: Doubleday,
    Page, 1908 NUC. London: A. Constable, 1908 BMC NUC.

    BKM 27 1908 male hero.
    PW—male hero
    TLS—male hero ex-convict
    ACAD-o
    ATH wearisome male

    004423   THE BATTLE-GROUND. London: A. Constable,
    1902 BMC. New York: Doubleday, Page, 1902 NUC.

    "Romance of the War of the Rebellion" U.S. Civil War
    BKM May 1902- revealed nothing.
    ARENA 1902 revealed nothing
    ATH 6-28-02 revealed nothing

    004424   THE BUILDERS. London: J. Murray, 1919
    BMC. Garden City, N.Y.: Doubleday, Page, 1919 NUC.

    Va. pols. study of a sweet woman devoted to good works
    who is yet mean and stingy and selfish. Still she can
    always appear right. TLS
    Presents the misunderstood man ATH
    "takes sides with misunderstood man" BAKER, 32, 202
    Angelica Blackburn dominates the novel-fine complete
    character. All seen through Caroline Meade's eye 32,
    mature, wise trained nurse, had faced a great
    tragedy-goes to care for Angelica's ill daughter.
    Characters full grown when we meet them-same at end as
    beginning inspite of coming of war. NYT 11-2-19 609
    SP- are far sighted idealists who favor intervention
    and world peace. Conflict between Angela, frail
    looking and beautiful, posing as Martyr wife, but
    infinitely selfish, and Caroline Meade, courageous and
    high minded, loves A's magnanimous husband. Caroline
    is deceived by her pose for a long time. A. does not
    allow her husband's freedom.

    004425   THE DELIVERANCE; A ROMANCE OF THE
    VIRGINIA TOBACCO FIELDS. New York: Doubleday, Page,
    1904 NUC. London: A. Constable, 1904 BMC.

    NYT- blind woman deceived by family into believing she
    is still wealthy, Confederate States are still a
    nation, and she still has 300 slaves. "Caustic
    comments on marriage and husbands"
    LBKM -0

    004426   THE DESCENDANT: A NOVEL [ANONYMOUS]. New
    York: Harper, 1897 NUC. London and New York: Osgood,

McIlvaine, 1897 BMC.

MIchael Akershem illeg. first resents his parents,
then society that outlaws him. Va.-moves to NY.,
writes for a radical journal, becomes ed. at 26. But
still angry. Loves Rachel Gavin, a young artist-a girl
of genius. She's a Bohemian and he's very much against
marriage so they live together. He's happy with her
but still no peace for him. Meets a different
woman-the "best domestic type." Instead of realizing
what Rachel's sacrifice was, he begins to question her
easy giving in. This woman domesticates his mind,
changes his ideals. CR 26,30:353.
Study of heredity. Michael Akershem "escapes from
bondage in small Virginia village," becomes a
journalist in New York. Atacks the social order
ferociously. Attacks all social institutions. LW
28:164.

004427   LIFE AND GABRIELLA; THE STORY OF A
WOMAN'S COURAGE. Garden City, N.Y.: Doubleday, Page,
1916 NUC. London: J. Murray, 1916 BMC.

"Gabrielle turned her back resolutely upon her
traditions...set about to achieve independence and
usefulness." "refuses to be a victim" as her mother
was (Her mother reveres a husband whom she has built
up in her memory) and as her sister is (married to a
faithless man). She goes to work in face of her
mother's protests. Leaves her work to marry, but the
marriage fails. Refusing to be a victim she takes her
children and goes back to work. At 38 she's a
successful New York business woman does fall in love
but not with a Southern gentleman type but a man who
respects her as a "new woman." PW:89 1/15/1916 187-8
NYT
TLS
SR-refuses to be victimized by life no matter how
heavily handicapped.
BKM (Florence F. Kelly)-one of three family
biographies Glasgow intends. 1st, already pub., had
Virginia who was a victim (an earlier era). When
Glasgow writes 3rd, heroine will be more advanced than
Gabriella. F.F.K. says Gabriella is not in advance
guard of feminism but rather is part of group which
supports it and enjoys what has been won.

004428   THE MILLER OF OLD CHURCH. London: J.
Murray, 1911 BMC. Garden City, N.Y.: Doubleday, Page,
1911 NUC.

Va, story of two men and game laws PW 6-3-11
BKM 33 (1911) 531-2
Social classes in the So. Molly Merryweather-illeg.,
orphan, is complex-wild, loveable, gentle, passionate,
cold and hard. She longs unutterably to be free and
see life. Inherits money, travels but finds she's left
"life" at home behind her. ? BKM
Sense of humor ATH
Molly daughter of a poor white woman, artist father.
Father loved mother but marr. outside the question. So
left Molly a secret trust fund. Reviewer reads the
novel as an epic of the New South-Molly is the best of
upper and lower So. classesmarries the miller.? BKM
NYT Several soc classes trying to adjust to new econ
conditions in So-several good characters. Jonathan Gay
returns for abroad to claim his inheritance (Old So.
mansion) treated with distrust because of Molly who
"seems to care only to revenge upon the whole masc.
sex the wrong her mother suffered." Threads of past
woven into story great portrayal of character.

004429   PHASES OF AN INFERIOR PLANET. New York
and London: Harper, 1898 NUC. London: W. Heinemann,
1898 BMC.

SP 81:494. "Feverish", artistic heroine marries
scientist. They "lacerate each other's emotions."
LIT 3:524. NY boarding house, Bohemian.
ACAD 54:295. Gloomy.
ACAD 55:290. "Extraordinary and pitiless analysis of a
woman of the time." Unrelieved misery. "Mariana passes
through all the deep experiences of life and finds
nothing but illusion. She wins such a love as might be
thought to redeem any existence from despair, yet it
leads but to deeper sorrows. Motherhood brings no
consolation. It seemed inexplicable to her that women
went on travailing and giving birth." Ends in her
death. I think the hero, a priest suicides too.
ATH 112:605. Their child died. They suffered poverty.
Algarcife, her husband, is a literary man. He becomes
a priest at end of of book.
CR 33:512. "In different forms we all know the
type-the slight, dazzling restless woman whose
brilliancy is the result of her unstable nervous
equilibrium."

PW-she had come to New York from Virginia, living on a
small income, training her voice for opera.
Young woman loves luxury. Considers herself a genius.
Weds a poor scientist. She's miserable, leaves him.
Becomes very rich as a singer. Husband gives up
science becomes a priest. Years later she returns he
forgives but she dies. LBKM 15:121
"An inarticulate moan at the pain of living." She
deserts her husband solely because of poverty. But
author is sympathetic towards her. BKM 8:493.

004430   THE ROMANCE OF A PLAIN MAN. New York:
Macmillan, 1909 NUC. London: J. Murray, 1909 BMC NUC.

While he achieves, she's unhappy. When he fails she's
a true helpmate; when he's ill she's happy PW 5-22-09
Sally Mickleborough marries Ben Starr but Ben knows he
doesn't satisfy her ideal. Tries to get rich and busy,
they become two strangers. Ruin in his business brings
them together. Once more he's off to get rich, blind
to wife's loneliness. LBKM
hero narrates "the curious emptiness of the position
of the rich American woman has never been more
tellingly emphasized" "no function in life" Sally,
naturally energetic is utterly bored, welcomes chances
to maintain husband and child when his business
ruined. SP

004431   VIRGINIA. A NOVEL. Garden City, N.Y.:
Doubleday, Page, 1913 NUC. London: W. Heinemann, 1913
BMC.

"the changing So. particularly the influence upon the
women of the South of the feminist mvt." NYT.
"Telling picture of the intellectual change which has
taken place since the early eighties. Virginia
Pendleton, a lovely southern girl, marries when very
young, Oliver Treadwell, a playwright, Virginia is the
old-fashioned type of woman who lives solely for her
husband and children, and when the latter are grown-up
finds herself without occupation, bewildered by the
independence of thought and action of the new
generation and mentally outgrown by her husband. A
woman of the early eighties still, while he is a man
of the twentieth century." PW.
Virginia is "true" woman; raised to be the ideal. "Out
of her love, her self abnegation,...comes a
slow-growing crescendo of misery" "The Feminist note
is commendably mellow" ATH
"woman's position in modern life." NYT 1913, 225
"The ideals of a generation past, of woman's
subordinate place, of her sole duty of love and
self-immolation for her family meet in conflict with
the spirit of the new age, which asks a place for
woman side by side with man in the work of the world."
NYT 1913 231
"tremendous difference between girl of the 80's and
the girl of today" NYT 1913, 244
"a more powerful argument for justice to women than
all the suffrage pleas in one-and this despite the
fact that Miss Glasgow does not deal at all with
suffrage." NYT 1913, 402
Intimate study of Virginia. A Southern gentle woman
gracious, dutiful, presiding over home and children.
soft not being a rebel when her illusions are
shattered; wears a mask of outward serenity but aches
inside for her husband's infidelities and
disillusionment in her children. NYT

004432   THE VOICE OF THE PEOPLE. New York:
Doubleday, Page, 1900 BMC NUC.

NYT 1900:259. "None of the women are as lofty in soul
and as richly endowed as the Rachel of the Descendant.
They are high-bred, fascinating Southern women,
belles before marriage, loyal wives and devoted
mothers thereafter." All the characters see love in
its proper proportion; their happiness is in no way
dependent on it. Not a "sex novel." Eugenia recognizes
the limitations of her marriage, but is not
introspective. Virginia. Politics. Hero is somewhat
brutal.
BKM 11:397. Career of hero from plough to governor's
chair.
SP 85:117. Eugenia "quite content" with her marriage
although reader regrets her fate.

004433   THE WHEEL OF LIFE. New York: Doubleday,
Page, 1906 NUC. London: A. Constable, 1906 BMC NUC.

PW-"study of temperament" "half doz. mismated men and
women" Chief woman is from Va., pub. book of poems,
chooses least worthy of her suitors"
NYT-friendship between two women, Laura and Gerly
ATH-women are excellent.

GLASIER, KATHARINE SAINT JOHN (CONWAY) BRUCE. United
Kingdom.

004434   AIMEE FURNISS, SCHOLAR. A STORY. BY
KATHARINE ST. JOHN CONWAY. London: "Clarion" Office,
1896 NUC.

GLASPELL, SUSAN. See MATSON, SUSAN (GLASPELL) COOK.

GLAZEBROOK, ETHEL.

004435   THE DOWER OF EARTH. London: Percival,
1891 BMC NUC.

Modern story of Stella Graham who gave up man she
loved to marry according to her father's wishes. We
trace the sorry results of her mistake. Iphigenia is
badly treated, ill, dies in a fall; suicide? ACAD
Stella is a patient Griselda, emulates lady of
Shallott in the end. ATH 97 436
Stella is attracted to this husband Mortimer Ashton
because he's a success in politics too. But he's
coarse and egotistical. A year or two proves him a
real brute. She poisons herself. She's half bewildered
by a violent headache when she does it. "She does not
consider the effect on her father of the action of his
only child." 3-21-91, SR 358

GLEASON, ADELE. B. 1850.

004436   THE GEORGIA BELLE. New York: C. Francis,
1895 NUC.

GLENTWORTH, MARGEURITE LINTON. B. 1881. United States.

004437   THE TENTH COMMANDMENT; A ROMANCE. Boston:
Lee and Shepard, 1902 NUC. London: Gay and Bird, 1902
BMC.

BOOK NEWS 12-02 actress "whose marriage fails to
satisfy her aspirations" "question of divorce and
remarriage is fearlessly handled" author's POV?
NYT-leaves husband and 4 kids after nine years-doesn't
like them any more.

004438   A TWENTIETH CENTURY BOY. London: Gay and
Bird, 1901 BMC. Boston: Lee and Shepard, 1901 PW.

story of the boy mostly; his sister sounds interesting
"to be regarded with awe" but review focuses on the
boy. NYT

GLENWOOD, IDA, pseud. See GORTON, CYNTHIA M. R.

GLOVER, ELIZABETH, pseud. See BENNETT, MARY E.

GLYN, ALICE CORALIE CARR.

004439   A DRAMA IN DREGS: A LIFE STUDY. BY
CORALIE CARR GLYN. London: Simpkin & Marshall, 1897
BMC NUC.

004440   THE IDYLL OF THE STAR-FLOWER: AN ALLEGORY
OF LIFE. [London]: D. Nutt, 1895 BMC.

Allegory of rel and purity and true and false love. SR
80:277.
Norse hero sets out on quest for "white star flower
which shall be the healing of all nations." Eric
Sunlocke's many perilous advents. ACAD 48:183

GLYN, ANNA L. United Kingdom.

004441   FIFTY POUNDS FOR A WIFE. Bristol: J. W.
Arrowsmith, [1892] BMC. New York: H. Holt, 1892 NUC.

ATH 99:402.
CR 7-9-92 p 16. Objective tale of crime focussed on
Winifred, who is "an intermittent maniac who has
murdered her mother and who...falls in love with and
abducts herself." Gerald rescues her from "inhuman
whipping" by buying (50 lbs) her from proprietor of
traveling shows.

004442   A PEARL OF THE REALM: A STORY OF NONSUCH
PALACE IN THE REIGN OF CHARLES I. New York: Dodd,
Mead, 1896 NUC. London: Hutchinson, 1897 BMC.

Title refers to a palace. There's a Queen Henrietta
Maria and a little heroine Margarie and a wicked
guardian. London in time of Earl of Arundel. ACAD
51:327

GLYN, CORALIE CARR. See GLYN, ALICE CORALIE CARR.

GLYN, ELINOR (SUTHERLAND). 1864-1943. United Kingdom.

004443   BEYOND THE ROCKS: A LOVE STORY. London:
Duckworth, 1906 BMC. New York and London: Harper, 1906
NUC.

PW-young woman married to man of 50.
NYT-sells herself to a grocer to support father, falls
for lord, gets rid of husband thru friend's switching
of letters.
TLS-written in a girls' school manner.

004444   THE CAREER OF KATHERINE BUSH. New York:
D. Appleton, 1916 BMC NUC. London: G. Newnes, [1929]
BMC.

"what distinguishes Miss Bush is the masc. char. of
her method-courage and deliberation." "triumph of
char. which transforms the shorthand typist, daughter
of auctioneer, into a duchess." "the doctrine of
aristocratic heredity is entirely demolished by the
story." The duke dismisses all the soulless mindless
aristocratic women who fling themselves at men. "Never
once do we think of Katherine as an adventuress for
her logical brain, transparent honesty, strong common
sense, true appreciation of values that true success
in women can never be based on deceit or intrigue nor
female charm. Even the most brilliant marriage is dust
without love." TLS
Begins as stenog. for a London money lender; sees life
is a game at which the strong win; determines to win.
Becomes secretary to a great lady; a Duke proposes.
"Her conscience forces her to tell him of her early
affair." He loves her the more for honesty. PW
NYT-She rises from lower middle class family to
peerage.

004445   THE DAMSEL AND THE SAGE; A WOMAN'S
WHIMSIES. New York and London: Harper, 1903 NUC.
London: Duckworth, 1903 BMC.

A girl like Elizabeth visits sage, they exchange ideas
on men and women. She has great intuition and
courageous logic that outwits the sage's efforts to
argue women's proper place. 10-17-03 PW

004446   ELIZABETH VISITS AMERICA. London:
Duckworth, 1909 BMC NUC. New York: Duffield, 1909 NUC.

letters to Dearest Mama-TLS
"comments upon men-women relations, divorce, Mormonism
"impertinent and vivacious." ACAD

004447   FAMILY. New York: D. Appleton, 1919 NUC.

"Romance of Eng soc" "a man's devotion to the purity
of his name and descent" PW
Amaryllis Ardayne marries a wealthy man who doesn't
"unfreeze her." So she looks elsewhere. Harietta
Boleski is a vamp married twice. NYT

004448   GUINEVERE'S LOVER. New York: D. Appleton,
1913 NUC.

PW "Love story with scenes in the English country.
Guinivere at the age of 16, is forced into marriage
with a man of fifty. Story has to do with a younger
man, whom she meets after her marriage and who falls
in love with her." 83:156.

004449   HALCYONE. New York: D. Appleton, 1912
NUC. London: Duckworth, 1912 BMC NUC.

PW-love story
ATH

004450   HIS HOUR. London: Duckworth, 1910 BMC
NUC. New York: D. Appleton, 1910 NUC.

BM Wild young Russian prince and young English
widow-pilgrimage of passion.
TLS

004451   THE LETTERS OF HER MOTHER TO ELIZABETH.
London: J. Lane, 1901 NUC.

004452   LETTERS TO CAROLINE. London: Duckworth,
1914 NUC BMC.

ATH-Series of deprecating and insulting letters of
advice to schoolgirl from godmother.

004453   THE MAN AND THE MOMENT. New York: D.
Appleton, 1914 NUC. London: Duckworth, 1915 BMC.

Woman leaves husband day after wedding; years later
meet, reconciled. TLS

"she's a doormat" type of mid-victorian fiction" Ath
PW"86 10-3-14:1119-"At a critical time in their lives,
young lord Arronstown and Sabine meet. She is being
wooed by a man she does not love; he is planning to
escape from a liaison that bores him. They think that
a formal marriage, like a business contract, will take
each of them out of the dilemma. Whether the
arrangement worked out as planned or in a more intense
fashion, covers five years' time and makes the story."

004454   ONE DAY: A SEQUEL TO "THREE WEEKS"
[ANONYMOUS]. New York: Macaulay, 1909 NUC.

004455   THE PHILOSOPHY OF LOVE. London: G.
Newnes, [c1920] NUC BMC. Auburn, N.Y.: Author's Press,
[c1923] NUC.

004456   THE POINT OF VIEW. New York: D. Appleton,
1913 NUC.

PW "A young English girl goes to Rome with her
conventional aunt and uncle. She is engaged to a
narrow minded curate, but when she meets a Russian
nobleman, she realizes that she cares nothing for the
curate, and she and her Russian proceed to make short
work of her relatives' conventions and prejudices."
84:1244.
Stella Rawson engaged to English curate. But falls in
love with Russian noble while in Rome. NYT

004457   THE PRICE OF THINGS. London: Duckworth,
[1919] BMC. Auburn, N.Y.: Author's Press, [c1919] NUC.

Story of an heir and a great estate. A Romantic
Russian talks of free love, Harietta Boleshi, a
souless German spy. TLS
a melange of erotics; impotent husband wants heir gets
a cousin who resembles him to take his place in bed.
SP
Wife falls in love with that substitute. LBKM

004458   THE REASON WHY. London: Duckworth, [1911]
BMC NUC. New York: D. Appleton, 1911 NUC.

Girl cares for her half brother, marries in order to
get help for him (he's crippled) story tells how
husband and wife find real love. PW 9-16-11
Zara 23, beautiful and virtuous, had been married to a
man "whose toy she was," has a poor opinion of men.
Marries for money for brother's sake; is cold to
husband. Gradually falls in love with him but he
refuses to respond. Meantime she gets paler, sicker.
He suspects her of infidelity, leaves Heroine,
red-gold haired-a countess, a widow of foreign birth.
Weds to help brother, Zara hates and despises all men
because of first husband. She scorns her new husband
but learns he's fine and learns to love him. ACAD.

004459   RED HAIR. Auburn, N.Y.: Author's Press,
[c1905] NUC. (First published as: The Vicissitudes of
Evangeline.)

004460   THE REFLECTIONS OF AMBROSINE, A NOVEL.
New York and London: Harper, 1902 NUC. London:
Duckworth, 1902 BMC.

NYT 11-15-02-- sounds promising but review not
helpful. Diary of a young girl, unhappy marriage.

004461   THE SEQUENCE, 1905--1912. London:
Duckworth, 1913 BMC NUC.

Guinevere is married but loves another man. Her son
makes the discovery. She decides to part from lover;
he marries another two days after her husband dies.
The son in turn has "a tremendous affaire with the
lover's wife. The two are drowned; the lovers united.
ACAD
Guinevere Bokum tells her story, wed at 17 to mid-aged
man; she obeyed parents in doing so, was afraid,
bullied and dominated by him. Has one son for whom she
has little affection. Very conscious of her kind of
marriage. Falls in love but will not "stoop to
dishonor." Her lover marries on rebound, but never
consumates the marriage because he discovers his new
wife has Negro blood in her. Guinevere's husband dies.
Her sister Letia very attractive worldly woman with
far out views on women. LBKM

004462   THE SEVENTH COMMANDMENT. New York:
Macaulay, [c1902] NUC.

004463   THREE WEEKS. New York: Duffield, 1907
NUC. London: Duckworth, 1907 BMC NUC.

"sold at the rate of 2,000 a day...because of its

purple reputation. Though it was prosecuted by the New
York Society for the Suppression of Vice,...the work
is a sexual hoax...rapturous sighs, lingering looks,
burning thoughts and asterisks."
Begins as a story of bold passion, at very end turns
into a melodrama. Lady a passionate Slav nature,
married to brutal husband. They live together for
three weeks. The lady goes home, has a son, and is
murdered by her husband. PW
sudden passion of two strangers for each other and
their abandonment, high born heroine. ACAD
Five days after meeting, a woman who witholds her
identity lives with a man. He is not to fetter her in
any way only to take it all as "an episode," and
permit her to go when she's ready. Passionate older
woman, young man. She provides every luxury. Author
glorifies their passion. She has no moral sense. NYT
"Chooses a most unusual theme, treated with extreme
frankness of opinion and in a vigorous, virile style
of writing...how a young man's soul was developed and
ennobled through an illicit passion indulged with a
very remarkable woman." R OF R

004464   THE VICISSITUDES OF EVANGELINE; A NOVEL.
London: Duckworth, 1905 BMC. New York and London:
Harper, 1905 NUC.

"outspoken diary of her feelings, her influence on
men." PW
All the audacities of 12 up-to-date women. red-haired,
exciting, unconv. Evangeline tells her own
story-frankly, brought up in a worldly atmosphere an
adventuress, her naturalness never warped by conv.
Disrespect of conv. NYT 156, 05
red-haired adventuress-improper. ACAD 241, 05
Age 20, she states outright she's to become an
adventuress, part innocence, part brazen air of the
modern minx. another Elizabeth. Athen 05:395.

004465   THE VISITS OF ELIZABETH. London:
Duckworth, 1900 BMC. Boston: C. E. Brown, [c1901] NUC.

SR 90:728. Enfant terrible. Series of letters to her
mother. wholesome and delectable.
ATH 116:790. English and French country houses.
ACAD 59:626. Ends with her engagement. "Young
aristocrat prattling to its mama." An ingenue rather
than an enfant terrible. Patrician. 17 years old.
"the enfant terrible" startling audacity

004466   WHEN THE HOUR CAME. London: G. Newnes,
[1915] BMC.

004467   YOUR AFFECTIONATE GODMOTHER. New York: D.
Appleton, 1914 NUC.

PW 85:5-2-14 1444.-Matter-of-fact, yet startling
advice to young girl who is about to be introduced
into society. This advice is upon the subjects of
personal conduct at home, on the street, in the
drawing room, upon personal habits, dress, religion,
matrimony, the selection of a husband, bearing towards
other people, etc. The title is drawn from the fact
that each chapter is in the form of a communication to
a young girl named Caroline and is signed "Your
affectionate godmother, E. G."

GLYNN, BARBARA.

004468   SHADOWED: A NOVEL. London: J. Ouseley,
1908 BMC.

TLS-Jewelry robbery with unusual amount of character
study.

004469   THE SOUL OF A WOMAN. London: Digby, Long,
1906 BMC.

TLS-Foolish, impossible. Two sisters one pregnant gets
sister's lover to marry her, dies, other sister
triumphs.

GLYNN, KATE A. United States.

004470   THE GIRL FROM OSHKOSH. BY IKE. Chicago:
E. A. Weeks, [c1896] NUC.

GODFREY, ELIZABETH, pseud. See BEDFORD, JESSIE.

GODFREY, HAL, pseud. See ECCLES, CHARLOTTE O'CONOR.

GODFREY, MRS. TOM.

004471   THE HUMBUG. London: Hurst & Blackett,
1912 BMC.

ATH-Woman of forty impersonates invalid's wife. People
around her are the humbugs.
TLS-O

004472   THE MARRYING OF GWENDOLINE JANE. London:
Hutchinson, 1905 BMC.

004473   A MODERN HAGAR. London: J. Long, 1908
BMC.

TLS-Notion of a childless wife in her intense longing
entertaining a proposal such as the title suggests

004474   SUNBEAM. London: Ward, Lock, 1904 BMC.

GODKIN, GEORGINA SARAH. United Kingdom.

004475   CAPTAIN VIVANTI'S PURSUIT. London: E.
Stock, 1907 BMC.

Historical novel and love story of Alice Herbert and
the Capt. TLS

004476   IL MAL OCCHIO; OR THE EVIL EYE. London:
S. Sonnenschein, 1894 NUC BMC.

Religious troubles of Italy in 17th century focus on
heroine who thinks for herself. SP 74:59.

GODSTOWE, ELIZABETH, pseud. See EWELL, ALICE MAUDE.

GOETCHIUS, MARIE LOUISE, pseud. See HALE, MARICE RUTLEDGE
(GIBSON).

GOLDIE, BERTHA BARRE.

004477   THE DISCIPLINE OF CHRISTINE. London: A.
Rivers, 1904 BMC.

ATH-conv.
TLS-Conv
ACAD-interesting female child

GOLDIE, BERYL.

004478   THE LEAVEN OF LOVE. London: G. Routledge,
1900 BMC.

ATH 1-26-01

004479   MARIAN VOYNE OR THE GREAT LIE. London: G.
Richards, 1904 BMC.

GOLDIE, HENRIETTA TAUBMAN.

004480   A PILGRIM OF LOVE. London: Digby, Long,
1905 BMC.

004481   THE VEILED LIFE. London: W. Heinemann,
1914 BMC.

Laura a kitchenmaid "conquers by humility" ends up
marrying a rough man. Dr.- friend educates her by
sending her books. "charming little heroine." LBKM
From cottage, to kitchen-maid in a "big house" to
"sophisticated philandering" with the gentleman she
eventually marries, to attempted suicide, elopement,
divorce, remarriage. "In spite of her unworthiness,
the author rewards the heroine with health and
happiness." SR
ATH 144:622-wooing and marriage of a kitchenmaid. Also
her experiences in service, She marries a doctor.
TLS-while in service is wooed by an agent of the
estate. Then she returns to her mother, illness and
poverty and finally accepts him. He is a brutal
husband and she suffers from his ill treatment. A
"long and particular account of two confinements"
(review cites this as example of a story "overloaded
with small and even petty details;" author's
"femininity is immature.") The doctor she eventually
marries attended her during her confinements and
illness.

GOLDRING, MAUDE.

004482   DEAN'S HALL. London: J. Murray, 1908 BMC.

TLS-Quaker types.
ATH-O

004483   THE DOWNSMAN: A STORY OF SUSSEX. London:
J. Murray, 1911 BMC.

Focuses upon a man. Socialist. ATH

004484   THE TENANTS OF PIXIE FARM. London: J.

Murray, 1909 BMC.

SR-rural romance.
Focuses on a man and a house. TLS

004485   THE WONDER YEAR. A NOVEL. London: E.
MacDonald, [1914] BMC.

LBKM- the awakening of a village to new ideas.
ATH-study on unconventional lines of the influence of
20th century ideas on two young women.

GOLDWIN, AGNES.

004486   IN DUE SEASON. London: Digby, Long, 1894
BMC.

SR 78:303. Alice Evans, past 30, desires to be a
hospital nurse. Persevering, she is "constantly driven
back by physical unfitness from the tasks to which she
would soonest put her hand to than the uncongenial
drudgery of the schoolroom. Dr. Arkwell hero, whose
strength of mind and integrity of purpose do not
absolve (him) from certain weaknesses which not every
young novelist would have ventured to link together."
SP 73:498. Rev. says love of doctor for young woman he
meets in consulting room and hers for him, a married
man, is theme of book. Both are noble, nothing
improper.

GOODELL, EMILY FAIRBANKS.

004487   CHOSEN. BY MRS. CONSTANS L. GOODELL. New
York: F. H. Revell, [1902] NUC.

Brief talks on religious subjects.

GOODELL, MRS. CONSTANS L. See GOODELL, EMILY FAIRBANKS.

GOODLOE, A. CARTER. See GOODLOE, ABBE CARTER.

GOODLOE, ABBE CARTER. B. 1867. United States.

004488   CALVERT OF STRATHMORE. BY CARTER GOODLOE.
New York: C. Scribner's Sons, 1903 NUC.

Hist PW 2-21-03

004489   COLLEGE GIRLS. New York: C. Scribner's
Sons, 1895 NUC. London: Downey, 1896 BMC.

Stories concerning romances-chiefly. PW: 10-5-95:583

004490   THE STAR GAZERS. BY A. CARTER GOODLOE.
New York: C. Scribner's Sons, 1910 NUC.

Sent romance PW

GOODLOE, CARTER. See GOODLOE, ABBE CARTER.

GOODRICH, EDNA. B. 1883. United States.

004491   DEYNARD'S DIVORCE. Boston: R. G. Badger,
[c1912] NUC.

PW-divorce, actress

GOODWIN, DORA MIRANDA MERRILL. B. 1869. Nationality
Unknown.

004492   THE DAUGHTER OF ANGY. Boston: R. G.
Badger, [c1911] NUC.

Mother-daughter. PW 10-14-11

GOODWIN, MAUD (WILDER). 1856-1935. United States.

004493   CLAIMS AND COUNTERCLAIMS. London and New
York: Doubleday, Page, 1905 BMC NUC.

Centers on hero, a doctor. PW 8-19-05.
Heroine seems a lackluster. The story centers on the
Doctor and a male friend. NYT 05:543

004494   THE COLONIAL CAVALIER; OR, SOUTHERN LIFE
BEFORE THE REVOLUTION. New York: Lovell, Coryell, 1894
BMC NUC.

004495   FLINT, HIS FAULTS, HIS FRIENDSHIPS, AND
HIS FORTUNES. Boston: Little, Brown, 1897 NUC.

A tale of today. Flint's faults are not unattractive;
friendships are free and unfettered; his fortunes-what
he deserves. LW 28:465.
BKM 6:473. Editor of a great daily. He is pessimistic,
prematurely old, and comes to a place to have

experiences that will alter these views. He and a
woman meet, love each other, each against her/his
will. Woman is relieved to observe that the landlady's
daughter also loves Flint. But he is totally unaware
of it. Tragedy follows.
NYT 1898:416. A newspaper editor, in love with
himself, comes to Nepang on vacation. Tragic
conclusion.

004496   FOUR ROADS TO PARADISE. New York:
Century, 1904 NUC.

NYT-0
PW-4 men in love with a woman.

004497   THE HEAD OF A HUNDRED: BEING AN ACCOUNT
OF CERTAIN PASSAGES IN THE LIFE OF HUMPHREY HUNTOON,
ESQR., SOMETYME AN OFFICER IN THE COLONY OF VIRGINIA.
EDITED BY MAUD WILDER GOODWIN. Boston: Little, Brown,
1895. London: J. M. Dent, 1896 BMC.

Based upon research of early Va. colonial records.
Uses actual names. Includes a scandal, rigors of river
life in the new country. CR 24:180
Humphrey tells his own story. Flouted by Betty Romney,
he came to new colony. Betty later comes on a ship of
"wives" but she's really escaping an arranged
marriage. Indian massacre. LW 26:201
NYT 1900:375. Heroine is shipped to Virginia in one of
the first shiploads of wives in order to escape
marrying a man of title whom she hates, her father's
choice. Story is of her marriage in Virginia, and how
couple comes to know and love each other.
LW 31:257. Narrated (?) by young Englishman who is MD
by profession and soldier of fortune "by practice."
Historical romance-reigns of James and Charles at
beginning of 17th. Set in Virginia sweet and pure
story of a timid man and his love. BKM 4:417

004498   SIR CHRISTOPHER; A ROMANCE OF A MARYLAND
MANOR IN 1644. Boston: Little, Brown, 1901 NUC.
London: Ward, Lock, 1904 BMC.

TLS-trad. hist.

004499   VERONICA PLAYFAIR. Boston: Little, Brown,
1909 NUC. London: F. Warne, [1912] BMC NUC.

Historical romance. First person narrative. Character
placed in Swift's, Pope's, Franklin's world. NYT

004500   WHITE APRONS: A ROMANCE OF BACON'S
REBELLION, VIRGINIA, 1676. Boston: Little, Brown,
1896. London: J. M. Dent, 1896 BMC.

BKM 3:455. Hist rom and love story.
LIT w 27:203. U. S. Bacon's Rebellion Penelope crosses
ocean to intercede with king to get lover's pardon;
succeeds.

GORDON, CAROL, pseud. See GATTLE, CAROLINE A.

GORDON, E. A. See GORDON, ELIZABETH ANNA.

GORDON, ELEANOR LYTLE (KINZIE). 1835-1917.

    004501   ROSEMARY AND RUE. New York: E. P. Dutton,
    1906 NUC.

GORDON, ELIZABETH ANNA.

    004502   CLEAR ROUND! OR, SEEDS OF STORY FROM
    OTHER COUNTRIES. BEING A CHRONICLE OF LINKS AND RIVETS
    IN THIS WORLD'S GIRDLE. BY E. A. GORDON. London: S.
    Low, 1893 BMC NUC. London: S. Low, Marston, [1895]
    NUC.

GORDON, HELEN (VAN METRE) VAN ANDERSON. B. 1859. United
States.

    004503   CARROL'S CONVERSION; A STORY OF LIFE. BY
    HELEN VAN ANDERSON. New York: N. Y. Magazine of
    Mysteries, [c1904] NUC.

    004504   THE ILLUMINED LIFE. Chicago: A. C.
    McClurg, 1912 NUC.

    004505   IT IS POSSIBLE: A STORY OF LIFE. BY HELEN
    VAN ANDERSON. Chicago: New Era, 1891 NUC.

    004506   THE JOURNAL OF A LIVE WOMAN. BY HELEN VAN
    ANDERSON. Boston: G. H. Wright, 1895 NUC.

GORDON, JULIEN, pseud. See CRUGER, JULIE GRINNELL
(STORROW).

GORDON, MRS. JAMES EDWARD HENRY.

    004507   EUNICE ANSCOMBE. London: S. Low, 1892
    BMC.

    ATH 99:401.
    SP. Characters of the children are interesting, but
    not hero or heroine.
    ACAD. A male journalist.
    SR-three women in love more or less with hero, who has
    only a passion for himself.

GORDON, NANCY MACKAY. United States.

    004508   HER BUNGALOW: AN ATLANTIAN MEMORY.
    Chicago: Hermetic Pub. Co., 1898 NUC.

GORE, ALICE AUGUSTA.

    004509   CHEQUERED COURTSHIP. London: Digby, Long,
    [1892] BMC.

    SR 74:744. Heroine has many admirers.
    German characters and scenes. Characters meet to
    discuss merits of various composers and complicated
    relationships. ACAD 43:151

GORE, SUSAN FRANCES (RICHARDS). United States.

    004510   AS THE TWIG IS BENT, A STORY FOR MOTHERS
    AND TEACHERS. BY SUSAN CHENERY. Boston: Houghton,
    Mifflin, 1901 NUC.

GORST, MRS. HAROLD E. See GORST, NINA C. F. (KENNEDY).

GORST, NINA C. F. (KENNEDY). United Kingdom.

    004511   AND AFTERWARDS? London: Greening, 1901
    BMC.

    "a women's revenge and opinions on life and men and
    manners." sexual ethics ATH 10-5-01.

    004512   THE LEECH. BY MRS. HAROLD E. GORST.
    London: Mills and Boon, [1911] BMC NUC.

    Misery of poor: Susannah a widow dies in agony. Mrs
    Charlotte Barnes her sister-in-law "leeched" her
    before her death. Her daughter, Elvina, works in
    library, draper's show room, gets ill from exhaustion,
    anemia, is burnt to death. TLS
    Charlotte Barnes, deserted-her greediness. LBKM
    Charlotte seeks asylum in sister-in-law's house, then
    takes over; the sister in law dies. Her daughter
    Elvina now at the mercy of her aunt and her aunt's
    miserable daughter. Then the story becomes a
    Cinderella type, but the prince arrives too late. ACAD
    "tragic picture of hardship and temptations besetting
    the career of a London shop-girl."

    004513   THE LIGHT. BY MRS. HAROLD E. GORST.
    London: Cassell, 1906 BMC NUC. New York: B. W. Dodge,
    1907 NUC.

    Story of the pregnancy and motherhood of an unwed
    servant who struggles to care for her blind baby.
    Moral redemption.
    ACAD-tale of moral redemption of servant girl in and
    out of work house with blind baby.
    TLS-interludes of female humanity are admirable.
    BKM-moral of the tale interferes with story.
    Unwed mother struggles to keep her self respect and
    support child. Pictures of maternity ward include
    statistics. "novel with a purpose"
    Sixteen year old unwed mother, loses faith, other
    woman helps to restore her faith, workhouse methods
    pictured. PW 11-23-07

    004514   POSSESSED OF DEVILS. London: J. Macqueen,
    1897 BMC.

    Demoniacal heroine. Lady Radclyffe hates her husband.
    She feels misunderstood; sees visions. Gets Francis
    Ingelow to elope with her. "From the cradle, the
    female infant, child, girl, woman, is not, and never
    has been, what she appears. She is a creature evolved
    out of an age of shams and unrealties." (quote from
    novel) ACAD 52: Fic Sup:37

    004515   THE SOUL OF MILLY GREEN. London: Cassell,
    1907 BMC.

    The gradual downfall of a girl of the lower cockney
    class from a flighty girl to a draggled and
    disreputable woman precipitated by a respectable man.
    TLS

Story dedicated to "the average respectable man." ATH
Decline and fall of a woman with "but a pretty face to
recommend her " Author tries to teach men about the
harm of breaking the 7th Commandment. Milly can't
perform her household duties. She's unfit as a mother
and wife, child taken from her. Critic: "training in
women's natural duties" needed

004516   THE THIEF ON THE CROSS. London: Nash,
1908 BMC.

TLS-"sordid erring life of a daughter of the slums. As
a novel it needs relief; as a "human document" it is a
moving and painful study, uncompromising in its
realism."
BKM-Eve Ridgefoote, daughter of a filthy drunken
mother, lives on the street, goes to prison, has
children and cares for them under circumstances "where
infanticide would appear almost laudable," the story
of the short life of a girl of the slums, a person of
courage.

004517   THIS OUR SISTER. BY MRS. HAROLD E. GORST.
London: Digby, Long, 1905 BMC NUC.

Nell's father murdered her mother. She's left with an
infant brother who dies in spite of her sacrifices.
Becomes an artist's model-artist has other designs.
Nell is briefly happy-commits suicide. Sordid poverty,
free from sentiment. ACAD 05:785.
Much understanding of Nell, nothing sentimental here.
LBKM
TLS-says we don't get to know the character Nell.
05:218.
ATH-does sell herself only to come home and find the
baby dead , becomes a model, falls in love with
artist, who casts her off in her hour of need. 05:171.

GORTON, CYNTHIA M. R. United States.

    004518   LILY PEARL AND THE MISTRESS OF ROSEDALE.
    BY IDA GLENWOOD. EDITED BY MAJOR JOSEPH KIRKLAND.
    Chicago: Dibble, 1892 NUC.

GOULD, ELIZABETH LINCOLN. D. 1914. United States.

    004519   CAP'N GID. [Philadelphia]: Penn, 1916
    NUC.

        male hero

    004520   GRANDMA. [Philadelphia]: Penn, 1911 NUC.

GOULD, ELIZABETH PORTER. 1848-1906. United States.

    004521   A PIONEER DOCTOR; A STORY OF THE
    SEVENTIES. Boston: R. G. Badger, 1904 NUC.

    WOMAN'S JOURNAL--young woman becomes doctor and goes
    to Syria to heal women.
    PW-does English suitor dissuade her?

GOULD, JENNIE W. United States.

    004522   TRUTH IS STRANGER THAN FICTION. BY ZELMA
    HOPE. [Port Henry, N.Y.:]: W. Lansing, 1891 NUC.

GOULD, MRS. HOWARD. See GOULD, VIOLA KATHRINE (CLEMMONS).

GOULD, VIOLA KATHRINE (CLEMMONS). United States.

    004523   THE CRYSTAL ROAD. BY MRS. HOWARD GOULD.
    New York: Lane, 1914 NUC.

    PW 86 11/28/14:1837 "Romance of the young supposed
    Indian, Rushing Water. The squaw of a chief, having
    borne no son, is driven by taunts to a white hunters'
    settlement. Here she steals a child, and returning to
    her tribe, passes him off as her own. Here Rushing
    Water grows up, in all things meeting the Indian
    standard. He rescues a beautiful French captive and
    takes her safely to the coast. From here adventure
    leads him over seas to France, where he learns about
    his parentage. Back he comes to the colonies and
    appears before the delighted Valerie in his true name
    and position."
    NYT 1914:540. Story is a demonstration that "blood
    will tell."

GOWING, EMILIA AYLMER (BLAKE).

    004524   AS CAESAR'S WIFE. London: J. Long, [1902]
    BMC.

    ATH 3-29-02--

004525   BY THAMES AND TIBER. London: J. Long,
1903 BMC.

dream shows heroine in Nero's time and modern times.
ATH 121:300
Story of a marriage of a woman whose mother came from
eminent Roman house; lost in catacombs, she has the
dream. TLS 1903:27

004526   GODS OF GOLD. London: F. V. White, 1896
BMC.

ATH 109:12. Society belle Ruby Lynndale is jilted by
aristocratic lover. She goes to the aid of the poor in
the East End. Falls for a priest, he runs away to
avoid temptation. ATH 109:12

004527   A KING'S DESIRE. London: J. Long, 1904
BMC.

LBKM-?
TLS-"harmless tale"

004528   LORD OF HIMSELF. London: J. Long, 1905
BMC.

Centers on a male poet. ATH 1905:173

004529   MERELY PLAYERS. London: White, 1897 BMC.

At 18, Ena Clair appears on the stage for the first
time as Juliet and Desdemona. Falls in love with young
actor who's involved with a bad woman, Lady Diana, who
manages to separate the two. "Then author lets loose
the small-pox" it blinds Ena's father getting him out
of trouble; it kills off Lady Diana, Lovers reunited.
She writes a play in blank verse, they wed. SR 84:449

004530   A SPIDER'S WEB. London: T. Burleigh, 1900
BMC.

SP 85:309. Wicked Russian heroine.
ATH 116:307. Nihilists, intrigue, etc.

004531   A TOUCH OF THE SUN. London: T. Burleigh,
1899 BMC.

English woman marries Indian Prince. Much discussion
of the differences between European and Oriental ideas
of marriage. L 4:317
Aimee Hildsbrand--the daughter, bitter of the
treatment her mother got vows the man she loves will
never marry the woman he prefers. Keeps her vow of
revenge. Harem in India depicted. Melodrama. LBKM
15:152
The irreconcilability of race with race. ATH 113:12

GRAEME, ALASTER, pseud. See MARRYAT, MRS. FREDERICK
TOWNSHEND.

GRAHAM, ALICE.

    004532   AN ODD SITUATION. London: J. Ouseley,
    [1911] BMC.

    Coincidences abound TLS

GRAHAM, EFFIE. See GRAHAM, SARAH EFFIE.

GRAHAM, MARGARET ETHEL BLAIR (OLIPHANT) MAXTONE.

    004533   A CHEF D'OEUVRE. BY E. BLAIR OLIPHANT.
    Bristol: J. W. Arrowsmith, 1893 BMC. (Bound with A Gem
    of Cremona by B. M. vere.)

GRAHAM, MARIE. United States.

    004534   A DEVOUT BLUEBEARD. New York: Abbey
    Press, [c1900] NUC.

GRAHAM, MRS. HENRY. See ASKWITH, ELLEN GRAHAM.

GRAHAM, MRS. JOHN E. See GRAHAM, SARAH MELISSA CARY
DOWNING.

GRAHAM, SARAH EFFIE.

    004535   AUNT LIZA'S "PRAISIN GATE". BY EFFIE
    GRAHAM. Chicago: A. C. McClurg, 1916 NUC.

    Old colored woman in Kansas worked for suffrage,
    though she was crippled and could not go beyond her
    own gate. PW

    004536   THE PASSIN-ON PARTY. BY EFFIE GRAHAM.
    Chicago: A. C. McClurg, 1912 NUC.

GRAHAM, SARAH MELISSA CARY DOWNING. United States.

004537   THE TOLTEC SAVIOR; A HISTORICAL ROMANCE
OF ANCIENT MEXICO BY MRS. JOHN E. GRAHAM. New York: G.
W. Dillingham, [1901] NUC.

6-8-01 PW

GRAHAM, WINIFRED. See CORY, MATILDA WINIFRED MURIEL
(GRAHAM).

GRAND, MADAME SARAH, pseud. See MACFALL, FRANCES ELIZABETH
(CLARKE).

GRAND, SARAH, pseud. See MACFALL, FRANCES ELIZABETH
(CLARKE).

GRANGE, AMY MARY.

004538   A MODERN GALAHAD. BY M. E. GRANGE.
London: Catholic Truth Society, 1895 BMC NUC.

004539   VICTIMS OF FASHION: A NOVEL. London: R.
Bentley, 1894 BMC.

SR 78:75. Brother and sister, American, octaroon, he
with brains, she without; both beautiful, captivate
English society. When secret of blood comes out, their
engagements are cancelled. He is ambitious, but she is
relieved because she has a black American lover who
wants to marry her. Lady Peggy would not have broken
off if he hadn't kept it a secret.
SP 72:119-reviewer says that Horace is already husband
of Lady Betty when news leaks out. Aurelia marries her
old saloon-keeping sweetheart, Jos Crawford.
ACAD 46:115. Her lover is Joscelyn Crawford, a
homely-bred yankee. Horace and Aurelia are wealthy,
are launching themselves on English society at the
death-bed request of their father. They are also
illegitimate with a strain of black blood.
ATH 103:770. Author's view "a little outside the
ordinary groove."

GRANGE, M. E. See GRANGE, AMY MARY.

GRANGE, MRS.

004540   A MAID OF THE WEST. London: Hurst and
Blackett, 1895 BMC NUC.

ATH 104:788. Pleasant love story

GRANGER, GRACE.

004541   THE LIGHT OF THE GODS. New York:
Cosmopolitan Press, 1911 NUC.

GRANT, DOUGLAS, pseud. See OSTRANDER, ISABEL EGENTON.

GRANT, ETHEL (WATTS) MUMFORD. 1878-1940. United States.

004542   DUPES. BY ETHEL WATTS MUMFORD. New York
and London: G. P. Putnam's Sons, 1901 BMC NUC.

Like the Bostonians. CR
NYT: Questionable: really about drying of public by
rel. fraud. Mme. Bouzales.

004543   OUT OF THE ASHES. BY ETHEL WATTS MUMFORD.
New York: Moffat, Yard, 1913 NUC.

Modern heroine...engaged in levying blackmail...a
thoroughly sophisticated widow. Mrs. Marteen no
innocent, she's a widow with a debutante daughter and
she knows what she's doing. It's her profession. The
account of her suffering as a woman and mother wins
the reader's sympathy, despite her unconventional way
of earning a living. NYT 13:472.

004544   WHITEWASH. BY ETHEL WATTS MUMFORD. Boson:
D. Estes, [1903] NUC. London: Ward, Lock, 1905 BMC.

GRANT, MARJORIE. Nationality Unknown.

004545   VERDUN DAYS IN PARIS. London: W. Collins
Sons, [1918] BMC NUC.

D 640 WWI- personal narratives.

GRANT, MRS. COLQUHOUN.

004546   THE MARRIAGE OF LORD VERRINER. London: J.
Long, [1910] BMC NUC.

TLS-light rom.

THEIR HEART'S DESIRE. New York: Dodd,
004547   Mead, 1909 PW. London: J. Long, 1910 BMC.

Christ story. 12-4-09. PW

GRANT, PEGGY. United States.

004548   THE GATE OF DREAMS; A STORY OF THE NEW
FOREST. London: A. Melrose, 1915 NUC BMC.

Janet Blake left to disagreeable artist father on
mother's death; her girl and boy love, her woman's
passion. TLS

GRANT, SADI.

004549   FOLLY AT CANNES. A NOVEL. London: Digby,
Long, 1902 BMC.

004550   A GUARDSMAN JAPANESE. London: Digby,
Long, 1905 BMC.

Kidnapping a wife. TLS 179,05

004551   A JAPANESE HOUSE-PARTY. London: Digby,
Long, 1904 BMC NUC.

004552   LOBELIA OF CHINA. London: Digby, Long,
1907 BMC.

Half Chinese, expert in drugs, kills the squire
accidentally just when he was going to marry her. TLS

004553   A NEW WOMAN SUBDUED. London: Digby, Long,
1898 BMC.

ACAD 55:158. Beatrice Smith-Gore. Captain Orchardson.
She belonged to 2 fashionable clubs and lived in a
dingy room.

004554   PLAIN WILLIAM. London: Digby, Long, 1916
BMC.

TLS-Dorinda meets tramp secretly, marries cousin,
William kills him, marries Dorinda, she has a baby,
goes to India, further love and secrecies.

004555   THE SECOND EVIL. London: J. Long, [1906]
BMC NUC.

Sisters, boarding school life, teashop, trip to Japan.
TLS
One has a flirtation with a man who is not prepared to
marry a pauper. Her only chance to marry is to a
vulgar elderly admirer. The two go to Japan.

004556   TREPASSERS WHO WERE PROSECUTED. London:
Digby, Long, 1899 BMC.

GRANVILLE, MARGARET. Nationality Unknown.

004557   DAINTY INIQUITY; A NOVEL. New York: G.W.
Dillingham, 1896 NUC.

PW 1-18-96. Her life is first wrecked by a false
marriage; her experience after this is neither
instructive nor entertaining.

GRAVES, CHARLOTTE ELIZABETH. B. 1846. United States.

004558   MAUD HARCOURT; OR HOW SHE BECAME AN
ARTIST. Syracuse, N.Y., 1897 NUC.

Career of art student in N.Y.-many adventures. LW
28:377

GRAVES, CLOTILDE INEZ MARY. 1863-1932. United Kingdom.

004559   BETWEEN TWO THIEVES. BY RICHARD DEHAN.
London: W. Heinemann, 1912 NUC BMC. New York: F. A.
Stokes, [1912] NUC.

SP--anti-war, title refers to Napoleon III and the
English army contractor. Heroine is Ada Merling who
organizes nursing in Crimea.

004560   THE DOP DOCTOR. BY RICHARD DEHAN. London:
W. Heinemann, 1910 NUC BMC. New York: G. H. Doran,
[c1910] NUC.

SP--About a military siege, horrors of war.

004561   DRAGON'S TEETH: A NOVEL. London: Dalziel,
1891 BMC.

004562   A FIELD OF TARES: A NOVEL. New York:
Harper, 1891 NUC.

Heroine a widow and adventuress. With female partner,
robs a man of much money. The two women part. She
starts a new life, marries but her past catches up to
her. Turns to crime again. All remedies are futile.
PW

004563   A GILDED VANITY. BY RICHARD DEHAN.
London: W. Heinemann, 1916 BMC. New York: G. H. Doran,
[c1916] NUC.

English social life. BKM Elizabeth turned from Watt,
man she loved to marriage with Marquess. Not happy.
Marquess' first wife, whom he believed dead appears.
In spite of advice, that her marriage be made legal E.
went out into her freedom. PW 90 11-11-16:1611.
LBKM--Farcical plot.
NYT

004564   MAIDS IN A MARKET GARDEN. BY RICHARD
DEHAN. London: W. H. Allen, 1894 NUC. New York: Wycil,
1912 NUC.

PW--6 women go to Cornwall to farm and support
themselves, eschewing masculine society. By end of
year only one is left true to her principles. POV?
SR 78:489. 4 young women embark on a business of fruit
growing and market gardening under supervision of
middle aged Rosevear Trevelyan. They are to keep the
insidious man as well as the destructive wireworm out
of this Eden. They have had one previous failure, the
United Gentlewomen's Work Emporium--failed from
neglect. They all fall in love--tragic consequences to
one of them.

004565   THE MAN OF IRON. BY RICHARD DEHAN.
London: W. Heinemann, [1915] NUC BMC. New York: F. A.
Stokes, [1915] NUC.

BKM--1915. Irishman and French girl in Franco-Prussian
War.
Bismarck, Franco-Prussian War. NYT

004566   ONE BRAVER THING. BY RICHARD DEHAN. New
York: Duffield, 1910 NUC.

Wife's gradual awakening to the fact that she loves
her husband and he needs her. PW
BKM 32 1910-11--Lynette has horror of all men, during
Boer War she is nurse of wounded in hospitals meets
surgeon. Falls in love with man who dies. Consents
finally to marry Saxham the surgeon in name only. Last
100 pages of book devoted to st. of marriage.
NYT--Title changed to "One Braver Thing" in U. S.
which refers to Saxham's refusal to reveal to the wife
he loves the baseness of his rival.

004567   "THAT WHICH HATH WINGS--" A NOVEL OF THE
DAY. BY RICHARD DEHAN. London: W. Heinemann, [1918]
BMC NUC. New York and London: G. P. Putnam's Sons,
1918 NUC.

PW--Very doubtful. Chief woman character is consenting
victim of a German's passion.
SR--Painted women. Young boy scout.

004568   A WELL MEANING WOMAN. London: Hutchinson,
1896 BMC.

SR-No depth, no purpose; farce repartee.
ATH 108:832. Story of a matchmaker, Lady Baintree, and
disasters she effects. Farce.
Points to a serious moral but treats marr. arranger
humorously-Lady Baintree and her machinations and
counseling. LBKM 11:124

GRAY, ANNABEL, pseud. See COX, ANNE.

GRAY, ANNIE JOSLYN.

    004569   FIREWEED. BY JOSLYN GRAY. New York: C.
    Scribner's Sons, 1920 NUC.

    PW-Is won from her selfishness thru love for man.
    NYT June 27, 1920, p. 17. Spoiled and beautiful Erica
    divorces husband who contests; she is denounced at
    trial by his lawyer. Meets same later while travelling
    in Europe, gradually is regenerated and she and lawyer
    marry.

    004570   THE JANUARY GIRL. BY JOSLYN GRAY. New
    York: C. Scribner's Sons, 1920 NUC.

    PW-city girl's struggle against prejudice in New

England town.
PZ7

    004571   KATHLEEN'S PROBATION. BY JOSLYN GRAY. New
    York: C. Scribner's Sons, 1918 NUC.

    PW-Nurse who felt only for herself, story of her
    career and atonement.
    NYT. Characters taken from life in studies of the
    college training school for nurses.
    PZ7

    004572   RUSTY MILLER. By JOSLYN GRAY. New York:
    C. Scribner's Sons, 1919 NUC.

    Girls PW
    PZ7

GRAY, CHARLOTTE ELVIRA. 1873-1938. United States.

    004573   AS HIS MOTHER SAW HIM. New York: Meridian
    Press, [c1917] NUC.

    Jesus Christ-Fiction

    004574   THE INN BY THE SEA. Cincinnati: Jennings
    & Graham, [c1914] NUC.

    "Portia Dennison is living on a farm with her uncle,
    aunt and cousin Donald when Elmer Hamlin comes to
    board. He greets her as an old friend, calling her
    Pearl Overton, to the girl's intense annoyance. This
    confusion continues and is much increased when Donald
    goes to town and sees Pearl Overton. Who the two girls
    are and how they learn the value of life's ordinary
    stations, duties and opportunities, make the plot and
    its complications. " PW 3-14-14 965

    004575   THE JERICHO ROAD. Cincinnati: Jennings
    and Graham, [c1912] NUC.

    PW-?

    004576   "OUT OF THE MIRE". Cincinnati: Jennings
    and Graham, [c1911] NUC.

    Girl rises out of poverty. PW 10-14-11

GRAY, ELIZABETH H. Nationality Unknown.

    004577   OLD NINETY-NINE'S CAVE. Boston: C. M.
    Clark, 1909 NUC.

    About Mississ. settlers

GRAY, ESCA.

    004578   BELFIELD: A NOVEL. London: Skeffington,
    1896 BMC.

    ATH 108:673. Belfield is intended by author to be "the
    perfect woman nobly planned." Her conversation is
    "stilted," "second-rate," trite. Petty jealousies of
    ministers, deacons, retired shopkeepers. "Ill-bred"
    people.
    ACAD 50:490. Daughter of Dissenting minister, a
    Dissenter and a mystic.

    004579   THE FAIRY STEPMOTHER. London: J. Clarke,
    1897 BMC.

GRAY, JOSLYN. See GRAY, ANNIE JOSLYN.

GRAY, MARY AGATHA. United States.

    004580   DERFEL THE STRONG; A ROMANCE OF THE DAYS
    OF KING HENRY VIII. London: R. & T. Washbourne, 1914
    BMC.

    PW 85 5/9/14 1554 "Tells of Henry VIII's efforts to
    rid himself of Katherine of Aragon and of his wooing
    of Anne Boleyn. Both women and the king are
    conspicuous figures in the tale, which follows the
    fortunes of the two queens even to their deaths. There
    are adventures galore and a happy love story also in
    the book."

    004581   "LIKE UNTO A MERCHANT". New York:
    Benziger, 1915 NUC.

    Mystery 4-17-15 PW

    004582   THE TEMPEST OF THE HEART. New York:
    Benziger, 1912 NUC.

    Near-priest turns to art, returns to God. 12-16-11 PW

004583　　　　THE TOWERS OF ST. NICHOLAS; A STORY OF
THE DAYS OF "GOOD QUEEN BESS". New York: P. J. Kenedy,
[c1913] NUC.

004584　　　　THE TURN OF THE TIDE. A STORY OF HUMBLE
LIFE BY THE SEA. New York: Benziger, 1910 NUC.

Hilda Moncrieff marries old miser, has unhappy life
but her love is steadfast and all ends happily. PW

GRAY, MAXWELL, pseud.　See TUTTIETT, MARY GLEED.

GRAY, PHOEBE.　United States.

004585　　　　THE GOLDEN LAMP. Boston: Small, Maynard,
[c1916] NUC. London: Jarrolds, [1917] BMC.

Mystery--2 baby boys left on Banford's doorstep.
Mystery solved through courage and generosity of
Margaret Lake and her own romance with Dr. Theodore
Acres. PW 89 2-19-16:605.
NYT--Serious purpose, anti-saloon life, heroine is the
one who declares her love. City is uplifted from
drunkenness and vice through her working.
About fortunes, baby heirs. TLS
ATH--Prohibition and baby.

004586　　　　LITTLE SIR GALLAHAD; A NOVEL. Boston:
Small, Maynard, [c1914] NUC. London: S. Paul, [1915]
BMC.

Story of childhood and youth. NYT
Anti-saloon propaganda, beaten by drunken father. But
sentimental LBKM
PW 86 12-24-14:1978--"Mary Alice Brown was taking home
washing when some rude boys upset her sled and basket.
Francis Willet,
he called himself, came to the rescue, and from that
incident started a friendship which became more when
they grew up."

GRAYSON, PAULINE.　United States.

004587　　　　GASPAR DESMOND'S PASSION; [ALSO, KREUTZER
SONATA BEARING FRUIT]. New York: J.S. Ogilvie, 1891
NUC.

004588　　　　THE SOCIAL EVIL; OR, THE WOMAN LALARGE.
New York: J.S. Ogilvie, 1893 NUC NUC.

Bringing into the world more children than parents can
afford is the evil. Wants births regulated by law and
so decrease the large class that becomes criminal
because it has no other method of existing. PW 3-25-93

GREEN, ANNA KATHARINE.　See ROHLFS, ANNA KATHARINE (GREEN).

GREEN, ANNE SANFORD.

004589　　　　POKAHUNTAS, MAID OF JAMESTOWN. Culpeper,
Va.: Exponent Press, 1907 NUC.

GREEN, E. EVERETT.　See GREEN, EVELYN EVERETT.

GREEN, EDITH M.

004590　　　　ELIZABETH GREY. Edinburgh and London: W.
Blackwood, 1905 BMC.

True picture of a living woman. Down to last shilling,
bombards editors with her MS with no success retires
to a farm with writer who becomes successful. ACAD
05:367.
Lives by her pen, her courage and humor. LBKM
27,28:104.

GREEN, EVELYN EVERETT.　1856-1932.　United Kingdom.

004591　　　　ADVENTUROUS ANNE. London: S. Paul, 1916
BMC.

TLS

004592　　　　AFTER WORCESTER, THE STORY OF A ROYAL
FUGITIVE. London: Nelson, 1901 NUC BMC.

004593　　　　AFTERTHOUGHT HOUSE. London: Christian
Knowledge Society, [1894] BMC.

004594　　　　ARNOLD INGLEHURST, THE PREACHER: A STORY
OF THE FEN COUNTRY. London: J. F. Shaw, [1896] BMC.

004595　　　　BARBED WIRE. London: S. Paul, 1914 BMC.

ATH--Heroine steals clothes from friend after losing

fortune gambling to win favor of grandfather. Inherits
his fortune.

004596　　　　BILLY'S BARGAIN. London: S. Paul, [1920]
BMC.

TLS--war and love.

004597　　　　BLACKLADIES. London: Hutchinson, 1914
BMC.

ATH--Heroine's father, charged with murder of her
mother, living at Blackladies, a haunted house.
TLS--Heroine finds ghost in shape of a nun whom she
constantly sees and embraces, and who is really her
father, an ex-convict.

004598　　　　THE CACTUS HEDGE. BY CECIL ADAIR. London:
S. Paul, 1919 BMC.

004599　　　　CAMBRIA'S CHIEFTAIN. New York: T. Nelson
and Sons, [1903] BMC.

ATH--Hist. for young.

004600　　　　CANTACUTE TOWERS. BY CECIL ADAIR. London:
S. Paul, 1911 BMC.

004601　　　　CAROL CAREW; OR, WAS IT IMPRUDENT?
London: S. W. Partridge, [1907] BMC.

004602　　　　THE CASTLE OF THE WHITE FLAG; A TALE OF
THE FRANCO-GERMAN WAR. New York: Nelson and Sons, 1904
NUC BMC.

Children in historical setting. PW 12-5-03.
Pretty tale of Franco-German War. PW, Xmas Supplement,
p.19.

004603　　　　THE CHATTERTON MYSTERY. London: J.
Clarke, 1896 BMC.

SP 77:344. Managing mother and submissive daughter,
but rebellion.

004604　　　　THE CHURCH AND THE KING: A TALE OF
ENGLAND IN THE DAYS OF HENRY VIII. London: T. Nelson,
1892 BMC NUC.

PW-Struggle over the establishment of the Church of
England.

004605　　　　THE CITY OF THE GOLDEN GATE. BY E.
EVERETT GREEN. London: S. Paul, [1909] BMC. New York:
Dodge, 1909 NUC.

Romance of San Francisco earthquake. PW

004606　　　　CLANRICKARD COURT. London: A. Melrose,
1907 BMC.

004607　　　　A CLERK OF OXFORD, AND HIS ADVENTURES IN
THE BARONS' WAR. London, New York: T. Nelson, 1898 BMC
NUC.

004608　　　　CLIVE LORIMER'S MARRIAGE. London: S.
Paul, 1911 BMC.

First wife turns up. TLS
2 heroines, one angelic, one demonic. ATH

004609　　　　CO-HEIRESSES. BY E. EVERETT GREEN.
London: S. Paul, [1909] NUC BMC.

Entertaining story of an inheritance left to 2 girls.
TLS

004610　　　　CONFIRMED BACHELOR. London: Hutchinson,
1915 BMC.

Simple love story. TLS

004611　　　　THE CONSCIENCE OF ROGER TREHERN. London:
R. T. S., [1903] BMC.

004612　　　　DARE LORIMER'S HERITAGE. London:
Hutchinson, 1891 BMC. Boston: Bradley & Woodruff,
[1892?] NUC.

Story of a headstrong boy with an inherited temper.
Often melancholy: SP
Male hero suspected of complicity in his brother's
death. PW

004613　　　　DASHING DICK'S DAUGHTER. London: S. Paul,
1916 BMC.

TLS--Love and spies.
ATH--Sally, when her father dies goes to England to
find his friends. Adventures.

004614   THE DEAN'S DAUGHTER. BY CECIL ADAIR.
London: S. Paul, [1910] BMC.

004615   THE DEFENCE OF THE ROCK. London: T.
Nelson, [1906] BMC.

004616   DEFIANT DIANA. London: S. Paul, 1913 BMC.

Stone workers--Diana, wilful headstrong, is uncrowned
Quarry Queen, possessing the confidence of the stone
workers. ACAD
Much of story relates her submission to the new master
of the estate of her family. ATH

004617   A DIFFICULT DAUGHTER. London: Sunday
School Union, [1895] BMC.

004618   A DIFFICULT HALF-DOZEN; A STORY. London:
Jarrolds, [1919] BMC.

004619   A DISPUTED HERITAGE. London: Pilgrim,
[1911] BMC.

004620   THE DOCTOR'S DOZEN. Edinburgh: Oliphant,
1892 BMC.

004621   DOMINIQUE'S VENGEANCE: A STORY OF FRANCE
AND FLORIDA. London: T. Nelson, 1897 BMC.

SP 77:902. France at close of 16th century. Male hero.

004622   THE DOUBLE HOUSE. London: S. Paul, 1914
BMC.

ATH--Hero and heroine live in double house. Unsolved
murders, love affairs.

004623   DUCKWORTH'S DIAMONDS. London: S. Paul,
[1912] BMC.

ATH

004624   DUFF DARLINGTON: OR AN UNSUSPECTED
GENIUS. London: S. W. Partridge, [1895] BMC.

004625   DUFFERIN'S KEEP. London: Hutchinson, 1905
BMC.

Wooing story. TLS

004626   ELEANOR'S HERO. London: Sunday School
Union, [1900] BMC.

ATH 115:812. For teenage girls.

004627   THE ERINCOURTS. London: Marshall, [1907]
BMC.

Innocent little tale. TLS

004628   ESTHER'S CHARGE. London: T. Nelson, 1899
BMC NUC.

004629   EUSTACE MARCHMONT, A FRIEND OF THE
PEOPLE. London: J. F. Shaw, [1895] BMC. Boston: A. I.
Bradley, [1895] NUC.

English family on west coast takes interest in working
people and in religion. Hero known as friend of the
people. Heir to fine estate, falls in love with cousin
Bride. She tries to influence the people toward
religion; the perils and consequences that result are
the story. LW 26:122
Time about 1835 PW 4-13-95:123

004630   EVIL MAY-DAY. A STORY OF 1517. London and
New York: T. Nelson, [1893] NUC 1894 BMC.

004631   THE EVOLUTION OF SARA. London:
Hutchinson, 1911 BMC.

Self sacrificing to elderly husband. TLS
Sara leads a solitary life as a child; on father's
death takes on burden of mother and invalid brother.
ATH

004632   EYES OF ETERNITY. London: S. Paul, 1918
BMC.

004633   FALCONER OF FALCONHURST. Edinburgh:
Oliphant, 1892 BMC NUC.

SP 69:474. Pleasant romance.

004634   FALLEN FORTUNES. New York: T. Nelson,
1902 PW. London: T. Nelson, [1902] NUC 1903 BMC.

Adventures of a gentleman of quality in the reign of
Queen Anne.

004635   THE FAMILY: SOME REMINISCENCES OF A
HOUSEKEEPER. London: Religious Tract Society, [1894]
BMC.

004636   A FIERY CHARIOT. London: Hutchinson,
[1900] BMC.

004637   FIREBRAND. London: Mascot Novels, [1919]
BMC.

004638   FLATS. Edinburgh: Oliphant, 1894 BMC.

ACAD 46:230. Love story.

004639   FOR THE FAITH: A STORY OF THE YOUNG
PIONEERS OF REFORMATION IN OXFORD. London: Nelson,
1902 NUC BMC.

004640   FRANCESCA. BY CECIL ADAIR. London: S.
Paul, [1912] BMC.

004641   THE FREEDOM OF FENELLA. London: S. Paul,
1918 BMC.

Orphaned drudge in aunt's household, old stuff. TLS
Develops into independent young woman.

004642   FRESH FROM THE FENS: A STORY OF THREE
LINCOLNSHIRE LASSES. BY E. WARD. London: Seeley, 1891
BMC.

004643   GABRIEL GARTH, CHARTIST. London: A.
Melrose, [1902] BMC.

004644   GALBRAITH OF WYNYATES. London: S. Paul,
[1912] BMC.

ATH--Love story.

004645   GOLDEN GWENDOLYN. London: Hutchinson,
[1893] BMC NUC. Boston: A.I. Bradley, 1893 NUC.

She has golden hair and much money. Her guardian
gambles away her inheritance. To escape the
consequences he tries to drive her insane, locks her
up, has her hypnotized. But G's lover saves her.
Sensational. LW 93,333

004646   A GORDON HIGHLANDER. London: T. Nelson,
1901 BMC. New York: 1901 NUC.

004647   GOWRIE'S VENGEANCE: THE ROMANCE OF A
CONSPIRACY. London: T. Nelson, [1908] BMC NUC.

Scotland-history-fiction, James VI

004648   A GREAT INDISCRETION. London: Isbister,
1895 BMC.

004649   GREEN DUSK FOR DREAMS. BY CECIL ADAIR.
London: S. Paul, 1918 BMC.

004650   THE GUARDIANSHIP OF GABRIELLE. London:
Hutchinson, 1908 BMC.

TLS--Sweet simple girl.

004651   GUY FULKES OF THE TOWERS. London:
Hutchinson, 1906 BMC.

TLS--Male, conventional romance.

004652   HALF-A-DOZEN SISTERS. London: Leisure
Hour Monthly library., [1909] NUC BMC.

004653   THE HEIR OF HASCOMBE HALL. A TALE OF THE
DAYS OF THE EARLY TUDORS. London and New York: T.
Nelson, 1900 BMC NUC.

004654   THE HEIRESS OF SWALLOWCLIFFE. London: S.
Paul, 1915 BMC.

004655   HERNSDALE'S HEIR. London: S. Paul, 1915
BMC.

A pretty story. Conventional and artificial. TLS

004656   A HERO OF THE HIGHLANDS; OR THE ROMANCE
OF A REBELLION, AS RELATED BY ONE WHO LOOKED ON.
London: T. Nelson, 1903 BMC NUC.

004657   THE HERONSTOKE MYSTERY. London: R. T. S.,
[1915] BMC.

004658   HILARY QUEST. London: Pilgrim Press, 1908
BMC.

004659   THE HOUSE OF SILENCE. London: Hutchinson,
1910 BMC.

Secretary to author, inspires him; they become engaged
but he marries an heiress. Silence (the secretary)
inherits a house, lives alone, develops her writing
talents. PW 8-26-11.

004660   IN FAIR GRANADA; A TALE OF MOORS AND
CHRISTIANS. London: T. Nelson, 1902 BMC NUC.

004661   IN NORTHERN SEAS. London: T. Nelson,
[1905] BMC.

004662   IN PURSUIT OF A PHANTOM. London: Leisure
Hour Monthly Lib., [1905] BMC NUC.

004663   IN TAUNTON TOWN: A STORY OF THE REBELLION
OF JAMES DUKE OF MONMOUTH IN 1685. London and New
York: T. Nelson, 1896 BMC NUC.

Ill fated rising of Monmouth. PW 10-12-95:631

004664   IN THE DAYS OF CHIVALRY: A TALE OF THE
TIMES OF THE BLACK PRINCE. London and New York: T.
Nelson, 1893 BMC 1895 NUC.

004665   IN THE WARS OF THE ROSES: A STORY FOR THE
YOUNG. London: Nelson, 1892 NUC. London: T. Nelson,
[1906] BMC.

Historical romance, time of Henry VI. SP 67,791

004666   INCHFALLEN. London: Ward, Lock, 1913 BMC.

004667   THE JILTING OF BRUCE HERIOT. London: R.
T. S., [1904] BMC.

004668   JOY'S JUBILEE. London: T. Nelson, 1898
BMC.

004669   JUDITH: THE MONEY-LENDER'S DAUGHTER.
Edinburgh: Oliphant, 1895 BMC. Boston: A. I. Bradley,
1896 NUC.

SP 76:455. "A woman among a thousand." Leonard, hero,
goes to a money-lender.
LW 27:138. Unscrupulous rival contrives to bring a
murder charge against him. Noble Judith never doubts
him.

004670   KEITH'S TRIAL AND VICTORY. London: Sunday
School Union, [1894] BMC.

004671   THE KING'S BUTTERFLY. London: E. Nister,
[1900] BMC. New York: E. P. Dutton, [1900] NUC.

004672   LADY ELIZABETH AND THE JUGGERNAUT.
London: Hodder and Stoughton, 1906 BMC.

TLS--Crusade against the motor car.

004673   THE LADY OF SHALL NOT. London:
Hutchinson, 1909 BMC.

Lady Sheila Knott widowed on wedding day tries to run
her husband's estate. TLS

004674   THE LADY OF THE BUNGALOW. London: S.
Paul, [1911] BMC.

Romantic triangle. TLS

004675   THE LORD OF DYNEVOR: A TALE OF THE TIMES
OF EDWARD THE FIRST. London and New York: T. Nelson,
1892 BMC NUC.

PW-Story of the Welsh struggle against English
conquest.

004676   MADAM OF CLYST PEVERIL. London: A.
Melrose, [1905] BMC.

004677   THE MAGIC ISLAND. BEING THE STORY OF A
GARDEN AND ITS MASTER. London: Hutchinson, 1906 BMC.

TLS--Pretty, idyllic friendship.
ATH

004678   MAID OF THE MOONFLOWER. BY CECIL ADAIR.
London: S. Paul, 1917 BMC.

004679   MARCUS QUAYLE, M.D. London: Hutchinson,
1913 BMC.

A woman in sympathy with the Suffrage movement refuses
to marry a doctor with old fashioned views. ATH
Two heroines One of them airs her views on the subject
of the woman movement at great length. In fact the
book may be called a suffrage novel. TLS

004680   MARRIED IN HASTE. London: Hutchinson,
1907 BMC.

Doreen woos an elderly stranger? TLS

004681   THE MASTER OF FERNHURST. London: J. F.
Shaw, [1900] BMC.

004682   THE MASTER OF MARSHLANDS. London: Ward,
Lock, 1906 BMC.

TLS--Diluted sensation for nice young people.

004683   MAUD MELVILLE'S MARRIAGE: A STORY OF THE
SEVENTEENTH CENTURY. London and New York: T. Nelson,
1893 BMC NUC.

Separated from husband immediately, loses trace of
him, falls into disfavor with her Puritan relations.
PW 10-7-93.

004684   MISS LORIMER OF CHARD. London: Melrose,
1907 BMC.

Typewriter works for the poor, loves a man who has no
sympathy with charity ends in tragedy. TLS

004685   MISS MALLORY OF MOTE. London: Hutchinson,
1912 BMC.

ATH--Woman who is tricked by man is scorned by
neighbors. Two unconventional characters.
TLS--Woman with a past inherits a fortune and settles
in country village.

004686   MISS MARJORIE OF SILVERMEAD. London:
Hutchinson, 1899 BMC. Philadelphia: G. W. Jacobs,
[1901] NUC.

Mystery, a lunatic. Ends in three happy weddings after
many love difficulties. SP 83:844.

004687   MISS URACA. Edinburgh and London:
Oliphant, 1894 BMC.

004688   THE MIST POOL. BY CECIL ADAIR. London: S.
Paul, 1915 BMC.

004689   MONKS--LYONNESS. BY CECIL ADAIR. London:
S. Paul, 1920 BMC.

004690   MONSTER'S MISTRESS. London: S. Paul, 1919
BMC.

Pretty tale of old man, dogs and children. TLS

004691   A MOTHERLESS MAID. London: A. Melrose,
[1906] BMC.

004692   MRS. DESMOND'S DAUGHTER. London: Morgan
and Scott, [1919] BMC.

004693   MRS. ROMAINE'S HOUSEHOLD. Edinburgh and
London: Oliphant, 1891 BMC. Boston: Bradley and
Woodruff, 1891 NUC.

Clare Chesterton becomes a governess in this household
after her mother dies. Eventually she becomes the
strongest influence on the family. Everyday events, a
love story and a tragedy. PW

004694   MY LADY JOANNA. BEING A CHRONICLE
CONCERNING THE KING'S CHILDREN. London: J. Nisbet,
1902 BMC.

ATH 10-18-02.

004695   THE MYSTERY OF ALTON GRANGE. London: T.
Nelson, 1899 BMC.

004696   NAMESAKES: THE STORY OF A SECRET. London:

Hutchinson, [1892] BMC.

004697   THE NIECE OF ESTHER LYNNE. London:
Hutchinson, 1903 BMC NUC.

004698   ODEYNE'S MARRIAGE. London: J. F. Shaw,
[1900] BMC.

004699   OLD MISS AUDREY: A CHRONICLE OF A QUIET
VILLAGE. London: Religious Tract Society, 1892 BMC.
New York: Revell, [189-?] NUC.

004700   OLIVE ROSCOE: OR THE NEW SISTER. London
and New York: T. Nelson, 1896 BMC NUC.

PW 11-14-96. Olive always believed she was an orphan
until she learned she had a father and brother. Her
experiences in her new home.
Bright courageous heroine, a recluse, a three-cornered
house, a colliery, a heroical invalid. CR 26,30:441.
Juv?

004701   OLIVIA'S EXPERIMENT. London: Hutchinson,
1901 BMC.

004702   OUR GREAT UNDERTAKING: A GRANDMOTHER'S
STORY. London: Hodder and Stoughton, 1906 BMC.

004703   A PAIR OF ORIGINALS: A STORY. BY E. WARD.
London: Seeley, 1892 BMC.

004704   A PAIR OF PICKLES. Edinburgh: Oliphant,
1892 BMC. Boston: Bradley, 1899 NUC.

004705   PATRICIA PENDRAGON: A NOVEL. BY E. WARD.
London: F. V. White, 1911 BMC.

004706   THE PRICE OF FRIENDSHIP. London: S. Paul,
1913 BMC.

Man impersonates friend to save friend's sister and
estate from unscrupulous uncle. He falls in love with
the sister.

004707   PRINCESS FAIRSTAR. New York: Dutton, 1901
PW. London: E. Nister, [1901] BMC.

004708   QUADRILLE COURT. BY CECIL ADAIR. London:
S. Paul, 1913 BMC. New York: International Fiction
Library, [c1929] NUC.

004709   THE QUALITIES OF MERCY. BY CECIL ADAIR.
London: S. Paul, [1911] BMC.

004710   A QUEEN OF HEARTS. London: F. V. White,
1909 BMC.

For girls. TLS

004711   RALPH ROXBURGH'S REVENGE. London: Sunday
School Union, [1895] BMC.

004712   RINGED BY FIRE: A STORY OF THE
FRANCO-PRUSSIAN WAR. BY E. EVERETT GREEN. London:
Nelson, [1904] BMC [1905] NUC.

004713   RONALD KENNEDY; OR A DOMESTIC DIFFICULTY.
London: S. W. Partridge, [1893] BMC.

004714   RUTH RAVELSTAN, THE PURITAN'S DAUGHTER.
London: T. Nelson, [1907] BMC NUC.

004715   THE SAILS OF LIFE. BY CECIL ADAIR.
London: S. Paul, 1915 BMC. New York: Brentano's, 1915
NUC.

004716   THE SECRET CHAMBER AT CHAD. London and
New York: T. Nelson, 1894 BMC NUC.

004717   THE SECRET OF MAX-SHELLING. New York:
Dutton, 1901 PW. London: J. F. Shaw, [1902] BMC.

004718   THE SECRET OF WOLD HULL. Chicago: A. C.
McClurg, 1905 NUC. London: Hutchinson, 1905 BMC.

A contracted marriage; wife hears mysterious rumors
about husband's life. PW
NYT--matrimonial bargain lacking? Sentiment.

004719   SHADOW-LAND; OR, WHAT LINDIS
ACCOMPLISHED. London: J. F. Shaw, 1892 BMC.

004720   SHUT IN: A TALE OF THE WONDERFUL SIEGE OF
ANTWERP IN . . . 1585. London: T. Nelson, 1894 BMC
NUC.

004721   THE SIGN OF THE RED CROSS: A TALE OF OLD
LONDON. BY E. EVERETT GREEN. London and New York: T.
Nelson, 1897 BMC NUC.

Time of London plague. A love story. Climax comes with
London fire. LW 28:27.
PW 12-12-96. Plague in London. Two young women who
nursed victims. Description of fire which followed.

004722   THE SILVER AXE. THE NARRATIVE OF RUPERT,
EARL OF HERONDALE. London: Hutchinson, 1900 BMC.

004723   THE SILVER TEA-SHOP. London: S. Paul,
1920 BMC.

TLS--Ordinary and pretty.

004724   "SISTER". A CHRONICLE OF FAIR HAVEN. BY
E. EVERETT GREEN. London and New York: T. Nelson, 1898
BMC NUC.

SR 85:566. Lovers parted by misunderstanding: marry
when they are middle-aged. For girls.

004725   SMOULDERING FIRES; OR THE KINSMEN OF
KINTHORNS. London: T. Nelson, [1905] BMC.

004726   A SOLDIER'S SON AND THE BATTLE HE FOUGHT.
London: J. F. Shaw, [1896] BMC.

004727   THE SQUIRE'S HEIR, OR THE SECRET OF
ROCHESTER'S WILL. London: A. Melrose, [1903] BMC.

004728   ST. DUNSTAN'S CLOCK, A STORY OF 1666. BY
E. WARD. London: Seeley, 1893 BMC.

004729   ST. WYNFRITH AND ITS INMATES: THE STORY
OF AN ALMSHOUSE. London: Jarrold, [1893] BMC.

ACAD 45:123. Almshouse life. "Sad story of Sarah
French."

004730   A STEPMOTHER'S STRATEGY. London:
Hutchinson, [1895] BMC.

004731   THE SUNNY SIDE OF THE STREET. A STORY OF
PATIENT WAITING. London: Religious Tract Society,
[1895] BMC.

004732   SUPERFLUOUS SISTERS. London: Hutchinson,
1907 BMC.

Sisters of husband react to new wife. TLS

004733   THE TEMPTATION OF MARY LISTER. London: S.
Paul, 1917 BMC.

A family feud leading up to the heroine's
impersonation of a dead friend and namesake whose
desire for vengeance she has solemly promised to
satisfy.

004734   THE THREE GRACES. London: A. Melrose,
[1904] BMC.

ATH--For young people.

004735   TOM HERON OF SAX. A STORY OF THE
EVANGELICAL REVIVAL OF THE EIGHTEENTH CENTURY. London:
Religious Tract Society, [1893] BMC. New York: Hunt
and Eaton, n.d. NUC.

Days of Wesley and Whitehead. He's a wild dare-devil
young blacksmith, influenced by minister. His stormy
rel. experiences recounted. Aim-to show first days of
Methodism. PW 11-11-93.

004736   TRUE STORIES OF GIRL HEROINES. New York:
E. P. Dutton, 1901 [?] NUC. London: Hutchinson,
[1901?] BMC NUC.

004737   UNDER THE INCENSE TREES. BY CECIL ADAIR.
London: S. Paul, 1914 BMC.

004738   UNDER TWO QUEENS. London: J. F. Shaw,
[1904] BMC NUC.

004739   URSULA TEMPEST. London: R. T. S., [1910]
BMC.

ATH--Against Christian Science, spirituality,
hypnotism. Biblical criticism is a sin. Woman suffrage
treated with less hostility and the lives of educated
girl--workers are described in a pleasant and
sympathetic manner.

004740   WHERE THERE'S A WILL. London: Hutchinson, [1902] BMC.

004741   WHITE WYVILL AND RED RUTHVEN. A STORY OF THE STRIFE OF THE ROSES. London: E. Nister, [1902] BMC.

004742   THE WIFE OF ARTHUR LORRAINE. A NOVEL. London: F. V. White, 1910 BMC.

ACAD--Mrg. as it should be.

004743   THE WILFUL WILLOUGHBYS; A CATHEDRAL CITY STORY. Edinburgh: Oliphant, 1893 BMC.

LW 27:47. Three heroines and their love stories.

004744   A WILL IN A WELL. London: S. Paul, 1910 BMC.

TLS--Inheritance romance.
ACAD.--ditto
LBKM--ditto

004745   THE WOOING OF VAL: THE STORY OF SIX DAYS. London: Hutchinson, 1900 BMC.

004746   WYHOLA. Edinburgh: Oliphant, 1892 BMC.

ACAD. Romance of Wyhola, a "rustic, passionless beauty" of Puritan upbringing.

GREEN, EVELYN EVERETT AND H. LOUISA BEDFORD.

004747   HIS CHOICE--AND HERS. THE STORY OF AN EPISODE. London: Christian Knowledge Society, [1895] BMC.

Hero Cyril Benson is a preacher-crusader vs vice. Sylvia O'Connor a lively Irish heroine. The two fall in love, have the usual difficulties. He dies before Sylvia really makes up her mind. He has been an episode, for there's a hint she'll marry Jim.

GREEN, EVELYN EVERETT, jt. au. See BEDFORD, H. LOUISA AND EVELYN EVERETT GREEN.

GREEN, HELEN. B. 1882. United States.

004748   THE MAISON DE SHINE; MORE STORIES OF THE ACTORS' BOARDING HOUSE. New York: B. W. Dodge, 1908 NUC.

NYT-

004749   MR. JACKSON. New York: B. W. Dodge, 1909 NUC.

GREEN, M. P. United States.

004750   DEAD IN THE EYE OF THE LAW. BY GAY PARKER. London: F. Warne, [1892] BMC. Chicago: Melbourne Pub. Co., 1892 NUC.

004751   THE FIGHT FOR DOMINION: A ROMANCE OF OUR FIRST WAR WITH SPAIN. BY GAY PARKER. New York: E. R. Herrick, [c1899] NUC.

Historical romance. Spanish don and Englishman rivals for a senorita. Time of Spanish dominion in Florida. Gen. Oglethorpe, Governor of Georgia is a prominent character. PW 55:775

004752   LA BELLE CREOLE. BY GAY PARKER. Chicago: E. A. Weeks, [1893] NUC.

PW. Ross and DeJarnette are friends in the Barbados; the latter dies and Ross impersonates him. Sensational events are a sequel, particularly those in New Orleans with Lucille de Guarcia (La Belle Creole)

GREEN, MARYON URQUHART. United Kingdom.

004753   THE FOOL OF FAERY. BY M. URQUHART. London: Mills and Boon, [1910] BMC NUC.

TLS Married woman and government clerk; sounds like focus is on him.
ATH she "unconsciously feeds his love" but her heart is with her husband

004754   THE ISLAND OF SOULS: BEING A SENSATIONAL FAIRY-TALE. BY M. URQUHART. London: Mills & Boon, 1910 BMC.

004755   THE MODELLING OF THE CLAY. BY M.

URQUHART. London: E. Nash, 1909 BMC.

004756   OUR LADY OF THE MISTS: A ROMANCE OF MEMORY. BY M. URQUHART. London: Hurst and Blackett, 1907 BMC.

young girl has visions of the Madonna "psychologic" TLS

004757   A TRAGEDY IN COMMONPLACE. BY M. URQUHART. London: Methuen, 1905 BMC.

Sophia has to bear the brunt with poverty year after year. her husband's no help with the six children. Yet the father wins their love. Sophia's devotion to household makes her squalid, her fault-finding, a disease. There's a miserable life long feud between her and her daughter. Behaves unpardonably to her daughter. We're given the gradual demoralization of the mother- looked upon sympathetically. ACAD 907,05 Husband weak, improvident, wife hard on herself and others, rigi d conception of duty. Sophia loses her youth with her children, always finding fault-this alienates the children; long struggle with daughter TLS 250,05
Ages quickly; husband with narrow mind, gives birth to an ugly daughter and several commonplace sons and a crippled boy. The girl grows up a wild genius but hates mother. Later struggle, daughter leaves. Mother dies unreconciled with anyone.

004758   THE WHEEL: A BOOK OF BEGINNINGS. BY M. URQUHART. London: Hurst and Blackett, 1907 BMC.

dual nature of a boy to manhood; two women who influence him LBKM brief desc. 4-07,35
a clear-eyed "boy-girl" but only a minor char ACAD focuses on hero TLS

GREENE, AELLA. 1838-1903. United States.

004759   CULMINATIONS: A NOVEL. [Springfield, Mass.]: [C. W. Bryan], 1892 NUC.

GREENE, ALICE CLAYTON.

004760   MIRIAM AND THE PHILISTINES. London: L. Parsons, 1920 BMC.

TLS-lived with another man and went back to her husband.
ATH -Brought up by, family disowned father as member of touring company. when he dies goes to live with grandmother. Her views of life at odds with conv. soc. and has courage of her convictions

GREENE, BELLE C. See GREENE, ISABEL CATHERINE (COLTON).

GREENE, FRANCES NIMMO. 1850-1921. United States.

004761   THE DEVIL TO PAY. New York: Scribner's Sons, 1918 NUC.

PW- Murder mystery.
NYT May 5, 1918, p 207; murder myst., as seen through eyes of 20 year old young man devoted to his older sister and determined to solve the mystery for her sake.

004762   INTO THE NIGHT: A STORY OF NEW ORLEANS. New York: T. Y. Crowell, [1909] NUC. London: Methuen, 1910 BMC.

Mafia in New Orleans 10-2-09
BM Mafia plotting in New Orleans
TLS Mafia ends in a murder
ATH. number of Italians lynched. Mafia steps in for revenge "Interest centers on a derelict babe raised by a citizen among his own children and finds an heroic death." Char. study of strong man and woman who enter into an ideal union."

004763   ONE CLEAR CALL. New York: Scribner's Sons, 1914 NUC.

BKM 40 1914-15
"Hamilton, a young physician, is seriously injured in an automobile accident caused by trying to avoid a beggar. A grateful patient, a woman with a mystery, cheers his convalescence and wins his love. Among Hamilton's friends are the Garnetts, an old couple with a black-sheep son. Hamilton is the means of influencing Garnett to right some of his wrongs toward others. It falls out that the woman of mystery is Garnett's wife. She decides to return to him, but his death makes the sacrifice unnecessary." PW 86

10/17/14:1245
NYT 1914:488. Plot of the novel turns on Garnett
Story of a man with short time to live who tries to
compensate for his evil life BKM

004764   THE RIGHT OF THE STRONGEST. New York:
Scribner's Sons, 1913 NUC.

BKM v. 37 1913 rev takes side of man
"Mary Elizabeth, after 10 years of careful schooling
in the city, comes back to the Alabama mountains to
teach and help her people. STory of her father's fate,
unknown to her, makes some of the natives hate and
fear her. Into the hills comes John Marshall, seeking
to add to his great wealth. He has discovered that he
can develop a great water power and that the legal
process, will be easy, but he reckons without the
mountain spirit and Mary Elizabeth, who loves him but
opposes him. Before the climax is reached he has to
deal with love, hate, and a mountain feud." PW.

GREENE, FRANCES NIMMO AND DOLLY WILLIAMS KIRK.

004765   WITH SPURS OF GOLD: HEROES OF CHIVALRY
AND THEIR DEEDS. Boston: Little, Brown, 1905 NUC.

GREENE, ISABEL CATHERINE (COLTON). United States.

004766   MR. AND MRS. HANNIBAL HAWKINS. BY BELLE
C. GREENE. New York: American Pub. Corp., [c1897] NUC.

GREENE, MARY ELLEN (BROWN). B. 1848. Nationality Unknown.

004767   THE DOOR WHERE THE WRONG LAY. Boston: C.
M. Clark, 1909 NUC.

Father turns out daughter who marries against his
will. PW 6-26-09

GREENE, NANCI LEWIS. United States.

004768   NANCE: A STORY OF KENTUCKY FEUDS.
Chicago,: F. T. Neely, [c1893] NUC BMC.

GREENE, SARAH PRATT (MACLEAN). 1856-1935. United States.

004769   DEACON LYSANDER. New York: Baker &
Taylor, [1904] BMC NUC.

PW- silly
NYT

004770   EVERBREEZE. New York and London: D.
Appleton, 1913 BMC NUC.

Two American women go "to vegetate" in the country.
TLS
"By author of "Cape Cod Folks." Geraldine Keever with
her compaion, Bertha Russ, goes to Tyne Valley for her
health, and there becomes so interested in the odd
people round her, including an "Irish" cook of Arabian
extraction, and a gentlemen hermit, that she forgets
to be sick. Love affairs for both girls follow, and
come to a happy conclusion." PW

004771   FLOOD TIDE. New York: Harper, 1901 BMC
NUC. Sydney: Angus & Robertson, 1902 BMC.

004772   THE LONG GREEN ROAD. New York: Baker &
Taylor, 1911 NUC.

NYT-rel. male hero.
Focuses on a man and religion. 11-18-11 PW

004773   THE MORAL IMBECILES. New York and London:
Harper, 1898 NUC.

BKM 8:166. Family members, quite conventional and
ordinary, dominated by a disagreeable young woman.
NYT 1898:631. Heroine is plain, capable. She becomes
manager of millionaire household; is loved and admired
by all including trillionaire suitor of daughter,
marries son. Daughter takes possession, in turn, of
heroine's humble Vermont farm, marries her brother.
Silly.

004774   POWER LOT. New York: Baker & Taylor,
[1906] BMC NUC. Toronto: Musson Book, [1906] NUC.

PW-Island romance.

004775   STUART AND BAMBOO: A NOVEL. New York and
London: Harper, 1897 BMC NUC.

"The beauty of human sympathy and universal
sisterhood" is the theme. A young woman accustomed to

luxury comes to the slums with $1.75. Works and
eventually dies there. CR 28,31:340.
Yarmouth. PW 52:672.
LIT 2:326. Study of life manners and passions in
American seaport town. Margaret Stuart with mysterious
past comes to Yarmouth to live and work. Stays at Mrs.
O'Ragan Stuart's boarding house which houses a variety
of people. Mrs. Stuart refers to any one not Celtic
and Roman Catholic as a Bamboo.

004776   VESTY OF THE BASINS: A NOVEL. New York:
Harper, 1892 NUC BMC.

CR 5-6-92. Cape Cod. Community beyond the pale, so low
in social status. Crippled English nobleman meets
Vesty there, romance.

004777   WINSLOW PLAIN. New York and London:
Harper, 1902 BMC NUC.

BOOK NEWS 12-02 Patience "is broad and liberal in the
midst of a straitened creed-ridden circle".

GREENLEAF, SUE. United States.

004778   DON MIGUEL LEHUMADA, DISCOVERER OF LIQUID
FROM THE SUN'S RAYS; AN OCCULT ROMANCE OF MEXICO AND
THE UNITED STATES. New York: B. W. Dodge, [c1906] NUC.

Pub in 1901 under title "liquid from the sun's rays".

004779   LIQUID FROM THE SUN'S RAYS. New York and
London: Abbey Press, [c1901] NUC.

004780   WED BY MIGHTY WAVES; A THRILLING ROMANCE
OF ILL-FATED GALVESTON. Chicago: Laird & Lee, [1901]
NUC.

Galveston, Tex-Storm, 1900

GREENSLET, ELLA STOOTHOFF (HULST). B. 1873. United States.

004781   THE NIGHTINGALE; A LARK. BY ELLENOR
STOOTHOFF. Boston: Houghton Mifflin, 1914 NUC.

Hilda Manely is a pampered spoiled wife who comes to
realize her selfishness and uselessness. Essentially
she's a woman of strong purpose. To save what's left
of her marriage tells husband she's going to Europe
and he must ask no questions. He under- stands her
"irresistible longing to roam the world." She has many
varied and bizarre advents. "There's a deep-lying
wisdom behind this eccentric move to leave her
husband." She se ts a date to return-when she hears
first nightingale. Away many months. Husband patient
in her "break for freedom" BKM 40 1914-1915
"The lark is not another name for the nightingale; it
describes Hilda's stay abroad. She goes there to rest
from society and her husband, and to get what
adventure her second-hand car can keep up with. She
really is a lovely woman, but she has got tired. In
Italy she hears a nightingale sing. In England her
husband joins her, bringing the precious bird in a
cage, the harbinger of their second honeymoon." PW 86
10/24/14;1344

GREENWOOD, GRACE, pseud. See LIPPINCOTT, SARA JANE
(CLARKE).

GREGG, HILDA CAROLINE. 1868-1933. United Kingdom.

004782   THE ADVANCED-GUARD. BY SYDNEY C. GRIER.
Edinburgh and London: W. Blackwood, 1903 BMC NUC.

"perverse and original wife" unconven. end. ACAD
64,318
Review ACAD 64, 342 focuses on hero
two women, one early Vict. type, the other energetic,
brave ATH 121, 430
Penelope is an old fashioned woman, marries a no-good
because he needs woman TLS 137,03

004783   BERRINGER OF BANDEIR. BY SYDNEY C. GRIER.
Edinburgh and London: W. Blackwood, 1919 BMC.

Plots, conspiracies, advents, etc TLS

004784   A CROWNED QUEEN: THE ROMANCE OF A
MINISTER OF STATE. BY SYDNEY C. GRIER. Edinburgh and
London: W. Blackwood, 1898 BMC NUC.

SP 81:410. Ruritania. Lord Cyril and Queen Ernestine.
Sequel to An uncrowned king.
LIT 3:604. Cyril leaves her court without remorse when
ambition calls.
LBKM 15:23. She is shrewish, willful, but abases

herself when in love with Cyril. She is willing to
give up her kingdom, go anywhere with him, but he has
cooled and refuses her in a humiliating way.

004785   ENGLAND HATH NEED OF THEE. BY SYDNEY C.
GRIER. Edinburgh and London: W. Blackwood, 1916 BMC.

    TLS-India-frontier
    ATH-nothing here

004786   FOR TRIUMPH OR TRUTH? A TALE OF THRILLING
ADVENTURE. BY SYDNEY C. GRIER. London: J. F. Shaw,
[1904] BMC.

004787   THE GREAT PROCONSUL. THE MEMOIRS OF MRS.
HESTER WARD, FORMERLY IN THE FAMILY OF WARREN
HASTINGS. BY SYDNEY C. GRIER. Edinburgh: W. Blackwood,
1904 BMC NUC. London:

    LBKM Diary of Mrs. Ward who lived thru some startling
    adventures
    ACAD-hist novel of Warren Hastings

004788   THE HEIR. BY SYDNEY C. GRIER. Edinburgh:
W. Blackwood, 1906 BMC NUC.

    TLS adventure story over rival claims to a throne
    ATH Strong hearted women
    BKM strong hearted women

004789   THE HERITAGE. BY SYDNEY C. GRIER.
Edinburgh and London: W. Blackwood, 1908 BMC NUC.

    TLS-Eirene, wife of Jeffany inherrits money to restore
    he husband's house to the throne of Emathia. Restless
    after 7 years of mrg she bolts to the Balkans with her
    husband, a friend and sister Zoe who is a writer. Seq.
    to The Heir.
    ACAD-0
    ATH 0

004790   HIS EXCELLENCY'S ENGLISH GOVERNESS. BY
SYDNEY C. GRIER. Edinburgh and London: W. Blackwood,
1896 BMC NUC.

    ACAD 50:199
    LBKM 10:119. Heroine has a B. A., goes to Bagdad as
    teacher of 10 year old Azim Bey, a most precocious
    child who becomes devotedly attached to her.
    Adventures
    ATH 107:839. Her name is Cecil, Her lover is a doctor,
    also at the court.
    ACAD 50:198. The women of the harem are very jealous
    of her; Azim is very jealous of the doctor. These
    feelings result in situations which reach the
    magnitude of international incidents.

004791   IN FURTHEST IND. THE NARRATIVE OF MR.
EDWARD CARLYTON OF THE HONOURABLE EAST INDIA COMPANY'S
SERVICE. BY SYDNEY C. GRIER. Edinburgh and London: W.
Blackwood, 1894 BMC NUC.

    ATH 104:672. The English in India in the 17th century.
    Historical romance. 1st person narration of hero.
    LBKM 7:56. Carefully researched. The breaking of new
    ground in fiction in describing the company's
    activities. One of the most ingenious imitations of an
    actual record ever written.

004792   THE KEEPERS OF THE GATE. BY SYDNEY C.
GRIER. Edinburgh and London: W. Blackwood, 1911 NUC
BMC.

    Indian frontier and mutiny TLS

004793   THE KINGDOM OF THE WASTE-LANDS. BY SYDNEY
C. GRIER. Edinburgh and London: Blackwood, 1917 BMC.

    Rebels and perils and advent TLS

004794   THE KINGS OF THE EAST: A ROMANCE OF THE
NEAR FUTURE. BY SYDNEY C. GRIER. Edinburgh and London:
W. Blackwood, 1900 BMC NUC. Boston: L. C. Page, 1902
NUC.

    LBKM 18:97. Cyril becomes head of Israel syndicate.
    International intrigue. Cyril's ambitious hopes end in
    disaster, but he "wins the hand" of Queen Ernestine.
    SP 84:558. Thru the syndicate the Jews of all nations
    hope to purchase Palestine.

004795   LIKE ANOTHER HELEN. BY SYDNEY C. GRIER.
Edinburgh and London: W. Blackwood, 1899 BMC NUC.
Boston: L. C. Page, 1902 NUC.

    In letter form. Bengal in the terrible years 1755-7.

The early letters from her boarding school. Then the
gruesome experiences of the writer Sylvia Freyne. The
Fall of Calcutta, English revenge. LIT. 5:134
Sophie Freyne "like another Helen finds another Troy"
and writes about it. LBKM 16:171 also SP 83:192.
Letters between two young women concerning Black Hole
incident in India in 18th BAKER 03 117

004796   ON THE WINNING SIDE. BY SYDNEY C. GRIER.
London: J. F. Shaw, [1904] BMC.

004797   ONE CROWDED HOUR. BY SYDNEY C. GRIER.
Edinburgh and London: W. Blackwood, 1912 BMC.

    ATH hist rom with love interest.

004798   THE PATH OF HONOUR. BY SYDNEY C. GRIER.
London: W. Blackwood, 1909 BMC.

    Honour beaut. serious, anxious to reform men. The
    course of the wooing of her is the story, hist rom TLS
    two young soldiers in India ACAD

004799   PEACE WITH HONOUR. BY SYDNEY C. GRIER.
Edinburgh and London: W. Blackwood, 1897 BMC. Boston:
L. C. Page, 1902 NUC.

    The heroine is a doctor attached to the Ethiopian
    Mission. There's a Brit officer who is at first
    completely prejudiced against New Women. ACAD 52 Fic
    Sup 106.
    "She accompanies a Eur. mission to the court of a
    semi-civilized state in Central Asia." ATH 110:744.
    SP 81:473. On a mission to Ethiopia are Georgia
    Keeling, M.D., and Major Richard North. He once loved
    her as a boy but she did not reciprocate. Also, she is
    now a "new woman" which he abhors.
    Story is of their relationship and mission's
    adventures, political intrigue, etc. LIT 3:116.
    BOOK NEWS 11-1902-young woman doctor who goes to
    Abyssinia to practice in the Sultan's harem.

004800   THE POWER OF THE KEYS. BY SYDNEY C.
GRIER. London and Edinburgh: W. Blackwood, 1907 BMC
NUC.

    The British in India LBKM 11-07, 99

004801   THE PRINCE OF THE CAPTIVITY: THE EPILOGUE
TO A ROMANCE. BY SYDNEY C. GRIER. Edinburgh: W.
Blackwood, 1902 BMC. Boston: L.C. Page, 1902 NUC.

    --concerns mrg. choice of heroine LBKM 7-02
    2 disagreeable American girls.
    ATH 5-31-02 American heroine best of the characters.

004802   THE PRINCESS'S TRAGEDY. BY SYDNEY C.
GRIER. Edinburgh and London: W. Blackwood, 1918 BMC.

    TLS 18th century princess of high born spirit

004803   THE PRIZE. BY SYDNEY C. GRIER. Edinburgh
and London: W. Blackwood, 1910 BMC NUC.

    TLS sequel, heroine adv. spirited firebrand fighting
    for house of Theophoms in Emathia
    ACAD Danae, a woman of spirt and resource. trilogy-the
    Heir-the Heritage before Danae, heroine, "a wild cat"
    whose adventures end happily in marriage. LBKM

004804   THE REARGUARD. BY SYDNEY C. GRIER.
Blackwood: 1915 NUC BMC.

    hero devotes self to natives of East Indies becoming
    their "beneficent Sovereign" He is a minister whose
    daughters are suppressed. The middle daughter "a dowdy
    shrinking little woman" achieves great fame as a
    novelist writing under pseudonym TLS

004805   A ROYAL MARRIAGE. BY SYDNEY C. GRIER.
Edinburgh and London: W. Blackwood, 1914 BMC.

    ATH hist rom. love-tale of an Eng princess in 18th c
    Germany

004806   THE STRONG HAND. BY SYDNEY C. GRIER.
Edinburgh and London: W. Blackwood, 1920 BMC.

    TLS-Hist rom

004807   AN UNCROWNED KING: A ROMANCE OF HIGH
POLITICS. BY SYDNEY C. GRIER. Edinburgh: W. Blackwood,
1896 BMC. New York: G. P. Putnam, 1896 NUC.

    ACAD 50:528. Not a romance. Political intrigue in the
    Balkans. Lord Carleon, Englishman, accepts a crown in

Thracia.
PW 11-14-96. He has liberal political ideas, is
interested in reform.
Lord Carleton of England House of Peers fills Throne
of Thracia. Involves a revolution. Falls in love with
Nadia O'Malachy whose parents are spies. She's rude,
rough. Refuses to share the throne. Carleton loses it;
tries war to regain it. At the end Nadia
succombs-agrees to be his doormat. LBKM 11:152
Prime minister of Thracia offers crown to English man.
He accepts, but when he falls in love with a spy's
daughter things get hairy. She is Nadia O'Malachy. SP
78:569

004808   THE WARDEN OF THE MARCHES. BY SYDNEY C.
GRIER. Edinburgh: W. Blackwood, 1901 BMC. Boston: L.C.
Page, 1902 NUC.

ATH 5-18-01
NYT 8-30-02 hist--

004809   WRIT IN WATER. BY SYDNEY C. GRIER.
Edinburgh and London: W. Blackwood, 1913 BMC NUC.

Governor Eyre of Jamaica in early 60s basis of this
story-very true to hist detail with a sub-plot
concerning two young women.
SP
An Englishman marries a woman who is anti-black
without telling her he has a strain of Asiatic blood
in him ATH

004810   A YOUNG MAN MARRIED. BY SYDNEY C. GRIER.
London: Hutchinson, 1909 BMC NUC.

hist war rom TLS
wife appears in every battle in which husband's
engaged SP

GREGG, HORTENSE GARDNER. United States.

004811   JAC AND GILL; OR, A SISTER'S FIDELITY. A
NOVEL. Norway, Me.: Advertiser Book Print, 1898 NUC.

GREGOR, MRS. JAMES.

004812   WHOSE WAS THE BLAME? A WOMAN'S VERSION OF
THE KREUTZER SONATA. London: S. Sonnenschein, 1894
BMC.

GREVILLE, BEATRICE VIOLET (GRAHAM) GREVILLE. 1842-1932.

004813   THE FIGHTERS. A NOVEL. London: Chapman
and Hall, 1907 BMC.

Hist rom ACAD
Story of the Penninsular war.
Heroine, an adventuress, marries British officer to
spy on our troops. SP

004814   THE HOME FOR FAILURES. London:
Hutchinson, 1896 BMC NUC.

ATH 109:12. Oriza, discontented with life offers her
house to miscellaneous collection of men and women.
She has a friend, the Hon. Rachel Cator, who has good
sense, vitality, rides a bike, "which latter is
becoming a tiresome intrusion in a class of fiction
that aspires above all to be modern."
Trag end. Oriza opens her home to lonely people,
failures. Her friend Hon. Rachel Cator and her bike.
ATH 109:12

004815   THAT HATED SAXON. London: Ward and
Downey, 1892 NUC 1893 BMC.

Two English men take up quarters in Irish country home
for hunting season with family of two beautiful young
women. After many halts and starts, the unions are
made and the Saxon no longer hated. SR 75:518.
Mona Murphy-"wild Irish girl in the early stages of
development." ACAD 43:322.

GREVILLE, HENRI, pseud. See DURAND, ALICE MARIE CELESTE
(FLEURY).

GREY, EVELYN.

004816   OUTRAGEOUS FORTUNE: BEING THE STORY OF
EVELYN GREY, HOSPITAL NURSE. London: Greening, 1900
BMC.

ACAD 58:334. Story of Evelyn Grey, Hospital nurse, a
seducer, misfortunes and ultimate happiness.
She has misfortunes which involve a seducer but
eventual happiness.

GREY, ROWLAND, pseud. See BROWN, LILIAN KATE ROWLAND.

GRIER, JULIA.

004817   SOULS ADRIFT. London: Digby, Long, 1909
BMC.

Rel. story TLS

GRIER, SYDNEY C., pseud. See GREGG, HILDA CAROLINE.

GRIFFIN, E. ACEITUNA. See GRIFFIN, EDITH ACEITUNA.

GRIFFIN, EDITH ACEITUNA. B. 1876.

004818   LADY SARAH'S DEED OF GIFT. BY E. ACEITUNA
GRIFFIN. Edinburgh and London: W. Blackwood, 1906 BMC.

ACAD-? young wife given money by older woman to leave
husband during contest of wills "wife gave in".
TLS-money from aunt of husband as an experiment in
human nature,reconciliation at end.

004819   MRS. VANNECK. BY E. ACEITUNA GRIFFIN.
London: E. Nash, 1907 BMC.

Beautiful, unscrupulous young widow avenges her half
sister by scheming with a young peer. TLS

004820   A SERVANT OF THE KING. BY E. ACEITUNA
GRIFFIN. Edinburgh and London: W. Blackwood, 1906 BMC.

ACAD tr hist rom.
ATH tr. hist rom

004821   THE TAVISTOCKS. BY E. ACEITUNA GRIFFIN.
London: T. W. Laurie, [1908] BMC.

TLS- two married sisters get in trouble while husbands
are away.

GRIFFIN, MRS. ELLEN M. See HOEY, ELLEN MARY (GRIFFIN).

GRIFFITH, CECIL. See BECKETT, CECIL (GRIFFITH).

GRIFFITH, HELEN (SHERMAN). 1873-1961. United States.

004822   ROSEMARY FOR REMEMBRANCE. Philadelphia:
Penn, 1911 NUC.

usual rom involved story. PW 10-28-11

GRIFFITH, MRS. L. W.

004823   ARTHUR. London: G. Routledge, 1920 BMC.

ATH-Little boy.

GRIFFITH, SUSAN M. B. 1851. United States.

004824   AN HUNDRED-FOLD; OR MRS. BELMONT'S
HARVEST. Richmond, Va.: Presbyterian Committee of
Publication, [c1898] NUC.

PW-step mother wins over children of clergyman,
California.

GRIFFITHS, GERTRUDE. United Kingdom.

004825   THE LURE OF THE MANOR. BY GERTRUDE
GRIFFITHS (MRS. PERCIVAL GRIFFITHS). London:
Skeffington, [c1919] BMC NUC. New York: Duffield, 1920
NUC.

A pleasing romance about gentle folks. TLS
NYT 7/11/20 p. 21. Romance, two heroines, three maiden
aunts.

004826   THE WEDDING GOWN OF "OLE MISS": A ROMANCE
OF VIRGINIA. BY GERTRUDE GRIFFITHS (MRS. PERCIVAL
GRIFFITHS). London: Skeffington, [c1918] BMC NUC.

TLS-Rom. tr.

GRIFFITHS, MRS. PERCIVAL. See GRIFFITHS, GERTRUDE.

GRIMSHAW, BEATRICE ETHEL. 1871-1953. Australia.

004827   BROKEN AWAY. London and New York: J.
Lane, 1897 BMC NUC.

About literary and professional people and the
Rivingtons on holiday and the madness of the writer
Moore who believes Rivington has stolen his brains. SP
79:628.

Two would be eminent writers, one a homicidal maniac.
ATH 109:611.
Stuart Rivington's wife tells him his latest novel is
weak; he believes. Move away from Dublin to get fresh
inspiration. Meet the insane rival novelist. PW
51:609.
Author's (male) writing career begins to fail. He
becomes worried about his health. Dr. says he's
homicidal. This author is Alfred Moore. Stuart
Rivington writes himself dry, wife suggests a rest so
they go off to the mts. His writing immediately
improves. Along comes Moore who believes Stuart has
stolen his brains. Tries to kill him but he survives
to write his greater novel. NYT 5-22-97.

004828   GUINEA GOLD. London: Mills & Boon, 1912
BMC. New York: Moffat, Yard, 1912 NUC.

TLS- search for gold.
SP- Mrs Carter "the Queen of the Northwest Island" is
a benevolent Amazon unfeminine type.
PW 83 3/8/13 : p. 877 "Another story of New Guinea by
author of "When the red gods call." George Scott, an
engineer from Belfast, through a strange chance learns
of a rich vein of gold in New Guinea. He sells his
business and leaving his fiancee goes out to find it.
His adventures with descriptions of the natives and
Europeans in this distant land make up an interesting
story, in which Scott has to face a conflict between
love and honor, and one of the characters proves that
the age of chivalry is not dead."
And there's the other woman, her beauty, helpless
clinging "the incarnation of a man's ideal-a type
apparently destined to become as extinct as a dodo" "a
man's woman" Charinian her name.
Mrs. Carter, queen of the Northwest Island, by virtue
of her motherliness is "not wholly masculine" NYT
Three men seek gold; we learn about their conflicts
and struggles. parallel story-love interest LBKM

004829   KRIS-GIRL. London: Mills & Boon, [1917]
BMC NUC.

Christine and chaperone and advents in Malaya TLS

004830   MY LADY OF THE ISLAND; A TALE OF THE
SOUTH SEAS. Chicago: McClurg, 1916 NUC.

Love, advent. shipwreck, etc. PW
love, adventure, shipwreck, etc male hero NYT

004831   NOBODY'S ISLAND. London: Hurst &
Blackett, 1917 NUC BMC. Garden City, N.Y.: Doubleday,
Page, 1922 NUC.

marital problems come out all right TLS
Is somewhere in Pacific. Australian mother brings wife
Edith a widow to this little known island. She flies
from trial after her husband's death under suspicious
circumstances, but she's recognized, but all turns out
ok. LBKM
"A lady suspected of having poisoned her husband
betakes herself to Pacific island and marries an old
flame" BAKER 32, p. 217

004832   RED BOB OF THE BISMARCKS. London: Hurst &
Blackett, 1915 BMC NUC.

a capital advent story about men TLS

004833   THE SORCERER'S STONE. London: Hodder &
Stoughton, [1914] BMC. Philadelphia: J.C. Winston,
[c1914] NUC.

ATH-Australian male narrator, concerning a diamond
owned by a New Guinea sorcerer.
PW 85 5/30/14 p. 1775 "The Marquis and Flint go into
the interior of New Guinea in search of a native
sorcerer. the first time he exhibits his magic to them
they discover that the crystal he uses is really a
magnificent diamond which they resolve to appropriate.
Then begins a series of adventures which keeps the
reader breathless and which only end with the last
page." PW

004834   THE TERRIBLE ISLAND. New York: Ridgway,
[c1919] NUC. London: Hurst and Blackett, 1920 BMC NUC.

TLS- male, mostly, adv.
ATH-woman walks out of the sea and tells of island.
party explores it.

004835   VAITI OF THE ISLANDS. London: A.P. Watt,
[1906] BMC. New York: A. Wessels, 1908 NUC.

half-civilized daughter of an English man and a Moon

princess. She can play piano and command an unruly
native crew, wield a belaying pin. many advents.
Marries, but reviewer says-how long can her husband
survive the marriage. marooned on a leper island seeks
prehistoric skulls in caves. ACAD
fearless reckless TLS
acts as a skipper on her father's yacht goes in search
of pearls.
PW Beaut intell. half breed heroine captain of her
father's ship.
NYT daring reckless and conscienceless as a pirate.
Maori princess. "unique and perilous adventures"

004836   WHEN THE RED GODS CALL. London: Mills &
Boon, 1911 BMC. New York: Moffat, Yard, 1911 NUC.

Two loves in the life of Hugh Lynch in So Pacific
setting. TLS
complications in a mixed marriage.One part is hero's
narrative; the other, the heroine's; white man marries
native woman (New Guinea), then falls in love with a
white woman. ATH
Critic says there's little difference in the two
views. SR

GRIMSHAWE, HELENA.

004837   TRAPPED BY AVARICE. London: Digby, Long,
1896 BMC.

ATH 108:156.
ACAD 50:490. Stolen necklace, crime on Lake Erie,
bogus will, happy ending.

GRIMWOOD, ETHEL SAINT CLAIR. United Kingdom.

004838   MY THREE YEARS IN MANIPUR AND ESCAPE FROM
THE RECENT MUTINY. London: R. Bentley, 1891 BMC NUC.

004839   THE POWER OF AN EYE: A NOVEL. BY MRS.
FRANK ST. CLAIR GRIMWOOD. London: F. V. White, 1892
BMC. New York: United States Book, [c1892] NUC.

GRIMWOOD, MRS. FRANK SAINT CLAIR. See GRIMWOOD, ETHEL SAINT
CLAIR.

GRINNELL, ELIZABETH (PRATT).

004840   FOR THE SAKE OF A NAME: A STORY OF OUR
TIMES. Elgin, Ill.: D.C. Cook, 1900 NUC.

004841   JOHN AND I AND THE CHURCH. New york: F.
H. Revell, 1897 NUC.

GRISSOM, IRENE (WELCH). B. 1873. United States.

004842   A DAUGHTER OF THE NORTHWEST. Boston:
Cornhill, [c1918] NUC.

Novel of the lumber industry. PW

004843   THE SUPERINTENDENT. New York: Alice
Harriman, 1910 NUC.

Story of a wise super. (male). PW

GRISWOLD, HATTIE (TYNG). 1840-1909. United States.

004844   FENCING WITH SHADOWS. Chicago: Morrill,
Higgins, [c1892] NUC.

Touches on all the perplexing problems: socialism,
philanthropy, religious doubts. LW 93,57

GRISWOLD, LATTA. 1876-1931. United states.

004845   THE INN AT RED OAK. New York: R. J.
Shores, [c1917] NUC.

PW-mystery.

GRISWOLD, SARAH ELIZABETH. United States.

004846   OUT OF LAW INTO GOSPEL; OR, GOD IN MAN.
Chicago, Ill.: F. M. Harley, 1893 NUC.

GRONER, AUGUSTA. See GRONER, AUGUSTE.

GRONER, AUGUSTE. 1850-1922.

004847   THE MAN WITH THE BLACK CORD. BY AUGUSTA
GRONER. New York: Duffield, 1911 NUC. (Tr. Grace
Isabel Colbron.)

PW-mur. mystery.
NYT-Joe Muller. Vienna detective and new adventures.

detective PW 4-1-11 LBKM NYT

004848   MENE TEKEL; A TALE OF STRANGE HAPPENINGS.
BY AUGUSTA GRONER. New York: Duffield, 1912 NUC. (Tr.
Grace Isabel Colbron.)

PW det.
NYT-det., males

GROOM, MRS. C.

004849   LOVE IN THE DARKNESS. By MRS. SYDNEY
GROOM. London: Skeffington, [1918] BMC.

TLS-English girl marries Australian millionaire when
her love is elsewhere.

004850   SHADOWS OF DESIRES. London: Skeffington,
[1919] BMC.

Gentle widow and reckless selfish daughter. TLS

GROOM, MRS. SYDNEY. See GROOM, MRS. C.

GROSS, ANNA GOLDMARK. United States.

004851   THE GNOMES OF THE SALINE MOUNTAINS: A
FANTASTIC NARRATIVE. New York: Shakespeare Press, 1912
NUC.

Scene is laid in the old world, with the great cities,
watering places and rural resorts of Austria & Germany
as background to the romance. Real life is pictured,
notwithstanding the introduction of the gnomes. PW

GROSS, MYRA GERALDINE. Nationality Unknown.

004852   THE STAR OF VALHALLA; A ROMANCE OF EARLY
CHRISTIANITY IN NORWAY. New York: F. A. Stokes, [1907]
NUC.

Old hist. romance of Christian maid and Olaf. PW
6-1-07

GROSSMANN, EDITH SEARLE. Nationality Unknown.

004853   THE HEART OF THE BUSH. London: Sands,
1911 BMC. New York: J. Lane, 1911 NUC.

ATH Life in New Zealand.
Husband and wife grow apart; she helps him understand
why PW 3-4-11
New Zealand forest-setting.
Heroine raised in England after mother died. Returns
to father with her English arist. notions. Must adjust
to the bush. Two men rival for her. NYT

004854   IN REVOLT. London and Sydney: Eden, 1893
BMC.

004855   A KNIGHT OF THE HOLY GHOST. London:
Watts, 1907 BMC.

"Too highly wrought" written "in view of a strong
reactionary tendency towards re-subjection" of women.
ACAD

GROSVENOR, CAROLINE SUSAN THEODORA (STUART-WORTLEY).
1858-1940.

004856   THE BANDS OF ORION. London: W. Heinemann,
1906 BMC NUC.

ACAD-Triangle
BKM-modern love story; young widow, ¾ male vagabond
who must have freedom to wander broad-minded generous
young woman--no marriage.

004857   LAURA. London: W. Heinemann, 1911 BMC.

Laura Cardew
Laurie's hatred of poverty makes her acquiesce to "go
with the property", that is she and property go to man
chosen for her. In the end she's converted-learns love
means more than wealth. TLS
Marries for money, young man she loves comes along to
complicate her life. ATH
SR A Becky Sharpe with a most unmaidenly career.

004858   THE THORNTON DEVICE. London: A.
Constable, 1907 NUC BMC.

Madeline involved with married man.? TLS
ACAD-Young woman comes to live with man and his wife,
is seduced by their neighbor, becomes pregnant, then
what?

GROVE, JESSICA, jt. au. See RACSTER, OLGA AND JESSICA
GROVE.

GROVES, FREDA MARY.

004859   MY LADY ROSIA. London: R. & T.
Washbourne, 1914 BMC. New York: Benziger, 1914 PW.

ACAD 87:185. Hist. rom., 14th c., traditional.

GRUNDY, MABEL SARAH BARNES. United Kingdom.

004860   "CANDYTUFT-I MEAN VERONICA". London:
Hutchinson, 1914 BMC NUC. Toronto: McClelland,
Goodchild and Stewart, [n.d.] NUC.

ATH-concerns a woman's artistic temperament which
nearly ruins hers and her husband's lives.
TLS-banal
Dual personality: Candytuft represents her real
nature; Veronica, her aspirations. Does not appreciate
husband. She's bedridden because of an accident.
"clamours for a nice cultivated person of the opposit
sex" to keep her company. Husband supplies one. Then
the fun begins. But review says no more. ATH

004861   DIMBIE AND I-AND AMELIA. New York: Baker
and Taylor, [1907] NUC.

sent story of paralyzed wife, husband's and servants'
devotion. PW

004862   A GIRL FOR SALE. London: Hutchinson, 1920
BMC.

TLS-ad in paper. WW's success in ejecting an
overbearing aunt from Quinton's home.

004863   GWENDA. New York: Baker and Taylor, 1910
BMC NUC.

PW-series of mushy letters to her aunt.
discontented young bride. BKM
NYT-letters reveal growing unhappiness of country girl
married to wealthy Londoner with whom she was utterly
in love. Love and marriage go down in disaster but out
of the ruins rises a genuine happiness.

004864   HAZEL OF HEATHERLAND. Baker and Taylor,
[1906] NUC.

PW-22 year old woman visits worldly aunt

004865   HILARY ON HER OWN. London: Hutchinson,
1908 BMC. New York: Baker and Taylor, 1908 NUC.

"Hilary Forrest, a bright and animated young girl,
grows tired of the dull and monotonous life in
Derbyshire and despite all protest goes to London in
search of a position as secretary. She tells of her
experiences in looking for the secretaryship and how
she fared on her thirty shillings a week." BKM v.28,
1908-9.
TLS-tired of domesticity, becomes a secretary
resolving in a love story of the usual sort.
BKM-experiences end in matrimony.

004866   MARGUERITE'S WONDERFUL YEAR. Bristol: J.
W. Arrowsmith, 1906 BMC. London: Hutchinson, [190-?]
NUC.

The year just before the wedding after which nothing
is the same: despair, suffering, loneliness. ACAD
TLS-tender domestic

004867   PATRICIA PLAYS A PART. London:
Hutchinson, 1913 BMC NUC. New York: Dodd, Mead, 1914
NUC.

An heiress who amuses herself travelling as if she
were no heiress at all. TLS
PW "Patricia Hastings, lovely, rich orphan, objects to
being wooed for her money, so she determines to leave
her English home and go to Mentone, stay at a second
class pension, and be liked for herself. Of course a
nice man finds her, and the rest of the tale is just a
love story of the right sort, for, after a
misunderstanding which seems gigantic to the lovers,
but is by no means unsurmountable, the wedding-bells
peal and everyone is happy." 85:764.

004868   A THAMES CAMP. Bristol: J. W. Arrowsmith,
[1902] BMC. Bristol: J. W. Arrowsmith, [191-?] NUC.

004869   THE THIRD MISS WENDERBY. London:

Hutchinson, 1911 BMC. New York: Baker and Taylor, [1911] NUC.

Diana governess falls for married man, unhappy for a year, finds real happiness with an old friend PW 11-18-11
An "old story" TLS
happy end-BKM

004870   TWO IN A TENT-AND JANE. Bristol: J. W. Arrowsmith, 1913 BMC NUC. London: Simpkin, Marshall, 1913 BMC. (new editin of "A Thames Camp")

004871   TWO MEN AND GWENDA. London: [1910] NUC.

TLS-letters describing unhappy marriage.
ATH--Natural and generous young woman marries a man involved in society. She becomes rapidly disillusioned. Triangle ensues.

004872   AN UNDRESSED HEROINE. London: Hutchinson, 1916 BMC NUC.

TLS-dowdy vs. beautifully dressed. Effect on romance.
ATH-dowdy vs. beautifully dressed. Effect on romance.

004873   THE VACILLATIONS OF HAZEL. Bristol: J. W. Arrowsmith, 1905 BMC. London: Hutchinson, [1917] NUC.

Hazel vacilates between two lovers. TLS

GUEST, FLORA (BIGELOW). Canada.

004874   THE JEWELLED BALL. Montreal: Cambridge Corp., [1908] NUC.

NYT-Conv.

GUEST, GILBERT, pseud. See BRENAN, FLORENCE MACCARTHY.

GUILFORD, L. T. See GUILFORD, LINDA THAYER.

GUILFORD, LINDA THAYER. 1848-1899. United States.

004875   MARGARET'S PLIGHTED TROTH. BY L. T. GUILFORD. Cleveland, O.: W. M. Bayne Printing, 1899 NUC.

GUNN, JEANNIE (TAYLOR).

004876   WE OF THE NEVER-NEVER: A NOVEL. BY MRS. AENEAS GUNN. London: Hutchinson, 1908 BMC NUC. New York: Macmillan, 1910 NUC.

TLS-Gushing story of cattleman's wife. Northern territory, Australia-Desc. & travel. Frontier and pioneer life-Australian.

GUNN, MRS. AENEAS. See GUNN, JEANNIE (TAYLOR).

GUTTENBERG, VIOLET.

004877   A MODERN EXODUS. A NOVEL. London: Greening, 1904 BMC.

LBKM -Jewish people in England.

004878   NEITHER JEW NOR GREEK. A STORY OF JEWISH SOCIAL LIFE. London: Chatto & Windus, 1902 BMC NUC.

ACAD. Adeline, like most Jewish girls of the present day, had been taught to place her affections in accordance with her parent's wishes.

004879   THE POWER OF THE PALMIST. London: Chatto & Windus, 1903 BMC.

Mysticism. ACAD 64, 178
Sensational, musical maniac, motor accident disposes of one bad husband. TLS 03,59

GUYSE, ELEANOR. Nationality Unknown.

004880   A MOVABLE QUARTETTE. New York: Abbey, [190-] NUC.

GUYTON, EMMA JANE (WORBOISE). 1825-1887. United Kingdom.

004881   CHARLES EVERSLEY'S CHOICE. A TRUE STORY. BY EMMA JANE WORBOISE. London: Clarke, 1895 BMC.

GWYN, ANNE BAXTER.

004882   IN A TURKISH GARDEN. London: Greening, 1910 BMC.

TLS-"nice little story," rom.

GWYNNE, AGNES. Nationality Unknown.

004883   THE BATHING-MAN. London and New York: J. Lane, 1916 BMC NUC.

NYT-Male hero and his problems
TLS-male hero and his problems

GYP, pseud. See DE JANVILLE, SYBILLE GABRIELLE MARIE ANTOINETTE (DE RIQUETTI DE MIRABEAU) MARTEL.

H., A. K., pseud. See HOPKINS, ALICE (KIMBALL), Also SANDERS, ELLA KATHERINE.

H., S. M., pseud. See HANBURY, SARAH MATILDA.

HAAS, CAROLINE HOOK. United States.

004884   A WHITE SLAVE OF THE NORTH; OR, LUCY MANCHESTER. Atlanta, Ga.: Foote and Davies, 1895 NUC.

HACK, ELIZABETH JANE (MILLER). B. 1878. United States.

004885   THE CITY OF DELIGHT; A LOVE DRAMA OF THE SIEGE AND FALL OF JERUSALEM. Indianapolis: Bobbs-Merrill, [1908] NUC. London: J. Clarke, 1908 BMC.

PW-Young Jewish woman involved in intrigue learns way of Christ.
Jerusalem-Siege A.D. 70-Fic. BKM

004886   DAYBREAK; A STORY OF THE AGE OF DISCOVERY. BY ELIZABETH MILLER (MRS. OREN S. HACK). New York: C. Scribner's Sons, 1915 NUC.

BKM 41 1915 Female spy disguised as male page in historical novel.
She rescues a Spanish nobleman PW 4-10-15
Antonia de Aragon, king's niece, one of four "intrepid knightly damsels who followed the queen through the wars." Story opens with siege of Granada destined to fall because of "woman & the unending mischief of her degradation." NYT
Rescues a young Spaniard from a Moorish prison. BKM

004887   SAUL OF TARSUS; A TALE OF EARLY CHRISTIANS. Indianapolis: Bobbs-Merrill, [1906] NUC BMC. London: Stead's Publishing House, 1909 BMC.

Trad., Historical-- TLS
Paul, St, apostle-Fic.

004888   THE YOKE; A ROMANCE OF THE DAYS WHEN THE LORD REDEEMED THE CHILDREN OF ISRAEL FROM THE BONDAGE OF EGYPT. Indianapolis: Bobbs-Merrill, [1904] NUC BMC.

NYT
Hist nov- PW

HACK, MRS. OREN S. See HACK, ELIZABETH JANE (MILLER).

HACKLEY, SARAH BELL. Nationality Unknown.

004889   THE TOBACCO TILLER. Boston: C. M. Clark, 1909 NUC.

HADSELLE, CELIA ANTOINETTE CHAPMAN. United States.

004890   SCRAPS: NEW AND OLD. BY MRS. C. A. C. HADSELLE. Pittsfield, Mass.: Sun Print Co., 1900 NUC.

HADSELLE, MRS. C. A. C. See HADSELLE, CELIA ANTOINETTE CHAPMAN.

HAGUE, GERTRUDE. Nationality Unknown.

004891   COUNTESS HELENA: A NOVEL. New York: G. W. Dillingham, 1900 NUC.

NYT 1900:516. There is a streak of insanity in Helena's noble family. She is brought up to believe in arranged marriages and to expect infidelity from husband. She is married to a count who is drunk at the ceremony and whose entire family is mad.

HAHN, COUNTESS HAHN. See HAHN, IDA MARIE LUISE SOPHIE FREDERIKE GUSTAVA VON HAHN.

HAHN, IDA MARIE LUISE SOPHIE FREDERIKE GUSTAVA VON HAHN. 1805-1880.

004892   THE HEIRESS OF CRONENSTEIN. BY THE COUNTESS HAHN-HAHN. New York: Benziger, 1900 NUC. (Tr.

Mary A. Allies)

PW—Her devotion to the church and efforts to "reclaim the soul of a former playmate." Moral purpose. Germany.

HAIDHEIM, L., pseud. See AHLBORN, LUISE (JAEGER).

HAINES, ALICE CALHOUN. United States.

    004893   FIRECRACKER JANE; A NOVEL. New York: H. Holt, 1918 NUC. London: Hurst and Blackett, [1919] BMC.

    PW—Romance of US Army on Mexican border.
NYT—Conflict between US and Mexican Rep. "in which women must win by intrigue the influence and independence that society accords them as their birthright in our northern world." Daughter of a U.S. officer marries a Mexican, then war.
Fiery spirited American young woman red haired, elopes to Mexico with a cousin (male) partly out of pique because father remarries. "In Mexico (where they have different trads. about women) she has thrilling adventures." All ends well. TLS
Runs off with romantic Spaniard "all but coming to a bad end." Rescued by lover in aeroplane. ATH
Her adventures include the murder of her husband, her capture and escape from brigands and rescue. SR

HALDANE, WINIFRED AGNES. United States.

    004894   A CHORD FROM A VIOLIN. Chicago: Laird and Lee, [c1896] NUC.

    PW 3-7-96. Romance, of Hester, a great singer, whose father had owned a rare violin, which she had had to sell when he was dying. Hears it at a concert years later and meets its owner.

HALE, ANNE GARDNER. 1823-1914. United States.

    004895   THE CLOSED BALCONY. Boston: C. M. Clark, 1907 NUC.

    Family story—illness. PW 12-7-07

HALE, BEATRICE (FORBES-ROBERTSON). B. 1883. United States.

    004896   THE NEST-BUILDER. New York: F. A. Stokes, [c1916] NUC.

    Marriage of a steadfast home-loving woman and a brilliant dynamic man. PW
NYT—He cares for life only as it helps him express beauty in art forms. She is the creator of the race, all other things subservient to nest building. Study of their discovery of this space in their marriage, etc.

HALE, LOUISE (CLOSSER). 1872-1933. United States.

    004897   THE ACTRESS; A NOVEL. New York and London: Harper, 1909 NUC. London: A. Constable, 1909 BMC.

    gives up sweetheart for stage. Tells her stage and domestic experiences. TLS
Rhoda Miller tells us about her successful career in verse. She has a chance to marry but a leading part in London appeals to her more. Returns to Aaron in the end. ACAD
Realistic intimate chronicle of her life as actress-this the strength of the work. Evenually loses interest in stage, marries the man "that part is in the nature of an anti-climax" BKM
"Focus of book actress' way of life, career, success, work" NYT

    004898   HER SOUL AND HER BODY. New York: Moffat, Yard, 1912 NUC. London: G. Routledge, 1913 BMC.

    NYT—Realistic story of young woman in her mid-teens who goes to Boston to study for the stage. An accounting of the work, unpleasant experience of the city, etc., before she became successful two or three years later.
"Realistic story, experience of a girl barely past her middle t eens, who goes from a new England village to Boston to study elocution, develops a talent for dancing, and finally, after two or three years and much dearly bought experience, finds herself on the road to success." NYT
"The pitfalls are so plainly described that women who want to help young girls in their fight for goodness have a few duties pointed out to them by this

plain-speaking book." Mrs. Hale is herself an actress of ability. IND
"Poignant truths about life and wickedness and goodness that will perhaps be rather upsetting to commonly held opinions." --NYT

    004899   THE MARRIED MISS WORTH; A NOVEL. New York and London: Harper, 1911 BMC NUC.

    Marriage and career clash, resolution? Actress marries leading man; happy till she gets a better part. He won't play lesser role, separate; she finally resigns to be full-time wife. PW
Two talented actors, husband and wife, how much should they sacrifice of careers to remain together? Answer woman will find her true happiness in sacrificing her career for the marriage. BKM
"It may carry a moral unawares, but it is the reader who finds it in the story. Not the author who presents it." NYT

    004900   A MOTOR-CAR DIVORCE. London: Duckworth, 1906 BMC. New York: Dodd, Mead, 1906 NUC.

    "John and I are going to get a divorce and an automobile." Opening sentence.
NYT—travel book hung on rejection of div.

HALE, MARICE RUTLEDGE (GIBSON). B. 1884. United States.

    004901   ANNE OF TREBOUL. BY MARIE LOUISE GOETCHIUS. New York: Century, 1910 BMC NUC.

    Anne's great longing to be loved; has child (not wed), her passion for her child. She's "starved hunch backed." PW
BKM—Hunchback invited to village fete by handsome man does not realize he does it to spite village belle. He does not love her and so she, against all advice, refuses to marry him. As the son grows older, father looks at him and finally reveals his identity, persuades him to leave mother and go to sea with him.

    004902   THE BLIND WHO SEE. BY MARIE LOUISE VAN SAANEN. New York: Century, 1911 BMC NUC.

    NYT—wife, restless leaves blind violinist husband and goes to Paris with another man. Eventually her husband has a concert there and she leaves other man to rejoin her husband.
Nona is young ardent wife of blind violinst who craves "some more virile element in her life than her husband's genius." She meets it in a man who sweeps her off to Paris. She's "caught in the toils of physical passion and flagrantly breaks her vows." She forgets all about her husband. Soon learns her illicit relation is just physical, returns to husband who loves and needs her more than ever. BKM 34:443-4

    004903   CHILDREN OF FATE. BY MARICE RUTLEDGE. New York: F. A. Stokes, [c1917] NUC.

    004904   WILD GRAPES. BY MARIE LOUISE VAN SAANEN. New York: Moffat, Yard, 1913 NUC.

    Emily and Lucia "exquisite parasites-useless devouring." None have time for husbands who support them. Behind the study of these women is the life of David Ghent-his career. On page 134 "enters a woman at last." He becomes the "typical American husband." She gets him to spend large sums of money on her. She (Lucia) and he make a secret marriage, soon after which she's off to Europe with her mother. Left in the states, he works hard to support her; gets ill. He keeps making fortunes for her while she squanders money and is off flirting, ignores him even when he comes. She plots a divorce by spreading bad rumors about him. Finally he discovers she's unfaithful, wakes up. BKM
"indictment of one form of American married life."

HALE, SARAH. B. 1856. United States.

    004905   MERCEDES. A STORY OF MEXICO. Louisville, Ky.: Baptist Book Concern, 1895 NUC BMC.

    She's a young Mexican woman who converts from RCsm to Protestantism; everyday life of people in Mexico. RC Church and priests in Mexico. PW 4-13-95:624

HALES, A. M. M. See HALES, ADA MATILDA MARY.

HALES, ADA MATILDA MARY. B. 1878.

    004906   LESLIE. BY A. M. M. London: Lynwood, 1913 BMC.

He loves Audrey but marries Maud. (Hero dies in the end). Maud suspects his love is directed elsewhere. TLS

004907   THE PURITAN'S PROGRESS. BY A. M. M. HALES. London: A. Melrose, 1920 BMC.

TLS-Heroine escapes from stupid home to wider world. Has phases of Puritanism and Nietzscheanism. ATH-Goes to Oxford, returns and puts Nietzschean ideals into pratice by "giving herself" to married man. Reverts to original Puritanism in end. L_BKM-Study of the effects of Christian restraint on a nature originally with the non-moral bias of a free Greek. Frances is an "eerie shadow" but book is an interesting experiment.

HALEY, MARY MURKLAND.

004908   A DORNFIELD SUMMER. Boston: Little, Brown, 1902 NUC.

PZ7

HALKETT, CONSTANCE CRAIGIE.

004909   SCANDERBEG: A ROMANCE OF CONQUEST. London: Bliss, Sands and Foster, 1895 BMC.

Historical romance of Alex the Great-his power, passion, conquests and self indulgence. ACAD 48:127

HALL, AMANDA BENJAMIN. B. 1890. United States.

004910   BLIND WISDOM. Philadelphia: G. W. Jacobs, [c1920] NUC.

PW-three American sisters of different temperaments and psychology of their marriages.

004911   THE LITTLE RED HOUSE IN THE HOLLOW. Philadelphia: G. W. Jacobs, [c1918] NUC. London: Hurst and Blackett, [1919] BMC.

NYT May 12, 1918 p 224. Fatherless family, the Haggans, love story of two oldest girls.

HALL, ELIZA CALVERT, pseud. See OBENCHAIN, ELIZA CAROLINE (CALVERT).

HALL, EUGENE pseud. See BAKER, EMMA EUGENE HALL.

HALL, EVELYN BEATRICE. B. 1868. United Kingdom.

004912   BASSET, A VILLAGE CHRONICLE. BY S. G. TALLENTYRE. New York: Moffat, Yard, 1910 NUC. London: Smith, Elder, 1910 BMC. (London edition has title: Early-victorian.)

village of early Victorian period and its inhabitants PW

004913   EARLY-VICTORIAN; A VILLAGE CHRONICLE. BY S. G. TALLENTYRE. London: Smith, Elder, 1910 NUC.

TLS-not much here
LBKM- Patient heroine.

004914   LOVE LAUGHS LAST. BY S. G. TALLENTYRE. Edinburgh and London: W. Blackwood, 1919 NUC BMC. New York: G.H. Doran, [c1919] NUC.

Early 19th village life reconstructed. A sea-going hero, good character of Camilla King, his mother, "linked with the loving and so often inconsequent mothers of all ages;" left poor when husband dies. Two heroines her son faces: Theodora-chilly, ambitious, blue stocking. Nancy-sweet courageous. Theodora declines a proposal. Holds Bible classes for servants and reading classes for young women; intelligent. Recites Horace. LBKM
Author stresses the conventions that force her principal character into a loveless marriage. Women are independent and self reliant. SP

004915   MATTHEW HARGRAVES. BY S. G. TALLENTYRE. London: Smith, Elder, 1914 NUC BMC. London and New York: G. P. Putnam's Sons, 1914 NUC.

Matthew Hargraves, son of the landlord of the Hope and Anchor, goes up to London and marries. He and his wife take into their coldly correct home a girl named Patty, whom Matthew gradually comes to recognize as the embodiment of the sympathetic qualities that are lacking in his prim wife. However, Matthew himself is a thoroughly conventional sort of person; so he goes on living his correct existence, and Patty passes from his life with the realization on the part of each of them that his union with his wife has been a mistake. PW
NYT-Matthew at all times occupies center stage-a fine character

HALL, GERTRUDE. See BROWNELL, ANNA GERTRUDE (HALL).

HALL, GRACE. Nationality Unknown.

004916   LETTERS FROM G. G. [ANONYMOUS]. New York: H. Holt, 1909 NUC.

Full of adorable nonsense. NYT

HALL, HELENE, pseud. See BOYNTON, HELEN (MASON).

HALL, MARGERY WATSON (DRIVER). B. 1864. United States.

004917   THE RESPONSIBILITY OF RUFFLES. BY MARGERY WATSON. Boston: Pilgrim Press, [c1913] NUC.

PW 84 11/8/13:1534 "A story of a number of interesting people at a quaint country village on Cape Cod. The heroine is a frank, healthy girl, considerably athletic, a bit slangy, but womanly, unselfish, and lovable, while the hero, or at least the central male figure, is "Danny," aged five, a boy with a remarkable talent for mischief."

HALL, RUTH. B. 1858. United States.

004918   THE BLACK GOWN. Boston: Houghton, Mifflin, 1900 NUC.

LW 31:268. Dutch Albany, "hero with three loveresses is a delightful person."
NYT 1900:738. Romance, historical. Black gown is robe of Jesuit priest, a disguise for hero's escapades. Albany in "primitive times." 1750?

004919   A DOWNRENTER'S SON. Boston: Houghton, Mifflin, 1902 NUC.

Attempt to abolish rents--PW.

004920   THE GOLDEN ARROW; A STORY OF ROGER WILLIAMS'S DAY. Boston: Houghton, Mifflin, 1901 NUC.

004921   THE PINE GROVE HOUSE. Boston: Houghton, Mifflin, 1903 NUC.

Centers on a group of people in a hotel NYT 03,672 Heroine, simple, high minded, heroic. PW 10-10-03

HALL, VIOLETTE. United States.

004922   CHANTICLEER; A PASTORAL ROMANCE. Boston: Lothrop, [1902] NUC.

HALLOWAY, MARY.

004923   CROSS ROADS; OR ISABEL ALISON'S HISTORY. Philadelphia: American Sunday School Pub. Union, [c1891] NUC.

Must leave comfortable home at early age to earn her living. Becomes a governess, a teacher. Has many problems. PW 10-24-91.

HALLOWELL, ALICE. United States.

004924   FORGETMENOT; OR, SUNSHINE IN AFFLICTION. A STORY FROM LIFE. Washington, D. C.: Gibson, 1893 NUC.

004925   THE STOLEN BABY, MARION CLARKE: A TOUCHING, TRUE, AND THRILLING STORY OF TODAY. New York: [The Evangelist Press], 1899 NUC.

Verse and prose, story of kidnapped child based on real incident of Baby Clarke that hit the NY newspapers. NYT 9-2-99,501

HALLOWES, FRANCES S.

004926   THE ENEMY: A STUDY IN HEREDITY. London: Headley, [1908] BMC.

004927   THE HATE OF HATE. London: Headley, 1901 BMC.

004928   THE PATRIOTISM OF DENYS MAHON. London: Headley, [1913] BMC.

004929   ZALZALAH! A STORY OF THE INDIAN
EARTHQUAKE. London: Headley, [1907] BMC.

HALSTEAD, ADA L., pseud. See NEWHALL, LAURA EUGENIA TERRY.

HALSTED, LENORA B. United States.

     004930   A VICTORIOUS LIFE. New York: Metropolitan
     Press, 1910 NUC.

     Old couple adopt waif who becomes serious student,
     goes to Washington in time of Civil War, labors to see
     wrong righted in government affairs, becomes a woman
     minister. PW
     NYT-her story, Bertha Henley. Her 1st marriage,
     disagreeable (her husband tricked her into a mock
     ceremony.) She wrote verse and achieved money and
     fame. Marriage got worse and she finally got a
     divorce. Then she married a Congressman but this also
     was not happy; he was killed by a bullet. She married
     again, this time a really good man, he died. Then she
     became a minister.

HAMBLIN, JESSIE DE FOLIART. United States.

     004931   A NEW WOMAN. Chicago: C.H. Kerr, [c1895]
     NUC.

     PW 5-9-96. The experiences of two titled Englishmen
     who make a bet that they will find no trouble in
     becoming engaged in a short time to American
     heiresses.

HAMER, PAULINE.

     004932   WILL-O'-THE-WISP. London: S. H.
     Bousfield, [1904] BMC.

HAMER, SARAH SELINA. Nationality Unknown.

     004933   DEAN-HURST. London: C. H. Kelly, 1895
     BMC.

     004934   MILLICENT'S MISTAKE. New York: A. D. F.
     Randolph, [1891] NUC. Edinburgh: Oliphant, Anderson &
     Ferrier, 1892 BMC.

     ACAD 42:128. "Annie Swan" school of fiction. She had
     been all but married to another man prior to her
     marriage to Caleb. Complications which are eventually
     overcome. "Simple wholesome story."

     004935   SWIRLBOROUGH MANOR. Edinburgh: Oliphant,
     1893 BMC.

HAMILTON, ADELAIDE DOUGLAS.

     004936   LEONE; A TALE OF THE JESUITS. EDITED BY
     LADY DUNBAR OF MOCHRUM. London: J. Long, 1906 BMC.

     ACAD-male adventure.

HAMILTON, ANNIE E. (HOLDSWORTH) LEE. United Kingdom.

     004937   BELHAVEN. BY MAX BERESFORD. London: Hurst
     and Blackett, 1892 BMC.

     ACAD 42:127. Scotch seaside town. hero villain is a
     murderer, swindler, expert in poisons and sentimental
     humbug; receives a horrible and original fate in
     America. Sybil is his daughter and the heroine.

     004938   THE BOOK OF ANNA. London: Hutchinson,
     1913 BMC.

     Sensations and thoughts of an introspective and
     imaginative girl who wants to write, "an unimportant
     small girl." TLS

     004939   DAME VERONA OF THE ANGELS. A STUDY IN
     TEMPERAMENT. London: Methuen, 1912 BMC.

     TLS-heroine a born mystic.
     ACAD-she is also illegitimate. Mother is separated
     from her father, chooses to become a nun but dies,
     presumably from fasting, when she is about to take her
     vows.

     004940   A GARDEN OF SPINSTERS. BY ANNIE E.
     HOLDSWORTH. London: W. Scott, 1904 BMC. Leipzig: B.
     Tauchnitz, 1904 NUC.

     004941   THE GODS ARRIVE. BY ANNIE E. HOLDSWORTH.
     London: W. Heinemann, 1897 BMC. New York: Dodd, Mead,
     1897 NUC.

Katharine aspires to be a labor-leader. Peggy is a
horse-breaker. SR 84:501.
Katharine waits a long while to get things straight
with her lover because he rips a letter (in his
pocket) while addressing a public meeting. He failed
to see the confession of love on the overleaf. ATH
110:450.
Katharine Fleming a "modern woman" carefully studied.
She is a leader of a labor mvt. and a successful
journalist. "The argument is in favor of love and
marriage for women against the deteriorating influence
of public or prof. life." PW 52:672.
Katharine loves Franklin because he gives himself to
the people . ACAD 52 Fic sup 77.
SP 80:126. Katharine and Richard are fellow workers in
the cause of Labour. Richard "has a conception of
woman's province and woman's duties not uncommon among
those who hold his views, and K., who has to earn a
living by paragraphing and reporting for women's
journals, does not satisfy it. Does he, can he love
her, is the question...all the more puzzling because
her abilities are superior to his, and her grip of the
question which is the main interest of her life far
more complete...pathetic glimpses of what may be
called the woman's Grub street."
LW 29:154. She is forced to go back to family farm and
work at making it pay. Feels it is work below her
powers. But when the half gods go and love, sacrifice
and Duty arrive, "she finds, as some happy people do,
that in losing her life she has saved it."

004942   GREAT LOWLANDS. BY ANNE E. HOLDSWORTH
(MRS. LEE HAMILTON). London: Hodder & Stoughton, 1901
BMC. Leipzig: B. Tauchnitz, 1902 NUC.

Depressing atmosphere of vulgarity. ATH

004943   THE IRON GATES. London: T.F. Unwin, 1906
BMC.

TLS-slum workers.
ATH-workers dominated by the memory of a dead woman
who gave a broken heart and life to the cause, she
becomes a cult, was a victim of a selfish husband.
Momerie is an unqualified cur and cad. Zo dancer in
music hall-finest character, some sordid misery of
outer London. SR

004944   JOANNA TRAILL, SPINSTER. BY ANNIE E.
HOLDSWORTH. London: W. Heinemann, 1894 NUC BMC. New
York: C. L. Webster, 1894 NUC.

SR 78:241. The sin of a woman and the treatment of
it--by men and by women. Grave. Morally right.
SP 73:416. Joanna is 30+ years old, has always been
dependent, inherits. She wants to be useful with her
new life, undertakes the care of an "untaught,
undisciplined creature" who had been greatly wronged.
ACAD 46:209. Pioneer Series. "Ladies of Pioneer Clubs
and Pioneer literature are too fond of giving
themselves and their cause away by this kind of
exaggeration" (an exaggeratedly vile male.) Joanna
meets Mr. Boas, becomes interested in his schemes and
takes on the rescue of Christine. She had been a
dependent of her sister and brother-in-law with no
will of her own. Boas is a philanthropist. She dies of
diptheria. Christine is rejected heartlessly by her
lover when he learns of her past.

004945   LADY LETTY BRANDON. London: J. Long, 1909
BMC.

Married to passionless judge "she pants to know what
love means,to have her life, to break her social
fetters. "Author wholely sympathetic. Lady Letty
travels with a woman friend under another name, falls
in love with an artist and marries him (bigamy) . Then
she starts a double life-is wife to both. TLS

004946   THE LITTLE COMPANY OF RUTH. London:
Methuen, 1910 BMC.

TLS - Sentimental, romance.

004947   MICHAEL ROSS, MINISTER. BY ANNIE E.
HOLDSWORTH. New York: Dodd, Mead, 1902 NUC.

NYT

004948   A NEW PAOLO AND FRANCESCA; A NOVEL. BY
ANNIE E. HOLDSWORTH. New York and London: John Lane,
1904 BMC NUC.

A passionate pretty baby is Janice. 4 people, each
loves the one who loves another. ACAD 1905:150.

004949   THE VALLEY OF THE GREAT SHADOW. BY ANNIE
E. HOLDSWORTH. (MRS. LEE-HAMILTON). London: W.
Heinemann, 1900 BMC. Chicago: H. S. Stone, 1900 NUC.

LBKM 18:63. Hotel in a Swiss valley. In spite of 6
deaths and 3 severe illnesses, is essentially
cheerful.
SP 84:849. Four marriages at the end.
ATH 115:493. "Does not err on the side of
cheerfulness." Health resort for consumptives (already
written about by B. Harraden) "curious combination of
lung-disease and love-making."

004950   THE YEARS THAT THE LOCUST HATH EATEN. BY
ANNIE E. HOLDSWORTH. London: W. Heinemann, 1895 BMC.
New York and London: Macmillan, 1895 NUC.

Priscilla Momerie, clergyman's daughter marries
without father's approval a young grocer's son spoiled
for work by a Camb. ed. They move to a flat of the
Regents' Buildings in London, occupied by working
people. She is a successful novelist; he's always on
the verge of publishing. Her disenchantment with her
husband, his paralysis upon the death of her child,
rejection of her MS., poverty, misery. PW
12-14-95:1145
SR 81:131. Story of a weak husband and a sad,
disillusioned wife, and a painter who paints her
portrait from memory.
ACAD 49:281. Momerie thinks himself a genius but does
nothing. Priscilla is a genius, or related to it, has
real literary ability, but he ignores it and permits
her to scrub, pot-boil and kill herself to provide the
necessities of life. Then she expects child and seeks
happiness in it by working doubly hard. Child is born
weak and sickly, Momerie gets paralysis, an affliction
not disturbing to him as he can watch wife work
without reproach.
LW 27:121. Reminds one of African Farm. Sad slow
martyrdom of Priscilla Momerie. In youth she is full
of hope, enthusiasm for the masses. Leaves her
father's rectory against his will to elope with a
writer, who is also a snob. She's disillusioned in him
especially when he shows no love for their child. The
child dies. Even though she has a chance for a truer
love, she rejects it. She's broken by then, dies. "The
ignoble strain that underlies the veneer of culture in
the man who cannot even guess the torture he inflicts
upon a generous soul is terribly traced." ATH 106:867

HAMILTON, CATHERINE JANE.

004951   A FLASH OF YOUTH. London: Sands, 1900
BMC.

SP 84:638. Alethea, an amateur curate comes to help a
country clergyman in his parish. She marries, leaves
her husband when she finds him making love to another,
goes into rescue work.

004952   FROM HAND TO HAND, OR, THE ADVENTURES OF
A JUBILEE SIXPENCE. London: S. W. Partridge, [1895]
BMC.

HAMILTON, CICELY MARY. B. 1875. United Kingdom.

004953   DIANA OF DOBSON'S. New York: Century,
1908 BMC NUC.

PW-inheritance, blows it, romantic ending.
NYT-a suitor, impressed with remarks Diana made during
her two week spree posing as a young widow, vows to
live only on money he can earn. They meet again, she
as a shop girl once more and decide they can live
together.
The attractive and clever Diana grows restless and
unhappy in the monotony and narrowness of her life as
one of the London shopgirls. "I sometimes feel-I feel
tonight"--Diana says--"as if I would give my immortal
soul to live, just live--for a week." Inherited three
hundred pounds. One short month of Paris gowns, a trip
to Switzerland, and two love affairs. Penniless
returns to London, to secure another position, suffers
many hardships. Outcome happy. Right man appears. BKM
27:1908.

004954   JUST TO GET MARRIED. London: Chapman and
Hall, 1911 BMC NUC.

Georgina Vicary surrenders to Adam to be free of her
dependence upon her aunt. She confesses the truth to
him. They marry. TLS
Pictures a wife dependent on relatives with no
marketable talent and no future but marriage. An

eligible man appears and all wait expectantly while
she angles for him feeling bitter and ashamed even as
she does so. The man proposes and she learns that her
methods were intolerable. She tells the man the truth
and parts. LBKM
Woman in revolt, her back against the wall,
hysterical, rude, truthtelling. Twice she lashes out
about not caring for him, breaks off engagement. It
turns out they really do care for each other. ACAD

004955   A MATTER OF MONEY. London: Chapman and
Hall, 1916 BMC.

TLS-Matrimonial unfaithfulness-wife is victim.
ATH-Liaison between struggling M.D. and foolish wife
of wealthy patient. They are discovered, divorce
threatens, but she finds a way of ending the miserable
situation.

004956   SENLIS. London: W. Collins, [1917] BMC
NUC.

004957   WILLIAM--AN ENGLISHMAN. London:
Skeffington, [1919] BMC. New York: F. A. Stokes,
[c1919] NUC.

William drawn by chance into Socialist circle, meets a
militant suffragette, marry (1914) go to a cottage in
Forest of Arden for honeymoon--(in France). Know
nothing of outbreak of war. Find everyone cleared out
of the area. Then meet up with German soldiers and
learn of the war. William marched away with captives,
later escapes, all his terrible fears as to what may
happen to G. become fact. He escapes, finds her. They
run along the road but motor-bicycle knocks her down,
crushes her side. Yet she goes on for days before she
dies. Returns to England tells pacifist friends, joins
up, is killed. His vow for revenge goes nowhere.
Change of heart of pacifist. TLS
Psychological effects of war shown dramatically. SP
PW-Two on honeymoon in Belgium are surprised by war
and advance of Germans in this country.

HAMILTON, EDITH HENRIETTA (FOWLER). B. 1865. United
Kingdom.

004958   A CORNER OF THE WEST. BY EDITH HENRIETTA
FOWLER. London: Hutchinson, 1899 BMC. New York:
Appleton, 1899 NUC.

Lavinia Garland is 30. "Amusing combination of old
maid and baby," her cousin Alison-irresponsible. LBKM
17:59
Petronel is slangy cigarette smoking hoyden who
ultimately weds a Peer. Then there's Allison Royce who
loves Dr. Jim Carey who is engaged to her aunt for 9
years. Lavinia, the aunt, lets him go. She was
dutifully caring for her old tyrant of a mother. SP
83:499
Hamlet of Devonshire, Eng. Stress upon influence of
mothers. PW 56:1155
NYT 1900:5. 3 heroines, their love affairs. Allison a
niece of Lavinia who is spiritless and loses her man.
Petronel is fast, vulgar.
BKM 10:501. English novel. Petronel is a child.
Lavinia self-sacrificing, all of them virtuous and
sweet.

004959   FOR RICHER FOR POORER. London: Hurst and
Blackett, 1905 BMC.

004960   HUGH'S BURDEN BUNDLE. London: Religious
Tract Society, [1897] BMC.

004961   PATRICIA. BY EDITH HENRIETTA FOWLER (HON.
MRS. ROBERT HAMILTON). New York: G. P. Putnam's sons,
1915 NUC. London: G. P. Putnam, 1915 BMC.

Story of intrigue and rom 3-13-15. PW
Patricia Vaughn at 28 has already done a lot of
literary work. A noted publisher asks her to write a
biography of her father. But he wants her to use
certain of her father's letters that will show that
the correspondent of said letters was mixed up in
several intrigues. Patricia agrees "having a weak
standard-The std. of a girl's honor. And being a
genius she writes it well." Ends up wealthy, married
to the son of man father corresponded with. NYT
"The book-so resolutely on the other side of the
angels, such sound domestic morals" She is an
outspoken young woman but doesn't do anything too
different. Assured (by husb.) at end, when pregnant
that sex of child need not concern her-boy or girl
will inherit alike. SP

004962   THE PROFESSOR'S CHILDREN. London:

Longmans, 1897 BMC.

004963　　　THE WORLD AND WINSTOW. BY EDITH HENRIETTA
FOWLER. London: Hodder and Stoughton, 1901 BMC. New
York: Dodd, Mead, 1901 BMC.

004964　　　THE YOUNG PRETENDERS. BY EDITH HENRIETTA
FOWLER. London and New York: Longmans, Green, 1895 BMC
NUC.

　　SR. child life.

HAMILTON, HELEN.

004965　　　THE ICONOCLAST. London: C. W. Daniel,
[1917] BMC.

ATH-Newspaper induces schoolmistress and clerk to
discuss sex and plan a romantic holiday. They are
relieved when it doesn't happen.
A newspaper that profoundly affects a high school
teacher Maud Larkin. She reads that teaching is the
withered Vestal Hood. Plunges into a romantic
adventure upon the call of vital human needs. Wants to
leap out of dead and monotonous respectability. Kindly
satiric. TLS

004966　　　MY HUSBAND STILL; A WORKING WOMAN'S
STORY. London: G. Bell, 1914 BMC NUC.

ATH-Theme is, in part, necessity of access to divorce
for poor as well as rich. Husband a brute, she kept
the children.

HAMILTON, HON. MRS. ROBERT. See HAMILTON, EDITH HENRIETTA
(FOWLER).

HAMILTON, KATE WATERMAN. B. 1841. United States.

004967　　　THE PARSON'S PROXY. Boston: Houghton,
Mifflin, 1896 NUC. London: A. Melrose, [1898] BMC.

LIt W 27:153. One of his backwoods flock knocks down
minister and then, repentant, offers to preach for him
while he is laid up.
PW 2-22-96. His experiences while substituting for the
parson are the story.

HAMILTON, LILLIAS.

004968　　　A NURSE'S BEQUEST. BY LILLIAS HAMILTON,
M.D. London: J. Murray, 1907 BMC.

Workhouse life and nurses there. Theory about pauper
children comes through the story: send them to Canada
as infants, raise them on farms in manual trades.
They'll be productive and farms self-supporting
settlements.
ACAD-story of a young woman in a workhouse infirmary.

004969　　　A VIZIER'S DAUGHTER. A TALE OF THE HAZARA
WAR. BY LILLIAS HAMILTON, M.D. London: J. Murray, 1900
BMC NUC.

SP 85:807. Rev. states she was court physician to the
ameer of Afghanistan. Story is of Gul Begum, daughter
of a mountaineer who has many difficult experiences,
is sold as a slave. She enables the secretary of the
Ameer to escape to India, plans and carries it out
dressed as a boy. Is killed there.

HAMILTON, LOUISE FRANCES PAINE. United States.

004970　　　ROMANCE OF GRAYLOCK MANOR. Chicago: Rand,
McNally, [c1899] NUC.

Young orphaned woman marries judge. Their happy
marriage at the Manor just begins when he's called off
to Civil War, dies leaving her to raise son. PW
56:1157

HAMILTON, M., pseud. See LUCK, MARY CHURCHILL
(SPOTTISWOODE-ASHE).

HAMILTON, MARY AGNES (ADAMSON). B. 1884. United Kingdom.

004971　　　DEAD YESTERDAY. London: Duckworth, [1916]
BMC NUC. New York: G. H. Doran, [c1916] NUC.

Daphne and Nigel, love idyllic for a time. She comes
to believe he is incapable of the depth of feeling
which would insure their happiness and breaks with
him. PW
NYT-description of pre-war English society. A group of
egoists. Daphne is more earnest than others. Middle
aged woman a writer and pacifist is author's

mouthpiece.
TLS-group of journalists and artists, male and female,
upon whom 1914 descends and for various reasons have
to meet it at home. Test of character. The group is
educated, clever, artistic, emancipated and bored.
ATH-outbreak of war comes to mother as frustration of
her life work.

004972　　　FULL CIRCLE. London: W. Collins, [c1919]
BMC NUC.

TLS-Bridget is persuaded by Socialist poet Elstree to
be his mistress. He develops a passion for her
brother's girl. Part two of novel Bridget has become
successful modern woman. Works, not embittered like
her brother but aware that life could not be defined
by any of one's limited syntheses.
ATH-4 years after leaving her, Elstree returned to
Bridget and asked marriage. She made him wait six
weeks, by which time he was engaged to someone else.

004973　　　THE LAST FORTNIGHT. London: W. Collins,
[1920] BMC.

TLS-mother in law and son and daughter. Daughter
deserved better husband. Ill disposed. Sad, unusual
story.
ATH-wife rescues a lame white kitten which she sees as
a symbol of her misery. They drown it. She drowns
herself.

004974　　　LESS THAN THE DUST. London: W. Heinemann,
1912 BMC. Boston: Houghton, Mifflin, 1912 NUC.

ATH- husband is subject of book.
Heroine loves her sister's husband; she's of the
strenuously idle rich. SR

004975　　　YES. London: W. Heinemann, [1914] BMC
NUC.

LRKM-male hero and Joan who is womanly and
self-sacrificing. Both artists.
TLS-the acceptance of the commonness of her lot was in
itself greatness.
Joan is exasperating. SP

HAMILTON, MRS. LEE. See HAMILTON, ANNIE E. (HOLDSWORTH)
LEE.

HAMLET, EDITH. See LYTTLETON, EDITH SOPHY (BALFOUR).

HAMLIN, MYRA LOUISA (SAWYER). 1856-1927. United States.

004976　　　CATHARINE'S PROXY. Boston: Little, Brown,
1902 NUC.

PZ7

HAMMOND, FRANCES, pseud. See CROAL, FRANCES A.

HAMMOND, L. H. See HAMMOND, LILY (HARDY).

HAMMOND, LILY (HARDY). 1859-1925. United States.

004977　　　IN THE GARDEN OF DELIGHT. BY L. H.
HAMMOND. New York: T.Y. Crowell, [c1916] NUC.

Story of young love told in first person by occupant
of a wheelchair. PW

004978　　　THE MASTER-WORD; A STORY OF THE SOUTH
TODAY. BY L. H. HAMMOND. New York: Macmillan, 1905
NUC.

Wife of 8 years discovers husband is father of
"mulatto" child hates, then forgives him; story has to
do with her relation to the child. The child hates her
blackness. "Author has written with sincerity and high
purpose." NYT 05:130. Viry-mother is three parts
white. Father is southern gentleman.

HANBURY, SARAH MATILDA.

004979　　　DOROTHY SADDINGTON. London: Skeffington,
1895 BMC.

reviewer refuses to review so amateurish a book. ACAD
48:222

004980　　　THE "NAUSICAA"; A LOVE STORY. BY S. M. H.
London: Skeffington, 1891 BMC.

HANCOCK, ELIZABETH HAZLEWOOD. 1871-1915. United States.

004981　　　BETTY PEMBROKE. New York: Neale, 1907

NUC.

Love-mystery. PW 12-28-07.
Sweet winsome. NYT

HANDASYDE, pseud. See BUCHANAN, EMILY HANDASYDE.

HANKS, BEULAH DOWNEY. United States.

004982   FOR THE HONOR OF A CHILD. New York:
Continental, 1899 NUC.

Young American woman realizes after marriage and a
child that she loves another man. Ends in tragedy.
Serves to warn against marrying for social or economic
reasons. PW 55:289
Margaret Laurence, poor, falls in love with Fairfax
Marmion, also poor. He leaves without confessing his
love. She marries a wealthy Spaniard who subjects her
to absolute torture. There's no question of divorce.
She bears her grief for her lovely son's sake. This
child even becomes close friends with Fairfax on his
return. BKM 9:185

HANNIS, MARGARET, jt. au. See WINN, MARY POLK AND MARGARET
HANNIS.

HAPGOOD, NEITH BOYCE. B. 1872. United States.

004983   THE BOND. BY NEITH BOYCE. New York:
Duffield, 1908 NUC. London: Duckworth, 1908 BMC.

PW-analysis of modern marriage.
TLS-Teresa kept her spinster quarters when she married
in case--, although she did not, like her Aunt Sophy,
regard marriage as a hideous bondage.
NYT-bickering quarreling jarring and nagging-an
unpleasant marriage.
Teresa, married to artist, is an artist. They're both
temperamental. She becomes jealous of another woman,
leaves her husband to go to Switzerland has a
near-serious flirtation. Couple reconciled. LBKM

004984   THE ETERNAL SPRING. BY NEITH BOYCE. New
York: Fox, Duffield, 1906 NUC. London: Hurst and
Blackett, 1907 BMC.

PW-love relationship among Americans summering in
Italy.
NYT-values are youth and young love. Cad of a hero
whose "creator evidently admires him very much." "Our
1 comfort is heroine is difficult and unpleasant. Sure
to plant a few thorns among the roses of wedded life."
Man and three ladies in Italy. TLS

004985   THE FORERUNNER. BY NEITH BOYCE. New York:
Fox, Duffield, 1903 NUC BMC. London: Hurst & Blackett,
1907 BMC.

Marital infidelity, marital incompatibility. Wife
gives her husband affection as long as he can give her
wealth. Finds her husband repellant. He's blind to her
moods. He's in business and she's a businessman's
widow. He loses money, goes off to start new business,
she forms indiscrete friendships , joins him, quarrels
she pours out all her anger. The wholly different
directions of their thoughts, feelings. Divorce not
necessary, he dies while away, she's spared that last
farewell. BKM
Insatiable passion for money making in a man; equally
insatiable passion for pleasure and self indulgence in
a woman. Ends in tragedy. PW 11-14-03
ATH-marriage in which wife is neglected by husband.

004986   A PIONEER OF TO-DAY. London: Hurst and
Blackett, 1907 BMC.

Sober realism of an unsuccessful marriage. TLS

HARBAND, BEATRICE M. Nationality Unknown.

004987   DAUGHTERS OF DARKNESS IN SUNNY INDIA. New
York and London: F. H. Revell, [1903] BMC NUC.

004988   JAYA: WHICH MEANS VICTORY. THIS IS THE
STORY OF A HINDU GIRL OF HIGH DEGREE, TELLING OF HER
LIFE'S STRUGGLES AS A MAIDEN, WIFE, AND WIDOW. London,
New York: Marshall, [1914?] BMC NUC.

Missions--Fic.; Women-missions-India.

004989   UNDER THE SHADOW OF DURGAMMA. A STORY OF
SOUTHERN INDIA. Melbourne: Religious Tract Society and
Sunday School Union of Victoria, [1901] NUC.

HARBERT, ELIZABETH MORRISSON (BOYNTON). 1845-1925. United

States.

004990   "AMORE". New York: Lovell, Gestefeld,
[c1892] NUC.

PW-minister and his wife's good works, her methods
startling to some straight-laced people.

HARDEN, ELIZABETH.

004991   OUR IMMORTAL BATTLE. London: Simpkin,
1915 BMC.

about two brothers-TLS

004992   THE SPINDLE. London: J. Long, 1912 BMC.

TLS-seaside town with melodrama scandals. Clemency, a
lady doctor, keeps outside petty circles and closes
book with self-sacrifice.
ATH-relinquishes lover

HARDING, D. C. F. See HARDING, DOLORES CHARLOTTE FREDERICA.

HARDING, DOLORES CHARLOTTE FREDERICA. B. 1888. United
Kingdom.

004993   AFFAIRS OF MEN. London: J. Long, 1912
BMC.

ATH-crude and tame presentation of flirtation and
illicit love making.

004994   THE GREAT EXPERIMENT. London: J. Long,
[1911] BMC.

story of a woman's love affair written in the form of
letters by the woman before she drowned herself. TLS

004995   ORANGES AND LEMONS. BY D. C. F. HARDING.
London, New York: Cassell, [1916] NUC BMC.

TLS-Delores, the last of an ancient family with no
money becomes a famous and wealthy dancer, gambles,
loses her money and her baby and dies of consumption.
Clever and appealing study of artistic temptation.

HARDING, EMILY GRACE.

004996   A NOBLE SACRIFICE. London: W. Scott,
[1897] BMC.

HARDING, JANE. B. 1889. United Kingdom.

004997   THE PUPPET. London: T. F. Unwin, 1917
BMC.

Turns on a preposterous will. TLS
In the manner of Jane Eyre. ATH

HARDING, MRS. AMBROSE.

004998   A DAUGHTER OF DEBATE. London: T. W.
Laurie, [1914] BMC.

LBKM - Alice Ashton, niece of the governor of Dominica
is very concerned with the way whites treat Negroes of
the West Indies and protests her uncle and cousin's
ways. Story discovers whether or not her trust in
blacks is well placed. Dr. Hampton, an ambitious
black, plays a strange part in her life.
TLS-her "inflated enthusiasms" about the blacks lead
to the "direst trouble."

004999   THE DOMINANT CHORD. London: T. W. Laurie,
[1912] BMC.

TLS-jealous frenzy of West Indian beauty over her
half-sister who wins her lover.
SP-"touches on the colour problem. People with strong
views will not be pleased."

HARDY, IZA DUFFUS. D. 1922. United Kingdom.

005000   A BUTTERFLY, HER FRIENDS AND FORTUNES, A
NOVEL. London: Chatto & Windus, 1903 BMC.

a "butterfly" and her two lovers. ATH

005001   HIS SILENCE. London: Digby, Long, 1907
BMC.

focuses on a man-TLS

005002   IN THE SPRINGTIME OF LOVE. London: C. A.
Pearson, 1895 BMC.

005003   THE LESSER EVIL. London: Chatto and Windus, 1901 BMC.

woman discovers she's married to a bigamist-ATH

005004   LOVE IN IDLENESS. London: Digby, Long, 1908 BMC.

TLS-takes place in the "orange belt of Florida, where two beautiful maidens amuse themselves with various young men who come to learn the business."
ACAD-Want vengeance on men but end up marrying?

005005   MACGILLEROY'S MILLIONS. London: Simpkin, Marshall, [1900] BMC.

SP 84:880. Ingenious story of inheritance and its effect on the heirs.
ATH 115:780. He is an escaped convict with 18 years still to serve if he doesn't claim it in one year, it goes to heroine.

005006   MAN, WOMAN AND FATE. London: Chatto and Windus, 1902 BMC.

ATH 4-12-02 "sensational domestic" Author's p.o.v.?

005007   THE MASTER OF MADRONO MILLS. A ROMANCE OF THE REDWOODS. London: Digby, Long, 1904 BMC.

005008   THE MYSTERY OF A MOONLIGHT TRYST. London: Digby, Long, 1908 BMC.

005009   THE REASON WHY. THE STORY OF A GIRL'S HEART. London: Digby, Long, 1905 BMC.

005010   THE SILENT WATCHERS. London: Digby, Long, 1910 BMC.

TLS-murder myst.

005011   THE STRANGE DISAPPEARANCE OF JOHN HAVERSHAM. London: Digby, Long, 1909 BMC.

Traditional mystery. TLS

005012   A TRAP OF FATE. London: Digby, Long, 1906 BMC.

005013   A WOMAN'S LOYALTY - A NOVEL. London: F. V. White, 1893 BMC.

Val Charitis, poet, learns he'll inherit estate only on death or second marriage of aunt. He poisons her and confesses it all to his fiance. She agrees to keep silent as long as no one else is accused of the crime. When someone is accused, she threatens to speak, he tosses her in the river. But she doesn't die, ends up marrying the accused and Val gets his. SR 75:270. Her name is Clemaine Everard. ACAD 43':390.

HARDY, ROBINA FORRESTER. D. 1891. United Kingdom.

005014   TIBBY'S TRYST: OR "I WILL LIFT UP MINE EYES UNTO THE HILLS". Edinburgh and London: Oliphant, Anderson and Ferrier, 1891 BMC.

Tibby Rutherford and Hugh Ellerslie are lovers. They marry and live happily. ACAD

HARE, CHRISTOPHER, pseud. See ANDREWS, MARIAN.

HARGRAVE, KATHARINE EDITH SPICER-JAY. 1896-1915. Nationality Unknown.

005015   AS A TREE FALLS. BY L. PARRY TRUSCOTT. London: T. F. Unwin, 1903 BMC.

005016   BROTHER-IN-LAW TO POTTS. BY L. PARRY TRUSCOTT. London: T. W. Laurie, [1915] BMC.

Potts narrow minded evangelist makes life miserable for wife and two daughters, but story centers on a young man and his ideal love. TLS
Potts aspires to an ideal girl, meets and saves a different one. LBKM

005017   CATHARINE. BY L. PARRY TRUSCOTT. London: T. W. Laurie, [1907] BMC.

Incredibly close seclusion for 18 years-prepared for nunhood. An artist paints her, comitted to awaken her. He's hit by lightning and dies. ACAD
Vowed to spinsterhood but her heart is won. TLS
SR-Enters into an "irregular union" with a man when she can not overthrow her vows. Sad story she finally sees the light, ends in a "higher note of happiness for the ill-starred lovers."

005018   HILARY'S CAREER. BY L. PARRY TRUSCOTT. London: T. W. Laurie, [1913] BMC.

Hilary is a male whose mother wants him to be a sailor; father wants him to be a publisher. When the marriage of his parents is shown to be illegal, his mother, "having full control, is able to gratify his own yearning for the sea." ATH
Father decides he should be a journalist, like himself. The battle begins, but neither gives way. Unfairness of the law which gives father right to decide is shown up vividly. Then it turns out that husband's wife #1 is really alive. LBKM

005019   THE MARRIAGE OF AMINTA. BY L. PARRY TRUSCOTT. Edinburgh and London: W. Blackwood, 1906 BMC.

ACAD-lunatic family
TLS-amusing fantasia, comedy: young ward and his guardian

005020   THE MOTHER OF PAULINE. BY L. PARRY TRUSCOTT. New York: D. Appleton, 1904 NUC. (Published in England as Motherhood.)

Cooper, "The Sex Problem Novel," BKM v.20 1904. Story of unwed mother.
"instincts of motherhood stronger than her love for Everhard, stronger even than her fear of social ostracism" refuses to give up child-everything works out.
NYT-another Hester.

005021   MOTHERHOOD. BY L. PARRY TRUSCOTT. London: T. F. Unwin, 1904 BMC.

LBKM -difficult subject well handled.
ATH-she harmed her daughter in confessing.
ACAD-belated marriage, subsequent expiation, Pauline, with her thousand and one scruples, becomes tiresome. Too many scruples, too little humor.

005022   MR. SAFFERY'S DISCIPLE. BY L. PARRY TRUSCOTT. London: T. W. Laurie, [1908] BMC.

TLS-schoolmaster and young boy.
ACAD-both in love with a woman who deserts them both for a former love.
ATH--0

005023   OBSTACLES: A NOVEL. BY L. PARRY TRUSCOTT. London: Chapman and Hall, 1916 BMC.

TLS-Susannah becomes a munitions worker to see what it is like to be poor before marrying poor soldier. Gwenny is also a munitions worker who has a drunken mother, their relationship is well described.
LBKM-Is close friends with her father, meets him every Saturday afternoon for tea.

005024   THE POET AND PENELOPE. BY L. PARRY TRUSCOTT. London: T. F. Unwin, 1902 BMC.

005025   THE QUESTION. BY L. PARRY TRUSCOTT. London: T. W. Laurie, [1910] BMC.

ATH-irony and sentimentality; she refuses to marry a musician until he proves himself, her indiscretion makes a fiasco of his first performance. There's a literary lady "whose passion for taking notes impedes her progress in authorship"
LBKM--Triangle.

005026   STARS OF DESTINY. BY L. PARRY TRUSCOTT. London: T. F. Unwin, [1905] BMC.

intellectual widow-TLS 295:05
Old triangle treated well; love on higher plane: man-a writer sensitive, a gifted woman older than he, married to a man she never sees (in asylum) spiritual, intelligent; they feel it is whole love. have transcended sex. Comes a shallow young woman, awakens animal in the man. The older woman realizes then love had not been whole. Good study ATH

HARGREAVES, C. Y. See HARGREAVES, CARRIE Y.

HARGREAVES, CARRIE Y.

005027   PAUL ROMER: A NOVEL. BY C. Y. HARGREAVES. London: A. and C. Black, 1893 BMC.

SP: love story, simple.

005028   POSTE RESTANTE: A NOVEL. BY C. Y.
HARGREAVES. London: A. & C. Black, 1894 BMC NUC.

SP 73:923. Two men who look alike, Englishmen in
Venice.

HARGROVE, ETHEL C.

005029   THE GARDEN OF DESIRE; A STORY OF THE
ISLE OF WIGHT. London: Grafton, 1916 BMC.

Agnes Lister at 25 feels she's in a rut in her small
village in Isle of Wight; determines not to stagnate
but change her life. At this time gets a proposal, but
refuses, for this isn't at all what she wants. She
wants to go to London and write. Does get the money to
go; uphill work at first; lives in woman's hostel, is
art student, a pavement artist, member of woman's
club, member of Socialist group and an author. Does
meet the right man in the end. LBKM

HARKER, L. ALLEN. See HARKER, LIZZIE ALLEN (WATSON).

HARKER, LIZZIE ALLEN (WATSON). 1863-1933. United Kingdom.

005030   ALLEGRA. BY L. ALLEN HARKER. London: J.
Murray, 1919 BMC NUC. New York: C. Scribner's Sons,
1920 NUC.

"young actress trained for five years in the
well-known Westingley Repertory theatre" "passionately
devoted to her art" TLS
Throws up a playwright, an author-wisely sticks to the
stage. ATH
"throws over the playwright who dramatized a trashy
novel and made it worth her taking the principal part,
then falls in love with the original author; but her
revulsion is complete when he sends her the rest of
his works. Allegra wisely sticks to the stage." BAKER
32:227
SR-Conflict between passion for art and love. She is
an actress.
BKM-Resentful of the intrusions of human intercourse
except as they lead to the advancement of her career,
which she chooses over love. Thoroughly likeable.
Egotistic. Her dog patiently listens to endless
outpouring of her mind.
NyT-"Author has had the good sense to avoid the
conventional 'happy ending' which in this instance
would have led to almost certain misery." 2-8-20:71

005031   CONCERNING PAUL AND FIAMMETTA. BY L.
ALLEN HARKER. London: E. Arnold, 1906 BMC. New York:
C. Scribner's Sons, 1906 NUC.

005032   THE FFOLLIOTS OF REDMARLEY. BY L. ALLEN
HARKER. London: J. Murray, 1913 BMC. New York: C.
Scribner's Sons, 1913 NUC.

He's a bookworm with a "charming" wife and a family of
six. His girls are open-air tomboy types. "a chapter
on women's suffrage is full of unexpected fun"? ATH
Slow awakening of a young girl to an understanding of
herself, her choice of suitors. Happy end. BKM
Combines story of social and political rise of a young
man with account of a delightful family. TLS
PW-By author of "Miss Esperance and Mr. Wycherly."
"English family made up of delightful and amusing
people, are the Ffolliots, young and old. The
adventures and scrapes of the children and the love
story of a boy, who works his way up from the shop to
Parliament, makes this a really delightful book, full
of human nature and interest, without any more
startling incidents than occur in most people's
lives." 83:2204

005033   HIS FIRST LEAVE. BY L. ALLEN HARKER.
London: E. Arnold, 1907 BMC. New York: C. Scribner's
Sons, 1908 NUC.

Heroine really nice-TLS
PW-womanly wife

005034   JAN AND HER JOB. BY L. ALLEN HARKER. New
York: C. Scribner's Sons, 1917 NUC. London: J. Murray,
1917 BMC.

Sister's death leads to Jan's taking care of the
children alone, then with the right man. PW
Competent, managing woman took care of father since
age 12, looked after sister's two motherless children
(sister worried into grave by rascal) Her friend Meg
helps her with the children. Meg is just as competent.

One of the children, Fay, is a niece very difficult to
handle. TLS
"Young woman who has to take charge of a batch of
children thru the death of her sister and her
brother-in-law's defection." BAKER 32:227
Janet Ross-NyT 4-8-19:131

005035   MASTER AND MAID. BY MRS. L. ALLEN HARKER.
London: J. Murray, 1910 NUC BMC. New York: C.
Scribner's Sons, 1911 NUC.

BM-witty, flirting good looking Irish girl in school
master's household.
TLS ditto
ATH-surrounded by admirers.
the maid who charms everyone and disturbs many men. PW

005036   MISS ESPERANCE AND MR. WYCHERLY. BY L.
ALLEN HARKER. New York: C. Scribner's Sons, 1908 NUC.
London: J. Murray, 1908 BMC NUC.

PW-children brought up by bachelor don with a strong
desire for drink, and a spinster.
TLS-"Cranfordy" old maid
ATH-but has a feeling of possiblity
NYT-Interesting relationship

005037   MR. WYCHERLY'S WARDS. BY L. ALLEN HARKER.
London: J. Murray, 1912 BMC. New York: C. Scribner's
Sons, 1912 NUC.

TLS-Miss Esperance is dead. A little niece is heroine.
"Charming."
SP-professor and his benevolence and his efficient
housekeeper

005038   A ROMANCE OF THE NURSERY. BY L. ALLEN
HARKER. London and New York: J. Lane, 1903 BMC NUC.

HARKER, MRS. L. ALLEN. See HARKER, LIZZIE ALLEN (WATSON).

HARKNESS, MARGARET ELISE.

005039   THE HOROSCOPE. BY JOHN LAW. Calcutta,
London: [1914] NUC.

HARLAN, MRS. M. R. B. 1879. United States.

005040   IN THE LAND OF EXTREMES. BY MARIE
COTTRELL. New York: Cochrane, 1909 NUC.

teacher. PW 7-3-09

HARLAND, MARION, pseud. See TERHUNE, MARY VIRGINIA (HAWES).

HARPER, CARRIE ANNA, jt. au. See DIX, BEULAH MARIE AND
CARRIE ANNA HARPER.

HARPER, ELLA JEANNETTE. United States.

005041   OUR THANKSGIVING. Indianapolis: Carlon
and Hollenbeck, 1893 NUC.

HARPER, FRANCES ELLEN (WATKINS). 1825-1911. United States.

005042   IOLA LEROY; OR, SHADOWS UPLIFTED.
Philadelphia, Pa.: Garrigues, 1892 NUC.

Concerns emancipation of slaves through the war days
"to the time of higher education and professional
callings for the colored people." Written by a Black
Woman, "ardent worker for the cause of her peple."
NATION 56,147

HARPER, OLIVE, pseud. See D'APERY, HELEN (BURRELL).

HARPER, SARAH JANE. B. 1863. United States.

005043   A NOVELETTE: MARTHA MYNHEER. BY DEAN
HUMPHREYS. Albany, N.Y.: C.F. Williams, 1911 NUC.

005044   A NOVELETTE: THE BLACK HAND. BY DEAN
HUMPHREYS. Albany, N.Y.: C. F. Williams, 1911 NUC.

HARRADEN, BEATRICE. 1864-1936. United Kingdom.

005045   THE FOWLER. Edinburgh: W. Blackwood, 1899
BMC. New York: Dodd, Mead, 1899 NUC.

NYT 5-6-99,299: nurse Isabel-fine study has not
appeared in fiction before. "Large splendidly
educated, independent, self willed heroine Nora
Penhurst" succumbs to the offensively unattractive
Theodore Bevan. She alone falls in his power. Finally
marries. Nurse Isabel born to be fashionable,
circumstances force her to nursing. Keen humor.

The Fowler is a man with power to control women. His
power is not defined, but Nora is his third victim.
She's intelligent, brilliant, but under his power
turns against her father, her lover, gives up all her
ideals until she reads the diary the Fowler keeps and
is able to free herself. His object is to tame people
and to break their individuality. Nurse Isabel is a
strong character. She's a woman of the world who takes
up nursing without any real vocation for it. LIT
An intellectual seduction. Nora is modern to her
fingertips with a great joy of life. Theodore Bevan is
decadent and evil. He's Byronic, (like Mischa Fox.)
Can make self pathetic and therefore attract women. He
sets his trap for Nora. Doesn't seduce her, just
strips her soul of all its beauty. Lures her from
women friends, lover, father. But she wins back her
individuality and self at the end. Had become
fascinated with him because he was so different. LBKM
16:47
His object was to annex young women's souls. SP 83:615
Study of the attraction of evil. CR 34:634

005046   THE GUIDING THREAD. New York: F. A.
Stokes, [c1916] NUC. London: Methuen, 1916 BMC.

NYT-Joan's husband loved her dearly, was kind to her
in his own queer way, but he had robbed her of every
particle of individuality. She was uneducated, but
with a good mind, he had married and trained her to be
a Renaissance scholar. For seven years they had worked
together, he sheltering her from all outside influence
until one day she saw a parrot and understood that
that had been her life. Leaves husband to become her
own person, goes to U. S.
LBKM-Bitter scene in which he slaps her face, she
walks out, not angry or desperate but elated by the
freedom.
BKM--When she decides to leave, she burns all her
work, seven years of notes, telling Horace that none
of it was really hers. Horace had depended on the
notes which a lifetime would hardly replace.

005047   HILDA STRAFFORD; A CALIFORNIA STORY. New
York: Dodd, Mead, 1897 NUC.

So. Calif. ranch life-Eng settlers there. Poor
Englishman in bad health settles in a dusty colorless
part of So. Calif. Hilda comes from England to marry
him. Is immediately disheartened by the place. His
nervousness makes things worse-he's dying but she
doesn't know, she's homesick, a dam bursts and
destroys their lemon crop. One day she tells Robert
she doesn't love him and wants to go back to England;
he dies that night. After that she feels less homesick
because she met Ben. But he blames her for hurrying
Robert's death. So Hilda goes back to England. NYT
5-8-97.
Young Calif. ranchers.-"Life on a Calif. ranch as seen
by a clever, emotional woman. Two stories: includes
"The Remittance Man."SR 83:616.
Young Englishman comes to California for his health.
Starts a ranch. After a few years Hilda, his betrothed
comes. But she's unsuited to the isolated life. Things
go well for a while, but then she condemns him for
putting her in exile. He dies broken hearted. Then
Hilda and her husband's best friend present a delicate
situation. The man understands her feelings but is
indignant with her. Loves her but is loyal to his
friend. They separate, She returns to England. SP
78:447.
Hilda's bitter hy. She is "consumed with regret for a
life she deems misspent and with longing to be home
again." ACAD 51:303.
Cultivation of lemon trees of no interest to her. ATH.
109:41 3.
She's a strong woman of bounding health. He was
already in ill health when he came to Calif. BKM
5:343.

005048   HILDA STRAFFORD AND THE REMITTANCE MAN.
TWO CALIFORNIAN STORIES. Edinburgh: W. Blackwood, 1897
BMC.

005049   INTERPLAY. London: Methuen, 1908 BMC. New
York: F. A. Stokes, [1908] NUC.

Harriet Rivers-woman of extraordinary talent and depth
of emotion. Many questions and problems of the day
such as women's movement. BKM
TLS-unconventional
"an unhappily married woman elopes with a lover, but
her husband refuses to divorce her until her lover's
death...theme, which is...equal morality for men and
women. There is discussion of all the "woman
questions," including the suffrage right." R OF R
BKM 28 1908-9 "The principal theme of Miss Harraden's

new book is the influence of personality upon
personality in shaping life's course. The romantic
interest centres in the love of a famous Arctic
explorer for an American, Harriet Rivers, a woman of
extraordinary talent and depth of emotion. Miss
Harraden brings into her story many questions and
problems of the day, among which is the woman's
suffrage movement."
SR-friendship between divorced woman and young
unconventional woman. Insistence of the author on the
"conception of woman as an independent being." Depth
of cha racter.

005050   KATHARINE FRENSHAM; A NOVEL. Edinburgh
and London: W. Blackwood, 1903 NUC BMC. New York:
Dodd, Mead, 1903 NUC.

Woman of high temper thwarts chemist husband. He tells
son he must have separation, that night she dies.
Katharine brings them cheer and warmth. She works with
specimens for scientist. PW
Warring temperaments spoiling each other's lives. NYT
Clifford feels responsible for wife's death for in a
dream he uttered his long repressed bitterness and she
heard. ACAD
Woman wrecks hero's mind and career. In a dream he
finally expresses his resentment. The revelation kills
her. Then Katherine steps in. ATH
Heroine is broad minded, direct, downright woman of
business Clara is an egoist. TLS

005051   OUT OF THE WRECK I RISE. London, New
York: T. Nelson, [1912] BMC NUC. New York: F. A.
Stokes, [1912] NUC.

PW-male hero who can't help stealing; two women.
TLS-who stifle their jealousy and work together to
save him.
SP-Tamar a shopkeeper who deals in jewels and Nell, a
widow, practical philanthropist. He has thrown both
over in the past, they work together to save him from
business scandal, but at last moment he throws it all
away. We are left in the dark.
NYT-B H has developed in the past four years to a
militant suffragist.
NYT--Two women are his victims. He is physically
slight, conclusion is inevitable.

005052   THE SCHOLAR'S DAUGHTER. New York: Dodd,
Mead, 1906 NUC. London: Methuen, 1906 NUC BMC.

PW-daughter rebels at working on father's dictionary
is surrounded by men (even servants in house); makes
acquaintance of celebrated actress.
NYT-who is actually her mother who left her husband
years before.
ACAD-reviewer hopes parents do not get back together,
can't blame wife for leaving.
TLS-superficial
LBKM-love story and reunion

005053   SHIPS THAT PASS IN THE NIGHT. London:
Lawrence and Bullen, 1893 BMC. Chicago: Donohue,
Henneberry, [1893] NUC.

LW 25:70. Hero does not suicide, an act of
self-sacrifice, because his mother wants him to live
for her sake.
CR-Sombre, hero and heroine are invalids; theme is the
loneliness of the individual. Modern
PW-They are at a winter resort for consumptives in
Alps. Her health has broken down from over work; she
is an author and a teacher. Languid, unconsumated love
story in Alpine health resort. Theme-the hollowness of
modern society. Leading motif: regeneration of
heroine's character by sights of human pathos. BAKER
03, 123
Bernardine Holme exhausted from "teaching, writing
articles for newspapers, attending socialist meetings
and taking part in political discussions "goes for
holiday. Meets a man for whom she is an equal
intelligent match. Returns to London, writes books,
discovers (as he does that) she loves the man. About
to wed, gets run over and dies in hospital. ACAD
43:390.

005054   SPRING SHALL PLANT. London, New York:
Hodder and Stoughton, [1920] BMC NUC.

TLS-story of rebellious and gifted child Patuffa.
SP-Expelled from many girls' schools at last makes
good in Dresden, to the advantage of her musical
talent.
LBKM-Incorrigible "scores" every time over adults.

005055   WHERE YOUR HEART IS. New York: Dodd,

Mead, 1918 NUC. (English ed. title: Where Your Treasure Is)

005056   WHERE YOUR TREASURE IS. London:
Hutchinson, 1918 BMC NUC.

PW-The gradual ennobling effect of war on a grasping
woman.
TLS-T. Scott, as she is known, is a Jewish dealer in
precious stones and antiquities. Thornton family. Rev.
very upset.
SR.- Mental odyssey. She is not grasping; she is
self-centered and consumed with interest in her
business. Friendship with Thornton's widow and family
begins to draw her out.
NYT-Tamar Scott, or T. Scott as her business
associates know her is a middle-aged Jewish dealer in
precious stones and antique jewelry, sullen and
"uncommonly rude at times." Becomes more outgoing and
warm gradually through friendship.

HARRIMAN, ALICE. See BROWNE, ALICE (HARRIMAN).

HARRINGTON, KATHERINE, pseud. See BENNETT, MRS. ROLF.

HARRIOTT, CLARA MORRIS. 1848-1925. United States.

005057   LEFT IN CHARGE. BY CLARA MORRIS. New
York: G. W. Dillingham, [c1904] NUC. London: T. F.
Unwin, 1904 BMC.

NYT-

005058   THE NEW "EAST LYNNE". BY CLARA MORRIS.
New York: C. H. Doscher, [c1908] NUC.

PW-menage a trois-wife believed dead-other two
marry-wife returns five years later as governess for
her children.

005059   A PASTEBOARD CROWN, A STORY OF THE NEW
YORK STAGE. BY CLARA MORRIS. New York: C. Scribner's
Sons, 1902 NUC. London: Isbister, 1902 BMC.

story of an actress. Falls in love with manager, a
married man. BOOK NEWS
NYT-Becomes mistress of manager. Continues after
discovering he already had a wife. She doesn't suffer
from her immoral act, loses nothing in character,
contrasted with sister whose life is one of domestic
monotony.

005060   A SILENT SINGER. BY CLARA MORRIS. New
York: Brentano's, 1899 NUC. London: Isbister, 1904
BMC.

005061   THE TROUBLE WOMAN. BY CLARA MORRIS. New
York and London: Funk and Wagnall, 1904 NUC.

A short story, quaint in its character, which tells of
the coming and going of the gaunt, sad-eyed figure
known as the "trouble woman." BKM
"powerfully realistic narration" of a woman with an
overwhelming troubled life who is a source of strength
in community. ARENA, 1904.

HARRIS, A. L. See HARRIS, ADA L.

HARRIS, ADA L. Nationality Unknown.

005062   THE FATAL REQUEST. BY A. L. HARRIS.
London: F. Warne, 1891 BMC. New York: Cassell, [c1891]
NUC.

Silas Buritt injured in railroad accident asks friend
to kill him. Afterwards the death is thought to be
murder till the truth comes out. ATH 98 318
Silas's remains recovered from accident show bullet
wound. PW 017
Contains a forgery, a murder, a ghost, a railroad
accident. SR 9-26-91, 365
SP-A shocker, but contains a lot of comedy. Part of it
in form of man's diary.

005063   A WIDOW ON WHEELS. BY A. L. HARRIS.
London: Hutchinson, 1896 BMC NUC.

HARRIS, CORRA MAY (WHITE). 1869-1935. United States.

005064   A CIRCUIT RIDER'S WIDOW. Garden City, NY:
Doubleday, Page, 1916 NUC.

Mary guide, mother, philosopher and friend to whole
community-PW
very human study of wife (later widowed) and her
religious attitude toward husband's Methodism. TLS

Corra writes about her own and husband's life-ATH
actual experience of Methodist circuit rider and
wife-PW
BKM-difficult

005065   THE CO-CITIZENS. Garden City NY:
Doubleday, Page, 1915 NUC. London: Wayfarer, [1919]
BMC.

woman leaves her money for the suffrage cause. what
the funds went to makes an amusing story. PW 9-11-15
Sara Mosely leaves her money to the cause of gaining
woman's suffrage in her very conservative district.
There's only one suffragist there; the state has a low
literacy, the public school lasted only five months.
The farmers were against schools. The Co-Citizens
League under able leadership of Mrs. Susan Walton gets
to work. All the wives who had done nothing but attend
husbands come to meetings. How the women won, the
methods they used is the story. NYT
"the original of Susan Walton was Mrs. Willian H.
Felton, Georgia's pioneer suffragist."

005066   EVE'S SECOND HUSBAND. Philadelphia:
Altemus, [c1911] NUC. London: Constable, 1911 BMC.

Widow who knows men are not to be respected even if
one loves them; remarries and struggles with husband
over the "infidelities of his political and marital
life" PW 3-11-11
TLS-Matter of fact Tennessee woman tells her views
with mixture of frankness and sent
ATH-woman has an unfaithful husband solves her
problem.
BKM-runs up bills for thousands of dollars so he can't
afford other woman. Loves him, but comments on
shortcomings of men, "being a good woman does not pay
except in goodness."

005067   HAPPILY MARRIED. New York: G. H. Doran
Co, [c1920] NUC. London: Hodder and Stoughton, [1920]
BMC.

TLS-message is to be a canny wife.
NYT-Virtuous wife deals successfully with other woman.

005068   IN SEARCH OF A HUSBAND. Garden City, NY:
Doubleday, Page, 1913 NUC. London: G. Richards, [1913]
BMC.

PW-"Scene is a Southern town where the preoccupation
of the young woman is to lay traps for as many male
hearts as possible. Joy Marr lives with her father and
brother and she and her brother make a bargain, he
with designs upon a certain lady, she with an eye to a
handsome newcomer. It is the queer twists which fate
gives to this compact between brother and sister that
make the story's background. Joy, drawn irresistibly
by David Brock, the newcomer, yet hesitates to accept
him because she has set her mind upon money; and so
she carries on a dangerous flirtation with another
man. But the fiddler must be paid--and paid he is."
84:1529
"Mrs. Harris's story is a study of the parasite woman.
Joy Marr is that type of southern belle, much featured
in fiction, who sees that ease, comfort and the good
things of life generally, are to be obtained not thru
personal effort but thru the beneficence of a man. She
accordingly directs her effort toward the acquisition
of that man. She determines at a very early age to
marry-and to marry well. Her schemings toward that
end, her failures and her final success make up that
story." BRD 6
Story opens with her debut; her one ambition is to
make a rich match but falls in love with a poor man.
Still determined to marry money. Sees time goes by-no
success. Makes one more desperate effort to get a rich
man, learns he has no interest in marriage. Returns to
marry poor man.
BKM-A virgin adventuress who, being good, has no
conscience about attaining her ends. Unwillingly falls
in love with a poor man but does not give up pursuit
of ambitious marriage. Years pass and she does not
succeed. One last attempt sends her back to poor man.

005069   JUSTICE. New York: Hearst's International
Library, 1915 NUC BMC.

"brings out the unreason, inequality and onesexedness
of human justice as represented by law." NYT

005070   MAKING HER HIS WIFE. Garden City, NY:
Doubleday, Page, 1918 NUC. London: T. Nelson, [1924]
BMC.

PW-John and Olive marry. She is restless, he is

determined to reduce her to his ideas of wifely duty. Conflict.
NYT-John "100 percent prig;" Olive "silly and spineless." They separate but eventually re-unite, "but the reader remains skeptical as to their future hapiness...but does not take sufficient interest in them to care whether they were wretched or not."

005071   THE RECORDING ANGEL. London: Constable, 1912 BMC. Garden City, N. Y.: Doubleday, Page, 1912 NUC.

wanderer returns to his native town in Georgia and stirs up the town. ATH
A blind old lady dictates sketches of townspeople to her derelict husband who secretly sells them for drink money. These made into a play that brings the town to a Renaissance. Hint of relationship between Jim Bone and a woman sounds interesting . Get other reviews. BKM
NYT-faults and foibles of women are her dearest game

HARRIS, CORRA MAY (WHITE) AND FAITH HARRIS LEECH.

005072   FROM SUNUP TO SUNDOWN. Garden City, New York: Doubleday, Page, 1919 NUC.

Letters between a mother "who runs a big farm and knows how and a recently married daughter who is helping her husband run his farm and does not know how." PW
Letters on the subjects of pigs, the war, management of husbands, effect of cooking on a wife's disposition, etc. NYT 6-8-19 321.

HARRIS, FRANCES ALLEN. United States.

005073   AMONG THE MEADOWS; A NOVEL. New York: Neale, 1905 NUC.

PW-Depicts farm life in the blue-grass region of Ky.

HARRIS, LINNIE SARAH. B. 1868. United States.

005074   SWEET PEGGY. Boston: Little, Brown, 1904 NUC.

PW-love story, but wife becomes public singer after mrg.
NYT-o

HARRIS, MARY KERNAHAN.

005075   DR. IVOR'S WIFE. BY MRS. MARY HARRIS. London: G. Allen, 1914 BMC.

LBKM-delicate situation handled with reticence. Margaret, teacher, marries her favorite pupil's truculent parent. Growth of a love both are too proud to admit. Her confession, which she is tricked into by her sister. His conversion.
ATH-what began as a marriage of convenience becomes a real marriage.

HARRIS, MIRIAM (COLES). 1834-1925. United States.

005076   A CHIT OF SIXTEEN, AND OTHER STORIES. New York: G. W. Dillingham, 1892 NUC.

short stories

005077   THE TENTS OF WICKEDNESS. New York: D. Appleton, 1907 NUC BMC.

Catholic girl, innocent, finds a friend among people of the smart set of New York. 10-5-07 PW
TLS- "Life of romance of a R. C. girl introduced into the frivolities and scandals of a wealthy entourage in New York."
ATH pure girl in vulgar soc, sectarian nature.

005078   AN UTTER FAILURE: A NOVEL. New York: D. Appleton, 1891 NUC. London: Allen & Storr, 1891 BMC.

American heroine raised without restraints of relatives goes to Florence, marries a count. Story recounts marital problems. PW
LW 23:11. Rachel marries an Italian she doesn't love. She loves her children but doesn't know how to be a mother. She leaves her family for their sake. Later, chancing to see her son's ordination, she dies of joy.

HARRIS, VIRGINIA FISHER. United States.

005079   TILLIE: A LOVE STORY. Tyler, Texas: Lee & Burnett, 1903 NUC.

HARRISON, CONSTANCE (CARY). 1843-1920. United States.

005080   A BACHELOR MAID. BY MRS. BURTON HARRISON. New York: Century, 1894 NUC. London: T. F. Unwin, 1895 BMC.

CR 21:227. Article on author, who describes heroine as fin-de-siecle. Discusses suffrage, "I pride myself upon the diplomatic way I touch a very delicate subject."
PW-concerns the woman question. Pure and noble woman animated by desire to benefit her sex, yet hardly understanding the things to be accomplished or the means of their accomplishment.
"An efficient antidote against the recent outbreak of the New Woman. It's key note is womanliness." Sara Stauffer, the apostle of Woman's Rights whose pretenses are false, seeks, by fair means or foul, what she denounces--matrimony. NY upper class.
The love of woman for man--the healthy ennobling love that foste ll the virtues-will endure and triumph in the end." CR 13:25
Morison Irving rejects her fiance because she thinks that a woman ought to live her own life and cannot do so if she is married. At the end she is glad to take him back. SP 75:469.

005081   THE CARLYLES; A STORY OF THE FALL OF THE CONFEDERACY. BY MRS. BURTON HARRISON. New York: D. Appleton, 1905 BMC NUC.

Hist. 11-4-05 PW

005082   THE CIRCLE OF A CENTURY. BY MRS. BURTON HARRISON. New York: Century, 1899 NUC.

Old New York in time of hardship and glory. "The doings of 1789 find their echo in the life of today." CR 35:1157
Sequence of love stories. PW 56:868
LW 31:70. New York City area, in the 18th c and now.

005083   THE COUNT AND THE CONGRESSMAN. BY MRS. BURTON HARRISON. New York: Cupples & Leon, [c1908] NUC.

PW rom.
BKM rom.

005084   AN ERRANT WOOING. BY MRS. BURTON HARRISON. New York: Century, 1895 NUC.

Widower and daughter who was hurt in love finds new love. Set in U.S., then England then Spain. Pauline Standish, cultured, unsent American gives up a wealthy American man for a poor foreigner. He's a Saxon who speaks Spanish and Arabic. Very unlike her. Differences between English and American conventions. CR. 24:197
Experiences of a European journey. And about a couple whose grandfather wants them to marry but who find others to love. LW26:217.
Love stories hung on a travel log of Europe. Sir Piers and Roger Woodbury and a dark and a fair maiden. BKM 2:54

005085   GOOD AMERICANS. BY MRS. BURTON HARRISON. New York: Century, 1898 NUC BMC.

PW. Hero is young lawyer, marries NY society girl. American idealism in him contrasted with European comfort and conventionality which many Americans seek in preference to their birthright. After problematic episodes they become good Americans.
Peter Davenant, chief character. Ambitious, strong. Attracted to a "Feeble Fickle Feminine" woman. She becomes a model wife "after undergoing a desperate surgical operation" (?). Her name is Sybil. BKM 8:495.
NY-man of purpose loves a woman who seeks only pleasure. NYT 6-24-99,405.

005086   LATTER-DAY SWEETHEARTS. BY MRS. BURTON HARRISON. London: T.F. Unwin, 1906 BMC. New York: Authors & Newspapers Assoc., 1906 NUC.

ACAD pleasant romance
TLS pleasant romance.

005087   A PRINCESS OF THE HILLS; AN ITALIAN ROMANCE. BY MRS. BURTON HARRISON. London: C.H. Kelly, 1901 BMC. Boston: Lothrop, [c1901] NUC.

A peasant girl of the Alps and an American "heroine of modern fiction" "make it warm for as many men and more breaking their hearts and mending them." BOOK NEWS short desc. Critic makes it questionable NYT '01

005088   A SON OF THE OLD DOMINION. BY MRS. BURTON HARRISON. Boston and London: Lamson, Wolffe, 1897 BMC NUC.

Hist. facts combined with fiction. Story of Va. just after the Revolution. A young heir gives up his estate in Eng. for American freedom. LW 28:288
Va. Rev. Days-hist rom CR 28,31:201
Love story, stirring picture of the times. Historical personages as characters. NYT 8-28-97,7
NYT 1898:415. Virginia before the Revolution, Washington.

005089   SWEET BELLS OUT OF TUNE. BY MRS. BURTON HARRISON. London: T. F. Unwin, 1893 BMC. New York: Century, 1893 NUC.

Characters are ill bred ill educated snobs-their spats bickerings and strivings, their outer flashiness, Mr. and Mrs. Vernon's estrangement. NATION 57:452.
Eleanor Halliday of an old Knickerbocker family marries a man who is a social climber. The career of this couple-her disillusionment in finding him selfish, ordinary. Her sister's love story, satirical sketches of English and American society. PW 10-21-93.
Fashionable world of New York, the 400. Very unfavorable view of dog eat dog social climbing. Women ready to sell themselves for wealth. Money the only value. Low sordid world. LW 93, 348.
Opens with wedding; bride the heroine. Divorcee, important character. Bride is Eleanor Halliday; Hildegarde de Lancey. Husband attracted to divorcee. When wife learns she will be making trip to Europe with them, she won't go; they go without her. She follows and his mother in England makes everything right. CR 20,23: 391-392.
SR. Satire of vices of American society. Virtuous wife, unfaithful husband who eventually is penitent and reformed.
SP 72:866. He has an affair with a divorcee.

005090   SYLVIA'S HUSBAND. BY MRS. BURTON HARRISON. New York: D. Appleton, 1904 BMC NUC.

NYT ?.

005091   TRANSPLANTED DAUGHTERS. London: T.F. Unwin, 1909 BMC.

a woman marries off her three daugherts TLS
"Seamy side of Eur-Amer marriage" two fail ATH
Cinderella type of story SP

005092   A TRIPLE ENTANGLEMENT. BY MRS. BURTON HARRISON. London: T. F. Unwin, 1898 BMC. Philadelphia: J. B. Lippincott, 1899 NUC.

SP 81:991. Two male friends, one cruelly duped by the other. Eventually, however, he is rewarded.
ATH 112:748. They love an English girl and she loves them. No entanglement in the traditional sense.
Enid Severn is secretly engaged to a bad man. Doesn't know he's bad; falls for another man. But the new lover finds out that Algy-the bad one-is unscrupulous though he finally frees Enid from the engagement. Then Enid and Stuart lose track of each other. She becomes a governess, alone. He gets engaged to another. Then they meet, part. On the last page they get together. BKM 9:474
Spanish setting, intricate plot--many characters. Young people who don't get what they want, settle for less. NYT 5-20-99,333

005093   THE UNWELCOME MRS. HATCH. A DRAMA OF EVERY DAY. BY MRS. BURTON HARRISON. New York: C.G. Burgoyne, 1901 NUC. New York: D. Appleton, 1903 BMC NUC.

Divorce in New York PW 6-27-03
Unfaithful husband, divorce, she returns after 12 years, begs to see her daughter, must disguise herself to be with her daughter on her wedding day; ends up dying in her daughter's arms. NYT 511 03

005094   A VIRGINIA COUSIN AND BAR HARBOR TALES. BY MRS. BURTON HARRISON. Boston: Lamson, Wolffe, 1895 NUC.

HARRISON, EDITH (OGDEN). D. 1955. United States.

005095   CLEMENCIA'S CRISIS. Chicago: A. C. McClurg, 1915 NUC.

Conflict between a vow to church & love; chooses love

005096   THE LADY OF THE SNOWS. Chicago: A. C. McClurg, 1912 NUC.

PW sounds like romance.

005097   PRINESS SAYRANE; A ROMANCE OF THE DAYS OF PRESTER JOHN. Chicago: A. C. McClurg, 1910 NUC.

Hist romance PW
Egypt 12th-14th cent. hist romance. NYT

HARRISON, ELLANETTA. United States.

005098   THE STAGE OF LIFE; A KENTUCKY STORY. Cincinnati: R. Clarke, 1903 NUC.

HARRISON, IDA (WITHERS). 1851-1927. United States.

005099   BEYOND THE BATTLE'S RIM; A STORY OF THE CONFEDERATE REFUGEES. New York: Neale, 1918 NUC.

PW-Story of Civil War.

HARRISON, KATHLEEN ELIZABETH.

005100   THROUGH UNSEEN PATHS. London: Sonnenschein, 1899 BMC.

Socialistic ideas. Also Squire's daughter who marries without the Squire's permission is reconciled to him when her child is born. LIT 5:349
She loses her memory; along with her child brought to a convent. When the child grows up the two are reconciled to Squire. SP 83:259

HARRISON, LILLIAN.

005101   THE PUPPET-SHOW; A NOVEL. London: J. Richmond, [1917] BMC.

Focuses on a professor and his loves TLS

HARRISON, MARIE.

005102   THE WOMAN ALONE. London: Holden & Hardingham, [1914] BMC.

ATH. Study of a woman doctor whose instincts led her to seek motherhood without marriage.
ATH 144:97. Author shows a woman doctor with a working-class practice has child, deliberately, without marriage which she is notinterested in. Her friends stand by her and "her patients accept the fact of her unorthodox motherhood." Shows "some of the causes which lie at the roots of feminine unrest today."

HARRISON, MARY SAINT LEGER (KINGSLEY). 1852-1931. United Kingdom.

005103   ADRIAN SAVAGE; A NOVEL. BY LUCAS MALET. New York and London: Harper, 1911 NUC. London: Hutchinson, 1911 BMC.

mother is a poet. He loves a very intelligent widow of 40; most of story a kind of diary of her feelings. PW 11-14-11
Joanna Smirthwaite-"unlovely, cramped and ardent" The story is ugly and brutal. TLS
Adrian loves Gabrielle St. Leger, widow (husband was twice her age; her marriage miserable. She is in no hurry to remarry, she's well off, young, devoted to daughter "attracted to the Feminist mvt."). Wealthy Joanna is "repellently plain, destitute of charm, tact, or experience" She believes Adrian loves her. This illusion dominates her whole life. She pours out all her feelings in her diary. SP
The manner of Joanna's enlightenment is singular ATH
She dreams that he told her he could never love her. kills self?SR

005104   THE CARISSIMA: A MODERN GROTESQUE. BY LUCAS MALET. London: Methuen, 1896 BMC. Chicago: H. S. Stone, 1896 NUC.

ATH 108:832. Charlotte Perry is the Carissima. Male narrator. Style recalls Henry James. Six principal actors: narrator, his friend Leversedge and Mrs Perry are the good angels; Charlotte, her father, and Percy Gerrard the bad.
ACAD 50:457. Leversedge found the remains of a caravan in S. Africa and a surviving dog eating a baby. He fired but hit rope dog was tied by; he rushed away with dog in pursuit; haunted by dog's ghost

thenceforth. Returns to Europe, is affianced to the Carissima, her parents and they go to a lakeside hotel. Carissima informs Hammond, the narrator, that she had a passion for him. He was tempted but when he saw that the toe of her shoe turned up, he was able to refuse. She "half-married" Leversedge. Her father was "ratfaced"; she had a "moon-clock" mother.
SP 77:771. Charlotte "eclipses even Jessie Enderby in her odious selfishness."
PW 11-7-96. Picture of "The chief wonder of the age, the modern young woman, who differs as much from all bygone types of womanhood as our modern modes of locomotion do from those obtaining in the days of Abraham! What such a woman did to the man who loved her and to the man she made think she loved him." She's a study of certain kind of modern womanhood—"complicated in emotions and desires but simple in action." LW 28:52
Man confesses to the young woman that he loves that he's haunted by the vision of a dog. She gets help from a male friend to make the vision seem more real. LBKM 11:124
Story of a horribly weird obsession that saps the man of strength by its terror. He loves La Carissima, worshiped by her mother. She is ultra sophisticated and modern. How will she react to his vision? She's artificial calculated, not a bit natural or spontaneous. BKM 4:564

005105   DAMARIS; A NOVEL. BY LUCAS MALET. (MRS. MARY ST. LEGER HARRISON). New York: Dodd, Mead, 1916 NUC. London: Hutchinson, 1916 BMC NUC.

PW 90:1167 10/7/16 5 yr old girl Damaris grieves for father's lover who fled back to her husband. Father sends for Mrs Perreira for girl and goes on a journey elswhere, foreswearing women forever.
TLS-Author seems to want us to believe in women as snares, as a drug, toy, lovely thing of evil etc.
BKM Father loved Mrs Perreira but she was married so he married someone. Then her husband died and she remembered. Then his wife died, leaving him Damaris. Still has raging passion for Mrs Perreira, whom he asks to visit to advise him on Damaris' education. Damaris loves Mrs. perreira but women of the post wage campaign to get rid of her. She is a generous and beautiful woman.

005106   DEADHAM HARD: A ROMANCE. BY LUCAS MALET (MARY ST. LEGER HARRISON). London: Methuen, [1919] BMC NUC. New York: Dodd, Mead, 1919 NUC.

Damaris Verity the eduction of a "vice-reine," her illeg brother, other ruling arist. review doesn't make the time of the novel clear nor the plot. TLS
mid- Victorian times. She's only child of Anglo-Indian, distinguished pol. officer; learns at 18 of "illeg" half-brother; conflict between loyalty to father and to brother and her harmonizing of these emotions are the story. SP
She marries SR
NYT 509 10-5-19

005107   THE FAR HORIZON. BY LUCAS MALET (MRS. MARY ST. LEGER HARRISON). London: Hutchinson, 1906 BMC NUC. New York: Dodd Mead, 1907 NUC.

older man and morals PW
Poppy St. John audacious, unconventional actress married to failing playwright, offers frank comradeship to older man. She's contrasted to Serena Longrove "typical middle-class English woman, limited, narrow." We get Serena's hopeless pursuit of hero as a Vict. woman might pursue a man." NYT
BKM 24 1906-7 actress
TLS-heroine is a good hearted courtesan rescued by male.
ATH o
BKM Her husband is a drunk who writes worthless plays, she knows other men, finally a 70 yr old Spaniard, a retired bank clerk.

005108   THE GATELESS BARRIER. BY LUCAS MALET. London: Methuen, 1900 BMC. New York: Dodd, Mead, 1900 NUC.

LBKM 19:24. Agnes, a ghost, is heroine, a shy haunting beauty and a young man to whom she appears, leading him back to his true self.
SP 85:246. "Story of a spiritual infidelity."
NYT 9-5-20, Reprint, story of dead woman who defies laws of life and death to be with her lover again.

005109   THE GOLDEN GALLEON. BY LUCAS MALET (MRS. MARY ST. LEGER HARRISON). New York: Hodder and Stoughton, [c1910] NUC.

Miranda Povey, a spinster living in London. Falls in love; "her spiritual devel. after she learns of the unworthiness of the man is vividly and sympathetically drawn." sent. story of old maids. NYT

005110   THE HISTORY OF SIR RICHARD CALMADY. A ROMANCE. BY LUCAS MALET. New York: A.L. Burt, [c1901] NUC. London: Methuen, 1901 BMC NUC.

"Honoria splendid in her freedom"
"Sex problem novel" BKM 1904 554
"He is a prism by which all the many colors in a woman's sexual personality may be set forth"-most importantly upon Katherine, the perfect mother Helen, the perfect sensualist Honoria, the perfect virgin all treated sympathetically (sympathy lacking in portrait of hero). Katherine: majestic, calm dignity, candid pearl of womanhood; Helen: (Richard's evil genius), selfish, artistic temperament takes the most enjoyment from life; the three women are the novel ACAD '01

005111   THE SCORE. BY LUCAS MALET (MRS. MARY ST. LEGER HARRISON). London: J. Murray, 1909 BMC. New York: E.P. Dutton, 1909 NUC.

two stories "Miserere Nohis" and "The courage of her convictions"
Story 2 actress at zenith of career refuses marriage to M.P. because of his career, sees the marriage won't work. PW 8-21-09
Story 2 Poppy St. John "slangy inpulsive desentimentalized actress" TLS
story 2 Poppy is well over 30 with a good deal of self respect and no illusions. loves her work; story 1 man filled with futile passion for a woman; nearly crushes her to death in his arms to prove his power of conquest when she rejects him "love and brutality are interchangeable"NYT
Story 1 Man urged to murder by his reputed father, a man who turns out to be his real father. Prompted by false information that that man did his mother wrong. SP

005112   THE TALL VILLA. BY LUCAS MALET (MARY ST. LEGER HARRISON). London: W. Collins, Sons, [1902] BMC. New York: G.H. Doran, [c1919] NUC.

Rom. of wife and ancestral ghost.

005113   THE WRECK OF THE GOLDEN GALLEON. BY LUCAS MALET (MRS. MARY ST. LEGER HARRISON). London: Hodder & Stoughton, 1910 NUC BMC.

TLS- two older women keep a lodging house in London, are disillusioned in a young lodger.
ATH silly old maids love starved.

HARRISON, MRS. BURTON. See HARRISON, CONSTANCE (CARY).

HARRISON, MRS. DARENT.

005114   MASTER PASSIONS. London: T. F. Unwin, 1899 BMC.

Hero is an artist who is summoned to West Indies to look after father's estate. Madge Wilton's musical career in Germany-well off, becomes a fine pianist. Life in the Conservatorium. SP 82:723

005115   THE STAIN ON THE SHIELD. London: J. Long, 1906 BMC.

TLS-male hero conv rom.
ATH-has a Scotch woman doctor.

HARRISON, NELLIE FORTESCUE. See MACMILLAN, NELLIE FORTESCUE (HARRISON).

HARRISON, S. F. See HARRISON, SUSIE FRANCES (RILEY).

HARRISON, S. FRANCES. See HARRISON, SUSIE FRANCES (RILEY).

HARRISON, SUSIE FRANCES (RILEY). 1859-1935. Canada.

005116   THE FOREST OF BOURG-MARIE. BY S. FRANCES HARRISON (SERANUS). London: E. Arnold, 1898 BMC NUC.

LIT 3:604. Canada. French Canadian types. Contact between simplicity of Mikel and flashy civilization of his grandson Magloire, who has been to Milwaukee and returned to regenerate his fellow-citizens.
ACAD 55:377. No heroine, no love interest.

005117   RINGFIELD; A NOVEL. BY S. F. HARRISON, "SERANUS". Toronto: Musson Book, [1914?] NUC. London:

Hodder & Stoughton, [1914] BMC.

HARROD, FRANCES (FORBES-ROBERTSON). United Kingdom.

005118   THE HIDDEN MODEL. London: Heinemann, 1901
BMC NUC.

heroine commits a crime ATH 7-20-01

005119   THE HORRIBLE MAN. A NOVEL. London: S.
Paul, 1913 BMC.

unreal characters: an artist, the squire, his
daughters ATH
The horrible man Crawley is a land agent and lawyer;
he has all the vices. He is all bad; the heroine, all
good. She turns into a milk-white hound"! Gets her
revenge that way. Springs at his throat. Dead bodies
of the man and dog are found; heroine returns home,
marries a man who was sole witness to the deed.
"allegory of the rise of the militant female against
horrible men?" SR

005120   MOTHER EARTH; A SENTIMENTAL COMEDY.
London: Heinemann, 1902 BS. New York: J.F. Taylor,
1902 BMC NUC.

ATH 12-6-02 conv. heroine

005121   THE POTENTATE. A ROMANCE. BY FRANCES
FORBES ROBERTSON. London: A. Constable, 1898 BMC NUC.
New York: Mershon, [c1898] NUC.

SP 80:629. Portrait of Italian Renaissance despot who
combined culture with cruelty. Also young hero and
heroine and their love story.
LIT 2:647.
ACAD 53:487 She is learned and about to enter a
religous order.
BKM 8:257 No woman who loved him could be considered
sane, as the author considers the women in her story.
NyT 1898:597 Hero's father has been killed by
villainous duke. He tries to kill him, kills his "evil
genius" who turns out to be the father of the woman he
loves. The duke wants her as his mistress.

005122   THE TAMING OF THE BRUTE. London: Methuen,
1905 BMC.

Rom hist. ACAD 448,05
Cecilie marries and tames the man LBKM 27-8, 106
Defies convention; on hearing of the gossip about a
man she once knew goes off to reclaim him TLS 161,05
ATH 05, 555

005123   THE WANTON. London: Greening, 1909 BMC.

love-hist TLS
Story of love treachery LBKM

005124   WHAT WE DREAM. London: Duckworth, 1903
BMC.

Delicate, fragile, bloodless ATH 122, 647
TLS 320,03

005125   THE WHITE HOUND. BY FRANCES
FORBES-ROBERTSON. New York: Dodd, Mead, 1913 NUC.

"Written by the sister of the well-known actor,
Johnston Forbes-Robertson. Scene is rural England. An
old scholar has perfectly normal wife and two
daughters, who live conventionally and have no desire
to do or be anything unusual. The third daughter is
different; she knows about things before they happen,
is rather wild and will not be trammeled to
conventions. The father dies, and the white hound
comes into the story, its connection with the girl
making a mystery round which the plot develops." PW

HART, ELIZABETH.

005126   IRRECONCILIABLES. London: A. Melrose,
[1916] BMC.

TLS ? Irish story, one of the heroines makes the
proposals.

HART, ETHEL GERTRUDE. Nationality Unknown.

005127   THE DREAM GIRL. Garden City, N.Y.:
Doubleday, Page, 1912 NUC.

"Max Herrick had been badly burned saving a child from
fire, and even after his life is safe, there are six
months of invalidismto be faced. To cheer him his good

comrade Polly Carr sugges ts a correspondence with a
friend of hers whom she describes as a sort of dream
lady. Book is made up of Max's letters and the girl's
reply, a surprise for Max as to the identity of Polly,
and the dream girl being the denouement." PW
Young man, semi invalid writes to girl living in the
hills that he has never seen. They have a mutual
friend, a typewriter. NYT
Polly and the dream girl are the same person. Polly
wants to find out the other side of Max's character.
NYT

HART, FRANCES NEWBOLD (NOYES). 1890-1943. United States.

005128   MARK. BY FRANCES NEWBOLD NOYES. New York:
E.J. Clode, [c1913] NUC.

PW 83 3/1/13:767 "Mark Spencer comes to England from
Australia, where he had lived far from all intercourse
except that of his parents. He is an Arcadian who
thinks the world all joy and he meets Priscilla
Hampden, and they play together until an unprincipled
woman steps in to part them. Mark's first knowledge of
evil is also his last, for he shoots himself."
He's innocent, beautiful as a Greek God; almost
entirely dialogue. NYT

005129   MY A.E.F.; A HAIL AND FAREWELL. BY
FRANCES NEWBOLD NOYES. New York: F.A. Stokes, [c1920]
NUC.

PW-plea to AEF that they give honest picture of what
happened "over there" from a Y girl who served in
France.

HART, MABEL. Nationality Unknown.

005130   FROM HARVEST TO HAY-TIME. London: Hurst
and Blackett, 1892 BMC.

Rose Purley runs her widowed mother's farm, gives work
to a tramp who is ill with sunstroke. The illness
makes him lose his memory. She's loved by local M.D.
and loves this young cultured Hercules-the tramp. ACAD
also ATH 98 682

005131   IN CUPID'S COLLEGE. London: Hurst and
Blackett, 1894 BMC.

SR 77:312. Heroine very beautiful but mentally
deficient in some way. Nevertheless, engaged but
engagement broken when she falls in love with another
man and attacks his fiance. The first man marries
someone else; the two of them share their home with
heroine--for life.
SP 72:475. She has so little mind that she only just
escapes idiocy. Concern of her mother for finding
someone to take care of her after her death. She has
an income of 8,000 lbs a year.
ATH 103:310. Ethel bears the penalty of her father's
vice. She has very little brain power, vapid of speech
and eccentric in action, but gentle, sensitive and
mostly devoid of malicious tendencies. A compensating
passion of love between Ethel and her mother.

005132   SACRILEGE FARM. London: W. Heinemann,
1902 BMC. New York: D. Appleton, 1903 NUC.

Young wife so ill treated she revolted. Husband found
dead. the family covers up the crime by burning the
house. But a servant, an ex mistress really killed
him--NYT 03, 377

005133   SISTER K. London: Methuen, [1909] BMC
NUC.

Hilary Gale hospital nurse and Sister K and their two
loves TLS
"wholesome and pleasant" ATH
Good detailed desc. of nursing profession SP

HART, MRS. ALFRED.

005134   A DOUBLE RUIN: A NOVEL. London: Eden,
1892 BMC.

ACAD 42:191. A sad story, both "delicate" and
"powerfully told."

HARTE, EDITH BAGOT.

005135   BIANCA. London: T. F. Unwin, 1893 BMC.

Italian heroine, English hero love each other. She's
daughter of a Marchesse, of a renowned family. She
"behaves with unaccountable wrong headedness in regard

to her marriage." SR 76:680.
SP 72:18. Heroine marries second time under the
impression her husband is dead. The bigamy is
concealed.

005136   A DARING SPIRIT. London: Digby, Long,
1901 BMC.

005137   IN DEEP WATERS. London: Digby, Long, 1902
BMC.

005138   THE PRICE OF SILENCE; A NOVEL. London:
Greening, 1906 BMC.

005139   THE WHEEL OF FATE. London: W. H. Addison,
1897 BMC.

005140   WRONGLY CONDEMNED: A NOVEL. London:
Jarrold, 1896 BMC.

SR- "Greenback" series. Quaker brother and sister on
trial for murder. Real criminal confesses at last
moment.
ACAD 50:128. Henry is secretly married to Ruth, the
sister, and they have a child. In spite of this he
engages himself to Rita. When Rita discovers truth,
she kills him. Suspicion falls on Ruth and her
brother.

HARTIER, MARY.

005141   CHAPEL FOLK. London: J. Clarke, 1898 BMC.

SP 81:914. Devonshire. Mid 19th c. Dissenters.
Minister as hero. His love story.
Young man's father becomes rich. The son becomes a
dissenting minister in western England, marries Grace,
and lives happily.
LIT 4:209
Dialect: West Country

HARTILL, MARIE.

005142   ANNE GREENFIELD, ONDERWIJZERES. South
Africa: T. M. Miller, 1915 BMC.

005143   THE SEED OF PARADISE. London and New
York: Hodder & Stoughton, 1915 BMC NUC.

HARTLEY, C. GASCOIGNE.   See LEWIS, CATHERINE GASQUOINE
(HARTLEY) GALLICHAN.

HARTLEY, OLGA.   United Kingdom.

005144   ANNE; A NOVEL. Philadelphia: J. B.
Lippincott, 1920 []NUC. London: W. Heinemann, 1920
BMC.

TLS-Love and religion.
SP Love and religion.
LBKM Heroine is a Peter Pan, refuses to grow up; as a
mother, in need of a nurse; as a wife in need of a
governess.
SR-She shapes up.
NYT 12-19-20 p 26 "Violent tempered erratic heroine."

HARTT, IRENE WIDDEMER.

005145   ON THE CHARLESTON. New York: Abbey Press,
[1900] NUC.

PW 8-3-01 Naval service in Philippines.

HARVEY, ANNIE JANE (TENNANT).   D. 1898.   United Kingdom.

005146   IVAN ALEXANDROVITCH: A SIBERIAN ROMANCE.
London: T. F. Unwin, 1897 BMC.

Great wealth and luxury in Siberia. Also the Buriatis
a savage tribe who chase escaped convicts. Ivan a half
reclaimed savage. First appeared in Parisian ballroom,
then with new bride at Govt. House, then naked among
the savages, recognized by wife ACAD 51:449

005147   THE VYVYANS: OR THE MURDER IN THE RUE
BELLECHASSE. BY ANDREE HOPE. London: Chapman and Hall,
1893 BMC. Chicago: Rand, McNally, 1893 NUC.

HARVEY, EMELINE DAGGETT.   United States.

005148   GOLD DUST. Chicago: Lotus, 1892 NUC.

PW-sensational story of American life. First scene is
Toronto, later Chicago, culminating in the Haymarket
Riot of May 4, 1887.

HARVEY, EMMA MAY (BATES).   B. 1868.   United States.

005149   GREATER THAN CAESAR. Boston: J. H. Earle,
1902 NUC.

HARVEY, MARIE.

005150   A DAUGHTER OF THE HEATHER. London: J.
Long, [1918] BMC.

Inclined to worldliness during her education at
Edinburgh. Estranged, then reconciled with lover. ATH
TLS-Scottish melodrama.

005151   SATAN, K. C. London: J. Long, 1909 BMC.

About a man with a hideous face TLS

HARWOOD, FRYNIWYD TENNYSON (JESSE).   1889-1958.   United
Kingdom.

005152   THE MAN WHO STAYED AT HOME. BY BEAMISH
TINKER. London: Mills and Boon, [1915] NUC BMC.

Popish Plot, 1678-Gt. Brit.

005153   THE MILKY WAY. BY F. TENNYSON JESSE.
London: W. Heinemann, 1913 NUC BMC. New York: G. H.
Doran, [c1914] NUC.

BKM-unsuccessful illustrator falls in with piper and
other woman's baby in shipwreck. They join strolling
players, touring England country towns.
Happy tale of delightful young vagrants-a child, his
nurse, two students SP
a man about town besides young woman who tells the
story ATH
Picaresque full of frank irresponsibility, gaiety,
comradeship , adventure. Viv tells the story. She and
Peter are commissioned to do a colour book of
Provence. She's an artist; he writes. She's a
strolling player, an open air model. journalistic
detective even a pavement artist. Always natural. She
and Peter are friends. Ends in wedding. TLS

005154   SECRET BREAD. BY F. TENNYSON JESSE.
London: W. Heinemann, 1917 BMC NUC. New York: G. H.
Doran, [c1917] NUC.

the secret bread is an estate; 80 years of the hero's
life TLS 5-17 272
Illeg son "elevated above his legitimate brethren"
BAKER 32,268
Whole life of a man in Cornwall-the hatred between
legitimate and illegitimate sons-whole career to
death's door. NYT

HASANOVITZ, ELIZABETH.

005155   ONE OF THEM; CHAPTERS FROM A PASSIONATE
AUTOBIOGRAPHY. Boston: Houghton Mifflin, 1918 NUC.

PW-story of pilgrimage from Russia to America, life in
the garment factories of NY to her exp with fellow
workers, labor leader and employers.
NYT Sept 22 '18 p 399. Story of Russian Jewess, told
by herself. Was a teacher in Russia, hates the
prejudice there. Forced her parents to consent to her
coming to U.S. by means of a hunger strike. Learned
dressmaking and joined Garment Workers Union.
Anti-capitalism, pro-union, she loses her health,
disillusioned in America, book closes with her
unemployed.
HD 8039 1. clothing trade-NY
(c)2.Trade-unions-NY(c)3.Strike and lockouts

HASELDEN, FLORENCE TAYLOR.   United States.

005156   MARION. New York: Broadway, [c1908] NUC.

Story of adoption, mistaken identity, a fortune--all
that. BKM

HASKELL, HELEN EGGLESTON.

005157   O-HEART-SAN: THE STORY OF A JAPANESE
GIRL. Boston: L. C. Page, 1908 NUC.

Barely saved from suicide; becomes a trained nurse NYT
PW-becomes a trained nurse in Jap. hospital-friendship
with American girl-exchange of ideas
NYT--dainty little tale

HASLETT, HARRIET HOLMES.   B. 1866.   United States.

005158   IMPULSES; STORIES TOUCHING THE LIFE OF

SANDY IN THE CITY OF ST. FRANCIS. Boston: Cornhill, [c1920] NUC.

HASTINGS, ELIZABETH, pseud. See SHERWOOD, MARGARET POLLOCK.

HATCH, MARY R. (PLATT). B. 1848. United States.

005159   THE MISSING MAN. Boston: Four Seas, [c1892] NUC.

PW-Wealthy banker who apparently has committed forgery disappears. Later reappears with explanations which are accepted by his business associates. Then a rugged mill-worker claims he is the missing man; the deserted wife supports his claim. Hypnotism is an element of the story.

005160   THE STRANGE DISAPPEARANCE OF EUGENE COMSTOCKS. BY MRS. MARY R. P. HATCH. New York: G. W. Dillingham, 1895 NUC.

Bank robbery in Vanceport, Maine. A beautiful woman plays a strange part in the plot. Comstocks is the bank teller. PW 2-16-95:321

HATHAWAY, JUDITH.

005161   A GIRL WITH NO NAME. London: Digby, Long, [1892] BMC.

Heroine lives with one uncle who goes mad. Then lives with another. Takes positions as companion. Falls in love. ACAD 43:238
autobiography. ATH 101, 150

HATTON, BESSIE.

005162   ENID LYLE. London: Chapman and Hall, 1894 BMC.

SR 77:641. Story of a convent friendship.
SP-Philip introduced to his unacknowledged child, Mary. Harry marries Enid.

005163   THE MASTER PASSION. London: C. A. Pearson, 1901 BMC.

Heroine's rebellious childhood, life in convent, peculiar, flew into passions loves poetry more than anything else in the world when she's all grown up. ACAD 01
ATH 3-16-01. Passionate girl raised by unsympathetic aunt, in convent. Falls in love with married man. Wife dies; marries him. Melodrama.

HAVERFIELD, E. L. See HAVERFIELD, ELEANOR LUISA.

HAVERFIELD, ELEANOR LUISA.

005164   AUDREY'S AWAKENING. London: H. Froude, 1910 BMC.

005165   BADMANSTOW. London: G. Allen, 1902 BMC.

ATH 11-29-02-not too helpful.

005166   BECAUSE OF JOCK. London: G. Allen, 1905 BMC.

"Fan" the type of woman all good girls should despise." ACAD. 1107,05
Story centers on Jock, Fan is superseded by another woman after Jock marries Fan.--LBKM 29-30, 41
TLS 305,05

005167   THE CONQUEST OF CLAUDIA. London: H. Frowde, 1910 BMC.

005168   THE CONTEST. London: G. Allen, 1906 BMC.

TLS o

005169   DAUNTLESS PATTY. London: H. Frowde, 1909 BMC.

005170   DONALD. London: T. Nelson, [1906] BMC.

005171   THE GHOST OF EXLEA PRIORY. London: t. Nelson, [1905] BMC.

005172   THE GIRL FROM THE BUSH. London: Collins, [1920] BMC.

005173   A HUMAN CYPHER. London: Hodder & Stoughton, 1909 BMC.

Trag of young wife who counts for nothing in the household. TLS
Ursula Bryanston well bred, beautiful and the misunderstanding between her and husband, the devel of her char. under the stress of trouble and loneliness and the clearing up of the misunderstanding. In the interim, they part for a year. She lives alone in London, she acquires knowledge of art and sociology. TLS

005174   AN IMPOSSIBLE FRIEND. London: J. Nisbet, 1911 BMC.

005175   JOAN TUDOR'S TRIUMPH. London: H. Milford, 1918 BMC.

005176   THE MASCOTTE OF SUNNYSIDE. London: Collins, [1906] BMC.

005177   THE SOW'S EAR. BY E. L. HAVERFIELD. London: G. Allen, 1904 BMC NUC.

ACAD-two men invest in coal field.

005178   THE SQUIRE. London: G. Allen, 1903 BMC.

005179   SYLVIA'S VICTORY. London: H. Froude, 1911 BMC.

HAWEIS, MARY ELIZA (JOY). 1852-1898.

005180   A FLAME OF FIRE: A NOVEL. London: Hurst and Blackett, 1897 BMC.

"Another addition to the foolish effusions with which women writers attack the eternal marr. question. The usual hysteria over the inequality of the sexes is painfully prominent." Wife goes one better than husband. Loves a soldier. "Aglae's unfortunate tendency to run away with any of her male friends." The results are Platonic, however. SR 84:122.
SP 80:889. In her foreward, Mrs. H. says "I wrote this story to indicate the helplessness of womankind." Her heroine marries, suffers. Son atones for the sin of the father.

HAWES, AMELIA APPLETON (PRENDERGAST). D. 1917. United States.

005181   THAT OTHER WOMAN. BY AMELIA APPLETON. New York: F. T. Neely, [1899] NUC.

A young man's mother won't consent to his marriage because his fiance's father might be a bigamous one. PW 55:902

HAWKER, BESSY.

005182   OVERLOOKED; A STORY OF NORTH DEVON. London: W. Gardner, 1898 BMC.

SP 81:609. Tale, gentle and simple, of life in North Devon.
ATH 112:710. Rosamond loves actor whose career is ended by illness. Together they operate a home for unfortunate actors.

HAWKER, MORWENNA PAULINE. 1865-1908. United Kingdom.

005183   CECILIA DE NOEL. BY LANOE FALCONER. London and New York: Macmillan, 1891 BMC NUC.

Relates experiences of several guests at World Manor and its Ghost...there is a plot, no love-making. ATH 98,646
Different kind of ghost--meets 6 people. Three are appalled by it; Cecilia who is more into human love--rather than formal rel. like the others--gets comfort from the ghost and teaches the ghost what God is. ACAD
Cecilia believes love rules the world. LBKM 11-91,70

005184   MADEMOISELLE IXE. BY LANOE FALCONER. London: T. F. Unwin, 1891 BMC. New York: Cassell, [c1891] NUC.

She's a Russian nihilist; leaves comfort of home to devote herself to suffering humanity. Belongs to a society that decides a certain count should die and she should kill him. She follows him to England. Becomes governor in home he visits. Fires at him at ball but misses, arrested, escapes. Contrast between narrowness of English and large experience and still larger sympathies of this woman. CR
So cool a hand as hers should have taken more accurate aim. LW 22:111

005185   SHOULDER TO SHOULDER. A TALE. BY L. F.
London: Griffith and Farran, [1891] BMC.

HAWKESWOOD, MRS. URBAN.

005186   AN AMERICAN COUNTESS. London: J.
Macqueen, 1900 BMC.

SP 85:54. She is married for her money, husband sets
up separate house for his mistress, his mother's maid
and a lady.
ACAD 58:390. The mistress is also a lady.

HAWKINS, BATTIE.

005187   NEW WINE: NEW BOTTLES. A NOVEL. London:
Digby, Long, 1898 BMC.

ACAD 54:105. Love.
ATH 112:347. Bride stands "like a white goddess of war
on her bed." (book.) She shoots her "would-be
ravisher, a Roman Catholic priest."

HAWKINS, MAY ANDERSON. United States.

005188   A WEE LASSIE; OR, A UNIQUE REPUBLIC. BY
MRS. MAY ANDERSON HAWKINS. Richmond, Va.: Presbyterian
Com. of Publication, [1902] NUC.

HAWTHORNE, HILDEGARDE. See OSKISON, HILDEGARDE (HAWTHORNE).

HAWTREY, EDITH.

005189   MY SILVER SPOONS. London: H.J. Drane,
[1901] BMC.

Attempts to keep a friendship Platonic rather than
have it degenerate into vulgar passion 9-3-01 ATH

HAWTREY, VALENTINA. United Kingdom.

005190   HERITAGE: A NOVEL. New York: Duffield,
1912 NUC. London: Constable, 1912 BMC.

PW-man who hates women quarrels with his heir,
marries, has child.
TLS-st of temperament, unsympathetic to men.
NYT- story of 20 years of marriage.
SP-Catherine refuses to bring her son up in the
Pimblett mould. She is only one unaffected by
fascination of Pimblett Court. St. of her child.
BKM- Grim study of a woman ruthlessly married by a
woman hater in order to revenge himself on his nephew,
who has enraged him by visiting his mother, a now
successful actress who ran away from his equally
contemptible father. Picks her out like a horse,
judging her points for future motherhood of his heir
BKM v. 36 1912-13-woman's martyrdom to brute
Martin Pimblett raised by stern father to despise and
distrust women. Marries only to get an heir SR

005191   IN A DESERT LAND. London: Constable, 1915
BMC. New York: Duffield, 1915 NUC.

Restlessness of married woman shows up in generation
after generation of her descendents PW 11-27-15
1rst Eleanor of 14th, a genius; then to a man then a
woman; a man, then a present-day Eleanor. Study of
frustration. Eleanor I has burning ambitions for son
but he failed. June dreamed of being a martyr, almost
marries but recoils and kills self. The present
Eleanor successful in her real life? TLS
Joins a nunnery ATH
rel. aspirations of a family thru generations SP

005192   IN THE SHADE. London: J. Murray, 1909
BMC.

SR. Woman is acquitted of murdering her husband,(which
she really did) assumes another name, meets and
becomes engaged to man who has been imprisoned and
also uses an assumed name. Her sister and his brothers
force revelation; they all get married, 1st couple has
daughter. Marriage between a woman who had murdered
her husband and been acquitted and a man who had been
in prison for fraud. They are happy but a "shadow
falls at the end."
Henrietta Harris. We first meet her after her
acquittal; her family's reactions. They do not really
believe her innocent; she resents them; they move away
where they'll be unknown. Later Henrietta admits she
did murder. Makes a second marriage after an
unconventional betrothal; their behavior as each
learns of the other. They settle happily, have a
daughter. the rest of the story concerns the daughter

and the effect of the revelation of her mother's crime
on her. TLS
She did poison husband "suffers no great pangs of
conscience" ATH

005193   A NE'ER-DO-WEEL. BY VALENTINE CARYL.
London: T.F. Unwin, 1903 BMC NUC.

005194   PERRONELLE. London and New York: J. Lane,
1904 BMC NUC.

LBKM-Young woman married against her will breaks away
for other man, fought against penance imposed by
church, works as servant for four years, finally ends
up on church steps with dead child in her arms ready
for penance.
ATH-o
TLS-o
ACAD-a story of expiation of sin
NYT-hist. of "young wife's misery, sin and punishment

005195   RODWELL. London: J. Murray, 1908 BMC NUC.

TLS male hero.
ACAD-Rodwells are charming gentry with gambling taint,
he marries three women, spends all their money and is
usurped from his home by a farmer's son.
ATH-First wife attempts to save young heiress from her
own fate by death bed promise from son that he will
not marry her. So, the widower Rodwell marries her
instead and dissipates her fortune. Tragedy lies in
the effect of this marriage on her character.
Catastrophe results.

005196   A ROMANCE OF OLD WARS. New York: H. Holt,
1906 NUC.

PW-hist romance.

005197   SUZANNE. London: J. Murray, 1906 BMC NUC.

ACAD---Man keeps his fiance waiting, goes to
war-marries-brings wife (Suzanne) home, tragic
ending-fiance is angry.
TLS-Painstaking tale.
ATH-Suzanne is driven out of the castle after his
death. Suzanne is a peasant.

HAY, AGNES GRANT.

005198   ARCHIBALD MENZIES. MYSTIC. London: J.
Milne, 1908 BMC.

TLS- Superficial. Rel.
ACAD-superf. rel.

005199   MALCOLM CANMORE'S PEARL. London: Hurst
and Blackett, 1907 BMC.

A "Sunday" book. ACAD
Historical romance. TLS

HAY, MARIE. See VON HINDENBERG, AGNES BLANCHE MARIE (HAY).

HAYCRAFT, MARGARET SCOTT (MACRITCHIE).

005200   THE CLEVER MISS JANCY. London:
Hutchinson, [1892] BMC.

005201   GILDAS HAVEN: A STORY. London: Jarrold,
1896 BMC.

SR-Dissenting heroine and high-church hero,
differences united in mrge finally as they work as
missionaries in Egypt.
ATH 107:441. Or is it Africa? Anyway, heathen offer
neutral ground for working out their differences. I
think she is reconciled to him. Pleasant.

005202   HIS RUSTIC WIFE. London: J. Clarke, 1895
BMC.

005203   LINDENHOLM. [London]: Religious Tract
Society, [1893] BMC.

005204   MISS ELIZABETH'S NIECE. London: S. W.
Partridge, 1898 BMC.

005205   RUNNELBROOK VALLEY. A TEMPERANCE STORY.
London: R. Culley, [1897] BMC.

005206   SILVERBEACH MANOR. London: G. Cauldwell,
[1891] BMC.

005207   SUNWOOD GLORY, OR THROUGH THE REFINER'S
FIRE. London: J. Nisbet, 1892 BMC.

SP 69:474. Heroine, proud of her aristocratic birth in toppling family, finally marries one of her father's tenants.

005208   SYBIL'S REPENTANCE; OR A DREAM OF GOOD.
London: C. H. Kelly, 1892 BMC.

Sybil Agmere because she loves the woman who adopted her conceals knowledge of her grandfather's will. PW 7-29-93

005209   UNA'S MARRIAGE. London: S. W. Partridge, 1898 BMC.

HAYDEN, ELEANOR G. United Kingdom.

005210   FROM A THATCHED COTTAGE. Westminster: A. Constable, 1902 BMC. New York: T. Y. Crowell, [1903] NUC.

Mid class English family and a curse. PW

005211   LOVE THE HARPER. London: Smith, Elder, 1914 BMC NUC.

SR-half sisters, Ruth and Phyllis, love the same man, John, a farmer. Ruth has been married (she's a secretary in London), has a child, her husband in Australia. John's brother has just come from Australia and tells Ruth her husband is dying of consumption. She goes to Australia to bury him, returns and marries John.
ATH-Ruth was told by husband when he married her that he already had a wife, untrue, but for years she believed it a bigamous marriage.

005212   ROSE OF LONE FARM. London: Smith, Elder, 1905 BMC.

Lovely, innocent Rose is in search of her parentage-in the process sleeps in workhouses, gathers with tramps, etc. ACAD

005213   TURNPIKE TRAVELLERS. London: A. Constable, 1903 BMC.

Berkshire village folk. ACAD

HAYLLAR, FLORENCE H. B. 1868.

005214   NEPENTHES. Edinburgh: W. Blackwood, 1907 BMC NUC.

ACAD-an Indian woman is shipwrecked, survives and goes to door of family where husband and wife are fighting over a child who has just died from fever and one who is sick. Wife thinks she's death. Then what. BKM

HAYMOND, MRS. W. E. United States.

005215   AGNES CHESWICK; A NOVEL. New York: I. H. Blanchard, [1901] NUC.

HAYWARD, GERTRUDE M. See CRAMPTON, GERTRUDE M. (HAYWARD).

HAYWARD, RACHEL, pseud. See CHAMBERS, ROSA.

HAZE, JOSEPHINE.

005216   A WOMAN AND A LITTLE DARK MAN: A FIN-DE-SIECLE ROMANCE. London: Digby, Long, 1896 BMC.

SR Aristocratic paupers turned dairy-keepers. Feeble love story.

HEANLEY, CHARLOTTE ELIZABETH.

005217   THE GRANITE HILLS. London: Chapman and Hall, 1920 BMC.

TLS-careful human study of Lilla, who married a farmer below her in Cornwall. Passion for a wandering novelist. Sincere, quiet.
ATH-tragedy is averted and there is the slow building of a heroine at one with Cornish sea and granite hills.
Psychological study. LBKM

HEARN, MARY ANN. 1834-1909.

005218   NINETEEN HUNDRED? A FORECAST AND A STORY. BY MARIANNE FARNINGHAM. London: J. Clarke, 1892 BMC.

005219   A WINDOW IN PARIS. BY MARIANNE FARNINGHAM. London: J. Clarke, 1898 BMC NUC.

Historical romance. Plea for universal peace. LIT 4:71.

005220   A WORKING WOMAN'S LIFE; AN AUTOBIOGRAPHY. BY MARIANNE FARNINGHAM. London: J. Clarke, [1907] NUC BMC.

HEATH, E. CROSBY. See HEATH, ELLA CROSBY.

HEATH, ELLA CROSBY.

005221   ENTER AN AMERICAN. BY E. CROSBY-HEATH. London: Methuen, [1915] NUC BMC.

Brings light into women's lives in boarding house. ATH

005222   HENRIETTA TAKING NOTES. BY E. CROSBY HEATH. London and New York: J. Lane, 1912 BMC NUC.

Girls book? 11 yr old girl gives account of her literary home. PW 11-4-11
passion for the stage ATH

HEATH, HELENA.

005223   PROPULSION OF DOMENICA. A NOVEL. London: J. Ouseley, 1908 BMC.

TLS-left her uncle's farm where she kept house, established a refuge in London, married.
ATH-Opens a lodging house for factory girls which "results in an unexpected and violent fiasco." She "recovers her ground," "wiser but not permanently sadder." Eventually marries the hard working curate of this slum district.

HEATHCOTE, MILLICENT. Nationality Unknown.

005224   ENTERTAINING JANE. London: Mills and Boon, [1914] BMC NUC.

ATH-young woman tries to earn her living first as a typist then as an entertainer. When she fails handsome hero rescues her in nick of time.

HEAVEN, LOUISE (PALMER). B. 1846. United States.

005225   AN IDOL OF BRONZE. London: Greening, 1901 BMC. Toronto: G. N. Morang, 1901 NUC.

Castilian young woman with advanced ideas. BOOK NEWS 2/1902

HECTOR, ANNIE (FRENCH). 1825-1902. United Kingdom.

005226   BARBARA, LADY'S MAID AND PEERESS. BY MRS. ALEXANDER. London: F. V. White, 1897 BMC. Philadelphia: J. B. Lippincott, 1898 NUC.

It is eventually proven that Barbara is Constance's half sister and more rightly the heir than Rex for all his machinations. ATH 110:558.
Barbara is first an apprentice to a milliner and dressmaker. Then becomes a lady's maid. Becomes friends with the young woman she serves. It turns out she's really from noble parents. ACAD 52:672.
SP 81:473. Vicissitudes of noble family. Romance.
LW 29:28. Heroine and two suitors.

005227   BROKEN LINKS: A LOVE STORY. BY MRS. ALEXANDER. New York: Cassell, [c1894] NUC.

CR 24:54. When 1st wife shows up, he uses her as an excuse to get rid of 2nd who has not conceived and he has therefore been morose. But he soon regrets this but cannot get her back.

005228   BROWN, V.C. BY MRS. ALEXANDER. London: T. F. Unwin, 1899 BMC. New York: R. F. Fenno, 1899 NUC.

He goes in search of his mother. When he wins military distinction, he is introduced to his general's wife who turns out to be his mother. He also learns he's a Viscount, marries and lives happily. LIT 4:316
She was a famous Hungarian actress. SP 82:206

005229   A CHOICE OF EVILS: A NOVEL. BY MRS. ALEXANDER. London: F. V. White, 1894 BMC NUC.

SP 73:565. Unwitting bigamous husband. He is able to get a divorce from first wife when she shows up, but is disappointed in the matter of a remarriage to his 2nd wife. She has found him to be not the kind, generous man she thought him to be during courtship, but a selfish prig. She refuses the 2nd marriage

ceremony, being legally free. She then goes on to
marry another.
ATH 104:381. "There are readers who will doubt whether
she was justified in refusing to return to her bondage
when the worthless stone of offense was removed from
her path."

005230   THE COST OF HER PRIDE. BY MRS. ALEXANDER.
London: F. V. White, 1898 BMC. Philadelphia: J. B.
Lippincott, 1899 NUC.

SP 81: "Mr. George Farrant is the sort of husband who
makes the magnanimity of the heroine almost
incredible."
ATH 112:748. While waiting for her divorce, she
"accepts the guardianship of the invalid daughter of
her rival. "Who gets the divorce? He is a rake.
PW-she gets a divorce from him. He is unfaithful.
LW 29:435. Leslie marries wrong man out of pride.
Divorces an d remarries.

005231   THE CRUMPLED LEAF: A VATICAN MYSTERY. BY
MRS. ALEXANDER. London: H.J. Drane, [1911] BMC.

Rome, conversion, divorce. ATH

005232   A FIGHT WITH FATE. BY MRS. ALEXANDER.
London: F. V. White, 1896 BMC. Philadelphia: J. B.
Lippincott, 1896 NUC.

SR-Beatrice, with tyrannical employer marries an earl
at conclusion. Also an heiress.
ATH 107:579
SP 77:187. She is a companion and secretary to older
woman. There is also an Australian millionaire. Rev.
says she's too good for Lord Lynford.
LW 27:202. The Australian, it turns out, is also a
Lynford and Beatrice is his grandniece. There's some
incident which is improper, casts a shadow on the
story.

005233   FOR HIS SAKE: A NOVEL. BY MRS. ALEXANDER.
London: F. V. White, 1892 BMC. Philadelphia: J. B.
Lippincott, 1892 NUC.

SP 69:420. Romance, Sybil marries a man she no longer
loves, out of duty, but he is soon dead and she is
free to marry her new choice.
PW-She becomes a writer of children's books.
ATH 100:349. Sybil's grandmother hates her, she is an
orphan; she "strikes up an acquaintance which is
destined to cost her dear." "When the time of trial
comes, she is capable of a profound act of
self-sacrifice."
ACAD:one man conveniently dies so she eventually gets
the other.

005234   FOUND WANTING: A NOVEL. BY MRS.
ALEXANDER. London: F. V. White, 1893 BMC.
Philadelphia: J. B. Lippincott, 1893 NUC.

Villain gains affections of May Riddell; then
announces that he's about to marry. Wants May to come
live with them, be his secretary, a sort of spiritual
friend. May refuses-in fact she isn't even tempted.
Her friend Mme. Falk is a journalist. Before all this
happened, she was living in comfort with her father.
His death made her penniless. Became a companion to a
woman in Scotland. PW 7-15-93.
London, Paris. Mr. Oglivie married May's best friend,
Frances Conroy. He offers to arrange a menage a trois.
SR 76:471.

005235   A GOLDEN AUTUMN: A NOVEL. BY MRS.
ALEXANDER. London: F. V. White, 1896 BMC.
Philadelphia: J. B. Lippincott, 1897 NUC.

PW 12-5-97 Marriage; he an army officer who has wasted
his inheritance, she an orphan from the middle class
with a fortune. "Her money is a constant source of
trouble; at last they quarrel so seriously that he
rejoins his regiment in India at the opening of a new
campaign. He gets a fortune, is innocently compromised
with a woman. She divorces him. Seven years later they
get together, then "a golden autumn."
Celia Rivers is married to a weak impatient man,
Derek. He leaves her when she reminds him that she
brought fortune to him. Derek is trying to improve his
wife's "middle-class" defects. She's oo gauche. ATH
109:146

005236   KITTY COSTELLO. BY MRS. ALEXANDER.
London: T. F. Unwin, 1904 BMC.

Victorian p.o.v. ATH

005237   MAMMON: A NOVEL. BY MRS. ALEXANDER. New
York: J. W. Lovell, [c1891] NUC. London: W. Heinemann,
1892 BMC.

ATH 99:210. Ward with money and her guardian. Their
love story.
SP-All the characters' actions except Claudia's are
inspired by concern for money.
LW 23:127. Claudia refuses to marry father's choice
because he is marrying her for money. Father is
enraged and leaves his money to him and appoints him
Claudia's guardian. Eventually thy fall in love and
marry.

005238   A MISSING HERO. BY MRS. ALEXANDER.
London: Chatto and Windus, [c1900] NUC 1901 BMC. New
York: R. F. Fenno, [c1900] NUC.

NYT-sentimental. ATH - 1-26-01

005239   MRS. CRICHTON'S CREDITOR: A NOVEL. BY
MRS. ALEXANDER. London: F. V. White, 1897 BMC.
Philadelphia: J. B. Lippincott, 1897 NUC.

An unhappy married woman and a sympathetic Scot.
Husband dies in the end. SR 84:46.
The Scot's mother interferes in the relationship
between her son and Gwendoline Crichton. The two
apparently keep a platonic relationship. ATH 109:739.
London middle-class.

005240   THE SNARE OF THE FOWLER. BY MRS.
ALEXANDER. London: Cassell, 1892 BMC. New York:
Cassell, [c1892] NUC.

ATH 100:479. "Myra escapes the machinations of her
enemies and marries the right man.
ACAD 43:480. She is believed illegitimate by her aunt
who gets a poor teaching job for her but takes her
back on discovering she is an heiress. Myra escapes,
is on her own, eventually inherits.
A persecuted heroine. A wicked widow wants the heroine
to marry her son (the villain) because the heroine is
about to come into a fortune but the heroine is
interested in a young artist. SR 1-21-93, 75
Myra Dallas refuses to marry the son, overcomes the
disgrace and charge of illegitimacy, triumphs in the
end-gets the inheritance. CR 14, 21:61

005241   THE STEP-MOTHER. BY MRS. ALEXANDER.
London: F. V. White, 1899 BMC. Philadelphia: J. B.
Lippincott, 1900 NUC.

The usual roles are reversed. She is good to the boy
whose father neglects and dislikes him. Her name is
Deen. SP 83:574.
"It is pleasant to believe that the traditional
estimate of stepmothers is often falsified by kindness
as genuine and devotion as unselfish as are exhibited
in the present story." Her love for the step-son
almost estranges her from husband. She's cultured,
broad minded. much conflict about the boy. PW 56:699

005242   STRONGER THAN LOVE. BY MRS. ALEXANDER.
New York: Brentano's, 1902 NUC. London: T. F. Unwin,
1902 BMC.

ATH-8-30-02-Conventional, unhappy wife.
NYT-7-26-02-not helpful.

005243   THROUGH FIRE TO FORTUNE. BY MRS.
ALEXANDER. London: T. F. Unwin, 1900 BMC. New York: R.
F. Fenno, 1900 NUC. (U. S. ed. Title: Thro' Fire to
Fortune)

Sp 84:143. Cara an apprentice at milliner's. Took
advantage of fire there to escape drunken stepmother;
being thought dead. Under an assumed name gets maid's
job with actress and then goes on stage. It is
discovered she is an heiress to a peer, has three
suitors, chooses 1.
LBKM 17:190. Cara becomes a successful actress, Mrs.
Bligh, a retired actress is her teacher, guide and
friend.

005244   A WARD IN CHANCERY: A NOVEL. BY MRS.
ALEXANDER. London: Osgood, McIlvaine, 1894 BMC. New
York: D. Appleton, 1894 NUC.

SR 77:285. Penniless girl suddenly rich, impoverished
again in last chapter, but there is a man.
SP 72:590. Courageous work in that the heroine is
plain without being astoundingly clever or blood
curdlingly wicked. Lives in Bohemian Paris until she
inherits at 19 and then must move to Philistine
uncle's in Bayswater.

005245   WELL WON: A NOVEL. BY MRS. ALEXANDER.
London: F. V. White, 1891 BMC. New York: J. A. Taylor,
1891 NUC.

Lots of characters, rapid movement of plot. There is a
brute of a husband and a much-enduring wife who
finally revolts. PW 03
Comedy of errors involving a forged bill. BOOK NEWS
111:138

005246   WHAT GOLD CANNOT BUY: A NOVEL. BY MRS.
ALEXANDER. London: F. V. White, 1895 BMC. Chicago: M.
A. Donohue, [18--?] NUC.

Kate Hilton undertakes to live in her mother-in-law's
house under a pseudonym for the purpose of reconciling
her husband to his mother. They have been estranged as
a consequence of their marriage. Kate succeeds. ATH
105:246

005247   A WINNING HAZARD. BY MRS. ALEXANDER.
London: T. F. Unwin, 1896 BMC. New York: D. Appleton,
1896 NUC.

SR-Wholesome.
ATH 107:31. Irish family, father failed as solicitor.
Romance.
ACAD 50:306. "As ever...she has chosen a good sweet
girl as her heroine."
PW 5-9-76 They come to London to make a living.
SP 77:249. Happy ending for heroine: comes into a
fortune and marries her lover.

005248   THE YELLOW FIEND. BY MRS. ALEXANDER. New
York: Dodd, Mead, 1901 NUC. London: T. F. Unwin, 1901
BMC.

HEDDLE, ETHEL FORSTER.

005249   CAROLA'S SECRET. London: S. W. Partridge,
[1903] BMC.

005250   CLARINDA'S QUEST: A STORY OF LONDON.
London: Blackie, 1910 BMC.

Girl heroine facing want. For girls. ACAD

005251   COLINA'S ISLAND. Edinburgh and London:
Oliphant, Anderson and Ferrier, 1900 PMC.

005252   GIRL COMRADES. London: Blackie, 1907 BMC.

005253   A HAUNTED TOWN. London: W. Gardner,
[1898] BMC.

SP 81:746. Portraits of old Scottish ladies. Love
interest.

005254   THE HOUSE OF SHADOWS. London: Odhams,
[1920] BMC.

005255   MARGET AT THE MANSE. London: W. Gardner,
Darton, 1899 NUC BMC.

Pleasant sketches of dwellers of Fife. BAKER 03,208
LBKM 17:155. Tales of Fifeshire fishing village.

005256   MARTIN REDFERN'S OATH. London: S. W.
Partridge, [1892] BMC.

005257   THE MYSTERY OF ST. RULE'S. London:
Blackie, 1902 BMC NUC. New York: Scribner, 1902 PW.

005258   AN ORIGINAL GIRL. New York: H. M.
Caldwell, 1901 [?] NUC. London: Blackie, 1902 BMC.

005259   THE PRIDE OF THE FAMILY. London: J.
Bowden, 1899 BMC.

Heroine rescues hero from drowning. Becomes a
typewriter to earn her living. SP 82:492
Loss and recovery by marriage of a family mansion.
ACAD 56:360
Family pride represented by two women-one young, one
old. ATH 113:394

005260   THE SECRET OF THE TURRET. London: I.
Pitman, 1905 BMC.

LBKM - story for young girls.

005261   SO SHALL HE REAP. London: J. Bowden, 1900
BMC.

LIT 6:89 Colin, driven into world as a boy with stolen

money, his career.

005262   STRANGERS IN THE LAND. London: Blackie,
1903 BMC NUC.

2 spinsters journey to Java accompanied by a girl LBKM
6-03,115

005263   THREE GIRLS IN A FLAT. London: 1896 NUC.

SP 77:902. Mabel is too selfish, lacks courtesy.

005264   THE TOWN'S VERDICT. London: Blackie, 1904
BMC.

LBKM 0
ATH--male student suspected of murder.

HEDGES, FLORENCE EDYTHE BLAKE. United States.

005265   I AM: A NOVEL OF PSYCHOTHERAPY. Boston:
Roxburgh, [c1910] NUC.

Focuses on a man-three women of different natures
affect him. PW

HEILGERS, HENRIETTA.

005266   STEPHEN THE MAN. London: J. Long, 1909
BMC.

Jealousy between a wife, a former mistress who had a
son and the whiskey Lord TLS

HEILGERS, LOUISE. United Kingdom.

005267   BABETTE WONDERS WHY. London: Dryden, 1916
BMC.

TLS-Gushing, conventional account of daughter of
uncovenanted birth and subsequent married unhappiness.
ATH.

005268   THE NAKED SOUL, THREE YEARS IN A WOMAN'S
LIFE. London: S. Swift, [1912] BMC NUC.

ATH-Sordid diary.
ACAD-Warped and bilious outlook of a selfish and
disappointed woman. Similar to the Dangerous Age.

005269   AN OFFICER'S WIFE. London: H. Jenkins,
1918 BMC.

Nothing new. TLS

005270   SACKCLOTH AND SATIN. London: Dryden, 1916
BMC.

005271   THAT RED-HEADED GIRL. London: H. Jenkins,
1917 BMC NUC.

Julia of the bonnet shop; Sheila, the red-head, and
their marital difficulties with Dick and Eliot. TLS
Sheila is an artist's model-behaves badly towards her
male and female friends (?). ATH

HEIMBURG, W., pseud. See BEHRENS, BERTHA.

HEKKING, AVIS.

005272   IN SEARCH OF JEHANNE: A ROMANCE. London:
J. Long, 1907 BMC.

Historical romance ACAD

005273   A KING OF MARS. London: J. Long, 1908
BMC.

ACAD-anti-war society.

HELLIS, NELLIE.

005274   WHERE THE BROOK AND THE RIVER MEET.
London: W. Gardner, 1894 BMC n.d. NUC. New York:
Whittaker, 1895 PW.

NYT 1898:416. Free from sensationalism, healthy homes
and lovable men and women, country gentle-folk.
Marjorie Doyne is engaged to med student, but when
father returns to England from Australia after the
death of Marjorie's stepma and brings home all the
children, Marjorie takes care of them, gives up her
boyfriend (who marries another) and is never sorry. PW
11-2-95:743

HELM, FLORA. United States.

005275   BETWEEN TWO FORCES: A RECORD OF A THEORY
AND A PASSION. Boston: Arena, 1894 NUC.

PW-Cecelia becomes an inmate of the Rencliffe
household. Younod, the son, believes she has inherent
forces and wants to use them to test his psychological
theories. Her cousin Leitz objects; she mediates. Then
what? Supernatural and the labor question.

HEMENWAY, HETTY. See RICHARD, HETTY LAWRENCE (HEMENWAY).

HENDERSON, FLORENCE LESLIE.

005276   A ROOM IN THE ROOF; BEING THE STORY OF
HE, SHE, AND IT. Westminster: Church Of England
Temperance Society, [1902] BMC.

005277   WAS SHE RIGHT? London: J. Masters, 1893
BMC.

Young woman goes to West Indies. Meets the hero there.
There's an uprising on one of the Islands. Marry-happy
ever after. ATH 101:119.

HENDERSON, MRS. S. E.   United States.

005278   JELARD. Logansport, Ind.: Longwell and
Cummings, 1892 NUC.

HENNIKER, FLORENCE ELLEN HUNGERFORD (MILNES).   D. 1923.
United Kingdom.

005279   BID ME GOOD-BYE. London: Bentley, 1892
BMC NUC.

ACAD 41:515. Heroine's "palpable lovemaking" "seems a
little inexplicable" "scenery is more pleasing then
the people"
SR - Mary loves a cad; he dies; she takes care of his
dog and remains unmarried until death.

005280   FOILED. London: Hurst and Blackett, 1893
BMC NUC.

Leontine Hesseltine is treated as a child-woman by
husband, a drunkard. Then there's a suicide (Anthony
Gore), a woman of the world attracted to the husband.
Society in a vulgar perspective. ACAD 43:56.
ATH 100:850. Renee Gore is passionate, loving woman.
Her husband is an ass whom she barely tolerates, she
"betrays him and commits forgery" for another man who
is not worth it, in reviewer's opinon. There is "no
small element of propriety in the book" and "a good
deal of passion."
SR. "Virtue triumphs." A husband, on learning of
wife's love for another, arranges a revolver accident
for himself.

005281   OUR FATAL SHADOWS. London: Hurst and
Blackett, 1907 BMC.

Letters. TLS

005282   SECOND FIDDLE. London: E. Nash, 1912 BMC.

TLS-pathetic heroine is at first second fiddle to
bride of her guardian and then after their death is
neglected wife of a stockbroker.
ATH-she fails to fully value herself, is neglected by
her friends.
LBKM-her husband is unfaithful; "at least in bodily
fidelity." She comforts and shares the pain of the
woman who has striven to take him away from her.

005283   SIR GEORGE: A NOVEL. London: R. Bentley,
1891 BMC NUC.

Uncle, nephew and nephew's fiance all love each other.
Nephew goes to India; uncle and fiance fall in love.
Harold returns and is shocked. The three go their
separate ways. Olive dies, uncle goes blind, Harold
marries. ATH 97 729
Uncle, Sir George Gresham, loves his nephew Harold who
is off to India in first part of book. At 20 he's
engaged to Olive. Since she's not well enough to make
the trip, they postpone wedding for three years till
his return. Then she and Sir George become fond of
each other. SR 6-27-91, 780

005284   SOWING THE SAND. London and New York:
Harper, 1898 BMC NUC.

SP 81:185. Wild oats, Ouida-esque. Hussars. Heroine is
married and has a cheek not untouched by crowsfeet.
LIT 2:590.

ACAD 53:521. Story about Charley Crespin, his
experience in the army, the "notorious Mrs. Eden," his
return home and patching up his life. His sister
Mildred is the heroine. He makes an attempt at suicide
which fails.

HENOCH, EMILY I.

005285   WHEN CUPID MOCKS; OR, AN OLD MAID'S
INFATUATION. London: H. J. Drane, [1906] BMC.

HENRY, MARY H.

005286   THE BENHURST CLUB, OR, THE DOINGS OF SOME
GIRLS. BY HOWE BENNING. Boston: Pilgrim Press, 1897
NUC.

LW 29:236. The story of a number of young women who
establish a "working girl's club" which would be
helpful and companionable to members in various
situations.

005287   GOSHEN HILL; OR, A LIFE'S BROKEN PIECES.
BY HOWE BENNING. New York: American Tract Society,
[c1895] NUC.

Helen Edwards craves more than her farm life at Goshen
Hill offers. Gets teaching post in Ill. Then mother
gets ill, returns home, makes a new plan for life on
the homestead and rescues Zoe Moore from dangers of
New York life. PW 12-26-95:704

HENSEL, OCTAVIA, pseud. See FONDA, MARY ALICE (IVES)
SEYMOUR.

HENSHAW, HELEN.   1876-1908.

005288   THE PASSING OF THE WORD. Cedar Rapids,
Ia.: Torch Press, 1910 NUC.

"Described as a romance of college life: It deals
mainly with the psychological development of the
principal character, Marian Mansfield." BKM v. 31,
1910.
NYT-filled with Christian spirit altho the girls are
allowed to indulge in plenty of wholesome fun.

HENSHAW, J. W. See HENSHAW, JULIA WILMOTTE (HENDERSON).

HENSHAW, JULIA WILMOTTE (HENDERSON).   1869-1937.

005289   WHY NOT, SWEETHEART? BY J. W. HENSHAW
(JULIAN DURHAM). London: T. F. Unwin, 1901 BMC NUC.
Toronto: G. N. Morang, 1901 NUC.

HERBERT, AGNES.

005290   THE ELEPHANT. London: Hutchinson, 1916
NUC BMC. New York: F. A. Stokes, [1917] NUC.

005291   THE MOOSE. London: A. & C. Black, 1913
BMC NUC.

HERBERT, ALICE.   United Kingdom.

005292   GARDEN OATS. London and New York: J.
Lane, 1914 BMC NUC.

SR-147:50-One of the "fleshy school of fiction."
"Garden Oats" a woman's wild oats, sown by heroine
before and after marriage." She describes her
sensations with gusto: book ends with repentance and
determination to turn over a new leaf.
ATH-mildly wild oats-ends happily settled as wife and
mother.
TLS-a wildly controlled character, a "vulgarity" which
at close of story "may lead her yet farther astray."
"militancy in love"-Dawson, "the Revolt of Phoebe
PW-Novel traces the development of a girl from early
school days to marriage and a little after. Her real
difficulties begin after her marriage, when many
pitfalls are prepared for this, at times petulant, but
always sweet natured heroine, who feels for a while
that her husband (the only man she could really love)
does not understand her as completely as she had
hoped.

005293   THE MEASURE OF OUR YOUTH. London, New
York: J. Lane, 1909 BMC NUC.

Centers on hero and his loves-PW
Story of a male flirt caught at the end by "mere
beauty"-ACAD

HERBERTSON, AGNES GROZIER.

005294   A BOOK WITHOUT A MAN! London: E. Stock,
1897 BMC.

Rose, Morda, The Limpet and Eena the emancipated one
talk about men and many subjects. ACAD 52 Fic Sup 78
SP 81:473. Four heroines. One was writing a book
without a man but she did not finish it, she married a
curate and left it to him.

005295   DEBORAH. London: Methuen, 1911 BMC.

Deborah Clarke changed places with Sarah Cubitt and
became domestic servant to an eccentric recluse . Deb
"obliged to leave her husband changes places with her
servant." She can't act the part makes a second
marriage after #1 dies. ATH

005296   THE HOUSE OF BRICKS. London: Blackie,
[1917] BMC.

005297   PATIENCE DEANE, A STUDY IN TEMPERAMENT
AND TEMPTATION. London: Methuen, 1904 BMC.

TLS-teacher, tale of thoughtful workmanship. Capable
self-reliant person plans to marry a man for his money
until he insults her.

005298   THE PLOWERS: A NOVEL. London: Greening,
1906 BMC.

TLS-Female heroine raised by a misogynist.

005299   THE SHIP THAT CAME HOME IN THE DARK.
London: Methuen, 1912 BMC.

TLS-Marg. takes place of her cousin Marj. married to
blind man. Marj. who does not love her husband goes
off with another man. Marg does love him.
ACAD-Dan the husband learns and is in a bad temper,
Marj is unreformed and Marg is about to marry someone
else when book ends.

005300   THE SUMMIT. London: Hutchinson, 1909 BMC.

"a drunken wife, a slatternly home, children that
despise their parents"-TLS
Pathetic relationship between husband and wife. ATH

HERBERTSON, JESSIE LECKIE. United Kingdom.

005301   BORROWERS OF FORTUNE. London: W.
Heinemann, 1912 BMC.

TLS-story of a cultured girl in village on whom was
shadow of her past as a governess.
SP-girl cruelly wronged

005302   CROFTON'S DAUGHTER. London: Methuen, 1919
BMC.

Julia Crofton, orphaned, faced with problem of the
life to which she must devote herself. TLS
She has courage, "an unashamed ardent nature."
Father's lasting influence. He had made his own
unfulfilled love affair so glamorous in her eyes that
she takes her own conquest of an elderly married man
too seriously.
Bohemian qualities from father war vs unimaginative
respectability of mother's people. She compels
sympathy by her hardy self-analysis and by bravely
repudiating promise to elope." TLS

005303   JUNIA. London: Chatto and Windus, 1908
BMC.

TLS-story of two women (both egotist and friends).
Author sees the world as it is felt by women, analysis
of what is happening in conversation-not an exchange
of information but a measuring of strengths.
ACAD-"vulgar, sordid, unpleasant"

005304   MORTAL MEN. London: W. Heinemann, 1907
BMC.

four school mistresses in Miss Rean's school and
Jessica who has an affair with brother of
head-mistress-ACAD. A girl who must have love at any
price willing to sacrifice all for it.

005305   THE STIGMA. A NOVEL. London: W.
Heinemann, 1905 BMC.

Susan illegitimate daughter of woman of pleasure.
After mother dies she must fend for self; she's an
artist but eyesight is poor. Moves in with relatives,
takes job as "warder to imbeciles" marries a young

doctor. ACAD
Her chief desire-to be self-sufficient, scorns her
father's offers of assistance (she's illegitimate)
even when she decides to marry, she fears "she's
evading her life" analytical skill in drawing the
heroine's individuality, intensity, we get her
innermost thoughts. ATH

005306   YOUNG LIFE. New York: Duffield, 1911 NUC.
London: W. Heinemann, 1911 BMC.

awakens only when she finally marries. PW 1-28-11
ATH-love and temptation and the claims of young life
on elders.
The young girl is insignificant to the story: really a
foil to Mary Leverson. "with the aid of a socially
impossible musician sacrifices the pride that has been
her existence for one crowded hour of living." SR

HERRICK, CHRISTINE (TERHUNE). B. 1859.

005307   MY BOY AND I. BY HIS MOTHER. Boston:
Estes, [c1913] NUC.

"no masculine help in bringing up her child" NYT
1913:581

HERRICK, HULDAH, pseud. See OBER, SARAH ENDICOTT.

HERRING, FRANCES ELIZABETH (CLARKE). 1851-1916. Canada.

005308   ENA. London: F. Griffiths, 1913 BMC NUC.

005309   THE GOLD MINERS; A SEQUEL TO THE PATHLESS
WEST. London: F. Griffiths, 1914 BMC NUC.

TLS-Anglo-Canadian author. Race for gold in 19th
century.

005310   IN THE PATHLESS WEST WITH SOLDIERS,
PIONEERS, MINERS AND SAVAGES. London: T. F. Unwin,
1904 NUC BMC.

PZ3 British Columbia-Description and Travel; Indians
-British Columbia.

005311   NAN AND OTHER PIONEER WOMEN OF THE WEST.
London: F. Griffiths, 1913 NUC BMC.

HERRINGTON, MRS. M. J. Nationality Unknown.

005312   THE STORY OF A TELEGRAPH OPERATOR. BY M.
L. New York: J. S. Ogilvie, 1893 NUC.

She wants a college education, but must work for
western union in New York. Later transfered to Penn.
Then Kansas where a disappointing experience concludes
the story. PW 7-29-43

HERVEY, AUGUSTA.

005313   THE LAST DAY OF HER LIFE. London:
Skeffington, 1894 BMC.

HESS, ISABELLA ROSA. B. 1872.

005314   SAINT CECILIA OF THE COURT. Edinburgh and
London: Oliphant, [1905] BMC. New York: F. H. Revell,
[c1905] NUC.

Pathetic story of a poor little girl-for girls. NYT
648, 05
brief desc BKM 22 (1905) 293

HESTON, WINIFRED ESTELLE THOMAS. United States.

005315   A BLUESTOCKING IN INDIA; HER MEDICAL
WARDS AND MESSAGES HOME. BY WINIFRED HESTON, M.D. New
York: F. H. Revell, [c1910] NUC. London: A. Melrose,
1910 BMC.

letters of a woman medical missionary in India-passion
for her work. NYT
Fiction?

HEWITT, E. M. See HEWITT, ETHEL MAY.

HEWITT, ETHEL MAY.

005316   THE EFFACEMENT OF ORIEL PENHALIGON.
London: S. Low, 1892 BMC.

005317   IN A CINQUE PORT: A STORY OF WINCHELSEA.
BY E. M. HEWITT. London: R. Bentley, 1894 BMC NUC.

SP 73:247. Romance in Winchelsea.

HICKOX, ADELAIDE, pseud. See SMITH, MRS. C. B.

HICKSON, MRS. MURRAY, pseud. See KITCAT, MABEL (HICKSON).

HIEMENZ, CLARA. United States.

005318   CRESS. St. Louis: Nixon-Jones, [c1906]
NUC.

HIGBEE, D. See GEPPERT, DORA (HIGBEE).

HIGGINS, ELIZABETH. See SULLIVAN, ELIZABETH (HIGGINS).

HIGGINS, MARY ALPINE.

005319   MISCHIEVOUS ETHEL COOPER, OR IN THE POWER
OF A VILLAIN. New York: J. S. Ogilvie, 1902 NUC.

HIGGINSON, ELLA (RHOADS). B. 1862. United States.

005320   MARIELLA OF OUT-WEST. New York and
London: Macmillan, 1902 BMC NUC.

Sensitive clever girl in uncongenial surroundings out
of place, misunderstood LBKM 1-03,168

HIGGINSON, MRS. S. J. See HIGGINSON, SARAH JANE (HATFIELD).

HIGGINSON, SARAH JANE (HATFIELD). United States.

005321   THE BEDOUIN GIRL. MRS. S. J. HIGGINSON.
New York: J. Selwin Tait, [c1894] NUC. London:
Isbister, 1894 BMC.

LW 25:139. Bedouin child escapes from her persecutors
and finds shelter with a Turk and an Arab. The Arab
adopts her and turns out to be her father. The Turk
"adores, betrays, and finally marries her."
PW-Feydeh is fleeing from an Arab who would forcibly
make her his wife. "Scenes from Eastern life, as women
of the Orient know it at present."

HILDYARD, IDA (LEMON).

005322   A DIVIDED DUTY. BY IDA LEMON. London:
Warne, 1891 NUC. Philadelphia: J. B. Lippincott, 1892
NUC.

Young Englishwoman Leslie Mansell living as governess
in Paris. Miss Duckworth, eccentric becomes a painter.
And a handsome young man with divided duty between
devotion to brother and loyalty to Leslie. PW
12-12-91.
Divided duty also would leave Leslie to sacrifice
lover for father. Both opt for each other. ACAD
Principally character studies. SP 67, 297 Also ATH 98
220.
Heroine is typical "ministering angel." Miss Bender's
thirst for vengeance and her power of "tracking her
victim to earth only to be equaled by that of hero."
But she spots the wrong man. Miss Duckworth gives up
being a governess to take up art in Paris but succeeds
only in being "untidy and impractical." SR
8-22-91:226.
CR 17:140. Heroine leaves home to make her own living.
Works as a governess but boards elsewhere. Romance
with young man she meets there. Complications over her
father who is serving a prison term for murder. All is
resolved.
IND 44:413. Heroine's life in Paris. "Shadow of crime
rests on father, shifts to lover." Happy ending.
LW 23:26. Suitable for girls. Moral. Heroine-Leslie
Mansell.

005323   MATTHEW FURTH. BY IDA LEMON. New York:
Longmans, Green, 1895 NUC.

East end novel. Selina earns money by pawning
neighbor's treasures. SR 80:247
Matthew is a dock worker recently promoted to
stevedore with higher wages. Marries Selina Pask even
though she knows he's killed a man over another woman.
Their marriage is not happy. He wanders off. She's
left alone to have child. She dies. SP 75:492
LW 27:251. London stevedore's marriage, deserted her
before baby is born. Returned too late.

HILL, CECILIA. United Kingdom.

005324   THE CITADEL. London: Hutchinson, 1917
BMC.

Catherine Buckland returns to the Citadel of Dinant at
the moment of German bombardment. TLS
A school teacher. "The invisible citadel which

overshadows the character is the church of Rome."
Begins with Catherine's childhood in Dinant, Belgium
and her schoolteaching. She and sister visit
successful schools. Then start their own. Catherine
finds exquisite relief from monotony of parents and
school in music. Dies at Dinant? TLS

005325   STONE WALLS. London: Hutchinson, [1919]
BMC NUC.

Petra, lonely child, instinctively an artist. Great
love of music--that love frightens mother and sets
stepfather against her. Her first struggle for life
when her violin and music taken away by her father. At
end just begins to tear down the walls that separate
her from her art. TLS
She's a musical genius. ATH
Repressed. Later teens were spent in benumbing apathy.
LBKM
She has one friend, Leonard Brook. Happy end. SR

005326   WINGS TRIUMPHANT. London: Hutchinson,
[1918] BMC.

TLS-Theodora and RC

HILL, ETHEL.

005327   THE UNLOVED. London: Greening, 1909 BMC.

Mary Primrose has much to say to her neighbors about
the position of women. She moves to London inspired by
social mission. Liberty and love are the two
requisites of life she believes. She returns to home
town, offers herself as mistress to a man, has a
child. Her lover turns out to be a thief who throws
her out. But we leave her with "the perfect peace that
has come to my soul, and the true harvest of
womanhood." TLS
Heroine falls madly in love, lives with a man
dispensing with the formality of the marriage-bond. He
turns out to be married and a thief; novel ends with
his suicide and birth of their child. "Frankly, a
woman ought to be ashamed to have written this novel."
ACAD

005328   THE WOMAN-FRIEND AND THE WIFE. London:
Greening, 1907 BMC.

Estrangement and renewed love. TLS

HILL, GRACE LIVINGSTON. See LUTZ, GRACE (LIVINGSTON) HILL.

HILL, MARION. 1870-1918. United States.

005329   GEORGETTE. Boston: Small, Maynard,
[c1912] NUC.

PW-actress who chooses home.
NYT-she is sent to a farm in the Poconos for her
health.

005330   THE LURE OF CROONING WATER. Boston:
Small, Maynard, [c1913] NUC. London: J. Long, 1913
BMC.

PW-Published originally under the title of Georgette.
A bright young actress likes men at her feet. Three
very different types succumb. Story concerns her
entanglements with the three.
ACAD-weary of town life, seeks rest and change in new
surroundings.
Actress, suffering from nervous strain, is ordered to
rest in the country where she causes mischief. ATH
Georgette Verlaine, American actress has a breakdown,
ordered to farm, causes an almost tragic imbroglio
there. Humorous. TLS

005331   MCALLISTER'S GROVE. London: J. Long, 1917
BMC. New York: D. Appleton, 1917 NUC.

High spirited NY woman invests all her savings and
buys Florida orange grove. Laurie McAllister shakes
off grandfather's attempt to master her. Problems of
orange farm, diseased trees. A crack shot with a
revolver. TLS
She also supports her grandfather. Told to give up the
project; won't. Staunchly independent. She wins
through; quiet love story in bkgd. LBKM
Knows oranges as well as Sanskrit. NYT
Annie Laurie McAllister invests last cent in Florida
orange grove, swindled. Ends up wedding man with fine
grove nearby. PW

005332   THE PETTISON TWINS. New York: McClure,
Phillips, 1906 NUC.

005333   A SLACK WIRE. London: J. Long, 1916 BMC.

TLS-marriage of Olaf Gibson, an acrobat, to quiet
sober businessman. Turns out happily.
ATH-she satisfies the family by using her talent to
quell a strike.

005334   SUNRISE VALLEY. Boston: Small, Maynard,
[c1914] BMC NUC. London: J. Long, 1914 BMC.

PW-Charming girl, brought up in luxury has to earn her
living and goes to Sunrise Valley, a little place in
Pennsylvania, to teach. Here she boards with the
Aldriches and soon learns to love the mother and
daughter, but quarrels constantly with the grave,
stern son. She makes good in her teaching, solves a
mystery of many years standing and falls in love in
spite of her self, with young Aldrich, learning that
snobbishness can't live in a wholesome atmosphere like
the Aldrich farm.
LBKM-chooses to teach in West and leaves luxurious
comfort of her aunt's NY residence.
TLS-Essentially a traditional romance.

005335   THE TOLL OF THE ROAD. New York: D.
Appleton, 1918 NUC. London: J. Long, [1918] NUC BMC.

PW--Gertrude Hall, a conventional schoolteacher, joins
a theatrical co. Story of how her character is
developed and how, finally, she chooses career over
wifehood.
ATH-Horrified at first by Bohemianism of the players,
comes to recognize merit of wider charity than
Puritanism. Mental growth.
NYT-6-16-18 p.278-She is piqued into joining the
company by her finance's refusal to permit her.

HILL, MILDRED.

005336   HIS LITTLE BIT O' GARDEN. London: H. R.
Allenson, [1913] BMC.

Religious tone; set partly in England and partly
mission work in Africa. TLS

HILTON, ALICE HOWARD.   United States.

005337   A BLONDE CREOLE; A STORY OF NEW ORLEANS.
Chicago: Stein, [c1891] NUC. New York: J.S. Ogilvie,
[1892] NUC.

PW-Lucia Corletti's an Italian with a fair complexion.
Two love episodes in her life: the romance of an
octaroon and a tragedy founded on a sensational murder
and a suicide.

005338   PAOLA CORLETTI, THE FAIR ITALIAN. New
York: F.T. Neely, [c1896] NUC. London: J. Henderson,
[1897] BMC.

She's a count's daughter. Count has married a wealthy
American woman to restore his fortune. This woman died
when her child was very young. Paola is lonely till
she marries. Pathetic scenes of their lives. Creole
life introduced. PW 51:737

HINCKLEY, HENRIETTA R.   United States.

005339   FROM OUT OF THE WEST. Boston: Mayhew,
1905 NUC.

HINE, MURIEL.   See COXON, MURIEL (HINE).

HINKSON, KATHARINE (TYNAN). 1861-1931. United Kingdom.

005340   THE ADVENTURES OF ALICIA. London: F.V.
White, 1906 BMC.

ACAD beautiful heroine etc
ATH beautiful heroine etc

005341   THE ADVENTURES OF CARLO. London: Blackie,
1900 BMC.

005342   BETTY CAREW. BY KATHARINE TYNAN (MRS. H.
A. HINKSON). London: Smith, Elder, 1910 BMC NUC.

TLS-Nice young people of good soc. status
LBKM nice young people of good soc. status

005343   THE CURSE OF CASTLE EAGLE. BY KATHARINE
TYNAN. New York: Duffield, 1915 NUC.

courageous Irish girl and her adventures 4-10-15 PW
delightful romance for young readers NYT

005344   A DAUGHTER OF KINGS. New York: Benziger,
1905 NUC. London: E. Nash, 1905 BMC NUC.

love story of ordinary sort PW 6-3-05
ATH 05, 587

005345   A DAUGHTER OF THE FIELDS. BY KATHARINE
TYNAN. London: Smith, Elder, 1900 BMC NUC. Chicago:
A.C. McClurg, 1901 NUC.

heroine from French convent comes home. mother runs a
farm, she too. LBKM 1-01
SP 85:807. Irish. Meg returns from French convent
school to find her newly widowed mother trying to
manage a failing farm. She wants Meg to take her place
in country society, but Meg refuses and takes over
running of farm with much success. Her romance and
ultimate marriage.

005346   THE DAUGHTER OF THE MANOR. London:
Blackie, 1914 BMC.

005347   THE DEAR IRISH GIRL. BY KATHARINE TYNAN.
London: Smith, Elder, 1899 NUC BMC. Chicago: A. C.
McClurg, 1899 NUC.

Biddy O'Connor and love at first sight and a happy
ending with a lady novelist's perfect hero-Maurice
O'Hara. LIT 4:317
Plot is traditional, but characters given fresh
touches. Biddy is untidy. The hero is interested in
archeology. And there's Miss Lucy Holt, the famous
Amazon "who had fought the league with a courage and
ferocity unequalled by the most militant of
landlords." She's an "overbearing, mannish, eccentric
elderly spinster," but sympathetically drawn. SP 82:93
Raised by father but more by herself in Dublin.
Neglected. Her father's a doctor. Biddy doesn't know
how to keep house. ATH 113:141
Portrait of captivating girl; sentimental love story.
BAKER 03,240

005348   DENYS THE DREAMER. A NOVEL. BY KATHARINE
TYNAN. London: W. Collins, Sons, [1920] BMC NUC. New
York: Benziger, 1921 NUC.

TLS Male
SR Male

005349   DICK PENTREATH. BY KATHARINE TYNAN.
London: Smith, Elder, 1905 BMC NUC. Chicago: A.C.
McClurg, 1906 NUC.

Susan is terrible, despised any assistance in her
upbringing an unusual type. "we are afraid of Susan"
"New trend for Tynan" 1201,05 ACAD
ATH 05, 829 says o about women

005350   FOR MAISIE: A LOVE STORY. BY KATHARINE
TYNAN. London: Hodder and Stoughton, [1906] NUC BMC.
Chicago: McClurg, 1907 NUC.

Rough uncultured man's love and self sacrifice for
adopted daughter PW 9-21-07
TLS
ATH
"pretty little love story" SP

005351   FOR THE WHITE ROSE. New York: Benziger,
1905 NUC.

005352   FORTUNE'S FAVOURITE. London: F. V. White,
1905 BMC.

everybody's amiable and all ends happily ACAD 760,05

005353   FREDA. BY KATHARINE TYNAN. London and New
York: Cassell, 1910 BMC NUC.

TLS poor little orphan gets all she wants
LBKM

005354   THE FRENCH WIFE. Philadelphia:
Lippincott, 1904 PW. London: F.V. White, 1904 BMC.

PW discovery that mrg. is not legal nor are children.
Husband is let to "act hastily," wife disappears
ATH-"love always leads to mrg and mrg never ends in
repentance"
TLS-Sunny world of Ireland
ACAD-the wife who disappeared is grandfather's 1st
wife; heroine wishes to discover heirs and restore
estate but it burns down

005355   A GIRL OF GALWAY. BY KATHARINE TYNAN.

London: Blackie, 1902 BMC NUC.

005356   THE GOLDEN LILY. New York: Benziger, 1902
NUC.

005357   THE GREAT CAPTAIN; A STORY OF THE DAYS OF
SIR WALTER RALEIGH. New York: Benziger, 1902 NUC.

PW-hist novel

005358   HER LADYSHIP. BY KATHARINE TYNAN. London:
Smith, Elder, 1907 BMC NUC. Chicago: McClurg, 1908
NUC.

Irish TLS

005359   HER MOTHER'S DAUGHTER. London: Smith,
Elder, 1909 BMC NUC.

Widow treated harshly by her husband's brothers TLS

005360   HONEY, MY HONEY. BY KATHARINE TYNAN.
London: Smith, Elder, 1912 BMC NUC.

ATH love story

005361   THE HONOURABLE MOLLY. BY KATHARINE TYNAN.
London: Smith, Elder, 1903 BMC. London: Murray, 1919
NUC.

three unsophisticated poor Irish women; one set of
twins; one wants to start a flower farm; five happy
couples at the end ACAD
Molly's successful struggle for an ind. career vs the
efforts of her very conventional guardian ATH 122,750

005362   THE HOUSE. BY KATHARINE TYNAN. London: W.
Collins, [1920] BMC NUC.

ATH-rom between an heir working incognito on a farm
and a medical student who is temporarily acting as a
milkmaid

005363   THE HOUSE OF THE CRICKETS. London: Smith,
Elder, 1908 BMC NUC.

TLS-escape of two daughters from father's tyranny into
a wider world.
ACAD-seeks fame and fortune, gets a man instead
SR 0
ATH 0

005364   THE HOUSE OF THE FOXES. London: Smith,
Elder, 1915 BMC NUC.

curse on old country house TLS

005365   THE HOUSE OF THE SECRET. BY KATHARINE
TYNAN. London: J. Clarke, 1910 BMC NUC.

TLS orphan girl living by herself

005366   JOHN BULTEEL'S DAUGHTERS. London: Smith,
Elder, 1914 BMC NUC.

LBKM there is a certain mystery about their bluff
congenial former father.
ACAD 86:404. Missing page from the church registry.

005367   JOHN-A-DREAMS. London: Smith, Elder, 1916
BMC NUC.

TLS-love story

005368   JUDY'S LOVERS. London: F.V. White, 1904
BMC.

ATH- tr. rom.
ACAD

005369   JULIA. BY KATHARINE TYNAN. London: Smith,
Elder, 1904 BMC NUC. Chicago: A. C. McClurg, 1905 NUC.

Charming Irish story. Julia is ugly to all except Sir
Mortimer, when he leaves, she's sent to a convent to
which he returns to rescue her NYT 375,05
ATH 0
ACAD 05, 15 review says Julia is uninteresting and
yellow in complexion

005370   A KING'S WOMAN. BEING THE NARRATIVE OF
MISS PENELOPE FAYLE, NOW MISTRESS FROBISHER,
CONCERNING THE LATE TROUBLOUS TIMES IN IRELAND.
London: Hurst & Blackett, 1902 BMC.

ATH 8-9-02 not helpful

005371   KIT. London: Smith, Elder, 1917 BMC NUC.

daughter of sailor, ends up with childhood sweetheart
TLS

005372   KITTY AUBREY. London: J. Nisbet, 1909
BMC.

LBKM- Young woman becomes M.D. "if it does not
inculcate any heroic ideals of the suffragettes, it
depicts a capable, young woman who has a soul above
clothes and jewels"
"little lady doctor" turnes herself around everyone's
heart, marries. TLS
"devoted to philanthropy and medicine" ATH

005373   A LITTLE RADIANT GIRL. London: Blackie,
1914 BMC 1915 NUC.

TLS Self-sacrificing matchmaker, romance

005374   LOVE OF BROTHERS. BY KATHARINE TYNAN.
London: Constable, 1919 BMC NUC. New York: Benziger,
1920 NUC.

Murder trad TLS

005375   LOVE OF SISTERS. BY KATHARINE TYNAN.
London: Smith, Elder, 1902 NUC BMC.

ATH 10-2502 Two youthful and two elderly sisters;
younger set have "commonplace love troubles;" elders
are modelled on Misses Jenhyns of Cranford. Eldest
sister ministers to needs of distressed ladies in a
home. "Blend of primness and rollicking joviality".

005376   LOVERS' MEETINGS. London: T.W. Laurie,
[1914] BMC NUC.

005377   THE MAN FROM AUSTRALIA. BY KATHARINE
TYNAN. London & Glasgow: W. Collins Sons, [c1919] BMC
NUC.

chief interest is setting SP

005378   MARGERY DAWE. London: Blackie, 1916 BMC
NUC.

005379   MARY GRAY. BY KATHARINE TYNAN. London and
New York: Cassell, 1908 BMC 1909 NUC.

TLS-traditional love story.
supports self and brothers and sisters. PW 7-3-09

005380   A MESALLIANCE. BY KATHARINE TYNAN. New
York: Duffield, 1913 NUC.

BKM-love story of an old bachelor
widow summons a man to her country place (?) Lizzie
Harding. NYT
hero comes to look upon cousin's marriage especially
the wife with a different view? "Ralph Bretherton is
summoned to the lovely country place, Littlecombe, by
the widow of his favorite cousin. His acquaintance
with his cousin's widow..." PW 84 11/29/13:278

005381   A MIDSUMMER ROSE. London: Smith, Elder,
1913 BMC NUC.

LBKM -an heir, his cousin and his cousin's wife. love.
a postponed inheritance SP
pretty love story, hero gives up woman he loves to
save the good name of another woman who saves him the
sacrifice by falling in love with someone else. ATH SR

005382   MISS GASCOIGNE. BY KATHARINE TYNAN.
London: J. Murray, 1918 BMC NUC.

TLS Romance

005383   MISS MARY. London: J. Murray, 1917 BMC
NUC.

simple country Irish girl becomes great lady a pretty
story TLS
Ireland LBKM

005384   MOLLY; MY HEART'S DELIGHT. London: Smith,
Elder, 1914 BMC NUC.

LBKM-Molly's story, with quotations from her diaries
and letters, from 15- until a woman, pure and sweet.

005385   MRS. PRATT OF PARADISE FARM. KATHARINE
TYNAN. London: Smith, Elder, 1913 BMC NUC.

she's a dear soul but some suspect she killed her
husband even though she was acquitted. She's under 30,
takes lodgers like the "irritatingly exemplary
couple-the Greville's who eloped." ACAD
"charming country story. Shadow of suspicion over Mrs.
Pratt lifted at the end" SP
Sentimental LBKM

005386   MY LOVE'S BUT A LASSIE. BY KATHARINE
TYNAN. London: Ward, Lock, 1918 BMC [192-] NUC.

TLS-Sens.
LBKM dainty love story

005387   OH, WHAT A PLAGUE IS LOVE! BY KATHARINE
TYNAN (MRS. H. A. HINKSON). London: A. and C. Black,
1896 BMC NUC. Chicago: A. C. McClurg, 1900 NUC.

SR-Lady killer father and his high-spirited children.
Irish. Genial.
ACAD 49:465. Father is so chivalrous and attractive to
women that he is always becoming involved in
delightful love affairs which his strong-minded
daughters do not allow to develop into marriage.

005388   PARADISE FARM. BY KATHARINE TYNAN. New
York: Duffield, 1911 NUC.

PW-- love story
NYT Love story

005389   PAT. New York: Benziger, 1913 NUC.

005390   PEGGY THE DAUGHTER. BY KATHARINE TYNAN.
London and New York: Cassell, 1909 BMC NUC.

NYT sweet and fragrant sent. Irish girl rescues father
from prison

005391   PRINCESS KATHARINE. BY KATHARINE TYNAN.
New York: Duffield, 1911 NUC. London: Ward, Lock, 1912
BMC.

girl rehabilitates mother who drinks 3-4-11 PW
TLS-Irish rom.
ATH-daughter, educated above her early surroundings,
returns to find her mother sunk into drink,
slovenliness, etc.-devotes her-self to her mother.
"just and gentle" picture

005392   THE QUEEN'S PAGE. A STORY OF THE DAYS OF
CHARLES I OF ENGLAND. New York, Cincinnati: Benziger,
1900 NUC.

005393   THE RATTLESNAKE. London: Ward, Lock, 1917
BMC NUC.

sensational story of villain with hypnotic powers TLS

005394   A RED, RED ROSE. London: E. Nash, 1903
BMC.

cheerful happy ending type of love story 8-03, 537 NYT
Homely natural story LBKM 4-03,32

005395   ROSE OF THE GARDEN; THE ROMANCE OF LADY
SARAH LENNOX, A NOVEL. BY KATHARINE TYNAN. London:
Constable, 1912 BMC. Indianapolis: Bobbs-Merrill,
[c1913] NUC.

PW 4 10/25/13: 1388 "Tells the story of lovely Lady
Sarah Lennox, a well-known figure of the court of
George III. Much of the book, though in fiction form,
is, however, historically accurate, being made up of
extracts from the heroine's letters to an intimate
friend."
BKM-hist rom. Lady Sarah Lennox, gives in to passion
for her cousin, but repents for years.
ATH novel of Lady Sarah Lennox who had a lover, left
her husband , daughter, etc.
TLS- extracts from life and letters
SR repented for years in self imposed almost-solitary
confinement.

005396   A SHAMEFUL INHERITANCE. BY KATHARINE
TYNAN. London and New York: Cassell, [1914] BMC NUC.

LBKM-hero's mother committed terrible crime, lives
near him, disguised, works as nurse. He gets sick and
she comes for him, he discovers her identity, she
disappears, he finds her.
TLS His father killed himself. STory is the effect of
disclosure of all this on young hero.

005397   SHE WALKS IN BEAUTY. BY KATHARINE TYNAN.

London: Smith, Elder, 1899 NUC. Chicago: McClurg, 1900
NUC.

Widow with three gorgeous daughters--their love
cross-purposes, misunderstandings, etc. Ends in many
wedding bells. Archibald Graydon and Molly, Pamela and
Sylvia. Rose-coloured plot. SP 83:876
Quiet Irish village. ACAD 57:632
Romance with happy ending. Three Irish girls. BAKER
03,240
ACAD 58:106. For girls. Saccharine Romance.
CR 37:86. Irish. Heroine's love story with happy
ending.

005398   "SINCE FIRST I SAW YOUR FACE". London:
Hutchinson, 1915 BMC.

simple tale of Irish peer TLS

005399   THE SQUIRE'S SWEETHEART. London: Ward,
Lock, 1915 BMC.

Old squire, young maid TLS

005400   THE STORY OF BAWN. BY KATHARINE TYNAN.
London: Smith, Elder, 1906 BMC NUC. Chicago: A.C.
McClurg, 1907 NUC.

Irish story-not promising 3-16-07 PW
NYT

005401   THE STORY OF CECILIA. London: Smith,
Elder, 1911 BMC NUC. New York: Benziger, 1911 NUC.

love and sacrifice 11-18-11 PW

005402   THE STORY OF CLARICE. London: J. Clarke,
1911 BMC.

Story of woman who marries a man thinking he's her
dead lover, the lover does indeed return. There's a
daughter too. TLS LBKM
SP-love and inheritance.

005403   THAT SWEET ENEMY. BY KATHARINE TYNAN
(MRS. HINKSON). London: A. Constable, 1901 BMC.
Philadelphia: J.B. Lippincott, 1901 NUC.

grand, proud, ready tongued Aunt Theodosia and her
adopted children BKM Apr '01
NYT ends in 4 happy marr

005404   THREE FAIR MAIDS; OR, THE BURKES OF
BERRYMORE. BY KATHARINE TYNAN. New York: Scribner,
1901 PW. London: Blackie, 1901 BMC NUC. (NUC:
Derrymore.)

005405   A UNION OF HEARTS. BY KATHARINE TYNAN
(MRS. HINKSON). London: J. Nisbet, [1900] NUC [1901]
BMC.

10-19-01 ATH

005406   THE WAY OF A MAID. BY KATHARINE TYNAN
(MRS. HINKSON). London: Lawrence and Bullen, 1895 NUC
BMC. New York: Dodd, Mead, 1895 NUC.

The maid is an Irish RC. who has "unaccountable fits
of depression." Her best friend is the daughter of a
Prot. woman who does work in the community, especially
helpful in ironing out the differences brought on by
different religions. PW 10-12-95:632
ATH 107:14. Old-fashioned style. Pure, wholesome with
a lively heroine.
LBKM 10:24. Irish girls' book.

005407   THE WEB OF FRAULEIN. London: Hodder and
Stoughton, 1916 BMC.

TLS- anti German
LBKM Anti German-essence of evil in the fraulein

005408   THE WEST WIND. London: Constable, 1916
BMC NUC.

TLS-RC.
ATH-RC.

HINKSON, MRS. See HINKSON, KATHARINE (TYNAN).

HINKSON, MRS. H. A. See HINKSON, KATHARINE (TYNAN).

HINMAN, ELIZABETH TROWBRIDGE (EGLESTON). B. 1881.
Nationality Unknown.

005409   NAYA; A STORY OF THE BIG HORN COUNTRY.

New York: Rand, McNally, 1910 NUC.

Story of a young woman, daughter of Indian princess.
PW

HIRSCH, CHARLOTTE (TELLER). B. 1876. United States.

005410   THE CAGE. BY CHARLOTTE TELLER. New York:
D. Appleton, 1907 BMC NUC.

girl full of ideas and enthusiasm who loves a
socialist. concerns Hay market riots PW 3-2-07
A minister, his daughter, daughter's companion who
shares work with poor Frederica Hartwell NYT

HITCHCOCK, MARY E.

005411   TALES OUT OF SCHOOL ABOUT NAVAL OFFICERS
(AND OTHERS). BY A WOMAN WHO HAS LIVED ON A
MAN-OF-WAR, MARY E. HITCHCOCK (MRS. ROSWELL D.
HITCHCOCK). New York: Gotham Press, [c1908] BMC NUC.

HITCHCOCK, MRS. ROSWELL D. See HITCHCOCK, MARY E.

HOARE, EDITH G.

005412   A FAULTY COURTSHIP: A TYROLESE ROMANCE.
London, New York: F. Warne, 1899 BMC.

Good account of a chamois-hunt. Good setting. SP
83:57.
Gretchen Forbach's stormy courtship. Set in Tyrol. The
village's feasts, market days, etc. ACAD 56:684

HOBBES, JOHN OLIVER, pseud. See CRAIGIE, PEARL MARY TERESA
(RICHARDS).

HOBHOUSE, VIOLET.

005413   AN UNKNOWN QUANTITY. London: Downey, 1898
BMC.

SP 80:864 Kilmeny, "brilliantly attractive girl" with
a hatred of death (although not a coward) and unable
to love, eventually casts fear of death out and
discovers she has a heart after all.
LIT 3:256. Ireland, England, Sicily.
ACAD Emotional, often religious.
ATH 111:251. She is maliciously locked up in a church,
dies of pneumonia.

005414   WARP AND WEFT: A STORY OF THE NORTH OF
IRELAND. London: Skeffington, 1899 BMC NUC.

No. Ireland. High minded heroine estranged from her
true love by trickery, weds a rich man to help
finances of father. Esther McVeagh. SP 82:312
Life in Antrim (?) BAKER 03,237

HOBSON, CORALIE (VON WERNER). B. 1891. United Kingdom.

005415   THE REVOLT OF YOUTH. BY MRS . C. HOBSON.
London: T.W. Laurie, 1919 BMC NUC.

Louie Swan. First person narrative. Young woman, moody
at home, unsuccessful as actress, incapable of
friendship and love; extremely sordid story of the
morals and miseries of a 3rd rate touring co. Air of
veracity. TLS
"Feminist views are largely reflected in the book."
ATH
Goes on stage, fails as Ophelia, returns to relatives,
marries. Theme awakening of womanhood. Study of
unrest. LBKM
The sexual instinct is highly developed in the
heroine. A rebel all her life. SR

HOBSON, HARRIET MALONE. United States.

005416   THE COMRADE OF NAVARRE; A TALE OF THE
HUGUENOTS. Philadelphia: Griffith and Rowland Press,
[1914] NUC.

PW-"Marsac, Comte de Brunnetere, was son of a papist
mother and Huguenot father. Marsac promised his father
to be true to the Protestant cause, but his brother
Berthon kept his mother's faith. Narrative follows
Marsac as comrad of Henry of Navarre through the
bloody religious wars. The king is his idol, but when
Henry turns Papist, Marsac renounces his allegiance.
Although a tale of war, story is a sermon for peace."

005417   SIS WITHIN. Philadelphia: G.W. Jacobs,
[1913] NUC.

"Most unusual novel...moving human plot materialized

from the psychic world" Maria Daviess
PW 84 11/1/13:1433 "Novel with an intense love story
running through it, in which the higher woman in
Diantha King is brought out by her love for a man who
had been tempted, had fallen, repented, and then risen
again to the very loftiest manhood. Sis, of "Jinks'
inside," is the central figure in this story and we
watch her development from her first explosive words
of the opening chapter until, after many ups and still
more downs, she at last comes into her own."

HOBSON, MARGARET.

005418   THE BEAUTIFUL HAND OF THE DEVIL. New
York: Abbey Press, 1900 [c] NUC.

HOBSON, MRS. C. See HOBSON, CORALIE (VON WERNER).

HOCKING, SALOME. See FIFIELD, SALOME (HOCKING).

HOCKLIFFE, MARIAN.

005419   THE REFINER'S FIRE: A NOVEL. London:
Cassell, 1898 BMC.

ACAD 55:334. English country life and rivalry between
2 lovers.
ATH 112:891. Young people and their love affairs,
healthy, no sense of humor.

HODGE, ALMA, jt. au. See SCOTT, FLORENCE MARY SEYMOUR AND
ALMA HODGE.

HODGKINSON, FLORENCE.

005420   THE CONVENT BELLE. London: Mascot Novels,
[1914] BMC.

005421   HIS FAIR LADY. London: Mascot Novels,
[1915] BMC.

005422   THE INTERRUPTED HONEYMOON. London: Adine,
[1919] BMC.

HODGSON, AGATHA.

005423   LOVE IN A COTTAGE; OR MAKING THE MOST OF
A SMALL INCOME. London: Ward and Downey, [1891] BMC.

Auto form. How to manage on 250 pounds a year. All the
practical financial details set down by young couple
before children come. SP 66, 488

HODGSON, GERALDINE EMMA. B. 1865.

005424   ACROSS THE FOREST AND FAR AWAY. Clifton:
Simpkin, Marshall, 1911 BMC.

005425   ANTONY DELAVEL, LL.D. London: J.
Macqueen, 1900 BMC.

SR 90:691. Antony writes books.
ATH 116:721. Incompatible heroine and aunt, Griselda
went out in canoe when aunt begged her not to and
drowned.
LIT 7:446. Antony is a prig. Heroine is interesting.

005426   IN THE WAY OF THE SAINTS. London, New
York: Longmans, Green, 1913 BMC NUC.

005427   IN THE WILDERNESS OF THIS WORLD. London:
Lawrence and Bullen, 1899 BMC.

SP 81:992. Magnanimous and self-effacing schoolmaster
hero.
ACAD 55:378. Simple and rough country folk. "Wherever
two or three are gathered together, there are the
seeds of a tragedy in the midst of them."
ATH 112:892. Melancholy life of school master whose
unselfishness is both bane and blessing.

005428   THE SUBTLE THING THAT'S SPIRIT. London:
A. Treherne, 1902 BMC.

005429   A TRAGEDY OF ERRORS. London: G. Allen,
1900 BMC.

LIT 7:446. Small child with stern father brought up by
uncongenial aunt. She is drowned in adolescence.

HODSDON, HELEN MERRILL. United States.

005430   THE LITTLE WINDOW. New York: T. Y.
Crowell, [c1913] NUC.

Spinster's home closed to younger sister because of

marriage to "ne'er-do-well." Welcomes home the
"outcast & her little ones." PW 84 9/6/13:621

HOEY, ELLEN MARY (GRIFFIN). United States.

005431   MOLL PITCHER'S PROPHECIES; OR, THE
AMERICAN SIBYL. BY MRS. ELLEN M. GRIFFIN. Boston,
Mass.: Eastburn Press, 1895 NUC.

HOFFMAN, MARIE E. United States.

005432   LINDY LOYD; A TALE OF THE MOUNTAINS.
Boston: M. Jones, 1920 NUC.

PW-Forced into a secret marriage with disreputable
moonshiner. Freed at last by husband's death to marry
man she loves.
NYT 6/27,20, p. 17. Traditional love story.

HOLBROOK, AMELIA WEED. United States.

005433   ONE OF THE MCINTYRES. Chicago: Waifs'
Mission & Training School, American Youth Dept., 1896
NUC.

005434   'WHIZ': A STORY OF THE MINES. Chicago:
Laird and Lee, [c1898] W.

HOLBROOK, ELIZABETH. United States.

005435   OLD 'KASKIA DAYS: A NOVEL. Chicago:
Schulte, 1893 NUC.

Story built around the Jesuit mission-Kaskaskia
founded in late 1600s. Includes a love story and
Indians in Illinois. PW 7-15-93.

HOLDEN, MARTHA EVERTS. 1844-1896.

005436   A STRING OF AMBER BEADS. Chicago: E. A.
Weeks, [c1893] NUC.

CR 21:166. Earnest expression of her views on life,
Martha Everts Holden.

HOLDING, ELISABETH (SANXAY). 1889-1955. United States.

005437   INVINCIBLE MINNIE. New York: G. H. Doran,
[c1920] NUC. London: Hodder & Stoughton, [1920] BMC.

NYT 1920:237 "harsh tones.. softened with humor and
charity. The author never sits in judgement of the
Minnies of the world." Author an American, lived most
of her life near NYC. First novel.
Minnie and Frances (Frankie) are sisters. Minnie is
stolid, slow-witted bovine, plods contentedly taking
care of dreary farmhouse, bed-ridden grandmother,
unpaid bills. Frances cannot accept this life, gets a
little bit of business training, goes to New York,
marries a shiftless and incompetent idler. Mrg. might
have been ok, however, had not Minnie run
amuck-plunging, trampling in a grotesque nightmarish
fashion, tragic, pitiful. Wrecks all lives she touches
including her own, and to the last casts blame on
everyone but herself Cooper, p. 1290, BKM
BKM- she is monster, alludes to her maternity?
TLS--She is a vampire type, preying on her sister, her
husbands, and child.
Frances and Minnie, sisters, are two strong
characters, in opposition with each other. When their
father dies, Frances is unable to attend medical
school as she had planned. She strongly desires a
career, something which Minnie is not sympathetic to.
Minnie, unlike Frances, is neither bright nor capable;
she is, however, clever and determined. She seduces
the man Frances is engaged to and marries him; she
then marries a second man in order to support the
first husband and herself. After bringing much
unhappiness to a number of people, she ends up
happily, running a boarding house. She is not
particularly maternal but remains in possession of her
child. (Book)

HOLDING, ELIZABETH E. United States.

005438   JOY, THE DEACONESS. New York: Hunt &
Eaton, 1893 NUC.

Mehitable Joy Lawrence trained in hospital work
accepts a position in the Deaconess Home in a large
city. Her career. Glimpses of the nature and methods
of the Order of American Deaconesses. PW 6-24-93

HOLDSWORTH, ANNIE E. See HAMILTON, ANNIE E. (HOLDSWORTH)
LEE.

HOLDSWORTH, ETHEL CARNIE. United Kingdom.

005439   HELEN OF FOUR GATES. BY AN EX-MILL GIRL
[ANONYMOUS]. New York: E. P. Dutton, [c1917] NUC.
London: H. Jenkins, 1917 BMC NUC.

Helen's father lost woman he loved because she was
told there's madness in his family. The man who told
ended up marrying that woman. Helen was their child,
but raised by the 1st man, father swears revenge on
her. Tells Helen's lover there's madness in her
family, forces her to marry another man but she
eventually gets back to her original lover TLS
No. country setting, wild passionate Helen believes
the man is her real father LBKM NYT

005440   THE HOUSE THAT JILL BUILT. London: H.
Jenkins, 1920 BMC.

TLS-Jilted by a man for someone with 500 lbs. Jill
inherits 10,000 lbs and builds a house in Ireland for
tired mothers

005441   THE MARRIAGE OF ELIZABETH. London: H.
Jenkins, 1920 BMC.

TLS-Poor village folk. John marries Eliz to keep
promise to dead wife he adored. She learns of promise
after marriage. She also has had confidence of wife
and her unfaithfulness. Happiness eventually.
LBKM-Formula writing.

005442   THE TAMING OF NAN. New York: E. P.
Dutton, [1919] NUC. London: H. Jenkins, 1920 BMC.

"Nan is a hooligan, a shrew, cruel, foul mouthed"
pitiless, callous. Her husband has all the virtues.
They have a daughter. Daily life of this family, cruel
Nan is tamed from wild beast of a woman. but it's "no
softened picture of womanhood." but her furies can
never be rooted out. Husband knows he'll have to give
space to these furies. In the intervals Nan will
grapple with them herself.? TLS
in self defense he strikes her (?) ATH
"let her own five sons die of neglect" This stone age
woman turns into a house-angel after 20 yrs of marr" ?
LBKM
tamed when she finds rel. BAKER 32,244
SR-Virago eventually tamed by husb. who has lost both
legs.
NYT Jan 25 '20 p 43. "Stone age woman needs to be
clubbed into submission."
PW. Lancashire working folk

HOLDSWORTH, GLADYS BERTHA (STERN). B. 1890. United
Kingdom.

005443   CHILDREN OF NO MAN'S LAND. BY G. B.
STERN. London: Duckworth, [1919] BMC NUC.

SP-hard fate of Germans brought up in England. Hero,
instead of being sent to trenches where he longs to
be, is sent to internment camp.
LBKM-position of Jews in the war

005444   GRAND CHAIN. BY G. B. STERN. London:
Nisbet, 1917 BMC NUC.

focus on a man, first as a boy surrounded by "odious"
women, a tyrant of a mother, a spy of a aunt and
vulgar aunts. His father was a neer do well. These
women make the boy feel he's contaminated. But it's
the sister who takes the easy way. But mother cares
only for son she wants to hold. The son must atone for
father's desertion. Story skips to 20 years later.
He's a widower with four modern children whom he
fears? TLS

005445   LARRY MUNRO. London: Chapman & Hall, 1920
BMC NUC. (American ed. title: The China Shop.)

TLS - 3 generations of Larries
LBKM- 3 generations of Larries.

005446   A MARRYING MAN. BY G. B. STERN. London:
Nisbet, [1918] BMC NUC.

SR- Gareth Temple, with a good deal of the feminine in
his nature accidentally gets into a compromising
position with Kathleen Morrison and proposes. She
refuses but sets up housekeeping with him instead.
Housekeeping persists long after Kathleen is heartily
sick of Gareth. He meets and falls in love with
Patricia and they marry after the two women have
talked it over-once more his futility asserts itself.
On last page Kathleen says "and I stood this sort of

thing for sixteen years." Character study.

005447   PANTOMIME. A NOVEL. BY G. B. STERN.
London: Hutchinson, 1914 BMC [1931] NUC.

LBKM-Jewish heroine is brought up in well-to-do
circumstances, then her family falls into financial
misfortune, she, her mother and uncle moving from
hotel to hotel, scrimping and saving. She yearns for
happiness, seeing herself play Principal Girl to
Principal Boy. Wanting a lover, she finds a
philanderer. Seeking a career, she joined the Academy
of Histrionic Art only to find her acting does not
impress. But she falls in love with a fellow student
and elopes. They are stormbound in Dover en route to
Paris, she gets cold feet and slips away to return to
London. He has preceded her.

005448   SEE-SAW. London: Hutchinson, 1914 BMC
[1931] NUC.

ATH-The effect of marriage on a talented woman with a
career. Study.
ATH 144:453. "His exuberance, simplicity, and strength
seemingly dominate Jaconne, while in reality it is his
weakness that holds her." Jaconne is "riotously happy,
enjoying the freedom of unconventional theatrical
life," believes this will continue after marriage.
"Attitude presented toward life is not always
well-balanced."
TLS " Ultimate victory of the superficial and selfish
artist husband."

005449   TWO AND THREES. BY G. B. STERN. London:
Nisbet, [1916] BMC NUC.

TLS-male hero, fun
ATH-male hero, fun

HOLLAND, ANNIE J.   Nationality Unknown.

005450   TALITHA CUMI; A STORY OF FREEDOM THROUGH
CHRISTIAN SCIENCE. Boston: Lee and Shepard, 1904 NUC.

HOLLAND, ANNIE JEFFERSON.   United States.

005451   THE REFUGEES: A SEQUEL TO "UNCLE TOM'S
CABIN". Austin, Texas: Published For Author, 1892 NUC.

HOLLAND, ELIZABETH, pseud.   See OWEN, ETHEL.

HOLLAND, JANE JANSEN.   United States.

005452   JANE JANSEN: A STORY OF A WOMAN'S
HERITAGE IN THE HEART OF APPALACHIA [ANONYMOUS].
Greensburgh, Pennsylvania: Oliver Pub. House, 1895
NUC.

HOLLEY, MARIETTA. 1844-1926.   United States.

005453   AROUND THE WORLD WITH JOSIAH ALLEN'S
WIFE. New York: G.W. Dillingham, [1905] NUC. London:
T.F. Unwin, 1905 BMC.

NYT 775,05 describes the book in terms of the travels.

005454   JOSIAH ALLEN ON THE WOMAN QUESTION. New
York: F. H. Revell, [c1914] BMC NUC.

005455   JOSIAH'S ALARM, AND ABEL PERRY'S FUNERAL.
BY JOSIAH ALLEN'S WIFE. Philadelphia: J. B.
Lippincott, 1895 NUC.

His alarm has to do with a furnace that burns almost
no coal but provides much heat. After using much coal,
decides what he has is a potash stove-kettle once
belonging to Washington. Abel's funeral and monument
planned by his son-in-law. PW7-20-95:106.

005456   SAMANTHA AT CONEY ISLAND AND A THOUSAND
OTHER ISLANDS. BY JOSIAH ALLEN'S WIFE (MARIETTA
HOLLEY). New York: Christian Herald, [c1911] NUC.

005457   SAMANTHA AT THE ST. LOUIS EXPOSITION. BY
JOSIAH ALLEN'S WIFE (MARIETTA HOLLEY). New York: G.W.
Dillingham, [1904] NUC. London: T.F. Unwin, 1904 BMC.

005458   SAMANTHA AT THE WORLD'S FAIR. BY JOSIAH
ALLEN'S WIFE (MARIETTA HOLLEY). New York, London, and
Toronto: Funk and Wagnalls, 1893 NUC BMC.

005459   SAMANTHA IN EUROPE. BY JOSIAH ALLEN'S
WIFE (MARIETTA HOLLEY). New York, London, and Toronto:
Funk and Wagnalls, 1896 NUC BMC.

005460   SAMANTHA ON CHILDREN'S RIGHTS. BY JOSIAH

ALLEN'S WIFE (MARIETTA HOLLEY). New York: G. W.
Dillingham, [c1909] NUC.

BKM views on training children Samantha advocates
children's rights

005461   SAMANTHA ON THE RACE PROBLEM. BY JOSIAH
ALLEN'S WIFE (MARIETTA HOLLEY). New York: Dodd, Mead,
[c1892] NUC. London: B. F. Stevens, [1892] BMC.

005462   SAMANTHA ON THE WOMAN QUESTION. BY
MARIETTA HOLLEY "JOSIAH ALLEN'S WIFE". New York: F. H.
Revell, [c1913] BMC NUC.

PW 84 9/20/13 p767 Samantha, well-known through her
adventures told in "Samantha at the Centennial," here
advocates votes for women and temperance with her
old-time vigor and humor.

005463   SAMANTHA VS. JOSIAH; BEING THE STORY OF A
BORROWED AUTOMOBILE AND WHAT CAME OF IT. New York:
Funk & Wagnalls, 1906 NUC.

NYT-cars and spiritualism

HOLLINGER, LIBBIE ISRAEL.

005464   THE DUKE AND THE HUMANITARIAN; A
SATIRICAL STORY. Boston: Arena, 1896 BMC.

PW 12-5-96. The reformer is hung as an anarchist. The
duke spends his American wife's millions and deserts
her. A plea for the working poor.

HOLLINS, DOROTHEA.

005465   THE MARRIAGE OF TRUE MINDS. BY THEOPHILA
NORTH. London: G. Richards, 1900 BMC.

ACAD 59:384. True love, happy ending.

HOLLIS, GERTRUDE.

005466   HUGH THE MESSENGER: A TALE OF THE SIEGE
OF CALAIS. London: Christian Knowledge Society, [1905]
BMC.

005467   IN A ROYAL NURSERY. London: Christian
Knowledge Society, [1911] NUC BMC.

Adventures of the children of Charles I during the
Great Rebellion.

005468   IN THE DAYS OF S. ANSELM. London:
Christian Knowledge Society, [1901] BMC.

005469   JEM FORSTER'S REVENGE. London: Christian
Knowledge Society, [1913] BMC.

005470   JENKYN CLYFFE, BEDESMAN. London:
Christian Knowledge Society, [1910] BMC NUC.

English History Henry IV 1399-1413

005471   THE KING WHO WAS NEVER CROWNED; A TALE OF
THE FIFTEENTH CENTURY. London: Christian Knowledge
Society, [1904] BMC.

005472   THE LOST EXILE. A TALE OF SIBERIA.
London: Christian Knowledge Society, [1912] BMC.

005473   LOVE'S VICTORY. London: Holden and
Hardingham, [1916] BMC.

Orphan girl raised as atheist, falls in love with a
clergyman who saves her life twice. ATH
She grows up in wealth; her name is Cecil. She has "no
particular scruples" except to revolt against
other-worldliness. Is flung into arms of an unworthy
man, rescued by a good one. TLS

005474   MY LORD OF READING; A TALE OF THE
REFORMATION. London: S.P.C.K., [1915] BMC [1929?] NUC.

005475   PHILIP OKEOVER'S PAGE-HOOD; A STORY OF
THE PEASANTS' RISING. London: Christian Knowledge
Society, [1907] BMC NUC.

English History 1377

005476   A SLAVE OF THE SARACEN; A TALE OF THE
SEVENTH CRUSADE. London: T. Nelson, [1904] BMC.

005477   SPURS AND BRIDE; HOW THEY WERE WON. A
TALE OF MAGNA CHARTA. London: Christian Knowledge
Society, [1903] BMC.

005478　　　TWO DOVER BOYS; OR, CAPTURED BY CORSAIRS. London: Blackie, 1911 BMC 1913 NUC.

English fiction 1509 two boys

005479　　　UNCLE MICHAEL'S STORY. A TALE OF THE RIVER AMAZON. London: S.P.C.K., [1920] BMC.

HOLLIS, MARGERY.

005480　　　STAPLETON'S LUCK. London: R. Bentley, 1897 BMC.

The dissenter "trying to reconcile bigotry with a tender heart". SR 84:475.
Ralph Stapleton in Aust. He lost employer's money on way to bank. Lost his job. The long effort to recover the money. ATH 110: 347.
Story ends well. LIT 1:22.
SP 81:448. Hero is robbed. Suspense, will he recover money? Romance, too.

005481　　　THROUGH THICK AND THIN. London: R. Bentley, 1893 BMC NUC.

Gay Rushton, daughter of a blackguard, devotes self to mother through thick and thin. Father deserts the family and is reported dead. Mother (Sophy) marries again. Gay learns father is alive, hides the information from her mother. Gay's lover is a journalist. SR 75, 407.
Sensational parts. "Miss Fanny Gresham of the Bijou Theater." ATH 101, 533.

005482　　　UP IN ARMS. London: R. Bentley, 1896 BMC NUC.

ATH 107:146. "A gentler, milder, and more irreproachable story of conjugal revolt has never been penned." "Noel is no hierophant of Feminism; she couldn't be imagined with a cigarette." Sir Piers "is anything but a bad baronet." Long-deferred reunion.
ACAD 49:260. He is converted, by separation, from a cold fortune-hunter into a loving husband.
SP 76:306. Noel is "repentant," She learns on her wedding day that he has married her for her money. She avails herself of a "recent legal judgement empowering a wife to live her own life without molestation."

HOLME, CONSTANCE. See PUNCHARD, CONSTANCE (HOLME).

HOLMES, ALEC, pseud. See SCOTT, AIMEE BYNG (HALL).

HOLMES, ELEANOR. Nationality Unknown.

005483　　　A BREACH OF PROMISE. London: Hurst and Blackett, 1907 BMC.

Traditional type of story. TLS

005484　　　LIFE'S FITFUL FEVER. London: Hurst and Blackett, 1898 BMC.

ACAD 54:125. The struggles of two sisters, left to fight their own way. Younger sister a journalist (Betty.)
SR 86:320. Wholesome, for the younger person.
LBKM 15:24. The literary one is the heroine, the other takes up singing and is a villain. There are other villains, all duly punished.

005485　　　THE PRICE OF A PEARL. A NOVEL. London: Hurst and Blackett, 1894 BMC. New York: Harper, 1894 NUC.

SR-modern. Heroine is not a type most women would want to identify with.
SP 72:590. Pearl has three suitors: Mr. Lewis (a middle-aged banker), Bertie Meredith (a nice but unattractive scion of a ducal house); and Hector (a medical student with a brilliant future.) She favors the latter when suddenly he finds himself penniless and alone. Rev. doesn't think she treated any of them well, but he is charmed by her.
ACAD 45:225. "She is not at all considerate, and in a sense is even selfish." She gets Hector, the man she loves, finally. Bertie's self-sacrifice?
ATH 103:407. Male characters almost without exception display a sensitiveness that is quite feminine in its intensity.

005486　　　THROUGH ANOTHER MAN'S EYES: A NOVEL. London: Hurst and Blackett, 1893 BMC.

The ill-fated marriage of Lizzie Pitt. Also all the

impediments that separate Magdalen Dumaresq from Colonel Gwynne. SP 70:548.
A forged will, a well dressed villain. SR 76:444.
Villains are black but the end is sunny. ACAD 43:369.
Mother, a blameless bigamist. "Study in limp...dependence on others." ACAD 43:390.
Retiring clergyman loves an heiress but her money comes between them. SP 84:500.

005487　　　TO-DAY AND TO-MORROW. London: Hurst and Blackett, 1895 BMC.

Reformed rake whose past troubles him. Mayor Heronden. SR 80:322.
Miss Helmsby is too perfect, too unreal. SP 75:275
At 44 he's still a desperate flirt yet kind guardian of his dead brother's child. A saint-sinner type. Centers on three women, one of past, Miss Helmsley, and Miss Katrinka whom he marries. It takes a young woman to reform a rake. ATH 106:188

HOLMES, GEORGIANA (KLINGLE).　United States.

005488　　　THE CHARLATAN'S PROPHECY. BY GEORGE KLINGLE. Boston: R. G. Badger, [c1915] NUC.

Romantic love story.

005489　　　THE ILLUMINED CROSS. BY GEORGE KLINGLE. New York: F. A. Stokes, 1898 [c] NUC.

HOLMES, MARA GORDON.

005490　　　SILVIA CRAVEN; OR THE SINS OF THE FATHERS. London: E. Stock, [1895] BMC.

She and brother have to earn own livings are orphaned. She becomes a governess; he a curate. She is an angel given to helping others. In the end she at 23 "falls a victim to her altruism; brother marries. ACAD:47:312. She dies of consumption after nursing a sick child. ATH 105:405.

HOLMES, MARGARET. See BATES, MARGRET HOLMES (ERNSPERGER).

HOLMES, MARGRET. See BATES, MARGRET HOLMES (ERNSPERGER).

HOLMES, MARY CAROLINE. 1859-1927. United States.

005491　　　THE KNOCK ON THE DOOR; A STORY OF TO-DAY. New York and London: F. H. Revell, [c1918] NUC. London: Oliphant, [1919] BMC.

PW-religious quest

005492　　　"WHO FOLLOWS IN THEIR TRAIN?" A SYRIAN ROMANCE. New York: F. H. Revell, [c1917] NUC.

HOLMES, MARY JANE (HAWES). 1825-1907. United States.

005493　　　THE ABANDONED FARM AND CONNIE'S MISTAKE. BY MRS. MARY J. HOLMES. New York: G.W. Dillingham, [1905] NUC.

Romance, two stories, Connie's secret-sham marriage.

005494　　　DOCTOR HATHERN'S DAUGHTERS: A STORY OF VIRGINIA, IN FOUR PARTS. By MRS. MARY J. HOLMES. New York: G. W. Dillingham, 1895 NUC.

Annie Hathern and her twin sister's experiences during Civil War-the coming of her step-mother. marriage of her sister, her own romance. PW 7-20-95:107

005495　　　THE MERIVAL BANKS. New York: G. W. Dillingham, [1903] NUC.

Also a love affair but concerns an island town. PW 9-19-03

005496　　　MRS. HALLAM'S COMPANION, AND THE SPRING FARM, AND OTHER TALES. BY MRS. MARY J. HOLMES. New York: G. W. Dillingham, 1896 NUC.

005497　　　PAUL RALSTON: A NOVEL. BY MRS. MARY J. HOLMES. New York: G. W. Dillingham, 1897 NUC.

Missionary's daughter comes from Africa to N.E. for a summer with her aunt. She's been sent from Africa because there's a man that has a strange hold on her. There's a murder and a trial. PW 52:738.

005498　　　RENA'S EXPERIMENT. New York: G. W. Dillingham, [1904] NUC.

NYT-doubtful, problem of inheritance to be gained thru

marriage of two people who have never met. Look-a-like cousin.

005499   THE TRACY DIAMONDS. BY MRS. MARY J. HOLMES. New York: G. W. Dillingham, 1899 NUC.

Mrs. Tracy comes to a boarding house on Albany-Boston road with her daughter. Places her diamonds in the safe to which three people know the combination. They are stolen. PW 56:649

HOLMES, MARY JOHNSON. United States.

005500   A FAIR PURITAN: A NEW ENGLAND TALE. New York: Hurst, 1891 NUC.

005501   THE HOUSE OF FIVE GABLES. New York: Hurst, 1892 NUC.

HOLROYD, CAROLINE C.

005502   SEETHING DAYS. A ROMANCE. London: A. D. Innes, 1894 NUC BMC.

HOLT, ADELAIDE. Nationality Unknown.

005503   OUTSIDE THE ARK. New York and London: John Lane, 1913 NUC BMC.

Hugh-critic turned playwright. Margaret, great actress, brilliant mind, has a lover, auto accident leaves her crippled. Iris hates her Sunday school life drowned a baby, comrades with Godrey. Three people outside the arc, different. Hugh writes a play for Margaret-role of cripple- a big success after his death; he refused to have it end in suicide. Hugh marries Iris who begins to be jealous of Margaret Stair; she reads his mail, spies on him. He knows she does; is very patient. She's devastated to learn he's innocent makes him go away while baby being born-won't have him around for months. He dies at sea. She lives to raise child and start a school.
PW"Hugh Inskip, a prominent man of letters, marries a young wife, whom he does not understand, because she is continually posing and never her natural self. She is also jealous of the beautiful actress, Margaret Stair, for whom Inskip is writing a play, and makes use of an ingenious and shady trick to spy upon her husband's motives. But Iris, the wife, is not entirely a malignant figure--for her frail beauty and helplessness makes an appeal for sympathy. Scene of the novel changes at times from the hub of London life to the peaceful quiet of a country vicarage, where the father of Iris lives." 83:1565

005504   THE VALLEY OF REGRET. New York and London: J. Lane, 1911 BMC NUC.

a tragic misalliance, concerns heredity-PW 5-6-11 husband kills a man who insults wife. While he's in prison, she meets and helps a doctor working in slums. They love each other but Betty returns to husband when he's released. "victory over temptation" LBKM
The tragedy of Betty. ACAD
pictures of slum life. Reviewer says the end is obscure as to whether husband dies. SP
Husband drinks and squanders money; husband and wife part. ATH
after five years in prison he returns and is forgiven-ATH

HOLT, EMILY SARAH. B. 1836. United Kingdom.

005505   ALL'S WELL; OR, ALICE'S VICTORY. Boston: Bradley and Woodruff, [1892] PW. London: Shaw, [1893] BMC.

PW-persecution of the Protestants under Queen Mary, 1556-58. Heroine is Alice Benden, one of the Canterbury Martyrs who was burned at the stake. She was delivered to justice by her own husband--her story is pathetic.

005506   COUNTESS MAUD, OR THE CHANGES OF THE WORLD. A TALE OF THE FOURTEENTH CENTURY. London: J. F. Shaw, [1892] BMC NUC.

SP Hist. romance of time of Richard II.
PW-historical romance, 14th c. London

005507   ONE SNOWY NIGHT; OR LONG AGO AT OXFORD. Boston: Bradley and Woodruff, [1893] NUC. London: J.F. Shaw, 1893 BMC.

30 Germans under leadership of Gerhardt who wanted to evangelize England came to Oxford in 1159. Story built on this incident --Christian attitude of England toward the German movement. Oxford's rel. life, especially Jewish mvt. 12-2-93 PW

HOLT, MINA. United Kingdom.

005508   SPECK BLACKNESS. Bristol: J. W. Arrowsmith, 1919 BMC.

Told by a dog. TLS

HOME, FRANCES.

005509   AGAINST THE ODDS. London: Jarrold, 1897 BMC.

Man struggles vs great odds to recover his reputation. Honor keeps him from showing he was more sinned against than sinning. Also portraits of Salvation Army people. Heroine Ina. SP 79:253 .

005510   AN AWAKENED MEMORY. London: Ward, Lock, 1909 BMC.

Mrs. Barnes aims to "put her memory to sleep." She drinks and so does her medical student husband. She's determined to obliterate the past but has an awakening memory of their only child Dorothy. "Quiet, thoughtful work" TLS

005511   THE EXPERIENCE OF DOROTHY LEIGH. London: G. Routledge, 1899 BMC.

Her life as a hospital nurse. Also the efforts of an alcoholic to reform himself. LIT 5:82
She eventually weds the Resident Surgical Officer for whom she first felt aversion. Heroine helps reform the alcoholic named Barnes. SP 83:259

005512   HUGH BROTHERTON, CURATE. London: Ward, Lock, 1903 BMC.

HOME, HENRIETTA.

005513   THE FLEDGLINGS. London: E. Mathews, 1912 BMC.

005514   VISIONS FOR COMPANY. London: A. Melrose, 1912 BMC.

ATH-Psych study of childhood and girlhood
TLS-"gentle" Eleanor. Sounds mostly like a girl's book.
Eleanor orphaned as a child, rich, lovely with adopted parents until the hero arrives. "She's introspective, self analytical, impractical and on the edge of morbidity." ACAD

HOOD, AGNES ELIZA (JACOMB). B. 1866. United Kingdom.

005515   ESTHER; A NOVEL. BY AGNES E. JACOMB. London: W. Heinemann, 1912 NUC BMC. New York: H. Ober, 1911 NUC.

TLS-minister favors his calling over claims of his wife. She "falls"
ATH-Sees his love for his wife a flaw that makes invalid his purity as a priest.
SP-She falls when he leaves for Africa for the good of his soul. He realizes his vanity, forgives her and all seems restored. Disagreeable.

005516   THE FAITH OF HIS FATHERS: A STORY OF SOME IDEALISTS. BY A. E. JACOMB. London: A. Melrose, 1909 BMC. New York: Dodd, Mead, 1909 NUC.

Man and woman marry vs. father's wish. PW 9-18-09
Effect of Puritanism-narrow and unbending-upon a group of characters. TLS
Father a hard nosed Methodist raising son and daughter by the book forces son to marry barmaid he's slept with. The mother begins to hate the relationship, watches son deteriorate. Her daughter Rachel falls in love with a near atheist, and father breaks them up. Mother rebels-takes daughter's side, daughter marries. Son kills his wife. Mother-a finely wrought study "loses her reason"-ATH
"written with considerabel power"-SP

005517   THE FRUITS OF THE MORROW. BY AGNES E. JACOMB. London: Methuen, 1914 BMC.

SR-Illegitimacy of older son made public by succession to barony.

005518   JOHNNY LEWISON. A NOVEL. BY AGNES E.

JACOMB. London: A. Melrose, 1909 BMC.

Jewish: Christian marriage. Wife revolts vs. "materialism and luxury with which Johnny's father oppresses her." She turns to Dick Chard, her old friend. Johnny's frustrated happiness. All real people. Author's attitude "is almost too subtle" ATH Mother catches Johnny for her daughter. Marjorie once engaged falls for a much less worthy man. SP

005519   THE LONELY ROAD. BY AGNES E. JACOMB. London: A. Melrose, 1911 BMC.

Husband of "lower station" marital unhappiness. Her love cools as she finds him crude . End is sad. TLS Correct, conventional Helen Andrews passes from rule of father to marriage with a man "aflame with primitive passion, unrefined. Full length presentation of a correct suburban wife in an intolerable position." LBKM
End is "unnecessarily tragic". ATH

HOOKER, FORRESTINE (COOPER). 1867-1932. United States.

005520   THE LONG DIM TRAIL. New York: A. A. Knopf, 1920 NUC. London: Mills and Boon, 1922 BMC.

PW-Western written by a frontier woman.

HOOPER, I.

005521   HIS GRACE O' THE GUNNE. London: A. and C. Black, 1897 NUC 1898 BMC.

SP 81:88. The narrative of Lurlin Kirke, who was "apprenticed to the master of a thieves' school at a tender age and at 21 stood so high in his calling that he was engaged to further the interests of a wicked nobleman in the West Country." He was to act as tutor to a crippled child and to poison. He cannot do this and attempts but fails to save the child's life. He does save Celia's life in an heroic act. "His isolation after the death of the only human being who loved him."

005522   THE MINISTER'S CONVERSION. London: A. and C. Black, 1898 BMC.

SP 81:656. Heroine & 3 lovers. Minister denounces wife from pulpit. Reconciliation follows.
LIT 3:605. Devonshire rivalry for the love of a country girl of a worthless gypsy lad, a freethinker and Socialist, and a nonconformist...compromised herself with the gypsy...the elders of the church serve as chorus characters show an oily hypocrisy.
ACAD 55:120. He was called upon in the course of his duty to admonish his wife publicly. His conversion followed.
ACAD 55:247.
SR 86:891 "shows how, in the midst of his agony at humiliating the woman he loves, there is the savage joy of denouncing what he considers her guilt. Her lover springs to her side and faces the congregation with her."

005523   NELL GWYN'S DIAMOND. London: A. and C. Black, 1899 BMC NUC.

Adventure. LIT 5:349
Aysgarth tries to regain fortune by finding Charles the second's stolen diamond. A woman commits cold-blooded murder. Abbess -a good villain. We are outraged by the tale of her sainthood. LBKM 17:62 Historical romance. 17th.
SR 89:86. A jewel which brings bad luck, adventures.

005524   THE SINGER OF MARLEY. London: Methuen, 1897 BMC NUC.

LBKM 14:132. Sir Lucius consented to a trick which saw his daughter married to an importer, knowing that she would be widowed in 6 months. Lux is sold as a slave in Martinique?

HOOPES, MARY HOWARD (PETERSON). United States.

005525   THE COMMODORE. BY MAUD HOWARD PETERSON. Boston: Lothrop, Lee & Shepard, [1914] BMC NUC.

PW 86 10/21/14:1404 "Tells of the development of the hero, known by his early pet name, the "Commodore," from a little boy born in the "Service" (U.S. Navy) to an officer upon the threshold of a career in that service. A love that at first runs a troublous course comes to the young man, but the sympathy of the Commandant's wife, his "Mentor," tides him over his

discouragement. Underlying the romance is author's belief that the Service will work into an element making for the peace of all nations."
NYT 1914:557

005526   THE MASTER-MAN [ANONYMOUS]. New York and London: J. Lane, 1906 BMC NUC.

About a male physician in small town. BKM
PW--Story of male doctor; niece has 2 lovers, keeps house for uncle, chooses son of woman the doctor loves. He is also a doctor & becomes the "master-man." Written by a woman.
ATH O
BKM-sweet, clean, harmless

005527   THE POTTER AND THE CLAY. A ROMANCE OF TODAY. BY MAUD HOWARD PETERSON. Boston: Lothrop, [c1901] NUC. London: C. H. Kelly, 1901 BMC.

Girl trained among soldiers by a soldier; two men vie for her. NYT
ATH 11-2-01

005528   THE SANCTUARY. BY MAUD HOWARD PETERSON. Boston: Lothrop, Lee and Shepard, [c1912] NUC. London: A.F. Bird, [1912] BMC.

PW triangle.
NYT-of modern social interest, brotherhood keynote of story. Complicated love situation. Psych. study. Blair Martin, millionaire's daughter, learns her lesson about the problem of wealth and misery from Hector Stone, the evangelist of brotherhood. She goes to the island of the angels where Cecile Stone is chatelaine. TLS

HOOVER, BESSIE RAY. B. 1874. United States.

005529   OPAL. New York and London: Harper, 1910 BMC NUC.

Plain working folk, a dutiful daughter, etc. NYT Romantic story of a teacher. PW

005530   PA FLICKINGER'S FOLKS. New York and London: Harper, 1909 BMC NUC.

HOPE, ANDREE, pseud. See HARVEY, ANNIE JANE (TENNANT).

HOPE, ETHEL PENMAN. B. 1885. Canada.

005531   DR. PAUL. Toronto: McClelland, Goodchild & Stewart, [c1918] NUC. New York: G. W. Doran, 1919 PW.

Physician (male) gives up liquor-PW
Undesirable father-a drunkard who dies of it. His fiance (Virginia) assists him in the final grappling. BKM 10/19
A man suddenly turned woman hater lives a hermit's life; even women servants must remain unseen or lose their jobs. Women are not to be mentioned in his presence. Virginia Molson engaged to Dr. Paul. Both of their fathers are doctors and alcoholics. Dr. Paul drinks, injures and loses hand as consequence (end of surgical career). Feels she's failed him because she broke engagement on hearing he drank; he becomes hermit. She tries to win him back. Humor. NYT 9-28-19 504

005532   EYES OF THE LAW. Toronto: McClelland and Stewart, [1920] BMC NUC.

005533   A HILLSIDE CHRISTMAS; THE STORY OF A SMILING HEART. Toronto: McClelland, Goodchild and Stewart, [c1917] BMC NUC.

005534   THE WAYS OF THE HEART. London: Hodder and Stoughton, [1911] BMC.

HOPE, FLORA.

005535   ROSAMOND. London: Lynwood, [1912] BMC.

HOPE, FLORENCE.

005536   THE TWO POWERS. London: J. Long, 1910 BMC.

TLS-unhappy marriage- R. C.

HOPE, FRANCES ESSEX THEODORA. United Kingdom.

005537   SHEPHERDLESS SHEEP. BY ESSEX SMITH. London: T.F. Unwin, 1914 BMC [n.d.] NUC.

ACAD 86:430. Male hero, a man who falls into the position of being an orator for the League of Lonely Souls, and is immediately successful, but knows himself to be a hypocrite. Saved by a woman's love. Study of the lonely souls who haunt the lecture halls and streets of London in search of some new gospel. "Moving study of a lonely, tempted spinster."

005538   WIND ON THE HEATH. BY ESSEX SMITH. New York: J. Lane, 1912 NUC BMC.

About a clerk who turns gypsy 12-2-11 PW

HOPE, GRAHAM, pseud. See HOPE, JESSIE GRAHAM.

HOPE, JESSIE GRAHAM. United Kingdom.

005539   AMALIA. BY GRAHAM HOPE. London: Smith, Elder, 1907 BMC.

005540   A CARDINAL AND HIS CONSCIENCE. BY GRAHAM HOPE. London: Smith, Elder, 1901 BMC.

005541   THE GAGE OF RED AND WHITE. BY GRAHAM HOPE. London: Smith, Elder, 1904 BMC.

005542   THE HONOUR OF "X". BY GRAHAM HOPE. London: Smith, Elder, 1908 BMC.

BKM-Russian spy falls in love but cannot marry because of the Nihilist Inner Circle's denial of mrg to its members.
ATH "nest" (the woman) is likely to live happily ever after

005543   THE LADY OF LYTE. BY GRAHAM HOPE. London: Methuen, [1905] BMC NUC.

005544   MY LORD WINCHENDEN. BY GRAHAM HOPE. London: Smith, Elder, 1902 BMC.

005545   THE TRIUMPH OF COUNT OSTERMANN. BY GRAHAM HOPE. London: Smith, Elder, 1903 BMC. New York: H. Holt, 1903 NUC.

Hist novel TLS 104,02

HOPE, LILITH. Nationality Unknown.

005546   THE ANVIL. London: Chapman & Hall, 1914 BMC.

ATH-Career of pleasure-loving half English half Spanish girl who wants to be a famous dancer like her sister.
TLS Her regeneration, fell into white slave peril and escaped. Was governess, teacher also.

005547   BEHOLD AND SEE! London: Hurst & Blackett, 1917 BMC NUC.

Sister Rose-Eng. nun caught by German invasion in Belgium; conflict: her vocation and womanhood. Closes with "redemption" ? TLS
Raped by German; conflict between her vocation and her child. LBKM
Keeps her child and goes back to the world. ATH

005548   SIMOON. London: S. Swift, [1913] BMC.

1rst person narrative by a "neurotic" woman ATH
"a shallow selfish" woman keeps a school, quarrels with husband over her devotion to a declassee friend, "discovers her heart." Her husband dies; novel closes sadly. "Study not without poignancy and insight of neurotic femininity with its power to attract men side by side with its lack of balance without his protection." Miriam is the heroine TLS

HOPE, MARGARET.

005549   CHRISTINA HOLBROOK. London: Methuen, 1912 BMC.

TLS-Somber, marries a man younger than herself and is so afraid of its turning out badly that she helps it to happen.
ATH o

005550   LITTLE MRS. LEE. London: Methuen, [1915] BMC NUC.

clinging, alluring, selfish, without a soul but winning of all hearts especially male. Runs away from husband "good riddance" TLS

A hard working and serious minded lady secretary adopts this adventuress. ATH

005551   MESSENGERS. London: Methuen, 1914 BMC.

ATH-woman is sent to prison for stealing a ring. Unable to conceal guilt from daughter, and at the sight of d's misery, she runs away from home in vain hope that she may retrieve the past.
TLS Her miserable end on an open hillside, abandoned by friends and family. Unrelieved gloom.

005552   NINA AND HER COUSINS. London: Digby, Long, 1912 BMC.

HOPE, ZELMA, pseud. See GOULD, JENNIE W.

HOPKINS, ALICE (KIMBALL). B. 1839. United States.

005553   A DAUGHTER OF THE DRUIDS. BY A. K. H. Boston: [A. K. Mudge], 1892 BMC NUC.

PW-Alice deKymber has a love of astronomy. Her experiments lead her to be suspected of witchcraft. She must flee England, eventually meets a scientific man, romance.

005554   MONA THE DRUIDESS: OR, THE ASTRAL SCIENCE OF OLD BRITAIN. Boston: Eastern, 1904 NUC.

PW- Vindication of ancient ceremonial worship.

HOPKINS, LOUISE MARTIN. B. 1860. United States.

005555   SIGNAL-LIGHTS; A STORY OF LIFE ON THE PRAIRIES. Boston: C. M. Clark, 1906 NUC.

PW-old-fashioned historical novel about Indians, etc.

HOPKINS, MARGARET SUTTON (BRISCOE). B. 1864. United States.

005556   THE IMAGE OF EVE. A ROMANCE WITH ALLEVIATIONS. BY MARGARET SUTTON BRISCOE. New York and London: Harper, 1909 BMC NUC.

Typical romantic 11-13-09 PW

005557   LINKS IN A CHAIN. BY MARGARET SUTTON BRISCOE. New York: Dodd, Mead, 1893 NUC.

CR 21:374. Guardian-ward he marries her hoping she will love him eventually.
PW-Man's disinterested love for a selfish, heartless woman.

HOPKINS, MRS. HERBERT MUELLER. See CAVENDISH, PAULINE BRADFORD (MACKIE) HOPKINS.

HOPKINS, PAULINE ELIZABETH. United States.

005558   CONTENDING FORCES: A ROMANCE ILLUSTRATIVE OF NEGRO LIFE NORTH AND SOUTH. Boston: Colored Co-operative Pub. Co., 1900 NUC.

HOPKINS, UNA NIXON. Nationality Unknown.

005559   A WINTER ROMANCE IN POPPYLAND. Boston: R. G. Badger, 1911 NUC.

Love story with a misunderstanding that gets cleared up. PW 3-18-11.

HOPPIN, EMILY HOWLAND. United States.

005560   FROM OUT OF THE PAST: THE STORY OF A MEETING IN TOURAINE. New York: Dodd, Mead, [c1893] NUC. London: B. F. Stevens, [1893].

Successful artist, Allan Doane meets an old love-Margaret Rivers, recently widowed, and her beautiful daughter, Hester. They travel through the South of France. PW 5-13-93.
Does not know who he loves more. CR 20, 23:70.
"Story ends as it should" BOOK NOTES 130:459.

005561   UNDER THE CORSICAN. New York: J. S. Tait, [c1894] NUC.

Days of the French Empire, historical romance. LW 26:105.
Young inkeeper's daughter is party to plot against Napoleon. She's messenger for a group of spies. PW 2-2-95:266

HORN, KATE.

005562   BECAUSE OF PHOEBE. London: S. Paul, 1915
BMC.

Pretty tale Phoebe's relation to her mother and their
two love stories. TLS

005563   THE BRIDE OF LOVE. London: S. Paul,
[1912] BMC.

ATH-too awful to review or commend
LBKM-silly romance.

005564   COLUMBINE AT THE FAIR. London: S. Paul,
1913 BMC.

Country vicarage and its surroundings. Effie eldest
daughter wayward. Gets little sympathy from mother who
is jealous of her. Hugh her lover is faithful to the
end. The changes in Effie from selfishness to
maturity. ACAD
Returns home after seeking adventure in London,
returns under tragic circumstances. TLS

005565   THE CORONATION OF GEORGE KING: A
LINCOLNSHIRE IDYLL. London: S. Paul, [1911] BMC.

005566   EDWARD AND I AND MRS. HONEYBUN. A ROMANCE
OF MARRIED LIFE. 1910 NUC. London: S. Paul, 1910 BMC.

Romantic story of couple who adjust to loss of wealth
PW
TLS-romantic story of couple who adjust to loss of
wealth.
NYT impossible but readable, sent

005567   THE FLUTE OF ARCADY. London: S. Paul,
1914 BMC.

LBKM-romance.

005568   FRIVOLE. London: S. Paul, 1914 BMC. New
York: Brentano's, 1914 NUC.

ACAD 86:430. She is weaned by her parents away from a
Socialist who desires her money.

005569   HANDLEY'S CORNER. London: S. Paul, 1919
BMC.

Molly at the sea side watering place, the social
welter, married, etc. TLS
War setting traditional love story ATH

005570   THE LOVE-LOCKS OF DIANA. London: S. Paul,
[1911] BMC.

Diana Ponsonby, drudge work in boarding house to pay
father's debt, later "serves as a decoy in a beauty
shop"-dances there (?) and a villain and a true love.
LBKM

005571   LOVE'S LAW. London: S. Paul, 1916 BMC.

TLS-Suburban society, heroine surrounded by sordid
views and ambitions.
LBKM- Author wishes to reinforce belief in universal
motherhood .

005572   THE MULBERRIES OF DAPHNE. London: S.
Paul, [1910] BMC.

TLS- Daphne runs away from family and society to live
in a cottage. She was being sold into a marriage,
works as a housekeeper. Anti-Jewish?
A young woman runs away from Mayfair to try the simple
life, with astonishingly good results. SP

005573   SHIPS OF DESIRE. London: Cassell, 1908
BMC. New York: Cassell, 1909 NUC.

TLS-love story
ATH 25 and 35 yr old women loved by and love 32 yr old
man
Noble soldiers, love, jealousy PW 4-24 '09

005574   SUSAN AND THE DUKE. A MERE LOVE STORY.
London: S. Paul, 1912 BMC.

She is soft gentle, clinging type that the dukes
apparently admire. In contrast to her there is the
bold bad brilliant beautiful woman who tries to rob
Susan of the dukes. But Susan marries one at the end.
ATH Love Story.
TLS love story.

005575   THE WHITE OWL. London: S. Paul, [1911]
BMC.

fresh pleasant rustic TLS
ACAD Story divided between mother and daughter "mother
is supposed to be devoting herself exclusively to
novel writing" ATH
Demeter woman-famous writer, on her husband's death
hands her child Persephone over to an aunt takes up
residence in Sicily to devote herself exclusively to
her art ATH

005576   "WHO'S THAT A-CALLING?" London: S. Paul,
[1920] BMC NUC.

TLS-purpose to show evils of drug habit which shadows
lives of heroine under her mother's influence and of a
shell-shocked officer-until love triumphs.
LBKM-widowed mother has had her brought up in country
and then summons her to London. Her mother has a flat,
where drugs are used and holds Kitty prisoner there
until Anthony, the shell-shocked new drug taker helps
her escape.

HORSMAN, EDITH E.   Nationality Unknown.

005577   FIVE MINUTES' FOLLY; OR NEIGHBOURS THREE.
London: Jarrold, 1901 BMC.

005578   LISA'S AWAKENING; THE STORY OF A PSYCHE
OF TO-DAY. Edinburgh: W. P. Nimmo, [1905] BMC.

005579   THE TWO ALTHEAS: A HOME CHRONICLE.
London: Jarrold, 1896 BMC. Boston: Estes and Lauriat,
[c1897] NUC.

HORSWELL, MAUD.

005580   AN UNUSUAL ROMANCE. London: E. Stock,
1916 BMC.

TLS-Secret heir.

HORT, DORA.   Nationality Unknown.

005581   TIURI; A TAHITIAN ROMANCE. London: T. F.
Unwin, 1893 BMC NUC.

Seamy side of relations between Europeans and natives.
The heroines are "a little more advanced and
emancipated than the English girl Maud Field." One
Tahitian wife dies because of her husband's
domineering nature, and the young woman who began by
loving this man ended up in sympathy with Tiari, the
wife. ATH 102:768
ACAD 45:10. Tahiti. "degradation of native races at
the hands of their conquerors." whether the primitive
relations between the sexes are not, on the whole,
happier than...super-civilized communities. Tiari, a
half-caste loves frenchman Selwin, "a paragon of
virtue but..." He marries her, his "priggish
philistinism loses him his wife."

HOSIE, LILLIE C.

005582   THE ROBBER TROOPS OF CIRCUMSTANCES: A
NOVEL OF TO-DAY. London: H. J. Drane, [1900] BMC.

SR 89:816. Factory workers in a nitro-glycerine plant.
ATH 116:53. Scotland. Mean and tyrannical
administration. Two suicides, harrowing episodes.

HOSKEN, ALICE CECIL (SEYMOUR).   United Kingdom.

005583   THE ADVENTURESS. BY CORALIE STANTON. New
York: T. J. McBride, 1907 NUC.

This ex-cafe singer marries rich banker; he kills
self; she's very rich; we follow her amazing career of
crime; gets men to work for her when they can't repay
loans PW 3-23-07

HOSKINS, BERTHA LADD.   United States.

005584   THE DOUBLE FORTUNE. New York: Neale, 1909
NUC.

Traditional detective 5-8-09 PW

HOTCHKISS, LOUISE SARAH.   United States.

005585   THEIR OWN WEDDING. Boston: G. H. Ellis,
1900 NUC.

HOUCHEN, M. A.

005586   CASTLE LACY; OR, FAMILY PORTRAITS IN PEN
AND PENCIL; AN UNCONVENTIONAL CHRONICLE. London:
Digby, Long, [1895] BMC.

HOUGHTON, BEATRICE YORK. United States.

005587   THE SHELLEYS OF GEORGIA. Boston: Lothrop,
Lee & Shepard, [1917] NUC.

Rose Shelley learns that her fiance has seduced a poor
mountain girl. She tries to make him understand his
obligation toward Minnie. Even secretly educates
Minnie so she'll be suitable as a wife. The man comes
to love Minnie; Rose marries another. PW

HOUGHTON, LOUISE (SEYMOUR). 1838-1920. United States.

005588   THE CRUISE OF THE MYSTERY IN MCALL
MISSION WORK. New York: American Tract Society,
[c1891] NUC.

The mystery is a mission boat. Story written to aid
building of such a boat for mission work on French
rivers.

HOUGHTON, LUCILE WAND (CAPLINGER). B. 1881. United States.

005589   A VENTURE IN IDENTITY. Garden City, N.Y.:
Doubleday, Page, 1911 NUC.

Justine becomes engaged with the proviso that four
years elapse before the wedding. Her fiance returns to
Montana; she stays on the continent. She loses her
memory; meets a man who looks like the portrait of her
fiance. NYT

HOUK, ELIZA PHILLIPS THRUSTON. 1833-1914. United States.

005590   LOUISA VARENA; OR LOVE'S RECOMPENSE.
[Dayton, Ohio]: [U. B. Publishing House], [c1905] NUC.

Christian Science problems.

HOUMAS, MOUNT, pseud. See GILL, MARY (GILL).

HOUSMAN, CLEMENCE ANNIE. United Kingdom.

005591   THE UNKNOWN SEA. London: Duckworth, 1898
BMC NUC.

005592   THE WEREWOLF. London: J. Lane, 1896 BMC
NUC. Chicago: Way and Williams, 1896 NUC.

LBKM -man saved from female werewolf by brother at
expense of his own death.
BKM 3:68. Miss Housman. Man saves his brother from
werewolf woman at expense of his own life.

HOUSTON, MARGARET BELL. United States.

005593   THE LITTLE STRAW WIFE. New York: H. F.
Fly, [1914] NUC.

HOUSTOUN, MATILDA CHARLOTTE (JESSE) FRASER. 1815?-1892.
United Kingdom.

005594   THE WAY SHE WON HIM. A NOVEL. London: F.
V. White, 1891 BMC NUC.

She's a music hall singer. Mystery of her parentage
solved; she marries and her marriage is tame. ACAD
She's illegitimate. The way she wins him is that he
falls in love with her. Ettie Cranston singer at
Coventry Music Hall and Charlie Alston, officer. Older
man tries to get her as his mistress. Ettie turns out
to be daughter of this older man's wife. (I assume
she's his second wife though the reviewer doesn't
say.) Ettie does accept a large inheritance from this
older man. SR 2-21-91, 232

HOWARD, BLANCHE WILLIS. See VON TEUFFEL, BLANCHE WILLIS
(HOWARD).

HOWARD, CONSTANCE ELEANORA CAROLINE AND ADA FIELDER KING.

005595   MASTER OF HER LIFE. London: F. V. White,
1891 BMC.

Stella Lancaster loves in her youth, but aunt drives
her and lover apart, she weds a Russian artist and
learns slowly to love him very much. All the while
she's pursued by a Grand Duke who hunts her everywhere
and tries to ruin the husband. But he gets his in the
end. ACAD
A thin sensational story. ATH 9858
Takes place in Russia. The Grand Duke is shattered to

pieces in an explosion. SR 10-17-91, 450

HOWARD, ISABEL.

005596   WOUNDED PRIDE. London: J. Long, 1899 BMC.

Young woman resents the conduct of her fiance before
they were married. He had loved another woman. ACAD
57:541
"Happy weddings with the pluming and preening of self
congratulatory brides." ATH 114:755

HOWARD, MABEL HARRIET (MACDONNELL).

005597   THE FAILURE OF SUCCESS. BY LADY MABEL
HOWARD. New York: Longmans, 1901 PW. London: Longmans,
1901 BMC NUC.

Holds onto fortune not her own. Her mind of interest.
12-14-01 ATH

005598   AN IRISH HOME. London: Longmans, Green,
1920 NUC BMC.

005599   THE UNDOING OF JOHN BREWSTER. London:
Longmans, 1899 BMC NUC.

Jilted, broken hearted, wrecked in faith and in
mind--all because he fell in love with an Italian
Roman Catholic woman. LIT 5:6 25
LBKM 17:154. Carmella is torn between church and John,
finally choosing church which undoes him.
PW. He develops religiously and joins the church.
(Rome)

HOWARD, MAUDE LESSEUER. United States.

005600   MYRIAM AND THE MYSTIC BROTHERHOOD. New
York: J. W. Lovell, [c1912] NUC.

Story of the occult, 3-20-15 BKM

HOWARTH, ANNA. South Africa.

005601   JAN: AN AFRIKANDER. London: Smith, Elder,
1897 NUC BMC.

He commits suicide. His friends remember him well.
ACAD 52 Fic Sup 92.
Jan Vermaak, an Eng. father & Kaffir mother,
nonetheless an heir to an estate and title in England.
ATH 110:669.

005602   KATRINA: A TALE OF THE KARROO. London:
Smith, Elder, 1898 NUC BMC.

SP 81:744. South Africa, the Dutch. Brother takes up
his brother's responsibilities, even marrying his
swindled and jilted fiancee. They grow to love each
other; his father grows to appreciate his true worth.
ACAD 55:515.
ATH 112:861. Katrina's development from a girl to an
earnest, helpful woman.

005603   NORA LESTER. London: Smith, Elder, 1902
BMC.

ATH 3-29-02 study of relations between Dutch and
English in South Africa.

005604   SWORD AND ASSEGAI. London: Smith, Elder,
1899 BMC.

Historical romance of the Kaffir wars of the 1830s.
LIT 5:546
S. Africa. Struggle of Eastern Province farmers
against their savage neighbors. True S.A. life on farm
and veldt. SR 88 Nov. 4 Supplement, iii
Historical: Kaffir Wars of 19th c. BAKER 03,241
LBKM 17:122. South Africa, from Kaffir outbreak in
1834 to 1850's. Fortunes of Brownlou and Farrer
families, adjacent farms.

HOWE, CORA E. United States.

005605   THE PILGRIMS' CHRISTMAS. Sandy Creek,
N.Y.: News Book Print, 1899 NUC.

HOWE, FRANCES S. B. 1842.

005606   14,000 MILES, A CARRIAGE AND TWO WOMEN.
[Fitchburg]: Private printing [Sentinel Print. Co.],
1906 NUC.

Drives through N.E. 3-2-07
"Reports of an unbroken series of annual drives

through New England, NY and Canada". Written for
Boston Evening Transcript and Leominster Daily
Enterprise.

HOWE, MAUD. See ELLIOTT, MAUD (HOWE).

HOWE, SUSAN HOWARD (JEWETT). B. 1872. United States.

    005607   KATE FORD'S FAMILY. Cincinnati: Editor
    Pub. Co., 1899 NUC.

HOWELL, CONSTANCE.

    005608   CHESTER CHASE. London: Everett, 1914 BMC.

    ATH - Hero and three heroines. At close he has been
    discarded by all three. One has become an imprisoned
    suffragette, another wife of a baronet.

    005609   COY, A NOVEL. London: Digby, Long, 1903
    BMC.

    005610   MANY DAYS AFTER. A NOVEL. London: Digby,
    Long, 1900 BMC.

    ATH 116:342. Gloomy story. Two men independently
    contemplate suicide, one murders the other and kills
    himself after the marriage of their children to each
    other.

    005611   MARRIED IN INDIA: A STORY OF ANGLO INDIAN
    LIFE IN THE SIXTIES. London: Ouseley, [1910] BMC.

    BM love one for all time is the theme.
    ACAD o
    ATH o

    005612   MRS. CHARTERIS. London: J. Ouseley,
    [1911] BMC.

    injustice and unwisdon of divorce laws TLS
    Mrs. C. deserted by her husband goes thru a form of
    marriage with another man who discovering the
    deception, leaves her. POV ATH

HOWELL, JEANNE M. United States.

    005613   A COMMON MISTAKE. New York: Merriam,
    [1892] NUC.

    PW-aims to show the corrupt morals of society, tragic
    conclusion. Heroine desires much admiration, expects
    suitors to be constant.
    LW 25:219. Headstrong girl chooses as her life's motto
    "Je m'amuse." Recounts girlhood days of frivolity,
    social distractions, forever unsatisfied until she
    lies dead from an overdose of chloral.

HOWELL, MARY HUBBARD. Nationality Unknown.

    005614   IN ONE GIRL'S EXPERIENCE. Philadelphia:
    American Sunday School Union, [c1891] NUC.

    Honor, trained in a fashionable finishing school, is
    orphaned at age 18 and completely incapable of earning
    her own living. Finally finds a home where she can be
    useful. PW 10-24-91.

    005615   ON LONEMAN'S ISLAND. Philadelphia:
    American Sunday School Union, [c1897] NUC.

    Lighthouse on the island. Father its keeper, mother
    and Bethia hungering for a change. Young man sick with
    smallpox comes on a boat with parents who plead for
    shelter. PW 52:819

HOWLAND, FRANCES LOUISE (MORSE). 1855-1944. United States.

    005616   CLIVEDEN. BY KENYON WEST. Boston:
    Lothrop, [1903] NUC.

HOY, MARY LAVINIA THOMPSON. Nationality Unknown.

    005617   ADRIENNE. BY MRS. FRANK L. HOY. New York:
    Neale, 1906 NUC.

    "A southern story of Civil War days in which the fair
    play-day world is transformed for a group of
    irresponsible Southern girls into a dreary world of
    waiting & anxiety." BRD

HOY, MRS FRANK L. See HOY, MARY LAVINIA THOMPSON.

HOYER, MARIA A.

    005618   GOOD DAME FORTUNE. London: Hurst and

Blackett, 1894 NUC BMC.

    SR 77:203. Romance, younger hero and heroine, 2 kindly
    older people.
    SP 72:799. Wealthy middle-aged bachelor in search of
    his family.
    ATH-a happy romance.

    005619   WHAT HAPPENED AT MORWYN. London: Digby,
    Long, [1893] BMC.

    A tear jerker. SR 76:711
    A bank fails and brings disgrace, ruin and death. ATH
    102:731.
    SP 72:58. Heroine pays off dead father's debts by
    illustrating botanical works.
    ACAD 45:10. "Painter of specimen flowers". "Distances
    all rivals at her work."

HOYT, ELEANOR. See BRAINERD, ELEANOR (HOYT).

HUARD, FRANCES (WILSON). B. 1885. United States.

    005620   LILIES WHITE AND RED. New York: G.H.
    Doran, [c1919] NUC.

    Two stories of life in France NYT
    One has to do with old woman who leads a most quiet
    life till the war and her great act of heroism for
    France. The other about a little boy who sees the
    horrors of the war that Germans are capable of. NYT
    5-25-19 295

HUDSON, HELEN.

    005621   FLAMES IN THE WIND. London: Hodder and
    Stoughton, [1918] BMC.

    LBKM male, adventure in Australia.

HUDSPETH, ROSA. United States.

    005622   IN THE MARKET PLACES: A FEW CHAPTERS
    CONCERNING CAROLYN ANSELM'S JOURNALISTIC CAREER.
    Omaha, Neb.: Douglas Print, 1900 NUC.

    005623   THE JUGGERNAUT OF THE MODERNS: A NOVEL.
    Boston: Arena, 1896 NUC.

    PW 10-17-96. "The author desires to impress the theory
    of but one standard of morals for men and for women.
    She illustrates her idea by the story of a beautiful
    and unprotected stenographer in a law firm in the
    rural west."

HUESTON, ETHEL (POWELSON). B. 1887. United States.

    005624   EVE TO THE RESCUE. Indianapolis:
    Bobbs-Merrill, [c1920] BMC NUC. London: Hutchinson,
    [1927] BMC.

    PW-Hated duty, helped others by convincing them they
    shouldn't act out of a sense of duty. adventures,
    light wholesome girl, peacemaker.

    005625   LEAVE IT TO DORIS. Indianapolis:
    Bobbs-Merrill, [c1919] BMC NUC. London: Methuen, 1920
    BMC.

    TLS

    005626   PRUDENCE OF THE PARSONAGE. Indianapolis:
    Bobbs-Merrill, [c1915] BMC NUC. London: E. Nash, 1916
    BMC.

    Jolly, wholesome story. The Book rev PW Aug 15
    One of the "girliest girls of fiction" NYT

    005627   PRUDENCE SAYS SO. Indianapolis:
    Bobbs-Merrill, [c1916] NUC BMC. London: Hodder and
    Stoughton, 1917 BMC.

    "Five daughters of Methodist parson who managed to get
    a great deal of enjoyment out of life for themselves
    and others. Romances for all young people." PW 90:686
    9/2/16
    NYT-for young girls.
    LBKM - dom. romance.
    Plenty of wholesome good spirits and sent and smoothly
    running love affairs TLS

    005628   SUNNY SLOPES. Indianapolis:
    Bobbs-Merrill, [c1917] NUC BMC. London: Skeffington,
    [1918] BMC.

    Minister and wife in St. Louis he gets TB-they move to

New Mexico. wife's sister Connie is a reporter PW
Two sisters: Carol fights for her husband's life.
"Struggles to keep from acquiring a lord and master."
BKM
NYT 326, 9-2-17
TLS-brave life of dying minister

HUGHES, DOROTHEA PRICE.

005629   TOWARDS THE LIGHT. A NOVEL. London:
Hodder and Stoughton, 1906 BMC.

TLS-Young woman loves artist, misunderstanding, he
marries another. years later, now a widow, she nurses
his wife, whose alcoholism has forced him to leave
her. Religious motif.

HUGHES, MRS. REGINALD. United States.

005630   SYBIL TREVYLLIAN. BY LYNDON (MRS.
REGINALD HUGHES). New York: Ward and Drummond, [c1892]
NUC.

PW-Sybil loses her father whom she idolizes; her
brother loses woman he loves to soldier. Sybil devotes
her life to helping others; is the means of bringing
happiness to soldier's widow and her child. "not
intended for very young readers."

HUGUENIN, ADELE. B. 1856. France.

005631   JONQUILLE; OR, THE SWISS SMUGGLER. BY T.
COMBE. London: Percival, 1891 BMC. (Tr. Beatrix L.
Tollemache)

NATION 145:401. Manuel is hero, meets Jonquille after
he takes to smuggling. She is called the captain of a
band of smugglers. They marry, but the same
restlessness which led Manuel to smuggling affects him
again, ending is tragic.
Jonquille is the wife of Manuel, a man who smuggles
tobacco between Switzerland and France. He's a
successful smuggler, but a poor husband. SR 12-26-91,
728

005632   A QUESTION OF LOVE, A STORY OF
SWITZERLAND. BY T. COMBE. Boston: Roberts, 1891 NUC.
(Tr. Annie R. Ramsey)

Pretty love tale set in Switzerland. Zoe grows up with
two aged men and old aunt. Love comes. PW 3-23-91.
Cousin sees she needs company her own age. Invites his
cousins. Zoe becomes engaged to one but love waits for
there's another suitor. LW

HULING, CAROLINE A.

005633   LETTERS OF A BUSINESS WOMAN TO HER NIECE.
New York: R.F. Fenno, [c1906] NUC.

Letters on clothing, relations of men and women in
offices.

HULL, E. M. See HULL, EDITH MAUDE.

HULL, EDITH MAUDE. United Kingdom.

005634   THE SHEIK; A NOVEL. BY E. M. HULL.
London: E. Nash, [1919] BMC NUC. Boston: Small,
Maynard, [1921] BMC NUC.

Diana Mayo--meant to be a boy--brought up and dressed
as one by much older brother. willful, headstrong,
meets her match in the sheik (she and brother, they
travel to Algeria) who kidnaps her. She hates the
taming process. End? TLS

HUME, ETHEL DOUGLAS.

005635   THE MULTIPLICITIES OF UNA. Edinburgh and
London: W. Blackwood, 1911 BMC.

Girl's visit to Malaya and her multiple loves. TLS

HUMPHREY, MRS. FRANK POPE. United States.

005636   PHOEBE TILSON. Chicago: Rand, McNally,
[c1898] NUC. London: Ward, Lock, 1898 BMC. (BMC: Frank
Hope Humphrey [pseud.].)

LW 29:455. She is jilted at the altar; dismisses her
guests and is solitary for months. Regenerated by the
other woman's child "who happens to her house."

HUMPHREY, ZEPHINE. See FAHNESTOCK, HARRIETTE ZEPHINE
(HUMPHREY).

HUMPHREYS, DEAN, pseud. See HARPER, SARAH JANE.

HUMPHREYS, ELIZA MARGARET J. (GOLLAN). D. 1938. United
Kingdom.

005637   ASENATH OF THE FORD, A ROMANCE OF RED
EARTH COUNTRY. BY "RITA". London: Griffith, Farran,
[1892] BMC. New York: J. A. Taylor, [1892] NUC.

ATH 100:813. Romance. Diary form. Unfortunate loves of
women in family, Asenath is more fortunate.
Lugubrious story. when nothing dreadful is happening,
the heroine asks herself "what next misfortune is to
befall us?" There's a ghost and a wise woman, a
runaway horse, a runaway woman, a runaway girl, storm
at sea, many many deaths, misunderstandings and
wickednesses. SR 1-28-93,100
Asenath ends up happily in love. ACAD 43:170

005638   BETTY BRENT, TYPIST. BY "RITA". London:
T.W. Laurie, [1908] BMC.

TLS-Secretary spends weekend in country house with
society. Simple minded heroine.
Simplistic story of good Betty among bad people LBKM

005639   CALVARY. A TRAGEDY OF SECTS. BY "RITA".
London: Hutchinson, 1909 BMC.

religious novel about a peasant TLS

005640   THE COUNTESS PHARAMOND; A SEQUEL TO
"SHEBA." BY RITA. New York: U. S. Book, [c1891] NUC.
London: F. V. White, 1893 BMC.

She's a soc. leader in Paris. At one of her receptions
Paul Meredith an old acquaintance is the indirect
cause of trag. and sensational incidences. PW 1-14-93
Sheba Ormatroyd passes through three vols. of
"unmitigated misery" until she's utterly happy as the
Countess Pharamond on the last page. SR 75, 488.
Marries a man who moves from being an opera singer to
an Earl, includes a poisoning and a suicide. ACAD
43:390
"The atrocities of Mr. Mixon the publisher." sequel to
"Sheba" Countess is foil to Sheba. Countess wicked,
cold. Sheba's successful novel condemned by the
leading critical journal on the strength of a few
botannical errors that have nothing to do with plot
style, char." ATH 101, 406

005641   DIANA OF THE EPHESIANS: A NOVEL. BY
"RITA". London: S. Low Marsten,, [1919] BMC NUC. New
York: F.A. Stokes, [c1920] NUC.

A Professor acknowledges his daughter born of a Greek
woman brings her to England. She's "ugly" in face and
form arrogant, loathed by all, upsets the country
house. (17 yrs old) announces she's writing the
greatest novel, plays Bach. "Impossible and
breathlessly melodramatic career" TLS
PW-Woman's struggle for fame and position.

005642   EDELWEISS. BY "RITA". London: S. Paul,
[1912] BMC.

005643   THE ENDING OF MY DAY, THE STORY OF A
STORMY LIFE. BY RITA, AUTHOR OF "SHEBA" "THE COUNTESS
PHARAMOND" "MISS KATE" "ASENATH OF THE FORD". London:
F. V. White, 1894 NUC BMC.

SR 77:446. Belle Ffolliott, extracts from her journal.
Belle's comments on Society, folly and immorality. She
marries, and "though innocent in the narrowest sense
of the word, is publicly and disgracefully divorced."
Marries the correspondent, Latin and Greek were
tolerably familiar to her.
ACAD 45:367. "She was quite innocent of anything worse
than taking up with certain fads of the women's rights
kind."
ATH 103:342.

005644   A GENDER IN SATIN. BY "RITA". London: T.
F. Unwin, [1895] BMC. New York: G. P. Putnam's Sons,
1895 NUC.

A wicked woman who wears charming negligees, a wicked
man, a pure woman, a humble husband.SR79:733
An ambitious doctor who uses women to get on with his
career. Thinks of all women as a gender in Satin.
Grantley Dering's (the doctor) best friend Christopher
Hope, an artist, loves a young woman who does not love
him. But he marries knowing this. Later Paula the wife
meets Grantly and comes under his spell. She confesses
to her husband who is noble enough to rise to the

occasion and "to wait" till she can release herself
from Grantley's power.CR. 24:132 SP 76:746. Paula,
married, falls for fin-de-siecle doctor, also married,
selfish and cynical. Paula's fine husband saves her
from herself and story closes with the hope that she
will come to love as well as respect him.

005645   GOOD MRS. HYPOCRITE. A STUDY IN
SELF-RIGHTEOUSNESS. BY "RITA". London: Hutchinson,
1897 BMC 1899 NUC. New York: F. M. Buckles, 1899 NUC.

Catherine McPherson is self righteous. Other
characters are her brother James, niece Margaret, a
Scot servant, and Tibble Minch. LW 30:279
An uncongenial maiden aunt as useful companion,
deaconess, scripture reader; grotesque matrimonial
aspiration, pilfering to catastrophe of overturned
lamp. ACAD 52 Fic Sup 66
Catherine Macpherson a religious hypocrite. Scotch, in
dialect. A very negative picture. ATH 110:286

005646   A GREY LIFE, A ROMANCE OF MODERN BATH.
London: S. Paul, 1913 BMC.

Three uneventful years in a girl's life; Rosaleen Le
Suir tells her story TLS

005647   GRIM JUSTICE. THE STUDY OF A CONSCIENCE.
London: G. Nash, 1912 BMC.

TLS-male hero non-conformist.
ATH male hero

005648   "HALF A TRUTH." BY "RITA". London:
Hutchinson, 1911 BMC.

the fashionable set, etc. TLS
Father, daughter, stepdaughter the fashionalbe set,
etc. travel ATH

005649   THE HOUSE CALLED HURRISH. BY RITA.
London: Hutchinson, 1909 BMC.

Lady Moonrake is a morphia addict who dies. TLS
Her companion Judith Sarsefield is the heroine. Style:
three forms: (1) narrative (2) diary of heroine (3)
diary of hero SP

005650   THE HOUSE OPPOSITE. BY "RITA". London: E.
Nash, 1912 BMC.

005651   A HUSBAND OF NO IMPORTANCE. BY RITA.
London: T.F. Unwin, 1894 BMC. New York: G. P. Putnam's
Sons, 1894 NUC.

ACAD 46:372. Wife is a novelist with the purpose of
reforming society, neglects her house and husband, who
she thinks is insignificant. He writes a play which
holds her up to scorn; she bursts into tears and
renounces all her "new-womanish" ways.
LBKM 7:26. Rita is attempting satire but is not
successful, satirization of the modern woman.
Anti-semitic jibes.

005652   THE INK-SLINGER. London: S. Paul, 1915
BMC.

Attack on publishing business. Hero is the center TLS

005653   THE IRON STAIR: A ROMANCE OF DARTMOOR. BY
"RITA" (MRS. DESMOND HUMPHREYS). New York and London:
G.P. Putnam's Sons, 1916 BMC NUC.

Geoffrey serving sentence for his brother's crime.
Renee, wife of real forger helps Geoffrey escape.
Renee's marriage has been a tragedy. PW 1/29/16: 343
NYT-male adv.
TLS

005654   THE JESTERS. BY "RITA". London:
Hutchinson, 1903 BMC.

Brief desc. ACAD 65, 328
Soul for mischief and a genius for plotting ACAD 65,
442
Lady Betty tries an experiment with a man but reviewer
won't say what it is?LBKM 11-03, 104
Titled lady of easy virtue ATH 122, 610

005655   JILL-ALL-ALONE. London: S. Paul, 1914
BMC.

ACAD 86:691. Jill grew up alone in the woods, a free
spirit. then the squire desires her, he is foiled, but
Jill dies.

005656   A JILT'S JOURNAL; A NOVEL. BY "RITA".
London: T. Unwin, 1901 BMC. New York: A. L. Burt,
[1902] NUC.

heroine confides her views on men discovers a volume
of mother's letters (mother is unknown to her). they
greatly influence her.Does she follow her mother's way
as a heartbreaker? ATH 10-5-01

005657   JOAN AND MRS. CARR. BY "RITA". London: F.
V. White, 1896 BMC.

SR-Mrs. Carr is a mondaine who comes into 5,000 a
year.
ATH 107:616. Sir Anthony is attracted to her rather
than the 18 yr old Joan, much to his aunt's distress.
Irish.
ACAD 49:506. She has a "dark passage in her early
life". Joan comes to live with her a noble character.
"There is occasionally a gleam of humor, as where the
author describes the proceedings of an advanced
woman's club." It seems Mrs. Carr may be Joan's
mother.

005658   KITTY THE RAG. BY "RITA". London:
Hutchinson, 1896 NUC BMC. New York: R. F. Fenno,
[c1897] NUC.

She's selfish and cruel as a child and ambitious. At 8
she has every one doing her bidding. She's opposite
her mother Hermia, Lady Ellingsworth. (father was a
peasant.). Hermia is cold and proud, forced to marry a
commonplace noble. She was away from Ireland for yrs.
Returns and everything reminds her of the trag of her
youth.-the peasant. ATH 109:146.
ACAD 50:594. Like Peg the Rake.

005659   THE LAIRD O' COCKPEN. A NOVEL. BY "RITA".
London: F.V. White, 1891 NUC BMC. New York: United
States Book, [1891] NUC.

Athole Lindsey comes to Scotland, she's Scottish by
birth. We get her reactions, descriptions, of
Inverness and Oban. We meet the Laird and Athole's
cousins. In Scotland dialect. ATH 97 470
Scottish penniless lass courted and abandoned by
careless lover. The virtuous Laird weds her. Then when
Laird her husband supposed dead, she realizes she
loves him and rejects the lover's attention. LW
Athole is her name, sensitive, impressionable; then
her husband "returns from the dead." ACAD
The lover also involved with Dora, the siren.
Athole Lindsay and Douglas Hay-both keep diaries. SR
5-19-91, 596

005660   LIE CIRCUMSPECT. London: Hutchinson, 1902
BMC.

ATH 6-7-02 not helpful

005661   THE MAKE-BELIEVERS. BY "RITA". London: S.
Low, 1920 BMC.

TLS male hero

005662   THE MAN IN POSSESSION. BY "RITA". New
York: Hovendon, [1891] NUC. London: F. V. White, 1893
BMC.

Tom Rivers, a woman hater, before he meets Kate
O'Brien. He's rich, a reformer. She is a gifted
actress with a beautiful voice. The rival is a rake.
SR 76,18.
LW 23:279. English house party. High-spirited Kate,
romance.
PW-Identifies author as Mrs. Otto Booth. Love story
involving father and daughter whose house is being
taken for back taxes.

005663   A MAN OF NO IMPORTANCE. BY "RITA".
London: Hurst & Blackett, 1907 BMC.

005664   THE MASQUERADERS. BY "RITA". London:
Hutchinson, 1904 BMC.

ATH-pair of poverty-stricken musical friends take
disguise, gain fame and money.
TLS pair of men.

005665   MASTER WILBERFORCE; A STUDY OF A BOY. BY
"RITA". London: Hutchinson, 1895 BMC. New York: G. P.
Putnam's Sons, 1895 NUC.

Professor and mild wife have different ways of raising
their son, who nevertheless turns out ok. But when he
falls in love with a young unsuitable woman, the

father interferes. The young woman dies as a result
and the boy's spirit is destroyed. At this point the
professor says "I believe in mothers." CR. 24:408
Professor believes a child should be raised without
restraints. Theory tested on their son and on an
adopted daughter. Couple's name: Wilberforce. PW
7-27-95:140
ACAD 49:74. Study of a child of quick intelligence,
his relationship with a stray Gypsy boy, not for
children.

005666   NAUGHTY MRS. GORDON. A ROMANCE OF
SOCIETY. BY RITA. London: F. V. White, 1894 BMC.

005667   AN OLD ROGUE'S TRAGEDY. BY RITA. London:
Hutchinson, 1899 BMC.

Natural and simple Molly Ronayne and Aunt Patricson.
LIT 4:665
Aunt Patricson is the old rogue. LBKM 16:113

005668   ONLY AN ACTRESS. BY "RITA". London: S.
Paul, [1911] BMC.

005669   PEG, THE RAKE. BY "RITA". London:
Hutchinson, 1894 BMC. [New York]: [P. F. Collier],
1895 NUC.

SP 73:923. Light reading. Bohemian elements. Peg is a
wild Irish girl type but is a woman of 40.
ATH 104:824. "The indignation she displays in the
matter of her jewels may be condoned, but the
unwomanly taunt on her tyrant's childlessness goes far
to reconcile the reader to the bitterness of fortune
which shortens her life." Peg's ill-starred marriage
with Sir Jasper Lustrell is elaborate in its detail of
self-infed suffering
Heroine is mid-aged, single. She is vulgar, loud,
undignified, yet neither uninteresting nor unloveable.
Sympathetic portrayal. SR 79:22.
Irish, Miss Emilia O'Hara, 40. Very lively with a
mysterious past. A thorough woman of the world,
clever, well educated. Proves more than a match to
stepmother her father hoped would tame her whims and
escapades. She does eventually marry, to escape the
annoyance of her home. But she's miserable. To get her
free, author reveals her secret marriage of twenty
years earlier which Emilia didn't know about! ACAD
47:53

005670   PETTICOAT LOOSE. A NOVEL. BY RITA.
London: Hutchinson, 1898 BMC.

LIT 3:605. Heroine is successful on stage. Novel is
named after racehorse that figures in 1st and last
chapters.
ACAD 55:157. Brianna loved late. Men only succeeded in
impressing the tedious idiocy of their sex upon the
indifference of her own. Three lovers persevered. In
the end one is dead, the other is dying, and the third
is taking her for a walk.
ATH 112:709. The villain exercised hypnotic influence
on her, culminating in downright rape, morbid and
unpleasant.

005671   THE PHILANTHROPIC BURGLAR. London:
Odhams, [1919] BMC.

Trad detective ATH
A "travestied" male detective LBKM

005672   THE POINTING FINGER. BY "RITA". London:
E. Nash, 1907 BMC NUC.

plot and incident brief description LBKM 3-07, 278

005673   PRINCE CHARMING. A FANTASTIC EPISODE IN
COURT DRESS. BY "RITA". London: Sands, 1901 BMC.

7-27-1 ATH

005674   QUEER LADY JUDAS. BY "RITA". London:
Hutchinson, 1905 BMC NUC.

Vanity of modern woman TLS 115, 05

005675   THE RUBBISH HEAP. BY "RITA" (MRS. DESMOND
HUMPHREYS). New York and London: G.P. Putnam's Sons,
1917 BMC NUC.

Complicated plot ties male recluse, two Victorian
"maiden ladies" their nephew recently from France, the
stray farm child he brought with him, an old second
hand shop and an unexpected romance. NYT 5-20-17 202
Trad romance complications PW
Two "old maids" upset by nephew's art BKM

TLS Romance but not love

005676   SABA MACDONALD. BY "RITA". London: Hurst
& Blackett, 1906 BMC.

TLS-Young girl's education in the 50's, cramped and
confining.

005677   THE SILENT WOMAN. BY "RITA". London:
Hutchinson, 1904 BMC.

Dr. Quarn is sapping the life of his invalid wife with
the medicine he prescribes. Sounds sensational LBKM
223, v. 27-8

005678   THE SIN OF JASPER STANDISH. BY "RITA".
London: A. Constable, 1901 BMC 1902 NUC. New York: R.
F. Fenno, 1902 NUC.

005679   THE SINNER. BY "RITA". London:
Hutchinson, 1897 BMC. Chicago: [c1897] NUC.

The patient and hospital nurse and the rich uncle from
Colo. arriving just in time. Doctor poisons wife.
Nellie Nugent is the wife's nurse. ACAD 52 Fic Sup
101.
The doctor has a weakness for women. Ruins several;
marries for money, then proceeds to kill her off so he
can marry another. Routine of hospital life well
described. Deborah Gray is also a nurse. The wife who
dies is Mrs. Langrishe. ATH 110:878 Ireland.
LW 29:124. Two trained nurses are heroines. Ex-lover
of one is a villainous doctor who poisons his wife.

005680   SOULS: A COMEDY OF INTENTIONS. BY "RITA".
New York: Brentano's, 1903 NUC. London: Hutchinson,
1903 BMC NUC.

novel of smart set. caustic attack on society as
rotten at the core. NYT 845,03

005681   VANITY! THE CONFESSIONS OF A COURT
MODISTE. BY RITA. London: T. F. Unwin, 1900 BMC NUC.
New York: F. M. Buckles, 1900 NUC.

SP 85:665. Narration of a Court dressmaker.

005682   A WOMAN IN IT. A SKETCH OF FEMININE
MISADVENTURE. BY "RITA". London: Hutchinson, 1895 BMC.
Philadelphia: J. B. Lippincott, 1895 NUC.

PW 12-5-96. Nina Garbett, volatile Irish girl, tells
in diary, her successes, failures as a companion to a
woman of rank and in other business and social
ventures. She goes by name of Mrs. Noel Grace because
of her part in sensational divorce proceedings.
Begins in the Divorce Court where the decision goes
against her. She's left without income and reputation.
Gets help from a woman who keeps a boarding house--a
job as companion to invalid woman. But this woman's
husband goes mad for Nina and kills off his wife.
Things get rough there, so Nina leaves and becomes a
kind of beauty products demonstrator. Somewhere along
the line she deserts another young man who loves her.
SR 80:587
Nina Garbett. Ends with Bertha Planefield who tells
her: "Where our sisters are friendless, desperate,
forsaken--there, Nina lies our country and our work."
ACAD 48:408
She's an Irish dare-devil, lonely and unscrupulous.
Very sympathetic. Bertha is her rich breezy American
good angel. ATH 106:381
A divorcee whose early life was a series of
misadventures; who meets a good man she protects from
herself, and later a pure friendship enters her life.
LW 28:279
SR-offends propriety, but good purpose. "No one,
certainly, will feel any desire to imitate the career
of the adventuress, whom she describes. And though her
Noel Gray seems as little likely as any human being to
give help to the friendless, desperate, forsaken of
her sex, it was at least a laudable ambition.

005683   A WOMAN OF SAMARIA. BY "RITA". London:
Hutchinson, 1900 BMC.

LIT 6:372. Vicar's daughter betrayed and abandoned,
obliged to flee home. Her career in the world, stage
life.

HUMPHREYS, ELIZA MARGARET J. (GOLLAN) AND LOUISA ALICE
BAKER.

005684   LOOKING-GLASS HOURS. BEING THE TRUE AND
FAITHFUL REFLECTIONS OF TWO FEMININE MINDS-WHAT LED
THEREUNTO-AND THE RESULT THEREOF. BY "RITA" AND

"ALIEN". London: Hutchinson, 1899 NUC BMC.

Letters: gradual estrangement and final reconciliation of a husband and wife. LIT 5:570

HUMPHREYS, MARY GAY. D. 1915. United States.

005685   JACK RACER. BY HENRY SOMERVILLE. New York: McClure, Phillips, 1901 NUC.

005686   RACER OF ILLINOIS. BY HENRY SOMERVILLE. New York: McClure, Phillips, 1902 NUC.

HUMPHREYS, MRS. DESMOND. See HUMPHREYS, ELIZA MARGARET J. (GOLLAN).

HUNGERFORD, MARGARET WOLFE (HAMILTON). 1855?-1897. United Kingdom.

005687   AN ANXIOUS MOMENT. London: Chatto and Windus, 1897 BMC NUC.

005688   THE COMING OF CHLOE. BY MRS. HUNGERFORD (THE DUCHESS). London: F. V. White, 1897 BMC. Philadelphia: J. B. Lippincott, 1897 NUC.

Widow Mrs. Fitzgerald in Ire. has two daughters, small income, so she takes in a boarder-Chloe Jones who's really someone else. Much love making and marr. ACAD 52 Fic. Sup 66.
She's an adventuress who is married. CR 26,30:252.
Three daughters and mother live in respectable poverty, To their home comes Chloe Jones-really Lady Burlingham, woman of the world, wit, she stirs things up in the quiet Irish village. All ends well. NYT 4-17-97.

005689   A CONQUERING HEROINE. BY THE DUCHESS. London: F. V. White, 1892 BMC. New York: Tait, [c1892] NUC.

PW-House party to which comes the heroine "in the guise of a charming Irish girl." "She breaks up several promising flirtations, and causes general unhappiness by her witching ways before she makes her final choice and dismisses her unlucky victims." ACAD "she (perhaps unconsciously) plays it very low down upon other girls who have not her natural charms and advantages."

005690   THE HOYDEN: A NOVEL. BY THE DUCHESS (MRS. HUNGERFORD). Philadelphia: J. B. Lippincott, 1893 NUC. London: Heinemann, 1894 BMC.

SR 77:16. Girl bride married for her money rebels, smites husband on both cheeks and leaves. This causes him to fall in love with her and beg her pardon.
ACAD 45:54. Mrs. H. has tried to portray in Marian Bethune a wicked woman, but she lacks "discretion and finesse" so that her depravity is ineffective.
Everything in the present tense. Flirts, prudes, low comedy gentleman plus an "extra spice of bad taste" LW 93, 239.
The hoyden is a young woman with money who marries an impoverished English lord who tells her he doesn't love her but needs her money to pay his debts. Their marriage is full of jealousy and then love. PW 7-1-93.

005691   LADY PATTY: A SKETCH. BY THE DUCHESS. London: F. V. White, 1892 BMC. Philadelphia: J. B. Lippincott, 1892 NUC.

ATH 100:93. Helen Gifford is central character, she resists influences of her mother (Lady Patty), an aunt, and an uncle, all who try to shape her life.
SP: Helen's blind to her mother's faults and scheming.

005692   LADY VERNER'S FLIGHT: A NOVEL. BY THE DUCHESS (MRS. HUNGERFORD). London: Chatto and Windus, 1893 BMC. New York: J. A. Taylor, [1893] NUC.

Triangle: Sir Verner is a monstrous husband, boasts to his wife of his infidelities, even tries to get her seduced so he can get a divorce. Lady Verner so long the Patient Griselda decides to act. She leaves him. There's a better man for her-Mr. Drayton. SP 70:396.
She becomes a housekeeper for a handsome squire when she leaves her husband. PW 2-18-93.
She is Rhoda. Husband has spent her fortune, beats her. Because she leaves him at same time a man who loves her leaves the country, gossip starts up. SR 75, 380
Ends in a second marriage. ACAD 43:346.

005693   A LONELY GIRL. London: Downy, 1896 BMC. Leipzig: B. Tauchnitz, 1897 NUC.

Irish country house, a clumsy joker Owen Magrath and his banjo, the loud matron Madame O'Flaherty, and the lonely girl made unlonely by love. ATH 109:13
The hated elderly relative-an uncle, the beautiful lonely country girl. The woman of the world married with a couple of lovers, the true hearted merry little fascinator, the reckless rake, the villain, a bushel of jewels. LW 28:254
PW 9/26/96. Ireland. Amber, until the death of her father, had never been recognized by Sir Lucien Adare and re and her other cousins.

005694   A LONELY MAID. BY MRS. HUNGERFORD ("THE DUCHESS"). Philadelphia: J. B. Lippincott, 1896 NUC.

005695   LOVICE. BY MRS. HUNGERFORD ("THE DUCHESS"). London: Chatto and Windus, 1897 BMC. Philadelphia: J. B. Lippincott, 1897 NUC.

Altercations and misunderstandings of a frank pair of lovers, Digby Devereux and Louie Crichton. But for Lovice--she wastes her time with a man who has only good looks on his side. Jilts her when his money runs low to wed a rich woman. Apparantly she's married when she feels this attraction. Confesses to husband upon her death bed. ATH 109:647.

005696   A MAD PRANK. BY THE "DUCHESS". London: F. V. White, 1893 BMC. New York: J. A. Taylor, 1893 NUC.

Gay, pretty story. Heroine dresses as a housemaid, attends a ball in order to see the man she has been matched up with-to marry. Then she insists on keeping the disguise when he comes to her home. The complications that follow. ACAD 44:228.

005697   NOR WIFE NOR MAID: A NOVEL. BY MRS. HUNGERFORD ("THE DUCHESS"). London: Heinemann, 1892 BMC. New York: J. W. Lovell, [1892] NUC.

ATH 99:434. Bigamy
LW 23:375. Very moral. Husband and wife believed first wife to be dead, they separate at once on hearing of her existence. But 2nd wife is pregnant, 1st wife is overcome by tragedy, hit by a railway car, leaving her fortune to child-to-be.

005698   NORA CREINA: A NOVEL. BY "THE DUCHESS" (MRS. HUNGERFORD). New York: Hovendon, [c1892] NUC. London: F. V. White, 1893 BMC.

SP 69:857. Romance, constant round of love scenes, parties, picnics, etc. "Inoffensively vulgar."
Two Irish sisters with an ogre for a stepfather, who wastes their income. When he marries, he takes a wife who cares for Sophie and Nora Carew. Nora loves a no-good man who throws her over when he learns she has no money. (He in turn is jilted)then Nora loves a worthy man. Sophie is a sunny lass who loves Denis. ACAD 43:170

005699   THE O'CONNORS OF BALLINAHINCH. BY MRS. HUNGERFORD ("THE DUCHESS"). New York: Hovendon, 1892 [c] NUC. London: Heinemann, 1893 BMC.

ATH 100:850. An Irish story which doesn't take sides politically. Nora loves an unfaithful man, whose worth, or lack of it, is obvious to all around her. Romance.
The Father sells his favorite hunter to Sir Heriot who loves one of the daughters. this Lord surpasses even the father who is described in heroic terms. Another man, a very ugly one loves the other Miss O'Connor. SP 70 491
Irish. SR 75, 381
Three daughters Molly the youngest and most fascinating-her love affairs are the focus. Also those of Geraldine and Kitty. ACAD 43:369

005700   PETER'S WIFE: A NOVEL. BY THE DUCHESS (MRS. HUNGERFORD). London: F. V. White, 1894 BMC NUC. Philadelphia: J. B. Lippincott, 1894 NUC.

SP 73:851. Wife married to perfectly good husband twice her age, is tempted by former love, finally sticks to marriage.
ACAD-conventional, dull.

005701   A POINT OF CONSCIENCE. BY MRS. HUNGERFORD ("THE DUCHESS"). London: Chatto and Windus, 1896 BMC. Philadelphia: J. B. Lippincott, 1896 NUC.

LBKM 10:26. Tangled loves, melodrama.
ATH 107:310. Country house people.
ACAD 49:342. Cassie wears knickerbockers. Maden and

her passionate story is more "dangerous ground" than usual for author.

005702   THE RED HOUSE. BY "THE DUCHESS". Chicago: Rand, McNally, 1894 NUC.

SR 77:203. The Red House Mystery? 1893? London? Chatto & Windus? Darkham murders his wife and is attempting to murder a rival when his idiot son murders him.

005703   THE RED HOUSE MYSTERY: A NOVEL. London: Chatto and Windus, 1893 BMC. Leipzig: Tauchnitz, 1894 NUC.

005704   THE THREE GRACES: A NOVEL. BY THE DUCHESS. London: Chatto and Windus, 1895 BMC. Philadelphia: J. B. Lippincott, 1895 NUC.

three young sisters-last name Grace, their fatuous and "cross-grained" father. A blind girl betrothed to one man, on recovering her sight finds she loves his brother. SP 74:907

005705   A TUG OF WAR: A NOVEL. London: F. V. White, 1895 BMC. Leipzig: B. Tauchnitz, 1895 NUC.

A villain seeks to gain an inheritance by foul means. Succeeds in "cutting his own throat." ACAD 48:202 Irish. two gentle maidens Kathleen and Ellen. ATH 106:155

005706   AN UNSATISFACTORY LOVER: A NOVEL. BY MRS. HUNGERFORD ("THE DUCHESS"). London: F. V. White, 1894 BMC NUC.

SP-romance of wild Irish girl Terry and quiet Englishman who overcomes all doubt when he expertly subdues a horse.
ACAD-Mrs. Hungerford supplies the masterful lover.
PW-5-2-96. Irish, witty, hot-tempered heroine and two younger brothers on a decaying home (parents dead.) She accepts rich cold Englishman for brother's sake. There is a handsome, witty, impoverished Irish cousin which makes trouble.

HUNGERFORD, MRS. See HUNGERFORD, MARGARET WOLFE (HAMILTON).

HUNT, ISOBEL VIOLET. 1866-1942. United Kingdom.

005707   THE CELEBRITY AT HOME. BY VIOLET HUNT. London: Chapman and Hall, 1904 BMC NUC.

BKM-family story.
ATH-Diary of a 14 year old daughter of male novelist who poses in the world as a bachelor and neglects his wife and children; "wide-awake and intensely disenchanted maiden."
ACAD-a "trifle."
Flapper woman. Child-woman-devil. "It's nice to do what you like even if it isn't good for you." EGOIST

005708   THE CELEBRITY'S DAUGHTER. BY VIOLET HUNT. London: S. Paul, [1913] BMC NUC. New York: Brentano's, 1914 NUC.

"Dull vulgarity. Not one single soul in this prof-pol-artistic circle is a lady or gentleman." ATH Miss Tempe Taylor at 18 declares herself quite mature and excessively English. She is "one of the most perfectly impossible young women who have ever been evolved in fiction." She has a wide knowledge of life. Comic history of her social rise; ends up marrying the prime minister, though her background is shady. SR Her mother is an actress, father a writer-ran away with a peeress. She has a love affair with the correspondent in a divorce case, is paid off to have nothing more to do with him. Last two pages becomes an heiress, engaged to Prime Minister. TLS

005709   THE DOLL; A HAPPY STORY. BY VIOLET HUNT. London: S. Paul, [c1911] BMC NUC.

Man married to divorcee Minnie Agate; disagreeable tangle of relationships. TLS
Two different types of women: Mrs. Hawtayne charming dependable and Isabel brusque hearty, wears tailor-made suits. Mrs. Hawtayne divorced. Can't make a go of second marriage. Divorce threatens but the couple are reconciled. ACAD
Loses her child in first marriage, plans the second to prevent losing her child Isabel. ATH
Minnie Hawtayne is a rebel defying conventions. Her daughter Isabel long separated from her makes a visit upon her coming of age. Minnie has divorced. Disagreeable entanglements involving her and daughter and two men work out in the end. Decadent people. SR

005710   A HARD WOMAN: A STORY IN SCENES. BY VIOLET HUNT. London: Chapman and Hall, 1895 BMC NUC. New York: D. Appleton, 1895 NUC.

"A story in Scenes"-series of lively dialogues developing the story of a clever, but selfish and shallow woman and her gradual moral descent." BAKER 03, 128
The form "an interlacing of scenes which are either narrative, or formal or informal dialogue" experimental. Neville is the heroine's foil; she's a model who becomes an actress. Mrs. Munday-vulgarity, infidelity- is the heroine. SR 80:656
Lydia Munday. the seamy side of London fashionable life. SP 75:771
Author a genius at dialogue. Heroine-clever, a ready tongue, selfish. Loses part of her fortune, has no money to pay bills, borrows from hairdresser, money lender. ATH 106:603
ACAD 49:32. "downfall and failure of a brilliant and successful woman." Lydia, like Dodo. "In the final scene, when she and her husband are left at last alone with the truth-and very little else, one's pity comes very near to liking after all." Variety of styles used appropriate to different episodes: male narrator, purely dramatic.
LW 27:92 Lydia is despicable.

005711   THE HOUSE OF MANY MIRRORS. BY VIOLET HUNT. London: S. Paul, [1915] BMC NUC. New York: Brentano's, 1915 NUC.

BKM-Minute psychological analysis of London society; woman determined to regain an estate for her husband that he lost in marrying her. She has a managing mind. NYT
"Miss Hunt brilliantly makes credible the heroism, from love of her husband and obsession with the idea of his succession to his uncle's estate, of this restless, naturally selfish, and useless woman." Serious, not satiric portrayal. Even withholds that she's very ill in order not to spoil her plan. TLS Rosamond Pleydell. ACAD
ACAD praises Hunt as equal to Bronte, Eliot.
BKM-Story of a wife's utterly useless sacrifice to see that her husband is provided for after her death. She is a strong woman, retired from the stage, with money married to a man whom she loves but cannot earn a living and whom she believes has been disinherited by his uncle because of her past. Her husband does not impose his values on her, although she lives in many ways that he would believe, if done by him, would sully his good name.

005712   THE HUMAN INTEREST. A STUDY IN INCOMPATIBILITIES. BY VIOLET HUNT. London: Methuen, 1899 BMC.

Phoebe Ellis has read Ibsen, wants to start a salon, is miserably married, wants a grand passion. She runs away from gray Newcastle, meets an artist who is her great love. Divorce and happy end for Phoebe. Egidea is a successful novelist, a different character. "The wife is so sadly comic," says author. LIT 5:495
She's too cultivated for her phillistine world. She gains our sympathy. The landscape artist has not allowed human interest in his work or life. Phoebe throws herself at him. LBKM 17:60
She meets a novelist (woman.) Decides to put Doll's House into practice. Disguises herself as a French General and leaves home . Takes a new name. Meets misogynist artist. SP 83:573
Farcical plot, satire of some modern types, the literary woman innocent of wordly knowledge, egoist, painter, etc. BAKER 03,128
CR 36:91. "Satire on the problem novel describing the vague longings of a discontented wife, and the affinity she so wonderfully discovers in a lonely country village."
LW 31:74. English Emma Bovary. Five characters in novel. Heroine who thinks she has mistaken her vocation, brutish husband, interfering husband's parent, wise and sympathetic woman of the world, and a lover.

005713   THE LAST DITCH. BY VIOLET HUNT. London: S. Paul, [1918] BMC NUC.

Letters of women, "aristocrats of the bluest blood," Lady Arles and her daughter, Lady Venice St. Remy and their set. Dabbed in futuristic art, becomes engaged to a labour leader "on condition that he never so much as attempts to kiss her." When he did so attempt, she married another man the same evening. One of Lady Arles' daughters becomes a bus conductor. Aristocracy in the last ditch. LBKM

005714   THE MAIDEN'S PROGRESS: A NOVEL IN
DIALOGUE. BY VIOLET HUNT. London: Osgood, McIlvaine,
1894 BMC.

SP 73:279. Moderna does everything, tries everything,
gets bored with everything. Remains a bachelor girl
for 9 years during which time she wants to see the
world for herself, acquire her own experience, make
her own mistakes. Her parents acquiesce contentedly.
ATH 104:218. Eventually marries a cousin.
LBKM 7:10. Novel is free from narrative and
description, almost entirely in dialogue, an
adaptation of the French form used by Gyp and M.
Lanedan.
CR 25:326. Novel has an atmosphere of success, is of
the world, worldly, lively heroine meets no obstacles.
"Though written by a woman has no ethical mission
whatsoever."
LW 25:259. Moderna comes to agree with Lord Coniston
who has "never seen any good come of the modern spirit
of dissatisfied curiosity and ruthlessness in women
who want to be different to other women, who can't
conform to what the wisdom of the ages has decreed for
them. It's bad form to say the least of it."
PW-Moderna is a fin-de-siecle girl of the Dodo type.
She becomes tired of independence.

005715   SOONER OR LATER, THE STORY OF AN
INGENIOUS INGENUE. BY VIOLET HUNT. London: Chapman and
Hall, 1904 BMC NUC.

ATH--o

005716   THEIR LIVES. BY VIOLET HUNT. London: S.
Paul, [1916] BMC NUC. New York: Brentano's, [1916?]
NUC.

Different in style: not dramatic; almost entirely
descriptive. Relation between Christina and Virgilia,
sisters. Christina the older dominates: daughters of
pre-Raphaelite artist. Christina cheapens her own
value in the matrimonial market both by her somewhat
repulsive love affair with a man old enough to be her
father and her attempts to attract men. NYT,
135,4-15-17

005717   UNKIST, UNKIND! A ROMANCE. BY VIOLET
HUNT. London: Chapman and Hall, 1897 BMC.

Wild heath country of Northumberland. A dark romantic
story of Sibella the learned young sect'y of Sir
Anthony who loves the secluded life and loves Sir
Anthony. She despises all that is "vain and worldly
and modern" LBKM 13:49.
Narrator is a governess, quick-witted, though plain.
Sibella Drake adept at alchemy, astrology and
demonology, completely devoted to her teacher and
master. When a woman of fashion threatens to take him,
Sibella "wreaks deadly vengeance" on her. SP 79:692.
Janet Freeman tells the story. Sibella is the "unkist
and unkind." ends in dual trag. Janet is companion to
Lady Darcie wife of Anthony. ATH 110:559.
Lady Darcie childlike surface, hard underneath. A
flirt "deserves all she got." Sibella-a study in
morbid psych. LIT 1:274.
SR 85:215. Tragedy. "Passion-smitten" Sibella, black
cats, poison rings, love potions, murder. Narrated by
Miss Freeman, who describes herself as "commonplace,
with susceptibilities presumably a little coarsened by
the winning of her bread as a 'hack'".
BkM 6:563. A long way from the company of highly
sophisticated modern women she (VH) was born to
analyze and depict. Old world. Ends in murder.
Sibella, secretary of Sir Anthony, spends her days
gladly among the dead, and most humanly in love with
her master.

005718   THE WAY OF MARRIAGE. BY VIOLET HUNT.
London: Chapman and Hall, 1896 BMC.

ATH 108:900. "Marriages galore, mostly unequal unhappy
mrges" Hardness and brilliance in character
delineation, cynical p.o.v.
ACAD 50:528, Private marital histories of a group of
dinner guests, narrated by a novelist, Mr. St. Jerome.
"Nine Pereira" powerful; "The story of Mrs. Arne" "A
highly original horror," stories in which Miss Augusta
Tempest figures are "excellent comedy."
Several women: on eve of marr. one finds her husband
has a past; one rebels vs her family that made her a
slave; one sends a younger lover off sees he consoles
himself easily. SP ;78 446

005719   THE WHITE ROSE OF WEARY LEAF. BY VIOLET

HUNT. New York: Brentano's, 1908 NUC. London: W.
Heinemann, 1908 BMC NUC.

BKM-modern Jane Eyre.
PW-rolling stone who has had many occupations and
succeeded in them. "Another of the many books that
picture the unnatural social conditions of the hour."
TLS-"Unemotional non-moral, frank yet with a pathetic
mouth and a femininity which subdues." Mr. Dand and
Amy, housekeeper-companion, their intimacy carried to
a tragic close.
ACAD-dies bearing his child, he kills himself.
SR-good figure and bad complexion.
Occupation-dressmaker, typewriter, amanuensis in
Russia, nurse in S. Africa, stage, philanthropy and
lectures on social problems. Talent for organization.
BKM-she is passionless and loathes attentions of men.

005720   THE WIFE OF ALTAMONT. BY VIOLET HUNT. New
York: Brentano's, 1910 NUC. London: W. Heinemann, 1910
BMC NUC.

Restless girl married to her father's cook sees a ship
launched; stirred by this event, she begins her
strenuous career. She often shows "lack of
refinement."
TLS-wife of murderer provides a home for his mistress
and her two children; he dies in prison; has a love
affair with a man engaged to someone else. Then two
women and children live in a house on his estate.
NYT-she desired her husband hanged.

005721   THE WORKADAY WOMAN. BY VIOLET HUNT.
London: T. W. Laurie, [1906] BMC NUC.

TLS-portrayal of workaday young women.
TLS-portrayal of workaday young woman.

HUNT, ISOBEL VIOLET, jt. au. See HUNT, MARGARET (RAINE) AND
ISOBEL VIOLET HUNT.

HUNT, MARGARET (RAINE). 1831-1912. United Kingdom.

005722   A BLACK SQUIRE. London: Chapman and Hall,
1894 BMC.

ATH 104:825. "Underbred" heroine Gulielma with social
aspirations. Lover has "finer sensibilities." Pleasant
and easy reading.

005723   MRS. JULIET. BY MRS. ALFRED W. HUNT.
London: Chatto and Windus, 1892 BMC NUC.

ATH 100:914. romance, with such trad themes as a
clandestine marriage, interception of love letters,
etc.
Juliet Craddock twice suspected of murder. Might have
been spared this had she revealed her secret marriage.
SP 70 396
She marries a soldier at the beginning of the book. He
leaves immediately after the wedding-not to return
till the end of the book. In the meantime she's
uncomfortable in being dependent on her aunt, Juliet
is suspected of her aunt's death. Then she becomes a
companion to an old woman who also dies. Juliet goes
on trial again. But, of course, she's innocent. SR
1-21-93, 75.
The Aunt, Mrs Caradoc is a wealthy vulgar Philistine,
oppressive toward Juliet. Her husband reappears at the
end. ATH 43:126

HUNT, MARGARET (RAINE) AND ISOBEL VIOLET HUNT.

005724   THE GOVERNESS. BY MRS. ALFRED HUNT AND
VIOLET HUNT. London: Chatto & Windus, 1912 BMC NUC.

TLS-conv. plot
ATH-conv. plot

HUNT, MRS. ALFRED. See HUNT, MARGARET (RAINE) AND ISOBEL
VIOLET HUNT.

HUNT, MRS. ALFRED W. See HUNT, MARGARET (RAINE).

HUNT, VIOLET. See HUNT, ISOBEL VIOLET, Also HUNT, MARGARET
(RAINE) AND ISOBEL VIOLET HUNT.

HUNTINGTON, FAYE, pseud. See FOSTER, THEODOSIA MARIA
(TOLL).

HUNTINGTON, GLADYS THEODORA (PARRISH). Nationality Unknown.

005725   CARFRAE'S COMEDY. BY GLADYS PARRISH.
London: W. Heinemann, 1915 BMC. New York: G. P.
Putnam's Sons, 1916 NUC.

An actress Blanche Benvell in Carfrae's comedy,
divorced, lives in a convent, exquisite, tender,
simple, trusting, childlike able to remain herself
under all circumstances, she lives peacefully as a
boarder at the convent. Divorced but would never
consider remarr. Rel. her strength. Friends visit her
at convent. TLS SR
Gradually unrest builds in her, realizes her love for
Julian. But gives him up painfully and her rel.
doesn't make it less painful. SR
Blanche ethereal, mystical type; to act in play.
Carfrae makes his drama from her own life which she
has told him. PW 89:2/19/1916 p 608
NYT An adorably feminine soul, enmeshed in scruples.
Is Divorced, making her home in a convent, three men
after her. rem.? (doesn't intent to)

HUNTINGTON, HELEN, pseud. See BARKER, HELEN MANCHESTER
(GATES) GRANVILLE.

HUNTINGTON, MARY H. United States.

005726   THE STRANGE ENVELOPE; OR, TWICE MARRIED.
A NOVEL. BY MRS. MARY H. HUNTINGTON. New York:
American News, [c1893] NUC.

The envelope conceals the reason why Judge Vennor of a
proud family of Florida was not twice wed. The judge
opposes his daughter's wish to marry, but her schemes
bring him in line with her view. PW 10-28-93.

HUNTLEY, FLORENCE (CHANCE). D. 1912. United States.

005727   THE DREAM CHILD. Boston, Mass.: Arena,
1892 NUC.

The Variens lose their small girl in an accident. Mrs.
Varien out of grief begins to live her real life in
sleep. For 18 years takes up her dream just where it
ended the night before. She's always with her child
Stella in her dreams. eventually leaves this life for
her "spirit mate." PW 8-26-93

005728   THE GAY GNANI OF GINGALEE; OR, DISCORDS
OF DEVOLUTION; A TRAGICAL ENTANGLEMENT OF MODERN
MYSTICISM AND MODERN SCIENCE. Chicago: Indo-American
Book, 1908 NUC.

Theosophy-NYT
PZ 3

HUNTLY, HOPE. See HUNTLY, KATE HOPE.

HUNTLY, KATE HOPE.

005729   THE BIRTHRIGHT OF GRIMALDI. London: K.
Paul, 1913 BMC.

Anti-vivisectionist novel. TLS

005730   FAIR MONACO: GUILTY OR NOT GUILTY? York:
J. Sampson, 1891 BMC.

005731   KAMI-NO-MICHI; THE WAY OF THE GODS IN
JAPAN. BY HOPE HUNTLY. London: Rebman, 1910 BMC NUC.

TLS--Female missionary impressed by Japanese religion.
ATH--conversations between English missionary and
Japanese heroine on Shintoism with latter holding her
own.
Breaks engagement; becomes missionary in Japan; learns
that rel. there is as good as Christianity. PW
3-18-11.

005732   OUR CODE OF HONOUR: A ROMANCE OF THE
FRONTIER WAR. London: S. Low, 1899 BMC.

Anglo-Indian romance; heroine uses slang. SP 82:560
Condemns the theory "that every married woman is fair
prey if she yield to aught save brute force."
SR 87:473. A loveless marriage and lawless affinities.

005733   THE WAY OF THE GODS IN JAPAN. BY HOPE
HUNTLY. Boston: Badger, 1911 NUC.

005734   WEDLOCK, AND ITS SKELETON KEY. London: S.
Low, 1891 BMC.

Anti-divorce novel about a man who was instrumental in
getting divorce reform laws passed and whose wife was
the first to take advantage of the law that gave
permission to divorced people to remarry . Also her
daughter gets mixed up with a divorced man. ACAD

HURD, GRACE MARGUERITE. United States.

005735   THE BENNETT TWINS. New York: MacMillan,
1900 BMC NUC. London: Macmillan, 1900 NUC.

Boy and girl in New York studying art (she-singing) on
their own, atmosphere of art-student life, hard work,
enthusiasm, "new" book for young people. CR '01
Eighteen students live in "The Hive" (NY Studio Bldg)
BKM 12:303. Humorous and healthy. Orphans go to New
York with $100; Don longing to be an artist, Agnes a
singer. They meet failure with humor; rev. is sure of
their ultimate success.
NYT 1900:700. Agnes and her brother in New York on
their own. He an art student, she a music student. She
is inclined to mother him, but she is not sentimental,
no romance.

HURD, MARIAN KENT, jt. au. See STOKELY, EDITH KEELEY AND
MARIAN KENT HURD.

HURLBUT, ELLA CHILDS. United States.

005736   MRS. CLIFT-CROSBY'S NIECE. New York:
Tait, 1893 NUC.

Moral: "never adopt a child." This niece because of
heredity develops into a "selfish, calculating,
deceitful young woman." "For all her beauty and charm
every one connected with her must have been glad when
death cut her off at 19." LW 93, 258.
Dr. adopts the child when mother dies in New York
hospital and doctor learns father, too, is dead. PW
7-8-93.

005737   PHILIPPA; OR, UNDER A CLOUD. BY ELLA. New
York: Cassell, [c1891] NUC.

Silly sentimental love story. IND
"A cloud" hangs over mother and daughter. Mother is
pale weak restless; Philippa is strong; unselfish.
Marries in the end but "cloud" still there. PW
American girl travels with terrified little mother
thru Europe. Pursued by gossip, denied friends and
lovers devoted to making mother's life less painful.
At last happiness comes to her LW

HUSELTON, ESTELLE ZINKHAN. United States.

005738   THE TUTORED SOUL. Boston: Sherman,
French, 1916 NUC.

Girl searching for the "why" of things searches for
answer from standpoint of reason and finally finds it
through the friendship of a man who has found that
"service is the active principle of happiness." PW
90:799 9/16/16

HUSTED, LILLIA SHAW. United States.

005739   THE BRIDE IN BLACK. Boston: Four Seas,
1920 NUC.

PW-Story of a masked bride who runs away on her
wedding night.
NYT 1920:240-Plus many other sensational happenings.

HUSTON, ETHELYN LESLIE. B. 1869. Canada.

005740   THE TOWERS OF ILIUM. New York: G. H.
Doran, [c1916] NUC.

June married in a moment of weakness. Discovers
marriage illegal because of technicality. Refuses to
have it legalized, preferring to face maternity
without marriage to a life with a man who was not her
ideal. PW
Somber work depicting the hardships women and her
children face without the benefits of financially
secure husbands; at the sametime the auther is
outspoken about the immorality of most women's
marriages which are for financial security and not a
great love. June refuses to marry, supports her
invalid father and herself by a succession of jobs:
running a nursing home, editing a medical dictionary,
and free-lance art work. She is tricked into a
marriage but renounces her husband and raises her
child without marriage. She has a close friend who is
a woman M.D. Ellen Key and George Eliot are frequently
quoted. She finally meets a man whom she can love
(Book)

HUTCHESON, MARIE.

005741   BARDOSSI'S DAUGHTER. London: Hutchinson,
1895 BMC NUC.

local color; Cheribina the nurse. SR 80:447

Artist's life in Florence Bardossi is a sculptor. His daughter Sylvia has three lovers, one a desperate villain. She eventually weds Lawrence Trent, an American art student. ACAD 48:244
SP 76:746. Romance. Sculptor: daughter Sylvia. Father fears for her future. Not a tragedy. Hunchback has a "hopeless passion" for her.

005742   BRUNO THE CONSCRIPT. London: Hutchinson, [1894] BMC NUC.

SR 78:415. Beatrice and Adele love Bruno, the former selfishly. He marries Beatrice. Tuscany.
SP-Bruno is an artist whose career is arrested by conscription. Purpose of the novel is anti-conscription.

HUTCHINGS, EMILY GRANT. United States.

005743   JAP HERRON; A NOVEL WRITTEN FROM THE OUIJA BOARD. New York: M. Kennerley, 1917 NUC.

"This book was supposed to have been dictated to the ouija board by Mark Twain to Mrs. Lola V. Hays and written down by Mrs. Emily Grant Hutchings." Publisher's letter
"Ouija board is competing with typewriter." Real author is Mark Twain who wrote through Mrs. Hutchings. Story of boy of lowly birth becomes noble man similar settings to Twain's. NYT 336, 9-9-17

HUTCHINSON, EDITH STOTESBURY. B. 1877. United States.

005744   A PAIR OF LITTLE PATENT LEATHER BOOTS. Philadelphia: J. B. Lippincott, 1913 NUC.

PW 83 3/15/13 p 985 "Letters written from Bob to Jack tell how the charm of a pair of little patent leather boots enticed a man half way across the continent of Europe. The incidents of the road, the varied types of people described, the illusive heroine, the "other man" and the final destiny of the little patent leather boots make an interesting story."

HUZARD, ANTOINETTE (DE BERGEVIN). B. 1874.

005745   THE DOCTOR WIFE: A NOVEL. BY COLETTE YVER. London: Hutchinson, 1909 BMC. (Tr. Anna, Comtesse de Bremont.)

woman doctor-the innumerable difficulties to be overcome by women in professions. NYT
conflict between a wife's duty to her (doctor) husband and the calls of her professional life. TLS

005746   A KING'S CALLING. BY COLETTE YVER. London: T. Nelson, [1913] NUC BMC. (Tr. by Hugh M. Miller)

romance dealing with court life in Lithuania; introduces socialism and bureaucracy. ATH
The king hires a socialist to be the science-governess of the heiress. Clara comes suspicious of monarchy but modifies her opinion.

005747   LOVE VS. LAW. (LES DAMES DU PALAIS). BY COLETTE YVER. New York and London: Putnam, 1911 NUC BMC. (Tr. by Mrs. Bradley Gilman)

women lawyers-the innumerable difficulties to be overcome by women in professions. NYT
Marriage and career question; the woman is "plain" woman lawyer, better lawyer than husband serious study of the problem. "a very modern type of French heroine." PW

005748   MIRABELLE OF PAMELUNA. BY COLETTE YVER. New York: C. Scribner, 1919 NUC. (Tr. by Lucy Humphrey Smith)

War story: family of French bookseller. Involves charming scenes of family reunions, picnics of two families, two love plots, an old French legend and battle scenes of heroism. Shows that the legend of French heroism is still alive. NYT

HYDE, MARY ELLEN (BURKE). B. 1854. United States.

005749   THE SINS OF THE FATHERS. Boston: Sherman, French, 1914 NUC.

PW 86 12/5/14:1893 "Even the events of Richard Cole's death (he was murdered by an unknown person) failed to make public the facts of his double life. These were known only by the woman involved and Gibson, his confidential clerk. Young Robert Cole, the legitimate

heir, had altruistic ideas. Stanton, old Cole's other son, was employed in the Cole works through Gibson's influence, to keep his mother silent. He was a drinker and lead disturbances among the men. Stanton's mother finally told him the truth. In a drunken rage, he tried to kill Robert Cole and himself. Before he died, he confessed to the murder of the elder Cole. Robert Cole recovered and went on with his work, hoping that the curse had been lifted from his family."

HYLAND, M. E. F.

005750   THE DREAM WOMAN. BY KYTHE WYLWYNNE. London: T. F. Unwin, 1901 BMC.

Husband fabricates an heroic past so heroine (a writer) will write a book about him. LBKM

005751   THE LOG OF THE SCARLET HOUSE. London: Christian Knowledge Society, [1905] BMC.

005752   THE PRIZE AND THE BLANK. London: Christian Knowledge Society, [1913] BMC.

005753   THE VISION OF ANGELS. London: J. Blackwood, [1896] BMC.

IKE, pseud. See GLYNN, KATE A.

ILES, SYBIL M.

005754   THE SCHOOL OF LIFE. A STUDY OF THE DISCIPLINE OF CIRCUMSTANCE. London: E. Stock, 1905 BMC.

Estrangement of a man and his wife who went on the stage TLS 05, 31

IMHAUS, ELIZABETH VIGOUREUX. United States.

005755   EXILED BY THE WORLD; A STORY OF THE HEART. New York: Mutual, [1901] NUC. London: Gay & Bird, 1902 BMC.

Actress

INCE, MABEL EMILY. United Kingdom.

005756   THE COMMONPLACE AND CLEMENTINE. London: Chatto and Windus, 1914 BMC.

TLS-man and woman brought up as brother and sister develop a "passionate" attachment ending in marriage. Story of feeling and sentiment.

005757   THE WISDOM OF WAITING. London: Chatto & Windus, 1912 BMC.

TLS-rapprochement of husband and wife ater years of separation.
ATH-O

INCHBOLD, A. C. See INCHBOLD, A. CUNNICK.

INCHBOLD, A. CUNNICK. United Kingdom.

005758   THE LETTER KILLETH: A ROMANCE OF THE SUSSEX DOWNS. London: S. W. Partridge, [1905] BMC.

005759   LOVE AND THE CRESCENT, A TALE OF THE NEAR EAST. BY A. C. INCHBOLD. London: Hutchinson, [1918] BMC. New York: F.A. Stokes, [c1920] NUC.

PW-deals with persecution of the Armenians. NYT 7/18/20 p 29 by the Turks before outbreak of a WW1. Young MD, his sister, her rival lovers, conventional romance.

005760   LOVE IN A THIRSTY LAND. London: Chatto and Windus, 1914 BMC.

SR 147:314 Julie is forced by parents into a convent, her suffering portrayed. She is taken to Holy Land by nuns; her lover follows, searching for her, aided by an American feminist journalist who is visiting the Holy Land to inquire into the position of women in the East. Portrays the "bitterness and rancour of opposing creeds" in Holy Land.

005761   PHANTASMA. London & Edinburgh: W. Blackwood, 1906 BMC NUC.

ACAD-Napoleon in Egypt. Romance of Napoleon and daughter of a Mameluke Bey

005762   PRINCESS FEATHER. London: Hutchinson,

1899 BMC.

Sussex rural life. Very refined young woman weds
Michael Tagg, a boor and a brute. "The horrible
auction of wives...is doubtless drawn from credible
tradition; the newspapers report such occurrences even
to-day." Elizabeth against this bkgd-her tragic
situation and her bkgd which insists she submit to her
duty as a wife however disgusting to her. After he
dies she has a peaceful life. LBKM 17:61
ACAD 58:14. "Mr. Inchbold's concern is to make us feel
what it was to be a peasant's wife in years before the
battle of Trafalgar. He succeeds. The picture is
sinister, but it convinces." Sussex. Elizabeth, a
foundling, carefully brought up, clever, refined,
reliable, is a lady's maid. On a visit with her
mistress to a country house, she met and married the
captain of the sheep shearers. He was bestial,
drunken, beat her, finally sold her in a wife auction
to a soldier.

005763   THE ROAD OF NO RETURN. London: Chatto &
Windus, 1909 BMC.

Hist rom of Russia TLS
Husband imprisoned becomes a monk, thus annulling
marriage. Wife beocmes a disciple of Tolstoy ATH
Plot concerns Russian revolutionaries Vounia one the
them. Vounia Petrovna Martinoff joins pilgrimage to
Holy Land to hide; she believes she murdered an
official who insulted her SP

005764   SALLIE OF PAINTER'S BAKERY. London: R. T.
S., [1920] BMC.

005765   THE SILVER DOVE. London: Hutchinson, 1900
BMC.

LBKM 19:27. Temperance story. Young wife runs away
from drunken husband, robs a shop and is condemned to
prison. The shock straightens him out.
ATH 116:476.
LIT 7:372. He is good husband except for drinking.

INGELOW, JEAN. 1820-1897. United Kingdom.

005766   A MOTTO CHANGED: A NOVEL. New York:
Harper, 1894 NUC.

INGLIS, JOHN, pseud. See CLIFFORD, MRS. W. K.

INGRAHAM, FRANCES C., pseud. See BELL, CLARA INGRAHAM.

INGRAM, ELEANOR MARIE. 1886-1921. United States.

005767   THE FLYING MERCURY. Indianapolis:
Bobbs-Merrill, [c1910] NUC.

Motor-car love story PW
love and motor cars NYT

005768   FROM THE CAR BEHIND. Philadelphia and
London: J. B. Lippincott, 1912 BMC NUC.

PW-Two male racers
ATH sent.

005769   THE GAME AND THE CANDLE. Indianapolis:
Bobbs Merrill, [1909] NUC.

Advent and intrigue in Russian court PW 10-16-09

005770   JOHN ALLARD; OR, THE GAME AND THE CANDLE.
London: T.W. Laurie, [1912] BMC.

TLS-male hero.

005771   A MAN'S HEARTH. Philadelphia and London:
J. B. Lippincott, 1915 BMC NUC.

TLS-Artificial, male hero,
seems to be anti-divorce NYT

005772   STANTON WINS. Indianapolis: Bobbs
Merrill, [c1911] NUC.

auto story PW 5-13-11

005773   THE TWICE AMERICAN. Philadelphia and
London: J.B. Lippincott, 1917 BMC NUC.

Man's success story, leader of South American state;
when Germans invade gets that state to join allies.
Subplot is a love story NYT

005774   THE UNAFRAID. Philadelphia and London:

J.B. Lippincott, 1913 BMC NUC.

TLS-Montenegro. "Pure romance"
PW 84 10/18/13:1286 "Scene is laid in mountains of
Montenegro. Delight Warren, an American girl of wealth
and position, two handsome Montenegrin officers, and
Jack Rupert, of auto racing fame, are the principal
characters. A six weeks' courtship and betrothal,-an
accident to the bridegroom,-a secret auto journey
made by Delight with the irrepressible Jack Rupert at
the wheel, -an abduction,-a series of exciting
episodes in a castle on the Albanian frontier,-and a
thrilling climax make the tale. By author of "From the
car behind."

IOTA, pseud. See CAFFYN, KATHLEEN MANNINGTON (HUNT).

IRELAND, MARY ELIZA (HAINES). B. 1834. United States.

005775   WHAT I TOLD DORCAS: A STORY FOR MISSION
WORKERS. New York: E. P. Dutton, 1895 NUC BMC.

"seeks to unite all denominations in the noble work of
missions" Mrs. Atheling active mission worker tells
her experiences. PW 12-7-95:1079
LW 27:47. Written to be read at missionary and sewing
society meetings.

IRETON, KATHLEEN.

005776   RITUALISM ABANDONED; OR A PRIEST
REDEEMED. London: J. Clarke, [1899] BMC.

SP 84:176. Nonconformist Minister and daughter redeem
priest.

IRON, RALPH, pseud. See SCHREINER, OLIVE EMILIE ALBERTINA
(SCHREINER) CRONWRIGHT.

IRONS, GENEVIEVE.

005777   A DAMSEL WHO DARED. A NOVEL. London:
Sands, [1909] BMC.

Dares to join Church of Rome, is cast off by family
TLS

005778   IN THE SERVICE OF THE KING. London:
Catholic Truth Society, 1912 BMC.

005779   A MAIDEN UP-TO-DATE: A NOVEL. London:
Sands, [1908] BMC.

005780   THE MAKING OF MOLLY. London: Catholic
Truth Society, 1908 BMC.

005781   THE MYSTERY OF THE PRIEST'S PARLOUR.
Edinburgh: Sands, [1911] BMC [n.d.] NUC. St. Louis: B.
Herder, [n.d.] NUC.

Roman priest suffers for another's crime. TLS

IRONSIDE, JOHN, pseud. See TAIT, EUPHEMIA MARGARET.

IRVINE, A. M. See IRVINE, AMY MARY.

IRVINE, AMY MARY. B. 1866. United Kingdom.

005782   THE DREAMS OF ORLOW. BY A. M. IRVINE.
London: G. Allen & Unwin, 1916 BMC. London: W. Rider,
1919 NUC.

005783   THE FRANTIC MISFORTUNES OF A NURSE; OR,
THE PROBATIONER. London: S. W. Partridge, [1916] BMC.

005784   THE PROBATIONER. London: S. W. Partridge,
[1910] BMC.

005785   ROGER DINWIDDIE, SOUL DOCTOR. London: T.
W. Laurie, [1907] BMC.

005786   THE SPECIALIST: A NOVEL. BY A. M. IRVINE.
New York and London: J. Lane, 1904 BMC NUC.

NYT O
TLS O

IRVING, E. M. BELL. See IRVING, EVA MARGARETTA BELL.

IRVING, ELIZABETH. United States.

005787   A NEW WORLD; OR, THE WAY TO WIN. Le Roy,
Ill.: 1905 NUC.

Rel. love story--PW 12-2-05

IRVING, EVA MARGARETTA BELL.

005788   MAYFIELD. THE STORY OF AN OLD WEALDEN
VILLAGE. BY E. M. BELL-IRVING. London: W. Clowes, 1903
NUC BMC.

DA 690 Mayfield, Eng.

IRVING, THEO.

005789   HALF WAY TO HADES. London: J. Milne, 1901
BMC.

IRWIN, FLORENCE. B. 1869. United States.

005790   THE MASK; A NOVEL. Boston: Little, Brown,
1917 NUC.

Allison, keenly intell., sheltered life, marries,
lives in shabby New York boarding house. Husband
erratic, brings shabby friends home, selfish, gambles
away their money. Has a son who dies in an accident
caused by husband. Her slow disillusionment thru all
this and out of sorrow, a building of their relation
in her helping him to forgive himself about child's
death. PW
Saves him from utter ruin. In her misery she turns to
writing. Both now are writers. NYT 10-14-17 401

005791   POOR DEAR THEODORA! New York and London:
G.P. Putnam's Sons, 1920 BMC NUC.

SP-social snubs and job of governess.
PW-young woman conquers discouragement and hardship
and wins happiness.
NYT 1920:168. She is a companion. Description of her
work in two families, Red Cross work during war,
romance.

005792   THE ROAD TO MECCA. New York and London:
G. P. Putnam's Sons, 1916 BMC NUC.

Ellie Prentess of "crude" birth has social
aspirations, models herself after a fashionable couple
with whom she travels to Europe. At end great rich
society hostess-but unhappy. PW
NYT cold, ambitious woman portrayed going thru steps
of becoming a social success.

IRWIN, GRACE. See IRWIN, MARY GRACE.

IRWIN, GRACE (LUCE). D. 1914. United States.

005793   THE DIARY OF A SHOW GIRL. New York:
Moffat, Yard, 1909 NUC.

Woman starving on shop-girl salary, gets job in chorus
line, rises to fame and fortune "retains her good
name, marries well" PW 4-10-09
BKM-"a tale of theatrical life in New York....whose
success is due more to the nimbleness of her wits than
her feet" BKM v. 29, 1909

IRWIN, INEZ (HAYNES). B. 1873. United States.

005794   ANGEL ISLAND. BY INEZ HAYNES GILLMORE.
London: G. Bell, 1914 BMC. New York: H. Holt, 1914
NUC.

BKM-"an impressive and rather daring Allegory, yet
treated in such a view of poetic imagery and shown
through such a rainbow mist of shimmering light, that
one scarcely realises until sober second thought that
it says things in regard to feminism which it would
not be easy to say in any less indirect way." Five
sailors are thrown on a remote island inhabited by a
superior race of women. Their feet do not touch earth,
they glide on iridescent wings, super women: half
birds, half angels. Woman is but little lower than the
angels, but men are primitive, cave men, regardless of
surface differences. All five men, including a scholar
who claims women should have their rights, resort to
cave man methods in trying to get the women they want.
Then they are captured and shorn of their wings; they
miss their freedom but accept their new burdens and
responsibilities until their revolt when the fathers
wish too soon to clip their daughter's wings. Symbolic
foreshadowing in the triumph of eugenics in birth of a
son with wings.
ACAD 87:81, Strike for their right to fly and win.
Allegory of the whole problem of women -Hartley
"A novel interpreting in symbolic form the changing
relationships between men and women in marriage. It
tells how five winged women, individual and free, come
flying to five strong modern men wrecked on a deserted
island. Woven into the romance are the opposing forces

of the old ideals of capture and the new ideals of
freedom." NYT 7-11-15.
"Five beautiful winged women hover over the island
where five men have been shipwrecked. The fierce
attraction, the longing to capture, the right and
wrong of the old and ever-new conflict between man and
woman are the threads from which the romance is
woven." PW

005795   THE HAPPY YEARS. New York: H. Holt, 1919
NUC.

005796   JANEY; BEING THE RECORD OF A SHORT
INTERVAL IN THE JOURNEY THROUGH LIFE AND THE STRUGGLE
WITH SOCIETY OF A LITTLE GIRL OF NINE. BY INEZ HAYNES
GILLMORE. New York: H. Holt, 1911 NUC.

005797   JUNE JEOPARDY. BY INEZ HAYNES GILLMORE.
New York: B. W. Huebsch, 1908 NUC.

The story describes the exciting events of one evening
in and around Boston. It deals with a necklace of
priceless diamonds for the possession of which a gang
of robbers had been plotting for many years. BKM
27,1908.
NYT-light comic romance.
Thethry, whose mother died when she was 10 and whose
father is a jewel thief, has spent most of her life in
a convent. She buys a house on Beacon Street in
Boston, invents a past, and brings five young working
women into the house to live with her. The book opens
with a discussion amongst the six women of men. They
are agreed that all men who think that "women's place
is in the home" or that any other activity makes a
woman "unfit for the position of wife and mother" are
impossible for them as companions or lovers. Thirsting
for adventure, Thethry leaves the group for an evening
walk. The story relates the night's adventures which
involve a diamond necklace, a gang of jewel thieves,
and six men who pass the tests the women have devised
for them. Romantic comedy.

005798   THE LADY OF THE KINGDOMS. New York: G. H.
Doran, [1917] NUC.

Two young women revolt vs. restrictive Cape Cod home.
Southward Drake captures all men's hearts but remains
indifferent to marriage. Hester Crowell, unattractive,
yearns for a child. They go to New York. Southward
shoots her lover when she finds him with another
woman. Hester claims the right to maternity without
marriage. Both find happiness. Southward marries man
she shot; Hester in the love of her child and
(perhaps) marriage to the one man who really cares for
her. PW
Close friends. Southward very attractive but won't
marry, dislikes children. Hester has no suitors.
(Mother nags her about her appearance) but wants a
child. NYT

005799   THE NATIVE SON. San Francisco: A. M.
Robertson, 1919 NUC.

005800   THE OLLIVANT ORPHANS. BY INEZ HAYNES
GILLMORE. London: Methuen, 1915 BMC. New York: H.
Holt, 1915 NUC.

Six young Americans, three girls, three boys, comedy
of youthful energy, high spirits, and
purposefulness-TLS
Two years in the lives of a down-and-out family of six
orphans, how they cooperate, adjust. three girls,
three boys. Book opens with their return from mother's
funeral all modern young people: Bechie struggles for
employment which seems everywhere to be denied to a
"homely" girl. Ann's excursion into the Bohemian set,
"Lainey's revolt" NYT

005801   PHOEBE AND ERNEST. BY INEZ HAYNES
GILLMORE. New York: H. Holt, 1910 NUC. London:
constable, 1911 BMC.

Home and school life of brother and sister. Pleasant
tales ACAD
She gushes ATH

005802   PHOEBE, ERNEST AND CUPID. New York: H.
Holt, 1912 NUC.

IRWIN, M. E. F. See MONSELL, MARGARET EMMA FAITH (IRWIN).

IRWIN, MARY GRACE. B. 1891.

005803   BROWN-EYED SUSAN. BY GRACE IRWIN.
Arlington, N. J.: Little Book Publisher, 1917 NUC.

Teacher-traditional romance:mother fails to understand
the needs of her daughter. NYT
Susan Yorke teaches in city public school. an
"open-eyed" study of the relation between modern young
woman and her mother. They love each other, but fail
to enter into each other's feelings. The book has a
romantic ending. NYT

IRWIN, VIOLET MARY. B. 1881. United States.

    005804   THE HUMAN DESIRE. Boston: Small, Maynard,
    [c1913] NUC.

    Berenice in cloistered seclusion of Italian convent.
    Desire for motherhood. A nun, hardly more than a
    child, in an Italian convent, runs away into world she
    knows nothing of. Wants to gather up children and
    bring them back to convent. NYT

    005805   WITS AND THE WOMAN. Boston: Small,
    Maynard, [c1919] BMC NUC.

    "shop girl to whom adventures come thick and fast"-PW
    Clarissa Kendall, ex department store saleswoman tells
    her own "cyclone of adventures"-She's an expert in
    slang. "A career of social adventure whose pace and
    convolutions make a whirlwind seem slow and straight."
    NYT 9-14-19:467

IVES, SARAH NOBLE.

    005806   THE KEY TO BETSY'S HEART. New York:
    Macmillan, 1916 BMC NUC.

JACBERNS, RAYMOND, pseud. See ASH, GEORGINA M. I.

JACK, ELLEN E. B. 1842. United States.

    005807   THE FATE OF A FAIRY. Chicago: W.B.
    Conkey, [c1910] NUC.

    Children's? PZ3

JACKSON, GABRIELLE EMILIE (SNOW). B. 1861. United States.

    005808   THE DAWN OF WOMANHOOD. New York: F. H.
    Revell, [c1908] NUC.

    HQ 1229 Young Women; Conduct of Life. (Fic.?)

    005809   THE MAID OF MIDDIE'S HAVEN; A STORY OF
    ANNAPOLIS LIFE. New York: McBride, Nast, 1912 NUC.

    005810   PEGGY STEWART. New York: Macmillan, 1911
    BMC NUC.

    girls book 11-18-11 PW

    005811   PEGGY STEWART AT HOME. New York:
    Macmillan, 1912 BMC NUC.

    Girls' book

    005812   THREE GRACES AT COLLEGE; A SEQUEL TO
    THREE GRACES. New York: D. Appleton, 1904 NUC.

    college stories

    005813   THREE LITTLE WOMEN'S SUCCESS; A STORY FOR
    GIRLS. Philadelphia: J.C. Winston, [c1910] NUC.

    girls' book

JACKSON, IDA.

    005814   MARJORY MAXWELL, THE MAJOR'S DAUGHTER.
    Edinburgh: D. M. Small, 1898 BMC.

    ACAD 53:625. Tender little love tale. Marjorie and
    minister.

    005815   WHEN HYACINTHS BLOOM. Edinburgh and
    London: Oliphant, 1898 BMC.

    PW-Boston. A. L. Bradley. Romance of a governess.
    Scotland.

JACKSON, LUCIE E.

    005816   FEODORA'S FAILURE. Philadelphia: D.
    McKay, [c1907] NUC. London: Ward, Lock, 1907 BMC.

    Fails to raise motherless brothers & sisters
    effectively. 7-6-07 p 27

    005817   THE FINDING OF CAMILLA. London: Ward,

Lock, 1909 BMC.

    005818   FOR MURIEL'S SAKE. London: Ward, Lock,
    1905 BMC.

JACKSON, MARGARET (DOYLE). B. 1868. United Kingdom.

    005819   A DAUGHTER OF THE PIT. Boston: Houghton,
    Mifflin, 1903 NUC. London: Cassell, 1903 BMC.

    Teacher's struggles in mining town--PW 2:28:03
    NYT-review focuses on descriptions of the coal mines.
    1903:137

    005820   THE HORSE-LEECH'S DAUGHTER. Boston:
    Houghton Mifflin, 1904 NUC.

    PW-woman with insatiable greed for money.
    NYT-Exaltation of hard working American husband.

    005821   WHEN LOVE IS KING. New York: G. W.
    Dillingham, [1905] NUC. London: T. F. Unwin, 1905 BMC.

    Typical love story-PW
    Adventures of two men-NYT

JACOB, CARRYE SILVEY. United States.

    005822   LOVE CAN CONQUER PRIDE. Nashville, Tenn.:
    University Press, 1893 NUC.

JACOB, MRS. ARTHUR. See JACOB, VIOLET MARY AUGUSTA
FREDERICA (KENNEDY-ERSKINE).

JACOB, VIOLET MARY AUGUSTA FREDERICA (KENNEDY-ERSKINE).
1863-1946. United Kingdom.

    005823   FLEMINGTON. BY VIOLET JACOB (MRS. ARTHUR
    JACOB). London: J. Murray, 1911 BMC NUC.

    005824   THE HISTORY OF AYTHAN WARING. BY VIOLET
    JACOB (MRS. ARTHUR JACOB). New York: Dutton, 1908 NUC.
    London: W. Heinemann, 1908 BMC.

    PW-Love story, character study.
    TLS-Story of relentless hatred of Hester Bridge for
    Aythan Waring who will somehow succeed to her
    property. "Infects Eustace his life long friend and
    transforms her into an evil genius. Rev. cannot find
    hatred credible, wishes there were more atmosphere
    (desc. of bonnets, etc)
    SR 0
    BKM 0
    ATH-Hester's "delineation is a sombre study of the
    madness which
    SP Hester is woman Aythan and Eustace's adopted father
    married. He dies intestate and she has his property
    for rest of life. P.O.V.?
    NYT 0

    005825   THE INTERLOPER. BY VIOLET JACOB (MRS.
    ARTHUR JACOB). New York: Doubleday, page, 1904 NUC.
    London: W. Heinemann, 1904 BMC.

    LBKM-love story
    ATH love story
    TLS 0
    ACAD-Portrait of a woman which will be a permanent
    addition to national gallery of characters in fiction.
    The interloper is a young man who returns from Spain
    with the man who has always passed as his father-all
    unconscious of the blot on his birth.

    005826   IRRESOLUTE CATHERINE. London: J. Murray,
    1908 BMC NUC. New York: Doubleday, Page, [1909] PW.

    ATH-Heroine farm servant
    Young working farm maid and two very different types
    of suitors. PW 3-27-09, BKM, NYT

    005827   THE SHEEP-STEALERS. New York and London:
    G. P. Putnam's Sons, 1902 NUC. London: W. Heinemann,
    1902 BMC.

    ATH9-20-02

JACOBI, MARY (PUTNAM). United States.

    005828   FOUND AND LOST. New York, London: G. P.
    Putnam's Sons, 1894 NUC.

    LW 25:353. Intense feeling, unique subject. First
    appeared in Atlantic Monthly, a Sermon at...published
    in Putnam's monthly.

JACOBS, CAROLINE EMILIA. 1872-1909.

005829   JOAN OF JUNIPER INN. BY EMILIA ELLIOTT.
Philadelphia: G. W. Jacobs, [1907] BMC NUC.

Fun loving story of widow and children who run an inn.
PW 9-7-07

005830   JOAN'S JOLLY VACATION. BY EMILIA ELLIOTT.
Philadelphia: G. W. Jacobs, [1909] NUC.

005831   PATRICIA. BY EMILIA ELLIOTT.
Philadelphia: G. W. Jacobs, [1910] NUC.

Children's. PW

005832   A TEXAS BLUE BONNET. BY EMILIA ELLIOT.
Boston: L. C. Page, 1910 NUC.

Western girl's adjustment to life in Boston. PW

JACOBS, ESTHER.

005833   LOVE AND LAW: A STORY OF THE JOY AND WOE
IN A SINGER'S LIFE. New York: G.W. Dillingham, 1895
NUC.

Esther Jacobs is plaintiff in breach of promise case
against Henry Sire. Her life, written by herself, her
career as an opera singer. Fiction? PW 2-16-95:322

JACOMB, A. E.   See HOOD, AGNES ELIZA (JACOMB).

JACOMB, AGNES E.   See HOOD, AGNES ELIZA (JACOMB).

JAMES, DOROTHY A BECKETT (TERRELL).   United Kingdom.

005834   EMANCIPATION; THE STORY OF A GIRL WHO
WANTED A CAREER. BY DOROTHY A BECKETT TERRELL. Funk &
Wagnalls, 1914 PW. London: Cassell, [1914] BMC.

NYT—Experieces of a young woman in search of a career.

005835   OH, MARY! BY DOROTHY A BECKETT TERRELL
(MRS. JOHN JAMES). Liverpool: Books Ltd., [1920] BMC
NUC.

LBKM—rom fantasy

005836   SISTER-IN-CHIEF. BY DOROTHY A BECKETT
TERRELL. London and New York: Cassell, 1912 BMC NUC.

JAMES, FLORENCE ALICE (PRICE).   1857-1929.   United Kingdom.

005837   ABBOT'S MOAT. BY FLORENCE WARDEN. London:
F. V. White, 1913 BMC.

Daring jewel robbery with romances between four young
people. ATH

005838   ADELA'S ORDEAL. BY FLORENCE WARDEN. New
York: International News, [c1893] NUC. London: W.
Stevens, [1894] BMC.

PW—Adela, the adopted daughter of Hamo's father, is
betrothed to Hamo. He is called away by machinations
of former lover and during his absence she learns he
is supposedly implicated in two crimes.

005839   THE ADVENTURES OF A PRETTY WOMAN. BY
FLORENCE WARDEN. London: S. Paul, 1909 BMC.

Traditional mystery. TLS

005840   THE BAD LORD LOCKINGTON. BY FLORENCE
WARDEN. London: J. Long, 1912 BMC.

005841   THE BARONET'S WIFE. BY FLORENCE WARDEN.
London: T. F. Unwin, 1908 BMC.

Crime and mystery. SP
About a criminal of good social position. TLS
Woman, a Lady (baronet's wife), unknown to husband
becomes a fence. ACAD
Woman involved in numerous robberies. ATH

005842   BEATRICE FROYLE'S CRIME. BY FLORENCE
WARDEN. London: C.A. Pearson, 1903 BMC.

Widow with a child, repudiated by relatives, passes
off her child as a daughter of the viscount. The count
believes it. ATH

005843   THE BEAUTY DOCTOR. BY FLORENCE WARDEN.
London: Greening, 1911 BMC.

Netta, assistant to a Bond Street beauty doctor.

Marries a viscount. TLS
Love, kidnapping, intrigue, sensation. ACAD

005844   THE BEAUTY OF THE FAMILY. A NOVEL. BY
FLORENCE WARDEN. London: F. V. White, [1910] BMC.

005845   BLINDMAN'S MARRIAGE. BY FLORENCE WARDEN.
London: T. W. Laurie, [1907] BMC NUC.

Jennifer marries to escape convent but loves a wanted
man. TLS

005846   THE BOHEMIAN GIRLS. A NOVEL. BY FLORENCE
WARDEN. London: F. V. White, 1899 BMC.

SP 81:873. Four young women driven to earning a living
in London; three on the stage. Finally all find
shelter in matrimony.
ACAD 55:480. They smoked, betted, drank champagne and
played billiards.

005847   THE CASE FOR THE LADY. A NOVEL. BY
FLORENCE WARDEN. London: Greening, 1910 BMC.

TLS—marriage to an adventuress with a secret past
(music-hall stage).
LBKM—romance.

005848   THE CASE OF SIR GEOFFREY. BY FLORENCE
WARDEN. London: J. Long, 1908 BMC.

Traditional murder mystery. TLS

005849   THE COLONEL'S PAST. BY FLORENCE WARDEN.
London: Ward, Lock, 1910 BMC NUC.

TLS—traditional love story.

005850   CROSS-FIRES. BY FLORENCE WARDEN. London:
Cassell, 1915 BMC.

Traditional mystery. ATH
Focuses on hero and gang of thieves. TLS

005851   THE DAZZLING MISS DAVISON. BY FLORENCE
WARDEN. London: T.F. Unwin, 1908 BMC NUC. New York:
H.K. Fly, [1910] NUC.

Lovely, intelligent, refined, pickpocket and
shoplifter. How does she pay for her fine clothes? Is
she under some crook's hypnotic control? NYT
TLS—Mystery over Rachel's income--happy ending. She
appears to reader and to her lover to be an
unscrupulous thief.

005852   A DESPERATE GAME, A NOVEL. BY FLORENCE
WARDEN. New York: A. L. Burt, [1902] NUC.

005853   A DEVIL'S BARGAIN. BY FLORENCE WARDEN.
London: J. Long, 1908 BMC.

TLS—male hero-wicked Jewess.

005854   THE DISAPPEARANCE OF NIGEL BLAIR. BY
FLORENCE WARDEN. London: Ward, Lock, 1911 BMC.

Sensational mystery. TLS

005855   DOCTOR DARCH'S WIFE; A STUDY. BY FLORENCE
WARDEN. London: F. V. White, 1896 [c] BMC. New York:
P. F. Collier, 1896 BMC NUC.

ATH 108:792. Mental attitudes and moral development of
heroine. The supposed wife of the doctor is
mysterious, a combination of childish charm and
innocence along with lack of morality and kindness.
A Lady Audley type--commits bigamy, attempts murder.
SR 83:393

005856   DOLLY THE ROMP. BY FLORENCE WARDEN.
London: F. V. White, 1897 BMC.

005857   THE EMPRESS OF THE ANDES. BY FLORENCE
WARDEN. London: T. W. Laurie, [1909] BMC.

005858   THE FACE IN THE FLASHLIGHT. BY FLORENCE
WARDEN. London: J. Long, 1905 BMC.

005859   THE FARM IN THE HILLS. BY FLORENCE
WARDEN. London: Sands, 1899 BMC NUC.

Story of crime in the wild Welsh hills. ATH 113:685

005860   THE FIGHT FOR A SOUL. BY FLORENCE WARDEN.
London: Digby, Long, 1912 BMC.

005861　　　A FIGHT TO A FINISH. BY FLORENCE WARDEN.
London: Chatto & Windrus, 1901 BMC.

005862　　　THE FINANCIER'S WIFE. BY FLORENCE WARDEN.
London: T. W. Laurie, [1906] BMC.

TLS-old wife pops up.

005863　　　FROM STAGE TO PEERAGE. AN AUTOBIOGRAPHY.
BY FLORENCE WARDEN. London: Digby, Long, 1911 BMC.

005864　　　THE GIRL WITH THE HAUNTING EYES. BY
FLORENCE WARDEN. London: Ward, Lock, 1920 BMC NUC.

TLS-murder and love.

005865　　　THE GIRLS AT THE GRANGE: A NOVEL. BY
FLORENCE WARDEN. London: F. V. White, 1897 BMC 1898
NUC.

first part: 4 orthodox conv. girls and an "obstinant
mouse-like mother" 2nd part: "a gambling hall located
in a Kent country house." They were invited by a
Jewish moneylender to lend the place respectability
while the gambling goes on. ACAD 52:27.

005866　　　GIRLS WILL BE GIRLS. BY FLORENCE WARDEN.
London: F. V. White, 1898 BMC.

ATH 111:19. High-spirited Drage girls. The firm of
Drage & Janion are into fraudulent transactions. A
farmer is murdered.

005867　　　THE GOOD SHIP "DOVE". BY FLORENCE WARDEN.
London: Ward, Lock, [1919] BMC.

Traditional mystery. TLS

005868　　　GRAVE LADY JANE. A NOVEL. BY FLORENCE
WARDEN. New York: J. A. Taylor, 1892 NUC. London: F.
V. White, 1893 BMC.

Heroine is 32, early disappointment in love. Is
persuaded through motives of revenge to give her
fortunes to an ecclesiological institute. Her lawyer
brings about a surprising end. PW 5-6-93
She's called upon to be mother of some young children.
"Her dormant sympathies" are awakened. ACAD 43:543
Set in Ilchester, England. Heroine 32 disappointed in
love "assumes a grave and austere appearance, with the
habits of a miser."Induced through motives of revenge
to bestow her fortunes upon an ecclesiological
institution." Her lawyer works things out; they wed.
BOOK NEWS 130:459

005869　　　THE GREY MOTH. BY FLORENCE W RDEN.
London: Ward, Lock, 1920 BMC.

TLS-also known as the Cobra, a masterful and
exceptionally although not impossibly wicked old
woman. Baffles investigation. There is a love story,
too.

005870　　　THE HALF-SMART SET. BY FLORENCE WARDEN.
New york: Stokes, [1908] PW. London: J. Milne, 1908
BMC.

PW-startling story of marriage.
TLS-young wife who learns virtue.
ACAD-author gives a temperate unbiased view of vulgar
set and narrow minded Puritans.

005871　　　THE HARLINGHAM CASE. BY FLORENCE WARDEN.
London: Ward, Lock, [1918] BMC.

TLS-murder mystery

005872　　　THE HEART OF A GIRL. BY FLORENCE WARDEN.
London: Chatto and Windus, 1903 BMC.

Modern day romance. Hearts of several girls: turbulent
and passionate, shallow and selfish. Loving and
capricious. LBKM

005873　　　HEIRESS OF DENSLEY WOLD. BY FLORENCE
WARDEN. London: Cassell, 1907 BMC.

Rascal uses her as decoy for purpose of fleecing her
wooers. TLS

005874　　　HIGHEST REFERENCES. BY FLORENCE WARDEN.
New York: J. W. Lovell, [1891] NUC. London: Railway
and General Automatic Library, [1892] BMC.

005875　　　A HOLE AND CORNER MARRIAGE. BY FLORENCE
WARDEN. London: C. A. Pearson, 1902 BMC.

Girl proposes marriage as means of escape from
detestable bridegroom. LBKM 10-02
ATH-Domestic sensational melodrama, " for firesides of
respectabe drawing rooms."

005876　　　THE HOUSE BY THE RIVER. BY FLORENCE
WARDEN. London: T.F. Unwin, 1905 BMC. New York: J.S.
Ogilvie, 1905 NUC.

A typewriter goes to work for invalid in house by
river, mysteries abound. PW

005877　　　THE HOUSE IN THE HILLS. BY FLORENCE
WARDEN. New York: R. F. Fenno, 1899 NUC.

Gruesome mystery and false trails. Reginald Masson
goes into welsh hills to find his brother. LW 30:407

005878　　　A HOUSE WITH A HISTORY. BY FLORENCE
WARDEN. London: F. V. White, 1901 BMC.

White slaver, exploits white penitents at the mangle
and wash tub. ATH

005879　　　AN IMPOSSIBLE HUSBAND. BY FLORENCE
WARDEN. London: J. Long, 1904 BMC.

ATH-American heiress, strong-willed, married to
aristocratic Englishman who has no affection for her.
Happy ending.

005880　　　THE INN BY THE SHORE. A NOVEL. BY
FLORENCE WARDEN. London: Jarrold, 1897 BMC NUC.

ATH 108:597. "Quiet little old maid" turns out to be a
criminal. Sensational, similar to The House on the
Marsh.
ACAD 50:326. Nellie and her uncle staying at inn. When
jewelry starts disappearing, Nellie is suspected, then
a murder.
She's a kleptomaniac, pulls off a great escape at the
end of Chap 2. SP:78:600

005881　　　JOAN, THE CURATE. BY FLORENCE WARDEN.
London: Chatto and Windus, 1898 BMC. New York and
London: F. M. Buckles, 1899 NUC.

SP 81:446. South Coast smugglers.
1748. She's so capable and useful in her father's
parish that she's called the curate. England, time of
free traders, considered by the government to be
smugglers. PW 55:574.

005882　　　KITTY'S ENGAGEMENT; A NOVEL. BY FLORENCE
WARDEN. London: F. V. white, 1895 BMC 1897 NUC. New
York: D. Appleton, 1895 NUC.

Combines story of middle-class life and murder. Set
about Holland Park. ACAD 47:254
The villain is rather a vulgar good-looking young man.
ATH 105:245
He, Charles Arnside murdered his wife; three years
later almost marries Kitty (a very weak woman) she
loves one man, "but lets herself be ordered to marry
another." LW 26:90

005883　　　A LADY IN BLACK. BY FLORENCE WARDEN.
London: International News, 1895 [c] NUC. London: F.
V. White, 1896 BMC.

005884　　　LADY JOAN'S COMPANION. BY FLORENCE
WARDEN. London: Digby, Long, 1902 BMC.

She's cold, strong, stern and dowdy by day and a
creature of imperial beauty when her hairpins are out.
LBKM 12-01

005885　　　LADY LEE. BY FLORENCE WARDEN. London:
T.W. Laurie, [1908] BMC.

TLS-love story.

005886　　　LADY RODWAY'S ORDEAL. BY FLORENCE WARDEN.
London: Ward, Lock, 1909 BMC.

Traditional murder story. TLS

005887　　　LADY URSULA'S HUSBAND. BY FLORENCE
WARDEN. London: Ward, Lock, 1914 BMC.

ATH-male hero, thief, and his reformation under
influence of his wife.

005888　　　LAIDLAW'S WIFE. BY FLORENCE WARDEN.
London: J. Long, 1911 BMC.

005889   LAW NOT JUSTICE. BY FLORENCE WARDEN.
London: Hurst and Blackett, 1906 BMC.

ATH-absolute doormat.

005890   A LIFE'S ARREARS. BY FLORENCE WARDEN.
London: Cassell, 1908 BMC. New York: Cassell, 1909 PW.

TLS-32 yr. old heiress inherits money, saves a man
from suicide whom she then marries.
Jane is 32 becomes wealthy goes to Monte Carlo-lots of
exciting advents. PW 7-3-09

005891   THE LIGHT IN THE UPPER STOREY. BY
FLORENCE WARDEN. London: Ward, Lock, 1917 BMC NUC.

German spy story. TLS

005892   THE LITTLE GREY MOUSE. BY FLORENCE
WARDEN. London: F. V. White, 1915 BMC.

005893   LITTLE MISS PRIM. A NOVEL. BY FLORENCE
WARDEN. London: F. V. White, 1898 BMC NUC.

ACAD 53:495. Governess and lady-help engaged to
doubtful family, but she wraps them around her finger
and finds a ring for it too.

005894   LORD PETWORTH'S DAUGHTER. BY FLORENCE
WARDEN. London: Ward, Lock, 1913 BMC.

005895   LORD QUARE'S VISITOR. BY FLORENCE WARDEN.
London: J. Long, [1915] BMC.

Conventional murder story. TLS

005896   LOVE AND LORDSHIP. BY FLORENCE WARDEN.
London: Chatto and Windus, 1906 BMC.

005897   THE LOVE THAT LASTS. BY FLORENCE WARDEN.
New York: Street and Smith, [1899] NUC. London: Ward,
Lock, [1900] BMC.

LBKM 19:28. Scotland. Sensational. Alison married to
man who had sunstroke in Africa and suffers from
delusions. She is loved by Fergus.
SP 85:416. Hero marries heroine for her money. His old
love occupies a wing of his house, goes about
disguised as a boy and makes trouble.
ACAD 59:242. Alison eventually marries Fergus after
her luckless mock-marriage.
LIT 7:239. Her husband is a villain, Gothic like,
brings her to a house which will be her home and
forbids her to enter a portion of it because there was
nothing to see.

005898   THE LOVELY MRS. PEMBERTON. BY FLORENCE
WARDEN. New York: F. M. Buckles, [1901] NUC. London:
J. Long, 1901 BMC NUC.

005899   LOVE'S SENTINEL. BY FLORENCE WARDEN.
London: J. Long, 1913 BMC.

To appease a dying friend, young clergyman agrees to
marry one woman though he loves another. ATH

005900   A LOWLY LOVER. BY FLORENCE WARDEN.
London: F. V. White, 1900 BMC.

LW 84:95. Character study of Bram.

005901   MAD SIR GEOFFREY. BY FLORENCE WARDEN.
London: Everett, 1907 BMC.

Pretty comedy, merry marriage bells. TLS

005902   THE MAJOR. BY FLORENCE WARDEN. London: F.
V. White, 1913 BMC.

005903   THE MAN WITH THE AMBER EYES. BY FLORENCE
WARDEN. London: J. Long, 1907 BMC NUC.

Murder story. ACAD

005904   THE MARRIAGE BROKER. BY FLORENCE WARDEN.
London: T.W. Laurie, [1907] BMC NUC.

Exposes people who live well because they're in the
business of bringing about good marriages. LBKM
8-07:184

005905   MARRIED BY STEALTH. BY FLORENCE WARDEN.
London: Ward, Lock, 1918 BMC.

TLS-trite romance.

005906   THE MASTER-KEY. BY FLORENCE WARDEN.
London: C. A. Pearson, 1898 BMC NUC.

SP 80:52. Sensational melodrama. Widow is schemed
against by heir apparent; her baby son apparently
destroyed and then accusations brought against her for
its destruction. Happy ending.
ATH 111:816.

005907   THE MATHESON MONEY. BY FLORENCE WARDEN.
London: J. Long, 1910 BMC.

TLS-murder.

005908   THE MILL HOUSE MYSTERY. BY FLORENCE
WARDEN. London: Jarrold, [1911] BMC.

005909   THE MILLIONAIRE'S SON. BY FLORENCE
WARDEN. London: Ward, Lock, 1908 BMC.

TLS-traditional.

005910   THE MIS-RULE OF THREE. BY FLORENCE
WARDEN. London: T.F. Unwin, 1903 BMC. New York: Wycil,
1903 NUC.

3 bachelors. PW
3 bachelors, a baby and a beautiful girl. NYT

005911   MISS FERRIBY'S CLIENTS. BY FLORENCE
WARDEN. London: T. W. Laurie, [1910] BMC NUC.

TLS-Male secretary is rescued at the end.
Miss Ferriby is a wealthy philanthropist whose income
is augmented by her popularity amongst society as a
fortune teller and by her even more clandestine
activities as a leader of a gang of criminals. The
qualities which contribute to her success on all three
fronts are a keen and shrewd intelligence, personal
magnetism and bravery in the face of danger. She is
undone by an infatuation for her young male secretary,
a passion which is unrequited. She is described as a
dwarf possessing much physical strength, a voice which
could be either full of feminine charm or masculine
authority, and although her face and hands are young
and beautiful, her hair is gray. (Book)

005912   MOLLIE THE HANDFUL. BY FLORENCE WARDEN.
London: F. V. White, 1912 BMC.

ATH-Mollie and her two male guardians.

005913   MORALS AND MILLIONS. BY FLORENCE WARDEN.
London: F.V. White, 1901 BMC.

005914   MY CHILD AND I. A WOMAN'S STORY. BY
FLORENCE WARDEN. London: F. V. White, 1894 BMC NUC.
Philadelphia: J. B. Lippincott, 1894 NUC.

SR-sensational plot, good son and bad son.
SP 72:882. The bad son, she eventually learns, is not
her son, but in spite of his being a thief, murderer
and liar she loves him and he absorbs her completely.
ACAD-he murders her husband, destroys his will which
left everything to her. She still loves him.
Perdita Fairbrace marries at a very early age. Brief
happiness. Then authenticity of marriage is
questioned. Husband dies, child born and taken away
from her. Perdita tells the history of her son. PW
12-9-93.

005915   MY LADY OF WHIMS. BY FLORENCE WARDEN.
London: Chatto & Windus, 1907 BMC.

Mystery. ACAD

005916   THE MYSTERY OF DUDLEY HOUSE. London: F.
V. White, 1897 BMC.

A murder. "Mrs. Higgs turns out to be a man." ATH
109:241.

005917   THE MYSTERY OF FOURWAYS. BY FLORENCE
WARDEN. New York: R. F. Fenno, 1900 NUC.

005918   THE MYSTERY OF THE INN BY THE SHORE. A
NOVEL. BY FLORENCE WARDEN. New York: R. Bonner, 1895
NUC.

005919   A MYSTERY OF THE THAMES. BY FLORENCE
WARDEN. London: Ward, Lock, 1913 BMC.

4 mysterious deaths. ATH

005920   A NIGHT SURPRISE. BY FLORENCE WARDEN.

London: Ward, Lock, 1919 BMC.

Traditional murder. TLS

005921   NO. 3 THE SQUARE. BY FLORENCE WARDEN.
London: J. Long, 1903 BMC NUC.

Horror story. LBKM 8-03:189

005922   THE OLD HOUSE AT THE CORNER. BY FLORENCE
WARDEN. London: Chatto & Windus, 1906 BMC NUC.

005923   ONCE TOO OFTEN. BY FLORENCE WARDEN.
London: J. Long, [1901] BMC.

005924   OUR WIDOW. A NOVEL. BY FLORENCE WARDEN.
New York: International News, [c1895] NUC. London: F.
V. White, 1896 BMC. (Published in the same year under
title: Three Wayward Girls   NUC)

SR-Family of innocent sisters; their loves and
marriages as happy conclusion.
ATH 107:31. Father is a villain, meets financial ruin.
Daughters are hoidens, but come to recognize the uses
of a chaperone.
ACAD Frivolity-"They all get good husbands in the
end."
SP 76:928. Comedy. Fast girls sowing their wild oats,
protected by their own innocence and good feeling.

005925   AN OUTSIDER'S YEAR. BY FLORENCE WARDEN.
London: J. Long, 1903 BMC.

An uncertain race course of marriage. ACAD

005926   A PASSAGE THROUGH BOHEMIA. BY FLORENCE
WARDEN. London: Ward and Downey, 1893 BMC. New York:
Hovendon, [c1893] NUC.

Father and son, Father an Earl, are opposites. Their
conflict leads to a fight; father accidentally killed.
Son Victred Speke hides out in a traveling show-as a
giant. Also in the show there's a dwarf "Red Jack" a
woman disguised as a man. She's an eloquent speaker.
Father uses her to stir up revolt of the poor, the two
love each other, but she dies of consumption. He
eventually marries Lady May. ACAD 44:107

005927   A PATCHED-UP AFFAIR. BY FLORENCE WARDEN.
London: C.A. Pearson, 1901 BMC.

Marriage with an up to date revenge. ACAD

005928   A PERFECT FOOL. BY FLORENCE WARDEN.
London: F. V. White, 1894 BMC NUC. New York:
International News, [c1894] NUC.

Mother and daughter lose all. Take position of
housekeepers for a man who, they discover, is keeping
the son of a friend as prisoner ostensibly because
this son is mad. He's really not, the plot is
discovered. This son is rich, weds daughter Christine
Abercarne. ACAD 47:31.
Beautiful woman lives in a palace where there's a
master, a deaf and dumb lunatic who turns out to be
normal. Tissue of improbabilities. SP 74:28.
SR-heroine picks out someone who appears to be a
lunatic but is in fact an heir.

005929   THE PLAIN MISS CRAY. BY FLORENCE WARDEN.
London: F. V. White, 1900 BMC NUC. New York: F. M.
Buckles, 1900 NUC.

BKM 12:302. Sensation. Bigamy, murder, etc.
SP 84:675. Heroine, wife of criminal, marries Irish
landlord to induce police to believe he is dead. Falls
for new husband, but eventually falls back to old one.
ATH 115:587. Narrated by Miss Cray. She has a younger
sister, I believe the one who marries in "formal
bigamy."

005930   PLAYING THE KNAVE. BY FLORENCE WARDEN.
London: T.W. Laurie, 1905 BMC.

One of those assumed identity stories. LBKM

005931   PRETTY MISS SMITH: A NOVEL. BY FLORENCE
WARDEN. London: W. Heinemann, 1891 BMC NUC. New York:
United States Book, [c1891] NUC.

"Wild dance of grotesque improbabilities." She's rich.
By the will, she must live in a house attached to a
brewery. ACAD
Driven mad by would-be heir: he forces owls down her
chimney to torment her. SR 71:571

005932   THE PRICE OF SILENCE. BY FLORENCE WARDEN.
London: Ward, Lock, 1916 BMC.

Murder, traditional. ATH

005933   RALPH RYDER OF BRENT; A NOVEL. BY
FLORENCE WARDEN. London: R. Bentley, 1892 BMC NUC. New
York and London: Street and Smith, [189-?] NUC.

ATH 99:338. Mystery.
CR 18:275. Male hero. Sensational. Mother left father
and child; drink makes a lunatic of him. She has him
locked up in barn with keeper, obliterates any trace
of her connection with him. Son comes of age and ?
LW 23:295. Son looks exactly like father, keeps being
mistaken for him.
SP 68:498. He is merely a puppet. Heroine is Nanny,
who suspects her husband of bigamy and of killing his
child.

005934   THE REAL MRS. DAYBROOK. BY FLORENCE
WARDEN. London: J. Long, 1906 BMC.

TLS-novel of incident.

005935   ROGUES FALL OUT. BY FLORENCE WARDEN.
London: Ward, Lock, 1908 BMC.

TLS-Mystery.

005936   ROOM NINETEEN. BY FLORENCE WARDEN.
London: Ward, Lock, 1915 BMC.

Fight intrigue over an estate. TLS
Simple and sentimental. SP

005937   A SCARBOROUGH ROMANCE. THE STRANGE STORY
OF MARY GLYNDE. BY FLORENCE WARDEN. London: F. V.
White, 1894 BMC.

005938   SEA MEY ABBEY. BY FLORENCE WARDEN. New
York: J. W. Lovell, 1891 [c] NUC.

Lame girl raised in convent is transferred to Sea Mey
Abbey, home of her father who is leading the life of
an outlaw. Survives life of every kind of crime and
"manages to work out her own salvation in her own
way." CR 17:313

005939   THE SECRET OF LYNNDALE. A NOVEL. BY
FLORENCE WARDEN. London: F. V. White, 1899 BMC.

Mystery involves two brothers--one good and one a
villain. ATH 113:685
Meg Wellington visits home in Midlands where a ghost's
appearance indicates a disgrace in the family. ACAD
56:534

005940   A SENSATIONAL CASE. BY FLORENCE WARDEN.
New York: International News, 1894 [c] NUC. New York:
Ward, Lock, 1898 BMC.

SP 81:410. Opens with acquittal of Linley Daxon,
charges of arson and murder.
LIT 3:328. He is then approached by stranger who wants
him as cardsharp partner.

005941   SERLE'S SECRET. BY FLORENCE WARDEN.
London: Everett, [1909] BMC.

The secret makes a marriage wretched. TLS

005942   A SHOCK TO SOCIETY. BY FLORENCE WARDEN.
London: F. V. White, 1892 NUC BMC. New York: Lovell,
Coryell, [c1892] NUC.

ACAD. Marriage of earl's daughter to farmer's son.
It is that Decima Uyastme, an earl's niece, marries a
young farmer-her equal in all but rank PW 2-4-93

005943   SIR MORCAMBE'S MARRIAGE. BY FLORENCE
WARDEN. London: Ward, Lock, 1909 BMC.

005944   SIR PENYWERN'S WIFE. BY FLORENCE WARDEN.
London: Ward, Lock, 1915 BMC.

Traditional detective. TLS

005945   THE SOCIALISM OF LADY JIM. BY FLORENCE
WARDEN. London: Digby, Long, 1908 BMC.

005946   A SOCIETY SCARE. BY FLORENCE WARDEN.
London: Hurst and Blackett, 1909 BMC.

Jewel thefts. TLS

005947   SOMETHING IN THE CITY. BY FLORENCE
WARDEN. London: J. Long, 1902 BMC NUC. New York: F. M.
Buckles, 1902 NUC.

Mystery-PW.

005948   A SPOILT GIRL. A NOVEL. BY FLORENCE
WARDEN. London: F. V. White, 1895 BMC. Philadelphia:
J. B. Lippincott, 1895 NUC.

"horses and mischief and dare-devil pranks, masterful
love and men boxing girls' ears" LW 26:332
SR-Harrington and her brothers grew up flourishing
revolvers, cheating at cards. Finally three left the
country; other two reformed.
ATH 107:14. Barbarians, impossible to believe in.
ACAD 49:33. Harry is not spoilt; "their presentation
is capital." She is made for better things, which she
discovers when she meets the new vicar.

005949   A SPORTING OFFER. BY FLORENCE WARDEN.
London: Ward, Lock, 1918 BMC NUC.

TLS- mystery.

005950   A TERRIBLE FAMILY. BY FLORENCE WARDEN.
London: W. Stevens, 1893 BMC. New York: International
News, [1893] NUC.

The impoverished Hoad-Bleans rent their home to the
terrible family-the Rhadegunds. This family is very
wealthy, consists of four handsome sons. The
Hoad-Bleans consist of many daughters. PW 8-19-93.

005951   THE THINGS THAT WOMEN DO. BY FLORENCE
WARDEN. London: F. V. White, 1912 BMC.

TLS-who murdered the poacher?
ACAD-Sebastian accused-saved by friendship of brave
and fearless damsel.

005952   THOSE WESTERTON GIRLS. BY FLORENCE
WARDEN. London: R. Bentley, 1891 NUC BMC. New York: J.
W. Lovell, [1891] NUC.

Country life and a rector who gets the speculation
fever so that he commits forgery. Saved from prison by
his daughter's lover whose name he forged. ACAD
Rector's three daughters run the farm successfully
while he wastes money. One marries a man who comes to
the farm to be taught farming. BOOK NEWS 111:138

005953   TOM DAWSON. BY FLORENCE WARDEN. London:
Chatto & Windus, 1904 BMC.

005954   TOWN LADY AND COUNTRY LASS. BY FLORENCE
WARDEN. London: F. V. White, 1900 BMC.

SP 85:214. Reign of George II. Romance.

005955   TWO LADS AND A LASS, AND OTHER STORIES.
BY FLORENCE WARDEN. London: F. V. White, 1896 BMC.

005956   THE VEILED LADY. BY FLORENCE WARDEN.
London: J. Long, 1909 BMC.

Mild mystery murder story. TLS

005957   A VERY ROUGH DIAMOND. BY FLORENCE WARDEN.
London: J. Nisbet, 1899 NUC BMC.

Title refers to a young man who is polished by the
heroine-his progress "from bearishness to the attitude
of a lover." ATH 114:551
SP 84:212. Heroine and two suitors; literary man and
agricultural.

005958   WEDDED, BUT NOT A WIFE. BY FLORENCE
WARDEN. London: F. V. White, 1911 BMC.

Thieves, adventure. ATH

005959   WHAT OUGHT SHE TO DO? BY FLORENCE WARDEN.
London: Chatto & Windus, 1904 BMC.

ATH-woman accused of theft, rescued by three young
men, one proposes immediately.

005960   WHEN THE DEVIL DRIVES. BY FLORENCE
WARDEN. London: Ward, Lock, 1910 BMC.

TLS-murder, det.

005961   THE WHITE COUNTESS. BY FLORENCE WARDEN.
London: J. Long, 1907 BMC.

Mystery. ACAD

005962   WHO WAS LADY THURNE? BY FLORENCE WARDEN.
London: J. Long, 1905 BMC.

ATH-melodrama of 1st wife who really isn't dead.

005963   WHY SHE LEFT HIM. BY FLORENCE WARDEN.
London: J. Long, 1914 BMC.

ATH-Gypsy girl married to a viscount and former
fiance, a desperate ruffian.

005964   A WILD WOOING. A NOVEL. BY FLORENCE
WARDEN. London: F. V. White, 1893 NUC BMC.

Freda Mulgrave's mother died when Freda was two.
Raised in French convent to age 18. She's summoned
home after that because her father opposes her plan to
enter nunnery. Her many vivid advents.
SP 70 746. Smugglers, secret passages, mistaken
identities, etc. ACAD 43:322.
Her father is the leader of smugglers. She's lame, but
brave, determined. Falls in love. ATH 101:374

005965   THE WILES OF WILHELMINA. BY FLORENCE
WARDEN. London: F. V. White, 1913 BMC.

She tries to get her three nieces married; she's a
widow. Gets 3 proposals herself. ATH

005966   A WILFUL WARD: A NOVEL. 1891 BS. London:
1891 NUC.

005967   THE WOMAN WITH THE DIAMONDS: A NOVEL. BY
FLORENCE WARDEN. London: F. V. White, 1895 BMC.

005968   A WOMAN'S STORY. BY FLORENCE WARDEN.
London: R. A. Everett, [1903] BMC.

005969   THE WRAITH OF OLVERSTONE. BY FLORENCE
WARDEN. London: Ward, Lock, 1916 BMC.

TLS-conventional mystery.

005970   THE YOUNGEST MISS BROWN. BY FLORENCE
WARDEN. London: Chatto & Windus, 1905 BMC.

Wooing story. TLS

JAMES, GERTIE DE S. WENTWORTH. United Kingdom.

005971   BARTER. London: Everett, [1912] BMC.

005972   THE CAGE UNBARRED: BEING THE STORY OF A
WOMAN WHO WAS DULL. London: Everett, [1913] BMC.

Hypochondriacal suburban wife so bored with her
marriage that husband trumps up a case of infidelity
so she can divorce him. Loses the man she expected to
marry; after a while returns to her now successful
husband. The cage is matrimony. TLS

005973   THE CHILD MARKET. London: T. W. Laurie,
[1918] BMC.

TLS-Theme is motherhood legitimate and illegitimate,
moral pointing to former.

005974   THE CURTAIN. London: Everett, [1915] BMC.

SR 147:118. Serious, about a young woman who can find
no happiness because she has been brought up on
knowledge of evil.
ATH-Brought up by a woman who educated her as "a
disciple of truth by raising the curtain of
convention." She is incapable of love until
forgetfulness blots out the past.

005975   THE DEVIL'S PROFESSION. London: Everett,
[1914] BMC.

ATH-woman steno-typist, whose work affects her
eyesight, enters the service of a medical man and is
employed in an asylum.
TLS-Lionne discovers that the patients are made to
appear insane by the injection of a drug. He is a
scoundrel, she likes his kisses, but when he snubs
her, she leaves.

005976   DIANA OF WEST KENSINGTON. London: C. H.
White, [1909] BMC.

005977   THE ESCORT; A FARCICAL COMEDY. London:
Everett, [c1912] BMC NUC.

ATH-grass widow, faced with becoming a rich man's mistress or escort (in male attire), chooses latter.

005978   FLOSSIE. THE STORY OF A COMMON GIRL. London: Everett, [1911] BMC.

005979   THE GIRL WHO WOULDN'T WORK. London: Everett, [1913] BMC.

005980   GLORIOUS MAN. London: C. H. White, [1910] BMC.

005981   GOLDEN YOUTH. London: T. W. Laurie, [1916] BMC.

A mid-aged wife recovers temporarily a season of youth and love. A lady detective is a prominent character. TLS
Drama set in beauty parlor. Various types of clients and treatment. ATH

005982   GREEN GRAPES. London: T. W. Laurie, [1918] BMC.

TLS-Unattractive tale of wealthy young widow incognito at Gray's Inn, her relationship with two or three men and the God of drink. (Bacchus).
ATH Morals are free and easy.

005983   THE HOUSE OF CHANCE. London: Everett, [c1911] BMC NUC. New York: W. Ricky, 1912 NUC.

PW-actress, impersonation.

005984   THE LESSON; A STORY OF LOVE, OF BOHEMIA, AND OF HUMAN PHILOSOPHY. London: Everett, [c1911] BMC NUC.

005985   MAIDEN MADNESS; A NOVEL. London: T. W. Laurie, [1919] BMC.

A forced marriage and illicit passion. TLS

005986   THE MAN MARKET. London: T W Laurie, [1917] BMC.

Young couple marry in haste, live extravagantly for first year. Having to budget lessens their affection for each other. They drift apart but after several years are reconciled. ATH

005987   MAN-MADE MORALS. London: Everett, [1915] BMC.

A liaison of a wife with an aristocrat boot shopkeeper. TLS
Husband, away on expedition, woman remarries when she falls in love. Learns later she's not a bigamist; husband number one died before second marriage. ATH

005988   THE MODERN MAGICIAN. London: T W Laurie, [1920] BMC.

TLS-37 year old man undertakes search for eugenically fit mother (not a success)
ATH-heroine is reduced to earning her living as an escort. Above faddist marries her and disappointed takes her to a doctor who thinking her unhappily mated arranges an informal exchange of husbands.

005989   THE PICCADILLY PURITAN. London: Fawcett, [1917] BMC NUC.

Alice seemed to be a "pick up" turns out to be a Puritan. TLS

005990   PINK PURITY. London: J. Milne, 1909 BMC.

Lil Carlingbord is "a female sinner at 15," a very objectionable young woman. TLS

005991   THE PRICE. London: Everett, 1911 BMC NUC. London and New York: M. Kennerley, 1911 NUC.

Aviation novel. Wife meets woman assumedly her husband's first wife; takes a lover, "comes to grief at the end because she insists on kissing her lover in a monoplane," TLS
Story of social climber. NYT
The couple crash in a plane. NYT

005992   PURPLE PASSION. London: T.W. Laurie, [1915] BMC.

005993   RED LOVE. London: T.W. Laurie, [1908] BMC.

TLS- sexual antagonism, passions. Lacks taste.

005994   SCARLET KISS; THE STORY OF A DEGENERATE WOMAN WHO DRIFTED. London: T.W. Laurie, [1910] BMC NUC.

LEKM-spinster of 30, editor of low-class paper Home Comfort. Marries but does not settle down to an uneventful life.

005995   THE SECRET FLAT. London: T.W. Laurie, [1914] BMC.

The sexual infatuations of the successful composer of love lyrics, her troubles and divorce do not make a pleasant story. TLS
The heroine tells her story. Treats the 7th commandment as though it now were an historical scrap of paper. War comes, loses means of livelihood, lover leaves for front, husband divorces her, refugee doesn't stay with her (another man.) ACAD

005996   STRINGS. London: Everett, [1914] BMC.

ATH: a man seeks the supremest satisfaction by leaving home and plunging into dissipation--only to return.

005997   A VERY BAD WOMAN. London: T.W. Laurie, [1919] BMC NUC.

005998   VIOLET VIRTUE. London: T.w. Laurie, [1916] BMC.

TLS-At 18 heroine marries rich older man; after unhappiness runs away and falls in love, divorces and remarries (happy) end of her career.

005999   WHITE WISDOM. London: Everett, [1913] BMC.

TLS- office of the Flashlight and the girls employed in the folding dept. Not a nice story.

006000   THE WIFE WHO FOUND OUT. London: T.W. Laurie, [1915] BMC.

Couple takes in a refugee. Very indulgent and faithful wife. TLS

006001   THE WILD WIDOW. London: T. W. Laurie, [1908] BMC. New York: Empire Book, [c1908] NUC.

Collects husband's life insurance, plays roulette at Monte Carlo and wins, invests in stocks. But there's a secret @ whether or not she's a widow? NYT ACAD
BKM-defrauds an insurance co., wins at Monte Carlo, speculates on the market, wins wealth and society.
ATH-vividly presented.

JAMES, KATHERINE.

006002   BEFORE THE DAWN. London: Chapman and Hall, 1913 BMC.

1849, Italy, two brothers who are look-alikes. Melodrama. Historical romance. ACAD

006003   THE CITY OF CONTRASTS: A STORY OF OLD PERUGIA. London: Chapman & Hall, 1915 BMC.

Fighting, feasting, treason. TLS
Focus on Andrea of Perugia. ATH

JAMES, M. H.

006004   BOGIE TALES OF EAST ANGLIA. Ipswich: Pawsey and Hayes, 1891 BMC.

JAMES, MARTHA, pseud. See DOYLE, MARTHA CLAIRE (MACGOWAN).

JAMES, MRS. JOHN. See JAMES, DOROTHY A BECKETT (TERRELL).

JAMES, WILHELMINA MARTHA.

006005   ANOTHER MAN'S BURDEN: A TALE OF LOVE AND DUTY. BY AUSTIN CLARE. London: S. P. C. K., [1892] BMC.

PW-Hero's father leaves him a legacy of debt with a dying request that he repay it. He does so; another love requires an even greater sacrifice; his nobility is finally rewarded.

006006   ANOTHER PAIR OF SHOES; A NORTHUMBRIAN

STORY. BY AUSTIN CLARE. London: S.P.C.K., [1911] BMC.
New York: E.S. Gorham, [n.d.] NUC.

006007   BY LANTERN LIGHT: A TALE OF THE CORNISH
COAST. BY AUSTIN CLARE. London: S. P. C. K., [1893]
BMC.

006008   THE CONSCIENCE OF DR. HOLT. BY AUSTIN
CLARE. London: J. Long, 1908 BMC.

TLS-o
ATH-Daughter of a dying man asks a young doctor to let
him die before he can write a will which will cause
her mother a grave injustice. MD falls in love with
her immediately.

006009   COURT CARDS, CHIEFLY THE KNAVE OF HEARTS.
A ROMANCE OF THE LITTLE GAME PLAYED BETWEEN ENGLAND
AND SCOTLAND AT THE CLOSE OF THE SIXTEENTH CENTURY. BY
AUSTIN CLARE. London: T.F. Unwin, 1903 BMC.

Historical romance-Baker 32, 104.

006010   "CROOKED S": THE STORY OF A SQUARE PEG IN
A ROUND HOLE. BY AUSTIN CLARE. London: Griffith &
Farran, [1891] BMC.

006011   AN ILL MATCHED PAIR: THE STORY OF A
MARRIAGE OF CONVENIENCE. BY AUSTIN CLARE. London: S.
P. C. K., [1896] BMC.

006012   THE LITTLE GATE OF TEARS. A ROMANCE OF
THE ISLAND OF GUERNSEY. BY AUSTIN CLARE. London: J.
Long, 1906 BMC.

TLS-Love story

006013   A LOCAL LION: THE STORY OF A FALSE
ESTIMATE. BY AUSTIN CLARE. London: S. P. C. K., 1891
BMC NUC. (NUC shows subtitle: Story for Young Men and
Maidens.)

006014   ONE STEP ASTRAY. BY AUSTIN CLARE. London:
S. P. C. K., 1894 BMC.

006015   OUT OF THE NET; OR, THE CHANGE IN ROBERT
HOLT. BY AUSTIN CLARE. London: S. P. C. K., [1899]
BMC.

006016   RANDAL OF RANDALHOLME: A TYNEDALE
TRAGEDY. BY AUSTIN CLARE. London: Chatto & Windus,
1904 BMC.

006017   A REAL REPENTANCE: A STORY OF
OBERAMMERGAU. BY AUSTIN CLARE. London: Griffith,
Farran, [1894] BMC NUC.

SR:story about the play.

006018   THE SHADOW OF A CLOUD. BY AUSTIN CLARE.
London: S.P.C.K., [1907] BMC.

006019   THE SIEGE PERILOUS. BY AUSTIN CLARE.
London: S. P. C. K., [1897] BMC.

Hero is an infantry man. On being ordered abroad,
sends sister and brother to Scot. border. He runs away
with an acting company. Then becomes a school teacher.
Simple life story. LIT 1:148.

006020   STANDARD-BEARERS: A STORY OF CHURCH
DEFENSE. BY AUSTIN CLARE. London: S. P. C. K., [1891]
BMC.

006021   THE TIDEWAY: A NOVEL. BY AUSTIN CLARE.
London: Chatto & Windus, 1903 BMC NUC.

Man marries under false pretenses (his money not
rightly his); he dies. "The number of undesireable
husbands who are killed off by ruthless novelists is
appalling to contemplate, by the way." Heroine has
"too many good points." ATH 121 300

006022   UNDER THE DOG-STAR: A TALE OF THE
BORDERS. BY AUSTIN CLARE. London: S. P. C. K., [1895]
BMC.

JAMES, WINIFRED. See DE JAN, WINIFRED LEWELLIN JAMES.

JAMESON, ANNIE EDITH (FOSTER). 1868-1931. United Kingdom.

006023   THE ART OF LIVING. SOCIAL PROBLEMS SOLVED
IN A NOVEL STORY-A NEW IDEA. BY J. E. BUCKROSE.
London: "The Gentlewoman Offices", 1903 BMC NUC.

006024   AUNT AUGUSTA IN EGYPT. BY J. E. BUCKROSE.
London: Mills & Boon, [1915] BMC.

006025   A BACHELOR'S COMEDY. BY J. E. BUCKROSE.
New York: Hodder & Stoughton, G. H. Doran, [c1912]
NUC. London: Mills & Boon, 1912 BMC NUC.

PW-the making of a man, a vicar
TLS-the making of a man, a vicar

006026   BECAUSE OF JANE. BY J. E. BUCKROSE. New
York: Hodder & Stoughton, G. H. Doran, [c1913] NUC.
London: Mills & Boon, [1913] NUC BMC.

Jane, an enfant terrible-helps save a marriage;
humorous.
PW 84 8-16-13 458 "Jane, aged six, is in full charge
of her aunt's love-story. She decides that she had
better be married and sets out to find a suitable
partner. During her activities Aunt Beatrice is caused
considerable embarrassment, and so is Jane's mother, a
thoroughly self-satisfied lady of extreme virtue, but
in the end the little girl's wishes are fulfilled."

006027   THE BROWNS. BY J. E. BUCKROSE. New York:
Hodder & Stoughton, G.H. Doran, [c1912] NUC. London:
Mills & Boon, [1912] BMC NUC.

mother and daughter; mother of joyous disposition;
daughter has violent battle with her conscience.
concerns a will and an old woman who changes it at the
last minute so that Miss Brown and Mrs. Brown need to
connive to get the money. They do, but daughter feels
guilty. Everyday people and narrow quiet lives NYT
ATH love story and inheritance.
TLS love story and inheritance.

006028   DOWN OUR STREET; A PROVINCIAL COMEDY. BY
J. E. BUCKROSE. London: Mills & Boon, [1911] BMC NUC.
New York: G. P. Putnam's Sons, 1911 NUC.

average kindly people 5-13-13 PW
Story centers on Mrs Bean who makes church suppers,
etc. succeed s because she'll do what others don't
quite like to do. TLS

006029   GAY MORNING. BY J. E. BUCKROSE. London:
Mills and Boon, [1914] BMC NUC. New York: Hodder &
Stoughton, [c1914] NUC.

ATH-Trad. romance and family.
TLS 13:40

006030   THE GIRL IN FANCY DRESS. BY J. E.
BUCKROSE. London: Hodder & Stoughton, [1920] BMC. New
York: G. H. Doran, [c1921] NUC.

TLS soc. com.

006031   A GOLDEN STRAW. BY J. E. BUCKROSE.
London: Mills & Boon, [1910] BMC NUC.

TLS-female is unable to marry either of her two lovers
ATH st of a secret mrg of a high minded emotional
woman to a weak musician.
SP St of a good hearted but dishonest businessman who
makes a fortune on patent soap.

006032   THE GOSSIP SHOP. BY J. E. BUCKROSE.
London and New York: Hodder & Stoughton, 1917 NUC BMC.
New York: G. H. Doran, [c1917] NUC.

A "Cranford" full of gentle little ladies, neat
houses, cream, kindness and delicate ways. Title seems
hard for there's not a malicious person in sight. They
were all "dears" in Wendlebury. Delia Lambert, her
gypsy ways, her cigarettes, her unconventionality. It
is she that attracts the man from the side of sweet
Pauine Westcott. TLS
Serious only a few pages at a time. Clever, enjoyable
LBKM
Charming, humorous SP
PW-love and romance
NYT-Wendlebury another Cranford, gossip initiated by
heroine in all innocence comes close to ruining a
man's life.

006033   THE GREY SHEPHERD. THE GROWTH OF A
LEGEND. BY J. E. BUCKROSE. London: Hodder & Stoughton,
1916 BMC NUC.

TLS Male hero
LBKM male hero

006034   A LITTLE GREEN WORLD; A VILLAGE COMEDY
WITHOUT A PLOT AND WITHOUT A PROBLEM. BY J. E.
BUCKROSE. London: Hutchinson, 1909 BMC. New York and

London: G. P. Putnam's Sons, 1913 NUC.

humorous story about a village TLS
Lydia Bell is high spirited, heroine-like LBKM
PW 9-20-13 766 "author of "Down Our Street", here
records the happenings in an English rural community,
where most of the inhabitants have social aspirations
which cause much heart burning and many humorous
situations. Into this society come Lydia Bell and her
mother, having just lost their money, and Lydia's
attractiveness and love of fun add to the social
disquiet particularly after the two most eligible men
fall in love with her."
Pleasant, delightful, healthful NYT

006035   LOVE IN A LITTLE TOWN. BY J. E. BUCKROSE.
London: Mills & Boon, [1911] BMC NUC. New York and
London: G. P. Putnam's Sons, 1911 NUC.

Straight love story PW 9-30-11

006036   MARRIAGE WHILE YOU WAIT. BY J. E.
BUCKROSE. London and New York: Hodder & Stoughton,
1919 NUC BMC.

Sophia Hastings and Captain Brooke marry. when he
comes back from service nerve wrecked, they face the
real trial and drift very near to disaster. TLS SP

006037   THE MATCHMAKERS. BY J. E. BUCKROSE. New
York: G. H. Doran, [c1916] NUC. London: Hodder &
Stoughton, [1916] BMC.

Cheerful pleasant story of our Miss Peggy and the
matchmakers of Pendleton who get her married to a rich
young man. Ends happily for everyone. sweet and sent.
NYT 2-11-17 47.
Villagers of a small town try to marry off the
Rector's daughter BKM
TLS "dear"

006038   THE PILGRIMAGE OF A FOOL. BY J. E.
BUCKROSE. London: Mills & Boon, 1910 BMC.

TLS-male hero seeks God

006039   THE ROUND-ABOUT. BY J. E. BUCKROSE.
London and New York: Hodder & Stoughton, 1916 NUC BMC.

The women of the Taylor family do a round about in the
20th. Lucy in Mid-Vict. times marries whom she
pleased; her daughter learns a trade and goes to war
as a nurse. PW
NYT O
TLS-father is an offensive bully.

006040   THE SILENT LEGION. BY J. E. BUCKROSE.
London and New York: Hodder & Stoughton, [c1918] NUC
BMC.

PW-Barbara returns to family from work in hospital to
help out with mother who has lost son in war and with
finances from war-ruined father. Meets Julian, family
does not approve and she feels it her duty to take
care of mother. Mother helps out and brings a
reconciliation
NYT Nov 8 '18 p. 471. Silent legion is the Br.
Middle-class, silently enduring the sacrifices they
are called on to make in wartime.

006041   SPRAY ON THE WINDOWS. BY J. E. BUCKROSE.
London: Mills & Boon, [1915] BMC NUC. New York: G. H.
Doran, [c1915] NUC.

dreams of marr. finds it sordid, considers leaving. PW
4-17-15
Ann Middleton dreams of marriage; tries to find a
husband but she's from poor family tho she's
beautiful, so she gets out-becomes a secretary. Then
she does marry, marr. fails but happy end (?) Ann
develops from a rather selfish girl to a noble woman
NYT
Ann "whose fate is to be slowly purged thru prosaic
suffering", at first is mean. Ann is the virgin
huntress type of Man and Superman. TLS
Heroine strong but stronger still is her wish to
comfort men hurt in battle with life, Mrs. Walker is
the older woman dispensing wise sayings. ATH

006042   THE TALE OF MR. TUBBS, A STORY OF A
KNIGHT WITHOUT ARMOUR. BY J. E. BUCKROSE. London:
Hodder & Stoughton, 1918 BMC NUC. New York:

TLS male hero, farce

006043   THE TOLL-BAR. BY J. E. BUCKROSE. London:

Hutchinson, 1907 BMC. New York and London: G. P.
Putnam's sons, 1912 NUC.

man in love with daughter of man he suspects murdered
his father LBKM 5-07,70
PW-Char. portraiture of drunken husband, colorless
wife and their daughter
NYT-gloomy dark book, altho heroine and hero are
united in end

006044   VOICES. BY J. E. BUCKROSE. London:
Hutchinson, 1908 NUC BMC.

TLS- Esther could hear voices, sect of hearers
developed, finally she confessed it was all humbug.
ATH-aunt brings the girl to her senses
SP faith healer. Esther had ordinary abilities but was
possessed with ambition to distinguish herself. Rival
of her prettier sister.

006045   WAR-TIME IN OUR STREET. THE STORY OF SOME
COMPANIES BEHIND THE FIRING LINE. BY J. E. BUCKROSE.
London and New York: Hodder and Stoughton, 1917 NUC
BMC.

006046   THE WOLF. BY J. E. BUCKROSE. London:
Hutchinson, 1908 NUC BMC.

TLS-married couple, inheritance insanity.
BKM married couple, inheritance insanity.

006047   THE WOOD END; A NOVEL. BY J. E. BUCKROSE.
London: Hutchinson, 1906 BMC NUC.

TLS- and ATH-idyllic courtship in the woods.

006048   YOUNG HEARTS. BY J. E. BUCKROSE. London:
Hodder & Stoughton, [c1920] BMC NUC. New York: G. H.
Doran, [c1920] NUC.

TLS- romantic comedy, family.
SP

JAMESON, E. M., pseud. See JONES, ELAINE ANTHONY.

JAMESON, EVA.

006049   WHEN THE DREAM IS PAST. London: J.
Nisbet, 1902 BMC.

ATH-4-5-02 not helpful.

JAMESON, MARGARET STORM. B. 1897. United Kingdom.

006050   THE HAPPY HIGHWAYS. BY STORM JAMESON. New
York: Century, 1920 NUC. London: W. Heinemann, 1920
BMC NUC.

TLS-Talk talk talk of Yorkshire studs in London on
every controversial subject. Margaret's sad
development. Narrated by Joy Hearne.
LBKM-Margaret dominates story. Lives with the students
until her marriage, when she marries one man altho
loving another. Unconv.

006051   THE POT BOILS; A NOVEL. BY STORM JAMESON.
London: Constable, [1919] BMC NUC.

presentation of opinions of Bolshevism and Neitzsche
thru chars. an attempt to show the notions of the
English cultured class-the intelligentsia-on
Fabianism, feminism. Story of young woman in Northern
univ; her career there and in London. Till she
marries. Reveals an erotic very, high browed student
life *she proceeds to London has a "good time" doing
the School of Economics and writing for suffragette
newspapers. Her tendency to erotic dreams. *suggests
unmarried students slept together "the sanity of the
new Renaissance." TLS

JAMESON, STORM. See JAMESON, MARGARET STORM.

JAMIESON, JANE H.

006052   MR. MACKENZIE'S WEDDING: A SHORT
CHRONICLE OF COLSTON. Edinburgh and London: Oliphant,
1893 BMC NUC.

Two stories "readable, wholesome" about wooing and
wedding. AcaD 44:108.

JAMISON, CECILIA VIETS. 1837?-1909. United States.

006053   LADY JANE. BY MRS. C. V. JAMISON. New
York: Century, 1891 NUC. London: Osgood, McIlvaine,
1891 BMC.

BMC shows "Lady Jane" as title.

006054   THISTLEDOWN. BY MRS. C. V. JAMISON. New
York: Century, 1903 NUC BMC.

Story of a male acrobat. PW 10-17-03

006055   TOINETTE'S PHILIP. BY MRS. C. V. JAMISON.
New York: Century, 1894 NUC BMC. London: Osgood,
McIlvaine, 1896 BMC.

JAMISON, MRS. C. V. See JAMISON, CECILIA VIETS.

JANIS, ELSIE. 1890-1956. United States.

006056   LOVE LETTERS OF AN ACTRESS. New York and
London: D. Appleton, 1913 NUC BMC.

series of letters between actress and all kinds of men
who love her. She marries none talks of career as
first love; still at end has dream of the man that
takes her away from it all-passionate love. But awakes
to reality that there's none such.
"Love story told in form of letters received and
written by a popular American actress. It is not a
love story in the sense of two people meeting and
marrying happily, but rather the record of the men,
who loved the actress, no one of whom was "Mr Right."
The character of the different men is revealed by
their letters, while her point of view, her hopes,
ideals and ambitions are shown in her replies." PW
5-31-13:1957

006057   A STAR FOR A NIGHT; A STORY OF STAGE
LIFE. New York: W. Rickey, 1911 NUC BMC.

JANVIER, MARGARET THOMSON. 1845-1913. United States.

006058   UMBRELLAS TO MEND. BY MARGARET
VANDEGRIFT. Boston: R. G. Badger, 1905 NUC.

JARBOE, MARY HALSEY (THOMAS). United States.

006059   'GO FORTH AND FIND.' BY THOMAS H.
BRAINERD. New York: Cassell, [c1895] BMC NUC.

006060   ROBERT ATTERBURY: A STUDY OF LOVE AND
LIFE. BY THOMAS H. BRAINERD. New York: Cassell,
[c1896] NUC.

PW 4-4-96. Illustration of author's views on mrge, 3
couples in story, story shifts from Calif. to Japan to
Boston. Chief characters are a young woman whose
mother is insane, and Robert who has inherited
consumption. They love each other, do not believe they
should marry, devise "a plan of living by which they
can be together, of which the book tells."

JARMAN, LIZZIE SUE GILBERT. United States.

006061   SHADOW OF ABSENT LOVE. BY MRS. L. GILBERT
JARMAN. Memphis, Tenn.: Southern, 1903 NUC.

JARMAN, MRS. L. GILBERT. See JARMAN, LIZZIE SUE GILBERT.

JAY, EDITH KATHARINE SPICER. Nationality Unknown.

006062   THE APOTHEOSIS OF MR. TYRAWLEY. BY E.
LIVINGSTON PRESCOTT. London: R. Bentley, 1896 BMC. New
York: Harper, 1896 NUC.

SR Handsome adventurer reforms for the love of a young
woman.
BKM 3:457. He is a gambler, and he has rescued her
from drowning.

006063   DEARER THAN HONOUR: A FOOL'S TRAGEDY. BY
E. LIVINGSTON PRESCOTT. London: Hutchinson, 1898 BMC.

LIT 2:704. Engaged man is persuaded by rival that
there is hereditary insanity in family. He commits a
theft and serves a prison sentence to protect girl
from himself. Finds out truth years later.
LEKM 14:81. Noble sacrificing hero. His life as a
convict, nine months of solitary, hard labour, and a
social pariah when he comes out. "Convict fiction."

006064   DONNY'S CAPTAIN. BY E. LIVINGSTON
PRESCOTT. London: R. T. S., [1903] BMC.

006065   HELOT AND HERO: A NOVEL. BY E. LIVINGSTON
PRESCOTT. London: Simpkin, Marshall, 1899 BMC.

Col. Niven's eldest son dies while gambling with a
card-shark called Blount, who also dies. The Col.

kidnaps Blount's son and makes him a "helot" to
prevent his own son from becoming a gambler. LIT 4:583

006066   HIS FAMILIAR FOE. THE STORY OF THE
DEGRADING INHERITANCE OF CAPTAIN ROBERT DUCIE OF H. M.
SILVER LANCERS. BY E. LIVINGSTON PRESCOTT. London: G.
Richards, 1901 BMC.

006067   ILLUSION: A ROMANCE OF MODERN EGYPT. BY
E. LIVINGSTON PRESCOTT. London: Simpkin, Marshall,
1899 BMC.

Plot to ruin a gallant young officer by injection that
produces the effects of drunkenness. SP 83:702

006068   A MASK AND A MARTYR. BY E. LIVINGSTON
PRESCOTT. London: E. Arnold, 1896 BMC NUC.

SR-Capt. Harradyne, resigned from Army with rumours of
war; his brother officers sent him a white feather. He
was, altho a Sunday school teacher, seen coming out of
public houses and was believed to be a drunk and a
wife-beater. His wife never went out. He was convicted
of stealing a jewel. He was seen frequently with fresh
wounds and bruises. what was going on? His wife was a
violent drunk, and he was protecting her. She finally
dies and he enlists as a private, dies fighting in
Egypt.
ATH 107:440. "Since 'Poor Nellie'-a book of a very
different method and manner with a somewhat similar
motive-we have seen nothing at all in fiction that
seems at all to touch the real aspect of the subject."
Author fails to make the husband completely
sympathetic-a few jarring notes.
ACAD 49:382. "A life which can only be described as a
hell on earth"-for him.
SP 76:487. Violet is a "raving murderess" when drunk.
"Even when she is perfectly sane and comparatively
sober, she is so selfish as to be absolutely incapable
of arousing devotion..."

006069   THE MEASURE OF A MAN. BY E. LIVINGSTON
PRESCOTT. London: J. Nisbet, 1898 BMC. New York: R. F.
Fenno, 1899 NUC.

SP 81:745. "Highly-coloured romance...redolent of the
old yellow-back sentimentality."
LIT 3:423. Hero is a non-com sgt.
SR 86:513. He is self-imagined martyr, his wife a
lady.
A plain sergeant is injured, found by young highly
educated woman who helps him. Love develops between
them. He educates himself to rise to her level. PW
55:646.
"One naturally judges the author to be... an army
officer." LW 30:235.
Country life in England and social world of London.
Hero, a sergeant, loves a young woman whose background
is a mystery. They marry secretly-Then separate. He's
off to India-She to establish her place in landed
society.- "her right of birth." Meets different kinds
of men; when husband returns, sees he's different, but
chooses him as the finer one. NYT 6-24-99, 407.

006070   THE MOST SECRET TRIBUNAL. BY E.
LIVINGSTON PRESCOTT. London: G. Richards, 1903 BMC.

006071   THE QUEEN'S OWN TRAITORS. BY E.
LIVINGSTON PRESCOTT. London: Hutchinson, 1904 BMC.

006072   THE RIP'S REDEMPTION: A TROOPER'S STORY.
BY E. LIVINGSTON PRESCOTT. London: J. Nisbet, 1897
BMC.

Young man finds his allowance cut off, joins army.
Degenerates. A letter from the sweetheart of a dead
friend starts him on the way up. ACAD 52 Fic Sup 111.
"Details of contemporary life among the troopers of
the first and second Life Guards have formed the
subject of more than one novel by Mr. Prescott." ATH
110:416.

006073   A SMALL SMALL CHILD. BY E. LIVINGSTON
PRESCOTT. London: J. Bowden, 1898 BMC.

006074   WITH CORDS OF LOVE. BY E. LIVINGSTON
PRESCOTT. London: R. T. S., [1904] BMC. London:
'Leisure Hour' Library Office, [1907] NUC BMC.

JAY, W. M. L., pseud. See WOODRUFF, JULIA LOUISA MATILDA
(CURTISS).

JEANS, ALICE.

006075   MINGLED SEED. London: J. Ouseley, [1913]
BMC.

Italy of the past, Mafia of Sicily, corruption, many
facts and much explanation. Francesco a principal
character ACAD

006076   THE REFORMER'S WIFE. London: Murray &
Evenden, 1912 BMC.

ATH-evils of factories
TLS-tale of early movements against factory abuse,
artless

006077   THE STRONGER WINGS. London: E. Stock,
1909 BMC NUC.

hist rom. TLS

JENKINS, HESTER DONALDSON. 1869-1941.

006078   BEHIND TURKISH LATTICES: THE STORY OF A
TURKISH WOMAN'S LIFE. Philadelphia: J. B. Lippincott,
1911 NUC. London: Chatto and Windus, 1911 NUC BMC.

HQ 1707 Turkey-Soc. life and custom; women in Turkey

JENKINSON, EMILY J. B. 1879. United Kingdom.

006079   BARBARA LYNN, A TALE OF THE DALES AND
FELLS. London: E. Arnold, 1914 NUC BMC.

SR 147:510. Two sisters in Westmorland, schoolmaster
marries wrong one. unhappy ending.
TLS Barbara (the one he didn't marry) a "great spirit
in a great body". Terrible old woman who rules from
her bed both of her great granddaughters, Lucy and
Barbara.

006080   SILVERWOOL. New York: Baker & Taylor,
[1910] NUC. London: E. Arnold, 1910 BMC NUC.

rivalry among sheep farmers, love triangle PW
ACAD Silverwool is a sheep

006081   THE SOUL OF UNREST; A NOVEL. London: E.
Arnold, 1912 BMC NUC. New York: Duffield, 1913 NUC.

ATH-poor and rich
TLS young woman stirred to service in slums
PW 84 8/9/13:424-"Inis Glora, a wild island of the
North Sea, where Bride grew up in the ruined castle of
the Macdonalds, and where she developed a love of all
things beautiful both spiritual and natural, and Angel
Meadow, a dreadful slum in a manufacturing town, where
she went to help the poor, are the two settings in
which this story of present-day social and industrial
conditions is developed."

JENNER, KATHERINE LEE (RAWLINGS). United Kingdom.

006082   LOVE OR MONEY: A NOVEL. BY KATHERINE LEE
(MRS. HENRY JENNER). London: Bentley, 1891 BMC NUC.
New York: D. Appleton, 1892 NUC.

She's "scheming worldly, imperturbable in her self
reliance and utterly destitute of a conscience." Gets
in serious trouble. Is sentenced to be hanged. ATH 98
579
IND 44:413. Life of church people in English parish.
Two daughters of rector are opposites, one living for
love, one for money.
CR 17:224. Oldest daughter of clergyman marries
nobleman for his money, soon runs through his fortune.
She determines then to go to continent with another
man, but forgets something and returning to home
finds her husband has shot himself. She is accused of
his murder and finally exonerated.
LW 23:58. Characters are "super-angelic" or
"super-diabolic." Really is no love.
PW-Clergyman with 11 children and a limited income. A
daughter is suspected of killing her husband and is
tried.
Portrait of young woman completely selfish egoist with
no moral sense-Phil Ferrars. She "feels her life in
every limb." Her seductive devilries; lovely and
wicked black sheep of family; father a Vicar. "We're
compelled to believe in her". Able novel well written.
ACAD

006083   WHEN FORTUNE FROWNS: BEING THE LIFE AND
ADVENTURES OF GILBERT COSWARTH. London: H. Cox, 1895
BMC.

JENNER, MRS. HENRY. See JENNER, KATHERINE LEE (RAWLINGS).

JENNINGS, MARY ELIZABETH. United States.

006084   ASA OF BETHLEHEM AND HIS HOUSEHOLD. B.C.
IV--A.D. XXX. New York: A. D. F. Randolph, 1895 NUC.

006085   THE BRAVE LITTLE MAID OF GOLDAU. New
York: A. D. F. Randolph, [c1892] NUC.

JEPHSON, HARRIET JULIA (CAMPBELL).

006086   LETTERS TO A DEBUTANTE. BY LADY JEPHSON.
Philadelphia: J. B. Lippincott, 1905 NUC. London: E.
Nash, 1905 BMC.

Conventional advice--courtesy book. NYT 620,05
Social ethics.

JEPHSON, LADY. See JEPHSON, HARRIET JULIA (CAMPBELL).

JESSE, F. TENNYSON. See HARWOOD, FRYNIWYD TENNYSON (JESSE).

JEWELL, A. IRENE. United States.

006087   MURIEL STERLING: A TALE OF THE AFRICAN
VELDT. BY MRS. FLETCHER WEBSTER JEWELL. New York:
International Book, 1900 NUC BMC.

JEWELL, LOUISE POND.

006088   THE GREAT ADVENTURE. New York: F. A.
Stokes, [c1911] NUC BMC. London: G. Bell, 1916 BMC.

Woman looks forward to death "with eagerness and
curiosity." When she comes close to dying feels real
excitement for the great adventure. NYT

JEWELL, MRS. FLETCHER WEBSTER. See JEWELL, A. IRENE.

JEWETT, SARAH ORNE. 1849-1909. United States.

006089   THE COUNTRY OF THE POINTED FIRS. Boston:
Houghton, Mifflin, 1896 NUC. London: T. F. Unwin, 1896
BMC.

LW 27:457. Dunnet Landing.
NYT Dec 12, 1896, p2. Fisher-folk in a Maine village.

006090   THE TORY LOVER. London: Smith, Elder,
1901 BMC. Boston: Houghton, Mifflin, 1901 NUC.

ATH 2-8-02 Book panned by Flora Mail Holly as an
historical novel see BKM p 195-6 Oct 1901
hist rom conventional DIAL
Heroine is sweet brave charming winsome loveable sane
gentle BOOK BUYER '01

JOCELYN, MRS. ROBERT. See RODEN, ADA MARIA (JENYNS)
JOCELYN.

JOHN, ALIX, pseud. See JONES, ALICE.

JOHN, EUGENIE. 1825-1887.

006091   A BRAVE WOMAN. BY E. MARLITT. New York:
Allison, [1891] NUC. (Tr. Margaret P. Waterman)

Countess Von Mainau is a 2nd wife. Husband loves
another woman and she's loved by Jesuit priest. She
has many enemies-close only to stepson. Wins over
husband in the end. CR

JOHNES, WINIFRED WALLACE (TINKER). United States.

006092   MEMOIRS OF A LITTLE GIRL. New York &
London: Transatlantic, 1896 NUC.

006093   MISS GWYNNE, BACHELOR: A NOVEL. New York:
G. W. Dillingham, 1894 NUC.

JOHNSON, ANNA. B. 1860. United States.

006094   AN ABUNDANT HARVEST. BY HOPE DARING.
Cincinnati: Jennings & Graham, [1904] NUC.

006095   AGNES GRANT'S EDUCATION. BY HOPE DARING.
Cincinnati: Jennings & Pye, [1902] NUC.

"efforts to fit herself for a teacher's profession" PW

006096   THE APPOINTED WAY; A TALE OF THE
SEVENTH-DAY ADVENTISTS. BY HOPE DARING. Philadelphia:
Griffith & Rowland Press, 1905 NUC.

pretty rel story PW 10-14-05

006097   ENTERING INTO HIS OWN. BY HOPE DARING.
New York: American Tract Society, [1903] NUC.

006098   FATHER JOHN; OR, RUTH WEBSTER'S QUEST. BY HOPE DARING. New York: American Tract Society, [c1907] NUC.

006099   THE GORDONS. BY HOPE DARING. New York: American Tract Society, [c1912] NUC.

006100   MADELINE, THE ISLAND GIRL. BY HOPE DARING. New York: Eaton & Mains, [c1906] NUC.

PW-young girl's story, inheritance etc.

006101   PAYING THE PRICE! BY HOPE DARING. New York: American Tract Society, [c1914] NUC.

self willed girl willing to marry for money learns better. (learns what) ? PW 1-16-15

006102   TO THE THIRD GENERATION. BY HOPE DARING. New York: American Tract Society, [1901] NUC.

a temperance story

006103   VALADERO RANCH. BY HOPE DARING. New York: American Tract Society, [c1911] NUC.

006104   A VIRGINIAN HOLIDAY. BY HOPE DARING. New York: American Tract Society, [c1909] NUC.

Story of treachery, love and kindness PW

JOHNSON, ANNIE FELLOWS. See JOHNSTON, ANNIE (FELLOWS).

JOHNSON, CORINNE.

006105   MARY KINGWOOD'S SCHOOL; A REAL STORY IDEALLY PRESENTED. New York: A. S. Barnes, [c1906] NUC.

JOHNSON, ELIZABETH WINTHROP. B. 1850. United States.

006106   ONE CHANCE IN A HUNDRED: A NOVEL. Boston: R.G. Badger, [c1911] NUC.

"a great deal of lawless loving" PW 12-2-11

006107   ORCHARD FOLK: TWO CALIFORNIA STORIES. New York: Continental, 1898 NUC.

JOHNSON, FANNY KEMBLE. See COSTELLO, FANNY KEMBLE (JOHNSON).

JOHNSON, LILLIAN (HARTMAN). United States.

006108   CHRISTMAS THORNS. Durango, Colorado: [c1895] NUC.

JOHNSON, MARY KELLOGG. B. 1836. United States.

006109   MAC: A DOG'S TRUE STORY. Boston: H. H. Carter, 1895 NUC.

JOHNSON, MRS. A. E.

006110   MARTINA MERIDEN; OR, WHAT IS MY MOTIVE? Philadelphia: American Baptist Pub. Soc., [1901] NUC.

JOHNSON, VIRGINIA WALES. 1849-1916. United States.

006111   A BERMUDA LILY. New York: A.S. Barnes, 1912 NUC.

PW-Young woman disappointed in love devotes her life to raising flowers.

006112   A ROYAL PHYSICIAN. London: T. F. Unwin, 1891 BMC NUC.

Setting is Tyrol. Lena is granddaughter of castle custodian loved by woodcarver artist. A man returns to Tyrol who loves her, tries to kill the artist but only injures his eyes. Artist's sight saved by a famous royal physician. SP, 66 732
Conventional story. ATH 97 245
Story of the Tyrol. ACAD

006113   A WORLD'S SHRINE. London: Gay and Bird, 1902 BMC.

Fic?

JOHNSTON, ANNIE (FELLOWS). 1863-1931. United States.

006114   ASA HOLMES; OR, AT THE CROSSROADS. Boston: L.C. Page, 1902 NUC.

NYT 6-28-02 elderly philosophical man.

006115   FLIP'S "ISLANDS OF PROVIDENCE". Boston: L.C. Page, 1904 NUC.

young man's experience looking for work PW 9-19-03

006116   GEORGINA OF THE RAINBOWS. New York: Britton, [c1916] NUC BMC.

006117   GEORGINA'S SERVICE STARS. New York: Britton, [c1918] NUC BMC. London and New York: D. Appleton, 1920 NUC BMC.

006118   IN THE DESERT OF WAITING; THE LEGEND OF CAMEL-BACK MOUNTAIN. Boston: L. C. Page, 1904 NUC.

006119   IT WAS THE ROAD TO JERICHO. New York: Britton, [c1919] NUC.

006120   THE JESTER'S SWORD, HOW ALDEBARAN, THE KING'S SON, WORE THE SHEATHED SWORD OF CONQUEST. Boston: L. C. Page, 1909 NUC.

006121   MARY WARE IN TEXAS. Boston: L. C. Page, 1910 NUC.

006122   MARY WARE'S PROMISED LAND. Boston: L. C. Page, 1912 NUC BMC.

PW--Gives up man she loves for sake of her work-later marries when it does not interfere with it.

006123   MISS SANTA CLAUS OF THE PULLMAN. BY ANNIE FELLOWS JOHNSON. New York: Century, 1913 NUC.

006124   TRAVELERS FIVE ALONG LIFE'S HIGHWAY: JIMMY, GIDEON WIGGAN, THE CLOWN, WEXLEY SNATHERS, BAP. SLOAN. Boston: L.C. Page, 1911 NUC.

JOHNSTON, GRACE L. KEITH. United Kingdom.

006125   BY FANCY LED. BY LESLIE KEITH. London: H. Marshall, 1901 BMC.

006126   CYNTHIA'S BROTHER. BY LESLIE KEITH. London: Religious Tract Society, [1901] BMC.

006127   THE DECEIVER. BY LESLIE KEITH. London: Religious Tract Soc., [1905] BMC. London: 'Leisure Hour' Library Office, [1907] NUC.

wife, really the second wife, sees that long-dead wife #1 has a fortune coming to her. She poses as wife #1 for benefit of her sick blind child. When child dies, she repents. Kills herself? ACAD 1265,05

006128   FOR LOVE OF PRUE. BY LESLIE KEITH. London: A. D. Innes, 1895 BMC.

Prue's romance and that of her cousin Rosa Brower, "robust and sensible-minded" Scene a remote Scotch Island. Prue Chillingworth, young widow, is independent. "Her wish to pauperize her less fortunate brethren has serious consequences." ATH 106:788 ACAD 49:75. Her warm heart and kindness turn her nephew's hatred to love; for love of her he returns to his wife, stops drinkingand attempts to make her happy.

006129   THE HALLETTS: A COUNTRY TOWN CHRONICLE. BY LESLIE KEITH. London: R. Bentley, 1891 BMC NUC.

Mary Kelyrge, heiress to Hallett estate. Solicitor gets her wed to his son, but real heir turns up . Doesn't take the place from Mary but weds Hester, sweet daughter of bad solicitor. ACAD
The Halletts are lawyers, father and son, both a bit crooked. An estate has been left to a grandson if he turns up in a year. SR 6-13-91, 723

006130   IN SPITE OF HERSELF. BY LESLIE KEITH. London: R. Bentley, 1892 BMC.

ACAD 42:260. Story of selfish wife and unselfish husband. "wholesome."
ATH 100:317. "a delightful story, especially for such as believe the marrying of young spinsters is the aim and end of every good matron's existence." Concerns seven sisters

006131   THE INDIAN UNCLE. BY LESLIE KEITH. London: R. Bentley, 1896 BMC NUC.

SR-Comes home after 40 yrs of successful fortune hunting disguised as Mr. Menteith. Detected by old Mrs

Gordon and her servant, but they keep the secret.
ATH 108:220. Scotch.

006132   'LISBETH. BY LESLIE KEITH. New York:
Cassell, [c1893] NUC. London: Cassell, 1893 BMC NUC.

SR 77:203. Male hero marries a woman he does not
completely love; she has never known another bachelor
except her brother. Effie, whom the hero loved and who
has a pulmonary condition, worked out their problems
before she drowned.
ACAD 45:185. Carstairs is a sensitive young author.
Elizabeth is a fine heroine. The Mitchell family is
abominable.
SP 72:342. LW 25:121
Domestic story-five elderly Scotswomen live in London,
their quarrels, character, talk. BAKER 03:209.

006133   A LOST ILLUSION. BY LESLIE KEITH. London:
Methuen, 1891 BMC. New York: United States Book,
[1891] NUC.

Loveday Penn-gentle, loyal, virginal, etc. Husband
develops into better person. SP 66, 764
She's raised by strict Quakers. Marries a brute. After
marriage learns of wrongs he's done. Runs away-returns
only to comfort his last hour. A worthier man awaits
her. LW

006134   THE MISCHIEF-MAKER. BY LESLIE KEITH.
London: R. Bentley, 1898 BMC NUC.

LIT 2:676. Scotch town. Title refers to Jennet Laidlaw
who rules the town with a "reign of malevolence."
Archie and Nancy and their love, she loves a
morpho-maniac, Archie loves her.
SR 85:693. Mrs. Laidlaw a "burly, bold, and boisterous
old woman, outspoken and masterful." "It is the
passion of this incorrigible old lady to rule her
world and hunt the rebels." She is not punished. Told
in 1st person by a spectator.

006135   "MY BONNIE LADY": A NOVEL. BY LESLIE
KEITH. London: Jarrold, 1897 BMC.

Feud between the Mintos and the Inglisses-Scot. The
laird of Minto and his wife driven to their graves
over the feud concerning a right of way. SR 83:673.
The Bonnie lady tries to reconcile them by playing
part of servant in one of the houses. SP 79:803.

006136   NEAR OF KIN. BY LESLIE KEITH. London:
Hurst and Blackett, 1903 BMC.

Clergyman's wife smokes, writes books vs. her
husband's preachings. But repents and dies. About
arist. LBKM 6-03, 115

006137   NOT EVEN A TRAGEDY. BY LESLIE KEITH.
London: G. Richards, 1904 BMC.

ATH-safe domestic.
TLS 0

006138   ON ALIEN SHORES. BY LESLIE KEITH. London:
Hurst and Blackett, 1900 BMC.

LBKM 18:190. Girl brought up in rich home marries a
Scotsman. Business takes him to China for 2 years. The
story is of her life in Edinburgh with his mother and
sister during that time. Portraits of the 3 women and
Scotch life-a woman's book.
SP 85:181. Character study, especially of mother.
SR 90:304. Susie has none of the masculine and
repulsive qualities with which latter-day novelists
endow their heroines.
ACAD 58:34

006139   OUR STREET. BY LESLIE KEITH. London:
Religious Tract Society, [1892] BMC. New York: F. H.
Revell, [189-?] NUC.

SP 69:474. He writes; she keeps house in "poorer"
neighborhood.

006140   PENANCE. BY LESLIE KEITH. London: Hodder
& Stoughton, 1901 BMC.

Young widow with child in shipwreck saves self but not
child. ATH 12-21-01

006141   A PLEASANT ROGUE. BY LESLIE KEITH.
London: Hurst & Blackett, 1902 BMC.

ATH 19-18-02--love story.

006142   A RASH VERDICT. BY LESLIE KEITH. London:
R. Bentley, 1897 BMC.

Margaret Thrale, niece of leather merchant, comes to
love Mr. Gale, a young lawyer. She cannot inherit from
her uncle if she marries Mr. Gale because this lawyer
refused to transact certain dishonest business for the
uncle. SR 84:269.
But she never really loved him, and anyway he dies.
LBKM 13:107.
Her married sister with whom she lives fears she'll
marry the man because she's been forbidden to. LIT
1:53.

006143   A TROUBLESOME PAIR. BY LESLIE KEITH.
London: R. Bentley, 1894 BMC.

SR 78:216. Esther and Agnes, and their marital
fortunes. Also their half-sister Mary who married a
parson for his sermons and when she discovered he
didn't write them, didn't speak to him for 20 years.
Rev. calls her an addled Heavenly Twin.
SP 73:280. Mary tries to fill her life with pets and
flowers. Finally consents to take up her cross in the
shape of the man she pities and is bound to by
marriage vows, though she can't possibly esteem or
love him.
ACAD 46:99. Mary is "too strong to attempt any risky
experiment in the way of emancipation."
ATH 104:153. All the fuss about Esther and Aggie's
unchaperoned condition seems old-fashioned.

006144   WAYFARERS ALL. A NOVEL. BY LESLIE KEITH.
London: Jarrold, [1899] BMC.

Different characters in a lodging house. Two children
play an important part. SP 83:614.
Domestic life and characters in London boardinghouse.
BAKER 03 209

006145   WHEN THE BOUR-TREE BLOOMS. London:
Religious Tract Society, [1894] BMC.

JOHNSTON, MARY. 1870-1936. United States.

006146   AUDREY. London: A. P. Watt, 1901 BMC.
Boston: Houghton Mifflin, 1902 NUC.

BKM Mar 1902
BOOK NEWS free spirit-tragic ending
Virginia-Colonial Hist-Fiction

006147   BY ORDER OF THE COMPANY. Westminster:
Constable, 1900 BMC NUC. (American ed. title "To Have
and To Hold")

LBKM 17:27. Historical romance.
SP. Early Virginia. English edition of TO HAVE AND TO
HOLD

006148   CEASE FIRING. London: Constable, 1912
BMC. Boston: Houghton Mifflin, 1912 NUC.

Continues The Long Roll; concerns the Civil War from a
Southern woman's point of view. The whole life of a
dying nation is depicted (the South) Struggle of South
seen in an intimate way. anti war; sees it as sad and
senseless. LBKM
"It wasn't worth it" runs through the account of the
war SR
U S Hist- Civil War
BKM v. 36 1912-13
ATH Civil War Desiree' is married a few years, throws
herself in to the struggle, dies, fittingly, at her
husband's side. "War in its horrible reality, yet with
compensating beauties."
PW-??wife follows husband to battle, lives in a cave
and nurses him when wounded
TLS anti-anti war
SP she is hellishly murdered
BKM-0
NYT-not a romance altho a beautiful love story runs
thru the agony and stupidity of war.

006149   FOES; A NOVEL. New York and London:
Harper, [1918] NUC.

PW-Stewart uprising in Scotland
NYT Nov 3 '18 p466 Elspeth drowns herself. A study in
hate between two men. Glenfernie and Ian. Greek
tragedy.

006150   THE FORTUNES OF GARIN. Boston: Houghton
Mifflin, 1915 NUC. London: Constable, 1915 BMC.

hist romance 10-23-15 PW

006151   HAGAR. Boston: Houghton Mifflin, 1913
NUC. London: Constable, 1913 BMC.

BKM-glowing argument for feminism. Hagar is highly
intelligent, becomes a successful author. Works for
the fem. movement. Story of inner growth and
convictions of a feminist.
PW 84 11/8/13:1529 "Story of girl's life-a girl born
in Virginia in the years following the war, when woman
was still a being set apart on a pedestal, content for
the most part to be more worshiped than understood.
Through the changing eighties and nineties, Hagar
moulded her character and her life. A visit to New
York marked the end of her petted but repressed
childhood and brought her to full realization of her
human opportunities and responsibilities. Her
awakening and development are described with
understanding, and the old Southern prejudice against
the Woman Movement is strongly drawn."
Hagar Ashendyne raised by weakly rebellious mother
among her starchly traditional Virginia family. She's
very intelligent, when mother dies, she goes to
boarding school, has an adolescent love affair with a
teacher, goes to New York, makes a start on her
literary career. Later we see her in London, a
successful novelist, falls in love with ex-con now
editor of a socialist paper, but he's married; becomes
involved in feminist movement. Status of
woman-important central theme. "the inner growth and
conviction of a feminist." BKM
"Miss Johnston's first story of modern life is an
interpretation of the woman movement. Hagar Ashendyne,
her heroine, is a Virginian, bred in the ancient
southern traditions, educated at one of the old-time
finishing institutions, and destined for the
time-honored "woman's-sphere." "If you could only make
your mind submissive," is her grandmother's plaint.
But Hagar's mind is not of the submissive type. She
breaks with family enters into the larger life that is
opening out to women everywhere. Hagar marries late,
after making a name as a novelist, and love is
accepted by her as the crown of life, not as its end,
long sought and long desired." BRD

006152   THE LAIRD OF GLENFERNIE. London:
Constable, 1919 BMC.

Friendship of two men turns to hatred when one
"betrays" the woman the other loves and she drowns
self TLS
Adventures of a Jacobite hero BAKER, 32,271

006153   LEWIS RAND. Boston: Houghton Mifflin,
1908 NUC BMC. Toronto: W. Briggs, 1908 NUC.

U S Hist 1789-1809 fic
PW-hist romance male hero
SR- wife with views entirely opposed to his.
ATH 0
NYT-male hero
focuses upon an ambitious man in Jefferson's time LBKM

006154   THE LONG ROLL. Boston: Houghton Mifflin,
1911 BMC NUC. Toronto: W. Briggs, 1911 NUC.

story of Civil War Stonewall Jackson LBKM
"War whose wounds are dressed by love"
U S Hist-Civil War SR

006155   MICHAEL FORTH. London: Constable, 1910
BMC. New York and London: Harper, [c1919] NUC.

story of reconstruction of South PW
Development of hero: story of South in background.
Religious, social and commercial conditions in
Virginia after Civil War BAKER, 32, 271
TLS-spiritual quest of Michael Forth and Miriam Dallas
SR-doesn't say much, nothing about Miriam

006156   THE OLD DOMINION: AN ACCOUNT OF CERTAIN
PRISONERS OF HOPE. A TALE OF COLONIAL VIRGINIA.
London: A. Constable, 1899 BMC.

Historical romance-dark and tumultuous: slave
plottings, a slave insurrection, the crushing of these
revolts. Patricia and Landless are separated at the
end. LBKM 16:82 130 (Same as prisoners of Hope.)
Landless, the hero, sold into slavery. He's son of a
Puritan gentleman. Works in fields, then as secretary
in Col. Vernay's house. Falls in love with the
daughter Pat. He leads a revolt, saves Pat but
commands her to desert him in the end. She does. Good
depiction of slave quarters. SR 87:632

006157   PRISONERS OF HOPE: A TALE OF COLONIAL

VIRGINIA. Boston: Houghton, Mifflin, 1898 NUC.

SP 81:782. "Romantic and tragical love-story of
Godfrey Landless and Patricia Verney, he a convict
Roundhead, she a Royalist beauty." Virginia.
BKM 8:254. A small cloud of danger hangs over the
Virginia settlers--the slave quarters and with them,
the indentured servants, of whom Landless is one.
NYT 1898:644. Virginia in time of Charles II. Written
in the manner of Scott. Uprisings of Indians, slaves,
indentured servants.

006158   SIR MORTIMER, A NOVEL. New York and
London: Harper, 1904 BMC NUC. Toronto: Poole, 1905
NUC.

PW--hist novel
NYT-A tale of men.
Gt Britian- Navy-Hist-Fiction

006159   SWEET ROCKET. New York and London:
Harper, [c1920] NUC. London: Constable, [1920] BMC
NUC.

PW A great love and a great quest
BKM. Small remote plantation, blinded son of the
family returns there to end his days with Platonic
companion, Marget. Spiritual atmosphere, Sweet Rocket
becomes a center of occult benignant force.
NYT-11-21-20 p21 mystical influence of Sweek Rocket,
views of people there on the evolution towards a new
world.

006160   TO HAVE AND TO HOLD. Boston: Houghton,
Mifflin, 1900 NUC. Toronto: G. N. Morang, 1900 BMC.

BKM 11:91. Happiness for Ralph and Jocelyn. Patricia
is Virginia aristocrat. Historical romance. Reviewed
by Katharine P. Woods.
CR 36:351. Ralph tossed dice and they decreed he
should get a wife from among the boatload of women
arriving. He chooses a young woman who is a king's
ward, fleeing from a forced marriage. Her English
lover is in hot pursuit, duels, adventures.
SR 89:306. "Intensely masculine quality." Patience is
wife to Ralph in name only.

006161   THE WANDERERS. Boston: Houghton Mifflin,
[1917] NUC. London: Constable, 1917 BMC.

episodes telling changes in love relations between men
and women from prehistoric to modern times PW
"A presentation in 19 episodes, of the gradual spread
of culture and the emanc. of women from primeval times
until the French Revolution." BAKER, 32, 270
Nineteen studies show points in history NYT
SF-An attempt to present primitive culture in the form
of romance. Theme is the gradual emancipation of
women, from most early times thru French Revolution.
Eternal duel of sex. Early episodes written in style
of sagas.
SR Portrays cave women living separate and ind. from
man with their children.

006162   THE WITCH. London: Constable, 1914 BMC.
Boston: Houghton Mifflin, 1914 NUC.

LBKM- Rev. infers they die.
PW 86 10/31/14:1403 "Tale of Elizabethan times. Joan
Heron, a girl of original nature and Dr. Aderhold, a
thinker in advance of his period, are suspected of
atheism and sorcery. They are arrested and tried, the
man for practice of the black art, and the girl for
witchcraft. They are sentenced to death, but escape
and take ship for Virginia, Joan disguised as the
physician's boy. On the ship Joan's identity and sex
are suspected and the sailors, ascribing the bad
weather to her witchcraft, set the couple adrift in an
open boat. Their adventures continue in the Bahamas
and later on their love story comes to a close in
England."
In times of Eliz's reign: orphaned girl inexperienced
concerning cruelty of religious intolerance. After
father died, lives alone in cottage. She had a cat,
has been seen talking to a man who was reputed to have
communication with devil. But he was one of "pillars
of soc" who lusted for Joan Heron who rejected him.
One night makes a scene at her house; from neighbors
view, it sounds as though she's consorting with
demons. Also her friendliness with an agnostic scholar
puts her in line for accusations. Both Joan and he
condemned to burn. (But she makes her escape disguised
as a man. Both escape, join Indians, marry. Tribe
attacked, further escape. Leave son behind dead.)
Eventually return to London and martyred. Long
melodramatic sequence BKM

BKM 40 1914-15 Eng. witch hunt

JOHNSTONE, EDITH.

006163   THE DOUCE FAMILY. London: T. Fisher
Unwin, 1896 BMC.

They are "self-righteous, handsome, intolerably
obtuse." Opposite to their brother's victim. SR 83:393

006164   THE GIRLEEN. London: Blackie, 1896 BMC.

006165   A SUNLESS HEART [ANONYMOUS]. London:
Ward, Lock and Bowden, 1894 BMC.

SP 73:248. "The author is certainly a woman" "painful"
"repellent" "an impeachment of the cruelty & tyranny
of man" Lotus is "an embodiment of wronged & suffering
womanhood." Other reviewers have compared it to
African Farm but rev. says it lacks the intellectual
content.
ACAD 46:83. Powerful. Gaspar and Gasparine, brother
and sister. He dies. also Mona.
ATH 104:153. Shows influence of French novel.
Nauseating.
LBKM 6:184. love of brother and sister whose story
forms first part of book told at a "white heat."
LBKM 6:5(Apr) Author is an Irish woman. Gasparine
outlives the brother she loves; is mad with grief. A
woman named Lotus comes to her rescue. She's a
lecturer in a Scotch college; sooths Gasparine. Tells
her own life: "her soul was born old and outraged by
man"s villainy". LW 28:58

JOLY, MRS. JOHN SWIFT.

006166   THOSE-DASH-AMATEURS. London: J. Long,
1918 NUC BMC.

TLS-Satirizes titled ladies who go to Bologne to act
as nurses. Makes up for damages to her sex in
portrayal of Janet, the professional nurse who is far
seeing, competent and firm.

JONATHAN, D.D., BROTHER. See PIERCE, ZERELDA F.

JONES, ALICE. 1853-1933. Canada.

006167   BUBBLES WE BUY. Boston: H. B. Turner,
1903 NUC. London: G. Richards, 1903 BMC.

Romance of love and superstition. Art student marries
rich, rejects her love; husband turns out to be mad,
the mad husband kills her child; she consigns him to
an asylum. NYT 393 03

006168   FLAME OF FROST. New York and London: D.
Appleton, 1914 BMC NUC.

PW 86 9/19/14:774 "Fred Norval, a young mining
engineer, intends to marry a beautiful heiress. Unable
to raise funds for a diamond quest, he starts off
unaided, promising to bring his sweetheart a diamond
for each finger. Stunned while excavating, Norval is
rescued by a girl, Iseult, who lives alone in the
Canadian wilds with her uncle, a reputed magician.
Through Iseult Norval learns of rich treasure fields,
and pursues the search in a series of adventures
involving mysterious Indian secrets. Norval learns to
love Iseult, but she teaches him that there is a curse
upon the diamonds."
NYT-best character development is of Iseult. The
"flame of frost" is an incredible diamond an Indian
woman has given her and has the repute of evil power.

006169   GABRIEL PRAED'S CASTLE. Boston: H. B.
Turner, 1904 NUC. London: G. Richards, 1904 BMC.

NYT-rich American is swindled in Paris; daughter helps
him see the truth.

006170   ISABEL BRODERICK--"BUBBLES WE BUY".
London and New York: J. Lane, 1904 BMC.

TLS-married to an insane artist. Complex.

006171   MARCUS HOLBEACH'S DAUGHTER. New York and
London: D. Appleton, 1912 NUC BMC.

PW-romance.
NYT-love story.
Canadian mining camp. ATH
Heroine the only child of a well-to-do errant father.
TLS

006172   THE NIGHT-HAWK; A ROMANCE OF THE '60'S.

BY ALIX JOHN. London: W. Heinemann, 1901 BMC. New
York: F. A. Stokes, [c1910] NUC.

"Wife of a year brought face to face with husband's
early life in the shape of his son by a handsome
mulatto." CR '01
NYT 01
U. S. Civil War-fiction.

JONES, ALICE ILGENFRITZ. D. 1906. United States.

006173   BEATRICE OF BAYOU TECHE. Chicago: A. C.
McClurg, 1895 NUC.

Slavery; brings out the deeper meanings of freedom.
Treats the life of a slave-who is a white girl.
Beatrice is at first ignorant of her "race," is
treated as part of master's family. Obtains freedom,
goes thru various episodes that test her character.
"Important contribution to the hy of the best phases
of slavery." LW 36:458.
She's talented and highly educated. After she's freed
she must still face the prejudices in NO. and SO. PW
11-2-95:74
BKM 4:433. Beatrice is a slave-child who is related by
blood to plantation family. Protest against slavery.
Colorful portrait of life with her grandmother. Then
hero is introduced and there is much travelling.

006174   THE CHEVALIER DE ST. DENIS. Chicago: A.
C. McClurg, 1900 NUC.

PW-historical romance. Hero "spent his manhood's
career in pioneering movements in the New world."

JONES, AMANDA THEODOCIA. 1835-1914.

006175   A PSYCHIC AUTOBIOGRAPHY. New York:
Greaves, [1910] BMC NUC. London: W. Rider, [1911] BMC
NUC. (BMC: Theodosia)

Account of women's company for working women destroyed
by men

JONES, CLARA AUGUSTA. Nationality Unknown.

006176   FOUND DEAD; OR, THE CHARLES RIVER
MYSTERY. BY HERO STRONG. New York: Street and Smith,
[1892] NUC.

JONES, CONSTANCE EVAN.

006177   CAPRICE: A STUDY IN EMOTIONS. London: J.
Nisbet, 1905 BMC.

006178   A MATTER OF TEMPERAMENT. London: J.
Nisbet, 1906 BMC.

TLS-Male orphan adopted discovers his origin.
LBKM -ditto

006179   THE TEN YEARS' AGREEMENT: AN EXPERIMENT
IN MATRIMONY. London: J. Nisbet, 1907 BMC.

Story of incompatibility ACAD
A woman with views insists on a ten year contract TLS

006180   WOMAN'S LOOKING GLASS: A SPINSTER'S
CHRONICLE. London: J. Nisbet, 1909 BMC.

Margaret Darcy spinster lives a dreary sheltered life
never moving from London, in shadow of hyprochondriac
aunt upon whom she's dependent. She's a slave. In her
30's fall for a dr. first man she meets beyond her
household. He's not attracted to her but advises aunt
to take her out. Margaret wealthy at aunt's death,
free and now sought after. At the end she's still
alone for the doctor she loves is engaged. Study of
frustrated love. Author's view is caustic vs men: "men
are narrow bigoted selfish vain" ACAD

JONES, D. EGERTON. See CALLAHAN, DORIS EGERTON (JONES).

JONES, DORA M. United Kingdom.

006181   AT THE GATES OF THE MORNING: A STORY OF
THE REFORMATION IN KENT. London: C. H. Kelly, 1898
BMC.

006182   CAMILLA OF THE FAIR TOWERS. London: A.
Melrose, 1920 BMC.

TLS-historical, male hero.

006183   A CASE OF CONSCIENCE. Edinburgh and
London: Oliphant, Anderson, 1891 BMC.

006184   DR. BRENT'S NEIGHBOURS: A TALE OF TWO
HOMES DURING THE GREAT WAR. London: C. H. Kelly, 1895
BMC.

006185   THE DUKE'S WARD: A ROMANCE OF OLD KENT.
London: Oliphant, Anderson, [1896] BMC.

   SP 77:773. Hist. Rising of Wat Tyler.

006186   A MAID OF NORMANDY: A ROMANCE OF
VERSAILLES. Edinburgh: W. Blackwood, 1906 BMC.

   ACAD-traditional historical romance.

006187   A SOLDIER OF THE KING; BEING SOME
PASSAGES IN THE LIFE OF MR. JOHN GIFFORD, SOMETIME
MAJOR IN THE SERVICE OF HIS MAJESTY KING CHARLES I,
AND AFTERWARDS MINISTER OF A CONGREGATION OF CHRIST'S
PEOPLE AT BEAFORD. London, Paris, New York: Cassell,
1901 NUC BMC.

   Historical novel. ATH 4-13-01

006188   A WOMAN'S WORD. Edinburgh: Oliphant, 1892
BMC.

   problems that arise from rigid adherence to a promise.
   Pleasant ACAD 43:32

JONES, E. B. C. See LUCAS, EMILY BEATRIX COURSOLLES
(JONES).

JONES, E. BRANDRAM.

006189   IN BURLEIGH'S DAYS. London: J. Long, 1916
BMC.

   TLS-historical, narrative by male
   ATH-historical, narrative by male

006190   THE SECOND CECIL. London: J. Long, 1917
BMC.

JONES, ELAINE ANTHONY.

006191   A HOUSE DIVIDED. BY E. M. JAMESON.
London: Hodder and Stoughton, 1905 BMC.

   ATH 05,794

006192   PEGGY PENDLETON. BY E. M. JAMESON.
London: Hodder and Stoughton, 1906 BMC. (Cover title
"Peggy Pendleton's Plan")

006193   THE PENDLETON TWINS. BY E. M. JAMESON.
London: H. Frowde, Hodder and Stoughton, 1904 BMC.

006194   THE PENDLETONS. BY E. M. JAMESON. London:
Hodder & Stoughton, 1904 BMC.

JONES, ENID (BAGNOLD). United Kingdom.

006195   THE HAPPY FOREIGNER. BY ENID BAGNOLD.
London: W. Heinemann, 1920 BMC NUC. New York: Century,
1920 NUC.

   ATH-Fanny an English girl goes to France at end of war
   to drive car for French army. She falls in love but it
   comes to nothing. She remains from 1st to last an
   unknown young woman, secret, folded within herself, a
   happy foreigner. She is almost without fear, nothing
   can cast her down. A new heroine, a pioneer who sees,
   feels, thinks, hears, yet is herself full of the sap
   of life.
   LBKM Aug 1920 p 178.
   SR-the heroine gets herself openly married in the face
   of London?

JONES, GERTRUDE (WARDEN). United Kingdom.

006196   AN ACTRESS'S HUSBAND. BY GERTRUDE WARDEN.
London: C.H. White, 1909 BMC.

   Michal Garth poisoned her husband; goes on to be a
   great actress; falls in love; later learns she really
   didn't poison her husband. TLS ATH

006197   AN ANGEL OF EVIL. London: W. Stevens,
[1897] BMC.

006198   BEAUTY IN DISTRESS. A STORY OF THE STAGE.
BY GERTRUDE WARDEN. London: Digby, Long, 1903 BMC.

   Two sisters a year apart in age and a man who plays
   two parts; he goes through a mock marriage with one;

actually marries the other. LBKM 12-03:154

006199   BEYOND THE LAW. BY GERTRUDE WARDEN.
London: Ward, Lock, 1902 BMC.

   ATH 8-16-02--male and professional nurse do people in
   for a price.

006200   THE CRIME IN THE ALPS: A NOVEL. BY
GERTRUDE WARDEN. London: F.V. White, 1908 BMC.

   TLS-sensation

006201   THE DANCING LEAVES. BY GERTRUDE WARDEN.
London: Ward, Lock, 1908 BMC.

   TLS-love story.

006202   DIANA OF DARTMOOR. BY GERTRUDE WARDEN.
London: Digby, Long, 1913 BMC.

   She's beautiful, boyish, innocent. Her guardian is a
   Saint on the surface. In reality he's a gambler and
   swindler besides. The machinations of a 15 year old
   blackmailing stable boy are the center of the tale.
   ATH
   LBKM-Sensational-murder, love. Captain Torrens
   succeeds in marrying daughter whose father he has
   killed.

006203   FIVE OLD MAIDS. A STORY OF THE SOUTH
COAST. London: W. Stevens, 1895 BMC.

006204   THE GAME OF LOVE. BY GERTRUDE WARDEN.
London: Digby, Long, 1904 BMC.

   LBKM Two men fighting over a woman.

006205   THE GRAY WOLF'S DAUGHTER. BY GERTRUDE
WARDEN. New York and London: International News,
[c1894] NUC.

   Sir Philip Cranston called grey wolf because he
   forbids his gypsy wife from meeting with her people.
   Sir Philip shoots father-in-law meeting secretly with
   the wife. An old gypsy woman curses Sir Philip-the
   curse described in story of his daughter. PW
   9-14-95:332

006206   HAUNTED. BY GERTRUDE WARDEN. London:
Ward, Lock, 1911 BMC.

   A shocker TLS
   ACAD

006207   THE HAUNTED HOUSE AT KEW. London: W.
Stevens, [1893] BMC.

006208   A HEART OF STONE. BY GERTRUDE WARDEN.
London: Digby, Long, 1905 BMC.

006209   HER FAIRY PRINCE. BY GERTRUDE WARDEN.
Philadelphia: J. B. Lippincott, 1895 NUC. London: W.
Stevens, [1896] BMC.

006210   MERELY MAN. BY GERTRUDE WARDEN. London:
J. V. White, 1909 BMC.

   Adventure and romance TLS

006211   THE MILLIONAIRE AND THE LADY. BY GERTRUDE
WARDEN. London: J. Long, 1907 BMC.

   Mystery, sensational ACAD

006212   THE MOTH AND THE FOOTLIGHTS. BY GERTRUDE
WARDEN. London: Digby, Long, 1906 BMC.

   TLS-Young actress who loses heart and money but is
   rescued by young MD.

006213   NOBODY'S WIDOW. BY GERTRUDE WARDEN.
London: Digby, Long, 1903 BMC.

   Girl-widow and her supposed late lamented husband
   brief description. LBKM 8-03:189.

006214   THE NUT BROWN MAYD; A RIVIERA MYSTERY. BY
GERTRUDE WARDEN. London: F.V. White, 1907 BMC.

   ACAD
   TLS

006215   THE PATH OF VIRTUE. A ROMANCE OF THE
MUSICAL COMEDY STAGE. BY GERTRUDE WARDEN. London: F.V.
White, 1912 BMC.

ATH sensational rom of the stage.

006216   ROBERT, THE DEVIL. BY GERTRUDE WARDEN.
London: Digby, Long, 1906 BMC.

TLS-Young woman married for her money by diabolical
man.
Vague review says nothing about women chars. SR

006217   SCOUNDREL OR SAINT? BY GERTRUDE WARDEN.
London: Digby, Long, 1902 BMC.

006218   THE SECRET OF A LETTER. BY GERTRUDE
WARDEN. London and New York: International News,
[c1894] NUC.

PW-Hero loves young French woman of mystery.

006219   THE SENTIMENTAL SEX. BY GERTRUDE WARDEN.
London: J. Lane, [1896] BMC.

Colonial seeks his ideal woman, a beautiful poetess
who is up-to-date. He marries her and comes to a bad
end.
ATH 108:155. She is very modern; he is old-fashioned
and puritanical, rough and honest backwoodsman.
"Clever comedy which develops into a tragedy."
LW 27:267. He suicides.
CR 29:117. "Immensely amusing" "As good as anything
Gyp has done and fully as naughty, though not as
nasty." "Cattle-raiser, she a poetess of passion, won't
allow her to look at pictures and statues not fully
clothed. Wants her to write a book of love poems
inspired by him. A young woman starts a flirtation
with him, makes wife jealous until an old lover kisses
her-then a catastrophe.

006220   SET TO PARTNERS. BY GERTRUDE WARDEN.
London: Digby, Long, 1902 BMC.

006221   THE SEVERN AFFAIR. BY GERTRUDE WARDEN.
London: J. Long, 1909 BMC.

Love and mystery. TLS
Antonio Canning is the unconventional slangy heroine,
changes from hatred to devotion of her guardian. LBKM

006222   STAND AND DELIVER! THE ADVENTURES OF A
CLEVER WOMAN. BY GERTRUDE WARDEN. London: F.V. White,
1910 BMC.

TLS-An adventuress and swindler. POV?

006223   A SYNDICATE OF SINNERS. BY GERTRUDE
WARDEN. London: Digby, Long, 1901 BMC.

PW 4-13-01

006224   TWO GIRLS AND A SAINT. BY GERTRUDE
WARDEN. London: F.V. White, 1915 BMC.

Two sisters and a cleric who loves one and distrusts
the other. TLS

006225   A WISE AND A FOOLISH VIRGIN. A NOVEL. BY
GERTRUDE WARDEN. London: F.V. White, 1904 BMC.

TLS-Mildish melodrama

006226   THE WOOING OF A FAIRY. BY GERTRUDE
WARDEN. London: Hurst and Blackett, 1897 BMC.

"Worthless" ATH 109:309.

006227   THE WORLD, THE FLESH AND THE CASINO. BY
GERTRUDE WARDEN. London: J. Long, 1909 BMC.

Love and gambling TLS

JONES, JANE.

006228   THE PRISON HOUSE. Edinburgh: W.
Blackwood, 1900 BMC.

SP 84:929. Hedonist hero marries Puritan, marriage
does not succeed. He elopes to Paris, has 2 children,
she won't give him a divorce. When at last he returns
to England in broken health, she reconciles.
SR 90:181. passionate governess Eve Hepburn, satirical
references to the clergy.
ATH 116:148. Rev. thinks must be pseud for male.
ACAD 58:534. Marriage is prison for him.

JONES, KATHARINE. B. 1868. Nationality Unknown.

006229   THE MAN WHO REAPS; A STORY. New York: D.
Fitzgerald, [c1912] NUC.

PW-mystery, male, psychic.

JONES, MABEL CRONISE. B. 1850. United States.

006230   ACHSAH, THE SISTER OF JAIRUS. New York:
Broadway, [c1911] NUC.

006231   IN DAYS OF OLD WHEN KNIGHTS WERE BOLD.
New York: Broadway, [c1911] NUC.

006232   SIX OF THEM AND THE OTHER THREE.
Cincinnati: Standard, [1902] NUC.

JONES, MARY TUPPER. United States.

006233   THE SYSTEM'S HAND. Chicago, Ill.: Midwest
& Producing Co., 1920 NUC.

PW-det. story dealing with conditions prevalent in
industrial history.

JONES, MARY WHITMORE.

006234   THE GRINDING MILLS. London: Isbister,
1903 BMC.

ATH 122,544

006235   TIME AND TIDE. London: H. J. Drane, 1907
BMC.

JONES, S. CARLTON. See JONES, SUSAN CARLETON.

JONES, SUSAN CARLETON. 1864-1926. United States.

006236   THE LA CHANCE MINE MYSTERY. BY S.
CARLETON. Boston: Little, Brown, 1920 NUC BMC. London:
Duckworth, 1921 BMC.

PW-Manager of an isolated gold mine and his dream
girl.
BKM action packed, she is under suspicion of being an
adventuress.
NYT 1920:23
Male narrator, partner in a gold mine in the north.
Story of adventure, Paulette the heroine has a
mysterious past and can shoot wolves and men from the
back of a pair of horses out of control.

006237   THE MICMAC. BY S. CARLETON. New York: H.
Holt, 1904 NUC BMC.

PW-"Clever young girl" love is the chief theme.

006238   OUT OF DROWNING VALLEY. BY S. CARLETON
JONES. New York: H. Holt, 1910 NUC.

JONES, SUSAN CARLETON AND HELEN MILECETE. B. 1864. United
States.

006239   THE CAREER OF MRS. OSBORNE. BY
CARLETON-MILECETE. New York, London: Smart Set, 1903
NUC.

Bored wife goes off with sister to London, poses as a
beauty, meets a former lover, dances flirts; all ends
in comedy? PW 10-10-0
Masquerades as the beauty, Mrs. Osborne for the sake
of an old lover, "eats the apples of Sodom" but finds
the taste of ashes, returns to husband. Riotous times
of these two sisters NYT 755,03

JONES, VICTORINE CLARISSE (JACQUET). United States.

006240   MISS HOGG, THE AMERICAN HEIRESS: A NOVEL.
New York: G. W. Dillingham, 1900 NUC.

CR 36: 574. Publisher's announcement:filled with human
interest and human sin.
PW-heroine is self-willed, ill-bred, persuades mother
to accompany her to London to buy a title.

JONSON, DOROTHY (FORSYTH).

006241   AS A MAN IS ABLE: A STUDY IN HUMAN
RELATIONSHIPS. BY DOROTHY LEIGHTON. London: W.
Heinemann, 1893 BMC.

Title alludes to E. B. Browning's poem, refers to idea
that women love more passionately and durably than
men. Iris Hope loves Vere Vandeleur as only a woman
can. His family objects to their relationship so they
send him off to India. He takes Iris with the idea of

marrying her in Paris, but it can not be done-legally.
Iris decides they don't need to part just because of
senseless regulations and red tape. As they travel, he
worries that they are not married. She says: "it's
ever so much nicer-more ideal-to be bound only by
love." It's freer. They go on to India, directly to
the camp where there is no one to marry them. There
three years a cousin of hers falls in love with her.
Then Vere inherits money, travels home to get it,
meets and loves Beatrice but returns to Iris, who
discovers that love, gives him up, meets Beatrice and
they become great friends-Beatrice learns only on
wedding day that Iris and Vere love each other, she
kills herself. SR 76:242.
Iris Hope loves Vere Vandeleur. When he doesn't get a
job in diplomatic service, he goes to plantation in
India with Iris. They aren't married. Try to get
married in Paris-on the way-but difficulties prevent
them. Later he loves and marries a different woman.
When he confesses to her she poisons herself because
she knows Iris; in fact, Iris saved her life. SP 71,
312
Iris' friend is Beatrice. Iris and Vere had lived
together. ACAD 44:168. The man blamed.

006242   DISILLUSION: A STORY WITH A PREFACE. BY
DOROTHY LEIGHTON. London: Henry, 1894 BMC.

SP 72:564. Linda is a type-writer and a member of the
Spade Club (a combination of the Pioneer Club and the
Fabian Society). She and Mark collaborate on a play.
He marries heartless Celia who eventually leaves with
another man. He gets from the Divorce Court a decree
nisi and proposes to Linda, but before the decree is
final, Celia returns disillusioned but not repentant,
and he is forced to tell Linda that he still loves
Celia. Women and men discuss things which they should
not.
ACAD 46:275. The women Spades accept the woman
question but not divided skirts and platform speaking.
They sought to elevate woman as a whole, and raise
man's ideal of her. Celia dies, future for Mark and
Linda is unclear. Embarrassing scenes at the end.
ATH-Linda is a comrade. Has short hair.
SR 78:415. Mark and Celia marry. He is a Socialist and
has told her that the legal marriage bond is
meaningful only in supporting views about property.
They should be bound in marriage only by their
conscience. She runs away with another man; Mark is
hurt because she didn't take him into her confidence.
Celia's remarks are "original, pungent and
entertaining," although she lacks morals.

JORDAN, ELIZABETH GARVER. 1867-1947. United States.

006243   THE GIRL IN THE MIRROR. New York:
Century, 1919 NUC BMC. London: Hodder & Stoughton,
[1925] BMC.

Love and mystery in New York theatre world PW
Barbara weds, off to Japan on honeymoon, leaving her
brother (whom she worries about) in the charge of
theatre friends; the brother Laurie is 23, a
successful playwright he sees a face in the mirror,
takes it down. Meets Miss Mays. Sees the same
reflection; this time the woman holds a gun. Therein
is the mystery's beginning. NYT 8-24,19 426

006244   MAY IVERSON TACKLES LIFE. New York and
London: Harper, 1912 BMC NUC.

006245   MAY IVERSON-HER BOOK. New York and
London: Harper, 1904 NUC.

PW stories of school girl life
NYT girls book

006246   MAY IVERSON'S CAREER. New York and
London: Harper, 1914 BMC NUC.

"The grown-up May Iverson, who always had a talent for
writing, comes to New York and starts as a newspaper
woman. There is sharp contrast between the point of
view she gained at the convent and the human
experiences she is "up against." She grows to be more
interested in what she sees than in her own attitude
towards it. Then she is beginning to really live. A
book and a play she has written are a success-but she
ends her professional career at the beginning of her
own love story." PW 86 11/7/14:1448.
NYT 1914:516."The publication of these rose-colored
romances will no doubt greatly increase the number of
would-be newspaperwomen." At 25 she leaves her
professional life behind her for marriage. Successful
journalist, novelist, dramatist. Short stories.

006247   TALES OF THE CLOISTER. New York and
London: Harper, 1901 BMC NUC.

All on theme "tragedy behind those quiet walls" women
who have put the world from sight, "repression of
natural emotion. CR -01
NYT 01 suggests the stories are sentimental.

006248   THE WINGS OF YOUTH; A NOVEL. New York and
London: Harper, [1918] BMC NUC.

PW-Barbara and her brother, tired of Midwest town,
come to New York to earn a living for one year without
communicating with one another. Barbara's pockets
picked, she accepts aid from Robert Warren. At end of
year brother is a playwright, Barbara is Mrs. Warren.
NYT P. 142 Mar 31, 1918 200w Ends with love affair for
Barbara and successful career for Lawrence.

JORDAN, KATE. See VERMILYE, KATE (JORDAN).

JORDAN, MARGARET OLIVE.

006249   GOD'S SMILES AND A LOOK INTO HIS FACE.
New York, London: F. T. Neely, [1901] NUC.

JORDAN, MODESTE HANNIS. United States.

006250   SIDNEY; A LOVE STORY OF THE OLD SOUTH.
New York: Cosmopolitan Press, 1912 NUC.

006251   THE STUDIO BABY AND SOME OTHER CHILDREN.
New York: Cosmopolitian Press, 1912 NUC.

JOSIAH ALLEN'S WIFE. See HOLLEY, MARIETTA.

JOURDAIN, ELEANOR FRANCES, jt. au. See MOBERLY, CHARLOTTE
ANNE ELIZABETH AND ELEANOR FRANCES JOURDAIN.

JOYCE, LILIAN ELWYN (ELLIOTT). B. 1884. United Kingdom.

006252   BLACK GOLD. BY L. ELWYN ELLIOTT. New
York: Macmillan, 1920 NUC.

PW-story of an opera company which is taken up the
Amazon to gather in the gold of the Brazilians.

JUDAH, MARY JAMESON AND MAY LOUISE SHIPP.

006253   THE OUTCOMINGS OF ADDISONVILLE: A STORY.
Indianapolis: 1892 W.

JUDSON, JEANNE MARGARET ANTONIA. B. 1890. United States.

006254   BECKONING ROADS. New York: Dodd, Mead,
1919 NUC.

NYT-Marquita Shay, orphaned, raised by father's friend
on Alberta ranch entirely surrounded by men.
Beautiful, all the men love her at 17. Tried school,
didn't like it, ran away from it by getting married.
Goes to live with her parents; father is a crook and
mother an invalid and fanatic. Runs away to an old
friend in New York. This friend, Rose Chisholm, is
divorced, spends most of her time in bars. Thru Rose
she meets a gambler who employs her to buy and sell
stocks for him in her name. Goes on to be a cloak
model. Then returns to domesticity.

006255   THE STARS INCLINE. New York: Dodd, Mead,
1920 NUC.

PW-young woman artist in New York in circle of clever
and eccentric Bohemians.

JUDSON, KATHARINE BERRY. United States.

006256   WHEN THE FORESTS ARE ABLAZE. Chicago: A.
C. McClurg, 1912 NUC.

PW-female schoolteacher takes up a claim in the middle
of a forest reserve.
NYT-With the intention of remaining there for five
years and thereby taking title to the property under
the Homestead Act. Passed thru many terrifying
experiences, the climax of which was the great forest
fire.

JULIAN, MARY.

006257   WHERE JASMINES BLOOM. London: Hodder &
Stoughton, [1917] BMC.

India TLS

JUNEAU, MAY, pseud. See FISLER, MAY (LEWIS).

JUSTICE, MAIBELLE HEICKS (MONROE). B. 1871. United States.

006258   LOVE AFFAIRS OF A WORLDLY MAN. Chicago:
F. T. Neely, 1894 NUC.

PW-separated from his actress-wife,an Anglo-Indian
girl. Heroine will not consent to his obtaining a
divorce from her, and although she finally dies, it is
not in time to avert tragedy.

JUSTIN, EDITH.

006259   MAIDS-A-WAITING. London: Drane's, [1913]
BMC.

Two orphaned, penniless; take a cottage in Cornwall;
take in boarders. Eventually they both settle happily.
ATH

JUTA, RENE. United Kingdom.

006260   CAPE CURREY. New York: H. Holt, 1920 NUC.
(London ed. title "The Tavern.")

006261   "THE TAVERN". London: W. Heinemann, 1920
BMC NUC.

NYT 8-22-20, p 27. Nickname for Dr. James Barry is
Cape Currey. Dr. Barry is "an undersized, odd,
strutting little fellow whose quick tongue and rasping
wit..." He is central character.
LBKM-Hero is surgeon-major, Dr. James Berry, a notable
figure in S. African society a century ago who fought
a duel and turned out to be a woman. She has a leper
son.
SR 0
Author is S. African.

KALOR, MARY FIELDING.

006262   YOUNG SPROUTS. Philadelphia: The Union
Press, [1901] NUC.

KANE, ALICE L. United States.

006263   ECHOES FROM THE SPIRIT WORLD [ANONYMOUS].
Topeka, Kansas: Crane, 1899 NUC.

KARNEY, EVELYN STORRS.

006264   BROKEN SNARES: HARD QUESTIONS, HEALTHFUL
WORDS. London: R. Scott, 1908 BMC.

006265   THE DUST OF DESIRE; OR IN THE DAYS OF
BUDDHA. London: R. Scott, 1912 BMC.

Buddhism-Fic

KATHARINE, pseud. See STEPHENS, LOUISE G.

KATYDID, pseud. See MACKINNEY, KATE (SLAUGHTER).

KATZENBERGER, FRANCES ISABELLE. United States.

006266   HE WOULD HAVE ME BE BRAVE: A STORY TAKEN
FROM LIFE. Dayton, Ohio: Groneweg Print Co., 1893 NUC.

006267   THE THREE VERDICTS: A STORY. Cincinnati:
Editor Pub. Co., 1898 NUC.

KAUFFMAN, CATHERINE. United States.

006268   AS NATURE PROMPTS: A NOVELETTE.
Cleveland, O.: Cleveland Print and Pub. Co., 1891 NUC.

KAUFFMAN, RUTH.

006269   HIGH STAKES; AN ADVENTURE. London: Mills
& Boon, [1915] BMC.

Trad. adventure story. TLS

KAUFMAN, JESSIE. United States.

006270   A JEWEL OF THE SEAS. Philadelphia and
London: J.B. Lippincott, 1912 NUC BMC.

PW-Myst., theft
BKM Myst., theft Hawaii

KAUP, ELIZABETH BARTOL (DEWING). B. 1885. United States.

006271   A BIG HORSE TO RIDE. BY E. B. DEWING. New
York: Macmillan, 1911 NUC BMC.

A famous dancer-successful; effect of marriage on
career. Her career is the prime factor of her life.
Rose Carson's stormy childhood, brilliant career as
dancer, actress, her moral and physical development to
womanhood. Marries young to man she finds unbearable,
separates, has a violent affair with a young man who
turns out to be too self-controlled for Rose. She
sends him off. He returns two years later now more to
her liking. TLS
Life is the big horse. The artist's isolated work and
struggle the whole technical side of her profession.
Work is the prime fact of her life. BKM
Simulates memoir form. Precocious at 13. Ecstasy of
1st public appearance. At 27 unhappily married.

006272   OTHER PEOPLE'S HOUSES. BY E. B. DEWING.
New York: Macmillan, 1909 NUC BMC.

TLS-story of social manners and character. Woman
novelist chief figure (genius)
ACAD-2nd woman is older. Novelist's idea of a
non-moral Superwoman. Novelist's energies drive her
beyond her physical capacity.
Heroine a woman writer who has achieved enormous
success with her first book. Emily Stedman descendent
from a long line of learned people, becomes tired of
her role as spectator of life-striking and absorbing
study of character. Loves her cousin. NYT

KEATE, EDITH MURRAY. United Kingdom.

006273   A GARDEN OF THE GODS. London: A. Rivers,
1914 BMC NUC.

LBKM-Romantic allegory
TLS-Limpid and pleasant

KEATING, ANNE (TRAVIS). B. 1875. United States.

006274   MAKING AN AMERICAN GENTLEMAN. BY ANNE
TEQUAY. Boston: Roxburgh, [c1920] NUC.

KEATS, GWENDOLINE. D. 1910. United Kingdom.

006275   ON TRIAL. BY ZACK. Edinburgh & London: W.
Blackwood, 1899 BMC. New York: Scribner, 1899 NUC.

Direct and simple picture of Devonshire village life
and of Phoebe and her lover-in dialect. When his
battalion is put on the alert for active service, he
writes to tell her he's afraid. She steals the money
for him to buy his discharge. LIT 5:447
She's turned out of her uncle's house as a
consequence. She was a servant there; her parents
turned her out. Her lover Dan Pizott never even offers
to share the blame. SP 83:498
History of a coward. ACAD 57:455.
LW 31:21. Rural England. Moral coward permits his
sweetheart to steal for him and thereby wreck her
life. Cheats his uncle, lies, sneaks. Despises himself
but cannot change. He's finally murdered by a man
worse than he.
Country girl commits a felony for the sake of a weak
lover, who makes her life a wreck, and he is too
cowardly to stand by her. BAKER 03 131

006276   THE WHITE COTTAGE. BY ZACK. Westminister:
A. Constable, 1901 BMC. New York: Scribner, 1901 NUC.

Widow, "A man incurably weak in soul" one feels a dim
suspicion that Luce (heroine) is not quite normal"
"The book leaves a bad taste" BOOK NEWS
Luce refuses the offer to "make her an honest woman"
ACAD
Luce marries the reckless daredevil rather than the
honest man who turns out to be a bigamist. Another
would make her an honest woman by marrying
her-adopting child but Luce refuses. NYT

KEAYS, H. A. See KEAYS, HERSILIA A. MITCHELL (COPP).

KEAYS, H. A. MITCHELL. See KEAYS, HERSILIA A. MITCHELL
(COPP).

KEAYS, HERSILIA A. MITCHELL (COPP). 1861-1910?. United
States.

006277   HE THAT EATETH BREAD WITH ME. BY H. A.
MITCHELL KEAYS. London, New York: McClure Phillips,
1904 BMC NUC.

Katherine, the first wife, impossibly angelic, calls
on second wife after the divorce. Protest vs American
divorce laws-They are too easy? ACAD 1905:84.
The iniquity of the system of easy divorce in U S-ATH
1905:106 .

PW-the effect of divorce on the children. anti-divorce

006278   I AND MY TRUE LOVE. BY H. A. MITCHELL
KEAYS. Boston: Small, Maynard, 1908 NUC.

PW-unhappy marriage.
BKM-parents reunited wife's mistake.

006279   IT WAS A BOY. Bristol: Arrowsmith, 1905
BMC.

arrival and development of a baby-ATH

006280   LITTLE LORDS OF CREATION. BY H. A. KEAYS.
Chicago: H. S. Stone, 1900 BMC NUC.

006281   THE MARRIAGE PORTION; A NOVEL. BY H. A.
MITCHELL KEAYS. Boston: Small, Maynard, [c1911] NUC.
London: G. Richards, [1912] BMC.

A young widow abhors the kinds of marriage she sees
around her. Determines not to marry again but is at
last overruled. PW 10-14-11.
TLS-conscientious serious study of relationship of man
and woman.

006282   "ME AND MY TRUE LOVE". Bristol: J. W.
Arrowsmith, 1909 BMC.

Man and woman "resolutely determined to
perform...parts assigned to them." TLS

006283   MRS. BRAND; A NOVEL. BY H. A. MITCHELL
KEAYS. Boston: Small, Maynard, [c1913] NUC.

PW "Overholt, minister in a prominent church, Mrs.
Brand, wife of the wealthiest member, who shortly
after the story opens, dies and leaves her his
fortune, Dr. Challoner, a fine, devoted physician, are
the chief characters. Overholt has a wonderful mental
picture of himself always before him in which he feels
the right emotions, does the correct thing, and is
really a wonderful person. He is able to impose this
picture on some other minds, but finally comes
absolutely to grief. Church politics and a decadent
church in contrast to ascendant religion is the
theme." 3-14-14:966.

006284   THE ROAD TO DAMASCUS; A NOVEL. BY H. A.
MITCHELL KEAYS. Boston: Small, Maynard, 1907 NUC BMC.
London: G Richards, 1912 BMC.

ATH-co education-daring thesis-author on side of
angels-virtue triumphs.
Woman adopts and rears illegitimate child of her
husband. PW 12-28-07.
Keeps the secret from husband, rears the child as her
own. Adopted son grows up with many of father's
traits. NYT
Richarda Homphrey, married two years, visited by woman
whose child was fathered by Richarda's husband. This
woman begs her to take child. Her marriage seems
doomed, but drawn to child. Keeps secret from him.
Child wants to know who he is; antagonisms between the
three. Good psychological study. She keeps truth from
both. NYT

006285   THE WORK OF OUR HANDS. BY H. A. MITCHELL
KEAYS. London, New York: McClure, Phillips, 1905 BMC
NUC.

husband and wife do reform work. PW 10-14-05.
Ideals of wife conflict with easy-going morally lax
husband. Wife is devoted to the cause of downtrodden
mill workers. Husband objects to her taking into their
home a woman of ill repute.

KEDDIE, HENRIETTA. 1827-1914. United Kingdom.

006286   THE AMERICAN COUSINS: A STORY OF
SHAKESPEARE'S COUNTRY. BY SARAH TYTLER. London: Digby,
Long, 1897 BMC.

Geneology and love. Geo. and Beville Sheldrake visit
Shakespeare country to be in touch with their
ancestors in Eng. ACAD 52 Fic Sup 162.
Marriages result from the visit. ATH 110:852.
LIT 2;179. Complications arising from class divisions.
Son makes improper mrge to daughter of merchant.
Old-fashioned. Happy ending.
SR 85:502. Family relents.

006287   ATONEMENT BY PROXY. BY SARAH TYTLER.
London: Digby, Long, 1902 BMC.

006288   A BANISHED LADY. BY SARAH TYTLER. London:

Digby, Long, 1909 BMC.

TLS-

006289   BENEATH THE SURFACE. A STORY OF TRUST AND
TRIAL. BY SARAH TYTLER. London: Sunday School Union,
1894 BMC.

006290   THE BRACEBRIDGES. BY SARAH TYTLER.
London: J. Long, 1906 BMC.

TLS-sedate story of domestic life.

006291   A BRIAR ROSE. BY SARAH TYTLER. London: J.
Long, 1907 BMC.

Humdrum, harmless. TLS

006292   A BUBBLE FORTUNE. BY SARAH TYTLER.
London: Hutchinson, 1893 BMC. Philadelphia: J.P.
Lippincott, 1896 NUC.

SP 72:591. Impersonation of rightful heir by hero
Harry.
LW 27:202. Nice every-day kind of people inherit a
country estate. Rightful heir appears; they go back to
their mediocre jobs, but mrge. gets it all back
together. Temptation of a man for a fortune that
should by his; the help of his worthy daughter and her
marriage to the heir. ACAD 44:483.Lower middle class
family get inheritance; then loses it. The effect on
father and daughters. ATH 102:803

006293   THE COUNTESS OF HUNTINGDON AND HER
CIRCLE. BY SARAH TYTLER. London: I. Pitman, 1907 BMC
NUC. Cincinnati: Jennings & Graham, 1907 NUC.

006294   THE COURTSHIP OF SARAH. BY SARAH TYTLER.
London: J. Long, [1902] BMC.

006295   A CRAZY MOMENT. BY SARAH TYTLER. London:
Digby, Long, 1899 NUC BMC.

Young childless woman kidnaps a baby who, when she's
grown up, runs off on learning the truth. ATH 114:831
SP 84:23. Childless wife kidnaps baby of a working
man's wife while husband is in service. When daughter
is older she discovers her real parentage and returns
to first mother.
LIT 6:113. "Miss Tytler does not believe over much in
maternal instinct or filial instinct either. When the
real mother and child are thrown together, in
ignorance of their relationship, she makes them rather
dislike one another." Disclosure comes at awkward
moment for daughter.

006296   DAUGHTER OF THE MANSE. BY SARAH TYTLER.
London: J. Norris, 1905 BMC.

Scottish story TLS 227,05
BAKER 13-157
ATH 05,178

006297   FAVOURS FROM FRANCE. BY SARAH TYTLER.
London: Digby, Long, 1904 BMC.

Story of a family, a "faded" second wife. LBKM 27-8,
226
BAKER 13-157

006298   FOUR RED ROSES. BY SARAH TYTLER. London:
J. Long, 1904 BMC.

ATH-four young women speedily find husbands.

006299   FRIENDLY FOES. BY SARAH TYTLER. London:
Digby, Long, 1903 BMC.

Freddy a girl in this murder story--brief desc ACAD
64,204
Short desc LBKM 4-03,35.
Squire's daughter marries ed. butler's son who was
edu. at her father's expense. ATH 121,399

006300   THE GIRLS OF INVERBARNS. BY SARAH TYTLER.
London: J. Long, 1906 BMC.

TLS-three old maids. Bachelors.
ATH-prim old maids. Love stories.

006301   HEARTS ARE TRUMPS. BY SARAH TYTLER.
London: J. Long, 1904 BMC.

LBKM-old fashioned, suitable for young girls.
ATH-0

006302   HIS REVERENCE THE RECTOR. BY SARAH
TYTLER. London: J. Long, 1905 BMC.

006303   A HONEYMOON'S ECLIPSE. BY SARAH TYTLER.
London: Chatto and Windus, 1899 NUC BMC.

The 1850s. Wife returns to her family after a petty
squabble very soon after honeymoon. Reunion in the
end. Scot. Husband is a minister. SP 83:755
Tina and Allan Farquharson. ACAD 57:456
She stoops to marry a minister in order to wed as
young as her sisters had. He's awkward and dull. They
part immediately. After long years a better
understanding. She's kind of spoiled to begin
with--head strong. ATH 114:652
Quiet tale of middle-class life. Adversity and poverty
sober up a silly wife. BAKER 03 224

006304   HONOR ORMTHWAITE; A NOVEL. BY THE AUTHOR
OF "LADY JEAN'S VAGARIES" [ANONYMOUS]. New York:
Harper, 1896 NUC.

LBKM 10:150. Lady Ormthwaite abandoned her dissipated
husband and gave their child to a cousin to care for.
Remarries, believing both are dead. Child turns out to
be alive; she eventually sends for her, passing her
off as a dependent to husband, then confesses to him,
he is very angry, turns out to be a niece of husband.

006305   IN CLARISSA'S DAY. BY SARAH TYTLER.
London: Chatto & Windus, 1903 BMC NUC.

Two women at Oxford--their adventures and loves. ACAD
64,50
Scene laid in Oxford and London, during the reign of
George I.

006306   INNOCENT MASQUERADERS. BY SARAH TYTLER.
London: J. Long, 1907 BMC.

Two orphan girls and the discovery of their parentage.
ACAD
BAKER-well born brought up on farm, not by a lady.
13-157

006307   JEAN KEIR OF CRAIGNEIL. BY SARAH TYTLER.
London: J. Long, 1900 BMC.

SP 85:938. An heiress and her two suitors.
ATH 116:851. Her studies of feminine character have
been gaining in interest of late. Rustic lady...old
fashioned education, inherits money. Thrown into
troublesome relations with young male neighbors--a
trial of her discretion and generosity.

006308   KINCAID'S WIDOW. BY THE AUTHOR OF
"CITOYENNE JACQUELINE" [ANONYMOUS]. London: Smith
Elder, 1895 BMC NUC.

Based on two historical crimes: one in which a wife
kills her husband through the hands of the serving man
who is broken on the wheel; the other, a niece who
stabs to death her uncle and seducer. Point of view is
to demonstrate the domestic cruelty of the Scotch
lord. Sympathy is with the women. ATH. 107:82.

006309   LADY JEAN'S SON: A NOVEL. BY SARAH
TYTLER. London: Jarrold, 1897 BMC.

Sequel to "Lady Jean's Vagaries." Edinburgh, 18th.
Involves the celebrated Douglas case.-a famous trial.
Outcome of the case involved with two love stories.
ACAD 51:328.
Jeanie is advocate's daughter, Lady Marget is almost
engaged to Jock Douglas, the defender. The case is
succession case. And his jr. counsel has his eye on
Jean. Lady Marget will give up Jock if he's an
imposter. ATH 109:207.
SP 80:889. Scotland. Famous Douglas case.

006310   LADY JEAN'S VAGARIES: A NOVEL
[ANONYMOUS]. London: R. Bentley, 1894 BMC. (Author
Sarah Tytler (Henrietta Keddie) per Acad. 51:328.
Authorship formally acknowledged on frontispiece of
sequel Lady Jean's Son.)

Sister of tyrannical Duke. She goes off to France
dressed as a man. Then she marries secretly not in
church but by a parson. For this she's spurned by
brother when she has twin sons, he calls them
illegitimate. SR 79:295.
Sympathetic study. ATH 105:181.

006311   LOGAN'S LOYALTY. BY SARAH TYTLER. London:
J. Long, 1900 BMC.

SP 84:419. Marriage between Scottish Baronet and
crofter girl. Daughter, devoted to her mother's
memory, runs away and marries a crofter. At father's
deathbed promises to bring her son up to fill his
rank. Husband is estranged by this and enlists. All
works out.
ATH 115:330. Father married a "barnyard beauty."
Unable to educate her, he degenerates into a captious
critic of her incompetence. She dies of a heart attack
after a stormy interview with him. Logan, 12 years
old, becomes her champion and marries her cousin.
Later realizes she has misjudged her father.
ACAD 58:206. Dialect has English translation in
parentheses.

006312   A LONELY LASSIE. BY SARAH TYTLER. London:
Religious Tract Society, 1893 BMC.

006313   A LOYAL LITTLE MAID. A STORY OF MAR'S
REBELLION. BY SARAH TYTLER. London: Blackie, 1899 NUC
BMC.

006314   "THE MACDONALD LASS". A STUDY FROM LAST
CENTURY. BY SARAH TYTLER. London: Chatto and Windus,
1895 NUC BMC.

Story of Flora Macdonald who saved the life of the
young Pretender, Charles Edward. The harm to the
Jacobite cause. She tells the story. Her independence.
SP 75:698. about 1750 in Long Island and SKYE.
Flora Macdonald's rescue of Pr. Charles after Culloden
1746. BAKER 03,224

006315   THE MACHINATIONS OF JANET. BY SARAH
TYTLER. London: J. Long, 1903 BMC.

Janet comes into a fortune, endeavors to be useful to
the less fortunate. ACAD 64,486
Wholesome with a few slaps at modern ideas. LBKM
7-03,152

006316   MAJOR SINGLETON'S DAUGHTER. BY SARAH
TYTLER. London: Digby, Long, 1904 BMC.

006317   MANY DAUGHTERS. BY SARAH TYTLER. London:
Digby, Long, 1900 BMC.

SP 85:182. A thoughtful woman's idea of the ultimate
ideal for the perfect and complete education of her
sex. Would cover the ground not only of Newnham and
Girton but include domestic science as well.
ATH 116:53. The Woman's Institute of Technical
Knowledge and its Productions. Slight plot.
ACAD 58:55H. Heroine Delia, has Cambridge degree in
math, applies it to cooking.
LIT 7:142. "We would have thought the day for such a
novel...had passed, but the demands for fiction are
many, and, no doubt, although we have not heard of it,
the rather long drawn-out twaddle of Many Daughters
finds amused readers."

006318   MISS NANSE. BY SARAH TYTLER. London: J.
Long, 1899 BMC.

Two old Scotch gentlewomen who have lost their
fortunes take up high-class dressmaking. Includes a
villain and a mystery.   LIT 4:375
In Cranford trad. Cranford-like but then villainy
takes over. All comes out right. LBKM 16:22
"Homely dignity of provincial gentlewomen" in the
tradition of Cranford. The two brothers of these
sisters return from India rich. The dress-making
business is closed. Miss Nanse and Miss Mattie. SP
82:385
Miss Nanse's faithful love for old Peter Purnes of the
post office. ATH 113:334
Domestic tale of pleasant characters. BAKER 03,224

006319   A MORNING MIST. BY SARAH TYTLER. London:
J. Clarke, 1892 BMC.

006320   MRS. CARMICHAEL'S GODDESSES. BY SARAH
TYTLER. London: Chatto and Windus, 1898 NUC BMC.

SP 81:378. Wholesome story of 90 years ago when widow
turned to cabinet-making to support herself and
daughters, was very successful. Brought her daughters
up like goddesses.
LIT 3:328. "Written in the Scotch language, with
translations of all the hard words given in brackets."
ATH 112:383.
LBKM 15:24. Keeps her daughters free of all taint from
the shop, as though she expected them to marry dukes,
which they didn't but she was satisfied. Capable,
managing woman, proud equally of her family and the
honour of her business.

006321　　THE POET AND HIS GUARDIAN ANGEL. BY SARAH TYTLER. London: Chatto & Windus, [1900] NUC 1901 BMC.

Cowper, Mrs. Unwin, and their circle at Olney, 1760-80 fiction.

006322　　QUEEN CHARLOTTE'S MAIDENS. BY SARAH TYTLER. London: Blackie, 1901 NUC. (Charlotte, Queen Consort of George III, Fic.)

Charlotte, Queen Consort of George III, fiction.

006323　　RACHEL LANGTON. BY SARAH TYTLER. London: Ward and Downey, 1896 NUC BMC.

ATH 107:474. Didactic. Superiority of middle class to gentry. Injustice of land distribution. Essex is an enthusiastic young actress.
ACAD 49:506. Rachel is strong-minded, quixotic, her convictions open to reconsideration. Had a low opinion of the stage as a career for women until she met Essex who later marries her son. "The description of Sophy Green, the advanced woman, is a piece of genuine comedy."

006324　　RIVAL CLAIMANTS. BY SARAH TYTLER. London: Digby, Long, 1901 BMC.

Historical romance with bright heroine. Ath 3-30-01

006325　　SIR DAVID'S VISITORS. BY SARAH TYTLER. London: Chatto & Windus, 1903 BMC.

006326　　STEPMOTHER IN AMBUSH. BY SARAH TYTLER. London: Digby, Long, 1905 BMC.

006327　　THREE MEN OF MARK. BY SARAH TYTLER. London: Chatto & Windus, 1901 BMC.

12-7-01 ATH

006328　　THE TWO LADY LASCELLES. BY SARAH TYTLER. London: Digby, Long, 1908 BMC.

TLS-fireside tale.

006329　　THE WITCH-WIFE. BY SARAH TYTLER. London: Chatto and Windus, 1897 NUC BMC.

Late 17th. "Merciless torture of innocent women in the British Isles." Sonsie Sibbie, heroine and martyr whose only sins were her love of animals and knowledge of herbs, her self reliance and lack of relatives. Depressing. SP 79:77.
Grim days of witch burning. BAKER 13,156.
SR 85:89: Scotland. Sibbie discovers by herself the merciful uses of morphia, chloroform, hypnotism. Is burned as witch. For girls. Kills herself among the flames.
ATH 111:19. "Sibylla Bethune is a dignified and gracious woman, whose knowledge and spirit are too rare for the atmosphere of dull fanaticism in which she lives, and whose end...is alleviated by the skill which provides her with an anaesthetic counter-poise to her suffering."

006330　　WOMEN MUST WEEP. BY SARAH TYTLER. London: J. Long, [1901] BMC.

Young woman comes to learn she's not the true daughter of the mother she loves. Meets her real mother, who tries to recover her. ATH 8-31-01

006331　　A YOUNG DRAGON. BY SARAH TYTLER. London: Chatto and Windus, 1900 NUC BMC.

SR 90:336. Anne, niece of old maid.
ATH 115:615. Anne's "soul revolts at the marriage of her gentle aunt to a rough farmer." His better character evolves.

KEELER, LUCY ELLIOT. 1864-1930.

006332　　IF I WERE A GIRL AGAIN. New York: F.H. Revell, [c1904] NUC. Edinburgh: Oliphant, [1904] BMC.

KEELER, MARY ADELAIDE. Nationality Unknown.

006333　　JUST A SUMMER AFFAIR. London, New York: F.T. Neely, [c1897] NUC.

PW 98-romance two suitors, a summer in Greenwich.

KEELING, ELSA D'ESTERRE. D. 1935. United Kingdom.

006334　　APPASSIONATA: A MUSICIAN'S STORY. London: Heinemann, 1893 BMC. New York: R. Bonner, 1893 NUC.

A young woman's devotion to her art-she's gifted in music-causes her marr. to be a very unhappy one. She's of a passionate ill-regulated nature. PW 12-16-93.
SR 77:446. Finnish heroine refuses to obey "Russian husband's just command." "She is punished by a seven years' situation" before they are reunited.
ACAD 45:98 "it was love of freedom rather than of music that made Selma keep her devoted lover waiting so many years before she would marry him."
LBKM 8:126. "Story of an artist, a beautiful finlander, of her love for her art, her infatuation for a sister artist, her very moderate affection for her husband, and the tragedy of her life, brought about directly by the treachery of the woman she had loved not wisely but too well, and by the stubborn prejudice of her husband... Her after life, bereft of art, and love, and even justice, fills us with indignation...Miss Keeling tells us of a man knowingly marrying a girl who loved art better than himself, of how he put cramping fetters on her, and in punishment of a freak in which there was something noble, punished her brutally, and with quite special meanness. Things were to improve, it is suggested at the end. We doubt it."

006335　　OLD MAIDS AND YOUNG. London and New York: Cassell, 1895 BMC NUC.

Onora and Mariabella are two "old maids" of traditional type and Cambridge female students. Far too many characters. ATH 106:897.
SR 81:81. A "tangled" tale of all sorts of women mingled in confusion; strange young lady is introduced midway thru book. Rotha as a child and grown up. Sweet and frivolous bride.
ACAD 49:10. Studies, also of the old maids, Miss Onora and Miss Mariabella.
SP 76:897. Miss Onora and Miss Mariabella both "good portraits."
PW 2-29-96. Study of diverse femininity in youth and middle age.

006336　　ORCHARDSCROFT: THE STORY OF AN ARTIST. London: T. F. Unwin, 1892 BMC. New York: Cassell, [c1892] NUC.

LBKM 3:92. Monstrous male.
ACAD 42:586. Life of two children of the slums who rise to something better, one through genius. They marry.
heroine Ally, wife of English gardener out of work because he drinks. Ally supports family by washing. She's Irish ignorant and untrained. Another tenant of the tenement house is a deserted woman who leaves her daughter with Ally and kills herself. Ally leaves the child at a rich family's house. Later her own son meets this girl May. LW 93, 148
Begins with a strike. Ally is rewarded for depositing child on the doorstep by a lucky chain of events that lead to husband's job as gardener at Orchardscraft. Their son becomes an artist who studies in Italy. SR 75, 299.

006337　　THE QUEEN'S SERF. BEING THE ADVENTURES OF AMBROSE GWINETT IN ENGLAND AND SPANISH AMERICA. London: T. F. Unwin, 1898 BMC NUC.

LIT 3:329. Historical romance. Archaic dialect.
ACAD 55:548. Reign of Queen Anne.
SR 86:447. A man cut down from a hanging and revived is under English law a queen's serf and obliged to leave the country until he can prove his innocence.

006338　　A RETURN TO NATURE: A KENTISH IDYLL. London: Jarrold, Daffodil, 1896 BMC.

Heroine becomes a governess in a remote Kentish village. Dirck is her American student. Finds a lover in the country. Was at Cambridge. LBKM 13:49
A quiet work about an American boy who wins his grandfather's love. Iveydene society. SR 84:756

KEITH, ALYN YATES, pseud. See MORRIS, EUGENIA LAURA (TUTTLE).

KEITH, KATHERINE. United States.

006339　　THE GIRL. New York: H. Holt, 1917 NUC.

In the manner of personal revelation, thru choice of significant incident reveals the life of American girl of the day. PW
Marion Crosby from childhood to young womanhood.

Series of impressionistic pictures representing
incidents in her life. She has a vivid imagination,
may be neurotic intense, learns, in the hands of older
women, to be ashamed of her "darker sides." Then come
lovers and an inconclusive end. NYT

KEITH, LESLIE, pseud. See JOHNSTON, GRACE L. KEITH.

KEITH, MARIAN, pseud. See MACGREGOR, MARY ESTHER (MILLER).

KELLEY, EMMA DUNHAM. United States.

006340   MEGDA. BY "FORGET-ME-NOT" (EMMA DUNHAM
KELLEY). Boston: J. H. Earle, 1891 NUC.

KELLEY, ETHEL MAY. B. 1878. United States.

006341   OUTSIDE INN. Indianapolis: Bobbs-Merrill,
[c1920] NUC BMC.

PW-young woman runs restaurant not for profit but for
humanity.
NYT 1920:236-But the food is so good she is also
financially successful. She adopts a daughter, had an
unhappy love affair, and finds marriage at end, but
"what attention is it possible to give to trifles such
as these when on the very next page, so to speak, one
may read of cream soup and breasts of duck, and squab
chickens..."

006342   OVER HERE; THE STORY OF A WAR.
Indianapolis: Bobbs-Merrill, [c1918] NUC BMC.

PW-love and war. When husband dies in war, she decides
to raise infant son as soldier.
NYT-She does not "let" her Tommy go to war, she sends
him to war.

006343   TURN ABOUT ELEANOR. Indianapolis:
Bobbs-Merrill, [1917] NUC BMC.

Three young men and three young women determined to
remain unmarried, adopt a child-each will care for
Eleanor two months of year; collectively responsible
for her education and care. She develops into a
beautiful person and the three men fall in love with
her. She ends up with one of them. PW

KELLNER, ELISABETH WILLARD (BROOKS). D. 1916. United
States.

006344   AS THE WORLD GOES BY. Boston: Little,
Brown, 1905 BMC NUC.

Actress and young daughter, divorcee (husband too
conventional.)PW 5-6-05
Daughter of actress separated from her husband. Mother
drives at break-neck speed, they learn fencing
together; there's a bit of jealousy in the mother
toward her daughter's youth. Discourages her
daughter's marriage to a Polish opera star (he's 40),
girl goes to college, gets a Ph.D., meets the Pole
again, mother killed in auto accident. "Romance of the
intense subjective order which through its
misunderstanding purifies."

KELLOGG, MARGARET AUGUSTA. United States.

006345   LEO DAYNE: A NOVEL. Boston: James H.
West, 1899 NUC.

NE. She is an impulsive, independent young woman. She
has two lovers neither worthy of her. She gives up
one; the other gives her up when he learns she has
abandoned the old faith for the new. LW 30:409
She becomes a forewoman of a tailoring place after her
father commits suicide and she, mother and brother
move to a manufacturing town. Study of conditions of
wage earners, religious and charitable work done for
them. PW 56:816

KELLY, ELEANOR MERCEIN.

006346   KILDARES OF STORM. New York: Century,
1916 BMC.

Touches on several "problems," blacks, poor whites,
heredity. Set in Kentucky. Kate Kildare marries into
the rough, gambling drinking family at 17. Her husband
is a ruffian. She turns to the gentle Fr. doctor who
was forced to kill a man. Story opens with his release
from prison. Splendid creation. Kate is the center.
(Review says 0 about husband.) NYT 2-4-17,40
Kate's lover goes to prison for murdering husband. Her
life devoted to management of plantation and bringing
up two daughters. Romance of two daughters and her

renewed romance with earlier lover. PW 90:1284
10/14/16

006347   WHY JOAN? New York: Century, 1919 BMC.

NYT-life in Kentucky.
NYT 3-30-19, 169 Crucial periods in Joan Darcy's life;
begins when she's 18, graduated from convent school,
not beautiful, very clever but shy. Her mother of
strong character has been dead for two years; father
who raises her is weak. He remarries, loses the money
her mother left her. She manages to forgive him and be
civil to her step-mother. "Serious, readable."
City life in Ky just before WW1. PW

KELLY, FLORENCE (FINCH). 1858-1939. United States.

006348   THE DELAFIELD AFFAIR. Chicago: A.C.
McClurg, 1909 NUC.

Story of a fraud, business man. PW
Adventures. NYT

006349   THE FATE OF FELIX BRAND. Philadelphia: J.
C. Winston, [c1913] NUC BMC.

Henrietta Marne, a young business woman who supports
her semi-invalid mother and pleasure-craven daughter.
Secretary, works hard, wins a reasonable amount of
success. She instinctively resists Felix Brand a dual
personality whose primary personality is the evil one.
NYT

006350   RHODA OF THE UNDERGROUND. New York:
Sturgis and Walton, 1909 NUC. London: Gay and Hancock,
1910 BMC.

Civil War heroine, daughter of abolistionist, runs
slaves with father: underground railroad. PW
Her principles force her to assist in the escape of
the black servants of her lover.
TLS-abolition-tender love story.
NYT-young woman devotes herself to abolition. Frees
the slaves of a man in love with her, goes to jail for
her activities.

006351   WITH HOOPS OF STEEL. London: B. F.
Stevens and Brown, 1900 BMC. Indianapolis:
Bowen-Merrill, [c1900] NUC.

ATH-western-all men.
PW-ranchmen, three close friends.

KELLY, JOAN COLLINGS. B. 1890. United Kingdom.

006352   BEAUTY FOR ASHES; A NOVEL. BY JOAN
SUTHERLAND. London: Hodder & Stoughton, [1920] BMC
NUC. New York: G. H. Doran, [c1922] NUC.

TLS-Desmond, Madge's lover wishes to marry someone
else after her divorce. Goes to India and dies.

006353   BEYOND THE SHADOW. BY JOAN SUTHERLAND.
London: Mills & Boon, 1914 BMC.

Involves an actor who loses his memory while playing
Othello and gains it back years later when he plays
the same role. TLS

006354   CAVANAGH OF KULTANN. BY JOAN SUTHERLAND.
London and New York: Harper, 1911 BMC.

Focuses on a man in India TLS

006355   COPHETUA'S SON. BY JOAN SUTHERLAND.
London: Mills and Boon, [1914] BMC NUC.

TLS Passionate and exotic foreigner, strong silent
Englishman and beautiful Eng. girl. Author is "unaware
that nowadays it is rather romantic and attractive to
be illegitimate."

006356   THE DAWN. BY JOAN SUTHERLAND. London and
New York: Harper, 1912 BMC.

TLS-Alec Carlyon and wife in Persia. Daughter of
politician. brings to him promise of new "dawn." Also
had passion for him which didn't wait for wife to fade
out (which she finally does)

006357   DESBOROUGH OF THE NORTH-WEST FRONTIER. BY
JOAN SUTHERLAND. London: Hodder & Stoughton, [1920]
BMC.

TLS-male-love and adv.
LBKM male-love and adv.

006358   THE EDGE OF EMPIRE. BY JOAN SUTHERLAND.
London: Mills & Boon, [1916] BMC NUC.

TLS Lewis is married to Henriette, an impossible wife,
loves Grizel, they are an ideal couple. Reader,
however, feels over-whelmed by their weakness in
tolerating Henriette until she finally dies.

006359   THE HIDDEN ROAD. BY JOAN SUTHERLAND.
London: Mills and Boon, [1913] BMC NUC.

Misunderstandings between hero and heroine set in
Tibet. SP
The cool Englishman on imperial work in the East. TLS

006360   IN THE NIGHT. BY JOAN SUTHERLAND. London:
Mills & Boon, 1920 BMC.

From play by Cyril Harcourt.

006361   THE LOCUST. BY JOAN SUTHERLAND. London:
Mills & Boon, 1917 BMC.

Focus on Colin a man, scientist, his travels,
research. TLS

006362   WINGS OF THE MORNING. BY JOAN SUTHERLAND.
London: Hodder & Stoughton, 1919 BMC.

War story "the welter of blood and adjectives in some
places goes to show that 'horrible imaginings' can
exceed even the loathsome realities of the trenches."
"The fault of the war," says the author "lay with the
politicians who had gambled with public moneys, kept
their mistresses with public funds, and betrayed the
people who had elected them." TLS

006363   WYNNEGATE SAHIB. BY JOAN SUTHERLAND.
London: Hodder & Stoughton, [1918] BMC NUC.

TLS-Love and male hero.

KELLY, M. AGNES. Nationality Unknown.

006364   HIS REBEL SWEETHEART. New York: Abbey
Press, [1902] NUC.

Revolutionary War

KELLY, MINNIE HARDING.

006365   DICK'S LOVE; OR, THE SHADOW OF CAWNPORE.
London: Simpkin, Marshall, 1914 BMC.

006366   FRANK HERON'S WIFE. A LOVE STORY. London:
R.T.S., [1909] BMC.

Sandringham series of Penny stories.

006367   GLORY; OR, THINGS TO COME. London:
Marshall, [1916] BMC.

006368   THE GOLDEN CITY. London: R.T.S., [1920]
BMC.

006369   "IT'S A LONG WAY--"; A ROMANCE OF THE
GREAT WAR. London: Simpkin, Marshall, 1915 BMC.

006370   THE LIGHTS OF UPTON POINT. London:
Religious Tract Society, [1903] BMC.

006371   PHILLIP COMPTON'S WILL. London: Religious
Tract Society, [c1910] BMC.

006372   ROY: A VILLAGE STORY. London: Religious
Tract Society, [1906] BMC.

006373   THE SECRET OF OAKLANDS. London: Religious
Tract Society, [1919] BMC.

006374   SHEWING THE WHITE FEATHER. London: H.J.
Drane, [1905] BMC.

006375   "WATCH". London: Marshall, [1914] BMC.

006376   THE WOODROUGH BROTHERS. London: Charles
and Dible, [1908] BMC.

KELLY, MRS. TOM.

006377   HIGHLAND LOCHS AND GLENS. London: H. J.
Drane, [1894] BMC.

006378   A LEDDY IN HER AIN RICHT: A BRIEF
ROMANCE. London: Hurst and Blackett, 1897 BMC.

Old-fashioned plot. A king comes to his own again.
Happy end. not in dialect. SR 83:230.
A runaway daughter, a love match, much shooting. ACAD
51:304.
Jaquetta doesn't know she's a Lady. Raised by
gamekeeper. ATH 109:376.

KELLY, MYRA. 1876-1910. United States.

006379   HER LITTLE YOUNG LADYSHIP. New York: C.
Scribner's Sons, 1911 NUC. London: Chapman and Hall,
1911 BMC.

Love and intrigue. PW

006380   THE ISLE OF DREAMS. New York: D.
Appleton, 1907 NUC BMC.

Woman artist who is successful only to find one man
has been buying her paintings. She then goes to Europe
for further study; her lover sells all her pictures;
her self confidence is restored. PW 4-6-07.

006381   ROSNAH. New York: D. Appleton, 1908 NUC
BMC.

Lady Rosnah impersonates another woman. TLS
Takes place of Sheila at family reunion.. Nothing
here. BKM
Impersonation, comedy. PW BKM NYT

006382   WARDS OF LIBERTY. New York: McClure, 1907
NUC.

BKM-young life of the ghetto as author came to know it
as a teacher in NY's east side.

KELSEY, JEANNETTE GARR (WASHBURN). B. 1850. United States.

006383   CLOUDED AMBER. BY PATIENCE WARREN.
Boston: R.G. Badger, [c1915] NUC.

Young woman's friendship with older actress PW 12-4-15

006384   WEATHERING THE STORM. BY JEANNETTE G.
WASHBURN KELSEY (PATIENCE WARREN). [Philadelphia]:
[privately printed], 1920 NUC.

KELSTON, BEATRICE.

006385   ALL THE JONESES. London: J. Long, 1917
BMC.

Amusing account of an inheritance. TLS LBKM

006386   BERTHA IN THE BACKGROUND. London: J.
Long, 1920 BMC.

TLS-Miss Agobeg main character.
SR-Miss Bishop visits friend Hilary, a novelist. Spy
mania. Bertha is always in the background,
communicating words of wisdom by telegram when called
upon.

006387   THE BLOWS OF CIRCUMSTANCE. London: J.
Long, 1915 BMC.

From girlhood, unique and striking personality. TLS
Emotional woman, goes on stage, marries to escape
suitors. "Ultimately finds herself in the dock." ATH
TLS-strong sombre insightful Amelie Gayne actress.

006388   THE EDGE OF TO-DAY. London: J. Long, 1918
BMC.

Isabel Beamish, bred in old-fashioned home, ignorant
of the world and of passion, marries a man she only
likes. All the vileness of animal love is on the
husband's side. Passion comes from elsewhere. She's
about to confess (her passion for another?) when she
sees husband kissing her sister's shoulder. A child
comes into the story. Incomplete plot. TLS
She's severe in judgement of husband, commits serious
indiscretions, receives decidedly more favours from
fortune than she deserves. ATH
Married, unhappy, she feels restraints on her freedom,
then she falls in love-determined to elope. Then sees
husband kissing her sister. Leaves but not with lover,
sets out to earn her living as a dancer. There is an
"accidental baby"? another marriage on the last page.
SR

006389   SEEKERS, EVERY ONE. London: J. Long, 1913
BMC.

Alicia Gunning after one baffling failure seeks
distraction on the stage. Her life with a provincial
touring company. TLS

006390   A THREE-CORNERED DUEL. London: J. Long,
1912 BMC.

TLS-Betty and Phyllis, twins, hoodwink poor Paul.
ATH-O

KEMP, GERALDINE.

006391   INGRAM. A NOVEL. London: Chapman & Hall,
1902 BMC.

ATH 11-30-01

006392   A MODERN MERIBAH: A NOVEL. London:
Skeffington, 1897 BMC.

Salvator is the hero, a perfect man. Knows god's
mysteries, Rites and ceremonies and his prayers. ACAD
52: Fic Sup 117.
SP 81:993. Story of founder of a theosophical
monastery in the Spanish Pyrenees and Englishman who
is novitiate in the monastery.

KENDALL, MAY.

006393   WHITE POPPIES: A NOVEL. London: Ward,
Lock and Bowden, 1893 BMC.

3 young women: one is murdered, one commits suicide;
the third considers suicide but it's hinted her death
was natural--all this at the end. #1 Had been too fond
of pleasant food and drink joined Salvation Army. #2
Advocated Spencer and attacked rel.& pol. #3 Loves a
man she claims to have known in the last world. SR
76:628
Hero pays father's debts out of profits as a reporter
in this tale of death and doom. "Henrietta, a plain
and passionate blue stocking is slighted by several
professors and left on the plain road to the Open
Door." ACAD 44:544
Frank loves Vi Romilly who loves John who loves Elsie
Everard who loves him but doesn't love Beau Austin. Vi
gives it up, joins Salvation Army, dies in drunken
scuffle, And all other kinds of love crisscrossing.
Henrietta Morland loves several professors, commits
suicide. ATH 102:730
LBKM 6:127. Intellectual Henrietta. She suicides.

KENDELL, JANE ANNE TORREY. B. 1868. Nationality Unknown.

006394   ALICE IN SUNDERLAND. BY JANE ANNE TORREY.
New York: Cochrane, 1909 NUC.

Experiences of a country schoolteacher. BKM v.30
1909-10

KENEALY, ANNESLEY.

006395   THE POODLE-WOMAN. A STORY OF "RESTITUTION
OF CONJUGAL RIGHTS". London: S. Paul, 1913 BMC.

"a votes-for-women novel" concerning the Cockspur's
marriage. "Throughout that curiously uninstructed
outlook upon practical life that marks some suffragist
writers." TLS

006396   THUS SAITH MRS. GRUNDY. London: J. Long,
1911 BMC.

Young woman rebels vs Mrs Grundy and goes off with
duke's son and then a sailor "unwholesome" story. TLS

006397   A "WATER-FLY'S" WOOING: A DRAMA IN BLACK
AND WHITE MARRIAGES. London: S. Paul, 1914 BMC.

ACAD 87:541 Waterfly is African halfcaste, and English
white girl marries him for his money, tragedy follows.
He is despicable. Sensational.
ATH 144:649 Deals with "deplorable effects" of
inter-racial marriages.

KENEALY, ARABELLA. D. 1938. United Kingdom.

006398   AN AMERICAN DUCHESS: A NOVEL. London:
Chapman & Hall, 1906 BMC.

TLS-anti feminism

006399   CHARMING RENEE. London: Hutchinson, 1900
BMC. New York and London: Harper, 1900 NUC.

SP 85:532. Hero shuts himself up for a crime he didn't

commit. Renee marries him. He marries her without love
for family reasons.
ATH 116:475. She conquers him with love.
ACAD 59:282. She's incredibly beautiful, physically a
goddess.

006400   "DO THE DEAD KNOW"? London: S. Paul,
[1915] BMC.

TLS Crime and mystery.

006401   DR. JANET OF HARLEY STREET. London:
Digby, Long, [1893] BMC NUC. New York: D. Appleton,
1894 NUC.

The heroine leaves her husband-a dissolute French
Marquis-Dr. Janet protects her. "After sundry exciting
events the heroine is united to a man whom she loves."
BAKER.
PW-Phyllis at 17 is married to French roue; his kiss
disgusts her and she runs away to London. Dr. Janet
Doyle takes her in, encourages her to become a
physician. "Endeavors to teach her the true position
and true mission of womanly women. The plot is made
the means of conveying in many telling sentences that
women should be ashamed to aim at being 'undeveloped
man,' or feminine or neuter instead of becoming
womanly in the highest sense." Young woman on wedding
day so revolted by her husband's kiss that she runs
away, never to return.
Dr. Janet befriends her and gets her into medical
profession. She meets a man also in the profession
whom she loves but can't marry. Reviewer feels the
author deprecates marriage. SP 70 825.
Phyllis Eve 19 marries elderly Marquis. Deserts him
hour after ceremony, "pleading for a recognition of
women's equality with man" ACAD 44:70.

006402   THE HONOURABLE MRS. SPOOR: A NOVEL.
London: Digby, Long, [1895] BMC NUC.

Woman of "evil life" "coarse" "meaningless
repulsiveness" "grossness" SR 79:870
She has a most disreputable past, marries a man of
good position. But she's stifled by the respectability
of her new life. Escapes to the woods where she sings
and acts up with "drunken abandonment." Meets a young
woman she fears knows all about her and will tell all.
So she leaves husband. ACAD 48:47
Made understandable, pitiable. ATH 105:769

006403   THE IRRESISTIBLE MRS. FERRERS. New york:
Dillingham, [c1912] NUC. London: S. Paul, [c1912] NUC
BMC.

LBKM Triangle. Mrs. Ferrers is a dangerous woman with
whom the husband is infatuated.
NYT- Mrs. Ferrers is as virtuous as she is lovely and
her pride in her reputation is an ally when she falls
in love with another woman's husband. Triangle with a
new twist.

006404   KING EDWARD INTERVENES: A NOVEL. London:
J. Long, [1910] BMC NUC.

TLS-Russian archduke and his wife become tenants of
honest country squire, sensational

006405   LADY FITZ-MAURICE'S HUSBAND: A NOVEL.
London: Chapman & Hall, 1906 BMC.

TLS dual personality, unfaithful wife elopes with her
own husband.
ATH characters are conventional.

006406   THE LOVE OF RICHARD HERRICK. A NOVEL.
London: Hutchinson, 1901 BMC.

ATH 3-1-02 anti-feminist--heroine loses "love" because
of her involvement in her work.

006407   THE MARRIAGE YOKE. London: Hurst &
Blackett, 1904 BMC.

ATH-Anti-feminist

006408   THE MATING OF ANTHEA. London: J. Long,
[1911] BMC. New York: J. Lane, 1911 NUC.

Guardian raised her so that she could neither read nor
write. New method of educating the 20th cent woman and
its results in Anthea PW 10-7-11
The new method is eugenics-training for the
"motherhood of noble human types." Part of the plan is
she doesn't read or write, doesn't know what love is.
The experiment fails but "all goes well for Anthea."

006409   MOLLY AND HER MAN OF WAR. London: R.
Bentley, 1893 BMC.

ATH 103:176. Adventures of three up-to-date young
people on a cruise, romance, happy ending.
ACAD 45:186. "A daring and sometimes savage satirist,
fun and humor. "One cannot help wishing that all
modern women, who believe in the potentialities and
rights of their sex, took their creed in this healthy,
lightsome fashion."

006410   THE PAINTED LADY. A NOVEL. London: S.
Paul, [1913] NUC BMC.

about a house, the head of which founds a Eugenic
village. His plans are upset by news concerning his
nephew and an inheritance.ATH
Ursula inherits because the title descends through the
female line and the fortune of Lady Germayne that
supported the model village of Eugenia passes on to
her now that her mother perished in San Francisco
earthquake. TLS

006411   A SEMI-DETACHED MARRIAGE: A NOVEL.
London: Hutchinson, 1899 BMC. London: Hutchinson,
[1901?] NUC.

Celia Welldron and Sir Latimer agree to such a
marriage: that is to marry and keep up two separate
establishments. She's rich. He's villainous. The
marriage goes bad. Celia weds Mr. Right. LIT 4:477.
She's a millionaire's daughter. Father left his
partner orders to marry her at his death. She becomes
attracted to a decadent baronet, marries him, but it
turns out he's a bigamist. She loses her baby, the
baronet dies, she marries her father's partner. Sir
Latimer is the villainous one. SP 82:616
She makes the part-time marriage with the decadent
baronet, Sir Latimer. ACAD 56:583

006412   SOME MEN ARE SUCH GENTLEMEN: A NOVEL.
London: Digby, Long, [1894] BMC.

Lois Clinton, sweet and womanly lives with grandma in
ancient manor house. Starves herself so grandma can
eat, thinks she sees ghosts. Dr. comes to care for
grandma, comes to care for Lois. But there's a rival.
ATH 47:166

006413   THE THINGS WE HAVE PRAYED FOR: A NOVEL.
London: Hurst & Blackett, 1915 BMC.

Worldy prosperity for one woman (this brings misery)
and a serene and restful home life for another. Shows
how aspirations of mother influence daughters. The
reasonable harmonious couple have a happy daughter.
ATH

006414   THE WAY OF A LOVER: A NOVEL. London:
Hurst and Blackett, 1914 BMC.

ACAD 87:462. Is there a woman MD or is Kenealy an MD?
Anyway, a surgeon gives his bride a scientifically
equipped nursing home.
ATH 144:308 Modern views of husband have bad effect on
mrg. Wife is a nurse.

006415   THE WHIPS OF TIME: A NOVEL. London: J.
Long, [1908] BMC NUC. Boston: Little, Brown, 1909 NUC.

Pschy study of children "switched" from real to other
parents. PW 4-3-09
Heredity, study TLS
"Author's peculiar theory with relation to athletic
women has assumed a milder and more reasonable form."
ATH
BKM

006416   WOMAN AND THE SHADOW: A NOVEL. London:
Hutchinson, 1898 BMC. Chicago: R. McNally, [c1898]
NUC.

LIT 2:450. Major Kershaw, engaged to Lady Alice, who
regrets having lost a prince with a large income, is
loved by Millicent, an heiress, who gives her fortune
to Alice so that she will be satisfied and goes
herself out to be a governess.
ACAD 53:255. Eventually the major gets a divorce, and
he and Millicent marry.

006417   THE WOMAN-HUNTER. London: S. Paul,
[c1912] BMC NUC.

TLS-Nerissa's two experiences in love.

ATH Good and courageous heroine tames strong and
virulent hero.
ACAD-Two halves of book; 1st, Nerissa is married to
man who abstains from her, finally joining a Trappist
monastery. Second half; she meets another man whom she
reforms and marries, her husband dying conveniently.

006418   WOMAN'S GREAT ADVENTURE: A NOVEL. London:
Hurst & Blackett, 1917 BMC.

Story of Nurse Stella; author intends her as a
selected mother-richly endowed in mind and body-of a
child best fitted to develop the best human chars. She
marries a baronet, he returns from war, their
differences, happy end? TLS

KENNARD, CHARLOTTE.

006419   HONOUR OR DESIRE. London: Digby, Long,
1904 BMC.

KENNARD, MARY E.   United Kingdom.

006420   AT THE TAIL OF THE HOUNDS. A NOVEL. BY
MRS. EDWARD KENNARD. London: F. V. White, 1897 BMC
NUC.

A hunting novel. "The atmosphere of the stables and
the rapture of 'kills' invade the love story." of
widow Mrs. Wentworth and Major Gruffoldi. ACAD 52 Fic
Sup 105.
SP 81:412. Hunting novel.

006421   THE CATCH OF THE COUNTY. BY MRS. EDWARD
KENNARD. London: F. V. White, 1894 NUC. London: F. V.
White, 1895 BMC.

SR 78:628. Male heir and his love affair. Hunting
scenes. He is momentarily diverted from parson's
daughter by circus rider disguised as Russian
princess.

006422   FOOLED BY A WOMAN: A NOVEL. London: F. V.
White, 1895 BMC.

Bianca, bad and beautiful Italian widow, fools George.
She murdered her mother-in-law, makes it look as tho
George did it. He is arrested, tried, condemned. Twice
the gallows refuse to work to hang him. Saved by new
evidence. SR 80:217

006423   THE GOLF LUNATIC AND HIS CYCLING WIFE. BY
MRS. EDWARD KENNARD. New York: Brentano's, 1902 NUC.
London: Hutchinson, 1902 BMC.

LBKM 5-02 Nature failed in bringing wife into world
with temperament of a man and husband should have been
a little girl.

006424   THE HUNTING GIRL: A NOVEL. BY MRS. EDWARD
KENNARD. London: White, 1893 BMC NUC. New York: J. A.
Taylor, [c1893] NUC.

Auto form. Told by an unscrupulous, vulgar beautiful
woman who plays with men. Is a come-on for her card
shark uncle. Rose Darlington. In the end she captures
a fine young man and lives happily ever after. In
spite of all her "moral deficiencies." SP 71, 585.
Marries wealthy Archie. The first words "I am a horrid
girl." SR 76:497

006425   IN THE TOILS OF THE CHARMER. BY MRS.
EDWARD KENNARD. Chicago: Rand, McNally, [1898] NUC.

PW Devonshire. Heroine refuses man her father wishes
her to marry and falls for an unknown hermit. Their
rom.

006426   JUST LIKE A WOMAN: A NOVEL. BY MRS.
EDWARD KENNARD. London: F. V. White, 1894 NUC.

ATH 103:641. Eve breaks her engagement to a general,
travels to Norway, meets a "moral Ibsen with the thews
and presence of Balder the Beautiful."
SP-part travel, part romance, Norway.
ACAD-society novel. Eve Carlingford, widow, her
romance.

006427   MORALS OF THE MIDLANDS: A SPORTING TALE.
London: Hutchinson, 1899 BMC.

"Hard riding and wayward affections." ACAD 56:460.
A long suffering wife and a handsome but commonplace
husband. An ill-sorted union. ATH 113:559
Hunting society-its manners and foibles. BAKER 03 132

006428   THE MOTOR MANIAC. A NOVEL. London: Hutchinson, 1902 BMC.

006429   A PROFESSIONAL RIDER. BY MRS. EDWARD KENNARD. London: A. Treherne, 1903 BMC NUC.

006430   A RIVERSIDE ROMANCE. London: F. V. White, 1896 BMC. London: F. V. White, 1898 NUC.

SR Gruesome romance. Strong heroine who fishes for salmon in Norway tries to marry her half-brother, "is crushed under a cliff, locked in the arms of a peculiarly objectionable mother."
ATH 107:310. "It is the unhappy fate of Mrs. Carson (the mother) who has long made the remote Fosdalen her refuge from a world which has used her ill, and to which her secret sense of criminality has placed her in antagonism, to crush the innocent hopes of a pair of happy lovers, her own daughter and her husband's son." He is illegitimate.
ACAD 49:302. Agatha's mother is strongly opposed to her daughter's marrying, has had her own painful experiences; she says "every sensible woman should bring up her daughters to look upon man as their natural enemy. Here Mrs. Kennard's pet hobby, the naughtiness and wickedness of man considered as a husband displays itself."

006431   A SON OF THE FLEET. London: F. V. White, 1903 BMC.

About the Navy, a sick boy and his recovery and flirtations. ACAD 64,610
ATH

006432   THE SORROWS OF A GOLFER'S WIFE. BY MRS. EDWARD KENNARD. London: F. V. White, 1896 BMC NUC.

SR-Golf-widow, along with her cook, takes to the links, leaving dinner to look after itself. Cures husband.
ATH 108:347. "Jack gets off better than he deserves; but this only illustrates the eminently womanlike and excellent qualities of his spirited yet faithful spouse."

006433   THAT PRETTY LITTLE HORSE-BREAKER: A NOVEL. BY MRS. EDWARD KENNARD. London: F. V. White, 1891 BMC NUC. London: F. V. White, 1892 NUC.

Hunting story Katherine Herrick: father financially ruined self, killed self. She knew she understood horses better than most men, becomes a horsebreaker rather than depend on charity of friends. Of her two lovers, one backs out on learning she has no money, the other, true. ACAD
Also ATH 98 448.
Becomes a lady rider and horse-breaker in a large horse-market. Takes lots of risks in her work. PW

006434   TONY LARKIN, ENGLISHMAN. BY MRS. EDWARD KENNARD. London: Hutchinson, 1900 BMC.

SP 84:710. English country life, hero distinguishes himself in Africa in big game hunting and military expedition. "Two most remarkable blacks, Zourinetta and her husband Sakki, whose manners--apart from a slight ferocity on the part of Sakki, would adorn the choicest circles, and whose conversation is superior to that of most of the Englishmen in the book."

006435   WEDDED TO SPORT: A NOVEL. BY MRS. EDWARD KENNARD. London: F. V. White, 1892 BMC. New York: National Book, [c1892] NUC.

ATH 100:515. Caustic view of sporting society.
CR 18:190 One of her "racy tales." Heroine writes two successful novels, "Such is Man" and "Such is Woman."
ACAD 42:480. "She (Mrs Kennard) holds a perpetually standing brief for that portion of the feminine world which, if not altogether meriting the contemptuous title of "the shrieking sisterhood," is at all events dissatisfied with the conditions under which the Almighty has placed it, and would fain change the order of things by protesting, or would in any case protest..." Story of Bligh Burton, a governess, her unhappy marriage, her flight from her husband, her love for another. Husband dies.
Blanche and her cousin share interest in sports, but he marries a woman of different interests--to his regret. Scene: midlands, Eng. PW 6-22-95:967.

KENNARD, MRS. ARTHUR. See KENNARD, NINA H.

KENNARD, MRS. EDWARD. See KENNARD, MARY E.

KENNARD, NINA H.

006436   DIOGENES' SANDALS. London and Sydney: Remington, 1893 BMC.

Studies held together with up-to-date knowledge and a thread of romance. ACAD 44:129.

006437   THE SECOND LADY DELCOMBE. BY MRS. ARTHUR KENNARD. London: Hutchinson, 1900 BMC. Philadelphia: J. B. Lippincott, 1900 NUC.

LBKM 18:97. The sporting world and the socially fashionable world, stripped of grace and glamour.
CR 37:467. She marries for money and then falls in love with her husband.
ATH 115:618. She "receives her husband's divorced wife...two ladies remain for several days under the same roof." "The Delcombes move in a society where divorce appears to be as common an event as matrimony and both institutions are regarded with a fine impartiality by those concerned." Original charming heroine.
ACAD 58:14. Not sensational. Clever character studies of women.

KENNEDY, SARA BEAUMONT (CANNON). D. 1921. United States.

006438   CICELY: A TALE OF THE GEORGIA MARCH. London: Hodder and Stoughton, 1911 BMC. Garden City, N.Y.: Doubleday, Page, 1911 NUC.

PW 10-7-11: Hist rom of Civil war

006439   JOSCELYN CHESHIRE. A STORY OF REVOLUTIONARY DAYS IN THE CAROLINAS. New York: Doubleday, Page, 1901 NUC BMC.

PW-6-1-01
Love and war, delightful, NYT

006440   THE WOOINGS OF JUDITH. London and New York: Doubleday, Page, 1902 BMC NUC.

Judith marries; her husband goes off to war and is reported dead; she remarries; the "dead" husband writes to the new one, but he keeps it secret. All ends well as Judith learns to really love #2. LBKM 10-03,54

KENNEDY, SARA MACKENZIE.

006441   ST. VALENTINE'S DAY. London: Burleigh, 1900 BMC.

006442   THE WINTER OF OUR DISCONTENT. Mussoorie: F. Bodycot, 1911 NUC.

KENNY, LOUISE M. STACKPOOLE.

006443   AT THE COURT OF IL MORO. London: J. Long, 1911 BMC.

TLS-Brilliant court of Beatrice D'Este and her husband in 15th century. Hero is an Eng. who loves Beatrice.

006444   CARROW OF CARROWDUFF. London: Greening, 1911 BMC.

006445   DAFFODIL'S LOVE AFFAIRS. London: Holden and Hardingham, [1913] BMC.

First-person narration of some love affairs Ath

006446   HEART OF THE SCARLET FIRE. London: Heath, Cranton, [1916] BMC.

TLS-Love story
ATH-Love story

006447   THE KING'S KISS. AN HISTORICAL ROMANCE. London: Digby, Long, 1912 BMC.

TLS- Story of marriage by wife; grants a king a kiss to save her cousin's life.

006448   LOVE IS LIFE. London: Greening, 1910 BMC.

TLS-Hist rom., forced wedding leading to love.

006449   MARY: A ROMANCE OF THE WEST COUNTRY. London: R.& T. Washbourne, 1915 BMC. St. Paul: B. Herder, 1915 NUC.

006450   THE RED HAIRED WOMAN; HER AUTOBIOGRAPHY. London: J. Murray, 1905 NUC BMC. New York: Dutton,

1906 PW.

ACAD—Irish woman and her family and lovers.

KENT, ANNABELLE.

006451   ROUND THE WORLD IN SILENCE. New York:
Greaves, 1911 NUC.

KENT, ELIZABETH. Nationality Unknown.

006452   THE HOUSE OPPOSITE; A MYSTERY. New York:
G.P. Putnam's Sons, 1902 BMC 1903 NUC.

ATH 12-13-02--dull

006453   WHO? New York and London: G.P. Putnam's
Sons, 1912 BMC NUC.

PW—Murd myst.
NYT—Murd myst.

KENT, NORA. B. 1899. United Kingdom.

006454   THE GREATER DAWN. London: L. Parsons,
1920 BMC.

TLS—Male MD hero
ATH Lavender, heroine writes songs

KENT, WINNIFRED. United States.

006455   SELL NOT THYSELF: A NOVEL. Chicago: Laird
and Lee, [c1894] NUC.

PW—Stella Dinsmore, a young woman of limited means who
has a cherished project advertises and makes a
matrimonial alliance which is purely a business
transaction. She also deals with other questions of
interest to women.
"A mother confessor." SP 75:405.

KENTON, EDNA. 1876-1954. United States.

006456   CLEM. New York: Century, 1907 BMC NUC.

Wholly unconventional woman. Review BKM 26(1907) 163
Mentioned in BKM 26 (1907) 3
a girl, fine by nature "crudely reared in the wild
environment of western ranch and mining camp," comes
to Chicago. Clem Merrit seen by the new world of conv.
soc. as "loud, overbearing, shriekingly insistent;"
others through slights and snubs try to make her see
herself as others see her so she won't accept the
proposal of a man of exclusive family. She does gain
self knowledge that makes her reject the man and
becomes assured of her superiority to petty world.
Thus she's free to choose the right man. Good psych.
study. BKM
"Remarkable facility of heroine for shifting
affection" NYT

006457   WHAT MANNER OF MAN? Indianapolis:
Bowen-Merrill, [1903] NUC BMC.

Artist marries young woman he must paint. She soon
learns he wants her as a model, not wife, runs off. He
is remorseful to have tortured a young woman only to
portray pain.
Artist who will use any means for his art-finds
perfect maiden but in order to paint her must marry
her just to paint the portrait that will make him
famous. As she learns he doesn't love her, her face,
expression change from that ideal look he sought. She
goes off to die. He finally by her death, is reached
in his heart. NYT 03,118

KENYON, CAMILLA EUGENIA LIES. B. 1876. United States.

006458   SPANISH DOUBLOONS. Indianapolis:
Bobbs-Merrill, [c1919] NUC BMC.

Adventurous journey to Pacific for treasure PW "For a
century or so after Robinson Crusoe, writers thought
advent. stories had to be about men." Virginia Harding
"heroine in a muddy blouse" accompanies Aunt Jane on a
treasure digging expedition. Her aunt has a map she
received from a dying sailor. "Two heroes bring beauty
and brains respectively." PW Book Rev
Heroine tells the story. "a search for hidden
riches... planned and directed by women, and the
adventurous young woman captures a sweetheart as well
as locating the treasure." BKM, Nov Dec 19, 385 NYT
511, 10-5-19

KENYON, EDITH C. D. 1925. United Kingdom.

006459   THE ADVENTURES OF TIMOTHY. London:
Religious Tract Society, [1907] NUC BMC.

Charles I

006460   THE ASHES OF HONOUR. London: Holden and
Hardingham, [1914] BMC.

006461   THE HAND OF HIS BROTHER; OR, GALAHAD'S
SIN. London: Gay and Bird, 1898 BMC.

SR 85:266.

006462   LOVE'S GOLDEN THREAD. London: S.W.
Partridge, [1905] BMC.

006463   LOVE'S TRIUMPH. London: "Leisure Hour"
Library, [1914] BMC.

006464   MOLLY'S CHARM. London: "Leisure Hour"
Library, [1914] BMC.

006465   THE MYSTERY OF BLACKSTONE MINE. London:
Holden and Hardingham, [1914] BMC.

006466   NOBLY DONE. London: R.T.S., [1909] BMC.

006467   SIR CLAUDE MANNERLY. London: Ward, Lock,
1905 BMC.

006468   THE SQUIRE OF LONSDALE. London: F. Warne,
1897 BMC NUC.

There is a question about who is the squire. Then
there's Mary, rector's daughter with her rival lovers,
one good doctor and one bad. The bad tries all sorts
of tricks, even attempts murder. Mary's "plain" sister
Lois also has her romance. SP 78:775

006469   TWO GIRLS IN A SIEGE; A TALE OF THE GREAT
CIVIL WAR, FOUNDED UPON FACTS CONTAINED IN OLD BOOKS
RELATING TO THE PLACE AND THE PERIOD. London: Leisure
Hour Monthly Library, [1905] BMC. London: Religious
Tract Society, 1908 NUC.

Gt Brit Civil War 1642-49

006470   THE WINNINGS OF GWENORA. London: Holden
and Hardingham, [1913] BMC.

Welsh.
She has 3 suitors, narrowly escapes marriage with an
old squire, finds happiness with the man she loves.
ATH

006471   THE WOOING OF MIFANWY. A WELSH LOVE
STORY. London: Holden & Hardingham, [1912] BMC.

ATH Love story
TLS Love story
Welch setting; story of an inheritance. Mifanwy is
very mid-Victorian: she's stiff, she weeps. ACAD

KEON, GRACE, pseud. See DOONAN, GRACE (WALLACE).

KERN, MARGARET.

006472   THE RUSTLE OF HIS ROBE. New York: F.
Neely, 1901 PW.

KERNAHAN, MARY JEAN HICKLING (GWYNNE). 1857-1941. United
Kingdom. Identified as Jeannie Gwynne Bettany Kernahan in
BMC.

006473   AN ARTIST'S MODEL. London: F. V. White,
1906 BMC.

TLS—True acct of model's shocking her relatives.

006474   ASHES OF PASSION. London: J. Long, 1909
BMC.

marriage intrigue and revenge TLS
Christobel Moore actress, vain. married to good
natured man who trusts her blindly. Loves a man who is
husband's friend. He takes off, meets a woman whom he
wishes to marry. Christabel starts a scandal LBKM
Absolutely heartless heroine SP

006475   THE AVENGING OF RUTHANNA. London: J.
Long, 1900 BMC.

LBKM 18:156. Book 1 & 2. In Book 1, Ruthanna is loved
and left in Book 2 she is avenged. She is ignorant,
trusting, loving and faithful; Victoria is clever,

inscrutable, loving, unfaithful. Cecil is a mixture of
strengths and weaknesses, evoking by turns sympathy,
contempt, irritation, etc.
SP 85:54. Cecil has sinned only against her peace of
mind. Odious characters.
ACAD 59:14. "Upshot is of an advanced order."

006476   A BEAUTIFUL SAVAGE. London: F. V. White,
1904 BMC.

006477   THE BLUE DIAMOND. London: Everett, [1914]
BMC.

ATH-Detective story with love interest. Solved by a
boy detective. Heroine works to clear her father's
name.

006478   A CASE FOR THE COURTS. London: F. V.
White, 1907 BMC.

the regular fare of romance and intrigue ACAD

006479   THE CHANCE CHILD. London: Everett, [1914]
BMC.

ATH Society and the stage.
ATH 144:96 and her search for love,
TLS Philista Follingay, beautiful and accomplished
actress, apparently rich, is followed by detectives
and "all her doings are strange." Edwin Strood poet in
love with her.

006480   DEVASTATION. London: J. Long, 1904 BMC.

LBKM-"has taken note of some of the tendencies of the
time"
TLS -Husband fails to drown his wife in 1st chapter
shoots her and himself later.

006481   THE DISAPPEARANCE OF THE DUKE. London: F.
V. White, 1907 BMC.

gruesome exper TLS

006482   A FAIR SINNER. BY MRS. COULSON KERNAHAN.
London: Everett, [1913] BMC NUC.

006483   THE FATE OF FELIX. London: J. Long, 1905
BMC.

overly sensational ACAD 199,05
bigamy and hypnotism ATH 269,05

006484   FRANK REDLAND, RECRUIT. A NOVEL. London:
J. Long, 1899 BMC.

Fanchette's mother lives in a villa in Redland. How
Frank Redland fell in love with "the kittenish"
Fanchette and his uncle, the squire, with Fanchette's
mother. LIT 4:346
Fanchette-an impossible ingenue very innocent at one
moment and a very wise woman the next. Title
misleading; plot is fantastic.SR 87:439

006485   THE FRAUD. London: Hodder and Stoughton,
1907 BMC.

Male secretary really writes the novelist's
novels.LBKM 11-07 99
Harriet Blair wife learns of "ghost" falls in love
with him. They are kindred souls end? SR
Our sympathy is with Mrs Blair and the secretary TLS

006486   THE GATE OF SINNERS. London: Everett,
1908 BMC.

TLS-Myst. of young widow, affairs of her nieces and
nephews.

006487   THE GO-BETWEEN. London: Everett, 1912
BMC.

TLS-0

006488   THE GRAVEN IMAGE. London: J. Milne, 1909
BMC.

Faylande Heath is a companion to daughter of a
sinister man who operates on criminal's faces to make
them unrecognizable. TLS

006489   THE HIRED GIRL. London: Everett, [1912]
BMC.

006490   THE HOUSE OF BLIGHT. London: Everett,
1911 BMC.

Sensational, haunted house TLS

006491   THE MYSTERY OF MAGDALEN. London: J. Long,
1906 BMC.

TLS- begins in a rollicking way, becomes dull, ends in
murder.
ATH 0

006492   THE MYSTERY OF MERE HALL. BY MRS. COULSON
KERNAHAN. London: Everett, [1912] BMC NUC.

Daughter of farmer and wife (who is of illegitimate
birth) turns out to be of royal blood. She contrasted
to another young woman, a prisoner to her stern
grandfather. One man deceives both girls. All ends
happily after villain killed off. ATH
Grim mystery, tangled plot. Seventeen year old convent
bred girl lives with her weird grandfather, finds Mere
Hall oppressive, runs away only to get into other
trouble LBKM

006493   NO VINDICATION. London: J. Long, [1901]
BMC.

ATH 8-24-07

006494   QUIXOTE OF MAGDALEN. London: Everett,
1909 BMC.

A man who betrayed a woman sets out to find and marry
her TLS

006495   THE SIN OF GABRIELLE. London: J. Long,
1908 BMC.

TLS an immoral heroine is finally blown up in a
chateau.
ACAD 0
BKM-Melodrama

006496   THE SINNINGS OF SERAPHINE. BY MRS COULSON
KERNAHAN. London: J. Long, [1906] BMC NUC.

TLS four murders, poison ring

006497   THE STOLEN MAN. BY MRS. COULSON KERNAHAN.
London: Everett, [1916?] BMC NUC.

rom-usual stuff; two sisters and a man TLS

006498   THE THIRTEENTH MAN. BY MRS COULSON
KERNAHAN. London: Everett, 1910 BMC NUC. New York: G.
W. Dillingham, [c1910] NUC.

TLS-melodrama
ATH-melodrama
Gothic like tale of a man's fiendish effort to
inherit. PW 3-11-11
NYT

006499   THE TRAP. London: Everett, 1917 BMC.

TLS-Boarding house keeper who blackmails his guests.

006500   TREWINNOT OF GUY'S: A NOVEL. BY MRS.
COULSON KERNAHAN. London: J. Long, 1898 BMC NUC.

SP 81:412. "Seamy side of medical life."
ATH 111:563. Old fashioned plot.
LBKM 14:49. Hero is a male medical student.
PW-He is impecunious, must eke out ways to complete
his courses. Love story.

006501   UNDER THE SEAL OF THE CONFESSIONAL.
London: Everett, 1910 BMC.

TLS artist and his daughter, ambles pleasantly

006502   AN UNWISE VIRGIN. London: J. Long, 1903
BMC.

Theme of demoniacal possession, blood curdling
episodes ATH 121 , 236

006503   THE VAGRANT BRIDE. London: Everett, 1911
BMC.

irresponsible young woman, descendant of gypsies,
learns respect thru love SP
Tale of mystery and terror ATH

006504   A VILLAGE MYSTERY. London: F. V. White,
1905 BMC.

ATH 642,05

006505   THE WHISPERER. London: F. V. White, 1905
BMC.

ATH 05,75

006506   THE WOMAN WHO UNDERSTOOD. London:
Everett, [1916] BMC.

TLS 0
ATH-"Foolish babyish woman runs away from an austere
disapproving daughter and her husband with a man with
whom she has a Platonic rel. Then daughter falls in
love, leaving husband to woman he has loved in silence
for twenty years.

KERNAHAN, MRS. COULSON. See KERNAHAN, MARY JEAN HICKLING
(GWYNNE).

KERR, AMABEL (COWPER). 1846-1906.

006507   A MIXED MARRIAGE. London: Art and Book,
1893 BMC. London: Art and Book, 1902 NUC.

006508   THE WHOLE DIFFERENCE. London: Sands, 1902
BMC. St. Louis: Herder, 1904 NUC.

Also Sands 1902

KERR, SOPHIE. 1880-1965. United States.

006509   THE BLUE ENVELOPE; A NOVEL. Garden City,
New York: Doubleday, Page, 1917 NUC. London: J. M
Dent, 1919 BMC.

Leslie must learn a profession and support herself for
two years before receiving her fortune. Stenographer
sent to Washington with a formula kidnapped by secret
agents PW 91:633 2/24/17

006510   THE GOLDEN BLOCK. Garden City, New York:
Doubleday Page, 1918 NUC. London: J. M. Dent, [1919]
BMC.

PW-Margaret Bailey is a business success but she fears
she must relinquish the partnership she wins thru a
big deal because her employer wishes to marry her.
Danger is averted when she welcomes back a man whom
she has come to love. She supports her family.
NYT. Margaret loves the world of business and is
exceedingly competent in it. She points out to her
admiring male associates that there is "no sex in
brains." She saves the Golden Block Co. and becomes a
full partner. She is not interested in marriage or
love, but there is an inference a the end of book that
she will eventually marry.

006511   LOVE AT LARGE: BEING THE AMUSING
CHRONICLES OF JULIETTA CARSON. New York and London:
Harper, [1916] BMC NUC.

A young woman solves her marriage problems by writing
stories to get even with people. In one she attacks a
woman who's after her husband. PW
NYT-nine stories, well to do ch's in a NY suburb much
humor
TLS-not all that amusing.
BKM- Pictures New York suburbia as a community of
women where men are in actuality aliens to life of
women. Comedy, but psychologically insightful.

006512   PAINTED MEADOWS. London: Hodder &
Stoughton, [1920] BMC. New York: G. H. Doran, [c1920]
NUC.

TLS-wife clings to memory of 1st husband (unworthy)
until she finds true value of husband.
NYT 1920:302 small town in southern U.S.

006513   THE SEE-SAW; A STORY OF TO-DAY. New York:
Doubleday-Page, 1919 NUC.

End of story: Marcia Crossey takes husband back after
he divorced her, married again, divorced number two
wife. Married five years, he drinks, attracted to
woman, falls for his wife's friend. Marcia leaves him,
divorces him, he remarries and is unhappy. His second
wife divorces him. He returns to Marcia. NYT p178
4-6-19
Married life "among Amer. prosperous and fast-living
younger set", business, clubs, soc life crowd out
domestic happiness PW

006514   SHOOTING STARS: A STORY OF TO-DAY.
London: Hurst and Blackett, [1919] BMC.

Marriage, divorce, 2nd marr.of husband, return to
first wife. TLS

KERRUISH, JESSIE DOUGLAS. United Kingdom.

006515   THE GIRL FROM KURDISTAN. London: Hodder
and Stoughton, 1918 BMC NUC.

TLS-Jenny Macroy with a passion for adventure &
domination attempts to improve the East. Title refers
to mistress of Rudolf Schlichting. POV?

006516   MISS HAROUN AL-RASCHID. New York: G. H.
Doran, [c1917] NUC. London: Hodder & Stoughton, [1917]
BMC NUC.

Tells her own story: daughter of Oxford prof and
Eastern woman. With half sister and bodyguard she has
many advents. in Turkey till she marries lover who
pursues her and discovers her mother. PW
"At one moment drastic with sister who wants to
collapse into the snow on a mountain journey; at
another she deftly revives memories of a long standing
blood-feud to save a village from massacre, frustrates
a deep-laid plot of Turkish spies." All set in context
of archeological expedition TLS
Assists him in arch. search. wit and great courage,
knowledge of East. Acts part of corpse, allows self to
be nailed into a coffin to save a whole community.
LBKM

KETTLE, MARY ROSA STUART. D. 1895. United Kingdom.

006517   THE MAGIC OF THE PINE WOODS: A TALE OF
THE DORSET DUNES. London: T. F. Unwin, 1891 BMC NUC.

Dorsetshire dunes. Story of reconciliation. Pinewoods
has a garden in its clearing the restoration of which
coincides with the reconciliation. Several other
characters: Misses Avenell and their nieces. ATH 97
763
Sweet pretty story, attractive young women and their
aunts and love entanglements, one siren Melanie who
flirts a lot, then gives that up. ACAD

006518   ROSE, SHAMROCK AND THISTLE: A STORY OF
TWO BORDER TOWERS. London: T. F. Unwin, 1893 BMC.

About border country. Irish lady stops a feud; money
troubles between Scot Laird and his neighbor, an
English settler. Union of hearts at the end. ATH 101,
602.
LW 25:58. Life on the Scottish border.
PW-Romance between English heroine, Scotch hero, with
Irish matchmaker.

KEY, HELEN ABERCROMBIE.

006519   A DAUGHTER OF LOVE. BY MRS. K. J. KEY.
London: Hutchinson, 1913 BMC. New York: Duffield, 1914
NUC.

PW 85 5/2/14 p.1445 "A daughter of unwedded parents
rises to be the wife of a peer. She is also the mother
of an illegitimate child and in the end is united with
this daughter's father. Left alone and penniless, Mary
is obliged to go out to service as general housemaid,
and it is during this time that she meets the man who
leads her astray. When cast out by her mistress she at
last finds refuge with a French lady who makes a
friend of her and her daughter is brought up under the
influence. Later she again meets her old lover, but
only after he has met and become devoted to his
daughter to whom the truth is at last revealed."
Characters are cheerfully impossible. Hero a socialist
of great wealth. Heroine is dazzling but
"illegitimate." ATH
romance, fairy tale TLS

KEY, MRS. K. J. See KEY, HELEN ABERCROMBIE.

KEYES, FRANCES PARKINSON (WHEELER). 1885-1970. United
States.

006520   THE OLD GRAY HOMESTEAD. Boston: Houghton
Mifflin, 1919 NUC. London: Hodder & Stoughton, 1919
BMC.

Country life in N.E. NYT
The Grays and their 8 children, poor till a
benefactress comes and helps them out NYT 295 5-25-19

KEYNES, HELEN MARY. B. 1892. United Kingdom.

006521   HONOUR THE KING. A ROMANCE. London:

Chatto & Windus, 1914 BMC.

ATH Hist rom-Charles I

006522   THE SPANISH MARRIAGE. A ROMANCE. London:
Chatto and Windus, 1913 BMC.

Negotiations for marriage of Prince Charles with the
Infanta of Spain in time of the Stuarts. ATH LBKM

KIDD, BEATRICE ETHEL. B. 1867.

006523   THE CASSOWARY: A STORY. BY MARK
WINTERTON. London: Jarrolds, [1918] BMC.

KIDSON, ETHEL.

006524   HERRINGFLEET. London: Chapman & Hall,
1912 BMC.

TLS-chronicle of seacoast town.

KIELER, LAURA ANNA SOPHIA MULLER.

006525   THY PEOPLE SHALL BE MY PEOPLE; OR KAREN
JURGENS OF EGTVED. FROM THE DANISH. . . BY BERNO
(CLARA BENER). London: Jarrold, [1906] BMC.

KIESOW, E. (LOUGH).

006526   MARGARET HETHERTON. London: T. F. Unwin,
1901 BMC.

KIISEL, LOUISE. United States.

006527   SPIRIT GOLD. Boston, Mass.: Stratford,
1920 NUC.

PW-regeneration of a man.

KILVERT, MARGARET (CAMERON). 1867-1947. United States.

006528   THE BACHELOR AND THE BABY. BY MARGARET
CAMERON. New York and London: Harper, 1908 NUC BMC.

PW-comedy, male left holding a baby.
BKM-comedy. Male left holding a baby.

006529   THE CAT AND THE CANARY. BY MARGARET
CAMERON. New York and London: Harper, 1908 NUC.

PW-marital comedy.

006530   THE GOLDEN RULE DOLLIVERS. BY MARGARET
CAMERON. New York and London: Harper, 1913 BMC NUC.

PW 84 9/27/13:949 They give lifts to other folk in
their new car. TLS

006531   THE INVOLUNTARY CHAPERON. BY MARGARET
CAMERON. New York and London: Harper, 1909 NUC BMC.

Women past 30 chaperones girl of 17 in S. A.; in
letters. 10-23-09 PW
SR-travel story.

006532   THE PRETENDER PERSON. BY MARGARET
CAMERON. New york and London: Harper, 1911 NUC BMC.

Widow. Woman's letter to sick man "everything finished
merrily." PW 10-28-11

KIMMELL, MARY FORWARD. Nationality Unknown.

006533   TANTALUS. Boston: C. M. Clark, 1909 NUC.

NYT-male hero obscure romance.

KIMMINS, GRACE THYRZA.

006534   POLLY OF PARKER'S RENTS. London: J.
Bowden, 1899 BMC.

KING, ADA FIELDER, jt. au. See HOWARD, CONSTANCE ELEANORA
CAROLINE AND ADA FIELDER KING.

KING, E. STERLING. See KING, ELISHA STERLING.

KING, ELISHA STERLING. B. 1862. United States.

006535   THE WILD ROSE OF CHEROKEE; OR, NANCY WARD
"THE POCAHONTAS OF THE WEST." A STORY OF THE EARLY
EXPLORATION, OCCUPANCY, AND SETTLEMENT OF THE STATE OF
TENNESSEE. A ROMANCE FOUNDED ON AND INTERWOVEN WITH
HISTORY. BY E. STERLING KING. Nashville: University
Press, 1895 NUC.

KING, FLORENCE M. Nationality Unknown.

006536   WOMANLIKE. London: Cassell, 1893 BMC.

KING, GEORGIANA GODDARD. 1871-1939.

006537   THE WAY OF PERFECT LOVE. New York:
Macmillan, 1908 NUC.

KING, GERTRUDE. Nationality Unknown.

006538   THE LANDLUBBERS. New York London:
Doubleday, Page, 1909 NUC BMC.

Four people in a life boat, two women, a teacher and
an adventuress. PW 4-10-09
Woman remains on abandoned boat because she would take
her life anyway. Meets and loves a man, fellow
survivor. NYT

KING, GRACE ELIZABETH. 1852-1932. United States.

006539   THE PLEASANT WAYS OF ST. MEDARD. London:
Constable, 1916 BMC. New York: H. Holt, 1916 NUC.

Sad picture of New Orleans defeated in Civil War TLS
Family in suburbs of N.O.; hero and heroine
highminded, proud, ruined.? TLS

KING, JANE M.

006540   KEEPING HOUSE: A STORY ON HOME
MANAGEMENT. BY THE AUTHOR OF "A LETTER FOR YOU," "A
HAPPY MOTHERS' MEETING" [ANONYMOUS]. London: W.
Gardner, 1910 BMC.

KING, K. DOUGLAS. See KING, KATHERINE DOUGLAS.

KING, KATHERINE DOUGLAS. D. 1901. United Kingdom.

006541   A BITTER VINTAGE. London: C. A. Pearson,
1899 BMC.

English travelling circus. Love tale of Tony and
Caryl. LIT 5:57
Tragic end. LBKM 17:89 1

006542   FATHER HILARION. London: Hutchinson, 1897
BMC.

He had wed an actress and seduced her sister, so he
does penance by working with the poor whom he despises
because of his arist.ideas. As "Father", his advice is
sought by a cousin Lady Janet whose son is infatuated
with a young woman. Turns out "Father" is first
repulsed by her poverty. Then falls madly in love with
her.-a school mistress. SR 84:177

006543   THE SCRIPTURE READER OF ST. MARK'S. BY K.
DOUGLAS KING. London: Hutchinson, [1895] BMC. New
York: Merriam, [c1896] NUC.

He's a strong austere man, falls for a woman "of vile
antecedents" and lives with her till a husband appears
out of her unknown past. BAKER,13,131 is she punished?
SR-Alexandra, affectionate and clinging, heartless and
cruel actions. Gloomy.

006544   URSULA. BY K. DOUGLAS KING. London: J.
Lane, 1900 BMC NUC.

SP 84:929. Russia, sensational.
ATH 115:714. Noble Russians, English relatives,
Southern Russia.
ACAD 58:470. Ursula independent, spirited, capable.
Visits relatives in Russia.
ACAD 58:553. Ursula is narrator. Her Russian
adventures include murder, mystery, lovers. Ends with
her marriage.

KING, MADGE.

006545   COUSIN CINDERELLA: A NOVEL. London: R.
Bentley, 1892 BMC.

ATH 100:126. Americans in London. Camma "wears a
strange talisman and hankers after the unseen," Lyle
has "a taste for morphine" Beulah (cousin Cinderella)
has "somewhat uncanny fascinations."
SP:Beulah is a manager, unlike the real Cinderella in
that she is selfish and clever, gets all the rewards.
She replaces a "girl of enchanting beauty" as heroine
in 2nd stage of book.
ACAD 42:108. Beulah is a Becky Sharp. "She is an
extremely clever person, and she does not make the

common mistake of exhibiting her cleverness for mere
ostentation; she knows that her resources are great,
but she uses them with economy and refrains from
profligate extravagance of expenditure." She is
"admirable."
SR. Mr. Basset, a rich American, his cousin Naomi
(beautiful but stupid) are in London to introduce
Naomi to society. She had her debut in Boston but no
success because of her stupidity, she failed to make
an impression.

KING, MARY RAYNER HYMAN. B. 1875. United States.

006546   THE JUDGMENT. New York: Cochrane, 1911
NUC.

Marries man of wealth to save mother from dying of
"hysterics" NYT

KING, MAUDE EGERTON (HINE). 1867-1927. United Kingdom.

006547   THE ARCHDEACON'S FAMILY. London: J.
Murray, 1909 BMC.

Careers & love affairs of several men. TLS

006548   BREAD AND WINE; A STORY OF GRAUBUNDEN.
Boston: Houghton, Mifflin, 1902 NUC.

006549   CHRISTIAN'S WIFE: A STORY OF GRAUBUNDEN.
London: Smith, Elder, 1902 BMC. London: Vineyard Pr.,
[19--] NUC.

ATH 12-27-02 "Relation of the rise, course, and
conclusion of a brief quarrel between a Swiss peasant
and his wife."

006550   THE CONVERSION OF MISS CAROLINE EDEN.
London: J. M. Dent, 1900 BMC.

LIT 7:528. Elderly spinster, church of England,
impressed by modern Congregational minister.

006551   ROUND ABOUT A BRIGHTON COACH OFFICE.
London: J. Lane, 1896 BMC. New York: Macmillan, 1896
NUC.

ACAD 49:11. Male narrator, recollections of small
fishing village.

KING, PAULINE. United States.

006552   ALIDA CRAIG. New York: G. H. Richmond,
1896 NUC. London and New York: E. Mathews, 1896 BMC.

PW 5-16-96. Story of a successful young woman painter,
Alida, in New York. Among her friends and patrons is a
man who, after confessing his love for her, tells her
of his previous engagement.

KING, RACHEL.

006553   THE COMMON PROBLEM. London: Lynwood, 1912
BMC.

Modern "unheroic" characters, artists. ACAD
ATH O
Written by Lady Ann "old maid in old-maidish style."
About the art world of London. Also an account of how
Lord Kingsford tries to keep his wife (a country
parson's daughter) out of the succession. TLS
Concerns a succession to a peerage. SP

KING, VERONICA.

006554   EURASIA: A TALE OF SHANGHAI LIFE. BY
WILLIAM A. RIVERS. Shanghai: Kelly and Walsh, [1907]
NUC.

006555   LORD GOLTHO; AN APOSTLE OF WHITENESS.
London: Hutchinson, 1895 BMC.

"evangelical hypocrite"-his sensual thoughts, his
"white evenings" a "picture of loathsomeness."
Heredity makes his son Felix what he is. Lucy Davenant
is the child-wife. ACAD 47:422

KINGSBURY, ELIZABETH. United States.

006556   TALE OF AN AMATEUR ADVENTURESS: THE
AUTOBIOGRAPHY OF ESTHER GRAY. ABRIDGED AND EDITED BY
ELIZABETH KINGSBURY. Cincinnati, Ohio: Editor Pub.
Co., 1898 NUC.

Daughter of an Indiana editor, "relates her efforts to
gain a living as journalist, business woman, book

agent, guide at the World's Fair of Chicago, as
private secretary, actress, and travelling companion."
PW

KINGSBURY, SARA. B. 1876. United States.

006557   THE ATONEMENT. Boston: Eastern Pub. Co.,
[c1905] NUC.

Marian, niece of millionaire, turns from life of
luxury to work among the poor renounces her betrothed
who betrayed a young sweat-shop worker.

KINGSCOTE, ADELINE GEORGINA ISABELLA (WOLFF). D. 1908.
United Kingdom.

006558   ANGLO-AMERICANS. BY LUCAS CLEEVE. London:
T. F. Unwin, 1903 BMC NUC.

006559   THE ARBITRATOR. BY LUCAS CLEEVE. London:
Digby, Long, 1909 BMC.

Heiress wants a man who cares not for her wealth "but
who only looked at me as a woman and found me wanting"
TLS

006560   AS THE TWIG IS BENT. BY LUCAS CLEEVE.
London: Digby, Long, 1901 BMC.

Heroine's lengthy conversations on moral issues. ATH

006561   BILLY'S WIFE. BY LUCAS CLEEVE. London: J.
Long, 1906 BMC.

TLS-unhappy marriage, spirited wife, concession to
sentiment at the end.

006562   BLUE LILIES. BY LUCAS CLEEVE. London: T.
F. Unwin, 1902 BMC.

LBKM 5-1902-Problem novel. Heroine manages her affairs
too successfully to be appealing.
ATH 6-14-1902-unhappy marriage. Stays with husband.

006563   BRUISED LILIES. BY LUCAS CLEEVE. London:
F. V. White, 1909 BMC.

Dorothy Trevelyan married to man she doesn't love;
loves another but social demands keep her from
happiness. TLS

006564   THE CARDINAL AND LADY SUSAN. BY LUCAS
CLEEVE. London: Greening, 1908 BMC.

TLS-Lady Susan's amorous escapades and relationship to
the Cardinal, whose old love's daughter she is.
ACAD-shockingly advanced young woman. What happens?
SF-she falls in love with Cardinal, marries in a fit
of pique, marriage not a success, then what?

006565   THE CHILDREN OF ENDURANCE. BEING THE
STORY OF A LATTER-DAY PROPHET. BY LUCAS CLEEVE.
London: T.F. Unwin, 1904 BMC.

006566   THE CONFESSIONS OF A CLIMBER. BY LUCAS
CLEEVE. London: Digby, Long, 1906 NUC BMC.

TLS-Male social climber.

006567   THE CONFESSIONS OF A WIDOW. BY LUCAS
CLEEVE. London: F.V. White, 1907 BMC.

Married to old man 10 yrs, lives now on farm she keeps
meeting old lovers who propose to her. Declines all
offers, decides to devote herself to the poor. She's
averse to marrying again because of the first
marriage. ACAD

006568   COUNSELS OF THE NIGHT. BY LUCAS CLEEVE.
London: T.F. Unwin, 1906 NUC BMC.

ACAD-sons and grandson of murderer have dreams of
same.

006569   DOLLAR CITY. A NOVEL. BY LUCAS CLEEVE.
London: Digby, Long, 1907 BMC.

A millionaire builds a city for rich men where women
will love men for themselves. No politics allowed. In
the end the city fails. SR

006570   A DOUBLE MARRIAGE. BY LUCAS CLEEVE.
London: T.F. Unwin, 1906 BMC.

TLS-marriage, separation, reconciliation.
ATH-incredible plot, they meet again and marry without

recognizing each other.

006571   THE DREAMER. BY LUCAS CLEEVE. London:
Digby, Long, 1905 BMC.

ACAD-male hero, 2nd marriage to his housekeeper,
abandons her and child by 1st marriage for married
woman of society. This is his awakening and end of
story.

006572   DUCHINKA. BY LUCAS CLEEVE. London: J.
Long, 1908 BMC.

ACAD-her affianced husband gambles and loses her at
the gaming tables.
TLS-0

006573   EILEEN. BY LUCAS CLEEVE. London: J. Long,
1903 BMC.

Eileen, married devours novels on the sex question;
morbid story of matrimonial infidelity. ACAD
Marital difficulties are eventually straightened out.
LBKM
She has yearnings toward the smart set, husband is
fond of a widow. ATH

006574   EPICURES. BY LUCAS CLEEVE. London:
Downey, 1896 BMC.

ATH 108:156. Sickly and negative. Eileen,
misunderstood was an epicure, study of her character
and tiresome relations with first her husband and
subsequently her lover.

006575   THE FOOL KILLER. BY LUCAS CLEEVE. London:
T.F. Unwin, 1904 BMC.

LBKM-mother and daughter-their loves, pierces human
nature.
ATH-shallow, young man marries woman 15 years older
and expects her to foot the bill for honeymoon.
TLS-written in diary form by woman, she finally kills
herself.
ACAD-unfaithful to her 1st husband, marries
foolkiller. Author raises Claire to thinking,
reasoning woman only to make her commit suicide at the
end. Characters are very real and well drawn.

006576   THE FOOL'S TAX. BY LUCAS CLEEVE. London:
T.F. Unwin, 1907 BMC.

American girl marries a French count, compares
American/French attitudes, divorce, etc. with America
showing up best. ACAD

006577   FREE SOIL. FREE SOUL. BY LUCAS CLEEVE.
London: Digby, Long, 1903 BMC.

BAKER-heroine rescues her lover from death, becomes
his wife and at last an honest woman. Historical
romance. ACAD Nothing short of an earthquake was
needed to bring about the wedding LBKM

006578   FRIENDS OF FATE: A NOVEL. BY LUCAS
CLEEVE. London: Greening, 1910 BMC.

Lawyers and scandal. TLS

006579   FROM CROWN TO CROSS. BY LUCAS CLEEVE.
London: Hurst and Blackett, 1903 BMC.

006580   HER FATHER'S SOUL. BY LUCAS CLEEVE.
London: J. Long, 1907 BMC.

Mysticism, reincarnation. TLS

006581   HIS ITALIAN WIFE. BY LUCAS CLEEVE.
London: J. Long, [1902] NUC BMC.

006582   THE HOVERERS; A TALE. BY LUCAS CLEEVE.
London: Greening, 1908 BMC.

TLS- feminine, heroine hoverers are upper class who
emigrate rather than eye an old carcass.
ACAD-she emigrates, I think, and a male admirer
follows her.

006583   THE INDISCRETIONS OF GLADYS. BY LUCAS
CLEEVE. London: J. Long, 1903 NUC BMC.

Phoebe a florist and a typist, resists the advances of
employers, marries but not happily? Lady Gladys'
indiscretions seem to be contagious; sensational
episodes. ACAD

006584   LADY SUSAN AND NOT THE CARDINAL. BY LUCAS
CLEEVE. London: F. V. White, 1910 BMC.

TLS-Sequel to Lady Susan and the Cardinal, She now
leaves her husband and marries someone else.
ACAD-Cardinal is not her husband. Her 1st husband dies
and she marries an Englishman (Cardinal spurned her.)
Behaving "a little wildly" in London, she realizes she
always ought to have a keeper which her husband
provides--domestic bliss.

006585   LADY SYLVIA. BY LUCAS CLEEVE. London: J.
Long, 1904 BMC.

006586   LAZARUS: A TALE OF THE EARTH'S GREAT
MIRACLE. BY LUCAS CLEEVE. London: Hutchinson, [1897]
BMC. New York: E. P. Dutton, 1897 NUC.

SR 83:593 Carries on about the tale in sermon-like
manner. Follows New Testament narrative closely.
SP 79:283.

006587   LOVE AND THE KING. BY LUCAS CLEEVE.
London: J. Long, 1906 BMC.

006588   THE LOVE LETTERS OF A FAITHLESS WIFE. BY
LUCAS CLEEVE. London: F.V.white, 1911 BMC.

Inspite of her philanderings we learn she's been in
love with he husband all the while. ACAD

006589   MADEMOISELLE NELLIE. BY LUCAS CLEEVE.
London: J. Long, 1905 BMC.

006590   THE MAGIC OF ROME. BY LUCAS CLEEVE.
London: Digby, Long, 1902 BMC.

006591   THE MAN IN THE STREET. BY LUCAS CLEEVE.
London: T.F. Unwin, 1903 BMC NUC.

Actress subject to hypnotic influence. ACAD
2 women and a man a tangle of love and politics. Man
on street watches, wins the heart of one of the women.
politics and occultism. At the end an M.P. cries as no
woman ever has? LBKM
Hero's affection wavers between tragic actress and a
moderate English woman. ATH 121:205.

006592   MARY ANNE OF PARCHMENT BUILDINGS. BY
LUCAS CLEEVE. London: Digby, Long, 1901 BMC.

006593   THE MASCOTTE OF PARK LANE. BY LUCAS
CLEEVE. London: Greening, 1907 NUC BMC.

A Kaffir girl guides a man to an undiscovered diamond
mine. He's Jewish. "Her dark and guilty past kept her
from marriage to a man of more suitable antecedents."
Inner life of a jeune fille. SR

006594   MOSTLY FOOLS AND A DUCHESS. BY LUCAS
CLEEVE. London: F.V. White, 1901 BMC.

006595   NATHAN TODD. A STORY OF MODERN VIRGINIA.
BY LUCAS CLEEVE. London: Digby, Long, 1907 BMC.

2 Russian women cut off from community became friends
with schoolteacher (male) who won't read Bible in
school. He loves the daughter-but the two women return
to Russia and the daughter marries. ACAD

006596   AN OLD MAN'S DARLING. BY LUCAS CLEEVE.
London: T.F. Unwin, 1908 BMC.

TLS-marriage of young woman to old count.

006597   THE ONE MOMENT. BY LUCAS CLEEVE. London:
J. Long, 1909 BMC.

Concerns the affinity theory of marriage (a pair
agrees to part when one has an affinity elsewhere.)
Mr. and Mrs. Carlyon Smith try it and fail. Two other
women play with it. TLS

006598   OUR LADY OF BEAUTY. BEING THE STORY OF
THE LOVE OF CHARLES VII, KING OF FRANCE, AND AGNES
SORELLE, DEMOISELLE DE FROMENTEAU. BY LUCAS CLEEVE.
London: Digby, Long, 1904 BMC.

LBKM-historical feminine heroine. Agnès Sorelle.
ACAD-who loved Charles VII of France and yielded her
purity to ave France. A woman of charm, beauty, wit,
diplomacy, wisdom, bravery, pure in heart.
ATH-0

006599   PLATO'S HANDMAIDEN. BY LUCAS CLEEVE.
London: J. Long, [1901] BMC.

Heroine starts a hat shop comes to financial ruin. ATH

006600   THE PROGRESS OF PRISCILLA. BY LUCAS
CLEEVE. London: T.F. Unwin, 1905 NUC BMC.

006601   THE PURPLE OF THE ORIENT. BY LUCAS
CLEEVE. London: J. Long, [1902] BMC NUC.

ATH 10-25-02-not helpful-Biblical?

006602   THE REAL CHRISTIAN. BY LUCAS CLEEVE.
London: J. Long, [1901] BMC.

006603   ROSABEL. A STORY OF THE GREATER LOVE. BY
LUCAS CLEEVE. London: Greening, 1910 BMC.

TLS-likeness of two twin brothers. Wife can't tell
them apart.

006604   THE ROSE GERANIUM. BY LUCAS CLEEVE.
London: T.F. Unwin, 1907 BMC.

Domestic drama. SR

006605   SAINT ELIZABETH OF LONDON. BY LUCAS
CLEEVE. London: J. Long, 1905 BMC.

Daughter of a divorced woman married to a brute
accepts her suffering as expiation for mother's sins.
(She's devout.) ACAD
Good woman, bad husband, woman too saint-like? LBKM

006606   THE SECRET CHURCH. BY LUCAS CLEEVE.
London: Digby, Long, 1906 BMC.

TLS-romance, anarchists.

006607   SELMA. BY LUCAS CLEEVE. London: J. Long,
1907 BMC.

Rival claims of love and money. Selma a singer he
marries for love. Lena a singer he marries for money.
TLS

006608   SEVEN NIGHTS IN A GONDOLA. BY LUCAS
CLEEVE. London: T.F. Unwin, 1906 BMC.

TLS-Love triangle.

006609   SOUL-TWILIGHT. BY LUCAS CLEEVE. London:
J. Long, 1906 BMC.

TLS-marital infidelity on both sides.

006610   STOLEN WATERS. BY LUCAS CLEEVE. London:
T.F. Unwin, 1905 BMC.

Martha, daughter of minister, seduced, child dies
purified by suffering; but emphasis on another
minister whose sin (of drinking) is hidden till he
reveals it to his congregation. ACAD

006611   THE WATER-FINDER. BY LUCAS CLEEVE.
London: Hutchinson, 1897 BMC.

He is Mike Openshaw. The son of a local magnate
inherits a gold mine in Aust. but there's no water
nearby. Comes back to England, convinces Mike to look
for water. Mike finds it comes back to discover the
man who employed him is now his rival in love. ACAD
51:353.

006612   WHAT A WOMAN WILL DO: A SOCIETY DRAMA.
London: F. V. White, 1900 BMC.

Woman lets her husband divorce her so that he can
marry an heiress and supply her with money he does not
have-for the children. ACAD 57:602.

006613   WHAT MEN CALL LOVE. A STORY OF SOUTH
AFRICA IN THE DAYS OF CETEWAYO. BY LUCAS CLEEVE.
London: F.V. White, 1901 BMC.

Lazy husband, negatively portrayed, hard working wife.
Mental and moral problems of marriage. Author's
political opinions expressed in unacceptable way. ATH

006614   WHAT WOMAN WILLS. BY LUCAS CLEEVE.
London: J. Long, 1908 BMC.

TLS-love story.

006615   WOMAN AND MOSES. BY LUCAS CLEEVE. London:
Hurst and Blackett, 1902 BMC.

Divorce.

006616   THE WOMAN WHO WOULDN'T: A NOVEL. BY LUCAS
CLEEVE. London: Simpkin, 1895 BMC. London: Simpkin,
Marshall, Hamilton, Kent, 1896 NUC.

Offends propriety, even more so than The Woman Who
Didn't. "Lucas Cleeve is a type of that mentally
diseased class which finds 'Purity' in a systematic
disuse of the sexual aspect of the physical human
being." She presents the "pure" Opalia as sweet in
temper and superb in health. Detailed picture of her
marriage. Husband succumbs to Lady Morris; Opalia
"sacrifices her noble ideal in the interests of her
husband's morals." "An essay in what one might call
serious pornography." SR 80:387
Young woman wants a platonic relationship but he can't
find satisfaction in such an arrangement. He loves
Opalia but is tempted by "the purely animal woman"
ACAD 48:314
A "nympholeptic" story ATH 106:382

006617   A WOMAN'S AYE AND NAY. BY LUCAS CLEEVE.
London: J. Long, 1908 BMC.

TLS-"This may be described as a suffragette novel, for
it opens at a moment when a woman's enfranchisement
bill has just become law ("that dire catastrophe" says
the author)- shows what mighthappen if one candidate
makes love to his opponent's wife, now a free and
independent elector."

006618   THE WORLD'S BLACKMAIL. A NOVEL. BY LUCAS
CLEEVE. London: F. V. White, 1900 BMC.

SR 90:432. California hero and his wife. He encounters
financial disaster in London, returns to California
but on last page intends to conquer London. "The good
genius of the book is a sympathetic literary woman."
ATH 116:438. This woman gives him very good and honest
counsel.

006619   YOLANDE THE PARISIENNE. A DREAM OF THE
TWENTIETH CENTURY. BY LUCAS CLEEVE. London: J. Long,
1900 BMC.

ACAD 59:444. Can't be compared, unless with Corelli's
Sorrows of Satan.
ACAD 59:517. Hero, through the agency of death and the
devil, is introduced to Eve, a recluse in the Sphinx.
A harlot has suicided for him; he further complicates
her existence.

KINGSLEY, FLORENCE (MORSE). 1859-1937. United States.

006620   AND SO THEY WERE MARRIED. New York: Dodd,
Mead, 1908 NUC.

"Mrs. Kingley writes in a humorous vein of the trials
of a young married couple. Though they start life with
the wrong idea, matters are eventually happily
readjusted." BKM 28 1908-9.

006621   BALM IN GILEAD. New York and London: Funk
& Wagnall, 1907 NUC.

006622   THE CROSS TRIUMPHANT. Philadelphia: H.
Altemus, 1899 NUC. London: G. Redway, [1899] BMC.

ACAD 59:262. Bible story, 17 years after the
Crucifixion.

006623   FRANCESCA. Boston: R. G. Badger, [c1911]
NUC.

Romance involving Italian girl PW 10-28-11

006624   THE GLASS HOUSE. New York: Dodd, Mead,
1909 NUC.

Wife of struggling architect, faithful, cares for
three children. Old friend convinces her to write. She
gives up her housework and care of children till one
gets into trouble. "Plea for mothers to do their job"?
PW 4-17-09 "better than House of Mirth" "cruel naked
verities" "women are wonderfully drawn" BKM

006625   THE HEART OF PHILURA. New York: Dodd,
Mead, 1914 NUC.

"Further adventures of the "Miss Philura" of the
Transfigurations of Miss Philura ...solves the
village mystery."
BKM 42 1915-16
Trad stuff NYT
BKM sent romance.

006626   HURRYING FATE AND GERALDINE. New York: F.
Bigelow Corp., [c1913] BMC NUC.

"The Farieighs were poor with only an old house and
ten acres of ground going to rack and ruin and
Geraldine's salary as a primary teacher, between them
and abject poverty. A lawyer turns up with an old
unpaid note of Grandfather Osborne's and tells them he
is about to sell the place for a client and pay the
note. Geraldine writes to the client who comes to see
her and being an impressionable young man, he promptly
falls captive to her beauty and charm. How she
overcomes her prejudice against him, after first
having masqueraded as one of his own lawyers, makes an
entertaining little tale." PW 84 11/1/13:1434
Amusing story of a girl, a garden and a young man. NYT

006627   THE INTELLECTUAL MISS LAMB. New York:
Century, 1906 BMC NUC.

BRD 1906 "This bit of satire has for its heroine a
very pretty professor of physiological psychology at a
woman's college. She regards men, women, and children
as so many "types" which she desires to study and
include in her next book. The man is not a bit
dismayed, when, in answer to a proposal, she informs
him that he "had completey confused his primary
inferences." "The ending of the romance is not unlike
those in which the heroine is somewhat less learned."
BKM v. 24 1906-7.

006628   KINDLY LIGHT. Philadelphia: H. Altemus,
[1904] NUC.

PW

006629   MISS PHILURA'S WEDDING GOWN. New York:
Dodd, Mead, 1912 NUC.

Book--Very sentimental romance.

006630   THE NEEDLE'S EYE. New York and London:
Funk & Wagnall, 1902 BMC NUC.

Altruism, old man and young boy. ARENA 1902.

006631   NEIGHBORS. New York: Dodd, Mead, 1917
NUC.

"little old maid dressmaker" and townsfriends. PW
more of Philura and her community-a strange assortment
of people like the dressmaker. NYT

006632   PAUL, A HERALD OF THE CROSS. Toronto and
London: W. Briggs, [1897] BMC. Philadelphia: H.
Altemus, 1897 NUC.

SR 90:180. Life of St. Paul
Chief events of St. Paul's life followed and expanded.
ACAD 57:746

006633   THE PRINCESS AND THE PLOUGHMAN. New York
and London: Harper, 1907 BMC NUC.

"Mary falls romantically in love with a
sister-student"?PW 6-1-07

006634   PRISONERS OF THE SEA: A ROMANCE OF THE
SEVENTEENTH CENTURY. Philadelphia: D. McKay, 1897 NUC.
London: Ward, Lock, [1897] BMC.

Adventures of Huguenot castaways on a beautiful Medit.
Island. Their adventures There. PW 52:673
LIT 3:160. 17th c. hist rom. love Interest, adventure.
ACAD Huguenots and identity of Man with the Iron Mask.
BKM 6:475.

006635   THE RESURRECTION OF MISS CYNTHIA. New
York: Dodd, Mead, 1905 NUC. London: Hodder and
Stoughton, 1905 BMC. (Eng. ed. title: The Resurrection
of Cynthia Day.)

At 35 with one year to live changes her whole way of
life is cured at the end?PW 10-7-05
She breaks loose from tradition, training; casts off
her black clothes for colors-but that's about as
daring as she gets. An old love affair rekindled and
anyway the doctor was wrong. NYT 651,05

006636   THE RETURN OF CAROLINE. New York and
London: Funk and Wagnalls, 1911 BMC NUC.

006637   THE SINGULAR MISS SMITH. New York and
London: Macmillan, 1904 NUC BMC.

PW club woman works as servant in order to understand
conditions better.
NYT -o
TLS-closes with a romance.

006638   THE STAR OF LOVE. New York and London: D.
Appleton, 1909 NUC BMC.

TLS-Esther at the court of Xerxes
about Hebrew Queen Ester 10-16-09 PW

006639   STEPHEN, A SOLDIER OF THE CROSS.
Philadelphia: H. Altemus, 1896 NUC. London: Sunday
School Union, [1896] BMC.

SR London, The Sunday School Union, 1896. Biblical.

006640   THOSE BREWSTER CHILDREN. New York: Dodd,
Mead, 1910 NUC.

"Described as 'the love story of an almost old maid';
mixed in with the lives of three lively human
youngsters, and flavoured with a very light and clever
plea for the proper method of bringing up chidren."
BKM, v. 31. 1910

006641   THOSE QUEER BROWNS. New York: Dodd, Mead,
1917 NUC.

Annie Smith woman with ideals of altruism and the new
socialism considers many problems of the day PW
9-21-07
Sociological studies in New York slums. wife and
professor husband devote lives to people of New York
slums.

006642   TITUS, A COMRADE OF THE CROSS. Chicago:
D. C. Cook, 1895 NUC. London: Ward, Lock, 1896 BMC.

006643   TO THE HIGHEST BIDDER. New York: Dodd,
Mead, 1911 NUC.

Woman auctions herself for service as maid in order to
raise money for mortgage Pw 1-28-11

006644   TOR, A STREET BOY OF JERUSALEM.
Philadelphia: H. Altemus, [c1904] NUC.

006645   THE TRANSFIGURATION OF MISS PHILURA. New
York and London: Funk & Wagnalls, 1901 NUC.

006646   TRUTHFUL JANE. New York: D. Appleton,
1907 NUC BMC.

Governess, poor relation to rich family; leaves
because of injustices, becomes lady's companion in
U.S. The lady is a smuggler. She twice refuses her
suitor. PW 2-2-07
Then searches a long time for employment, position as
house maid for a while. Inherits a fortune and
marries. BKM

006647   VERONICA. New York: D. Appleton, 1913 BMC
NUC.

"Veronica, a princess of Herod's court, living in the
palace, is secretly infected with leprosy. Story is
interwoven of a lover's quest of Veronica and hers for
healing. She hears of Jesus and the cures He has
wrought, and summons Him. But He is not to be
commanded compelled nor bribed. In the end His noble
patience touches Veronica, she follows Him to
Golgotha, and when He falls under His burden offers
her handkerchief to wipe the blood and sweat from His
face. He returns the gift and Veronica is cured. by
Author of "Titus, a comrade of the cross." PW 83:1187.

006648   WILHELMINA CHANGES HER MIND. Boston:
Small, Maynard, [c1912] NUC.

PW love story

KINGSLEY, FLORENCE (MORSE), jt. au. See FREEMAN, MARY
ELEANOR (WILKINS) AND FLORENCE (MORSE) KINGSLEY.

KINKAID, MARY HOLLAND (MACNEISH). B. 1861. United States.

006649   THE MAN OF YESTERDAY; A ROMANCE OF A
VANISHING RACE. New York: F.A. Stokes, [1908] NUC.

PW-Heroine daughter of Indian mother and white father
abandoned by white husband.
BKM 27, 1908- who intended to bring her East but
didn't and didn't return. she has a child and when it
is born sends for him three times (but does not say
she is pregnant, only sick). He does not come and she

has the child adopted by the tribe, thereby legally
cutting off any claim by the father.
NYT-psych st- she has a college education (as does the
Indian who loves her) and possesses the strong
intellectual qualities of the modern woman.

006650   WALDA; A NOVEL. New York and London:
Harper, 1903 NUC BMC.

Trained to become prophetess in her community and to
reject love and marriage. Must struggle between love
and her religious beliefs 3-28-03 PW
Love and Marriage discouraged in this religious
community, her awakening, final decision to forsake
religion for her love, is excommunicated. NYT 03, 308

KINKEAD, ELEANOR TALBOT. See SHORT, ELEANOR TALBOT
(KINKEAD).

KINKEAD, NELLIE TALBOT. See SHORT, ELEANOR TALBOT
(KINKEAD).

KINTZEL, MRS. A. G. See KINTZEL, MRS. ALBERT GASTON.

KINTZEL, MRS. ALBERT GASTON. B. 1854. United States.

006651   LADY CENTURY. BY MRS. A. G. KINTZEL. New
York: Broadway, [1904] NUC.

006652   LEAVE ME MY HONOR. BY MRS. A. G. KINTZEL.
New York: Broadway, [1904] NUC.

NYT-heroine is a "constitutional flirt," loved and
understood by all three of her husbands, whom in their
turn she, also, loved.

KIPPEN, JANE M.

006653   FLORENCE STANLEY: OR FORGIVING BECAUSE
MUCH FORGIVEN. London: Partridge, [1891] BMC.

006654   THE LAIRD'S DEED OF SETTLEMENT; OR, THE
SECRET OF THE VAULT. London: Digby, Long, [1893] BMC.

Old fashioned plot centered around this vindictive
Laird, a high-spirited young man, a good young woman.
ACAD 43:390.
Cousin Janet loves Kenneth who never knows it. ATH
101:407.

KIRBY, AUGUSTA KLEIN.

006655   ANATOLE: A ROMANCE OF THE SEA. New York:
Dutton, 1904 PW. London: J. M. Dent, 1904 BMC.

KIRBY, ELIZABETH. United Kingdom.

006656   THE ADORABLE DREAMER. New York: G. H.
Doran, [c1920] NUC.

PW-temperamental girl and her pursuit of truth and
happiness.
NYT 9-12-20 p 26. She is a novelist, loved by all
kinds of young men but she yearns for a middle-aged
explorer who ignores her, being much more interested
in the author of "Garbage." Penelope looks for a
"Cause" and adventure. "Light little story."

006657   THE BRIDEGROOM. London: Sidgwick &
Jackson, 1916 BMC NUC.

006658   LITTLE MISS MUFFET: A LOVE STORY FOR
GROWN-UPS. New York: Moffat, Yard, 1919 NUC.

Leaves home to follow writing career but finds true
satisfaction in love in the end. NYT

006659   LITTLE MISS MUFFET: A WHIMSICAL
INVENTION. London: Duckworth, 1918 BMC.

TLS-taken to a home for a rest cure, Sleeping Beauty
is aroused by kisses of young doctor.
LBKM-whimsical. Miss M's pilgrimage from vicarage
through journalistic life in London to goal of love.
Diary form. Cynical postscript entitled anti-climax.

006660   PENELOPE. London: Hodder & Stoughton,
[1920] BMC NUC.

TLS-young modern woman who couldn't help posing but
really wanted a husband and children
LBKM-main character is Sir Anthony Faire, an old man
playing at youth and self-deceived.

KIRBY, MARGARET.

006661   AN ENGLISH GIRL IN THE EAST. A TALE OF
JAPAN AND INDIA. London: A. Melrose, [1913] BMC.

Social life of Europeans in Japan and India-Japanese
customs--along with a thread of romance. ATH

KIRK, DOLLY WILLIAMS, jt. au. See GREENE, FRANCES NIMMO AND
DOLLY WILLIAMS KIRK.

KIRK, ELEANOR, pseud. See AMES, ELEANOR MARIA
(EASTERBROOK).

KIRK, ELLEN WARNER (OLNEY). B. 1842. United States.

006662   THE APOLOGY OF AYLIFFE. Boston: Houghton
Mifflin, 1904 NUC.

PW doesn't sound promising.
NYT-sweet lovable girl who lives to help others.

006663   CIPHERS. Boston: Houghton, Mifflin, 1891
NUC.

New York society; centered around Mrs. Lee Childe; LW
Her reappearance in society celebrated with a
brilliant reception of authors, artists, etc. who
figure in the story-some as cyphers. PW
Romance CR 17:181

006664   GOOD-BYE, PROUD WORLD. Boston: Houghton
Mifflin, 1903 NUC.

Newspaper woman for 10 years, indispensible to
management of the business. Also inherits an estate
which she manages PW 10-03-03
WOMAN'S JOURNAL 10-3-03
BKM (1903) 18, 330
Heroine at first, editor of woman's column in
newspaper. Works hard enough to kill six women but
gives it all up for housework. Story centers on
house.--NYT 03,661

006665   MARCIA, A NOVEL. Boston: Houghton,
Mifflin, 1907 NUC.

"loving freedom, Marcia sets aside the judgement alike
of old friends and new and follows her own life of
purpose." "vivid picture of a free woman, mistress of
her own destiny" WOMAN'S JOURNAL 12-14-07
Inherits large estate, works to support self and keep
it by writing marries the right man. PW 3-23-07
Autobiographical, college bred, independent, refuses
ancestral riches, works as secretary. NYT

006666   OUR LADY VANITY. Boston: Houghton
Mifflin, 1901 NUC.

PW 9-14-01
Joan neglects her child, she lives for adulation,
wants the world at her feet. Carries on an intrigue
while married, does as she pleases, till father
discovers the intrigue, puts her in her place. She
dies. NYT

006667   A REMEDY FOR LOVE. Boston: Houghton,
Mifflin, 1902 NUC.

Widower and two daughters--ATH 121 45
NYT 7-5-02--Romance.

006668   THE REVOLT OF A DAUGHTER. Boston:
Houghton, Mifflin, 1897 NUC.

Scene US, then Italy. The daughter of an Italian
father and a mother twice widowed. Two men that love
the widow and her daughter-the many innocent cross
purposes. PW 52:368.

006669   A REVOLUTIONARY LOVE-STORY, AND THE HIGH
STEEPLE OF ST. CHRYSOSTOM'S. Chicago: H. S. Stone,
1898 NUC.

NYT 1898:422. Revolutionary Love Story: Connecticut
love gone awry; Cicely faded away and died.
Revolution. High Steeple: English village: hero
becomes life-long cripple because of his rival for
heroine.

006670   THE STORY OF LAWRENCE GARTHE. Boston:
Houghton, Mifflin, 1894 NUC.

PW-ought a girl marry a divorced man whose wife is
still living? Constance ponders, and, it seems,
decides to do so when his wife enters her fifth
marriage.
The soul-life of a child. Also the author has felt

obliged to introduce the new woman. A young woman marries a man after he is divorced. CR 23:437.

KIRKE, GENEVIEVE. Nationality Unknown.

006671   AN UNWEDDED WIFE. Chicago: Morrill, Higgins, 1892 NUC.

PW-Jessie a typewriter loves her employer a married man. Story of her life before and after yielding to temptation.

KIRKLAND, WINIFRED MARGARETTA. 1872-1943. United States.

006672   THE CHRISTMAS BISHOP. Boston: Small, Maynard, [c1913] NUC.

"Story of a great-hearted Episcopal bishop who passes a certain Christmas of his life in what seem to him three hopeless attempts to make things go right for the three human beings with whom in succession his day is chiefly passed. How his influence made itself felt in reality, in contrast to his own ignorance of its value, is the burden of the story." PW 11-15-13 1588

006673   THE HOME-COMERS. Boston: Houghton Mifflin, 1910 NUC.

sent. story PW

006674   INTRODUCING CORINNA. New York: F.H. Revell, [c1909] NUC.

head of boarding school; saves it; girls book?

KIRLEW, MARIANNE.

006675   HER PATH TO THE STARS. London: Gay and Bird, 1907 BMC.

006676   IVYHOLME; OR, THE SECRET OF THE SANDHILLS. London: R. Culley, [1907] BMC.

KIRSCHNER, LULA. 1854-1934. Russia.

006677   BLANCHE: THE MAID OF LILLE; TR. FROM THE GERMAN OF OSSIP SCHUBIN. Boston: Priv. print [Colonial Press], 1902 NUC. (Tr. Sarah H. Adams)

006678   BORIS LENSKY. FROM THE GERMAN. BY OSSIP SCHUBIN. New York: Worthington, 1891 NUC. (Tr. Elsie L. Lathrop)

Violinist, selfish, vain, famous. A man of insatiable appetite for excesses. Loves same woman son loves after wrecking many women's lives. DIAL 6-91. Daughter plans own death. Compared to Anna. NATION 8-6-91, 107.
Last days of great genius depicted with much realism. PW

006679   BROKEN WINGS. BY OSSIP SCHUBIN. New York: P. F. Collier, [c1893] NUC.

006680   CHORDS AND DISCORDS, A STORY OF SOULS ASTRAY. New York: P. F. Collier, 1894 NUC. (English Version of Ossip Schubin's "Woher Tönt Dieser Missklung Durch Die Welt?" Tr. A. H. L.)

006681   THE CLOSING DOOR. BY OSSIP SCHUBIN. London: J. M. Dent, 1896 BMC. (Tr. from the German by Marie D. Gurney)

006682   COUNTESS ERIKA'S APPRENTICESHIP. TR. FROM THE GERMAN OF OSSIP SCHUBIN. Philadelphia: J. B. Lippincott, 1891 BMC NUC. (Tr. Mrs. A. L. Wister)

Story opens when she's 11. Her father dislikes her. When mother dies, adopted by grandmother and introduced to Berlin society. PW
NATION 54:115. German aristocratic society and its intrigues.
ACAD 41:178. She is "united at last to the only man who commands our admiration in these pages."
Social life of German princes and princesses in Berlin and Venice. Author "pushes heroine to verge of a precipice finds her willing to go over, draws her back" to marry an honest man. IND

006683   FELIX LANZBERG'S EXPIATION. BY OSSIP SCHUBIN. New York: Worthington, 1892 NUC. (Tr. Elsie L. Lathrop)

PW-Marriage of Linda to a man "under the shadow of an early sin," her discovery, his expiation.

006684   THE HAND OF DESTINY. BY OSSIP SCHUBIN. New York: Worthington, 1892 NUC. (Tr. Mary A. Robinson)

LW 23:310. Austrian society in Rome. Young Austrian falls in love with girl of the middle class, does not offer marriage and his attentions are compromising. Her brother calls him out in a duel; the brother is killed. She realizes how little her admirer was worth.

006685   A LEAFLESS SPRING. BY OSSIP SCHUBIN. Philadelphia: J. B. Lippincott, 1893 NUC. (Tr. from the German by Mary J. Safford)

Englishman considers himself ruined goes to Paris to study art to make a living. Meets an Italian model. Later marries a respectable English woman. End is sensational and tragic. PW 3-18-93.
The model is unhappily married and doesn't live with her husband. He didn't wait for explanations when he learned she had a husband. Rushed into marriage with the English woman. He's stabbed on honeymoon by model's husband.

006686   ONE OF US. BY OSSIP SCHUBIN. New York: P. F. Collier, 1893 NUC. (Tr. Mrs. Ellen Waugh)

006687   THE STORY OF A GENIUS; FROM THE GERMAN OF OSSIP SCHUBIN. New York: R. F. Fenno, 1898 NUC. (Tr. E. H. Lockwood)

PW-male violinist from broken home. Friend steals his love and his musical work. Genius gives up; his life a failure.
Gesa von Zuylen is a waif, but a genius in music. Annette is his fiance. Alphonse his friend who steals Annette while Gesa is on tour. Also steals Gesa's opera. When Gesa returns Annette is dying and his friend is famous for the opera.

KITCAT, MABEL (HICKSON).

006688   CHRONICLES OF TEDDY'S VILLAGE. BY MRS. MURRAY HICKSON. London: Ward, Lock, 1899 BMC. London: 1898 NUC.

006689   A LATTER-DAY ROMANCE. London: Bliss, Sands and Foster, 1893 BMC.

A woman's mistake. Had agnostic and rationalistic training. Book suggests it is to blame? She leaves husband for another man. ACAD 44:565. Melancholy and unwholesome.
SR Lillian married to blind husband, is restless. He "more than less deliberately" suicides. Her lover is worthless.

KLICKMANN, FLORA. United Kingdom.

006690   THE AMBITIONS OF JENNY INGRAM; A TRUE STORY OF MODERN LONDON LIFE. London: R. T. S., [1905] BMC. London: "Leisure Hour" Library Office, [1907] NUC.

006691   BETWEEN THE LARCH-WOODS AND THE WEIR. London: R. T. S., [1917] BMC. New York: F. A. Stokes, [1918] NUC.

006692   THE FLOWER-PATCH AMONG THE HILLS. London: R. T. S., [1916] BMC. New York: F. A. Stokes, [1916?] NUC.

ATH 0
Country life in Surrey and Monmouthshire.

KLINGLE, GEORGE, pseud. See HOLMES, GEORGIANA (KLINGLE).

KNAPP, ADELINE. 1860-1909. United States.

006693   THE WELL IN THE DESERT. New York: Century, 1908 BMC NUC.

PW-Male hero.
BKM- male hero.

KNAPP, HARRIET LORETTA. United States.

006694   MIRIAM'S TOWER. New York: G. W. Dillingham, 1897 NUC.

Allegory: Miriam lives with Peace. Is tempted by a stranger to explore Elysian Fields. Her lover leaves her. Back to Tower to live with Despair till Hope comes. PW 51:394

KNAPP, MARGARET LIZZIE. B. 1863. United States.

006695   BUT STILL A MAN. Boston: Little, Brown,
1909 NUC.

   Story of a male minister PW 2-13-09

KNAPP, MARY CLAY. United States.

   006696   WHOSE SOUL HAVE I NOW? A NOVEL. Boston:
   Arena, 1896 NUC.

   PW 6-13-96. Author believes material age is passing.
   Life of the heroine proves that the perfect woman
   exists only when the material development equals the
   higher mental and spiritual, and that by intimate
   association with such a woman a man who is purely
   material and selfish may, through the triumph of his
   sense of justice, become a humanitarian and bless the
   world by pure disinterested service.

KNEELAND, CLARISSA ABIA. B. 1878.

   006697   SMUGGLER'S ISLAND AND THE DEVIL FIRES OF
   SAN MOROS. Boston: Houghton Mifflin, 1915 BMC NUC.
   London: T. Nelson, 1919 BMC.

   Mod Swiss family Robinson. PW 11-13-15

KNIGHT, ADELE FERGUSON. B. 1867. United States.

   006698   MADEMOISELLE CELESTE, A ROMANCE OF THE
   FRENCH REVOLUTION. Philadelphia: G.W. Jacobs, [1910]
   NUC. London: Hutchinson, 1911 BMC.

   Begins with rescue of heroine from guillotine. TLS
   LBKM-rom.
   hist rom. PW
   NYT love story

   006699   THE RIGHT TO REIGN. A ROMANCE OF THE
   KINGDOM OF DRECQ. Philadelphia: G.W. Jacobs, [1912]
   NUC.

KNIGHT, MAUDE C.

   006700   CHANCE THE CHANGELING. London: Greening,
   1907 BMC NUC.

   Mystery and adventure. TLS.
   two men who are twins.

KNIGHTS, LILIAN R.

   006701   THE ROSE OF DAWN; A FIRST CENTURY STORY.
   London: Jarrold, 1898 BMC.

   SR 86:512. Ladylike Romans and ancient Britons.

KNOCKER, GRATIANA LONGWORTH.

   006702   THE WITCH OF WITHYFORD: A STORY OF
   EXMOOR. BY GRATIANA CHANTER. London: J. M. Dent, 1896
   BMC. New York: Macmillan, 1896 NUC.

   LW 27:219. Real witch, spells, familiars etc. in
   connection with murder, child-stealing. Happy ending.

KNOLLYS, B. S. See WOLSELEY, BEATRICE S. (KNOLLYS).

KNOOP, GERTRUDE.

   006703   DUKE RODNEY'S SECRET. BY PERRINGTON
   PRIMM. London: Jarrold, 1901 BMC.

   006704   THE GIRL AT RIVERFIELD MANOR. BY
   PERRINGTON PRIMM. London: F. V. White, 1900 BMC.

   SP 84:387. Irene. Australia and England.
   ACAD 58:206. Pleasant love story.

006705   IVY CARDEW. A NOVEL. London: Jarrold,
1901 BMC.

KNOWLES, JOSEPHINE PITCAIRN.

   006706   FELIX MORGAINE. London: Methuen, 1919
   BMC.

   LBKM male rector.

   006707   THE UPHOLSTERED CAGE. London: Hodder &
   Stoughton, [1912] BMC NUC.

   Fic? Woman-social and moral questions; woman-England.
   "Considers the problem of the unmarried daughter, the
   sheltered woman of no vocation who lives with her

parents in the home signified by the "upholstered
cage." NUC

KNOWLES, MABEL WINIFRED. 1875-1949. United Kingdom.

   006708   THE AMBITIONS OF JILL. BY MAY WYNNE.
   London: J. Long, 1920 BMC.

   TLS love and inheritance.

   006709   A BLOT ON THE ESCUTCHEON. BY MAY WYNNE.
   New York: R.F. Fenno, [190-] NUC. London: Mills &
   Boon, 1910 BMC.

   PW-historic romance
   TLS-male hero, hist
   LBKM male hero, hist

   006710   THE BRAVE BRIGANDS. BY MAY WYNNE. London:
   S. Paul, [1913] BMC.

   hist rom; ATH

   006711   THE CLAIM THAT WON. BY MAY WYNNE. London:
   Everett, [c1912] BMC NUC.

   ATH- historic male hero.
   TLS historic male hero

   006712   THE CURSE OF GOLD. BY MAY WYNNE. London:
   Aldine, [1919] BMC.

   006713   THE DESTINY OF CLAUDE. BY MAY WYNNE.
   London: S. Paul, [1913] BMC.

   Fr. in 16th -hist rom. ATH
   Claude is a young and adventurous demoiselle, runs
   away from home to escape the convent. Goes to Henry
   II's court in Paris with a friend. Enters Marie
   Stuart's service. Flood of exciting adventures TLS

   006714   FOES OF FREEDOM. BY MAY WYNNE. London:
   Chapman & Hall, 1916 BMC.

   006715   FOR CHARLES THE ROVER; A ROMANCE. BY MAY
   WYNNE. London: Greening, 1909 BMC. New York: R.F.
   Fenno, [1911] NUC.

   Charles Stuart 1720-1788

   006716   FOR CHURCH AND CHIEFTAIN. BY MAY WYNNE.
   London: Mills and Boon,, [1909] BMC NUC.

   trad hist rom TLS
   Lovers and advent ACAD
   Ireland-Hist-Fic Elizabeth 1558-1579

   006717   FOR FAITH AND NAVARRE. BY MAY WYNNE.
   London: J. Long, 1904 BMC.

   ACAD-historic romance.

   006718   THE GALLANT GRAHAM. A ROMANCE. BY MAY
   WYNNE. London: Greening, 1911 BMC.

   Hist. rom TLS TLS Hist. rom.

   006719   A GALLANT OF SPAIN. BY MAY WYNNE. London:
   S. Paul, [1920] BMC.

   006720   THE GIPSY COUNT. BY MAY WYNNE. New York:
   John McBride, 1909 NUC.

   Trad. hist romance NYT Story of chivalry. PW 4-17-09

   006721   THE GIPSY KING. BY MAY WYNNE. London:
   Chapman & Hall, 1917 BMC.

   Trad hist rom TLS

   006722   THE GOAL. BY MAY WYNNE. London: Digby,
   Long, 1907 BMC.

   Unexciting traditional story TLS

   006723   HENRY OF NAVARRE; A ROMANCE OF AUGUST,
   1572. BY MAY WYNNE. New York: G. P. Putnam's Sons,
   1908 NUC. London: Greening, 1909 BMC.

   Trad hist rom LBKM
   Romance BKM
   From the play "Henry of Navarre" by William Devereux
   BMC

   006724   THE HERO OF URBINO. BY MAY WYNNE. London:
   S. Paul, 1914 BMC.

Traditional historical romance. ATH
ATH hist romance, Italy and the Borgias.

006725   "HEY FOR CAVALIERS!" A ROMANCE. BY MAY
WYNNE. London: Greening, 1912 BMC NUC.

TLS-Romance of Civil War

006726   THE HONOUR OF THE SCHOOL. BY MAY WYNNE.
London: Nisbet, [1918] BMC.

006727   HONOUR'S FETTERS. BY MAY WYNNE. London:
S. Paul, [1911] BMC.

Historical romance TLS

006728   JANIE'S GREAT MISTAKE. BY MAY WYNNE.
London: Odhams, [1920] BMC.

006729   THE KING OF A DAY: A ROMANCE. BY MAY
WYNNE. London: Jarrolds, [1918] BMC.

TLS-historical, male.

006730   A KING'S TRAGEDY. BY MAY WYNNE. London:
Digby, Long, 1905 BMC.

006731   LET ERIN REMEMBER. BY MAY WYNNE. London:
Greening, [1908] BMC.

TLS-Ireland in 12th century.
SR-Love and War.

006732   THE LYONS MAIL; A ROMANCE...FOUNDED ON
THE CELEBRATED PLAY ["LE COURRIER DE LYON"] BY E.
MOREAU. BY MAY WYNNE. London: Jarrold, [1917] BMC.

006733   MAID OF BRITTANY. BY MAY WYNNE. London:
Greening, 1906 BMC.

TLS Historical Romance. Romance of war of 1870 LBKM

006734   MARCEL OF THE "ZEPHYRS". BY MAY WYNNE.
London: Jarrold, [1917] BMC.

006735   THE MASTER WIT. A STORY OF BOCCACCIO. BY
MAY WYNNE. London: Greening, 1911 BMC.

Story of Boccaccio TLS

006736   MISTRESS CYNTHIA. BY MAY WYNNE. London:
Greening, 1910 BMC NUC.

TLS-Historical romance. Gt. Britain history fic.
1727-60

006737   PENANCE. BY MAY WYNNE. London: [Mascot
Novels], [1917] BMC.

006738   A PRINCE OF INTRIGUE. A ROMANCE OF
MAZEPPA. BY MAY WYNNE. London: Jarrolds, [1920] BMC
NUC.

TLS-hist. rom.

006739   QUEEN JENNIE. BY MAY WYNNE. London:
Chapman & Hall, 1918 BMC.

TLS-Spirited heroine, champion of the Stuart cause
becomes bride of King Robert Bruce.
LBKM-Leads the band of Highland Rovers on midnight
forays. Wife in name only of so-called King Robert
Bruce but in reality Queen of his adherents.

006740   THE RED FLEUR-DE-LYS. BY MAY WYNNE.
London: S. Paul, 1912 BMC.

TLS-Historical romance.
ATH-Historical romance.

006741   THE REGENT'S GIFT. BY MAY WYNNE. London:
Chapman & Hall, 1915 BMC.

Traditional historical romance TLS

006742   ROBIN THE PRODIGAL: A ROMANCE. BY MAY
WYNNE. London: Jarrolds, [1919] BMC.

Her 34th historical romance.

006743   RONALD LINDSAY. BY MAY WYNNE. London: J.
Long, [1905] BMC NUC.

Historical romance LBKM Scotland Fict. 1689

006744   A RUN FOR HIS MONEY. BY MAY WYNNE. Aldine
Pub Co.: [1919] BMC.

006745   SCOUTS FOR SERBIA: A STORY OF WAR AND
ADVENTURE. BY MAY WYNNE. London: T. Nelson, [1919]
BMC.

006746   THE SECRET OF THE ZENANA. BY MAY WYNNE.
London: Greening, 1913 BMC.

Mrs. Merrington is a prisoner in an Indian Rajah's
Zenana (?) for 20 years. During this time raises a
daughter Angela. She's about to be married off to an
Indian potentate when a Scot disguised as a woman
enters the zenana and rescues her. Thrilling meoldrama
of 18th century. ACAD

006747   THE SILENT CAPTAIN. BY MAY WYNNE. London:
S. Paul, 1914 BMC.

ATH- historical romance-16th century France.

006748   A SPY FOR NAPOLEON: A ROMANCE. BY MAY
WYNNE. London: Jarrolds, [1917] BMC.

"A story of the First Consulate in which a woman plays
the chief part in many intrigues between France and
England ATH
"The heroine is one of Napoleon's spies under Fouche
at the time of the Cadoudal- Pichegru conspiracy."
BAKER 32 512

006749   THE STORY OF HEATHER. BY MAY WYNNE.
London: J. Nelson, [1912] BMC.

006750   STRANDED IN BELGIUM. BY MAY WYNNE.
London: Blackie, [1918] BMC.

006751   SYMPATHY. BY MAY WYNNE. London:
Skeffington, 1901 BMC.

006752   THE TAILOR OF VITRE. BY MAY WYNNE.
London: Gay & Hancock, 1908 BMC.

TLS- old fashioned historical romance.
ATH. Old fashioned historical romance.

006753   THE TAINT OF TRAGEDY. BY MAY WYNNE.
London: [Mascot Novels], [1917] BMC.

006754   THE TEMPTATION OF PHILIP CARR. BY MAY
WYNNE. London: S. Sonnenschien, 1905 BMC.

About a man missioner TLS 187,05

006755   THREE'S COMPANY. BY MAY WYNNE. London:
Blackie, [1917] BMC.

006756   WHEN TERROR RULED. BY MAY WYNNE. London:
Greening, 1907 BMC.

KNOWLING, MERIEL (BUCHANAN). B. 1886.

006757   TANIA. A RUSSIAN STORY. London: H.
Jenkins, 1914 BMC.

ACAD 86:494 Triangular romance-nothing more.

006758   WHITE WITCH. BY MERIEL BUCHANAN. London:
H. Jenkins, 1913 NUC BMC.

Comedy of errors; Austrian high life. Marie Bernadine
marries & falls in love with husband. Several mixed up
couples: "fresh, young, idyllic." ACAD
Two sisters contrasted: Eileen outspoken and selfish;
Marie Bernadine, reserved and unselfish. Their love
tangles. SP
3 couples; for none of whom there is a promise of
happiness. ATH

KNOX, JANETTE HILL. B. 1845. United States.

006759   JUSTA HAMLIN'S VOCATION. New York and
London: Abbey Press, [1902] NUC.

KOCH, MARY.

006760   PAUL JEROME. A NOVEL. London: Greening,
1906 BMC.

TLS-mild tale of impulsive girl who married the wrong
curate.

KOPPKE, GEORGENIA JOSEPHINE LUKE. United States.

006761   BOWS OF WHITE RIBBON: A ROMANCE OF THE

SPANISH-AMERICAN WAR. Chicago: Woman's Temperance Pub. Association, [c1899] NUC.

KORTRECHT, AUGUSTA.

006762   A DIXIE ROSE IN BLOOM. Philadelphia and London: J. B. Lippincott, 1910 BMC NUC. (BMC: A Dixie Rose.)

Girls' story. PW

KOVALEVSKY, SOPHIA. See KOVALEVSKYAYA, SOF'YA VASIL'EVNA (KORVIN-KRUKOVSKAIA).

KOVALEVSKYAYA, SOF'YA VASIL'EVNA (KORVIN-KRUKOVSKAIA). 1850-1891.

006763   VERA BARANTZOVA. FROM THE RUSSIAN OF SOPHIA KOVALEVSKY. London: Ward & Downey, 1895 NUC BMC.

The changes in a Russian arist. family because of emancipation of serfs. Vera's love affair with an older teacher. Her second marr. to a Nihilist. Attached to the cause and goes to Siberia to live among the exiles. SP 74:302

006764   VERA VORONTZOFF. Boston: Lamson and Wolffe, [c1896] NUC BMC. (Tr. Anna Von Rydingsvard)

BKM 3:556. Romance. Vera formed a friendship which was developing towards love with Stepan, an older man with liberal ideas for governmental reform in Russia. He is exiled, dies a year later. She receives a letter from him which influences her to do something great for Russian liberty. She will work in Siberia for the exiles.

KRAUSE, LYDA FARRINGTON. 1864-1939. United States.

006765   CHRISTINE'S INSPIRATION. BY BARBARA YECHTON. New York: J. Pott, 1892 NUC.

PW Woman artist "sacrifices her work and fame in the cause of a grief-stricken friend." "An Easter story with a moral."

006766   FORTUNE'S BOATS. BY BARBARA YECHTON. Boston and New York: Houghton, Mifflin, 1900 NUC.

LW 31:268. Wholesome. Five sisters and their mother and saintly uncle living in NYC flat. Inspiring. For girls?
PW. One is a companion, another a journalist who writes a novel, another an interior decorator, another works with the poor. Their love stories, too.

006767   HONOR D'EVEREL. BY BARBARA YECHTON. New York: Dodd, Mead, 1903 NUC.

Honor takes care of 8 younger siblings. Rejects lover to take her flock to US to be educated. 10-10-03 PW

006768   A LITTLE TURNING ASIDE. BY BARBARA YECHTON. Philadelphia: G. W. Jacobs, 1898 NUC.

History of a self-willed young artist who prefers art to duty-Hetty's career. Girls?
Hetty Drayton believes she will be a great artist; because of ambition. "deserts her only relative in her time of need and is brutally cruel." About to compete for a prize, is blinded. How Dr. Dennis and his mother brought a change in Hetty. BOOK NEWS 98-99:306

006769   YOUNG MRS. TEDDY. BY BARBARA YECHTON. New York: Dodd, Mead, 1901 NUC.

PW
Sentimental. NYT

006770   A YOUNG SAVAGE. BY BARBARA YECHTON. Boston: Houghton, Mifflin, 1899 NUC.

The Latimers, reduced gentlefolk, rel., refined. Mrs. Latimer, the invalid and center of all activity "rules by never asserting herself." Sharley is powerless because she does assert herself. And Little John (Junanita Kyle) is fascinating. Teddy falls in love with her. It's a goody-goody type of story. BKM 1:281 Juanita Kyle is the young savage. She rides, shoots, leads a free unconv. life in Colo. How she's tamed by Latimers in NYC. esp. by Mrs. Latimer. PW 56:1226 Juv?

KRIKORIAN, JESSIE.

006771   A DAUGHTER OF MYSTERY. London: Grifith,

Farran, 1892 BMC.

ATH 100:155. Cleopatra Gunn "believes herself to be a limb of Satan in spite of all her friends' efforts to humanize her." Witchcraft and the supernatural.
SP 69:651. She seems to possess supernatural powers.
ACAD 42:88. She is in love with the squire who is already married. She mesmerizes his wife and causes her to throw herself in front of an engine. He remains true to dead wife. Filled with remorse, and foiled, she chooses the same death. Her grandmother, Granny Gunn, has already been murdered by the villagers for possessing the evil eye.

KROUT, CAROLINE VIRGINIA. 1853-1931. United States.

006772   DIONIS OF THE WHITE VEIL. BY CAROLINE BROWN. Boston: L.C. Page, 1911 NUC.

Young woman forced to be nun, has many advents of pioneer woman in Louisiana, leaves convent for love-PW 7-29-11

006773   KNIGHTS IN FUSTIAN: A WAR TIME STORY OF INDIANA. BY CAROLINE BROWN. Boston and New York: Houghton, Mifflin, 1900 NUC.

NYT 1900:276. American historical romance. Civil War. The Knights of the Golden Circle, a secret society of the Secessionists, conspiracy. No heroes. Author exalts the heroism of the women they outstrip the men in valor and determination and (I infer) intelligence.

006774   ON THE WE-A TRAIL: A STORY OF THE GREAT WILDERNESS. BY CAROLINE BROWN. New York: Macmillan, 1903 NUC BMC. London: Macmillan, 1903 NUC.

Book of Revolution, canoes, scalps ACAD 65, 586

KRYSHANOVSKAYA, V. I. See KRYZHANOVSKAIA, VERA IVANOVNA.

KRYZHANOVSKAIA, VERA IVANOVNA.

006775   THE TORCH-BEARERS OF BOHEMIA. BY V. I. KRYSHANOVSKAYA. London: Chatto and Windus, 1916 BMC. New York: R. M. McBride, 1917 NUC. (Tr. Juliet M. Soskice)

Historical romance of the struggle for national and religious liberty in the time of the martyr Hus. (1369). NYT

KURZ, ISOLDE. 1853-1944.

006776   TALES OF FLORENCE. London: A. Melrose, 1919 BMC. (Tr. Lilian Dundas.)

Two romances, the better one "The Marriage of the Dead."
Original date of pub. 1890.
BAKER 32 285

KYLE, RUBY BERYL. United States.

006777   PAUL ST. PAUL, A SON OF THE PEOPLE: A NOVEL. Buffalo: C. Wells Moulton, 1895 NUC.

He is a celebrated tenor, said to be son of Spanish Don Carlos who claimed Spanish throne. Young woman comes into his life, becomes his ward; also becomes a famous opera singer; is about to marry him, learns he's her half brother. PW 2-16-95:322.

L., M., pseud. See HERRINGTON, MRS. M. J.

LACOSTE, LUCIE. D. 1931. United States.

006778   MIMINETTA. New York: Avondale Press, 1917 NUC.

Mother love.

LADD, ANNA COLEMAN (WATTS). 1878-1938. United States.

006779   THE CANDID ADVENTURER. Boston: Houghton, Mifflin, 1913 NUC.

PW 83 3/15/13 p.985 "Hero is a young artist whose relations with two women, one a young and beautiful New England widow, the other his Polish model, make the story's incidents. Scene is laid in his Cambridge (Mass.) studio, in Rome and Paris. Ending is happy."

006780   HIERONYMUS RIDES; EPISODES IN THE LIFE OF A KNIGHT AND JESTER AT THE COURT OF MAXIMILIAN, KING OF THE ROMANS. London: Macmillan, 1912 BMC NUC.

NYT, ATH, TLS—historical romance.
Fantasy concerning Italy and Germany and Renaissance
politics with glimpses of imperial pageantry, court
intrigues, fugitive romances, etc. SR

LAFFAN, BERTHA JANE (GRUNDY) LEITH ADAMS. D. 1912. United
Kingdom.

006781   BONNIE KATE: A STORY FROM A WOMAN'S POINT
OF VIEW. BY MRS. LEITH ADAMS (MRS. R. S. DE COURCY
LAFFAN). London: K. Paul, 1891 BMC NUC.

006782   COLOUR SERGEANT, NO. 1 COMPANY. London:
Jarrold, 1894 BMC.

Military life in Ireland. Opens with a flogging but
for the most part is not violent. The Sergeant turns
out, of course, to be a gentleman. A romance included.
SP 74:139

006783   THE CRUISE OF "THE TOMAHAWK": THE STORY
OF A SUMMER'S HOLIDAY IN PROSE AND RHYME. BY MRS. R.
S. DE C. LAFFAN...ASSISTED BY "STOKE" AND "BOW".
London: Eden, Remington, 1892 BMC.

006784   A GARRISON ROMANCE. London: Eden,
Remington, 1892 BMC NUC.

ATH 99:275. military life.
SP 69:74. Military romance. Question of whether a girl
should marry a man she doesn't love to help her
family.
ACAD 41:251. Problem is solved when he accidentally
learns she loves another by his jumping overboard,
having willed all to her.

006785   THE OLD PASTURES. A STORY OF THE WOODS
AND FIELDS. London: K. Paul, 1895 BMC.

SR—heroine from Birmingham. Her romance with squire's
son
ATH 107:82. Unsuccessful attempt at dialect.
Warwickshire. She is a bookseller's daughter, has a
social conscience.

006786   THE PEYTON ROMANCE. BY MRS. LEITH ADAMS
(MRS. R. S. DECOURCY LAFFAN). London: K. Paul, 1892
BMC NUC.

ATH: Sentimental romance of a young girl.

006787   THE PRINCE'S FEATHERS. A STORY OF LEAFY
WARWICKSHIRE IN THE OLDEN TIMES. London: Digby, Long,
1899 BMC.

LIT 6:89. Idyll, pretty, dainty. Bessie comes back an
honest woman to her mother.
Warwickshire. Mystery of Bessie's origin. ACAD 57:682

006788   THE VICAR OF DALE END: A STUDY. London:
Digby, Long, 1906 BMC.

TLS—tragic fate through a scapegrace son.

LAFFAN, MRS. R. S. DE C. See LAFFAN, BERTHA JANE (GRUNDY)
LEITH ADAMS.

LAFFAN, MRS. R. S. DE COURCY. See LAFFAN, BERTHA JANE
(GRUNDY) LEITH ADAMS.

LAGEN, M. J. See LAGEN, MARY JULIA AND CALLY THOMAS RYLAND.

LAGEN, MARY JULIA AND CALLY THOMAS RYLAND. B. 1856.
Nationality Unknown.

006789   DAPHNE AND HER LAD. BY M. J. LAGEN AND
CALLY RYLAND. New York: H. Holt, 1904 NUC.

NYT—two editors of women's pages correspond, at first
casually then passionately, he finally visits her and
discovers she has a drunken husband.

LAGERLOF, SELMA OTTILIANA LOUISA. 1858-1940.

006790   THE EMPEROR OF PORTUGALLIA. Garden City,
N.Y.: Doubleday, Page, 1916 BMC NUC. London: Hodder
and Stoughton, [1916] BMC. (Tr. by Velma Swanston
Howard.)

Swedish peasant life. TLS
Episodes; in beginning father whose child is his sole
source of delight; at end, death of father brought on
by beloved daughter who returned after 15 years of
absence and silence. Hates rather than sympathizes
with him? TLS

"Girl goes out into the world to earn money to save
parents home. After few letters containing needed
money, nothing more is heard from her. Father refuses
to believe ill of her, tells neighbors she is reigning
over her empire of Portugallia."   PW 90:1356
10/21/16.
NYT she has gone wrong; father gone mad.

006791   FURTHER ADVENTURES OF NILS. London:
Hodder and Stoughton, 1911 BMC. Garden City, N.Y.:
Doubleday, Page, 1911 NUC. (Tr. Velma Swanston
Howard.)

006792   GOSTA BERLING'S SAGA. London: Chapman and
Hall, 1898 NUC BMC. (Tr. from the Swedish by Lillie
Tudeer)

ACAD 55:480. An unfrocked priest, and the wife of
Major Samzeiuls, the most powerful woman of Varmland,
yet unhappy.
A series of stories set around this outcast priest,
reveller, drunkard hero. Flavor of Scandinavian
superstitions. The devil and bonds written in blood.
Passionate loves and hates. LBKM 16:83.
Sweden, early 19th. He is a crazy priest without a
post because of drunkeness. Margarita Samzeiuls
elderly Amazon who rules the countryside, owns 7
foundries, smokes a clay pipe...her wild crew of
cavaliers. SP 83:139.
Shows close union of people to nature, the power of
pagan myths, and reliance of men upon the rule of
women for their safety. Marguerite is driven out of
her position of power by her husband and the
Cavaliers. What follows is a year of ruin, the subject
of the story. SR 87:120

006793   THE HOLY CITY, JERUSALEM II. Garden City,
N.Y.: Doubleday, Page, 1918 BMC NUC. (Tr. Velma
Swanston Howard.)

PW—story centers on Gertrude. Also Barbra, wife of
Ingmar who has left her to follow Gertrude.
NYT p 167 Apr 14, 1918 1750 w. Story of the Gordon
colonialists in Jerusalem. Dissensions of various
groups. Gertrude almost loses her mind. Ingmar saves
her. Barbra is his wife. Goes through period of
suffering while Ingmar, Bo and Gertrude are in Sweden.

006794   JERUSALEM. London: W. Heinemann, 1903 BMC
NUC. Garden City NY: Doubleday, Page, 1915 NUC. (Tr.
by Jessie Brochner.)

A story full of delicate, quiet perception about a
farmer. ACAD 65, 150
Rel. revival of a Swedish community. Father of hero
postpones marriage for economic reasons till child is
born and marries the mother after she serves the term
for killing the child. Hero jilts his sweetheart,
marries for a farm, makes a pilgrimage, returns to
wife who has allowed the rumor that her coming child
(that she fears is an idiot) is not his. Strong women.
ACAD 65,233
LBKM 9-03,221
History of a whole parish, the idealism of these
simple people, an epic of Swedish life. PW 10-2-15
TLS—love of home vs. rel, idealism and emigration to
Holy Land.

006795   THE LEGEND OF THE SACRED IMAGE. New York:
H. Holt, 1914 NUC. (Tr. Velma Swanston Howard.)

006796   LILIECRONA'S HOME. New York: E. P.
Dutton, 1914 NUC. (Tr. Anna Barwell.)

BKM 39-1914
Swedish village life—much in detail. Good study of a
little girl who "acts as buffer between a woman and
her stepdaughter." ATH

006797   THE MIRACLES OF ANTICHRIST: A NOVEL.
Boston: Little, Brown, 1899 NUC. London: Gay and Bird,
1899 BMC. (Tr. from the Swedish by Pauline Bancroft
Flach NUC)

A false Christ whose kingdom was only this world
answers all mundane prayers—for wealth, happiness,
justice, love, etc. But cannot help one wanting
forgiveness. LBKM 16:111.
A saga. How he crosses the lives of others and through
suffering, finds himself. ACAD 56:191
The New Socialism shown to be a failure because it is
of this world. "The lesson is that man was not created
for personal happiness, but to leave the world a
holier place." PW 55:544

006798   THE OUTCAST. London: Glydendal, [1920]

NUC. Garden City, N.Y. and Toronto: Doubleday, Page, 1922 NUC.

006799   THE STORY OF GOSTA BERLING. London: Gay and Bird, 1898 NUC BMC. Boston: Little, Brown, 1898 NUC. (Tr. Pauline Bancroft Flach BMC)

BKM 8:253. Gosta Berling, the disgraced priest, is the strongest and weakest of men. The major's wife is the strongest and weakest of women. Fragments, book reads backward as lucidly as it reads forward. From book: she is a doughty woman. She's not afraid of a thundering drinking song...as bold as a man and as proud as a queen. Songs she loves, and sounding fiddles and the hunting horn. She likes wine and games of cards. Gosta is the best speaker, dancer, singer, musician, hunter, drinking companion, and card player in all Sweden. They meet.
NYT 1898:826. He is won back to virtue.
LW 29:396

006800   THE WONDERFUL ADVENTURES OF NILS. London, New York: Doubleday, Page, 1907 BMC NUC. (Tr. Velma Swanston Howard)

LAHEE, M. R.

006801   SYBIL WEST: A LANCASHIRE STORY. Oldham: W. E. Clegg, 1892 BMC.

LAING, JANET. United Kingdom.

006802   BEFORE THE WIND. London and Toronto: J. M. Dent, 1918 BMC. New York: E. P. Dutton, [c1918] NUC.

PW-Ann has lost family after outbreak of war, goes to Scotland as companion to two old ladies. Stirred by Ann's patriotism, they open their house to "wracstraws" to economize on servants. Soldier recuperates from wounds disguised as a wrackstraw in order to do some detective work. Love for Ann.
ATH-one of servants is a German spy.
NYT May 12, 1918 p. 224. O

006803   THE BORDERLANDERS. London: J. M. Dent, 1904 BMC.

ATH-people insane, heroine delightfully impulsive.
TLS-inmates of a home for eccentrics, diary of heroine who works there and has a grand passion for the mistress.
ACAD-witty, style reminiscent of Rhoda Broughton.

006804   THE MAN WITH THE LAMP. London: J. M. Dent, 1919 NUC BMC. New York: E. P. Dutton, 1919 NUC.

War story: focuses on a prussian man who breaks down before war is done. BKM 10-19
He's a German pianist who searches for his old tutor with whom he had a relation of "spirit and sense." The search takes on a sense of "the unearthly, the disembodied" He finds him and tells him the story of being forced to enter the U-boat service. He needs a spiritual renewal. NYT 12-28-19 787

006805   THE WIZARD'S AUNT. A NOVEL. London: J. M. Dent, 1903 BMC.

Heroine is "self willed, yet attractive." ATH 121,460
An entangled plot. TLS 138,03

LAKE, MARY. B. 1873. United States.

006806   THE DRUG SLAVE. London, New York: Cassell, 1913 BMC NUC.

LAMB, MARY ELIZABETH (JORDAN). B. 1839. United States.

006807   IRENE LISCOMB; A STORY OF THE OLD SOUTH. New York: Broadway, [c1908] NUC.

006808   THE MYSTERY OF WALDERSTEIN: A STORY FROM THE LIFE OF TWO PRUSSIAN OFFICERS. Chicago: Donohue, Henneberry, [c1894] NUC.

LAMONT, FRANCES, pseud. See MOBERLY, CHARLOTTE ANNE ELIZABETH AND ELEANOR FRANCES JOURDAIN.

LA MOTTE, ELLEN NEWBOLD. 1873-1961. United States.

006809   THE BACKWASH OF WAR: THE HUMAN WRECKAGE OF THE BATTLEFIELD AS WITNESSED BY AN AMERICAN HOSPITAL NURSE. New York and London: G.P. Putnam's Sons, 1916 BMC.

Terrible in its realism, dreadful description of gas gangrene. Author's abhorrence of war. ATH
D 640 WWI--Personal narratives.

LANCASTER, G. B., pseud. See LYTTLETON, EDITH JOAN.

LANDA, GERTRUDE (GORDON). United Kingdom.

006810   THE CASE AND THE CURE. London: Sands, 1901 BMC.

12-21-01 ATH

LANDI, COUNTESS ZANARDI. See LANDI, KAROLINE FRANZISKA M. ZANARDI.

LANDI, KAROLINE FRANZISKA M. ZANARDI. B. 1882.

006811   THE ROYAL OUTCAST: A ROMANCE OF TODAY. BY COUNTESS ZANARDI LANDI. London: E. Nash, 1916 BMC. (BMC: Caroline)

TLS-male hero; hist. rom.

LANDON, MARY.

006812   'MID PLEASURES AND PALACES. London: T. F. Unwin, 1907 BMC NUC.

More a travel book. TLS
A narrative of travel in Siam and Japan. BMC

LANDRUM, GRACE WARREN.

006813   CHARLOTTE. New York: G. H. Doran, [c1919] NUC.

PW-biog. of a young woman.
CT 275 Charlotte S. Robertson 1900-17

LANE, ANNA (EICHBERG) KING. 1853-1927. United States.

006814   ACCORDING TO MARIA. BY MRS. JOHN LANE. London: J. Lane, 1910 BMC. New York: J. Lane, 1910 NUC.

TLS-satire of social climber.
ACAD-denounces arid life of society.
ATH-
NYT-

006815   KITWYK. BY MRS. JOHN LANE. London and New York: J. Lane, 1903 BMC NUC.

006816   MARIA AGAIN. BY MRS. JOHN LANE. London: J. Lane, 1915 BMC. New York: J. Lane, 1915 NUC.

Mother of married daughter has unique views on love, life, literature and manners. PW 9-11-15
All her witty comments. Life and social aspirations of Maria as a middle-aged mother of a married daughter. NYT
"A grandmother but no grandma" drives car, holds "shameless and worldly points of view." Good natured social satire. LBKM
"Epitome of the smart, pseudo-fashionable, up-to-date woman--vain, heartless. "The kind for whom life is endurable only "in the swim." Always doing the smart thing; two horrors--being middle class and getting old. Maria satirized? SR

006817   WAR: PHASES ACCORDING TO MARIA. BY MRS. JOHN LANE. London and New York: J. Lane, 1917 BMC NUC.

Maria prepares for Zeppelin raids, visits a submarine, "does her 'bit' of warwork" pro-war. PW
SR A sort of feminized John Bull--ignorant, prejudiced, narrow, conservative but practical. Believes in the higher classes.
LBKM & TLS-catty little comedy.

LANE, ELINOR (MACARTNEY). B. about 1864-D. 1909. United States.

006818   ALL FOR THE LOVE OF A LADY. New York: D. Appleton, 1906 NUC. London: Hodder and Stoughton, 1906 BMC.

TLS-agreeable romance.
NYT-O

006819   THE APPLE-TREE COTTAGE. New York and London: Harper, 1910 BMC NUC.

BKM-love story.

006820   KATRINE: A NOVEL. New York and London:
Harper, 1909 BMC NUC.

Romance of a woman's triumph and a man's awakening to
the stern realities of life. R OF R
Sweet, good, gifted becomes opera star. Her studies,
loves. PW
Chooses honeymoon. BKM NYT

006821   MILLS OF GOD: A NOVEL. New York: D.
Appleton, 1901 BMC NUC.

Extra-marital love, married to wrong man, heroine
sticks to her marriage, sees her lover marry a younger
woman. A woman of great emotion and intellect has an
illegitimate son, raises him as a child of her
husband. BOOK BUYER
Elinor fine, strong, unconventional. CR

006822   NANCY STAIR; A NOVEL. New York: D.
Appleton, 1904 BMC NUC. London: W. Heinemann, 1905
BMC.

Lord Stair's tempestuous wooing of the half-gypsy
(Nancy's parents.) Ma dies in childbirth. Father
travels for 5 years. Her loving kindness, her
education as a gentleman in classics and logic; her
poetry; her law training, bravery, honesty; saves
Danvers at his trial by her woman's wit. Brought up by
men. End is conventional. ACAD 1905:149.

LANE, LORIS.

006823   A HERO'S ARMOUR. Bristol: J. W.
Arrowsmith, [1895] BMC.

LANE, LYDIA SPENCER (BLANEY).

006824   I MARRIED A SOLDIER; OR, OLD DAYS IN THE
OLD ARMY. Philadelphia: J.B. Lippincott, 1893 NUC.

Life led by army personnel and their wives and
families 1856-79, the privations and dangers. CR
14,21:45

LANE, MRS. JOHN. See LANE, ANNA (EICHBERG) KING.

LANE, MRS. QUINCEY.

006825   THE FANSHAWE TREASURE. London: Simpkin &
Marshall, 1894 BMC.

LANE, ROSE (WILDER). B. 1887. United States.

006826   DIVERGING ROADS. New York: Century, 1919
BMC NUC.

NYT-story of Pacific Coast.
Honest portrayal of the woman alone, Helen Davis is
engaged but young man too poor to marry yet.
So she decides to work. Learns telegraphy. But is
bored with it. Story follows her unsophisticated
reactions to city life. Then she gets a good job in
San Francisco and meets a rich man. We get her
reactions, the broad understanding that comes with her
marriage, the years of hard work as a business woman
when she's alone-separated. Works as real estate agent
in the oil fields, advertising writer, newspaper
reporter. A human being, not a puppet. NYT 4-13-19:200

LANG, LOUISA LOCKHART (STEUART). United Kingdom.

006827   BUBBLES AND TROUBLES. BY MRS. L. LOCKHART
LANG. London: A. Rivers, 1910 BMC NUC.

TLS-young married pair and baby.

006828   KNIGHT CHECKS QUEEN. BY MRS. L. LOCKHART
LANG. London: A. Rivers, 1911 NUC BMC.

Anne Maitland is impulsive, wayward, "bursting with
life" when she marries. She's thus freed from tyrant
father. She becomes a world-famous singer. TLS
Heroine "goes through a form of marriage with a man of
science in order to have liberty to train her voice."
She reaches almost to a prima donna, but husband's
financial breakdown causes her "to earn money by
performing as a gymnist in tights." Heroine is high
tempered but decidedly likeable. ATH

LANG, MRS. L. LOCKHART. See LANG, LOUISA LOCKHART
(STEUART).

LANGBRIDGE, ROSAMOND. B. 1880.

006829   THE AMBUSH OF YOUNG DAYS. London:
Duckworth, 1906 BMC.

ACAD-character study of women in squalid residential
hotel.
BKM-select private temperance hotel run and owned by
Mrs. Hanrahan. Love story of poor Myrtle Hanrahan and
sorrowful history of Miss O'Shaugnessy. Pathos and
humor, well written.

006830   THE FLAME AND THE FLOOD. London: T.F.
Unwin, 1903 BMC.

Heroine must choose between love of an actor and the
child of the man who is her husband. ACAD

006831   IMPERIAL RICHENDA: A FANTASTIC COMEDY.
London: Rivers, 1908 BMC NUC.

BKM-she applies as housemaid at a hotel and runs
it-mystery here.
Comedy in Ireland. She (of the title) is an
adventurous young woman, becomes waitress in hotel to
escape marriage. In the end she marries the insipid
Amersham. ATH

006832   THE STARS BEYOND. London: E. Nash, 1907
BMC.

Defies marriage convention. Verity is offensive-for
her a husband represents a fleeting mood, children,
fleeting emotions; leaves husband just before child
born. Divorce. TLS

006833   THE THIRD EXPERIMENT. London: T.F. Unwin,
1904 BMC.

ATH-interesting women, class of shopkeepers.

LANGER, ANGELA. 1886-1916. United Kingdom.

006834   RUE AND ROSES. London: W. Heinemann, 1913
NUC BMC. New York: G.H. Doran, [c1913] NUC.

An unmarried woman lays her soul bare. NYT
Lonely and poor German girl Sincere record in simple
language. TLS
"Anna, the girl who writes the book, is a German whose
parents are very poor. She goes out into service and
in spite of her drudgery writes real poetry. When love
comes it is very different from her dreams but is the
means of further intellectual and emotional
development for her." PW 8-23-13.
Anna as a girl scrubs floors, minds children and
writes poems and dreams of a past lover. Of humble
birth but ambitious, a friend helps her with her
poetry and education. This friend does not offer to
marry her or go beyond friendship. He believes she's
the kind of woman that love kills. ACAD

LANGFORD, GRACE.

006835   WERONA; A ROMANCE OF AUSTRALIAN DOMESTIC
LIFE. London & Sydney: Remington, 1893 BMC.

Heroine Pauline-beautiful and proud. Sweet, loveable
Joyce, the first a tragic, the second a comic figure.
SP 71:312.

LANGLOIS, DORA.

006836   IN THE SHADOW OF PA-MENKH. London: S.
Low, 1908 BMC.

TLS--a hunt for gold in Egypt with love interest.

LANGTRY, LILLIE. See DE BATHE, EMILIE CHARLOTTE (LANGTRY).

LANGWORTHY, FERRIER. Nationality Unknown.

006837   JEM-A-DREAMS. SHE DREAMS OF A HERO.
London: Holden and Hardingham, [1916] BMC NUC.

006838   SLAVES OF CHANCE; A NOVEL. London: L.
Smithers, 1899 BMC. Boston: L. C. Page, 1900 NUC.

PW-widow and 5 daughters, poor, in London. Mother's
desire that they marry throws them in the way of many
temptations. One runs away and makes her living in an
unusual way.

LANSDOWNE, JANE. D. 1908. United Kingdom.

006839   THE SHADOW OF EVERSLEIGH. New York:
Benziger Brothers, 1908 NUC.

PW-seventeenth century

LANSFELDT, LAURIE.

006840   THE ALIEN OF THE FAMILY. London: J.
Clarke, 1894 BMC.

006841   UNKNOWN TO HERSELF. London: J. Clarke,
1897 BMC.

LIT 2:148. Hypnotism.

LANYON, MRS. H. SANT MARTIN.

006842   SARAH, P. G. London: T.F. Unwin, 1900
BMC.

ACAD 59:604. Young orphan advertises for a companion,
her various experiences as a paying guest.

LANZA, CLARA (HAMMOND). B. 1859. United States.

006843   THE DWELLER ON THE BORDERLAND.
Philadelphia: J. J. McVey, 1909 NUC.

Young tutor, wife, child move to NYC; he becomes tutor
to a beautiful woman painter of ability but doesn't
tell her he's married. Through her adopts RC--no
longer on the border. PW
NyT-becomes a priest.

006844   A GOLDEN PILGRIMAGE: A NOVEL. Chicago:
Laird and Lee, 1892 NUC.

PW-Story of a heroine ambitious for wealth and
position, a cruel girl. Hero and his rival have
misplaced their love.
LW 23:261. Grim study of a mercenary marriage. Selfish
and exacting heroine.

006845   HORACE EVERETT: A NOVEL. New York: G. W.
Dillingham, 1897 NUC.

His mother is his problem. She neglects him as he
grows up. He goes to New York to meet his father's
wealthy relatives. Here he begins to make a career.
His mother shows up. She had remarried, was deserted
and robbed. Horace gives up his fiance. Gives mother a
home. PW 51:394.

LAPAGE, GERTRUDE.

006846   THE CHILDREN OF THE THORNWREATH. San
Francisco: P. Elder and M. Shepard, 1902 NUC.

LAPAUZE, JEANNE (LOISEAU). 1860-1921.

006847   PASSION SLAVE. Paris: 1892 BMC. Paris: A.
Lemerre, 1892 NUC.

006848   THE POWER OF THE PAST. BY DANIEL LESUER.
London: E. Nash, 1906 BMC.

ACAD-portrayal of a young woman.
ATH-motor car race. Story largely concerned with
French law of legitimization.

LARGE, MARY HARRIOTT. United States.

006849   THE TWELFTH JUROR. Boston: C. M. Clark,
1908 NUC.

PW-murder in Ky.

LARYMORE, CONSTANCE (BELCHER).

006850   A RESIDENT'S WIFE IN NIGERIA. New York:
E. P. Dutton, 1908 NUC. London: G. Routledge, 1908
BMC.

DT 360 Nigeria description & travel

LA SELLE, EVELYN. United States.

006851   THE BLACK SHEEP. BY QUI. Raleigh, N.C.:
Edwards and Broughton, 1895 NUC.

LATHBURY, EVA. United Kingdom.

006852   THE LONG GALLERY. New York: H. Holt, 1909
NUC.

Typical romance. PW 3 unusually attractive women. BKM

006853   THE MOVING CAMP. London: A. Rivers, 1911
BMC NUC.

Morag O'Brien exercises vague uncanny influences. TLS
A kind of beautiful white devil. Keen analysis of
feminine motives, but sometimes cruel. SR

006854   MR. MEYER'S PUPIL. London: A. Rivers,
1907 BMC.

Child kidnapped to keep the mother from running off?
LBKM 12-07:1.46.
Girl-fresh,curious mind; her teacher kidnaps her to
prevent mother from fleeing with a lover. Wife-well
drawn, much vitality with no good way in her life to
use it? ACAD
Serena Denny, the pupil, a minx, governess,
husband-hunter (Becky Sharpe type) what happens to
her? Lady Violet's story

006855   THE PEOPLE DOWNSTAIRS. London: A. Rivers,
1908 BMC.

ACAD-unconventional, great, psychological drama, 2
women, but what?
SR-a brace of fanciful wives and commonplace husbands,
yet they are patient enough to listen to the long and
egotistical harangues of their wives. About what?

006856   THE SINKING SHIP. London: A. Rivers, 1909
NUC BMC. New York: H. Holt, 1909 NUC.

Heroine an actress turns very serious about her act
and its purpose. PW 12-4-09.
Vanda Conquest and husband are both actors. A young
playwright is first attracted to Vanda then to her
daughter. TLS
Vanda woman of genius doomed to marriage with man she
doesn't love and who never loved her. LBKM
Character study of an actress at a critical point in
her artistic career. At high point of success feels
she's on the brink of a sudden downfall. Tries to
assure her place by developing her tragic powers as an
actress.

LATHROP, ANNIE WAKEMAN. Nationality Unknown.

006857   THE AUTOBIOGRAPHY OF A CHARWOMAN AS
CHRONICLED BY ANNIE WAKEMAN. London: J. Macqueen, 1900
NUC BMC. (Published in U.S.A. with Title: A Gentle
Woman of the Slums; Being the Autobiography of a
Charwoman.)

LBKM 18:189. "Faithful picture." She is fatalistic,
accepting the inevitable, her story is sadder than she
knew.
SP 85:85. She is a housekeeper at 16, betrayed by man
she works for, he repudiates their child.
Hand-to-mouth struggle for rest of her life. First
marriage, although bigamous, is to a good man. When he
dies, she marries a brute who illtreats and deserts
her. "Cheerful patience of the poor" demonstrated.
ATH 115:116. Cockney dialect, or something that is
meant to represent it. "It can hardly be thought that
the charwoman's life has received the most appropriate
or most interesting form of expression."

006858   A GENTLEWOMAN OF THE SLUMS: BEING THE
AUTOBIOGRAPHY OF A CHARWOMAN, AS CHRONICLED BY ANNIE
WAKEMAN. Boston: L.C. Page, 1901 NUC.

Unconsciously heroic. Betrayed, but never pitied.
Unwed mother raises child; respected, not sent. Never
repents relation with man who betrays her and deserted
her. Marriage, slums, the terrible economics.

LATHROP, ELISE L.

006859   A TRANSPLANTED AMERICAN. London: J. Long,
1911 BMC.

TLS-Story of social antagonisms. Italian sailor and
American girl.
ATH-happy ending-baby?

LATHROP, LORIN ANDREWS. 1858-1929. United States.

006860   THE GIRL ON THE HILLTOP. BY KENYON
GAMBIER. New York: G.H. Doran, [c1920] NUC.

NYT:448 7/25/20 p28. Romance. Roger, the hero, is
"handed about by three girls."

006861   THE WHITE HORSE AND THE RED-HAIRED GIRL.
BY KENYON GAMBIER. New York: G.H. Doran, [c1919] NUC
BMC.

Brisk exciting wartime romance-Mary Travers matches
her wits against the Germans in occupied Belgium in

her effort to save her brother who is reported
"missing" but whom she suspects is alive. NYT 3-23-19,
142.

LATIMER, MARY ELIZABETH (WORMELEY). 1822-1904. United
States.

006862   THE PRINCE INCOGNITO. Chicago: A. C.
McClurg, 1902 NUC.

Un-civil marriage, wife disguises as boy.
Historical fiction.

LAUDER, MARIA ELISE TURNER. Canada.

006863   AT LAST. Buffalo: C.W. Moulton, 1894 NUC.

LW 27:251. Ardently religious widow and her son, a
musical prodigy. Home in Toronto. Mother dies in
France.
Rome. Lovers meet after a separation of several years,
lose each other by death. PW 2-16-95:322
Noble and unselfish work of the women's Christian
Temperance Union. Set primarily in France and the
Riviera. PW 12-21-95:1181

LAUGHLIN, CLARA ELIZABETH. 1873-1941. United States.

006864   CHILDREN OF TO-MORROW. New York: C.
Scribner's Sons, 1911 NUC.

East side NY slums and young men and women interested
in literature and art, but more in bettering social
conditions. PW 8-26-11
A loose jointed story, many characters: actresses,
shop girls. BKM
Author has great deal to say about hardships which the
NY working girl faces, the perils, the way they're
underpaid. NYT

006865   DIVIDED; THE STORY OF A POEM. New York:
F.H. Revell, [1904] BMC NUC.

BKM-love and fame?

006866   EVERYBODY'S LONESOME; A TRUE FAIRY STORY.
New York: F.H. Revell, [c1910] NUC. London: G.P.
Putnam's Sons, 1911 BMC.

006867   FELICITY, THE MAKING OF A COMEDIENNE. New
York: C. Scribner's Sons, 1907 NUC.

Life of a successful actress, Fame and love
"completes" felicity. PW 3-23-07.
Career of actress from precocious childhood as a
repressed youngster when she escapes through
playacting. Shows the toil, sacrifice, demand of
acting, the isolation, loneliness of the successful
star, the slim chance she has of love. All well worth
the heavy price. No mention of marriage. BKM
Felicity Fergus. NYT

006868   THE GLEANERS; A NOVELETTE. New York and
London: F. H. Revell, [c1911] NUC.

Sentimental story. PW

006869   THE HEART OF HER HIGHNESS. New York and
London: G.P. Putnams Sons, 1917 NUC 1918 [] BMC.

TLS Duchess Mary's heart torn between politics and
love finds at last a combination of both.
Historical romance. Mary of Burgandy almost sacrifices
love for good of country through a marriage of
convenience. PW

006870   "JUST FOLKS." New York: Macmillan, 1910
BMC NUC.

Betts Tully, probation officer in Chicago slums. PW
All part of the experience of a brave young woman;
series of scenes in lives of the struggling millions:
love story of mid-aged Liza Allen. SP
A probation officer of Chicago Juvenile Court who
lives among the people she serves, very realistic.

006871   THE KEYS OF HEAVEN. New York: G.H. Doran,
[c1918] NUC.

PW-male hero.
Romance which ends in the great war. Triangle. NYT
3-24-1918

006872   THE LADY IN GRAY; A STORY OF THE STEPS BY
WHICH WE CLIMB. New York: F.H. Revell, 1908 NUC.

006873   MILADI; BEING SUNDRY LITTLE CHAPTERS
DEVOTED TO YOUR DAY-DREAMS, DEAR MILADI, AND YOUR
REALIZATIONS--HARKING BACK TO YOUR EDUCATION, YOUR
EXPERIENCE IN THE INDUSTRIAL WORLD AND YOUR DECISION
IN FAVOR OF THE CLAIMS OF HOME, AND COMING DOWN TO THE
DEVELOPMENT OF YOUR LOVE, THE BUILDING OF YOUR HOUSE
O'DREAMS, AND YOUR MOTHERHOOD. Chicago: F.H. Revell,
[1903] NUC.

006874   THE PENNY PHILANTHROPIST; A STORY THAT
COULD BE TRUE. New York: F. H. Revell, [c1912] NUC.

PW-story of Haymarket slums, 18 yr. old female keeps a
"news emporium," sets aside a penny a day for
philanthropy. NYT

006875   WHEN JOY BEGINS; A LITTLE STORY OF THE
WOMAN-HEART. New York: F.H. Revell, 1905 BMC NUC.

Widow adopts son. Brief description. BKM

006876   WHEN MY SHIP COMES HOME. New York: F.H.
Revell, [c1915] NUC.

LAURENCE, FRANCES ELSIE (FRY). B. 1893. Canada.

006877   HALF A GIPSY. BY CHRISTINE FIELD. London:
A. Melrose, [1916] BMC NUC.

TLS-Mollie is governess in love with singer who is
half gypsy.
ATH-love story. English governess in Russia.

LAUT, A. C. See LAUT, AGNES CHRISTINA.

LAUT, AGNES CHRISTINA. 1871-1936. Canada.

006878   THE FREEBOOTERS OF THE WILDERNESS. New
York: Moffat, Yard, 1910 NUC BMC. Toronto: Mission
Book Co., 1910 NUC.

Dick and Eleanor Wayland fight a corrupt senator--it's
her fight especially. PW

006879   HERALDS OF EMPIRE. BEING THE STORY OF ONE
RAMSAY STANHOPE LIEUTENANT TO PIERRE RADISSON IN THE
NORTHERN FUR TRADE. BY A. C. LAUT. Toronto: W. Briggs,
1902 BMC NUC. New York: D. Appleton, 1902 NUC.

NYT 5-17-1902-author is in love with her hero.

006880   LORDS OF THE NORTH; A ROMANCE OF THE
NORTHWEST. BY A. C. LAUT. London: B.F. Stevens and
Brown, 1900 BMC. New York: P.F.Collier, [c1900] NUC.

Adventures in fur trading.
Northwest Territory, Canada-History-Fiction
NYT 1900:939. Historical romance, 1815. Northwest Co.
vs. Hudson Bay Co.

006881   THE NEW DAWN. New York: Moffat, Yard,
1913 NUC.

BKM-male businessman rises to incredible success then
loses wife and fortune and discovers he has missed all
that was worthwhile. Dies of a heart attack while wife
is rushing back to him.
PW "characters are a strong man who allows nothing to
stand in the way of his success, and his wife, who,
seeing her husband's disregard for the moral law of
business, attempts to throw aside the moral law of
life. A girl artist saves her from herself and awakens
her soul to a new dawn of spiritual life, while to the
man comes the realization that he is part dreamer,
part fool, and that man can conquer a man."

LA VOIE, JULIA. United States.

006882   A TALE HALF TOLD. New York: Broadway,
[c1904] NUC.

LAW, CISSIE.

006883   PIERCE MORAN. London: Digby, Long, 1893
BMC.

Born without a soul, gets one from a young girl who
then becomes mere intelligence (sans emotions and
spirituality). Lolo the girl's sister combats and
conquers this dark force. ACAD 43:542.

LAW, JOHN, pseud. See HARKNESS, MARGARET ELISE.

LAW, LEDA.

006884   AND THE WORLD SAITH. London: Digby, Long,

1895 BMC.

Immoral characters. Leading idea is "that the woman
who longs to sin and refrains through cowardice and
not through virtue is a poorer kind of creature than
the woman who bravely sins and takes the
consequences." "The day of such books is drawing to an
end and a purer taste is reasserting itself." ACAD.
47:154

LAWLESS, EMILY. 1845-1913. United Kingdom.

006885   GRANIA, THE STORY OF AN ISLAND. BY THE
HON. EMILY LAWLESS. New York & London: Macmillan, 1892
NUC. London: Smith, Elder, 1892 BMC.

LW 23:139. Isle of Arran. Desolate, narrow life of
meager population. "The utmost that a woman can hope
for is that her "man" shall not drink, or beat her, or
neglect to provide for his children." Grania, strong
and able "has but two outlets for her affection-her
consumptive sister and her lover, whose worthlessness
she suspects and despises, but will not admit, even to
herself." "He stands as her one chance for the
future." She dies in the sea trying to get through a
dense fog in an effort to bring the priest to her
dying sister; her lover being too cowardly to go
himself. NATION 145:401. no plot. Great sympathy for
Irish peasantry.
ATH 99;496. Tragic story of two sisters.
SP: He refuses to accompany her on way to get priest
although she begs him to. He kissed her once, between
two drags on his pipe; her passion was awakened then
and she knew what love could be like, while knowing it
would not be like that with him.

006886   MAELCHO, A SIXTEENTH CENTURY NARRATIVE.
BY THE HON. EMILY LAWLESS. New York: D. Appleton, 1894
NUC. London: Smith & Elder, 1894 BMC.

SR 78:716. Story of the Irish rebellion 1577-1582.
Essentially the work is a character study of the Saxon
and Celtic temperament. Unrelieved portrayal of the
horrors of war. No love story.

006887   TRAITS AND CONFIDENCES. BY THE HON. EMILY
LAWLESS. London: Methuen, 1898 BMC.

LAWRENCE, ALBERT, pseud. See LAWRENCE, ALBERTA ELIZA INEZ
(CHAMBERLAIN).

LAWRENCE, ALBERTA ELIZA INEZ (CHAMBERLAIN). B. 1875.
United States.

006888   THE TRAVELS OF PHOEBE ANN. BY ALBERT
LAWRENCE. Boston: C. M. Clark, 1908 NUC.

Older woman 4-3-09 PW

LAWRENCE, EDITH, pseud. See BAILEY, EDITH LAWRENCE (BLACK).

LAWRENCE, ELIZABETH. United States.

006889   A HEROIC SINNER AND THE PILGRIM SPINSTER:
A ROMANCE. BY GORHAM SILVA. Albany, N.Y.: Granite Pub.
Co., 1893 NUC.

006890   THE WORM THAT CEASED TO TURN. BY GORHAM
SILVA. New York: J. S. Ogilvie, [c1895] NUC.

"painful experience of a middle aged bachelor living
in the country who takes a girl from the poorhouse as
his wife" PW 8-17-95:222

LAWRENCE, ROSAMOND (NAPIER). B. 1878. United Kingdom.

006891   THE FAITHFUL FAILURE. BY ROSAMUND NAPIER.
New York: G. H. Doran, [1910?] NUC. London: Duckworth,
1910 BMC.

Sentimental brother and sister. PW 10-28-11
Discovers on honeymoon she doesn't love husband. SP
"Two lovers rob every moment of the last drop of
gladness." Two "militant souls meet defeat with a
jest." A genuine Bohemian runs through the work. NYT
Beautiful picture of sisterly devotion. Review focuses
on the heroes. NYT
TLS-typical romance.

006892   THE HEART OF A GIPSY. London: Duckworth,
1909 BMC.

Tender simple little wife. TLS
Two young women: Bunny Thompson and adopted "gypsy"
sister Meridiana. LBKM
Conflict between her love for a man and a beech tree

(?) (The tree is the only parent she has known) child
of nature. Comes to London to be surgeon's wife. Out
of her element. Breaks away, returns to nature.

006893   TAMSIE. New York: Hodder & Stoughton,
[1912] NUC. London: Hodder & Stoughton, [1912] BMC.

PW-gypsy like female hero
TLS-Tamsie is a tomgirl and bluestocking; in the end
marries the stag fellow.
LBKM-her guardian loves her but because of age and
poverty leaves for Egypt alone. David Guest travels
with the gypsies. They meet, form a band through their
unhappiness.

006894   TESS HARCOURT. London, New York: Hodder &
Stoughton, [1913] BMC NUC.

NYT-loves and is loved by man with invalid wife. Is
involved in some way with community work .
The "Ring" provides motives for this story. SP
(Wagner's)
"Should be read on a piano stool." Man married to
alcoholic woman loves Tess. The story of love and
suffering and renunciation. TLS

LAWSON, JESSIE (KERR). 1838-1917.

006895   THE CURSE THAT CAME HOME. Edinburgh:
Oliphant, Anderson and Ferrier, 1894 BMC.

ACAD 46:252. Scotland. Nephew steals will that would
have left father's money to his step-daughter; she is
left in poverty.

006896   DR. BRUNO'S WIFE: A TORONTO SOCIETY
STORY. BY MRS. J. KERR LAWSON. London: Simpkin,
Marshall, Hamilton, Kent, [1893] NUC BMC.

006897   EUPHIE LYN; OR, THE FISHERS OF OLD
INWEERIE. Edinburgh: Oliphant, Anderson and Ferrier,
1893 BMC.

006898   A VAIN SACRIFICE. Edinburgh: Oliphent
Anderson and Ferrier, 1892 BMC.

ACAD 41:443. Vice of selfishness is contrasted with
the virtue of self-sacrifice.

LAWSON, LAURA BURNETT. United States.

006899   LEONORA; A TALE OF THE GREAT SMOKIES. New
York: Neale, 1904 NUC.

LAWSON, MINNIE. United States.

006900   MONEY TO LOAN ON ALL COLLATERALS: A TALE
OF THE TIMES. Detroit, Mich.: Excelsior Publishing
Company, [c1895] NUC.

illustrates the rapacity of collateral loan agents and
the misery of the borrowers. LW 26:283

LAWSON, MRS. J. KERR. See LAWSON, JESSIE (KERR).

LAYARD, NINA FRANCES.

006901   SONGS IN MANY MOODS. BY NINA FRANCES
LAYARD. [AND] THE WANDERING ALBATROSS. BY ANNIE
CORDER. London and New York: Longmans, Green, 1897
NUC.

LEA, FANNY HEASLIP. 1884-1955. United States.

006902   CHLOE MALONE. Boston: Little, Brown, 1916
BMC NUC. London: J. M. Dent, [1919] BMC.

NYT-Sweet romance

006903   THE DANGER ZONE. London: A. Melrose, 1911
BMC.

Marr. of clever complex woman to simple husband. Later
she meets the man who "awakens her dormant fires" TLS

006904   QUICKSANDS. New York: Sturgis and Walton,
1911 NUC.

Woman out of love with husband, in love with another.
Must decide between. 4-22-11 PW
Husband good natured, from wretched beginnings; wife
of sophisticated background and interests. At first
she's attracted to his simple nature. The other man is
an author. End not revealed. NYT

006905   SICILY ANN, A ROMANCE. New York and

London: Harper, 1914 BMC NUC.

TLS-Sweet young romance in Honolulu.
PW 86 10/17/14:1246. "She was pretty and sweet and not
at all a flirt. A young man who was rich, but not of a
true Virginia family, like Sicily Ann's, wanted to
marry her. Her mother objected, and because she could
not send him off, she sent Sicily Ann to Honolulu on a
visit. The young man followed. So did the mother, and
arrived in time to see the chap as a real hero worthy
to marry her daughter."
NYT1914:475 "dainty"

LEAMON, SARAH CANNON. United States.

006906   THE HART JEWELS. Cincinnati: Press of
Jennings and Graham, [1905] NUC.

006907   A MINISTER'S PROBATION. Nashville, Tenn.:
Barbee and Smith, 1899 NUC.

006908   TAUGHT BY EXPERIENCE. Cincinnati: Curts
and Jennings, [c1900] NUC.

LEAN, FLORENCE (MARRYAT) CHURCH. 1837-1899. United
Kingdom.

006909   AN ANGEL OF PITY. BY FLORENCE MARRYAT.
London: Hutchinson, 1898 BMC.

SP 81:184. Manifesto against vivisection. Rose,
heroine, is a hospital nurse. Protests a surgeon's
experiments on a pauper patient. The surgeon falls for
her and then wants to marry her. She is committed to
her profession and has no interest in marriage, but he
offers to make her head of a nursing home, so she
accepts. After marriage, she discovers he wants her to
be a decorative accessory. She submits, but despite
his reassurances, continues to worry that he has
dabbled in vivisection. She discovers his secret
laboratory, the horror of it is described, he
retaliates by operating on her pet dog. She breaks in,
puts dog out of pain, throws knife at her husband,
hits his hand. He gets sick, she nurses him. He
repents, establishes the nursing home, and forswears
vivisection.
ATH 11:786. Revenge on pet because she has refused to
live with him as his wife.

006910   AT HEART A RAKE. BY FLORENCE MARRYAT.
London: H. Cox, 1895 BMC. New York: Cassell, [c1895]
NUC.

Lady Phyllis becomes V.P. of Pushahead club. Her
husband carries on with another woman. SR 80:386.
"But every woman is at heart a rake," "unsavory"
"unspeakably distasteful" "nauseous" SP 75:561
"much female smoking, drinking and bad language."
Cissy Barnard gets beat up by husband, elopes with
kind Jack Austin. A lady cyclist Lady Phyllis
separates from husband because of incompatibility. On
p. 494 they get back together for their child's sake.
ACAD 48:267
Continues her parable vs men especially military men,
who make the worst husbands. But draws the line at
separation for frivolous reasons-as in Lady Phyllis'
case. ATH 106:188
Lady Phyllis McNaughton joins a woman's club vs her
husband's wishes PW 8-3-95:162

006911   A BANKRUPT HEART. BY FLORENCE MARRYAT.
London: F. V. White, 1894 BMC. New York: C. B. Reed,
1894 NUC.

SR-ruined country maid attempts suicide when lover
marries. She is rescued, has adventures, foils the
villain, kills her self with carbolic acid sheepwash.
ACAD 46:131. She sacrifices herself for the happiness
of the lover who has jilted her.

006912   THE BEAUTIFUL SOUL. BY FLORENCE MARRYAT.
London: Digby, Long, 1894 BMC. New York: Cassell,
[c1895] NUC.

Felicia Hetherington is a wealthy spinster of 35.
She's plain, gets engaged to a young journalist of 24,
who proceeds to make love to 19 year old Mab Selwyn.
Matters are well-arranged by the end. ACAD 47:55
She witnessed the accident in which the young man lost
a leg, took him to hospital. He urged marriage. The 19
year old almost breaks up the relationship. PW
5-18-95:774

006913   THE BLOOD OF THE VAMPIRE. BY FLORENCE
MARRYAT. London: Hutchinson, 1897 BMC. Leipzig: B.
Tauchnitz, 1897 NUC.

SP 81:447. "Vulgar people with loose principles."
Heroine is daughter of a quadroon and Jamaican planter
whose grandmother has been bitten by a vampire. She
has inherited the vampire's power without its
inclination.

006914   THE DEAD MAN'S MESSAGE; AN OCCULT
ROMANCE. BY FLORENCE MARRYAT. New York: C. B. Reed,
1894 NUC.

006915   THE DREAM THAT STAYED. BY FLORENCE
MARRYAT. London: Hutchinson, 1896 BMC. Leipzig: B.
Tauchnitz, 1897 NUC.

ATH 108:752. "No person of refinement or taste will
read beyond the first chapter. General Raynam, whose
wife many years ago has deserted him, has a daughter
engaged to Sir Guy. All three go to Scotland where Sir
Guy falls for and engages himself to another woman who
turns out to be the illeg. daughter of Mrs. Raynam who
is now posing as a widow. The general feels that May,
the illegitimate daughter, has no right to Sir Guy
because of her illegitimacy. May od's on chloral. Sir
Guy after an attack of brain fever finally marries
Mary. Mrs. Raynham loses her mind; "We are expected to
sympathize with her." "If a woman plays battledore and
shuttlecock with the seventh commandment in the
irresponsible, motiveless way that she does, she ought
to take the consequences."

006916   A FATAL SILENCE. BY FLORENCE MARRYAT.
London: Griffith and Farran, [1891] BMC NUC. New York:
Street & Smith, [1902] NUC.

Many characters; in dialect. ATH 98 859.
Village school teacher marries a wealthy man believing
her husband dead. Story tells of persecution of Miss
Stafford by church warden, his colleague and their
wives. She leaves the village, returns as wife of a
chief landowner. ACAD 40:557
PW-Paula changed her name and became a teacher in a
village school in order to bury her past. But her
actions were misunderstood and she accepted dismissal
by the parish committee rather than reveal her
history. She marries a farmer, further developments.

006917   THE FOLLY OF ALISON. BY FLORENCE MARRYAT.
London: F. V. White, 1899 BMC.

She forgets her loyal lover, transfers her attentions
to a man she hardly knows but to whose character she
is harshly awakened when he attempts to compromise
her. She's a great heiress. But she ends up marrying
Lucian and telling him all about bad Granville Baird.
ATH 114:615

006918   THE HAMPSTEAD MYSTERY. A NOVEL. BY
FLORENCE MARRYAT. London: F. V. White, 1894 BMC NUC.

SR 77:96. Bride killed day after wedding by family
friend who has had a secret passion for her. He takes
to opium, wife discovers and protects him. Husband
becomes a priest until by chance murderer of his wife
confesses to him; then he marries and goes to the
colonies.

006919   HOW LIKE A WOMAN! A NOVEL. BY FLORENCE
MARRYAT. London: Griffith, Farran, 1892 BMC. New York:
Lovell, Coryell, [c1894] NUC.

006920   IN THE NAME OF LIBERTY. BY FLORENCE
MARRYAT. London: Digby, Long, [1897] BMC.

Story of the lost heir who returns. Maurice Farrell is
a wicked anarchist; his wife Jane is a private
detective. Maurice and friends try to blow up the
Earl-stopped by the detective. Maurice rehabilitated.
ACAD 51:519
PW-an indictment of socialism. Hero is a journalist
who has joined the socialists through a misfortune.
Also his wife, Lord Innisfale, and several detectives.

006921   IRIS THE AVENGER. BY FLORENCE MARRYAT.
London: Hutchinson, 1899 BMC. Leipzig: B. Tauchnitz,
1899 NUC.

Iris Bevan is a governess, actress, typist, marries an
Earl on whom she is resolved to wreak vengeance for
the betrayal of her sister. But husband turns out to
be only the friend of the betrayer. SP 82:687

006922   THE NOBLER SEX. BY FLORENCE MARRYAT.
London: F. V. White, 1892 BMC. New York: U.S. Book,
1892 NUC.

CR 18:202. People of varying "degrees of depravity."
LW 23:311. "A woman destitute of moral fiber" marries
a man she cannot love, then loves a man she cannot
marry, then lives with a man while her divorce is
pending, then marries him and later divorces him.
"There are points in the history so analagous to Miss
Marryat's own career as to give it the atmosphere of
personal reminiscence, and altogether the record is as
distasteful as it is objectionable."
PW Written in first person. Heroine is novelist,
actress, and public speaker.
ACAD 42:190 "Heroine seems to imagine that the
defilement which involves all the other characters
leaves her pure, but her conduct will scarcely support
that view in the eyes of most readers."

006923   PARSON JONES. BY FLORENCE MARRYAT.
London: Griffith and Farran, 1893 BMC. New York:
Cassell, [c1893] NUC.

Quiet Welsh village. The parson first has a conflict
with a member of the "Literalists," later an even
stronger temptation. Struggle with his conscience.
Finds peace. PW 6-10-93.
Goes to New Zealand as a missionary. SR 76:47.
Raised by parents to enter the church-no choice;
married off by mother-no choice. Has his awakening. CR
20, 23:86.

006924   A PASSING MADNESS. BY FLORENCE MARRYAT.
London: Hutchinson, 1897 BMC. Leipzig: B. Tauchnitz,
1897 NUC.

A young doctor must protect his sweetheart against her
brother, twin to her other sister and prone to
homicide. SR 84:205.
Involves a large fortune. ACAD 51:449.

006925   A RATIONAL MARRIAGE. BY FLORENCE MARRYAT.
London: F. V. White, 1899 BMC. New York: F. M.
Buckles, 1899 NUC.

Joan Trevor, independent, insists on earning her own
way-is bored living with relatives. Her grandfather
promises to leave his granddaughters 7,000 pounds a
year each if they don't marry. Joan therefore makes a
rational marriage with a journalist-can't live in same
house. Problems arise from secret marriage-then
grandfather told and he relents. SP 83:95
BKM 11:191. Strong-minded young woman has ideas about
reformation of marriage. Persuades Larry to secretly
marry her and sign a contract that the marriage will
be secret, rational and platonic. Amusing account of
their honeymoon and her realization that she has been
all wrong.
PW-she is a secretary, is expecting an inheritance for
which she must be single, one of the causes of the
secret marriage.

006926   THE RISEN DEAD. BY FLORENCE MARRYAT.
London: S. Blackett, 1891 BMC. New York: U. S. Book,
[1891] NUC.

Thrilling episodes: a near suicide, secret marriage,
murderous duel and the mystery of the risen dead all
involving aristocrats. ATH 98:188
Also bigamy; a wife thought dead comes to life. Ends
with marriage and reconciliation. LW
Ingenious series of complications and situations. SR
72:54

006927   SAINT AND SINNER. BY FLORENCE MARRYAT.
London: Holden & Hardingham, [1914] BMC.

006928   A SOUL ON FIRE. BY FLORENCE MARRYAT.
London: Bliss, Sands, 1898 BMC. Leipzig: B. Tauchnitz,
1898 BMC NUC.

SP 81:411. Brutal and selfish professor dies on p. 36.
Rest of story is of his spirit experiences, remorse,
etc.

006929   THE SPIRIT WORLD. BY FLORENCE MARRYAT.
London: F. V. White, 1894 BMC NUC. New York: C. B.
Reed, 1894 BMC NUC. (Fiction?)

006930   THE STRANGE TRANSFIGURATION OF HANNAH
STUBBS. BY FLORENCE MARRYAT. London: Hutchinson, 1896
BMC. Leipzig: B. Tauchnitz, 1896 NUC.

ACAD 49:382 "Emphasizes the deterioration of Marryat
as a novelist." Hannah is a domestic servant taken in
hand by Signor Ricardo because she has hypnotic
powers. The spirit of the she-devil who was his former
wife possesses her; much havoc until she again returns
to herself and dies.

SP 76:899. The wife was an adulteress. Rev. infers
that this has passed to Hannah.

006931   THERE IS NO DEATH. BY FLORENCE MARRYAT.
London: K. Paul, 1891 BMC NUC. New York: J. W. Lovell,
[c1891] NUC.

Story of ghosts and mediums, ghost of a child that
died, ghosts that appear daily by regular appointment.
"Makes one's head reel" "incredible". LW

006932   WHY DID SHE LOVE HIM? A NOVEL. BY
FLORENCE MARRYAT. London: F. V. White, 1898 BMC.

LEBAUDY, MME. JULES GUSTAVE.

006933   CHRISTINE MYRIANE. London: Digby, Long,
[1898] BMC. (Tr. S. Cazaly)

ACAD 54:11. Tr. Sarah Cazaly. "Love story set in
official circles in the south of France, and embracing
some of the events of the Franco-Prussian war."
SR 86:248. "Picture of the French 'jeune fille' and
her inner life and possibilities." Wooden love affair,
Christiane develops in an unexpected way.

LEBLANC, GEORGETTE. 1869-1941.

006934   THE CHOICE OF LIFE. New York: Dodd,Mead,
1914 NUC. London: Methuen, 1914 BMC. (Tr. A. Tiexeira
de Mattos.)

NYT-idealistic older woman attempts to enlarge and
mold the life of a peasant girl, Roseline. She wishes
to train her to work to deliver other women who are
still oppressed by circumstances or people, author
believes women should be free from chains of
traditional conventions, the burden of their own
apathy, should be aroused to self-expression, courage,
sympathy. Freedom of life, thought, and love. She
believes Roseline will find vividness, education and
power in love. Is defeated because Roseline lacks
force necessary for great feeling. She finds herself
in a quiet contentment caring for a cat, flowers and
the customers of a village shop.
TLS-"One must be an ardent feminist not to feel, after
reading the book through, that there is a little too
much scent in the room."

LE BLOND, ELIZABETH ALICE FRANCES (HAWKINS-WHITSHED) BURNABY
MAIN. B. 1860. United Kingdom.

006935   ADVENTURES ON THE ROOF OF THE WORLD. BY
MRS. AUBREY LE BLOND (MRS. MAIN). London: T. F. Unwin,
1904 NUC BMC.

DQ823 Alps, description and travel; mountaineering

006936   THE STORY OF AN ALPINE WINTER. BY MRS.
AUBREY LE BLOND. New York: Macmillan, 1907 PW. London:
G. Bell, 1907 BMC NUC.

Winter life in Alpines.
SR-love story. Mostly travel and description.

LE BLOND, MRS. AUBREY. See LE BLOND, ELIZABETH ALICE
FRANCES (HAWKINS-WHITSHED) BURNABY MAIN.

LE BRETON, FARREN, pseud. See BLAKE, MABEL P.

LECKEY, PHOEBE (BAKER). B. 1882. United States.

006937   THE BECKONING HEIGHTS. BY PHOEBE FABIAN
LECKEY. New York: Neale, 1908 NUC.

BKM-young woman comes to live in Va, ancestral home
and laughs at reports that it is haunted. She and her
"noble lover" are chief characters.

LE CONTE, CAROLINE EATON. B. 1863. United States.

006938   THE STATUE IN THE AIR. New York:
Macmillan, 1897 NUC BMC.

Gods on Olympus, monsters, men like beasts, beasts
like men. LW 28:376.
An allegory of the scheme of redemption. The statue is
the unattainable ideal. PW 52:606.
CR 32:76 Allegory involving love and chaos and the
valley of Callithera.

LEE, ALICE LOUISE. B. 1868. United States.

006939   CAP'N JOE'S SISTER. New York: F. A.
Stokes, [1912] BMC NUC.

PW-fisher folk ?? sounds sentimental.
NYT-simple folk

006940   A FRESHMAN COED. Phliadelphia: Penn, 1910
NUC.

006941   A JUNIOR CO-ED. Philadelphia: Penn, 1912
NUC.

006942   A SENIOR CO-ED. Philadelphia: Penn, 1913
NUC.

006943   A SOPHOMORE CO-ED. Philadelphia: Penn,
1911 NUC.

Coeds write a girls' edition for local paper; wins
support for coed. PW 10-21-11

LEE, ANNE. B. 1871. United States.

006944   A WOMAN IN REVOLT. New York: D.
Fitzgerald, [c1913] NUC.

PW "heroine, a musical genius, arrogates all the
liberty of action demanded by the disciples of
individualism. Through the suffering consequent upon
flying in the face of accepted institutions, she
learns the greatest of all lessons; that the good of
the race is paramount to the happiness of the
individual." PW 84:1962.
"Expresses the most advanced phase of feminine
evolution, having for a background the working of the
social evil in which the woman's side of the subject
is particularly emphasized." NYT 1913:547.

LEE, GEORGINA.

006945   INHALING. London: Chatto & Windus, 1911
BMC.

Biddy Winter loved her husband but he dominated her
too much. Her friends persuade her she has no indep.
Their views on female emancipation were extravagant.
Ends in compromise. TLS

LEE, HELENA (CRUMETT).

006946   ACROSS SIBERIA ALONE; AN AMERICAN WOMAN'S
ADVENTURES. BY MRS. JOHN CLARENCE LEE. New York and
London: J.Lane, 1914 NUC.

"Author in her journey from Shanghai to Moscow, came
safely through experiences which at times made her
regret her daring. Thanks to a count, a countess and
other distinguished persons by whom she was
entertained, she saw Siberian life more intimately
than a mere tourist. A mysterious letter in Russian
accompanying her passport startles all its readers and
occasions many complications." PW
DK 755 Siberia--Description and travel.

LEE, JENNETTE BARBOUR (PERRY). 1860-1951. United States.

006947   THE AIR-MAN AND THE TRAMP. New York: C.
Scribner's Sons, 1918 NUC.

PW-love, inheritance, war
NYT-May 5, 1918, p 212. Artificial romance. Gabriell
Eaton, a tired working woman who has spent herself
working for her invalid mother and is strangely
desolate after her mother's death, inherits a
neglected old estate and decides to live on it.

006948   AUNT JANE. New York: C. Scribner's Sons,
1915 NUC. London: Methuen, 1916 BMC.

The heroine mid-aged is in charge of an endowed
hospital in an inland city. Her capabilities and
personality and her delayed love story form the theme.
BKM v.42 1915-16.
Woman runs a hospital masterfully, there's a belated
romance. PW
Tactful, efficient, strong willed, a wisp of a love
plot-NyT
She loves a romance and gets so involved in others is
unaware that millionaire patient is in love with her.
TLS--Awful "Angel" type, soupy nurse whom even the
doctors stand in awe of.

006949   BETTY HARRIS. Methuen: 1912 BMC.

ATH-millionaire's child abducted.
TLS-12 year, brought back by fruit seller.
SP-immigrants in Chicago.

006950   THE CHINESE COAT. New York: C. Scribner's

Sons, 1920 NUC.

NYT 9-26-1920:23.-Symbolic, wife's desire for a
Chinese coat, she and husband's pursuit of it as final
fulfillment of their lives.

006951   THE GREEN JACKET. New York: C. Scribner's
Sons, 1917 NUC. London: Skeffington, [1918] BMC.

Milly Newberry detective becomes tired of turning over
criminals to police. Decides to punish them
herself-those she catches. Solves a crime of missing
jewels that baffled detective agencies for yrs.
PW-head of Millicent Newberry Detective Agency,
started by herself. A detective with a
difference-those that employ her must agree that she
alone will decide what's to be done with the culprit.
(believes too many people go to prison.)
TLS-Heroine solves a mystery which New York's finest
detective agency failed in. she mixes philanthropy
with detection and is knitting (I always have a piece
of knitting in hand-a new piece for every case).
Review disappointed in her management of her love
affairs.
SP-She makes an original bargain with the authorities
as to the future of the criminals tracked down by her.

006952   HAPPY ISLAND: A NEW "UNCLE WILLIAM"
STORY. New York: Century, 1910 BMC NUC.

006953   KATE WETHERILL: AN EARTH COMEDY. New
York: Century, 1900 BMC NUC.

PW-New England heroine, educated, marries factory
employee. Soon disillusioned in her marriage, sordid
conditions of her life drive her to verge of suicide.
CR 37:85. Novel in 3 parts, Hell, Purgatory, Paradise.
Study of a woman's temperament. Kate married to a
clod, a factory foreman whose pleasure is to eat and
watch a ball game. She had mistaken passion for love.

006954   MR. ACHILLES. New York: Dodd, Mead, 1912
NUC.

006955   A PILLAR OF SALT. Boston: Houghton
Mifflin, 1901 NUC.

The moral is that the education and environment fo men
and women are too one sided and separate; that both
need practical co-ed in order to supplement and help
each other. The one lost in general ities, the other
in petty causes.WOMAN'S JOURNAL 3-16-01:83
The tired, practical, poverty-threatened wife of a
visionary-NATION 01
Husband and wife never understand each other; work for
different goals. BKM

006956   THE RAIN-COAT GIRL. New York: C.
Scribner's Sons, 1919 NUC. London: Hurst and Blackatt,
[1921] BMC.

factory village life; stenographer at "the works"
"optimist"-PW
NYT-Isabel Merton, a "phenomenal stenographer, an
artist in costume and coiffure, able to visualize mill
girl's transformation and sketch it on paper and then
bring it about, a natural dancer, intuitively master
of merchandising, a community organizer and an
adorable lady love...opens a cooperative laundry." Pro
cooperative enterprise.

006957   SIMEON TETLOW'S SHADOW. New York:
Century, 1909 BMC NUC. London: Hodder and Stoughton,
1909 BMC.

the shadow is a young man who works for big railroad
businessman. PW 3-3-09.

006958   THE SON OF A FIDDLER. Boston: Houghton,
Mifflin, 1902 NUC.

006959   THE TASTE OF APPLES. New York: Dodd,
Mead, 1913 NUC. London: Skeffington, [1919] BMC.

PW "Visionary old New England shoemaker and his brisk
Yankee wife are treated to a trip to England, and the
latter keeps house a la New England there in one of
the oldest nooks of the country. Her husband meets
dukes and beggars on the same plane of sympathetic
friendliness and is met by them in the same spirit.
The record of their experiences makes wholesome,
pleasant reading." PW 84:951.

006960   UNCLE WILLIAM: THE MAN WHO WAS SHIF'LESS.
New York: Century, 1906 BMC NUC. London: Hodder and
Stoughton, [1916] BMC.

PW-nice old man's story
NYT

006961   THE WOMAN IN THE ALCOVE. New York: C.
Scribner's Sons, 1914 NUC.

Man scrimps, builds bankroll; wife a faded drudge.
Discovers her twin in fabulous restaurant-what the
wife could have been if he weren't so tight. BKM
"Story of married life, showing how a self-centered
lawyer finds in his supposedly scrimping, practical
wife, a very different sort of person." PW
BKM-Husband had always kept tight rein on purse
strings, never allowing his wife who was forcd to
scrimp and save to guess the wealth he was piling up.
Then business one day brought him into an exclusive
resort of pleasure where he sees a woman who could be
his wife if she had had all the countless little
comforts and luxuries which he could so easily have
given.

LEE, KATHERINE, pseud. See JENNER, KATHERINE LEE
(RAWLINGS).

LEE, MARGARET. 1841-1914. United States.

006962   ONE TOUCH OF NATURE. New York: J. A.
Taylor, [c1892] NUC.

PW-Rose is brought up by professor of mathematics who
believes restraint is detrimental to the individual.

006963   SEPARATION. New York: F. M. Buckles, 1902
NUC.

BOOK NEWS 02

LEE, MARIAN, pseud. See COMSTOCK, ANNA (BOTSFORD).

LEE, MARY CATHERINE (JENKINS). D. 1927. United States.

006964   IN THE CHEERING-UP BUSINESS. Boston and
New York: Houghton, Mifflin, 1891 NUC. London: Lily
Series, 1891 BMC.

Young woman of 17 tells the story. There's a doctor, a
"stick" who won't marry till his mother dies: LW
Well-written: all ends in gloomy failure: IND
Rebecca Parmelee orphan, thrown out by step-mother
tries to make her own living. Can't get work. Aunt
asks her to come live with her and cheer her up.
Rebecca starts that business. Goes to Quaker
settlement in New Jersey. Sounds juvenile. PW 2-22-91.

006965   AN ISLAND PLANT: A NANTUCKET STORY.
Nantucket [Mass.]: Goldenrod Literary and Debating
Society, 1896 NUC.

006966   LOIS MALLET'S DANGEROUS GIFT. Boston:
Houghton, Mifflin, 1902 NUC.

Great beauty of Quaker-PW

006967   A SOULLESS SINGER. Boston and New York:
Houghton, Mifflin, 1895 NUC.

Woman has a beautiful voice but fails to succeed
because she "sings without soul." Gives up music,
tutors a boy who has a fine voice. Wants to adopt him
since his family and hate the stage. Ends
up loving the father and finding she really can sing
now. CR 23:460
Her whole existence is centered upon being a singer.
Acquires skill and technique but her singing lacks
passion. A summer in a secluded Quaker settlement by
the sea and her meeting with a young boy with a
marvellous voice introduce her to feelings that give
her voice soul. BKM 4:346

LEE, MARY (CHAPPELL). 1849-1932. United States.

006968   GARRET GRAIN; OR THE HOUSE BLESSED. BY
MRS. FRANK LEE. Boston: Congregational Sunday School
and Pub. Society, [c1894] NUC.

PW-story of happy Christian farming family.

LEE, MARY HOLLAND. United States.

006969   MARGARET SALISBURY. Boston: Arena, 1894
NUC.

PW-Margaret on a visit to a friend in New England is
made subservient to hypnotic influence of Miss
Appleton. Discovers she has psychic power. There is a

hero also.

LEE, MRS. FRANK. See LEE, MARY (CHAPPELL).

LEE, MRS. JOHN CLARENCE. See LEE, HELENA (CRUMETT).

LEE, MRS. NORMAN.

006970   THE ANGEL AND THE ANIMAL. London: Digby,
Long, 1916 BMC.

TLS-Story of woman who after a happy marriage yearns
again for passion, loses her heart to French doctor,
he marries elsewhere. Illicit passion.

LEE, NORA.

006971   SISTER GWENDOLEN; A LOVE SKETCH. London:
Roxburghe Press, [1896] BMC.

LEE, SUSAN RICHMOND. United Kingdom.

006972   ALIX OF THE GLEN: A NOVEL. BY CURTIS
YORKE. London: J. Long, 1905 BMC.

Everyone at cross purposes, conventional love story.
ACAD ATH

006973   THE ALTERNATE LIFE: A ROMANCE. BY CURTIS
YORKE. London: Hutchinson, 1916 BMC.

006974   BECAUSE OF THE CHILD: A STORY WITHOUT A
PLOT. BY CURTIS YORKE. London: Jarrold, 1897 BMC.

Dot Fraser at 18 - young girl's book-sequence novels.
SR Depressing. A dreadful little girl. An unfortunate.
ATH 108: 7 yrs. old, too good not to die, but she
lives and is the means of doing a lot of good.

006975   BUNGAY OF BANDILOO. AN EPISODE. BY CURTIS
YORKE. London: Hurst and Blackett, 1903 BMC.

LBKM-a humorous account of a socialist breaking into
high society.

006976   CARPATHIA KNOX. A NOVEL. BY CURTIS YORKE.
London: Jarrold, [1900] BMC.

006977   DANGEROUS DOROTHY. A NOVEL. BY CURTIS
YORKE. London: J. Long, 1912 BMC.

ATH-witty and sent. badinage.
SR-Romance.

006978   DARRELL CHEVASNEY: A NOVEL. BY CURTIS
YORKE. London: Jarrold, 1894 BMC.

ACAD 45:226. Maysel broke her engagement to Darrell
and married someone else. He married her sister,
became a highway robber, choked his wife to death when
she discovered it. Not one of Maysel's six sons lives
to maturity.

006979   DELPHINE. A NOVEL. BY CURTIS YORKE.
London: J. Long, 1904 BMC.

BKM-love story with maddening little heroine.
ATH-rescued from poverty by love.

006980   DISENTANGLED. BY CURTIS YORKE. London:
Hutchinson, 1915 BMC.

006981   ENCHANTED. BY CURTIS YORKE. London: J.
Long, [1916] BMC.

006982   A FLIRTATION WITH TRUTH. BY CURTIS YORKE.
London: J. Macqueen, 1897 BMC.

006983   THE GIRL AND THE MAN. BY CURTIS YORKE.
London: J. Long, [1904] BMC 1906 NUC.

TLS-owners of adjacent Canadian mines; they become
partners.
BKM-she learned everything about mining from her
uncle, promised him at deathbed to find in Canada the
lost silver lode.
Woman in mining camp. PW 4-10-09

006984   THE GIRL IN GREY. BY CURTIS YORKE.
London: J. Long, [1914] BMC.

ATH-young woman wishes revenge on evil man, instead
falls in love with him.

006985   HER MEASURE. A NOVEL. BY CURTIS YORKE.
London: Hutchinson, 1915 BMC.

006986   HIS HEART TO WIN. BY CURTIS YORKE.
London: Jarrold, 1893 BMC. London: Jarrold, 1899 NUC.

Jilted by Esther Fairfax, Dorian Keith forms a
relationship with young Mollie that ends in his
proposing marriage though he tells her he doesn't love
her. Things don't go well especially since Esther
shows up. Then Esther dies. Dorian is jealous for no
good reason, loses his job, gets ill, etc. Hard times
teach him he really loves his wife. SR 76:76.
Dorian and Mollie lead a life of poverty and struggle.
ATH 102:156.

006987   IRRESPONSIBLE KITTY. BY CURTIS YORKE.
London: J. Long, [1906] BMC.

TLS-younger sister left as a charge to neglected older
sister by mother. Jealousy, dainty love story.
ATH-older sister attempts to pass off Kitty's child by
a secret marriage as hers and her husband's.
Misunderstandings, reconciliation./

006988   JOCELYN ERROLL. A NOVEL. BY CURTIS YORKE.
London: Jarrold, 1900 BMC.

He gives up his position as clergy because he has
formed a creed of his own. He weds serious Beatrice.
Also Pauline, a villain, involved with him. SP 83:994
Novel of purpose. Clergyman and free thinking wife
brought back to rel. Heartless siren brought to
calamity. BAKER 03,190

006989   JOYCE. A NOVEL. BY CURTIS YORKE. London:
Hutchinson, 1918 BMC.

TLS-love affairs of Joyce and her friend Caprice who
states conjugal adoration has long since become a
"back number." Joyce revises her lover's novel without
his knowledge.

006990   THE LEVEL TRACK. A NOVEL. BY CURTIS
YORKE. London: Hutchinson, [1919] BMC.

Married problems and reconciliations. TLS
Sunshiny heroine. ATH

006991   THE MEDLICOTTS: AN UNEVENTFUL FAMILY
CHRONICLE. BY CURTIS YORKE. London: Jarrold, 1895 BMC.

English family life in large mansion in
Bloomsbury.-three generations. Grandmother the
"presiding genius." ACAD 48:160

006992   A MEMORY INCARNATE. A NOVEL. BY CURTIS
YORKE. London: Hurst and Blackett, 1902 BMC.

006993   MISS DAFFODIL. A LOVE STORY. BY CURTIS
YORKE. London: J. Long, 1911 BMC.

For girls. TLS
A Love Story. ATH

006994   MOLLIE DEVERILL. A NOVEL. BY CURTIS
YORKE. London: J. Long, [c1909] BMC NUC. Boston: D.
Estes, [c1909] NUC.

Mollie marries vs her will, story of her adjustment to
meet husband's wishes. PW
Ravishing self-willed girl marries man twice her age.
The pair end in each other's arms. TLS
After several escapades on her part, one which costs
her her child. NYT

006995   OLIVE KINSELLA. BY CURTIS YORKE. London:
J. Long, 1905 BMC.

A mystery, a secret room, a disappearance. An
irritating heroine. ACAD 05:63.
3 sets of husbands and wives misunderstanding each
other. Two sets make up, Olive remains misunderstood.
ATH 140:05.

006996   ONCE! A NOVEL. BY CURTIS YORKE. London:
Jarrold, 1892 BMC.

ACAD murder and sudden death, grisly.
Married man makes love (in his own house) to his
cousin. His wife takes chloral and elopes with a
lover. Also other characters
SP 70, 397

006997   ONLY BETTY. BY CURTIS YORKE. London: J.
Long, 1907 BMC. London: J. Long, [1908] NUC.

Well educated girl must earn her way, takes charge of

young girl for three months. PW 4-10-09.
Welsh nurse housekeeper. TLS

006998   THE OTHER SARA. BY CURTIS YORKE. London:
J. Long, 1908 BMC NUC. Boston: D. Estes, [c1908] NUC.

TLS-vulgar but good-hearted woman comes into money,
doesn't sound promising.
SR-conventional and pleasant

006999   PATRICIA OF PALL MALL. BY CURTIS YORKE.
London: J. Long, 1910 BMC.

Romantic stuff. TLS
Girl left an old house. ATH

007000   QUEER LITTLE JANE. BY CURTIS YORKE.
London: J. Long, 1912 BMC.

TLS-unsophisticated Jane goes to Canadian ranch.
ATH-runs away goes to Canada to find friend who is
engaged to another.

007001   A RECORD OF DISCORDS. BY CURTIS YORKE.
London: Jarrold, 1894 BMC.

ATH 104:491. Vampire woman, Katrine Delahaye.

007002   A ROMANCE OF MODERN LONDON. A NOVEL. BY
CURTIS YORKE. London: F. V. White, 1892 BMC NUC.

ATH 99:112. concerns relationship of adopted brother
and sister.
SP. tangled loves, mistaken marriages, eventually
straightened out by a few convenient deaths.
ACAD: written with a serious purpose.

007003   SHE WHO MEANT WELL. A NOVEL. BY CURTIS
YORKE. London: Hutchinson, 1917 BMC.

A very pretty romance. TLS
Marriage brought about by deception between a young
woman and a crippled man. She of title is sister who
brought about the marriage ATH

007004   THEIR MARRIAGE. A NOVEL. BY CURTIS YORKE.
London: J. Long, 1908 BMC.

TLS-typical nice young couples happiness simple.

007005   THOSE CHILDREN. BY CURTIS YORKE. London:
F. V. white, 1896 BMC.

007006   TWO ON AN ISLAND! AN EPISODE. BY CURTIS
YORKE. London: F. V. white, 1892 BMC.

007007   THE UNKNOWN ROAD. AN EVERYDAY STORY. BY
CURTIS YORKE. London: Hutchinson, [1920] BMC.

TLS-orphan works, becomes manager of antique shop,
marries.

007008   VALENTINE: A STORY OF IDEALS. BY CURTIS
YORKE. London: Jarrold, 1897 BMC.

She's 7 in chap. 1. Story follows her life yr. by yr.
ACAD 52:Fic Sup:97.
Her ideals are destroyed in her teens. She has her
consolation prize-a man-far from the fancies she wove.
ATH 110:669
SP 81:473. Development of a girl thru womanhood.

007009   THE VISION OF THE YEARS. BY CURTIS YORKE.
London: J. Long, 1913 BMC.

Berenice, 27, "not good looking" lives in Bloomsbury
lodging-house, looking for another job. Traditional
end. TLS
The vision occupies half of the book. ACAD

007010   WAYWARD ANNE. BY CURTIS YORKE. London: J.
Long, 1910 BMC. Boston: D. Estes, [c1910] NUC.

TLS-Anne and Brian writers-their romance. Sentimental
and silly.

007011   THE WOMAN RUTH. BY CURTIS YORKE. London:
J. Long, [1914] BMC.

ACAD 87:495-slandered young woman, her friends support
her, love episode comes to nothing, unhappy ending.

007012   THE WORLD AND DELIA. BY CURTIS YORKE.
London: J. Long, [1907] NUC BMC.

Girl of 20, husband of 40, several step children;

married love-story refreshing. LBKM 3-07:278.
Marriage grows into love. Delia cramped by her two
aunts, seeks freedom as girl-wife.
Girl marries much older man to escape life with
prudish aunts. The couple learn to love each other
after many trials. PW 4-10-09

LEE, SUSAN RICHMOND AND MRS. E. M. DAVY.

> 007013   TWO LOVES. BY CURTIS YORKE & E. M. DAVY.
> London: Hurst & Blackett, 1904 BMC.
>
> LBKM--light, full of incident.

LEE, VERNON, pseud. See PAGET, VIOLET.

LEECH, FAITH HARRIS, jt. au. See HARRIS, CORRA MAY (WHITE)
AND FAITH HARRIS LEECH.

LEEDS, DUCHESS OF. See OSBORNE, KATHERINE FRANCES.

LEEDS, LUCY A.

> 007014   CHATEAU BLUEBEARD. London: H. J. Drane,
> [1912] BMC.
>
> Clever tale @ a marriage, a castle, a count, and
> Bluebeard theme. Happy ending. TLS
> ATH 0
>
> 007015   MR. MASSITER. London: Lynwood, 1913 BMC.
>
> TLS-silly and horrid women.
> Miles Hillington marries Fan "a girl he had wronged."
> Author upholds this marriage as a solution for the
> wrong, though Fan is of very low class. Miles is a
> physical wreck at the end. ACAD.

LEEDS, VIRGINIA NILES. Nationality Unknown.

> 007016   THE DAUGHTER OF A HUNDRED MILLIONS. New
> York: F.T. Neely, 1897 NUC. London: F.T. Neely, 1897
> BMC.
>
> Heiress engaged to English Lord fears he's after her
> money. He has same fear. They discover they really
> love each other. PW 52: 1100
>
> 007017   THE HONOR OF A GENTLEMAN: A NOVEL. New
> York and London: F. T. Neely, [1899] NUC.
>
> "33 distinct descriptions of toilettes... NY
> society... The leading ladies possess as rich and
> varied a wardrobe as a modern actress.. A contribution
> to clothes philosophy." NYT 7-8-99, 453

LEESON, MAUDE. United Kingdom.

> 007018   THE DISCRETION OF DECIMA. London:
> Blackie, 1913 NUC BMC.
>
> 007019   GOD'S PRICE. London: G. Allen and Unwin,
> 1920 BMC.
>
> TLS-Valerie and unfaithful husband, returns on page 1.
> SP-divorce and remarriage
> ATH-religious view of divorce.
> SR-
>
> 007020   THE MARRIAGE OF CECILIA. London: T. F.
> Unwin, [1914] BMC NUC. New York and London: G. P.
> Putnam's Sons, 1914 NUC.
>
> TLS-"The marriage entered into quixotically on his
> part, opens for her an avenue of escape." A child is
> born.
> PW:85 3/21/14:1022 "Story based on a marriage which is
> entered into as a mere form, the parties separating
> immediately after the ceremony, believing they will
> never meet again. Of course, Fate decrees differently
> and brings them together under circumstances which,
> while making each realize how necessary to his or her
> happiness is the other, yet enforces restraint. The
> doubts, misgivings and tussle with self which each
> endures make the story which ends happily."
>
> 007021   THE STEPSISTER. London: Blackie, 1915
> BMC.
>
> SR 147:774. "The Flapper will hail it as a safe novel
> to give to her mother--or maiden aunt, should she
> possess one of these, nowadays, rare specimens."
> ACAD 87:239. Girl's book.
> TLS--Girl's book.

LE FEUVRE, AMY. D. 1929. United Kingdom.

> 007022   A BIT OF ROUGH ROAD. London: R.T.S., 1908
> BMC.
>
> 007023   BRIDGET'S QUARTER DECK. London: Hodder
> and Stoughton, 1905 BMC.
>
> 007024   THE BURRIED RING. London: Hodder and
> Stoughton, 1905 BMC.
>
> 007025   THE CHATEAU BY THE LAKE. London: Hodder
> and Stoughton, 1907 BMC.
>
> Love, rel, sensation LBKM 11-07,99
>
> 007026   A CHERRY TREE. London: Hodder and
> Stoughton, 1901 BMC. London: Pickering, [n.d.] NUC.
>
> 007027   A COUNTRY CORNER. London: Cassell, 1909
> BMC.
>
> Suitable for girls TLS
>
> 007028   DADDY'S SWORD. London and New York:
> Hodder and Stoughton, 1915 BMC NUC.
>
> 007029   A DAUGHTER OF THE SEA. New York: T.Y.
> Crowell, [1902] NUC. London: Hodder & Stoughton, 1902
> BMC.
>
> Independent young woman PW
> ATH 11-8-02 Disguised, heroine and four kindred souls
> have occupation of rescuing sailors on stormy nights.
> Keeps this secret from her husband-is discovered, all
> ends happily
> DIAL 11-16-02 single handed does her work.
>
> 007030   THE DISCOVERY OF DAMARIS. London: R. T.
> S., [1920] NUC.
>
> 007031   FOUR GATES. London and New York: Cassell,
> 1912 BMC NUC.
>
> ATH lives of four girls.
>
> 007032   A HAPPY WOMAN. London: R. T. S., 1918
> BMC.
>
> TLS simple, wholesome
>
> 007033   HAREBELL'S FRIEND. London: R. T. S.,
> [1914] BMC.
>
> 007034   HEATHER'S MISTRESS. New York: T. Y.
> Crowell, 1901 NUC. London: R. T. S., [1901] BMC.
>
> Twin sisters PW 10-05-01
>
> 007035   HER HUSBAND'S PROPERTY. London: R. T. S.,
> 1913 BMC.
>
> gentle harmless ATH
>
> 007036   HERSELF AND HER BOY. London: Cassell,
> 1914 BMC.
>
> TLS Wholesome domestic novel.
>
> 007037   HIS LITTLE DAUGHTER. London: R. T. S.,
> 1904 BMC.
>
> 007038   JOAN'S HANDFUL. London: Cassell, 1915
> BMC.
>
> 007039   JOYCE AND THE RAMBLER. London: Hodder &
> Stoughton, 1910 BMC.
>
> TLS-domestic.
>
> 007040   LADDIE'S CHOICE. BY MARY THURSTON DODGE.
> New York: Dodd, Mead, 1912 NUC. London: R. T. S.,
> [c1912] BMC NUC.
>
> PW 9/27/13:951 "A widowed organist, devoted to art,
> resolutely un worldly, and as resolutely set on
> finding the highest sort of happiness in life; three
> vigorous and active boys, who are very real boys; an
> English cathedral town and a circle of delightful
> friends, including a pair of very devoted lovers-all
> these form the constituents of the story."
> Young Agnes raises three boys, cares for Mr. Vanasour,
> organist.
> All about Dad and the three boys, Chummie who has a
> beautiful voice, costs of living in the city. All very
> churchy and about hating money, built in allegory of
> Princesses, pilgrim's Progess a kind of theme, about

going to school.

007041   A MADCAP FAMILY; OR, SYBIL'S HOME.
London: S.W. Partridge, [1916] BMC.

007042   THE MAKING OF A WOMAN. London: Hodder and
Stoughton, 1903 BMC.

"Enfranchisement of an artist who becomes a
missionary" ACAD 65,572

007043   THE MENDER. London: R. T. S., 1906 BMC
NUC.

007044   ODD. London: R. T. S., [1919] BMC.

007045   ODD MADE EVEN. London: R. T. S., [1902]
BMC.

007046   OLIVE TRACY. London: Hodder and
Stoughton, 1901 BMC NUC. New York: Dodd, Mead, 1901
NUC.

LBKM 19:89. Domestic. Wholesome. Olive realizes she
loves man after she has refused him twice. Suffers for
a year.
3-9-01 PW
TLS Introducing the S. African war, wholesome and safe
for girls.

007047   ON THE EDGE OF THE MOOR. BY THE AUTHOR OF
PROBABLE SONS, THE ODD ONE, DWELL DEEP, ETC.
[ANONYMOUS]. New York: F.H. Revell, [c1897] NUC.

Miss Rhoda Carlton sets up her little establishment on
the edge of the moor. Earns 140 pounds year. Sets
herself to redress wrongs of tyrannical landlord. SP
79:530

007048   SOME BUILDERS. London: Cassell, 1913 BMC.

Pretty milk and water love story with happy ending ATH

007049   TERRIE'S MOORLAND HOME. London: Morgan
and Scott, [1918] BMC.

007050   TESTED! Philadelphia: Heidelburg Press,
1911 NUC. London: S. W. Partridge, [1912] BMC.

Sequel to "Robin's Heritage"

007051   TWO TRAMPS. London: Hodder and Stoughton,
1903 BMC. New York: F. H. Revell, [1903] NUC.

LEFROY, ELLA NAPIER.

007052   JANET DELILLE. BY E. N. LEIGH FRY.
London: Hurst and Blackett, 1894 BMC.

SR 77:500. Janet is an artist, the widow of a
brilliant painter and a worthless man. Story opens
with her happy Bohemian existence, living with Katie,
a younger woman who has been left in her charge. Katie
marries the wrong man, is soon bored and restless; a
friend of Janet's, an older man, lives in same area.
ACAD 45:391. This friend went to India and died, never
knowing Janet loved him. She is left with her art.
ATH 103:506.

007053   THE MAN'S CAUSE. BY ELLA NAPIER LEFROY.
("E. N. LEIGH FRY"). London: J. Lane, 1899 BMC.

Young woman prefers the son of a clerical sensualist
to a blameless young Baronet, who tells the heroine
all about his rival's bad past who in turn tells the
young woman. But the letter doesn't reach the young
woman till months after she's wed. Drowns herself.
Warns parents about morals of prospective sons-in-law.
SP 83:449
"A serious novel, embodying a plea for the better
understanding and consideration of women." ACAD 57:776
"Advocates the cause of women against husbands who
have sown wild oats." Heroine is new woman. She hears
of a woman about to marry a man with a past, writes to
her. "Tedious conversations about women's suffrage.
Author's distorted code of ethics." SR 88:400
LW:31:119. Injustice to women. Attacks double
standard, the marriage of daughters to men with
licentious pasts. Concrete examples of the possible
disastrous results.
ACAD 58:126. Mrs. Chesney, a widow, recently set free
from the smothering horror of an uncongenial marriage.
Attends a houseparty, comments on guests.

007054   A SCOTS THISTLE. BY E. N. LEIGH FRY.
London: R. Bentley, 1892 BMC NUC.

ATH 99:275. romance for girls.
SP

LE GATE, ROSA BOTTOMS. United States.

007055   MAGNOLIA BLOOMS. Evansville, Ind.: Keller
Printing, 1896 NUC.

LEGGE, MARGARET. United Kingdom.

007056   THE PRICE OF STEPHEN BONYNGE. London: A.
Rivers, 1913 BMC.

Bohemian life in Eng. setting; artists; conflict
between morality and the artistic temperament. Heroine
dies. ATH
London Art Institute-their bohemian relationships. TLS

007057   THE REBELLION OF ESTHER. London: A.
Rivers, 1914 BMC NUC.

LBKM-Esther, made perpetually unhappy by her father's
temper, goes to live with an aunt in London. She
discovers she has literary abilities and she falls in
love, seriously, with a married man. Modern. What
then?
SR 147:544. They live together without mrg, but author
does not follow them beyond this decision.
ATH Choice between man and mother who needs her
sympathy and protection at home.
TLS: She returned home. "Strong and emanicapated to do
sucessful battle for her poor crushed mother."

007058   A SEMI-DETACHED MARRIAGE. London: A.
Rivers, 1912 BMC.

TLS She leaves her husband to lead her own life and
join women's movement gets into intimate corresp. with
someone who turns out to be Dick, her elderly husband.
LBKM Janet is strong, sensible, self-reliant.

007059   THE WANE OF UXENDEN. A NOVEL. London: E.
Arnold, 1917 BMC NUC.

occultism. TLS Hermoine Cheadle is a journalist, a
fine modern-spirited woman of exceptional ability,
goes back to her country home after a trag. There
she's confronted with the wreckage of a past age. Old
families going extinct. But here finds peace and
strength to go on. Attack on occultism LBKM

LEGH, M. H. CORNWALL. See LEGH, MARY HELENA CORNWALL.

LEGH, MARY HELENA CORNWALL. United Kingdom.

007060   AT THE FOOT OF THE RAINBOW: A TALE OF
ADVENTURE. London: W. Gardner and Darton, 1900 BMC.

007061   GOLD IN THE FURNACE. BY M. H. CORNWALL
LEGH. London: Religious Tract Society, [1900] BMC.
London: Leisure Hour Library, [1906] NUC.

007062   AN INCORRIGIBLE GIRL. BY M. H. CORNWALL
LEGH. London: Religious Tract Society, [1899] BMC.
London: Leisure Hour Library, [1909] NUC.

LEIGH, ESME.

007063   MERMAID: A SKETCH. Glasgow: D. Bryce,
1893 BMC.

Uncompromising optimism. Unsmooth love of Phyllis
Tempeat and Dicky Fayrefaxe. He's ordered to service,
thought killed. Baronet comes along, etc. but all put
right. ATH 102:622.

LEIGH, LEOTI. United States.

007064   NONIE. Cincinnati: Editor Pub. Co.,
[c1899] NUC.

LEIGH, ROSE ANNA. United States.

007065   MARGUERITE; OR, A WILD FLOWER. Dallas,
Texas: Showalter-Lincoln, [c1893] NUC.

LEIGHTON, DOROTHY, pseud. See JONSON, DOROTHY (FORSYTH).

LEIGHTON, MARIE FLORA BARBARA (CONNOR). United Kingdom.

007066   THE AMAZING VERDICT. London: G. Richards,
1904 BMC. London: G. Newnes, 1918 NUC.

TLS-mur. myst.

007067   BLACK SILENCE. London: Ward, Lock, 1913
BMC.

Sensation, melodrama ATH
LBKM-relation between two men.

007068   THE BRIDE OF DUTTON MARKET. London: Ward,
Lock, 1911 BMC.

A remarkably successful lady detective is one of the
principal chars. ATH

007069   BUILDERS OF SHIPS. London: Ward, Lock,
1911 BMC NUC.

Romantic stuff ACAD

007070   CONVICT 100. London: Ward, Lock, 1920
BMC.

TLS male heroes.

007071   CONVICT 413 L. London: Ward, Lock, 1910
BMC.

TLS Murd & Infidelity

007072   DARK PERIL. London: Hodder and Stoughton,
1916 BMC.

LBKM-Two cousins look alike, young missionary loves
one, complications.

007073   DEEP WATERS. London: Ward, Lock, 1909
BMC.

Mrs Femming discovers that her husband is a forger TLS
Misfortunes of love end in wedding bells LBKM

007074   THE DUCHESS GRACE. London: Ward, Lock,
1918 BMC NUC.

TLS-Mur myst in which murderer is known in 5th chapter
and rest of book concerned with wrongfully condemned
heroine's miseries in prison. Lover finally achieves
her freedom.
LBKM-Descriptions of female convict prison are grimly
realistic.

007075   DUCKS AND DRAKES. London: Ward, Lock,
1913 BMC.

"Sensational tale of the owner of a large shop who
plays ducks & drakes with his fortune." ATH

007076   EVERY MAN HAS HIS PRICE. London: Ward,
Lock, 1917 BMC NUC.

Sensational murder TLS

007077   AN EYE FOR AN EYE. London: Ward, Lock,
1909 BMC.

Crammed with incidents TLS
Sensational plot, escape, mystery etc. LBKM

007078   THE FIRES OF LOVE. London: Ward, Lock,
1915 BMC.

Murder, mystery, marriage in the end. TLS

007079   THE GATES OF SORROW. London: Ward, Lock,
1915 BMC.

Geraldine Croy's mother is in prison for murder.
Accepts a marr prop. (he knows about her mother)
learns mother escaped prison, burned in railroad
accident. All turns out well. TLS

007080   GERALDINE WALTON - WOMAN! London: Ward,
Lock, 1914 BMC.

LBKM-sensation. Geraldine is sister of Stephen who has
been missing for seven years and is missing again on
the night of the party celebrating his return.
ATH-Cardsharper is invited to impersonate him.
TLS-Geraldine is a millionaire. She marries, at end,
engineer making 100 lbs a year.

007081   THE GIRL OF THE YELLOW DIAMONDS. London:
C. A. Renfson, 1920 BMC.

007082   GREED. London: Ward, Lock, 1911 BMC NUC.

Story of blackmail, murder mystery TLS LBKM

007083   GUILTY OR INNOCENT? London: Ward, Lock,
1918 BMC.

TLS- tr mys

007084   THE HAND OF THE UNSEEN, A ROMANCE OF REAL
LIFE. London: Ward, Lock, 1918 BMC.

TLS murd myst. Ellaline comdemned to penal servitude

007085   THE HARVEST OF SIN. London: J. Bowden,
1898 BMC.

112:787. Heroine's father was divorced before she was
born.
London family refined reduced to poverty because
father dies, son goes away. Daughter goes on stage,
meets a wealthy man, persuaded by mother to marry him
but his crime affects her tragically. Meant to show
that no refined woman can be an actress. PW 55: 370.

007086   THE HEART'S AWAKENING. A NOVEL. London:
Chapman & Hall, 1893 BMC.

Shallow Deliah Manifold. Strong minded eldest Miss
Manfield. SP 70:396.
Deliah first engaged to peasant's son who has been to
Oxford; throws him over for Earl. Married she flirts
with the peasant, now a parson. Throws herself at him
within an hour of her husband's death. But he rejects
her for her sister. Deliah weds another. SR 76 443
Deliah Roxby's development. Acts in passion, but
learns she has a soul. Study of the changes in her.
Esther Ricardo, beautiful, fierce, cruel, greedy,
unscrupulous way she amasses a fortune, murdered. ACAD
43:346.

007087   HER CONVICT HUSBAND. London: Ward, Lock,
1913 BMC.

007088   HER LADYSHIP'S SILENCE. London: Cassell,
1907 BMC.

Gambling, murder, gang of thieves-everything ACAD ATH
TLS
Much action, advent TLS

007089   HER MARRIAGE LINES. London: Ward, Lock,
1912 BMC.

007090   HIDDEN HANDS. London: G. Newnes, [1918]
BMC.

007091   HUMAN NATURE. London: Ward, Lock, 1916
BMC.

TLS tr myst.
ATH tr myst.

007092   IN GOD'S GOOD TIME. London: G. Richards,
1903 BMC.

Murder, blackmail, etc ACAD 64, 366 ATH 121, 750

007093   IN THE GRIP OF A LIE. London: J. Long,
[1916] BMC.

TLS Murd Myst., heroine sent to jail.

007094   JOAN MAR, DETECTIVE. London: Ward, Lock,
1910 BMC.

007095   JUSTICE! London: Ward, Lock, 1910 BMC.

TLS murder
ACAD murder

007096   THE LADY OF BALMERINO; A ROMANCE OF THE
GRAMPIANS. London: Trischler, 1891 BMC.

SP. Fugitives from France carrying Marie Antoinette's
diamonds stay with a farmer who is actually a Jacobite
in hiding. His son has become the Chief of a band of
caterans. His daughter is meeting him secretly. Father
thinks it an assignation, kills son without
recognizing him, band kills father. By end of story
nearly everyone has been killed except daughter and a
young farmer who becomes her successful suitor.
ATH 99:177. A dozen murders involving French woman
entrusted with Marie Antoinette's jewels staying at
home of Jacobite outlaw, whose daughter is lady of the
title.

007097   LUCILE DARE, DETECTIVE. London: Ward,
Lock, 1919 BMC NUC.

Takes on several disguises to solve crimes. Vivid advents. " In the course of tracking down the murderer of her friend's father,she finds professional duty, friendship and love hard to reconcile." TLS

007098   THE MAN WHO KNEW ALL. London: J. Long, [1916] BMC NUC.

TLS-A tangle of mrgs.
LBKM-a tangle of mrgs.

007099   THE MARKED WOMAN. London: Hodder & Stoughton, 1916 BMC.

TLS heroine is shot in the side at one point and at another pinked in the arm in a duel with her step-sister. Villainess was of such muscular strength that she had grappled with two men more than once in a life-death struggle and come out victorious.
ATH Story culminates in desperate duel between fem. villain and gentle heroine.

007100   THE MISSING MISS RANDOLPH. London: Ward,lock, 1912 BMC.

ATH-heroine has adventurous career.

007101   "MONEY". London: Ward, Lock, 1909 BMC.

Story of intrigue, love, disapearances TLS
Brutal mtds of successful businessmen in seeking gold in Aust. LBKM.

007102   THE MYSTERY OF THE THREE FINGERS. London: J. Long, 1916 BMC.

TLS murder & abduction. Heroine starts as worker within a lace factory ends as a peeress.
ATH a girl from Br. Columbia eventually unmasks the villian.

007103   A NAPOLEON OF THE PRESS. London: Hodder and Stoughton, 1900 BMC.

SP 85:665. Career of a newspaper owner.
LIT 7:510. Self made man.

007104   THE OPAL HEART. London: Ward, Lock, 1920 BMC.

TLS Lady detective.

007105   PUT YOURSELF IN HER PLACE. London: Ward, Lock, 1908 BMC.

TLS-?

007106   RED GOLD. London: Ward, Lock, 1919 BMC.

About a young actress "Angel May" and her kidnapped adopted child TLS
She falls in love with a clergyman, abductions, etc SR

007107   THE RED-PAINTED BOX. BEING THE NARRATIVE OF A CURIOUS EXPERIENCE IN THE LIFE OF THE REVEREND MARK BESSEMER. London: J. Macqueen, 1897 BMC.

SR 85:88. Murder story. Hero is "a great fool" but author pities him and gives him a happy ending.

007108   SEALED LIPS. London: Ward, Lock, 1906 BMC.

007109   THE SHAME OF SILENCE. London: J. Long, [1917] BMC.

Traditional melo-drama TLS
Crime, etc. ATH

007110   THE SILVER STAIR. London: Ward, Lock, 1914 BMC.

LBKM-Sensational tale of passionate love and hate, crime and punishment.

007111   THE STORY OF A GREAT SIN. London: Ward, Lock, 1916 BMC.

LBKM-Lovers kept apart by reticence of someone guilty of a crime.

007112   THE TRIANGLE. London: Ward Lock,, 1912 BMC NUC.

ATH Sens melodrama.

007113   UNDER THE BROAD ARROW. London: Hodder & Stoughton, [1914] BMC.

007114   VENGEANCE IS MINE. London: Ward Lock,, 1917 BMC NUC.

Trad crime story TLS ATH

007115   THE WAY OF SINNERS. London: Ward, Lock, 1914 BMC.

LBKM-Young woman renounces comfort and luxury to join young man and elderly woman in religious campaign.
ATH a "Money Queen" poses for a time as a baron, plays chief part.
ATH 144;562. Female millionaire. "story relates how she wreaked her vengeance upon those who tried to get rid of her while she was confined in a home for inebriates."
TLS- woman of power.

LEITH, ALICIA AMY.

007116   A PLANT OF LEMON VERBENA: A SOMERSETSHIRE IDYLL. London: Gibbings, 1895 BMC.

in dialect. Set in West Somerset. SR 80:247
"Romance of her youth told by an old woman" The beautiful Breton Sailor who came, made promises, left. How she followed, found him and suffered. ACAD 48:183.

LEITH, MARY CHARLOTTE JULIA.

007117   A BLACK MARTINMAS. A STORY. London: Lynwood, 1912 BMC.

ATH-placid domestic.

007118   CHAMPION SANDY: A STORY. BY MRS. DISNEY LEITH. Aberdeen: A. Murray, 1910 BMC. Dumfries: R. G. Mann, 1910 BMC.

007119   LACHLAN'S WIDOW. London: Lynwood, 1913 BMC.

Goody-goody story of country folk, much dialect (Scot.). Lachlan's widow married him on his death bed, took charge of her 3 step-children, managed her father's house. Eventually father remarries and so does Mollie. ACAD

LEITH, MRS. DISNEY. See LEITH, MARY CHARLOTTE JULIA.

LEMON, IDA. See HILDYARD, IDA (LEMON).

LEMORE, CLARA. See ROBERTS, CLARA (LEMORE).

LENNOX, AGNES GORDON. Nationality Unknown.

007120   BROWNIE. New York: J. Lane, 1916 BMC NUC. London: J. Lane, 1916 BMC NUC.

Brownie and Ian love each other but Rita is still Ian's wife in the eyes of the world. Brownie wants to defy the world, but Ian won't let her. He goes on trip to Tibet, when he recovers from fever and hears of Rita's death it is time for him to see thru the disguise of his servant's nephew. PW 90:687 9/2/16.
NYT Melodramatic romance.
LBKM 0
ATH-Brownie is one of world's temptresses to men who have time and money to waste and lack courage to run away.

007121   A GIRL'S MARRIAGE. London: J. Lane, 1914 NUC. New York: J. Lane, 1914 BMC.

PW 85 5/16/14 1652--"Fay Beaumont and her brother make a compact never to marry. Later on, she learns that he is only prevented from marrying Mollie de Lisle by this promise. She proposes a secret marriage with Lord Malcolm Kinross, in order to clear Pat's path. She takes the step without any notion of the obligations entailed, and is filled with horror on learning to what she has pledged herself. Lord Malcolm is killed in a motor accident. Second part of book tells of Fay's marriage to Dick Garnett, entered into in a spirit of friendship and of her finding out that friendship is not satisfying."
LBKM Fay is incredibly naive about mrg. Second husband is permitted no more than friendship, love is born out of jealousy at end of book and makes Fay a human being.
SR 147:609--0
TLS 13:166--0

LENORE, pseud. See ROWLAND, K. ALICE.

LENTON, JESSIE (POPE). D. 1941. United Kingdom.

007122   THE SHY AGE. BY JESSIE POPE. London: G.
Richards, 1914 BMC.

ACAD 87:495. Boys and their pranks

007123   THE TRACY TUBBSES. BY JESSIE POPE.
London: Mills and Boon, [1914] NUC BMC.

LBKM-comic view of young married couple

LEONARD, MARY FINLEY. B. 1862.

007124   EVERYDAY SUSAN; A STORY FOR GIRLS. New
York: T. Y. Crowell, [c1912] NUC.

For younger readers?
PZ7

007125   THE SPECTACLE MAN; A STORY OF THE MISSING
BRIDGE. Boston: W. A. Wilde, [c1901] NUC.

007126   SUSAN GROWS UP. New York: T. Y. Crowell,
[c1914] NUC.

007127   THE WAYS OF JANE; A STORY WITH WHICH THE
WISE AND PRUDENT HAVE NO CONCERN. New York: Duffield,
1917 NUC.

PW 91:1108 4/7/17
Told by a girl of 7 or 8 about her aunt Angela's
several romances; the question of her ownership of a
church is settled. NYT 6-3-17, 218.

LEONARD, MARY HALL. 1847-1921. United States.

007128   A CODE OF HONOR. Cincinnati, Ohio: Editor
Pub. Co., 1897 NUC.

007129   THE DAYS OF THE SWAMP ANGEL. New York:
Neale, 1914 NUC.

007130   A DISCOVERED COUNTRY. Cincinnati: Editor
Pub. Co., 1900 NUC.

LEROY, AMELIE CLAIRE. B. 1851. United Kingdom.

007131   ARRESTED: A NOVEL. BY ESME STUART.
London: F. V. White, 1896 BMC. New York: Appleton,
1897 NUC.

A buried treasure found by man who is suspected of
murder and must therefore leave the woman he loves.
She tries to establish his innocence. BKM 5:523
Oliver Englefield, country-town bank clerk is
disgruntled about his love life and his career. Elsie
Kennerly, mistress of Yule Farm. And Tim who saves
Oliver from the gallows. SR 84:205
A man innocently imprisoned for murder; a heroine
persecuted by a man in his absence. ATH 109:309

007132   A BRAVE FIGHT, AND OTHER STORIES. BY ESME
STUART. London: J. Nisbet, 1892 BMC.

Short stories

007133   BY REEDS AND RUSHES: A STORY. BY ESME
STUART. Edinburgh and London: Oliphant, 1898 BMC.

ACAD 53:576. Love story of farm families.

007134   BY RIGHT OF SUCCESSION. BY ESME STUART.
London: Ward and Downey, 1893 BMC.

Two beautiful orphaned "illegitimate" young women, an
inheritance, a wicked relative who sends them off. Her
son who loves one of them, discovery of a marriage
certificate. SR 76:243.
Grace and Sibyl Gordon. ACAD 44:189.

007135   A CHARMING GIRL. BY ESME STUART. London:
Greening, 1907 BMC.

Everyone thinks she's an angel. TLS
ACAD-story for a schoolgirl.

007136   CHRISTALLA: AN UNKNOWN QUANTITY. BY ESME
STUART. London: Methuen, 1900 BMC.

LBKM 19:27. Her life from child to success in the
History Tripos. Also a mother who causes son's death
by deserting him and his father.
SP 84:454. No love interest.

SR 89:499. "Delicious and engaging old maid, 11 years
of age." She takes a first class at Cambridge.

007137   CLAUDEA'S ISLAND. BY ESME STUART. London:
Low, 1893 BMC. Chicago: F. T. Neely, 1895 NUC.

SRev 77:151 "Lovable bright girl" dies at end of book.
Two lovers and Gina, Claudea's foil and rival.
SP 72:379. She owned the island. Her preacher-lover's
earnestneess contrasted with her larger nature.
Herbert Ravencroft breaks engagement to the Hon.
Georgina Ashton. Gets interested in a young woman, a
nature girl type who loves the sea.
The girl dies; the engagement is renewed. ACAD 44:585.
Claudea's "a healthy mind in a beautiful body." Her
end is sad and heroic. ATH 102:803

007138   THE CULTURE OF CHRIS. BY ESME STUART.
London: Jarrolds, [1919] BMC.

007139   THE FOOTSTEPS OF FORTUNE. BY ESME STUART.
London: J. Nisbet, 1896 BMC.

SP-South African goldfields.

007140   FOR LOVE AND RANSOM. BY ESME STUART.
London: Jarrold, [1905] BMC.

007141   HARUM SCARUM: A POOR RELATION. BY ESME
STUART. London: Jarrold, 1896 BMC.

SP 76:777. Colonial heroine, Antonia, unconventional,
entertaining exploits, wholesome high spirts, Not a
problem novel.

007142   HARUM SCARUM MARRIED. BY ESME STUART.
London: Jarrolds, 1918 BMC. (First pub. under title
Two Troubadours.)

007143   HARUM SCARUM. THE STORY OF A WILD GIRL.
BY ESME STUART. New York: International News, [c1895]
NUC.

Penniless young Australian relation incenses her aunt,
an English duchess, with her free ways-eats in the
kitchen, rides bare back, ignores class distinctions,
is fearlessly truthful. PW 7-20-95:189

007144   HARUM SCARUM'S FORTUNE. BY ESME STUART.
London: Jarrold, [1909] BMC.

007145   IN THE DARK. BY ESME STUART. London: J.
Long, 1899 BMC.

Love, adventure, anarchy. Denis Courthouse and Violet
Drake comeout all right, but not Lucia. Durand is the
villain. English Dr. kidnapped in Venice, brought to
Paris, kept prisoner. Treasure hunting, mysterious
gondoliers, murder attempts, etc. LBKM 16:171
"Suppressed sensationalism." SP 83:259

007146   INSCRUTABLE; A STORY. BY ESME STUART. New
York: J. A. Taylor, [1892] NUC. London: Bliss, Sands,
1894 BMC.

Upon his ma's death, Lancelot Dighton becomes heir
expectant of uncle's fortune, learns of a mystery
concerning his uncle. Sensational details of his own
romance too. PW 1-14-93
SR 77:313. Mystery, hero is penniless author.
SP. Puzzling relations of Lancelot Garrick and Hilda.
ATH 103:343. A shocker

007147   THE KNIGHTS OF ROSEMULLION. BY ESME
STUART. London: National Society's Depository, 1898
BMC.

007148   MARRIED TO ORDER: A ROMANCE OF MODERN
DAYS. BY ESME STUART. London: H. Cox, 1895 BMC.

Young man wandering in No. Country finds his way to a
palace of the King of Rothbery. It's present time. The
palace is a ruin, but life within carried on
luxuriously. There's a Princess. The young man meets
the princess later when she's sent out into the world
to make a fortune to save the palace. SP 75:176.
Penelope Winskell marries Philip Gillbanks to save
father from ruin. Then she loves another man. But her
husband was all but murdered by her father. He's left
blind. She devotes herself to him or wants to, but he
refuses to be her burden. There the tale ends. ACAD
48:127
Sensational episodes ATH 105:798

007149   A MINE OF WEALTH. BY ESME STUART. London:
Hurst and Blackett, 1896 NUC BMC.

ATH 107:578. Villain of a 40 yr old woman and 20 yr
old daughter. She has married the wrong man who had
married the wrong woman. They have a twenty yr old
son. Wrong man and woman die. Romance. Also a gold
mine.
ACAD 49:423. Mrs. Beddoes, the widow, is
"strong-minded, somewhat unscrupulous," whose temper
has been tried by a disappointment

007150   MONA: A MANX IDYLL. BY ESME STUART.
London: Jarrold, [1905] BMC.

Love story of the old sort. LBKM Christmas issue.
1905, p. 26

007151   OUT OF REACH. A STORY. BY ESME STUART.
London & Edinburgh: W. & R. Chambers, 1894 BMC.

007152   THE POWER OF THE PAST. A NOVEL. BY ESME
STUART. London: R. Bentley, 1894 NUC BMC.

SR. 77:694-heroine has youthful affair, shoots her
former lover when he tries to blackmail, eventually
kills herself in remorse.
SP 72:907. Ahah! She regrets the laudanum, decides to
walk it off, rev. says conclusion is vague but "we
infer that Inez is successful...and lives happily ever
afterwards." She had confessed to her husband-who was
such a terrible prig-that she was in despair.

007153   SENT TO COVENTRY. BY ESME STUART. London:
J. Long, 1898 BMC.

SP 81:914. Devonshire. Heroine's family socially
ostracized after father's loss of money. In style of
Charlotte Yonge.
Dagmar von Wurm, wealthy widow of a husband who died
shortly after their marriage freeing her from an
unhappy relationship, goes to live in a quiet town.
Her child died too. Her brother joins her. There's
gossip. A doctor wins her at the end. But she also
makes some sacrifice. ATH 113:109.

007154   THE SILVER MINE. AN UNDERGROUND STORY. BY
ESME STUART. London: National Society, [1891] BMC.

007155   THE STRENGTH OF STRAW. BY ESME STUART.
London: J. Long, 1900 BMC.

007156   THE STRENGTH OF TWO: A NOVEL. BY ESME
STUART. London: F. V. White, 1898 BMC.

ACAD 53:347. Temperately sensational. Gambler and his
daughter, Joy, young squire, Sir Ivor, dwarf, rich old
aunt, etc. Spirited.
ATH 111:531.

007157   THE TAMING OF TAMZIN. BY ESME STUART.
London: G. G. Harrap, 1920 BMC.

007158   TANGLED THREADS. BY ESME STUART. London:
S. W. Partridge, 1897 BMC.

007159   THROUGH THE FLOOD; THE STORY OF AN
OUT-OF-THE-WAY PLACE. BY ESME STUART. New York: T.
Whittaker, 1892 NUC.

Ada Dacre disinherited because of her elopement. Has
three children, dies, husband's sister raises the
children not knowing the mother's history. That she's
an aristocrat, who wed a farmer. PW 12-9-93

007160   TWO TROUBADOURS. A STORY. BY ESME STUART.
London: Smith, Elder, 1912 BMC.

007161   VIRGINIE'S HUSBAND. A NOVEL. BY ESME
STUART. London: A. D. Innes, 1892 BMC.

ATH- Girls' story. Love after marriage.

007162   A WOMAN OF FORTY; A MONOGRAPH. BY ESME
STUART. London: Methuen, 1893 NUC BMC. New York:
Appleton, 1893 NUC.

More beautiful than young woman of 20 and more
attractive but when in competition with youth, her
years count against her. "An opportune attack of
diptheria cuts the knot of her perplexities, and
perhaps it is as well for her that it does." LW 93,
451.
Magdalen Cuthbert. ACAD 44:383. Griselda Foy is 20.
SR 77:16. Magdalen reawakens to a "2nd summer of
love." Man is engaged to a younger woman.
SP 72:137. she is tempted to win him over and make
another woman suffer as she has, but decides against

it. A "one-character" novel.
CR 21:54. She braves diptheria and worldly censure to
nurse him-both die.

LESLIE, EMMA. United Kingdom.

007163   LADY MARJORY: A STORY OF METHODIST WORK A
HUNDRED YEARS AGO. London: C.H. Kelly, 1892 BMC. New
York: Hunt and Eaton, 1893.

Goes with father, Earl of Arran to America. He's
condemned to labor as a convict slave. Romance in her
life and events of American history before Revolution
and early history of Methodism. PW 9-16-93

007164   THROUGH STORM TO CALM; A TALE OF LAST
CENTURY. London: Religious Tract Society, [1897] BMC.

SP 80:148. Methodist revival, from that pov.

LESLIE, HENRIETTA, pseud. See SCHUETZE, GLADYS HENRIETTA
(RAPHAEL).

LESUER, DANIEL, pseud. See LAPAUZE, JEANNE (LOISEAU).

LETCH, GERTRUDE.

007165   JOAN HARCOURT: THE STORY OF A PLAIN
WOMAN. London: H. J. Drane, [1910] BMC.

LETHBRIDGE, SYBIL CAMPBELL. United Kingdom.

007166   THE JOURNEY HOME. London: Skeffington,
[1919] BMC.

Mattie Jameson's intense love for nephew conflicts
with that of love of husband. TLS
Strong psych study. Violet's indifference to conv.
Runs off with a man. They die. Their son Johnny
adopted. TLS 649

007167   LET BE. London: Methuen, [1916] BMC NUC.

TLS-Study of an episode in the life of a well matched
couple. his infidelity.
LBKM Study of an episode in the life of a well matched
couple.

007168   LOVE AND MY LADY. London: Holden and
Hardingham, [1913] BMC.

Heroine writes in 1st person; concerns Emperor of
Medovia and similar personages. ATH

007169   THE MARAUDERS. London: Mascot Novels,
[1917] BMC.

007170   MIDDLE LIFE. London: Holden & Hardingham,
[1915] BMC.

Middle-aged heroine with sense of humor, Anne-Marie
Dasant (42) candid, sensible, shrewd personality.
Romance comes to her. But the author "makes no trite
or facile appeals to sentiment." TLS

007171   MISFITS. London: Skeffington, [1920] BMC.

TLS-Love
ATH-Spinster endowed with beauty, charm and ability
dissuades women from mrg., arousing in them serious
views of life. Heroine has thrown over three fiances
at her instigation, is in turn jilted. From this
experience, oddly enough, she learns to set a fairer
value on male sex in general and her underrated pa in
particular.

007172   ONE WOMAN'S HERO. London: Methuen, 1917
BMC NUC.

Letters from wife of soldier to her woman friend. Her
life and feelings during past 18 months of war TLS

007173   THE SHORELESS SEA. A NOVEL. London:
Holden and Hardingham, 1912 BMC.

TLS A man and his 2nd wife on their honeymoon meet his
first wife and her lover. The lover makes love to
second wife and first wife gets engaged to second
wife's father.
ATH-a man and his second wife on their honeymoon meet
his first wife and her lover. The lover makes love to
second wife and first wife gets engaged to second
wife's father.

007174   THE SINS OF THE CHILDREN. London: Holden
& Hardingham, [1918] BMC.

TLS-Edith, pregnant, asks Adolph, a German, to marry
her. Refuses, Joe strikes him and he falls over a
cliff. He doesn't like Edith, but she threatens etc
and he marries her. Adolph hadn't really died and
shows up years later to wreak vengeance.

LETTS, W. M. See LETTS, WINIFRED M.

LETTS, WINIFRED M. B. 1882. United Kingdom.

    007175   CHRISTINA'S SON. London: Gardner, [1915]
NUC BMC.

    Chr. marries a man she liked not loved, became "a
common place woman, a unit in that vast army of sober
matrons" Her maternal passion centered on son, his
mrg. shipwrecked, trag. involved. ATH
SP-He marries a heartless woman who neglects, deserts
and drives him to an untimely end. Symp. study of
parents and children. She had artistic leanings but
trad brought her to mrg. with older man who soon dies,
leaving her without means.

    007176   DIANA DETHRONED. BY W. M. LETTS. London:
J. Lane, 1909 BMC NUC.

    Frank, naive, devoted to routine, incapable of real
love, engagement ends disastrously, marries cousin,
baby dies, husband becomes an addict. Then her heart
awakens 6-26-09 PW

    007177   THE ROUGH WAY. BY W. M. LETTS. London: W.
Gardner, Darton, [1913] NUC BMC. Milwaukee: Young
Churchman Co., [1913?] NUC.

    ATH male hero who is tempted
"Story of a man who hesitates at the cross-roads of
life, shall he choose the easy, pleasant way, or the
rougher, lonelier way of duty? Inclination and his
love for an actress, a frank hedonist, turn him toward
the primrose path, but circumstances bar that road,
and he follows the stonier, finding happiness in the
journey." PW

LEVERSON, ADA. 1865-1933. United Kingdom.

    007178   BIRD OF PARADISE. London: G. Richards,
1914 BMC. New York: W. W. Norton, [1952] NUC.

    LBKM- 6 heroes and heroines
ATH Ends in almost perfect happiness of three married
couples.

    007179   THE LIMIT. London: G. Richards, [1911]
BMC NUC.

    An actress and a poet-two women minor chars? TLS
Whole book concerns a timid husband a wife and other
man (artist) Wife and artist think they love each
other till he "said the wrong thing" and wife stays on
with husband. ? LBKM

    007180   LOVE AT SECOND SIGHT. London: Chapman &
Hall, 1916 BMC.

    TLS-- Nothing here.
ATH O
SP-- 0

    007181   LOVE'S SHADOW. London: Richards, 1908
BMC.

    TLS-- 0
ACAD--frothy love story.
ATH--Leverson "after her own fashion is a feminist and
seldom gives her sex the worst of the situation.
Egotisms and fidgetiness in their more masc.
manifestations engage her and she describes them, if
anything, a little too well."
SP--a satire.

    007182   TENTERHOOKS. London: G. Richards, [1912]
BMC NUC.

    ATH offered fullness of life for which she hungers,
wife rejects it because it would mean degradation of
fool she has married.
TLS a greater ass than he was in "love's shadow"
SP-She is tied to an insufferably fatuous and errant
husb.

    007183   THE TWELFTH HOUR. London: E. G. Richards,
1907 BMC NUC.

    LBKM 8-07,180

A comedy of manners TLS
More or less decorous flirtations of married women ATH

LE VOLEUR, pseud. See CAREY, ROSA NOUCHETTE.

LEWALD, FANNY. See STAHR, FANNY LEWALD.

LEWIS, CATHERINE GASQUOINE (HARTLEY) GALLICHAN. 1867-1928.

    007184   LIFE THE MODELLER. London: J. Macqueen,
1899 BMC.

    Mary Braithwaite-well educated daughter of rich
shopkeeper. Heroine Margaret Harvey's love affairs. SP
82:917

    007185   THE WEAVER'S SHUTTLE. BY C. GASCOIGNE
HARTLEY. London: Greening, 1905 BMC.

LEWIS, ELIZABETH PORTIA (GOODSON). United States.

    007186   LORENZO OF SARZANA. Boston: R. G. Badger,
1907 NUC.

    Boston girl goes to Italy to study painting; Mary
Mortimer a painter and Marguerite her companion; Mary
learns the man she loves is married, but also
discovers she loves another BKM

LEWIS, EMILY GWYNNE.

    007187   AS ONE FLESH. London: J. Ouseley, 1909
BMC.

    An impetuous young woman marries a man knowing of his
past, suspects he's unfaithful, runs off, earns her
living in America and England, finally marries the
man's brother. TLS

    007188   GRAHAM GARTHMORE, VICAR. London: Murray
and Evenden, [1913] BMC.

    Religious tale ATH

    007189   TEMPORARY INSANITY. London: Murray and
Evenden, [1913] BMC.

    "a feminine Jekyll and Hyde." heroine cuts her
husband's throat because he got drunk and tried to
kiss her. Marries again. Author sympathetic-there is
no responsibility for murder when murderer is not
sane. The changes in the heroine's temperament are
rapid and startling. ACAD
Goes through series of shocks that cause her to
remember. Then one shock brings oblivion. Meantime she
remarries, gets a fortune and a title. ATH

LEWIS, GLADYS ADELINA.

    007190   GEORGES LEWYS' THE "CHARMED AMERICAN"
(FRANCOIS L'AMERICAIN) A STORY OF THE IRON DIVISION OF
FRANCE. New York: J. Lane, 1919 NUC.

    "These notes from the trenches were written by
Francois Xavier, a naturalized American, but a native
of France from the Alsatian border. He had served his
military term in the Iron division of France and was
"gruelled, sinewed and hardened" in the practice of
arms before he came to America and became a citizen.
When the war broke out he became once more a French
patriot, returned to his division, and for thirty-two
months was in the thick of the struggle bearing a
charmed life and returning unscathed to his wife and
two children in San Francisco, decorated with the
Croix de guerre. The notes present such a story of
"the horrible realities of war," that the publishers
deferred their publication till the return of our own
troops. The translator vouches for the absolute
truthfulness and the writer himself says at the end:
"Every word in those notes of mine is true, so help me
Heaven! and any one having cause to doubt has never
been on the front. War is not a pleasure, or a
necessity,-it is a curse." BRD, 1919.

LEWIS, HARRIET NEWELL (O'BRIEN). 1841-1878. United States.

    007191   BEATRIX ROHAN: A NOVEL. New York: R.
Bonner's Sons, 1892 NUC.

    PW-guardian holds ward prisoner to gain her fortune.
Her escape and subsequent adventures.

    007192   CECIL ROSS; A SEQUEL TO EDITH TREVOR'S
SECRET. New York: R. Bonner's Sons, 1892 NUC.

    PW-Cecil disappeared in 1st novel, is now discovered

and sensational facts of her imprisonment revealed.
Lady Edith is seen at a disadvantage and her secret
disclosed.

007193   EDITH TREVOR'S SECRET: A NOVEL. New York:
R. Bonner's Sons, 1892 NUC.

PW-her machinations after she is widowed from
ill-judged marriage.

007194   GUY TRESILLIAN'S FATE: A SEQUEL TO
TRESILLIAN COURT. New York: R. Bonner's Sons, 1893
NUC.

After the wreck in Sicilian waters and the robbing of
his birthright by Jasper Lowder. Sensational
consequences under which Lowder is revealed. PW
7-29-93

007195   THE HAUNTED HUSBAND: A NOVEL. New York:
R. Bonner's Sons, 1893 NUC.

Sylvia Monk hates Bernice, the wife of her former
betrothed. She visits an Indian ayah and concocts a
plot against Bernice. Counterplotting by Bernice's
stepbrother brings strange issues-like spectral
visitation. PW 1-14-93

007196   NEVA'S THREE LOVERS: A NOVEL. New York:
R. Bonner's Sons, [c1892] NUC.

PW-Octavia, an adventuress marries wealthy widower who
is called to India shortly after wedding. She has
scheme for gaining control of his wealth;
complications.

007197   TRESILLIAN COURT. New York: R. Bonner's
Sons, 1893 NUC.

Two men look alike. Story of an impersonation for an
inheritance. PW 7-15-93

LEWIS, MARTHA LEWIS (BECKWITH) EWELL. 1841-1902. United
States.

007198   TWICE TRIED; OR, ASA WARREN'S METAL.
Philadelphia: Silver-line Pub. Co., [c1899] NUC.

007199   THE WIFE'S VOW. Philadelphia: W. S.
Fortescue, [c1895] NUC.

PW-4-18-96. two murders, committed by poison, are the
leading events in a story of New York. A young man
just married is suspected of poisoning his mother; he
flees the city and is a wanderer for a few years
before his innocence is discovered. Maria, an Italian
servant, is the culprit.

LEWIS, MARY H. MILTON.

007200   CHARRED WOOD. London: Heath, Cranton,
[1916] BMC.

LEWYS, GEORGES, pseud. See LEWIS, GLADYS ADELINA.

LEYLAND, MARIE LOUISE (MACK) CREED. 1874-1935. Australia.

007201   ATTRACTION. BY LOUISE MACK. London: Mills
and Boon, [1913] BMC NUC.

Ambitions, self-confident aggressive male. ATH.
A masterful man subdues Teresa Martindale, wins and
keeps her love through poverty to success. TLS

007202   AN AUSTRALIAN GIRL IN LONDON. BY LOUISE
MACK. London: T. F. Unwin, 1902 BMC NUC.

007203   CHILDREN OF THE SUN. BY LOUISE MACK.
London: A. Melrose, [1906] BMC.

TLS--Trad. love story.

007204   GIRLS TOGETHER. BY LOUISE MACK (MRS. J.
PERCY CREED). London: Pilgrim Press, [1903] NUC.

007205   THE HOUSE OF DAFFODILS. London: Mills and
Boon, 1914 BMC.

Mary Houghton's harmless sentimental story. TLS
Nothing new. ACAD.

007206   IN A WHITE PALACE. London: Rivers, 1910
BMC.

TLS--woman falsely charged and sent to prison
impersonates another and gets job as secretary to man

who convicted her--he's blind. Eventually marry and he
discovers her innocence and recovers his sight.

007207   THE MARRIAGE OF EDWARD. BY LOUISE MACK.
London: Mills and Boon, [1913] BMC NUC.

Loveless marriage for money of a woman to a much older
man she hardly knows--who fall in love. ATH
Sprightly communications from a literary young woman
in London. TLS

007208   THE MUSIC MAKERS; THE LOVE STORY OF A
WOMAN COMPOSER. BY LOUISE MACK. London: Mills and
Boon, [1914] BMC NUC.

ATH--established and successful woman composer
produces friend's opera. Through misunderstanding he
thinks she has tried to claim it as hers. All cleared
up.

007209   THE RED ROSE OF A SUMMER. BY LOUISE MACK.
London: Rivers, 1909 BMC NUC.

Venice love story. TLS
Young widow's friendship-turned love with a youth she
calls Boy.

007210   THE ROMANCE OF A WOMAN OF THIRTY. BY
LOUISE MACK. London: A. Rivers, 1911 NUC.

Alec is 5 yrs. younger than Daisy Underdown, widow.
She tells the story. TLS
Study of a woman who confesses to a passion for
romance. "Subjective study of the working of a woman's
mind." Ultimately makes a choice, gives her hand to
the man who most needs her care. "A slight story" LBKM

007211   TEENS, A STORY OF AUSTRALIAN SCHOOLGIRLS.
BY LOUISE MACK (MRS. J. PERCY CREED). London: A.
Melrose, [1903] NUC BMC.

007212   THEODORA'S HUSBAND. London: A. Rivers,
1909 BMC.

Theo. penniless married Sir George. Falls out of love,
secret meetings with an inventor of an airship. PW
SR--former lover shows up at bad time forcing her to
keep secrets. There is a female troublemaker. Results
are flight for the young wife, imprisonment for the
husband.
She loves an aviator though she's married. The
problems clear up. TLS

007213   WIFE TO PETER. BY LOUISE MACK. London: A.
Rivers, 1911 BMC NUC.

007214   THE WORLD IS ROUND. BY LOUISE MACK.
London: T. F. Unwin, 1896 BMC.

SR Book is better than its cover (Little Novel Series)
ACAD 50:96. Jean, a writer, and her two lovers.

LIBBEY, LAURA JEAN. 1862-1924. United States.

007215   THE ALPHABET OF LOVE: A THRILLING
ROMANCE. New York: N. L. Munro, 1892 NUC. London:
Aldinde, [1896] BMC.

007216   THE BEAUTIFUL COQUETTE; OR, THE LOVE THAT
WON HER. New York: N. L. Munro, 1892 NUC.

007217   THE CRIME OF HALLOW-E'EN; OR, THE HEIRESS
OF GRAYSTONE HALL. A THRILLING LOVE STORY. New York:
J. B. Ogilvie, 1891 NUC.

007218   DAISY GORDON'S FOLLY; OR, THE WORLD LOST
FOR LOVE'S SAKE. New York: N. L. Munro, 1892 NUC.
London: Aldine, 1896 BMC.

007219   DORA MILLER; OR, A YOUNG GIRL'S LOVE AND
PRIDE. New York: N. L. Munro, 1892 NUC.

007220   FLORABELL'S LOVER; OR, RIVAL BELLES. A
NOVEL. New York: R. Bonner's Sons, 1892 NUC.

CR 17:314. Traditional romance.
PW-misunderstandings after the wedding

007221   HE LOVED BUT WAS LURED AWAY. New York: J.
S. Ogilvie, 1891 NUC.

007222   LITTLE LEAFY, THE CLOAKMAKER'S BEAUTIFUL
DAUGHTER: A ROMANTIC STORY OF A LOVELY WORKING-GIRL IN
THE CITY OF NEW YORK. New York: N. L. Munro, 1891 NUC.

007223   LITTLE RUBY'S RIVAL LOVERS; OR, A CRUEL

REVENGE. New York: N. L. Munro, 1892 W.

007224 LYNDALL'S TEMPTATION; OR, BLINDED BY
LOVE. A STORY OF FASHIONABLE LIFE AT LENOX. New York:
N. L. Munro, 1892 NUC.

007225 A MASTER WORKMAN'S OATH; OR, CORALIE THE
UNFORTUNATE. A LOVE STORY PORTRAYING THE LIFE,
ROMANCE, AND STRANGE FATE OF A BEAUTIFUL NEW YORK
WORKING-GIRL. New York: J. S. Ogilvie, 1892 NUC.

007226 OLIVE'S COURTSHIP: A NOVEL. New York:
American News, 1892.

007227 ONLY A MECHANIC'S DAUGHTER: A CHARMING
LOVE STORY OF LOVE AND PASSION. New York: N. L. Munro,
1892 NUC.

007228 WE PARTED AT THE ALTAR: A NOVEL. New
York: R. Bonner's Sons, 1892 NUC.

PW-Frederick marries Doris for a motive other than
love. She learns truth after wedding but
"circumstances" separate them. Years later they meet;
he is engaged to another; she reveals her identity.

007229 WHEN LOVELY MAIDEN STOOPS TO FOLLY; OR,
'WHEN LOVELY WOMAN STOOPS TO FOLLY.' A NOVEL. New
York: American News, [c1896] NUC.

LICHTENSTEIN, JOY. B. 1874. United States.

007230 FOR THE BLUE AND GOLD; A TALE OF LIFE AT
THE UNIVERSITY OF CALIFORNIA. San Francisco: A. M.
Robertson, 1901 NUC.

LILJENCRANTZ, OTTILIA ADELINA. 1876-1910. United States.

007231 RANDVAR THE SONGSMITH; A ROMANCE OF
NORUMBEGA. New York and London: Harper, 1906 NUC BMC.

America-Desc. & explor-Norse-Fiction
PW myth and hist. rom.

007232 THE THRALL OF LEIF THE LUCKY; A STORY OF
VIKING DAYS. London: C. F. Cazenove, 1902 BMC.
Chicago: A. C. McClurg, 1902 NUC.

Am-Desc & explor-Norse-fiction

007233 THE VINLAND CHAMPIONS. New York: D.
Appleton, 1904 NUC BMC. London: Ward, Lock, 1905 BMC.

007234 THE WARD OF KING CANUTE; A ROMANCE OF THE
DANISH CONQUEST. Chicago: A. C. McClurg, 1903 NUC.
London: Ward, Lock, 1904 BMC NUC.

Canute, the great, king of Eng. and Denmark, 995-1035
woman disguised. becomes Canute's page, goes into
battle with him, saves his life, is wounded, in the
end sees justice done for her father's murder and
marries. NYT 03,324

LILLIE, LUCY CECIL (WHITE). B. 1855. United States.

007235 A FAMILY DILEMMA: A STORY FOR GIRLS.
Philadelphia: Porter and Coates, [c1894] NUC.

LW 25:470. Inheritance problem, between two women,
both fine characters. Fortune is used by Jean in
founding a model academy.

007236 FOR HONOR'S SAKE: A SEQUEL TO "THE
SQUIRE'S DAUGHTER". Philadelphia: Porter and Coates,
[c1891] NUC.

LW 23:26. Sequel to the Squire's Daughter. Dolly Kent,
the heroine is constantly imposed on, even to the
extent of initially refusing the man she loves because
it's possible her cousin loves him. Story concludes
with her married and in possession of a fortune.

007237 A GIRL'S ORDEAL. Philadelphia: H. T.
Coates, 1897 NUC.

LW 29:102 Sensational. Too many characters, not true
to life, too complicated.
Constance Reade is made to feel she's a burden to her
father and her step-mother. She therefore goes to live
as a companion to a wealthy young woman her own age.
PW 52:673

007238 PHIL AND THE BABY, AND FALSE WITNESS: TWO
STORIES. New York: Harper, 1891 NUC.

Phil and baby in a traveling show, separated reunited;

PW 3-28-91.
False witness: evil results of careless speech. LW

LINCOLN, JEANIE THOMAS (GOULD). 1846-1921. United States.

007239 A JAVELIN OF FATE. Boston: Houghton,
Mifflin, 1905 BMC NUC.

Widow wants to revenge herself vs. man who once
deserted her. PW 12-2-05

007240 THE LUCK OF RATHCOOLE: BEING THE ROMANTIC
ADVENTURES OF MISTRESS FAITH WOLCOTT (SOMETIMES KNOWN
AS "MISS MOPPET") DURING HER SOJOURN IN NEW YORK AT AN
EARLY PERIOD OF THE REPUBLIC. Boston:
Houghton-Mifflin, 1912 NUC. London: Constable, 1912
BMC.

PW-love story.
TLS-love story.

007241 A PRETTY TORY: BEING A ROMANCE OF
PARTISAN WARFARE DURING THE WAR OF INDEPENDENCE IN THE
PROVINCES OF GEORGIA AND SOUTH CAROLINA, RELATING TO
MISTRESS GERALDINE MONCRIFFE. Boston and New York:
Houghton, Mifflin, 1899 NUC.

Savannah 1780-81. Two men in love with the pretty
Tory. PW 56:1159
CR 36:182. Historical romance. American Revolution.
Geraldine saves her lover from destruction.

007242 AN UNWILLING MAID: BEING THE HISTORY OF
CERTAIN EPISODES DURING THE AMERICAN REVOLUTION IN THE
EARLY LIFE OF MISTRESS BETTY YORKE, BORN WOLCOTT.
Boston: Houghton, Mifflin, 1897 NUC.

LINCOLN, MAY, pseud. See BROUGHTON, IDA MAY (LINKINS).

LINCOLN, NATALIE SUMNER. 1881-1935. United States.

007243 C.O.D. New York and London: D. Appleton,
1915 NUC BMC.

Mystery-murder PW 4-3-15
Detective-trad. NYT

007244 I SPY. New York and London: D. Appleton,
1916 BMC NUC.

Mystery story PW Spy story NYT

007245 THE LOST DESPATCH. New York and London:
D. Appleton, 1913 BMC NUC.

Civil war, Nancy Newton, a spy for confederate Army, a
love affair with a union officer complicates the plot.
She disguises self as union trooper. meets a union
secret agent, knocks him down with butt of revolver,
escapes. Later she's arrested at a ball, found guilty,
but Lincoln pardons her. She knows telegraphy NYT
"A story constructed with Washington as the central
locus, and with the web of circumstance weaving itself
around Miss Nancy Newton, a rebel spy who falls into
danger through the strange disappearance of an
important despatch. Miss Newton, made to swear
allegiance to the Confederacy by her dying father,
acts as a bearer of secret information to Richmond.
Loved by a Union officer, Major Robert Goddard, she
finds herself in a distressing predicament upon her
arrest under the double and sinister charge of treason
and murder." BRD

007246 THE MAN INSIDE. New York and London: D.
Appleton, 1914 BMC NUC.

PW 85 3/21/14:1022 "Cynthia Carew, one of the most
popular belles of Washington, returning home from a
ball discovers to her horror that she is not the sole
occupant of the family carriage, but that huddled in
the corner of the seat is the dead body of her uncle,
Senator James Carew. Washington is in a ferment of
excitement over this mysterious murder. Efforts of the
detectives to discover who killed Carew disclose an
international intrigue involving Japan, Panama,
Columbia and the United States. Story is one of
thrills, and the mystery is not solved until the very
end of the book."

007247 THE MOVING FINGER. New York and London:
D. Appleton, 1918 BMC NUC.

PW-Murd myst, Secret Service. baffled, who solves
mystery?
NYT-Sick man, Bruce Brainerd, is murdered. Vera Deane,
a trained nurse, who is taking care of him is one of

the suspects.

007248　　　THE NAMELESS MAN. New York and London: D.
Appleton, 1917 BMC NUC.

Murder mystery Trad LBK
Detective NYT

007249　　　THE OFFICIAL CHAPERON. New York and
London: D. Appleton, 1915 BMC NUC.

About a missing necklace PW 9-25-15
Mrs. Calderon Fordyce injured in railroad accident is
hunchbacked. Can't chaperone her daughter around soc,
hires Marjorie Langdon 24. But thefts lead to her
dismissal. Her honesty proven in the end. NYT

007250　　　THE RED SEAL. New York and London: D.
Appleton, 1920 BMC NUC.

PW Soc life and crime
NYT 4/11/20 Barbara Macintyre has been burglarized;
suspect falls dead in court, it is revealed that he is
actually her fiance in disguise, she demands an
autopsy.

007251　　　THE THREE STRINGS. New York and London:
D. Appleton, 1918 BMC NUC.

PW murd myst
NYT Dec 29 18 p582. Evelyn Preston finds a dead
stranger in her parlor.

007252　　　THE TREVOR CASE. New York and London: D.
Appleton, 1912 BMC NUC.

PW mur. mys.
TLS Mur mys.
ATH mur mys.

LINDEN, ANNIE. Nationality Unknown.

007253　　　GOLD: A DUTCH INDIAN STORY FOR ENGLISH
PEOPLE. London: J. Lane, 1896 BMC. New York: Century,
1896 NUC.

SR-"hilarious realism." For example, uncle with coarse
underlip, blue and wet, on many chins etc. "And after
this we have to stand by while he of the underlipped
makes love to the dainty heroine, as uncles, it
appears, are encouraged to do in Holland." Adventures
for gold mixed with supernatural. Accounts of ordinary
Dutch.
ATH 108:189. Tale of adventure. Contains incident of
deserted Malay girl who hearing the carriage of a
European drive past with new bride flung her baby
against the wall. It fell dead and she was never sane
again. Dutch East Indies. Heroine organizes a rescue
party and saves hero who has been lost searching for
gold.
ACAD 50:219 "Abundance of reference to illicit
intercourse between European men and native women."
BKM 4:370
Dutch East India, Java. The relations of Dutch to
native women, endless murders. Jan Van Reimskerk's
search for gold. CR 26,30:58.
The search leads to death or madness for the crew, Jan
escaping by the skin of his teeth. LW 28:43

007254　　　A WOMAN OF SENTIMENT. London: Methuen,
1904 BMC.

TLS-disillusioned wife in fash. social world of
Holland. Married to unfaithful husband tries to
convert him to her concept of love, fails; plays then
at flirtation and finds herself in love, finally and
unhappily after much struggle remains with husband

LINDSAY, CAROLINE BLANCHE ELIZABETH (FITZROY). 1844-1912.
United Kingdom.

007255　　　BERTHA'S EARL: A NOVEL. London: R.
Bentley, 1891 NUC BMC.

Bertha Millings supports herself and her sister by
painting. The Earl she marries is undemonstrative
about his love and rather "stupid." SP 66 896
(she's of "low-birth.") Their marriage is full of
trouble partly because of husband's personality,
partly because of his sister's interference. A good
duchess sets things right. ACAD
Sentimental ATH 97 696
The Earl is a dry stick and the wrong side of 50. An
anonomyous letter about a young doctor interested in
Bertha also brings problems. SR 6-6-91, 688

007256　　　A TANGLED WEB. London: A. and C. Black,
1892 BMC.

LBKM 3:92. Lady Grissel is bored with her castle in
Scotland and in revolt against arranged betrothal to
her cousin so escapes to London and lives under name
of Marjory Smith, from Australia. Meets cousin, they
fall in love.
ATH 100:660.
ACAD romance

LINLEY, LAURA.

007257　　　OUT OF THE VORTEX: THE TRUE RECORD OF A
FIGHT FOR A SOUL. London: K. Paul, 1916 BMC.

LINTON, E. LYNN. See LINTON, ELIZABETH (LYNN).

LINTON, ELIZABETH (LYNN). 1822-1898. United Kingdom.

007258　　　DULCIE EVERTON. BY E. LYNN LINTON.
London: Chatto and Windus, 1896 NUC BMC.

ATH 108:447. Country lives and squirearchy. Portrayal
of idealized society. Dulcie's husband tempted by
adventures but finally rewon.

007259　　　IN HASTE AND AT LEISURE; A NOVEL. London:
W. Heinemann, 1895 BMC.

Attacks "members of the Pioneer club and other
propagandistic feminine clubs" as "centers of social
and moral contamination" Phoebe Barrington marries at
16 after running away from home. Husband is 17-parents
ship him off to Africa. Phoebe attracted to Excelsior
club where she's transformed into "a fiend of a
woman"-A grotesque New Woman. Author "over-shoots her
mark." "This is a pity for the new developments of
militant femininity provide material for good satire;
and unfortunately the book consists not of satire but
of clumsy invective." SP 74:584
Heroine involved in fem. activities of Excelsior club
where women "united on great question of the
diabolical nature of husband, the degrading
institution of marriage, the shameful burden of
matrimony, women's claims to be a county Councillor, a
voter, a lawyer a judge, an M.P." Neglects her child,
destroys husband's love almost wrecks marriage
BKM2:531. Satire, weird exaggerations. Author "revels
in their depravities."

007260　　　THE NEW WOMAN; IN HASTE AND AT LEISURE.
BY E. LYNN LINTON. New York: Merriam, [c1895] NUC.

007261　　　THE ONE TOO MANY. BY E. LYNN LINTON.
London: Chatto and Windus, 1894 BMC. Chicago: F. T.
Neely, 1894 NUC.

SP 72:443. Dedicated to "the sweet girls still left
among us who have no part in the new revolt, but are
content to be dutiful, innocent, and sheltered."
Portrays graduates of women's colleges as smokers,
drinkers, and flirts. "There ought to be exultation in
Girton, Newnham, and Holloway over the self-inflicted
defeat of so doughty an assailant as Mrs. Lynn
Linton."
ATH 103:342.

007262　　　THE SECOND YOUTH OF THEODORA DESANGES. BY
MRS. LYNN LINTON. London: Hutchinson, 1900 BMC NUC.

LINTON, MRS. LYNN. See LINTON, ELIZABETH (LYNN).

LIPPINCOTT, SARA JANE (CLARKE). 1823-1904. United States.

007263　　　STORIES AND SKETCHES. BY GRACE GREENWOOD.
New York: Tait, [c1892] NUC.

Short stories.

LIPPMANN, JULIA MATHILDE. 1864-1952. United States.

007264　　　"BURKESES AMY". New York: H. Holt, 1915
NUC.

Young woman raised in wealthy circumstances decides
against travelling in Europe to work with father in
the thick of NY east side tenement district. NYT

007265　　　THE INTERLOPERS. Philadelphia: Penn, 1917
NUC.

007266　　　MAKING OVER MARTHA. New York: H. Holt,
1913 NUC.

PW 84 11/8/13:1530 "Martha is a big, kindly Irish

charwoman, with a generous fund of strength, common
sense, and good humor. When she arrives from New York
with her family in a New England village, her
neighbors all take a hand at "Making over Martha" to
the New England pattern. But Martha, with her
competent meeting of every situation, unconsciously
"makes over" several of the villagers, and helps a
very pretty love affair to a satisfactory conclusion.
She is the same Martha of "Martha-by-the-day."

007267   THE MANNEQUIN. New York: Duffield, 1917
NUC.

Woman mistaken for a model, taken aboard ship--all
ends in pleasant romance. PW
Incredible plot--a dressmaker promises a mannequin to
a rich client for her son's amusement. Heroine is
kidnapped, put on yacht where she meets a man--love
follows. NYT 6-3-17 218

007268   MARTHA AND CUPID. New York: Holt, 1914
NUC.

PW 86 10/31/14:1403 "The "Martha" of author's previous
novels marries in this one. As Mrs. Slawson she looks
at family life through those shrewd, wise, kindly eyes
that see so much--and yet see so little of gloom.
Children come to Martha and one of them, a daughter is
wayward, but Cora's baby sets matters right.
NYT 1914:504. "Big, loveable Irish woman."

007269   MARTHA BY-THE-DAY. New York: H. Holt,
1912 NUC. London: G. Richards, 1913 BMC.

PW-romance of a governess.
NYT-conventional theme (love story) and unusual
character (Martha, who controls plot)
Motherly Irish charwoman, saves friendless girl from
being run over, promotes her marriage, "homely
philosophy." ATH
Martha Slawson does laundry work.

LISLE, DAVID, pseud. See WARDELL, MRS. VILLIERS.

LISTER, EDITH.

007270   ON STRONGER WINGS. London: Cassell, 1893
BMC.

English life. Artist unjustly deprived of estates,
gets them in the end. He's Herbert Vernay. Also love
interest: Maude Melville. ACAD 44:412.

LITCHFIELD, GRACE DENIO. 1849-1944. United States.

007271   THE BURNING QUESTION. New York and
London: G. P. Putnam's Sons, 1913 BMC NUC.

London A runaway wife; leaves baby daughter too;
yearns to be a great violinist. Husband pursues her;
she has her maid tell him she's dead. At very end
resurrected for happy close. ATH

007272   IN THE CRUCIBLE. New York, London: G. P.
Putnam's Sons, 1897 NUC BMC.

Young woman marries wrong man because Mr. Right thinks
himself a murderer. Truth comes out. The husband is
the guilty one but the couple resolve to be quiet and
good. Eventually the way is cleared by the husband's
suicide. SR 84:299.
A good young man and a bad young man both love the
beauty. The good one blamed for the crime done by the
bad one. Also an earthquake LBM 12:129.
She is Leigh Cameron. Doesn't marry man she loves
because she believes he's involved in a crime. Is
lonely and miserable, marries, by chance, the real
criminal while still loving #1. Then she is in the
crucible-her joyless, loveless life with a man she
can't love or respect. Learns sympathy and charity
from the ordeal. CR 26, 30:354.
SP 80:313. Leigh, Washington social belle, marries the
wrong man because he has gained an advantage over
another. An earth-quake straightens everything out.

007273   THE LETTER D. New York: Dodd, Mead, 1904
NUC.

PW-rivalry over a woman BKM 20 1904

007274   THE MOVING FINGER WRITES. New York and
London: G. P. Putnam's Sons, 1900 NUC.

Conversations between Mr. Alden and sister-in-law
heroine loves an insane man? Suicide. CR, 1901.
PW-Agnes, heroine, constant companion to classics

father. By chance picks up a book of modern poetry,
then meets the poet. Agnes' influence on his loving,
selfish, unreliable, and jealous wife. Tragic climax
arising from secret in the life of the poet.

007275   THE SUPREME GIFT. Boston: Little, Brown,
1908 NUC.

"The news of her father's bankruptcy is carried to
Joan Kildon while she is attending a fashionable
reception in Washington. Not only is all his own money
involved, but the savings of many poor people, which
had been intrusted to him and on which he had paid
large interests. Out of pity for the poor unfortunates
Joan pledges herself to pay off her father's debts.
She attempts to pawn a necklace, but is informed that
it is worthless, the diamonds having already been
removed by her father and replaced with paste. Some
relatives are killed in an automobile accident and Jan
is advised that she has come into a fortune which will
almost liquidate the debts. At the last moment she
discovers that this is not the case, but that her
cousin Archibald Hallam is the real heir. She tries to
persuade him to devote this to her father's cause,
which he promises to do provided she will marry him.
In order to accomplish her purpose she gives up the
man she really loves and promises to marry her cousin.
He finally relents and gives back her promise, but not
until it is too late. Joan dies before she and the man
whom she loves have been reunited." BKM v.27 1908.

LITTLE, ALICIA HELEN NEVA (BEWICKE). D. 1926. United
Kingdom.

007276   A MARRIAGE IN CHINA. BY MRS. ARCHIBALD
LITTLE (A. E. N. BEWICKE). London: W. Heinemann, 1899
NUC.

Much information about China. SP 82:312
Mr. Fortescue is a consul in China. He has two
children by a Chinese woman; when he's in England
falls for Miss Grey but leaves in order to avoid
entanglement. Later she comes to China to do
missionary work, they meet, he offers marriage. They
adopt the two children. The Chinese wife marries a
Portuguese. ATH 109:504

007277   A MILLIONAIRE'S COURTSHIP. London: T. F.
Unwin, 1906 BMC.

TLS-0
ATH-traditional love story.

007278   OUT IN CHINA! BY MRS. ARCHIBALD LITTLE.
London: A. Treherne, 1902 BMC NUC.

A novel <>.

LITTLE, FRANCES, pseud. See MACAULAY, FANNIE (CALDWELL).

LITTLE, M. See LITTLE, MAUDE.

LITTLE, MAUDE. United Kingdom.

007279   AT THE SIGN OF THE BURNING BUSH. BY M.
LITTLE. New York: H. Holt, 1910 NUC. London: Chatto &
Windus, 1910 BMC.

About three divinity students and the women that
influence their lives. PW, LBKM

007280   THE CHILDREN'S BREAD, A ROMANCE. London:
Chatto & Windus, 1912 BMC.

TLS-son seeks vengeance for mother's betrayal.
ATH-son seeks vengeance for mother's betrayal.

007281   THE ROSE-COLOURED ROOM. London & Toronto:
Sidgwick & Johnson, 1915 BMC. New York: Scribner's,
1915 NUC.

Straight story of a widow & three daughters and love.
PW 9-4-15
Glasgow. Man falls in love with married woman. Builds
a rose-coloured room in his house for her.
Work seems to focus upon him. NYT
And his failure at whatever he engages in. Another
character Grace Morland teacher of gymnastics. TLS

007282   A WOMAN ON THE THRESHOLD. London: Chatto
& Windus, 1911 BMC.

Theodosia heroine has two selves, one an aspiring
imaginative spirit of the rebel, the other timid and
conventional. The two men who love her embody these
antagonistic forces. ATH

The heroine writes a novel: the hero is herself,
rebellious vs commonplace domestic surroundings.
Theodosia suppresses her writing gift, marries a
conventional school master. Then she has a son who
lives the life she portrayed in her novel. Dosey
Haining's literary ambitions end with the marriage
bell. Her son fulfills in almost every particular the
actions fore ordained by his mother for the hero of
her unwritten novel. LBKM
Author is concerned with the artistic temperament.
Heroine is a woman of genius whose natural development
has been checked by circumstances. Domestic
occupations prevent her from writing. ATH

LITTLE, MRS. ARCHIBALD. See LITTLE, ALICIA HELEN NEVA
(BEWICKE).

LITVINOVA, IVY (LOW). United States.

007283   GROWING PAINS. A NOVEL. BY IVY LOW.
London: W. Heinemann, 1913 BMC NUC. New York: G. H.
Doran, 1913 NUC.

PW 5-31-13 1958 "Gertrude Wilson is the heroine, and
the book relates her development from childhood to
womanhood. Her questions and doubts, her schoolgirl
devotion to an older girl, her dreams of life,
seekings after their realization, and then the
awakening, when real love and happiness come. There is
much charm in the relation and the reader learns how
empty is existence without a definite object."
Gertrude has a "violent adoration for an elder girl"
ATH
"too frank and too outspoken" LBKM
"Primarily, this novel is a study of the development
of a soul from childhood to maturity. Incidentally it
gives an extraordinarily vivid picture of London
middle-class life...without father, mother, brother or
sister, and not in the least understood by the Aunt
Mary who gives her a home, the inevitable result is
that Gertrude seeks an outlet for the love she would
naturally have given her own people, in many
'unnatural' directions. Sacrifice to her means
sacrament. At the end of the story we leave her
radiantly happy." BRD

007284   THE QUESTING BEAST. London: M. Secker,
1914 BMC.

LBKM-Rachel Cohen is a typist whose landlady boards
her for nothing so she can write successful novels.
Reviewer calls her unlikeable and hints that her
emotional involvements are most interesting part of
book.
ATH 143:131. Study of a literary woman's temperament,
handling delicate subjects, Unconventional.
TLS 13:41 Rachael "frankly a female rake," "erotic
career," she ends up "comfortably as a successful
novelist at 27."

LIVESAY, JESSIE E.

007285   THE LITTLE TIN GODS. A NOVEL. London:
Hurst & Blackett, 1901 BMC.

007286   THE SHADE OF THE ACACIA. London: J. Long,
1907 BMC.

Life in a fox hunting county; man falls in love with
his best friend's wife. ACAD
All the women are half bad. Cynical gay old lady of
over 76. A jealous mean-souled, vulgar woman. Young
wife who "forces her husband's dearest friend to
become an adulterer."
"Repulsive" women. SR

007287   SINK RED SUN. London: Heath, Cranton &
Ouseley, [1914] BMC.

ATH-heroine for love of her sister administers poison
to her husband. Later, in remorse takes some herself,
finds it was harmless. India.
TLS-hysterical story.

007288   SONS OF THE BLOOD. London: F. V. White,
1910 BMC.

TLS-romantic melodrama.
ACAD-

LIVINGSTON, MRS. C. M. See ALDEN, ISABELLA (MACDONALD) AND
MARCIA (MACDONALD) LIVINGSTONE.

LIVINGSTONE, ALICE. Nationality Unknown.

007289   A SEALED BOOK. New York: R. F. Fenno,

[c1906] NUC. London: Ward, Lock, 1906 BMC.

Mystery-2-9-07 PW
Gloomy mystery. NYT
Woman marries secretly a man with a past: spends part
of her time with husband part at home as unmarried
daughter. Later her daughter grows up to be a musician
in the service of her pastor father?
ACAD-sensational intrigue. Conventional-heroine.
TLS-
ATH-

LIVINGSTONE, MARCIA MACDONALD, jt. au. See ALDEN, ISABELLA
(MACDONALD) AND MARCIA MACDONALD LIVINGSTONE.

LIVINGSTONE, MRS. C. M. See ALDEN, ISABELLA (MACDONALD) AND
MARCIA (MACDONALD) LIVINGSTONE.

LLOYD, ADELE TOWSON. United States.

007290   "AND NE'ER FORGET WILL I". Chicago:
Private printing, 1912 NUC.

LLOYD, AGNES EVANS.

007291   HEERA SINGH. A SEQUEL TO "THE SQUIRE'S
MANUSCRIPT". Chester: Phillipson and Golder, 1900 BMC.

007292   THE SQUIRE'S MANUSCRIPT: A TALE WITH A
PURPOSE. Chester: Phillipson and Golder, 1896 BMC.

LLOYD, BEATRIX DEMAREST. United States.

007293   THE PASTIME OF ETERNITY. New York: C.
Scribner's Sons, 1904 NUC.

PW-centered on a man.
NYT-grotesque characters.
BKM 1904-vulgar wife, husband and other woman have
artistic temperaments. Conventional morality would not
keep them apart, something else does.

LLOYD, EDITH M. J.

007294   WAS IT DESTINY? London: R. T. S., 1913
BMC.

Girl raised with two boys becomes a famous singer.
Becomes engaged to one admirer, really loves another.
The first killed in bob-sled accident.

LLOYD, THEODOSIA.

007295   INNOCENCE IN THE WILDERNESS; A ROMANCE.
London: Chatto & Windus, 1912 BMC.

TLS-story of man who does socialist writing, sister
works in settlement and another woman who becomes an
embroideress.
ATH-women stand out against shadowy background of men.
Woman develops character and powers in artistic and
journalistic world of London.
LBKM -0

LOANE, M. E.

007296   THE COMMON GROWTH. London: E. Arnold,
1911 BMC. New York: Longmans, Green, 1911 NUC. (BMC:
Essays on social subjects.)

Essays on social subjects.

007297   THE QUEEN'S POOR: LIFE AS THEY FIND IT IN
TOWN AND COUNTRY. New York: Longmans, Green, 1905 PW.
London: E. Arnold, 1905 BMC NUC.

Nurse's experience with English poor. PW 11-18-05.

LOCKE, GLADYS EDSON. B. 1887. United States.

007298   RONALD O' THE MOONS. Boston: Four Seas,
1919 NUC.

007299   THAT AFFAIR AT PORTSTEAD MANOR. Boston:
Sherman, French, 1914 NUC.

PW 86 8/1/44:356 "The theft of a necklace is followed
by the murder of Lord Portstead. The recovery of the
necklace only adds to the mystery of the murder. Three
people are eager to shoulder the guilt, which
complicates the plot beyond the detectives' powers of
solution. Unknown to the others, the heroine has been
for years involved in unhappy circumstances. These
change at last, and she is not only able to tell the
truth about the crime, but to bring happiness to
herself and the others.

NYT-Woman detective solves crime; male guest who is student of Sherlock Holmes furnishes humor by his attempts."

LOCKE, SOPHIA MARY, pseud. See YOUNG, AMELIA SOPHIA COATES AND BLANCHE MARY LOFTUS TOTTENHAM.

LOCKETT, JEANNIE.

007300   JUDITH GRANT: A NOVEL. London: Hutchinson, 1892 BMC.

ATH 100:736. Romance. Middle-aged man jilted by one woman recovers and marries another. Marriage takes place "under very peculiar circumstances."
SR 74:716. He and 18 year old girl are suiciding in the same pool. They talk it over, marry, she gets an education, they fall in love.
She and Sir Robert Dene meet at Dead Man's Pool, both ready to drown themselves because they're unhappy. They marry in an unusual manner to save her reputation. Then they part for three years to meet again at the same spot. The point is to give life three more years of trial. When they meet, each is again ready to die, but this time in order to secure the happiness of the other. ACAD 43:32

LOCKETT, MARY F. Nationality Unknown.

007301   CHRISTOPHER. BY "THE PRINCESS". New York, London: Abbey Press, [1902] NUC.

LOCKHART, CAROLINE. B. 1875. United States.

007302   THE FIGHTING SHEPHERDESS. Boston: Small, Maynard, [1919] NUC BMC. London: Hodder & Stoughton, [1925] BMC.

"Struggle of a girl of low origin vs. the pettiness of a small town in the West." PW
Adopted by kind old scholar who later is murdered; Kate is suspected but then she triumphs over all. NYT

007303   THE FULL OF THE MOON. Philadelphia: J. B. Lippincott, 1914 BMC NUC.

ATH-American girl sees a bit of Texas before accepting hand of patient lover.
PW 3-14-14:966-"By author of "Me-Smith" etc. Romance of Nan, a fresh, warm-hearted Western girl. When Nan tires suddenly of her humdrum existence and wishes to see life, incidents both humorous and tragic follow quickly. She soon learns the bitter taste of life in the raw. Her adventurous spirit eventually leads her into an unpleasant complication, the climax of which is a tense and wholly unexpected scene. When she needs him most, she finds among her admirers the man to count on."

007304   THE LADY DOC. Philadelphia & London: J. B. Lippincott, 1912 NUC BMC.

A verbal war between two women involving scissors and a flowerpot. ACAD
PW-? graduate of a fake medical college, greedy and incompetent.
ATH-Charlatan-self aggrandizement.
NYT-Dr. Emma Harpe is thoroughly repulsive--no male author would dare present such a character.

007305   THE MAN FROM THE BITTER ROOTS. Philadelphia and London: J. B. Lippincott, 1915 BMC NUC.

Love, adventure, danger. 10-30-15 NYT
NYT-wholesome breezy Western.

007306   "ME-SMITH". Philadelphia and London: J. B. Lippincott, 1911 NUC BMC.

ATH-life on a Texas cattleranch.

LODGE, HARRIET (NEWELL). B. 1848. United States.

007307   A BIT OF FINESSE: A STORY OF FIFTY YEARS AGO. Indianapolis: Bowen-Merrill, 1894 NUC.

PW-Abigail's mother died in childbirth; reared by grandmother. Then father remarries and she goes to a new home.
Gail Raymor's mother died when Gail was an infant, raised by Grandma. Moves to a city in Ohio Valley, meets Chester Nevelle, a manufacturer. A designing woman--Laura Winthrop--tries to break them up with a bit of finesse and would have succeeded if it were not for a parrot. LW 26:251

LODGE, MRS.

007308   THE DARINGFORDS: A NOVEL. London: Digby, Long, 1900 BMC.

007309   DAVID PALMERE. A NOVEL. London: Digby, Long, 1900 BMC.

ACAD 58:410. Romance, wedding.

007310   THE MYSTERY OF BLOOMSBURY CRESCENT. London: Digby, Long, [1896] BMC.

SR-Crime story. Hypnotist is foiled and hero and heroine marry.
ACAD-Belated exponent of hypnotism and mesmerism.

007311   THE MYSTERY OF MONKSWOOD. London: Digby, Long, 1899 BMC.

Heroine loves a young man, then marries an old Peer and discovers the two are father and son. The Peer is jealous, carries her off to house where his first wife (that he believed dead) is masquerading as a ghost. The ghost stabs the heroine. SP 83:225

007312   THE RECTOR'S TEMPTATION. London: Digby, Long, 1902 BMC.

007313   A SON OF THE GODS. London: Digby, Long, 1898 BMC.

ACAD 53:660. Miss Dustan who at times felt her youth had been wasted and at others believed herself young, beautiful and irresistible.

LOGAN, BELLE V. 1864-1957. United States.

007314   HER SHATTERED IDOL. Chicago: Morrill, Higgins, [c1893] NUC.

LOGAN, SUSAN CONSTANCE.

007315   EVERYDAY LIFE. London: H. J. Drane, [1905] BMC.

LOHN, AGNETTE MIDGARDEN. United States.

007316   THE VOICE OF THE BIG FIRS. [St Paul]: [Printed by the Pioneer Co.], [c1918] NUC.

PW-adventure and loves of four young people among firs in Oregon.

LOMBARDI, CYNTHIA. See LOMBARDI, GEORGINA MARIE (RICHMOND).

LOMBARDI, GEORGINA MARIE (RICHMOND). D. 1942. United States.

007317   A CRY OF YOUTH. BY CYNTHIA LOMBARDI. New York and London: D. Appleton, 1920 BMC NUC.

TLS priest
PW young American woman living in Rome teaching and man pledged to monastic life. She takes job at castle of Belmontes, a myst., she never sees them.

LONG, FANNY F. 1859-1935. United States.

007318   BEN ABBOTT: A TEMPERANCE STORY. New York: Eaton and Mains, 1896 NUC.

PW 10-17-96. 18 yr. old hero fights intemperance in his own family, his older brother is inebriate.

LONG, GABRIELLE MARGARET VERE (CAMPBELL) COSTANZO. 1888-1952. United Kingdom.

007319   "BECAUSE OF THESE THINGS". BY MARJORIE BOWEN. London: Methuen & Co,, [1915] BMC NUC.

Man marries passionate Italian, carries her to Scotland. Kills her and son when he thinks she's unfaithful. TLS

007320   BLACK MAGIC. A TALE OF THE RISE AND FALL OF ANTICHRIST. London: Rivers, 1909 NUC BMC. New York: Hodder & Stoughton, [1913] NUC.

History of a refractory young nun Ursula and of a "effeminate and hysterical artist" Dirk and a diabolic Pope. The heroine robs, bribes the college of Cardinals, works to excommunicate the Emperor; story of witches, relics, violence "Pope Joan in Masquerade" TLS

007321   THE BURNING GLASS. BY MARJORIE BOWEN.
London: W. Collins sons,, [1918] NUC BMC. New York: E.
P. Dutton, [1920] NUC.

TLS Julie de Lespinasse is heroine.
PW-Hist. rom. about Julie de Lespinasse, celebrated
French wit and writer.
NYT Mar 21 '20 p1. Emphasis is on the clincial details
of comsumption, her agony.

007322   THE CARNIVAL OF FLORENCE. BY MARJORIE
BOWEN. London: Methuen, 1915 BMC. New York: E. P.
Dutton, 1915 NUC.

hist rom TLS
Major char: Madonna Aprilis-the conflict within her
between "the call of her blood" and the stern voice of
Savonarola. "storm-driven" TLS

007323   THE CHEATS; A ROMANTIC FANTASY. BY
MARJORIE BOWEN. London: W. Collins, Sons, [1920] BMC
NUC.

TLS hist. rom., male heroes

007324   DEFENDER OF THE FAITH. BY MARJORIE BOWEN.
London: Methuen, [1911] BMC NUC.

Hist rom about William and Mary. TLS

007325   THE GLEN O' WEEPING. London: Rivers, 1907
NUC BMC.

Hist. novel LBKM 6-07, 108
TLS: Massacre of Glenroe

007326   GOD AND THE KING. BY MARJORIE BOWEN.
London: Methuen, [1911] BMC NUC.

Rev. of 1688 TLS
Wm & Mary. ACAD
Sequel to Defender of the Faith. ATH
NYT- About William and Mary.
Hist novel SP.

007327   GOD'S PLAYTHINGS. BY MARJORIE BOWEN.
London: Smith, Elder, 1912 BMC NUC. (Tales)

Blood curdling episodes, " deathbed scenes of
repentant and non-repentant sinners and unfortunates"
like Don Juan, Lucrezia Borgia. ACAD
The execution of Madame du Barry. SP

007328   THE GOVERNOR OF ENGLAND. BY MARJORIE
BOWEN. London: Methuen, [1913] BMC NUC. New York: E.
P. Dutton, 1914 NUC.

Historical romance concerning Oliver Cromwell ACAD

007329   I WILL MAINTAIN. BY MARJORIE BOWEN.
London: Methuen, [1910] BMC NUC.

TLS- Struggle of Protestantism.
Netherlands- History
Historical romance NYT

007330   KINGS-AT-ARMS. BY MARJORIE BOWEN. London:
Methuen, [1918] BMC NUC. New York: Dutton, 1919 PW.

Historical romance set in Sweden PW
TLS historical, male hero.
Struggle between Karl of Sweden and Peter of Russia.
the women are the beautiful, high spirited Aurora,
mistress of the King and Katherina, camp follower who
becomes mistress then wife of Peter. NYT

007331   A KNIGHT OF SPAIN. BY MARJORIE BOWEN.
London: Methuen, [1913] NUC BMC.

Historical romance of Spain's Philip II and his half
brother Don Juan. Beautiful Juan deals with traitors,
loves passionately, rides away from each occasion. But
story gets gloomy. ATH, SR

007332   THE LEOPARD AND THE LILY. BY MARJORIE
BOWEN. New York: McClure, Phillips, 1907 NUC. London
and New York: Doubleday, Page, 1909 BMC NUC.

TLS-historical male hero.
SR historical male hero.
Brittany-Hist. Gilles de Bretayne 1425-50
BKM v. 30 1909-10- egoist? loves a married man.
Unbridled passions. Woman of fierce jealousy & pride
hist. PW 9-11-09
Heroine wants money and freedom, comes into a fortune

but made "to pay" in the end? Killed, trampled by
horse BKM, NYT

007333   LOVER'S KNOTS. BY MARJORIE BOWEN. London:
[Everett's Library], 1912 BMC.

007334   THE MASTER OF STAIR. BY MARJORIE BOWEN.
New York: McClure, Phillips, 1907 NUC.

Bloody historical advent 5-4-07 PW
Scotland-Hist
Stair, John, earl 1648-1707

007335   A MOMENT'S MADNESS. BY M. BOWEN. London:
Cassell, [1908] NUC.

007336   MR. MISFORTUNATE. BY MARJORIE BOWEN.
London: W. Collins, [c1919] BMC NUC.

Traditional historical romance TLS
Court life of Prince Charles. LBKM, SR
Romanticized version of life of young Pretender BAKER,
32, p. 69

007337   MR. WASHINGTON. BY MARJORIE BOWEN.
London: Methuen, [1915] BMC NUC.

About Revolutionary war. TLS

007338   PRINCE AND HERETIC. BY MARJORIE BOWEN.
London: Metheun, [1914] NUC BMC. New York: E.P.
Dutton, [1915] NUC.

LBKM-Historical romance, Philip of Spain and William
of Orange.
16th C. historical romance, review focuses on the
Prince. His wife is "deformed of temper and of face,"
but no more is said about her. NYT

007339   THE QUEST OF GLORY. BY MARJORIE BOWEN.
London: Metheun, [1911] NUC 1912 BMC. New York: E.P.
Dutton, 1912 NUC.

TLS- Male hero historical romance.
Concerns a Marquis of mid 18th who leaves rank of
nobility to write philosophy. NYT

007340   THE RAKE'S PROGRESS. BY MARJORIE BOWEN.
London: W. Rider, 1912 BMC.

007341   THE SOLDIER FROM VIRGINIA. BY MARJORIE
BOWEN. New York: D. Appleton, 1912 NUC BMC. London: T.
Nelson, [1925] BMC.

NYT-history G. Washington

007342   THE SWORD DECIDES! A CHRONICLE OF A QUEEN
IN THE DARK AGES: FOUNDED ON THE STORY OF GIOVANNA OF
NAPLES. BY MARJORIE BOWEN. New York: McClure, 1908
NUC. London: A. Rivers, 1908 BMC.

PW historical novel.
TLS chronicle of a Queen in the Dark Ages based on
Giovanna of Naples. Refuses to marry rightful heir and
declares herself queen. Later entices him to visit
her. He is strangled in her presence and flung from
her bedroom window. Fighting ensues Ludovic comes to
avenge, falls for Giovanna and until he "asserts his
manhood" plots continue. SR-Giovanna "thirsts for
powers, and resents the dominion of a husband." Author
insists she is charming but not passionate.
ATH- Rev. thinks her "ruin" is not "complete enough
for poetic justice"
traditional historical romance LBKM

007343   THE THIRD ESTATE. BY MARJORIE BOWEN.
London: Methuen, [1917] BMC NUC. New York: E.P.
Dutton, [1918] NUC.

Story of estates general 1789-91 BAKER 32, p. 69
PW-Hist-French Revolution Marquis marries Pelagie for
her fortune, runs off with her sister. Pelagie kills
herself and sister seeks protection of Italian
nobleman. Marquis marries in his own rank. POV?
NYT Sept 1, '18 p. 374. 0

007344   THE TWO CARNATIONS. BY MARJORIE BOWEN.
London: Canell, 1913 NUC BMC. New York: P.R. Reynolds,
1913 NUC.

Fr. Rev; heroine in love with a Frenchman, pursued by
an Englishman who wins her in the end. ATH
She narrowly escapes the guillotine TLS

007345   THE VIPER OF MILAN: A ROMANCE OF
LOMBARDY. BY MARJORIE BOWEN. New York: McClure-

Phillips, 1906 NUC. London: A. Rivers, 1906 NUC BMC.

PW- Historical romance.
NYT-author is 15 years old, no love, unhappy ending.?
ATH o
LBKM- Lombardi-Hist-fic

007346   "WILLIAM BY THE GRACE OF GOD--." BY
MARJORIE BOWEN. London: Methuen, [1916] BMC NUC. New
York: E.P. Dutton, [1917] NUC.

TLS- story of William of Orange.
Traditional historical romance. PW

LONG, HELEN BEECHER. United States.

007347   THE GIRL HE LEFT BEHIND. New York: G.
Sully, [c1918] NUC.

PW- man at war, secretary saves his business from
unscrupulous man.
WWI-fic

007348   HOW JANICE DAY WON. New York: Sully &
Kleinteich, [c1916] BMC NUC.

Janice in prohibition campaign believed a theft was
connected to drinking in town PW 90:8/19/16 p.568
NYT- Funny, not always intentionally. Janice reforms
town in which Lake View Inn had been granted a bar
license. She is a school girl.

007349   JANICE DAY. New York: Sully & Kleinteich,
[c1914] NUC.

"Janice is sent to board with some shiftless relatives
while her father is in Mexico. Her own ambition to do
something and her father's example and precepts, impel
her to do her utmost to improve her surroundings.
Gradually her influence effects many reforms. The
young school teacher, whom she inspires to nobler
work, falls in love with her, but she makes him prove
his worth before she accepts him." PW 86 10/1-/14:1205
p. 27

007350   JANICE DAY, THE YOUNG HOMEMAKER. New
York: G. Sully, [c1919] NUC.

007351   THE MISSION OF JANICE DAY. New York:
Sully & Kleinteich, [c1917] NUC BMC.

She's older now than in earlier book about her. Goes
into Mexico under actual peril to rescue her father
captured by a bandit, straightens out Uncle's
financial problems, and has time for a romance. NYT
138 4-15-17

007352   THE TESTING OF JANICE DAY. New York:
Sully & Kleinteich, [c1915] NUC.

Gets her first auto, arrested for speeding. PW 9-25-15
Love entanglements, etc. NYT

LONG, LILY AUGUSTA. D. 1927. United States.

007353   APPRENTICES TO DESTINY. New York: Merrill
and Baker, [c1893] NUC.

CR 21:237. Life in the midwest.

007354   THE FULLERTON CASE. BY ROMAN DOUBLEDAY.
London: E. Nash, 1920 BMC.

TLS-tr. det.
SR-0

007355   THE GREEN TREE MYSTERY. BY ROMAN
DOUBLEDAY. New York and London: D. Appleton, 1917 NUC
BMC.

"Upon the body of a man found dead by the roadside is
a notebook in which is written a confession that he
has killed the deservedly unpopular rich man of the
village. The search for an adequate motive opens up so
many possibilities that the daughter of the murdered
man employs a detective to discover the truth." BRD
1917

007356   THE HEMLOCK AVENUE MYSTERY. BY ROMAN
DOUBLEDAY. Boston: Little, Brown, 1908 NUC.

BRD- "A new edition of a popular mystery story in
which a young attorney comes to sudden death, the
supposition being that his rival and enemy killed him.
The story involves two women suspected of
participation in the crime, while a third one who had

really slain the man by accident was wholly
unconscious of the deed. A young newspaper reporter
unravels the tangle which suspicion and doubt are
alone responsible for. "This is, we think, the best
detective story by an American author that has
appeared in recent years." ARENA 39:733. Je. '08.
200w.

007357   THE RED HOUSE ON ROWAN STREET. BY ROMAN
DOUBLEDAY. Boston: Little, Brown, 1910 NUC.

"A young man who crosses half of the continent to urge
a fair Priscilla to reconsider her refusal to marry
his friend no sooner sets foot in the town and
delivers his message than he is plunged into a mystery
that is robbing the family of the young woman in
question of honor and friends. His part in removing
the cloud of suspicion is a bold one with no end of
surprising adventure. As for the romance, any John
Alden sympathizer will undertake to venture a prophecy
at the start." BRD

007358   THE SAINTSBURY AFFAIR. BY ROMAN
DOUBLEDAY. Boston: Little, Brown, 1912 NUC.

"A young lawyer, the hero of this mystery story, is
called upon one day to defend a prominent citizen of
Saintsbury against a notorious blackmailer, and the
next is sought to take up the case of a youth of the
town who confesses to the murder of the criminal in
question. The situation that develops affords several
novel aspects; among them first, a criminal's use of
hypnotism in fastening his crime upon an innocent man
with the result that the latter believes himself to be
guilty, and, second, the use, not of Puddin'head
Wilson's thumb print, but of tooth marks in an apple
as a means of identifying the real criminal. A
romance, more than ordinarily sprightly, touches up
the amateur sleuth's victory with an additional
highlight." BRD

LONG, MAE VAN NORMAN. United States.

007359   THE WONDER WOMAN. Philadelphia: Penn,
1917 NUC.

LONGNOR, LETTICE.

007360   THE MANUSCRIPT OF LETTICE LONGNOR, BEING
THE ADVENTURES OF A LADY OF THE 17TH CENTURY. EDITED
BY HER DESCENDANT ELIZABETH LONGNOR. London: H.J.
Drane, [1909] BMC.

Abduction, rescue, love--ATH

LOOMIS, ANNIE ELISABETH. 1850-1940. United States.

007361   MORRIS JULIAN'S WIFE. A NOVEL. BY
ELIZABETH OLMIS. New York: R. Bonner, 1892 NUC.
London: Hutchinson, 1893 BMC.

PW-35 year old man marries a schoolgirl, Satia. At
first seemed ideal, then she has a revulsion of
feeling and acts unconventionally. After remorse and
atonement on husband's part, reunion.
Satia Maynard, married, in love, wealthy. She is
"crushed out of herself by the very weight of his
indulgence." Leaves him, goes to Europe. Leaves her
son. "A more utterly foolish and conceited little
egotist than Satia does not exist in fiction." Then
the chase of husband after wife begins. It lasts for
years. Even includes his being a judge and trying his
long-lost wife for murder. SR 75, 325
She deserts him because he's oppressive and indulgent,
wants "to cultivate her own individuality" wants
"breathing space."
Travels in Europe. ATH 101, 308

007362   THE SYLVESTER QUARRY, SEQUEL TO "OVER AT
LITTLE ACORNS". BY ELISABETH OLMIS. Richmond, Va.:
Presbyterian Com. of Pub., [1901] NUC.

LOOSE, KATHARINE RIEGEL. B. 1877. United States.

007363   HEARTS CONTENDING: A NOVEL. BY GEORG
SCHOCK. New York and London: Harper, 1910 BMC NUC.

LORD, ALICE EMMA (SAUERWEIN). 1848-1930. United States.

007364   THE DAYS OF LAMB AND COLERIDGE. New York:
H. Holt, 1893 BMC NUC.

Historical romance built around facts concerning the
lives and friends of the two authors. PW 12-2-93

LORIMER, NORMA OCTAVIA. B. 1864. United Kingdom.

007365   CATHERINE STERLING. London: W. Heinemann,
1903 BMC.

Marriage without benefit of clergy. ACAD 64, 462
Man has wife in insane asylum, he dies, she's a widow
in all but name ACAD 64, 533
High-souled hero and heroine see foolishness of
marriage, live together unmarried, bound by love.
Catherine arrives in Japan, finds father dead. She's
alone with no money lives with a man whose wife is an
incurable lunatic. Later he dies, she returns to
London, falls in love but won't tell her prudish lover
about her past, end is unexpected. LBKM 6-03-110
ATH 121, 651

007366   THE GOD'S CARNIVAL. London: S. Paul, 1916
BMC. New York: Brentano's, 1916 NUC.

NYT-Male hero. Italian waiter's marriage to German
bride. Story of their son.
TLS-Male hero. Italian waiter's marriage to German
bride. Story of their son
WWI-fic

007367   JOSIAH'S WIFE. London: Methuen, 1898 BMC.

ACAD 53:149. Camela enjoys a year's holiday from her
Baptist husband, goes to Sicily, meets Platonic
affinity. Husband wants divorce, affinity insists that
he first should also have a year's holiday. On his
return he finds Camela chastened and penitent.
ACAD 53:371. She is not c & p. Husband has been
changed by year in Europe, more sophisticated, etc.,
so that Camela no longer wants divorce. She has the
artistic temperament, wants to live life fully.
ATH 111:338. "A reader may well start with the feeling
that here will be one more instance of the woman of
the late 19th c, always out of harmony with her
surroundings, and especially her husband." "The wife,
who has or supposes she has, the artist nature,
confides the workings of her untrammelled,
uncomprehended soul to her piano in outbursts of
Chopin or wild Hungarian melodies. This is the way of
the highly strung complex young woman of fiction just
now, and we know who is mainly responsible for her.
Camela Accomes, with time and trial, slightly toned
down." "The springs of her warped nature are revealed,
and one has to excuse her caprices a little." "The
relations that subsist between the husband and wife
are of a kind not easily treated in the English
novel." They are American.

007368   A MENDER OF IMAGES. A NOVEL. London:
Hutchinson, [1920] BMC NUC. New York: Brentano's,
[c1921] NUC.

TLS-romance
ATH- Author shows ill treatment of women and animals
in Sicily.

007369   MIRRY-ANN: A MANX STORY. London: S. Paul,
1900 BMC. New York: D. Appleton, 1900 NUC.

LBKM- Mirry-Ann is an educated woman Methodist
preacher living simply on Isle of Man. She loves Dick
Schofield, a "nursery-governess" who works for a woman
farmer, but believes she cannot accept his love. John
Thomas, owner of a fishing boat also loves her, loses
his eyesight saving her life. On religious principles
feels she must marry him. But story ends on a happy
note.
LBKM 17:28. Manx. Thread of tragedy, love story.
SP 84:317. Three suitors of supposedly illegitimate
heroine who turns out to be the legitimate half-sister
of one.
ATH 115:301. Village girl of superior education and
sister of bachelor squire contrasted. Village girl
discovers she is legitimate.
ACAD 58:146. Mirry-Ann is introduced as a preacher.
The squire's sister believes her religion humbug, that
she likes dress of the preacher.
LIT 6:190. Happy ending for Mirry-Ann.

007370   ON DESERT ALTARS. London: S. Paul, 1915
NUC BMC. New York: Brentano's, [1915] NUC.

BKM 41 1915 marital infidelity.
psychol development of Alice Lindsay. In order to save
her husband's life, "makes a bargain with another
man." Story concerns husband's learning of what she
did." NYT
Gives herself to a millionaire as the price of getting
her husband a livelihood Alice's emancipated
wanderings with another lover TLS
A wife's infidelity made heroic and pardonable.

Husband ill needs to move to better climate; sells
self to wealthy Jew: she has a child which is his.
Husband learns, turns out wife and child. She lives
with former admirer but all forgiven , reconciliation
BKM

007371   ON ETNA: A ROMANCE OF BRIGAND LIFE.
London: W. Heinemann, 1904 BMC. New York: H. Holt,
1904 NUC.

ATH- young woman who thinks brigands are fascinating
is carried off by them.
PW-? kidnapped by Mafia, falls for Chief.
NYT
ACAD-romance

007372   THE PAGAN WOMAN. London: Chatto & Windus,
1907 BMC.

Two women one of the philosophy that you let others do
the unpleasant work that needs doing; the other-you do
the work that needs to be done. A professional woman
#1 (the pagan) gets the man from the other who served
him for years. Author makes pagan woman sympathetic;
In Martha we get the everyday trag of "unfulfilled
womanhood." In Marion the modern woman's claim to life
"life to the dregs, sometimes at the cost of others"
ACAD
Housekeeper marries elderly scholar. Marion Houston,
the pagan and intelligent. Martha-old maid "crushed by
household duties" Marion is aggressive toward men. We
get the course of their two lives to a final tragedy
what is it? Contrast between the two. SR

007373   THE SECOND WOMAN. A NOVEL. London: S.
Paul, 1912 BMC.

TLS-love story.
ATH-woman decides if another woman gains her husband's
love, she will give him up. She does so. Many
complications. Tangled situation.

007374   A SWEET DISORDER. London: A. D. Innes,
1896 BMC.

SR-Daisy and a blind lover. Molly who tries
governessing and concludes "Hell must be full of other
people's children."
ATH 108:188. Imitates Mrs. Hungerford. Molly is
heroine, wrote a novel. Ingenuous, gushing.
ACAD 49:361. Molly and Daisy go to London, Molly to
earn her living as governess or journalist. She
struggles, for awhile is a waitress and also a
skirt-dancer. In the end she confessed to Dacre that
love was almost as good as independence.

007375   THERE WAS A KING IN EGYPT. London: S.
Paul, 1918 BMC. New York: Brentano's, 1918 NUC.

PW-Love story
TLS-conventional plot
NYT-0

007376   A WIFE OUT OF EGYPT. London: S. Paul,
[1913] BMC NUC. New York: Brentano's, 1914 NUC.

Heroine, a beautiful Syrian, engaged to an Englishman
but the racial bar separates them; she eventually
marries another man ATH
Mass of information on Egypt racial bar is the real
theme TLS

007377   WITH OTHER EYES. London: S. Paul, [1919]
BMC NUC. New York: Brentono's, [c1920] NUC.

Conventional TLS
ATH-love story which gives an answer to problem
whether women should be stuck with men they no longer
want merely because they have been in war.
PW-Char. development thru war experience.
NYT 6/27/20. Daughter and widowed mother travel; meet
father and son. Father and mother marry, children
don't because he is a young and ambitious MD.
Evangeline later meets Alex, a woman who has run away
from her husband with whom she had migrated to Canada
and had wasted their money. She is on her way back to
England to open a boarding house. "The fortunes of the
two women are more or less interwoven."

LOTHROP, HARRIET MULFORD (STONE). 1844-1924. United
States.

007378   THE JUDGES' CAVE: BEING A ROMANCE OF THE
NEW HAVEN COLONY IN THE DAYS OF THE REGICIDE, 1661. BY
MARGARET SIDNEY. Boston: Lothrop, [c1900] NUC BMC.

PW-story of the fugitive judges Goffe and Whalley, historically accurate.

007379   A LITTLE MAID OF BOSTON TOWN. BY MARGARET SIDNEY. Boston: Lothrop, Lee & Shepard, [1910] NUC.

18th rom. mostly for children. NYT
PZ3

007380   THE OLD TOWN PUMP: A STORY OF EAST AND WEST. BY MARGARET SIDNEY. Boston: Lothrop, 1895 NUC BMC.

PW 3-7-96, Rumor of attack on Miss Nancy Harkness, patron saint of N. England village, on Thanksgiving. Untrue, mystery is revealed after the principal characters emigrate to West, a graphic description being given of a race for possession in the boomers' section.

007381   SALLY, MRS. TUBBS. BY MARGARET SIDNEY. Boston: Lothrop, [1903] NUC.

Dreads being an old maid, prevails upon Tubbs to marry her, humorous? PW 10-3-03
Set on marriage, expert laundress, would marry by 50 so she won't be an old maid. Is this a satire? NYT 03, 745
Sally 49 energetic, industrious--fears being old main--proposes. humor older woman--WOMAN'S JOURNAL 10-17-03

LOUD, EMILY SYRENA. United Kingdom.

007382   TAURUA; OR WRITTEN IN THE BOOK OF FATE. Cincinnati: Editor Pub. Co., 1899 NUC.

Life on S. Sea island. Adventures of an English woman thrown by chance among the natives. They adopt her. The rituals and customs of these people. Arava's release. LIT 5:134
Idealistic picture of South Seas. BAKER 03,252

LOUGHEAD, FLORA (HAINES) APPONYI. B. 1855. United States.

007383   THE ABANDONED CLAIM. Boston and New York: Houghton, Mifflin, 1891 NUC. London: A. P. WattDuckworth, 1891 BMC.

Hope, Ned and Martin Austin left orphans (oldest is 15.) They enter a claim for government land and successfully cultivate the land. PW 12-5-91.

007384   THE BLACK CURTAIN. Boston and New York: Houghton, Mifflin, 1898 NUC. London: Duckworth, 1899 BMC.

LW 29:404. An artist who is color blind and a singer who has lost her voice both take up the same government claim on land in Cal. Dispute follows, she wins, they fall in love with each other.
A young woman singer has lost her voice, a male artist lost his sight. They settle on the same plot in California. Argue about their rights, end up in love. LIT 4:240.
Both are squatters. He builds a log cabin; she a paper house. Miss Judith seems to be in the wrong in most of the arguments. At the end the black curtain is drawn; he sees, her voice returns. LBKM 15:187

007385   A CROWN OF THORNS. San Francisco: C.A. Murdock, [c1891] NUC.

CR 17:167. Young San Franciscan woman attends meeting in which Society for the Prevention of Cruelty to Children is investigating Chinese adoption of babies for immoral purposes. Finds her own child in act of having her feet crushed, child she had 4 years earlier abandoned and whom she now courageously acknowledges to be her own.

LOUTHAN, HATTIE (HORNER). B. 1865. United States.

007386   IN PASSION'S DRAGNET: A NOVEL. Boston: R. G. Badger, 1903 NUC.

PW-Plea for co-ed.
NYT-plea for woman's independence and education so that she is less vulnerable.

007387   A ROCKY MOUNTAIN FEUD. Boston: C. M. Clark, [c1910] NUC.

007388   "THIS WAS A MAN"...A ROMANCE. Boston: C. M. Clark, 1906 NUC.

Story of a hero of Colarado PW 1-26-07
Melodrama, mixed identities NYT

LOVE, MARGARET (BROWN). United States.

007389   TOM HUSTON'S TRANSFORMATION. New York: Abbey Press, [1900] NUC.

LOVEDAY, ELLEN BEAUMONT.

007390   THE ROAD TO HILLSBROW. London: Chapman & Hall, 1914 BMC.

ATH-male hero, composer and his struggles.
TLS-Dickensian.
TLS 13:275 Essay on the good will of the human family.

LOVEJOY, MARY EVELYN WOOD. B. 1847. United States.

007391   DANDELION; OR, OUT OF THE SHADOWS. London and New York: F. T. Neely, [c1899] NUC.

LOVELL, INGRAHAM, pseud. See BACON, JOSEPHINE DODGE (DASKAM).

LOW, IVY. See LITVINOVA, IVY (LOW).

LOWE, CORINNE MARTIN. B. 1882.

007392   CONFESSIONS OF A SOCIAL SECRETARY. New York and London: Harper, [1917] NUC.

007393   SAUL. New York: J.A. McCann, 1919 NUC. London: Constable, 1920 BMC.

Jewish home life. PW
Focuses upon an East Side Jewish boy, man. PW Book Review
Wife-highest type of Jewess-"pure and aspiring." BKM 9-21-19 NYT 453
TLS- success in dress making.
ATH He's unfaithful, nearly ruined, wife takes him back and manages all.
SR-Saul attempts to free himself of the sewing machine in the sweat shop and rise to designer. Along with this passion is another, his reliance on Hannah Sadowsky, whom he loves, marries, almost deserts & returns to in his hour of defeat.

LOWENBERG, MRS. I. United States.

007394   THE IRRESISTIBLE CURRENT. New York: Broadway, [c1908] NUC.

PW religious romance.
BKM-Jewish woman's parents will not allow her to marry outside her faith

007395   A NATION'S CRIME; A NOVEL. New York: Neale, 1910 NUC.

Series of misalliances-3rd and 4th generation of them, but anti-divorce PW

007396   THE VOICES. San Franscisco: H. Wagner, 1920 NUC.

TLS-Woman born with the word "mission" on her lips, listens to inner voices, becomes political and industrial leader.

LOWNDES, MARIE ADELAIDE (BELLOC). 1868-1947. United Kingdom.

007397   BARBARA REBELL. BY MRS. BELLOC-LOWNDES. London: W. Heinemann, 1905 BMC NUC. New York: B.W. Dodge, 1907 NUC.

Barbara, mother, married to scoundrel who won't divorce her. Remained his wife in name only the rest of her life. Her god-daughter, Barbara Robell also married to a scoundrel, leaves him, she falls in love. She lives with him, but the memory of her mother draws them apart. Later husband dies and she does marry the lover. Review BKM 145, vol. 29-30
Starts with Barbara at 10 in French courts 1870. Marries a cousin, separates, comes to London where her real life begins PW 5-18-07

007398   THE CHINK IN THE ARMOUR. BY MRS. BELLOC LOWNDES. London: Methuen, [1912] BMC NUC. New York: Scribner's, 1912 NUC.

PW-?
TLS--Murder mystery. Character study of relations between men and women.

ATH-0
ACAD-two women in a gambling center, one is murdered,
the other almost.
BKM- Anna Wolsky, confirmed gambler disappears at a
casino. Young English-woman, her friend, risks her
life to solve the mystery
NYT-0

007399   THE END OF HER HONEYMOON. BY MRS. BELLOC
LOWNDES. New York: C. Scribner's Sons, 1913 NUC.
London: Methuen, 1914 BMC NUC.

LBKM-Nancy's bridegroom disappears. She is consoled by
an American.
SR 147-:376. He shows up, in last few pages, explains.
TLS 13:141
"Scene is laid in Paris in an exposition year, central
figures are an English girl, Nancy Dampier, and a
family of Americans who meet by chance at a little
hotel in the Latin Quarter. Nancy arrives late at
night with her husband, after a three weeks honeymoon
in Italy. They are unable to get a large room and are
obliged to take two small ones, widely separated.
After bidding her husband good-night, Nancy never sees
him again, and it is this mystery the story is
occupied in unraveling." PW 84 9/20/13p768.
Mystery; husband missing on honeymoon in Paris. Story
follows the step-by-step search for him NYT

007400   FROM THE VASTY DEEP. BY MRS. BELLOC
LOWNDES. London: Hutchinson, [1902] BMC NUC. New York:
G.H. Doran, [c1921] NUC. (Am. ed. title: From Out The
Vasty Deep.)

TLS- Spiritualism; a modern girl with great powers as
a medium makes a discovery of murder.
SP Bubbles

007401   GOOD OLD ANNA. BY MRS. BELLOC LOWNDES.
London: Hutchinson, 1915 BMC NUC. New York: G.H.
Doran, [1916] NUC.

German Anna servant during war became tool in German
organization bringing suffering and disaster to the
family she loved PW
NYT-because she is so dumb. so are the two women.
BKM-Rev feels implication is every German in England
is likely to be connected with the spy system. Anna's
sympathies are with German, but it is unconsciously
that she becomes a spy and a conspirator. Hangs
herself in her cell.
Anna is a "good stupid old deluded" servant in this
spy story TLS
She does spy work SP
War setting, study of town's reactions to naturalized
aliens like Anna. Sympathetic toward Anna too. Stupid,
used by Germans as spy SP

007402   THE HEART OF PENELOPE. London: W.
Heinemann, 1904 BMC NUC.

loves one man, marries another with whom she works in
an Eastside Settlement till he dies. Then she's
attracted to a 3rd man. What is the tragedy at the
end? LBKM 27-8, 223.
TLS-

007403   JANE OGLANDER. BY MRS. BELLOC LOWNDES.
London: W. Heinemann, 1911 BMC NUC. New York: C.
Scribner's Sons, 1911 NUC.

Story of Circe-like woman PW 4-29-11
Jane jilted? inconclusive end what will Jane do? TLS
"best type of modern young woman of culture". Mrs.
Maule "eats the souls of men" and gets her just
reward. She's the Circe-like woman? LBKM
Jane:self reliant, reserved. Jane and Mrs. Maule are
friends till Jane's fiance falls under Mrs. Maule's
spell. Jane accepts this, even tries to persuade Mr.
Maule to divorce his wife so wife can marry the man
?ACAD
"It does not seem to occur to the Author that Athena's
husband was justified in putting choral crystals into
her chocolate at night to kill her." SP
Maule-wicked-married to old man, chases after other
men. Goes after her friend's fiance. "Her plan fails
in the end. He's ready to return to Jane. "Just what
Jane does we are not told"
ATH-Maule "a masterpiece" woman without conscience,
self centered but possessing passion and charm. The
book is really hers.

007404   LILLA: A PART OF HER LIFE. BY MRS.
BELLOC-LOWNDES. London: Hutchinson, 1916 BMC NUC. New
York: G.H. Doran, [c1917] NUC.

Lilla Singleton's husband reported dead in action; she
meets and marries after a short courtship. Husband one
returns alive. "Lilla solves her problem by
undertaking relief work in France." The men go their
ways. PW
1rst marriage had meant the stifling of individuality
to Lilla. Nevertheless she's strong with a deep
capacity to love-not ruined in her 9 years of
marriage. She's then widowed, goes into war work
marries again NYT 4-1-17 114

007405   THE LODGER. BY MRS. BELLOC LOWNDES.
London: Methuen, [1913] BMC NUC. New York: C.
Scribner's Sons, 1913 NUC.

"During the last fortnight four very curious murders
have been committed within a comparatively small
area." On the victim's dress, in each case is pinned a
three-cornered piece of paper, on which is written in
red ink the words "The Avenger." This is the situation
set forth in the beginning of this story which is not
a detective tale, but is told from the point of view
of persons who believe they know the murderer, but are
not sure enough to act. The chief actors are the
Buntings, London lodging-keepers, and their stranger
lodger." PW 3-7-14 768
The Detective relegated to a minor place. SP
Series of murders by a homicidal maniac and the misery
of the couple with whom he lodges who know his secret.
ATH
based upon Jack the Ripper "crude and coarse" LBK
Scarifies and thrills horror upon horror, a grisly
tale TLS

007406   THE LONELY HOUSE. BY MRS. BELLOC LOWNDES.
London: Hutchinson, 1920 NUC BMC. New York: G.H.
Doran, [c1920] NUC.

TLS-? helpless heroine
ATH-male det
NYT 9-12-20 p. 27 Lily's adv in this house. "gruesome"
love complications and murder by a man SR

007407   LOVE AND HATRED. BY MRS. BELLOC LOWNDES.
London: Chapman & Hall, 1917 BMC NUC. New York: G.H.
Doran, [c1917] NUC.

PW-Laura and Godfrey unhappily married. Laura and
Oliver in love; Kathy and Godfrey in love. Godfrey
dies "accidentally." A year later, just after he has
married Laura, police discover Oliver killed Godfrey.
He is shot while hunting to avoid publicity and trag.
for Laura.
NYT p. 130 Mar 24, 1918 Actually, he shoots himself
but death is made to look like accident. Neither Laura
nor her mother ever discover the true nature of the
two deaths.

007408   MARY PECHELL. BY MRS. BELLOC LOWNDES.
London: Methuen, 1912 BMC NUC. New York: C. Scribner's
Sons, 1912 NUC.

BKM v. 36 1912-13
ATH-reminded of Cranford by love story of old maid.
TLS-Mary is a modern girl of the best kind.
SP-0
ACAD-two rivals which does she choose?

007409   OUT OF THE WAR? BY MRS. BELLOC LOWNDES.
London: Chapman & Hall, 1918 BMC NUC.

TLS German spy tricked American girl.

007410   THE PHILOSOPHY OF THE MARQUISE. BY MRS
BELLOC LOWNDES. London: G. Richards, 1899 NUC BMC.

The whole novel in dialogue. The Marquise is Fr.
visits an English country house. Interwoven life
stories, humorous and tragic -all suggested, inferred
rather than definitely stated. LIT 4:527
Also the Dean, Lady Moon and Jenny. A cynical note
throughout. LBKM 16:170.
Comedy and satire. Three women who used to be
schoolmates meet in middle-age. All reveal their
contemptible personalities. SP 82:758

007411   PRICE OF ADMIRALTY. London: G. Newnes,
[1915] BMC.

with "Why They Married"

007412   THE PULSE OF LIFE; A STORY OF A PASSING
WORLD. BY MRS. BELLOC LOWNDES. London: W. Heinemann,
1908 NUC BMC. New York: Dodd, Mead, 1909 NUC.

Romance of royalty figure. PW 2-13-09

present day old Catholic nobility in England focuses
on the hero. NYT
ACAD-old fashioned love story.
BKM
TLS-0

007413   THE RED CROSS BARGE. BY MRS. BELLOC
LOWNDES. London: Smith, Elder, 1916 BMC NUC. New York:
G.H. Doran, [1918] NUC.

TLS-male German MD in war
ATH-male German MD in war
PW - love and war and Germans.
NYT-Jeanne Rouannes in charge of Red Cross barge.
Noble, patriotic heroine. Dr Max Keller, German
surgeon and product of German training that Germans
are superior to every other people comes to
disillusionment.

007414   STUDIES IN WIVES. BY MRS. BELLOC LOWNDES.
London: W. Heinemann, 1909 BMC. New York: M.
Kennerley, [c1910] NUC.

six stories of unhappy marriage. Author preoccupied
with the war between the sexes. All but one husband is
in the wrong and so are the wives. In each story of
wrong husbands the case involves another woman. A
"cool patient investigation" TLS
"one tragedy of a leasehold marriage in which the wife
will not consent to a renewal" LBKM
Subtle characterization: a contract marriage with
option of renewal.
"Six short stories dealing with various phases of
married life." BKM v. 31, 1910

007415   THE UTTERMOST FARTHING. BY MRS. BELLOC
LOWNDES. London: W. Heinemann, 1908 BMC NUC. New York:
M. Kennerley, [c1910] NUC.

TLS-Wife goes off with man, dies of heart disease on
journey, he arranges to protect her reputation.
ATH-Wife goes off with man, dies of heart disease on
journey, he arranges to protect her reputation.

007416   WHEN NO MAN PURSUETH; AN EVERYDAY STORY.
BY MRS. BELLOC LOWNDES. London: W. Heinemann, 1910 BMC
NUC. New York: M. Kennerley, 1911 NUC.

TLS--Wedding bells at end.
LBKM--Wedding bells at end.
queer family, suspicion of plot to kill wife NYT

LOWNDES, MRS. BELLOC. See LOWNDES, MARIE ADELAIDE (BELLOC).

LOWTH, ALYS.

007417   A DAUGHTER OF THE TRANSVAAL. London:
Hutchinson, 1899 BMC NUC.

Race hatred in girls' school in a Cape Colony. There
are daughters of Dopper farmers, of Johannesburg Jews,
French missionary, English officer. Succession of
encounters of force as well as wits between English
and Dutch girls. Author is apparently prejudiced
against the Boer girls. SP 83:789
LIT 6:24. "Strange book about a girls' school in Cape
Colony, where the young ladies spend most of their
spare time discussing with great violence--verbal and
physical--the question of Boer against Briton in S.
Africa." Author is a Briton, and "distributes her
heroines and villainesses accordingly."

007418   DOREEN COASTING. WITH SOME ACCOUNTS OF
THE PLACES SHE SAW AND THE PEOPLE SHE ENCOUNTERED.
EDITED BY ALYS LOWTH. London: Longmans, Green, 1912
NUC BMC.

Irish, series of letters, her travels, observations,
photos of Victoria Falls, etc. Fiction? ACAD
DT 365 Africa, Description & travel voyage to East &
So. Africa

LUCAS, EMILY BEATRIX COURSOLLES (JONES). B. 1893. United
Kingdom.

007419   QUIET INTERIOR. BY E. B. C. JONES.
London: R. Cobden-Sanderson, [c1920] BMC NUC. New
York: Boni & Liveright, [1921] NUC.

TLS-clash of female temperaments, witty Bohemian
lives.
SP-Heroine is a tepid conscientious objector. She and
her sister live so quietly in their interiors that
they feel no necessity for doing war work. Author does
not manage to make her a sympathetic figure.
ATH-Fastidious girl. She is an emancipated daughter in

an upper middle class family, Claire Norris has charm.
In giving up Clemence, man she loved, to her sister,
Claire discovered her inner world, and she at last
feels in harmony with life.
LBKM -0

LUCK, MARY CHURCHILL (SPOTTISWOODE-ASHE). Fl. 1895-1914.
United Kingdom.

007420   ACROSS AN ULSTER BOG. BY M. HAMILTON.
London: W. Heinemann, 1896 BMC. New York: E. Arnold,
1896 NUC.

SR-Seduction of a peasant girl by a curate.
ATH 108:126. Pioneer Series. Ellen is a mother before
she is 17. "Her youth excites disgust in the reader."
Ireland. Sordid, repellent.
ACAD 50:129. "The brothers, bent on revenge, waylay
Duffin (the curate) one night and thrash him until he
dies, letting his body slip into a bog. All this is
truly Irish.
BKM 3:552.

007421   BEYOND THE BOUNDARY. BY M. HAMILTON.
London: Hurst and Blackett, 1902 BMC.

007422   CUT LAURELS. BY M. HAMILTON. London: W.
Heinemann, 1905 BMC NUC.

Frailty of a man; supreme nobility of a woman.
Katharine separated 18 years from her husband who is
prisoner of Arabs. She's been working, saving money as
a dressmaker all these years with her daughter. He
brings back an Arab wife and two children, asks his
wife who her companion is: doesn't remember he has a
daughter. She forgives him. They start life fresh
again. ACAD 175,05
Jack goes to Egypt to make a fortune, is imprisoned.
Wife and daughter run a famous dressmaking
establishment. Wife finds that to save his life he
married and has a son. She forgives him-in time. After
a break of 20 years they start out again. TLS 27-8,30
Wife goes to Egypt on hearing of her husband's
release, learns he has a mistress and two children. We
follow Katharine's mind from point to point TLS 1905,
58
he returns with his two half-caste sons to England
269,05 ATH

007423   THE DISHONOUR OF FRANK SCOTT. BY M.
HAMILTON. London: Hurst & Blackett, 1900 BMC. New
York: Harper, 1900 NUC.

Strong novel for strong men and women BOOK BUYER 01
LBKM 19:27. Bigamy. Two wives, one passionate, the
other not.
ATH 116:374. He ruined "three lives" (maybe 4) Engaged
to Violet, daughter of his chief, he falls for Barbara
and persuades her to break off engagement with native
doctor. India. He is a "mixture of moral cowardice and
false tenderness."
NYT 1900:701. He marries Barbara as soon as they reach
India, clandestinely. Violet is expected to die. Her
father persuades Fluffy to become her "nominal"
husband. He needs money, talks to Barbara, she agrees.
Then Violet's health improves and she is pregnant.
Barbara can't stand it and tells her father. Then
Violet dies and Fluffy returns to Barbara.

007424   THE FIRST CLAIM. BY M. HAMILTON. London:
Methuen, 1906 BMC. New York: Doubleday, Page, 1907
NUC.

TLS-Woman torn between fat, pompous, old husband and
child of 1st husband whom she had deserted. Second
wife of 1st husband mistreats the child and turns her
into a horrible little girl. Shall she (mother)
reawaken the scandal of her marriage to forcibly
rescue hateful child?
Wife 17 married to old man, leaves him and her child,
elopes and marries another, returns and steals her
child +PW3-16-07
Gwen. NYT

007425   THE FREEDOM OF HENRY MEREDYTH. BY M.
HAMILTON. New York: D. Appleton, 1897 NUC. London: W.
Heinemann, 1898 BMC.

He's divorced, wants to marry again but his ex wife
and daughter protest. He's "a dull dog." His daughter
is "vicious-tempered, obstinant and wrong headed. LBKM
13:50
A divorced husband and what he does with his freedom
and what his daughter Vivien and cousin and former
lover Alison Carnegie do with it. ACAD 52 Fic Sup 87
Miss Urquhart "is a passionate feminist." ATH 110:878

SR 85:336 Henry, after 18 years of marriage is central
character. He has a divorced wife and children. She
stands between him and heroine.

007426   THE GENERAL'S WIFE. BY M. HAMILTON.
London: S. Paul, 1916 BMC.

TLS-another soldier married to worthless wife.

007427   THE LOCUST'S YEARS. BY M. HAMILTON.
London: Skeffington, [1919] BMC.

Marriage of Susan shy author of 40 to a young rich man
17 years younger than she. The marriage works. TLS
Then her love does not stand the test of matrimony SP

007428   MCLEOD OF THE CAMERONS. BY M. HAMILTON.
London: W. Heinemann, 1897 BMC. New York: D. Appleton,
1897 NUC.

The heroine is Christina and she's made sympathetic.
Raised by her cruel parents Lord & Lady Lorimer, she's
anxious to get away. So elopes with the first man
who'll marry her. He's lower class, a seaman, crude in
his habits. Christine has to put up with a lot from
him-bad table manners, dress, no culture, etc. Meets
Andrew McLeod, an officer and they talk books. But
there's something strange about him. Lives in fear of
going mad. One mad moment he tries to kill Christina.
He has lucid moments, is hospitalized. NYT 2-7-97
She's extremely young when she married this impossible
man. She struggles to makes the best of it. SR 83:452
Christina Stoddart meets McLeod who is a kind of
woman-hater but takes to her. They become friends. PW
51:49
Christina Stoddart is married to a clod. She married
when she was barely out of school and on the occasion
of his leaving for China. When they meet again 3 years
later, she's even more intell. and refined, so the
disillusionment in her husband is complete. She has a
friend, McLeod who is her intell. companion, but he is
increasingly losing his sanity and becoming a
homocidal maniac. She helps him thru his illness in
the face of gossip-to his suicide. In the meantime she
made the best of her marriage. SP 78:176
Rare: "The woman who marries beneath her." She's an
earl's niece; husband an engineer. He's shown as
gauche. CR 26,30:250.
He goes mad and dies violently. BKM 5:167

007429   MRS. BRATT. BY M. HAMILTON. London: S.
Paul, 1913 BMC.

Mr. Brett forgives her for a serious fault, but never
ceases to remind her of it. Also concerns their
daughter "who has played with many men" ATH
Both mother and daughter plunge into illicit unions
for happiness. Mother most sympathetic. We learn first
of her long martyrdom with a monotonously fiendish
husband-a kind of penance for an early lapse which had
parted her from her daughter. Loves a much younger man
who has been discarded by her daughter. TLS

007430   ON AN ULSTER FARM. BY M. HAMILTON.
London: R.A. Everett, [1904] NUC [1905] BMC.

007431   POOR ELISABETH. BY M. HAMILTON. London:
Hurst and Blackett, 1901 BMC. London: 1901 NUC.

A really vain man. A miserable book, no ray of joy.
Ely always shocks her husband. Dies 8-10-1 ATH

007432   A SELF-DENYING ORDINANCE. BY M. HAMILTON.
New York: D. Appleton, 1895 NUC BMC. Heinemann, 1896
BS.

SR--Nice and natural heroine, unfaithful husband and
faithful wife.
ATH 107:212. Heroic Joanna, pure. Romance is
high-strung, impassioned. Contrasts of worldliness
etc.
ACAD 49:260. Joanna is engaged to Nicholas who elopes
with a married woman. Joanna broken-hearted. He
returns to Ulster with her creating a scandal because
of the baby. Her husband will not give her a divorce.
Nicholas' brother buys her off and induces Nicholas,
who is in debt, to emigrate and work. Joanna offers to
go with him. They are married against everyone's
advice.
SP 76:244. Joanna is a hoyden.

007433   THE WOMAN WHO LOOKED BACK. BY M.
HAMILTON. London: S. Paul, [1914] BMC NUC.

LBKM-Sara married Oliver Moore and then it is
discovered that a 1st Mrs. Moore exists. She looks at

her past and yearns for a former lover. Oliver gets a
divorce and they end up staying together.
ATH 144:526. Married for 12 years before discovery of
1st wife. Chooses to remain with husband because of
her love for her children (scene with daughters). Book
has "sub-acid flavour."

LUDLUM, JEAN KATE. United States.

    007434   BARCLAY'S DAUGHTER. New York: National
    Temperance Society, 1893 NUC.

    007435   JOHN WINTHROP'S DEFEAT: A NOVEL. New
    York: R. Bonner's Sons, 1891 NUC.

    Set in New York and Paris. Harry Graham recklessly
    squanders his and his wife's fortunes. John Winthrop,
    lawyer, saves them. PW 10-24-91.
    Widow ends up marrying Winthrop. BOOK NEWS 111:135

    007436   LIDA CAMPBELL; OR, DRAMA OF A LIFE. A
    NOVEL. New York: R. Bonner's Sons, 1892 NUC.

    PW-"Strangely endowed" woman writes a novel hoping "to
    ventilate her ill-balanced action and strange theory
    of being." Sensational incidents involved in her
    attempts to publish.

    007437   UNDER A CLOUD: A NOVEL. New York: R.
    Bonner's Sons, 1891 NUC.

LUEHRMANN, ADELE. United States.

    007438   THE CURIOUS CASE OF MARIE DUPONT. New
    York: Century, 1916 BMC NUC.

    Mystery. Marie dancer "once notorious in Paris." Loss
    of memory PW 90:8/19/16 p. 568
    NYT-Marie is beautiful and clever young woman; people
    suspect her of being a Parisian dancer who was
    supposedly murdered.
    BKM-when Gavoch sees her dance he remembers seeing her
    in a vile Montmartre cafe-the mistress of a notorious
    Rumanian prince & a leader of the demi-monde.

    007439   THE OTHER BROWN. New York: Century, 1917
    NUC BMC.

    Traditional detective. PW
    Mystery about dual personality. BKM
    Psychological detective yarn. NYT 9-2-17,322

    007440   THE TRIPLE MYSTERY. New York: Dodd, Mead,
    1920 NUC.

    PW-Mystery involving death of three men.
    NYT 1920:320

LUFFMANN, LAURA BOGUE. Nationality Unknown.

    007441   A QUESTION OF LATITUDE. London: J. Lane,
    1912 BMC. New York: J. Lane, 1912 BMC NUC.

    NYT-modern Australia, heroine seems to be a
    below-stairs person.
    Life in Australia. 12-2-11. PW.
    Love story of loveable woman. TLS
    Sordid realities. SP
    Terminates in a bush honeymoon. ATH

LUND, KATHLEEN A.

    007442   IN AND OUT OF THE WOOD. London: Heath,
    Cranton, [1919] BMC.

    Hero tells life story of heroine includes a family of
    dwarfs (?) TLS Nothing here.

    007443   MRS. DUSTY-FUSSER, HOW SHE SWEPT INTO
    SOCIETY. London: Dean & Son, [1909] BMC.

    007444   OLIVER IN WILLOWMERE. London: Heath,
    Cranton & Ouseley, [1914] BMC.

    ATH Romance. Oliver an evangelist.

    007445   THE PUPIL OF A LITTLE MONK. London:
    Heath, Cranton, [1916] BMC.

LUPTON, ANNE.

    007446   MRS. LINCOLN'S NIECE. London: Digby and
    Long, [1892] BMC.

    Louisa deVere beautiful secretly married, kidnapped by
    wicked Baron who keeps her imprisoned (but doesn't

touch her) till she escapes and rejoins husband after various experiences. ACAD.

LUSK, ALICE FREEMAN.

007447   A WOMAN'S ANSWER TO ROOSEVELT; A STORY ON RACE SUICIDE. Los Angeles, Cal.: Commercial Printing House, 1908 NUC.

PW-desc of woman with eleven children, endless labor, early death, wealthy husband quickly marries another. PW-Description of woman with 11 children, endless labor, early death, wealthy husband quickly marries another.

LUST, ADELINA (COHNFELDT). B. 1860. United States.

007448   A TENT OF GRACE. London: A. P. Watt, [1899] BMC. Boston: Houghton, Mifflin, 1899 NUC.

German story. A pastor and his wife rescue a Jewess from murder at the hands of village rowdies. Jette is raised as a Jew, but "in the end prejudice prevails and the hapless Jette is practically beaten to death by the brutal peasants." SP 83:613
Jette grown up is very beautiful. A wealthy Jew wants to marry her, but she loves the pastor's son, so she refuses the wealthy one. Ends in tragedy. BKM 9:379
Conflict in her between rel. and love. PW 55:645
Hebrew heroine sheltered by Christian clergyman who enables her to practice her fate. But she meets a horrible death because of hatred of Gentiles "partly acting through the embittered will of her own people." NYT 6-24-99,408

LUTES, DELLA (THOMPSON). D. 1942. United States.

007449   JUST AWAY; A STORY OF HOPE. Cooperstown, N.Y.: Crist, Scott & Parbhall, 1906 NUC.

007450   MY BOY IN KHAKI: A MOTHER'S STORY. New York and London: Harper, [1918] NUC.

NYT Aug 25, 1918, p 366. Mother overcomes grief and sees vision of achievement in sacrifice of son to war. Inspirational. "Women behind and men at the front...Theirs must be the fight but ours must be the spirit with which they gain victory."

LUTTON, ELIZABETH MILLER. United States.

007451   THE CRACKER BOX SCHOOL. Chicago: Reilly & Britton, [c1917] NUC.

Teacher-trad. romance.

LUTZ, ELLEN A. United States.

007452   ONE WOMAN'S STORY; OR, THE CHRONICLES OF A QUIET LIFE AS TOLD IN DOROTHEA'S DIARY. Cincinnati: Cranston and Curts, 1895 NUC.

LUTZ, GRACE (LIVINGSTON) HILL. 1865-1947. United States.

007453   ACCORDING TO THE PATTERN. BY GRACE LIVINGSTONE HILL. Philadelphia: Griffith & Rowland Press, 1903 NUC.

Young loyal wife 10-31-03 PW

007454   THE ANGEL OF HIS PRESENCE. BY GRACE LIVINGSTON HILL. Philadelphia: American Baptist Society, [1902] NUC. (Bound with Gabriel the Acadian by Edith M. Nicholl Bowyer.)

PW--Religious young loyal wife.

007455   AUNT CRETE'S EMANCIPATION. Boston, Mass.: Golden Rule Co., [c1911] NUC.

007456   BECAUSE OF STEPHEN. BY GRACE LIVINGSTON HILL. Boston: Golden Rule Co., [1904] NUC.

007457   THE BEST MAN. Philadelphia and London: J.B. Lippincott, 1914 BMC NUC.

"Cyril Gordon, of the U.S. Secret Service, is sent to New York to secure a paper that has been stolen by some financiers. He gets the paper and has to fly for his life; seeing a carriage, he jumps in, disguising himself as he is driven along. When the carriage stops he finds himself at a church, where he is hustled up the aisle and married to a charming girl, before he can explain. What happens then makes the rest of this exciting and amusing tale." PW

007458   CLOUDY JEWEL. BY GRACE LIVINGSTON HILL (MRS. LUTZ). Philadelphia and London: J.B. Lippincott, 1920 BMC NUC.

PW-two college age motherless children select an aunt to keep house for them for the four years. She brings religion to them. She was formerly family drudge. Romance too.
NYT 12-19-20 p. 26

007459   "A DAILY RATE". BY GRACE LIVINGSTON HILL. Philadelphia: Union, [c1900] NUC.

PW-Celia, sales woman and boarder at a slovenly house. She inherits a little money and takes charge of house, improving food, manners, morals.

007460   DAWN OF THE MORNING. Philadelphia and London: J.B. Lippincott, 1911 BMC NUC.

Jemina Quaker girl's dreaded bridegroom dies on morning of wedding, replaced by younger brother. When she learns whom she's married-runs off. Whole book is the search for her and reconciliation with husband. 6-3-11 PW
Jemina's unhappy childhood, brooding over mother. NYT

007461   THE ENCHANTED BARN. Philadelphia and London: J.B. Lippincott, 1918 BMCNUC.

PW-love
NYT-June 9, 1918, p266-Heroine is a stenographer and chief support of ill mother and five sisters and brothers. They live in a barn as a temporary expedient, she is kidnapped on business trip to Washington, romance between her and owner of barn, solving all problems.

007462   EXIT BETTY. BY GRACE LIVINGSTON HILL (MRS. LUTZ). Philadelphia and London: J.B. Lippincott, 1920 BMC NUC.

TLS romance sent
PW-runs away before wedding to man her step-mother has chosen.

007463   THE FINDING OF JASPER HOLT. Philadelphia and London: J.B. Lippincott, 1916 BMC NUC.

Western adventure surrounding a wallet and a highway man PW
Western adventure surrounding a wallet and a highway man TLS

007464   THE GIRL FROM MONTANA. Boston: Golden Rule Co., 1908 NUC. Philadelphia: J. B. Lippincott, 1922 BMC.

orphan girl rides the wilds of Montana PW 1-30-05

007465   LO, MICHAEL! Philadelphia: J. B. Lippincott, 1913 BMC NUC.

"Mikky," a little newsboy, saves the life of Starr, the baby daughter of a rich banker, from an angry mob. Through the banker's help and his own indomitable energy "Mikky" rises to power, always remembering the poorer class from which he arose. The story of how he and Starr eventually struggled through class prejudice to happiness, is developed through a series of incidents which test the character of each." PW 6/7/13 2006

007466   LONE POINT: A SUMMER OUTING. London: Baptist Tract and Book Society, 1898 BMC. Philadelphia: A. J. Rowland, [c1898] NUC.

Domestic novel, religious theme, love story on seaside. BOOK NEWS 98-99:306

007467   THE MAN OF THE DESERT. New York: F. H. Revell, [c1914] NUC.

"Hazel, a daughter of luxury, while traveling in Arizona flees fom the importunities of an unwelcome suitor and is lost in the desert. Her rescue by the missionary is the beginning of a love story which ends happily, when the society girl has fitted herself for a life of service." PW:86 9/15/14:628.
NYT

007468   MARCIA SCHUYLER. Philadelphia and London: J.B. Lippincott, 1908 BMC NUC.

PW-awful love story
BKM-awful love story

356

007469   MIRANDA. Philadelphia and London: J.B.
Lippincott, 1915 BMC NUC.

Pioneer advent love story PW 5-1-15
About settling of Oregon NYT

007470   THE MYSTERY OF MARY. Philadelphia and
London: J. B. Lippincott, 1912 NUC.

007471   THE OBSESSION OF VICLONA GRACEN.
Philadelphia and London: J.B. Lippincott, 1915 NUC.

ATH-sent elderly aunt unmarried acquires good
influence over nephew and friends
Young woman inherits money raises her nephew alone PW
10-9-15

007472   PHOEBE DEANE. Philadelphia: J.B.
Lippincott, 1909 NUC. London: Hodder & Stoughton,
[1921] BMC.

a fairy tale kind of story of rescue of Cinderella NYT
BKM romance

007473   THE RED SIGNAL. Philadelphia and London:
J.B. Lippincott, 1919 BMC NUC.

American girl foils whole network of German
spies-Hilda Lessing. She's then prisoner. But she gets
help from a young engineer in getting secret
information she gathered to Washington. NYT
Spirited young American woman vs spies. TLS
"Hilda Lessing serves her country by foiling a
diabolical plot which threatens the safety of the
nation." PW

007474   THE SEARCH. Philadelphia and London: J.B.
Lippincott, 1919 BMC NUC.

TLS-for girls Soldier ready to sacrifice life for
officer, his rival in love PW
War story of an evil man who tries to wreck the
reputation of one young man and to marry a sweet girl.
Characters are types.NYT 691, 11-30-19

007475   THE STORY OF A WHIM. BY GRACE LIVINGSTON
HILL. Boston: Golden Rule Co., [c1903] NUC.

007476   AN UNWILLING GUEST. BY GRACE LIVINGSTON
HILL. Philadelphia: American Baptist Pub. society,
[1902] NUC.

007477   A VOICE IN THE WILDERNESS: A NOVEL. New
York and London: Harper, [1916] BMC NUC.

NYT-young school teacher in Arizona, has adventures
and a pretty love story; she has a mission to civilize
a part of the wild west.
TLS-0

007478   THE WITNESS; A NOVEL. New York and
London: Harper, [1917] NUC.

Focuses on a man who finds himself thru religion PW

LUTZ, MRS. See LUTZ, GRACE (LIVINGSTON) HILL.

LYALL, DAVID [pseud.]. "David Lyall" works under this
pseud. are attributed in BMC to Annie S. (Swan) Smith; in
NUC to Helen Buckingham (Mathers) Reeves.

007479   ANOTHER MAN'S MONEY. BY DAVID LYALL.
London: R.T.S., 1902 BMC. London: The 'Leisure Hour'
Library Office, [1907] NUC BMC.

007480   AT THE ELEVENTH HOUR. BY DAVID LYALL.
London: Isbister, 1899 BMC.

007481   BOND OR FREE. BY DAVID LYALL. London:
Hodder and Stoughton, 1913 BMC.

Calladine family-things go better for them, father
gets a promotion, mother who drinks is cured, oldest
daughter drudge of the house is married. TLS

007482   THE CORNER-STONE. THE RECORD OF AN OLD
HOUSE. BY DAVID LYALL. London: Hodder & Stoughton,
1904 BMC.

TLS-wholesome record of an old house.
ACAD.

007483   AN ENGLISH ROSE. BY DAVID LYALL. London:
Cassell, 1918 BMC.

TLS-harmless romance.

007484   THE FIGHTING LINE. BY DAVID LYALL.
London: Religious Tract Society, 1908 NUC.

007485   THE FLOWERS O'THE FOREST. BY DAVID LYALL.
London: Hodder and Stoughton, 1900 BMC.

SP 85:938. War stories, narrated by David Lyall, war
correspondent of the St. George's Gazette.

007486   "FOR BETTER, FOR WORSE;" A STORY OF
MARRIED LIFE. BY DAVID LYALL. London: C. H. Kelly,
1914 BMC.

ATH-Young couple's marriage.

007487   THE GOLD THAT PERISHETH. BY DAVID LYALL.
London: Leisure Hour Monthly Library, [1905] NUC BMC.

007488   THE GRAVEN IMAGE. BY DAVID LYALL. London:
Hodder and Stoughton, [1919] BMC.

Selfish bully of a husband. Saintly wife. TLS

007489   HANDICAPPED. BY DAVID LYALL. London and
New York: Hodder and Stoughton, 1914 BMC NUC.

Stories of the Salvation Army rescue work BMC
ATH-A collection of human documents illustrating power
of Christianity.
Salvation army-fic

007490   THE HERITAGE OF THE FREE; OR MORE THAN
CONQUERORS. BY DAVID LyALL. London: Hodder and
Stoughton, 1905 BMC.

007491   THE HOUSE NOT MADE WITH HANDS. BY DAVID
LYALL. London: Hodder and Stoughton, [1912] BMC NUC.

TLS- rich manufacturer and influence of a gentle woman

007492   IN A STRANGE LAND. BY DAVID LYALL.
London: Hodder and Stoughton, [1917] BMC.

Typical love story except that heroine's mother-in-law
is a German Jew who hates her daughter-in-law's race
and loves the Fatherland. TLS

007493   THE INTERVENING SEA. BY DAVID LYALL.
London: Leisure Hour Monthly Library, [1906] NUC BMC.

007494   THE LAND OF BEULAH. BY DAVID LYALL.
London: Hodder and Stoughton, 1916 BMC.

TLS-trite plot
ATH-trite plot, traditional

007495   THE LOOP OF GOLD. BY DAVID LYALL. London:
Cassell, 1920 BMC.

TLS-Vain selfish wife at War Office while husband is
in battle.

007496   MARRIED QUARTERS: A STORY FOR THE TIMES.
BY DAVID LYALL. London: Hodder and Stoughton, [1919]
BMC.

marriage difficulties helped by Quaker. TLS
SP-unequal war marriage.

007497   THE ONE WHO CAME AFTER; A STUDY OF A
MODERN WOMAN. BY DAVID LYALL. London: Hodder and
Stoughton, 1910 BMC.

TLS-Christine runs away from her husband a few weeks
after marriage because she was bored. Women's rights
play a (minor) part. She comes back.
ATH-Abrupt change from militant suffragist to ardent
theosophist.

007498   THE RISE OF PHILIP BARRETT. BY DAVID
LYALL. London: Hodder and Stoughton, 1915 BMC NUC.

007499   ROSS DURHAM, SURGEON. BY DAVID LYALL.
London: Hodder and Stoughton, 1907 BMC.

Lots of people but no strong heroine. TLS

007500   THE SHIPS OF MON DESIR. BY DAVID LYALL.
London: Hodder and Stoughton, 1910 BMC.

TLS-Mon Desir is a hostel for young English women,
their stories.

007501   THE SIGN OF THE GOLDEN FLEECE. BY DAVID

LYALL. London: Hodder and Stoughton, 1906 BMC NUC.

TLS-loveable old maid Miss Bethia Hardcastle.

007502   A STRONG MAN'S LOVE. BY DAVID LYALL.
London: S W Partridge, [1906] BMC.

Margaret Dunsmore tires of her husband's political
ambitions, ready to sacrifice these for fast society.
SR
TLS-Story of two marriages and their interaction.

007503   THE TWO MISS JEFFREYS. BY DAVID LYALL.
London: Hodder and Stoughton, 1899 BMC.

LIT 6:264. Short story, grouped around firm of
lawyers.

007504   A WASTREL REDEEMED. BY DAVID LYALL. New
York: F. H. Revell, 1895 NUC.

LYALL, EDNA, pseud. See BAYLY, ADA ELLEN.

LYLE, MARIUS, pseud. See SMYTH, UNA MAUD LYLE.

LYNCH, GERTRUDE. United States.

007505   THE FIGHTING CHANCE: THE ROMANCE OF AN
INGENUE. New York and London: Smart Set, 1903 NUC.

Modern romance set in Washington politics. PW 9-5-03

LYNCH, HANNAH. C. 1862-1904. United Kingdom.

007506   AUTOBIOGRAPHY OF A CHILD [ANONYMOUS]. New
York: Dodd, Mead, 1899 NUC. Edinburgh and London: W.
Blackwood, 1899 BMC.

Ferocious brutality toward a helpless child, a girl
whose mother was filled with vindictive animosity
toward children, so that she beat them, banged them on
the ground, battered them. She's Irish. At 8, moves
from this mother to nuns of Ladies of Mercy where
she's starved and mistreated. LIT 4:477
Angela has an inhuman mother, cruel sisters and a
heartless teacher but grows up to a normal womanhood.
Is beaten even tortured by the Sisters of an English
convent. Only her first five years were happy and
indulged. This enables her to avoid being warped by
what followed and explains her outbursts of anger and
resentment against her treatment. LBKM 16:55
Told by mature woman who can forgive her mother now.
ACAD 56:526
CR 36:30. Cold brutal mother. Kind stepfather. English
convent school years, sufferings from injustice.

007507   CLARE MONRO: THE STORY OF A MOTHER AND
DAUGHTER. London: J. Milne, [1900] BMC.

ACAD 59:384. Mother and daughter, tragic.

007508   DAUGHTERS OF MEN. New York: J. W. Lovell,
[c1892] NUC.

LW 23:245. Athens and the Isle of Terror. Two love
stories woven together; in one the man wavers between
three women. One, a gentle Greek maiden shoots him
through the shoulder for deserting her; he likes her
better for it. CR 8-6-92, p.66. Romance between
daughters of Greek scholar and young Turk. Greek
hatred of Turks is theme.
ACAD 41:27. Photini Natzelhuber, the pupil of Liszt
and the rival of Rubenstein, a genius, a coarse
sensualist, half mad and wholly kind-hearted. She
ruins the life (at all events the moral life) of
Rudolph Ehrenstein, a simple impressionable Austrian,
and allows him to be entangled in a liaison with her,
in which "cognac plays a far more important part than
passion."
SRev 73:688. Inarime has been trained intellectually
and gymnastically on the most approved classic lines."

007509   DENYS D'AUVRILLAC. A STORY OF FRENCH
LIFE. London: J. Macqueen, 1896 BMC.

SR-Domestic life, in contrast to British conception of
its liveliness.
ATH 108:899. Troubles and unhappy love of an English
girl studying art in France. Characters are not gay
Bohemians but serious, almost Germanic types.
ACAD 50:490. She is loved by two Frenchmen.

007510   JINNY BLAKE. London: Dent, 1897 BMC.

How a high-spirited, idealistic young woman was tamed
and disillusioned. Her chaperone Lady Jewsbury, her

patient lover John Trowbridge. ACAD 51:545.

007511   AN ODD EXPERIMENT. London: Methuen, 1897
BMC.

A justice-loving woman receives and reclaims her
husband's mistress. SR 84:450
Struggle of middle-aged woman for love of her husband.
She goes to see the other woman. Insists that Blanche
come to stay with them. Blanche is a young woman. The
Raymonds. ACAD 51, Fict Sup 6-19-97, 18

007512   THE PRINCE OF THE GLADES. London:
Methuen, 1891 BMC.

Story of Irish Fenian mvt. Camilla Knoys "a veritable
hero in petticoats." The motive is revolutionary. ACAD
A beautiful "but rather chilly" woman-chilly to all
but causes, is completely involved in the movement to
the extent of a 60 mile midnight ride. Miss Knoys is
this Diana-like woman. ATH 97 307
She falls in love with Godfrey O'Moore but he goes to
prison and his brother is attracted to her. Godfrey,
consequently shoots his brother. 5-9-91, SR, 565

007513   ROSNI HARVEY: A NOVEL. London: Chapman
and Hall, 1892 BMC.

ATH 100:625. Ireland and Greece. Rosni reads Greek and
German philosophers in the original language. She and
her cousin Annie go to Greece.
ACAD 42:454. "Her one great pleasure lay in her
studis. As a girl-character Rosni is just a little
over-drawn on the intellectual side." She marries a
Greek.
SRev 74:594. Rosni would like to be a medical student.
Her parents and brother are dead by end of the first
volume.

LYNCH, HARRIET LOUISE (HUSTED). 1864-1943. United States.

007514   A LITTLE GAME WITH DESTINY. BY MARIE ST.
FELIX. New York: Nocton, 1892 NUC.

"The girl who plays the little game of destiny
confides her repulsive history to the pages of her
journal. She is but sixteen when her story begins, and
for several years afterwards leads a dual life. To her
parents, rich Boston people of social importance, she
is an innocent school-girl pursuing her studies; to a
certain fast set she is 'Mrs. Gammell,' the mistress
of an elderly married man who has ruined her, and a
reckless drinker and gambler. Her career henceforth is
a downward one to the end, no detail of which is
spared the reader. the story is said to be 'a vivid
picture of what is happening about us every week of
the year.'" Publishers Weekly.

007515   PATRICIA: A SEQUEL TO "TWO BAD BROWN
EYES". BY MARIE ST. FELIX. New York: Merriam, [c1895]
NUC.

007516   TOLD BY TWO; A ROMANCE OF BERMUDA. BY
MARIE ST. FELIX (MRS. JEROME MORLEY LYNCH). Chicago:
M. A. Donohue, [c1901] NUC.

--8-31-01 PW

007517   TWO BAD BROWN EYES. BY MARIE ST. FELIX.
New York: Merriam, [c1894] NUC.

PW-possessor of eyes in title is a respectable country
girl seduced by a clergyman who repents, is filled
with horror at her immorality, and deserts her. She
drifts into a life of sin and Bohemian Paris. Fifteen
years later she returns to Chicago during Columbian
Fair; meets clergyman's daughter, and takes vengeance
in a horribly cruel, wicked way.

LYNCH, LAWRENCE L., pseud. See VAN DEVENTER, EMMA MURDOCH.

LYNCH, MRS. JEROME MORLEY. See LYNCH, HARRIET LOUISE
(HUSTED).

LYNCH, VIRGINIA. United States.

007518   DR. TOM GARDNER: A STORY FROM LIFE. New
York, Chicago, London: F. T. Neely, [c1900] NUC.

LYND, SYLVIA (DRYHURST). 1888-1952. United Kingdom.

007519   THE CHORUS: A TALE OF LOVE AND FOLLY.
London: Constable, 1915 BMC. New York: E. P. Dutton,
[1916] NUC.

TLS-passion of a 40 year old wealthy craftsman in

metal work for a 16 year old who has "all the
possibilities of a wanton." Reader gathers from final
chapter that they are realized. Wife's friends discuss
liaison and are the chorus, separate the two, he goes
back to his wife, she "comes to a bad, but gracefully
indicated, end."
"Beautiful child of 16 falls in love. Left destitute,
to go to the bad on the streets of London" PW 90:1284
10/14/16
NYT-a novel of startling power. Involves Nelly Hayes
of mysterious parentage, Arthur Hamel a successful
artist who plays havoc with her life. He does finally
resist her appeal, but hurts her bitterly. Also about
Mrs. Hamel and Hilda, Kelly's friend who is a strong
beautiful modern girl one closes the book with a dull
heartache.

LYNDON, pseud. See HUGHES, MRS. REGINALD.

LYNN, ETHEL GRACE ALSPICE.

007520   THE ADVENTURES OF A WOMAN HOBO. BY ETHEL
LYNN, M.D. New York: G.H. Doran, [c1917] NUC.

adventures of couple on a tandem bike PW
Dr. Ethel Lynn out of work in Chicago in 1908 because
of depression and suffering from TB must get to
California. With no money available, she and husband
go by bike and on freight cars.
Diary form. all ends well. NYT 258, 7-8-17
Account of the experience of the author and her
husband in traveling by bicycle from Chicago to
California. NUC
F 95 West-Desc and trav non-fiction?

LYNN, EVE.

007521   THE JOY OF HELL. London: H.J. Drane,
[1906] BMC.

LYNN, MARGARET. United States.

007522   FREE SOIL. New York: Macmillan, 1920 NUC.

PW-Story of free soil struggle in Kansas
NYT 12-19-20 P24. Brave people fighting for freedom
thru dangers and conspiracies.

LYON, ANNA E. United States.

007523   PRUDENCE PRATT. BY MRS. DORE LYON. New
York: G. V. Blackburne, 1903 NUC.

NY smart set. PW 6-27-03
Some discussions "in bad taste." Innocent old
fashioned love story. Much about clothes. 03 NYT 653

LYON, GILBERTA M. F.

007524   ABSENT, YET PRESENT. London: Digby, Long,
[1894] BMC.

Man sworn to keep a secret but it makes him appear a
scoundrel to the woman he loves. SP 74:401
Laura Markham throws over man she loves to marry her
uncle for his money. The young man, in the meantime,
loses his sight. (He'sthe one who swears to keep a
secret) ACAD 47:31
SR-simple, old-fashioned love story.

007525   FOR GOOD OR EVIL. London: Gay and Bird,
1893 NUC BMC.

Zelia Langton and Pansy Bruce cousins. The first good,
the second bad-almost elopes. But Zelia brings her
cousin around to be good and both end happily. ATH
102:879.
SP-Pansy, born naturally good, looks after Zelia, who
would like to be good until she is safely married to a
nice man.

007526   ONE HOUR OF MADNESS. London: Digby, Long,
[1895] BMC NUC.

ACAD 49:195. Scotland. In that hour Lord Malreward
married the wrong woman. They grow farther apart; she
elopes and comes to grief in every way. He had wanted
to elope but Lady Nan had refused: he would now marry
her except he gets sick and dies.

LYON, LUCILE GRINNAN. United States.

007527   "THE GREENWOODS". New York: Neale, 1915
NUC.

"A love story with a study of an unusual child." BKM

41 1915
Mischevious little girl called "The Greenwoods."
8-21-15 PW

LYON, MRS. DORE. See LYON, ANNA E.

LYONS, MARGARET REDIC. Nationality Unknown.

007528   TRIXEY, THE MANICURE GIRL. BY MARGARET
REDIC. New York: Broadway, [c1908] NUC.

LYSTER, CORA.

007529   PAUL HEINSIUS: A STUDY FROM LIFE. London:
T. Unwin, 1896 BMC.

SR-one of the ideas of the plot is entirely revolting.
Study of Paul and his betrothed, the latter from her
letters only.
ATH 107:616. "Breaks fresh ground." A cold and
observant eye carefully noting the squirmings of a few
Germanic characters. Unpleasing subject, unsavory.
Heinsius is a cashier, has disease and pain?
ACAD 50:218. "The illustration of human frailty as
exhibited in the male species." He neglects the woman
to whom he is engaged, seduces his nurse, finally is
scorned by the girl he has ruined, rejected by his
betrothed wife, and utterly befooled by a clever woman
he had supposed to be another of his victims.
CR 29:59. "Valuable commentary on Turkish life and
customs."

LYTTLETON, EDITH JOAN. 1874-1945. New Zealand.

007530   THE ALTAR STAIRS. BY G. B. LANCASTER. New
York: Doubleday, [1908] PW. London: Hodder &
Stoughton, [1908] NUC BMC.

PW-male adventure.
TLS-trading and love in the S. Pacific.
BRD- "A novel which tells a tale of the South seas, in
which a dominating man suddenly finds himself in love
with a woman who is bound to another. The hero holds
for months in his power the man to whom the woman he
loves is bound, but ultimate happiness comes out of it
all."- NYT
"The grip of the story can in no way be conveyed by an
outline of the plot, each incident being so firmly
built into the general structure that the whole must
be envisaged in detail to be appreciated. It would
seem as if there might be less wading in gore without
sacrificing the sweep and vigor of the story." NATION.
87:553. D. 3. '08. 250w.

007531   FOOL DIVINE. BY G. B. LANCASTER. London:
Hodder and Stoughton, [1917] BMC. New York: G. H.
Doran, [c1917] NUC.

Man loves Cuban woman, marital problems,
reconciliation. PW

007532   THE HONOURABLE PEGGY. BY G. B. LANCASTER.
London: Constable, 1911 BMC.

Motor-car story. TLS

007533   JIM OF THE RANGES. BY G. B. LANCASTER.
London: Constable, 1910 BMC. London: Constable, 1911
NUC.

BM Australian adventure.
TLS-Australian adventure. Male.

007534   THE LAW-BRINGERS. BY G. B. LANCASTER.
London, New York: Hodder and Stoughton, [c1913] BMC
NUC.

Canadian Northwest. Two mounted police and their
different attitudes toward their work as law-bringers.
Two women--Jennifer conventional "good" woman. Andree
untamed daughter of white man, Indian wife. Focus is
on the affection between the two men. NYT
"The story is mainly that of two men of the police of
north-west Canada. ...Of the two, whose fortunes are
intimately connectedin love and service, one has a
reckless past, especially with women, and finally
redeems it after a great struggle. The other is a man
of sterling quality, a steady worker whose only
mistakeis falling in love with a girl unworthy of
him." (ATH) BRD 1913.

007535   THE SAVIGNYS. BY G. B. LANCASTER. London
New York: Hodder and Stoughton, [1918] NUC BMC.

007536   SONS O' MEN. BY G. B. LANCASTER. London:
A. Melrose, [1904] NUC BMC. New York: Doubleday, Page,

007537   THE SPUR; OR THE BONDAGE OF KIN SEVERNE.
BY G. B. LANCASTER. New York: Doubleday, Page, 1906
NUC.

NYT-male hero, but there is a heroine. Rev. not
informative but sounds promising from its tone.
"Any one who knows aught of Australian or island life,
of sheep farms, or copra gatherers and traders, will
respond to this vivid writing..." (OUTLOOK) BRD 1906

007538   A SPUR TO SMITE. BY G. B. LANCASTER.
London: A. Melrose, [1905] BMC NUC.

About a sheep herder.

007539   THE TRACKS WE TREAD. BY G. B. LANCASTER.
New York: Doubleday, Page, 1907 NUC. London: Hodder
and Stoughton, 1907 BMC.

Adventure. 10-19-09. PW

LYTTLETON, EDITH SOPHY (BALFOUR).   B. 1865.   United Kingdom.

007540   THE TOUCH OF SORROW. BY EDITH HAMLET.
London: J. M. Dent, 1896 BMC. New York: H. Holt, 1896
NUC.

Study of influence of grief on a young woman. At first
is happy, selfish, thoughtless. Feels nothing for the
grief of others. Death of her child makes her
understand. CR 26,30:253
LBKM 10:175. Stella felt she deserved life's
treasures, rebellious until given a grief she has to
face, which softens her.
SR-Death of her baby is the "Touch of sorrow." Rev.
finds it not believable that this wrought a change.
SP 77:375. Rev. finds change unlikely.
BKM 4:163. Rev. finds too much insight into
obstetrics, a subject "best left in the shadow."

M., A. S., pseud. See MACNEILL, NEVADA.

MABEL, pseud. See PARKS, MABEL E.

MABIE, LOUISE (KENNEDY). D. 1957. United States.

007541   THE LIGHTS ARE BRIGHT. "FOUR BELLS AND
THE LIGHTS ARE BRIGHT." NIGHT CALL OF LOOKOUT ON THE
ORE-BOATS OF THE GREAT LAKES.) A NOVEL. New York and
London: Harper, 1914 NUC BMC.

Story of Middle West business competition, Lake City
Steel versus the Trevor Works. The former initiates a
series of persecutions amounting to a plot to drive
the other out. One of their agents, Hubert,
complicates matters by falling in love with Theodora
Trevor, owner of the Works, but earlier he has flirted
with Miss Beach, secretary, as a means to his end.
Lake City Steel comes near winning but Miss Beach
turns witness against them. Theodora finds her true
love in the faithful manager of her business. PW
NYT-Theodora at 18 is owner and operator of immense
mines of iron ore and a big steel works on Lake Erie.
Her father has left her with a sense of responsibility
and obligation that the property be administered to
serve society in every sense. Rival concern attempts
to gain control of the Trevor works; suave man has
been assigned to task of influencing her to sell.
Rivalry in love between him and her forceful manager.

007542   THE WINGS OF PRIDE. New York and London:
Harper, 1913 BMC NUC.

PW-"Scene opens in New York, where Olive Muir,
beautiful, arrogant and spoiled, lives with her mother
with every luxury surrounding her. Mrs. Muir asks
Alice Prentice, a girl from Ohio, to visit them
against Olive's wishes, and she makes Alice miserable.
Then just as she repents of her hardness she learns
that Alice is her sister, Mrs. Muir only her adopted
mother and disreputable Mr. Prentice is her father.
What she then does, how she goes to her own mother,
and the part a fine young lawyer and some grafters
play in her life make the rest of the story." 83:1100.
The humiliating discovery of her real origin changes
her completely and sends her to Ohio to take up her
duties to others. Falls in love with a Western lawyer.

MACALEESE, SUSAN ELIZABETH. United States.

007543   THE AMBITIONS OF A WORLDLY WOMAN. BY
ALICE E. MURRAY. New York: F. Neely, [1901] NUC.

PW 8-17-01

MACALILLY, ALICE. Nationality Unknown.

007544   HERCULES CARLSON. Cincinnati: Jennings &
Pye, [1903] NUC.

Concerns a boy. 12-12-03 PW

007545   HILDA LANE'S ADOPTIONS. Cincinnati:
Jennings & Graham, [c1905] NUC.

Misunderstanding keeps Hilda from the man she loves
for twenty years. She adopts a boy and a black girl;
educates them. The girl gives her life to white fever
sufferers, the boy discovering upon marriage that he's
part black gives his life to uplifting the blacks. BRD

007546   THE LARKINS WEDDING. New York: Moffat,
Yard, 1905 NUC.

Widow; humorous story PW 10-7-05
NYT 650,05

007547   TERRA COTTA; A STUDY OF LIFE IN THE CLAY.
Cincinnati: Jennings & Pye, [1903] NUC.

Mystery and crime PW 2-14-03

MACALPINE, AVERY. See MACALPINE, STELLA AVERY FARRINGTON.

MACALPINE, STELLA AVERY FARRINGTON. United States.

007548   A MAN'S CONSCIENCE: A NOVEL. BY AVERY
MACALPINE. London: S. Low, 1891 BMC. New York: Harper,
1891 NUC.

Young man of good birth loves a farmer's daughter.
Mother interferes. He goes off to Europe. The young
woman marries a minister. He does send her a letter
upon learning, but it's intercepted by a revengeful
postmaster. SR 8-22-91,228

MACANDREW, MERCEDES.

007549   A COAT OF MANY COLOURS; WOVEN FROM
HONORIA'S LETTERS TO THE BEST FRIEND, AND PATCHED WITH
PIECES FROM A CERTAIN NOTEBOOK. BY THE AUTHOR OF
HONORIA'S PATCHWORK [ANONYMOUS]. London: Chapman &
Hall, 1905 BMC.

Honoria has some good ideas, fond of books, has an
honest, inquiring mind. ACAD 05:1098.

007550   HONORIA'S PATCHWORK. London: Chapman &
Hall, 1904 BMC.

007551   WHAT MATTERS [ANONYMOUS]. London: Chapman
& Hall, 1911 BMC.

MACARTHUR, ADELLA R. United States.

007552   'THAT ROMANIST': A NOVEL. Boston: Arena,
1896 NUC.

PW 11-7-96. Romance, in which religious differences
between Catholic and Protestant are overcome.

MACARTHUR, RUTH ALBERTA (BROWN).

007553   LITTLE MOTHER. Philadelphia: Penn, 1916
NUC. London: G.G. Harrap, 1917 BMC.

P27

MACAULAY, ALLAN, pseud. See STEWART, CHARLOTTE.

MACAULAY, FANNIE (CALDWELL). 1863-1941. United States.

007554   THE HOUSE OF THE MISTY STAR; A ROMANCE OF
YOUTH AND HOPE AND LOVE IN OLD JAPAN. BY FRANCES
LITTLE (FANNIE CALDWELL MACAULAY). New York: Century,
1915 NUC. London: Hodder & Stoughton, 1915 NUC.

2 spinsters, a teacher and a missionary and a young
couple. Sweet, harmless book. Heroine, fat & nearly
60.
Setting is Japan; Miss Ursula Jenkins. Taught here 30
of her 58 years. Taught English. Finds joy in her
garden. She learns of another woman in distress (Jane
Grey) and brings her to her house. A young troublesome
Japanese American girl also comes to live at her
house. She meets her man through the two older women.
Amusing and charming. NYT
Slight pretty. TLS

007555   THE LADY AND SADA SAN; A SEQUEL TO THE

LADY OF THE DECORATION. BY FRANCES LITTLE. New York: Century, 1912 NUC.

PW-
NYT

007556   THE LADY MARRIED. BY THE AUTHOR OF "THE LADY OF THE DECORATION" [ANONYMOUS]. London: Hodder & Stoughton, 1912 BMC.

Sequel to Lady of decoration. Descriptions of Japan and revolution in Peking. SP
ATH-trivial and sentimental letters.

007557   THE LADY OF THE DECORATION. BY FRANCES LITTLE. New York: Century, 1906 BMC NUC. London: Hodder and Stoughton, 1906 BMC NUC.

PW-Kentucky widow goes to Japan to teach. Kentucky woman's experiences as kindergarten teacher in a mission school in Japan and later as a nurse in the Russo-Japanese War. Sentimental and romantic. (Book)

007558   LITTLE SISTER SNOW. BY FRANCES LITTLE. New York: Century, 1909 NUC. London: Hodder & Stoughton, 1909 NUC BMC.

Yuki San--mixed marriage idea.
Study of Japanese girl from childhood to betrothal in grave Japanese style to suitor of parents' choice. Yuki then meets an American. Her diary, "that naive, pathetic, exquisite confession" "a powerful brief for the emancipation of women of the Orient from the unnatural laws governing marriage." TLS

MACAULAY, MARGARET.

007559   THE SENTENCE ABSOLUTE. London: J. Nisbet, 1914 BMC.

ATH male hero helped out by sympathetic heroine.

MACAULAY, R. See MACAULAY, ROSE.

MACAULAY, ROSE. 1881-1958. United Kingdom.

007560   ABBOTS VERNEY; A NOVEL. BY R. MACAULAY. London: J. Murray, 1906 BMC NUC.

Study of temperament--focuses on a man. LBKM
heroine is a bore. TLS

007561   THE FURNACE. London: J. Murray, 1907 BMC NUC.

Dregs of society in an Italian town. ACAD
Brother and sister in Italy. TLS

007562   THE LEE SHORE. BY R. MACAULAY. New York: G. H. Doran, [c1912] NUC. London: Hodder & Stoughton, [1912] BMC.

"Novel won first prize in the $5000 Prize Novel Award made by Hodder & Stoughton. Story of a man determined to be happy. An aristocrat by birth and training, a vagabond by nature, Peter Margerison preferred the chance-met adventurers of the highroad to more normal and well-regulated persons. He rebelled against conventions, and fled from cities to the freedom of the road, his lee shore. Tale is full of lovable men and women, an atmosphere of holiday care-freeness, and sun-bathed landscapes of Italy's coast towns." PW
ATH-Peter loses all including wife and reputation but refuses to grow up and becomes a tramp hawking his own embroidery. Brother is Hilary.
TLS-dear little breakable piece of weakness, his disreputable brother and happy go lucky optimistic wife are the menage.
SP-Vyvian is unspeakable.
SR-Peter is main character. He marries Rhoda but loves Lucy who is married to Denis. Rhoda runs off with former lover, leaving him with his son Thomas and his dog, then he goes for a tramp with Rodney. He almost runs off with Lucy but doesn't because of Denis.

007563   THE MAKING OF A BIGOT. London: Hodder and Stoughton, [c1914] BMC NUC.

SR 147- supp 21 Mar 18. Male hero who likes everyone, is sure there is some truth in every opinion. Realistic character study.
ATH 143:377-he decides, finally, on looking at other people, that one cannot succeed without becoming an absolute bigot.

007564   NON-COMBATANTS AND OTHERS. London and New York: Hodder & Stoughton, [1916] BMC NUC.

TLS-civilians during war. Alix is heroine.

007565   POTTERISM, A TRAGI-FARCICAL TRACT. New York: Boni & Liveright, [c1920] NUC. London: W. Collins, 1920 NUC BMC.

TLS-pro love and truth. Potterism is a disease which affects humanity. Anti-Potterite hero is male.
SP-All women characters are modern. Mother is a novelist, Jane a journalist. Katherine a scientist. Potter family have a publishing firm, invincibly successful, "flaunting the banner of the great sentimental public," advances triumphantly. Jane marries Hobart, a true Potterite but grows to love Arthur Gideon an anti-P. Hobart was pushed downstairs and died. Who did it? Jane is a daughter of the Potter Pr., determined to take and keep best of life, greedy, lazy, spoiled child.
SR-Jane's mother writes sentimental spiritual novels. After Hobart dies Jane & Gideon become engaged; his paper, the Weekly Facts, has been destroyed and he goes to Russia to gather facts, but never returns. NYT 10-31-20 p. 22. Novel in 6 books, 1st and last author narrator, other 4 by different characters. One of these is a burlesque of the Florence Barclay-Ethel Dell-Ruby Ayres school of fiction.

007566   THE SECRET RIVER. BY R. MACAULAY. London: J. Murray, 1909 NUC BMC.

007567   THE VALLEY CAPTIVES. BY R. MACAULAY. New York: H. Holt, 1911 NUC. London: J. Murray, 1912 BMC.

John is tougher than her brother. PW 5-6-11
Story of hatred, fear and murder--morose tale of Wales. TLS
Story centers on Teddy Vallon, the man. SR

007568   VIEWS AND VAGABONDS. BY R. MACAULAY. New York: H. Holt, 1912 NUC. London: J. Murray, 1912 NUC BMC.

PW-personalities vs principles.
TLS-male aristocrat sets up as blacksmith and marries village girl.
ATH-she is inarticulate, self sufficient but shut-in, unapproachable, husband could not know her mind. Triumph of characterization.
SP-Louie is a millhand. She gets fed up with her husband's pompous friends and family, goes to the vagabonds, the Crevequers. She tells him off and parts--finally he becomes a human being and they are united. She and the Crevequers stand out against a company of shrewd and amiable worldlings, faddists and social experimentalists. (Life is not a solemn thing).

007569   WHAT NOT: A PROPHETIC COMEDY. London: Constable, 1919 NUC BMC.

A prophecy : what Civil Service life will be, street aeroplanes in London. A bevy of young people-their lives and loves. Kitty Grammond among them-elegant, adventurous immensely efficient enjoys many freedoms. Helps run the Ministry of Brains (registers mental category of all in England, tells each whom to marry and whom not.) Kitty's brain of highest order. A minister of Brains (a deficient) shouldn't marry. But they marry and it works. The truth ruins the Ministry of Brains. SP
Reviewer can't decide whether the work is serious or not or whom or what is satirized. LBKM
Satire upon the future menace of official control, centering in the Ministry of Brains that tries to eliminate the unintelligent. BAKER

MACBETH, MADGE HAMILTON (LYONS). B. 1878?. Canada.

007570   KLEATH. Boston: Small, Maynard, [c1917] NUC BMC. Toronto: Musson Book, [c1917] NUC.

Story of a man with a secret past. Wife shows up when he's on trial. PW
Yukon, Kleath, a linotype operator, comes North to be free. But gets involved with two women, one siren, one angel. NYT 259 7-8-17

007571   THE WINNING GAME. New York: Broadway, 1910 NUC.

NYT Wife devoted to Alcoholic husband, reforms him.

MACCAHAN, BELLE TRAVERS. Nationality Unknown.

361

007572   THE PRESHUS CHILD. New York: Cochrane,
1909 NUC.

    Wholesome story about an adoption. NYT

MACCALEB, IDA HARWOOD. United States.

    007573   TRIUMPHS AND FAILURES. New York:
    Broadway, [c1905] NUC.

MACCALL, FLORINDA.

    007574   DOUBLE BONDS. London: Cassell, 1909 BMC.

    Happiness and misery of Silver Mackay of Australia.
    TLS

MACCALL, SIDNEY, pseud. See FENOLLOSA, MARY (MACNEIL).

MACCARTER, MARGARET (HILL). 1860-1938. United States.

    007575   THE CORNER STONE. Chicago: A. C. McClurg,
    1915 NUC.

    007576   THE COTTONWOOD'S STORY. Topeka, Kan.:
    Crane, 1903 NUC.

    007577   IN OLD QUIVIRA. Topeka, Kan.: Crane, 1908
    NUC.

    007578   A MASTER'S DEGREE. Chicago: A.C. McClurg,
    1913 NUC. London: C.F. Cazenove, 1913 BMC.

    PW 84 10/11/13:1246 Kansas college; two young men come
    to study: don't realize they're related. "Scene is
    laid in a Kansas college, where Dean Pennelben fights
    big fight for the people of the plains. There are
    three love stories interwoven through the tale and
    strange events that lead them all to a happy ending."

    007579   PAYING MOTHER; THE TRIBUTE BEAUTIFUL. New
    York & London: Harper, [c1920] NUC.

    007580   THE PEACE OF THE SOLOMON VALLEY. Chicago:
    A.C. McClurg, 1911 NUC.

    1. Solomon valley, Kansas

    007581   THE PRICE OF THE PRAIRIE, A STORY OF
    KANSAS. Chicago: A. C. McClurg, 1910 NUC.

    Kansas pioneer life -PW
    NyT

    007582   THE RECLAIMERS. New York & London:
    Harper, [1918] BMC NUC.

    PW Rom in Kansas
    Subject is reclaiming US desert land. Geraldine Swaim,
    beautiful, business-like, firm of purpose, owns 1200
    acres in Kansas. She was raised in luxury but seeks an
    independent existence "in the land of sagebrush,
    sandstones and blowouts." Learns her land is a blow-up
    (worthless) becomes a math teacher; overcomes
    prejudice of the town and its gossip. She braves all
    this and succeeds. There is a hero. NYT

    007583   VANGUARDS OF THE PLAINS: A ROMANCE OF THE
    OLD SANTA FE TRAIL. New York & London: Harper, [1917]
    BMC NUC.

    Trad advent story of Indians, etc. with Gail and
    Beverly (?) as heroes PW
    historical novel of the trade achievements in settling
    the west, of commerce. Story starts when her o is a
    boy. His household goes west. NYT

    007584   A WALL OF MEN. Chicago: A.C. McClurg,
    1912 NUC.

    PW--Kansas
    NYT--hist., founding of a commonwealth

    007585   WINNING THE WILDERNESS. Chicago: McClurg,
    1914 NUC.

    PW 86 10-10-14:1205--"Asher Aydelot, a former United
    States soldier, and his wife take up a homestead claim
    in Kansas. They win out in a long fight with nature,
    and learn also to love the prairies. Their boy has the
    same love of the soil, but he enlists in the Spanish
    war, goes to the Philippines and later to the Boxer
    war. At length he answers the call of the prairie,
    where a Kansas girl is waiting for him."

MACCARTHY, EMMA W. United States.

007586   CONGRESSMAN JOHN AND HIS WIFE'S
SATISFACTION: A NOVEL. New York: G. W. Dillingham,
1891 NUC.

    Mrs John Fairfax is ambitious for her husband but in
    the end loses all taste for political prominence.
    Washington scene. Beautiful Marguerite Howard comes to
    live with them. Her romance with a Russian baron.
    Crime, suicide, revenge. PW 3-7-91.

MACCARTHY, MARY (WARRE CORNISH).

    007587   A PIER & A BAND. A NOVEL OF THE NINETIES.
    London: Chatto & Windus, 1918 BMC. London: M. Secker,
    1931 NUC.

    TLS-heroine and author both chuck the hero.
    SR-argument over making neighborhood into a resort
    puts Antony & Perdita into relationship of Romeo and
    Juliet. Perdita, not really of her family's mind (it's
    not houses that spoil the landscape, its ugly houses)
    finds a more congenial partner. Antony settles down to
    a bachelorhood of keeping his property safe from
    tourists. Author: "he had achieved his object; few
    people enjoyed the place." Perdita's character and
    relationship with selfish father.

MACCARTNEY, CATHERINE ROBERTSON. United States.

    007588   THE HERO OF THE AGES: A STORY OF THE
    NAZARENE. New York, Chicago, Toronto: F. H. Revell,
    [c1896] NUC.

MACCARTY, IDA HELEN. B. 1876. United States.

    007589   MARIAM'NE OF THE CEDARS. New York:
    Shakespeare Press, 1911 NUC.

MACCAULEY, CLARICE VALLETTE. United States.

    007590   THE GARDEN OF DREAMS. Chicago: McClurg,
    1912 NUC.

    PW--"idyllic love story"
    NYT

MACCHESNEY, DORA GREENWELL. 1871-1912. United States.

    007591   BEATRIX INFELIX: A SUMMER TRAGEDY IN
    ROME. New York and London: J. Lane, 1898 BMC NUC.

    LIT 3:136. Beatrice and Horatia in Rome, with
    Beatrice's mother, a novelist. Horatia, a native of
    New England, narrates story. Beatrice hopes for
    Nirvana after death, Horatia not troubled by religious
    aspirations. Beatrice and her loves, none of which she
    can accept, finally she overdoses on chloral.
    ACAD 53:469. Beatrice a Marie Bashkirtseff type:
    unhappy, unsatisfied.
    SR 85:664. Beatrice is forced into a loveless marriage
    by her mother.

    007592   THE CONFESSION OF RICHARD PLANTAGENET.
    London: Smith, Elder, 1913 BMC NUC.

    hist rom--white-washes Richard of Gloucester ACAD

    007593   CORNET STRONG OF IRETON'S HORSE; AN
    EPISODE OF THE IRONSIDES. New York & London: J. Lane,
    1903 BMC NUC.

    hist. 3-28-03 PW
    hist. ACAD 226 v64 and 390
    Cavaliers vs puritans LBKM 4-03, 30
    ATH, 121, 494

    007594   KATHLEEN CLARE: HER BOOK, 1637-1641.
    EDITED BY DORA GREENWELL MCCHESNEY. Edinburgh: W.
    Blackwood, 1895 BMC NUC.

    historical romance: fall of Stafford and love affair
    of young girl. SR 80:247.
    Day by day account of life at Dublin Castle. A love
    story of cross purposes, whole issue of King vs
    Parliament. Her hero's trial and imprisonment. ACAD
    48:183

    007595   LONDON ROSES. AN IDYLL OF THE BRITISH
    MUSEUM. London: Smith, Elder, 1903 BMC NUC.

    romance begins in a library ACAD 64, 610
    homesick for the states ACAD 65, 37
    her wisdom; they meet in the British Museum ATH 122,87

    007596   MIRIAM CROMWELL, ROYALIST: A ROMANCE OF

THE GREAT REBELLION. Chicago: Way and Williams, 1897
NUC. Edinburgh and London: W. Blackwood, 1897 BMC.

Dramatic war scenes. SR 83:278.
Daredevil Rupert is hero. Miriam is Cromwell's niece.
She loves him but he's devoted to King. Chance takes
her to Charles' court at Oxford. Author's view
impartial. ACAD 51:103.

007597 RUPERT, BY THE GRACE OF GOD; THE STORY OF
AN UNRECORDED PLOT SET FORTH BY WILL FORTESCUE; EDITED
AND REVISED BY DORA GREENWELL MCCHESNEY. London:
Macmillan, 1899 BMC NUC.

Historical romance. Civil Wars of 17th Century England
told by Will Fortescue. Battle scenes. LIT 5:303
plot to put Prince Rupert on English throne in place
of Charles I. LBKM 16:113
Action packed historical romance. "A tour de force,
for a woman at least, to fight over again these
battlefields"-of the Cavaliers and Roundheads. NYT
7-22-99,485
Intrigue, war, adventure. BAKER 03,139

007598 THE WOUNDS OF A FRIEND. London: Smith,
Elder, 1908 BMC NUC.

TLS--Rom. adv. male heroes. A romance of Eng. and
America, dealing with Raleigh's lost colony of Roanoke

007599 YESTERDAY'S TOMORROW: A ROMANCE OF THE
RESTORATION. London: J.M. Dent, 1905 BMC NUC.

hist. rom ACAD 05,127
ATH 05,204

MACCHESNEY, ELIZABETH STUDDIEFORD.

007600 UNDER THE SHADOW OF THE MISSION: A MEMORY
OF SANTA BARBARA. BY L. STUDDIEFORD MCCHESNEY. London:
Methuen, 1897 NUC.

Invalids in Esperanza hotel--a novel without a story.
Ultimata, the speaker, through her love of daughter,
nature, paints her own portrait. Discussion on women's
place, theology. Holds certain belief most fiercely.
There's a militant aspect . All her
friends--especially the women--are intensely
interesting. She says that falling in love with women
has been her life -long weakness. Her appreciation of
women is intense. Very beautiful relation between her
and daughter. SR 83:588
Conversations of a chorus of women and two men. All
characters have symbolic names. ACAD 51:425

MACCHESNEY, L. STUDDIEFORD, pseud. See MACCHESNEY,
ELIZABETH STUDDIEFORD.

MACCHETTA, BLANCHE ROOSEVELT (TUCKER). 1853-1898. United
States.

007601 HAZEL FANE. A NOVEL. BY BLANCHE
ROOSEVELT. London: Chapman and Hall, 1891 BMC NUC.

Jacob Brent accused of murdering brother but is
innocent. Found guilty-circumstantial evidence.
Powerful argument vs capital punishment. ACAD
There is also Hazel's romance and brilliant talk. ATH
98 615
English country soc. plot culminates in a murder,
trial. Jacob's brother defrauded him of an estate. SR
11-7-1891, 533
SP-purpose of novel is the institution of a Court of
Criminal Appeal. Story of 2 brothers.

007602 A RIVIERA ROMANCE "RIEN NE VA PLUS". BY
BLANCHE ROOSEVELT. London: Downey, 1899 NUC BMC.

Vulgar story of gamblers in Monte Carlo told through
diaries of hero and heroine. SP 83:648

MACCLELLAN, HARRIET (HARE). United States.

007603 BROKEN CHORDS CROSSED BY THE ECHO OF A
FALSE NOTE. BY MRS. GEORGE MCCLELLAN (HARFORD
FLEMMING). Philadelphia: J. B. Lippincott, 1893 BMC
NUC.

A young woman entered convent; took her vows, forced
to leave but keeps her vows in spirit by refusing to
marry, meeting him daily as friend-a strained
situation. They prize their friendship (which lasts
thru their whole lives) above all else. CR 22:161.
Clergyman's daughter runs away from home and becomes
an actress. Marries a man to "save herself from
disgrace." He dies. The man who disgraced her loves

another woman who throws him over when she learns his
secret-"sends him to make reparations." He marries the
clergyman's daughter. There are complications and
unhappiness but all ends well. PW 1-7-93.

MACCLELLAN, MRS. GEORGE. See MACCLELLAN, HARRIET (HARE).

MACCLELLAND, M. G. See MACCLELLAND, MARY GREENWAY.

MACCLELLAND, MARY GREENWAY. 1853-1895. United States.

007604 BROADOAKS. BY M. G. MCCLELLAND. St. Paul:
Price-McGill, [c1893].

Virginia; title refers to a home of heroine with two
suitors-a northeast engineer and a gallant Southern
man. The two are contrasted. PW 6-10-93

007605 MAMMY MYSTIC. BY M. G. MCCLELLAND. New
York: Merriam, [c1895] NUC.

Mystic is a quardroon slave, marries a Scandanavian
though law forbids such a marriage. when her child is
born, substitutes it for her mistress' dead child;
that child grows to womanhood, marries, has a daughter
Eugenia in whose life "the effects of this act are
seen and the laws of heredity traced." PW
12-14-95:1147

007606 MANITOU ISLAND. BY M. G. MCCLELLAND. New
York: H. Holt, 1892 NUC.

CR 8-20-92 p 91. Dilapidated Southern mansion
surrounded by swamp lands, a blighted family. Gloomy
plot, insanity. Dr Irene best character.
LW 23:310. Insanity, murder and harrowing mystery.

007607 A NAMELESS NOVEL. BY M. G. MCCLELLAND.
New York: S. H. Moore, [1891] NUC.

Contest to name the novel. One of chief chars is a
Black man with blue gums whose ancestors killed mules
by biting them. IND.

007608 THE OLD POST-ROAD. BY M. G. MCCLELLAND.
New York: Merriam, [c1894] NUC.

LW 25:282. Blighted romance of young woman who enters
a convent after discovering her lover is a highwayman.
He remorses and later gives money to convent where she
is praying for him.
CR 25:237. Historical romance. Maryland in 1790's.
Band of highwaymen, gentlemen of high connections.
Their identity is discovered. Tragedy of young woman.

007609 ST. JOHN'S WOOING: A STORY. BY M. G.
MCCLELLAND. New York: Harper, 1895 NUC.

Texas. St. John, English, drifts down to Texas, gets
lucky, falls in love, marries, lives happily. LW 26:42
PW-romance. English hero on Texas ranch.

MACCLUNG, NELLIE LETITIA (MOONEY). 1873-1951. Canada.

007610 DANNY AND THE PINK LADY. London: Hodder &
Stoughton, 1908 BMC.

TLS--Sent

007611 IN TIMES LIKE THESE. New York: D.
Appleton, 1915 BMC NUC. Toronto: G.J. McLeod & Allen,
1915 BMC NUC.

HQ 1221 woman-social and moral questions

007612 THE SECOND CHANCE. New York: Doubleday,
Page, 1910 NUC. London: Hodder & Stoughton, [1910]
BMC.

TLS sent stuff PW TLS.
heroine Searle Watson a good angel, wholesome
countrified story set in Canada LBKM

007613 SOWING SEEDS IN DANNY. New York:
Doubleday, Page, 1908 NUC. London: Doubleday, Page,
1908 BMC.

MACCLUSKY, H. M. See MACCLUSKY, HENRIETTA MARIA EVANS.

MACCLUSKY, HENRIETTA MARIA EVANS. B. 1844.

007614 THE WAY OF LIFE. BY H. M. MCCLUSKY. New
York: M. E. Munson, [1905] NUC.

MACCOMAS, INA VIOLET. B. 1889. United Kingdom.

007615　　　　　ASHES OF VENGEANCE. A ROMANCE OF OLD
FRANCE. BY H. B. SOMERVILLE. London: Hutchinson, 1913
BMC. New York: McBride, Nast, 1914 NUC.

thrilling story of vendetta & love ATH

007616　　　　　THE MAN'S STORY. BY H. B. SOMERVILLE.
London: Hutchinson, [1919] BMC NUC.

007617　　　　　THE MARK OF VRAYE. BY H. B. SOMERVILLE.
London: Hutchinson, 1917 BMC.

trad hist rom TLS

007618　　　　　SOME WOMEN AND TIMOTHY. BY H. B.
SOMERVILLE. London: Hutchinson, 1915 NUC BMC. New
York: E.P. Dutton, [1915] NUC.

all the women bring out his friendly genial qualities
TLS

MACCONNELL, SARAH WARDER. United States.

007619　　　　　MANY MANSIONS. Boston: Houghton Mifflin,
1918 NUC.

PW-love story.
NYT-brought up in gloomy boarding house, earns living
as interior decorator.

007620　　　　　WHY, THEODORA! Boston: Small, Maynard,
[1915] BMC NUC.

Thinks for self, unconventional. Makes her own way has
a painter lover who goes to prison. PW 10-16-15
Fanciful tale.
An intimate study of the soul of the heroine. BKM 42
1915-16

MACCORD, LOTTIE. United States.

007621　　　　　ONLY A HORSE: OR, TOM'S REFORM. Emporia,
Kan.: McCord & McCord, 1905 NUC.

PW adventures of 2 horses, designed to encourage
gentleness towards animals

MACCRACKIN, JOSEPHINE (WOEMPNER) CLIFFORD. B. 1838. United
States.

007622　　　　　'ANOTHER JUANITA,' AND OTHER STORIES. BY
JOSEPHINE CLIFFORD. Buffalo: C. Wells Moulton, 1893
NUC.

MACCULLOCH, CATHARINE (WAUGH). B. 1862.

007623　　　　　MR. LEX; OR, THE LEGAL STATUS OF MOTHER
AND CHILD. Chicago, New York: F. H. Revell, 1899 NUC.

From list of books related to woman's question and
suffrage. WOMAN'S JOURNAL. 12-2-11
A legal treatise in form of fiction. LC card.

MACCULLOUGH, MYRTLE (REED). 1874-1911. United States.

007624　　　　　AT THE SIGN OF THE JACK O'LANTERN. BY
MYRTLE REED. New York & London: G.P. Putman's Sons,
1905 BMC NUC.

funny story about a house PW 9-9-05
story has its serious side--troublous processes of
young married life; but the humor of it all over
shadows the more serious aim NYT 674,05.
bustle, noise, confusion ACAD 1009,05.

007625　　　　　FLOWER OF THE DUSK. BY MYRTLE REED. New
York & London: G. P. Putnam's Sons, 1908 BMC NUC.

ATH--blind man deceived with good intentions by his
family
BKM

007626　　　　　LATER LOVE LETTERS OF A MUSICIAN. BY
MYRTLE REED. New York: G. P. Putnam's Sons, 1900 NUC
BMC.

007627　　　　　LAVENDER AND OLD LACE. BY MYRTLE REED.
New York & London: G. P. Putnam's Sons, 1902 BMC NUC.

"An American Cranford" placid New England Life,
dainty? LBKM 3-3:250.
"old maid" love of son of man who should have married
her, "crude treatment" "comic relief...is dreadful"?
ATH, 121, 286
　　　　　　　　　　＊

007628　　　　　LOVE LETTERS OF A MUSICIAN. BY MYRTLE

REED. New York and London: G. P. Putnam's Sons, 1899
NUC BMC.

Violinist writes letters to a woman he never hopes to
win nor is she expected to read them. His illness
brings her to his side. PW 56:777

007629　　　　　MASTER OF THE VINEYARD. BY MYRTLE REED.
New York & London: G. P. Putnam's Sons, 1910 BMC NUC.

Rosemary's lover jilts her but she takes him back.
ACAD
Obscure criticism, but mentions the "beautiful white
witch" SR BM--A homily against divorce.
PW--a romance.

007630　　　　　THE MASTER'S VIOLIN. BY MYRTLE REED. New
York & London: G. P. Putnam's Sons, 1904 BMC NUC.

NYT-sent.
ACAD-sent.

007631　　　　　OLD ROSE AND SILVER. BY MYRTLE REED. New
York & London: G. P. Putnam's Sons, 1909 BMC NUC.

2 heroines one 40 one 20-Isabel; young violinist of 30
loves both. humor 10-2-09 PW.
Rose Bernard the woman of 40 finds a lover at the end.
TLS.
He is the young violinist who was first attracted to
Silver (Isabel). BKM.

007632　　　　　THE SHADOW OF VICTORY; A ROMANCE OF FORT
DEARBORN. BY MYRTLE REED. New York & London: G. P.
Putnam's Sons, 1903 NUC BMC.

historical romance PW 9-5-03.
historical romance NYT 845, 03.
historical romance. LBKM 10-03, 54.

007633　　　　　A SPINNER IN THE SUN. BY MYRTLE REED. New
York & London: G. P. Putnam's Sons, 1906 BMC NUC.

PW-Mystery of a veiled lady- portrayal of old maid
etc.
NYT-husband has deserted her because of burned face,
has worn a veil for 25 years, lover kills himself from
remorse. Happy at end removes veil was never burned.
ACAD

007634　　　　　A WEAVER OF DREAMS. BY MYRTLE REED. New
York & London: G. P. Putnam's Sons, 1911 BMC NUC.

A crippled man & a lame woman were old lovers "things
end happily for them" PW 9-16-11.
"The Eternal Feminine represented by an inordinate
love for clothes and an intense consciousness of moral
superiority to man plays a prominent part." ATH
TLS
ACAD

MACDONALD, JULIA.

007635　　　　　"IF ONLY!" London: W. Stevens, 1920 BMC.

007636　　　　　THE SINS OF THE FATHERS. Bombay: Times
Press, 1906 BMC.

007637　　　　　WHILE THE MUSIC LASTS. London: Holden and
Hardingham, [1913] BMC.

Covers 3 generations, career of male artist, Owen
Montgomery who marries a barmaid against his parents'
wishes. He's quickly disillusioned with her. Only his
music has a good influence on her. Therefore he
destroys his violin. Part II deals with their children
after they part. LBKM TLS

MACDONALD, LUCRETIA S.

007638　　　　　CHECKERBERRY. New York: Cochrane, 1908
NUC.

The heroine is Rachel who in her infancy was kidnapped
to be trained for circus. Falls into hands of a
winsome spinster who transforms her house into a home
for both her and 11 other young orphaned girls in whom
she is interested. BKM v.29, 1909.

MACDONALD, LUCY MAUD (MONTGOMERY). 1874-1942. Canada.

007639　　　　　ANNE OF AVONLEA. BY LUCY MAUD MONTGOMERY.
Boston: L.C. Page, 1909 NUC. London: I. Pitman, 1909
BMC.

Teacher (Anne of Green Gables) marries man who has all

the books she wants & more. PW 9-4-09
Anne has a vivid imagination and expresses
broad-minded views. LBKM

007640   ANNE OF GREEN GABLES. BY LUCY MAUD
MONTGOMERY. London: Pitman, 1908 BMC. Boston: L.C.
Page, 1908 NUC.

Sent domestic tale. TLS
Age 11-17, focus on first two years. She is adopted
educated; becomes a school teacher, supports another
woman. Written for adults LBKM
A vivacious, spunky girl growing up. SP
PW-A child is adopted; includes a cross narrow minded
spinster.

007641   ANNE OF THE ISLAND. BY LUCY MAUD
MONTGOMERY. Boston: Page, 1915 NUC BMC. London: I.
Pitman, 1915 BMC.

007642   ANNE'S HOUSE OF DREAMS. BY LUCY MAUD
MONTGOMERY. New York: F. A. Stokes, [c1917] NUC.
London: Constable, 1917 BMC.

TLS Happy marriage
Anne of Green Gables gets her dream house. PW
NYT 8-26-17:318

007643   CHRONICLES OF AVONLEA IN WHICH ANNE
SHIRLEY OF GREEN GABLES AND AVONLEA PLAYS SOME PART.
BY LUCY MAUD MONTGOMERY. London: S. Low, 1912 BMC.
Boston: L.C. Page, 1912 NUC.

007644   FURTHER CHRONICLES OF AVONLEA WHICH HAVE
TO DO WITH MANY PERSONALITIES AND EVENTS IN AND ABOUT
AVONLEA. BY LUCY MAUD MONTGOMERY. Boston: Page, 1920
BMC NUC.

007645   THE GOLDEN ROAD. BY LUCY MAUD MONTGOMERY.
Boston: L.C. Page, 1913 NUC BMC. London: Cassell, 1914
BMC.

PW 84 10/11/13:1246 "The happy, fun-loving group
introduced in 'The story girl' travel down 'the golden
road' to the parting of ways in this new story. Old
friendships are renewed with the simple folk of Prince
Edward Island. The adventurings of the King family, as
chronicled in a daily newspaper, which is aided and
abetted by the heathen Peter, with its headline
features of the long-expected romance which enters
into the life of pretty Aunt Olivia, the return of a
prodigal, which strangely enough causes temporary
anguish instead of joy to one childish heart, and what
happens to the Awkward Man make the story's
incidents."
ATH Young people run a magazine in Canada.

007646   KILMENY OF THE ORCHARD. BY LUCY MAUD
MONTGOMERY. Boston: L. C. Page, 1910 NUC. London: I.
Pitman, 1910 BMC.

Deaf mute girl learns to speak through her love for a
teacher. PW
LBKM oh no, thru shock of fear for her lover.
ATH she is a musical genius. Sent.
BKM teacher is the young man

007647   RAINBOW VALLEY. BY LUCY MAUD MONTGOMERY.
New York: F.A. Stokes, [1919] NUC. London: Constable,
1920 BMC.

Anne of Green Gables story, focuses upon her six
children's antics; oldest is 13 PW
Humorous conversations, incidents. NYT 9-21-19:485

007648   THE STORY GIRL. BY LUCY MAUD MONTGOMERY.
Boston: L.C. Page, 1911 NUC. London: I. Pitman, 1911
BMC.

Tells weird tales. PW 6-3-11
"Fascinating little girl." Her best quality is her
voice. "It makes words live." "When you go away from
her you find out she isn't a bit pretty after all."
LBKM

MACDONALD, M. P. See MACDONALD, MARGARET P.

MACDONALD, MARGARET P.

007649   TREFOIL; THE STORY OF A GIRL'S SOCIETY.
BY M. P. MACDONALD. London, New York: Thomas Nelson,
1900 NUC BMC.

MACDONALD, MRS. M. United Kingdom.

007650   ON THE BREEZY MOOR: FACT AND FICTION. St.

Louis: B. Herder, [1915] BMC. London: Sands, [1915]
BMC.

2 stories.

MACDONELL, ANNE.

007651   THE STORY OF TERESA. London: Methuen,
1902 BMC NUC.

LBKM-1902-epic of a woman's life-a Hardy woman.
ATH 3-8-02-not helpful-Teresa "almost as rare as
Hardy's Sue".

MACDONNELL, MRS. A. J.

007652   DID SHE DO RIGHT? A ROMANCE OF THE 20TH
CENTURY. London: S. Paul, 1909 BMC.

Romance of 2 women in Rome. TLS
Whole review discusses grammar. ACAD
unwitting rivalry of 2 friends one young one 35, who
both love same man. LBKM

MACDOUGALL, ELLA L. (RANDALL). United States.

007653   FROM SIDE STREETS AND BOULEVARDS: A
COLLECTION OF CHICAGO STORIES. BY PRESERVED WHEELER.
Chicago: R. R. Donnelley, 1893 NUC.

007654   HENNESSEY, OF LAKE COUNTY. BY PRESERVED
WHEELER. Antioch, Illinois: Burke and Storms, 1894
NUC.

007655   ONE SCHOOLMA'AM LESS. BY PRESERVED
WHEELER. Chicago: R. R. Donnelley, 1895 NUC.

MACDOUGALL, SYLVIA (BORGSTROM). Nationality Unknown.

007656   THE BAY OF LILACS: A ROMANCE FROM
FINLAND. BY PAUL WAINEMAN. London: Methuen, 1907 BMC.

007657   BY A FINNISH LAKE. BY PAUL WAINEMAN.
London: Methuen, 1903 BMC NUC.

007658   A DUCHESS OF FRANCE. ROMANCE OF OLD
VERSAILLES. BY PAUL WAINEMAN. London: Hurst and
Blackett, 1915 BMC.

007659   A HEROINE FROM FINLAND. BY PAUL WAINEMAN.
London: Methuen, 1902 BMC.

007660   A ROMAN PICTURE. BY PAUL WAINEMAN.
London: Methuen, 1914 BMC.

007661   THE SONG OF THE FOREST. BY PAUL WAINEMAN.
London: Methuen, 1904 BMC.

007662   THE WIFE OF NICHOLAS FLEMING. BY PAUL
WAINEMAN. London: Methuen, 1910 BMC.

MACELRATH, FRANCES.

007663   THE RUSTLER: A TALE OF LOVE AND WAR IN
WYOMING. New York & London: Funk & Wagnalls, 1902 NUC
BMC.

Life of cowboy. ATH 121, 12

MACELROY, LUCY (CLEAVER). 1860-1901. United States.

007664   ANSWERED: A ROMANCE OF THE SILENT YEARS.
Franklin, Ohio: Editor Pub. Co., 1896 NUC.

007665   JULETTY; A STORY OF OLD KENTUCKY. New
York: T. Y. Crowell, [c1901] NUC.

Heroine is a moonshiner. CR 01

007666   THE SILENT PIONEER. New York: T. Y.
Crowell, [1902] NUC.

MACEWEN, CONSTANCE. See DICKER, CONSTANCE (MACEWEN).

MACFADDEN, G. V. See MACFADDEN, GERTRUDE VIOLET.

MACFADDEN, GERTRUDE VIOLET. United Kingdom.

007667   HIS GRACE OF GRUB STREET. BY G. V.
MCFADDEN. London and New York: J. Lane, 1918 NUC BMC.

PW-18th century romance male hero.
NYT 12-8-1918:546--heroine is spirited.

007668   THE HONEST LAWYER. BY G. V. MCFADDEN. New
York and London: J. Lane, 1916 BMC NUC.

Romance. Woman proposes, lawyer rejects her, at length
find themselves to be soulmates. PW 91:304 1/27/17.
TLS-there is a high spirited arrogant young woman in
conflict with him.
ATH-does not sound promising. She possesses ancient
family privileges, asks a lawyer to marry her,
subsequently sends him to the stocks. He commits a
technical felony for her sake and is sentenced to
deportation for life. She marries him in prison and
has him pardoned.

007669   MAUMBURY RINGS. BY G. V. MCFADDEN.
London: Hodder & Stoughton, [1920] NUC [1921] BMC.

007670   THE PREVENTIVE MAN. BY G. V. MCFADDEN.
London and New York: J. Lane, 1920 BMC NUC.

TLS-adventure & smuggling.
LBKM-hero does not have strength and spirit of
previous novels, as the Honest Lawyer.
NYT 1920:223. Love story.

007671   THE TRUSTY SERVANT. BY G. V. MCFADDEN.
London and New York: J. Lane, 1920 BMC NUC.

TLS-melodramatic, but a hoyden daughter Josian.
ATH-sale of criminal's body, executed, to sculptor as
model. Life has not quite left.

MACFALL, FRANCES ELIZABETH (CLARKE). 1862-1943. United
Kingdom.

007672   ADNAM'S ORCHARD: A PROLOGUE. BY SARAH
GRAND. London: W. Heinemann, 1912 BMC NUC. New York:
D. Appleton, 1913 NUC.

"The character of Lena Kedlock is, perhaps, the most
complex and appealing, but the denouement leaves us
somewhat in doubt about her later life." LIT D 46:478
Mr 1 '13
"Novel by author of "the heavenly twins," dealing with
modern problems. Scene is rural England, and the
characters embrace a whole community from duke and
duchess down to the humblest agricultural laborer.
Adnam Pratt, son of a tenant on the estate, develops
an ability for intensive farming and makes a small
orchard so richly productive that surprise, jealousy,
romance, and intrigue get their grip on the entire
community. Story is ably worked out, and is a strong
appeal for the "back-to-the-soil" movement." PW
ATH-Land question and male hero
TLS-all the modern problems, all the cries and causes,
expounds her views, feminism.

007673   BABS THE IMPOSSIBLE. BY SARAH GRAND. New
York and London: Harper, 1900 NUC. London: Hutchinson,
1901 BMC.

adolescent little Pagan, don't know what Babs will do
at the end because she is adolescent--capable of
anything, full of doubt. BKM 13 1901 185-6.

007674   THE BETH BOOK. BY SARAH GRAND. New York:
D. Appleton, 1897 NUC. London: W. Heinemann, 1898 BMC.
(Bookseller adds "Being a Study from the Life of
Elizabeth Caldwell Maclure, a Woman of Genius.")

300 pages given to childhood. "irrelevant and foolish
drivel." Later she is "freed of her impossible
innocence" in regard to matters of sex. Then claims
her health suffers when she submits to husband. Then
leaves her husband to become a great writer and
speaker. Beth from all sides "personified feminine
childhood." Her mother prefers her brother. Her father
is unfaithful. Her husband a doctor in hospital where
vivisection is practiced-apparently. "Holds an
appointment to a hospital for specific disease"
"Apparently she must preach her wonderful doctrine of
the equality of the sexes" at the cost of her art.
Review by Frank Danby. SR 84:557.
Husband is a detestable brute, gross. If by genius is
meant persistant energy-no woman of genius shown. LBKM
13:106.
Marries an odious sensualist at 16. No heroine so
completely described as Beth. SP 79:691.
"Biog of a girl who believes she has genius-a New
Woman". "moralizing tirades about modern soc. the
masculine regime, etc. BAKER 03, 116
Life for her "one continuous misery." Marries without
love, spied on by husband, a vivisectionist. Leaves
him-becomes a novelist meets Amer artist in London
boarding house. He's ill; she nurses him, provides for
him. Divorce not stated becomes speaker on women's
rights. NYT 12-4-97,11.

007675   A DOMESTIC EXPERIMENT. BY THE AUTHOR OF
"IDEALA: A STUDY FROM LIFE" [ANONYMOUS]. Edinburgh and
London: Blackwood, 1891 BMC NUC.

Agatha is disgusted with her husband and attracted to
Paul Oldham. "She goes a great deal too far with him."
She's a clear-sighted, cultured woman. ACAD.
Her husband is foolish though good-natured. Agatha
loves another but is saved from disaster.
"Distasteful" SP 66:700.
"vulgar, foolish, impossible." ATH 97:278.

007676   THE HEAVENLY TWINS. BY MADAME SARAH
GRAND. London: W. Heinemann, 1893 BMC. New York:
Cassell, [c1893] NUC.

Attacks the double standard. Evadne Colquhoun refuses
to be wife to her husband when she learns he slept
with other women in the past. Author believes men no
less than women should be expected to be virgins. SP
70 395
Author moves from "snarling" to "wrath." The
diabolical pranks of the twins from cradle to grave
plus Evadne's story. Subject: elevation of man's moral
status to that of woman. Remove double standard by
women refusing to marry men who have had sex and that
women must have full knowledge of sex. Evadne gives in
to pressure of her family to return to husband and a
mere appearance of wedded life. Nation 57, 374.
But he is not to touch her. This lasts several years.
One of her friends (a woman) is married to a man with
a dissipated past, has a child that looks like a
"speckled toad," learns her husband had a child before
marriage, gets ill, dies. Heavenly twins, Diavolo and
Angelica, grow up. And there's a young married woman
who disguises herself as a man and visits a young
tenor, who learns her identity and is killed off by
pneumonia. Angelica weeps at his grave. CR 20, 23:220
First published at author's own expense: CR. 20, 23:92

007677   SINGULARLY DELUDED, A ROMANCE. BY THE
AUTHOR OF "IDEALA", ETC. [ANONYMOUS]. Edinburgh: W.
Blackwood, 1893 BMC. New York: G. Munroe, [c1895] NUC.

Suspenseful, nightmarish adventures of heroine in
pursuit of a man she thinks is her husband gone mad.
She keeps up with them with an extraordinary
endurance. A fire at sea is a fine description
involving several characters. Travels from England to
France. PW 6-10-93

007678   THE WINGED VICTORY. BY SARAH GRAND. New
York: D. Appleton, 1916 NUC. London: W. Heinemann,
[1916] BMC NUC.

energetic English woman devotes self to improving
conditions of farmers. Wavers between love and
ambition. NYT
Ella and Lord Melton secretly marry. Discover they are
both the Duke's children. Melton kills self. PW
90:1282 10/14/16
TLS-Ella works for the lace workers. Duke and duchess
set her up in London with lavish townhouse and place
of business. She sells lace here and becomes a
celebrity. Also close companionship with the duke. An
attack is made on her honor, she kills the person
involved. Then there is talk about her being mistress
to duke. Marries heir, discover they are sister and
brother.
ATH-She plans to free the lace trade from the sweating
conditions. Meanwhile Duke attends her, scandal, she
decides to marry son of duke one week hence.

MACFARLANE, ISABELLA.

007679   A ROYAL KNIGHT; A TALE OF NUREMBURG. New
York: G. W. Dillingham, [1905] NUC.

historical romance 4-8-05 PW
historical romance 304,05 NYT

MACGARY, ELIZABETH VISERE.

007680   AN AMERICAN GIRL IN MEXICO. New York:
Dodd, Mead, 1904 NUC BMC.

F 1215 Mexico-Social life & customs

MACGEE, AGNES POTTER. United States.

007681   DOROTHY ANGSLEIGH; A STORY OF WAR TIMES.
Chicago: W. B. Conkey, 1907 NUC.

Civil war period. Adopted woman marries soldier; he
deserts her; she becomes a nurse & discovers her
father & his luxurious home. PW 5-11-07

MACGEOCH, DAISY.

007682   TWO EYES OF GREY. London: Cassell, 1914
BMC.

TLS-- Foolish melodrama based on song of same title.

MACGILL, MARGARET (GIBBONS). United Kingdom.

007683   AN ANZAC'S BRIDE. London: H. Jenkins,
1918 BMC.

begins & ends in bliss, stupid misunderstandings bring
misery in between. TLS

007684   THE BARTERED BRIDE. London: H. Jenkins,
1921 BMC.

TLS-Molly runs from brutal stepfather, then drunken
fiance & again from him after he has forced her to
marry him. Faithful young miner in background.
TLS-Canadian

007685   THE ROSE OF GLENCONNEL. London: H.
Jenkins, 1917 BMC.

TLS--Stranded as a child in mining camp, has many
advents. finds herself heir to fortune.
Heroine sweet & child like in this tale of love &
adventure. LBKM

007686   WHOM LOVE HATH CHOSEN. London: H.
Jenkins, 1920 BMC.

Course of true love, etc. trad TLS

MACGLASSON, EVA WILDER. See BRODHEAD, EVA WILDER
(MACGLASSON).

MACGOWAN, ALICE. B. 1858. United States.

007687   JUDITH OF THE CUMBERLANDS. New York and
London: G.P. Putnam's Sons, 1908 BMC NUC.

PW-impassioned love, mountain feud and dew.
NYT-compound of womanly weakness and strength.
Selfless and pure devotion. Novel based partly on the
author's experiences at Roan Mountain, N. C.

007688   THE LAST WORD. Boson: L.C. Page, 1903
NUC. London: Hutchinson, 1903 BMC.

Young woman goes to NY to be a writer, becomes an
author, marries man who illustrated her book. ACAD
65,108
Cycle of experiences of newspaper woman, becomes
engaged to manager, throws him over because of his
views regarding the subject of women, finally converts
him and marries him on the understanding that she's to
retain her profession and her independence instead of
making sunshine for his exclusive benefit. Her friend,
strong in classics, biology, astronomy. ATH 122,448.
WOMAN'S JOURNAL 10-11-1902. Lively heroine travels on
horseback through Texas, returns to NY to begin a
journalistic career. Marries. Conflict between
individuality and love. BOOK BUYER 02.
NYT 9-27-02. A romance: man (who turns out to be head
of publishing company) loses money and becomes a
cowboy. She distinguishes herself as a writer and they
write a book together. 2 strong wills in opposition.

007689   THE SWORD IN THE MOUNTAINS. New York and
London: G.P. Putnam's Sons, 1910 BMC NUC.

BM-Civil War Romance.
PW-Civil War Romance.

007690   THE WIVING OF LANCE CLEAVERAGE. New York
& London: G.P. Putnam's Sons, 1909 BMC NUC.

Tenn mts. hero wins beauty who makes him miserable;
separate; when he's in trouble she proves loving. PW
simple, strong, direct, TLS
Focuses on the diction. NYT
Depicts the struggle of a young married couple, both
strong characters, but wilful and headstrong. BKM 30
1909-10

MACGOWAN, ALICE AND GRACE (MACGOWAN) COOKE.

007691   RETURN: A STORY OF THE SEA ISLANDS IN
1739. London: Hodder and Stoughton, 1905 BMC. Boston:
L.C. Page, 1905 NUC.

Strenuous heroine "oversteps the extreme limits of

readers' forebearance" NYT 195 05.
neo-historic Colonial So. Carol. Grows through days of
bitterness into noble womanhood NYT 05, 392 BAKER
32-113.
Passionate, self-willed woman flees Charlestown; her
lover humilated her-he left her to wait at the church
and wrote that she jilted lots of men, so he's jilting
her. ATH 05, 607.

MACGOWAN, ALICE, jt. au. See COOKE, GRACE (MACGOWAN) AND
ALICE MACGOWAN.

MACGREGOR, A. LYNDSAY. See MACGREGOR, ANNIE LYNDSAY.

MACGREGOR, ANNIE LYNDSAY. United States.

007692   'BOUND, NOT BLESSED'. BY A. LYNDSAY
MACGREGOR. New York: G. W. Dillingham, 1892 NUC.

PW-Unhappy marriage of good wife and scoundrel
husband.

MACGREGOR, MARY ESTHER (MILLER). 1876-1961. Canada.

007693   DUNCAN POLITE, THE WATCHMAN OF GLENORO.
BY MARIAN KEITH. London: Hodder and Stoughton, 1905
BMC. New York: Revell, [1905] NUC.

About a lumberjack and a preacher. 6-3-05 PW
NYT 450,05

007694   THE END OF THE RAINBOW. BY MARIAN KEITH.
New York: Doran, [c1913] NUC.

PW 85 5/2/14 p.1445 "Roderick McRae set out when only
six to find it, he searched for many years and then
found something better. Scenes are laid in Canadian
village of Algonquin, where live Lawyer Ed, the
eternally light-hearted, who helps everyone, Angus
McRae, Roderick's father, who devotes his life to
helping the poor and the sinning, Helen Murray the
young school teacher who helps Angus and teaches
Roderick what the true crock of gold is, and many
other characters."

007695   IN ORCHARD GLEN. BY MARIAN KEITH. New
York: Doran, [1918] NUC.

Scotch inhabitants of Ontario. PW
Wartime story. TLS
Christina Lindsay not beautiful, but all
self-sacrificing, her loves and self-sacrifices. Life
in Canadian village. NYT 5-18-19 289

007696   'LIZBETH OF THE DALE. BY MARIAN KEITH.
New York: Doran, [c1910] NUC. London: Hodder &
Stoughton, 1911 BMC.

"Old maid" with 8 nieces and nephews and they all have
a jolly time. 4-8-11 PW

007697   THE POT O'GOLD: AT THE END OF THE
RAINBOW. BY MARIAN KEITH. London: Hodder and
Stoughton, 1914 BMC.

ATH-simple-hearted Scottish and Irish people living in
Canadian town.

007698   THE SILVER MAPLE. A STORY OF UPPER
CANADA. BY MARIAN KEITH. London: Hodder & Stoughton,
[1906] BMC. New York: Revell, [c1906] NUC.

PW-historical novel-male hero.
NYT-historical novel-male hero.

007699   TREASURE VALLEY. BY MARIAN KEITH. London,
New York: Hodder & Stoughton, [1908] BMC. New York: G.
Doran, [c1908] NUC.

TLS-Canada-male hero from England.
Lively optimism. 11-13-09 PW.

MACHA, VERA.

007700   ONE OF MANY. London: Digby, Long, 1900
BMC.

ATH 115:780. Modern domestic life in England, tone of
melancholy, autobiographical form.
ACAD 58:490. Many love affairs of heroine, most of
them unfortunate.
LIT 7:123. Ester Armytage, becomes a governess,
considers it a calling.

MACHAR, AGNES MAULE. 1837-1927. Canada.

007701   THE HEIR OF FAIRMOUNT GRANGE. London: Digby, Long, [1895] BMC.

desc of St. Lawrence and Quebec area. Ethel Howard loses then gets back an English estate after drunken heir dies. Her love who gives her up when she loses wealth, then seeks her out in Canada when she gets it back. gives her heart to Norman who rescues her from drowning. ACAD 47:377

007702   ROLAND GRAEME, KNIGHT. A NOVEL OF OUR TIME. New York: Fords, Howard & Hulbert, [c1892] NUC.

He's a very idealistic socialist involved in strikes and the labor question. Story follows the successive stages of his changing ideas. CR 14,21:19 DIAL 13:310. Socialistic tract. Setting is large American manufacturing town. Male hero. "Lack of restraint."

MACHELL, MRS. G.

007703   DURING ONE SUMMER: A NOVEL. London: A. H. Stockwell, 1918 BMC.

MACILWRAITH, JEAN NEWTON. 1859-1938. Canada.

007704   THE CURIOUS CAREER OF RODERICK CAMPBELL. Boston: Houghton, Mifflin, 1901 NUC. Westminster: A. Constable, [1901] BMC.

American hero of revolution. PW 3-23-01 BKM too.

007705   A DIANA OF QUEBEC. London: Smith, Elder, 1912 BMC. Toronto: Bell & Cockburn, 1912 NUC.

TLS old fashioned romance
ATH-old fashioned romance
Canadian romance-young impressionable Nelson SP

007706   THE MAKING OF MARY. BY JEAN FORSYTH. London: T. F. Unwin, 1895 BMC NUC. New York: Cassell, [c1895] NUC.

Very little concerns the "making" of Mary. She's raised on shores of Lake Michigan. A blunt, callous waif-drives her guardians to distraction with her flirtations. Other characters: the Scotch editer-Mr. Gemmill, his wife who is into theosophy, etc. ATH 106:156
Mary Mason orphan gets passed around till she secures a home in Michigan. She's a strange child and her "mother" Mrs. Gemmill tries to tame her. But she "bosses the show," flirts outrageously (when she's grown up) takes a place in a nursing institution, gets small pox, loses her beauty. We're left to speculate the effect. ACAD 48:143
Many theories go into the "making" PW 8-3-85:161

MACIVOR, MARY A. United States.

007707   THE UPPER TRAIL. Boston: Roxburgh, [c1912] NUC.

PW-Western heroine is a "little southern school teacher with a strong will and prejudices"

MACK, LOUISE. See LEYLAND, MARIE LOUISE (MACK) CREED.

MACKARNESS, MATILDA ANNE (PLANCHE). 1826-1881. United Kingdom.

007708   A WOMAN WITHOUT A HEAD. London: Hutchinson, 1892 BMC.

MACKAY, ANNIE E. United States.

007709   A LATTER DAY SAINT. BY MRS. ALFRED ALMOND MCKAY. New York, Chicago, Toronto: F. H. Revell, [c1893] NUC.

MACKAY, HELEN GANSEVOORT (EDWARDS). B. 1876. United States.

007710   ACCIDENTALS. London: A. Melrose, [c1915] NUC BMC. New York: Duffield, 1915 NUC.

007711   CHILL-HOURS. London: A. Melrose, 1919 NUC BMC. New York: Duffield, 1920 NUC.

007712   THE COBWEB CLOAK. New York: Duffield, 1912 NUC. London: A. Melrose, [c1912] BMC.

PW-sounds awful.
NYT-sounds awful.

007713   HALF LOAVES; A STORY. New York: Duffield, 1911 NUC. London: Chatto & Windus, 1912 BMC.

TLS-wife can no longer stand being taken for granted and goes to Italy.
ATH-meets and loves a man there.
Wife wants a great love; husband only capable of half-loaf. PW 3-25-11
Florida Marvin renounces her half-loaf (who wasted affections on various amours) and goes to live by herself in Italy. There she meets a modern St. Francis who gets her involved with working with the poor. At the end-the very end returns to her half loaf! NYT

MACKAY, ISABEL ECCLESTONE (MACPHERSON). 1875-1928. Canada.

007714   THE HOUSE OF WINDOWS. London, New York: Cassell, 1912 BMC NUC.

PW-2 sisters adopt baby, adventure and mystery.
TLS-becomes a shophand in the store whose owner is her father although neither knows it because she was kidnapped as a baby.
ATH-promising.
NYT-Canadian store. A woman is the kidnapper, whose husband and daughter have been ruined by the business methods of the store.

007715   MIST OF MORNING. New York: G. H. Doran, [c1919] BMC NUC.

Semi-humorous romance of country life. NYT
England just before war-a romance. PW
Hero-an inventor who becomes engaged to a young woman under rather unusual circumstances. A comedy of manners ends with the war. NYT 537, 10-12-19
TLS-portrait of men and women. Conv.

007716   UP THE HILL AND OVER. New York: G.H. Doran, [c1917] NUC. London: Goodchild & Stewart, [1918] BMC.

TLS-love story. But also a character study of woman drug addict. Esther loves a man whose wife disappeared and who turns out to be Esther's drug addict Stepmother. "An overdose clears the way for a happy end." PW
The man is Dr. Coombe who comes to a small town in Canada after suffering a nervous breakdown, makes a hit with the community and with Esther.
NYT 127,4-8-17. (the 2 accounts don't agree).

MACKAY, KATHERINE DYER.

007717   ROSE STEWART'S LOVE STORY. A ROMANCE OF CULLODEN. Stirling: Eneas Mackay, 1903 BMC.

007718   THE STONE OF DESTINY. New York and London: Harper, 1904 BMC NUC.

Story of a marriage of different natures PW

MACKAY, LYDIA MILLER.

007719   THE RETURN OF THE EMIGRANT. Edinburgh: W. Blackwood, 1907 BMC.

Centers on the hero Colin nothing new ACAD, TLS doesn't say much else SP

MACKAY, MARY. 1855-1924. United Kingdom.

007720   ANGEL'S WICKEDNESS: A TRUE STORY. BY MARIE CORELLI. New York: W. R. Beers, 1900 NUC.

007721   BARABBAS: A DREAM OF THE WORLD'S TRAGEDY. BY MARIE CORELLI. London: Methuen, 1893 BMC. Philadelphia: J. B. Lippincott, 1894 NUC.

Melodramatic: Biblical. Offense against good taste. SP 71:689.
Hero is the robber released instead of Christ. Story covers three days from Christ's arraignment before Pilate to his rising from the grave. LW 93:386.
Judas, Mary, Peter, etc. SR 76:546.
CR 21:166. Bible story, new element being Judith Iscariot, a sister of Judas.

007722   BOY, A SKETCH. BY MARIE CORELLI. London: Hutchinson, 1900 BMC. Philadelphia: J. B. Lippincott, 1900 NUC.

NYT 1900:419. Study of child of besotted father and stupid mother. Spinster takes interest in him but mother, jealous, sends him to school in France. He develops his father's tendencies, although his good

side is brought out later when spinster is his friend
in need. Disgraced, he enlists and is killed in the
Transvaal War.
LW 31:147. Mother is a slovenly fool.

007723   THE DEVIL'S MOTOR; A FANTASY. BY MARIE
CORELLI. New York: 1910 NUC. [London]: Hodder and
Stoughton, 1910 BMC NUC.

Fantasy about the Devil. PW

007724   THE DISTANT VOICE: A FACT OR A FANCY? BY
MARIE CORELLI. Philadelphia: J. B. Lippincott, 1896
NUC.

007725   GOD'S GOOD MAN: A SIMPLE LOVE STORY. BY
MARIE CORELLI. New York: A.L. Burt, [c1904] NUC.
London: Methuen, 1904 BMC NUC.

PW-doesn't sound like anything here.

007726   HOLY ORDERS: THE TRAGEDY OF A QUIET LIFE.
BY MARIE CORELLI. New York: Frederick A. Stokes,
[1908] NUC. London: Methuen, 1908 NUC BMC.

PW-drink problem, male clergyman hero.

007727   INNOCENT, HER FANCY AND HIS FACT; A
NOVEL. BY MARIE CORELLI. London and New York: Hodder &
Stoughton, 1914 BMC NUC. New York: G. H. Doran,
[c1914] NUC.

Innocent: well read. Robin, not so. She admires his
looks. She's not pretty. Opposes love, marriage. Briar
Farm, the man she thinks is her father is dying. Tells
her @ real father (brought her to farm one night of
thunder.) So at 18, no name, past. Robin wants to
marry her; she is against it. more than marrige for
women- anti marriage; Father dies; she off to London,
work. Becomes an author (anon) success; lit.
crit.Learns @ parents: Ma, selfish love affair Pa
artist. Dies like Lily Bart. She happens to room with
woman who was engaged to her father. Romantic theme:
Brontesque. Meets descendent of Knight of Briar Farm,
falls in love. He's an artist, paints her. he says her
love destroys her; love improves his work. Jocelyn
would break up; to him it's an affair. She dies in
process of returning to Briar Farm, mad. (Book).
Of strange unknown ancestry, no schooling raised by
foster father, absorbed in dreams. Chief joy is
treasure chest of old books. Teaches self to read
English and Norman Fr. Becomes enamored with life of
past. At 20 writes a novel that all England proclaims
to be the work of genius. Goes off to London after
foster father dies, happens to room with her real
father's former betrothed; marvellously artificial and
sensational. Famous in London, jealous of real Ma,
cast off by Lover-artist striking her a death blow by
doing so. BKM v.40, 1914-15.

007728   JANE: A SOCIAL INCIDENT. BY MARIE
CORELLI. London: Hutchinson, 1897 BMC NUC.
Philadelphia: J. B. Lippincott, 1897 NUC.

At 57 she inherits a fortune and comes out. what Jane
Belmont thought of London society and vice versa.
Under the guidance of Mrs. Maddenham-a kind of society
promoter, but Jane throws out royalty from her house
when she sees they are vulgar. Returns to her country
house. CR 26,30:218.
PW 12-12-96. Staid English woman inherits a fortune
and is incited to make social experiment in London
society.

007729   THE LIFE EVERLASTING. A REALITY OF
ROMANCE. BY MARIE CORELLI. New York: Hodder &
Stoughton, [c1911] NUC. London: Methuen, [1911] BMC
NUC.

Strange Love affair of both mortal & immortal passion.
PW

007730   THE MASTER-CHRISTIAN: A QUESTION OF THE
TIME. BY MARIE CORELLI. London: Methuen, 1900 BMC NUC.
New York: Dodd, Mead, 1900 NUC.

LW 31:200. An assault on the pretenses and
superficialities of the Christian Church through
history.
NYT 1900:670

007731   THE MIGHTY ATOM. BY MARIE CORELLI.
London: Hutchinson, 1896 BMC NUC. Philadelphia: J. B.
Lippincott, 1896 NUC.

BKM 4:260.

007732   THE MURDER OF DELICIA. BY MARIE CORELLI.
London: Skeffington, 1896 BMC NUC. Philadelphia: J. B.
Lippincott, 1896 NUC.

Heroine-a famous author earning piles of money, wins
all admiration. Brings the most distinguished
Personage of the Realm to her feet, gets 8000 pounds
advance for her novel. She killed by disappointment in
her husband. LW 28:254
NYT 10-31-1896. p. 5. Delicia is a very financially
successful writer. She marries a cad who does not work
and supports him. when he becomes unfaithful with
others, she dies of a broken heart.
PW 10-17-96. "The author claims that there are a large
proportion of men who live by their wives' earnings
and yet deride women in public and consider them
'unsexed' when their merits are publicly
acknowledged." Delicia was a successful novelist,
freely placed her income at her husband's disposal,
adoring him completely. Disillusionment concerning him
killed her.

007733   THE SILENCE OF THE MAHARAJAH. BY MARIE
CORELLI. New York: Merriam, [c1895] NUC.

English in India. Love of Indian Prince for wife of
Englishman. His delicacy contrasted to husband's
brutality. PW 4-20-95:653

007734   THE SORROWS OF SATAN; OR, THE STRANGE
EXPERIENCE OF ONE GEOFFREY TEMPEST, MILLIONAIRE. BY
MARIE CORELLI. London: Methuen, 1895 BMC NUC.
Philadelphia: J. B. Lippincott, 1896 NUC.

Unsuccessful literary hack forms a bond like that of
Faust to a Prince. Pw 12-7-95:1075
Devil is the hero, a pathetic rendering. BAKER,03,94
BKM 4:424. Heroine Mavis Clare writes successful
books. Lucio Romanas comes to London, he is Latin.
Lady Sibyl falls under his spell kills herself with
poison, after writing 75 page note of farewell,
warning others of the devil and decrying contemporary
social evils.

007735   THE SOUL OF LILITH. BY MARIE CORELLI.
London: R. Bentley, 1892 BMC NUC. New York: J. W.
Lovell, [c1892] NUC.

CR 18:249. El Rami, an East Indian performs many
experiments attempting to explain supernatural in
turns of natural, including one involving a young girl
whom he keeps in a trance except when he sends her in
search of existence of the "soul."
LIT world 23:175. "theosophy, ancient Egyptian
religion, mysticism, astrology, palmistry, magnetism,
spiritualism and trickery of every kind"
SP 68:612.
SR 73:515. Irene Vassilius was a genius, an author
whose books were unfairly reviewed by male critics
because she was a woman. "And at last she condescended
to marry a very handsome clever good rich man, who
understood, and frequently told her, how very much he
was her inferior, morally and intellectually. She
being a woman of genius and he only a duke."

007736   THE STRANGE VISITATION OF JOSIAH MCNASON,
A GHOST STORY. BY MARIE CORELLI. New York:
International News, [c1904] NUC. London: G. Newnes,
1904 BMC NUC.

007737   TEMPORAL POWER; A STUDY IN SUPREMACY. BY
MARIE CORELLI. London: Methuen, 1902 BMC NUC. New
York: Dodd, Mead, 1902 NUC.

BOOK NEWS-power of kings-political theory.

007738   "THREE WISE MEN OF GOTHAM." A "NEW"
READING OF AN OLD RHYME. BY MARIE CORELLI.
Philadelphia: J. B. Lippincott, 1896 NUC.

007739   THE TREASURE OF HEAVEN, A ROMANCE OF
RICHES. BY MARIE CORELLI. New York: Dodd, Mead, 1906
NUC. London: A. Constable, 1906 NUC BMC.

PW-story of wealthy 70 yr. old man.
NYT-love and money don't mix.

007740   THE YOUNG DIANA; AN EXPERIMENT OF THE
FUTURE. BY MARIE CORELLI. New York: G.H. Doran,
[c1918] NUC. London: Hutchinson, 1918 BMC NUC.

PW-humorously realistic novel of womankind.
NYT-Nov.24 '18 p509. Diana May, at 40, unmarried,
lives with her parents and takes care of them.
Although she is intelligent, generous, a fine

musician, they are conscious that all their friends
regard her as an old maid and they are not grateful
for her care. An independent friend urges her to move
in with her in London and look for work, which she
finally does. Then, through being a subject of an
experiment she becomes endowed with youth, beauty, and
an ethereal quality which raises her above such
trifles as human vengeance or love. There is a great
deal about the despicable qualities of men.

007741   ZISKA: THE PROBLEM OF A WICKED SOUL. BY
MARIE CORELLI. London: Simpkin, Marshall, 1897 BMC
NUC. New York: Stone & Kimball, 1897 NUC.

Transmigration of souls. Wicked Egyptian Anerexes
reaped the reward of ancient sins "by finding his
beloved Ziska become a skeleton under his touch,"
himself alive about to be entombed. LW 28:254.
She is reincarnation of famous Egyptian dancing woman
of the 18th Dynasty. A famous painter is reincarnation
of Anerexes. She recognizes this man as one who
murdered her in her former life. Gets her revenge. PW
51:681.
NYT 1898:416. Theosophy, the occult, and Christianity.
Unwholesome: High and lofty Denzil Murray, a Scot.
Armand Gervais a Fr. Artist. They are rivals for the
magnificent Princess Ziska. The two men are close
friends. Much happens at a masked ball. The two men
swear to kill each other. The princess destroys both
because she's really an incarnation of an ancient
Egyptian?NYT 5-15-97,5.

MACKAY, MRS. ALFRED ALMOND. See MACKAY, ANNIE E.

MACKELLAR, DOROTHEA. See MACKELLAR, ISOBEL MARION DOROTHEA,
Also MACKELLAR, ISOBEL MARION DOROTHEA AND RUTH BEDFORD.

MACKELLAR, ISOBEL MARION DOROTHEA. Australia.

007742   OUTLAW'S LUCK. BY DOROTHEA MACKELLAR.
London: Mills and Boon, [1913] BMC NUC.

Kid Prevost Argentine;focus on hero-card player, cool,
in control, honorable, horse tamer, horse lover. Story
of his career. Slipped into evil ways-horse thief.
Katharine Hammond capable, courageous. SP

MACKELLAR, ISOBEL MARION DOROTHEA AND RUTH BEDFORD.

007743   THE LITTLE BLUE DEVIL. BY DOROTHEA
MACKELLAR AND RUTH BEDFORD. London: A. Rivers, 1912
BMC NUC.

TLS-male hero
ATH-male hero.

007744   TWO'S COMPANY. BY DOROTHEA MACKELLAR AND
RUTH BEDFORD. London: Rivers, 1914 NUC BMC.

ATH-Love affairs of Australian mining engineer.

MACKENZIE, HANNAH B.

007745   AFTER TOUCH OF WEDDED HANDS. Edinburgh
and London: Oliphant, 1891 BMC.

Couple marry with understanding she doesn't love him
but marrying for some obligation. Relation gets colder
after marriage. She's an atheist; he a devout
minister. Separate; she gets ill, reconciled. She
gives in to husband's rel. ACAD

007746   CROWNED VICTOR: A STORY OF STRIFE.
Edinburgh and London: Oliphant and Anderson, 1894 BMC.

Vicious medical student tamed by young woman.
Eventually becomes a hero-loses his life to save
another. SP 80:559
Young woman daughter of English professor inspires two
students. One becomes a rich businessman; the other a
doctor. She is a trained nurse in Edinburgh. Chooses
one of the men. PW 52:707.

007747   HECTOR MACRAE: A MODERN STORY OF THE WEST
HIGHLANDS. London: Simpkin, Marshall, 1898 BMC.

LIT 2:591. Old-fashioned sensation.
ATH 111:532. Modern Scotland. Arabella appears as a
spirit in a house but is a woman seeking revenge of a
sordid crime.

MACKENZIE, JEAN KENYON. 1874-1936. United States.

007748   BLACK SHEEP: ADVENTURES IN WEST AFRICA.
Boston: Houghton Mifflin, 1916 NUC.

Young missionary in African jungle writes letters to
her father-describes the people, with full
appreciation for their personalities. PW
DT 569 1. Cameroons-Descr. & travs. 2.
Missions--Cameroons.

MACKENZIE, SIBELL LILIAN (BLUNT).

007749   THE DAYS OF FIRE. London: P. Welby, 1908
BMC.

TLS-Historical, male hero

007750   THE DECOY. A ROMANCE. London: E.
Macdonald, 1914 BMC.

LBKM-Hero is head of a gang of slavers, handsome,
heartless, frankly evil. He falls in love with a slave
child, sends her to the slave college at Tyre. Their
love then brings out all that is fine in his nature,
transforming him. Phoenician customs, strange code of
honor, unchivalrous treatment of women & sacred bond
of friendship existing among men all described.
ACAD 86:369.

007751   THE GOLDEN GUARD. London: G. Allen, 1912
BMC.

ATH Love story.
TLS-Love story.

007752   OUT OF THE DARK. London: E. Mathews, 1910
BMC.

Fantasy: heroine falls in love with mysterious (Aros,
the King) person whom she encounters in an underground
rock chamber. Later meets him in London Society. Her
love will release him from doom. They live together,
travel, criticized by conven. people. ACAD
Suggestion of vampirism SR.

007753   SONS OF THE MILESIANS. London: E. Nash,
1906 BMC.

tales

007754   SWORD-OF-THE-CROWN. RENDERED INTO ENGLISH
BY THE COUNTESS OF CROMARTIE. London: E. Mathews, 1910
BMC.

LBKM-King Arthur rom.

007755   THE WEB OF THE PAST. London: E. Nash,
1905 BMC.

MACKIE, PAULINE BRADFORD. See CAVENDISH, PAULINE BRADFORD
(MACKIE) HOPKINS.

MACKIN, MARIE. United States.

007756   THE MYSTERY OF THE MARBLETONS: A ROMANCE
OF REALITY. New York: Abbey Press, [c1900] NUC.

MACKINNEY, ALICE JEAN CHANDLER (WEBSTER). 1876-1916.
United States.

007757   DADDY-LONG-LEGS. BY JEAN WEBSTER. New
York: Century, 1912 BMC NUC. London: Hodder &
Stoughton, 1913 BMC.

Letters from a charity orphan girl to her unknown
guardian; her sweet good years at college. ATH
Jerusha Abbott, orphan, goes to college to begin a
career in writing on condition that she will write her
guardian without expecting reply. Does so; even
illustrates her letters. The result is the expected
one. TLS

007758   DEAR ENEMY. BY JEAN WEBSTER. New York:
Century, 1915 BMC NUC. London: Hodder & Stoughton,
[1915] BMC.

Sallie McBride, used to wealth & luxury in charge of
orphanage. 113 orphans; introduces modern ideas for
reform of orphanages. Engaged to congressman who has
wife in insane asylum. NYT
Breaks all traditional rules about orphanages; does
101 radical & astounding things. Treats her charges as
individuals. NYT
Her letters to 2 or 3 friends. Does marry dr. in the
end. TLS
TLS-society girl takes position of orphanage
superintendent. She proposes novel & revolutionary
reforms to trustees.

007759   THE FOUR-POOLS MYSTERY. New York:

Century, 1908 NUC. London: Hodder & Stoughton, [1916]
BMC.

PW Mostly men

007760   JERRY. London: Hodder & Stoughton, [1916]
BMC.

007761   JERRY, JUNIOR. BY JEAN WEBSTER. New York:
Century, 1907 BMC NUC.

007762   JUST PATTY. BY JEAN WEBSTER. New York:
Century, 1911 BMC NUC. London: Hodder & Stoughton,
1915 BMC.

007763   PATTY AND PRISCILLA. London: Hodder &
Stoughton, [1915] BMC.

007764   THE WHEAT PRINCESS. BY JEAN WEBSTER. New
York: Century, 1905 BMC NUC. London: Hodder &
Stoughton, 1916 BMC.

Wheat famine in Italy with its relationship to
American Business. PW 10-28-05

007765   WHEN PATTY WENT TO COLLEGE. BY JEAN
WEBSTER. New York: Century, 1903 BMC NUC.

Humorous experiences of college girl who gets into all
kinds of scrapes. 4-4-03 PW
Likes to get into scrapes, plays practical jokes-no
real student. NYT 1903, 96

MACKINNEY, ANNIE BOOTH, jt. au. See COOKE, GRACE (MACGOWAN)
AND ANNIE BOOTH MACKINNEY.

MACKINNEY, KATE (SLAUGHTER). B. 1857. United States.

007766   THE SILENT WITNESS; A TALE OF A KENTUCKY
TRAGEDY. BY KATE SLAUGHTER MCKINNEY (KATYDID). New
York: Neale, 1906 NUC.

Murder story PW 2-9-07

007767   THE WEED BY THE WALL. BY KATE SLAUGHTER
MCKINNEY (KATYDID). Boston: R. G. Badger, [c1911] NUC.

Story of a man's sins and redemption. PW 12-23-11

MACKIRDY, MRS. ARCHIBALD. See MACKIRDY, OLIVE CHRISTIAN
(MALVERY).

MACKIRDY, OLIVE CHRISTIAN (MALVERY). D. 1914.

007768   BABY TOILERS. BY OLIVE CHRISTIAN MALVERY
(MRS. ARCHIBALD MACKIRDY). London: Hutchinson, 1907
BMC NUC.

007769   LOVE'S SOLDIER. A NOVEL. London: Cassell,
1913 BMC.

"Robert Hayes is very lonely, his mother having
recently died, when he finds little Elizabeth Morris,
a waif of London slums, and takes her home. The child
tells him her pitiful story, showing by her beauty and
latent refinement that she was born to better things.
Robert educates the child and they are devoted to each
other. Business calls him to America, where he is
reunited to the girl he has long loved, and Elizabeth
finds her long lost father. Curtain goes down on
peace, wealth and happiness for everyone." PW

007770   THE SOUL MARKET, WITH WHICH IS INCLUDED
"THE HEART OF THINGS". BY OLIVE CHRISTIAN MALVERY
(MRS. ARCHIBALD MACKIRDY). London: Hutchinson, 1906
BMC. New York: McClure, Phillips, 1907 NUC.

007771   THE SPECULATOR. London: T. W. Laurie,
[1908] BMC.

TLS-young wife, who to make money for herself and her
children, went on to the Stock Exchange as Mr. Otto
Martini; husband, arriving home from Arabia, a distant
diplomat, was horrified to hear the story. Mild
entertainment.
ACAD-light and easy reading.

007772   THIRTEEN NIGHTS. London: Hodder and
Stoughton, 1908 BMC.

007773   A YEAR AND A DAY. BY OLIVE CHRISTIAN
MALVERY. London: Hutchinson, 1912 BMC NUC.

ATH articles-virulent attack on the medical
profession, a special exception being made in favour
of women doctors. Non-fiction?

MACKOWAN, EVAH MAY (CARTWRIGHT). B. 1885. Canada.

007774   GRAYDON OF THE WINDERMERE. New York: G.H.
Doran, [c1920] NUC. Toronto: McClelland & Stewart,
[c1920] NUC.

PW-love on a ranch in Saskatchewan.

007775   JANET OF KOOTENAY; LIFE, LOVE & LAUGHTER
IN AN ARCADY OF THE WEST. New York: G. H. Doran,
[c1919] NUC. Toronto: McClelland & Stewart, [c1919]
NUC.

Enthusiastic girl, runs an 80 acre farm (fruit) in the
far west.PW
Janet Kirk, teacher, reporter, homesteader letters to
friend Nan. A neighbor farmer helps her out; (not
sentimental).
NYT-469,9-14-19 there's much gossip till they marry.

MACKUBIN, ELLEN. D. 1915. United States.

007776   THE KING OF THE TOWN. Boston and New
York: Houghton, Mifflin, 1898 NUC.

NYT 1898, p.102. Reformed sinner is colorful preacher
in mining town.
LW 29:203. Military port in Montana. Major is forced
to reveal the king's past. Edith Lorimer believes in
him.

MACLAGAN, BRIDGET, pseud. See TURNER, MARY BORDEN.

MACLANE, MARY. 1881-1929. United States.

007777   I, MARY MACLANE; A DIARY OF HUMAN DAYS.
New York: F. A. Stokes, [c1917] BMC NUC.

"Morbid, analytical to the swirling point, weird,
stubborn, selfish, conceited, what a magnificent
Russian revolutionist she might have been!" PW

007778   MY FRIEND ANNABEL LEE. Chicago: H. S.
Stone, 1903 NUC.

Title refers to a statue to whom the author pours out
her views on all subjects. PW

007779   THE STORY OF MARY MACLANE. BY HERSELF.
Chicago: H. S. Stone, 1902 BMC NUC. London: G.
Richards, 1902 BMC.

"Heavy responsibility rests on the man who allowed a
poor girl to parade a girl's green sickness and shout
in the streets the symptoms which should have been
whispered in the consulting room." BKM v.6, 1902.
"Unprecedented egotism, atheist, her young woman's
body she worships." BOOK NEWS 02.
Young woman in Western small town thoroughly bored &
unhappy. "Had I been born a man I would by now have
made a deep impression on the world." Marriage rites
are superfluous. Loves porterhouse steak & onions. NYT

MACLAREN, AMY. United Kingdom.

007780   BAWBEE JOCK. London: J. Murray, 1910 BMC.
New York & London: G. P. Putnam's Sons, 1911 NUC.

BM-- Highland romance.
TLS simple love story.
Scottish love story: sweet simple PW 3-25-11
Old fashioned heroine NYT

007781   DONALD'S TRUST. London: G. Newnes,
[c1916] BMC NUC.

007782   FROM A DAVOS BALCONY. London: Duckworth,
1903 BMC NUC.

007783   THE HEIR OF DUNCARRON. New York & London:
G. P. Putnam's Sons, 1912 NUC.

heiress, debts, love, etc. PW
heiress, debts, love, etc. NYT

007784   THE HOUSE OF BARNKIRK. London: Duckworth,
1905 BMC.

mother & 3 children ACAD 520, 05

007785   THROUGH OTHER EYES. London: J. Murray,
1914 BMC NUC. New York & London: G. P. Putnam's Sons,
1914 NUC.

"Scene is English countryside, Maisie Yorke, an only

child, has always queened it over her little world,
where she will succeed her father as owner of the
manor. Then her father thinking she needs a woman's
curbing influence marries again, a woman, who
irritates the girl and in whom she can see no good. It
is this inability to see with another's eyes which
develops the hard streak in the girl's nature, which
it takes the love of a delightful youth, the birth of
little twin half-brothers and her stepmother's death,
to dissipate and make her realize her shortcomings."
PW 85 4-11-14:1263.
LBKM-The central figure is Sunshine, a frail gentle
invalid who watches Maisie flirting with a village
youth who grows serious about her only to lose her to
someone else. But all ends well & Sunshine too finds a
man who brings gladness into her heart.

007786   WITH THE MERRY AUSTRIANS. London: J.
Murray, 1909 BMC. New York & London: G. P. Putnam's
Sons, 1912 NUC.

NYT love story.
pretty little romance. TLS

007787   THE YOKE OF SILENCE. London: Mills &
Boon, [1911] NUC BMC. New York & London: G. P.
Putnam's Sons, 1911 NUC.

Disputes between husband & wife, an adventuress who
causes them, & a child who reunites the couple. SR
PW-Separation& reunion of husband & wife.
NYT-melodrama

MACLAREN, EMILY.

007788   THE HARP OF LIFE. London: Gay & Hancock,
[1913] BMC.

007789   OUT OF THE DUST OF BATTLE. London: Murray
& Evenden, [1920] BMC.

TLS romance
TLS-war Canadian girl nurses hero at the front.
ATH-love is dominant interest

007790   THE SOUL OF ANNE. London: Murray &
Evenden, [1914] BMC.

ATH. A woman, deserted by her husband for many years,
returns to him out of a sense of duty.
TLS He is a bigamist, a swindler, etc., but still she
is puzzled about her duty to him. An accident finally
disposes of him, releasing her to her true lover.

007791   THE WEB OF CIRCUMSTANCE. London: Murray
and Evenden, [1914] BMC.

TLS historical romance. Rome

MACLAUGHLIN, MRS. W. J. United States.

007792   THE DIARY OF A UTAH GIRL. New York:
Broadway, [1911] NUC.

MACLAURIN, KATE L.

007793   THE LEAST RESISTANCE. New York: G. H.
Doran, [c1916] NUC.

Evelyn Lane marries drunken actor. She leaves him.
Takes up acting but has no love for it-to support
herself, drifts along, has one success in her
profession, dies. PW
NY-She always followed line of least resistance.

MACLAWS, EMILY LAFAYETTE. United States.

007794   JEZEBEL: A ROMANCE IN THE DAYS WHEN AHAB
WAS KING OF ISRAEL. BY LAFAYETTE MCLAWS. London: A.
Constable, [1902] BMC. Boston: Lothrop, [1902] NUC.

NYT 8-2-02 not helpful.

007795   MAID OF ATHENS. BY LAFAYETTE MCLAWS.
Boston: Little, Brown, 1906 BMC NUC.

PW-Byron.
NYT--Sent. love story.

007796   THE WELDING. BY LAFAYETTE MCLAWS. Boston:
Little, Brown, 1907 NUC.

Career of business man and politics. 11-02-07. PW

007797   WHEN THE LAND WAS YOUNG. BEING THE TRUE
ROMANCE OF MISTRESS ANTOINETTE HUGUENIN AND CAPTAIN

JACK MIDDLETON IN THE DAYS OF THE BUCCANEERS. BY
LAFAYETTE MCLAWS. London: A. Constable, [1901] BMC.
Boston: Lothrop, [c1901] NUC.

Woman masquerades as a man, fences with a duke. ACAD
01
A ready tongue and brave; captured by Spaniards, taken
to Florence, dons a man's court suit given for her
fencing prowess, escapes, meets a pirate-attacks and
disarms him. Pretends to be a Fr. count, swears like a
pirate, self-possessed, quarrelsome, she rules the
ship. Beautiful, dauntless, incredible Antoinette. NYT
01

MACLAWS, LAFAYETTE. See MACLAWS, EMILY LAFAYETTE.

MACLEAN, ANNIE MARION. D. 1934. Canada.

007798   CHEERO! New York: Woman's Press, 1918
NUC.

PW-Humble story of Jane's illness & convalescence.
Jane and her hospital adventures in pursuit of health.
(ad, NYT)

MACLEAN, CAROLINE BRETT.

007799   THE STORY OF STELLA: A NOVEL. London: S.
Sonnenschein, 1905 BMC.

MACLEAN, CLARA VICTORIA (DARGAN). United States.

007800   LIGHT O' LOVE. New York: Worthington,
1891 NUC.

Christine Trescott becomes a governess in a rich
family where the total lack of sympathy changes her
from a loving to an embittered person. Then she
marries an older man who is killed on the way home
from the wedding. Then she's a kind of prisoner in her
husband's home and suffers from the coldness of her
sister-in-law, a rel. fanatic. Through her physician,
Light of love breaks into her "rebellious soul." PW
12-12-91.
LW 23:59. Mystery, noble heroine, sinister villain,
malicious woman, and a mother's love.

MACLEAN, MAGGIE.

007801   A ROMANCE OF SKYE. Edinburgh: Oliphant,
Anderson and Ferrier, [1893] BMC.

MACLEOD, A. IAN, pseud. See RANDALL, MRS. HENRY W.

MACLEOD, CLARA NEVADA. United States.

007802   THEN, AND NOT 'TIL THEN: A NOVEL. New
York: Authors' Pub. Association, [c1897] NUC.

"The foundation of a true society will be laid only
when the husbands and fathers are as pure as they wish
their daughters to be: then and not until then."
Sensational. LW 28:479.

MACLEOD, DELLA CAMPBELL. United States.

007803   THE MAIDEN MANIFEST. Boston: Little,
Brown, 1913 NUC. Toronto: McClelland & Goodchild, 1913
BMC.

"Impressionable young man, while looking at a blue
frock hanging in a Fifth Avenue cleaner's window
suddenly has a vision of its fair owner. The vision
recurs at intervals, and so ensnares the young man's
heart that he resolves to find this fascinating,
tantalizing "Dream Girl", as he comes to call her.
Thereupon begins his quest, which leads him into a web
of difficulties and sadly upsets his order of life,
until his ideal girl is discovered in a real one." PW
"marshmallowy" NYT

MACLEOD, IRENE RUTHERFORD. See DE SELINCOURT, IRENE
RUTHERFORD (MACLEOD).

MACLEOD, MRS. ALICK, pseud. See MARTIN, CATHERINE EDITH
MACAULEY (MACKAY).

MACMAHON, ELLA J. United Kingdom.

007804   THE COURT OF CONSCIENCE. London: Chapman
& Hall, 1908 BMC.

TLS? Audrey's marriage to Mildmay before she knew he
had divorced his last wife.
ACAD. She leaves him but his wife dies & they reunite.

007805 THE DIVINE FOLLY. London: Chapman and
Hall, 1913 BMC.

Ruth Frere, so good, a saint-her spiritual influence
over all SP
sordidness of high life ATH
Blanche Adeane cannot forgive her erring husband; she
has only cold contempt for him. He disregards her
feelings. Things get worse between them when she
learns her husband's most recent affection is for her
intimate friend Elma Fancourt. LBKM
Blanche discovers her friend Elma Fancourt "has been
false" with her husband. TLS

007806 AN ELDERLY PERSON AND SOME OTHERS.
London: Chapman & Hall, 1906 BMC.

tales

007807 FANCY O'BRIEN. London: Chapman and Hall,
1909 BMC.

lower class Irish woman Bridget wronged by rogue of
title, treated despicably, sympathetc treatment of her
ATH

007808 FORTUNE'S YELLOW: A NOVEL. London:
Hutchinson, 1900 BMC.

SP 84:489. Mrs. Headington turned down Arthur 21 years
ago and married for position. Meets again and hopes he
will renew his suit. He falls for the daughter.
Complications. They eventually marry.

007809 THE HEART'S BANISHMENT. London: Chapman &
Hall, 1907 BMC.

ACAD-hero is a minister & playwright.
Clergyman & actress-TLS
no help. SR

007810 AN HONOURABLE ESTATE. London: Hutchinson,
1898 BMC. London: Mills & Boon, [191??] NUC BMC.

SP 81:346. Brenda married to a man she doesn't love is
tempted by a man with whom she becomes infatuated. A
severe illness and her husband Jimmy's heroism
reconcile her to her lot.
ACAD 54:219. Motto of story is "Il y a toujours l'un
qui baise et l'autre qui tend la joue." The adventures
of Rev. James Vincent among the fair. Florence and
Ireland.

007811 JEMIMA. London: Chapman & Hall, 1903 BMC.

ATH. hero who does not believe women worth taking
seriously; she sets him straight.

007812 THE JOB. London: J. Nisbet, 1914 BMC.

ATH Ireland. Irish inability to cope with modern
industry male hero.
TLS-suitable for young people.

007813 JOHN FITZHENRY, A STUDY. London: Mills &
Boon, 1920 BMC.

TLS Male hero ch st
SP male hero ch st

007814 A MODERN MAN. New York & London:
Macmillan, 1895 NUC. London: J. M. Dent, 1895 BMC.

He's a successful, self assured young lawyer. Merton
Byng. friend of father's has two daughters. Byng "has
promised himself the eldest." Muriel, placid, amiable,
rich. But they don't get tog ether yet. He goes off
and has an affair with a Welsh young woman Miss Sibyl,
is ready to give up Muriel "to do the right thing" but
Miss Sibyl announces she's already engaged. So he goes
back and marries Muriel who knows about the affair but
doesn't fuss about it "like the women in books
now-a-days." CR 24:178

007815 A NEW NOTE. London: Hutchinson, 1894 BMC.
New York: R. F. Fenno, [c1895] NUC. (Published
anonymously in England.)

SP 78:627. Victoria, a violinist, secretly writes an
opera, Sappho, which takes London by storm. Although
there are two men she is interested in, she is
uncommitted at close of book.
ACAD 46:348.
Victoria Leathley energetic, strong in purpose, of
wealthy family but wants her own career. Her violin
recital at St. James Hall was not a great success,
composes an opera which is very successful. Then she
falls in love with a vulgar man being more attracted
to his sensuousness than to her wholesome young
suitor. SP 74:270.
LW 27:365-clever modern young woman musician; her
independence and self-sufficiency collapse before
Loevicio.
PW 5-2-96. She is a violinist and composes an opera
which is a great success. Falls for the man who sings
the tenor role.

007816 THE OTHER SON: A NOVEL. London: Chapman &
Hall, 1904 BMC.

ATH-male heroes
ACAD-male heroes

007817 OXENDALE. London: Chapman and Hall, 1905
BMC.

Life long friends plan to marry await inheritance,
which becomes a complicated matter ACAD 1201, 05 LBKM
v29-30, 90

007818 A PITILESS PASSION. New York and London:
Macmillan, 1895 NUC. London: Hutchinson, [1896] BMC.
(Hutchinson ed.: A Pitiful Passion.)

Georgie Fitzroy is married to a man who soon learns
she's an alcoholic and who becomes interested in
another woman. He's English of good social
position-Norman Grain. PW 12-14-95:1146
LBKM 10:162. A wife's craving for drink. The husband,
a cad, on discovering his wife's weakness, is chiefly
concerned with the scandal. Tragic.
ACAD 49:238. Norman "behaves nobly and even resists
the temptation to seek a new home with Magdalen
Ponsonby, a self-sacrificing woman of a high type, who
loves him as deeply as he loves her." "Perishes while
heroically endeavoring to save his worthless and
wretched wife from a fire." "We can sympathize with
him in his anger at the deliberate concealment
practiced on him."
LW 27:220. Pitiless.

007819 A RICH MAN'S TABLE: A COMEDY OF VALUES.
London: Mills & Boon, [1916] BMC.

TLS-male hero.

007820 THE STRAITS OF POVERTY. A STUDY OF
TEMPERAMENT. London: Chapman & Hall, 1911 BMC.

marital difficulties of a "nice" wife and an ambitious
man. TLS
nothing promising. SP
2 constrasting & mutually antithetical types of men
seen thru a woman's eyes. Chooses the self made
bounder, over the gentleman; has problems in her
marriage. Does not on the whole repent her choice. ATH

007821 SUCH AS HAVE ERRED. London: Hutchinson,
1902 BMC.

ATH 10-18-02--husband refuses to divorce "the woman
who called herself his wife" & loving another
"detailed to her very innocent ears his not too
reputable story"

007822 THE TOUCHSTONE OF LIFE. London:
Hutchinson, 1897 BMC. New York: F. A. Stokes, [c1897]
NUC.

Governor and prime minister of a colony both in love
with the same woman are brothers, but only one of them
knows this. ATH 109:537.
Hero Ivor Clay, 37, millionaire leader of New Britain.
He is the illeg. son of an Earl. The legitimate son
becomes governor of New Britain. PW 52:232.
Ivor Clay refuses to cowtow to his father. Makes a
million on his own. BKM 6:166.
Cambridge, Eng. and Eng. colony of New Britain. Ivor
Clay learns he's illeg. renounces fortune his father
left him goes to New Britain becomes a millionaire,
returns to Eng. falls in love with Susan Romer who is
engaged to his half-brother. She rides 16 miles one
dark night on her bicycle to warn him against a
conspiracy to murder him; saves his life. This
incident stands out as an "unconscious tribute to the
widespread popularity of the wheel." NYT 10-2-97,7.

MACMANUS, L. United Kingdom.

007823 LALLY OF THE BRIGADE; A ROMANCE. Boston:
L. C. Page, 1899 NUC. London: T. F. Unwin, 1899 BMC.

Historical romance. Fights, hair breadth escapes in
Cremona. The Brigade is the Irish Brigade in the war
of the Spanish Succession. SP 83:193

007824   THE RED STAR. London: T. F. Unwin, 1894
BMC. New York: G. P. Putnam's, 1895 NUC.

SR 82:72. Pahlen marries Polish countess on Tsar's
orders; he informs her immediately after the ceremony
that he has a 1st wife. She disguises as a boy and
becomes an aide-de-camp; he resumes his duties in
army. Eventually they fall in love. 1st wife dies.
ATH 107:512. Autonym Series. Everlasting duel of sex
against the grim background of war in all its horror.
LW 27:218. She is a lieutenant on the general's staff.
1806.
Capt. of Imperial Russian guard must marry Countess
Halka for political reasons but convinces her to live
apart since he's married. PW 10-5-95:585

007825   THE SILK OF THE KINE. New York: Harper,
1895 NUC. London: T. F. Unwin, 1896 BMC.

ATH 107:803. Cromwellian period in Ireland. Heroine
has adventures, is almost kidnapped as slave. Margery
Guire (heroine?) has thrilling adventures; but, rev.
says., one must be a student of Irish history in age
of Cromwell to understand them intelligently.
SP 77:186. She is rescued by English officer. Hates
him, but eventually rom.

MACMILLAN, JENNIE. United States.

007826   THE MOCKING BIRD'S BREED. New York: R. J.
Shores, [c1918] NUC.

PW-love story
NYT-Story of racial prejudice, the hero of which is
the son of a Cherokee Princess, his love story.

MACMILLAN, MRS. ALEC. See MACMILLAN, NELLIE FORTESCUE
(HARRISON).

MACMILLAN, NELLIE FORTESCUE (HARRISON).

007827   THE EVOLUTION OF DAPHNE. A NOVEL. BY MRS.
ALEC MACMILLAN (NELLIE FORTESCUE HARRISON). London: F.
V. White, 1897 BMC. New York: P. F. Collier, 1897 NUC.

007828   THE WEIRD WELL: A STORY. BY MRS. ALEC
MACMILLAN. London: Greening, 1899 BMC.

Heroine is Vera Polowski. ACAD 57:430

MACNAB, FRANCES, pseud. See FRASER, AGNES.

MACNAB, WINIFRED M.

007829   CROWNS. London: Lynwood, 1912 BMC.

TLS-succession.

MACNAMARA, RACHEL SWETE. United Kingdom.

007830   THE AWAKENING. A NOVEL. London: H.
Jenkins, 1914 BMC NUC.

ATH 143:473. Story of a young woman's marriage to a
sensualist, he is crippled, she finds a better mate.
TLS-story of her sexual awakening, a pretty tale on
conventional lines.

007831   THE BELOVED SINNER. New York and London:
Putnam's Sons, 1919 NUC.

Romance, true love conquers misunderstanding. PW
NYT-178,4-6-19. English well to do people. Focus on
Desiree, her meeting with an unconventional sculptor,
her friend Princess Pafnuty who takes her dancing
barefoot in the park in moonlight. Desiree ends up
marrying owner of the park.

007832   THE CROWDED TEMPLE. London: Hurst &
Blackett, [1920] BMC.

TLS-pretty and sentimental. Efforts to bring parents
back together.
ATH-suggestions of incest between father and
daughter-but author is not able to tackle the subject.

007833   DRIFTING WATERS. London: Chapman & Hall,
1915 BMC NUC. New York & London: G.P. Putnam's Sons,
1915 NUC.

Anne Tudor's mother had miserable life with father who
was unfaithful and who abandoned her; then her own

marriage, problems, reconciliation. TLS
"Girl's rebellion against jealous proprietorship of
mother's love, much in mother's marriage to account
for her bitterness of soul and to explain her
tyrannous affection that demands daughter's devotion.
When Anne's fancy is caught, clandestine expression of
her attachment makes the plot and the several trials
of her dignity." PW 89:3/11/16:935
NYT-mother divorces father and then clings to only
child. Daughter marries secretly, then stays with
mother until death. What is fate of marriage? I think
all is cleared up at last.

007834   THE FRINGE OF THE DESERT. A NOVEL. New
York and London: G.P. Putnam's Sons, 1913 NUC. London:
H. Jenkins, 1913 BMC NUC.

"Mildred Ivors had been brought up by two elderly
cousins in a diet English village. When she was twenty
she received a letter from her mother telling her she
was to spend six months with her, then six months with
her father in Egypt, and when she was twenty-one she
could choose to live with either one of them or map
out a career for herself. Book tells of the year thus
spent and then what happens when her father marries
again without telling the woman that his first wife
lives. It is a story of conflicting temperaments that
nothing could reconcile." PW
Mother devoted to golf. Reviewer won't tell end. ACAD
Disappointed woman, turned to dogs, cigarettes and
outdoor games (sympathetic view) ATH
Mildred Ivors and Hesper Marlowe, modern in the best
sense. LBKM
Artistic man married to woman who is not artistic.
She's practical, critical. They have a daughter
Mildred who combines these traits. They separate.
Hesper Belhasard Marlowe believes the wife is dead,
falls in love with Ivors who postpones telling her the
truth. They are married. NYT

007835   THE GREEN SHOES OF APRIL. London: Hurst &
Blackett, [1919] BMC.

Disappearance of a wife of an unsuccessful marriage.
Madeline Lysaught turns up after her husband
remarries. All ends well. TLS

007836   LARK'S GATE; A NOVEL. London: Hurst &
Blackett, 1918 BMC.

TLS-Rosny experiences passion, separation, motherhood,
loveless marriage, divorce. Her ambitious mother had
wanted a son and 17 yr. old Rosny, going to the
country farm, Lark's Gate, at her doctor's request,
was impulsive ignorant, romantic and with little
knowledge of parental love or care.
ATH-their marriage is prevented by father (the farmer)
and they are separated.
SR-mother takes baby telling R. it is dead. Finally R
& J are reunited and marry.

007837   A MARRIAGE HAS BEEN ARRANGED. London: E.
Arnold, 1917 BMC NUC.

Toye Tempest-hard, pleasure loving, selfish,
unmaternal wife, moved to passion but to nothing else;
"she is simply repellent." TLS
Her selfish soullessness. Her creator does not mean
her to be attractive.
She is unrelievedly detestable, odious, red-haired,
golden eyed, sharp tongue, baffling personality. LBKM
No man capable or strong enough to be her equal mate.
Her heartless egoism. Toye alone is vital, absorbs the
reader's interest. We have no sympathy for her
victims. What effect the changed atmosphere of war has
on Toye we are left to conjecture. SR

007838   MORNING JOY. London: Hurst & Blackett,
[1918] BMC.

Desiree "spring incarnate, vivid, fragrant, glowing,"
goes to London, captures all hearts. Breaking of 8th
command. TLS
Her flowery sweetness, her loves. LBKM

007839   SEED OF FIRE. Edinburgh & London: W.
Blackwood, 1910 BMC.

TLS-sister of an archeologist in Egypt called by the
desert loves an Arab.
ACAD-an accomplished woman of the world.
ATH-she leaves the Arab after a few clinches etc. and
recalls it as green passion.
SR-she also rejects another admirer, a colleague of
her brother.

007840   THE SIBYL OF VENICE. Edinburgh: W.
Blackwood, 1908 BMC.

TLS-6 stories of a Venetian wisewoman. Her love
potions, etc.
Pia La Strega is the main character. Her spells and
charms. ATH

007841   SPINNERS IN SILENCE. Edinburgh: W.
Blackwood, 1911 BMC.

Pretty love story of Lutie Bagenal. TLS

007842   THE TORCH OF LIFE. New York & London:
G.P. Putnam's Sons, 1914 NUC.

PW 86 9-19-14:775--"For 10 yrs. Titian Fleury has been
the wife of a man hopelessly paralyzed owing to an
accident on their wedding day. Then he dies and at the
age of twenty-nine she finds herself free to discover
the world of which she has heard men speak. She has
ten spurned and thwarted years to avenge. Her
ingenious and impulsive nature cries aloud for
happiness and love and she finds it, this time a love
with wings."
NYT-husband has denied her all contact with others.
Finds a good man's love after a too avid enjoyment of
some of the pleasures she has been denied.

007843   THE TRANCE. Edinburgh: W. Blackwood, 1908
BMC.

TLS-love story sent.
SR -puzzling.
ATH-20 year trance.
SP-begins after her child is born.

MACNAUGHTAN, S. See MACNAUGHTAN, SARAH BROOM.

MACNAUGHTAN, SARAH BROOM. 1864-1916. United Kingdom.

007844   THE ANDERSONS. BY S. MACNAUGHTAN. London:
J. Murray, 1910 BMC NUC. New York: E.P. Dutton, 1911
NUC.

BM-Clydeship builders who come into society.
TLS-
ATH
SP-Flora is a managing, spirited young woman and there
are strong positive older women.
The peculiarities of Scottish life and character. LBKM

007845   THE EXPENSIVE MISS DU CANE. BY S.
MACNAUGHTAN. New York: P.R. Reynolds, 1906 NUC.
London: W. Heinemann, 1907 BMC NUC.

Shrewd comments on women and life. TLS
Miss Florrie Ellis-frankly a husband hunter. Charlotte
Balfour certain type of a modern girl. Super
self-confidence. Desire to live a strenuous life.
Keen, intellectual, self reliant. Boundless energy,
speaks on subject of raising children; wins from us
something more than respect. Hetty Du Cane is main
character. Her friendship with Lady Clitheroe (Agnes),
love for Geoffrey. Sweet reserved womanhood, yet comes
to be called expensive, why? "Nicest women...remain
unmarried;" study of several types of women. SP
NYT-ironic, 2 people meet at a houseparty, fall in
love, at final hour he realizes she is not wealthy and
withdraws. Study in temperament.

007846   THE FORTUNE OF CHRISTINA M'NAB. BY S.
MACNAUGHTAN. London: Methuen, 1901 BMC. New York: D.
Appleton, 1901 NUC.

007847   FOUR-CHIMNEYS: A NOVEL. BY S.
MACNAUGHTAN. London: T. Nelson, [1912] BMC NUC.

SP-sacrificial wife.

007848   THE GIFT; A NOVEL. BY S. MACNAUGHTAN.
London: Hodder & Stoughton, 1904 BMC NUC.

BKM-leads to God.
TLS-independent social worker who is not interested in
marriage but who becomes so deeply in love with
celibate clergyman that she cannot stay away from
him-leads to painful humiliating scene and tragedy.
ACAD-1 of the ever-growing class of women who seem to
be avoiding marriage.

007849   A LAME DOG'S DIARY; A NOVEL. BY S.
MACNAUGHTAN. London: Heinemann, 1905 NUC BMC. New
York: Dodd, Mead, 1906 NUC.

PW-young man who has lost his leg in war starts a

diary with widow of small town happenings.

007850   PETER AND JANE; OR THE MISSING HEIR. BY
S. MACNAUGHTAN. London: Methuen, 1911 BMC. New York:
Dodd, Mead, 1911 NUC.

Peter inherits a fortune, searches for brother. TLS
Along with a healthy love story. ATH
PW-inheritance.
NYT-modern,heroine, interesting older women
characters.

007851   SELAH HARRISON. BY S. MACNAUGHTAN.
London: R. Bentley, 1898 BMC. London and New York:
Macmillan, 1899 NUC.

Gloomy story of a minister who works in Kent, falls in
love with a squire's daughter, has no hope of winning
her love, goes off to do missionary work in Taro.
Marries but is unhappy--always loved the squire's
daughter. ATH 113:527
SP 81:346. Biographical romance. Trial and
self-sacrifice of missionary in the South Seas.
LIT 3:136. He is Scotch.
SP 85:825. His austere youth, passion for Constance
and marriage with Janet. His mother's name was
Marjory, a carnal name, and she signed herself M.
Harrison hoping it would be thought to stand for Mary
or Martha.

007852   SNOW UPON THE DESERT. BY S. MACNAUGHTAN.
London: Hodder and Stoughton, [c1913] BMC NUC.

A voyage to India, financial difficulties of a young
woman, sentimental difficulties of another, the
bewildering unconventionality of Hecules, the young
woman. Author "lays bare the foibles of her own sex
with dreadful understanding and sincerity." SP
Englishwoman whose finer instincts are warped by
social influences amid which she is forced to live.
ATH
Disgusted with girls' school having ideals worth
having from father. NYT
Focuses upon two women, one single, the other married.
TLS
BKM-Mrs. Antrobus is most beautiful English woman in
India. Her husband goes his own way and is more than
willing that she should go hers. She is an enigma; the
author portrays her through the eyes of the men
surrounding her. One kills himself. What is her last,
strange odyssey?
BKM 38- married woman who fascinates other men.

007853   SOME ELDERLY PEOPLE AND THEIR YOUNG
FRIENDS. BY S. MACNAUGHTAN. London: Smith, Elder, 1915
NUC BMC. New York: E.P. Dutton, [19--?] NUC.

Contrasts between seniors and juniors. Traditional
stuff. TLS
Julia is 40. Sisters and friends older, she lives in
comfortable house, servants, butler, gives big
dinners, drinks. LBKM
Clemmie extreme modernity. LBKM
Suffragette theme included. No plot, characters and
conversations. 4 elderly, 3 young. ATH
Julia gives financial assistance to unhappily married
sister. The young people Jim and Jack (2 women)
intelligent, independent journalist and dramatic
critic. Clemmie joins suffragettes. Gentle satire,
kindly. SP

007854   THEY WHO QUESTION. BY S. MACNAUGHTAN. New
York: Macmillan, 1914 NUC. London: Smith,Elder, 1916
BMC NUC.

TLS-published anonymously in 1914, embodies much rel.
thinking.
Much about religion TLS
Much about religion ATH
ACAD 0
NYT-Theme is doubt and religion.
BKM Sept 1916 p.162

007855   THREE MISS GRAEMES. BY S. MACNAUGHTAN.
London: J. Murray, 1908 BMC NUC. New York: E.P.
Dutton, 1908 NUC.

TLS-sounds frothy.
ACAD-after a few ups and downs wedding bells.
Three girls educated, in an unusual way. PW
Raised on lonely Scottish Island by pa. when he dies,
they go off to London to find employment. Their
efforts to understand modern London. Helen chief
heroine. NYT

007856   US FOUR. BY S. MACNAUGHTAN. London: J.

Murray, 1909 BMC NUC.

LBKM-4 sisters, Tabby, Jumpy, Jock & Poppy.
Unconventional view.
SR-portrayal of character, nurse and governess but not
of parents.

MACNEILL, CORA.   United States.

007857   "MISSOURA". Minneapolis: Mizzoura Pub.
Co., 1898 W.

MACNEILL, NEVADA.   United States.

007858   THE BANKER AND THE TYPEWRITER
[ANONYMOUS]. New York: G. W. Dillingham, 1895 NUC.

007859   THE DISAGREEABLE MAN: A NOVEL. BY A. S.
M. New York: G. W. Dillingham, 1895 NUC.

007860   LA NOUVELLE FEMME. BY A. S. M. New York:
G. W. Dillingham, 1896 NUC.

007861   A MARRIAGE ABOVE ZERO: A NOVEL. BY
NEVADA. New York: G. W. Dillingham, 1894 NUC.

PW-heroine loves a senator, a married man. Scene
shifts from Washington to Mexico, where she discovers
she is daughter of rich hidalgo. Wins senator from
wife and marries him.

007862   THE RED ROSE OF SAVANNAH: A NOVEL. BY A.
S. M. New York: G. W. Dillingham, [c1894] NUC.

PW-an orphan at 17, Elsie finds employment in
Washington office. Her supervisor leaves her after
mock marriage. She learns in Chicago of his
wickedness. The way his sins are told makes the book
almost unsuitable for circulation.

007863   ROB ROCKAFELLOW: A BOSTON SOCIETY MAN'S
DIARY. BY A. MANN. New York: G. W. Dillingham, 1894
NUC.

007864   THE YELLOW ROSE OF NEW ORLEANS: A NOVEL.
BY A. S. M. New York: G. W. Dillingham, 1895 NUC.

MACNEILL, ORANGE.   United States.

007865   A JESUIT OF TO-DAY. New York: J. Selwin
Tait, [c1895] NUC.

LW 27:76. Written to promote Roman Catholic Church.
Male hero

MACPHERSON, JEAN.

007866   DIDUMS: A SILHOUETTE. London: J. Long,
1899 BMC.

Soulful young woman in love with her brother-in-law.
Her adventures and early death. LIT 4:640
Two sisters-orphans. Elder is heartless, marries rich,
abandons younger to a life of a drudge. Husband of
elder becomes disillusioned with her--attracted to
poor Didums, then loves her. SP 82:648

MACPHERSON, MISS, pseud.   See PINCKNEY, SUSANNA SHULRICK
HAYNE.

MACQUEEN, ANNE, jt. au.   See COOKE, GRACE (MACGOWAN) AND
ANNE MACQUEEN.

MACQUOID, KATHARINE SARAH (GADSDEN). 1824-1917. United
Kingdom.

007867   APPLEDORE FARM. New York: Lovell,
Coryell, [c1892] NUC. London: Ward and Downey, 1894
BMC.

CR 18:118. Englishman marries, then doesn't know what
to do with his wife.
LW 23:279. Heroine loves wrong man, is subsequently
sorry and recoils into love for a most respectable
husband.
West of England. Farmer's daughter philanders with
young collegian, then marries a sturdy honest
Englishman of her own class. CR 24:248

007868   BERRIS. New York: J. W. Lovell, [1892]
NUC. London: Ward and Downey, 1893 BMC.

CR 18:202. Berris hates poverty she and her sister
live in. Inherits a paltry sum, marries the lawyer
involved, but wants more than he provides, decides
that "sooner or later she will have it" succeeds. Rev

does not like her.
She is beautiful but poor, lives with sister in a
small Yorkshire town. Wants her beauty to pay off in
rich husband. Marries a young up and coming soliciter.
He's assumed drowned. Marries another. Husband #1
shows up. SR 75, 270
Berris Bedale-beautiful, vain, frivolous contrasted
with sister, good woman happily married. Realizes the
goodness of husband #1 only after he's dead but makes
the most of husband #2. ACAD 43:302
LW 23:311. She marries a man whose "frank brutality
terrifies her into self-control and silence." "We
leave her a chastened sinner and a reasonably good
wife."
Berres Bedale, orphan, inherits money, marries a
lawyer, but marriage goes poorly. When he dies, she
remarries for "wealth and social rank". Contrast
between the two marriages. PW 2-9-95:298

007869   CAPTAIN DALLINGTON. Bristol: J. W.
Arrowsmith, 1907 BMC.

highwayman-romance TLS
ACAD. male blackguard hero.

007870   DRIFTING APART: A STORY. London:
Percival, 1891 NUC BMC.

Two unconnected stories. Title story a French love
story. "Hetty's Revenge" set in Yorkshire fishing
town, England. ACAD Also ATH 97 533

007871   HIS HEART'S DESIRE: A ROMANCE. London:
Hodder and Stoughton, 1903 BMC NUC.

historical romance ACAD 64, 486
historical romance LBKM. 7-03, 148
ATH 121, 750
TLS 152, 93

007872   HIS LAST CARD. London: Ward and Downey,
1895 BMC NUC.

A scamp and gambler disowned by family is rude to a
young woman in public. When he calls on her, she shows
him the door. He pursues her through the time she
believes her husband to be dead , right up to the time
they are both grandparents. ATH 106:787
ACAD 49:10. Reconciliation of wife and husband under
auspices of grandchild.
SP 76:273. Vengeance of a man who attempted to kiss a
girl he had never seen before and was rebuffed in
indignation, the woman refusing to have anything more
to do with him. His relentless persecution of her
throughout her life, robbing her of her "poor weak
husband" then her daughter and very nearly her
granddaughter.

007873   IN AN ORCHARD: A NOVEL. London: Bliss,
1894 BMC.

SP-pretty, pleasant.
ACAD-flighty Gabrielle but perfectly pure. Brief
marriage.

007874   MAISIE DERRICK. New York: Lovell,
Coryell, [c1891] NUC. London: A. D. Innes, 1892 BMC.

007875   MOLLY MONTAGUE'S LOVE STORY. London:
National Society's Depository, [1911] BMC.

007876   THE STORY OF LOIS. London: J. Long, 1898
BMC NUC.

ACAD 53:370. Lois' determination to become an actress
despite Indian father's fears. Meets failure and a
scoundrel, then success and a husband.
ATH 111:688. Lois is motherless (rev. suggests mother
died of boredom) raised by well-meaning inept male
parent. "Receives at the outset of her professional
life one of those bitter blows which harden the best
of women. She has the necessary self-respect to reject
the tardy reparation offered by the wicked Baronet,
and there are hopes at the fall of the curtain that a
certain elderly faithful friend will afford her the
needed consolation for her bitter experiences."
PW-"the girl loves her art beyond all other love, and
neither titles nor unflagging devotion change her from
her artistic purpose."

007877   A WARD OF THE KING: A ROMANCE. London: J.
Long, 1898 BMC. New York: F. M. Buckles, 1899 NUC.

LIT 3:606. Brittany, reign of Francis I. Mainly a love
story.
ATH 112:927. Jeanne d'Acigne, a widow is heroine.

16th French Count Laval the villain. Countesse Jeanne
improvement on the traditional heroine of romantic
fiction. The hero d'Orbec. LBKM 15:188.

MACVANE, EDITH. B. 1878. United States.

007878   THE ADVENTURES OF JOUJOU. Philadelphia
and London: J.B. Lippincott, 1906 NUC.

007879   THE BLACK FLIER. New York: Moffat, Yard,
1909 NUC.

Bridegroom discovers marriage license incorrect, goes
off to make it right, kidnapped-all made right. PW
6-26-09.
Kidnapped by young woman, poses with him as man and
wife; the law is after her. Adventure. Mix-ups. BKM

007880   THE DUCHESS OF DREAMS. Philadelphia and
London: J.B. Lippincott, 1908 NUC. London: J. Milne,
1908 EMC.

TLS-adventure of a fake duchess?
ACAD-American actress impersonates a duchess to help a
woman get into exclusive society. A Russian spy
blackmails her etc.

007881   HER WORD OF HONOR. Boston: Little, Brown,
1912 NUC.

PW-love story.

007882   TARANTELLA. Boston: Houghton Mifflin,
[1911] NUC. London: Hurst & Blackett, 1912 EMC.

Victim of an unfortunate marriage. Freed from toils of
a worthless husband. PW 10-21-11.
Theme: the right of a woman to happiness. Wife tied to
loathsome husband because rel. keeps her bound. Goes
to Italy to seek freedom from her marriage from the
church. There Cynthia Godfrey meets a man she loves.
Scandal caused by the man's sister forces Cynthia to
withdraw her application for annulment. But in the
end, she is freed. NYT
TLS-love story.
ATH-love story.

007883   THE THOROUGHBRED. New York: G.W.
Dillingham, [c1909] NUC.

Wife of title sticks with husband wrongly accused of a
crime. PW 3-20-09.
Scandal of embezzling. BKM NYT

MACVOY, RUTH SHARTEL. United States.

007884   THE TRAITOR'S SON; A NOVEL. New York:
Neale, 1915 NUC.

historical romance 11-27-15 PW

MADDOX, PEARL GROVES.

007885   THE PRECIPICE. BY MRS. PEARL GROVE
MADDOX. Baltimore: McLean, 1917 NUC.

Faith in God straightens out Doris Chartain's marriage
problems. PW

MADESANI, GRAZIA COSIMA (DELEDDA). 1871-1936.

007886   AFTER THE DIVORCE, A ROMANCE. BY GRAZIA
DELEDDA. New York: H. Holt, 1905 NUC EMC.

BKM 21 (1905) 270
Husband sentenced to 27 yrs in prison; murdered his
uncle. The couple were married by a civil service.
Wife convinced to remarry by church ceremony. Husband
refuses to divorce but has no power to stop the new
marriage. Wife soon impatient with her new husband who
drinks a lot. She's now judged as a bigamist, has a
child. The true murderer is discovered. Husband
returns with no wish to see his former wife. The 2nd
husband is killed. The original couple have been
meeting? Attitude of author NYT 267,05. Manifesto vs
divorce

007887   ASHES (CENERE), A SARDINIAN STORY. BY
GRAZIA DELEDDA. London and New York: J. Lane, 1908 NUC
EMC.

PW- Primitive passions, illicit love sordid crimes
TLS-Male hero
ACAD--who is illegitimate son of a young woman who has
been betrayed and banished from her father's house.
She drifts, finally abandons her child, son hopes she

is dead, meets her, provides her with lodging, loses
the woman he loves, hears his mother is ill but she
has in fact killed herself. He is left with
overwhelming self reproach.
BKM O
ATH O
NYT 13:267 5/9/08

007888   AN INNOCENT BARABBAS. BY GRAZIA DELEDDA.
New York: National Alumni, [1907] NUC. (Tr. James C.
Brogan)

007889   NOSTALGIA. BY GRAZIA DELEDDA. London:
Chapman and Hall, 1905 BMC. (Tr. Helen Hester
Colville.)

ACAD-young wife unhappy living with husband and his
family, then small apartment, returns to family home
in country, prepared to remain until husband can
afford better, loves him too much, returns to spacious
apt, has child and then learns of sordid arrangement
husband has made with rich woman to obtain it. Then
what?
BKM-subtle analysis of a woman's character.

MADISON, LUCY FOSTER. 1865-1932. United States.

007890   BEE AND BUTTERFLY; A TALE OF TWO COUSINS.
Chicago: M. A. Donohue, [c1913] NUC.

007891   A COLONIAL MAID OF OLD VIRGINIA.
Philadelphia: Penn, 1902 NUC.

007892   A DAUGHTER OF THE UNION. Philadelphia:
Penn, 1903 NUC.

007893   A MAID OF SALEM TOWNE. Philadelphia:
Penn, 1906 BMC NUC.

PW-historical. Witch saved at last moment.

007894   PEGGY OWEN & LIBERTY. Philadelphia: Penn,
1912 NUC.

MADISON, MARIE. United States.

007895   THE WITCH: A NOVEL. New Haven, Conn.: New
Haven Pub. Co., 1891 NUC.

MAGEE, HARRIET CECIL. United States.

007896   SAVED TO SERVE. Philadelphia: American
Baptist Pub. Society, 1895 NUC.

PW 2-1-96. After an illness he devoted his life to
service of Christ. Romance & history of S. S. Brigade,
also.
LW 27:235. New England. Religious tone.

MAGEE, VIOLET.

007897   SCHOLAR'S MATE: A STORY. London: Downey,
1895 EMC.

unmarried woman of 35 is the heroine; Mollie Dorothea
is fascinating. "With such a husband as she is
fortunate enough to get, her treachery is slightly
revolting." SR 80:88
"An Oxford beauty flirts away her time with successive
generations of undergrads until finally at the age of
34, she consents to marry a middle aged professor."
When an old beau shows up, she becomes close with him
"devoid of any actual breach of the commandments."
ACAD 47:522
"She displays little restraint in her conduct." ATH
105:670 Reviewer believes the author is male.
SP 76:901. Adultery. Fin-de-siecle. Smart, clever.

MAGOUN, JEANNE BARTHOLOW. B. 1870. United States.

007898   THE LIGHT. New York: M. Kennerley, 1911
NUC.

Letters that show conversion to woman suffrage; writer
of letters responds to anti-suffrage tracts. FRANKLIN,
138

007899   THE MISSION OF VICTORIA WILHELMINA. New
York: B. W. Huebsch, 1912 BMC NUC. London: G. P.
Putnam, 1912 BMC.

TLS-Diary of silly girl who trusted a conventional
villain, mawkish.
ACAD--author knows right from wrong and does not raise
inclination to a God. Girl betrayed and deserted, had
no mother to advise her.

NYT-Illeg child lived one day but accomplished her
mission which was to set straight her mother's heart.
She is then able to face the world bravely, calmly. A
N.Y. working girl with an active spirit and eager
mind. Diary form.

MAGRUDER, JULIA. 1854-1907. United States.

007900   AT ANCHOR, AND HONORED IN THE BREACH: TWO
NOVELS. Philadelphia: J. B. Lippincott, 1891 W.

007901   A BEAUTIFUL ALIEN. Boston: R. G. Badger,
1900 NUC.

Swedish Italian young woman fresh from convent married
to a wealthy American. She's very unhappy. Albert
Noel, a lawyer comes into her life and saves her from
utter despair. Her awakening. PW 56:329

007902   DEAD SELVES. Philadelphia: J. B.
Lippincott, 1898 W. London: J. Bowden, 1898 BMC.

LIT 3:606. Book opens on heroine's marriage. Title
refers to past selves of a developing individual, the
stepping stones of their path. Both hero and heroine
change. J. Bowden, London.
SR 86:447. Powerful, original. She was married in her
youth to a semi-imbecile. She is now a widow and has
an imbecile child. Duncan Fraser, a brilliant
scientist, has exhausted his fortune on his research,
is on the verge of a great discovery. He has nothing
but contempt for the widow who has so degraded
herself, but he offers marriage as a business
transaction; her money for position and protection.
She accepts.
LBKM 14:138. A study of her development. 2 loveless
marriages, indifferent motherhood, her dawning love
for her husband, the slow awakening of her
womanliness, the rousing of heart and conscience, her
eager clinging to her husband's mother, the final
triumph of duty and of love." Relationship with
mother-in-law.
Rhoda Gwyn married an imbecile for his money and had
an imbecile child. when husband died she married
Duncan Fraser so that she'll have prestige of his
name, and he will have her money for his scientific
experiments--a kind of marriage of convenience. He
hates her. Then a few years go by. She begins to take
an interest in his work and the world. Reads Eliot.
Husband buys her all of Eliot's works, reads Jane
Eyre. Makes friends with a Mrs. Fraser to whom she can
really talk. She and husband very gradually overcome
their coldness toward each other. There's a setback
when she decides to bring her child to their home, and
her illness from which she recovers. But they end
happy. CR 26,30:214.

007903   A HEAVEN-KISSING HILL. Chicago and New
York: H. S. Stone, 1899 NUC.

Poor artist paints a picture bought by a woman for
$100. She inspires him in his work as does a proud
society girl. Title refers to a painting he makes to
express a line of Shakespeare's poetry. PW 55:575

007904   HER HUSBAND; THE MYSTERY OF A MAN.
Boston: Small, Maynard, [c1911] NUC. London: G.
Richards, 1912 BMC.

ATH-tedious love-making. Wayward and unconventional
young American woman, her Scotch husband and his twin
brother.
BKM 34 (1912) 658 wife's desertion.

007905   JEPTHAH'S DAUGHTER. New York: R. Bonner's
Sons, 1894 NUC. (Bound with Yet She Loved Him by Kate
Brew Vaughn.)

007906   A MANIFEST DESTINY. New York and London:
Harper, 1900 NUC.

BKM 11:191. "The name of Julia Magruder stands for
that which is saccharine and sentimental." Heroine
marries wrong man for money and position; he dies and
after a suitable interval she marries right one, who
has waited.
NYT 1900:163. Suffering, beautiful heroine marries
wrong man. Learns wealth does not bring happiness. He
perishes in hunting accident and reunion with right
one. Will appeal to 16 year old girls.

007907   THE PRINCESS SONIA. New York: Century,
1895 BMC 1896 NUC.

Young American woman studies art in Paris Latin
Quarter-meets Russ. princess upon whom story focuses.

PW 10-12-95:633

007908   A REALIZED IDEAL. Chicago & New York: H.
S. Stone, 1898 NUC.

LW 29;183. Man attending wedding of his friend looks
in bride's face and realizes she is his ideal. He
leaves immediately for Africa and returns 2 years
hence when husband is dead and he takes his place.

007909   STRUAN. Boston: R. G. Badger, 1899 NUC.

Jenny wins Struan by her outspoken passion. At first
she's frank and brave. Later becomes all pettiness and
vulgarity. SR 88:82
LW 29:437. High minded musician twice marries the
wrong woman. In end he is widower & ready for #3.
PW-story of his 2nd marriage and how he and a 19 year
old country girl with a good voice solve their
differences as husband and wife.

007910   A SUNNY SOUTHERNER. Boston: L. C. Page,
1901 NUC.

Heroine tramps and rides, fancies herself progressive,
falls in love with a student disguised as a worker.
"Written for a woman's newspaper and experience tells
us that dull heroes are best beloved by modern women"?
NYT '01

007911   THE VIOLET. New York, London, and Bombay:
Longmans, Green, 1896 NUC BMC.

SR Woman with brutal husband vows to live a single
life after husband dies. Second mrge in last chapter.
ATH 108:597 Namby-pamby. "Sickly sentimental" heroine.
CR 29:257. She gets position as chaperone in New York.
Louise's guardian falls in love with her; gradually
her past is revealed.

MAIN, MRS. See LE BLOND, ELIZABETH ALICE FRANCES
(HAWKINS-WHITSHED) BURNABY MAIN.

MAIRET, MADAME JEANNE, pseud. See BIGOT, MARIE (HEALY).

MAITLAND, ELLA FULLER. United Kingdom.

007912   BLANCHE ESMEAD: A STORY OF DIVERSE
TEMPERAMENTS. London: Methuen, [1906] BMC NUC.

ACAD-spineless wife married to boorish minister. His
death cures her neuralgia.
TLS-superficial, traditional.
ATH-clash of temperaments, calls her "wifey."

007913   BY LAND AND BY WATER. London: W. Gardner,
Darton, [1911] BMC NUC.

007914   PAGES FROM THE DAY BOOK OF BETHIA
HARDACRE. London: Chapman and Hall, 1895 NUC BMC.

diary of a love sick young woman out-of-the-way in
London who tries to "cheat her hunger for love" by
garden work, tells about her friend's lives. It has a
"rare old world charm" At the end Bethia finds love
and can forget her herbs and her garden. ATH 106:351

007915   PRIORS ROOTHING. London: Smith, Elder,
1903 BMC NUC.

A country story. ACAD 65,292
Noisy vulgarity of Dolly and Victoria.
Review in LBKM 12-03,150
life of a parish; some "vulgar" people TLS 280,03

007916   THE SALTONSTALL GAZETTE. CONDUCTED BY
PETER SALTONSTALL, ESQ., AND WRITTEN BY VARIOUS HANDS.
London: Chapman and Hall, 1896 NUC BMC.

MAITLAND, VICTORIA.

007917   THE HUB OF LIFE. London: 1908 NUC.

007918   SO VERY HUMAN: A TALE. London: Century,
1909 BMC.

MAJOR, GERTRUDE KEENE.

007919   THE REVELATION IN THE MOUNTAIN. New York:
Cochrane, 1909 NUC.

BX 8645 Mormons & Mormonism

MAKEPEACE, CARRIE JANE. B. 1849. United States.

007920   THE WHITEST MAN. Boston: R. G. Badger,

1905 NUC.

MALET, LUCAS, pseud. See HARRISON, MARY SAINT LEGER (KINGSLEY).

MALLANDAINE, CATHARINE E. (SMITH).

007921   'AGAINST THE GRAIN'. New York: E. & J. B. Young, 1902 PW. London: Christian Knowledge Society, [1902] BMC.

007922   A BROKEN CUP. London: Christian Knowledge Society, [1905] BMC.

007923   THE CAVERN OF LAMENTS: A STORY OF SARK. London: J. Long, 1904 BMC.

ATH-ordinary love story.
TLS-concerning social relationships and family misunderstandings.

007924   IN LUCK'S WAY. London: Christian Knowledge Society, [1901] BMC.

007925   JASPER'S SWEETBRIAR; OR, "TO HAVE AND TO HOLD". London: Christian Knowledge Society, [1898] BMC.

SP 81:628 Lucy marries a fisherman, Jasper, below her in education. Estrangement and reconciliation.

007926   LIKE CURES LIKE. London: Christian Knowledge Society, [1901] BMC.

007927   A STEP IN THE DARK. London: Christian Knowledge Society, [1903] BMC.

007928   THE WILL AND THE WAY. London: Christian Knowledge Society, [1902] BMC.

MALLARY, M. JEANIE.

007929   A SEEMING TRIFLE. New York: American Tract Society, [c1892] NUC.

PW-Olive fights in a Christian way for George's sobriety.

MALLET, MAUD. United Kingdom.

007930   THE FLY IN THE BOTTLE. London: Mills & Boon, [1920] BMC [19--] NUC.

TLS-Anna is mistress to owner of petite maison not in a position to marry. Longs to escape. Becomes engaged to young man but not telling him truth. Discovered, and she resigns herself to bottle.

007931   THE LOVE CHIT. London: Mills & Boon, [1920] BMC.

TLS-love.
ATH-sets out to marry man with millions, is quite successful.

MALLING, INGRID MATHILDA (KRUSE). 1864-1942.

007932   THE GOVERNOR'S WIFE; PICTURES FROM THE IMPERIAL COURT OF FRANCE 1806-1807. New York: T. M. St. John, 1904 NUC. (Tr. Henriette Langaa St. John)

P23
Madame Junot 1784-1838

007933   THE IMMACULATE YOUNG MINISTER. A NOVEL. London: Constable, 1913 BMC. (Tr. Arthur G. Chater.)

Concerns men who dominated affairs in Prince Florizel's time and of an unusual marriage. ATH

007934   LADY ELIZABETH PERCY. Kobenhavn, Kristiana, 1905 BMC. Stockholm: Bonnier, [1905] NUC.

Time of Charles II, Eng. Fic.

007935   A ROMANCE OF THE FIRST CONSUL. London: W. Heinemann, 1898 BMC. (Tr. Anna Molboe)

SP 81:836. Historical romance. Young heiress is hypnotized by Bonaparte into leaving her fiance, becomes a Royal mistress, eventually suicides by drowning.
LIT 3:256. She regrets nothing, loves Bonaparte with a perfect passion and had pre-decided that she will not live when the first brightness has passed, will not tolerate a single flaw in her romance. When first

shadow falls, she takes her remedy.

MALLOWAN, AGATHA MARY CLARISSA (MILLER) CHRISTIE. B. 1891. United Kingdom.

007936   THE MYSTERIOUS AFFAIR AT STYLES. A DETECTIVE STORY. BY AGATHA CHRISTIE. New York and London: J. Lane, 1920 NUC BMC.

PW-det.
NYT 12-26-20 p. 26. M. Poirot.

MALVERY, OLIVE CHRISTIAN. See MACKIRDY, OLIVE CHRISTIAN (MALVERY).

MANDER, JANE. New Zealand.

007937   THE STORY OF A NEW ZEALAND RIVER. New York and London: J. Lane, 1920 BMC NUC.

TLS-Opposition between Alice's traditional beliefs and modern opinions of Shaw and Wells.
ATH O
LEKM-Ultra modern in attitude
PW-Isolated lumber camp in New Zealand.
NYT 1920:240. Alice develops from a "reserved, ultra-conventional and somewhat Puritanical type" to being "able to look on with-out any attempt at interference while (her) 18-year old daughter goes to live with a married man."(Author approves). Her daughter Asia devotes herself to educating the people and to Socialism.

MANIATES, BELLE KANARIS. United States.

007938   AMARILLY IN LOVE. Boston: Little, Brown, 1917 NUC.

PW a girls' book

007939   AMARILLY OF CLOTHES-LINE ALLEY. Boston: Little brown, 1915 BMC NUC. London: Hodder & Stoughton, 1917 BMC.

Amarilly Jenkins in her teens, eldest of 8, the mainstay of the Jenkins; very sugary TLS
Raises her family out of proverty. Bought a farm. Artist friend (male) sends her through college. Home from college wants to be independent. Writes a successful play. Her family stays in the country; she moves to the city. NYT 318 8-26-17
Little scrub girl "uplifted" fast by young woman then by young artist. He helps her in theatre. NYT
Story of rescue work in the slums from which develops a happy love story. BKM
Heroine" finds her ambitions awakened when scrubbing in the theatre."
From the slums; family consists of widowed mother eight children-all of whom work except the baby. WOMAN'S EDUC. ASSOC. April 1915 No 31
Amarilly is "keen precocious and ambitious." Thru her efforts, people get interested in her family, give aid, give her an ed.
NYT

007940   DAVID DUNNE; A ROMANCE OF THE MIDDLE WEST. Chicago: Rand, McNally, [c1912] NUC.

NYT-male career

007941   MILDEW MANSE. Boston: Little, Brown, 1916 BMC NUC.

Joan Lynn an enterprising optimist, came to board at the Manse and helped the family out of many difficulties. PW 89 1/1/16 p23
NYT Capable 20 year old, an expert advertising manager, diplomatist, real estate promoter, etc. Silly wholesome book about "haphazard" large family.

007942   OUR NEXT-DOOR NEIGHBORS. Boston: Little, Brown, 1917 BMC NUC.

Five children left in care of neighbors because parents were too busy doing research BKM Amusing

007943   PENNY OF TOP HILL TRAIL. Toronto: Copp, Clark, [c1919] NUC BMC. Chicago: Reilly & Lee, [1919] BMC.

NYT a mystery story.

007944   SAND HOLLER. Chicago: Reilly & Lee, [c1920] NUC.

PW-Rural south. Kenneth Lloyd is a beautiful Southern

woman with a cetain perversity. Kate Jonas finds it
better to be married and bossed than never to be
married at all, Olive Ogden causes complications.

MANIFOLD, AMY.

007945   BESSIE DREW; OR, THE ODD LITTLE GIRL.
London: S. W. Partridge, [1899] BMC.

007946   FOR HAL'S SAKE. London: Digby, Long, 1892
BMC.

ATH 100:220. "trivially pretty." "A group of children
who perform the acts of grown-up men and women in a
childish way" "pathetic" story of Hal and his sister.

MANN, A., pseud. See MACNEILL, NEVADA.

MANN, MARY E. (RACKHAM). United Kingdom.

007947   AMONG THE SYRINGAS. London: T. F. Unwin,
1901 BMC.

Barbara: idle, ignorant, untruthful. wilful, selfish
so human BKM 5-01
Motto of book "who's born a woman is born a fool" is
Barbara the fool? ACAD 01
"A woman unrestrainedly herself" ACAD 01
ATH-5-11-01

007948   ASTRAY IN ARCADY. London: Methuen, [1910]
BMC NUC.

TLS-Letters from a famous authoress, Charlotte Poole.
ATH-Concerning the inhabitants of an incredibly dull
village.
SR--Writing incredibly dull letters in spite of her
incredible literary success.

007949   AVENGING CHILDREN. London: Methuen,
[1909] BMC NUC.

Grace Blore is pretty, brainless, a coward, is dutiful
to her father, but a "heartless rebel" outside the
family. She loves one man, but gets engaged to man her
father chooses. She counts on man she loves to
extricate her, but he marries another and he commits
suicide. Another char Eleanor "a mature woman who
suffers a change for the worse." TLS
ATH 0
Patriarchal father of one family-bully and tyrant
especially to daughter. Grace Blore is a coward at
home, desperately afraid of her father. But faced with
prospect of a marriage to a man she doesn't want,
persuades a man she does love to run off. They're
caught and Grace returned to her father's house. She's
finally bullied into rebellion. SP

007950   THE CEDAR STAR. New York: R. F. Fenno,
[c1897] NUC. London: Hutchinson, 1898 BMC.

SP 80:174. Ted Harringay marries the wrong woman. When
he, she, and the woman he loves are upset boating,
even though she directed him to save the other woman
first, which he does, when the wife rises to the
surface, and clutches him, he sticks her off and lets
her drown. On learning, on their marriage eve, the
price of their marriage, his second wife flees. She
later on forgives him and is about to send for him,
but he has died in S. Africa.
ACAD 53:93. Betty, wilful, has her own way as a child
and continues until she suffers and is sorry.
ACAD 53:202. Story of 4 children in a rectory, growing
up without a mother. 2nd half of story focuses on
Betty's womanhood.
SR 85:565. Betty is an artist, a promising painter.
She falls for her cousin's husband, Edward Harringay.
They are on the point of eloping when three of them
are overturned in boat, wife drowns. Betty, shocked,
returns, flees to her work. A year later he seeks her
out, renews his suit, they marry. Truth on wedding
night.
LBKM 14:23. Betty is "selfish, passionate,
domineering, a prey to sudden gusts of temper, and of
emotion, but withal generous, brave, and true as
steel."

007951   THE EGLAMORE PORTRAITS. London: Methuen,
[1906] BMC NUC.

ACAD. Silly flighty little wife and mother-in-law
problem.
TLS-Slight and light.
ATH

007952   THE FIELDS OF DULDITCH. London: Digby,

Long, 1902 BMC NUC.

007953   FORTUNE'S CAP. London: Hurst and
Blackett, 1905 BMC NUC.

About Tillie and the fortune she gets ACAD 1081,05
LBKM v29-30, 91
A maid receives a hugh fortune-story of her education.
ATH 68, 05

007954   GRANDPAPA'S GRANDDAUGHTER. London: Mills
& Boon, 1915 BMC.

Artificial story of 2 grand daughters; one
conscientious-the other uncontrolled. TLS

007955   GRAN'MA'S JANE. London: Methuen, 1903 BMC
NUC.

A Norwich lass with degenerate relatives. ACAD 65,
500.
Charming idyl, heroine embodiment of young joy and
love and innocence ATH 122,610
Mrs. Wylde's son is a spendthrift, a drunk, married to
an infant wife who gives birth while outside a public
hanging takes place; new mother dies, father too drunk
to understand son drives his mother mad. TLS 328,03

007956   THE HEART-SMITER. London: Methuen, 1908
BMC.

TLS-love
BKM
BAKER 13-304

007957   IN SUMMER SHADE. A NOVEL. New York:
Harper, 1892 NUC. London: H. Henry, 1893 BMC.

Lively scenes and bright conversations of a large
family. The Burne family. Father degraded the family
by marrying a gypsy. Daughter Mary Burne is beautiful.
Her beauty attracts many men and causes jealousies. PW
1-7-93.
Her sister Holly married an aristocrat whose brother
loves Mary but Mary loves Bob Barton more, but Bob is
killed. So then gossip about Mary's past (that is in
actuality Holly's past) gets in the way of the
wedding. All ends well. SR 75:127.
Heroine "one of those self-reliant, plain spoken,
impulsive Bohemian girls"-Mary Eurne. ACAD 43:195.
"Whole hy of the sister's adventure in London." ATH
101:181.

007958   THE MATING OF A DOVE. London: T. F.
Unwin, 1901 BMC.

ACAD: about Monica and her marriage to Rev. Bell not
success. She would have given him a dozen times over
to have her mother back.
ATH 3-8-02 "class distinctions"

007959   THE MEMORIES OF RONALD LOVE. London:
Methuen, 1907 BMC.

A child's life in early 19th ACAD
TLS
ATH Painful story of an illeg child who finally goes
to his father and is accepted by Eleanor, his father's
wife. She treats him tenderly, forgives husband's sin
and his relation with poor Nancie (ma. of Child) SP

007960   MOONLIGHT. London: T. F. Unwin, 1898 BMC.

Title refers to hero. Wrecks the happiness of the
woman he loves. LBKM 15:119
SP 81:873. Heroine, reduced to poverty, works in
"monster shop, the humours and squalors of which are
described with considerable skill." "Intrinsically
painful theme." Also relationships with two men.
ACAD 55:548. She works in a grocery and drapery shop.
She is removed by a rich uncle. She marries the wrong
man upon discovery that her aunt, as well as she,
loves the right man. Tragic ending.
ATH 112:925. "Seems calculated to please women more
than men."

007961   MRS. DAY'S DAUGHTERS. London and New
York: Hodder & Stoughton, [c1913] BMC NUC.

Tragedy of hereditary weakness in dealing with money.
Father, then son are financially disgraced. Mrs Day
must take over grocery Shop. Her two daughters Bessie
and Deleah very different; Bessie-weak, idle;
Deleah-Excellent charming. SP
Bessie, lazy selfish, hysterical; mother and sister
independent women. ATH

007962   OLIVIA'S SUMMER. London: Methuen, 1902
BMC 1903 NUC.

007963   OUT IN LIFE'S RAIN. London: Hutchinson,
1899 BMC.

007964   THE PARISH NURSE. London: Methuen, 1905
BMC NUC.

Emily-capable, strong, independent falls for a regular
bully! He dominates her, bullies her and she loves it.
And she shows the poor people as ignorant,
mean-souled, ungrateful. ACAD 984,05
Emily-capable, cares for sick children, woman with
cancer, capitulates to the strong man, calls him her
master. Masterful man is back. Because of her strength
and ind., this capitulation is extreme. TLS 250,05
Feels his "intensity and desire to protect" fascinated
to yield to a will stronger than hers. ATH 05,235

007965   THE PATTEN EXPERIMENT. London: T. F.
Unwin, [1899] BMC.

Patten is a minister who wants to see for himself how
a farm laborer manages to support a family on 11
shillings a week. His relatives help in the
experiment. LIT 5:374
Amusing. SP 83:499
They hungered, quarrelled, got headaches, indigestion,
but they kept out of debt. ACAD 57:485
LBKM 17:123. Humorous account of prosperous family's
attempt to survive as agricultural laborers for a
week. Romance too

007966   THE PEDLAR'S PACK. London: Mills & Boon,
[1918] BMC.

007967   PERDITA: A NOVEL. London: R. Bentley,
1893 BMC.

Perditta Sant's husband disappears on wedding day. She
has good reason to believe he's dead. He's the same
man arrested for swindling in wife's presence. He's a
bigamist. He reappears at the end. But story concerns
the two women. They are drawn together. We also get
Perditta's romances because she believes she's a
widow. Widowed, Perditta is poor, gets a job as
teacher at girls' school, the mistress of which is
wife #1. About to marry, husband she thought dead
appears. He murders wife #1; taken to jail; hint that
she will now marry man she loves. SP 76 303.
The other woman Pauline Ashford. A woman's school in
London suburb. Painter finally wins Perditta . ATH
102;415

007968   ROSE AT HONEYPOT. London: Methuen, [1906]
BMC NUC.

ACAD-love affair between married woman and gamekeeper
she meets while staying in the country.
TLS-innocent helpless heroine tragi-comedy
ATH-mixture of sent. & comedy; we should mildly shake
Rose.

007969   THE SHEEP AND THE GOATS. London: Methuen,
1907 BMC NUC.

Witty and sparkling Amanda-ACAD
Minister champions young woman-Daisy-of his parish,
gives her a home TLS
Amanda-a siren, a minx; series of ineffectual
flirtations falls for school-master but he's
worthless, another lover distracted by Daisy
Meers-mere good looks. Amanda & Daisy vie for this
man; comic but "no lack of serious relief" "Daisy is
dreadful" End?
Rebellious sister of the rector, Mother whose ambition
would destroy her daughter's life. Ends in rector's
marr. but to whom?

007970   SUSANNAH. London: Henry, 1895 BMC. New
York: Harper, 1896 NUC.

Mrs. Foote takes charge of the heroine "who is thrown
upon the world." Her son Paragon. ACAD 48:431
She's a new kind of heroine, shows individuality in
speech and manner. All her moods. She tends her drug
ridden brother in the lodging house in Great Kirby St.
Ends betrothed to a young doctor. ATH:106:679.
Young lady becomes a servant to nurse her dying
brother, "loses a doubtful lover and gains a true one"
A household tyrant, female, supplies comedy.
BAKER,03,141
SP 77:562. Susannah impoverished works in a variety of
positions after a short stay with a miserly jealous

older woman friend. Her experience as maid-of-all-work
in a boarding house is unhappy.
BKM 3:557. Her brother is an opium wreck; his friends
insult her. One, a doctor, takes an interest. They are
eventually married.
CR 29:59.

007971   THERE ONCE WAS A PRINCE. London: H.
Henry, 1896 BMC.

007972   THERE WAS A WIDOW. London: Methuen,
[1911] BMC NUC.

Widowed Julia Delane with three children "too weak to
fend for herself" "muddlehead" TLS
Her difficulties in supporting herself, how a rich
cousin tyrannized her, how a gruff going doctor won
her ACAD
Julie Delane is loveable, 30, penniless widow, with no
way to support herself. Her brother arranges for her
to be housekeeper to a young doctor who took over her
husband's practice. Through a jealous woman, their
relation misinterpreted; scandal follows; he must
leave. Takes another job as housekeeper; Things get
worse till the end, which the reviewer refuses to
disclose. SP
She is "stupid and as insensitive as a conscientious
cow" also volatile (?) on the way to a second
marriage. ATH
"Excellent novel" Author has a very warm regard for
poor Julia Delane. SR

007973   THROUGH THE WINDOW. London: Mills & Boon,
1913 BMC.

007974   THE VICTIM. London: Hodder & Stoughton,
1917 BMC.

Mother deserts husband for another man. Victim-the
daughter born out of wedlock who was handed over to
foster mother. In her charge becomes a drugge. The
mother deserted in turn is taken back by husband. Yrs
later, when husband dies, meets her lover, together
they search for their child. TLS
The wages of sin is death is the theme SP.

007975   WHEN A MAN MARRIES. New York: Hodder &
Stoughton, [1916] BMC NUC.

TLS-silly romance
ATH story of a man's pitifully mistaken mrg told by
the woman whom it injures.

007976   WHEN ARNOLD COMES HOME. London: Henry,
1897 BMC.

007977   A WINTER'S TALE. London: R. Bentley, 1891
BMC. Leipzig: B. Tauchnitz, 1891 NUC.

Erica Birch very ind. Knows real affection from sham
affection, finds it. ACAD
A chilling dreadful kind of novel. Penny is murdered.
Hercourt is mad. (Erica escapes from him.) Did Penny
really propose to the Squire. SP 66, 700

MANN, MARY (RIDPATH). B. 1867. United States.

007978   THE UNOFFICIAL SECRETARY. Chicago: A. C.
McClurg, 1912 NUC.

PW love story in Paraguay, travel described in
letters.
NYT travel & romance.

MANN, RUFUS, pseud. See SHALER, SOPHIA PENN (PAGE).

MANNING, FRANCES DUNCAN. B. 1877. United States.

007979   MY GARDEN DOCTOR. BY FRANCES DUNCAN.
Garden City, New York: Doubleday, 1914 NUC.

PW 85 4/11/14 p.1262 "Heroine had had a complete
breakdown and found it hard to rally, in spite of her
youth, until she took a sudden interest in an old
German neighbor working in his garden. This stirred
longings for a garden of her own, so she and her nurse
took a little place in New Hampshire and Caroline
began to make a garden. Working out-of-doors with
growing things restored her health and poise while a
man whose love of nature made him understand and help
her need was the doctor who made all her future
bright."

007980   ROBERTA OF ROSEBERRY GARDENS. BY FRANCES
DUNCAN. Garden City, New York: Doubleday, Page, 1916
NUC BMC. London: Constable, 1916 BMC.

Roberta is secretary to owner of gardens (nurseries)
learns the trade and more worldly things. PW
Love story as well NYT, TLS
ATH Pretty story of woman into horticulture.

MANNING, GLORIA. B. 1881. Nationality Unknown.

007981   IMPROPER PRUE. New York: B. W. Dodge,
1909 NUC.

"Prudence is a charming and audacious young woman who
gains for herself the title of Improper Prue through
her love of saying and doing unconventional things."
BKM 29:1909

MANNING, MARIE. D. 1945. United States.

007982   JUDITH OF THE PLAINS; A NOVEL. New York &
London: Harper, 1903 BMC NUC.

Noble figure of girl throbbing with passion and life.
PW 10-31-03
Tall, "half breed" noble woman towers over women of
the East. Review in NYT 03,834

007983   LORD ALINGHAM, BANKRUPT. New York: Dodd
Mead, 1902 NUC. London: B. F. Stevens & Brown, 1902
BMC.

MANNIX, MARY ELLEN. 1846-1939. United States.

007984   CHRONICLES OF 'THE LITTLE SISTERS'. Notre
Dame, Indiana: Ave Maria, [c1899] NUC.

007985   A LIFE'S LABYRINTH. Notre Dame, Indiana:
Ave Maria, [c1901] NUC.

ATH 2-8-02 Old fashioned story--but rev. does not say
much.

MANSFIELD, CHARLOTTE. B. 1881. United Kingdom.

007986   THE DUPE: A BRITISH AND SOUTH AFRICAN
STORY OF THE YEARS 1914 AND 1915. London: Simpkin,
Marshall, 1917 BMC.

She is an American widow whose husband left her plans
for a flying gun. Marries a ruthless German. Her
friend Dawn Mather proves to be a good counter plotter
vs German spy husband. TLS
Reviewer focuses on the war in the novel. LBKM.

007987   FOR SATAN FINDS.... London: Holden and
Hardingham, [1917] BMC.

TLS-Her hands are idle in the veld, his on board ship
back to England. They agree to start "fresh".

007988   THE GIRL AND THE GODS. London: Hermes
Press, 1906 BMC.

007989   GLORIA: A GIRL OF THE SOUTH AFRICAN VELD.
London: Holden & Hardingham, 1916 [JBMC. London:
Simpkin, Marshall, Hamilton, [1917] NUC.

Diamond mines and illicit diamond buying. TLS

007990   LOVE AND A WOMAN. London: T. W. Laurie,
[1909] BMC.

Eileen Manners "forward minx" becomes mistress of
married man, an eminent politician. He commits suicide
so she can marry cousin. TLS
Author makes the relation between Eileen and the
politician fierce, sympathetic. Sir Hartley dies
voluntarily so that Eileen may marry her cousin-doctor
who is in love with her. ACAD.

007991   RED PEARLS. A NOVEL. London: Holden &
Hardingham, [1914] BMC.

Love and quest of hero for the pearls. ATH
For a beautiful but so far cold woman TLS

007992   SEX AND SILLER, A NOVEL. London: R.
Holden & Hardingham, 1920 BMC NUC.

007993   STRINGS. London: W. Westall, [1920] BMC.

LBKM: lurid nonsense. Perenza is utterly selfish,
glorifies in cruelty for art's sake. Violin maker, he
makes love to an Eng. woman to get a rare violin and
abandons her. Years later he takes demonaic possession
of his hitherto unclaimed son on verge of mrg. Unclear
then, but impression is that he strings his fiddle

with the entrails or nerves of the mother and a
similar fiddle for his son, made of the body of the
bride and strung with hair.
SR-0

007994   TORN LACE. London: W. Scott, 1904 BMC.

MANTLE, BEATRICE. United States.

007995   GRET: THE STORY OF A PAGAN. New York:
Century, 1907 BMC NUC.

Daughter of lumber jack "runs wild among the rough
men," knows the lumber business well. Then she rebels
when her father tries to tame her. She rashly marries
a no-good to assert her indep. BKM 26 (1907) 270-1
Returns home ignoring the marriage. When 2 business
men come to the area to start a shingle business, she
uses her know-how to make the business a success. The
business brings a new social set to the area. Errol
Ludlowe comes and Gret really falls for him. She
refuses to let her early blunder get in her way-can't
see why that marriage binds her. Marries him, but trag
comes when he learns about the marriage. BKM
NYT

007996   IN THE HOUSE OF ANOTHER. New York:
Century, 1920 BMC NUC.

PW- Myst, woman, injured in accident, wakes up in
strange surroundings. How she works out her fate.
NYT 10-17-20 p.11. "a tangled web" written "solely to
divert".

MAPES, ELLA (STRYKER). B. 1870. United States.

007997   BECAUSE OF POWER. New York: G. W.
Dillingham, 1903 NUC. London: T. F. Unwin, 1903 BMC.

Youthful romance. Becomes a living tragedy. PW 5-23-03

MARAINI, YOI. Nationality Unknown.

007998   A CHILD WENT FORTH. BY YOI PAWLOWSKA.
London: Duckworth, 1914 BMC NUC.

SR 118:54. Child study, but author does not give
sequel of the woman, leaving her at the door of
boarding school.

007999   THOSE THAT DREAM. London: Duckworth, 1912
BMC NUC.

TLS Two female characters of arresting personality,
one is too ethereal; sedate impassive style.

008000   A YEAR OF STRANGERS. BY YOI PAWLOWSKA.
London: Duckworth, 1911 BMC NUC.

MAREO, CAMILLE, pseud. See BOREL, MARGUERITE (APPELL).

MARCH, CATHERINE.

008001   A BARREN VICTORY. BY CARL SWERDNA.
London: W. Stevens, [1897] BMC.

008002   CHERRY BLOSSOM. BY THE AUTHOR OF "MADAM'S
WORD" [ANONYMOUS]. London: W. Stevens, [1892] BMC.

008003   A DESPERATE GAME. BY CARL SWERDNA.
London: W. Stevens, [1895] BMC.

008004   A LONG LANE. BY THE AUTHOR OF "CHERRY
BLOSSOM" [ANONYMOUS]. London: W.Stevens, [1893] BMC.

A beautiful heiress marries her trustee. Selina, a
widow. SP 76::423.

008005   MY LADY'S WAY. BY CARL SWERDNA. London:
W. Stevens, [1905] BMC.

008006   NOT A SAINT. BY THE AUTHOR OF "PRUE"
"CHERRYBLOSSOM" ETC. [ANONYMOUS]. London: W. Stevens,
[1894] BMC.

008007   "ON LONDON STONES". London: J. Clarke,
1897 BMC.

SP 80:123. Ninon Varondie, heroine, strong-willed.
Father is important leader of secret political
society. Randal and Jacelyn are lovers.
LIT 2:452 Major Woodcourt also likes Ninon. Rev. is
not sure she would make a "comfortable wife".

008008   PRUE. BY THE AUTHOR OF "CHERRY BLOSSOM"
[ANONYMOUS]. London: W. Stevens, [1896] BMC.

MARCH, CLARICE.

008009   MARRED BY MEDDLING. London: Digby, Long,
1894 BMC.

MARCH, ELEANOR SUTCLIFFE. Nationality Unknown.

008010   A STUMBLER IN WIDE SHOES [ANONYMOUS].
London: Hutchinson, 1896 BMC. New York: H. Holt, 1896
NUC.

BKM 4:163. Conventional plot in Amsterdam. "It is
rather a fad, since the star of Zangwill rose above
the literary horizon, to be interested in the Jews;
and accordingly, in her poverty, Myrtle's residence is
fixed near the Jewish quarter in Amsterdam."
PW 6-27-96. Rupert rescues Eng. woman from drowning.
An artist, he spends a short time in England on her
brother's farm in training, marries her and returns to
Holland. Rupert's father with his extravagant habits,
a Jewish money lender and his beautiful daughter, play
a large part in their married life, the latter trying
in vain to capture Rupert's heart.

MARCH, ELLA.

008011   MY SUITORS. London: Digby, Long, [1891]
BMC.

ATH 99:563. Romance of a governess.
ACAD 41:562. Who marries a baronet.

MARCHAND, ANNABELLA BRUCE.

008012   DIRK, A SOUTH AFRICAN. New York:
Longmans, Green, 1913 NUC. London: Longmans, 1913 BMC.

Tant Gezina saw the hand of God in everything--never
loses faith. Dirk has an incorruptible conscience. He
dies. ATH
"Gives vivid and interesting picture of the old Boer
life and manner in the South Africa of thirty years
ago. It tells the story of a South African Boer family
of primitive ways and of its ruin by an unscrupulous
travelling dealer, and of the revenge planned by the
surviving member of the family." PW 2-27-13;951

MARCHANT, BESSIE. See COMFORT, BESSIE (MARCHANT).

MARCHBANK, AGNES. Nationality Unknown.

008013   AN ANGEL'S VISIT AND A GUID TOCHER.
London: W. W. Gibbings, 1892 BMC.

008014   THE COVENANTERS OF ANNANDALE. Paisley: J.
& R. Parland, [1895] BMC.

008015   RUTH FARMER: A STORY. New York: Cassell,
[c1896] NUC. London: Jarrold, 1896 BMC.

ACAD 49:506. Totally misunderstood by her husband. She
leaves; it is believed that she has drowned. He is at
the point of marrying another when he becomes
disenchanted by his bride and convinced that his wife
is alive. She has endured poverty, almost lost her
child. By end of book they are reunited.
SP 77:344. She goes thru some strange experiences.

008016   SOME EDINBURGH BOHEMIANS. Auchterarder:
Torani, [1891] BMC.

008017   A SWATCH O' HOMESPUN. Edinburgh: R. W.
Hunter, [1896] BMC.

MARCY, MARY EDNA (TOBIAS). B. 1877. United States.

008018   OUT OF THE DUMP. Chicago: Charles H.
Kerr, 1909 NUC.

First person narrative of hard life in Stockyards
region of Chicago. It tells of death of father due to
a rotten chute, experience of family with charities.
Author convinced all this wretchedness is due to
capitalism. NYT

MAREAN, BEATRICE. United States.

008019   HER SHADOWED LIFE; A ROMANCE OF ST.
AUGUSTINE. Chicago: E. A. Weeks, [c1893] NUC.

PW-Secret mrg of heroine, then, believing herself a
widow marries again. Return of 1st husband plunges her
into a course of deceit until 2nd widowhood brings
freedom.

008020   THE TRAGEDIES OF OAK HURST: A FLORIDA
ROMANCE. Chicago: Donohue, Henneberry, 1891 NUC.

008021   WON AT LAST: A NOVEL. Chicago: Donohue,
Henneberry, 1892 NUC.

MARKS, JEANNETTE AUGUSTUS. B. 1875. United States.

008022   THE END OF A SONG. Boston: Houghton
Mifflin, 1911 NUC. Mauve Library, 1911 BMC.

Homey story of Welsh life. PW 3-18-11

008023   LEVIATHAN, THE RECORD OF A STRUGGLE AND A
TRIUMPH. New York: Hodder and Stoughton, [c1913] NUC.
London: Hodder & Stoughton, 1914 BMC.

ATH 143:472. Woman marries young professor with opium
habit and reforms him.
PW. Story of the struggle of John Dean against the
drug habit. Margaret Richards marries him, knowing he
takes the drug, but hoping to help him in his fight,
which old Francis, his colored servant has loyally
made with him for some years. It is a desperate
battle, and the victory is hard-won, but it is won in
the end. In telling her tale, author reveals much of
the drug evil in America and the methods of those
selling the stuff.

MARKS, MARY A. M. (HOPPUS). Nationality Unknown.

008024   DAVID PANNELL, A STUDY OF CONSCIENCE.
London: Hutchinson, 1894 BMC.

SR 78:490. Moral flabbiness in male author analyzed.
ACAD-setting is Rome.

008025   DR. WILLOUGHBY SMITH. A NOVEL. London: R.
Bentley, 1892 BMC.

ATH 99:496.
SP Story of a male murderer, an ordinary upright man
who, without any knowledge that he would do so,
committed a crime. Study of his character, incipient
insanity, after the crime.
SR 73:392. Killed his best friend; he coveted his
wife.

008026   THOROUGH; A NOVEL. London: Bentley, 1894
NUC BMC.

SR-77:641. Irish social life during days of Cromwell.
SP-too much history, too little fiction. Dull.
ACAD-too much history, too little fiction.

MARLITT, E., pseud. See JOHN, EUGENIE.

MARLOWE, MARY (O'SHANASSY). Australia.

008027   THE WOMEN WHO WAIT. London: Simpkin,
Marshall, 1918 BMC NUC.

TLS-demonstration of chastening influence of war on
feminist.

MARQUIS, RENIA (MELCHER). B. 1881. United States.

008028   THE TORCH BEARER. New York and London: D.
Appleton, 1914 NUC.

Sheila Caldwell thru childhood, her rich possibilities
as writer, persuaded to marry by young man. Comes to
realize she sacrificed her rare individuality to a
self centered arrogant man who jealously refuses to
recognize a woman's right to self expression. Bored,
she tries desperately to write knowing her husband
objects. One day while she's writing, nurse takes son
out, gets very ill. In a morbid mood she vows never to
write if his life spared. As it turns out husband
mellows; son inherits ma's rare gift. At least she's
been a torch bearer. BKM
"Sheila Caldwell, a girl of rare literary gift and
passionate idealism, realizes too late that her
husband is intellectually and spiritually her
inferior: This tragedy is intensified when she
realizes that the companionship of another man with
talents and interests similar to her own brings
relief. Striving for spiritual self-adjustment, she
seeks happiness in art, almost forgetting the prior
claims of motherhood. Her struggle to keep her
womanhood reproachless, and yet to hold fast to the
new found love makes the story, and Sheila is finally
able to declare, "I'm glad I've lived." PW
Sheila, after birth of son, out of despondency, is
writing secretly against her husband's wishes (he
refuses to recognize a woman's right to

self-expression) when a nurse takes her son out and he
gets a contagious disease. She, feeling guilty, vows
never to write again if he lives. Many years later,
she and her husband reflect that her talent has not
been lost because her son has it; she is a
torch-bearer.
BKM 40 1914-15

MARR, KATE THYSON. D. 1907. United States.

008029   BOUND BY THE LAW. New York: G. W.
Dillingham, 1898 NUC.

PW-Geraldine gives husband her love and her fortune.
Utterly heartless, he squandered both. Bears all
rather than disgrace her children with a divorce.
Then, when all money is gone, he refuses to support
her and proposes a legal separation. Her struggles to
feed and clothe her children.

008030   CONFESSIONS OF A GRASS WIDOW, A NOVEL.
New York and London: F. T. Neely, [c1900] NUC.

Adventures of a fair divorcee along with letters from
Dodo "a startlingly audacious young woman" restless
and unhappy in her marriage. LBKM Oct '01

MARRIAGE, CAROLINE.

008031   THE LUCK OF BARERAKES. London: W.
Heinemann, 1903 BMC.

Murder in remote village of 100 years earlier. ACAD
65,38
A woman to save her good name marries a murderer? The
misery of her life. In dialect ACAD 65,68
Centers on a murder done in the past. ATH 122,120
Illeg. child, woman first asks for marriage then
refuses what is given grudgingly, finally accepts it.
TLS 217,03

MARRIOTT, CONSTANCE (SUTCLIFFE).

008032   OUR LADY OF THE ICE. A STORY OF THE ALPS.
BY CONSTANCE SUTCLIFFE. London: Greening, 1901 BMC.

MARRYAT, FLORENCE. See LEAN, FLORENCE (MARRYAT) CHURCH.

MARRYAT, MRS. FREDERICK TOWNSHEND. Nationality Unknown.

008033   ROMANCE OF THE LADY ARBELL. BY ALASTER
GRAEME (MRS. FREDERICK TOWNSHEND MARRYAT). London: F.
V. White, 1899 NUC BMC.

Appallingly gloomy historical romance. Very
sympathetic heroine who is extremely unhappy. LIT
4:581

MARSDEW, THALIA.

008034   IDONEA. London: Eden, Remington, 1891
BMC.

SP 68:721. Reviewer finds it "incredible" that Idonea,
critical of her father's attitude toward her mother
and relationship with another woman, should become
involved with a married man. "Granted the liaison,
however, the tragic deaths of Idonea and her infant
are quite natural events." Idonea's "moral and
phsycial struggles."
SP 73:128. She lived with a married man on weekends.

MARSH, FRANCES.

008035   THE IRON GAME. A STORY OF THE
FRANCO-PRUSSIAN WAR. London: A. C. Fifield, 1909 BMC.

Concerns war TLS
Heroine is a surgical nurse in Fr. Antiwar novel
showing horrors of warfare. SP

008036   A ROMANCE OF OLD FOLKESTONE. London: A.
C. Fifield, 1906 BMC.

TLS-conventional romance.

MARSHALL, BEATRICE. United Kingdom.

008037   HIS MOST DEARE LADYE: A STORY OF MARY,
COUNTESS OF PEMBROKE, SISTER OF SIR PHILIP SIDNEY.
London: Seeley, 1906 BMC. New York: Dutton, 1906 NUC.

008038   OLD BLACKFRIARS; A STORY OF THE DAYS OF
SIR ANTHONY VAN DYCK. London: Seeley, 1901 BMC. New
York: E. P. Dutton, 1902 NUC.

008039   AN OLD LONDON NOSEGAY. GATHERED FROM THE
DAY-BOOK OF MISTRESS LOVEJOY YOUNG, KINSWOMAN BY
MARRIAGE OF THE LADY FANSHAWE. London: Seeley, 1903
NUC BMC. New York: E. P. Dutton, 1903 NUC.

Domestic life in London at time of Civil War.
LBKM-book for girls.

008040   THE QUEEN'S KNIGHT ERRANT: A STORY OF THE
DAYS OF SIR WALTER RALEIGH. New York: E. P. Dutton,
1905 NUC. London: Seeley, 1905 BMC.

Historical romance of sensation. 204,05 NYT

008041   THE SEIGE OF YORK. A STORY OF THE DAYS OF
THOMAS LORD FAIRFAX. London: Seeley, 1902 BMC NUC. New
York: P. Dutton, 1903 PW.

Woman "keenly alive to the lower orders of creation."
Historical romance. NYT 03 288

MARSHALL, EMMA (MARTIN). 1830-1899. United Kingdom.

008042   ABIGAIL TEMPLETON; OR BRAVE EFFORTS. A
STORY OF TODAY. London and Edinburgh: W. & R.
Chambers, 1896 BMC.

PW 11-14-96. Girl's book.

008043   BETTER LATE THAN NEVER. London: Griffith,
Farran, [1898] BMC.

ACAD 53:496. Old fashioned pure love story.
SP 85:825. Nice moral book for girls.

008044   BOSCOMBE CHINE. London: 1893 NUC.

Story of Bournesmouth over 50 yrs. Covers the reign of
Victoria. SP 76:131

008045   THE BRIDE'S HOME. London: J. Nisbet,
[1893] BMC.

008046   BRISTOL BELLS. A STORY OF THE EIGHTEENTH
CENTURY. London: Seeley, 1892 BMC NUC.

LW 23:213. Story of Chatterton. Historical romance.

008047   BY THE NORTH SEA; OR, THE PROTECTOR'S
GRANDDAUGHTER. London: Jarrold, 1896 BMC. New York:
Whittaker, 1896 NUC.

SP 76:557. Fictionalized account of life of Mrs.
Bridget Bendyst, grand daughter of Oliver Cromwell.
PW 11-14-96. In diary form by Albinia Ellis who lived
in the household. Combines facts and fiction.
Mrs. Bridget Bendyst (daughter of Cromwell) "made
herself conspicuous by her manual labor, her eccentric
dress." LW 28:128

008048   CASTLE MEADOW; A STORY OF NORWICH A
HUNDRED YEARS AGO. London: Seeley, 1897 BMC NUC. New
York: Macmillan, 1897 NUC.

"The childhood and boyhood of "Old" Chrome, the
painter and of William Crotch, the composer." CR
28,31:34.
Wm. Crotch, a musician-his life and times. BAKER 03
143.
Norwich end of 18th. Focus of story is Hyacinth the
19th cent. type "but not a young woman who screamed at
the sight of a spider or caterpillar, nor went into
hysterics if she thought she did not receive
sufficient admiration." She's an "angel of goodness"
to a trying old father. There are rivals for her love.
Her godmother-"a new woman of the most advanced order,
single-handed chases away 4 ruffians who have been
hired to steal Hyacinth... and frightens <Hyacinth's>
imprudently ardent old lover into an attack of
paralysis. NYT 10-2-97,7.

008049   CROSS PURPOSES; OR THE DEANES OF DEAN'S
CROFT. London: Griffith, Farran, Browne, [1899] BMC.
(BMC - Completed by Beatrice Marshall and Evelyn E.
Green)

008050   AN ESCAPE FROM THE TOWER: A STORY OF THE
JACOBITE RISING OF 1715. London: Seeley, 1896 BMC NUC.
New York: Macmillan, 1896 NUC.

ACAD 50:112. Lady Nithsdale rescues her husband from
the tower. "Stirring heroism"; he by contrast seems
"almost weak".

008051   THE FIRST LIGHT ON THE EDDYSTONE. A
STORY. London: Seeley, 1894 BMC.

008052   A HAUNT OF ANCIENT PEACE; A STORY.
London: Seeley, 1897 BMC.

Little Gidding settlement of 17th. semi-hist. Sermons
of John Donne; tries to give a true sense of the time.
ACAD 51:76.
Nicholas Ferrar's life and times. BAKER 03,143.
It is Nicholas Ferrar's house at little Gidding and
his friends are Geo. Herbert and John Donne. LBKM
11:126.

008053   HURLY-BURLY; OR AFTER STORM COMES A CALM.
London: J. F. Shaw, [1892] BMC.

008054   IN THE CHOIR OF WESTMINSTER ABBEY: A
STORY OF HENRY PURCELL'S DAYS. London: Seeley, 1897
BMC NUC. New York: Macmillan, 1897 NUC.

Hist. rom. about the days of Purcell, the Jacobites,
Queen Mary, etc. SP 79:801
Henry Purcell-his life and times. BAKER 03, 143
LIT 3:83. Prose poem. Narrated by female servant in
Henry Purcell's household.

008055   IN THE PURPLE. London: Nisbet, 1891 BMC.

Heroine is a rich baroness. SP

008056   IN THE SERVICE OF RACHEL, LADY RUSSELL. A
STORY. London: Seeley, 1893 BMC NUC. New York:
Macmillan, 1893 NUC.

Historical romance early 1600s. Scenes of Lady
Russell's home life taken from her real letters. Her
happy home life. Mingles hy and fiction. LW 1893,26.
PW 17th century love story woven into historical
events. Lord Russell was executed in connection with
plot against King Charles.

008057   KENSINGTON PALACE IN THE DAYS OF QUEEN
MARY II. New York: Macmillan, 1894 NUC. London:
Seeley, 1895 BMC NUC.

LW 25:470. Hist rom. Ch. study of Queen Mary the
Second.
Life and times of Queen Mary. BAKER 03, 143

008058   LADY MAUDE'S HELP; OR THE STORY OF
CHRISTIAN MOSS. London: T. Nelson, 1898 BMC.

008059   THE LADY OF HOLT DENE. London: Griffith,
Farran, [1897] BMC.

A man at his death arranges for relatives to raise his
daughter whom he had kept secluded. There's also an
excellent Bishop. SP 79:903.

008060   LADY ROSALIND, OR FAMILY FEUDS. London:
J. Nisbet, 1897 BMC.

Proud young Eng. woman disciplined by misfortune not
of her own making. Rosalind Penfold faces knowledge of
her father's double life, his death, many other
trials. Her cousin, not her own brother is her
father's successor. Though "it is not her destiny to
marry, finds a measure of happiness in dignified
spinsterdom." SP 79:565.
Her father dies when he's in debt. She's anxious to
clear his name, her fiance leaves her, she learns her
father's money went to blackmail-he had been married
secretly, the two children of that marriage are now
put in Rosalind's care.

008061   THE LADY'S MANOR, OR BETWEEN BROOK AND
RIVER. A TALE. London: J. Nisbet, 1896 BMC. New York:
E. P. Dutton, [n.d.] NUC.

"Whether Myrtle learned the great lesson that there
are better things than `intellectual culture' we do
not know, for the end of story leaves her still
learning the lesson." SR 80 844
Myrtle Cameron seeks a superior education. Is coached
by Miss Brown for Oxford, but Miss Brown "prizes
womanly graces more." Myrtle is an heiress.

008062   A LITTLE CURIOSITY. London: Shaw, [1896]
BMC.

008063   LIZETTE AND HER MISSION; OR, OVER THE
MOOR. New York: E. P. Dutton, [1894] NUC. London:
Nisbet, 1895 BMC.

PW-Lizette acts as mediator between her uncle and his
step son. Girls book?

008064   THE MASTER OF THE MUSICIANS. A STORY OF
HANDEL'S DAYS. London: Seeley, 1896 BMC NUC. New York:
Macmillan, 1896 NUC.

008065   MOTHER AND SON, OR, "I WILL". London:
"Home Words" Pub. Office, [1894] BMC.

008066   MY LADY BOUNTIFUL. London: J. Nisbet,
[1891] BMC NUC. New York: T. Whittaker, [189-] NUC.

Heroine is rich. She and her young brother become
their uncle's charge on their mother's death, though
the uncle never forgave their mother for her marriage.
SP 68 570

008067   NATURE'S GENTLEMAN; OR "MANNERS MAKYTH
MAN". London: J. Nisbet, 1893 BMC.

PW-England rural life. Virtuous woodcarver hero and
the girl he loves who is a silly flirt.

008068   ONLY SUSAN; HER OWN STORY. London: J.
Nisbet, 1896 BMC. New York: E. P. Dutton, [1896] NUC.

SR-Saintly Joan dies, giving Susan who is more lovable
a chance for happiness. Follows heroine thru love to
matrimony.
SP 77:623 Susan is a "Cinderella"., her narration.
PW 10-24-96. Becomes a famous painter, but is always
"only Susan" throughout her life, the one from whom
every sacrifice is expected and received.

008069   THE PARSON'S DAUGHTER: HER EARLY
RECOLLECTIONS, AND HOW MR. ROMNEY PAINTED HER. A STORY
[COMPLETED BY BEATRICE MARSHALL]. London: Seeley, 1899
BMC. New York: E. P. Dutton, 1899 NUC.

008070   PAT'S INHERITANCE. London: J. Nisbet,
[1892] BMC.

His only inheritance is his good name-how he keeps it
untarnished through poverty and troubles Pw 12-2-93

008071   PENSHURST CASTLE IN THE TIME OF SIR
PHILIP SIDNEY. London: Seeley, 1894 BMC NUC. New York:
Macmillan, 1894 NUC.

Sir Philip Sidney is central character. Two love
stories. Based upon history. Lw 93,468

008072   PETER'S PROMISES, OR LOOK BEFORE YOU
LEAP. London: J. F. Shaw, [1893] BMC.

008073   A ROMANCE OF THE UNDERCLIFFE; OR, THE
ISLE OF WIGHT IN 1799. London: Seeley, 1891 BMC NUC.

008074   ROSE DEANE: OR, CHRISTMAS ROSES. Bristol:
J. W. Arrowsmith, [1899] BMC NUC.

Ultra sent heroine droops and dies for no reason
except that she burned her hand. Many tears. SP 82:917

008075   SIR BENJAMIN'S BOUNTY. London: J. Nisbet,
1896 BMC. Boston: A. I. Bradley, 1896 NUC.

SR-Shopkeeping society in provincial town. Schoolboy
fraud.

008076   THE THIN END OF THE WEDGE. London:
Jarrold, [1900] BMC.

008077   TIME TRIES. London: J. Nisbet, 1899 BMC.

008078   THE TWO HENRIETTAS. London: Partridge,
[1896] BMC.

One goes to London to earn a living for herself and
sister when her father dies. She writes. The other
writes because she's restless, bored and ambitious.
No. 1 gets on well; No. 2 writes a problem novel, pays
for the publishing, but doesn't do well. Love affairs
for both. SP 78:571

008079   UNDER THE DOME OF ST. PAUL'S; A STORY OF
SIR CHIRSTOPHER WREN'S DAYS. London: Seeley, 1898 NUC.
New York: Macmillan, 1898 NUC.

008080   UNDER THE LABURNUMS: A STORY. London: J.
Nisbet, 1898 BMC NUC. New York: E. P. Dutton, [19--?]
NUC.

SP 81:717. Story of old-fashioned single woman taking
charge of spirited young girl. For young readers.

008081   THE WHITE KING'S DAUGHTER: A STORY OF
PRINCESS ELIZABETH. London: Seeley, 1895 NUC. New

York: Macmillan, 1895 NUC.

Hist. rom. Puritans from p.o.v. of Orthodox churchmen.
SR 79:839
Chas I's daughter Princess Elizabeth, Parliament vs
king. Lady Herietta Pole at Court. SP 74:89

008082   WINCHESTER MEADS IN THE TIME OF THOMAS
KEN, D.D. SOMETIME BISHOP OF BATH AND WELLS. London:
Seeley, 1891 BMC NUC. New York: E. P. Dutton, 1891
NUC.

Late 17th, Winchester in days of Chas. II, James II,
Wm III: SP 4-25-91,572
Time of Bishop Thomas Ker: CR

008083   WINIFREDE'S JOURNAL OF HER LIFE AT EXETER
AND NORWICH IN THE DAYS OF BISHOP HALL. New York:
Macmillan, 1891 NUC. London: Seeley, 1892 BMC NUC.

LW 23:26. Girls book. Time of Charles I. Orphan girl
SP. She is a Royalist, has two lovers.
Historical facts about the bishop worked into a
romance. ATH 98 859.
journal begun in 1637, ends in 1686. PW D12

008084   THE YOUNG QUEEN OF HEARTS; A STORY OF THE
PRINCESS ELIZABETH AND HER BROTHER HENRY, PRINCE OF
WALES. New York: Macmillan, 1898 NUC. London: Seeley,
1898 BMC.

NYT 1898:458. Eng. in Queen Anne's reign. Story of the
lives of Princess Elizabeth and Prince Henry. Much
historical detail, also a pretty, wholesome love
story.

MARSHALL, EMMA (MARTIN) AND EMILY DIBDIN.

008085   A PINK OF PERFECTION. London: J. Nisbet,
1900 BMC.

MARSHALL, ETHEL.

008086   HOPE IS KING. London: R. T. S., 1911 BMC.

Man inherits curse of drink. TLS

MARSHALL, FRANCES (BRIDGES). United Kingdom.

008087   ANTONIA'S PROMISE. BY THE AUTHOR OF
"JOSEPH'S LITTLE COAT" [ANONYMOUS]. London: R. T. S.,
[1898] BMC.

008088   THE BISHOP'S DELUSION. BY ALAN ST. AUBYN.
London: Ward and Downey, 1896 BMC.

SP 76:641. "The relapse of a negro into heathen
degradation, a man to all appearance profoundly
affected by culture and religion." Topic has been
treated by Grant Allen, but St. Aubyn has her own
approach.

008089   BONNIE MAGGIE LAUDER. BY ALAN ST. AUBYN.
London: F. V. White, 1899 BMC.

Mother and daughter love same man who marries
daughter. He had been engaged to the mother. SP 83:129

008090   BROKEN LIGHTS. BY THE AUTHOR OF "A FELLOW
OF TRINITY" [ANONYMOUS]. London: R. T. S., [1892] BMC
NUC. New York: F. H. Revell, [1893] NUC.

008091   A CORONATION NECKLACE. BY ALAN ST. AUBYN.
London: F. V. White, 1905 BMC.

008092   THE DEAN'S LITTLE DAUGHTER. BY THE AUTHOR
OF "A FELLOW OF TRINITY" [ANONYMOUS]. London: Society
for Promoting Christian Knowledge, [1891] BMC.

008093   A FAIR IMPOSTOR: A STORY OF EXMOOR. BY
ALAN ST. AUBYN. London: F. V. White, 1898 BMC NUC.

SR 85:470. Heroine engaged to man she does not love.
Eventually some papers prove he is a villain and she
is disengaged and ready for the right man.
Set in Exmoor. Celia Carmichael daughter of a withered
rector who had married his housekeeper. A Princesse
who rents a house at Stoke Edith plays a negative
part.
ACAD 53 FIC SUP 122

008094   FOR THE OLD SAKE'S SAKE. BY ALAN ST.
AUBYN. Chicago and New York: Rand, McNally, 1891 NUC.

LW 23:89. Letitia, older sister, postpones her
marriage because her orphaned half-sister Cynthia is

left to her care. Fiance goes off for several years as
missionary; when he returns, Letitia has aged. Cynthia
matured and his heart does not remain constant, altho
he insists on keeping his vow. Then something happens.
PW-Sister leaves home; it is supposed he has murdered
her and he is tried. Letitia gives him up to sister.

008095   FORTUNE'S GATE. BY ALAN ST. AUBYN.
London: Chatto and Windus, 1898 BMC.

ACAD 53:393. Andrew goes to Cambridge. His life there,
Newnham. Title refers to a pill, with which he hoped
to make a fortune.
ATH 112:154. "Alan St. Aubyn still works the vein of
academic fiction." Philippa, Andrew's sister, had won
a couple of scholarships, unprecedented, to Newnham.
She pays for Andrew's boat club out of her scholarship
money. She is a science student, deciphers a symbol in
a formula for a pill. For a while, she and Andrew are
tempted to become wealthy quacks.
LIT 3:113. young man of humble origins at Cambridge in
fast set. Love of a good woman, a hospital nurse,
helps him regain his old ideals. Pictures of life at
Newnham.
LBKM 14:50. "Picture given of the miserable life of
poor women students is ridiculously over-drawn." Peggy
O'Neill, "an incorrigible flirt, a very mean kind of
flirt" robs purses, then becomes elevated idealistic
nurse. This is "too much." "Tinsel is tinsel to the
end."

008096   THE HARP OF LIFE. BY ALAN ST. AUBYN.
London: F. V. White, 1908 BMC.

TLS-Cambridge Univ. Life-two women students.

008097   IN THE FACE OF THE WORLD. A NOVEL. BY
ALAN ST. AUBYN. London: Chatto and Windus, 1894 BMC
NUC.

SP 73:408. Renounces his father's wealth, feeling it
ill-gotten (a brewery) and settles down with poor
people only to see how desperately they need the money
he has relinquished.
ACAD-sticks it out and "achieves a vast amount of
good;" through his example "makes a saint" of the
heroine.
LBKM Gets title, money, and renounced sweetheart at
the end.

008098   IN THE SWEET WEST COUNTRY. BY ALAN ST.
AUBYN. London: F. V. White, 1895 BMC. London: F. V.
White, 1897 NUC.

SR-Farmer's daughter is wooed by title; she renounces
him for his family's sake and each marries someone
else happily.

008099   JOSEPH'S LITTLE COAT. BY THE AUTHOR OF "A
FELLOW OF TRINITY" [ANONYMOUS]. London: R. T. S.,
[1891] BMC.

Pathetic story of what a loving child may do to bring
a father to better thoughts. SP 68:28

008100   THE JUNIOR DEAN: A NOVEL. BY ALAN ST.
AUBYN. London: Chatto and Windus, 1891 BMC NUC.

University life-ATH 98:859.
Molly Gray is a student at Ladies' College at Newnham.
She's engaged to a junior dean of the college her
brother attends. Her brother and then the junior dean
get mixed up with Rosey, a wicked actress "in a shady
house" where gambling takes place. Brachenbury, a
wicked sort, introduced Molly's brother to this life.
The junior dean happened to save Rosey's life-so she
loves him. Many mixups between Molly and the dean, but
all ends happily. SR 11-28-91, 615.
ACAD 41:84. Life at Cambridge. The subject of women's
higher education is treated with a judicious lightness
of touch and playful irony.

008101   THE MAIDEN'S CREED. London: Digby, Long,
1901 BMC.

008102   MARY UNWIN. BY ALAN ST. AUBYN. London:
Chatto & Windus, 1899 BMC.

She is a poor rector's daughter wooed unsuccessfully
by Geoffrey Colleton who tries to marry an heiress to
avoid work, is spurned, returns to Mary who at this
moment receives a large inheritance. LIT 4:428
Domestic tale of country parson's family where love
and poverty run a hard race. BAKER 03 173

008103   THE MASTER OF ST. BENEDICT'S. BY ALAN ST.

AUBYN. London: Chatto and Windus, 1893 BMC. Chicago and New York: Rand, McNally, 1893 NUC.

University life. Wyatt Edgall is an alcoholic. Cuts his own throat when he gets the Dts. He's the master of the title. The Newnham girls are prigs at the start of the novel, but become more noble. Pamela Gwatkin and Capability Stubbs especially. Pamela is shown much stronger than her brother. Lucy Rae, on the other hand is made contemptible SP 70, 259.
Sens novel. LW 93, 163.
Lucy Rae, grandniece of old master becomes a student. Her ambition: to try for a Tripos. Story traces her life as a student. PW 4-15-93
Lucy studies to be a teacher. She learns about Wyatt to whom she was attracted. Wyatt kills self. She marries in the end. SR 75, 155.
Cambridge. Anthony Rae, the old master "dies a-babbling." Rachel his wife after 40 years of marriage to him and 40 years of waiting for her lover, makes a happy marriage. Descriptions of woman's life at Newnham are the best parts. ACAD 43:282.

008104   MAY SILVER. BY ALAN ST. AUBYN. London: F.V. White, 1901 BMC.

008105   MODEST LITTLE SARA. BY ALAN ST. AUBYN. London: Chatto and Windus, 1892 BMC. Chicago and New York: Rand, McNally, 1892 NUC.

"The devices of a handsome and unscrupulous young lady, resident in Cambridge, who teaches music, fascinates undergraduates, and manages to levy a considerable amount of blackmail from them." Also the record of her engagement to the wrong man. ACAD 43:151.
ATH 101,50 Her mother is in dire financial trouble; therefore Sara accepts a man she detests and then jilts him. The young woman described is Georgina.

008106   MRS. DUNBAR'S SECRET. BY ALAN ST. AUBYN. London: Chatto and Windus, 1899 BMC.

Man and wife both make bigamous marriages. Author believes that only the wife's child by the second marriage is illegal. Mrs. Dunbar is found out, but the man escapes detection. SP 83:789.
A marriage mixup begun by fact that a young couple each marry again in the lifetime of the other. ATH 114:797

008107   THE OLD MAID'S SWEETHEART: A PROSE IDYL. BY ALAN ST. AUBYN. London: Chatto and Windus, 1892 BMC. London: 1892 NUC.

ATH 100:253. Central character, Letitia Primrose is a 50 year old spinster. "He had to bring out all the oddities of demeanor and costume, the obtuseness and the matter-of-fact prosaic commonplace of an old maid of 50, and still at the same time to make her thoroughly lovable and sympathetic; to point the tragedy of her life while allowing her to be in some measure ridiculous."
Sp 69:504. the minister she is engaged to falls in love with her young and beautiful sister. Sister, after attempting suicide, confesses all to Letitia, who stands by bravely as sister and minister are married.

008108   ORCHARD DAMEREL. BY ALAN ST. AUBYN. London: Hurst and Blackett, 1894 BMC NUC.

SR-78:300. Robert Lyon, a minister, marries, has financial problems which work out. Lady Aylmerton's niece married an aged solicitor to escape her bullying and Hugh Damerel. Story is also about Mrs. Penrose and her three daughters, Bertha, Phyllis and Joan. Joan marries Robert; Phyllis marries Hugh.
ATH 103:506. Gushing story told with girlish simplicity.

008109   THE ORDEAL OF SARA. BY ALAN ST. AUBYN. London: F.V. White, 1904 BMC.

008110   A PRICK OF CONSCIENCE. BY ALAN ST. AUBYN. London: Digby, Long, 1900 BMC.

SP 85:343. Wicked heroine who reforms and gives up her lover to another woman.
ATH 116:342. She prefers a soldier to her husband. Then there is complication of the governess.

008111   A PROCTOR'S WOOING. BY ALAN ST. AUBYN. London: F. V. White, 1897 BMC NUC.

One of her Cambridge novels. Newnham girls SR 83:128.

Their visits to St. Crispin's, of a duel. ATH 109:13.

008112   PURPLE HEATHER: A STORY OF EXMOOR. BY ALAN ST. AUBYN. London: J. Long, 1907 BMC.

008113   THE RED VAN. BY ALAN ST. AUBYN. London: Digby Long, 1906 BMC.

TLS-0

008114   THE SCARLET LADY. BY ALAN ST. AUBYN. London: F.V. White, 1902 BMC.

008115   THE SENIOR TUTOR, A STORY OF A CAMBRIDGE COURT (THE BISHOP'S DELUSION). BY ALAN ST. AUBYN. London: F.V. White, 1904 BMC.

008116   A SILVER CORD. BY THE AUTHOR OF "THE DEAN'S LITTLE DAUGHTER" [ANONYMOUS]. London: Society For Promoting Christian Knowledge, [1895] BMC.

008117   THE SQUIRE OF BRATTON. BY THE AUTHOR OF "THE DEAN'S LITTLE DAUGHTER" [ANONYMOUS]. London: S. P. C. K., [1893] BMC.

008118   TO HIS OWN MASTER. A NOVEL. BY ALAN ST. AUBYN. London: Chatto and Windus, 1893 BMC NUC. New York: Cleveland, 1893 NUC.

SR 77:150. Romance of a curate. One of the women who interests him has been to Girton; she marries the rector.
LBKM 6:127. There is also a woman who is the villain, with a "ferocious and sensual nature" "whom we are asked to think particularly fascinating." The Girton girl, with a strong resolute and generous character is also a nursery governess and "faithless lover." Stephen Dashwood is followed through life by misfortunes mostly from circumstances. Mary Grove's desertion, his dealings with the Grove family, the father who has ruined three women. "The Girton girl who has given up a certain first in order to tend a drunken father and a forlorn mother." Stephen and Mary, the Girton girl, don't marry. He's a curate in the East-End and "she accepts the freedom which he offers...and consoles herself quickly." ATH 102, 658.

008119   TO STEP ASIDE IS HUMAN. BY ALAN ST. AUBYN. London: F. V. White, 1896 BMC NUC.

ATH 107:711
ACAD 49:423. Bet Lampen marries an invalid for his money, after his death falls desperately in love with heir to the estate, nearly succeeds in marrying him. Dick Lampen, a shallow young doctor.

008120   A TRAGIC HONEYMOON, A NOVEL. BY ALAN ST. AUBYN. London: F. V. White, 1894 NUC BMC.

Nancy has numerous conquests-everyone falls for her. SP 74:72.
Nancy Coulcher is the beauty, two plain sisters Lucy and Augusta. Nancy is a bride and widow within 48 hrs. ACAD 47:54
SR 78:689. Clergyman's daughter marries rich man she doesn't love. She tells him the night after their marriage; he suicides, leaving her a rich widow. Story ends with the understanding that she will marry the man she loves, a pious curate.

008121   THE TREMLETT DIAMONDS. BY ALAN ST. AUBYN. London: Chatto and Windus, 1895 BMC NUC.

Based upon a real jewel theft. Lionel Tremlett hides the diamonds on the day of his wedding. Hires a detective to find evidence against Edith Darcy who is tried for the crime. SP 74:723
Tremblett is a drunken country squire. There's also a Dora Bellow and a Capt. Stanhope. The two women marry the two men. ACAD 47:521

008122   WAPPING OLD STAIRS. BY THE AUTHOR OF "JOSEPH'S LITTLE COAT" [ANONYMOUS]. [London]: Religious Tract Society, [1895] BMC.

008123   THE WOOING OF MAY. BY ALAN ST. AUBYN. London: White, 1897 BMC.

Tries to hold 3 lovers. When she is about to wed one, one of the others causes an accident that leaves her a cripple for life. Then she marries the 3rd. She's shallow and selfish. Includes love stories of her two sisters, a murder trial, clairvoyance. SR 84:398.
SP 80:148. An unconscionable flirt.

MARSHALL, MARGUERITE MOOERS. B. 1887. United States.

008124   THE DRIFT. New York and London: D. Appleton, 1911 BMC NUC.

Letters of young writer in love with married man; he plans a divorce but finds his wife is pregnant. The writer kills herself 9-9-11 PW
After they fall in love she goes to New York to do literary work; in the meantime he'll try to get a divorce. NYT

MARSHALL, MRS. CHARLES.

008125   A PARISH SCANDAL. A TALE OF MODERN MANNERS. London: E. Stock, 1901 BMC.

ATH 2-8-02: Sordid tale of persecution of innocent curate and woman by gossips, rescued by Sister Cecilia committing a murder which is alluded to as a fanatical act.

MARSLAND, CORA. B. 1859. United States.

008126   THE ANGEL OF THE GILA: A TALE OF ARIZONA. Boston: R. G. Badger, [c1911] NUC.

NYT-Mass. teacher in Arizona mining town and her efforts with cowboys, saloon keepers, Mormons, young Indians and mining town riff-raff. Also a pale love story.
Esther a teacher converts a mining town to self respecting decent town. PW 1911 12-16

MARTENS, MARY E.

008127   A DAUGHTER OF SIN. A SIMPLE STORY. London: E. Stock, 1915 BMC.

Dedication to those women of Napal "who have suffered under an injust, one-sided and most iniquitous law" "question of the relation between white women and black men" TLS

008128   A WOMAN OF SMALL ACCOUNT. A SOUTH AFRICAN SOCIAL PICTURE. London: W. Scott, 1911 BMC.

Author is "obsessed with the subject of women's rights and wrongs and belabors her plot with talk of suffrage." "Men may be on the whole a bad lot-that is the impression one gets, but the calm and flawless superiority of Hester, the heroine,...is very fatiguing." She becomes a famous author."TLS
S. African Hertes has strong enough veiws on the sex question to break up her home. "a powerfully drawn character." ACAD

MARTIN, AMARALA (ARTER). United States.

008129   A FEATHER'S WEIGHT: A STORY OF MYSTERY. New York and London: Abbey Press, [c1900] NUC.

MARTIN, CAROLINE. United States.

008130   THE BLUE RIDGE MYSTERY: A NOVEL. New York: Robert Lewis Weed Co., [c1897] NUC.

PW ´ 98. 1860 in S. Carolina. Heroine's mother cruelly murdered;she is adopted, Her romantic story.

MARTIN, CATHERINE EDITH MACAULEY (MACKAY). 1847/48-1937. Australia.

008131   THE SILENT SEA; A NOVEL. BY MRS. ALICK MACLEOD. New York: Harper, 1892 NUC. London: R. Bentley, 1892 BMC.

ATH 100:550. Salt-bush country of South Australia. "Insipid" heroine Doris.
SP 69:775. Mining town.
ACAD 42:408. Young woman is in love with "boy ten years younger than herself."
Aust gold region. Silent Sea is a desert plain. Helen Paget charming woman of 30 contrasted to young delicate Doris. LW 93, 26

MARTIN, CLARA I. United Kingdom.

008132   A LITTLE AVERSION. Bristol: J.W. Arrowsmith, [1912] BMC NUC.

ATH- conv and uninteresting ch's, heroine left penniless-18th century.
SP 0
ACAD-

MARTIN, DOROTHEA HENESS (KNOX). United States.

008133   THE HEART OF WASHINGTON. Washington, D. C.: Neale, 1909 NUC.

Imaginative story of George's first love. PW 8-7-09.

MARTIN, DOROTHY.

008134   FATHER FOX: A STORY OF THE PRESENT DAY. London: E. Stock, 1899 BMC.

ATH 115:173. He seeks to bring money to Anglican Church by trapping young women in a nunnery. If they don't bring money, they are not nicely treated. Anti-Romanism.

MARTIN, EMILY.

008135   EVEN MINE OWN FAMILIAR FRIEND. London: S. Low, 1892 BMC.

ACAD 41:346. Two men love Una, one has been bound by her father not to reveal it to her, giving the wrong man an advantage. Una is a "woman of character," "strong-minded determination," end is better than the beginning.
SR 73:338. She divorces him and marries a doctor.

MARTIN, GEORGE (MADDEN). 1866-1946. United States.

008136   ABBIE ANN. New York: Century, 1907 BMC NUC.

008137   THE ANGEL OF THE TENEMENT. New York: Bonnell, Silver, 1897 NUC. London: Bairnie Series, 1899 BMC. (Bairnie Series are dainty books for children - BMC)

008138   EMMY LOU, HER BOOK AND HEART. New York: McClure, Phillips, 1902 NUC. London: Hodder and Stoughton, 1903 BMC.

Child's developing character and intelligence. LBKM 11-03, 103.
PZ 7

008139   EMMY LOU'S ROAD TO GRACE; BEING A LITTLE PILGRIM'S PROGRESS. New York and London: D. Appleton, 1916 NUC BMC.

Chronicles the gropings of little Emmy Lou among the perplexities of creeds. PW 90:1460 10/28/16.
Listed as adult fic.--PW PZ 7

008140   THE HOUSE OF FULFILLMENT. London: Hodder & Stoughton, 1904 BMC. New York: McClure, Phillips, 1904 NUC.

PW--sounds like Pollyanna goodie heroine
NYT ?
TLS 0

008141   LETITIA: NURSERY CORPS, U.S.A. New York: McClure, 1907 NUC.

008142   SELINA: HER HOPEFUL EFFORTS AND HER LIVELIER FAILURES. New York: D. Appleton, 1914 BMC NUC.

"Selina, a girl just out of school in a small Southern town starts to make a living." WOMAN'S EDUC ASSOC 4-1915. No. 31
Heroine "undertakes to settle the question whether or not daughters are expected to solve their economic problems thru marriage". She's average in beauty, etc, has to earn a living PKM
"Whereas "Emmy Lou" turned the flashlight on the public school, Selina does the same service for the home and outside world. Selina's father has to keep his nose to the grindstone constantly, and even then the bills are never all paid. After her graduation Selina begins to teach, but that does not mend matters materially. She has lovers and therein some members of her family see the solution. But Selina has advanced ideas for a girl of the 80's and vows that, when she marries, it will not be to solve the economic problem". PW 86 11/7/14:1450.
NYT 1914:517--"She stands in the faint dawn of the revolt of women...but is not at all aware that she is one of those who are blazing the way for a new order of things." Wholesome, not too serious.
BKM 40 1914 -15 rev not too helpful

MARTIN, H. R. See MARTIN, HELEN (REIMENSNYDER).

MARTIN, HELEN (REIMENSNYDER). 1868-1939. United States.

008143   BARNABETTA. New York: Century, 1914 BMC
NUC.

"Author of "Tillie: a Mennonite maid" again takes a
Pennsylvania Dutch heroine. Barnabetta Dreary has been
household drudge to her father and brothers for five
years, when Mr. Dreary marries again, a woman with an
income of her own which he expects to take charge of.
The new Mrs. Dreary has very different ideas, and with
good natured determination sees them carried out. She
relieves Barnabetta of the work and sends her to
school and college where a new world is opened to the
girl. It is the picture of this awakening and
development and the part two men play in her new life
which is drawn sympathetically here." PW 3/28/14 1113

008144   THE CROSSWAYS. New York: Century, 1910
BMC NUC.

BKM v. 31 1910 wife almost killed by misunderstanding
of doctor husband-male attitude toward marriage. She
is physically delicate and he thinks he is acting for
her own good when he heaps all the burdens of
housework on her. She is almost killed by it but in
spite of physical weakness finally bends him to her
will.
NYT--an attempt to mold his high-strung cultured bride
into household drudge who is the Dutchman's ideal
woman. Happy ending is hardly credible. Refuses to pay
out money for woman's work.
Southern woman, cultured, falls in love with her
doctor, marries him knowing only the one side of
him-the professional side. the other side comes out
after marriage. Story follows this conflict of
temperaments: "her desperate battle to keep her self
respect." PW

008145   THE ELUSIVE HILDEGARDE: A NOVEL. BY H. R.
MARTIN. New York: R. F. Fenno, 1900 NUC.

NYT 1900:407. Hildegarde eccentric and unconventional
is attempting to educate herself to teach. She marries
her stepbrother Lyon Kent. Her mother has used her to
get money from her stepfather.

008146   FANATIC OR CHRISTIAN? A STORY OF THE
PENNSYLVANIA DUTCH. Garden City, N.Y.: Doubleday,
Page, 1918 NUC. Toronto: T. Langton, [1918?] NUC.

PW--Family has amassed fortune thru factory. Stella is
traditional, Gertie has been to college and wants to
apply modern welfare methods to factory. David, a
factory reformer, discovers he has always loved
Gertie, and proves to be the real heir of the Swartz
fortune.
NYT--Stella and Gertie battle over father's fortune;
Stella is scheming and selfish, Gertie champions
factory people. Episode in early part of father's life
upsets all Stella's plans. Socialist p.o.v.

008147   THE FIGHTING DOCTOR. New York: Century,
1912 BMC NUC.

PW--public spirited male MD
NYT--heroine is school teacher. Dr is not flawless, he
says he would not send his children to same school
with black children.

008148   HER HUSBAND'S PURSE. Garden City, N.Y.:
Doubleday, Page, 1916 NUC. London: C. Brown, 1916 BMC.

Margaret Berkeley moves from southern home to Penn
Dutch household when she marries. She must fight for
her self respect and the rights of her children vs the
iron hand of her husband's two spinster sisters? PW
NYT--Her husband was a rat, a weasel and a money slot,
his two sisters the same but with abysmal ignorance,
as well. Myst, knownonly to her friend, why she
married him. She is treated like a breeder allotted
$10 a month and expected to account for every penny.
Most of book is taken up with her adjustment to these
circumstances.

008149   HIS COURTSHIP. New York and London:
McClure, Phillips, 1907 NUC BMC.

Young college professor woos a Penn. Dutch woman who
is far above her surroundings PW 5-4-07
Eunice, from earliest childhood made a drudge is
discovered by professor to have a keen mind. She's
self-educated really an heir to a fortune. BKM

008150   MAGGIE OF VIRGINSBURG; A STORY OF THE
PENNSYLVANIA DUTCH. New York: Century, 1918 BMC NUC.

PW--Maggie and Henry rebel against sordidness and
meanness of surroundings and leave Virginia. She
becomes secretary to bishop and then teacher in church
school; both are radicals and story is a criticism of
Christian Church. Biological basis for their rebellion
against Virginia-myst. of their birth.
NYT Nov 17 '18 p. 470. 0

008151   MARTHA OF THE MENNONITE COUNTRY. Garden
City, N.Y.: Doubleday Page, 1915 NUC. London: C.
Brown, 1915 BMC.

Penn Dutch BKM 41 1915
romantic story of a male teacher-writer PW 3-13-15
a famous novelist gone dry, so he comes to Pa. to
teach for a while. An heiress, too, comes. She's
determined to have a teaching career and to be
President of girl's college. Takes job as asst.
Principal in high school. The two know each other, but
are not yet aware that they do. Martha (tragic part of
story) drudge, of good mind-as the novelist discovers.
NYT

008152   THE PARASITE; A NOVEL. Philadelphia and
London: J.B. Lippincott, 1913 BMC NUC.

"New story by author of "Tillie, a Mennonite maid."
deserts the field of her former books. Joan Laird is
married to Judge Randall only in name. He wants some
one to take care of his little boy and she wants a
home. The judge and his first wife were divorced four
years before Joan enters the agreement which she
carries through bravely, winning a great triumph in
the end." PW
"Is Joan the impoverished hanger on less a parasite
than Catherine the splendid self sufficient?" NYT
reveals author's socialist ideas ATH
"strong story of Joan Laird and Judge Randall married
only in name." "startling" "unexpected" "Joan the
impoverished hanger-on," "Catherine, the splendid and
self sufficient" NYT 1913, 101
NYT, 1913, 39
"The heroine, the parasite of the title, is a southern
girl who visits about from one good family to another
on the lookout for a suitable opportunity to marry.
The hero is a disillusioned man who has been married
and divorced and who marries a second time only to
provide a mother for his small son. The situation that
develops after the union of these two is that in which
husband and wife fall in love after marriage." BRD

008153   THE REVOLT OF ANNE ROYLE. New York:
Century, 1908 BMC NUC.

"The scene is laid in a Pennsylvania city. Anne is a
winsome little girl who leads a lonely and unhappy
life under the iron rule of her father. In spite of
all she develops into a very charming young woman.
Among her lovers are the rector and curate of the
fashionable church of the town." BKM 28 1908-09.
NYT 0
"quite startling views on marriage" unmarried woman
should be free to have a child "no questions asked";
gifted Anne "beautifully and consistently drawn":
raised by domineering aunt and father who hates the
sight of her, good scholar at college, accepts an
unworthy suitor out of sheer loneliness; discovers her
true feelings, her "revolt" follows. Ends in great and
unselfish love? for child out of wedlock? BKM v.29
1909.

008154   SABINA: A STORY OF THE AMISH. New York:
Century, 1905 BMC NUC.

18 year old Amish girl comes in contact with young
artist from outside world, becomes dissatisfied with
her life PW 10-7-05
Finally thru illness loses the memory of the two years
during which she loved him. NYT 644,05

008155   THE SCHOOLMASTER OF HESSVILLE. Garden
City, N.Y.: Doubleday, Page, 1920 NUC.

PW--story of a plain little girl
NYT 9-12-20 p. 27. John Wimmer is passionately in love
with Irene Laub "of a coarse fibre" and is married to
Minnie Maus, a "Mennonite and his subordinate in
school." His struggles with himself.

008156   THOSE FITZENBERGERS. Garden City, N.Y.:
Doubleday, Page, 1917 NUC. London: J.M. Dent, [1919]
BMC.

Pennsylvania Dutch story. Satiric, small town life and
its narrowness. BKM

008157   TILLIE A MENNONITE MAID: A STORY OF THE
PENNSYLVANIA DUTCH. New York: Century, 1904 NUC.
London: Hodder & Stoughton, 1905 BMC.

"Tillie is the daughter of an ignorant farmer and she
boasts of two lovers, a pertinacious Dutchman, and a
school master, graduated from Harvard. The story is
written to amuse." BKM, v. 29, 1904
"defies her father and makes a strong educated woman
of herself". PW
NYT "love for her teacher, Miss Margaret...grew into a
passion" .
Women are beasts of burden, their lives hideously
narrow. Tillie, intelligent and determined, sees all
the injustice and opposes it. She's victorious in the
end. The father is an ultra-patriarch that Tillie
opposes. ACAD 1905:665.

008158   UNCHAPERONED: A NOVEL. BY HELEN
REIMENSNYDER. New York: R. F. Fenno, [1896] NUC.

LW 27:252. Three women, Miss Matthews, her niece, Miss
Rankin, and a man, Dr. Forney, at a secluded summer
boarding house.

008159   WARREN HYDE. BY THE AUTHOR OF
"UNCHAPERONED" [ANONYMOUS]. New York: R. F. Fenno,
[c1897] NUC.

He "has been divorced from the beautiful wife whom he
loved, with little explanation to the public, is free
to marry Nelda Chase, who has scruples as to the
remarriage of divorced persons, because the divorce
cloaked a radical flow in the first contract the pair
being, without knowing it, brother and sister." LW
29:91.

008160   WHEN HALF-GODS GO; BEING THE STORY OF A
BRIEF WEDDED LIFE AS TOLD IN INTIMATE AND CONFIDENTIAL
LETTERS WRITTEN BY A BRIDE TO A FORMER COLLEGE MATE.
New York: Century, 1911 BMC NUC.

Sex inequality-other cultures BKM 33 (1911) 201
Letters to old friend. Edith marries musician, happy
till the other woman shows up, struggle of wife to
keep her husband's loyalty. PW 2-18-11
Theme:...mutual attitude of a man and a wife in
courtship and marriage. form: letters move from
Mennonite world to application of her theme to
universal level. Soon after Edith marries discovers
her husband weak. Endures his platonic passion for
another woman which soon wanes Then the real god
arrives. "psychol study" BKM
Husband shrugged off by the other woman who learns
what real love is.

MARTIN, MABEL WOOD. B. 1880. United States.

008161   THE GREEN GOD'S PAVILLION; A NOVEL OF THE
PHILLIPINES. New York: F.A. Stokes, [c1920] NUC.

BKM? Reviewer says "little American schoolteacher
yearns to do something for the native and finds it so
terribly useless. There are big men and women moving
among the riotously beautiful & appallingly horrible
scenes" "hopelessness of a Caucasian ever doing
anything really worthwhile for the Asian, who himself
seems so little to desire or deserve it."

MARTIN, MARY EMMA. United Kingdom.

008162   BRITOMART. A NOVEL. BY MRS. HERBERT
MARTIN. London: R. Bentley, 1893 BMC NUC.

SR 77:203. Heroine is illegitimate heir to uncle of
Geoffrey who had been counting on that inheritance to
marry Viola.
SP 72:137. Penrose reminds Geoffrey of Spenser's
girl-knight.
ACAD: She has the "strongest powers of will and sense
of duty coupled with an almost uncomfortably bold
habit of plain speaking."

008163   FORTUNE AT THE HELM. London: Hurst and
Blackett, 1899 BMC.

Welsh girl driven from home because of her evil
drunken father. Marries a servant. Gaynor Williams is
friendless in London- her struggles, adventures and
perils. SP 83:193
Alone in London and meets emancipated young American
artist and her male friend. Focus on Gaynor-girl to
woman. Wins a gallant lover.

008164   GENTLEMAN GEORGE: A STORY WITHOUT A
HEROINE. London: Hurst and Blackett, 1897 BMC.

Plain tale of a middle-aged man and a small boy. SR
83:453. Man of good birth sinks to poverty but
content. At 50 he's still an innocent, Kind person.
LBKM 11:183.
Was from good family and good education. Abandonned
all. Buried self in Midland slums doing odd jobs. But
retains his finer qualities. SP 79:309.

008165   A GIRL'S PAST; A NOVEL. BY MRS. HERBERT
MARTIN. London: F. V. White, 1893 BMC NUC.

Minister has three daughters, Gwen, the eldest. She's
unconventional in character and appearance. Fascinates
Brooke Graham. Can't marry because she had been
pressed into a girl marriage, was rescued at the
church door, but marriage not annulled. That husband
returns, hurt in accident, nursed by Gwen, dies, she
weds Brooke. ACAD 43:458.
Gweneth Lane's father; a minister who likes a nip now
and then and fails to provide a good living for his
family. She's pensive, reserved and this nature
attracts the young squire. But she must first go thru
two years of unhappy marriage with a "bounder" because
of her past. She has a shocking little crippled sister
who gets better. The thing in her past is embarrassing
but not improper. SR 75, 633.

008166   HER DEBUT. BY MRS. HERBERT MARTIN.
London: Hurst and Blackett, 1895 BMC NUC.

The appearance of a young woman as concert pianist.
She had an unfortunate love affair but now knows the
man "could never have fulfilled the ideal of her life"
SR 79:870
Erma Laniska can feel but not speak. Is a woman who
suffers in silence. We pity and admire her. SP 74:55
Ermengarde Laniska daughter of a foreign countess, an
adventuress, who marries an English landowner, has a
child, but is fatally shocked when her husband the
count turns up. Erma is a dark beauty, careless of her
appearance. Early resolved to be a great singer and to
that end, runs away from home. For a time love
distracts her. Returns to her training, makes her
debut. Her "dead" father is one of the violinists.
ACAD 48:28
Heroine is Polish. Very self-conscious at first but
also proud and independent. Suffers from the schemings
of her mother. Set in part in Bloomsbury boarding
house. ATH 105:734.

008167   JOCK'S WARD. BY MRS. HERBERT MARTIN.
London: C. A. Pearson, 1899 BMC. New York: 1900 NUC.

"A London street-Arab who constitutes himself
protector of a broken-down shoemaker." Their
adventures in their country retreat. LIT 4:558
Touching story of a boy. BAKER 03,143
NYT 1900:694. Ezia sentenced to six months hard labor
because his child had died without a doctor. He
believed in faith-healing. Jock, a London street Arab
who knew the shoemaker, and his son, protested in
court. When he came out of jail he was suicidal and
Jock looked after him, leading to regeneration.

008168   LINDSAY'S GIRL: A NOVEL. BY MRS. HERBERT
MARTIN. London: Jarrold, 1896 BMC. New York: R. F.
Fenno, [c1896] NUC.

SR-"Greenback Series", popular ed.
ACAD 50:95. Valentine Lindsay is strong, robust, but
even she is overcome by the secret of her birth.
SP 76:928. She is illegitimate. She marries her
guardian, a good serious older man whom she comes to
love.
PW 5-2-96. Guardian marries her to protect her. World
is unkind to her but she outlives it all.

008169   A LOW-BORN LASS: A NOVEL. London: Hurst
and Blackett, 1898 BMC.

SR 85:264. Stormy, unhappy life of Sukey Rogers.
ACAD 53:149. Loved one man and married another.
ATH 111:245. Character of a factory girl.

008170   A MAN AND A BROTHER: A NOVEL. London:
Ward and Downey, 1892 BMC.

ACAD 41:369. he is exploited by his brother and
participates in something dishonorable.
SP- man struggling to raise himself from alcohol and
opium.
SR. 73:393. Margery, the heroine is "robust,"
"modern," "who enjoys life thoroughly." "She enters on
a career that is nearly as hazardous (as becoming a
step-mother of 8 children), and her enterprise is

crowned with the success that generally attends audacity."

008171   MANY A YEAR AGO. London: Ward and Downey, 1892 BMC.

100 years ago. Rev. Stephen Wingate's rebellious politics concerning separation of church and state land him in prison where he dies of gaol-fever. Daughter Nancy supplies the romance. Her father taught her Latin and Greek "which do not prevent her from making good bread." Happy marriage for her. SR 1-14-93, 45
Wingate is released "only to die of prison fever." ACAD 43:126

008172   A MUSICAL GENIUS; A STORY. London: Blackie, 1896 BMC.

008173   OUT OF THE WORKHOUSE. London: Bentley, 1896 BMC.

ATH 108:481. Old Peter Lucas transformed from pauper to man of wealth.
Concerns a rugged old peasant Peter Lucas-ignor., crafty, narrow. And his will. SP 78:278

008174   SUIT AND SERVICE: A NOVEL. London: Hurst and Blackett, 1894 BMC.

SP 73:565. "Shy, awkward Rachel, who is made miserable by the consciousness that her reserved, indeed repellant, manner, altogether belies her real feelings," makes a successful marriage to a coachman. ACAD 46:252. Coachman inherits an estate.

008175   WON BY GENTLENESS. London: Cassell, 1900 BMC.

MARTIN, MRS. CHARLES.

008176   THE GUERDON OF FAITH. London: J. Long, 1911 BMC.

TLS-Beatrice & Philip blackened by false suspicions. ATH-a drugtaker robs parents, confesses to daughter who assumes the blame.

008177   MISS PAUNCEFORT'S PERIL. London: J. Long, 1901 BMC.

All about heroine's problem of marrying a divorced man. She's a Roman Catholic. ATH 11-2-01.

MARTIN, MRS. HERBERT. See MARTIN, MARY EMMA.

MARTIN, VIOLET FLORENCE AND EDITH ANNA OENONE SOMERVILLE.

008178   BEGGARS ON HORSEBACK. A RIDING TOUR IN NORTH WALES. BY MARTIN ROSS AND E. OE. SOMERVILLE. Edinburgh and London: W. Blackwood, 1895 BMC NUC.

DA 740 Wales, North-Desc and travel.

008179   A PATRICK'S DAY HUNT. BY MARTIN ROSS AND E. OE. SOMERVILLE. Westminister: A. Constable, [1902] BMC NUC.

008180   THE SILVER FOX. BY MARTIN ROSS AND E. OE. SOMERVILLE. London: Lawrence & Bullen, 1898 BMC NUC. London, New York & Bombay: Longmans, Green, 1900 NUC.

SR 85:402. A bounder and two women.

MARTIN, VIOLET FLORENCE, jt. au. See SOMERVILLE, EDITH ANNA OENONE AND VIOLET FLORENCE MARTIN.

MARTINDALE, ELIZABETH.

008181   MARGARET HEVER. London: Duckworth, 1909 BMC.

Margaret's problem in choosing between two men--Nell Hawthorne "makes a good deal of trouble." TLS
Margaret marries the mature historian. ATH

MARTINDELL, CHARLOTTE S. United States.

008182   THE DIARY OF A BRIDE. New York: T. Y. Crowell, [c1905] NUC.

Thoughts of a loving wife. PW 10-14-05.

MARTYN, MRS. GEORGE.

008183   A LIBERAL EDUCATION. London: F. Warne,

[1894] BMC.

Set in England west country, then India. Story of a good lad who gets better and better and of the sweet young woman he loves. Nation 56,395.
Hector Argentine cut off without a penny because of his youthful follies; he's an undergrad. Eventually saved by Daisy Lambert. ACAD 44:509.

008184   WORSE THAN A CRIME: THE HISTORY OF A MISTAKE. London: Digby, Long, 1896 BMC.

ACAD 50:257. Tangle of matches and marriages of country middle-class people.

MARX, MAGDELEINE, pseud. See PAZ, MAGDELEINE (LEGENDRE).

MASON, CAROLINE (ATWATER). 1853-1939. United States.

008185   THE BINDING OF THE STRONG: A LOVE STORY. New York: F.H. Revell, [c1908] NUC. London: Hodder & Stoughton, [1908] BMC.

TLS-Milton

008186   CONSCRIPTS OF CONSCIENCE. New York: F.H. Revell, [c1919] NUC.

PW-Plea in story form for volunteers for medical mission work in the Orient.

008187   HOLT OF HEATHFIELD. New York: Macmillan and London, 1903 BMC NUC.

008188   A LILY OF FRANCE. Philadelphia: Griffith & Rowland, 1901 NUC.

CR-historical novel in which heroine is more emancipated than newest woman of today.
Netherlands-hist-1556-1648

008189   THE LITTLE GREEN GOD. New York: F.H. Revell, [1902] BMC NUC.

008190   THE MINISTER OF CARTHAGE. Philadelphia: Curtis, 1899 NUC.

Attacks clergy who look for prosperous parishes and parishes that look for pew-filling preachers. And a love story. PW 55:544

008191   A MINISTER OF THE WORLD. New York: A. D. F. Randolph, [c1895] NUC.

Stephen Castle minister of N.E. parish persuaded by beautiful New York woman to take a parish there. Stephen's mother dies from the shock in the different kind of living she finds in New York. He soon comes to his senses, resigns and marries the girlhe didn't know he loved. LW 26:251

008192   THE MYSTERY OF MISS MOTTE. Boston: L.C. Page, 1909 NUC.

mystery romance BKM
Heroine persuaded by mother never to marry because of mystery concerning her birth NYT

008193   WAXWING. New York: F.H. Revell, [c1905] BMC NUC.

008194   WHEN SHE CAME TO HERSELF. BY ALISON BROOKE. Philadelphia: American Baptist Publication Society, [c1901] NUC.

008195   THE WHITE SHIELD. Philadelphia: Griffith & Rowland Press, 1904 NUC.

NYT--female Christian who undergoes suffering and tortures for her faith; slaps a priest who touches her, is thrown to the tigers, survives.

008196   A WIND FLOWER: A NOVEL. Philadelphia: A. J. Rowland, [c1899] NUC.

NE-a quaker and a high church priest are character studies. Shows changing views concerning rel. doctrines. PW 55:575
Fierce spiritual conflict in Francis Norman from high to low church ideas. He loves the windflower-Eunice Herendeau but she's fickle and doesn't support him so he ends up with her sister Mary-a steadier sort. LW 30:140
Eunice, a Quakeress, struggles between love and her faith. Sad conclusion. NYT 6-24-99,408

008197   A WOMAN OF YESTERDAY. New York:
Doubleday, Page, 1900 NUC. London: Hodder & Stoughton,
1901 BMC.

LW 31:268. Anna Mallison, austere, ardent. Missionary.
Early part of the century. Anna comes to accept her
love of literature and art as not sinful.
PW Brought up in strict orthodoxy, gradual change in
point of view.

MASON, EDITH HUNTINGTON.   United States.

008198   THE GREAT PLAN. Chicago: A.C. McClurg,
1913 BMC NUC. London: C.F. Cazenove, 1913 BMC.

"An American girl plots the political enfranchisement
of her down-trodden German sisters, who have no votes,
and takes up her residence in a castle."
"An American girl's deeply laid plot for the political
enfranchisement of her down trodden German sisters who
had no vote or other women's rights." NYT 1913 550

008199   THE POLITICIAN. Chicago: A.C. McClurg,
1910 NUC.

ambitious politician marries wealthy woman; problem of
his career and fear of his neglecting his wife ? PW
BKM -renounces marriage because politicians must
neglect their wives
NYT-she has a bad quarter of an hour and marries
someone else.

008200   THE REAL AGATHA; THE UNUSUAL ADVENTURES
OF TWO YOUNG MEN AND AN HEIRESS. Chicago: A.C.
McClurg, 1907 NUC.

Mystery PW 12-7-07
BKM 27 1908--comedy-author's pov? no one knows which
is the real one (she will inherit a lot) suitors have
to take a chance.

MASON, EVELEEN LAURA. B. 1838. United States.

008201   AN EPISODE IN THE DOINGS OF THE DUALIZED.
[Boston]: [Press of Fish & Libby], 1898 NUC.

MASON, GRACE (SARTWELL). B. 1877. United States.

008202   THE GOD PARENTS. Boston: Houghton
Mifflin, 1910 NUC.

"Well poised" young woman about to make her 14th trip
to Europe, hurried off by young man: chaperoned they
spend three weeks camping, save a boy, fall in love?
PW
BKM-She learns it is rather pleasant to be dictated to
provided the right man does the dictating.

008203   HIS WIFE'S JOB. New York and London: D.
Appleton, [c1919] BMC NUC.

"ornamental and useless wife who when husband went to
war went to work and made good and upon her husband's
return became his real partner" PW
Anne Henderson opens a shop with her friend Marian
Beal on 5th Ave. Got into financial difficulties.
Later goes off to the war with her husabnd presumbaly
to do war work. He had been bored with her as
housewife. Now his feelings are changed. NYT 6-22-19,
339

008204   THE SHADOW OF ROSALIE BYRNES. New York
and London: D. Appleton, 1919 BMC NUC.

mystery beginning with love at first sight, war
marriage PW
Rosalie Byrnes entertains soldiers with her singing.
Love at first sight marriage. Family against her
because she was in chorus line; try to break up
marriage. But all comes out well in the end. NYT
11-9-19 641

MASON, MRS. SHIERS.

008205   HUBERT SHERBORNE, PRIEST. BY TARIKA.
London: Simpkin, Marshall, 1901 BMC.

008206   THE LOVES OF STELLA. London: S. Paul,
[1912] BMC.

TLS-love story
ATH-love story

MASSON, ROSALINE ORME.

008207   IN OUR TOWN. London: Hodder & Stoughton,

1901 BMC.

008208   LESLIE FARQUHAR. London: J. Murray, 1902
BMC.

brought up by father, always out-of-doors, living like
a boy, reviewer asks why author doesn't let Leslie
marry the poet LBKM 1-03,169.
"One can hardly believe that there is such a thing as
a grown-up girl who has never thought of marriage, and
if there is such a thing one cannot believe that she
would be attractive." ATH 121, 365.

008209   NINA. London: Macmillan, 1911 BMC NUC.

sentimental story of identity of orphaned girl TLS
Gentle domestic story ACAD
gentle domestic story ATH

008210   OUR BYE-ELECTION. Bristol: J.W.
Arrowsmith, 1908 BMC.

TLS-Comedy, male heroes

008211   THE TRANSGRESSORS. London: Hodder and
Stoughton, 1899 BMC.

LBKM 17:118. Modern Edinburgh. A judge, Lord Graham, a
divinity student, John Innes, and Betty Graham are
central characters. Tragedy. John suicides.
"Young men in love are supposed to discuss their
religion." SP 83:961

MASTERMAN, J., pseud. See RYBOT, VICTORIA (BAKER).

MASTERS, CAROLINE.

008212   THE DUCHESS LASS. London: F. Warne, 1896
BMC NUC.

ATH 108:833. Penniless after death of her parents, she
lives with her father's family, who have always looked
down on her mother's side as North Country mill hands.
Goaded by their treatment, she herself becomes a
Lancashire weaver.
Frances Carroll argues with her aunt and thus leaves
her uncle and aunt's house to make her living-weaving
as her mother did before she married. Love story too.
PW 51:340
Factory life in North of England. Heroine is daughter
of a mill woman who had married a gentleman. So she
takes up her mother's work in the mill. SP 78:552

008213   THE SHUTTLE OF FATE. London: F. Warne,
1895 BMC NUC.

Lancashire story. Dialect, strikes, a stern parent, a
repentant prodigal, young manager, love, etc. ATH
106:831
PW 1-4-96. A strike at a Lancashire Mill. Hard father,
wicked son, young woman whose parents are a mystery
and mill manager who loves her.

008214   THE WORLD'S COARSE THUMB. London: F.
Warne, 1897 BMC NUC.

PW-Hero's attempt to clear his father's name. Also his
romance. Lancashire.

MASTERSON, KATE. B. 1870. United States.

008215   THE DOBLEYS. New York: G. W. Dillingham,
[c1900] NUC.

MATEER, ADA (HAVEN).

008216   SIEGE DAYS: PERSONAL EXPERIENCES OF
AMERICAN WOMEN AND CHILDREN DURING THE PEKING SIEGE.
New York: F.H. Revell, [c1903] NUC.

MATHERS, H. See REEVES, HELEN BUCKINGHAM (MATHERS).

MATHERS, HELEN. See REEVES, HELEN BUCKINGHAM (MATHERS).

MATHESON, C. M. See MATHESON, CHARLOTTE MARY.

MATHESON, CHARLOTTE MARY. B. 1892. United Kingdom.

008217   CHILDREN OF THE DESOLATE. BY C. M.
MATHESON. London: T.F. Unwin, 1916 BMC.

TLS -study of a woman an artist. Unhappy marriage.
Naomi Peel almost overthrows her mentally as well as
physically.

008218   THE GENERATION BETWEEN. BY C. M.

MATHESON. London: T. F. Unwin, [1915] NUC BMC. New
York: Brentano's, 1915 NUC.

Heroine is of generation between woman being confined
in home/out in world. In between two worlds, Thomasine
Latimer marries in a hurry to please father.
Miserable, runs away from husband she doesn't love,
child she didn't want, house work she didn't like.
Runs to a settlement where women run things. Author
shows problems of such a community. Thomasine unhappy
here. Author makes her discover she is all wrong
returns her to duty-husband and child. TLS
NYT-Thomasine is personification of all unrest and
rebellion of women today. She resents giving up her
plans for her brother's education for their careers.
She decides to make gardening a profession-anything to
avoid being the conventional daughter at home. Loves
and enjoys freedom, egotistic, unconcerned with larger
aims of women; she impetuously leaves her child and
husband for Dyleshort, an all women's community
founded by a woman with the purpose of developing a
nation within the nation where women with no thought
of rivalry with man should fulfill a magnificent
ideal, which ideal would in time become the standard
of the country.

MATHESON, E. REID, pseud. See MIDGLEY, MRS. LLEWELLYN.

MATHEWS, AMANDA. See CHASE, AMANDA (MATHEWS).

MATHEWS, FRANCES AYMAR. 1865-1925. United States.

008219   BILLY DUANE; A NOVEL. New York: Dodd,
Mead, 1905 NUC.

Couple becomes estranged because mother must be abroad
with sick child. In the meantime he's immersed in
politics, she returns and problems keep them apart. PW
3-11-05
Very brief desc BKM 21 (1905)321
Wife takes son abroad, meets and likes a pianist;
Husband now mayor of New York. Wife involved in
gambling scandal; New York society with its intrigues
and divorces; estrangment of the Duanes. Loves to play
roulette NYT 173.05

008220   A CHRISTMAS HONEYMOON. New York: Moffat,
Yard, 1912 NUC.

PW-Unhappy marriage
NYT-Christmas story

008221   FANNY OF THE FORTY FROCKS. Philadelphia:
J. C. Winston, [c1913] BMC NUC.

Goes to New York to seek fortune; finds self in
England, gets involved in a diplomatic intrigue-saves
a duke from French plot.

008222   THE FLAME DANCER. New York: G. W.
Dillingham, [c1908] NUC. London: T. Unwin, 1908 BMC.

A story of mystery, Oriental mysticism, and romance in
which is introduced the Chinese art of See-foo-tee, or
double hypnotism.
BKM v.28 1908-09.
NYT--a tangled tale.
Story about priceless jewels. TLS

008223   IF DAVID KNEW; A NOVEL. London: T. F.
Unwin, 1910 BMC. New York: G. W. Dillingham, [c1910]
NUC.

Woman addicted to morphine keeps this a secret from
husband. PW
NYT Woman addicted to morphine keeps this a secret
from husband.

008224   THE MARQUISE'S MILLIONS; A NOVEL. New
York and London: Funk and Wagnalls, 1905 BMC NUC.

Two old French women eccentrics-all about an
inheritance and a young woman's effort to get it. PW
4-29-05
NYT 342,05
ACAD 1033, 05

008225   A MARRIED MAN: A NOVEL. Chicago and New
York: Rand, McNally, [c1899] NUC. London: T. F. Unwin,
[1899] BMC.

Paul Amory, U.S. Senator, falls in love for the first
time with a widow of 40--Mrs. Tremlowe. They wed in
Paris. Paul soon learns she's an adventuress. But he
does nothing till he meets 23 year old Leah
Livingston. When Leah learns he's married she backs

off and a suitor for her comes on the scene. Then Mrs.
A dies. He rushes to Leah but learns she's dead. But
he revives her. LW 30:449
BKM 11:95. Paul marries wrong woman. Dreams of right
one. They meet; love. But they abhor divorce. Then
wife dies, problem is solved.

008226   MY LADY PEGGY GOES TO TOWN. London: B. F.
Stevens & Brown, [1901] BMC. Indianapolis:
Bowen-Merrill, [c1901] NUC.

One of our problematic women who catches the man and
toys with him. Peggy's metamorphosis into a man BOOK
NOTES 12 '01
"If she ends as wife, she's more fortunate than she
deserves to be" NYT
BKM 13 1901 307 masquerades as a boy.

008227   MY LADY PEGGY LEAVES TOWN. New York:
Moffat, Yard, 1913 NUC.

"This Lady Peggy is the descendent of the heroine of
"Lady Peggy goes to town". The modern girl is quite as
daring as her ancestress, and proves it by going west
with her aunt and representing herself as a young
widow, taking the name of a former admirer who was
killed in the Philippines. Her comedy takes on a grim
aspect when the man turns up, hunted as a spy selling
secrets to Japan, and hearing her called Mrs. Gratiot,
claims her as his wife. She helps him escape, but he
drags her away with him, and before she is rescued she
goes through a series of adventures which are
certainly unexpected and exciting." Young girl goes
west, establishes herself as widow of former admirer
believed dead who then shows up hunted as a spy and
claims her, she disguises herself as a boy etc. PW
4-5-13:1238.
"The new Lady Peggy is still English in character, but
somewhat Americanized by an international marriage of
her ancestors. She lives in New York. Tiring of the
social gayeties of her 'set' she leaves town (and a
score of broken hearts), deciding to live the simple
life out west." (NYT)
"This simple life proves to be a series of astonishing
adventures involving tragedy as well as comedy and the
curtain falls on Lady Peggy again in tame New York
happily settled in life." BRD

008228   THE NEW YORKERS, AND OTHER PEOPLE. New
York: Godfrey A. S. Wieners, 1900 NUC.

CR 37:468 Short stories.

008229   PAMELA CONGREVE; A NOVEL. New York: Dodd,
Mead, 1904 NUC.

PW Actress
NYT Young woman, half dead, vows vengeance on fiance
who allowed her father to hang for his murder. Starts
as barmaid, becomes an actress and finally is able to
bring him to a tragic death.

008230   THE STAIRCASE OF SURPRISE. New York: D.
Appleton, 1905 BMC NUC.

Advent-war PW 11-4-05

008231   THE UNDEFILED: A NOVEL OF TO-DAY. London
and New York: Harper, 1906 BMC NUC.

NYT 0
ATH 0 "Four persons are the principals in this story.
The plot turns on the neglect of a gifted wife by her
young husband, who is a successful novelist. He flirts
with a young artist to such an extent that his wife
decides to leave him. In order to save his career she
does not carry her resolution into effect. She does,
however, accept a position as secretary to a very
wealthy western young man. Unforeseen events arise and
many exciting adventures are experienced, but the
deserving receive their reward at last." BKM v.24
1906-7.

MATHEWS, GERTRUDE (SINGLETON). B. 1881.

008232   TREASURE. New York: Holt, 1917 NUC.

Search for a lost mine in So. America related by the
hero. NYT

MATHEWS, MRS. W. G.

008233   AN ABUNDANT HARVEST. London: Murray &
Evenden, [1914] BMC.

MATLACK, MARGARET MOORE.

008234   SERGEANT JANE. Boston: Little, Brown,
1920 NUC.

MATSON, SUSAN (GLASPELL) COOK. 1882-1948. United States.

    008235   FIDELITY; A NOVEL. BY SUSAN GLASPELL.
    Boston: Small, Maynard, [c1915] BMC NUC.

    BKM 41 1915
    Ruth Holland young woman and the 11 years of her life
    with her lover; the attitude of society toward them;
    develops early a taste for something different. PW
    5-8-15
    Young woman runs away with married man. They try to
    live a sane, normal life against a world that would
    deny them happiness. Ruth, daughter of an important
    family in Mid West town, the older man, married in
    name only. Stuart, their secret meetings, her double
    life at parties, with the girls, with him. Their
    discovery that he has bad lungs and must go to
    Arizona. They live in Arizona 11 yrs. Ruth's father's
    death brings them back. Story concerns the town
    against them; she has not found happiness, shows the
    difficult material life of the two, their love has
    diminished. NYT
    When the man freed (divorced) he expects Ruth to marry
    him but Ruth refuses (marr. would spoil what once was
    beautiful to her)

    008236   THE GLORY OF THE CONQUERED; THE STORY OF
    A GREAT LOVE. BY SUSAN GLASPELL. New York: Stokes,
    [1909] NUC BMC.

    BKM v. 29 1909
    devotion of wife to famous Chicago man of science who
    goes blind. TLS
    Husband scientist, wife painter-their sufferings. Her
    child dies at birth, he goes blind, later dies; she
    becomes irreligious and bitter till she paints
    husband's portrait. It's a success; she's "clarified
    in her mind." ATH
    Ernestine Stanly repeats mother's error of marrying a
    scientist;is a successful artist, a triumph in Paris.
    Husband can't understand the artistic temperament. One
    day he goes blind-he's at the end of his career. She
    puts art aside, trains self to continue his research.
    Makes great discoveries in the lab. All this while
    husband knows nothing about the change. On graduation,
    she suffers a temporary breakdown. later he dies. She
    takes up her art again. paints him-her great opus. NYT

    008237   THE VISIONING; A NOVEL. BY SUSAN
    GLASPELL. New York: Stokes, [1911] NUC. London: J.
    Murray, 1912 BMC.

    Woman does and says unexpected things in army camp,
    rescues girl from suicide, they become friends.
    BKM 33 (1911) 419-20
    Marries a Socialist PW 5-6-11
    Katy Jones, an army girl, one day saves another young
    woman from suicide, gets her to come home and remain
    with her. Katy gives her clothes, money. This Annie
    comes to have faith in people thru Katy's care. Katy
    also meets a strange young man, wise, a kind of
    hermit. Thru him she gets new values. She plans to
    marry this man who was once in army prison for
    striking an officer yet she's appalled that her
    brother is about to marry Annie who also is outside
    the army tradition. Katy learns to see the wrong in
    army life and to have vision of a world of peace.
    Author is explicitly against US Army. NYT
    TLS- girl saved from suicide and housed by Katie. Army
    life is the atmosphere.
    ATH-treats girl "with past" like a sister

MATTHEWS, MARY ANDERSON. United States.

    008238   LOVE VS. LAW. New York: Broadway
    Publishing, [c1905] NUC.

    "Establishes a successful practice" "pleads before U S
    Senate for equal suffrage" secures majority vote.
    5-20-05 WOMAN'S JOURNAL

MATTHEWS, SUE FROMAN. United States.

    008239   A BEGGAR'S STORY. New York, Chicago,
    Toronto: F. H. Revell, [c1894] NUC.

    008240   GRANDMOTHER, A TALE OF OLD KENTUCKY. New
    York: J.S. Olgivie, [c1911] NUC.

    Heredity story. PW 9-30-11.

    008241   SIC VITA EST (SUCH IS LIFE). New York: G.

        W. Dillingham, 1896 NUC.

MATTHEWS, VICTORIA (EARLE). United States.

    008242   AUNT LINDY: A STORY FOUNDED ON REAL LIFE.
    BY VICTORIA EARLE. New York: 1893 W.

MATURIN, EDITH (MONEY).

    008243   PETRONEL OF PARADISE. London: E. Nash,
    1907 BMC.

    Love complications. LBKM 1907:213.
    "A bit of an angel with the spice of a
    devil"-romantic, sentimental, and gushing. ACAD.
    ATH

    008244   PETTICOAT PILGRIMS ON TREK. BY MRS. FRED
    MATURIN. London: E. Nash, 1909 BMC NUC.

    008245   THE THIN RED LINE OF HEROES. London: G.
    Richards, 1903 BMC.

    Social side of army life; a woman blossoms into a
    "real live Mrs. C.O." ACAD 64:204

MATURIN, MRS. FRED. See MATURIN, EDITH (MONEY).

MAUD, CONSTANCE ELIZABETH. United Kingdom.

    008246   ANGELIQUE. London: Duckworth, 1912 BMC.

    008247   A DAUGHTER OF FRANCE. London: Methuen,
    [1908] BMC NUC.

    TLS-young Fr. wife with dominating husband flees. Then
    what?
    BMC-reconciliation sent.
    Rom. love story. Misunderstanding, separation,
    reconciliation. NYT, 3-20-09

    008248   AN ENGLISH GIRL IN PARIS. London and New
    York: J. Lane, 1902 BMC NUC. (Published anonymously in
    England.)

    NYT-7-19-02 Comedy about Eng. vs Fr.

    008249   FELICITY IN FRANCE. London: W. Heinemann,
    1906 BMC. New York: C. Scribner's Sons, 1906 NUC.

    ACAD boyish aunt of 60 travels with niece.

    008250   MY FRENCH FRIENDS. London: Smith, Elder,
    1904 BMC.

    ACAD small beer.

    008251   MY FRENCH YEAR. London: Mills & Boon,
    [1919] BMC NUC.

    008252   NO SURRENDER. London: Duckworth, 1911
    BMC. New York: J. Lane, 1912 NUC.

    Author says her characters move among events that are
    historically true and that events touching prison and
    law court experiences related to women are factual.
    Relates to Suffragist and Suffragette movements. ATH
    "2 typical heroines of the suffragette movement--one a
    mill hand and the other a woman of wealth and rank.
    The characters are a little too obviously "made to
    order" but the story is nevertheless very
    interesting..."FRANKLIN
    PW-theme is women's suffrage.
    ACAD-an argument from beginning to end.
    SR-tract, only incidentally a novel heroines go to
    prison, etc.
    LBKM-witty and incisive

MAUDE, ELSIE.

    008253   THRICE WEDDED. AN ADVENTURESS'S VOW.
    London: Drane's, [1913] BMC.

    Adventurer kidnaps a married woman, imprisons her,
    gets this wife's husband to marry the adventuress,
    commits suicide--after which the husband remarries his
    wife. ATH

MAUDE, ETHEL. Nationality Unknown.

    008254   BELINDA-AND SOME OTHERS. Bristol: J. W.
    Arrowsmith, [1892] BMC. New York: D. Appleton, 1898
    NUC.

    Short stories.

MAUDE, MRS. W. See MAUDE, SOPHIE DORA (SPICER).

MAUDE, SOPHIE DORA (SPICER).

008255   THE CHILD COUNTESS. BY MRS. W. MAUDE.
London: R. Washbourne, 1893 BMC.

008256   THE DUCHESS OF YORK'S PAGE. London: R & T
Washbourne, 1900 BMC.

008257   A RUNAWAY MARRIAGE. London: Catholic
Truth Society, 1894 BMC.

MAULE, MARY KATHERINE (FINIGAN). B. 1861?. United States.

008258   A PRAIRIE-SCHOONER PRINCESS. Boston:
Lothrop, Lee & Shepard, [c1920] NUC. London: Hodder &
Stoughton, 1927[] BMC.

MAURICE, GABRIELLE FITZ.

008259   MRS. FITZ-MAURICE ON LEAVE. London:
Greening, 1908 BMC NUC.

ACAD--Spends her time in the arms of other men while
her husband is away and is able to convince her
husband of the justice of it.

MAXTON, CLUNIE.

008260   HEIR TO A MILLION. London: H.J. Drane,
[1907] BMC.

MAXWELL, BEATRICE ETHEL HERON. D. 1927.

008261   THE ADVENTURES OF A LADY PEARL-BROKER.
London: New Century Press, 1899 NUC.

Exciting story-she sells pearls on commission. Runs
risk of being robbed of 20,000 pounds of jewels at a
time. ACAD 57:372
Series of efforts to rob her. No character study. ATH
114:586

008262   THE QUEEN REGENT. London: Ward, Lock,
1903 BMC.

MAXWELL, BEATRICE ETHEL HERON AND FLORENCE E. EASTWICK.

008263   THE FIFTH WHEEL. BY BEATRICE
HERON-MAXWELL AND F. E. EASTWICK. London: Ward, Lock,
1916 BMC NUC.

ATH-murder mystery, traditional.

008264   A WOMAN'S SOUL. London: H. Marshall, 1900
BMC.

SR 90:592. Daphne has brains and heart above average.
ATH 116:507. She marries a marquis for his title and
money, has a lukewarm affection for him. She is too
soulful for him.
ACAD 59:362. Incompatibility, separation and tragedy
deeper than either follow her ill-advised marriage.
LIT 7:421 Extracts from Daphne's & Laurence's
diaries. "Plenty of rather artificial tragedy."

MAXWELL, ELLEN BLACKMAR. See BARKER, ELLEN (BLACKMAR)
MAXWELL.

MAXWELL, HELEN.

008265   A DAUGHTER OF THOR: THE STUDY OF A MODERN
WOMAN. London: Brown, Langham, 1905 BMC.

ACAD: half-pagan heroine.

008266   EVE AND THE WOOD GOD. London: Brown,
Langham, 1906 BMC.

A man hypnotizes Eve to love him. SR

MAXWELL, MARY ELIZABETH (BRADDON). 1837-1915. United
Kingdom.

008267   ALL ALONG THE RIVER. BY M. E. BRADDON.
London: Simpkin, Marshall, Hamilton, Kent, 1893 BMC
NUC. New York: Cassell, 1893 NUC. (Published
anonymously in England.)

Isola Disney lives a lonely life while husband a Major
serves in Burma. A fascinating rake comes to town and
Isola is fascinated. Whether she "falls" or not is in
question, but she is trapped on his yacht, does escape
and returns home with love of husband intact. There's
real confusion as to whether she slept with the guy.

Perhaps intentional-author wants us to like her.. SP
71, 146.
Child-wife left alone immediately after marriage. ATH
101, 760.
CR 21:272. Two people who loved well but not wisely
and paid the death penalty for their unsanctioned
love.
History of Isola Disney--sympathetic. Left
alone-husband in Burmah, she falls for Lord
Lostwithiel. Husband returns; she lies to him. Truth
doesn't come out until her death when her husband
forgives her. Author forgives her; we're meant to; but
reviewer refuses to. SR 76:102

008268   THE BLUE BAND; OR, A STORY OF WOMAN'S
VENGEANCE. New York: [n.d.] NUC.

008269   THE CHRISTMAS HIRELINGS; A NOVEL. BY M.
E. BRADDON. New York: Harper, 1894 NUC. London:
Simpkin, Marshall, 1894 BMC NUC.

008270   THE CONFLICT. BY M. E. BRADDON. London:
Simpkin, Marshall, 1903 BMC NUC. Leipzig: B.
Tauchnitz, 1903 NUC.

Short desc ACAD 64,414
Weird story about an evil man whose spirit inhabits
other people's bodies ATH 121, 650

008271   DEAD LOVE HAS CHAINS. BY M. E. BRADDON.
London: Hurst and Blackett, 1907 NUC BMC. Leipzig: B.
Tauchnitz, 1907 NUC.

Passionate, half understood, love of past wrecks her
later love; brief desc LBKM 7-07,148
Painful story of modern life. SP.

008272   DURING HER MAJESTY'S PLEASURE. BY M. E.
BRADDON. London: Hurst & Blackett, 1908 NUC BMC.
Leipzig: B. Tauchnitz, 1908 NUC.

TLS conv.
ATH conv.

008273   GERARD; OR, THE WORLD, THE FLESH, AND THE
DEVIL. A NOVEL. BY THE AUTHOR OF "LADY AUDLEY'S
SECRET," ETC. [ANONYMOUS]. London: Simpkin and
Marshall, 1891 NUC BMC. Leipzig: B. Tauchnitz, 1891
NUC.

Imitates Faust story in every detail. Set in London in
modern time. SP 67 762
Gerard Hillertson: LW
Heroine Margaret, like that of Goethe except that
she's "gerettet" in this world with over a million
dollars. ATH 98 614

008274   THE GHOST'S NAME. New York: The Dramatic
Mirror, [c1891] NUC.

008275   GRACE DARNEL. BY MISS M. E. BRADDON. New
York: F. M. Lupton, 1894 NUC.

008276   THE GREEN CURTAIN. BY M. E. BRADDON.
London: Hutchinson, 1911 NUC BMC.

TLS focuses on a man. Story of Eng stage ATH

008277   HER CONVICT. BY M. E. BRADDON. London:
Hurst and Blackett, 1907 BMC NUC.

Crime story TLS

008278   HIS DARLING SIN. BY M. E. BRADDON.
London: Simpkin, Marshall, [1899] BMC NUC.

Traditional detective story. SP 83:662.
Widow inherits between 20 and 50,000 pounds a year.
She's a woman brought up to do without things. Also a
murder. ACAD 57:485
His darling sin is Kate Delmaine of the chorus at the
Spectator Theatre. He is murdered by Kate's husband.
ATH 114:718

008279   IN HIGH PLACES. BY M. E. BRADDON. London:
Hutchinson, 1898 BMC NUC.

SP 81:345. Romance of the reign of Charles I. Male
hero. Braddon has written over 100 novels and has
abandoned the sensational for the placid historical
romance.
LIT 3:499.
LBKM 15:19. He is illegitimate son of Buckingham.

008280   THE INFIDEL; A ROMANCE. BY M. E. BRADDON.
New York: Harper, 1900 NUC. London: Simpkin, Marshall,

008281   THE INFIDEL; A STORY OF THE GREAT
REVIVAL. BY M. E. BRADDON. London: Simpkin, Marshall,
[1900] BMC. Leipzig: B. Tauchnitz, 1900 NUC.

LW 31:223. Reign of George II. Story of beautiful and
virtuous woman, her marriage to wealthy profligate out
of kindness on his deathbed, her conversion to
Methodism and Church of England and refusal to marry a
man she loves because of former marriage.
PW-Antonia and her father William Thornton, pursued
the profession of letters. They wrote plays and
essays, made translations and furnished smart
paragraphs for the society journals. Antonia raised
like a boy, an atheist with high ideals.

008282   LONDON PRIDE; OR, WHEN THE WORLD WAS
YOUNGER. London: Simpkin, Marshall, 1896 BMC NUC.

SR-Heroine in London during time of plague.
ATH 108:521. Lord Farefam "finds himself burdened with
a divided duty between his wife and her sister
Angela." Angela is a "delightful and irreproachable
heroine." Passion.
SP 77:595.

008283   A LOST EDEN. London: Hutchinson, 1904 NUC
BMC.

LBKM complicated plot but promising heroine.
ATH 0
TLS-governess whom artist refuses to marry.
ACAD--Jane Eyre again.

008284   MARY. BY M. E. BRADDON. London:
Hutchinson, 1916 BMC NUC.

TLS-betrayed in her girlhood, at last finds it
possible to accept the love of a man.
ATH-she becomes a reader to wealthy invalid through
friendship of male social worker; inherits invalid's
money.

008285   MIRANDA. BY M. E. BRADDON. London:
Hutchinson, 1913 NUC BMC.

She's up-to-date. Her life traced from early childhood
to second marriage. A great love and sympathy exist
between her and mother who is opposite her restless,
energetic daughter. ACAD
Miranda-strange mingling of this century and the 19th,
precocious, well educated. Reads Newman, Darwin,
Spencer; but she's a bit prudish-reads only the
classics; marries. SP
Marries but discovers her husband is a murderer. Left
happy at Trownham. TLS

008286   OUR ADVERSARY. BY M. E. BRADDON. London:
Hutchinson, 1909 BMC NUC.

Centers on male preacher. TLS
Sensational LBKM

008287   THE ROSE OF LIFE. BY M. E. BRADDON. New
York: Brentano's, 1905 NUC. London: Hutchinson, 1905
NUC BMC.

Wife "turns nun" PW 8-12-05
About an egotistical poet, rescues a young woman from
suicide, takes her home to his wife. (another woman in
the story suffers an unhappy marr.) and falls in love
with her; tragic end comes to the poet NYT 555 05
Poet saves Helen, gets her a governess position. His
wife, he discovers, has already been married! and all
ends happily! TLS 05:160.
Poet-attractive in his egotism, discovered swindling
one of his friends. His simple-minded devoted wife is
sympathetic rather than irritating. Bigamous marr. ATH
651,05

008288   ROUGH JUSTICE. BY M. E. BRADDON. London:
Simpkin, Marshall, 1898 BMC NUC. Leipzig: B.
Tauchnitz, 1898 NUC.

SP 80:309. Villains, murder, mystery. Oliver Greswold,
a social reformer and philanthropist, murders his
cousin who had inherited a fortune he had counted on
coming to him and which reverts to him on her death.
Suspicion falls on her former lover. The highly
accomplished detective, Mr. Faunce, solves the crime,
and Oliver is forced to write a confession in front of
Wentworth's betrothed. Satisfied of his innocence, she
consents to the burning of the document and Oliver
continues his philanthropy.
ACAD 53:149. "Hero is a Cambridge man who tracks down

real criminal and wrings a confession from him" (what
happened to detective?).
ATH 111:244. "The rough justice which leaves the two
betrayers of Lillian Carford to their conscience."
(Greswold & Wentworth.) Lillian "is parting in misery
from her only lover when she is struck down by the
felon shot of Greswold." Greswold: "I was justified in
suppressing a useless life."

008289   SONS OF FIRE. BY THE AUTHOR OF "LADY
AUDLEY'S SECRET" ETC. [ANONYMOUS]. London: Simpkin,
Marshall, [1895] BMC NUC.

Mrs. Wornock's great faith in spititualism though she
had been deceived by mediums in the past and two men
who look alike. No plot. Allan Carew and Geoffrey
Wornock look alike. Similarities and differences in
them. They argue over the same woman-Suzette St.
Vincent. Geoffrey goes half mad, attempts to kill
Allan. Good complex character-Mrs. Worock, Geoffrey's
mother. ACAD 48:407
SR-Country house romance.

008290   THOU ART THE MAN. BY THE AUTHOR OF "LADY
AUDLEY'S SECRET", ETC. [ANONYMOUS]. London: Simpkin
and Marshall, [1894] BMC NUC.

SR 78:566. Sibyl is in love with epileptic lunatic;
her mother loved her father who also was one. She
helps him escape when it appears he committed a
murder; the murderer helps her. Coralie sounds
interesting; her diary is part of the story, in which
she speculates on the probable death of her father.
Victorian Detective Fiction: Coralie Urquhart, lady's
companion, is the detective.

008291   UNDER LOVE'S RULE. BY THE AUTHOR OF "LADY
AUDLEY'S SECRET" ETC. [ANONYMOUS]. London: Simpkin,
Marshall, 1897 BMC NUC.

Her 58th novel. Maiden aunt devotes self to her
frivolous sister's three children. Ends up marrying
the engineer from India. There is Miss Warren the
governess who does good work in West End London slums.
The household is that of the Lerich's. The money goes;
Mr. Lerich kills himself. The aunt teaches the wife,
her sister, to adjust. SR 83:399.
A condemnation of the high and smart rich set. The
"feather brained" hostess who neglects her children is
contrasted to her sister who is not married to a rich
man and loves the kids. ATH 109:536.
SP 80:147. Weak man and his empty-headed wife inherit
wealth, have three spoiled sons. Ellinor, the wife,
grows in character and shows she can a mother's
duty.

008292   THE VENETIANS: A NOVEL. BY M. E. BRADDON.
London: Simpkin, Marshall, 1892 BMC NUC. New York:
Harper, 1892 NUC. (Published anonymously in England.)

SP -Hero commits unpremeditated murder, escapes.
Becomes engaged, discovers fiancee's brother is the
man he has killed. The secret leaks out.

008293   WHEN THE WORLD WAS YOUNGER. BY MISS M. E.
BRADDON. New York: R.F. Fenno, [c1897] NUC.

Historical novel. Young woman whose father serves
Charles I, educated in Fr. convent, goes to Eng.,
nurses brother-in-law in plague, moves to country
home. LW 28:478

008294   THE WHITE HOUSE. BY M. E. BRADDON.
London: Hurst & Blackett, 1906 NUC BMC.

TLS-fem hero marries a missionary.

MAXWELL, SYBIL.

008295   IN A BLACK MANTLE: AN HISTORICAL NOVEL.
London: Griffith and Farran, 1892 BMC.

MAY, DANAE.

008296   THE INCONSEQUENCES OF SARA. London: A.
Treherne, 1902 NUC BMC.

LBKM 5-02 "clever undisciplined young woman...not
truthful but makes a difference".
ACAD-reads Aurelius for pleasure and writes persiflage
for money.

MAY, FLORENCE LAND. B. 1871. United States.

008297   THE BROKEN WHEEL. Boston: C.M. Clark,
[c1910] NUC.

Political corruption in San Francisco.
NYT-post earthquake. Unscrupulous man's operations.
Woman question?

MAY, GEORGIANA MARION (CRAIK). 1831-1895. United Kingdom.

008298   THE HOUSE OF SWEET MEMORIES. London:
Griffith, Farran, 1892 BMC.

008299   PATIENCE HOLT. BY GEORGIANA M. CRAIK
(MRS. A. W. MAY). London: R. Bentley, 1891 NUC BMC.

SR 74:171. Patience proposes. Her husband turns out to
be a boor; she is impatient with his stupidity. Her
mother an impoverished widow, was more anxious for
Patience to marry an intelligent man with nothing than
the dull but kind heir of their landlord. Reviewer
finds this unnatural.
Her father is a very conventional Quaker whom she
shocks by her manners. Story concerns her relationship
to Ralph whom she snubs time and time again and then
weds. ACAD
She's misunderstood by her family. At school shocks
all by bathing near nude in fountain. Marries squire's
son out of gratitude. He saved her life. ATH 98 448
Old squire left widowed raises son in protected
environment then plots to get him wed to Patience a
very highly spirited young woman very different from
the shy Ralph. SP 67, 762.
Little understanding of her by Ralph either.

008300   POOR OLD NEPTUNE. London: Griffith,
Farran, Browne, [1897] BMC.

MAY, MRS. A. W. See MAY, GEORGIANA MARION (CRAIK).

MAY, SOPHIE, pseud. See CLARKE, REBECCA SOPHIA.

MAYES, HELEN.

008301   LOVE IN THE FJORDS. London: J. Ouseley,
[1913] BMC.

"A poor little romance" and descriptions of Norway.
ATH, TLS

MAYNARD, CORA. United States.

008302   THE LETTER AND THE SPIRIT. New York:
Stokes, 1898 NUC.

LW 29:434. Mismatched couples in marriage. Walter and
Mrs. Worthington contemplate running away, but decide
they would grow tired of each other. He is married to
cold religious woman.
PW-emptiness of modern social life.

008303   SOME MODERN HERETICS: A NOVEL. Boston:
Roberts, 1896 NUC.

BKM 4:370. Many characters, clever sayings.
PW 10-10-96. Winifred Gray, novelist and dramatist and
somewhat of an anarchist, in other people's opinion,
meets Vida, daughter of a millionaire whom Gray has
mortally offended. Revenge, love, strike, etc.

MAYNARD, LUCY.

008304   THE PHILANTHROPIST. London: Methuen, 1898
BMC.

ACAD 53:495. Life in an Orphan Asylum. Strong love
interest by way of relief. Touches of satire.
ACAD 54:221. "The melancholy of the teaching
profession lies heavily on this book." The lovers
marry and become proprietors of a boys' school on Lake
Geneva. The philanthropist appears to be a fake, the
discovery of which is part of the plot.
ATH 111:768. Sentimental. Penrose, after leaving the
orphanage, earns a meager living by doing
philanthropic work in E. London.
LBKM 14:167. Author's purpose is "to show up the
hideousness of life in benevolent institutions."

MAYNARD, SARA KATHERINE (CASEY). United Kingdom.

008305   LIBBY ANN. BY SADIE KATHERINE CASEY.
London: W. Heinemann, 1913 BMC NUC.

Irish girl acts as second mother to her many small
brothers and sisters. ATH
"A particularly aggravating self-satisfied managing
female, even as a child." receives many proposals. TLS

MAYNE, ETHEL COLBURN. D. 1941. United Kingdom.

008306   THE CLEARER VISION. London: T. F. Unwin,
1898 BMC.

LBKM 15:87. Powerful, "unusual courage of unreserve,"
soul feminine cut deep down the middle. The writer's
attitude is "the tone of disparagement, as if love,
and wifehood, and motherhood were but a poor business
for a woman."

008307   THE FOURTH SHIP. London: Chapman & Hall,
1908 BMC.

TLS-? Allegory, 1st part takes place in 1850's. Story
of a woman who does not marry.
ACAD Ends up an old woman living with the man she once
loved and his wife and children. End of book focuses
on one of the daughters.
ATH-final part of book attempts to contrast Mid
Victorian and late Victorian ways of girls.

008308   GOLD LACE, A STUDY OF GIRLHOOD. London:
Chapman & Hall, 1913 NUC BMC.

Flirtations between service men and "girls who are so
pathetically easy to come at" in Ireland. ATH
"Illuminating discussion of women's significance in
the world" LBKM
Feelings and relations between the young women and men
at naval station and garrison town. Rhoda is a Shavian
and "something of a feminist" She thinks herself
superior to the young officers she meets in Ireland.
TLS

008309   JESSIE VANDELEUR. London: Allen, 1902
BMC.

A moral degenerate-pursues the quest of personal
happiness; steals plot of her lover's book. destroys
his ms. No pity for him at his death and when all is
told to 2nd love, it doesn't matter.

008310   ONE OF OUR GRANDMOTHERS. London: Chapman
& Hall, 1916 NUC BMC.

TLS-She is a piano player, born of stupid Eng father
and coarse Irish step-mother. The year is 1860 and she
struggles to get out of her commonplace surroundings
so she can pursue her music.
LBKM-She yearns for more freedom than 1860 can give
her.
ATH Psych st. Passionate struggle against and
dependence on father or husband.

008311   THINGS THAT NO ONE TELLS. London: Chapman
& Hall, 1910 NUC BMC.

MAYO, ISABELLA (FYVIE). 1843-1914. United Kingdom.

008312   A BLACK DIAMOND; OR THE BEST AND THE
WORST OF IT. BY EDWARD GARRETT. London: Home Words
Pub. Office, [1894] BMC.

008313   CHRYSTAL JOYCE: THE STORY OF A GOLDEN
LIFE. BY EDWARD GARRETT. London: Partridge, [1899]
BMC.

008314   A DAUGHTER OF THE KLEPHTS; OR A GIRL OF
MODERN GREECE. London: W.R. Chambers, [1897] BMC.

Story of the Greek war of 1805-24. BAKER 03,213
Modern Greece. Patience Hedges is Greek by birth.
Raised in England became a waif, saved by woman who
left her a legacy. Parents discovered; returns to
Greece at time of struggle for independence. Finds
herself in the thick of it. "Devotes her fortune to
the national cause" and escapes disaster in the
disguise of a pallibar. ACAD 52 Fic Sup 39

008315   HER DAY OF SERVICE. BY EDWARD GARRETT.
Edinburgh and London: Oliphant and Anderson, 1894 BMC.

008316   A NINE DAYS' WONDER; OR THE MYSTERY OF
THE HOUSE: A TALE OF THE TURF. BY EDWARD GARRETT.
London: "Home Words", [1897] BMC.

008317   RAB BETHUNE'S DOUBLE: OR LIFE'S LONG
BATTLE WON. BY EDWARD GARRETT. Edinburgh and London:
Oliphant, 1894 NUC BMC.

MAYO, MARGARET (LILIAN CLATLIN). 1882-1951. United States.

008318   BABY MINE. New York: Dodd, Mead, 1911
NUC. London: Cassell, 1911 BMC.

Novelized farce. PW 11-4-11

Novel adapted from play of same name. BMC

008319   POLLY OF THE CIRCUS. New York: Dodd,
Mead, 1908 NUC. London: Cassell, 1909 BMC.

PW-romance between Polly & young parson, she is not
good enough for him etc.
BKM

MAYOR, F. M. See MAYOR, FLORA MACDONALD.

MAYOR, FLORA MACDONALD. B. 1872. United Kingdom.

008320   THE THIRD MISS SYMONS. BY F. M. MAYOR.
London: Sidgwick & Jackson, 1913 NUC BMC.

Henrietta Symons depressing life-history of an unloved
"superfluous" woman; her deterioration is described
"with keen penetration and much literary skill." SP
Her life a series of dull periods; all possibilities
of happiness atrophied. Old age finds her "hopeless,
selfish, stupid". ATH
63 years of an unmarried well to do daughter of a
mid-Victorian country soliciter. Her morbid childhood,
a plain record of her life, her relations to her
married sisters. TLS

MEAD, EMILY W. B. 1820.

008321   IN THE BEGINNING: A BOOK FOR THE NEW ERA.
[Santa Cruz, Cal.]: [Sentinel], [1910] NUC.

MEAD, MOIRA.

008322   PASTE. ADAPTED FROM THE FILM PLAY OF
BANNISTER MERWIN. London: Mills & Boon, 1916 BMC.

MEADE, L. T., pseud. See SMITH, ELIZABETH THOMASINA
(MEADE).

MEADE, LAURA T., pseud. See SMITH, ELIZABETH THOMASINA
(MEADE).

MEADE, MRS. L. T., pseud. See SMITH, ELIZABETH THOMASINA
(MEADE).

MEADOWS, ALICE MAUD. D. 1913.

008323   BLIND MAN'S BUFF. London: Everett, 1907
BMC.

008324   CUT BY SOCIETY. London: Digby, Long, 1906
BMC.

TLS-unsatisfactory mrgs.

008325   DAYS OF DOUBT. London: Ward, Lock, 1901
BMC.

A man and his double (a woman). ATH 3-16-01

008326   THE DUKEDOM OF PORTSEA. London: T.W.
Laurie, [1909] BMC.

Story of parentage. Review dwells on author's split
infinitives! TLS

008327   THE EXTREME PENALTY. London: Digby, Long,
1906 BMC.

008328   THE EYE OF FATE. London: Ward, Lock,
[1899] BMC.

Murder, conviction of the innocent, ultimate
confession of the guilty. ATH 114:891

008329   A GHOST FROM THE PAST. London: T.W.
Laurie, [1911] BMC.

Another first wife shows up. TLS

008330   HER SOUL'S DESIRE. London: T.W. Laurie,
[1910] BMC.

TLS-trad. love story.

008331   THE HOUSE AT THE CORNER. London: T.W.
Laurie, [1908] BMC.

TLS-unscrupulous M.D.
SR.-unscrupulous M.D.

008332   I CHARGE YOU BOTH. London: Digby, Long,
1905 BMC.

Lena's husband is put in an asylum; she takes an

alias, exploits her beauty, becomes a bigamist and a
murderer! TLS 1905:187

008333   THE INFATUATION OF MARCELLA. London:
Digby, Long, 1909 BMC.

An "uncomfortable" story--marriage of a farmer's niece
to a Lord doesn't succeed. TLS

008334   AN INNOCENT SINNER. London: Digby, Long,
1910 BMC.

TLS-young wife in league with gang of criminals.

008335   A MILLION OF MONEY. New York: Brentano's,
1907 NUC. London: Sisley's, 1907 BMC.

NYT-four marriages and three murders.

008336   THE MOTH AND THE FLAME. London: J. Milne,
1908 BMC.

TLS-widow marries.
ACAD-misunderstandings finally cleared up.

008337   THE ODD TRICK. London: J. Long, [1908]
BMC NUC.

TLS-male rascal.

008338   ONE LIFE BETWEEN. London: Ward, Lock,
[1901] BMC.

ATH 1-4-02

008339   OUT FROM THE NIGHT. London: Ward, Lock,
1899 BMC NUC.

008340   THE ROMANCE OF A MADHOUSE. Bristol: J. W.
Arrowsmith, [1891] BMC.

Young lawyer meets beautiful young woman unjustly
accused of murder and confined to institution on
grounds of insanity. Convinced of her innocence, sets
out to clear her and succeeds. Wedding. ACAD

008341   THREE LOVERS AND ONE LASS. London: Digby,
Long, 1908 BMC.

TLS-typ. rom.

008342   A TICKET-OF-LEAVE GIRL. London: Digby,
Long, 1911 BMC.

TLS-crime story. Brenda wrongly suffers five years of
imprisonment.

008343   WHEN THE HEART IS YOUNG. London: Digby,
Long, 1895 BMC.

"some mild love making." sent. ACAD. 47:502

008344   THE WICKED WORLD. London: T.W. Laurie,
[1910] BMC.

TLS-typical rom.

MEAKIN, ANNETTE M. B.

008345   A RIBBON OF IRON. New York: E.P. Dutton,
[1901] NUC. Westminster: A. Constable, 1902 BMC.

An account of a journey on the Trans-Siberian railway.

MEARNS, LILLIAN HATHAWAY. United States.

008346   A PHILIPPINE ROMANCE. New York: Aberdeen,
[c1910] NUC.

MEARS, A. GARLAND. See MEARS, AMELIA GARLAND.

MEARS, AMELIA GARLAND.

008347   MERCIA, THE ASTRONOMER ROYAL: A ROMANCE.
BY A. GARLAND MEARS. London: Simpkin, Marshall,
Hamilton, Kent, 1895 NUC BMC.

2002 AD-all done by electricity. No more
wars-tournaments where the opponent is paralyzed in
right arm, not killed. Mercia becomes Empress of India
SR 80:277

008348   TALES OF OUR TOWN. London: Simpkin,
Marshall, [1893] BMC.

MEARS, LOUISE.

008349   CONCERNING SOME FOOLS AND THEIR FOLLY. BY NEWTON SANDARS. London: Sands, 1901 BMC.

Two sisters (both actresses) wed clergymen, both refuse to play part of clergyman's wife, one leaves husband, neither believes in marriage. ATH Jan 1902

MEARS, MADGE. Nationality Unknown.

008350   THE CANDID COURTSHIP. London and New York: J. Lane, 1917 NUC BMC.

"Story represents modern feminist p.o.v." Joan, a leader in feminist mvt., remains true to her principles. Refuses to marry a man because of his past, tho she broadens her views later and accepts the man PW
"A feminist love story" BKM
Ideal of universal sisterhood; careful study of young womanhood. TLS
Setting: boarding house in Hygate: heroine meets architect who has had an affair; he confesses this, she rejects him: "his standard of morality has not been as high as her own". Circumstances bring a satisfying basis of agreement. ATH NYT

008351   THE FLAPPER'S MOTHER. London: J. Lane, 1918 BMC NUC. New York: J. Lane, 1918 BMC NUC.

Concerns whether desertion and insanity are sufficient grounds for dissolving a marr. ATH
"The blundering stupidity of our marr. laws" a loveable woman with a despicable husband, he left her without a word. She's forced to take boarders. She falls in love with his cousin they wait 6 ysears. (lsw say one must wait 7.) The flapper Vera falls for married man with insane wife (law says he can't divorce her). She disregards marriage, but doesn't find happiness in her unconv. position. She's 17. takes a lover ATH.
SR
"Indictment of the law of divorce" NYT
TLS-Vicar has three daughters & one son. They are strapping athletes, he is sensitive, delicate. Vicar not disturbed by this arrangement of tastes in his children. Rev. thinks heroine Vera & Ritchie the married philanderer who betrayed her both contemptible.

008352   THE JEALOUS GODDESS. London: J. Lane, 1915 NUC BMC. New York: J. Lane, 1915 NUC.

Young couple has serious misunderstanding as they adjust to marr. and a baby 6-26-15 PW
The jeal. goddess-work or Art
Make up in the end but there's psych realism here. TLS
Art demands all. Both devoted to art but home life hampers them, then marriage does. Girl wants only to paint, finds herself about to be an unwilling mother. She becomes desperately dependent. He proceeds with his work. Then they give up ideas of future glory; choose the artist's life of work well done. "The book is a strong protest vs the idea that marriage and maternity are the chief and only aims of women. It asks, if things were equal between men and women would women ever want to marry" SR

008353   THE SHELTERED SEX. London and New York: J. Lane, 1916 NUC BMC.

Ruth goes off with Jolivard to escape from her restricted life. he will help her get work. Train wreck. J. Hurt--Ruth holds his job for him. "They were just pals" After several years Ruth's brother wants her to join him in Australia. J & R decide they can not separate so they marry and go to Australia. PW 90:9/2/16 p687.
NYT-Principal theme deadly Br. vice of respectability. Author seems to believe Br. philistinism is root of woman's enslavement. J. has a secret wife but she gets a divorce in U.S. At first, while they were pals, otherwise was believed & Ruth was ostracized.

MEARS, MARY MARTHA. B. 1876. United States.

008354   THE BIRD IN THE BOX. New York: F. A. Stokes, [1910] NUC.

Heroine without parents grows up healthy in freedom of the open air with grandfather. A young inventor comes to the small fishing town. She learns to love him but he leaves. She then leaves the town with her grandpa, to seek her fortune in New York. Here leads a hard life yet ends up marrying a millionaire. The young inventor reappears. She uses her husband's money to help him with an invention. (Title describes a gift from husband that she holds as symbol for her marriage.) What follows is "her indiscretion," much disaster, but "author makes her seem glad to be a bird in the box." ? BKM
Young girl brought up among fishermen in Maine leads a "wild unsatisfied" life, meets an inventor. She follows him to New York, discovers he's married. She marries a business man, but is unhappy. Her thoughts are with the inventor. PW
BKM v 32, 1910-11.

008355   THE BREATH OF THE RUNNERS; A NOVEL. New York: F. A. Stokes, [1906] NUC.

Beulah & Enid, careers of two young women as sculptors-from year when they first felt the ambition, thru years of toil, discouragement, uncertain progress. Beulah flings away a golden opportunity rather than take unfair adv. of her friend Enid; the other destroys Beulah's work because she's jealous of Beulah's success. "true contentment (for Beulah) in a husband's love. BKM.

008356   EMMA LOU-HER BOOK. New York: H. Holt, 1896 NUC.

BKM 3:269. Diary of 18 yr. old. "inane"
PW 3-28-96. Teaches school, does copying for a minister, occasionally writes his sermons, has lofty views.

008357   ROSAMOND THE SECOND, BEING THE TRUE RECORD OF THE UNPARALLELED ROMANCE OF ONE CLAUDIUS FULLER. New York: F. A. Stokes, [1910] NUC.

Fantastic tale: scientist conceited can't win Rosamond, makes model of her in wax, run by electricity, converses with her. But she's predictable and loving compared with the real Rosamond. PW.
NYT--He fashioned her not to contradict him, but finds opposition dearer then he had imagined. Meanwhile the 1st Rosamond discovers something.

MEDINI, F. ROENA. See MEDINI, FRANCES ROENA.

MEDINI, FRANCES ROENA. B. 1856.

008358   EDALAINE: A METRICAL ROMANCE. BY F. ROENA MEDINI. New York: G. W. Dillingham, 1892 NUC.

PW Happy family disillusioned with the Fourierites. Two sisters love the same man.

MEEHAN, ELEANOR (CHILDS).

008359   MEMORIES OF A RED-LETTER SUMMER. Cincinnati: R. Clarke, 1903 NUC.

MEEKER, NELLIE J. Fl. 1883-1902. United States.

008360   BEVERLY OSGOOD; OR, WHEN THE GREAT CITY IS AWAKE. A NOVEL. BY JANE VALENTINE. New York: G. W. Dillingham, 1900 NUC.

PW-Nina Palermo, innocent, poor, is victim of "evil circumstances" in NYC.

008361   IN THE MARKET PLACE. BY JANE VALENTINE. London and New York: Abbey Press, [1902] NUC.

008362   JONAS BRAND; OR, LIVING WITHIN THE LAW. BY JANE VALENTINE. New York and London: Abbey Press, [1901] NUC.

MEGUIRE, EMMA ELISE (GEISELMAN). B. 1847. Nationality Unknown.

008363   THE MAKIN'S OF A GIRL. Boston: R. G. Badger, 1911 NUC.

Father-daughter relation is "unusual" a girl who uses "original methods to solve problems," her travels in Europe. PW

MEIGS, CORNELIA LYNDE. B. 1884. United States.

008364   THE KINGDOM OF THE WINDING ROAD. London: Macmillan, 1915 BMC.

Experiences of a beggar and his travels. ATH

008365   THE PIRATE OF JASPER PEAK. BY ADAIR ALDON. New York: Macmillan, 1918 NUC.

MELERA, MARGUERITE (YERTA) YERTA, jt. au. See YERTA,

GABRIELLE AND MARGUERITE (YERTA) YERTA-MELERA.

MELLOR, DORA.

008366   BEAUTY RETIRE; AN HISTORICAL ROMANCE.
London: Greening, 1909 BMC NUC.

Hist. rom of Hetty, a country curate's daughter her
migration to London, her love, her life as a slave in
Jamaica. Time of James II. TLS

MELNEC, S., pseud. See BOETTGER, CLEMENTINE.

MELTON, FRANCES JONES. United States.

008367   A DAUGHTER OF THE HIGHLANDERS. Boston:
Roxburgh, [c1910] NUC.

Hist. PW

MENDL, GLADYS, pseud. See SCHUETZE, GLADYS HENRIETTA
(RAPHAEL).

MENTOR, HILARY.

008368   FATES WHIRLPOOL. London: Heath, Cranton,
1917 BMC.

"Illegitimate young woman; her "chequered" love
affairs. TLS

MENTOR, LILLIAN FRANCES. Nationality Unknown.

008369   THE DAY OF THE RESIS. New York:
Dillingham, 1897 NUC.

Party of Americans search for and find the land of On
in Africa. They are well met, but escape with
diamonds; the day of the title refers to the day all
Onites over 65 are killed. PW 51:394

MENZIES, AMY CHARLOTTE.

008370   ABNEGATION. London: J. Long, [1915] BMC.

TLS, war, hero a baronet, brave on battle field.

008371   LOVE'S RESPONSIBILITIES. London: Holden &
Hardingham, [1914] BMC.

MERCIER, ANNE.

008372   ARUM FIELD; OR LIFE'S REALITY. London: W.
Gardner, 1891 BMC NUC.

SP 68:503. Arum falls in love with a poet who also
gambles and forges to pay his debts.

MEREDITH, ALBERTA.

008373   A CLERICAL COURTSHIP. London: Simpkin &
Marshall, 1893 BMC.

MEREDITH, ELLIS. See CLEMENT, ELLIS (MEREDITH).

MEREDITH, ISABEL, pseud. See AGRESTI, OLIVIA ROSSETTI AND
HELENE ROSSETTI ANGELI.

MEREDITH, KATHARINE MARY CHEEVER. United States.

008374   DRUMSTICKS. A LITTLE STORY OF A SINNER
AND A CHILD. New York, London: Transatlantic, 1895
NUC.

A man, a wife, and a woman who is "Drumsticks'"
mother. The child reconciles man and wife. Child
rescued from bad mother, given a good home by man and
wife, but dies. Charlotte Poole "is content to be a
good wife and mother." CR 24:281

008375   GREEN GATES: AN ANALYSIS OF FOOLISHNESS.
New York: D. Appleton, 1896 NUC BMC.

BKM 3:552. Modern and quite impudently French. No
plain speaking--coquettish. Young women who are "brown
and little devils" who die, "leaving jewelled hat pins
sticking in their hats and perfume in coquettish
garments."
PW 6-13-96. Long Island country house. Love of young
woman for married man.
Sad tale of a crippled heroine--her puzzling
personality. Haunting. LW 28:228
Morality is of the lowest ebb.

008376   THE WING OF LOVE. New York: McClure,
Phillips, 1905 NUC.

Bohemian life; about a widow and her young daughter.
PW 4-29-05
NYT 1905:381.

MEREDITH, LOUISE.

008377   A WOMAN'S MISTAKE. London: A.H.
Stockwell, [1916] BMC.

TLS Tale of farming life.

MERINGTON, MARGUERITE. D. 1951. United States.

008378   SCARLETT OF THE MOUNTED. New York:
Moffat, Yard, 1906 BMC NUC.

PW-Klondike mining camp romance.
NYT-Klondike mining camp romance.

MERIVALE, JEAN.

008379   CROSS-PURPOSES: A STORY OF THE
FRANCO-GERMAN WAR. London: E. Stock, 1903 BMC.

MERREL, CONCORDIA. United Kingdom.

008380   JULIA TAKES HER CHANCE. London: Selwyn &
Blount, 1920 BMC. New York: T. Seltzer, 1921 NUC.

TLS Love and romance
ATH--but after failing at acting she is offered
brilliant matrimonial proposal which she turns down.
Becomes typist and confidential clerk, finally marries
employer.
LBKM-Is great success as actress but escapes it and
mrg into obscurity where she found something better
than fame or titles. She is full of rollicking
laughter and life.

MERRICK, HOPE (BUTLER-WILKINS). D. 1917. United Kingdom.

008381   MARY-GIRL. A POSTHUMOUS NOVEL. London: W.
Collins, Sons., [c1920] BMC NUC.

TLS-Ezra, Pa, sends Mary to work. She has a downfall
for which is repentent.
LBKM-Rev implies Ezra & Mary are husband and wife.
They are Quakers and have great ambition to rebuild
barn used for meeting house. Manor Family needs
someone to suckle (nurse) a new baby, dr. suggests
Mary, Ezra consents, bldg. is started with 1st
paycheck. Agony, shame & trouble follow. There is an
episode concerning Mary & Latimer: "Had Mary been
younger, one might have thought her lapse with Latimer
probable...She had not hated Ezra nor even thought of
leaving him."
NYT 7/11/20 p27

008382   WHEN A GIRL'S ENGAGED. London: Chatto &
Windus, 1905 BMC.

MERRILIES, MEG, pseud. See GERMAINE, LOTTIE.

MERRIMAN, EFFIE (WOODWARD). B. 1857. United States.

008383   THE CONWAYS. Boston: Lee & Shepard, 1893
NUC.

PW-Western village life, pleasant characters, town
improvements.

MERRON, ELEANOR. United States.

008384   AS THE WIND BLOWS: A NOVEL. New York:
Lovell, Coryell, [c1895] NUC.

Dorothea Willis an impulsive sensitive child raised by
two aunts, both of whom crush her individuality. Then
she makes a friend at school and lives and travels
with her. Loves her brother, cares for him until he
dies from paresis-though she found him unreliable in
every way. PW 10-19-95:674
LW 27:251. Varying divorce laws in states, man
appearing as husband of two wives because of this

METCALFE, EDITH.

008385   THE HANDLE OF SIN. London: Ward, Lock,
1917 BMC.

Career of a weak young man. TLS
Brother and sister commit forgery. LBKM

008386   PYRAMIDS OF SNOW. London: Ward, Lock,
1903 BMC.

Two brothers; one is a ne'er do well. LBKM 10-03:106.

METHLEY, ALICE A.

008387   THE IDENTITY OF JANE. London: J. Long,
1905 BMC.

Finds her parentage TLS 05, 67

008388   THE KEY OF LIFE. London: T. F. Unwin,
1909 BMC.

Eliz Cathcart's betrothed-thought dead-comes to life
blind after 10 yrs imprisonment. happy end. ACAD
SP

008389   LA BELLE DAME. London: J. Long, 1906 BMC.

ACAD Heroine steals family jewels, commits murder,
drugs niece and tries to force her into mrg and
finally poisons herself.
ATH--Heroine steals family jewels, commits murder,
drugs niece and tries to force her into mrg and
finally poisons herself.

METHLEY, VIOLET MARY. United Kingdom.

008390   THE LOADSTONE. London: Hurst & Blackett,
1914 BMC.

ACAD 86:595 male hero and pretty love story. Napoleon
at Longwood.

008391   A MAN'S HONOUR. London: Hurst & Blackett,
1920 BMC NUC.

TLS-domestic triangle
ATH Love

008392   WHYS AND WHEREFORES. London: Skeffington,
[1919] BMC. (BMC: Tales and studies.)

Tales & Studies

METZ, FREDA VIRGINIA. United States.

008393   ROSELIN; OR, A RUBY NECKLACE. Hammond,
Ind.: W.B. Conkey, 1913 NUC.

Misunderstanding and mystery, involving a ruby
necklace and a drowned child. PW 84:2176.

MEYER, ANNIE (NATHAN). 1867-1951. United States.

008394   HELEN BRENT, M.D.: A SOCIAL STUDY
[ANONYMOUS]. New York: Cassell, [c1892] NUC. London
and New York: Gay and Bird, 1893 BMC.

CR 7-16-92 p 30. She loves a lawyer, but he cannot
reconcile her public life with his private
requirements. She refuses to give up her career for
marriage. He marries someone else who finally runs
away because she is tired of his neglect of her for
his career.
LW 23:198. She becomes head of a Hospital and College
for Women. By end of story Harold sees the fallacy of
his reasoning.

008395   ROBERT ANNYS: POOR PRIEST. A TALE OF THE
GREAT UPRISING. New York and London: Macmillan, 1901
NUC BMC.

Rose is a woman of passion who loves love and power;
Mathilda is a woman of affection. Rose is "sex
incarnate, vital;" She thrills responsively to passion
whenever she finds it. BKM 13:576-8.
ATH 6-22-01; BOOK BUYER 1902. NYT

MEYER, LUCY JANE (RIDER). 1849-1922. United States.

008396   DEACONESS STORIES. Chicago: Hope, [c1900]
NUC.

008397   MARY NORTH. A NOVEL. New York: F.H.
Revell, [c1903] NUC BMC.

Romantic young woman deluded into a bogus marriage.
Soon disillusioned, she leaves him and moves to
Chicago. LBKM 6-03:116.
A sham marriage, awakening, heroine's misery, escape;
struggle of earlier lover to find her. ATH 122:282.

MEYER, NICO BECH. United States.

008398   A STORY FROM PULLMANTOWN. Chicago: C H.

Kerr, 1894 NUC.

MEYNELL, VIOLA. See DALLYN, VIOLA (MEYNELL).

MEYRICK, DIANA.

008399   PEACE ALLEY. London: Sidgwick and
Jackson, 1910 BMC.

TLS-Village of sweet old maids but too much love
interest.

008400   PHYLLIS AND FELICITY. London: Sidgwick
and Jackson, 1911 BMC.

Two stepsisters get to know each other after they are
grown up. The story ends with their marriages. TLS
Close understanding after youth is past ATH

MICHAELIS, KARIN. See STANGELAND, KATHARINA MARIE BECH
(BRONDUM) MICHAELIS.

MICHAELS, JANIE CHASE. United States.

008401   A NATURAL SEQUENCE: A STORY OF PHOENIX,
ARIZONA. Bangor, Maine: C. H. Glass, 1895 NUC.

MICHELL, SYBIL C.

008402   INGA OF MORDANGER. London: J. Ouseley,
[1910] BMC.

TLS simple Norwegian girl comes to Eng. as companion,
decoyed into bad mrg, gets back to Norway and old
lover.

MICHELSON, MIRIAM. 1870-1942. United States.

008403   ANTHONY OVERMAN. London and New York:
Doubleday, Page, 1906 BMC NUC.

BKM 24 1906-7--focus on woman reporter, reviewer
doesn't like her.
PW-heroine is "keen, alert, self reliant, brilliant,
up-to-date". "yields to her great love for socialist
hero's fine character but he tells her she will only
take her place in his great scheme for a better
world."
NYT-Male reviewer doesn't like her-she is a "woman
after all," giving up her yellow journalism (making
ruthless copy out of people) and editorship of large
paper to "marry her hopelessly unworldly altruist"?

008404   IN THE BISHOP'S CARRIAGE. Indianapolis:
Bobbs-Merrill, [1904] NUC BMC. London: A. Constable,
1904 BMC.

BKM 19 1904--female "Raffles"-thief, confidence woman,
goes straight (mostly), becomes an actress.

008405   THE MADIGANS. New York: Century, 1904 BMC
NUC.

PW story of family life, maiden aunt.
NYT-family of six girls, father wanted a son.

008406   MICHAEL THWAITE'S WIFE. New York:
Doubleday, Page, 1909 NUC.

BKM v. 30 1909-10 twins-one substitutes as wife for
another.
Twin women, so different Tess and Trix one deserts
husband for man involved in good works; when she dies,
sister takes her place as wife of original husband now
almost blind. PW 6-12-09
As children, changed names and personalities for a day
Trix, brilliant, selfish; Tess good. Tess thrust into
posing as wife of sister's husband. She really loves
the man. Happiness comes to her. BKM
"Involuntary deception of a husband by substitution of
his wife's twin sister for the wife herself-" does it
to save her sister's good name. Set in NYC. BKM

008407   A YELLOW JOURNALIST. New York: D.
Appleton, 1905 NUC BMC.

Woman star reporter; love story peripheral
review BKM 22 (1905) 373-4

MIDDLEMASS, JEAN. United Kingdom.

008408   AT THE ALTAR STEPS. London: Digby, Long,
1910 BMC.

TLS-ordinary love story.

008409   BLANCHE CONINGHAM'S SURRENDER. London: F. V. White, 1898 BMC.

ACAD 53:229. Central character is a vengeful moneylender, surrounded by aristocrats. ATH 111:401. Blanche, widow with son, marries a villain who sends boy to a school where he dies. Eventually husband dies and Blanche marries right man.

008410   CLAUDE AND MAUDE. London: Henry, [1893] BMC.

008411   COUNT REMINY. London: J. Long, 1905 BMC.

Sensational mystery. TLS 1905:52

008412   AN EVIL ANGEL. London: Digby, Long, 1908 BMC.

TLS-Conventional type explaining murder of Lord Vessey on his wedding day.

008413   THE FALKNERS OF GREENHURST. London: Digby, Long, 1904 BMC.

008414   FALLEN FROM FAVOR. London: Digby, Long, 1902 BMC.

ATH 2-1-1902

008415   A FELON'S DAUGHTER. London: Digby, Long, 1906 BMC.

TLS-Mild little tale.

008416   HIS LAWFUL WIFE. London: Digby, Long, 1901 BMC.

ATH 8-17-01

008417   HOW I BECAME EMINENT. London: Eden, Remington, 1892 BMC.

ACAD 42:455. "Considerable element of burlesque." Harry gives up large income for glories of the stage, "becomes a leading star in the provinces," is exploited by an American.

008418   HUSH MONEY. London: Digby, Long, [1895] BMC.

008419   IN STORM AND STRIFE: A NOVEL. London: Digby, Long, 1899 BMC.

Sir George Godfrey resolved to marry his rustic sweetheart before he was 21. Some villains, a cousin and heir presumptive, a diamond robbery, an abduction. SP 82:94

008420   LOVES OLD AND NEW. London: Digby, Long, 1908 BMC.

TLS Murd myst, female hero

008421   MIGNON'S PERIL. London: Digby Long, 1909 BMC.

Mystery TLS

008422   THE MYSTERIOUS MRS. NUTFORD. London: [Aldine Masterpieces Of Modern Fiction], [1896] BMC.

008423   THE MYSTERY OF CLEMENT DUNRAVEN; A NOVEL. London: Digby, Long, [1894] BMC NUC.

SP 72:119. Baronet, a villain, but viewed sympathetically by wife and other characters through bigamy, murder, and letting his father-in-law stand trial because his own feelings are too fine. He feels duty driven to do certain unpleasant things. ACAD 46:27.

008424   THE QUEEN WASP. London: Digby, Long, 1900 BMC.

ATH 115:714. Lives of business people in the city. The fortunes and affections of some anxious females are involved in the operations and conduct of these businessmen.

008425   RUTH ANSTEY. London: Digby, Long, 1904 BMC.

008426   SHE'S FOOLING THEE! London: Aldine Masterpieces Of Modern Fiction, [1895] BMC.

008427   A VENEERED SCAMP. London: J. Long, 1906 BMC.

TLS-Sensational novel, mur.
ATH-Sensational novel, mur.

008428   VENGEANCE IS MINE; A NOVEL. London: Aldine Masterpieces Of Modern Fiction, [1895] BMC.

008429   A WHEEL OF FIRE. London: Digby, Long, 1901 BMC.

ATH 2-16-01

008430   A WOMAN'S CALVARY. London: Digby, Long, 1903 BMC.

ATH 121:651

008431   THE YELLOW BADGE. London: Digby, Long, 1899 BMC.

Susie Maclaren sets out to convert an aggressive criminal type of man, Bill Rees. Also the fortunes of Jack Gillespie unjustly accused of a crime and consequently disinherited. ATH 114:797 SP-modern, ex-convicts, "works," and love affairs.

MIDDLETON, JESSIE ADELAIDE.

008432   ANOTHER GREY GHOST BOOK, WITH A CHAPTER ON PROPHETIC DREAMS AND A NOTE ON VAMPIRES. London: E. Nash, 1914 BMC NUC.

008433   THE GREY GHOST BOOK. London: E. Nash, 1912 NUC BMC.

008434   THE WHITE GHOST BOOK. London and New York: Cassell, 1916 BMC [] NUC.

MIDGLEY, MRS. LLEWELLYN.   United Kingdom.

008435   THE UNCONSCIOUS QUEST. BY F. REID MATHESON. London and Toronto: Sidgwick and Jackson, 1913 NUC BMC.

widow doesn't know her own mind. NYT Dorothea widowed after 20 years of marriage is 40ish. travels, falls in love with a young man (he could be her son) "amiable, silly old woman" Another presents her as a strong soul reasserting her individuality at end returns home, forgets the young man as easily as she had her husband. TLS

008436   THE WORLD'S VOICES. BY E. REID MATHESON. London: Sisley, [1908] BMC.

nun leaves convent, almost penniless becomes nurse. TLS

MIGHELS, ELLA STERLING (CLARK). 1853-1934. United States.

008437   THE FULL GLORY OF DIANTHA. BY MRS. PHILIP VERRILL MIGHELS. Chicago: Forbes, 1909 NUC.

Bookkeeper, strong, healthy, wants an innocent "unsullied man", rejects suitors, moves west to find her man. PW 5-15-09 Returns to one she rejected BKM Idea that love does not equal compatibility in marriage. NYT

MIGHELS, MRS. PHILIP VERRILL. See MIGHELS, ELLA STERLING (CLARK).

MIGNON, pseud. See BASELEY, MRS.

MIKOULITCH, V., pseud. See VESELITSKAIA, LIDIIA IVANOVNA.

MILBURN, LUCY MACDOWELL.

008438   LOST LETTERS FROM LESBOS. Chicago: R. R. Donnelly, 1902 NUC.

"Sappho's" prose love letters to an Egyptian prince presented as real-mostly concern Greece and her reading. NYT 1903:21

MILECETE, HELEN. Nationality Unknown.

008439   A DETACHED PIRATE; THE ROMANCE OF GAY VANDELEUR. London: Greening, 1900 BMC. Boston: Little, Brown, 1903 NUC.

Divorce and reconciliation. Gay is the heroine 6-6-03 PW

For a while a gay divorcee, husband learns he accused
her wrongly, they reunite in spite of the fact that
she was engaged to another in the interim and has
several risque adventures and a stay with the circus
as a bareback rider. NYT 03 369
SR 90:691. Gay is married to Colonel Gore, divorces
him, has adventures. Told in a series of letters from
Gay to a friend. Title is not so mystifying as
character of the rebellious heroine. Could not stand
dull routine of domestic life.
ATH 116:790. After her divorce she seeks shores of a
new continent, uses her maiden name. Actually she
still loves husband, and eventually friend succeeds in
reunion. Husband stern yet devoted.
Gay found mrg. to Colonel Gore dull and "playing the
part of a woman so cumbersome to my development (I am
quoting the new woman's jargon now) that I decided to
be a man." (Book)

008440   A GIRL OF THE NORTH; A STORY OF LONDON
AND CANADA. London: Greening, 1900 NUC BMC.

SP Mrs. Phillips tries experiments with (her) conjugal
relations in order to avoid the monotony of married
life.
SR 89:625. Author's "blase youthfulness, and weariness
of mere domestic joys." "Lame protest against
convention in the relation of men and women."
ACAD 58:410. Laura Archer, Canadian, rich. Trip to
London. Canadian lover. She is part French, English,
and Indian.

MILECETE, HELEN, jt. au. See JONES, SUSAN CARLETON AND
HELEN MILECETE.

MILES, EMMA (BELL). 1879-1919.

008441   THE SPIRIT OF THE MOUNTAINS. New York: J.
Pott, 1905 NUC.

Mountaineer's lives. PW 11-18-05

MILLARD, SARAH M. United States.

008442   M. OF B. [ANONYMOUS]. Council Bluffs,
Iowa: S. M. Millard, [c1893] NUC.

MILLER, ADDIE LETTIE (PECK). B. 1867. United States.

008443   LETTIE; OR THE WHIRLWIND'S CAPER.
Naugatuck, Conn.: The Author, 1916 NUC.

Lettie leaves her husband on their wedding day. Story
follows her career of independence to their
reconcilation.

MILLER, ALICE (DUER). 1874-1942. United States.

008444   THE BEAUTY AND THE BOLSHEVIST. New York
and London: Harper, [c1920] BMC NUC.

PW-Comedy, clash between her capitalist father and
radical young editor.

008445   THE BLUE ARCH. New York: Scribner's
Sons., 1910 NUC.

"Heroine is an astronomer, and devotes herself to her
work against the wishes of her family. She is
unconventional also in that she does fully half of the
wooing herself. But whatever she does is done quite
simply and without bravado, and her gentle candor
cannot fail to charm." FRANKLIN.
Nina Sinnott finishes college-wants to devote life to
astronomy. Her family oppose her, but she persists in
her ambition. Becomes secretary to a brilliant
astronomer, a college teacher.-- PW

008446   THE BURGLAR AND THE BLIZZARD; A CHRISTMAS
STORY. New York: Hearst's Internat'l Lib., [c1914]
NUC.

PW 86 12/5/14:1894 The burglar plus his innocent
sister and a young millionaire are captured by a
blizzard and held in a countryhouse. Here they spend
the xmas holiday, while romance and justice accomplish
their separate ends.

008447   CALDERON'S PRISONER. New York: C.
Scribner's Sons, 1903 NUC.

Two up-to-date society novelettes.
1. Young woman restless with a persistent love, bored
with New York travels to South America, gets involved
in a revolution, taken prisoner. 2. Falls out of love
with husband; they argue and separate over issue of

how much freedom a husband should have. He dies in
shipwreck, remaries? NYT 03, 927
Contents-Calderon's prisoner-Cyril Vane's wife.

008448   THE CHARM SCHOOL. New York and London:
Harper, [c1919] BMC NUC.

Humorous man of 25 inherits a fashionable school for
girls and tries to run it. A 17 yr old girl takes over
and teaches him something he didn't know.PW
He Changes curriculum convinced the girls need to
learn fascination; Not scholarship. BKM Nov-Dec 1919.
TLS-He runs school on lines of producing charming
mrgble women and theory that if a student were to fall
in love with him he would sublimate this into love of
their work. which he considers unlikely.
LBKM-Run not as an intro to a college career. Austin,
possessing the "most extraordinary beauty," has
complications.

008449   COME OUT OF THE KITCHEN! A ROMANCE.
London: Hodder & Stoughton, [1916] BMC. New York:
Century, 1916 BMC NUC.

Well-to-do American rents a country house: his
servants behave in surprising ways.--TLS
Man buys a house, employs the servants already there.
They are a mysterious crew and the man learns the
secret to profit by it. PW
NYT He is from North, he rents an old dilapidated
Southern mansion, brings his lawyer, his hopefully
future mother in law and her daughter.
BKM-The owners are the servants, go along with the
farce in order to rent the house. He falls in love
with Jane-Ellen the cook.

008450   THE HAPPIEST TIME OF THEIR LIVES. New
York: Century, 1918 BMC NUC. London: Hodder &
Stoughton, [1919] BMC.

PW-Mother and girl friend scheme to marry Mathilde
properly.
NYT May 19, 1918, p. 231. Satire, contrasting types of
women, examination of the question of women's
relationship to men and to society.
Records the simultaneous love affairs of three
generations to show that real love can occur at any
stage of maturity.--TLS

C08451   LADIES MUST LIVE. New York: Century, 1917
BMC NUC.

Nancy Almer, marries; but enjoys capturing other men.
Christine Fenimer single has same pleasure but she's
poor while Nancy is married to a rich man. Contest
between them over a rich man. Christine gets him and
even tho he loses his money, keeps him. PW
Rivalry of two woman for rich man
SP-Ladies represented as pursuing young men without
regard to either morality or reticence.

008452   LESS THAN KIN. New York: H. Holt, 1909
NUC.

Ingenious love story mistaken identity PW 6-12-09
Focuses upon a man BKM
Focuses upon a man NYT

008453   THE MODERN OBSTACLE. New York: Scribner's
Sons, 1903 NUC. London: G.P. Putnam's Sons, 1904 BMC.

Worldly, scintillating heroine, must have money (the
obstacle) yet hates the crude ambition of marrying
wealth; rejects love to marry wealth, on night of
betrothal writes to her love. Author shows all this as
a kind of modern enslavement. NYT
Lack of money in marriage and how love overcomes it.
PW 5-9-03

008454   THINGS. New York: C. Scribner's Sons,
1914 NUC.

PW 85 5/2/14 p. 1446--"Mrs. Royce, a devoted mother
with great executive ability, manages her household
and family so completely that unconsciously she keeps
everyone at a nervous tension which reacts unfavorably
upon their health. Thinking that her young daughter is
overwrought, she consults a nerve specialist, who
after carefully observing the girl and other members
of the household, advises Mrs. Royce to go away and
leave them alone for a while as she is really the
cause of the overstrain noticeable in them all. Upon
her return she finds them all very well and happy but
glad to see her, and she realizes that "things," not
ideas, have filled her life and occupied her mind."

MILLER, ANNIE (JENNESS). B. 1859. United States.

008455   THE PHILOSOPHER OF DRIFTWOOD: A NOVEL. BY
MRS. JENNESS MILLER. Washington, D.C.: Jenness Miller
Publications, 1897 NUC.

A daughter learns to understand why her mother
divorced her father when she herself has to break her
engagement to one man because she really loves someone
else.

MILLER, ELIZABETH (YORK). United States.

008456   THE BLUE AURA. New York: E.J. Clode,
[c1917] NUC.

Dora Trelawney toe dancer, starving; marries manager
of vaudeville group in London; many complications
before she makes a resolution. PW
Chorus girl-"a fierce little rowdy alley cat prowling
after a bone"; "the author dislikes her own heroine."
PW
Turco, male clown, is another character. NYT

008457   BRIDE OF AN HOUR. London: D.C. Thomson,
[1920] BMC.

008458   THE FORBIDDEN SACRIFICE. London: Simpkin,
Marshall, [1916] BMC NUC.

Wife adopts a most questionable line of conduct to
save husband threatened by TB. SP
TLS-borrows money from former lover for operation.

008459   HIS FORBIDDEN WIFE. London: D.C. Thomson,
[1920] BMC.

MILLER, EMILY CLARK (HUNTINGTON). 1833-1913. United
States.

008460   THE KING'S MESSENGERS. New York: Hunt and
Eaton, 1891 NUC.

Title refers to group of boys, a club formed by
Richard Halford to carry out the idea of duty to Lord
Jesus. PW 10-24-91.

MILLER, ESTHER. United Kingdom.

008461   A BLOSSOM IN THE WILDERNESS. London:
Hodder and Stoughton, 1912 BMC.

008462   CASSERLEY'S WIFE. London: S. Paul, 1913
BMC.

Lord Casserly marries his fiance's sister in mistake
for his fiance who was thought by her sister to be
dead. The sister shows up. ATH TLS

008463   THE FORTUNE-TELLER. London: Hodder &
Stoughton, [1911] BMC.

008464   KIND HEARTS ARE MORE THAN CORONETS.
London: Hodder & Stoughton, [1911] BMC.

008465   LIVING LIES. London: Methuen, 1907 BMC.

Man lets another "take the rap"; his wife and sister
know he's guilty. ACAD TLS ATH

008466   THE MOTH AND THE STAR. London: Hodder &
Stoughton, [1911] BMC.

008467   THE MYSTERY OF BLACKWATER GRANGE. London:
Hodder & Stoughton, 1912 BMC.

008468   A PROPHET OF THE REAL. New York: J.F.
Taylor, 1902 NUC. London: W. Heinemann, 1902 BMC.

ATH 2-15-02

008469   ROSABEL. Philadelphia: J.B. Lippincott,
1904 NUC. London: W. Heinemann, 1904 BMC.

NYT Hatred between mother & daughter who contest for
same man.

008470   SHOULD SHE HAVE SPOKEN? London: Ward,
Lock, [1900] BMC.

SP 85:54. Heroine on wedding eve finds out there is a
first wife. She is subsequently murdered and heroine
suspects her husband. He is innocent and his marriage
to 1st wife was bigamous.

008471   THE SPORT OF THE GODS. London: A. D.

Innes, 1897 BMC.

Detective. SR 84:46
Turns on idea that wife can't testify against husband.
For a long time they are separated, she thinking he's
guilty. Then a new witness shows up. ATH 109:178

008472   THE ST. CADIX CASE. London: Innes, 1898
BMC.

LIT 3:87.
ACAD 53:521. Heroine's lover is murdered on the day he
marries her.
ATH 111:786. Romance and happy ending.
SR 86:53. She is tried for his murder, acquitted,
marries a doctor.

008473   A VENDETTA IN VANITY FAIR. London: W.
Heinemann, 1905 BMC NUC.

ATH-Two fashionable rivals (female) try to "best" one
another.

008474   WHEN THE HEART IS YOUNG. London: Hodder &
Stoughton, [1911] BMC.

008475   WILLOWWOOD. London: Harper, 1899 BMC.

Wicked woman ruins two men. Frances Deltry punished at
the end. A second plot concerns an agnostic's
conversion. LIT 5:233
Her husband disfigured by an explosion in S. Africa.
Wife upset; he suggests she take a trip. Meets a man
she loves, carries on, says she's a widow, doesn't
change her name, marries the guy. Her first husband
runs into her and her new husband at a party, shoots
self. Consadine breaks with her. Apparently this is
all the punishment she gets. LBKM 16:140

008476   THE WOMAN WINS. London: ["Daily Mail],
[1911] BMC.

MILLER, HARRIET (MANN). 1831-1918.

008477   WHAT HAPPENED TO BARBARA. BY OLIVE THORNE
MILLER. Boston: Houghton, Mifflin, 1907 NUC.

She's 14-17, Trials & Triumphs at school; becomes a
maid, helps to run a newspaper-finally "wins her
heart's desire." PW 5-11-07
"Unhappiness comes from her naughtiness." NYT

MILLER, IRENE. Nationality Unknown.

008478   SEKHET. London and New York: J. Lane,
1912 BMC NUC.

Evarne Stornway comes under influence of Egyptian
goddess when in Egypt. She is goddess of Love and
Cruelty. Evarne consents to live with her male
guardian. They part, she struggles in careers in
theatre and as a model, "with a very painful and
dramatic ending to her career." TLS
PW-final tragedy.
ACAD-Raised by her father in condition of pure
physical beauty as conceived by Greeks-no tight
clothes etc. Left at 16 to care of old vile friend who
helps her for several years and casts her off when
tired of her. Tries to make her way in London in
theatrical Co, as a needlewoman, finally an artist's
model. Terrible tragedy at end.
BKM -Evarne, who cannot live without love is finally
to marry Lord Winborough's nephew. Lord Winborough
turns out to be former lover who has cast her off; he
will tell nephew and prevent mrg; she murders him but
it turns out she has murdered nephew by error.
Successful artist's model; murderess BKM 35 (1912)
190-1
NYT Sekhet is an Egyptian goddess of love and cruelty.
Evarne goes mad at end.

MILLER, MARY ELIZA BAKEWELL (GAUNT). 1872-1942. Australia.

008479   DAVE'S SWEETHEART. London: E. Arnold,
1894 BMC NUC.

SR 78:331. He is a murderer, persuades her to marry
police captain to better himself. She deserts him
eventually for Dave and he does likewise eventually.
She dies of hunger and exposure. Australia.
SP 72:443. Stepmother of Jennie is "a woman of great
brilliance and force, almost pathetic from her
helplessness to cure the the the evils against which she
is studying."

008480   DEADMAN'S. London: Methuen, 1898 BMC. New

York: New Amsterdam Book Co., [1898?] NUC.

LIT 3:606. Hero, tragedy bestowed by advice of
platonic friend.
ACAD 54:295. Deadman's was a camp where human nature
was rough, elemental, profane. A colonial novel.
SR 86:513. Marriage of young man to girl of low birth
whom he believes he has ruined. He doesn't want to
marry, but the woman he loves platonically has a
morality which absolutely requires it. Then he falls
really in love with someone else. But his wife was
already married to a convict, so all works out.
Australian gold fields. Centers on love between a
married man, commissioner of the field and a young
woman, Wenny. LW 30:140.

008481   EVERY MAN'S DESIRE. BY MARY GAUNT.
London: T. W. Laurie, [1913] BMC NUC.

West coast of Africa; two ill-matched couples. ACAD
England's burden of "ruling Africa" is harder to bear
since women arrived SR

008482   KIRKHAM'S FIND. London: Methuen, 1897 BMC
NUC.

Phoebe; the fight with "black-fellows" SR 84:475.
Aust. Phoebe Marsden wants to be ind. keeps bees.
Includes much of Aust. life, search for gold, fights
with the aborigines. ACAD 52 Fic Sup: 61.

008483   THE MOVING FINGER. BY MARY GAUNT. London:
Methuen, 1895 BMC NUC.

Blood curdling Aust. story of the blackest crimes and
the grandest heroism. ATH 106:382

008484   THE MUMMY MOVES. BY MARY GAUNT. London:
T. W. Laurie, [1910] BMC. New York: E. J. Clode,
[c1925] NUC.

TLS--Murd. myst.
ACAD-- murd. myst.

008485   THE UNCOUNTED COST. BY MARY GAUNT. New
York: E. J. Clode, [1910] NUC. London: T. W. Laurie,
1910 BMC.

Heroine is a novelist who believes in trial marr.
Learns to her grief that her theory is unworkable (?)
PW
TLS-Two heroines, Anne lives with Bullen 2 yrs and he
does not think experiment successful. Kitty married
woman thinks virtue is dull and is, quoting her
"playing at half a love with half a lover." They all
have adventures in Africa.
ACAD-They are besieged by Blacks. Capt. Bullen is
killed by one who was educated at Oxford and whom he
had flogged. Cunningham, formerly in love with marr.
woman falls for Anne, her cousin.
NYT 0
Story seems to center on a male char. Cunningham but
has two female chars. Mrs. Pearce who has a serious
flirtation with this man while her husband is away and
Anne, Mrs Pearce's friend who is a successful novelist
"always yearning for new experiences."

008486   A WIND FROM THE WILDERNESS. BY MARY
GAUNT. London: T. W. Laurie, [1919] BMC NUC.

Stella Chapman-disaster upon disaster follows her.
Author allows the various chapters to be told by diff.
chars. TLS
In China and Tibet "A self-possessed and attractive
young doctor in Yang Ching" Stella is the dr. SP
China in early days of war; missionary compound.
Rosalie Grabme D does not profess to be a Christian;
is there to heal bodies. She describes the poverty and
suffering. An uprising, wanderings in Tibet, three
left two women and a man struggle on through Arctic
wastes; unhappy end. LBKM
SR Two people, Tibet etc.

MILLER, MINNIE (WILLIS) BAINES. B. 1845. United States.

008487   HIS COUSIN, THE DOCTOR: A STORY. BY
MINNIE WILLIS BAINES. Cincinnati: Cranston and Stowe,
1891 NUC.

Anti-Christian Science love story. PW
It's his cousin Sadie that he finds on his return to
town. She's now Dr. Sarah Katherine Spencer, a
professional of the healing art after the doctrines of
Christian Science. LW

008488   MRS. CHERRY'S SISTER; OR, CHRISTIAN

SCIENCE AT FAIRFAX. Cincinnati: Jennings and Pye,
[c1900] NUC.

MILLER, MRS. JENNESS. See MILLER, ANNIE (JENNESS).

MILLER, OLIVE THORNE, pseud. See MILLER, HARRIET (MANN).

MILLER, SARA.

008489   UNDER THE EAGLE'S WING. Philadelphia:
Jewish Publication Soc. of America, 1899 BMC NUC.

NYT 1900:163 Listed under fiction 229 pp.

MILLIN, SARAH GERTRUDE (LIEBSON). 1889-1968. South Africa.

008490   THE DARK RIVER. London: W. Collins' Sons,
1919 BMC NUC. New York: T. Seltzer, 1920 NUC.

TLS: John marries Black woman in S. Africa and has 4
children; then without mentioning it marries Hester.
Story of Hester, Alma & Ruth, three sisters. Love,
romance.
ATH: Story is really of Alma who seemed so made for
life & somehow just missed it, until nothing was left
for her but Van Reede
SR:Turns on relation between white male and native
woman.
PW-6 characters 3 men & 3 women and their sombre
testing. No hero or heroine, no romance. Style is
combination of Hardy, James & Hauptmann.

MILLS, DOROTHY RACHEL MELISSA (WALPOLE). B. 1889. United
Kingdom.

008491   CARD HOUSES. London: E. Mills, 1916 BMC.

008492   THE LAUGHTER OF FOOLS. London: Duckworth,
[1920] BMC NUC.

TLS-Louise becomes a widow after an earlier elopement,
returns to London. Then a vivid picture of all the
paraphenalia of the latest decadence-drugs, alcohol;
Black masses, orgies, Lurid but a social document of
the times (1916-20).

MILLS, ESTELLA J. Nationality Unknown.

008493   STORM-SWEPT; OR, SAVED TO SERVE. Boston:
J. H. Earle, 1897 NUC.

MILLS, JANE DEARBORN. United States.

008494   THE MOTHER-ARTIST. BY JANE DEARBORN MILLS
(MRS. JAMES E. MILLS). Boston: Palmer, 1904 NUC.

MILLS, MRS. JAMES E. See MILLS, JANE DEARBORN.

MILLS, THEODORA FLOWER.

008495   HANDS OF HEALING; AN IDYLL. Bristol: J.W.
Arrowsmith, 1914 BMC.

ATH-Woman broken by sorrow finds happiness and romance
in her garden.

MILMAN, HELEN. See CROFTON, HELEN ROSE ANNE (MILMAN).

MILN, LOUISE (JORDAN). 1864-1933. United States.

008496   AN ACTOR'S WOOING: BEING THE CONFESSIONS
OF A CHAPERON. London: Osgood, McIlvaine, [1896] NUC
BMC.

008497   THE FEAST OF LANTERNS. London: Hodder &
Stoughton, [1920] BMC. New York: F. A. Stokes, [c1920]
NUC.

TLS-First half describes life and family of Chinese
grande dame.
Second half describes descendant Tien Tzu's trip to
England.
SP-

008498   HUMPTY-DUMPTY: THE STORY OF TWO MEN WHO
RODE STRAIGHT. London: Hodder & Stoughton, [1919] BMC.

Based on the comedy by Horace Annesby Vachell.

008499   THE INVISIBLE FOE; A STORY ADOPTED FROM
THE PLAY BY WALTER HACKETT. BY LOUISE JORDAN MILN
(MRS. GEORGE CRICHTON MILN). London: Jarrolds, [1918]
BMC. New York: F. A. Stokes, [c1920] NUC.

ATH-nothing here.
NYT 7/18/20 p 29. Romance, with hero unjustly accused

of embezzlement. Also heroine and her father have psychic powers, he communicates truth to her after his death.

008500   MR. WU. BY LOUISE JORDAN MILN (MRS. GEORGE CRICHTON MILN). New York: A. L. Burt, [c1918] NUC. London: Cassell, 1918 BMC.

Based on the play by H. M. Vernon and H. Owne. China-Fic.

008501   THE PURPLE MASK; ADAPTED FROM THE PLAY "LE CHEVALIER AU MASQUE" OF MM. PAUL ARMONT AND JEAN MANOUSSI. New York: F. A. Stokes, [c1918] NUC. London: Hodder & Stoughton, [1918] BMC.

Adapted from play "le Chevalier au Masque" of M. M. Paul Armont and Jean Manoussi.

008502   "WERE MAN BUT CONSTANT". London: Jarrolds, [1918] BMC.

TLS-Pursuit of money
ATH-Portrait of predatory men.

008503   A WOMAN AND HER TALENT. London: W. Blackwood, 1905 BMC.

Ugly scenes and painful pictures-of how the wheels of domesticity go round in times of storm and stress. Helen goes to Vassar, marries, suffers a "torrent of mud". At Vassar she astonished her profs with her brilliance, was encouraged to pursue her studies chose marriage. All goes well till husband realizes she can write better than he. Helen becomes famous, supports the family while her husband wastes money. Husband wrecks the home, their son. Very sordid arguments betweem them. ACAD. 664,05
Talented girl at Vassar, a genius. Professors eager to study with her. also a talent of loving "biggest sort of intellect" writes well, talked well, a moving influence. Bad marriage distressing deterioration of a husband; deserts her. LBKM 27-8,173
About Amer College life. ATH 0 747, 05

MILN, MRS. GEORGE CRICHTON. See MILN, LOUISE (JORDAN).

MILTON, GLADYS ALEXANDRA.

008504   THE HOOFSLIDE. BY ANTHONY CARLYLE. London: Mills and Boon, 1920 BMC.

MINER, LUELLA. 1861-1935.

008505   TWO HEROES OF CATHAY; AN AUTOBIOGRAPHY AND A SKETCH. New York: F. H. Revell, [c1903] NUC.

MINIKEN, BERTHA M. M.

008506   AN ENGLISH WIFE. London: Digby, Long, [1896] BMC.

008507   MARJORIE'S MISTAKE. Edinburgh: G.A. Morton, 1905 BMC.

Sentimental old-type story TLS 1905:163.

008508   THROUGH LIFE'S ROUGH WAY. London: Digby, Long, 1900 BMC.

MINITER, EDITH MAY (DOWE). B. 1869. United States.

008509   OUR NATUPSKI NEIGHBORS. New York: H. Holt, 1916 NUC.

"Polish immigrant family. Father a tyrant drives his family, starves them; some die; his recreation-to beat his wife and children. Several of the children did well-one went to Harvard, another became a teacher. Document of Polish immigrants in N.E. NYT Contrast between immigrants and native born inhabitants of New England town. PW 90:1357 10-21-16 NYT Contrast between immigrants & native born inhabitants of New England town.

MINNETT, CORA.

008510   THE DAY AFTER TO-MORROW. London: F. V. White, 1911 BMC.

Tale of 1975, aviation is universal. America is a monarchy. "immense benefits have followed from the political equality of woman." Heroine is a great Parliamentary leader and orator. On eve of being appointed governor-General of Australia she proved to be a murderess. Goes off scene exclaiming that if the

man she loved were damned "and I could join him in any hell where he would love me, it would be heaven." TLS

008511   THE GIRDLE OF KAF. London: W. J. Ham-Smith, 1912 BMC.

ATH--Message from spirit world to widow.
TLS--message from spirit world to widow.

008512   THE MODEL MILLIONAIRE. London: W. J. Ham-Smith, 1911 BMC.

A young idealist gets a fortune to carry out his philanthropic scheme. TLS

MINOGUE, ANNA CATHERINE. B. 1874. United States.

008513   CARDOME: A ROMANCE OF KENTUCKY. New York: P.F. Collier, [c1904] NUC.

Civil war story. PW 4-15-05

008514   THE WATERS OF CONTRADICTION. New York: P.J. Kenedy, [c1912] NUC.

MIRRLEES, HOPE.

008515   MADELAINE, ONE OF LOVE'S JANSENISTS. London: W. Collins Sons, 1919 BMC.

Set in mid-17th cent. France intense feelings of this young woman of unusual temperament-ardent, instinctive subtle. intelligent. She's obsessed with growing up to be an intimate friend of Madamoaselle de Scudery. When she finally does meet her, she's disillusioned, disappointed. TLS
"Madeline apes Mlle de Scudery with the devoted folly of youth until she is completely divorced from reality." BAKER 32 345

MITCHELL, AGNES C.

008516   A BOND OF BLOOD. London: J. Leng, [1920] BMC.

008517   A BRIDE BETRAYED. London: J. Leng, [1920] BMC.

008518   THE SPINNING OF FATE. London: Cassell, 1907 BMC.

Mother, 2 sons and daughter but centers on son. TLS. Three type of womanhood.

MITCHELL, ELIZABETH HARCOURT (ROLLS).

008519   THE KING'S STIRRUP: A TALE OF THE FOREST. London: Christian Knowledge Society, [1896] BMC NUC.

NYT 1898:416. Story of a dog and his master in the days of King William. Also a romance and religious sent.

MITCHELL, FRANCES MARIAN. United States.

008520   JOAN OF RAINBOW SPRINGS. Boston: Lothrop, Lee & Shepard, [1911] NUC.

11 yr. old waif makes "high talk" about the Bible, Christian Science. She has a grand vocabulary tho she says she hasn't read very extensively. NYT

MITTON, G. E. See SCOTT, GERALDINE EDITH (MITTON).

MIX, JENNIE IRENE. United States.

008521   AT FAME'S GATEWAY; THE ROMANCE OF A PIANISTE. New York: H. Holt, 1920 NUC.

PW-Girl from oil town comes to New York for musical fame.
NYT 1920: 321. She is a musical prodigy. Usual love interest and traditional ending, but story is more about her music, and her teacher, Anton Brandt.

MOBERLY, CHARLOTTE ANNE ELIZABETH AND ELEANOR FRANCES JOURDAIN.

008522   AN ADVENTURE. BY ELIZABETH MORISON AND FRANCES LAMONT. London: Macmillan, 1911 BMC. New York: Macmillan, 1911 NUC.

Two English ladies see apparition of Marie Antoinette. PW 5-20-11.

MOBERLY, L. G. See MOBERLY, LUCY GERTRUDE.

MOBERLY, LUCY GERTRUDE. B. 1860.

008523   AFTER LONG YEARS. London: Ward, Lock,
1915 BMC.

008524   ANGELA'S MARRIAGE. London: Ward, Lock,
1908 BMC.

TLS-obvious love-romance.

008525   CHRISTINA. London: ward, Lock, 1912 BMC.

ATH-O.

008526   CLEANSING FIRES. London: Ward, Lock, 1914
BMC.

ATH-2 heroines, 1 a hospital sister, the other
secretly married and widowed in 1st chapter.
TLS-romance.

008527   THE COST. London: Mills & Boon, 1911 BMC.

Story of a betrayed girl whose child is placed in a
sisterhood. ATH
Well-bred country girl betrayed by fellow-lodger in a
London boarding house. Ought she to tell a worthy man
of this if she meets one? Problem treated
conventionally (?) ATH

008528   DAN AND ANOTHER. London: Ward, Lock, 1907
BMC.

Edith's husband adopts her illegitimate child (one she
had before her marriage). Edith doesn't know who the
father of the child is. ACAD
Mrs. Edith Burnett is horribly bored. SR

008529   DIANA. London: Ward, Lock, 1907 BMC.

Fresh unsophisticated orphan's complications with
rival guardians. TLS

008530   FORTUNE'S FOUNDLING. London: Ward, Lock,
1911 BMC.

An infant heir stolen; an attempt to incarcerate the
mother in an asylum. ATH

008531   A GREAT PATIENCE. London: S.W. Partridge,
1902 BMC.

008532   HEART OF GOLD. BY L. G. MOBERLY. London:
Ward, Lock, 1911 BMC NUC.

Nancy Marchmere, factory girl with voice of gold,
becomes great diva. TLS

008533   THE HIGHWAY. London: Methuen, 1915 BMC.

The lot of the poor, duty of the rich; influence that
taught a rich and selfish heroine to think of others.
TLS
A woman's spiritual development. A wealthy young woman
reads a diary about suffering of poor person. ATH.

008534   HIS LITTLE GIRL. London: Ward, Lock, 1912
BMC.

TLS--Sens.

008535   HOPE, MY WIFE. London: Ward, Lock, 1906
BMC.

LBKM-man promises to marry a girl to take care of her.
She turns out to be unattractive and of an unsettling
temper. Happy ending.

008536   IN THE BALANCE. BY L. G. MOBERLY. London:
Ward, Lock, 1910 BMC NUC.

TLS-man told he has one year to live.

008537   JOY. London: Ward, Lock, 1910 BMC.

TLS-little girl deserted by her father eventually
regains her heritage from a false claimant.

008538   THE KEY OF GOLD. London: Ward, Lock, 1918
BMC.

TLS-is love.

008539   THE LITTLE OLD MAN WITH THE TIRED FACE.
Toronto: Warwick & Rutter, [1917] BMC.

008540   MAID MARJORY. London: Ward, Lock, 1916
BMC.

ATH--O.

008541   MAN AND WOMAN. London: Methuen, 1914 BMC.

ATH-heroine is 27 year old man-hater who is converted
on a trip to India.

008542   PHYLLIS. London: ward, Lock, 1911 BMC.

Phyllis' mother murdered her (Phyllis's) father and is
sentenced to 20 years in prison. Phyllis believes her
mother is innocent but there's the slow realization of
her mother's guilt. LBKM

008543   SECOND BESTS. A THING OF SHREDS AND
PATCHES. London: Mills & Boon, [1916] BMC.

TLS-love story?

008544   THE SIN OF ALISON DERING. London: Ward,
Lock, 1909 BMC.

Alison impersonates a young widow who died. She's
welcomed and accepted by the husband's relative;
sympathetically drawn. All turns out well. TLS
The disguise works well; she begins to fall in love
with husband thought dead. At end he returns. LBKM

008545   SUNSHINE ALL THE WAY. London: Ward, Lock,
1918 BMC.

TLS-sunny sent heroine.

008546   A TANGLED WEB. London: Ward, Lock, 1908
BMC.

TLS-interrupted wedding, mystery.
ATH-women who forget their marriages, etc.

008547   THAT PREPOSTEROUS WILL. London: Ward,
Lock, 1906 BMC.

TLS-will with a condition of marriage.

008548   UNTIL SEVENTY TIMES SEVEN. London: Ward,
Lock, 1913 BMC.

008549   VERE. London: Ward, Lock, 1920 BMC.

TLS-pretty rom.

008550   A VERY DOUBTFUL EXPERIMENT. London: Ward,
Lock, 1909 BMC.

Lady secretary inherits large fortune, convinces
scientist-boss to marry her. TLS

008551   VIOLET DUNSTAN. London: Ward, Lock, 1912
BMC.

008552   A WAIF OF DESTINY. London: Ward, Lock,
1910 BMC.

TLS-gentle heroine, mystery and crime. Sensational
exploits. Young woman of extraordinary vitality, made
to stay a night with an unknown corpse, is injured in
railroad collision, assumes identity of fellow
passenger who is killed, escapes a house by climbing
down a water pipe, is run over while hypnotized, twice
in hospital. She's a spy in the pay of a certain
foreign power. She possesses hypnotic powers. Everyone
resists this adventuress but one man.-- ACAD

008553   A WOMAN AGAINST THE WORLD. London: Ward,
Lock, 1909 BMC.

Margaret Merivale, penniless, takes position of
nurse-companion. Doesn't tell she's suspected of
murdering her husband 10 yrs earlier. She and Sir
Bayan become lovers (he has a mad wife; she's nurse
companion to his child.) Ends happily.--TLS

MOLESWORTH, MARY LOUISA (STEWART). B. 1842. United
Kingdom.

008554   THE BEWITCHED LAMP. London and Edinburgh:
W. and R. Chambers, 1891 BMC. London: 1891 NUC.

008555   THE GRIM HOUSE. BY MRS. MOLESWORTH.
London: J. Nisbet, 1899 NUC BMC.

008556   IMOGEN; OR ONLY EIGHTEEN. BY MRS.

MOLESWORTH. London: W. & R. Chambers, 1892 BMC. New York: T. Whittaker, [1892] NUC.

ATH 100:443. She is the victim of an ugly trick played by two girls.

008557   THE LAUREL WALK. London: Isbister, 1898 BMC. Philadelphia: D. Biddle, 1898 NUC.

ACAD 55:158. "A very pleasant story for young women who fancy home life is dull and want things to happen."

008558   LEONA. BY MRS. MOLESWORTH. London: Cassell, 1892 BMC. New York: Cassell, [c1892] NUC.

LEKM 3:29. Sentimental, hero is a soldier, "surface picture of sayings and doings of nice people." SP.
PW-"Study in the temperaments, motives, hopes trials and temptations of young girls." "a warning against interference on the part of good, well-meaning women in the heart histories of their girl relatives."

008559   MEG LANGHOLME; OR THE DAY AFTER TOMORROW. BY MRS. MOLESWORTH. London: W. and R. Chambers, 1897 NUC BMC. Philadelphia: J. B. Lippincott, 1897 NUC.

Pretty love story ends in marr. told by the bride. Includes the mysterious. And an abduction. SP 79:626. A will that says she must marry a certain man before he's 30 causes her to be abducted. PW 52:1101

008560   NURSE HEATHERDALE'S STORY. London: Macmillan, 1891 BMC NUC. New York and London: Macmillan, 1893 NUC. (Bound with Little Miss Peggy)

After one nurse deserts four children, this one takes over and lives with them for many years. She tells their stories. PW

008561   PHILIPPA. BY MRS. MOLESWORTH. Philadelphia: J. B. Lippincott, 1896 NUC. London: W. & R. Chambers, 1897 BMC.

Heroine acts as maid to her sister when that sister goes to visit rich relatives. This sham becomes an obsession to her, it plagues her. ACAD 51:146

008562   SHEILA'S MYSTERY. BY MRS. MOLESWORTH. London: Macmillan, 1895 BMC NUC.

Story for girls LW 26:217

008563   THE STORY OF A YEAR. BY MRS. MOLESWORTH. London: Macmillan, 1910 BMC NUC.

ACAD-wife and daughter fend for themselves due to loss of husband's fortune. Plucky she embroiders while he is in W. Indies.

008564   SWEET CONTENT. London: Griffith and Farran, 1891 BMC. New york: E. P. Dutton, [1891?] NUC.

008565   WHITE TURRETS. BY MRS. MOLESWORTH. New York: T. Whittaker, [1895] NUC. London: W. and R. Chambers, 1896 BMC NUC.

Miss Winifred Maryon hates domestic duties of running a large estate "wants to make herself of real use in the world". Becomes assistant secretary in charitable organization. Then supernatural is introduced. SP 75:529
"Intended as a warning to girls who turns their backs upon obvious duties to search for a career." ACAD 48:222

MOLESWORTH, MRS. See MOLESWORTH, MARY LOUISA (STEWART).

MOLYNEUX, ANNA MARY VIVIENNE.

008566   PRIEST OF ST. AGATHA'S. London: Sands, 1902 BMC.

MOLYNEUX, THERESA.

008567   THE DEFEAT OF AVARICE; A NOVEL. London: Digby, Long, [1898] BMC.

SR 86:217. Rev. couldn't finish it. Seems to be a love story, almost illiterate.

008568   A LADY'S CONFESSIONS. London: Digby, Long, [1897] BMC.

MONNIOT, MLLE. V. See MONNIOT, VICTORINE.

MONNIOT, VICTORINE. B. 1824.

008569   MADAME ROSELY. BY MLLE. V. MONNIOT. New York: Cassell, 1893 NUC. (Tr. Elvira Quintero and Jean Mack)

"A picture of Fr. domestic life of which little is seen in the usual French novel." Young French woman married to banker writes letters from Paris to mother in Marseilles. BOOK NEWS 130:460
Fr. Young woman marries older widow with two children. Story follows her life in letters to mother. Ends in a miracle, LW 93,193
By returning good for evil she wins over her step children and their grand mother. CR 20,23:69

MONROE, ANNE SHANNON. 1877-1945. United States.

008570   EUGENE NORTON: A TALE OF THE SAGEBRUSH LAND. Chicago: Rand, McNally, [c1900] NUC. London: A. E. Hubsch, [1900] BMC.

PW-young American singer returns home after her first triumph in Berlin and marries a man connected with mining interests to please her father. She departs for lonely life in West. Eugene, an MD full of noble ideals, heard her sing in Berlin and has followed her to U.S.

008571   HAPPY VALLEY; A STORY OF OREGON. Chicago: A.C. McClurg, 1916 NUC.

Regeneration of a male drinker-PW

008572   MAKING A BUSINESS WOMAN. New York: H. Holt, 1912 NUC.

Leaves country town, goes to Chicago to escape boredom and achieve independence. Built for success in the intricate ways of the business world. Likes the business world.--NYT
HF 5391 1. Woman-Employment 2. Business.
A young woman whose business assets are good sense, good health and the ability to use a typewriter goes to Chicago to earn her living, fiction.
PW-the story of the rise of a typist to success in the business world.

MONROE, HARRIET (EARHART). 1842-1926. United States.

008573   THE HEROINE OF THE MINING CAMP. Philadelphia: Lutheran Soc., [c1894] NUC.

PW Jennie in Colorado mining area, goes there to teach school. Also romance.

MONSELL, MARGARET EMMA FAITH (IRWIN). United Kingdom.

008574   COME OUT TO PLAY. A NOVEL. BY M. E. F. IRWIN. London: Constable, 1914 BMC. New York: G. H. Doran, [1915] NUC.

LBKM-Life story of a young man about town, truffles. Didn't take life seriously until it was too late.
ATH-Comedy culminating in nightmare.
TLS-suicide.

008575   HOW MANY MILES TO BABYLON? BY M. E. F. IRWIN. London: Constable, 1913 BMC NUC.

fairy-changeling-like heroine. Set in Cornwall and Ireland. wild elf like Irish girl, her struggles with conventions in which she wins and with love, in which she loses. ATH

008576   OUT OF THE HOUSE. BY M. E. F. IRWIN. London: Constable, 1916 BMC NUC. New York: Doran, [19--?] NUC.

Carolin Pomfret avoids an arranged marriage: a few days before the wedding she walks out of the house to meet Kalmeny. PW
London, story begins when she's five, orphaned, comes to live with aunts and cousins-all women. Their principal interests are whist and rereading family diaries (insanely proud of their family). Carolin sheltered. One event in her young life-the visit of Uncle Philip.
TLS-She is emancipated from Pomfrets by Irish violinist.

MONTAGU, LILIAN HELEN. 1874-1963.

008577   BROKEN STALKS. BY LILY H. MONTAGU. London: R.B. Johnson, 1902 BMC NUC.

ATH 10-25-02. temperance novel.

008578   NAOMI'S EXODUS. London: T.F. Unwin, 1901
NUC BMC.

Lives of English working girls-young girl from ghetto
in west London. ACAD
Young girl breaks with all her old ties successfully.
ATH 3-16-01

MONTAGU, LILY H. See MONTAGU, LILIAN HELEN.

MONTAGUE, ELIZABETH MAY. United States.

008579   BESIDE A SOUTHERN SEA; A NOVEL. New York:
Neale, 1905 NUC.

Lonely married woman of 27 and her relation to her
brother-in-law who turns up when she's loneliest and
in whom she confides. NYT
"The heroine is a woman who never learned to love the
man whom she married when but a mere girl. Her
husband's brother, in whom her affections seem
centered, is the hero." BKM v 23, 1906

MONTAGUE, MARGARET PRESCOTT. 1878-1955. United States.

008580   IN CALVERT'S VALLEY. New York: Baker and
Taylor, 1908 NUC.

Concerns a murder. TLS
Hester is "sweet and fine." ACAD
BKM: tragedy and expiation
NYT: Male hero

008581   LINDA. Boston: Houghton, Mifflin, 1912
NUC. London: Constable, 1913 BMC.

She is "very feminine." SP
Southern country girl, uneducated; charming story
"prettily told" along traditional lines. ATH
Linda Stillwater ignorant mountain girl, loves nature,
is optimistic. Marries a middle aged man only because
he threatens to beat her mother if she doesn't. when
her father learns the husband has another wife, he
demands Linda's return. She goes off alone to wander
in the woods; everyone befriends her, has her child
without scandal, goes to Boston, is adopted by a kind
old lady, educated, brought into society, gets 2
proposals. BKM
PW- runs away from husband.
NYT Happy ending shines all the way back to the 1st
page.

008582   THE SOWING OF ALDERSON CREE. New York:
Baker & Taylor, [1907] BMC NUC.

Story focuses on the father who is murdered and on the
avenging son. PW 4-20-07

008583   UNCLE SAM OF FREEDOM RIDGE. Garden City,
N. Y.: Doubleday, Page, 1920 NUC.

PW-Patriotism.
NYT 7/18/20 p.5 spirit of the post war nation.

MONTGOMERY, FLORENCE. 1843-1923. United Kingdom.

008584   BEHIND THE SCENES IN THE SCHOOLROOM.
BEING THE EXPERIENCES OF A YOUNG GOVERNESS. London:
Macmillan, 1913 BMC NUC.

Girl governess is "faultless and sentimental." ATH

008585   COLONEL NORTON. London: R. Bentley, 1895
BMC. New York and London: Longmans, Green, 1895 NUC.

At first Maud Egerton is frivolous, selfish, flighty;
when we meet her again as Lady Manorlands-a wife and
mother-she's inspiring and serious. It's not till late
in the novel that she recounts the sacrifice which
brought about the change in her. SP 75:115
The change in her is brought by an act of heroism. LW
26:170

008586   PREJUDGED. London and New York:
Macmillan, 1900 NUC BMC.

SR 90:559. Old-fashioned romance.
ACAD 1-5-01

MONTGOMERY, K. L., jt. pseud. See MONTGOMERY, KATHLEEN AND
LETITIA MONTGOMERY.

MONTGOMERY, KATHLEEN AND LETITIA MONTGOMERY.

008587   THE ARK OF THE CURSE. BY K. L.
MONTGOMERY. London: Hurst & Blackett, 1906 BMC.

ACAD-the Cagots
TLS-Elizabethan
ATH-Cagots are the accursed race of France.

008588   THE CARDINAL'S PAWN: HOW FLORENCE SET,
HOW VENICE CHECKED, AND HOW THE GAME FELL OUT. BY K.
L. MONTGOMERY. London: T.F. Unwin, 1903 BMC. Chicago:
A.C. McClurg, 1910 NUC.

A tale of the Florence and Venice of the Renaissance.
The Cardinal's pawn is a girl of wit and daring. In
order to save her brother from death at the hands of a
faithless wife who wishes to be rid of him so that her
social ambitions may be realized, the girl enters the
Cardinal's game disguised as the brother she would
save. BKM
BKM-novel of incident and intrigue and involving a
woman with an identical twin brother.
ATH-woman is disguised as male-she is very clever.
TLS-a really good book.

008589   COLONEL KATE. BY K. L. MONTGOMERY.
London: Methuen, [1908] NUC BMC.

TLS--Scotch-tale of Charles Edward's rising,
adventure, woman of action who is taken prisoner,
brutally maltreated by her husband , involved in
daring conspiracies in return for which she is named
(title) by Chavalier.
SR--0
ATH--0

008590   THE GATE-OPENERS. BY K. L. MONTGOMERY.
London: J. Long, 1912 BMC.

TLS-Welsh toll-gate riots of 1843 and Rebekah, the
leader of them.

008591   LOVE IN THE LISTS: A PENSION COMEDY. BY
K. L. MONTGOMERY. London: T.F. Unwin, 1905 BMC.

Love comedy-farce.

008592   MAIDS OF SALEM. BY K. L. MONTGOMERY.
London: J. Long, 1915 BMC.

NE witch hunt, the raw vehemence of the time. TLS

008593   MAJOR WEIR. BY K. L. MONTGOMERY. London:
T.F. Unwin, 1904 BMC NUC.

LFKM- male hero.
ATH
TLS-o

MONTGOMERY, LETITIA, jt. au. See MONTGOMERY, KATHLEEN AND
LETITIA MONTGOMERY.

MONTGOMERY, LUCY MAUD. See MACDONALD, LUCY MAUD
(MONTGOMERY).

MONTRESOR, F. F. See MONTRESOR, FRANCES FREDERICA.

MONTRESOR, FRANCES FREDERICA. D. 1934. United Kingdom.

008594   THE ALIEN; A STORY OF MIDDLE AGE. BY F.
F. MONTRESOR. New York: D. Appleton, 1901 NUC. London:
Methuen, 1901 BMC.

PW-11-16-01
ATH-11-2-01

008595   AT THE CROSS-ROADS. BY F. F. MONTRESOR.
London: Hutchinson, 1897 BMC. New York: D. Appleton,
1897 NUC.

Jack Cardew young author, engaged to Gilian Molyneux.
He's imprisoned for embezzling insurance co for
insurance of a MS. he alleged to have been burned by
accident. Out of prison, makes fortune in Africa,
returns and marries Gilian. Jack's reparation is
stopped by the fact that Gilian's mother withheld
evidence at the time of the crime. Gilian hates her
mother for this. SP 79:692.
Gilian believed in him inspite of her family. When
they marry and child dies, they draw apart for a
while, but he saves her this time (reviewer says it's
not clear from what). ACAD 52 Fic Sup 106.
Gilian "modern to the finger tips, hard in
grain...entirely destitute of the "clinging" ways of
the maiden of earlier days." ATH 110:630.
"Heroine is a very mod. figure, hard grained but

capable of intense passion, showing her strength of
devotion by waiting 7 yrs for her convict lover and
then exerting herself to prove his innocence." BAKER
03,149.
LW 29:28.

008596   THE BURNING TORCH. BY F. F. MONTRESOR.
London: J.Murray, 1905 BMC. New York: E.P. Dutton,
1907 NUC.

Dolores many abnormal traits. Sees visions, foretells
disasters inner fires consume her. PW 9-14-07.
A prophetess, but no one listens. LBKM 8-07,177
A modern Cassandra-dies in the end. A book of
numberless catastrophies. ACAD
Awkward, timid eccentric orphan girl, Dolores Ellerson
has the power of clairvoyance. Forsees impending
disasters. Made an attractive heroine. She ought to
have married Gregory but she has promised another man
never to be engaged to anyone but him.

008597   THE CELESTIAL SURGEON. BY F. F.
MONTRESOR. London: E. Arnold, 1904 BMC. New york:
Longmans Green, 1905 NUC.

ATH-uninteresting heroine.
TLS-o

008598   FALSE COIN OR TRUE? BY F. F. MONTRESOR.
London: Hutchinson, 1896 BMC. New York: D. Appleton,
1896 NUC.

ATH 108:382. Study of French Magician Moreze. Romance
of Linda, a workhouse girl he has rescued from the
streets and uses in his act.
ACAD 50:326. A Scotsman, Maclean, loves her, she
returns his love. He publicly denounces Moreze for his
exploitation of her. She leaves Moreze to marry
Maclean but goes back to nurse Moreze in his illness.
BKM 3;450. Moreze complex person.
CR 29:143.
A conjuror, hypnotist finds in Linda great
possibilities as a medium. She learns the art. There's
a rival for M. Moreze's affection, but he gives her
up. Then a Scot falls for Linda but he doesn't like
her work. SP 78:877
She's a kitchen drudge in London, saved from
starvation and trained to prof. of high class medium.
LW 28:28

008599   A FISH OUT OF WATER. London: J. Murray,
1910 BMC.

ATH-young woman cutting loose from her family.

008600   INTO THE HIGHWAYS AND HEDGES. BY F. F.
MONTRESOR. London: Hutchinson, 1895 BMC. New York: D.
Appleton, 1895 NUC.

Barnabas, a preacher has a "call to convert a young
woman of beauty and fortune. The conversion ends with
her repudiating her family, traveling with him while
he talks to the masses and falling in love with him,
throughout the book. Includes sens episodes about
diamonds and a murder trial SR 79:703
Margaret Deane becomes "nominally" his wife. There's
another man-more worldly-interested in her. He is
contrasted to Barnabas Thorpe. SP 75:376
Barnabas catches Margaret on rebound by rel. She
leaves a house of luxury to follow his ascetic life.
She was married to him "but did not love him as a man"
till she saw him ready to sacrifice himself for
another. ACAD 47:233
Impressionable, cultivated Margaret weds a street
preacher. He's unlearned, quixotic. His rival is a
keen, hard headed Jew. Mary afterwards learns to love
her husband. BAKER 03 149

008601   THE ONE WHO LOOKED ON. BY F. F.
MONTRESOR. London: Hutchinson, 1895 BMC. New York: D.
Appleton, 1895 NUC.

Susie looks on a chapter of her life involving Sir
Charles, M.P., a part of her life that influenced her
very much. SR 80:881
She learns he's been faithful to an early love, an
invalid girl whom an accident kept him from marrying.
Death of Susie's uncle brought her to home of her
guardian, Sir Charles. Juv PW 12-7-95:1081
BkM 4:432. Less religious than Into the Highways and
Hedges. Gentle and tolerant P.O.V.

008602   THE STRICTLY TRAINED MOTHER. BY F. F.
MONTRESOR. London: J. Murray, 1913 BMC 1916 NUC.

2 daughters possessing every virtue but tact manage

their old mother without understanding her, with
regard only to her health. The mother escapes to her
grand-daughter; reconciled to daughters in the end.
ACAD
A chicken pecked mother, throws off her bondage, and
rebels against her tyrannical daughters. SP
Mrs. Betterton. All her life under someone's thumb.
Husband tyrannized her. Daughters tyrannized her
without knowing it. Escapes to her granddaughter (a
modern type) whose mother had married writer that Mr.
Betterton opposed. LBKM SR

008603   THROUGH THE CHRYSALIS. BY F. F.
MONTRESOR. London: J. Murray, 1910 BMC NUC.

TLS-a Becky Sharpe type who does not have a downfall,
who is well liked by the reader. Babette.
ATH-Irresponsible father-she snatches at luxury but
works her way through the meshes she had wound around
her life. Maybe marries at end someone else?
Babette, story is prettily developed. --LBKM
Story of her parentage. SR

008604   WORTH WHILE. London and New York: E.
Arnold, 1896 BMC NUC.

PW 6-6-96. Love story of a middle-aged clerk brought
up in workhouse. Tells his story in form of letters to
an imaginary mother from a child. Also, novelette
"Lady Jane," a sad revelation of family history.

MOODY, HELEN (WATTERSON). 1860-1928. United States.

008605   A CHILD'S LETTERS TO HER HUSBAND. New
York: Doubleday, Page, 1903 NUC. London: W. Heinemann,
1904 BMC.

Child of 10 writes to imaginary husband. PW 9-19-03

MOOR, CHARLOTTE.

008606   MARINA DE LA REY. London: Digby, Long,
1903 BMC NUC.

A governess. TLS 1-03:8

008607   MISS VAUGHAN. London: Bennett, 1911 BMC.

So. African escapade "in which title-role is played by
a young man of quixotic impulse." ATH

MOORE, AULA. United States.

008608   A KING'S HEART: AN AMERICAN FAIRY STORY.
BY AULA EUFAULA. [Houston, Texas]: [c1894] NUC.

MOORE, BERTHA PEARL. 1894-1925. United States.

008609   SARAH AND HER DAUGHTER. BY BERTHA PEARL.
New York: T. Seltzer, 1920 NUC. London: L. Pearsons,
1921 BMC.

PW-Life of NY ghetto family and younger generation in
America. Sarah, learning of an American institution
dealing with refractory husbands takes Elias to court,
is astonished and distressed when he is committed for
10 days. Is disgraced in eyes of her neighbors. (Elias
would not work on Jewish Sabbath.) She works by the
day, and when she has work, 8 yr old Minnie has to do
all work at home. Poverty. Mother-daughter
relationship. She has outbursts of anger at Minnie and
then regrets.
BKM Sarah becomes temporarily insane at death of
husband and then becomes a money-mad mistress of a
sweatshop in which her own children are employed and
exploited. Minnie, sensitive, revolts and leaves home
at 16. She attempts to find a living wage, must
constantly struggle against sexual exploitation by
men, never finds the "love" which she feels is the one
sure prize in the world. Struggles helplessly and
hopelessly, her health ruined, reaches a nadir of
bitterness and despair in hospital. She then decides
she may as well fling decency aside, becomes a
mistress, withdraws from this only to marry a squalid
man.
NYT 1920:253

MOORE, CAECILIA.

008610   THE SHADOW OF THE DRAGON. London: Chapman
and Hall, 1913 BMC.

Horrors of white slave traffic in the East. The way a
woman is decoyed by an unscrupulous man and woman and
sold to brothel-keeper. An heroic deliverer comes in
the nick of time. Serious subject treated too lightly.

ACAD
Author feels readers should become suffragettes to
stop the practice. SP
Hespie McLeod, orphan, on her way to her uncle in
Australia. A fellow traveler offers to show her a bit
of life and offers her congenial employment. Taken to
Shanghai and sold into slavery. Author has a very poor
opinion of men. Focus on the heroine's career; the
purpose is to plead a cause. TLS
"A story concerned with the white slave traffic in
Shanghai. The horrors detailed are indeed terrible,
but there is no reason why, as the author appears to
think, readers should become suffragettes." SP
12-20-13

MOORE, DOROTHEA.

008611   BROWN: A STORY OF WATERLOO YEAR. London:
J. Nisbet, 1905 BMC. New York: Eaton & Mains, 1907 PW.

Historical romance. PW 12-28-07

008612   CAPTAIN NANCY: A STORY OF THE
'FORTY-FIVE. London: J. Nisbet, 1914 BMC.

008613   CECILY'S HIGHWAYMAN. London: J. Nisbet,
1914 BMC.

008614   EVELYN: A CHRONICLE. London: T. Nelson,
[1904] BMC.

008615   THE HEAD GIRL'S SISTER. London: Nisbet,
[1918] BMC.

008616   HEAD OF THE LOWER SCHOOL. London: Nisbet,
[1919] BMC. New York: G. P. Putnam's Sons, 1920 NUC.

008617   JEPTHAH'S LASS: THE STORY OF A ROUGH
NIGHT. London: S.W. Partridge, [1907] BMC.

008618   KNIGHTS OF THE RED CROSS. London: T.
Nelson, 1907 BMC.

008619   A LADY OF METTLE. London: S.W. Partridge,
[1910] BMC.

008620   THE LUCAS GIRLS; OR THE MAN OF THE
FAMILY. London: S.W. Partridge, [1911] BMC.

008621   THE LUCK OF LEDGE POINT: A TALE OF 1805.
London: Blackie, 1910 BMC.

008622   THE MAKING OF URSULA. London: S.W.
Partridge, [1910] BMC.

008623   MISTRESS DOROTHY. THE STORY OF A BRAVE
HEART. London: National Society's Depository, [1902]
BMC.

008624   MY LADY BELLAMY. A STORY OF ADVENTURE.
London: J. Nisbet, 1909 BMC NUC.

008625   NADIA TO THE RESCUE. A TALE OF THE LAND
OF THE CZAR. London: J. Nisbet, 1912 BMC.

008626   A NEST OF MALIGNANTS: A STORY OF THE
CIVIL WAR. London: S.P.C.K., [1919] BMC.

008627   PAMELA'S HERO: A TALE OF THE GORDON
RIOTS. London: Blackie, 1908 BMC.

008628   ROSEMARY THE REBEL. London: S.W.
Partridge, [1913] BMC.

008629   WANTED, AN ENGLISH GIRL: THE ADVENTURES
OF AN ENGLISH SCHOOLGIRL IN GERMANY. London: S.W.
Partridge, 1916 BMC.

008630   WHEN THE MOON IS GREEN. London: S.W.
Partridge, [1917] BMC.

MOORE, E. HAMILTON. United Kingdom.

008631   THE GARDEN OF LOVE: AN IDYLL IN PROSE.
London: E. Macdonald, 1914 BMC.

LBKM-Male artist hero. Love tragedy-flirts with one
and falls for the other.
ATH 144:306.0

008632   THE RUT. London: E. Macdonald, 1913 BMC.

Young woman of 18 drifts into marriage. Doesn't
realize her life is in a rut, that she has never
lived. Awakens at middle age and becomes infatuated
with a man; he's amused by her "love", husband is cold

and unforgiving, children are curious. ATH
Futile, hopeless story. NYT

MOORE, EDITH.

008633   A WILFUL WIDOW. London: Constable, 1913
BMC.

Shows inefficacy of present-day charity. wealthy young
woman becomes a socialist. ATH
Mary Lavender, the widow whose great fortune will be
forfieted if she becomes a socialist. She does and
testator's design is thwarted. TLS

MOORE, EDITH MARY.

008634   THE BLIND MARKSMAN. London: Hodder &
Stoughton, [1920] BMC.

TLS-Theodora as companion first to despotic old lady,
next to intellectual feminist. Marriage at end. POV?
LBKM dedicated to E. Carpenter.
SP-dreary girl after melancholy youth marries weak and
unsuccessful man. Ch. st., depressing.
LBKM-Jane, ugly and original, married 1st to heavy
male and enslaved by his heavier mother is lively and
pert. Ideal lover comes on stage.

008635   THE IDEALIST AND MARY TREHERNE. London:
G. Allen, 1910 BMC.

TLS
ATH
Happily ever after story. SR

008636   THE LURE OF EVE. London: Cassell, 1909
BMC NUC. New York: Cassell, 1909 PW.

No soul, makes life hard for husband, "too outspoken
for open shelf fiction." PW 10-30-09.
Beautiful, impassive Annabel Summers is married to a
writer who hopes to learn the Secret of Woman. He
finally does and achieves his great novel woman and
Destiny. TLS
Arthur Laine, budding novelist, has great theories of
new world in which women will play leading part. But
he has no firsthand knowledge of women. Marries a
conventional girl with no mind who is no inspiration
to him. Their disillusionment with each other grows.
Lora is the real woman in the work. Intense well
written. LBKM

008637   THE SPIRIT AND THE LAW. London: Chapman
and Hall, 1916 BMC.

TLS-reflective silent shoemaker with a passion for
drink married to a "slut" and liaison with pure minded
farmer's daughter.
LBKM--They are Greek drama figures of tragedy. Both
find courage to follow their own law.

008638   TEDDY R.N.D. London: Hodder & Stoughton,
[1917] BMC.

About a young boy to time he enters war. TLS

008639   THE WRONG SIDE OF DESTINY. London:
Cassell, 1909 BMC.

Rose Esquilant, noble and pure-minded, loves a man not
her husband. She tells her son David
about her love. He shoots himself! TLS
Rose married very young a man of business some years
her senior. Duty to boys keeps her from the man she
loves. Her sons grow up. She accepts one living with a
woman who writes. But son misunderstands her, shoots
self. LBKM

MOORE, JUSTINA. Nationality Unknown.

008640   IMMANUEL. BY MARTIN J. PRITCHARD. London:
W. Heinemann, 1896 NUC.

008641   THE OTHER MAN: A NOVEL. BY MARTIN J.
PRITCHARD. London: Hutchinson, 1902 BMC.

008642   THE PASSION OF ROSAMUND KEITH. BY MARTIN
J. PRITCHARD. London: Hutchinson, 1899 BMC. Chicago:
H. S. Stone, 1899 NUC.

Describes specimans of the old and new women. Miss
Keith travels with her uncle through So. Europe.
Snowbound in a monastery in Albania where she finds a
long lost lover. PW 55:906

008643   WITHOUT SIN. A NOVEL. BY MARTIN J.

PRITCHARD. London: W. Heinemann, 1896 BMC. Chicago: H. S. Stone, 1896 NUC.

LW 27:330. "contempt for conventionality" London, characters are "mostly disagreeable Jews or members of a fast English set and the central figure is that of a sweet and beautiful girl who is the victim at once of a most singular hallucination and of the depravity of man. We do not care to relate in these columns the events..."
CR 29:209. Mary Levinge, beautiful, Jewish, "neurotic," "apparently subject to epileptic seizures, believes herself destined to become the mother of Israel's true Messiah." Her father is a Bond Street art dealer.
BN-"Ruffian she had the misfortune to sit for her picture and all of the rest of the rabble rout arouse little interest, but considerable nausea, in the reader whose taste is not for ugly perversity."

MOORE, M. LOUISE. United States.

008644   AL-MODAD; OR, LIFE SCENES BEYOND THE POLAR CIRCUMFLEX. A RELIGIO-SCIENTIFIC SOLUTION OF THE PROBLEMS OF PRESENT AND FUTURE LIFE. BY AN UNTRAMMELED FREE-THINKER. Shell Bank, Cameron Parish, La.: M. Louise Moore and M. Beauchamp, 1892 NUC.

MOORE, MARY.

008645   MIRTH IN HEAVEN. London: H.J. Drane, [1908] BMC.

MOORE, MONICA, pseud. See WILSON, MONA.

MOORE, MRS. STUART. 1875-1941. United Kingdom.

008646   THE COLUMN OF DUST. BY EVELYN UNDERHILL. London: Methuen, [1909] BMC NUC.

SR-Doctrine that there is something peculiarly ennobling to the female in bearing an illeg child appears-medley of occultism mysticism and shrewd observance of feminine follies.
Supernatural realities in modern London. A "spirit" takes hold of Constance Tyrrel. "It is isolated, energetic, and desirous of advent, hungry, restless." She has a niece Vera and later we get "an extremely frank confession relating to Vera." TLS

008647   THE GREY WORLD. BY EVELYN UNDERHILL. New York: Century, 1904 NUC. London: W. Heinemann, 1904 BMC.

PW- A waif who dies enters spirit world and re-enters this worl d as a child. Goes back and forth.
NYT
Outspoken on sex; chars. do supremely shocking things, about Bloomsbury NYT 05, 150
Gray world a different novel? about transition between life and death in a child?

008648   THE LOST WORD. BY EVELYN UNDERHILL. London: W. Heinemann, 1907 BMC NUC.

The agitation in two lovers described with insight, but seems to focus on hero. LBKM 3-07, 273
Centers on Paul, his visions and dreams ACAD
Centers on a man, an architect. SR

MOORE, NANCY.

008649   THE NIGHTINGALE. London: Constable, 1914 BMC.

ATH young woman traveling for her health, innocuous, conclusion is reunion with husband.

MOORE, SUSAN TEACKLE (SMITH). United States.

008650   RYLE'S OPEN GATE. Boston: Houghton, Mifflin, 1891 NUC.

Mother and son spend time in a Dutch house in Long Island. Their household and acquaintances. IND
Mother and son, "Robin and I," spend summer in fisherman's cottage. The fisherman is called Ryle. His conversations with acquaintances in dialect. Record of daily life of mother and son, their visitors. SR 9-5-91, 279
Some dialect BOOK NEWS 107:478

MOORER, LOUISA HAYNES. United States.

008651   SEQUOYAH-A ROMANCE UNDER WESTERN SKIES. New York: Broadway, [c1911] NUC.

MORAN, JEANNIE WORMLEY (BLACKBURN). 1842-1929. United States.

008652   MISS WASHINGTON OF VIRGINIA. A SEMI-CENTENNIAL LOVE-STORY. BY MRS. F. BERGER MORAN, NEE JEANNIE BLACKBURN. Philadelphia: J.B. Lippincott, 1893 NUC. London: S. Low, [1912] BMC.

MORAN, MRS. F. BERGER. See MORAN, JEANNIE WORMLEY (BLACKBURN).

MORDAUNT, ELEANOR, pseud. See BOWLES, EVELYN MAY (CLOWES) WIEHE.

MORDAUNT, ELENOR, pseud. See BOWLES, EVELYN MAY (CLOWES) WIEHE.

MORDAUNT, ELINOR, pseud. See BOWLES, EVELYN MAY (CLOWES) WIEHE.

MORGAN, EMILY MALBONE. 1862-1937. United States.

008653   THE FLIGHT OF THE "SWALLOW". New York: A. D. F. Randolph, [c1894] NUC.

LW 25:218. French refugee in New England in colonial days. Attempts to earn his living by giving dancing lessons, is driven out of church. Inherits a fortune, leaves, sends church $1,000.

008654   A LADY OF THE OLDEN TIME. Hartford, Conn.: Belknap and Warfield, [c1896] NUC.

PW 12-5-96. Ideal character.

008655   MADONNAS OF THE SMOKE; OR, OUR "MARY'S MEADOW". New York: A. D. F. Randolph, [c1893] NUC.

Group of young women in large manufacturing city form a working woman's club. After they see a photo of Raphael's madonna, they take that name. One project: they rent a meadow. PW 6-10-93. Story tells of their use of the meadow.

008656   A POPPY GARDEN. Hartford: Belknap and Warfield, 1892 NUC.

"solitary spinster with a love story running thru it, tender and suggestive" set in New England. BOOK NEWS 130:458.

008657   PRIOR RAHERE'S ROSE. [New Haven]: [c1892] NUC.

time is 19th century. The story based on sad episode in life of child patient of St. Bartholomew's hospital. PW 4-1-93

MORISON, CAROLINE WOOD, jt. au. See COOKE, GRACE (MACGOWAN) AND CAROLINE WOOD MORISON.

MORISON, ELIZABETH, pseud. See MOBERLY, CHARLOTTE ANNE ELIZABETH AND ELEANOR FRANCES JOURDAIN.

MORLEY, LOLA.

008658   LIFE'S WHEEL. London: Digby, Long, 1898 BMC NUC.

ACAD 53:521. Hero is a duke. Mysteries, birthmarks, detectives.

MORLEY, MARGARET WARNER. 1858-1923.

008659   LITTLE MITCHELL: THE STORY OF A MOUNTAIN SQUIRREL. Chicago: A.C. McClurg, 1904 NUC. London: Methuen, 1907 BMC.

MORRIS, ANNA VAN RENSSELAER. United States.

008660   THE APPLE WOMAN OF THE KLICKITAT. New York: Duffield, 1918 NUC.

PW-- Experiences of a woman who develops an orchard in Washington.

MORRIS, CLARA. See HARRIOTT, CLARA MORRIS.

MORRIS, ELSIE LOUISE.

008661   WOMAN OF THE HOUR, PAST-PRESENT-FUTURE. BY DR. ELSIE LOUISE MORRIS. Los Angeles: Austin, 1919 NUC.

MORRIS, EUGENIA LAURA (TUTTLE). B. 1833. United States.

008662   A HILLTOP SUMMER. BY ALYN YATES KEITH.
Boston: Lee and Shepard, [c1894] NUC.

LW. New England country life.
PW - Life of Hilltop people described somewhat in the
style of Cranford.

008663   A SPINSTER'S LEAFLETS: WHEREIN IS WRITTEN
THE HISTORY OF HER "DOORSTEP BABY," A FANCY WHICH IN
TIME BECAME A FACT AND CHANGED A LIFE. BY ALYN YATES
KEITH. Boston: Lee and Shepard, 1894 NUC.

Old maid in New England village, her longing for
motherhood, her care of an orphan boy. PW 12-16-93.
Lit W 25:37, Lonely spinster adopts little
boy--tender, pathetic

MORRIS, MARY HUSBAND. United Kingdom.

008664   THE PASTARD. London: Heath, Cranton &
Ouseley, [c1913] BMC NUC.

Adventure & smuggling in days of George III. Hero, a
smuggler, becomes an Admiral. ATH TLS

MORRISON, ADELE (SARPY). B. 1842. United States.

008665   A NEW ENGLAND PRIMROSE. Chicago: Branch,
[c1918] NUC.

NYT-Love story in New England.

MORRISON, DEBORAH, pseud. See CLARK, SUSIE CHAMPNEY.

MORRISON, MARY GRAY. Nationality Unknown.

008666   THE SEA-FARERS: A ROMANCE OF A NEW
ENGLAND COAST TOWN. New York: Doubleday, Page, 1900
NUC.

NYT 1900:365. Scapegrace son and friend believed
drowned off New England coast. Merchant father sees
ghost of him ghost for $5000, money disappears,
marries the friend, becomes a pirate, robs his father,
is caught by Italians, is pardoned and returns home
for happy ending.

MORROW, HONORE (MACCUE) WILLSIE. 1880?-1940. United
States.

008667   BENEFITS FORGOT; A STORY OF LINCOLN AND
MOTHER LOVE. BY HONORE WILLSIE. New York: F. A.
Stokes, [c1917] NUC.

Son's recognition of mother PW

008668   THE FORBIDDEN TRAIL. BY HONORE WILLSIE.
New York: F. A. Stokes, [c1919] NUC. London: T.
Butterworth, 1920 BMC.

ATH Sounds like male heroes and love.
LBKM Sounds like male heroes and love.
Two westerners experiment with solar heat and thwart
enemy schemes to steal results of their work. PW
Roger Moore and Ernest Wolf; The heat will help
irrigate deserts. NYT 670,11-23-19

008669   THE HEART OF THE DESERT (KUT-LE OF THE
DESERT). BY HONORE WILLSIE. New York: F. A. Stokes,
[1913] BMC NUC. London: T. Butterworth, 1921 BMC.

PW 84 9/27/13 p. 953 "In the Arizona desert a delicate
girl and a masterful Indian, who has kidnapped her.
Although the Indian, a university man and companion of
the girl's friends, treats his captive with the upmost
respect and tenderness, still she hates him bitterly.
By degrees the desert works its spell, and when after
weeks of pursuit Rhoda's friends find her, she refuses
to go back with them, and marries her Indian."
The Indian takes his captive to his Pueblo village.
NYT

008670   LYDIA OF THE PINES. BY HONORE WILLSIE.
New York: F. A. Stokes, [c1917] NUC. London: Hodder &
Stoughton, [1923] BMC.

Lydia goes away to college. Returns to Missouri Lake
County. Inspires Billy to attack liquor interests and
Indian land graft. PW 91:685 3/3/17
"heroine blazes her own trail to success" Story of a
personality   Lydia dominates the book. We get about
ten years of her life, her relations with all kinds of
people. The big issues of the community she faces like
the treatment of Indians in a nearby reservation. She
inspires a cleaningup of political graft; inspires a

Congressional Investigation of the way whites took
Indian land. She voices "the feeling of the feminist
toward public affairs: I did it because I felt
responsible..." marries in the end. NYT 2-25-17 62

008671   STILL JIM. BY HONORE WILLSIE. New York:
F. A. Stokes, [1915] BMC NUC. London: G. Richards,
1916 BMC.

Mostly about Jim whom Penelope marries after her
husband of an unhappy marriage dies. PW 4-24-15
NYT
TLS Male Hero

MORSE, HARRIET CLARA. Nationality Unknown.

008672   A COWBOY CAVALIER. Boston: C. M. Clark,
1908 NUC.

NYT typ love story

MORSE, LUCY (GIBBONS). B. 1839. United States.

008673   RACHEL STANWOOD: A STORY OF THE MIDDLE OF
THE NINETEENTH CENTURY. Boston and New York: Houghton,
Mifflin, 1893 NUC BMC.

Quakers in New York 1850-60. Hers and husband's home
is a station of the underground railroad. Their
children consider "nigger" a bad swear word and tell
their friends they belong to the Abolitionist Church.
LW 93, 369
Famous figures like Garrison, Mrs. Child figure in the
story. PW 10-28-93.

MORSE, MARGARET FESSENDEN. B. 1877. United States.

008674   ON THE ROAD TO ARDEN. Boston: Houghton
Mifflin, 1909 NUC.

A romantic narrative of a springtime excursion out
into the countryside taken by two wilful maids. BKM v.
29, 1909

008675   THE SPIRIT OF THE PINES. Boston:
Houghton, Mifflin, 1906 NUC.

PW-Love story, renunciation
NYT-"White Terror"?

MORTLAKE, G. N., pseud. See STOPES, MARIE CHARLOTTE
CARMICHAEL.

MORTON, MARTHA. 1865-1925. United States.

008676   HER LORD AND MASTER. Philadelphia: D.
Biddle, [1902] BMC NUC. (BMC: Victoria Morton.)

International romance. Miss Indiana's captivating
vulgarity-vulgar as Daisy Miller is vulgar; Eng., Amer
romance and marr. meeting with mother-in-law NYT
03,83. The play "Her Lord and Master" by Martha
Morton, was first produced in New York, during
...1902... Miss Victoria Morton...now presents 'Her
Lord and Master' as a novel"-foreword. NUC

MORTON, MARY A. United States.

008677   ABBIE SAUNDERS: A STORY OF PIONEER DAYS
IN MINNESOTA. Fresno, Cal.: Published For Author, 1892
NUC.

MORTON, VICTORIA. United States.

008678   THE WHIRLPOOL. New York: E. P. Dutton,
[c1916] NUC.

Criminals and law courts and a woman's redemption. BKM
Bella sentenced to reformatory by Judge. Ten years
later meets and falls in love with him. Years pass to
free old pal she speaks out. Judge resigns in order to
work with her to secure second chance for convicts. PW
90:1613 11/11/16
NYT Bella was in a gambling estab. after reform
school. Book begins with her going to Maine woods
where she meets judge. He/she or both are breaking
down. She is regenerated thru love.

008679   THE YELLOW TICKET. FROM THE PLAY OF THE
SAME NAME BY MICHAEL MORTON. New York: H. K. Fly,
[c1914] BMC NUC.

Jewish woman carries a yellow ticket (issued to
prostitutes though she really isn't one) PW 2-13-15.

MOSELEY, ELLA LOWERY. United States.

008680   THE WONDER LADY. Boston: Lothrop, Lee and
Shepard, [1911] NUC.

Romantic story of a mysterious woman do-gooder and the
doctor who seeks her. PW 8-26-11

MOSS, MARY. 1864-1914. United States.

008681   THE POET AND THE PARISH. New York: H.
Holt, 1906 BMC NUC.

PW--Male hero-unhappy marriage.
NYT-Beastly poet husb-wife is a prurient prude?

008682   A SEQUENCE IN HEARTS. Philadelphia and
London: J. B. Lippincott, 1903 NUC.

Marriage and baby (she raises by the books) change
frivolous Violet into a common place woman (She was
full of unrest) Her women friends look on and
criticize. PW 10-10-03
BKM 1903, 18 314
Heroine poses for woman who makes poster ads. Another
char is an "abominably perfect young wife and mother."
NYT 03 786

MOULE, MARGARET.

008683   THE THIRTEENTH BRYDAIN: A NOVEL. London:
Jarrold, 1897 BMC.

A man must perish because he is no. 13. Drinks a
poisoned cup of coffee meant for someone else. SP
79:566.

MOUNTAIN, ISOBEL. Nationality Unknown.

008684   A MAIDEN IN MALAYA. London: A. Melrose,
[1919] BMC NUC.

Social life in Malaya. The rising vs. the British in
1916. TLS
Elizabeth Tain drifts into a marriage without quite
wishing it; falls in love with a man on way to visit
brother in Malaya. SR

008685   SALAAM. London: A. Melrose, 1917 BMC.

A woman's engagement and marriage in India. TLS

008686   TIGRESS! London: Heath, Cranton, [1920]
BMC.

TLS-Young officer pursued to the point of scandal by
girl who wants to force him to marry her. POV?
SP-His restoration to health by Anglo-Indian friend,
Mrs Merton, is theme.

MOUNTAIN, LUCENA BELLE (WALKER). B. 1877. United States.

008687   JOY DELLE. Cincinnati: Jennings and
Graham, [c1912] NUC.

MOUTON, EUGENIE. United States.

008688   JOSEPHINE JOSEPH: TEXAS SKETCHES.
Cincinnati: Editor Pub. Co., 1900 NUC.

MOYER, ALICE CURTICE. Nationality Unknown.

008689   A ROMANCE OF THE ROAD; MAKING LOVE AND A
LIVING. Chicago: Laird & Lee, [c1912] NUC.

PW-Story of a widow who travels for a commercial
house.
NYT- Purports to be real, about persons who discuss
the work with the author and give her photographs.
About a Chicago business house in which most of the
work is done by women who work together and come
together socially. There are two or three men (not
employed by the house) who figure as suitors.

MUCKLESTON, EDITH MARGARET (WHERRY). United States.

008690   THE RED LANTERN; BEING THE STORY OF THE
GODDESS OF THE RED LANTERN LIGHT. BY EDITH WHERRY.
London: J. Lane, 1911 BMC. New York: J. Lane, 1911
NUC.

Eurasian woman loved by man she's repelled by (he's
ugly) Tragic PW 4 -1-11
Chinese story at time of Boxer Rising ATH
BKM 33 (1911) 317
Eurasian; to placate old grandmother on her death bed,
Mahlee tries to cut off her "indecently large feet,"

dies. Her after-life is part of the story! ACAD
Used by a Boxer leader (a man she loves) for his pol.
purposes as a reincarnation of a kind of Joan of Arc
of China. She uses that position for power(?) LBKM
She's half Chinese, wholely Chinese by training.
Grandmother sold her to a foreign Mandarin who forbade
her to bind the girl's feet BKM

008691   THE WANDERER ON A THOUSAND HILLS. BY
EDITH WHERRY. New York and London: J. Lane, 1917 BMC
NUC.

TLS-Chinese girl marries, her girl baby is destroyed
by in-laws. She adopts a European boy who rises to the
pinnacle of Ch. scholarship. Ends in trag.
Male hero PW 91:1229 4/14/17
English boy, Chinese foster mother BKM
Young Chinese woman loses her husband and child,
wanders off, finds an English child. Story concerns
this boy who grown to manhood can't accept European
ideas, and becomes a religious fanatic. NYT
Chinese life and custom; struggle in soul of this man
between call "of the blood" and circumstance. NYT
5-6-17 183

MUENSTERBERG, MARGARETE ANNA ADELHEID. B. 1889. United
States.

008692   ANNA BORDEN'S CAREER. A NOVEL. New York
and London: D. Appleton, 1913 BMC NUC.

TLS-Heiress is social success in Berlin, then becomes
a hospital nurse, an actress, a factory hand, a
champion of the Toilers' Brotherhood. Marries its
labor hero John Bruce, ending tragic and melodramatic.
POV
"... is loved by an Englishman but refuses him because
she could never be afraid of him...nurse...sampling
other activities even down to the squalid
depths...career is active and eventful, but she fails
because she always loves the thrill of the moment but
not the cause... closes in a hopeful fashion". PW
"Miss Muensterberg's heroine seems to typify the
modern feminine unrest. She is the daughter of a
millionaire, who tires of society and tries in turn
many occupations. She is successively, a nurse, an
actress, a factory worker, and the wife of a strike
leader. In none of these ventures, however, does she
find any permanent satisfaction. Her inherent
restlessness drives her on to new experiments. BRD
"a firm and consistent analysis of an all too
prevalent and a none too wholesome type," NYT 18:478
"A dissatisfied woman's life" "plunges from one ardent
enterprise into another and finally into a daring
marriage." "the feminine warrior" her ailment "the
thrill mania" "thirsts for experiences" "love affairs
a pleasant source of thrill" "She shattered fetters
and became a trained nurse...tried
footlights...married...life slammed the door in her
face" But she opened it and entered. NYT 1913 478

008693   RED POPPIES: A NOVEL. New York and
London: D. Appleton, 1915 BMC NUC.

"Modern painter in society and bohemia." BKM 41 1915
The painter is male. TLS
About a male artist PW. 2-6-15

MUHLBACH, LOUISE, pseud. See MUNDT, KLARA (MUELLER).

MUIR, DOROTHY ERSKINE.

008694   SUMMER FRIENDSHIPS. London: G. Richards,
1915 BMC.

Letters of a tour in Scotland TLS

MUIR, OLIVE BEATRICE. United States.

008695   THY NAME IS WOMAN: A NOVEL. New York: G.
W. Dillingham, 1894 NUC.

008696   WITH MALICE TOWARD NONE. Chicago: Rand,
McNally, [c1900] NUC.

PW-Lal North became an actress after father's death,
married an actor in the same company. Soon after she
hears he is already married. Her ideal in life is
honor. She acts.

MULCAHY, ELIZA LORETTA MACCABE. B. 1863.

008697   WANDEWANA'S PROPHECY AND FRAGMENTS IN
VERSE. Baltimore: J. Murphy, [c1905] NUC.

MULHOLLAND, CLARA.

414

008698   THROUGH MIST AND SHADOW. Dublin: Sealy,
Bryers, 1909 BMC.

melodrama of fainting heroines. TLS

MULHOLLAND, ROSA. See GILBERT, ROSA (MULHOLLAND).

MULLINS, ISLA MAY (HAWLEY). 1859-1936. United States.

008699   ANNE'S WEDDING; A BLOSSOM SHOP ROMANCE.
Boston: Page, 1916 NUC.

PW 90:1124 9/30/16

008700   THE BLOSSOM SHOP: A STORY OF THE SOUTH.
Boston: L.C. Page, 1913 NUC.

PW 83 6/21/13 2162 "Mrs. Grey and her little blind
daughter Eugene support themselves by sending to
northern florists, wild smilax and the beautiful cape
jessamine which grow abundantly in their Alabama home.
Then a fire is the means of bringing to light a will
which endows them with wealth and the opportunity of
going to a great occulist with Gene. When they return
to the South, Gene can see, and Mrs. Grey has
consented to marry the man who has long loved her."

008701   TWEEDIE: THE STORY OF A TRUE HEART.
Boston: Page, 1919 NUC.

Girls?

MULTIPLE AUTHORS.

008702   THE AFFAIR AT THE INN. BY KATE DOUGLAS
WIGGIN, MARY FINDLATER, JANE FINDLATER, ALLAN MCAULAY.
Boston: Houghton Mifflin, 1904 NUC.

008703   DAUGHTERS OF AESCULAPIUS; STORIES WRITTEN
BY ALUMNAE AND STUDENTS OF THE WOMAN'S MEDICAL COLLEGE
OF PENNSYLVANIA, AND EDITED BY A COMMITTEE APPOINTED
BY THE STUDENTS' ASSOCIATION OF THE COLLEGE.
Philadelphia: G. W. Jacobs, 1897 NUC.

008704   THE MODERN MARRIAGE MARKET. BY MARIE
CORELLI, LADY JEUNE, FLORA ANNIE STEEL, SUSAN,
COUNTESS OF MALMESBURY. London: Hutchinson, 1898 BMC
NUC. London: J. B. Lippincott, 1900 NUC.

PW-not fiction. 4 articles on marriage, with as many
different points of view.

008705   ROBINETTA. BY KATE DOUGLAS WIGGIN, MARY
FINDLATER, JANE FINDLATER AND ALLAN MCAULAY. London:
Gay & Hancock, 1911 BMC. Boston: Houghton Mifflin,
[1911] NUC.

Widow at 22 searches for relatives in England--?W
4-4-11

008706   SHROUDED IN MYSTERY. BY SARAH, ELEANOR
AND HARRIET STREDDER. London: H. J. Drane, [1901] BMC.

008707   THREE GIRLS IN A FLAT. BY ENID YANDELL,
JEAN LOUGHBOROUGH, LAURA HAYES. [Chicago]: [Knight,
Leonard], [c1892] NUC.

MUMFORD, ETHEL WATTS. See GRANT, ETHEL (WATTS) MUMFORD.

MUMMA, ROSA MEYERS. United States.

008708   ANGELA: A SALVATION ARMY LASSIE. New
York: Neale, 1907 NUC.

Woman killed a man hides identity in Salv. Army. PW

008709   FALLINA; A TALE OF MODERN AMERICAN SOCIAL
LIFE. Boston: Roxburgh, 1906 NUC.

PW "The story of an unhappy marriage with some good
'hits' upon the laxity of our present divorce laws."

MUNCIE, ELIZABETH (HAMILTON).

008710   FOUR EPOCHS OF LIFE. New York: Greaves,
[c1910] BMC NUC.

Man and woman both doctors and the good they did. "The
author, a physician, deals with the question of sex."
PW

MUNDT, KLARA (MUELLER). 1814-1873.

008711   A CONSPIRACY OF THE CARBONARI. BY LOUISE
MULBACH. New York: F.T. Neely, 1896 NUC. (Tr. Mary J.

Safford)

PW-Napoleon. Secret Society of the Carbonari plan to
assassinate him. A beautiful woman and her father,
spies in the service of Napoleon, discover them.
Historical novel: conspiracy of Fouche to kidnap
Napoleon. BOOK NEWS 96-7:136

MUNGER, DELL H. B. 1862. United States.

008712   THE WIND BEFORE THE DAWN. Garden City,
New York: Doubleday, Page, 1912 NUC. London: Hodder &
Stoughton, 1912 BMC.

Kansas prairie farm: the work and struggle the soul
and body-killing grind and monotony of a woman's part
in it because husbands "own" their wives and treat
them like beasts giving them no freedom. Heroine,
gifted. She at last wins respect and real love of
husband. ATH
Elizabeth Farnshaw flings away her ambitions on a
selfish tyrannical man, marries him, tries to change
him. Is miserable. Falls in love with her husband's
partner. He "sacrifices himself that the gates of
liberty may be opened to her. Learns that in her own
words, "There is no other way...A woman to be free
must have money of her own. She must not be supported
by a man."--LBKM
BKM v36 1912-13-prairie school teacher marries, has
love affair with other man who leaves her money,
separates from husband and because of money (freedom)
consents to live with him again. Described as a
woman's movement book.

MUNN, MARGARET (CROSBY). United States.

008713   THE PATH OF STARS. New York: Dodd, Mead,
1903 NUC.

heroine has voice that thrills Liszt, but ill health
spoils her career; later conquers her illness, becomes
opera singer-her final life work. PW 10-17-03
Heroine-an introspective and morbid turn of mind
reluctant to love-has much to say on the subject.

MUNN, MARGUERITE (BRYANT). United Kingdom.

008714   THE ADJUSTMENT. BY MARGUERITE BRYANT.
London: W. Heinemann, 1912 NUC BMC. New York:
Duffield, 1912 NUC.

PW-very complicated
TLS Christine marries and redeems a social outcast,
reunites her mother and father
ATH A thoughtful and subtle study of character and
life.
NYT Highly emotional situations handled in a
repressed, tense way.
ATH "It is the heroine who, in ignorance, effects the
'adjustment,' by reforming and marrying the man whom
her father had deeply wronged. An interesting feature
is the meeting and gradually growing friendship of
this father and daughter. She never sees him until she
is nineteen and then meets him in society under an
assumed name. The principal situation is improbable,
but if that is once granted, events follow each other
and the plot develops naturally enough."

008715   THE ADVENTURES OF LOUIS DURAL. London:
S.C. Brown, Langham, 1905 BMC.

008716   ANNE KEMPBURN: TRUTHSEEKER. BY MARGUERITE
BRYANT. New York: Duffield, 1910 NUC. London: W.
Heinemann, 1910 BMC.

Heroine wants to make a better world. Story concerns
constructive mission work with the poor and Anne's
career.
SR-Seeks the meaning of life through socialism and
statistics. Marries a wealthy young secretary
TLS-Career as secretary
ACAD-she studies relationship between capital and
labour to get position
NYT all the sent. interest gravitates to Naomi her
older sister "and of Anne we remember nothing more
weakly feminine than the impassioned handshake with
which she and the long suffering Max cement their
matrimonial pact." She is keenly interested in
economic theory and the regeneration of society.
Becomes sec. of labor leader whose sister has a post
of importance. Anne's sister is a famous singer. SP

008717   CHRISTOPHER HIBBAULT: ROADMAKER. BY
MARGUERITE BRYANT. London: W. Heinemann, 1908 BMC. New
York: Duffield, 1909 NUC.

Story of a young man PW 2-13-09
About men and the mastery of a beautiful girl LBKM,
BKM, SP, NYT
TLS - Male hero

008718   THE DOMINANT PASSION. BY MARGUERITE
BRYANT (MRS. PHILIP MUNN). London: Hutchinson, 1913
NUC BMC. New York: Duffield, 1913 NUC.

Dominant passion of genius-as it concerns 4 persons
ATH
Man a scientific genius; Honor a literary genius.
Andrea Bredon artistic genius. Laurence, music genius.
for Andrea: art "crushes out human sympathies and
moral responsibilities." TLS
"Story of a London artist, Andrea Bredon, whose
passion of creation dominates his life. For his sins
against his fellows he feels regret, but sins against
art fill him with misery. He alienates his son and
comes between his cousin Anthony and his wife, a
beautiful woman whose inspiration Andrea believes he
needs in his work. She averts a tragedy only by
destroying the manuscript of her book, the thing
dearest to her in the world." PW:94 11-29-13:273.
BKM-He ruins the career of his son, a musician whom he
believes he needs as a model. when Honor learns of a
crowning act of cruelty of his to his son and of his
duplicity in estranging her from her husband, she
returns to Italy and him. Andrea's art falls to pieces
and he determines to make peace with Honor, whatever
the cost.
BKM 38- Male artist almost ruins marriage of female
novelist by his selfishness.

008719   FELICITY CROFTON. BY MARGUERITE BRYANT
(MRS. PHILIP MUNN). New York: Duffield, 1916 NUC BMC.
London: W. Heinemann, 1916 BMC.

BKM-filled with individual significance. Felicity has
a daughter Veronica. About another woman-Stella-there
is a mystery.
NYT Felicity widow and mother of 18 year old daughter,
at 38 she exhibits energy and interest in life and fun
(Rev. thinks author makes too much of this-it is not
unusual for 40 yr old American woman to skate,
toboggan, dance, etc.) Love interest is completly
unimportant. Stella profits from Felicity's loyalty to
a young man and her sacrifice in this matter which is
a ystery. Stella is morbid but (according to rev) best
portrayed in book.
TLS Felicity takes blame for drug taking of young
man's wife (Stella?)

008720   A GREAT RESPONSIBILITY. BY MARGUERITE
BRYANT. London: Hurst and Blackett, 1895 NUC BMC.

Sir Cecil Lestrange is bitterly sad that child of his
only son (now dead) is a girl. Sets out to make her
"masculine by training." When she's 16, she gets not a
governess but a tutor whom she eventually loves. Cecil
the young woman "is much more a boy than a girl" more
interested in horses than gossip. "A fine
individuality" SP 74:584
Sir Cecil wished to train her with a sense of a man's
responsibility to family name and estates. She shocks
London society. ACAD 47:376
"Thanks to her upbringing she remains to the end
curiously unconscious of her sex" ATH 105:469.

008721   MORTON VERLOST. London: A. and C. Black,
1895 BMC.

ACAD 49:32. Male hero. Involves a magical ring and
Blacks in the West Indies.
Grew up estranged from father. He also loved a woman
who became his step mother. Marries a woman (without
love on either side) Then she falls in love. He gets
out of the way by becoming involved in a rising of
natives on a mysterious island. ATH 106:678.
Man's past has fatal influence upon him. BAKER '03,
82.

008722   THE PRINCESS CYNTHIA. BY MARGUERITE
BRYANT. London: Cassell, 1901 BMC. New York: Funk &
Wagnalls, 1901 NUC.

Preference for ind. and brutality in her admirers!
12-28-01 ATH

008723   THE SEEKERS: AN EXPLANATION. London: St.
Catherine Press, [1916] BMC.

008724   THE SHADOW ON THE STONE. BY MARGUERITE
BRYANT (MRS. PHILIP MUNN). New York: Duffield, 1917
NUC BMC. London: Methuen, 1918 BMC.

Two men and Pauline Paget, set out to establish a
model republic and succeed in spite of enemy's effort
to wreck the scheme. PW

008725   A WOMAN'S PRIVILEGE. BY MARGUERITE
BRYANT. London: A. D. Innes, 1898 BMC NUC.

LIT 3:257.
ACAD 53:522. An actress, an inheritance.
ACAD 54:106. Plot to get money left to her father.
Francis, her cousin one of the plotters. Her friend,
Richard Carroll, goes to Egypt to solve mystery, he
has adventures there.

MUNN, MRS. PHILIP. See MUNN, MARGUERITE (BRYANT).

MUNOZ, ANITA CLAY. Nationality Unknown.

    008726   IN LOVE AND TRUTH; OR THE DOWNFALL OF
    SAMUEL SEELE, HEALER. New York and London: Abbey
    Press, [c1901] NUC.

MURDOCH, GLADYS H.

    008727   COTTON IS KING. London: Sands, [1912]
    BMC.

    ATH-- male hero
    TLS-- But he is really concerned with relations
    between himself and his wife.

    008728   MISTRESS CHARITY GODOLPHIN. London: J.
    Murray, 1914 BMC.

    SR 147:645--Hist rom. Monmouth, trial of Alice Lisle,
    execution by burning.
    ACAD 86:562--Rev.'s sympathies are more with Lisle
    than with hero or heroine of story.

    008729   STERLING SILVER. London: G. Allen, 1910
    BMC.

    TLS-too much action.

MURDOCK, LOUISE R. (SAUNDERS). B. 1872. United States.

    008730   ALMETTA OF GABRIEL'S RUN. New York:
    Meridian Press, [c1917] NUC.

MURFREE, FANNY NOAILLES DICKINSON. United States.

    008731   FELICIA: A NOVEL. Boston: Houghton,
    Mifflin, 1891 NUC BMC. (Eng. ed. title: "A Singer's
    Wife: a Novel".)

    Society woman (young) of western town, marries opera
    star and travels with him. He's devoted to his art.
    She tries to be "the woman behind" but can't. Trouble
    between them. Well written. HARPERS 's 83 642.
    Novel gives us a year in her life. Daughter of
    aristocrat, she's proud of her family. Marries Hugh
    Kennell only after hesitation. Cares nothing for his
    profession; is lonely, has given up home, etc. Ashamed
    of him in costume. Doesn't like his friends; hates
    living in hotels-wants a home. He's too busy to see
    how unhappy she is. Crisis comes when she's aware a
    woman singer interested in him. Crisis hurts his
    career temporarily. He fears for his career; she fears
    losing him. Novel ends there. LW
    Sister of Mary N. Murfree, Charles Egbert Craddock
    ATH 99:225. "Incompatibility of the artistic with the
    domestic life."
    ACAD 41:60. Strong minded heroine marries a singer
    against the wishes of friends and family. She is
    miserable in marriage when it develops his art is more
    important to him and she has been cast off by her
    friends. His tragic death concludes story.

    008732   A SINGER'S WIFE: A NOVEL. London:
    Cassell, 1891 BMC. (Am. ed. title: Felicia, a Novel.)

MURFREE, MARY NOAILLES. 1850-1922. United States.

    008733   THE AMULET; A NOVEL. BY CHARLES EGBERT
    CRADDOCK. New York and London: Macmillan, 1906 BMC
    NUC.

    British frontier life 1763; artifical nature of 18th
    soc. SP
    PW-frontier & Indians, love story etc.

    008734   THE BUSHWHACKERS, AND OTHER STORIES. BY
    CHARLES EGBERT CRADDOCK. Chicago: H. S. Stone, 1899
    NUC. London: Ward, Lock, 1899 BMC.

    008735   THE FAIR MISSISSIPPIAN. A NOVEL. BY

416

CHARLES EGBERT CRADDOCK. Boston: Houghton, Mifflin, 1908 BMC NUC.

NATION 88:42 1/14/09
DIAL: 46:86 2/1/09
PW house myst
Mrs. Honoria Faurie, widow, employs a young man (10 yrs younger) to tutor her sons. The tutor becomes an important part of household-love follows. NYT

008736   HIS VANISHED STAR. BY CHARLES EGBERT CRADDOCK. Boston: Houghton, Mifflin, 1894 NUC BMC.

ATH 104:672.
LW 25:212. Moonshiners.
PW-horrors of illicit whiskey distilling and its consequences.

008737   IN THE "STRANGER PEOPLE'S" COUNTRY: A NOVEL. BY CHARLES EGBERT CRADDOCK. New York: Harper, 1891 NUC BMC. London: J.R. Osgood, 1891 BMC.

NATION 54:153. Frontier story. Man of science who desecrates graves and romantic outlaw, Fee Guthree. Story concerns Shaddock and his investigations of ancient graves of pigmy peoples, horse stealers. Heroine: Letitia Pettingill: ACAD
Smokey Mountains people concerned about their relationship to these pigmy people whose graves are nearby. Other characters: Rhodes on an election campaign; Adelaide Yates. The traditional perfect woman, eternally faithful; Letitia, exasperating and fascinating; Fee, in love with her: LBKM
in dialect ATH 98 830.
Picture of mountain hillbillies in Tennessee.

008738   THE JUGGLER. BY CHARLES EGBERT CRADDOCK. Boston: Houghton, Mifflin, 1897 NUC. London: Gay and Bird, 1898 BMC.

Tenn. mts. young man comes to this area to take up a whole new life. He's been "buried-"reported dead and now must take a new identity. LW 28:478.
Tragedy and a love story. PW 52:820.
Tragic, gruesome ending. ATH 113:494.
SP 81:52. Royce is on a Mississippi steamer with a friend when it sinks. His friend has robbed him of his clothes, money he was carrying for the firm, and drowned. Royce decides to bury his identity and poses as a conjuror in Tenn. He eventually excites suspicion and jealousy. When he feels that his alias is threatened, he suicides by allowing himself to be stabbed in his act.
CR 32:215.
Hero lives among mountain people for fear of unjust accusation that he robbed his employers. Kills self at end by contriving to have his friend kill him unknowingly. Thinks he's about to be apprehended. Was wrong. NYT 12-4-97:15.

008739   THE MYSTERY OF WITCH-FACE MOUNTAIN, AND OTHER STORIES. BY CHARLES EGBERT CRADDOCK. Boston: Houghton, Mifflin, 1895 NUC BMC.

008740   THE ORDEAL; A MOUNTAIN ROMANCE OF TENNESSEE. BY CHARLES EGBERT CRADDOCK. Philadelphia and London: Lippincott, 1912 BMC NUC.

PW In attempt to recover kidnapped child mother and former lover become reconciled

008741   A SPECTRE OF POWER. BY CHARLES EGBERT CRADDOCK. Boston: Houghton, Mifflin, 1903 NUC.

PW hist. romance

008742   THE STORM CENTRE; A NOVEL. BY CHARLES EGBERT CRADDOCK. New York and London: Macmillan, 1905 BMC NUC.

Hist. rom. of civil war PW 7-1-05
NYT 1905:480 LBKM 29-30:40

008743   THE STORY OF DUCIEHURST. A TALE OF THE MISSISSIPPI. BY CHARLES EGBERT CRADDOCK. New York: Macmillan, 1914 BMC NUC.

PW 86 8/15/14:482 "Instead of the familiar comedy, the resemblance between the Ducie twins, Randal and Adrian, makes for tragedy.Their plantation, Duciehurst, is illegally held by Floyd Rosney, who persuaded Paula to break her engagement with Randal Ducie to marry him. Paula is unhappy, and on an impulse restores some hidden papers and jewels to Randal, and goes back to her uncle's home. Her husband concludes that she has eloped with Randal. Unable to

distinguish between the twins, he kills Adrian in revenge. Floyd Rosney dies making his escape, and Randal marries a nobler and more constant woman than Paula."
Trad mystery, intrigue legal entanglement. BKM

008744   THE STORY OF OLD FORT LOUDON. BY CHARLES EGBERT CRADDOCK. New York and London: Macmillan, 1899 NUC BMC.

Historical romance about the Cherokee Indians, the Scot Alexander McLeod and Odalie McLeod. LIT 4:556. Odalie brings her gentle ways and artistic tastes into the wilderness and makes an ideal home. BKM 9:184
Play? Early Tennessee attack by Cherokees, NYT 2-25-1899 115

008745   THE WINDFALL: A NOVEL. BY CHARLES EGBERT CRADDOCK. New York: Duffield, 1907 NUC BMC. London: Chatto and Windus, 1907 BMC.

Moonshiner country, hero runs a traveling show. PW 4-27-07
BAKER 32:119
NYT

MURPHY, AGNES G.

008746   ONE WOMAN'S WISDOM. London: Routledge, 1895 BMC.

MURPHY, EMILY (FERGUSON). 1868-1933.

008747   JANEY CANUCK IN THE WEST. BY EMILY FERGUSON. London: Cassell, 1910 BMC NUC.

LBKM-travel in Canadian West

008748   OPEN TRAILS. BY JANEY CANUCK (EMILY FERGUSON). New York and London: Cassell, 1912 NUC BMC.

008749   SEEDS OF PINE. BY JANEY CANUCK. London and New York: Hodder & Stoughton, [1914] BMC NUC.

NYT-Author Canadian newspaperwoman; travels and sketches of Canada

MURPHY, EVA (MORLEY). United States.

008750   LOIS MORTON'S INVESTMENT. Topeka, Kan.: Crane, 1912 NUC.

MURRAY, ALICE E., pseud. See MACALEESE, SUSAN ELIZABETH.

MURRAY, DORA.

008751   A PRECIOUS JEWEL. London: Digby, Long, [1892] BMC. (The original name of the book, "The Sins of the Fathers," remains as a running title. BMC)

ACAD 42:168. Romance involving inheritance threatened by discovery of illegitimate birth. All works out.

MURRAY, EUNICE GUTHRIE. B. 1877.

008752   THE HIDDEN TRAGEDY. London: C. W. Daniel, [1917] BMC.

ATH Relates to work for woman suffrage; there is a love interest
Developes into what is really an "out of date" suffrage novel. Scot girl ed. at Girton takes to philanthropic work. TLS

008753   THE LASS HE LEFT BEHIND. London: A. H. Stockwell, [1918] BMC.

MURRAY, KATE.

008754   THE BLUE STAR: A ROMANCE OF TODAY. London: E.G. Richards, 1907 BMC.

Man purchases "dead" body of Henrietta, transmits her vitality to a young man weary of life; makes her a raving beauty. TLS.
French girl "restored to life after a long trance with amazing beauty and complete absence of soul." Author follows her career as far as conventions allow. SR

008755   THE SPIRIT OF THE HOUSE, BEING AN ACCOUNT OF CALDICOTT COURT--AN IMAGINARY HOUSE--AND OF SOME WHO DWELT THERE. London: Hodder and Stoughton, 1915 BMC.

Two women love one man; one loves him well enough to give him up to the other. TLS

Man engrossed in his house and garden. ATH

MURRAY, ROSALIND. B. 1890. United Kingdom.

008756   THE LEADING NOTE. London: Sidgwick &
Jackson, 1910 BMC NUC.

TLS-A Russian (a follower of Tolstoi) makes profound
impression on young woman.
SP-She is daughter of rich widower; Ortshoff's ideas
disturb her and when she sees him a year later begs
him to take her to Russia with him. He refuses.
Carola.
SR--C

008757   MOONSEED. London: Sidgwick & Jackson,
1911 BMC.

LBKM. Chloe, strange, suppressed, sensitive, eager for
beauty loves artist who loves her honest, proud out of
doors sport loving cousin. Both find him unworthy. She
makes a sober mrg with sober middle-aged man but the
freshness of her life is gone, not to be restored.
Birth and death of love sad story. TLS
Chloe Warburton secretive, outspoken, jealous and
unselfish "a three-cornered nature." Spends her life
in a dumb resentment vs the scheme of things. She
loves a young man but repels him so with her rudeness,
he turns to another, Augusta "a manly Amazon. The
young man Claude proves to be a cowardly man,
confesses it to Augusta, threatens suicide. She has
contempt for his weakness. It is Chloe who goes to
save Claude from himself. She in turn is repelled by
him, goes off, later marries another man. Five yrs
later, meets and falls under Claude's spell, then
depises husband. "A study of discontent" SP

008758   UNSTABLE WAYS. London & Toronto: Sidgwick
& Jackson, 1914 BMC.

SR 118 supp 24 Oct p7--Giocosa is discontented,
suicides. Rev. likens her to modern emancipated girl,
whose freedom has brought unhappiness. Sees novel as
criticism of the woman's movement, what is the author
doing?
ACAD 87:264--"A few thrashings in her youth and a
masterful lover would probably have saved her from her
sad fate." She is morbidto a degree; her outlook on
life is not vicious, but unhealthy. "It is evidently
the author's intention to portray to what lengths
discontent and restlessness, so evident in a certain
section of womanhood today, can lead their victim."
TLS-13:386-She is a foreign woman, not belonging to
any race or country not brought up in the security of
convention, and lacking the strength needed for a life
of freedom, which her parents had. The world seemed
"at times so alluring, at times so frightening". "She
had not the courage, the passion, and the purpose that
they must have who would be a law unto themselves; and
she was too restless and individualistic for the sheep
folds...She played about with men she could not love;
she found nothing real and nothing worth living for;
she was, if we may put it bluntly, a very selfish,
shallow and silly young person. And therefore, when
she comes to grief and is released by death, which she
so dreaded, from life, of which she could make
nothing, we are left unmoved, either in idea or heart.
She is, we feel not worth our troubling about."

MURRELL, CORNELIA RANDOLPH. B. 1851. Nationality Unknown.

008759   THE WHITE CASTLE OF LOUISIANA. BY M. R.
AILENROC. Louisville, Ky.: J. P. Morton, 1903 NUC.

Hist-PW
Louisiana-Social life & custom.

MURTAUGH, MARY G.

008760   SNATCHES FROM A DIARY, 1917-18. Boston:
Four Seas, 1918 NUC.

NYT Tells the author's emotions regarding an American
girl whose soldier lover is at war.

MUZAKOVA, JOHANA (ROTTOVA). 1830-1899.

008761   MARIA FELICIA ("THE LAST MISTRESS OF
HLOHOV") A STORY OF BOHEMIAN LOVE. BY CAROLINE SVETLA.
Chicago: A.C. McClurg, 1898 NUC. (Tr. Antonie Krejsa)

PW-Bohemia during rule of Maria Teresa and Joseph II.
Maria, daughter of an aristocrat, devotes her life to
rights of masses and justice for a persecuted
religious society. Love story too. Bohemia in second
emperor Joseph's reign. BOOK NEWS 98-99:306.

MUZZY, ALICE M. Nationality Unknown.

008762   THREE FAIR PHILANTHROPISTS. New York:
Abbey Press, [c1901] NUC.

MYDDLETON, FAY. Nationality Unknown.

008763   "IMPOSSIBLE PETER". London: W. Collins
Sons, [1918] BMC NUC.

TLS-Love and inheritance

008764   SOURIS. A NOVEL. London & Dublin:
Maunsel, 1915 BMC.

A handsome artist wooing village maid; at end the
great recital where glimpse of his wife restores the
soul to his music. Maureen (Souris-Sweet Soul) wants
to live but is crushed. LBKM

MYERS, ANNA BALMER. United States.

008765   PATCHWORK; A STORY OF "THE PLAIN PEOPLE".
Philadelphia: G. W. Jacobs, [c1920] NUC.

PW-Rom, Penn Dutch
NYT 1920:321 "Perfectly innocuous little story" about
Phoebe, her voice lessons in Philadelphia, and her
loves.

MYLECHREEST, WINIFRED BROOKS.

008766   THE FAIREST OF THE STUARTS. London: S.
Low, 1912 BMC NUC.

TLS-hist. rom.

NALKOWSKA, SOFJA RYGIER. See NALKOWSKA, ZOFIA RYGIER.

NALKOWSKA, ZOFIA RYGIER. 1885-1954. Poland.

008767   KOBIETY-WOMEN. A NOVEL OF POLISH LIFE. BY
SOFJA RYGIER-NALKOWSKA. New York and London: G. P.
Putnam's Sons, 1920 BMC NUC. (Tr. Michael Henry
Dziewicki)

TLS-Exposure of the fem. mind, women need men's love,
but they always lose, no matter how much supremacy
they seem to have. Altho they have loss, they also
have honor, a quality men don't share. Story of three
women.
PW (v98, no 18, Nov 6, 1920, p 73)--Identifies author
as "brilliant Polish woman." Unusual study of woman's
psych. Told in first person, she dislikes all
colorless people. Unfolds the reactions of a woman to
her environment. In the manner of Marie Bashkirtseff.
NYT 10-24-20 p. 25.
PW-Analysis of feminine psychology.

NAPIER, EVA MARIA LOUISA (MACDONALD). 1846-1930. United
Kingdom.

008768   "AS THE SPARKS FLY UPWARD." London: H. J.
Drane, [1905] BMC.

Review compares author with Corelli; doesn't say much
about this satire. ACAD 882,05
A perfect heroine dies at the end? LBKM 213, 27-8

008769   CAN MAN PUT ASUNDER? BY LADY NAPIER OF
MAGDALA. London: J. Murray, 1911 BMC NUC.

The round of balls and teas of high society. ACAD.
Shona Barcaldine doesn't think about marriage, but
when several seasons go by and no "husband" comes
forth, her parents worry. She's perfectly content to
live with her parents. When she learns her parents are
anxious, she rushes into a loveless marriage. And
there's another woman in her husband's life. How does
it end? LBKM
"Personal aspect of the divorce question" heroine
repents her hasty marriage ATH

008770   FIONA. London: J. Murray, 1909 BMC.

Fiona's lover rescues her from a whale; commonplace
romance TLS
Fond of painting. LBKM

008771   HALF A LIE. London: J. Murray, 1916 BMC.

TLS--girl's life marred by scandal of alleged
flirtations with chauffeur.
SR-Girl who harks back to stage, her half lie
(designed to save herself) nearly wrecks reputation of

high born girl. Virtue triumphs and all ends well.

008772   HOW SHE PLAYED THE GAME. London: J.
Murray, 1910 BMC.

TLS--High spirited-girl used to luxury becomes poor
and a companion.
ATH-to a vulgar lady. After a few rom. adv. marries a
Scots lover.

008773   MUDDLING THROUGH. London: J. Murray, 1912
BMC.

TLS--story of a widow and her wooer.

008774   A STORMY MORNING. London: J. Murray, 1908
BMC.

TLS-Love in high soc.
SR-
ATH

008775   TO THE THIRD AND FOURTH GENERATIONS.
London: J. Murray, 1913 BMC.

Seduction, ghosts, illegitimate infant, death in a
convent. ATH
Hildegard Mauleverer makes a loveless marriage with a
marquess and forces her daughter into a loveless
marriage with a Russian prince. TLS

NAPIER, ROSAMOND. See LAWRENCE, ROSAMOND (NAPIER).

NAPIER OF MAGDALA, LADY. See NAPIER, EVA MARIA LOUISA
(MACDONALD).

NASH, CELIA.

008776   QUEENS AND KNAVES: A NOVEL. London:
Digby, Long, [1898] BMC.

ACAD 53:93. Wicked Jew Steinsen and his victims, his
ultimate downfall.

NEAL, ELIZABETH.

008777   COMING OF AGE. London: Hurst and
Blackett, 1895 BMC.

Death of baby baronet and substitution of him for his
Italian foster brother. A melo-drama but with humorous
characters like Lady Rosalie Finch. SP 75:561
Capt. Dalrymple tried for forgery-wife and daughters
show little interest. "Genteel melodrama."ATH 106:350

008778   FRIEND OR RIVAL. London: Hurst and
Blackett, 1896 BMC.

ATH 107:114. Narrated by plain older sister of
beautiful Vera. Sympathetic account of Nihilists and
their persecutions.
ACAD 49:134. Vera has two lovers; trickery on the part
of Sergius who allows his love for Vera to take
precedence over his desire to rescue or avenge his
Russian mother who was banished to Siberia at his
birth. He persuades Percival, the other lover, to make
the trip to Russia in his place.
SP 76:307. Percival has always taken 2nd place in
their scholastic rivalry. Vera has a secret.

008779   IN HER OWN RIGHT. London: Oliphant,
Anderson and Ferrier, 1892 BMC.

008780   MY BROTHER BASIL. Edinburgh and London:
Oliphant, Anderson, 1891 BMC. New York: A. D. F.
Randolph, [1892] NUC.

Man ignorant of parentage turns out to be heir to
great estate and displaces the wicked heir-apparent.
ACAD

008781   SIFTED AS WHEAT. Edinburgh and London:
Oliphant, 1893 BMC.

008782   WITNESS MY HAND: A FENSHIRE STORY.
London: Cassell, 1894 BMC.

008783   THE WOOING OF CHRISTABEL. Edinburgh:
Oliphant, Anderson and Ferrier, 1892 BMC.

NEEDELL, MARY ANNA (LUPTON). B. 1830. United Kingdom.

008784   THE HONOUR OF VIVIEN BRUCE. A NOVEL.
London: F. V. White, 1899 BMC.

Attack on her poor writing. ATH 114:220.

008785   JAMES VANSITTART'S VENGEANCE; A NOVEL. BY
MRS. J. H. NEEDELL. New York: D. Appleton, 1895 NUC.

008786   PASSING THE LOVE OF WOMEN: A NOVEL. BY
MRS. J. H. NEEDELL. London: F. Warne, 1892 BMC. New
York: D. Appleton, 1892 NUC.

ATH 100:625. Title refers to friendship between two
male cousins. Margery Denison lacks "femininity,"
"fails to stir deep interest."
LW 23:354. They are both in love with her.
"a kind of David and Jonathan love between two cousins
who have been attached to the same girl" CR. 14, 21:61

008787   STEPHEN ELLICOTT'S DAUGHTER: A NOVEL. BY
MRS. J. H. NEEDELL. London and New York: F. Warne,
1891 BMC. New York: D. Appleton, 1891 NUC.

CR 17:36 "Tale of fraud and felony committed by father
and son" and the effects on their lives. Moral theme.
Steps in a man's descent to crime and his break with
his sister: SP 66, 596.
Characters highly stylized BAKER 03, 153;
concerns heredity. Hester Ellicott's mother died at
Hester's birth: raised by father, a self made rich
farmer. They are close. She's the studious type,
marries squire's son. Effect of heritage on the pair;
LW.
Winifred is the proud sister. ACAD
The sufferings of a woman who watches her husband sink
low into immoral life. ATH 97 307

008788   UNEQUALLY YOKED. BY MRS. J. H. NEEDELL.
Edinburgh and London: Oliphant, Anderson, 1891 BMC.
Boston: A. I. Bradley, 1898 NUC.

A domestic novel; cultured man, vulgar, ignorant woman
marry-both unhappy. BAKER 03, 153
She married him to be secure and to amuse herself;
instead she finds she's shut away in the country -her
husband away doing parish work most of day. He loves
her but just isn't the demonstrative type. An old
lover shows up. Gossip. Focus on behavior and
character of heroine. ACAD
PW-marriage of son of rector to his social inferior.
Warning to young people against this kind of marriage.
Happy ending after all.

008789   UNSTABLE AS WATER. BY MRS. J. H. NEEDELL.
London and New York: F. Warne, 1902 BMC NUC.

008790   THE VENGEANCE OF JAMES VANSITTART. BY
MRS. J. H. NEEDELL. London: Hutchinson, 1895 BMC. New
York: D. Appleton, 1895 NUC.

A vengeance that survives a generation and is taken
out on an innocent young man simply because he is his
father's son; also a pair ofportraits in contrast:
selfish weak Maurice Vansittart (whose uncle seeks
vengeance) and his wife Diane moved by duty rather
than love and whose situation is pitiable. SP 74:907
Noble young woman weds a hateful man to save her
father from ruin and save her brothers and sisters.
But the man Maurice is merely dependent on uncle. She
is Diana Charteris. When they wed, uncle casts them
out. Maurice collapses; wife battles adversity. ACAD
47:522
"The life of woman with a man whom she has never loved
and cannot respect is described in detail." PW
6-15-95:939.
He wants to revenge himself on his brother who wronged
him, but the brother dies so he plots his revenge vs
his brother's son. Accepts him, gives him life of
luxury, sees him marry a woman whose family is
destitute and who marries him only for money. Then he
cuts him off. The rest of the novel is a fine study of
the wife Diana Charteris-all the hardships. Her
splendid nobility. BKM 4:417

NEEDELL, MRS. J. H. See NEEDELL, MARY ANNA (LUPTON).

NEEDHAM, ELIZABETH ANNABLE. B. 1844. United States.

008791   MRS. WHILLING'S FAITH CURE. BY MRS. GEO.
C. NEEDHAM. Boston: Bradley and Woodruff, [c1891] NUC.

NEEDHAM, HANNAH.

008792   "AN HELPMEET". London: W.&G. Foyle, 1919
BMC.

Anti-feminist novel. TLS

NEEDHAM, MRS. GEO. C. See NEEDHAM, ELIZABETH ANNABLE.

NEFF, ELIZABETH (HYER). D. 1942. United States.

008793   ALTARS TO MAMMON. New York: F.A. Stokes,
[1908] NUC.

PW-hero a clergyman.
BKM-hero a clergyman

008794   MISS WEALTHY, DEPUTY SHERIFF. New York:
F.A. Stokes, [1912] NUC.

pW-silly

NEILD, AGNES L.

008795   ROUGH-HEWERS. London: Murray and Evenden,
[1913] BMC.

Domestic life in the North, depressing. ATH

NEILL, MAIDIE.

008796   TENNESSEE LEE. BY TYDANCE BRUCE. New
York: F. T. Neely, [c1902] NUC.

NEISH, ROSALIE.

008797   THE OTHERS-BY ONE OF THEM. Bristol: J.W.
Arrowsmith, [1898] BMC. (Tales (BMC))

SP 81:Gentle satire of family with six children,
placid matron, complacent egotistical politician.

NELSON, KATHLEEN GRAY. United States.

008798   TUEN, SLAVE AND EMPRESS. New York: E.P.
Dutton, 1898 NUC. London: Sands, 1899 BMC.

PW - Sold by her father as a slave and then adopted by
that family, presented to emperor and marriage
follows.

NELSON, ROBERTA BERESFORD. 1864-1910. United States.

008799   ONCE UPON A TIME: STORIES. Franklin,
Ohio: Editor Pub. Co., 1895 NUC.

NEPEAN, EDITH.

008800   GWYNETH OF THE WELSH HILLS. London: S.
Paul, 1917 BMC.

TLS: country story Wales.
SP: melodrama.
Joins a band of gypsies but essentially a traditional
love story. LBKM

008801   WELSH LOVE. London: S. Paul, 1919 BMC.

Traditional love story. TLS

NEPEAN, ELEANOR.

008802   SEA AND SWORD. London: Digby, Long, 1915
BMC.

Tale of days when Eng. Pirates took Span. nobles
prisoners. Time of Inquisition. A young woman
masquerades as the captain of a pirate ship. TLS

008803   THE STAIN. London: Hurst & Blackett, 1919
BMC.

A baronet's wife takes her husband's cousin as a
lover. Her child is born (the lover is the father)
after the husband dies and results in her lover's loss
of inheritance. TLS

NEPEAN, EVELYN MAUD (REID). United Kingdom.

008804   MY TWO KINGS. 1674-1686, 1916. BY MRS.
EVAN NEPEAN. London: A. Melrose, 1917 BMC NUC. New
York: Dutton, 1918 NUC. (Am. ed. title: My Two Kings;
a Novel of the Stuart Restoration.)

PW-author believes she is Charlotte Stuart, a cousin
of Charles II & this is an account of her other life.

NEPEAN, MRS. EVAN. See NEPEAN, EVELYN MAUD (REID).

NESBIT, E. See BLAND, EDITH (NESBIT).

NETHERSOLE, S. C. See NETHERSOLE, SUSIE COLYER.

NETHERSOLE, SUSIE COLYER. B. 1869. United Kingdom.

008805   THE GAME OF THE TANGLED WEB. London:
Mills & Boon, 1916 BMC.

TLS-Prunella and her husband adopt a tinker's boy
after her son dies. Meticulous record, son is only an
average type. Prunella dies at same time.

008806   MARY UP AT GAFFRIES AND LETITIA HER
FRIEND. London: Mills and Boon, 1909 BMC.

Independent and intell. woman of Kent where their
labor is valuable. Mary is strong, proud,
selfpossessed, capable, discovers she's illeg.
splendid women, worthless men. TLS
"women give their lives mainly to expiating the
transgressions of their menkind being"ATH
Quiet account of country life; Mary is "delightful".
SP

008807   RIPE CORN. A NOVEL. London: Mills & Boon,
1911 BMC.

"The reader hates Missie Victoria" Jane Tallboys
marries Jim in the end ? TLS
Story of village life; not much here SP

008808   TAKE JOY HOME: A NOVEL OF COUNTRY LIFE.
London: Mills & Boon, 1919 BMC.

She marries old man, he dies, marries man of her
choice. TLS
Nothing new ATH

008809   WILSAM. BY S. C. NETHERSOLE. New York:
Macmillan, 1913 NUC. London: Mills & Boon, [1913] BMC
NUC.

PW 83 5/31/13:1960 "Wilsam: goods driven ashore where
no wreck or ship is visible, hence called goods of
God's mercy. A waif cast up by the sea on the Kentish
coast is the heroine. She finds relatives, one a
feeble-minded aunt with whom she lives, others a
grasping uncle and his wife, and their two sons. She
grows into girlhood and womanhood, marrying one of her
cousins, and always through her life there is the deep
murmur of an undercurrent of tragedy and always she
justifies the title wilsam. Setting is a vivid picture
of the coast of Kent and the hop country."
Changes point of view with each chapter; farmer class.
Tragedy at end after Mercy Pardilov's marriage. SP
Shipwreck, tiny girl survivor, washed ashore into arms
of person her mother, dying, consigned her to. They
name her Wilsam. Her father had wronged her mother's
sister, then run away with her (Mercy's mother) It was
Hannah Anseed, the sister's friend who saw her through
her pregnancy. Hannah makes the man she marries accept
the child, no questions asked. Hannah cares for the
sister Milly after her year in an asylum, now docile
as a child. Her boy and Mercy grow up together not
knowing they are brother and sister. We watch Milly
grow up, through drudgery, obstacles, heartaches
bitter trials of married life. Husband causes death of
their child, becomes a raving creature-goes mad. At
the end she has a chance for a belated and crippled
happiness. BKM

NEVADA. See MACNEILL, NEVADA.

NEVILL, FLORENCE. Nationality Unknown.

008810   WHAT DREAMS MAY COME: A STUDY IN FAILURE.
Boston: Sherman, French, 1910 NUC. London: R. Scott,
1914 BMC.

ATH- a thoughtful attempt to solve problem of
suffering and to point out sin of self-murder.

NEVILLE, JULIA.

008811   THE SLEEPING VILLAGE. A TALE OF RUSSIA.
London: J. Long, [1912] BMC.

ATH-love story.

NEW, CATHERINE (MACLAEN). Canada.

008812   A WOMAN REIGNS. Indianapolis:
Bowen-Merrill, 1896 NUC. (The Fate of a Fatalist: pp.
73-112.)

NEWBERRY, FANNIE ELLSWORTH (STONE). 1848-1942. United
States.

008813   BRIAN'S HOME. Boston: Congregational
Sunday School and Publishing Society, [1892] NUC.

LW 23:246. Story of a family of children. wholesome.

008814   BUBBLES. Boston: A. I. Bradley, 1897 NUC.

BKM 6:562. ?worldly woman who gave her honor to a man
she loved?

008815   BY STRANGE PATHS. London: A. Melrose,
1898 BMC.

ACAD 54:245. Heroine applies for position of
housekeeper, marries not long after.
ATH 112:489. Denver, Col. Keen appreciation of a
woman's troubles and difficulties. "Heroine is
depicted as a kind of Parthenia and hero as modern
Ingomar."
SR 86:480. Priggish and goody-goody.

008816   THE HOUSE OF HOLLISTER. Boston: A. I.
Bradley, 1895 BMC.

The Hollisters are wealthy mill owners-the elite of
Stillmere, one of whom tries to prevent a boss
lumberman from moving in next door. PW 10-5-95:585.

008817   THE IMPRESS OF A GENTLEWOMAN. Boston:
Bradley and Woodruff, [c1891] NUC. London: Hutchinson,
[1894] BMC.

Romance ACAD 41:34.
A refined Christian woman goes to a rough wild town
and works wonders in reforming the people; writing is
weak. IND.
Town of Action. Mrs. Raymond betters the conditions;
socially, morally, and physically. PW 9-12-9 1

008818   JOYCE'S INVESTMENTS. Boston: A. I.
Bradley, 1899 NUC.

She's heiress to a large fortune gotten dishonestly by
her father. She takes her mother's name, goes to
father's factories, introduces new methods, builds new
houses for the workers, improves their lives. She
succeeds in all and weds the man of her choice. LW
30:377

008819   NOT FOR PROFIT. Boston: A.I. Bradley,
[c1894] NUC.

LW 25:302 New England spinster, Thirza Bascom,
inherits money and opens a boarding house in Chicago
for benefit of guests.

008820   THE ODD ONE. Boston: A. I. Bradley, 1893
NUC.

Because she's different from her four sisters,
Elizabeth Merritt is called the odd one and for this
is chosen to go with invalid uncle to California. The
trip and her unusual action after her return. PW
9-2-93.

008821   SARA, A PRINCESS. Boston: Bradley &
Woodruff, [c1892] NUC.

PW-Heroine is fisherman's daughter, has had some
education. An orphan, with a young family dependent on
her, she doesn't lose sight of her high aims and
glowing aspirations.

008822   A SON'S VICTORY: A STORY OF THE LAND OF
THE HONEY-BEE. Boston: Pilgrim Press, [c1897] NUC.

008823   STRANGE CONDITIONS. Boston: A. I.
Bradley, [c1896] NUC. London: Hodder and Stoughton,
1898 BMC.

LIT 3:525. Heroine "regenerates the family whom she
serves."
PW-10-10-96. Young woman because of health changes
employment from office work to housekeeper. Head of
household a wealthy widower. They marry. First wife,
long believed dead, shows up.

008824   THE WRESTLER OF PHILIPPI; A TALE OF THE
EARLY CHRISTIANS. Elgin, Ill.: D. C. Cook, [1896] NUC.

NEWBIGGING, ANNA CHRISTENA (ISAACSON). B. 1869. United
States.

008825   A CRY OF THE SOUL; A ROMANCE OF 1862.
Boston: Sherman, French, 1917 NUC.

A woman's Mormon faith keeps the couple apart till she
gives it up. PW

NEWCOMBE, ELIZABETH.

008826   THE IRONY OF FATE: A NOVEL. London:
Digby, Long, 1895 BMC.

NEWHALL, LAURA EUGENIA TERRY. B. 1861. United States.

008827   THE BRIDE OF INFELICE: A NOVEL. BY ADA L.
HALSTEAD. [San Francisco: Bancroft], [1892] NUC.

NEWLIN, KATHARINE. Nationality Unknown.

008828   THE LELY OR THE LADY. A STORY OF AMERICAN
DOLLARS AND AN HEIRLOOM PICTURE. London: Cassell, 1913
BMC.

"Tells of the visit of an American heiress to the
house of an English lord, who owns a famous painting.
This picture is the cause of much trouble and
excitement, and changes hands more than once in the
story. Linda Roland, the American pulling all the
strings by which her English friends dance to her
tune, and which bring a surprising denouement." PW

008829   PENELOPE INTRUDES. A STORY FOR GIRLS.
London: Cassell, [1911] BMC. New York: Cassell, [1912]
NUC.

PW-American girl in England.

NEWMAN, MARY WENTWORTH. Nationality Unknown.

008830   BEGUN IN JEST. London: J. Murray, 1891
BMC.

Mabel Lieth raised in rich family has no training to
support self, but in part to show she can and in part
to get away from the man she loves (whom she believes
loves her sister) she takes a job as a governess
posing as a poor woman. Her first position is a
failure; her second more successful. The love
entanglements are worked out. Light and humorous
reading. SP 67 927
Makes five conquests in the three months, but a few of
these turn to other women very rapidly. She's
bold-interrupts conversations, gives opinions when not
asked, argues with male strangers, dresses boldly. No
less than four sets of lovers paired off at the end.
SR 12-12-91, 670
ATH 99:12 "Mabel's experiment of acting as an amateur
governess."

008831   HIS VINDICATION. Westminster: A.
Constable, 1896 BMC.

SR-Grown-up fairy-tale with happy ending for all the
good characters.
ACAD 50:305. Vindication of Latimer who died by his
own hand and whose fortune has been invested in a
ruinous mine. Vindication worked out by Barbara, his
ward, and Noel, his son. Interesting development of
Barbara's character.

008832   JAN. London: Christian Knowledge Society,
1891 BMC.

008833   JOHN MAILLARD. London: Christian
Knowledge Society, [1894] BMC.

SR-young clergyman and his relations with his
vicarage.

008834   THE PARTING WAYS. London: Christian
Knowledge Society, [1897] BMC.

008835   WHAT CAME BETWEEN. London: Christian
Knowledge Society, [1893] BMC.

NEWTON, ALMA. United States.

008836   A JEWEL IN THE SAND. New York: Duffield,
1919 NUC.

PW-a talented young woman wins her way in the world.
NYT Jan 25 '20 p. 39. She is sensitive, craves beauty
and perfect experience. She doesn't find perfect love,
men see in her another Lilith. She loses her grip on
life, an accident disfigures her. Her spiritual and
mystical vision overcome her circumstances.
Realistic story of career of brilliant woman whose
talents bring her in touch with people who have no
appreciation of her. The story involves her efforts to
get away from these "friends." NYT 10-19-19, 572

008837   THE LOVE LETTERS OF A MYSTIC. New York:
J. Lane, 1916 NUC.

letters between two parted lovers conv stuff NYT
Written from Capri by a violinist, to recall to the
woman he loves the happiness they had together, and to
hunt for the reason for her coldness. The explanation
brings happiness at the end. PW

008838   MEMORIES. New York: Duffield, 1917 NUC.

diary of woman whose love is unrequited; helps man
marry woman he loves, without bitterness PW
spiritual theme. Narrator (a woman, Zarah Kreeshna),
loves the same man her best woman friend loves. The
man loves her friend, Sarah. Spiritual experience of
the love torn woman. NYT

NEWTON, ELIZABETH.

008839   UNDER THE LINDEN. A NOVEL. BY GILLAN
VASE. London: Digby, Long, 1900 BMC.

ACAD 58:126. Sentimental German story. Romance, two
twin sisters, double suicide.
LIT 6:336. Germany, German characters. Cruel treatment
at Town Orphanage.

NEWTON, LUCY HAY.

008840   A GIRL OF YESTERDAY. London: Hurst &
Blackett, 1896 BMC.

SR- Unhappy marriage. Wife compromises herself with
worldly man; husband reappears and they are reunited.
ATH 107:60. Innocent friendship with cad, her eyes are
opened before any catastrophe occurs.

008841   SOMEWHERE IN SCOTLAND, AUGUST TO
DECEMBER, 1914. BY MRS. F. HAY-NEWTON. London: J.
Murray, 1917 NUC BMC.

Effect of war on Scot. village. TLS
CR compares it to other works says little. Diary of
Miss Mysie Cuningham. TLS

NEWTON, MRS. F. HAY. See NEWTON, LUCY HAY.

NICHOLAS, ANNA. United States.

008842   THE MAKING OF THOMAS BARTON.
Indianapolis: The Bobbs-Merrill Company, [c1913] NUC
BMC.

Short stories? "Miss Lucyann...stole the family
Bible...the Postmistress...undeniable abuse of her
official position." NYT 1913 502

NICHOLL, EDITH M. See BOWYER, EDITH M. (NICHOLL).

NICHOLS, LAURA D.

008843   A NORWAY SUMMER. Boston: Roberts, 1897
NUC.

Ellen records her impressions of Norway and a love
story-hers-with Sidney. BKM 6; 258

NICHOLSON, CELIA ANNA. United Kingdom.

008844   MARTIN, SON OF JOHN. London: Sidgwick &
Jackson, 1918 BMC.

Wife deserts him; son murders him. SR

NICHOLSON, EDITH MAUD.

008845   BENT ON CONQUEST. London: Hurst and
Blackett, 1892 BMC NUC.

ACAD 42:308. "Tangled love affairs satisfactorily
adjusted" charming butler turns out to be employer's
heir.

NICHOLSON, JESSIE L.

008846   AFTER LONG WAITING. London: Hurst and
Blackett, 1897 BMC NUC.

Improbable plot concerning "lost or stolen children"
SR 83:278
A child is kidnapped, then found. "The finding...is a
great disappointment." Two love stories that end in
marriage. SP 78:810
Lost for 16 yrs. He shows up but there are still many
complications. ATH 109:112

008847   'TWIXT WILL AND WILL NOT. London: Hurst

and Blackett, 1895 BMC.

Rhoda and sister Fannie, merry and whole-some. SR
80:447 Rhoda Heriot takes job of governess, falls in
love with landowner Burke. But there's a mystery about
him. She throws him over only to discover he's a much
better man than she had dreamed. All works out. ACAD
48:243
ATH 107:146. "Commonplace "heroine; repellantly
angular middle-aged suitor.
SP 76:779. Rhoda is plain, straightforward, foil to
Charles Burke.

NICHOLSON, LUCY.

008848   THE TEMPERAMENT OF THOMASINA. London:
Methuen, 1916 BMC.

ATH-T's father trains her to be practical; she
develops a turn for poetry.

NICHOLSON, MEREDITH. 1866-1947. United States.

008849   BLACKSHEEP! BLACKSHEEP! New York: C.
Scribner's Sons, 1920 NUC.

008850   A HOOSIER CHRONICLE. Boston: Houghton
Mifflin, 1912 NUC BMC.

008851   THE HOUSE OF A THOUSAND CANDLES.
Indianapolis: Bobbs-Merrill, [1905] NUC BMC. London:
[Daily Mail Sixpenny Novels #35], [1908] NUC.

008852   LADY LARKSPUR. New York: C. Scribner's
Sons, 1919 NUC.

008853   THE LITTLE BROWN JUG AT KILDARE.
Indianapolis: Bobbs-Merrill, [1908] NUC. (Eng. ed.
title: The War of the Carolinas.)

008854   THE LORDS OF THE HIGH DECISION. New York:
Doubleday, Page, 1909 NUC. London: Doubleday Page,
1909 BMC.

008855   THE MADNESS OF MAY. New York: C.
Scribner's Sons, 1917 NUC.

008856   THE MAIN CHANCE. Indianapolis:
Bobbs-Merrill, [1903] NUC BMC.

008857   OTHERWISE PHYLLIS. Boston: Houghton
Mifflin, 1913 NUC. London: Constable, 1913 BMC.

008858   THE PORT OF MISSING MEN. Indianapolis:
Bobbs-Merrill, [1907] NUC BMC. London: Gay & Bird,
1907 BMC.

008859   THE PROOF OF THE PUDDING. London: Hodder
& Stoughton, 1916 BMC. Boston: Houghton Mifflin, 1916
BMC.

ATH-flirty heroine has love affair with hard drinking
drug merchant, he gets a divorce but is saved and
recaptured by wife. Heroine becomes serious minded
prosperous.
BKM-

008860   A REVERSIBLE SANTA CLAUS. Boston:
Houghton Mifflin, 1917 NUC.

008861   ROSALIND AT RED GATE. Indianapolis:
Bobbs-Merrill, [1907] NUC. London: Everett, 1908 BMC.

008862   THE SIEGE OF THE SEVEN SUITORS. Boston:
Houghton Mifflin, 1910 NUC. London: Constable, 1910
BMC.

008863   THE VALLEY OF DEMOCRACY. London and New
York: A Melrose, 1919 BMC.

008864   THE WAR OF THE CAROLINAS. London,
Edinburgh, and New York: T. Nelson, [1909] NUC BMC.
(Am. ed. title: The Little Brown Jug at Kildare.)

No. Carolina-So. Carolina

008865   ZELDA DAMERON. Indianapolis:
Bobbs-Merrill, [1904] NUC BMC.

NICHOLSON, VICTORIA MARY SACKVILLE-WEST. B. 1892. United
Kingdom.

008866   HERITAGE. BY V. SACKVILLE-WEST. London:
W. Collins Sons, [c1919] BMC NUC. New York: G.H.
Doran, [c1919] NUC.

Traces Spanish heredity. 2 narrators: A begins by
telling how B told him a story. Then A picks up the
story for himself; then B comes in again by means of
letters to A. B a priggish pedant who "noses about the
psychology of a splendid woman rather than falling in
love with her and saving her from marrying a brute who
had a hold over her, the hold was the drop of Spanish
blood." B transformed from prig to man, wins the young
woman back in the end. "We suspect something subtler
than the story brings out." TLS
Ruth Penniston (2 sides to her nature) wild Sp
passionate side leads her to marry her wild cousin.
Sussex side loves a quiet middle-aged Englishman. SP
No central point only many points of significance. 1st
narrator Malory a voyeur relates an experience with
English family the Penniston's. The strangeness of the
family is that the great grand mother was a Spanish
dancer. That wild blood runs in Ruth and Ruth's
cousin. 2nd narrator the listener visits the family
one year later. Ruth miserable with cruel husband.
This narrator wishes the husband dead so Ruth can
marry Malory. Ruth shoots husband but doesn't kill
him. 3rd part journal sent by Mallory to his friend.
Tells of next 10 years. How he (Mallory) asked Ruth to
leave her husband, she refused. Mallory returns to
find husband left out of fear of Ruth. Can now marry
Mallory fear of what? SP LBKM
Reviewer likes the book, but finds it disjointed. BKM
9-19

NICKLIN, CONSTANCE.

　　008867　　　　THE HOUR AND THE WOMAN. London: Methuen,
1910 BMC.

　　TLS-she hunts the opposite sex, she is plain,
unsuccessful. A gloomy book.
ATH-Repellent woman in charge of small girl whom she
alternately loves and jealously hates makes herself
indispensible to child in order to marry father.
SR-Has set her heart on marriage-any marriage and is
repeatedly disappointed. Heart overflows with rancor
and bitterness.

NIGHTINGALE, HELEN MARGARET.

　　008868　　　　SAVILE GILCHRIST, M.D. London: J. Long,
1906 BMC.

　　TLS-fictionalized version of surgeon's life.

NIXON, LOUISA.

　　008869　　　　A MINISTERING ANGEL. London: Simpkin,
1906 BMC.

　　Crammed with earls & baronets. Dull, childish. TLS

NIXON, MARY F. See ROULET, MARY F. (NIXON).

NIXSON, EDITH MAY MAYER.

　　008870　　　　GOLDEN VANITY. BY MAISIE BENNETT. London:
Mills & Boon, 1912 BMC.

　　TLS-Orphanage to domestic service to stage; finally
united with lover.

NOBLE, ANNETTE LUCILE. 1844-1932. United States.

　　008871　　　　A CRAZY ANGEL. New York & London: G. P.
Putnam's Sons, 1901 BMC NUC. (with the collaboration
of Grace Lathrop Collin.)

　　ATH 3-8-02. Conventional, American heiress and her
love story.

　　008872　　　　EUGENE'S QUEST. New York: American Tract
Society, [1906] NUC.

　　008873　　　　JACOB'S HEIRESS. Philadelphia:
Presbyterian Board of Publication and Sabbath School
Work, [c1894] NUC.

　　PW-Historical romance-16th century persecution of
Protestants in Holland and France.

　　008874　　　　LOVE AND SHAWL-STRAPS. New York, London:
G. P. Putnam's Sons, 1894 NUC. (with the collaboration
of Pearl Clement Coann.)

　　CR 25:370. Doctor and his sister travel for his
health, meet a lot of people interested in
love-making. End up taking home two old women without
"entanglements"

008875　　　　THE PARSONAGE SECRET. New York: J. B.
Dunn, 1898 NUC.

008876　　　　THE PROFESSOR'S DILEMMA. New York,
London: G. P. Putnam's Sons, 1897 BMC NUC.

　　Fresh, high spirited tale of two elderly aunts and
their entanglement with a professor. LBKM 13:106.
The two women are off to Egypt to join their brother.
Prof. tries to decide between them. LW 28:343.
Professor Reid. Jean penrose is the one. PW 52:111.
The other gets a husband too. LIT. 1:148.
Comedy: Americans touring Egypt. ATH 113:239.

008877　　　　RACHEL'S FARM. New York: American Tract
Society, [c1894] NUC.

　　PW-Rachel an orphan, worked as a typewriter for her
uncle, but was constantly made aware of her dependent
position. Accepts the offer of an aunt to make her
farm her home, learns the daily work of the farm,
eventually inherits it and puts it to use.

NOEL, AUGUSTA.

008878　　　　THE WISE MAN OF STERNCROSS. London: J.
Murray, 1901 BMC.

　　ATH 6-15-01

NOMAD, pseud. See SMITH, ADELE CRAFTON.

NOOT, JUDITH. B. 1859. Nationality Unknown.

008879　　　　LADY DEAN'S DAUGHTER, OR THE CONFESSION
OF A DYING WOMAN. New York: Cochrane, 1909 NUC.

　　Husband, believing he has married his sister leaves
her. Child kidnapped; she must work. Happy ending. PW
4-17-09
"Wife's horrible plans for revenge upon a husband who
had deserted her;" plans wreck five lives. BKM

NORFLEET. MINNIE TISING.

008880　　　　WHIRL AROUND THE WORLD. Versailles, Mo.:
Versailles Statesman, 1918 NUC.

　　Trip around the world.

NORMAN, MRS. GEORGE, pseud. See BLOUNT, MELESINA MARY.

NORRIS, KATHLEEN (THOMPSON). 1880-1966. United States.

008881　　　　HARRIET AND THE PIPES. London: J. Murray,
1920 BMC. Garden City: Doubleday, page, 1920 NUC.

　　TLS-Richard Carter's love story. Wife is soulless,
beautiful and they divorce. Harriet 29 years old is
governess in family.
ATH-finally marries Richard.
PW-Gives herself to a poet and adventurer, how she
meets the consequences and finds real love.
NYT 8-1-20 p. 24 She's actually innocent, traditional
plot of governess marrying into family of wealth.

008882　　　　THE HEART OF RACHEL. London: J. Murray,
1916 BMC. Garden City, N.Y.: Doubleday, Page, 1916
NUC.

　　marries for comfort, miserable marriage, divorce, 2nd
marriage for love ATH
Rachael divorces Clarence. Marries Dr. Gregory comes
to believe all divorces are wrong leaves Gregory PW
90:8/19/16:569.
PW 9 0:8/19/16 600-1 "burden of Rachael's philosophy
and apparently the author's is that divorce for any
reason is wrong."
NYT--What is the menacing tragedy of the closing
chapter? She has two sons by 2nd marriage. After 8
years of marriage to their father, she discovers he's
infatuated by someone else.

008883　　　　JOSSELYN'S WIFE. Garden City, New York:
Doubleday, Page, 1918 NUC. London: J. Murray, 1919
BMC.

　　PW-great love conquers all.
NYT Sept 29 '18 p. 410. Studies art, but mostly
romance is theme.
A good murder story and a love story of a too too
faithful wife. TLS

008884　　　　MARTIE, THE UNCONQUERED. Garden City, N.
Y.: Doubleday, Page, 1917 NUC. London: J. Murray, 1918
BMC.

TLS-Moral is need of giving girls a training or
profession. Struggles of Martie, throughout life to
earn a living without it. Further complicated by her
R.C.ism. which prohibits her marrying a divorced man.
Martie Monroe, youngest daughter of a shiftless So.
farmer grows up in a stifling environment.
Disappointed in her first love, plunges into marriage,
and motherhood finds her penniless in New York.
Widowhood brings her back to home town. The claims on
her clash: family, son, a rich admirer and "her own
hungry longing for ind. self expression. The last
claim proves the strongest and she leaves to live her
own life." PW
At end, put aside two men's offers of marriage, goes
to New York to live with son, works on newspaper to
support self and him with very good prospects for
advancement and happiness NYT 8-5-17 286

008885   MOTHER; A STORY. New York: Macmillan,
1911 BMC NUC.

Margaret becomes a companion to a wealthy woman, sees
in this society same ideas as hers on children and
marriage; love makes her see things a new way. She
goes home full of love for mother. 11-18-11 PW

008886   THE RICH MRS. BURGOYNE. New York:
Macmillan, 1912 BMC NUC.

ATH- Another love story.
NYT-heroine is Ida Tarbell's type-going back to doing
the job of being a woman better.
PW-sounds like a strong heroine.
BKM-Widow with children believed to be rich settles
into California town filled with women leading aimless
lives. To surprise of all she becomes a worker and
reformer. Concludes with her marriage to an old
sweetheart.

008887   SATURDAY'S CHILD. New York: Macmillan,
1914 NUC. London: Macmillan, 1914 BMC.

Susan Brown works in an office. All the men love her;
flies from these admirers; becomes companion to
novelist who offers to divorce wife for her. She
agrees to go with him before he's divorced. Chance
keeps them from going off together. Ends up marrying
one of original suitors. (Reviewer is angered at the
casual way Norris presents such a woman as all right.)
BKM
"Like the child in the rhyme, Susan "has to work for
her living"; she has far to go through poverty and
wealth to happiness. Her choice of lovers falls on the
least attractive of three; but she finds it wise in
the end. Before she reaches this, she holds many
views, and learns that love is service and sacrifice."
PW 86 8/29/14:590.
NYT-Susan works first as a bookkeeper, then as
companion, then gets married and is happy doing her
housework as wife.

008888   SISTERS. London: J. Murray, 1919 BMC.
Garden City, N.Y.: Doubleday, Page, 1919 NUC.

SR-3, live in West U.S. revolves around married life
of younger.
Alix marries a man who loves her sister Cherry
Strickland. Cherry is married to an engineer, dislikes
rough mining life. Alix kills herself, cripples
Cherry's husband. TLS
love between sisters, father and daughters, friends.
Love, licit and illicit between men and women. Cherry
and Alix Strickland are the sisters: scene California.
Alix is a busy wholesome young woman. Her sister more
beautiful, engaged at 18. Hurries into marriage to man
she and family hardly know. She's soon miserable till
Alix comes to her rescue. NYT 491 9-28-19

008889   THE STORY OF JULIA PAGE. London: J.
Murray, 1915 NUC BMC. Garden City, N.Y.: Doubleday,
Page, 1915 NUC.

neglected slum child grows to be a fine woman, married
to man insanely jealous of her dead lover. Separation
and reconciliation ATH
Story starts her life at 4, in rooms over a saloon
natural inclinations different: to be a lady. Climbs
to success, but is ever stained by one act in her past
NYT
Woman works in neighborhood house, marries happily but
has bad memories of her poor and unhappy childhood
home. PW 9-11-15
She understands her husband, he doesn't understand
her, they separate Ending?
ending not clear SP

008890   THE TREASURE. New York: Macmillan, 1914
BMC NUC.

ATH-shocked by her daughter's proposing to a man.
"Tells the experiences of the Salisbury family, first
with the old-fashioned, tyrannical maid, then with an
efficient, college-trained young woman, who makes
domestic science a profession. Poor Mrs. Salisbury
finds it difficult to reconcile her ideas of mistress
and "help" to this superior young person's attitude,
and yet she acknowledges the girl's ability. Story is
amusing but also states some of the vexed household
questions and gives a possible solution." PW 85
3/7/14:769.
BKM 39 1914 servant who is a "young woman with a
college education in domestic science" - what Gilman
has advocated.

008891   UNDERTOW. Garden City, N.Y.: Doubleday,
Page, 1917 NUC. London: C. Brown, 1917 BMC.

Albert and Nancy Bradley lose their idealism with
their growing wealth. Live too fast to enjoy children.
House burns down, better ideals return. PW
The early years of their marriage are sane and happy.
Then like a curse they are caught up with "keeping up"
with the suburban neighbors. All their values are
perverted as a consequence. NYT 4-1-17, 113

NORRIS, MARY HARRIOTT. 1848-1919. United States.

008892   THE GRAPES OF WRATH. A TALE OF NORTH AND
SOUTH. Boston: Small, Maynard, 1901 BMC NUC.

008893   THE GRAY HOUSE OF THE QUARRIES. Boston:
Lamson, Wolffe, 1898 NUC BMC.

NYT 1898:416. Character study of young American woman
reared in family following New England traditions but
living in Dutch village in Catskills. Question of
consanguineous marriage for sake of keeping parcels of
land in family.
PW-greed and avarice of Dutch settlers contrasted with
liberality of Susannah's family.

008894   JOHN APPLEGATE, SURGEON; A NOVEL. St.
Paul, Minn.: Price-McGill, [c1893] NUC.

He loves Margaret Huntington adopted daughter of a
doctor. He's testing which is stronger heredity or ed.
PW 2-18-93

008895   LAKEWOOD: A STORY OF TO-DAY. New York and
London: F. A. Stokes, [c1895] NUC BMC.

Portia Max-how she maintains her social position after
her loss of fortune, her unconventional love affair.
Well-known high society of New York and Boston. PW
12-7-95:1082.
ACAD 49:134. Several romances amongst wealthy families
staying at a New York winter resort.

008896   THE STORY OF CHRISTINA. New York: Neale,
1907 NUC.

Heiress becomes a "self-controlled useful woman" PW
7-6-07
NYT-pursued for her inheritance.

008897   THE VEIL: A FANTASY. Boston: A. G.
Badger, 1907 NUC.

PW-mystery ghosts.
BKM-3 houses vacant and then leased by people whose
lives become peculiarly associated.
NYT-young woman visits owner of three houses and meets
three tenants.

NORRIS, ZOE ANDERSON. United States.

008898   THE COLOR OF HIS SOUL. New York and
London: Funk & Wagnalls, 1902 NUC.

Expression of soc. & matrim. theories of a radical
professor.

008899   THE QUEST OF POLLY LOCKE. New York: J. S.
Ogilvie, 1902 NUC.

search for ideal man on the Riviera. NYT 8-23-02

NORTH, LEIGH, pseud. See PHELPS, ELIZABETH STEWARD.

NORTH, MARY M. United States.

008900   A PRAIRIE-SCHOONER: A ROMANCE OF THE
PLAINS OF KANSAS. Washington, D. C.: Neale, [c1902]
NUC.

NORTH, PLEYDELL, pseud. See EASTWICK, MRS. EGERTON.

NORTH, THEOPHILA, pseud. See HOLLINS, DOROTHEA.

NORTON, M. F. LATHAM. See NORTON, MARY FRANKLYN LATHAM.

NORTON, MARY FRANKLYN LATHAM. B. 1891. United States.

008901   THE ROSE OF AUZENBURG. BY M. F.
LATHAM-NORTON. New York: Broadway, [c1911] NUC.

NOYES, FRANCES NEWBOLD. See HART, FRANCES NEWBOLD (NOYES).

NUTT, JANE A.

008902   FOR KING AND COUNTRY; OR KINTAIL PLACE.
London: S. Sonnenschein, 1891 BMC.

Young French girl narrates story of struggle in France
between the Republic and LaVandee. Her sympathy is
with the monarchy. She ultimately finds happiness and
shelter in England. notes, maps. ACAD
Historical novel. Royalist rising in La Vendee against
the revolutionary powers in France. English
involved-hero and heroine. SR 3-28-91, 388

NYE, ISABEL CLIFTON. United States.

008903   DELPHA; OR MARRIAGE AS A FAILURE AND A
SUCCESS. A DRAMATIC LOVE STORY FOUNDED ON LIFE. BY
ROLDAH. New York: G. W. Dillingham, 1896 NUC.

PW 5-16-96. Marries a man who becomes a convicted
thief; after 9 years of separation meets a manly
lawyer. conflict between what she thinks is right and
her love.

NYLEN, IRENE. United States.

008904   MAN'S HIGHEST DUTY, A STORY AND A
MESSAGE. New York City: L. Schmoeger, [c1920] NUC.

PW- Story of the after effects of the world war

O., T. W., pseud. See YOUNG, VIRGINIA C.

OAKLEY, HESTER CALDWELL. United States.

008905   AS HAVING NOTHING. New York and London:
G. P. Putnam, 1898 NUC BMC.

LW 29:268. Old fashioned love story in modern setting.
PW Two heroines living in New York. Elizabeth studied
art in Europe, has her own studio, and becomes a very
successful book illustrator. Supports her mother.

OBENCHAIN, ELIZA CAROLINE (CALVERT). B. 1856. United
States.

008906   AUNT JANE OF KENTUCKY. BY ELIZA CALVERT
HALL. Boston: Little, Brown, 1907 NUC. London:
Cassell, 1909 BMC.

gives her readers the good gospel of women's rights.
Point of view of a wise old woman with a young heart
as she speaks of her youth, prime and neighbors: the
women who buy a church organ tho men oppose, the
rebellion of Milly Amos-who refuses to sing "sweet Day
of rest" in church because there is no day of rest for
housewife. Seems to have flavor of Cranford. NYT
WOMAN'S JOURNAL 4-27-07
her recollections-pretty little pictures TLS
Cheery stories "staunch friend of all women" LBKM

008907   THE LAND OF LONG AGO. BY ELIZA CALVERT
HALL. Boston: Little, Brown, 1909 NUC. London and New
York: Cassell, 1910 BMC NUC.

another Aunt Jane novel: her stories, her gossiping
NYT
TLS -"tender" recollections

008908   SALLY ANN'S EXPERIENCE. BY ELIZA CALVERT
HALL. Boston: Little, Brown, 1907 NUC.

at head of title:From "Aunt Jane of Kentucky"
published three times by WOMAN'S JOURNAL. Concerns
injustice of marriage law in Kentucky. BKM. v. 32
1910-11
NYT-This is 1st chapter of Aunt Jane of Kentucky
published separately. Tells how Sally Ann rebuked men
of Goshen church for presuming to judge the woman

treasurer who borrowed funds when her daughter was
dying in Louisville and her stingy husband refused her
car fare. "a delightfully funny suffrage story" "plain
tale of plain people"
ad WOMAN'S JOURNAL 11-19-10

008909   TO LOVE AND TO CHERISH. BY ELIZA CALVERT
HALL. Boston: Little, Brown, 1911 NUC.

man sets aside political career because he knows his
wife would sacrifice herself if he won (she's a
mountain girl and could not fit the role of governor's
wife) PW 5-6-11
She knows she's too "simple" to fill role as his wife;
he knows he can't do without her.

OBER, SARAH ENDICOTT. 1854-1932. United States.

008910   GINSEY KREIDER. BY HULDAH HERRICK.
Boston: Pilgrim Press, [c1900] NUC.

PW-Kentucky mountains. Ginsey rescued from something
which could have ruined her at 14. Plea for more
education and religious instruction in this area.

O'BRIEN, ALICE.

008911   ANTHONY BLAKE'S EXPERIMENT [ANONYMOUS].
London: R. Bentley, 1896 BMC.

LBKM 10:21. Deceived woman enters convent for life,
never acknowledging herself to son as his mother.
SR-She was a French singer
ATH 108:347. Anthony was a novelist who dissected and
exploited Armande who loved him. Gave her an irregular
marriage and took her to England.
SP 77:596

O'BRIEN, ANNIE GEORGINA.

008912   A TWENTIETH CENTURY HERO. BY THE HON.
GEORGINA O'BRIEN. London and Dublin: Maunsell, 1913
BMC NUC.

SR 147 supp 21 Mar p. 10. A man decoys a girl into
mock-marriage; when she escapes, he follows and
murders her. Skilled lawyers get him off and he
thereafter appears nightly at music halls extolled as
a hero.
one "hero" disappears from heroine's farm in part I.
saves her in III. The villain really is the
hero-satirical title. ATH

O'BRIEN, FLORENCE ROMA MUIR WILSON. B. 1891. United
Kingdom.

008913   IF ALL THESE YOUNG MEN. BY ROMER WILSON.
London: Methuen, [1919] NUC BMC.

war-its effect on modern young people in England.
Josephine Miller talks about war, belongs to
intellectual set; all war seems an intrusion on the
lives of these "creatures of fine feeling" No plot,
ends inconsequently; characters talk and analyze their
emotions at time of national peril. LBKM

008914   MARTIN SCHULER. BY ROMER WILSON. London:
Methuen, 1917 [?] NUC [1918] BMC. New York: H. Holt,
1919 NUC.

"This novel is a study of the artistic temperament as
exemplifiedin a young German composer. The scene is
laid in Heidelberg, Leipsic, Berlin, and the Black
Forest, and the action takes place prior to the great
war. The plot is of the slightest-the interest centers
in the character of Martin, whose career we follow
from his boyhood in the Heidelberg home to his death
in the Berlin opera house, in 1914, when his last
opera "The peahens," is produced. His secretary, his
friends, the woman whom he loves, are all the slaves
of his moods, used to foster his creative energy, yet
they all feel his magnetism and shrink from no
sacrifice to serve him." BRD

O'BRIEN, HON. GEORGINA. See O'BRIEN, ANNIE GEORGINA.

O'BRIEN, MARGARET E. United States.

008915   JUDITH, THE DAUGHTER OF JUDAS: A TALE.
Philadelphia: J. B. Lippincott, 1891 NUC BMC.

O'BRIEN, MARY MARVIN (HEATON) VORSE. D. 1955. United
States.

008916   AUTOBIOGRAPHY OF AN ELDERLY WOMAN.
Boston: Houghton Mifflin, 1911 NUC.

youth to age; growing old gracefully. Grand children.
PW 10-7-11

008917   THE BREAKING IN OF A YACHTSMAN'S WIFE.
Boston: Houghton Mifflin, 1908 NUC.

PW-amusing.
BKM-amusing.

008918   GROWING UP. New York: Boni & Liveright,
[c1920] NUC. London: Brentano's, 1923 BMC.

PW-NY family.
NYT 1920:25 humorous account of children, their
pranks, etc.

008919   THE HEART'S COUNTRY. Boston: Houghton
Mifflin, 1914 NUC.

BKM 39 1914. Not too helpful.
PW 85 5/2/14 p.1449. "Story of the love-life of a
charming and sensitive girl, impulsive, eager for joy,
yet with her impulses. The story of her development
from childhood to her happy marriage is told with
intimacy of understanding, humor and tenderness. Ellen
Payne is so full of eager life that she frequently
shocks the prim New England village of 50 years ago in
which she lives. Then comes the charming city youth
who wins her love, and through whom she learns what
pain is. In the end she finds that Alec Yorke, her
life-long friend, is the real meaning of her life."

008920   I'VE COME TO STAY: A LOVE COMEDY OF
BOHEMIA. New York: Century, 1918 BMC NUC.

Heroine won't marry till she has "played and played
and played." Greenwich Village artist life. NYT
Humorous. Camilla Deerfield paints-successfully:
resides in comfortable studio next door to male friend
who writes. A cat brings them together. Then there's
Sonya the anarchist—a child who moves in with the
young man. All ends happily. NYT 4-27-19, 249

008921   MEN AND STEEL. New York: Boni &
Liveright, [c1920] NUC. London: Labour, 1922 BMC.

PW lives in the world of steel.
HD 5325 1. Steel 1919-20. 2. Steel industry & trade.

008922   THE NINTH MAN, A STORY. New York &
London: Harper, 1920 BMC NUC.

PW-story of a captured city in which the conquerer has
appointed every 9th man to name someone for death.
City is saved by one of its humblest citizens.
NYT 12-19-20 p.24

008923   THE PRESTONS. New York: Boni & Liveright,
1918 BMC NUC.

Mother writes family chronicle-middle class Americans,
provincial. But nothing new. TLS
Sent account of woman's daily life. ATH
Old fashioned narrator-conventional story. BKM
PW Everyday life of average American family.

008924   THE VERY LITTLE PERSON. Boston: Houghton,
1911 BMC NUC.

Incidents in the life of a girl baby and especially of
the parents' lives during the first year or two after
her birth. NYT

O'BRIEN, MRS. WILLIAM. See O'BRIEN, SOPHIE RAFFALOVICH.

O'BRIEN, SOPHIE RAFFALOVICH.

008925   ROSETTE; A TALE OF PARIS AND DUBLIN. BY
MRS. WILLIAM O'BRIEN. London: Burns and Oates, 1907
BMC.

She becomes a nun; "her vocation is her one romance."
SR:TLS

008926   UNDER CROAGH PATRICK. BY MRS. WILLIAM
O'BRIEN. London: J. Long, 1904 BMC.

O'CONNOR, ELIZABETH (PASCHAL). United States.

008927   DOG STARS: THREE LUMINARIES IN THE DOG
WORLD. BY MRS. T. P. O'CONNOR. New York: G.H. Doran,
[c1915] NUC. London: T. F. Unwin, [1916] BMC.

008928   I MYSELF. BY MRS. T. P. O'CONNOR. London:
Methuen, 1910 BMC NUC. New York: Brentano's, 1911 NUC.

008929   LITTLE THANK YOU. BY MRS. T. P. O'CONNOR.
London: G. P. Putnam, 1912 NUC BMC. New York: 1913
NUC.

Pleasant, everyday life. young widow loved her first
husband but falls in love all over again. Title is the
nickname of her son who plays an important part in the
novel. Happy story of happy people. LBKM, NYT
"Little Thank You is the small son of lovely Nancy
Drummond, who was made a widow when only eighteen, her
husband being killed hunting. She has to support
herself, so goes to New York, where she meets Billy
Winthrop, son of a man who loved her mother, and Billy
loses his heart to her at first sight. Story tells of
his siege of the citadel of her affections and the
part dear Little Thank You plays in it." PW, 1913.

O'CONNOR, LUCY VIOLET (BULLOCK-WEBSTER).

008930   THE IDEA OF MARY'S MEADOW. London: A.
Rivers, 1912 BMC.

008931   MARY'S MEADOW PAPERS. BY MRS. ARMEL
O'CONNOR. London: A. Rivers, 1915 BMC NUC.

O'CONNOR, MARY HAMILTON. Nationality Unknown.

008932   THE VANISHING SWEDE: A TALE OF ADVENTURE
AND PLUCK IN THE PINE FORESTS OF OREGON. New York: R.
G. Cooke, 1905 NUC.

Adventure. PW 5-13-05

O'CONNOR, MRS. ARMEL. See O'CONNOR, LUCY VIOLET
(BULLOCK-WEBSTER).

O'CONNOR, MRS. T. P. See O'CONNOR, ELIZABETH (PASCHAL).

O'DONNELL, JESSIE FREMONT. United States.

008933   A SOUL FROM PUDGE'S CORNERS: A NOVEL. New
York: G. W. Dillingham, 1892 W. (Listed PW. Sept. 3,
1892)

OEMLER, MARIE (CONWAY). 1879-1932. United States.

008934   THE BUTTERFLY MAN: A NOVEL. London: W.
Heinemann, 1918 BMC. (Am. ed. title: Slippy McGee...
.)

TLS-Sweetening influence of priest on hero.

008935   THE PURPLE HEIGHTS. New York: Century,
1920 BMC NUC. London: W. Heinemann, 1921 BMC NUC.

PW-rise of country boy who was dunce in school. Nancy
Simms untrained and rebellious.
NYT 10-24-20 p. 23- They are "forced" into a marriage,
separate, he lives in Paris, she in New York. He has
affair she has "romance" is thinking of having
marriage annulled. then what?

008936   SLIPPY MCGEE, SOMETIMES KNOWN AS THE
BUTTERFLY MAN. New York: Century, 1917 BMC NUC.

trad story BKM
burglar and his comrade a priest help each other.
Priest saves the thief's life-gets doctor who
amputates a bad leg. his rehabilitation physical and
moral by the priest and others NYT 4-29-17, 166

008937   A WOMAN NAMED SMITH. New York: Century,
1919 BMC NUC. London: W. Heinemann, 1920 BMC.

set in So. Pw
"a new efficient business woman" PW
a mystery tale concerning jewels and ghosts and a
double love story. All concerned parties are in Hynds
House occupied by two "damyankee" business women who
take in boarders. They manage to overcome the
resentment of the community; solve the mystery, find
the right mates. NYT 11-30-19 701
TLS -romance
SR-woman is left an old house by distant relative who
hated her neighbors. Terms of will she must turn it
into a boarding house and she in time solves family
mystery. Good fun.

OHL, MAUDE ANNULET (ANDREWS). 1866-1943. United States.

008938   THE WIFE OF NARCISSUS. BY ANNULET
ANDREWS. New York: Moffat, Yard, 1908 NUC.

PW-Artist married to intensely selfish poet, great
unhappiness.

"The life of a young girl, Sophia Van Cort, told by herself in the form of a journal. The scene of the story is in New York of to-day. She becomes associated with a man who poses as a poet of passion and with whom she becomes infatuated. She tells of her meeting with this "Beautiful Being" whom she calls "Narcissus," of her marriage to him and of the Bohemian life they lead." BKM v.35 1907?

OKELEIGH, CREDITA.

008939   A WREATH OF ROSEMARY; OR, MELODIES FROM FAR AWAY. London: Drane's, [1914] BMC.

OLDER, CORA MIRANDA (BAGGERLY). United States.

008940   ESTHER DAMON. BY MRS. FREMONT OLDER. New York: C. Scribner's Sons, 1911 NUC.

breaks away from strict home, becomes "outcast" of society. Influenced toward good by the "worst kind of man" who establishes a miniature republic; tries to reform a town. PW 6-10-11
Rural New York in 1870's NYT

008941   THE GIANTS. BY MRS. FREMONT OLDER. New York: D. Appleton, 1905 BMC NUC.

about business (monopolies) PW 10-7-05

008942   THE SOCIALIST AND THE PRINCE. BY MRS. FREMONT OLDER. New York and London: Funk & Wagnalls, 1903 NUC BMC.

Rich girl torn between two loves. PW 3-7-03
Socialist (male) makes love like a brute; Heroine drains life of sensation, fears nothing so much as boredom, daringly reaches for every new experience. She becomes ruthless; he will lead her into something more than disregard for convention. Never was vanity so supreme; NyT 03 225

OLDER, MRS. FREMONT. See OLDER, CORA MIRANDA (BAGGERLY).

OLDMEADOW, ANNIE CECILIA (DAWSON).

008943   A BOX OF CHOCOLATES. London: G. Richards, 1913 BMC.

Purpose: "earnest supplication to militant suffragettes to desist from their diabolical deeds." The workings of Catherine Hanley's mind and her evolution from "a crazy to a sane woman" Reviewer goes on to say the appeal will do no good "woman who will sacrifice human lives, destroy valuable property, throw honest workers out of employment...are beyond appeals and can only bedealt with by drastic measures." ACAD 6-14-13 752
Story involves a bomb; story dedicated "to the militant suffragists" TLS.

O'LEARY, AGNES MARIE. United States.

008944   BEYOND THESE VOICES: A NOVEL. New York: Broadway, [1909] NUC.

OLIPHANT, BLOSSOM DRUM. United States.

008945   A DOG-DAY JOURNAL. BY BLOSSOM DRUM. New York, London: Abbey Press, [1901] NUC.

008946   MRS. LEMON'S NEIGHBORS. New York: Neale, 1905 NUC.

OLIPHANT, E. BLAIR. See GRAHAM, MARGARET ETHEL BLAIR (OLIPHANT) MAXTONE.

OLIPHANT, MARGARET OLIPHANT (WILSON). 1828-1897. United Kingdom.

008947   THE CUCKOO IN THE NEST. BY MRS. OLIPHANT. London: Hutchinson, 1892 BMC NUC. New York: U. S. Book, [c1892] NUC.

ATH 100:413. Patty is strong, fiery heroine, marries Sir Giles for his fortune, routs friends of the family at the reading of Giles' will. Later marries for love.
LW 23:497. Patty is a barmaid.
SP 69:793.Patty is a barmaid.
SP 69:793. Patty, a barmaid marries Sir Giles' son, a loutish half-imbecile. Established as the mistress of her father-in-law's house, her future is jeopardized by her husband's alcoholism.
Scheming sharp tongued Patty Hewitt, inn-keeper's daughter, marries a feeble minded son of Sir Giles. Endures through the marriage his early death-before getting title, gets Sir Giles to make her heir, fights those who contest that will. She is a fighter, but she comes to realize she has no one, nor does she know how to enjoy her fortune. Finally leaves it all to marry an old beau and live in his modest house. CR 20,23:69

008948   DIANA; THE HISTORY OF A GREAT MISTAKE. BY MRS. OLIPHANT. New York: U. S. Book, [c1892] NUC.

ACAD 42:167. Diana, "mistress of Trelawny Chase, is a practical minded woman of 30. unmarried and disinclined to marry."
Analysis of relations of six people. Diana is rich, supports two selfish women. Hero loses her because thru his error he makes it seem as though he wants one of the other women. CR 14, 20:62

008949   DIANA TRELAWNY: THE HISTORY OF A GREAT MISTAKE. Edinburgh: W. Blackwood, 1892 BMC NUC.

ATH 100:188-Diana is adored by Pandolfini, a passionate Italian. The mistake results in his being "bound in honour for life to a limp and selfish little nobody in white muslin." He marries a woman he doesn't love because of a friend who has interceded for him, but with the wrong woman.
PW-Diana is a school teacher who was bequeathed a large fortune. She is 30 when story opens, kind to all about her. She has sent her aunt and niece to Italy for their health and then follows them.
Fresh wholesome love story. English party including Diana Trelawny visit Pisa. Centers on a mistake. That involves Diana and Count Pandolfini. LW 26:365.

008950   DIES IRAE: THE STORY OF A SPIRIT IN PRISON [ANONYMOUS]. Edinburgh & London: W. Blackwood, 1895 BMC.

008951   THE HEIR PRESUMPTIVE AND THE HEIR APPARENT. BY MRS. OLIPHANT. New York: J. W. Lovell, [1891] NUC. London: Macmillan, 1892 BMC.

LBKM 3:90. Heroine marries heir presumptive, then father marries.
They're cousins. The second born in father's old age and forgotten by mother during her madness. Crisis comes when he becomes ill and mother regains her senses to rush to him. LW
The first is John Parke. PW 6-25-91.
But central character scheming Mrs. Parke who is wed to the first and doesn't want to lose fortune. Practically a murderess- attempts murder of the heir apparent, a young boy. Searching and truthful study of her. SP 70,17
"The strange history of Lady Frogmore's matrimonial experience is a little too obstetrical in parts." SR, 1-14-93,44

008952   A HOUSE IN BLOOMSBURY. A NOVEL. BY MRS. OLIPHANT. London: Hutchinson, 1894 BMC. New York: Dodd, Mead, 1894 NUC.

ATH 104:347. Mr. Mannering and his daughter live in lodging house as do Miss Bethune and Gilchrest, her servant.
SP 73:408. a lodging house. Mrs. Mannering, a supposedly childless wife; Miss Bethune a supposed spinster; both have children from whom they have been parted.

008953   JANET. London: Hurst and Blackett, 1891 NUC BMC.

Janet Summerhays is vain. Her position as governess soon turns humdrum. She attracts the attention of two men who rival for her affections. Brings on tragedy when she indiscreetly reveals a family secret she discovered. SP 66, 595
ACAD Only sympathetic character is mother who kept the family secret so long.
ATH 97 278. Placid story except for early part of part III. A mysterious person and how his presence will effect the others. Heroine English, pretty, etc., but also a flirt and a liar.
Two men, one a rogue, the other a fool from Oxford. SR 5-9-91, 565.

008954   LADY WILLIAM. BY MRS. OLIPHANT. London: Macmillan, 1893 BMC. New York: Macmillan, 1893 NUC.

SR 77:529. Lady William's daughter can't inherit until Lady William proves the legality of her marriage.
SP 78:341. An interrupted romance which ends well.
ACAD 45:225. ATH 103:175

008955   THE MARRIAGE OF ELINOR. BY MRS. OLIPHANT.
London and New York: Macmillan, 1892 BMC NUC.

ATH 99:396. Hasty marriage; leisurely repentance.
Dolly is a modern type.
SP: Fin de siecle heroine. Wilful. Leaves her husband.
SR 73:422. raises her son by herself. Husband returns
eventually, to worship at her feet, along with her son
and cousin.
Elinor Dennistoun marries a fast man despite
objections of friends. they marry but are miserable.
So they separate. PW 4-22-93

008956   OLD MR. TREDGOLD. A STORY OF TWO SISTERS.
BY MRS. M. O. W. OLIPHANT. New York: Longmans, Green,
1895 NUC. London: Longmans, 1896 BMC.

ATH 107:439. Story of two sisters, one a modern young
woman, Stella, a comrade to her suitor, etc., and what
the rev. calls her nobler sister Katherine. Father is
a vulgar moneymaker.
SP 76:486. "Stella shrieks and fusses too much even
for masculine nerves."
LW 27:59. "A spoiled child"

008957   THE RAILWAY MAN AND HIS CHILDREN. London:
Macmillan, 1891 BMC. New York: Macmillan, 1891 NUC.

Railroad man risen from the ranks wins love of young
cultured wife late in life. BAKER.
Evelyn Ferrance "elderly" had made an unromantic
marriage. Interesting details of this domestic
problem. ATH 98 82 9.
He is John Rowland. Meets Evelyn when she's middle
aged. They marry. Story relates her problems with his
grown children. PW 10-24-91.
SP-story of a middle-aged woman's marriage to a man
with two older children by a first marriage.
Since that marriage he has risen in wealth and social
position. He has not seen the children in years. When
they come together as a family, he is disappointed in
them; she appreciates and understands them, but they
don't entirely trust her; near tragedy. ACAD 41:130.
Best character is the wife.

008958   SIR ROBERT'S FORTUNE: THE STORY OF A
SCOTCH MOOR. BY MRS. OLIPHANT. New York: Harper, 1894
NUC. London: Methuen, 1895 BMC.

Gloomy, Lily Ramsay, heiress makes a secret marriage
to Ronald Lumsden, young lawyer. Her uncle tried to
prevent the marriage because Ronald is unprincipled
though he loves Lily. Then she has a child SP 75:215
Contrasts old girl with new. Lily is of the old; Helen
the new. Lily can't see why Helen is so taken with
rakish man she loves. "Lily's way wins out." She loves
a prudent youth, but uncle vs marriage. Packs the two
young women off to tower in the moors. Lily marries
secretly. But Ronald has an eye on her fortune, so
after baby is born, steals it. Eventually loses Lily's
love. Ronald dies. ATH 106:315
LW 25:371. Scotland. Secret marriage; he a fortune
hunter.

008959   THE SORCERESS: A NOVEL. BY MRS. OLIPHANT.
London: F. V. White, 1893 BMC. New York: J. A. Taylor,
[1893] NUC.

"Adventurous as Laura is, Mrs. Oliphant claims our
sympathy for her resourcefulness and courage." The men
are not to be pitied. ATH 101, 307
Sets out to marry Colonel Kingsward. Schemes takes
risks. SP 70:547.
Miss Bee Kingsward and her idiotic lover. "Words,
words, words." SR 75, 325.
Makes misery between lovers, then makes love to the
young woman's brother. Throws him over and goes after
the father. ACAD 43:302.

008960   THAT LITTLE CUTTY. DR. BARRERE. ISABEL
DYSART. London and New York: Macmillan, 1898 BMC NUC.

ACAD 54:295. 3 short stories.

008961   TWO STRANGERS. BY MRS. OLIPHANT. London:
T. F. Unwin, 1894 BMC. New York: R. F. Fenno, [c1895]
NUC.

008962   THE UNJUST STEWARD; OR THE MINISTER'S
DEBT. BY MRS. OLIPHANT. London and Edinburgh: W. and
R. Chambers, 1896 NUC BMC. Philadelphia: J. B.
Lippincott, 1896 NUC.

ATH 108:780. Scotland-Fife. "sufficiently removed from
the commonplace banalities, the sexual problems, and

the topical ingenuities of the day." Spirited heroine.
She and her brother overhear a "momentous interview"
between their father and mother.
ACAD 50:489. Father has borrowed money from friend for
their education. The friend dies and minister tells
executor debt was 50 lbs rather than 300. Remorse,
confusion, everything ok.

008963   THE WAYS OF LIFE. TWO STORIES. BY MRS.
OLIPHANT. London: Smith and Elder, 1897 NUC BMC. New
York and London: G. P. Putnam, 1897 NUC.

Both concern prosperous men who have lived productive
lives but are at the point when "it would be better
for them not to be." LBKM 12:128.
Both have wife and children; both face financial
disaster. Mr. Dalyell alienates with the methods he
chooses to save his credit.Mr. Sanford, the painter is
the more sympathetic. SP 78:771.
"Mr. Sanford" is an artist of 60 who was a great
success but now out of demand. His paintings don't
pay; he has no money. If he dies his family will have
insurance. Dies by accident. "Mr. Robert Dalyell."
Scottish business man.-a speculator who loses heavily.
So his family will get insurance, pretends to be dead.
Wife marries his best friend. Then he really dies. BKM
6:66.
Artist finds his paintings aren't selling any more.
Just then killed in accident and family can live on
insurance. NYT 7-24-97,7.

008964   WHO WAS LOST AND IS FOUND. BY MRS.
OLIPHANT. Edinburgh and London: W. Blackwood, 1894 BMC
NUC. New York: Harper, 1895 NUC.

ATH 104:671. Mrs. Ogilvy has patiently awaited for
years the return of her son. When he comes, he is
either a murderer or returns with one or both. Terror
reigns.
PW-she is hiding them from her neighbors and the law
and is in constant fear both for them and from them.
Robert Ogilvy runs off, gets mixed up with criminal
types out west. Returns to waiting mother, leader of
gang in pursuit who forces himself into her home, uses
violence. Then Robert asserts himself. Maternal love
and self sacrifice. ACAD 47:31

OLIPHANT, MRS. See OLIPHANT, MARGARET OLIPHANT (WILSON).

OLIPHANT, MRS. M. O. W. See OLIPHANT, MARGARET OLIPHANT
(WILSON).

OLIVE, CLAUDE, pseud. See OLIVER, EMMA C.

OLIVER, AMY ROBERTA (RUCK). B. 1878. United Kingdom.

008965   ARABELLA THE AWFUL. BY BERTA RUCK.
London: Hodder & Stoughton, [1918] BMC NUC.

008966   THE BACK NUMBER. BY BERTA RUCK. New York:
1919 NUC.

008967   THE BOY WITH WINGS. BY BERTA RUCK (MRS.
OLIVER ONIONS). New York: Dodd, Mead, 1915 NUC.

Girl falls in love with airman. Rival-man's machine.
War calls husband away. Gets leave-when he meets next
flight "reader knows who passenger is and why she has
come." PW 89 1/29/16 p345
Gwenna comes to London from Wales, gets job as steno
and leaves it for more exciting one as secretary to
the Aeroplane Lady, head of an aircraft factory. Falls
for Paul; when their love is consumated she refuses to
leave him and takes his mechanic's place in plane.
They are shot down and die.

008968   THE BRIDGE OF KISSES. BY BERTA RUCK.
London: Hutchinson, 1917 BMC. New York: Dodd, Mead,
1920 NUC.

"Joey" Dale, heroine, tells her own story. rushes into
marriage with wealthy architect, falls in love with
another man. TLS

008969   THE COURTSHIP OF ROSAMUND FAYRE. BY BERTA
RUCK. London: Hutchinson, 1915 BMC NUC.

About a girls' club. Rosamund a secretary; writes love
letters for her employer. The fiance falls in love
with her thru her letters. TLS
LBKM

008970   THE DISTURBING CHARM. BY BERTA RUCK.
London: Hodder & Stoughton, [1919] BMC. New York:
Dodd, Mead, 1919 NUC.

Trad: about a love charm. TLS
Trad: about a love charm PW

008971   THE DREAM DOMESTICATED. BY BERTA RUCK.
New York: Harper's Bazar, 1918 NUC.

008972   THE GIRL WHO PROPOSED! London: Hodder &
Stoughton, [1918] BMC.

008973   THE GIRLS AT HIS BILLET: A NOVEL. BY
BERTA RUCK. London: Hutchinson, 1916 BMC NUC. New
York: Dodd, Mead, 1916 NUC.

TLS soldier rom. Three sisters in sleepy Eng. town
experience the change that comes with the troops'
arrival. PW
Humorous; Eng. village in wartime "whipped cream
fiction." Three blonde sisters live in dull little
hamlet with Aunt Victoria "an old maid who has got
married to another old maid" when war brings soldiers
into the previously all-female household. NYT 4-1-17.

008974   THE GREAT UNMET. BY BERTA RUCK. New York:
Harper's Bazar, 1918 NUC.

008975   HIS OFFICIAL FIANCEE. BY BERTA RUCK (MRS.
OLIVER ONIONS). New York: Dodd, Mead, 1914 NUC.
London: Hutchinson, 1914 BMC.

NYT-story of a typewriter engaged to head of firm.
NYT Apr 28, 1918, p.202.-Monica Trout, 1st person
narrative, is paid to pose as head of firm's fiancee
for one year.
LBKM-light, amusing.
ATH-Typist becomes engaged to the "governor" on
understanding that it would be broken off in 1 yr.
TLS-- Romance
Typist gets raise to play part of her boss's fiancee
and ends up marrying him. NYT
Monica Trout herself tells the story.

008976   IN ANOTHER GIRL'S SHOES. BY BERTA RUCK
(MRS. OLIVER ONIONS). New York: Dodd, Mead, 1916 NUC.
London: Hodder & Stoughton, [1917] BMC.

Vera movie-actress puts Rose in her place as widowed
war-bride. Captain turns up. Vera's divorce not legal.
PW 90 8/26/19 p.648.
NYT
LBKM--2 women exchange places, Rose with actress who
must meet soldier husband's family, etc.
Comedy Rose Whitelands, young and refined governess is
adopted as a widow of a couple's son. TLS

008977   THE LAD WITH WINGS. BY BERTA RUCK (MRS.
OLIVER ONIONS). London: Hutchinson, 1915 BMC NUC.

A typewriter Gwenna Williams loves and is loved by
famous airman, marries. TLS

008978   THE LAND-GIRL'S LOVE STORY. BY BERTA
RUCK. London: Hodder & Stoughton, [1919] BMC. New
York: Dodd, Mead, 1919 NUC.

An idyll about Joan and her chum Elizabeth TLS
SP
Humorous story of the war in which two Eng. girls
become farmerettes. NYT
The author is "afire with admiration for the woman's
land army" Joan Mathews and Elizabeth weare do office
work in London. Joan is pretty and in love; Eliz is
boyish and hates men. They join the land army after
Joan's boyfriend is unfaithful and Joan loses her job.
In Wales they work on farm. In the end both marry.
Eliz proposes to the man she weds. NYT

008979   MISS MILLION'S MAID; A ROMANCE OF LOVE
AND FORTUNE. BY BERTA RUCK (MRS. OLIVER ONIONS). New
York: Dodd, Mead, 1915 NUC. London: Hutchinson, 1916
BMC.

Beatrice Lovelace told she's too good for her
neighbors (by her family) is lonely and bored,
especially after her servant friend, Miss Million
inherits a million. Beatrice leaves home to do maid's
work. Eventually becomes her friend's maid. girls? NYT
TLS- comedy rom.

008980   RUFUS ON THE REBOUND. BY BERTA RUCK. New
York: Harper's Bazar, 1918 NUC.

008981   SWEETHEARTS UNMET. BY BERTA RUCK. New
York: Dodd, Mead, 1919 NUC. London: Hodder &
Stoughton, [1920] BMC.

TLS-rom

PW-dealing with young people in a large city.
NYT-Young romantic love.

008982   THE THREE OF HEARTS. BY BERTA RUCK (MRS.
OLIVER ONIONS). New York: Dodd, Mead, 1917 NUC.
London: Hodder & Stoughton, [1918] BMC.

TLS Farcical rom.
NYT-Humorous. regimental dance; male hero, finds
himself fiance of three young women.

008983   "THRIFTLESS GOLD". BY BERTA RUCK. New
York: 1919 NUC.

008984   THE WOOING OF ROSAMUND FAYRE. BY BERTA
RUCK (MRS. OLIVER ONIONS). New York: Dodd, Mead, 1915
NUC.

Same as Courtship of R. F. ?
Busy rich young woman has her secretary Rosamund write
love letters for her. PW 10-9-15
Sacchrine rom. the rich woman is absorbed "in modern
kinds of good work." Sometimes she reads the letters
before they go out, sometimes not. Rosamund's own
personality gets into the letters; as a consequence
the man rushes home. Light gay, ends as many novels of
the time do. "like a secret sob, the deep note of
passionate patriotism." NYT

008985   THE WRONG MR. RIGHT: A NOVEL. BY BERTA
RUCK. London: Hodder & Stoughton, [1919] BMC. New
York: Dodd, Mead, 1922 NUC.

008986   THE YEARS FOR RACHAEL. BY BERTA RUCK.
London: Hodder & Stoughton, [1918] BMC. New York:
Dodd, Mead, 1918 NUC.

PW-engaged for 10 yrs, at outbreak of war goes to
London which proves to be a great turning point in her
career.
TLS-From the woman's pov. He had cut up his love
letters to her to make into book. She was conductor on
omnibus (journalistic stunt) when he came back into
her life and she threw him over.
NYT 12-15-1918 p.553. Gwen Brook, in her own voice,
relates 10 year engagement, she becomes a successful
journalist.

OLIVER, EMMA C.   United States.

   008987   LIFE AS HILDA FOUND IT. BY CLAUDE OLIVE.
   [Centreville, Miss.]: [c1897] NUC.

OLIVER, LAETITIA SELWYN.

   008988   THE EXPIATION OF LADY ANNE. London: H.J.
   Drane, 1905 BMC.

   TLS-commonplace tale of a family curse, etc.
   BKM

   008989   THE SCARLET CRESCENT. London: H.J. Drane,
   1906 BMC.

OLIVER, MABEL.

   008990   THE SMUGGLER'S DAUGHTER. London: H.J.
   Drane, [1910] BMC.

OLIVER, TEMPLE, pseud. See SMITH, JEANIE OLIVER (DAVIDSON).

OLMIS, ELISABETH, pseud. See LOOMIS, ANNIE ELISABETH.

OLMSTEAD, FLORENCE.

   008991   THE ONE FOUNDATION: A NOVEL [ANONYMOUS].
   London: Hodder & Stoughton, 1907 BMC.

   BKM-young woman saved by man marrying her.

OLMSTEAD, FLORENCE. United States.

   008992   ANCHORAGE. New York: C. Scribner's Sons,
   1917 NUC.

   Focuses on Paul, semi invalid first cared for by older
   woman then infatuated by and marries an irresponsible
   young woman. She leaves; he writes; happy end. PW
   The older woman is Louisa-"middle-aged, commonsense
   spinster" who "would be amusing if we did not hear
   quite so much about her." The young woman is Hilda
   Fordham, full of energy who becomes impatient with her
   restricted life, tied to an invalid. NYT 5-20-17:195

   008993   A CLOISTERED ROMANCE. New York: C.
   Scribner's Sons, 1915 NUC.

About a couple of Nuns who help a romance grow. PW
4-17-15
Amusing tale of different Sisters of the Poor who run
a home for aged. NYT

008994   FATHER BERNARD'S PARISH. New York: C.
Scribner's sons, 1916 NUC.

A poor parish and a love triangle. PW, NyT

008995   MRS. ELI AND POLICY ANN. Chicago: Reilly
& Britton, [c1912] NUC.

Pw-Love and family, conv.

008996   ON FURLOUGH. New York: C. Scribner's
Sons, 1918 NUC.

Pw-love and war
NYT Sept 15, '18, p 392. Recuperating soldier in
Virginia, younger and older woman.

008997   STAFFORD'S ISLAND. New York: C.
Scribner's Sons, 1920 NUC.

PW love story on Island off coast of Ga.

O'NEILL, MOIRA, pseud. See SKRINE, NESTA (HIGGINSON).

O'NEILL, ROSE CECIL. B. 1874.

008998   THE LADY IN THE WHITE VEIL. New York and
London: Harper, 1909 BMC.

Reviewer rejects the book without saying much about
it. BKM Mystery PW

008999   THE LOVES OF EDWY. Boston: Lothrop, 1904
NUC.

NYT--young woman goes on stage, is loved by two men,
then what.

ONIONS, MRS. OLIVER, pseud. See OLIVER, AMY ROBERTA (RUCK).

OPENSHAW, MARY. See BINSTEAD, MARY (OPENSHAW).

ORCUTT, EMMA LOUISE. United States.

009000   THE DIVINE SEAL. Boston: C. M. Clark,
1909 NUC.

Fantasy in futuristic terms-beautiful girl rescued
from man-serpent creature. PW

009001   ESTHER MATHER: A ROMANCE. New York:
Grafton Press, 1901 NUC.

ORCUTT, H. E. See ORCUTT, HARRIET E.

ORCUTT, HARRIET E. United States.

009002   THE EMPIRE OF THE INVISIBLES. BY H. E.
ORCUTT. New York: Metaphysical, 1899 NUC.

009003   A MODERN LOVE STORY, WHICH DOES NOT END
AT THE ALTAR. Chicago: C. H. Kerr, 1894 NUC BMC.

Pw-a not-so-young heroine devoted to art and
theosophy, who hates housekeeping refuses to marry
minister she loves on grounds of losing her
independence. Chapters record their conversations on
the subject, the history of their eventual marriage
and its results. POV?

ORCZY, BARONESS. See BARSTOW, EMMA MAGDALENA ROSALIA MARIA
JOSEFA BARBARA ORCZY.

ORCZY, BARONESS EMMUSKA. See BARSTOW, EMMA MAGDALENA
ROSALIA MARIA JOSEFA BARBARA ORCZY.

O'REILLY, ELEANOR GRACE.

009004   JOAN AND JERRY. London: W. & R. Chambers,
1891 NUC. New York: T. Whittaker, [1892] PW.

PW-Joan and Jerry, two cousins called derisively
Beauty and Brains by an aunt, meet for 1st time in
London lodging-house. Joan runs lodging house, their
friendship.

009005   WHEN WE WERE YOUNG. London: W. & R.
Chambers, 1892 BMC. New York: T. Whittaker, 1893 PW.

Olivia St. Leger brought a precious amethyst ring to

her marriage. It was handed down for generations, then
lost, then found by Lou Delamere and her twin brother.
PW 12-2-93

ORGAN, MARGARET (STEPHENSON). B. 1840. United States.

009006   THE LAST BATTLE-GROUND. New York: G.T.
Long, [c1910] NUC.

Novel about dangers of alcohol PW 1-14-11

ORLOVA, OL'GA.

009007   VANYA: A TALE OF SIBERIA. Edinburgh: R.
Grant, 1898 BMC NUC. (Tr. by E. H. N.)

Prison life in Siberia. ACAD 56:94.

ORME, ELIZA.

009008   LADY FRY OF DARLINGTON. London: Hodder
and Stoughton, 1898 NUC BMC. (Biography? Fry, Sophia,
1837-1897.)

ORMEROD, MAUD W. United States.

009009   MADAM PARADOX: A NOVEL. New York: D.
Biddle, [c1899] NUC.

She is Katharine Randolph who writes for a magazine
under the name of Madame Paradox. Husband believed
dead, falls in love with editor, husband returns a
physical wreck. She cares for him while editor waits.
Also concerns an artist drawn to two women--one
beautiful model, the other a simple unsophisticated
young woman. BKM 10:187

O'ROURKE, KATE PEIRNE.

009010   THE NOBLE AND HIS DAUGHTER. Los Angeles,
Cal.: [J. B. Cummings], 1911 NUC.

ORPEN, ADELA ELIZABETH RICHARDS. United Kingdom.

009011   THE CHRONICLES OF THE SID; OR THE LIFE
AND TRAVELS OF ADELIA GATES. London: Religious Tract
Society, 1893 BMC NUC.

009012   CORRAGEEN IN '98: A STORY OF THE IRISH
REBELLION. London: Methuen, 1898 BMC NUC.

SP 81:446. Sentimental. Laura, wife of a Loyalist,
"aspired to play the part of Madame Roland without the
subsequent tragedy, and came within an ace of
forfeiting her life and that of her child for
philandering with disaffection."
LIT 3:524. "Never since Eve ate the fateful apple has
woman been brought under the sway of pure reason" says
Mrs. Orpen.
Irish rebellion of '98 in unflattering terms--pro Eng.
LBKM 15:152.

009013   THE JAY-HAWKERS. A STORY OF FREE SOIL AND
BORDER RUFFIAN DAYS. New York: D. Appleton, 1900 BMC
NUC.

NYT 1900:544. Missouri & Kansas in "free soil" days.
Jay-Hawkers raided slaves and brought them to free
territory. Young Northerner blunders into a murder.

009014   PERFECTION CITY. London: Hutchinson, 1897
BMC. New York: D. Appleton, 1897 NUC.

Olive a young bride comes to a communist settlement.
She's a rebel. Madame Morozoff-Smith study of a woman
who embraces a cause for the sake of a man. LBKM
12:19.
Nebraska Olive: a rebel, an inconvertible heretic.
Gentle satire, but Olive is very sympathetic char. BKM
5:523.
SP 80:454. Cooperative community in Kansas. Madam
Morozoff-Smith is the founder. Olive comes to the
community as a young bride; M. M-S is in love with her
husband. The community crashes when she is unable to
separate him from Olive.

ORR, CHRISTINE GRANT MILLAR. B. 1899. United Kingdom.

009015   THE GLORIOUS THING. London: Hodder &
Stoughton, 1919 BMC NUC.

Middle-class life in Edinburgh during war. TLS

ORRED, META. Nationality Unknown.

009016   "GLAMOUR". A ROMANCE. Philadelphia:

Lippincott, 1896 BMC 1897 NUC.

Hero is Maurice-much affected by Influence, Evil and Unknown Sorrow. Also by a ring of a wicked ancestress. "Allegory is stalking about but we cannot quite track her down." LBKM 12:19

ORSHANSKI, G. (YSTRIDDE) YSTRIDDE.

009017   AN EXILE'S DAUGHTER. London: J. Long, 1911 BMC.

Fortunes of a country vicar's granddaughter in Russian Revolution. TLS
An anarchist included. TLS

009018   A TARTAR'S LOVE. London: J. Long, 1913 BMC.

A Tartar lad works for Russians to earn money to marry. Contrasts in temperaments. ATH

009019   THREE DUKES. New York and London: G. P. Putnam's Sons, 1904 NUC. London: T. F. Unwin, 1905 BMC.

Young governess for mad nobleman whose mad wife beats her child; three heroines governesses in Russia. NYT 05,20
Wife full of small deceits toward her husband; beats her grown daughter; true picture of woman's side of life. ACAD 1905:150
ATH 1905:172

ORZESZKO, ELIZA. See ORZESZKOWA, ELIZA (PAWLOWSKA).

ORZESZKOWA, ELIZA (PAWLOWSKA). 1842-1910. Poland.

009020   THE ARGONAUTS. BY ELIZA ORZESZKO. New York: C. Scribner's Sons, 1901 NUC. (Tr. Jeremiah Curtin)

"Strong food for mature men and women" BOOK BUYER 1-02
Ultimate male chauvinist business man destroys his family.

009021   THE INTERRUPTED MELODY. BY ELIZA ORZESZKO. London: A. Melrose, 1912 BMC NUC. (Tr. from Polish by M. Ochenkowska)

ATH-Duke and maid of low degree meet, are attracted, separate.
TLS-He makes love to her incognito.

009022   MEIR EZOFOVITCH: A NOVEL. New York: W.L. Allison, [c1898] NUC BMC. (Tr. Iza Young)

ACAD 53:575. Jewish life in Poland. Sad.
PW-persecution of Karaites by Talmudists. Meir, an orthodox Jew, attempts to stop the persecutions, is cast out by his family and becomes a wanderer. ATH112:895 Jewish question. Town of Berditchev almost all Jews, two factions. Orzeszk "champion of religious toleration" but "she does not fail to give a lurid picture of the greed and squalor of the Hebrew towns and the fanaticism and intolerance of the Kahal." Jewish hero, sympathetic.

009023   THE MODERN ARGONAUTS. BY ELIZA ORZESZKO. London: Greening, 1901 BMC NUC. (Tr. from Polish by Count S. C. DeSoissons)

009024   AN OBSCURE APOSTLE: A DRAMATIC STORY. London: Greening, 1899 BMC NUC. (Tr. from Polish by C. S. DeSoissons)

Deals with Polish Jewry. ACAD 57:513
LBKM 17:154. Hebrew community in remote Polish town, Szybow. Meir is hero.
SP 84:59. "Uncompromising avoidance of the amenities of romance."

OSBORN, MRS. PETER E. United States.

009025   THE DANBURY FAIR. BY AUNT DEBBY. Danbury, Conn.: Danbury Medical Print., 1894 NUC.

OSBORNE, KATHERINE FRANCES. B. 1862.

009026   CAPRICCIOS. BY THE DUCHESS OF LEEDS. London: Hodder and Stoughton, 1898 NUC BMC.

OSBORNE, MRS. D. C. United States.

009027   UNDER GOLDEN SKIES; OR, IN THE NEW ELDORADO. A STORY OF SOUTHERN LIFE BY A SOUTHERN

AUTHOR. Raleigh, N. C.: Edwards and Broughton, 1898 NUC.

OSGOOD, GRACE ROSE. B. 1881. Nationality Unknown.

009028   AT THE SIGN OF THE BLUE ANCHOR: A TALE OF 1776. Boston: C. M. Clark, 1909 NUC.

OSGOOD, IRENE (DE BELLOT). 1875-1922. United States.

009029   AN IDOL'S PASSION. New York: Transatlantic, 1895 NUC.

SP 77:186 "the poorest trash"

009030   THE INDELICATE DUELLIST [ANONYMOUS]. London: J. Richmond, 1914 BMC.

009031   A MOTHER IN DREAMS. London: J. Richmond, 1912 BMC.

009032   SERVITUDE. New York: [Trow Press], 1908 NUC. London: Sisley's, [1908] BMC.

Adventure story PW 4-10-09
Horrors of Algerian life in early 1800's--slavery. BKM BKM V. 29 1909. Free and independent American girl, love story. Horrors of slavery in Africa.
TLS-Christian slaves in Algiers in 19th century. Not suitable for young.
ACAD-unredeemed horrors.
BKM-0
ATH-0

009033   THE SHADOW OF DESIRE. New York: Cleveland, 1893 NUC.

Ran away with a man at 17, married again shortly after his death, marrying again at the end, #2 was killed in a duel by her lover. Her name is Ruth. SR 76, 47.
"It simply astounds us that any woman could write such a book." ACAD 44:108.
Ruth Bronson-overly passionate "undue strength of her physical passions. "weaned to nobler aspirations" patiently by husband. ATH 102, 61
"Unpleasantly suggestive." One woman, married a second ttime "gives back kisses hot and fast" to the hero with a "voluptuous heavy red mouth." When he kills her husband, she repulses him, marries a third. SP 71, 314.
Ruth Parker widowed at 18 after a year of marriage to a man twice her age with whom she had eloped and who led a dissolute life. She doesn't profit by this experience "but leads a stormy life, always influenced by her spasmodic and uncontrolled affections." PW 6-10-93.

009034   TO A NUN CONFESS'D. LETTERS FROM YOLANDE TO SISTER MARY. London: Sisley's, 1906 BMC.

TLS-Gushing letters about a liaison with a man with whom she proposes to go over a cliff in a motor car. Unhappy wife writes to nun friend. Woman's soul bared; self analysis by a victim of hopeless love. PW 4-10-09

009035   WHERE PHARAOH DREAMS. BEING THE IMPRESSIONS OF A WOMAN-OF-MOODS IN EGYPT. London: J. Richmond, 1914 BMC. Philadelphia: J. B. Lippincott, [1914?] NUC.

LBKM-fantasies in Egypt; reviewer not sure of their meaning.
ATH-Impressions of a woman of moods.

OSKISON, HILDEGARDE (HAWTHORNE). D. 1952. United States.

009036   A COUNTRY INTERLUDE; A NOVELETTE. BY HILDEGARDE HAWTHORNE. Boston: Houghton, Mifflin, 1904 NUC.

"Summer love story on the Hudson." PW
NYT-dainty tale, full of nature.

OSMOND, SOPHIE.

009037   AN AUSTRALIAN WOOING. Letchworth: Garden City Press, 1916 BMC.

TLS-an advertisement for Australia. The adventuress of the story is an Australian and is mortally wounded fighting Germans from an aeroplane with an Austral. invention, a gyrating hand grenade.

OSTLERE, EDITH.

009038   FROM SEVEN DIALS. London: Duckworth, 1898

BMC.

SR 86:764. London slum inhabitants.

OSTLERE, MAY.

009039   DEAD! London: Trischler, [1891] BMC.

OSTRANDER, FANNIE ELIZA. United States.

009040   WHEN HEARTS ARE TRUE: A NOVEL. Chicago:
Laird and Lee, [c1897] NUC.

Althea Dunning learns at her uncle's death that he has
lost his fortune and that there is insanity in the
family. Her romance follows. PW 51:370.

OSTRANDER, ISABEL EGENTON. 1883-1924. United States.

009041   ANYTHING ONCE. BY DOUGLAS GRANT. New
York: W. J. Watt, [c1920] NUC.

009042   ASHES TO ASHES. New York: R. M. McBride,
1919 NUC. London: Hurst & Blackett, [1921] BMC.

Murder mystery from point of view of the murderer. We
know his identity from the start. The suspense comes
in what clue he's left that will bring his discovery.
NYT 12-28-19 782

009043   AT ONE-THIRTY; A MYSTERY. New York: W. J.
Watt, [c1915] NUC. London: Simpkin, Marshall, 1916
BMC.

Last case detective Damon Gaunt ever took. Let
beautiful and high-minded murderer escape. Knew too
much money and influence on the other side to trust
her to a trial. Retired after his failure. PW 89
1/29/16:346

009044   BOOTY. BY DOUGLAS GRANT. New York: W. J.
Watt, [c1919] NUC.

Mystery PW

009045   THE CLUE IN THE AIR. A DETECTIVE STORY.
New York: W. J. Watt, [c1917] NUC.

TLS-Detective male heros.
Trad detective PW

009046   THE FIFTH ACE. BY DOUGLAS GRANT. New
York: W. J. Watt, [c1918] NUC.

009047   THE HERITAGE OF CAIN. New York: W. J.
Watt, [1916] NUC. London: Hurst & Blackett, [1922]
BMC.

Mystery PW 90:1358 10/21/16

009048   HOW MANY CARDS? New York: R. M. McBride,
1920 NUC. London: Hurst & Blackett, [1922] BMC.

PW mur. mystery.

009049   ISLAND OF INTRIGUE. New York: R. M.
McBride, 1918 NUC. London: Skeffington, [1919] BMC.

PW-Mystery.
Kidnapping of oil-King's daughter nothing here. TLS
Maida Waring takes a pleasure trip by auto and
yacht-or so the story seems to say, till we realize
she's been kidnapped by a gang masquerading as friends
of the family. All turns out well. Told in first
person. Rescued by hero but not in a way that presumes
on the readers' credulity. NYT

009050   THE MAN WHO CONVICTED HIMSELF. BY DAVID
FOX. New York: R. M. McBride, 1920 NUC.

009051   THE PRIMAL LAW. New York: M. Kennerly,
1915 BMC NUC.

Mary escapes mill life by leaving town with a man; 10
years of "cosmopolitan" career with several men. Uses
all her money to help poor children as reparation for
the way she earned it. PW 2-20-15
As factory worker. Set in mill town; heroine 16 has
been working in factory 8 yrs. But wants education and
happiness. Goes with a man who promises to hire a
teacher for her and buy her clothes. Goes from man to
man. End: returns to mill town to use the money she
has and to work to better condition of mill-children.
NYT

009052   THE SECOND BULLET. BY ROBERT ORR

CHIPPERFIELD. New York: R. M. McBride, 1919 NUC.
London: Skeffington, [1920] BMC.

009053   THE SINGLE TRACK. BY DOUGLAS GRANT. New
York: W. J. Watt, [c1919] NUC.

PW-Story of a rich girl who undertakes hard work in a
mining camp (Alaska)
"This is the story of the heroine who goes into
primitive regions to save the family fortune. Janetta
has been one of the idle rich till she is told, on her
twenty-first birthday, that she has been living for
some time on her brother's income...how Janetta goes
up, into the Klondike, outwits the family enemies,
falls in love with the stalwart foreman and, with his
able assistance, saves the mine." NYT 6-6-20, 302.

009054   SUSPENSE. New York: R.M. McBride, 1918
NUC. London: Skeffington, [1919] BMC.

PW-Mys. story. Betty risks life by becoming secretary
to Mrs. Otterbury, head of a band of crooks, to
recover papers by means of which she has been
blackmailing Betty's father. Det. falls for Betty.
NYT June 9, 1918 p266-0
Betty Shaw, lonely young woman with an aura of mystery
about her- sinister birth scar on cheek. When strange
things happen at Mrs. Otterbury's (where Betty is in
service) she reveals all the "courage, sangfroid and
tenacity of a professional detective." A professional
detective provides a satisfactory climax for her
career. TLS.

009055   THE TWENTY-SIX CLUES. New York: W. J.
Watt, [c1919] NUC. London: Hurst & Blackett, [1921]
BMC.

Murder Mystery PW
NYT: Thrills, surprise, suspense, male detective's
viewpoint; murder of a young married woman; no clues
no motives.

009056   UNSEEN HANDS. BY ROBERT ORR CHIPPERFIELD.
New York: R. M. McBride, 1920 NUC.

PW--Detective story.
"This story of Mr. Chipperfield's is placed before us
as a mystery in which every member of a wealthy family
seems to be menaced. The mother and the eldest son
have each died under peculiar circumstances shortly
before the opening of the story. We are instantly met
with strange, murderous intention being disclosed in
regard to the father and the second son. Such intimate
knowledge of the family life is disclosed that we are
forced to the conclusion that it is an 'Inside job.'
The problem is to find the person with motive and
means for such gradual but wholesale murder."(Boston
Transcript) BRD

O'SULLIVAN, E. C. United States.

009057   MR. DIMOCK. BY MRS. DENIS O'SULLIVAN. New
York and London: J. Lane, 1920 BMC NUC.

PW-international romance, male hero entangled with
many ladies from different countries.
NYT 12-26-20 p. 24

O'SULLIVAN, MRS. DENIS. See O'SULLIVAN, E. C.

OTTMANN, NINA.

009058   THE STOLEN GOD AND OTHER EXPERIENCES OF
PALACE LIFE. Carey Press, 1915 BMC.

Intimate account of Indian palace life from point of
view of medical missionary. SP

OUIDA, pseud. See DE LA RAMEE, MARIE LOUISE.

OVERTON, ELLA EDERSHEIM.

009059   A LADY BORN. New York: E. & J. B. Young,
1893. London: Christian Knowledge Society, [1893] BMC.

Two sisters consider themselves "ladies born." Though
in humble circumstances, orphaned. One becomes a
successful house decorator, the other, a
governess-unsuccessfully because she puts on airs.
Both learn the truth about their mother's real station
in life. PW 12-2-93

009060   THE SCHOOLMISTRESS OF HAVEN'S END.
London: Religious Tract Society, [1900] BMC.

OVERTON, GWENDOLEN. B. 1876. United States.

009061 ANNE CARMEL. New York and London: Macmillan, 1903 BMC NUC.

The sex question, a strong and thoroughly fearless woman she pursues her man who's in no position to marry, and she's too fine to demand it. The community condemns her but she ignores it; when the man returns married, she promises to go off with him. At very end she stays to save her brother's reputation (a minister) or is it that the man is not as strong as she would like? BKM 18 (1903)
Young priest and sister-unconventional experiences. PW 6-20-03
To marry would ruin her lover's life so she dispenses with the ceremony. ACAD 65,19
BKM 18

009062 THE CAPTAIN'S DAUGHTER. New York and London: Macmillan, 1903 BMC NUC.

LBKM-Suitable for younger readers.
ATH Suitable for younger readers

009063 CAPTAINS OF THE WORLD. New York: Macmillan, 1904 NUC BMC. London: Macmillan, 1904 NUC.

Love between a working man and his employer's daughter, a strike. LBKM 27-8,68
NYT-0

009064 THE GOLDEN CHAIN. New York and London: Macmillan, 1903 NUC BMC.

Amusing, idlyllic story of Mexico's borderland, love, etc.   NYT 03 784

009065 THE HERITAGE OF UNREST. New York: Macmillan, 1901 BMC NUC. London: Macmillan, 1901 NUC.

"savage, tumultuous, throbbing" Felipa, a half breed, educated must tame her nature to the demands of civilized life. BOOK BUYER 6-01.
Problem of heredity-unrest; Felipa intell. holds center-power of heredity, mother's savage race calling. Felipa strong with her Apache undersoul, her thirst for cruelty, indifference to the presence of suffering, wild moments of atavism, her truth, courage, absolute loyalty. Not loveable-admirable ends in death. Heredity vs environment author is unsparing in her denunication of our actions toward Indian. DIAL 7-01
"The heritage" may be taken as meaning the national heritage that comes to us from our blundering and dishonorable treatment of Indian Wards"

OVINGTON, MARY WHITE. 1865-1951. United States.

009066 THE SHADOW. New York: Harcourt, Brace & Howe, 1920 NUC.

PW-Southern girl aristocrat in childhood is placed on doorstep of Negro cabin.
NYT 6/27/20 Hertha is brought up in black family, believing that she is one of them. While she is a maid in a white household, she gets a letter informing her that she is "white", the illegitimate daughter of a deceased white woman, and she has inherited $2,000 dollars. Miss Witherspoon decides to take her to Boston and see to her "proper development"; she runs away in railroad station in New York and becomes independent. Factory work, stenography, typing. Rejection of suitor when he denounces the Negroes. Her black brother Tom in a lynch mob and her affirmation that he is her brother and she is colored.

OWEN, ALICE. United States.

009067 THE ROOT OF ALL EVIL. New York: Broadway Publishing, [c1909] NUC.

Moral-vs money-hunger. PW 11-20-09

OWEN, CAROLINE DALE, pseud. See SNEDEKER, CAROLINE DALE (PARKE).

OWEN, ETHEL.

009068 THE EVOLUTION OF A WIFE: A ROMANCE. BY ELIZABETH HOLLAND. London: J. Milne, 1896 BMC.

Fortunes of a convent-bred young woman. Marie-her many lovers, her vanities. SR 83:278
SP 77:944. Marie de Hauteville, a flirt, marries Rudolf who has saved her life. He is passionate and occasionally drinks too much so she leaves him. For a time she "remains unmarried." Then she marries him a second time; I believe satisfied his passion. Reissue of "The Evolution of a Wife."

009069 THE GENTLEMAN HELP. A NOVEL. Bristol: J. W. Arrowsmith, [1910] BMC.

"Beautiful and immoral stepmother"; "siren widow"; neglects her stepchildren. She resides in a separate wing of the house. SR
TLS-silly.
ACAD-silly.

OWEN, MARGUERITE (DE GODART) CUNLIFFE. 1859-1927. United Kingdom.

009070 THE CRADLE OF THE ROSE. BY THE AUTHOR OF THE MARTYRDOM OF AN EMPRESS [ANONYMOUS]. London and New York: Harper, 1908 BMC NUC.

"Lady Clanvowe, the heroine, is the wife of an English diplomat. When her husband is called to Asia on a public mission she returns to her native Brittany. Here she studies the conditions of her people and eventually becomes the instigator of an insurrection, the object of which is to overthrow the French Republic. Her chief accomplice is a young Breton, a nobleman and ex-naval officer, Count Olier de Frehel. Their plans fail and the two plotters, who have fallen in love with each other, meet their fate together as, pursued by the officers of the law, they plunge into the river." BKM v.28 1908-9.

009071 A DOFFED CORONET. BY THE AUTHOR OF THE MARTYRDOM OF AN EMPRESS [ANONYMOUS]. London and New York: Harper, 1902 BMC NUC.

009072 EMERALD AND ERMINE: A TALE OF THE ARGOAT. BY THE AUTHOR OF THE MARTYRDOM OF AN EMPRESS [ANONYMOUS]. London and New York: Harper, 1907 BMC NUC.

Mystery love-BKM

009073 GREY MIST: A NOVEL. BY THE AUTHOR OF THE MARTYRDOM OF AN EMPRESS [ANONYMOUS]. New York and London: Harper, 1906 BMC NUC.

PW-story of kidnapped baby boy.

009074 MOONGLADE: A NOVEL. BY THE AUTHOR OF THE MARTYRDOM OF AN EMPRESS [ANONYMOUS]. New York and London: Harper, 1915 BMC NUC.

Marguerite de Plenhoel-romantic adventure. PW 3-6-15
Heroine--sprightly, impulsive, high sense of honor & justice but essentially a romance. NYT

009075 SNOW-FIRE, A STORY OF THE RUSSIAN COURT. BY THE AUTHOR OF THE MARTYRDOM OF AN EMPRESS [ANONYMOUS]. New York and London: Harper, 1910 BMC NUC.

TLS-two women and two men.
BKM-love story.
court romance-NYT

009076 THE TRIBULATIONS OF A PRINCESS; WITH PORTS. FROM PHOTOS. BY THE AUTHOR OF THE MARTYRDOM OF AN EMPRESS [ANONYMOUS]. London and New York: Harper, 1901 NUC BMC.

woman of the world. Picture of army nursing-its hardships and dangers, daredevil adventures, feats of horsemanship. Dashing courageous woman likes danger in her sports. Raised as a boy. Contracted to a marriage at 15.

009077 THE TRIDENT AND THE NET: A NOVEL. BY THE AUTHOR OF THE MARTYRDOM OF AN EMPRESS [ANONYMOUS]. New York and London: Harper, 1905 BMC NUC.

Centers on hero; mother a bad influence, sister helps save him. PW 9-16-05
Brother and sister devotion; she's simple: he's complex, tyrannical mother-her passionate devotion and persecution-NYT 643, 05

OWEN, MARY ALICIA. B. 1858.

009078 THE DAUGHTER OF ALOUETTE. London: Methuen, 1896 BMC NUC.

ACAD 50:347. Her husband is "a well-conducted red Indian."

OWINGS, MRS. OSMOND YOUNG. United States.

009079 PHOEBE; A NOVEL. New York: Cosmopolitan Press, 1912 NUC.

OXENDEN, MAUD. United Kingdom.

009080 INTERLUDES. London: E. Arnold, [1896] BMC NUC.

009081 A REPUTATION FOR A SONG. London: E. Arnold, 1898 BMC.

LIT 3:136. The sending of a foolish wife back to her husband.
ACAD 53:310. About a man who made a great sacrifice to a sick man's whim.

009082 THE STORY OF ESTHER. London: W. Blackwood, 1908 BMC.

TLS-Griselda
ACAD--? gives up a life of her own for her nephew, sends her nephew's father to his death for his sake (he is evil), son follows in father's footsteps and turns on Esther when he discovers truth. Great tragedy. She dies.

PACHECO, MARY. United States.

009083 THE NEW DON QUIXOTE. New York: Abbey Press, [c1900] NUC.

PADON, ELLA FLORENCE. United States.

009084 IN CHARGE OF THE CONSUL. Boston: R. G. Badger, 1907 NUC.

BKM-Five American girls; adventure and love affairs during a year in Germany, uncle is American Consular.

PAGE, ANNE.

009085 AN AFTERNOON RIDE: A SOUTH AFRICAN SKETCH. London: Roxburghe Press, [1897] BMC.

Lurid story of a husband's straying love. ACAD 52 Fic sup:114

PAGE, EDITH M.

009086 A MATRIMONIAL FREAK: A NOVEL. London: Digby, Long, [1897] BMC.

"Marriage" between a young woman of 17 and an Oxford undergrad conducted by themselves in an empty church.
ACAD 52 Fic Sup 116
LIT 2:148. Heroine Tricked into sham mrge. with cousin.

PAGE, GERTRUDE. See DOBBIN, GERTRUDE (PAGE).

PAGET, MRS. GERALD.

009087 GOING THROUGH THE MILL. London: Brown, Langham, 1908 BMC.

TLS "A lady of the world, 40 yrs old, well connected and with much intelligence and readiness of speech," is stimulated and emancipated by the Great Teacher (a woman) and the narrator throws off all merely conventional views and champions the claims of woman."
ATH- Great Teacher "Ideal" whose love toward humanity cannot be claimed by any one person appears to her in her astral body and sends her a dream which depicts a young woman sentenced to death by a jury of unrefined men. Dream prophesies the appointment of female judges.

PAGET, VIOLET. 1856-1935. United Kingdom.

009088 ARIADNE IN MANTUA. A ROMANCE IN FIVE ACTS. BY VERNON LEE. Oxford: Blackwell, 1903 BMC NUC. Portland, Me.: T. B. Mosher, 1906 NUC.

009089 THE LEGEND OF MADAME KRASINSKA. BY VERNON LEE. Portland, Me.: T. B. Mosher, 1903 NUC.

009090 LOUIS NORBERT. A TWO-FOLD ROMANCE. BY VERNON LEE. London: J. Lane, 1914 BMC. New York: J. Lane, 1914 NUC.

SR 147:742. Series of letters. Medieval setting. Psychological happening between a people of the present day. Young archeologist investigates Venetia

Hammond's ancestor, invents rather than disappoint her.
ACAD 86:827. O
ATH 143:754 O

009091 PENELOPE BRANDLING: A TALE OF THE WELSH COAST IN THE EIGHTEENTH CENTURY. BY VERNON LEE. London: T. F. Unwin, 1903 BMC NUC.

A gothic type of novel. LBKM 10-03,64
Intrigues suspense.

009092 SISTER BENVENUTA AND THE CHRIST CHILD: AN EIGHTEENTH CENTURY LEGEND. BY VERNON LEE. New York: M. Kennerly, [1905] NUC. London: E. G. Richards, 1906 BMC.

PAHLOW, GERTRUDE CURTIS BROWN. 1881-1937. United States.

009093 THE CROSS OF HEARTS DESIRE. New York: Duffield, 1916 NUC. London: Methuen, 1918 BMC.

TLS-New York in 1914. A good male German. A Victorian heroine who finds remedy of discontent lies in service.
NYT-Marcia; Taught that "woman's beauty is her power," is brought up traditionally, is a statuesque beauty but nonentity, She meets an idealistic young man, turns on charm as she has been taught, he is utterly bored by her. In second chapter she goes to NY to work; story is of her development from a beautiful bore to an alert and interesting person.

009094 THE GILDED CHRYSALIS; A NOVEL. New York: Duffield, 1914 NUC.

PW:86 8/29/14:596 "The heroine, brought up in luxury, marries a college professor and goes to live in a college town. Before she is a real mate of her husband, they have many scenes, and, on her part, foolish indiscretions. She runs away from him; and during this time spent in working for good people in a farm house, she finds herself."
NYT O

009095 THE GLORY OF GOING ON. New York: Duffield, 1919 NUC.

"Strong girl and her struggle thru life" PW
An independent young woman first single, then married. NYT
Boston: heroine gives up all social prospects mapped out for her by her education; wants to make a place for herself as a singer. At first she fails, disillusioned she marries-a Dictator who forbids her to sing in slum settlement. This domestic Napoleon makes her life miserable. Hilda gets a divorce and lives with her two children and meets the man she really loves, a novelist. But he's killed in war. No happy end; The heroine goes on with her music, determined to make a career. NYT 10-12-19 537

PAIN, AMELIA (LEHMANN). D. 1920. United Kingdom.

009096 SAINT EVA. London: Osgood, 1897 BMC. New York: Harper, 1897 NUC.

A very painful story of a saintly country girl-Eve Corona. She falls in love with a man who is incapable of a true love. She has an invalid mother to support. He-Clayton Seaford-throws her over. But she is not "ruined." Eva dies.
Her life history. She's nun-like, is kissed by Clayton Seaford who rides off. Takes her kisses seriously, kills self. ACAD 51 :376.
Her girlhood at Springfield-her dreary existence. Her first sexual feelings. Sensitive nature. ATH 109:503. BKM 5:437.
London good soc. in town and country and Italy world of good breeding, current fashions in art, etc-a society novel. Eva began in Italy, Ital. father and philistine Brit. mother raised in primitive Eng. home. Her emotions, her misery her destruction by lightning. Rosalind is compelled by Clayton Seaford to love him. Then he neglects her. She could have turned to the young physician who loves her, but didn't. Unconv. love of solitude, sensitive appreciation of beauty. NYT 5-8-97.

PAIN, NANCY AND WINIFRED ROSE.

009097 CRYING FOR THE MOON. London: T. W. Laurie, [1914] BMC.

LBKM-Two unconventional young women living alone, at the suggestion of the rector's wife, hang a man's hat in the hall to ward off burglars. They then create an imaginary lodger "Reginald," supplied with little luxuries. Then a real Reginald comes into their home. A tangle of love stories, not all of which gets straightened out.

PAINE, HARRIET ELIZA. 1845-1910.

009098   THE UNMARRIED WOMAN. BY ELIZA CHESTER. New York: Dodd, Mead, 1892 NUC.

Her conviction is women shoud marry to avoid the feverish longing to do some work that will justify their lives and to avoid the feeling of hopelessness that they can't help others. CR 14, 20:161.

PAINTER, LYDIA (HOYT) FARMER. 1842-1903. United States.

009099   AUNT BELINDY'S POINTS OF VIEW, AND A MODERN MRS. MALAPROP: TYPICAL CHARACTER SKETCHES. BY LYDIA HOYT FARMER. New York: Merriam, [c1895] NUC.

Two women discuss women's clubs and women's suffrage. Aunt Belinda and her husband argue the "woman question" from all sides among other issues of the day. PW 6-15-95:937

009100   THE DOOM OF THE HOLY CITY: CHRIST AND CAESAR. BY LYDIA HOYT FARMER. New York: A. D. F. Randolph, [c1895] NUC.

LW. 27:60. Palestine, AD64. Love story of some Jewish young women. Two sold as slaves to the Romans, one rescued from the lions by her Roman lover.

PALATIONAS, DOROTHY. United States.

009101   WHEN HE FOUND HIMSELF. Columbus, Ohio: Heer Press, 1918 NUC.

PALMER, LYNDE, pseud. See PEEBLES, MARY LOUISE (PARMELEE).

PALMER, MARY A. United States.

009102   MARIAN: A STORY OF THE SOUTH. New York: Neale Publishing Company, 1917 NUC.

South family and their slaves, Marian makes a bad marriage but is reunited with her true love. PW

PALMER, MAUD CLAYTON.

009103   JUDITH CARRINGTON'S ROMANCE. BY MRS. CLAYTON PALMER. London: Simpkin, Marshall, 1910 BMC.

TLS-harmless.
ACAD-harmless.

009104   ONLY PRETENDIN'. London: H. J. Drane, [1912] BMC.

009105   THE STORY OF ANGELINA WACKS. London: W. Gardner, 1913 BMC.

009106   SUPPOSIN'. London: Gardner, Darton, [1914] BMC.

PALMER, MRS. CLAYTON. See PALMER, MAUD CLAYTON.

PALMER, WILLIAM SCOTT, pseud. See DOWSON, MARY EMILY.

PAMPLIN, MAY EREHOS.

009107   TITANIA; OR, AN OLD FASHIONED GIRL'S IDYLL. A LOVE STORY. Manchester: Brook & Chrystal, 1892 BMC.

PANGBORN, GEORGIA WOOD. B. 1872. United States.

009108   ROMAN BIZNET. Boston: Houghton, Mifflin, 1902 NUC.

Man and his son in North country. ATH 121:11

PANSY, pseud. See ALDEN, ISABELLA (MACDONALD), Also ALDEN, ISABELLA (MACDONALD) AND MARCIA (MACDONALD) LIVINGSTONE.

PANTON, JANE ELLEN (FRITH). 1848-1923.

009109   THE BUILDING OF WHISPERS. BY THE AUTHOR OF "LEAVES FROM A LIFE" [ANONYMOUS]. London: Heath, Cranton and Ouseley, [1915] BMC.

The lady of the Abbey in times of French Revolution tells the story; in part focus is on Whispers, a house "the hy of themaking and ending of a home" Then her

disembodied spirit reigns in the house. ? TLS

009110   THE CANNIBAL CRUSADER: AN ALLEGORY FOR THE TIMES. Bristol: J. W. Arrowsmith, 1908 BMC.

TLS exposure of shams of soc. respectability by a youth from a primitive island.
ATH-Critical of the "existing order of things"

009111   FRESH LEAVES AND GREEN PASTURES. BY THE AUTHOR OF "LEAVES FROM A LIFE" [ANONYMOUS]. New York: Brentano's, 1909 NUC. London: E. Nash, 1909 BMC.

009112   LEAVES FROM A GARDEN. BY THE AUTHOR OF "LEAVES FROM A LIFE," "FRESH LEAVES AND GREEN PASTURES," "COUNTRY SKETCHES IN BLACK AND WHITE" [ANONYMOUS]. London: E. Nash, 1910 NUC BMC.

009113   LEAVES FROM THE COUNTRYSIDE: AN EPISODE. BY THE AUTHOR OF "LEAVES FROM A LIFE" [ANONYMOUS]. London: Heath, Cranton and Ouseley, 1914 BMC.

ATH Lives in rural Dorsetshire
TLS- Chatty agreeable discourse by lady visiting friends and a local mystery.

009114   THE RIVER OF YEARS. BY THE AUTHOR OF "LEAVES FROM A LIFE" [ANONYMOUS]. London: Heath Cranton, [1916] BMC.

TLS Story of her life, efforts in a special line of journalism, marriage and desertion by a painter.
ATH Descriptions of her home life and education. Regards her husband's failings in a convincing philosophic spirit. quiet and thoughtful.

009115   ROUND ABOUT A RECTORY. BY THE AUTHOR OF "LEAVES FROM A LIFE" [ANONYMOUS]. London: S. Swift, [1912] BMC NUC.

Study of parochial life in a rural backwater with shrewd comments on the poor law. SP

PARADISE, DOROTHEA CHESTER. Nationality Unknown.

009116   IF THERE MUST BE BATTLES; LETTERS OF PEGGY POLLOCK. London: T. F. Unwin, 1915 BMC [1916] NUC.

TLS-sentimental letters to a soldier

PARHAM, HELENA BEATRICE RICHENDA.

009117   IN PART TO BLAME. BY HAINE WHYTE. Bristol: J. W. Arrowsmith, [1892] BMC.

ACAD 42:128. Don Francisco Freitas is a murderer, bigamist assaulter of women. Spanish-American. There is also a poet.
SR-In the end he is gulled into a marriage, "paid in his own coin."

009118   PEARLE: OR, "IN HIS NAME," AND OTHER TALES. BY HAINE WHYTE. Bristol: J. W. Arrowsmith, [1893] BMC.

009119   WHERE WAS THE SIN? OR THE VALUE OF LOVE. BY HAINE WHYTE. Bristol: J. W. Arowsmith, [1891] BMC.

PARISH, JULIA ROYCE. 1844-1918. United States.

009120   DIADAMA VAN DYNE. [AND] THISTLEDOWN. [Bay City, Mich.]: [J. P. Lambert], 1899 NUC.

PARK, MRS. KENDALL.

009121   RIQUILDA; A ROMANCE OF BARCELONA. Murray and Evendon, [1912] BMC.

ACAD-0
Historical romance-TLS
ATH-Historical romance

PARKER, AGNES. United States.

009122   THE REAL MADELEINE POLLARD: A DIARY OF TEN WEEKS' ASSOCIATION WITH THE PLAINTIFF IN THE FAMOUS BRECKINRIDGE-POLLARD SUIT. AN INTIMATE STUDY OF CHARACTER. New York: G. W. Dillingham, 1894 NUC.

PW-purports to have been written by a female detective who gained access to the home in which Miss Pollard resided during the trial, won her affection and confidence, and by a constant scrutiny of her words and actions tried to determine the exact sort of woman she really was. POV?

PARKER, BESSIE.

009123   MISS LOMAX: MILLIONAIRE. London: W.
Blackwood, 1905 BMC.

Has wealth, wit; changes places with a friend and
becomes a governess. BKM 29-30:41

PARKER, CLARA. United States.

009124   AN EVENTFUL NIGHT: A COMEDY OF A WESTERN
MINING TOWN. New York: Doubleday and McClure, 1900
NUC.

PARKER, FRANCES. B. 1875. United States.

009125   HOPE HATHAWAY; A STORY OF WESTERN RANCH
LIFE. Boston: C. M. Clark, 1904 NUC.

PW-Refuses to marry man her parents have chosen,
leaves home and becomes school teacher.

009126   MARJIE OF THE LOWER RANCH. Boston: C. M.
Clark, 1903 BMC NUC.

009127   WINDING WATERS, THE STORY OF A LONG TRAIL
AND STRONG HEARTS. Boston: C. M. Clark, 1909 NUC.

Western PW 11-20-09

PARKER, GAY, pseud. See GREEN, M. P.

PARKER, LOTTIE BLAIR. C. 1885-1937. United States.

009128   HOMESPUN; A STORY OF SOME NEW ENGLAND
FOLK. New York: H. Holt, 1909 NUC.

Story of Northeast PW 6-19-09;NYT

PARKER, MARGARET.

009129   THE DESIRE OF THEIR HEARTS: A NOVEL.
London: Jarrold, 1899 BMC.

Marjorie desires money most and she gets it in the
form of a very large inheritance which is taken from
her later when a newer will is found. So her fiance
leaves her. She studies art in Rome and gains an
elderly suitor. LBKM 16:113
Thinks of painting Tennyson's women as she envisioned
them. ACAD 56:244
She's a governess at first. ATH 113:375. Suitable for
girls.

PARKER, MARIA HILDRETH. United States.

009130   THE COUNTRY HOME; OR, EVENTS OF A SEASON.
Lowell, Mass.: Citizen Newspaper, 1894 NUC.

PARKER, MARY MONCURE (PAYNTER). 1862-1941. United States.

009131   A FAIR MAID OF FLORIDA. A STORY OF THE
SPANISH POSSESSION OF THE FLORIDAS IN THE EIGHTEENTH
CENTURY. Chicago: 1898 NUC.

009132   A GIRL OF CHICAGO. New York and London:
F. T. Neely, [1901] NUC.

PW 8-17-01

PARKER, NELLA.

009133   THE MISTAKE OF MONICA. London: G.
Routledge, [1899] BMC.

She's into music. Pushed into marriage to please her
aunt. "After supporting the wrong man in comfort until
he becomes insupportable," she turns her attention to
a former lover and all is made right when her husband
bicycles into a stone wall. LIT 4:502
She's married to a bad husband. ATH 113:335

PARKES, ALICE.

009134   ERMENGARDE. A STORY OF ROMNEY MARSH IN
THE THIRTEENTH CENTURY. BY MRS. HADDON PARKES.
London: E. Stock, 1893 BMC.

Much history research. Historical romance of mid 13th
century. Etoile carried off by wicked knight. ATH
102:879

PARKES, ELIZABETH (ROBINS). 1862-1952. United States.

009135   CAMILLA. BY ELIZABETH ROBINS. London:

Hodder & Stoughton, New York: Dodd, Mead, 1918 NUC.

at 28 she travels to continent & Eng.-we learn of her
past-her childhood, early marriage, estrangement and
divorce. Now she's engaged but demands a moratorium
before marriage. Her fiance is against this. She
returns to US to think things over. Here she meets
husband (who had remarried and divorced) they're
almost reconciled when he says "women as companions
are a failure" SP
PW novel of divorce and perplexities of a divorce.
TLS-She cannot enter into another relationship because
of memories of the past. Finally does.
NyT-0

009136   COME AND FIND ME! BY ELIZABETH ROBINS.
New York: Century, 1908 NUC. London: Heinemann, 1908
BMC.

BKM v. 27 1908
PW-Hildegarde in North looking for her father; love
story.
TLS-gold rush
SR-excellent female character
ATH-photographic impressions

009137   THE CONVERT. BY ELIZABETH ROBINS. New
York: Macmillan, 1907 NUC. London: Methuen, 1907 BMC
NUC.

novel "centered in the first suffragette agitations"
the movement itself. Review BKM 26 (1907) 405-6
plea for woman suffrage. "Striving appeal for
suffrage" "a tract in fiction" "plea for radical
enlargement of woman's sphere in the affairs of
national government" no love motif. Vida
levering-psych study: leads aimless life in social
circle . She hears of the sexless suffragettes who
spit at police, hears one speak-by accident-amazed at
her; goes to more meetings-becomes active in mvt.

009138   A DARK LANTERN: A STORY WITH A PROLOGUE.
BY ELIZABETH ROBINS (C. E. RAIMOND). New York and
London: Macmillan, 1905 NUC BMC.

"problem of separate standard of morality for man and
woman" Katharine offered a morganatic marriage (no
claim to husband's wealth) "double standard" Review
BKM 21 (1905) 516-7
emotional girl allows herself to be dominated by a dr.
Earlier she loved a German prince but refused to
descend to a morganatic marriage; sacrifices her life
to a brutal selfish man PW 6-10-05
ends with reunion of husband and wife-long in strife.
Dowager opposes the morganatic marriage of her god
daughter. Kath loves a prince, wastes much of her
youth on this fantasy. Marries a dr. and their
marriage full of pain for her. He's brutal "a plea for
experimental marriage"? strips all disguise from the
love-passion in women-the operation of love in the
case of a steady, sensible woman and a real man. ACAD
543,05
a terrible fellow, growls, knocks women. Is it
supposed to be humorous? Does Robins believe Katherine
would love such a man? LBKM 27-8, 102
Katherine declines a morganatic marriage makes a
different arrangement. a plea for experimental
marriage? TLS 153, 05
She marries the brute. ATH 05, 651

009139   THE FLORENTINE FRAME. BY ELIZABETH
ROBINS. New York: Moffat, Yard, 1909 NUC. London: J.
Murray, 1909 BMC.

LBKM- he loves mother but marries daughter due to a
misunderstanding. mother & daughter love same man.
Both think he loves the daughter they force him to
marry. He only learns after mother died, that she
loved him and he her. see "Feminine Unrest & some
Recent Novels" BKM 30 Dec. 1909, 382-3
Isabella Rosco, widow of bad husband; Eugenia her
daughter. They become rivals. TLS
Mother gives up the man for daughter's sake , Genie
learns the husband really loved her mother. ATH
mother never had a chance to live, unhappily married,
remained with husband because of daughter Genie
(modern girl) falls in love over and over always the
pursuer. Always writing love letters knows what she
wants "goes after it with a directness which makes one
shudder" view of novel is the popular idea that "the
best thing a woman has on earth is her play
attractiveness" and that this is short lived "one
peerless moment of actual perfection...when the
feminine first comes to flower...its little day of
ravishment, and then--"

009140   GEORGE MANDEVILLE'S HUSBAND. BY C. E.
RAIMOND. London: W. Heinemann, 1894 NUC BMC. New York:
D. Appleton, 1894 NUC.

SR 78:241. story of artist married to novelist and
their child Rosina. She was disagreeable, vain,
foolish, he very weak and somewhat of a maunderer; she
kept the upper hand. He says to Rosina, "I'd rather my
daughter scrubbed floors than write books." Her father
is the only sympathetic figure in her world; her
critical attitude toward mother is inevitable.
SP 73:144. George is coarse, strong-minded, selfish,
undiscriminating. She is stout, frowsy, slatternly, at
dress rehearsal of her play, roaring directions at
all." To sit down daily to the task of being George
Eliot to rise up the average lady novelist to the end,
must, even if only dimly comprehended, be a
soul-tragedy of no mean proportion." She cared nothing
for Rosina and was totally blind to her illness.
ACAD 46:252. The development of Lois Carpenter. After
her marriage she adopted the name George Mandeville
and determined to be a novelist, with the missions of
progress and women's emancipation.
ACAD 46:252. "With the exception of a play, which
fails, she obtains considerable success as a writer,
and entirely eclipses the personality of her rather
invertebrate and weak-willed husband."
ATH 104:250. "The chief merit of the book lies in the
portrait of the husband, a man whose artistic
aspirations (and even whose interest in life) are
utterly killed by the hideous existence to which he is
condemned...his scrupulous cleanliness and his love of
personal seemliness throw up the unfeminine squalor of
George Mandeville's person and mind; and a very just
effect is conveyed by the gradual metamorphosis of his
Bohemian and unconventional joyousness into the
straitest conventionality by contact with his wife's
unconventional ideas and manners. Very charming, too,
is the alliance of the father with his only daughter,
and there is much pathos in their furtive conclaves in
the box-room. The disclosure, however, by the mother,
which finally kills and disgusts the daughter..."
LBKM 7:26-satire on the modern woman.

009141   THE MAGNETIC NORTH. BY ELIZABETH ROBINS
(C. E. RAIMOND). New York: F. A. Stokes, [1904] NUC.
London: W. Heinemann, 1905 BMC NUC.

BKM 19 1904-not helpful
NYT -0
LBKM- main characters are men, but there are women;
minor characters.
TLS- doesn't mention women. Story of klondike.

009142   THE MESSENGER: A NOVEL. BY ELIZABETH
ROBINS. London: Hodder & Stoughton, [1919] BMC. New
York: Century, 1919 NUC.

Nan Ellis, pacifist lover who gives up pacifism when
he meets up with German brutality. Greta: German
governess, spy who matches skill and daring with
Scotland yard. TLS
Greta Van Schwartzenberg, governess is a spy working
for people who trust her. But the employer's secretary
suspects. To avoid scandal for the employer, Sir
William, Greta is only deported when found out. But
she comes back; quick wit, power of self command, lack
of scruples. Nan Ellis "adores" Greta. Nan is American
follows Greta all over the place. Gets involved in
padifism divided in her sympathies. NYT 10-12-19, 531
TLS-governess-spy. visit of American girl Nan Ellis to
the spy in prison terrible in its realism and suicide
of principal char. is quite a relief.

009143   THE MILLS OF THE GODS. BY ELIZABETH
ROBINS. New york: Moffat, Yard, 1908 NUC. London: T.
Butterworth, 1920 BMC.

"A story of tragedy with its scenes laid on the
continent. It te
l ls how a woman of the world after thirty years has
her revenge for the ill treatment she received at the
hands of an Italian nobleman." BKM 28 1908-9

009144   MILLY'S STORY, THE NEW MOON. BY C. E.
RAIMOND. London: W. Heinemann, 1895 BMC NUC.

Milly Munroe, wife of successful London doctor,
believes
gloss on G.E. Raimond's "New Moon" SR 79:979. in
omens. The estrangement between herself and husband
she believes is due to the fact that he is scientific,
she's imaginative. Tries to learn science. Then gets
jealous of one of his patients. ACAD 48:159

009145   MY LITTLE SISTER. BY ELIZABETH ROBINS.

New York: Dodd, Mead, 1913 NUC.

R OF R v 47, 1913, p. 630
"conveys vividly the undescribable horror of white
slavery. Bettina after a "watched and exquisite
childhood" pushed into this "ghastly pit"; . She's too
sheltered, ignorant, a hot house flower. NYT
2 sisters visit London at the invitation of an aunt,
but the woman who meets them traffics in white
slavery. The older escapes tries to rescue her sister.
The novel attacks the sheltered life system of
education for young girls. BKM
"white slave traffic" "Suddenly one of the chief
figures in the book, a charming girl, is swept into
the marshes of the traffic.The earth opens and
swallows her; that is all." NYT, 1913, 40 Much fuller
review. NYT 1913, 90.

009146   THE NEW MOON. BY C. E. RAIMOND. London:
W. Heinemann, 1894 BMC. New York: D. Appleton, 1895
NUC.

Sentimental story of a man married young to a foolish
invalid wife who is full of unscientific beliefs and
superstitions, First person narrative. A woman without
vitality or energy, inert clinging wife; the other
woman a complete contrast. The other is Dorothy Lance.
Ends with a fire-the impression of "gloom,
dissatisfaction and general uncertainty." ATH 105:670
"story of a perfect friendship. There's a poor
marriage; then another woman comes to love the husband
not knowing he's married. They know they love each
other, but "are good friends and companions only." The
wife does not die in order to make the lovers happy.
LW 26:171

009147   THE OPEN QUESTION: A TALE OF TWO
TEMPERAMENTS. BY C. E. RAIMOND. London: W. Heinemann,
1899 NUC BMC. New York and London: Harper, 1899 NUC.

Val brims with life, wants to experience everything.
Buoyant irresponsible fascinating egotism. Her lover
Ethan is a decadent weakling. Morbid, unwholesome,
demoralizing. LBKM 15:113
Three questions: of immortality, duty to unborn child;
right of suicide. Ohio town after Civil War. The Gano
family--very proud. Ethan Gano dies in the war, leaves
a son for his mother to raise. (His wife is dead.)
This child raised by the unusually strong mother who
faced loss of wealth, etc. He loves Val--the strong
buoyant woman--his opposite. With TB inherited in
both, risk to children is great, but they marry. They
pledged to die together if she gets pregnant--to die
before child is born. This they do after their
marriage. LW 30:52
Mrs. Gano dominates the book--a very strong woman. (In
dying pulled the sheet over her face.) She rules,
she's the main element of sanity. But when she dies,
sanity goes. CR 34:157
Uncommonly intelligent young woman wed to her cousin,
wealthy and gifted agree to suicide to avoid
perpetuating TB. Agreed before their marriage.
Respected Gano family snobs. Their inbreeding. She is
valerie yearned for love, fame as a young woman. All
her aspirations crushed by circumstances and
environment except her yearning for love. Loves Ethan.
Agree to marry but to suicide if child comes to kill
the child. NYT 2-18-99,98
SP 81:836. The marriage of first cousins. The question
at issue is better left to the family doctor.
LIT 3:498. Several open questions. Should cousins
marry? Is there a future world in which lovers will be
reunited? Under either hypothesis, is it lawful for a
couple to commit double suicide? Valerie and Ethan, in
spite of warning, marry for one year, with suicidal
past at end. Contract of pair and strong grandmother.
ACAD 55:332. Six central characters, all women, from
the Gano family, the strongest being Mrs. Gano, the
grandmother, and Val. Suicide was intended if needed,
and then it was needed. But Ethan wishes to trust to
luck and the idea is abandoned. But before her child
is born, Val returns to it and insists. At end they
sail out to sea. Open question might be did they
suicide?
ATH 112:891. Mrs. Gano, the true heroine.

009148   UNDER HIS ROOF. BY ELIZABETH ROBINS.
London: woods, [1912] BMC.

009149   UNDER THE SOUTHERN CROSS. BY ELIZABETH
ROBINS. New York: F. A. Stokes, [1907] BMC NUC.

fervid love making. saucy and cool headed woman PW
12-14-07
Young woman tells her advents of a sea and land trip
from San Francisco to N.Y. via Panama. Her problem how

to dispose of passionate Young Baron ?
BKM 27 1908 "Ultra-independent" heroine meets on ocean liner man with traditional old-fashioned ideas of women's dependence upon man written with "half-veiled touch of satire."

009150   "WHERE ARE YOU GOING TO...?" BY ELIZABETH ROBINS. London: W. Heinemann, 1913 BMC NUC. Leipzig: B. Tauchnitz, 1913 NUC.

See My Little Sister. The horror of kidnapping in the white slave traffic. The heroine and her sister are carried off. SP
She is of genteel breeding and exceptional innocence; is actually kidnapped. SR
Bettina's sister tells the story. kidnapped by woman disguised as aunt. TLS

PARKES, MRS. HADDON. See PARKES, ALICE.

PARKMAN, SUSAN.   Nationality unknown.

009151   TWO NOBLE WOMEN. New York: American Tract Soc., [c1897] NUC.

Wife of famous judge and wife of humble tinner join forces for social betterment of several of the poor woman's neighbors "who have fallen from grace." PW 51:519

PARKS, MABEL E. B. 1862.

009152   A SOUL'S LOVE LETTER. BY MABEL. Westwood, Mass.: Ariel Press, 1904 NUC.

"Her demands for social justice reveal the reformer" ARENA 1905

PARMELE, MARY (PLATT). 1843-1911. United States.

009153   ANSWERED IN THE NEGATIVE. New York: Parmele and Chaffee, [c1892] NUC.

PARR, LOUISA (TAYLOR). D. 1903. United Kingdom.

009154   CAN THIS BE LOVE? A NOVEL. BY MRS. PARR. London: Longmans, 1893 BMC. New York: Longmans, Green, 1893 NUC.

Stella Clarkson, daughter of a poor clerk inherits fortune on condition she is raised after age 5 by guardians. Though her life is very different from that of her family, she remains close to them. First she thinks she loves her guardian's son, then she meets a man she loves without question. LW 93, 335 Also SR 76:388

009155   DUMPS AND I. London: Methuen, 1891 BMC.

009156   THE SQUIRE. BY MRS. PARR. London: Cassell, 1892 BMC. New York: Cassell, [c1892] NUC.

PW-Heroine is daughter of physician, leaving her a stepmother and large debts. Squire is a bachelor for mysterious reasons.
CR 9-24-92, p 164. Rejected male hero, his devotion to sweetheart's daughter.
ATH 100:188, Portrait of a "quiet man with strong feeling," an "educated modest gentleman."

PARR, MRS. See PARR, LOUISA (TAYLOR).

PARR, OLIVE KATHARINE. 1874-1955. United Kingdom.

009157   THE DARTMOOR WINDOW AGAIN. BY BEATRICE CHASE (OLIVE KATHARINE PARR). London and New York: Longmans, Green, 1918 BMC NUC.

PR 6031 Dartmoor, Eng.

009158   THE HEART OF THE MOOR. BY BEATRICE CHASE. London: H. Jenkins, 1914 NUC BMC.

SR 147 supp 21 Mar p 8. Two women who have been "ill-wished" and are convinced that their lovers and husbands are doomed to violent deaths. Dartmoor.

009159   THE LITTLE CARDINAL. New York: Benziger, 1912 NUC.

PW-Male sent
ATH Male sent.

009160   PEARL; OR, A PASSING BRIGHTNESS. Edinburgh: Sands, 1906 BMC NUC.

009161   A RED-HANDED SAINT. New York: Benziger, 1909 NUC. London: Washbourne, 1909 NUC.

SP-R. C. Tract
NYT-The heroine (see title) is a murderess who becomes a prison visitor on her release from jail. Novel dealing with the London slums.

009162   THROUGH A DARTMOOR WINDOW. BY BEATRICE CHASE. London and New York: Longmans, Green, 1915 BMC NUC.

Wholesome desc. of rural life PW 8-14-15
"My own intimate daily life" literary mode of quasi-confidential chat" SR
The weather, dogs, cats, etc of Dartmoor ACAD

009163   THE VOICE OF THE RIVER. A DARTMOOR STORY. London: G. Routledge, 1903 BMC. New York: E. P. Dutton, 1903 BMC.

009164   WHITE KNIGHTS ON DARTMOOR. London: Longmans, Green, 1917 BMC.

009165   A WHITE-HANDED SAINT. London: R. & T. Washbourne, 1913 BMC NUC.

First person-told by heroine to saint of title who is a priest with a paralyzed arm. Their many conversations because she's an impetuous pagan. ATH.

PARRISH, GLADYS. See HUNTINGTON, GLADYS THEODORA (PARRISH).

PARSONS, CAROLINE. United States.

009166   ESTHER HILLS, HOUSEMAID. New York, London: Abbey Press, [1901] NUC.

PARSONS, CORNELIA MITCHELL. United States.

009167   THE QUAKER CROSS; A STORY OF THE OLD BOWNE HOUSE. New York: Natl. Americana Society, 1911 NUC.

009168   A SECRET OF THE SEA. New York: J. S. Ogilvie, [c1896] NUC.

PARSONS, FLORENCE MARY (WILSON). 1864-1934.

009169   OVER THE EDGE. London: E. Macdonald, 1915 BMC.

Christian Guildersleeve (the heroine) loves John but finds out he's married. Marries his brother. "a feeble literary reflection of his elder" Hopes and regrets, envy and egotism, fancied slights and, idolization turned to hate...all these things darken her diseased mind." until "it is no longer a mind but a mood. The world seems against her." TLS

009170   SIR JULIAN THE APOSTATE. BY MRS. CLEMENT PARSONS. London: W. Heinemann, 1903 BMC NUC.

Ella's husband is paralyzed; her attraction for Julian ACAD 64,634 ACAD, 65,83
TLS 201,03

PARSONS, MRS. CLEMENT. See PARSONS, FLORENCE MARY (WILSON).

PARUK, OLGA.

009171   BEWARE OF PURDAH-A STUDY OF MAHOMMEDON MARRIAGE. London: Simpkin, Marshall, Hamilton, Kent, 1916 NUC BMC. (Tales)

ATH-Describes suffering auth. says she knows from experience to await English women entering Moslem mrg. ATH 8/16 fic?

PASTON, GEORGE, pseud. See SYMONDS, EMILY MORSE.

PATCH, KATE (WHITING). 1870-1909. United States.

009172   BECAUSE YOU ARE YOU. New York: Dodd, Mead, 1913 NUC.

From Jane Spindler's cottage, one can see the sea and ships. Pretty tale--tired school teacher sent by doctor to rest. Goes to board with a delightful spinster --living out there restores her health, meets a man; tells her own story. NYT

PATERSON, ISABEL (BOWLER). 1885-1960. Canada.

009173   THE MAGPIE'S NEST. New York: J. Lane, 1917 NUC. London: J. Lane, 1917 BMC NUC.

Girl born in Rockies comes to NY makes her fortune and
finds a true love." The latter part of the story is
in obedience to the conv. happy end," but most of the
novel is "tense, full, eager, devouring youth" PW
Indep. Fascinating young artist-Hope Fielding. We
leave her at the gate of her paradise? TLS
Search for happiness only to be found in magpie's nest
which is always out or reach. ATH
"It is difficult to fancy any imprudence of which she
was not guilty, or any accepted code of womanly virtue
that she was not willing to throw over the windmills."
but her author loves her. Heroine shudders at
"essential brutality" of the permanence of marriage.
Most families have at least one divorce. NYT 139
4-15-17
"Hope had many lovers, was married and divorced." PW
91: 1059 3/31/17

009174   THE SHADOW RIDERS. London: J. Lane, 1916
BMC NUC. New York: J. Lane, 1916 NUC.

Canadian N.W. Duty is a word obsolete for the
characters; the situations "go far toward indicating
that the age old ideals of feminine conduct are fast
crumbling to dust." NYT 4-15-17,138
PW 89: 2/26/16: 692 NYT Canadian writer. 1st novel.
Her., Lesle y Johns is fine and vital, possessing much
cultiv. and knowledge. TLS Auth narrowly feminine in
her outlook-regards men as a bad lot auth.C Perhaps it
is that secret sense of guilt in common makes for the
solidarity of men as a sex; they are all outlaws
together." Deals with 2 mrgs. BKM O
ATH heroine is a journalist.

PATERSON, MARGARET.

009175   PEGGOTTS; OR THE INDIAN CONTINGENT.
London: W. Blackwood, 1907 BMC.

    LBKM 179 8-07
    Family letters TLS

009176   REALITY. Edinburgh: W. Blackwood, 1908
BMC.

    TLS--trad, quiet
    ATH

PATRICK, DIANA, pseud. See WILSON, DESEMEA (NEWMAN).

PATTERSON, MARJORIE. D. 1948. United States.

009177   THE DUST OF THE ROAD. A NOVEL. New York:
H. Holt, 1913 NUC. London: Chatto & Windus, 1913 BMC.

PW 9/27/13 952 "Romance of the stage. Tony, the
heroine, is a lovable American girl who goes to
England and has experiences with a Shakespearean
touring company. She and her solemn dog, Samuel
Pickwick, are a most engaging pair and together go
blithely their way. The hero is a morose, red-headed
sculptor, who is also by turns actor and dramatist."
She finally sacrifices her career on the altar of
love. ATH
Unconventional, ambitious, on the stage. Tony loves
her work. NYT

009178   FORTUNATA; A NOVEL. New York and London:
Harper, 1911 BMC NUC.

"an Italian Becky Sharpe" NYT
Girl of 18 lives in palace, spends money lavishly,
associates with unhealthy companions marries an
Englishman and is "forced to live with his hum-drum
mother and daughter" ends in tragedy; she remains
erratic throughout. PW 2-25-11

009179   A WOMAN'S MAN. New York: G. H. Doran,
[c1919] NUC. London: W. Heinemann, 1920 BMC.

Artist drowns his ambitions in sensuality. PW
Story of Armand de Vaucourt and the many women in his
life, their influence. In the end the beneficent
influence of an adopted orphan girl. NYT 675, 11-23-19
TLS Written in person of husband, a selfish and
unfaithful literary man. Contrasted with wife
Bernadette who is good. Symp with wife. Analysis of
his char. and record of sordid details of life.
ATH.Psych story thru out life he is influenced by
women, pious and austere men, viperish and unmoral
publisher's wife, good natured Princesse and neglected
little Bernadette.
BKM-He has a relationship with a siren in Paris, but
disgusted with her, he marries Bern. and they live
together quietly for ten years. He does some good work

and wins fame as man of letters but hankers after his
life in Paris. "On the brink of a new erotic
experience, his wife dies; and at a stroke his eyes
are opened." Realizes she had always been his
strength, etc.

PAUL, FORD, pseud. See PIPER, ANNA W. FORD.

PAUL, MARJORIE. United States.

009180   THE PASSING OF ALIX: A NOVEL. Boston:
Arena, 1895 NUC.

Alix marries a French marquise and finds life with him
degrading. Shows the perils of American women marrying
Eur artists PW 10-26-95:709

PAULINA ELIZABETH OTTILIA LOUISA, QUEEN CONSORT OF CHARLES
I, KING OF RUMANIA. 1843-1916. Europe.

009181   THE DREAMER OF DREAMS. BY THE QUEEN OF
RUMANIA. London and New York: Hodder and Stoughton,
[1915] NUC.

009182   EDLEEN VAUGHN: OR PATHS OF PERIL. A
NOVEL. BY CARMEN SYLVA. New York: Cassell, [c1891]
NUC. London: F. V. White, 1892 BMC.

The novel overflows with action, sentiment, and
moralizing. There's enough incident for a dozen
stories: wicked son and fond mother, step mother, a
witch, insanity, suicide, love, marriage, crime. LW
Theme: maternal passion: all incidents show the
misplaced love of Edleen for her no-good son, commits
crimes for him and he commits all crimes including
murder. NATION 53, 471
SF 68:750. "There is a certain coarseness of
suggestion in various passages which has the effect of
rendering the book repellant." "The fiction of the
last quarter of a century has proved that women will
rush in where the average man would fear to tread..."
ACAD 41:586. Story of maternal devotion to a worthless
son which is so extreme that mother allows a servant
to go to prison, robs her husband, and finally goes to
a premature grave. All to no avail; her incorrigible
son is finally deported.
She realizes the mistake she has made while dying. SR
73:687.

009183   HOW I SPENT MY SIXTIETH BIRTHDAY. BY
"CARMEN SYLVA". Guildford: Astolat Press, 1904 NUC.
(Tr. by H. E. Delf)

009184   SUFFERING'S JOURNEY ON THE EARTH. BY
CARMEN SYLVA. London: Jarrold, 1905 BMC. (Tr. from
Leidens Erdengang by Margaret A. Nash)

PAULL, M. A. See RIPLEY, MARY ANNA (PAULL).

PAWLOWSKA, YOI. See MARAINI, YOI.

PAXTON, MARY W.

009185   JENNY'S BAWBEE: A NOVEL. London: Downey,
1896 BMC.

ATH 108:220. Scottish. Medical students. Quiet, sober
novel of manners.
ACAD 50:178. Wicked guardian (Mesmeric) wants to marry
Jenny for her money. She is in love with a med.
student Ulric, who rescues her from the guardian after
her long struggle.

PAYNE, MARY E. Nationality Unknown.

009186   VIOLA LIVINGSTONE OR WHAT'S IN A NAME?
New York and London: Abbey Press, [1901] NUC.

PAZ, MAGDELEINE (LEGENDRE).

009187   WOMAN. BY MAGDELEINE MARX. New York: T.
Seltzer, 1920 NUC. London: G. Allen & Unwin, 1921 BMC.
(Tr. A. S. Seltzer)

NYT 1920:25. Author defends 1) multiple love relations
for women and 2) financial independence. She cries out
against the "fallacy of the maternal instinct." Rev.
hates this book.
BKM-Unnamed heroine is narrator. Leaves home, gets
room in boarding house and gets job in factory. She
meets Monia, a young Russian at the boarding house,
takes him out for a walk and just as he is saying
goodby, she asks him to live with her. He marries her,
they have a child, then she has a lover, tells her
husband that she loves him even more. Their marriage
continues, undiminished until both husband and lover

go to the front. She writes both every day. Husband is killed, then lover. She reflects that somewhere in the world there are persons for whom she is waiting but she will come to know.

PEACOCKE, ISABEL MAUD. See CLUETT, ISABEL MAUD (PEACOCKE).

PEAKE, C. M. A. See PEAKE, CHARLOTTE M. A.

PEAKE, CHARLOTTE M. A. B. 1862. United Kingdom.

009188   ELI OF THE DOWNS: A NOVEL. BY C. M. A. PEAKE. London: W. Heinemann, 1920 BMC NUC. New York: G.H. Doran, [c1920] NUC.

TLS Male shepherd.
PW Also a sailor.
NYT 9-12-20 p27

PEARD, FRANCES MARY. 1835-1923. United Kingdom.

009189   THE ABBOT'S BRIDGE. London: National Society's Depository, [1891] BMC. New York: Thomas Whittaker, [1891?] NUC.

Historical romance time of Edward III. Boy escapes from cruel step mother. His adventures on the road with wolves, robbers, etc. PW 10-31-91.

009190   THE BARONESS: A DUTCH STORY. London: R. Bentley, 1892 BMC NUC.

IND 44:413. "Breach is finally healed by love."
LW 23:43.
ATH 99:113. Marriage between Dutch baron and half French woman has not been happy, she has taken the "advice of a sinister friend" and obtained a separation. Under Dutch law this is possible if husband has been violent, and after 5 years the marriage is dissolved by default if husband and wife do not appear in court. Story opens here.
ACAD: Who is Hilvardine Steen? Character carried over from Near Neighbors? She remains the baroness' faithful friend throughout her troubles.

009191   THE CAREER OF CLAUDIA. London: R. Bentley, 1897 BMC.

A landscape gardener, completely self sufficient, her onslaught on the old ways, her belief in her own powers-The New Woman LBKM 12:18.
She's well ed. competent, convinced and dedicated to devoting herself to a prof. Becomes a landscape gardener, goes to live with three "old maid" aunts. Soon has a suitor-about whom Claudia is annoyed because he's the sterling sort. Is attracted to a rake type. Novel shows "the entire inadequacy of the higher ed...to cope with the weapons wielded by men and women"? CR believes it's anti women's rights, but shows no evidence. SP 78:447.
She does marry. "We like her much better at her landscape gardening, and so too, we suspect, did the author." "The magazine public would never tolerate a girl who succeeded at landscape gardening." ACAD 51:400.

009192   CATHERINE: A NOVEL. New York: Harper, 1893 NUC. London: Innes, 1894 BMC.

ACAD 46:226. Love story of volatile heroine who is injured in the field and disfigured for life, jilted by one lover but loved by other.
Old fashioned pious story. Young woman gives up young soldier; engaged to rich man who loves only her pretty face. An accident mars her face; she loses his love. The difficult adjustments she must make; in end accepts the old lover who always loved her for herself. LW 93 114.
Catherine Armstrong falls from horse, small English villiage, early 1800s. PW 2-11-93.

009193   DONNA TERESA. London: Macmillan, 1899 BMC NUC.

Young widow in Italy. Her marriage to a noble was a disaster. She's English. Teresa now is free has money wants to give her sister Sylvia a good time. Sylvia's lover soon falls in love with Teresa but Teresa is not interested. Sylvia learns, is brokenup, killed accidentally. We leave Teresa at 25. SP 83:961
Man engaged to a woman, falls in love with her sister. BAKER 03 161
LBKM 17:153. She marries her sister, who is a border-line idiot to a prig with an important future, slurring over her sister's foolishness.
ATH 115:43. Author is always safe for young readers.

Sylvia is a "pathetic nonentity."

009194   THE FLYING MONTHS. London: Smith, Elder, 1909 BMC. Leipzig: B. Tauchnitz, 1909 NUC.

Cordelia, companion in Italy and India to volatile Nesta Hastings, marries. TLS
A widow, heartless and young contrasted to straight clear-eyed loveable Cordelia. ACAD
Two women rivals for man's affection. ATH
Nesta is "impossibly odious". SP

009195   AN INTERLOPER: A NOVEL. London: R. Bentley, 1894 BMC. New York: Harper, 1894 NUC.

SR 78:184. Nathalie marries to help her family financially. When her husband is accused of theft, she stands by him and sees him through.
ACAD-he is weak and foolish.
ATH-her husband's family, initially at least, is not nice to her.

009196   NUMBER ONE AND NUMBER TWO. London: Macmillan, 1900 BMC. Leipzig: B. Tauchnitz, 1901 NUC.

SP 85:937. Bride Kennedy, an independent orphan, travelling in Egypt. She has been disappointed in love and henceforth wants only the admiration of men, but eventually succumbs to number two.
Hurt by #1, she leads #2 a dog's life. LBKM 2-01
Heroine utterly bored with English country life and a parson brother-in-law; escapes to Egypt with a companion. Complex characterization. ACAD 01

009197   THE RING FROM JAIPUR. London: Smith, Elder, 1904 BMC. Leipzig: B. Tauchnitz, 1905 NUC.

ATH-military in India. Unsmooth course in marriage "characterization of more than ordinary merit."
ACAD-wife bored with husband, unsympathetically treated.

009198   THE SECRET OF THE ORGAN LOFT. London: W. Gardner and Darton, [1891] BMC.

009199   THE SWING OF THE PENDULUM. London: R. Bentley, 1893 BMC NUC. New York: Harper, 1894 NUC.

(1) English travel in Norway (2) back in England there's a flirt, a lovely maiden, a flippant matron, foolish boy lover, a cynic. SR 76:546.
Anne Dalrymple "Beautiful, intelligent, incomprehensible"-who will she marry? ACAD 44:564.
PW-Norway

PEARL, BERTHA, pseud. See MOORE, BERTHA PEARL.

PEARN, VIOLET A.

009200   LOVE ON THE HAPPY HILL. London: A. Melrose, 1911 BMC.

LBKM-Male hero who is disenchanted with life by selfish, shallow wife; uplifted by idyllic love and life of his daughter.
Edith goes to Australia with father, rejects Gerald. Meantime Amy traps him. She's "unsufferably vain, vulgar and selfish." Marries her, comes to learn love makes everything good TLS

009201   SEPARATE STARS. London: J. Murray, 1910 BMC.

Joan (would be artist) marries Roger who plays cricket. They never understand each other. Then Roger is killed; Joan raises her son to be an artist. But he has different ideas about art from hers, so as a mature woman she takes up art seriously. The story ends there.
TLS Conflict of art vs love and life. Joan is a painter with high ideals of devotion to her art, she first surrenders to love of good husband whom she loses. Hopes for her son are shattered.
ATH She hopes that her gift would pass to him, trained him etc, he is nothing but a craftsman. She refuses second offer of mrg. to take up her art again. She is disconcerted by son's choice of subject matter for his canvases.

PEATTIE, ELIA (WILKINSON). 1862-1935. United States.

009202   THE ANGEL WITH A BROOM. Chicago: R.F. Seymour, for the Cordon, [1915] NUC.

009203   ANNIE LAURIE & AZALEA. Chicago: Reilly & Britton, 1913 NUC.

PW 8-23-13 505-"Annie Laurie Pace, is invited by Mrs.
Carson, to join her daughter Carin and Azalea McBirney
in instruction under Miss Parkhurst. At first she is
unwelcome, but after a healthy explosion which clears
the air, the three girls become the best of friends.
Annie meets with trouble and loses her inheritance,
and the girls help to bring the defaulters to a
realization of their crime and restore the fortune."

009204   AZALEA AT SUNSET GAP. Chicago: Reilly &
Britton, [c1914] NUC.

009205   AZALEA: THE STORY OF A GIRL IN THE BLUE
RIDGE MOUNTAINS. Chicago: Reilly & Britton, [c1912]
NUC.

009206   AZALEA'S SILVER WEB. Chicago: Reilly &
Britton, [c1915] NUC.

009207   THE BELEAGUERED FOREST. New York: D.
Appleton, 1901 BMC NUC.

heroine marries a man she hardly knows (who is mad)
and never loves. Lives among 70 loggers BOOK NEWS.
Sept 01
Regina-lonely sensitive, would be artist learns her
art is futile, marries drug addict; record of her
growth and her husband's deterioation. ends with her
exit from the woods (husband a lumberjack). Regina's
evolution, her brief marriage CR
Regina keeps a studio, artist, lives a Bohemian life,
loses the little money she has. Marries a man because
his life as lumberjack promises excitement-she doesn't
love him. He turns out to be on opium. She helps him.
Loves the pines. One day finds her husband dead. She
walks out of the forest. NYT '01
ACAD-begins with "my 1st proposal of marriage" "Marie
Bashkirtseff-Rhoda Broughton heroine"- development of
a strong woman's character "artistic neurotic"
ATH-husband has morphia habit.

009208   CASTLE, KNIGHT & TROUBADOUR, IN AN
APOLOGY AND THREE TABLEAUX. Chicago: Blue Sky Press,
1903 NUC.

009209   EDDA AND THE OAK. Chicago: Rand McNally,
[c1911] NUC.

009210   THE EDGE OF THINGS. Chicago, London: F.H.
Revell, 1903 BMC NUC.

Calif. desert ranch, its painful loneliness; hero
finds happiness in "unusual ways" NYT 03,653 USF 1:241
USF 2:209

009211   HOW JACQUES CAME INTO THE FOREST OF
ARDEN: AN IMPERTINENCE. Chicago: Blue Sky Press,
[c1901] NUC.

009212   THE JUDGE. Chicago and New York: Rand,
McNally, 1891 NUC. London: Everett, [1907] BMC.

LW 29:140. Judge has a monomania for bloodshed,
beginning with animals proceeds to human beings . Even
his daughter is in danger. At last truth comes out via
a reporter when daughter's lover is being tried for
murder judge committed. She hides with her father
until he dies.
PW-He suicides.

009213   LOTTA EMBURY'S CAREER. Boston: Houghton
Mifflin, 1915 NUC.

009214   THE NEWCOMERS. Boston: Houghton Mifflin,
1917 NUC.

a family moves to small town, at first unwelcomed, but
make friends, etc. PW

009215   THE PRECIPICE: A NOVEL. Boston: Houghton
Mifflin, 1914 NUC.

"A novel dealing almost wholly with the feminist
problems of to day. In its chief character it
dramatizes the opposing calls to woman of love and the
independent career and attempts to reconcile the two.
it pictures other phases of the modern feminine unrest
in other characters" NYT 7-11-15
BKM 39 1914-Hero and heroine refuse to give up careers
for marriage. They keep careers and marry one residing
in Washington D C and the other in Oregon.
"The feminist movement is the mainspring of this
story. Kate Barrington goes to the university against
all the traditions of her little home town and her
father and mother. When she returns, she finds herself

antagonistic to her father's tyranny toward women, and
after her mother's death goes back to Chicago as a
social worker. The aspirations, doubts, dreads,
discontent and frank hope of the present-day woman are
all depicted in Kate, who hesitates long between love
and what she considers her larger duty, but finally
finds a way to reconcile the two."__PW.

PECK, THEODORA AGNES. B. 1882. United States.

009216   HESTER OF THE GRANTS. A ROMANCE OF OLD
BENNINGTON. New York: Fox, Duffield, 1905 NUC.

historical 5-20-05 PW
381,05 NYT
girl patriot quite as daring as the usual historical
novel heroine but a bit more winsome.

009217   THE SWORD OF DUNDEE. A TALE OF "BONNIE
PRINCE CHARLIE". New York: Duffield, 1908 NUC.

TLS-hist, gallant heroine who convoys the prince
across the sea
ATH-heroine is a compromise between Jenny Cameron and
Flora Macdonald and wields the sword with effect.

009218   WHITE DAWN; A LEGEND OF TICONDEROGA. New
York: F.H. Revell, [c1914] NUC.

"A romance of love and war. the plot, for the most
part, is laid in the Champlain valley, in the days
when the armies of Wolfe and Montcalm were striving
for supremacy in the northern part of the continent.
the author crowds her book with action, and depicts
scene after scene resounding with the clash of arms."
PW 86 9/5/14:630
NYT-but heroine plays important part in the war.

PECK, WINIFRED FRANCES (KNOX). United Kingdom.

009219   TWELVE BIRTHDAYS. London: J. Murray, 1918
BMC.

PEDLER, MARGARET (BASS). D. 1948. United Kingdom.

009220   THE HERMIT OF FAR END. London: Hodder &
Stoughton, 1919 BMC. New York: G. H. Doran, [1920]
NUC.

PW-Male hero, living alone paying for another's sin.
NYT 4/4/20 Mystery and a love story
Traditional stuff involving romance of woman with
hermit.TLS

009221   THE HOUSE OF DREAMS-COME-TRUE. New York:
G. H. Doran, [c1919] NUC. London: Hodder & Stoughton,
[1919] BMC.

PW-Devonshire today
NYT 8-1-20 p. 24 "half a dozen time honored types"
"light"
Traditional love melodrama. TLS

009222   THE LAMP OF FATE. London: Hodder &
Stoughton, [1920] BMC. New York: G. H. Doran, [c1921]
NUC.

TLS-pretty

009223   THE SPLENDID FOLLY. London: Mills and
Boon, 1918 BMC. New York: G. H. Doran, [c1921] NUC.

TLS-Diana, singer, and her love

PEEBLES, MARY LOUISE (PARMELEE). 1833-1915. United States.

009224   A QUESTION OF HONOUR. BY LYNDE PALMER.
New York: Dodd, Mead, [c1893] NUC.

009225   WHERE HONOUR LEADS. BY LYNDE PALMER. New
York: Dodd, Mead, [c1894] NUC.

PW-sequel to "Question of Honor." Hero and heroine
have returned to Penfield center, ten years after
their mining experience in the West. Honor is still
the question, involves Schuyler Prage and a murder
trial.

PEEKE, MARGARET BLOODGOOD (PECK). 1838-1908. United
States.

009226   BORN OF FLAME: A ROSICRUCIAN STORY.
Philadelphia: J. B. Lippincott, 1892 NUC.

LW 23:213 Mystic doctrines, Eastern men and women in
the Adirondacks.

PW-Story opens in Rosedale insane asylum with death of Clothilde and transmittal of a packet of letters to Dr. Grotius which reveals her fatal secret. His diary. Many mystical doctrines.

009227   ZENIA, THE VESTAL; OR, THE PROBLEM OF VIBRATIONS. Boston, Mass.: Arena, 1893 NUC.

She's an American woman who falls in love with a master of theosophy. Learns she was once a vestal virgin in the time of ancient Egypt. Dedicates herself to vestal service. PW 8-19-93

PEEL, DOROTHY CONSTANCE (BAYLIFF). United Kingdom.

009228   THE HAT SHOP. BY MRS. C. S. PEEL. London: J. Lane, 1914 BMC NUC. New York: J. Lane, 1914 NUC.

what occurs there ACAD
Business side of carrying on a fashionable modiste's establishment plus a love story. But interest is in showing the energy and capital vital to the enterprise as well as experience. SP
Mrs. Earl of good family has gone into the trade. Roona the shop assistant-her struggle to live on 12 shillings a week TLS
PW-"This is a tale of a young widow of good family, who endeavors to add to her not very adequate income and at the same time to find herself a stimulating occupation by opening a hat-shop in the West End of London. Besides glimpses of all the members of the staff we see the customers-from both sides of the counter."

009229   MRS. BARNET-ROBES. BY MRS. C. S. PEEL. London: J. Lane, 1915 BMC NUC. New York: J. Lane, 1915 NUC.

Nettie young woman (a dressmaker) is seduced, made pregnant, abandoned. She's determined that her child not be hurt. Buys a wedding ring, takes name Mrs. Barnet and opens a modest dressmaking establishment. (got help from church). Meanwhile, the man thinks of her, tries to send her money, marries, has a daughter too. Book concerns the two daughters, Gladys Barnet and Anthea Selincourt. GLADYS-Illeg. devoted to mother, happy, normal, healthy prosperous. earns a good income as fashionplate artist sets mother up on Sloane St in shop. Marries the man of her choice. ANTHEA-legal, neurotic aversion for step mother. falls in love with married man, kills self when she fails to seduce a married man. ACAD
Anthea, an intense ego, "a masterful portrait- she "lives, vital and vivid upon the page" NYT

009230   A MRS. JONES. BY MRS. C. S. PEEL. London and New York: J. Lane, 1916 NUC BMC.

"Dot financially compelled to find an occupation. Farquhar promised her the happiness she longed for. She determined to do right by her husband even if it broke her own heart." PW 90:1124 9/30/16
TLS-Unhappy marriage caused her to take sent journey. She remarks later "I have taken nothing from my husband that he ever had." Several women who are hungry dissatisfied wives. Men are ninnies.
ATH-Her restlessness appears to be due to lack of abiding principle.

PEEL, MRS. C. S. See PEEL, DOROTHY CONSTANCE (BAYLIFF).

PELTON, MABELL SHIPPIE CLARKE.

009231   A TAR-HEEL BARON. Philadelphia and London: J. B. Lippincott, 1903 BMC NUC.

focus on hero--3-14-03 PW
NYT-03 225, about a German Baron and two women in his life.

PEMBERTON, CAROLINE H. United States.

009232   STEPHEN THE BLACK. Philadelphia: G. W. Jacobs, [c1899] NUC.

Study of conditions of slaves 30 years after freedom. Stephen is educated, becomes a school teacher for Blacks. Inter-racial marriage a chief theme. PW 56:1161
LW 31:76. The bad conditions in the South for the Blacks after the Civil War.

009233   YOUR LITTLE BROTHER JAMES. Philadelphia: G. W. Jacobs, 1896 NUC.

PEMBERTON, HARRIET LOUISA CHILDE.

009234   THE SILENT VALLEY. AN EPISODE. London: Constable, 1912 BMC.

TLS-The home of Averil who has something unique and universal which inspired poets and painters.
ATH-The home of Averil who has something unique and universal which inspired poets and painters.

PEMBERTON, JEANNETTE. United States.

009235   BUFFETING. New York: Dodd, Mead, [c1892] NUC.

Mother and two daughters left penniless after father's death but Mother is too proud to close up the big house though they can't afford to heat it all. Servants are kept, because the women can't do the work. One daughter loathes this false luxury and envies poor who don't give a damn for appearances. She wants to go into a learned profession, but rather than shock her mother, becomes a governess. Tells the story of her struggle in first person. CR 14,20:216.

PENDER, MARGARET T. (O'DOHERTY). 1850?-1920. United Kingdom.

009236   THE GREEN COCKADE: A TALE OF ULSTER IN 'NINETY-EIGHT. BY MRS. M. T. PENDER. Dublin: Sealy, 1898 BMC NUC.

Thrilling incidents, escapes, daredevil exploits. Historical romance. SP 83:93
Includes a love story, suicide of villain. ATH 113:79.

009237   MARRIED IN MAY. BY MRS. M. T. PENDER. Dublin: M. Lester, 1920 BMC NUC.

PENDER, MRS. M. T. See PENDER, MARGARET T. (O'DOHERTY).

PENDERED, MARY LUCY. 1858-1940. United Kingdom.

009238   AT LAVENDER COTTAGE. London: Mills and Boon, 1912 BMC NUC.

gentle humorous details of rural life with Miss Patty (maiden-lady-gardener-in-a-village type) ending up wedded. SR
ATH- Spinster, small nephew visit, mild romance of village life
TLS-love story about a rustic coquette SP

009239   DAISY THE MINX. A DIVERSION. London: W.J. Ham-Smith, 1911 BMC.

a music hall artist but the regular fare of love, impersonation, etc. ACAD

009240   DUST AND LAURELS. A STUDY IN NINETEENTH CENTURY WOMANHOOD. London: Griffith and Farran, 1893 BMC. New York: D. Appleton, 1894 NUC.

Should be called a Study in 19th Century Vulgarity. Vera writes books, promotes a woman's Free College between books. Has an "ugly flirtation" and becomes a "mere wife" (quote from book.) Not meant as a negative character. BKM 4:49.
Heroine is coarse and repellant. Passion as a study is unwholesome even if it is finally restrained. In the end she weds a good man. LW 26:42.
A too keen appreciation of masculine charms. She's a brilliant social success, famous author. Marries a man inferior to herself in order to escape from a temptation from which her better self revolts. Veronica Grace ATH 102:285.
vera Grace--middle aged single-meets Sylvia Grant at University Extension Meeting. They become friends, Vera comes to live in Sylvia's home. Vera has many involvements with men, including a Capt. Dalton who dies. she becomes a famous novelist, marries a don. SR 76:243.
She flirts outrageously. Inherits money--founds a Free College for women. Is a great literary success as author of "Fractions" the world at her feet. ACAD 44:250

009241   AN ENGLISHMAN. London: Methuen, 1899 BMC.

Michael Rolf is a grocer in Market Grazen. Marries Maria Lovel his child's governess after she refuses a better offer. He inherits wealth in the end. LIT 5:546
Market Grazen is the agricultural town. Maria is of aristocratic birth, highly educated. Doesn't come as governess because she must. She wants to earn her own living. She's disgusted at first, but ends up loving

and marrying Michael. Unusual: a refined, distinctly
patrician woman wedded to a grocer. ACAD 57:573
LW 31:74. Heroine marries into class lower than hers.
There is a butcher who is a violinist and well-read.
Rev. finds it not likely.

009242   LILY MAGIC. London: Mills and Boon, 1913
BMC.

Amaryllis Whyte, a most attractive heroine. LBKM
She and brother (orphans) move into a town and make
all the people good. SR
Amaryllis pure sweet 16 TLS

009243   MICHAEL ROLF, ENGLISHMAN. New York:
Doubleday and McClure, 1899 NUC. (Eng. ed. title: An
Englishman.)

009244   MUSK OF ROSES. FROM THE EGO BOOK OF DELIA
WYCOMBE. London: Cassell, 1903 BMC.

retired singer married to gentleman farmer-a
philistine who falls asleep during her performance. A
third party-a sensual young musician, woman's
unrequited passion ACAD 65,507
Diary. Includes gardening; portrayal of a very modern
woman, DelATH, 122, 715

009245   A PASTORAL PLAYED OUT. London: W.
Heinemann, 1895 BMC. New York: Cassell, [c1895] NUC.

A baby-murder by the worried heroine. Glyda was young
and inexperienced--only 17 when she fell. Then she
murdered her child. Became a dazzling woman of the
world. A great actress. He sees her. SR 79:661
She writes a Ballad of Woman, ACAD 47:398
This lovely cottage maiden rapidly develops views on
the wrongs of her own sex. Before we are done with her
she is on the platform reciting a Ballad of Woman, her
own composition, in a clinging fire-red silk dress.
Man is the monster and marriage the bugbear. Conway
Etheredge is the villain--cause of Glyda's grief.
Through him she's reduced to washerwoman. Then
rescued. ATH 105:533
Glyda Mariold--healthy country girl who consents to
live with love--no wedding. Because of debts, he
marries a Russian princess.Gylda has no blame for him.
At the end is reunited with him when the Russian wife
goes into theosophy and decides Gylda is the better
mate for the husband. PW 3-30-95:513

009246   PHYLLIDA FLOUTS ME. London: Mills & Boon,
1913 BMC.

Phyllida reads poetry and dreams of an ideal
lover-nothing like her farmer friend John Martin. His
sister-angered that Phyllida should take John so
lightly, disguises herself as a man-the type that will
appeal to Phyllida. Tries to win Phyllida's affection.
The result of the experience is the most amazing ten
days of her life. Phyllida's disappointment in her
ideal man with his exaggerated passions brings her
back to John. LBKM

009247   PLAIN JILL: A MERE LOVE STORY. London:
Chapman & Hall, 1915 BMC.

009248   THE SECRET OF THE DRAGON. A ROMANCE
ANCIENT AND MODERN. London and New York: Harper, 1911
BMC.

Story of the occult TLS

009249   THE SECRET SYMPATHY. London: Chapman &
Hall, 1916 BMC.

TLS-old plot with long lost heir but treated
interestingly Katherine and her young sister Winnie
live independently together.
LBKM-Katherine becomes a chauffeuse

009250   THE SILENT BATTLEFIELD. London: Chapman &
Hall, 1918 BMC NUC.

"Illegitimate child whose mother "makes good" in a
country shop which the son expands into a great
business" SP
Seems to focus on hero and mother's plans and
sacrifices for his future
TLS- male hero

PENDERED, MARY LUCY AND ALICE STRONACH.

009251   THE CHAMPION. London and New York:
Harper, 1902 BMC.

ATH 5-24-02--not helpful

PENN, RACHEL, pseud. See WILLARD, CAROLINE MACCOY (WHITE).

PENNELL, ELIZABETH (ROBINS). 1855-1936.

009252   THE FEASTS OF AUTOLYCUS: THE DIARY OF A
GREEDY WOMAN, EDITED BY ELIZABETH ROBINS PENNELL.
London: J. Lane, 1896 BMC. New York: Merriam, 1896
NUC.

SP 77:598. Collection of her articles on meals and
recipes.

009253   THE LOVERS. Philadelphia: J. B.
Lippincott, 1917 PW. London: W. Heinemann, 1917 BMC
NUC.

Their story, includes letters that show his training
as artist. Both are artists PW

009254   OUR HOUSE AND THE PEOPLE IN IT. Boston:
Houghton Mifflin, 1910 NUC. London: T. F. Unwin, 1910
BMC.

experience with domestic and other help, socialists,
suffragettes. PW
non-fiction? DA 684

PENNINGTON, JEANNE GILLESPIE. United States.

009255   THE SEA OF CIRCUMSTANCE. New York and
London: Abbey Press, [1902] NUC.

PENNINGTON, PATIENCE, pseud. See PRINGLE, ELIZABETH WATIES
(ALLSTON).

PENNY, F. E. See PENNY, FANNY EMILY (FARR).

PENNY, FANNY EMILY (FARR). d. 1939. United Kingdom.

009256   DARK CORNERS. London: Chatto & Windus,
1908 BMC NUC.

TLS- India
ACAD
ATH

009257   DESIRE AND DELIGHT. BY F. E. PENNY.
London: Chatto & Windus, 1919 BMC NUC.

India. matrimonial parting and reconciliation. TLS
Rosemary goes to India to marry Maurice Edenhope of
the Indian Medical Service but misses him-he goes off
on trip for a year. The horrors he saw change him, but
he keeps his promise, marries her as a formality,
ignores her, leaves her. She puts him out of her life;
changes her name; takes off wedding ring; becomes a
V.A.D. nurse; when her husband is himself again,
reconciliation comes. TLS
she sees the change, thinks it's fatigue, suggests the
wedding wait.
Pits her wit and courage vs a harem gang. Plays on
their superstition by posing as white witch. Beats
them at their own game; thrilling romantic drama LBKM

009258   DIAMONDS. BY F. E. PENNY. London: Hodder
& Stoughton, [1920] BMC.

SP history India

009259   DILYS: AN INDIAN ROMANCE. London: Chatto
& Windus, 1905 BMC.

heiress lost, living among the poor, found, married.
ACAD 10 83, 05
Gipsy TLS 305,05

009260   A FOREST OFFICER; BEING EPISODES IN THE
LIFE OF JIM BURNS. London: Methuen, 1900 BMC.

SP 85:892. Hero's courtship in last chapter, rest of
book is adventures of his in India.

009261   THE INEVITABLE LAW. BY F. E. PENNY.
London: Chatto & Windus, 1907 BMC 1909 NUC.

about Indian law and politics ACAD
TLS-focuses on Rama, an Indian; blind heroine-her
"tactless insistence" is exasperating. Reviewer dwells
on style

009262   LOVE BY AN INDIAN RIVER. London: Chatto &
Windus, 1916 BMC.

TLS-Anglo-Indian-Main theme superstitions. there is an

American woman who runs a fruit canning business.
LBKM-also has a love affair
ATH-exhibits courage in time of danger

009263   LOVE IN A PALACE. London: Chatto &
Windus, 1915 BMC.

can't see bride till after wedding; learns then she's
blind. Realizes his duty is to love and cherish her
the more. TLS
"story of the inner life of the harem showing how
western tendencies are gradually forcing their way in"
"intimate life of the women in their seclusion" "the
secondary wives in Indian houses" SR

009264   LOVE IN THE HILLS. London: Chatto &
Windus, 1913 BMC.

India-military station social life, races, jungles,
storms, animals. Nonia Armscote has had previous
marriages; she loves animals, is never free of love
affairs. Hero a soldier of solid character. there is a
scheming adventurer. ACAD
Her husband turns up-plot centers on legality of this
earlier unfortunate marriage. LBKM

009265   A LOVE OFFENSIVE. BY F. E. PENNY. London:
Chatto & Windus, 1918 BMC NUC.

TLS-war and India.

009266   A LOVE TANGLE. London: Chatto & Windus,
1916 BMC. New York: Dutton, 1917 NUC.

TLS-heroine is Indian trained on European lines.
3 different romances in So. India: Two involve English
women; the third, a Hindu. PW
War background NYT 250 7-1-17

009267   THE MALABAR MAGICIAN. BY F. E. PENNY.
London: Chatto & Windus, 1912 NUC BMC.

TLS-1 female character. she an Indian
ATH-

009268   MISSING! London: Chatto & Windus, 1917
BMC.

a Rajah missing, war, court life TLS
ATH-0
"the ranee and her Rajput husbands are drawn with
insight" BAKE R 32, 381

009269   A MIXED MARRIAGE. London: Methuen, 1903
BMC NUC.

brief description ACAD 64, 106 Lorina marries a
Prince, black.
Bride of Mohammedan finds life in India unacceptable
ATH 121, 300

009270   THE OUTCASTE. BY F. E. PENNY. London:
Chatto & Windus, 1912 BMC NUC.

TLS-same as usual
SP same as usual

009271   THE RAJAH. London: Chatto & Windus, 1911
BMC.

focuses on the Rajah TLS
Rajah comes to England to be educated, returns home
with a young woman as secretary and Pauline
Dersingham, the young woman's sister. Picture of harem
life ruled by 4 "mothers" of the Rajah is vivid SP

009272   THE ROMANCE OF A NAUTCH GIRL: A NOVEL. BY
MRS. FRANK PENNY. London: S. Sonnenschein, 1898 BMC
NUC.

LIT 3:40. Anglo-Indian. Murder and disappearance of
doctor's brother. He was buried by natives inside the
body of a buffalo.
ATH 111:689. Author has "great sympathy with the
natives, and even those of mixed blood...yet he (a
mix) is represented as being on the best of terms with
all the residents, and to be the beloved of a European
young lady of pure English blood! The stay-at- home
reader is thus given an altogether false idea..."

009273   SACRIFICE. London: Chatto & Windus, 1910
BMC.

BM. Indian life-serious study.
TLS-of religious attitudes

009274   THE SANYASI. London: Chatto & Windus,
1904 BMC 1911 NUC.

BKM _ Indian mystic hero
ATH 0

009275   THE TEA PLANTER. BY F. E. PENNY. London:
Chatto & Windus, 1906 BMC NUC.

ACAD--pleasant reading of a family in the sun of
Ceylon.
TLS--pleasant reading of a family in the sun of
Ceylon.

009276   THE UNLUCKY MARK. London: Chatto &
Windus, 1909 BMC NUC.

Story of racehorsing TLS
mixed marriage racial and social difficulties in India
LBKM

PENNY, MRS. FRANK. See PENNY, FANNY EMILY (FARR).

PENROSE, MARY ELIZABETH (LEWIS). B. 1860. United Kingdom.

009277   AS DUST IN THE BALANCE. BY MRS. H. H.
PENROSE. London: A. Rivers, 1905 BMC.

unhappy marriage and a man the wife should have
married; all treated very differently. ACAD 1131,05
Has her sister's contempt, leaves her husband-an
impossible prig
ATH 05, 794

009278   THE BRAT. A TRIFLE. BY MRS. H. H.
PENROSE. London: Mills & Boon, 1913 BMC.

three little friends, the Brat is 9, the youngest, the
governess and her romance ATH
She's the target of their torment. She's faded,
broken-spirited, middle-aged, with a grey background
of lost love. She has most trouble with the brat yet
he brings a bit of joy in her life. LBKM, TLS

009279   BURNT FLAX. BY MRS. H. H. PENROSE.
London: Mills and Boon, 1914 BMC.

LBKM-Life and loves of the Fitzpatricks, a wealthy
Irish family, the discontent of the tenants (Col.
Fitzpatrick has to flee the country at one point).
Maurice Dinnon, the Fitzpatrick's agent, who sees both
sides. He is engaged to Fitzpatrick's daughter and
loved secretly by Anastasia, a peasant girl.
ATH-Ireland.

009280   CHARLES THE GREAT. A VERY LIGHT COMEDY.
BY MRS. H. H. PENROSE. London: Methuen, 1912 BMC.

SP-Portrait of a country squire who believes himself
to be a genius.
LBKM - modern comedy.

009281   DENIS TRENCH. A PLOTLESS HISTORY OF HOW
HE FOLLOWED THE GLEAM AND WORKED OUT HIS SALVATION. BY
MRS. H. H. PENROSE. London: A. Rivers, 1911 BMC NUC.

Grace Diston "the insufferably perfect literary lady"
who marries and who shows him up as a prig and "poor
drunken Stella" ?TLS
Concerns Denis, women seem peripheral ACAD
Focus upon a hero from age 9 to becoming a successful
novelist LBKM
MRS. Stella Trench is an alcoholic. She parted from
her husband on her wedding day. ? SR

009282   A FAERY LAND FORLORN. BY MRS. H. H.
PENROSE. London: A. Rivers, 1912 BMC NUC.

ATH-0
LEKM- he bequeaths his child to former love who had
always wanted a fairy child. Mother does not object.

009283   THE GIVEN PROOF. BY MRS. H. H. PENROSE.
London: T.W. Laurie, [1907] BMC.

Murder and knavery Theodosia has some grandeur-has a
lover who asks her to leave her husband. TLS

009284   THE GREY ABOVE THE GREEN. BY MRS. H. H.
PENROSE. London: Hodder & Stoughton, [1908] BMC.

TLS-doubtful
ATH-Young woman becomes a successful dramatist and is
finally reunited with her childhood sweetheart

009285   THE HOUSE OF RENNEL. BY MRS. H. H.

PENROSE. London: A. Rivers, 1913 NUC BMC.

two brothers; one married; one a single man, a scamp.
gets his sister-in-law's maid pregnant; the maid dies;
sister-in-law raises child as her own. the problems
that arise. ATH

009286   THE LOVE THAT NEVER DIES: A STUDY. BY
MRS. H. H. PENROSE. London: Jarrold, 1898 BMC.

ACAD 54:296. Love and sentiment. She marries the wrong
man.
LBKM 15:59. Hero brought up by 4 aunts; discovers
truth about his mother after he is 21. Unhappy
marriage-all deepening into tragedy.

009287   THE MODERN GOSPEL. BY MRS. H. H. PENROSE.
London: A. Constable, 1898 BMC.

LIT 3:606. An anti-vivisection tract of 313 pages,
with a slap at the modern woman thrown in.
ATH 112:346. Heroine is narrator.
SR 86:280.

009288   RACHEL THE OUTSIDER. BY MRS. H. H.
PENROSE. London: Chapman & Hall, 1906 BMC.

ACAD-orphan who becomes successful novelist and
happily married. Pleasant reading
TLS-old fashioned domestic
ATH-0
BKM-searching novel of character unusual personality.

009289   A SHELTERED WOMAN. BY MRS. H. H. PENROSE.
London: A. Rivers, 1911 BMC NUC.

LBKM-Cecily, left 3 months after marriage by husband
is wrongfully accused by his aunts of infidelity.
Refuses to clear herself in order to protect her
sister-in-law Violet, who was divorcing her husband.
Later husband comes back to Cecily and asks for truth,
she tells, he forgives but determines to stop Violet's
divorce. The agony of what she had endured in vain, of
betraying her friend to her husband whom she should
have have been able to trust was too much-Cecily died
of shock.
Husband is away, wife has innocent relations with a
young poet. Scandal follows. Husband shown "to be a
prig" Ends unhappily TLS
young woman the scapegoat for her unscrupulous sister
in law. SP
Frustrated by too narrow an upbringing ATH

009290   SOMETHING IMPOSSIBLE. AN EXTRAVAGANZA. BY
MRS. H. H. PENROSE. London: Mills & Boon, 1914 BMC.

ATH 144:212. Male MD gets wish to be changed into
handsome Adonis.

009291   TWO YOUNG PIGEONS, ETC. BY MRS. H. H.
PENROSE. London: Mills & Boon, 1915 BMC.

Letters from a man to his fiance, newly widowed. But
focus is on two children, the pigeons TLS

009292   THE UNEQUAL YOKE: A STUDY IN
TEMPERAMENTS. BY MRS. H. H. PENROSE. London: A.
Rivers, 1905 BMC.

minister and wife who has no sympathy with his cramped
theology, shocks the parish. Study in temperaments
given with feeling and insight TLS 05, 91

PENROSE, MRS. H. H. See PENROSE, MARY ELIZABETH (LEWIS).

PENTREATH, DOLLY.

009293   BENEATH THE MOON. Truro: J. Pollard, 1899
BMC.

ACAD 58:34. Melodrama. India. "The heroine is a
fragile adventuress, whose husband, realizing his
perils, contrives to be drowned and then Lady Eleanor
begins adventuring in earnest."

PERCEVAL, HONOR, pseud. See POWYS, NORAH.

PERCIVAL, DOROTHY. Nationality Unknown.

009294   FOOTSTEPS. London: J. Lane, 1918 BMC NUC.
New York: J. Lane, 1918 NUC BMC.

PW English girl on Canary Island.
TLS-She has met only the worst of men until in Las
Palmas she meets a young engineer.
SR-Analysis of her attitude toward a sex which

inspires her with distrust, Tolerance of her
unpleasant but harmless admirer seems drawn from life.
NYT Dec. 8 '18 p. 538. Daphne "has become embittered,
degenerated into a sort of "feminist and old maid."
She and her indolent father, in the Canaries to
retrieve his fortune, do not prosper. Her hatred of
men grows, she is forced to take in a boarder (male),
her father wishes to marry her to a brutal
Spaniard-there is an "exciting climax."

PERCY, VICTORIA FREDERICA CAROLINE.

009295   MEGGIE. A DAY DREAM. London: Smith,
Elder, 1908 BMC.

PERKINS, ANNIE STEVENS. United States.

009296   APPOINTED PATHS. Boston: J. H. Earle,
1896 NUC.

PERKINS, MARGARET MOWER.

009297   THE GREATER WATERLOO; A LOVE STORY. BY
ROBERT RICHARDSON. London: T.F. Unwin, 1905 BMC. New
York: G.W. Dillingham, [1905] NUC.

Complicated story set in London and Canada involving
Gretchen and Karl, their grandfathers, a villain who
steals Karl's play, a threat of breach of promise,
etc. NYT 9-9-05, 589.

PERKINS, ROSE.

009298   BARBARA LAVENDER. London: H. J. Drane,
[1906] BMC.

TLS-o

009299   THE HOUSE OF HARDALE. London: J. Long,
1900 BMC.

SP 84:675. Melodrama. Exchange of children.

PERKS, LILY.

009300   FROM ARCADY TO BABYLON. London: D. Stott,
1892 BMC.

ATH 100:661. Four young women of an "innocent and
engaging type of socialism.

009301   GIFTS AND WEIRDS. London: R. Bentley,
1896 BMC.

ATH 107:546. Several people who are in love, some
marry, some don't. The Orkneys.

009302   A LATE SPRINGTIME. London: T. F. Unwin,
1895 BMC.

Honor Dare is an orphan with money, loved by Philip
Lorraine who is poor. But Bessie Lawson alone knows
he's going to be rich. Because Bessie lies about
Honor's feelings for him, Philip marries Bessie. Then
Philip and Honor discover their love, and he wants her
to sleep with him but they wait until Bessie dies in a
train crash. And Honor has her late springtime. SR
79:518

009303   LIFE'S COUNTERPOINT. London: C. A.
Pearson, 1903 BMC.

Politics, music, love, Italy and a passionate unstable
woman. LBKM 11-03, 106
Becomes a great opera singer. Review is vague TLS 288,
03

PERKS, MRS. J. HARTLEY.

009304   AMONG THE BRACKEN. London: A. Constable,
1896 BMC.

SR Has a "saucy and athletic" heroine, more
interesting than the "soon-to-perish introspective and
diary-keeping young woman." Ailie has two lovers,
decides to run away with one, then discovers she
prefers the other.
ATH 107:712. Scotland. painstaking dialect of the
locals.
SP 77:219. Sarah, Alison's sister, is a nurse and
unhappily married. Alison chooses suitor from
professional class which she hates. Their father is a
doctor.

PERLEY, MRS. T. E. United States.

009305   FROM TIMBER TO TOWN, DOWN IN EGYPT. BY AN
EARLY SETTLER [ANONYMOUS]. Chicago: A. C. McClurg,
1891 NUC.

In dialect, pioneers in Illinois ("record of a
vanishing dialect.") Their camp meetings, arguments
about baptism. Sons get to Legislature of the state
though father never "cud larn ter spell." LW
Move from Kentucy to Illinois, see timber claims
(theirs) grow into a town. IND

PERONNE, pseud. See THOMPSON, ELLEN PERRONET.

PERRIN, ALICE (ROBINSON). 1867-1934. United Kingdom.

009306   THE ANGLO-INDIANS. London: Methuen,
[1912] BMC NUC. New York: Duffield, 1913 NUC.

ATH-Life in India.
SP-3 daughters facing return to England with retiring
parents, youngest one loves India. Working out of
their lives. Study of the domestic side of life in
India.
ACAD- Matrimonial angling of mother, youngest daughter
gets job as typewriter, eventually marries capt. from
India.
"Story of how Mr. Fleetwood and his daughters return
to England after his retirement from the Indian Civil
Service. Here they find that things are very different
instead of being people of importance, they are
practically nobodies. In spite of this, the three
girls make good marriages, and one, at least, returns
to India, which had called her ever since she left."
PW 8-9-13, 426

009307   THE CHARM. New York: D. Fitzgerald,
[1910] NUC. London: Methuen, 1910 BMC.

"peculiar" characters PW 9-9-11
Eurasian woman commits suicide to allow husband to
return to earlier love, a white woman NYT
BM English man marries an Eurasian widow,
TLS
ACAD
SP- auth pov?
SR-Teresa gets a love potion (which is really a
poison) puts some of it in his teacup makes him sick
she takes the rest.

009308   A FREE SOLITUDE. London: Chatto & Windus,
1907 BMC NUC.

Study of Eurasians and England; conflict between love
of woman and country ACAD
Myra, Eurasian, fiary temper, ambitious TLS

009309   THE HAPPY HUNTING GROUND. London:
Methuen, 1914 BMC. Leipzig: B. Tauchnitz, 1914 NUC.

LBKM-after an unhappy affair in London, heroine goes
to India with the businesslike intent of putting
herself on the marriage market. Author tells this
frankly and sympathetically, making this strange
situation seem natural and seemly. But she accepts
proposal of her prey almost by accident, her resolve
having failed. He takes her as his wife hoping love
will follow. there is an older woman who married for a
home and plays her part dutifully without ever loving
her husband.
SR-0
TLS: Illustration of dilemma of moneyless girl: to
marry or not to marry.

009310   IDOLATRY. New York: Duffield, 1909 NUC.
London: Chatto & Windus, 1909 BMC NUC.

girl seeks mother in missionary work in India. PW
3-13-09
Anne Criviner is conventional; review says no more
about her TLS
She begins as selfish rich girl; radically changed by
love for a missionary ATH

009311   INTO TEMPTATION. London: F. V. White,
1894 BMC.

SR 77:203. Autobiography of young woman, married to
old man in India, and a young man.
SP 72:187. "The heroine marries a foolish and
disagreeable man in order to get away from a home
where she meets with no kindness, goes out to India,
engages in some pronounced flirtations in what we hope
is a gross caricature of Indian society, loses, or
rather is freed from her husband, and comes back to
England to receive another offer from a man she almost
loves. Shall she accept him or go to live in a flat in
London?...she answers in favor of the flat--for the
present." 1st person narration.
ACAD 45:286. Husband dies.

009312   LATE IN LIFE. London: Hurst and Blackett,
1896 BMC.

SR-Two sisters, a pretty one who is killed in an
accident, and a plain one. The doctor loved the 1st
"late in life," eventually marries the second.
ATH 107:75. Average people. Nina is selfish.
ACAD 50:28. Anglo-Indian.
Dr. George Barr works for years in India to support a
widowed sister. When she remarries, he's able to take
a holiday. Falls in love with young Ella who is
already engaged. Is loved by her older sister Emily. A
carriage accident solves things. Ella dies; Emily and
Dr. Barr find love late in life. SP 78:671

009313   RED RECORDS. London: Chatto and Windus,
1906 NUC.

009314   SEPARATION. London: Cassell, 1917 BMC.

heroine is "a study in the odious" who makes her
husband give up work in India he loves. TLS
The woman is "selfishly happy amidst London society"
Daughter marries a Hindu ATH

009315   THE SPELL OF THE JUNGLE. London: A.
Treherne, 1902 BMC. New York: Duffield, 1910 NUC.

Ray at 19 sets out to her father in India; father
considers her a nuisance decides to spring her on his
woman-hater friend.
LBKM 2-01, 215
Heroine almost sacrificed to a tiger. ATH, 121, 11

009316   STAR OF INDIA. London: Cassell, 1919 BMC.

Stella Carrington 17 bored almost to despair in
genteel village yearns for India (she's half Indian)
marries elderly Colonel. InnIndia sees women and
children massacred. Knows now she was wrong to come,
falls in love with young writer. Jealous husband
orders writer out. 2nd part deals with young woman
bent upon political reform. TLS

009317   THE STRONGER CLAIM. London: F. Nash, 1903
BMC. New York: Duffield, 1910 NUC.

sympathetic story of Indians of India and prejudice of
English. ACAD 65,507
mixed marriage with usual tragic results; the half
caste Eurasia LBKM 12-03,153
BKM-English man with wife discovers in India that he
is half Eurasian. When a riot breaks out he is unable
to act as an Englishman and is run over by the mob.
Author-pov?-anti mixed mariage, as is Candles In the
wind.

009318   THE VOW OF SILENCE. London: Cassell,
[1920] BMC NUC.

TLS love in India.

009319   THE WATERS OF DESTRUCTION. London: Chatto
& Windus, 1905 BMC NUC.

hero torn between two women, one English, the other a
Hindu girl-widow, the 2nd is thrust upon him and he
must marry or she'll drown herself. Disillusion comes
after two years . Author shows such marriage to be
disastrous. This wife dead; hero marries the English
woman. ACAD 1081, 05
more sophisticated Inidan man, lonely in an isolated
station, marries a native girl.? ATH 05, 575
more an anti-mixed-marriage story than a sympathetic
study?

009320   THE WOMAN IN THE BAZAAR. London: Cassell,
1914 BMC 1926 NUC.

LBKM-Innocent, the daughter of a vicar, Raefella is
married to Capt. Coventry, a selfish husband. Disaster
when roue comes on the scene, but husband awakes to
sympathy in full knowledge of Raefella's tragedy, so
happy ending.
ATH 144:533-His 2nd marriage might also have been a
disaster if he had not awakened by seeing "his
abandoned first wife playing the part of a
courtesan"."Painful theme-the future of a divorced
woman abandoned by her lover." TLS 13:506

PERRY, STELLA GEORGE (STERN). B. 1877. United States.

009321   THE KIND ADVENTURE. New York: F. A.
Stokes, [c1914] NUC.

009322   MELINDY. New York: Moffat, Yard, 1912
NUC.

009323   PALMETTO: THE ROMANCE OF A LOUISIANA
GIRL. New York: F. A. Stokes, [c1920] NUC.

NYT 12-5-20 p. 20. First novel. Louisiana bayous.
Romance. Palmetto is "bewitching, vital as a flame,
full of wild grace."

PETERSEN, MARIE BJELKE. 1816-1959. Australia.

009324   THE CAPTIVE SINGER. London: Hodder &
Stoughton, [1917] BMC.

The singer is a male. Iris the heroine; the novel is
full of raptures. TLS
Iris's love redeems him. LBKM

009325   THE IMMORTAL FLAME. New York and London:
Harper, [c1919] NUC BMC.

NYT-Jan 18 '20 p 33. Romantic love, then religion.
Two men desperately love a fascinating woman. PW

PETERSON, MARGARET ANN. 1883-1933. United Kingdom.

009326   BLIND EYES. London: A. Melrose, 1914 BMC
NUC. Chicago: Browne & Howell, 1914 NUC.

ATH-1 girl dies in the dock of a criminal court, the
other finally is about to marry a man who loves her.
"Pretty Cynthia Weston, raised by an indulgent older
sister in a typical well-to-do English home, reaches
maturity still a child in her outlook on life and its
responsibilities. She is suddenly sobered by a serious
proposal of marriage, which she declines after her
sister tries to explain to her the meaning of love.
She rebelliously leaves her sister's home to make her
own way in the world. She goes to London, and there,
through her own experiences and those of three other
girls with whom she is thrown, learns the answer to
her fierce questionings." PW 86 10/24/14:13
SR-0
Cynthia Weston 17 lives in a fairy land of illusion.
Toys with boys and men in complete ignorance, of the
facts of life. Becomes engaged but does not really
care for the man. The man's sister discovers how
innocent Cynthia is, amuses herself in "tearing aside
the veil of illusion" so ruthlessly that Cynthia
breaks engagement, develops a morbid frame of mind and
narrowly misses spoiling her whole life. "Full of
suggestion on some intimate questions of sex psych."
cruelty of letting young women grow up ignorant of
sex. BKM

009327   BUTTERFLY WINGS. London: Hurst and
Blackett, 1916 BMC.

TLS--rom
BKM-Billy, by-passed by Peggy whose unstable nature
led to another choice becomes friends with Stella. She
is an artist, good but unconventional, and when she
decides she loves him, she tells him. He, to avoid
hurting her conceals he still loves Peggy. When Peggy
disillusioned with her 1st choice seeks out Billy,
whom she really loves, she finds him living with
Stella. Then tradegy, but war straightens out all.

009328   THE DEATH DRUM. London: Hurst & Blackett,
1919 BMC.

Mingling of races: Englishman and native woman they
have a white son, black daughter. White man loves and
deserts the daughter. Juanita and her white brother
swears vengeance. TLS
LBKM-Love and revenge of half caste married to English
woman who loves him and whom he comes to love but who
is victim of his revenge.

009329   FATE AND THE WATCHER. London: Hurst &
Blackett, 1917 BMC.

English woman a flirt and an Indian prince who takes
her in earnest. ATH

009330   JUST BECAUSE. London: A. Melrose, 1915
BMC.

marriage misunderstanding, reconciliation. TLS

009331   THE LOVE OF NAVARRE. London: A. Melrose,
1915 BMC.

009332   LOVE'S BURDEN. London: Hurst & Blackett,
1918 BMC.

TLS-Margot has deep feeling and appreciation for her
mother, who has carried love, self sacrifice and
humility to excess. she marries and goes to India with
Derek-a distorted mind. character study of her
marriage
ATH-he is a neurotic spiritualist.
LBKM-His obsession in Eastern black magic ends in
murder and madness. After a short and disillusioning
experience in a London sisterhood, found happiness.
Had learned the unwisdom of futile self sacrifice.
SR-Convent of the Lonely Hearts. Marries her true
love.

009333   THE LURE OF THE LITTLE DRUM. New York:
G.P. Putnam's, 1913 NUC. London: A. Melrose, 1913 BMC
NUC.

married woman is attracted to keeper of a harem,
enters it, tries to escape, is tortured in "repellent
scene" Cooper, Morality and fiction in some recent
novels. BKM, Feb. 1914. India. Esther is lured by the
endless beating of little drums which has an effect
upon her; she finds herself responding to some call of
the blood. She fights against it, tells her husband,
but he does not take her seriously. One night, under
the influence of the drum she leaves home and goes
straight to Ishut Khan and his harem. Husband falls
ill and knows not of her departure; when he recovers,
his relatives tell him she had died of cholera.
Meanwhile, her madness has turned to hatred, and Ishut
Khan, unable to tolerate a white woman's loathing,
tortures her in a barbaric and repellant way.
Degradation, suffering, escape, final agony.
"The $1,250 prize story. In this story of India the
plot turns on the destructive fascination exercised by
an unprincipled native ruler upon an English girl,
married to a man who is completely devoted to her. In
spite of advice and warnings she leaves her husband
for the Indian prince. Too late she learns the evil
nature of the latter, escapes from the harem and tries
to return to her husband." PW 11/8/13: 1531
Esther Williams, husband appeals to the good; the
Prince to her evil side. can give no real love to
husband leaves him for harem. She dies in the end in
childbirth (husband's child) as does her child. ACAD
she's attracted to evil; almost hypnotized by this
Prince. Author shares the disgust of other characters
for this attraction. NYT
Sympathetic toward the woman. TLS

009334   MOON MOUNTAINS. London: Hurst & Blackett,
[1920] BMC NUC.

TLS-male hero

009335   THE SWORD-POINTS OF LOVE. London: Hurst &
Blackett, [1919] BMC.

Mavis is a lively irresponsible young woman
half-forced into marriage. Her husband rough, coarse,
takes her to Uganda. He's brutal to her and savage in
his treatment of the natives. Closes in tragedy? TLS
opens on light note. Mavis seems trivial but after
marriage, gains our sympathy. "Blazes out fiercely vs
her captor's brutality." From then on we follow her
suffering course with compassion. Brooding over the
house in Uganda is cruelty, terror and squalor.
Husband a brute she's wretched, lonely shut up in
wilderness forced to watch him savagely flog the
natives, holds back her hatred in the interest of her
unborn child. Husband dies, but no conv. happy end.
LBKM

009336   "TO LOVE". London: Hurst & Blackett, 1915
BMC.

Joan Rutherford from village, betrayed by cad, marries
young doctor who sees her through her suffering TLS
She's well educated; tires of having nothing to do,
demands liberty of salaried occupation, indulges in
casual amorous advents; struggle of an untrained woman
to earn a living. The sordid conditions of such a
life.

009337   TONY BELLEW. London: A. Melrose, 1914
BMC.

ATH-Hero returns to India without knowing that his
mother was Indian.
ATH 144:531. His mother killed herself, his adopted
mother never loved him. told him of his Indian blood
when he became engaged to English girl.

TLS-Illustration of the tragedy of the color problem.

PETERSON, MAUD HOWARD, pseud. See HOOPES, MARY HOWARD
(PETERSON).

PETTUS, MAIA. B. 1875. United States.

009338   MEDA'S HERITAGE. New York: Neale, 1906
NUC.

"Love and religion are interwoven into this story of
Southern life. the heritage which fell to the heroine
was her mission to preach the gospel and to take up
the work laid down when death claimed her father. She
wins success only after having trodden a path beset by
obstacles and drawbacks."BKM v. 24 1906-7

009339   PRINCESS OF GLENNDALE; A STORY OF THE
SOUTH. Washington: Neale, 1902 NUC.

PHELPS, ELEANOR GAYLORD.

009340   AS A FALLING STAR. Chicago: A. C.
McClurg, 1901 NUC.

PW 10-26-01
ATH 12-21-01

PHELPS, ELIZABETH STEWARD. United States.

009341   ALLENDALE'S CHOICE: A VILLAGE CHRONICLE.
BY LEIGH NORTH. Milwaukee, Wis.: Young Churchman, 1895
NUC.

009342   ARTHUR NORRIS; OR, A MODERN KNIGHT. BY
LEIGH NORTH. Milwaukee: Young Churchman, 1915 NUC.

2 friends, marry, become missionaries in China PW
5-15-15

PHELPS, ELIZABETH STUART. See WARD, ELIZABETH STUART
(PHELPS).

PHELPS, SYDNEY K.

009343   FROM BLUE SKY TO GREY. London:
Skeffington, 1904 BMC.

009344   HIS 'PRENTICE HAND. London: J. Long, 1900
BMC.

ATH 115:561. Mr. Swinford, a converted stockbroker
"poaching on the manors of the clergy is odious." =The
best character is an entirely up-to-date, not to say
slangy young woman who acts as temporary governess in
the evangelist's family, when he lost the wife whom he
tormented...and now seeks to replace."
ACAD 58:334. Ralph Vivian, curate and Ethel happily
married at end.

PHILLIMORE, MRS. C. E.

009345   A MILLION FOR A SOUL: A NOVEL OF
ANGLO-INDIAN LIFE. London: J. Long, 1915 BMC.

India: heroine under stress of work takes to drinking.
She's mared. ultimately reclaimed. TLS

009346   TWO WOMEN AND A MAHARAJAH. London: J.
Long, 1906 BMC.

about two Eurasian marriages, and about Constance, a
fine character "failure of mingled blood" TLS
Brief Description LBKM 3-07,278
ATH - O

PHILLIPS, F. EMILY.

009347   A COUNTY SCANDAL. London: J. Macqueen,
1899 BMC.

Scandal involves money matters. ACAD 56:534
Allegra raised in luxury but wholly isolated from
people. She is well-educated by her guardian whose
heir later becomes her guardian. This heir (Marmaduke)
is a cad. ATH 113:749

009348   THE EDUCATION OF ANTONIA. London:
Macmillan, 1895 BMC.

"Essentially a woman's book, it is written in the main
from the standpoint of impotent sympathy with the
sufferings of women who, handicapped by disabilities
of sex, have to compete with men in the struggle for
life." The tone is "often bitter." "Another
omnipresent fault is that inartistic excess of details

of minor feminine experience of which we have
complained before" Antonia expresses all the author's
ideas. SP 75:937.
ATH 107:82.
ACAD 49:75. "interest in Antonia's career is
thoroughly well sustained.

009349   THE KNIGHT'S TALE. Edinburgh: W.
Blackwood, 1897 BMC. Chicago: Way and Williams, 1897
NUC.

Focus upon a man who is an idealist as well as a
person of action, a fighter in the Garibaldian wars.
LBKM 12:44.
Mainly a study of a woman-Veronica loves and marries
Louis-at ceremony he is bound and under sentence of
immediate execution. (He's a communist) We see Paris
behind barricades through her eyes
Paris during the commune and Veronica's rescue of her
lover, defends him to his party at the sacrifice of
her personal reputation. ATH 109:611.
SP 80:148. Hist. rom, capture of Paris by Versailles
troops.

009350   THE MAN OF THE FAMILY: A STORY OF
FORTUNAUS AND THE BARBARIANS. London: Macmillan, 1898
BMC NUC.

ACAD 53:495. An artist, Sebastian, and a teacher,
Barbara, who had gained his attention by her brave
action during a fire. I think she preferred her work.
ACAD 54:13. Title refers to Barbara, who is supporting
her family, a Board school teacher. She is given a 2
week holiday in Paris after the fire at school, it is
then that she meets Sebastian, "the soft dilettante
for whom this strong, clever, independent young
warrior is to become willing to lay down her arms."
ATH 111:688. Sebastian's parents do not approve of his
marrying lower-classed Barbara. Sad and embittering
for her.
SR 85:825. "has the undercurrent of vehement assertion
that women really have a sense of honour and a sense
of humour that one so commonly detects in women's
novels."
LBKM 14:110. "The only strong character in a group of
invertebrates."

PHILLIPS, MABEL KATHERINE.

009351   THE SUPREME POWER. London: J. Long, 1910
BMC.

TLS religious atmosphere

PHILLIPS, MRS. ALFRED. 1822?-1876. Nationality Unknown.

009352   THE BIRTH OF A SOUL. A PSYCHOLOGICAL
STUDY. London: W. H. Allen, 1894 BMC. Chicago: Rand,
McNally, 1894 NUC.

ACAD 46:472. Alix, Jewish heroine, has been left her
grandfather's fortune if she doesn't marry a
Christian. She almost marries Lord Southcombe who has
plenty. He dies and it is subsequent to this that her
soul is born.

009353   A RUDE AWAKENING. A ROMANCE. London:
Trischler, 1891 BMC.

Too preachy. The two sinners are treated
sympathetically. SP 67, 681
Mary Prior is illegitimate. She learns this when she's
about to marry. Raised by father for years. Tries to
break off marriage, but truth makes no difference to
fiance. ACAD
"Decidedly painful...void of offense". ATH 99:113

009354   A SPINSTER'S DIARY. Bristol: J. W.
Arrowsmith, 1892 BMC.

SR 73:363. Hypnotist is one of the characters.

PHIPPS, SARAH E. United States.

009355   THE OLD HOUSE BY THE SEA. New York and
London: F. T. Neely, [1901] NUC.

PW 8-17-01

PICHLER, LOUISE.

009356   A DAUGHTER OF ROME: A ROMANCE OF THE
FATHERLAND. London: Digby, Long, 1893 BMC. (Tr. by J.
M. Colles)

PICKARD, FLORENCE (WILLINGHAM). 1862-1930. United States.

009357   BETWEEN SCARLET THRONES. Boston:
Stratford, 1919 NUC.

NYT 2-1-20:65. 4 years of research in preparation.
Filled with uncurbed human passions, etc. Bible tale.

009358   THE IDES OF MARCH. London and New York:
F.T. Neely, [1899] NUC.

LW 30:251 8/5/1899

PICKERING, PERCIVAL, pseud. See STIRLING, ANNA MARIA DIANA
WILHELMINA (PICKERING).

PICKETT, ANITA (TRUEMAN). B. 1881. United States.

009359   ANTON'S ANGELS: A ROMANCE. BY ANITA
TRUEMAN. New York: Alliance, 1900 NUC.

PICKETT, LA SALLE CORBELL. 1848-1931. United States.

009360   THE BUGLES OF GETTYSBURG. Chicago: F. G.
Browne, 1913 BMC NUC.

Brief romance commemorating the battle. NYT

PICKTHALL, MARJORIE LOWRY CHRISTIE. B. 1883. Canada.

009361   BILLY'S HERO; OR, THE VALLEY OF GOLD.
London: S. W. Partridge, [1908] BMC. Toronto: Musson,
[1908] NUC.

009362   LITTLE HEARTS. London: Methuen, 1915 BMC
NUC.

Hero is focus of novel. TLS
Improbable tale; all sorts of impossibilities. Focus
on Michael. SR

009363   THE STRAIGHT ROAD. Toronto: Musson,
1908?[] NUC. London: S. W. Partridge, [1909] BMC NUC.

PICTON, NINA. United States.

009364   AT THE THRESHOLD. BY LAURA DEARBORN. New
York: Cassell, [c1893] NUC.

Ideas on immortality, the judgment and eternal
happiness. A soul enters immortal life, passes thru
successive spheres and is left at the threshold of the
"Eternal City." PW 2-11-93.

PIERCE, LUCIE FRANCE. United States.

009365   THE WHITE DEVIL OF VERDE: A STORY OF THE
WEST. New York: G. W. Dillingham, 1898 NUC BMC.

NYT 1898:826. Story of Western life.
PW-Marcia, a progressive New Yorker, goes west to
recuperate. She discovers a lost mine and locates a
claim. Her efforts to protect her interests and hold
the claim win her the name of "The White Devil of
Verde."

PIERCE, ZERELDA F. United States.

009366   THE CHURCH REPUBLIC: A ROMANCE OF
METHODISM. BY BROTHER JONATHAN, D.D. New York: Wilbur
B. Ketcham, [c1892] NUC.

PIERSON, JANE SUSANNA (ANDERSON). B. 1854. United States.

009367   THE COMING OF THE DAWN. Cincinnati:
Standard, [c1917] NUC.

Russian Jew and Christian woman in love, but he can't
marry her because of his rel. and devotion to Russian
people. Dies in the end. PW
purpose to break down anti-semitism. Both her parents
and his oppose the marriage. She starts a mission in
the Ghetto to help the Jews. He goes to help Jews in
Russia; caught in a program sent to Siberia but
escapes. Joins the Siberian army to free the oppressed
people there. NYT
Story of Russia and America NYT

PINCKNEY, SUSANNA SHULRICK HAYNE. B. 1843. United States.

009368   DOUGLAS, TENDER AND TRUE. BY MISS
MCPHERSON. St. Louis: Nixon-Jones Print. Co., 1892
NUC.

009369   IN THE SOUTHLAND. Washington: Neale, 1906
NUC.

PINKERTON, LULU.

009370   GOD JOINED THEM. A NOVEL. London: Murray
& Evendon [sic], [1915] BMC.

Villain, beautiful girl, lost heir, etc. TLS

009371   THE POWER OF GOLD. London: Murray &
Evenden, [1915] BMC.

Soc. novel. ATH

PINNIX, HANNAH COURTNEY. 1851-1931. United States.

009372   CHANEY'S STRATAGEM. Boston: C. M. Clark,
1909 NUC.

NYT: babies changed in the cradle

PINSENT, ELLEN FRANCES (PARKER). 1866-1949. United
Kingdom.

009373   CHILDREN OF THIS WORLD. London: Methuen,
1895 BMC NUC.

Rachel is a child of light rather than one of this
world like her friend Janet. Both are "intellectual,
upright and thoroughly modern in their outlook." One
has "grit," the other none. Rachel's "self chosen end
is impressive." ATH 105:502

009374   JENNY'S CASE. London: S. Sonnenschein,
1892 BMC NUC.

ATH 100:414. Tale of sordid treachery and cureless
suffering. Jenny's ruin. Peasant class.
ACAD 42:282. Jenny is a farmer's maid-of all work, she
is seduced by local policeman on a promise of
marriage. She leaves the village to have her child in
a distant town, and is driven for a time upon the
streets for a livelihood. The local poacher, who loved
her returns from his regiment and kills the cop, sinks
into alcohol and dies himself. Jenny disappears.
SR: story is entirely limited to peasant life and is
concerned only with its unpleasant aspects. Absence of
moralizings.

009375   JOB HILDRED, ARTIST AND CARPENTER. BY DR.
RICHARDS; EDITED BY ELLEN F. PINSENT. London and New
York: E. Arnold, 1897 BMC NUC.

LW 29:10. Village painter is sponsored by lady who
guides his life. He breaks away, marries girl in
village but cannot find happiness. He ends in
madhouse.

009376   NO PLACE FOR REPENTANCE. London: T. F.
Unwin, 1896 BMC. New York: A. D. F. Randolph, [c1896]
NUC.

SR Clergyman with dipsomania. Depressing but
inevitable ending.
ACAD 50:129. Fights against it in vain. He is
energetic in saving others from drinking.
ACAD 50:159: Artistic rather than controversial p.o.v.
Quiet rural town. Dialect of Lincolnshire-"excellent."

PIPER, ANNA W. FORD. United States.

009377   PEAK'S ISLAND, A ROMANCE OF BUCCANEER
DAYS. BY FORD PAUL. Portland, Me.: The Author, 1892
NUC.

PIPER, MARGARET R. See CHALMERS, MARGARET REBECCA (PIPER).

PIRKIS, CATHARINE LOUISA. United Kingdom.

009378   A BRIDE OF A SUMMER'S DAY. London: [1891]
NUC.

009379   THE EXPERIENCES OF LOVEDAY BROOKE, LADY
DETECTIVE. London: Hutchinson, 1894 BMC.

SR 77:477. "A small, keen, not very pretty (we think)
not very young (we are sure) lady detective who is
always called in at the last moment in extremely
obscure cases which have baffled the best experience
and ingenuity of all the professional males of
Europe."

009380   A RED SISTER: A STORY OF THREE DAYS AND
THREE MONTHS. London: S. Low, 1891 BMC NUC.

Lady Jean Herrick rejects poor clergyman for
millionaire's heir thinking the old father will soon
die. But he lives 20 years more. Her own son loves a

poor woman. Lady Jean breaks them apart and the young
woman becomes a Red Sister but rescued before taking
final vows. Then husband gets ill at same time old man
is dying. So she poisons the old man. Husband dies.
She's wealthy, but falls in hands of a villain who
suspects, tells her son. She kills self. Son and young
woman reunited. ACAD.
"She's an out-and-out bold bad woman". Son's fiance
saw her mix the poison. Through help of old lover who
became priest, gets her shut up in convent. SR
12-5-91, 642

PITFIELD, ADA.

009381   THE BACHELORS OF WESTCOMBE. London: Gay
and Hancock, 1909 BMC.

The first years of marriage between a man of 40 and a
woman 15 years younger. All is mended happily. TLS
Husband and wife trample on each other; but all is
love in the end. ATH

009382   A BREATH OF SCANDAL. London: Gay and
Hancock, 1914 BMC.

ATH-Romance of a young heiress who insists on seeing
the world accompanied only by an old servant.
TLS-Her independent spirit bows to a man.

009383   PRINCESS OF THE SANDHILLS. London: Gay
and Bird, 1908 BMC NUC.

ATH- sent puppets.

009384   THE SILENCE OF GRAY'S INN. London: Gay
and Hancock, 1911 BMC.

"A very nice little heroine." TLS
Pretty tale about a woman who fills many positions and
ends happily married. ATH

PITKIN, HELEN. B. 1877. United States.

009385   AN ANGEL BY BREVET: A STORY OF MODERN NEW
ORLEANS. Philadelphia and London: J. B. Lippincott,
1904 NUC.

Young Creole girl who uses "conjur" men and women to
win her love, a widow-modern, advanced with heterodox
idea. NYT 1905:54
PW-love story.

PITT, SARAH.

009386   A LIMITED SUCCESS. London: Cassell, 1897
BMC.

New minister Rev. Trent promoted to rich parish. He
comes already engaged to a poorer woman of the poorer
parish-Alice Chadwick. He meets brilliant socialite
Kate Craven. The two contrasted. Also his widowed
sister fresh home from Aust. with ideas and manners of
a free woman. ACAD 52: Fic Sup 102
LIT 2:117. Central figure is minister who courts
working-class girl, and then gaining an advance in
position, he shuns her and falls for someone else.
Denies to fiancee his relationship with former lover,
all comes out after mrge. Ultimate reconciliation
wherein he regains his wife's love if not respect.

009387   THE WHITE HOUSE AT INCH GOW. London:
Cassell, 1891 BMC NUC.

LW 23:26 Romance of Nell, a motherless heroine.
"Simple faith and enduring constancy win their
reward."
IND 44:2, Scotch social life.
ACAD 41:35. Concerns a middle class family and their
ups and downs. Happy ending.

PITTMAN, H. D. See PITTMAN, HANNAH (DAVIESS).

PITTMAN, HANNAH (DAVIESS). B. 1840. United States.

009388   GO FORTH AND FIND. BY H. D. PITTMAN.
Boston: R. G. Badger, 1910 NUC.

NYT-story of true love.

009389   THE HEART OF KENTUCKY. BY MRS. H. D.
PITTMAN. Washington: Neale, 1908 NUC.

PW-Murder, unfaithful husband
NYT-O

PITTMAN, MRS. H. D. See PITTMAN, HANNAH (DAVIESS).

PLANTZ, MYRA (GOODWIN). 1856-1914. United States.

009390   A GREAT APPOINTMENT. New York: Hunt and
Eaton, 1895 NUC.

Bishop gives a great appointment to Wilbur by sending
him to poorest congregation in Michigan. His devoted
sister becomes his housekeeper. PW 10-19-95:675
LW 27:236. Methodist minister and his sister go to
Michigan woods to carry the gospel to miners and
lumbermen. They build a little community of good will.

PLAYNE, CAROLINE ELISABETH.

009391   THE ROMANCE OF A LONELY WOMAN. London: T.
Unwin, 1904 BMC.

ATH-?consumptives in Algiers
TLS-young widow earning her living attached herself to
three people and lost them all

009392   THE TERROR OF THE MACDURGHOTTS. London:
T.F. Unwin, 1907 BMC.

TLS- a woman from a fictitious South American republic
"where war has been foresworn and the reign of love
inaugurated" comes to Northern part of Scotland where
feuding has gone on for years. "Expresses an idea that
is at once revolutionary and the soundest practical
wisdom." Terror in title is the state of mind of
people at war.
SR-Sincere

PLEYDELL, KATHLEEN (GROVE) MANSEL.

009393   A VOICE FROM OBLIVION. London: Digby,
Long, 1908 BMC.

TLS Hermione, heroine, is nurse and benefactor among
Arabs. divorces her husband, makes love with another
man, feeble and rather sickly story"
ATH-Slight story of an unhappy marriage between
libertine and sentimentalist

PLYMPTON, A. G. See PLYMPTON, ALMIRA GEORGE.

PLYMPTON, ALMIRA GEORGE. B. 1852. United States.

009394   A BUD OF PROMISE: A STORY FOR AMBITIOUS
PARENTS. BY A. G. PLYMPTON. Boston: Roberts, 1895 NUC.

An ambitious professor and Bud, his overworked son.
Bud contrasted with Teddy whose parents are sensible
and unambitious. Ends in disaster for Bud, health for
Ted. LW 26:428

009395   IN THE SHADOW OF THE BLACK PINE; A
ROMANCE OF THE MASSACHUSETTS BAY COLONY. BY A. G.
PLYMPTON. Boston: Small, Maynard, 1901 BMC NUC.

009396   OLD-HOME DAY AT HAZELTOWN. BY A. G.
PLYMPTON. Boston: Little, Brown, 1906 NUC.

PW-Sentimental story,

POLLARD, ELIZA FRANCES. United Kingdom.

009397   A DAUGHTER OF FRANCE. A STORY OF ACADIA.
London: T. Nelson, 1900 BMC.

Early history of Acadia when Charles de la Tour was
governor. Historical romance. PW 56:819

009398   THE DOCTOR'S NIECE. London: Blackie,
[1901] BMC.

009399   ESTHER DUNBAR; OR VENGEANCE IS MINE.
London: S. W. Partridge, [1897] BMC.

"Illegal wedding of hero to spotless heroine" and
later marr. to heiress who can save his father's name.
And the wealthy uncle from Amer. "with money for all
the virtuous chars." SR 84:475 for young people.

009400   FOR THE EMPEROR. London: T. Nelson,
[1909] BMC NUC.

Historical romance-experiences of a young woman during
the French invasion and retreat from Moscow. NUC

009401   FOR THE RED ROSE. London: Blackie, [1902]
NUC. London: Blackie, 1903 BMC.

Story of War of the Roses. NUC

009402   FORTUNE'S WHEEL. London: S. W. Partridge, [1899] BMC.

The good young man punished for a crime he didn't commit. S. African gold mines. Marriage of Jocelyn Carmichael to a different male character--Frank Thornton. LIT 5:623

009403   A GENTLEMAN OF ENGLAND: A ROMANCE OF THE TIME OF SIR PHILIP SIDNEY. London: W. H. Addison, 1897 BMC. London: Partridge, [1911] NUC.

009404   A GIRL OF THE EIGHTEENTH CENTURY. London: T. Nelson, [1906] BMC.

009405   A GIRL'S STRONGHOLD. London: S. W. Partridge, [1909] BMC.

009406   THE GREEN MOUNTAIN BOYS: A STORY OF THE AMERICAN WAR OF INDEPENDENCE. New York: Dodd, Mead, 1895 NUC. London: S. W. Partridge, [1896] BMC.

PW 10-24-96. "With a little love and romance thrown in, the story has to do with the wild deeds of the Green Mountain boys in Vermont in the war for independence."

009407   A HERO KING: A ROMANCE OF THE DAYS OF ALFRED THE GREAT. London: S. W. Partridge, 1898 BMC NUC.

009408   THE KING'S SIGNET; OR THE STORY OF A HUGUENOT FAMILY. London: Blackie, 1900 BMC. London, 1900 NUC.

009409   THE KNIGHTS OF LIBERTY. London: T. Nelson, [1904] BMC.

009410   THE LAST OF THE CLIFFORDS. New York: T. Nelson and Sons, 1903 NUC. London: T. Nelson, 1903 BMC.

009411   THE MINISTER'S MONEY. London: S. W. Partridge, 1896 BMC.

009412   MY LADY MARCIA; A STORY OF THE FRENCH REVOLUTION. London: T. Nelson, 1901 BMC.

009413   A NEW ENGLAND MAID; A TALE OF THE AMERICAN REBELLION. Boston: H. M. Caldwell, [1911] PW. London: Blackie, 1911 BMC.

NYT--She is a sister of Benedict Arnold; "an old maid by birth, devoted from the cradle to prunes and prisms and doomed to be admired only by her inventor."
Historical romance. PW 9-23-11
About sister of Benedict Arnold. NYT

009414   "NOT WANTED"; OR, THE WRECK OF THE "PROVIDENCE". London: Partridge, [1891] BMC NUC.

009415   THE OLD MOAT FARM: A STORY OF QUEEN ELIZABETH'S DAYS. London: Blackie, 1906 BMC NUC.

009416   ROGER THE RANGER: A STORY OF BORDER LIFE AMONG THE INDIANS. London: S. W. Partridge, [1893] BMC.

009417   A SAXON MAID. London: Blackie, [1901] BMC NUC.

009418   THE SCARLET JUDGES; A TALE OF THE INQUISITION IN THE NETHERLANDS. London: S. W. Partridge, [1900] BMC.

LBKM 19: Christmas Supplement, p. 20. Countess Teresa, noble, brave, endures suffering and is spared punishment of the judge.

009419   THE SILVER HAND: A STORY OF INDIA IN THE EIGHTEENTH CENTURY. London: Blackie, 1909 BMC.

009420   THROUGH LIFE'S SHADOWS. London: S. W. Partridge, [1893] BMC.

009421   TRUE UNTO DEATH: A STORY OF RUSSIAN LIFE AND THE CRIMEAN WAR. London: S. W. Partridge, [1894] BMC.

SR 78:691. English governess of independent character accepts position with wealthy Russian family. She responds to her student Viera's views on the oppressiveness of the Russian government, and together they develop and promulgate these views. The government retaliates first by banishing Viera from her home, then sending her to Siberia. The governess goes with her and stays with her until her death.

009422   UNDER THE WAR-CLOUDS. A TALE OF 1870. London: Sunday School Union, [1895] BMC.

009423   THE WHITE DOVE OF AMRITZIR. A ROMANCE OF ANGLO-INDIAN LIFE. London: Partridge, [1896] BMC.

009424   THE WRECK OF THE "PROVIDENCE". London: S. W. Partridge, [1900] BMC.

POLLITT, MRS. J. MILTON.

009425   DOROTHY PENROSE. A NOVEL. London: Eden, Remington, 1893 BMC NUC.

Seventeenth century historical romance. Jealousy parts the lovers for a long time and leads to tragedy. Days of Stuarts; superstitions, haunted chambers, rogues and vagabonds. ACAD 43:150.

POMEROY, MARY SHEPARDSON. Nationality Unknown.

009426   LOVE'S CRUCIBLE. Boston: Sherman, French, 1911 NUC.

Woman travels about with a man for years; later finds forgiveness for her erratic life. PW 12-2-11

POOL, MARIA LOUISE. 1841-1898. United States.

009427   AGAINST HUMAN NATURE: A NOVEL. New York: Harper, 1895 NUC.

" An English spinster appears as a force" but principal character a N.Carolina girl who is converted at a revivalist meeting and herself-wants to save souls. She marries the minister, then learns to love him. LW 26:458
Alminy Drowdy, N.E. spinster, goes to N.C. to take charge of daughter of man she loved who is now dead. She's conventional; the young woman freer-Temple Crawford. Temple and Alminy are contrasted. Temple marries the minister, "preaches and works among the poor." PW 10-19-95:675
Daughter of Mass. Yankee and a Louisianin grows up in the wild mts. of N.C. Temple Crawford believes it's mad to marry since her mother was so miserable. Then she "experiences religion" under the preaching of an evangelist of the Mercers but it's really love. BKM 2:332
CR 29:56. Spinster from NE in North Carolina mts. Cultured minister marries untamed mountain heroine, religion a mutual interest, union is successful.

009428   BOSS AND OTHER DOGS. New York: Stone and Kimball, 1896 NUC.

009429   DALLY. New York: Harper, 1891 NUC.

Widow in Massachusetts takes in waifs. Dally is one-half savage, untutored. Asks for whiskey on her arrival. ACAD.
She's from North Carolina. Story in dialects. NATION 8-13-91, 125.
Becomes a terror in the neighborhood. But through love is reformed. PW 4-1-91.

009430   DOLLY. London: Osgood and McIlvaine, 1891 BMC.

009431   FRIENDSHIP AND FOLLY: A NOVEL. Boston: L. C. Page, 1898 NUC. London: J. Long, [1900] BMC.

NYT 1898:644. In 1870 there was published a New York magazine called Galaxy, which contained shocking stories of old-fashioned bad heroines. MLP wrote stories of this sort for Galaxy. Then she started publishing novels about ten years ago with modern heroines. This novel is a reversion to the old style, in spite of fact that she rides a bicycle. She is bewitching, irresistible, and detestable; the hero is her helpless victim.
LW 39:371. She is heartless and fascinating, attracting men and leaving them until a bicycling accident finishes her career.
ATH 90:790. "Poor puppet-like Carolyn."

009432   A GOLDEN SORROW. Chicago: H. S. Stone, 1898 NUC.

Geneviève Leete, fascinating; Faxon Shepard, the nice man. They meet in Florida, but Jose Mendoza hypnotizes Geneviève into marrying him so the lovers don't get together till the last page.
PW-St. Augustine, Florida. Heroine is loved by 3 men.

Her mother is scheming, mercenary.
Genevieve Leete 25 is in St. Augustine for the winter
with her Ma; falls in love with a man who she believes
is not rich. Mother marries her off to wealthy
Spaniard, but it is soon discovered that a mock
marriage she made as a young girl was real; it is
annulled; and she marries the man she loves. NYT
1-14-9,20

009433   IN A DIKE SHANTY. Chicago: Stone and
Kimball, 1896 NUC.

BKM 3:539. New England country people. Light touch,
final tragedy inappropriate.
LW 27:234. Two women on Cape Cod for the summer. Their
adventures.

009434   IN BUNCOMBE COUNTY. Chicago: H. S. Stone,
1896 NUC BMC.

PW 11-7-96. Two women resting during a summer find a
gifted young man of original character, who proves to
have artistic gifts, and they take him away from his
native hills to give him an opportunity to become a
painter.

009435   IN THE FIRST PERSON: A NOVEL. New York:
Harper, 1896 NUC.

PW 11-14-96. Wilhelmina is 23 in New England when her
voice is discovered by a great prima donna; she
induced her to leave home and study. "The girl's
mother, a dreamy Second Adventist, under a kind of
hypnotic control exercised by her husband, is a strong
power in Wilhelmina's life. Studies, triumphs,
jealousies, a secret mrge, etc., are all lived through
by Wilhelmina, who at last goes to Europe with her
mother to study singing."
New England, heroine's own story. Wilhelmina Armstrong
has a beautiful voice becomes understudy of a prima
donna. The tawdry love of a tenor for her. Goes to
Paris to study. She refuses to marry the man her
father chooses. He dies of drinking. Mother is a
gentle woman. LW 28:39.
Billy is a farmer's daughter (first person narr.)
whose voice and dramatic talents are discovered by an
opera singer who takes her in charge. CR 26,30:439
NYT Dec 12, 1896, p2. Billy has a fine voice and
studies under Leonora Runciman. As her understudy, she
soon is looked on as a rival by Leonora, who drops
her. In despair she secretly marries Vale, a tenor.
Then her father, a horse dealer, dies and Billy
returns home to care for her mother and the farm. She
advertises for a boarder. L. Runciman shows up,
looking for a place to die. Her husband, an
ex-convict, is with her. She had abetted him at
forgery.

009436   KATHARINE NORTH: A NOVEL. New York:
Harper, 1893 NUC.

Divorce ends a marriage "brought about by unhallowed
means." Katharine married at 18 to a Deacon. LW
93:147.
Mrs. Llandaff is a public speaker-speaks on working
women. Katharine had run away after a forced ceremony
of marriage to an elderly deacon. NATION 56, 297
Mother persuades her to become fourth wife of old
deacon. Directly after marriage ceremony she takes off
with another young woman to a summer resort on
Massachusetts Bay and becomes a waiter in a
restaurant. Meets her aunt a speaker on women's wrongs
who strongly influences her life. PW 3-18-93.
N.E. Katharine loathes the old deacon. CR 20, 23:50

009437   THE MELOON FARM: A NOVEL. New York and
London: Harper, 1900 NUC.

NYT 1900:466. All her stories are pleasant and
wholesome. Hero is a farmer. His housekeeper has been
an opera singer who knew international fame and then
failure. She is still young and =highly original."

009438   MRS. GERALD: A NOVEL. New York: Harper,
1896 NUC.

BKM 3:539. Judith loves a man other than her husband.
Question is never one of disloyalty. Follows
"demented" husband thru moonlit African deserts to
help him keep an appointment.
LW 27:267. He suicides.
PW 7-18-96. He is insane. "Another of the author's
strong studies of woman's complex nature."
BN-Judith's worthless father died; Judith was
suspected of killing him. She married a man she didn't
love to protect the reputation of the man she loved,

also for his money to help support her mother. They
make a trip to Africa; hereditary insanity breaks out.

009439   MRS. KEATS BRADFORD: A NOVEL. New York:
Harper, 1892 NUC.

LW 23:261. Sequel to Roweny in Boston. She tries to
lead a separate life from her husband for a time
because he is jealous of her art. They are reconciled.
CR 118:176. Pursues her career, first with husband in
Paris, and then alone for two years in Boston.

009440   OUT OF STEP: A NOVEL. New York: Harper,
1894 NUC.

CR 25:428. Salome, trained as a Puritan, doesn't have
their code of honor. Develops an abnormal conscience.
She has a magnanimous rival. Second part of story
concerns her marriage.
LW 25:267. After marriage, she realizes it cannot last
because they do not regard abstract truth in the same
way. She chooses death as a way out and refuses to go
South as her doctor has advised. Mrs. Keats Bradford
is a friend and influence.
PW-a sequel to The Two Salomes. Her dual nature. Mrs.
Bradford has become a celebrated portrait painter; her
portrait of Salome shows him his wife's perverted
nature as he has never before realized it.

009441   THE RED-BRIDGE NEIGHBORHOOD: A NOVEL. New
York and London: Harper, 1898 NUC.

CR 32:357. A very mean family called Nawns.
LW 29:124. She is married to a man who is more of a
miser than his father. Reserved about it, but begs
minister to pray with her that her son won't have the
same temperament. He does & he doesn't. Character
study of her.
NYT 1898, p.199. Olive and Isabel both love Robert; he
marries Olive who is grieving over losing him. Rev.
finds her a paragon, but Robert drifts back to Isabel.
"There is a burglary, a divorce, and unlimited moral
squalor." Olive retains compassion for Robert but not
love.

009442   ROWENY IN BOSTON: A NOVEL. New York:
Harper, 1892 BMC NUC.

LW 23:110. Record of the lives of common workers in
the city.
CR 17:314. 9 year old girl from Georgia raised to
drink, swear, and do just as she pleased (Dally) in
staid circles in N. E. village.
In this novel heroine goes to Boston to study art,
takes herself much too seriously. NATION 145:362.
Moral is that when woman and man are competing for
woman's affection, it is always the masc. which
prevails.

009443   SAND 'N' BUSHES. Chicago: H. S. Stone,
1899 NUC.

Amusing story of two young women who buy horses at an
auction in Boston and proceed to ride out to Cape Cod.
PW 55:728.
Amabel Waldo. LW 30:183.
Two women close to 30 travel from Boston to uppermost
Cape Cod on horseback. They know nothing of the
horses. One carries a kitten. Gossip about them. Comic
Amabel loses her skirt. She's a reformer. Makes parts
of the skirt into pants, buys a man's saddle. Light
reading. NYT 5-13-99 309

009444   THE TWO SALOMES: A NOVEL. New York:
Harper, 1893 NUC.

Sad, serious story of an "abnormal" young woman. She
"commits a grave offense," confesses to mother not
because she repents but because she senses others see
it as wrong. The mother tries to give her daughter a
conscience. Another character, Mrs. Darrah is a
novelist. LW 93 367
A young woman with two heredities, Spanish and
Puritan. Story ends with a question. NATION 57:292.
Salome Gerry. Doctor orders her to Florida. In
sunshine, she gets better. Mother can't understand
her. Has no conscience, delibertely forges a check to
save father. Author makes the young heroine
sympathetic and attractive. CR 20, 23:255.

POOLE, EVA TRAVERS EVERED.

009445   HIS TROUBLESOME SISTER. London: Digby,
Long, 1894 BMC.

ACAD 45:514. Tangled loves.

ATH 103:539. Charged with religious and other
platitudes.

POOLE, MARY BELLE. United States.

009446   DOWN FATE'S WALK: A MODERN SOCIETY NOVEL.
[New Orleans, La.]: [Men and Masters Magazine], 1896
NUC.

009447   WHAT THE YEARS BROUGHT: A NOVELETTE. New
Orleans: Current Topic Pub. House, 1894 W.

POOR, AGNES BLAKE. 1842-1922. United States.

009448   BROTHERS AND STRANGERS. Boston: Roberts,
1893 NUC.

The Butler brothers are strangers to each other.
Arthur about to marry Sophy Curtis meets Flora
Shepherd, sister of his brother's (Orlando) wife.
Falls in love with her, finds he can't marry Sophy,
but Flora refuses him because she sees how fickle he
is. He must wait years during which time he becomes
more tender and kind before Flora will have him. LW
93, 333.
Set in Boston and New York.
Two brothers from poor family: one works hard and
saves; the other studies for ministry, marries, has
many children, no money. Mother expects first to help
out the second. Refuses at first, but made to see he's
wrong. CR 20, 23:255.

009449   UNDER GUIDING STARS; A MASSACHUSETTS
STORY OF THE CENTURY END. New York and London: G.P.
Putman's Sons, 1905 BMC NUC.

NYT-brother's wife, a young person "born to command"
and her in-laws.
PW-a shop girl who controls her mother-a mental
healer.
"strong minded" heroine.
WOMAN'S JOURNAL 10-21-05

POORE, IDA MARGARET (GRAVES). B. 1860. United Kingdom.

009450   MY SISTER BARBARA. London: Downey, 1897
BMC.

Subtitle: "Passages from the Diary of Diana Russell,
kept for the benefit of her husband, Captain Geoffrey
Russell, R.E. during his absence with a Special
Commission in Central Asia." She joins sister and
grandmother at Sandbury Common, meets the gentry.
She's a witty observer; her sister falls in love. ACAD
52 Fic sup 121.
LIT 2:452. Pretty love story of girl and good American
painter.

009451   RACHEL FITZPATRICK. BY LADY POORE. New
York and London: J. Lane, 1920 NUC. London: J. Lane,
1920 BMC.

TLS-romance.
ATH-Irish, she cannot stand English family she lives
with in London, escapes from Uncle who takes her to
Germany, meets her old governess and they travel home
together. Eventually marries.
SR-O
NYT 7-25-20, p27

POORE, LADY. See POORE, IDA MARGARET (GRAVES).

POORE, LOUISA C.

009452   MOTIVES. London: E. Stock, 1910 BMC.

TLS-male hero

POPE, JESSIE. See LENTON, JESSIE (POPE).

POPE, MARION (MANVILLE). B. 1859. United States.

009453   UP THE MATTERHORN IN A BOAT. New York:
Century, 1897 NUC BMC.

Humorous account of a sky-boat, a sort of flying
machine. Two Americans and a dog. Perils and
adventures. PW 52:639.

POPE, MARTHA GRACE. United States.

009454   VICTORIA. Boston: Sherman, French, 1915
NUC.

Her development from an untried girl to a woman. PW
5-15-15

POPHAM, FLORENCE. Nationality Unknown.

009455   THE HOUSEWIVES OF EDENRISE. New York:
Appleton, 1902 NUC. London: W. Heinemann, 1902 BMC.

BOOK NEWS 12-02 "the appearance of Mrs. Greenlaw gave
them something to gossip about" satire.
ATH 12-13-02--dull
NYT 11-8-02. Not dull, portrayal of housewives--slice
of life? "a modern Cranford"

009456   THE PARAMOR PAPERS. Bristol: J. W.
Arrowsmith, 1905 BMC.

009457   A SUMMER HOLIDAY. Bristol: J. W.
Arrowsmith, 1907 BMC.

Newly married woman and group take a Swiss holiday
that begins with gymnastics. They behave as they
should not; platonic friendships threaten to become
more. ACAD
Three couples, on holiday. TLS

POPP, ADELHEID (DWORAK). 1869-1939.

009458   THE AUTOBIOGRAPHY OF A WORKING WOMAN.
London: T.F. Unwin, 1912 BMC NUC. Chicago: F.G.
Browne, 1913 NUC. (Tr. E. C. Harvey)

LBKM-tr from German. Struggle from childhood to
results of years of self-culture and unfailing
courage.
HD 6149 1. Woman-employment-Germany 2. Socialsim in
Germany
conditions of women's work in Vienna-similarities with
New York are profound. NYT

PORTER, ELEANOR (HODGMAN). 1868-1920. United States.

009459   CROSS CURRENTS: THE STORY OF MARGARET.
Boston: W.A. Wilde, [c1907] NUC. London: G.G. Harrap,
1928 BMC.

Girl reared in luxury spends some time among poor. PW
11-2-07
"The story of a little girl of wealth who was lost and
found by a little waif of the slums, taken to his
meager attic and forced to grow up among the sordid
conditions of sweat shops and dirty streets. The book
is a revealing child--labor document."

009460   DAWN. Boston: Houghton Mifflin, 1919 NUC.

PW-male hero. Blind boy realizes he'll never to able
to fight in the war. 821, I,1919.
hired girl . But really the autocratic ruler of the
family.

009461   JUST DAVID. Boston: Houghton, Mifflin,
1916 NUC. London: Constable, 1916 BMC.

Boy and his father. PW NYT TLS

009462   KEITH'S DARK TOWER. London: Constable,
1919 BMC.

Male hero blind. TLS Am.ed. title Dawn.

009463   MARY MARIE. London: Constable, [1920]
BMC. Boston: Houghton, Mifflin, 1920 NUC.

TLS-gushing story of divorce and reconciliation.
NYT-1920:27 child of divorced parents, a Pollyanna who
suffers because of their acts.

009464   MISS BILLY. Boston: L.C. Page, 1911 NUC.
London: S. Paul, 1914 BMC.

LBKM-Billy is alone in the world at 18 (acts more like
12), writes to family friends and asks if she can live
with them. Delightful.
charming girl grows up-problem in deciding among many
lovers. PW 6-3-11.

009465   MISS BILLY-MARRIED. Boston: Page, 1914
BMC NUC. London: S. Paul, [1915] BMC.

PW 85 3/7/14:769 "Heroine of the Miss Billy books is
again the chief figure. Story tells of her marriage,
the trying times she has when the cook leaves, of her
small son and her absorption in him to the exclusion
apparently of her husband and the sad time they had
until Billy realized that she could be a devoted
mother and a devoted wife at the same time, and the
happiness that came to them and various other people

that Billy took a hand at helping.
Her comings goings sayings doings. All sugar. TLS

009466   MISS BILLY'S DECISION. Boston: L.C. Page,
1912 NUC. London: S.Paul, [1915] BMC.

PW-silly love story.
Billy is cultured, rich, composes songs, benevolent,
independent, domesticated, vivacious. On father's
death goes to live with father's male friend and two
bachelors. (They expect a boy.) 2 engagements follow.
Then "Mary Jane" comes on the scene. He is an opera
tenor? SP

009467   OH, MONEY! MONEY! London: Constable, 1918
BMC. Boston: Houghton Mifflin, 1918 NUC.

PW-romance, Frank James and Flora each receive 100,000
from cousin.
NYT-he would leave vast fortune to the one who made
best use of 100,000. Flora wins. Extremely moral
little story.

009468   THE ROAD TO UNDERSTANDING. Boston:
Houghton, Mifflin, 1917 NUC. London: Constable, [1917]
BMC.

Traditional romance. Marriage problems, separation,
reconciliation. TLS
Self improvement scheme on the part of the wife. ATH
Helen Barnet poor nursemaid marries a rich cultured
man. Marriage brings disillusionment on both sides. He
has only a small income. She wanted wealth. She's
coarse to him. Things get very bad; a child makes them
worse. But they get on the long road of understanding.
NYT 5-13-17 186

009469   THE STORY OF MARCO. New York: A.L. Burt,
[c1911] NUC. London: S. Paul, [1920] BMC.

TLS-9 year old boy.
a gypsy male violinist. 11-18-11 PW

009470   THE TURN OF THE TIDE; THE STORY OF HOW
MARGARET SOLVED HER PROBLEM. Boston: W.A. Wilde,
[c1908] NUC. London: G. G. Harrap, 1928 BMC.

PORTER, GENE (STRATTON). 1868-1924. United States.

009471   AT THE FOOT OF THE RAINBOW. New York:
Outing, 1907 NUC. London: Hodder and Stoughton, [1913]
BMC.

009472   A DAUGHTER OF THE LAND. London: J.
Murray, 1918 BMC. Garden City, N.Y.: Doubleday, Page,
[c1918] NUC.

PW-Family of 16. The nine sons are at 21 to be given
200 acres, the seven daughters six weeks in normal
school and a bolt of cloth and dress to be married in.
Kate, the youngest rebels against this. Reviewer says
"Every feminist will rejoice in the sudden emergence
of Mrs. Bates, the overworked and repressed mother of
the 16."
TLS-Kate leaves home for her independence as a school
teacher. She starts a saw mill, happy 2nd marriage.
NYT Aug 4, 1918, p. 338. What she wanted from life was
"a man, a farm, and a family," and she finally gets
them.
Brutal father; heroine self confident not sentimental
as earlier novels. SR
"Taffy of the feminine sort, made by women for women."
BKM June 1919:421.

009473   FRECKLES. London: Doubleday, Page, 1904
BMC. New York: Doubleday, Page, 1904 NUC.

009474   A GIRL OF THE LIMBERLOST. New York:
Doubleday, 1909 NUC. London: Doubleday, 1909 BMC.

children's book. PW 8-28-09
Almost tragic efforts of a brave young woman to win an
education and develop her musical talents. She's
practically alone for her mother's grief over
husband's death has estranged her from the girl. The
girl succeeds, even in softening her mother's stoney
heart. For young readers. NYT

009475   THE HARVESTER. Garden City. N.Y.:
Doubleday, Page, 1911 NUC. London: Hodder and
Stoughton, 1911 BMC.

Romantic story of the woods and an ideal girl. PW
8-26-11. NYT

009476   LADDIE; A TRUE BLUE STORY. Garden City,

N.Y.: Doubleday, Page, 1913 NUC. London: J. Murray,
1913 BMC.

Concerns a wealthy English family whose daughter is
wooed by Laddie. Little sister tells the story; she
idealizes her oldest brother Laddie who is now in
love. Little home circle where keynote of life is
love. NYT BKM

009477   MICHAEL O'HALLORAN. London: J. Murray,
1915 BMC. Garden City, N.Y.: Doubleday, Page, 1915
NUC.

009478   THE SONG OF THE CARDINAL: A LOVE STORY.
Indianapolis: Bobbs Merrill, [1903] BMC NUC. London:
Hodder and Stoughton, 1913 BMC.

PORTER, HELEN.

009479   THE SECOND BLOOM: A TALE OF THE BEGINNING
OF THE NINETEENTH CENTURY. London: Greening, 1906 BMC.

Romance. LBKM 2-07:236
thrills, love story, male hero the focus. ACAD

PORTER, JESSIE.

009480   BETTY AT BAY; A COMEDY OF TODAY. London:
Jarrolds, [1919] BMC.

Pleasant love story. SP
Wife's problem with father in law. SR

PORTER, MARY (BIDDER).

009481   IN THE SHADOW OF THE CROWN. BY MARY
BIDDER. London: A. Constable, 1899 BMC.

PORTER, REBECCA NEWMAN. B. 1883. United States.

009482   THE GIRL FROM FOUR CORNERS; A ROMANCE OF
CALIFORNIA TO-DAY. New York: H. Holt, 1920 NUC.

PW-Freda Bayne brought up in coarse surroundings makes
her way in San Francisco.
NYT 8-1-20 p. 26. Works 1st as a hairdresser, then in
bookstore. Romance, choice between two men.

PORTER, ROSE. 1845-1906. United States.

009483   A DAUGHTER OF ISRAEL. New York: E. P.
Dutton, 1899 NUC.

009484   MY SON'S WIFE. New York: A. D. F.
Randolph, [c1895] NUC. London: J. Nisbet, 1896 BMC.

Old grandmother writes the story of her
daughter-in-law's childhood, girlhood and happy
life-for her granddaughter. Information from diaries.
"Sweet" PW 11-2-95:746
SR - Diary of a model young woman with comments by her
admiring mother-in-law.

009485   ONE OF THE SWEET OLD CHAPTERS: A
FRAGMENT. New York: F. H. Revell, 1896 NUC.

009486   SAINT MARTIN'S SUMMER OR, THE ROMANCE OF
THE CLIFF. New York: F. H. Revell, [c1891] NUC.

Complications over a will; tangled love affairs:
Margaret Boscawen believes herself the heir of a
mansion in Cornwall. A rival heir comes forth, and he
and the local curate are rivals for Margaret's love.
Focus on the development of her character thru
suffering. PW 4-8-91.

PORTSMOUTH, MARIANNE.

009487   DOCTOR JOHN. London: H. J. Drane, [1903]
BMC.

Idle husband lays down all pretensions to manliness to
loaf while his wife works. LBKM July 1903:152.

POST, EMILY (PRICE). 1873-1960. United States.

009488   THE EAGLE'S FEATHER. New York: Dodd,
Mead, 1910 NUC.

Vera lives with a married artist genius who's writing
a great tragedy. Though he loves her, he tells her to
go--just so he can finish his play, use her pain as
model. PW
BKM 32, 1910-11. Married to a poet (mad) who uses her
(cruelly) for artistic inspiration. How does it end? "
"Male poet working on his magnus opus. He's married,

RC so cannot divorce, Vera, woman he loves, risks all
to live with him. They're happy till he's near
finishing his tragic poem. In order to have the right
subject for his poem, tells the woman he doesn't love
her. In her agony, he gets the subject he needs. He
becomes famous, realizes what he's done, she's left.
He loved her all along but chooses art over love. NYT

009489   THE FLIGHT OF A MOTH. New York: Dodd,
Mead, 1904 NUC.

PW 22 year old widow rebels against conventions until
she meets a man who is able to prepare her to be
fettered by love and law.

009490   PURPLE AND FINE LINEN. New York: D.
Appleton, 1905 BMC NUC.

Camilla develops from child to woman. Young and
thoughtless marries a rich man who treats her as a
plaything. Another man awakens her on the brink of
marital shipwreck.

009491   THE TITLE MARKET. New York: Dodd, Mead,
1909 NUC.

American and foreign marriage business totally
exposed. Nina the younger heroine has excellent chance
of finding out the Italian ideas on subject and the
business attitude toward marriage in the proposals
from Italian nobles.
BKM v.30 1909-10. International marriage

009492   WOVEN IN THE TAPESTRY. New York: Moffat,
Yard, 1908 NUC.

POST, HELEN (WILMANS). 1831-1907.

009493   THE CONQUEST OF DEATH. BY HELEN WILMANS.
Seabreeze, Fl.: International Scientific Assoc.,
[c1900] NUC. London: E. Bell, 1902 BMC.

009494   LIMITLESS MAN. BY HELEN WILMANS. London:
E. Bell, 1902 BMC.

POTTER, FRANCES BOARDMAN (SQUIRE). 1867-1914. United
States.

009495   THE BALLINGTONS, A NOVEL. BY FRANCES
SQUIRE. Boston: Little, Brown, 1905 NUC.

"A story of modern social relations in connection with
married life. 2 families are concerned, in one the
husband is the financial power, in the other it is the
wife. The interest is centered in the spiritual
awakening of Agnes Ballington, her struggle for the
rights of the soul, and the steady involvement of
other homes and other individuals." BKM v.23,1906
Two marriages. In one woman gets no money, forced to
use deception to help her mother. In the other, rich
woman can't get husband to leave his position to live
on her income. Study of how far a husband or wife must
respect each other's individuality and grant freedom
in marriage is theme. PW 10-7-05.
2 married couples. In one husband holds the purse, in
the other the wife does. Tyranny of withholding, of
giving. First one studied thoroughly--affect upon
wife, gradual disillusion of the marriage. Story of
unhappy loves, of interesting middle-age. NYT 672,05

POTTER, MARGARET. See BLACK, MARGARET HORTON (POTTER).

POTTER, MARGARET HORTON. See BLACK, MARGARET HORTON
(POTTER).

POWELL, ELLA MAY. B. 1863. United States.

009496   WINONA: A STORY OF TO-DAY. New York: A.
Lovell, [c1891] NUC.

009497   WOMEN WHO LAUGH. New York, London:
Transatlantic, 1895 NUC.

POWELL, FRANCES, pseud. See CASE, FRANCES POWELL.

POWELL, TALLULAH MATTESON. United States.

009498   AN ENGLISH GIRL IN AMERICA. Chicago: F.
T. Neely, [c1892] NUC.

POWER, EDITH MARY.

009499   A KNIGHT OF GOD. Edinburgh: Sands, 1909
BMC.

POWER, EDITH MARY. B. 1870. United Kingdom.

009500   HER FATHER'S SHARE: A NOVEL. New York:
Benziger, 1916 NUC.

Story of orphans and disguises. PW
Young Irish girl visits relatives in Portugal. BKM

POWER, EILEEN EDNA. B. 1889.

009501   THE PAYCOCKES OF COGGESHALL. London:
Methuen, [1920] BMC NUC. (Biography ?)

POWERS, CAROL (HOYT). United States.

009502   THE ISLE OF WHIMS. Boston: R. G. Badger,
[c1913] NUC.

PW 11-15-13 1590. "Whimsical story of a summer home on
a New England island. A happily married young woman
feels quite competent to arrange the matrimonial
affairs of her friends and hits upon two of them as
the especial object of her care. First she throws them
together, then has qualms of fear that they are not
suited to each other, but the young couple go calmly
on their way to their chosen goal."

POWYS, NORAH.

009503   IN A COUNTRY TOWN: A STORY UNFOUNDED ON
FACT. BY HONOR PERCEVAL. London: R. Bentley, 1897 BMC.

"Unsatisfactory" psych. novel. ACAD 51:520.
Miss Brunhild Fayne derives pleasure in caring for the
child that she believes is an illeg. child of one of
her admirers; moral lessons are obvious. ATH 109:611.

POYNTER, ELEANOR FRANCES. United Kingdom.

009504   AN EXQUISITE FOOL [ANONYMOUS]. London:
Osgood, McIlvaine, 1892 BMC NUC. New York: Harper,
1892 NUC.

LBKM 3:91. "Study of character" of "unhappy and
brilliant" woman, Helen Bromley, who is "fastidious,
elegant, and with fine perceptions where dress,
society and literature are concerned." The only man
she ever loved told her this was a pretty coating for
a vulgar soul. She has a sordid history, Euphemia, her
daughter by 1st marriage is wholesome, stupid.
A woman believes husband is dead, marries a second
time. Is then pursued by husband #1 who hounds her to
death. Fine analysis of character of mother and her
daughter and the man who hesitates marrying the
daughter. Ends tragically. Reviewer sees no way to
explain title. LW 93 12
George Lidderdale returns from a dinner party where he
met a woman he had not seen for 15 years. He brings
out letters that renew the story of their
acquaintance. CR 14 old series 22, new 19.(Hard to
reconcile this with notes from LW)
Heroine with brilliant possibilities. Ruined by
selfishness and bad luck. Sordid. ATH 101,14

009505   MICHAEL FERRIER. London and New York:
Macmillan, 1902 NUC BMC.

ATH 5-10-02 not helpful.

PRAED, MRS. CAMPBELL. See PRAED, ROSA CAROLINE
(MURRAY-PRIOR).

PRAED, ROSA CAROLINE (MURRAY-PRIOR). 1851-1935. Australia.

009506   "AS A WATCH IN THE NIGHT": A DRAMA OF
WAKING AND DREAM IN FIVE ACTS. By MRS. CAMPBELL PRAED.
London: Chatto and Windus, 1901 BMC NUC.

SP 85:754. Reincarnation. Heroine has a dual
existence; a lady of fashion with an interest in
politics and a Roman matron in the time of Domitian.
ATH 90:753. She has a studio in Chelsea, is friend of
one man, the mistress of another. She has two
historical pasts.

009507   THE BODY OF HIS DESIRE. A ROMANCE OF THE
SOUL. London: Cassell, 1912 BMC NUC.

PW psychic.
TLS-psychic.
LBKM-Neseta, the heroine is not a character in the
usual sense but a mysterious incarnation of Rev.
Chalmers (an evangelist) physical revolt against the
asceticism of his teaching.

009508   BY THEIR FRUITS: A NOVEL. BY MRS.
CAMPBELL PRAED. London, Paris, New York, Toronto,

Melbourne: Cassell, 1908 NUC BMC.

Twin sisters: one evil, one good. Bad one marries,
good one takes her place.
PW-twin sisters, 1 with drug habit, other loves and
yields to sister's husband.
TLS-0
ATH-0

009509   CHRISTINA CHARD. BY MRS. CAMPBELL-PRAED.
New York: D. Appleton, 1893 NUC. London: Chatto and
Windus, 1894 BMC.

SR-77:476. Australian young woman, comes into a
million and is introduced to London society.
"Christina Chard is represented as being one of those
neurotic and abnormal women who are the daughters of
much reading of that strange and sickly book The
Heavenly Twins."
ACAD 45:391. She was betrayed at 17. Her nature is
softened by the death of her little daughter Ralda,
whom she discovers in a strange way (her betrayal had
given her an intense hatred for mankind.) Lady St.
Helier wants to found a salon, start cooperative
nurseries for the poor, and organize guilds for the
employment of women.
ATH 103:407. The story of a woman's vengeance.
LBKM 7:57. Christina has an occult power over mankind,
Ralda has a visionary nature.
LW 25:41.

009510   DECEMBER ROSES. BY MRS. CAMPBELL-PRAED.
New York: D. Appleton, 1892 NUC. Bristol: J. W.
Arrowsmith, [1893] BMC.

"Violet's renunciation is made a little too morbid by
her religious scruples" "Eleanor needlessly delayed a
union she had every reason to welcome." ACAD 44:338.
LW 23:278. Divorced Australian woman meets a former
lover. Their love for each other is renewed; story is
of the "conscientious scruples and struggles" of
herself and the woman he is engaged to.
PW: love story of a 40 year old man and 32 year old
woman.

009511   DWELLERS BY THE RIVER. BY MRS. CAMPBELL
PRAED. London: J.Long, [1903?] BMC NUC. (Tales.)

009512   FUGITIVE ANNE: A ROMANCE OF THE
UNEXPLORED BUSH. BY MRS. CAMPBELL PRAED. London: J.
Long, [1902] BMC NUC.

About Australian marriage laws; wife takes to the bush
her body painted black- to escape husband. Her
fantastic adventures in the bush-there she meets an
explorer-their adventures are unique, chaste, but
thrilling. ACAD 64,130 Married 4 months, slips out of
window port aboard ship to escape her bully husband.
But she didn't die, lives an exciting life wandering
in the bush, takes position of High Priestess,
marriage to a faithful lover. The wicked husband made
away with at right moment. ATH 121,108
Runs from odious husband in company of a black, meets
Danish explorer, becomes a priestess. Husband gets
what he deserved. Anne weds the explorer. TLS 03,25

009513   THE GHOST. BY MRS. CAMPBELL PRAED.
London: R.A. Everett, 1903 BMC NUC.

Publishes a novel not her own to rescue alcoholic
aunt. The ghost (writer) appears when she's a success.
ACAD 64,486
ATH 121, 810 0
Treated OK, marries her publisher. TLS, 155,03

009514   THE INSANE ROOT. A ROMANCE OF A STRANGE
COUNTRY. BY MRS. CAMPBELL PRAED. London: T.F. Unwin,
1902 BMC. New York: Funk & Wagnalls, [1902?] NUC.

ATH 2-15-02-tedious heroine. No real and alive people
at all.
NYT 02

009515   LADY BRIDGET IN THE NEVER-NEVER LAND; A
STORY OF AUSTRALIAN LIFE. London: Hutchinson, 1915 BMC
NUC.

NYT-30 yr. old wife, tired of social life and
dependence on her aunt, thoughtlessly marries an
Australian and goes with him to Moongarr . Story of
their marriage.
Heroine's thrilling adventures in England and
Australia. NYT
The never-never land is Australia. Lady Bridgett's
temperament clashes with her husband's. Things made
worse for they are squatters. He must be right; she

sentimental and flighty, takes part in all the newest
movements. But she changes in the novel. . TLS

009516   THE LOST EARL OF ELLAN: A STORY OF
AUSTRALIAN LIFE. BY MRS. CAMPBELL PRAED. London:
Chatto & Windus, 1906 BMC NUC.

TLS- male hero. conv.
ATH-2 sisters in love with him.

009517   THE LUCK OF THE LEURA. BY MRS. CAMPBELL
PRAED. London: J. Long, [1907] BMC NUC.

Australian bush life. Short stories on one theme: the
terrible side of Australian bushlife...from the
woman's point of view. Its strains and demands on
women settlers. SR

009518   MADAME IZAN: A TOURIST STORY. BY MRS.
CAMPBELL-PRAED. London: Chatto and Windus, 1899 NUC.
New York: D. Appleton, 1899 NUC.

Story of travel--mostly in Japan. Madame Izan and her
companion Mrs. Bax. LIT 4:556.
Heroine is blind, married to a Japanese from whom she
was immediately separated by her family. The husband
attaches himself to her as a guide (unknown to her.)
She also meets, in her travels, a young Australian
millionaire who loves her. Climax is unconventional.
SP 82:560
Theodosia Gotch tries to save the geishas. Satire too
severe. SR 87:761
Pretty, sentimental love affair between Englishwoman
and a Japanese noble. BAKER 03,253

009519   THE MAID OF THE RIVER. AN AUSTRALIAN
GIRL'S LOVE STORY. BY MRS. CAMPBELL PRAED. London: J.
Long, [1905] BMC NUC.

Innocent girl rejects nice man for scoundrel who
betrays her by mock marriage; scandal and desertion
follow. Wants legitimacy for her child but it turns
out the man has a mad wife. What's different is that
when the wife dies, the girl (Nuni) brings an action
of breach of promise. ACAD 880,05
LBKM v.29-30,43
Successfully sues her betrayer for breach of promise.
ATH 203,05

009520   MRS. TREGASKISS. A NOVEL OF
ANGLO-AUSTRALIAN LIFE. BY MRS. CAMPBELL-PRAED. New
York: D. Appleton, 1895 NUC. London: Chatto and
Windus, 1896 BMC NUC.

A type of the new woman shrinking from wifehood and
motherhood. Raised in England, though born in
Australia. She marries a rough Australian rancher
after her father loses his money, commits suicide and
the chances of her making a brilliant marriage
disappear. Opens when she's had several children, is
enduring her husband. Almost elopes with a man she
falls in love with. The death of her child alone
prevents her. PW 12-7-95:1083
Agony of a sensitive and cultivated woman forced to
live out her life on a distant station (ranch in
America) with no social or cultural opportunities.
SR-Australia. Unhappy wife resists, stays with
husband, dreary ending.
ATH 107:212. She has a dull, unfaithful husband, she
is highly-strung, imaginative, has affair another man.
Husband and wife are reunited through remorse and
self-reproach over the death of their daughter.
ACAD 49:301. One gets an intimate acquaintance of the
habits and daily routine of women's lives in the bush.
SP 76:486. His remorse; he is alcoholic as well as
unfaithful. Gives up both, Clare, on the verge of
eloping, decides to stay with him and their other
child. She had a bad father and unfaithful lover.

009521   THE MYSTERY WOMAN. London: Cassell, 1913
BMC NUC.

Treats subject of occultism seriously; also contains
an anarchist plot. SP
Heroine astounds society by her performances as a
palmist; finally commits suicide as a wonderful
sacrifice for her beloved. ATH
Stanmount sisters-one marries rank; one trade: the 3rd
the mystery woman Althea is business-like and
practical, a clairvoyant of unquestionable
performances and extraordinary powers. Her tragic end
comes because in her is reincarnated the soul of the
Delphic Pythia. TLS

009522   NULMA; AN ANGLO-AUSTRALIAN ROMANCE. BY
MRS. CAMPBELL-PRAED. London: Chatto and Windus, 1897

BMC. New York: D. Appleton, 1897 NUC.

Beautiful, unsophisticated daughter of self-made
colonial near to governer's circle. Meets the new
chief justice. This man Kennard is involved with his
secretary's wife-Margot Keefe. But he now falls for
Nulma. Margot causes trouble between them so that
Nulma becomes engaged to an elderly admirer. A good
solution presented. Nulma is innocent, brilliant and
impulsive, contrasted to the worldly clever exotic
Margot. Both sympathetic, Margot a victim of a
marriage of conven ience made hastily to a jealous
boor. The other woman portrayed sym. SP 78:771 1870.
Aust..
"In the first bloom of womanhood" comes in contact
with decadent from Eng. learns to love an unworthy
man. BAKER 03 253.

009523   NYRIA. BY MRS. CAMPBELL PRAED. London:
T.F. Unwin, 1904 BMC NUC.

ATH-psychic
ACAD. Story of a slave girl spiritual.

009524   OPAL FIRE. BY MRS. CAMPBELL PRAED. London
and New York: Cassell, 1910 BMC NUC.

BM Australia, love
TLS-Australia, love .
ATH- Young woman engaged to young man: they are
separated and he appears false. Her father tricks her
into a conventional marriage, years later he shows up,
she's a mother and what happens then? Sad story with
more than a touch of the cruelty of the world's wild
places.
Life in Australia bush; disaster of a child. SP

009525   THE OTHER MRS. JACOBS; A MATRIMONIAL
COMPLICATION. BY MRS. CAMPBELL PRAED. London: J. Long,
1903 BMC NUC.

Susan is Mrs. Jacob's companion; she's egotistical.
ACAD 150 v65
Bitter matrimonial complications. LBKM 225,9-03
Bohemian Life. Heroine writes novels. Susan her
companion. ATH 122,280

009526   OUTLAW AND LAW MAKER. BY MRS.
CAMPBELL-PRAED. London: Chatto and Windus, 1893 BMC.
New York: D. Appleton, 1894 NUC.

PW-Old-fashioned story of love, adventure, and
disguised gentlemen outlaws. Young English woman
visits her sister in Australia. Hears all about a
local hero called Moonlight. She has two lovers-one
the safe true type, the other more dashing who is one
and the same as Moon light. CR 23:158.
Life and politics in Australia. BAKER '03 253
Irish hero-in army. Almost arrested for turning troops
to Fenianism becomes a brigand, goes to Australia.
Farmed by day and highway robbed by night, became M.P.
Then minister-though he's still sought. Becomes a
peer, betrayed, about to be arrested, drowns self. SR
76 628.
Elsie Valient, unconventional-all her lovers: one she
treats cooly, one gives her diamonds, the third kisses
her passionately, the fourth drugs her. She's
attracted to the hero Morris Blake. She doesn't marry
any of the four. Don't know how it ends. ACAD 44:508.

009527   THE ROMANCE OF A CHALET. A STORY. BY MRS.
CAMPBELL-PRAED. London: F. V. white, 1892 BMC.
Philadelphia: J. B. Lippincott, 1892 NUC.

ATH 99:12. romance, self-sacrifice
CR 17:69. Heroine is American traveling in Europe
whose mother is insane and has murdered another woman.
She does not learn of this till conclusion, and then
decides to join an RC nunnery.
ACAD 4:35. She is asked by Sir Rupert to be his wife,
he had hesitated before because there is insanity in
his family. She accepts, and for awhile they are happy
until another cloud comes over this love. Story is sad
from this point on. Heroine is rich and travels alone
except for her dog.
Mrs. Ruth Elliott tells the story of Constance Van
Klaft, a wealthy American girl she met in France and
Switzerland traveling with her St Bernard. Constance
becomes engaged to an English noble but then learns he
broke off the engagement because he discovered
insanity in his family. When she discovers the same in
hers, Constance makes new plans for her life. PW
12-5-91.
She was ready to marry him though there is insanity in
his family, but when she hears the same about her
relations, gives up idea of marriage. she's not told

yet, when later she's about to marry a Roman prince,
learns about her mother and retires to convent. SR
12-12-91, 670

009528   THE ROMANCE OF A STATION. AN AUSTRALIAN
STORY. BY MRS. CAMPBELL PRAED. London: Trischler,
[1891] BMC NUC.

009529   THE ROMANCE OF MADEMOISELLE AISSE. BY
MRS. CAMPBELL PRAED. London: J. Long, [1910] BMC NUC.

TLS-historic, woman of the Regency, tempted by three
men and three passions.
SR-0

009530   THE SCOURGE-STICK. BY MRS. CAMPBELL
PRAED. London: W. Heinemann, 1898 BMC. New York: J.
Chartress, 1898 NUC.

ACAD 53:255. In the form of a woman's autobiography.
Esther Zamiel, Vassal, Vrintz, author, with a "triune
personality" passionately devoted to art in various
forms.
ACAD 53:395. Hector Vassal, an elderly admirer. She
marries him when she fails as an actress. He is cold
and ruthless; they are unhappy and she meets someone
else. when Hector is dying, he loses his mask of
respectability and has Esther read indecent French
novels to him by the hour.
ATH 111:432. Hector is an "elderly sensualist of
peculiar malignity," she nearly loses her health and
her mind, takes up writing and through this meets
Hector's nephew, Robert Vassal, a publisher's reader,
who falls for her. "One of Esther's morbid fancies is
that the invisible embodiment of generations of hatred
makes ever a third in her meetings with her husband or
her lover."
LBKM 14:23. A repressed and sentimental woman, a bore.

009531   SISTER SORROW: A STORY OF AUSTRALIAN
LIFE. London: Hutchinson, 1916 BMC.

TLS-Wilkins enslaves his wife Delores because she is a
pure psychic. He is Satanically evil. Narrated by
Agatha, Delores' friend. Delores is a likeable
governess.

009532   SOME LOVES AND A LIFE: A STUDY OF A
NEUROTIC WOMAN. London: F.V. White, 1904 BMC.

Heroic neurotic, morphine addict; strong interest in
characterization. Enlists our sympathy. ATH 106,05

009533   THE SOUL OF COUNTESS ADRIAN. A ROMANCE.
BY MRS. CAMPBELL PRAED. London: Trischler, 1891 BMC.
New York: U. S. Book, [c1891] NUC.

This soul becomes a vampire spirit and inhabits
Beatrice Brett's body. Beatrice is a young American
actress, a star in London. Her lover suffers from the
change in her until she is exorcized by a mystic.
Includes Mrs. Alexander's "Heart of Oak" and "Sophy".
PW 6-6-91.
Lover quick to see the difference. LW Also ACAD.
The soul belongs to a dead Countess who loved the
artist. 5-9-91, 571 SR
The countess has no soul. She is a "beautiful human
animal with unusually developed sensuous instincts"
Dies, transfers her passionate nature to rival which
quality "proves repellant to the gentleman". After the
rival is exorcized and proper again she lives happily
with the man. BOOK NEWS 107:47 9

PRAGA, MRS. ALFRED.

009534   LOVE AND 200 POUNDS A YEAR. London: T. W.
Laurie, [1913] BMC.

Two sisters--one marries a rich man whom she doesn't
love and is discontent; the other marries for love and
200 pounds a year and is very happy. ATH
Cynthia Rafferty wishes to prove that marriage on 200
pounds a year can include good meals, well-kept house,
servant, pretty things--the refinements. Science of
household management a marvel of practical sense. LBKM

PRATT, AGNES LOUISE. United States.

009535   AUNT SARAH: A MOTHER OF NEW ENGLAND.
Boston: Richard Badger, 1906 NUC.

PW-Civil War

PRATT, CORNELIA ATWOOD. See COMER, CORNELIA ATWOOD (PRATT).

PRATT, GRACE TYLER. United States.

009536   THE BAINBRIDGE MYSTERY; THE HOUSEKEEPER'S
STORY. Boston: Sherman, French, 1911 NUC.

Eliza Carter, middle-aged, becomes housekeeper to Mr.
Mader who is murdered. She discovers the murderer. PW

PRATT, LUCY. B. 1874. United States.

009537   EZEKIEL. New York: Doubleday, Page, 1909
NUC.

Story of a Black boy

009538   FELIX TELLS IT. New York and London: D.
Appleton, 1915 BMC NUC.

Ten year old Felix writes a book on The Nature of
Fathers and Mothers. NYT

PRATT, SARAH WILDER. United States.

009539   THY BROTHER LEONIDAS. Chicago: Universal
Truth Pub. Co., [1900] NUC.

PW-Romance illustrating power of a religion similar to
Bhuddism in which love is the keynote.

PRENTISS, CAROLINE (EDWARDS). B. 1872.

009540   LOVE AND LAUGHTER. New York and London:
G. P. Putnam's Sons, 1917 NUC.

PRESCOTT, AUGUSTA. Nationality Unknown.

009541   THE STAIRWAY ON THE WALL. New York: Alice
Harriman, 1911 NUC.

Woman proposes to a man to avoid a detested man;
mostly mystery and murder. PW 4-29-11.

PRESCOTT, E. LIVINGSTON, pseud. See JAY, EDITH KATHARINE
SPICER.

PRESTON, ANNA. B. 1887. Canada.

009542   THE GLORY AND THE DREAM. New York: B.W.
Huebsch, 1915 NUC.

An Irish boy and his imagination. NYT
NYT-. 6 year old male hero.
BKM- 6 yr. old male hero.

009543   THE RECORD OF A SILENT LIFE. New York:
B.W. Huebsch, 1912 NUC. London: M. Secker, 1913 BMC.

PW-dumb young woman but very intelligent inherits and
becomes interested in philantrophy
NYT-without power of speech but develops into a source
of strength.
"The record covers many years of the life of a woman
born dumb. her own affliction gives her a sympathy for
all suffering and when she is left with a great house
and an independent fortune she makes her home a haven
for all outcasts and failures. She takes them as
boarders but allows them to make their own terms and
announces in her advertisement, "children pets, old
people , and invalids not only admitted, but invited."
Her story is made up of a chronicle of the lives of
the queer derelicts of humanity who find their way to
her door. It is written with the realism of a diary
and the detail of a pathological study; yet the result
is cold and detached." ATH 1913,1;251 Mr 1 50w
"An excellent piece of literary work, but not
convincing as a true record of the existence of a
woman born without speech. The characters are original
and well-drawn." BOSTON TRANSCRIPT p7 D 21 12 180w
"A strange unclassifiable book, seeming at first
intolerably and offensibly gloomy, this Record
gradually enfolds the reader in a poignant interest."
NY TIMES 18:66 F 9 13 220w.
Original and kindly portrayal of a vigorous but dumb
woman her life from childhood; desires to be wanted,
fills her house with stray boarders. SP 110:932.

PRESTON, LAURA FITZHUGH. B. 1846. United States.

009544   UNCLE BOB: HIS REFLECTIONS. New York:
Grafton Press, [1904] NUC.

Preacher's musings PW 10-14-05

PRICE, ELEANOR CATHERINE. United Kingdom.

009545   ANGELOT: A STORY OF THE FIRST EMPIRE.
London: G. G. Harrap, 1902 BMC. New York: T. Y.

Crowell, [1902] NUC.

009546   BROWN ROBIN. London: Isbister, 1899 BMC.

009547   THE HEIRESS OF THE FOREST. A ROMANCE OF
OLD ANJOU. London: Isbister, 1900 BMC. New York: T. Y.
Crowell, 1901 NUC.

SP 85:464. Romance of old France. Kidnappings,
convents.
PW 2-23-01

009548   IN SLIPPERY PLACES. Oxford: A. R.
Mowbray, 1905 BMC NUC.

009549   IN THE LION'S MOUTH: THE STORY OF TWO
ENGLISH CHILDREN IN FRANCE, 1789-1793. London and New
York: Macmillan, 1894 BMC NUC.

Historical romance of French Revolution. Brother and
sister-English orphans sent to live in French village
by guardian at time of first stirrings of revolution.
The two side with aristocrats. They're separated;
she's captured and awaits death. But saved, the two
return to England. SP 74:139
Time of French Revolution. Two English children go to
France, many stirring adventures. The young man
marries. The young woman remains true to the memory of
a young man she rejected. CR 23:203
Conventional story-two English children in French
Revolution. Times of Burke. BAKER 03, 165

009550   JOHN'S LILY. London: Wells Gardner,
[1894] BMC.

SR-children's story.

009551   THE LITTLE ONE. London: Bentley, 1891 BMC
NUC.

Agnes D'Alby a minister's daughter attracted to a
scoundrel, Gilbert, Mrs. Murray's son. She elopes with
him, learns he's married, returns home and dies.
Gloomy story but well written. SP 1-31-91 , 150 also
ACAD 97 50
Minister of Langholm-two granddaughters. Nora is a
novelist of enormously high standards; lives with
father and sister Agnes 17. (Nora is past 20). They
are all the world to her. Then she ignores them for "a
violent and enthusiastic love for Mrs. Murray," a
newcomer. Mrs. Murray's son seduced Agnes (the little
one). Grandfather dies at time Agnes left. Nora full
of grief comes home after sister dies. Her novel
contained an elopement like Agnes. SR 1-10-91, 48

009552   MISS LATIMER OF BRYANS. London: R.
Bentley, 1893 BMC NUC.

Well-written. Heroine with best intentions makes a
mess of her life and that of others. Chooses an
unworthy man, rejects one who is worthy and who loves
her. And tries to match the rejected one to Maggie
Farrant. The rejected lover accepts the arrangement
because he knows Maggie is mixed up with the man Miss
Latimer chooses. SP 70, 258; SR 75, 181.
"There is a good deal of the 'feminine' kind of man
now so much in vogue." ATH 101, 245.

009553   OFF THE HIGH ROAD: THE STORY OF A SUMMER.
London: Macmillan, 1899 BMC NUC.

Viola Fairfax runs off to keep from marrying a man
chosen by her bad guardian in order to keep her
fortune in the family. She goes to a country town
where she advertises for a house off the high road.
Mrs. Downes who rents her a cottage has a son who
falls in love with Viola. LIT 4:346
She assumes a different name.
Midland landscape. SP 82:278

009554   THE QUEEN'S MAN: A ROMANCE OF THE WARS OF
THE ROSES. London: A. Constable, 1905 BMC NUC.

Historical romance. ACAD 1905:948.
ATH 1905:467

009555   TINA THE WANDERER. London: Christian
Knowledge Society, [1901] BMC.

PRICE, ELIZABETH ROBINSON (WALKER). B. 1863. United
States.

009556   FREDERICA DENNISON, SPINSTER. Boston:
Pilgrim Press, [c1916] NUC.

"Influence of young woman who is a genius at making

friends and helping her companion." BKM 1917:543
Diary of woman who went to Lansing to study music; a
genius at making friends. PW

PRICE, ELLA PERRY. United States.

009557   THE CRY HEARD. Cincinatti, O.: Curts and
Jennings, [c1898] NUC.

Purpose-to interest young people in missionary work.
PW 55:252.

009558   HER REALM. Cincinatti: Curts and
Jennings, [1903] NUC.

"A high type of womanhood"

PRICE, HILDA P. (CUMINGS). United Kingdom.

009559   NO GRAVEN IMAGE. BY HILDA P. CUMINGS.
London: J. Murray, 1916 BMC NUC.

TLS-relationship of two men.
ATH-relationship of two men.
a young Angelican divine. BKM

PRICE, MARGARET BARNES.

009560   DADDY'S WIDOW: A LONG ISLAND STORY. New
York: Broadway, [1916] NUC.

Several people's love stories. PW

PRICHARD, KATHARINE SUSANNAH. See THROSSELL, KATHARINE
SUSANNAH (PRICHARD).

PRICHARD, SARAH JOHNSON. 1830-1909. United States.

009561   SHAWNIE WADE. Boston: R. G. Badger, 1909
NUC.

So. girl of fiery temper and indomitable spirit comes
to No. School, changes places with a slave playmate
who is her counterpartin looks. Afterwards no one
believes she is not the slave.

PRIMM, PERRINGTON, pseud. See KNOOP, GERTRUDE.

PRIMROSE, DEBORAH.

009562   A MODERN BOEOTIA; PICTURES FROM LIFE IN A
COUNTRY PARISH. London: Methuen, 1904 BMC NUC.

PRINCE, HELEN CHOATE (PRATT). B. 1857. United States.

009563   AT THE SIGN OF THE SILVER CRESCENT.
Boston: Houghton, Mifflin, 1898 NUC. London: Gay and
Bird, 1898 BMC.

LIT 3:500. Modern French story, upholding virtue. Gay
and Bird, London.
CR 32:298. Idyllic romance.
NYT 1898:257. Author shows an abhorrence for Catholics
and Jews. The priest makes a woman a profligate and at
the same time plays the role of detective. Final
triumph of virtuous Protestants & Catholics.
PW-Aristocratic girl marries wealthy Jew for money for
her family; after marriage does not hesitate to show
her contempt for him. He drifts to another woman who
also wants his money.

009564   THE STORY OF CHRISTINE ROCHEFORT. Boston:
Houghton, Mifflin, 1895 NUC. London: Longmans, 1895
BMC.

Young woman leaves husband-dazzled by Socialist. At
the end he's beaten to bits and she returns with
relief to her husband. SR 80:119
Christine D'Arcy of noble family now poor makes a
marriage of convenience to a wealthy manufacturer for
the sake of her family. Awakened by ardent young
socialist, but returns to husband. SP 75:186
Theme: "struggle of a woman, hampered by a traditional
idea of herself, to slow self-realization." Problems
of strikes, labor, capital and the church included. CR
23:435
She takes the side of workers against her husband-a
manufacturer. "Wild, impractical notions of equality."
Is converted to love of him and capitalism. ACAD
48:144
French provincial life, a strike, anarchism, and a
love story. Christine is all shiny idealism, her
husband's passion for her; her respect for him; her
idealized love for another man; and her greater
growing love for husband, the small things of their
wedded days, etc. BKM 4:264

009565   THE STRONGEST MASTER. Boston: Houghton,
Mifflin, 1902 NUC.

BOOK NEWS 11-1902. Young man who has a passion for
reform of marriage.
NYT 10-25-02. Lives with woman without marriage
ceremony, she has baby goes wild for a time. "As far
as we can understand it, Chris and Clytie are made man
and wife in an orthodox manner".

009566   A TRANSATLANTIC CHATELAINE. Boston:
Houghton, Mifflin, 1897 NUC. London: Watt, [1897] BMC.

Silvia has an unsatisfactory father; marries a man who
goes off an d is killed in Civil War; has a lawsuit
with her in-laws; goe s to France where things go
worse for her. SP 70:717.
Selfish father; mother died young. She learns to shun
love as a tragic thing. Civil war comes. Her father
goes but marries her off first (in case he should
die). Her new husband goes off to war too. Husband
dies; her feelings of patriotism lead her to use her
fortune to restore an impoverished French noble.
Unhappy but finds comfort in philosophy. CR 26,30:270.
Sylvia Huntington marries a man who fetters her mind
and soul to the end. LW 28:164.
ATH 111:434. American widow marries a French title and
regrets.

PRINCESS, pseud. See LOCKETT, MARY F.

PRINDIVILLE, KATE GERTRUDE. Nationality Unknown.

009567   TWO OF THE GUESTS. New York: J. Pott,
1905 NUC.

Romantic love story in letters: PW 4-8-05
Group of guests and what they all think about each
other. NYT 1905:247.

PRINDLE, FRANCES WESTON (CARRUTH). B. 1867. United States.

009568   THOSE DALE GIRLS. BY FRANCES WESTON
CARRUTH. Chicago: A.C. McClurg, 1899 NUC.

Wealthy father dies, the two must earn own living.
Success as bakers. "They are regular manufacturers"
love interest NYT 408, June 24 '99

009569   THE WAY OF BELINDA. BY FRANCES WESTON
CARRUTH. New York: Dodd, Mead, 1901 NUC.

Bohemian life and world of journalism. BOOK NEWS May,
1901
BKM 13 (1901) 286-7
Courage of her convictions. PW 3-30-01
Slum sister, refuses to marry in her class, marries
reporter, but is it a pretty story as NYT suggests.
'01

PRINGLE, ELIZABETH WATIES (ALLSTON). 1845-1921.

009570   A WOMAN RICE PLANTER. BY PATIENCE
PENNINGTON. New York: Macmillan, 1913 BMC NUC.

Manages two large plantations with skill and
"indomitable persistence"

PRITCHARD, MARTIN J., pseud. See MOORE, JUSTINA.

PRITCHARD, MRS. ERIC.

009571   THE CULT OF CHIFFON. London: G. Richards,
1902 BMC NUC.

PROCTER, MRS. JOHN.

009572   AN OAK OF CHIVABY. London: Digby, Long,
[1897] BMC.

PROCTOR, GERTRUDE AMELIA. United States.

009573   GLEAMS OF SCARLET; A TALE OF THE CANADIAN
ROCKIES. Boston: Sherman, French, 1915 NUC.

NYT Story of girl and brother in West. He is on trial
for a serious crime but is innoc. Woman physician
takes her back East and helps her to an education
which trains her art.

PROST, YVETTE.

009574   THE SAVING PRIDE. New York: Dodd, Mead,
1912 NUC. (Tr. Frank Alvah Dearborn)

PW-Love story

PROTHERO, JOHN KEITH, pseud. See CHESTERTON, ADA ELIZABETH
(JONES).

PROTHEROE, HOPE.

009575   HIS LORDSHIP'S BABY. London: J. and J.
Bennett, [1912] BMC.

TLS-sensational
ATH-sensational

009576   ONE MAN'S SIN. London: J. Long, 1908 BMC.

TLS-religion, male hero.

009577   THE SHADOW OF A DWARF. London: Century
Press, 1911 BMC.

About a devilish dwarf. ATH

PROUTY, OLIVE (HIGGINS). 1882-1974. United States.

009578   BOBBIE, GENERAL MANAGER. A NOVEL. London:
E. Nash, 1913 BMC. New York: F. A. Stokes, [1913] NUC.

Almost persuaded she's a genius; ends in marriage. NYT
"The story of a very fine tom-boyish girl who
successfully manages and mothers a family of brothers
and sisters, some younger, some older than herself.
Bobbie spends one tragic term in a boarding-school to
which her family in mistaken kindness send her,
feeling that she ought to acquire some of the
attributes of a lady. Bobbie who has already developed
the much more valuable attributes of a woman is
decidedly out of place in the frivolous, fashionable
atmosphere and when family circumstances call her home
she comes again into her own element. She sees her
family married; marries herself and continues to be to
husband, brothers and sisters and nieces a wise and
kindly general manager. "It is the world of Little
women that she depicts. The story itself with its
various love episodes is interesting." BRD

009579   THE FIFTH WHEEL; A NOVEL. New York: F. A.
Stokes, [c1916] NUC. London: Cassell, 1918 BMC.

The "real" Ruth refuses the rich marriage planned by
sister-in-law. The other Ruth gives in. She's a
nobody, so the man's mother gets her son to jilt Ruth.
Ruth manages her own life then; then mother gets to
like her, leaves her money. Ruth marries another man.
PW
NYT Narrated by two sisters, Ruth and Lucy Ruth
rejects debutante role, marriage of convenience, goes
to little university town and begins to define her own
life. Falls in love but did not marry because he
objects to her activism in suffrage. Years later he
feels differently and They get back together.
TLS-She is an orphan. Financially independent and not
neccessary to the happiness of any household.
Discovers she is in fact dependent on her brother's
charity. Goes to New York, becomes a suffragist, and
altho marries in end, discovers a different view as to
place of women in life.

009580   THE STAR IN THE WINDOW; A NOVEL. New
York: F. A. Stokes, [c1918] NUC BMC. London: W.
Collins, [1920] BMC.

TLS Reba strives successfully for right to live her
own life, rev. says, but is far from feminist, has
gentle loving spirit of self sacrifice with
unrecognized powers behind it.
ATH-Adventures in Boston. Even in her own family
becomes person of importance. Finds a lover, too.
PW- love. But Reba rebels at 25, leaving her New
England family for the "Alliance" in Boston.

PRYCE, D. HUGH. See PRYCE, DAISY HUGH.

PRYCE, DAISY HUGH. United Kingdom.

009581   DEYNCOURT OF DEYNCOURT. London: J. Long,
1907 BMC.

Nothing new. ACAD
Concerns estates. TLS

009582   A DIAMOND IN THE DUST. London: Digby,
Long, 1909 BMC.

ACAD-conventional
A first wife turns up but all ends in love and
happiness. TLS

009583   THE ETHICS OF EVAN WYNNE. London:
Everett, [1913] BMC.

009584   GODDESSES THREE: A NOVEL. London:
Bentley, 1896 BMC.

ATH 108:481. Two sisters and a cousin. London and
Austria. Cheerful ending, in spite of sense of
tragedy.
ACAD 50:280. Villains are done in in a holocaust of a
fire. Plot turns on hereditary madness, scheming 2nd
wife of baron.
SP 77:401. Evangela, English cousin of two sisters, is
heroine. Her love story.

009585   HILL MAGIC. London: Heath, Cranton and
Ouseley, [1914] BMC.

009586   LOVE'S MIRAGE; BEING A STORY OF THE POWER
OF THE PAST. London: Greening, 1902 BMC.

009587   THE MARRIAGE OF COUNT MALORTO. London:
Everett, [1911] BMC.

The count kidnaps Anne who learns to love him. TLS

009588   THE PASHA. London: G. Allen, 1901 BMC.

009589   THE PRECIPICE. BY D. HUGH PRYCE. London:
Everett, [c1911] BMC NUC.

009590   VALDA HANEM: THE ROMANCE OF A TURKISH
HARIM. London: Macmillan, 1899 BMC NUC.

She's the beautiful Circassian wife of a Turkish Pasha
living in Cairo. Army Captain falls in love with her.
Disguises self as a workman installing lights in the
palace, wins her admission that she loves him. Pasha
learns; she dies of brain fever; the Captain returns
to England. It is the Pasha and not the Captain who
grieves for her most. SP 83:701
An enlightened Pasha, monogamist; despicable
Englishman's intrigue with Mrs. Pasha. BOOK NEWS 355
Intimate description of a harem. British officer's
intrigue with the Pasha's beloved wife. BAKER 03 166

PRYCE, GWENDOLEN.

009591   JOHN JONES, CURATE. London: T. F. Unwin,
1901 NUC.

ATH: 8-3-01

009592   A LONG SHADOW. London: Cassell, 1912 BMC.

TLS-unconfessed crime shadows a man's life.
ATH-unconfessed crime shadows a man's life.
LBKM-unconfessed crimes shadows a man's life.

009593   A SON OF ARVON. London: T. F. Unwin, 1906
BMC.

TLS-0
ATH-Traditional love story.

PRYDE, ANTHONY, pseud. See WEEKES, AGNES RUSSELL.

PRYOR, MRS. ROGER A. See PRYOR, SARA AGNES (RICE).

PRYOR, SARA AGNES (RICE). 1830-1912. United States.

009594   THE COLONEL'S STORY. BY MRS. ROGER A.
PRYOR. New York: Macmillan, 1911 BMC NUC.

Pre-Civil war, romance. PW 4-1-11, TLS, SR

PUDDICOMBE, ANNE ADALIZA (EVANS). 1836-1908. United
Kingdom.

009595   BY BERWEN BANKS; A ROMANCE OF WELSH LIFE.
BY ALLEN RAINE. London: Hutchinson, 1899 BMC. New
York: A. L. Burt, [c1899] NUC.

Careful study of Welsh manners and customs. A Senior
Wrangler who quotes poetry and sketches. LIT 4:347.
Hero meets young yoman, talks her into a secret
marriage and then goes off to Australia leaving her
bound to secrecy. When he returns, he doesn't even
recognize her. But she forgives him. LBKM 15:188
Valmai is the heroine; Gwynne Ellis, L.Caradoc Wynne
are the two men. ACAD 56:192
Wynne doesn't recognize her because he lost his
memory. Happy end. ACAD 56:327.
Idyllic peasant life in Wales--some melodrama in which
a higher class is involved. BAKER 03,167

009596   A CHANGE AT DAWN. BY ALLEN RAINE. London:
"Daily Mail", [1904] BMC.

009597   GARTHOWEN; A STORY OF A WELSH HOMESTEAD.
BY ALLEN RAINE. New York: D. Appleton, 1900 NUC.
London: Hutchinson, 1900 BMC.

LBKM 18:63. Two brothers love heroine; she eventually
chooses the unselfish and less worldly one.
ATH 115:395. Morna and her adopted mother Sara, a
gentle mystic.

009598   HEARTS OF WALES: AN OLD ROMANCE. BY ALLEN
RAINE. London: Hutchinson, 1905 BMC.

009599   MIFANWY (A WELSH SINGER). BY ALLEN RAINE.
New York: D. Appleton, 1897 NUC.

009600   NEITHER STOREHOUSE NOR BARN. BY ALLEN
RAINE. London: Hutchinson, 1908 NUC BMC.

TLS-love story.
BKM-love story.

009601   ON THE WINGS OF THE WIND. BY ALLEN RAINE.
London: Hutchinson, 1903 BMC.

009602   QUEEN OF THE RUSHES; A TALE OF THE WELSH
REVIVAL. BY ALLEN RAINE. London: Hutchinson, 1906 BMC.
Philadelphia: G.W. Jacobs, [c1906] NUC.

ATH -miracles
LBKM-miracles

009603   TORN SAILS; A TALE OF A WELSH VILLAGE. BY
ALLEN RAINE. London: Hutchinson, 1898 BMC. New York:
D. Appleton, 1898 NUC.

ACAD 53:285. Love story in Welch village which moves
through pain to bliss.
LW 29:253. Love and optimism.

009604   UNDER THE THATCH. BY ALLEN RAINE. London:
Hutchinson, 1910 NUC BMC.

TLS-male doctor
LBKM-daughter gives mother an overdose when she asks
to relieve her of terrible and fatal pain.
ATH-but it turns out that she really didn't give an
overdose as she intended.

009605   A WELSH SINGER: A NOVEL. BY ALLEN RAINE.
London: Hutchinson, 1897 BMC. (Am. ed. title: Mifanwy
(A Welsh Singer))

"Artless loves and career of a Welsh shepherdess
turned public singer" SR 84:475.
Her name is Mifanwy. She's very successful in London.
ACAD 52 Fic sup 62. ,
At 15 can't read or write. Leaves home, joins circus.
Friends get her voice training. Meets a young man from
her past now a famous sculptor in London PW 52:328.
Idyllic Welsh life and melodramatic episodes in
London. Heroine a shepardess becomes a popular
contralto. BAKER 03, 167.
Ierian Gwylit and Mifanwy tend sheep. Laissabeth a
"bad" girl is M's rival. Laissabeth is wicked enough
to push sheep over cliff so children will be beaten
for it. M. has a beaut. voice; Ierian carves. M. first
joins circus. Then becomes a great singer. They are
separated while still young. At time of their greatest
artistic achievement reunited. NYT 9-11-97,3.

009606   A WELSH WITCH; A ROMANCE OF ROUGH PLACES.
BY ALLEN RAINE. London: Hutchinson, 1902 BMC. New
York: D. Appleton, 1902 NUC.

009607   WHERE BILLOWS ROLL: A TALE OF THE WELSH
COAST. BY ALLEN RAINE. London: Hutchinson, 1909 BMC.

PUGH, BARBARA TUCKER. United States.

009608   CHRONICLES OF A COUNTRY SCHOOL TEACHER.
Baltimore, Md.: Saulsbury, [c1919] NUC.

PW Story about Indiana school life yrs ago.

PUGH, HELEN PROTHERO (LEWIS). United Kingdom.

009609   AS GOD MADE HER. London: Hutchinson,
[1919] BMC.

Wholly self sacrificing heroine. TLS

009610   HOOKS OF STEEL. London: Hutchinson, 1894

BMC NUC.

SP 72:590. Mad uncle and his niece who converses in
Shakespearean quotations, her two lovers, one a prig,
the other a cad. A naivete of absurdity, laughable yet
likeable.
ACAD 45:286. Romance.

009611   A LADY OF MY OWN. London: Hurst and
Blackett, 1891 BMC.

She marries a miserable man. At end struck by
lightning. SP 67, 104
Wife hurried to grave by politician husband. She's
delicate and sensitive just as her daughter is.
Hyacinth gets similar treatment from her father.
Leaves home when he strikes her. Returns and forgives
after much wandering. ACAD
Opens with much sentiment-gets better ATH 98 349
Persis Shipley, heroine. Struck by lightning in her
own boat on her own lake before she's 20. SR 5-23-91,
627

009612   LOVE AND THE WHIRLWIND: A NOVEL. London:
Hutchinson, 1916 BMC.

TLS-Companion's adventure in family of mother and two
violent but good-hearted sons ends in tragedy. Mother
is feeble minded. One of sons thinks he killed
other--and so does everyone else till end of book.
Dorinda, Wales.
Wild Wales, many characters, much happens, nothing
here. LBKM

009613   THE PEEPSHOW. London: Hutchinson, [1917]
BMC.

Poor relation tries to straighten out lives of her
rich kin. TLS

009614   THE RUDDER AND THE ROCK. London: Hurst
and Blackett, 1907 BMC.

Problem of identity/wooing. TLS

009615   THE SILVER BRIDGE. London: Hutchinson,
1918 BMC.

TLS-romance, inheritance

009616   THRALDOM. London: J. Long, 1903 BMC.

Centers on a child--her dignity, helplessness and
waywardness and a stepmother. Father and nurse can't
protect her. Wicked stepmother's relation to the
organist. ATH 122:310
Mirabel wants to live her own life, get away from
everything, she's "selfish, thoughtless, and
deceitful", at the end she goes the old way--a
particular kind of wickedness. TLS 1903:243

009617   TOBIAS AND THE ANGEL. London: J. Milne,
1908 BMC.

TLS-sentimental love story

009618   THE UNGUARDED TAPER. London: J. Long,
1906 BMC.

TLS-heroine on her own after father's death,
"spiritism."

PULLEN, ELISABETH (JONES). United States.

009619   MR. WHITMAN: A STORY OF THE BRIGANDS.
Boston: Lothrop, [1902] NUC.

NYT 6-14-02

PULLING, J. K. See PULLING, JOAN KING.

PULLING, JOAN KING.

009620   IN LEADING STRINGS. BY J. K. PULLING.
London: Sidgwick and Jackson, 1920 BMC. New York:
Moffat, Yard, 1922 NUC.

TLS-male hero.

PULVER, MARY BRECHT. United States.

009621   THE SPRING LADY. Indianapolis:
Bobbs-Merrill, [c1914] BMC NUC.

PW:86 9/19/14:776. "Rita runs away from the artificial
and luxurious life of New York and from a

busines-engrossed husband to the little village of
Sweethills. Here she meets the village "masher," a
tragic little dressmaker, Cynthia, a sweet young
country girl, and Paul, a poet who makes love to her.
Village gossip dallies with her good name and a New
York acquaintance discovers her retreat, but despite
all Rita finds happiness which her husband is summoned
to share."

PUNCHARD, CONSTANCE (HOLME). 1881-1955. United Kingdom.

009622   BEAUTIFUL END. BY CONSTANCE HOLME.
London: Mills & Boon, [1918] BMC NUC.

TLS-male musician.
Name of a farm. ATH
Daughter-in-law makes an old man absolutely miserable
SR, BAKER 32:245

009623   CRUMP FOLK GOING HOME. BY CONSTANCE
HOLME. London: Mills & Boon, [1913] BMC NUC.

Crump is a stately ancestral home. Young woman engaged
to master of Crump--not out of love, but for love of
the land she feels is hers but has no claim to.
Deborah saved from making this wrong marriage by the
man's death. Comes to love the new master of Crump and
all ends well. LBKM TLS

009624   THE HOMECOMING. BY CONSTANCE HOLME. New
York: R.M. McBride, 1916 NUC.

Story of restless Julian. PW

009625   THE LONELY PLOUGH. BY CONSTANCE HOLME.
London: Mills & Boon, [1914] BMC NUC.

ATH-a land agent, his business and love affairs.
TLS 13:238. Doesn't say anything about the women.

009626   THE OLD ROAD FROM SPAIN. BY CONSTANCE
HOLME. London: Mills & Boon, [1916] BMC NUC.

TLS-family,mystery.

009627   THE SPLENDID FAIRING. BY CONSTANCE HOLME.
London: Mills & Boon, [1919] BMC NUC.

Story of a tenant farming family--then bitterly hard
times. The terrible hatred between the wife &
sister-in law, Sarah & Eliza. TLS

PURDON, K. F. See PURDON, KATHERINE FRANCES.

PURDON, KATHERINE FRANCES. B. 1852. United Kingdom.

009628   DINNY OF THE DOORSTEP. BY K. F. PURDON.
London: T. F. Unwin, 1918 BMC. Dublin: Talbot Press,
1918 NUC BMC.

Irish poor, but no criticism of the system--just wants
us to sympathize "the poor are awfully good to each
other"; one gets used to poverty, etc. TLS
"Brings out strongly the obstacles to genuine sympathy
between people of different classes and the consequent
failure of many well-meant efforts to do good." ATH

009629   THE FOLK OF FURRY FARM. BY K. F. PURDON.
London: J. Nisbet, [1914] BMC NUC.

PW 86 9/5/14:630. "Concerns tight-fisted old Michael
Hefferman's attempt to get him a young wife. A wooing
by proxy, a daylight ghost, the exploits of a cattle
thief go to making up this tale of homely life in an
unspoiled section of Ireland. Michael finds happiness
at last, not as he had expected, but in the
companionship of a little child."
NYT-Furry Farm is down-at-the heels, had once been
great.
LBKM-Furry Farm is down-at-the heels, had once been
great.
SR 147:407. Ireland (Meath).

009630   THE LAUNDRY AT HOME. BY K. F. PURDON.
London: W. Gardner, [1902] BMC NUC.

PURDY, JENNIE BOUTON. Nationality unknown.

009631   THE DARK STRAIN. BY SHUBAEL. London and
New York: Abby Press, [1903] NUC.

PUTNAM, EFFIE DOUGLASS. Nationality unknown.

009632   CIRILLO. New York: Life Publishing Co.,
1903 NUC BMC. London: J. Henderson, 1903 BMC.

PUTNAM, NINA (WILCOX). 1888-1962. United States.

009633   ADAM'S GARDEN; A NOVEL. Philadelphia and
London: J. B. Lippincott, 1916 BMC NUC.

Story of a will and love or salvation. PW
NYT-Adam is principal character a sort of wasteful
vagabond, but heroine is an aeroplane girl.
Preposterous.
TLS-He finds a vacant city lot where he raises flowers
and cultivates humanity.

009634   ESMERALDA; OR EVERY LITTLE BIT HELPS.
Philadelphia and London: J. B. Lippincott, 1918 NUC.

PW-Western woman comes East.

009635   THE IMPOSSIBLE BOY. Indianapolis:
Bobbs-Merrill, [c1913] BMC NUC.

009636   IN SEARCH OF ARCADY. Garden City, New
York: Doubleday, Page, 1912 NUC.

PW-love story
NYT-English earl comes to US in search of a wife and
becomes a gypsy chair peddlar.

009637   IT PAYS TO SMILE. New York: G. H. Doran,
[c1920] NUC.

PW-Freedom Talbot, N. Eng. spinster breaks from the
bonds of her quiet home and tradition in an
unconventional way. Conducts the affairs of her
charge, Peaches, on a Western ranch, tangle of a
criminal mystery.

009638   THE LITTLE MISSIONER. New York and
London: D. Appleton, 1915 BMC NUC.

Girl with ambitions to be a missionary turns to love.
Mod. American love story BKM 41 1915
"Clean, straight, young enthusiast" loves her garden
best TLS

QUEEN OF RUMANIA. See PAULINA ELIZABETH OTTILIA LOUISA,
QUEEN CONSORT OF CHARLES I, KING OF RUMANIA.

QUI, pseud. See LA SELLE, EVELYN.

QUIGLEY, DOROTHY.

009639   TWO OF THE BEST. New York: E. P. Dutton,
[c1901] NUC.

Children's book. NYT

QUILP, JOCELYN.

009640   BARON VERDIGRIS. A ROMANCE OF THE
REVERSED DIRECTION. London: Henry, 1894 BMC NUC.

QUIN, TETH, pseud. See QUINN, ETHEL.

QUINN, E. HARDINGHAM. See SCOTT, PATRICIA ETHEL
(STONEHOUSE).

QUINN, ETHEL. Australia.

009641   THE WELL-SINKERS. AN AUSTRALIAN PASTORAL.
BY TETH QUIN. London: T. F. Unwin, 1899 BMC NUC.

Life in arid regions of Central Australia. Artist
comes and falls in love with the well-sinker's niece,
then he returns to   Paris and dies. Unhappy end. LIT
5:375
Depressing-drought, disaster, death. SP 83:536
Dull, colourless life in a remote station in New So.
Wales. BAKER 03,253

RACSTER, OLGA AND JESSICA GROVE.

009642   THE PHASES OF FELICITY: A NOVEL OF SOUTH
AFRICA. London: G. Allen & Unwin, 1916 BMC NUC.

TLS-roving in S. Africa as 1. teaching music 2.
writing for newspaper 3. loving Bromley.
LBKM 0

RADFORD, DOLLIE. B. 1858.

009643   ONE WAY OF LOVE: AN IDYLL. London: T. F.
Unwin, 1898 BMC NUC.

Sacha is a lonely young woman living with her dull
aunt and uncle. Along comes a man of the world who
seduces her, goes off to someone else and she is "left

to her lost illusions." That's the end of the story.
LIT 4:239.

RADFORD, MRS. C. H.

009644   JENNY OF THE VILLA. London: E. Arnold,
1900 BMC.

ATH 116:612. Politics. Jenny is daughter of a
tradesman.

RADIUS, ANNA (ZUCCARI). 1846-1918.

009645   THE SOUL OF AN ARTIST. San Francisco: P.
Elder, [c1905] NUC. (Tr. from the Italian of Neera
(pseud.) by E. L. Murison.)

RAE, LETTICE MILNE.

009646   MR. SUFFER-LONG. London: R. T. S., [1920]
BMC.

TLS-for young readers

009647   THE STRANGER ON THE AVENTINE. London: Gay
and Hancock, 1913 BMC.

Rome in early Christian days. TLS

RAE, LUCY M.

009648   ADAM STUART. London: Ward, Lock, 1908
BMC.

TLS-character study of male surgeon

009649   THE HEART OF A GREAT MAN. London: F. V.
White, 1903 BMC.

Scientist from whom spy woman tries to discover plans
for Russian Government. ACAD 64:610.

RAE, MRS. MILNE.

009650   A BATTLE IN THE SMOKE; A TALE OF
ANGLO-INDIAN LIFE. London: Hodder and Stoughton,
[1912] BMC.

TLS-India, mixed up love.

009651   BRIDE LORRAINE. London: R.T.S., 1911 BMC.

Romance-TLS
Marries a man she doesn't love (because of father's
dying wish) "having already given her affections to a
rake"; ends happily. ATH

009652   THE WHIPPING BOY. London: Gay and
Hancock, [1914] BMC.

RAFFALOVICH, VERA FRIEDLANDER.

009653   PASSION'S QUEST. London: Selwyn and
Blount, 1920 BMC.

RAFFENSPERGER, ANNA FRANCES. United States.

009654   LED IN UNKNOWN PATHS. New York: T. Y.
Crowell, [1891] NUC.

Semi-rel novel from mother's diary LW

RAGSDALE, LULAH. See RAGSDALE, TALLULAH.

RAGSDALE, TALLULAH. United States.

009655   THE CRIME OF PHILIP GUTHRIE. Chicago:
Morrill, Higgins, 1892 NUC.

PW Dr Guthrie is a specialist in mental diseases. The
heroine, high-spirited, and angry with her lover,
impulsively marries him. What follows is "a strange
and weird study of a singular psychological condition
in both the husband and wife."

009656   MISS DULCIE FROM DIXIE. BY LULAH
RAGSDALE. New York and London: D. Appleton, 1917 BMC
NUC.

Problems between So. women and No. relatives solved;
concerns Dulcie Culpepper and an inheritance PW
Diary. She's a gifted dressmaker and an actress. A
success. Critics praise her. The men love her. NYT
326, 9-2-17

009657   NEXT-BESTERS. BY LULAH RAGSDALE. New

York: C. Scribner's Sons, 1920 NUC.

NYT 7/25/20 p 26. For girls, two young sisters, their
romance, etc. sent.

009658   A SHADOW'S SHADOW. BY LULAH RAGSDALE.
Philadelphia: J. B. Lippincott, 1893 NUC.

Heroine goes on stage because her "furious ardor, her
nervous force, her eating, burning restlessneess found
an outlet only in that great source that serves as a
safety value for so many overcharged natures." CR
14,21:19

RAIMOND, C. E., pseud. See PARKES, ELIZABETH (ROBINS).

RAINE, ALLEN, pseud. See PUDDICOMBE, ANNE ADALIZA (EVANS).

RAIT, JANET ELDER.

009659   ALISON HOWARD. Westminster: H. Constable,
1903 BMC.

ACAD 65,60
Allison inherits a fortune but must earn her own
living for two years and give half her income
thereafter to charity; sees much poverty, works as
clerk in employ. office. LBKM 9-03 220
Difficulties of a class of women who must make their
own living and are unprepared to do so; several poorer
women ATH 122, 310

RAMSAY, RINA. United Kingdom.

009660   BARNABY, A NOVEL. London: Hutchinson,
1910 BMC.

LBKM-Susan impersonates a widow and discovers husband
is alive. Real wife also shows up.
ATH-husband collaborates with her imposture, falls for
her, is not really married.

009661   THE IMPOSSIBLE SHE. London: Constable,
1912 BMC NUC.

TLS-hunting and romance.

009662   THE KEY OF THE DOOR. London: Hutchinson,
1908 BMC.

TLS-retired general is accosted by female who says
she's his wife.
ATH-has he forgotten?

009663   MISS DRUMMOND'S DILEMMA. London: R.
Bentley, 1896 BMC.

LBKM 10:121. Ranee is left with wrong person, a woman
who cares for the mentally afflicted, when her parents
go to India. Ranee becomes engaged and Mrs. Yool warns
fiance of her "condition."
ATH 107:776 Not sensational, pleasant.
SP 77:778. Ranee's mother is insane, her mother and
father are loyal and devoted to each other. Tom
returns to Ranee in spite of Mrs. Yool's warning.

009664   THE STRAW. London: Hutchinson, 1909 BMC.
New York: Macmillan, 1909 NUC.

BKM, 29:1909-married to a brute; somebody shoots him;
tries to reform him (he's involved with another
woman). As she does this she's in love with another
man. Her marriage goes bad; husband knocks her out
with a blow; husband murdered.

009665   THE WAY OF A WOMAN. New York: Dodd, Mead,
1911 NUC.

Actress "plays" the part of a widow whose husband
shows up; they fall for each other. PW 5-13-11.

RAMSDEN, HELEN GUENDOLEN (SEYMOUR). 1846-1910.

009666   SPEEDWELL. BY LADY GUENDOLEN RAMSDEN.
London: R. Bentley, 1894 BMC.

SR 77:557. Attractive widow doing good works in the
London slums thinks herself invulnerable to love until
attractive ego-less young man comes along. But then he
turns to her niece; she has a cruel awakening, but man
gets neither of them.
ACAD 45:287. Little love-story, like Edna Lyall.

RAMSDEN, LADY GUENDOLEN. See RAMSDEN, HELEN GUENDOLEN
(SEYMOUR).

RAMSEY, ALICIA (ROYSTON). 1864-1933. United Kingdom.

009667   THE ADVENTURES OF MORTIMER DIXON. London:
S. Paul, [1913] BMC NUC.

Exciting tale of Chinese intrigue in London told by
newsman. Morty who is "beautiful" in person, loved by
women. He's nearly poisoned.

009668   MISS ELIZABETH GIBBS. London: Mills &
Boon, [1915] BMC NUC.

How she thought it would be delicious to sit in a big
office and be an editor. How she became editor of the
Universe "a magazine for advanced women." Her exper in
the main office, her splendid success. TLS

RAMSEY, OLIVIA.

009669   CALLISTA IN REVOLT. London: J. Long, 1914
BMC.

ATH:Callista is in care of eccentric grandmother and
prim cousin. When grandmother dies, cousin becomes
lively and Callista is left alone.
TLS-Cousin creates a stir by the abandonment of her
stage dancing. Innocuous. Happy close.

009670   THE GIRL FROM GATFORD. London: J. Long,
1909 BMC.

Young girl in her teens "very fascinating and very
'coming on'" and her amorous liaison with a married
man. TLS
Almost incest. ATH

009671   A GIRL OF NO IMPORTANCE. London: J. Long,
1913 BMC.

An Earl falls in love with 16 yr old RC with mystic
powers. A second heroine "who figures as a boy" ATH

009672   THE MARRIAGE OF LIONEL GLYDE. London: J.
Long, 1908 BMC.

TLS-Viola forced by poverty to marry austere Rev.
Glyde, finds satisfaction with Sir Gilbert Lavent.
"not of an improving character -quite the reverse."
SP. Husb. kills himself (why?) and Viola and her lover
live happily ever after.

009673   THE OTHER WIFE. London: J. Long, 1911
BMC.

Pamela Charette refuses to marry man she loves because
he's Roman Catholic, marries instead a pious worldly
man, whose "dead" wife shows up. Later she rescues a
child from gypsies that turns out to be her first
lover's child. "all ends in rapture" TLS

009674   THE ROMANCE OF OLGA AVELING. London: J.
Long, 1910 BMC.

TLS- conv rom.

009675   THE SECRET CALLING. London: J. Long,
[1914] BMC.

ATH Two young women, one loved by an artist, the other
involved in an arranged marriage with a baron.

009676   SYLVIA AND THE SECRETARY. London: J.
Long, 1909 BMC.

Secretary of elderly man has a cativating wife. TLS

009677   TWO MEN AND A GOVERNESS. London: J. Long,
1912 BMC.

TLS she has choice of becoming wife of one man or
mistress of another in Balkan state.
ATH she has choice of becoming wife of one man or
mistress of another in Balkan state.

RAND, JOSEPHINE. United States.

009678   SARDIS AND THE SPIRIT-GUEST: THE STORY OF
A DREAM. New York: E. P. Dutton, 1897 NUC.

RAND, KATHARINE ELLEN. United States.

009679   THE CHILDHOOD OF AN AFFINITY. Boston:
Arena, 1893 NUC.

PW-Relationship between a boy and girl until their
marriage. Psychological study.

RANDALL, MRS. HENRY W.

009680   HACK'S BRAT. BY A. IAN MACLEOD. London:
Hodder & Stoughton, 1916 BMC.

TLS-little girl fathered in mining camp in Australia.
Story of her development, relationship with her father
& career as a singer.
Adopts and marries her. Before this, however, he is
obsessed by training her voice and she breaks off from
him. ATH

RANDLE, LALAH RUTH.

009681   MY MOUNTAIN TOPS, THE ROMANCE OF A
JOURNEY ACROSS THE CANADIAN ROCKIES. New York: Neale
Publishing, 1912 NUC.

RANDOLPH, EVELYN SAINT LEGER (SAVILE). United Kingdom.

009682   THE BLACKBERRY PICKERS. BY EVELYN ST.
LEGER. New York and London: G. P. Putnam's Sons, 1912
BMC NUC.

009683   DAPPER. BY EVELYN ST. LEGER. London:
Christian Knowledge Society, [1908] BMC.

009684   DIARIES OF THREE WOMEN OF THE LAST
CENTURY. EDITED BY EVELYN ST. LEGER. Bristol: J. W.
Arrowsmith, [1907] BMC NUC.

Woman writes to dead lover; her niece and grandniece
marry, are estranged, return to husbands? ACAD
Three generations of women to the modern young lady.
TLS

009685   THE SHAPE OF THE WORLD. BY EVELYN ST.
LEGER. New York and London: G. P. Putnam's Sons, 1912
BMC NUC.

PW- p.o.v. symp to martyr wife who truimphs
ATH-carries hereditary imbecilities into the realism
of farce. Witty.
ACAD-Men are ogres not human. In Javelins family all
men end their lives miserably-hereditary-daughter
breaks thru.
BKM-For ten generations the Javelins have succeeded in
Making miserable the women who married them.
Christopher's father has sulked himself to death
because he could not make his wife jealous. Chris Jr
married to a patient woman repeats pattern until he
falls in a rage, undergoes an operation on his brain
and is cured.
NYT However, Lady Javelin Jr. becomes a successful
playwright.

009686   THE TOLLHOUSE. BY EVELYN ST. LEGER. New
York: E.P. Dutton, [1915] NUC. London: Smith, Elder,
1915 BMC.

Told in 1rst person by a woman in far off country town
of Eng. She encourages enlistment in the war, becomes
a kind of patriotic leader. NYT
Pro-war SP

RANKIN, MARGARET M.

009687   MORAG MACLEAN. A PERTHSHIRE STORY OF
FIFTY YEARS AGO. London: Sunday School Union, [1895]
BMC.

RANSOM, OLIVE, pseud. See STEPHENS, KATE.

RAPHAEL, ALICE PEARL. B. 1887. Nationality Unknown.

009688   THE FULFILLMENT. New York: Sturgis &
Walton, 1910 NUC.

"The heroine is an ardent, brilliant, and
high-spirited girl, who soon after her marriage to a
titled Russian finds herself at odds with a husband of
narrow prejudices and limited views. The interest of
the story centres in her audacious plan of escape from
her unhappiness, the strange experiences that result,
and her final conclusions regarding the obligations of
a wife to her husband and society." BKM 31 1910
Married woman seized with "the modern unrest" leaves
husband and son to pursue artistic ambitions in Paris;
ending drives home old-fashioned morals? PW
NYT-Marries an artist in Paris until her son grows up
finds her, she is spurned by son and husband and sinks
into remorse.

RAPHAEL, MARY F.

009689　　AS CHANCE WOULD HAVE IT. London: Duckworth, 1917 BMC.

Young widow learns husband alive after she remarries; the shock kills her. TLS
Four men offer themselves to waitress in London to rescue her from menial employment and unwelcome attention of a dissolute nobleman. She agrees, chooses one, marries. "Author's point of view is a little old fashioned" in the working out of the story. LBKM.

009690　　PHOEBE MAROON. London: Heath, Cranton and Ouseley, [1914] BMC.

ACAD 86:399. Artist's model, keeps house for him for a time, eventually marries an Irishman.
ATH 143:467. Refuses to marry artist after his wife dies because she believes marriage a barrier to art.

RAU, RENTALA VENKATASUBBA.

009691　　KAMALA'S LETTERS TO HER HUSBAND. Mylapore, Madras: English Publishing House, 1902 BMC NUC.

RAWSON, MAUD STEPNEY.　United Kingdom.

009692　　THE APPRENTICE. London: Hutchinson, 1904 BMC.

LBKM-Hist. Heroine falls thru passion but reviewer said had not the excuse of ignorance and therefore not a victim leaves audience irritated and scandalized.
ATH 0
TLS 0
ACAD-Story of boat builders, his daughter and an apprentice; restoration of the marshes, imminent tragedy near end, does not mention heroine.

009693　　THE EASY GO LUCKIES; OR ONE WAY OF LIVING. London: Methuen, 1908 BMC.

TLS -amusing family party
SR

009694　　THE ENCHANTED GARDEN. London: Methuen, 1907 BMC.

Unhappy marr. woman goes to Spain to escape her husband's infidelities, falls in love at the first opportunity. Her husband shoots him. the pryings and probings of a woman's soul sympathetically told. ACAD
Joanna Hurst at 35 SP

009695　　HAPPINESS. London: Methuen, 1909 BMC.

Stella Marcett's image "smirched" because of a passionate love scene. There are several other passionate scenes. TLS.
"Sex-problems are handled with candour" ATH

009696　　JOURNEYMAN LOVE. London: Hutchinson, 1902 BMC.

ATH 6-7-02-hist. novel.

009697　　THE LABOURER'S COMEDY. London: A. Constable, 1905 BMC NUC.

Brave Pamela is a journalist, supports her inventor husband. But her strength gives out. As does her deep belief in her husband's ultimate success; the hopes, joys, sorrows. ACAD 1361,05
A friend saves them-financially.
TLS- Young couple, financially reversed, he an inventor, she goes to work on a group of women's papers, she is courageous, spirited.

009698　　A LADY OF THE REGENCY. BY MRS. STEPNEY RAWSON. London: Hutchinson, 1900 BMC. New York: Harper, 1901 NUC.

PW 2-23-01
Unhappy Princess of wales-faithful to unfaithful husband, alien in her adopted land. Another character-June is strong and bright realizes her love was childish; good character study of women characters as well as hist. period. NYT 01
LBKM 18:127. Historical romance. regency, 1800-1820. Queen Charlotte, Princess Charlotte, Princess Caroline. June Cherier is the heroine, who comes from a Yorkshire home to London, becomes attached to the Court and finds herself surrounded by intrigue. Caroline Amelia Elizabeth, Queen Consort of George IV, 1768-1821-fic.

009699　　THE MAGIC GATE. London: Hutchinson, 1917 BMC.

Study of a provincial Eng. community during the war. TLS
Jennet extremely self possessed woman. She becomes acting mgr. of an amazing American "Lady Paramount." She comes to the village to manage the Lady's estate. She wrestles with the village problems. Reviewer interprets her as symbol of Eng. TLS
"Driven along all the time in top gear" ATH.

009700　　MORLAC OF GASCONY. London: Hutchinson, 1915 BMC NUC.

Trad hist rom. TLS

009701　　THE PRICELESS THING. London: S. Paul, [1914] BMC NUC.

LBKM-rom. myst. Heroine applies for position of librarian in cousin's country mansion exciting tale.
ACAD 86:627. She is librarian. Combination of a detective story, love story, ghost story.
TLS 13:249

009702　　SPLENDID ZIPPORAH. London: Methuen, 1911 BMC.

Zipporah Londesbury musician, tours, teaches, free lances, runs the Londesbury orchestra; conducts her own orchestra TLS
After going into Society, she wearies of it "with some daring companions started forth to seek an independent living." author's "consciousness of feminine emancipation" ATH.
" A most ungentle giantess" "the woman artist on her own who finds art and professional ambition not all sufficing" SR
Zipporah Londesbury, a tall handsome young musician wants to conduct an orchestra and achieves her purpose. She also goes up in a Suffragist's baloon, a deed of great courage. LBKM
She is 6'2", whistles, sleeps on floor, is gawkey. her room at college is like a man's. virtuoso of cello. At 25 goes out on world tour. Meets a feminist . Very positive portrayal of feminist. Becomes music teacher, rebuffs offer of marr. her art makes her avoid ties. She Conducts orchestra, has second friend-a male "comrade". Interest in Commadine mostly musical-has a voice. At end he must reach top to be equal to her. Whole music career shown. "I am Eng. I can play the cello and bass well, the piano a little, the horn tolerably. The clarinet fairly, the viola a bit, the oboe ditto and the drums. I have some acquaintance with the flute; the bassoon I am now studying and I can conduct a band." (Book)

009703　　TALES OF RYE TOWN. London: A. Constable, 1905 BMC NUC.

009704　　THE THREE ANARCHISTS. London: S. Paul, [1912] BMC NUC.

ATH i.e., love, birth & death and their influence on a young wife. Married to a bleak and sordid man. She is too patient. Psych study Tragedy.
SP-Plucky heroine married to and released from a curmudgeon. Dreary but good work in this study.

009705　　THE WATERED GARDEN. London: S. Paul, [1913] BMC NUC.

How the heroine Bettina Gale arranges a garden and a home for a "socially pushing employer" SP ATH
Light Comedy of manners-of a garden, polite love affairs, aeroplane. The kind of men and women we know. LBKM
Bettina's career from time she becomes a secretary-gardener to her own inheritance of the house of her employer. The story is just that, an account of her very busy whirlwind of a life. TLS

RAWSON, MRS. STEPNEY.　See RAWSON, MAUD STEPNEY.

RAY, ANNA CHAPIN.　1865-1945.　United States.

009706　　ACKROYD OF THE FACULTY. Boston: Little, Brown, 1907 NUC.

Story of a professor with a poor social background, PW 4-13-07
Daughter of department chairman, Connie Everest, and a young professor in department -Ackroyd. NYT

009707　　THE BRENTONS. London: W.J. Ham-Smith,

1912 BMC. Boston: Little, Brown, 1912 BMC NUC.

PW-he is a minister but cannot reconcile scientific
and religious principles; she is shallow, selfish,
socially ambitious.

009708   THE BRIDGE BUILDERS. Boston: Little,
Brown, 1909 NUC.

Mother's jealousy of her daughter. PW 2-20-09
Jessica risks her life to save a young engineer as old
bridge falls. BKM
Gay, unconventional,capable, careless of her
appearance. NYT

009709   BY THE GOOD SAINTE ANNE; A STORY OF
MODERN QUEBEC. Boston: Little, Brown, 1904 NUC.

PW-St. Anne de Beaupre love story?
NYT-0

009710   THE DOMINANT STRAIN. Boston: Little,
Brown, 1903 BMC NUC.

Mistake a woman makes in trying to change a man after
marriage. Cotton Mather. Historical 6-6-03 PW
Should a woman marry a man who has inherited the
appetite for drink; does and has troubles. NYT 03 409

009711   EACH LIFE UNFULFILLED. Boston: Little,
Brown, 1899 NUC.

Tom Heaton is blind, struck just at the point when he
shows great promise as an author. He loves Elinor but
once he's blind feels he can't ask for her love in
return. So she doesn't know the conflict in him.
Becomes his friend and comrade, loves his cousin, but
is also unfulfilled. BKM 9:378.
She is studying for a career in music. A vivid picture
is given of her debut as a singer. PW 55:616
Elinor Tiemann. Hero blinded, separated from woman he
loves, but becomes a strong fine human being. Heroine
"of the spiritually blind who know not their own
defect." NYT 4-15-99,246

009712   HEARTS AND CREEDS. Boston: Little, Brown,
1906 BMC NUC.

PW-disastrous marriage between Protestant & Catholic.
NYT-Arline's ambitions for a salon come close to
wrecking her husband's and brother's careers?

009713   NATHALIE'S CHUM. Boston: Little, Brown,
1902 NUC. London: H.Frowde, 1909 BMC.

009714   NATHALIE'S SISTER, THE LAST OF THE
MCALISTER RECORDS. Boston: Little, Brown, 1904 NUC.
London: H. Frowde, 1910 BMC.

009715   ON BOARD THE BEATIC. Boston: Little,
Brown, 1913 NUC. Toronto: McClelland & Goodchild, 1913
BMC.

"Romance of a trip across the Atlantic, with a London
and Belgium background as well. A middle-aged Captain
of industry, Carl Clode, and Aileen Warbarton, a
self-assured, independent woman of thirty-two, are the
principals, but there are other characters, each with
a distinct personality. Aileen Warburton believes that
her freedom is the greatest thing in life to her, but
learns that loneliness and so-called freedom often go
together and there is something better and greater for
her. By author of The Brentons." PW
Reached 32 without marrying, thinks so exceedingly
well of herself that she has doubts about allowing
anybody to stand with her at the apex of her world.
NYT
Romance of a self-assured, independent woman of
thirty-two and a middle-aged captain. NYT 1913,202

009716   ON THE FIRING LINE; A ROMANCE OF SOUTH
AFRICA. Boston: Little, Brown, 1905 NUC.

South African War-1899-1902
Love and combat: Boer war,

009717   OVER THE QUICKSANDS. Boston: Little,
Brown, 1910 NUC.

Donald & Hilda (cousins) visit Quebec, make friends.
There's a tragedy(?) but a happy end. PW
NYT-0.

009718   QUICKENED. Boston: Little, Brown, 1908
NUC.

PW-male hero saved by Catholicism.
BKM-male hero saved by Catholicism.

009719   SIDNEY: HER SENIOR YEAR. Boston: Little,
Brown, 1910 NUC.

College senior: delightful times. PW

009720   TEDDY: HER DAUGHTER. A SEQUEL TO TEDDY:
HER BOOK. Boston: Little, Brown, 1901 BMC NUC. London:
H. Frowde, 1911 BMC.

009721   URSULA'S FRESHMAN. Boston: Little, Brown,
1903 NUC.

Quick tempered. Her cousin is the Yale freshman? PW
10-17-03.

009722   A WOMAN WITH A PURPOSE. Boston: Little,
Brown, 1911 NUC. London: S. Paul, [1911] BMC.

Dorcas Sloane, graduate of Smith, refuses to marry
till she makes something of herself. PW 2-18-11.
Becomes a novelist, marries, is estranged from her
husband, who treats her like a plaything. ATH
Heroine a fine creature capable of furious temper.
Fails as writer, marries a man with whom she's
unhappy. All ends in perfect reconciliation. Tried to
support herself by her pen and in failing retained her
high ideals and her respect for her own opinions. NYT

RAY, MAUDE MASSEY. United States.

009723   LILLIAN AND LUCILE: A NOVEL. Atlanta,
Ga.: Franklin Print. and Pub. Co., 1899 NUC.

RAYMOND, EMMA FRANCES HARMON. United States.

009724   A ROMANCE OF NEW MEADOWS. Lewiston,
Maine: Lewiston Journal Co., 1900 NUC.

RAYMOND, EVELYN (HUNT). 1843-1910.

009725   AMONG THE LINDENS. Boston: Little, Brown,
1898 NUC.

PW Young woman struggles against poverty in New York
City flat. Rescue of an old man leads to "ideal
existence among the lindens."

009726   THE BRASS BOUND BOX. Boston: Dana Estes,
[c1905] NUC.

009727   A DAUGHTER OF THE FOREST. Philadelphia:
Penn Publishing, 1902 NUC.

009728   THE DOINGS OF NANCY. Boston: D. Estes,
[1904] NUC.

009729   AN HONOR GIRL. Boston: Lee and Shepard,
1904 NUC.

PW-having won a scholarship to college, she must
return home to help family.

009730   JESSICA TRENT: HER LIFE ON A RANCH.
London: Shurmer Sithrop, [1902] BMC. New York and
London: Street and Smith, [1902] NUC.

009731   THE SUN MAID; A STORY OF FORT DEARBORN.
London: J. M. Dent, 1900 BMC. New York: E. P. Dutton,
[c1900] NUC.

Story of a woman raised by Indians-ATH 2-23-01. Lives
to be 100.

RAYMOND, FRANCES. United States.

009732   MAYLOU. New York: G. W. Dillingham, 1898
NUC BMC.

PW-woman who is mistress to man and fond of luxury and
amusement. Meets a man who believes her pure; on the
eve of their marriage her past is revealed. Rest of
book devoted to her repentance.

RAYNER, E. See RAYNER, EMMA.

RAYNER, EMMA. D. 1926. United States.

009733   THE DILEMMA OF ENGELTIE; THE ROMANCE OF A
DUTCH COLONIAL MAID. Boston: L. C. Page, 1911 NUC.
London: Cassell, 1912 BMC.

TLS-historical romance

009734   DORIS KINGSLEY, CHILD AND COLONIST. New
York: G. W. Dillingham, [1901] NUC. London: T. F.
Unwin, 1901 BMC.

PW 10-26-01.

009735   FREE TO SERVE; A TALE OF COLONIAL NEW
YORK. BY E. RAYNER. Boston: Copeland and Day, 1897
NUC. London & Boston: G. P. Putnam, 1900 BMC.

N. Y. early 18th, hist. rom. The lives of two brothers
and the handmaid who is "free to serve but not to
plight her troth till the end." PW 52:741.
Brother and sister leave ancestral home in Eng. to
seek their fortunes in US. He's a no good who has run
up debts and she saves him from prison. When they get
to New York, Aveline must go into service as a
bondswoman to pay their passage. Sold for five years
to a Dutch family who are fond of her. The two sons
love her. Aveline Nevard loves one. Ends in happy
coupling. BKM 6:357.
CR 32:265. Heroine, an 18th c. gentlewoman, is brought
by circumstances to the position of bond-servant on
the plantation of a Dutch patroon in New York.
NYT 1898:415 New York during colonial times. STory of
an indentured servant, actually a slave.
    ATH 2-2-01
N. Y. (City)-hist-fic

009736   HANDICAPPED AMONG THE FREE. New York:
Dodd, Mead, 1903 NUC BMC. London: Hodder and
Stoughton, 1903 BMC.

PW aBout a black man 3-31-03.
LBKM 1903; 52
ATH 122:478

009737   IN CASTLE AND COLONY. Chicago: H. S.
Stone, 1899 NUC BMC.

Historical fiction. Swedish colony in U.S. 1641 in
Delaware. Agneta Botorpa finds happiness and freedom
for which she and mother left Sweden. LW 30:267
Agneta had been engaged since she was five, but when
father gone, her mother objects to the
arrangement--Agneta by now is 18. Mother and daughter
go to U.S. Agneta has two fine suitors one of whom
sacrifices himself in war for the other. BKM 9:186
Settlement of Swedes and Finns in Delaware. NYT
8-5-99,515

009738   VISITING THE SIN: A TALE OF MOUNTAIN LIFE
IN KENTUCKY AND TENNESSEE. Boston: Small, Maynard,
1900 NUC BMC. London: G.P. Putnam's Sons, 1901 BMC.

NYT 1900:864. Savagery of mountain life. Naomi is
heroine.

RAYTHORNE, VALERIE.

    009739   THE MYSTERY OF RUSHBROOKE. London: Digby,
    Long, 1912 BMC.

RE, LUCY. See BARTLETT, LUCY RE.

REA, ALICE.

    009740   DALEFOLK. London: Hurst and Blackett,
    1895 BMC NUC.

    Cumberland country-thorough and intimate knowledge of
    its life. The old superstitions of this mountain area.
    Half mad parson appeals to curse and the victim of it
    turns out to be his best friend. SP 74:616
    Concerns two generations. Curse laid upon one, removed
    in the next. ACAD 47:233

REA, HOPE.

    009741   THE POSSESSION OF ELIZABETH. A TALE.
    London: A. Treherne, 1902 BMC.

REA, LORNA. United Kingdom.

    009742   SIX MRS. GREENES. New York: Harper, 1919
    PW. London: W. Heinemann, 1929 BMC.

    "Analysis and contrasts with irony and pleasant humor.
    6 women all wives or widows and members of one family,
    from old Mrs. Greene, all but bedridden though still
    active in mind, to the latest married of her
    grandchildren." BAKER 32 401

READ, GEORGIA WILLIS. United States.

    009743   MEDOC IN THE MOOR. Boston: Sherman,

French, 1914 NUC.

PW:86 9/19/14:776 "A Brenton romance. Terese, the
courageous and strong hearted old peasant woman, the
real heroine of the tale, through the alchemy of her
unselfishness, changes a deepest sorrow into happiness
for the others. Anton, Louise, Gabriel, the
millionairess (with her broad acres and old
bonnets)-all the village bring their tangles, good and
bad, to Terese, who sets them right again. Monsieur
and Mademoiselle themselves would have made a sorry
enough affair of their love but for her."
NYT-Terese is most important character, an innkeeper.
Breton village.

READ, MRS. CARTER.

    009744   HIS WIFE'S SISTER. London: J. Long, 1915
    BMC.

    Millionaire marries one sister, then the other. TLS
    Self sacrifice of sister who gives her skin to her
    brother--he needs grafting. ATH

READE, AMYE. Nationality Unknown.

    009745   SLAVES OF THE SAWDUST. London: F. V.
    White, 1892 NUC BMC. New York: J. W. Lovell, [c1892]
    NUC.

    LW 23:245. Descriptions of tortures young children go
    through to fit them for performances.
    ATH 99:338. Exploitation of children in circus life.

READE, MRS. R. H.

    009746   THE GOLDSMITH'S WARD: A TALE OF LONDON
    CITY IN THE FIFTEENTH CENTURY. London: Chapman and
    Hall, 1891 BMC NUC.

READER, EMILY E. Nationality Unknown.

    009747   PRIESTESS AND QUEEN: A TALE OF THE WHITE
    RACE OF MEXICO. BEING THE ADVENTURES OF IGNIGENE AND
    HER TWENTY-SIX FAIR MAIDENS. London, New York:
    Longmans, Green, 1899 BMC NUC.

    Written in blank verse. LIT 4:528.
    The perils of Indigene and her 26 fair maidens, their
    captivity and their deaths. Inigigene of the white race
    in Mexico was an ideal queen. Somehow some men's suits
    are found and the women won't dally with equipment not
    their own. Review says this court is therefore no
    place for New Women. SR 88:241.

REANEY, ISABEL (EDIS). B. 1847. Nationality Unknown.

    009748   CLAUD DARREL'S HEIR. London: R.T.S.,
    [1910] BMC.

    009749   A DAUGHTER'S INHERITANCE. London: Heath,
    Cranton and Ouseley, [1913] BMC.

    ATH-Inherited weakness for strong drink. Degraded by
    the habit. Is spirited and has good intentions, story
    is of her efforts to obtain a living without a
    character and regain her self-control.

    009750   DR. GREY'S PATIENT: A NOVEL. London:
    Bliss, 1893 BMC.

    Young beautiful woman rushes about the country alone,
    faces many perils, the worst from the "libertine
    propensities of an individual who eventually turns out
    to be her father." Glory St. Clair. SP 71, 772.
    Heroine has a mother who is an alcoholic, finds
    salvation at a mission service. 76 SR 681.
    The doctor celebrating his silver wedding anniversary
    is called to deliver a child and asked to kill it by
    the father. The child Glory St. Clair "put off," grows
    up not knowing parents. Complicatins. ACAD 44:435.
    She was a Nurse (Glory) ATH 102:657

    009751   THE FACE AT THE WINDOW. Glasgow: Scottish
    Temperance League, [1900] BMC.

    009752   GLADYS' VOW. A STORY OF TODAY. London: J.
    Clarke, 1892 BMC.

    009753   MOLLY BROWN, A GIRL IN A THOUSAND.
    London: R.T.S., [1909] BMC.

    009754   POOR MRS. EGERTON; A STUDY IN ATMOSPHERE.
    London: Cranton & Ouseley, [1914] BMC.

    ATH-life in a small community of widowed women in

reduced circumstances.

009755   THE ROMANCE OF AN EMERGENCY. London: H.J. Drane, [1901?] BMC NUC.

ATH-1-25-02

009756   UNDER ORDERS; NOT HIS OWN MASTER. BY MRS. G. S. REANEY. Chicago: Advance Pub. Co., 1900 NUC. London: C. J. Thynne, 1900 BMC.

PW-young missionary. Tierra del Fugo. Gives up girl he loves when she makes it a question of choice between her and his work.

009757   UNTIL CLAIMED. London: R. T. S., [1913] BMC.

REANEY, MRS. G. S. See REANEY, ISABEL (EDIS).

REBBECK, MRS. ELIZABETH. See REBEK, LILLIE.

REBEK, LILLIE.

009758   THE HOME OF THE DRAGON, A TONQUINESE IDYLL TOLD IN SEVEN CHAPTERS. BY ANNA CATHARINA. London: T. Unwin, 1893 BMC NUC.

009759   THE STRAGGLERS; A TALE OF PRIMAL ASPERITIES. BY MRS. ELIZABETH REBBECK (ANNA CATHARINA). London: F. Griffiths, 1910 BMC NUC.

TLS-study of a marriage.
ATH-From a woman's p.o.v. in a "man's country." Mary Faire "carries on the battle;" Hetty Culver gives in. SP

REDDEN, HELEN PINKERTON.

009760   M'CLELLAN OF M'CLELLAN. London: Bliss, 1895 BMC.

A man and a woman love but don't believe the other loves in return. The young man an orphan turns out to be a laird. The young woman becomes a successful painter. And all goes well. ACAD 47:312
The fate of a large family of a Scot farmer, but women characters most interesting. ATH 103:373

REDFIELD, MARTIN, pseud. See BROWN, ALICE.

REDFORD, ELIZABETH ADAMSON. United States.

009761   NEITHER DO I. New York: B'Way, 1911 NUC.

Changes the legend of Mary Magdeline; is duped by Prince Herod; thinks he'll marry her; "when she leaves the palace, it is to become Mary of Magdala." NYT

REDGRAVE, SUSAN.

009762   JANE'S HUSBAND; OR, TWO IN A CARAVAN. London: S. Low, [1916] BMC.

TLS-love story. ATH

REDIC, MARGARET, pseud. See LYONS, MARGARET REDIC.

REDWOOD, ETHEL BOVERTON.

009763   WANDERINGS AND WOOINGS EAST OF SUEZ. London: J. Long, 1913 BMC.

Young woman and her aunt travel in far east. She finds love and happiness. ATH
To Far East and back. LBKM

REED, CARMEN. United States.

009764   THE KNIGHTS OF THE SILVER STAR. New York: Guild Pub. Concern, [c1897] NUC.

REED, FANNIE KIMBALL. B. 1870. United States.

009765   A CHOPIN NOCTURNE, AND OTHER SKETCHES. Cleveland: Privately Printed For Author, 1900 NUC.

REED, FLORIDA PRESLEY. United States.

009766   VESTA; OR, THE HIDDEN CROSS. Atlanta, Ga.: Foote and Davies, 1894 NUC.

REED, HELEN LEAH. 1860(?)-1926. United States.

009767   BRENDA'S WARD: A SEQUEL TO "AMY IN ACADIA". Boston: Little, Brown, 1906 NUC.

PW-young wife takes care of lovable girl.

009768   MISS THEODORA: A WEST END STORY. Boston: R. G. Badger, 1898 NUC.

NYT 1898:50. Impecunious aunt of fine old family and her nephew, a romance. She is snubbed by Brahmin relatives, he doesn't go to Harvard, marries a Western girl. They all move to Denver. Aunt is happy there.
LW 29:371. A "still life" on the order of Cranford. Quiet, uneventful, realistic environment, individuals, West End in Boston.

009769   NAPOLEON'S YOUNG NEIGHBOR. Boston: Little, Brown, 1907 NUC.

Historical romance for young people. PW 11-2-07

REED, LAURA (COATES). United States.

009770   WEST AND EAST; AN ALGERIAN ROMANCE. Chicago: C. H. Sergel, [1892] NUC.

PW-Love story on shipboard.

REED, MYRTLE. See MACCULLOUGH, MYRTLE (REED).

REESE, ALICE. United States.

009771   HURRAH FOR AMERICA: A TALE OF WELSH LIFE. Dayton, Ohio: U.S. Pub. House, 1898 NUC.

REESE, CARA. United States.

009772   "AND SHE GOT ALL THAT!" WOMAN'S SPHERE IN LIFE'S BATTLE. New York: F. H. Revell, 1897 NUC.

LW 29:205--Wife of working-man husband is dissatisfied; leaves husband to study nursing. By this she is almost entirely " weaned" from husband and home, goes abroad as nurse companion. Her only child dies, her husband badly injured in mill accident. She returns home to care for him and reunites in a "chastened life and mended home."

REEVE, KATHARINE ROOSEVELT. United States.

009773   COVERT-SIDE COURTSHIP. Philadelphia: J.B. Lippincott, 1909 NUC.

She races her own horse, has two lovers, one who at first thought she was a boy. PW

REEVES, AMBER. See WHITE, AMBER (REEVES) BLANCO.

REEVES, HELEN BUCKINGHAM (MATHERS). 1853-1920. United Kingdom.

009774   BAM WILDFIRE. A CHARACTER SKETCH. BY HELEN MATHERS. London: T. Burleigh, 1898 BMC NUC.

ACAD 53:681. Bam is heroine. "Treats of the fringe of society in a tone to which the bookstall censor can hardly take exception."

009775   BECKY. BY HELEN MATHERS. London: C. A. Pearson, 1900 BMC.

SP 84:526. "Glorification of robust and bibulous virility." Picture of a pioneer and empire builder, Africa.
ATH 115:525. Youthful heroine and her friends, modern slang.
ACAD 58:450. "Though very high-spirited, she is one of the many women who enjoy being beaten by the right man."

009776   CINDERS. A NOVEL. London: C.A. Pearson, 1901 BMC NUC.

How the women do talk, with vehemence, slang. What freedom! ATH 5-18-01

009777   DAVID LYALL'S LOVE STORY. BY THE AUTHOR OF THE "THE LAND O' THE LEAL" [ANONYMOUS]. London: Hodder and Stoughton, 1897 NUC BMC. Toronto: Copp Clark, 1898 BMC.

ACAD 53:3. Love for Euphan and the winning of her. Journalism. He is "grave, mildly humorous, and pious." ACAD 53:202. Scotch journalist in London. He and his editor are too good; love is in background.
ATH 111:532. Focus is on Scotch folk in London, a study in "Scotch pathos."

009778   DIMPLES. London: Simpkin, Marshall, 1903
BMC.

009779   THE FACE IN THE MIRROR AND OTHER STORIES.
London: Digby, Long, 1903 BMC.

009780   THE FERRYMAN. London: Methuen, 1905 BMC.

Euthanasia ATH 05,366

009781   GAY LAWLESS. BY HELEN MATHERS. London: S.
Paul, 1908 BMC NUC.

TLS-passion of heroine for racing, horses etc.
SR- love story
BKM-0

009782   GRIFF OF GRIFFITHSCOURT. BY H. MATHERS.
London: Methuen, 1903 BMC NUC.

Couple "eating each other...like delicate cake."
sentimental ACAD 65, 212
Dan (a woman) watches over her sister; she's a wilful
tom-boy, strong and purposeful story contains an
unpleasant, nasty incident. LBKM, 10-03, 53
ATH-"out of taste" "much to dislike" 122, 610

009783   "HONEY". BY HELEN MATHERS. London:
Methuen, 1902 BMC NUC.

ACAD-"rebel against all that is conventional"
ATH 9-20-02 might pass for a novel of the 60's but
does not have vigor of Miss Broughton, etc. Not
amusing, dons male attire.

009784   THE JUGGLER AND THE SOUL. BY HELEN
MATHERS. London: Skeffington, 1896 BMC.

The spiritual side of a good man transformed into "the
bad, dead Jasper." "revolting" "incredible." Ninga is
allied to a "worse than living death." She makes a
second marriage to a scientific man (Sabine) who
brings an animal back to life. Lots of preaching and
protesting. SP 78:552
Anglo-Indian young woman Ninga left by father in care
of a scientist who can bring the dead to life. He and
his two students vie for Ninga's love. ATH 109:44

009785   LOVE, THE THIEF. BY HELEN MATHERS.
London: S. Paul, 1909 BMC NUC.

Kit Mallory is bright, flippant but mostly detective
murder story. LBKM
"shocker" "passionately unconventional people" ATH

009786   THE LOVELY MALINCOURT; A NOVEL. BY HELEN
MATHERS. London: Jarrold, 1895 BMC. Chicago: C. H.
Seigel, 1899 NUC.

Lesley Malincourt plays havoc with men's hearts until
Major Kilcurry. He fights a duel for her. ACAD 48:243
Lives in country, sent by father to London to see how
bad it is so she'll come home and marry a squire. But
she meets a handsome, intelligent Major in Lond. ATH
106:286
SP 76:556. Daughter, unmanageable, is sent to London
by father, he thinking a little neglect will bring her
around. She, being very beautiful, extends her field
of suitors and becomes more unmanageable than ever.

009787   A MAN OF TO-DAY. A NOVEL. BY HELEN
MATHERS. London: F. V. White, 1894 BMC. Philadelphia:
J. B. Lippincott, 1894 NUC.

SR 77:615. Old-fashioned. Slangy young people and
moralizing.
CR-romance.
PW-hero is a Russian fatalist and pessimist. Story
deals with Dennison family and Easter, whose life is
"spoiled by the man of today."

009788   MY JO, JOHN: A NOVEL. BY HELEN MATHERS.
London: F. V. White, 1891 BMC. New York: J. W. Lovell,
[1891] NUC.

Colonel and Mrs. John Andrews have a serious
misunderstanding-Married 20 years. Pleasant and
readable. ACAD
Separate, go separate ways, reunite. CR 17:19

009789   PIGSKIN AND PETTICOAT. BY HELEN MATHERS.
London: E. Nash, 1907 BMC. Leipzig: B. Tauchnitz, 1907
NUC.

Much femininity-TLS

009790   THE REBEL. BY HELEN MATHERS. New York: A.
E. Cluett, 1896 NUC. M. Kenner and Golberg, 1896 BS.

009791   "SIDE-SHOWS". London: Simpkin, Marshall,
1904 BMC.

009792   THE SIN OF HAGAR. London: Hutchinson,
1896 BMC NUC.

ATH 107:775. Hagar, a hypnotic medium had been
"utilized" by her father until she loathed him. After
his mysterious murder she moved into home of Lord
Straubenzee and his impressionable daughter Nadege.
Mischief followed; Hager used hypnotic power on her.
Romance.
ACAD 50:95 She attempted to gain the love of Will
Cassilis, married, through her powers. Finally kills
herself. "More sinned against than sinning." father
dehumanized her.

009793   A STUDY OF A WOMAN; OR VENUS VICTRIX. A
NOVEL. BY HELEN MATHERS. London: F. V. White, 1893
BMC.

Analysis of the character of an introspective person,
who, under the tension of keen suffering and
suspicion, imagines herself guilty of a crime which
she neither conceived nor compassed. ACAD 43:262

009794   TALLY HO! BY HELEN MATHERS. London:
Methuen, 1906 BMC NUC.

ACAD--horse, heroine, marriage etc

009795   T'OTHER DEAR CHARMER; A NOVEL. BY HELEN
MATHERS. London: F. V. White, [1892] BMC. New York: J.
W. Lovell, [c1892] NUC.

CR 7-16-92. Traditional romance

009796   VENUS VICTRIX, A STUDY OF A WOMAN. BY
HELEN MATHERS. New York: U. S. Book, [1892] NUC.
London: F. V. White, 1893 BMC. (Eng. Ed. title: A
Study of a Woman; or Venus Victrix, a Novel.)

009797   WHAT THE GLASS TOLD: A NOVEL. London: F.
V. White, 1893 BMC. Leipzig: B. Tauchnitz, 1893 NUC.
(Leipzig ed. bound with A Study of a Woman,)

Fr. man loves married woman but doesn't try to seduce
her. ACAD 44:270

REEVES, HELEN BUCKINGHAM (MATHERS).   See Also LYALL, DAVID
[pseud.].

REEVES, MRS. E. M.   United States.

009798   UNDER THE STARS AND STRIPES. Castalia, S.
Dak.: Published By Author, 1891 NUC.

REEVES, MRS. S. K.   Nationality Unknown.

009799   DONALD PATTERSON'S DAUGHTER.
Philadelphia: American Sunday School Union, 1893 NUC.

She's Helen, born in humble town in the West where her
father is minister. A record of his good work there
and her development. PW 10-14-93.

REICHARDT, ANNIE.

009800   GIRL-LIFE IN THE HAREM; A TRUE ACCOUNT OF
GIRL-LIFE IN ORIENTAL CLIMES. London: J. Ouseley, 1908
BMC NUC.

"not to tell a sensational tale but to delineate
faithfully a Moslem interior and a few months of
girl-life in a Damascus harem. As I myself have known
it." Author's statement about her novel. TLS

REID, CHRISTIAN, pseud. See TIERNAN, FRANCES CHRISTINE
(FISHER).

REID, ELIZABETH.

009801   GEORGE MARKHAM. A ROMANCE OF THE WEST.
London: Sonnenschein, 1898 BMC.

ACAD 55:548. Sensational, sentimental romance of the
West.
Young man weds elderly adventuress and is wretched
ever after. SP 83:280.

REID, SYBIL BEATRICE.

009802   MY DEAR GRENADIER. London: J. Macqueen,

1896 BMC.

SR-Is a 6'1" heroine; her death clears the way for the minor heroine's (the narrator), marriage.
ACAD 49:424. The narrator, Patricia, has 7 brothers. A number of them are devoted to Beatrice, the grenadier, as Patricia is herself. Patricia acts heroically in regard to Edward, to whom Beatrice is engaged. "homely, gossiping narrative".

009803   SWEET PEAS: AN EVERYDAY STORY. London: Remington, 1894 BMC.

REIFSNIDER, ANNA CYRENE (PORTER). 1850-1932. United States.

009804   BETWEEN TWO WORLDS. BY MRS. CALVIN KRYDER REIFSNIDER. St. Louis: A. C. Reifsnider Book Co., 1897 NUC.

009805   RUBY GLADSTONE; OR, A RETURN TO EARTH. St. Louis: A. C. Reifsnider Book Co., 1893 W.

009806   UNFORGIVEN. St. Louis, Mo.: A. C. Reifsnider Book Co., [c1893] NUC.

Julia Hudson is a very gifted woman. "The author seems to have aimed to prove through her that a woman's greatest happiness is found in congenial work." PW 6-10-93.

REIFSNIDER, MRS. CALVIN KRYDER. See REIFSNIDER, ANNA CYRENE (PORTER).

REIMENSNYDER, HELEN. See MARTIN, HELEN (REIMENSNYDER).

REMICK, GRACE MAY.

009807   JANE STUART, COMRADE. Philadelphia: Penn, 1916 NUC.

Slight story of friendship between women. PW

RENELL, KATHARINE.

009808   SHIBBOLETH! THE STORY OF A MISTAKE. London: Digby, Long, [1897] BMC.

RENNIE, ELIZABETH WHITAKER.

009809   A FIERY SWORD. New York and London: Abbey, [1902] NUC BMC.

ATH-the theme sustains the fallacy of a platonic affection between those "unevenly yoked." Subject is handled in a "daring and masterly manner."

RENNISON, RENNIE.

009810   GEORGE'S GEORGINA. London: Simpkin, Marshall, 1905 BMC.

009811   MIXED RELATIONSHIPS. London: Simpkin, Marshall, 1905 BMC.

RENO, ITTI (KINNEY). B. 1862. United States.

009812   AN EXCEPTIONAL CASE: A NOVEL. Philadelphia: J. B. Lippincott, 1891 NUC.

Father tries to marry off daughter for business reasons. But the suitor insults her so she won't have him. Therefore, he ruins the father's business. Also shoots himself in her sight so that the world will learn what she's done and no one will wed her. PW 3-2-91.
Heroine wants most to paint. Offered in marriage, refuses, devotes life to painting. CR

RENSINK, MRS. J. W. United States.

009813   THE WORLD'S FAIREST; OR, TRUE HEARTS AT HOME. Chicago: Donohue, Henneberry, [c1893] NUC.

REPPLIER, AGNES. 1855-1950. United States.

009814   IN OUR CONVENT DAYS. New York: Houghton, Mifflin, 1905 NUC. London: A. Constable, 1905 BMC.

Sketches, recollections of girl's school. NYT 1905:797

REUSS, JESSIE.

009815   DISTANT LAMPS. A NOVEL. London: Jarrold, 1903 BMC.

REVERE, M. P., pseud. See WILLIAMSON, ALICE MURIEL (LIVINGSTON).

REYNOLDS, AMY DORA.

009816   AN ABSENT HERO. London: Mills and Boon, 1914 BMC.

TLS-He never comes on the scene, his personality is seen through the other characters. In the last sentence reader is permitted to hear his laugh outside in the garden.

009817   AS FLOWS THE RIVER. London: Chapman and Hall, 1911 BMC.

Boy-girl romance, emphasis on spiritual. ATH

009818   THE BOOK OF ANGELUS DRAYTON. London: J. Long, 1904 BMC.

TLS--diary of a male, nature.

009819   FETTERS ON THE FEET; A NOVEL. London: E. Arnold, 1917 BMC.

Quaker girl leaves her home to become a companion to strong-minded Mrs Fletcher, pagan in her religious outlook. TLS
Leaves not out of spirit of revolt but to avoid attentions of cousin Alec who wanted her to do mission work with him in Uganda. From Mrs. Fletcher's ideas, she's left dazed ? TLS
Margaret Greenfield seeks after God. LBKM

009820   THE FORSYTHE WAY. London: Chapman and Hall, 1910 BMC.

TLS- male hero romance
ATH- male hero romance
Intrigue concerning inheritance. SR

009821   THE GIFTED NAME. London: Hodder and Stoughton, [1912] BMC.

TLS-family of Farland, represented by famous novelist Hester. Includes one of the "most offensively horsey young women we have ever met in fiction"

009822   THE GRANITE CROSS. BY MRS. FRED REYNOLDS. London: Chapman and Hall, 1913 NUC BMC.

Cornish life; Matthew Treen fisherman aspires to be an artist, goes to London meets Judith Marston. She's attracted to him; they become engaged. Sees her mistake Matthew returns to village. Focus is on him.

009823   THE GREY TERRACE. London: Chapman and Hall, 1912 BMC.

TLS-
ATH-
ACAD-Keith, an M.D., strikes a man who then dies, his friend Jeanne, also an M.D.-certifies otherwise. BKM-Keith has romance with Maisie, Jeanne is a particularly interesting study, a wholly loveable woman.

009824   HAZEL OF HAZELDEAN. London: Hurst and Blackett, 1906 BMC.

NYT-Traditional love story.
ACAD-trivial, little girl raised as boy for purpose of inheritance, scoffs at feminine limitations.
TLS
ATH-

009825   THE HORSESHOE. London: Chapman and Hall, 1911 BMC.

Cornish fishing talk -TLS
Love triangles -ACAD

009826   THE HOUSE OF REST. London: Hurst and Blackett, 1907 BMC.

Leone founds a home for the weary. TLS The humors of her guests and her own love story after 10 years of struggle with poverty in London, Leone Lorraine inherits money. Opens a house of rest for unfortunates. Then she marries. The two carry on the good work she started.

009827   THE HUT ON THE ISLAND: THE STORY OF A WEEK'S HOLIDAY. London: Gall and Inglis, [1902] BMC.

009828   THE IDYLL OF AN IDLER; BEING SOME
ADVENTURES OF A CARAVAN IN CORNWALL. London: Everett,
1910 BMC.

009829   AN IDYLL OF THE DAWN. London: J. Bowden,
1898 BMC.

SP 81:782. Study of childhood from the point of view
of a precocious child.

009830   IN SILENCE. London: Hurst and Blackett,
1906 BMC.

TLS-unrealistic treatment of a deaf child female
ATH-becomes the founder of an institution for the
training of children like herself. Mrs. Reynolds has
made a real study of a deaf mute's character and has
handled the subject with loving care.

009831   IN THE YEARS THAT CAME AFTER. London:
Hutchinson, 1899 BMC.

Two sisters, Greta and Irene--one becomes a famous
writer, the other marries a curate. The two are
contrasted. LIT 5:623
SP 84:637. Wales. Greta, brilliant, writes an
anonymous novel which is a success, and so powerful
that her liberal father forbids her to read it.
LBKM 17:121. Greta, her literary adventures and her
romance. Sub plot mystery about her father.

009832   THE LADY IN GREY. London: Hurst and
Blackett, [1909] BMC.

Sentimental love story-TLS

009833   LETTERS TO A PRISONER. London: Chapman an
Halld, 1912 BMC.

ATH-from a wife

009834   LLANARTRO. A WELSH IDYLL. London: Gay and
Bird, 1895 BMC.

A girl, a bull, two men who love her. One gives blood
to the other to save his life after he was attacked by
the bull. SR 80:447
Welsh. Meg paints well. SP 75:153

009835   LONG FURROWS. London: Mills and Boon,
1915 BMC.

Widow Esther Lane; her son a bank clerk. He confesses
to embezzlement. She and he escape from justice,
wander off as tramps, settle in a village. Along comes
a man her age with a daughter her son's age. TLS

009836   LOVE'S MAGIC. London: Hurst and Blackett,
1908 BMC.

Opal Fielding, her education and her loves and
marriage. LBKM
TLS-sentimental story of girl ending in betrothal.
ATH-.

009837   THE MAKING OF MICHAEL. London: G. Allen,
1905 BMC.

ACAD -story of a boy.

009838   THE MAN-WITH-THE-WOODEN-FACE. BY MRS.
FRED REYNOLDS. New York: Fox, Duffield, 1903 NUC.
London: Hutchinson, 1903 BMC.

"old maid" recovers her girlhood when she gets
attentions of the man whom she eventually marries
sent. NYT O3, 570
ATH 121, 717 O
TLS-03, 138

009839   A QUAKER WOOING. London: Hutchinson, 1905
BMC.

Quaker's love for a merry female non-Quaker.
Delightful, charming. ATH 607,05

009840   ST. DAVID OF THE DUST. London: Hurst and
Blackett, 1908 BMC.

TLS-little boy, mysticism, love
SR -little boy, mysticism, love
ACAD-little boy, mysticism, love

009841   A TANGLED GARDEN: A NOVEL. London:
Hutchinson, 1896 BMC.

ATH 108:597. Domestic novel, doctor with dipsomaniac
wife whom he rescues from the flames, writer with
illegitimate child whom Mona mothers etc.
A man with a past the legacy of which is little Robin
whose ma is dead. He betrayed another man's wife.
Story of the child's life and death. ACAD 51:175

009842   THESE THREE. London: Hodder and
Stoughton, 1907 BMC.

three women Faith, Hope and Charity run a farm; their
=domestic heroism" LBKM 11-07, 99
saved by a chivalrous farmer. Effect of hard life on
wife raised to be soft. TLS SR

009843   THE WOMAN FLINCHES. London: Chapman and
Hall, 1913 BMC.

Lonely girl misunderstood by parents is heroine. The
vagaries of her dissipated father and love affairs of
her mother make up the story-as they appear to her.
ATH
Daughter writes about mother and father's abuse of
mother. Slowly works out a reconciliation. At the end
they are kneeling together at her side. TLS

REYNOLDS, BESSIE.

009844   LOAVES AND FISHES. London: E. Stock, 1899
BMC.

Struggles of a hard working dissenting minister and
his wife to show the kind of life such ministers and
their families lead, the poor conditions. LIT 5:596
SP 84:318. Struggle of Nonconformist clergyman and
wife to live on 100 lbs a year.

REYNOLDS, GERTRUDE M. (ROBINS). D. 1939. United Kingdom.

009845   ALSO RAN. BY MRS. BAILLIE REYNOLDS.
London: Hutchinson, 1920 BS. New York: G. H. Doran,
[c1920] NUC.

TLS-heroine a war nurse falls in love with patient but
marries his brother to save father's good name.
NYT-Oct 3, 1920, p 25. Two murders, mystery

009846   BEWARE OF THE DOG. BY MRS. BAILLIE
REYNOLDS. London: Mills & Boon, 1910 BMC. New York:
Brentano's, [1911] NUC.

Male detective-NYT

009847   BROKEN OFF. BY MRS. BAILLIE REYNOLDS.
London: Hodder and Stoughton, 1907 BMC. New York:
Brentano's, 1907 NUC.

Feelings of a pair-the man worships her, she's
repulsed by him. Their changing emotions. TLS
Broken engagement "a feminine novel" . SR

009848   A CASTLE TO LET. BY MRS. BAILLIE
REYNOLDS. New York: G. H. Doran, [1917] NUC. London:
Cassell, 1917 BMC.

A romance of an English heiress and a cave. PW
TLS-
LBKM-mystery of a cave near castle that a rich woman
rents. She's determined to solve it. LBKM.
Young English woman studies at Oxford, makes friends
with Hungarian woman, accompanies her to her ancestral
home-a castle, nearby is a cave reportedly inhabited
by a terrible dragon. Secret of cave discovered. ATH
BAKER 32 404

009849   THE COST OF A PROMISE; A NOVEL IN THREE
PARTS. BY MRS. BAILLIE REYNOLDS. London: Hodder and
Stoughton, 1914 BMC. New York: G. H. Doran, [c1914]
NUC.

LBKM-Germaine, whose childhood mentor was a socialist,
and whose father claimed to be a descendent of
Charlotte Corday, tried to serve a scapegrace uncle by
exacting Corday's crime against his step-brother, "who
to protect her future made her promise never to
disclose her frustrated crime." She grew up with the
revolutionary strain finding its outlet in Women's
Suffrage.
ATH 144:283 Reviewer finds it incredible that heroine
could prove to be an efficient guide on the question
of suffrage.
"The promise was made when Germaine was a child.
Excited by the socialist ideas she heard, she
attempted to murder the young squire. He, a kind and
wise man, foresaw how this deed might ruin her life;
and he made her promise never to tell of it. Through

her girlhood, Germaine kept the promise. When she felt
she must tell her fiance, the squire released her from
the promise. The contrast between this man's behavior
under the knowledge, and the squire's, showed Germaine
which was her real lover." PW 86 10/10/14:1206
TLS-She is a "born suffragette", makes public speeches
on the subject.
NYT-Goes into an office to support herself and her
mother rather than becoming a "down-trodden"
governess. She is a militant suffragist; one chapter
devoted to a violent political marriage.

009850   THE COURT FAVORITE. London: Mill and
Boon, 1915 BMC.

009851   THE DAUGHTER PAYS. BY MRS. BAILLIE
REYNOLDS. New York: Doran, 1915 NUC. London: Cassell,
1916 BMC.

Woman jilts man for a richer lover. Years later
arranges for marriage of her daughter Virginia to 1st
suitor now bent on revenge, daughter's brave soul wins
the love of the grim misogynist. PW 90: 980 9/23/16
NYT-she reforms him TLS

009852   A DOUBTFUL CHARACTER. BY MRS. BAILLIE
REYNOLDS. London and New York: Hodder and Stoughton,
[c1913] BMC NUC.

Man of title convicted of manslaughter and suspected
of murder. ATH
Heroine has happy end-Una Martindale alone except for
friend-a male whose past is a doubtful one-which is
eventually cleared up. TLS

009853   THE DREAM AND THE MAN. London: J. Murray,
1902 BMC.

Combines supernatural and modern themes LBKM, 1-03,168

009854   A DULL GIRL'S DESTINY. BY MRS. BAILLIE
REYNOLDS. New York: Brentano's, 1907 NUC. London:
Hutchinson, 1907 BMC.

heroine is a brilliant novelist and successful, quiet
on surface, way ahead of her family. BKM 2 6 (1907)
105
Mrs. Lebreton: journalist; Avril Eden success in
Literature. Avril is opposite of dull. Writes under a
pen name considered author of great classics. Marries
but conceals secret of authorship from professor
husband. NYT

009855   THE GIRL FROM NOWHERE. BY MRS. BAILLIE
REYNOLDS. New York: Hodder and Stoughton, [c1910] NUC.
London: Hodder and Stoughton, 1910 BMC NUC.

Focus upon a man who had saved a woman would-be
suicide. PW 2-25-11
Felix is about to take poison when Veronica (who
throws self ou t of upper window) lands on his
balcony. She's escaping an uncle who "sold her" to a
music-hall agent. Felix is an anarchist just out of
prison. "So he spirited her away in a barge." Review
unclear after this description of the opening except
that the girl really has a title we learn. SR
TLS- typical romance
ATH-typical romance

009856   HER POINT OF VIEW. BY G. M. ROBINS (MRS.
BAILLIE REYNOLDS). London: Hurst and Blackett, 1896
NUC BMC.

LBKM 10:176. Stella, a violinist is loved by two
writers, one a distinguished novelist whom she plans
to marry. The other, who had formerly rejected her
because of her lack of position or money, goes mad
with jealousy, lures her to his quarters where "the
leering Beardsleyism of the "Yellow Book" jostled the
medievalism of an ivory inlaid bureau," etc. Attempts
to force her into a relationship but novelist rescues
her.
SR "Surrender so absolute that it shook him body and
soul"
ATH 108:347. "Overflowing with sentimentality, nice
principles"
ACAD 50:159. Her point of view had changed.

009857   THE IDES OF MARCH. BY G. M. ROBINS. New
York: J. W. Lovell, [1891] NUC. London: Hurst and
Blackett, 1892 BMC.

There's an old prophecy about the Westmorelands that
affects their lives and loves. A group of young people
love and blunder until all is disentangled and the
right ones joined. ATH 98 859

Elderly man of ancient lineage fears his son will have
no heir. Hears a prophecy concerning this peril.
Determines to marry off his son, a misogynist, before
ides of March. Then he meets Hope Merion who jilted
his best friend; when young Westmoreland learns the
truth about the supposed jilt, all is ok. SR 12-19-91,
699
SP-family prophecy of extinction. Father is anxious
that his son will marry and have children, but son is
interested only in love-making.
LW 23:246. Romance, male hero.
PW Prophecy about extinction of a family and father's
efforts to avoid it.
ACAD 41:60. Hope breaks off her engagement when she
learns her fiance has treated a member of her sex
dishonourably. Soldier in So. army killed. Widow
believing herself ill gives away her six children.
Recovers, visits them. Little record of who's who so
that when they are grown, a sister almost marries a
brother.

009858   IN THE BALANCE. London: 1893 BMC. Hurst
and Blackett,

009859   THE KING'S WIDOW. BY MRS. BAILLIE
REYNOLDS. London: Cassell, 1919 BMC. New York: G. H.
Doran, [c1919] NUC.

fairy tale world of princes, princesses, -TLS
Evadne married by proxy to a young king whom she has
never seen won't believe reports of his death; he
returns to the throne after imprisonment. PW
Nordernreich, King's widow, warlike, treacherous,
orders assassinations, plots to gain control of the
country Pannonia by marrying Evadne to her pawn. The
widow had ordered the assassination of the man
Evadne's married to but he lives. NYT 359, 7-6-19

009860   THE LONELY STRONGHOLD. BY MRS. BAILLIE
REYNOLDS. London: Cassell, 1918 BMC. New York: G. H.
Doran, [c1918] NUC.

ATH-male hero.
PW- love story
TLS- love story
NYT-May 26, 1918 p 242. Olwen Innes, tired of her bank
job, takes up post as companion, falls in love with
son of family, one of two twins, Then, during the war,
with an inheritance she obtained a house and used it
as a hospital. At end of war Ninion(twin) returns from
being prisoner and they are reunited.

009861   A MAKE-SHIFT MARRIAGE. BY MRS. BAILLIE
REYNOLDS. London and New York: Hodder and Stoughton,
[c1912] BMC NUC.

Man marries a woman on the rebound. Vivien is the
woman who refused him (she's fluffy); Astrid is the
unloved wife with fine mind and rare character. Her
mother-in-law comes to her aid. Mrs. Brandon a rare
mother-in-law in fiction-NYT
"A most extraordinary and vivid novel of the marriage
problem." . NYT 1913 353
ATH-editor, deserted by fiance marries his typist and
then falls in love with her.
LBKM-

009862   THE MAN WHO WON. BY MRS. BAILLIE REYNOLDS
(G. M. ROBINS). London: Hutchinson, 1905 BMC NUC. New
York: Brentano's, 1907 NUC.

Millie is fully an individual. At 16 she shrinks from
Bert's passion. Years later she contemptuously rebukes
him until he disciplines himself to be acceptable to
her. Millie also takes eager delight in work:
architecture. Does a determined passion in a man
arouse the same in a woman? At 16 Millie shrinks from
it; years later, she's at first repulsed, then she's
all afire. Millie takes eager delight in her work-real
work. ACAD-857,05
Bert, violent, is contemptuously rebuked by Millie.
Disciplines himself to be acceptable to her. LBKM
29-30, 42
Evolution of full manhood and womanhood in Bert and
Millie. High-spirited complex. ATH 05,366
orphan and cruel stepmother. Studies to be an
architect, self supporting does marry. PW 6-1-07

009863   NIGEL FERRARD. London: Hurst and
Blackett, 1899 BMC.

Young woman while sleepwalking saw a man murdered.
Fell through skylight where she was watching.
Injured--loses memory. Marries the murderer, later
regains her memory. But as it turns out he wasn't the
murderer anyway. LBKM 15:152

SP 81:782. Highly sensational, ignoble, deception
practiced by the hero.
ATH 112:861.Involves an operation done by two surgeons
in the middle of the night, one intends to and does
kill patient but convinces other that it was his
fault, witnessed by small girl who grows into
beautiful creature who doesn't remember that night
until...
Heroine completely loses her memory after witnessing a
murder in her early youth. SP
LIT 3:523. 14 year old girl sleepwalking witnesses a
crime. Loss of memory. She is abducted to prevent
disclosure. Guardian marries ward and then his fraud
is discovered.

009864   THE NOTORIOUS MISS LISLE. BY MRS. BAILLIE
REYNOLDS. London and New York: Hodder and Stoughton,
[1911] BMC NUC.

Gaenor Lisle woman involved in a divorce case
innocently. Problems with her new husband worked out.
PW 10-28-11

009865   "OPEN, SESAME!" BY MRS. BAILLIE
REYNOLDS. New York: Doran, [1918] NUC. London:
Skeffington, [1919] BMC.

War experience of those who stayed home. PW

009866   OUT OF THE NIGHT. BY MRS. BAILLIE
REYNOLDS. London and New York: Hodder and Stoughton,
[1910] BMC NUC.

heroine, Vernon Wilmot: adventures, misunderstandings
end in happiness? PW
TLS-she leaves Vancouver when her estate manager falls
in love wth her. His wife has deserted him. He comes
to England for his wife meets with repulse and
tragedy.
LBKM-o
ATH-She works among the poor.
NYT-o

009867   PHOEBE IN FETTERS. London: J. Murray,
1904 BMC. London: Hodder, [n.d.] NUC.

BKM-defense of marriage as sacred and indissoluble.
ATH-wife yet not a wife. Review does not agree with
BKM.
ACAD-wife is not turned on physically by husband until
passion awakes.

009868   THE PRISONER OF THE GARRET. London: S. W.
Partridge, [1915] BMC.

009869   THE SILENCE BROKEN: A STORY OF THE
UNEXPLAINED. London: Hurst and Blackett, 1897 BMC.

A ghost in order to convince her husband that she died
"true" has an artist paint her portrait.(?) ATH
109:834

009870   THE SUPREME TEST. BY MRS. BAILLIE
REYNOLDS. New York: Brentano's, 1908 NUC. London:
Hutchinson, 1908 BMC.

PW-triangle
TLS-high spirited heroine
young girl awakens mid-aged man to his narrowness. BKM
Miss Kythe West visits her less fortunate friend
Frieda Medway (housekeeper for a church warden).
They're both young. The Warden is shocked at Kythe's
unconventional views. She reforms him to something
like a human being. NYT

009871   "THALASSA!" BY MRS. BAILLIE REYNOLDS. New
York: Brentano, 1906 NUC. London: Hutchinson, 1906
BMC.

PW-young girl orphan
TLS- conventional
A Jane Eyre kind of story not promising. BKM 25 (1907)
182 Frail but self reliant woman comes to serve as
governess for child of an isolated man who has some
dark secret in his life. Wins the man but on learning
the secret is forced to seek self support where he
will not find her; love compels her to return. BKM
A strenuous hero woos defenseless orphan by scorn and
jeers: He's convinced only a pure man can woo a pure
woman. Author's view not clear.

009872   TO SET HER FREE. BY G. M. ROBINS. London:
Hurst and Blackett, 1895 NUC BMC.

Detective. SR 80:514
Heroine unwittingly made the tool of a villain. ATH

106:564
SP 76:247. Nihilists and detectives. Miss Trevaunance
entangled in a compromising secret.

009873   A WAYWARD GIRL. London: S. W. Partridge,
[1913] BMC.

REYNOLDS, KATHARINE (YIRSA). B. 1883. United States.

009874   GREEN VALLEY. Boston: Little, Brown, 1919
NUC BMC.

Romance in country setting. PW
Love story of a town--all about Green Valley. PW Book
Review 1919:817
Idyl-peaceful serene setting for Nan and man she
loves. Simple, unselfish, untroubled people. NYT

REYNOLDS, MINNIE JOSEPHINE. B. 1865.

009875   THE CRAYON CLUE. New York: M. Kennerley,
1915 BMC NUC.

Billy Pen (a woman) fights vs the school board; goes
to state legislature, goes all the way with her fight
vs corruption PW 6-12-15
Graft and corruption become really tiresome when
teachers forced to use greasy crayons. This is Billy's
clue that sweeps her into a great campaign for honest
government. She takes the stump, preaches a great
sermon at a Presbyterian Church demonstrates "what a
woman can do once she is roused." "The author has been
given a lion's share of the credit in getting an
amendment for equal suffrage through Colorado Senate."
NYT
Prominent worker for the cause; book is a "good
campaign document". NYT

REYNOLDS, MRS. BAILLIE. See REYNOLDS, GERTRUDE M. (ROBINS).

REYNOLDS, MRS. FRED. See REYNOLDS, AMY DORA.

RHOADES, NINA. B. 1863.

009876   THE OTHER SYLVIA. Boston: Lothrop, Lee &
Shepard, [1910] NUC.

Children's. PW

009877   RUTH CAMPBELL'S EXPERIMENT: A STORY.
Boston: W. A. Wilde, [1904] NUC.

PW-young woman must support herself.

009878   SILVER LININGS. New York: McClure,
Phillips, 1903 NUC.

Blind girl who suffers greed of sister's husband. PW
10-3-03, NYT 1903:773

009879   THAT PRESTON GIRL: A STORY. Boston: W. A.
Wilde, [c1905] NUC.

RHODES, HATTIE H. Nationality Unknown.

009880   ONE AMERICAN GIRL. BY VIRGINIA WEBB. New
York: G. W. Dillingham, [1901] NUC.

PW 3-2-01

RHODES, KATHLYN. United Kingdom.

009881   AFTERWARDS. London: Hutchinson, 1915 BMC.
New York: Duffield, [1917] NUC.

Doctor shoots girl on her request, to save her from
fate worse than death. She profaned an Indian temple.
LBKM Mrs. Carstairs victim of cruel persecution. Dr
Anstice clears her name. PW 90:980 9/23/16

009882   THE CITY OF PALMS. London: Hutchinson,
[1919] BMC.

Traditional melodrama TLS

009883   THE DESERT DREAMERS. London: Hutchinson,
1909 BMC.

focuses on Allison, a man. TLS
Man marries, wife dies; grieves for four years, weds
another who turns out to be wife's sister. ATH

009884   FLOWER OF GRASS. London: Hutchinson, 1911
BMC.

Phyllida Gordon married has a "liaison" in Egypt with

an Orienta. TLS
Third edition of "Flower of Grass"

009885   THE GOLDEN APPLE. London: Hutchinson,
[1920] BMC.

TLS-love and society in Egypt.

009886   HEADMISTRESS HILARY. London: J. Nisbet,
1914 BMC.

009887   THE LURE OF THE DESERT; A NOVEL. London:
Hutchinson, 1916 NUC BMC.

  TLS- tale of revenge
  ATH- tale of revenge

009888   THE MAKING OF A SOUL. London: Hutchinson,
1914 BMC.

  ACAD 86:526. Antonia, a typist, married to a man who
  does not love her and considers her his intellectual
  inferior. She is persuaded to leave her husband by
  other woman, but a year or so later, he repentant,
  they are reconciled.
  TLS-Owen Rose (husband) "dainty satire on the futility
  of the intellectual man without perception."

009889   MANY WATERS. London: Digby, Long, 1899
BMC.

  Love story concerning Stella and a Miss Brandon and a
  young man. ACAD 57:682

009890   SANDS OF GOLD. London: Hutchinson, 1918
BMC. New York: Duffield, 1919 NUC.

  TLS-insane asylum in Egypt. Relationship of a placid
  love affair between doctor and girl and hectic
  emotions of a neurotic English woman and insane Greek
  youth.
  LBKM-Greek youth is hero of a love passion. Something
  in Dr. Preston's past which makes it impossible for
  him to be anything but a mad doctor or to think of
  love and marrige.
  Set in Far East, surgeon "because of an imagined wrong
  swears himself to celibacy. PW, NYT
  NYT 3-30-19, 159 Egypt, set in "lunatic asylum"; story
  conerns Celia, daughter of Superintendent, who ends
  unhappily but helps save hero's love affair with
  Denise "the good, pure woman of Victorian fiction".

009891   THE STRAIGHT RACE. London: Holden and
Hardingham, [1916] BMC.

  Young friendless woman must earn own living from shop
  to stage-the temptations and trials of stage life. The
  rake livens the story, but is murdered in the middle.
  ATH
  Dierdre Granville-trials of chorus girl wooed by
  theatrical manager. Ends happily.

009892   SWEET LIFE. A NOVEL. London: Hutchinson,
1908 BMC 1916 NUC.

  TLS- love
  ATH-first part describes the struggles and ultimate
  failure of a well-educated girl to earn her living in
  London. Painful subject. Second half melodramatic and
  improbable.

009893   THE WAX IMAGE AND OTHER STORIES. London:
Holden and Hardingham, 1912 BMC.

009894   THE WILL OF ALLAH. Boston: D. Estes,
[1908] NUC. London: Hutchinson, [1908] BMC.

  Cynthia marries a hunchback. Her repulsion yields to
  affection. TLS
  TLS--love story
  ATH--love story

RHONE, MRS. D. L. See RHONE, ROSAMOND (DODSON).

RHONE, ROSAMOND (DODSON). B. 1855. United States.

009895   AMONG THE DUNES. BY MRS. D. L. RHONE. New
York and London: F. T. Neely, 1897 NUC BMC.

  NYT 1898:257. Question of Nordoff's heir. Africa.
  Kathlot, a Gypsy woman in Jutland and in a harem.
  "Exuberant fancy".

009896   THE DAYS OF THE SON OF MAN: A TALE OF
SYRIA. New York & London: G. P. Putnam's Sons, 1902
BMC NUC.

RHYS, GRACE (LITTLE). 1865-1929. United Kingdom.

009897   THE BRIDE. London: Methuen, 1909 BMC.

  Esther Carey & mother, driven from country home
  because of misfortune, settle in London. Esther
  marries a sculptor after her break with a man she was
  engaged to. Sculptor absorbed in his work. TLS
  Heroine loses her luxurious life (father commits
  suicide.) ATH

009898   THE CHARMING OF ESTERCEL. London: Dent,
1913 BMC. New York: E. P. Dutton, 1913 NUC.

  Elizabethan Ireland-strange beliefs in powers of
  charms. A slight love story. ATH
  Focus on Estercel and his great white horse. TLS

009899   THE DIVERTED VILLAGE: A HOLIDAY BOOK.
London: Methuen, 1903 BMC.

  Agreeable account of how "Eve & I" settled down in a
  Norfolk village. TLS 1903:75

009900   MARY DOMINIC. London: J. M. Dent, 1898
BMC. Leipzig: B. Tauchnitz, 1899 NUC.

  SP 81:694. Fallen heroine, badly treated by peasant
  father. Ireland.
  LIT 3:574. Powerful, nothing so fine since Grania.
  Ireland at the time of the land league & the secret
  society formed out of Irish agitation; Leeson its
  leader. And Mary seduced by Hugh Latimor whom she yet
  feels pity for at his death. LBKM 15:117
  She's 15, wild, untaught, rustic, full of romantic
  illusions. At 17, she and child thrown out to fend for
  herself. ATH 113:12

009901   THE PRINCE OF LISNOVER. London: Methuen,
1904 BMC.

  ATH-male Irish hero.

009902   THE WOOING OF SHEILA. London: Methuen,
1901 BMC. New York: H. Holt, 1901 NUC.

  ATH 8-24-01.
  Sentimental: NYT

RICE, ALICE CALDWELL (HEGAN). 1870-1942. United States.

009903   THE HONORABLE PERCIVAL. New York:
Century, 1914 NUC. London: Hodder & Stoughton, 1915
BMC.

  PW 86 10/24/14:1343 "As a solace for having been
  jilted by a quite correct English fiancee, the
  Honorable Percival is taking a trip around the world.
  He presents a front of icy indifference to all his
  fellow travelers until Bobby boards the liner at San
  Francisco. Bobby means mischief. She is American,
  pretty, daring. The Honorable Percival, for all his
  disapproval of her, wakes up. Things happen fast on
  that liner, and Bobby doesn't lose a moment. It is the
  honorable Britisher that loses."
  LBKM-Bobby doesn't want him. Humorous-Percival's inane
  vanity.

009904   LOVEY MARY. London: Hodder and Stoughton,
1903 BMC. New York: Century, 1903 NUC.

  NYT 1903:140: sounds like a children's book.

009905   MR. OPP. London: Hodder and Stoughton,
1909 BMC. New York: Century, 1909 BMC NUC.

  Sentimental story. TLS LBKM NYT

009906   MRS. WIGGS OF THE CABBAGE PATCH. New
York: Century, 1901 BMC NUC. London: Hodder &
Stoughton, 1902 BMC.

009907   A ROMANCE OF BILLY-GOAT HILL. London:
Hodder & Stoughton, 1912 BMC. New York: Century, 1912
NUC.

  TLS-Kentucky, young lovers, old professor.
  NYT-love story.

009908   SANDY. London: Hodder & Stoughton, 1905
BMC. New York: Century, 1905 NUC.

  Boys' adventure? PW 4-29-05
  Sandy falls in love, marries--novel focuses upon him.
  NYT 1905:316

RICE, FANNIE BOND. Nationality Unknown.

009909   A SAINT OF THE TWENTIETH CENTURY. Boston:
R. G. Badger, 1910 NUC.

About a pastor. PW NYT

RICE, RUTH LITTLE (MASON). 1884-1927. United States.

009910   THE TRAILERS: A NOVEL. New York: F. H.
Revell, [c1909] NUC.

Story of a religious idealist and the woman who works
with him. PW 2-27-09 BKM

RICHARD, HETTY LAWRENCE (HEMENWAY). 1890-1961. United
States.

009911   FOUR DAYS; THE STORY OF A WAR MARRIAGE.
BY HETTY HEMENWAY. Boston: Little, Brown, 1917 NUC.

Their four days of marriage before the wife sends
soldier off with a smile. PW

RICHARD, MARIE E. United States.

009912   THE COUNTRY CHARGE. Philadelphia:
Lutheran Soc., [1897] NUC.

Theme: "No matter what other quality a minister has,
he/she must love the weakest of his <her> flock" to be
a real minister. PW

RICHARDS, CLARICE (ESTABROOK). B. 1875. United States.

009913   A TENDERFOOT BRIDE; TALES FROM AN OLD
RANCH. New York: F. H. Revell, [c1920] NUC.

PW-Eastern bride in the West. Portrayal of easy
unconventionality and tragedy of lives lived beyond
pale of 10 commandments. All-night dances, rides with
half-tamed horses.
BKM-covers a 16 year period, from time she arrived in
a lawless land to pastoral age of sheep and herders
and farmers.

RICHARDS, DR., pseud. See PINSENT, ELLEN FRANCES (PARKER).

RICHARDS, LAURA ELIZABETH (HOWE). 1850-1943. United
States.

009914   THE ARMSTRONGS. Boston: D. Estes, [c1905]
NUC.

009915   A DAUGHTER OF JEHU. New York and London:
D. Appleton, 1918 BMC NUC.

PW-orphaned girl returns to home town and earns living
by running a livery stable.
NYT Nov. 17 '18 p 494. She was also a cab driver.
Insisted on being independent and living alone. Sweet
and sent.
Old fashioned provincial folk; school of Cranford. TLS

009916   GEOFFREY STRONG. Boston: D. Estes,
[c1901] NUC.

Two "old maids" living contentedly, one sworn to
spinsterhood (?) sentimental. NyT '01 Julia Ward
Howe's daughter.

009917   GRANDMOTHER, THE STORY OF A LIFE THAT
NEVER WAS LIVED. Boston: D. Estes, [c1907] NUC.

Old man marries young woman. His daughter nicknames
her grandma. BKM

009918   THE HURDY-GURDY. Boston: D. Estes, [1902]
NUC.

009919   JIM OF HELLAS; OR, IN DURANCE VILE.
BETHESDA POOL. Boston: Estes & Lauriat, 1895 NUC.

(1)New Eng. Jim a Greek sailor wins a middle-aged
spinster. (2) The troubling of Bethesda Pool brings
together two elderly and two young lovers. PW
5-4-95:708

009920   LOVE AND ROCKS. Boston: Estes and
Lauriat, 1898 NUC.

Romance on N. England coast of two students
vacationing; he a Harvard student of surgery; she a
Smith student trying to decide between literature and

medicine as a career. PW

009921   MISS JIMMY. Boston: D. Estes, [c1913]
NUC.

PW 83 5/31/13:1961 "Miss Jimmy went away for five
years, became a nurse and when her sister was ill
returned to her native village and took it, as well as
the bovine Sylphine and her mean-spirited husband in
charge. Her cheery helpfulness makes a difference to
every one she comes near, while her unfailing sense of
humor keeps her sweet. She reforms the village
scapegrace, helps a lovelorn maiden, and also finds
her own mate while ministering to her neighbors."
see PW vol. 84, p.546
"This is a story of a Maine village, in which Jemima
Dolly, famiarly known as Miss Jimmy comes home after
some years spent in a city as a trained nurse, finds
plenty to do on her native heath, and does it with
birdlike alertness, a constant sense of humor, the
breeziest of spirits, and a capacity that is always
equal to the occasion." NYT

009922   MRS. TREE. Boston: D. Estes, [1902] NUC.

BOOK NEWS 02
NYT 02 not helpful.

009923   MRS. TREE'S WILL. Boston: D. Estes,
[c1905] NUC.

009924   ON BOARD THE MARY SANDS. Boston: D.
Estes, [c1911] NUC.

Quaint advents. NYT

009925   PIPPIN, A WANDERING FLAME. New York and
London: D. Appleton, 1917 BMC NUC.

Male hero. Boy thief goes to prison, released, becomes
an honest vagabond. NYT 137 4-15-17

009926   "UP TO CALVINS". Boston: D. Estes,
[c1910] NUC.

Story of a good farm couple who do endless good
things. PW
Humorous adventures of Calvin. NYT

009927   THE WOOING OF CALVIN PARKS. Boston: D.
Estes, [c1908] NUC.

"Portraying the simple life of the quaint "Down East"
characters Calvin Parks is an interesting character
who has bought out the candy route. His faithful old
horse takes him from village to village, where he
dispenses of his wares and gossips by the way." BKM28
1908-9

RICHARDS, MARIAN EDWARDS. Nationality Unknown.

009928   ZANDRIE. New York: Century, 1909 BMC NUC.

Wild freedom loving girl wants to care for her
crippled knight. PW 9-18-09. NYT

RICHARDSON, ANNA STEESE (SAUSSER). 1865-1949.

009929   ADVENTURES IN THRIFT. Indianapolis:
Bobbs-Merrill, [1916] BMC NUC.

Woman undertakes to run her house for 1/3 less; tests
all the modern methods, marketing, cooperative buying
stores, clubs, commercial kitchens. PW
NYT-enables Claire to marry man whose income she had
formerly thought was impossible to live on.

RICHARDSON, DOROTHY. 1875-1955. United States.

009930   THE LONG DAY. THE STORY OF A NEW YORK
WORKING GIRL, AS TOLD BY HERSELF [ANONYMOUS]. New
York: Century, 1905 BMC NUC.

True picture of unfortunate underpaid working girl in
factory; meets all types of working women. "The
working girls are responsible"? PW 10-14-05
BKM 22 (1905)403 Used to Teach, lured to city by ads
of self-supporting women doing well: factory work, the
horrible conditions that goad the women into
prostitution; years of struggle but works her way up
to respected business woman. NYT 672, 05.

RICHARDSON, DOROTHY MILLER. 1873-1957. United Kingdom.

009931   BACKWATER. London: Duckworth, [1916] BMC
NUC. New York: A.A. Knopf, 1917 NUC.

009932 HONEYCOMB. London: Duckworth, 1917 BMC NUC. New York: A.A. Knopf, 1919 NUC.

1895-Hastings at Sea: Ma kills self. Mrs. Corrie: unhappy conv. soc. childlike woman. Mrs. Kronin pursues all pleasures. Mr. Corrie reveals limits of men's minds

009933 INTERIM. London: Duckworth, [1919] BMC NUC. New York: A.A. Knopf, 1920 NUC.

Most continuously and intensely alive. Sensible to all impressions. Nothing escapes her; responds to all stimuli; all life is exciting business. Bloomsbury boarding house. All seen from inside. Intense realization of the moment. TLS
NYT 1920:320. Miriam acutely self-conscious young woman. Dread and distrust of people. "Nebulous inner life."

009934 POINTED ROOFS. London: Duckworth, 1915 BMC NUC. New York: A.A. Knopf, 1919 NUC.

Miriam is a teacher in Hanover for six months-her relations to her girl students, to Fraulein Pfaff, her school teacher life.

009935 THE TRAP. London: A.A. Knopf, 1919 NUC. London: Duckworth, 1925 BMC NUC.

009936 THE TUNNEL. London: Duckworth, 1919 BMC NUC. New York: A.A. Knopf, 1919 NUC.

"discrepancy between what she has to say and traditional forms. Believes in a live novel-one that actually grows. As Miriam says,"To write books knowing all about style would be to become like a man." Cuts out she & him and all the old deliberate business-what's left is denuded, unsheltered, unbegun and unfinished consciousness of Miriam which endlessly reflects. No theme, no story. We're invited to follow all the impressions that flicker through her mind, that wake other thoughts and thread together past & present. We think as she thinks, we're seated in her mind. Succeeds in achieving a sense of reality far greater than trad novel does. TLS
Assists 3 dentists- all details of her work. No conventional romance. She is a militant feminist. Man is the enemy. "At best a complacent tyrant who abuses his place in the sun." Well educated, well read. SP

RICHARDSON, HENRY HANDEL, pseud. See ROBERTSON, ETHEL FLORENCE LINDESAY (RICHARDSON).

RICHARDSON, JERUSHA DAVIDSON (HUNTING).

009937 A DRAMA OF SUNSHINE, PLAYED IN HOMBURG. London: T.F. Unwin, 1903 BMC.

Restless highstrung queen of fashion, wants to manipulate destinies and order careers. ACAD 65,84 Resents husband for injuring their child in a drunken rage. ACAD 65,149
LBKM 9-03,222 Fashionable vulgarity. Heroine of rapid manners. ATH 122,247

009938 GATES OF BRASS. London: Digby, Long, 1909 BMC.

A world famous prima donna and her daughter just out of college. TLS

009939 THEY TWAIN. London: T.F. Unwin, 1904 BMC.

ATH- tiresome imagined marital differences.
TLS-careful study of a marriage, especially good portrayal of the woman.
ACAD-hoydenish wife who figures as an exclamation of horror through many pages.

RICHARDSON, MARY RALEIGH.

009940 MATILDA AND MARCUS: A NOVEL. London: Simpkin, 1915 BMC.

TLS-author is venting her enthusiastic feminism. Matilda is an idealist, married to Marc a poet, she is unhappy, arranges to marry Sir Henry.

RICHARDSON, ROBERT, pseud. See PERKINS, MARGARET MOWER.

RICHARDSON, TERESA EDEN (PEARCE SEROCOLD). D. 1918.

009941 DORA HENDERSON. London: Heath, Cranton & Ouseley, [1914] BMC.

009942 AN ENGLISH GIRL IN TOKYO. London: Heath & Cranton, [1913] BMC NUC.

Russo-Japanese War. A shadowy English heroine. Banal, sentimental. ATH
Violet Courtley visits Tokyo; brother is at the Embassy; falls in love with war correspondent. TLS

RICHBERG, ELOISE O. RANDALL. United States.

009943 BUNKER HILL TO CHICAGO: A STORY. Chicago: Dibble, 1893 NUC.

RICHINGS, EMILY A.

009944 BROKEN AT THE FOUNTAIN. London: Heath, Cranton, [1916] BMC.

TLS-Historical novel.
ATH-chief character is secretly married to prince. Her coronation takes place after her death.

009945 IN CHAUCER'S MAYTIME. London: T. F. Unwin, 1902 BMC NUC.

ATH 12-20-02 historical novel.

009946 SIR WALTER'S WIFE: A STORY OF TWO REIGNS. London: H. Drane, 1900 NUC BMC.

SR 89:368. Serious historical research has gone into the writing. She tells of Raleigh's & Throckmorton's love--she rejects intrigue.
A story of Sir Walter Raleigh and Elizabeth Throckmorton; for marrying whom he was forbidden the court of Queen Elizabeth. NATION

009947 WHITE ROSELEAVES; A STORY OF THE YORKIST COURT. London: H. J. Drane, [1912] BMC.

ATH-historical novel of Elizabeth, Queen of Ed IV.

RICHMOND, GRACE LOUISE (SMITH). 1866-1959. United States.

009948 BROTHERLY HOUSE. Garden City, N.Y.: Doubleday, Page, 1912 NUC.

PW-family unity.
NYT-Christmas story.

009949 THE BROWN STUDY. Garden City, N.Y.: Doubleday, Page, 1917 NUC BMC. London: Hodder & Stoughton, [1920] BMC.

Man goes to minister the poor vs. wife's objection, but she soon joins him. PW NYT

009950 A COURT OF INQUIRY. New York: Doubleday, Page, 1909 NUC. London: Doubleday, Page, 1909 BMC.

Group of men and women discuss everything. PW 10-16-09

009951 THE ENLISTING WIFE. Garden City, New York: Doubleday, Page, 1918 NUC.

NYT-story for bride-wives.
NYT-p 189 Apr 21,1918 210w

009952 THE INDIFFERENCE OF JULIET. New York: Doubleday, Page, 1905 NUC. London: Hodder & Stoughton, [1919] BMC.

Gushy story of sensible married life. PW 4-22-05 NYT 1905:245

009953 MRS. RED PEPPER. Garden City, N.Y.: Doubleday, Page, 1913 NUC. London: Hodder & Stoughton, [1919] BMC.

PW 83 5/31/13:1962 "Dr. and Mrs. Redfield Pepper Burns, whose courtship was recorded in "Red Pepper Burns" are again the chief characters. They are so happily married themselves that they do their utmost to marry off another couple most successfully."

009954 RED AND BLACK. Garden City, New York: Doubleday, Page, 1919 NUC. London: Methuen, 1920 BMC.

Further experiences of Red Pepper Burns. PW
Not as sentimental as earlier stories. Dr. Pepper is middle aged and his friendship with the new minister (Black.) NYT 12-21-19:769.

009955 RED PEPPER BURNS. Garden City, New York: Doubleday, Page, 1910 NUC. London: Hodder & Stoughton,

1910 BMC.

About a good doctor (male) PW
Story of a male country doctor. NYT

009956   RED PEPPER'S PATIENTS WITH AN ACCOUNT OF
ANNE LINTON'S CASE IN PARTICULAR. Garden City, New
York: Doubleday, Page, 1917 BMC NUC. London: Methuen,
1919 BMC.

He's now a doctor in a suburban town. We meet his
patients. His private life seems separate till the
connections to his work are made clear. NYT
9-23-17:361

009957   ROUND THE CORNER IN GAY STREET. London
and New York: Doubleday, Page, 1908 BMC NUC.

009958   THE SECOND VIOLIN. New York: Doubleday,
Page, 1906 NUC. London: Doubleday, 1906 BMC.

PW-sentimental family story.

009959   STRAWBERRY ACRES. Garden City, N.Y.:
Doubleday, Page, 1911 NUC. London: Hodder & Stoughton,
[1919] BMC.

009960   THE TWENTY-FOURTH OF JUNE, MIDSUMMER'S
DAY. Garden City, N.Y.: Doubleday, Page, 1914 BMC NUC.

PW:86 8/29/14:596 "A young man with real stuff in him,
but dilettante tastes. His idea of the occupation of a
real gentleman is to amass wealth in the leisurely
care of his country estates; this is the life for
which he is preparing himself in spite of his
grandfather, when--enter Roberta. Now, Roberta is a
lady of charm and good sense. It becomes plain to her
admirer that she will not throw herself away on a man
who does not earn enough to buy gasoline, so to speak.
Therefore, this man makes good, and Roberta is happy,
and the grandfather is proud."
NYT-O
"Reeks with good influences."
"Novel of moral domestic class." TLS
Simple pure paragon of a heroine. BKM

009961   UNDER THE CHRISTMAS STARS. Garden City,
N.Y.: Doubleday, Page, 1913 NUC.

PW 84 11/15/13:1590 "Molly is different from the wives
of the other Fernald boys who come together with their
families for Christmas at the old New England
homestead. For Ralph was not contented, like his
brothers, with a prim, narrow-minded woman for a wife.
Suspicion had been aroused by the mere knowledge that
Molly was a Westerner, but suspicion was changed to
open hostility, and open hostility to a family quarrel
at the sight of her. The men, attracted by her
genuineness, avowed her charming!--their wives
disliked her Western ways. How a little child, born
under the Christmas stars, united this divided family
and changed a quarrelsome meeting into the jolliest of
reunions makes the story."

009962   UNDER THE COUNTRY SKY. Garden City, NY:
Doubleday, Page, 1916 NUC. London: J. Murray, 1916
BMC.

"After college, Georgiana yearns for "life" that her
little country town doesn't offer. The family has
little money. A writer comes to stay; she loves him
but he goes away. But he really was a great surgeon
and much comes of their relationship." PW
NYT-love story.
ATH-

009963   THE WHISTLING MOTHER. London: C. Brown,
1917 BMC. Garden City, N.Y.: Doubleday, Page, 1917
NUC.

009964   WITH JULIET IN ENGLAND. London and New
York: Doubleday, Page, 1907 BMC NUC.

RICHMOND, LILLY.

009965   SALLY: A SYDNEY TALE IN THREE PARTS.
Melbourne: G. Robertson, 1897 NUC.

RICKARD, JESSIE LOUISA (MOORE).   B. 1879.   United Kingdom.

009966   CATHY ROSSITER. BY MRS. VICTOR RICKARD.
London and New York: Hodder & Stoughton, [1919] NUC
BMC.

LBKM-harps upon women's rights. 2 familiar
types-overstrung idealist and hard-mouthed lady

medico. Lovable and irresponsible Cathy calls in
Monica the doctor, a mere opportunist, who confines
her to a private madhouse "and the scene it affords
together with maddening assurances and blarney, the
franker threats of stricter treatment, the farce of
the magistrate 's visit of inspection...best and
truest writing in the book." She is rescued by Robert
PW-she seeks to better social conditions in England.
NYT-Mar 21 '20 p4. Cathy, after staying for a while
with George (a pacifist) and his mistress, married
Jack Lorrimer. He and Monica Henstock eventually
contrive to get her locked up in an insane asylum. An
ex-drug addict came to her rescue.
High strung, unstable; her friend Dr. Monica Henstock,
Cathy wild enthusiasms. Dabbles with labor agitators
but marries a stable sort of Colonel gets into
scrapes, gets ill. Certified as insane and put in
asylum. Her sufferings there fully described. Rescued.
TLS
SP-is in asylum through scrupulous plotting of woman
doctor in love with her husband.

009967   DREGS. London: A. Rivers, 1914 BMC.

ATH-high-spirited and unruly boy, bad company. Double
love-tale.
TLS-his downward career, rescued from depths of
poverty and degradation by a Eurasian whom he had
married and deserted.
Focuses on a Heart of Darkness type story and hero.
LBKM

009968   THE FIRE OF GREEN BOUGHS. London:
Duckworth, 1918 BMC NUC. New York: Dodd, Mead, 1919
NUC.

TLS-idealistic clergyman and irresponsible clever girl
in raided London.
TLS-Sylvia has burned an official letter which
involved a poor woman in trouble with the authorities,
hid a dying German washed ashore. Flouted rules and
conventions. Title refers to sacrifice of youth in
war-author blames it on selfishness of the old who are
protected by their impotence.
SP-an impassioned impeachment of the elder generation.
Sylvia was brought up by a miserly uncle, had no
useful accomplishments, a failure as a war worker, is
a liar and a thief, has courage and a spirit of
humanity. A young wounded officer unhinged from the
horrors of the war kills himself.
set in London and Ireland. PW
Theme: the young have been sacrificed by and for the
advantage of the old-the old meaning all men above
military age. Young Englishman comes home disfigured
wishing he had died with the first. BKM June' 19, 457
Finds sacrifice of the war a futile one. Sylvia Tracy
shelters a German officer, lies to the authorities,
thwarts the search for him (author obviously admires
her for this). She's denounced as pro-German; novel
traces her different jobs in one of the ministries,
later as secretary in London. NYT

009969   THE FRANTIC BOAST. London: Duckworth,
[1917] BMC NUC.

Two wives leave their husbands in Burma, go to London.
Lisa Weston is sick of hers. Judith Coleston couldn't
stand hers; she was in love with a journalist. (She's
the principal character.)
TLS
Author interjects her own views of marriage. ATH

009970   THE HOUSE OF COURAGE. London: Duckworth,
1919 BMC NUC. New York: Dodd, Mead, 1919 NUC.

Secure world of Irish town plunged into war. The women
who waited for their men to return. TLS
Sufferings of German p.o.w.s-the one different aspect.
SP

009971   THE LIGHT ABOVE THE CROSSROADS. London:
Duckworth, [1916] BMC NUC.

TLS- male spy.
NYT-young attache at British embassy in Berlin.
NYT-June 30,1918,p.302. Detailed account of what has
led to Marcus becoming a spy when asked to do so by
his chief. His best friend is a German. Author has
tenderness for Germans and Germany.
pW- male hero and war.
Story of an intelligence officer in the war. LBKM SP

009972   A RECKLESS PURITAN. London: Hodder &
Stoughton, [1920] BMC. New York: G.H. Doran, [c1921]
NUC.

TLS-Irish girl married to Englishman returns home 1 day to find another woman in house. Leaves, story is about her struggles. Works for a woman of many causes, spends a month in jail for alleged theft.

009973   YOUNG MR. GIBBS. London: E. Nash, 1911 BMC.

Comedy of wife who persisted in being young and vivacious though she had a grown son. TLS Son's efforts to keep her from bringing ridicule upon him. LBKM

RICKARD, MRS. VICTOR. See RICKARD, JESSIE LOUISA (MOORE).

RICKER, SARAH B. United States.

009974   IN THE SIXTIES. New York: Abbey Press, [1903] NUC.

RICKERT, EDITH. See RICKERT, MARTHA EDITH.

RICKERT, MARTHA EDITH. 1871-1938. United States.

009975   THE BEGGAR IN THE HEART. BY EDITH RICKERT. New York: Moffat, Yard, 1909 NUC. London: E. Arnold, 1909 BMC.

See BKM, vol 30, 1909-10
Female vagabond, potter, middle-aged heroine gives herself to nobleman for life. PW 10-23-09
Settles in London. Petty Zou is her name; she's wooed by a Lord who does finally get a yes from her. Elderly heroine-"exceedingly modern" ATH

009976   FOLLY. BY EDITH RICKERT. New York: Baker & Taylor, [1906] NUC. London: E. Arnold, 1906 BMC NUC.

BKM 23 1906 Loveless marriage-defies conventions but returns to husband after death of other man.
PW-Husband's virtues madden spirited young wife, falls for poet; leaves husband to nurse him.
NYT Triangle
ACAD 0
ATH Book opens with strain of rejoicing that Folly can regard her first born without actual detestation. Husband forgives her her poet and gladly accepts her back.

009977   THE GOLDEN HAWK. BY EDITH RICKERT. New York: Baker and Taylor, 1907 NUC. London: E. Arnold, 1907 BMC.

Heroine is wild enough in her way till it's crushed out of her by her lord and master? ACAD
A picaresque kind of novel concerning Trillon romantic SP

009978   OUT OF THE CYPRESS SWAMP. BY EDITH RICKERT. London: Methuen, 1902 BMC NUC.

ATH 3-29-02- "author's chief care is centered on her hero"

009979   THE REAPER. BY EDITH RICKERT. London: Arnold, 1904 BMC. Boston: Houghton, Mifflin, 1904 NUC.

Hero's mother is a drunkard Asla "defies widowhood"
Story of fisher folk LBKM, v27-28,179
PW-"fine char. study of strong and weak women"
NYT-hero's mother drinks
TLS-0

RIDDELL, CHARLOTTE ELIZA LAWSON (COWAN). 1832-1906. United Kingdom.

009980   THE BANSHEE'S WARNING, AND OTHER TALES. London: Remington, 1894 BMC.

009981   DID HE DESERVE IT? London: Downey, 1897 BMC.

The "shop" of the literary trade. He married young, supports family of nine as a journalist. Writes a bitter review of a friend's book; friend kills self. Daughter loses faith in him. But she marries happily. He buys into a publishing business and weds a rich widow. ACAD 51:496.
Wrote a scathing review though he admired the book. ATH 110:186

009982   THE HEAD OF THE FIRM. BY MRS. J. H. RIDDELL. New York: J. W. Lovell, [c1891] NUC. London: W. Heinemann, 1892 NUC.

CR 18:165. He goes wrong and is rescued and forever

after cared for by sweet and "phenomenally good" heroine.
SP 69:824. She is a "daughter of the people." Success does not spoil her. Strong and kind.
LBKM 3:29. Aileen, a "superior coster" girl gains a fortune and becomes educated for society. The head of the firm, a generous kind man ends up in "fraudulent bankruptcy."
ATH 100:443
PW-She is a Vender of fruits and vegetables. She inherits money and hires a governess to educate her for her new position.
ACAD 42:332. She marries Philip Vernbum.

009983   A MAD TOUR; OR, A JOURNEY UNDERTAKEN IN AN INSANE MOMENT THROUGH CENTRAL EUROPE ON FOOT. BY MRS. J. H. RIDDELL. London: R. Bentley, 1891 NUC BMC. New York, Chicago: U. S. Book, [c1891] NUC.

CR 18:190. Woman of mid age and young youth set out on walking tour; she has many apprehensions about succeeding physically. She is the one who endures and ends up as his nurse.
PW "light and amusing"

009984   MY FIRST LOVE, AND MY LAST LOVE [A SEQUEL]. BY MRS. J. H. RIDDELL. New York: J. W. Lovell, [1891] NUC. London: Hutchinson, [1891] BMC. (Eng. ed.: My First Love. A Novel.)

A successful English lawyer daydreams about two women in his past. PW 7-25-91.
Sweetly sentimental; told by hero. Loved a young woman who was forced to marry man of her own class. He married a woman he didn't love. They are one and the same? LW
Story from a man's point of view. GODEY'S 123, 270

009985   A RICH MAN'S DAUGHTER. BY MRS. J. H. RIDDELL. New York: International News, [c1895] NUC. London: F. V. White, 1897 BMC.

Claud Dagley a shilling doctor, his "delicate brutalities"; A reformed wife beater, and the heroine, a weak character. SR 84:475
Mrs. Vink, wife of wife-beater, is a cheat and a liar "deserves the frequent drubbings her husband gives her." Her husband is a drinker as well. Focus of story the doctor himself a cad and an egoist. ACAD 52:Fic. Sup. 46
PW3-21-96. Young doctor who desires wealth and power persuades youngest daughter of rich man to secretly marry him.

009986   A SILENT TRAGEDY: A NOVEL. London: F. V. White, 1893 BMC.

Walter Pernon becomes chaplain of a leper hospital making a forced declaration that he's a leper. Becomes one, dies. ACAD 43:459

RIDDELL, MRS. J. H. See RIDDELL, CHARLOTTE ELIZA LAWSON (COWAN).

RIDDING, LAURA ELIZABETH.

009987   BY WEEPING CROSS. London: Hodder and Stoughton, 1899 BMC.

Simple story of life in 15th cent Fr-with horrors hard by. BAKER 03 169
Concerns love and rel. persecution-a Cistercian abbey in So. Fr. is center of the locale of the story. ACAD 57:602

RIDEOUT, MRS. JACOB BARZILLA. United States.

009988   SHE BEATS THE DEVIL [ANONYMOUS]. Los Angeles, Cal.: C. W. Palm Co., 1898 W.

RIDGEWAY, ALGERNON, pseud. See WOOD, ANNA COGSWELL.

RIDLEY, ALICE (DAVENPORT). D. 1945. United Kingdom.

009989   ANNE MAINWARING. London: Longmans, 1901 BMC. New York: Longmans, Green, 1901 NUC.

LBKM May 01
BKM 13 (1901)503
Heroine "stormy, strenuous" feels she's destined to be a great artist, but married young to a man socially her inferior. Her friendship with Lady Katherine and its downfall. BOOK NEWS 6-01
Friendship for another woman. Anne, a thorn in her mother's side ATH

009990   A DAUGHTER OF JAEL. London: Longmans,
Green, 1904 BMC NUC.

Heroine decides to kill her grandfather who humiliates
her brother. She does so, keeps her secret, avoids
soc. devotes self to brother. Then she falls in love.
Does she tell the man? (reviewer won't say) Author is
sympathetic. Presents her as strong minded,
sufficient, with the highest motives. NyT 05,21
Author is sympathetic to this woman who murders.
Heroine has the courage to take what seems to her the
only way to save her brother and the courage to keep
her secret and bear the guilt alone. And years later
she's tempted to use the same method when a woman
threatens to win her husband, but she doesn't.
Frances-a masterful study. LBKM 27-8,p.222
PW -kills her grandfather for sake of her brother;
grandfather-cruel old miser who has starved and beaten
the children. Is later tempted to kill woman who moves
in with her and husband.
ATH O
TLS-was entirely justified in killing her grandfather.
Her punishment wasw temptation to kill the other
woman-agonies of guilt.

009991   MARGERY FYTTON. London: Chapman & Hall,
1913 NUC BMC. New York: Duffield, 1913 PW.

PW 8-9-13 426 "Margery, a child of ten, believes
herself to be the beloved daughter and heiress of Hugh
Fytton, but when her beautiful mother dies Hugh
discovers from some old love letters of his wife that
the little girl is not of his race at all. The poor
child cannot think why her father has turned against
her, and she hates the youth who is the possessor of
the beautiful house which should have been hers. The
heir, her supposed cousin, is in misery over the whole
matter too, and such is the situation when at
twenty-one, by her father's command, Margery learns
the secret of her birth. This is the main thread of
the story."

009992   THE SPARROW WITH ONE WHITE FEATHER. BY
LADY RIDLEY. London: Smith, Elder, 1905 BMC 1906 NUC.
New York: Dutton, 1906 NUC.

Father is completely estranged from the daughter he
loved once he learns he's not her father. Dies without
reconciling this attitude. Learns from father's
solicitor at age twenty five the truth; breaks
engagement. SP
Husband discovers wife's infidelity after years of
married life, effect of the discovery on him and her
daughter. "author impartial throughout" TLS

009993   THE STORY OF ALINE. London: Chapman and
Hall, 1896 NUC BMC.

LBKM 11:96, Mrge, love, friendships, benevolence gave
her pain. Her grief and capacity for suffering,
delicate & sensitive work.
ATH 108:871. Her husband's illness makes a strain on
her fortitude. Painful subject handled with
"commendable restraint."
She has nothing in common with her husband who is
athletic and not intellectual. She has a friend in
Gerald Eversley. Then she she invites a niece to come
live with her. This young woman looks like her aunt
and soon wins Gerald's attention. At this same time,
the husband is badly crippled in an accident. The
crisis brings out Aline's passion for happiness. She
does all she can to keep them apart and when the
husband kills himself, it's too late. Gerald and her
niece are engaged. A few years later when she's about
to marry someone else, she calls Gerald back into her
life and resumes a relationship with him. SP 78:176

RIDLEY, LADY. See RIDLEY, ALICE (DAVENPORT).

RIDLEY, WINIFRED.

009994   THE OMEN. A ROMANCE AND A TRAGEDY.
London: J. Ouseley, [1912] BMC.

RIGGS, KATE DOUGLAS (SMITH) WIGGIN. 1856-1923. United
States.

009995   BLUEBEARD; A MUSICAL FANTASY. BY KATE
DOUGLAS WIGGIN. HEREIN LIES THE STORY OF THE
MIRACULOUS DISCOVERY IN A HAT BOX OF AN UNPUBLISHED
OPERA BY THE LATE RICHARD WAGNER, DEALING IN THE MOST
UNIQUE AND CLIMACTERIC MANNER WITH FEMINISM, TRIAL
MARRIAGE, BIGAMY AND POLYGAMY; ITS LIBRETTO AND
LEIT-MOTIVE HAVE BEEN STUDIED WITH PASSION AND ARE NOW
REVEALED WITH RELIGIOUS ZEAL. BY KATE DOUGLAS WIGGIN.
New York and London: Harper, 1914 NUC BMC.

ML65 Music-anecdotes, facetiae, satire.

009996   A CATHEDRAL COURTSHIP, AND PENELOPE'S
ENGLISH EXPERIENCES. BY KATE DOUGLAS WIGGIN. Boston:
Houghton Mifflin, 1893 NUC. London: Gay and Bird, 1893
BMC NUC.

Two American women's experiences in England; all the
humor that is to be found in the English. NATION
56:475.
Penelope Hamilton, an artist. Celia Van Tyck and
Catherine Schuyler tour the English Cathedral towns.
Catherine meets a young architect who saves her from
an embarrassing situation, the consequences of which
each records in separate accounts. Both Heroines marry
US American heroes. ACAD 44:208
Fresh, humorous vivacious-both stories, ATH 102:189.

009997   THE DIARY OF A GOOSE GIRL. BY KATE
DOUGLAS WIGGIN. Boston: Houghton, Mifflin, 1902 NUC.
London: Gay & Bird, 1902 BMC.

NYT 5-17-02 farm life.

009998   FINDING A HOME. BY KATE DOUGLAS WIGGIN.
Boston: Houghton, Mifflin, [c1907] NUC.

From the author's book entitled "Timothy's quest"

009999   MARM LISA. BY KATE DOUGLAS WIGGIN.
Boston: Houghton Mifflin, 1896 NUC. London: Gay and
Bird, [1896] BMC.

Adopted child-half witted. Mrs. Grubb who adopts her
is an irresponsible humanitarian--she cares for
humanity. Not individuals. Merciless indictment of the
type. SP 78:447.
She's a congenital idiot. In the hands of Mrs. Grubb
she gets poor care. But Mistress Mary, who is part of
a woman's community that cares for such people, takes
her in hand. Story of Liza's mental growth under the
care of these women and Liza's act of heroism.
Treatment of Mrs. Grubb is "goodnatured satire." ACAD
51:146.
She's 10, psychology of a dark soul. She's a "spirit
in prison" with only one ray of light-a vision of
duty. "Exquisitely symbolic character study...of a
feeble-minded child." Her mistress cares for humanity
but not individuality. Rescued by another woman. BKM
4:571.

010000   MOTHER CAREY'S CHICKENS. BY KATE DOUGLAS
WIGGIN. Boston: Houghton Mifflin, 1911 NUC.

Father dies straight off, Mrs Carey left with 4
children (but his memory a spiritual presence). Poor,
she still takes in a little cousin. LBKM
"Luscious sentimentality" SP

010001   NEW CHRONICLES OF REBECCA. BY KATE
DOUGLAS WIGGIN. Boston: Houghton Mifflin, 1907 BMC
NUC. London: A. Constable, [1909] BMC.

Rebecca "hot tempered, impulsive and adventurous" with
literary ambitions is precocious masterful, great in
courage and has a warm heart. Leader of the girls at
school. Always writing stories. Her diary of "queer"
thoughts is the best part. SR

010002   THE OLD PEABODY PEW: A CHRISTMAS ROMANCE
OF A COUNTRY CHURCH. BY KATE DOUGLAS WIGGIN. London:
A. Constable, [1907] BMC NUC. Boston: Houghton
Mifflin, 1907 NUC.

010003   PENELOPE'S ENGLISH EXPERIENCES. BY KATE
DOUGLAS WIGGIN. Boston: Houghton Mifflin, 1900 NUC
BMC. London: Gay and Bird, 1901 BMC.

010004   PENELOPE'S EXPERIENCES IN SCOTLAND. BEING
EXTRACTS FROM THE COMMONPLACE BOOK OF PENELOPE
HAMILTON. BY KATE DOUGLAS WIGGIN. London: Gay and
Bird, 1898 BMC. London: Bell, 1898 NUC.

SP 80:796. Much like Mrs. Cotes travel-fiction.
Penelope and two friends, Salemina, a middle-aged
Bostonian spinster, Francesca, a vivacious New Yorker;
their enthusiasm for things Scottish. Witty.
ATH 112:32.

010005   PENELOPE'S IRISH EXPERIENCES. BY KATE
DOUGLAS WIGGIN. Boston: Houghton Mifflin, 1901 NUC.
London: Gay & Bird, 1901 BMC NUC.

Three women (one married, one engaged and one "to be
settled" travel in Ireland) meet a stranded yankee

girl and befriend her BOOK NEWS 6-'01
Sequel to "Penelope's Progress"

010006   PENELOPE'S POSTSCRIPTS; SWITZERLAND:
VENICE: WALES: DEVON: HOME. BY KATE DOUGLAS WIGGIN.
Boston: Houghton Mifflin, 1915 NUC. London: Hodder &
Stoughton, 1915 BMC.

Tells of her husband; home, three babies. NYT
Little accounts of her travels SP

010007   PENELOPE'S PROGRESS: BEING SUCH EXTRACTS
FROM THE COMMONPLACE BOOK OF PENELOPE HAMILTON AS
RELATED TO HER EXPERIENCES IN SCOTLAND. BY KATE
DOUGLAS WIGGIN. London: A.P. Watt, 1897 BMC. Boston:
Houghton Mifflin, 1898 NUC.

CR 33:101. Sounds like same as Penelope's experiences.

010008   REBECCA OF SUNNYBROOK FARM. BY KATE
DOUGLAS WIGGIN. London: Gay & Bird, 1903 BMC. Boston:
Houghton Mifflin, 1903 BMC NUC.

010009   THE ROMANCE OF A CHRISTMAS CARD. BY KATE
DOUGLAS WIGGIN. Boston: Houghton Mifflin, 1916 NUC.
London: Hodder & Stoughton, [1916] BMC.

Christmas cards bring two men back to their native
village. One renews a romance broken off by his
departure PW 90:1360 10/21/16
ATH-0

010010   ROSE O' THE RIVER. BY KATE DOUGLAS
WIGGIN. Boston: Houghton Mifflin, 1905 NUC. London:
Hodder & Stoughton, 1909 BMC NUC.

Pretty love story. PW 10-7-05
NYT 635,05
ACAD 05, 1008
LBKM 05, v 29-30
TLS 05 305

010011   THE STORY OF WAITSTILL BAXTER. BY KATE
DOUGLAS WIGGIN. Boston: Houghton Mifflin, 1913 NUC.
London: Hodder & Stoughton, [1913] BMC.

Stepsisters-their problems as young women Patience;
fiery, red hair -unconventional NYT 1913, 518
Waitsell is a young woman; her half-sister Patience
daughters of stern Deacon whose 3 wives die joyously
to get away from him. Neither of daughters meek; can't
be dutiful easily. Both revolt, one impulsively; the
other calmly, "sometimes a little too sweet" heroine
refuses to submit to injustice-surprising for the time
about 1840. NYT
Waitsell was a drudge to her father; story of that
drudgery, father's strict morals and narrow outlook.
TLS

010012   SUSANNA AND SUE. BY KATE DOUGLAS WIGGIN.
Boston: Houghton-Mifflin, 1909 NUC. London: Hodder &
Stoughton, 1909 BMC.

"Susanna leaves her pleasure-loving husband and their
son John and makes her home in a Shaker community with
her little daughter Sue. The story tells of the
problems of married life and the conflicting duties
which assail Susanna's conscience, and especially of
the help and inspiration which she received from the
Shakers and from her little girl." BKM, 30, 1909-10
Woman leaves husband with one child, takes Sue, has
happy life with Shakers, feels guilty, returns, all's
well. 10-9-09 PW
She settles down with the Shakers till peace of mind
returns. Study of Shakers who renounce the world and
never marry. The "tragedy" that occurs when two Shaker
young people fall in love, run away to marry. LBKM

RIIS, STELLA EUGENIE (ASLING). B. 1877. United States.

010013   CROWNED AT ELIM. BY STELLA EUGENIA
ASLING. New York: Smith and Wilkins, 1903 NUC.

Historical romance 12-12-03. PW

RINEHART, MARY (ROBERTS). 1876-1958. United States.

010014   THE AFTER HOUSE: A STORY OF LOVE, MYSTERY
AND A PRIVATE YACHT. Boston: Houghton Mifflin, 1914
NUC. London: Simpkin, Marshall, [1915] BMC.

Trad murder story TLS
"Ralph Leslie, just through his medical course and
anything but prosperous, has his capital reduced to
the vanishing point by an attack of typhoid. In order
to get a sea trip and make a little money, he ships as

cabinboy on the Turner's yacht. Turner is dissipated
and his wife and her sister have much to bear from
him, and the trip is far from pleasant even before
tragedy steps in. In one night the captain, a guest,
and a maid are all murdered, and no one knows by whom.
The mystery is a hard one to solve, suspicion pointing
first to one, then another, the solution being a
complete surprise."

010015   THE AMAZING ADVENTURES OF LETITIA
CARBERRY. Indianapolis: Bobbs-Merrill, [c1911] NUC.
London: Hodder & Stoughton, [1919] BMC.

NYT-Witty, adventurous old woman, unashamed of her
spinsterhood.She is a patient in a hospital, solves a
murder mystery. She has two friends of same age.
Tish-Lizzie-Aggie
mystery involving three "old maids" PW 12-1-11

010016   THE AMAZING INTERLUDE. London: J. Murray,
1918 BMC. New York: G. H. Doran, [c1918] NUC.

PW-Sara Lee living in conv. mid-west town is stirred
to help behind lines in France. She asks Ladies Aid
Society to send her over to start soup kitchen. She is
sweet, simple, finds love in Henri, a Belgian officer.
Does not ask but tells her fiance that she is going to
France.
NYT May 12, 1918, p.218-0
American young woman runs a house of mercy-dispenses
soup near the front line SP
Leaves quiet backwater existence finds happiness in
caring for war wounded and finds love. ATH
Sara Lee Kennedy serious, quiet, conscientious. "By no
means fashionable;" confident. Sponsored by Ladies
Working Party in US smuggled across channel assisted
by a Belg. officer and friend she nurses soldiers.
Happy end. SR

010017   BAB, A SUB-DEB. New York: G. H. Doran,
[1917] NUC. London: Hodder & Stoughton, [1920] BMC.

010018   THE CASE OF JENNIE BRICE. Indianapolis:
Bobbs-Merrill, [c1913] BMC NUC. London: Hodder &
Stoughton, [1919] BMC.

PW 83 3/1/13:768 "Scenes are laid in Pittsburgh during
the flood of 1907. A startling case of mistaken
identity; a network of incriminating circumstances
pointing to the guilt of the actress's husband; a
chain of evidence establishing a substanial alibi;
clues galore indicating a score of possibilities; a
jury trial; a strange love plot-all these go to make
this tale of mystery."

010019   THE CIRCULAR STAIRCASE. Indianapolis:
Bobbs-Merrill, [1908] NUC. London: Cassell, 1909 BMC.

PW-told by a middle-aged spinster who buys large
house. Mystery
Trad.
Detective TLS

010020   DANGEROUS DAYS. London: Hodder &
Stoughton, [1919] BMC. New York: G. H. Doran, [c1919]
NUC.

PW Effect of War on Amer society World War; 1916-18.
Male hero is a munitions company owner married to a
shallow woman Natalie. She spoils their son; she "has
no interest in the war" She's compared to Audrey
Valentine who is noble,etc. We get the love affair of
the son. Ends in tragedy. The idea of the book is that
people are totally indifferent to the war until the
U.S. got involved.
NYT 7-6-19,357

010021   "ISN'T THAT JUST LIKE A MAN"! New York:
G. H. Doran, [c1920] BMC NUC.

010022   K. London: Smith, Elder, 1915 BMC.
Boston: Houghton Mifflin, 1915 NUC.

Nurse-doctor mystery 8-7-15 PW
Anguish of marital infidelities, dreams of girlhood
unfulfilled,raw life-centers on K PW Book Rev Sept 15
LBKM Two MD's one a U.S. superman and one naughty, and
two nurses.
SP Chief theme is development of Sidney Page's rom.

010023   LONG LIVE THE KING! Boston: Houghton
Mifflin, 1917 NUC. London: J. Murray, 1917 BMC.

About a Eur. court, a king, his escapades intrigues of
court. PW
A Crown Prince of ten who wants a dog NYT

TLS-Hist, Male Hero

010024   THE MAN IN LOWER TEN. Indianapolis:
Bobbs-Merrill, [1909] NUC. London: Cassell, 1909 BMC.

    Detective PW 3-20-09

010025   A POOR WISE MAN. New York: G. H. Doran,
[c1920] NUC. London: Hodder & Stoughton, [1920] BMC.

    TLS-Lily and her revolt, after hard work in the war,
against luxurious home and tyrannical grandfather
leading to strange company and disaster.
    PW-She is tool of unscrupulous labor leader, arm of
innocent son of capitalism and star of a poor man's
life. Problem between labor and capital and futility
of mob violence.
    BKM-She and Willy (poor young man) have been
companions in non-belligerant war work. Akers, a
revolutionary radical is the villain.
    NYT 10-17-20 p.20 Her revolt is short-lived and
mistaken.

010026   THE STREET OF SEVEN STARS. Boston:
Houghton Mifflin, 1914 NUC. London: Cassell, 1915 BMC.

    Harmony Wells "young clever, but poor musician" falls
in love, story of claims of love and of art. TLS
PW 86 10/3/1123 "Suddenly Harmony realized that her
money was alost gone. She was studying in Vienna, and
dreamed that she would be a great violinist. It was
almost worse than if she had never started her work.
She would not give it up, and decided to stay and earn
more money to go on with it. She went hunting work and
found-Peter. He was nearly as poor as she, a student
and an American, too. He gave her sympathy and
chivalry, and that his little money between them.
Their home in the Street of Seven Stairs sheltered
tired Dr. Anna and Jimmie, a waif. The neighbors could
not believe that they were poor and happy and good,
all at once. The gossip spoiled their companionship
for a time, but not for all time, one may be sure."

010027   TISH. Boston: Houghton Mifflin, 1916 BMC
NUC. London: Hodder & Stoughton, [1917] BMC.

    Advents of three "dear old things""old maids" LBKM
Elderly spinsters Tish, Aggie and Lizzie-auto racing
scheme and her unconventional adventures. PW
90:8/5/16:438
    NYT-Lizzie is the narrator. One of the stories
involves a woman chauffeur.

010028   THE TRUCE OF GOD. New York: G. H. Doran,
[c1920] NUC.

    PW-Christmas story rom. chivalry in France.

010029   WHEN A MAN MARRIES. Indianapolis: Bobbs
Merrill, [c1909] NUC. London: Hodder & Stoughton,
[1920] BMC.

    NYT Woman narrator, friend is still miserably in love
with his divorced wife, she suggests a party, his
strait laced aunt (and his sole source of income)
arrives, divorce is concealed by narrator posing as
his wife for a few hours but their house is put under
quarantine.
    trad. mystery PW 12-4-09

010030   WHERE THERE'S A WILL. Indianapolis:
Bobbs-Merrill, [c1912] NUC. New York: A. L. Burt,
[1914] NUC.

    PW Fem hero.
    NYT Heroine, a spring-house girl in a sanitarium, has
strong individuality and pungent humor. The adventure
portrayed is most exciting time of her long and
diplomatic career.

010031   THE WINDOW AT THE WHITE CAT.
Indianapolis: Bobbs-Merrill, [c1910] NUC. London: E.
Nash, 1911 BMC.

    Mystery murder PW

RION, HANNA. See VER BECK, HANNA (RION).

RIPLEY, MARY ANNA (PAULL). B. 1838.

010032   HILDEBRAND AND CICELY; OR, THE MONK OF
TAVYSTOKE ABBAYE. BY M. A. PAULL. Cincinnati, O.:
Cranston and Curts, 1895 NUC.

    He is an English Augustinian monk of the 16th century
who sought shelter in the abbey. He keeps his vows

though sorely tempted by Cicely. PW 12-28-95:1211

010033   LED BY LOVE. London: Hodder, 1894 BMC.

010034   LOVE UNFEIGNED; OR "LET LOVE BE WITHOUT
DISSIMULATION". London: Jarrold, 1891 BMC.

010035   THE MYSTERY OF THE MOUNT; OR THE STORY OF
MAY'S SIXPENCE. London: T. Nelson, 1898 BMC.

RITA, pseud. See HUMPHREYS, ELIZA MARGARET J. (GOLLAN),
Also HUMPHREYS, ELIZA MARGARET J. (GOLLAN) AND LOUISA
ALICE BAKER.

RITCHIE, BARBARA LOGIE.

010036   THE TENANT OF SEA COTTAGE. London: Drane,
[1916] BMC.

    TLS-Lady burglar (time honored?) and her accomplice,
an artist.

RITCHIE, MRS. DAVID GEORGE. United Kingdom.

010037   THE HUMAN CRY. London: Methuen, 1912 BMC.

    TLS-satire of "half-educated woman of our times."
ATH-unrest is motive force of three characters-woman
becomes dupe of an imposter. Young woman with
hereditary taint feels she is unfairly handicapped.
SP-Eva is the pseudo-educ. woman who is mean and has a
number of religious crazes and final overwhelming (too
much) tragedy. Mossmore (an ambitious radical) says
"women of good education need protection as much as
men of no education." She also ridicules the
sentimental radical. The dominant theme is hereditary
insanity and sad fate of heroine who is--who? Violet?

010038   MAN AND THE CASSOCK. London: Methuen,
1908 BMC NUC.

    SR-unpromising-consumptive Anglican priest and his
selfish sister who wants him to get married.
    SP-

010039   THE NEW WARDEN. London: J. Murray, 1918
BMC.

    TLS-love
    SP-love
    NYT-romantic love.

010040   THE TRUTHFUL LIAR. London: Methuen, 1903
BMC NUC.

    A dean with contempt for women; a woman of judgment,
knowledge and humor narrowly escapes falling victim to
a blackguard. ATH 122:715.
    One heroine, tall, serious, full of faith and all
virtue; the other-doubting, flippant and "in the
horrid phrase of the past, a new woman." Author drives
home her own philosophy. Modern audacious novel. TLS
1903:273

010041   TWO SINNERS. London: Smith Elder, 1915
BMC. New York: E. P. Dutton, [1915?] NUC.

    Ursula loses chance to marry to care for other two
sisters. PW 7-31-15
    The sins are pride, hardness of heart. NYT
    Some satiric sketches. Maud forced to face
srinsterhood or marry a wealthy man she likes but
doesn't love; becomes engaged to him, but finds she
can't go through with the marriage; learns to love him
after long separation. But author doesn't show what
makes Maud Monckton change. TLS ATH

RITCHIE, MRS. RICHMOND. See SARTORIS, ADELAIDE.

RIVERS, RUTH. Nationality Unknown.

010042   SHE WAS A WIDOW. London: J. Long, 1911
BMC.

    "She was also a mercenary, deceitful. sensual woman
interested above all other things in the effect of her
lures upon the sex- instinct of the men she met. This
story is a nauseous delineation in the first person of
a type of char. that our plain-speaking forefathers
would have summed up in one word." SR

RIVERS, WILLIAM A., pseud. See KING, VERONICA.

RIVES, AMELIE. See TROUBETZKOY, AMELIE (RIVES) CHANLER.

RIVES, HALLIE ERMINIE. See WHEELER, HALLIE ERMINIE (RIVES).

ROADS, ETHEL. B. 1890. United States.

010043   THE ROMANCE OF A GUARDSMAN. [Reading,
Pa.]: [Press of Reading Eagle], [c1917] NUC.

ROBB, HELEN R. United States.

010044   GREGORY, THE ARMENIAN: A SON OF THE KING.
Boston: Pilgrim Press, [c1898] NUC.

Protestant life in Armenia during Russo-Turkish war
1877-78 to 99 LW 30:23

ROBBINS, ALICE EMILY. United Kingdom.

010045   THINGS THAT PASS. London: A. Melrose,
1912 BMC NUC.

TLS-highly moral tale of upper-class life.
ACAD-highly moral tale of upper-class life. Opens with
Mary West, a new bride, coming to her new farm home.
She's one of those people meant to serve others. Lena
Williams comes to work at the farm; becomes Mary's
daughter-in-law. The story covers many years. LBKM

010046   A TOUR AND A ROMANCE. London: A. Melrose,
1911 BMC NUC. New York: Baker & Taylor, 1911 NUC.

More of a tour than a romance. PW 9-16-11
Joana at first considers culture, money and position
above love, but finds her destiny in an Englishman.
ACAD

ROBBINS, EMMA SHELTON. United States.

010047   OH, YOU ENGLISH! New York: Neale, 1915
NUC.

Amily at her father's death left the Ozarks and went
to NY to earn her living. After escaping perils of
many kinds. She married Lord Richard and discovered
her English relatives (from father's side.) PW
89:2/5/16:392

ROBBINS, MABEL HOTCHKISS. United States.

010048   THE GENIUS OF ELIZABETH ANNE. Boston:
Pilgrim Press, [c1916] NUC.

Humble life in a crowded city, the trials and triumphs
of Elizabeth. PW BKM

010049   THE HEART OF A MOTHER-TO-BE. Boston:
Pilgrim Press, [c1917] NUC.

Diary telling dreams, hopes and fears preceding
motherhood. PW

ROBBINS, MRS. S. S. See ROBBINS, SARAH (STUART).

ROBBINS, SARAH (STUART). B. 1817.

010050   HULDAH BRENT'S WILL. BY MRS. S. S.
ROBBINS. Boston: Bradley and Woodruff, [c1891] NUC.

She's 82. Makes a will that involves Paul Ainsworth.
The story tells of lawyer's temptations, fate and
their effect on Paul. PW 4-4-91.

ROBERTS, CLARA (LEMORE). D. 1898. United States.

010051   AT WAR WITH DESTINY. BY CLARA LEMORE.
London: W. Stevens, [1896] BMC.

010052   A BONDAGE WITHOUT FETTERS. BY CLARA
LEMORE. London: W. Stevens, [1898] BMC.

010053   A COVENANT WITH THE DEAD: A NOVEL. BY
CLARA LEMORE. London: Griffith, Farran, [1892] BMC.
Philadelphia: J. B. Lippincott, 1892 NUC. (Published
anonymously in England.)

LW 23:214. Brave little Dolly.
CR 7-23-92 Son of lord marries actress. Tangle of
son's marriages, straightened out by father
ACAD 41:562. Hero marries a woman with whom he has
been stranded over night, although he already has a
wife (he dies immediately after the wedding). His
brother married a woman who already had a husband.

010054   GWEN DALE'S ORDEAL [ANONYMOUS]. London:
W. Stevens, [1891] BMC.

010055   A LITTLE USURPER [ANONYMOUS]. London: W.
Stevens, [1900] BMC.

010056   THE LOVE OF AN OBSOLETE WOMAN. CHRONICLED
BY HERSELF [ANONYMOUS]. Westminster: Constable, 1897
BMC.

PW "The story of 6 years in the life of a woman who
insists that woman is only half of man, that she does
not know the meaning of the word life until she has
lived in close, constant, and unrestricted communion
with her other half. She is 27 when she finds this
'other half' in her theatrical manager, a married man.
The writer has set out to prove a theory, but has
succeeded only in writing an unhealthy & unnecessary
book."
Starts with the first meeting with her lover. Writes
only of him, ends when he dies. SR 83:725

010057   MADGE DALE'S MARRIAGE PORTION
[ANONYMOUS]. London: W. Stevens, [1891] BMC.

010058   PENHALA: A WAYSIDE WIZARD. BY CLARA
LEMORE. London: Hurst and Blackett, 1895 BMC NUC.

Hero's "sorrows under false accusation" passion,
mystery, romance with a Nihilist for an evil genius up
to the happy end. SR 79:230
SP 73:734. Nihilist scoundrel, wicked squire, mock
marriage.
ACAD: Cornish

010059   PUT ASUNDER. BY THE AUTHOR OF "GWEN
DALE'S ORDEAL" [ANONYMOUS]. London: W. Stevens, [1895]
BMC.

ROBERTS, ELLEN. United States.

010060   ONE OF EARTH'S DAUGHTERS. Boston: Arena,
1893 W.

ROBERTS, HELEN C. Nationality Unknown.

010061   THE DISCREET ADVENTURE. London: T. F.
Unwin,, [1917] BMC NUC.

Character study of Alberta Upwey, a woman with a
superior attitude toward "social inferiors," worships
Art. "We are meant to sympathize with her throughout."
Story concerns the way she and her two sisters live
their lives. LBKM
What does she do? Becomes a governess suspected of
having designs on her employer's unmarried brother.
She's shocked to learn her employers not a married
couple. He has a mad wife.? ATH

010062   A FREE HAND. London: Duckworth, 1914 BMC
NUC. New York: [n.d.] NUC.

LBKM-Detailed study from childhood to middle age.
Reviewer states hero's mother and his first wife, his
daughter and his second wife kept him in harness all
his life as a seaside dentist, which, except for one
moment, he bears with a quiet heroism. Author's real
talent lies in the powerful vision of his first wife,
a strange heroine. His folly is marrying a woman who
loved her profession more than her husband.
SR 147:609. First wife an actress, who left him. He
tries to find solace in their little daughter. Ridley
Courage-hero.
TLS: Alison told him when they married that she did
not believe in it, and that there might come a time
when she would want her independence.

010063   OLD BRENT'S DAUGHTER. London: Duckworth,
1912 BMC.

TLS-Well educated daughter of a well-to-do butcher.
ACAD Class differences sensationalism she meets man of
ancient family. amor vincit.

010064   SOMETHING NEW. London: Duckworth, 1913
BMC.

Tessa Harting shocked by death of sister's fiance on
his wedding eve, decides to "find herself." gives up
her soft-well-fed kind of life for harder life with
workers. ACAD ATH

ROBERTS, INA BREVOORT (DEANE). B. 1874. United States.

010065   THE LIFTING OF A FINGER. Philadelphia: J.
B. Lippincott, 1901 NUC.

ROBERTS, LIBBIE M.

010066   THE PADRE'S MISSION. [Los Angeles]:
[Provident Print Shop], [c1911] NUC.

In verse. NUC

ROBERTS, MARGARET. 1833-1919. United Kingdom.

010067   LILIAN AND LILI. BY THE AUTHOR OF "THE
ATELIER DU LYS" [ANONYMOUS]. London: A. D. Innes, 1892
BMC.

Lili is the daughter of a reckless Englishman and Fr.
mother. Her father lost the fortune that went to
Lilian, daughter of young brother. The two cousins
meet in England. Fr. manners keep them apart for Lili
is glad to return to France and give up the claim for
the inheritance. ACAD, ATH 98 859
Second to Lili in interest is Mitchell the cat. SR
11-7-91,533

010068   NICCOLINA NICCOLINI. BY THE AUTHOR OF
"MADEMOISELLE MORI" [ANONYMOUS]. London: Gardiner,
Darton, [1897] NUC BMC. (NUC does not indicate
anonymous publication.)

Young English widow in Italy. The growing up of little
Lina and her love affair. ACAD 52 Fic sup 97.
Lina loses her parents, left unknown runs wild,
dominates other children finally restored to step
grandmother. ATH 782:110.
SP 81:221. Italy. The marriage of an Italian man to a
young English woman.
LIT 2:451. "Love could hardly be altogether absent
from any typical study of a woman, but it is of the
essence of this con-ception that love takes a
subordinate place, and it is here but slightly touched
on." In this author's stories her heroines are endowed
with talent, the improvement of which is one main
object of their lives. "This gives an independence and
complete-ness to a woman's career which it is hard for
her to attain in any other way." Niccolina is an
orphan of an Italian painter and Eng. Mother.

010069   NOT ONE OF US. BY THE AUTHOR OF
"MADEMOISELLE MORI" [ANONYMOUS]. London: National
Society, [1892] NUC BMC. New York: T. Whittaker,
[1892] NUC. (NUC does not indicate anonymous
publication.)

010070   THE SECRET OF MADAME DE MONLUC. BY THE
AUTHOR OF "MADEMOISELLE MORI" [ANONYMOUS]. London:
Methuen, 1891 BMC 1894 NUC. (NUC does not indicate
anonymous publication.)

ACAD. 41:60. Old French nobility; she could not stand
any breath of discredit to family. Locked her
granddaughter in a convent, but she is freed to marry.

010071   A YOUNGER SISTER. BY THE AUTHOR OF "THE
ATELIER DU LYS" [ANONYMOUS]. London: Longmans, Green,
1892 BMC NUC.

ATH 100:58. contrast between two sisters. Father is
pedant, a kind egoist. Lake District.
LW 23:245. Guenola, the younger sister is the "fin de
siecle young woman." She finds life in country home
beyond bearing, at last is free to earn her own
living. After experiencing some of the difficulties of
being a woman worker, she is less self-confident and
better appreciates home and love.
CR 8-6-92 Two sisters, one her father's devoted and
adored companion, the other longing to study Greek and
math and therefore considered selfish. Older one
accepts marriage offer and leaves country, younger
makes sacrifice and remains as companion of
narrow-minded father.
SP 68:889. Story concludes with her marriage and her
position in her husband's printing shop as manager of
employees there.

ROBERTS, MARY ELEANOR (ROBERTS). B. 1867.

010072   CLOTH OF FRIEZE. Philadelphia and London:
J. B. Lippincott, 1911 NUC.

ROBERTS, NINA.

010073   "ODETTE." A ROMANCE. London: A. H.
Stockwell, [1920] BMC.

ROBERTSON, ALICE ALBERTHE. B. 1871. United States.

010074   BLACK BUTTERFLIES: A NOVEL. BY BERTHE ST.
LUZ. New York: R.F. Fenno, 1905 NUC.

Story of Hindu mysticism PW 7-22-05

010075   TAMAR CURZE. BY BERTHE ST. LUZ. New York:

R. F. Fenno, [c1908] NUC.

PW- Half woman, half tiger wins cousin's love, wife
dies, he repulses her, tiger kills him
BKM evil influence

ROBERTSON, ESTHER. B. 1844. United States.

010076   THE WORLD WELL LOST. New York: Benziger,
1898 NUC.

PW-marriage of Catholic woman to Protestant husband,
promise that half the children be raised in each
religion. Reclaims promise on deathbed. Both children
become Catholic, the daughter a nun.

ROBERTSON, ETHEL FLORENCE LINDESAY (RICHARDSON). 1870-1946.
United Kingdom.

010077   THE FORTUNES OF RICHARD MAHONY. BY HENRY
HANDEL RICHARDSON. New York: H. Holt, 1917 NUC.
London: Heinemann, [1917] NUC BMC.

First vol. of trilogy, followed by "The Way Home" and
"Ultima Thule" NUC
ATH-Male hero.
Man and wife in Austraila. He sets up medical
practice. They return to Eng. PW
Changes in the town parallel changes in the man TLS
Edinburgh man off to gold rush in Aust., but can't mix
with the low life, can't make friends. Wife gets him
to start a practice. Holds deep resentment for Aust.
Then has an urge to return to England. Wife is a
capable housewife. SP

010078   THE GETTING OF WISDOM. BY HENRY HANDEL
RICHARDSON. London: W. Heinemann, 1910 NUC BMC. New
York: Duffield, 1910 NUC.

Development of unusual girl 12-16. Laura Rambotham
goes to boarding schhool in Aust. We get her thoughts,
emotions attitudes. PW
ACAD-unpleasant girl.
ATH-Temperament of an unusual sort. Remarkable study;
anatomical

010079   MAURICE GUEST. BY HENRY HANDEL
RICHARDSON. London: W. Heinemann, 1908 BMC NUC. New
York: P. R. Reynolds, 1908 NUC.

TLS-Male musician ? depressing.
BKM-Fem musician too
ATH-he is overmastered by a passion for a "worthless
Cleopatra," kills himself.
Music student in Germany. NYT

ROBERTSON, FRANCES FORBES. See HARROD, FRANCES
(FORBES-ROBERTSON).

ROBERTSON, HELEN FIELD. B. 1896.

010080   THE LETTERS OF A WOMAN WHO WAS. BY THE
WOMAN [ANONYMOUS]. Minneapolis, Minn.: W. H.
Robertson, 1917 NUC.

ROBERTSON, MAUDE.

010081   A WOMAN OF MOODS. London: Simpkin,
Marshall, [1903] BMC.

LBKM-Runaway mrg, separation after four months, meet
in Paris one year later, cold formal antagonism, keep
their secret-then what?
ATH-Her new fiance dies, she and husband reconciled.
Studies of French and American women; is well written.

ROBINS, ELIZABETH. See PARKES, ELIZABETH (ROBINS).

ROBINS, G. M. See REYNOLDS, GERTRUDE M. (ROBINS).

ROBINSON, F. MABEL. See ROBINSON, FRANCES MABEL.

ROBINSON, FRANCES MABEL. United Kingdom.

010082   CHIMAERA: A NOVEL. London: W. Heinemann,
1895 BMC.

Joe's life: struggles to be a sculptor burdened by a
vulgar wife. Becomes in the end a comedian. SR 80:55
Fannie Star, the wife, is amiable not a modern heroine
type ACAD 47:541
Joe learns at 22 that he is illegitimate, his mother
having eloped with a young soldier because her husband
was brutish. Joe joins the army because he's hurt by
the news. Army life described vividly. Meets his
comrade's sister, a servant, "indulges in a warm

flirtation though he still loves a young woman of his own class." When he learns she's engaged, becomes engaged to servant girl. ATH 105:836

010083   HOVENDEN, V. C.: THE DESTINY OF A MAN OF ACTION. A NOVEL. BY F. MABEL ROBINSON. London: Methuen, 1891 BMC.

Althea Rodriguez, half English and half Jewish, a temptress of violent passions. First loves Hovenden but when he loses his fortune she turns her love to a surgeon who drags her down to low life of Bohemia and leaves her down and out. She returns to Hovenden now a cripple and dies. ACAD
He is tender to her on her return. SP 67 926
Hovenden loses a leg. ATH 98 682
Hovenden, Victoria Cross winner, marries Althea on his return from war. Hovenden eventually marries another woman. SR 11-28-91, 615
CR: 17:37 Male hero. War with Zulus, elopement with married woman, monastary and finally marriage to old flame.
LW 23:110. Male hero, his life in army, loses his leg in civilian life, then he runs away with another man's wife. Repents, joins monastary, finally marries cousin who promises to be mother to his illegitimate child.

ROBINSON, MARGARET BLAKE. United States.

010084   THE LEFT-SIDE MAN. New York: J. S. Ogilvie Pub. Co., 1902 NUC.

Review describes the hero, an Irish patriot, says nothing of the heroine except she's well balanced, sensible. NYT 1903:18

010085   SOULS IN PAWN. A STORY OF NEW YORK LIFE. New York: F. H. Revell, [1900] BMC NUC.

ROBINSON, NELLIE GRACE. B. 1874. United States.

010086   PHILO'S DAUGHTER: THE STORY OF THE DAUGHTER OF THE THIEF WITH WHOM CHRIST WAS CRUCIFIED. Cincinatti: Jennings & Graham, [c1908] NUC.

Loyal daughter and father-time of Christ. PW 1-2-09

ROBINSON, SUZANNE (ANTROBUS), United States.

010087   THE KING'S MESSENGER: A NOVEL. BY SUZANNE ANTROBUS. New York and London: Harper, 1901 NUC.

Heroine leaves husband to bear a secret packet to the New France; falls in love with another man. BOOK NEWS Oct, 1901
Really sent. hist. study NYT

ROBSON, ISABEL STUART.

010088   MRS. PEDERSON'S NIECE. London: Cassell, 1901 BMC.

010089   THE ODDITY, A STORY OF HIGH SCHOOL LIFE. London: Jarrold, [1901] BMC.

010090   THE OLD HOUSE AT RUNGATE. London: R. Culley, 1901 BMC.

010091   THEODORA; OR, GOLDEN OPPORTUNITIES. London: R. Culley, 1902 BMC.

010092   THE TROUBLESOME BEVANS; OR, LAURENCE, THE HERO OF GREAT MORVANS. London: R. Culley, [1906] BMC.

010093   WHAT GLADYS DID. London: R. Culley, 1904 BMC.

ROCKWOOD, CAROLINE WASHBURN. United States.

010094   AN ADIRONDACK ROMANCE. New York: New Amsterdam Book Co., [c1897] NUC.

010095   AN EAST FLORIDA ROMANCE. New York: New Amsterdam Book Co., [c1897] NUC.

010096   IN BISCAYNE BAY. New York: Dodd, Mead, 1891 BMC NUC.

CR 17:324. Light romance with many photos of Florida. Two very happy romances, one between Tom and Nan who buy a yacht and cruise along Southern California. PW 12-19-91.

RODEN, ADA MARIA (JENYNS) JOCELYN. B. 1860.

010097   A BIG STAKE: A NOVEL. BY MRS. ROBERT

JOCELYN. London: F. V. White, 1892 BMC. Philadelphia: J. B. Lippincott, 1892 NUC.

PW Story of Aline and Valda, step mother and daughter, after father's death, their relationship, Valda's unconscious rivalry in Aline's romances, come to a good understanding of each other.
ATH 100:414. Efforts of mother to "utilize her daughter's wealth and social advantages."
ACAD 42:308. She "repents of her schemings."
SR. Lacks incident, mainly conversations between the two women, nothing approaching romance.

010098   A DANGEROUS BRUTE: A SPORTING SKETCH. London: Hutchinson, [1895] BMC.

ATH 107:48. Hawthorne a huge brown gentleman of a horse; his owners and their characters.
ACAD 49:134. For the hunting set. He had an incorrigible temper along with his other fine qualities.

010099   DRAWN BLANK: A NOVEL. BY MRS. ROBERT JOCELYN. London: F. V. White, 1892 BMC NUC. Philadelphia: J. B. Lippincott, 1892 NUC.

LW 23:89. Two baby girls exchanged at birth. Man marries one for her money, switch is discovered, he has drawn a blank.
Exchange of babies in order to get inheritance. Young woman grows up impersonates heiress but lack of scar on her foot gives up the game. ATH 98, 758
Nurse Grant substitutes her own baby for Lord Leftbury's daughter. PW 11-14-91.

010100   FOR ONE SEASON ONLY: A SPORTING NOVEL. London: F. V. White, 1893 BMC.

Large hands, loud voice, decided opinions daring manners. "She almost takes one's breath away." ACAD 44:337.
Big framed, honest, sportswoman, rough manner, mannish ways. ATH 102:353
New kind of heroine, six foot two inches. SR 76:388
Modern capable young woman, self-reliant, calls a spade a spade. Georgina Pembrooke is a paying guest for horse season at Macfluster Hall. There she hunts and wages a campaign against her host because he neglects his daughter, Charlotte. Georgina helps get rid of an unsuitable suitor for Charlotte. Also arranges that father will pay for London trip for the neglected Charlotte. SP 71, 435

010101   HENRY MASSINGER: A NOVEL. London: F. V. White, 1899 BMC.

He is a faith-healer. SP 82:830
Doris and her mother are "womanly women... Of the type we hope to survive." ATH 113:779

010102   JUANITA CARRINGTON: A SPORTING NOVEL. London: Digby, Long, [1896] BMC.

SR-Aristocracy-pure hero and heroine, wicked dark lady.
ATH 107:474. Romance
ACAD 49:423. Wholesome, does not have the atmosphere of the stable as many sporting novels have.

010103   LADY MARY'S EXPERIENCES: A NOVEL. London: White, 1897 BMC.

010104   MISS RAYBURN'S DIAMONDS. London: F. V. White, 1898 BMC.

ATH 112:347. She is a plain heroine with a short and dumpy figure. Mary Mortlock persuades her husband to steal the diamonds and pay his creditors and then replace them.
ACAD 54:193. Loved by Jim for herself and by his brother for her diamonds.

010105   ONLY A FLIRT: A NOVEL. London: F. V. White, 1897 BMC.

Sibyl Desmond is pursued by Capt Darrington who is twice her age, she's 16. He has no thought of marr. She knows what he is but loves him still. ATH 109:739

010106   ONLY A HORSE DEALER: A NOVEL. BY MRS. ROBERT JOCELYN. London: White, 1893 BMC NUC.

Pleasant; concerns hunting and horse-dealing and ghosts, unconventional heroine Helen Clinbarton. SP 70 259. Elizabeth Bevan, horse-dealer's sister-married, proprietor of her household. SR

75:155.
Crosspurposes in love affairs: ACAD 43:218.
Two sisters one of 17, one of 22. ATH 101:214.

010107   ONLY A LOVE STORY. London: Hutchinson,
1897 BMC.

Veronia Brackendale edu. in a "manly" fashion. Weds
Col. Radcliffe instead of Reggie who proposed. Reggie
goes off and weds Alice Carr who is much too good for
him. ATH 110:852

010108   PAMELA'S HONEYMOON: A NOVEL. London:
Hutchinson, [1894] BMC.

ACAD 45:391. Love story.
ATH 103:574. Sprightly story of a honeymoon.

010109   A REGULAR FRAUD. A NOVEL. London: F. V.
White, 1896 BMC.

SR-Young man staying at country house and dressing as
a young woman.
ATH 107:616. Cecil, 19, is "felt to be an undesirable
encumbrance when his mother is compelled to become the
adviser and companion" of three girls. Bicycling
brings on confusion and confession. Romance.

010110   RUN TO GROUND; A SPORTING NOVEL. London:
Hutchinson, 1894 BMC.

SR 78:717. Russian princess runs to ground her enemy
with her mesmeric powers. Heroine is Violet, ingenue,
and her love affairs.
Lt. Goring is accused of cheating at cards. He dies.
Princess Dagmar Saravaski who loved him comes to
England under an assumed name, settles near the
accuser. Through her mesmeric powers finds the guilty
one and clears Goring's name. ACAD 47:9
Hypnotism brings to light a crime committed five years
earlier. A too perfect heroine and her love affair. SP
74:28

010111   THE SEA OF FORTUNE. London: Digby, Long,
1901 BMC.

RODNEY, MARY.

010112   IN THE MOUNTAIN'S SHADOW; A TALE OF LIFE,
LOVE AND ADVENTURE ON A WESTERN RANCH. Boston: C. M.
Clark, 1908 NUC.

RODZIEWICZ, MARYA. See RODZIEWICZOWNA, MARIA.

RODZIEWICZOWNA, MARIA. 1863-1944. Lithuania.

010113   ANIMA VILIS. A TALE OF THE GREAT SIBERIAN
STEPPE. BY MARYA RODZIEWICZ. London: Jarrold, [1900]
BMC. New York: Dodd, Mead, 1900 NUC. (Tr. S. C. De
Soissons)

ACAD 58:314. Author is a Pole, rich, free and
independent, having never met her ideal, according to
Count de Soissons' preface. Poles in Siberia.
ACAD 58:450. Unfortunate hero, reduced at last to life
in Siberia, marriage to Marya, who awakens like the
country in the 1st week of spring. She says (from
book) "do you know that there are some days when one
is afraid to touch a knife?", commenting on effect of
Siberia on human beings. Speaks of her "perpetual
martyrdom, this longing which must be overcome."
LIT 6:444. Hero incredibly unfortunate. Siberian
steppes, effect on human lives. Marya and Antony
survive a blizzard.
PW-"Anima Vilis" is spirit of the woman who after
persecuting him for years allows him happiness with
her rival.

010114   DEVAYTIS: A NOVEL. London: Digby, Long,
1901 BMC. London: Digby, Long, 1901 NUC. (Tr. Count S.
C. de Soissons.)

010115   DISTAFF; A NOVEL. BY MARYA RODZIEWICZ.
London: Jarrold, 1901 BMC NUC. (Tr. S.C. de Soissons)

a Russian new woman, at 17 leaves home secretly for
the university there follow several years of ind
comradeship, study of medicine. BKM, London 7-01

ROE, MRS. J. HARCOURT. Nationality Unknown.

010116   A MAN OF MYSTERY. London: J. Blackwood,
[1893] BMC.

Mr. Fellerman, alias Lord Mountain, at 7 was saved
from shipwreck, raised a Buddhist (the son of Eng.

peer). Wants to spread the faith. Goes to England,
organizes a woman's college for those who will preach
the faith. Falls in love with one. SR 76:302

010117   ROMANCE OF MRS. WODEHOUSE. London:
Hutchinson, 1896 BMC.

SR Pleasant story. Old lover, who lives near her.
ATH 108:560. She has a past. There is also the mystery
of Mabel's origin, a runaway bride & groom.

010118   THE SILENT ROOM. London: Skeffington,
[1895] BMC.

Godfrey Wilkinson and his solitary vigils, mystery SR
79:489

ROE, MYRTLE LELBEE. See ROE, MYRTLE LOUIE (BODLE).

ROE, MYRTLE LOUIE (BODLE). B. 1876. United States.

010119   THROUGH THE NARROWS. BY MYRTLE LELBEE
ROE. Boston: Sherman, French, 1912 NUC.

Orphan mystery. PW 12-23-11
NYT-love story.

ROE, V. E. See ROE, VINGIE EVE.

ROE, VINGIE EVE. 1879-1958. United States.

010120   A DIVINE EGOTIST. New York: Dodd, Mead,
1916 NUC.

BKM-Velving Craith is a novelist who after
transforming a broken down farm into a model
settlement frees her town from corrupt politicians.
She is aided by a drunkard whom she rescues from the
gutter. She thrashes a vile politician with one hand.
Adopts a blind baby. Marries the regenerated drunk in
last chapter.

010121   THE HEART OF NIGHT WIND; A STORY OF THE
GREAT NORTH WEST. New York: Dodd, Mead, 1913 NUC.
London: Gay & Hancock, [1928] BMC.

Heroine "becomes the protegee of a very remarkable and
exceptional old woman who is cook, mother, and
general-in-chief of a certain lumber camp in Oregon."
She knows no other world but that of lumber camp. then
she meets a handsome man from the East. NYT

010122   THE MAID OF THE WHISPERING HILLS. New
York: Dodd, Mead, 1912 NUC. London: Gay & Hancock,
1915 BMC.

PW Girl is leader of band of French Canadians in the
wilderness.
NYT Romance-three men vying for her etc.
18th c. hist romance; Terror of Indians TLS

010123   THE PRIMAL LURE: A ROMANCE OF FORT LU
CERNE. BY V. E. ROE. New York: Dodd, Mead, 1914 NUC.
London: Gay & Hancock, [c1915] BMC.

BKM-Lois LeWayne is suspected of stealing ledgers of a
Hudson Bay Co. trading post. Kept in local prison.
Cruel consequences follow. Lois had loved Angus, the
Scotch agent who was her accuser.
hero had done a great wrong to strong
heroine-unwittingly; superstrong heroine and
hero-setting Hudson Bay Territory TLS
"Pestilence and predacious Indians supply the heroine
with opportunity for exhibiting qualities rare among
the honorable, let alone thieves." "heroine is a
superwoman" of "inexhaustible energy" many sensational
instances including "an Indian doctress's performance
of the operation of transfusion of blood"
"By author of "The maid of the whispering hills." From
the hour when McConnel, the masterful young factor at
a tiny Hudson Bay Post, seizes Lois, the darkeyed,
beautiful French Canadian girl, and throws her into
prison there begins a drama, first of hate, then of
love, devotion and self-sacrifice. They are strong,
passionate, primitive people in that little log-built
stockade, hedged round by the dangers and privations
of the grim wilderness. They do not play at fighting
and they do not play at loving; and the story of two
of these forest folk, two splendid specimens, is
vividly told." PW 85 3/7/14:770

010124   THARON OF LOST VALLEY. New York: Dodd,
Mead, 1919 NUC. London: Cassell, 1920 BMC.

Lawless cattle rustlers PW
TLS-Primitive woman of the wild, a wonderful shot and

horsewoman, who is taught womanhood by love.

ROGERS, ALICE ASHMORE.   Nationality Unknown.

010125   A WAITING RACE. New York and London:
Abbey Press, [1902] NUC.

ROGERS, ANNA (ALEXANDER).   D. 1908. United States.

010126   PEACE AND THE VICES. New York: C.
Scribner, 1904 NUC.

PW-husband is alcoholic.

ROGERS, BESSIE STORY.   United States.

010127   AS IT MAY BE; A STORY OF THE FUTURE.
Boston: R. G. Badger, 1905 NUC.

"year 2905 ... shows how sickness and consequently
doctors have been eliminated not thru spiritual
freedom but through liberty that results from
nourishing the body according to a set of Utopian
principles."

ROGERS, GRACE DEAN (MACLEOD).   B. 1865. United Kingdom.

010128   JOAN AT HALFWAY. New York: G. H. Doran,
[c1919] BMC NUC.

Nova Scotia--farm life--the Wisdom family. Young Joan
Wisdom in her middle teens comes to live with
relatives and learns all about the family
history--helps to right some long standing wrongs. NYT
11-16-19; 656
TLS-sunshine girl.

ROGERS, MARIAN.

010129   NOT BY MAN ALONE. London: Digby, Long,
[1898] BMC.

SR-innocent convicts and forbidden banns.

ROGERS, MARY HULBERT.   Nationality Unknown.

010130   CHILDREN OF THE NIGHT. New York:
Duffield, 1911 NUC.

Optimistic reminiscences of blind woman. PW 10-21-11
Middle-aged woman talks to her secretary. She's blind.
Will dictate her whole life but digresses. NYT

ROHLEDER, GRACE IRENE.

010131   WOMAN ON THE BENCH. Washington, D. C.:
1920 NUC.

PW pov? Auth is member of bar in DC

ROHLFS, ANNA KATHARINE (GREEN).   1846-1935. United States.

010132   AGATHA WEBB. BY ANNA KATHARINE GREEN. New
York: G. P. putnam's sons, 1899 NUC BMC.

Many murders-the beautiful Agatha Webb, her servant,
husband, lovers. Traditional detective. BKM 9:90
SP 85:246. Murder mystery.
ATH 116:148. Agatha is the good woman or grand woman
as her friends call her. There is a girl adventuress.
LIT 7:107. "Most mischiefs... traceable to a sinister
young woman with extraordinary attractions."

010133   THE CHIEF LEGATEE. BY ANNA KATHARINE
GREEN. Toronto: McLeod & Allen, [1906] NUC [1907] BMC.
New York and London: Authors & Newspapers Association,
[1906] NUC [1907] BMC.

disappearance of new bride TLS

010134   THE CIRCULAR STUDY. New York: McClure,
Phillips, 1900 NUC BMC. London: Ward, Lock, 1900 BMC.

LW 31:223. Mr. Gryce.
PW and Mr. Sweetwater. Wealthy NY man murdered in his
study.
"mystery story whose crime discovered to have been
committed in self defense, involves a dramatic tale of
revenge and love" BRD

010135   CYNTHIA WAKEHAM'S MONEY. BY ANNA
KATHARINE GREEN. New York, London: G. P. Putnam's
Sons, 1892 NUC. London: Ward, Lock, 1904 BMC NUC.

ATH 100:586. Two sisters and their "strange dwelling."
Hiram Huchins is a "villain of a new and rather

alarming type."
CR 18:118. Lawyer seeks and finds heirs of above, two
young women, falls in love with one. There is a
mystery in her life, involving a scar on her face.

010136   DARK HOLLOW. BY ANNA KATHARINE GREEN.
London: E. Nash, 1914 BMC NUC. New York: Dodd, Mead,
1914 NUC.

"A dark hollow on the edge of town crossed by a
footbridge, upon which, one night, a woman searching
for her lost child, sees silhouetted against the sky,
an upraised arm and a head surmounted by a peculiar
cap, and she hears a blow. At that instant a man is
murdered. Between that startling glimpse and the next
time the woman sees that curious cap, many events of
great importance to the woman and those dearest to her
occur, and after twelve years she finds herself once
more involved in that tragic mystery on the solving of
which depends her child's happiness. "

010137   THE DOCTOR, HIS WIFE, AND THE CLOCK. BY
ANNA KATHARINE GREEN (MRS. CHARLES ROHLFS). New York,
London: G. P. Putnam's Sons, 1895 NUC. London: T. F.
Unwin, 1895 BMC.

Detective. Murder in New York. ACAD 48:244

010138   DOCTOR IZARD. BY ANNA KATHARINE GREEN.
(MRS. CHARLES ROHLFS). London: S.S. McClure, [1894]
BMC. New York: G.P. Putnam's Sons, 1895 NUC.

ATH 107:378-mass of crude horrors.
Detective: murder, grave-robbing, etc. LW 26:217

010139   THE FILIGREE BALL: BEING A FULL AND TRUE
ACCOUNT OF THE SOLUTION OF THE MYSTERY CONCERNING THE
JEFFREY-MOORE AFFAIR. BY ANNA KATHARINE GREEN.
Indianapolis: Bobbs-Merrill, [1903] BMC NUC. London:
T. F. Unwin, 1904 BMC NUC.

mystery 3-28-03 PW
murder NYT 03 251

010140   THE GOLDEN SLIPPER, AND OTHER PROBLEMS
FOR VIOLET STRANGE. BY ANNA KATHARINE GREEN (MRS.
CHARLES ROHLFS). New York: G. P. Putnam's Sons, 1915
BMC NUC.

successful detective. she falls in love PW 11-27-15
TLS-Violet is an American detective.

010141   THE HOUSE IN THE MIST. BY ANNA KATHARINE
GREEN. Indianapolis: Bobbs-Merrill, [1905] BMC NUC.

010142   THE HOUSE OF THE WHISPERING PINES. BY
ANNA KATHARINE GREEN. New York and London: G.P.
Putnam's Sons, 1910 NUC. London: E. Nash, 1910 BMC
NUC.

mystery-detective PW
NYT young woman's sister is killed. She is suspected
by sister's fiance. Who solves mystery?

010143   INITIALS ONLY. BY ANNA KATHARINE GREEN.
New York: Dodd, Mead, 1911 NUC. London: E. Nash, 1912
BMC.

murder mystery 10-7-11 PW
ATH male criminal hero followed by detective

010144   LOST MAN'S LANE: A SECOND EPISODE IN THE
LIFE OF AMELIA BUTTERWORTH. BY ANNA KATHARINE GREEN
(MRS. CHARLES ROHLFS). New York and London: G. P.
Putnam's Sons, 1898 BMC NUC.

NYT 1898:268. Amelia Butterworth & Gryce join forces
in detection, she seeming to play largest part.
LW 29:187. A.B. "is, in some respects an even more
original conception than Doyle's Sherlock Holmes. She
is, furthermore, a much more canny character, and so
one will wonder that her friend, Mr. Gryce, should
wish he could dare to offer her his heart and hand."
PW-she is assisted by Gryce.
ACAD 53:659
CR 32:413

010145   MARKED "PERSONAL". BY ANNA KATHARINE
GREEN (MRS. CHARLES ROHLFS). New York, London: G. P.
Putnam's Sons, 1893 BMC NUC.

Young man forced to marry a certain woman, then they
fall in love. NATION 57:104.
Man murdered on wedding day. Son and young second wife
employ people to solve the crime. 6-3-93PW
Tale of revenge. Two gold prospectors kill a boy for

food. The rest of the party condemn the two to suffer
any punishment the boy's father decides, but
punishment postponed 12 years while they search for
gold. After that each receives a card marked personal
to meet the avenger. CR 20, 23:29 9.

010146   THE MAYOR'S WIFE. By ANNA KATHARINE
GREEN. Indianapolis: Bobbs-Merrill, [1907] NUC. London
Daily Mail: [1909] BMC.

painful story of the depressed mayor's wife. PW
5-11-07
Detective BKM

010147   THE MILLIONAIRE BABY. BY ANNA KATHARINE
GREEN. London: Chatto & Windus, 1905 BMC NUC.
Indianapolis: Bobbs-Merrill, [1905] BMC NUC.

detective, kidnapping NYT 393,05

010148   MISS HURD, AN ENIGMA. BY ANNA KATHARINE
GREEN (MRS. CHARLES ROHLFS). New York, London: G. P.
Putnam's Sons, 1894 BMC NUC.

LW 25:352. She makes repeated attempts to run away
from her devoted husband, always meekly returning when
he seeks her out. After a final escape there is a
suspicion that he has murdered her.
PW-when she runs away she earns her living by various
means.
She's a married woman who leaves husband exchanging
wealth for obscurity and poverty. She makes many such
flights because she dislikes her husband who has
complete control over her each time he finds and
returns her home. SR 79:165

010149   THE MYSTERY OF THE HASTY ARROW. BY ANNA
KATHARINE GREEN. New York: Dodd, Mead, 1917 NUC.

Trad detective PW
old detective Gryce solved mystery of beautiful woman
shot by an arrow. NYT

010150   ONE OF MY SONS. BY ANNA KATHARINE GREEN
(MRS. CHARLES ROHLFS). New York and London: G.P
Putnam's Sons, 1901 NUC. London: Ward, Lock, 1904 BMC.

detective story- 11-23-01 PW

010151   THAT AFFAIR NEXT DOOR. BY ANNA KATHARINE
GREEN (MRS. CHARLES ROHLFS). New York, London: G. P.
Putnam's Sons, 1897 BMC NUC.

Detective Gryce and "the still more astute Miss
Butterworth." LBKM 12:43.
Miss Butterworth sees a man and a woman arrive at house
next to hers, then discovers the woman dead,
investigates: "sets to work to unravel the mystery and
bring the murderer to justice, does her work with
great ability." There's a friendly competition between
the spinster and the prof. detective Mr. Gryce. He is
beaten because he's over confident. SP 78:774.

010152   THREE THOUSAND DOLLARS. BY ANNA KATHARINE
GREEN. Boston: R. G. Badger, 1910 NUC.

traditional detective PW 10-30-09

010153   TO THE MINUTE, SCARLET AND BLACK; 2 TALES
OF LIFE'S PERPLEXITIES. BY ANNA KATHARINE GREEN (MRS.
CHARLES ROHLFS). New York and London: Putnam's Sons,
1916 NUC.

1. Mysterious house Judith's grandfather left her;
former lover wants house 2. Dr. returns home to find
two women and a man gambling in his dining room-stakes
men's lives pW 90:1121 9/30/16
NYT -0
SR-0
two stories, one includes a capable girl who helps
solve the mystery LBKM

010154   THE WOMAN IN THE ALCOVE. BY ANNA
KATHARINE GREEN. London: Chatto & Windus, 1906 BMC.
Indianapolis: Bobbs-Merrill, [1906] BMC NUC.

"This story is told by a young girl who has just
become engaged To a splendid fellow while attending a
ball in New York City. right after the engagement a
woman, who has attracted much attention by the wearing
of a large celebrated diamond, is murdered and the
young fiance, against whom all suspicions point, is
held responsible. The young woman does her best to
prove his innocence, and while the plot, as unraveled
by her, does not give the facts, it swerves the
detectives from the wrong tracks and enables them to

bring the real criminal to justice. Arthur I. Keller
has illustrated the book." BKM 23 1906

010155   A WOMAN OF MYSTERY. London: Collier, 1909
BMC NUC.

mystery disappearance of bride TLS

ROHLFS, MRS. CHARLES. See ROHLFS, ANNA KATHARINE (GREEN).

ROLAND, ALICE KATE.   United States.

010156   LATTER-DAY SINNERS. New York: Neale, 1906
NUC.

010157   ROSALIND MORTON; OR, THE MYSTERY OF IVY
CROWN. A KENTUCKY STORY. Louisville, Ky.: C. T.
Dearing, 1898 NUC.

ROLDAH, pseud. See NYE, ISABEL CLIFTON.

ROLLINS, ALICE MARLAND WELLINGTON. 1847-1897. United
States.

010158   THE STORY OF AZRON. New York: [Press of
J. J. Little], 1895 NUC.

ROLLINS, CLARA HARRIOT (SHERWOOD). B. 1874. United States.

010159   THREADS OF LIFE. Boston: Lamson, Wolffe,
1897 NUC.

"Heart histories" of two cultured talented women. In
learned witty fashion discuss the nature of men and
women, their privileges, rights and duties. One is 27
single; the other 38, a widow and grandmother. PW
52:1103.
LW 29:203. Witty. Mrs Farnham. Miriam Sard. Farm near
Concord, Mass.

ROOF, KATHARINE METCALF. United States.

010160   THE GREAT DEMONSTRATION. New York and
London: D. Appleton, 1920 BMC NUC.

PW-love story and psychic phenomena

010161   THE STRANGER AT THE HEARTH. Boston:
Small, Maynard, [c1916] BMC NUC.

Nina and Daniel love each other but have said goodbye
because they dare not even be friends. Husband tries
to kill wrong person and then commits suicide. PW
90:1461 10/28/16
NYT-alien races threatening to fill the role of cuckoo
in our national nest. The heroine, an expatriated
American, now an Italian countess observes America's
deterioration--in manners and more.

ROOSEVELT, BLANCHE, pseud. See MACCHETTA, BLANCHE ROOSEVELT
(TUCKER).

ROOSEVELT, FLORENCE.

010162   THE SIREN'S NET: A NOVEL. TRANSCRIBED
FROM LIFE. London: T. F. Unwin, 1905 BMC NUC.

Story of the difficulties and risks in a career of
opera singer. LBKM 28-9,68

ROPER, CHARLOTTE.

010163   ZIGZAG TRAVELS. London: T. F. Unwin, 1895
BMC.

ROPER, THERESA (KETCHESON). B. 1867.

010164   REBOUNDING VENGEANCE, AN INDIAN ROMANCE,
AND THE EVOLUTION OF NEWPORT, OREGON. [Corvallis,
Or.]: [Gazette-Times Press], [c1919] NUC.

RORISON, EDITH S.

010165   THE SWIMMERS. London: W. Heinemann, 1906
BMC NUC.

TLS-book for girls.

010166   A TASTE OF QUALITY. London: J. Long, 1904
BMC NUC.

LBKM-0
ACAD-family story.

ROSE, GINA.

010167   THE BEAUTIFUL ARABELLA PHIPPS AND OTHERS.
London: E. Stock, 1914 BMC.

ROSE, HELOISE (DURANT).   United States.

    010168   A DUCAL SKELETON. London and New York: F.
    T. Neely, [c1899] NUC.

    Two illeg. children of a duke; later mother is
    discovered. Treatment of family towards them. NYT
    6-10-99,383

ROSE, WINIFRED, jt. au. See PAIN, NANCY AND WINIFRED ROSE.

ROSEBORO´, VIOLA.   United States.

    010169   THE JOYOUS HEART. London and New York:
    McClure, Phillips, 1903 BMC NUC.

    Pagan woman. PW 5-2-03
    Woman with undying spirit of joy of life. NYT 1903:325
    LW 34:210 8/1903

    010170   PLAYERS AND VAGABONDS. New York, London:
    Macmillan, 1904 BMC NUC.

    010171   STORMS OF YOUTH. New York: C. Scribner,
    1920 NUC.

    PW-story of love and politics in a small town in the
    border country between North and South.
    NYT 1920:30 male hero.

ROSEMARY, pseud. See WATSON, MARGARET.

ROSMAN, ALICE GRANT.

    010172   MISS BRYDE OF ENGLAND. London: A.
    Melrose, [1915] BMC.

    Helen and her brother escape a tyrannical father move
    to London and pursue their careers in the literary and
    artistic society. TLS

    010173   THE TOWER WALL. London: Hodder &
    Stoughton, 1916 BMC.

    TLS-Central interest is heroine´s mother and
    sacrifice.

ROSS, M. A. See ROSS, MERIEL AIMIE.

ROSS, MARTIN, pseud. See MARTIN, VIOLET FLORENCE AND EDITH
ANNA OENONE SOMERVILLE, Also SOMERVILLE, EDITH ANNA AND
VIOLET FRANCES MARTIN.

ROSS, MERIEL AIMIE.   United Kingdom.

    010174   LADY BEATRIX AND THE FORBIDDEN MAN
    [ANONYMOUS]. London and New York: Harper, 1902 BMC.

    ATH 9-6-02

    010175   THE PAWNS OF FATE. BY M. A. ROSS. London
    and New York: Harper, 1911 BMC NUC.

    Hon. Sybil Colquhoun married, widowed. TLS
    At 21, marries a man of 63; he dies; she then loves a
    young man who marries another. So Sybil "sought refuge
    in slumming." Sensational story. SP
    Happy ending. ATH: Raises questions concerning the
    moral basis of society.

    010176   SIR ANTHONY AND THE EWE LAMB. BY THE
    AUTHOR OF "LADY BEATRIX AND THE FORBIDDEN MAN"
    [ANONYMOUS]. London and New York: Harper, 1903 BMC.

    Clever story of a flirt. ACAD 65:38.
    "The ewe lamb is an irresponsible idiot of a girl the
    book describes as winsome." LBKM 1903:87
    ATH 121:780

ROSSETTI, CHRISTINA GEORGINA. 1830-1894. United Kingdom.

    010177   MAUDE; A STORY FOR GIRLS. London: J.
    Bowden, 1897 BMC NUC.

    "fumblings...of a half-learned art and half-developed
    power." Author did wisely in throwing it aside as
    "unworthy" of publication. Record of a
    half-hysterical, self occupied person who dies early
    "somewhat to the relief of the reader." Better it was
    buried with her as her manuscript poems were. LW
    28:244

ROSSI, LOUISE.

010178   AN UNCONVENTIONAL GIRL. London: Lawrence
and Bullen, 1896 BMC.

    SR-For sometime past she has been conventional in
    fiction. Reads as a child, reads erotic poetry as a
    schoolgirl, ends as a famous novelist.
    ATH 107:60. Writes a book, lives alone and smokes
    cigarettes. "Nowadays these proceedings are rather
    conventional than otherwise".
    ACAD 50:160. Linda L´Estrange, a lonely life.

ROSSO, MARGUERITE.

    010179   IN THE COILS OF THE SERPENT. London: H.
    J. Drane, [1899] BMC.

    Melo. The Serpent is a Svengali-like Amer. yachtsman
    who has Sir Montague and his two sons in his power. SR
    88:807
    Melodrama about mental control. ACAD 57:746.

ROTH, AMELIA M. A.   United States.

    010180   AN HEIRESS IN NAME ONLY; OR THE
    ADVENTURES OF GWENDOLYN. Baltimore, Md.: Saulsbury,
    [c1919] NUC.

    PW-unhappy heiress.

ROULET, MARY F. (NIXON). D. 1930. United States.

    010181   GOD, THE KING, MY BROTHER. BY MARY F.
    NIXON. Boston: L.C. Page, 1900 NUC. London: Ward,
    Lock, 1901 BMC.

    PW-historical romance. Spain during reign of Pedro the
    Cruel. Twin-brothers, English, are heroes.
    ATH 8-24-01

    010182   A HARP OF MANY CHORDS. BY MARY F. NIXON.
    St. Louis: B. Herder, [c1899] NUC.

    010183   THE WAIF OF RAINBOW COURT. St. Louis: B.
    Herder, 1912 NUC.

ROUSE, ADELAIDE LOUISE. D. 1912. United States.

    010184   THE DEANE GIRLS. A HOME STORY. New York:
    A. L. Burt, [1895] NUC. London: Hodder and Stoughton,
    1895 BMC.

    Eight daughters of poor clergyman help out by
    teaching, journalism, taking in boarders-till most of
    them wed. PW 6-15-95 940

    010185   HER FATHER´S FAMILY. New York: American
    Tract Society, [1903] NUC.

    010186   THE LETTERS OF THEODORA. New York and
    London: Macmillan, 1905 BMC NUC.

    Heroine hack writer and lecturer ex college teacher
    living in New York, her trials as a writer, lecturer,
    almost marries a congressman for his money but
    repents. marries Latin professor "Merges her literary
    ambitions in his career"PW 3-4-05
    College instructor, now free lance writer, moves to NY
    without giving her boyfriend her address, finds that
    the literary world there not waiting for her. Runs
    into John (her boyfriend) teaching at Columbia. ind
    spirit of this woman-will have none of him. Becomes a
    lecturer, breaks engagement to a congressman, goes
    abroad, John in pursuit. Finally marries but has her
    own ideas about wifehood. *NYT 287,05 ACAD 420,05

    010187   UNDER MY OWN ROOF. New York and London:
    Funk & Wagnalls, 1902 BMC NUC.

    NYT 9-6-02 Spinster who contracts to build her own
    house wrote (journalist in youth) for a living.
    Finally marries next door neighbor sort of sweet

ROUSE, LYDIA L. Fl. 1881-1894. United States.

    010188   EBB AND FLOW. New York: Hunt and Eaton,
    1892 NUC.

    PW-Story of Jessie, Alternating joys and sorrows.

    010189   KATHIE´S MARGARET. Philadelphia: American
    Baptist Soc., [c1894] NUC.

    PW-Scotch home life. Kathie´s husband is killed by
    alcohol; she is left with two young children, one of
    whom is Margaret, the other heroine of the story.

ROWE, HENRIETTA (GOULD). 1835-1910. United States.

010190   A MAID OF BAR HARBOR. Boston: Little,
Brown, 1902 BMC NUC.

Dial 8-02 evolution of Bar Harbor.

010191   QUEENSHITHE. Buffalo: C. W. Moulton, 1895
NUC.

ROWLAND, HELEN. B. 1876. United States.

010192   THE DIGRESSIONS OF POLLY. New York: Baker
and Taylor, [1905] NUC.

Polly and fiance discuss cigarette smoking, art of
proposing, making over of a wife, etc. Modern girl,
liberal views. NYT 1905: 393.
Brief description. BKM 21 (1905) 319

010193   REFLECTIONS OF A BACHELOR GIRL. New York:
Dodge, [c1909] NUC. London: S. Paul, [1909] BMC.

010194   THE SAYINGS OF MRS. SOLOMON: BEING THE
CONFESSIONS OF THE SEVEN HUNDREDTH WIFE AS REVEALED TO
HELEN ROWLAND. New York: Dodge, [c1913] NUC. London:
Simpkin, Marshall, [1920] BMC.

010195   THE WIDOW, TO SAY NOTHING OF THE MAN. New
York: Dodge Publishing, [c1908] NUC. London: S. Paul,
[1909] BMC.

"In which the widow and the bachelor discuss matrimony
in all places and all occasions of meeting. After
their philosophising and soliloquising, the question
being whether single or married life is preferable,
they decide in favour of the latter by taking the step
themselves." BKM v28 1908
NYT-

ROWLAND, JANE.

010196   TOM GENUFLEX; OR 'LIFE'S LITTLE DAY'. BY
AUNT CHERRY. Llwyn-y-brain: 1909 BMC.

Girls' school life. TLS

ROWLAND, K. ALICE. United States.

010197   FICKLE FATE. BY LENORE. Birmingham, Ala.:
Roberts, 1892 NUC.

ROWLANDS, EFFIE ADELAIDE, pseud. See ALBANESI, EFFIE
ADELAIDE MARIA.

ROWLANDS, LILIAN BOWEN.

010198   THE PASSION OF MAHAEL. London: T. F.
Unwin, 1902 BMC.

ACAD-extra-marital affair
ATH 8-9-02 - central figure is male.

010199   THE PITEOUSNESS OF PASSING THINGS.
London: New Century Press, 1900 BMC. London: 1900 NUC.

LIT 7:51. Peasants, Martha, illegitimate child.
"Idealistic old adopted father" asks if she loves him,
if she yearns for him; she says no, she can't say she
cares for him any longer. Depressing.

ROWSELL, MARY CATHERINE. United Kingdom.

010200   THE FRIEND OF THE PEOPLE; A TALE OF THE
REIGN OF TERROR. London: T. F. Unwin, 1894 BMC. New
York: F. A. Stokes, [c1895] NUC.

SR 78:390. Historical romance, French Revolution. Two
half brothers.
ACAD 46:251. Impersonation of one by the other.
Historical romance. Male look-a-likes, one
aristocratic, the other illegitimate. PW 4-20-95:656.

010201   THE GREEN MEN OF NORWELL, AND OTHER
STORIES. London: Simpkin and Marshall, [1896] BMC.

010202   HONOUR BRIGHT, A STORY OF THE DAYS OF
KING CHARLES. London: E. Nister, [1899] NUC BMC. New
York: E. P. Dutton, [1899?] NUC.

010203   MONSIEUR DE PARIS: A ROMANCE. London:
Chatto & Windus, 1907 BMC NUC.

Tale of mean people. ACAD

010204   PETRONELLA AND MADAME PONOWSKI. London:
Skeffington, 1891 BMC. (Two tales)

ACAD 41:11. Petronella: Jacobite girl and her
Hanoverian lover. Quarrel about politics and are not
reunited until middle-aged. Madame Ponowski: Heroine
is a murderer; collects victims heads in a cabinet.

010205   THE WILD SWANS: OR, THE ADVENTURE OF
ROLAND CLEEVE. London: S. W. Partridge, [1905] BMC.

ROY, GORDON, pseud. See WALLACE, HELEN.

ROY, LILLIAN ELIZABETH (BECKER). 1868-1932. United States.

010206   THE SEEDLINGS' HARVEST. New York: Wessel
and Bissell, 1910 NUC.

Sentimental religious story. PW

ROY, OLIVIA.

010207   THE AWAKENING OF MRS. CARSTAIRS.
Edinburgh: G. A. Morton, 1904 BMC.

LBKM-diary in which is revealed a lawless, consuming
passion. She "left her home a cold, passionless girl
liking her husband as a friend"

010208   THE HUSBAND HUNTER. London: T. W. Laurie,
1907 BMC.

"Nothing very exciting" Joanna is quite a nice young
lady. TLS

ROYCE, MARJORY.

010209   THE DESPERATE MARRIAGE. London: Hodder &
Stoughton, [1919] BMC.

Love entanglements that work out. TLS
Violet Hedley, governess, loves employer whose wife
married him for money, loves child whom the mother
neglects. When her employer leaves, the wife
discharges Violet. She hurriedly marries a soldier. On
wedding morning hears from the employer that wife is
dead. Reviewer won't tell the end. LBKM

010210   DINAH LEAVES SCHOOL. London: Hodder &
Stoughton, 1913 BMC.

010211   A DREAM CHILD COME TRUE. London: Hodder &
Stoughton, 1918 BMC.

TLS-two boys, adoption.

010212   THE GIRL WITH NO PROPOSALS: AN EPISODE OF
1913. London: Hodder & Stoughton, 1918 BMC.

Contrast of twins Edith and Phillipa. For 26 years
live contentedly in quiet rectory; father's cousin, a
match maker, comes along and gets one married. LBKM
TLS-love and sentimentality.

ROZANT, INA.

010213   AN ACTRESS'S PILGRIMAGE. London: T.
Sealey Clark, 1906 NUC BMC.

010214   LIFE'S UNDERSTUDIES: A NOVEL. London: T.
S. Clark, [1907] BMC NUC. New York: M. Kennerley,
[1915?] NUC.

Actress whose husband becomes insane, tells world and
her child her husband is dead. He goes out of her life
when he learns this. PW 7-10-09

RUCK, BERTA. See OLIVER, AMY ROBERTA (RUCK).

RUDD, JEAN PORTER. United States.

010215   BAS' THERES: A NARRATIVE-DRAMA OF TIROL.
Norwich, Conn.: Bulletin Press, 1897 NUC BMC.

010216   THE TOWER OF THE OLD SCHLOSS. New York:
G. P. Putnam's Sons, 1896 NUC.

LW 27:365. Love story in Germanic style, wholesome.

RUDOLF, MRS. E. DE M.

010217   THE BLUE CARNATION. London: Ward Lock,
1916 BMC.

TLS-Gentle unassuming story Millicent is a student at
a horticultural college. Her pa is trying to cultivate

a blue carnation, rom.
ATH-She has taken up horticulture as a career. The
Hero cultivates title and becomes famous.

010218   CURTIS & CO. London: Ward, Lock, 1917
BMC.

Two women left in poverty; one marries a clergy man,
the other a shop keeper. "When a motor accident lays
him up she herself takes the business bravely in hand
so effectively that it is doubtful whether she or he
should be called the Co." TLS

RUFFIN, M. E. HENRY. See RUFFIN, MARGARET ELLEN (HENRY).

RUFFIN, MARGARET ELLEN (HENRY). B. 1857. United States.

010219   THE NORTH STAR; A TALE OF NORWAY IN THE
TENTH CENTURY. BY M. E. HENRY-RUFFIN. Boston: Little,
Brown, 1904 NUC.

NYT Hist. romance

010220   THE SHIELD OF SILENCE. BY M. E.
HENRY-RUFFIN. New York: Benziger, 1914 NUC.

PW 85 5/2/14 p1448

RUGER, FLORENCE WHITE. B. 1858. United States.

010221   CONSTANCE D'BROLIE. New York, London:
Abbey Press, [1902] NUC BMC.

RUMSEY, FRANCES. United States.

010222   LEONORA; A NOVEL. New York and London: D.
Appleton, 1910 BMC NUC.

NYT-Story of divorce but author is not pro or con.
Leonora's parents are divorced, she spends three
months time alternately and hates it all; violently
opposed to divorce but falls in love with divorced
man.

010223   MR. CUSHING AND MLLE. DU CHASTEL. New
York and London: J. Lane, 1917 NUC 1918 BMC.

TLS-Two men, two women, their relations treated in
pompous Jamesian style.
SR. Mlle du Chentel, French orphan, was married in
aunt's house by Amer., who then brought her to U.S.
Analysis of their mrg. Separation. An attempt with
another Amer. Mr Irish, failure. She returns to Paris
to live in poverty and retirement. Book ends with
first husband (Mr. Cushing) proposing that they should
remarry at Whatene's risk.
French wife with Am husband finds life incomplete and
forms liaisons. Husband gives her her freedom PW
91:1228 4/14/17
International marriage Amer-French and its problems,
psychological analysis NYT 4-22-17 163

RUNA, pseud. See BESKOW, ELISABETH MARIA.

RUNKLE, BERTHA. See BASH, BERTHA (RUNKLE).

RUSSEL, FLORENCE KIMBALL.

010224   BORN TO THE BLUE; A STORY OF THE ARMY.
Boston: L. C. Page, 1906 NUC.

PW-military hero.

RUSSELL, ANNA VIRGINIA.

010225   A STORY TOLD BY PINS. New York: Neale,
1908 NUC.

RUSSELL, DORA. United Kingdom.

010226   A COUNTRY SWEETHEART. London: Chatto and
Windus, 1894 BMC. Chicago: Rand, McNally, [1895] NUC.

SP-73:565. Bigamous husband.
ATH 104:381. Women who propose to men. Vulgar
characters elbow out the more refined.

010227   THE CURATE OF ROYSTON. London: Digby,
Long, 1906 BMC.

010228   A DAUGHTER OF DARKNESS. London: Digby,
Long, 1905 BMC.

010229   THE DRIFT OF FATE. London: Chatto and
Windus, 1895 BMC.

Estate is mortgaged to man who threatens to foreclose
unless Nell becomes his wife. Nell Drummond prepares
for the marriage to save her father. She buys a knife.
but instead of using it, deserts her husband. She
dresses in men's clothes and on her wedding day walks
out. SP 70:115
She's 19, becomes a governess-companion; then she's
loved by her young student's cousin which brings woe
to employer and to his daughter. But the heroine does
not suffer; these actions enable her fortune. ATH
105:605

010230   AN EVIL REPUTATION: A NOVEL. London:
Griffith, Farran, 1892 BMC.

ACAD 42:211. Lonely house on seacoast with "evil
reputation" for tragedy. "Beautiful young married
woman is the victim, but she survives almost unheard
of cruelties to bring retribution on her guilty
husband and his accomplice. Sensational.
SR. 74:310. Husband and his accomplice think they have
killed her, but she recovers. She is then twice
abducted by them. He is arrested on the day of his
wedding to another woman; she is rescued and marries
someone else.

010231   A FATAL PAST: A NOVEL. New York: J. W.
Lovell, [1891] NUC. London: Simpkin, Marshall, [1896]
BMC.

SR-Blameless heroine, romance.
ATH-Secrets from the past
SP 76:580. Lady Ennismore in trying to shoot her first
husband whom she hates shoots her second cousin whom
she doesn't hate.
Lady Ennismore married with several children. Man she
wed at 16 turns up. Son of first marriage claims her
name and fortune. Her second marriage declared
illegal. PW.
She tried unsuccessfully to kill husband number 1 when
he turned up, kills husband she loves by mistake. She
also dies. LW

010232   A GREAT TEMPTATION. London: F. V. White,
1894 BMC.

SR 78:331. Laura is educated, writing a novel. She
marries a solicitor, tires of him, loves Sir Ralph.
leaves her husband but that is all. Her husband dies
of typhoid fever.
ATH 103:342. Her husband identifies a dead woman with
a disfigured face as Laura and remarries.

010233   HER PROMISE TRUE. Chicago: Rand, McNally,
[c1898] NUC. London: Digby, Long, 1899 BMC.

LW 29;204. Villainous aunt intercepts correspondence
between niece and lover. She marries wrong man. She
then discovers deception, runs away with lover, ends
in tragedy.
Lovers estranged because of intercepted letters Belle
Wayland runs off from husband with her lover from whom
she was separated. Her lover dies before they can wed.
She returns to England, dies in childbirth. SP 83:759.

010234   A HIDDEN CHAIN: A NOVEL. London: Digby,
Long, 1894 BMC. Chicago: Rand, McNally, [1896] NUC.

SR 78;129. Eva married to tyrant clergyman. He goes
off to Africa for many years; she assumes him dead; he
turns up day before wedding.
ACAD-D. Russell is the heir of M.E. Braddon.
Clair horsewhips a treacherous banker.

010235   HIS WILL AND HERS. Chicago: Rand,
McNally, 1894 NUC.

PW-Laura because of contents of letter written by
father who has just died gives up man she loves and
marries one she doesn't care for. Before she has a
chance to degenerate into a humdrum matron, former
lover takes action--pathetic love story.

010236   THE LAST SIGNAL. New York: J. A. Taylor,
[1892] NUC. London: F. V. White, 1893 BMC.

PW Miriam shields her sister from disgrace, almost
destroying her own married happiness. England
Theme seems to be "the sheltering of faithless wives
and murderers." Two sisters, one wed to old man; the
other single. The single one plans to elope but her
lover thinking he sees her with another man, shoots
him. SR 75, 352
Miriam is the single one; Joan is unhappily married
and involved with someone else. Joan ends up marrying
a Sir James Mackennon. ATH 43:282

"two shallow young women who respect neither parents nor husbands" Completely self indulgent. Both carry on with other men though engaged or married. They are made to suffer. ATH 101, 245

010237   A MAN'S PRIVILEGE. London: Digby, Long, [1895] BMC. Chicago: Rand, McNally, [1897] NUC.

SR. Romantic complications
ACAD 49:10. She marries a murderer but he suicides and she marries right man.

010238   MISS CHURCHILL. London: Digby, Long, 1907 BMC.

010239   THE OTHER BOND. New York: J. A. Taylor, [1892] NUC. London: Digby, Long, [1895] BMC.

PW-Male hero unable to marry the woman he loves because he is bound to another, years later they are united.

010240   THE SECRET OF THE RIVER. London: Hurst and Blackett, 1891 BMC.

010241   THE SILENT WATCHERS. London: Digby, Long, 1903 BMC.

010242   A TORN-OUT PAGE. Chicago: Rand, McNally, [1897] NUC. London: Digby, Long, 1899 BMC.

PW-Daughter of an English admiral has at 16 a secret and unhappy marriage. She afterwards conceals it from her father, the "torn-out page" of her life.
SP 84:95 Isabel is kidnapped by Spaniard for ransom.

RUSSELL, FRANCES E. United States.

010243   A QUAINT SPINSTER. Boston: Roberts, 1895 NUC.

Priscilla Trippings inherits a fortune, "sets up a home for the sisterhood." Together with Misses Lawrence, Pressie, Meekson, and Gildersleeve, she conducts night-classes and cooking schools. Their home becomes a center of great influence. CR. 23:438.

RUSSELL, LINDSAY PATRICIA. 1870-1949.

010244   EARTHWARE. London: Cassell, 1918 BMC.

TLS-The develop. of a woman thru a hard childhood, a hard married life and for a time a freer outlook in London.

010245   THE ETERNAL TRIANGLE. London: Ward, Lock, 1915 NUC BMC.

010246   THE GATES OF KUT. London and New York: Cassell, [1917] BMC NUC.

010247   THE GATES OF SILENCE. London: Ward, Lock, 1915 BMC.

010248   THE INTERIOR. London: Ward, Lock, 1916 BMC.

LBKM Tangled love affairs in Aust.

010249   LAND O' THE DAWNING. London: Cassell, [1917] BMC.

ATH. Heroine takes part in Sinn Fein rebellion.

010250   SONS OF ISCARIOT. London: Ward, Lock, 1916 BMC.

TLS-Austral fem. 9-21-16
TLS-experience of inmorality of RC priesthood. Girl betrayed by priest.

010251   SOULS IN PAWN. London: Ward, Lock, 1913 BMC.

Roman Catholic priest-scandalous story of chastity and sobriety ignored. attacks RC. LBKM

010252   THE WOMAN WHO LIVED AGAIN. London: Hurst and Blackett, 1916 BMC.

ATH She is used by Germans as spy.

010253   THE YEARS OF FORGETTING. London: Ward & Lock, 1914 BMC.

ATH-Australia. Young woman deceived by priest.

Struggles to make a living for herself and her child. She is loved unavailingly by faithful man. Priest becomes a bishop. Tragic ending.
TLS Morbid.

RUSSELL, MARIE.

010254   MARJORIE. London: F. Griffiths, 1913 BMC NUC.

010255   RUSSIAN REBELS. London: F. Griffiths, 1914 BMC.

TLS Story of imaginative Edna, governess in Russian family without conv. ending in marriage.

RUSSELL, MARION.

010256   AN EXCELLENT MYSTERY. London: S. Swift, 1912 BMC.

ATH-flees an uncongenial home and marries a man she does not love, he deserts, she divorces, left with prospect of happier union.

010257   FIVE WOMEN AND A CARAVAN. London: E. Nash, 1911 BMC.

RUSSELL, MARY ANNETTE (BEAUCHAMP) ARNIM RUSSELL. 1866-1941. United Kingdom.

010258   THE ADVENTURES OF ELIZABETH IN RUGEN. BY THE AUTHOR OF "ELIZABETH AND HER GERMAN GARDEN" [ANONYMOUS]. New York and London: Macmillan, 1904 BMC NUC. Leipzig: B. Tauchnitz, 1906 NUC.

BKM Middle-aged woman-emancipated cousin?
NyT A more "veritable" benefactress than Anna
BKM-Elizabeth attempts to persuade cousin to laugh at her husband rather than take him seriously, attempts to bring them together; takes a month's vacation each year from husband and children.

010259   THE BENEFACTRESS. BY THE AUTHOR OF "ELIZABETH AND HER GERMAN GARDEN" [ANONYMOUS]. London and New York: Macmillan, 1901 BMC NUC.

Unmarried woman comes into money and establishes her estate as a home for unmarried women who are impoverished. BOOK BUYER 1-02
Heroine marries and single women are ugly, DIAL

010260   THE CARAVANERS. BY THE AUTHOR OF "ELIZABETH AND HER GERMAN GARDEN" [ANONYMOUS]. New York: Doubleday, Page, [c1909] NUC. London: Smith, Elder, 1909 BMC 1910 NUC.

Diary of man concerning Eng. and German manners. PW
NYT Portrait of a disagreeable man. Attempts to celebrate his twenty-fifth anniversary (on the basis of two wives) with a trip, but is so unpopular with fellow travellers who have borne other discomforts stoically that they give up the journey after a week andthe Baron is forced to do the same. One of the points of disagreement is over the women's share of the work of the trip-he does not agree with Englishmen.
Germans in Eng. TLS
Merciless ironical studies of male weaknesses and pomposity especially that of the narrator oblivious to his faults; gradual revolt of oppressed wife of German husband. ATH
Interesting group of Pilgrims including fascinating Frau Von Eckthum whom the speaker misunderstands to be attracted to him.

010261   CHRISTINE. BY ALICE CHOLMONDELEY. New York: Macmillan, 1917 NUC. London: Macmillan, 1917 BMC.

Writes to mother from Germany where she studies violin, tells of her art, people, love for German officer.: just before and after outbreak of war. She dies in hospital. PW
Acclaimed a genius by her music master; she's 22. in preface we're told of the death of this letter writer, daughter of the author. Letters are convincingly real. TLS
Dead of pneumonia; becomes disillusioned in the German people SP
"excitingly independent,shocking," The shock of change the war bring to the relations. SR
Mother sacrifices for her daughter's year of study. Shrewd statements about the Kaiser, state of mind of Germans. NYT 8-15-17285

010262　　　　CHRISTOPHER AND COLUMBUS. BY THE AUTHOR
OF "ELIZABETH AND HER GERMAN GARDEN" [ANONYMOUS].
London: Macmillan, 1919 BMC. Garden City, New York:
Doubleday, Page, 1919 NUC.

Two young women part-German live in Eng. Their
guardian offended by their presence sends them off to
Amer. A kind of Sir Galahad takes charge SP LBKM
"Good deal of sentiment" BAKER, 32, p. 15

010263　　　　ELIZABETH AND HER GERMAN GARDEN
[ANONYMOUS]. London: Macmillan, 1898 BMC NUC. New
York: Macmillan, 1898 NUC.

SP 81:467. Elizabeth has left her town flat and is
staying alone, getting house fixed up for husband and
children. Refers to her husband as "the man of wrath."
Descriptions of gardening and neighbors. North
Germany.

010264　　　　FRAULEIN SCHMIDT AND MR. ANSTRUTHER;
BEING THE LETTERS OF AN INDEPENDENT WOMAN. BY THE
AUTHOR OF "ELIZABETH AND HER GERMAN GARDEN" AND "THE
PRINCESS PRISCILLA'S FORTNIGHT" [ANONYMOUS]. New York:
C. Scribner's Sons, 1907 NUC. London: Macmillan, 1907
NUC.

Elizabeth child of German scholar, jilted by Eng
lover, has the wit to find comedy in her external
circumstances and courage to keep her soul alive. Thru
poverty, sickness and sorrow. "Her life is splendid"
ACAD
Contains letters of an ind. woman Maria to Mr. A. They
were engaged, broke off, but correspond. Called
Rose-Marie but she is really Eliz- TLS
She has a fine taste in letters and music. Rose-Marie
Schmidt meets Anstruther, fall in love, secretly
engaged, jilts her for rich girl, tries to carry on
with both. Her love turns to contempt. She finally
chooses poverty and indep. to renewal of old
relations. Letters include lit. crit., vivid
unconventional talk. She's completly cured of the past
love for him.

010265　　　　IN THE MOUNTAINS [ANONYMOUS]. Garden
City, New York: Doubleday, Page, 1920 NUC. London:
Macmillan, 1920 BMC NUC.

TLS diary of a woman living in a Swiss chalet with two
widows. Their relationship. Finally her uncle, a 60 yr
old arrives.
ATH Auth is sent, but witty, a good story.
SR-Has come there for healing resources of Nature
after war. Two widows join her by chance. Jewhes
marries the man.
PW-Unhappy woman goes to Swiss chalet where dwellers
are set on their feet and made useful once more to
themselves and the world
NYT 10-3-20 p24. Cultured woman living alone in Swiss
mts. recovering from losing all she loved in war. Two
women find her place by chance and become permanent
guests. Diary form. Story of her recovery there, with
them, from her grief.

010266　　　　THE PASTOR'S WIFE. BY THE AUTHOR OF
"ELIZABETH AND HER GERMAN GARDEN" [ANONYMOUS]. London:
Smith, Elder, 1914 BMC NUC. Garden City, New York:
Doubleday, Page, 1914 NUC.

ATH 144:353 Eng. wife of German pastor. She has six
children in seven years; two have survived, her health
is shattered for a long period of time, she is finally
estranged from husband.
TLS 13:450 Book divided in three parts. First is
Ingeborg's meeting with Herr Dremmel. Second opens on
her exhausted and ill, she regains her strength, but
refuses to have sex with Dremmel, who during the past
two years has been "generally kind and liking his wife
better than anything except manure." End of part two
she is strong and well but "an unnoticed piece of
sisterly furniture." Part three tells of new man, her
affair, her penitent return to husband-to love and
live with him forever "Herr Dremmel went on writing-he
had forgotten Ingeborg." The end.
NYT 1914:517 "The woman belonging to him is, except
for her sex, negligible."
BKM v. 40 1914-15
PW 86 11/14/14:1568 "Ingeborg was an English bishop's
daughter and his right hand, so when she found herself
alone in London she was fairly intoxicated with the
freedom. On an impluse she joined a traveling tour for
the Continent, whereon Herr Dremmel marked her for his
own. Ingeborg's share in the courtship consisted
chiefly of "buts" which the good Herr never even
heard. Consequently Ingeborg became the pastor's wife
and we see the Teuton-British problem through her

eyes. At one time it becomes too much for her and she
yields to an indiscretion which has a most
characteristic and humorous denouement."
Eng. Ingeborg Bullavant on tour in Switz, gets engaged
to German pastor she's known for two days. After ten
years of marriage and six children runs off to Venice
with artist believing he wants to paint her. *Husband
pays no attention to her-he's absorbed in manure (his
way of communicating with his flock to become a farmer
like them). Along came the artist. Ingeborg takes off
leaving a note-Finds artist's intentions are no good,
returns full of remorse which husband can't understand
because he never read the note, so busy was he with
his manure. BKM

010267　　　　THE PIOUS PILGRIMAGE. BY THE AUTHOR OF
ELIZABETH AND HER GERMAN GARDEN [ANONYMOUS]. Boston:
R. G. Badger, 1901 NUC.

010268　　　　THE PRINCESS PRISCILLA'S FORTNIGHT. BY
THE AUTHOR OF "ELIZABETH AND HER GERMAN GARDEN"
[ANONYMOUS]. London: Smith, Elder, 1905 BMC NUC. New
York: C. Scribner's Sons, 1905 NUC.

Another Elizabeth. Priscilla feeling her soul starved
runs away from court "her opinion on saintly
wives-identical with Mrs Deland's"; Priscilla's
awakening to the life she chose, the chores of
everyday life. NYT 794,05
BAKER 32-15

010269　　　　THE SOLITARY SUMMER. BY THE AUTHOR OF
"ELIZABETH AND HER GERMAN GARDEN" [ANONYMOUS]. London:
Macmillan, 1899 BMC. New York: Macmillan, 1899 NUC.

NYT 1900:404. Continuation of Elizabeth and her German
Garden. Partnership of the gardener with experience
and no ideas and Elizabeth with the reverse-their
bungling, this time on a larger scale.
Female hermit meditates on nature and life in her
secluded garden. There's both humor and seriousness in
her commentary. Stresses value of communication with
nature. BAKER 03, 66
Elizabeth still has her garden, is still talkative,
Convinces us that the ideal is to spend a summer in a
garden alone with a few books. No. Germany. She and
husband agree to a summer apart from the world. ACAD
56:604

RUSSELL, MRS. H. E.

010270　　　　JOYCE MARTINDALE. London: Remington, 1894
BMC.

ACAD 45:166. Australia. "Powerful and sometimes
trenchant opinions on social subjects." Concerns a
curate believing in celibacy and in love with Joyce.
ATH-Joyce rejects his suit.

010271　　　　TOO EASILY JEALOUS. AN AUSTRALIAN
ROMANCE. London: Eden, 1892 BMC.

ATH 100:859. North Queensland. Romance.
Ethel Stanhope married for a while and happy is
accused of unfaithfulness by husband who listens to
gossip. She leaves Australia for Eng. (home). Hearing
he's dead, she marries. He reappears. Both she and
second husband die. ACAD 43:56

RUSSELL, RAYMOND, pseud. See FEARING, LILIAN BLANCHE.

RUSSELL, RITA.

010272　　　　IN A WEB OF GOLD. London: Digby, Long,
[1897] BMC.

RUSSELL, VIOLET.

010273　　　　HEROES OF THE DAWN. Dublin and London:
Maunsel, [1913] BMC NUC. New York: Macmillan, 1914
NUC.

RUTHERFORD, C. See RUTHERFORD, CONSTANCE.

RUTHERFORD, CONSTANCE. Nationality Unknown.

010274　　　　THE BLAZING STAR. London: E. Macdonald,
1914 BMC.

ATH-traditional historical romance.

010275　　　　THE STRAIGHT FURROW. BY C. RUTHERFORD.
London: A. Melrose, [1920] BMC NUC.

TLS-romance.

RUTLEDGE, MARICE. See HALE, MARICE RUTLEDGE (GIBSON).

RYAN, MARAH ELLIS (MARTIN). 1860(?)-1934. United States.

010276   THE BONDWOMAN. Chicago: Rand, McNally,
1899. London: T. F. Unwin, [1899] BMC.

The heroine is fiercely resentful for the wrongs of
slave women in the U.S.. She buys a plantation in time
of Civil War, becomes a spy, uses every means to ruin
her federal lover whom she believes to be the owner of
an octoroon. Unexpected end. LW 30:408
She's a French marquise, widow of 20, full of ideas,
fine ed. Learns she's an Octoroon. Comes upon her own
identity while trying to free her fellow-women from
the consequences of slavery. PW 56:777.

010277   A CHANCE CHILD, COMRADES, HENDREX AND
MARGOTTE, AND PERSEPHONE: BEING FOUR TALES. Chicago:
Rand, McNally, 1896 NUC.

BOOK NEWS 1. model and a sculptor. 2. war story. 3.
Swedish love story. 4. Negro dialect.

010278   A FLOWER OF FRANCE: A STORY OF OLD
LOUISIANA. Chicago: Rand, McNally, 1894 NUC.

LW 25:303. New Orleans, adventure, happy ending.
PW-Zizi, an African slave, incurs the displeasure of
her master and is branded with the fleur-de-lis. Her
vengeance. Her final act of restitution.

010279   THE FLUTE OF THE GODS. New York: F. A.
Stokes, [1909] BMC NUC.

"Romance of the Am. Indians of the desert" BKM 30
1909-10
Life of Indians in Amer as fiction 10-9-09 PW

010280   FOR THE SOUL OF RAFAEL. Chicago: A. C.
McClurg, 1906 NUC. London: C. F. Casenove, 1906 BMC.

hist. tale TLS
Marries a man whom she does not love and who is
despicable. Made an oath to his dying mother to be
responsible for his soul. How does she keep the oath?
BKM 24, 1906
NYT

010281   THE HOUSE OF THE DAWN. Chicago: A. C.
McClurg, 1914 BMC NUC.

PW:86 11/14/14:1574 "Tale of love and religion in
Spanish Mexico A high born Castilian girl found her
soul in the Indian country in the House of Dawn, a
sanctuary of sun worship. The world, her former world,
said she had lost it; but the world does not always
know."
Hist rom of inquisition days told in first person by
woman who follows her betrothed to the new world NYT

010282   INDIAN LOVE LETTERS. Chicago: A. C.
McClurg, 1907 NUC.

Educated Indian drifts back to Indian ways tho he
loves a New York girl. Letters are to her-he's dying
of a fatal disease. 3-16-07 PW

010283   MY QUAKER MAID. Chicago: Rand, McNally,
[c1906] NUC.

010284   A PAGAN OF THE ALLEGHANIES. Chicago:
Rand, McNally, 1891 BMC NUC.

CR 17:100. Young man from East and Pagan, a young man
reared in coal region of Pennsylvania without
"knowledge of his birth or education," but who
nevertheless has acquired an education from nature, a
perfect moral code and a belief in transmigration, and
a young woman who is in love with him.
Uncle sends nephew to Alleghanies to look over
property. Nephew meets a relative, radical. The Pagan.
Both of them fall in love with Krin, the unhappy wife
of a distiller. Story tells of the effect of the
unspoken love on the three. Remarkable book. LW

010285   SQUAW ELOUISE. Chicago: Rand, McNally,
1892 NUC.

PW. Story of an Indian girl who loves and is deceived
by a white man.
North Pacific Indians. Purpose "alliances between the
races are degrading to both." LW '93, 58

010286   THAT GIRL, MONTANA. Chicago: Rand,
McNally, 1901 NUC.

12-7-01 PW

010287   TOLD IN THE HILLS: A NOVEL. Chicago:
Rand, McNally, 1891 NUC.

Jack Genesee hero combines best of white and "Indian
Traits." Raised by Indians; based on a superstition in
Montana silver mine area; Kentucky people go there for
the summer. Their adventures and hy of their guide
(Jack) and a noble woman. PW 3-14-91.

010288   THE TREASURE TRAIL; A ROMANCE OF THE LAND
OF GOLD AND SUNSHINE. Chicago: A. C. McClurg, 1918 BMC
NUC.

PW Search for gold and Germ-Mex plots against U.S.
before dec. of war.

010289   THE WOMAN OF THE TWILIGHT; THE STORY OF A
STORY. London: C. F. Cazenove, 1913 BMC. Chicago: A.
C. McClurg, 1913 NUC.

PW 83 5/10/13:1688 "Scene is alternately a Mexican
settlement in California and fashionable sets in
eastern cities. Through her marriage in her girlhood
to a man who has since deserted her, the heroine, an
artist of genius, is debarred from union with the man
she comes to love in later life. Those bars she and
her lover strive for a time to ignore. Depicts the
views both of the individual who claims the right of
personal happiness, and the conventions which, blind
though they necessarily are, yet serve the interests
of the civilization which the individual seeker after
happiness has accepted."
Very sympathetic view of the heroine Monica Wayne. NYT
"Man and Woman who seek happiness outside the law
(Marriage)" Heroine's "flaming indignation against
certain hideously unjust laws" NYT 1913, 340
"The story opens in the Mexican village in southern
California in which McLane Sargent first saw the woman
who inspired the story which made him famous and which
he called, symbolically, "The woman of the twilight."
The scene shifts to the Atlantic coast and to
fashionable New York. Here some years later, Sargent
meets Monica Wayne, but does not recognize her as "La
Querida" the little wild girl of Mexican experience.
In the working out of events, the plot of his story is
in some measure repeated in his own life; Monica
passes out of his world, becoming to him another Woman
of the Twilight." BRD

RYAN, MARGARET. United States.

010290   SUE TERRY; OR, TWO HEARTS--TWO MINDS--TWO
WOMEN'S WAYS. New York: M. W. Hazen, 1904 NUC.

RYBOT, VICTORIA (BAKER). Nationality Unknown.

010291   A DEVOTED COUPLE; A NOVEL. BY J.
MASTERMAN. London: R. Bentley, 1894 BMC. New York:
Harper, 1894 NUC.

SP 72:475. Story of a family, six sons, John Bulls of
the sort to uphold England's power and glory wherever
they go.
ATH 103:342.

RYCE, JOHN, pseud. See BROWNE, ALICE M.

RYCROFT, CISSIE.

010292   A SUNBEAM FROM ITALY: THE LIFE STORY OF
VESTA DE TIVOLI. London: Digby, Long, 1904 BMC.

LBKM-mild love story.

RYLAND, CALLY THOMAS, jt. au. See LAGEN, MARY JULIA AND
CALLY THOMAS RYLAND.

RYLEY, ELIZABETH.

010293   THE SOUL OF JUNE COURTNEY: A NOVEL.
London: Duckworth, 1917 BMC.

How she found her soul and became a woman instead of a
souless butterfly. Through war work but mostly through
love. TLS SP SR

RYLEY, MADELEINE LUCETTE. 1868-1934. United States.

010294   AN AMERICAN CITIZEN: A NOVEL. New York:
G. W. Dillingham, 1898 NUC.

NYT 1898:416. Based on play.
PW Inheritance based on American hero becoming a

493

British citizen.
Set in New York and on Riviera. Novel is by author of play by the same name. ACAD 57:254.

RYND, EVELYNE ELSIE.   United Kingdom.

010295   IN THE CITY OF UNDER. London: E. Arnold, 1914 BMC NUC. New York: Longmans, Green, [1914] NUC.

ATH-fantasy. Good for children. Hermes as a hawker. Young boy hero.
PW 86 11/14/14:1574 "Pseudo fairy tale of a boy who had to come back from India to live in a dilapidated house in the street called Down. He was very lonely at first, but a friendship with the Hawker opened up a whole new world."
Fanciful tale, allegorical. NYT

010296   MRS. GREEN. New York: Putnam's Sons, 1901 NUC. London: J. Murray, 1901 BMC NUC.

PW 8-10-01

010297   MRS. GREEN AGAIN. London: J. Murray, 1915 BMC 1916 NUC.

010298   OTHERLAND. London: W. Gardner, 1907 BMC.

S., A. E., pseud. See STAPLEY, ANNIE E.

S., E. A. B., pseud. See SHACKELFORD, ELEANOR A. B.

SABINE, JULIA A. United States.

010299   AT THE END OF THE RAINBOW. New York: T. Whittaker, 1892 NUC.

LW 23:330. English girl goes to Colorado as a "lady-help" of American family; convinces them all of the beauty of the church of England.

SADLEIR, MARIE M.

010300   SUCH IS THE LAW! A STORY. London: Greening, 1899 BMC.

Concerns the law that gives a man the right to will his property away from his wife and children. The author opposes the law. LIT 5:326.
Lavender and Sydney Weston. Apparently he is unfaithful. ATH 114:487.

010301   AN UNCANNY GIRL. London: D. Stott, 1894 BMC.

SR-gloomy, but a happy ending.
ATH-old-fashioned wickedness.

SADLER, CORA G. Nationality Unknown.

010302   THE PENDULUM: A NOVEL. Boston: Sherman French, 1912 NUC.

PW-woman loses her mind through husband's blow; avenged by her son

SADLER, S. H.

010303   THE BOTHERS OF MARRIED LIFE. London: S. Sonnenschein, 1903 BMC.

TLS 03 99

010304   HENRIETTA. London: G. Routledge, 1907 BMC.

010305   THE LITTLE HAIR TRUNK. London: Heath, Cranton, [1919] BMC.

010306   THE LOVE AFFAIR OF MR. WILKINSON. London: Heath, Cranton & Ouseley, [1915] BMC.

010307   TRUNKLES. London: J. Ouseley, [1912] BMC.

SADLIER, ANNA THERESA. 1854-1932. Canada.

010308   ARABELLA. St. Louis, Mo.: B. Herder, 1907 NUC.

010309   COUSIN WILHELMINA. St. Louis, Mo.: B. Herder, 1907 NUC.

010310   GERALD DE LACEY'S DAUGHTER; AN HISTORICAL ROMANCE OF COLONIAL DAYS. New York: P. J. Kenedy, 1916 NUC.

Traditional historical romance of William of Orange. PW

010311   THE LOST JEWEL OF THE MORTIMERS. St. Louis, Mo.: B. Herder, 1904 NUC.

010312   THE PILKINGTON HEIR. New York: Benziger, 1903 NUC.

Historical novel. PW 2-14-03. For Catholic young people.

010313   THE RED INN OF SAINT LYPHAR. New York: Benziger, [c1904] NUC.

Bloody histical study of French Revolution. PW 3-4-05

010314   THE SILENCE OF SEBASTIAN. Notre Dame, Ind.: Ave Maria, [c1913] NUC.

Wife deserts husband. He remarries has a son. At his death, he tells son to seek that first wife to discover whether his second marriage was indeed legal. He-the son-is sworn to secrecy. ATH

010315   THE TALISMAN. New York: Benziger, 1903 NUC.

Historical Catholic theme. 2-14-03 PW

010316   THE TRUE STORY OF MASTER GERARD. New York: Benziger, 1900 NUC.

NY in days of Wm. of Orange. PW 56:1301

010317   WAYWARD WINIFRED. New York: Benziger, 1905 NUC.

Story for girls.

SAGER, JULIET GILMAN. B. 1873. United States.

010318   ANNE, ACTRESS; THE ROMANCE OF A STAR. New York: F.A. Stokes, [1913] BMC NUC.

Anne North successful actress, who has struggled for years to educate her daughter. Elsie at 18 joins mother in New York goes on stage. Anne must face conflict between her ambition and love for selfish daughter. A fine man loves Anne and helps her find happiness PW 84 10/4/13 P. 1141
"the anxieties heart burnings and jealousies of the the profession" "actress who is at the same time a mother" NYT 1913, 577
Anne now a leading lady in a stock company in Brooklyn. Was left a widow with a child when she was very young, places her child with a relative. Daughter, now 18 comes into her life just at the point when she falls in love. Daughter, too, on stage, plans to use mother's influence. The man now loves the daughter instead. The daughter wins the man and mother's place on stage. BKM

SAHN, LOUISE.

010319   LUTES AND RIFTS. A NOVEL. London: E. Stock, 1898 BMC.

LIT 2:537. Unoriginal.
SR 85:601. After years of estrangement sister and brother come together.

SAINT AUBYN, ALAN, pseud. See MARSHALL, FRANCES (BRIDGES).

SAINT AUBYN, DAISY.

010320   A GARLAND OF THORNS. A NOVEL. London and Sydney: Eden, 1893 BMC.

SAINT CLAIR, AGATHA.

010321   THE EXILE. London: E. Stock, 1908 BMC.

TLS-love story, male hero

SAINT CLAIR, NONINE.

010322   IN SUNNY AUSTRALIA: A NOVEL. London: Gay and Bird, 1896 BMC.

SAINT CLAIR, STELLA.

010323   PHILIPPA IN NAPLES; OR, LOVE TRIUMPHANT. London: A.H. Stockwell, [1920] BMC.

SAINT CLAIRE, EMILY.

010324   A RUINED LIFE. London: Digby, Long,
[1894] BMC.

    ATH 104:887. Old-fashioned attempt to write a romance.

SAINT CLAIRE, MAY.

    010325   A STORMY PAST. London: Digby, Long,
    [1896] BMC.

SAINT FELIX, MARIE, pseud. See LYNCH, HARRIET LOUISE
(HUSTED).

SAINT JOHN, ISABELLA.

    010326   A JOURNEY IN WAR TIME. London and New
    York: J. Lane, 1919 BMC.

    Account of a journey taken by a mother to find her son
    missing in action PW

SAINT LEGER, EVELYN, pseud. See RANDOLPH, EVELYN SAINT
LEGER (SAVILE).

SAINT LUZ, BERTHE, pseud. See ROBERTSON, ALICE ALBERTHE.

SAINT MICHAEL, ELIZABETH.

    010327   BURNT OFFERINGS. London: G. Allen, 1914
    BMC.

    ATH. The life-story of a love-child, the daughter of
    an English artist and a Japanese mousme. (tearoom
    girl).
    ATH 144:98 Moralizing and sentimental. Hannah cannot
    be happy in either England or Japan.

SALE, EDITH (TUNIS). United States.

    010328   RED ROSE INN. Philadelphia: Lippincott,
    1911 NUC.

    In letters decides between two suitors. NYT PW 6-3-11

SALZSCHEIDER, FLORENCE LUCIE (DICKINSON). United States.

    010329   PANDORA. A NOVEL. BY MRS. SALZSCHEIDER.
    San Francisco: Whitaker & Ray, 1901 NUC.

SALZSCHEIDER, MRS. See SALZSCHEIDER, FLORENCE LUCIE
(DICKINSON).

SAMPSON, EMMA (SPEED). B. 1868.

    010330   MAMMY'S WHITE FOLKS. Chicago: Reilly &
    Lee, [c1919] NUC.

    Foundling raised by doctor's "Mammy." PW

SAMPSON, JANE FELTON. United States.

    010331   CHRONICLES OF OLD RIVERBY. Boston:
    Sherman, French, 1913 NUC.

    PW 12/20/13 2178 "Rachel Winn, a young girl in search
    of health, goes to Old Riverly, a village so primitive
    that its only means of communication with the outside
    world, is a ramshackle stage. Here she meets many
    quaint characters and her experiences with them make
    the story."

SAMPTER, JESSIE ETHEL. 1883-1938.

    010332   THE SEEKERS. New York: M. Kennerley, 1910
    NUC.

SANBORN, KATHERINE ABBOTT. 1839-1917. United States.

    010333   ABANDONING AN ADOPTED FARM. New York: D.
    Appleton, 1894 NUC BMC.

    010334   ADOPTING AN ABANDONED FARM. New York: D.
    Appleton, 1891 NUC BMC.

    Tired of city and of apartments, a woman buys a farm
    for a bargain. Runs it successfully. Experiences at
    auctions, buying a horse, raising chickens, etc. PW
    7-25-91.

    010335   A TRUTHFUL WOMAN IN SOUTHERN CALIFORNIA.
    London: Sampson Low, 1893 BMC. New York: Appleton,
    1893 NUC BMC.

    Leaves her farm in Gooseville, Mass. because she's ill
    and sojourns through various resorts in Caifornia. PW

8-12-93

SANBORN, MARY FARLEY (SANBORN). 1853-1941. United States.

    010336   THE CANVAS DOOR. New York: B. W. Dodge,
    1909 NUC. London: A. Rivers, 1910 BMC.

    TLS-Allegra preaches paganism, makes love to Boy, is
    familiar with Medieval England and execution of Marie
    Antoinette.
    Fantasy. PW 12-11-09

    010337   THE FIRST VALLEY; A NOVEL. Boston: Four
    Seas, 1920 NUC.

    PW-picturing experiences of a girl in the realm beyond
    death.

    010338   IT CAME TO PASS. Boston: Lee and Shepard,
    1892 NUC.

    LW 23:230. Sisters, at home with widowed father.

    010339   LYNETTE AND THE CONGRESSMAN. Boston:
    Little, Brown, 1905 BMC NUC.

    Romantic love story. PW 10-14-05

    010340   PAULA FERRIS. Boston: Lee and Shepard,
    1893 NUC.

    "...a woman has permitted a man to tell her he loves
    her and has answered that she loves him" has been
    "passionately kissed, etc. and returns to loving her
    husband and to being loved by him without a sign of
    regret or shadow of remorse." The author believes in
    women like Paula who can experience "outlaw passion"
    and remain pure and good. The reviewer sees her as
    "hysterical," idle and self indulgent. LW 24:258.
    "...a woman has permitted a man to tell her he loves
    her and has answered that she loves him," has been
    "passionately kissed, etc. and returns to loving her
    husband and to being loved by him without asign of
    regret or shadow of remorse." The author believes in
    women like Paula whoutlaw passion" and remain pure and
    good. The reviewer sees her as "hysterical," idle and
    self indulgent. LW 24:258.

    010341   THE REVELATION OF HERSELF. New York:
    Dodd, Mead, 1904 NUC.

    PW-letters to a man.
    NYT?-sounds doubtful.

SAND, GEORGE, pseud. See DUDEVANT, AMANTINE LUCILE AURORE
(DUPIN).

SANDARS, NEWTON, pseud. See MEARS, LOUISE.

SANDARS, VIRGINIA FRANCES ZERLINA. B. 1828.

    010342   A LIFE'S DEVOTION. BY LADY VIRGINIA
    SANDARS. London: Hurst and Blackett, 1891 NUC BMC.

    "Utterly unremarkable" ACAD.
    Bridget and Shelah are two characters. SP 67, 77
    Life's devotion is Hugh's for Shelah. Irish. ATH 97
    728
    Time of Crimean war. Bridget is Shelah's nurse. Shelah
    is a well protected daughter of Irish peer. Hugh
    Carmichael is in love with her. Scene changes from
    Ireland to London. "Healthy pleasant reading." SR
    7-11-91, 54

SANDEMAN, MINA.

    010343   CHARMING MISS KYRLE. London: J. Long,
    1899 BMC.

    She and her young widow mother exchange advice on love
    affairs. ACAD 57:513.
    LBKM 17:122. Romance of Lord Pangbourne and Miss
    Kyrle, villainous machinations of others to prevent
    it.

    010344   THE INFATUATION OF AMANDA. London: Digby,
    Long, [1898] BMC.

    ACAD 53:229. Amanda loved the curate. But she
    discovered after their marriage that he had for her
    only a "tepid toleration." Also, he went to stage
    shows and joined a stage crowd. Once he had an "acme
    of rage." Amanda killed him.
    SR 85:470. Amanda is not beautiful. She goes mad when
    she kills him.

010345   THE ROSY CROSS AND OTHER PHYSICAL TALES.
Westminster: Roxburghe Press, 1896 NUC BMC.

010346   SIR GASPARD'S AFFINITY. London:
Digby, Long, 1897 BMC.

   Lurid. A governess thoroughly Eng. ACAD 52 Fic sup
   105.
   LIT 2:451. Narration of grandmother to her
   grandchildren. Suitable for young girls. "breezy.
   charming."

010347   AN UNCONVENTIONAL MAID. A NOVEL. London:
Skeffington, 1904 BMC.

   ATH-plain and piquant, astonishes with the brilliant
   audacity of her views, marries a famous scientist who
   is an ardent anti-vivisectionist.
   ACAD-in form of autobiography, humorous.

010348   WICKED ROSAMOND. London: J. Long, 1899
BMC.

   Uses poison to remove the object of her hate. Her fate
   provides a salutary moral. SP 82:459
   Story of a perverted nature. Tries to poison her
   husband by means of poisoned gloves a music-hall woman
   gave her. They were made from a recipe of Catherine de
   Medici. ACAD 56:244.
   Her daughter is angelic. Set in Brighton. ATH 113:271

010349   THE WORSHIP OF LUCIFER: A NOVEL. London:
Digby, Long, 1897 BMC.

SANDERS, E. K. See SANDERS, ELLA KATHERINE.

SANDERS, ELLA KATHERINE.

010350   ANGELIQUE OF PORT-ROYAL, 1591-1661. BY A.
K. H. London: Skeffington, 1905 BMC NUC.

010351   FENELON. HIS FRIENDS AND HIS ENEMIES.
1651-1715. London and New York: Longmans, Green, 1901
BMC NUC.

010352   FOR PRINCE AND PEOPLE: A TALE OF OLD
GENOA. BY E. K. SANDERS. London and New York:
Macmillan, 1897 NUC.

   Oberto goes out to seek his fortune. Discovers he's
   the heir of Andrea Doria. ACAD 52 Fic sup 123.
   SP 80:175. Hist. rom. of Italian Renaissance. The
   revolt of the Fieschi, Genoa. Male hero.
   LIT 2:355. No female amongst principal characters. No
   love, no mrge. Rivalry between two families.

010353   THE FOREST PLAYFELLOW: A STORY. London:
A. Constable, 1907 BMC.

   Story from a young boy's point of view. TLS

SANDERS, HELEN FITZGERALD. United States.

010354   THE DREAM MAKER. Boston: Cornhill,
[c1918] NUC.

010355   LITTLE MOTHER AMERICA. Boston: Cornhill,
[c1919] NUC.

   Story of patriotism and war. PW NYT

010356   THE WHITE QUIVER. New York: Duffield,
1913 NUC.

   PW-"Story of the Piegans before they felt the
   influence of the white man. It pictures the Indian as
   he was, every myth, custom and ceremonial described
   having been gleaned from patriarchs of the tribe. It
   recounts the love of White Quiver for Dawn Mist who
   was spirited away by an enemy and how White Quiver
   sought her far and wide."

SANDERSON, ETHEL LEGROS.

010357   THE STORY OF LEAH. London: W. Stevens,
[1895] BMC.

SANDS, BEATRICE. United States.

010358   WEEPERS IN PLAYTIME. New York: J. Lane,
1908 NUC.

   PW- child born of bigamous marriage, placed in home,
   mother works to befriend children in these
   institutions at last discovers her child.
   NYT-purpose novel-institutionalized children are the

weepers.

SANDYS, OLIVER, pseud. See EVANS, MARGUERITE FLORENCE
HELENE (JERVIS).

SANFORD, M. BOURCHIER. See SANFORD, MARY BOURCHIER.

SANFORD, MARY BOURCHIER. Canada.

010359   THE ROMANCE OF A JESUIT MISSION: A
HISTORICAL ROMANCE. BY M. BOURCHIER SANFORD. New York:
Baker and Taylor, [c1897] NUC.

   NYT 1898:415. 17th c. Fort Ste Marie, Canada, mission
   to Huron Indians.

SANGSTER, MARGARET ELIZABETH (MUNSON). 1838-1912. United
States.

010360   EASTOVER PARISH, A TALE OF YESTERDAY. New
York: F.H. Revell, [c1912] NUC.

   PW-virtuous community life.

010361   ELEANOR LEE: A NOVEL. New York: F.H.
Revell, [1903] BMC NUC.

   Works among poor, rehabilitates drunken husband. Civil
   war period. PW 10-3-03.
   Touches upon many modern women's subjects. Women's
   clubs, work among the poor. NYT 03,783.

010362   FAIREST GIRLHOOD. Chicago: F.H. Revell,
[c1906] NUC. London: Oliphant, [1906] BMC NUC.

010363   JANET WARD, A DAUGHTER OF THE MANSE. New
York: F.H. Revell, [c1902] BMC NUC.

010364   WHEN ANGELS COME TO MEN. New York and
London: F.H. Revell, [1903] BMC NUC.

SANGSTER, URANIA NOTT. United States.

010365   THE POWER OF GOLD: A ROMANCE OF LONDON,
ENGLAND. BY (RENA) URANIA NOTT SANGSTER. Buffalo,
N.Y.: Matthew-Northrup Works, 1909 NUC.

   Fortunes of a couple in New York and London; their
   dire perils; happy end. PW

SARCEY, YVONNE.

010366   THE ROAD TO HAPPINESS (LA ROUTE DU
BONHEUR). London: A. Melrose, 1910 BMC. (Tr. by
Constance Williams.)

SARTORIS, ADELAIDE.

010367   A WEEK IN A FRENCH COUNTRY HOUSE. BY MRS.
RICHMOND RITCHIE. New York: Macmillan, 1902.

SATTERLEE, ANNA ELIZA (HICKOX). B. 1851. United States.

010368   THE WONDER GIRL: A TOURIST TALE OF
CALIFORNIA. Boston: Sherman, French, 1915 NUC.

   She sings, dances, and tours California. PW 12-18-15

SATTERTHWAIT, ELISABETH CARPENTER. United States.

010369   A SON OF THE CAROLINAS: A STORY OF THE
HURRICANE UPON THE SEA ISLANDS. Philadelphia: H.
Altemus, 1898 NUC BMC.

   PW-old fashioned love story of Northern Quakeress and
   a new man of the South.

SAUNDERS, ANNA M. United States.

010370   GOLDEN-ROD: A STORY OF THE WEST. BY A
DAUGHTER OF NEBRASKA [ANONYMOUS]. Lincoln, Nebraska:
Golden-rod Pub. Co., [c1896] NUC.

SAUNDERS, FRANCES WILCE.

010371   STORIES FOR MEN AND WOMEN. London:
Sonnenschein, 1896 BMC.

SAUNDERS, MARGARET ELSIE (CROWTHER) BAILLIE. B. 1873.
United Kingdom.

010372   BECKY & CO.: A NOVEL. London: Hutchinson,
[1919?] BMC NUC.

   TLS-cultured milliner with business establishment
   wherein she houses her woman workers and Franciscan

nuns.
SP-there is a love story.

010373   THE BELFRY. London: Hodder & Stoughton,
[1914] BMC NUC.

LBKM-wife marries man who is committed to mental
asylum, told his case is hopeless. Finding no pleasure
in society, she is about to join a High Church nunnery
when in Bruges she meets a dramatist whose genius
stirs her and she becomes selflessly and passionately
attached. He thinks nothing of her sacrifice. Her
husband recovers, begs her forgiveness. To tell him
might shatter his newly gained health.
ATH 144:232. Returns to husband. She has collaborated
on play with other man, no credit given her for it.

010374   BLACK SHEEP CHAPEL. London: Hurst &
Blackett, [1918] BMC. New York: G. H. Doran, [c1919]
NUC.

Religious story and a mystery. ATH
Saints and sinners, ritualism. SR
And commerce. PW
TLS-religion

010375   THE BRIDE'S MIRROR. London: Hutchinson,
1910 BMC.

BM-"a society love affair."
ATH-free love and wife beating and atheism are subject
matter.

010376   CAPTAIN THE CURE. London, New York:
Hodder & Stoughton, 1915 NUC BMC.

Priest turns soldier. LBKM

010377   THE DISTAFF DREAMERS: A SOBER COMEDY.
London: Hutchinson, 1916 BMC NUC.

TLS-0 love story.
ATH-0 love story.

010378   THE GREAT FOLK OF OLD MARYLEBONE. London:
H. J. Glaisher, 1904 BMC NUC.

010379   LADY G. London: Hutchinson, 1912 BMC.

TLS-heavy on plot, heroine is a female jailbird with
several aliases.
ATH-many thrills in thief's career as she climbs to
fabulous heights of social success.
LBKM-confesses to her husband to save him from death,
leads to her downfall. When she leaves jail she finds
a young woman-suicide in good clothes, exchanges
clothes, has then to assume responsibility for
child--by chance marries suicide's father.

010380   LITANY LANE, A NOVEL. London: Hutchinson,
1909 BMC 1910 NUC.

LBKM-male fights for soul of dancer.
Life of slum girl; separated from husband she becomes
a rage--dancer and mimic. Three men struggle for her:
one for her mind; one for her charms; a priest for her
soul. "Startling marriage to Sir Nigel". "Triumphs as
artist." TLS
ATH adds little

010381   LONDON LOVERS. London: T. F. Unwin, 1906
BMC NUC.

010382   THE MAYORESS'S WOOING. London:
Hutchinson, 1908 BMC NUC.

TLS-niece of mayor woos MD who exposes a drug which
mayor has made his fortune on. Discovers he is the
mayor's son.
BKM-she is a pawn.
ATH-

010383   THE PRINCE'S SHADOW. London, New York:
Hodder and Stoughton, [c1913] BMC NUC.

Exiled Italian prince marries young woman from London.
ATH
The womanly self-abnegation of women in court life.
Males treated with brisk tolerance-no heroes. TLS

010384   SAINTS IN SOCIETY. London: T. F. Unwin,
1905 NUC BMC. New York and London: G. P. Putman's
Sons, 1906 NUC.

A Labour leader plummeted to success; his cockney wife
really rises to the occasion. He later takes to

morphine and dies. She remarries, this time a baronet.
She addresses a crowd of unemployed in her husband's
stead? ACAD 1106,05
Chloris, the wife, is discontented, vulgar? ATH 05,642
PW-married couple meet temptations of worldly success.
NYT-wife Cockney girl of low origins who transforms
herself into hard-working sincere woman.

010385   A SHEPHERD OF KENSINGTON. London: Hodder
& Stoughton, 1907 BMC NUC.

London society- TLS

010386   YOUNG MADAM AT CLAPP'S. London:
Hutchinson, 1917 BMC.

SAUNDERS, MARGARET MARSHALL. 1861-1947. United States.

010387   DEFICIENT SAINTS. A TALE OF MAINE. BY
MARSHALL SAUNDERS. Boston: L. C. Page, 1899 NUC BMC.
London: G. Bell, 1903 BMC.

Mrs. Hypolyta Prymmer--cold, hard self righteous
church woman--her widowhood, courtship and realization
of her deficiencies. PW 56:736
BKM 10:501. Bangor-Puritan mother-in-law, Mrs. Prymmer
and unkindness to daughter-in-law. Miss Gastonguay "a
little gentlemanly short-legged lady in a broadcloth
coat." Captain White tames Hypolyta then marries her.

010388   THE GIRL FROM VERMONT. THE STORY OF A
VACATION SCHOOL TEACHER. BY MARSHALL SAUNDERS.
Philadelphia: Griffith and Rowland Press, 1910 NUC.

NYT-Anti child labor theme. Heroine is in profession
of organizing children's playgrounds and vacation
schools. Wins love of town's wealthiest manufacturer
and reforms him and his business.

010389   HER SAILOR. A LOVE STORY. BY MARSHALL
SAUNDERS. Boston: L. C. Page, 1900 NUC.

LW 31:26. Heroine at early age marries a sea captain,
finally grows to love him.

010390   THE HOUSE OF ARMOUR. BY MARSHALL
SAUNDERS. Philadelphia: A. J. Rowland, 1897 NUC.

010391   ROSE A CHARLITTE: AN ACADIAN ROMANCE. BY
MARSHALL SAUNDERS. Boston: L. C. Page, 1898 NUC BMC.
London: Methuen, 1899 BMC.

NYT 1898:501. Idyl of Acadia which is also an
exposition of the Acadian people and their
intrepretation of their history. M.S. is from Nova
Scotia.

SAUNDERS, MARSHALL, pseud. See SAUNDERS, MARGARET MARSHALL.

SAUNDERSON, IRENE.

010392   A WELSH HEROINE. A ROMANCE OF COLLIERY
LIFE. London: Lynwood, [1911] BMC.

SAVAGE, AMY.

010393   BETTY'S HUSBAND [ANONYMOUS]. London: G.
Richards, 1902 BMC.

SAVI, E. W. See SAVI, ETHEL WINIFRED (BRYNING).

SAVI, ETHEL WINIFRED (BRYNING). 1865-1954. United Kingdom.

010394   BABA AND THE BLACK SHEEP. London: Hurst &
Blackett, 1914 BMC.

ACAD 86:762. India. Jean lived alone, in charge of a
plantation, after her father's death. Love story
involving John and Max.
ATH-she is regarded by the natives as an arbitrator
and a magistrate.
TLS-they admire and respect her; she is 22. Romance
between her and the black sheep, a self-exiled
Englishman.

010395   BANKED FIRES. BY E. W. SAVI. New York and
London: G.P. Putnam's Sons, 1919 BMC NUC.

Anglo-Indian story: must choose between husband and
child. She insists on going home to England with her
child vs. her husband's wishes. He's devoted to his
career in India. TLS
Joyce Meredith "puts her child first and her husband
nowhere." LBKM
She's 15 years younger than husband, "brainless."
NYT Calls the tale conventional; with various couples

paired off in the end. NYT 10-19-19 584

010396   A BLIND ALLEY. London: Digby, Long, 1911
BMC.

010397   THE DAUGHTER-IN-LAW. London: Hurst &
Blackett, 1913 BMC.

Marriage of English woman to a rich Zengali, her
unhappiness and escape. ATH

010398   MISTRESS OF HERSELF. London: Hurst &
Blackett, [1918] BMC.

TLS-love story.
ATH-2 daughters; 1 is fashionable and artificial,
other (who is the heroine) has advanced views, is too
aggressive, rev. feels.

010399   THE REPROOF OF CHANCE. London: Digby,
Long, 1910 BMC.

TLS-simple, wholesome, love story.
Love, misunderstanding, etc. ACAD
Woman goes far to wreck her own life and his-the man
who loves her. LBKM

010400   SINNERS ALL. London: Hurst & Blackett,
1915 BMC.

Duty of restitution by a son in India to a
stepdaughter in England of a fortune, ends up falling
in love with her, marrying, etc. TLS

010401   WHEN THE BLOOD BURNS. BY E. W. SAVI. New
York and London: G.P. putnam's Sons, 1920 BMC NUC.

TLS- love and passion, without marriage. Marcelle,
typist, goes to India with David to discuss it. Her
mother (who in youth had done the same) died of heart
disease. Happy ending.
ATH-while in India, where passing as a respectable
couple, secret leaks out and they are cold-shouldered.
Man's devotion not proof to this test and Marcelle
breaks connection, thereby being thrown on her own
resources.
NYT Sept. 19, 1920, p.22. Marcelle is illegitimate.

SAVILE, HELEN V.

010402   LOVE, THE PLAYER. London: 1899 NUC.

Country life in Ireland and elsewhere. The heart-story
of a woman. LIT 5:134
Lurid melodrama. Woman betrayed, her rejected suitor
vows revenge, her twin sister shot by mistake (Janet
Brady adopts her sister's illegitimate child, is much
scorned for this action.) She dies in that shooting.
SP 83:225
Tragic: Irish life, unpleasant people--the rector and
his wife. BAKER 03 173

SAVORGNAN, CORA A. (SLOCOMB) BRAZZA. B. 1862. United
States.

010403   AN AMERICAN IDYLL. BY THE COUNTESS DI
BRAZZA (CORA SLOCOMB). Boston: Arena, 1896 NUC BMC.
(Published also under title: Ampharita: an American
Idyll.)

Scientist goes to study the Pima Indians in Mexico.
Ampharita, a Piman maiden helps him with his research.
Is also his servant. PW 51:337

SAWKINS, MRS. LANGFIELD.

010404   THE AGITATOR IN DISGUISE. London: Heath
Cranton & Onseley, [1914] BMC.

ATH-historical romance, Ireland. Male hero.

010405   LADYE BERTHA OF ROMROW. A ROMANCE OF THE
GOLDEN AGE. London: F. Griffiths, 1913 BMC.

Romance of a history student who shows no small
imagination and literary gifts. TLS

SAWTELL, ELLA.

010406   THE BREATH OF SCANDAL. London: Greening,
1909 BMC.

Husband becomes a famous singer; Hazel, deserted and
misunderstood hides self in London. She has a career
as famous violinist cut short by her death. TLS

SAWTELLE, MARY P.   United States.

010407   THE HEROINE OF '49: A STORY OF THE
PACIFIC COAST. BY MRS. M. P. SAWTELLE. [San
Francisco]: [Printed By Francis Valentine], [c1891]
NUC.

SAWTELLE, MRS. M. P.   See SAWTELLE, MARY P.

SAWYER, EDITH AUGUSTA. B. 1869. United States.

010408   MARY CAMERON: A ROMANCE OF FISHERMAN'S
ISLAND. Boston: B. H. Sanborn, 1899 NUC.

Maine. She visits Boston and learns all about women's
issues but "fortunately her native good sense eschews
the wisdom of female voting." Pure simple natural etc.
love story. LW 30:250
Off Maine coast. She's 18. Womanly beyond her years.
Her loneliness on this remote island, trip to Boston.
Ends in love. NYT 9-2 -99,581
CR 36:472. Romance in Maine.

SAWYER, JOSEPHINE CAROLINE. B. 1878. United States.

010409   ALL'S FAIR IN LOVE. New York: Dodd, Mead,
1904 BMC NUC. London: B. F. Stevens & Brown, 1904 BMC.

Historical-PW

010410   EVERY INCH A KING: A ROMANCE OF HENRY OF
MONMOUTH, SOMETIMES PRINCE OF WALES. New York: Dodd,
Mead, 1901 NUC.

Concerns Henry III.

SAWYER, RUTH. B. 1880. United States.

010411   HERSELF, HIMSELF AND MYSELF; A ROMANCE.
New York & London: Harper, [1917] NUC.

Nora's dreams; finds himself in the end. PW
Sugary. Nora Kelly lost husband and child comes to
U.S. becomes a nurse to a child (herself) whose
parents die and leave the child to Nora and 3
musicians. Then they went to Ireland and found
Himself. NYT

010412   LEERIE. New York and London: Harper,
[c1920] BMC NUC.

PW-heroine is nurse serving in war zone.
NYT 8-15-20. sentimental. Love story incidental. Story
is of Leerie as a nurse, first in a sanitarium where
she broke rules and anything else necessary to give
the best care to her patients and her subsequent loss
of professional reputation, then as army nurse, having
postponed her wedding to work in France.

010413   THE PRIMROSE RING. New York and London:
Harper, [1915] BMC NUC.

Story of a nurse and house surgeon who try to save the
ward for incurables. They're transported to
Land-of-hearts desire. PW 5-15-15
Sent. fairy tale like story NYT

010414   SEVEN MILES TO ARDEN. New York & London:
Harper, [1916] BMC NUC.

Patsy is an actress always 7 miles from happiness till
she meets a tinker. PW
NYT-fairy story for grown ups.

SAXBY, JESSIE MARGARET (EDMONDSTON). 1842-1940.

010415   A CAMSTERIE NACKET. BEING THE STORY OF A
CONTRARY LADDIE ILL TO GUIDE. Edinburgh: Oliphant,
Anderson and Ferrier, 1894 BMC.

ACAD 46:100. A Shetland manse and a rebellious urchin.

010416   HER FIRST PLACE. London: Christian
Knowledge Society, [1891] BMC.

010417   LUCKY-LINES, OR, WON FROM THE WAVES.
Edinburgh and London: Oliphant, Anderson and Ferrier,
1893 BMC.

A mysterious bag with secret contents; two men and two
women-Yaspard, Magnus, Helen, Annie and sensational
situations. ACAD 44:168

010418   QUEEN OF THE ISLES, ETC. London: S. W.
Partridge, [1897] BMC.

010419   SISTERS-IN-LOVE. London: S. W. Partridge,
[1895] BMC.

SAYLOR, EMMA ROSALYN (SUTEMEIER). B. 1863. United States.

010420   THE LAST MILE-STONE. San Francisco: P.
Elder, 1917 NUC.

Letters to Jerry from Edith. He's a friend; husband in
sanitorium. She starts a home for aged in california.
Trip to Honolulu. Husband dies (insane), story ends
with last milestone of contentment for Jerry and
Edith. PW

SCAMMON, LAURA EVERINGHAM. United States.

010421   SPOON-RIVER DAN. Kansas City [Mo.]:
Hudson-Kimberly, 1894 NUC.

SCANLAN, ANNA C. D. 1894. United States.

010422   DERVORGILLA; OR, THE DOWNFALL OF IRELAND.
Milwaukee, Wis.: J. H. Yewdale, 1895 NUC BMC.

SCANNELL, FLORENCE.

010423   CINDERELLA'S SISTERS. London: Heath,
Cranton & Ouseley, [1914] BMC.

TLS-Romance a la Cinderella

010424   PETER'S PREDICAMENT: A SEQUEL TO
CINDERELLA'S SISTERS. London: Heath, Cranton, [1919]
BMC.

Centers on the hero, Peter. TLS
SP-Sobering effect of war.

SCARBOROUGH, MILDRED.

010425   THE SIGNAL LIGHT: A TALE OF THE
CONNECTICUT RIVER. Philadelphia: American Baptist
Publication Society, 1904 NUC.

SCARFOGLIO, MATILDE (SERAO). 1856-1927.

010426   AFTER THE PARDON. BY MATILDE SERAO.
London: E. Nash, 1908 NUC 1909 BMC. New York:
Stuyvesant Press, 1909 NUC.

Maria Quasco deserts husband to live with another man.
He pardons her but there is no happiness when they
come back together. She returns to husband when her
passion for her lover burns out. "considerable
psychological insight" ATH

010427   THE BALLET DANCER, AND ON GUARD. BY
MATILDE SERAO. New York and London: Harper, 1901 NUC.
London: W. Heinemann, 1901 BMC. (Tr. from the Italian)

Italian ballet dancer "homely", powerful psychological
study. BOOK NOTES Dec '01

010428   THE CONQUEST OF ROME. BY MATILDE SERAO.
New York and London: Harper, 1902 NUC. London: W.
Heinemann, 1902 BMC.

010429   THE DESIRE OF LIFE. BY MATILDE SERAO.
London: S. Paul, [1911] BMC NUC. (Tr. from the Italian
by William Collinge)

"unpleasant" account of two Italian semi-adventurers.
TLS
English girl commits suicide as a result of the misery
inflicted on her by lover who won't free himself from
another woman. ATH

010430   FAREWELL LOVE! A NOVEL. BY MATILDE SERAO.
New York: Minerva Pub. Co., [1892] NUC BMC. (Tr. from
the Italian by Mrs. H. Harland.)

SR 77:313. Anna, passionate heroine "flies with one
man and marries another." The man she eloped with
delivered her into the hands of her guardian whom she
subsequently married. She was unhappy, he found her a
"bore," she shot herself.
ACAD 45:346. Anna is "the victim of neurotic
degeneracy," much in common with Hedda Gabler altho
Addio Amore published in 1887, before Hedda. James S.
Little LBKM Anna Acquaviva.

010431   THE LAND OF COCKAYNE; A NOVEL. BY MATILDE
SERAO. New York and London: Harper, 1901 NUC. London:
W. Heinemann, [n.d.] BMC.

Passion for gambling; heroine? CR '01

unrelieved horror, but mostly a study of the gambling
mania in Naples. ACAD '01

010432   SOULS DIVIDED. BY MATILDE SERAO. London:
S. Paul, [1919] BMC NUC. New York: Brentano's, 1920
NUC. (Tr. from the Italian by William Collinge.)

PW-Romance about Italian young woman.
NYT-Mar 21 '20 p1. In form of letters (seldom used
now), from hero to heroine, passionate love.
Unrequited.
Letters-passionate outpourings of violent love of
Paolo for Diana Sforza on hearing her singing. She's
poor and an orphan. She's promised to an elderly man.
TLS
"luscious and emotional" two lovers who are never
united. "The lady marries an English diplomatist and
when he dies is unable to trace her love, pines away
and dies" BAKER 32 429

SCARRITT, ELIZABETH MARINER. Nationality Unknown.

010433   QUID EST. New York and London: Abbey
Press, [1902] NUC.

SCHALLENBERGER, V., pseud. See SIMMONS, VESTA S.

SCHAUFFLER, RACHEL CAPER. B. 1876. United States.

010434   THE GOODLY FELLOWSHIP. New York:
Macmillan, 1912 BMC NUC.

BKM 35 (1912) suggests a strong heroine. Rash young
woman starts out.
PW-to encircle globe, stops with missionaries.
ATH-designed for the good young person.
TLS-American missionary life in Persia.
LBKM-American missionary marries a gruff antipathetic
man who proves too strong for her.
NYT-1st character-she is in a dirty Persian guest
house talking with her Moslem courier who refuses to
do what she wants done while a dirty curious hostile
crowd collect and finger her clothes. She is next in a
hand-to-hand struggle with a Persian in a deserted
mountain defile where he has misled her.

SCHEM, LIDA CLARA. 1875-1923. United States.

010435   THE GREATER JOY; A ROMANCE. BY MARGARET
BLAKE. New York: G. W. Dillingham, [c1912] NUC BMC.

PW-Doctor-nurse "not for young readers."

010436   THE HYPHEN. New York: E. P. Dutton,
[c1920] NUC.

PW-Psych of a German-American and others of foreign
origin who are in the process of becoming American.
NYT 10-31-20 Male hero. "There is only one way for
those of German blood who are guiltless to prove their
innocence, and that is to go and fight Germany."

010437   MATTHEW FERGUSON. BY MARGARET BLAKE. New
York: G.W. Dillingham, [c1914] NUC BMC.

PW 85 5/30/14 1772-"Matthew Ferguson's success came
from his scheme of self-aggrandizement which he called
the system of scientific egoism for the advancement of
the individual. How he meets the powers behind the big
R.R. Trust, wins their approval and incidentally an
enormous salary--how he finds Doris Diberto and saves
her from a fate worse than death by a marriage of form
only; how his marriage is consummated: his agony upon
discovering his child's resemblance to another man,
his accusation of his wife and ultimate belief in her
with his final break with his system make the story."
ATH 144: 178 O

010438   THE VOICE OF THE HEART. A ROMANCE. BY
MARGARET BLAKE. New York: G.W. Dillingham, [c1913] NUC
BMC.

"Story of a girl who is married by a musician because
he wishes to develop her voice. Another musician,
Richard Pryce, loves Betty, and she loves him, but an
apparently insuperable obstacle had separated them.
Three years of suffering ensue. Betty's husband
treating her most cruelly, but in the end she brushes
aside all stumbling blocks and seizes her happiness. "
PW
"Romance of a girl who believes marriage is a bond of
friendship and comradeship, but not of love." NYT 1913
202
"A cleverly worded plea for the recognition of passion
as a vital necessity in rounding out a perfect
marriage. The biggest thing in sex fiction." NYT 1913

579
Heroine "determined to marry no man who would ask of his wife anyything but affection, companionship and respect, bars as illicit the call of the flesh until her lover finds the key to her humanity." NYT 354 (1913)

SCHERR, MARIE. United States.

010439   THE IMMORTAL GYMNASTS. BY MARIE CHER. New York: Doran, [c1915] NUC. London: W. Heinemann, 1915 BMC.

Magic Shop. juv.
BKM-rom.
Bina is one of the gymnasts TLS
Fantasy in part. ATH

SCHNEBLY, FRANCES MARGARET. B. 1867. Nationality Unknown.

010440   THE VITAL TOUCH: A STORY OF THE POWER OF LOVE. Chicago: Laird and Lee, [c1912] NUC.

PW-love story of a would-be priest.
NYT-love story of a would-be priest.

SCHNEIDER, MARTHA LEMON. United States.

010441   A GOVENMENT COUNTESS: A NOVEL OF DEPARTMENTAL LIFE IN WASHINGTON. BY MARTHA LEMON SCHNEIDER (MRS. CHARLES W. SCHNEIDER). Washington, D.C.: Neale Publishing, 1905 NUC.

SCHNEIDER, MRS. CHARLES W. See SCHNEIDER, MARTHA LEMON.

SCHOCK, GEORG, pseud. See LOOSE, KATHARINE RIEGEL.

SCHOEFFEL, FLORENCE BLACKBURN (WHITE). 1860-1900. United States.

010442   SADDLE AND SENTIMENT. BY WENONA GILMAN. New York, London: Outing, [c1892] NUC.

010443   A WANDERING BEAUTY; OR, THE TEMPTATIONS OF A GREAT CITY. BY WENONA GILMAN. New York: Munro's Pub. House, 1891 NUC.

SCHOFIELD, LILY.

010444   CASSANDRA BY MISTAKE. London: Methuen, 1914 BMC.

ATH-psychology professor brings up his ward in an experimental way in order to test certain theories. ATH 144:477. He removes her from all society, hoping to prove that her "spirit writing" can be definitely cited as not being from any "mundane source." She murders a dumb attendant in defending herself from assault and rest of story "is concerned with saving her from the gallows."

010445   ELIZABETH, BETSY, AND BESS. London: Duckworth, 1912 BMC.

ATH-story of a schoolgirl.
TLS-has a vitality which puts it outside the class of girls books, vital significant portrait of spirited woman between 13-18
LBKM-easy, light style, entertaining. Love story present.
Youth of imaginative Irish girl. Concerns R.C. and Protestantism. SP

010446   I DON'T KNOW. London: Duckworth, 1913 BMC.

Soul of drowned seaman enters another man's body.
Consequence a Jekell-Hyde personality. ATH

SCHOONMAKER, NANCY (MUSSELMAN). B. 1873. United States.

010447   THE ETERNAL FIRES. New York: Broadway, [c1910] NUC.

"Relating the sad experiences of a young Kentucky girl who, rebelling against the narrow life she is compelled to lead among the farming people of Kentucky, decides to see and know something of the broader life in the outside world. She completes a college course, and then goes abroad for several years." BKM V 31, 1910
NYT-In Paris she becomes inspiration for artist, is disillusioned in that relationship and finally agrees to marry American businessman suitor.
Reviewed in Forerunner by C. P. Gilman

SCHREINER, OLIVE EMILIE ALBERTINA (SCHREINER) CRONWRIGHT. 1855-1920. South Africa.

010448   DREAM LIFE AND REAL LIFE; A LITTLE AFRICAN STORY. BY RALPH IRON. Boston: Roberts, 1893 NUC. London: T. F. Unwin, 1893 NUC BMC.

010449   DREAMS. Boston: Roberts, 1891 NUC. London: T. F. Unwin, 1891 NUC BMC.

Subject is women's rights. A woman's 11 dreams. ACAD.
A classic of feminism: Wellington

010450   TROOPER PETER HALKET OF MASHONALAND. London: T. F. Unwin, 1897 NUC BMC. Boston: Roberts, 1897 NUC.

"A completely conscientious exposition of its author's rel. & political views." Peter is 21, slum-bred, physically weak. Alone at a fire he has a vision of JC. This meeting leads to his freeing a black man. He dies. Africa. SR 83:389.
Review by Frank Danby. Purpose novel-vs the imperalism of England in S. Africa. CR 26,30:285.
"Suppressed in Eng." LW 28:83.
Black and white problem in S. Africa. J. C., the principal spokesperson. BAKER 03, 242.
NYT 1898:414. English soldier in Africa who for first time experiences religious feeling, wanders the veldt bent on saving souls, dies on mission of mercy.

SCHREINER, TIN, pseud. See BRODERICK, THERESE.

SCHUBIN, OSSIP, pseud. See KIRSCHNER, LULA.

SCHUETZE, GLADYS HENRIETTA (RAPHAEL). B. 1884. United Kingdom.

010451   A MOUSE WITH WINGS. BY HENRIETTA LESLIE. London and Glasgow: Collins Clear-Type Press, [1920] BMC.

TLS-feminist point of view, but not limited to questions of suffrage. Olga has an unhappy marriage, raises her son to be not like husband. She is a Fabian and a pacifist. Son loves Beryl, a militant suffragist, but he enlists in war and is killed. Olga is horrified by his enlistment. Olga meets a Fabian man she likes.
ATH-Beryl is a "mouse" or a suffragette released under the "cat and mouse" act. Arnold has been trained by his mother to the end that he should not resemble his sport-loving "normal" father. The two women are temperamentally antagonistic but agree in their hatred of war.

010452   PARENTAGE. BY GLADYS MENDL. London: Chapman & Hall, 1913 BMC.

2 parts: promise, fulfillment; development of Peter Deeping, his upbringing by parents who want to mould his character to suit themselves. Peter meets Unity Jane--an American girl educated in Paris--strong enough to make him rebel against his parents. ACAD

010453   THE ROUNDABOUT. BY GLADYS MENDL. London: Chapman and Hall, 1911 BMC.

The Story of a woman's friendships between two art students and the unhappy marriage of one (Jessica) of them to a man who drinks. "Too much rhetoric". TLS
Jessica falls in love with another man. All works out peacefully(?) LBKM

010454   THE STRAIGHT ROAD. BY GLADYS MENDL. London: Chapman & Hall, 1911 BMC.

Woman discovers love outside her marriage but she keeps to the straight road of duty. TLS
path of restitution of men and women. ATH

010455   WHERE RUNS THE RIVER? BY HENRIETTA LESLIE. New York: Dutton, 1916 PW. London: J. M. Dent, 1916 BMC NUC.

Fluvia lives a strange, lonely childhood with her guardian, an old man she calls Wisdom, in the mountains of Wales. First loves artist, then older man, settles for a musician. PW
NYT-215,6-3-17
TLS-sentimental romance.

SCHULDER, IRENE DICKSON. Nationality unknown.

010456   VIRGINIA RUSSELL. New York: Cochrane, 1908 NUC.

SCHULTZ, JEANNE. B. 1870.

010457   JEAN DE KERDREN. New York: Appleton, 1892
NUC. London: Nelson, 1916 BMC.

NUC: Published in Paris, Firmin-Didot 1887 under pseud
Philippe Saint Hilaire
LW 23:278. Male hero, marries governess out of pity,
they grow to love each other after. Then she dies of
consumption and he becomes a priest.
CR 318:118. Male with passion for sea has vowed never
to marry, but does to protect woman from insult. They
later fall in love, but "their happiness is
short-lived."
Man marries a woman out of chivalry; they learn to
love each other; she dies of consumption. He becomes a
priest. NATION 56, 297

010458   STRAIGHT-ON: A STORY FOR YOUNG AND OLD.
BY THE AUTHOR OF "COLETTE" [ANONYMOUS]. New York: D.
Appleton, 1891 NUC.

Philip Bailleul's development as a young man, school
experiences, his aspirations for ideals set down by
model of his father whose motto straight on was given
to the boy at the father's death. NATION 53,512

SCHURMANN, HELEN. United States.

010459   THE SOLITARY SURVIVOR, AND OTHER STORIES.
Indianapolis: 1896 W.

SCHUSTER, ROSE.

010460   THE ROAD TO VICTORY. London: Chapman and
Hall, 1913 BMC NUC.

Frederick the Great--his conversion from arrogant fop
to hard-headed businessman. TLS

010461   THE TRIPLE CROWN. London: Chapman & Hall,
1912 BMC NUC.

TLS-historical book
ATH-historical book

SCHWARTZ, JULIA AUGUSTA. B. 1873. United States.

010462   ELINOR'S COLLEGE CAREER. Boston: Little,
Brown, 1906 NUC.

PW-Tactless genius

010463   VASSAR STUDIES. New York and London: G.
P. Putnam's Sons, 1899 NUC BMC.

12 studies: 12 types of students. "To embody in
literary form for the alumnae of a particular
institution, memories and impressions of their college
days." Author's purpose. Rev. says 300 pages without
incident or a single male figure makes appallingly
dull reading. Not really fiction. SP 83:474

SCIDMORE, ELIZA RUHAMAH. 1856-1928.

010464   AS THE HAGUE ORDAINS: JOURNAL OF A
RUSSIAN PRISONER'S WIFE IN JAPAN [ANONYMOUS]. New
York: H. Holt, 1907 NUC.

Journal of wife of Russian prisoner in Japan; is nurse
in hospital. She's quick of mind, fearless; reports
the horrors of war. NYT
DS 517, 9 1. Japan Desc and Travel 2. Russo Japanese
War 1904-05

SCOTT, AIMEE BYNG (HALL). United Kingdom.

010465   THE EMPORIUM. A NOVEL OF MODERN SOCIETY.
BY ALEC HOLMES. London: G. Allen, 1912 BMC.

010466   THE SONG OF THE STARS; A NOVEL. BY ALEC
HOLMES. London: G. Allen and Unwin, 1917 BMC NUC.

SCOTT, C. A. DAWSON. See SCOTT, CATHARINE AMY (DAWSON).

SCOTT, CATHARINE AMY (DAWSON). United Kingdom.

010467   AGAINST THE GRAIN. A CHARACTER STUDY.
London: W. Heinemann, 1919 BMC.

Escapades of boy, then man. Harry King. TLS
Prize fighters. Sexual triumphs of a man. Women who
lay their hearts at his feet. LBKM

010468   THE AGONY COLUMN. London: Chapman & Hall,

1909 NUC BMC.

The woman finds no appeal in the common duties of
life. She's an idealist, lives a dream, yearns for
what she doesn't have, ignores what's present; married
to mid-aged soldier. Her life's a mess. Falls in
love--for him wrecks her marriage. Frances Morgan very
sympathetic. TLS
Husband refuses to believe he was the father of their
2nd child. Frances neglects home, absorbed in
friendship with young Jew. Husband believes they're
lovers. Husband after absence in Africa, ready to take
her back though convinced she's guilty (she's not).
Frances rejects him. Still in contact with the young
Jew but he's married. They seem to have had a platonic
relationship. ATH
"The author leaves the heroine in a hopeless plight."
SP

010469   THE BURDEN. BY C. A. DAWSON SCOTT.
London: W. Heinemann, 1908 BMC. New York: R. Reynolds,
[c1908] NUC.

TLS-"an attempt to justify a young wife's infidelity
to an elderly husband." "Stodgy."
SR-character study. Author condones heroine who "knew
that she had ripened into a womanhood more kindly and
tolerant than if she had remained the cold and gentle
wife of the old scholar."
ATH-reveals to guardians of husband's will the truth
so that her child's father (the heir apparent) will
not be deprived of his rightful inheritance.

010470   THE CADDIS-WORM; OR, EPISODES IN THE LIFE
OF RICHARD AND CATHERINE BLAKE. London: Hurst &
Blackett, 1914 BMC.

LBKM-like the title, Catherine, married to a
domineering dr., has created a sheath, symbolizing the
virtues civilization considers praiseworthy--meekness,
unselfishness, etc. Behind the sheath Catherine held
herself aloof. But when her children begin to suffer
from their father's domination, she emerges and does
battle. Mother and children win their own
independence.
ACAD 87:121. Catherine has no voice in her children's
affairs until it is discovered that his 1st wife was
not dead when they married, the children are not
legitimate--and therefore her concern--not husband's.
TLS 13:311

010471   THE HEADLAND. London: W. Heinemann, 1920
BMC. New York: A. A. Knopf, 1920 NUC.

TLS-Roma, keen-witted denizen of London studios. Tavis
Hawke, young farmer, the natural man calling to the
natural woman, Hendre Pendragon, heir, small
red-haired man of 40, a perfect son, clear minded,
studious, Roma feels him safe and pleasant to accept
as husband. He has a monstrous passion to which he
periodically succumbs and has struggled against all
his life. Horrible achievement. Mystery of the blood?
SP-covers three days.
ATH-Roma decides she loves Tavis, passion.
LBKM-3 day's action seen through Roma's eyes. She sees
Hendre whose sole joy in life is gratification of vile
unnatural impulses and Clarice, both loving the dark
because their deeds are evil.

010472   MADCAP JANE; OR, YOUTH. London: Chapman
and Hall, 1910 BMC.

LBKM young wife bored runs away and works as servant
in her mother-in-law's household. Finally returns.
SR-not a serious work.

010473   MRS. NOAKES. AN ORDINARY WOMAN. London:
Chapman & Hall, 1911 BMC NUC.

Middle class woman yearns for the best but has to take
2nd best. Husband ruins the faith she once had in him.
Son turns out badly. "Sincere actuality of the
capacity of an ordinary woman for love and suffering."
TLS

010474   THE ROLLING STONE; A NOVEL. BY C. A.
DAWSON-SCOTT. New York: A. A. Knopf, 1920 NUC.
(English title "Against the Grain.")

PW-unconventional man after years of wandering comes
back to quiet life in England.
NYT Feb 8 '20 p. 70. Harry King, from 6 to 36,
character study. Interesting but not attractive hero.
Self-centered, doing wrong was getting caught. Can't
be faithful to a woman, unable to settle down. Book
suggests he is on verge of settling but reader cannot

believe he is capable of staying settled. His
character doesn't change.

010475   THE STORY OF ANNA BEAMES. London: W.
Heinemann, 1907 BMC NUC.

Spinster of 35 "given to all good works." Keeps house
for brother-vicar. She learns of attentions of local
Don Juan to a young woman and foils his plan. Falls a
victim to the man. In a month he throws her downstairs
and she dies in giving birth to the child. "Treated
with the freedom characteristic of feminine fiction."
ACAD
Seduced by the scoundrel, she dies after he throws her
downstairs after a sordid marriage. TLS
Succumbs to an unworthy passion at 35, falls for an
adventurer, a short and unhappy marriage. SP

010476   TREASURE TROVE. BY C. A. DAWSON SCOTT.
London: W. Heinemann, 1909 BMC. New York: Duffield,
1909 NUC.

Story of money. TLS

010477   WASTRALLS. A NOVEL. BY C. A.
DAWSON-SCOTT. London: W. Heinemann, [1918] BMC NUC.

SR-Tragedy of ill-mated pair in rural Cornwall. Sabina
works wastralls (farm) with skill of a man, refusing
offers of marriage until she weds a farm hand of
foreign blood. Sabina is crippled by an accident but
insists on managing farm, control of which her husband
desires. Passion and moody fits overrule him and
tragedy results. Character study.

SCOTT, CHRISTABEL.

010478   IONA: A ROMANCE OF THE WEST. London: E.
Stock, 1896 BMC.

SCOTT, E. C. See SCOTT, ELLEN (CORRIGAN).

SCOTT, ELLEN (CORRIGAN). 1862-1936. United States.

010479   THE LOYALTY OF ELIZABETH BESS. BY E. C.
SCOTT. New York: Macmillan, 1918 NUC.

SCOTT, FLORENCE MARY SEYMOUR.

010480   GWLADYS PEMBERTON. London: Smith, Elder,
1896 BMC.

LBKM 10:88. Heroine and two other characters dead by
end of book. A wicked father, a vicar.
SR Gwladys dies nursing a fever-struck village.
ACAD 50:48. No love interest. Gwladys is handsome and
clever, has original and unconventional ideas.

SCOTT, FLORENCE MARY SEYMOUR AND ALMA HODGE.

010481   THE COMING OF THE KING. London: J. M.
Dent, 1898 BMC.

SCOTT, FRANCES.

010482   THE WORLD'S OLD STORY. London: Digby,
Long, 1900 BMC.

ATH 115:142. Youth, courtship, marriage, honeymoon,
domestic bereavement and troubles.

SCOTT, FRANCINA. Nationality Unknown.

010483   ROMANCE OF A TRAINED NURSE. New York:
Cooke and Fry, 1901 NUC.

Studies, graduates, fills several positions PW
3-30-01.

SCOTT, GERALDINE EDITH (MITTON). D. 1955. United Kingdom.

010484   A BACHELOR GIRL IN BURMA. BY G. E.
MITTON. London: A. & C. Black, 1907 NUC BMC.

010485   A BACHELOR GIRL IN LONDON. BY G. E.
MITTON. London: A. & C. Black, 1898 NUC BMC.

LIT 2:537. Comes to London to make fortune in
journalism, stays at single women's club. Eventually
makes fortune by marriage.
ACAD 54:58. Portrayal of large number of single women
working in an effort to live decently. Description of
the drudgery of her job as typist.
LBKM 14:80. "Accurate and convincing", portrayal of
"London girl bachelordom" with its "utter loneliness."

010486   THE CELLAR-HOUSE OF PERVYSE: A TALE OF
UNCOMMON THINGS FROM THE JOURNALS AND LETTERS OF THE
BARONESS T'SERCLAES AND MAIRI CHISHOLM. BY G. E.
MITTON. London: A. & C. Black, 1917 BMC NUC.

SR-the journals of two women who were given special
permission to go into the firing line to treat the
wounded on the site rather than be transported. What
was to be a week's experiment was extended for two
years. They drove motorcycles, ambulances, cared for
injured in midst of shelling, lived in a cellar which
they were bombed out of three times.

010487   FIRE AND TOW. BY G. E. MITTON. London:
Hutchinson, 1899 NUC BMC.

010488   THE GIFTS OF ENEMIES. London: A. & C.
Black, 1900 BMC.

LBKM 18:156.
SP 84:603. Hero impoverished at death of father.
Through influence of heroine, Betty Ventris, widow of
speculator and gambler, he becomes financially
successful journalist. She is a curious specimen of
the modern woman, for in spite of a somewhat showy
exterior and flirtatious manner, she is a disciple of
Maeterlink, cherishes high ideals and revolts against
the materialistic atmosphere her marriage has thrown
her into.
ATH 115:561. First few chapters devoted to cricket.
Study of Neil's character. ACAD 58:334. Tim Ventris
bet that he would marry the 1st girl he saw in a hat
trimmed in blue.
ACAD 59:53. Rosa Wybrow begins the tale by killing a
man. Neil is a professional cricketer.

010489   HAWK OF THE DESERT: A NOVEL. BY G. E.
MITTON. London: J. Murray, 1917 BMC.

Adventure: German spies TLS
ATH

010490   THE OPPORTUNIST. BY G. E. MITTON. London:
A. & C. Black, 1902 BMC NUC.

ATH 3-8-1902 Political novel

010491   THE TWO-STRINGED FIDDLE. BY G. E. MITTON.
London: J. Murray, 1919 BMC NUC.

Horror story TLS
Includes a young widow and her son interested in
big-game shooting. ATH

SCOTT, GERTRUDE FISHER.

010492   JEAN CABOT IN CAP AND GOWN. Boston:
Lothrop, Lee and Shepard, [1915] NUC.

PW 86 8/12/14:517 Jean's last year in college and her
plans and hopes for the future.

010493   JEAN CABOT IN THE BRITISH ISLES. Boston:
Lothrop, Lee and Shepard, [1913] NUC.

College story, vacation travelling

SCOTT, HARRIET. United States.

010494   HENRIETTA: A NOVEL. Minneapolis, Minn.:
1892 NUC.

SCOTT, JESSIE. United States.

010495   RUNNYMEDE; A ROMANCE OF AUSTRALIA. San
Francisco: Whitaker and Ray, 1903 NUC.

SCOTT, LEADER, pseud. See BAXTER, LUCY E. (BARNES).

SCOTT, META C.

010496   BENJAMIN'S SACK: TOLD FROM
NORTHUMBERLAND. London: Ward, Lock and Bowden, 1896
BMC.

LBKM 11:50. Margaret stole money from a woman her
brother loved for his sake. A rival tells the woman
and he takes the blame himself to protect the memory
of his sister. The woman sends him away, but ends up
taking him back.
ATH 108:753. Agnes must marry a Roman Catholic by the
time she is 25 or lose her inheritance. She is in love
with a parish clergyman who tries to augment his
income by writing a novel.
ACAD 50:560. Clergyman is Benjamin; the publishers
want 50 lbs to publish his novel. Margaret is

Benjamin's sister, burglarizes Agnes's house to get the 50 lbs. All ends well.

SCOTT, PATRICIA ETHEL (STONEHOUSE). 1870-1949. Australia.

010497 THAT WOMAN FROM JAVA. BY E. HARDINGHAM QUINN. London: Hurst and Blackett, 1916 BMC.

TLS-Eleanor has been dragged thru the divorce court by the treachery of a friend--comes to live in Java. Happy ending with son of Javan friend.

SCOTT, ROSE LAURE (ALLATINI).

010498 DESPISED AND REJECTED. BY R. ALLATINI. London: C. W. Daniel, [1918] NUC.

"Immediately suppressed on publication" NUC
TLS--A plea for pacifism and for tolerance of those abnormal in their affections. "Not recommended for general reading."
ATH--Many conscientious objectors would scorn to descend to petty lying; secrecy and subterfuge characters indulge in.

010499 HAPPY EVER AFTER. London: Mills and Boon, 1914 BMC.

ATH heroine yearned for marriage of love, lost it through writing a story containing biographical details
TLS Olive had literary ambitions, wanted to be a novelist. Story is her "emotional history from childhood."

010500 PAYMENT: A NOVEL. London: A. Melrose, 1915 BMC.

daughter "doomed to existence with a mother whose chief interest is to kill time" goes to fortune tellers ATH

010501 REQUIEM. London: M. Secker, 1919 BMC.

crowded with characters but focuses on young male Bohemian a glutton for sensation. Cecile, a model, Olivia Armstrong a writer TLS

010502 ROOT AND BRANCH. BY R. ALLATINI. London: G. Allen and Unwin, [1917] BMC NUC.

a study of a Jewish family, several generations, euthanasia large company of characters TLS

SCOTT, WINIFRED MAY.

010503 LOVE AND THE MAN. London: Drane, [1915] BMC.

Woman achieves immense success as an authoress. writes of her passion for a married man; "emotion is overdone" TLS

010504 THE SERPENT; A TALE OF THE CHILTERN HILLS. London: Lynwood, [1911] BMC.

diamond fields in South Africa

SCUDDER, VIDA DUTTON. 1861-1954. United States.

010505 THE DISCIPLE OF A SAINT: BEING THE IMAGINARY BIOGRAPHY OF RANIERO DE LANDOCCIO DEI PAGLIARESI. New York: E. P. Dutton, 1907 NUC. London: J. M. Dent, 1907 BMC.

Imaginary study (biography) of Catherine's secretary. 5-4-07 PW

010506 A LISTENER IN BABEL: BEING A SERIES OF IMAGINARY CONVERSATIONS HELD AT THE CLOSE OF THE LAST CENTURY AND REPORTED BY VIDA D. SCUDDER. Boston: Houghton, Mifflin, 1903 NUC.

The great questions of the day: heroine of high ideals thrown into relations with capital, labor, co llege, church. PW 10-24-03

SEABROOK, PHOEBE HAMILTON. United States.

010507 A DAUGHTER OF THE CONFEDERACY: A STORY OF THE OLD SOUTH AND THE NEW. Washington: Neale Publishing, 1906 NUC.

Civil War family novel. 2-23-07 PW

SEAMAN, AUGUSTA (HUIELL). 1879-1950. United States.

010508 THE BOARDED-UP HOUSE. New York: Century, 1915 BMC NUC.

010509 THE CRIMSON PATCH. New York: Century, 1920 BMC NUC.

010510 THE GIRL NEXT DOOR. New York: Century, 1917 BMC NUC.

010511 JACQUELINE OF THE CARRIER PIGEONS; A STORY OF THE SIEGE OF LEYDEN. London: Sidgwick and Jackson, 1910 BMC. New York: Sturgis and Walton, 1910 NUC.

Historical romance. PW

010512 THE LASS OF RICHMOND HILL. London: Cassell, [1917] BMC.

010513 MAMSELLE OF THE WILDERNESS; A STORY OF LA SALLE AND HIS PIONEERS. [New York]: Sturgis and Walton, 1913 NUC.

PW 83 6/14/13 "Fortunes of the young hero and heroine are bound up with one of the daring episodes of early American history--La Salle's attempt to found a colony at the mouth of the Mississippi. Little Mamselle is sent to America from a convent, not knowing who or what she is. In the new world she meets with many adventures and after she is grown-up the mystery surrounding her is cleared away, but she elects to discard the title which is hers and stay in America with the man she loves."

010514 MELISSA ACROSS THE FENCE. New York: Century, 1918 BMC NUC.

010515 THE SAPPHIRE SIGNET. New York: Century, 1916 BMC NUC.

010516 THE SLIPPER POINT MYSTERY. New York: Century, 1919 BMC NUC.

010517 THREE SIDES OF PARADISE GREEN. New York: Century, 1918 BMC NUC.

010518 WHEN A COBBLER RULED THE KING. New York: Sturgis and Walton, 1911 NUC.

Historical romance. PW 4-22-11

SEARCHFIELD, EMILIE.

010519 JACOB WINTERTON'S INHERITANCE. BY THE AUTHOR OF "MY BROTHER JACK" [ANONYMOUS]. London: C. H. Kelly, 1892 BMC.

CR 21:166. Simple, pious country family.

SEARLES, FLORA M. United States.

010520 THE SCARLET RIBBON. Boston: J. H. Earle, [c1900].

SEARS, CLARA ENDICOTT. B. 1863. United States.

010521 THE BELL-RINGER: AN OLD TIME VILLAGE TALE. Boston: Houghton, Mifflin, 1918 NUC.

PW-romance

SEARS, MARGARET L. United States.

010522 MENOTOMY: A ROMANCE OF 1776. Boston: R. G. Badger, 1908 NUC.

PW-historical romance

SEATON, ROSE.

010523 ROMANCES AND POEMS. London: Simpkin and Marshall, [1891] BMC NUC.

SEAWELL, MOLLY ELLIOT. 1860-1916. United States.

010524 BETTY AT FORT BLIZZARD. Philadelphia and London: J. B. Lippincott, 1916 BMC NUC.

Romance of army frontier life. PW 90:1286 10/14/16 NYT-Romance of army frontier life.

010525 BETTY'S VIRGINIA CHRISTMAS. Philadelphia and London: Lippincott, 1914 NUC.

PW 86 10/10/14:1207. "Colonel Beverly had been obliged

to sell his old Southern mansion to a Northerner.
Philip Fortescue, the son, an officer in the United
States army, falls in love with mischievous and
charming Betty, the Colonel's granddaughter. The hitch
comes when Betty cannot bear to desert "gran'dad," but
the Colonel, Aunt Tulip and Uncle Caesar are persuaded
to come and live with her in the old mansion; so
wedding bells ring out merrily."
NYT 1914:476--"pretty" "sentimental"

010526   THE CHATEAU OF MONTPLAISIR. New York: D.
Appleton, 1906 BMC NUC.

PW-comedy
NYT-older woman who is unconventional

010527   CHILDREN OF DESTINY. New York: D.
Appleton, 1893 NUC BMC.

A family's tendency to early death. Richard Skelton of
the Old South, slaveowner. NATION 56, 31
Luxurious living in the South. Richard Skelton and
Sylvia Shapleigh love each other. An involved plot. PW
4-1-93.

010528   DESPOTISM AND DEMOCRACY; A STUDY IN
WASHINGTON SOCIETY AND POLITICS [ANONYMOUS]. New York:
McClure, Phillips, 1903 BMC NUC.

010529   THE DIARY OF A BEAUTY: A STORY.
Philadelphia and London: J. B. Lippincott, 1915 BMC
NUC.

Story of a beautiful girl an old "spinster" and a
young man. 3-27-15 PW
Pleasantly written tale told by the beauty who wins
and loses fortunes. Was a post mistress, taken under
wealthy spinster's wing. Inherits money inspires an
artist to write a play. Hopes to star in it. NYT

010530   THE FORTUNES OF FIFI. Indianapolis:
Bobbs-Merrill, [1903] BMC NUC.

Pretty love story. PW 9-12-03
NYT 03, 654

010531   FRANCEZKA. Indianapolis, Ind.:
Bowen-Merrill, [c1902] NUC. London: B. F. Stevens and
Brown, 1902 BMC.

centers on Count de Saxe. Actress is introduced. PW
NYT 10-25-02 Historical novel.
Historical romance about an actress. ACAD 438 v64
O ATH 122, 151

010532   THE HISTORY OF THE LADY BETTY STAIR. New
York: C. Scribner's Sons, 1897 NUC BMC.

1798 Hist. rom. court of future Chas. X of France.
Lady Betty is a spirited woman. Strikes Bastien when
he kissed her. Loved and was separated from de
Bourmont. But they meet on the battlefield in Algeria
where" she fell bleeding from a dozen wounds" but
lives for the happy end. BKM 6:257.
ACAD 53:1. French refugees in Edinburgh in 1798-1827.
ATH 111:597. Through a misunderstanding she does not
marry hero, joins a convent.

010533   THE HOUSE OF EGREMONT: A NOVEL. New York:
C. Scribner's Sons, 1900 NUC. Toronto: Copp, Clark,
1900 BMC.

010534   THE IMPRISONED MIDSHIPMEN. New York: D.
Appleton, 1908 BMC NUC.

010535   THE JUGGLERS: A STORY. New York:
Macmillan, 1911 BMC NUC.

historical romance; includes an opera singer; rescues
two men. PW 12-30-11

010536   THE LADIES' BATTLE. New York: Macmillan,
1911 BMC NUC.

010537   THE LAST DUCHESS OF BELGRADE. New York:
D. Appleton, 1908 BMC NUC.

PW-historical
BKM-after husband treats her horribly he finds out how
good she is to him.

010538   THE LIVELY ADVENTURES OF GAVIN HAMILTON.
London and New York: Harper, 1899 BMC NUC.

First a Lt. then a peer-dashing courageous fellow.
Hist. rom. of the wars of Frederick the Great. PW

56:736
Bold Scot, hero of 7 years war BAKER 03 218

010539   THE LOVES OF THE LADY ARABELLA. New York:
Macmillan, 1898 BMC NUC.

SP 81:446. adventures of young naval officer at end of
last century. Lady Arabella, "the human counterpart of
a man-slaying tigress, a highly impossible
anti-heroine."
She makes men mad. Two came under her spell-who would
rather die than wed her. Includes a devoted,
ever-wrangling couple-Sir Peter & Lady Hawkshaw.
Plenty of action. LBKM 15:155.
Most of the story focuses upon a Lieutenant in the
English Navy, swearing, gambling and fighting. Lady
Arabella is really cold, loveless. BKM 8:493.

010540   THE MARRIAGE OF THEODORA. New York: Dodd,
Mead, 1910 NUC.

Duty to father and husband. PW
NYT-duty to father and husband

010541   PAPA BOUCHARD. New York: Scribner's, 1901
NUC.

10-12-01 PW
Papa is emancipated. NYT

010542   THE ROCK OF THE LION. New York and
London: Harper, 1898 BMC NUC.

1779-1783 Amer. midshipman served under Paul Jones is
now a prisoner of war. Has to do with Gibraltor. PW
52:1136
ACAD 55:201. Siege of Gibralter. Paul Jones.

010543   THE SECRET OF TONI. New York: D.
Appleton, 1907 BMC NUC.

Sentimental romance about a soldier. PW 2-2-07
Romance of four with happy endings. NYT

010544   THE SON OF COLUMBUS. New York and London:
Harper, 1912 BMC NUC.

010545   THE SPRIGHTLY ROMANCE OF MARSAC. New
York: C. Scribner's Sons, 1896 NUC.

PW 10-17-96. Two journalists, Parisians, impecunious
and reduced to the last extremity, invent a rich uncle
in America. Their credit is restored, etc., then uncle
becomes a reality.

010546   A STRANGE, SAD COMEDY. London: Warne,
1896 BMC. New York: Century, 1896 NUC BMC.

BKM 4:74. of the South.
PW 5-16-96. Virginia in 1864, then Newport in 1874.
Eccentric hypochondraic and French adventuress. Brings
out "freedom and perfect modesty of well-bred Southern
girls as compared with the acquired manners of
recently enriched New Yorkers."

010547   THE VICTORY. New York: D. Appleton, 1906
BMC NUC.

PW-Civil War romance.

010548   A VIRGINIA CAVALIER. New York: Harper,
[c1896] NUC.

Story of George Washington from his first military
instruction to Braddock's defeat. BKM 5:261

SEDGWICK, ANNE DOUGLAS. See DE SELINCOURT, ANNE DOUGLAS
(SEDGWICK).

SEEGMILLER, WILHELMINA. 1866-1913.

010549   SING A SONG OF SEASONS. Chicago: Rand,
McNally, [c1914] NUC.

SEGAL, JOSEPHINE.

010550   THE JUDGE'S DECISION. Philadelphia: Press
of Review Pub. and Print. Co., 1907 NUC.

SEIBERT, MARY FRANCES. United States.

010551   "ZULMA": A STORY OF THE OLD SOUTH.
Natchez, Miss.: Natchez Print. and Stationery Co.,
1897 NUC.

SEIVER, JULIA A. B. United States.

010552   BIRKWOOD: A NOVEL. Boston: Arena, 1896
NUC.

PW 10-3-96. "The main thought throughout this book is
the equality of the sexes and the development of the
race intellectually, morally, and physically, that
future generations may receive their just birthright."
BOOK NEWS "Strong, healthy"

SELKIRK, EMILY. Nationality Unknown.

010553   THE STIGMA. Boston: G. P. Putnam's Sons,
1906 NUC. London: H. B. Turner, 1906 BMC.

PW-young woman school teacher with negro blood;
tragedy
NYT-O
"The race problem is the foundation upon which Miss
Selkirk has laid her story. One of the chief
characters is a mulatto girl, who finds her "stigma"
of blood such a curse that she commits suicide. A
villainous white man is another important character. A
romance between a Southern man and woman runs through
the tale. "BKM 23 1906

SELLINGHAM, ELLA J. H. United States.

010554   THE HERO OF CARILLON; OR, FORT
TICONDEROGA IN 1777. Ticonderoga, N.Y.: W. T. Bryan,
1897 NUC.

SENIOR, FRANCESCA DOROTHY PONSONBY. B. 1884.

010555   CAPRICE, HER BOOK. London: A. & C. Black,
1910 BMC NUC.

TLS-village life.
NYT

010556   THE CLUTCH OF CIRCUMSTANCE; OR, THE GATES
OF DAWN. London: A. & C. Black, 1908 BMC NUC.

PW-historical romance.
TLS-King Arthur.
SR-King Arthur.

SERANUS, pseud. See HARRISON, SUSIE FRANCES (RILEY).

SERAO, MATILDE. See SCARFOGLIO, MATILDE (SERAO).

SERGEANT, ADELINE. See SERGEANT, EMILY FRANCES ADELINE.

SERGEANT, EMILY FRANCES ADELINE. 1851-1904. United
Kingdom.

010557   ACCUSED AND ACCUSER. London: Methuen,
1904 BMC NUC.

TLS-o

010558   ALISON'S ORDEAL; A STORY FOR GIRLS.
London: J. Nisbet, 1903 BMC.

Raised along unusual lines by absent-minded parent;
she is self-reliant. ATH 122, 851

010559   ANTHEA'S WAY. London: Methuen, 1903 BMC.

Very brief description. ACAD 64, 106
Anthea raised on moral stories, rigid ideas of right
and wrong and a belief in self-sacrifice but she grew
courageous, large-hearted, honest, her pluck when
things hurt, loyalty to gipsy child, sensible
behavior. LBKM 3-03, 253

010560   BARBARA'S MONEY. London: Methuen, 1902
BMC.

ATH 8-16-02

010561   BENEATH THE VEIL. London: J. Long, 1903
BMC.

Half sisters: one good, one bad. The seamy sides of
modern life. ACAD 64, 438
One sister disguises as other, weds. The groom on
discovery has an apoplectic fit; careers of two step
sisters. LBKM 6-03, 116

010562   BLAKE OF ORIEL. BY ADELINE SERGEANT.
London: F. V. White, 1899 NUC BMC.

Hero begins as prize winner in Board school, goes on
to University. But he's a liar and thief. Becomes
leader of a cult of higher life among undergrads. His
downfall. Dangers of mere intell. ed. SP 83:449.
Exploits hard working mother, abandons shopgirl, Anne
Egerton is a young woman of birth and fortune who
falls victim to him. Ethel the shopgirl, Liz the
factory hand. ATH 114:416.
University don really a cad and a thief. Found out
only after his death. BAKER 03:174

010563   A BROKEN IDOL. London: Hurst and
Blackett, 1893 NUC BMC.

Winifred Considine marries a carpenter, is artistic
and intell. She's an M.P.'s daughter. She seems
inapproachable to Will, a socialist leader. young
woman Liz comes between them for a time but their
marriage goes smoothly enough. Portrait of Liz is a
good one. She believes Will has been unfaithful and
she hates Winifred. Another fine portrait is Elma
Considine, Winifred's younger sister. She's wilful and
ambitious and heartless.
Passion and marriage of Will Hardinge and Winifred
Coinsidine. He's a socialist leader. She's upper class
attracted to him. Their differences and difficulties.
Undisciplined, violent Liz has her revenge on Will.
Also a good study of Elma Considine, vain, ambitious.
ACAD 43:478

010564   BROOKE'S DAUGHTER. BY ADELINE SERGEANT.
New York: U. S. Book, [1891] NUC.

She's clever, attractive, raised in convent, no
knowledge of parents. Mother takes her out, explains
separation from father, that kept her in convent till
grown up. She's to spend a year with one, then the
other, then decide. But brings them together instead.
CR

010565   CASPAR BROOKE'S DAUGHTER. London: Hurst
and Blackett, 1891 BMC 1909? [] NUC.

Leslie Brooke is 19, just out of convent where she was
sent when her parents argued and separated. She is to
spend a year with each and then decide on one to live
with. Actually brings them together. There's a nurse
who is a spy and Leslie's aunt, a doctor. ACAD Also
ATH 98 318

010566   CELIA'S FORTUNE. London: Digby Long, 1904
BMC.

010567   THE CHOICE OF EMELIA. London: J. Long,
1906 BMC.

TLS-Sensation novel young wife is nearly murdered by
father-in-law.
ATH-o

010568   CHRISTINE; A NOVEL. BY ADELINE SERGEANT.
New York: Tait, Sons, 1892 NUC. London: Hurst and
Blackett, 1894 BMC NUC.

heroine goes to Egypt upon uncle's invitation. Arrives
to find him dead and herself with a large inheritance.
Then there's the scoundrel who would cheat her of it,
the hero who protects her and the flirt who goes after
the hero. SP 71, 947
Her uncle, long estranged from her immediate family,
invites her to spend a winter with him. He's a
military man and plans to marry her to his protege, a
young soldier. But he dies before she arrives. Then
she loses an inheritance PW 3-18-93
Gilbert Greville is the hero; Paul Floriam, the bad
guy. ATH 102:693

010569   THE CLAIM OF ANTHONY LOCKHART. London:
Hurst and Blackett, 1897 BMC.

Villain's mangled corpse found at foot of cliff, while
the good folk live happily on. SR 84:631.
Many typical sensational ingredients: missing will,
venal dr., murder. Earl of Morven finds his brother,
the Kleptomamiac, is chained up in doctor's cellar. SR
79:409

010570   THE COMING OF THE RANDOLPHS. London:
Methuen, 1906 BMC.

TLS-conv. domestic

010571   THE COMMON LOT. London: A. Melrose,
[1899] BMC.

Ursula Keane uses her small income to support step
mother and step brothers and sisters after her father
dies. Ultimately marries a Dr. "a polemic in favour of
feminine duty." First when she's well off and "goes

her round of the Girls' Friendly and Mothers' meetings
elevating the masses with moral recitations." Then
when she's poor and supports family. ATH 113:621
A strong good natured woman forsakes ambitions to care
for an ungrateful family. Rewarded by love of a good
man. BAKER 03 174

010572   THE CONSCIENCE OF GILBERT POLLARD.
London: Hodder and Stoughton, 1900 BMC.

    ACAD 59:444. "Somewhat old-fashioned."

010573   CYNTHIA'S IDEAL. London: Hodder and
Stoughton, 1903 BMC.

    Subtle analysis of changes in Cynthia's character and
    the forces molding it. She finds herself and the right
    man. LBKM 10-03, 57

010574   DAUNAY'S TOWER; A NOVEL. BY ADELINE
SERGEANT. London: F. V. White, 1900 BMC. New York: F.
M. Buckles, 1901 NUC.

    ATH 116:373. Annabel has for some reason been kept a
    mystery by her father until she is 18, when he visits
    her for the 1st time and orders her to marry a cousin
    she doesn't know. She refuses. He then tells people
    she is dead, shortly thereafter dying himself and
    leaving inheritance a problem.
    R 37:466. Heroine goes from workhouse drudge to idol
    of society
    PW--2-23-01

010575   A DEADLY FOE: A ROMANCE OF THE NORTHERN
SEAS. London: Hutchinson, 1895 BMC.

    He is Oliver Dyson, meets the hero in imaginary polar
    region, leaves the hero to die, but Frank Lovell
    escapes. Heroine is Nelly Dene. ACAD 48:359
    Hero rescued by missing father-in-law who had
    disappeared years before. A tearful heroine. ATH
    106:896

010576   DR. ENDICOTT'S EXPERIMENT. BY ADELINE
SERGEANT. London: Chatto and Windus, 1894 BMC. New
York: Cassell, [c1895] NUC.

    ATH-grotesque scene in churchyard.
    ACAD 46:471. Story of a doctor who operates on wife's
    friend with cancer cure and then she is struck down by
    carriage, depriving him of proof of his cure.
    LBKM 7:57. Sensational, in Miss Sergeant's
    earlier...and more successful manner. Dr. attempts to
    disinter the body, is surprised by husband, in scuffle
    he dies. More events follow.
    The doctor finds what he believes is a cure for
    cancer, uses it on a friend's wife, but she dies in a
    carriage accident. Her husband won't allow an autopsy,
    so the doctor digs up the corpse in order to see
    whether his cure worked. At the grave he meets the
    husband and in the fight, kills him. "Ghoulish." SP
    74:28.

010577   AN EAST LONDON MYSTERY. London: Hurst and
Blackett, 1892 BMC.

    ATH 99:497. Melodrama. Romance of the slums. a
    "woman's brave devotion," girl of the slums defends
    her weak, worthless husband. Strong, she is tutored by
    a governess to compensate.

010578   THE ENTHUSIAST. London: Methuen, 1903
BMC.

010579   ERICA'S HUSBAND. London: Hurst and
Blackett, 1896 BMC.

    SR
    ACAD 49:237. Erica is left fatherless in mining camps
    under guardianship of Dick Vandeleur. Cyril Fane
    schemes to marry her for her money, but is eventually
    overthrown.
    SP 76:487. The Sierras. She and Dick marry in the end.
    First part of book spirited.

010580   THE FAILURE OF SIBYL FLETCHER; A NOVEL.
BY ADELINE SERGEANT. London: Heinemann, 1896 BMC.
Philadelphia: J. B. Lippincott, 1896 NUC.

    LBKM 10:21. Combines her introspective and sensational
    styles. "Sybil's love is so much more than undignified
    as to be degrading." Her subjugation to Michael Drage,
    a monster and a bully.
    SR Pleasant.
    ATH 108:317. "The experiment of marrying an uneducated
    peasant, although of gentle blood, deserved failure."

Sibyl is "not a failure, though she fails," she is
"noteworthy." Asked Sibyl to marry him or he would
drown them both. She chose marriage, and grew to
genuinely love him. He regretted having threatened her
and could not believe in her love, thinking it only a
fulfillment of a promise. All is finally cleared.
PW 3-28-96. She is a painter in water-colors,
successful, lives in artistic apartments in London.
She is engaged to a writer. He breaks engagement for
other woman and then sybil's failure comes and she
loses her health and her power to paint. Seeks rest in
obscure village where she meets Michael. Eventually,
when they understand each other, "her genius blossoms
anew."

010581   THE FUTURE OF PHYLLIS. London: J. Long,
1902 BMC.

    The cruel transference of a gentlewoman (one by
    instinct and eduation, not birth) to position of
    housekeeper. ATH 121, 45

010582   GILBERT POLLARD. London: Hodder and
Stoughton, [1912] BMC.

010583   A GREAT LADY. London: Methuen, 1901 BMC.

    8-17-01 ATH

010584   THE IDOL-MAKER. A NOVEL. BY ADELINE
SERGEANT. New York: D. Appleton, 1896 NUC. London:
Hutchinson, 1897 BMC.

    BKM 4:371 Conventional, semi-religious novel. Good
    guardian and ward.
    PW 10-10-96. Hero has strong missionary purpose to
    convert the heathen. A young noble has a passion for
    missionary work among Hindoos. Goes around smashing
    old idols. Returns to England to discover his uncle is
    in the idol business for export. ACAD 51:232

010585   AN IMPETUOUS GIRL. London: Hurst and
Blackett, 1906 BMC.

010586   IN THE WILDERNESS. London: A. Melrose,
[1896] BMC.

    SR Mild type of new woman...Janet works in East End
    until marriage with former lover whose wife has died.
    At same time adopts child from slums.
    ATH 108:636. "The matter is already somewhat out of
    fashion."
    SP 77:649. Illustrates the thesis that all souls who
    have work of the "higher kind" to do, go through a
    period of loneliness, a "sojourn in the wilderness."
    Janet comes out of it "purified and strengthened. She
    goes to an older woman for counsel.
    Frivolous girl robs her friend's lover. Mrs Gordon's
    agony over her unattractive daughter who decides to
    devote herself to the Whitechapel poor. ACAD 51:46

010587   IN VALLOMBROSA: A SEQUENCE. London: F. V.
White, 1897 BMC.

    Cecily Marchmont and her husband separated by mutual
    consent and with grave cause. When he returns ill with
    a mortal disease, she admits her love for Frank
    Wycherley. SP 79:629.
    She's estranged from husband. Then he comes to
    Vallomberosa to ask forgiveness. Then dying begs her
    to marry the man that loves her. Wants her to be
    happy. ACAD 51, June 12 1897 Fiction supplement.

010588   AN INDEPENDENT MAIDEN. London: J. Long,
1906 BMC.

010589   KITTY HOLDEN. London: Hurst and Blackett,
1895 BMC.

    Story of Kitty, her child that she thought dead, her
    husband who keeps some secret from her, has committed
    some crime-at first for her benefit he thinks-but we
    trace his downfall. SP 74:432
    She's married at a registrar's office, then the
    ceremony. The ceremony found invalid. Also includes a
    supposed foundling, an attempted murder, etc. SR
    79:421

010590   THE LADY CHARLOTTE. A NOVEL. BY ADELINE
SERGEANT. Chicago and New York: Rand, McNally, [1897]
NUC. London: Hutchinson, 1898 BMC.

    English society. Young literary aspirant tries to lie
    his way into literary society and to steal some
    valuable memoirs. LW 28:377
    Lady Charlotte Byng, a great traveller. Writes books,

is a reader for publishing houses. She rows and is a
first-class shot. Her secretary, a young man, gets
hold of private papers of hers, writes a book about
her. Publishers send it to her to read. Her
punishment of the dishonorable writer is swift and
sure. PW 52:299
SP 80:451. Arthur Ellisoin, an unscrupulous literary
man, managed to steal family papers of employers of
his admirable and hard working female cousin,
Charlotte Byng, a publisher's reader, is sent by
accident the Ms. in which these documents are
incorporated. Armed with a revolver, she goes to his
rooms and forces him to give up the papers and sign a
confession. He then od's on chloral.
BKM 14:190. Her husband, her publishers, the male
world in general are made to tremble at her nod. She
is central character. Esther Ellisoin, a college
graduate and a new woman one of the best character
studies in the book.

010591   LOVE STORY OF MARGARET WYNNE. BY ADELINE
SERGEANT. Chicago: Rand, McNally, [c1898] NUC. London:
F.V. White, 1899 BMC.

Melodramatic. Heir to baronetcy makes a bigamous
marriage. Blackmailed by her first husband, the Fr.
wife drugs her father-in-law and forges a check. The
heir's brother learns of this, promises to keep the
secret, is considered the culprit and makes no denial.
This brother eventually inherits the fortune. SP
83:206
Margaret is a penniless niece, companion to a
tyrannous aunt upon whose death Margaret becomes
wealthy. Her faith in Baynard's innocence is justified
in the end. BAKER 03 174

010592   THE LOVE THAT OVERCAME. London: Methuen,
1903 BMC.

Short description. ACAD 65, 38
Old fashioned love story. LBKM 188, 8-03

010593   MALINCOURT KEEP. London: J. Long, 1904
BMC.

010594   MARGARET WYNNE. BY ADELINE SERGEANT.
Chicago: Rand, McNally, [c1898] NUC.

PW-Margaret and her aunt spend a month's vacation at
English rural boarding house. She meets and believes
in hero who falls under suspicion of forgery.

010595   MARJORY MOORE'S LOVERS. London: F. T.
Neely, [1897] BMC.

"English novelists-mostly women, we regret to
say-continue to put forth indecent and prurient
stories," so a work like this one is refreshing,
"wholesome, uplifting." CR 28,31:34.
Country girl had a musical career, makes a wrong
marriage. suffered, found her true mate. LW 28:399.

010596   MARJORY'S MISTAKE. London: Hurst and
Blackett, 1895 BMC.

She marries the wrong man-Archie Severne, mean
treacherous coward. Should have married Felix Hyde who
has all the virtues. Marjory's nature is impulsive,
reckless, artistic. SP 75:405
Marjory Moore is a budding musical genius. A noted
Q.C. takes her where she'll be properly trained, but
she falls in love. She's warned against Archie but
marries. He goes from bad to worse, must leave the
country. She turns to old faithful lover Felix. They
wed when Archie dies. ACAD 48:243
ATH 107:47. Hero and heroine are musicians.
PW 4-18-96. Has talent for music. Rich squire with son
who prefers medicine to music has passion for music,
educates Marjory, and then, by terms of his will,
tries to force marriage between Marjory and his son.

010597   THE MARRIAGE OF LYDIA MAINWARING: A
NOVEL. London: Hutchinson, 1902 BMC.

ATH 4-26-02--Active plot, not much characterization.

010598   MASTER OF BEECHWOOD; A NOVEL. BY ADELINE
SERGEANT. London: Methuen, 1902 BMC.

010599   MISS BETTY'S MISTAKE. A STORY. London:
Hurst and Blackett, 1895 BMC.

ACAD 53:369. She is betrayed. A daughter loves a
father and a mad mother who are not her parents.
ATH 111:596. Betty, I think, is the mother and Lina
the daughter. Father writes popular novels. Lina

marries happily at end.
LBKM 14:139. Betty marries into a bad set and gets out
of it. She is admirable. "Situations a little too
advanced"

010600   MISS CLEVELAND'S COMPANION. London: F.V.
White, 1901 BMC NUC.

SP 85:891. Miss Cleveland, an heiress and Tressel
Oliver her companion, their romances. Less sensational
than usual.

010601   THE MISSING ELIZABETH; A NOVEL. London:
Chatto and Windus, 1905 BMC.

Story of a convict and a child. LBKM 141:27-8
Child is his daughter; he has been in prison for
years, now searches for her. ATH 1905:42

010602   THE MISTRESS OF QUEST: A NOVEL. BY
ADELINE SERGEANT. London: Hutchinson, [1895] BMC. New
York: D. Appleton, 1895 NUC.

Family in Cumberland. Young Julian meets with her
artist friend. ACAD 48:67
Heroine is Lisbeth Verrall strong, human,
unconventional. ATH 105:669
Lisbeth fine and noble is contrasted with her half
sister Alys, selfish artistic. Murder, poison, idiocy,
insanity. LW 26:233
3 women and 3 men. Happy end for Lizbeth. BOOK NEWS
157:27

010603   MRS. LYGON'S HUSBAND. London: Methuen,
1905 BMC.

Woman released from asylum seeks her husband and
daughter. Husband who confined her is an "unmitigated
villain." ATH 1905:202

010604   MY LADY'S DIAMONDS. New York: F.M.
Buckles, 1901 NUC. London: Ward, Lock, 1901 NUC BMC.

10-19-01 PW

010605   THE MYSTERY OF THE MOAT. BY ADELINE
SERGEANT. London: Methuen, [1905] BMC NUC.

010606   NEAR RELATIONS: A STORY. London: Hodder
and Stoughton, 1902 BMC.

010607   NELLIE MATURIN'S VICTORY. London: Hodder
and Stoughton, 1905 BMC.

Pleasant healthy story. ATH 1905:190

010608   NO AMBITION. Edinburgh: Oliphant,
Anderson and Ferrier, 1895 BMC. Bardley, 1897 NUC.

modern girl's world of school and college and
professional ambitions. The Denbigh family.
Disappearance of Clarice's husband. LBKM 9:65
ACAD 49:33. Heroine wins a scholarship at Girton, but
when she sees financial hardship it will entail on
family if she takes it, she gives it up without giving
the real reason. Then looked on as spiritless by
members of her family.

010609   OUT OF DUE SEASON: A MEZZOTINT. BY
ADELINE SERGEANT. London: Heinemann, 1895 BMC. New
York: D. Appleton, 1895 NUC.

Study of somber village working man and wife. Wife is
shallow and pretty. She runs off, he follows and
rescues her from Soho slums. SR. 80:386
Gideon and Emmy Blake. She runs off with an officer
who then deserts her. "She falls into the lowest
depths of degradation." Their union and their tragic
death in a storm. ACAD 48:336
Results of a bad marriage. Includes the death of the
child. ATH 106:528
"He suffers vicariously for his wife's sins and
reclaims her from the streets of London" PW
9-14-95:332

010610   THE PASSION OF PAUL MARILLIER. BY ADELINE
SERGEANT. London: Methuen, [1908] NUC BMC.

TLS
ACAD- inheritance.

010611   THE PROGRESS OF RACHEL. London: Methuen,
1904 BMC.

LBKM-Unattractive wealthy young woman married by man
out of pity.

ATH-Careful and thoughtful study of character.

010612   THE QUEST OF GEOFFREY DARRELL. London:
Methuen, 1907 BMC.

Murder, mystery--ACAD.

010613   REPARATION: A NOVEL. London: Hutchinson,
1905 BMC.

010614   A RISE IN THE WORLD. A NOVEL. BY ADELINE
SERGEANT. New York: F. M. Buckles, 1900 NUC.

. She was not beautiful says author.
SP 84:176. Elizabeth married the heir of a peer, to
the distress of his family, but she developed to fill
her position. Her husband became less a person,
plagued with jealousy, etc. died. Eliz. dropped her
title, married a doctor, and devoted her life to
philanthropy.
ACAD 58:84. Opens with committee meeting of Society
for the Help of Friendless Girls. A servant-girl case
is brought forward.

010615   ROGER VANBRUGH'S WIFE. London:
Hutchinson, 1896 BMC NUC.

ATH 107:647. Melodrama. French count has influence
over noble colonel. Trouble between colonel and his
Polish wife comes of this
ACAD 49:260
SP 76:273 Improbable plot.

010616   A ROGUE'S DAUGHTER. BY ADELINE SERGEANT.
New York and London: F. A. Stokes, [c1895] NUC.

ACAD 49:466. Heroine, adventures, ultimate marriage.
SP 76:580. conventional
CR 29:143

010617   THE SIN OF LABAN ROUTH. London: Digby
Long, 1905 BMC.

010618   SIR ANTHONY. London: Hurst and Blackett,
1892 BMC.

ATH 100:586. Tangled loves of young people; everything
gets worked out.
SP. Father keeps two children of previous marriage as
part of his household under fiction that he has
adopted them with intention of springing it on his
wife that they will disinherit children of their
marriage. Goes on this way for 20 years.
PW - Second wife, when she begins to suspect the
truth, poisons Sir Anthony. (NY J.A. Taylor <1892> c.
1891-Sir Anthony's Secret)

010619   SIR ANTHONY'S SECRET; OR, A FALSE
POSITION. BY ADELINE SERGEANT. New York: J. A. Taylor,
[1891] NUC.

010620   THE SIXTH SENSE: A NOVEL. London:
Hutchinson, 1905 BMC.

Doctor's patient (a "foolish" woman) kills her doctor
and goes mad. TLS 1905:83.

010621   A SOUL APART: A NOVEL. London: Hurst and
Blackett, 1902 BMC.

010622   ST. MAUR. London: Hurst and Blackett,
1894 BMC.

SP-melodrama.
ACAD 46:229. In the style of M.E. Braddon. Kidnapping,
conspiracy, inheritance, old-fashioned villainy.

010623   THE STORY OF A PENITENT SOUL. BEING THE
PRIVATE PAPERS OF MR. STEPHEN DART [ANONYMOUS]. New
York: J. W. Lovell, [c1891] NUC. London: Bentley, 1892
BMC NUC.

SP 69:296. Story of a man and wife and her
minister-lover, Stephen Dart. She confesses her sin to
her husband on her death bed; he takes a "terrible
vengeance" on Dart. Book focuses on Dart, himself the
product of an illegitimate union, for which he blames
his disposition to sin.
ACAD 42:88. "Their subsequent expiation forms one of
the saddest pages in modern fiction, while the revenge
exacted by the husband is Italian-like in its
diabolical cruelty."
ATH 100:188. Papers purportedly of the late Mr. Dart
which "trace the paralysis of will, the moral diseases
of a being weakened and tainted at the source of
life." His revelations are "unwholesome and depressing

reading." Painful, tragic.
CR 18:118. Father-son problem of hereditary vice.

010624   THE STORY OF PHIL ENDERBY. London: J.
Bowden, 1898 BMC.

SP 81:746. "Melodramatic idyll of the Fen country in
which the grandson of a boat-builder, thanks to the
ineffectual villainy of a saturnine uncle, becomes a
successful landscape painter, and enjoys the privilege
of removing the gravestone erected to his own memory."

010625   THE SURRENDER OF MARGARET BELLARMINE. A
FRAGMENT. EDITED BY ADELINE SERGEANT. New York:
International News, 1894 NUC. London: International
News, 1894 BMC.

SR 77:500. Diary of young widow who writes poetry and
meditates on religious topics.
SP 72:475. Finds peace and happiness at last in
Christianity and renunciation.
ACAD 45:392. Psychological study. Margaret's spirit
crushed by cold calculating husband. Awakens after his
death, but lover proves dishonorable and she breaks
engagement.
ATH 103:407. Unlike the author's sensational novels.
Surrender, I think, to religion.

010626   SYLVIA'S AMBITION. London: Hodder and
Stoughton, 1901 BMC.

Wants to be an actress, does so at end of book. ACAD
01

010627   THIS BODY OF DEATH, A STORY. London:
Hurst and Blackett, 1901 BMC. (NUC: This Story of
Death: A Story. London, 1901.)

010628   TOLD IN THE TWILIGHT. London: F. V.
White, 1896 BMC.

Short stories.

010629   THE TREASURE OF CAPTAIN SCARLETT. London:
Hutchinson, 1901 BMC. London: 1901 NUC.

Peggy's perverse and uncalled for misunderstandings
with her lover, absurdities of her conduct; Eleanor's
sense of duty. 5-25-01 ATH

010630   UNDER SUSPICION. London: Methuen, 1904
BMC.

TLS-young woman suspected of two things.

010631   A VALUABLE LIFE. A NOVEL. BY ADELINE
SERGEANT. Chicago: Rand, McNally, [c1897] NUC. London:
F.V. White, 1898 BMC.

ATH 112:251. Father abandons daughter in burning ship;
subsequently borrows money from her when he learns she
was saved and has been adopted by rich people.
PW-he is a minister who thinks he is so valuable to
the people that his life must be saved over his
daughter's. When she meets him later, he is more
selfish and also dishonest.

010632   THE WATERS OF OBLIVION. London: J. Long,
1904 BMC.

TLS- male hero in financial world.

010633   THE WORK OF OLIVER BYRD: A NOVEL. London:
J. Nisbet, 1902 BMC.

LEKM 1902 "An editor...is held up to the public
gaze...assumes a power which he does not possess and
takes advantage of the brains of his
contributors...wrecking the lives of the women he
comes in contact with and flourishing."

010634   THE YELLOW DIAMOND. London: Methuen, 1904
BMC.

ATH- murder mystery and male detective.

SERJEANT, CONSTANCE.

010635   HIS CAPTAIN. London: S. W. Partridge,
[1906] BMC.

010636   IN THE ANARCHISTS' DEN. London: Marshall,
[1904] BMC.

010637   A TALE OF RED PEKIN. London: Marshall,
[1902] BMC NUC.

010638   A THREEFOLD MYSTERY: A TALE OF MONTE
CARLO. London: Elliot Stock, 1894 BMC.

SR 77:557. Two young women at Monte Carlo; Paul, lover
of one shoots himself rather than face disgrace of
forgery. He turns up years later and all ends happily.
SP 1st person narration by one of the two sisters. He
becomes a preacher.

010639   WHEN THE SAINTS ARE GONE. London: J.
Long, 1908 BMC. London: Nicholson, [19-?] NUC.

SERRELL, EDITH, jt. au. See BERNARD, MARGUERITE AND EDITH
SERRELL.

SETON, CHRISTINE.

010640   AN AMATEUR PROVIDENCE. London: E. Arnold,
1902 BMC.

ATH 11-29-02--"Weak & foolish heroine."

SETON, CHRISTINE AND ESTRA WILBRAHAM.

010641   TWO BABES IN THE CITY. London: E. Arnold,
1901 BMC.

SETON, JULIA. B. 1862. United States.

010642   DESTINY: A NEW-THOUGHT NOVEL. New York:
E. J. Clode, [c1917] NUC.

Audrienne Lebaron, high minded, dissatisfied with her
aimless life, comes to NY to study. Her married
friends don't take marriage seriously. She falls in
love and, though he dies, remains married to his
memory. PW
Audrienne refuses marriage because of ambition; goes
to city to be a great writer. But simple country
training has not prepared her. Enters mysticism
school; observes experiments with the soul. The doctor
(her husband) killed, she devotes her life to
publicity work in the psychic realm. PW NYT

SEVERNE, FLORENCE.

010643   THE DOWAGER'S DETERMINATION. London:
Digby, Long, 1897 BMC.

She's Lady Raymore and is determined her grandson
marry and break the hereditary strain of madness.
Lilian Jardine is the victim. But the grandson does go
mad, tries to kill Lilian, kills self. ACAD 51:232

010644   IN THE MESHES. London: Osgood, 1894 BMC.

SR 77:588. Young woman in London trying to make ends
meet in various positions, becomes lover of married
doctor and is persuaded to continue the relationship
after she learns of his wife, who is dying-then she is
suspected of murder. POV?
SP-did the MD poison her accidentally?
ACAD 45:392. The doctor married "an unattractive
Jewess for her money." He doesn't get very much of it
and "begins a course of systematic cruelty to her."

010645   JOSE: A STUDY OF TEMPERAMENT. London:
Digby, Long, 1903 BMC.

A child who has trouble with her stepmother. ACAD
64:204
Stepmother, jealous stepdaughter, faithful husband
unfaithful wife. TLS 1903:51

010646   UNEVEN GROUND. London: D. Stott, 1891
BMC.

"of the family magazine type" ATH 98 717
SR-Story of a jilted girl who grows to love the rival
of her idol.

SEYMER, GERTRUDE CLAY KER.

010647   THE BLACK PATCH. A SPORTING NOVEL.
London: G. Routledge, 1894 BMC.

ATH 104:888. Vivacious. Clara, daughter of
horse-loving father and sharing his love has detective
powers equal to "any hero of Scotland Yard" daringly
solves a mystery involving horses and cures her father
of his desire that "had he but had a son".
Sporting novel: changing of twin colts at birth. The
fraud detected by young woman. SR 79:134

010648   "SINCE FIRST I SAW YOUR FACE". London: G.

Routledge, [1899] BMC.

SP 81:472. Twins. One addicted to gambling, the other
to winning back the lost fortune. Saved by a young
heiress's mrg. proposal.

SEYMOUR, BEATRICE KEAN (STAPLETON). D. 1955. United
Kingdom.

010649   INVISIBLE TIDES. London: Chapman and
Hall, 1919 NUC. New York: T. Seltzer, 1921 NUC.

"novel of gloom" Rosamund finds the war inspiring;
Pamela finds the war delightful. The author would like
to put them in their place? TLS
wife, husband, lover. Lover killed in war, wife
returns to husband. "It is a careful and rather too
sombre-study of temperament even of nerves ... not so
much what characters are as what takes place within
them" BAKER 32 430
SP-heroine returns to husband after death of lover.
"future of this presumed ill-assorted pair fills the
reader with the utm ost foreboding."
LBKM-Helena's relationship with Hilary has obvious
sympathy and understanding of author. Reviewer wonders
why Helena returned to husband.

SEYMOUR, MRS. H. M. United States.

010650   "FEALTY AND DUTY" (FOY POUR DEVOIR); OR,
"THE SNAP SHOT".   A SOCIETY NARRATIVE. Rome, N.Y.:
Citizen Office, [c1898] NUC.

SHACKELFORD, ELEANOR A. B. United States.

010651   VIRGINIA DARE: A ROMANCE OF THE SIXTEENTH
CENTURY. BY E. A. B. S. New York: Thomas Whittaker,
1892 NUC.

She's daughter of Gov. White of Va. She was 10 days
old when he left for England in 1587. She was captured
by Indians. Story ends when she marries Iosco who
becomes a Christian to marry her CR 14, 21:61

SHACKELFORD, ETHEL. United States.

010652   THE JUMPING-OFF PLACE. London: Hodder and
Stoughton, 1913 BMC. New York: G.H. Doran, [c1913]
NUC.

"with her nerves all unstrung from the shock of her
parents' tragic death in a wreck following close upon
her separaton from her husband, lovely Mrs. Evan-Stone
goes to a Montana mining camp in search of health and
distraction. Unknown to her, her husband is there, and
while, during the two months she stays she never sees
him, still that two months suffices to clear away
their difficulties and finally unites them. How this
happens is entertainingly told." PW 5/17/13 1822

010653   THE LIFE OF ME. New York: Dodge, [c1910]
NUC.

BKM-autobiography of a baby.
NYT

SHAFER, SARA (ANDREW). D. 1913. United States.

010654   BEYOND CHANCE OF CHANGE. New York and
London: Macmillan, 1905 BMC NUC.

Nice family story PW 3-11-05
NYT 295,05

010655   THE DAY BEFORE YESTERDAY. New York:
Macmillan, 1904 BMC.

NYT-story of village life and children.

SHAFFNER, LILLYAN.

010656   SUZANNE. Chicago: Monarch Book Co.,
[c1906] NUC.

SHAKESPEAR, OLIVIA.

010657   THE DEVOTEES. London: W. Heinemann, 1904
BMC.

LBKM-Traditional love story
ACAD-Princess Libanoff outrages all convention, is
beyond logic and laws.

010658   THE FALSE LAUREL. London: Osgood, 1896
BMC.

LBKM 10:120. Daria is all intellect and no emotion.
Marries without love, destroys her poems because they
are not as good as her husband's, leaves her home to
write great plays, wrestles with insanity and poverty,
suicides. Review says three main characters are all
abnormal; author is too solemn, Daria couldn't die
soon enough, for rev.
SR She goes mad.
ATH 108:188, "Hidden tragedy of Daria's missed life."
POV?

010659   THE JOURNEY OF HIGH HONOUR. London:
Osgood & McIlvaine, 1895 BMC.

LBKM 7:92. Unhappy marriage; one finds a more suitable
mate, Elizabeth's "emancipated flight to London."
A pretty-pretty book. Elizabeth Jordan and Felicia
Noble are close as sisters. Eliz 10 yrs. older,
stately, intelligent, wealthy. Marries, husband falls
for sister Felicia. But all comes out OK. SR 79;134
Author is a pretty writer; the book a pretty-pretty
book. Felicia responds to Elizabeth's husband,
complications; Elizabeth behaves well. Felicia is very
pretty, and not naughtier than we like. The male
character--the author is only joking in pretending to
regard him as a human being. SR 79:134

010660   LOVE ON A MORTAL LEASE. A NOVEL. London:
Osgood & McIlvaine, 1894 BMC.

SR 78:304. Rachel insists she is pure even after she
has lost her honour.
ATH 104:29. She is clever, in the 2nd part of book is
story of her marriage, study of effects of wealth on
literary ambition.

010661   RUPERT ARMSTRONG. London & New York:
Harper, 1898 BMC.

A daughter's devotion to her artist father and her
attempt to renew his faith in his ideals. LIT 4:316.
Loves her father above all else. He is Rupert. Agatha
hates her mother who has "sucked the spirituality from
her husband." Agatha is brutally frank to her mother
in their encounters—a kind of duel between them.
Agatha's friend Clare Garton marries an elderly
officer who becomes a kind of Bluebeard. She leaves
him, elopes with another man. SP 83:171.
Agatha does not succeed in rehabilitating her father.
She's physically unattractive, uncompromising in her
attempts to change her father. ATH 113;270

010662   UNCLE HILARY. London: Methuen, [1910] BMC
NUC.

TLS-male hero, marries, first wife shows up.
SR-Mother and daughter both make several marriages
without formality of divorces. They leave the men and
they seem to choose them. POV

SHALER, SOPHIA PENN (PAGE). United States.

    010663   THE PRELUDE AND THE PLAY. BY RUFUS MANN.
    Boston: Houghton, Mifflin, 1900 NUC.

SHAND, CHRISTINE R.

    010664   MISS PILSBURY'S FORTUNE. London: Mills
    and Boon, [1909] BMC.

    Wealthy girl escapes marrying a Marquis to marry her
    Quaker friend. TLS
    Her wealth leaves her free to form a marriage of
    affection. ATH

SHAPIRO, ANNA RATNER. United States.

    010665   THE BIRTH OF UNIVERSAL BROTHERHOOD.
    Kansas City, Mo.: Burton, [c1916] BMC NUC.

    Story of betrayal and things made right. PW

    010666   RED RUTH; THE BIRTH OF UNIVERSAL
    BROTHERHOOD. Chicago: Arc Pub. Co., 1917 NUC.

    NYT-theme is birth of universal brotherhood. Red Ruth,
    the heroine preaches a gospel of right living and
    loving. At end of story characters are engaged in
    effort to organize world for peace and harmony and
    universal brotherhood. NYT p 117 Mar 17, 1918
    First published as "The Birth of Universal
    Brotherhood."
    Plea for universal brotherhood. Gimbel family
    represents the ideal ? PW

SHARBER, KATE (TRIMBLE). B. 1883. United States.

010667   AMAZING GRACE, WHO PROVES THAT VIRTUE HAS
ITS SILVER LINING. Indianapolis: Bobbs-Merrill,
[c1914] BMC NUC.

PW 86 11/14/14:1574 "Grace, daughter of an
aristocratic Southern family, is society reporter on
the Herald. Her sole fortune consists of a package of
love letters written by a celebrated novelist, Lady
Frances Webb, to her distinguished ancestor, James
Christie, the artist. Yet sentimental scruples prevent
Grace from turning the letters into money. While on an
assignment, she meets Maitland Tait, a young
Englishman, who holds a secret of great interest to
her paper. They are mutually attracted, but Tait is
led to believe that she is encouraging him for
business reasons only. This misunderstanding is
happily cleared up and it is disclosed that Maitland,
too, has an important personal interest in the
letters."
Autobiographical, refuses to make public love letters
of the past that would bring money. All comes out
right for her. NYT
To the scandal of her family, Grace Christie a
Southern girl keeps her independence, is a reporter
for Oldsburg Herald, won't marry. She inherits old
love letters between her famous ancestor and an
equally famous English novelist woman. Is offered a
lot of money by publisher, but burns them. inspired by
a young man who comes into her life. BKM

010668   THE ANNALS OF ANN. Indianapolis:
Bobbs-Merrill, [c1910] NUC.

Diary of love affairs of marriageable friends (she's
young-the "gawky age") NYT
Ann at "gawky age" is intensely interested in grown-up
love affairs. Her view of love episodes in her diary.
PW

010669   AT THE AGE OF EVE. Indianapolis:
Bobbs-Merrill, [c1911] NUC.

Young woman loves lawyer discovers he's tyrannical in
time; goes thru year of misery. 11-4-11 PW

SHARKEY, EMMA AUGUSTA (BROWN). B. 1858. United States.

010670   MAM'SELLE, A MODERN HEATHEN. THE 94TH
NOVEL OF THE CELEBRATED SOUTHERN AUTHORESS, E. BURKE
COLLINS. Philadelphia: W. J. Benners, 1895 BMC NUC.

Young woman raised in back woods of Louisiana is
nevertheless a genius of acting. The 94th novel of the
celebrated Southern authoress, E. Burke Collins
<pseud.>. NUC

SHARP, EVELYN. B. 1869. United Kingdom.

010671   AT THE RELTON ARMS. London: J. Lane, 1895
BMC. Boston: Roberts, 1895 NUC.

She's a "bachelor," irresponsible, full of daring
remarks; considers and rejects a proposal to elope
with her friend's husband. SR 80:20
Lady Joan Relton unconventional love-making and
advanced young women. ACAD 48:107
A man speaks about Society and is constantly falling
in love with the young woman he speaks to. But Lady
Joan sees thru him. ATH 106:316

010672   THE MAKING OF A PRIG. New York & London:
J. Lane, 1897 BMC NUC.

The heroine is not really a prig but a lively,
insolent, outspoken modern young woman, moody. She
pursues a young man frankly, refuses him when she gets
him, then is sorry she let him go. Much of lovers'
quarrels. LBKM 13:50.
Katharine finds home life uncongenial. On grounds that
her father could use help, she goes to London to earn
her living. Lives in a boarding house for prof. women,
esp. journalists. Becomes asst. mistress in girls'
school. A young man with whom she has a Platonic
relation helped her get the job. They are engaged but
she soon discovers what he's like and lets him go.
Gets herself in a compromising position ("subtle
satire on the selfishness of men") Almost weds boy
from home town but he goes off and kills himself; she
marries "a philandering barrister." SP 70:691.
Katherine Austen's life in London with the working
women. Reviewers have most trouble with the title. LIT
1:114.
SR 85:305. Kitty, in spite of her sincerity, gaiety,
intelligence, is self righteous and therefore finally
a failure in the eyes of Paul, the sentimental hero,

and her women students.
Tries a platonic relationship which fails. Her aunt in
London "takes an interest in women's rights" BOOK NEWS
658.

010673   THE MAKING OF A SCHOOL GIRL. London:
Marshall & Russell, 1897 BMC. New York and London: J.
Lane, 1897 NUC.

010674   NICOLETE: A NOVEL. London: Constable,
1907 BMC. New York: Brentano's, 1908 NUC.

Artistic girl; a woman's book, savoring of "The
injured female:"sympathetic to Nicolete-ACAD.
Part 1 childhood of heroine. Part 2 "Study of an
artistic temperament hampered by environment and the
possession of a conscience." I-happy period of
childhood ends with mother's tragic death. Knows how
to draw well, but made a drudge by brothers and a
sister, all of whom are now cared for by a prim maiden
aunt. Contemplates a marriage to secure her family but
"marriage fills her with dismay." Gets out of it by
way of an unexpected legacy; travels two years with
parents in Italy. The will says she's to remain
unmarried; she falls in love. Keeps to the conditions
of the will?
BKM-young girl from large family, mother dies, she is
strong force, congenial companionship with her father,
develops into a "s trong woman-fearless and
original-with a heart full of love for humanity." Love
affair too.
NYT-her story from six to marriage; a genius but
womanly.

010675   REBEL WOMEN. New York: J. Lane, 1910 NUC.
London: A. C. Fifield, 1910 BMC NUC.

Concerns militant English suffragists, their feelings
and experience-flinging selves vs. barred doors of
Parliament, marching, meeting against orders from
police, street gatherings. Suggests the working people
of London strongly supported the suffragists; is
fiction. NYT
Stories "give insight into the soul of the women's
movement in England." WOMAN'S JOURNAL 12-17-10
Sketches of suffragette meetings in England "written
by an enthusiastic supporter of the cause"

010676   SOMEWHERE IN CHRISTENDOM. London: G.
Allen and Unwin, [1919] BMC NUC.

An allegory showing how a country avoids war. Critical
of Britian "the author finds exquisite humour in the
thought of a man willing to die for his country." TLS

010677   THE WAR OF ALL THE AGES. London: Sidgwick
and Jackson, 1915 BMC.

010678   THE YOUNGEST GIRL IN THE SCHOOL. New York
and London: Macmillan, 1901 NUC BMC.

Little girl in large family of boys comes into contact
with "girl nature" for the first time at school. 12
year old adolescent.

SHARP, HILDA MARY. United Kingdom.

010679   A PAWN IN PAWN. London: T. F. Unwin, 1920
BMC NUC. New York and London: G. P. putnam's Sons,
1920 NUC.

TLS-story of illegitimate girl adopted by a poet
genius. Story is told by his friend, a journalist.
ATH-she develops a remarkable gift for poetry. From
whence, environment or heredity?
PW-she is left penniless when her benefactor is
believed to be lost at sea.
NYT 1920:30. He had adopted her with intent to pass on
inheritance to her, but died without leaving a will.
She also is faced with a charge of plagiarism.

010680   THE STARS IN THEIR COURSES. New York and
London: Putnam's Sons, 1917 NUC. London: T. F. Unwin,
1917 BMC.

Male hero. A gambler and his love problems. TLS
Two young men who are his heirs. LBKM

SHARP, KATHARINE (DOORIS). 1845-1935. United States.

010681   SUMMER IN A BOG. Cincinnati: Stewart &
Kidd, [c1913] NUC.

PW 83 5/3/13: "outdoor papers mingled with the humor
of everyday life. Some of the chapters are: Haunts of
the fringed gentian: Snakes and botanizing: Finding

Phryma; The woman botanist, etc."

SHAW, ADELE MARIE. United States.

010682   THE COAST OF FREEDOM. A ROMANCE OF THE
ADVENTUROUS TIMES OF THE FIRST SELF-MADE AMERICAN. New
York: Doubleday, Page, 1902 NUC. London and New York:
Hodder & Stoughton, 1903 BMC.

SHAW, ADELE MARIE AND CARMELITA BECKWITH.

010683   THE LADY OF THE DYNAMOS. New York: H.
Holt, 1909 NUC.

Heroine-brainy, studies dynamos becomes comrade to
hero in his work. She's an inventor in Ceylon. PW
4-10-09

SHAW, JESSIE MACGREGOR. Nationality Unknown.

010684   BY THE CLOSEST TIES. Philadelphia: Union
Press, [1899] NUC.

Husband conceals fact that he was married before but
wife died. A son of that marriage (unknown to the man)
shows up to be recognized and the secret is out. The
wife smooths things out well. PW 56:819

SHAW, MRS. DONALD.

010685   SUNSET. London: W. J. Ham-Smith, 1913 BMC
NUC.

Set in California. SP
Wife learns of husband's past, refuses to live with
him, separate five years during which husband has
amatory experiences with a beautiful Mexican girl who
saves his life. ATH

010686   THE VIRGIN ROYAL. London: F. Palmer, 1912
BMC.

ATH-mother of a soldier.

SHEARD, VIRNA (STANTON). 1865(?)-1943. Canada.

010687   BY THE QUEEN'S GRACE: A NOVEL. Toronto:
W. Briggs, 1904 BMC. New York: F.A. Stokes, [1905]
NUC.

Hist. romance PW 2-25-05
NYT 324, 05 Long love story of court and queen's maid
of honor. A gentle girl...with an unbending will BKM
21 (1905)218

010688   A MAID OF MANY MOODS. New York: J. Pott,
1902 NUC. London: S. Bagster, 1902 BMC.

010689   THE MAN AT LONE LAKE. New York and
London: Cassell, 1912 BMC NUC.

PW-Love story.
LBKM- An unconventional love story in the silent
north.

SHEFFIELD, RENA CARY. United States.

010690   THE GOLDEN HOLLOW. New York: J. Lane,
1913 NUC.

Barbara Kavazze writes to a man whose books make her
think he will understand her. She's "naturally
domestic," finds herself taking care of house and
children of her guardian. Has an adventurous gypsy
side to her nature...So she writes to the Captain. He
meets her, they fall in love. NYT
PW 10-25-13:392 "Anonymous letters written by a girl
to a man whose books reveal a kinship with her own
mind. How she breaks her engagement to her older
cousin Mac, gives up his children for whom she had
cared and provided so long and marries Dan Calderwood,
the man of her choice, makes up an entertaining
romance."

SHELDON, MARY BOARDMAN. Nationality Unknown.

010691   COFFEE AND A LOVE AFFAIR: AN AMERICAN
GIRL'S ROMANCE ON A COFFEE PLANTATION. New York: F. A.
Stokes, [1908] NUC.

BKM-romance

SHELDON, MRS. GEORGIE, pseud. See DOWNS, SARAH ELIZABETH
(FORBUSH).

SHELDON, RUTH LOUISE. United States.

511

010692   DOLLY, A DAUGHTER OF NEW ENGLAND. Akron,
O.: Saalfield, [c1905] NUC.

"lively girl...expelled...goes abroad..." Madcap girl
unprincipled in her love affairs makes bad marriage,
widowed. PW 7-1-05
Brief discription-BKM 21 (1905) 657

010693   FLEXIBLE MORALS. New York: H. I. Kimball,
1898 NUC.

A very young woman weds, is neglected then abandoned
by husband. "A marriage of this kind is given as a
just cause for flexible morals on the part of the
woman." Much "moralizing." BKM 9:186.
Tells her own story. LW 30:123.

010694   RED, WHITE, and BLUE DAYS. New York: H.
I. Kimball, 1898 NUC.

SHELLEY, BERTHA.

010695   ENDERBY. London: Methuen, 1906 BMC.

ATH-emotional fervour, real passion.

010696   THE EVOLUTION OF EVE. London: Methuen,
1913 BMC.

Contrast between heroine's open and rough world of
Australia and more complex world of London--into which
she is thrown. She remains "faithful to her ideals."
ATH
An unsophisticated young woman marries the wrong man.
After stern experience, marries the right one. TLS

SHENSTONE, MILDRED.

010697   A PAINTER'S HONEYMOON. London: T. Unwin,
1896 BMC.

SR-Book is better than its cover (Little novels
series)

010698   THE PAVILIONS OF LOVE. London: E. Arnold,
1903 BMC.

Love and the supernatural-ACAD 64:486. ATH 121:779
Gets her man by hanging over cliff till he swears
he'll marry her. Afterwards pretends suicide, steals
the second Mrs. Rackstraw's child. TLS 155:03

SHEPHERD, EDITH WOODELL. Nationality Unknown.

010699   A MAID OF MOODS: A TALE OF THE MAINE
WOODS. Boston: C. M. Clark, [c1910] NUC.

SHEPHERD, ELIZABETH LEE (KIRKLAND). B. 1872. United
States.

010700   BOSS. BY ODETTE TYLER. New York and
London: Transatlantic, 1896 NUC.

SHEPHERD, MARGARET LISLE. B. 1859.

010701   MY LIFE IN THE CONVENT; OR THE MARVELLOUS
PERSONAL EXPERIENCES OF MARGARET L. SHEPHERD (SISTER
MAGDALENE ADELAIDE). Columbus, O.: [c1893] NUC.

"Real" experiences of RC woman, betrayed by a priest
enters convent. "The story of convent life is a
succession of vulgar, revolting episodes." She left
the convent, joined Salvation Army and then became a
lecturer vs. Romanism. Autobiography? Not PZ in NUC.
PW 3-11-93

SHEPHERD, MAY F. United States.

010702   SADIE; OR, HAPPY AT LAST. New York:
Broadway, [c1911] NUC.

SHEPPARD, ANTOINETTE. United States.

010703   THE HEROINE OF SANTIAGO DE CUBA (A
SEQUEL); OR, WHAT FOLLOWED THE SINKING OF THE
MERRIMAC. New York: Abbey Press, [c1900] NUC.

SHERWOOD, MARGARET POLLOCK. 1864-1955. United States.

010704   THE COMING OF THE TIDE. Boston: Houghton,
Mifflin, 1905 NUC. London: A. Constable, 1905 BMC.

Sentimental romance. PW 10-21-05

010705   DAPHNE: A PASTORAL OF ITALY. London:
Chatto and Windus, 1907 BMC.

Young girl's weeks in Italy, a pretty tale. LBKM Nov.
1907:100

010706   DAPHNE: AN AUTUMN PASTORAL. Boston:
Houghton, Mifflin, 1903 NUC.

Fanciful idyl. PW 11-7-03
NYT 1903:806

010707   AN EXPERIMENT IN ALTRUISM. BY ELIZABETH
HASTINGS. New York and London: Macmillan, 1895 NUC.

Satire on several altruistic types: the anarchist who
plays with his children while plotting murders and
while his wife does all the work at home; woman doctor
struggling for sanitary reforms; Janet, the doubter
who refuses to try to elevate the masses. The effect
of these and other types on a tailoress, the "victim
of all this experiment in Altruism." Book ends on word
of hope -in spite of the satire. CR 23:432.

010708   HENRY WORTHINGTON, IDEALIST. New York,
London: Macmillan, 1899 BMC NUC.

Relation of father & son. LBKM 17:90
Prof. of sociology wants the college to refuse a grant
"ground out of the victims of dept. store methods."
The heroine is the grantor's daughter. PW 56:653
He revolts vs industrial conditions. Author implies
that "all stores in which women clerks are paid wages
on which no woman can decently live and forced by a
system of fines to stand all day despite the seats
placed behind their counters, all stores in which
goods are bought at starvation prices from sweatshops"
are not to be allowed. Love story Annice Gordon
11-4-99, 741 NYT
SP 84:23. Life in U. S. university town. Heroine
Annice takes position as saleswoman in her father's
"semi-fraudulent establishment." Henry and Annice, rev
says, will have "a severe struggle in their joint
life" because of offending university and her wealthy
father.
SR 89:534. Henry is professor of economics, is
passionate about the human side of it. Annice shares
his idealism.

010709   A PURITAN BOHEMIA. New York and London:
Macmillan, 1896 NUC.

PW 12-5-96. New England city. After 5 years study
abroad, Anne, an artist, settles here to work. "She is
loved by another artist who achieves success about the
same time she does. The question is, should an artist
marry? Anne says "no" and sticks to her resolve."
Woman's Bohemia in a Puritan city, not a happy place,
but a place of "earnest, sad ascetic," women. Study of
the minds of these idealists: Anne Bradford living to
paint; Helen Wistar wants to share her life with
artists; Mrs Kent who works for the poor. It's a place
where "man is a memory, a shadow, rarely a reality."
CR 26,30.93
Anne Bradford 27 artist won't marry Howard Stanton.
Boston bldg. only for women artists. Thence: "it used
to be the bad boy who ran away from home. Now it's the
good girl in search of philanthropic adventure."
(quote from book) LW 28:43
A different Bohemia, an austere land in Amer. of
ideals and hard work. "Study of the earnest women who
voluntarily follow an intellectual, artistic or
philanthropic mission. In the Rembrandt Studios. This
rev. says the women are all unhappy and unfulfilled
because they are devoting themselves to art
completely. Anne Bradford rejects the lover that comes
after her. BKM 4:570

010710   THE STORY OF KING SYLVAIN AND QUEEN
AIMEE. New York and London: Macmillan, 1904 NUC.

NYT-idyllic love story

010711   A WORLD TO MEND; THE JOURNAL OF A WORKING
MAN. Boston: Little, Brown, 1920 BMC NUC.

PW-reflections of a man who, stung by the war, begins
to find a finer citizenship for himself and others.
NYT 11-14-20. Diary form. Reflections on social
problems, philosophy. Least among the problems is the
sex problem.

010712   THE WORN DOORSTEP. Boston: Little, Brown,
1916 NUC BMC. London: Hodder and Stoughton, 1917 BMC.

NYT-war widow, her journal of a retreat in a small
English village. Record of a year, she cannot shut out

people who come to her doorstep.
Diary of a woman who lost husband in war, takes a home in English midlands; intimate memories. TLS

SHEW, ELIZABETH LEILA.

010713   IF MEN WERE WISE. A NOVEL. London: Bentley, 1894 BMC.

SP 72:795. Tragic termination to story of unconventionally religious man and heroine.
ATH 103:609. Mary Ford, a school teacher whose husband had deserted her, goes to British Columbia and meets Lawrence Wrayburn, a free-thinker from England who has been jilted. She passes as a single woman, they fall in love, her husband shows up.

SHIELDS, GERTRUDE MARGARET. B. 1890. United States.

010714   CASTE THREE. New York: Century, 1918 BMC NUC.

NYT-Male hero, works, marries, becomes good citizen, author feels his "settling down" is a waste.

SHIPE, MARY MAGDALENE. United States.

010715   CLINTA; OR, THE INSIDE OF LIFE. BY MRS. M. M. SHIPE. Baltimore: W. J. C. Dulany, 1899 NUC.

SHIPE, MRS. M. M. See SHIPE, MARY MAGDALENE.

SHIPLEY, HESTER E., pseud. See WILLIAMS, SARAH STONE.

SHIPP, MAY LOUISE, jt. au. See JUDAH, MARY JAMESON AND MAY LOUISE SHIPP.

SHIPTON, HELEN. United Kingdom.

010716   THE HERONS. New York & London: Macmillan, 1894 NUC.

Fortunes of 2 brothers. Edmond and Cosmo Heron. ACAD 48:518.
Old England country family, one son at home, the other away-vanished. Reconciliation in the end. LW 26:459
SR-family of men. Tragic elements.
ATH 107:115. Bad older brother, good self-sacrificing one.

SHIPTON, HELEN.

010717   ALSTON CRUCIS. London: Hurst and Blackett, 1893 BMC.

Hero is half English aristocrat, half gypsy. Sets out to vindicate innocent father of crime and find guilty party. His-Harold Marleward's -own right to his name is in jeopardy. SP 70 130.
His father's funeral opens the book. His father's crime was murder. His son establishes his innocence and clears his name of the charge of illeg. ACAD 43:10

010718   THE FAITH OF HIS FATHER. London: Christian Knowledge Society, 1897 BMC.

010719   A HERO'S EXPERIMENT. London: Christian Knowledge Society, 1894 BMC.

010720   THE LAST OF THE FENWICKES. London: Hurst and Blackett, 1891 BMC.

010721   A MASTERFUL MAN. London: Christian Knowlege Society, [1899] BMC.

010722   OUT IN THE WORLD. London: Christian Knowledge Society, [1893] BMC.

010723   SPITEWINTER. London: Christian Knowledge Society, [1892] BMC.

010724   THE STRONG GOD CIRCUMSTANCE. London: Methuen, 1900 BMC.

LBKM 118:28. The disgrace and exile of an innocent, proud, and active-brained man.
ACAD 58:389. He is a university coach wrongly suspected of fraudulent conduct.

010725   TEN TALENTS. London: Christian Knowledge Society, [1895] BMC.

010726   THE TOUCHSTONE. London: Isbister, 1899 BMC.

010727   TWILIGHT. London: A. D. Innes, 1891 BMC.

Louis Lorimer is a weak man who causes much grief especially to Katherine Lyndhurst, deserts her on eve of wedding day, causing her to live in a kind of twilight world. Story of her awakening from it. ATH 98, 759

010728   "TWO FRIENDS AND A FIDDLE". London: Christian Knowledge Society, 1891 BMC.

010729   WORLD'S GAIN. London: Christian Knowledge Society, 1896 BMC.

SHIPTON, HELEN, jt. au. See COLERIDGE, CHRISTABEL ROSE AND HELEN SHIPTON.

SHOLL, A. M. See SHOLL, ANNA MACCLURE.

SHOLL, ANNA MACCLURE. United States.

010730   THE ANCIENT JOURNEY. BY A. M. SHOLL. New York: Longmans, Green, 1917 BMC NUC.

"By the ancient journey is meant the journey to God"-foreword.

010731   BLUE BLOOD AND RED. BY GEOFFREY CORSON. New York: H. Holt, 1915 NUC. London: Hodder and Stoughton, 1915 BMC. (Eng. ed.: Carmichael: Blue Blood and Red.)

010732   THE GREATER LOVE. New York: Outing, 1908 NUC. London: T. F. Unwin, 1909 BMC.

PW-"there is no escape from the consequences of an offence against the laws governing the sexes, no matter how extenuating the circumstances may be".
NYT-Mother-daughter relationship. Mother and daughter returned to mother's home; they cultured, town provincial, she keeping secret irregularity of daughter's birth. "But then a vulgar woman steps in with a final result which is logical and satisfactory." A study of a mother's love for her daughter.
"The story is based on the love of Eleanor Valgrave, who leaves her home in America and goes to Paris to study art, for an English officer who is married to an insane woman," BKM v27, 1908
A famous painter, Eleanor Hatherley, with her illegitimate daughter, Constance, returns from Paris to her conventional provincial American family. The story concerns the effect of Constance's illegitimacy, on herself and lovers. TLS
subject "rarely touched upon"; "the passionate love of a woman for her girl-child." Their devotion to one another. ACAD
Widow returns from Paris to N.E. but secret of illegitimate daughter comes out. Town turns from welcoming kindness to harsh treatment. For a time daughter sides vs her. ATH

010733   THE LAW OF LIFE. New York: D. Appleton, 1903 NUC. London and New York: W. Heinemann, 1904 BMC.

college education for women vs. co-ed. Marries professor: restless housewife. BKM 18 (1903) 300-2
Barb marries professor 25 years older because he's lonely; tries to be a wife but all ways seem closed when baby dies. Takes part in campus social life, meets and loves man her own age but she pities her husband too much to ask for divorce. At end the young man forced to resign his post leaves. The book leaves a feeling of revolt because it is so true to life. BKM 1903 302
Marriage young girl: old scholar NYT 9-03, 644
Mismarriage of an intellectual young woman to her old guardian (a math scholar); loves a young man who leaves. ARENA 1904
ATH-the law of life compels her to stick with fuddy duddy so his feelings won't be hurt.

010734   THE PORT OF STORMS. New York: D. Appleton, 1905 BMC.

Woman represents true womanliness, PW 3-11-05

010735   THIS WAY OUT. New York: Hearst's International Library, 1915 BMC NUC.

Margaret Carpenter woman detective-as a vocation "laying bare of mysteries and tracking of criminals" are something she does on the side. She does her detective feats mainly by virtue. Story told by man who is first her suitor, later her husband, "of her powers of psychological analysis" NYT

SHOOK, MARTHA CAROLINE (DIAL). B. 1838. United States.

010736   ALONG THE KING'S HIGHWAY; OR, THE
INVISIBLE ROUTE; A ROMANCE OF THE SOUTHERN UNITED
STATES. BY JOHN CORNELIUS. San Antonio:
Maverick-Clarke Litho Co., [c1912] NUC.

SHORE, FLORENCE TEIGNMOUTH. United Kingdom.

010737   CIRCE'S DAUGHTER. BY PRISCILLA CRAVEN.
London: Hurst & Blackett, 1913 BMC NUC. New York:
Duffield, 1913 NUC.

PW 84 9/20/13 p. 769 "Scene is laid in London. Claudia
Iverson marries a rising barrister believing that they
are deeply in love with each other only to find that
her husband is absorbed in his career and incapable of
much affection. She is a most attractive woman; other
men find her so, and she is confronted with the
problem of maintaining her ideals amid temptations. A
fine man helps her, and in the end she finds true
happiness."
"The problem of the neglected wife." "mother..a
tarnished reputation". "Pat...the third and youngest
daughter.. is blessedly sexless...finds life full of
splendid things quite outside of sentiment." NYT 1913

010738   LIFE'S COMPASS. BY PRISCILLA CRAVEN.
London: Alston Rivers, 1910 BMC.

TLS Leigh sacrifices everything for a great
passion—turns out a failure.

010739   A LIGHTED CANDLE. BY PRISCILLA CRAVEN.
London: A. Rivers, 1909 NUC BMC.

Ghita Streatfield has a worthless father; she prepares
to sell herself to the highest bidder. At 18 she's
callous. She struggles with poverty. Ends "Chastened,
happy and rich." TLS

010740   LOVE AND THE LODGER. BY PRISCILLA CRAVEN.
Digby, Long, 1909 BMC.

The Matrimomal campaign of Mrs. Macstinger TLS
Kentish town shown in the raw: "bare brutality of the
slum." One character is a landlady—"a slut." ACAD

010741   THE PRIDE OF THE GRAFTONS. BY PRISCILLA
CRAVEN. New York: Appleton, 1909 NUC.

Mannish daughter. PW 10-9-09
Ghita Grafton assumes responsibility of mother and
sister when father dies. promises to marry only on
account of her suitor's money. BKM NYT

010742   THE ROSE WITH A THORN. BY PRISCILLA
CRAVEN. New York: Appleton, 1911 NUC. (Eng. ed. title:
The School of Love.)

Woman maries man involved in "base" divorce case;
separates from husband until "barely diverted tragedy
set right" PW 6-3-11

010743   THE SCHOOL OF LOVE. BY PRISCILLA CRAVEN.
London: T.W. Laurie, [c1911] BMC NUC.

Marriage in fashionable society. TLS
"Author is no suffragist." SP ATH

SHORE, STELLA.

010744   WHEN LOVE WAS ALL. London: A. H.
Stockwell, [1920] BMC.

TLS--love and war.

SHORT, ELEANOR TALBOT (KINKEAD). United States.

010745   THE COURAGE OF BLACKBURN BLAIR. BY
ELEANOR TALBOT KINKEAD. New York: Moffat, Yard, 1907
NUC.

PW 11-16-07

010746   FLORIDA ALEXANDER, A KENTUCKY GIRL. BY
ELEANOR TALBOT KINKEAD. Chicago: A. C. McClurg, 1898
NUC.

PW—returns to her father's house after an absence
which is a mystery. Father has married again.
Florida's character is illuminated by conversations of
young step-sisters. "Narrowing or broadening effects
of marriage is again discussed."
A very intellectual and beautiful woman, a tragic
incident in her life. LW 30:38

010747   'GAINST WIND AND TIDE. BY NELLIE TALBOT
KINKEAD. New York: Rand McNally, 1892 NUC.

Set in Ky. Woman's plot to avenge the murder of her
husband by winning the love of the murderer "recoils
back on herself." Loses her own heart, ends in trag.
PW 1-7-93

010748   THE INVISIBLE BOND. BY ELEANOR TALBOT
KINKEAD. New York: Moffat, Yard, 1906 NUC.

PW—Powerfully magnetic woman ruthlessly loves and
leaves men.
BKM 23 1906-"lawless passion" dies - how? author's
pov?
NYT-two women and the effect each has on the hero's
career.
BKM. Study of an adventuress, a Becky Sharp or Lily
Bart.

010749   THE SPOILS OF THE STRONG. BY ELEANOR
TALBOT KINKEAD. (MRS. THOMPSON SHORT). New York: James
A. Mccann, 1920 NUC.

010750   YOUNG GREER OF KENTUCKY: A NOVEL. BY
ELEANOR TALBOT KINKEAD. Chicago and New York: Rand,
McNally, 1895 NUC.

He's at Harvard, then at a German universtiy. Returns
to home town, makes friends among the cultured, is
estranged thereby from parents and Dorinda who loves
him. But learns in time what's true from what's
artificial. PW 12-7-95:1079.

SHORT, MRS. THOMPSON. See SHORT, ELEANOR TALBOT (KINKEAD).

SHORTALL, KATHERINE.

010751   A "Y" GIRL IN FRANCE. LETTERS OF
KATHERINE SHORTALL. Boston: R. G. Badger, [c1919] BMC
NUC.

PW-letters

SHORTER, DORA (SIGERSON). 1866-1918.

010752   THROUGH WINTRY TERRORS. London: Cassell,
1907 BMC NUC.

Daughter closed out, abused by father when she gets
home late; she rushes out. Artist walks the street all
night so she can sleep in his room; father still
insists they marry. Then grow to love each other. LBKM
12-07:149.
Sentimental, pitiful. ACAD

SHOTLAND, JULIA ELIZA. United States.

010753   RESTDALE. New York: Burre, [c1906] NUC.

PW-Life in the country--young girl--happy home, love
story, ideal mother.

SHUBAEL, pseud. See PURDY, JENNIE BOUTON.

SHUEY, LILLIAN (HINMAN). 1853-1921. United States.

010754   DAVID OF JUNIPER GULCH: A STORY OF THE
PLACER REGIONS OF CALIFORNIA. Chicago: Laird and Lee,
[c1894] W.

PW-story of Hulda Hardy, her sacrifice for a woman
friend, her experiences as a school teacher in
California. Happy ending.

010755   DON LUIS' WIFE: A ROMANCE OF THE WEST
INDIES FROM HER LETTERS AND THE MANUSCRIPTS OF THE
PADRE, THE DOCTOR CACCAVELLI, MARC AURELE, CURATE OF
SAMANA. Boston and London: Lamson, Wolffe, 1897 NUC.

Experiences of a N. E. woman, wife of an adventurer on
San Domingo Island. Problems of mixed marriage
confessed to priest. PW 52:1103.
BKM 7:171. Purports to be actual record of N. Eng.
girl wed to wealthy resident of San Domingo. Her
narration, minor flirtations, insults of husband's
family, etc. LIT W 29:140.

SHUGERT, FANNY ALRICKS. United States.

010756   THE DAY BREAKETH. A TALE OF JERUSALEM AND
ROME IN THE DAYS OF CHRIST. Philadelphia: H. Altemus,
1898 NUC.

LW 29:253. Biblical, conventional.

SHULER, MARJORIE. United States.

010757   FOR RENT-ONE PEDESTAL. New York: National
Woman Suffrage pub. Co., 1917 NUC.

"Story of a young woman who lost her position as
teacher because she made a speech for suffrage, how
she gave her whole time to the cause, and made many
conversions including that of a certain college
professor. Told in the form of letters to an intimate
friend" PW 91:1022 3/24/17

SHUTE, MRS. A. B. E.

010758   THE CROSS ROADS. London: E. Nash, 1917
BMC.

Heroine's overwhelming success as an actress. SP

010759   THE UNCONSCIOUS BIGAMIST. London: J.
Long, 1911 BMC.

Heroine unhappily married takes a second husband when
she hears her husband has been killed in Boer war. ATH

SICHEL, EDITH HELEN. 1862-1914.

010760   WORTHINGTON JUNIOR. A STORY OF CONTRASTS.
London: S. Sonnenschein, 1893 BMC.

Good character study. Author tries to be too
up-to-date. ATH 102:878.
SR: Histories of Maurice and Algy.

SICKERT, ELLEN MELICENT (COBDEN). 1848-1914. Nationality
Unknown.

010761   SYLVIA SAXON. EPISODES IN A LIFE. BY
ELLEN MELICENT COBDEN (MILES AMBER). London: T. F.
Unwin, [c1914] BMC NUC.

SR 118:118. Brought up to believe in material vs.
spiritual values. Husband and lover are failures,
motherhood a matter of resentment. At end she is
taking "plunge into the larger world where women
consider freedom the ultimate goal." Rev. hates her.
POV of author?
ACAD 87:155. Sylvia's mental and spiritual
development-her search for the meaning of life. Cold
and depressing work.
ATH 144:96
TLS 13:334. Sylvia's "last episode" "regrettable,"
Rev. feels she softens in character as book develops.

010762   WISTONS: A STORY IN THREE PARTS. BY MILES
AMBER. London: T. F. Unwin, 1902 BMC. New York: C.
Scribner's Sons, 1902 NUC.

ATH 2-15-02 "Hardy-like" male is an "artist-egoist"
NYT 3-22-02 not helpful
Esther and Rhoda are sisters brought up in the country
but given an education by their father. Their mother
was a gypsy. Esther marries an egotistical novelist
and finally leaves him. Rhoda chooses not to marry but
lives with a man, becomes pregnant, and leaves him,
claiming the baby as her own. He subsequently tracks
her down and kills her. (Book)

SIDGWICK, CECILY (ULLMANN). D. 1934. United Kingdom.

010763   ANNE LULWORTH. BY MRS. ALFRED SIDGWICK.
London: Methuen, [1917] BMC NUC.

Anxious love making and a happy end. TLS
She's a secretary. SP

010764   ANTHEA'S GUEST. BY MRS. ALFRED SIDGWICK.
London: Methuen, [1911] BMC NUC.

Lydia Jordan, the viper adventuress; fine Anthea.
Story focuses on Lydia-TLS
"Anthea must give way to Lydia who can deceive, lie
and be altogether dishonorable" critic is really upset
with this one. ACAD
Anthea is a graceful confident resolute young woman.
At 18 determined to go to Germany to study music and
languages. She meets Lydia in Germany (Lydia was a
known flirt). Takes her back to England with her.
Lydia becomes a governess, Anthea refuses a marriage
proposal-wants to be free for several years to be
mistress of her uncle's estate. Then Lydia loses her
job, plots, flirts, marries the uncle. Lydia an
unscrupulous adventuress but author makes her
"extremely human and interesting" SP

010765   BELOW STAIRS. BY MRS. ALFRED SIDGWICK.
London: Methuen, [1913] BMC NUC.

Adventures of a modern servant girl-Priscilla Day's
different mistresses, the hardships and dangers. SP
Her heart is eventually won by an old love. LBKM
Priscilla Day-her everyday trials in the burden of
service. She's companionable and loveable.

010766   THE BERYL STONES. BY MRS. ALFRED
SIDGWICK. New York: Longmans, Green, 1903 NUC. London:
E. Arnold, 1903 BMC.

Ursula steals the stones to feed dying father; seen by
a man who "schemes to bend her will," goes to London,
becomes a successful actress. ACAD 65, 443
We forgive her theft that places her in villain's
hands (blackmail) earlier struggles for existence-ATH
en 122, 610
NYT 1-30-04-Melodrama heroine who is starving steals
jewels, after a lot of action all is well.

010767   COUSIN IVO. BY MRS. ANDREW DEAN. London:
Black, 1899 BMC NUC.

Bright witty story set in a German castle. LIT 4:428
A villianous German count, Hilda (whose diary is
included) and atypical English gentleman. LBKM 16:56
Young English peer employed to find heir of a
childless millionaire gets involved with a wicked
count. SP 82:350
Cousin Ivo is the wicked count. He's always drugging
drinks or pushing princesses into wells. Ends as
victim of a thunderbolt. ACAD 56:383

010768   CYNTHIA'S WAY. BY MRS. ALFRED SIDGWICK.
London: E. Arnold, 1901 BMC. New York: Longmans,
Green, 1901 NUC.

NYT-02 heiress in disguise takes job as governess,
marries

010769   THE DEVIL'S CRADLE. BY MRS. ALFRED
SIDGWICK. New York: W.J. Watt, [c1918] NUC.

PW-English widow in Germany during war.
NYT Jul 14,1918,p.314. Anglo-German marriage, in
tradition of the anonymous "Christine". Anti-German,
but unlike other books in tradition, it is a happy
marriage; only when her husband dies is she in danger
and must escape the country.
WWI-fiction.

010770   THE GRASSHOPPERS. By MRS. ANDREW DEAN
(MRS. ALFRED SIDGWICK). New York: F. A. Stokes,
[c1895] NUC. London: A. & C. Black, 1895 BMC. (BMC:
Grasshopper.)

Mrs. Frere and her daughter Nell, selfish and
extravagant, ruin the father. At first we hold them in
contempt for father's early death; then as they
realize what they've done they are presented more
sympathetically. Also Hilary Frere strong, learns the
hard lessons of life. SP 75:275
Mother and two daughters accustomed to luxury thrown
penniless on the world by death of father. Tale of
pinching poverty. Mother and Nelly have most problems.
Hillary very practical. ACAD 47:334.
Key note: ladies without money are the most helpless
the most pitiable creatures in the world. The sudden
plunge of three delicately pictured women into the
abyss of poverty, privation, and dependence. Hillary
Freres intellectual evolution. She alone of the 3 has
the capacity of fighting her way back to independence.
She considers the doctrines of feminism. ATH 105:533
Satire of the vulgarities and stupidities of English
and more especially of German society. Title refers to
widow and two daughters. Improvident, who take refuge
with German relatives in Hamburg. Widow dies; one
daughter marries man her sister rejects--for a home.
Hilary is then free to earn a poor living till she
weds. BKM 4:414
LW 27:46. Tract on the evils of bringing up women in
ignorance of money matters, and educating them in
utter inability to earn their own living, if worse
comes to worse. Tragedy of a widow and her two
daughters left penniless with husband's death.
Conventional mother was a governess, a German, who
married an Englishman. Hilary--different--insists upon
college, dresses differently, does strange
unconventional things. PW 6-1-95:865

010771   IN OTHER DAYS. BY MRS. ALFRED SIDGWICK.
London: Methuen, [1915] BMC NUC.

Story of mother and daughter and the reconciliation of

a couple.TLS
Subtle study of various characters to show misfortunes
of attractive people who have come down in the world.
Reviewers don't give any real sense of the novel.
Insist author has no purpose except to entertain in a
quiet manner. SP

010772   THE INNER SHRINE. BY MRS. ALFRED SIDGWICK
(MRS. ANDREW DEAN). London and New York: Harper, 1900
BMC NUC.

LBKM 19:92. Two heroines, rivals, both loveable. A Mr.
and Mrs. Clatworthy; he is eccentric, trying various
money-making schemes.
SP 85:717. Tragedy. Celia is a governess. Clatworthy
makes trouble. Lady Helen defends Celia & her husband,
knowing they are innocent, loves them both, but dies,
knowing he loves Celia. Then they marry.
ATH 0-12-01

010773   IRON COUSINS. BY MRS. ALFRED SIDGWICK.
New York: W. J. Watt, [c1919] NUC.

PW-English governess in German family before the war.
NYT-6/27/20 p 17. Picture of life in middle-class
German family.

010774   KAREN. BY MRS. ALFRED SIDGWICK. London:
W. Collins, [1918] BMC NUC.

ATH-picture of German social life.

010775   THE KINSMAN. BY MRS. ALFRED SIDGWICK.
London: Methuen, 1907 BMC. New York: Macmillan, 1907
NUC.

Story of an imposter. PW 2-9-07
Two men so alike even the women in love with them
can't tell them apart? ACAD
Sensational extravagance fantastic comedy. An
intricate plot of mixed identities. Pamela's
unconventional courtship? What is it? How large a part
does she play? Amusing story-focuses on the two men.
BKM
Story seems to focus on the identity question.

010776   LAMORNA. BY MRS. ALFRED SIDGWICK. London:
Methuen, [1912] BMC NUC.

ATH-two sisters on a trip-one goes on a weekend with
married man.
TLS-then marries another. He finds out, what next?
SP-Lamorna combines the best domestic virtues with
artistic temperament. She is raised by aunt who has
married off two daughters but is keeping Lamorna on
(she is 23) to do her odd jobs, secretarial work,
governess etc. Lamorna inherits 4,000 pounds, takes
her minx-like cousin Pansy, who is English, on a trip
to Italy where Pansy commits an indiscretion. The
villain attempts to blackmail Lamorna into marriage
but she is not that self sacrificing and marries a
young artist.
ACAD-Lamorna is a real artist

010777   THE LANTERN BEARERS. BY MRS. ALFRED
SIDGWICK. London: Methuen, 1910 BMC NUC. Leipzig: B.
Tauchnitz, 1911 NUC.

Suburban poverty: mid aged husband loses job. Men are
automatons, who sleep, commute, return home angered
because they're worked like machines. Women are snobs,
complacent. The exception is Mrs. Bryne: doesn't want
her daughter to be like other suburban women. Helga is
the young daughter. Isolation of suburbs. The dancing
clique. The religious clique. The lonely clique to
which Mrs. Bryne belongs. Mr. Byrne a hopeless man.
Mrs. Bryne the strength-practical optimism.
Ma-daughter relationship their different outlooks on
the manner in which Helga should conduct herself. A
hopeless courage in their lives. Her feelings of young
love, the motherly sort of love Mrs. Bryne has for her
weak husband.
TLS-love story.
ACAD-love story.
LBKM-love story.

010778   LESSER'S DAUGHTER. BY MRS. ANDREW DEAN.
New York: G. P. Putnam's Sons, 1894 NUC BMC.

ACAD 46:"powerful and enthralling study of one of the
many phases of contemporary Judaism."
ATH 104:709. Jew in mixed marriage and his heartless
wife and shallow daughter.
LBKM 7:56. Corona, haughty vulgar Austrian marries
small ugly but wealthy Jew. He is meek; she is not. He
is constantly snubbed and spends most of his time

reading a history of Europe to make up for his
cultural deficiencies. He dies of an aneurism.

010779   MR. BROOM AND HIS BROTHER: A STORY IN TWO
PARTS. BY MRS. ALFRED SIDGWICK. London: Chapman &
Hall, 1915 NUC BMC.

2 fairy tales.

010780   MRS. FINCH-BRASSY. BY MRS. ANDREW DEAN.
London: R. Bentley, 1893 BMC.

Satire of people in a small town of Whincliffe: the
vulgar Mrs. Finch-Brassy who paints herself, her
entertaining, a bachelor's party, star crossed lovers,
death of a school boy at the end. SR 76:2 73.
Concerns many families. Main character is restless,
self asserting, tries to dominate people, tries to
trap a young man into marriage by writing him an
acceptance letter to a proposal he never made.
Unattractive character. ACAD 44:189.
"Thoroughly disagreeable" an individual, rather than a
type. ATH 102, 155

010781   THE PROFESSOR'S LEGACY. BY MRS. ALFRED
SIDGWICK. London: E. Arnold, 1905 BMC. New York: H.
Holt, 1905 NUC.

Complicated first year of marriage. PW 11-11-05
Anglo-German marriage; German wife marries Englishman
with a daughter. He dies. The wife offends
conventionalities? NYT 797,05

010782   THE PURPLE JAR. BY MRS. ALFRED SIDGWICK.
London: Hutchinson, [1919] BMC NUC. (Am. ed. title:
Iron Cousins.)

Governess in Hamburg, almost falls in love but this
man "loses his purple" in her eyes. Marries a strong
man, returns home. Anti-German. TLS
American edition title: Iron Cousins.

010783   SALT AND SAVOUR. BY MRS. ALFRED SIDGWICK.
London: Methuen, [1916] BMC NUC.

ATH-anti-German.
WWI-fiction.

010784   THE SALT OF THE EARTH. BY MRS. ALFRED
SIDGWICK. New York: W.J. Watt, [c1917] NUC.

German-English marriage of today, Brenda Muller.
English born girl of German descent, had visited
Germany, loved it; marries German, moves to Berlin but
it's so different. A year of bickering about her
English habits, domineering husband, intruding
in-laws, husband, unfaithful, loss of baby-did her
best to adjust. Story leaves her safe in England
without husband facing a happy future. PW

010785   THE SEVERINS. BY MRS. ALFRED SIDGWICK.
London: Methuen, 1909 BMC NUC.

Conflict between Bohemian and conventional manners in
a modern family. LBKM
Unlikely people. ATH
Contrasts British conventionality and semi-continental
Bohemianism in two families. Severins. Mother and 6
children. Nonconformists except for one son.
Outrageously unconventional who keep company with
Russian anarchists. Selma: modern rebel, goes to Paris
to study art. Clotilda, separated from husband plans
to elope with another man. Author makes these people
attractive at same time shows Bohemianism as squalid?
Other family--the Wallinghams. SP

010786   A SPLENDID COUSIN. BY MRS. ANDREW DEAN.
London: Unwin, 1892 BMC. New York: Cassell, [c1892]
NUC.

Title refers to a person who is much admired but does
not deserve the admiration. LW 93, 41
Theodora run over in a fog. She thinks of nothing but
her violin ACAD 43:56
Completely wrapped up in her art, sacrifices mother,
cousin, husband to her art. Treats others as though
"they were born to serve her interests" but finds
she'll never achieve anything with her art for all she
sacrificed. ATH 101, 50
She is Theodora Legh. She has no heart. She wants only
to play piano and have her own way. Steals her cousin
Jane's lover. Wrecks others' lives, then her own. LW
26:332.

010787   A WOMAN WITH A FUTURE. BY MRS. ANDREW
DEAN (MRS. ALFRED SIDGWICK). New York and London: F.

A. Stokes, [c1895] NUC. London: Black, 1896 BMC.

LBKM 10:58. Hesperia is idle, shallow, vulgar,
uneducated, false, cold, cowardly, and insolent.
SR-she is a charming Hedonist. "The author like most
straitlaced women, is very hard upon her own
sex"..."understands men very little and women not at
all."
ATH 107:648. "understanding but no sympathy can be
accorded her." She is married. "Formerly it (fiction)
was nearly always about a young woman whose history
invariably ended with her marriage." "A future still
more heartless, hollow and sensual suggests itself as
likely to be the consumation of her career."
ACAD 49:444. "The heroine is not without charm, and
too shrewd to have given herself away as she does in
the last chapter."
PW 6-6-96. She leaves her husband and goes away with
an adventurer with millions.

SIDGWICK, ETHEL. B. 1877. United Kingdom.

010788   THE ACCOLADE. London and Toronto:
Sidgwick & Jackson, [1915] BMC NUC. Boston: Small,
Maynard, [c1916] NUC.

NYT
male hero who resists temptation of another woman. BKM
The Ingestre family. Grandmother-actress Marian
Fenelly but focuses on a male genius. TLS
John married wrong woman, Ursula. She attempts to make
him believe that Helena young and direct is engaged to
her brother's friend, Quentin. Results in suicide of
the girl who loves Quentin. John works out his
problems and considers only Helena's happiness. PW
89:2/19/16:608.

010789   DUKE JONES: A SEQUEL TO "A LADY OF
LEISURE". London & Toronto: Sidgwick & Jackson, [1914]
BMC NUC. Boston: Small, Maynard, [1915] NUC.

SR 118:491. Mild, absurd, male hero who, loving one
woman, he served and married another.
ATH 144:477. Elusive style.
TLS 13:494. Rev. thinks he really didn't mind making
an honest woman of Lisa.
Lifts a little man to heroic heights. Centers on
Violet? PW Review Oct. 1915
Story concerns a honeymoon; bride's Ma mid-aged so
avid of the power fast slipping from her waning beauty
as to be jealous of her own daughter, jealous to the
point of positive dislike. All characters carefully
elaborated. NYT

010790   HATCHWAYS. Boston: Small, Maynard,
[c1916] NUC. London: Sidgwick & Jackson, 1916 BMC NUC.

Dutchess's determination to marry her sons
appropriately. Study of temperaments and of mothers.
PW 90:1615 11/11/16
NYT. Heroine is Ernestine Redgate.
A kind of social novel into which a French man comes.
Various types. Nothing new. SP

010791   HERSELF. Boston: Small, Maynard, [c1912]
NUC. London: Sidgwick & Jackson, 1912 BMC NUC.

PW-young woman victim of scandal-making, teacher in
French school.
ATH 0
ACAD 0
SR-daughter of heroic Brian, attracted to other
splendid rogues, in the end marries satisfactory
husband
LBKM-someone has a black face. Patrick is pitiful, in
love with Harriet. Death claims him. Harriet lives
through the bad days. There is Geoffry Horn, Bertha
Lindt the musician, Ann Maskery, Dr. Gudgeon too.
NYT 0

010792   JAMESIE. London: Sidgwick & Jackson, 1918
BMC. Boston: Small, Maynard, [c1918] NUC.

PW-sequel to Hatchways. Effect of war on 8 year old
son of Bess and Iveagh. Study of character. Jamesie is
suddenly, brutally killed by the war. Author's pov is
that war-not Germany-is a fiend incarnate. Rev.
comments that Deland has also expressed this new way
of looking at the war.
TLS-0
NYT Aug. 25,1918,p.361.Story is told through
collection of letters and brief notes, intimate and
informal, between characters . Characters include a
range of feminists, from militant suffragist to
conservative. Jamesie dies in the English Channel, on
a boat that is torpedoed. This rev. feels that the

enemy is not war (which he says is only background,
although several characters are killed by it) but
fate-an influence of Sidgwick's Greek studies.

010793   A LADY OF LEISURE. London and Toronto:
Sidgwick and Jackson, 1914 BMC NUC. Boston: Small,
Maynard, [c1914] NUC.

ACAD 86:237. Sidgwick's style is elusive and reticent,
according to this rev. and others.
TLS 13:77 Violet and Alice have brains.
The whims of a daughter of a great London surgeon.
Overcomes their objections, enters dressmaking
establishment. LR
PW 86 9/26/14:968 "Vivid and sometimes amusing
experiences of an English girl who entered a London
dressmaking establishment to satisfy a whim. Here she
learned something about her own world and much about
this new one that had stirred her curiosity. The
people that she met were individuals, not types. Among
them was her lover, who did not know that she was an
heiress until her father told him so."
NYT-Violet Ashwin, a perfect mistress of herself &
every situation. Her sister Margery is infatuated with
an animal-tragedy is averted.
SR 147:443.0.
LBKM-the revelation of woman to woman. Sidgwick:
"Margery was basely in love with a beautiful animal,
and many have been likewise ; men very openly and
exultantly, and women in secret, and tormented."
Violet converts everyone except her mother (who seems
stupid to reviewer) to her views.

010794   LE GENTLEMAN: AN IDYLL OF THE QUARTER.
London: Sidgwick & Jackson, 1911 BMC 1912 NUC. Boston:
Small, Maynard, 1912 NUC.

Pretty story of French & English people. Meysie
Lampeter a merciless picture of the silly affected
type of English woman? Gilberte sane, practical,
intelligent, French. TLS
Meysie, English butterfly girl with artistic ambitions
but no feeling or depth of character. She's engaged.
Her fiance meets Gilberte, student at Sorbonne. Meysie
in the meantime is attracted to an artist. End? LBKM
A Lady student's art career in Paris. Tale of simple
piety. SR
NYT 0
PW Triangle

010795   PROMISE. London: Sidgwick & Jackson, 1910
BMC 1912 NUC. Boston: Small, Maynard, 1912 NUC.

TLS-male genius.
ATH-male genius.

010796   SUCCESSION. A COMEDY OF THE GENERATIONS.
(A CONTINUATION OF "PROMISE"). London & Toronto:
Sidgwick & Jackson, 1913 BMC NUC. Boston: Small,
Maynard, [c1913] NUC.

A continuation of Promise.
Antoine, a musical genius-his temperament and
experiences. NYT

SIDGWICK, MRS. ALFRED. See SIDGWICK, CECILY (ULLMANN).

SIDNEY, MARGARET, pseud. See LOTHROP, HARRIET MULFORD
(STONE).

SIEGEL, HENRIETTA. United States.

010797   THE SIN OF IGNORANCE. New York: Broadway,
[1904] NUC.

SIEVEKING, ISABEL GIBERNE.

010798   THE GREAT POSTPONEMENT. BY I. GIBERNE.
London: J. Ouseley, [1912] BMC NUC.

ATH-A warning to English women about to marry
Frenchmen, something about internal regulations.
TLS-unhappy marriages.
ACAD-0

SILBERRAD, U. L. See SILBERRAD, UNA LUCY.

SILBERRAD, UNA LUCY. B. 1872. United Kingdom.

010799   THE AFFAIRS OF JOHN BOLSOVER. London: T.
Nelson, [1911] BMC.

010800   CO-DIRECTORS. London: Hodder & Stoughton,
1915 BMC NUC.

They are an inventor and Ely Thain who has inherited

an interest in the co. that puts the inventor's invention on the market . Author has made Ely male like. They have "almost identical moral qualities." Both have a vast capacity for orderly work." We fancy Elizabeth may have got herself drawn as a protest vs the type of woman who feels she is not necessary to anybody." She's 35. They fight against mischance and opposition to the invention. Critical of the antagonism in business caused by the competitive spirit. ATH
NYT-heroine is not young, or pretty. She has a head for business, has inherited a business from her brother which involves her with a middle-aged unromantic (like herself) inventor. Romance develops.

010801   CUDDY YARBOROUGH'S DAUGHTER. London: Constable, 1914 BMC NUC. New York: G.H. Doran, [c1914] NUC.

LBKM-genial Cuddy, father of 10 year old Violet Jane, mother dead. Sam, Cuddy's old friend, visits them at Countershell. Violet's Aunt Maud is a beautiful and thoughtless creature whom Sam once loved.
ATH-contrast between sweet Violet and selfish Maud. Father and daughter.

010802   CURAYL. New York: Doubleday, Page, 1906 NUC. London: A. Constable, 1906 BMC NUC.

PW-unhappy marriage; awakening. Married for husband's money. ACAD
TLS-O superficial, conv.
ATH O

010803   DESIRE. BY U. L. SILBERRAD. New York: Doubleday, Page, 1908 NUC. London: A. Constable, 1908 BMC 1909 NUC.

PW-wholly unconventional woman.
TLS-finds her role and her love in business. Helpful intelligent. A good comrade.
ACAD O
Desire, a woman, frank, courageous heroic. Review says nothing else about her. LBKM

010804   THE ENCHANTER. London: Macmillan, 1899 BMC NUC.

Biographical type. Begins with small boy and girl. Later their adventures in Hunza, India. Return to England. SP 83:754
Mysteries of sorcery and magic. Maledict Screed's influence over John Forsyth's mind. Portrait also of a man of simple views and love of nature--Nicholas Pycroft. SR 88:839.
LBKM 117:120. Two enchanters: Nicholas whose family is into occult research and he a scientist, and Screed, thief, vampire, etc.
ACAD 58:34. Nicholas is very good, becomes a great scientist, his romance.

010805   THE GOOD COMRADE. New York: Doubleday, Page, 1907 NUC. London: A. Constable, 1907 BMC.

Daughters of a proud family. One breaks tradition, takes job as housekeeper. PW 10-5-07.
Struggle between her necessities and her honor, her poverty-sharpened wits and her real nature?
LBKM8-07,178
Julia hates conventions; she has our complete sympathy. We praise the development of the natural woman in Julia. She steals a secret of the new explosive to please the man she loves to prove to him she could succeed where he failed. ACAD
Julia Polkington, positively portrayed, steals a formula to pay a debt.

010806   GREEN PASTURES. London: Hutchinson, [1919] NUC BMC.

Historical romance, traditional stuff. TLS

010807   IN THE COURSE OF BUSINESS. London: Daily Mail, [1904] BMC.

010808   THE INHERITANCE. London: Hutchinson, 1916 BMC NUC.

TLS-male legitimate & female illegitimate are joint heirs to property. She is a vagabond, a coiner, wanted by the law. They eventually marry. 17th C.

010809   JIM ROBINSON. London: Hutchinson, [1920] BMC NUC.

TLS-male hero.

ATH-reappearance of an old acquaintance, that inventive chemical genius who has been in more than one novel has added to his scientific acquirements the art of washing up. Also a strong-minded woman of mature years, generous and devoted and incredibly unrestrained in language.

010810   KEREN OF LOWBOLE. New York: G.H. Doran, [c1913] NUC. London: Constable, 1913 BMC NUC.

PW 8/9/13 "Keren is the daughter of a gipsy and an alchemist who lives in an ancient forest, helping her father at the furnace and learning much of his art, but not its deepest and most terrible secrets. Scene is England at the time of the witchcraft delusion which hangs, an ominous cloud, over Keren. Her father lives for revenge, but why and upon whom is not revealed until the story's end. Keren is discovered by strangers lost in the forest, visits relatives and there meets enemies, escapes arrest as a witch, and at last finds her true love."
Daughter of an Egyptian witch who escaped the fire by suicide. Story tells of her father's tardy revenge on his Dutch enemies and her hasty flight from the cruel ignorance of Colchester. Time of witchhunts. TLS

010811   THE LADY OF DREAMS. New York: Doubleday, Page, [1900] BMC NUC.

ATH 116:721. Sombre, contemporary life in E. London. ACAD 59:551. Agnes' uncle has delerium tremors, more than once attempts murder on his death bed. Succeeds once. Agnes kills him. She marries the hero, a big-hearted doctor who works in the slums. She doesn't love him and later falls for another. Subsequent tragedy.
LIT 7:528. Mrs. Tancreed (Agnes) "found she could not love the husband who loved her so fondly."
PW-she has become "strangely elusive and dream-like" under the strain of caring for her uncle.

010812   THE LYNDWOOD AFFAIR. London: Hutchinson, 1918 BMC NUC.

ATH-murder mystery.

010813   THE MYSTERY OF BARNARD HANSON. London: Hutchinson, 1915 BMC NUC.

Detective tradition. TLS SP

010814   ORDINARY PEOPLE. London: Constable, 1909 BMC NUC.

Catherine Santerre. Wife returns to husband incognito (dyes her hair) as a clerk unrecognized after their separation early in marriage. ATH
Story of a man brought up to be timid by a domineering mother, makes a nonsensual marriage, when his mother dies. The wife has had an affair in her youth-misunderstanding, separation, reunion. ACAD
LBKM-marriage problem. Something in her past she disguises herself and works in his office as a typist.

010815   PETRONILLA HEROVEN. BY U. L. SILBERRAD. New York: Doubleday, Page, 1903 NUC. Westminster: A. Constable, 1903 BMC.

Illeg child gets a peculiar education. 12-5-03. PW ACAD 65, 292. Obscure brief description. Illegitimate of birth, she bears it with a haughty air. ACAD 65,327 Review LBKM 12-03,148
solitary upbringing on a farm, yet a shrewd observer of life. ATH 122,513
Her dull life, good character portrayal but much of murder, suicide, jewels, and the rest? TLS, 273,03

010816   PRINCESS PUCK. New york: Doubleday, Page, 1901 NUC. London: Macmillan, 1902 BMC.

ATH 2-15-02. "Bill is a capital study in girlhood...somewhat of a new departure in treatment...regular hoiden without mere pertness and flippancy."

010817   THE REAL PRESENCE. London: Hodder & Stoughton, [1912] BMC.

010818   SAMPSON RIDEOUT, QUAKER. London and New York: T. Nelson, [1911] BMC NUC.

Traditional historical romance about Quakers. ACAD

010819   SUCCESS. London: Constable, 1912 BMC NUC. New York: 1913 NUC.

TLS- male hero with mouse-like cousin Nan.
SP-but she refuses to marry him and he should have a
sensible person to look after him.
ACAD 0
SP-story is of his failure in industrial world and his
eventual success not through fame. Focus is on him,
Nan seems to be auxiliary.
"Hero is a young inventor in employ of firm of
government engineers. He invents a new and most deadly
weapon of war and is accused of selling it, not to his
own employers, but to certain foreign powers. Effect
is to discredit him and make it impossible for him to
earn his living in his chosen profession. Story hinges
upon this point of patriotism and honor, and also
shows how inefficient a skilled man may appear in this
day of specialized labor, if he works at a task for
which his education unfits him. By author of The Good
Comrade."

010820   SUCCESS OF MARK WYNGATE. BY U. L.
SILBERRAD. New York: Doubleday, Page, 1902 NUC.
Westminster: A. Constable, 1902 BMC.

Strong resolute woman in love with a machine of a man.
tragic end. Sacrifice of her life to his
(scientist-chemist) success. LBKM 2-03,214
ACAD 1902-man and woman, both chemists, in
partnership. Description of Bachelor hall, residence
for women workers. Woman rarely finds work sufficient
in itself-penalty of her sex?
ATH 10-11-22. Daughter takes father's place in job at
welding-forge after he becomes sick and dies. Becomes
co-operator with scientist-inventor. Cold
scientist-tragic end.
BKM 12-02-a novel without love-making heroine without
coquetry. Judith is a creature of unusual physical
mental and emotional strength. She can forge iron
bars, her recreation is pure mathematics. At one point
teaches in London and lives in Bachelor's Buildings,
negative portrayal of young working women--all her
work is for hero-quote from book, "success except for
him never occurred to her."

SILKE, LOUISE C.

010821   STEADFAST AND TRUE; A TALE OF THE
HUGUENOTS. London: Religious Tract Society, [1897]
BMC.

SP 80:148. French Huguenots, refugees in English home.

SILVA, GORHAM, pseud. See LAWRENCE, ELIZABETH.

SIME, J. G. See SIME, JESSIE GEORGINA.

SIME, JESSIE GEORGINA. B. 1880. Canada.

010822   SISTER WOMAN. BY J. G. SIME. London: G.
Richards, 1919 BMC NUC.

30 Stories bound together with one theme "the needs of
women with those instincts that urge women to find an
expression of themselves in action rather than in
words." Almost all are working in Canada. "With
instructive demands for happiness beyond the narrow
limits of their daily drudgery." The motive power
behind them all-the need to give which is thwarted.
(?) TLS
"Stories convey an idea of women's desire for freedom
and self expression." SP

SIMMINS, META.

010823   THE GATES OF SILENCE. London: G. Newnes,
[1915] BMC.

010824   THE SECOND LADY KENDAL. London: G.
Newnes, [1912] BMC.

SIMMONS, VESTA S. United States.

010825   GREEN TEA: A LOVE STORY. BY V.
SCHALLENBERGER. New York: Cassell, [c1892] NUC.
London: T. F. Unwin, 1892 BMC.

ATH 99:339. California romance.
PW-Gives her heart, at 16, to brother of her most
intimate friend.

010826   A VILLAGE DRAMA. New York: Cassell,
[c1896] NUC. London: Bliss, Sands, 1896 BMC.

ATH 107:744. Study in "male flirtation." Pitiable
heroine. Her attempts to put love philtre in his water
jug.
ACAD 49:486. "Painstaking attempt to catch and

faithfully interpret the outwardly uneventful life" in
Spriggs. A backward village in California.

SIMMS, MARGARET D. United States.

010827   WHAT WILL SHE DO? A ROMANCE OF SOUTHERN
LIFE. New York and London: Abbey Press, [c1900] NUC.

SIMON, EMMA (COUVELY). 1848-1934.

010828   TRUE DAUGHTER OF HARTENSTEIN. A NOVEL. BY
E. VELY. New York: R. Bonner's Sons, 1892 NUC. (Tr.
Mary J. Safford)

PW Hertha, penniless on death of her father, the
count. Her romance, adventures and heroism.

SIMONTON, IDA VERA. 18??-1931. United States.

010829   HELL'S PLAYGROUND. New York: Moffat,
Yard, 1912 NUC. London: Gay & Hancock, 1915 BMC.

W. Africa: the degeneration of the white man in the
tropics due to absence of white women and to drink,
but mostly because he gets involved with a native
woman. Author attacks the foreign administration in
the Congo. She pictures the native women as mere
chattels, merchandise to be sold or leased by father
or husband to the highest foreign bidder. One
beautiful native woman is whipped to death because
she's unfaithful to her white master. LBKM
ATH-W. Coast of Africa.
Shows the horrors of slave trade. TLS
BKM v.36 1912-13. Frankness of utterance. Critique of
colonial rule, male colonialist's involvement with
black woman-portrayal of black women as Chattel in
African society.
NYT-failure of craftsmanship.

SIMPSON, KATHERINE.

010830   THE FUGITIVE YEARS. London: J. Long, 1912
BMC.

ACAD-Phoda is and always has been crazy about her
selfish cousin who seeks her out only when he needs
her. Finally offers her position of his mistress (his
wife in asylum) which she refuses despite free love
ideas she shares with friend. The end is not
unexpected.

SIMPSON, LUCIE.

010831   THAT AMBITIOUS SHE. A NOVEL. London:
Greening, 1906 BMC.

TLS---girl in London society.

SIMPSON, VIOLET A. United Kingdom.

010832   THE BEACON-WATCHERS. London: Chapman and
Hall, 1913 BMC NUC.

Development of the child Sara, her hurried unfortunate
marriage. But she wins out in the end. ACAD

010833   THE BONNET CONSPIRATORS: A STORY OF 1815.
London: Smith, Elder, 1903 BMC.

Smuggling adventure--historical romance. ACAD 64-342
ACAD 64,510
LBKM 6-03, 112
ATH 121, 493.

010834   FLOWER OF THE GOLDEN HEART. London:
Chapman and Hall, 1913 BMC.

Era of Charles II; Lord Gaye's passion for Ester,
leads him to desert his wife. Great Plague SP
TLS

010835   IN FANCY'S MIRROR. Edinburgh and London:
W. Blackwood, 1911 BMC.

Young woman's complete loss of memory. TLS
"Strange education of Victorine Carysfort and the
highly unsuitable marriage which was arranged"; loss
of memory helps her to assert self and choose the
right person. LBKM

010836   THE KEYS OF MY HEART. London: Chapman &
Hall, 1915 NUC BMC.

Francesca Bellares--independent, young: all she does
is help hero, saves marriage. TLS
Makes a comfortable living by private demonstrations

in cookery. ATH

010837   OCCASION'S FORELOCK. London: E. Arnold, 1906 BMC.

TLS-secretary (male or female?) to a politician.

010838   THE PARSON'S WOOD. London: E. Nash, 1905 BMC.

Seventeenth century story. ACAD 1905:1361

010839   THE SOVEREIGN POWER: A ROMANCE OF GEORGIAN DAYS. London: Smith, Elder, 1904 BMC.

LBKM-historical romance.
ATH -historical romance.
ACAD-historical romance.

SINCLAIR, B. M.   See SINCLAIR, BERTHA (MUZZY).

SINCLAIR, BERTHA (MUZZY). 1874?-1940. United States.

010840   CABIN FEVER. A NOVEL. BY B. M. BOWER. Boston: Little, Brown, 1918 NUC BMC.

PW-male hero who leaves his wife and child-get together in end.
NYT-begins with divorce of Marie & Bud who in 2nd year of their marriage have cabin fever. He joins Cash Markham, a prospector and soon cabin fever affects this relationship. He discovers a baby who becomes a bond between the two men, they becoming both anxious and devoted fathers.

010841   CHIP, OF THE FLYING U. BY B. M. BOWER (B. M. SINCLAIR). New York: G.W. Dillingham, [1906] NUC. London: T. Nelson, [1920] BMC.

"The scenes of this story are laid on a western ranch, the Flyint U. Chip, the hero, is sent to the station to bring the proprietor's sister, who is coming to spend the summer with her brother, the owner of the ranch. The sister is young and fair, and is, also, a physician. She overcomes the prejudice of all the cowboys, particularly of Chip, when she saves the life of his favourite horse, and when she sets a broken collar-bone and treats a badly sprained ankle for him. That he eventually wins her for his wife may be surmised before the reader reaches the end of the story." BKM v.23 1906

010842   FLYING U RANCH. BY B. M. BOWER. New York: G.W. Dillingham, [1914] NUC BMC.

PW 85 3/28/14:1109 "Introduces characters of Chip of the Flying U. Accident keeps the Old Man in Chicago and Weary is in charge of the ranch. Dunk Whittaker, a disreputable character, former partner of the Old Man, to get square buys the next ranch and stocks it with sheep, the cowman's special abomination. The sheep are driven into Flying U to graze, at last the Happy Family rebels and things happen fast and furious to Dunk Whittaker, putting a wholesome fear of the law into him and causing his departure."

010843   THE FLYING U'S LAST STAND. BY B. M. BOWER. Boston: Little, Brown, 1915 BMC NUC.

"Little Doctor" is Old Man Chip's young sister. Woman land agent unscrupulous and determined takes large part. She has a colony of homeseekers (mostly women school teachers) file claims against the land needed by the Flying U Ranch for grazing. In the controversy the Ranch wins out. NYT

010844   GOOD INDIAN. BY B. M. BOWER. Boston: Little, Brown, 1912 NUC BMC. London: Methuen, 1919 BMC.

PW-male hero, Western. Focus on male cowboy. TLS

010845   THE GRINGOS. A STORY OF THE OLD CALIFORNIA DAYS IN 1849. BY B. M. BOWER. Boston: Little, Brown, 1913 NUC. London: Methuen, 1923 BMC.

PW:84 1-/18/13:1288 "Scene is the ranch of Don Andres Picardo. Here come two Americans or gringos as they are called. Dade and his friend Jack Allen, whom he has just rescued from a disgraceful death at the hands of the Vigilance Committee in San Francis co. They are accepted hospitably by Don Andres and given employment, and naturally they both fall victims to the beauty of their host's daughter, Senorita Teresita, to the intense jealousy of another suitor, Don Jose. A stage set with one maid and three lovers

promises plenty of excitement, and the promise is fulfilled."
"For a time Jack, the younger and more dashingly attractive of the two, seems to be the accepted lover. But he incurs the enmity of Don Jose, a Mexican who also loves the girl, and finds himself precipitated into a duel, of which the heartless senorita approves. At its end, when Jack, having his enemy at his mercy, grants him his life, both young Americans, convinced of the girl's shallowness, are content to ride away." BRD

010846   THE HAPPY FAMILY. BY B. M. BOWER (B. M. SINCLAIR). New York: G.W. Dillingham, [c1910] NUC. London: T. Nelson, [1920] BMC.

Story of cattle country, cowboy adventures. PW

010847   HER PRAIRIE KNIGHT AND ROWDY OF THE "CROSS L." BY B. M. BOWER (B. M. SINCLAIR). New York: G.W. Dillingham, [1907] NUC. London: T. Nelson, 1921 BMC.

Western love story. BKM

010848   THE HERITAGE OF THE SIOUX. BY B. M. BOWER. Boston: Little, Brown, 1916 NUC BMC. London: Hodder and Stoughton, [1923] BMC.

Fake bank robbery for film purposes, precedes a real one. Family sworn in as deputy sheriffs follow the trail. PW 90:974. NYT 9/23/16

010849   JEAN OF THE LAZY A. BY B. M. BOWER. Boston: Little, Brown, 1915 NUC BMC. London: Methuen, [1918] BMC.

Becomes movie star to establish father's innocence; more a detective story. PW 10-9-15
Chances to do some horse-riding stunts before manager of film company, joins the co. featured as Jean of the Lazy A. with the money she earns from making movies gets father out of prison.
BKM-needs money to get her father out of jail (he is of course innocent). She is the best rider and lariat thrower in the state and joins a moving picture company and does stunts before the cameras, risking her life for an ever-increasing salary.

010850   LONESOME LAND. BY B. M. BOWER. London: S. Paul, 1912 BMC. Boston: Little, Brown, 1912 NUC.

PW-unhappy wife married to man who has morally deteriorated in the West.
ATH-through drink-there is a chivalrous cowboy.
BKM-neglect and physical violence to wife. Husband finally killed by sheriff's bullet. Valerie marries cowboy who has befriended her throughout her marriage. NYT O

010851   THE LONESOME TRAIL. BY B. M. BOWER (B. M. SINCLAIR). New York: G.W. Dillingham, [c1909] NUC. London: T. Nelson, [1920] BMC.

Western PW 3-20-09.

010852   THE LONG SHADOW. BY B. M. BOWER. New York: G.W. Dillingham, [c1909] NUC. London: T. Nelson, [1921] BMC.

Western. PW 10-30-09.

010853   THE LOOKOUT MAN. BY B. M. BOWER. Boston: Little, Brown, 1917 NUC.

Story of a man at a Forest Reserve station who falls in love. PW

010854   THE LURE OF THE DIM TRAILS. BY B. M. BOWER. New York: G.W. Dillingham, [1907] NUC. London: T. Nelson, [1921] BMC.

Western adventure. 11-2-07 PW

010855   THE PHANTOM HERD. BY B. M. BOWER. Boston: Little, Brown, 1916 NUC BMC. London: Hodder, Stoughton, [1922] BMC.

Story of rancher who writes a screen story. PW NYT

010856   THE QUIRT. BY B. M. BOWER. Boston: Little, Brown, 1920 NUC.

PW-Lorraine's mother had left Quirt Ranch and her husband while Lorraine was a child. She worked (Lorraine) in the movies. when her mother remarried,

she decided to return to the ranch and her father.
Experiences chilling adventures more horrible than
movies (witnesses a cold-blooded murder.)
NYT 1920:22

010857   THE RANCH AT THE WOLVERINE. BY B. M.
BOWER. Boston: Little, Brown, 1914 NUC BMC. London: E.
Nash, 1916 BMC.

TLS-Western, love story.
PW 86 9/26/14:965 "Story of ranch life and
cattle-stealing in Idaho, Ward Warren had started life
with big notions and for a while he fared well until
fortune began to use him for a football. He told Billy
Louise all this and she believed in him. Billy Louise
was a plucky girl who ran the ranch for her mother
after her father died. Billy looked out for every one,
crude pioneer Marthy, and particularly Ward Warren
when he got into difficulties. Finally Ward and Billy
discover that they are essential to each other's
happiness."
NYT 1914:463

010858   THE RANGE DWELLERS. BY B. M. BOWER (B. M.
SINCLAIR). New York: G.W. Dillingham, [1907] NUC.
London, New York: T.F. Unwin, 1907 BMC.

Adventures of a prodigal son. 3-2-07 PW

010859   RIM O' THE WORLD. BY B. M. BOWER. Boston:
Little, Brown, 1919 NUC BMC. London: Hodder and
Stoughton, [1922] BMC.

Feud on Idaho ranch. NYT
Love and family feud PW

010860   SKYRIDER. BY B. M. BOWER. Boston: Little,
Brown, 1918 NUC BMC. London: Methuen, 1920 BMC.

Traditional heroine; western setting near Mexico. BKM
TLS O
PW-male aviator, Johnny.
NYT-Dec. 15 '18 p 554. When he tells heroine he would
like to fly in war and fight Germans, she calls him
crazy and idiotic. It is no surprise to the reader
when her sense of honor proves to be of a sufficiently
Germanic quality to permit her to read another
person's letters without a qualm. However, she uses a
revolver with considerable ability, and we are
evidently expected to like her.

010861   STARR OF THE DESERT. BY B. M. BOWER.
Boston: Little, Brown, 1917 NUC BMC. London: Hodder
and Stoughton, [1923] BMC.

Helen May moved to N. Mexico, because of ill health;
complications involving a Mexican revolt. PW
She and her family unhappy in New Mexico till they
meet up with Starr, Texas ranger and secret service
agent, there to investigate movement to return 3
states to Mexico. NYT 190, 5-13-17.

010862   THE THUNDER BIRD. BY B. M. BOWER. Boston:
Little, Brown, 1919 NUC BMC. London: Hodder and
Stoughton, [1923] BMC.

Western-further aeronautic adventures of Johnny
Jewell. PW
Skyrider Johnny Jewell wins his airplane. Mary V.
Selmer is the young woman he loves who makes many
demands. NYT 7-6-19,359

010863   THE UPHILL CLIMB. BY B. M. BOWER. Boston:
Little, Brown, 1913 NUC. London: Methuen, 1923 BMC.

"By author of Good Indian. Ford Campbell, cowboy with
a capacity for drink, marries a girl one evening, and
next morning can't remember why, what she looked like,
nor where she went. None of his friends can help him.
Then he meets a girl who exerts a refining influence
over him, sympathizing with him, even while condemning
his faults. He starts his uphill climb toward
amounting to something, becomes foreman of the Double
Cross Ranch, makes good after a hard fight, and then
discovers the connection between his wild marriage and
the present." PW.

SINCLAIR, EDITH.

010864   HIS HONOUR AND HIS LOVE. Edinburgh and
London: W. Blackwood, 1911 BMC.

Historical romance. TLS

SINCLAIR, MAY. 1870-1946. United Kingdom.

010865   AUDREY CRAVEN. Edinburgh & London:
Blackwood, 1897 BMC. New York: H. Holt, 1906 NUC.

Audrey is vain, ignorant, callous. A chameleon type.
Her char. "laid bare mercilessly-but sympathatically."
Can't help being what she is. She jilts two men who
love her, becomes mistress of a man who doesn't. But
Audrey does not take the "irrevocable step" -only
because Langley Wyndham has a purely prof. interest in
wanting her as model for heroine of his new book.
Cruelly misused by him. Katherine Haviland-good,
devoted to brother, falls for Hardy, a drinker. SR
83:588.
A sympathetic portrayal; ultimately marries a chinless
country gentleman with a small fortune in goose
farming; she has beauty, charm but is selfish
insincere and mendacious. Her relations with several
men.
PW-"Earlier book by author of Divine Fire." At 25
mistress of her own person, her own income, her own
house" inordinate spiritual and physical vanity.
NYT-writer made her love him so that he could use her
as material; marries a dullard?

010866   THE BELFRY. New York: Macmillan, 1916
NUC.

NYT Tasker Jevons and Viola Thesiger go to Bruges to
see the Belfry. Jevons dominates the story; Walter
Furnival narrates it.
Rev. thinks V. is outrageously selfish, psych study.
Viola, typist. "Just because they wanted to look at
the belfry of Bruges, she and Jevons (struggling
writer) traveled to Belgium together". Later married.
In time Jevons little vulgarities almost brought her
to breaking point. War changed all this as his big
qualities came through. PW 89:2-19-16:609.
BKM Conclusion begs the question of how V. is to live
with his vulgarity.

010867   THE COMBINED MAZE. New York and London:
Harper, 1913 NUC. London: Hutchinson, 1913 BMC NUC.

John Ransome, clerk, devotes evenings to building up
his body, Winnie Dymond also at a desk all day
(independent), Violet her friend. NYT
PW 3-1-13 768 "Tells of fine youth, much given to
exercise, who lives with his mother and tippling
father, keeper of a small drug store in London. At the
gymnasium Ranny Ransome meets a sweet, wholesome girl,
Winny Dymond, and is on the point of telling her of
his love when he comes in contact with her friend,
Violet Usher. Ranny is captivated by her, never
realizing that she is absolutely without moral sense
and they are speedily married. Violet repents almost
immediately. She hates her children, neglects her
home, and finally runs away with another man. Winny
stands by Ranny, and just as he has saved enough to
pay for a divorce he has to use the money to bury his
father. Again he saves, he and Winny are about to be
happy, when Violet comes back."
Husband takes her back out of duty. SP
"An indictment of the Eng. divorce law" Edna Kenton PW
3/22/13 p. 1137
Winnie "perfectly able...to accompany herself home."
Violet "had a roving eye" "Winnie...practised the
revived Greek Gospel of physical fitness" The novel is
"a modern revival of the olympic games" NYT 1913, 130.
BKM v. 37 1913
Cockney London of underpaid overworked clerks and shop
girls. There's only one clean influence here-a
cooperative club for both men and women, a
well-equipped gymnasium, swimming tanks, a respectable
gathering place for evenings. The big function when
the sexes compete (the combined maze of their
marching) symbol for relation between sexes. Strong
Winny Dymond meets Ransome who realizes too late what
a prize she is. She is clean, wholesome womanhood,
natural with men-opposite Violet Usher "sex incarnate"
Whom he marries and regrets marrying. NYT

010868   THE CREATORS; A COMEDY. New York:
Century, 1910 NUC. London: Constable, 1910 BMC NUC.

Serious writer-men and women. The question explored
"Is it possible for the man or woman of genius to
marry and sacrifice neither family or success in
creative work?" PW
ACAD-Characters are self convicted of vacuity and
conceit.
BKM-Irony
"Strain of being novelist and wife and mother." R. B.
JOHNSON

010869   THE DIVINE FIRE. New York: H. Holt, 1904
NUC. Westminster: A. Constable, 1904 BMC NUC.

Outspoken about sex, characters do and say shocking
things women play with fire. Lucia must come down from
her pedestal to inspire the poet. BKM (1905)21
We see Lucia thru the poet's eyes, Kitty, Poppy,
Flossie are other kinds. Review makes it all sound
good but doesn't get down to specifics; centers on the
poet? NYT 150,05
PW Ch. study of male poet
NYT 0
LBKM 0
TLS 0
Lucia's friendship with Kitty is strong good
relationship to Miss Roots, Flossie intell,
aggressive, active interest independent of men, can
view them in a detached way, Supports self by teaching
piano. Proposes to the man in the end.

010870   THE FLAW IN THE CRYSTAL. New York: E. P.
Dutton, [c1912] NUC.

"Woman cloaks with a mantle of spirituality an affair
with the husband of another woman" NYT 1913,130.
BKM v. 36 1912-13-theme is the healing power young
woman discovers she has. Comes from sexual purity. She
heals those who are going mad, but in one case the
strength of madness of the man causes her power to
weaken and she effects only a temporary cure. She
realizes she must give up on him or his madness will
be transferred to her. He goes to an asylum; the
married man who loves her goes back to his wife,
cured, and she remains alone.
NYT in a state of peace or is it lassitude?

010871   THE HELPMATE. New York: H. Holt, 1907
NUC. London: A. Constable, 1907 BMC NUC.

Resentment of man's past; satire of conv. good wife. R
OF R
BKM 26 (1907) 276-278
Anne is a terrible indictment of the conventionally
good woman-all superficial virtue and hidden faults.
Edith a delicate contrast, an invalid unselfish, quick
witted tries to warn Anne that her treatment of her
husband is wrong. Anne does understand finally TLS
analysis of the "good woman" Ann Majendie marries, in
love, discovers a sordid chapter in husband's past.
She sets herself up on a pedestal condemning him at
every turn as inferior, Eventually he becomes what she
believes he is. In the end Ann develops into a
perfectly rational human being. NYT
Wife "who had her grievance (against husband) nursed
through 400 pages" NYT 1913 130.

010872   THE IMMORTAL MOMENT: THE STORY OF KITTY
TAILLEUR. New York: Doubleday, Page, 1908 NUC. (Eng.
ed. title: Kitty Tailleur.)

BKM 28 1908-9 Woman with tarnished past loves and is
loved by man who on learning the "truth" renounces
her-for sake of child-she acquiesces and kills
herself. 1. She tells him the truth. 2. He decides
against mrg. 3. She then kills herself.
Pub in England under title "Kitty Tailleur"

010873   THE JUDGMENT OF EVE. New York: Ridgway,
[c1907] NUC. London and New York: Harper, 1907 BMC
1908 NUC.

"Aggie Purcell, the belle in a country town of
England, hesitates a long while in making up her mind
which man to marry among a number of suitors, none of
whom she really loves. The choice lies between a
prosperous sheep-rancher from Australia and a
struggling London clerk of literary tendencies. Aggie,
who also has glimmerings of the intellectual life,
shrinks from the sheep-rancher and marries the
poetical clerk. They attempt to live the intellectual
life in a London flat." V.27 1908 BKM
NYT-The clerk is not a success (as the rancher is) and
Eve is worn down with maternal cares and dies
prematurely leaving her husband with the care of their
children. How good was her judgment?

010874   KITTY TAILLEUR. London: A. Constable,
1908 BMC NUC. (Am. ed. title: The Immortal Moment.)

Am. ed.: The Immortal Moment.
ACAD- Meets man whom she loves decides not to reveal
her past to him, he brings his children to her, she
realizes she cannot escape her past, commits suicide.
SR-?

010875   MARY OLIVIER; A LIFE. London and New
York: Cassell, [1919] BMC NUC.

Her first recollections-at two being taken in mother's
bed, at mother's breast. At 12 doesn't know how babies
get born. At 14-They still haven't told her-adores and
hates mother. Sees family as abnormal-except for Aunt
Charlotte who made love to every man she met. She's
one of the loveless. Revenges self by reviving in
restrospect all the bitter moments.-rejection of love,
humiliations, disappointments. TLS
Mary is a gifted thinker, poet, still at mother's side
at 27; only in her studies and poetry breaks away.
Finds it easier to sacrifice self-give up love than
free self.
Mrs Oliver fragile as a bird but "holds her four
children with a grip so strong that not one of them
can make a career, marry or develop, an ind.
personality." PW Book Review 1919, 96 I, 743
Reviewed by Gertrude Atherton

010876   MR. AND MRS. NEVILL TYSON. Edinburgh &
London: W. Blackwood, 1898 BMC.

SP 81:745. Husband, self-made, is jealous of his own
child. Weak wife "practically abandons child rather
than incur his wrath and displeasure." He abandons her
when child dies. She clings to his friend, he being
all she had left of her husband. Welcomes him back and
saves him from burning to death while in drunken
stupor. She ages, he no longer is attracted to her,
and leaves again, permanently. She dies alone. LIT
3:604.
ACAD 55:478. Molly is a fool. When nursing her baby
seemed to lessen her beauty, he obliged her to give
the baby to someone else's care where it died of
neglect. She lost all her beauty saving him in the
fire. He was repelled by her scarred face; she knew
it; although his soul was filled with tenderness for
her.
Mrs. Tyson an enigma. She's naive, innocent on one
hand; on the other--the little ways that scandalise
the county, the unaccountable speeches. The husband is
a subtly unfeminine characterization of a man to the
author's credit, says the reviewer. His wife is
disfigured. He has a lover. SR 88:305.

010877   THE ROMANTIC. New York: Macmillan, 1920
NUC. London: W. Collins, [1920] BMC NUC.

TLS-Sharlie falls for two men, both liars and skunks.
Auth analyzes their characters. Both romantic on
surface but basically motivated only by desire for
power. While second deserts wounded men on field
Sharlie does not. First man was married.
SP Charlotte (Sharlie) and her friend Gwennie are farm
workers . As their group traveled to Belgium, they
thought it most romantic thing that ever happened.
Conway keeps going out, unaware that danger will
affect his physical condition. Begins to resort to
cruelty after each failure, which enables him to try
again. He is shot in back by wounded German he has
left to die.
ATH-He is unable to have sex with Sharlie. (Rev. says
Sharlie is obsessed with her sex-experiences)
LBKM He is seen not thru author's eyes-but Sharlie's.
Break from conventional writing.
NYT 10-17-20 p 10. WwI-Fic

010878   SUPERSEDED. New York: H. Holt, 1906 NUC.

"Two sides of a Question" one part of this two part
story. The centripetal and psychic life of independent
womanhood. Two heroines, at first in restricting
circumstances want more; one woman of fortune flees; a
teacher ATH 3-16-01
(Am. reprint of earlier work) See BKM review, v. 24
1906.
Older woman (teacher) portraying "the anguish of
discovering one has outlived one's usefulness."

010879   TASKER JEVONS: THE REAL STORY. London:
Hutchinson, 1916 NUC BMC.

Tasker & Viola marry. He is a genius. He saves life of
Viola's military brother who had despised him. Tasker
seems to be main focus.
LBKM-He is egotist, a bounder also innocent easy to
see why V loved him and Thesigers did not find him
"Canterbury." V's love strained at that
point-disapproval of brother. Tasker lost his hand in
rescue.
SP-Tasker has no social or educational advantages. He
is under sized and has a freakish irregularity of
features. Viola met him, loved him, and arranged
things so they would have to marry in spite of
family's disapproval. He is a new type of hero. She is
put off by his poor taste for awhile.

010880   THE THREE SISTERS. London: Hutchinson,
1914 BMC NUC. New York: Macmillan, 1914 NUC.

ATH 144;424. Father has more or less been responsible
for death of 1st two wives, 3rd has left him. He is
bent on reducing to a minimum the matrimonial
possibilities of his children.
TLS 13:142. Their "sex histories." "The intimate
history of the ordinary woman, who loves and
marries-or does not marry- surprises, and even in a
sense shocks, far more than the most scandalous
chronicle...""One realizes...how tragically women are
the victims of their very sex." "Cruel and true"
ending.
NYT 1914:486 Grim and ruthless
PW 86 11/7/14:1451 "These daughters of a Garthdale
vicar represent distinct attitudes toward life, and
marriage in particular. Alice, the youngest, is
aggressive; Mary the oldest, is meek. Between is
Gwenda, the most unselfish and with the largest view.
In their village is only one man, Rawcliffe, suitable
for any of them to marry. Alice is infatuated with
him. He is most attracted to Gwenda, but is a cad
without courage to make convincing love to her in the
situation. He allows her to go away in order to leave
Alice the field. But Mary takes this chance and
succeeds in marrying him. Meantime Alice brings the
family to the edge of tragedy. Gwenda returns and sees
Alice safely married. One hopes that the life of dull
duty with her father that Gwenda settles into will not
last."
"A sympathetic and probing study of feminine psych"
One sister gets offer of marriage from man she
believes her sister loved. So she goes away, but
instead of marrying sister number two, he marries
number three. BKM
"Lays bare the secret places of the souls of three
sisters." their objective-the snaring of men. Alice
does it directly; Mary is the hypocrite (seeming so
innocent) Gwenda too, snares the man she wants but
sacrifices him and self. SR

010881   THE TREE OF HEAVEN. London and New York:
Cassell, [1917] BMC NUC.

All that happens happens near the ash tree. Frances
Harrison has five children. We see them first in peace
time (3 sons and a daughter) Then the vortex of the
years 1910-14 when Frances' belief that nothing will
ever happen, is shaken by women's movement., pol.
troubles. Children swept into the vortex. Critic
suggests author is "ashamed of what Eng was doing in
those yrs. Then the war and the ways the war "took"
the family. Frances "tight little mind" TLS
Subtle analysis skillfully interweaves episodes such
as agitation of militant suffragists. ATH
The moral anguish of a C.O. BAKER 32, 437
Dorothea Harrison 18 tall, upright, robust,
undismayed, competent. Takes the measure of
Victorianism as well as free love and turns to work
and study, leaves college with a first-class in Econ.
It's her misfortune to fall for a man who opposes
women's rights. (She's caught in a suffrage raid and
spends three months in Holloway jail.) War comes,
volunteers for active service, wants to go to front,
but Frank Drayton says it's no place for women. "Even
after Drayton's death, his will survives to hold her
in London." Wellington
"Spirit of revolt...suffragist caught in a raid...in
the end subdued by Masculine ideas of duty" Wellington
LBKM-Rev. says war is background and remains
background because individuals are more important than
cosmic events. Dorothea is a suffragist.
NYT Study of the psychological effects of war on the
individuals in a family. Dorothea joins the Women's
Service Corp. She has been jailed as a militant
suffragist. The movement, already well-organized at
onset of war "presented their late enemy, the
Goverment, with an instrument of national service made
to its hand."

010882   TWO SIDES OF A QUESTION. New York:
Taylor, 1901 NUC. London: A. Constable, 1901 BMC.

010883   THE TYSONS (MR. AND MRS. NEVILL TYSON).
New York: B. W. Dodge, 1906 NUC.

3-people by their speech and acts shock the neighbors
3-30-07 PW
BKM woman married to brute egoist both die.
Shows how Nevill Tyson, a male novelist "wronged and
bullied and, in a way, killed the wife who loved him."
Wellington

SINDICI, MARIA MAGDA STUART.

010884   VIA LUCIS; A NOVEL. BY KASSANDRA VIVARIA.
London: W. Heinemann, 1898 BMC. New York: G. H.
Richmond, 1898 NUC.

SP 81:781. A life history. In her audacity and
unconventionality she (K.V.) reminds us most of all
of...Atherton. Arduina, daughter of English-American
mother and a declasse Italian count, is brought up by
her father and a tipsy governess. Agonizing childhood.
Sent to a convent school, wants to start a female
order of Jesuits. Is loved by her best friend's
husband, when she dies they marry, love dies first in
him, then her. Small step-daughter is a consolation.
ACAD 54:105. Rev. says author has entered a convent
whose rules will not permit her to see her book in
print. "An impassioned analysis."
ATH 112:346. Should not be dismissed with phrase
morbid and modern. "Minute and exhaustive mental
analysis." Rev. feels Arduina is a progressive human
being, and her emotional and physical exhaustion at
book's end is only a temporary state.
BKM 8:68.
CR 33:297. Morose and brutal father. She spent one
year in school working out the details of the new
female order. Met Prospero that summer, and after much
conflict between the worldly and the spiritual, she
becomes engaged to him. Then, persuaded by priest to
give him up, she also gives up plans for order. Then
she finally marries Prospero; he is 17 years older
than she. Two years later she discovers he has wearied
of her.
LBKM 14:163. Flings herself with enthusiasm into each
life in turn, only to find disappointment and
disillusionment. Arduina is left among the shadows.
NYT 1898:501. Modern, morbid, depressing. Rome.
Arduina, "queer, morbid, passionate, sullen,
intelligent, visionary, introspective daughter of roue
and consumptive Anglo-American woman." After mother's
death raised by a drunken governess. Then a convent
school. More, but rev. doesn't say what, finds her a
bore.

SINGLETON, ESTHER. 1865-1930. United States.

010885   A DAUGHTER OF THE REVOLUTION. New York:
Moffat, Yard, 1915 NUC.

Writes but must sell estate PW 11-27-15
Young woman goes to New York to start a new career.
"Her self-confidence proves justifiable." her first
article is published in newspaper; her first essay in
a magazine. But she's more interested in soc. life of
New York. opera, meeting of D.A.R. NYT

SINGMASTER, ELSIE. 1879-1958. United States.

010886   BASIL EVERMAN. Boston: Houghton Mifflin,
1920 NUC.

PW- life in college town
NYT Mar 4/2 1920 Mary Lister, a narrow-minded Puritan
is married to college president in small town, but
still grieves inconsolably for her brother, Basil, who
has died 20 years ago and is a completely different
kind of person. He is main character, has left a
legacy which comes to affect many.

010887   EMMELINE. Boston: Houghton, Mifflin, 1916
NUC.

During battle of Gettysburg, Emmeline cooked for the
rebels (in her house). She actually grows to like her
enemies. Led to the rescue of her own wounded brother.
PW
NYT-sincere and simple story

010888   JOHN BARING'S HOUSE. Boston: Houghton
Mifflin, 1920 NUC.

010889   KATY GAUMER. Boston: Houghton, Mifflin,
1915 NUC.

Love story of the Pennsylvania Dutch--BKM 41 1915
Ambitious young woman--NYT

010890   THE LONG JOURNEY. Boston: Houghton
Mifflin, 1917 NUC.

Adventure in Mohawk Valley two centuries ago. NYT

010891   WHEN SARAH SAVED THE DAY. Boston:
Houghton Mifflin, 1909 NUC.

010892   WHEN SARAH WENT TO SCHOOL. Boston:
Houghton Mifflin, 1910 NUC.

SISSON, S. ELIZABETH. Nationality Unknown.

010893   DOROTHY; A TALE OF TWO LANDS. Cincinnati:
Jennings and Graham, [c1906] NUC.

PW-Fifteen year old girl orphan and her plight,
complicated love affairs, happy ending.

010894   GATHERED THISTLES OR, A STORY OF TWO
HOUSEHOLDS. Fremont, Neb.: Hammond, 1897 NUC.

010895   RICHARD NEWCOMBE. New york: Eaton and
Mains, [1900] NUC.

NYT 1900:666. Opens with a double marriage, history of
the two families. Pious wife and a worldly wife. They
go West to seek their fortunes (1840s). They have many
children.
PW-Richard, oldest son of worldly family, shows bad
influence of early training.

SIVITER, ANNA (PIERPONT). B. 1859. United States.

010896   NEHE: A TALE OF THE TIMES OF ARTAXERXES.
Boston: W. A. Wilde, 1901 NUC.

PW 10-5-01

SIVITER, ANNA (PIERPONT) AND FRANCES P. SIVITER.

010897   ON PAROLE. New York: Holt, 1916 NUC.

Boy's story--PW.

SIVITER, FRANCES P., jt. au. See SIVITER, ANNA (PIERPONT)
AND FRANCES P. SIVITER.

SIZER, KATE THOMPSON.

010898   THE FRUIT-GATHERERS. London: C. H. Kelly,
1896 BMC.

010899   LUDWIG'S TREASURE. London: C. H. Kelly,
1897 BMC.

010900   "MAYFLOWER" PILGRIMS. London: C. H.
Kelly, [1898] BMC.

010901   NORTHWARD HO! London: C. H. Kelly, 1895
BMC.

010902   THE WOOING OF OSYTH, A STORY OF THE
EASTERN COUNTIES IN SAXON TIMES. London: Jarrold,
[1893] BMC.

PW 10-24-96. Betrothed to King Sighere, St Osyth
refuses to marry him and enters the convent, where
afterwards she is martyred by the Danes. Sighere
marries her cousin.

SKENE, F. M. F. See SKENE, FELICIA MARY FRANCES.

SKENE, FELICIA MARY FRANCES. 1821-1899. United Kingdom.

010903   HIDDEN DEPTHS, A TALE FOR THE TIMES. BY
F. M. F. SKENE. Chicago: Rand, McNally, 1894 NUC.

SKILES, MAY EVELYN. Nationality Unknown.

010904   A SINGULAR METAMORPHOSIS. New York: Abbey
Press, [1902] NUC.

"A Story of 83 pages, in which a mystery is intimated
in the 1st chapter." BKM (Books rec'd.) Jan 1903

SKINNER, CONSTANCE LINDSAY. D. 1939. United States.

010905   "GOOD-MORNING ROSAMOND"! Garden City, New
York: Doubleday, Page, 1917 NUC.

PW 91:1278 4/21/17 Widow gives up mourning one morning
when she's free from the supervision of grim old
servants. The day full of comedy of errors proves to
be such as her town has never seen. Humorous

SKINNER, GERTRUDE, pseud. See TEASDALE, MINNIE.

SKINNER, HENRIETTA CHANNING (DANA). 1857-1928. United
States.

010906   ESPIRITU SANTO: A NOVEL. New York and
London: Harper, 1899 BMC NUC.

Sentimental. She smiled at the priest on the day she
was baptized. LIT 4:558.
Love story of Espiritu Santo, the heroine and the

angelic Teodora. LBKM 16:170. She and the young tenor
are too good for earth, die at end.

010907   FAITH BRANDON, A NOVEL. New York and
London: D. Appleton, 1912 BMC NUC.

TLS-marriage of American girl to Russian prince.
NYT-love story

010908   HEART AND SOUL, A NOVEL. New York and
London: Harper, 1901 BMC NUC.

IND 53:2305 9/26/01
LW 32:142 9/1/01

010909   THEIR CHOICE: A NOVEL. New York:
Benziger, 1913 NUC.

PW 83 3/1/13:768 "Diary of a charming American woman
of thirty-five, who goes to Holland with her brother's
family, only believing that her youth is quite past,
and that she is merely a middle-aged woman to all who
meet her. A fine Austrian, delegate to the Hague,
Peace Conference, finally convinces her that she is
mistaken."

SKOTTOWE, BRITIFFE CONSTABLE, jt. au. See SNEYD, PAMELA AND
BRITIFFE CONSTABLE SKOTTOWE.

SKRAM, BERTHA AMALIE (ALVER). 1846-1905. Norway.

010910   PROFESSOR HIERONIMUS. London and New
York: J. Lane, 1899 BMC NUC. (Tr. from the Danish by
Alice Stronach and G.B. Jacobi)

Married young, went around world with Sea Captain
husband. When bored, left him, was an inmate of a
lunatic asylum. SP 83:419.
He is a fanatic and a tyrant of the insane and weak.
All must cringe before his power. He rules over an
insane asylum where a woman who is sane is maltreated.
She comes for expert help for her nervousness. Is
treated as insane, put in with lunatics and dangerous
maniacs. LBKM 16:56
Dr. mistakes rebelliousness for madness. Sufferings of
the tortured wife. SP 82:419
"Revolting details of the mental conditions and
treatment of lunatics in an asylum." SR 87:728

SKRINE, MARY JESSIE HAMMOND (TOOKE). B. 1856. United
Kingdom.

010911   BEDESMAN 4. London: Duckworth, 1914 BMC.
New York: Century, 1914 NUC BMC.

TLS
PW 85 4/18/14 p. 300. "David, son of an English
quarryman, is a brilliant lad. His little sister,
Emily, a plodding faithful child, adores him. Oxford
professor secures David an appointment to a free
school and the lad absorbs the new atmosphere like a
sponge. He takes a scholarship and goes to Oxford,
where he meets and falls in love with Gwen, a
beautiful, high-born girl. There is a dramatic scene,
when David looks up from the dinner table, at this
aristocrat's house, to discover his sister Emily the
maid-servant who is waiting on the table. David proves
that he has the soul of a gentleman and Gwen, that she
is a real aristocrat."
TLS-Sugary romance

010912   BILLIE'S MOTHER: A NOVEL. New York:
Century, 1915 NUC. London: E. Arnold, 1915 BMC.

Sentimental story PW 2-27-15.
Mother protects her son against a bad father who is a
murderer serving a prison sentence. She hides her
child. NYT
A very melodramatic tale, wife who returns to husband
at end, promises to wait for him to complete his
second prison term. SP
"Development of a young girl's character". BKM

010913   THE DEVOUT LADY: A STUDY IN FOUR
CENTURIES. London: Constable, 1917 BMC NUC.

010914   THE HERITAGE OF ELISE. London: E. Arnold,
1917 BMC.

Village girl takes to the streets but unknown to her
she's an heiress. TLS

010915   THE HOUSE OF THE LUCK. London: Smith,
Elder, 1906 BMC NUC.

ACAD-story of a boy.

About a child. ATH SR

010916   A ROMANCE OF THE SIMPLE. London: E. Arnold, 1911 BMC NUC.

Focuses upon a "half-witted" son. TLS

010917   A STEP-SON OF THE SOIL. London: E. Arnold, 1910 BMC NUC.

ATH-country folk
SP-little boy hero.

010918   THE WORLD'S DELIGHT. London and New York: J. Lane, 1902 BMC NUC.

SKRINE, NESTA (HIGGINSON). United Kingdom.

010919   AN EASTER VACATION. BY MOIRA O'NEILL. London: Lawrence and Bullen, 1893 NUC BMC. New York: E. P. Dutton, 1894 NUC.

Mac an invalid boy. "Weak invertebrate Mrs. Forsyth" and Maisie "who gave the Cambridge tone...has all the qualities to be desired of a heroine who does not live by beauty alone." ACAD 43:322.
A leap year dance. No plot "man, from woman's point of view is treated with quiet sagacity and humor." ATH 101, 435
PW-Pupil and master at a resort.

010920   THE ELF-ERRANT. BY MOIRA O'NEILL. London: Lawrence and Bullen, 1895 BMC NUC. New York: Dodd, Mead, 1895 NUC.

SLADE, CHRISTINE JOPE.

010921   THE BREAD AND BUTTER MARRIAGE. London: Hodder & Stoughton, [1920] BMC.

010922   THE KEYS OF HEAVEN. London: Hodder & Stoughton, [1920] BMC.

010923   LOVE IN A MUDDLE. London: Hodder & Stoughton, [1920] BMC.

010924   MONTY'S GIRL. London: Hodder & Stoughton, [1920] BMC.

010925   WEDDING RINGS FOR THREE. London: Hodder & Stoughton, [1920] BMC.

SLATER, CATHERINE PONTON.

010926   MARGARET POW LOOKS BACK. London: Hodder & Stoughton, 1920 BMC.

TLS Sequel. Amusing talk of Scotswoman

010927   MARGET POW COMES HOME. London: Hodder & Stoughton, 1914 BMC.

TLS story of Scottish maid, a sequel.

010928   MARGET POW IN FOREIGN PARTS. London: Hodder & Stoughton, [1912] BMC [1913] NUC.

SLATTERY, MARGARET. United States.

010929   THE COSTLY STAR. Boston: Pilgrim Press, [c1917] NUC.

Estranged couple reunited by son. PW

SLEIGHT, MARY BRECK. D. 1928. United States.

010930   AT THE MANOR WHEN THE BRITISH HELD THE HUDSON. New York: R.F. Fenno, [c1912] NUC.

NYT patriotic, historical.

010931   AN ISLAND HEROINE: THE STORY OF A DAUGHTER OF THE REVOLUTION. Boston: Lothrop, [c1898] NUC.

PW-Margaret is heroine, grand daughter of Quaker. Her courtship, much historical information of British occupation of Long Island.

SLOAN, ANNIE LEE. B. 1861. United States.

010932   THE CAROLINIANS: AN OLD FASHIONED NOVEL OF STIRRING TIMES IN THE EARLY COLONY OF CAROLINA. New York: Neale, 1904 NUC.

Hist. rom. NYT 278,05

SLOCUM, CORA. See SAVORGNAN, CORA A. (SLOCOMB) BRAZZA.

SLOOT, NICOLINA MARIA CHRISTINA. 1853-1927.

010933   THE RESIDENT'S DAUGHTER. BY MELATI VAN JAVA. London: Henry, 1893 BMC. (Tr. A. Teixeira de Mattos.)

Colonial life in the Indian possessions of Holland: Java, Batavia. The heroine is a "half-caste", marriage de convenance. But love comes. SR 76:273.
Etty Klovens marries an East Indian government official. The resident's daughter is a child of his former wife-a Javanese woman. ACAD 44:190.
A melati is a favorite flower in Java. Dutch shown as vulgar, materialistic. Etty is a study of "heartless selfishness". Heroine is resident's daughter half-caste. ATH 102:284."Not afraid to make a half-caste girl the heroine."

SLOSSON, ANNIE (TRUMBULL). 1838-1926. United States.

010934   ANNA MALANN. Hartford, Conn.: Case, Lockwood and Brainard, 1894 NUC.

010935   AUNT ABBY'S NEIGHBORS. New York: F.H. Revell, 1902 BMC NUC.

Abby's views on sects, heaven, tithes, friendship etc. PW

010936   AUNT LIEFY. New York: A. D. F. Randolph, [c1892] NUC.

PW transformation of an irreligious and selfish woman to a kindly person.

010937   A DISSATISFIED SOUL, AND A PROPHETIC ROMANCER. New York: Bonnell, Silver, 1908 NUC.

NYT-Ghost

010938   THE HERESY OF MEHETABEL CLARK. New York: Harper, 1892 NUC.

LW 23:214. She is transformed by severe illness to wider experience of spiritual love.
CR 17:314. Story is narrated by male driving a car of tourists thru NE. He is not aware of the deeper significance of his story
PW Before illness she was a narrow Puritan. Her new and unorthodox religion arouses wrath of townspeople. "Pathetic last scene"

010939   WHITE CHRISTOPHER. New York: J. Pott, 1901 NUC. London: S. Bagster, 1901 BMC.

PW 3-9-01

SMART, MRS IRWIN.

010940   EBB AND FLOW, A NOVEL. London: G. Routledge, 1912 BMC.

Nan Ironside leaves home, moves to London, marries, desperate poverty, quarrel, parting, reconciliation. TLS
PW-Love story unhappy mar. reunion.
SR-Married a weak man who with two whiskeys on an empty stomach accused her of nagging and she threw a bread knife at him. He went off to fight the Boers, she achieved literary success but remained faithful to his memory. When he returned, short one leg, they reunited.
LBKM-Story of Nancy from babyhood to reconciliation. Also a painful earlier love.

010941   ONE LIFE AND THE NEXT. London: Sisley's, [1908] BMC.

TLS-Three love stories.

SMEATON, ANNIE.

010942   GORDON OGILVY. Edinburgh: Oliphant, Anderson, 1905 BMC NUC.

010943   IN THE SUPERLATIVE: A LOVE STORY. Edinburgh: Oliphant, Anderson & Ferrier, 1907 BMC.

010944   ON WINGS OF FIRE. A ROMANCE OF MOROCCO OF TO-DAY. London: J. & J. Bennett, [1912] BMC.

ATH-Rom

SMEDLEY, CONSTANCE. See ARMFIELD, ANNE CONSTANCE (SMEDLEY).

SMEETH, HELEN MARIE. B. 1865. Nationality Unknown.

    010945   THE LOG OF THREE ACROSS THE SEA. Chicago: Henneberry, 1910 NUC.

SMITH, ADELE CRAFTON.

    010946   CONCERNING A MARRIAGE. BY "NOMAD". London: Hurst & Blackett, 1904 BMC.

    LBKM Loveless marriage
    TLS-Careful and sincere.

    010947   REMINISCENCES OF A PRIMA DONNA. BY NOMAD. London: A. H. Stockwell, 1912 BMC.

    010948   A STRANGE WILL AND ITS CONSEQUENCE. BY NOMAD. London: A. H. Stockwell, [1913] BMC.

    010949   THE WOMAN DECIDES. BY "NOMAD". London: J. Ouseley, [1912] BMC.

    ATH Gushy, old fashioned.

SMITH, ALICE M. DEW.

    010950   CONFIDENCES OF AN AMATEUR GARDENER. London: Seeley, 1897 BMC.

    010951   THE DIARY OF A DREAMER. London: T. F. Unwin, 1900 BMC.

    CR 37:568. In the style of Elizabeth and her German garden, she is a nature lover.
    PW Diary. Mostly about domestic affairs. Everyday life of married woman.

SMITH, ALICE (PRESCOTT). B. 1868. United States.

    010952   THE LEGATEE. Boston: Houghton, Mifflin, 1903 NUC.

    Focus on hero's adventures PW 4-4-03
    The heroine flits from one man to another; later becomes "serious and much less entertaining." NYT 03 256
    "...The Legatee is really no worse than 99 per cent of the increasing flood of novels which now reaches us from across the Atlantic." ATH 121, 751

    010953   MONTLIVET. Boston: Houghton, Mifflin, 1906 NUC BMC. London: Constable, 1906 NUC.

    PW-Hist. novel.
    ACAD Hist nov.-heroine in male disguise rescued by hero-her mind tempered in a masculine school but essentially feminine and loveable

    010954   OFF THE HIGHWAY. Boston: Houghton, Mifflin, 1904 NUC.

    NYT-The author seems to desire to point out the folly of a too critical masculine attitude toward women.

SMITH, ANNIE H.

    010955   ROSEMARY LEIGH; A STORY OF THE SOUTH. New York: Neale, 1905 NUC.

SMITH, ANNIE LAURA.

    010956   ROSINE; THE STORY OF A FAIR YOUNG GIRL. BY CATHERINE VON SCYLER. New York and London: Broadway, 1903 NUC.

    The attempted revenge and horrid fate of a woman scorned; pleaded with man she loved to love her; he saw her as a friend; she steals his children after he's married. NYT 03, 913

SMITH, ANNIE S. (SWAN). 1859-1945. United Kingdom.

    010957   AN AMERICAN WOMAN. BY ANNIE S. SWAN. London: Hutchinson, 1900 BMC. New York: Dutton, [n.d.] NUC.

    ATH 116:819 Wealthy heroine.

    010958   ANNE HYDE, TRAVELLING COMPANION. London: Hodder & Stoughton, 1908 BMC.

    TLS-Angel of mercy and her employers

    010959   THE ANSWER TO A CHRISTMAS PRAYER. BY ANNIE S. SWAN. [New York]: [P. F. Collier], [1894] NUC.

    010960   THE AYRES OF STUDLEIGH. BY ANNIE S. SWAN. Edinburgh: Oliphant, 1891 BMC. Cincinnati: Cranston and Stowe, [1891] NUC.

    Love stories of several couples in Warwickshire, England. PW

    010961   A BACHELOR IN SEARCH OF A WIFE, AND ROGER MARCHAM'S WARD. BY ANNIE S. SWAN. Edinburgh: Oliphant, 1892 BMC NUC.

    010962   A BITTER DEBT, A TALE OF THE BLACK COUNTRY. London: Hutchinson, 1893 BMC.

    "A justice, his sharp little niece, and the workaday above-her-station heroine he marries." ATH 10 2:879.

    010963   THE BONDAGE OF RICHES. London: S. W. Partridge, [1912] BMC.

    010964   THE BRIDGE BUILDERS. BY ANNIE S. SWAN. London: Hodder & Stoughton, [1913] NUC BMC.

    American learns a colleague plans to destroy bridge-tracks him down to kill him but forestalled in Paris, reunited with his love who has accepted someone else. ATH

    010965   THE BROAD ROAD. London: Hurst and Blackett, 1908 BMC.

    Love, tangles, Jewish theme. LBKM
    TLS-Jewel Robbery

    010966   THE BURDEN-BEARERS. London: Hutchinson, 1900 BMC.

    010967   CHRISTIAN'S CROSS; OR, TESTED BUT TRUE. London: Hodder & Stoughton, 1905 BMC.

    010968   CORRODING GOLD. London: Cassell, 1914 BMC.

    ATH Effect of sudden wealth on middle-class family

    010969   THE CURSE OF COWDEN. London: Hutchinson, 1897 BMC.

    010970   ELIZABETH GLEN, M.B.: THE EXPERIENCES OF A LADY DOCTOR. London: Hutchinson, 1895 BMC.

    She makes a fortune as a doctor. Very sympathetic with her patients. Marries in the end. SR 80:21
    Beautiful woman doctor. She's an exceptional practitioner with great sympathy for her patients. She amasses a fortune and a victoria. Finally retires to marry a good nobleman. SR 80:21
    Settles down professionally in Bloomsbury after she takes her degree. Ministers to minds as well as bodies. SP 75:468
    Dr. Glen says all men doctors would go on treating the body when the mind is the problem as in Nora Fleming's case. ACAD 48:28

    010971   THE FAIRWEATHERS. A STORY OF THE OLD WORLD AND THE NEW. London: Hodder and Stoughton, 1913 BMC.

    Four orphan young women brought up without professions. Janet Fairweather goes to Canada to earn her living. All four Janet, Bella, Madge and Nancy make successful marriages in the end. SP

    010972   THE FARRANTS. A STORY OF STRUGGLE AND VICTORY. London: C. H. Kelly, 1913 BMC.

    010973   A FAVORITE OF FORTUNE. London: Cassell, 1912 BMC.

    ATH rom and inher.

    010974   FETTERED YET FREE; A STUDY IN HEREDITY. BY ANNIE S. SWAN. New York: Dodd, Mead, 1895 NUC.

    Scotland: fettered by love of drink-hereditary, but frees himself through noble efforts. PW 10-12-95:636 BKM 2:435. Fife, Scotland.

    010975   A FOOLISH MARRIAGE: AN EDINBURGH STORY OF STUDENT LIFE. BY ANNIE S. SWAN (MRS. BURNETT-SMITH). London: Hutchinson, 1894 BMC. Toronto: W. Briggs, [1894] NUC.

SR-goody-goody heroine, two lovers.
ACAD-left penniless, supports herself by helping aunt
run a boarding house for med students, one is the
hero.

010976   THE GUINEA STAMP; A TALE OF MODERN
GLASGOW. BY ANNIE S. SWAN. Cincinnati: Cranston and
Curts, 1892 NUC. Edinburgh: Oliphant, 1892 BMC.

010977   HANDS ACROSS THE SEA. London: Oliphant,
[1919] BMC.

Life of Scot family in Canada simple, charming TLS

010978   HESTER LANE. London: Hodder & Stoughton,
1908 BMC.

TLS-mild agreeable tale of how young woman started an
employment agency.
BKM-abandons business when she becomes engaged.

010979   THE INHERITANCE. London: Hodder &
Stoughton, 1909 BMC.

010980   KINSFOLK. London: Hutchinson, 1896 BMC.

ATH 108:220. Scottish. Domestic tale of middle-aged
bachelor clergyman in Glasgow.
ACAD 50:160. Deceptions practised on him by his
kinsfolk.

010981   THE LAST OF THEIR RACE. London: Hodder &
Stoughton, [1911] BMC.

Courageous highland girl is head of house because of
aged father and a brother disgraced. ATH

010982   LETTERS TO A WAR BRIDE. BY ANNIE S. SWAN.
London: Hodder & Stoughton, [1915] BMC NUC.

010983   A LOST IDEAL. BY ANNIE S. SWAN. Edinburgh
& London: Oliphant, 1894 BMC. New York: Ward, Lock &
Bowden, [c1894] NUC.

SP 73:928. Good wife married to artist leaves him when
she overhears him making love to an old flame who is
rejecting his advances. Later their reconciliation and
her improvement of him as a man and an artist.
LBKM 7:57. There is a Miss Ryder writing her 37th
three volume novel.
PW-he is an author.

010984   LOVE GIVES ITSELF: THE STORY OF A BLOOD
FEUD. London: Hodder & Stoughton, 1915 BMC.

010985   LOVE GROWN COLD. London: Methuen, 1902
BMC.

010986   LOVE, THE MASTER KEY. London: Hodder &
Stoughton, 1905 BMC.

010987   LOVE UNLOCKS THE DOOR. London: Hodder &
Stoughton, 1907 BMC.

010988   LOVE'S BARRIER. London: Cassell, 1910
BMC.

BM for home reading
TLS-For home reading

010989   LOVE'S CROWN. SONGS OF MEMORY AND HOPE.
Edinburgh: W. P. Nimmo, [1913] BMC.

010990   LOVE'S MIRACLE. London: Hodder and
Stoughton, 1910 BMC.

010991   THE MAGIC OF LOVE. London: Hodder &
Stoughton, 1909 BMC.

010992   MAITLAND OF LAURIESTON; A FAMILY HISTORY.
BY ANNIE S. SWAN. London and Edinburgh: Oliphant, 1891
BMC. Cincinatti: Jennings and Pye, [n.d.] NUC.

A family history: Presbyterian farmer sees son grow to
give up farm and become agnostic--but he's
Christianized by pious wife. BAKER 03,223
Scotch. Wife is Agnes Laurie. Son becomes agnostic in
part because father is so strict. PW
Death of their child also helps reform him. SR
1-3-91,20

010993   MARGARET HOLROYD; OR, THE PIONEERS.
London: Hodder & Stoughton, 1910 BMC.

TLS a story of "the Woman's Cause"
LBKM-and its effect on various lives, those who are

awakened by it, those who become weary and drop out.

010994   MARY GARTH: A CLYDESIDE ROMANCE. London:
Hodder & Stoughton, 1904 BMC.

010995   A MASK OF GOLD. THE MYSTERY OF THE
MEADOWS. London: Hodder & Stoughton, 1906 BMC. London:
Oliphant, [1953] NUC.

010996   MEG HAMILTON, AN AYRSHIRE ROMANCE.
London: Hodder & Stoughton, 1914 BMC.

TLS Popular, wholesome. Mrg preserves her virtue in
spite of living in midst of waste, gambling, and
impending ruin.

010997   MEMORIES OF MARGARET GRAINGER,
SCHOOLMISTRESS. London: Hutchinson, 1896 BMC. London:
Hutchinson, [n.d.] NUC.

She is a schoolmistress. In each of the 11 chapters
she describes one of her female pupils--all
individuals and interesting. Many love stories. These
stories make up her auto-biography. SP 78:98
SR-Lives and destinies of some of her pupils. Virtuous
examples.
ATH 107:33. Good reading for young people.
ACAD 49:424. "The business of a schoolmistress has
from all time been considered appropriate to women."

010998   MRS. KEITH HAMILTON, M.B. MORE
EXPERIENCES OF ELIZABETH GLEN. London: Hutchinson,
1897 BMC.

"Experiences of a Lady Doctor" continued. Now she is
retired and plans to establish a home for women who
work in dress-making establishments. SP 79:566.

010999   THE MYSTERY OF BARRY INGRAM. London:
Cassell, 1910 BMC.

TLS-Innocent Fugitive from justice.

011000   NANCY NICOLSON; OR, WHO SHALL BE HEIR?
London: Hodder & Stoughton, 1906 BMC.

011001   THE NE'ER-DO-WEEL. London: Hutchinson,
[1897] BMC.

Donald Orde generally misbehaves as a boy but grows to
be good, noble a pillar of soc. ACAD 52:Fic sup. 97.
Unwittingly commits bigamy, but it's his wife's fault.
She pretends to commit suicide. Ends up in Parliament.
ATH 110:745.

011002   NOT YET: A PAGE FROM A NOBLE LIFE.
London: Hutchinson, [1898] BMC.

011003   THE OLD MOORINGS. A STORY OF MODERN LIFE.
London: R. Culley, [1909] BMC NUC.

011004   PRAIRIE FIRES. London: Cassell, 1913 BMC.

Set in England and Canada ATH

011005   RHONA KEITH. London: Hodder & Stoughton,
1910 BMC.

011006   THE RULING PASSION. London: People's
Friend Library, [1920] BMC.

011007   SHEILA. BY ANNIE S. SWAN (MRS. BURNETT
SMITH). Cincinnati: Cranston and Stowe, [1891] NUC.

Sheila Murray's father dies; mother remarries. When
mother and step-father die, Sheila owns Dalmore
(estate). There's a bitter feeling because a young boy
loses the expected inheritance. But all ends happily.
PW 9-12-91.

011008   A SON OF ERIN, BY ANNIE S. SWAN (MRS.
BURNETT SMITH). London: Hutchinson, 1899 BMC.

011009   SONGS OF MEMORY AND HOPE. BY ANNIE S.
SWAN. Edinburgh: W. P. Nimmo, [1911] BMC. New York: H.
M. Caldwell, [c1911] NUC.

011010   THE STEP-MOTHER. London: Hodder &
Stoughton, 1915 BMC.

011011   A STORMY VOYAGER. London: Hutchinson,
[1896] BMC.

ATH 108:899. Domestic for family reading, although
wife runs away from her husband, nothing really bad
happens and she comes to see the error of her ways.

011012   TO FOLLOW THE LEAD. London: C. H. Kelly,
1911 BMC.

011013   A VICTORY WON. London: Hutchinson, 1895
BMC.

011014   WHAT SHALL IT PROFIT? OR, RODEN'S CHOICE.
BY ANNIE S. SWAN. London: S. W. Partridge, [1910] BMC.
[n.d.] NUC.

011015   WHO SHALL SERVE? A STORY FOR THE TIMES.
London: Oliphant, 1891 BMC.

Dorothea Redmond and James Wentworth improve the
social conditions of strikers in a shipyard in Malden.
After the owner's attempts to avoid a strike fail. PW
12-19

011016   THE WOMAN'S PART. London: Hodder &
Stoughton, [1916] BMC.

011017   WOVEN OF THE WIND. London: Hodder &
Stoughton, 1912 BMC.

011018   WYNDHAM'S DAUGHTER. A STORY OF TO-DAY.
London: Hutchinson, 1898 BMC.

LIT 2:591. Socialism in London.
ACAD 53:55. "Dedicated to those among my young sisters
who are discontented with their lot, in the hope that
the true record of Joyce Wyndham's experience may help
them to take up with cheerfulness the duty which lies
nearest."
ATH 111:433. Heroine is a revolted daughter who takes
up Socialism and lives in a settlement in London.
Learns her lesson and returns to fold.

011019   YOUNG BLOOD. London: Hodder & Stoughton,
[1917] BMC.

SMITH, ANNIE S. (SWAN). See Also LYALL, DAVID [pseud.].

SMITH, AUGUSTA A. VARTY.

011020   MATTHEW TINDALE. A NOVEL. London:
Bentley, 1891 BMC.

Blacksmith's daughter betrayed by idle young squire
who loves a cultured woman of his own class. Matthew
Tindale the blacksmith and the young squire meet at
cliff's edge. There's a murder. ATH 98:859
SP-novel begins much resembling Adam Bede. Maggie is
Hetty, Matthew is Adam. But he is Maggie's brother,
Sidney is her lover. But this beginning is an
"expedient to prepare the ground for another story
infinitely richer in both moral and intellectual
fascination." Matthew, a kind and controlled man
realizes that in a moment of passion he has killed
someone, and that to spare someone else, he can't
confess.
SR 73:74. Maggie was in love with her seducer,
Aschenburg. Matthew goes to prison, faces trial
without talking.

SMITH, CARRIE CLAY. United States.

011021   PASSING SHADOWS AND A LIFE'S SORROW.
Macon, Missouri: Times Pub. House, 1892 NUC.

SMITH, CATHERINE GRANT FURLEY.

011022   QUIXOTE, THE WEAVER. London: Hurst and
Blackett, 1892 BMC NUC.

SP 69:419. Scottish manufacturing town. Factory life.
Head of factory is Quixotic, treats employees as human
beings.
ACAD 42:210. he is a socialist, misunderstood and
disliked for his actions. he is supported by his wife
and Lindsay Lorimer, a violinist "of lofty
aspirations."

011023   AN UNSOUGHT HERITAGE. London: Hurst and
Blackett, 1896 BMC.

SMITH, CICELY FOX. D. 1954. United Kingdom.

011024   THE CITY OF HOPE. A STORY OF THE NEW
WEST. London & Toronto: Sidgwick and Jackson, 1914 BMC
NUC.

LBKM-Rev. says it's 1st novel, by a woman. Mark, an
Englishman, makes his way in Canada as a farmer.
ATH-Hardships endured because of fraudulent sale of
land to his father who thinks it will be good for his

son.

011025   PEREGRINE IN LOVE. A COMEDY. London:
Hodder & Stoughton, [1920] BMC.

TLS-Male hero & simple girl.

011026   SINGING SANDS: AN EPISODE. London: Hodder
& Stoughton, 1918 BMC.

TLS-Eng heroine in British Columbia falls in love.

SMITH, CLARA AND THEODORA BOSANQUET.

011027   SPECTATORS. London: Constable, 1916 BMC.

SMITH, CONSTANCE ISABEL. B. 1894. United Kingdom.

011028   ADAM'S FIRST WIFE. London: A. Melrose,
[1920] BMC NUC.

TLS-Left by her lover, marries farmer. Eventually
lover comes back. Life on the farm. Is she a
librarian?

SMITH, CONSTANCE ISABELLA STUART. United Kingdom.

011029   THE BACKSLIDER: A STORY OF TODAY. London:
Bentley, 1896 BMC.

SP 77:943. Classed as "novel of reaction" as opposed
to "novel of revolt." Katherine, modern, writes a
"hill-top" novel, published anonymously. Marries a
scholar. Authorship is made known to her husband by a
former lover; estrangement and reconciliation. Other
feminist characters (I guess the debating society)
unconverted.
Young woman, intelligent, raised among "bad bold"
people writes a "very naughty" book. Repents the
publication, but it goes into 7 editions. There's a
villain who knows she wrote it and a husband who
doesn't. Lives in a university town. Ends in
confession and forgiveness. Serious. SR 83:100.

011030   CORBAN. London: Hurst & Blackett, 1901
BMC.

ATH 7-13-01

011031   A CUMBERER OF THE GROUND; A NOVEL. New
York: Harper, 1894 NUC. London: Methuen, 1894 BMC.

SR 78:130. Heroine marries out of duty although loving
another. Many times tempted but steadfastly loyal.
SP 72:119. She has promised Brian's mother she would
marry, so she does, even though she and Lyon know they
love each other.
CR 25:331. She leaves her husband, is persuaded to go
back, more trouble.
LW 25:282. He was "faithful to the highest needs of
the one woman he loved."

011032   LOVE HATH WINGS. London: Isbister, 1899
BMC.

One young man wants a rich woman to marry him and help
in his philanthropic works, but he doesn't; young
woman seeks to marry rich to help her poor family, but
doesn't. The loves of the two are true-basically. LBKM
16:141

011033   THE MAGIC WORD. London: Isbister, 1900
BMC.

SP 84:778. South American republic, political
adventure.

011034   ONE WAY OF LOVE. London: Hurst and
Blackett, 1893 BMC.

SP 69:824. "Amiable and unselfish" heroine with "good
sense." Anxiety caused by her sister and two brothers.
Her progress from poverty to a desire for Chippendale
to a realization that she can be happy in ordinary
surroundings with a man she loves.

011035   PRISONERS OF HOPE. London: A. D. Innes,
1898 BMC.

SP 81:565. "Merciless study in feminine meanness."
Linda marries Richard, a philanthropic slum-worker in
the East End. Discovers she cannot stand the life,
manipulates her husband so that she spends more and
more time away from it. Richard forgives her; at the
conclusion she says, "I wish I were a different sort
of woman. I should like to have made you happy. But

it's useless pretending...I would care, as you want me
to care--if I could; but I can't. There is no more to
be said about it."
LIT 3:472. When smallpox epidemic breaks out and she
wants to run away, he considers her cowardice unworthy
of a clergyman's wife.
Linda Ainslie marries a clergy opposite to her in
nature. Joins him in his work in the slums. But soon
tires of the slums and of him. Then a wordly admirer
comes along. SR 87:217.

SMITH, ELISE HOWARD. B. 1893. United States.

011036   A KNIGHT OF TODAY. Philadelphia: J. C.
Winston, 1919 NUC.

Love story: theme "the danger of a girl's ignorance of
vital truths". PW
"The girl who knew too little." NYT

SMITH, ELIZABETH THOMASINA (MEADE). 1854-1914. United
Kingdom.

011037   THE A.B.C. GIRL. London: F.V. White, 1910
BMC.

011038   THE ADVENTURES OF MIRANDA. London: J.
Long, 1904 BMC.

BKM Trad. Love Story

011039   AN ADVENTURESS. BY L. T. MEADE. London:
Chatto and Windus, 1899 BMC NUC.

She assumes identity of an heiress who dies young.
Takes over her whole life. Is punished at the
end--loss of memory and "a mod ified kind of idiocy."
LB 17:63
SR 89:23. She personates an heiress but part way
through gives up and sinks into partial insanity.

011040   THE AIM OF HER LIFE. London: J. Long,
1908 BMC.

011041   ALL SORTS. London: J. Nisbet, 1899 BMC
NUC.

Widow and daughter down to last pennies start a
boarding house in Bloomsbury. Their
housekeeper-partner "draws up a tariff on such a basis
as to render profit impossible." SP 83:702
Westerna Wickham determines to support self and mother
when their money gone. Society is outraged by her
actions. Friends scorn her except two. All sorts come
to her boarding house, lovers among them. ATH. 114:831

011042   AT THE BACK OF THE WORLD. London: Hurst &
Blackett, 1904 BMC.

LBKM love story

011043   AYLWYN'S FRIENDS. BY L. T. MEADE. London:
W. & R. Chambers, 1909 BMC NUC.

011044   A BAND OF MIRTH. London: W. & R.
Chambers, 1914 BMC.

011045   BELINDA TREHERNE. London: J. Long, 1910
BMC.

TLS ghost story
LBKM-young woman answers ad for governess with strong
nerves.

011046   BESS OF DELANY'S. London: Digby, Long,
1905 BMC.

factory life; splendid heroine persuades the man she
loves to marry her friend who is too weak to do
factory work, sympathetic description of factory
workers, a strike. Bess and man she loves now married
to her friend do good work LBKM v 29-30

011047   BETTER THAN RICHES. London: W. & R.
Chambers, 1917 BMC.

011048   BETTY OF THE RECTORY. BY MRS. L. T.
MEADE. New York: Grosset & Dunlop, [c1908] NUC.
London: Cassell, 1908 BMC.

PW-ideal clergyman's wife
TLS-ideal clergyman's wife

011049   BETTY VIVIAN: A STORY OF HADDO COURT
SCHOOL. Philadelphia: Lippincott, 1909 PW. London: W.
& R. Chambers, 1909 BMC.

011050   THE BLUE DIAMOND. BY L. T. MEADE. London:
Chatto & Windus, 1901 BMC NUC.

011051   BLUE OF THE SEA. London: J. Nisbet, 1909
BMC.

011052   A BRAVE POOR THING. BY L. T. MEADE.
London: Isbister, [1899] NUC 1900 BMC.

SP 88:675. Story of a typewriter girl.

011053   BRIDE OF TO-MORROW. London: "Daily Mail",
[1904] BMC.

011054   BROTHER OR HUSBAND. London: F.V. White,
1909 BMC.

story of scandals, TLS
"a deceased-wife's-sister novel" SP

011055   THE BURDEN OF HER YOUTH. London: J. Long,
1903 BMC.

goes to London to make her own way; story closes in
marriage. ACAD 65,60

011056   BY MUTUAL CONSENT. London: Digby, Long,
1903 BMC.

case of exact likeness two men, one a scoundrel. LBKM
1903 29

011057   CASTLE POVERTY. London: J. Nisbet, 1904
BMC.

011058   CATALINA: ART STUDENT. BY L. T. MEADE.
London and Edinburgh: W.&R.Chambers, 1896 BMC.
Philadelphia: J.B. Lippincott, 1897 NUC.

Love plays no part. Catalina is young art student.
Much more resolute and strong than mother and sisters.
Her relationship to the old scholar; her successes.
ACAD 51:146

011059   CAVE PERILOUS. London: Religious Tract
Society, [1898] BMC.

SP 81:716. Bread riots. For young readers.

011060   THE CHATEAU OF MYSTERY. London: Everett,
1907 BMC.

011061   THE CLEVEREST WOMAN IN ENGLAND. London:
J. Nisbet, 1898 BMC. Boston: A. I. Bradley, 1899 NUC.

SP 81:531. Dagmar, modern emancipated woman married to
an uncompromising prig, Geoffrey, a literary man. She
is brilliant, high minded.
LIT 3:423. She devotes all her energies to the cause
of her sex and its wrongs, and is the idol of the
female multitude, while her husband holds views
diametrically opposed to hero. Dagmar dies of smallpox
before her troubles come to a head.

011062   THE COLONEL AND THE BOY. London: Hodder &
Stoughton, [1906] BMC.

011063   THE COLONEL'S CONQUEST. BY LAURA T.
MEADE. Philadelphia: G.W. Jacobs, [1907] NUC.

about a boy and his mother PW 8-31-07
"story of a frivolous mother's awakening to
womanliness and mother love through the devotion of
her little lame child. Book contains a lesson for
grown up readers even tho written for the young" BRD

011064   THE CONFESSIONS OF A COURT MILLINER. BY
L. T. MEADE. London: J. Long, [1902] BMC NUC.

ACAD o
ATH 9-27-02 "carelessly written records of wildly
improbable events" "cheap stuff"

011065   CORPORAL VIOLET. London: Hodder &
Stoughton, [1912] BMC.

TLS-soldier hero

011066   COSEY CORNER: OR, HOW THEY KEPT A FARM.
London: W. & R. Chambers, 1901 BMC.

011067   THE COURT-HARMAN GIRLS. New York: Dutton,
1908 PW. London: W. & R. Chambers, 1908 BMC.

011068   THE COURTSHIP OF SYBIL. London: J. Long,

1908 BMC.

TLS

011069   THE CURSE OF THE FEVERALS. London: J.
Long, 1907 BMC.

011070   THE DARLING OF THE SCHOOL. London: W. &
R. Chambers, 1915 BMC.

011071   THE DAUGHTER OF A SOLDIER, A COLLEEN OF
SOUTH IRELAND. BY MRS. L. T. MEADE. New York: Hurst,
[c1915] BMC NUC.

011072   DAUGHTERS OF TODAY. London: H. Frowde,
Hodder & Stoughton, 1917 BMC.

011073   DESBOROUGH'S WIFE. London: Digby, Long,
1911 BMC.

man married poor woman tries to marry rich one as well
TLS

011074   THE DESIRE OF MEN: AN IMPOSSIBILITY.
London: Digby, Long, 1899 BMC.

About hypnosis and the transfusion of the vital
principles. SP 83:500.
Eugenia holds her grandfather's hands, looks into his
eyes intensely and transforms this 75 year-old to a
young man of full vigour-immortal. The power comes
from Dr. Jellybrand. ACAD 57:310
LIT 6:51. Man runs inexpensive boarding house serving
luxurious food, makes old boarders young, through
occult powers.

011075   A DOUBLE REVENGE. London: Digby, Long,
1902 BMC.

011076   DRIFT. London: Methuen, 1902 BMC.

ATH 3-22-02 not helpful

011077   DUMPS: A PLAIN GIRL. BY L. T. MEADE. New
York: E.P. Dutton, 1905 NUC. London: W. & R. Chambers,
1905 BMC.

011078   ELIZABETH'S PRISONER. London: S. Paul,
1914 BMC.

ATH-Hides an escaped convict in her studio.

011079   ENGAGED TO BE MARRIED. A TALE OF TODAY.
London: Griffith, Farran, [1895] BMC.

SP 76:642. Three young women in a flat. Helen,
practical and absorbed in her work. Dorothea, her
sister, an artistic genius. Emany, quiet, engaged to
be married with a poor, dependent family at home, is
the heroine. "A story we heartily recommend to young
ladies of the would-be intellectual and self-sufficing
type."

011080   THE FACE OF JULIET. London: J. Long, 1906
BMC.

LBKM conv love story

011081   FOR DEAR DAD. London: W. & R. Chambers,
1911 BMC.

011082   THE FOUNTAIN OF BEAUTY. BY L. T. MEADE.
London: J. Long, [1909] BMC NUC.

about a jewel TLS

011083   FROM THE HAND OF THE HUNTER. London: J.
Long, 1906 BMC.

TLS-mother by a piece of culpable folly has killed her
own daughter.

011084   THE GIRL AND HER FORTUNE. London: Hodder
& Stoughton, 1906 BMC.

2 delightful orphaned ladies-neither of them has a
lover in the end--TLS

011085   A GIRL FROM AMERICA. New York: Dutton,
1907 PW. London: W. & R. Chambers, 1907 BMC.

011086   THE GIRL FROM SPAIN. London: Digby, Long,
1911 BMC.

TLS-Spanish girl in England rectory with scenes of
journalistic life.

011087   A GIRL IN TEN THOUSAND. BY L. T. MEADE.
Edinburgh and London: Oliphant, [1896] BMC. New York:
T. Whittaker, 1897 NUC.

ATH 108:901. For girls.
SP 77:622. Effie wants to nurse, but has
responsibilities at home (mother is feeble). She goes,
but after a time has to give up nrsg. "to retrieve the
family fortunes, ruined by an unconscionable brother."

011088   A GIRL OF TODAY. London: J. Long, 1910
BMC.

TLS

011089   THE GIRLS OF ABINGER CLOSE. London: W. &
R. Chambers, 1913 BMC.

011090   THE GIRLS OF MERTON COLLEGE. BY MRS. L.
T. MEADE. New York: Hurst, [1911] BMC NUC.

011091   THE GIRLS OF ST. WODE'S. BY L. T. MEADE.
London and Edinburgh: W.&R. Chambers, 1898 BMC. New
York: Mershon, [1902?] NUC.

SP 81:808. Shows her readers, most of them, it is to
be presumed, likely to be girls, one aspect of the new
order of things, the careers open to women. St. Wode's
is a women's college.

011092   GIRLS OF THE FOREST. BY L. T. MEADE.
London: W. & R. Chambers, 1902 BMC NUC. New York: E.P.
Dutton, 1912 [?] NUC.

011093   A GOLDEN SHADOW. London: Ward, Lock, 1906
BMC.

TLS-Typical L.T. Meade

011094   GOOD LUCK. BY L. T. MEADE. London: J.
Nisbet, 1896 BMC. Boston: 1897 NUC.

London East End workers: Grannie Reed earns a scant
livelihood by needlework. Chiefly by her wonderful
feather stitch, a family tradition. Loses use of her
arm. ACAD 51:146

011095   GREATER THAN GOLD. London: Ward, Lock,
1915 BMC.

teaches the value of a good heart. TLS

011096   A HANDFUL OF SILVER. Edinburgh and
London: Oliphant, 1897 BMC. New York: E.P. Dutton,
1898 NUC.

LIT 3:18. "Silly and unwholesome." Dorothy refuses to
marry man
She loves because dead father has left large debt
which she feels she must pay herself. If she allowed
her husband to do it, it would destroy their
relationship.
ATH 111:19. Audrey is wildly devoted to someone who
loves her cousin. Her struggling, suffering mother,
"ever sinning for the sake of the beloved child, whom
she nevertheless recognizes to be a light weight in
the scales."
PW-mother appropriates inheritance actually her
niece's for the sake of her daughter. Consequences of
her dishonesty.

011097   THE HEART OF HELEN. London: J. Long, 1906
BMC.

TLS 2 girls and Russian revolutionaries

011098   HEPSY GIPSY. London: Methuen, 1891 BMC.

011099   HER HAPPY FACE. London: Ward, Lock, 1914
BMC.

ATH-Happiness threatened by sins of her mother, but
she becomes a "happy wife."

011100   HETTY BERESFORD. London: Hodder &
Stoughton, 1908 BMC.

TLS-poor little girl

011101   THE HILL-TOP GIRL. BY L. T. MEADE.
London: W. & R. Chambers, 1906 BMC NUC. New York: A.
L. Burt, [192-?] NUC.

011102   HIS MASCOT. London: J. Long, 1905 BMC.

Caryl introduced as a thief, steals and lies, must marry or she'll be exposed. 881,05 ACAD

011103   HOLLYHOCK: A SPIRIT OF MISCHIEF. London: W. & R. Chambers, 1916 BMC.

011104   THE HOME OF SILENCE. London: Sisley's, 1907 BMC.

Molly-strong ACAD
love story TLS

011105   THE HOME OF SWEET CONTENT. London: F.V. White, 1906 BMC.

TLS

011106   THE HOUSE OF BLACK MAGIC. London: F.V. White, 1912 BMC NUC.

011107   I WILL SING A NEW SONG. London: Hodder & Stoughton, 1909 BMC.

woman married to musician unhappily till her "secret" cleared up TLS

011108   IN AN IRON GRIP; A NOVEL. London: Chatto and Windus, 1894 BMC NUC.

Sensational, concerns the stage. Esther Claymore and Frank Forbes marry. Esther learns her wicked uncle stole her mother's diamonds, so she forged his name on a check. The uncle came after her, locked her up. She escapes, gets five years at old Bailey. Came out none the worse but had many adventures in prison. SR 79:229.

011109   IN THE FLOWER OF HER YOUTH. London: J. Nisbet, 1906 BMC.

TLS-Typical L. T. Meade

011110   JILL, A FLOWER GIRL. BY L. T. MEADE. London: Isbister, [1893] BMC. New York: T. Whittaker, 1893 NUC.

Jill Robinson makes a precarious living selling flowers to the rich in the West End. Story tells of her heroic act concerning her alcoholic mother. PW 8-5-93.

011111   JILL. BY L. T. MEADE. New York: U. S. Book, [c1892] NUC.

011112   JILL THE IRRESISTIBLE. New York: Hurst, [1915] BMC.

011113   KINDRED SPIRITS. London: J. Long, 1907 BMC.

mystery about a Scottish estate TLS

011114   LADY ANNE. London: J. Nisbet, 1910 BMC.

011115   THE LADY CAKE-MAKER. London: Hodder & Stoughton, 1904 BMC.

011116   THE LADY OF DELIGHT. London: Hodder and Stoughton, 1907 BMC.

Dorothea & her grandfather TLS

011117   A LIFE FOR A LOVE; A STORY OF TO-DAY. BY L. T. MEADE. New York: U. S. Book, [c1891] NUC. London: Digby, Long, [1894] BMC.

ACAD 46:552. Man marries daughter, lives with her a year so her father can collect his life insurance and pay off 80,000 lb debt. He returns from the Antipodes three years later, his health broken, reunion with wife, then he dies. She's noble.
Plot to insure son-in-law for a large sum and then get rid of him by a fraudulent announcement of death. Wyndheim offers to do the disappearing in order to marry the villain's daugther Esther. ATH 105:13 Montimer Pagent represents a once great ship-building company. Sets in motion a sinister scheme. His daughter is loved by a parson who gives a life for love. PW 3-16-91.

011118   LIGHT O' THE MORNING; THE STORY OF AN IRISH GIRL. BY L. T. MEADE. London & Edinburgh: W. & R. Chambers, 1899 BMC. New York: Dutton, 1900 NUC.

011119   LITTLE JOSEPHINE. London: J. Long, 1907 BMC.

TLS-nice girls do not marry bad rich young men.

011120   LITTLE WIFE HESTER. London: J. Long, 1905 BMC.

marital difficulties but all comes out all right. heroine considerable force "wrong headedness" ATH269,05

011121   LORD AND LADY KITTY. London: F.V. White, 1912 BMC.

ATH-fairy tale
TLS-fairy tale

011122   THE LOVE OF SUSAN CARDIGAN. London: Digby, Long, 1907 BMC.

mild story TLS

011123   LOVE TRIUMPHANT. London: T.F. Unwin, 1904 BMC.

011124   LOVEDAY: THE STORY OF AN HEIRESS. London: Hodder & Stoughton, 1905 BMC.

011125   LOVE'S CROSS ROADS. London: s. Paul, [1912] BMC.

ATH-for girls
SP-for girls

011126   A MADCAP. BY MRS. L. T. MEADE. Rahway, N.J.: Mershon, [1904] NUC. London: Cassell, 1904 BMC.

011127   MADGE MOSTYN'S NIECES. London: W. & R. Chambers, 1916 BMC.

011128   THE MAID INDOMITABLE. London: Ward, Lock, 1916 BMC.

011129   A MAID OF MYSTERY. London: F.V. White, 1904 BMC.

011130   THE MAID WITH THE GOGGLES. London: Digby, Long, 1906 BMC.

TLS-Private sensational history of female "model" typist in a detective firm.

011131   MARGARET. London: F.V. white, 1902 BMC.

ATH 7-12-02 "mild domestic fiction"

011132   MARY GIFFORD, M.B. London: Wells Gardner, 1898 BMC.

SP 81:914. Woman doctor, "energetic, rather than attractive." "Display of expert knowleage somehow detracts from the charm of the story."
ACAD 55:378. Heroine, is bachelor of medicine. Heroine's narrative.
ATH 112:861. She establishes a dispensary at Hoxton and accomplishes much.
She's a doctor. The old doctor admires her, She fell in love with John Erle. The old Dr. is Dr. Follett. LBKM 15:187

011133   THE MEDICINE LADY. BY L. T. MEADE. London: Cassell, 1892 BMC. New York: Cassell, [c1892] NUC.

LBKM3:61. She uses the drug timialy at first with much success. When the story closes, with her child dying, she loses her mind.
CR 18:248. Story of woman who has been passing out "lymph" a medicine her dying husband commanded her not to use, confesses To a mob in street that it is imperfect and that she has killed her child with it. She is stabbed by man in crowd.
LW 23:407. Story opens with Cecilia Harvey, a young nurse on probation in a hospital. she fails to get the position because she is impulsive and sensitive. Dr Digby takes an interest in her and they marry.
ACAD 40:585. she tries the medicine on herself, first, and is cured.

011134   MERRY GIRLS OF ENGLAND. BY L. T. MEADE. London: Cassell, 1896 BMC. Boston: A.I. Bradley, [1897] NUC.

SP 77:903. Story of three girls running a farm and making it pay.

011135   MICAH FARADAY, ADVENTURER. London: Ward,

Lock, 1910 BMC.

TLS-murder

011136   MISS GWENDOLINE. London: J. Long, [1911]
BMC.

011137   MOTHER AND SON. London: Ward, Lock, 1911
BMC.

morbidly sentimental TLS
woman has child and heir after 7 years of marriage,
but boy dies when father's away; she substitutes
another child. Loves and raises him; later has
children of her own. LBKM

011138   NANCE KENNEDY. London: S.W. Partridge,
[1910] BMC.

011139   THE NECKLACE OF PARMONA. London: Ward,
Lock, 1909 BMC.

011140   THE NEW MRS. LASCELLES. London: J.
Clarke, 1901 BMC.

011141   NURSE CHARLOTTE. London: J. Long, 1904
BMC.

011142   OCEANA'S GIRLHOOD. BY MRS. L. T. MEADE.
New York: Hurst, [c1909] NUC.

011143   OLD READYMONEY'S DAUGHTER. London:
Partridge, [1905] BMC.

011144   ON THE BRINK OF A CHASM; A RECORD OF PLOT
AND PASSION. BY L. T. MEADE. London: Chatto and
Windus, 1898 BMC. New York: F. M. Buckles, 1899 NUC.

LIT 3:280. Nurse betrays murderer and rescues
child-baronet.
ATH 112:61. She has studied under a great Parisian
doctor, understands mesmerism. She uses the boy to
avenge herself on the villain she loves.
Nurse uses hypnotism to rescue young boy from brain
specialist's plot to be rid of him so that the
specialist can inherit a large sum of money. PW
56:1270

011145   THE ORACLE OF MADDOX STREET. BY MRS. L.
T. MEADE. London: Ward, Lock, 1904 BMC NUC.

011146   THE OTHER WOMAN. BY L. T. MEADE. London:
W. Scott, 1905 BMC NUC.

011147   OUT OF THE FASHION. BY L. T. MEADE.
London: Methuen, 1892 BMC. New York: Cassell, [c1892]
NUC.

LW 23:246. Three sisters without money run an ideal
boarding house. 4th sister does not join them because
of disapproval of her lover who thinks it's
unfashionable. She marries him and her sisters
prosper.

011148   THE PASSION OF KATHLEEN DUVEEN. London:
S. Paul, 1913 BMC.

Crime of young man indirectly responsible for his
young wife's death, Ireland. ATH

011149   PETER THE PILGRIM. BY. L. T. MEADE.
London: W. & R. Chambers, 1903 BMC NUC.

011150   PETRONELLA; AND THE COMING OF POLLY. BY
L. T. MEADE. London: W. & R. Chambers, 1904 NUC.

011151   A PLUCKY GIRL. BY LAURA T. MEADE.
Philadelphia: G. W. Jacobs, [1900] NUC.

011152   PRETTY-GIRL AND THE OTHERS. Edinburgh: W.
& R. Chambers, 1910 BMC.

011153   A PRINCESS OF THE GUTTER. BY L. T. MEADE.
London: W. Gardner, 1895 BMC. New York and London:
G.P. Putnam's Sons, [c1896] NUC.

ATH 108:522. Cockney dialect. Story of Miss Prinsep
who worked in East End for good of the masses.
ACAD 108:114. She is a graduate of Girton, inherits a
fortune. Since it was amassed by grinding down the
poor, she chooses to live in "evil and unsanitary
surroundings" working at returning it to them in the
form of better homes and advantages of civilization.

011154   THE PRINCESS OF THE REVELS. BY L. T.
MEADE. London: W. & R. Chambers, 1909 BMC. New York:

New York Book, 1910 NUC.

011155   THE PURSUIT OF PENELOPE. London: Digby,
Long, 1909 BMC.

Lady detective clears up the terrible secret
accusation hanging over Mrs. Forbes' marriage. TLS

011156   THE REBELLION OF LIL CARRINGTON. BY L. T.
MEADE. London: Cassell, 1898 BMC. London and New York:
F. T. Neely, [1898] NUC.

SR 86:859. Intended to convey a moral lesson to young
girls.

011157   THE RED CAP OF LIBERTY. BY L. T. MEADE.
London: J. Nisbet, 1907 BMC NUC.

hist romance TLS

011158   THE RED RUTH. London: T. W. Laurie,
[1907] BMC.

sensational mystery TLS

011159   RESURGAM. London: Methuen, 1903 BMC.

story of couple who go mountain climbing, stay
overnight because of fog, scandal, must marry after an
estrangement.-LBKM 10-3,63

011160   ROSA REGINA. A STORY OF GIRLS.
Philadelphia: Lippincott, 1910 PW. London: W. & R.
Chambers, 1910 BMC.

011161   ROSEBURY. London: Chatto & Windus, 1903
BMC.

passionate nature, absence of moral instincts commits
two of the worst crimes possible yet treated
completely sympathetically ATH 121, 334

011162   RUFFLES. London: S. Paul, [1911] BMC.

15 year old girl is "a female Sherlock Holmes" ATH

011163   SARAH'S MOTHER. London: Hodder &
Stoughton, 1908 BMC.

TLS-mother daughter relationship mother dying while
daughter vacations, high minded
ATH-mother daughter relationship mother dying while
daughter vacations, high minded.

011164   THE SECRET OF THE DEAD. London: F.V.
White, 1901 BMC.

011165   SILENCED. London: Ward, Lock, 1904 BMC.

011166   THE SIREN: A NOVEL. London: F. V. White,
1898 BMC.

ATH 112:384. Vera, the siren, is half Russian, and a
Nihilist with strong Socialistic tendencies. Her
father, an English Colonel, learns of her existence
when she comes of age. Her Nihilist leaders order her
to rid him of his money and take his life. She takes
the money but kills herself rather than him.
ACAD 53:496. Society story, Russian secret police,
tragic ending for heroine.

011167   A SISTER OF THE RED CROSS. A TALE OF THE
SOUTH AFRICAN WAR. BY MRS. L. T. MEADE. London: T.
Nelson, 1901 BMC NUC.

hospital nurse in So Africa.
So Africa-hist 1899-1902

011168   A SOLDIER OF FORTUNE. BY L. T. MEADE.
London: Chatto and Windus, 1894 BMC. New York: R. F.
Fenno, [c1895] NUC.

SP 72:722. Hero is a journalist, heroine turns him
down at book's end. Rev. doesn't like Phyllis, finds
her selfish, why has Meade concentrated on her rather
than the hero?
Young man after university education, starts out in
life with full love of father, mother and 3
self-sacrificing sisters. His adventures, women he
meets, etc. CR 24:408.

011169   A SON OF ISHMAEL; A NOVEL. BY L. T.
MEADE. London: F. V. White, 1896 BMC NUC. New York:
New Amsterdam Book, [c1896] NUC.

ATH 108:481. Old fashioned melodrama. Husband is

secretly connected with a gang of burglars.
SP 77:684. In "House on the Marsh" category. Wife has
employed a detective to discover her brother's
murderer. He identifies her husband, but is wrong, it
was another member of the gang. Husband wants to get
out of gang but head won't let him.

011170   THE SORCERESS OF THE STRAND. BY L. T.
MEADE. London and New York: Ward, Lock, 1903 BMC 1904
NUC.

011171   THE SOUL OF MARGARET RAND. London: Ward,
Lock, 1911 BMC.

Margaret Rand finds woman to impersonate her in order
that she can inherit money TLS

011172   THE STORMY PETREL. London: Hurst and
Blackett, 1909 BMC.

Ireland potato famine TLS
focus on Kathleen OHara ACAD

011173   A STUMBLE BY THE WAY. London: Chatto &
Windus, 1902 BMC.

011174   A SWEET GIRL GRADUATE. BY L. T. MEADE.
London: Cassell, 1891 BMC NUC. New York: Burt, [1897]
NUC.

SP-"describes life in one of the two colleges where
the higher education of women has been followed more
seriously and more successfully than anywhere else, as
far, at least, as England is concerned." Newnham.

011175   THE TEMPTATION OF OLIVE LATIMER. BY MRS.
L. T. MEADE. New York: Mershon, [c1899] NUC. London:
Hutchinson, 1900 BMC.

SP 85:19
ACAD 58:430. Domestic

011176   THAT BRILLIANT PEGGY. London: Hodder &
Stoughton, 1903 BMC.

LBKM-novel about the "shortcomings" of the heroine who
has many faults but is "charming"

011177   THIS TROUBLESOME WORLD. BY L. T. MEADE.
London: E. Arnold, 1893 BMC. New York: Macmillan, 1893
NUC. (Published anonymously in England.)

SR 77:178. Villainous baronet, murdered in the first
volume.
ACAD 45:31. By a doctor whose wife he has seduced. His
daughter is accused and stands trial; his wife finally
convinces him to save daughter by confessing.

011178   THROUGH PERIL FOR A WIFE. London: Digby,
Long, 1902 BMC.

011179   TWENTY-FOUR HOURS. A NOVEL OF TO-DAY.
London: F.V. White, 1911 BMC.

story of man who takes bank funds ACAD

011180   VICTORY. London: Methuen, 1906 BMC.

ATH-anti-vivisectionist.

011181   VIRGINIA. London: Digby Long, 1905 BMC.

011182   THE VOICE OF THE CHARMER. London: Chatto
and Windus, 1895 BMC.

hypnosis, the wicked hero-John Ward swindles people.
His young wife becomes his "instrument" he reduces her
to a state of slavery. Gets her to commit fraud with
him. She's tortured by what she does till she "kills
her conscience." In the end comes to herself, makes
restitution, she and husband swept away in a flood. SP
75:937.
SR-Forged wills, disguised identities; charmer is male
villain with occult powers.

011183   WAGES. A NOVEL. BY L. T. MEADE. London:
J. Nisbet, 1900 BMC. Boston: [c1900] NUC.

ACAD 59:262. Concerned with drug habit, morphia, eau
de cologne, brandy, laudanum, and society women. The
doctor himself is a victim.

011184   THE WAY OF A WOMAN. London: F. V. White,
1897 BMC.

Quintin Garstin is a preacher on opium, was married to

"passionate and brazen" Dolly who died. Is loved by
Marjory whom he jilted earlier to marry Dolly. She
does everything to help him with his habit and hidden
sin. He's a great preacher. ACAD 52 Fic sup 42.

011185   WHEELS OF IRON. London: J. Nisbet, 1901
BMC.

011186   THE WHITE TZAR. London: Marshall,
Russell, [1896] BMC.

011187   WILD HEATHER. BY L. T. MEADE. London and
New York: Cassell, 1909 BMC NUC.

011188   A WILD IRSIH GIRL. BY L. T. MEADE.
London: W. & R. Chambers, 1910 BMC. New York: Hurst,
[c1910] NUC.

011189   WILD KITTY. BY L. T. MEADE. London &
Edinburgh: W. & R. Chambers, 1897 BMC. Chicago: M. A.
Donohue, [1902] NUC.

011190   THE WITCH MAID. London: J. Nisbet, 1903
BMC.

011191   THE WOOING OF MONICA. London: J. Long,
[1914] BMC.

SP 84:176. Very wealthy heroine and scheming guardian.

SMITH, ELLEN ADA.

011192   THE BUSYBODY. London: J. Long, 1910 BMC.

TLS-Two male business partners, but narrator Anne
Arden is a novelist and journalist who plays
substantial part in book. Character study of male and
female.
ATH-She retires to a remote village to recover from a
disappointment in love. Writes about inhabitants.

011193   THE DESPOT. London: J. Long, [1915] BMC.

Beauty specialist, remedies for mental illness. TLS

011194   FIRST IN THE FIELD. London: Digby, Long,
1905 BMC.

A wooing tale TLS 131, 05

011195   THE FULFILLING OF THE LAW. London:
Hutchinson, 1903 BMC.

Love of the land about a farmer ACAD 12-03,155
ATH 122, 850
Barbara strangely married and strangely tamed? TLS 03,
378

011196   IN HER OWN WAY. London: Hutchinson, 1904
BMC.

LBKM young woman seeking to atone for her's father
dishonesty, rejects attention of young doctor.
ATH-Devotes last year of her life to wooing Dr so he
can inherit her money-conventional conclusion.

011197   JOHN PARAMOR'S PURPOSE. London: E.
Arnold, 1917 BMC.

Self grasping character; poetic justice meted out TLS
Focus is on John TLS

011198   THE LAST STRONGHOLD. London: J. Long,
[1912] BMC NUC.

TLS-is a quiet mind and conscience which Lucy, having
lost, attempts to regain by filling her house with
people who need to be fed and looked after.
ATH-Little plot

011199   THE ONE IN POSSESSION: A NOVEL. London:
Jarrolds, [1919] BMC.

Enid Moberly starving accepts help from a man "a
fantastic marr. adventure." TLS
She's made possessor of an estate, her husband the
farm bailiff ATH
Dispute over inheritance Tragic end SR

011200   THE ONLY PRISON. London: J. Long, 1913
BMC.

Man, a literary agent, wins a young woman's complete
trust. When the man's wife dies and he's free to
marry, his past stands in the way ATH
One heroine an art student; the other a writer-her

lover acts as secretary and agent. TLS

011201   THE PRICE OF CONQUEST. London: J. Long, 1914 BMC.

ATH-Male hero-musician, discovers a girl with musical talent, gives her lessons, becomes her guardian, she becomes famous, they marry.
ATH 143:472. When he thinks she is outstripping him in skill and personality, his emotions subtly analyzed. Both violinists.
TLS "Dainty and whimsical tale."

011202   THE PRIDE OF THE TRISTAN HERRICKS. London: Digby, Long, 1905 BMC.

011203   STRESS. London: J. Long, 1916 BMC.

TLS Polish exiles in London-Male hero politician.

011204   THE UNGOVERNED MOMENT. London: Hutchinson, 1907 BMC.

Betty's struggle for work in London, her relation with an editor TLS

SMITH, ELSIE KATHLEEN SETH. Nationality Unknown.

011205   DON RAIMON: A STORY OF RAYMUND LULL. London: S.P.C.K., 1919 BMC NUC.

<Missionary Stories>

011206   A SON OF ODIN. A TALE OF EAST ANGLIA. London: Jarrold, [1909] BMC NUC.

011207   THE WAY OF LITTLE GIDDING. London: H.R. Allenson, [1914] BMC NUC.

ATH Hist romance 17th century, religion.

SMITH, EMMA JOSEPHINE. B. 1844. United States.

011208   UNRAVELING A MYSTERY. New York: Cosmopolitan Press, 1911 NUC.

PW love stroy of a young man

SMITH, EMMA POW. See BAUDER, EMMA POW (SMITH).

SMITH, ESSEX, pseud. See HOPE, FRANCES ESSEX THEODORA.

SMITH, GERTRUDE. 1860-1917. United States.

011209   DEDORA HEYWOOD. New York: Dodd, Mead, 1896 NUC.

LW 27:172. Semi-religious study, half-cold love story against a background cf village character and prejudice.
PW 3-21-96. New England village. Dedora and David have been separated for 20 years over religious differences, barely get together again when separated by death.

011210   THE QUEEN OF LITTLE BARRYMORE STREET. New york: F. H. Revell, [1902] BMC NUC.

SMITH, HARRIET (LUMMIS). D. 1947. United States.

011211   AGATHA'S AUNT. Indianapolis: Bobbs-Merrill, [c1920] BMC NUC.

PW-Agatha masquerades as her great aunt. Comedy.

011212   OTHER PEOPLE'S BUSINESS: THE ROMANTIC CAREER OF THE PRACTICAL MISS DALE. Indianapolis: Bobbs-Merrill, [c1916] BMC NUC.

Persis 36 yr old spinster dressmaker had a lover. PW 90:981 9/23/16
Persis Dale is a doctor of affairs-she knows how to take care of whatever happens-brave fine humorous-manages everything. NYT

SMITH, ISABEL. Fl. 1900-1913. United Kingdom.

011213   THE ADVENTURES OF A RUNAWAY BRIDE. London: J. Ouseley, [1910] BMC.

ACAD-silly rom.

011214   THE JEWEL HOUSE. London: J. Long, 1907 BMC.

Pretty country romance Brief desc LBKM 148,7-07

011215   MATED. London: Digby, Long, 1911 BMC.

ACAD-Julia trifles with a chauffeur, is not pregnant but perhaps fears the same. Is left property and income if she marries in the year, manages to do so successfully.
Julia Romney companion her troubles and happy marriage. TLS

011216   THE MINISTER'S GUEST; A NOVEL. New York: D. Appleton, 1900 NUC. London: T. F. Unwin, 1900 BMC.

LBKM 18:189. Wholesome. Nannie visits nonconformist rector, a family friend, at request in mother's will. Her love story.

011217   NEVERTHELESS. London: A. Rivers, 1913 BMC NUC.

Man whose wife is in an asylum, falls in love with another woman and asks her to live with him. ATH
A woman torn between conventional promptings and natural inclinations-Sara Gale is poor learns she loves a man whose wife is in an asylum. Law allows husband no out. She decides to live with him not knowing wife dead at that moment. One character is a platform champion of women's rights. LBKM "Thoughtful treatment of subjects like female suffrage, nonconformity and divorce."

SMITH, JEANIE OLIVER (DAVIDSON). 1836-1925. United States.

011218   DONALD MONCRIEFF. A COMPANION BOOK TO "THE MAYOR OF KANEMETA". Buffalo: C. W. Moulton, 1893 NUC.

CR 21:908. Sequel to the Mayor of Kanameta. Earnest desire to get something done for "abandoned and sin swept districts of cities."

011219   A FOREST IDYL. BY TEMPLE OLIVER. Boston: Sherman, French, 1913 NUC.

PW 84 12/20/13:2178. Tells how a man is healed mentally and physically by contact with nature and how a fine woman is willing to face misinterpretation for his sake.

011220   THE MAYOR OF KANEMETA. New York: American News, 1891 NUC.

LW 23:58. Utopian socialist settlement. Miriam Rice is heroine. Zurisky is anarchist-villain.
CR 21:408. Plea for effort to help "abandoned and sin swept districts of cities."

SMITH, LILLA MAY (HALL). B. 1860. Nationality Unknown.

011221   DOWN OUR WAY. New York: Dodd, Mead, 1911 NUC.

Gawky Kentucky woman-plain, courageous, gets sickly husband and her brood out of one difficulty after another. PW 9-16-11

SMITH, MARGARET.

011222   FRERE'S HOUSEKEEPER. London: Hurst & Blackett, 1906 BMC.

ACAD-? wedding bells at end.
TLS-Slum bred woman weds country squire. She has a very defiant spirit. Well written.
ATH-Driven from home, works caring for children in a shiftless household. Much disillusioned young woman.

SMITH, MARGARET SCOTT.

011223   ALBERTA AND THE OTHERS: A TRUTHFUL STORY OF WESTERN CANADA. London and Toronto: Sidgwick and Jackson, 1914 BMC.

ACAD 87:264. Family moves from England to Western Canada.

SMITH, MARION COUTHOUY. United States.

011224   DR. MARKS, SOCIALIST. Cincinnati: Editor Pub. Co., 1897 NUC.

SMITH, MARY E. United States.

011225   AMBITION'S CONTEST; OR, FAITH AND INTELLECT. BY CHRISTINE FABER. New York: P. J. Kenedy, [c1896] NUC.

011226   A CHIVALROUS DEED AND WHAT CAME OF IT. BY CHRISTINE FABER. New York: P. J. Kenedy, 1891 NUC.

011227   A FATAL RESEMBLANCE: A NOVEL. BY CHRISTINE FABER. New York: P. J. Kenedy, 1900 NUC.

011228   AN ORIGINAL GIRL. BY CHRISTINE FABER. New York: P. J. Kenedy, 1901 NUC.

011229   REAPING THE WHIRLWIND: A STORY OF TODAY. BY CHRISTINE FABER. New York: P. J. Kenedy, 1905 NUC.

A woman's deceit and vanity. PW 7-1-05

SMITH, MARY ELIZABETH. 1880-1915. United States.

011230   IN BETHANY HOUSE; A STORY OF SOCIAL SERVICE. New York: F.H. Revell, [c1912] NUC.

NYT Religious tract

SMITH, MARY ELLIS. United States.

011231   A MODEL ACTRESS. [Chicago]: [Vollrath and Veronee], [c1892] NUC.

SMITH, MARY PAULINE. United States.

011232   GUY'S FORTUNE. BY M. B. EAGAN. St. Louis, Mo.: B. Herder, 1900 NUC.

SMITH, MINNA CAROLINE. B. 1860. United States.

011233   MARY PAGET: A ROMANCE OF OLD BERMUDA. New York: Macmillan, 1900 NUC BMC.

LW 31:140. Pretty romance. SP 84:387. Historical romance in style of Hungerford. Heroine is abducted, escapes, and reunion with hero. ACAD 58:206. Based on historical documents. Narrated by Mary, wife of one of the men who in 1609 was wrecked in the Sea Venture on Smith's Island.

SMITH, MRS. BURNETT. See SMITH, ANNIE S. (SWAN).

SMITH, MRS. C. B.

011234   IN THE EARLY DAYS. BY ADELAIDE HICKOX. New York: Broadway, [c1910] NUC.

SMITH, MRS. G. CASTLE.

011235   MARY PILLENGER, "SUPREME FACTOR". BY BRENDA. London: G. P. Putnam's Sons, 1912 BMC.

Anti-socialism; pro-Army and Navy and King; plea for boy-scout movement. Mary develops from uncouth washerwoman to neat, trim respectable member of society. ACAD
Mary hardworking washerwoman with family of six-how her family "stirred out of squalor and laziness." ATH

011236   THE SECRET TERROR. BY BRENDA. London: S. Paul, 1909 BMC.

Terror of intemperance TLS
Woman alcoholic; mother keeps daughter's "vicious behavior" a secret ATH

SMITH, MRS. H. SCOTT.

011237   A FAR CRY. London: J. Long, 1913 BMC.

011238   FATE'S LEGACY; A TALE OF ANGLO-INDIAN LIFE. BY FRANK DESMOND. London: J. Ouseley, 1908 BMC.

TLS-stereotyped story of taint of hereditary madness as bar to marriage.

SMITH, MRS. LABAN EDWARD.

011239   IN SOCIAL QUICKSANDS. London and New York: F. T. Neely, [1898] NUC.

PW-Heroine, adopted daughter of western mineowner, is vulgar and bad like her dead mother.

SMITH, MRS. POCA T. United States.

011240   MARGOLEEN. Clarkeville, Tenn.: W. P. Titus, 1897 NUC.

SMITH, MRS. RUFUS W. See SMITH, OREON (MANN).

SMITH, MYRA MALINDA JOHONNOT. United States.

011241   DEMANDS OF SOCIETY. Boston, Mass.: A. I. Bradley, [c1899] NUC.

SMITH, NORA ARCHIBALD. D. 1934. United States.

011242   UNDER THE CACTUS FLAG: A STORY OF LIFE IN MEXICO. Boston: Houghton Mifflin, 1899 NUC. London: Gay & Bird, 1899 BMC.

SMITH, OREON (MANN). United States.

011243   THE NOVICE. BY MRS. RUFUS W. SMITH (NEE OREON MANN). La Grange, Georgia: Cox and Ward, 1894 NUC.

SMITH, S. JENNIE. D. 1904. Nationality Unknown.

011244   MADGE, A GIRL IN EARNEST. Boston: Lee & Shepard, 1902 NUC.

"Scorns patronage of arisocratic relatives and supports family" PW

SMITH, SARA TRAINER. United States.

011245   OLD CHARLMONT'S SEED-BED. New York: Benziger, 1900 NUC.

SMITH, SARAH. 1832-1911. United Kingdom.

011246   HALF BROTHERS. BY HESBA STRETTON. London: Religious Tract Society, [1892] BMC. New York: Cassell, [c1892] NUC.

LW 93,42 Sophy Goldsmith marries a young man who takes her to Italy and deserts her. She dies at childbirth; her son raised and persecuted by peasants. The husband learns Sophy is dead, marries a woman of his own class. While travelling in Italy they meet his son. The adjustments of their future lives is the story. They have a son Philip.
CR 18:276. Two half-brothers and an inheritance.

011247   JESSICA'S MOTHER. BY HESBA STRETTON. Philadelphia: H. Altemus, [c1898] NUC. London: Religious Tract Society, [1904] BMC.

011248   THE SOUL OF HONOUR. BY HESBA STRETTON. London: Isbister, 1898 BMC.

SMITH, SHEILA KAYE. See FRY, SHEILA KAYE (SMITH).

SMITH, SYBIL CORMACK.

011249   THAT WHICH WAS WRITTEN. London: Methuen, 1913 BMC.

So African farms. English woman is complete success in her housekeeping; Dutch Family are in a complete muddle. Concerns gold and heroine's love affairs. SP Woman seduced in her youth almost hides the fact from her fiance but confesses. Her lover returns but dies and the new pair marry. ATH.
Nance Burke, a nurse, is "really offensive"

011250   THE VELDT WOMAN. London: Murray & Evenden, [1911] BMC.

She is one of many whose lives are blighted by a sordid young man. Sombre ATH

SMITH, VIRGINIA MACKAY. United States.

011251   THE LITTLE GREY LADY. New York: E. S. Gorham, 1914 NUC.

SMITHSON, ANNIE MARY PATRICIA. B. 1883. United Kingdom.

011252   BY STRANGE PATHS. London: T. F. Unwin, 1919 BMC. Dublin: Talbot Press, 1919 BMC NUC.

TLS-Conversion to RC
ATH-Heroine is Irish, earns living as a nurse in Eng. hosp. Becomes member of Gaelic League, finally marries a Nationalist. Critical of England.

011253   HER IRISH HERITAGE. Dublin: Talbot Press, 1917 BMC. New York: P. J. Kenedy, 1918 NUC.

PW-Clare, Irish politics of 1916.

SMYTH, EDITH E.

011254   A DOUBLE MISTAKE. London: Marshall, Russell, [1898] BMC.

SMYTH, UNA MAUD LYLE. United Kingdom.

011255   SINS OF THE MOTHERS. BY MARIUS LYLE.
London: A. Melrose, [1918] BMC.

011256   UNHAPPY IN THY DARING. BY MARIUS LYLE.
London: A. Melrose, [c1916] BMC NUC. New York and
London: G. P. Putnam's, 1916 NUC.

BRD- "A story with an Irish setting in which the
characters are two half-sisters and the husband of one
of them. Shelagh Lynch is a beautiful girl, fond of
society and passionately fond of riding. Hester, her
younger half-sister, while unattractive in person is
superior in mentality. She is however unscrupulous and
uses her cleverness to win the interest of Rupert
Standish, her sister's husband. Their common
intellectual interests draw them together and while
Shelagh is recovering from a hunting-field accident,
husband and sister do not scruple to deceive her and
betray her trust. Hester pays the price for her
villainy, but Rupert, for whom the author seems to
have a feeling of tender regard, goes unscathed,
accepting his wife's forgiveness as only his honest
due."
"There are passages which violate, I do not say
morals, but taste; they present ignoble things in a
vulgar way." H.W. Boynton - BKM 44:645 F '17 580w
"A study in morbid psychology, a woman near of kin to
a hobgoblin, she is none the less projected from the
book, a creature vividly alive." NATION 103:543 D 7
'16 350w
"The story is very detailed-far too much so for its
matter. It touches on many subjects, as the love for
and power of money; the sex question; the Irish land
tangle; but having touched them it leaves them. In
spite of some situations of interest and suspense, the
characters are for the most part unreal."--NYT 21:283
J1 16'16 250w
"There are interesting pictures of Irish country life
and society, together with brief but interesting
allusions to the superstitions associated with the
dwellings of the old families. The plot, which tends
to the tragic, is strongly developed, though without
arousing tragic emotion." (Springfield Republican p13
Je 25'16 200w) BRD

SNEDEKER, CAROLINE DALE (PARKE). 1871-1956. United States.

011257   THE COWARD OF THERMOPYLAE. Garden City,
New York: Doubleday, Page, 1911 NUC.

Historical romance: time of Ancient Greece. PW 4-29-11

011258   SETH WAY; A ROMANCE OF THE NEW HARMONY
COMMUNITY. BY CAROLINE DALE OWEN (MRS. CHARLES H.
SNEDEKER). Boston: Houghton Mifflin, 1917 NUC.

Jessonda Macleod goes to New Harmony community to
teach music. At 19 she is "in thought and principles
much in advance of the woman of her time." Seth put
off by this at first.? PW

011259   THE SPARTAN. Garden City, New York:
Doubleday, Page, 1912 NUC. London: Hodder and
Stoughton, 1912 BMC. (Published in 1911 under title:
The Coward of Thermopylae.)

Published in 1911 under title "The Coward of
Thermopylae."

SNEDEKER, FLORENCE WATTERS.

011260   A FAMILY CANOE TRIP. New York: Harper,
1892 NUC.

CR 18:262. Three week vacation on lakes George and
Champlain.

SNEDEKER, MRS. CHARLES H. See SNEDEKER, CAROLINE DALE
(PARKE).

SNEYD, PAMELA.

011261   NEEDS MUST. A NOVEL. London: Osgood, 1894
BMC.

SR 77:330. Revendeuse of clothing; mystery over jewel
in one article. There is not a lady in the book. We
are allowed to see the foolish side alone of the men.
ATH 103:538. There is also a woman who plays poker and
picks up a husband on the Underground Railway. A main
character.

SNEYD, PAMELA AND BRITIFFE CONSTABLE SKOTTOWE.

011262   AN ISHMAELITE INDEED. London: Hurst &
Blackett, 1893 BMC.

Miss Beatrix Spenlowe, the Ishmaelite, is a smart
American adventuress. goes to England "to make a
success in literature using family secrets" so that
people can tell who the characters of her novel
"Joachina" are. Then she tries to and nearly succeeds
in winning over her friend's fiance. "probably a study
of heredity." Her mother had deserted husband for a
man who tired of her.

SNOW, ELLEN. United States.

011263   THE CONFESSION OF SEYMOUR VANE. New York:
R. F. Fenno, [c1908] NUC.

"A series of letters written by Seymour Vane, a man
apparently very much in love with his wife, to his
friend Leila Carlton.
letters of husband who loves wife, to his friend Leila
Carlton." BKM

011264   THE EVOLUTION OF ROSE. Boston: R. G.
Badger, 1907 NUC.

BKM-Diary from young woman coming out in society, love
affair with Episcopalian curate.
NYT-O

SNOW, ISABEL, pseud. See DI CADHILAC, MARGARET ISABELLA
(COLLIER) GALLETTI.

SOLDENE, EMILY.

011265   YOUNG MRS. STAPLES. London: Downey, 1896
BMC.

ATH 108:753. Interesting heroine suicides.

SOLOMON, JESSICA.

011266   THE FLITTING OF ANGELINA; A NOVEL.
London: J. Ouseley, 1908 BMC.

011267   ISABEL MCDONALD. London: Heath, Cranton
and Ouseley, [1915] BMC.

Lives a dull life with her family; loves a doctor who
marries someone else, TLS
"Girl of the modern order of things" her ideas
conflict with those of her aunt and uncle. ATH

011268   THE UNSELFISHNESS OF SUSAN. London: Cope
and Fenwick, [1916] BMC.

SOMERS, KATE.

011269   DR. WEEDON'S WAIF. London: Digby & Long,
[1893] BMC.

SOMERS, SUZANNE.

011270   A SERPENT IN HIS WAY. London: J. Long,
1906 BMC.

ACAD-mystery and adventure.
TLS-Irish family ill-treatment of dependent female
relative.
ATH-nothing here.

SOMERSET, ISABELLA CAROLINE (SOMERS-COCKS). 1851-1921.
United Kingdom.

011271   SKETCHES IN BLACK AND WHITE. London: T.F.
Unwin, 1896 BMC.

SR-pitiful scenes of lower classes, grim account of
woman who killed her baby. Story of unfortunate young
woman.
ACAD 49:302. First sketch is episode in life of a slum
boy; second is tale of seduction.

011272   UNDER THE ARCH. BY LADY HENRY SOMERSET.
New York: Doubleday, Page, 1906 NUC. London: Hurst and
Blackett, 1906 BMC.

PW-novel of modern London
NYT-"heroine will find happiness when she finds
someone to love and take care of."

SOMERSET, LADY HENRY. See SOMERSET, ISABELLA CAROLINE
(SOMERS-COCKS).

SOMERVILLE, DORIS.

011273   GREEN CHALK. London and New York: J. Lane, 1913 BMC NUC.

PW 11/1/13 1436. "A dilettante, Stein, with 200 pounds a year, pays for the educational development of a pavement artist on condition that his (Stein's) name shall be signed on each picture, and that he he shall receive all the profits accruing. When the beautiful woman, whom Stein marries, discovers the secret, she also realizes that it was not the artist she had loved, but the pictures."
Nephew upset to learn uncle leaves wealth to Miss Claudia Badminton-Dale; gets an artist to paint an "ideal" portrait of woman and to sign his own name to paintings. Claudia shows up--she's like the portrait and she had fallen in love with the artist. NYT

SOMERVILLE, E. OE. See MARTIN, VIOLET FLORENCE AND EDITH ANNA OENONE SOMERVILLE, Also SOMERVILLE, EDITH ANNA AND VIOLET FLORENCE MARTIN.

SOMERVILLE, EDITH ANNA OENONE AND VIOLET FLORENCE MARTIN.

011274   DAN RUSSELL THE FOX; AN EPISODE IN THE LIFE OF MISS ROWAN. BY E. OE. SOMERVILLE AND MARTIN ROSS. London: Methuen, [1911] BMC NUC. New York: G.H. Doran, [1912] NUC.

The heroine is "a capable, highly educated young woman-an orphan of considerable means—who suddenly succumbs to the Passion of the Chase...Half-way on the road to becoming a blue stocking, she is rapidly converted into an Amazon." (SP) "A chance acquaintance with an Irish widow, who talks much of hunting...brings her, under the wing of a married cousin, to the west of Ireland. Here she not only learns to ride, but is so enthralled by the passion for hunting that she finds an epitome of all manly virtues in the amateur whip." (SR) BRD 1913.

011275   IN MR. KNOX'S COUNTRY. BY E. OE. SOMERVILLE AND MARTIN ROSS. London: Longmans, 1915 BMC NUC.

Adventures of an Irish magistrate. PW 9-14-15. "There is just enough of sentiment to make our laughter the more full; and there is a setting of cliff and sea and the halloo of the hounds and country races, and trouble, upon an Homeric scale, with the plumber or with the refractory tackle of an unpunctual yacht."-(SR) BRD 1915

011276   MOUNT MUSIC. BY E. OE. SOMERVILLE AND MARTIN ROSS. New York and London: Longmans, Green, 1919 BMC 1920 NUC.

PW-Ireland
NYT-3/28/20 Christian, heroine, good horse woman, her love story, Irish politics.

011277   NABOTH'S VINEYARD. A NOVEL. BY E. OE. SOMERVILLE AND MARTIN ROSS. London: S. Blackett, 1891 BMC NUC.

011278   THE REAL CHARLOTTE. BY E. OE. SOMERVILLE AND MARTIN ROSS. London: Ward and Downey, 1894 BMC. London, New York & Bombay: Longmans, Green, 1901 NUC.

SR 78:45. An attempt at Irish wit with an unhappy ending.
ACAD 46:45. Charlotte "never marries; she has no domestic ties; but circumstances turn her into a landowner and a man of business. Given these conditions in a woman of violent nature, under whose not very admirable social polish lurks a coarse, hungry, self-seeking real ego, and what can the end be but unsatisfactory? Returned love would probably have saved her...it was only when she was undeceived by a cruel disenchantment that her inner nature rose in strength and Charlotte showed herself the selfish and brutal woman she was." Francie "flits to her fate"--a tragic one.

011279   SOME EXPERIENCES OF AN IRISH R.M. BY E. OE. SOMERVILLE AND MARTIN ROSS. London, New York: Longmans, Green, 1899 BMC NUC. (Illus. by E. Oe. Somerville)

SOMERVILLE, EDITH ANNA OENONE, jt. au. See MARTIN, VIOLET FLORENCE AND EDITH ANNA OENONE SOMERVILLE.

SOMERVILLE, H. B., pseud. See MACCOMAS, INA VIOLET.

SOMERVILLE, HENRY, pseud. See HUMPHREYS, MARY GAY.

SORIN, SCOTA, pseud. See TROOP, EDNA WILLA (SULLIVAN).

SOUTAR, LUCY H.

011280   A HIGHLAND WEB. Edinburgh: G. A. Morton, 1905 BMC.

SOUTHEY, ROSAMOND. Nationality Unknown.

011281   HUGH GORDON: A SOUTH AFRICAN NOVEL. London: Duckworth, 1915 BMC.

Traditional novel of war and love. TLS

011282   THE LAST BOUT. London: Duckworth, [1918] BMC NUC.

TLS-war and romance. Heroine is virile in her resourcefulness but truly feminine in love.
LBKM-Virile heroines Tony and Cecil.
SR

011283   ROGER'S LUCK. London: W.J. Ham-Smith, 1912 BMC.

TLS- male hero
ATH-Sara a bright patch in drab setting.

SOUTHWART, ELIZABETH. United Kingdom.

011284   THE STORY OF JENNY; A MILL GIRL'S DIARY. London: Macdonald, 1920 BMC NUC.

TLS-from Boer War thru Armistice. "The new realism" close and intimate record.

SOUTHWICK, LELLIE C. United States.

011285   A NEIGHBORHOOD OF GIRLS. Springfield, Mo.: Jewell, 1896 NUC.

SOUTHWORTH, EMMA DOROTHY ELIZA (NEVITTE). 1819-1899. United States.

011286   BRANDON COYLE'S WIFE. A SEQUEL TO A SKELETON IN THE CLOSET. BY MRS. E. D. E. N. SOUTHWORTH. New York: R. Bonner's Sons, 1893 NUC.

011287   BROKEN PLEDGES: A STORY OF NOIR ET BLANC. Philadelphia: T. B. Peterson, [c1891] NUC.

011288   DAVID LINDSAY: A SEQUEL TO "GLORIA". BY MRS. E. D. E. N. SOUTHWORTH. New York: R. Bonner's Sons, 1891 NUC.

011289   "EM": A NOVEL. BY MRS. E. D. E. N. SOUTHWORTH. New York: R. Bonner's Sons, 1892 NUC.

011290   EM'S HUSBAND: A NOVEL. BY MRS. E. D. E. N. SOUTHWORTH. New York: R. Bonner's Sons, 1892 NUC.

011291   GERTRUDE HADDON: "ONLY A GIRL'S HEART." BY MRS. E. D. E. N. SOUTHWORTH. New York: R. Bonner's Sons, 1894 NUC.

011292   GLORIA: A NOVEL. BY MRS. E. D. E. N. SOUTHWORTH. New York: R. Bonner's Sons, 1891 NUC.

011293   LILITH: A SEQUEL TO "THE UNLOVED WIFE". BY MRS. E. D. E. N. SOUTHWORTH. New York: R. Bonner's Sons, 1891 NUC.

011294   ONLY A GIRL'S HEART: A NOVEL. BY MRS. E. D. E. N. SOUTHWORTH. New York: R. Bonner's Sons, 1893 NUC.

011295   THE REJECTED BRIDE. "ONLY A GIRL'S HEART." BY MRS. E. D. E. N. SOUTHWORTH. New York: R. Bonner's Sons, 1894 NUC.

011296   A SKELETON IN THE CLOSET: A NOVEL. BY MRS. E. D. E. N. SOUTHWORTH. New York: R. Bonner's Sons, 1893 NUC.

011297   THE UNLOVED WIFE: A NOVEL. BY MRS. E. D. E. N. SOUTHWORTH. New York: R. Bonner's Sons, 1891 NUC.

SOUTHWORTH, MRS. E. D. E. N. See SOUTHWORTH, EMMA DOROTHY ELIZA (NEVITTE).

SPADONI, ADRIANA. B. 1883. United States.

011298   THE SWING OF THE PENDULUM. New York: Boni & Liveright, [c1919] NUC. London: Hutchinson, [1921] BMC.

PW-Life-story of a modern Am. woman portrays man's
attitude towards sex and the true relationship between
man and woman. She had a hatred for teaching school
and feared she would be forced to. A social reformer.
Weak and sensual husband.
BkM-Jean Norris is clever, ambitious college grad.,
contempuous of the old-fashioned woman. Marries a
Bounder, leaves him and goes East to work. Organizing
a national movement for women. Is mistress to
unhappily married man; they part because he will not
give mistress his child. Eventually finds an older man
she loves.
NYT Mar 21 '20 p1. Jean, from her graduation from
University of California to time of her second
marriage when she is 39, a successful social worker in
NY. First job is assistant in a library. Then becomes
a newspaper reporter. No romantic love in second
marriage.

SPARHAWK, FRANCES CAMPBELL. B. 1847. United States.

011299   DOROTHY BROOK'S VACATION. New York: T. Y.
Crowell, [c1910] NUC.

Girl's book-PW

011300   HONOR DALTON: A NOVEL. New York: F. H.
Revell, [1903] BMC NUC.

Strong novel of character a man and a woman neither
"deflected from the paths of right even by an intense
love." PW 9-12-03.
Honor's efforts to pay back money her father
embezzled. NYT 03, 754.
Honor proud of her good name, disgraced by her father.
ACAD 65, 572

011301   ONOQUA. Boston: Lee and Shepard, 1892
NUC.

CR 7-16-1892. Story of the wrongs of Indian life on
the reservation.
LW 23:261. Onoqua is Indian, educated in an Eastern
school, returns to tribe hoping to teach them what she
has learned. She is helped by an Indian of another
tribe whom she eventually marries. "Their experiences
show that unless work can be provided for the returned
students, they must leave the tribe to find it, or
fall back into the ways they have tried to outgrow.
Enforced idleness robs them of ambition and skill; but
no people can learn the arts and industries in a land
where neither are."

011302   SENATOR INTRIGUE AND INSPECTOR NOSEBY: A
TALE OF SPOILS. Boston: Red-letter Pub. Co., 1895 NUC
BMC.

The spoils system-how it works against educating and
civilizing the Indians. also a tragic love story. PW
6-9-95:870

011303   A WEDDING TANGLE. Boston: Arena, 1893
NUC.

SPARKS, ALICE WILKINSON. United States.

011304   MY WIFE'S HUSBAND: A TOUCH OF NATURE.
Chicago: Laird and Lee, 1897 NUC.

SPARROW, MARIA DUNTON. United States.

011305   HEREFORD: A STORY. Boston: R. G. Badger,
1910 NUC.

Poor whites in North Carolina; young northerner
(male?) comes to teach among them. PW

SPENDER, EMILY. B. 1841. United Kingdom.

011306   THE LAW BREAKERS. BY THE AUTHOR OF A
SOLDIER FOR A DAY [ANONYMOUS]. London: F. V. White,
1903 BMC.

Dominant theme-contrast between the masculine and
feminine outlook at the outset of marriage. Rhoda is
50-author "harps" on world's attitudes towards
spinsters; convinces her niece not to marry the man
she planned to for he could never be a "comrade."
Eventually finds her ideal.

011307   A SOLDIER FOR A DAY. A STORY OF THE
ITALIAN WAR OF INDEPENDENCE. London: F. V. White, 1901
BMC.

Italian girl of working class takes on brother's

(twins) disguise in army. ATH 4-6-01

SPENDER, LILIAN (HEADLAND). 1835-1895. United Kingdom.

011308   A MODERN QUIXOTE. London: Hutchinson,
1894 BMC NUC.

ACAD 46:490. Male artist who brings all kinds of
problems on himself by his constant befriending of and
generosity to the poor, etc.
LBKM 7:57. He is an advanced socialist. Happy ending.

011309   NO HUMDRUM LIFE FOR ME. A STORY OF AN
ENGLISH HOME. London: Hutchinson, 1892 BMC NUC.

011310   A STRANGE TEMPTATION. London: Hutchinson,
1893 BMC NUC.

Polly Smith is a dancer whose dying friend Azaela-also
a dancer-hears she has inherited a lot of money.
Azaela dies before she can carry out her wish and make
Polly her heir. Polly poses as Azaela (temptation)
gets inheritance, later marries a young squire. Her
career as a social beauty. She's finally unmasked by
a old love from her dance days, exiled from her home.
But still there's a happy end for her. SP 71,584
Azaela Deverill ACAD 44:482.

011311   THIRTEEN DOCTORS. London: Innes, 1895
BMC.

011312   A WAKING. London: Hutchinson, 1892 BMC
NUC.

See Zina's Awaking

011313   THE WOOING OF DORIS. London: Innes, 1895
BMC.

Her father is guardian to Roger, the young man she
loves. Because the father wastes Roger's inheritance,
Doris feels she can't marry Roger. Marries another,
but after this one dies, she and Roger are wed. ACAD
48:518
SP 76:779. Recent death of Mrs. Spender. Pleasant
romance.

011314   ZINA'S AWAKING, A NOVEL. BY MRS. J. KENT
SPENDER. New York: R. Bonner's Sons, 1892 NUC.

SR. She is a genius who has been trained in all the
philosophies.
ATH 99:693. "Retelling of The Doll's House," first
months of marriage, Zina's revolt. "morbidly
interesting"
SP 68:883. Zina's father and husband are "fine
studies...of cold selfishness." "Mrs Carruthers who
supports her ungrateful and critical husband by what
she knows to be third- rate literary hack work, with
unfailing cheerfulness and without a moment's recourse
to self-pity, is a charming creation."
ACAD 42:28. She has in fact three awakenings: her
father, her lover, and her husband, whose wife she
never is except in name. She is a woman of "noble
instincts;=is consoled by =earnest= Mary Carruthers.

SPENDER, MRS. J. KENT. See SPENDER, LILIAN (HEADLAND).

SPIELMANN, MABEL HENRIETTA (SAMUEL). 1862-1938.

011315   MARGERY REDFORD AND HER FRIENDS. London:
Chatto and Windus, 1908 BMC.

011316   MY SON AND I. London: G. Allen, 1908 BMC
NUC.

TLS-sentimental and light
SR-0
ATH-0

011317   THE STERNDALES OF STERNDALE HOUSE: A
NOVEL. London: Chatto and Windus, 1919 BMC.

History of family in different short stories. TLS
Several generations. LBKM
Doris Sterndale-"Certainly sympathetic" fools around
behind her husband's back. LBKM

SPINNER, ALICE, pseud. See FRASER, AUGUSTA ZELIA (WEBB).

SPOFFORD, HARRIET ELIZABETH (PRESCOTT). 1835-1921. United
States.

011318   THE ELDER'S PEOPLE. Boston: Houghton,
Mifflin, 1920 NUC.

PW-Stories of rural New England.
NYT 1920:198. New England village people, "simple, conventional tales."

011319   AN INHERITANCE. New York: C. Scribner's Sons, 1897 NUC.

There's insanity in the Camperdown family and a woman who discovers on her honeymoon that her husband married her for her money. But goes on believing so strongly in him as a person and doctor that she makes something of him. This couple, the Donners. Two plots. CR 28,31:187

011320   A LOST JEWEL. Boston: Lee and Shepard, 1891 BMC NUC.

Child stolen and restored. LW

011321   THE MAID HE MARRIED. Chicago: H. S. Stone, 1899 NUC.

Josephine Grey, beautiful, talented school teacher. Her rich aunt and uncle launch her into high society. She reigns queen for six months. About to wed a millionaire, remembers her true self and the doctor she loved. He's brought into high society too and given a wealthy practice. BKM 9:90

011322   THE MAKING OF A FORTUNE: A ROMANCE. New York and London: Harper, 1911 NUC.

Nice story of older rich husband and young beautiful woman and some jewels. 3-25-11 PW

011323   A MASTER SPIRIT. New York: C. Scribner's Sons, 1896 NUC.

PW 3-28-96. Romance of devoted Puritan with opera impressario. The tradegy provides her with the essential she needed to be a "master spirt," a great sorrow.

011324   PRISCILLA'S LOVE-STORY. Chicago: H. S. Stone, 1898 NUC.

LW 29:155. She loves a foolish boy, marries an older and wiser man, finds happiness in motherhood. PW-she is a music teacher in a college town, captivated a student with her beauty. Husband is the hero.

011325   THAT BETTY. New York: F. H. Revell, [1903] BMC NUC.

Maid tells story of her "master's" reborn faith. Peace on earth type. NYT 03 654

SPOTTISWOODE, SYBIL GWENDOLEN (LAMB). B. 1879. United Kingdom.

011326   CHRONICLES OF A GERMAN TOWN. BY THE AUTHOR OF "MARCIA IN GERMANY" [ANONYMOUS]. London: Methuen, 1915 BMC.

First pub. as "Lotteries of Circumstance"

011327   HEDWIG IN ENGLAND. BY THE AUTHOR OF "MARCIA IN GERMANY" [ANONYMOUS]. London: W. Heinemann, [1909] BMC NUC.

Mild humor ATH

011328   HER HUSBAND'S COUNTRY. London: W. Heinemann, 1911 BMC. New York: Duffield, 1911 NUC.

Internt'l marr leads to unhappiness and trag. PW 6-24-11
Patience Thaile escapes her dull and miserable Eng. home to Germany. Here she has the "best time of her life" marries a young man despite family's objections. Their national characteristics clash (He's Germ.) neither is to blame. LBKM
Patience sees that "a woman's position is not what she thinks it should be" in Germany. Believes she can make her own life better. Marries (with hesitancy) but learns her husband too is a tyrant and profligate. SP "finds out what her husband's Country really is so far as her sex is concerned." completely sympathetic. she's well on the way to revolting when he breaks his neck and the way made clear for another man. SR

011329   MARCIA IN GERMANY. AN INDISCREET CHRONICLE [ANONYMOUS]. London: W. Heinemann, 1908 BMC NUC.

TLS-Travel Tale

011330   THE TEST. London: Skeffington, 1918 BMC.

TLS-is war on a group of people who are cliches. SR

SPRENT, MABEL.

011331   LOVE'S APPRENTICESHIP. London: Methuen, 1913 BMC.

Australian Polly young woman impelled by desire for love and excitement plunges into the whirl of European life. Struggle between her own nature and Eng middle class conventions. ATH
Starts an independent life with her brother and a woman, Sylvia friend in Dresden. TLS

SPRINGER, FLETA CAMPBELL. United States.

011332   GREGG: A NOVEL. New York and London: Harper, [1919] BMC NUC.

Psychological mystery story of a man who was not understood. PW
Slow revelation of Gregg's character to his wife and male friend. Told through the voice of an elderly friend. Monica West is married to Gregg "an authentic work of art." A war book, scene changes from Paris to the Riviera to New York. NYT

SPRINGER, MARY ELIZABETH. United States.

011333   DOROTHY QUINCY: A STORY OF THE AMERICAN REVOLUTION. London and New York.: F. T. Neely, [1899] NUC.

She's John Hancock's wife in this historical romance; her suitors. Her first and second marriage. NYT 6-24-99, 408

011334   ELIZABETH SCHUYLER: A STORY OF OLD NEW YORK. New York: I. H. Blanchard, [1903] NUC.

History NYT 1903, 69

011335   "LADY HANCOCK": A STORY OF THE AMERICAN REVOLUTION. New York: I. H. Blanchard, [c1900] NUC.

SPURLING, CLARIBEL, jt. au. See CLAY, BEATRICE ELIZABETH AND CLARIBEL SPURLING.

SQUIRE, EILEEN HARRIET ANSTRUTHER (WILKINSON). B. 1884.

011336   THE FARM SERVANT. BY E. H. ANSTRUTHER. London: G. Allen & Unwin, [1916] BMC NUC.

TLS-study of character, with focus on Frank-Anna bears his child alone in village, he finally returns, they marry.

011337   THE HUSBAND. BY E. H. ANSTRUTHER. London and New York: J. Lane, 1919 BMC NUC.

SP. Penelope very modern, befriended by a cousin. Later goes to London to earn a living, liaison with cousin's husband, cousin dies.
NYT 7-11-20 p 25. Then Penelope and widower are left together.
Margery Dennithorne dies, repents treatment of husband. Phoebe "blunt tongue suffragette"? TLS
Margery prefers to be the Lady Bountiful of their great house while husband does soc. reform work in London.

SQUIRE, FRANCES. See POTTER, FRANCES BOARDMAN (SQUIRE).

SQUIRE, GEORGINA M.

011338   A SPRIG OF HONEYSUCKLE. A STORY OF EPPING FOREST. London: Blackie, [1892] BMC.

011339   TWO COUNTRY STORIES. London: Digby, Long, 1892 BMC.

STACEY, MARGARET (WESTRUP). United Kingdom.

011340   THE COMING OF BILLY. BY MARGARET WESTRUP. London and New York: Harper, 1905 BMC NUC.

Mostly about a boy 9-9-05 PW

011341   THE DEVIL'S PROBLEM. BY MARGARET WESTRUP. London: Hurst and Blackett, [1919] BMC NUC.

Penelope Glynn a complex character dreary
self-absorbed girl passionately fond of her seaside
world. At 25, marries (tho not yet awakened to
anything but pity) a helpless nerve-wracked soldier
whom she had nursed and saved. TLS
Never considers the true, full meaning of marriage.
Soldier recovers health. Not clear how the marriage
goes. TLS
Happy end-both confess their love. LBKM

011342   ELIZABETH IN RETREAT. BY MARGARET WESTRUP
(MRS. W. SYDNEY STACEY). New York: J. Lane, 1912 NUC.
London: J. Lane, 1912 BMC.

PW-wife is told husband has first wife, he immediately
has stroke, she nurses him for five years, and then
discovers she has been his lawful wife.
TLS-by author of "Elizabeth's Children" Prudence has
drink sodden husband and a son. Story is about them.
ATH-O

011343   ELIZABETH'S CHILDREN [ANONYMOUS]. London
and New York: J. Lane, 1903 BMC NUC.

Elizabeth of Visits of Elizabeth married adventure of
her sons.
PW 4-18-03
LBKM 8-03 183
Very brief description BKM 17 (1903) 429
Elizabeth a "feather headed" person. ATH 122, 248

011344   THE FOG AND THE FAN. London: Hurst and
Blackett, [1920] BMC.

011345   THE GREATER MISCHIEF: A NOVEL. BY
MARGARET WESTRUP. London and New York: Harper, 1907
BMC NUC.

PW-Young woman heroine
NYT-relations between mother and children
Audrey's home and family-TLS

011346   HELEN ALLISTON [ANONYMOUS]. New York and
London: J. Lane, 1904 BMC NUC.

PW-?
NYT-conventional
ATH-conventional

011347   THE MOULDING LOFT. BY MARGARET WESTRUP
(MRS. W. SYDNEY STACEY). London: Methuen, [1917] BMC
NUC.

Story with much conversation. Catherine Chator is a
kind of model. There may be insanity in her family.
TLS

011348   PHYLLIS IN MIDDLEWYCH. BY MARGARET
WESTRUP (MRS. W. SYDNEY STACEY). London: J. Lane, 1911
BMC. New York: J. Lane, 1911 NUC.

Mischief and gaiety of boys and girls. BKM

011349   ROGER INGRAM. BY MARGARET WESTRUP (MRS.
W. SYDNEY STACEY). London: Methuen, [1915] BMC.

Tibbie, shop girl marries an intelligent artist. TLS

011350   TIDE MARKS. BY MARGARET WESTRUP (MRS. W.
SYDNEY STACEY). New York: Macmillan, 1913 NUC. London:
Methuen, [1913] BMC NUC.

PW 84 11/8/13:1534. "Heroine is the child of a gipsy
mother and an ascetic poet, and the theme is the
willful avoidance of love by this girl. Phillippa
Hamilton left poor and alone seeks employment and
finds it at last with a most amusing family keeping a
cheap millinery shop in London. Discouraged, she
consents to marry Michael Brent in order to be his
housekeeper and from then on the story is concerned
with Brent's winning of her love and her many
misunderstandings of him before he succeeds."
Wife in name only who learns to love husband. Best
scenes: her work in hat shop. SP
Heroine has a highly introspective nature; bases her
researches on previous study of herself in the mirror.
She's a "typical flapper"-ATH
Audacious, she enters the most extraordinary adventure
with a casual air. Marries on condition that she'll
only be his housekeeper. He's madly in love with her.
versed in all the advanced thoughts of the age of
moral anarchy. Love awakens her at the end. LBKM

011351   THE YOUNG O'BRIENS, BEING AN ACCOUNT OF
THEIR SOJOURN IN LONDON. BY THE AUTHOR OF "ELIZABETH'S
CHILDREN" [ANONYMOUS]. London and New York: J. Lane,

1906 BMC NUC.

ATH-story about children and maiden aunt.

STACEY, MRS. W. SYDNEY. See STACEY, MARGARET (WESTRUP).

STACPOOLE, MARGARET (ROBSON) DE VERE. D. 1934. United
Kingdom.

011352   THE BATTLE OF FLOWERS. London:
Hutchinson, 1916 BMC NUC.

TLS-Heroine is Joan Candon, a journalist, a secretary
and finally proprietor of the Dial.
SP. A blind man is in love with her and Miss Flyte who
is plain and unselfishly devoted to him. He recovers
his sight whom does he chose? This is one of several
plots.

011353   LONDON 1913. London: Hutchinson, 1914 BMC
NUC. New York: Duffield, 1914 PW.

Adventures and misadventures of So African magnate and
daughter in London. NYT
LBKM-O
SR 147:149 Modern London society-all of it rotten.

011354   MONTE CARLO; A NOVEL. London: Hutchinson,
1913 BMC NUC. New York: Dodd, Mead, 1914 NUC.

English artist and her wife Julia Revell. Their
marriage was an elopement. Novel concerns the
conflicting elements of her nature; the conventional
side, her love for husband. She is a successful
novelist. SP
"Daughter of an English prelate has married an artist,
a gentleman by birth, but a bohemian. At Monte Carlo,
they fall in with a group of the artist's friends of
the baser bohemian sort which, together with some
other unfortunate occurrences, brings about a serious
breach until a gentleman adventurer in the pay of the
Austrian Secret Service affects a reconciliaton." PW
BKM-She has been brought up in the narrowest possible
manner and then suddenly rebelled and made a runaway
match. Bohemian life loses its glamour and recognition
of her blunder gives her material for a first novel.
She and her husband make a trip to MC on the first
royalties.
Heroine receives hundreds of dollars from her
publisher, would flee to Paris with husband. He loses
her money gambling and spends it on another woman. She
consoles herself with another man who helps reconcile
the two. The end brings more money. ATH

STAHR, FANNY LEWALD. 1811-1889.

011355   THE MASK OF BEAUTY: A NOVEL. BY FANNY
LEWALD. New York: R. Bonner's Sons, 1894 NUC. (Tr.
Mary M. Pleasants)

PW-Katherine, a widow, gives birth to daughter after
death of husband. Mother or daughter's extraordinary
beauty cause of many tragic incidents.

STAIRS, GORDON, pseud. See AUSTIN, MARY (HUNTER).

STALLARD, CONSTANCE LOUISA.

011356   THE FORD. London: E. Nash, 1917 BMC NUC.

Anti-Irish; priest who drinks; English depicted as
prigs. TLS

STANGELAND, KARIN MICHAELIS. See STANGELAND, KATHARINA
MARIE BECH (BRONDUM) MICHAELIS.

STANGELAND, KATHARINA MARIE BECH (BRONDUM) MICHAELIS.
1872-1950. Denmark.

011357   ANDREA: THE TRIBULATIONS OF A CHILD. BY
KARIN MICHAELIS. New York: McClure, Phillips, 1904
NUC. (Tr. from Danish by John Nilsen Laurvik.)

A dying child; speaks of her sorrow because of
difference between her parents, tries to find the
cause, mother reads part, is reconciled to husband.
NYT
Two parents each jealously devoted to Andrea, a grown
up daughter; the child dies, sorrow brings parents
together-sorrow that her last days made disagreeable
for the friction between them. ACAD 128, 05
TLS 05, 82

011358   THE CHILD: ANDREA. BY KARIN MICHAELIS.
London: Duckworth, 1904 BMC NUC. San Francisco: P.
Elder, [1916] NUC. (Tr. by J. N. Laurvik.)

540

011359   THE DANGEROUS AGE: LETTERS AND FRAGMENTS
FROM A WOMAN'S DIARY. BY KARIN MICHAELIS. London, New
York: J. Lane, 1911 NUC BMC. (Tr. by Marcel Prevost.)

Letters and fragments. Elsie Lindtner, 22 years wed,
so dissatisfied with husband with whom she never had
an angry word that she gets a divorce and goes to live
in the country. Solitude is all she wants. From this
retreat she writes to all her married friends who are
her age and as restless. Attempts a relationship with
a younger man, turns to husband who has since taken up
with a 19 year old, takes a trip around the world.
Critic upset for author presents Elsie's case as
universal. ACAD
"Preposterous obsession with the dangers of middle
age." "Passes through the dreaded furnace of her
40's."
Married for money, security (father went bankrupt),"
learned a pretty face is her fortune. In her teens
"sets her cap" for a rich elderly widow but actually
married Lindtner, a wealthy Dane. Married 22 years.
Chose him for money. After 22 years, leaves husband,
urge to live alone,moves to house on island secretly.
Really escapes boredom of her husband. Even at villa
bored. Jeanne becomes her salient interest
here-intimate confidante, but writes her old admirer
who sees how changed (old) she is. Eventually craves
her husband's boring company but he married. Takes a
cook's tour around the world with Jeanne. (Book)

011360   ELSIE LINDTNER, A SEQUEL TO "THE
DANGEROUS AGE". BY KARIN MICHAELIS. New York: J. Lane,
1912 NUC. London: J. Lane, 1912 BMC NUC. (Tr. by
Beatrice Marshall.)

PW-Single young woman adopts a street urchin and
devotes her life to him.
TLS-She is intensely egotistic, startingly frank,
futility of he life, until she adopts child. Includes
also 40 pages of a professors wife's letters to her
lover. "The duty of absolute self-effacement, provided
she has found love, seems to be Mme Michaelis' final
gospel for women."
ACAD-Elsie very different from character in Dangerous
Age. Finds consolation in following the fortunes of
her maid and a certain amount of happiness.
Keeps spark of her youth alive-gambles in Monte Carlo,
travels in Greece with Jeanne, fences in London, rides
in New York and adopts a small boy, street orphan.
Letters to Lili Rothe "ideal mother" who loves husband
and another man. Insists she loves both. Letters to
Magna Willman who has a child outside of her
marriage-proudly. (Book)

011361   THE GOVERNOR. BY KARIN MICHAELIS
STANGELAND. London and New York: J. Lane, 1913 NUC
BMC. (Tr. by Amy Skovgaard-Pedersen.)

Terse, sombre study of crime and passion, evil men and
women. Medieval setting in Holland Runow-weak
governor. Nightmarish. Beardsleyish "a powerful,
ruthless grotesque fantasy preaching evil." ACAD

STANIFORTH, EDITH. United Kingdom.

011362   IN SPITE OF ALL: A NOVEL. New York:
Benziger, 1917 NUC.

Sissy Wharton marries the man who was "won from her"
by another woman. when that woman died, she took him
back. PW
rivalry between two women NYT

011363   UNDER WHICH FLAG? A ROMANCE OF THE
BOURBON RESTORATION. London: R. & T. Washbourne, 1915
BMC.

TLS-Historical romance, Napoleon

011364   WAS IT A MARRIAGE? London: J. W.
Arrowsmith, 1915 BMC.

Not in legal sense but child accepted by father; she,
the child; her love affairs are the story. TLS
"A great wrong has been done to her mother which she
discovers just in time to wreck her new found
happiness." ATH

STANLEY, CAROLINE.

011365   THE PINK TULIP: A NOVEL OF TO-DAY.
London: Roxburghe Press, [1898] BMC.

STANLEY, CAROLINE (ABBOT). 1849-1919. United States.

011366   THE KEEPER OF THE VINEYARD, A TALE OF THE
OZARKS. New York: F. H. Revell, [c1913] NUC.

PW 11/15/13 1591 "Eleanor Dinwoody, a successful
Chicago teacher, is suddenly confronted with the
problem of the maintenance of her brother's family of
five. She engineered their migration to the highlands
of Missouri and pluckily shouldered the burden of
their support. In making them healthy and happy there,
she found it necessary to improve the school and the
church, and did it with a vigor that first astonished
and then delighted the easy-going "natives." A love
affair between her eldest niece Bess and Neil Gilmer
runs through the story, and at the end Neil's uncle,
who thought all women faithless or frail, surprises
himself and her by falling in love and marrying Nell."

011367   THE MASTER OF "THE OAKS". A NOVEL.
London: A. Melrose, [1912] BMC. New York: F. H.
Revell, [c1912] NUC.

NYT-Wholesome and charming
PW-Male hero with history of crime, disclosure-al6's
well.

011368   A MODERN MADONNA. New York: Century, 1906
BMC NUC.

"A story based upon a law which, until ten years ago,
was enforced in the District of Columbia. This law
permitted a man to will the custody of his child to
whomever he chose. The widow of a man, with whom she
was very unhappy, finds that her husband struck his
cruelest blow when he willed their baby to his
brother" How this affects the mother and her tragical
life is the story. BKM v. 24. 1906-7
WOMAN'S JOURNAL 12/8/1906 Women of Wash. aid mother
in getting law signed by president making parents
equal guardians. "novel is throughout a plea for equal
suffrage..."
NYT

011369   ORDER NO. 11; A TALE OF THE BORDER. New
York: Century, 1904 NUC.

PW-Hist novel
NYT anti-war Missouri-Hist-Civil War

011370   THEIR CHRISTMAS GOLDEN WEDDING. New York:
T. Y. Crowell, [1913] NUC.

Old couple separated-re-united in time for 50th
anniversary.

STANLEY, DOROTHY (TENNANT). United Kingdom.

011371   MISS PIM'S CAMOUFLAGE. BY LADY STANLEY.
London: Hutchinson, 1918 BMC. Boston: Houghton
Mifflin, 1918 NUC.

PW. Spinster of 50 works for war office, has many
exciting adventures.
TLS Can make herself and anything she touches
invisible. Visits Kaisar's bedroom where she nearly
shoots him etc.
NYT Perdita Prim. When she discovers her gift, she
goes to war office and volunteers her services. She is
sent to Germany. Exciting, interesting, not comic.
Anti-German pov.

STANLEY, LADY. See STANLEY, DOROTHY (TENNANT).

STANLEY, MARTHA MELEAN BURGESS. B. 1872. United States.

011372   THE SOULS OF MEN. New York: G. W.
Dillingham, [c1913] NUC.

PW 83 3/1/13:768 "Bob Mannering and his wife are
living in the wilds of the unsettled tobacco districts
of Cuba. Beth grows to hate the life, and when a
wealthy New York clubman, traveling in Cuba, is
attracted by her unusual voice and offers to help her
to go on the stage, she accepts and goes to New York.
She makes a brilliant success and the New Yorker
demands his price. Beth almost gives in, is saved by a
miracle, or what seems one to her, and returns to her
husband and happiness."

STANLEY, WINIFRED.

011373   A FLASH OF THE WILL. London: Chatto &
Windus, 1904 BMC.

ATH-Heroine described as a genius but according to rev
is priggish and neurotic 19th c type.
TLS unhappy mrg., temptations of heroine.

STANNARD, HENRIETTA ELIZA VAUGHAN (PALMER). 1856-1911.
United Kingdom.

011374   AUNT JOHNNIE. A NOVEL. BY JOHN STRANGE
WINTER. London: F. V. White, 1893 BMC NUC.
Philadelphia: J. B. Lippincott, 1893 NUC.

Light reading. Aunt Johnie is an unselfish,
tactful-busybody. Helps a lot of young people. By
daring strategy gets two families together that oppose
the marriage of their son and daughter. SP 70 :655.
Plot turns on a family feud. LW 93:292.
Widow of 50 makes all around her happy. PW 7-29-93.

011375   THE BINKS FAMILY. THE STORY OF A SOCIAL
EVOLUTION. BY JOHN STRANGE WINTER. London: F. V.
White, 1899 BMC. New York: G. W. Dillingham, 1900 NUC.

PW-rich dairy man and his family. His daughter's
marriage to a man with no history.

011376   A BLAMELESS WOMAN. BY JOHN STRANGE
WINTER. London, New York: International News, [c1894]
NUC. London: F. V. White, 1895 BMC NUC.

Hero a Russian prince, persuades Margaret North to
elope and live in Berlin. She finds out he has a wife.
Returns to England to her guardian whom she's deceived
saying she was studying German in Berlin. She's ill
for a while, then marries, has a family , but her
secret gets out. Husband sues for
divorce-successfully. ACAD 47:334.
Author holds her blameless. PW 5-18-95:777.
After living with a Russian count for two years in
Berlin under cover of a false marriage into which she
was duped, comes home and in the character of a
spotless maiden, marries a man she does not care for.
BAKER 03,189

011377   A BLAZE OF GLORY. BY JOHN STRANGE WINTER.
Philadelphia and London: J. B. Lippincott, 1902 BMC
NUC.

ATH 7-12-02-fainting love-sick girl.

011378   A BORN SOLDIER. BY JOHN STRANGE WINTER.
London: F.V. White, 1894 BMC NUC.

ACAD-hero unjustly accused and tried for heroine's
murder; at last moment she rushes into court and
explains it was another woman found in her clothes.
Excels in love and sport-not shown much in battle.
Philip Jervis makes love to a married woman, is
visited by a young woman in his barracks. Shows women
as slaves to the uniform. The married woman is a
revolting creature. The young woman is a fool. SP 74:368

011379   CAPTAIN FRASER'S PROFESSION. A NOVEL. BY
JOHN STRANGE WINTER. London: F. V. White, 1910 BMC.

TLS-a jewel thief.
ACAD-a jewel thief.
Ath

011380   THE CAREER OF A BEAUTY; A NOVEL. BY JOHN
STRANGE WINTER. London: F. V. White, 1900 BMC.
Philadelphia and London: J. B. Lippincott, 1901 NUC.

Marries without much love; falls in trance on wedding
day; dreams of a man in India who dreams of her. ATH
4-13-01

011381   CHERRY'S CHILD; A NOVEL. BY JOHN STRANGE
WINTER. London: F. V. White, 1904 BMC. Philadelphia
and London: J. B. Lippincott, 1904 NUC.

PW love story.
NYT-love story.

011382   CONNIE, THE ACTRESS: A NOVEL. BY JOHN
STRANGE WINTER. London: F. V. White, 1902 BMC.

011383   THE COUNTESS OF MOUNTENOY. BY JOHN
STRANGE WINTER. London: J. Long, 1904 BMC NUC.

LBKM - Love triangle.

011384   DICK THE FAITHFUL: A NOVEL. BY JOHN
STRANGE WINTER. London: F. V. White, 1905 BMC.

011385   EVERY INCH A SOLDIER. BY JOHN STRANGE
WINTER. Philadelphia: J. B. Lippincott, 1894 NUC.

LW 25:266. Cavalry officer charged with murder of a
woman, finally cleared. Garrison life, wicked women.

011386   EVERYBODY'S FAVORITE. A NOVEL. BY JOHN
STRANGE WINTER. London: F. V. White, 1897 BMC NUC.

Two brothers grow up and love one girl. ACAD 52 Fic
sup 73.

011387   EXPERIENCES OF A LADY HELP. BY JOHN
STRANGE WINTER. New York: Lovell, Coryell, [c1892]
NUC.

CR Sister governesses, both marrying titles.

011388   THE GHOST OF AN OLD LOVE: A NOVEL. BY
JOHN STRANGE WINTER. London: J. E. Nash, [1903] BMC.

011389   A GIRL IN LONDON. BY JOHN STRANGE WINTER.
London: R. A. Everett, [1903] BMC.

011390   GOOD-BYE. A NOVEL. BY JOHN STRANGE
WINTER. London: F. V. White, 1891 BMC. New York:
United States Book, [c1891] NUC.

Husband divorces wife on false evidence. She
disappears. He marries society girl he doesn't care
for and who feels only friendship for him. Then he
learns his wife was innocent. Goes in search of her
but she won't have him. The two women, old
acquaintances, become good friends. Husband left to
his own conscience. LW 1891, 241
The Adairs-eventually the second Mrs. Adair dies of
consumption and the first remarries Mr. Adair. SR
6-27-91, 781

011391   GRIP; A NOVEL. BY JOHN STRANGE WINTER.
London: F. V. White, 1896 BMC. New York: Stone &
Kimball, 1896 NUC.

An impetuous Yorkshire youth-"Bulldog"- family motto
is Grip. He's in a regiment in Ireland. Jilted by
girlfriend. Goes after her, arrested for another man
in Paris; in prison his companion turns out to be his
fiance's husband. Finally weds another. CR SP
26,30:387.

011392   HEART AND SWORD. BY JOHN STRANGE WINTER.
London: F. V. White, 1898 BMC. Philadelphia: J. B.
Lippincott, 1899 NUC.

ACAD 55:76. Love, regimental life, and the stage,
ending with divorce proceedings and death.
ATH 112:862. "To John Strange Winter position, birth,
and refinement are nothing compared to Bohemianism and
unconventionality. We find her, for instance, sneering
at the soldier husband who objects to his wife not
only being an actress, but giving her entire life and
sympathies to her calling." "An attempt to convince
readers that the profession is in every respect
superior to society. A book of merit, though it is not
wholesome reading for young folks."
Katherine Mollinder is famous in London as the most
remarkable actress of the day. While her fiance is
soldiering in India, she grows more and more devoted
to her profession. There is an elopement and an
"unconventional change of partners." A faint attack on
divorce laws. LW 30:267.
She also becomes a manager of a first class theater.
Her career and interests are so different from her
fiance's that they drift apart for a long while before
they eventually wed. Fine portrayal of "theatre life
and of the domestic life of an ambitious intelligent
actress of irreproachable character." PW 56:7
Military element but deals largely with the career of
an actress. One answer to question should wives work?
6-24-99, 408. NYT

011393   THE HEART OF MAUREEN. BY JOHN STRANGE
WINTER. London: C. H. White, 1910 BMC.

TLS-melodrama.
ACAD-melodrama.

011394   I LOVED HER ONCE. A NOVEL. BY JOHN
STRANGE WINTER. London: F. V. White, 1896 BMC.

ACAD 49:526. Story of a violinist of great talent,
unknown. His child starves to death. His wife never
forgives him and he falls in love with another, Mary
Hamilton. But she must marry the Baron to save her
father! Trag.

011395   I MARRIED A WIFE, A NOVEL. BY JOHN
STRANGE WINTER. New York & London: F. A. Stokes,
[c1895] NUC BMC. London: F. V. White, 1895 BMC.

ACAD 49:94. "It was necessary that J.S.W. should

return to that order of story which made her famous,
and her latest book belongs to that innocent type."
"Small beer" "for the young person." Heroine a
do-gooder among the poor.
CR 29:57. Two daughters, Eldest is an advocate of the
most advanced woman's rights; younger is a
philanthropist in the slums and the wife of the title.
She is married to an officer, "comes dangerously near
to bringing about a mutiny in the regiment by her
mistaken philanthropic activity among the wives and
children of the soldiers."

011396   IN LUCK'S WAY. BY JOHN STRANGE WINTER.
New York: J. W. Lovell, 1891 NUC. (Bound with
Moth-Mullein by S. Baring-Gould.)

Effie Staunton is a rich young woman who meets a poor
crossing-sweeper and his sister and helps them. PW 024

011397   IN THE SAME REGIMENT, AND OTHER STORIES.
BY JOHN STRANGE WINTER. London: F. V. White, 1898 BMC.

Short stories.

011398   INTO AN UNKNOWN WORLD. A NOVEL. BY JOHN
STRANGE WINTER. London: F. V. White, 1897 BMC NUC.
Philadelphia: J. B. Lippincott, 1897 NUC.

Marjory Dundas is an aristocrat. While traveling in
Europe with her sister and German governess, she falls
in love with a man of business. Marries him, realizes
the gap between her class and his but adjusts. For
seven years keeps away from her family. Slow
reconciliation follows and all kinds of success and
fortune for her husband. (MP, fortune.) LW 28:194.
Knows she must live in her husband's social world so
different from what she's used to. PW 51:651.

011399   THE IVORY BOX. BY JOHN STRANGE WINTER.
London: C. H. White, 1909 BMC.

Disappearance of Eunice; turns up as a Countess. TLS
"Girls' gift-book." ACAD

011400   JIMMY. A NOVEL. BY JOHN STRANGE WINTER.
London: F. V. White, 1903 BMC.

ACAD 65,14 about a robbery.

011401   JUST AS IT WAS: A NOVEL. BY JOHN STRANGE
WINTER. London: F. V. White, 1905 BMC NUC.

A confusion of lovers. TLS 187,05

011402   LADY JENNIFER. BY JOHN STRANGE WINTER.
London: C. H. White, 1909 BMC.

011403   THE LITTLE AUNT. BY JOHN STRANGE WINTER.
London: F. V. White, 1905 BMC.

TLS-"Girlish maiden of 40 marries "Him-of-the
Hawkeyes."

011404   LITTLE JOAN. A NOVEL. BY JOHN STRANGE
WINTER. Philadelphia: Lippincott, 1903 NUC. London: F.
V. White, 1903 BMC.

Engaged to one, loves another. NYT 03,841

011405   THE LITTLE VANITIES OF MRS. WHITTAKER. A
NOVEL. BY JOHN STRANGE WINTER. London: F. V. White,
1904 BMC. New York and London: Funk & Wagnalls, 1904
NUC.

NYT-anti-feminist; story of a new woman who returns to
traditional values.

011406   LOST: A SWEETHEART. BY JOHN STRANGE
WINTER. London: F. V. White, 1903 BMC.

011407   LOVE AND TWENTY. BY JOHN STRANGE WINTER.
London: J. Long, 1905 BMC.

011408   THE LOVE OF PHILIP HAMPDEN: A NOVEL. BY
JOHN STRANGE WINTER. London: F. V. White, 1907 BMC.

Adventures of a man. ACAD

011409   THE LUCK OF THE NAPIERS. A NOVEL. BY JOHN
STRANGE WINTER. London: F. V. White, 1911 BMC.

011410   LUMLEY, THE PAINTER. A NOVEL. BY JOHN
STRANGE WINTER. London: F. V. White, 1891 BMC. New
York: J. W. Lovell, [1891] NUC.

Flimsy society novel. LW 23:58 Hero is a genius.

011411   THE MAGIC WHEEL. BY JOHN STRANGE WINTER.
Philadelphia and London: Lippincott, 1901 NUC.

011412   A MAGNIFICENT YOUNG MAN. A NOVEL. BY JOHN
STRANGE WINTER. London: F. V. White, 1895 BMC NUC.
Philadelphia: J. B. Lippincott, 1895 NUC.

impossible adventures of a hero SR 80:386
Godfrey Bladensbrook decides to call himself William
Smith, thereby subjecting his young wife to injurious
suspicions and himself to 18 months in prison. ACAD
48:222.
Godfrey's mother was widowed. She raised him by
herself. ATH 106:286
Couple marry because they find themselves away
together overnight. Then Godfrey taken to prison for a
crime committed by a man by the name he assumed.
Serves the term not letting anyone know where he is in
order to keep his and wife's reputation clear. Returns
to wife, good reputation and a baby he didn't know he
had. LW 26:253

011413   THE MAJOR'S FAVORITE, A NOVEL. BY JOHN
STRANGE WINTER. London: F. V. White, 1895 BMC. New
York: J. S. Tait, 1895 NUC.

barrack life. His favorite is a St. Bernard who is
getting dangerous in his old age. The Marjor's two
daughers marry. The dog found poisoned was put to
death because of fear he had cancer and would bite out
of madness. ACAD 47:462

011414   THE MAN I LOVED. A NOVEL. BY JOHN STRANGE
WINTER. London: F. V. White, 1901 BMC.

ATH 9-28-01

011415   A MAN'S MAN. A NOVEL. BY JOHN STRANGE
WINTER. London: F. V. White, 1893 BMC 1894 NUC.

011416   THE MARRIED MISS BINKS. A NOVEL. BY JOHN
STRANGE WINTER. London: F. V. White, 1900 BMC NUC.

LBKM 19:29. Narrated by Anna Binks. Light and
wholesome.
SP 85:182. Her husband turns out to be an earl.
LIT 7:86. Foolish society women.

011417   MARTY. A NOVEL. BY JOHN STRANGE WINTER.
Philadelphia and London: J. B. Lippincott, 1903 NUC.
London: F. V. White, 1903 BMC NUC.

Woman supports family by selling second hand clothes,
well educated, marries "above" her, marriage doesn't
go well. PW 3-14-03
Study of mother and mother-in-law. NYT 03,191

011418   MARY HAMILTON'S ROMANCE. BY JOHN STRANGE
WINTER. New York: R. F. Fenno, 1898 NUC.

011419   A MATTER OF SENTIMENT: A NOVEL. BY JOHN
STRANGE WINTER. London: F. V. White, 1902 BMC. New
York: A. L. Burt, [1903] NUC.

011420   MERE LUCK. A NOVEL. BY JOHN STRANGE
WINTER. London: F. V. White, 1892 BMC NUC.

011421   MISS DERING'S PRICE: A NOVEL. BY JOHN
STRANGE WINTER. London: F. V. White, 1907 BMC.

Innocent midnight visit of man to his girl-cousin's
room. He falls dead; she throws the corpse out the
window and washes her hands. ACAD

011422   MISS PEGGY. THE STORY OF A VERY MODERN
GIRL. BY JOHN STRANGE WINTER. London: F. V. White,
1912 BMC.

011423   THE MONEY SENSE; A NOVEL. BY JOHN STRANGE
WINTER. London: G. Richards, 1900 BMC. New York: G. W.
Dillingham, [1900] NUC.

NYT 1900:408. Heroine, charming, has no sense of
money. Finally marries a title.
SP 84:318. First marries a "profligate good-natured
little Jew" and divorces him, then Silenus, a
fashionable portrait painter, horrible, old.
SR 90:53. "Extravagance is a vice pushed to the utmost
limit, leading her...to disgrace and the brandy
bottle."

011424   A MOTHER'S HOLIDAY. BY JOHN STRANGE
WINTER. London and New York: Ward, Lock, 1899 BMC NUC.

011425   MY GEOFF; OR THE EXPERIENCES OF A

LADY-HELP. BY JOHN STRANGE WINTER. London: F.V. White, 1892 BMC NUC.

ATH 100:126. Title is inaccurate, heroine was never a lady-help. Amusing.
ACAD. Heroine is like Jane Eyre. Romance.

011426   A MYSTERY OF MAYFAIR. BY JOHN STRANGE WINTER. London: F. V. white, 1908 BMC.

TLS-Suspense and mystery.

011427   A NAME TO CONJURE WITH; A NOVEL. BY JOHN STRANGE WINTER. London: F. V. white, 1899 BMC. Philadelphia: J. B. Lippincott, 1900 NUC.

Growth of the drink habit on a strong person. She's an overworked authoress who finds she depends upon green chartreuse to get through her work. Very sympathetic character. Mary Lessingham struggles to keep herself and her children living luxuriously as they are accustomed. LIT 5:374
She's famous as a novelist. Her husband is her business manager. She supports him and children. Feels her creative powers are failing but that drink helps. SP 83:417
A literary woman takes to alcohol as a stimulant...contracts the habit, with ruinous consequences. BAKER 03,189
History of a woman. Father loses mind and money. She makes comfortable home for them in cheaper part of town. She takes up writing. Marries a friend who helped her publish. Then years later he gets ill, she takes up the pen again. Fame comes, but the demands of fame on her health are great takes to alcohol. It inspires her; under the effects of liquor she wrote fluently and marvelously; without it she was incapacitated. Her trials, sorrows, temptations struggles. NYT 11-18-99 772

011428   ONLY HUMAN; OR, JUSTICE. A NOVEL. BY JOHN STRANGE WINTER. London: F. V. white, 1892 BMC. Philadelphia: J. B. Lippincott, 1892 NUC.

LW 23:88.
PW Lord Esseldine refused help to Mrs. Broughton when she appealed to him to spare her husband when his extravagance led to dishonesty and disgrace. Years later he regrets his insulting words.
CR 17:253 She goes to America with her daughter

011429   THE OTHER MAN'S WIFE. A NOVEL. BY JOHN STRANGE WINTER. London: F. V. white, 1891 BMC. New York: F. M. Lupton, [n.d.] NUC.

English army major ruins and deserts daughter of Corsican noble. Her two sisters organize a vendetta, follow him all over the world, trap him in London; one murders him. She tells her story to Ethel Mordaunt's friend. Ethel was forced by ambitious mother to marry that major. And her friend believes she (Ethel) killed the man because he's a bastard. CP.
Widowed Ethel is now free to marry the man she loves. SP 67 76
Also ATH 97 405.

011430   THE PEACEMAKERS: A NOVEL. BY JOHN STRANGE WINTER. London: F. V. white, 1898 BMC. Philadelphia: J. B. Lippincott, 1898 NUC.

NYT 1898:365. Florence, 24 year old working woman in London, rides bike. Unromantic, betroths herself on p. 10 in matter of fact way to young business man whose parents are founders of religious sect, "Peacemakers." They are subject of story, not her comfortable, happy marriage. Father is not a man of peace, all sham.

011431   THE PRICE OF A WIFE. BY JOHN STRANGE WINTER. Philadelphia: J. B. Lippincott, 1901 NUC.

A nurse whose father demands a price for her. NYT

011432   RED COATS. BY JOHN STRANGE WINTER. London: F. V. white, 1894 BMC.

011433   THE SAME THING WITH A DIFFERENCE: BEING THE CHRONICLE OF A SUBURBAN EPISODE. BY JOHN STRANGE WINTER. London: F. V. white, 1896 BMC NUC.

011434   A SEASIDE FLIRT: A NOVEL. BY JOHN STRANGE WINTER. London: F. V. white, 1897 BMC.

011435   A SELF-MADE COUNTESS. THE JUSTIFICATION OF A HUSBAND. BY JOHN STRANGE WINTER. London: F. V. white, 1900 BMC. Philadelphia: J. B. Lippincott, 1901 NUC.

LW 31:267. Charming Blanche...true and tender...little ambitions balanced by...wholesome aims and emotions. Not a single grain of impropriety.
PW-English widow and 3 daughters. The youngest helps a duke propose. Her marriage, her attempts to take her place in society.

011436   A SEVENTH CHILD. BY JOHN STRANGE WINTER. London: F. V. white, 1894 BMC NUC. New York: J. S. Tait, [c1894] NUC.

SP-7th child of parents, both of whom are seventh children. Makes her clairvoyant.

011437   SHE WAS CALLED NOEL, AND OTHER STORIES. BY JOHN STRANGE WINTER. London: F. V. white, 1900 BMC.

011438   A SIMPLE GENTLEMAN: A NOVEL. BY JOHN STRANGE WINTER. London: F. V. White, 1906 BMC.

ATH-not too promising.

011439   SISTER ANNE. BY JOHN STRANGE WINTER. London: F. V. white, 1904 BMC.

011440   SLY-BOOTS. BY JOHN STRANGE WINTER. London: J. Long, 1904 BMC NUC.

011441   THE SOLDIER AND A LADY. A NOVEL. BY JOHN STRANGE WINTER. London: F. V. white, 1899 BMC.

011442   A SOLDIER'S CHILDREN. BY JOHN STRANGE WINTER. London: Chatto and Windus, 1892 BMC NUC.

ACAD. Pleasant and touching. Virtuous and precocious children.

011443   THE SOUL OF HONOR. BY JOHN STRANGE WINTER. New York: R. F. Fenno, 1902 NUC.

BOOK NEWS 11-1902. Bank clerk "whose hobby is roses and joy bringing up two little girls."

011444   THE SOUL OF THE BISHOP. A NOVEL. BY JOHN STRANGE WINTER. London: F. V. white, 1893 BMC NUC. New York: J. S. Tait, [c1893] NUC.

Loyal Broad-church bishop wants to wed a woman who can't accept the 39 articles. SP 71, 753.
Her name is Cecil Constable. PW 11-11-93.
The book is plea for liberality in rel. First the wedding is postponed because she feels it's unjust that unbaptized babies can't go to heaven. Also ot her doctrines bothered her. Bishop convinces her that it's enough she believes in the fundamental Christian ideas. Then she breaks up the marriage because he believes she's agnostic. SR 76:497.

011445   THE STRANGE STORY OF MY LIFE, A NOVEL. BY JOHN STRANGE WINTER. London: F. V. white, 1896 BMC NUC. Chicago and New York: Rand, McNally, [c1897] NUC.

SP 77:821 "A good little thing" and her good fortune. All the characters are good. After her father's death, she is taken up by various people, each time more fortunate.
LW 29:102. Adventures of heroine in India, Italy, Servia. Her mrge to another after believing husband dead. He isn't. Happy end.

011446   THE STRANGER WOMAN. BY JOHN STRANGE WINTER. London: White, 1894 BMC. New York: J. S. Tait, 1894 NUC.

Vera Blount inherits uncle's cottage. Goes to live there, loves Roger Valliant. But there's a terrible barrier between them. Revealed in a letter that came with her inheritance. Happy ending. ACAD 47:32.

011447   A SUMMER JAUNT: BEING A RAMBLING AUTOBIOGRAPHY. BY JOHN STRANGE WINTER. London: F. V. White, 1899 BMC NUC.

Mr. and Mrs. John Strange Winter visit Dieppe for summer with characters from a previous book. SP 83:160

011448   THAT MRS. SMITH. A NOVEL. BY JOHN STRANGE WINTER. London: F. V. white, 1893 BMC.

011449   THOSE GIRLS. BY JOHN STRANGE WINTER. New York: U. S. Book, [c1892] NUC.

PW female student in seminary misbehaves and is consigned to a convent.

011450   THE TROUBLES OF AN UNLUCKY BOY. A NOVEL.
BY JOHN STRANGE WINTER. London: F. V. White, 1897 BMC.

011451   THE TRUTH-TELLERS, A NOVEL. BY JOHN
STRANGE WINTER. Philadelphia: J. B. Lippincott, 1896
NUC. London: F. V. White, 1896 BMC NUC.

ATH 108:220. Simple domestic story.
ACAD 50:178. They are a pair of terrible infants-"not
so smart, perhaps," as the Heavenly Twins, but "even
more down on the nail with their searching comments on
men and things."
SP 77:274. Artificial adjuncts to the feminine toilet
the targets, in the fashionable home and circle of
their maiden aunt.
PW 6-13-96. There are five.

011452   UNCLE CHARLES: A NOVEL. BY JOHN STRANGE
WINTER. London: Hurst & Blackett, 1902 BMC.

ATH 10-25-02 male gourmand.

011453   WEDLOCK. BY JOHN STRANGE WINTER. New
York: R. F. Fenno, 1898 NUC.

English middle-class life. Heroine married a second
time. Husband no. 1, a sailor, shows up. Surprising
end. PW 55:320.

STANTON, CORALIE, pseud. See HOSKEN, ALICE CECIL (SEYMOUR).

STANTON, ELIZABETH BRANDON. United States.

011454   "FATA MORGANA," A VISION OF EMPIRE--THE
BURR CONSPIRACY IN MISSISSIPPI TERRITORY AND THE GREAT
SOUTHWEST--NATCHEZ LOVE STORY OF EX-VICE PRESIDENT
AARON BURR: A HISTORICAL NOVEL. [Crowley, La.]:
[Signal Publishing Co.], 1917 NUC.

PW-historical male hero

STAPLETON, PATIENCE. 1863-1893. United States.

011455   ROSE GERANIUM. A TRAGEDY [ANONYMOUS].
Chicago: Morrill, Higgins, 1892 NUC.

PW-Love affair which ended in murder.

STAPLEY, ANNIE E.

011456   WHAT CAME TO ME IN THE SILENCE. BY A. E.
S. London: T. Burleigh, 1899 BMC.

STAPP, EMILIE BLACKMORE.

011457   THE SQUAW LADY. Philadelphia: D. McKay,
[c1913] NUC.

"Boys and girls of the Go-Hawk Tribe adopt old Mrs.
Shirley as their Squaw Lady, take turns staying with
her while her son is away, and have all manner of good
times with her, from cooky-baking to an amateur play."
PW

011458   THE TRAIL OF THE GO-HAWKS. Boston: C. M.
Clark, 1908 NUC.

011459   UNCLE PETER--HEATHEN. Philadelphia: D.
McKay, [c1912] NUC.

STAR, MARIA.

011460   ALISTAIR, A ROMANCE. London: Constable,
1911 BMC.

Reincarnation-TLS

STARK, HARRIET. United States.

011461   THE BACILLUS OF BEAUTY: A ROMANCE OF
TO-DAY. New York: F. A. Stokes, [c1900] NUC.

NYT 1900:718. Theme of turmoil beauty causes. Helen is
heroine..PW-German professor has discovered how to
produce perfect beauty by a bacillus.

STARKEY, HELEN. United States.

011462   PLATO PAVED THE WAY. New York: Neale,
1913 NUC.

STARR, MARGARET.

011463   SANE OR INSANE? OR HOW I REGAINED
LIBERTY. [Baltimore]: [Fosnot, Williams], [1904] NUC.

PW-experiences in an insane asylum.

STEARNS, AMANDA (AKIN).

011464   THE LADY NURSE OF WARD E. New York: Baker
and Taylor, 1909 NUC.

Chatty letters, civil war nurse PW 11-6-09

STEEL, FLORA ANNIE (WEBSTER). 1847-1929. United Kingdom.

011465   THE ADVENTURES OF AKBAR. New York: F. A.
Stokes, [1913] NUC. London: W. Heinemann, 1913 BMC.

011466   THE FLATTERER FOR GAIN. London: "Daily
Mail", [1904] BMC.

011467   THE GIFT OF THE GODS. New York: J.
Chartres, 1897 NUC. London: W. Heinemann, 1911 BMC
NUC.

Conflict between a woman's duty to law and husband's
ancestral home ATH
A woman's devotion to her "barren acres." Margaret
lives on a homestead in Scotland; she's a widow, to
her home comes a seaman who has suffered memory loss.
He loves her and there's trouble when he recovers his
memory. Review doesn't say what happens. "not a
loveable heroine" "her fierce love of the land is a
fine thing". SR

011468   THE HOSTS OF THE LORD. New York, London:
Macmillan, 1899 NUC. London: W. Heinemann, 1900 BMC.

LW 31:268. India. Italian-Indian (mixed) heroine whose
guardian is a priest.
SP 85:716. Indian revolt. She and two lovers are
killed.

011469   IN THE TIDEWAY. Westminster: Constable,
1897 BMC. New York: Macmillan, 1897 NUC.

Leisurely rich on vacation in the Hebrides. Heroine is
a beautiful wilful reckless lady of fashion who loves
her cousin but marries a wealthy man only to learn
shortly thereafter that he's an alcoholic. Her cousin
has married also out of love. Now she calls on him and
their relationship is revived. The husband is hussled
away. She's also pursued by another admirer. "Saved
from scandal by a boating accident in which she
drowns." SP 78:923.
N. W. Scotland. Lady Maud dies in the quicksand. ACAD
June 12, 1897, Fict. Sup. II.

011470   KING-ERRANT. London: W. Heinemann, 1912
BMC. New York: F. A. Stokes, [1912] NUC.

TLS-Male hero worship
NYT male hero worship
Hist romance of Babar. The founder of the Mogul
Empire, from his youth to death, 16th c clashing
customs. warring creeds, fanaticism, treachery, self
sacrifice, Mahometan religion, plurality of wives NYT
SP LBKM

011471   MARMADUKE. New York: F. A. Stokes, 1917
NUC. London: W. Heinemann, 1917 BMC NUC.

Trad love story involving castle and inheritance. PW
"Marrion Paul's fidelity to her chief" TLS
Her life of self-denial for his sake SP NYT

011472   MISS STUART'S LEGACY. BY MRS. F. A.
STEEL. New York & London: Macmillan, 1893 BMC NUC.

Life-military, civil, and native-in India. She's
unconventional and falseness of conventional sentiment
and morality is often pointed out. Much action, many
characters. BKM 5:57. Faizapore is the community.
LW 27:172. India, the indigo district of Faizapore.
Treachery, half-caste who saves his regiment at
expense of his own life.
Set in the wilds of Afganistan. Her legacy is money
and indecision-inherited. Her "half-caste lover who
saves the regiment." LW 93, 367.
She's educated in England, rejoins father in India. He
has remarried. Inherits-gives legacy to founding a
home for incurably ill children. PW 10-14-93.

011473   MISTRESS OF MEN: A NOVEL. London: W.
Heinemann, 1917 BMC 1918 NUC. New York: F. A. Stokes,
1917 NUC.

Nurjahan poor, born in caravan, left to die in sands,
rescued, desired by emperor. Becomes Empress of India
and virtually the ruler, skilled housewife, great

huntress, bold, ambitious "undaunted courage and
unsullied virtue" TLS
PW-17th c Indian is Mihrunnissa, "Queen of Women,"
Abandoned baby girl who became great beauty and after
20 yrs Empress of India and its ruler.
NYT-"The long struggle of a beautiful and highly
intellectual woman to overcome the artificial
disabilities imposed upon her simply and solely
because of her sex. Able, intelligent, a strong, just,
and thoroughly capable ruler, she could govern only
through her weak, amiable, and drunken husband."
Reigned in fact- if not in name-as prime minister.

011474   MUSIC HATH CHARMS. New York & London:
Macmillan, 1895 NUC.

011475   ON THE FACE OF THE WATERS, A TALE OF THE
MUTINY. Rahway, N.J.: Mershon, 1896 NUC. London: W.
Heinemann, 1897 BMC.

SR 82:569. At Delhi. Alice Gissing tempted Major
Erlton from his wife. She is a Becky Sharpe, carries
the book on her own shoulders. Dies midway thru book
an heroic death and when Mrs Erlton helps bury her,
"One is made to feel that the injured makes it
entirely convincing." She gives her life to save a
child. Remainder of the book devoted to Kate Erlton
and Jim Douglas; they remain "formless shadows."
Breathless adventures.
ATH 108:792. Insight into the native side of the
Indian Mutiny. "Regret to find that the author is
unable to shake herself free from the objectionable
habit prevalent among so many lady writers of dragging
in the sexual question freely. This blemish renders
the work unsuitable for young people." Historically
accurate.
ACAD 50:488. History overbalances the fiction. Alice
Gissing's relationship with the Major described "with
rare and even audacious sympathy." She is pregnant.
Fiction based on hy. of the Indian Mutiny. The sense
of its coming. The effects. Fine details and
scholarship as well as a work of great imagination.
LBKM 11:123
Alice Gissing and Kate Erlton contrasted. CR 26,30.75
India-hist-Sepoy Rebellion, 1857-1858-fic. Author
"stands second to no man in her military allure"
writes spectacular war scenes of Indian mutiny in
Delhi. Centers on James Douglas a spy for the English
Bureau of Information. Another man owes him gambling
debt. This man's wife offers her jewels in order to
avoid a scandal. But James refuses. Later he saves
this woman when the battle is on & then sticks it out
with her no-good cheating husband till he dies. Musket
fire, spurs, sabres, mutiny, battle- with those
subjects, which are apparently impossible to her sex,
Mrs. Steele shows powers which are marvelous."
NYT 2: 13-07,2

011476   THE POTTER'S THUMB: A NOVEL. London: W.
Heinemann, 1894 BMC. New York: Harper, 1894 NUC.

SR 78:74. Oriental intrigue; a potentate who is a
masher, an English heroine who marries three times,
and another who is more prosaic.
SP 73:87. India. Sensitive sympathetic portrayal of
Indian character. Conflict over preservation of a
sluice.
ACAD 46:63. Interesting female characters--Chadni, an
Indian courtesan, Beatrice a Eurasian, and Rose
Tweedie, an English girl.
LW 25:202.

011477   A PRINCE OF DREAMERS. London: W.
Heinemann, 1908 BMC NUC. New York: Doubleday, Page,
1909 NUC.

Hist. novel of India of 16th c., focuses upon the
Prince. One character, Atma Devi "claims and obtains
her father's office of bard and champion to the king."
LBKM

011478   RED ROWANS. BY MRS. F. A. STEEL. New York
and London: Macmillan, 1895 BMC NUC.

Story of Scotch Highlands. Paul McLeod first loves and
leaves Jeanie Duncan who attempts revenge but dies
loving him. After this he loves Marjorie Carmichael
who apparently falls prey to his charms at the same
time he's wooing Violet because she has the money that
will rehabilitate his estate. ATH 106:639
Marjory is educated as a boy by a scholarly uncle. At
17 she's learned in Greek and Latin, a math genius.
She studies to enter the university; at this point
meets Paul. Tragic end. PW 10-19:677.
Theme: can love exist free of "self-denying penance of
proprie ty and duty." English and Scots in Scotland.

"Mrs. Steel's work has a masculine force which is
shown not only in her independen ce of convention and
the stock phrase, but in her almost virile
appreciation of passion."
ACAD 49:32. Scotch Highlands. Paul McLeod, a
psychological study. Marjorie loves him, Tom must
console himself with her friendship, which, Marjory
writes, "is bigger than love."

011479   SALT DUTY. London: W. Heinemann, 1904
BMC.

011480   A SOVEREIGN REMEDY. London: W. Heinemann,
1906 BMC NUC. New York: Trow Press, 1906 NUC.

TLS-Fairy tale unreal heroine.
ATH-
Aura is a new type of woman; money-the remedy (but
responsible for evil) PW 1-26-07
New in that she's unworldly, has never seen money BKM
NYT

011481   THE SWIMMERS. New York and London:
Macmillan, 1895 NUC.

011482   VOICES IN THE NIGHT; A CHROMATIC
FANTASIA. London: W. Heinemann, 1900 BMC NUC. New
York, London: Macmillan, 1900 NUC.

LBKM 18:124. India. John Ellison is introduced at end,
a village jester, seems almost an emanation of the
dead hero. Krishu, a pure bred Brahmin with a desire
for progress, marries an English wife and discovers
life she leads him into is vulgar and coarse. Lesley
Drummond is made after the particularly disagreeable
pattern which Mrs. S. insists is typical of British
girls today.
SP 84:813. She is a governess and marries Jack
Raymond.
NYT 1900:383. Hero is in love with Leslie. They
prevent an attack on the hospitals. Krishu and his
wife are accepted by neither the natives nor the
English, the wife will have nothing to do with even
his mother.

STEEL, MRS. F. A. See STEEL, FLORA ANNIE (WEBSTER).

STEELE, ANNA CAROLINE (WOOD).

011483   CLOVE PINK: A STUDY FROM MEMORY. London:
Chapman and Hall, 1894 BMC.

SR-pretty love story of Diantha who remained true to
the memory of a dragoon and eventually died.

011484   LESBIA: A STUDY IN ONE VOLUME. London: G.
Bell, 1896 BMC.

LBKM 10:121. She is a bright-coloured stinging fly,
her love affair with Kenneth Ross. Reconciliation in
last chapters; rev. skeptical that it can last.
ATH 108:155. Her "abrupt regeneration" an "exceedingly
unconvincing miracle."
SP 76:777. Man with a heart married to a woman without
one. She considers herself more virtuous, as a woman
who needs admirers, to a woman who goes "all lengths"
with a lover. Husband may tend towards physical rather
than spiritual side of love.
ACAD 49:485. The Downs, horses. Staunch, persevering
Kenneth (hero), and irresponsible daughter of a
dancing mistress, Lesbia. Ending is unrealistic.

STEELE, CHRISTIE, pseud. See BERNARD, MARY N.

STEELE, FRANCESCA MARIA.

011485   BROTHER FRANCIS: A NOVEL. BY DARLEY DALE.
London: R.A. Everett, 1904 BMC.

011486   CHLOE. BY DARLEY DALE. London: Bliss,
Sands, 1897 BMC.

She plays the violin. Dr. who cares for her father
falls in love with her. An overdose of opium kills the
father-caused by a carelessly written prescription.
There's an impersonation too. Acad 52 Fic Sup. 84.
Dr. and brother are lookalikes; one is sent to prison
for a crime the other committed. ATH 110:524.
SP 81:380. Two brothers, one a country practitioner,
one a London physician, identical twins. Confusion.
Amusing.

011487   THE DAUGHTERS OF JOB. BY DARLEY DALE.
London: R.A. Everett, 1902 BMC.

011488   THE GAME OF LIFE: A NOVEL. BY DARLEY

DALE. London: Hutchinson, 1894 BMC. New York: P. F.
Collier, [c1894] NUC.

SP 73:247. Melodrama with Italian villain.
ACAD-there is a secondary character, Miss Frampton,
"the cultivated and witty bachelor lady-you cannot
call her an old maid."

011489   LOTTIE'S WOOING. BY DARLEY DALE. London:
Hutchinson, 1893 BMC. New York: Cassell, [c1893] NUC.

Charlotte Vaughan determines to marry a particular
man-who happens to love someone else. Tries all kinds
of tricks-including putting an announcement in the
London news that she has married him. The man is never
deceived by the tricks. But the more she fails, the
better a person she becomes and so finally does
attract and win him. SP 70, 708.
And Virginia Willoughby travels in a van on a tour
with a female cousin and with Lottie's brother but
weds a baronet whom she shot in the leg when he came
prowling around the caravan in a fog. SR 75,633.
Bribes a gypsy to say they're destined to wed; gets to
him as by mistake a letter in which she refuses a
proposal of marriage, sends announcements of their
wedding to Times. Wants this man because he's the
landlord and family in rough financial shape. ACAD
43:458

011490   NAOMI'S TRANSGRESSIONS. BY DARLEY DALE.
London and New York: F. Warne, 1907 BMC.

Naomi is disinherited unless she marries a cousin
she's never seen; plots with a friend to have cousin
refuse to marry her; she's a rel. enthusiast-enters
Cath. nunnery. PW 4-20-07
Terribly uninteresting, dull, lack luster is Naomi.
ACAD

011491   REUBEN FOREMAN, THE VILLAGE BLACKSMITH. A
NOVEL. BY DARLEY DALE. New York: R. Bonner's Sons,
1892 NUC.

011492   STELLA'S STORY: A VENETIAN TALE. BY
DARLEY DALE. London: J. S. Virtue, 1897 BMC.

Her lover marries another woman out of duty but
because of a mine explosion in which his wife died,
he's able to return and resume their relationship
after a short time. ATH 109:13
ACAD 50:490. Simple love story of Stella, Paul, and
Mary. Paul marries Mary, but she dies and he comes
back to Stella.

011493   THE VILLAGE BLACKSMITH. BY DARLEY DALE.
London: Hutchinson, 1892 BMC.

SP 69:775. Melodramatic comedy of ordinary village
folk.

STEELE, ROWENA (GRANICE). United States.

011494   WEAK OR WICKED? A ROMANCE. Lodi, Cal.:
Steele, 1893 NUC.

STEFFENS, JOSEPHINE BONTECOU. United States.

011495   LETITIA BERKELEY, A.M.: A NOVEL. New
York: F. A. Stokes, [c1899] NUC.

Psycho-physical study of a young woman whose
physiology triumphs over her psychology. Daughter of
professor of small N.E. college, bored with her narrow
life. Goes to New York and gets involved in social
life. Goes to Paris to study medicine. In New York she
had become involved with Philip Euston-been to his
apartment, slept with him. When she meets a man she
loves, she felt no love for Philip, she tells him
about Philip. Much discussion of sex being
sinless--author's view. The erotic in fiction, an
unhealthy story. BKM 9:91
The story dwells especially upon the difference of the
moral standards held binding upon man and woman. PW
56:179
Student days in Paris-meets anarchists and theorists
of both sexes. Mrs. Ball coarse but strong and shrewd
speaks blunt truth. Tells Philip bluntly that he's
illegitimate to force him to make reparation to
Letitia, whom he considers unworthy of him. She leaves
NY all but ruined, studies medicine in Paris, refused
his belated offer of marriage. Leaves town where
father is a Professor Emeritus to see what the world
was like. Gets mixed up with questionable crowd in NY
sins. To Paris and a wilder group, Anarchists and
others. Brainy. Meets Dr. she loves. Tells him all.
But they don't wed. NYT 9-19-99, 547

STEIN, GERTRUDE. 1874-1946. United States.

011496   THREE LIVES, STORIES OF THE GOOD ANNA,
MELANCTHA AND THE GENTLE LENA. New York: Grafton
Press, 1909 PW. London: J. Lane, 1920 BMC.

STEMPEL, MARY GAILLARD (TOBIN) MACCAN. United States.

011497   THE FINISHED WEB [ANONYMOUS]. New
Orleans: Current Topics Pub. Co., 1892 W.

STEPHENS, ETHEL STEFANA. See DROWER, ETHEL STEFANA
(STEVENS).

STEPHENS, KATE. 1853-1938. United States.

011498   LIFE AT LAUREL TOWN IN ANGLO-SAXON
KANSAS. Lawrence, Kansas: Alumni Assoc. of the
University of Kansas, 1920 BMC NUC.

PW-Story of the late 60's in Kansas.

011499   A WOMAN'S HEART: MANUSCRIPTS FOUND IN THE
PAPERS OF KATHERINE PESHCONET AND EDITED BY HER
EXECUTOR OLIVE RANSOM. London and New York: Doubleday,
Page, 1906 BMC NUC.

PW-secret marriage with priest which ends in tragedy.
NYT-he confesses, does penance, she dies, along with
her child. In form of her letters to priest,
persuading him to marry her, etc.

STEPHENS, LOUISE G. B. 1843.

011500   LETTERS FROM AN OREGON RANCH. BY
KATHARINE. Chicago: A. C. McClurg, 1905 NUC.

Adventures of Oregon settlers 4-22-05 PW.

STEPHENSON, CORA BENNETT. See CLARE, CORA ESTELLA BENNETT
(STEPHENSON).

STERLING, SARA HAWKS. United States.

011501   A LADY OF KING ARTHUR'S COURT: BEING A
ROMANCE OF THE HOLY GRAIL. Philadelphia: G.W. Jacobs,
1907 NUC BMC. London: Chatto & Windus, 1909 BMC.

Trad. hist. rom. TLS
Medieval romance 10-19-07 PW
BAKER 13-502

011502   SHAKESPEARE'S SWEETHEART. Philadelphia:
G.W. Jacobs, 1905 NUC BMC. London: Chatto & Windus,
1907 BMC.

About Ann Hathaway and the bard & Jonson. TLS
ACAD-semi true story of Anne Hathaway, spirited.

STERN, E. G. See STERN, ELIZABETH GERTRUDE (LEVIN).

STERN, ELIZABETH GERTRUDE (LEVIN). 1890-1954. United
States.

011503   MY MOTHER AND I. BY E. G. STERN. New
York: Macmillan, 1917 NUC.

melting pot idea as means of escape from Judaism.
Heroine grows away from Polish Jewish ghetto and
mother. Goes to college, marries in America. Escapes
from the drudgery, child-bearing, gossipy sisters of
the ghetto. "her escape linked with triumph in having
achieved modern womanhood." BKM
Everything contributes to making the gulf between
mother and daughter wide until the daughter leaves.
Daughter moves toward all that is American, beginning
with reading Little Women NYT 7-8-17, 258

STERN, G. B. See HOLDSWORTH, GLADYS BERTHA (STERN).

STERNE, STUART, pseud. See BLOEDE, GERTRUDE.

STERRETT, FRANCES ROBERTA. 1869-1947. United States.

011504   THE JAM GIRL. New York and London: D.
Appleton, 1914 BMC NUC.

"Judith Henderson, American heiress, has trouble with
the French customs when another American, Hiram
Bingham, Jr., comes to her rescue. They breakfast
together at a little inn and buy from the innkeeper
the recipe for a marvellous jam known as the "King's
Jam." PW

011505   JIMMIE THE SIXTH. New York and London: D.

Appleton, 1918 BMC NUC.

PW-male and war
of military stock, shocks relatives by becoming a
designer of women's clothes. Even his sweetheart casts
him off as a male dressmaker. Makes good in foreign
legion. TLS

011506   MARY ROSE OF MIFFLIN. New York and
London: D. Appleton, 1916 BMC NUC.

Mary with her "cheerful little personality" brings joy
to a city apartment house PW
NYT-Mary with her "cheerful little personality" brings
joy to a city apartment house

011507   NANCY GOES TO TOWN. New York and London:
D. Appleton, 1920 BMC NUC.

011508   REBECCA'S PROMISE. New York and London:
D. Appleton, 1919 BMC NUC.

Young girl "sacrifices the present" to provide for her
old age NYT

011509   UP THE ROAD WITH SALLIE. New York and
London: D. Appleton, 1915 NUC BMC.

young woman spends her inheritance giving her old aunt
pleasure 9-25-15 PW
Sallie's various pretty advents. NYT
"Judith Henderson, American heiress, has trouble with
the French customs when another American, Hiram
Bingham, Jr., comes to her rescue. They breakfast
together at a little inn and buy from the innkeeper
the recipe for a marvellous jam known as the "King's
Jam." PW
TLS-romance, wedding of two jam manufacturers and
their offspring.

011510   WILLIAM AND WILLIAMINA. New York and
London: D. Appleton, 1917 BMC NUC.

Helen school teacher, her housemaid Marietta, a
feminist, Williamina's desire to give to every body.
She's called Bill. legally adopted by William? PW
The new man, William found her; adopted her; they live
in a river shack happily. People began to say the girl
needed a mother. Reviewer calls William "a masculine
old maid." NYT
Humorous story of a man who tries to enlist in the
army. NYT

STETSON, CHARLOTTE PERKINS. See GILMAN, CHARLOTTE (PERKINS)
STETSON.

STETTHEIMER, ETTIE. United States.

011511   PHILOSOPHY: AN AUTOBIOGRAPHICAL FRAGMENT.
BY HENRIE WASTE. London: Longmans, 1917 BMC. New York:
Longmans, Green, 1917 NUC.

Henrie is an American woman studying in Germany, Univ.
of Freiburg, for Ph.D. Story traces the development of
her personality when love conflicts with her studies.
PW
The degree is to her a mere detail-what matters is the
mental quest. For her philosophy is the science of
wonder; she is ready "to adventure fearlessly wherever
the question mark will take her." Love comes-a fellow
student, but he leaves and she finishes her degree;
after which she's ready to take up the relationship.
She tells the story NYT

STEUART, MARIA.

011512   MODERN DAUGHTERS. London: S. W.
Partridge, [1915] BMC.

TLS-Love affairs of a group of people

STEVENS, E. S. See DROWER, ETHEL STEFANA (STEVENS).

STEVENS, MARY C.

011513   MARJORY WITH THE CHAMORROS. New York:
American Tract Society, [c1907] NUC.

STEVENS, MARY FLETCHER. United States.

011514   BY SUBTLE FRAGRANCE HELD. Philadelphia:
J. B. Lippincott, 1893 NUC.

Memories awakened by the fragrance of a perfume keep a
young woman from accepting an unworthy lover .
PW-proud society girl develops warm loving nature in

quiet country home. Love story.

STEVENS, NINA.

011515   THE PERILS OF SYMPATHY. London: T. F.
Unwin, 1902 BMC.

LBKM-Anglo Indian triangle, man comes to his senses
and marries English woman.

STEVENS, SHEPPARD, pseud. See STEVENS, SUSAN SHEPPARD
(PIERCE).

STEVENS, SUSAN SHEPPARD (PIERCE). B. 1862. United States.

011516   I AM THE KING: BEING THE ACCOUNT OF SOME
HAPPENINGS IN THE LIFE OF GODFREY DE BERSAC,
CRUSADER-KNIGHT. BY SHEPPARD STEVENS. London: Gay &
Bird, 1898 BMC NUC. Boston: Little, Brown, 1898 NUC.

SP 81:837. Historical romance.
PW-Richard I and Godfrey in the Holy Land captured by
Saracens. Godfrey pretends to be king to protect him.

011517   IN THE EAGLE'S TALON; A ROMANCE OF THE
LOUISIANA PURCHASE. BY SHEPPARD STEVENS. Boston:
Little, Brown, 1902 BMC NUC.

DIAL 33:67 8/1/02
LW 33:140 9/1/02

011518   THE SIGN OF TRIUMPH; A ROMANCE OF THE
CHILDREN'S CRUSADE. BY SHEPPARD STEVENS. London:
Chapman and Hall, 1904 BMC. Boston: L. C. Page, 1904
NUC.

PW-Historical novel.

011519   THE SWORD OF JUSTICE. BY SHEPPARD
STEVENS. London: Gay & Bird, 1899 BMC. Boston: Little,
Brown, 1899 NUC.

CR 36:90. Historical romance. Struggle of the French
and Spanish for Florida, love story.

STEWART, CHARLOTTE. 1863-1918. United Kingdom.

011520   BEGGARS AND SORNERS. BY ALLAN MCAULAY.
London and New York: J. Lane, 1912 BMC NUC.

LBKM-1950's Helen Murray visits Amsterdam after an
illness. Her experiences including torture, espionage,
and interview with the Pretender and mrg to her host.
NYT-not a romance, but intended to show the seamy,
darker side of political intrigues.

011521   BLACK MARY. BY ALLAN MCAULAY. London:
T.F. Unwin, [1901] BMC.

life of Mary-half-caste See BAKER 13, 296
"Kindly portraiture of Perthshire folk 100 years ago,
bringing out strongly their hardness and their
integrity. In the half caste daughter of a neer do
well emigrant to the W. Indies, a much idealized
picture is presented of invincible goodness and
generosity. Black Mary's life of hardship, peril and
disappointment nobly borne, is pathetic" BAKER 13,296

011522   THE EAGLE'S NEST. BY ALLAN MCAULAY.
London and New York: J. Lane, 1910 BMC NUC.

hist novel, self sacrificing heroine SP

011523   POOR SONS OF A DAY. BY ALLAN MCAULAY.
London: J. Nisbet, 1902 BMC NUC.

hist romance See BAKER 13, 296

011524   THE RHYMER. BY ALLAN MCAULAY. New York:
C. Scribner's Sons, 1900 NUC. London: T. F. Unwin,
1900 NUC BMC.

SP 84:558. Literary heroine corresponds with Robert
Burns, real heroine acts as intermediary,
complications.
ACAD 58:274. Marriage with Jean Armour and affair with
Clarinda.
ATH 115:459. One of the least creditable portions of
Robert Burns' life. The affair with Mysie, a sordid
tragedy.

011525   THE SAFETY OF THE HONOURS. BY ALLAN
MCAULAY. Edinburgh: W. Blackwood, 1906 BMC.

hist romance-Cromwell invasion

STEWART, EDITH ANNE.

011526   LOVE AND THE PEOPLE. London: Lynwood,
1911 BMC.

novel of social reform, slum settlement life;
working-class aspirations, marriage of a young woman
to an artisan. TLS
"Socialism and woman's rights have a large hearing
here." Heroine wants a fuller life than her father's
home offers ACAD
Heroine marries a working man who is killed. SP

STEWART, ELLA MAUDE. United States.

011527   MAJELLA; OR, NAMELESS AND BLIND. A STORY
OF THE SUSQUEHANNA. Philadelphia: J. B. Lippincott,
1893 NUC.

STEWART, GERALD, pseud. See BERRY, MARY LEE.

STEWART, MARTHA MORLEY.

011528   GREYHOUND FANNY. Chicago: R. R.
Donnelley, 1912 NUC.

Story of a dog

STEWART, MARY. United States.

011529   UNSPOTTED FROM THE WORLD. New York: R. L.
Weed, [c1897] NUC.

PW-two heroines brought up in isolation in Ozarks by
refined parents who have avoided human company. Their
love affairs, St. Louis and Europe.

STICKNEY, MARY ETTA (SMITH). United States.

011530   BROWN OF LOST RIVER: A STORY OF THE WEST.
New York: D. Appleton, 1900 NUC.

PW-Wyoming. Brown, a bronco breaker, and his romance
with Edith Ellery.

STILLMAN, ANNIE RAYMOND. B. 1855. United States.

011531   FOOL'S GOLD: A STUDY IN VALUES. A NOVEL.
Chicago: F.H. Revell, 1902 BMC NUC.

STILLSON, FLORENCE GEORGEANNA MERCHANT. United States.

011532   DORIS: A STORY OF 1778. Danbury [Conn.]:
Published For Private Circulation, 1891 NUC.

STIRLING, ANNA MARIA DIANA WILHELMINA (PICKERING).

011533   A LIFE AWRY. A NOVEL. BY PERCIVAL
PICKERING. London: Bliss, Sands and Foster, 1893 BMC
NUC.

Judy transformed from strong beautiful girl to plain
deformed woman by an accident. Lover returns after
years and is repulsed by the change. She conceals her
love for him so he tells her about his new love
interest. Nurses him through an illness, succeeds in
reconciling him and his new love after they have
differences. Kills herself in the end. The strain is
too much. Good character study. SP 71,753
Furious and passionate love of a crippled young woman
for her commonplace cousin who cares nothing for her.
Her friend Maud believes love is a disease. Is
completely bored with her husband. Two talk a lot
about love and men. SR 76 654
Focus is completely on Judy whose life begins with
such promise and brightness. BKM 5:88

011534   A PLIABLE MARRIAGE. BY PERCIVAL
PICKERING. London: Osgood, 1895 BMC.

owes much to John Oliver Hobbes and to "New Woman
vapours not even yet banished from our literary
atmosphere." Platonic marriage The young woman who
converses on improper topics, etc. SR 79:704
"experiment of a young gentleman and lady who agree
to go thru the ceremony of marriage as an unavoidable
concession to conventionality previous to their
becoming business partners for life and her entering
upon the duties of confidential housekeeper to look
after his estate and act as hostess to his guests."
But he really loves her, tries in a gauche way
(suggested by his wife's rival) to subjugate her. They
part. Reconciled in end. SP 74:692

011535   THE SPIRIT IS WILLING. BY PERCIVAL
PICKERING. London: Bliss, Sands, 1898 BMC.

ACAD 53:201. Misplaced affections, unhappy marriages.
Aunt Letitia, a "prim sharp-eyed old maid," chivalrous
weak nephew. Seacoast.
ATH 101:401. Heroine is married to a painter of severe
morals, a misalliance. She turns to another man. She
said to her husband, "I do not know how men are
constituted; but for women, love has to be created.
Yes, I tell you, planted, tended, compelled into
being. You do not know? Oh men like you never do know!
This love creating is an art, a knack which the worst
men possess, a talent which they perfect with care.
And so it is they win women's love, while men like you
go hungry."

011536   TOY-GODS. BY PERCIVAL PICKERING. London:
J. Long, 1904 BMC.

LBKM-Heroine niece of a charwoman, sharp, shrewd, not
meek, humor, ambitious.
ACAD-Story of her move from her mother's to her
father's class.
TLS-Move from "common" to "commonplace"--analytical
study.

STIRLING, ELIZABETH. See STIRLING, MABEL ELIZABETH.

STIRLING, MABEL ELIZABETH.

011537   BARBARA MARY. BY ELIZABETH STIRLING.
London: S. Paul, 1919 BMC.

Unhappy marr. (one prearranged by a will) heroine
moves in a rich, idle, pleasure loving world. Marriage
ends up happy. TLS
Sugary tale. LBKM

011538   SWEET ALOES. BY ELIZABETH STIRLING.
London: S. Paul, [1920] NUC BMC.

TLS Margaret is perfect comrade of all the young men
at an Indian station. Father is drunken. Good
character drawing of colonel, continually abusing his
wife and exhibiting good nature to rest of world,
particularly the women.
LBKM Father shoots man Margaret loves

STOCK, ETTA FLORENCE (NIGHTENGALE). B. 1858. United
States.

011539   THE REDEMPTION OF CHARLEY PHILLIPS.
Boston: Four Seas, 1919 NUC.

"Mod bus. man to whom life seemed empty" finds hope.
PW NYT

011540   TO EVERY MAN HIS WORK. Boston: Four Seas,
1919 NUC.

Two men discouraged find hope in work. PW

STOCK, GERTRUDE GEORGINA (DOUGLAS).

011541   A WASTED LIFE AND MARR'D. London: Hurst
and Blackett, 1892 BMC.

Story of a waif, Maud Deering, raised by a baker. Her
life is wasted and marr'd by her selfish father. ATH
98 859
Young wife shoots husband who shot her dog. SR
12-19-91,699
ACAD: Maud, daughter of English heir & Canadian girl,
is foisted off as foundling by father after her
mother's death. She eventually discovers her
parentage, but not a happy ending.

STOCKLEY, CYNTHIA. 1883-1936. United Kingdom.

011542   THE CLAW. London: Hurst and Blackett,
1911 BMC NUC. New York and London: G. P. Putnam's
Sons, 1911 NUC.

Deidre Saurin narrates her life in Africa. She learns
"the tyranny of love and the tragedy of marriage" and
her experiences with hyenas. TLS
Travels the veldt alone. Marries miserably to learn
the man she loves is really alive wins happiness in
the end. PW 5-13-11.
"Heroine's biting wit, her candor in love-a remarkable
woman." ATH, NYT
English girl riding in a post cart across Africa. Miss
Saurin saved by a chivalrous man who beats her black
driver (the driver was some kind of threat to Miss
Saurin). Back in society she's subject to much
scandal. (for what?)
Used to have an art studio in Latin quarter. She

dislikes the society she moves in; likes to shock
them. She falls in love but marries a different man,
Maurice Stair, her lover dies. Stair is a cad and a
liar. The marriage is a trick; Stair has pretended
that her lover died. The marriage is horrible. Poisons
him? Author of "Violence".

011543   THE DREAM SHIP. London: Constable, 1913
BMC NUC.

Wife deserts husband who does not understand her. She
was a "correspondent from the centers of storm." He, a
doctor, establishes her as a housekeeper in his
nursing home. ATH
Wife Val Valdana, journalist-writes from all corners
of the world. She's incapable of domesticity, can't
run the hospital. When her first husband turns up, she
runs off with her son and adopted daughter. Eventually
this husband dies; the doctor comes to have a proper
sense of her. Life begins again with hope. She's a
complex, rich, sympathetic character real, modern.
LBKM
Young brilliant, a writer using a pseud. Brilliant
journalist writing under a pseudonym and reporting
from all corners of the world cannot settle for
domestic work. Val Valdanha runs off with her son and
adopted daughter when her first husband turns up after
an absence because she knows he can never understand
her. When he dies, she marries a doctor who comes to
have a proper sense of her after his initial mistake
of expecting her to be housekeeper in his nursing
home.

011544   PINK GODS AND BLUE DEMONS. London, New
York: Cassell, [1920] BMC NUC. New York: G. H. Doran,
[c1920] NUC.

NYT 1920:320 Young, foolish and beautiful wife becomes
fascinated with valuable pink diamonds owned by
scheming roue. S. Africa.

011545   POPPY; THE STORY OF A SOUTH AFRICAN GIRL.
London: Hurst and Blackett, [1910?] NUC BMC. New York
and London: G. P. Putnam's Sons, 1911 NUC.

Marital complications: unfortunate life of heroine, a
double divorce and remarriage, ending unresolved. PW
BKM-0
NYT-Author portrays immorality and attempts to justify
it-all its art is given toward making attractive the
woman who has found in her passion adequate cause for
her fall.
Overworked orphan drudge-alluring beauty with artist's
temperament who wins fame as a writer, novelist. TLS
S. African story, heroine described as "superior" "her
sensuous and artistic temperament," sexuality plays
too prominent a part. ATH
BKM-v. 31 1910 Single parent-refuses to let the
world's scorn crush her.

011546   VIRGINIA OF THE RHODESIANS. London:
Hutchinson, 1903 BMC 1910 BMC. Boston: Estes, 1911
NUC.

Unconventional narrator of love stories of South
Africa; distaste for chaperone nonsense; her
personality connects the stories. Invites us "to learn
about women" thru her. ACAD 64, 534
Young woman-precociously cynical outlook. Setting is
Africa among people with questionable pasts pursuing
pleasure. Her inmost thoughts; hides from a gossiping
world. The hopelessness of winning the man she loves?
BKM 34 (1911) 77-8
Virginia tells stories in first person; same
characters woven through, but no sense of her given in
review. NYT

011547   WANDERFOOT (THE DREAM SHIP). New York and
London: G P. Putnam's Sons., 1913 NUC.

BKM-Val Valdana, a partial Oriental and wandering
widow who makes lunch of brandy, soda, and a sardine,
fingers are stained with nicotine and who habitaully
makes use of alcohol marries Westenra, a physician who
finds her the woman of his dreams but disapproves of
her otherwise. Then her no-good first husband turns
up, she leaves Westenra rather than tell him and
raises chickens and gardens, bringing two children
with her. Her daughter Haidee comes to womanhood, many
love affairs.
"Wanderfoot" is the nomme de plume of Valentine
valdana, a successful woman journalist who has lived a
strange, adventurous life. She had married, when very
young, a man who was absolutely worthless, who
deserted her and whose death in the Boer War was an
unmixed blessing. On a steamer bound for New York,

Valentine meets Dr. Westenra, they fall in love and
marry almost immediately and then after their son is
born Valdana turns up. Valentine and Westenra
separate, the latter ignorant of Valdana's being alive
and for five or six years both are very unhappy, but
at last their path is made smooth for them. By author
of "Poppy". PW 84 11/8/13:1533.
Most famous woman journalist in Europe. NYT

STODDARD, JANIE E. United States.

   011548   TEMPESTS OF THE PLAY GODS. New York:
   Neale, 1904 NUC.

STOKELY, EDITH KEELEY AND MARIAN KENT HURD.

   011549   MISS BILLY: A NEIGHBORHOOD STORY. Boston:
   Lothrop, [1905] NUC.

   Young woman changes a whole neighborhood. PW 4-22-05
   Book for girls, brief description in BKM 21 (1905)
   440.

STOLZENBERG, BETSEY (RIDDLE) VON HUTTEN ZUM. B. 1874.
United States.

   011550   ARABY. BY BARONESS VON HUTTEN. New York:
   Smart Set, 1904 NUC.

   PW-suicide?

   011551   THE BAG OF SAFFRON. BY THE BARONESS VON
   HUTTEN. London: Hutchinson, 1917 BMC NUC. New York: D.
   Appleton, 1918 NUC.

   Biog. of a minx with incidental portraits of other
   people in a distinctively feminine style. BAKER 32:256
   PW-Love. Cuckoo is Becky Sharp without her adroitness.
   NYT-portrait of cold, selfish, materialistic woman.
   Sudden and unexpected development of character at the
   end.

   011552   BEECHY; OR THE LORDSHIP OF LOVE. BY
   BETTINA VON HUTTEN. New York: F.A. Stokes, [1909] NUC.

   Beatrice in disguise of boy becomes a successful opera
   star in Rome; meets her fate. Marries and gives up
   career. BKM
   Brought up in slums, chooses stage career, keeps self
   unsullied and strong. Dons boy's clothes to sing in
   Carmen; finds them convenient. Sells papers on street
   in daytime. Becomes a great diva who conquers NY and
   London. Author makes her success believeable;
   fascinating study portrait painted very well. NYT

   011553   BIRD'S FOUNTAIN. BY THE BARONESS VON
   HUTTEN. London: Hutchinson, 1915 BMC NUC. New York: D.
   Appleton, 1915 NUC.

   BKM-Amy plays around with other man only to discover
   she and husband love each other.
   Amy Dorset 35, married 16 years beauty, wealth,
   position. But she had never had a love affair. She and
   husband placidly indifferent to each other. He's dull,
   much older, falls for a rake. Lawrence Croxley, "a
   homely middle aged spinster" who loves Amy and does
   her best to save her. Amy "silly useless butterfly,"
   weak, falls for this unworthy man. But even she "is
   admirably drawn and wins from the reader the pity the
   author evidently intended her to obtain." NYT

   011554   THE GREEN PATCH. BY BETTINA VON HUTTEN.
   New York: F.A. Stokes, [c1910] NUC. London:
   Hutchinson, 1910 BMC.

   A well bred man grows tired of family, leaves them.
   Daughter joins him and gets an unconventional
   up-bringing. Marries one man who loved her sister,
   falls in love with another. All turns out
   satisfactorily. PW
   NYT-he has 3 daughters, all who visit him from time to
   time in his Italian villa.

   011555   THE HALO. BY BETTINA VON HUTTEN. New
   York: Dodd, Mead, 1907 NUC. London: Methuen, 1907 BMC.

   Bridgit Mead-sulky, embittered, tired of poverty, sick
   of mother's nagging her to marry old wealthy men.
   Makes hasty engagement to drinker who is young and
   rich but soon falls in love with his father-who is
   married. Only the hand of death intervenes to keep
   them from going off together. Bridgit stronger
   passions that many women never heard of. TLS
   Victor famous violinist old but youthful. Wife
   charming peasant woman. Son Theo wayward. Lady Bridgit
   Mead ravishing promises to marry Theo but soon falls

550

for his father--twice her age and more. But father
makes her marry son when he learns of engagement. But
their passion lives, plan to elope. Death of wife
startles them. NYT
ACAD-ordinary love story, wife dies conveniently.

011556   HAPPY HOUSE. BY THE BARONESS VON HUTTEN.
London: Hutchinson, [1919] NUC BMC. New York: G.H.
Doran, [c1920] NUC.

A husband's unfaithfulness, projected divorce and final
return. TLS
SR-Mrs. Walbridge is a writer of popular sentimental
pre-Georgian romances, whose happy endings are no
longer in style. Her idle husband and not too amiable
children despise her books but spend her money. She
has necessary evidence for divorce but does not take
action because he is making such a fool of himself.
What happens?
PW-holds family together with her struggles.
BKM-Mrs. Walbridge capable, practical middle-aged
woman. Although her nearest approach to personal
tragedy is when her popularity wanes, she writes to
provide for her family. She has a swift rise to real
fame. The lord of the manor who loved her in her youth
is drawn to her daughter only to find he still loves
the mother. But she will not divorce husband, she
regards him as an investment she has paid for in heavy
installments until he has acquired the sentimental
value of a costly mistake. The lord stays around.
NYT-Mrs. Walbridge is over 50. "Perfect simplicity and
clear sightedness which enable her to see her
contemptible husband and selfish children precisely as
they are. She is at times a little exasperating in her
meekness, her sentimentality, and her continual
self-sacrifice."

011557   HE AND HECUBA; A NOVEL. BY BARONESS VON
HUTTEN. New York: D. Appleton, 1905 BMC NUC.

Story seems to focus upon a clergyman and several
women in his life. PW
Beautiful woman with no morals and a clergyman;
sordid, frank realism; feminine self-sufficiency and
passion, taste for ragged edges of propriety. Pastor,
husband of a faded wife and numerous neglected
children gives up life of passion for church till
Rosalba shows up. Pastor attracted, stirred up writes
a novel of his youth. A missing husband shows up. The
pastor feels guilt, the wife is broken. Tragic. NYT

011558   KINGSMEAD, A NOVEL. BY BETTINA VON
HUTTEN. London: Hutchinson, 1909 BMC. New York: Dodd,
Mead, 1909 NUC.

Characters of Pam and Halo come together in England.
PW
Pam has white hair, married a long time. Charming love
story. TLS
Mrs. Gilfin a widow loved by two men. BKM NYT

011559   THE LORDSHIP OF LOVE; A NOVEL. BY
BARONESS VON HUTTEN. London: Hutchinson, 1909 BMC.
Toronto: Musson Book, [1909] NUC.

Career and romance of an orphaned cast-off daughter of
a princely Roman house. Very sympathetic figure of her
struggling childhood and fame as a great singer. TLS
A woman singer genius, Beatrice Cavaleone: her taste
of musical Bohemia, year in convent, escape back to
music, her debut, instant success, a most
unconventional happy ending. Anglice Beechy is
Beatrice Cavaleone. TLS
Falls in love with married man but they do not give
way to their love. The friendship between the wife and
the singer is not very consistent with good taste. SP
LBKM-from slums to operatic artist via various jobs.

011560   MAG PYE. BY BETTINA VON HUTTEN. London:
Hutchinson, 1917 BMC. New York: D. Appleton, 1917 NUC.
(Eng. ed. title: Magpie)

She's a little girl, a kind of laundry maid who at 16
after some training has a picture on the line of the
Academy. Takes care of father-on opium. TLS
Also careful portrait of mother who after years of
suffering has her identity recovered. Artist husband
had gone under. ATH
(Maggie-Margaret Pye). Told by old bachelor-girl
whose artistic ed. he promotes. NYT
Makes her way to success and happiness by sheer force
of character. Her father loves one woman but marries
another who leaves when she realizes she can't make
him happy. Mag Pye's mother deserts her too. Years
later we find Mag Pye who can draw; given proper
instruction, her genius comes forth. Her genius runs

out; falls in love. BKM

011561   MARIA. London: Hutchinson, 1914 BMC NUC.
New York: D. Appleton, 1914 NUC.

SR-Maria, conventionally proper, loves and is loved by
a prince who cannot marry her because of difference in
their social status. Her sufferings make her a great
rather than a good singer.

011562   "MARR'D IN MAKING". BY BARONESS VON
HUTTEN. London: A. Constable, 1901 BMC. Philadelphia
and London: J. B. Lippincott, 1901 NUC.

problem novel. Mother dies in chapter 1 heredity the
problem that ends in the river. Beth heroine and
sinner by inheritance attractive. Suicide seems
unprepared for; a triumph of morals. ACAD
Beth, an instinctive liar, flirt, atheist. She's
married but reserves passion for an old flame who is
married. Considers eloping with him. Instead kills
herself. ATH

011563   MISS CARMICHAEL'S CONSCIENCE. A STUDY IN
FLUCTUATIONS. BY BARONESS VON HUTTEN. Philadelphia and
London: J. B. Lippincott, 1900 BMC NUC.

NYT 1900:408. Mary is fascinating but does not wreck
lives. Restores Jim to Eve, marries a crippled lord.
She's a vain heartless flirt. Her conscience awakens
when she loves a married man. LW 30:408
She has a beautiful voice. PW 56:775

011564   MRS. DRUMMOND'S VOCATION. London: W.
Heinemann, 1913 BMC.

011565   THE ONE WAY OUT. BY BETTINA VON HUTTEN.
New York: Dodd, Mead, 1906 NUC.

"The principal character in this amusing storiette
proposes to three girls in one evening and is three
times refused. He withholds the fourth proposal, the
one that would doubtless have been accepted. The
reasons which prompted his actions is the story. The
illustrations are by Harrison Fisher. The volume
presents a holiday appearance." BKM v.24, 1906-07.

011566   OUR LADY OF THE BEECHES. BY THE BARONESS
VON HUTTEN. Boston: Houghton, Mifflin, 1902 NUC.
London: W. Heinemann, 1907 BMC.

Lonely wife's letter to a writer (man) she never met
and his to her. Their meeting, friendship, love, brief
description. LBKM 5-07,70
"a disembodied friendship" thru letters. American
woman with a dislike for society. ACAD
Lady is an author-TLS
They meet but part-ATH
heroine married several years, husband a big-game
shooter, travels a lot, the sport bores her so she
stays home. She's a countess of 29 interested in
philosophy, nature, metaphysics, writes to author of a
philosophy work-Richard Saxe, 42, falls for her. They
meet by chance. They converse, "fantastic adventure in
friendship." She's drawn very sympathetically. She's
"superb," married woman carries on a "literary
flirtation".
DIAL-11-16-02--witty intelligent correspondence
between married woman and another man (doctor) leads,
finally to their meeting and declaration of love.
NYT-10-18-02-"as they are decent folks, and the lady's
husband is a good fellow, they presently part, never,
one hopes, to meet again."

011567   PAM. BY BETTINA VON HUTTEN. London: W.
Heinemann, 1904 BMC. New York: Dodd, Mead, 1905 NUC.

"destined to live life vastly different from that of
other girls." Pam is illegitimate, parents live
together though mother still married to another man.
BKM
"the couple...flaunt their perfect and radiant
happiness in the face of social ostracism." precocious
adolescent. Pam decides she'll accept love but will
never marry. Rejection of marriage, born out of
wedlock.

011568   PAM DECIDES; A SEQUEL TO "PAM". BY
BETTINA VON HUTTEN. New York: Dodd, Mead, 1906 NUC.

PW-now 27, living secretly writing cheap novels.

011569   SHARROW. BY BETTINA VON HUTTEN. London:
Hutchinson, 1912 BMC NUC. New York: D Appleton, 1912
NUC.

TLS-story of a house and the family whose lives it dominates.

011570   VIOLETT; A CHRONICLE. BY BARONESS VON HUTTEN. Boston: Houghton, Mifflin, 1904 NUC.

NYT-story of a male musician

011571   WHAT BECAME OF PAM. BY BARONESS VON HUTTEN. London: W. Heinemann, 1906 NUC BMC.

STONE, JANE, pseud. See TRIMBLE, JESSIE.

STONE, MARY E. See BASSETT, MARY E. (STONE).

STONE, MATILDA WOODS. United States.

011572   EVERY MAN HIS CHANCE. Boston: R.G. Badger, 1909 NUC.

Story of a town PW 1-16-09

STONE, PATTIE (WRIGHT). 1853-1931. United States.

011573   AS YE SOW; A ROMANCE OF COOSA VALLEY. New York: Neale, 1906 NUC.

STOOTHOFF, ELLENOR, pseud. See GREENSLET, ELLA STOOTHOFF (HULST).

STOPES, MARIE CHARLOTTE CARMICHAEL. 1880-1958. United Kingdom.

011574   LOVE LETTERS OF A JAPANESE, EDITED BY G. N. MORTLAKE. London: S. Paul, [1911] BMC NUC.

Correspondence between English woman and Japanese lover; "prolonged erotics." TLS

STORER, MARIA (LONGWORTH). 1849-1932. United States.

011575   THE BORODINO MYSTERY. St. Louis and London: B. Herder, [1916] NUC.

011576   THE VILLA ROSSIGNOL; OR, THE ADVANCE OF ISLAM. St. Louis, Mo. and London: B. Herder, 1918 BMC NUC.

STORY, EDITH MARY (STEANE). B. 1861. United Kingdom.

011577   BLACK HUMPHREY: A STORY OF THE OLD CORNISH COACHING AND KIDNAPPING DAYS. BY JAMES CASSIDY. London: W. Scott, [1911] BMC.

011578   FATHER PAUL. BY JAMES CASSIDY. London: Kegan Paul, 1908 BMC.

011579   THE GIFT OF LIFE: A ROMANCE. BY JAMES CASSIDY. London: Chapman and Hall, 1897 BMC.

STOTT, BEATRICE.

011580   CHRISTIAN DERRICK. London: Chatto and Windus, 1915 BMC.

Study of a misogynist. As a boy had no mother, disagreeable step mother. As adult his hate for his friend's wife conceals love. TLS

011581   ROSEMARY AND RUE. London: Sidgwick and Jackson, 1912 BMC.

ATH-Psychological study of a young woman.
TLS-Rosemary daughter of Rosamunda of former book. Wretched girlhood, falls from virtue, leads double life, marries a man she learns to abhor and enters on a career of misery. She lacks loveable qualities and is hard as nails. POV?

011582   ROSEMONDE. London: T. F. Unwin, 1903 BMC.

A man's unlovely soul dissected; the woman's soul more harmonious; He's wretched; She's a real woman. He tortures her mentally and physically. Psychological study of her undying passion for this cruel man who nevertheless loves her intensely. Very concentrated study of the two. ACAD 65, 622
LBKM-unhappy marriage, husband is Byronic, charming, selfish and distrustful of his wife even after she allows him to read her locked diary she has kept for years.

STOUT, ETHEL ALMAZ. United Kingdom.

011583   THE GOLDEN LURE. London: G. Newnes, [1917] BMC.

STOVALL, EUGENIA (ORCHARD). B. 1872?. United States.

011584   A SON OF CAROLINA. BY GENIE ORCHARD STOVALL. New York: Neale, 1909 NUC.

Woman steps over conventional bounds of taste, wealth, and tradition for the sake of worthless man. PW 11-13-09.
Couple adopt a child with part "negro blood"; she grows up a beauty; told the secret; dies in the end. NYT

STOVALL, GENIE ORCHARD. See STOVALL, EUGENIA (ORCHARD).

STOW, EDITH. United States.

011585   NANCY THE JOYOUS. Chicago: Reilly & Britton, [1914] NUC.

PW 86 8/1/14:357 "Nancy, learning by chance that marriage would injure her lover's advancement, renounces him without disclosing her reason. She avoids another match planned by a rich aunt by becoming missionary in the mountains. How the Bishop is concerned in the destiny of Nancy and John makes the story."

STRAHAN, KAY (CLEAVER). 1888-1941. United States.

011586   PEGGY-MARY. New York: Duffield, 1915 NUC.

Stenographer and her marital problems. PW 9-11-15 "Fluffy girly; girliness" NYT

STRAIN, E. H. See STRAIN, EUPHANS H. (MACNAUGHTON).

STRAIN, EUPHANS H. (MACNAUGHTON). D. 1934. United Kingdom.

011587   ELMSLIE'S DRAG-NET. BY E. H. STRAIN. London: Methuen, 1900 BMC.

LBKM 19:89. short stories.

011588   LAURA'S LEGACY. BY E. H. STRAIN. London: T.Unwin, 1903 BMC.

Laura just lost husband and son; "inherits" a baby girl who was the child of a nameless tramp who died. Lady Laura not told. She believes God brought her the child in her time of need. ACAD 65, 562

011589   A MAN'S FOES. BY E. H. STRAIN. London and New York: Ward, Lock and Bowden, 1895 BMC NUC.

Ulster 1688-89:groups of men bond together to resist King James' laws. Told by a wise narrator-a woman who describes loves and fortunes of her husband and her circle of Scotch and English colonists. ATH 106:527
Prots. vs Catholics in Ulster in 17th century. BAKER 03, 222
SR. Siege of Derry, purportedly written by wife of one of its defenders. No love story. Womanly women.
CR 29:58. Quick-witted heroine, outwits a soldier by wrapping him in her mantle, pistols and all, until husband arrives.
ACAD 49:282. Hardships of the citizens of Derry during siege of 1689. Mrs. Hamilton heroically saves her husband's life. True to fact.
BKM 3:160. Narrative of wife. After his rescue, he must escape, and she is left alone to defend her children. She resists temptation "when desertion of the cause would save her little ones from starvation." A "womanly woman."

011590   A PROPHET'S REWARD. Edinburgh: W. Blackwood, 1908 BMC.

TLS-political-18th c. Scotch.
ACAD-political-18th c. Scotch.
BKM-political-18th c. Scotch.
ATH Female heroine immersed in the terrors of the French Revolution.

STRANNIK, IVAN, pseud. See ANICHKOVA, ANNA MITROFANOVNA (AVINOVA).

STRATENUS, LOUISE ANTOINETTE. 1852-1908.

011591   SUSPECTED. London: Chapman and Hall, 1892 BMC. New York: B. Appleton, 1893 NUC. (Tr. S. Von Straalen)

ATH 100:221. Heroine is the type known as the "man's woman."
ACAD - Romance

SR 74:281 "striking study of a woman"
innocent man suspected of killing his rival for
beautiful woman's love. Germany. Heroine is poor
living with uncle. she loves the wrong man. PW 6-17-93
She lives with aunt and uncle who pick a good man for
her to wed, but she loves a cad. Then she sees the
worthiness of the young man chosen by her guardians,
but he's then suspected of killing the cad. All ok in
the end. CR 20,23:100

STRATFORD, BARBARA ELIZABETH (ERRINGTON) WINGFIELD. B.
1862. United Kingdom.

011592   BERYL IN INDIA. Liverpool: Books, Ltd.,
[1920] BMC NUC.

TLS-Fresh candid view of India and the Memsahib. Beryl
is a shuttlecock between husband and lover-no agony
involved, she just keeps changing her mind.

STRATTON, JENNIE M. United States.

011593   CECIL'S CROWN. Cleveland, Ohio: Williams,
1891 NUC.

STRAUSS, JULIET VIRGINIA.

011594   THE IDEAS OF A PLAIN COUNTRY WOMAN. BY
"THE COUNTRY CONTRIBUTOR" [ANONYMOUS]. London and New
York: Doubleday, Page, 1908 BMC NUC.

Attitudes, ideas "almost too healthy," praises
poverty, etc. ACAD

STRAY, ERMINA C. United States.

011595   THE GOLDEN LINK; OR, THE SHADOW OF SIN. A
STORY OF OUR TIMES. Almont, Mich.: Larger Hope Pub.
Co., 1891 NUC.

STREATFEILD, LILIAN CECIL.

011596   EVELYN'S QUEST. BY ELSIE FEILD. London:
H. J. Glaisher, 1906 BMC.

TLS-suitable for young readers, a young woman
searching for religion, working among the poor.

STREDDER, SARAH, ELEANOR AND HARRIET. See MULTIPLE AUTHORS.

STREET, LILIAN. United Kingdom.

011597   THE DISPUTED MARRIAGE. London: J.M. Dent,
1911 BMC. New York: E. P. Dutton, 1911 PMC.

Mod. society life; letters. ATH
Barbara Jack is made undesireable-a suffragette and
child hater. SR
ACAD-Letters, love-tale

011598   FITZJAMES. London: Methuen, 1900 BMC.

LBKM 18:189. Hero is famous much loved poet.
SP 85:182. Modern semi-society story.
ACAD 59:261. Also, he is an artist, critic and
musician. Adoring heroine. Marriage at end.

011599   THE GOODWOOD WEEK. London: Aldine, 1899
BMC.

011600   THE LITTLE PLAIN WOMAN AND OTHERS.
London: T. F. Unwin, 1895 BMC.

Concerns a literary woman. Other stories. "Second hand
George Egerton" SR:80:640
Concerns a literary woman described as young, small,
weird, electric: "what a colourless soulless face is
mine! I believe I am as sexless as you said!" she
exclaims to the man she loves; whileto the man who
loves her she confides, "I began life in hell, and I
haven't admired the road to heaven, so I am sitting on
the side to consider the next move." ATH 107:312. She
is uncomfortable in her love affairs, as in all other
affairs of her daily life. Everything goes wrong in a
dull, vague manner, and book ends with her as lonely
and unsatisfied as she was at start. 'and other
stories' are five very short sketches.

011601   NELL AND THE ACTOR. London: Skeffington,
1897 BMC.

An unpleasant doctor and an adventuress. Both killed
in the end. Nell marries an actor. SR 83:453
Nell is self-sacrificing. ATH 109:532
Two brothers, one a good man-Graham, the artist. The
other, bad, Paul, a science student. Nell loves Graham

but Paul loves Nell. Paul and his mistress plot to
poison Nell's mind against Graham, but they fail. Then
Paul's mistress tries to kill Nell. SP 78:775

011602   THE WORLD AND ONORA. London: Duckworth,
1898 BMC.

LIT 3:606. Portrait of ill-used wife relieved of her
burden.
ATH 112:485.
LBKM 15:58. She married a 40 year old baronet who was
cruel to her & killed her baby. She left him and fell
for a music-hall singer whom she married after her
husband died.

STRETTON, HESBA, pseud. See SMITH, SARAH.

STRICKLAND, MARGARET.

011603   ELUSIVE PEG: BEING SOME CHAPTERS IN THE
LIFE OF PEGGY VERDON, NEE O'HARA. London: Angold's,
[1917] BMC.

"Tomboy's escapades" as a girl and as a married woman.
TLS
She's Irish, wayward, irresponsible, tendency to
reckless gambling but made loveable. Marries a man
from respectable pious family; their financial
difficulties; "indulges in all manner of subterfuges
to secure money" comes to see her husband not as
virtuous as she thought. LBKM

STRICKLAND, TERESA HAMMOND. United States.

011604   UNDER THE BAN: A SOUTH CAROLINA ROMANCE.
Chicago: Rand, McNally, [c1898] NUC.

STRONACH, ALICE, jt. au. See PENDERED, MARY LUCY AND ALICE
STRONACH.

STRONG, CLARA LATHROP. United States.

011605   FORFEIT: A NOVEL. New York: Houghton
Mifflin, 1912 NUC.

NYT A man and woman in Puritan Massachusetts.
Condemnation of early Puritans.

STRONG, HERO, pseud. See JONES, CLARA AUGUSTA.

STRONG, ISOBEL, pseud. See FIELD, ISOBEL (OSBOURNE).

STRONG, LOUISE JACKSON. United States.

011606   THE SWOOP OF THE WEEK; OR, THE TREASURE
AT "MA'S LEGACY". Cincinnati: Jennings & Graham,
[c1913] NUC.

PW 83 3/15/13 p. 986 "Story of a party of boys, who,
seven in number, call themselves "The week." The
incidents of the book turn upon a camping trip, and a
hidden treasure in a nearby farm gives special
interest to the story. The events leading up to the
discovery of the treasure make exciting reading."

STROTHER, EMILY (VIELE). B. 1865. United States.

011607   EVE DORRE; THE STORY OF HER PRECARIOUS
YOUTH. New York: E. P. Dutton, [c1915] NUC. London: J.
M. Dent, 1916 BMC.

BKM 42 1915-16
Picture of French life PW 10-16-15
TLS-An Amer who marries a Fr. painter. Writes of her
ordinary doings and surroundings. Is suicidal,
BKM-Rev is furious. She smokes a lot.

STUART, DOROTHY MARGARET.

011608   MARTIN THE MUMMER. London: Constable,
1910 BMC NUC.

TLS-history.
Historical romance--ACAD
SR

011609   ST. LO, A NOVEL. London: Holder and
Hardingham, 1912 BMC.

ATH-male hero of 15th century.
TLS-male hero of 15th century.

STUART, ELEANOR, pseud. See CHILDS, ELEANOR STUART
(PATTERSON).

STUART, ESME, pseud. See LEROY, AMELIE CLAIRE.

STUART, FLORENCE. United Kingdom.

011610   PUNCHINELLO [ANONYMOUS]. J. Bowden, 1899
BS. Boston: L. C. Page, 1900 NUC.

Auto. form; inner life of a great 18th century
musician. Morbid. He's a hunchback. Marries girl but
he's so jealous he causes her death. LIT 5:374
Hunchback is a dwarf. LBKM 17:30.
Later learns from his wife's diary that she was
faithful and devoted. SP 83:259
A self-tormented artist, who is a dwarf. His deformity
preys on him so as to spoil his life. BAKER 03,67
NYT 1900:938. Crippled musician marries. Suspects wife
of lover. Finds lover dead and scars his face.

STUART, RUTH (MACENERY). 1856-1917. United States.

011611   CARLOTTA'S INTENDED. A NOVEL.
Philadelphia: J. B. Lippincott, [c1891] NUC.

LW 25:233. Romance of "little Irish shoemaker."

011612   THE COCOON: A REST-CURE COMEDY. New York:
Hearst's International Library, [1915] BMC NUC.

letters from a sanitorium to her husband and diary
entries PW 4-24-15
heroine apparently happily married has nervous
breakdown, sent to sanitorium from which she writes
letters to husband. She begins to have hysterics when
she believes that a fellow patient is receiving love
letters from her (the first woman's) husband, but of
course it isn't true ? BKM

011613   GEORGE WASHINGTON JONES, A CHRISTMAS GIFT
THAT WENT A-BEGGING. Philadelphia: H. Altemus, [1903]
NUC. London: C. H. Kelly, [1904] BMC.

011614   NAPOLEON JACKSON, THE GENTLEMAN OF THE
PLUSH ROCKER. New York: Century, 1902 BMC NUC.

"negro life in a humorous vein" PW
Good natured wife assumes role of provider DIAL
11-16-02

011615   THE RIVER'S CHILDREN: AN IDYL OF THE
MISSISSIPPI. New York: Century, 1904 BMC NUC.

Pagan worship of Mississippi River NYT 05, 43

011616   SONNY. New York: Century, 1896 NUC BMC,
NUC.

PW 11-21-96. Children's book.
"Growth and career of an only son in a middle aged
household." Begins with his birth, ends with his
marriage. Great love and trust of father for son. LW
28:59

011617   SONNY'S FATHER; IN WHICH THE FATHER, NOW
BECOME GRANDFATHER, A KINDLY OBSERVER OF LIFE AND A
GENIAL PHILOSOPHER, IN HIS DESULTORY TALKS WITH THE
FAMILY DOCTOR, CARRIES ALONG THE STORY OF SONNY. New
York: Century, 1910 NUC BMC.

011618   THE STORY OF BABETTE, A LITTLE CREOLE
GIRL. New York: Harper, 1894 NUC. London: Osgood and
McIlvaine, 1895 BMC.

011619   THE UNLIVED LIFE OF LITTLE MARY ELLEN.
Indianapolis: Bobbs-Merrill, [c1910] NUC.

left at altar, she goes crazy (?) prays for a baby.
Thinks a doll is her baby! Friends later persuade her
the doll died. PW

011620   THE WOMAN'S EXCHANGE OF SIMPKINSVILLE.
New York & London: Harper, 1899 NUC.

STURGE, M. CARTA. See STURGE, MARY CHARLOTTE.

STURGE, MARY CHARLOTTE.

011621   THE TIME SPELL OF THE CHATEAU D'ARPON. BY
M. CARTA STURGE. Bristol: Arrowsmith, 1898 BMC NUC.

STUTTLE, LILLA DALE AVERY. United States.

011622   MAKING HOME HAPPY. Battle Creek, Mich.,
Chicago: Review and Herald Pub Co., 1898 NUC.

011623   MAKING HOME PEACEFUL: SEQUEL TO "MAKING
HOME HAPPY". Battle Creek, Michigan: Home Life Pub
Co., [c1899] NUC.

STUYVESANT, ALICE, pseud. See WILLIAMSON, ALICE MURIEL
(LIVINGSTON).

SUKLOVA, MARIYA.

011624   THE LIFE-STORY OF A RUSSIAN EXILE. New
York: Century, 1914 BMC NUC. London: W. Heinemann,
1915 BMC. (Tr. Gregory Yarros.)

A peasant, a born revolutionary "frank revelation of a
revolutionary" Author herself exiled to Siberia for
her pol. views. SR

SULLIVAN, ELIZABETH (HIGGINS). B. 1874. United States.

011625   OUT OF THE WEST, A NOVEL. BY ELIZABETH
HIGGINS. New York and London: Harper, 1902 BMC NUC.

BOOK NEWS-heroine western stump-orator for Populist
Party, marries and sends husband to Congress, he
becomes corrupted. "Colorado Joan of Arc"
NYT-Not helpful
One part deals with marriage and poverty, the other
with marriage and wealth. ATH. 121, 431,1

SULLIVAN, MARGARET DAVIES. United States.

011626   GODDESS OF THE DAWN: A ROMANCE. New York:
Dillingham, [c1914] BMC NUC.

"Three men adore Doris, the "wellestar" girl. One is a
struggling young sculptor who will not ask her to
share his poverty. Another she finds does not meet her
ideal of the man she should marry. Her experience with
a third is tragical. A tale of how love really comes
and moulds and mars, with a happy ending telling how
it rewards."

SULLIVAN, MAY KELLOGG. United States.

011627   A WOMAN WHO WENT TO ALASKA. Boston: J. H.
Earle, [c1902] NUC.

Woman loves to travel, goes to Arctic circle WOMAN'S
JOURNAL 1-24-03. Fiction? F 909.

SULLIVAN, MRS. A. SHACKELFORD. United States.

011628   A QUESTIONABLE MARRIAGE. Chicago: Rand,
McNally, [c1897] NUC.

"...based upon complications incident to the Oklahoma
divorce law and the decision of the supreme court
declaring that law void." PW 51:921. point of view.

SUMERWELL, FLORIDA POPE. Nationality Unknown.

011629   FOUR IN FAMILY: A STORY OF HOW WE LOOK
FROM WHERE THE DOG SITS. Indianapolis: Bobbs-Merrill,
[c1911] NUC.

Nonsense story; dog narrator. BKM

SUMMERS, DOROTHY.

011630   A MAN'S LOVE. London: T. F. Unwin, 1907
BMC.

Saint-like Laurel, base Lilia; heroine is "dense"; the
type that's bound to be "treated cruelly"; nearly dies
of brain-fever. ACAD
Jealous husband. TLS
A charming devoted wife, an impulsive "horsey" girl is
skillfully drawn, a seductive American roue. SR

011631   THE PLAINS OF ALU. London: Everett, 1908
BMC.

TLS-high spirited heroine who saves her lover,
removing a spell by going to Egypt and restoring
Ramses head to his body.

011632   RENUNCIATION. London: T. F. Unwin, 1905
BMC.

Centers upon an athlete becoming a hideously deformed
cripple. ACAD 1155, 05

SUMNER, HELEN L. See WOODBURY, HELEN LAURA (SUMNER).

SUNDERLAND, URANIA BURNETT. Nationality Unknown.

011633   THAT WAGER OF DOT'S. BY PENELOPE
DALRYMPLE. New York and London: Abbey Press, [1901]
NUC.

SUPER, EMMA LEFFERTS. United States.

011634   ONE RICH MAN'S SON. Cincinnati: Cranston
and Curts, 1895 NUC.

How an heroic mother saved such a son "from temporal
and eternal ruin." PW 8-10-95:203

SURBRIDGE, AGNES. Nationality Unknown.

011635   THE CONFESSIONS OF A CLUB WOMAN. New
York: Doubleday, Page, 1904 NUC.

Conflict between meetings and domestic duties. BKM v.
19, 1904
BKM v. 20, 1904
NYT 0

SURGHNOR, MRS M. F. B. 1833. United States.

011636   UNCLE TOM OF THE OLD SOUTH: A STORY OF
THE SOUTH IN RECONSTRUCTION DAYS. New Orleans: L.
Graham, 1897 NUC.

SURREY, MARGARET.

011637   BY A BROAD WATER OF THE WEST. London:
RTS, 1910 BMC.

TLS-tender love story.

011638   AN IDYLL IN VENICE. London: RTS, [1906]
BMC.

011639   A MODERN ATALANTA: PASSAGES IN THE LIFE
OF A YOUNG HEIRESS. London: RTS, [1908] BMC.

TLS-Acted like her heathen namesake--mild tale.

011640   THE SOUL OF A GIRL. London: Marshall
Brothers, [1907] BMC.

Simple love story--TLS

SUTCLIFFE, CONSTANCE. See MARRIOTT, CONSTANCE (SUTCLIFFE).

SUTHERLAND, JOAN, pseud. See KELLY, JOAN COLLINGS.

SUTHERLAND, MILLICENT FANNY (SAINT CLAIR-ERSKINE)
SUTHERLAND-LEVESON-GOWER. B. 1867. United Kingdom.

011641   ONE HOUR AND THE NEXT. London: Methuen,
1899 BMC. New York: 1899 NUC.

The Labour problem-a strike. A school-master loves
Agnes; and a Christian Socialist who also loves her
while she loves Lester, a radical agitator. She types
for him and he regards her solely as a tool. He has a
wife he neglects. All remains that way. No one gets a
happy end. Agnes learns Lester has no love for her. Is
cold and hard to him. On the last page she is
miserable. LIT 5:448.
Agnes Strainer--enthusiastic, her boundless self
confidence, her blind love for Lester. LBKM 17:89
Asheton the good Socialist, Lester, the bad radical.
SR 88:558

SUTPHEN, ELEANOR AMERMAN. United States.

011642   YE NEXTE THYNGE. New York: F. H. Revell,
[c1897] NUC.

SUTTON, ELIZABETH M. Nationality Unknown.

011643   CELESTE. New York: G. W. Dillingham, 1895
NUC.

Marie Lascille, French peasant, leaves home with Count
who leaves her after a few years and marries another.
Marie lives free life in Paris, plots vs. the count.
Steals his child with intention of raising her to be a
prostitute. PW 2-16-95:324.

SVENSON, EMILY. See BAKER, AMELIA LOVISA (SVENSON).

SVETLA, CAROLINE, pseud. See MUZAKOVA, JOHANA (ROTTOVA).

SWABEY, HILDA M.

011644   THE CHIEF COMMISSIONER. London: Methuen,
1912 BMC NUC.

TLS-Hard and unyielding Indian civil servant and
relationship with his smart and self-assured daughter.
ATH Misogymist, he has become no more than a hard

working machine. e.Squabbles between himself and
daughter; she triumphs in some degree.
ACAD-She succeeds in conquering him; she is singularly
unloveable without sexual impulses. He had found his
wife so far beneath him he had left her and children
for India. Successful career. Then Dora shows up, he
had practically forgotten children as well as wife in
his ambitious projects.

SWAN, ANNIE S. See SMITH, ANNIE S. (SWAN).

SWAN, CAROLINE DAVENPORT.

011645   THE UNFADING LIGHT. Boston: Sherman,
French, 1911 NUC.

SWAN, ELIZA B. United States.

011646   THE OPAL QUEEN. Cincinnati: Robert
Clarke, 1897 NUC.

LW 23:151. Purpose is to persuade women to renounce
current fashions and wear classic Greek dress.
PW-South. Elise Archer. Danger of aesthetics becoming
more important than spirituality.

SWAN, MAGGIE.

011647   FOR THE SAKE O' THE SILLER. A FIFESHIRE
STORY OF FORTY YEARS AGO. Edinburgh & London:
Oliphant, 1893 BMC.

CR 21:272. Fifeshire story of 50 years ago. Effie

011648   A LATE AWAKENING. London and New York:
Ward, Lock, and Bowden, 1895 BMC 1896 NUC.

ATH 107:50. Nautilus Series. Cold Scottish parson and
his forlorn wife and their daughter who educates him
in humanity. Lady of the manse flees and dies in snow.
ACAD 49:114. She is driven out by his coldness. When
he is left with child, his emotional nature awakes.
Scot. "sudden marriage of a stern and obstinate parson
with the unknown and destitute daughter of his dear
friend." Unhappiness results in her leaving. He's
regenerated years later through the child he finds at
wife's death bed. CR. 26,30:255

011649   LIFE'S BLINDFOLD GAME. Edinburgh:
Oliphant, Anderson & Ferrier, 1895 BMC.

Mary Ellsworth mistress of a public school loves David
Grey, Presbyterian minister. For a time he is
attracted to another woman but comes to realize what a
gem Mary is. ACAD. 48:432
English conventional love story. BOOK NEWS 97-8, 637

011650   A NEGLECTED PRIVILEGE: THE STORY OF A
MODERN WOMAN. London: Ward, Lock, 1896 BMC.

ACAD 50:490. Story of a woman who ruined her husband
in her pursuit of freedom, and was sorry ever after.
Two sisters, very different. Elsie Blair marries
without "accepting the responsibility of marriage."
She leaves her doctor husband and refuses to return.
SP 78:61
ATH 108:834. Medical assistant and his affairs with
two daughters of his chief.

011651   THROUGH LOVE TO REPENTANCE. Edinburgh &
London: Oliphant, 1894 BMC.

SP-excellent purpose, but all the good people meet
with a bad end.

011652   A WAY IN THE WILDERNESS. London:
Partridge, 1892 BMC.

SWAN, MIRANDA ELIOT. United States.

011653   DAISY: THE AUTOBIOGRAPHY OF A CAT.
Boston: Noyes, [c1900] NUC.

SWAN, MYRA.

011654   BALLAST: A NOVEL. London: Longmans, 1901
BMC. New York: 1901 NUC.

Two step sisters one an alcoholic. The other
sacrifices lover to care for her sister who is an
alcoholic. ACAD 01
ATH 4-6-01

011655   GROUND IVY; A NOVEL. London: S. C. Brown,
Langham, 1905 BMC.

011656   SHALLOWS. London: Hurst and Blackett,
1894 BMC NUC.

SP-various loves and a happy ending.
ACAD-child reconciles parents after a long
estrangement.

011657   THE UNATTAINABLE. London: Chapman and
Hall, 1898 BMC NUC.

ACAD 55:158. Mary Allen, ambitious, went to London and
met a man who told her she would be successful in
music halls.
ATH 112:710. Can be read by girls.
SR 86:714. Man has passion for woman other than his
sickly wife. Wife dies and so does passion. It returns
at close of book, but this time desired woman is
unattainable.
Mary is the heroine; a fickle hero gives her a lot of
grief. LBKM 15:120

SWEETING, JEANNIE.

011658   RODRICK DALTON'S LAST STAKE, OR MADGE
LEIGH'S REDEMPTION. London: A. H. Stockwell, [1907]
BMC.

Moralizing melodrama--TLS

SWERDNA, CARL, pseud. See MARCH, CATHERINE.

SWETNAM, FLORA MAY (STAFFORD). B. 1874. United States.

011659   MISS PHENA. New York: American Tract
Society, [c1916] NUC.

Quiet but forceful spinster, a leader in more than one
movement in her community, influences young people PW

SWEYN, FRANCES.

011660   MILLICENT SIMONDS; OR, THROUGH CLEANSING
FIRES. London: Religious Tract Society, [1891] BMC.
New York: F. H. Revell, [1892] PW.

PW-Over-sensitive, she could not bear the "stigma" on
the Simonds' name.

SYKES, CHRISTINA ANNE JESSICA.

011661   ALGERNON CASTERTON. SOME EXPERIENCES
DURING THE FIRST TWENTY-FIVE YEARS OF HIS LIFE.
London: Bickers, 1903 BMC.

011662   THE MACDONNELLS. BY J. A. C. SYKES.
London: W. Heinemann, 1905 BMC NUC.

Mrs. Macdonnell a mother of the old school head of
family, youngest child is 20. She rules sternly. ACAD
495, 05.
ATH 555, 05.

011663   MARK ALSTON: AN IMPRESSION. London: E.
Nash, 1908 BMC.

TLS-domestic life of Ruskin.

SYKES, J. A. C. See SYKES, CHRISTINA ANNE JESSICA.

SYLVA, CARMEN, pseud. See PAULINA ELIZABETH OTTILIA LOUISA,
QUEEN CONSORT OF CHARLES I, KING OF RUMANIA.

SYLVERAN, ANNA. United States.

011664   NANCY'S EVENTFUL CHRISTMAS. [Lowell,
Mass.]: [1897] NUC.

SYLVESTRE, M. A., pseud. See DRAKE, MARY TYRWHITT.

SYMINGTON, MAGGIE.

011665   MY LOST MANUSCRIPT: THE ROMANCE OF A
SCHOOL. London: Wells Gardner, [1894] BMC.

SYMONDS, EMILY MORSE. D. 1936. United Kingdom.

011666   A BREAD AND BUTTER MISS: A SKETCH IN
OUTLINE. BY GEORGE PASTON. London: Osgood and
McIlvaine, 1895 BMC NUC.

She is 17, makes her debut in society on a few days'
visit with rich relatives. Returns home engaged. ATH
105:180
PW-Theodora, from large impoverished famiy, visits
worldly cousin and makes the "catch" of the season.

011667   THE CAREER OF CANDIDA. BY GEORGE PASTON.
London: Chapman and Hall, 1896 BMC NUC. New York: D.
Appleton, 1897 NUC.

As a child refuses to pray because she gets no
responses: boyish tastes and costume. At 16 is sick of
being told she's pretty. She goes to London where she
teaches gymnastics and fencing. Marries and becomes
completely disillusioned with her weak husband,
separation, then a platonic friendship. SR 84:501.
Fine, robust woman with no nonsense about her in spite
of her opinions. A new woman. ATH 109:112.
Leaves her husband, returns to gymnastics instruction.
Years later sees husband crippled. Begs to be allowed
to nurse him for evermore. LBKM 11:154.
Falls in love with a very weak, miserable, inconstant
dissipated young man (a Willy-boy). Leaves, supports
self and son. Sees husband crippled. Takes him home
and supports him too, but not happy. LW 28:73.

011668   A FAIR DECEIVER. BY GEORGE PASTON. London
and New York: Harper, 1898 BMC NUC. Leipzig: B.
Tauchnitz, 1898 NUC.

Lesbia lovely flirt but so witty and likeable. Her
elder sister--Magda. Ends in abrupt tragedy. SP 79:604
"Unconventional treatment of a somewhat hackneyed
theme."
She's engaged to a man who ought to marry her sister.
BAKER 03 158

011669   A MODERN AMAZON. A NOVEL. BY GEORGE
PASTON. London: Osgood and McIlvaine, 1894 BMC.

SP 73:248. "Hardly likely to be received with favor at
the Pioneer Club and other revolutionary centers."
Regina is a journalist.
ACAD 46:7. At 26 she marries Humphrey, although she
doesn't love him, has, in fact, never had romantic
feelings toward any man . She is advised by an eminent
specialist, Sir Gregory Linkwater, not to return to
her husband unless she can love him as a wife.
ATH 103:574. Marries him on the time-honoured one
condition of wilful and fastidious maidens. Wooed and
won by her husband after marriage, and is brought to
her senses by a strong dose of suffering and
humiliation. She is "just a little Ibsenite, a little
woman's Rights', a little emancipationist, but as
selfish in disposition and as farouche in manner as
the most unlovely of her type." Remarkably innocent
and unsuspicious.

011670   A STUDY IN PREJUDICES. BY GEORGE PASTON.
London: Hutchinson, 1895 BMC. New York: D. Appleton,
1895 NUC BMC.

"Clever satire on the average man who, in his heart,
holds the opinion that a woman should be the mere
reflex of her husband: that it is a little short of
heresy and sacrilege for her to think for herself."
Such a one marries then separates from his wife when
he learns she flirted before marriage. ACAD 47:480.
Cecily Tregarthen wants to escape the life of
drudgery, marries a very narrow minded egotist, a
writer. She is gleeful to discover her priggish
husband's "irregularities." ATH 106:528
Satire on the "old man," in contradistinction to the
new woman, whose ideal is a combination of "doll-wife
and cow-mother."
"Trampling on the sanctity of married life." Heroine
is addicted to improper flirting because she was
raised in a "frivolous vulgar circle." But she's
innocent at heart and intelligent. She is Cecily.
Falls for a straight guy, a writer, who hears about
her past and drops her. He likes his women to be old
fashioned. He of course has a past too. He is a study
of obstinate prejudice. BKM 4:416

011671   A WRITER OF BOOKS. BY GEORGE PASTON.
London: Chapman and Hall, 1898 BMC. New York:
Appleton, 1899 NUC.

SP 81:530. Cosima goes to Bloomsbury to write. After a
year she is discouraged and marries the wrong man,
later meets a man she can love. Leaves her husband and
goes back to writing. Quote from last Chapter: "love
may once have been a woman's whole existence, but that
was when a skein of embroidery silk was the only other
string to her bow. In the life of the modern woman,
blessed with an almost inexhaustible supply of
strings, love is no less episodical than in the life
of a man." Admirable, portrayal of the feminine side
of Grub Street. LIT 3:591
ACAD 55:246. "Is what people call a sex novel. The
vogue of the sex novel has certainly passed."
ATH 112:638. "The means she takes to prevent

reconciliation with her husband are original."
LBKM 15:56. "This writer of books gives the author the
opportunity of standing up valiantly for the dignity
and seriousness of fiction, the richest mine for the
historian and the sociologist of the future."
Cosima Chudleigh publishes her first book when she's
very young before she's had experiences. Tries to gain
such second-hand by living at a boarding house and
watching and studying people for copy. Then she
marries and lives with a husband she doesn't love and
then she meets a man she does love. Her husband is
dull with his habit of tuneless humming. Cosima
believes society should make the wedding ceremony as
prolonged an experience and as difficult an experience
as is divorce. BKM 8:184.
Her father was a librarian, sister and brother "made
studies at British Museum." The brother and sister
understand her as her husband never does. PW 55:252.
Cosima marries Tom but doesn't love him. She writes
novels. Bessy Heywood tigress who tortures her
victims. Episode in the life of a talented young
woman. NYT 2-11-99,86.

SYMONDS, MARGARET. See VAUGHAN, MARGARET SYMONDS.

SYMONS, BERYL MARY ELIZABETH (TAUBMAN). United Kingdom.

011672   A LADY OF FRANCE; A ROMANCE OF MEDIEVAL
PARIS. London: S. Paul, 1910 BMC.

ATH

SYNGE, MRS. HAMILTON.

011673   A SUPREME MOMENT. London: T. F. Unwin,
1905 BMC.

ACAD Awakening of a woman who has kept house for her
brother through a young woman who comes to live with
him. "It is a pity that the men in this story are
shadows."
TLS-Unfolding of a staid middle-aged woman who becomes
a new person by end of book without altering the facts
of her life.

SYNNOT, MRS. MARCUS.

011674   ANGUS FAULKENER: OR THE SPORT OF DESTINY.
London: S. Sonnenschein, 1898 BMC.

SYRETT, NETTA. United Kingdom.

011675   ANNE PAGE. London: Chatto & Windus, 1908
BMC NUC. New York: J. Lane, 1909 NUC.

TLS-Middle aged heroine with a Paris episode in her
past which author condones and even the vicar
questions that there are more than one path to heaven.
ACAD-She has invited a phys rel. with a painter,
refusing him mrg. The dr's wife also has a Parisian
liaison. "brutal mother" treated as if it were
perfectly all right.
BKM-She refuses to marry him but offers to live with
him for as long as their love lasts. A few yars later
she calmly leaves him and returns to her English
village. She is middle aged. "The heroine defies the
conventions and comes to no bad end." As curate's
daughter leads a narrow life, becomes a companion and
is left a fortune. Then she "throws herself at her
lover's head, but refuses to marry him." She reasons
that she has a right to arrange her own life and would
not bind anyone to her except by bond of love. Lives
with him three years. Author makes it seem "that the
man is lucky who receives such companionship as hers,"
and as though after such an exper. she could resume
her life among those who order their lives otherwise.
NYT

011676   BARBARA OF THE THORN. London: Chatto &
Windus, 1913 BMC.

Young woman is partly of Italian descent and doesn't
know it. When she's in Rome, she sees visions of
tragedies in her family over generations. ACAD
There's a love story complicated by two doctors who
threaten to wreck her natural and her unnatural life.
ATH
She's 28-has her liberty but no competence. Has these
remarkable psychic experiences in Rome. Later the man
she marries finds proof for these experiences in her
father's diary. She was in fact reliving early
experiences of her ancestors. LBKM
Keeps getting the vision of a murder. Young man and
his doctor friend help "cure" her. But her visions are
found to be real; ends well TLS

011677   A CASTLE OF DREAMS. London: Chatto &
Windus, 1909 BMC. Chicago: A. C. McClurg, 1909 NUC.

Girl frightens off suitors with wierd stories and
sounds? 8-21-09 PW
Bridget growing to womanhood alone in an old castle.
Her development (when a group of people come to
castle) and her love? TLS
Her refusal to grow up, to conform; rejects father's
choice of husband; frightens off suitors; chooses own
lover. BKM

011678   THE CASTLE OF FOUR TOWERS. London:
Duckworth, 1909 BMC NUC.

011679   THE CHILD OF PROMISE. London: Chapman and
Hall, 1907 BMC.

Man deserts one woman-Natasha ACAD
A Tolstoyan colony: Mary shares her husband's views on
socialism due to influence of Russian governess.
Natasha (child of promise) born to this couple,
dedicated to the cause. Natasha grows up less
idealistic but a socialist lecturer. Much of novel
concerns the level of her commitment as a socialist
platform speaker. TLS
Natasha & Val ignore "the claims of matrimony" in the
end they are lovers, he must leave for Vienna, but she
makes a success of her life-lectures on socialism.
Critic feels author "considers babies quite
incompatible with high intell development" SP

011680   THE DAY'S JOURNEY. London: Chapman &
Hall, 1905 BMC. Chicago: A. C. McClurg, 1906 NUC.

Cecily, brilliant, in a secluded married life finds
after a few yrs of marr. that her husband has a
mistress. As she makes this discovery, an old lover of
hers comes on the scene. She can mother her husband
who like a child returns to her penitent. ACAD 639 05
Faithful woman friend; author is very sympathetic
toward all three women even the female villain Story
ends sadly ATH 201,05
BKM-"A tale of jealousy, suspicion, misunderstanding,
separation, and eventually reunion. The hero, a man
who feels that his talent for literary work is being
thwarted at home, leaves his wife and forms a
friendship for a beautiful girl. During the separation
the wife writes a book which meets with wonderful
success. This book is the means of awakening the
husband to his sense of duty, and he returns to his
wife, who receives him, but on such terms as to teach
him a lesson in humility." v. 24 1906
NYT-When husband becomes unfaithful, old lover and
friend encourage wife to move to London and take her
place among men and women. She does, and writes a book
more successful than any of her husband's who
eventually tires of his sandalled love and asks wife
to accept him back. Then what.

011681   DRENDER'S DAUGHTER. London: Chatto &
Windus, 1911 BMC. New York: J. Lane, 1911 NUC.

Arist. raises girl to be his model wife, thinks she's
of peasant stock (wants to mix arist. blood with
healthy peasant blood) she grows up intense and high
spirited-she's really an arist-refuses to submit to
his theories, separation, both find suitable mates. PW
7-17-11
Nancy Drender is hot-tempered, a born rebel. LBKM
He's a "prig" our sympathy is with Nancy
Man educates a girl to be his wife in later years. She
marries him partly out of gratitude, mostly because
she's trained only to be a wife. She detests him: his
experiment fails. Marriage fails. Both find other
suitable mates. SP

011682   THE GOD OF CHANCE. London: Skeffington,
[1920] BMC NUC.

TLS-Deborah hates monotony of teaching, has natural
gift for acting. Finally makes break too late, her
voice has been ruined, but finds happiness in colony
of art lovers.

011683   GODMOTHER'S GARDEN. London: Blackie,
[1918] BMC.

011684   THE JAM QUEEN. London: Methuen, 1914 BMC.

LBKM-Sept'14. Expresses views that some
highly-educated women are foolish, neglectful mothers
with feminist fads are not to be re-spected,
institutes for the poor are powerful temptations for
their organizers.

011685　　　　NOBODY'S FAULT. London: J. Lane, 1896
BMC. Boston: Roberts, 1896 NUC.

ATH 107:343. Keynote Series. Story of an educated girl
in an uneducated family who is unable to escape and
find or make a world for herself.
ACAD 49:342. Bridget Ruan "took her life in her
hand...and made rather a hash of it."
SP 76:777. She goes to London and lives in lodgings,
teaching high school. The loneliness and dullness.
Meets Carey at a concert and loves him but he leaves.
Marries, cannot endure it, leaves her husband. Reverts
to her single life. Carey returns, and they plan to
live together when something happens which causes
Bridget to give up the idea.
PW 2-29-96. She writes stories, was born a genius and
a new woman.
LBKM 14:132. "As far as we know for the first time in
fiction, a true and faithful picture of the life of a
high-schoolmistress."

011686　　　　OLIVIA L. CAREW. New York: John Lane,
1910 PW. London: Chatto & Windus, 1910 BMC NUC.

N. E. School teacher with literary tendencies marries
an architect because she thinks he'll help her in her
ambitions. She neglects "her duties." Finds happiness
finally "in conventionaliy." PW
TLS-Development as an Englishman's wife in Siena,
Florence, Rome, has an affair? with novelist who
awakens in her sense of art, life, beauty. Author
thinks he is a cad.
ATH Unhappy mrg complicated by intervention of second
woman and later second man. Good female ch's. Dramatic
unexpected conclusion
SR She was revolted by realities of mrg, had unbounded
belief in her intellectual capacities, a prig. Is
finally brought to a sense of her pathetic futility.
Then comes regeneration.
NYT-Rev. thinks author a prig.

011687　　　　ROSANNE. London: Hurst & Blackett, 1902
BMC.

ACAD-Character studies of women
ATH 3-15-02 "neurotic female portrayed with minute
care" "writer must remember there are men as well as
women in the world."

011688　　　　ROSE COTTINGHAM; A NOVEL. New York: G. P.
Putnam's Sons, 1915 NUC. (Eng. ed. title: The
Victorians.)

"Rose girl with brains hedged in by brainless folk. On
leaving boarding school becomes a social failure. At
length found the world where she was not
misunderstood. Published successful novel, met man who
could appreciate her." PW 89: 1/29/16:348

011689　　　　ROSE COTTINGHAM MARRIED. London: T. F.
Unwin, [1916] BMC NUC.

NYT-Story of Rose from 9-20, Rose is in a constant
state of rebellion. Moves from narrow confines of
grandmother's home to intellectual, social and
Bohemian aspects of London.
In the 90's, young woman cultured, of good family
marries a brilliant young labor leader with
distressing table manners and no "family." She suffers
in the attempt to blend two entirely different ideals.
Loves him; tries to force herself into the mould.
Succeeds finally by changing the mould itself. LBKM

011690　　　　THREE WOMEN. London: Chatto & Windus,
1912 BMC NUC.

ATH-the world, the flesh, the devil permeated by the
emotions.
TLS-O
SP-"Rosamund is needlessly offensive, a suburban
Messalina. Katherine Verney, is also of a type-let us
say-the ultra-modern kind carried to the extremest
point. She perhaps conveys the most awful warning of
all, for she is the brilliant business woman who
deliberately stifles all her natural inclinations and
refuses to marry lest domestic life should interfere
with her business interests. Phillida tells the
man...she will become his mistress not his wife. For
this she is very properly punished by discovering that
the relationship of mrg. is not purely one of sex, but
that "the mutual society, help and comfort that the
one sought to have of the other" is unattainable save
by a legal tie. It is just as well that women who are,
to use the modern phrase, feminists, should have this
point brought home to them in fiction, tho, of course,
the novels which preach this moral must necessarily be

rather unpleasant reading."

011691　　　　THE TREE OF LIFE. London & New York: J.
Lane, 1897 BMC NUC.

A novel of Revolution. A woman's left grey and
suppressed. "She breaks her chains, and almost
finishes her husband." ACAD 52 Fic Sup 97.
Characters are very sym, especially Christine. Fine
male characterization too. "whole gallery of women at
college who are being trained as schoolteachers." ACAD
52 Fic Sup 111.
387 pages of discussion of sex question. Christine
Willowfield-as a child all joy crushed out of her by a
father who believes women have no reason. Then female
student life, unsuccessful, marriage, lover, deserts
husband (all our sympathy with her) LIT 1:211
LBKM 14:132. "We are truly sorry that N.S. has fallen
a victim to this epidemic of modernity." Christine at
college, unhappy marriage to Farborough. Both father
and husband are "impossibly heartless persons."
SR 85:306. Christine, daughter of a scientific man who
has always been totally absorbed in his work, marries
a socialist with the same trait. When their baby was
dying, he insisted on her keeping a speaking
engagement.

011692　　　　TROUBLERS OF THE PEACE. London: Chatto &
Windus, 1917 BMC.

The difficulties which may beset the mothers of modern
girls. Two principal mothers: Isabel Wickham (Joan's
mother), Margaret Courtenay (Sylvia's). Isabel no
friendship with Joan; Margaret friendship with Sylvia
is complete. Isabel successful-little time for family.
Joan grows up to be an antagonistic young woman. This
antagonism is worse just when her mother wants to draw
close. Joan attracted to every freedom in life-free
love, hunger striking, etc. TLS
"Conflict of wills between a selfish mother and an
equally selfish daughter" but mother lavishes
concessions; the daughter remains irreconcilable;
daughter's friends include Anarchist woman "Author is
unwavering in her faith that liberty has no dangers
which can outweigh its advantage."

011693　　　　THE VICTORIANS; A NOVEL. London: T. F.
Unwin,, [1915] BMC NUC.

Heroine: emot. clever, not pretty. Very full picture
of the school where she Rose Cottingham was educated
and more particularly of its mistress Miss Quayle. The
revolt of Rosie vs narrow Victorianism her intro to
the advanced thought of London. The beginning of her
fame as a writer. TLS
Minute account of Rose's life beginning 9-19. Helen
Ferguson her foil-self possessed where Rose is
sensitive emotional. TLS
"Condemns whole system of upbringing of children in
mid 19th." SP

011694　　　　THE WIFE OF A HERO. London: Skeffington,
[1918] BMC NUC.

TLS-Intellectual Anne marries a beautiful and brave
young man during war. He is lacking in everything
else. Anne's relationship with her mother-in-law, etc.
Irene Latter to escape uncongenial home married a
soldier. Anne Templeton, spoiled and adored by aunt,
highly educated, well read, married a beautiful man-no
intellect. They have nothing in common. She's relieved
to hear he's killed in war. Then hears he's alive.
Then a mistress of this man hearing that Anne doesn't
love husband proposes a "rearrangement of partners."
TLS

011695　　　　WOMEN AND CIRCUMSTANCE. London: Chapman &
Hall, 1906 BMC.

SZASZ, ELSA (BRANDT). B. 1875.

011696　　　　THE TEMPLE ON THE HILL; A TALE OF
TRANSYLVANIA. London: Sidgwick and Jackson, 1912 BMC
NUC.

ATH-Russian priest runs out of money trying to build
church. Tries to get parish to bring materials and
work. Ends with suicide of young girl who has played a
leading part. Roumanian writer writing in English.
ACAD

T., M. I., pseud. See TODD, MARY VAN LENNUP (IVES).

TABER, LOUISE EDDY. B. 1890. United States.

011697　　　　THE FLAME. New York: A. Harriman, 1911

NUC.

Story of love and wooing 10-14-11 PW
Marriage of rich American woman to impoverished
foreign noble. This fortune hunter chases Gwendolyn
Rolfe but she's saved from him by a music hall singer
that the prince had wronged in her earlier days.
Gwen finds happiness with another foreigner. NYT

TABER, MARY JANE HOWLAND. B. 1834. United States.

011698   BATHSHEBA'S LETTERS TO HER COUSIN DEBORAH
1831-1861. Philadelphia: J. C. Winston, 1913 NUC.

PW 84 9/27/13, 567

011699   A HONEYMOON SOLILOQUY. Philadelphia: J.
C. Winston, 1914 NUC.

TABER, SUSAN. United States.

011700   COUNTRY NEIGHBORS; A LONG ISLAND
PASTORAL. New York: Duffield, 1912 NUC.

PW-Young man provides for his family.

011701   THE JEWEL OF THEIR SOULS. New York:
Duffield, 1914 NUC.

NYT-Like A. D. Sedgwick in "courage with which she
faces the disagreeable qualities in her people."
Country house on the Hudson owned by a millionaire, a
ruthless man with strong-willed daughters.
Unconventional.

011702   UNEXPECTED AFFINITIES, A SERIO-COMEDY.
New York: Duffield, 1913 NUC.

"By author of "Country neighbors." Scene is New York,
and the plot involves a number of people such as one
is always meeting. Alice Harvey, a girl with high
ideals, and her frivolous married sister, Rosalie, are
the two principal women characters. Rosalie's husband,
Peter St. Clair, an artist, and Herbert Norton, a
millionaire, are the men most involved in the plot,
though some of the minor characters play telling
parts." PW

TADEMA, LAURENCE ALMA. D. 1940. United Kingdom.

011703   THE FATE-SPINNER. London: E. B. Mortlock,
1900 EMC NUC.

ATH 115:10. "Neurotic" heroine Ginerva, bedridden by
the death of her child for five days. Lonely husband
begins affair with Althea, the cheerful governess.
Ginerva almost elopes with husband's cousin, but at
last moment has premonition she won't be happy.

TADEMA, LAURENCE ALMA . D. 1940. United Kingdom.

011704   THE WINGS OF ICARUS: BEING THE LIFE OF
ONE EMILIA FLETCHER AS REVEALED BY HERSELF IN: I.
THIRTY-FIVE LETTERS WRITTEN TO CONSTANCE NORRIS
BETWEEN JULY 18TH 188- AND MARCH 26TH OF THE FOLLOWING
YEAR II. A FRAGMENTARY JOURNAL III. A POSTSCRIPT. New
York and London: W. Heinemann, 1894 BMC NUC.

ACAD 46:230. Emilia is a female prig...in her
"advancement," and her melancholy and her meditations.
"An early application of the slipper and an education
in sound religion and useful learning would have been
the making of her." She has a friend, Constance
Norris, who is a maumariee, "a pretty word for an ugly
thing of no particular time or language." She has a
love who is a poet. She adores Constance and then he
does. Pioneer Series.
LBKM 7:27. In form of letters and diary. Emilia has
"advanced ideas," renounces poet she loves when her
friend is heartbroken. Letters are to her "frivolous"
friend. She falls in love, becomes engaged altho he
doesn't love her, invites friend to visit, he and
friend fall passionately in love. She sees this and
wants to give him up, but can't carry it through, and
marries him, hoping that if they go off everything
will work out. At the end of the year she gives up,
brings him home with intention of freeing him to
friend. Too late. Tragedy.
PW-Her husband and her friend suicide.

TAGGART, MARION AMES. 1866-1945. United States.

011705   ASER, THE SHEPHERD. New York: Benziger,
1897 NUC.

011706   BETH'S OLD HOME. Boston: W. A. Wilde,

[c1915] NUC.

Woman Philanthropist

011707   BEZALEEL. New York, Cincinnati, Chicago:
Benziger, 1897 NUC.

011708   CAPTAIN SYLVIA. New York: Doubleday,
Page, 1918 NUC.

PW-girl's story. PZ7

011709   THE ELDER MISS AINSBOROUGH. New York:
Benziger, 1915 NUC.

Love of older sister for younger PW 2-27-15

011710   HER DAUGHTER JEAN; A STORY. Boston: W. A.
Wilde, [c1913] NUC.

PW 84 9/20/13:770 "Story centers around Jean, a young
girl who is strong of heart because her heart is a
loving one. Love for her mother gives her courage
through days of effort. She is a true sister also to
careless Rodney, steady Steve and little Dorcas, and
she willingly drops her beloved books and poetry
writing that she may grapple with the real problems of
life for her mother's sake."

011711   LOYAL BLUE AND ROYAL SCARLET; A STORY OF
'76. New York: Benziger, 1899 NUC.

Revolutionary War in New York City. 1775 to Cornwall's
surrender. Also love story. PW 56:778.

011712   THE UNRAVELING OF A TANGLE. New York:
Benziger, 1903 NUC.

Story of Intrigue-one woman against another. 3-14-03
PW

TAINTER, HELEN (DAVIES). United States.

011713   THE REVERIES OF A SPINSTER. BY HELEN
DAVIES. New York: F. T. Neely, 1897 NUC.

New York schoolteacher is lovely; she has an imaginary
lover, and then a very real one. She becomes a
professional musician and scorns love for art. PW
52:111.
Marjorie works hard but has her dreams. A spirit she
calls on named Sandalphon helps her bear her burden.
Is musical-becomes an accompanist. Gets her chance
when singer doesn't show up. Astonished the audience.
Then Marjorie found her true position and all the
fashionable world of New York wanted to hear her.
Becomes wealthy. NYT 8-7-97, 3.

TAIT, EUPHEMIA MARGARET. United Kingdom.

011714   FORGED IN STRONG FIRES. BY JOHN IRONSIDE.
Boston: Little, Brown, 1911 NUC. London: Methuen, 1912
BMC.

"The din and agony of warfare among the Boers and
English in Oom Paul's time form the background of this
tale which concerns itself mainly with forging the
character of a brave hearted English girl who nursed
the wounded fighters, and her lover a young Boer who
had been Oxford trained." BRD 1911.

011715   THE RED SYMBOL. BY JOHN IRONSIDE. Boston:
Little, Brown, 1910 NUC. London: E. Nash, 1911 BMC.

"Anne Pendennis, an English girl, and the
Grand-Duchess Anna Petrovna, a nihilist. Anne's
English lover, sent to Russia on special
correspondence duty, becomes involved in the intrigues
of the league of which the grand-duchess is the
leading spirit, and which makes use of the red symbol,
a five-petaled red geranium flower." BRD 1910

TALBOT, JEAN.

011716   FATE UNSEEN. London: Digby, Long, 1919
BMC.

Man wrongs a woman, makes things right after he spends
time in Canada, wife dies, the "illeg" child dies. TLS
LBKM-Male hero

TALBOT, MARJORIE. Nationality Unknown.

011717   MERRILL. BY MARJORIE TALBOT (G.L.S.,
'06). Boston: Mayhew Publishing, 1906 NUC.

TALCOTT, HANNAH ELIZABETH (BRADBURY). 1827-1893. United States.

011718   DOROTHY GRAY: AN INDIAN SUMMER IDYL. Boston: Damrell and Upham, 1891 NUC.

Good beautiful Quakeress on a paradise of a farm to which young artist comes and love follows. Much quotation from Browning. CR.
CR shows same publishing, title, date; but author as Mrs. H. B. Goodwin.

TALLENTYRE, S. G., pseud. See HALL, EVELYN BEATRICE.

TALLMAN, MYRTLE CATHERINE.

011719   THE TRAVELING TRIO. Lincoln, Nebr.: Woodruff-Collins Press, 1908 NUC.

PW-Story of an invalid who travels merrily and cheerfully.

TAMURA, NAOMI.

011720   THE JAPANESE BRIDE. New York: Harper, 1893 BMC NUC.

Frank pictures of Japanese home life in chapters like "Why do we marry?" "Courting" "The Honeymoon" PW 3-18-93

TANQUERAY, MRS. BERTRAM.

011721   THE CALL OF THE FUTURE. London: Hurst and Blackett, 1901 BMC.

9-21-01 ATH

011722   HOYA CORNEY: A NOVEL. London: Digby, Long, 1899 BMC.

He is a modern Cimabue, a genius in corduroy. A melodrama of the music halls. LIT 4:528
He marries Joan Wisconsin, daughter of a financier. SP 82:350

011723   THE ROYAL QUAKER. London: Methuen, 1904 BMC.

ATH-Heroine a natural daughter of a king becomes a Quaker-mixed personality of levity and seriousness. Long relationship up and down with man.
TLS-fictionalized account of Jane Stuart; rejects man on basis of a religion which she later accepts. Spiritual struggle.

TAPMAN, LILLIAN SMITH. United States.

011724   THE SUCCESS OF FAILURE. BY A WAYFARER [ANONYMOUS]. New York: Tapman, [c1913] BMC NUC.

Allegorical; young woman typifies Service; young man typifies love. There is a hospital of the New Birth. NYT

TAPNER, ETHEL GRACE.

011725   ONE EVENTFUL SUMMER: A ROMANCE OF NORTH DEVON. London: J. Long, 1907 BMC.

Heroine "a green eyed maiden" is a poet ACAD Phyllis tries to support mother by writing. Never conversed with any man except Ed. Goes forth to meet men so she can write. Man she meets wealthy, runs bogus paper in London promised to print her stuff. TLS

TAPPAN, EVA MARCH. 1854-1930. United States.

011726   DIXIE KITTEN. Boston: Houghton Mifflin, 1910 NUC.

011727   IN THE DAYS OF QUEEN ELIZABETH. Boston: Lee and Shepard, 1902 NUC.

Elizabeth-fiction 1533-1603

011728   IN THE DAYS OF QUEEN VICTORIA. Boston: Lee and Shepard, 1903 NUC.

Victoria 1819-1901 Fiction

011729   IN THE DAYS OF WILLIAM THE CONQUEROR. Boston: Lee and Shepard, 1901 NUC.

PW 9-14-01

011730   WHEN KNIGHTS WERE BOLD. Boston: Houghton Mifflin, 1911 NUC.

Historical romance of chivalry. PW 11-18-11

TARBELL, IDA MINERVA. 1857-1944. United States.

011731   THE RISING OF THE TIDE: THE STORY OF SABINSPORT. New York: Macmillan, 1919 NUC. London: Macmillan, 1919 BMC.

Pro-war story TLS
American awakens to her part in the war. PW
NYT 4-6-19, 173 Mid-west attitudes toward war, its changes, alterations. From indifference to establishment of munitions factory to protests by the local press. Reads best as a series of articles about the war.
WWI-Fiction

TARIKA, pseud. See MASON, MRS. SHIERS.

TASMA, pseud. See COUVREUR, JESSIE CATHERINE (HUYBERS).

TAUNTON, WINEFRIDE TRAFFORD.

011732   THE DOOM OF THE HOUSE OF MARSANIAC. London: Digby, Long, 1905 BMC.

011733   IGDRASIL. London: E. G. Richards, 1906 BMC.

TLS--romance
ATH--romance
LBKM romance

011734   MARKED WITH A CIPHER. London: Downey, 1901 BMC.

Bigamy ATH 2-16-01

011735   THE NIGHT DANCER. London: Simpkin, Marshall, 1912 BMC NUC. Boston: Estes, 1913.

PW 83 3/22/13 p. 1102 "Jerry the Loot, the Night Dancer, one of a notorious band of thieves, has been made so through the jealousy and desire for revenge of Rosa Craoock, at one time a good and clever woman, but dragged to the depths by her love for Jerry's father. At her death she leaves a letter telling the story of her life and divulging the secret of the Night Dancer's high birth. The rest of the tale is concerned with solving this mystery."

011736   THE REDEMPTION OF DAMIAN GIER. London: Digby Long, 1904 BMC.

TLS-Weird, under a progenital taint which makes him feline.
A tiger of a man.

011737   THE ROMANCE OF A STATE SECRET. London: Simpkin, Marshall, [1911] BMC. Boston: Estes, 1912.

PW-Hist.
NYT Hist

011738   SILENT DOMINION. London: Methuen, 1903 BMC.

Occult powers LBKM 5-03,77
ATH v. 121, 560

011739   THE THRESHOLD. London: J. Long, 1908 BMC.

Story of love and religious views. TLS

TAYLOR, BELLE GRAY. United States.

011740   CAPTIVE CONCEITS. New York: G. P. Putnam's Sons, 1896 NUC.

011741   THE SARDONYX SEAL: A ROMANCE OF NORMANDY. New York, London: G. P. Putnam's Sons, 1891 NUC.

Three villas on Normandy coast. Uncle and nephew in one. This uncle wears the seal representative of great English estate. In #2, aunt and niece on vacation; in third old woman with scientist brother to whom she devotes her life. The story of how the nephew and niece get together. Bewildering plot, mystery upon mystery, variety of dangers. NATION 5-7-91, 384 Many conversations about art and literature. PW 3-28-91.

TAYLOR, C. BRYSON. B. 1880. United States.

011742   IN THE DWELLINGS OF THE WILDERNESS. New York: H. Holt, 1904 BMC NUC.

NYT-Spirit of evil princess let loose.
PW-Adventure story in the Egyptian tombs.

011743   NICANOR, TELLER OF TALES: A STORY OF ROMAN BRITAIN. Chicago: A. C. McClurg, 1906 BMC NUC.

PW-Saga-like story of male
NYT-saga-like story of male

TAYLOR, ELLEN.

011744   A THOUSAND PITIES. London: T. F. Unwin, 1901 BMC.

TAYLOR, G. W. See BROSTER, DOROTHY KATHLEEN AND GERTRUDE WINIFRED TAYLOR.

TAYLOR, GERTRUDE WINIFRED, jt. au. See BROSTER, DOROTHY KATHLEEN AND GERTRUDE WINIFRED TAYLOR.

TAYLOR, I. E.

011745   A MAN FROM THE SHIRES. BY MRS. JOHN TAYLOR. Gay and Bird, 1905 BMC.

TAYLOR, IDA ASHWORTH.

011746   HILARY CAREW, FLORIST, A LOVE STORY. Edinburgh: Oliphant, Anderson and Ferrier, 1893 BMC.

TAYLOR, KATHARINE HAVILAND. 1888-1941. United States.

011747   BARBARA OF BALTIMORE. New York: G. H. Doran, [1919] NUC.

Southern family surrounded by mystery. PW
Aggressively moral. Family of Crane, Alex 21, Barbara 17-she's all goodness. Alex resents being poor. Family turns house into sanitorium (father is a doctor). First patient is wealthy man. Alex sets her cap for him. NYT 9-23-19, 684

011748   CECILIA OF THE PINK ROSES. New York: G. H. Doran, [c1917] NUC.

Father's fortune changes, can raise Cecilia Madden as a lady-as her dead mother wished. Sent to school, cautioned never to be ashamed of poor past. Meets a young man "from other world" frightens him away with her openness about her past. PW

011749   YELLOW SOAP. Garden City, N.Y.: Doubleday, Page, 1920 NUC.

PW-Poor boy brought up in atmosphere of soap rises. NYT 7/11/20 p. 23. His mother, a washerwoman, brings him with her when she washes other people's clothes. He is illegitimate but his mother says father was a "gent" and he shall be one, too.

TAYLOR, LYDIA JUTSUM.

011750   LAND OF THE SCARLET LEAF. BY MRS. ALFRED EDWARD TAYLOR. London: Hodder & Stoughton, [1915] BMC.

Companion to wealthy Canadian woman, marries and degenerates in Montreal's fashionable life, finds true love in the end. TLS
Woman in search of a husband. Delia chooses a rich man over the man she loves. Makes the choice with "wide-open eyes." After marr. gets extravagant, gambles, borrows money from man she loves, forges her husband's signature to check, When husband found dead, lover suspected. Story flouts poetic justice; husband who is "wronged, dies" wife reunited with lover. SP

TAYLOR, M. IMLAY. See TAYLOR, MARY IMLAY.

TAYLOR, MARY ARGYLE.

011751   DELFINA OF THE DOLPHINS. London: A.C. Fifield, 1912 BMC. London: Vineyard Press, 1912 NUC.

Italy-ACAD

TAYLOR, MARY (COLLIVER). United States.

011752   THE DIVORCE. Columbus, Ohio: 1895 NUC.

TAYLOR, MARY IMLAY. 1878-1938. United States.

011753   ANNE SCARLETT. BY M. IMLAY TAYLOR.

Chicago: A. C. McClurg, 1901 NUC.

011754   CALEB TRENCH. Boston: Little, Brown, 1910 NUC.

He works against class prejudice and corruption in the South. PW
BKM

011755   A CANDLE IN THE WIND. New York: Moffat, Yard, 1919 NUC.

Arthur Faunce "Coward's fight to make good" PW
Contemporary American life in US NYT
He leads an expedition to So. Pole. A woman's (Diane) love finally renews his courage. NYT 9-14-19

011756   THE CARDINAL'S MUSKETEER. BY M. IMLAY TAYLOR. Chicago: A. C. McClurg, 1900 NUC.

NYT 1900:408. France during Richelieu period. Hero is a musketeer.

011757   THE COBBLER OF NIMES. BY M. IMLAY TAYLOR. Chicago: A. C. McClurg, 1900 NUC.

PW-Idyllic love story. France under reign of Louis XIV.

011758   THE HOUSE OF THE WIZARD. BY M. IMLAY TAYLOR. Chicago: A. C. McClurg, 1899 NUC. London: Gay and Bird, 1900 BMC. (Gt. Brit.-hist-Henry VIII-fic.)

SP 84:318. Historical romance. Henry VIII. Love story too.
Betty Carew is maid to Katherine, divorced wife of Henry VIII, then to Ann Boleyn. Court intrigues, Betty's complicated love life. LW 30:456

011759   AN IMPERIAL LOVER. BY M. IMLAY TAYLOR. Chicago: A. C. McClurg, 1897 NUC. London: Gay and Bird, 1899 BMC.

Intrigue of Peter the Great to marry daughter of house of Totoff, the failure of it, consequent marriage to a peasant who became Catherine I of Russia. PW 52:1104
1703: viscount tells of his secretary who loves a young woman loved by the Russian Czar. How the Czar is foiled-especially by Najine's faithfulness to the diplomatic secretary. SP 83:140
NYT 1898:415. Russia, Court of Peter the Great. His romance and marriage to Catherine, a peasant girl with the "tigress in her nature, passionate, bold, ambitious, a peasant, a slave, and Empress of all the Russians."
LW 29:60. Historical romance. Peter the Great is hero, his love for French girl.

011760   THE IMPERSONATOR. Boston: Little, Brown, 1906 NUC. London: Gay & Bird, 1906 BMC.

PW-young woman takes place of friend on visit to aunt in Washington.
NYT-Succeeds and wins way from poverty in Paris to success in Wash. aunt sends real niece packing because she doesn't like her.
Pictures of society in Washington SP

011761   THE LONG WAY. Boston: Little, Brown, 1913 NUC.

PW 5-10-13 1690 "Scene is laid in Washington. Eva Astry, pretty,weak and selfish, throws her guilt upon her sister Rachel, accusing her of indiscretion with her own lover. Eva's husband insists that Belhaven, the man, marry Rachel at once and she consents to save her sister's reputation. By degrees Eva comes to realize her sin and unworthiness and the enormity of Rachel's sacrifice and does her best to make reparation. Belhaven, Astry and John Charter, who loves Rachel, play important parts in the drama, which finally works out with happiness in store for Rachel."

011762   MY LADY CLANCARTY. BEING THE TRUE STORY OF THE EARL OF CLANCARTY AND LADY ELIZABETH SPENCER. London: Gay & Bird, 1905 BMC. Boston: Little, Brown, 1905 BMC NUC.

Irish Jacobite peer and girl wife; hist. rom BAKER 13, 506

011763   ON THE RED STAIRCASE. BY M. IMLAY TAYLOR. Chicago: McClurg, 1896 BMC NUC. London: Gay and Bird, 1898 BMC.

Bloody hist. novel of reign of Russia's Peter the

Great. LW 28:127
Famous staircase in Kremlin. PW 51:78
NYT 1898:415. Russia. Hero rescues heroine from cruel
uncle. Adventures.

011764   THE REAPING. Boston: Little, Brown, 1908
NUC. London: Hutchinson, 1909 BMC.

PW-Woman marries for money, divorces, 1st love no
longer interested.
BKM-Central ch. seems to be a man loved by two women.
Focuses on politician and his two loves. TLS
Not much here except a divorce ATH

011765   THE REBELLION OF THE PRINCESS. BY M.
IMLAY TAYLOR. New York and London: McClure, Phillips,
1903 BMC NUC.

Female Russian princess is heroine 3-28-03 PW
Historical "gory" romance. NYT 03 285

011766   THE WILD FAWN. New York: Moffat, Yard,
1920 NUC.

PW-French young woman in Southern town and wife of one
of its most respected citizens.
NYT 7/11/20 p 25 She is a dancer, complications with
family, she develops a "soul"

011767   A YANKEE VOLUNTEER. BY M. IMLAY TAYLOR.
Chicago: A. C. McClurg, 1898 NUC. London: Gay and
Bird, 1899 BMC.

PW American Revolution, Mass. Told by John, a soldier.
Some love interest.

TAYLOR, MRS. ALFRED EDWARD. See TAYLOR, LYDIA JUTSUM.

TAYLOR, MRS. CHARLES TRACY. See TAYLOR, SOPHIE C.

TAYLOR, MRS. JOHN. See TAYLOR, I. E.

TAYLOR, NANCY LLOYD.

011768   BY STILL HARDER FATE. London: S.
Sonnenschein, 1898 BMC.

TAYLOR, SOPHIE C. Nationality Unknown.

011769   A DAUGHTER OF THE MANSE. BY MRS. CHARLES
TRACY TAYLOR. Philadelphia: J. C. Winston, [1909] NUC.

Young woman takes command "even preaches when her
preacher-father loses his voice and breaks down." PW
NYT love story

TAYLOR, UNA ASHWORTH.

011770   THE KING'S FAVORITE. London: Methuen,
1892 BMC.

ATH99:759. Simona, a religious neophyte is heroine.
Two evil men, Tristram and Prospero. Psychological.
SP 68:884. Dream-like. Spiritual beings in human form.
Simona is only one of the three who survives. She and
Prospero have been students of the monk Tristram who
has been for them the embodiment of God. He betrays
"the cause" and dies the "death of a renegade.= With
his death, Prospero experiences a "great void," and
his soul dies. Simona's faith is "steadied and
purified" by this revelation. Tragedy follows.
ACAD. Time period the Restoration.

011771   NETS FOR THE WIND. London: J. Lane, 1896
BMC NUC.

SR Stories, in the "ultra-fervid, neurotic style for
which Miss Olive Schreiner is partly responsible.
ATH 108:254. Women with intense loves either misplaced
or misunderstood.
SP Allegories.

TAYLOR, WINIFRED LOUISE.

011772   THE MAN BEHIND THE BARS. New York: C.
Scribner's Sons, 1914 NUC. London: Bikers, 1915 BMC.

TCHERNINE, ODETTE. United Kingdom.

011773   THOU SHALL NOT FAIL. London: A. Melrose,
[1917] BMC NUC.

TLS-Male hero

TEAL, ANGELINE (GRUEY). 1842-1913. United States.

011774   LILLIAN'S LOVERS (THE SPEAKER OF THE
HOUSE). A NOVEL. Chicago: Laird and Lee, [c1897] NUC.

Published 1894 as "The Speaker of the House."

011775   MURIEL HOWE. New York: Dodd, Mead,
[c1892] NUC. London: B. F. Stevens, [1892] BMC.

PW-Muriel is a school teacher. Becomes engaged and
finds she loves another man.
She was intended for life of missionary but proves to
be better suited for love and marriage LW '93, 43

011776   THE ROSE OF LOVE. New York: Dodd, Mead,
1893 NUC. London: B. F. Stevens, [1893] BMC.

Chicago and then California. Delphine Barbaseau is
about to marry. Learns her mother died in insane
asylum. Refuses to marry until doctor establishes
cause of mother's mental illness. PW 11-4-93.
CP 21:54. Insanity of heroine's mother holds up
marriage until it is determined it was caused by a
fall, not heredity.

011777   THE SPEAKER OF THE HOUSE, A NOVEL.
Chicago: Laird and Lee, [1894] NUC.

TEASDALE, MINNIE. B. 1880. United States.

011778   A LOOKING GLASS. BY GERTRUDE SKINNER.
Boston: Sherman, French, 1913 NUC.

"Story aiming to reflect for the nation its treatment
of the negro. There are no colored people in the book,
they are merely represented by the poor, while the
rich are those prejudiced against them." PW 5/31/13

TEETGEN, A. B. See TEETGEN, ADA B.

TEETGEN, ADA B.

011779   A WHITE PASSION. BY A. B. TEETGEN.
London: W. Gardner, [1913] BMC. Toronto: Bell &
Cockburn, 1913 [ ] NUC.

Founding of a prairie hospital in Alberta and a slight
love story. SP
Canada; prairie doctor starts a hospital, trials of
wives and mothers hundreds of miles away from medical
care. Alma Norway is a hospital matron. SR
Need for central treatment in hospital for the
scattered Canadian farming population. TLS

TELLER, CHARLOTTE. See HIRSCH, CHARLOTTE (TELLER).

TEMPEST, MARJORY.

011780   TILL THE DAY BREAK. London: F. Griffiths,
1911 BMC.

TEMPEST, OLIVE.

011781   UNDER EASTERN SKIES. London: J. Long,
1912 BMC.

Indian army law-no one must marry until he's attained
rank of captain. ATH

TEMPLE, CRONA, pseud. See CORFIELD, CLARA.

TEMPLE, URSULA.

011782   THE SQUIRE'S WILL. London: R. T. S.,
[1907] BMC.

TENCH, MARY FRANCES ALICIA.

011783   AGAINST THE PIKES. London: W. R. Russell,
[1903] BMC.

011784   A PRINCE FROM THE GREAT NEVER NEVER.
London: Hurst and Blackett, 1899 BMC.

Irish young woman restores order to a ramshackle
household. Molly Despard good angel to the community.
SP 82:94.
The Prince is her lover and Great Never Never is a
wilderness in Australia where the Prince goes
exploring while Molly waits.

011785   WHERE THE SURF BREAKS. London: Hurst and
Blackett, 1897 BMC.

Series of reminiscences of old servants and Irish
villagers. Excessive detail. ACAD 52: Fic Sup 58.
"Tender feeling and gentle humour." ATH 110:317

TENISON, E. M. See TENISON, EVA MABEL.

TENISON, EVA MABEL. United Kingdom.

011786   THE VALIANT HEART. BY E. M. TENISON. New
York: E. S. Gorham, 1920 BMC NUC.

PW religious rom.

TENNYSON, MARY H., pseud. See FOLKARD, MARY H.

TEQUAY, ANNE, pseud. See KEATING, ANNE (TRAVIS).

TERHUNE, MARY VIRGINIA (HAWES). 1830-1922. United States.

011787   THE CARRINGTONS OF HIGH HILL; AN OLD
VIRGINIA CHRONICLE. BY MARION HARLAND. New York: C.
Scribner's Sons, 1919 NUC.

Plantation life in Va. long before Civil War. PW
A love story of an older woman and a mystery about
Helen's (18-yr-old) mother-about the old South. NYT
9-21-19

011788   THE DISTRACTIONS OF MARTHA. BY MARION
HARLAND. New York: C. Scribner's Sons, 1906 BMC NUC.

PW-story of inexperienced bride.

011789   HIS GREAT SELF. BY MARION HARLAND.
Philadelphia: J. B. Lippincott, 1892 NUC. London: F.
Warne, 1892 BMC.

LW 23:110. Love story, heroine dies of a broken heart.
Virginia.
CR 17:276. Historical romance concerning unrequited
love of Evelyn Bird who died of a broken heart.
Virginia.

011790   A LONG LANE. BY MARION HARLAND. New York:
Hearst's International Library, 1915 NUC BMC.

Chronicle of old Dutch family. PW 11-27-15
Story of a village with a hard set of rules. (People
of "the Jersies") conflict between the old and new
ways. Tyrannical father, an unwed mother, various
persons. NYT

011791   MR. WAYT'S WIFE'S SISTER. New York:
Cassell, [c1894] NUC.

PW-minister, totally lacking in consideration of his
wife and five children. Wife adores him, sister keeps
household going, then has lover.

011792   THE ROYAL ROAD; OR, TAKING HIM AT HIS
WORD. BY MARION HARLAND. New York: A. D. F. Randolph,
[c1894] NUC.

PW-wife left, after 17 years of marriage, with six
children dependent on a married brother. She is proud;
husband, posing for years as a man too fine for daily
work, has embezzled and run with another woman.

011793   RUTH BERGEN'S LIMITATIONS: A MODERN
AUTO-DA-FE. BY MARION HARLAND. New York, Chicago,
Toronto: F. H. Revell, 1897 NUC.

011794   WHEN GRANDMAMMA WAS FOURTEEN. BY MARION
HARLAND. Boston: Lothrop, [1905] NUC.

TERRELL, DOROTHY A BECKETT. See JAMES, DOROTHY A BECKETT
(TERRELL).

TERROT, MRS. CHARLES E.

011795   THE ATHERSTONE BEQUEST. London: T.
Burleigh, 1900 BMC.

SP 84:881. An ugly duckling who is tiresome, family
bequest is disinterested affection.
ACAD 58:410. Much marrying. Last chapters are alive
with babies and complacent mothers.

011796   OUR PAYING GUEST AND OTHER STORIES.
London: Digby and Long, 1897 BMC.

TERRY, ELEANORE S.

011797   GOD'S GOOD WOMAN. London: J. Long, 1909
BMC.

Madge Graylands, wife of middle-aged farmer, weeps for
her first love, her husband's younger brother. TLS

011798   THE NEW DELILAH. London: W. Scott, 1904
BMC NUC.

NYT-The revelation of a degenerate life, on the eve of
suicide.
TLS-autobiography of a woman who jilted a poor curate
and married a baronet and regretted it.

TESKEY, ADELINE MARGARET. D. 1924. Canada.

011799   ALEXANDER MCBAIN, B.A.; A PRINCE IN
PENURY. New York: F. H. Revell, [c1906] NUC.

PW-temperance story.

011800   CANDLELIGHT DAYS. New York and London:
Cassell, 1913 NUC BMC.

Early settlers in Ontario-no plot. ATH
Focus on characters, a boy-man. LPKM
Pioneer days in Canada largely based on actual
reminiscenses of aged friends. TLS

011801   THE VILLAGE ARTIST. New York: F. H.
Revell, [c1905] NUC. Edinburgh: Oliphant, [1905] BMC.

Woman as "artist" who looks for good in all. PW
9-23-05

011802   WHERE THE SUGAR MAPLE GROWS: IDYLLS OF A
CANADIAN VILLAGE. New York: R. F. Fenno, 1901 NUC.
Toronto: Musson Book, [1913] BMC.

About a Canadian village "not unlike Cranford" SP

011803   THE YELLOW PEARL; A STORY OF THE EAST AND
THE WEST. New York: Hodder and Stoughton, [c1911] NUC.
London: Hodder and Stoughton, 1911 BMC.

Chinese-Amer girl finds much to admire and condemn in
U.S.-PW 10-28-11

TETERS, WILBERTINE. See WORDEN, WILBERTINE (TETERS).

THACKER, MAY DIXON. B. 1876. United States.

011804   THE STRENGTH OF THE WEAK. New York:
Broadway, 1910 NUC.

THANET, OCTAVE, pseud. See FRENCH, ALICE.

THAYER, EMMA (HOMAN). 1842-1908. United States.

011805   A LEGEND OF GLENWOOD SPRINGS. Chicago:
Colvin Pub. Co., 1900 NUC.

011806   PETRONILLA, THE SISTER. New York, London:
F. T. Neely, [c1897] NUC BMC.

PW '98. Heroine marries a lawyer of the Knickerbocker
set. She is from a rural village in the White
mountaints, but attended an exclusive Boston school.
Differences with husband included religion cause her
to leave him and enter a sisterhood, taking the name
of Sister Petronella.

THAYER, EMMA REDINGTON (LEE). B. 1874. United States.

011807   THE MYSTERY OF THE THIRTEENTH FLOOR. BY
LEE THAYER. New York: Century, 1919 BMC NUC.

Murder of lawyer, love story intertwined. PW BKM May
'19
NYT: 13th floor of office building-James Randolph
Stone's office murdered just after he makes a will.

011808   THE UNLATCHED DOOR. BY LEE THAYER. New
York: Century, 1920 NUC BMC.

PW-Love and myst in New York
NYT 1920:321. Young man suspected of murder of
beautiful woman next door.

THAYER, LEE, pseud. See THAYER, EMMA REDINGTON (LEE).

THEODOLI, LILY (CONRAD). Europe.

011809   CANDIDUCCIA; SCENES FROM ROMAN LIFE.
London: K. Paul, 1894 BMC NUC.

Clash of decaying feudalism vs modern ideas in a Roman
town. Politics separate Candiduccia from her lover;
her family is from the old, his from the new order.
Peppino who returns to her only after he betrays
Lauretta, deserts Candiduccia and throws over another
woman. Thorough knowledge of Italian scenery and

customs. SR 79:77
SP 73:925. Sombre story of Italian rural life. Heroine
is in love with liberal, Count and Countess try to
prevent her marriage to him; semi-tragedy results. He
betrays her.

011810   SCENES FROM ROMAN LIFE; UNDER PRESSURE.
London: Macmillan, 1892 BMC. New York: Macmillan, 1892
NUC.

LBKM 3:60. Roman society. Astalli family, devoted to
the Church, "austere" upbringing of their daughters
who "were not taught to please."
ATH 100:660. Ends happily with marriage for daughters.
Tyranny of head of family.
CR 18:274. Italy, marriage between two people of
opposing political beliefs.
LW 23:390. Daughters were not resigned to the will of
their parents.
ACAD-Author is American. Love story.
Customs, prejudices and virtues of aristocrats. Romans
in early days of united Italy. They shrink from the
new. NATION, 56,16.

THICKNESSE, LILY.

011811   EGERIA. London: Hurst and Blackett, 1896
BMC.

ATH 107:542. Painstaking realistic detail. The infant
terrible is mildly amusing. Adult characters do not
reflect much credit on civilization. Central figure is
not Egeria.
ACAD 49:153. Mark meets Egeria, separated for years
from her husband. Struggles to resist but can't. While
still under her spell meets Jocelyn who is engaged.
Mark eventually rises to nobility.

011812   STUFF O' THE CONSCIENCE. London: Harper,
1899 BMC.

Roland Withington is a dramatic genius, but success
does not make him happy. LIT 5:82
Story of Withington who becomes a great actor. But
gives up his work as petty and immoral. He's haunted
by the Infinite. Title refers to his struggle to win
the love of a high minded woman married to a hopeless
invalid. He (Roland) is married to a call ous society
woman. She stays married; he goes off to do
philanthropic works. LBKM 16:141 SP 83:23
He should have married Benita Norton. ACAD 57:15

011813   TWO SINNERS. London: Downey, 1897 BMC.

Doctor is hero. Mary Power has a past. "A few years
ago it was thought fair to take away the reputation of
any heroine...today such a proceeding is not
permissible." Mary has an unconvincing past. ATH
110:122
SP 80:454. Mary Power "preserves her pride and
independence under such trying circumstances." Dr.
Jodworth has an "affection" for her but is
"unnecessarily brutal in his persistent attempt to
ascertain from Mary what attractions she could see in
her former lover."
Hero is lady killer, Roger Tadworth.

THOMAS, ANNIE. See CUDLIP, ANNIE HALL (THOMAS).

THOMAS, BERTHA. United Kingdom.

011814   THE SON OF THE HOUSE. London: Chatto and
Windus, 1900 BMC.

LBKM 18:97. Oswald, who wishes to practice his
socialist ideals, is shut up in an insane asylum by
his sharp-witted mother. She convinces Ralph of his
brother's insanity.
ATH 115:395. Pleasant domestic, not a problem novel.

THOMAS, KATE, pseud. See BULL, KATHARINE THOMAS (JARBOE).

THOMAS, KATHERINE ELWES. United States.

011815   NOT ALL THE KING'S HORSES: A NOVEL OF
WASHINGTON SOCIETY. New York: Cassell, [c1896] NUC
BMC.

PW 10-31-96. Selfish woman determines to be leader of
Washington society. After she becomes a widow she gets
a multi-millionaire and succeeds.
NYT Dec 12, 1896, p2. Three months in the life of Mrs.
Oglethorpe, heartless queen of Washington society, a
widow who throws over an old lover for a wealthy
backwoodsman.

THOMPSON, ANNIE. Nationality Unknown.

011816   A MORAL DILEMMA, A NOVEL. London:
Longmans, 1893 BMC. New York: Longmans, Green, 1893
NUC.

A man returns to England to prove his innocence of a
crime, dies on the way having left the evidence with a
second man, John. But John does nothing because he
learns the woman he loves is in love with the real
criminal. Is afraid to disturb her happiness. Mary is
the heroine; she constrasted to Kate. Mary is sweet
and Kate is sharp-witted and sharp tempered. SP
70:364. Also LW 93:42.
In fact, Mary loves a third man. ACAD 43:238.
Alan Twiss is the man who dies. John Coyford, the man
with the information. Mary Forester the heroine. PW
1-21-93.

011817   THE NARROW MARGIN: A NOVEL. London:
Sisley's, [1907] BMC NUC.

Two women on a trip, one for health the other to
verify the death of her no-good husband. TLS
Three women, Elinor Fairfax, heroine, Fanny, her
"hysterical" charge, Mrs. Mark White, "fast and
brilliant"-SP

THOMPSON, ANNIE E. United States.

011818   ELSIE: A STORY FOR THE HOME. Boston: J.
H. Earle, 1892 NUC.

THOMPSON, ELLEN PERRONET.

011819   THE VEIL OF LIBERTY. A TALE OF THE
GIRONDINS. BY PERONNE. London: A. and C. Black, 1895
BMC NUC.

historical novel., 18th century. French Protestantism.
LBKM 9:64
SP 76:928. Adventures of a Huguenot family of Nismes
in Paris after the declaration of "equal civil
rights." One of the brothers joins the Girondins; the
sister, Sophie, is guillotined-others escape.

THOMPSON, JOAN.

011820   MARY ENGLAND. London: Methuen, 1919 BMC.

Drab struggle of farm life-its influence on Mary
fortified by inner goodness, resists evil. TLS
relations to two men. Squalor of her life and
upbringing. Unexpected ending? Not happy? LBKM

THOMPSON, LILIAN TURNER.

011821   APRIL GIRLS. BY LILIAN TURNER. London:
Ward, Lock, 1911 BMC.

011822   AUSTRALIAN LASSIE. BY LILIAN TURNER.
London: Ward, Lock, 1903 BMC.

011823   BETTY THE SCRIBE. BY LILIAN TURNER.
London: Ward, Lock, 1906 BMC. New York: Saafield,
[c1907] NUC.

At 16 raises three brothers and one sister. Writes; at
21 goes to seek fortune as a writer. "Betty absolutely
refuses to be a woman as the story closes." PW 6-22-07

011824   THE GIRL FROM THE BACK BLOCKS. BY LILIAN
TURNER. London: Ward, Lock, 1914 BMC.

011825   NOUGHTS AND CROSSES. BY LILIAN TURNER.
London: Ward, Lock, 1917 BMC.

011826   PARADISE AND THE PERRYS. BY LILIAN
TURNER. London: Ward, Lock, 1908 BMC.

011827   THE PERRY GIRLS. BY LILIAN TURNER.
London: Ward, Lock, 1909 BMC.

011828   RACHEL. By LILIAN TURNER. Liverpool:
Books, Ltd., [1920] BMC.

TLS 0

011829   STAIRWAYS TO THE STARS. BY LILIAN TURNER.
London: Ward, Lock, 1913 BMC.

011830   THREE NEW CHUM GIRLS. BY LILIAN TURNER.
London: Ward, Lock, 1910 BMC.

011831   WAR'S HEART THROBS. BY LILIAN TURNER.
London: Ward, Lock, 1915 BMC.

011832   YOUNG LOVE. BY LILIAN TURNER. London:
Ward, Lock, 1902 BMC.

THOMPSON, M. AGNES. United States.

   011833   METAIRIE, AND OTHER OLD AUNT TILDA OF NEW
ORLEANS SKETCHES. New Orleans, La.: [c1892] NUC.

THOMPSON, MARAVENE (KENNEDY). United States.

   011834   PERSUASIVE PEGGY. New York: F. A. Stokes,
[1916] NUC BMC. London: Hutchinson, 1916 BMC.

   "Peggy was pretty, persistent and progressive. Story
of amusing situations of young married couple and of
toppling over of Ed's prejudices under Peggy's
persuasiveness. PW 89:1/8/16:121
TLS-domestic bliss-sent

   011835   THE WOMAN'S LAW. New York: F. A. Stokes,
[1914] NUC. London: E. Nash, 1914 BMC.

   BKM-Woman whose husband has killed a man does all she
can to protect child from dishonor, involving helping
him to escape and later bringing his double, an
amnesia victim in to play his role with child.
TLS-Immediately upon her husband's telling her of the
murder, she jumped into her car and drove through the
streets of New York, picked up his double and brought
him home. "They learn to love each other."
PW. "The woman, for the sake of her son, pits her
daring and wit against the machinery of justice in an
attempt to save her worth-less husband from the
consequences of a crime. Her law-the woman's
law-dicates the protection of her child, even though
the law of the land be against her. While the culprit
flees the country she finds a double to impersonate
him. The strange consequences of the unusual situation
make a story full of action."

THOMSON, ANNIE D.

   011836   THE STORY OF KIRSTY'S LOVE. Edinburgh: A.
Elliot, 1897 BMC.

THOMSON, L. NORTON. See THOMSON, PRISCILLA (NORTON).

THOMSON, MRS. L. NORTON. See THOMSON, PRISCILLA (NORTON).

THOMSON, PRISCILLA (NORTON). B. 1836. United States.

   011837   LOOKING THROUGH THE MISTS; OR, EVERY
HEART KNOWETH ITS OWN SORROW. BY L. NORTON THOMSON.
New York: Neely, [c1900] NUC.

   011838   NOT TO HAVE AND TO HOLD. BY MRS. L.
NORTON-THOMSON. New York: Broadway, 1909 NUC.

THONGER, M. ELLEN. See THONGER, MARGARET ELLEN.

THONGER, MARGARET ELLEN. United Kingdom.

   011839   "THE BEES"; THE STORY OF THE "B" TRIPLETS
AND THEIR AUNT. BY M. ELLEN THONGER. New York and
London: G. P. Putnam's Sons, 1911 NUC. London: Chapman
& Hall, 1911 BMC.

   Children's TLS

   011840   JOCK AND I AND THE HYDRA. BY M. ELLEN
THONGER. London: Digby, Long, 1905 BMC NUC.

THORNE, MARION, pseud. See THURSTON, IDA (TREADWELL).

THORNTON, JEAN, pseud. See GANT, ANNA MARIA ELIZABETH.

THORNTON, MARY TAYLOR. Nationality Unknown.

   011841   DELPHINE DECIDES. London: S. Low, [1920]
BMC.

   ATH-Love affairs. Reviewer says she is agreeable young
woman, but there is something peculiar about her.
Novel of domestic life. Study of Philippa Ainley more
than Delphine who robs P.'s lover. TLS

   011842   WHEN PAN PIPES; A FANTASTIC ROMANCE OF
THE THIRTIES. London: S. Low, [1915] BMC. New York: G.
H. Doran, [1916] NUC.

   Children and fairies. PW
NYT-Children and fairies.

THROCKMORTON, JOSEPHINE HOLT. United States.

011843   DONALD MACDONALD. New York: Neale, 1907
NUC.

   West Point careers. PW 7-6-07

011844   SERGEANT JIMMY. Washington, D.C.: [c1911]
NUC.

THROPP, CLARA. United States.

   011845   A FEW LITTLE LIVES. New York: 1896 NUC.

THROSSELL, KATHARINE SUSANNAH (PRICHARD). B. 1884.
Australia.

   011846   THE PIONEERS. BY KATHARINE SUSANNAH
PRICHARD. London and New York: Hodder & Stoughton,
[1915] NUC BMC.

   Rev. PW:89 1/15/916 p. 190-1 Pioneer life in
Australasia. Mary helped two convicts escape justice.
She has mysterious past-years later convicts reappear.
Convict's daughter Deirdre sells herself to save her
father from return to prison. She was willing to pay
the highest price to shelter "the Schoolmaster" but
refused to pay when she found she had been cheated.
This left a cloud of pain and horror over all her
life. Mary meets convict while staying alone in woods.
(Donald has had to travel but has left her with a gun
telling her to shoot any man coming to her door.)
BKM-Deirdre avenges herself on the man who has
betrayed her into becoming his wife, he deserves to
die-and she kills him. She goes scot-free.
Convict life; escaped convict's gratitude to young
married woman who helped him. His daughter and her son
become lovers. ATH
"Australasian prize novel in Hodder and Stoughton's
All British 1,000 pounds prize novel competition."

   011847   WINDLESTRAWS. BY KATHARINE SUSANNAH
PTICHARD. London: Holden and Hardingham, [1917] BMC
NUC.

   TLS Male hero derelicts?

THRUMSTON, CORA M. United States.

   011848   POLLY AND I. Chicago: Donohue and
Henneberry, [c1893] NUC.

THRUSTON, LUCY MEACHAM (KIDD). B. 1862. United States.

   011849   CALLED TO THE FIELD; A STORY OF VIRGINIA
IN THE CIVIL WAR. Boston: Little, Brown, 1906 BMC NUC.

   PW-Story of Southern girl left alone with servants
during Civil War.
NYT-war from a woman's p.o.v.-but its watching and
waiting-tragedy.

   011850   A GIRL OF VIRGINIA. Boston: Little,
Brown, 1902 NUC BMC.

   NYT 6-21-02

   011851   JENIFER. Boston: Little, Brown, 1907 NUC.

   Story of a boy grown man who learns he's been selfish.
PW 5-11-07

   011852   MISTRESS BRENT: A STORY OF LORD
BALTIMORE'S COLONY IN 1638. Boston: Little, Brown,
1901 BMC NUC.

   Heroine manages estate lives own life. PW 10-12-01
Love is not her whole life, courage and enterprise to
manage her estates in the new world of colonial times.
Large brained and strong NYT

   011853   WHERE THE TIDE COMES IN. Boston: Little,
Brown, 1904 NUC.

   PW Va. love story.
NYT-conv. love story

THURSTON, I. T. See THURSTON, IDA (TREADWELL).

THURSTON, IDA (TREADWELL). 1848-1918.

   011854   THE BIG BROTHER OF SABIN STREET,
CONTINUING THE STORY OF THEODORE BRYAN "THE BISHOP'S
SHADOW". BY I. T. THURSTON. New York: F. H. Revell,
[c1909] NUC.

   Good work in slums done by Bishop's helper 9-11-09 PW

011855   RUTH PRENTICE. BY MARION THORNE. Boston:
Congregational Sunday School and Pub.Soc., [c1895]
NUC.

She returns home after mother died. Farmhouse and home
life had degenerated while she was living in N. Y.
with her aunt and getting ready for college. She
brings a great change to home and community. PW
10-19-95:677

011856   THE TESTING OF SIDNEY DEAN. Boston:
Pilgrim Press, [1904] NUC.

PW-Male hero.

011857   THE TORCH BEARER; A CAMP FIRE GIRLS'
STORY. BY I. T. THURSTON. New York: F. H. Revell,
[c1913] NUC.

PZ3

011858   A VILLAGE CONTEST; OR, NO SURRENDER;
SEQUEL TO A BACHELOR MAID AND HER BROTHER. BY I. T.
THURSTON. Boston: A. I. Bradley, 1899 NUC.

Romantic entanglement involving Sepha Dunlap, Helen
Dale, the Rev. Donald Keith & Max. PW 56:298

THURSTON, KATHERINE CECIL (MADDEN). 1875-1911. United
Kingdom.

011859   THE CIRCLE. New York: Dodd, Mead, 1903
NUC. Edinburgh: W. Blackwood, 1903 BMC.

(good feminist review by Eleaner Booth Simmons)
(1903) 17 BKM 192-3 Anna intense vitality: at 16
tingling with life, craves action, bored in the shop
with her father she's stifling with dullness, leaves
for advent. Studies for stage, has a brilliant career.
Then returns to papa because she feels guilty ends in
her marr.
Russian girl in London slums, deserts father to study
for stage, becomes a great actress, returns later to
her father's shop. PW 2-14-03
NYT 03,155
ACAD, 64, 115
Jewish widower driven to Eng to avoid persecution in
Russia, daughter Anna. He neglects her for his books
and his curio shop. Anna sees little of world, one
night she takes in a deformed fugitive who comes to
adore her, leaves her home reluctantly for a career,
later has a real love. Steps down from topmost height
of career to return to papa. LBKM 3-03-240 /
ATH 121, 269

011860   THE FLY ON THE WHEEL. New York: Dodd,
Mead, 1908 NUC. Edinburgh: W. Blackwood, 1908 BMC.

BKM(serialized)-Hedda Gabler type egoist-kills herself
rather than married man she loves-but was a last
minute decision.

011861   THE GAMBLER, A NOVEL. New York and
London: Harper, 1905 NUC. Toronto: F. H. Revell, 1905
BMC.

Long review woman gambler, gets in debt, about to
commit suicide, happy end. BKM (1905) 22, 361-4
Fearless, impulsive, high spirited passion for
gambling. PW 9-23-05
Young girl married to elderly man, inherited the
gambling passion from father. Story relates her career
as a widow. There is a hero. NYT 591,05
Ends in a death for which heroine feels responsible.
ACAD-A woman who has an inherited weakness for
gambling but much strength of char.
TLS---bewildering mixture.

011862   JOHN CHILCOTE, M.P. Edinburgh and London:
W. Blackwood, 1904 BMC 1905 NUC.

011863   THE MASQUERADER: A NOVEL. New York and
London: Harper, 1904 NUC.

Pub. in Eng under title John Chilcote, M.P.

011864   MAX. A NOVEL. New York: Harper, 1910 NUC.
London: Hutchinson, 1910 BMC.

Russian princess dresses as boy, runs off to Paris to
escape marriage to live as she pleases. Friendship
develops to love as Ned Blake comes to learn his
friend is female. PW

011865   THE MYSTICS: A NOVEL. New York and
London: Harper, 1907 NUC. Edinburgh: W. Blackwood,

1907 BMC.

About a group of rel. mystics. PW 4-13-07

THURSTON, MABEL NELSON. United States.

011866   ON THE ROAD TO ARCADY. New York: F. H.
Revell, [1903] BMC NUC.

Love and nature-PW 10-31-03.
NYT 03, 859

011867   SARAH ANN. New York: Dodd, Mead, 1917
NUC.

THYNNE, MOLLY.

011868   THE UNCERTAIN GLORY. London: Methuen,
1914 BMC.

ATH-Artistic life in Munich and London.
TLS-Pleasant young people, romance
Contrast of two women "a man's girl" and a girl's
girl". "A harmless book all about nice people." SP

TIBBITS, ANNIE O. United Kingdom.

011869   AT WHAT SACIFICE? London: Digby, Long,
1912 BMC NUC.

Effie Gale-Carew, spoiled and dearly loved by father
not by step brother and his wife, is suddenly faced
with death, mystery and suspicion so horrible she runs
off, lost for six years. At the end of that time her
lover meets her, finds her utterly changed for her
suffering. Both suffer more before they come together
at last. LBKM

011870   BROKEN FETTERS; A THRILLING STORY OF
FACTORY AND STAGE LIFE. London: [Mascot Novels],
[1917] BMC.

011871   THE GREY CASTLE MYSTERY. London: [Mascot
Novels], [1919] BMC.

011872   LOVE NOT ENOUGH. London: [Mascot Novels],
[1920] BMC.

011873   LOVE WITHOUT PITY. London: [Mascot
Novels], [1915] BMC.

011874   MARQUESS SPLENDID. London: Digby, Long,
1910 BMC.

TLS-traditional romance.
ACAD 7-9-10,35. Rev. analyzes the lack of ability in
women in general.
LBKM-He is a rogue but changes because he wants to
meet and marry a young woman he saved from the streets
at 12 and whom he hasn't seen since. Their meeting is
powerful and surprising.

011875   NO ROOF TO SHELTER HER. London: Aldine,
[1919] BMC.

011876   PAID IN FULL. London: [Mascot Novels],
[1920] BMC.

011877   THE PATH UNKNOWN. London: D. C. Thomson,
[1920] BMC.

011878   PRISONERS FOR LIFE. London: [Mascot
Novels], [1917] BMC.

011879   SILENT LIPS. London: [Mascot Novels],
[1919] BMC.

TICKNOR, CAROLINE. 1866-1937. United States.

011880   MISS BELLADONNA: A CHILD OF TO-DAY.
Boston: Little, Brown, 1897 NUC.

Spoiled "shrewd, selfish, hard, pretty," Her perfect
barbarity. Outspoken about her parents. She and
brothers and sisters are "advanced children." Religion
they have none; morals are their jest; sentiment and
imagination are strangers to them. Bored by Arabian
Nights, no patience with Santa Claus. "They refuse to
be civilized." Author exposes "the fallacy of an ed.
system which neglects educating the mind and soul, to
educate the body." NYT 10-30-97, 5.

TIDDEMAN, L. E. See TIDDEMAN, LIZZIE ELLEN.

TIDDEMAN, LIZZIE ELLEN. United Kingdom.

011881   MOLLY'S DECISION. BY L. E. TIDDEMAN.
London: Society for Promoting Christian Knowledge,
1911 NUC BMC. New York: E. S. Gorham, [n.d.] NUC.

011882   TENDER AND TRUE. BY L. E. TIDDEMAN.
London: 'Leisure Hour' Library Office, 1905 NUC BMC.

TIERNAN, FRANCES CHRISTINE (FISHER). 1846-1920. United
States.

011883   CARMELA. BY CHRISTIAN REID. Philadelphia:
H. L. Kilner, [c1891] NUC.

011884   THE CHASE OF AN HEIRESS. BY CHRISTIAN
REID. New York & London: G. P. Putnam's Sons, 1898 NUC
BMC.

NYT 1898:516. Romance in W. Indies. Leslie, the hero
is looking for an heir of Ancram's. She has run off
with a man to make her lover jealous, stabbed the man
she was travelling with when he tried to kiss her.
Katherine, the heroine, is the true detective who
tracks her down for Leslie. Everything straightens out
and ends with two marriages.

011885   A COMEDY OF ELOPEMENT. BY CHRISTIAN REID.
New York: D. Appleton, 1893 NUC.

Young woman sends her 15 year old girl cousin to tell
her lover she has changed her mind about eloping with
him. Six years later in Venice, the young cousin is
forced to elope in order to marry the man of her
choice; she's now very wealthy. 2-7-93. PW
Early days of St. Augustine. She had decided to wed
someone else with more money. A comedy of errors. CR
14, 20:216.
Miss Fanny Berian, belle from New York, about to elope
with one man stays on in Florida to marry a rich one.
Sends her young cousin to give the first man the news.
Years later Fanny is instrumental in getting the two
married. LW 93, 74.

011886   THE DAUGHTER OF A STAR. BY CHRISTIAN
REID. New York: Devin-Adair, [c1913] NUC BMC.

011887   A DAUGHTER OF THE SIERRA. BY CHRISTIAN
REID. St. Louis, Mo.: B. Herder, 1903 NUC.

011888   FAIRY GOLD. BY CHRISTIAN REID. Notre
Dame, Ind.: Ave Maria, [c1897] NUC.

011889   A FAR-AWAY PRINCESS. BY CHRISTIAN REID.
New York: Devin-Adair, [c1914] NUC BMC.

PZ3

011890   THE LAND OF THE SUN: VISTAS MEXICANAS. BY
CHRISTIAN REID. New York: D. Appleton, 1894 NUC.

011891   THE LIGHT OF THE VISION. BY CHRISTIAN
REID. Notre Dame, Ind.: Ave Maria, [c1911] NUC.

011892   A LITTLE MAID OF ARCADY. BY CHRISTIAN
REID. Philadelphia: H. L. Kilner, [c1893] NUC.

011893   THE LOST LODE. BY CHRISTIAN REID.
Philadelphia: H. L. Kilner, [c1892] NUC. (Bound with
Stella's Discipline by F. X. L.)

PW The lost lode: vein of ore in Mexican mine. Hero is
led to commit an act of treachery for it;is saved from
the consequences by the heroine.

011894   THE MAN OF THE FAMILY: A NOVEL. BY
CHRISTIAN REID. New York & London: G. P. Putnam's
Sons, 1897 NUC.

A buried treasure. The man is a young woman who
disguises herself as a man and searches and finds the
ancestral treasure. LW:28 478.
Wouldn't sacrifice her sister Diane to discharge a
debt. Yvonne who had always supplied the masculine
element in the family dresses as a man and travels by
steamship from New York to Haiti. Meets a man who for
several weeks has no idea she's a woman. Together they
find the treasure. After they find all the treasure
and get it home, he goes off. But she--much
later--manages a meeting. Plans a tea party where
she'll appear as Henri de Marsillac (her disguise).
BKM 6:258

011895   THE PICTURE OF LAS CRUCES: A ROMANCE OF
MEXICO. BY CHRISTIAN REID. New York: D. Appleton, 1896
NUC BMC.

LW 27:330. A gentle Mexican girl, the wife of Don

Luis, bears a striking resemblance to an ancestor's
portrait. He conceives that she possesses this
ancestor's "frailities," tragedy follows.
PW 5-23-96. American artist in Mexico, Ralph Ingraham,
meets Carmen, living embodiment of the Velasquez he
has gone there to see. Asks to paint her portrait and
falls in love with her.

011896   PRINCESS NADINE. BY CHRISTIAN REID. New
York and London: G. P. Putnam's Sons, 1908 NUC BMC.

PW-Complicated plot
BKM-Russian princess renounces her aspirations to a
throne and marries.

011897   THE SECRET BEQUEST. BY CHRISTIAN REID.
Notre Dame, Ind.: Ave Maria, [c1915] NUC.

011898   VERA'S CHARGE. BY CHRISTIAN REID. Notre
Dame, Ind.: Ave Maria, [c1907] NUC.

011899   THE WARGRAVE TRUST. BY CHRISTIAN REID.
New York: Benziger, 1912 NUC.

Problem of an inheritance. PW 12-2-11

011900   WEIGHED IN THE BALANCE. BY CHRISTIAN
REID. Boston: Marlier, Callanan, 1900 NUC.

PW-psychological study of heroine, an idealist who
finds the world's motives and standards in direct
contradiction to hers. Love, sorrow. Bohemian Paris,
American society.

011901   A WOMAN OF FORTUNE: A NOVEL. BY CHRISTIAN
REID. New York: Benziger, 1896 NUC.

PW 12-12-96. Romance of American heiress opposed to
marriage who meets an Irishman on board ship and is
converted to Catholicism

TIERNEY, CATHERINE A. United States.

011902   PAULE. Westfield, Mass.: C. A. Tierney,
[c1897] NUC.

TINAYRE, MARCELLE, pseud. See TINAYRE, MARGUERITE SUZANNE
MARCELLE (CHASTEAU).

TINAYRE, MARGUERITE SUZANNE MARCELLE (CHASTEAU). B. 1877.
France.

011903   BIRD OF THE STORM. London: Bohemian Pub.
Co., [1913] BMC.

011904   THE HOUSE OF SIN. BY MARCELLE TINAYRE.
London: Maclaren, 1905 NUC. (Tr. A. Smyth.)

011905   MADELINE AT HER MIRROR; A WOMAN'S DIARY.
BY MARCELLE TINAYRE. New York and London: John Lane,
1913 NUC BMC. (Tr. Winifred Stephens.)

PW 84 10/4/13:1142 A woman's diary, married when very
young, widowed, children grown; attractive,
intelligent. "Purports to be written by a young
Parisian widow, who jots down all her thoughts on her
children, her friends, her country house, Parisian
society, and modern existence in general."
BKM:changes her mind that children fill her life-wants
more. "one of the foremost names in French feminism."
R OF R 49:375.
"Nothing of interest as between one woman and another
is omitted." A widow...finds her children growing up
rapidly...keeping the robust health of her childhood."
NYT 1913 684
"This is not a novel, the author explains, but a
collection of impressions, of dreams, and of memories,
in which fiction mingles with fact." ...The narrator
is a well-to-do widow of thirty-five, the mother of
two children, and the fashions, entertaining, the
importunities of the country, foreign politics,
apartment-hunting for relatives, together with a
slight concern over advancing age (are) a few of the
topics chosen."--NATION

011906   SACRIFICE. BY MARCELLE TINAYRE. London:
A. Melrose, [1915] BMC 1916 [c] NUC. (Tr. M. Harriet
M. Capes.)

TLS-See review of La Veillee des Armes 7-15-15.

011907   THE SHADOW OF LOVE. BY MARCELLE TINAYRE.
London, New York: J. Lane, 1911 BMC NUC. (Tr. Alfred
Allinson)

NYT (1910)-Denise has been brought up on Philosophy

and science. Thesis is the right of the child not to
be born.
"We search our memories in vain for any fiction
matching it in its handling of the physical facts of
life....Two girls appear in the story, the one trained
by her father, a physician, to believe firmly in that
right, of all others most ignored, the "right of the
child not to be born," has reached the age of 27
years, a well-poised, calm young woman. How all that
her rearing and her own nature have carefully built up
within her soul crumbles at the touch of a love far
removed from passion, an almost maternal yearning over
a dying man, is the dominant theme of the story. The
other girl, Fortunade...is of the stuff of which
medieval saints were made. Her temperament is that of
a mystic, her longing is for the cloister." NYT
6-25-11, 403.
"If Mme. Tinayre makes her heroine succumb, in spite
of her forceful theories, to so vulgar a sentiment as
amorous pity, it is because her theories are too new
to have become an integral part of this heroine's
being. It is obvious that the author believes that the
woman of the future will not be subject to lapses of
this nature." NYT 4-10-10, 25.

011908   THE SWEETNESS OF LIFE. BY MARCELLE
TINAYRE. London: E. Nash, 1912 BMC NUC. (Tr. Lilian
Wiggins)

TLS-see original review (of Fr. ed) 7-6-1911

011909   TO ARMS! (LA VEILEE DES ARMES); AN
IMPRESSION OF THE SPIRIT OF FRANCE. New York: E. P.
Dutton, [c1918] NUC. (Tr. Lucy H. Humphrey.
Another English translation by Capes has title
"Sacrifice".)

NYT-Effect of World War I on small group of people in
Paris. Strongly patriotic.

TINCKER, M. A. See TINCKER, MARY AGNES.

TINCKER, MARY AGNES. 1831-1907. United States.

011910   GRAPES AND THORNS; OR, A PRIEST'S
SACRIFICE. BY M. A. TINCKER. New York: Christian Press
Assoc., 1909 NUC.

011911   SAN SALVADOR. Boston: Houghton Mifflin,
1892 NUC BMC.

LW 23:150. A secluded utopia fantastically concealed
in the heart of the Italian mountains. A mystical
community who "know each other by signs and songs"
"permeate Europe with a network of somewhat wild
benevolence;= and combine this occult religion with
olive pickling, lace making, and cold working. NATION
145:402 : An ideal community in Spain made up of
social outcasts.
PW-Tacita is the heroine who goes to San Salvadore
where she finds peace. Simplicity in way of life.

TINKER, BEAMISH, pseud. See HARWOOD, FRYNIWYD TENNYSON
(JESSE).

TINSLEY, LELIA MARY (TINSLEY). B. 1870. United States.

011912   SETTING THE GOLDEN EGG; BEING THE PRAYER
OF A WOMAN FOR THE UNION AND GROWTH OF SCIENCE AND ART
IN THIS DAY OF HUMAN UPHEAVAL. New York: Tinsley,
[c1916] NUC.

TIPPETT, ISABEL C.

011913   FLOWER OF THE WORLD. London: J. Long,
1909 BMC.

TLS-sounds promising has emancipated woman.
Feminine villian. ACAD

011914   GREEN GIRL. London: J. Long, 1913 BMC.

Life in Latin quarter, young woman dislikes being tied
by the marriage bond. LBKM
Janette Acklebourne goes to Paris to study art; there
met a man she travelled with. Later marries a rich man
against her better judgment, then rejoins the man she
met in France. TLS

011915   LIFE-FORCE. London: Everett, [1915] BMC.

A good many social problems; wife with drunken
husband, husband with mad wife; craving starved woman
who can't find a mate. Author is "advanced in her
outlook" TLS

011916   THE POWER OF THE PETTICOAT. London: J.
Long, 1911 BMC.

Sensational story involving RCsm-TLS

011917   THE PURPLE BUTTERFLY. London: J. Long,
1910 BMC.

TLS-Unprincipled Babette, flirt, etc. "unpleasant
heroine".

011918   THE WASTER. London: J. Long, 1912 BMC.

ATH-Charming idealizer of women
TLS-cute
ACAD-cute

TIPPETTS, KATHERINE (BELL). B. 1865. United States.

011919   PRINCE ARENGZEBA: A ROMANCE OF LAKE
GEORGE. BY JEROME CABLE. Glens Falls, N.Y.: W. H.
Tippetts Star Pub. Co., [c1892] NUC. (Beautiful Lake
George, pp. 124-154, by William Henry Tippetts.)

TITSON, MARIE.

011920   THE THREE SISTERS. London: Digby, Long,
1913 BMC.

TODD, MARGARET GEORGINA. 1859-1918. United Kingdom.

011921   AFTER MANY DAYS. BY GRAHAM TRAVERS. New
York: G. Putnam's Sons, 1895 NUC.

011922   THE EXAMINER'S CONSCIENCE. BY GRAHAM
TRAVERS. New York: G. Putnam's Sons, 1896 NUC.

011923   GROWTH, A NOVEL. BY GRAHAM TRAVERS
(MARGARET TODD, M.D.). London: A. Constable, 1906 BMC.
New York: Holt, 1907 NUC.

One of leading women-a successful actress 4-20-07 PW

011924   THE KNIGHT AND THE LADY. New York: 1895
NUC.

011925   MONA MACLEAN, MEDICAL STUDENT. A NOVEL.
BY GRAHAM TRAVERS. Edinburgh: Blackwood, 1892 BMC. New
York: D. Appleton, 1892 NUC.

SP 69:775. Women medical students. An "intellectual
comedy."
ACAD 42:504. Full of the "female medical movement".
Mona marries another doctor and they are practitioners
together. She tends a small shop in Scotland for 6
months. Becomes a medical student. Has early failures
then later successes in exams. marries a physcian and
is his "medical as well as wifely partner." LW 93,209

011926   THE WAY OF ESCAPE; A NOVEL. BY GRAHAM
TRAVERS (MARGARET TODD). New York: D. Appleton, 1902.
London: Blackwood, 1902 BMC.

LBKM-6-02 Theme is inability to escape anguish of
early affair, need more details.
ATH 5-17-02 not helpful.
DIAL 8-02-Sunday school story, religious-book is about
development of her character.

011927   WINDYHAUGH. A NOVEL. BY GRAHAM TRAVERS.
London: W. Blackwood, 1898 BMC. New York: D. Appleton,
1899 NUC.

SP 81:693. Mental, spiritual and physical development
of Wilhelmina from 7 to 20. She has a very lonely
childhood, going from Puritanical grandmother to
stepmother to her wastrel father to her marriage to a
Cambridge prig, who, she discovers does not feel she
is his intellectual equal. She leaves him, works as a
governess, studies science, becomes a successful
actress. Eventual reconciliation.
ACAD 55:376. "A kind of Sartor Resartus translated
into feminine and every day terms, with a woman
instead of a man as the central character; with the
trials, circumstances, and thoughts of the late
nineteenth century given in place of the abstract and
transcendental scenery of Carlyle." SR 86:859.
LBKM 15:85. By end of book has brought her husband to
his knees.
Wilhelmina is restless. Becomes an actress, quits
that, gets married, leaves husband. Then sends for him
when, because of heredity, she takes to "something
worse than Scotch drink." LIT 4:98.
Wilhelmina Galbraith--from "prim precocious repressed"
childhood to strong wise womanhood. Lots of problems
on the way: a gambling father, sordid poverty, an

unfaithful husband. Became a governess and then an
eager student. Nurses her dying father. Happily
married in the end. LW 30:54.
Wilhelmina Galbraith, pride makes her leave her
husband when she learns he married her for honor not
love. Author is too much Wilhelmina's advocate. NYT
3-4-99,133.

TODD, MARY VAN LENNUP (IVES). B. 1849. United States.

011928   AN AMERICAN ABELARD AND HELOISE; A LOVE
STORY. New York: Grafton Press, [1904] NUC.

"Revolt vs religion and conventional usage." She
reguses to accept the subject conditions of a wife.
Hero is an "involuntary martyr to progressive views of
womanly indep. with hope of home and marr.
indefinitely postponed." WOMAN'S JOURNAL 6-3-05
"indignant protest against various injustices of
modern times". BKM (1905) 21, 322
Romance of a modern clergyman and a woman with views
of her own on marriage and rights of women. She won't
marry him until "both have practically lived out their
views." They separate for three years of probation.
Not concluded. PW 4-1-05
Young minister loves a woman who's impatient with his
religious views, she takes off, he traces her, but
falls ill, decides to follow her religion for she
won't marry him. NYT 311,05

011929   AN AMERICAN MADONNA, A STORY OF LOVE. New
York: The Binghamton Book Mfg. Co., 1908 NUC.

011930   DEBORAH, THE ADVANCED WOMAN. BY M. I. T.
Boston: Arena, 1896 NUC.

PW 10-10-96. "A strong and pathetic story of life
among the Mormons during the early years of their
settlement on the shores of Salt Lake, written for the
purpose of asserting woman's coequality with man and
aiding in her release from that subjection to man's
use and passion which has been her lot for years."

011931   THE HETERODOX MARRIAGE OF A NEW WOMAN.
New York: R. L. Weed, [c1898] NUC.

LW 29:253. "Outcome is not at all startling after all
the protests of the mother & daughter." Substitution
of "till it shall please God to separate us."
PW-intellectual heroine. Her mother argues for the old
school of thought.

011932   JUST FRIENDS; A COMMON SENSE STORY. New
York: Calkins, 1908 NUC.

011933   A PREMATURE SOCIALIST, OUIDA'S WITTIEST
STORY BUILT INTO A COMEDY. New York: Broadway, [c1906]
NUC.

Based on an altruist.

011934   VIOLINA; OR THE PASSING OF THE OLD ADAM
AND EVE. A ROMANCE. New York: Broadway, 1904 NUC.

NYT-Young woman musician marries a scoundrel, leaves
him and returns to her musical career and a young man.

TOMKINSON, JULIA REDFORD.

011935   DORIS, A MOUNT HOLYOKE GIRL. New York:
American Tract Soc., [c1913] NUC.

"Simple story of a girl who went to Mt. Holyoke in the
early days of its career and was one of the first to
come under Miss Lyons' influence. Tells of her home
life on a New England farm, her education, life as a
teacher and happy marriage." PW

TOMPKINS, ELIZABETH KNIGHT. B. 1865. United States.

011936   THE BROKEN RING: A ROMANCE. New York,
London: G. P. Putnam's Sons, 1896 NUC BMC.

PW 6-6-96. Germany, love story of prince and princess.
Comic-operatic; about a merry war between two nations
and a princess captured and her jailer who loves her,
etc. CR 28,31:34

011937   HER MAJESTY: A ROMANCE OF TO-DAY. New
York, London: G. P. Putnam's Sons, 1895 NUC 1896 BMC.

A queen travels incognito among her people to discover
their needs, meets and loves a duke also travelling
incognito. Comes the revolution and she and the duke
get together. CR. 24:248
Queen Honoria. She is daring and relates to Hugo as a

comrade. LW 26:253
Marry, called back to rule. BOOK NEWS 157:24

011938   TALKS WITH BARBARA: BEING AN INFORMAL AND
EXPERIMENTAL DISCUSSION, FROM THE POINT OF VIEW OF A
YOUNG WOMAN OF TO-MORROW, OF CERTAIN OF THE
COMPLEXITIES OF LIFE, PARTICULARLY IN REGARD TO THE
RELATIONS OF MEN AND WOMEN. New York and London: G. P.
Putnam's Sons, 1900 W BMC.

NYT 1900:420. Doctor is her confidant. On the social
condition of women. Rev. thinks she's crazy and author
is unkind to her sex. PW-includes marriage, masculine
vs feminine honor, nice girls in real life vs nice
girls in novels.

011939   THE THINGS THAT COUNT. New York and
London: G. P. Putnam's Sons, 1900 NUC BMC.

NYT 1900:409. Heroine is young woman of small means
who lives by visits to her wealthy friends. Awakening,
regeneration, and love. LW 31:172. Her awakening is in
no way religious. Her discussions with men of "mutual
attraction, love and marriage," are a "little
shocking."
Evelyn-expensive tastes and a banjo. "The austere
reader is continually lacerated by Evelyn's manners."
"The imperfect heroine is one of the most popular
arrivals in recent literature," sees the error of her
ways in the end? CR 01

TOMPKINS, ELLEN WILKINS. United States.

011940   THE EGOTISTICAL I. New York: E. P.
Dutton, [c1913] NUC.

Young woman loved by old bachelor, as father loves a
daughter. Pleasant, sunshiny book NYT
BKM-semi invalid & elderly bachelor (of title) and the
youthful pessimist (female) and their conversations.

011941   THE ENLIGHTENMENT OF PAULINA. New York:
E. P. Dutton, [c1917] NUC.

She's poor marries rich man she dislikes. treats him
miserably. Then he embezzles, is a penniless criminal,
goes to prison. Eventually returns to husband. PW
"Loathes him from the bottom of her heart" After he
goes to prison, she goes to live with her mother's
friend where enlightment comes NYT

TOMPKINS, FLORENCE. Nationality Unknown.

011942   THE MAN IN THE MOON; OR, THE UNEXPECTED.
BY BERTRAM DENDRON. New York: Bonnell, Silver, [1901]
NUC.

TOMPKINS, JULIET WILBOR. 1871-1956. United States.

011943   AT THE SIGN OF THE OLDEST HOUSE; A MODERN
ROMANCE. Indianapolis: Bobbs-Merrill, [c1917] BMC NUC.

011944   DIANTHA. New York: Century, 1915 BMC NUC.

BKM 41 1915
Prince-princess story PW 5-29-15
Twin sisters-as babies very much alike then one grew
fat, sluggish colourless as other developed beauty.
(Sylvia) The former had hidden revolts, longing to be
like sister who was arrogant and spoiled. Diantha
ignored, saw men flock to her sister, ignore her. A
man finally really likes her, but Sylvia cuts her out.
Diantha gets sick but restored to beauty, while Sylvia
fades "one of the most interesting pieces of psych.
analysis that have been issued in months" BKM

011945   DR. ELLEN. New York: Baker & Taylor,
[1908] NUC.

PW-Woman M.D. sacrifices career to take her sister to
Sierras (TB). Sister does not know she is sick, Ellen
practices in West, problems.
BKM-Male quack comes into town, Ellen loses a patient
and soon after all her patients leave her to go to the
quack. Then what?
NYT Hero is worthy even of this superior woman,
strong, independent.

011946   EVER AFTER. Garden City, N. Y.:
Doubleday, Page, 1913 NUC NUC.

PW 83 5/31/13:1963 "Lucy Cuyler was rich, she was also
a Bostonian. Dana Malone was poor and a Californian.
Lucy could paint and Dana composed, but made little
money with his music. They married, thinking their
love would bridge the gulf made by Lucy's wealth, but

found that New England thrift and Western open-handedness could not understand each other. For a while this brought them unhappiness, but they solved their problem and proved that real love can sometimes do the apparently impossible."
She can give away thousands and never flinch, but she's a penny watcher. This trait runs in her family and causes problems in her marriage. NYT
problems of wife's independent fortune; meets him at an artist colony she established; he immediately squanders her money when they marry. She leaves; he wants to earn his own income. She tranfers whole fortune to him. BKM

011947   A GIRL NAMED MARY. Indianapolis: Bobbs-Merrill, [c1918] BMC NUC.

PW. Mother spends fortune searching for daughter Mary who disappeared at two. Loves all Marys she finds. At last finds her own, a stenographer proud and independent and fiercely loyal to stepmother. Wins her love thru understanding of her love affair.
NYT, Sept 29, '18, p 411. Mother was as a young woman a somewhat frivolous woman, but character develops through her "long inquiry into the lives and homes of working girls." Has spent her time and energy for causes that will benefit children and working women. When she finds her daughter, she discovers her to be a first-class working woman, as proud of her work as another woman might be of her wealth.

011948   JOANNA BUILDS A NEST. Indianapolis: Bobbs-Merrill, [c1920] BMC NUC. London: Page, 1921 BMC.

PW-Problems of homemaking, delights of remodeling a house. Joanna persuades publisher to let her spend half of week in a small country house she has bought. Arranges for a housekeeper-chaperone and a war veteran to stay with her; former is lazy, latter is from Civil war. Humorous.

011949   OPEN HOUSE. New York: Baker & Taylor, [1909] NUC.

BKM 4. 29-1909 woman becomes physician's assist, and marries him.
Change in woman who after years of luxury must earn own living. Takes job as physician's ass't but finds it hard to take orders. As she becomes capable, doctor finds there's more in life than medicine. BKM

011950   PLEASURES AND PALACES. London: Hodder & Stoughton, 1912 BMC. Garden City, N. Y.: Doubleday, Page, 1912 NUC.

"The home making adventures of Marie Rose"- subtitle. Her life a series of stays in hotels where she had no chance to do housekeeping. Takes a flat, sees how complicated life can be. There's a young man next door. ATH
PW-"an amusing little story in which love and home are triumphantly vindicated."
BKM 35 (1912) 316-17

011951   THE SEED OF THE RIGHTEOUS. Indianapolis: Bobbs Merrill, [c1916] BMC NUC.

Chloe rebels at her family's attitude that the world owes them a living because their father has been a great public worker. PW
Chloe rebels at her family's attitude that the world owes them a living be. their father had been a great public worker. NYT
BKM She becomes independent; Alex then sees she is too good for that and marries her.

011952   THE STARLING. Indianapolis: Bobbs-Merrill, [c1919] BMC NUC.

Selfishness of Prof. Cowthorne affects daughter Sarah & wife. PW
Sarah Cowthorne writes novels, she's a person who takes joy in things others take for granted. Her father, a great scholar, is a patriarchal figure who despises instinct-a complete rationalist. Both Sarah and her mother hunger for people's companionship; but the prof. keeps them enclosed. But Sarah has two men interested in her. "It is true, my dear, men are not much, but they are all we have in that line." Says her mother. NYT 9-14-19 467

011953   THE TOP OF THE MORNING. New York: Baker & Taylor, 1910 NUC.

"A series of sketches concerned with the doings of the

six genial and artistic friends who form a club known in their own circle as 'Us'." BKM v. 31, 1910

TOPHAM, ANNE. B. 1874. United Kingdom.

011954   THE BEGINNING AND THE END. London: A. Melrose, 1919 BMC.

Anne Arbuthnot artistic, orphan, schooled narrowly at a "young ladies's seminary," "gives herself" passionately to a young man when she's only 17. Careful study develops from troubled waters to happiness. Heroine-a "little too perfect." TLS
Reconstitutes her life and "makes good" SP. Careful study of her childhood and youth, rescue from despair by old nurse. Becomes a portrait painter, finally marries "leaving her seducer a prey to the agonies of remorse" LBKM

011955   DAPHNE IN PARIS. BY THE AUTHOR OF "DAPHNE IN THE FATHERLAND" [ANONYMOUS]. London: A. Melrose, 1913 BMC.

Mother sends Daphne to Paris so she'll forget the poor man she's in love with. Chaperoned by a (Betty) young woman who is as romantic as she. Has a chance to wed a "chinless" duke but chooses the poor man. Daphne speaks in own voice through most of novel. "Splitting her infinitives as only a woman can." ACAD 2-22-13 p. 240

011956   DAPHNE IN THE FATHERLAND [ANONYMOUS]. London: A. Melrose, 1912 BMC. New York: Brentano's, 1912 NUC.

ATH Combination of letters and diary of English girl visiting Germany.
SP-

011957   THE GOLDEN MOMENT. London: A. Melrose, 1915 BMC NUC.

The stage, the heroine a Germ. princess TLS
Eng man carries her off ATH

011958   JULIA AND I IN CANADA. BY THE AUTHOR OF "DAPHNE IN THE FATHERLAND" [ANONYMOUS]. London: A. Melrose, 1913 BMC.

Two Englishwomen and their brother struggle to set up a house in Montreal for a year. The problems of women finding living quarters- (men can live in boarding houses the world over). These women have to create own home, do all domestic work. Rickety buildings and flats of Montreal. SP
ACAD 86:16. Julia & Priscilla on a lecture tour in Eastern Canada. "teaching Canadians how to run Canada." Rev. finds them opinionated and priggish.

TORREY, JANE ANNE, pseud. See KENDELL, JANE ANNE TORREY.

TOSTI, BERTHE.

011959   THE HEART OF RUBY. London: Chapman & Hall, 1903 BMC. (Tr. Violet Hunt.)

TOTTENHAM, B. LOFTUS. See TOTTENHAM, BLANCHE MARY LOFTUS.

TOTTENHAM, BLANCHE MARY LOFTUS.

011960   A HEART'S REVENGE. London: Hurst and Blackett, 1894 BMC.

SP 72:444. Miserable tyrant drives son from home, wife to arms of lover.

011961   IN THE SHADOW OF THREE. London: Hutchinson, 1898 BMC.

Sp 81:445. Fall of Venice. Historical romance, last years of 18th century. Duels, tortures, imprisonments.

011962   MORE KIN THAN KIND. BY B. LOFTUS TOTTENHAM. London: Hurst and Blackett, 1892 BMC.

SP 69:297. romance involving an inheritance and question of illegitimate birth, but all works out for hero and heroine.

011963   THE UNWRITTEN LAW. London: A. & C. Black, 1895 BMC.

Ire. Rose Regan loves Brian Dermot but father wants her to wed Ned Donelly. Brian imprisoned for involvement in mvt. Doesn't show up at church. Since she's pregnant, she married Ned. Brian released

earlier than expected. Trag. ACAD 48:455
SP 76:386. Irish. "We are not entirely satisfied with
the way in which the plot is worked out. Surely the
typical Irish girl, with the best qualities that made
her countrywomen the admiration of the world, would
not have acted as she did."

011964   A VENETIAN LOVE STORY. London: Osgood and
McIlvaine, 1896 BMC NUC.

Italy, mid. ages. Fasoli a great artist. Carita D´Este
lurid portrait of a Venetian woman of beauty and of
atsolute lack of principle. SP 79:627
She marries a man after her husband is missing. The
second man is a better one; therefore we´re "apt to
condone the infidelty"- until the catastrophe of the
novel. ATH 109:12

TOTTENHAM, BLANCHE MARY LOFTUS, jt. au. See YOUNG, AMELIA
SOPHIA COATES AND BLANCHE MARY LOFTUS TOTTENHAM.

TOWGOOD, EDITH ETHEL. United Kingdom.

011965   THE GOAL OF FORTUNE. London: Sidgwick &
Jackson, 1911 BMC NUC.

LBKM-really expresses the woman's view, not based on
male models, delicate, precise, fidelity to observed
life, Alison has humour, brains and purpose but author
says it was "inevitable that she would fall in love
with her first serious wooer." An account of people
rather than events.
Alison comes close to her husband Arnold Vernon
finally in last chapter TLS
Married a man for whom she had only a friendly regard.
ATH

TOWNESEND, FRANCES ELIZA (HODGSON) BURNETT. 1849-1924.
United States.

011966   THE CAPTAIN'S YOUNGEST. BY FRANCES
HODGSON BURNETT. London: F. Warne, [1894] BMC 1899
NUC.

011967   THE DAWN OF A TO-MORROW. BY FRANCES
HODGSON BURNETT. New York: C. Scribner's Sons, 1906
NUC. London: F. Warne, 1907 BMC NUC.

Depressed man comtemplates suicide. LBKM 3,C7 276
Despair of poverty, old woman of the slums. TLS?
PW-Man about to commit suicide meets poor London girl,
helps others like her
NYT O

011968   THE DRURY LANE BOYS' CLUB. BY FRANCES
HODGSON BURNETT. Washington, D.C.: "The Moon", 1892
NUC.

011969   EMILY FOX-SETON; BEING THE MAKING OF A
MARCHIONESS AND THE METHODS OF LADY WALDERHURST. BY
FRANCES HODGSON BURNETT. New York: F. A. Stokes,
[c1901] NUC.

011970   HIS GRACE OF OSMONDE: BEING THE PORTIONS
OF THAT NOBLEMAN'S LIFE OMITTED IN THE RELATION OF HIS
LADY'S STORY PRESENTED TO THE WORLD OF FASHION UNDER
THE TITLE OF A LADY OF QUALITY. BY FRANCES HODGSON
BURNETT. New York: C. Scribner's Sons, 1897 NUC.
London: F. Warne, 1897 BMC.

LIT 2:17. Same story as "A Lady of Quality", but from
a different p.o.v., focussing on the hero. Clorinda,
when viewed thru his eyes loses some of her "wayward
and masterful individuality." "Unconventional
rebellious figure, noble in its physical strength and
beauty, defiant of social restrictions." Set in 18th.
Splendid, intelligent. NYT 11-20-97,8.
"A complementary or alternative version of the same
author's ´A Lady of Quality,´" Same chars. "The
astounding exploits of Clorinda Wildairs and her
adorable duke." SP 79:777.
Hero too idealized as is heroine. ACAD 52 FIc Sup 122.
Part 1 given to hy of this ideal hero-on his perfect
way to manhood-Oxford. In his youth he had heard of
Clorinda, seen her in boy's clothes. A woman of
unrivaled profanity. The duke-hero falls in love with
the swearing beauty. But he's scared off and she
marries someone else. His great remorse. CR 28,31:299.
"Crowned the follies of her youth with a capital
crime"-murder. She's "up to her knees in broken
commandments" but she's presented as a true woman,
wife, and tender mother, excellence in England's
womanhood.
Killed her lover-is made justifiable. Even her husband
says he would have done the same. This is the
husband's side of story. What should he do "when a

wife comes to him in silence without womanhood's
crown?" BKM 6:355.

011971   IN CONNECTION WITH THE DE WILLOUGHBY
CLAIM. BY FRANCES HODGSON BURNETT. London: F. Warne,
1899 BMC. New York: C. Scribner's Sons, 1899 NUC.

The claim is for damage done to their property during
the war of Secession--property in N. Carolina. LIT
5:623
Rural S. Tenn. Son of Town judge--a kind of clumsy
loser, leaves his family, goes to NC and becomes a
store keeper. Adopts an orphan girl; he becomes a
better person. Story covers many years. SP 83:919

011972   A LADY OF QUALITY: BEING A MOST CURIOUS
HITHERTO UNKNOWN HISTORY, AS RELATED TO MR. ISAAC
BICKERSTAFF BUT NOT PRESENTED TO THE WORLD OF FASHION
THROUGH THE PAGES OF THE TATLER AND NOW FOR THE FIRST
TIME WRITTEN DOWN. BY FRANCES HODGSON BURNETT. New
York: C. Scribner's Sons, 1896 NUC. London: F. Warne,
1896 BMC.

SR 81:627. Clorinda's mother dies in childbirth. She
lives with her father, a drunken bestial baronet, whom
she doesn't run into until she is six at which time
she curses him and beats him with his own hunting
crop. He is much affected and dresses her in breeches
and treats her as a son until she is 15 and decides to
be a lady. First marries an elderly title who dies.
Then on eve of a fantastic mrge, another beast of a
baronet, one who had seduced her as a child, threatens
her with a 6" lock of her hair. She asks him to tea,
reads sermons until he arrives, brains him and buries
him in the cellar. Marries and lives happily to a ripe
old age.
ATH 107:440. A law unto herself. Her sister defends
morality of her act and subsequent secrecy. "It is
idle to reflect whether such a woman could have had
her being, even in the 18th century."
SP 76:522. Keynote is strength of her indomitable
will.
BKM 3:156. "Granting that many a wretched woman has
killed her lover, no one of them all has as yet gone
on record that by so doing she has blotted out her own
shame. The belief that this can be done by the
shedding of blood is still a male article of faith.
The subsequent argument making the murder committed by
this lady of quality ´the accomplishment of love's
purification,´ and the primary, immediate, and
permanent cause of the spiritual transfiguration of
the murderess is equally insane and pernicious."

011973   THE LAND OF THE BLUE FLOWER. BY FRANCES
HODGSON BURNETT. New York: Moffat, Yard, 1909 NUC.
London: G. P. Putnam's Sons, 1912 BMC.

011974   THE LOST PRINCE. BY FRANCES HODGSON
BURNETT. New York: A. L. Burt, [c1910] NUC. London:
Hodder and Stoughton, 1915 BMC.

Hist. rom., focus on a boy Marco. NYT

011975   THE MAKING OF A MARCHIONESS. BY FRANCES
HODGSON BURNETT. New York: F. A. Stokes, [c1901] NUC.
London: Smith, Elder, 1901 BMC.

PW 10-5-01
Woman of 34 works helping house-wives with shopping,
choosing servants becomes a Lady herself. ATH 12-14-01

011976   THE METHODS OF LADY WALDERHURST. BY
FRANCES HODGSON BURNETT. New York: F. A. Stokes,
[c1901] NUC.

Older woman.

011977   THE ONE I KNEW THE BEST OF ALL: A MEMORY
OF THE MIND OF A CHILD. BY FRANCES HODGSON BURNETT.
New York: C. Scribner's Sons, 1893 NUC. London: F.
Warne, 1893 BMC.

Auto Story of Manchester girl who came to live in
North Carolina mountains because her brothers might
find work in the new world. To the time when an editor
accepts two stories by this girl of 15. NATION 57, 395
Her own life from third to 15th year. PW 10-28-93.

011978   THE SHUTTLE. BY FRANCES HODGSON BURNETT.
London: W. Heinemann, 1907 BMC. New York: F. A.
Stokes, [1907] NUC.

Modern young woman outspoken, well educated. knows the
facts. Bettina saves her sister from husband, who cuts
her off from family and takes over her income. Bettina
saves the estate, takes charge of all repairs, hires

and fires. Love: She is a millionairess he's poor but
has estate. No word of love between them; he goes off
to help sick in epidemic, she calls him back to life.
Vs. Nigel: Battle of wits; he's attracted to her real
villain. The scene where he has her trapped, but she's
self sufficient, hides from him, rescued. Internat'l
marr. Amer/Eng Diff in rights conventions, laws talk
of divorce. Melodrama with modern girl imposed upon
it.

011979   T. TEMBAROM. BY FRANCES HODGSON BURNETT.
New york: Century, [c1913] NUC. London: Hodder and
Stoughton, [1913] NUC BMC.

Began as newsboy, moved up to Harlem society reporter
and on to a large inheritance in England. NYT
PW:84 10/25/13:1384 "T. Tembarom" started in life as a
New York newsboy, and by hard work rose to the dizzy
heights of Harlem society reporter on a Sunday
newspaper. Then came to London solicitor who announced
that he was heir to $350,000 a year and vast estates,
and carried him off to England. T. Tembarom had fallen
in love with Little Ann at first sight in the dingy,
cheap New York boarding house. Little Ann was English,
had rare common sense and a heart of gold; and she
declared that "T. Tembarom" must do his honest best by
the new life which he did for a year and then found a
surprising way of renouncing his fortune and marrying
Little Ann."
SR 3 Jan '14 from shoe black to president.

011980   TWENTIETH THOUSAND. BY FRANCES HODGSON
BURNETT. London: F. Warne, 1891 BMC.

011981   THE WHITE PEOPLE. BY FRANCES HODGSON
BURNETT. New York and London: Harper, [1917] NUC.
London: W. Heinemann, 1920 BMC.

A young Scotch heiress and a famour writer BKM
As a lonely child she sees the White people who she
understands later are really the Dead who are not
really dead but part of all that is a continuity. The
novel attempts to assuage the effects of fear of
death. NYT 2-18-17,53

TOWNSEND, METTA (FOLGER). B. 1862. United States.

011982   IN THE NANTAHALAS: A NOVEL. New York:
Broadway, [1910] NUC.

TOWNSEND, VIRGINIA FRANCES. 1836-1920. United States.

011983   MOSTLY MARJORIE DAY. Boston: Lee and
Shepard., 1892 NUC.

penniless when pa dies, becomes rich woman's
companion. Suddenly inherits 60 million marries. IND.

TOWNSHEND, DOROTHEA (BAKER).

011984   CAPTAIN CHIMNEY-SWEEP. A STORY OF THE
GREAT WAR. London: T. Nelson, 1900 BMC.

011985   A LION, A MOUSE AND A MOTOR CAR: A
FANTASIA. London: Simpkin, Marshall, 1915 BMC NUC.

Pretty parson's daughter, social life, ends up the
wife of Sir Roger. TLS

011986   A LOST LEADER. A TALE OF RESTORATION
DAYS. London: Christian Knowledge Society, [1902] BMC
NUC.

011987   STRANGE ADVENTURES OF A YOUNG LADY OF
QUALITY, MDCCV. London: Digby, Long, [1893] BMC.

011988   WHITHER? THE STORY OF A FLIGHT. London:
S.P.C.K., [1918] BMC NUC.

TOWNSHEND, GLADYS ETHEL GWENDOLEN EUGENIE (SUTHERST)
TOWNSHEND. United Kingdom.

011989   MARRIED LIFE: THE ADVENTURES OF HERBERT
AND MARIANA. London: Hodder & Stoughton, 1914 BMC.

TLS-male narrator, who treats agreeable young couple
as "great big children."

011990   THE WIDENING CIRCLE: A ROMANTIC
CHRONICLE. BY THE MARCHIONESS TOWNSHEND. New York:
Appleton, 1920 NUC. London: E. Nash, [1920] NUC BMC.

LBKM-family story, humorous. Put down of father who is
a gambler in stocks.
NYT 10-24-20 p. 25 for girls.

TOWNSHEND, MARCHIONESS. See TOWNSHEND, GLADYS ETHEL
GWENDOLEN EUGENIE (SUTHERST) TOWNSHEND.

TOYE, NINA. United Kingdom.

011991   THE DEATH RIDER. London and New York:
Cassell, [1916] BMC NUC.

TLS Historical. Character study of a "peculiar aspect"
of Italy of Pope Julius II, which was the brutal ways
of Captain Malviso with women. really awful-the woman
humiliated in the first chapter, Fiametta designs a
gruesome revenge which is his nemesis.

TOZIER, JOSEPHINE. B. 1863.

011992   A SPRING FORTNIGHT IN FRANCE. London: C.
Brown, 1907 BMC. New York: Dodd, Mead, 1907 NUC.

TLS-travel novel

011993   SUSAN IN SICILY; HER ADVENTURES AND THOSE
OF HER FRIENDS DURING THEIR TRAVELS AND SOJOURNS IN
THE GARDEN OF THE MEDITERRANEAN. Boston: L. C. Page,
1910 NUC.

Travel and fiction. letters, PW

TRACY, VIRGINIA. United States.

011994   "PERSONS UNKNOWN". New York: Century,
1914 BMC NUC.

PW 86 10/24/14:1344 "Bryce Herrick, a young novelist,
watches upon the blind across the way the shadow of a
woman's violent gestures and listens to a man's loud
tones above the sound of the piano. Then a pistol is
discharged and the lights go out. Herrick investigates
and discovers the dead body of a man in the apartment.
He turns out to be a well-known publisher engaged to a
witty, high-spirited actress, Christina Hope. How
suspicion rests upon her, how Herrick finds her his
ideal as a heroine and sweetheart, and how the mystery
of the murder is satisfactorily removed, occupies the
rest of the tale."
NYT 1914

TRAHERNE, HARRIET MARGARET ANNE.

011995   THE GHOST OF TINTERN ABBEY. Clifton: J.
Baker, 1901 BMC.

011996   THE MILL ON THE USK: A WELSH TALE.
London: Keegan Paul, 1894 BMC.

SR 78:629. Welsh rivals in love with a beauty.

TRAIL, FLORENCE. 1854-1944. United States.

011997   UNDER THE SECOND RENAISSANCE: A NOVEL.
Buffalo: C. W. Moulton, 1894 NUC BMC.

LW 25:219. Heroine's family and lover hold the career
of an actress in abhorrence. "A defense of the
righteousness of the stage." All ends well.
PW-her trials and triumphs as an actress. Opposes
family in her choice.
Southern young woman goes on stage though family
opposes the idea. She's a success. Returns home when
brother is ill; family is convinced she failed. While
at home she falls in love, but returns to her work to
be free of its complications. He follows her and
eventually they marry. He is represented as enjoying
her triumphs. CR 23:203.

TRAIN, ELIZABETH PHIPPS. B. 1856. United States.

011998   THE AUTOBIOGRAPHY OF A PROFESSIONAL
BEAUTY. Philadelphia: J. B. Lippincott, 1896 NUC.

PW 3-14-96. American girl, educated in France, makes
debut in London, her lovers and adventures, marries an
American lawyer.
LW 27:154. Trans-Atlantic romance, hypnotism.

011999   A DESERTER FROM PHILISTIA. London: J.
Bowden, 1897 BMC.

Heroine is a rich successful and virtuous dancer. She
has educated her daughter in a convent. When Lisa
comes out, she condemns her mother for her profession
and destroys her mother's plans for marriage to
someone she loves because it would involve divorce.
She does all this, smugly feeling she has saved her
mother's soul. LBKM 14:133

012000　　　　DOCTOR LAMAR [ANONYMOUS]. New York: T. Y.
Crowell, [c1891] NUC.

Because of promise made to wife, doctor ends her life.
Author raises the pros and cons without committing
herself. PW
Gives poison to his wife dying of cancer. Rather than
keep it secret, mentions it to friends. LW

012001　　　　MADAM OF THE IVIES. Philadelphia &
London: J. B. Lippincott, 1898 NUC.

LW 29:199. Mad sensationalism. Jane Eyre plot in
modern New York setting, incidents are rearranged.
PW-Dorothy, the heroine, is narrator, answers an ad
for companion to elderly lady. There is a mystery in
her life and Dorothy brings about her reconciliation
with her son.

012002　　　　A MARITAL LIABILITY. Philadelphia: J. B.
Lippincott, 1897 BMC NUC. London: Ward, Lock, [1899]
BMC.

Two stories: character studies. 1-husband suffers for
his immoral wife and the pure-minded daughter.
2-Rochester and Jane Eyre motif. LIT 5:82
1-he takes wife's guilt upon himself. 2-Madame of the
Ivies. LBKM 16:110
Man goes to prison for ten years to protect his wife
from charge of forgery. LW 28:279
He serves 10 years, released, meets his daughter and
with her help and that of Charlotte Pendexter it is
proven that his wife did it. PW 51:651
A man serves a prison term for a crime committed by
his wife. She's vain, mercenary, a drug addict. Their
daughter who believes her father is innocent and a
beautiful woman who puts everything right. NYT 4-17-97

012003　　　　A QUEEN OF HEARTS. Philadelphia: J. B.
Lippincott, 1898 NUC.

BKM 6:474. Story of an actress, told by herself of her
childhood, marriage, career. Marriage unhappy.
LW 29:205. She is a ballet dancer.
At 37, mother of daughter about to be wed begins a
diary. Her father was an actor, opposed by her
mother's family. How she escaped the tyranny of a
strict family, became a dancer, brought up her
daughter in ignorance that she was a dancer, gave up
her own chance of happiness, for the daughter she
deserted. Apparently gave up her daughter and chance
of happiness because of her chequered past. PW 52:710.
Young girl (vagabond spirit) irks under the humdrum of
her life, deserts husband and children and becomes a
"danseuse" known as Mlle. Cleo. Daughter in convent
after husband's death doesn't know of her mother's
profession. BOOK NEWS 6-01

012004　　　　A SOCIAL HIGHWAYMAN. Philadelphia: J. B.
Lippincott, 1896 NUC. London: Ward, Lock, [1898] BMC.

ATH 112:489. Also contains A Professional Beauty.
Unbelievable incidents.
LBKM 15:25. 1- A modern Robin Hood, a dandified thief.
Narrated by his valet, to whom he was a hero. 2-
salvation of a woman through an honest love.
LW 27:77. Man who is likeable, a gentleman, is in
actuality a highway robber.
Well-educated, cultured young man lives in luxury in
New York, supports self by robbing jewels from
friends. PW 12-7-95:1085

TRAIN, ETHEL (KISSAM). 1875-1923. United States.

012005　　　　BRINGING OUT BARBARA. New York: C.
Scribner's, 1917 NUC.

Society girl decides to get out into the sane world PW
91:1111 4/7/17
She objects to the life and habits of her idle-rich
family. Home from boarding school, she "comes out", at
17. By 18 she has met an artist earnest like herself
who "rescues her." She has great talent for painting.
NYT 4-8-17, 131

012006　　　　"SON". New York: C. Scribner's Sons, 1911
NUC.

TRASK, KATE (NICHOLS). 1853-1922. United States.

012007　　　　FREE NOT BOUND. BY KATRINA TRASK. New
York and London: G. P. Putnam's Sons, 1903 BMC NUC.

Historical novel about woman married to N.E. minister.
She is excommunicated because of her convictions,
sticks to them, travels during war in search of

husband, captured by the Eng. etc., finally two are
reconciled but I think he changes his mind. ARENA 1904
"Free-thinking wife" separation come back together
with better understanding WOMAN'S JOURNAL 11-7-03
Very brief desc. BKM 18 (1903) 451
fearless man of stern theology married to a
free-thinker; story deals with the "mutually repellant
influence of these two unlike people;" a final accord
reached with integrity, both learn and bend after a
long separation. NYT 03, 794

012008　　　　IN MY LADY'S GARDEN; PAGES FROM THE DIARY
OF SIR JOHN ELWYNNE. BY KATRINA TRASK. London: J.
Lane, 1907 BMC NUC. New York: J. Lane, 1907 NUC.

012009　　　　IN THE VANGUARD. BY KATRINA TRASK. New
York: Macmillan, 1913 BMC NUC.

Anti-war Courage it takes for one man to realize what
he's doing is legalized murder and he refuses to
serve. BKM

012010　　　　THE INVISIBLE BALANCE SHEET. BY KATRINA
TRASK. New York: J. Lane, 1916 BMC NUC. London: J.
Lane, 1916 NUC.

Love is set off vs money: hero must remain unmarried
to get fortune. He chooses money and suffers for his
error. TLS
LBKM
Romantic stuff PW

012011　　　　JOHN LEIGHTON, JR.: A NOVEL. BY KATRINA
TRASK. New York and London: Harper, 1898 NUC.

LIT 2:452. Madelaine's unhappy marriage and her
solution.
NYT 1898 p 45. Story of a young man who cannot, unlike
his father, believe in a Calvinistic God. Falls in
love with the wife of a brute; they fall, she pulls
them out of their error. They find happiness in their
courage, etc. Anti-divorce. He is restored to
religion, once he sees God as loving and forgiving.
More a study of Madeleine, John's early love. She
married a man named Gray. Then she meets up with John
and they renew their love but are honorable. Then Gray
takes to drink and Madeleine stays on to help him,
John, a lawyer, goes off to save the world. ACAD 52
FIC SUP 121
Discussion of divorce. CR 28,31:278
"Men and women of the cultured circles of our complex
modern society." Hero revolts against Calvinism and
rise through agnostic ism into Christianity. Rev.
feels the episode of Stephanie Romaine shows "the
passion that degrades;" problem novel: "a higher
nature mated to a lower," and the "love that comes too
late." Author's solution is a unique one which the
reviewer withholds. NYT 10-30-97,5

012012　　　　THE MIGHTY AND THE LOWLY. BY KATRINA
TRASK. New York: Macmillan, 1915 NUC BMC.

012013　　　　WHITE SATIN AND HOMESPUN. BY KATRINA
TRASK. New York: A. D. F. Randolph, [c1896] NUC.

BKM 4:374. Righteous prig, Morton visits the poor and
preaches to working people. Asks daughter of a
millionaire to marry him. When she accepts, he adds
that she will have to give up all her money and live
in the tenements. She is willing to give up most of
it. He retracts his offer. After a few days she
capitulates and book ends happily.
Katharine van Santland is rich, aristocratic; Morton
Hunnewell is a reformer in the slums. He criticizes
her life. She loves him. Gives up her luxury for a
life of work in the slums. LW 28:145

TRASK, KATRINA. See TRASK, KATE (NICHOLS).

TRAVERS, GRAHAM, pseud. See TODD, MARGARET GEORGINA.

TRAVERS, HETTIE.

012014　　　　FROM AN INVALID'S WINDOW. London: R. T.
S., [1901] BMC.

012015　　　　THE GARNER. London: R. Scott, 1916 BMC.

012016　　　　THE SPICE GATHERERS. London: A. H.
Stockwell, [1917] BMC.

012017　　　　A STORMY PASSAGE. London: Digby, Long,
1913 BMC.

Alice Woodhouse's life; died at 22, set in 16th cent.
Chars black/white: sweet maidens and scheming

villains. ACAD TLS

TRAVERS, JOHN, pseud. See BELL, EVA MARY (HAMILTON).

TRAVERS, LIBBIE MILLER. United States.

    012018   THE HONOR OF A LEE. New York: Cochrane,
    1908 NUC.

    PW-Hist rom. civil war

TRAVIS, ELMA (ALLEN). 1861-1917. United States.

    012019   THE COBBLER. New York: Outing, 1908 NUC.

    "The chief character is the son of a village cobbler.
    He is rather a "literary genius," is unconventional
    and heedless. He marries the daughter of a wealthy
    neighbour without the knowledge of the girl's father.
    She, too, has her peculiarities, and it takes them a
    long time to discover they can live together happily."
    BKM v.27 1908
    NYT-She has an interest in astronomical investigation
    which takes her away from home much of the time. He
    needs companionship and finds it in two very different
    women. He is eventually reconciled to his wife.

    012020   THE PANG-YANGER. BY ELMA A. TRAVIS, M.D.
    New York: McClure, Phillips, 1905 NUC.

    A "soulless" woman deserts husband and child marries
    another-trusting to her husband's lack of proof of
    first marr. PW 11-11-05

TREGARTHEN, MONICA.

    012021   HER ANGEL FRIEND: A STORY IN TWO PARTS.
    London: Digby, Long, [1894] BMC.

    ATH 103:506. Doctor's hyper-sensitive wife dies
    because of one unkind word from him. Angel friend is a
    nurse who takes over doctor and his daughters.

TRELAWNEY, DAYRELL, pseud. See FOWLER, ADA DAYRELL.

TREMAYNE, SYDNEY, pseud. See COOKSON, SYBIL IRENE ELEANOR
(TAYLOR).

TREMLETT, MRS. HORACE. United Kingdom.

    012022   BIRDS OF A FEATHER. London: Hutchinson,
    [c1919] BMC NUC.

    Man from war office searching out German escaped POWs.
    TLS

    012023   CURING CHRISTOPHER. London: J. Lane, 1914
    BMC NUC. New York: J. Lane, 1914 NUC.

    ACAD 86:398. "One thing is certain, the author is no
    suffragist."
    PW 85 5/30/14 p. 1780 "Complaint of which Christopher
    finds it necessary to be cured is what, in a moment of
    the embarrassment, he describes as loss of memory, but
    is in reality an attack of infatuation for a musical
    comedy actress, followed by a very rough handling from
    one of the lady's most formidable admirers.
    Christopher's wife regards his condition as very
    grave, and he undergoes a good deal of discomfort in
    the course of his cure."

    012024   EMILY DOES HER BEST. London: J. Lane,
    1917 NUC BMC. New York: J. Lane, 1917 NUC BMC.

    Light amusing comedy TLS
    Pipsy, woman of uncertain char; has an entirely uncon,
    relation with a man-She meets this man's straight
    sister-Emily "spinster." Pipsy pretends to be the
    man's wife, But "in spite of her lack of morals" is
    candid, attractive-she openly admits to Emily that she
    and Emily's brother are not married, returns to
    Johannesburg as a newly appointed secret service
    Agent. LBKM
    Emily is 30 single because she never took to
    husband-hunting, she says. Brother lives with a woman,
    tries to hide this from Emily who is much more
    broadminded than he thinks. Emily finds romance at the
    end. NyT

    012025   GIDDY MRS. GOODYER. London: J. Lane, 1916
    BMC NUC. New York: J. Lane, 1916 BMC NUC.

    Maudie, bored with her husband goes to South Africa
    where one can get a divorce simply for the asking. And
    there's Kathleen Wormsley who believes in the "Power
    of Love" and found in a text the road to a chronic

condition of bliss. Humorous NYT 138-4-15-17
Mrs Goodyer attempts to outwit legal authorities in
Pretoria and get a divorce. Finally becomes
reconciled. PW 91:1228 4/14/17

    012026   LOOKING FOR GRACE. London: J. Lane, 1915
    BMC NUC. New York: J. Lane, 1915 BMC NUC.

    Mystery involving a widow NYT A war comedy LBKM

    012027   PLATONIC PETER. London: Hutchinson,
    [1919] BMC NUC.

    SR-Silly

TRENT, ELIZABETH.

    012028   KATHRYN. London: Heath, Cranton, [1916]
    BMC.

    ATH-Hypersensitive excitable heroine wins fiance's
    respect by rescuing child, altho afraid of spiders. S.
    Australia.

TREVELYAN, MARIE.

    012029   BRITAIN'S GREATNESS FORETOLD. THE STORY
    OF BOADICEA, THE BRITISH WARRIOR-QUEEN. London: J.
    Hogg, 1900 BMC NUC.

    LIT 7:528. Historical novel, Boadicea. Patriotic,
    Imperialistic.

TRIMBLE, JESSIE. B. 1873. United States.

    012030   THE NEW MAN. BY JANE STONE. New York: T.
    Y. Crowell, [1913] NUC.

    PW 84 10/11/13:1247 "Novelette concerning the love
    affairs of John Ridgeway, a wealthy New Yorker, and
    Mollie Preston, while a secondary plot deals with the
    much discussed white slave problem and has to do with
    Frances Stevens, daughter of a western senator, who is
    kidnapped while walking in Central Park. Ridgeway is
    dismayed at finding an obstacle to the smooth course
    of his love for Mollie in what he regards as her
    strong-minded views concerning the white slave
    traffic. Frances Stevens comes into the story just in
    time to save the day for Mollie and to bring the book
    to a satisfactory conclusion." Subplot concerns white
    slavery. Frances Stephens, daughter of a Western
    senator, is kidnapped in Central Park. It affects the
    main love plot in that Mollie Preston holds some very
    strong views on the subject of white slavery and her
    romance with John Ridgeway is jeopardized because he
    does not understand her attitude.

TROLLOPE, FRANCES ELEANOR (TERNAN). 1834-1913. United
Kingdom.

    012031   THAT WILD WHEEL: A NOVEL. London: R.
    Bentley, 1892 BMC. New York: Harper, 1892 NUC.

    CR 18:164. Story of the Hughes family "possessed of
    the idea that the women as well as the men in the
    family were to bear their share of the burdens." They
    worked, one kept a boarding school, another had a
    position in London. Then all of the family's
    enterprises failed and then a struggle for existence.
    LW 23:294 Barbara begins early in life to earn her
    living.
    ATH 99:788. Male painter and his niece Barbara, his
    chief admirer, "nice and natural."

TROOP, EDNA WILLA (SULLIVAN). United States.

    012032   BLACKBIRD, A STORY OF MACKINAC ISLAND. BY
    SCOTA SORIN. Detroit, Mich.: Citator, [c1907] NUC.

    012033   THE PENDULUM; A STORY. BY SCOTA SORIN.
    New York: Duffield, 1910 NUC.

TROUBETZKOY, AMELIE (RIVES) CHANLER. 1863-1945. United
States.

    012034   ACCORDING TO ST. JOHN. BY AMELIE RIVES.
    London: W. Heinemann, 1891 BMC. New York: J. W.
    Lovell, [c1891] NUC BMC.

    Artist life in Paris; Jean Carter from Virginia falls
    in love with an artist who is married. She admits to
    the wife she loves Andrean and Mrs. Farrance is very
    kind. Mrs. Farrance dies, Jean marries Andrean. Jean
    is a persecuted person, self torturing. After marriage
    imagines her husband still loves first wife. Reads a
    passage he wrote in his diary about the wife and takes

morphia to end her life. SR 11-21-91, 589
Jean Carter came to Paris to study violin and become a
famous violinist. Good psychological study of her.
Wife dreads death because she's been so unhappy; When
Andrean marries Jean, he immediately regrets the
marriage. She learns this, takes fatal dose of
morphine to free him. SP 67, 765 Title from scripture:
lay down one's life for one's friend.

012035   BARBARA DERING. A SEQUEL TO THE QUICK OR
THE DEAD? BY AMELIE RIVES. London: Chatto and Windus,
1892 BMC. Philadelphia: J. B. Lippincott, 1893 NUC.

"the American George Sand, as foolish admirers love to
designate her"-ACAD 42:604.
ATH 100:737. Sequel to "The Quick and the Dead."
Barbara is 29, less hoydenish. After much
selfsearching decides to marry. Story of hers and
another couple's marriage. Men "come off rather
badly." "Barbara is a sort of pioneer in an obscure
region." "Certain scenes and reflections...express
what many persons (women, perhaps, particularly) may
have felt in a dumb and groping fashion."
LW 23:403. Her friend is married to a man who is
unfeeling, Barbara's husband has an excess of feeling.
They discuss the problems of their marriages,
Barbara's husband is physically abusive at times (she
is too).
SP 69:777. rev. says Barbara has been criticized by
critics, some claiming that it is a portrait of the
author, which Rives has denied. rev. does not
understand with which sex her sympathies lie.
Criticizes her for developing in her work a strain of
morbidness.
Two years after she sends Jock Dering away, they are
reunited and married. They're unhappy because he's
unreasonable, exacting- "male to the core." "There is
a certain feminine quality without which the character
of no man is likeable"- says the author. He's fierce
about everything. Much friction between them. He
leaves her with her child, uncertain of his return.
"Outspoken" "few women could have written it" CR.
14,20:140

012036   A DAMSEL ERRANT. BY AMELIE RIVES
(PRINCESS TROUBETZKOY). London: Authors' Syndicate,
1897 BMC. Philadelphia: J. B. Lippincott, 1898 NUC.

Yovanne Savare rescues her lover from hanging after he
kills her father in battle--but the killing had most
to do with the father's carelessness. PW 52:741.

012037   THE ELUSIVE LADY. BY AMELIE RIVES
(PRINCESS TROUBETZKOY). London: Hurst & Blackett, 1918
BMC NUC.

TLS ghost story

012038   THE GHOST GARDEN; A NOVEL. BY AMELIE
RIVES (PRINCESS TROUBETZKOY). New York: F. A. Stokes,
[c1918] NUC.

PW-love story and a ghost.
NYT Sept 1, 1918 Two people staying at house
previously occupied by dead woman. He protects her
from ghost, but struggles with ghost tensely.

012039   THE GOLDEN ROSE: THE ROMANCE OF A STRANGE
SOUL. BY AMELIE RIVES (PRINCESS TROUBETZKOY). New York
and London: Harper, 1908 BMC NUC.

PW-Problem of Platonic relationship
BKM + 27 1908 confusing
TLS-love of an heiress and its disillusionment.
ACAD-sophisticated mind.
BKM-formerly married woman has platonic love; does not
want it soiled by mrg. He leaves her for a few months;
when he returns he no longer loves her. Motto of the
book "What the wind is to a bonfire and a match,
Absence is to love; it kindles a great passion and
extinguishes a small one."
NYT Meraud Cabell "study of psych and pathology of the
moods of the rather mature heroine."

012040   HIDDEN HOUSE. BY AMELIE RIVES (THE
PRINCESS TROUBETZKOY). Philadelphia and London: J. B.
Lippincott, 1912 BMC NUC.

PW-dual personality: two sisters? 1 woman?
ATH-Two souls are fighting for her body, her poetry
rivals. R. Burns.
BKM-0
NYT-Moina and Robina struggle over one body; hero
loves them both, Robina is a poet. Takes place in Blue
Ridge Mountains of Va. There is a Scotch grandfather
of heroine.

012041   MERIEL. A LOVE STORY. London: Chatto and
Windus, 1898 BMC.

ACAD 53:575. Love story.

012042   PAN'S MOUNTAIN. BY AMELIE RIVES (PRINCESS
TROUBETZKOY). New York and London: Harper, 1910 BMC
NUC.

BM Italian Romance
TLS Italian Romance
NYT She worships pagan gods, book is a tropical flower
of almost poisonous odour, shows outraged motherhood
can slay in a momentary passion of sex and rob the
brain of sanity.

012043   SHADOWS OF FLAMES; A NOVEL. BY AMELIE
RIVES (PRINCESS TROUBETZKOY). London: Hurst &
Blackett, 1915 BMC. New York: F. A. Stokes, [1915]
NUC.

BKM 42 1915-16
Married to an addict, then marries a man younger than
herself, the passion burns out. She gets a divorce. PW
9-4-15
Sympathetic story of a "happiness hunter" self
centered of rich passionate nature suffers thru her
mistakes terribly; married to morphine addict other
men in her life. NYT
Marries a drug addict, then an alcoholic, then an
Italian prince who promises to make a good husband.
ATH.

012044   TANIS, THE SANG-DIGGER. New York: Town
Topics, 1893 NUC.

At the end returns to the mountains. "Her lawless
lover makes this the price of her mistress' safety and
restoration to her husband." She must renounce the new
hopes of a new world-this "noble savage." ATH 102:767.
ACAD 45:10. Tanis a primeval pagan who knows and feels
physical passion but also knows this is only part of
ideal love, shows ideal picture of man and woman
through window to her physically beautiful but earthy
lover. He can't see it.
She is a "wild woodland beauty" who loves a man who
has already betrayed three women. She longs to be
civilized and tries to inspire Sam Rose in the same
direction, but fails. By a trick he wins her but only
after her love for him is dead. LW'93, 351.
She lives like a savage. Mostly in dialect. PW
10-14-93. Alleghany mountains. She digs sang-a
medicinal root. "Her primitive conceptions of human
relations, her fierce, but virginal, passion
"contrasted with high-born Southern Lady with whom she
goes to live. She gropes for something "higher". Makes
rapid progress, becomes sophisticated.

012045   TRIX AND OVER-THE-MOON. BY AMELIE RIVES
(PRINCESS TROUBETZKOY). New York and London: Harper,
1909 BMC NUC.

Woman of Va.; husband writes bad novels; she loves
horses "better than anything else in life" runs her
own farm and breeds horses NYT
Over the-Moon is her stallion.

012046   WORLD'S-END. BY AMELIE RIVES (PRINCESS
TROUBETZKOY). London: Hurst & Blackett, 1914 BMC. New
York: F. A. Stokes, [1914] NUC.

LBKM-Realistic novel written in a sentimental manner.
Phoebe is wooed by Richard, a dark soul, who then
deserts her and leads her to the point of suicide.
Then her cousin Owen rescues her, marries her, knowing
1st born will not be his child, but out of tact, he
does not let her know he knows this.
ATH 144:178. Story of their marriage.
PW 85 4/18/14 p. 1300 "Scene is laid on a Virginia
plantation. World's End. Phoebe Nelson is fascinated
by her cousin Richard, who all but ruins her prospects
of happiness. His uncle, Owen Randolph, sets to work
to rebuild her life, marries her and devotes himself
to making her happy, always hoping she will herself
tell him what he already knows of her relations with
Robert. Phoebe lives through some tragic months before
she finds peace and joy."
TLS 13:334 She is pregnant by Richard, which Owen
knows all along, waits for her to tell him.

TROUBETZKOY, PRINCESS. See TROUBETZKOY, AMELIE (RIVES)
CHANLER.

TROUBRIDGE, LAURA (GURNEY). United Kingdom.

012047   ALL'S WELL, BILLY. London: Methuen, 1918
BMC.

TLS Conv. rom.

012048   BODY AND SOUL. London: Mills and Boon,
1911 BMC.

Divine woman refines fascinating hero. TLS
Rosalyn 17 marries a Peer, he's atrocious but she
forgives all. LBKM SR

012049   THE CHEAT. London: Mills & Boon, 1909
BMC.

Valeria cheats at cards; a Duke proposes on condition
that she won't play anymore. TLS

012050   THE CREATURE OF CIRCUMSTANCE. BY LADY
TROWBRIDGE. London: Mills & Boon, 1911 BMC.

Sensational story of 2 women rivals for a man's love.
LBKM

012051   THE EVIL DAY. London: Methuen, 1915 BMC.

"That day women in mid age feel life is over and pant
for a lost passion." Heroine 40 married, revolts from
placid home and from too familiar husband for young
man. Husband treats her fairly when he returns to his
errant wife. TLS

012052   THE FIRST LAW. London: Mills and Boon,
1909 BMC.

A divorced disreputable wife and her violent death.
TLS

012053   THE GIRL WITH THE BLUE EYES. London:
Mills & Boon, 1912 BMC.

012054   THE HALF OF HIS KINGDOM: A ROMANCE.
London: Cassell, 1916 BMC.

TLS-aristocrat and heir.

012055   THE HOUSE OF CARDS. London: Hutchinson,
1908 BMC.

TLS-bad marriage.
BKM-young woman married to klepto, would-be lover
insists on her giving him chance after chance to
improve. Dies. All is well.

012056   A MARRIAGE OF BLACKMAIL. London:
Hutchinson, 1908 BMC.

TLS-conventional love story.

012057   THE MILLIONAIRE. London: T.F. Unwin, 1907
BMC.

2 married people fall in love (not with husband and
wife). The wife dies and the husband commits suicide
and all ends happily? ACAD
Man finds work for husband of Mrs. Sydney in Mexico
because he loves her. TLS

012058   MRS. VERNON'S DAUGHTER. London: Methuen,
1917 BMC.

Damaris is disillusioned to discover what her ideal
mother is really like. Has consolation in the love of
a man. TLS

012059   O, PERFECT LOVE. London: Methuen, 1920
BMC.

TLS-invalid war husband - she won't stay - in a year
she's learned her lesson and is back.

012060   PAUL'S STEPMOTHER AND ONE OTHER STORY.
London: G. Richards, 1897 BMC.

(1) Paul Wallender, old fashioned, middle-aged, likes
old-fashioned woman. Has pure mother for his ideal;
yet falls passionately in love with young step-mother.
Ends with her suicide when she hears of his death-tho
in fact he lives 20 years to mourn her. (2) "Poor
Roderick" Roderick is a cad. SR 83: 519

012061   STORMLIGHT. London: Mills & Boon, 1912
BMC.

012062   THIS MAN AND THIS WOMAN. BY LADY
TROUBRIDGE. London: E. Nash, 1914 BMC NUC.

ATH-unfortunate married life of young and
irresponsible couple. Happy ending.
TLS-pregnancy puts an end to thoughts of separation.

012063   THE UNGUARDED HOUR. BY LADY TROUBRIDGE.
London: E. Nash, 1913 BMC NUC.

Beautiful and high-born flirt loses her virtue but
marries happily in the end. TLS

012064   THE WOMAN THOU GAVEST. London: T.F.
Unwin, 1906 BMC.

TLS-villaninous guardian and her female ward.
LBKM-love story.

012065   THE WOMAN WHO FORGOT. A MODERN LOVE
STORY. London: Mills & Boon, 1910 BMC.

TLS-in midst of intimacy with man on train, there is
collision, she gets amnesia, marries him, husband
turns up, tragedy.

TROUT, GRACE WILBUR. United States.

012066   A MORMON WIFE. Chicago: E. A. Weeks,
[1896] NUC.

Before Polygamy was abandonned in Utah, woman learns
her husband in spite of promise to her-is about to
take a second wife. Ends in tragedy for her and her
children. PW 8-10-95:203

TROWBRIDGE, LADY. See TROUBRIDGE, LAURA (GURNEY).

TRUDGIAN, MRS. T. D.

012067   WITH DRUMS UNMUFFLED. BY L. A. BURGESS.
London: Mills and Boon, 1913 BMC.

A nursemaid in Gibralter. LBKM

TRUEMAN, ANITA. See PICKETT, ANITA (TRUEMAN).

TRUMAN, OLIVIA M.

012068   THE SPIRIT JUGGLER. London: F. V. White,
1907 BMC.

TRUMBULL, ANNIE ELIOT. 1857-1949. United States.

012069   A CAPE COD WEEK. New York: A. S. Barnes,
1898 NUC.

LW 29:253. Five young women spend a week in Cape Cod.
"The smell of a mysterious cigar on one of their last
evenings is the nearest approach made toward a hero."

012070   LIFE'S COMMON WAY. New York: A.S. Barnes,
1903 NUC.

A modern woman, the currents beneath a conventional
surface of N.E. life. PW 5-2-03
One woman married unhappily, another has a marriage
that makes her recklessly indifferent to public
opinion. 3 good characters: women. No marriage is
happy. NYT

012071   MISTRESS CONTENT CRADDOCK. New York: A.
S. Barnes, 1899 NUC. London: H. R. Allenson, [1899]
BMC.

Early settlers in Massachusetts-their fierce
puritanism. LIT 4:666
Two men wooing her. CR 35:748
Historical, N. England-Salem. Roger Williams a central
character. A romance too. NYT 6-24-99:408
NYT 1900:408. Massachusetts Bay Colony in Roger
Williams' time.
ATH 115:588. Careful study. Religious.

012072   WHITE BIRCHES: A NOVEL. BY ANNIE ELIOT.
New York: Harper, 1893 NUC.

American young woman and man meet on the occasion of
his sprained ankle, love. PW 3-18-93.
She was attending cows nearby. She got help. CR 14,
20:307.

TRUSCOTT, L. PARRY. See HARGRAVE, KATHARINE EDITH
SPICER-JAY.

TUCKER, BERYL.

012073   THE MAN WHO LIVED. London: W. Heinemann,

1908 BMC NUC.

LBKM

012074   THE RING: A ROMANCE. London: W.
Heinemann, 1908 BMC.

012075   THE WORLD AND MR. FREYNE. A FANTASTIC
ROMANCE. London: A. Melrose, 1913 BMC.

John Freyne came to life in a laboratory. Has neither
soul nor moral sense nor affection. Story records all
his deficiencies, brings tragedy into a woman's life.
Finally earns a soul and with it a dual personality.
SR

TUCKER, CHARLOTTE MARIA. 1821-1893.

012076   BATTLING WITH THE WORLD. BY A. L. O. E.
London: T. Nelson, [1904] BMC.

012077   THE BLACKSMITH OF BONIFACE LANE. BY A. L.
O. E. London and New York: T. Nelson, 1891 BMC NUC.

Hist rom, reign of Hen. IV, Eng. Hero is victim of
persecution of the time. SP 66,23

012078   THE FORLORN HOPE. BY A. L. O. E. New
York: T. Nelson, 1893 PW. London: T. Nelson, 1893 BMC.

Mid 19th abolition story with Wm. Garrison as hero and
"leader of the forlorn hope." Heroine associates with
him. Set in Va. PW 10-7-93

012079   THE IRON CHAIN AND THE GOLDEN. BY A. L.
O. E. New York and London: T. Nelson, 1892 NUC BMC.

PW Two Saxon priests, each representing differing
factions of Catholicism. Superstition is the iron
chain which imposes celibacy on priests, love the
golden.
SP-Hist rom. time of Norman kings

TUCKER, ELIZABETH S.

012080   THE MAGIC KEY. Boston: Little, Brown,
1901 BMC NUC.

TUPPER, EDITH SESSIONS. United States.

012081   HEARTS TRIUMPHANT. New York: D. Appleton,
1906 BMC NUC.

PW-Adventuress, hist.
NYT-conv. ch. types, rom.

012082   THE STUFF OF DREAMS. New York: B. W.
Dodge, 1908 NUC.

Focuses on a playboy and his lovely angels or
beautiful devils. NYT
PW-Love story

TURCZYNOWICZ, LAURA (BLACKWELL) DE GOZDAWA.

012083   WHEN THE PRUSSIANS CAME TO POLAND: THE
EXPERIENCES OF AN AMERICAN WOMAN DURING THE GERMAN
INVASION. New York and London: G. P. Putnam's Sons,
1916 NUC.

PW Amer. woman (married to Polish noble) kept prisoner
by Germans in her home for 7 mos. Her struggles, work
for Red Cross, fight for her children's lives-they
have typhus.

TURK, JEANNIE, jt. au. See TURK, SHEILA AGNES AND JEANNIE
TURK.

TURK, SHEILA AGNES AND JEANNIE TURK.

012084   THE MARRIAGE BOND ONLY DEATH CAN SUNDER.
London: H. J. Drane, [1912] BMC.

TURNBULL, CLARA. United Kingdom.

012085   THE DAMSEL DARK: A FOOL'S ROMANCE.
London: Melrose, 1912 BMC.

TLS- historical. Rosamund-Eleanor-Becket-Henry
ATH O
ACAD. Heroine in absence of her brother raises the
fortunes of her house and strikes terror into evil
doers. Unhorses her fighting uncle in a tourney before
the king.

012086   THE LOVE SPINNER. London: Methuen, [1919]

BMC NUC.

Jessie Hope Templeton "a maiden lady" owns a block of
houses. A self effacing sort, helps lovers unite, that
sort of thing. TLS

012087   LOVE WILL FIND OUT THE WAY. London:
Methuen, 1920 BMC.

TLS-historical romance.

TURNBULL, DORA AMY DILLON. D. 1961. United Kingdom.

012088   THE DEVIL'S WIND. BY PATRICIA WENTWORTH
(MRS. G. F. DILLON). New York and London: G.P.
Putnam's Sons, 1912 NUC. London: A. Melrose, 1912 BMC
NUC.

PW India, Triangle
TLS modern love story.
ATH modern love story. BKM

012089   THE FIRE WITHIN. BY PATRICIA WENTWORTH
(MRS. G. F. DILLON). New York & London: G.P. Putnam's
Sons, 1913 NUC. London: A. Melrose, 1913 BMC NUC.

Plenty of interest in babies; one woman has 23! ACAD
"David Blake, a doctor, makes out a death certificate
stating that old Mr. Mottisfont died of natural causes
when he knows that death was due to poisoning. He does
this for the sake of Mary Mottisfont, whom he loves,
and who asks him to do it to save her husband, towards
whom suspicion would point. After thus jeopardizing
his honor, David goes through a strange mental
experience, involving psychic phenomena, and through
the love of a fine woman, at last wins back his peace
of mind." PW 10/4/13 1142
Concerns a murder a false accusation as well as
relations between two sisters. TLS

012090   A LITTLE MORE THAN KIN. BY PATRICIA
WENTWORTH. London: A. Melrose, 1911 BMC NUC.

Historical: French Revolution, but a woman in disguise
as twin brother shows she's brave. PW 4-29-11.
Am. ed. title: More than Kin.
Revolution days in France & England. SP
Disguise of a wilful woman in boy's clothes. ATH

012091   A MARRIAGE UNDER THE TERROR. BY PATRICIA
WENTWORTH. London: A. Melrose, 1910 BMC. New York and
London: G.P. Putnam's Sons, 1910 NUC.

PW-French Revolution.
TLS-forced marriage between revolutionary leader and
aristocratic girl-love develops. NYT

012092   MORE THAN KIN. BY PATRICIA WENTWORTH. New
York and London: G.P. Putnam's Sons, 1911 NUC.

Published in England under title: A Little More than
Kin.

012093   QUEEN ANNE IS DEAD. BY PATRICIA
WENTWORTH. London: A. Melrose, 1915 BMC NUC.

Heroine overdone goodness. Hero villains, TLS

012094   SIMON HERIOT. BY PATRICIA WENTWORTH.
London: A. Melrose, [1914] BMC.

ATH-love story of young man working in London.

TURNBULL, FRANCESE HUBBARD (LITCHFIELD). D. 1927. United
States.

012095   THE GOLDEN BOOK OF VENICE: A HISTORICAL
ROMANCE OF THE 16TH CENTURY. BY MRS. LAWRENCE
TURNBULL. New York: Century, 1900 NUC BMC.

PW-in the quarrel between Paul the Pope and Paul the
Friar, wife sides with Pope and husband and his family
with friar.

012096   THE ROYAL PAWN OF VENICE. A ROMANCE OF
CYPRUS. BY MRS. LAWRENCE TURNBULL. Philadelphia and
London: J. B. Lippincott, 1911 BMC NUC.

Hist romance PW 6-3-11

012097   VAL-MARIA: A ROMANCE OF THE TIME OF
NAPOLEON I. BY MRS. LAWRENCE TURNBULL. Philadelphia:
J. B. Lippincott, 1893 NUC.

Felix, a young sculptor, adores Napoleon. His great
work turns out to be a statue of Napoleon that so

effects the emperor when he sees it that his whole
life passes before him. LW 93:162.

TURNBULL, MARGARET. D. 1942. United States.

012098   THE CLOSE-UP. New York and London:
Harper, [1918] BMC NUC.

PW- love in a motion picture studio. Kate goes west to
be a mummer, comes to love studio life and career.
NYT Dec 29˜18 p 582. No character delineation.
Probably Kate will marry Jeffrey, a secret service
agent. She has become a star.

012099   HANDLE WITH CARE; A NOVEL. New York and
London: Harper, [1916] BMC NUC.

"Young woman took hold of a man˜s life and made
something out of it...in the face of small town talk,
this took courage." PW 89 1/15/16 p.161
NYT-she is an assistant in the psychological division
of a research laboratory-an adjunct to a huge
institution for human wrecks, nervous and otherwise.
She is breaking down from overwork herself when she
ends up in Covered Bridge and meets the drunken
express agent who is the hero. Title describes him.
She decides to rest and recuperate. Touches on
alcoholism and deplorable prison conditions. Author of
Looking After Sandy.
TLS-she has been ordered to take 6 months rest after
death of her mother. Develops an antagonism for agent
which can only lead to the opposite.

012100   LOOKING AFTER SANDY; A SIMPLE ROMANCE.
New York & London: Harper, 1914 BMC NUC.

PW 86 9/26/14:969 "Sandy, aged eleven, to avoid the
poorhouse, runs away and finds a home in the family of
the Fire Chief of a Jersey town. Here she grows up
happily sharing good times and hard times with the six
other children. Sandy has many lovers, and two of them
leave town when rejected. Sandy goes away herself and
later writes a successful book, the dramatization of
which unites her with one of her old sweethearts."
TLS-of the bright domestic kind. Rises from shorthand
clerk to successful dramatist.
NYT 1914:462

TURNBULL, MRS. LAWRENCE. See TURNBULL, FRANCESE HUBBARD
(LITCHFIELD).

TURNER, LILIAN. See THOMPSON, LILIAN TURNER.

TURNER, MARGARET STORRS.

012101   MULBERRY SPRINGS. London: T. F. Unwin,
1917 BMC.

TLS Marie Louise Stefanie Hyrst is installed at a spa
belonging to her father˜s friend as Mrs Hillyer, a
sort of official entertainer. Guests decide she is
Princess Prisha V. in disguise.
LBKM Obsessed with marrying an Englishman.

TURNER, MARY BORDEN. 1886-1968. United Kingdom.

012102   COLLISION. BY BRIDGET MACLAGAN. London:
Duckworth, 1913 BMC NUC.

Anglo-Indian novel: Maggie ultra modern young woman
attractive in spite of the extreme folly of her ways,
especially in her conduct to her friend˜s husband(?)
SP
Adventures in India of a Suffragist leader and an ex
labour M.P. in sympathy with the cause. ATH

012103   THE MISTRESS OF KINGDOMS; OR SMOKING
FLAX; A NOVEL. BY BRIDGET MACLAGAN. London: Duckworth,
1912 BMC NUC.

ATH-Woman in India whose child˜s death leads her to
ultimate happiness.
TLS-After passages with a married lover goes to India
marries simple minded but devoted chaplain rebels but
is happy after child˜s death.
Rape in the South. Black authoress? Cooper. See
problem novel. BKM, 1904
The focus is on Barbara˜s development, beginning with
the death of her father during her first year in
college. Her first love is for an artist who is
married; later she loves and marries a man she meets
in India, but she doesn˜t feel the same passion she
had for the artist. She is restless and leaves India
for awile, but she grows to understand her husband and
herself more fully. They share the experience of the
birth of their child, but they are separated when the

child gets sick and Barbara fights a losing battle for
its life. A strong counter-theme is the penetrating
analysis of Barbara˜s relationship to her mother.
(Book)

012104   THE ROMANTIC WOMAN. BY BRIDGET MACLAGEN
(MARY BORDEN-TURNER). London: Constable, 1916 NUC BMC.
New York: A. A. Knopf, 1920 NUC. (English ed. title:
The Romantic Women.)

TLS--Joan Fairfax, American ends up marrying a Duke.
Not a romance.
ATH--War reunites their marriage.
PW--Disillusionment and gradual readjustment of
Chicago heiress who marries into British Military
aristocracy. Marital infideli ties.
BKM--She lives in a gutter of her own making,
spiritual and mental squalor of languid, corrupt
"best" people.
NYT--"Unblushing frankness." An atmosphere of "dull
discontent, poignant disillusionment" "depressing
picture of the utter cyni cism of English high
society" and "the rawness and childishness of the
ultra rich set of Chicago."

TURPIN, EDNA HENRY LEE. 1869-1952. United States.

012105   ABRAM˜S FREEDOM. Boston: Pilgrim Press,
[c1913] NUC.

PW 11/8/13 1833 "Southern story about a slave who
longed to be free and arranged with his bewildered but
kindly master to purchase his own liberty. But before
the necessary sum was earned there came the war, the
emancipation proclamation-and new problems. How these
affected the old negro and Emmeline, his sharp tongue
wife, is entertainingly set forth."

012106   HAPPY ACRES. New York: Macmillan, 1913
BMC NUC.

012107   HONEY-SWEET. New York: Macmillan, 1911
BMC NUC.

012108   TREASURE MOUNTAIN. New York: Century,
1920 BMC NUC.

PZ7

TUTTIETT, MARY GLEED. 1847-1923. United Kingdom.

012109   THE BLACK OPAL. BY MAXWELL GRAY. New
York: D. Appleton, 1918 NUC.

NYT Dec. 8 ˜18, p.546 Mystery without much
mysteriousness. Focus on the heroine˜s character.

012110   A COSTLY FREAK. BY MAXWELL GRAY. London:
K. Paul, 1894 BMC. New York: D. Appleton, 1894 NUC.

SR: 78:101. Elderly clergyman accused of stealing,
tried, and acquited.
SP-thoroughly healthy.

012111   THE DESIRE OF THE MOTH. BY MAXWELL GRAY.
New York: D. Appleton, 1913 NUC BMC.

Long-parted lovers meet after many years. Hero, a bank
clerk, wife Blanche, daughter Beatrice, go to
Switzerland. Blanche not "one of those horrid women
who was always wanting...to have votes...and to go to
prison instead of elevating their husband˜s minds by
staying at home...and having nothing to do. Woman˜s
sphere is the home." NYT

012112   THE DIAMOND PENDANT. BY MAXWELL GRAY.
London: Hutchinson, 1918 BMC NUC.

TLS-mystery

012113   FOUR-LEAVED CLOVER; AN EVERYDAY ROMANCE.
BY MAXWELL GRAY. London: W. Heinemann, 1901 BMC. New
York: D. Appleton, 1901 NUC.

PW 8-3-01
ATH 8-31-01
Heroine a doormat type. NYT

012114   THE GREAT REFUSAL. BY MAXWELL GRAY. New
York: D. Appleton, 1906 NUC. London: J. Long, 1906
BMC.

PW- male socialistic hero.
NYT-group of young men go to Africa to establish
Colony of Brotherhood. Not enough information on
women.

ATH-there is a woman who comes out first in Greats, distancing even those dominant males, works for a social settlement connected with a male university settlement in which the hero and his friends are concerned.
ACAD--male hero founds brotherhood in Africa.
TLS

012115   THE HOUSE OF HIDDEN TREASURE: A NOVEL. BY MAXWELL GRAY. London: Heinemann, 1898 BMC. New York: D. Appleton, 1898 NUC.

SP 81:154. Central figure is Grace, daughter of woman who made runaway marriage and was estranged from her father Sir Geoffery. Grace is victim of schemes of her cousin Brinson who wants inheritance. Relationship to her mother. Grace is a fast young lady of the 1850's. She dies.
LIT 3:230. She is a high-spirited reckless girl who devotes herself to a single life of self repression and self sacrifice.
SR 86:353. Grace is "human and lovable, all wildness and passion, with no drop of vicious blood." "Vivid colours of her youth and its doings." She marries grim grey Mark Hilton. Sent. and sensational. "Sketch of a particularly fascinating woman."
LBKM 15:23. Her motto; "De l'audace, de l'audace it tonjour de l'audace." Closing is "deeply pathetic." No other ending would have been satisfactory. Grace could not have taken a new role after creating for herself that of Hidden Treasure in the Old House.
PW-she becomes "the help and blessing of the whole countryside," after being steadied by her mother's troubles.

012116   IN THE HEART OF THE STORM; A TALE OF MODERN CHIVALRY. BY MAXWELL GRAY. London: K. Paul, 1891 BMC. New York: U. S. Book, [1891] NUC.

Concerns the Indian mutiny, though the author "continually finds the opportunity for talk on women's rights." BAKER 03, 16.
The intermingled fates of four people. An orphan, an old miller's daughter, Claude and Ada. Ada is frivolous at first-then shows strength of character. The young do not love "as their elders plan they shall" PW 3-16-91.
The harm a man can do an innocent woman that causes gossip about her. Author attacks the double standard. NATION 265, 10-1-91
So. English country people. ATH 97, 696
Tragedy of Jessie, a village girl innocent but self-condemned and terrified by gossip. Sympathetic view. Also brilliant adventures of Ada escaping from Sepoy Rebellion (Indian mutiny) in India. LW
Jessie Meade makes a secret marriage. 5-23-91, 626 SR

012117   THE LAST SENTENCE. BY MAXWELL GRAY. London: Heinemann, 1893 BMC. New York: Tait, [c1893] NUC.

A barrister's wife supposedly dies in a fire; but she lives and sees him courting another woman. The shock kills her. He condemns his own daughter (as judge) for child murder; but her innocence is proven to save her from death. BAKER 03 116
Punishment of Cecil Marlowe's weakness. Nursed by young peasant woman, marries her though she's of lower class, marriage goes poorly, leaves her and child, finds the woman he should have wed. Then wife dies. He marries. Years later as judge is called to pass sentence of death on his daughter by Renee the young peasant wife. She's convicted of murdering her child. (He's morally responsible for Renee's death.) SP 71, 147, CR 20,23:183. Also LW 93, 251.
Wife present in courtroom; he knows it's his daughter; collapses after sentence. Her name is Renee Keronac. From her father's lips Renee's and his child gets the death sentence. PW 5-13-93
Ends at gallows. SR 75:544

012118   LAYS OF THE DRAGON SLAYER. BY MAXWELL GRAY. London: Bliss, Sands, 1894 BMC.

012119   RIBSTONE PIPPINS; A COUNTRY TALE. BY MAXWELL GRAY. London and New York: Harper, 1898 BMC NUC.

SP 80:452. Rural idyll. Love story of a waggoner. Pleasant view of agricultural workers.
ATH 111:400. Pretty.
ACAD 53:201. Rustic idyll of West England. Hero is a carter. Dialect.

012120   RICHARD ROSNY. BY MAXWELL GRAY. New York: D. Appleton, 1903 NUC. London: W. Heinemann, [1903]

BMC.

Focuses on Richard unhappy man ACAD 64,278
LBKM 5-03,74
ATH 121,651 an unhappy 2nd marriage, exact details of the friction between mother and son and husband and wife.
TLS-03,96

012121   SOMETHING AFAR. BY MAXWELL GRAY. London: E. Arnold, 1913 BMC NUC.

Hero now old had loved a great Italian lady. They meet after many years; each has had marriage and children.
ATH

012122   THE SUSPICIONS OF ERMENGARDE. BY MAXWELL GRAY. London: J. Long, 1908 BMC. (Am. ed. title: The Suspicions of Mrs. Allonby.)

ACAD- silly love story.
SR
BKM
PW-young wife travels to Monte Carlo, has adventures, is rescued by husband who follows her in disguise.
TLS-silly, trite.

012123   SWEETHEARTS AND FRIENDS, A NOVEL. BY MAXWELL GRAY. London: Marshall, Russell, 1897 BMC. New York: D. Appleton, 1897 NUC.

A young woman becomes a doctor in the 1870s while friends and sweethearts look on with horror. ATH 110:630.
Amy Langston. Her brother refuses to see her while she is studying medicine. She's an advocate of female suffrage. Believes prof. woman should remain single. Theories tested by a young man who believes in clinging vine type of woman. PW 52:1161.
LW 29:124. "Amy finally comes to her own; and the purpose of the story becomes evident in showing that a mission, or a cause, or a profession, or an advanced theory fails to satisfy a woman, and that love and home are best afterall." Amy "tried to be a kind of independent modern woman."

012124   UNCONFESSED. BY MAXWELL GRAY. London: J. Long, 1911 BMC NUC.

ATH-story of two brothers.

012125   THE WORLD-MENDER; A NOVEL. BY MAXWELL GRAY. New York: D. Appleton, 1916 NUC. London: Hutchinson, 1916 BMC NUC.

Male politican NYT
Male politican TLS

TUTTLE, MARGARETTA MUHLENBERG (PERKINS). B. 1880. United States.

012126   HIS WORLDLY GOODS. Indianapolis: Bobbs-Merrill, [c1912] NUC.

PW-triangle
NYT-Love story.

TWEEDALE, VIOLET (CHAMBERS). 1862?-1936. United Kingdom.

012127   AND THEY TWO. London: G. Redway, 1897 BMC.

"The heroine is of a purity that faints at marriage and kills herself on her wedding day in a fury of spotlessness." SR 84:46.

012128   AUSTIN'S CAREER. London: J. Long, 1912 BMC.

TLS-male hero and his wasted life.
ATH entanglement in youth-honorable fulfillment. Bohemian life.

012129   THE BEAUTIFUL MRS. DAVENANT. A NOVEL OF LOVE AND MYSTERY. New York: F.A. Stokes, [c1920] NUC. London: H. Jenkins, 1920 BMC NUC.

TLS-ghost.
SR-2 unattached women living by themselves, ghost and murder.
NYT 12-26-20, p25. Old-fashioned type of romance treated in a modern way.

012130   AN EMPTY HERITAGE. London: J. Long, 1908 BMC.

TLS-male inheritance etc. ACAD

012131   THE GREEN LADY. London: H. Jenkins,
[1920] BMC.

    TLS-vampirism and dual personality.

012132   THE HAZARDS OF LIFE. London: J. Long,
1904 BMC.

    LBKM-1st wife shows up after all thought dead. RC
    faith. Then what?
    TLS-soulful brilliant woman who smokes marries
    Welshman; his family cannot adjust-then what?

012133   THE HEART OF A WOMAN. London: Hurst &
Blackett, 1917 BMC.

    Infidelities of a lord. TLS
    The typist-secretary has very definite opinions on
    many subjects and is an uncompromising Suffragist-one
    of the least artificia l characters. Novel deals with
    customs of certain sections of society.
    The customs of certain sections of society. One
    character is a typist-secretary who has very definite
    opinions on many subjects and who is a suffragist
    devoted to the cause.

012134   HER GRACE'S SECRET. Philadelphia: G.W.
Jacobs, [1901] NUC. London: Hutchinson, 1901 BMC.

    English socialist novel. Heroine finds her duties as a
    great lady empty compared to her love who is
    intellectually her equal. The lady's eloquence on many
    social issues. ATH 8-10-01

012135   THE HONEYCOMB OF LIFE. London:
Hutchinson, 1902 BMC.

    Independent heroine is several degrees too aggressive.
    LBKM 10-02.
    ATH 9-13-02 Illicit passions of several very
    dissipated people, including that of a young
    consumptive girl for her illegitimate father.

012136   THE HOUSE OF THE OTHER WORLD. London: J.
Long, 1913 BMC NUC.

    Haunted house that Sir Paul and Lady Ashton Heriot
    take on lease-the hauntings and tragic events. ATH TLS

012137   HYPOCRITES AND SINNERS. London: J. Long,
1910 BMC.

    TLS-anti-socialist.
    LBKM-anti socialist. Male hero.

012138   THE KINGDOM OF MAMMON. London: J. Long,
1899 BMC.

    Wicked and vulgar clergy. Dean Wedderburn tries to
    dissuade his wife from leaving to join another man by
    telling her it will hurt his career. She's also told
    she'll ruin the man's reputation, so she stays;
    husband becomes a bishop. This as he's being enthroned
    as Archbishop. SP 82:722

012139   LADY SARAH'S SON. London: J. Long, 1906
BMC NUC.

    TLS-story of illegitimate male.

012140   LORD EVERSLEIGH'S SINS. London: J. Long,
1905 BMC.

    Love entanglements. TLS 05 52
    Marriage of convenience, but wife develops a passion
    for her husband, that he does not respond to? ATH
    396,05

012141   LOVE AND WAR. London: Hurst & Blackett,
1916 NUC BMC.

    TLS-Lord Cressy is a pacifist when the great war
    comes.
    ATH-finally changes his mind.

012142   MRS. BARRINGTON'S ATONEMENT. London: J.
Long, 1907 BMC.

    Triangle. TLS
    TLS-gives her wandering husband a baby.

012143   THE PORTALS OF LOVE. London: J. Long,
1906 BMC NUC.

TLS-0

012144   THE QUENCHLESS FLAME. London: J. Long,
1909 BMC.

    Spanish woman is married to a brutal drunkard, falls
    in love with Englishman. Story switches to England and
    Lady Langdale and her fashionable world. The Spanish
    woman comes back into the story in a surprising way.
    TLS

012145   A REAPER OF THE WHIRLWIND. London: J.
Long, 1911 BMC.

    Marion marries Viscount not knowing there's madness in
    his family. Loves her son's tutor? Heredity, insanity,
    etc. ATH

012146   THE SWEETS OF OFFICE. London: J. Long,
1907 BMC.

    Political novel heroine a beautiful angel. TLS

012147   AN UNHOLY ALLIANCE. London: J. Long,
[1914] BMC.

012148   UNSOLVED MYSTERIES. London: Digby, Long,
[1895] BMC.

012149   THE VEILED WOMAN. London: H.Jenkins, 1918
BMC.

    TLS-politics of the novel center around feminism and
    suffrage. Rev. feels this out of date.

012150   WHAT SHALL IT PROFIT A MAN? London:
Digby, Long, [1897] BMC.

    The good society. The Squire, his wife, Lady Augusta.
    Mt. Royal, etc. ACAD 52: Fic Sup 122
    SR 85:470. Villain exerts influence over wife's aunt
    until he falls in river and drowns.

012151   WINGATE'S WIFE. London: J. Long, 1916 BMC
NUC.

    TLS-portrays women as victims of tyranny or cajolery
    of man. Wingate's wife kills (did she?) him when he
    shows up to threaten her married life after 20 years,
    she had deserted him.
    ATH-Gloria Power expresses author's views on feminism.
    What?

TWEEDIE, ETHEL BRILLIANA (HARLEY). D. 1940.

012152   BEHIND THE FOOTLIGHTS. New York: Dodd,
Mead, 1904 NUC. London: Hutchinson, 1904 BMC NUC.

012153   WILTON, Q.C.; OR, LIFE IN A HIGHLAND
SHOOTING BOX. BY MRS. ALEC TWEEDIE (nee HARLEY).
London: H. Cox, 1895 BMC NUC.

    Love and sport, a desc of golf, shooting and fishing.
    SP 74:763
    Highland sport novel with all necessary ingredients: a
    beneficent laird, some natives, people up from the
    city on holiday, lovers, a widow. LBKM 9:32

TWEEDIE, MRS. ALEC. See TWEEDIE, ETHEL BRILLIANA (HARLEY).

TWELLS, JULIA HELEN, JR. United States.

012154   BY THE HIGHER LAW. Philadephia: H. T.
Coates, [1901] BMC NUC.

    ATH 3-22-02 soc. novel.

012155   ET TU, SEJANE! A STORY OF CAPRI IN THE
DAYS OF TIBERIUS. London: Chatto & Windus, 1904 BMC.

    ATH-hist rom.
    ACAD

012156   A TRIUMPH OF DESTINY. Philadelphia: J. B.
Lippincott, 1896 NUC 1897 BMC.

    PW 12-5-96. Study of singularly complex character; an
    argument against mrge. Marries a man she is both
    attracted to and repulsed by. After a year they
    separate. After an experience with a country boy whom
    she thinks she loves, she reunites with her husb. and
    they agree to live as brother and sister.
    Phenix Loraine-a school girl's idol, but after one
    year married to him Helen Wentworth finds that none of
    his charms satisfy. Left him "to seek fresher
    experiences and develop more fully her own nature."

Next she loves a nature boy type-a cowboy. Then returns to a platonic relation with Phenix. LW 28:278 BN "He in the meanwhile having become a different man and having learned to appreciate his wife properly."

TWIGGS, SARAH LOWE.

012157   THE SUPREME ADVENTURE. Bryn Athyn, Pa.: Academy Book Room, 1919 NUC.

story of the future life PW

TWING, CAROLINN EDNA (SKINNER). B. 1844. United States.

012158   'LISBETH: A STORY OF TWO WORLDS. BY CARRIE E. S. TWING. Boston: Banner Of Light Pub. Co., 1900 NUC.

TWING, CARRIE E. S. See TWING, CAROLINN EDNA (SKINNER).

TYBOUT, ELLA MIDDLETON. United States.

012159   THE SMUGGLER. Philadelphia and London: J. B. Lippincott, 1907 NUC.

Three girls seeking health vacation in Canada met with all kinds of exper--PW 10-10-07
BKM-Adv. of 3 Am. girls in Canada who unwittingly entertain smugglers.
NYT-"The reader is spared the tedium of a triple love story."

012160   THE WIFE OF THE SECRETARY OF STATE. Philadelphia and London: J. B. Lippincott, 1905 NUC.

High pol. Washington life. PW 11-11-05

TYLER, ODETTE, pseud. See SHEPHERD, ELIZABETH LEE (KIRKLAND).

TYLER, PHILIPPA.

012161   THE LUSHINGTON MYSTERY ("THOU SHALT NOT ESCAPE---"). London: Heath, Cranton, [1919] BMC NUC.

Espionage, murder, suicide. SP

012162   THE MANATON DISASTER. London: Heath, Cranton, [1920] BMC.

TLS Love and inheritance
ATH Love and inheritance

TYLER, THERESE PAULINE (COLES). B. 1884. United States.

012163   THE DUSTY ROAD. Philadelphia and London: J. B. Lippincott, 1915 NUC.

Woman of position must strain to "put on appearance," set with temptations? PW 2-13-15
Development of heroine's char. BKM 41 1915 poverty, revolt, temptation, despair of idealistic young woman; must keep up appearances because family was well-off. Mother bitter; father drunk; brother intolerable. NYT What happens?
Story of Therese's different love relationships until she marries. Another woman with brutal husband who breaks her only solace- reading Ibsen. She has a "beautiful spiritual friendship with an author but the spirituality declines." TLS
Takes heroine thru three loves to the right one BKm

TYNAN, KATHARINE. See HINKSON, KATHARINE (TYNAN).

TYSON, ANNIE ARRINGTON. United States.

012164   DRAMANA; A ROMANCE OF THE STAGE. New York: Neale, 1903 NUC.

TYTLER, SARAH, pseud. See KEDDIE, HENRIETTA.

ULLMAN, ALICE WOODS. 1871-1959. United States.

012165   A GINGHAM ROSE. Indianapolis: Bobbs-Merrill, [1904] BMC NUC.

NYT-Sounds conv., love story, "up-to-date story of New York" BKM v. 19, 1904
"aspirants for fame" Arena 1904

UNDERDOWN, EMILY.

012166   THE CARVED BOX: A STORY FROM SWITZERLAND. BY NORLEY CHESTER. London: Blackie, [1894] BMC.

012167   CRISTINA. A ROMANCE OF ITALY IN OLDEN

DAYS. London: S. Sonnenschein, 1903 BMC.

BAKER '13:365 Historical romance.

012168   KNIGHTS OF THE GRAIL. LOHENGRIN: GALAHAD. BY NORLEY CHESTER. London: T. Nelson, 1907 BMC 1908 NUC.

012169   OLGA'S DREAM: A NINETEENTH CENTURY FAIRY TALE. BY NORLEY CHESTER. London: Skeffington, 1892 BMC NUC.

012170   A PLAIN WOMAN'S PART. BY NORLEY CHESTER. London: E. Arnold, 1900 BMC.

SP 87:747. Plain woman is narrator not heroine. Conflict in heroine over "very strong female affection and an illicit love affair."
ATH 115:618. Plain woman is "priggish and precise."

UNDERHILL, EVELYN, pseud. See MOORE, MRS. STUART.

UNDERWOOD, EDNA (WORTHLEY). B. 1873. United States.

012171   LETTERS FROM A PRAIRIE GARDEN. Boston: M. Jones Co., 1919 NUC.

Letters from a woman to a man she's never seen. PW

012172   THE WHIRLWIND. Boston: Small, Maynard, [c1918] NUC BMC.

PW-Hist court intrigue-central fig. Catharine of Russia.
NYT Aug 25, 1918, p366. Catharine is portrayed as all head and no heart, ambitious and able.

012173   THE WHIRLWIND OF PASSION. London: Hurst & Blackett, [1919] BMC.

Heroine is Catherine the Great of Russia. TLS
SR-Young Catherine the Great

UNDERWOOD, RUTH. Nationality Unknown.

012174   A LIVING LEGACY. Philadelphia: J. C. Winston, 1912 NUC.

PW--
NYT-romance

UPHAM, ELIZABETH.

012175   SUNSHINE AND COLLEGE GIRLS. New York: Morse, [1901] NUC.

College women about to graduate make several plans: write, live for public, live for worthy ideals- 2 most idealistic don't marry, other's ambitions wane. The two devote selves to the poor. NYT 01

URNER, MABEL HERBERT. 1881-1957. United States.

012176   THE JOURNAL OF A NEGLECTED WIFE. New York: B.W. Dodge, 1909 NUC.

Husband unfaithful, separation, adjustment, painfully real. PW 7-6-09
Feelings unshrinkingly revealed. Morbidly truthful. A woman of "unlovely middle-age lays bare her agony, her shame, her thwarted passion, her pitiful attempts to grow young, the slow breaking of her pride." NYT

012177   THE WOMAN ALONE. New York: Hearst's International Library, 1914 BMC NUC.

NYT 1914:461. Contemptible hero, oscillating between wife and mistress, unable to be faithful to either...whom one longs to kick, filled with most unpleasant scenes, painful ending, leaves a distinctly bad taste in one's mouth. Repeats the truth whenever there is a guilty passion the woman pays, and the woman alone.
Heroine loves married man whose conscience won't let him divorce. PW 3-6-15

URQUHART, M. See GREEN, MARYON URQUHART.

VACARESCO, HELENE. See VACARESCU, ELENA.

VACARESCU, ELENA. B. 1868.

012178   THE KING'S WIFE. BY HELENE VACARESCO. London: T. W. Laurie, [1907] BMC NUC.

Diary of King's son who becomes king. TLS

Story of court and Royal romance SP

012179   THE QUEEN'S FRIEND. BY HELENE VACARESCO.
London: T. W. Laurie, [1908] BMC.

TLS-Mrg. of fem Roumanian aristocrat to English peer
and its failure-she is as bad as an Oriental in his
family's eyes; author sympathetic with wife.
ACAD-O

012180   ROYAL LOVERS. THE ADVENTURES OF TWO
EMPRESSES. BY HELENE VACARESCO. London: Mills & Boon,
[1909] NUC BMC.

The intrigues, plans, failures and truimphs of two
royal women who have five marriagable daughters. Three
marry, two live their lives "by the prescribed rules
for royalties."? PW
European Court life. TLS

VADOS, pseud. See FARLEY, AGNES.

VAILE, CHARLOTTE MARION (WHITE). 1852-1902.

012181   THE M. M. C.: A STORY OF THE GREAT
ROCKIES. Boston: W. A. Wilde, [1898] NUC.

Title refers to a mine in Rockies and a man who
believed in his venture and with the help of a boy and
a school teacher, Alice Hildreth, realizes his dream.
LW 30:42.
PW-New England school teacher trapped in Colorado
mining camp by early onset of winter. Her struggle to
hold on to a claim for an old friend.

VAIZEY, JESSIE (BELL) MANSERGH. B. 1857. United Kingdom.

012182   THE ADVENTURES OF BILLIE BELSHAW. London:
Mills & Boon, 1912 BMC.

ATH male
SP

012183   BETTY TREVOR. BY MRS. GEORGE DE HORNE
VAIZEY. London: R. T. S., [1907] BMC. New York: G. P.
Putnam, 1917 NUC.

A clean wholesome tale with a host of interesting
characters. Betty longs to be pretty, meets a stranger
who turns out to be her brother's best friend and her
husband in the end. NYT 4-15-17, 138

012184   BIG GAME: A STORY FOR GIRLS. London:
R.T.S., [1908] BMC.

012185   A COLLEGE GIRL. BY MRS. GEORGE DE HORNE
VAIZEY. London: R. T. S., 1913 BMC. New York and
London: G.P. Putnam's Sons, 1916 NUC.

NYT 10/29/16 p.456

012186   THE CONQUEST OF CHRYSTABEL. London:
Cassell, 1909 BMC.

A love story involving a fortune. TLS

012187   CYNTHIA CHARRINGTON. London: Cassell,
1911 BMC.

Has a gambling spirit, chafes at restrictions in her
life; heartbreak comes in that she loves a man who
doesn't love her. Goes off to do settlement work. PW
11-18-11.
Beth the "Lady of all work." SP

012188   THE DAUGHTERS OF A GENIUS. A STORY OF
BRAVE ENDEAVORS. London: W. & R. Chambers, 1903 BMC.
Philadelphia: Lippincott, 1903 PW.

Father has daughters cultivate their individual
talents. They follow his advice. PW 11-7-03

012189   FLAMING JUNE. London: Cassell, 1908 BMC.

Astonishes the British natives. SP
One of series of books for young women. ATH
TLS-2 charming love stories.
ATH-2 charming love stories.

012190   GRIZEL MARRIED. BY MRS. GEORGE DE HORNE
VAIZEY. London: Mills & Boon, [1914] BMC NUC.

ATH-woman, after 10 years of marriage, longs for
romance. ATH 143:823.0
TLS-sequel to An Unknown Lover. Domestic, sweet
Grizel.

Pub. in US as Lady Cassandra.

012191   HARRIET MANNERING'S PAYING GUESTS.
London: Mills & Boon, [1917] BMC.

012192   THE HEART OF UNA SACKVILLE. London: S.W.
Partridge, [1907] BMC.

012193   A HONEYMOON IN HIDING. BY MRS. GEORGE DE
HORNE VAIZEY. New York: Cassell, 1911 PW. London:
Cassell, 1911 BMC NUC.

Honeymooners hide out at home. PW 4-29-11.

012194   A HOUSEFUL OF GIRLS. London: R. T. S.,
[1902] BMC.

012195   HOW LIKE A KING: THE WEEK-END OF MR.
SEPTIMUS EDWARD. London: S.H. Bousfield, 1905 BMC.
London: Cassell, [1907] NUC.

012196   THE INDEPENDENCE OF CLAIRE. London: R. T.
S., [1915] BMC.

012197   LADY CASSANDRA. BY MRS. GEORGE DE HORNE
VAIZEY. New York: G.P. Putnam's Sons, 1914 NUC.

PW 86 9/26/14:969 "Cassandra Raynor finds relief from
the tedium of married life in the companionship of
Dane Peignton. The freindship becomes love on both
sides. Yet Dane, almost by accident, engages himself
to a pretty young girl. Grizel Beverly, Cassandra's
sprightly friend, knows of her trouble, and by her
sympathy helps her to come to a better understanding
of the situation . Published in Great Britain under
the title Grizel married."
NYT-Grizel gets Cassandra back on the moral track.
Friendship between women appears to be belittled by
author as a release of petty ideas and talk a "good
husband" would not be able to bear.

012198   THE LADY OF THE BASEMENT FLAT. London:
Woman's Magazine and Girl's Own Paper, [1917] BMC.

She's a wealthy woman of 26 who disguises herself as
an elderly spinster to do good works for the
struggling poor. TLS

012199   THE LOVE AFFAIRS OF PIXIE. London: R. T.
S., [1914] BMC.

TLS-romance for girls.

012200   MANNERING'S PAYING GUESTS. London: Mills
& Boon, [1917] BMC.

012201   A QUESTION OF MARRIAGE. BY MRS. GEORGE DE
HORNE VAIZEY. London: Hodder & Stoughton, 1910 BMC.
New York and London: G.P. Putnam's Sons, 1911 NUC.

A girl who must never marry--stays engaged for 8
years; he goes off and marries another. They remain
friends; she does good works; is fulfilled without
marriage? Vanna Strangeways. PW 4-1-11
Young girl, cultured and beautiful, told by doctor
that marriage is out for her: marriage for her would
be a fate worse than death. The story studies the
gloomy effect of such news on her. Then she meets the
man and we get the long years of struggle against him
and herself. Side by side, story of her friend who has
an average marriage. At end, the first convinces her
suitor to go. She finds happiness in visits from this
friend. Lives a life of peace and happiness. (The
problem she has is hereditary insanity. NYT

012202   A ROSE-COLOURED THREAD. London: J.
Bowden, 1898 BMC.

SP 81:782. Cairo. "Tenderly handled romance of Janet
Graham." "Sufferings of governesses."
A plain governess is wooed by an English doctor. Then
an old love of his shows up and there are
complications. PW 55:371
Governess (plain) given up by suitor when a good
looking rich lover of his past comes along. SR 87:57

012203   SALT OF LIFE. BY MRS. GEORGE DE HORNE
VAIZEY. London: Mills & Boon, 1915 BMC NUC.

A family history. TLS
Happy ending. SP
Heroine wins a prize for her novel and a husband. ATH.
Family moves from Scotland to London.

012204   AN UNKNOWN LOVER. BY MRS. GEORGE DE HORNE
VAIZEY. New York: G. P. Putnam's Sons, 1913 NUC.

London: Mills and Boon, [1913] BMC NUC.

PW 83 6/7/13:2010 "Somewhat strained relations have
arisen between a widowed brother and his sister, who
has spent eight years keeping house for him. Both want
to change, and each fears to hurt the other. The
brother marries and Katrine, the sister, goes to India
to spend a year with friends. She has been exchanging
letters with a man she has never seen and their
meeting, round which there is some mystery, and the
development of their love story makes a very pleasant
tale."
They fall in love with each other's letters. SP

VAIZEY, MRS. GEORGE DE HORNE. See VAIZEY, JESSIE (BELL)
MANSERGH.

VAKA, DEMETRA. See BROWN, DEMETRA (VAKA).

VALENTINE, JANE, pseud. See MEEKER, NELLIE J.

VALJEAN, IRIS.

012205   THE JOURNAL OF IRIS VALJEAN. Kansas City,
Mo.: Hudson-Kimberly, 1903 NUC.

VALLINGS, GABRIELLE FRANCESCA LILIAN MAY. B. 1886. United
Kingdom.

012206   BINDWEED. London: Hutchinson, 1916 BMC
NUC. New York: Dodd, Mead, 1916 PW.

TLS--Eugenie trained by opera singer. Love vs. passion
(bindweed), worlds of genius and art and the peasant's
cottage.
ATH--pro "holy wedlock"--(auth)
Eugenie Massini, French convent-bred woman with a
wonderful voice, but jealous aunt watches over her;
murders a man she thinks is out to get Eugenie.
melodrama PW
The Aunt Victorine--goes insane. Eugenie comes under
the care of Mme. Perintot ex-opera singer who really
appreciates and devotes herself to Eugenie's talent. A
tenor interferes with these plans. NYT 5-27-17 211

012207   TUMULT: A ROMANCE. London: Hutchinson,
1918 BMC.

TLS-Superfluity and sensation. Theme is love of
natural beauty.
ATH-Heroine and hero represent struggle between
civilization and nature. Strange blend of actual and
mythical.
Fantasy involving Pan. SR

VALMER, LOUISE.

012208   THE TENOR'S MELODRAMA. London: S. Swift,
[1912] BMC.

TLS-he is married to a "vampire" wife (blameless,
loving but narrow partner) who stifles his genius. He
loves another.

VAN, JENNIE E., pseud. See VAN AMRINGE, JENNIE ELIZABETH
(WILMUTH).

VANAMEE, LIDA (OSTROM). United States.

012209   AN ADIRONDACK IDYL. New York: C. T.
Dillingham, [c1893] NUC.

Young woman gives up her lover when she learns he's
really engaged to another woman. All is put in order
when he shows proof that the other woman loves another
man. LW 93:387.

012210   TWO WOMEN; OR, "OVER THE HILLS AND FAR
AWAY". New York: Merriam, [c1895] NUC.

one is a widow, the other single-travel to Eurpoe for
self-improvement; reviewer says they're
husband-hunting. CR 24:232.
"A record of two women's friendship and of their
respective love stories" LW 26:203

VAN AMRINGE, JENNIE ELIZABETH (WILMUTH). B. 1855. United
States.

012211   WISE OLD DEACON; THE STORY OF A DOG. BY
JENNIE E. VAN. New York: Broadway, 1903 NUC.

VAN ANDERSON, HELEN. See GORDON, HELEN (VAN METRE) VAN
ANDERSON.

VAN BUREN, EVELYN. United States.

012212   PIPPIN. New York: Century, 1913 BMC NUC.

"Story of London streets. American girl pursuing
acting career meets Pippin who is trying to support a
consumptive younger brother; she has inherited the
fatal taste of her inebriate father; and she has been
trained by her associates to be an expert
pick-pocket." see Cooper First Novels.
Pippin (Victoria Alexandra) because of family's
poverty, she's a pick pocket, deft and successful at
that business. But her native instincts are honest.
Struggle to earn her living honestly, meeting with
young actress. NYT

VANDEGRIFT, MARGARET, pseud. See JANVIER, MARGARET THOMSON.

VANDELEUR, JUDITH.

012213   VAL: A STORY OF THE TIVY-SIDE. London:
Hurst and Blackett, 1896 BMC.

SR Two heroines: one a tomboy, the other whose shyness
was mistaken for coldness.
ATH 108:480. Wholesome childhood.
ACAD 50:238. Childhood to girlhood.

VANDERCOOK, MARGARET O'BANNON (WOMACK). B. 1876. United
States.

012214   THE LOVES OF AMBROSE. Garden City, N.Y.:
Doubleday, Page, 1914 NUC.

PW:85 3/14/14:968. "Quaint little Kentucky town, fifty
years ago is the scene. Ambrose Thompson, homely,
kindly, with a sense of humor, is the hero. His four
marriages are told about, why and how he married each
wife, beginning when he was twenty-one, and making his
final venture at seventy-six."
BKM-Four wives-spring, summer, autumn, and winter.

VAN DER VERE, LENORE.

012215   WAYFARERS. London: G. P. Putnam & Sons,
1912 BMC.

ATH-describes life in a sanitorium for phthisis.
Semi-insane and drunken Dr. and a Polish exile who
sacrifices his life for girl patient. Morbid.

VAN DE VELDE, MADAME.

012216   DOCTOR GREYSTONE. A STORY. London:
Trischler, [1891] BMC.

VAN DEVENTER, E. M. See VAN DEVENTER, EMMA MURDOCH.

VAN DEVENTER, E. MURDOCH. See VAN DEVENTER, EMMA MURDOCH.

VAN DEVENTER, EMMA MURDOCH. Fl. 1879-1912. United States.

012217   AGAINST ODDS. A ROMANCE OF THE MIDWAY
PLAISANCE. BY LAWRENCE L. LYNCH (E. MURDOCH VAN
DEVENTER). Chicago: Rand, McNally, 1894 NUC. London:
Ward & Lock, 1894 BMC.

012218   A BLIND LEAD; DARING AND THRILLING
ADVENTURES, CLEVER DETECTIVE WORK. BY LAWRENCE L.
LYNCH. <E. M. VAN DEVENTER>. Chicago: Laird & Lee,
[c1912] NUC.

012219   THE DANGER LINE. BY LAWRENCE L. LYNCH.
London: Ward, Lock, 1905 BMC.

012220   A DEAD MAN'S STEP. A DETECTIVE STORY. BY
"LAWRENCE L. LYNCH" (E. MURDOCH VAN DEVENTER).
Chicago: Rand, McNally, 1893 NUC. London: Ward and
Lock, 1893 BMC.

PW-murder, bank robbery, innocent man suspected, love
episodes.

012221   THE DOVERFIELDS' DIAMONDS: THE GREAT GEM
MYSTERY. BY LAWRENCE L. LYNCH. Chicago: Laird & Lee,
[1906] NUC. London: Ward, Lock, 1907 BMC.

PW-?
ACAD-typical stolen jewels mystery.

012222   HIGH STAKES. BY LAWRENCE L. LYNCH (E.
MURDOCH VAN DEVENTER). Chicago: Laird & Lee, [c1899]
NUC. London: Ward, Lock, 1901 BMC.

012223   THE LAST STROKE. BY LAWRENCE L. LYNCH (E.
MURDOCH VAN DEVENTER). Chicago: Laird & Lee, [c1896]
NUC. London: Ward, Lock, [1897] BMC.

PW 12-5-96. A crime and its detection.

012224   MAN AND MASTER: A TALE OF LOVE, INTRIGUE
AND MYSTERY. BY LAWRENCE L. LYNCH. Chicago: Laird &
Lee, 1908 PW. London: Ward, Lock, 1909 BMC.

PW-murder mystery.
BKM-murder mystery.

012225   MOINA; OR, AGAINST THE MIGHTY. BY
LAWRENCE L. LYNCH. London: Ward, Lock, 1891 BS.
Chicago: Laird & Lee, 1891 NUC BMC.

About a secret society in United States. ATH 97 405.
The mighty are the anarchists and socialists
throughout the world. Monica is the beautiful daughter
of an English gentleman secretly in League with
American anarchists. PW. danger of anarchism shown.

012226   NO PROOF. BY LAWRENCE L. LYNCH (E.
MURDOCH VAN DEVENTER). London: Ward and Lock, 1895
BMC. Chicago: Rand, McNally, [c1895] NUC.

detective. Bride of few weeks found dead. Murder or
suicide? PW 10-12-95:633.

012227   A SEALED VERDICT. BY LAWRENCE L. LYNCH.
London: J. Long, 1916 BMC.

TLS-murder mystery.

012228   A SLENDER CLUE; OR, THE MYSTERY OF MARDI
GRAZ. BY LAWRENCE L. LYNCH. London: Ward, Lock, 1891
BMC. Chicago: Laird and Lee, 1891 NUC.

012229   UNDER FATE'S WHEEL. A STORY OF MYSTERY,
LOVE, AND THE BICYCLE, ETC. BY LAWRENCE L. LYNCH (E.
MURDOCH VAN DEVENTER). London: Ward, Lock, [1900] BMC.
Chicago: Laird and Lee, [c1900] NUC.

SR 90:304. Crime, property, love and melodramatic
misery. Mad mesmerist.
ATH 116:276. Villain, a cyclist and hypnotist, kidnaps
child of the Western prairie, encourages her to become
a professional cyclist. Everyone cycles, including
heroine. New Era Cycle Club.
ACAD 59:212. On her deathbed Inez explains about her
bike ride in male attire, the "air gun with which she
did the deed."

012230   THE UNSEEN HAND. BY LAWRENCE L. LYNCH (E.
MURDOCH VAN DEVENTER). London and New York: Ward,
Lock, [1899] BMC NUC.

Conventional detective story with misleading clues.
LIT 5:375
Wealth, marriage and murder. ACAD 57:254

012231   THE WOMAN WHO DARED. BY LAWRENCE L.
LYNCH. Chicago: Laird & Lee, [1902] BMC. London: Ward,
Lock, [1902] BMC.

Detective story in the West.

012232   A WOMAN'S TRAGEDY; OR, THE DETECTIVE'S
TASK. London: Ward, Lock, [1904] BMC.

VAN DE WATER, VIRGINIA BELLE (TERHUNE). 1865-1945. United
States.

012233   IN THE WEB OF LIFE. New York: Hearst's
International Library, [1914] NUC.

PW 86 12/5/14:1895. "Ralph Morton gambles away money
intrusted to him to pay a debt and borrows from a
married woman. His older cousin Tom comes to the
rescue and promises to return the money in person, as
Ralph is called away. Thereupon develops a series of
misunderstandings. Tom's fiancee is suspicious and
Ralph plays false and engages himself to her, to be
thrown over later. Eventually Tom finds out that
Constance, a poor relation of Edith's, who has trusted
him throughout, is the woman he really loves."

012234   THE TWO SISTERS. New York: Hearst's
International Library, 1914 BMC NUC.

PW 85 5/30/14 p.1780 "Julia and Caryl Marvin find
their life with their stepmother impossible, so come
to New York to earn their living. Julia finds work in
a department store, but Caryl scorns anything of the
sort, takes a few lessons at a business college and is
engaged as stenographer by Kelley Delaine, a writer.
Empty-headed and pleasure-loving, Caryl accepts the
attentions of any man who will give her a good time,

while her sister is distracted with anxiety. Delaine
falls in love with Julia and tries to keep Caryl out
of harm, but unsuccessfully. She elopes with a man
whom she does not know is married, and Julia only sees
her again when she is dying, when Delaine has found
her and takes Julia, now his wife, to the hospital
where she is."

VAN DRESSER, JASMINE STONE. B. 1875. United States.

012235   GIBBY OF CLAMSHELL ALLEY. New York: Dodd,
Mead, 1916 NUC.

A Boy and his boat. PW, NYT

VAN DUESEN, REBECCA. Nationality Unknown.

012236   SEA BREEZES AND SAND DUNES. New York:
Abbey Press, [1902] NUC.

Happy summer of younger members of family. PW

VANE, CAPEL, pseud. See ALLPORT, ELLEN.

VANE, DENZIL, pseud. See DU TERTRE, FANNY.

VANE, DEREK. See BACK, BLANCHE EATON.

VAN FOSSEN, LOO B. United States.

012237   ABANDONED: A ROMANCE. BY LOUIS B. ZELCOE.
New York, London: F. T. Neely, [c1900] NUC.

VAN HOESEN, ANTOINETTE. See WAKEMAN, ANTOINETTE PRUDENCE
(VAN HOESEN).

VAN JAVA, MELATI, pseud. See SLOOT, NICOLINA MARIA
CHRISTINA.

VAN SAANEN, MARIE LOUISE, pseud. See HALE, MARICE RUTLEDGE
(GIBSON).

VANSITTART, SIBELL. United Kingdom.

012238   LOCKETT'S LEA. London: E. Arnold, 1914
BMC.

ATH Heredity. Life of daughter of notorious parents.
TLS Marion "sinks downward," fascinating personality."

VAN SLINGERLAND, NELLIE BINGHAM. B. 1850. United States.

012239   CUPID, THE DEVIL'S STOKER; OR, HEAVEN'S
GATE TO HELL; A ROMANCE OF HEREDITY IN ARGENTINA AND
OLD SPAIN. BY NELLIE BINGHAM VAN SLINGERLAND (NEILE
BEVANS). New York: Fifth Ave. Pub. Co., 1905 NUC.

012240   LOVE AND POLITICS: A SOCIAL ROMANCE OF A
PROMINENT ORATOR AND A SOCIETY QUEEN. BY NEILE BEVANS.
[Jersey City, N.J.]: Jersey City Printing, [c1899]
NUC.

VAN SLYKE, LUCILLE (BALDWIN). B. 1880. United States.

012241   LITTLE MISS BY-THE-DAY. New York: F. A.
Stokes, [c1919] NUC. London: Nisbet, 1920 BMC.

"Felicia Day returns to Brooklyn of her childhood to
find it's a slum. Poor little Felicia was left alone
and penniless in a strange world. The story of her
struggles as a by-the-day seamstress is delicately
done." "She is perhaps a shade bit too naive for even
the most sheltered maiden." Straightens out her life
and those of several others. Romance a part. PW Book
Rev
Works to save her house from auction PW
TLS fairy romance.

VAN STEINBURG, DORA F. United States.

012242   AUNT TIRZAH; A NOVEL. New York: Broadway,
[c1910] NUC.

VAN VORST, BESSIE (MACGINNIS). 1873-1928. United States.

012243   THE ISSUES OF LIFE. A NOVEL OF THE
AMERICAN WOMAN OF TO-DAY. BY MRS. JOHN VAN VORST.
London and New York: Doubleday, Page, 1904 BMC NUC.

"a novel of the 'American woman of today,' the
so-called 'new woman' who substitutes clubs and
personal freedom for the home". BKM
NYT-caricatures of "new woman"

012244   LETTERS TO WOMEN IN LOVE. BY MRS. JOHN
VAN VORST. New York: D. Appleton, 1906 NUC.

VAN VORST, BESSIE (MACGINNIS) AND MARIE VAN VORST.

012245   BAGSBY'S DAUGHTER. New York: Harper, 1901
NUC. London: G. Richards, 1901 BMC.

light love story BAKER 13-508

012246   THE WOMAN WHO TOILS. BEING THE
EXPERIENCES OF TWO LADIES AS FACTORY GIRLS. BY MRS.
JOHN VAN VORST AND MARIE VAN VORST. London: G.
Richards, 1903 BMC. New York: Doubleday, Page, 1903
NUC.

VAN VORST, MARIE. 1867-1936. United States.

012247   AMANDA OF THE MILL: A NOVEL. London: W.
Heinemann, 1904 BMC. New York: Dodd, Mead, 1905 NUC.

The terrible life of Southern cotton mills puts Amanda
on the way to becoming a prostitute. But her
successful rehabilitation of a male alcoholic brings
her his mother's gratitude and an inheritance. Amanda
now a wealthy woman works to reform life in the mills.
The underlying purpose of the author is to picture the
operatives in the cotton mills of the South, a girl,
simple and innocent is transformed into a woman of the
world. PW 9-6-13
BKM 21 (1905) 388-391
Amanda almost driven to prostitution by harsh working
conditions. Rehabilitates an alcoholic man who becomes
a labor leader. Mother of this no-good man makes
Amanda an heiress. 4-8-05 PW
Terrible life in the mills, Amanda leads them to
better conditions through education and wealth. NYT
260 05
Tragedy of poor white trash. Weakness of men and their
dependence on women for moral and spiritual strength.
ACAD 05,241
ATH 05,395

012248   BIG TREMAINE; A NOVEL. Boston: Little,
Brown, 1914 BMC NUC. London: Mills & Boon, 1915 BMC.

Exile, he returns to Virginia. TLS
Focus on hero. BKM
PW 86 10/10/14: 1209 "As a young man, Tremaine leaves
his Virginia home a self-confessed thief. Fifteen
years later he returns to re-establish himself in the
community, regain his mother's love and esteem, and
make himself a power for good. Then Isobel, the girl,
comes into his life. He feels a barrier between them
and does his best to appear mean in her eyes, and
nearly breaks her heart. In reality, his brother was
the thief. Julia, the brother's widow, knows this; but
she loves Tremaine and tries to win him from Isobel.
When Julia sees Tremaine giving up all he has gained,
and, the second time, going away silent, the force of
his sacrifice impels her to tell the truth, which
proved Isobel's early assertion that the Tremaine she
loved had never been a thief." NYT

012249   THE BROKEN BELL. Indianapolis:
Bobbs-Merrill, [c1912] NUC. London: Constable, 1913
BMC.

Beautiful Italian countess, estranged from husband
because he's unfaithful, seeks consolation in courting
temptation. Her morals are hopelessly mixed. ATH
She is smitten by a great love; travels from Naples to
a small village. TLS
PW triangle
NYT-love story.

012250   FAIRFAX AND HIS PRIDE; A NOVEL. London:
Chatto & Windus, 1913 BMC. Boston: Small, Maynard,
[c1920] NUC.

American sculptor struggles for fame. His first
marriage and his contemplation of a second one. TLS
PW-ambitious and idealistic artist in NY. Sculptor,
eventual success.
NYT 1920:170

012251   FIRST LOVE. Indianapolis.: Bobbs Merrill,
[c1910] NUC. London: Mills & Boon, 1910 BMC.

Young man loves older married woman, Virginia
Bathhurst attracted to him but has linked her life
with sottish middle age. She controls her feelings
wisely. Refuses to marry him when death of husband
sets her free. Author gives no real motives for this
decision. BKM
She marries an old admirer of her own age. He also
(now more mature) marries. NYT
BKM-v.32 1910-11. Love between male youth and older

woman who when death sets her free refuses to marry
him.
ATH -sacrifices her love for him for his sake etc.
Married woman's friendship with younger man and her
successful triumph over her affection. Even after her
husband dies. PW
"A very feminine, very sentimental idyll of an
emotional young idolatry for a married woman who
nurses him back from death's door and this fine
dis-illusioned woman's struggle against the temptation
of his chivalrous worship." BAKER 13,508

012252   THE GIRL FROM HIS TOWN. Indianapolis:
Bobbs-Merrill, [c1910] NUC. London: Mills & Boon, 1910
BMC.

BKM-v.31 1910-dance hall girl with sordid past.
TLS- romance.
BKM-the dance hall girl is justly notorious, marries
and lives happily ever after.
Millionaire marries ex drug-store counter woman who
became actress. PW
SR-

012253   HIS LOVE STORY. Indianapolis: Bobbs
Merrill, [c1913] NUC BMC. London: Mills & Boon, 1914
BMC.

PW 5/31/13 1964 "Captain Le Comte de Sabron, was poor,
with nothing but his profession, so he determined
never to fall in love, as he could not afford to
marry. He reckoned without lovely Julia Redmond, an
American girl visiting her aunt, for as soon as he saw
her he lost his heart. Anyway he need not tell his
love, and he rode off to Algiers and fighting. Then he
was badly wounded and lost in the desert, and Julia
went to find him and did it, which quite changed his
resolution about marrying."
He's poor, she's wealthy. NYT
French officer loves wealthy American woman, but he's
poor, so he can't propose. Then he's lost in battle;
she finds him, saves his life. SR

012254   IN AMBUSH. Philadelphia: J.B. Lippincott,
1909 NUC. London: Methuen, 1909 BMC.

BKM v.30, 1909-10: Heroine murders man who is too
pushy. Author's pov? What happens to her?

012255   MARY MORELAND; A NOVEL. London: Mills &
Boon, [1915] BMC. Boston: Little, Brown, 1915 BMC NUC.

BKM 41 1915-review doesn't tell all. Secretary resigns
rather than give in to her boss; becomes secretary to
an author. Ends up marrying the boss. PW 5-29-15
She wears a business suit; in NY. NYT
Secretary to three different employers. TLS
Secretary, the efficient type who knows her boss'
every mood, learns he's about to divorce. She takes
dictation concerning his plans. Then he turns to her
and says he loves her, wants her to go off with him.
Chance keeps them from such a move. She meets wife,
tries to convince husband to return to wife. BKM

012256   MISS DESMOND; AN IMPRESSION. New York:
Macmillan, 1905 NUC. London: W. Heinemann, 1905 BMC.

Maiden lady; sister is divorced and talked about;
chaperones niece in Switzerland; she awakens . Her
reward comes? PW 11-18-05
Brief description. BKM 22 (1905) 540
NYT--love story of a beautiful spinster of 30.

012257   PHILIP LONGSTRETH; A NOVEL. London and
New York: Harper, 1902 BMC NUC.

BOOK NEWS-torn between factory worker and woman of his
own class, finally chooses latter.
ATH 6-7-02. The close comes abruptly and leaves the
actual issue undetermined.
BKM-Amber Garland beautiful tawny-haired forewoman?

012258   THE SENTIMENTAL ADVENTURES OF JIMMY
BULSTRODE. New York: C. Scribner's Sons, 1908 NUC.
London: Methuen, 1908 BMC.

PW-study of a man with the heart of a child.
TLS
ATH

012259   THE SIN OF GEORGE WARRENER. New York
London: Macmillan, 1906 NUC. London: W. Heinemann,
1906 BMC.

BKM 23 1906-bored wife, awakening, extra marital,
extravagance drives husband to theft. Unhappy ending.

NYT 7-21-06 p. 461-sordid characters, unredeemed by
even a step in the right direction, bring down the
thunderbolt on that woman. 7-21-06 p. 461
TLS-character of Mrs. Warrener held and mastered the
interest throughout-- shallow stupidity to triumphant
independence.

012260   STORE-TREMAINE; FORTELLING FRA VIRGINIEN.
Chicago: J. Anderson, [c1917] NUC.

012261   THE TWO FACES. London: Mills & Boon, 1911
BMC.

Portrait painter TLS

012262   WAR LETTERS OF AN AMERICAN WOMAN. New
York and London: J. Lane, 1916 BMC NUC.

Express sympathy for France, thrill that comes from
seeing bravery of soldiers. PW
D 640 WWI personal narratives.

VAN VORST, MARIE, jt. au. See VAN VORST, BESSIE (MACGINNIS)
AND MARIE VAN VORST.

VAN VORST, MRS. JOHN. See VAN VORST, BESSIE (MACGINNIS),
Also VAN VORST, BESSIE (MACGINNIS) AND MARIE VAN VORST.

VAN WOGLUM, CHARLOTTE R. See BANGS, CHARLOTTE REBECCA
(WOGLOM).

VASE, GILLAN, pseud. See NEWTON, ELIZABETH.

VASSAL, GABRIELLE M.

012263   A ROMANCE OF THE WESTERN FRONT. London:
W. Heinemann, 1918 BMC.

TLS-love and war.

VAUGHAN, GERTRUDE ELIZA MARY. United Kingdom.

012264   THE BIRD OF LIFE. London: Chapman & Hall,
1917 NUC BMC.

From childhood to womanhood, Rachel Carwardine raised
by clerical uncle, marries clergy. Narrow rel. views
contrasted to free spirit of inquiry. Life of work and
charity idealized in Rachel. Leaves husband after two
drab years, without a word of warning , establishes "a
soul-affinity" with a dr. Becomes a famous author.
Author wishes us to treat the heroine with "a hushed
and reverent admiration." Faces the dilemma of loving
one man, returning to husband. War solves things. Both
men die. We leave Rachel in a rel. rhapsody with a
young son to give her life an aim and a meaning. TLS
Through school days, office work, efforts to become a
journalist. In her open letter, confesses to having
feigned suicide to defraud Venning of his rights as
father and husband. Never meant husband to see it, but
he does. SR
Husband forgives her, reconciled after 7 years in
hiding.

012265   THE FLIGHT OF MARJETTE. A STORY OF THE
SIEGE OF ANTWERP. London: Chapman and Hall, 1916 BMC
NUC.

TLS-young girl's diary of above event.

VAUGHAN, MARGARET SYMONDS. 1869-1925. United Kingdom.

012266   A CHILD OF THE ALPS. BY MARGARET SYMONDS.
London: T. F. Unwin, [1920] BMC NUC. New York: F.A.
Stokes, [1921] NUC.

TLS love story
ATH love story

VAUGHN, KATE (BREW). 1874-1933. United States.

012267   YET SHE LOVED HIM. BY MRS. KATE VAUGHN.
New York: R. Bonner's Sons, [1894] NUC. (Bound with
Jepthah's Daughter by Julia Magruder.)

PW-First story:Capt. St. John tries to rid himself of
a low-bred wife. Second story: founded on Hebrew
history.

VEITCH, SOPHIE FRANCES FANE.

012268   MARGARET DRUMMOND, MILLIONAIRE. London:
A. & C. Black, 1893 BMC.

ATH 103:176. Comes into money. She is high-spirited,
chivalrous. Novel is an indictment of the narrowness

and hypocrisy of Scottish clericalism.
Scotland. How she came to Moyle island and her
million. How she uses it for so many great purposes.
And then how she turns over control of it to husband
at the end. SP 71 688
The strifes and petty warfare of inhabitants of remote
island, property of Marg. Almost the whole book
devoted to her efforts to help the people, budgeting
etc. SR 16 571
She's self sufficent, determined to be a model
proprietor "Her powers of mind, her seriousness, her
information were altogether abnormal." BKM 5:58

012269   A MODERN CRUSADER. London: A. and C.
Black, 1895 BMC.

Arthur Reid minister saw woman die from drink, refuses
a legacy from a man who earned his wealth from alcohol
sales. Loses a woman because he gave up the legacy.
She married someone else but grows coarse. SR 80:694
Murder, suicide, depravity, revenge, all ills follow
the train of whiskey. ATH 106:867
SP 76:307. Purpose novel, but what purpose? There are
people who drink, but she is contemptuous of the
teetotalers. Crusader is Arthur Reid, a clergyman; he
is a prig.

VELY, E., pseud. See SIMON, EMMA (COUVELY).

VENN, MRS. See VENN, SUSANNA CARNEGIE.

VENN, SUSANNA CARNEGIE. Nationality Unknown.

012270   THE HUSBAND OF ONE WIFE. BY MRS. VENN.
London: Hurst and Blackett, 1894 BMC NUC.

SP 72:723. Psychological study of Victoria Goldenour,
wife of Dr. Garfoyle, bishop, "her kaleidoscopic moods
and contradictions." "He strives to save the wilful,
beautiful woman from herself; and he, "though he fails
in his purpose, never fails in the protecting love
which prompted it."
ACAD 45:471. Married 3 times. First died, then Dr.
Garfoyle (twice her age) then? Happy in her 1st and
3rd marriages.
ATH 103:609. Versatile character without a tinge of
coarseness. Third marriage to unimaginative but
unselfish agriculturist.
LW 25:302. Untactfully tells 3rd husband that "the"
husband was the 2nd, the real child of her heart was
child of her 1st husband.
PW-happy in her 3rd marriage.

012271   SOME MARRIED FELLOWS. BY THE AUTHOR OF
"THE DAILYS OF SODDEN FEN" [ANONYMOUS]. London: R.
Bentley, 1893 BMC.

University life. Contrast of two male types;
Chevington Applewood is selfless. Randal Keltridge is
morbid. Randal makes Helen miserable though his
intention is to make her happy. And we know
Chevington's character through his relationship to
Margaret. SP 70:395.
Helen's marriage is miserable. Because she's
intelligent, her husband suggests she take courses and
she does well. Tries philosophy because her
relationship is not meaningful. He leaves her, returns
after two years, but she's through. At very end united
at her brother's funeral. SR 75:182

VERA, pseud. See BERNSTEIN, HENNY.

VER BECK, HANNA (RION). 1875-1924. United States.

012272   THE GARDEN IN THE WILDERNESS. BY A HERMIT
[ANONYMOUS]. New York: Baker and Taylor, 1909 NUC.

012273   THE SMILING ROAD. BY HANNA RION. New
York: E. J. Clode, [c1910] NUC.

Unlovely sordid poverty. NYT
Libby Trevelyan married; husband leaves her after
getting money from her grandfather. She makes a new
life, helps her neighbors, befriends a man and through
this friendship comes happiness. PW

VERDENAL, MRS. DOMINIQUE FRANCOIS. Nationality Unknown.

012274   "LADIES FIRST!" A NOVEL. London: G.
Routledge, 1896 BMC. New York: Home Pub. Co., [1896]
NUC.

PW 2-29-96. California. "Ladies First" being the motto
of Nat Halsted, who carries these sentiments out in
his daily life, even to the exclusion of business
interests.

VERDIER, MARGUERITE LOUISE. United States.

012275   TWO LITTLE MAIDS: A TALE OF SOUTH
FLORIDA; AND CONCHITA: A MEXICAN ROMANCE. New York: W.
L. Allison, [c1894] NUC.

VERMILYE, KATE (JORDAN). 1862-1926. United Kingdom.

012276   AGAINST THE WINDS. BY KATE JORDAN.
Boston: Little, Brown, 1919 NUC BMC. London:
Hutchinson, [1919] BMC.

wife sacrifices self to help husband who drinks. TLS
Naomi Tway leaves home when she learns mother is
"secretly interested in a house of ill fame." Spec
Marries commercial traveller who takes to drink. She
falls for a millionaire but story ends with her caring
for husband dying. LBKM
Analytical novel; "Southern girl of high ideals"
leaves her sordid home and battles poverty, of an
unsuitable marriage and of an overwhelming love. PW
Begins as typist in a flour mill-hungers for travel
and adventure learns her mother a prostitute leaves.
Drifts into marriage. Well drawn characters. NYT

012277   A CIRCLE IN THE SAND. BY KATE JORDAN
(MRS. F. M. VERMILYE). Boston, and London: Lamson,
Wolffe, 1898 NUC.

Two women: one a journalist "awakened" writes a book.
The other all pink & white femininity and radiant
selfishness. Editor (male) becomes comrades with the
first, marries the second thinking she'll make the
best wife. But she fails miserably, goes on
stage-fails at that-dies after deserting husband. He
then turns to the journalist who "refuses to accept
the remains." BKM 9:186.
Anne Garrick-a new woman. LW 30:75.
Anne Garrick is a new woman, a journalist. Happy
mixture of the feminine and mental vigor. Loves a man
who disappoints her when he comes under the spell of a
flirt. He is a man of the world--equal to her in all
ways. She gets over him. Then loves a weaker man. This
relationship works out better. LW 30:75.
The streets, slums, drawing rooms of a great city.
"Young broad-minded professional woman at her desk in
the editorial office of a great daily." Episodes
include a miners' strike. PW 55:251.
"Anne Garrick, the heroine and successful woman
journalist, devoted to her calling, happy amid the
whirl and tension of a working life in a great city,
strong and self reliant, yet beautiful withal, and
intensely sympathetic, is an interesting but somewhat
idealized type of the awakened woman." Contrast to her
petted society beauty of a cousin-Olga. Loved by man
who wants an equal as lover but doesn't want her
messing in world affairs. He yields to a selfish, cold
woman. NYT 2-18-99,101.

012278   THE CREEPING TIDES, A ROMANCE OF AN OLD
NEIGHBORHOOD. BY KATE JORDAN. Boston: Little, Brown,
1913 NUC. London: S. Paul, [1915] BMC.

absorbing mystery-NYT
"Greenwich Village, that quaint backwater of New York,
is the setting for this story. To this haven drifts
John Cross, an English soldier concealing a shattered
reputation, and Fanny Barrett, hiding from an
obsessing terror. How the tides of exposure overwhelm
these two and how they finally won to peace and safety
make an interesting tale." PW 5-10-13:168.
Hero and young woman have reason to fear detection,
await the creeping tides of exposure. ATH

012279   THE NEXT CORNER. New York: Harper, 1920
PW. Boston: Little, Brown, 1921 NUC.

PW-Unfaithful wife is separated from Spanish lover
when the father of a woman he has ruined shoots him.
Returns to unknowning husband but lives in fear of
discovery.

012280   THE OTHER HOUSE: A STUDY OF HUMAN NATURE.
BY KATE JORDAN. New York: Lovell, Coryell, [c1892].

CR 18:274. An MD whose greatest success is with female
criminals is in love with woman next door. One night
she stands outside his window and confesses her life
story to him.
LW 23:375. He is married, falls "desperately in love
with a young woman of most 'shady' antecedents. He
ends in Molokai with death by "self-invoked" leprosy.
Marian is left to "lifetime of unavailing regret."

012281   TIME THE COMEDIAN. BY KATE JORDAN.

London: D. Appleton, 1905 BMC NUC.

woman is about to desert husband and child, man with
whom she is to elope learns the husband killed self on
hearing of her plan. Man refuses to marry her, gives
her an allowance, comes to love her daughter, but his
old letters to the woman keep him and the daughter
apart. BRD.

VERMILYE, MRS. F. M. See VERMILYE, KATE (JORDAN).

VERY, LYDIA LOUISA ANNA. 1823-1901. United States.

012282   A STRANGE DISCOURSE: A TALE OF NEW
ENGLAND LIFE. Boston: J. H. Earle, [c1898] NUC.

012283   A STRANGE RECLUSE; OR, YE DID IT UNTO ME.
[Salem, Mass.]: [Salem Press], [1899] NUC.

012284   SYLPH; OR, THE ORGAN-GRINDER'S DAUGHTER.
Boston: J. H. Earle, 1898 NUC.

VESELITSKAIA, LIDIIA IVANOVNA. 1857-1936.

012285   MIMI'S MARRIAGE. BY V. MIKOULITCH.
London: T. F. Unwin, [1915] BMC NUC. (Tr. from the
Russian by C. Hagberg Wright. "Eng. trans. first pub.
in 1893; second impression, 1915" NUC.)

LEKM 6:160. Brainless girl brought up to marry a rich
husband. Soulless stupidity. Vava grows into an
idealist, has a soul, thought of writing to Tolstoi.
"Sordid type of literature" Harmless but amusing
adventures of apretty young woman married to elderly
man. ATH

VIEBIG, CLARA. See COHN, CLARA (VIEBIG).

VILA, ANNIE FIELDS. B. 1844. United States.

012286   THE FORMER COUNTESS; A ROMANCE OF THE
FRENCH REVOLUTION. Boston: Sherman, French, 1912 NUC.

"Story of the French Revolution. Heroine is the young
Countess of Navarre, widowed through the malignity of
one of the Jacobins, who has planned to secure her for
himself. She and her family including her brother, the
Duke de Beaumont, and Chabert, his secretary, a man of
unusual charm and character, are obliged to seek
safety in flight. Before starting on their journey,
the Countess yields to Chabert's wishes, and his years
of devotion and marries him. Many trials are met and
overcome before the tale ends." PW

012287   INHERITED FREEDOM; DEDICATED TO THE
DAUGHTERS OF THE REVOLUTION IN AMERICA, THE D. R. AND
THE D. A. R. WRITTEN BY A DAUGHTER [ANONYMOUS].
Boston: W. B. Clarke, [c1905] NUC.

VILLARI, LINDA (WHITE) MAZINI. 1836-1915.

012288   EUROPEAN RELATIONS: A TIROLESE SKETCH. BY
TALMAGE DALIN. London: T. F. Unwin, 1891 BMC. New
York: Cassell, [c1891] NUC.

Sojourn among Australian Alps and a romance of Natalie
Berg. Acad
American family in Europe visiting relatives.
Difference between two sets of people. American young
woman falls for European cousin who is contrasted to
American man.

VILLARS, MEG. United Kingdom.

012289   BETTY-ALL-ALONE. New York: E.J. Clode,
[c1914] NUC. London: G. Richards, 1914 NUC BMC.

Searches for a husband, drawn into bohemian life in
Paris, finally finds the right man. PW 2-6-15.
Brave, adventurous spirit, high animal spirits. Great
sense of humor, in search of the Golden Male, born
wealthy, left penniless goes to work, boldly seeks a
rich husband, takes a job in America as newspaper
artist, another as a companion, finds the right man.
PW

012290   THE BROKEN LAUGH. London: G. Richards,
1920 BMC. New York: R.M. McBride, 1920 NUC.

Kissy Milliner. The natural child of Russian
aristocracy. A seduction. Nothing promising TLS
SR-Kissy-girl is victimized by a scoundrel, spends a
year in a disreputable Parisian hostel, lives with man
claiming to be his wife. They are very happy. War
comes, German occupation, she is killed in air raid on
eve of wedding. Thesis that wife who has no legal

claim is more amiable.
NYT 11-7-20 She is illegitimate daughter of
illegitimate mother; seduced while still a child and
then a servant to women in a brothel. Author is
sympathetic to her, but Kissy, although she doesn't
feel wicked, she doesn't feel worthy of the man.

VINCENT, JOYCE.

012291   SELBRIDGE & CO. Sydney: MacCartie, 1903
NUC.

ATH 122:282

VIOLETTA.

012292   THE HEIR OF INGLESBY. BY VIOLETTA.
London: Sonnenschein, 1893 BMC.

Hero Rudalpho di Como: Mother English, father Italian,
orphaned, becomes artist. Then in England discovers
his inheritance, marries Gwendalyn. ACAD 44:412

VISGER, JEAN ALLEN (PINDER) OWEN. 1841-1922.

012293   LOVE COVERS ALL. A STORY FOR OLDER GIRLS.
London: R. T. S., [1910] BMC.

012294   RUTH THORNTON; OR, TWO GIRLS AND A
SUMMER. London: R. T. S., [1915] BMC.

VIVARIA, KASSANDRA, pseud. See SINDICI, MARIA MAGDA STUART.

VON CLAUSSEN, IDA. United States.

012295   FORGET IT. New York: Broadway, [c1910]
NUC.

VON ESCHSTRUTH, NATALY. B. 1860.

012296   COUNTESS DYNAR; OR POLISH BLOOD: A NOVEL.
New York: R. Bonner's Sons, [1894] NUC. (Tr. Cora
Louise Turner)

CR True love on an unsmooth course.
PW. Count Gustav Dyner adopts under peculiar
circumstances the son of a Polish refugee. Years later
his daughter, the countess, questions her father's
action and the right of the Pole to her family titles.

012297   THE ERL QUEEN. New York: Worthington,
1892 NUC. (Tr. Emily S. Howard)

CR 18:164. German romance between young woman and man
of lower rank who raises himself by winning fame in
the wars, ends in marriage.

012298   HER LITTLE HIGHNESS: A NOVEL. New York:
R. Bonner's Sons, [1894] NUC. (Tr. Elise L. Lathrop)

PW-Count, a widower, falls in love with princess the
same age as his son.

012299   A PRIESTESS OF COMEDY. New York: R.
Bonner, [1893] NUC. (Tr. Elise L. Lathrop)

Wants to win a position in the "comedy" of social
life. She's the daughter of a vulgar, newly ennobled
millionaire. First marr: husband wastes her money.
Second marr: her nature has changed; she wins
happiness and social recognition. Germany. PW 8-19-93

012300   A PRINCESS OF THE STAGE: A NOVEL. New
York: R. Bonner's Sons, [1894] NUC. (Tr. Elise L.
Lathrop)

PW-Romance. Misunderstanding brings about Prince
Gregory's death, focus shifts to his heir.

012301   THE WILD ROSE OF GROSS-STAUFFEN. New
York: Worthington, 1892 NUC.

CR 17:209 Country maiden snubbed by count gets revenge
and they finally marry.

VON GOLDAECKER, D.

012302   A BUTTERFLY. London: J. Long, 1907 BMC.

Foolish, clumsy butterfly ACAD
"Selfish little flirt" well drawn "crudity about the
treatment" TLS

VON HEYKING, ELISABETH AUGUSTE LUISE HELENE MELUSINE
MAXIMILIANE (VON FLEMMING). 1861-1925.

012303   THE LETTERS WHICH NEVER REACHED HIM
[ANONYMOUS]. London: E. Nash, 1904 BMC. New York: E.
P. Dutton, 1904 NUC.

BKM-Woman's husband is insane, she writes to man in
military who might have been her husband but both men
die before knowing--"revelation of unhappiness and
anxiety bordering on the morbid."

012304   LOVERS IN EXILE. BY THE AUTHOR OF "THE
LETTERS WHICH NEVER REACHED HIM" [ANONYMOUS]. London:
E. Nash, 1914 BMC NUC. New York: Dutton, 1915 NUC.

Attacks German aristocracy. Ilse marries middle aged
German aristocrat. A few years pass; she falls in love
with another man, secures a divorce. The husband uses
all his power to make his now divorced wife and her
new husband miserable. NYT
LBKM-love story. Ilse marries a Von Zehren,
primitively old-fashioned, cannot keep her
individuality, falls for Wolf Von Walden, divorces,
remarries. The Von Zehrens finally ruin his diplomatic
career.
ATH 144:246-In spite of persecution she is happy.

VON HILLERN, WILHELMINE (BIRCH). 1836-1916.

012305   ON THE CROSS: A ROMANCE OF THE PASSION
PLAY AT OBERAMMERGAU. New York: G.G. Peck, 1893 NUC.

Romance interwoven with events of the passion play. PW
12-9-93

VON HINDENBERG, AGNES BLANCHE MARIE (HAY). 1873-1938.
Europe.

012306   A GERMAN POMPADOUR: BEING THE
EXTRAORDINARY HISTORY OF WILHELMINE VON GRAVENITZ,
LANDHOFMEISTERIN OF WIRTEMBERG, A NARRATIVE OF THE
EIGHTEENTH CENTURY. BY MARIE HAY. London: A.
Constable, 1906 NUC BMC.

ACAD-Historical account of wicked woman Wilhelmine Von
Gravenitz.
Historical romance about a wife who "gathers into her
hands the reins of government." She's a mistress,
feared as a witch with hypnotic powers over men. Takes
over all the property-her court vied with the glories
of Versailles. Then the duke casts her off. She's
tried for treason, grasping land, witchcraft, bigamy,
attempted murder yet she is eventually pardoned, lives
out her days in her Swiss castle.

012307   MAS'ANIELLO, A NEAPOLITAN TRAGEDY. BY
MARIE HAY. London: Constable, 1913 BMC NUC. Leipzig:
B. Tauchnitz, 1921 NUC.

Neopolitan history before Masaniello's revolution
against Spain in 1647. ATH TLS

VON HUTTEN, BARONESS. See STOLZENBERG, BETSEY (RIDDLE) VON
HUTTEN ZUM.

VON HUTTEN, BETTINA. See STOLZENBERG, BETSEY (RIDDLE) VON
HUTTEN ZUM.

VON KRUSENSTJERNA, ADA. B. 1854.

012308   LOOKING HEAVENWARD. London: R. T. S.,
[1910] BMC. (Tr. from the German by A. Duncan Dodds.)

VON SCYLER, CATHERINE, pseud. See SMITH, ANNIE LAURA.

VON SUTTNER, BERTHA FELICIE SOPHIE (KINSKY). 1843-1914.
Germany.

012309   "GROUND ARMS!" THE STORY OF A LIFE, A
ROMANCE OF EUROPEAN WAR. Chicago: A. C. McClurg, 1892
NUC. (Tr. from the German by Alice Asbury Abbott)

LW 23:213. Journal form. Begins with the journalist's
belief in the "grandeur" of war. She marries a
soldier, lives through a war (her husband is killed)
and "then out of her personal suffering questions the
justification of any war." Marrying again, she is once
more affected by war, and after her husband is shot,
falsely accused of being a spy, she spends rest of her
life working for international arbitration.
CR 17:314. Emphasis on the need for education for
women, "if the highest degree of civilization is to be
attained.= "Crusade against war," "claim of every
human being to the ownership and control of his own
life."
NYT-young woman daughter of general educated to war
and frustrated that "laurels of the battleground" are
denied her sex, marries young military officer; war

comes, she becomes a passionate advocate of peace.

012310   LAY DOWN YOUR ARMS; THE AUTOBIOGRAPHY OF
MARTHA VON TILLING. London: Longmans, 1892 BMC. New
York: Longmans, 1894 NUC. (Tr. by T. Holmes)

See Ground Arms
Remarkable book written and published in Germany.
Argument vs. war and the false ideas of patriotism in
first part; in second illustrations of horrors of war
in Germany and Austria. ATH 97 373

012311   WHEN THOUGHTS WILL SOAR; A ROMANCE OF THE
IMMEDIATE FUTURE. BY BARONESS BERTHA VON SUTTNER.
London: Constable, 1914 BMC. Boston: Houghton Mifflin,
1914 NUC. (Tr. Nathan Haskell Dole.)

Franka devotes herself to the uplift of woman and even
refuses a prince for the lover who shares her ideals.
PW 85:6/17/14:2027

VON TEUFFEL, BLANCHE WILLIS (HOWARD). 1847-1898. United
States.

012312   A BATTLE AND A BOY. BY BLANCHE WILLIS
HOWARD. New York: Tait, [1892] NUC. London: W.
Heinemann, 1894 BMC.

012313   DIONYSIUS THE WEAVER'S HEART'S DEAREST.
BY BLANCHE WILLIS HOWARD. New York: C. Scribner's
Sons, 1899 NUC.

Nelka says: "I cannot dig, to beg I am ashamed. I have
not learned to work. I am too cowardly to die...it is
a monstrous thing that girls are left so blind." BKM
10:384
Entered service of a Countess, becomes disciple of a
French Chef, betrayed by a valet, weds a postman. SP
83:790
She is a wild child, very bright, becomes a
professional cook. Enters Countess von Vallade's
household. Compared with Nelka, both 18, the Countess'
daughter. Nelka marries a man she doesn't love. Vroni
does not marry the father of her two children. When he
offers her marriage, she learns he's been false to her
and refuses him. BKM 10:384
ATH 115:618. Sad story of country girl in area of the
Danube.

012314   THE GARDEN OF EDEN. BY BLANCHE WILLIS
HOWARD. New York: C. Scribner's Sons, 1900 BMC NUC.
Toronto: C. Clarke, 1900 BMC.

The long-talked-of new woman.
NYT 1900:290. Monica deeply loves first one married
man, then another. Obviously Mme. v.T.'s aim is to
show a modern misconception of the 7th commandment, to
prove, in spite of the long established acceptance of
the contrary truth, that platonic love is not a mere
idle phrase, but a living fact that ought to be
recognized. CR 37:278. Protest against the world as it
is, against cruelty to the superfine and
supersensitive. Moral is one should accept suffering
undismayed. PW-question of divorce finds much
consideration. BKM 11-589. Lachrymose. Monica loves a
married man. Her mother, anti-divorce, persuades her
to leave the country. She later falls for another man
who brings her added sorrow.

012315   NO HEROES. BY BLANCHE WILLIS HOWARD.
Boston: Houghton Mifflin, 1893 NUC. London: Gay and
Bird, 1894 BMC.

ACAD 46:210. For boys-a boy hero.

012316   VRONI, THE WEAVER'S HEART'S DEAREST. BY
BLANCHE WILLIS HOWARD. London: F. Warne, 1899 BMC.

VOYNICH, E. L. See VOYNICH, ETHEL LILLIAN (BOOLE).

VOYNICH, ETHEL LILLIAN (BOOLE). 1864-1960. United Kingdom.

012317   THE GADFLY. BY E. L. VOYNICH. London: W.
Heinemann, 1897 BMC. New York: H. Holt, 1897 NUC.

SP 81:474. Very strong meat. We are doubtful about
recommending it to our readers. Tragic story of young
Italy. Relationship of Arthur Burton and Montanelli,
director of a Seminary, Bishop and Cardinal.
SR 85:88. Character of the Gadfly is incomprehensible.
Bkgd struggles of young Italy. Focus on the Gadfly, a
man of tremendous influence, a conspirator and
pamphleteer. It is his own father the Cardinal who
must virtually condemn his son to death at the point
they are reunited. The Gadfly wrote about the demands
of human beings more important than those of god. LBKM

13:22
Arthur Burton arrested for conspiring against Italian
government, imprisoned. Free he learns government got
information through priest to whom he confessed. Gemma
believes him to be a traitor to the cause she is
devoted to also, strikes him, gives him up. At same
time he learns he's illegitimate. Feigns suicide,
leaves for S. America. 13 years later returns
disguised as foe of church.
As Gadfly writes against Jesuits for Liberal party.
Gemma on the committee of the party. His father is now
a Cardinal and his enemy, but he loves him. ACAD
52:Fic. Sup. 74.
Zita who was his mistress and who abandoned him out of
jealousy of Gemma--a masculine character. CR 28,31:73

012318   AN INTERRUPTED FRIENDSHIP. BY E. L.
VOYNICH. London: Hutchinson, 1910 BMC. New York:
Macmillan, 1910 NUC.

LBKM-Gadfly, guide of South American Expedition, is
suspicious of others, although most of those in his
party become his devoted friends. 1 introduces him to
his crippled sister, she proffers her affection, but
his incurable suspicion prevents him from responding.
Tragedy.
BKM v.31 1910 Crippled girl in love.
TLS- friendship between Italian revolutionary and son
of marquis on an expedition in S. America.
ATH the girl undergoes an operation and is no longer
crippled, then she is run over and permanently
crippled. Gadfly through a misunderstanding refuses
her love.
SP
NYT 0
Lame girl, devoted brother and his friend in
S.America. Strong friendship. She becomes hard and
morbid. They discuss many social problems. PW

012319   JACK RAYMOND. BY E. L. VOYNICH. London:
W. Heinemann, 1901 BMC. Philadelphia: J. B.
Lippincott, 1901 NUC.

Woman gives up all for artist. Saccharine,
sentimental. ACAD 01
ATH-not much here either. 5-25-01

012320   OLIVE LATHAM. BY E. L. VOYNICH.
Philadelphia: J.B. Lippincott, 1904 NUC. London: W.
Heinemann, 1904 BMC.

NYT-heroic nature.
ATH-Russia-a female genius and her children
suppressed. At last is in England where she hovers on
borderline of insanity. Horrors.
TLS-nurse goes to Russia to take care of her
consumptive lover; she is dragged through months of
mental agony by his arrest and death in prison.
Chilling horror, perfect writing.

VYNNE, NORA. D. 1914. United Kingdom.

012321   THE BLIND ARTIST'S PICTURES AND OTHER
STORIES. London: Jarrold, 1893 BMC NUC.

012322   A COMEDY OF HONOUR. London: Ward, Lock
and Bowden, 1895 BMC NUC.

Witty: "delightful people are bound to come well out
of their scrapes" ACAD 48:542
ATH 107:50. Nautilus Series. A quartet of lovers, one
with an overstrained conscience, exemplifying various
standards of honor. Does not become tragedy.
SP 76:898. Lois steals Nellie's lover.
He decides to marry Millie; Lois and he can't give
each other up. They go to talk to Nellie; she has
married Fayne.

012323   HONEY OF ALOES, AND OTHER STORIES.
London: Ward, Lock and Bowden, 1894 BMC NUC.

012324   A MAN AND HIS WOMANKIND. London:
Hutchinson, 1895 BMC NUC.

"man is that ridiculous monstrous school-boy which so
delights the feminine heart" but "the humanity of his
womankind more than allows for his impossibility." SR
80:555
Ends in the middle. Dick Cedicsson demonstrates his
manhood. ACAD 48:292
Young man and his wife and the first few months of
their marriage-recommended to "heart-sick readers of
the modern novel." LW 26:428
very young man marries woman older who for years
earned her living as journalist. She has no taste for
housework-leaves all that to mother-in-law and

sister-in-law. PW 10-26-95:711
SP 76:114. The Cedicssons. A mother-in-law who knits
stockings a daughter-in-law who writes "analytic"
novels; both spoil the husband and do their best to
conceal from him the fact that he has a scandalous
father. They study themselves, Dick, and Irene, Dick's
"self-tormenting" sister. At one point Dick flares out
against their self-martyrdoms.
BKM 2:938. we are left not knowing what happened when
Dick found his old hair brush.

012325   THE PIECES OF SILVER. London: Melrose,
1911 BMC.

    Beatrice Stallingway is a woman's rights person. She
    and a man set out to reform the world. TLS
    Beatrice's fortunate escape from Giles Brodrick cheers
    the reader. LBKM
    "Clever and sanely conceived feminist novel."
    Heroine-hard working journalist and politician. ATH

012326   THE PRIEST'S MARRIAGE. London: T.
Burleigh, 1899 BMC. New york and London: Putnam, 1900
NUC.

    Almost all dialogue; title states the subject clearly.
    LIT 5:571
    "Is an ex-priest or a girl like Annie Fulton?" The
    riddle is solved by experiment. ACAD 57:574
    She marries the renegade priest. The wife retains our
    sympathy and interest to the last. ATH 114:797
    LW 31:139. Renounces his vows first, marries and
    becomes a Protestant layman. Happy at first, then
    periods swinging between passion and rejection. Then a
    return to his monastery, refusing her letters. She has
    a child and takes steps for a legal separation. On the
    last evening of the period allowed by the law for his
    return, he comes back. But she no longer loves him and
    so he goes back to monastery. He is in turn
    affectionate and repelled by her, believing as he does
    that love is fleshly, base. She's distrbed by this
    attitude.

012327   SO IT IS WITH THE DAMSEL. London: S.
Paul, 1913 BMC.

    A campaign versus social evils: white slave traffic,
    but with a happy ending. ATH
    A tract on White Slavery trade. Horrors of secret
    trade in South America. Young woman from middle class
    London. In the end, she escapes her bondage, meets up
    with the 2 agents of her flight.

012328   THE STORY OF A FOOL AND HIS FOLLY.
London: Hutchinson, [1896] BMC.

    "Record in repulsiveness" Mrs. Craigh's invalid
    husband wants to set her free to join her
    clerk-lover-though she fears her lover won't risk
    losing his job. Therefore, she arranges to compromise
    herself to get a divorce, but husband dies anyway. SR
    83:129
    ATH 108:417. Pair of plotting and self-interested
    lovers. Base characters, particularly George Abbott.
    Mrs. Craigh has Anthony in her thrall, she is
    monstrous yet human. Painful.
    ACAD 50:346. A very foolish hero. "Altho book is a
    failure, N.V. shows every sign of becoming the best
    woman writer since the too brief career of Emily
    Bronte."

VYSE, MAUD J.

    012329   A MODERN ATALANTA; AND OTHER STORIES.
    London: Kegan Paul, [1897] BMC.

WADSLEY, LUCY ELLEN.

    012330   BLUE BLOOD AND RED. London: E. Stock,
    1903 BMC.

    012331   THE LADY ALGIVE. A TALE OF PRIESTCRAFT.
    London: Digby, Long, 1902 BMC.

WADSLEY, OLIVE. D. 1859. United Kingdom.

    012332   BELONGING. A NOVEL. London and New York:
    Cassell, [1920] NUC.

    TLS-Sara Desanges, a widow, and two lovers, Julian and
    Charles. Charles is killed, Sara goes to a year's
    imprisonment.
    SP-Crime was committed by someone else, Julian?
    Account of her feelings under solitary confinement.
    NYT 9-26-20 p. 24. Low moral tone.

012333   CONQUEST. London: Cassell, 1915 BMC. New
York: Dodd, Mead, 1917 NUC.

    Love and prize fighting . TLS
    Story of a prize fighter . Scene in Paris and New
    York. PW
    Story begins when he's 10; concerns his "conquest of
    his work and of the woman he loves." NYT 10-7-17 389

012334   THE FLAME. London and New york: Cassell,
1914 BMC NUC.

    London slums, Paris schools, Italy-through all of it
    runs this flame-child of aristocratic and drunken
    parents. At 18 she's a mistress of a 40 year old man,
    later an assistant in a Paris magasin, then a
    celebrated caricaturist, finally a staid married
    woman-after a brief passionate episode with an Oxford
    youth. ATH.
    Toni Saumarez, mistress to man whose wife is mad. Rise
    of Toni, her career as famous Parisian caricaturist,
    marr. TLS
    PW Toni, from London slums, is not pretty but
    fascinating. Love comes but lover dies changing her
    life. She becomes a famous newspaper cartoonist in
    Paris, love comes again and brings her career to a
    close.
    NYT-Mother and father were incurable drunkards, raised
    by uncle after their deaths until he died and she was
    17. "The men who loved Toni were curiously negligent
    in the respect of providing for her future." "The
    book, like the heroine, is of the entirely emotional
    type."

012335   FRAILTY: A NOVEL. London and New York:
Cassell, [1917] BMC NUC.

    TLS Male hero-gypsy to millionaire; wife is an
    alcoholic.
    Husband, a reformed drug taker discovers after a few
    months of happy marriage that his young wife is an
    alcoholic. His disgust exaggerates her problem. But
    finally they make a joint effort to overcome their
    failings. LBKM

012336   INSTEAD. London: Cassell, 1919 BMC NUC.

    Annuzjata her loves and friendships in London and
    Europe. Overdone romance concerns a beautiful and
    talented male. TLS
    Becomes a waitress in Brazil. SP

012337   NEVERTHELESS. London: Cassell, 1918 BMC.

    TLS-Spoiled brat of a hero falls for woman 12 yrs his
    senior. He wishes to marry her, Viola makes excuse
    that her age would hamper their relation later on.
    Asks that they dispense with marriage. John believes
    her husband still alive. Later he discovers he is not
    and his career is threatened by scandal.
    ATH Hero is not worthy of sacrifices
    LBKM He takes all the two woman have to give and
    returns so little

012338   POSSESSION. London: Cassell, 1916 BMC.
New York: Dodd, Mead, 1917 NUC.

    TLS- rom.

    Valerie Sartin. Love Story of a London waif who grows
    into "a figure of romance and tragedy" BKM
    loved by several men. The book ends happily but
    "Valerie disappoints us" because of her flirtations
    and her indifference to her Child. NYT 89 3-11-17

012339   REALITY. London: Cassell, 1914 BMC.

    ATH Heroine at 18 was married to old man whom she
    loathed. Second marriage to vain and selfish musician.
    ATH 144;98. Tragedy of 2nd mrg.
    TLS 13:298

WAGGAMAN, MARY TERESA MACKEE. 1846-1931. United States.

    012340   CAPTAIN TED. New York: Benziger, 1910
    NUC.

    012341   CARROLL DARE. New York: Benziger, 1903
    NUC.

    His heroism in Revolutionary War 11-21-03 PW

    012342   CORINNE'S VOW. New York: Benziger, 1902
    NUC.

    --for Catholic readers.

012343   ERIC; OR, THE BLACK FINGER. Philadelphia:
H.L. Kilner, [c1910] NUC.

012344   GRAPES OF THORNS; A NOVEL. New York:
Benziger, 1917 NUC.

    PW 91:1279 4/21/17

012345   LISBETH; THE STORY OF A FIRST COMMUNION.
New York: P.J. Kenedy, [c1914] NUC.

    PZ 3

012346   NAN NOBODY. New York: Benziger, 1901 NUC.

012347   SANDY JOE. New York: Benziger, 1916 NUC.

012348   THE SECRET OF POCOMOKE. Notre Dame, Ind:
Ave Maria Press, [c1914] NUC.

012349   SHIPMATES. New York: Benziger, 1914 NUC.

    PW 86 11/14/14:1575-"Pip, a twelve year old boy, at
death's door in the city, is transferred by Judy, the
faithful maid, to a shack on the shore. Here he
regains his health and finds a friend in Roving Bob, a
lad of mystery."

012350   STRONG-ARM OF AVALON. New York: Benziger,
1904 NUC.

    PW historical novel.

012351   WHITE EAGLE. Nortre Dame, Ind.: Ave Maria
Press, [c1915] NUC.

WAGNALLS, MABEL. B. 1871. United States.

012352   MISERERE (A MUSICAL STORY). New York,
London: Funk and Wagnalls, 1892 NUC.

    PW-Heroine is a nun and a singer, becomes engaged to a
man with a tragic past which catches up with him.

012353   THE PALACE OF DANGER. A STORY OF LA
POMPADOUR. New York: Funk & Wagnall, 1908 NUC. London:
J. Long, [1909] BMC.

    PW-historical romance.
    NYT-historical romance.
    Hist tale of French Court TLS

012354   THE ROSE-BUSH OF A THOUSAND YEARS. New
York and London: Funk & Wagnall, 1918 BMC NUC.

    PW-religion & fallen woman.
    NYT-June 30, 1918. Artist's model turns to life of
toil and spiritual redemption.

WAGNER, BELLE M. United States.

012355   WITHIN THE TEMPLE OF ISIS. Denver:
Astro-philosophical Pub. Co., 1899 NUC.

WAINEMAN, PAUL, pseud. See MACDOUGALL, SYLVIA (BORGSTROM).

WAIT, FRONA EUNICE, pseud. See COLBURN, FRONA EUNICE WAIT
(SMITH).

WAITE, LUCY. United States.

012356   DOCTOR HELEN RAND. BY LOIS WRIGHT.
Chicago: physicians' Pub. Co., 1891 NUC.

WAKEFORD, MRS. T. M.

012357   A SOUTH AFRICAN HEIRESS. London: J. Long,
1913 BMC.

    Capetown Colonial love story; Florence heroine makes a
foolish marriage; realizes later she loves another
man. "writing is poor" ATH
    Difficulties of marriage in trite manner TLS

WAKEMAN, ANNIE. See LATHROP, ANNIE WAKEMAN.

WAKEMAN, ANTOINETTE PRUDENCE (VAN HOESEN). B. 1856. United
States.

012358   QUESTIONS OF CONSCIENCE: A NOVEL. BY
ANTOINETTE VAN HOESEN. Chicago, New York: G. M. Hill,
[c1900] NUC.

WAKLEY, ALINE A.

012359   A SON OF HELVETIA. A NOVEL. London:
Greening, 1907 BMC.

    Melodrama: an "imbecile heroine" ACAD
    Loveless marriage, separation, marries again. TLS

WALCH, CAROLINE C. Nationality Unknown.

012360   DOCTOR SPHINX: A NOVEL. New York: F. T.
Neely, [c1898] NUC.

    "Impressions and experience of young woman who is
making her way in the world without influential
friends and under the dual disability of lack of
training and an unusual amount of morbid
conscientiousness." BKM 9:186

WALFORD, L. B. See WALFORD, LUCY BETHIA (COLQUHOUN).

WALFORD, LUCY BETHIA (COLQUHOUN). 1845-1915. United
Kingdom.

012361   THE ARCHDEACON. BY L. B. WALFORD. London:
C. A. Pearson, 1898 BMC. New York: Longmans, 1899 NUC.

    Set in three views of Theo Yorke; first as undergrad
and his first meeting with a young woman; then as
Archdeacon; then as a simple parish priest. The young
woman reappears as a widow. At the end they marry. LIT
4:153.
    She is Irene Ravelston. She wanted society. Hero bred
for the church is full of high purpose. A day's events
changes all, becomes worldly, self-satisfied.
Reawakens in mid-life. NYT 2-18-99,100

012362   THE BLACK FAMILIARS. BY L. B. WALFORD.
London: J. Clarke, 1903 BMC NUC. New York: Longmans,
Green, 1903 PW.

    Mother hates her only daughter because her ambitions
for her husband had turned him to his daughter for
comradeship. First she plans a marriage for her
daughter; causes a rumor that her daughter is guilty
of heresy (time is the reformation), plot discovered,
commits suicide. NYT 03, 985

012363   A BUBBLE: A STORY. BY L. B. WALFORD.
Westminster: A. Constable, 1895 BMC. New York: F. A.
Stokes, [c1895] NUC.

    Genius named Dirom and General Manleverer's daugher SR
79:733
    LW 27:76. Heroine and two suitors, painful ending.
CR 29:58.

012364   CELIA: AND THE PARENTS. London: T.
Nelson, [1910] BMC.

012365   CHARLOTTE. London and New York: Longmans,
1902 BMC NUC.

    Coquette who meets a just fate NYT 4-26-02

012366   DAVID AND JONATHAN ON THE RIVIERA.
London: Methuen, 1914 BMC.

    TLS reverend and his friends.

012367   THE ENLIGHTENMENT OF OLIVIA. BY L. B.
WALFORD. New York and London: Longmans, Green, 1907
NUC BMC.

    Learns to appreciate her less intell. husband. No deep
psychol study. Olivia of wayward charm and
"spoilt-child fancies" human couple TLS
    Olivia "that dreary wind-bag of a woman" vacillates
between duty and pleasure. She's "anemic" "The book
may 'run through' innumberable' editions, it may
spread a virus of discontent in thousands of childish
minds." SR
    Olivia has literary tastes, comtempt for her
neighbors. She's indifferent to public-opinion
"awakened to her true position in the world and to her
husband."? BKM

012368   FREDERICK. BY L. B. WALFORD. London:
Smith, Elder, 1895 BMC. New York & London: Macmillan,
1895 NUC.

    LBKM 10:163. Loveable, aimless, idle eccentric hero.
Got up early one morning as a preliminary to extensive
reform.
    SR - A loveable fool.
    ATH He is taken in hand by "little" Ally.

012369   THE INTRUDERS. London and New York:

Longmans, 1898 BMC NUC.

SP 81:494. Country society a la Hungerford.
ACAD 55:29. Julian and Amelia, brother and sister, lived together for years. Then his marriage.
A quiet country town and the arrival of a young rich man. Also a sister completely devoted to her brother Julian Monteagle and "Molly's chilly marriage and early death." LIT 4:153.

012370   IVA KILDARE: A MATRIMONIAL PROBLEM.
London and New York: Longmans, 1897 BMC NUC.

Matrimonial schemes of a warm-hearted Irish widow. SP 79:692.
She and Reggie Goffe discover they love each other-on the night he's to leave for India. Meantime she's wooed by an ex business man wealthy Mr. Druitt. When Druitt learns on Reggie's return that Iva loves Reggie he gives them a fine manor. And Lady Tilbury proposes to Druitt who becomes her third husband. "Delightful." ACAD 52. Fic Sup 107.
SR 85:369. Devotion to the pursuit of lovemaking. Mother of heroine offers herself in marriage to disappointed suitors of her daughter.

012371   LEDDY MARGET. BY L. B. WALFORD. London, New York: Longmans, 1898 BMC NUC.

SP 80:832. Lovable unconventional old woman, climbing apple trees at 80.
ATH 112:190. Charitable to her neighbors. Pathetic piety of her peaceful end.
NYT 1898:492. Past 80, physically perfect, has a heart of gold, and lives to shower benefits on others. Dies and rises to heaven as a saint.

012372   LEONORE STUBBS. BY L. B. WALFORD. London and New York: Longmans, Green, 1908 BMC NUC.

Left a widow, penniless, returns home. Believed to be wealthy, she is pursued by suitors, finally marries rich man. BKM NYT
PW-Young Widow
TLS- "Dom. love story"
SR-A widow at 21, penniless, thrown back to her father who assumes her life is over. She resents his attitude
BKM-Two sisters still at home- She falls for one engaged to her sister. Her "moves are diagonal, not straightforward".
ATH conclusion is out of harmony with the beginning.
BKM-her father insists she keep her poverty a secret. She marries a rich man her father had picked out for one of her sisters.

012373   THE MATCHMAKER, A NOVEL. BY L. B. WALFORD. London, New York: Longmans, Green, 1894 NUC BMC.

SR 78:440. Matchmaking heroine, with suitable match for herself at end. The Carnousties spoil the existence of two of their daughters and destroy the third.
SP 73:850. Brave heroine.
ACAD: Mina, the youngest daughter, pays for her love affair with her life.
ATH 104:787. "A tale of domestic repression and its disastrous consequences. Though Mrs. Walford is probably the last person in the world who would consciously harbour such an aim, her description of the Carnoustie household is calculated to place a premium on filial revolt as compared with submission."
CR 25:328. Penelope is trying to make a match between Mina and Redwood, but Mina loves a Highlander. He misunderstands and in jealous rage shoots at couple killing Mina, then kills himself. Mrs. Carnoustie goes mad. Penelope marries Redwood.

012374   THE MISCHIEF OF MONICA. BY L. B. WALFORD. New York: J. W. Lovell, [1891] NUC. London: Longmans, 1891 BMC.

She's always witty, brilliant, sometimes willful. Background whole social world of balls and marriages and efforts to climb social ladder: LW
Monica Lavenham is noble, but worldly training has warped her. Heartlessly sets out to rob Daisy Schofield's lover-but sees what she's done; her character is transformed. ACAD Well written

012375   THE ONE GOOD GUEST: A NOVEL. BY L. B. WALFORD. London, New York: Longmans, Green, 1892 BMC NUC.

ATH 100:415. a family party.
CR 7-16-92 p 30. Four children, the oldest 21,

determine to live together with "such decorum and propriety" that no one can say that they need an older person's supervision. They do so, author sympathetic to them. Story is of a house party they give.

012376   ONE OF OURSELVES. BY L. B. WALFORD. London and New York: Longmans, 1900 BMC NUC.

ATH 90:754. Trio of vivacious girls in the modern key.
SP 85:937. Three impecunious orphan sisters, one almost makes a bigamous marriage, is resued by an actress and weds a peer

012377   A PINCH OF EXPERIENCE. BY L. B. WALFORD. London: Methuen, 1891 BMC. New York: J. W. Lovell, [1891] NUC.

Rhoda is a spoiled child. When she is bored in her country surroundings, her mother sends her to London. We read of her experiences in Cleaveland Square. PW
CR 17:182 Rhoda, American girl, visits ill lot of relations in England, is finally rescued by parents from their schemes.
ACAD 41:84. She is daughter of English squire, insists on visiting branch of family in London, is disillusioned by their vulgarity.

012378   "PLOUGHED", AND OTHER STORIES. London and New york: Longmans, 1894 BMC NUC.

SP-religious conversion of hero.

012379   A QUESTION OF PENMANSHIP: STORIES. BY L. B. WALFORD. London: Griffith, Farran, 1893 BMC NUC.

012380   SIR PATRICK: THE PUDDOCK. BY L. B. WALFORD. London: C. A. Pearson, 1899 BMC. New York: Longmans, Green, 1899 NUC.

He is homely; heroine has no brains--just looks, money and a friendly manner. He's a Scotch Baronet. SP 83:919
LIT 6:190. Romance between plain unstylish Sophy Gill and ugly-looking hero. Ireland.

012381   STAR. London: T. Nelson, 1911 BMC.

012382   STAY-AT-HOMES. BY L. B. WALFORD. London: Longmans, 1903 BMC.

Three daughters of an upper-class secluded family PW 7-18-03
Daughter of 27 sent to her romm for allowing a young man to join her in a walk? NYT 03,467
Study of influence of environment on char. of three women. A sprightly woman of 50. +TLS, 160,03

012383   SUCCESSORS TO THE TITLE. BY L. B. WALFORD. London: Methuen, 1896 BMC. New York: D. Appleton, 1896 NUC.

ATH 107:60. Young couple find themselves Lord and Lady St. Bees. Humorless account of their "rashly" taking on their social obligations unprepared.
SP 76:927.

WALKER, AGNESE LAURIE.

012384   HADASSAH QUEEN OF PERSIA. London: R. Scott, 1912 BMC.

012385   PAULINE MERRILL: A NOVEL. London: Greening, 1905 BMC.

WALKER, ETHEL.

012386   THE PRIEST AND THE ACTRESS AND OTHER TALES: BEING IDYLLS OF SEVEN DIALS. Westminster: Roxburghe Press, [1897] BMC.

WALKER, FRANCES M. COTTON. Nationality Unknown.

012387   CLOISTER TO COURT: SCENES FROM THE LIFE OF CHARLOTTE OF BOURBON, ABBESS OF JOUARRE, PRINCESS OF ORANGE. New York and London: Longmans, Green, 1909 NUC.

Hist novel life in nunnery. ATH

WALKER, MRS. FAURE.

012388   MISCONCEPTION. London: Chapman and Hall, 1898 BMC.

Woman with grown children believes the worst of her husband who had always been true. SP 82:59

ACAD 55:480. Misunderstanding of motives of Colonel who comes to plead another's cause to heroine. County families and well-bred people.

WALL, IDA BLANCHE (FORD). B. 1860. United States.

012389   COMEDY OF PETTY CONFLICTS. New York: Broadway, [c1908] NUC.

BKM-Portrayal of domestic life with its every-day joys and sorrows.

012390   ROMANCE AND TRAGEDY OF A SUMMER. BY MRS. D. H. WALL. New York and London: F. T. Neely, [1903] NUC.

012391   SISTER IN NAME ONLY. BY MRS. D. H. WALL. New York and London: F. T. Neely, [1902] NUC.

WALL, MARY.

012392   BACK TO THE WORLD. London: Chapman & Hall, 1916 BMC.

TLS-Story autobiographic of a 49 yr old woman just released from a lunatic asylum until her death.
ATH Period treated is Autumn 1914

012393   A WRITING-WOMAN'S ROMANCE. Manchester: H. Eva, [1908] BMC.

WALL, MARY VIRGINIA. United States.

012394   THE DAUGHTER OF VIRGINIA DARE. New York: Neale, 1908 NUC.

PW-History
BKM-History
NYT 0 Story of Pocahontas. Story based upon supposition that Pocahontas was daught er of V. Dare.

WALL, MRS. D. H. See WALL, IDA BLANCHE (FORD).

WALLACE, EDNA KINGSLEY. United States.

012395   THE QUEST OF THE DREAM. New York and London: G. P. Putnam's Sons, 1913 NUC BMC.

LBKM-letters from Doria to several persons. Love story. Doria has strong opinions. "womanly"-"an innocently naive word used by benighted masculines who neither know nor wish to know what a woman is but only what they would like her to be!"
PW 84 9/27/13:953 "Contains the communions of a girl with her ideal, and not a few experiences with the actual ultimately lifted into the realm of the ideal. There is suspense and heartache, and an apparently irremediable misunderstanding between the two chief characters, but in the end love triumphs. Pages are printed in two colors."
writes to her friend Barbara, to David and to her dream man, imaginary confidant. A very complex person; letters reveal her completely, modern indep. NYT
Letters-heart story of Doria French a composer. Gives her first affections to a mythical man of her own creation: abstracted man. Later an actual man comes into her life. "Moderate love story of an independent woman of today" BKM
NYT 1913 414
"A story told in letters. Most of the letters are written by Doria French in St. Paul to David Hartnell in New york; later by Doria West, in St. Paul. Some of them, however, at the beginning of the series, are written by Doria French to a mythical being called John, who represents "abstract man." To him she writes the things she can not say to David, the concrete man." BRD
ACAD 86:16. Series of letters. Doris in pursuit of her dream marries artist, he then wants to be rid of her while he perfects his technique, finally they get together. Rev. thinks this a mistake.

WALLACE, ELIZABETH. B. 1866.

012396   GARDEN OF PARIS. Chicago: A.C. McClurg, 1911 NUC.

WALLACE, HELEN. United Kingdom.

012397   BLIND HOPES. London: Cassell, 1909 BMC. New York: Cassell, 1909 PW.

Focuses on a man. TLS
Lady Lucy Heriot leaves husband to marry another man. Story seems to involve the inheritance of her estate after she dies. PW

BKM-male hero and his inheritance.

012398   THE COMING OF ISOBEL. London: Cassell, 1907 BMC NUC.

Loss of identity mystery. TLS

012399   THE GREATEST OF THESE. London: Hodder & Stoughton, 1901 BMC.

12-7-01 ATH

012400   HASTY FRUIT. London: E. Stock, 1906 BMC.

TLS-marriage, separation, reconciliation.
ATH-wholesome entertainment.

012401   HIS COUSIN ADAIR. BY GORDON ROY. Edinburgh: W. Blackwood, 1891 BMC NUC.

A family of entirely female poor relatives is tolerated and patronized by their cousins and neighbors. Constrast of Adair self sacrificing and Agnes who is not, (sisters) good character study too of cousin Isabel and actress Cicely Charleris-uses a strong narcotic. ACAD
Adair is the heroine, conventional foil to her sister Agnes and cousin Isabel. Agnes is worldly, marries an elderly manufacturer for his money; she stipulates "that he shall likewise marry her family and especially her mother into the bargain." SR 4-25-91, 501

012402   LIFE'S CHEQUER-BOARD. New York: Cassell, 1908 PW. London: Cassell, 1908 BMC.

PW-unjust will.
TLS-love story.

012403   LOTUS OR LAUREL? London: E. Arnold, 1900 BMC.

SP 84:710. Great violinist cannot bear that her daughter become a professional rival. She dies in an accident and daughter's genius comes to light. Reader is left in doubt as to whether she will continue her career or marry man she loves.
SR 90:180. Whether heroine finally chose lotus or laurel an open question.
LIT 7:86. Dramatic moment when mother asks Karola to postpone her career so as to leave her undisputed first place in the few years left to her; Karola refuses.

012404   MORNING GLORY. New York: Cassell, 1913 PW. London: Cassell, 1913 BMC.

Husband mistakes wife's brother for a lover; they part. Ends on note of discontent. ATH

012405   THE SONS OF THE SEIGNEUR. New York: Outing, 1907 NUC.

Historical romance. 6-8-07 PW

012406   TO PLEASURE MADAME. London: Cassell, 1907 BMC.

Historical romance. TLS days of Chas II

012407   THE YOKE OF CIRCUMSTANCE. London: Cassell, 1910 BMC. New York: Cassell, 1911 PW.

Woman marries a man she doesn't love for the sake of the family fortunes. NYT
TLS-Pleasant.

WALLACE, MARY, pseud. See DOONAN, GRACE (WALLACE).

WALLACE, MRS. A.

012408   IN THE SERVICE OF LOVE. London: J. Flack, 1892 BMC.

ACAD 41:442:wholesome. Young son after mother's death patiently and successfully wins father to temperance.

WALLER, M. E. See WALLER, MARY ELLA.

WALLER, MARY ELLA. 1855-1938. United States.

012409   A CRY IN THE WILDERNESS. Boston: Little, Brown, 1912 NUC. London: A. Melrose, 1912 BMC.

PW-26 years old woman goes to Canada, works as librarian on estaate.

TLS She is illegitimate and is wooed by-as it turns
out-her mother's husband.
NYT O

012410   A DAUGHTER OF THE RICH. BY M. E. WALLER.
Boston: Little, Brown, 1903 NUC. London: Ward Lock,
1904 BMC.

Happy summer for two young girls 10-24-03 PW
"Such a story as maiden aunt might choose for her
niece" 03, NYT 802

012411   FLAMSTED QUARRIES. Boston: Little, Brown,
1910 NUC. London: A. Melrose, 1911 BMC.

Heroine child of Irish immigrants in New York, social
and industrial questions of Amer. life. PW
BKM v. 32
"devoted" heroine, crime, redemption? TLS
Aileen-mischievous loveable tease of a child LBKM
"the carefully nurtured hatred of a woman vs another
whom she knew was the only woman her husband really
loved." ACAD

012412   FROM AN ISLAND OUTPOST. Boston: Little,
Brown, 1914 BMC NUC.

012413   MY RAGPICKER. London: A. Melrose, 1911
BMC. Boston: Little, Brown, 1911 NUC.

012414   OUT OF THE SILENCES. Boston: Little,
Brown, 1918 BMC NUC.

PW-Male heroes
NYT Nov 3 '18 p 470. Plea for full citizenship of Am.
Indian. "Tragedy of the half-breed, and especially of
the educated half-breed woman is lightly touched upon"
Hero urges Indians to join him in a "blood sacrifice,"
throwing themselves into war after the shameful two
year silence of their country. All go to trenches in
France.
Romance of Indians and the west TLS
Heroine in half-Scotch; hero killed SP LBKM
Focus on a boy-a man BKM

012415   SANNA; A NOVEL. BY M. E. WALLER. New York
and London: Harper, 1905 NUC.

A wild romping madcap of a girl PW 4-29-05
Races her skiff NYT 245,05
sea maiden, fearless Story "touched with sin" but
basically wholesome NYT 05,319
Locale-island in Alantic, 60 miles from U. S. coast.
Fr. Marquis endowed a school here where French taught.
Story concerns the new schoolmaster, mystery of his
birth. He loves "unconventional Sanna" Review says no
more about Sanna. ACAD
Susanna Oceana Landers lives on Island of Dukes. She
has three suitors. LBKM

012416   SANNA OF THE ISLAND TOWN. Boston: Little,
Brown, 1912 NUC. London: A. Melrose, 1912 BMC.

012417   THE WOOD-CARVER OF LYMPUS. BY M. E.
WALLER. Boston: Little, Brown, 1904 NUC. London: A.
Melrose, 1909 BMC.

Diary of crippled man TLS
adds little LBKM
Pub. US 1904
NYT-O

012418   A YEAR OUT OF LIFE. New York: D.
Appleton, 1909 BMC NUC. London: A. Melrose, 1909 BMC.

Nathalie, woman studies German, translates German
author, writes to him, he proposes, she realizes when
she meets him that it's the letter-writer not this man
she loves, rejects him. Later she realizes she loves
him, he rejects her ? PW 4-17-09
Nothing comes of the relation-no marr. BKM
"A sexless and well informed young person who is by no
means too scarce in our time and country." "Nathalie
goes on her emasculated way...certain to evolve into a
perfect specimen of old maid." NYT
LBKM-She is translating a German work and is in
correspondence over it with its German author. He
falls for her but she not for him but she thinks they
are friends inviting him to spend a day with her. He
replied that he would not, she had robbed him of a
year out of his life etc. She? Pov?

WALLING, ANNA STRUNSKY. B. 1879. United States.

012419   VIOLETTE OF PERE LACHAISE. New York: F.
A. Stokes, [1915] NUC.

"Records the spiritual devel. of a gifted young woman
who becomes an actress and devotes herself to the
social revolution." SR

WALLING, ELIZABETH (BACON). United States.

012420   PHEBE. [Wilmington, Del.,]: [c1895] NUC.

WALPOLE, MARY.

012421   THE LOVE SEEKERS. London: Greening, 1908
BMC.

TLS-love story.

WALTHER, ANNA HILDA LOUISE. B. 1878.

012422   A PILGRIMAGE WITH A MILLINER'S NEEDLE.
New York: F. A. Stokes, [c1912] NUC.

How she millinered her way thru France, Germany,
Russia and South Africa and love story. PW.

WALTON, CATHERINE AUGUSTA.

012423   DOCTOR FORESTER. London: R.T.S., [1906]
BMC. Philadelphia: American Sunday-School Union, 1907
PW.

Straight romance 11-16-07 PW

012424   GOLDEN THREADS FOR LIFE'S WEAVING.
London: R.T.S., [1906] BMC.

012425   THE LOST CLUE. London: R.T.S., 1907 BMC.
Philadelphia: American Sunday-School Union, 1908 PW.

Detective TLS
PW-myst involving money

WALTON, ELEANOR GOING. United States.

012426   SHE WHO WILL NOT WHEN SHE MAY.
Philadelphia: H. Altemus, 1898 NUC.

LW 29:322. Letters, telegrams, articles from NYT, and
photographs. Writers of the letters are a man and
woman. She rejected his suit because of her art and a
preference for a platonic relationship, then tragedy
which startles "like a flash of lightning."
PW-just as she has changed her mind, letter arrives
announcing his betrothal to another woman.

WALTZ, ELIZABETH (CHERRY). 1866-1903. United States.

012427   THE ANCIENT LANDMARK; A KENTUCKY ROMANCE.
New York: McClure, Phillips, 1905 NUC BMC.

ACAD brutal maltreatment of wife by husband permitted.
ATH-desc. of gradual revolt of an injured wife thru
efforts of hero to remove "ancient landmark" (matrim.
legislation) thru galvanizing community into action.
About divorce husband drug addict.
brief desc. BKM 22 (1905) 291
Husband's brutality divorce advocated by cousin from
Harvard- a young man PW 9-2305

012428   PA GLADDEN; THE STORY OF A COMMON MAN.
New York: Century, 1903 NUC. London: Hodder &
Stoughton, 1904 BMC.

His rel ideas PW 10-24-03
NYT 03, 787

WALWORTH, JEANNETTE RITCHIE (HADERMANN). 1837-1918. United
States.

012429   FORTUNE'S TANGLED SKEIN; A NOVEL. New
York: Baker & Taylor, [1898] NUC. London: F. Warne,
1899 BMC.

PW-Olivia's experiences as companion to half-crazed
woman in rural district of Mississippi. Adventure and
mystery. A mysterious death and suspicion of
murder. SP 83:722.   Scase solved with the
help of a Bohemian young woman detective. LW 30:91

012430   AN OLD FOGY. BY MRS. J. H. WALWORTH. New
York: Merriam, [c1895] NUC.

LW 27:75. High-bred Southern family, impoverished,
move to New York.

012431   ON THE WINNING SIDE: A SOUTHERN STORY OF
ANTE-BELLUM TIMES. [New York]: [R. F. Fenno], [c1893]

NUC.

LW 29:124. Story of ante-bellum Southern family.
Slavery is the issue.
PW- Son of the planter and son of the overseer in
college; the latter is excluded from good society but
overcomes social prejudice and is on the winning side
in both love and war. College town, Shingleton,
Missisippi.

012432   UNCLE SCIPIO: A STORY OF UNCERTAIN DAYS
IN THE SOUTH. New York: R. F. Fenno, [c1896] NUC.

PW 12-5-96. Love story in Miss. valley after Civil
War. Uncle Scipio is an old slave.
Miss., after Civil war. Northerner comes to look at
estate. Under guidance of an old black man he gets
insights into the life and ways, makes a good marr. LW
28:44

WALWORTH, MRS. J. H. See WALWORTH, JEANNETTE RITCHIE
(HADERMANN).

WARD, A. B. See BAILEY, ALICE (WARD).

WARD, DORA.

012433   THE MARRIAGE OF CLARYS. Letchworth:
Garden City Press, 1917 BMC.

TLS She's widowed halfway thru the book. Clara Bailey
is a nurse. TLS

WARD, E., pseud. See GREEN, EVELYN EVERETT.

WARD, ELIZABETH STUART (PHELPS). 1844-1911. United States.

012434   AVERY. BY ELIZABETH STUART PHELPS.
Boston: Houghton Mifflin, 1902 NUC. London: G.
Richards, 1903 BMC.

BOOK NEWS 12-02 Husband is so deficient in
demonstration of affections it nearly kills wife.
CR-recalls "Confessions of a wife"
Selfish man ignores wife's sickness, sees the light,
comes home to find her dead-but physician brings her
back. Husband an egoist, wife effaces herself over and
over. ACAD, 65,83

012435   CHAPTERS FROM A LIFE. BY ELIZABETH STUART
PHELPS. Boston: Houghton, Mifflin, 1896 NUC. London:
J. Clarke, [1897] BMC.

012436   A CHARIOT OF FIRE. BY ELIZABETH STUART
PHELPS. New York and London: Harper, 1910 NUC.

012437   COMRADES. BY ELIZABETH STUART PHELPS. New
York and London: Harper, 1911 NUC.

012438   CONFESSIONS OF A WIFE. BY MARY ADAMS. New
York: Century, 1902 NUC.

"A vivid expression of what it is to be a
highly-concentrated, double-distilled wife--and
nothing else. No shadow of interest had she Marna in
life except this man; no duty, no pleasure, no use, no
ambition, no religion, no business--nothing whatever
but one embodied demand for her man. He was indeed all
the world to her--and he didn't like it." GILMAN, THE
HOME, 228

012439   DONALD MARCY. BY ELIZABETH STUART PHELPS.
London: W. Heinemann, 1893 BMC. Boston: Houghton,
Mifflin, 1893 NUC.

American college life. Fay Fleet puts all the
authorities of Harle (Yale) to shame. They give a
prize to an oration that was cribbed. She discovers
it. In love, is guide, philosopher and friend as well
as brilliant companion. SP 71, 250.
The hero is frank and handsome. He gains the oratory
prize when Fay uncovers the plagiarism. He's Donald.
He had been suspended for cruel hazing. PW 5-6-93

012440   JONATHAN AND DAVID. BY ELIZABETH STUART
PHELPS. New York and London: Harper, 1909 NUC.

012441   THE MAN IN THE CASE. BY ELIZABETH STUART
PHELPS. London: A. Constable, 1906 BMC. Boston:
Houghton, Mifflin, 1906 BMC NUC.

PW-Mystery surrounds middle-aged woman who is about to
marry and then withdraws.
NYT-0
ATH 0
Joan Dare, "a spinster of good position." Her virtue

is suspected (?) and she's ostracized by the town. She
refuses to explain things to her loyal lover. Finally
"the mystery" is solved. 2 or3 other women "carefully
delineated". SR

012442   A SINGULAR LIFE. BY ELIZABETH STUART
PHELPS. London: J. Clarke, 1895 BMC. Boston: Houghton,
Mifflin, 1895 NUC.

Emanuel Bayard educated for ministry, well-traveled is
called to N E town as minister but the local council
finds his religious ideas unsound. Starts indep
Christian work in same town. PW 10-19-95:675
BKM 3:261. "novel of emotion" Spiritual Bayard must
choose between Helen and his mission of service. He
chooses the latter and eventually gets Helen too.
Helen is "womanly."

012443   THE SUCCESSORS OF MARY THE FIRST. BY
ELIZABETH STUART PHELPS. Boston: Houghton Mifflin,
1901 NUC.

"The story indicates clearly the folly of so-called
"education" when it leaves a young woman helpless and
dependent upon others in her effort to make a home."
WOMAN'S JOURNAL 4-3-01
The discomfort, derangement, estrangement, of wife and
husband wrought by presence of servants. The
seriousness of the problem. The daughter of the
household- domineering, selfish. A draining mother in
law. Problem novel: a debate in women's clubs:
relation of servant to mistress.

012444   THE SUPPLY AT SAINT AGATHA'S. BY
ELIZABETH STUART PHELPS. Boston: Houghton, Mifflin,
1896 NUC.

BKM 3:261. Spiritual appeal. A minister, his
congregation, the teaching of Christ.
LW 27:365. Message is the brotherhood of man.

012445   THOUGH LIFE US DO PART. BY ELIZABETH
STUART PHELPS. Boston: Houghton Mifflin, 1908 BMC NUC.

"The unhappy married life of Dr. Chanceford and
Carolyn Sterling, daughter of a wealthy resident of a
little New England coast town in which the action of
the story takes place. The young doctor is socially
his wife's inferior, and a tendency on his part to
drink heavily and to take undue interest in a certain
Mrs. Marriot gradually strains the family relations
almost to the breaking point." BKM v. 28 1908-9
TLS-0
NYT- Reconciliation, sacrificing wife

012446   TRIXY. BY ELIZABETH STUART PHELPS.
Boston: Houghton, Mifflin, 1904 NUC. London: Hodder &
Stoughton, 1905 BMC.

anti-vivisection; Trixy is a dog. TLS 124,05

012447   WALLED IN; A NOVEL. BY ELIZABETH STUART
PHELPS. London and New York: Harper, 1907 BMC NUC.

Tessa-vain, beautiful, heartless wife of crippled
prof. TLS
Husband is walled in after auto accident, falls for a
nurse. BKM
NYT- husband married to a flirt, half sister nurse
wins his love and mrg. after wife turns over in canoe.

WARD, FLORENCE GANNON HANFELD. B. 1860. Nationality
Unknown.

012448   UNDER THE NORTHERN LIGHTS. BY MRS. J.
CARLETON WARD. New York: A. Wessels, 1909 NUC.

Man makes unwise marriage to secretary addicted to
drugs that make her insane. He goes to Alaska, falls
in love with another woman. Happy end. 9-18-09 PW
Story seems to focus on him, the mad wife incidental?
BKM
Most of story takes place in Alaska the "heroine is
sweet and lonely and charming." NYT

WARD, FLORENCE JEANNETTE (BAIER). 1886-1959. United
States.

012449   THE SINGING HEART. New York: J. A.
McCann, 1919 NUC.

PW-young woman remains in small town to keep house for
father and brother.

WARD, J. OLIVE PATRICIA. See WARD, JANE OLIVE PATRICIA.

WARD, JANE OLIVE PATRICIA. B. 1882. United States.

    012450   THE HERD. BY J. OLIVE PATRICIA WARD. New
    York: Cochrane, 1908 NUC.

    PW-Dakotas, expose of wrong endured by farmers. "love
    motive"

WARD, JOSEPHINE MARY (HOPE-SCOTT). 1864-1932. United
Kingdom.

    012451   GREAT POSSESSIONS. BY MRS. WILFRID WARD.
    London: Longmans, 1909 BMC. New York and London: G. P.
    Putnam's Sons, 1909 NUC.

    Eng. House of mirth PW 11-6-09
    A Becky Sharpe type penitent in the end. Lady Rose
    Bright, a second char, has refreshing common sense
    "sweet" quiet. TLS
    the effect of large fortune upon this woman ATH
    Story opens, man leaves fortune not to wife but to a
    woman the wife never heard of. Later we learn this
    hero was blackmailed to change his will because of an
    earlier affair. It's that woman's daughter Molly
    Dexter who gets the money. When there's a later will
    discovered she holds fast to her wealth passionately
    "Type of adventuress rare in fiction" SP

    012452   HORACE BLAKE; A NOVEL. BY MRS. WILFRID
    WARD. New York: G. P. Putnam's Sons, 1913 NUC. London:
    Hutchinson, 1913 BMC.

    PW 1-31-14 375 "Story of a great genius and remarkable
    dramatist, who, having broken from Roman Catholicism
    as a young man under the influence of his
    father-in-law, not only breathed a flaming spirit of
    destructiveness through his brilliant plays, but
    during the twenty years of his greatness plumbed in
    his own person every depth of moral degradation, being
    only saved from the usual public consequences of his
    actions by the devotion of his wife.
    2 Parts: (1) his illness, return to R C sm & death.
    (2) the writing of his biography by his daughter and
    Stephen Tempest, the conflict between their desire for
    truth and their ideal conception of the man. The
    impression he left upon people. SP
    Irrelevant introduction of anti-suffrage propaganda.
    ATH

    012453   THE JOB SECRETARY, AN IMPRESSION. BY MRS.
    WILFRID WARD. New York: Longmans, Green, 1911 NUC.
    London: Longmans, 1911 BMC.

    Novelist writes of unhappy marr; story parallels his
    secretary's life and almost wrecks his own marr.-PW
    6-3-11
    She neither types nor writes shorthand Mrs. Carstairs,
    They discuss, shape his novel of Laura whose story
    really is Mrs. Carstairs', her biography SP
    Mrs. Carstaris is a runaway wife. ATH

    012454   THE LIGHT BEHIND. BY MRS. WILFRID WARD.
    London and New York: J. Lane, 1903 BMC NUC.

    Love and Friendship; PW 3-14-03
    Lady Cheriton, childless, plays the patron to many a
    youth, her lonely career; the perfect woman, nobly
    planned" but with a few feminine weaknesses" her death
    ATH 121 366
    Deeply wronged wife gets a separation. Heroine has the
    courage of her common sense faces scandal mongers
    bravely, dies at the end. NYT 03, 191
    Two women, one man, a husband. Lady Cheriton, the
    injured wife. "The author distributes to her own sex
    the noblest parts." LBKM 3-03,248

    012455   ONE POOR SCRUPLE; A SEVEN WEEKS' STORY.
    BY MRS. WILFRID WARD. London: Longmans, 1899 BMC. New
    York: Longmans, Green, 1899 NUC.

    "Free from the common faults of the lady novelist."
    Madge, Cecelia. Much about RC and London society. LIT
    4:478.
    Thesis: that modern woman cannot dispense with
    Christianity. Pleasure-seeking Irish adventuress.
    Celia Rupert, brilliant, pagan society beauty and her
    duel with Mrs. George Riversdale. The prize is Lord
    Bellasis. Madge Riversdale wins him though she's a RC
    and he's a divorced man. When Celia hears, believing
    also that she has inherited an incurable malady, she
    kills herself. Modern woman has not the courage to
    withstand tragedy without rel. SP 82:491
    Madge Riversdale, widow, worldly. After a separation
    mixes again with her husband's people. Loves and
    accepts proposal of a divorced man. But does not marry
    him in the end. Because he's divorced? ACAD 56:507

Madge Roman Catholic but has drifted from the church,
about to marry the divorced man, sister in law saves
her soul. Makes a loveless marriage to everyone's
approval, even the author's. LW 30:167
"A study of the question of marriage with a divorcee,
including the intimate delineations of Roman Catholic
life and ideas with portraiture of women characters."
BAKER 03 183
English aristocrat Roman Catholic families. NYT
6-24-99:407

    012456   OUT OF DUE TIME: A NOVEL. BY MRS. WILFRID
    PHILIP WARD. New York and London: Longmans, 1906 BMC
    NUC.

    PW Catholicism
    NYT Catholicism
    ACAD 0
    TLS--nothing here

WARD, MABEL HENSHAW. United States.

    012457   THE DIARY OF AN OLD MAID [ANONYMOUS].
    [Washington, D.C.]: [Published By Author], [c1895]
    NUC.

WARD, MARY AUGUSTA (ARNOLD). 1851-1920. United Kingdom.

    012458   BESSIE COSTRELL. London: Hodder and
    Stoughton, [1912] BMC.

    012459   CANADIAN BORN. BY MRS. HUMPHRY WARD.
    London: Smith, Elder, 1910 BMC.

    TLS-0
    LBKM-
    SP- male rivalry over widow

    012460   THE CASE OF RICHARD MEYNELL. BY MRS.
    HUMPHRY WARD. London: Smith, Elder, 1911 BMC. Garden
    City, N. Y.: Doubleday, Page, 1911 NUC.

    Mostly concerns rel: priest falls in love, a sin in
    the family brings tragedy. PW 11-11-11.

    012461   THE CORYSTON FAMILY; A NOVEL. BY MRS.
    HUMPHRY WARD. New York and London: Harper, 1913 BMC
    NUC.

    Almost every aspect of the conflict of old and
    new-attitudes concerning religion, divorce, women's
    place-especially. Strong Lady Coryston tries to
    shackle her sons, ends unhappily. They turn on her for
    devoting herself to politics rather than "the place
    for which (her) better, softer qualities fit her."
    Proves the futility of women in politics. ACAD
    Three sons and a daughter-she is dominated by mother
    as are two of the sons, all of whom turn against her
    political beliefs in some way. In part an
    anti-suffrage statement. SP
    PW:84 12/18/13:1289 "Presentation of the struggle
    between the aristocratic and radical elements. In
    three different directions fate is waiting for Lady
    Coryston; her eldest son defies her politically, her
    heir, Arthur, plans to marry the daughter of the man
    whom she hates bitterly; and her young daughter is
    already beginning to rebel against restraint. Her
    courtship by an influential young neighbor began in
    idyllic sweetness; then she started to think as well
    as to feel, and found that she had made a mistake. In
    the end Mrs. Ward resolves these discords into
    harmonics."

    012462   COUSIN PHILIP. BY MRS. HUMPHRY WARD.
    London: W. Collins Sons, [1919] BMC NUC. (American
    edition title: Helena.)

    Helena Pitstone is restless, contemptuous of
    authority-all that rebel women used to be before war
    but she surrenders-takes a husband she knows will be
    her boss. TLS
    The taming of a wild girl-thru love marriage and
    children. ATH
    New girl of the period. Smokes, drives, calls men by
    first name full of unrest, is bold but settles down to
    marriage ultimately.

    012463   DAPHNE; OR, "MARRIAGE A 'LA MODE". London
    and New York: Cassell, 1909 BMC NUC.

    Daphne Floyd wooed for her money marries Adonis like
    Roger Barnes. He's a fool; they're unhappy; her
    passion turns into tyranny, jealousy. Their marriage
    is ugly, made uglier by comparison to another ugly
    marriage and a good one. Their marriage is
    shipwrecked, their child dies, the husband turns to

drink and dies. Intended as indictment of injust
divorce laws and a certain attitude toward marriage.
She deserts her husband, obtains freedom. TLS
"Story more truly indicts economic conditions
governing marriage than it does American divorce
laws." ATH
Written to "expose the dangers of Feminism"? SP

012464   DELIA BLANCHFLOWER. BY MRS. HUMPHRY WARD.
New York: Hearst's International Library, 1914 NUC.
London: Ward, Lock, 1915 BMC.

Delia learns after her father's death that a guardian
will control the estate till she gives up the cause.
Gertrude dies unrepentant. Delia renounces her faith
in militant feminism. Aims of militants supported;
means condemned. Author skeptical that vote will
remove grievances of women. SP
NYT 1915
Delia, young, rich is "captured" by a militant
suffragist. Story shows her gradual liberation from
that spell, love comes to her.(?) Vivid description of
mob's attack on suffragists' raid on house of
Parliament. Author ponders the whole question of
women's rights. "Advanced views on women's rights and
mission." Admirable portrait of Gertrude Marvell
militant. Author sympathizes with her tho vs her
actions. Woman question is much bigger than the vote,
goes beyond it: the woman question is the "whole
future of women". TLS
Gertrude Marvell is a destructive fanatical woman.
Dies in fire she set in one of England's old houses to
dramatize women's suffrage.
PW 86 11/14/14:1575. "A chilvarous, middle-aged man
suddenly inherits the guardianship of an immature and
rather badly educated young woman. Winnington's
responsibilities towards Delia were clearly defined in
two directions. He was to have complete control of her
income until she was twenty-five; and he was to break
her connection with Gertrude Marvell, a militant. The
action, and discussion of the novel are concerned with
the militancy of the suffragette movement, a protest
against it, which closes in Gertrude Marvell's tragic
death, and the marriage of Delia and Winnington."

012465   DIANA MALLORY. BY MRS. HUMPHRY WARD.
London: Smith, Elder, 1908 BMC NUC.

TLS-doesn't seem to have anything
ACAD-
ATH-

012466   ELEANOR; A NOVEL. BY MRS. HUMPHRY WARD.
London: Smith, Elder, 1900 BMC. London & New York:
Harper, 1900 NUC BMC.

BKM 12:345. Eleanor, for 8 years after death of
husband and child, has steeped herself and numbed her
existence in intellectual endeavor until her health is
broken. Goes to Rome to recuperate and becomes
companion of her cousin Edward. He is self-centered,
arrogant, is writing a book. Eleanor falls for him and
throws herself into book, drawing on her little
remaining strength. She hopes not that he will love
her, but will be dependent on her. Then a friend of
his criticizes the book. Edward accepts the new views
and Eleanor finds herself deposed. He marries Lucy
Foster. Eleanor suffers much and dies.
Sp 85:625.
ATH 116:573. Friendship between Eleanor and Lucy.
Eleanor appeals to her, they run away together, he
follows, reconciliation, then marriage.
NYT 1900:761.
All of Italy is background to love triangle; aging
sickly widow Eleanor, cousin Edward, innocent young
American Lucy. Eleanor sees Lucy getting in way of
Edward's career (he's writing a book @ Italy) takes
her away; finally reunites the lovers. Eleanor also
loves Edward.
Negative depiction of hero who wrecks his wife's life.
BOOK BUYER 01
Hero a woman's man (?) dangerous as a husband, but
interesting as a friend. CR 01

012467   ELIZABETH'S CAMPAIGN. BY MRS. HUMPHRY
WARD. New York: Dodd, Mead, 1918 NUC.

NYT-Oct 13 '18 p 445-"Mrs Ward cares very greatly
about the war and very little about her characters."
WWI-Fiction

012468   ELTHAM HOUSE. BY MRS HUMPHRY WARD.
London: Cassell, 1915 BMC. New York: Hearst's
International Library, 1915 NUC.

Divorce said to have caused death of her child thru

neglect, deserted another PW 9-25-15
Caroline Marsworth runs away from her marriage with
Alec Wing, deserting her two children. The younger one
dies, people mistakenly think, because of her running
off. Husband divorces her. She marries Alec. Theme:
How will society receive them? Losses become an agony
for her because her personal defiance soon spends
itself. Dies of a mysterious diease--NYT

012469   FENWICK'S CAREER. BY MRS. HUMPHRY WARD.
New York and London: Harper, 1906 NUC. London: Smith,
Elder, 1906 BMC.

PW-male artist-
NYT-artist-poor wife-unselfish woman--triangle
TLS--really traditional
ATH-0

012470   FIELDS OF VICTORY. BY MRS. HUMPHRY WARD.
London: Hutchinson, [1919] BMC. New York: C.
Scribner's Sons, 1919 NUC.

D640 WWI-Personal narratives. Campaigns-France Letters
based on a journey through the outfields of France.
BMC

012471   A GREAT SUCCESS. BY MRS. HUMPHRY WARD.
New York: Hearst's International Library, 1916 NUC.
London: Smith, Elder, 1916 BMC.

Doris Meadows and the social set in England and
Scotland. Little promise here. PW LBKM ATH

012472   HARVEST. BY MRS. HUMPHRY WARD. London: W.
Collins Sons, [1920] BMC. New York: Dodd, Mead, 1920
NUC.

TLS-Woman torn between love and fear of revealing her
past. Suicide.
SP-story of triumphant feminism, labors and successes
on the land. Rachel, divorced, accepts in her
loneliness protection from a man who dies. With a
legacy she buys a farm, employs a woman assistant.
Farm prospers, but she suffers from disclosure of her
past. Glories and dangers of women's independence.
NYT 4/4/20 p1. Rachel Henderson, graduate of an
agricultural college and Janet Leighton, a classmate,
rent a farm and run it together successfully.
Disclosure of Rachel's past, which she beleved dead,
results ien tragedy for her.
Two women run farm "met in college...fallen in love
with each other...attracted to the loneliness of the
other."

012473   HELBECK OF BANNISDALE. BY MRS. HUMPHRY
WARD. London and New York: Macmillan, 1898 NUC.
London: Smith, Elder, 1898 BMC.

SP. 80:826. Agnostic heroine and Roman Catholic hero
love each other but cannot reconcile their
differences. Her agnosticism is in memory of her
father, an emotional position.
LIT. 2:702. She tries to accept faith, and when she
cannot, suicides. He becomes a Jesuit.
CR. 33:89. ATH. 111:751.
SR 86:511 "freedom is her being, and life must be
impossible so with such a husband." She experiences
enough of 'those facts' to see the incompatibility,
and she makes away with herself.

012474   HELENA. BY MRS. HUMPHRY WARD. New York:
Dodd, Mead, 1919 NUC.

BKM-Portrayal of modern young woman, but Mrs. W. has
no sympathy for this kind of woman and does not
understand her. "Young creatures must chuckle at such
imaginary pictures of herself as Helena and M.
Deland's The Rising Tide."
"Impetuous girl whose artfulness is increased by the
war-time experience." PW
Helena Masson falls in love with her guardian; story
concerns older (50) man's effort to extricate himself.
NYT
She was in canteen work and motor driving to help war
effort. Theme of kind of world young women are faced
with in war years when all the young men are gone. NYT
11-23-19 669

012475   THE HISTORY OF DAVID GRIEVE. BY MRS.
HUMPHRY WARD. New York and London: Macmillan, 1892
NUC. London: Smith, Elder, 1892 BMC.

IND 44:206 "Monochrome pessimism." Attack on orthodox
religion. Louie is seduced by a sculptor in Paris,
David arranges their marriage, but he is so terrible
she is led to suicide.

CR 17:63. he is brilliant, has advanced political and social ideas, and is very generous and sacrificing to women in his life,especially his sister Louie who is constantly raging at him and finally kills herself before his eyes.
ATH 99:142. Louie and her downfall most interesting part of book.
SP 68:268. Elise Delauney is the sculptor David lives with. There are two long quotations from the novel in this review illustrating the conflict between her art and her love for David. A sympathetic and attractive characterization. However, marriage to a woman he doesn't love seems to be the instrument of his redemption.

012476   LADY CONNIE. BY MRS. HUMPHRY WARD. New York: Hearst's International Library, 1916 NUC. London: Smith, Elder, 1916 BMC NUC.

PW 90:1127 9/30/76
NYT-she is accomplished, rich, charming, many men love her. Story of her relationship with two of them.
TLS-Focus is on character of Falloden.

012477   LADY MERTON, COLONIST. BY MRS. HUMPHRY WARD. New York: Doubleday, Page, 1910 NUC.

012478   LADY ROSE'S DAUGHTER; A NOVEL. BY MRS. HUMPHRY WARD. London: Smith, Elder, 1903 BMC. New York and London: Harper, 1903 NUC.

A brilliant woman-but incapable of individual or direct action "the very best of the anti-feminist type"; can only work thru men. "Lady Rose is the apotheosis of the parasite class. With all her charms and ability she remains the product of a slave-status, the typical expression of a passing order." Julie, penniless, enters society as companion to a lady; by her own social gifts becomes the center. Her employer jealous, fires her. Julie lies, intrigues, loves her cousin's fiance, has fits of morbid emotion. AtH 121, 430
Reluctantly, unlovingly becomes a wife: with her marriage begins a conflict, fierce and long TLS O 3
Theme: what women want. Julie-acute misery, "perished outright of her unhappy infatuation," but does survive. Lady Rose chooses exile with lover to respectable marriage with husband she dislikes. Julie intelligent, diplomatic, love purges her weaknesses, one of the men in her life dies, the other remains to "tame and console her"? ACAD 248 v64
LBKM 4-03, 19

012479   MARCELLA. BY MRS. HUMPHRY WARD. New York and London: Macmillan, 1894 NUC. London: Smith, Elder, 1894 BMC.

SR. 77:367. Marcella is an ardent Socialist. Her father is an "impecunious landlord with a disreputable history." Marcella crusades for socialism, becomes engaged to Lord Maxwell's son, although she tells him she has no room for love. Then a glamorous Socialist leader comes on the scene, leads to her breaking her engagement. Eventual disillusionment in and exposure of this man Wharton. Marcella is also a hospital nurse.
SP 72:586. Marcella is extremely complex, defies complete analysis. Hero is Aldous Raeburn, a rather shadowy romantic figure. Mrs. Ward expounds at length on Socialism
ACAD 45:363. Marcella is tried by the fires and comes back to Aldous Raeburn's love.
ATH 103:469.
LBKM 6:55. Mrs. Ward the gentle pioneer of timid souls--an introduction to socialism, but not for those who have already learned about it. She is fair-minded and impartial on the issue; Marcella remains an indefinite Socialist to the end.
LW 25:99.

012480   MARRIAGE A LA MODE. BY MRS. HUMPHRY WARD. New York: Doubleday, Page, 1909 NUC.

Heroine appears heartless and unscrupulous PW 6-5-09. Daphne, independent, up-to-date. She has depths to her nature "volcanic and primitive". She's a millionairess loved by a poor timid Englishman happy to be bought by her, be her slave. They marry she tires of him, leaves because she's a woman with "aggressive belief in woman's freedom and individualism." Book ends with an indictment of American divorce laws. LBKM
In Part Iv, their child dies calling for the father, father turns to drink, gets TB. She tries to help; he rejects her. Anti-American divorce. BKM
A British tirade vs the divorce laws of certain of our Western States. NYT

012481   THE MARRIAGE OF WILLIAM ASHE; A NOVEL. BY MRS. HUMPHRY WARD. New York and London: Harper, 1905 NUC. London: Smith, Elder, 1905 BMC.

Kitty Ashe beautiful, reckless but destructive. Author treats her sympathetically, part of a fast crowd, smokes, flirts, even writes a novel exposing her husband's political secrets. Husband tolerant to this point, leaves her. She runs off with another man; the lover treats her harshly, she dies painfully and penitently of TB. Kitty:bewitching, maddening, tragic, destructive, and self consuming; the worst thing possible for such a woman was the mushy husband who hardens at just the wrong time. NYT O5,146 ATH 333,05 "She stands for woman's greater individual freedom". Her problem is loneliness because of an all-too-busy husband, selfish, inconsiderate, neglects her crippled child. Without one redeeming trait. Letters to editor. NYT 226 C5   Doesn't love her child, the broken marriage is the husband's fault-he so absorbed with career. Kitty loves to shock, should have been given a thrashing. There is another man-very attractive-author too sympathetic toward Kitty. Her dangerous fascinations, love of excitement interrupt husband's career.

012482   THE MATING OF LYDIA. BY MRS. HUMPHRY WARD. Garden City, New York: Doubleday, Page, 1913 NUC. London: Smith, Elder, 1913 BMC NUC.

PW 83 3/29/13 p 1193. "Lydia Penfold, a young and charming artist, drawing in the Lake country for her living, is of a poetic and unworldly temper. Equally poetic and unworldly is Lord Tatham, a young landowner who falls in love with her. But she loves a briefless barrister, Claude Faversham. The old eccentric and tyrant, Edmund Melrose, who is immensely wealthy, and has a house full of art treasures, gets Faversham into his power and bribes him with the hope of a vast inheritance. In Lydia's eyes Melrose's wealth is poisoned and the novel is a study of rival passions between Faversham and Tatham and of conflict of conscience between Lydia and Faversham."
Study of effect of wealth on character "almost impossible perfection of Lydia" ACAD
Lydia Penfold emancipated, holds theory of comradeship between men and women. Sister Susan, feminist, writes tragedies. Lydia tempted to barter her independence and ideals for a coronet; refuses him tries to maintain a camaraderie with him and Faversham but ends up marrying him. SP ATH
"Initially attempts independence but loves and marries, with author's total approval. Heroine is "independent, intelligent, and strong spirited but ending is too much in accord with the conventions of romance" NYT 1913 200

012483   'MISSING'. BY MRS. HUMPHRY WARD. New York: Dodd, Mead, 1917 NUC. London: W. Collins, Sons, [1917] BMC.

Nellie Sarratt, wed three weeks, husband off to war. Sister tries to get her interested in a wealthy baronet. Husband reported missing. Sister learns he's OK, but doesn't tell Nellie. Only learns when he's dying. PW
After his death, she's self reliant. She becomes a nurse. We leave her "a working and individual woman who whether she ultimately marres the baronet or not, will never be a plaything or a parasite." TLS
LBKM Two sisters Barb-hard, cold Nellie-young clinging "describes the mental condition of such a woman in a sympathetic spirit." SR
Action from June 1915-May 1917 NYT

012484   SIR GEORGE TRESSADY. BY MRS. HUMPHRY WARD. London: Smith, Elder, 1896 BMC. New York: Macmillan, 1896 NUC.

LBKM 11:49. Sequel to Marcella. "Marcella in her mellower years is more distasteful than ever." Tressady hopelessly adores Marcella, is married to a vixen. Everyone behaves with propriety but her.
SR 82:397. Marcella is a paragon of matronly virtue, the mainstay of the lower classes in her patronage. Mrs Ward is a snob. See rev. for futher details of her social attitude.
ATH 108:414 Marcella is a "bundle of perfections."
ACAD 50:423.
BKM 4:245
CR 29:229. Marcella a "noble character."

012485   THE STORY OF BESSIE COSTRELL. BY MRS. HUMPHRY WARD. New York and London: Macmillan, 1895 NUC. London: Smith, Elder, 1895 BMC.

A sudden catastrophe in the lives of three with a bkgd
of misery of poor village life. Bolderfeld, laborer
for whom his savings of 70 pounds is his life. Isaac a
religious dissenter, fanatic. Bessie tempted, fell. CR
24:24
Grim, sombre, sin and suicide. ACAD 48:182
Story of a tempted woman told with full sympathy. "a
moral lapse having nothing to do with sex"? LW 26:250
sordid life of English village. Bessie is given an old
man's savings to guard. She steals it coin by coin,
treats the neighbors. When it's all gone, she kills
herself. Bessie's "feeble" love for her children, awe
for her stern husband. BKM 2:52
Woman borrows money she can't repay. Faced by husband
and accusers, kills self. BAKER 03, 183

012486   TESTING OF DIANA MALLORY. BY MRS HUMPHRY
WARD. New York and London: Harper, 1908 NUC.

BKM 28 1908 "Secondary character who is one of the few
New Women Mrs. Ward does not ridicule."

012487   THE WAR AND ELIZABETH. BY MRS HUMPHRY
WARD. London: W. Collins Sons, [c1918] BMC NUC.

Nationalistic, -LBKM
TLS-Elizabeth is a fine Greek scholar, a trained
accountant, knowledgeable in the details of farming,
gardening and estate agency. Also wifely and motherly.
Also patriotic, unlike her employer Squire Mannering
who, not a pacifist, felt it extremely inconsiderate
of rulers on both sides to let their war interfere
with his and his family's lives. She converts him.

WARD, MRS. HUMPHRY. See WARD, MARY AUGUSTA (ARNOLD).

WARD, MRS. J. CARLTON. See WARD, FLORENCE GANNON HANFELD.

WARD, MRS. WILFRID. See WARD, JOSEPHINE MARY (HOPE-SCOTT).

WARDE, EVELYN B.

012488   ELENA. London: Simpkin, Marshall, 1910
BMC.

TLS-Caesar and Lucrezia are protagonists.

WARDELL, MRS. VILLIERS. United Kingdom.

012489   THE IMPOSSIBLE MRS. BELLOW. BY DAVID
LISLE. New York: F. A. Stokes, [c1916] NUC. London: E.
Nash, 1916 NUC BMC.

Jack and Mrs. Bellew fell in love, but she recognized
how impersonal their marriage would be. Dr. Helstan
believed she had a tragic story as well as a past and
befriended her. PW 90:769 9/9/16
Betty Bellew, is "impossible" because she has a "past"
and is therefore a social outcast. In spite of this,
the story ends in her marriage to a man who accepts
the scandals in her history and the social ban she is
under. "The author's theory is apparently that
expressed by the American Senator Willard: 'It might
be better to realize that nature is very much the same
in both sexes, and to give women full credit for
temptations resisted....I find it very easy to
overlook a slip, even several slips, in a 'mere
woman.'" NYT, 9/10/1916, p.356.

012490   A KINGDOM DIVIDED. BY DAVID LISLE.
London: Methuen, 1912 BMC.

012491   A PAINTER OF SOULS. BY DAVID LISLE.
London: Methuen, [1911] BMC NUC.

BRD- "The dominant character in this book, and the one
that gives it its name, is a young Irish
portrait-painter, Miles Dering, whose strong
personality and high ideals are due in great measure
to the training given him by his uncle, who has been
in close sympathy with the Brook Farm community in
America. Dering's own life is clean and wholesome and
he insists on painting his subjects as they really
are, not as they pretend to be or wish to appear." "it
is a profound study of the crucial hours in the life
of a young woman, by a man who obviously understands
women fairly well." "Is one of the best of recent
stories of Rome."
"It is a considerable question whether to regard 'A
painter of souls,' by David Lisle as art criticism
sugared to the public taste with romance, or as
romance entangled with a mission to expound that
particular school of modern art, the spirit of which
is being expressed, perhaps, by Rodin."

012492   THE SOUL OF LIFE; OR, WHAT IS LOVE? BY
DAVID LISLE. New York: F. A. Stokes, [1913] NUC. (Eng.
ed. title: What is love?)

012493   WHAT IS LOVE? BY DAVID LISLE. London:
Methuen, [1913] BMC NUC.

Isola Dering actress in Paris: marries in the end. TLS

WARDEN, FLORENCE, pseud. See JAMES, FLORENCE ALICE (PRICE).

WARDEN, GERTRUDE. See JONES, GERTRUDE (WARDEN).

WARE, EVELYN WOODFORD. United States.

012494   THE ISLANDERS: A ROMANCE OF MARTHA'S
VINEYARD. Boston: A. Mudge, 1892 NUC.

WARING, ELEANOR HOWARD. Nationality Unknown.

012495   THE WHITE PATH; A NOVEL. New York: Neale,
1907 NUC.

PW-Man cannot get divorce from wife, he and talented
writer defy conventions and live together POV?

WARING, MALVINA SARAH (BLACK). 1842-1930. United States.

012496   THE SANDHILLER, A NOVEL. New York: Neale,
1904 NUC.

NYT-Toad's ancestry limits her marital opportunities.

WARNER, ANNA BARTLETT. 1827-1915. United States.

012497   PATIENCE. Philadelphia: J. B. Lippincott,
1891 NUC.

Year of her life; captivating heroine; wholesome
story; LW. Dies of a broken heart; IND
Patience Hathaway in small New England town drowns
herself for longing for a wider life and greater love
than her life offers. Repressed with her set smile. CR

012498   WEST POINT COLOURS: LIFE AT MILITARY
SCHOOL. New York: F. H. Revell, [1903] NUC. London: J.
Nisbet, 1903 BMC.

Life at West Point ACAD 65,622

WARNER, ANNE. See FRENCH, ANNE RICHMOND (WARNER).

WARREN, ADELE.

012499   GRAYBRIDGE HALL. A ROMANCE. London:
Skeffington, 1893 BMC.

Wild melodrama involving parson Grier, his wife and
Captain Kendal. Hero shot accidently at the end. SR
76:130.
An engaged couple, but the man goes off-no marriage.
ATH 101, 503

WARREN, CONSTANCE MARTHA (WILLIAMS). B. 1877. United
States.

012500   PEARLS ASTRAY. A ROMANTIC EPISODE OF THE
LAST DEMOCRACY. Boston: Small, Maynard, [c1920] BMC
NUC.

012501   THE PHOENIX. Boston: Houghton Mifflin,
1917 NUC.

Janet's marriage a mistake, she "almost succumbed to a
great temptation." Solution of her problem nursing in
a French Hospital PW

WARREN, CORNELIA. 1857-1921. United States.

012502   MISS WILTON. Boston: Houghton Mifflin,
1892 NUC.

LW 23:87. An adventuress who runs up debts in an
irresponsible fashion. She has antagonized Bessie
Folsom by her behavior (a music teacher), but they
become friends after she reforms her ways.
CR 17:276. She is left a large fortune which she
imprudently spends, is being blackmailed, must borrow
large sums.

WARREN, GERTRUDE L.

012503   THE MYSTERY OF HAZELGROVE. A NOVEL.
London: Digby, Long, 1895 BMC.

Heroine at a French boarding school. "is permitted a

freedom which we find it difficult to credit." Meets
the hero. Her father is mixed up in a forgery case.
ACAD 48:29

WARREN, MAUDE LAVINIA (RADFORD). 1875-1934. United States.

    012504   BARBARA'S MARRIAGES; A NOVEL. New York
    and London: Harper, 1915 BMC NUC.

    Barbara Langsworthy forced to marry middle-aged man
    who is killed on their wedding trip. Ten yrs later
    marries a cad-ends in divorce; marries again happily
    PW 4-3-15
    As a young woman very unhappy living with brother and
    his wife. Has no training.Marriage instead of freeing
    her "renders her a helpless thrall for six long
    years." Another man comes in her life; falls in love
    with him. He brings her much misery too. She gets rid
    of him and "we leave her to the enjoyment of a belated
    happiness which she has certainly earned." Symp.
    heroine: "developement from a bewildered girl to
    strong self reliant woman is well portrayed." NYT
    3 marriages. TLS

    012505   THE LAND OF THE LIVING; A NOVEL. New York
    and London: Harper, 1908 BMC NUC.

    BKM v. 28 1908 reactionary politics-males.
    PW-Irish girl in Chicago seeking her fortune.
    ATH

    012506   THE MAIN ROAD; A NOVEL. New York and
    London: Harper, 1913 BMC NUC.

    PW 10-11-13 1248 "Reveals, with all its lights and
    shades, a wonderful itinerary of a woman's journey
    from sentimentalism to passion, showing the broad
    highroad on which she started, confident of arriving
    quickly at a goal, the blind alleys where her
    inexperience led her, the long and weary detours she
    had to make. But there are pictured also the bright
    spots where she found happiness, the companionship of
    friends and the glory at the journey's end. The
    "Beloved"-there could be only one-would come some day
    and for him she kept such a wealth of affection as no
    woman she believed, ever gave a man. By author of
    "Peter, Peter."
    "Brought up on romances...her one idea in
    marriage...has a love affair...jilted...caught up in
    suffrage mvt...takes part in the garment strike...a
    good man's love crowns her life." 1913, NYT 642
    Women's Political World, Mar 1, 1914 "Janet Bellamy
    reared as, in her father's opinion, a sheltered
    daughter should be...A childhood on a Wisconsin farm,
    four years in the University of Chicago, a period in
    the home of a wealthy cousin, a later period in a
    social settlement, are the stages into which Janet's
    journey toward full self-realization is divided." BRD

    012507   PETER-PETER, A ROMANCE OUT OF TOWN. New
    York and London: Harper, 1909 BMC NUC.

    Man does housekeeping while wife teaches music; twins
    are born. Humorous. PW 6-5-09
    Couple used to luxury struggle with poverty. He cooks
    and washes dishes; she teaches French and music. Twins
    inspire him to write poems and verses about them.
    These bring success. BKM
    Nursery idyl NYT

WARREN, PATIENCE, pseud. See KELSEY, JEANNETTE GARR
(WASHBURN).

WARRY, C. KING.

    012508   THE SENTINEL OF WESSEX. London: T. Unwin,
    1904 BMC.

    LBKM-trad love story

WARWICK, ANNE, pseud. See CRANSTON, RUTH.

WASHBURNE, MARION (FOSTER). B. 1863. United States.

    012509   THE HOUSE ON THE NORTH SHORE. Chicago: A.
    C. McClurg, 1909 NUC.

    Story of heredity. 10-9-09 PW

    012510   A LITTLE FOUNTAIN OF LIFE. Chicago and
    London: Rand, McNally, [1904] NUC.

WASTE, HENRIE, pseud. See STETTHEIMER, ETTIE.

WASTENEYS, LADY.

    012511   LIFE'S WRECKAGE. London: Digby, Long,
    1908 BMC.

    TLS-Unfaithful husband, trag.

WATANNA, ONOTO, pseud. See BABCOCK, WINNIFRED (EATON).

WATERBURY, JENNIE BULLARD. United States.

    012512   A NEW RACE DIPLOMATIST: A NOVEL.
    Philadelphia & London: J. B. Lippincott, 1900 NUC BMC.

    ernational romance.
    PW-two young men, U.S. President and ambassador, in
    international relations "bring out the true American
    spirit."

WATERER, GLADYS.

    012513   THE THIRD CHANCE. A NOVEL. London: G.
    Allen, 1912 BMC.

    TLS Independent woman and her saving of a man (actor)
    from himself.
    ATH O

WATERHOUSE, MRS. J. M.

    012514   THE MEDHURSTS OF MINDALA: THE STORY OF
    THE DEVELOPMENT OF A SOUL. London: E. Stock, 1897 BMC.

    Australia- a girl's soul. ACAD 52 Fic Sup 114

WATERHOUSE, MRS. JOHN.

    012515   FOR MARJORY'S SAKE: A STORY OF SOUTH
    AUSTRALIAN COUNTRY LIFE. London: Digby, Long, [1893]
    BMC.

    Country life in South Australia. SP 71,276
    Domestic life upset by scandal. ACAD 44:365

WATKINS, MARY LINDSAY. Nationality Unknown.

    012516   MY LADY PRIMROSE; A LOVE STORY. New York:
    Neale, 1903 NUC.

WATSON, ALEXANDRA MARY CHALMERS. B. 1873.

    012517   THE CASE OF LETITIA. London: Smith,
    Elder, 1911 BMC NUC.

    "Purging trials of mental suffering on a girl's
    self-centered nature" TLS
    Marries a second time after first husband dies. ACAD
    Her marriage to a repulsive man and her recovery of
    her freedom and happy second marriage, tho the latter
    involves parting with her child. ATH.

    012518   "DENHAM'S;" OR, A WEB OF LIFE. London:
    Smith, Elder, 1912 BMC NUC.

    TLS Story of a coaching establishment.
    ATH, SP Story of a boy.

    012519   STEP-CHILDREN OF NATURE. London: H.
    Latimer, 1913 BMC.

    Vs cousins marrying. Concerns birth and childhood of
    illeg. heroine who falls in love with illegitimate
    male. ATH.

WATSON, AUGUSTA (CAMPBELL). 1862-1936. United States.

    012520   BEYOND THE CITY GATE: A ROMANCE OF OLD
    NEW YORK. New York: E. P. Dutton, 1897 NUC.

    Doesn't give a sense of the time or place. CR 28,
    31:34.
    Time when Wall Street was the boundary; Harlem a
    village in the distance. Freida Van Dycke-heroine, a
    lover who dies, a lover she weds and settles with.
    Captain Kidd also. LW 28:203.
    Manhattan 1700-Farms (with some having slave girls at
    work in them) lined the Bowery. Freida is gentle
    womanhood with her two rival lovers. NYT 5-15-97.

    012521   DOROTHY THE PURITAN: THE STORY OF A
    STRANGE DELUSION. New York: E. P. Dutton, 1893 NUC
    BMC.

    Old Salem days of rigid Puritanism. Dorothy is no
    Puritan in spirit-she is out of place in Salem. She
    likes to dance, is vain, much tempted, and has pluck.
    LW 93 226.
    Vivid and accurate description of the witchcraft

delusion. PW 6-17-93.

012522   OFF LYNNPORT LIGHT: A NOVEL. New York: E.
P. Dutton, 1895 NUC.

New England seafaring town. A young woman can't marry
the man she loves. He goes off, she's desperate.
Minister helps her out. She married minister. Old love
shows up. Saves minister's life at the cost of his
own. LW 26:253

012523   THE OLD HARBOR TOWN: A NOVEL. New York:
G. W. Dillingham, 1892 NUC.

LW 23:230. Romance of revolution. New London, Conn

WATSON, ELIZABETH SOPHIA (FLETCHER). D. 1918.

012524   THE HEART OF BABYLON. BY DEAS CROMARTY.
London: H. Marshall, [1900] BMC.

SP 85:892. Story of young draper's assistant from the
provinces in London. After many vicissitudes settles
down as partner in "monster shop" with his first
employer's daughter as wife & helpmeet. Character
study.
ATH 116:574. Meets a successful novelist and one,
imagines, proposes. His mother comes to London and
takes him home.
LIT 7:420. He is a Methodist, feels he has a mission
to rouse modern Babylon. YT 1900:408. True & honest
love surmounts all difficulties. Int

012525   A HIGH LITTLE WORLD AND WHAT HAPPENED
THERE. London: R. Bentley, 1892 BMC NUC.

ATH 100:32. Yorkshire folk, beset with tragedy upon
tragedy.
ACAD 42:149. Resemblances to Wuthering Heights. Hard
stoical people, Lady Hartley, the heroine in a certain
sense, has a brute of a son and a daughter who burdens
her with her grandchildren. Laura Garnett is a deaf
and dumb heiress and one of the central characters.

012526   LAUDER AND HER LOVERS: A NOVEL OF THE
NORTH. BY DEAS CROMARTY. London: Hodder and Stoughton,
1902 BMC.

ATH 121:173

012527   THIS MAN'S DOMINION: A STORY OF
SELF-WILL. BY DEAS CROMARTY. London: Methuen, 1894
BMC.

ATH 104:788. Anti-establishment. Characters all seem
to suffer from paralysis of the will. Meaning obscure.
Mr. Harley, a minister, and his flock. "The universe
and its progress weighs on them too heavily."

012528   UNDER GOD'S SKY: THE STORY OF A CLEFT IN
MARLAND. BY DEAS CROMARTY. London: A. D. Innes, 1895
BMC. London and New York: Macmillan, 1895 NUC.

Venice: a young woman of the moors and Rhoda. Their
motives are obscured so that in the end they marry men
we least expect them to SR 80:21
Wild No. Country of England and London as well. Main
interest is the country-woman Rhoda who "at length
fulfills her life's purpose. She and husband are grim,
determined, rugged, instinctive people-akin to the
soil of No. country. ATH 105:768

012529   WHEN HEARTS ARE YOUNG: AN IDYLL. BY DEAS
CROMARTY. London: J. Bowden, [1896] BMC [1897] NUC.

WATSON, HELEN H.

012530   ANDREW GOODFELLOW: A TALE OF 1805. London
and New York: Macmillan, 1906 BMC NUC.

ACAD 0
TLS-rom. of the days of Nelson
ATH rom. of the days of Nelson
"heroine too mature and intellectually alert for 17"
NYT Plymouth story of fortunes and fate of a
Lieutenant in British navy and the beautiful woman.

012531   THE CAPTAIN'S DAUGHTER. London: Mills and
Boon, 1909 BMC.

A homely romance TLS
Constance Roper can sail a boat but her aspirations
are literary. She "finds herself" as wife of
schoolmaster. (Before her marr. becomes a journalist,
discovers, rescues and nurses her wastrel brother.)
The marr. doesn't always go well. Constance leaves at

one point. She and husband get school in the black.
Light spirited, "up" to any occasion, strong. SP.

012532   LOVE, THE INTRUDER: A MODERN ROMANCE.
London: R. T. S., 1909 BMC.

Wholesome domestic story TLS

012533   THE OPEN VALLEY. London: Cassell, 1912
BMC.

TLS Male commits fraud, in youth, effect on his
family.
ATH Male commits fraud, in youth, effect on his
family.

012534   PEGGY, D.O. THE STORY OF THE SEVEN
O'ROURKES. London: Cassell, [1910] BMC.

012535   PEGGY, S.G., BEING THE FURTHER HISTORY OF
PEGGY, D.O. London: Cassell, 1911 BMC.

012536   REBECCA OF THE FELLS. London: R. T. S.,
1914 BMC.

ATH Invalid son of peer nursed to recovery by heroine.
TLS She is "self-schooled, self-scanned,
self-honoured, self-secure.

012537   WHEN THE KING CAME SOUTH. London:
Religious Tract Society, 1912 BMC NUC.

LPKM Molly, during Cromwellian period, adopts a male
disguise to deliver a message for her friend Ceciley
to her lover, is captured and becomes a prisoner of
war. Kept apart from her own lover for a long time
because of opposing political views.
Civil wars-(Eng) adv. and two love stories, told by
heroine. ATH
TLS-Story for girls, adv of Molly Fleming, adv in
boy's attire, bringing her own and her friend's love
to safety.

WATSON, KATHLEEN.

012538   THE GAIETY OF FATMA: A NOVEL. London:
Brown, Langham, 1906 BMC.

ACAD-half Arab heroine marries man she doesn't love,
almost marries another, then in Algeria marries her
hero.
TLS Fairy tale, magic
ATH Fairy tale, magic

012539   THE HOUSE OF BROKEN DREAMS: A MEMORY.
London: Brown Langham, 1908 BMC.

WATSON, LILY.

012540   A CHILD OF GENIUS. London: S. W.
Partridge, 1898 BMC.

012541   A FORTUNATE EXILE. London: Religious
Tract Society, [1896] BMC.

012542   A GARDEN OF GIRLS. STORIES ILLUSTRATING
THE BEATITUDES. London: R. T. S, [1893] BMC.

012543   THE HILL OF ANGELS. London: R. T. S.,
[1892] BMC. New York: F. H. Revell, [n.d.] NUC.

012544   IN THE DAYS OF MOZART: THE STORY OF A
YOUNG MUSICIAN. London: Religious Tract Society,
[1891] BMC. New York: F. H. Revell, [189-?] NUC.

012545   THE VICAR OF LANGTHWAITE. London: R.
Bentley, 1893 BMC NUC.

SR 77:529. Disputes of high church and dissenters,
impartial p.o.v. SP 72:798.
Carfax is a high churchman who falls in love with a
professor's daughter. He finally resolves to keep his
celibacy but he also leaves church to becomes a parish
priest in R. C. church ACAD 45:206.
"To hold up the mirror to a certain phase of Non
Conformist Life and thought." LIT 1:117

WATSON, MARGARET.

012546   DRIVEN! London: T. F. Unwin, 1905 BMC
NUC.

Peasants struggle to earn a decent wage ACAD 949, 05
ATH 05, 298

012547   HIS DEAR DESIRE. London: Smith, Elder,

601

1913 BMC.

Intimate, realistic study of country life in So.
Midlands. Focus on Bob Wyatt whose passion is the
mill; boy-manhood. Emily the over-perfect heroine.
ACAD

012548   UNDER THE CHILTERNS. A STORY OF ENGLISH
VILLAGE LIFE. BY ROSEMARY. London: T. F. Unwin, 1895
BMC NUC.

country people's ways and talk and the tragedies of
the Nutt family that focus on their efforts to keep
their cottage ATH105:470

WATSON, MARGERY, pseud. See HALL, MARGERY WATSON (DRIVER).

WATSON, MARIE. United States.

012549   THE TWO PATHS. BY MARIE WATSON, F.T.S.
Chicago: A. C. Clark, 1897 NUC.

WATSON, MARY DEVEREUX. D. 1914. United States.

012550   BETTY PEACH: A TALE OF COLONIAL DAYS. BY
M. DEVEREUX. Marblehead [Mass.]: M. H. Graves, 1896
NUC.

012551   FROM KINGDOM TO COLONY. BY MARY DEVEREUX.
London: Gay and Bird, 1899 BMC. Boston: Little, Brown,
1899 NUC.

Hist romance with women in disguise but same old rom.
stuff. NYT 988, 03
Brave little wilful Mistress Devereux. Quaint old town
of Marblehead in days of Revolution PW 56:1264
NYT 1900:324. Historical romance. American Revolution.
Two brave heroines, one forced into a marriage which
is happy.
ATH 115:143. Seige of Boston.

012552   LAFITTE OF LOUISIANA. Boston: Little,
Brown, 1902 BMC NUC.

Hist. NYT 7-5-02

012553   UP AND DOWN THE SANDS OF GOLD. BY MARY
DEVEREUX. Boston: Little, Brown, 1901 BMC NUC.

10-19-01 PW
Widow-can't forget husband tho he a scoundrel; sees
her mistake allows herself to be happy-remarries. NYT

WATSON, MRS. E. G. HERON.

012554   DOROTHY DAY. Edinburgh and London:
Oliphant, 1896 BMC.

012555   IN THE DEIL'S GRIP. Edinburgh: R. W.
Hunter, 1899 BMC.

012556   TWA BONNIE SCOTCH LASSIES. Edinburgh:
Turnbull & Spears, 1897 BMC.

WATSON, VIRGINIA CRUSE. B. 1872. United States.

012557   MIDSHIPMAN DAYS. BY ROGER WEST. Boston:
Houghton Mifflin, 1913 NUC.

WATTS, MARY (STANBERY). B. 1868. United States.

012558   THE BOARDMAN FAMILY. New York: Macmillan,
1918 BMC NUC.

TLS-Sandra becomes professional dancer to save family
income, engaged to Jewish manager, they go down in
Lusitania, she is saved but her feet are damaged.
Finds happiness elsewhere.
PW-Sandra, brought up in genteel family in Ohio, goes
to New York to become a dancer. Her development and
emancipation from traditions of her family.
NYT p 166 Apr 14,1918 3,000 w. Becomes successful as a
dancer.

012559   FROM FATHER TO SON. New York: Macmillan,
1919 NUC.

Young man of wealthy family learns the wealth came
from profiteering. PW
Covers years 1910-18 BKM
Stephen, the son, Lawson, the father, Edith-father's
sister; wife can't do anything but be charming,
spoiled daughter Hecter is contrasted to Edith, "born
executive", cool capable, breaks with her German
husband after dealing capably with his bullying.
Effect of war on these people. NYT 7-13-19 365.

012560   THE LEGACY; A STORY OF A WOMAN. London:
Macmillan, 1911 BMC. New York: Macmillan, 1911 NUC.

SP- an interesting presentation of uninteresting
things. Independent competent girl remarkable career
PW 5-13-11
Letty Breen from childhood to 2nd marr "sympathetic
biog" TLS BKM 33 (1911) 650-1
Letty's char., marries a clerk. Husband has accident,
left weak-minded, dies after three years, she marries
a man she doesn't love but who has money. ACAD
Passion is no part of her nature. Saved from
temptation to be false to her colourless husband.?
LBKM
Life of girl, friendless, poor, shows us her genealogy
to 4th generation-the clashing strains of her
heredity. BKM "A fine psych study, masterly
delineation" NYT

012561   NATHAN BURKE. New York: Macmillan, 1910
BMC NUC.

Centers on the man, a lawyer-his career PW
TLS -male
ATH -male .

012562   THE NOON-MARK. New York: Macmillan, 1920
NUC.

BKM-Heroine is a girl of the people who is
aesthetically crude but has integrity. Almost marries
son of aristocrat McQuairs but realizes in time she
will never be one of them and does not care to be.
NYT 11-14-20 p 22. Mid western city. Nettie is "easily
recognized type of American business woman, capable,
hard-working, intelligent, and dependable." She once
hoped to be the head of a business college, but she
marries, not clear with what, but she says "everything
anybody could want." Her cousin, a contrast to her,
feminine, ends up as a leader in the "Altruistic
Brotherhood."

012563   THE RISE OF JENNIE CUSHING. New York:
Macmillan, 1914 BMC NUC.

NYT 1914:458 Midwest. Jennie is in a reform school
from 12 to 18. Only a slight and slightly emphasized
love story, Jennie refuses to marry this lover. "Mrs.
Watts shows only the sillier and more hysterical side
"of the suffrage movement, which wearies and
disappoints Jennie."
TLS 13:519
PW 86 10/24/14:1346. "Jennie Cushing, abandoned at the
age of twelve, is sent to a reform school and later
takes a position as servant in a rural town. Her
strength, beauty and oddly unresponsive yet compelling
personality attract several suitors, to whose
attentions she is entirely indifferent. Later she
moves to the city, and as attendant to a young society
girl whose picture is being painted, meets Donelson
Meigs, wealthy young artist. In his love for her he
laughs at class barriers, but she refuses to marry
him, choosing to live with him unmarried. Always
master of herself, she has no qualms of conscience in
this course, nor does she falter later when it seems
right to her to give up her life's happiness."
ACAD 87:495. She goes from hired farm help to
manicurist, to artist's model, to suffragist's
secretary, to organizer of a model home for children.
ATH 144:533 0
Of questionable ancestry. Arrested for assaulting a
boy bigger than self to protect a cat. Committed to
State Reformatory. Later tries to learn, works as
drudge on farm, prospers as a manicure, three years of
real happiness with artist, awakens to the incongruity
of that relationship. Final attainment of content in a
life devoted to saving other homeless girls from
mistakes such as hers. Tragic, "a human soul, vital
unmistakably individual." As child saw no humor in
children teasing weaker children. Has innate chivalry
toward the helpless; never fears hard physical work,
Has ideals, inquenchable instinct for beauty. BKM
"A novel portraying the evolution of an American girl
and her relations with the social and economic
movements of the times and their influence upon her,
including her work with the suffragists. NYT 7-11-15.

012564   THE RUDDER; A NOVEL WITH SEVERAL HEROES.
New York and London: Macmillan, 1916 NUC BMC.

Eleanor a woman of charm and mental ability makes an
unfortunate marriage to a rich man's son who takes up
baseball because he has no talents. Eleanor makes the
best life she can, guiding herself by holding "the
rudder true" PW

NYT- A serious & sympathetic study of a woman who
marries a big man she thinks she will be happy with.
She makes a life out of the tangled mess that has
fallen into her hands. Altho mrg. ends in divorce, not
an unhappy ending.

012565   THE TENANTS; AN EPISODE OF THE 80´S. New
York: McClure, 1908 NUC.

PW Story of southern family and soc customs of 80´s.
NYT- a ch. study, interesting sounding women.

012566   VAN CLEVE. New York: Macmillan, 1913 BMC
NUC.

Young man obliged to support a family of foolish
goodhearted women and a pompous old man, his
grandmother, aunt, cousin and uncle. Ten years pass
before he and his love can marry. NYT
PW- Lorrie cannot see what a devoted husband Van Cleve
would make her because of her mistaken love for a
ne´er do well who is killed in the war and whose
reputation is concealed by generous act of her
brother. Ten years later truth dawns and she marries
Van Cleve.

WEAVER, ANNE. United Kingdom.

012567   "AS WE ARE MADE---". London: A. Melrose,
1917 BMC.

Girl comes from France to England to visit kinsfolk.
TLS

012568   THE COMPROMISING OF JANE. London: J.
Long, 1912 BMC NUC.

ATH-Amusing, improbable plot.

012569   THE CORMORANT. London: A. Melrose, 1919
BMC.

Cynara dismissed from job as private secretary because
she admits she stole pearls-but didn´t. Is adopted by
rich old woman, loved and then deserted by her lover,
flirts with lots of others, saved from one by air raid
alert. TLS
Red-haired joins government department as war worker;
at end established an innocent-marries.? SR

012570   THE DOOR THAT WAS SHUT. London: A.
Melrose, [1914] BMC NUC.

ATH Remarriage for sake of child.

012571   THE LITTLE BLIND GOD. London: A. Melrose,
[1915] BMC.

Days of duels and ladies´ honor TLS

012572   A MASQUERADE AND A MONASTERY. London: J.
Long, 1913 BMC.

German princess masquerades as a lady-in-waiting and a
gipsy to catch the Prince. Ends up in a monastary,
gets out. All ends well. ATH

012573   THIN ICE. London: J. Long, 1914 BMC.

ATH Society romance.

WEAVER, BAILLE GERTRUDE RENTON (COLMORE). United Kingdom.

012574   THE ANGEL AND THE OUTCAST. BY G. COLMORE.
London: Hutchinson, 1907 BMC.

Two sisters-one marries a baronet, the other becomes
an alcoholic. TLS
Parents; a brutalized father, a battered hopeless
mother. Two daughters: one fierce and uncouth one
sweetness and light. The sweet one adopted by rich
woman raised--protected. The other-goes to prison;
finds gin makes her forget her problems. Works in
slaughter house, the two meet and each on separate
occasions helps save the other. TLS
Sisters passionate, jealous love for the sister taken
from her. ATH
Yan: the unattractive "drunk-sodden" outcast. Lillian:
prig. Reform novel; descriptions of slaughterhouse;
tragedy comes to outcast; The two "well-realized
characters." SP

012575   THE CRIMSON GATE. BY G. COLMORE. London:
S. Paul, [1910] BMC.

ACAD-High spirited heroine marries cousin to discover

he has murdered her grandfather. He dies saving a
child from fire.
TLS-She has been a hospital nurse, is
anti-vivisection, for the poor and suffrage.

012576   A DAUGHTER OF MUSIC. BY G. COLMORE.
London: Heinemann, 1894 BMC. New York: D. Appleton,
1894 NUC.

SR 77:587. Rhoda and her miserly grandfather, a farmer
who denied Rhoda´s mother the drugs, food, etc. she
needed to stay alive. Her fiance, Paul Garnet, a
savage orphan with strange cruel patience. Anthony
Dexter, a musician who recognizes Rhoda´s musical
ability and who controls her with the power of his
music. The morbid child of Rhoda´s sin who dies in an
ecstasy of musical indulgence.
ACAD 45:413. Somber, powerful, like Wuthering Heights.
Her child is Anthony´s son. Rhoda´s life clouded and
empty.
ATH 103:506. Premise is that music can work moral
mischief. Intro. quotation: "the daughters of music
shall be brought low."
CR 25:330. She goes to Italy with Anthony as his
paramour, eventually becomes depressed with this
position and goes to London, living in poverty and
degradation. Paul finds her, brings her home where he
simultaneously punishes and protects her. where they
can go on side by side, together, yet forever apart.
Much earlier he had told her it was her potential
wickedness that fed his love.
PW-she goes to Venice with Anthony after she has
married Paul. Painful long expiation. Suggests she has
a dual personality.

012577   THE GUEST. BY G. COLMORE. London: E.
Arnold, 1917 BMC.

Journey of Harriet Marchant and Pauline Caillaux
across the dunes of Belgium to England at outbreak of
war. "Conflicting ideals of love and of force."TLS
They meet accidentally, Harriet befriends Pauline,
takes her to her home. A romance develops between
Pauline and Harriet´s brother, but all the while
Pauline is a spy, a German spy masquerading as French
woman. Pauline believes in force; Harriet´s an
idealist (Christian.) LBKM

012578   A LADDER OF TEARS; A NOVEL. BY G.
COLMORE. Westminster: A. Constable, 1904 BMC.

ATH-young woman married to old man and his half-witted
sons has a strong sense of wifely duty, sinks into
Nirvana in middle age.
TLS-imaginative biography, above all transparently
truthful about herself thru patient and intimate
unfolding of her mental and emotional history.
ACAD-carries her burden with emotional dignity and
lack of complaint. She has a healthy hopeful view of
life.

012579   A LIVING EPITAPH. BY G. COLMORE. London:
Longmans, 1891 BMC.

rival lovers of Miranda Dane; Letitia Letherbarrow
waits for vengeance, not suspecting her friend is her
enemy and vice versa. Fine, fascinating novel.
Nathaniel Ashe´s final act of renunciation. ACAD

012580   LOVE FOR A KEY. BY G. COLMORE. London:
Heinemann, 1896 BMC.

A marriage drama-the changes in husband and wife, the
estrangement. SR 83:725
"A woman´s weariness and disappointment." Annette Gray
marries for love; husband married her for money. She
is "plain and dowdy, " he´s good looking and popular.
When he loses his youth and beauty, he returns to her
on her deathbed. ACAD 51:425.
Story of a wife whose quiet nature gradually changes
the coarseness of her husband. ATH 199:649.

012581   THE MARBLE FACE. BY G. COLMORE. London:
Smith, Elder, 1900 BMC.

SR 90:797. Heroine narrator loves weak-minded man
whose mother is a fiend behind a marble face.
ATH 116.476, narrated in alternate chapters by hero
and heroine who lives next door. He is kept a prisoner
in house by his mother who holds some silly threat
over him.
LIT 7:325. Laura Lequesnay and Dormley Cotterel.
Secret misery of his life, Laura rescues him. High
tragedy. Vividness, power.

012582   PRIESTS OF PROGRESS. BY G. COLMORE.

London: S. Paul, 1908 BMC. New York: B. W. Dodge,
1908.

TLS--anti-vivisectionist, male hero.
Anti-vivisection and experimental surgery in attitude
of doctor hero. BKM SP

012583   THE STRANGE STORY OF HESTER WYNNE, TOLD
BY HERSELF; WITH A PROLOGUE. BY G. COLMORE. London:
Smith, Elder, 1899 BMC. New York: D. Appleton, 1899
NUC.

Sensational, machinations of a villain who wants the
locket Hester wears. LIT 5:161
Development of a young man who watched his father die
of DTs and who fears he inherited alcoholism. LBKM
17:31. The DTs scene is an introduction.
Heroine forced to wed that young man. Happy end. SP
83:94. Thrilling mystery. ACAD 57:160
LW 31:69. Hester is imprisoned by Jesse, her
guardian's son, in an attempt to force marriage on
her. He is member of secret Irish-American society and
desperately needs to repay moneys he has appropriated.
Hester is an heiress. She escapes; he is shot by
society's agent. She returns to true lover. She is
heir to large estate; doesn't know it; Mrs. Pimpernel
and son try to drive her mad and to force her to marry
the son. But ends well for Hester. NYT 9-2-99,581

012584   SUFFRAGETTE SALLY. BY G. COLMORE. London:
S. Paul, [1911] BMC.

"Simply a contribution to the campaign lit. of the
mvt. detailing recent events with vigourous
partisanship." TLS
Clear outline of militant mvt and "a vigourous
inspiring" story. Sally a servant, a drudge, goes to a
meeting hears a feminist speak "a new life opens out
before her." LBKM

012585   THE THUNDERBOLT. BY G. COLMORE. London:
T. F. Unwin, [1919] BMC NUC. New York: T. Seltzer,
1920 NUC.

Nurse and mother vie for child's affections. "The end
is revolting." TLS
PW-Dorrie, brought up in the "sheltered life," reaps
tragedy which this system leaves her defenseless
against. Grim, fine craftsman, cumulative power.
Becomes unsuspecting victim of MD's unscrupulous
experimentation.
NYT 1920:198. Is innoculated with what, VD? Sores
appear, first on arm, then on lip. Fiance breaks off
engagement. She mustn't be told.

012586   A VALLEY OF SHADOWS. BY G. COLMORE.
London: Chattto & Windus, 1892 BMC.

SP 69:298. Village of sleepy Dale, puritan types. Mr.
Hargreaves asks "a lady to leave because her
antecedents did not please him." "Gloomy."
ACAD. "oppressively somber" "pure tragedy" "not
contemporary realism"
SR. Lucy Saryll, "after 10 years peaceful of
existence" confessed that she had really murdered her
husband.

012587   WHISPERS. BY G. COLMORE. London: Hurst
and Blackett, 1914 BMC.

ATH-Mystery story with artist hero.
TLS-Story is about Mrs. Cayne and her tragic end.

WEAVER, EMILY POYNTON. 1865-1943. Canada.

012588   PRINCE RUPERT'S NAMESAKE, OR, AFTER THE
RESTORATION. Boston: Congregational Sunday School and
Pub. Society, 1893 PW. Edinburgh: Oliphant, 1894 BMC.

Time of restoration. Royalists meet problems
maintaining their property. Rescues from Plague and
London fire. PW 10-14-93

012589   THE RABBI'S SONS; A STORY OF THE DAYS OF
ST. PAUL. Boston: Congregational Sunday School and
Pub. Society, [1891] NUC. London: C. H. Kelly, 1891
BMC.

Two sons leave home because rabbi is so strict; they
become thieves and meet Paul who tells them of
Christianity. They and later the rabbi convert to
Christianity.

012590   THE RAINPROOF INVENTION; OR SOME TANGLED
THREADS. Boston: Congregational Sunday-School and Pub.
Society, [c1896] NUC.

The invention makes clothes waterproof. Manufacturer
tries to keep it secret; his daughter tangles things
up. BOOK NEWS 96-7; 141.
PW 10-10-96. Process of waterproofing clothing
closely-guarded secret of a manufacturer whose
daughter is a thoughtless and heartless coquette and
gets things tangled up.

012591   THE SEARCH FOR MOLLY MARLING. London: R.
T. S., [1903] BMC.

012592   THE TROUBLE MAN; OR, THE WARDS OF ST.
JAMES. London: R.T.S., [1910] BMC. Toronto: Musson,
[19--?] NUC.

WEBB, FRANCES ISABEL (CURRIE). United States.

012593   A BREATH OF SUSPICION: A NOVEL. New York:
F. I. Webb, [c1895] W.

Young woman marries in haste to get away from harsh
guardian. The marriage is broken temporarily by
separation because of a friend of the husband's who
causes a breath of suspicion. PW 2-16-95:321

WEBB, GLADYS MARY. See WEBB, MARY GLADYS (MEREDITH).

WEBB, MARY GLADYS (MEREDITH). 1883-1927. United Kingdom.

012594   THE GOLDEN ARROW. London: Constable, 1916
BMC NUC. New York: Dutton, [n.d.].

Woman's love and self sacrifice. BKM
Wales, Deborah Arden, great love for a man is
eventually returned in kind. NYT 5-6-17 183
TLS-family life in Wales, philosophizing, male hero,
love story.
LBKM-a study of sex in two contrasting marriages.

012595   GONE TO EARTH. BY GLADYS MARY WEBB. New
York: E. P. Dutton, [c1917] NUC. London: Constable,
1917 BMC.

Hazel Woodus drawn between two kinds of love-married
to one man loves another. At end loves husband, but
she dies. PW
Concerned especially with suffering inflicted on
animals and all defenseless creatures by man. Hazel,
focus of the book, is a strange girl of the woods "so
primitive that she is more like some incarnation of
the earth than a human being." One love is nature; her
one passion-pity for all suffering things. At each
step faced with pain of more and more cruelty. In her
search for security wavers between two men, one
represents emotion of body, the other soul. Meets a
horrible death in rescuing her tame fox from hounds.
TLS
In a rage with her father (whom she has no love for)
she says she'll marry the first man who proposes.
Marries a minister; the marriage is disastrous. LBKM

012596   THE HOUSE IN DORMER FOREST. BY GLADYS
MARY WEBB. London: Hutchinson, [1920] BMC. New York:
G. Doran, [1921] NUC.

TLS-Soul-destroying blight in the atmosphere. Darke
family. Depressing lives, none of them normal.
Catherine is cruel, Mrs. Darke is hated by servants
and children, dreaded by her failing mother.
ATH-most unsympathetic ch of all is Scripture-quoting
grandmother. Only sympathetic character is Sarah, a
servant. An ill omened house whose womenkind do no
useful work and yet never leave home, even for a
honeymoon.
LBKM-fierce human passions contained for years by
conventions and fanaticism. One daughter escapes to
freer world. Grandmother burns house down in end!

WEBB, VIRGINIA, pseud. See RHODES, HATTIE H.

WEBER, ALICE. Nationality unknown.

012597   AN AFFAIR OF HONOUR. London: Griffith,
Farran, 1892 BMC. Philadelphia: Lippincott, 1893 NUC.

012598   THE CLOCK ON THE STAIRS. London:
Griffith, Farran, 1892 BMC.

WEBER, ANTOINETTE.

012599   CHANGES AND CHANCES. London: E. Arnold,
1903 BMC.

Village life Austen-like ACAD. 178 69
A "feminine" novel. TLS 03, 59

WEBLING, PEGGY. United Kingdom.

012600   BLUE JAY. New York: P. R. Reynolds,
[c1905] NUC. London: W. Heinemann, 1906 BMC.

TLS-career of a young pro acrobat with pretty romance.
ATH--male hero.

012601   BOUNDARY HOUSE. London: Hutchinson,
[c1916] BMC NUC.

TLS--love story
ATH-She marries older man (who has tricked her) she
does not love, but endures her hard life and brings
happiness into lives of others.

012602   COMEDY CORNER. London: Hutchinson, [1920]
BMC NUC.

TLS-Romance

012603   EDGAR CHIRRUP. London: Methuen, 1915 BMC.
New York: G. P. Putnam's Sons, 1915 NUC.

Focuses upon an actor. 6-19-15 PW

012604   FELIX CHRISTIE. London: Methuen, 1912
BMC.

TLS--male hero
ATH
ACAD-
SP would be violinist who becomes a writer and loves
Pearl, "vulgar and little."-Reviewer is tired of her
and her surroundings.
LBKM-

012605   IN OUR STREET. London: Hutchinson, 1918
BMC NUC.

TLS-

012606   THE PEARL STRINGER. London: Methuen, 1913
BMC NUC.

Careers of two women, one a pearl stringer, the other
her friend Rose. We trace their story from shabby
little Colet Street. Rose Leonard is passionate,
impetuous "not too high principled" ; the other,
quietly virtuous. But virtue not rewarded. The other
establishes friendship with elderly man but there's no
thought of marriage; he dies, she's left a pearl
stringer. Rose finds happiness, the other doesn't. All
male characters of minor importance. ACAD
Rose has passionate love affair, comes to appreciate
husband though he's a dull middle-aged dentist. SP

012607   THE SCENT SHOP. London: Hutchinson,
[1919] BMC.

Life of whole family and others of half-gypsy- Half
chemist owner of shop. TLS

012608   A SPIRIT OF MIRTH. London: Methuen, 1910
BMC. New York: E. P. Dutton, 1911 NUC.

BM-Heroine is daughter of "The Human Eel."
Sentimental?
TLS-O
ATH-becomes star of variety stage, marries a wastrel,
he is reformed by conventional devices.
SP-
about a little girl who cares for "stupid boy;"
They're adopted. She's sunny, happy, loving, etc.
PW 3-18-11
BKM 33 (1911) 418 not helpful.
A fairy tale -SR

012609   THE STORY OF VIRGINIA PERFECT. London:
Methuen, 1909 BMC NUC.

Uncongenial marriage, treachery of husband, ATH
"A dangerous theme treated with fact." SP

012610   VIRGINIA PERFECT. London: Methuen, 1911
BMC.

WEBSTER, JEAN. See MACKINNEY, ALICE JEAN CHANDLER
(WEBSTER).

WEBSTER, NESTA HELEN.

012611   THE SHEEP TRACK, AN ASPECT OF LONDON
SOCIETY. New York: E. P. Dutton, 1914 NUC. London: J.
Murray, 1914 BMC NUC.

Shows improved conditions in women's work in last
decade for mid-class women, but if you're from high
society if goal is marriage "then the emancipation of
modern women counts for little or nothing." Marcia
Fayne "high bred" comes to live with aunts in England.
They are ultra-conservative and she finds them
hypocritical. Leaves for Bohemia in her "desperate
revolt vs narrow smugness of London." "Her audacious
experience as a bachelor girl could have been saved by
Time and marriage. BKM
NYT-Modern society life in London; heroine's father is
an intellectual recluse living in Nice with his books
and with Marcia. Marcia raised on the theory of
beauty-must be given no conception of the gross or
ugly. They live an isolated life til they move to
London. The rest of the book is an expose of shallow
London society.
BKM-Marcia Fayne is raised by misanthrope father to
know of nothing ugly. When she has reached brink of
womanhood, she is sent to three aunts in England. She
revolts against their smug conventionality and joins
group of Bohemians. She becomes disillusioned with
character of some of her closest friends and also
loses opportunity of making socially advantageous
marriage.
NYT-So therefore realizes, while sheep tracks may be
monotonous,they are more satisfactory than picking out
a path of one's one.
ACAD 86:563. A satire. London society is the
sheeptrack. Marcia must rise above sheep track or
perish. Epicteus: "Look to it that thou do nothing
like a sheep, or thus...had the man perished."
TLS-To stay on the track may bring boredom and misery;
to leave it may bring pleasures scarcely worth the
price in danger and loss of repute. "Amusing sensible
girl trying in vain to find her place."

WEED, MARIA.

012612   A VOICE IN THE WILDERNESS. Chicago: Laird
and Lee, [c1895] NUC.

"Warning against indiscriminate use of morphine to
make a patient's suffering endurable." PW 47:871. A
woman musical artist- becomes addicted, but is cured
by doctor whose wife had died of the habit.

WEEKES, A. R. See WEEKES, AGNES RUSSELL.

WEEKES, AGNES RUSSELL. United Kingdom.

012613   FAITH UNFAITHFUL. London: A. Melrose,
1910 BMC.

012614   JENNY ESSENDEN. BY ANTHONY PRYDE. London:
A. Melrose, [1916] BMC. New York: R. M. McBride, 1921
NUC.

ATH Strong realism
TLS O

012615   MARQUERAY'S DUEL. BY ANTHONY PRYDE. New
York: R. M. McBride, 1920 NUC. London: A. Melrose,
[1919] BMC. (Published anonymously in England.)

012616   YARBOROUGH THE PREMIER. A NOVEL. BY A. R.
WEEKES. New York and London: Harper, 1904 BMC NUC.

LBKM melod.

WEEKES, AGNES RUSSELL, jt. au. See WEEKES, ROSE KIRKPATRICK
AND AGNES RUSSELL WEEKES.

WEEKES, R. K. See WEEKES, ROSE KIRKPATRICK.

WEEKES, ROSE KIRKPATRICK. B. 1874. United Kingdom.

012617   B 14. A NOVEL. London: G. Allen & Unwin,
1920 BMC.

TLS-Melodrama
SP Feelings of a man imprisoned for manslaughter.

012618   CONVICT B 14; A NOVEL. BY R. K. WEEKES.
New York: Brentano's, [c1920] NUC.

012619   THE FALL OF THE CARDS. London and New
York: Harper, 1905 BMC.

012620   FELLOW PRISONERS. BY R. K. WEEKES.
London: A. Rivers, 1911 BMC NUC.

Convict and a soured cripple "charm of academic young
ladies of Cambridge-the heroines" TLS

012621   THE LAURENSONS. London: Constable, 1913 BMC.

Man intercedes for his brother with a woman he himself loves. ATH
Life in Jesuit college. TLS

012622   LOVE IN CHIEF; A NOVEL. New York and London: Harper, 1904 BMC NUC.

PW-Love story
NYT love story
ACAD love story.

012623   THE MASSAREEN AFFAIR. London: E. Arnold, 1917 BMC.

Claudia sets up house with her cousin, at first brother and sister relation. He's separated from wife. They fall in love and people give them grief. Finally wife commits suicide. TLS

012624   SEABORNE OF THE BONNET SHOP. BY R. K. WEEKES. London: H. Jenkins,, 1914 BMC NUC.

LEKM-0
ATH Male hero, romance

WEEKES, ROSE KIRKPATRICK AND AGNES RUSSELL WEEKES.

012625   THE TRAGIC PRINCE. London: A. Melrose, 1912 BMC.

TLS Succession.

WEEKS, HELEN MARIAN. B. 1840. United States.

012626   THE SEQUEL OF A WASTED LIFE: COMPRISING A STORY FOUNDED ON FACTS. BY DR. HELEN M. WEEKS. Girard, Pa.: Murphy and Nichols Printers, 1896 NUC.

WEIGALL, C. E. C. See WEIGALL, CONSTANCE E. C.

WEIGALL, CONSTANCE E. C. Nationality Unknown.

012627   FAR ABOVE RUBIES. London: S. W. Partridge, [1910] BMC.

012628   THE GATE OF HAPPINESS. BY C. E. C. WEIGALL. London: R.T.S., 1907 BMC. London: 'Leisure Hour' Library Office, [1909] NUC.

012629   HUTTON'S MILLION. London: "Leisure Hour" Library Office, [1915] BMC.

012630   IN ALL TIME OF OUR WEALTH. London: R. T. S., [1904] BMC.

012631   THE RED LIGHT. New York: Cassell, 1907 PW. London: Cassell, 1907 BMC.

Experiences & love story of a school girl in Malta. TLS

012632   THE SECRET OF TWO HEARTS. London: "Leisure Hour" Library Office, [1915] BMC.

012633   THE TEMPTATION OF DULCE CARRUTHERS. London: Cassell, 1893 BMC.

012634   A WIFE WORTH WINNING. London: S. W. Partridge, [1907] BMC.

tale of romance TLS

WEIMAN, RITA. 1889-1954. United States.

012635   PLAYING THE GAME: THE STORY OF A SOCIETY GIRL. New York: Cupples & Leon, [c1910] NUC.

Heroine has many experiences "that should not come to a young girl" PW

WEISS, SARA.

012636   DECIMON HUYDAS, A ROMANCE OF MARS; A STORY OF ACTUAL EXPERIENCES IN ENTO (MARS) MANY CENTURIES AGO GIVEN TO THE PSYCHIC SARA WEISS AND BY HER TRANSCRIBED AUTOMATICALLY UNDER THE EDITORIAL DIRECTION OF SPIRIT CARL DE L'ESTER. Rochester, N.Y.: Austin, 1906 NUC.

BF 1311 Spiritualism.

012637   JOURNEYS TO THE PLANET MARS; OR, OUR MISSION TO ENTO. New York: Bradford Press, [1903] NUC.

WELBORN, MINA WALKER.

012638   THE ROMANCE OF A TRUE MARRIAGE. London: A. H. Stockwell, [1911] BMC.

TLS-Mild and edifying-reformation of male.

WELLMAN, RITA. B. 1890. United States.

012639   THE WINGS OF DESIRE. New York: Moffat, Yard, 1919 NUC.

influence of women on artist's (male) life PW
about Greenwich Village. Reared to love beauty, young artist needs woman of the Rossetti type, a model, but then marries a more ordinary woman. young man force-fed culture by his mother, still becomes a famous artist in the end. Story traces his love affairs in New York especially. Goes off to Japan. NYT 11-2-19 626

WELLS, CAROLYN. D. 1942. United States.

012640   ABENIKE CALDWELL; A BURLESQUE HISTORICAL NOVEL. New York: R. H. Russell, 1902 NUC.

Burleque hist rom. NYT 03,135

012641   ANYBODY BUT ANNE. Philadelphia and London: J.B Lippincott, 1914 BMC NUC.

PW 3-14-14 968 "A murder is committed in the study of the Van wyck home, and the room is found securely bolted and locked on the inside, which seems to point to suicide. Valuable pearls and important papers, however, are missing, implicating three members of the household, one of whom is Mrs. Van Wyck, the charming but apparently guilty member of the family. Who was the criminal, and why? How was the escape made from the study? And what the method of killing? Fleming Stone, the detective, shows how easily these questions may be solved, and through his endeavors the murderer is discovered."
TLS 13:346 Anne marries rich old man for his money, he is murdered. She then marries male narrator of story.

012642   BETTY'S HAPPY YEAR. New York: Century, 1910 NUC BMC.

Really enjoys life and makes a lot of friends, simple "roguish" girl. PW

012643   THE PRIDE OF A MOMENT. New York: G. H. Doran, [1916] NUC. London: Hodder & Stoughton, [1920] BMC.

Mystery PW 90:8/19/16 p.569
NYT
TLS det.

012644   A CHAIN OF EVIDENCE. Philadelphia and London: J. B. Lippincott, 1912 NUC.

PW--Murd. mystery
NYT-Janet's great uncle is murdered, she lives alone with him, all the windows are locked and she is suspected of murder. Fleming Stone investigates.

012645   THE CLUE. Philadelphia: J. B. Lippincott, 1909 NUC. London: Hodder & Stoughton, [1920] BMC.

Trad. detective. PW 10-23-09

012646   THE CURVED BLADES. Philadelphia and London: J. B. Lippincott, 1916 BMC NUC.

Mystery. Fleming Stone called in to solve. PW 89 3/11/16:938
NYT-Shows us Fleming Stone in love-

012647   THE DIAMOND PIN. Philadelphia and London: J. B. Lippincott, 1919 BMC NUC.

Murder mystery-trad. TLS
Fleming Stone PW
BKM, May '19
NYT 3-30-19, 169 Eccentric woman who loved to play practical jokes found murdered. Jewels gone but no evidence that one could escape the room where the murder committed.

012648   THE DISAPPEARANCE OF KIMBALL WEBB. BY ROLAND WRIGHT. New York: Dodd, Mead, 1920 NUC.

"Mystery and adventure story centering about a man who

disappears as if by magic the night before his
proposed wedding to a beautiful young heiress. All
efforts to find him prove for weeks in vain. Some
think him spirited away by ghosts. Elsie, the heiress,
is implored by her relatives to marry some one else,
for if she does not marry soon, by the conditions of
the will, she loses her fortune. But for her there is
no one but Webb. Finally after desperate efforts, and
dreadful adventures, the mystery is solved at last.
Webb is brought back in time to save the fortune, and
the "master mind" who has spirited the bridegroom away
and kept him basely hid is one least expected." BRD

012649   THE DORRANCE DOMAIN. Boston: W. A. Wilde,
[c1905] NUC.

Old Lady, young grandchildren run a hotel. PW 10-28-05

012650   THE EMILY EMMINS PAPERS. New York and
London: G. P. Putnam's Sons, 1907 BMC NUC.

Young woman loves to travel and wander about PW
11-23-07

012651   FAULKNER'S FOLLY. New York: G. H. Doran,
[c1917] NUC.

Trad detective PW
Two women suspected of murder that happens in a
building named after architect (title) NYT

012652   IN THE ONYX LOBBY. New York: G. H. Doran,
[c1920] NUC. London: Hodder & Stoughton, [1920] BMC.

PW-myst.
TLS det.
NYT 9-12-20, p26. Roisterer murdered, chorus girl
suspected.

012653   THE MAN WHO FELL THROUGH THE EARTH. New
York: G. H. Doran, [c1919] NUC. London: G. G. Harrap,
1924 BMC.

Mystery-murder solved by the master detective Penny
Wise and asst. Zizi. PW

012654   THE MARK OF CAIN. Philadelphia: J. B.
Lippincott, 1917 BMC NUC. London: Hodder & Stoughton,
[1920] BMC.

Mystery detective Trad TLS
Another Fleming Stone mystery NYT

012655   THE MAXWELL MYSTERY. Philadelphia and
London: J. B. Lippincott, 1913 NUC.

PW 83 3/22/13 p.1103 "First scene is a gay house party
at a country place in New Jersey. On the second night,
the dance which is in progress is startlingly
interrupted by the announcement of what looks like a
double murder, committed in the library. It proves,
however, that only the man has been killed, the girl
being merely wounded and found unconscious with a
revolver in her hand. Many of the guests are suspected
at different times, but it is only when Fleming Stone,
the detective of "A chain of evidence," is called in
that the mystery is solved. Experiences of a beautiful
Russian. As a restless, motherless girl she becomes
the wife of a dissolute Russian army officer. Divorce
rescues her."

012656   PATTY AT HOME. New York: Dodd, Mead, 1904
NUC.

PW-Very unlikely, daughter of rich father furnishes a
home.

012657   PATTY-BRIDE. New York: Dodd, Mead, 1918
NUC.

PW Patty does war within and has an intrigue, marries
a captain.

012658   PATTY'S SUITORS. New York: Dodd, Mead,
1914 NUC.

Patty has lots of suitors but is determined not to
marry for awhile. PW 1-9-15

012659   RASPBERRY JAM. Philadelphia and London:
J. B. Lippincott, 1920 BMC NUC.

TLS F. Stone det.
ATH Aided by a preternaturally smart 16 year old who
finds clue in raspberry jam stain.
NYT 4/4/20 p1. Wife suspected of husband's murder.

012660   THE ROOM WITH THE TASSELS. New York: G.
H. Doran, [c1918] NUC.

NYT Oct 27 '18 p 459. Haunted house, occupied by group
of friends interested in spirits and the occult.
Former murder. Then a new and terrible crime.
Detective Pennington Wise and his assistant Zizi.

012661   THE STAYING GUEST. New York: Century,
1904 BMC NUC.

012662   TROTTY'S TRIP. Philadelphia: D. Biddle,
[1902] NUC.

012663   TWO LITTLE WOMEN ON A HOLIDAY. New York:
Dodd, Mead, 1915 NUC.

In NYC, a gay time, two young men come to rescue PW

012664   VICKY VAN. Philadelphia and London: J. B.
Lippincott, 1918 BMC NUC.

PW-tr. myst.
ATH Fleming Stone solve.

012665   THE WHITE ALLEY. Philadelphia and London:
J. B. Lippincott, 1915 BMC NUC.

Trad. detective 5-1-15 NYT

WELLS, FLORENCE. United States.

012666   TAMA; THE DIARY OF A JAPANESE SCHOOL
GIRL. New York: Woman's Press, 1919 NUC.

Diary of a Japanese schoolgirl. NYT

WELTY, CORA GOTTSCHALK. 1876-1951. United States.

012667   THE MASQUERADING OF MARGARET. Boston:
C.M. Clark, 1908 NUC.

Amish people, Margaret a city girl masquerades as an
Amish girl. Happy end. PW 4-3-09

WEMYSS, MARY C. E. United Kingdom.

012668   GRANNIE. BY MRS. GEORGE WEMYSS. New York:
Macmillan, 1914 NUC.

PW 85 4/4/14 p. 1163 "Grannie is an utterly delightful
old lady who thoroughly understands that while it was
her duty to bring up her children, it is her privilege
to spoil her grandchildren. She writes a book in which
she tells of her feelings for her thirteen
grandchildren, their fathers and mothers, the clever
things they say and do, and even their naughtinesses,
which are never really naughty to her. She also
assists the love affair of her oldest granddaughter,
and that of her youngest daughter, and it is all told
with an unfailing sense of humor and a wealth of
affection for children. By author of 'The professional
aunt'."

012669   GRANNIE FOR GRANTED. BY MRS. GEORGE
WEMYSS. London: Constable, 1914 BMC NUC.

LBKM- joys of being a grandmother.
SR 147 supp 21 Mar. p 10. Pretty, pleasant.

012670   IMPOSSIBLE PEOPLE. London: Constable,
1918 BMC NUC. Boston: Houghton, Mifflin, 1918 NUC.

TLS-rector, his wife and their community.
SR
NYT-John and Joanna are impossible but likeable. Her
house is persistently untidy, reviewer feels it "could
scarcely have been a very comfortable abode." After
their baby dies, they adopt a child. Story is of her,
her adopted parents, and her real parents, also
impossible.
PW-Unconventional. John, clergyman, and Joanna, wife,
and their conventional daughter Hope. Story is mainly
of John and Joanna.

012671   JAUNTY IN CHARGE. BY MRS. GEORGE WEMYSS.
London: Constable, 1915 BMC. New York: E. P. Dutton,
[1916] NUC.

NYT-story of a butler bringing up two little
girls-loveable, whims, etc.
Little story of the loves and lives of Pamela and
Sally. TLS
Heroine suffers because of unconventional upbringing
by butler mother put her children in charge of butler

when she died-didn't trust irresponsible husband. ATH
Romance and tears. Sentimental. SP

012672   A LOST INTEREST. BY MRS. GEORGE WEMYSS.
London: Constable, 1912 BMC. Toronto: McClelland,
[1912?] NUC.

TLS-pursuit of a young wife by a Lothario.
ATH-0
ACAD-husband sent to Africa during 1st 3 months of
marriage, is a lost interest to his grass widow.
Thanks to a cynical old sinner Georgina Blatherwake
she is able to look her husband in face on his return.
Best book of year. Witty and brilliant cleverness.
Wife is pawn of story.

012673   ORANGES AND LEMONS. London: Constable,
1919 BMC. Boston: Houghton, Mifflin, 1919 NUC.

SR-family
Traditional stuff involving uncle and two nieces. TLS
Conventional, mildly amusing love tale of Diana and
Elsie. NYT 355,6-29-19

012674   PEOPLE OF POPHAM. London: Constable, 1911
BMC. Boston: Houghton Mifflin, [1911] NUC.

romantic TLS
Small town. NYT

012675   PETUNIA. BY MRS. GEORGE WEMYSS. London:
Constable, 1916 BMC NUC. New York: Dutton, [1917] NUC.

Will-girl must not marry PW 91:1279 4/21/17.
Light and bright. SR
She is colorless, dull. Her father leaves everything
to her, not to his five sons, with the stipulation
that it's hers until she weds. The brothers get to the
business of finding her a husband. She finds her own.
NYT 7-8-17 259
TLS domestic comedy

012676   PRISCILLA. London: Constable, 1912 BMC.

ATH-prattle of a bride.
Married at 17, approaching maternity at 23. The book
is "the reflection of a state of mind." SP
Positively vulgar. Silly. SR

012677   THE PROFESSIONAL AUNT. London: Constable,
1910 BMC. Boston: Houghton Mifflin, 1910 NUC.

Dealing with the experiences of a charming young woman
whose married sisters have made her a professional
aunt: BKM v.31,1910.
TLS-weds her lover at the end
NYT-sunshiney.

012678   PRUDENT PRISCILLA. Boston: Houghton
Mifflin, 1912 NUC.

NYT-dumb Prisc.

WEMYSS, MRS. GEORGE. See WEMYSS, MARY C. E.

WENTWORTH, PATRICIA, pseud. See TURNBULL, DORA AMY DILLON.

WERNER, ALICE. 1859-1935. South Africa.

012679   O'DRISCOLL'S WEIRD AND OTHERS STORIES.
London: Cassell, 1892 BMC NUC.

WERNER, E., pseud. See BUERSTENBINDER, ELISABETH.

WEST, CONSTANCE.

012680   ASPIRATIONS. A STORY OF TO-DAY. London:
G. Richards, 1902 BMC.

WEST, FRANCES.

012681   A GIRL OF METTLE. London: Collins
Clear-Type Press, [1908] BMC.

WEST, KENYON, pseud. See HOWLAND, FRANCES LOUISE (MORSE).

WEST, LILLIAN (CLARKSON). B. 1869.

012682   AUNT HOPE'S KITCHEN STOVE AND THE GIRLS
AROUND IT. Cincinnati: Stewart & Kidd, 1911 NUC.

WEST, MARY. United Kingdom.

012683   A BORN PLAYER. New York and London:
Macmillan, 1893 NUC BMC.

Minister becomes actor and dies on eve of success.
BAKER 03, 185
Prejudices vs the stage, divisions of church of
England and nonconformity explored. LW 93, 75
Sees Edmund Kean as Lear. We follow his career to sad
end. SR 75:300.
Raised in rigid Wesleyan faith where theatre is
forbidden. Becomes a minister but just can't preach.
Died at the end of performance in Romeo and Juliet. CR
14, 20:363

012684   HESTER NEALE: A NOVEL. London: Simpkin,
Marshall, [1896] BMC.

WEST, MRS. RANYARD.

012685   MARGARET AND THE DOCTOR. London: Mills
and Boon, 1913 BMC.

Scottish tale-farmer marries servant lass whose
"modesty and charm conquer local prejudices" TLS

WEST, REBECCA, pseud. See FAIRFIELD, CICILY ISABEL ANDREWS.

WEST, ROGER, pseud. See WATSON, VIRGINIA CRUSE.

WEST, V. SACKVILLE. See NICHOLSON, VICTORIA MARY
SACKVILLE-WEST.

WESTBURY, ATHA.

012686   THE SHADOW OF HILTON FERNBROOK. A ROMANCE
OF MAORILAND. London: Chatto and Windus, [1896] NUC
BMC. New York: New Amsterdam Book, [1896] NUC.

ATH 107:61. "Wild incoherence," "harmless" and
"foolish"
ACAD 50:178. Maoriland. Crime and fighting. An escaped
convict impersonates another man, gets away with it
until a girl the man was once engaged to notices a
small difference.
SP 77:249. Also hypnotism.
SR Sumptuousness surrounds heroine.

WESTON, E. MARGARET.

012687   PAMELA'S CHOICE. London: Isbister, [1904]
BMC.

Mid-aged woman devotes fortune to women who are
willing to ignore the existence of men. One young man
to "reach" a young woman so committed disguises as an
old woman. The mid-aged woman becomes poor-gets a job
working for the diguised old lady' ATH 44,05

WESTON, KATE HELEN.

012688   THE MAN MACDONALD. London: Holden &
Hardingham, [1912] BMC.

Painful Eurasian problem. ATH 115
Eurasian Flora marries an Englishman. Author allows
death to save the happiness of her hero. LBKM

012689   THE PARTNERS. A TALE OF THE NOR'WEST
COAST OF AUSTRALIA. London: Hutchinson, 1911 BMC NUC.

Tale of northwest coast of Australia. ATH

012690   THE PRELUDE. London: Holden & Hardingham,
[1914] BMC.

ATH-An Australian story, in which the heroine, after
leaving her husband and child, is wrecked on an island
with a Socialist.
TLS-Reviewer does not like her. She buys a newspaper,
runs it, promotes Socialist lover. After both husband
and lover are dead she suddenly (according to rev)
remembers her child and selfishly takes him away from
her mother-in-law, back to a world of work.

WESTOVER, CYNTHIA M. See ALDEN, CYNTHIA MAY (WESTOVER).

WESTRUP, MARGARET. See STACEY, MARGARET (WESTRUP).

WETMORE, ELIZABETH (BISLAND). 1861-1929. United States.

012691   A CANDLE OF UNDERSTANDING. A NOVEL. BY
ELIZABETH BISLAND. New York and London: Harper, 1903
BMC NUC.

Girl grows up to be an actress. Gives up her career
for quiet happiness. PW 10-3-83
NYT 03,719-a story after Civil War, doesn't say much
about heroine, told from point of view of young girl.
Career of actress in disillusionary fashion.

012692   THE CASE OF JOHN SMITH: HIS HEAVEN AND
HIS HELL. BY ELIZABETH BISLAND. New York and London:
G. P. Putnam's Sons, 1916 BMC NUC.

Religion and an ordinary man. PW
NYT
"Shining One" is the leader-through visions-of Smith
and his wife. TLS

012693   A FLYING TRIP AROUND THE WORLD. New York:
Harper, 1891 NUC. London: Osgood and McIlvaine, 1891
BMC.

Miss Bisland is sent by prominent magazine to make a
tour around the world in order to beat Nelly Bly's
record for such a tour. Nellie Bly famous for her
tour. PW 6-6-91 well-written

WETMORE, ELIZABETH (BISLAND), jt. au. See BROUGHTON, RHODA
AND ELIZABETH (BISLAND) WETMORE.

WHARTON, ANNE HOLLINGSWORTH. 1845-1928. United States.

012694   AN ENGLISH HONEYMOON. Philadelphia: J. B.
Lippincott, 1908 NUC. London: W. Heinemann, 1909 BMC.

PW travel
NYT travel
DA630 Eng-Des & trad.

012695   ITALIAN DAYS AND WAYS. Philadelphia and
London: J.B. Lippincott, 1906 NUC.

PW-Travel and Love.

012696   A ROSE OF OLD QUEBEC. Philadelphia and
London: J. B. Lippincott, 1913 BMC NUC.

PW84 11/8/13:1534 "Uses the historical love affair
between Lord Nelson, then a young captain, and a
Quebec beauty. Their first meeting is at a ball given
in honor of the captain and crew of the "Albemarie,"
at which affair, Mary Thompson, the heroine,
dances...with Ensign Allan McGregor, who later plays
an important part in the romance. Old Quebec with its
many historical associations is the background..."

WHARTON, EDITH NEWBOLD (JONES). 1862-1937. United States.

012697   THE AGE OF INNOCENCE. New York: Appleton,
1920 BMC NUC.

PW young American woman, unhappily married to a Pole,
returns to face cramped viewpoint of NY society.
NYT 10-17-20 p1.

012698   THE CUSTOM OF THE COUNTRY. New York: C.
Scribner's Sons, 1913 NUC. London: Macmillan, 1913
BMC.

PW 84 11/1/13:1436 "Undine Spragg, the heroine,
presents a picture of unmitigated selfishness, and a
greed which she uses her beauty to satisfy. Her father
having made a fortune in Apex City, brings his wife
and daughter to New York where the latter begins her
career of climbing. She marries Ralph Marvell, son of
an old conservative New York family, flirts with
dissipated, wealthy, Peter Van Degen, leaves her
husband and goes to Europe. Ralph kills himself, and
Undine marries a French nobleman, divorces him and
marries Elmer Moffatt, a multi-millionaire, whom she
had married and divorced in Apex City days."
4 matrimonial ventures, deals with the break in each.
Purpose: to show the scandalous state of American
divorce laws--too easy (?) According to ACAD reviewer.
Heroine-3 divorces. Really attacks a class of social
climbers who make marriage a business. SP
"Undine...the most repellant heroine...monstrous. To
gratify all her wishes. Discontented. Bitterly
disappointed in her lack of social opportunities. Her
child's birth she resents." 1913, NYT 557
The author's theme is that it is the custom of the
country for mmen not to let their wives share in the
real business of life; that it is normal for a man to
work hard for a woman, but quite abnormal not to care
to tell her anything about it; that women do not take
an interest in the work of men because men do not take
enough interest in them. The central figure, a
selfish, ambitious, uncultivated woman, about whom the
theme is elaborated is, naturally, an unpleasant
individual to follow through the six hundred pages of
the book. Yet the portrayal is masterly and most
artistic." BRD
"Mrs. Wharton has painted Undine Spragg with an
unsparing mercilessness that almost makes the reader

wince. It is a splendid and memorable piece of work, a
portrait to form a worthy contrast to the equally
unforgetable one of Lily Bart." F.T. Cooper BKM 38:416
D '13
LBKM-Custom is rapid mating. Depicts troubles
inflicted on child by divorce. Inner misery of a woman
who is inferior to all the men she marries. No moral
drawn.

012699   ETHAN FROME. New York: C. Scribner's
Sons, 1911 NUC. London: Macmillan, 1911 BMC NUC.

Upon these innocent lovers come years of disease,
hopelessness. TLS
Centers on Ethan. ACAD
A man, a sickly wife and the woman Ethan loves and who
almost died in their attempt to commit suicide
together. SP

012700   THE FRUIT OF THE TREE. New York: C.
Scribner's Sons, 1907 BMC NUC. London: Macmillan, 1907
BMC NUC.

Set up like 3 separate stories. 1 conventional:
Justine in 2 & 3 makes a good heroine. TLS
BKM 273-5 (1907) 26 Man marries widow-owner of mill
but marriage goes bad. Wife Bessy self centered,
emotional. Justine Brent, nurse tries to bring them
together but falls for man (a reformist) and he for
her. Wife falls from horse. see notes
ACAD--a woman who is self-sacrificing but can't keep
it up, story of her relationship with man, another
strong working woman. Character study.

012701   A GIFT FROM THE GRAVE. London: J. Murray,
1900 BMC NUC.

See the Touchstone.

012702   THE HOUSE OF MIRTH. New York: C.
Scribner's Sons, 1905 NUC. London: Macmillan, 1905 BMC
NUC.

012703   MADAME DE TREYMES. New York: Scribner's
Sons, 1907 NUC. London: Macmillan, 1907 BMC.

Divorce. Woman wants divorce from intolerable husband,
his family seeks to get her son. PW 3-16-07
BKM 25 (1907) 303-4
France & American attitudes: divorce. LBKM 6-02,113
Injustice to women of France divorce laws; woman
remains in marriage rather than give up child. R OF R
35 1907
American with French Catholic husband, separated but
won't divorce for scandal will hurt her child. A
previous lover proposes and he helps her get an
undefended divorce--almost, for family really wants
the child. ACAD
The great force of the French family as an
organization. SP

012704   THE MARNE: A TALE OF THE WAR. London:
Macmillan, 1918 BMC NUC. New York: D. Appleton, 1918
NUC.

TLS-war and male hero.
NYT-Dec 8 '18 p 537. Critical of U.S. neutrality.
Short war story. LBKM
Troy Belknap loves France as few Americans do because
he spent his boyhood summers there. War comes. He goes
to France as ambulance driver. NYT

012705   THE REEF, A NOVEL. London: Macmillan,
1912 BMC. New York: D. Appleton, 1912 NUC.

BKM v.36
TLS-story of a woman who is too regulated and
repressed.
SR-Sophy meets Darrow while traveling alone in France;
they see sights of Paris together and spend 1 rainy
day in hotel. She goes to England, becomes governess
employed by Anna Leath who has become engaged to
Darrow. She becomes engaged to young Leath, and Darrow
and she feel they have to make a general confession of
their Paris adventure. Tragedy follows.
NYT 0
Darrow loves Mrs. Leath. Goes to Paris to her-to
propose. Just as he's about to arrive, she wires him
to postpone his visit. Irritated, he runs across Sophy
Viner, a paid companion to a friend of his, now out of
work. He shows her Paris; she's grateful. When he gets
the notice from Mrs. Leath, he destroys it, feeling
unworthy. Mrs. Leath sends another message 6 months
later. He goes and finds that Sophy is now governess
to Mrs. Leath's child and about to marry her brother.
Sophy renounces the marriage because she finds she

loves Darrow. Mrs. Leath learns the truth, forgives everyone. LBKM

012706   SANCTUARY. New York: C. Scribner's Sons, 1903 BMC NUC. London: Macmillan, 1903 BMC.

About heredity. PW 11-14-03
Responsibility to unborn--saves lover's children from weak mother, gives her own children a morally weak father. Superbly strong woman struggles with the inherited taint of her only son. NYT 836,03
Denis does wrong, confesses to fiance who at first wants to break off; then realizes she still loves him. For the sake of the children they might have, she marries Denis. She finds in her son the same weakness, but forewarned as no other woman might be, she checks it and saves him-breaking the heredity thing. LBKM 12-03,150
Mother found married life tragic; works to prevent her son from following in father's footsteps and does so. ATH 122,750

012707   SUMMER: A NOVEL. New York: D. Appleton, 1917 BMC NUC. London: Macmillan, 1917 BMC.

Charity Royall child of convict and dissolute Ma, raised by kind lawyer, becomes mistress to young man who leaves her pregnant. The lawyer gives her the protection of his name. PW
Small NE town. New York man dazzled her. Charity visits an insinuating lady-doctor. TLS
Old lawyer weds her out of compassion. SP
Her fall not allowed to ruin her life. Told with sympathy. SR

012708   THE TOUCHSTONE. New York: C. Scribner's Sons, 1900 NUC.

NYT 1900:302. Glennard publishes a number of letters anonymously to get money to marry Alexa, a treachery to a dead friend. How it affects him, their marriage, final tragedy.
SP 85:181 (A Gift From the Grave.) He publishes intimate letters to himself from a novelist, revealing her name but not his.
ACAD 59:173. Margaret Aubyn, a woman who combined personal shyness and intellectual audacity; has passion for Glennard who lacks the capacity to love so big a woman.

012709   THE VALLEY OF DECISION. New York: C. Scribner's Sons, 1902 NUC. London: J. Murray, 1902 BMC.

BKM, Apr, 1902.
ATH 6-14-02.

WHATHAM, MARGARET E.

012710   ADRIFT IN A GREAT CITY, A STORY. BY M. E. WINCHESTER. London: Seeley, 1893 BMC NUC.

012711   A DOUBLE CHERRY, A STORY. BY M. E. WINCHESTER. New York: Macmillan, 1894 NUC. London: Seeley, 1895 BMC NUC.

012712   LITTLE KING RANNIE, THE MISSING HEIR OF CAMBERLEY, A NOVEL. BY M. E. WINCHESTER. London: Digby, Long, 1899 BMC.

A shipwreck, missing heir, a boy who comes into his own. A novel-despite the title, insists the reviewer. SR 88:305

012713   A ROMANCE OF THE UNSEEN, A NOVEL. BY M. E. WINCHESTER. London: Digby, Long, 1900 BMC. (The running title is "The Harbour Bar" BMC)

ATH 116:545. The occult, Algernon, stupid but innocent, and his two wives.

012714   TEMPEST-TOSSED, A NOVEL. BY M. E. WINCHESTER. London: Digby, Long, 1899 BMC.

SP 84:176. Melodrama and the slums.
ACAD 58:84. Hero is an indolent young medical student.

WHEAT, LU. United States.

012715   AH MOY, THE STORY OF A CHINESE GIRL. New York: Grafton Press, [c1908] NUC.

Begins before her birth, with father's prayer for a son but affection grows between them. Her feet are bound; she is betrothed but fiance killed in Boxer Rebellion. Father, now poor sells her to slave dealer hoping she'll marry a rich merchant. But he gives her a knife to save herself from shame should things go bad. Carried off to Chinatown hell in San Francisco. Uses father's knife. NYT
"Ah Moy is a Chinese girl, beloved by her parents, and one who had led a happy life until a famine struck the land. when her father had reached the end of his resources it seemed that there was nothing left to be done, in order to protect his wife and their son, but to part with Ah Moy. She was a girl of great beauty and the slave dealer was willing to pay a big price for her, which sum would be sufficient to tide the family over until the rains came and they were once more able to return to the ancestral home." BKM v28 1908-9
Her owner takes her to San Francisco. Missionairies try to free her in court but lose case.

012716   HELEN; A STORY OF THINGS TO BE. New York: Grafton Press, [c1908] NUC.

"The scene is laid in Southern California and Helen is the only child of William Andrews, the owner of a ranch there. After her father's death Helen rents the ranch and goes to the city to study art." BKM 28 1908-9

012717   THE THIRD DAUGHTER; OR A STORY OF CHINESE HOME LIFE. Los Angeles: Oriental Pub. Co., [c1906] NUC.

WHEATLEY, LOUISE KNIGHT. United States.

012718   ASHES OF ROSES. New York: Dodd, Mead, [c1893] NUC. London: B. F. Stevens, [1893] BMC.

"Second glow of love in a man's heart." LW 93, 369. Told by daughter of his old sweetheart. The old man meets her and thinks again of his lost love. PW 10-14-93.
Ruth Penrose, the fourth, meets the old man who may have known her great grandmother. CR 20, 2 3:298.

WHEATON, EMILY. Nationality Unknown.

012719   THE RUSSELLS IN CHICAGO. Boston: L.C. Page, 1902 NUC.

WHEELER, CORA KELLEY. United States.

012720   MY ALLEGIANCE. Franklin, Ohio: Editor Pub. Co., 1896 NUC.

WHEELER, ESTHER GRACIE (LAWRENCE). United States.

012721   A WASHINGTON SYMPHONY. BY MRS. WILLIAM LAMONT WHEELER. New York, London: G. P. Putnam's Sons, 1893 NUC.

A young woman's relationship with a married man. Also two murders and a happy end. LW 93:179.
Mrs. Leigh-Scott brilliant talker, good listener-has all the virtues. CR 20, 23:87.

WHEELER, HALLIE ERMINIE (RIVES). 1876-1956. United States.

012722   AS THE HART PANTETH. BY HALLIE ERMINIE RIVES. New York: G. W. Dillingham, 1898 NUC.

PW-idealistic young man offers violinist platonic friendship. He believes marriage and home cares should not stand in way of highest art. She loves him but is too proud to tell him because of his belief.
Young woman is a violinist. Grows up with young man, a poet who is her friend, chaperone, critic. She becomes famous. Then he realizes he loves her, leaves because she's devoted to her art. She learns then that love comes first. BKM 8:494.

012723   THE CASTAWAY: THREE GREAT MEN RUINED IN ONE YEAR--A KING, A CAD, AND A CASTAWAY. BY HALLIE ERMINIE RIVES. Indianapolis: Bobbs-Merrill, [1904] BMC NUC.

PW Byron as hero.
NYT-0
TLS-Lord Byron

012724   A FOOL IN SPOTS. BY HALLIE ERMINIE RIVES. Saint Louis: Woodward and Tiernan Print. Co., [c1894] NUC.

Kentucky daughter of ex-Confederate officer marries New York artist. Her domestic infelicity is the story. PW 3-9-95:423.

012725 A FURNACE OF EARTH. BY HALLIE ERMINIE
RIVES. London: G. Richards, 1900 BMC. New York:
Camelot, 1900 NUC.

BKM 12:193. Physically passionate Margaret. Sample:
moods sometimes struck through her like the smell of
earth to a wild thing of the jungle. She has a lover
whom she loves passionately, but she has been taught
to despise her physical responses and yearns for
spiritual development. So she refuses him until a time
when, as a nurse on probation, he is brought to the
hospital seriously injured and she realizes she would
love him if he were a physical wreck.
Sp 85:464. "Purple patches," hero must be crippled
before heroine is persuaded her love is not too earthy
for marriage.
LIT 7:326. Erotic descriptions of their love, sensual.

012726 HEARTS COURAGEOUS. BY HALLIE ERMINIE
RIVES. London: B. F. Stevens & Brown, [1902] BMC.
Indianapolis: Bobbs-Merrill, [1902] NUC.

Virginia's love story; days of Revolutionary War. Full
of incidents, adventures. ATH, TLS

012727 THE KINGDOM OF SLENDER SWORDS. BY HALLIE
ERMINIE RIVES (MRS. POST WHEELER). Indianapolis:
Bobbs-Merrill, [c1910] NUC. London: Everett, 1911 BMC.

Concerns an inventor in Japan. TLS
NYT-love story.

012728 THE LONG LANE'S TURNING. BY HALLIE
ERMINIE RIVES (MRS. POST WHEELER). New York: Dodd,
Mead, 1917 NUC. London: Hurst & Blackett, 1918 BMC.

TLS-evil of drink.
Echo (the heroine) desired by two men, their struggle;
a murder, etc. PW
Evils of drink affect all the characters. BAKER
'32:409 BKM
A melodramatic temperance novel. NYT

012729 SATAN SANDERSON. BY HALLIE ERMINIE RIVES.
Indianapolis: Bobbs-Merrill, [1907] NUC. London:
Hutchinson, 1908 BMC.

"Conspicuous for very poor qualities, has to do with
the marriage of a blind girl to a criminal. One of the
chief episodes of the story is a game of cards for
money, played on the communion table of a church,
whose rector himself suggests the game and
participates in it!" R OF R v.37,1908
TLS-self sacrificing male hero; mistaken identity.
A college rake. PW 8-17-07

012730 SMOKING FLAX. BY HALLIE ERMINIE RIVES.
London, New York: F. T. Neely, [c1897] BMC NUC.

Elliott Harding is a Northerner who is against
lynching but comes to understand the So. point of view
when his betrothed is raped and murdered. PW 52:709

012731 THE VALIANTS OF VIRGINIA. BY HALLIE
ERMINIE RIVES (MRS. POST WHEELER). Indianapolis:
Bobbs-Merrill, [c1912] NUC BMC. London: Mills & Boon,
1913 BMC.

young man goes to Virginia after the company he works
for fails, discovers he owns a 1200 acre farm, falls
in love with a woman who at last consents to marry
him. NYT

WHEELER, HARRIET MARTHA. B. 1858. United States.

012732 THE WOMAN IN STONE; A NOVEL. New York:
Broadway, 1903 NUC.

WHEELER, HELEN MAUDE. Nationality Unknown.

012733 AN UP-TO-DATE PAUPER. Boston: C.M. Clark,
1907 NUC.

From poverty to struggle. Becomes singer. PW 12-28-07

WHEELER, IDA WORDEN. United States.

012734 SIEGFRIED, THE MYSTIC: A NOVEL. Boston:
Arena, 1896 NUC BMC.

PW 2-29-96. His mission is to lead people to be
stronger, braver, more loving, kind, etc.

WHEELER, MRS. POST. See WHEELER, HALLIE ERMINIE (RIVES).

WHEELER, MRS. WILLIAM LAMONT. See WHEELER, ESTHER GRACIE

(LAWRENCE).

WHEELER, PRESERVED, pseud. See MACDOUGALL, ELLA L.
(RANDALL).

WHEELWRIGHT, EDITH GRAY.

012735 ANTHONY GRAEME. London: R. Bentley, 1895
BMC NUC.

He's a don wrapped up in his books; therefore his
marriage fails. SR:80:447
Wife tries to get interested in philosophy. They drift
apart because he's a cold turkey. She leaves. He
realizes his loss, goes after her but it's too late.
She died rescuing a drowning child. He dies of a
broken heart. ACAD 48:336
N.E. story "unforseen growth of love in an
intellectual and unimpassioned nature." BAKER 03, 187

012736 A SLOW AWAKENING. London: Chatto &
Windus, 1902 BMC.

ACAD

012737 THE VENGEANCE OF MEDEA. London: Digby,
Lang, [1894] BMC.

SR-2 girls and an artist friend. Full of complications
and strange events.
ATH 104:825. "The most tiresome of the group is
addressed as Poetess or my Poetess by a youthful
female admirer perhaps seventeen times or thereabouts
in the course of a page." Characters lack worldly
wisdom.

WHERRY, ALBINIA LUCY (CUST). B. 1857.

012738 CHRONICLES OF ERTHIG ON THE DYKE. BY
ALBINIA LUCY CUST (MRS. WHERRY). New York and London:
John Lane, 1914 NUC BMC.

PW 86 10/10/14:1209 "Story not of a family, but of a
house. Letters and Mss. are from a house in Wales, and
date back to the seventeenth century. Written by such
different people as the first squire who knew the
debtors' price, the successful lawyer who bought up
the estate and established himself there, politicians
and courtiers, even the servants to each other, they
have human as well as historical interest."

WHERRY, EDITH. See MUCKLESTON, EDITH MARGARET (WHERRY).

WHERRY, MRS. See WHERRY, ALBINIA LUCY (CUST).

WHITAKER, EVELYN. Fl. 1891-1903. United States.

012739 BELLE. BY THE AUTHOR OF LADDIE
[ANONYMOUS]. London and Edinburgh: W. & R. Chambers,
1898 BMC. Boston: Little, Brown, 1898 NUC.

LW 29:456. Heir amuses himself with her but wants
financial marriage. When he does propose finally,
Belle rejects him in favor of an old comrade.

WHITAKER, LYDIA. United States.

012740 THE PROPHET OF MARTINIQUE; A LOVE STORY
EMBRACING A VIVID ACCOUNT OF THE HISTORIC DESTRUCTION
OF MONT PELEE. New York: J.S. Barcus, [c1906] NUC.

NYT-Volcanic eruption, male hero.

WHITBY, BEATRICE. D. 1931. United Kingdom.

012741 AFTER ALL. London: Hurst & Blackett, 1904
BMC.

012742 BEQUEATHED; A NOVEL. London: Hurst and
Blackett, 1900 BMC. New York and London: Harper, 1900
NUC.

NYT 1900:534. Ethel, sweet, womanly, marries, dies in
childbirth. Husband replaces her with her antithesis
and regrets until he dies. Daughter, too, a loveless
life, but wedding bells at end.
LBKM 18:127. Letice, daughter, is heroine.
SP 84:778. She is conventional type of modern heroine,
therefore not as attractive as her Victorian mother.
ATH 115:683. Author writes quiet studies in human
nature--especially in womankind. Mother & daughter are
full of tenderness and gentle influences.

012743 FLOWER AND THORN. New York: Dodd, Mead,
1901 NUC. London: Hurst & Blackett, 1901 BMC.

012744   IN THE SUNTIME OF HER YOUTH. London:
Hurst and Blackett, 1893 BMC NUC. New York: D.
Appleton, 1893 NUC.

Agnes and Elspeth Trevor-sisters. Grow up as tomboys,
mother is a worn anxious woman. Neither sister has
"suntime"; Agnes weds a selfish middle-aged man.
Elspeth is responsible for family when father dies.
Love stories for each. PW 1-21-93.
Celia is youngest. Agnes marries a man 40 years older
who is rich-for family's sake. Celia dies in a boat
accident caused by Agnes. Agnes' old husband dies and
she weds a younger man she was attracted to earlier.
Elsie eventually marries a bookworm. SR 75:127.
Cheerless. ACAD 43:195

012745   MARY FENWICK'S DAUGHTER, A NOVEL. London:
Hurst and Blackett, 1894 BMC NUC. New York: D.
Appleton, 1894 NUC.

SR 77:668. Romance, two suitors.
SP 72:907. Bab Fenwick had friendly feelings for both,
desired neither as a lover, yet accepted both.
"Absolutely incapable of any emotion warmer than
genial camaraderie."
ACAD 46:63. Bab is not a new woman "which follows from
the fact that she is a lady; but she is hoidenal,
first, in being very athletic, and, secondly, in not
ostensibly feeling the necessity of anything more than
comradeship with the opposite sex." Reviewer seems to
say that she broke her back, then was jilted, and
thrown, "in the condition of damaged goods, a penitent
and an invalid, on the hands of good cousin Jack."
Reviewer says process probably tamed her at least till
she got quite well.
ATH 103:675. Bab is a familiar type of English country
house life. Manly and chivalrous maiden. Unconscious
egotism with which this stupid girl tramples on all
the finer susceptibilities of the young man.
PW one of the mannish girls of today.
Called Bab-raised in open air riding horses that no
one could control. Didn't take men seriously, said
she'd marry her old friend Jack just to get rid of the
others. Jack proposed, but she learned she didn't want
him. Later she has an accident with a runaway horse.
Jack's devotion makes her realize she loves him. CR
23:7

012746   A MATTER OF SKILL. New York: Appleton,
1891. London: Hurst and Blackett, 1896 BMC NUC.

Helen Milford, proud indulged daughter, leaves home to
escape attentions of her father's curates. She
considers love a weakness and imagines herself
invulnerable. Then Albert Jones tries to win her. PW
7-25-96.
Meets her fate in Albert. LW

012747   ONE REASON WHY. New York: D. Appleton,
1891 NUC. London: Hurst and Blackett, 1892 BMC NUC.

Governess-heroine. SP 67 763
Sensitive, common sense type-Ursula, a put upon
heroine, rivals with a haughty damsel for heir's hand
and wins. ACAD
Ursula Nugent waits a long time to respond to eldest
son in whose house she is governess because she wants
to be sure of his love. (His earlier attachment to a
matron cools when she gets fat.) ATH 98 646
Also she thinks he might regret marrying below his
social class. PW 10-17-92.
Governess and young son of proprietor of house fall in
love. His mother burned to death, she's badly hurt
by a dog (the governess), and there's a ghost. Hero
and heroine argue and love. 11-14-91 SR, 561

012748   THE RESULT OF AN ACCIDENT. London:
Methuen, 1908 BMC.

TLS-from a woman's pov, the mother; provides a reason
why the average marriage is as successful as it is.
ATH O

012749   ROSAMUND. London: Methuen, [1911] BMC
NUC.

"Rosamund went out to India, as a beautiful bride and
returned as a widow with twins-broken down, hopeless,
reserved and cold-as depressed with her lot as the
reader will be by the record of it." TLS
Psychological problem. ATH

012750   SUNSET. New York: D. Appleton, 1897 NUC.
London: Hurst and Blackett, 1898 BMC NUC.

SR 85:119. Contrast in the methods of two sets of

parents in rearing their daughters.
ACAD 53:4. Frances refuses to marry man she loves
because he is poor. At 24, she is still in love with
him; he is a widower. However, he no longer wants to
marry her and goes to Australia, leaving his daughter
in her care. A few years later, he sends for his
daughter. Alone, 29 years old, in the sunset of her
life, she marries the vicar. "Careful and sympathetic
study."
BKM 7:354. The Beaumonts. She is extravagant, they
drift apart, she leaves him with another man. They
have a neglected daughter Alix. Frances comes to this
home on an indefinite visit.
Frances Blake was "a little too hard and worldly wise"
in her youth and as a consequence loses George Brand
who goes off to Austrralia. But in later life earns an
intelligent, patient lover. ATH 110:878.

012751   THE WHIRLIGIG OF TIME. London: Hurst &
Blackett, 1906 BMC NUC.

ACAD-tale of wives, one old, one new. Is author's pov
definitely with the new?
TLS-effect of marriage on an advanced woman.
ATH-feminist spinster marries selfish man with
children. Will please those who demand a quiet,
domestic narrative.

WHITCOMB, JESSIE (WRIGHT). United States.

012752   AS QUEER AS SHE COULD BE. BY JESSIE E.
WRIGHT. Philadelphia: Presbyterian Board Of
Publication and Sabbath- School work, 1895 NUC.

PW-6-27-96. Hilary loses her job on the newspaper in
Boston. Opens house on Cape Cod for "five Boston
Street Arabs."

012753   HIS BEST FRIEND. Boston: Pilgrim Press,
[c1898] NUC.

012754   MARJORIBANKS. BY ELVIRTON WRIGHT. Boston:
Congregational Sunday- School and Pub. Society,
[c1892] NUC.

WHITE, AMBER (REEVES) BLANCO. B. 1887.

012755   HELEN IN LOVE. London: Hurst & Blackett,
1916 BMC.

TLS-title applies to love of herself & her fancies.
Although she is also interested in young man whom she
invites to kiss her. She rides a motor bike.

012756   A LADY AND HER HUSBAND. London: W.
Heinemann, [1914] BMC.

TLS 13:104
PW 85 5/2/14 p. 1447 "Story of two strong
personalities clashing with each other in defense of
their antagonistic ideals. The woman's soul has been
suddenly awakened to altruistic activities. She
becomes an active worker among the forces for social
betterment. The man is an individualist. To him
success means the overcoming of his weaker
brethren-the expansion of his power at no matter what
cost to others. For a while this parts them, but they
come together again, each having conceded something
through love of the other."
BKM-Satire. Middle-aged woman finds herself at a loss
for something to do when daughter leaves home.
Daughter suggests she visit her husband's various
restaurants, finding out what, if anything, is wrong
with them. Applies the principles on which she has
been nurtured & brought up her daughters & brings
about a deadlock with her husband who has 2 sets of
standards, 1 for family & 1 for business. She,
however, holds the controlling share of stock in firm.
ATH 143:309 O.
LBKM-Mrs. Heyham, thru her Fabian daughter becomes
concerned with welfare of women working in her
husband's tea shops. Study of the ordinary man, kind
to family and beastly in other ways.

012757   THE REWARD OF VIRTUE. London: W.
Heinemann, 1911 BMC.

LBKM-Story of relations between mother & daughter. Her
mother, Evelyn Baker's mother, was her greatest
friend, which had worked out unfortunately, but when
her own daughter is born she does not think of this.
Jarring notes of her marriage.
Evelyn Baker whose mother said when she was born
"girls are so much easier" was doomed to lead a stupid
life. Married a man she didn't love, turned to good
works, grew tired of them, had a child, & thanked fate

it was a girl because "girls are..." Her story is
story of every woman.
Intimate story of a girl from childhood to marriage.
ATH.
"Heroine...is out for emotion...interested...in her
own sensations." R. B. JOHNSON.

WHITE, CAROLINE (EARLE). 1833-1916. United States.

012758   A MODERN AGRIPPA. PATIENCE BARKER: A TALE
OF OLD NANTUCKET. Philadelphia: J. B. Lippincott, 1893
NUC.

(1) Edith Merton possesses a mirror that reflects her
own shortcomings. (It's unlike Agrippa's mirror that
reflected evil thoughts and desires.) The glass plays
an important part in her romance. (2) The seven years
wooing of Captain Barker's daughter. PW 6-3-93. On old
Nantucket.
(1) falls in love with and encourages her best
friend's fiance. Refuses her friend's lover, makes a
better match. BOOK NEWS 130:458

012759   AN OCEAN MYSTERY. Philadelphia and
London: J.B. Lippincott, 1903 NUC.

American and French institutions compared. NYT 871, 03

WHITE, DOROTHY VERNON HORACE (SMITH).

012760   FRANK BURNET. London: J. Murray, 1909
BMC.

Story of a blacksmith's boy who becomes a famous
painter. TLS

012761   ISABEL. London: Mills and Boon, 1911 BMC.

012762   MISS MONA. London: Methuen, 1907 BMC.

WHITE, ELIZA ORNE. 1856-1947. United States.

012763   A BORROWED SISTER. Boston: Houghton,
Mifflin, 1906 NUC.

  PZ 7

012764   BROTHERS IN FUR. Boston: Houghton,
Mifflin, 1910 NUC.

  PZ 10

012765   THE COMING OF THEODORA. Boston: Houghton
Mifflin, 1895 NUC. London: Smith, Elder, 1895 BMC.

energetic sister-in-law raids a happy household. The
attempts to get her married to be rid of her. SR
70:640
She brings order and rebellion into her brother's
house. She's unselfish and insensitive, a genius for
managing. LBKM 9:65
She's been to college and taught political economy and
hy in a western college. Her brother and his wife are
artists. PW 10-5-95:588
14 months of her; has made a name and position for
herself in the world. Knows there is one way to do a
thing-hers. Wins Frank Compton's heart, but his small
daughter objects to the marriage. She gave up her name
and position to "help" her brother out of love for him
and "her longing for family ties." BKM 2:230
LW 27:87. Marie and Edward, two artists, are easy
going slipshod housekeepers. When Edward's sister,
Theodora, arrives, there is much friction.

012766   THE ENCHANTED MOUNTAIN. Boston: Houghton
Mifflin, [1911] NUC.

012767   THE FIRST STEP; A NOVEL. Boston: Houghton
Mifflin, 1914 NUC.

PW 85 4/4/14 p.1163 "The first step was when Isabel
began to repair the house she inherited. Carpenter,
plumber, and architect lead her into appalling expense
and humorous complications which are amusingly told,
and which effect surprisingly a rather unexpected
romance."

012768   JOHN FORSYTH'S AUNTS. New York and
London: McClure, Phillips, 1901 BMC NUC.

3 sisters live happily together. "A struggle for
independence lands Lucy in a greenhouse where for the
first time in her repressed life, she enjoyed ind.
Moral: refuse to marry if you feel attracted to do
so." The WOMAN'S JOURNAL 12-7-01
Life from the ingenuous point of view of women who

believe "thatamong polygamous men there exists even a
rarer man who having loved once, can never love
again." CR 02
Old fashioned spinsters. But one decides to become a
nurse. NYT

012769   LESLEY CHILTON. Boston: Houghton,
Mifflin, 1903 NUC.

Heroine has advanced ideas about higher ed for women.
BKM 18 (1903) 330.
Begins with discussion of the woman question. Heroine
but remains herself; active in woman suffrage club.
OMAN'S JOURNAL 10-10-03
Many witty conversations "which are not a contribution
to the solution of the woman question." PW 10-3-03.
Heroine uses her views to keep at bay an anti-suffrage
male, then she later marries him. NYT 661,03

012770   A LOVER OF TRUTH. Boston: Houghton
Mifflin, 1898 NUC. London: Smith, Elder, 1898 BMC.

SP 81:566. "Acute and sympathetic study of the growth
and expansion of a reserved, sensitive and high-minded
nature."
LIT 3:524. Jean Rycroft, neither conventional nor
abnormal. Her history, from childhood in New England
(Mass.) atmosphere of seriousness and restraint to
womanhood where she discovers her love for Alan a
delusion and gives it to another. "An intelligent
being whose actions and affections are deliberate and
conscious, is, in the last half dozen pages,
transformed into a creature of caprices as
inexplicable as they are unexpected."
ATH 112:641. Restraint and gloom. Bicycling in Mass.
Has to wait until the man she loves becomes a widower.
NYT 1898:686. Heroine, Jean, is a painter. Rev.
doesn't like her, thinks her attitude selfish because
she didn't marry the man "for whom she would have to
make a thousand daily sacrifices."
Jean Rycroft, an individual, extremely self conscious.
Decides on a career in art since she has no
inclination to marry. Convinces her sister of the
same. But gives up her pretense of a career when a
suitor shows up. BKM 8:492
Endowed with a larger share of morbid
self-consciousness than usually goes to the making of
the misery of her type and her friends. Author insists
upon Jean's individuality...but the reader will hardly
concede it. "It is quite in keeping that she should
expect her sister to remain unmarried simply because
she herself proposes an artistic career, in the
absence of any temptation to matrimony. It is equally
true to the type that she herself abandons this empty
pretence of a career at the first inducement to
marry."

012771   AN ONLY CHILD. Boston: Houghton Mifflin,
1905 NUC.

012772   THE WARES OF EDGEFIELD. Boston: Houghton
Mifflin, 1909 NUC.

Couple have difficulties. Children grow to maturity
cause further problems. Ends in murder. PW 10-9-09
Two generations of tangled love affairs. BKM

012773   WINTERBOROUGH. Boston: Houghton Mifflin,
1892 NUC.

LW 23:472. Story of Persis in N E town, beginning with
her defiance of her teacher at 13 and ending with her
engagement to him. Her literary aspirations and
disappointments.
PW-They have opposite views on most subjects.

WHITE, ELIZABETH STOUGHTON (GALE). United States.

012774   UNO WHO. New York: Abbey Press, [c1900]
NUC.

WHITE, GRACE (MILLER). United States.

012775   A CHORUS GIRL'S LUCK IN NEW YORK. A
THRILLING STORY FOUNDED ON THE PLAY OF THE SAME NAME.
New York: J.S. Ogilvie, 1907 NUC.

Founded on play by Albert Herman Wood.

012776   CONVICT 999. A THRILLING STORY FOUNDED
UPON THE PLAY OF THE SAME NAME. New York: J.S.
Ogilvie, 1907 NUC.

Play by Albert Herman Wood.

012777   EDNA, THE PRETTY TYPEWRITER. A THRILLING

STORY FOUNDED UPON A PLAY OF THE SAME NAME. New York:
J.S. Ogilvie, 1907 NUC.

Play by Albert Herman Wood.

012778   FROM THE VALLEY OF THE MISSING. New York:
W.J. Watt, [1911] NUC. London: Hutchinson, 1912 BMC.

Love-mystery-adventure kind of thing. PW 11-18-11.

012779   JUDY OF ROGUES' HARBOR. New York: H.K.
Fly, [1918] NUC. London: Hodder & Stoughton, [1925]
BMC.

012780   ROSE O' PARADISE. New York: H. K. Fly,
[1915] NUC. London: Mills & Boon, 1918 BMC.

Girl's story. Villains, hero, heroine. NYT
TLS-Jimmie, an heiress and musical genius, hides from
an enemy with a Jewish cobbler and his wife.
SR-she is a fiddler and composer.

012781   THE SECRET OF THE STORM COUNTRY. New
York: H.K. Fly, [c1917] NUC. London: Hodder &
Stoughton, [1924] BMC.

Continues story of Tess of the Storm Country made
famous by Mary Pickford's movie. Again concerns
squatterfolk on Lake Cayuga. Tess works hard at music
and studies. Makes a secret marriage with Cornell
student. Story moves back and forth from squatters to
rich Ithaca people.
NYT 7-22-17 274

012782   SECRETS OF THE POLICE. A THRILLING STORY
FOUNDED UPON THE PLAY OF THE SAME NAME. New York: J.S.
Ogilvie, 1906 NUC.

012783   STORM COUNTRY POLLY. Boston: Little,
Brown, 1920 NUC BMC. London: Hodder & Stoughton,
[1924] BMC.

PW-squatter settlement on Lake Cayuga threatened by
Marcus MacKenzie who wants to reclaim land.
NYT 1920:252. A Pollyanna, love story.

012784   TESS OF ITHACA. London: Mills and Boon,
[1909] BMC NUC.

Overly sentimental story of squatters and barefoot
Tess. TLS

012785   TESS OF THE STORM COUNTRY. New York: W.J.
Watt, [c1909] NUC. London: Hodder & Stoughton, [1924]
BMC. (Pub. London 1909 title: Tess of Ithaca.)

Daughter of squatter; ignorant but relatively ready to
sacrifice self for sister of man she loves? PW
NYT-fisherman squatters on Lake Cayuga. Loyal to her
father who is charged with murder of game warden. She
is dirty & uncouth.

012786   WHEN TRAGEDY GRINS. New York: W.J. Watt,
[c1912] NUC. London: C. Palmer & Hayward, 1916 BMC.

PW-American girl in Paris without money becomes a
night beggar.
NYT-strange.
TLS-American girl in Parisian underworld.

WHITE, HESTER.

012787   MOUNTAINS OF NECESSITY. Edinburgh and
London: W. Blackwood, 1901 BMC.

Flora "Stiff-necked" raises mountains of necessity
between self and husband. ATH 4-27-01

012788   THE STRENGTH OF A CHAIN. London: Heath,
Cranton & Ouseley, [1914] BMC.

ATH "A young artist takes a dislike to his friend's
fiancee, a strong-minded young woman with modern
ideas, and, at the suggestion of an older man who
calls himself a professor of science, makes psychic
experiments on her against her will. The author traces
the subsequent change in her character and attitude
towards her lover.
TLS The archeologist wants papers which are in her
possession.

012789   UNCLE JEM. London: T. F. Unwin, 1907 BMC.

Reviewer goes on and on about what a poor novel this
is. ACAD
Harmless tale TLS

WHITE, IDA BELLE.

012790   SPIRITS DO RETURN. Kansas City, Mo.:
White Pub. Co., 1915 NUC.

innocent man in prison. PW 10-30-15

WHITE, MARY K.   United States.

012791   TWICE LOYAL; A NOVEL. New York: Neale,
1917 NUC.

Civil war days. Catherine Hunter's sympathies are with
the No. but loves a So. Soldier. Her cousin loves a
No. soldier. Both couples end happily. PW

WHITE, MRS. JOHN.

012792   NESTA. A NOVEL. London: Simpkin and
Marshall, 1893 BMC.

WHITE, PEARL. B. 1889.

012793   JUST ME. New York: G. H. Doran, [c1919]
NUC.

Auto. of a moving picture actress PW

WHITE, ROMA, pseud. See WINDER, BLANCHE ORAM.

WHITEHOUSE, FLORENCE BROOKS. Nationality Unknown.

012794   THE EFFENDI; A ROMANCE OF THE SOUDAN.
Boston: Little, Brown, 1904 NUC.

NYT-harems, adventures, wedding bells.

012795   THE GOD OF THINGS; A NOVEL OF MODERN
EGYPT. Boston: Little, Brown, 1902 BMC NUC.

NYT 5-17-02-appears possibly to be anti-divorce for
any reason.

WHITELEY, ELIZABETH.

012796   THE DEVIL'S THRONE. London: Digby, Long,
1903 BMC.

extravagant fantasy ACAD 65, 572

WHITELEY, ISABEL (NIXON). 1859-1935. United States.

012797   THE FALCON OF LANGEAC. Boston: Copeland
and Day, 1897 NUC BMC.

First person narration. Historical romance with
elements of the weird. Hero imprisoned, his escape
from the villain. Catherine heroine and her rescue.
Idyllic love scenes. CR 26, 30:252.
Old French Chateau: knights and serfs and a maiden
making her escape from Malo in nun's garb.--LW 28:194.

012798   FOR THE FRENCH LILIES (A.D. 1511-1512).
St. Louis, Mo.: B. Herder, 1899 NUC.

WHITELEY, OPAL DE VERE GABRIELLE DE BOURBON DE LA TREMOILLE
STANLEY.

012799   THE DIARY OF OPAL WHITELEY. London: G. P.
Putnam's Sons, 1920 BMC NUC.

Between age 6 & 7

012800   THE STORY OF OPAL; THE JOURNAL OF AN
UNDERSTANDING HEART. Boston: Atlantic Monthly Press,
[c1920] NUC.

PS3545

WHITELL, EVELYN. United States.

012801   EXTRAORDINARY MARY. Los Angeles: Master
Mind, [1920] NUC.

012802   THE WOMAN HEALER. Los Angeles: Master
Mind, [c1920] NUC.

PW A New Thought novel.

WHITELOCK, L. CLARKSON. See WHITELOCK, LOUISE (CLARKSON).

WHITELOCK, LOUISE (CLARKSON). B. 1865. United States.

012803   HOW HINDSIGHT MET PROVINCIALATIS. BY L.
CLARKSON WHITELOCK. Boston: Copeland and Day, 1898

NUC.

WHITHAM, G. I. See WHITHAM, GRACE I.

WHITHAM, GRACE I. Nationality Unknown.

012804   BASIL THE PAGE: A STORY OF THE DAYS OF
QUEEN ELIZABETH. London: W. Gardner, 1908 BMC.

012805   CAPTIVE ROYAL CHILDREN. London: W.
Gardner, 1911 BMC. New York: F. A. Stokes, [1911] NUC.

Stories of royal children who have been prisoners in
England.

012806   HIS MAJESTY'S GLOVE: A STORY OF THE GREAT
REBELLION. London: T. Nelson, [1909] BMC NUC.

012807   THE LAST OF THE WHITE COATS: A STORY OF
CAVALIERS AND ROUNDHEADS. BY G. I. WHITHAM. London:
Seeley, 1906 BMC NUC.

Gt. Brit. Hist.-Civil War, 1642-49 PZ7

012808   THE LORD OF MARNEY, A TALE OF THE DAYS OF
ST. LOUIS OF FRANCE. London: Blackie, [1912] BMC.

012809   "MR. MANLEY." BY G. I. WHITHAM. London
and New York: J. Lane, 1918 BMC NUC.

PW-murder mystery.
TLS-Maude is heroine.
ATH-0
LBKM-Mr. M. solves it.
SP-0
NYT-June 9,1918, p266. Pretty love story. Maude, an
orphan, loyal, courageous, and sensible.

012810   THE NAMELESS PRINCE: A TALE OF
PLANTAGENET DAYS. BY G. I. WHITHAM. London: Blackie,
1912 BMC NUC.

012811   THE RED KNIGHT. A TALE OF THE DAYS OF
KING EDWARD III. London: Blackie, 1911 BMC.

012812   SIR SLEEP-AWAKE AND HIS BROTHER: A STORY
OF THE CRUSADES. London: Blackie, 1909 BMC.

012813   SQUIRE AND PAGE: A STORY OF OLDEN DAYS.
London: Blackie, 1906 BMC NUC.

012814   ST. JOHN OF HONEYLEA. BY G. I. WHITHAM.
New York and London: J. Lane, 1919 BMC NUC.

PW-male hero inherits estate with a curse on it.
NYT 1920:236. Mystery, and a love story.

WHITING, ANNA KATHARINE. Nationality Unknown.

012815   GLENWOOD. Boston: C.M. Clark, 1907 NUC.

WHITING, LILIAN. B. 1859.

012816   AFTER HER DEATH; THE STORY OF A SUMMER.
BY THE AUTHOR OF "THE WORLD BEAUTIFUL" [ANONYMOUS].
London: Sampson Low, Marston, 1897 BMC. Boston:
Roberts, 1897 BMC NUC.

Seven papers "rich in remembrance and regret and
speculation as to the other life." PW 51:779

WHITING, MARY BRADFORD. United Kingdom.

012817   A DAUGHTER OF THE EMPIRE. London: H.
Milford, 1919 BMC.

012818   DAUNTLESS HEART. London: S.P.C.K., [1915]
BMC.

012819   DENIS O'NEIL. London: R. Bentley, 1892
BMC NUC.

ATH 99:210. Convict doctor goes to Australia, woman
follows him, their misfortunes. "Unrelieved record of
misfortune."
SP 68:651. He is forced by a secret society by whom he
is captured to "remove" his uncle, an obnoxious
landlord. He only wounds him, but is deported. Woman
is a nurse, they work together in Australia until she
dies of diptheria and he is killed by a member of the
secret society.
SR 73:307. Fennians.

012820   JOSEE: AN AUSTRALIAN STORY. London:
Christian Knowledge Society, [1900] BMC.

012821   LOVE'S LESSON. London: National Society's
Depository, [1906] BMC.

012822   LOVE'S SACRIFICE. London: R. T. S.,
[1904] BMC NUC. London: Leisure Hour Library Office,
[1908] NUC.

012823   MERIEL'S CAREER. A TALE OF LITERARY LIFE
IN LONDON. London: Blackie, 1914 BMC.

SR 147:510 Meriel comes to London for a literary life,
she is a prig. Finances force her to work as editor of
"the New Girl," a "startling" American publication.
Her knowledge of human nature widens. Other literary
women characters, including a famous novelist.
ATH 143:495. Her employer has hired her solely so that
she could be advertised as the "youngest editress."
Learns that "love does count and that she is not a
great literary genius." "Should appeal to the 'young
person.'"
TLS "Author makes her succumb at the end, in the
proper feminine way, to love."

012824   THE MOULDING OF MARJORIE. London:
S.P.C.K., [1915] BMC.

012825   THE PLOUGH OF SHAME. London: J. M. Dent,
1906 BMC NUC.

ACAD--hist novel.

012826   ROSA'S MISTAKE; OR, THE CHORD OF SELF.
London: S. W. Partridge, [1907] BMC.

012827   A THORNY WAY. London: T. Nelson, 1892
BMC.

012828   THE TORCHBEARERS. London: J. M. Dent,
1904 BMC.

ATH 05, 204 0

012829   WALLABY HILL. London: Religious Tract
Society, [1895] BMC NUC.

WHITNEY, ADELINE DUTTON (TRAIN). 1824-1906. United States.

012830   BIDDY'S EPISODES. BY MRS. A. D. T.
WHITNEY. Boston: Houghton Mifflin, 1904 NUC.

PW-young girl concerned with social issues.
NYT-for young girls, sickly.

012831   A GOLDEN GOSSIP: NEIGHBORHOOD STORY
NUMBER TWO. BY MRS. A. D. T. WHITNEY. Boston: Houghton
Mifflin, 1892 NUC BMC.

CR 17:324. Miss Haven, who believes in positive value
of gossip if it is told truly and with good will
straightens out misunderstanding between embittered
woman and her niece.

012832   SQUARE PEGS. BY MRS. A. D. T. WHITNEY.
London: A. P. Watt, [1899] BMC. Boston: Houghton,
Mifflin, 1899 NUC.

Estabel Charlock wild, unbound by convention from
girlhood to womanhood sturdy, strong solid woman. Hero
to match; book leaves the two pledged to themselves
and to one another to try to "right some of the wrong
relations of men." Especially graspy capitalists. Two
reformers. She's a country girl, goes to Boston
private school--ambitious aunt, snobby classmates.
Against profit building speculation enriching
capitalists. NYT 11-4-99,740

WHITNEY, GERTRUDE CAPEN. 1861-1941. United States.

012833   ABOVE THE SHAME OF CIRCUMSTANCE. BY
GERTRUDE CAPEN WHITNEY (MRS. GEORGE ERASTUS WHITNEY).
Boston: Sherman, French, 1913 NUC.

PW 12/20/13:2180 "Story of the growth in character
attained by a woman who wins her way against heavy
odds from spiriting serfdom to spiritual freedom. The
Practice of the Presence of God is her talisman."

012834   THE HOUSE OF LANDELL; OR, FOLLOW AND
FIND. BY GERTRUDE CAPEN WHITNEY (MRS. GEORGE ERASTUS
WHITNEY). New York: R. F. Fenno, [c1917] NUC.

Agnes Landall, highly cultured, gifted with psychic
powers, advances toward spiritual enlightenment, but
then falls in love. PW
Book ends with a couple of weddings NYT 275,7-22-17

012835   I CHOOSE. Boston: Sherman, French, 1910
NUC.

BKM-Chooses to remain in prison to help her companions
altho wrongly accused of a crime and sentenced for
five yrs.
"The one who chooses to remain in prison in order to
help her companions is a poor woman who was wrongly
accused of a crime and imprisoned for a term of five
years."

012836   YET SPEAKETH HE. Boston: Sherman, French,
1910 NUC.

WHITNEY, LOUISA MARETTA (BAILEY). B. 1844. United States.

012837   GOLDIE'S INHERITANCE; A STORY OF THE
SIEGE OF ATLANTA. Burlington, Vt.: Free Press Assoc.,
1903 NUC.

Civil War.

WHITNEY, MRS. A. D. T. See WHITNEY, ADELINE DUTTON (TRAIN).

WHITNEY, MRS. GEORGE ERASTUS. See WHITNEY, GERTRUDE CAPEN.

WHITTEMORE, EMMA (MOTT). 1850-1931. United States.

012838   DELIA; FORMERLY THE BLUE-BIRD OF MULBERRY
BEND. BY MRS. E. M. WHITTEMORE. New York: The Door of
Hope, [c1893] NUC.

PW 10-10-96. Story of a young girl rescued by
missionaries. Proceeds from sale of book will be used
for similar purposes.

WHITTEMORE, MRS. E. M. See WHITTEMORE, EMMA (MOTT).

WHYTE, CHRISTINA GOWANS.

012839   THE FIVE MACLEODS. London: H. Frowde,
1909 BMC.

012840   FOR THE SAKE OF KITTY. London: Collins'
Cleartype Press, 1909 BMC.

012841   THE GIRLS NEXT DOOR. London: S. W.
Partridge, [1910] BMC.

012842   NINA'S CAREER. New York: Macmillan, 1907
NUC. London: H. Frowde, 1908 BMC.

Art student in London and Paris. PW 10-26-07

012843   THE STORY BOOK GIRLS. New York:
Macmillan, 1906 NUC. London: Hodder & Stoughton, 1906
BMC.

PW Two sets of sisters.

012844   UNCLE HILARY'S NIECES. London: H. Frowde,
1910 BMC.

WHYTE, HAINE, pseud. See PARHAM, HELENA BEATRICE RICHENDA.

WHYTE, VIOLET.

012845   A BROKEN PROMISE. London: C. A. Pearson,
1899 BMC.

Heroine is an "airy fairy", an early Victorian type.
Her father's dead; she's engaged to young Australian
sheep-farmer. While he's away; she flirts around.
Falls in love with another man. ATH 11 4:684.
SP 84:23. Publisher says Whyte is Stannard.
LIT 6:51. Dot, a coquette with craving for admiration
and affection. (Also says it is Stannard)

WICKSTEED, HILDA M.

012846   TITCH. London: Swarthmore Press, [1920]
BMC.

TLS dog
Story of a dog.

WIDDEMER, MARGARET. B. 1880. United States.

012847   I'VE MARRIED MARJORIE. New York:
Harcourt, Brace & Howe, 1920 NUC.

PW-War bride and returning husband problems.
NYT 8-22-20, p27. Sent.

012848   ROSAMUND-WHY NOT? London: Hodder &
Stoughton, 1916 BMC.

012849   THE ROSE-GARDEN HUSBAND. Philadelphia: J.
B. Lippincott Co., 1915 NUC. London: Hodder &
Stoughton, 1915 BMC.

"girl librarian" promoted to library teacher. BKM 41
1915
Librarian "on her way to being an old maid" PW 2-13-16
Dreams of and gets a rose garden husband. NYT
Marries a rich cripple rejuvenates him. A genre Amers
love drenched in sugar. TLS
Too much mother love keeps Allan Harrington a cripple.
When mother about to die, offers Phyllis Narcissa (the
librarian) a marriage in name only to care for Allan
who will shortly die. "Could I have a rose garden,"
she asks. thus the matter is settled. She's released
thereby from hard drudgery of library work. Love
brings miracle cure. BKM

012850   WHY NOT? New York: Hearst's Internat'l
Lib. Co., 1915 BMC NUC.

Inherits $3,000 takes a bungalow, adopts a child,
helps a lot of people. PW 9-25-15
"Pretty whimsies" sunny spirit NYT
Eng. ed. Rosamond-why Not?

012851   WINONA OF CAMP KARONYA. Philadelphia and
London: J. B. Lippincott Co., 1917 BMC NUC.

012852   WINONA OF THE CAMP FIRE. Philadephia and
London: J. B. Lippincott Co., 1915 NUC. London: 1916
BMC.

012853   WINONA'S WAR FARM. Philadephia and
London: J. B. Lippincott Co., 1918 BMC NUC.

PZ7

012854   WINONA'S WAY. A STORY OF RECONSTRUCTION.
Philadelphia and London: J. B. Lippinott Co., 1919 NUC
BMC.

012855   THE WISHING-RING MAN. New York: H. Holt,
1917 NUC. London: Hodder & Stoughton, [1918] BMC.

Sent rom. about a New England Summer colony before the
war. PW NYT
TLS-Conv. sent.

012856   YOU'RE ONLY YOUNG ONCE. New York: H.
Holt, 1918 NUC. London: Hodder & Stoughton, [1919]
BMC.

PW-family story.

WIGGIN, KATE DOUGLAS. See RIGGS, KATE DOUGLAS (SMITH)
WIGGIN.

WIGHT, EMMA HOWARD. United States.

012857   THE LITTLE MAID OF ISRAEL. St. Louis,
Mo.: B. Herder, 1900 NUC.

012858   PASSION FLOWERS AND THE CROSS: A NOVEL.
Baltimore, Md.: Calendar, 1891 NUC.

WIGRAM, EIRENE. United Kingdom.

012859   THE AFFAIR OF THE ENVELOPE. London:
Methuen, 1910 BMC.

TLS International politics with Madame Kampine's
career chief interest.
ATH-clever
SP. She is a nurse and a very financially successful
spy.
SR Lady Margaret wrote a novel which turns out to be
true.

012860   ALAN! ALAN! A STORY OF ENGLAND'S
WAR-TIME. London: J. Murray, 1915 BMC NUC.

Focuses on a hero, a murder, etc. TLS
Trial of Madelaine Leigh ACAD

WILBRAHAM, ESTRA, jt. au. See SETON, CHRISTINE AND ESTRA
WILBRAHAM.

WILCOX, ELLA (WHEELER). 1850-1919. United States.

012861   AN AMBITIOUS MAN. Chicago: E. A. Weeks,
[c1896] NUC. London: Gay & Hancock, 1908 BMC.

TLS-O
ACAD-man marries for wealth but loves woman who is

typewriter in his office. They succumb, she disappears. Later her daughter Joy is loved by man married to father's legit daughter who dies and Joy refuses to marry him although she was on the point of succumbing.
PW 6-20-96. He marries for money while loving another woman.

012862   THE DIARY OF A FAITHLESS HUSBAND. London: Gay and Hancock, 1910 BMC.

TLS--presents side of divorced husband.

012863   A DOUBLE LIFE. London: Gay & Bird, [1891] BMC. New York: J. S. Ogilivie, [1891] NUC.

John Chester a respectable citizen commits a crime, conceals his act for years, lives under an alias. Story deals with his life and with Erastus Lounsbury's mistaken marriage. PW

012864   EVERY DAY THOUGHTS IN PROSE AND VERSE. Chicago: W. B. Conkey, [1901] NUC.

City woman of empty boarding-house surroundings. BOOK NEWS Sept. '04

012865   SWEET DANGER. Chicago: M. A. Donohue, [c1902] NUC.

PW-Dolores and Helena shcool friends. Dolores, loving a man, lives with him but refuses to marry because of her mother's unhappy marriage. She "falls victim to impossible theories." Helena finds home and happiness.

012866   WAS IT SUICIDE? New York: F. T. Neely, 1897 NUC.

WILCOX, MARRION. 1858-1926. United States.

012867   VENGEANCE OF THE FEMALE. Chicago: H. Stone, 1899 NUC. London: Harper, 1899 BMC.

WILD, IDA. Nationality Unknown.

012868   DRUM'S HOUSE. London: Constable, 1913 BMC. New York: E.P. Dutton, 1914 NUC.

It's an old building inhabited by some amusing folk. The couple, The Millincoes, were gamblers, have "retired" for the sake of their two daughters. Story turns tragic, one of the daughters secretly wedded, falls in love with a married man. They are found dead in each other's arms. LBKM

012869   HOUSE-ROOM. New York and London: J. Lane, 1916 BMC NUC. London: J. Lane, 1916 NUC.

Virginia's husband in asylum. She makes life for herself, teaching cooking and being friends with Dr. Clewes. Everyone advises them they are justified in anything they do. She resists afraid to ruin Clewes' career. Looks for unvulnerable happiness in her sacrifice PW 90:1360 10/21/16
ATH O

012870   ZOE, THE DANCER. London and New York: J. Lane, 1911 BMC NUC.

Fourteen years in convent, goes out on her own, rejects offer of marriage to make her own way, becomes a famous dancer; marries but finds husband worthless, runs away to return to stage, great love comes in her life. Book closes on decision whether to go back to husband or break for good. PW 4-1-11
"It's a pity that the tone of the book is so vulgar" SR

WILKINS, MARY E. See FREEMAN, MARY ELEANOR (WILKINS).

WILKINSON, FLORENCE. See EVANS, FLORENCE (WILKINSON).

WILKINSON, FLORENCE M.

012871   STEPHEN ROCHFORD. London: Lynwood, [1916] BMC.

Minister and miseries inflicted on him by his flock.
TLS

WILKINSON, HELEN COSTERTON.

012872   A HOST OF THORNS. London: Simpkin, Marshall, [1900] BMC.

WILKINSON, MARGUERITE OGDEN (BIGELOW). 1883-1928.

012873   IN VIVID GARDENS; SONG OF THE WOMAN SPIRIT. BY MARGUERITE WILKINNSON (MARGUERITE OGDEN BIGELOW). Boston: Sherman, French, 1911 NUC.

WILLARD, CAROLINE MACCOY (WHITE). United States.

012874   KIN-DA-SHON'S WIFE: AN ALASKAN STORY. BY MRS. EUGENE S. WILLARD. New York: F. H. Revell, [c1892] NUC BMC. London: R.T.S., [1893] BMC.

PW Condition of the Eskimos. "Facts she had studied <for an earlier work of non-fiction> so carefully she has here woven into a story of love and suffering in this wild, strange country, where women are so yet little better than animals."
Torture and brutality endured by Eskimos in Alaska. "United with the poetic and fanciful speech of the Red Indian, the Alaskan possesses his ferocity of nature and his insensitivity to pain." The great family house where dozens live, young girls' imprisonment in caves for months merely for the purpose of making them more marriageable, girls of 12 wed to their grandfathers, boys to their grandmothers. CR 14,20:127

012875   A SON OF ISRAEL: AN ORIGINAL STORY. BY "RACHEL PENN". Philadelphia: J. B. Lippincott, 1898 NUC. London: J. Macqueen, 1898 BMC.

ACAD 53:285. Russian-Jewish love story. David and Olga, Jew and Christian, love and suffer.
SR 85:471. Jewish suffering in Russia.
LW 29:75. He is exiled to Siberia, but is brought back, happy ending.

WILLARD, KATE LIVINGSTON. United States.

012876   A COLONY OF GIRLS: A NOVEL. New York: Dodd, Mead, 1892 NUC.

LW 23:246. Light romance concerning a group of young girls in seaside town where there are no young men until a shipful arrive.

WILLARD, MRS. EUGENE S. See WILLARD, CAROLINE MACCOY (WHITE).

WILLCOCKS, M. P. See WILLCOCKS, MARY PATRICIA.

WILLCOCKS, MARY PATRICIA. B. 1869. United Kingdom.

012877   CHANGE. BY M. P. WILLCOCKS. London: Hutchinson, 1915 BMC NUC.

Author "shows an intimate sympathy in the varying stages of adolescence and can define truly the mind of a girl of 16, with its restless dissatisfaction, its self sufficiency" Love comes, then disillusionment. SP Woman astonishingly real; tolerant picture of the universal type "the managing woman" (manage and spoil men) Passionate Bess and her professor (a male) TLS

012878   THE EYES OF THE BLIND; A NOVEL. BY M. P. WILLCOCKS. London: Hutchinson, 1917 BMC NUC.

"Eager young beauty swayed by two lovers" minor char: "strong, steady woman takes the man she wants, has the child she wants without wasting regrets that she had not married." ? TLS
Char upon char, all kinds-their stories blended in a single tale. LBKM

012879   A MAN OF GENIUS; A STORY OF THE JUDGMENT OF PARIS. BY M. P. WILLCOCKS. London and New York: J. Lane, 1908 BMC NUC.

PW-Two men and a woman
TLS-glorification of that more than helf animal devotion to a man-woman's genius for self sacrifice.
SR-

012880   THE POWER BEHIND. BY M. P. WILLCOCKS. London: Hutchinson, 1913 NUC BMC.

Sophie Revel adopted by Dr. Revel and his severe wife. Dr. raises her to love beauty, but doesn't prepare her for life. He dies; she works on farm. "There are various indications that she has not escaped the spirit of unrest now hovering over the female population" the quote refers to author and "justifies" the lack of love plot in the novel. Reviewer feels author is much more interested in affairs of the mind. ACAD
Sophie married, unhappy 2nd marriage to an elderly doctor "the sacrifice of her small boy"? SP
Her guardian commits suicide ATH

From her birth to arrival of second son—That time
crowded with revolts. Gets liberal ideas from father
who raised her. Marriage finds her among strangers;
Husband dies; remarries an old man, father-like. LBKM

012881   THE SLEEPING PARTNER. BY M. P. WILLCOCKS.
London: Hutchinson, 1919 BMC NUC.

One male char becomes a "midwife of brain babies" but
dies; son a publisher's reader who "carefully analyzes
the feminine novelist of the hour, for it is women who
make sales if not reputations." Then Mrs. Colquhoun,
the novelist, comes on the scene. Her subject she says
is Man and woman—sex, no. Writes for well-to-do
suburban woman. Her "clients" from their own point of
view" What they crave is love stories with the woman
at the center, the motive power, with enough spice
about the atmosphere to suit married woman and enough
worship to suggest a lover who was quite unlike the
gentleman who supplied fur coats. Advance on the edge
of things, combined in a long drawn-out agony for the
man." That was Mrs. C's recipe. About the publishing
world—"diagnoses and idealizes publishers"? TLS
Focus on Silas Brutton a publisher "suffering from
morbid horror of sex". ATH
Silas' sex attitude warped by father who took him to a
prison to see a child molester. Contrast to brother
Ned who is all man. Silas finds happiness with a young
woman whose passion is biology Nan Carey. SR

012882   TOWARDS NEW HORIZONS. BY M. P. WILLCOCKS.
London and New York: J. Lane, 1919 BMC NUC.

Army discipline sneered at, made ridiculous; English
people encouraged to revolt to solve land question;
Sexual promiscuity is described as "simplicity of
outlook" or "free alliances"; marr. law denounced as
"the creation of an artificial class that has lost its
grip on reality" SR

012883   THE WAY UP. BY M. P. WILLCOCKS. London
and New York: J. Lane, 1910 BMC NUC.

Man so involved in setting up model factory he
neglects pleasure-loving wife. She leaves him, leads a
careless life. Death of son makes both of them "begin
to think." good characterization PW
LBKM Wife is very wealthy, he insists on living in
small house like other workmen, has acquired a factory
with his wife's money and wishes to turn it over to
workers. His mother is a strong ch. Wife is a
"pleasure-loving minx long held in check by her
affection for him."
SR-Philippa is at 1st Michael's right hand and then
his 2nd wife.
NYT-Elise kills herself, after searching in vain in
others for the love denied her by husband. Michael's
secretary is portrayed as being doubly outside of
woman's world, having neither love nor opportunity.

012884   WIDDICOMBE. BY M. P. WILLCOCKS. London
and New York: J. Lane, 1905 BMC NUC.

ACAD 05, 368
Village people discuss things that would astonish you,
3 couples TLS 153,05
Silphine full of joy of living; her fiance a prude.
They separate but then come back together. ATH 429, 05

012885   THE WILL TO LIVE. BY M. P. WILLCOCKS. New
York: Macmillan, 1913 NUC.

012886   THE WIND AMONG THE BARLEY. London: Mills
& Boon, 1912 BMC NUC.

012887   THE WINGLESS VICTORY. BY M. P. WILLCOCKS.
New York and London: J. Lane, 1907 NUC BMC.

A loveless marr. wife of wild nature "led to the brink
of doing wrong" Has a child, leaves her husband, is
again tempted. After much pain the pair is reunited.
PW 6-8-07
Wife has disastrous flirtations with other men because
she thinks her husband doesn't love her (actually he's
having business problems.) She leaves, the husband
"makes overtures for union" with another with Johanna.
This other woman visits the wife. The two are
contrasted. Other woman gives the wife the clue to
reunion with husband.
The wife is mod. heroine—craves power, restless, vain,
heartless egoism. LBKM 5-07-68
Wilmot Borlace (wife) marries only because she's tired
of the single life; fine analysis of char. TLS
Psychol study of a few years in a woman's life. SP.
NYT-descr. of the passage from old-fashioned spinster
to modern unmarried woman.

012888   WINGS OF DESIRE. BY M. P. WILLCOCKS.
London and New York: J. Lane, 1912 BMC NUC.

PW-Woman problem is the theme.
TLS-"Sets forth new independence of women; all the
women in it are moved to do something by themselves
with their lives and not be mere appendages to men."
Author does not admit possibility of a union of two
human beings equal and yet different. Ch. named Sara.
LBKM-Sara Bellen finds herself subservient to her
domestic tyrant of a father and Archer, her novelist
husband. She has no children, is indifferent to her
unfaithful husband. Is bitterly resentful of the
tyranny to the service of sex, had wanted a musical
career.
ATH O
ACAD Character study.
NYT Aims to be a novel in favor of the rights of
women—all female characters are intent on a
professional career. Mrg. vs career?

WILLIAMS, ELLEN.

    012889   ANNA MARSDEN'S EXPERIMENT. London:
    Greening, 1899 BMC.

    Anna Marsden is "an ugly journalist who thought that
    life would look more lively through masculine eyes.
    Her travestissement is so successful that no one
    recognizes her." She shares the lodgings of the man
    she loves who loves another woman, gets a job on a
    newspaper, and discovers that in her writing "a manly
    mode of expression comes much more easily to her than
    a feminine style." SP 83:536. When the man she loves
    dies, she runs into misfortunes, and eventually
    resumes her dress as a woman.

WILLIAMS, FRANCES FENWICK. Canada.

    012890   A SOUL ON FIRE. New York and London: J.
    Lane, 1915 NUC.

    Woman can "slay and terrify at will" yet stay within
    the law. Witch heritage. There is promise of
    salvation, for this witch-wife in a coming generation.
    10-2-15PW
    Direct descendent of a witch, holds much power.
    Beautiful young woman believes herself to be inheritor
    of a curse. Plot moves thru discovery of her powers,
    the damage she does, the causes of her power and the
    final "laying of her ghost." NYT

    012891   THEODORA; A SOUL ON FIRE. London and New
    York: J. Lane, 1915 BMC.

    Dark mysterious woman, several deaths were traced to
    her; she later owned herself to 9 murders.,
    reincarnation of the Witch of Caine. Brings in
    suffrage quest "which has, we could suggest, nothing
    necessarily to do with the reincarn. of medieval
    witches." TLS

WILLIAMS, GERTRUDE E.

    012892   CRIME'S CRY. London: Warren, 1912 BMC.

WILLIAMS, MARGERY. See BIANCO, MARGERY (WILLIAMS).

WILLIAMS, MARTHA MACCULLOCH. United States.

    012893   TWO OF A TRADE. New York: J. S. Tait,
    1894 BMC NUC.

    PW-Endymion Weeper, a literary aspirant, advertises
    and Mrs. Pascom responds. His plot is to use her as a
    literary model for his novel. Story is of how she
    fills the role.

WILLIAMS, MARY GERTRUDE. Nationality Unknown.

    012894   ALIAS KITTY CASEY; A NOVEL. New York: P.
    J. Kenedy, [c1911] NUC.

WILLIAMS, MAUD E.

    012895   THE SORROW STONES, AN UNFINISHED STORY.
    London and New York: Longmans, 1913 BMC NUC.

    Kit, a country boy with passion for learning whose
    life is wasted in war. ATH SR TLS
    PW:84 11/29/13:287. "Scene is the north of England,
    where the Hawkrigg had held the farm of Far Dyke for
    generations. All that are left of the family are old
    John and his wife and their grandson, little
    Christopher. The boy wants to be a scholar, not a

farmer..."

WILLIAMS, MRS. RHOBY S. United States.

  012896   NOT LIKE OTHER MEN. New York: J. S.
  Ogilvie, [c1896] NUC.

WILLIAMS, NELLA.

  012897   MY SISTER TAKES A REST CURE. London:
  Jarrolds, [1919] BMC.

  Letters and diary written by Margaret Maitland to
  father from France TLS
  ATH-depicts life in Fr. Sanatorium of young woman who
  has had a nervous breakdown. A slight love story also.

WILLIAMS, ROBERT DOLLY, pseud. See BLACK, MARGARET HORTON
  (POTTER).

WILLIAMS, SARAH STONE.

  012898   THE MAN FROM LONDON TOWN. BY SARAH STONE
  WILLIAMS (HESTER E. SHIPLEY). New York: Neale, 1906
  NUC.

WILLIAMSON, ALICE MURIEL (LIVINGSTON). 1869-1933. United
  Kingdom.

  012899   THE ADVENTURE OF PRINCESS SYLIVA. BY MRS.
  C. N. WILLIAMSON. London: Methuen, 1900 BMC. New York:
  Metropolitan Prss, 1909 NUC.

  SP 84:454. Sentimental comedy. Heroine under an
  assumed identity courts and captivates the emperor, to
  whom she is engaged.
  ATH 115:494. Will yield only to his love, a "bit of a
  hoiden."

  012900   THE BARN STORMERS: BEING THE TRAGICAL
  SIDE OF A COMEDY. BY MRS. HARCOURT WILLIAMSON. London:
  Hutchinson, 1897 BMC. New York: F. A. Stokes, [c1897]
  NUC.

  Squalid actualities and the humors of everyday life of
  a touring company in the states. Strong friendship
  between the heroine and Della Thomas, the Cinderella
  of the company. SP 79:778.
  Heroine sails alone to new world to seek her fortune.
  She's English. Her name is Monica. Joins the
  Barn-Stormers.
  LBKM 14:131.--Monica, convent-bred English girl joins
  Scott Ambler Comedy Company, an acting group. They
  tour in U S. Problems but in the end Monica has
  millions.
  PW-a lesson to other girls who would like to go on
  stage. An American millionaire solves all her
  problems.

  012901   A BID FOR A CORONET. New York: G.
  Routledge & Sons, 1901 PW. London: G. Routledge, 1901
  BMC.

  012902   THE BRIDE'S BREVIARY [ANONYMOUS]. London:
  Hodder & Stoughton, [1912] BMC.

  BKML-Diary form, strange marriage, gay, artless style.
  TLS -heiress and baronet
  LBKM-also story of her strange marriage

  012903   THE BRIDE'S HERO. BY M. P. REVERE. New
  York: F.A. Stokes, [1912] NUC.

  PW-story of a marriage.

  012904   THE CASTLE OF THE SHADOWS. BY MRS. C. N.
  WILLIAMSON. London: Methuen, 1905 BMC NUC. New York:
  Hudson Press, [1909] NUC BMC.

  sensational story of a castle LBKM 27-8, 33

  012905   THE FLOWER FORBIDDEN. London: Hodder &
  Stoughton, [1911] BMC NUC.

  012906   FORTUNE'S SPORT. London: C. A. Pearson,
  1898 BMC.

  SP 31:531. Sensational, abduction of a V.C. on the eve
  of his wedding.
  LIT 3:402. Expanded novelette. Happy ending.
  SR 86:680. Sensation novel of the Manville Fenn order.
  Hero saved by heroine with her camera.

  012907   THE GIRL OF THE PASSION PLAY. London:
  Hodder & Stoughton, [1911] BMC.

  012908   THE GIRL WHO HAD NOTHING. London: Ward,
  Lock, 1905 BMC.

  Joan servant turned out "flashes with brilliant
  audacity" thru the world of high finance, fashionable
  social and international politics" TLS 220, 05

  012909   THE HOUSE BY THE LOCK. BY MRS. C. N.
  WILLIAMSON. London: Ward, Lock, 1899 BMC. Chicago:
  B.W. Dodge, 1906 NUC.

  Heroine blackmailed into a loveless marriage with the
  villain to shield her brother from murder charge.
  Impersonation, headless corpses, sensational. SP
  83:536

  012910   THE HOUSE OF THE LAST COURT. BY DONA
  TERESA DE SAVALLO, MARQUESA D'ALPENS. New York:
  McClure, 1908 NUC. London: Hodder & Stoughton, 1908
  BMC. (NUC: Marchioness D'Alpens.)

  BKM-a widow and her daughter rent a house, their
  neighbors avoid them and they discover there is a
  mystery about the house which the daughter solves.
  ATH-O
  BKM-the court conceals a man who has been convicted of
  a crime. She clears all that up and they marry.
  TLS-mystery.

  012911   LADY MARY OF THE DARK HOUSE. BY MRS. C.
  N. WILLIAMSON. London: J. Bowden, 1898 BMC. Toronto:
  Musson, [19--] NUC.

  SP 81:283. Horror story. Stepmother attempts multiple
  ways of killing heroine so she won't get inheritance.
  The good triumph.
  SR 86:320, of the Sheridan Lefauve blood-curdling
  romance school. "Beautiful damsels are persecuted by
  fiendish stepmothers and dastardly villains. There are
  secret chambers, sliding panels, nails a la Jael for
  piercing the temples of sleepers, heroic lovers
  springing to the rescue through trap-doors, and
  beautiful disguised mothers who watch over outraged
  innocence."

  012912   THE LIFE MASK; A NOVEL. BY THE AUTHOR OF
  "TO M. L. G." [ANONYMOUS]. New York: F.A. Stokes,
  [1913] NUC.

  PW 3-18-13 878"Anita Durrand, known as Mrs.
  Lippincott, has a tragic secret, which she and her
  devoted servant seek to keep from the world. They take
  a house in Grenada, thinking that they are safe, but
  Hugh Shannon sees Anita, falls in love with her, and
  manages to make her acquaintance. Though she loves
  him, the girl refuses to marry him and will not
  explain her reason, until his sister comes, recognizes
  her and insists upon her telling him about herself.
  what the secret is and how the cloud is dispersed end
  the tale." "The story of a young woman who has spent
  ten years of her life in prison. Upon her release she
  feels that all avenues of happiness must be closed to
  her but finds gradually that the old love of life is
  returning. In a secluded corner of Spain where she
  goes with a devoted servant to seek peace in seclusion
  she finds the lover whom she feels she cannot marry
  because of the blot on her life. Then, in an
  unexpected manner, proof of her innocence comes." BRD
  1st person narrative of a young woman sentenced to
  life imprisonment for murder of her husband. Set free
  after 10 years because she's very ill. regains health,
  falls in love; about to do away with herself when she
  learns she's innocent. Scene Grenada; young woman with
  unhappy past, loves a man but can't accept him without
  telling him about her past. She was wed when but a
  girl to a middle aged Englishman, has spent 10 years
  in prison unjustly accused of murdering him. NYT

  012913   THE LITTLE WHITE NUN. London: F.V. White,
  1903 BMC.

  story of intrigue and love ACAD 64, 84
  melodrama ATH 721, 236

  012914   MY LADY CINDERELLA. BY MRS. C. N.
  WILLIAMSON. London: G. Routledge, 1900 BMC. New York:
  B. W. Dodge, 1906 NUC.

  ATH 90:754. All plot, no character study.
  LIT 7:420. Modern version of the myth. Consuelo is a
  nursery governess. Secret of her birth, etc.

  012915   THE NEWSPAPER GIRL. London: C. A.
  Pearson, 1899 BMC.

  An American heiress changes her name and goes to

London to work as a journalist. She gets completely involved in her work by disguising herself in different ways to get close to the stories. When she hears of a newspaper for sale, she buys it and makes her lover the editor. A fun book. LIT 4:556
Lucille Chandler. "Pictures of the inner workings of those journals which cater to feminine readers." SP 22:648
Melodramatic and realism - the methods and manners of journalistic life. BAKER 03,189

012916   ORDERED SOUTH. London: G. Routledge, [1900] BMC NUC.

SP: 84:526. Romance of an orphan and a baronet, plenty of sensational horrors.
ATH 115:494. Hero returns wounded from war, is experimented on by his beautiful cousin who successively commits forgery, larceny, burglary, arson, and murder.
PW-hero takes part of little girl in orphanage, through him she becomes a nurse. When he returns wounded, she helps him, saves his life from scheming relatives. Happy ending.

012917   PAPA. BY MRS. C. N. WILLIAMSON. London: Methuen, 1902 BMC NUC.

012918   PRINCESS MARY'S LOCKED BOOK [ANONYMOUS]. London: Cassell, 1912 BMC. New York: Cassell, 1913 NUC.

Fairy-tale-like love story. NYT

012919   QUEEN SWEETHEART. London: F.V. White, 1901 BMC.

012920   THE SEA COULD TELL. London: Methuen, 1904 BMC.

TLS-mystery of a yacht adrift with no one on it.

012921   THE SILENT BATTLE. BY MRS. C. N. WILLIAMSON. London: Hurst & Blackett, 1902 BMC. New York: Doubleday, 1909 NUC.

mystery, intrigue, etc. NYT

012922   TO M. L. G., OR, HE WHO PASSED [ANONYMOUS]. New York: F.A. Stokes, [1912] NUC.

012923   THE TURNSTILE OF NIGHT. BY MRS. C. N. WILLIAMSON. London: Hurst & Blackett, 1904 BMC NUC.

012924   'TWIXT DEVIL AND DEEP SEA. A NOVEL. London: C.A. Pearson, 1901 BMC.

012925   THE UNDERGROUND SYNDICATE. London: Hodder & Stoughton, [1910] BMC.

012926   THE VANITY BOX. BY ALICE STUYVESANT. Garden City, N.Y.: Doubleday, 1911 NUC. London: Hodder & Stoughton, [1913] BMC.

012927   WHAT I FOUND OUT IN THE HOUSE OF A GERMAN PRINCE. BY AN ENGLISH GOVERNESS [ANONYMOUS]. London: Chapman & Hall, 1915 NUC BMC. New York: F.A. Stokes, [1915] NUC.

012928   A WOMAN IN GREY. BY MRS. C. N. WILLIAMSON. London: G. Routledge, 1898 BMC NUC. New York: A. L. Burt, [n.d.] NUC.

SP 80:630. "The most extravagantly sensational novel that we have ever encountered. There is no relief in the breathless and kaleidoscopic procession of horror, sensation, and crime." Floria Amory leads an exciting life; one of her aliases is Consuelo Hope and she is a brilliant novelist.
ATH 171:757. Ultra-sensational.
PW-Lorn Abbey, known throughout England as the House of Fear. Terrence Amory discovers the identity of the "woman in grey" in the Tower Chamber.

012929   THE WOMAN WHO DARED. London: Methuen, 1903 BMC.

WILLIAMSON, EMMA SARA. Nationality Unknown.

012930   A CHILD WIDOW. London: Chatto and Windus, 1891 BMC NUC.

She's a child wife who becomes a child widow very shortly after her marriage, she's 17. Marries old dying father of man she loves to insure her lover getting inheritance. Her sister is much wiser. She

Millicent is both mother and sister to Nancy Bell. SP 67 133
Nancy's lover believes she married old man for money. He falls for Millicent and marries her. At the end it looks as though Nancy will wed a brave Colonel. ACAD also ATH 97, 728
Sens. plots, horrid murder. Millicent Bell and Nancy Bell, orphans, attempt to earn their living by taking boarders. That's the way the novel starts out; then it becomes packed with sens. events. SR 6-20-91, 749

012931   A PROVINCIAL LADY. BY MRS. F. HARCOURT WILLIAMSON. London: Hutchinson, 1896 BMC NUC.

ATH 109:311. Ambitious young widow and her unsuccessful attempts to enter society. She is "delightful," author is witty. There is a lover in the future, known to the reader only by his letters.
ACAD 49:302. Frothy and gossiping throughout.

WILLIAMSON, MARJORIE.

012932   I. Bristol: J. W. Arrowsmith, [1899] BMC.

69 tiny pages. Fragile, sentimental. ACAD. 57:184.

012933   JOHN FALINER'S DAUGHTER. London: Syd. H. E. Foxwell, 1902 BMC.

012934   WHO DID IT? London: Syd. H. E. Foxwell, 1903 BMC.

Murder TLS 03,107

WILLIAMSON, MRS. C. N. See WILLIAMSON, ALICE MURIEL (LIVINGSTON).

WILLIAMSON, MRS. E. K.

012935   THINGS AS THEY ARE. London: J. Long, 1912 BMC.

ATH-"This ought not to be."

WILLIAMSON, MRS. F. HARCOURT. See WILLIAMSON, EMMA SARA.

WILLIAMSON, MRS. HARCOURT. See WILLIAMSON, ALICE MURIEL (LIVINGSTON).

WILLIAMSON, MRS. N. B. See WILLIAMSON, NANCY BLASDEL GRAVES.

WILLIAMSON, NANCY BLASDEL GRAVES. B. 1838.

012936   LAMECH. BY MRS. N. B. WILLIAMSON. San Francisco: Whitaker & Ray, 1904 NUC.

WILLMOTT, NELLIE LOWE. United States.

012937   A DASH OF RED PAINT. New Haven, Conn.: E. B. Sheldon, 1894 NUC.

WILLSIE, HONORE. See MORROW, HONORE (MACCUE) WILLSIE.

WILLY, COLETTE, pseud. See DE JOUVENAL, SIDONIE GABRIELLE (COLETTE) GAUTHER-VILLARS.

WILMANS, HELEN. See POST, HELEN (WILMANS).

WILMARTH, CORA D.

012938   WIDOWS GRAVE AND OTHERWISE. PURLOINED BY AN EX-WIDOW AND PICTURED BY A VICTIM. [San Francisco]: [P. Elder], 1903 NUC.

WILSON, ANNELIZA CARRUTHERS. D. 1924. United States.

012939   AN IVY VINE, AND HOW IT GREW. BY ANNIE E. WILSON. Richmond, Va.: Presbyterian Com. of Publication, [1902] NUC.

012940   LOVE'S LEADING STRINGS. BY ANNIE E. WILSON. Philadelphia: American Baptist Soc., [1902] NUC.

012941   WEBS OF WAR IN WHITE AND BLACK. BY ANNIE E. WILSON. New York: Broadway, 1913 NUC.

WILSON, ANNIE.

012942   ALICE LAUDER: A SKETCH. London: Osgood, McIlvaine, 1893 BMC.

She sings in concert. Plot hangs on error made by hero on hearing she was engaged to professor of music-meaning engaged to sing at a concert in

Birmingham. The mistake leads the hero to flirt with
another woman. All turns out right. SR 76:711.
"The resolve of the heroine to put away her delights
of love in order to devote herself to the operatic
stage." ACAD 44:509.
Also fine study of Lizzie Austin-"her exuberant
spirits and outrageous outbursts of slang" discover s
man she loves was playing with her. ATH 102:910.

012943   TWO SUMMERS. London & New York: Harper,
1900 BMC.

SP 84:557. Mrs. J. Glenny Wilson. Spent at the
Antipodes by nice English people.
ACAD 58:356. One of the summers in South Pacific, one
in England. Little or no plot.

WILSON, ANNIE E. See WILSON, ANNELIZA CARRUTHERS.

WILSON, ANNIE HENRI.

012944   MR. MERCER OF NEW YORK: A NOVEL. New
York: Dillingham, 1896 NUC.

PW 8-22-96. Rich handsome young man weary of his fast
life retires to North Carolina mountains to
recuperate. He meets fresh and sweet girl who is later
"given to him by her poor and illiterate old parents
to do with as he pleased."

WILSON, AUGUSTA JANE (EVANS). 1835-1909. United States.

012945   DEVOTA. New York: G. W. Dillingham,
[1907] NUC. London: T. F. Unwin, 1907 BMC.

A proud woman separated from husband because of
misunderstanding. Comes to beg pardon. PW 7-13-07
She's a mystery. Comes to governor to plead for friend
condemned to death. We learn she's on intimate terms
with the governor and we learn what her mystery is?
BKM
A proud woman separates from husband because of
misunderstanding. Reconciled after many years. NYT

012946   A SPECKLED BIRD. New York: G. W.
Dillingham, [1902] NUC. London: Hutchinson, 1902 BMC.

WILSON, CATHERINE. United Kingdom.

012947   THE MODERN EVANGELINE. London: Gay and
Hancock, 1912 BMC NUC.

ATH-love story.

WILSON, DESEMEA (NEWMAN). United Kingdom.

012948   THE ISLANDS OF DESIRE. A NOVEL. BY DIANA
PATRICK. London: Hutchinson, [1920] BMC. New York:
E.P. Dutton, [1921] NUC.

TLS- Rose, unpalatable marriage. Then two daughters
(half-sisters) both actresses.

012949   THE WIDER WAY: A NOVEL. BY DIANA PATRICK.
London: Hutchinson, 1920 BMC. New York: E.P. Dutton,
[1920] NUC.

TLS-Veronica with a good stepmother is likeably
perfect. Career as school teacher, short marriage to a
German, friendship with Lord Swathe.
ATH-harmless, pretty and silly
LBKM-Original, promising, lively. Veronica does not
know who her father is-questions Swathe; he pales,
etc, writes a document and hides it. Veronica is
cornered by a complete bounder. Escapes to marry a
German.
PW- Because of passionate love barely escapes
disaster.
NYT 7-11-20 p31. The German dies, shortly after the
war begins.

WILSON, FLORA (HAYTER) BERESFORD MONTANARO.

012950   ROMANCE OF THE TAPE: FOUNDED ON FACT.
London & Sydney: Remington, 1893 BMC.

012951   SATAN'S COURIER; OR, THE COMPANY
PROMOTER: BEING THE SECRET HISTORY OF EVENTS WHICH LED
UP TO THE BOER WAR. London: Jarrold, [1904] BMC.

012952   A SOCIAL SCANDAL. Grimsby A. Gait, 1893
BMC.

WILSON, LEONA (DALRYMPLE). B. 1884. United States.

012953   DIANE OF THE GREEN VAN. BY LEONA

DALRYMPLE. Chicago: Reilly and Britton, [c1914] BMC
NUC.

PW 3-7-14 765 "Diane Westfall, heiress, with gypsy
tendencies, determines to make a trip from Connecticut
to Florida in a van, camping by the way. Philip
Poynter, who has met Diane casually, follows her trail
in a hay cart, partly for the joy of being near her,
partly to protect her from certain mysterious plots in
which her cousin Carl, a baron, a prince in disguise
and a few others are involved. It transpires,
eventually, that the question of who shall rule
Houdania is causing all the trouble."

012954   IN THE HEART OF THE CHRISTMAS PINES. BY
LEONA DALRYMPLE. New York: McBride, Nast, 1913 NUC.

PW 84 11/29/13:274. "Christmas story of how Jean
Varian went to tiny Westowe to appraise and criticise
her lover's mother, whom she had never seen and of
whom she was jealous. Of how Mrs. Loring, known as
Aunt Cheerful, took her in, not knowing who she was
and all the girl's bitter, lonely, jealousy was burned
away, and when Christmas came there was joy and a
surprising reunion."

012955   JIMSY, THE CHRISTMAS KID. BY LEONA
DALRYMPLE. New York: R. M. McBride, 1915 NUC.

012956   KENNY. BY LEONA DALRYMPLE. Chicago:
Reilly and Britton, [c1917] NUC BMC.

Kenny is a male artist and dreamer, runs off, meets
fairy-Joan. PW
He has a 23 year old son; Kenny is 44 but very young.
He's a kind of dreamer who comes to realize he's 44.
Joan, the one female character has stepped out of a
dream. Story traces relation of father and son. NYT
8-19-17 302

012957   THE LOVABLE MEDDLER. BY LEONA DALRYMPLE.
Chicago: Reilly and Britton, [c1915] BMC NUC.

Cheerful buoyant "ripples with humor" a male dr. NYT
romance sent story of Scot "meddler" 8-7-15 PW, Book
Review August.

012958   TRAUMEREI. BY LEONA DALRYMPLE. New York:
McBride, Nast, 1912 NUC.

PW--violin mystery-wedding bells
NYT-violin mystery-wedding bells
NYT-love, music, poetry

012959   UNCLE NOAH'S CHRISTMAS INSPIRATION. BY
LEONA DALRYMPLE. New York: McBride, Nast, 1912 NUC.

012960   UNCLE NOAH'S CHRISTMAS PARTY. BY LEONA
DALRYMPLE. New York: McBride, Nast, 1914 NUC.

012961   WHEN THE YULE LOG BURNS; A CHRISTMAS
STORY. BY LEONA DALRYMPLE. New York: R. A. Mcbride,
1916 NUC.

WILSON, MABEL FITZROY.

012962   ALL GLORIOUS WITHIN. London: S. Bagster,
[1905] BMC.

012963   HOW THE DREAMS CAME TRUE. BY THE AUTHOR
OF WHEN THE SWALLOWS COME AGAIN [ANONYMOUS]. London:
R. T. S., [1901] BMC.

012964   THE KING'S DAUGHTERS. London: S. Bagster,
[1905] BMC.

012965   WHEN THE WORLD WENT WRY. London: S.
Sonnenschein, 1905 BMC.

WILSON, MARIAN CALVERT. United States.

012966   MANUELITA: THE STORY OF SAN XAVIER DEL
BAC. New York: U. S. Book, [c1891] NUC.

CR 18:119 Romance of an orphan raised by a Catholic
priest in Mexico.
LW 23:262. Plot serves only as basis for providing
information about Franciscan mission to the Pinca
Indians. Manuelita marries a Spaniard who dies, gives
up her son to his father who has repudiated her. Does
mission work, son at last joins her.
PW-Her marriage results in a life of devotion to the
mission.

WILSON, MARY J.

012967   THE KNIGHT OF THE NEEDLE ROCK AND HIS
DAYS, 1571-1606. London: E. Stock, 1905 BMC.

Historical romance. 473,05 ACAD

WILSON, MONA.

012968   THE STORY OF ROSALIND RETOLD FROM HER
DIARY. BY MONICA MOORE. London: Sidgwick and Jackson,
1910 BMC.

TLS-unhappy marriage story.

WILSON, MRS. LESTER S. United States.

012969   MRS. SINCLAIR'S EXPERIMENTS. Kansas City,
Mo.: H. T. Wright, 1900 NUC.

PW-story told through letters of Stella Sinclair, a
widow of an unhappy marriage, who has little belief in
men's honor. Her experiments made on single and
married admirers confirm this.

WILSON, ROMER, pseud. See O'BRIEN, FLORENCE ROMA MUIR
WILSON.

WILSON, THEODORA WILSON. D. 1941. United Kingdom.

012970   THE BARGAIN: A STORY OF LOVE. London:
Hutchinson, 1909 BMC.

romance story TLS

012971   BESS OF HARDENDALE. London: Hutchinson,
1908 BMC NUC.

TLS-lost birthright, switched babies
ATH lost birthright,

012972   THE ISLANDERS: THE STORY OF A FAMILY.
London: Blackie, 1910 BMC.

012973   LANGBARROW HALL. New York and London: D.
Appleton, 1905 BMC NUC.

inheritance, love, jealousy NYT 197,05
ATH 05 460

012974   THE LAST WEAPON: A VISION. London: C.W.
Daniel, [1916] BMC NUC. Philadelphia: J.C. Winston,
[1917] NUC.

012975   THE MAGIC JUJUBES. London: A. Rivers,
[1906] BMC.

012976   A MODERN AHAB. London: S. Paul, [1912]
BMC.

ATH-"sent" baronet is opposed by a woman artist in his
appropriation of land for a deer run.
TLS-0

012977   MOLL O' THE TOLL-BAR. London: Hutchinson,
1911 BMC.

brave, magnetic young woman; historical romance public
whipping of women TLS
Moll has a strange power over the peasants of
Ullerdale. Some fear her, call her a witch. But she's
made admirable, "her betwitching beauty, her
independence, her deep love and intolerable hate"
"Moll and Doll are adorable" LBKM
a female quixote righting wrongs in the world of
social misery and oppression of late 17th early 18th
century. ATH

012978   THE NAVVY FROM KING'S. New York: Cassell,
1907. London: Cassell, 1907 BMC.

pretty harmless love story LBKM 7-07, 148

012979   NETHERDALE FOR EVER! London: Swarthmore
Press, [1919] BMC.

012980   SARAH THE VALIANT. London: A. Rivers,
1907 BMC.

012981   T'BACCA QUEEN; A NOVEL. London: E.
Arnold, 1901 BMC. New York: D. Appleton, 1902 NUC.

Carolina factory girl.

012982   URSULA RAVEN. London and New York:
Harper, 1905 BMC.

girls unconv. but never overstepping the limits of

good taste. All the characters are a little too good.
TLS 315,05
father ruined, she becomes school teacher, strong by
nature, finds happiness in the end ATH 05,607

012983   THE WEAPON UNSHEATHED: A SPIRITUAL
ADVENTURE. London: C.W. Daniel, [1916] BMC NUC.

upholds pacifism ATH

012984   THE WRESTLERS: FATHER, MOTHER, SON.
London: C.W. Daniel, 1916 BMC.

TLS--so religious and much suffering of Russian Marya,
embittered by her experiences in Siberia.

WINCHESTER, M. E. pseud. See WHATHAM, MARGARET E.

WINDER, BLANCHE ORAM.

012985   BACKSHEESH. BY ROMA WHITE. London:
Cassell, 1902 BMC.

ATH 11-8-02? Man marries Circassian in Egypt in Muslim
ceremony then wants to give hand and fortune to his
own kind. What then?

012986   THE CHANGELING OF BRANDLESOME. BY ROMA
WHITE. London: A. D. Innes, 1896 BMC.

SR-Hist romance, pretty.
ACAD 50:593. Stuart period, lancashire, male
foundling. Romance.

012987   THE ISLAND OF SEVEN SHADOWS. BY ROMA
WHITE. London: A. D. Innes, 1898 BMC.

SP 81:567. Breton coast, English characters.
Friendship between Mary and Joan: contrast of their
natures, the influences they have on others. Mary's
attitude toward four men. LBKM 15:153
LIT 3:604. Brittany. Island reclaimed by family. Mary
has an elusive, bewitching personality, no principles
and little character but she has charm.

012988   MOODS AND WINDS OF ARABY. London: Brown,
Langham, 1906 BMC.

012989   PUNCHINELLO'S ROMANCE. BY ROMA WHITE.
London: A. D. Innes, 1892 BMC NUC.

ACAD 41:539. Characters talk in epigrams or parables.
Dickensian in its "unchartered freedom of fantasy."
Two elderly sisters and their matchmaking.

012990   A STOLEN MASK. BY ROMA WHITE. London: A.
D. Innes, 1896 BMC.

ATH 107:710. Brilliant wayward heroine, Lois, manages
to keep clar of the worst degradation, altho she
falls, but not beyond recovery. Depiction of the seamy
side of emancipated or Bohemian life.

WINN, MARY POLK. United States.

012991   A MASTER OF THE INNER COURT. New York:
Broadway, [c1915] NUC.

WINN, MARY POLK AND MARGARET HANNIS.

012992   THE LAW AND THE LETTER; A STORY OF THE
PROVINCE OF LOUISIANA. Washington: Neale, 1907 NUC.

Story deals with an interesting experiment like that
of the practice of sending cargoes of maidens to be
married off by nuns to soldiers of French army? PW
4-6-07
Story of such a marriage-a woman substituted for the
chosen one and the mystery of that marriage. NYT?

WINSLOW, HELEN MARIA. 1851-1938. United States.

012993   CONCERNING POLLY AND SOME OTHERS. Boston:
Lee and Shepard, 1902 NUC.

story of a life, taken in early youth from squalid
tenement to noble womanhood in typical New England
family.

012994   PEGGY AT SPINSTER FARM. Boston: L.C.
Page, 1908 NUC.

012995   THE PLEASURING OF SUSAN SMITH. Boston:
L.C. Page, 1912 NUC. London: I. Pitman, 1912 BMC.

PW-40 year old woman, inherits money and goes to town.

012996   THE PRESIDENT OF QUEX. A WOMAN'S CLUB
STORY. Boston: Lothrop, Lee and Shepard, [1906] NUC.

"The inside life of an up-to-date woman's club is the
theme of this novel. The principal character in the
tale is a beautiful young woman, bereaved of all her
loved ones, who seeks to nurse her sorrow in the quiet
of her home. Her acceptance of the office of president
in Quex, the name of the club, changes her life. Two
romances are interwoven into the story. Mr. W.L.
Jacobs has drawn sixteen illustrations for the book."
BKM v.24 1906-07
NYT "it is obvious it has been written in defense of
women's clubs." Club works for community reforms

012997   SALOME SHEPARD, REFORMER. Boston, Mass.:
Arena, 1893 NUC.

She inherits a big factory, and a strike makes her
realize the need for reforms. Introduces model
housing, builds a hall with a library and classrooms
for the workers and establishes a system of profit
sharing. Love interest between her and the man who
becomes her agent. LW 93, 193.
Girlhood spent in studies and travels in Europe.
Expected to be an ornament, becomes awakened to human
rights. BOOK NEWS 130:461.

012998   SPINSTER FARM. Boston: L.C. Page, 1908
NUC.

"Giving the experiences of a maiden lady and her niece
Peggy on her farm in Massachusetts, where they go to
live in order to get away from the noise and bustle of
city life. interesting pictures of their farm life, of
their neighbours and of the surrounding country are
given. One of the amusing characters in the book is
Hiram, the hired man." BKM 27 1908

012999   A WOMAN FOR MAYOR; A NOVEL OF TODAY.
Chicago: Reilly and Britton, 1909 NUC.

City of Roma where women vote "Election of a woman as
reform Mayor" where city is corrupt, She's kidnapped;
(there actually was a woman mayor at the time.)
WOMAN'S JOURNAL 7-31-09
"based on the present-day suffrage question. Her theme
is that where women are given the right to vote women
will be elected to high offices. Her heroine is
elected to the office of Mayor and shortly afterward
marries her opponent in the campaign." BKM. v. 30
1909-10
New mayor cleans up town, gang kidnaps her, escapes,
drives out the gang, asked to run again. PW 7-3-09

013000   THE WOMAN OF TO-MORROW. New York: J.
Pott, 1905 NUC.

non-fiction? HQ 1221 Woman

WINSLOW, MARGARET E.

013001   MISS MALCOLM'S TEN: A STORY FOR THE
KING'S DAUGHTERS. Boston: Congregational Sunday School
Pub. Soc., [c1892] NUC.

LW 23:375. "Purpose to show that one may be very
enthusiastic in a good cause...and fall into grievous
errors." Several of the 10 girls did not understand
the "importance of the work they had pledged
themselves to." Some parts of book are in "bad taste."

WINSLOW, ROSE GUGGENHEIM. United States.

013002   THE GLORIOUS HOPE; A NOVEL. BY JANE BURR.
Croton-on-Hudson, N.Y.: James Burr, 1918 NUC. London:
Duckworth, 1921 BMC.

PW Country girl seeks artistic career in New York.
NYT Dec. 15 '18 p554. She marries Socialist artist who
never works. She leaves him and takes a job as typist
for $8.00 a week.

013003   LETTERS OF A DAKOTA DIVORCEE. BY JANE
BURR. Boston: Roxburgh, [c1909] NUC.

013004   THE PASSIONATE SPECTATOR. BY JANE BURR.
London: Duckworth, 1920 BMC. New York: T. Seltzer,
1921 NUC.

ATH-an argument for physical love freely indulged,
married or not.
LBKM-marriage will be freely repudiated, but even
within it there will be adventures. Will lead to
greater health and happiness.

WINSTANLEY, LILIAN. B. 1875. United Kingdom.

013005   THE SCHOLAR VAGABOND. London: Hutchinson,
1909 BMC.

An idyll of nature and open air TLS
LBKM adds little

013006   STOLEN BANNS. London: Hutchinson, 1907
BMC.

013007   THE WINGED LION. London: Hutchinson, 1908
BMC.

TLS-Gwendolen attracted by young Socialist M.P.
ATH-o

WINSTON, ANNIE STEGER.

013008   MEMOIRS OF A CHILD. New York: Longmans,
Green, 1903 BMC NUC.

A little So. girl's view of adults, etc. NYT 03, 735
Brief desc ACAD 65, 415 doesn't add much.
Interesting study of sub-conscious and
self-consciousness LBKM 11-05, 105.

WINSTON, N. B. See WINSTON, NANNIE B.

WINSTON, NANNIE B. United States.

013009   THE GRACE OF ORDERS. BY N. B. WINSTON.
New York: Abbey Press, [1901] NUC.

"The maiden aunt, Miss Rachel, is the best among the
womankind. Have readers to thank the incomparable Miss
Marlinspuyk for the racy and charming old maids who
are beginning to venture into the realm of fiction?"
NYT 2-8-02

013010   WATERS THAT PASS AWAY. New York: G. W.
Dillingham, 1899 NUC.

Helen Galbraith sacrifices honour to keep a job that
enables her to support her afflicted husband. She pays
the price with bitter remorse. CR 35:758
Conversations about art in U.S. wifely devotion, risky
situations. But sin shown as killing to the spirit;
abnormal diseased side of life. NYT 4-15-99,245

WINTER, ALICE (AMES). 1865-1944. United States.

013011   JEWEL WEED. Indianapolis: Bobbs-Merrill,
[1906] NUC BMC.

PW-marriage

013012   THE PRIZE TO THE HARDY. Indianapolis:
Bobbs-Merrill, [1905] BMC NUC.

"Mrs. Lyell, a typical characterzation of a class of
women whose study of transcendental philosophy and the
higher thought has served to destroy their
appreciation for home life" PW
heroine rescues hero from frozen lake
BKM 21 107 1905
Touch of Indian blood. NYT 05, 244

WINTER, ELIZABETH (CAMPBELL). 1841-1922. United States.

013013   THE SPANISH TREASURE. A NOVEL. BY
ISABELLA CASTELAR. London: J. Henderson, 1893 BMC. New
York: R. Bonner's Sons, 1893 NUC.

Relates the burying of a treasure in the west by one
of Columbus' crew. The heirs of this man try to find
it. Their thrilling adventures. One is a young
American woman. PW 2-11-93

WINTER, JOHN STRANGE, pseud. See STANNARD, HENRIETTA ELIZA
VAUGHAN (PALMER).

WINTER, LOUISE. United States.

013014   HEARTS AFLAME. New York and London: Smart
Set, 1903 NUC.

divorced woman's struggle to get back into society PW
9-05-03
BKM 03

WINTERGREEN, JANE.

013015   TWO IN A FLAT. London: Hodder &
Stoughton, [1908] BMC.

TLS-Pleasant chatty unoriginal record of daily life.
SR-Lady and maid, gentle satire
BKM o

WINTERTON, MARK, pseud. See KIDD, BEATRICE ETHEL.

WITHERSPOON, ISABELLA M. United States.

013016   RITA DE GARTHEZ, THE BEAUTIFUL
RECONCENTRADO: A TALE OF THE HISPANO-AMERICAN WAR.
Bellport, New York: Regent, 1898 W.

013017   THE TRAGEDY OF AGES. New York: F.T.
Neely, 1897 NUC. London: F. T. Neely, 1897 BMC.

Concerns "causes which lead women to shrink from the
duties and cares of maternity." PW 52:1105

WITTIGSCHLAGER, WILHELMINA. United States.

013018   MINNA, WIFE OF THE YOUNG RABBI, A NOVEL.
New York: Consolidated Retail Booksellers, 1905 NUC
BMC. London: Gay & Bird, 1906 BS.

TLS-improbable romance
"This story of Jewish life turns on the enforced
marriage of a young girl, twelve years of age, to a
Jewish student whom she has never met, and from whom
she flees soon after the wedding.... Minna's
tendencies toward nihilism cause her to be banished to
Siberia and result in the death of the Czar, whose
daughter she proves to be." BKM. v.23, 1906

WODNIL, GABRIELLE.

013019   BRINETA AT BRIGHTON. A BOARDING HOUSE
ROMANCE. London: S. Paul, 1913 BMC.

Boarding house romance. Brineta's romance and
introduction to the boarders. TLS

013020   MAGGIE OF MARGATE. A SEASIDE SENSATION.
London: S. Paul, [1912] BMC.

ATH-titled lady masquerades as a servant.
TLS-Romance

WOLF, ALICE S. United States.

013021   A HOUSE OF CARDS. Chicago: Stone and
Kimball, 1896 NUC.

LW. 27:250. North Carolina. Loys' mrge to Gregory, her
old friend, whom she thought she would eventually
love. He loved her and promised much for the future,
but from day-to-day was selfish and did not tell her
about hereditary insanity.
PW 4-4-96. She was a schoolteacher, she marries him
because she is having trouble with her eyes, they are
overworked and need rest. Too late the man she might
have loved comes into her life.
BOOK NEWS Miss Wolf is from San Francisco. She has
literary aspirations; he is out of sympathy with her
ambitions.

WOLF, EMMA. B. 1865. United States.

013022   FULFILLMENT; A CALIFORNIA NOVEL. New
York: H. Holt, 1916 NUC.

Two sisters live in cottage in San Francisco. Gwen
Heath, beauty and impetuous slips into a love affair
and marriage and a situation that offers nothing but
unhappiness and divorce. PW
NYT-Development of a selfish heroine into a noble
woman. At 24 she marries to avoid poverty tolerates
then hates husband, estranged, birth of child.
BKM-sounds like she gets back to husband. Sound moral
and conjugal principles. A sentimental and slightly
voluptuous tract.

013023   HEIRS OF YESTERDAY. Chicago: A. C.
McClurg, 1900 NUC BMC.

PW-young Jewish doctor in San Francisco before Spanish
American War prefers company of Gentiles to Jews. This
broken down by Gentile prejudice, Jewish
exclusiveness, and a spirited and idealistic young
Jewish woman.

013024   THE JOY OF LIFE. Chicago: A. C. McClurg,
1896 NUC.

BKM 4:375. Contrast of two men, Anthony and Cecil,
what they believe, their inner lives. Anthony is a

cynic.
PW 10-31-96. Both love same girl. Modern western city.

013025   OTHER THINGS BEING EQUAL. Chicago: A. C.
McClurg, 1892 NUC.

PW-Story of meeting of Ruth Levice, a Jewess, and Dr.
Kemp, Christian. Other things being equal, religious
creed should make no difference in married happiness.
Jews in San Francisco. Happy marriage of the Levice's.
Love story of Ruth and Dr. Kemp LW '93,12
Father has sole care of daughter up to 25, then turns
her over to mother. He is a pleasant tolerant person.
Father and daughter have a beautiful relation. At his
request she marries a man he chose-at his death bed.
CR.14,20:162

013026   A PRODIGAL IN LOVE: A NOVEL. New York:
Harper, 1894 NUC.

LW 25:219. "Exhibits one of the most extraordinary
developments of affection and aberration in its
leading characters of which we know." Constance, the
sister-mother is sincerely noble.
PW-home perplexities. Constance left in charge of
large family of sisters. Hall Kenyon fell in love with
one sister and married another. Constance is good to
sisters, equally to one who most injured her.

WOLFENSTEIN, MARTHA. 1869-1906. United States.

013027   IDYLLS OF THE GASS. Philadelphia: Jewish
Publication Society of America, 1901 BMC NUC.

Jewish boy wants to be a rabbi ACAD 65, 60; 65, 107.
Sketches of Jewish village life in Austria.

WOLFF, JETTA SOPHIA.

013028   NO PLACE FOR HER. London: Greening, 1902
BMC.

WOLSELEY, BEATRICE S. (KNOLLYS).

013029   MY BLACK SPIRIT. BY B. S. KNOLLYS. London
and Sydney: Remington, 1893 BMC.

WOOD, AIMEE M. United States.

013030   MUSICAL ROMANCES. Kansas City, Mo.: Life
Pub. Co., 1898 NUC.

WOOD, AMY MAUDE.

013031   LOVE'S AFTERMATH. London: H.J. Drane,
[1903] BMC.

for grils TLS 03 35

WOOD, ANNA COGSWELL. Fl.1891-1904. United States.

013032   DIANA FONTAINE: A NOVEL. BY ALGERNON
RIDGEWAY. Philadelphia: J. B. Lippincott, 1891 NUC.

013033   THE WESTOVERS. BY ALGERNON RIDGEWAY.
London: Digby, Long, [1894] BMC.

013034   WESTOVER'S WARD. BY ALGERNON RIDGEWAY.
London: R. Bentley, 1892 BMC NUC.

WOOD, ANNIE MARY.

013035   SAND-FACE: A STORY OF ANGLO-EASTERN LIFE.
London: Hodder and Stoughton, 1916 BMC.

TLS-Story of Chinese concession, devoted missionary
work.

013036   SEAS BETWEEN; OR, CALLED TO THE EAST AND
CLAIMED BY THE WEST. London: E. Stock, 1908 BMC.

SR. Missionary life in China. Good portrayal of
feminine characters, women genuinely absorbed in
religion. Rev believes this requires far greater
courage than writing a conventionally "daring" study
of illicit passions.

WOOD, EDITH (ELMER). 1871-1945. United States.

013037   HER PROVINCIAL COUSIN: A STORY OF
BRITTANY. New York: Cassell, [c1893] NUC.

CR 21:238. Brittany, quaint love story

013038   AN OBERLAND CHALET. New York: Wessels &
Bissell, 1910 NUC. London: T. Werner Laurie, [1911]

BMC.

DG 24 Switzerland-descr & trav

013039   THE SPIRIT OF THE SERVICE. New York and
London: Macmillan, 1903 BMC NUC.

LBKM-about war in Spain "spirited men and girls"
PW 11-7-03
NYT '03

WOOD, FANNY MORRIS. United Kingdom.

013040   FIVE YEARS AND A MONTH. [London]:
Duckworth, 1913 BMC NUC.

Unhappy marriage, callous husband, flirtatious wife
who dies on last page. SP
They separate, get involved with others in the
interim. TLS

WOOD, FRANCES HARIOTT.

013041   THE OLD RED SCHOOL-HOUSE. A CANADIAN BUSH
TALE. London: S. W. Partridge, [1898] BMC.

013042   PERISH THE BAUBLES. London: Simpkin,
Marshall, [1898] BMC.

013043   RIVULET COTTAGES. London: Christian
Knowledge Society, [1895] BMC.

    Tales

013044   SWALLOW CASTLE. London: Christian
Knowledge Society, [1899] BMC.

WOOD, JOANNA E. D. 1919. Canada.

013045   A DAUGHTER OF WITCHES. A ROMANCE. London:
Hurst and Blackett, 1900 BMC. Toronto: W.J. Gage,
[1900] NUC.

LBKM 19:28. Beautiful woman marries New England
minister, tempts him, leads him, ruining him before
his congregation. She loved a loveable rip of a cousin
and married the gentle minister   this brought out
her evil powers. She suffers tragically ithe end.
SP 85:309. Unnaturally unadulterated wickedness of
heroine.
ATH 116:276. She writes his sermons with hypnotic
suggestion. Learns to love her slave.

013046   FARDEN HA'. London: Hurst & Blackett,
1902 BMC.

ATH 1902-"man's attitude toward his friend" <and wife
who have had a child> should be "suffer in silence and
go on as if nothing had happened"

013047   JUDITH MOORE, OR, FASHIONING A PIPE.
Toronto: Ontario, 1898 BMC NUC.

013048   THE UNTEMPERED WIND. New York: J. S.
Tait, [1894] NUC.

LW 25:392. To show that a woman needs pity and
forgiveness as an unwed mother. Earnest. Retribution.
PW-"Myron Holder's fresh girlhood is wrecked by a
young medical student who loves and forgets. Her
efforts to earn a living for her little boy are
blocked by every woman from her own grandmother to the
last and least of village matrons. The story is strong
and wholly tragic to the end."
A girl has sinned-a whole town turns against her
hypocritically. They make her life unbearable; she's
tied here because she's poor and has an aged relative
to care for. CR 23:47.

WOOD, L. C. See WOOD, LYDIA COPE (COLLINS).

WOOD, LYDIA COPE (COLLINS). B. 1845. United States.

013049   FOR A FREE CONSCIENCE. BY L. C. WOOD. New
York: F. H. Revell, [1905] NUC.

Life of two young women. one dark haired and saucy, a
fair one who mothers her, a Quaker. NYT 542, 05

WOOD, MARY ROSALIE ALLING. United States.

013050   THE TURN OF THE CURRENT; A STUDY OF THE
NEW CONSCIOUSNESS. New York: Neale, 1904 NUC.

WOOD, S. ELLA. United States.

013051   SHIBBOLETH: A NOVEL. Chicago: W. B.
Conkey, [c1898] NUC.

WOOD, SABINE W. United States.

013052   THE CRADLE OF THE DEEP; AN ACCOUNT OF THE
ADVENTURES OF ELEANOR CHANNING AND JOHN STARBUCK. BY
JACOB FISHER. Boston: L. C. Page, 1912 NUC.

013053   THE MAN WHO SAW WRONG, BY JACOB FISHER.
Philadelphia: J C. Winston., [c1913] NUC.

"The story is concerned with two rival artists, each
of whom is trying for a salon prize. They employ the
same model, Adrea Varrick, a girl of great beauty. One
of the two, Julius Lavigne, is 'the man who saw
wrong,' which being interpreted means that he distorts
the lives and motives of everyone, especially his
subjects; he even looks into their souls and falsifies
those on his canvas." BRD 1913

013054   THE QUITTER, A NOVEL. BY JACOB FISHER.
Philadelphia: J. C. Winston, [c1914] NUC.

BRD- Like the princesses in the fairy tales of old,
Sophia Burton of this story sends her lover on a
quest. She will not marry him until he has proved
himself; and since she desires a coat made of baby
musk-ox skins she sends him off into the frozen north
in search of this contraband fur. Hallam succeeds in
getting what he goes after, but he never claims his
reward at Sophia Burton's hands; for up in the north
he finds Norma Leonard, an unsophisticated daughter of
the wilds, and when he does return with his prize he
brings a wife with him. "Aside from a somewhat
strained motive, the plot is well planned and the
story is entertaining. The girl of the north is at
least an original type." +-Boston Transcript p24 0
28'14 230w

WOODBURY, HELEN LAURA (SUMNER). United States.

013055   THE WHITE SLAVE; OR, "THE CROSS OF GOLD".
BY HELEN L. SUMNER. Chicago: C. H. Kerr, [c1896] NUC
BMC.

WOODBURY, MARY C. United States.

013056   HEREDITY; OR, HARRY HARWOOD'S
INHERITANCE. Boston: McDonald and Gill, 1892 NUC.

WOODCOCK, CATHERINE MARY ANTONY.

013057   PARADYSE TERRESTRE. BY C. M. ANTONY.
London: R. & T. Washbourne, 1914 BMC.

Supernatural stories of heavenly visions. TLS
<Miss-according to TLS>

WOODGATE, MILDRED VIOLET. B. 1904. United Kingdom.

013058   THE WORLD OF A CHILD. London: Heath,
Cranton & Ouseley, [1913] BMC.

Thoughts and doings and influence of her surroundings
upon her-up to age 8 TLS

WOODMAN, H. REA. See WOODMAN, HANNAH REA.

WOODMAN, HANNAH REA. B. 1870. United States.

013059   THE NOAHS AFLOAT; AN HISTORICAL ROMANCE.
BY H. REA WOODMAN. New York: Neale, 1905 NUC.

Modern version of Noah's trip PW 7-15-05
NYT 457,05

WOODMAN, MARY. United States.

013060   A TOUCH OF NEW ENGLAND; AN OLD FASHIONED
STORY FOR YOUNG AND OLD HEARTS. Boston: J. G. Cupples,
1903 NUC.

013061   A TOUCH OF PORTUGAL; OR, THE LITTLE COUNT
OF VILLA MONCAO. Boston: Atlantic Printing, 1910 NUC.

WOODROFFE, DANIEL, pseud. See WOODS, MRS. JAMES CHAPMAN.

WOODROW, MRS. WILSON. See WOODROW, NANCY MANN (WADDEL).

WOODROW, NANCY MANN (WADDEL). 1870-1935. United States.

013062   THE BEAUTY. BY MRS. WILSON WOODROW.
Indianapolis: Bobbs Merrill, [c1910] NUC.

husband learns wife's worth; she, his loveable

character-after much misunderstanding PW
BKM triangle in marriage. Husband leaves her for a few
months to allow her to choose. She creates a business
establishment teaching women how to dress, etc.; and
while thus occupied realizes she loves her husband.
NYT-She has too much strength of character to be
relegated to role of pretty plaything and the two pass
thru difficult times before they come to understanding
and happiness.

013063   THE BIRD OF TIME; BEING CONVERSATIONS
WITH EGERIA. By MRS. WILSON WOODROW. New York:
McClure, Phillips, 1907 NUC.

cultured New York men and women; subjects of
particular interest to women.

013064   THE BLACK PEARL. BY MRS. WILSON WOODROW.
New York and London: D. Appleton, 1912 BMC NUC.

PW-dancer pursued thru the West by theatrical
manager.??
NYT- 0
man doesn't take life seriously till another dies that
he might live. ATH
love story of a dancer in a mountain mining camp TLS

013065   THE HORNET'S NEST. BY MRS. WILSON
WOODROW. Boston: Little, Brown, 1917 NUC.

focuses on a Senator PW
underworld competes with law and order BKM
mystery story involving jewels and the Hornet who was
in reality Ashe Colvin. NYT 111,3-25,17

013066   THE NEW MISSIONER. BY MRS. WILSON
WOODROW. New York: McClure, 1907 NUC.

She's a minister gives up love for her career 10-26-07
PW
Frances Benton becomes a minister in Rockies, her work
and influence. She's not welcomed at first in mining
camp of Zenith. Ladies Aid Soc unfriendly. wins them
over by a pact, becomes head of Society. Devotes
energies to good works NYT
TLS-woman missioner in a mining village. Who against
much opposition won the hearts of the people

013067   SALLY SALT. BY MRS. WILSON WOODROW.
Indianapolis: Bobbs-Merrill, [c1912] NUC.

PW-widow who lives with another widow manages farm;
love stories
NYT romance

013068   THE SILVER BUTTERFLY. BY MRS. WILSON
WOODROW. Indianapolis: Bobbs-Merrill, [1908] NUC.

@ a silver mine BKM
PW-romance
BKM romance -

WOODRUFF, HELEN (SMITH). 1888-1924. United States.

013069   THE IMPRISONED FREEMAN. New York: G.
Sully, [1918] BMC NUC.

PW-Male hero, wronged by wife and injustice of laws.
NYT May 26, 1918, p. 249. of "atrocities which cry to
Heaven" Dramatic and tragic.

013070   THE LADY OF THE LIGHTHOUSE. New York: G.
H. Doran, [c1913] NUC.

NYT-Heroine works with the blind and "the lighthouse",
an institution for the blind which helps them become
self-supporting and therefore cheerful thru work.

013071   THE LITTLE HOUSE. New York: G. H. Doran,
[c1914] NUC.

PW 86 10/17/14:1249 "The Sorrylady's daughter, Rose,
had eloped with a yankee. The daughter died, and
Dorothy, her little girl, went South to cheer her
grandmother. Her love was lavished on the Sorrylady
and on the stern old Colonel, and she made them forget
old shadows."

013072   MIS' BEAUTY. New York: Alice Harriman,
1911 NUC. London: Hodder & Stoughton, 1913 BMC.

Sent. southern story PW 12-16-11
So Family; about "darkies" and their family devotion.
ATH.

013073   MR. DOCTOR-MAN. New York: H. Doran,

[c1915] NUC.

NYT-male char. study.

WOODRUFF, JANE (SCOTT).

013074   THE ROSES OF SAINT ELIZABETH. Boston: L.
C. Page, 1906 NUC.

Sent love story 9-16-05 PW

WOODRUFF, JULIA LOUISA MATILDA (CURTISS). 1833-1909.
United States.

013075   BELLERUE; OR, THE STORY OF ROLF. BY W. M.
L. JAY. New York: E. P. Dutton, 1891 NUC. London:
Griffith, Farran, 1891 BMC.

Pastor's wife tells of new experiences in husband's
new position but real interest is murder mystery and
an inheritance and lookalikes. SP 66, 699
Rolf Kenwood's male friend clears his friend's name of
murder charge after Rolf dies. They are lookalikes and
the friend (Captain Murray) impersonates Rolf to save
him. CR ACAD also ATH 97 307

WOODS, ALICE. B. 1871. United States.

013076   EDGES. Indianapolis: Bowen-Merrill,
[1902] NUC. London: B. F. Stevens & Brown, [1902] BMC.

DIAL 11-16-02 Bohemian life-two artists, male and
female, 1st in New England, she goes to Paris, he
follows, marries.
NYT 12-6-02 Heroine "is gifted with rare intelligence
which understands and delights in Walt Whitman &
Schopenhauer". She to he, "You like me of course...but
do hold fast to your own identity because if you don't
it's all off with my liking you."

013077   FAME-SEEKERS. New York: G. H. Doran,
[c1912] NUC.

PW-Bohemian student life in Paris.
NYT-novel with purpose warning against women seeking
fame and professional life.

WOODS, CHARLOTTE ELIZABETH.

013078   AN EVERY-DAY LIFE. Leadenhall Press,
1895. London: Published For The Authoress, 1895 BMC.
(A Religious work BMC)

WOODS, KATHARINE PEARSON. 1853-1923. United States.

013079   THE CROWNING OF CANDACE. New York: Dodd,
Mead, 1896 NUC. London: B. F. Stevens, 1896 BMC.

PW 10-24-96. Candace's 1st story a huge success, 2nd
one a failure. She learns who are her real friends,
and discovers that her devotion to her art has been
really selfishness. This awakening to love and duty is
the real crowning of Candace.
Joys, sorrows and tragedies of simple mining people
put together by Candace; the book is accepted by a
N.Y. publisher and the town celebrates Candace's
achievement. She is interviewed, flattered, beseiged
by publishers. Writes another novel in 6 wks. But it
proves a failure. A lesson to those who would rush
into print. BKM 5:262

013080   FROM DUSK TO DAWN. New York: D. Appleton,
1892 NUC.

PW-Story with ethical purpose concerning a
faith-healer, a theosophist, an orthodox clergyman, a
mesmerist, and a medium, their discussions on
improving the world.
Modern Religious novel. Each character represents a
phase of so called religion thought evolving toward
"vitalism." NATION 56, 20
Hero is a clergyman of Church of England. Disbelieves
utterly in spiritualism and tries to save daughters
from it. CR 14,20:216

013081   JOHN: A TALE OF KING MESSIAH. New York:
Dodd, Mead, 1896 NUC. London: B.F. Stevens, 1896 BMC.

PW 10-24-96. Ten years in the life of Jesus.

013082   THE SON OF INGAR. New York: Dodd, Mead,
1897 NUC. London: S. W. Partridge, 1898 BMC.

LW 29:188. Biblical story after death of Christ.

WOODS, MARGARET LOUISA (BRADLEY). B. 1856. United Kingdom.

013083　　　　ESTHER VANHOMRIGH. New York: J. W.
Lovell, [c1891] NUC. London: J. Murray, 1891 BMC.

LW 23:386. Psychological study of her relationship
with Swift. He is portrayed as consistently cold and
cruel, she as having a deep passion which could be
neither discouraged nor restrained. Author is partial
to Esther, too harsh with Swift, rev.feels.
Fiction story about Swift and Vanessa and 18th century
literary characters. BAKER 03,190
author sides with Vanessa rather than Stella. Make
Swift's letter from Vanessa to Stella an actual
interview. ACAD
Character of Esther (Vanessa) impulsive eager with
intellectual ambitions. friendship with Swift turns to
infatuation which she declares with little reserve.
(younger and more brilliant rival of Swift's
affection). Stella and she meet."Her ill fated
experiment in friendship" SP 67 890
Well done. Works with recorded facts, as well as whole
spirit of the time and of Swift. ATH 98 645
Makes Swift go thru the form of a private marriage
with Stella shortly before Vanessa's death and Stella
denies the fact to Vanessa in an interview between
them the day before Swift returns the latter's letter.
In this book it is her letters to him, not her letters
to Stella that he returns. Vanessa's illness and death
follow immediate upon the event. SR 11-28-91, 615

013084　　　　THE INVADER; A NOVEL. New York: Harper,
1907 NUC. London: W. Heinemann, 1907 BMC.

Dual personality in a woman who has
everything-scholarly attainment, strong char, loveable
domestic nature. The other is fun loving frivolous and
the one her Oxford husband prefers. PW 5-11-07
Because of an experience in hypnosis, "Milly shares
her life with clever, loose-living Mildred." She
marries and at times becomes Mildred. Husband comes to
love not Milly he married but the baser Mildred. She
has a child. Milly kills herself and this other. LBKM
6-07,110
Mildred-unscrupulous, gay coquette Milly-dull,
conscientious wife ACAD
Life at Oxford-mostly about women "amazons" and blue
stockings" among them-hocky-playing, at home in
science and slang. Mildred wearies of scholarly
husband, runs off with another man. SP.

013085　　　　THE KING'S REVOKE; AN EPISODE IN THE LIFE
OF PATRICK DILLON. New York: E. P. Dutton, 1906 NUC.
London: Smith, Elder, 1906 BMC NUC.

NYT-hist rom.
LBKM-

013086　　　　PASTELS UNDER THE SOUTHERN CROSS. London:
Smith, Elder, 1911 BMC NUC.

013087　　　　SONS OF THE SWORD, A ROMANCE OF THE
PENINSULAR WAR. New York: McClure, Phillips, 1901 NUC.
London: W. Heinemann, 1901 BMC.

　PW 12-7-01
　ATH 12-14-01

013088　　　　THE VAGABONDS. London: Smith, Elder, 1894
BMC. New York & London: Macmillan, 1894 NUC.

LW 25:463. Development of sister's executive ability.
LBKM 7:52. Tragic love story of middle-aged clown in
travelling circus. The wife he believed dead turned up
after he is married to a younger woman whom he loves
but she is in love with someone else.
English story of circus life, the climax of which is
Joe's saving his rival's life by killing the elephant
he (Joe) loves. He's the clown, greathearted. CR
23:474.

013089　　　　WEEPING FERRY, AND OTHER STORIES. London
and New York: Longmans, 1898 NUC.

WOODS, MARY A.

013090　　　　AD LUCEM: A NOVEL. Letchworth: Garden
City Press, 1914 BMC.

ATH 144:561. Group of cultured middle-class. Leader is
heroine, gives lectures on the Beautiful. Dies.
TLS because she discovers her marriage is bigamous.

WOODS, MRS. J. C. See WOODS, MRS. JAMES CHAPMAN.

WOODS, MRS. JAMES CHAPMAN. United Kingdom.

013091　　　　THE BEAUTY SHOP. BY DANIEL WOODROFFE.
London: T. Laurie, [1905] NUC BMC.

ACAD-Vicious modern social people cynical humour. Mrs.
Sali's beauty shop.
ATH-Wherein is sought physical beauty when time or
nature has proved unkind.

013092　　　　THE EVIL EYE. BY DANIEL WOODROFFE (MRS.
J. C. WOODS). London: W. Heinemann, 1903 NUC.

013093　　　　HER CELESTIAL HUSBAND. BY DANIEL
WOODROFFE. London: T. F. Unwin, 1895 BMC NUC.

Sybil Conyers quarrels with fiance. Then marries a
Chinese man-Leu-ching. "We wish we could describe it
as improbable, but there is no conceivable folly in
this way that Englishwomen have not ventured upon." SP
75:613
Her horror of Chinese customs, her gradual loathing of
her husband. Loses her mind, murders her husband,
dies. Shows the "absolute unwisdon, not to say
immorality of mixed marriages. No Engliswoman should
mate with the black man or the yellow man" ACAD 47 480

013094　　　　THE RAT-TRAP. BY DANIEL WOODROFFE.
London: T.W. Laurie, [1912] BMC.

ATH-man caught in mrg, shown way out by heroine.
SR-Heroine gets him on ship bound for west Indies, it
is shipwrecked and they are on an island of slaves
with violent owner. Dr. of violence and sudden death.
Wife (in Hanwell) is a homicidal maniac. An attack on
the conventional sanctity of the mrg. tie.

013095　　　　TANGLED TRINITIES. BY DANIEL WOODROFFE.
London: W. Heinemann, 1901 BMC. New York: Dodd, Mead,
1901 NUC.

"A curious study in a psychological and material sense
of a girl who is half white and the other half negro.
Asta Steele and her father, the vicar of Borth, the
vicar showing his negro origin, are two personages
apparently out of place in England. Asta is ever
longing for her home in Jamaica. She never is in touch
with her surroundings, nor for that is her father.
Between the two there is the sincerest affection. The
girl is in charge of a narrowminded aunt. In the
neighborhood are many people who make it a business to
be rude to Asta and her father. Asta resents this
constant snubbing...what is novel in the romance is
the treatment of the woman of a mixed blood, and it is
not a flattering one." NYT 9-21-01, 658.

WOODS, VIRNA. 1864-1903. United States.

013096　　　　AN ELUSIVE LOVER. London: A. Constable,
1898 BMC. Boston: Houghton, Mifflin, 1898 NUC.

SP 81:313. Hero, a Californian, has a dual
personality.
LIT 3:606. He is jealous of his other self, challenges
him to single combat. He is, eventually, charged with
Heroine is in love with that half of him which is a
German painter. Complications. Eventually entire
murder and brought to trial. Acquitted. personality is
merged into German painter.

013097　　　　A MODERN MAGDALENE. Boston: Lee and
Shepard, 1894 NUC.

PW-she elopes with married man. A few years of
happiness before his death. Little child, poverty,
vice and misery follow before release of death.

WOOLF, ADELINE VIRGINIA (STEPHEN). 1882-1941. United
Kingdom.

013098　　　　THE MARK ON THE WALL. Richmond: Hogarth
Press, 1919 BMC NUC.

013099　　　　NIGHT AND DAY. BY VIRGINIA WOOLF. London:
Duckworth, [1919] BMC NUC. New York: G. H. Doran,
[c1920] NUC.

PW-Practical woman and her intellectual friends.
NYT 12-5-70 p 20. She is writing the life of a poet;
work does not progress. Mary Datchet, whom all the
group leans on emotionally, is a "resolute" working
girl.
Victorianism gives place to the present; love affairs
of five people-"these active brains with no refuge of
inherited stds and acceptances to run to, must try
everything for themselves and will take nothing for
granted. Katharine Hilbery rooted in the Victorian Era
but shooting up into the untried future!-seeking

security from one man, daring in another." She & Ralph
Denkam are going to be honestly themselves. Mrs.
Sallie Seal. the suffragist. TLS
Katherine's attempt to reconcile the world of reality
with her dream world. Wealth, father a great poet,
practical, precocious. Her half unconscious protest vs
family trad. falls in love, realizes this is a
betrayal of her dream. ATH

013100   THE VOYAGE OUT. BY VIRGINIA WOOLF London:
Duckworth, 1915 BMC NUC.

"Never was a book more recklessly feminine" late
development of sheltered young woman. Rachel Vinrace
has only her music, goes on voyage to S. America.
spends a few months in a little port. The illogic of
her death leaves one desolated by a sense of fatality
of life TLS
NYT 1920:308 Rachel, 24, and a group of "smart"
people, their "clever" talk.

WOOLF, VIRGINIA. See WOOLF, ADELINE VIRGINIA (STEPHEN).

WOOLSEY, SARAH CHAUNCEY. 1835-1905.

013101   THE RULE OF THREE. BY SUSAN COOLIDGE.
Philadelphia: H. Altemus, [1904] NUC.

PW-stepmother and "unruly" daughters.

WOOLSON, CONSTANCE FENIMORE. 1840-1894. United States.

013102   HORACE CHASE: A NOVEL. New York: Harper,
1894 NUC. London: Osgood, 1894 BMC.

SR 78:331. Ruth falls for a business acquaintance of
her 19 year older husband. She flees to him only to
find he is in love with another. Story closes with her
"comfortably penitent" in her husband's arms.
ACAD-novel is full of studies of women, including a
sculptress who smokes.

WORBOISE, EMMA JANE. See GUYTON, EMMA JANE (WORBOISE).

WORDEN, HATTIE WELLER. United States.

013103   EDNA LEE: A NOVEL. Chicago: Scroll, 1900
NUC.

013104   EVA. A NOVEL. Lily Dale, N.Y.: Sunflower
Pub. Co., 1906 NUC.

WORDEN, WILBERTINE (TETERS). D. 1949. United States.

013105   THE SNOWS OF YESTER-YEAR: A NOVEL. BY
WILBERTINE TETERS. Boston: Arena, 1895 NUC.

Young couple both with TB in Colo. dying. The woman is
a gifted, well read, fearless thinker. She has a
friend who idolizes her and with whom the husband
falls in love. Death of the couple solves the problem.
PW 12-21-95:1184

WORKMAN, MARY CHRISTIANA (SHEEDY). 1859-1926. United
States.

013106   AN AMERICAN SINGER IN PARIS; A NOVEL. BY
MRS. HANSON WORKMAN. Cincinnati: Tribune printing,
1908 NUC BMC.

PW-Fem-Singer

WORKMAN, MRS. HANSON. See WORKMAN, MARY CHRISTIANA
(SHEEDY).

WORTH, PATIENCE. United States.

013107   HOPE TRUEBLOOD. BY PATIENCE WORTH,
COMMUNICATED THROUGH MRS. JOHN H. CURRAN. New York: H.
Holt, 1918 NUC. London: Skeffington, [1919] BMC.

PW-Autobiography of illegitimate Hope and her
sufferings until myst. is cleared.
NYT, June 2, 1918, p. 254. Patience Worth communicates
this story (as she has two previous works) through
Mrs. John H. Curran, by whose fingers it was spelled
out on a ouija board. Story is told in first person by
Hope Trueblood, in Eng. village during Victorian era.
Mysteries, humor, and a concept of God as universal
love.
Hope, illegitimate, tells her story-reactions to
strange grown-up world interspersed with torrents of
hysterical emotions.?TLS 140 SP

013108   THE SORRY TALE; A STORY OF THE TIME OF
CHRIST. BY PATIENCE WORTH, COMMUNICATED THROUGH MRS.

J. H. CURRAN. New York: H. Holt, 1917 BMC NUC. (BMC:
Imputed author Patience Worth)

Written in "strange farrago of strained and clipped
and grammarless utterances" interspersed with passages
of real beauty. Makes one of thieves on the cross son
of Tiberius and a slave girl BKM
640 pp spelled out on a ouija board by Patience from a
former life returned who now "speaks" to Mrs. Curran
at the rate of 2500-5000 words an evening (Often gives
poetry too-all flawless) In this tale "Patience works
her own will with the gospels; invents new miracle."
NYT 255 7-8-17

WORTHINGTON, ELIZABETH STRONG. United States.

013109   THE GENTLE ART OF COOKING WIVES. New
York: Dodge, [c1900] NUC.

013110   HOW TO COOK HUSBANDS. New York: Dodge,
1899 NUC. London: Siegle, Hill, 1908 BMC.

A 34 year old woman describes her difficulties in
choosing a husband. Having made her selection; she and
he have a misunderstanding. In the interim before they
are reconciled, she gives advice about managing a
husband and includes advice by married friends. PW
55:1001.

013111   THE LITTLE BROWN DOG: A TALE OF THE
PRESIDIO. San Francisco: Cubery, 1898 NUC.

WORTHINGTON, VICTORIA. United States.

013112   RANK VS. MERIT. New York: Home Book,
[1893] NUC.

PW-Love story. Son of lord marries gardener's
daughter. Marriage is annulled by family. She becomes
actress and singer. Final reconciliation.

WOTTON, MABEL E. United Kingdom.

013113   A GIRL DIPLOMATIST. London: Chapman and
Hall, 1892 BMC.

ATH 100:126. Love scenes "gushingly sentimental."
Romance. Hero is a prig, jealous, complications.
SR 74:281. Barbara Thorpe believes women should have a
wider sphere of action. She wants to be a diplomat.
Reviewer snickers, "her story tends to show," without
its being the author's intent, "diplomacy is not for
women."

013114   THE LITTLE BROWNS. London: Blackie, 1900
BMC.

WRAY, ANGELINA W. United States.

013115   BETTY TUCKER'S AMBITION. Boston: Lothrop,
[1913] NUC.

Betty-writer gets job on local paper.

013116   JEAN MITCHELL'S SCHOOL; A STORY.
Bloomington, Ill.: Public-School Pub. Co., 1902 NUC.

Ideal school.

WRENCH, MOLLIE LOUISE (GIBBS) STANLEY.

013117   BEAT: A MODERN LOVE STORY. London:
Duckworth, 1917 BMC.

Beat is her name. She's a blacksmith's daughter with a
stepmother, becomes the struggling guardian of her
younger sisters. Then comes a lugubrious love story.
TLS
From earliest years forced to make her own way
insatiable thirst for knowledge; her great
aim-college, just as she gets there her aunt dies and
she must care for sisters. Gives up studies, teaches
in London, struggling to keep a home together and
train her sisters. With the two oldest she fails; love
of luxury too strong for them. With youngest, she
succeeds. Story of unfulfilled loves-no happy end LBKM
Beat is a "Council school teacher" with two no-good
sisters. Beat hands over one of her lovers to one
sister who makes a bad wife. This sister is an invalid
and Beat and her former lover care for her SR.

013118   BURNT WINGS. London: J. Long, 1909 BMC.

Husband has "burned his wings" with another woman;
wife loves another man. Ends in reconciliation. TLS

013119   THE COURT OF THE GENTILES. London: Mills
& Boon, 1913 BMC.

"A little cloying in its intense femininity" ATH
The chief heroine is a brilliant novelist who marries
a wealthy cripple. We get their adventures in a No.
African desert. In III we have another heroine,
another novelist, even more brilliant. TLS

013120   THE DEVIL'S STAIRS. London: Duckworth,
1918 BMC.

TLS-Barbara and unhappy marriage. Depressing.
ATH-"Everybody slips who treads upon the devil's
stairs" They yield to passion in spite of a prior
marriage.
LBKM She is forced to marry lawyer she detests because
of his trickery. Spends a little time with man she
loves before wedding (wife in an asylum). Child born
is not husband's. A serious theme treated in a serious
fashion.
SR Herself the daughter of a liaison with her mother
and neighbor, she claims the right to choose a father
for her child. Lover is killed in war. Barbara's
childhood (soul destroying environment of home), as
nursery governess and secretary to feminist.

013121   LILY LOUISA. London: Methuen, 1915 BMC.

Girl becomes artist "rehash of old material" TLS

013122   LOVE'S FOOL; THE CONFESSIONS OF A
MAGDALEN. London: J. Long, [1909] BMC.

TLS-Sensuous throbbing passionate woman, a number of
men involved and a clairvoyant who was a "tiger."

013123   A PERFECT PASSION. London: J. Long, 1910
BMC.

TLS-Mary learns the lesson of self renunciation-

013124   PILLARS OF SMOKE. London: J. Long, 1912
BMC.

TLS-Farm life and village customs.
ATH Sister's self-sacrifice
ACAD Renounces marriage for sake of keeping her
brother sober. POV?

013125   POTTER AND CLAY. London: Methuen, 1914
BMC.

ATH-Country workers' lives.
ATH 143:469. Marah escapes at 17 from brutal father,
marries older man. Later on is awakened by his young
secretary. Husband and secretary go to Africa, when
latter dies, husband pretends it is his death, returns
to the village under secy's name wearing a black silk
mask on the pretence that half his face has been shot
away.
TLS Also Sapphira, whose motto is "taste and try."
Racy novel.

013126   A PRIESTESS OF HUMANITY. London: J. Long,
[1913] BMC.

Margot rescued from the streets, made housekeeper by a
writer (Clive) who later marries her. TLS "A lady
novelist rejoicing in the discovery of her affinity"
ATH

013127   RUTH OF THE ROWLDRICH. London: Mills &
Boon, 1912 BMC.

TLS-Young woman goes to London becomes journalist, 1st
book big success, 2nd a failure, returns home to arms
of her old love.
ATH o
LBKM-Intimate analysis of conflicting elements. She is
glad to exchange, finally, the obsession of an
all-possessing ambition for the peace and happiness of
a home with David. Ruth goes to London, because she is
painfully aware that her faculties will never have a
chance to blossom if she settles down as a wife.

WRIGHT, CAROLINE. B. 1886. Nationality Unknown.

013128   THE EVEN HAND. BY QUINCY GERMAINE.
Boston: Pilgrim Press, [c1912] NUC.

013129   RECOGNITION. A MYSTERY OF THE COMING
COLONY. London: Digby, Long, 1895 BMC.

WRIGHT, CLARA (PARRISH). B. 1861. Nationality Unknown.

013130   AN UP-TO-DATE COURTSHIP. New York:
Cockrance, 1909 NUC.

Exchange of letters between man and woman concerning
vital questions about their fitness for marriage. PW

WRIGHT, ELVIRTON, pseud. See WHITCOMB, JESSIE (WRIGHT).

WRIGHT, EMILY DUDLEY. B. 1860. United States.

013131   PADDIE. Boston: Stratford, 1920 NUC.

PW-

WRIGHT, HELEN SAUNDERS (SMITH). B. 1874. United States.

013132   THE VALLEY OF LEBANON. New York: R. J.
Shores, 1916 NUC.

Marg. Orth marries a physician. PW

WRIGHT, JESSIE E. See WHITCOMB, JESSIE (WRIGHT).

WRIGHT, JULIA (MACNAIR). 1840-1903. United States.

013133   ADAM'S DAUGHTERS. New York: American
Tract Society, [c1892] NUC.

PW-Mother and three daughters at first fail and
finally succeed in earning a living. Purpose is to aid
struggling women and to deter them from leaving rural
areas in hopes of better prospects in cities.

013134   THE CARDIFF ESTATE; A STORY. New York:
American Tract Soc., [c1897] NUC.

Theme of bettering the lower classes by rebuilding
dilapidated tenements. PW 52:610

013135   HER READY-MADE FAMILY. New York: National
Temperance Society, [c1896] NUC.

013136   THE HOUSE ON THE BLUFF; A WESTERN FLOOD
STORY. New York: American Tract Soc., [1896] NUC.

PW 10-17-96 Flood victims stay for a time with Madame
Baron. Their stories.

013137   A MODERN PRODIGAL. New York: National
Temperance Society, 1892 NUC.

013138   MR. GROSVENOR'S DAUGHTER. New York:
American Tract Soc., [1893] NUC.

Deborah becomes a working woman because of financial
reverses in her family. She works in a big city. The
way she adapts to the change is the theme. PW 5-13-93

013139   A NEW SAMARITAN. New York: American Tract
Soc., [1895] NUC.

Persis Thrale an heiress has a plan to help the poor
in a large city. PW 10-5-95:589.

013140   ON A SNOW-BOUND TRAIN. New York: American
Tract Soc., [c1893] NUC.

Snow-bound in North Pacific in mid-December near
Omaha. Train delayed several days. Passengers draw
together, read, sing, etc. PW 10-7-93.

013141   THE POOLES' MILLIONS; THE STORY OF A CARD
HOUSE. Boston: Congregational Sunday School Pub.
Society, [1896] NUC.

Warrine and LaRue are two young women forced into
marriage. Both have great struggles but both "come out
of the fire, sweet strong noble women." Both couples
hurt in crash. LW 28:12.
Daughter of spendthrift marries wealthy alcoholic.
When he commits suicide, she marries a sober
millionaire. BOOK NEWS 96-7:140.

013142   RAGWEED: A WEST WORLD STORY.
Philadelphia: Presbyterian Board of Publication, 1894
NUC.

Family of movers "squat on" Missouri River land
belonging to three orphans. True picture of these
caravan people who wander the west. The family is met
by a young woman relative of the owners who makes them
feel at home. She rehabilitates two of the children.
LW 26:90.

013143   TOWARD THE GLORY GATE; A STORY OF SOUL
GROWTH. Philadelphia: Union, [c1898] BMC NUC.

PW-Eight noble women discuss what God would have them make of themselves, also discuss art and literature. Heroine is the "commonplace girl in the group."

WRIGHT, LOIS, pseud. See WAITE, LUCY.

WRIGHT, LOUISE SOPHIE (WIGFALL). 1846-1915.

013144   A SOUTHERN GIRL IN '61; THE WAR-TIME MEMORIES OF A CONFEDERATE SENATOR'S DAUGHTER. BY MRS. D. G. WRIGHT. London and New York: Doubleday, Page, 1905 BMC NUC.

Review says much of civil war, little of the southern girl NYT 558, 05

WRIGHT, MABEL (OSGOOD). 1859-1939. United States.

013145   AT THE SIGN OF THE FOX; A ROMANCE. BY BARBARA, AUTHOR OF "THE GARDEN OF A COMMUNTER'S WIFE" ETC. New York: Macmillan, 1905 BMC. London: Macmillan, 1905 NUC.

Daughter must support family, opens a tea garden in Boston. PW 7-15-05
Was an art student before her father lost his fortune. Feminine, sentimental? NYT 476,05
Brooke is strong, resourceful, self reliant? LBKM 211, 27-8
Brave endeavors of a woman to a family after father falls into evil ways. Opens the tea shop. A lover watches nearby, saves her life marries her. ATH 05,397

013146   AUNT JIMMY'S WILL. New York and London: Macmillan, 1903 NUC.

Girl becomes artist "makes life happy for an interesting little cripple" PW 10-31-03

013147   THE GARDEN OF A COMMUTER'S WIFE. RECORDED BY THE GARDENER [ANONYMOUS]. New York: MacMillan, 1901 NUCB. London: Macmillan, 1901 NUC.

11-9-1901 PW about gardening

013148   THE LOVE THAT LIVES. New York: Macmillan, 1911 BMC NUC.

History of a family from wedding to children's betrothals; sentimental. ATH
Parents' plans for their children and the ways they actually turn out. NYT

013149   PEOPLE OF THE WHIRLPOOL, FROM THE EXPERIENCE BOOK OF A COMMUTER'S WIFE [ANONYMOUS]. New York and London: Macmillan, 1903 NUC BMC.

About suburban area invaded by whirlpool people--idle New Yorkers. NYT 1903:352
Written by mother of twins--ACAD 64:558
LBKM 7-03: 151

013150   POPPEA OF THE POST-OFFICE. BY MABEL OSGOOD WRIGHT (BARBARA). New York: Macmillan, 1909 NUC BMC.

Tracing of orphan's parentage and love story PW 7-1709

013151   PRINCESS FLOWER HAT. A COMEDY FROM THE PERPLEXITY BOOK OF BARBARA, THE COMMUTER'S WIFE. New York: Macmillan, 1910 NUC. London: Macmillan, 1910 BMC.

34 and has never thought of marriage though John has been waiting 15 years. The Princess buys a farm; John marries, the princess marries a neighbor? sounds sent. PW
Young woman sets up housekeeping on her own. Takes a cottage and her troubles with her garden, a pair of lovers, scandal-loving neighbors "charming" "tender" ACAD
In the background is Barbara Campbell, the commuter's wife, The princess buys a cottage near Barbara's suburban life. Wedding bell ending. NYT

013152   THE STRANGER AT THE GATE; A STORY OF CHRISTMAS. New York: Macmillan, 1913 BMC NUC.

"A story of Christmas" SR
PW 84; 12-6-13 1466 "An Oriental student of domestic life in varous countries presents a letter of introduction to a money absorbed business man shortly before the holidays. This letter comes from such an important factor in the man's life that he cannot ignore it and so, chafing at the idea of wasting time

he invites the scholar to his New York home."

013153   THE WOMAN ERRANT: BEING SOME CHAPTERS FROM THE WONDER BOOK OF BARBARA, THE COMMUTER'S WIFE [ANONYMOUS]. New York and London: Macmillan, 1904 BMC NUC.

NYT-Anti feminist "the author has something to say on the subject of the woman domestic in connection with the woman errant"
BKM v. 19 1904
BKM 20 1904 Negative view of women's clubs-very interesting .

WRIGHT, MARGARET.

013154   THE OTHER SELF; A STUDY IN THE SENSITIVE. London: Murray and Evenden, [1920] BMC.

TLS-Young woman chafing for freedom is crippled. Introspection follows. Her "other self" rejects love of a masterful man. Author sees in her creation "a parched, unhealthy state of mind, intensive and narrow in outlook," and one which the heroisms of the war have made a "curio" of the past.

WRIGHT, MARY (TAPPAN). 1851-1917. United States.

013155   ALIENS. New York: C. Scribner's Sons, 1902 NUC.

NYT 5-3-02 daughter of a scholar who has treated her as an intellectual person marries a man in the South with a Germanic idea of marriage, 2nd rate man, story of their marriage.

013156   THE CHARIOTEERS. New York and London: D. Appleton, 1912 BMC NUC.

PW-Love for a married man.
NYT-Octavia undertook to steer the chariot of her life with a high hand. Character study, college town.

013157   THE TEST. New York: C. Scribner's Sons, 1904 NUC.

"Proud young girl, refined and cultured, loved not wisely but too well. "A novel of American life of today" BKM, v. 20, 1904.
Becomes pregnant and learns on her wedding day man has become drunk and married another woman. Cooper. The Sex problem novel. BKM 19,1904

013158   THE TOWER; A NOVEL. New York: C. Scribner's Sons, 1906 NUC.

PW-Unmarried heroine of 38 in academic setting.
NYT-Meets old male friend for first time in twenty years-what then?
ATH O

WRIGHT, MRS. D. G. See WRIGHT, LOUISE SOPHIE (WIGFALL).

WRIGHT, ROWLAND, pseud. See WELLS, CAROLYN.

WUNDERLICH, JENNIE M. United States.

013159   SWEET BLOSSOMS 'NEATH FROSTED LEAVES. York, Pa.: P. Anstadt, 1899 NUC.

WYATT, EDITH FRANKLIN. 1873-1958. United States.

013160   TRUE LOVE: A COMEDY OF THE AFFECTIONS. New York: McClure, Phillips, 1903 NUC.

Satire on modern life in Chicago PW 3-7-03
Two sets of lovers, one trad, colorless, the other "sweet wholesome." The satire is levelled against the first.-NYT 03, 168

WYATT, LUCY MAY LINSLEY. Nationality Unknown.

013161   CONSTANCE HAMILTON. New York: Abbey Press, [c1901] NUC.

WYE, INA.

013162   MISS WENDER. London: Digby, Long, 1910 BMC.

"Does not deserve a husband" beautiful, noble, self sacrificing goes around breaking hearts, holds on to discarded lovers, lives in a cottage on one lover's estate while she keeps an eye on another man. Her mother is a divorced alcoholic. Eva stands by her mother, Eva is loved by one at the end, engaged to

another, but she loves a third. Novel ends with no
idea of whether or if she marries. SR
TLS--male dual personality.

013163   "WILD CAT": A TALE. London: Greening,
1905 BMC.

WYLDE, KATHARINE, pseud. See COLVILL, HELEN HESTER.

WYLDE, MRS. HENRY.

013164   IN QUEST OF A NAME. London: Tower, 1895
BMC.

Tower romances; heroine is 17. "Voluptuous Creole
girl" ruined by Spanish lover. Then she sets out to
deliberately betray all the men she can. Ends up
marrying Captain Harrigan, but she carries on with her
lovers anyway. Then the Spaniard discovers her and
kills her. A good young man marries the virtuous
heroine Isabel Davies. Ultra-sens. ACAD 48:29.

WYLIE, I. A. R. See WYLIE, IDA ALEXA ROSS.

WYLIE, IDA ALEXA ROSS. 1885-1959. United Kingdom.

013165   BRODIE AND THE DEEP SEA. BY I. A. R.
WYLIE. London: Mills & Boon, [1920] BMC NUC.

SP Mrg of grocer's son to girl of good family, story
of their adjustment to each other, wife's difficulties
and misery. Reconciled by husband's attempt to settle
labor difficulties.
ATH She is a V. A. D.

013166   CHILDREN OF THE STORM. New York: J. Lane,
1920 NUC.

PW-Love story of woman who married secretly outside
her social class. Tangle involves many people.
NYT 12-5-20 p18. Even though they are free of class
values, their marriage is destroyed by attitudes
toward them. Adam's taking charge and quelling labor
unrest really begs the question as a solution.

013167   THE DAUGHTER OF BRAHMA. BY I. A. R.
WYLIE. Indianapolis: Bobbs-Merrill, [c1912] NUC.
London: Mills & Boon, [1912] BMC NUC.

Sarasvati and the hero help prevent another mutiny in
India. NYT
SP-Sarasvati is a demi-goddess married to a English
man in England.

013168   DIVIDING WATERS. BY I. A. R. WYLIE.
London: Mills & Boon, [1911] NUC BMC. Indianapolis:
Bobbs-merrill, [c1911] NUC.

International marriage: English woman, German
husband-severe trials and trag. 9-30-11 PW
Hot-headed English heroine revolts from German husband
then becomes germanized. TLS
Nora Ingestre accepts job of companion to an invalid
girl to escape boredom of her home. Marries the girl's
brother (German). Comes to be incompatible with him,
leaves, returns to make a reconcilation at her death.
SP

013169   THE DUCHESS IN PURSUIT. London: Mills &
Boon, 1917 BMC.

013170   FIVE YEARS TO FIND OUT. BY I. A. R.
WYLIE. Indianapolis: Bobbs-Merrill, [c1914] NUC.

013171   THE HERMIT DOCTOR OF GAYA; A LOVE STORY
OF MODERN INDIA. BY I. A. R. WYLIE. New York and
London: G. P. Putnam's Sons, 1916 NUC.

No promise here PW
NYT He is major figure, but heroine, a dancer, is
splendid, courageous and human. Anglo-Indian setting.
She marries someone she doesn't love and so does
everyone else in the story.

013172   IN DIFFERENT KEYS. London: Mills & Boon,
1911 BMC.

013173   THE NATIVE BORN; OR THE RAJAH'S PEOPLE.
BY I. A. R. WYLIE. Indianapolis: Bobbs-Merrill,
[c1910] NUC.

Race question in India PW

013174   THE PAUPERS OF PORTMAN SQUARE. London:
Cassell, 1913 BMC.

Modern fairy tale, lack of money turns an idle spoiled
young couple into a caring careful model pair. ATH.
They were so "deteriorated" that they neglected their
child; when fortune goes, husband drives a cab.
They're regenerated. TLS

013175   THE RAJAH'S PEOPLE. BY I. A. R. WYLIE.
London: Mills & Boon, [1910] BMC NUC.

TLS -melodrama
ATH

013176   THE RED MIRAGE. BY I. A. R. WYLIE.
London: Mills and Boon,, [1913] BMC NUC.

Life in French Foreign Legion in No. Africa Colonel
Destinn and two other men.
rival over callous Sylvia Omney. LBKM
PW 86 10/17/14:1251 "Richard Farquhar, within a few
hours, learn that Sylvia, his sweetheart, loves
Arnaud, an officer in the French army, and that his
own father had betrayed his country and had murdered a
man. Farquhar buys the evidence of his father's guilt
by resigning his commission in the army. He also
assumes the blame of Arnaud's trickery to save Sylvia.
Into this darkness comes a sympathetic woman. The
delivery of a message to his lost father takes
Farquhar to the French posts on the borders of the
desert and here he finds the woman once more."

013177   THE SHINING HEIGHTS. BY I. A. R. WYLIE.
New York: J. Lane, 1917 NUC. London: Mills & Boon,
[1917] BMC NUC.

Focuses on a scientist, his experiences, etc. PW
And his wife's great faith in him TLS

013178   THE TEMPLE OF DAWN. BY I. A. R. WYLIE.
London: Mills & Boon,, [1915] BMC NUC. New York:
Doran, [1915] NUC.

Woman murderess PW 10-2-15

013179   TOWARDS MORNING. BY I. A. R. WYLIE.
London: Cassell, 1918 BMC. New York: J. Lane, 1918
NUC.

PW-Study of the making of a German soldier. Helmut is
taken from his mother and toys. Finally, a brutalized
soldier, he is ordered into a hut to debase a solitary
girl-she is a playmate whom he had loved. He is shot
for his disobedience.
NYT Sept 1, 1918 p 370. Also other characters who
rebel against brutalization by present regime.
WWI-Fic

013180   TRISTRAM SAHIB. BY I. A. R. WYLIE.
London: Mills & Boon,, [1915] BMC NUC.

TLS India, intensely passionate feelings, revels in
violence. Tristram is an MD, a large strong gentle
man, a woman's hero.
LBKM O

WYLLARDE, DOLF. D. 1950. United Kingdom.

013181   AS YE HAVE SOWN. London: Hurst &
Blackett, 1906 BMC. New York: J. Lane, 1907 NUC.

TLS O
ATH-virtuous wife in the suburbs.
BKM O-satire.
Society of lax morals; heroine of illegitimate
birth-much said on subject. Moral hideousness of
social-upper class.

013182   CAPTAIN AMYAS, BEING THE CAREER OF D'ARCY
AMYAS, R.N.R., LATE MASTER OF THE R.M.S. PRINCESS. New
York: J. Lane, 1904 NUC. London: W. Heinemann, 1904
BMC.

NYT-a cad with women. A book which should never have
been written.
ATH-returning from a voyage to discover his youthful
love pregnant from another, henceforth he abuses
sexually all females.

013183   THE CAREER OF BEAUTY DARLING. London: S.
Paul, 1912 BMC. New York: J. Lane, 1912 NUC.

TLS-squalid vulgarity of life behind the stage.
NYT-sordid & ugly life. At 14, foundling (adopted) is
victimized(?) by a strolling artist-from that time on
she drifts from 1 man to another, without thought or
passion. Portrayal of dread of motherhood.
BKM v 36 1912-13. Play-toy of a man-suicide as escape

from maternity. .
"This story adds to the numerous novels dealing with
the drab side of musical comedy."ATH
"A foundling on a doorstep, Beauty is adopted by a
commonplace woman who keeps her until she is 14; at
that age the girl is victimized by a strolling artist
and runs away to go on the stage. For the rest of her
life she drifts carelessly from one man to another,
without thought and without passion, tossed about
until the day of her death." NYT
"There is nothing very fresh or distinguished about
it." ATH 1912,2:626 N 23 20w
"Dolf Wyllarde has her faults and her limitations. Is
a better piece of work than Frank Danby's kindred
novel, in so far as it leaves the impression of
literal truth." F.T. Cooper. BKM 36:564 Ja '13 420w
"The story of her life and death is sordid and ugly
enough. That it has in it much of sober truth is
impossible to deny; in its very lack of contrast, of
suggestion, in its unrelieved and purposeless
grossness, it is probably a sufficiently ordinary
tale. The career of Beauty Darling offers a fairly
good treatment of a theme that ought to be and that
has been before this--handled much more than fairly
well." NYT 17:692 N 24 '12 250w
PW-involvement with man throws her on her own.
@ musical comedy stage-realistic picture. LBKM
"The heroine finds that the handicap of poverty and
friendlessnes is a fatal one in the theatre. Her
artistic success and moral downfall go hand in hand.
Beauty Darling is a woman of pleasure, the play-toy of
man and nothing else and her hideously spectacular
suicide <is> perpetrated as the only possible escape
from what she regards as the supreme disgrace of
maternity." LBKM

O13184   EXILE: AN OUTPOST OF EMPIRE. New York: J.
Lane, 1916 NUC. London: T.F. Unwin, [1916] BMC NUC.

Claudia Everard married to a chief justice who trusts
his secrets to Hervey. The husband then asks Claudia
to offer anything to get back the letter. PW
NYT-Hervey-Rochester type, Claudia has face and form
of a goddess and is cold as ice.
TLS O

O13185   THE GUARDIANS OF PANZY: A STORY. London:
Hutchinson, 1899 BMC.

Pansy is a girl? A Mrs. Hamilton is supposed to have
killed herself. LIT 4:428

O13186   HANDS ACROSS THE SEA! London: Holden and
Hardingham, [1914] BMC.

O13187   THE HOLIDAY HUSBAND. London: Hurst &
Blackett, [1919] BMC NUC. New York: J. Lane, 1919 NUC.

Vervain Chalmont, young struggling alone; a stolen
fortnight with a lover; the dark shadow cast upon her
thereafter. TLS
Grasps at happiness of a married holiday without
marriage on basis that she is alone, therefore harms
no one. Does have happy holiday but then begins to
trace the consequences of her actions upon others. A
friend not up to such an affair imitates her action.
Becomes a suffragette. Loss of her post. Gradual
development into womanhood. Holiday husband appears
again in a way. Most wounding to her future. Theme:
the double standard of sexual morality. TLS
Underpaid, underfed overworked executive secretary of
Colonial Women's League-semi charitable organization.
She's 20, bored to death, alone, spends two weeks with
a man, thought she'd hurt no one, but the affair gets
in the way of her making a more permanent relationship
with a different man later. Attractive, keeps our
sympathy. NYT 354,6-29-19

O13188   IT WAS THE TIME OF ROSES. London: Holden
& Hardingham, [1918] BMC.

SR 147:477. Life in West Indies. Eulalie the Creole,
the most interesting and vital of the characters,
unfortunately; must be destroyed before English man
and woman can live in happiness.

O13189   A LONELY LITTLE LADY. London: Hutchinson,
[1897] BMC.

LW 29:28. seduction of the mother of eight year old
daughter , her abandonment of her home. Not a child's
book. "tiny thing makes herself dear and important to
her elderly father." "sweet"

O13190   MAFOOTA; A ROMANCE OF JAMAICA. London:
Hurst & Blackett, 1907 BMC. New York: J. Lane, 1907

NUC.

Sex ed. in women unprepared for marriage. Woman's
husband is unfaithful; she assumes another woman's
identity; in her experience she grows TLS
BKM 26 (1908) 553-4
ACAD-overhearing that her husband is unfaithful, she
goes to Mafoota, Jamaica and lives there happily until
her husband arrives and there is a reconciliation.
BKM-young woman marries, finds herself relieved when
her husband has to cut their honeymoon short. Some
weeks later she is to meet him in Jamaica, but is
hoping perhaps something will happen to postpone it.
Arriving in Kingston, she overhears conversation about
her husband's life style, is horrified. She travelled
with a young invalid woman joining her uncle and who
had died on the boat-she assumes her name and joins
her uncle. Lives with the natives and is for the next
3 years given a new education about sex & life etc, in
awakening (she was prim & proper)...finally after 3
years she is reunited with husband.

O13191   THE PATHETIC SNOBS; BEING CERTAIN
HAPPENINGS IN THE SECOND YEAR OF THE WAR IN THE LIVES
OF VERY ORDINARY PEOPLE. London: Hurst & Blackett,
1918 NUC BMC. New York: J. Lane, 1918 NUC.

PW-Primrose defies mother & marries soldier beneath
her. But whose actual rank proves otherwise.
TLS-pathetic Miss Johns may in some ways claim to be
heroine of book. War is more atmosphere than real.
Snobbery is lightly satirized.
NYT Oct.6 '18 p429 O

O13192   THE PATHWAY OF THE PIONEER (NOUS OUTRES).
London: Methuen, 1906 BMC. New York: J. Lane, 1909
NUC.

Story of seven women who work, not a success story but
concerned rather with their disappointments.
ACAD-story of 7 women who work. Rev critical because
they are pitiful waifs rather than strong professional
women.
ATH-good theme weak handling.
PW-a story of 7 girls who have banded themselves
together for mutual help & cheer under the name nous
autres. They represent collectively the professions
open to women of no deliberate training, though well
educated. They are introduced to the reader at one of
their weekly gatherings and the author depicts the
home and business life of each one individually.

O13193   THE RAT-TRAP. New York and London: J.
Lane, 1904 NUC.

BKM 19 1904 Loveless marriage-other man-who arranges
death of husband (in battle)-are they then happy?
Frank & subtle analysis of woman's thoughts endowed
with vitality. Husband a drunk.
NYT-freedom from convention. See Uriah the Hittite.

O13194   THE RIDING MASTER. London: S. Paul, 1910
BMC. New York: J. Lane, 1911 NUC.

Mrs. Ainslie Devereaux, too dull for unfaithful
husband, learns to ride, play bridge, find comradeship
elsewhere. TLS
Review BKM 33 (1911) 192. Suggests possibilities but
not helpful.
Two enfants terribles. PW 2-11-11
Mrs. Devereux struggles to retain her husband's
affection and her friendship with the Major. More a
sporting story. LBKM
The riding master looks on and teaches riding to a
whole group of fashionable people whose lives form
various triangles. BKM
Many distressful dears, distasteful. Several plots: in
one a woman learns from husband's mistress how to
attract men, so she can win him back. SR
Adds little. NYT

O13195   ROSE-WHITE YOUTH. New York: J. Lane, 1908
NUC. London: Cassell, 1908 BMC.

PW-children's book? Precocious Captain Rugby's horse?
TLS-arresting study of a high spirited girl just
learning the meaning of womanhood.
BKM O
NYT O

O13196   THE STORY OF EDEN. New York: J. Lane,
1902 NUC. London: W. Heinemann, 1902 BMC.

ACAD-pre-marital affair, marriage, secret is kept but
woman not happy.
DIAL-marries reasonably happy in spite of her earlier

indiscretion.
ATH 3-1-02.

013197   TEMPERAMENT. A ROMANCE OF HERO-WORSHIP.
London: S. Paul, [1920] BMC NUC. New York: J. Lane,
1920 PW.

Sexual and artistic history of Jean Delamore. Musical
composer, she dies giving birth to illegitimate child.
LBKM-warmed-up version of Ouidaesque naughtiness.
SR Senitie-St. Joan the Undivine or Joan composes
light music, is a native of the tropics and cherishes
passion fruit. Her most serious affair, fatally
terminated, is with sexagenarian son of ducal house.
Justifies her nickname by making an edifying end, gets
religion after a fashion peculiar to herself.
NYT 8-22-20 p.26. Author says Joan was a genius. Rev.
says a queer child who develops into a queer woman.
Was taught to smoke at 12, gave herself willingly,
almost aggressively, to Lord Ossy, then is pregnant.

013198   THE UNOFFICIAL HONEYMOON. London:
Methuen, [1911] BMC NUC. New York: J. Lane, 1911 NUC.

NYT-story of an English army officer "a little
dried-up, Scotch Methodist missionary girl," cast on a
lonely island. She passes as a boy for a while. When
they are finally rescued they marry, having waited for
the law rather than the law he had wanted to live by
on the island. A love story, but peculiar.
Leslie-a missionary; Survivors of a shipwreck; thinks
of going off with nuns who sail by, but he stops her.
Marries her? BKM 34 (1911) 443
Man and woman on island, no chance of rescue, no
public opinion to concern them. Leslie Machelt-unusual
type of heroine. TLS
How would a man and woman act if there were no such
thing as public opinion. On island for 6 months. ACAD
Leslie raised strictly; the man, free thinking,
comradeship ensues. Love comes slowly and rescue at
the end. LBKM

013199   URIAH THE HITTITE. London: W. Heinemann,
1904 BMC.

See the Rat Trap.
LBKM-Evelyn Gregory and wife of his ADC fall in love,
ADC is sent to front (by E.G.) is killed and widow and
E.G. marry, live happily.
ATH O
TLS-searching passages concerning the nature of men
and women.

013200   WHERE THE LOTUS BLOWS. London: Holden and
Hardingham, [1914] BMC.

013201   YOUTH WILL BE SERVED. London: S. Paul,
1913 BMC. New York: J. Lane, 1913 NUC.

PW:84 10/18/13:1289 "A young English girl of nineteen
married to an army man, much older than herself, whose
duties keep him in India, is the heroine of the story,
and the interesting incidents of the tale circle round
the problem of wherein her chief duty lies--to be in
India with her husband or to lead a life of her own
choosing in her English home. Between a fascinating
husband, an adorable young son and an importunate
lover, Gillian's inclinations are torn asunder, and
the reader is interested up to the last page in
surmising what her choice is going to be."
BKM-as years go by with husband in army, she begins to
see that any restlessness will reflect on her son and
that her role in life is to become more and more
passive, sacrificing her own interests in order to
serve him.
Gillian. Young woman married to older soldier; she has
a son before she's 19. She learns he loves his
profession more than he loves her. She devotes herself
to her son until another man comes into her life. The
son unintentionally intervenes. ACAD
She's thwarted in her aspirations for a musical
career. ATH
Gillian Kirby married young an older man, a soldier
devoted to his work. She tries hard to keep from being
bored. Her youth had not been served-married too
young.

WYLWYNNE, KYTHE, pseud. See HYLAND, M. E. F.

WYNDHAM, ELEANOR.

013202   THE LILY AND DAVID. London: T.W. Laurie,
[1908] BMC.

TLS-Pure Lily struggles against hereditary gambling
trait and runs off with someone on her wedding day.

POV?

013203   THE WINE IN THE CUP. London: T.W. Laurie,
[1909] BMC.

WYNDHAM, MAUD WYETH.

013204   THE HERETIC'S DAUGHTER. London: Tylston &
Edwards, 1895 BMC.

Inez is loved by Father Juniper who does everything to
win her, but though she is often in danger, she is not
to be trapped. ACAD 48:456
Old time tale of persecuted maidens and perjured
priests, violence and hair breadth escapes in secret
underground passages. ATH 106:528
Sp 76:901. Escape of heroine from villainous priest
whose library contained books on "Socialism, labor
topics and atheism."

WYNMAN, MARGARET, pseud. See DIXON, ELLA HEPWORTH.

WYNNE, CONSTANCE. Nationality Unknown.

013205   THE WOMEN OF CEDAR GROVE. London: C.W.
Daniel, 1920 BMC NUC.

TLS-life of a poor street in a manufacturing
district-its social and industrial conditions, working
women, young and old, their problems and comradeship.

WYNNE, FLORENCE.

013206   THE KING'S COMING. AN HISTORICAL NOVEL.
London: Skeffington, 1904 BMC.

WYNNE, FREDA.

013207   THE PROFLIGATES. London: H.J. Drane,
[1906] BMC.

WYNNE, MAY, pseud. See KNOWLES, MABEL WINIFRED.

WYNNE, WINIFRED.

013208   THE INNOCENCE OF ISABEL. London:
Sisley's, [1909] BMC.

Story of fortune and love TLS

X, LADY.

013209   DECREE NISI. BY LADY X. London: J. Long,
1911 BMC.

Woman of "Diary of My Honeymoon" tells of marriage
(happy) to lawyer. TLS

013210   THE DIARY OF MY HONEYMOON. New York:
Macaulay, 1910. London and New York: J. Long, 1910
BMC.

Lady Cecelia "story of a sale by marriage of an Earl's
daughter to a rich money lender," the hard time she
went thru, the trag. that freed her. TLS
A degrading marriage ending in freedom ATH
In three months changed from childish girl to
self-reliant woman. Author conveys "the impression of
a tender dependent nature, cruelly flung back at every
turn, upon its own frail resources" the ills of the
marriage market. NYT

X, pseud. See ARMFIELD, ANNE CONSTANCE (SMEDLEY).

YARDLEY, MAUD H. Nationality Unknown.

013211   AT THE DOOR OF THE HEART. London: A.M.
Gardner, [1913] BMC.

013212   BECAUSE. London: S. Paul, [1913] BMC.

Pembrook newly married is suspected of murder. (He
visited an old flame who later took poison.) The
villain of the story has a letter that would prove
Pembrook's guilt, demands that the wife Grita give the
rest of her life to him for it; she does. There is a
happy ending. ACAD

013213   LOVE'S DEBT. London: Bohemian, [1913]
BMC.

013214   A MAN'S LIFE IS DIFFERENT; OR THE
SLEEPING FLAME. London: Greening, [1914] BMC.

ATH-"The hero who has used a girl badly in his youth,
meets her again some years after his marriage with

another." Description of "subsequent attitude of the
two women toward him."
TLS Both he and first woman die, clearing the way for
marriage of wife to devoted friend.

013215   MRS. JOHN. London: A.M. Gardner, [1919]
BMC.

013216   NOR ALL YOUR TEARS. New York: R.F. Fenno,
[c1908] NUC. London: Sisley's, [1908] BMC.

PW-Penniless orphan whose wrongs drive her to murder,
dies.
TLS-too little restraint, melodrama

013217   SINLESS: A NOVEL. London: Sisley's, 1906
BMC. New York: R.F. Fenno, [19--?] NUC.

Mixed up identities of two husbands and two wives. PW
8 10-07
BKM
Three men return from India, two of them were away
from wives for 10 years. One wife meets her husband.
Later they discover they aren't husband and wife.
Complications, tragedy follow. "Author's solution is
daring and unconventional." NYT
ACAD-Man returns and spends night with woman who is a
stranger but believes is his wife. She "trustingly
adopts him as her husband." End of Chapter 1. Then
what?
TLS-They now love each other-what next?
ATH-O

013218   SOULMATES. London: Greening, [1917] BMC.

Kay has love affair with a man whose wife is in an
asylum. He dies, she's pregnant, remarries, husband
leaves her on wedding day. Ends tragically. TLS
ATH-She loves a man whose wife is in asylum. Marries
another to conceal her trouble. He is killed by
accident, she suspected of his murder, dies with birth
of child. Sad.

013219   TO-DAY AND LOVE, A NOVEL. London: Hurst
and Blackett, 1910 BMC.

TLS- romance, ordinary

YCUL, NELLE.

013220   HIS WIFE BY FORCE, IN CROMWELL'S DAYS.
London: Remington, 1894 BMC.

ACAD 45:532. Rev. thinks author's name is Lucy Ellen.
Last name Ycul. Muriel, a Royalist is married by
force, yet also through affection.

YECHTON, BARBARA, pseud. See KRAUSE, LYDA FARRINGTON.

YEIGH, KATE (WESTLAKE). 1856-1906. Canada.

013221   A SPECIMEN SPINSTER. London: T.F. Unwin,
1905 BMC. Philadelphia: Griffith, 1906 NUC.

"Without any tendency toward bragging, a maiden lady
who has more money than she actually needs for her
personal wants tells how she lives her life for others
and the enjoyment it brings them and her. A pretty
love story runs through the book." BKM v. 24 1906-7
PW-Good deeds, loves children "Aunt Polly Wogg"

YERTA, GABRIELLE AND MARGUERITE (YERTA) YERTA-MELERA.

013222   SIX WOMEN AND THE INVASION. BY GABRIELLE
AND MARGUERITE YERTA. London: Macmillan, 1917 BMC 1918
NUC.

YERTA, MARGUERITE. See YERTA, GABRIELLE AND MARGUERITE
(YERTA) YERTA-MELERA.

YEZIERSKA, ANZIA. B. 1885. United States.

013223   HUNGRY HEARTS. Boston: Houghton Mifflin,
1920 NUC. London: T.F. Unwin, 1922 BMC.

PW-short story of New York Eastside by a former
sweatshop worker.
BKM-stories reek with the aching passion of a lonely
girl. Powerful indictment of the immigration problem.
Soldier who returns from war to find his mother with
household goods sitting in the street.

YONGE, CHARLOTTE MARY. 1823-1901. United Kingdom.

013224   THE CARBONELS. New York: T. Whittaker,
1895 NUC. London: National Society's Depository,

[1896] BMC.
1822 Capt. Carbonel went to live on inherited estate
in Uphill Priors among people considered a bad lot.
But through his reforms he accomplishes many changes
among the poor. PW 11-2-95:748
Historical social conditions of English rural
districts in early 1800s, the church, landlords. BKM
2:232

013225   THE CONSTABLE'S TOWER; OR, THE TIMES OF
MAGNA CHARTA. New York: T. Whittaker, 1891 NUC.
London: National Society, [1891] BMC.

historical romance time of Magna Carta: IND
hero is Hubert de Burgh. SP 67 844
Burgh, Hubert De D. 1243-fic. Gt. Brit-hist-John,
1199-1216-fic

013226   THE COOK AND THE CAPTIVE; OR, ATTALUS THE
HOSTAGE. New York: T. Whittaker, 1894 NUC. London:
National Society Depository, [1895] BMC.

SR 87:581. Historical romance. Romans in Gaul 530 A.D.
SP-missionary rescues male captive.
France-hist-Early Period to 987-fic

013227   THE CROSS ROADS; OR, A CHOICE IN LIFE.
London: National Society, [c1892] BMC. New York: T.
Whittaker, [1892] NUC.

LW 23:390. Romance of two English servants.

013228   FOUNDED ON PAPER; OR, UPHILL AND DOWNHILL
BETWEEN THE TWO JUBILEES. New York: T. Whittaker, 1897
NUC. London: National Society's Depository, [1898]
BMC.

Main story concerns Lucy Darling and Wilfred Truman
who learns to amend his faults of overconfidence and
jealousy. Sub plot: Eva and Alfred Greylark 17 and 19,
marry in a hurry because he's out of work. She's
industrious; he's lazy. He gambles. Tragic catastrophe
of murder and suicide. SP 79:802.

013229   GRISLY GRISELL; OR THE LAIDLY LADY OF
WHITBURN; A TALE OF THE WARS OF THE ROSES. London &
New York: Macmillan, 1893 BMC NUC.

Grisell Dacre daughter of a Scot lord. An explosion of
gunpowder disfigures her when she's 10. The boy
contracted to marry her is responsible. But contract
is cancelled anyway because families are on opposite
sides in War of Roses. First everyone despises her.
Then when her sweet nature wins their love she's
considered a witch. Escapes to foreign land. Returns
years later weds, loved, accepted. LW 93, 226.
Gives her energies to learning about herbs and
potions. CR 20, 23:71.
Gt. Brit-hist-wars of the Roses-fic.

013230   THE HERD BOY AND HIS HERMIT. New York: T.
Whittaker, 1899 NUC. London: National Society's
Depository, [1900] BMC.

NYT 1900:408. England during War of the Roses.

013231   THE LONG VACATION. New York & London:
Macmillan, 1895 BMC NUC.

Conversations between young people for the most part.
ACAD 48:43 2. Beloved rector from Vale breaks down
from overwork, taken by devoted sister to St. Andrews
Rock. Joined by various members of large family for
walks.
ATH 107:440. Steeped in the atmosphere of superhuman
purity and goodness, crowded with young girls.
People from other novels, and their descendants "meet,
converse, act in theatricals and further intermarry"
BKM 2:232
SR Second generation of the Underwood family.

013232   MODERN BROODS; OR, DEVELOPMENTS UNLOOKED
FOR. London and New York: Macmillan, 1900 BMC NUC.

SR 90:797. Contrast of today's young woman with
yesterday's, latter was better.
ATH 116:680. Magdalen is left in charge of four young
step-sisters.

013233   THE PATRIOTS OF PALESTINE; A STORY OF THE
MACCABEES. New York: T. Whittaker, 1898 NUC. London:
National Society's Depository, [1899] BMC.

PW-Biblical story. 174 B.C. The Maccabees are the
heros.

013234   THE PILGRIMAGE OF THE BEN BERIAH. London
and New York: Macmillan, 1897 BMC NUC.

Fills in The outlined story of Exodus. SP 79:379.
A single family of the tribe of Ephraim. ACAD 51:472.
The exodus, life in the wilderness, entrance of
children of Israel into the Promised land from the
view of a High Churchwoman, the author. "The influence
of the eternal womanly" in the doings of the
Israelites may be somewhat exaggerated." NYT 5-15-97.

013235   THE RELEASE, OR, CAROLINE'S FRENCH
KINDRED. London & New York: Macmillan, 1896 BMC NUC.

ATH 108:382. Written for young people. Heroine is
being educated in a French convent.
ACAD 50:178. French Revolution. Heroine is English at
time when French hatred of English was at its height.
Undergoes dangerous adventures, defies the French
fleet, heroic bravery, is safe at last in England.

013236   THAT STICK. London & New York: Macmillan,
1892 NUC BMC.

LW 23:75. Fine, upstanding male hero.
ATH 99:497. Lord Northmore "and his mouselike old maid
of a wife."
SP 68:469. Story of a law clerk who, by a series of
unexpected deaths, inherits a title.

013237   THE TREASURES IN THE MARSHES. London:
National Society's Depository, [1893] BMC. New York:
T. Whittaker, [c1893] NUC.

Two cousins, each on his own, discover ancient coins
in North Lynchford and Blackmead, South Lynchford. The
discovery inspires each to different kinds of action.
PW 10-14-93.

013238   TWO PENNILESS PRINCESSES. London:
Macmillan, 1891 BMC.

dull story: SP 66 596.
Eleanor and Jean Stewart daughters of James I
semi-captives in Dunbar castle, join older sister at
French court CR.
Their trip to France, a stay at a luxurious nunnery,
various advents including abduction, rescue, weddings.
ACAD Also ATH 97 84

013239   THE WARDSHIP OF STEEPCOMBE. New York: T.
Whittaker, 1896 NUC. London: National Society's
Depository, [1896] BMC.

LW 27:381. Combe family's involvement in the civil
strife.
PW 11-14-96.
Gt. Brit-hist-Richard II-1377-1399-fic.

YONGE, CHARLOTTE MARY AND CHRISTABEL ROSE COLERIDGE.

013240   STROLLING PLAYERS. A HARMONY OF
CONTRASTS. London and New York: Macmillan, 1893 BMC
NUC.

The Willinghams, well born family, lose their money,
organize a group of players and go about presenting
comedies to the rich. In the end return to their old
lives. Three weddings result from their experiment. LW
93, 194

YORKE, CURTIS, pseud. See LEE, SUSAN RICHMOND, Also LEE,
SUSAN RICHMOND AND MRS. E. M. DAVY.

YOUNG, AMELIA SOPHIA COATES AND BLANCHE MARY LOFTUS
TOTTENHAM.

013241   WHO WINS-LOSES. BY SOPHIA MARY LOCKE.
London: R. Bentley, 1893 BMC.

Narrater Miss Fletcher prominent in smart society,
listened to by characters like Gerald Legh. She's
maternal toward him; sympathetic character. ATH
102:156. Off for a year or two. Falls for a young
woman Alix Brown. But he's saved from her. Two
marriages. Dorothy, Legh's sister marries Sir Evan and
Gerald marries Mamia; this is the marriage that goes
bad. Mamia gets more and more eccentric and
unattractive. SR 76, 75

YOUNG, E. H. See YOUNG, EMILY HILDA.

YOUNG, ELEANOR DEY. United States.

013242   TWO PRINCETONIANS AND OTHER JERSEYITES.
Trenton, N.J.: MacCrellish and Quigley Printers, 1898

NUC.

YOUNG, EMILY HILDA. 1880-1949. United Kingdom.

013243   A CORN OF WHEAT. London: W. Heinemann,
1910 BMC.

TLS-Judith has a strong instinctive distaste for her
lovers and a love of nature, for motherhood, against
wifehood.
LBKM-about to have child and no longer loves the
father. Impulsively marries a draper-preacher just
before child is born. Can't stand the marriage and
flees. Contains interesting women characters.
ATH-Vehemently refused to marry the father, a tiresome
young socialist. Child dies at birth, egoist.
SR-When the child dies at birth, she wakes to the
cruelty of civilization, has thoughts of killing
herself.

013244   MOOR FIRES. BY E. H. YOUNG. London: J.
Murray, 1916 BMC. New York: Harcourt, Brace, [1927]
NUC.

TLS-unjustified self sacrifice. Helen, to save her
sister Miriam from a man promises him anything to save
her. He asks for marriage, she acquiesces altho
engaged to another. Married in fact, still loves
other, rev. is shocked
ATH-Has brooding melancholy associated with a Bronte
environment.
Minute study of the four Canipers who live with
stepmother on the breast of the moor, secluded,
mysterious influence of the moor on sensitive nature
of twins Miriam and Helen-develop in extreme ways,
complements of each other. Miriam hungered for
service; Helen has obsession to give; Miriam gossiped;
Helen gave, when Miriam in danger. Helen sacrifices
self and lover. Closing chapters delicate
psychological study of Helen's married life. LBKM

013245   YONDER. London: W. Heinemann, 1912 BMC.
New York: G. H. Doran, 1913 NUC.

SP Serious, good work. Two families, Edward and his
daughter Theresa; Clara caring for her weak and
drunken husband and strong willed sons. One of the
fathers kills the other. Theresa learns to let her
imagination rule rather than serve her. She marries
Alex, the son.
SR-fine character study of Theresa, Clara and Nancy
(Theresa 's invalid mother) Story ends with a murder
and a suicide.
LBKM-0
"The strong-natured girl is a decisive figure with her
all too modern contempt of convention and her longing
for all the sensations that life can bring." NYT(1913)
39 Jan. 26, 1913
"When Edward Webb asks his little daughter, what he
shall bring her she replies, "An adventure." In
pursuit of the adventure the little traveler in
dressmaker's fittings wanders all night on the
mountains and in the morning, almost exhausted,
reaches a friendly house. Three people live here, a
man, his wife, a fine woman, who tries to make him
amount to something, and their son, a poetic boy, at
swords points with his father. When the boy grows up
he falls in love with Edward Webb's daughter. But she
becomes engaged to a richer man. But it all comes
right in the end."

YOUNG, ETHEL WINIFRID.

013246   A WITCH OF THE WEST: A NOVEL. London:
Sisley's, [1908] BMC.

Neighbors believe Nora is a witch TLS

YOUNG, F. E. MILLS. See YOUNG, FLORENCE ETHEL MILLS.

YOUNG, FLORENCE ETHEL MILLS. 1875-1954. United Kingdom.

013247   THE ALMONDS OF LIFE. BY F. E. MILLS
YOUNG. New York: G.H. Doran, [c1920] NUC. London:
Hodder and Stoughton, [1920] BMC.

TLS"come to those who have no teeth." Triangle,
Gerda, John, Maud (noble wife, does not give John
divorce because of children).
SP-moral shows the unhappy consequences of a guilty
passion openly indulged.
LBKM-Unexpected depths of womanhood and disappointing
shallowness of an unusually lucky man, George, married
to a hearty, sensible woman, loves Gerda, married to a
man old enough to be her pa. Women whose lives he
spoils have to straighten things out for themselves,

with no help from him. NYT 9-12-20 p26

013248   ATONEMENT. BY F. E. MILLS YOUNG. London
and New York: J. Lane, 1910 BMC NUC.

ACAD-?
TLS-Male hero atones for yielding to his love for
Sylvia, marries Naomi.
LBKM-elemental passions in South Africa.
ATH-"The terror of a giddy girl whose sexual error
threatens to expose her has often been depicted but
one is unprepared to see her suicide followed by that
of an innocent man." Black sheep marries the "good"
heroine.
NYT-young man deliberately ensnared by engaged young
woman. He offers to marry her, she refuses, he urges
her to confess to her affianced. She again refuses.
Reviewer believes she atones bitterly at end of book.

013249   BEATRICE ASHLEIGH. BY F. E. MILLS YOUNG.
London: Hodder and Stoughton, [1918] BMC. New York:
G.H. Doran, [c1918] NUC.

PW-When father dies lives with uncle, rector in small
town, very different life. with war, becomes a nurse,
when Hugh comes back a cripple, love triumphs.
TLS-From atheism to religion
LBKM-0
NYT-War brings purpose to Beatrice's life.

013250   THE BIGAMIST. BY F. E. MILLS YOUNG.
London and New York: J. Lane, 1916 BMC NUC.

False marriage between Pamela and Arnott in which she
was the deceived one. Wife writes her. Pamela decides
to go on as they were. Refuses to appeal to the law
which was on her side. PW 90:1462 10/28/16
Pamela and Herbert-Arnotts of South Africa. Married
five years, has a daughter of four, happy. Letter
comes from his "real wife," woman claiming to be.
Husband is a bigamist. She can't give him up, but he
begins to respect her less for staying. The real wife
poses no further threat, but Pamela's old love shows
up. TLS
Decides to conceal the truth from friends, but things
go bad between them. Also husband is interested in a
third woman. The first wife dies and after a good deal
of humiliation and suffering the heroine, completely
disillusioned, marries the man for the sake of her
children. ATH

013251   THE BYWONNER. BY F. E. MILLS YOUNG.
London and New York: J. Lane, 1916 BMC NUC.

South Africa, nothing here: Adele becomes prey to a
handsome libertine PW
NYT-Most interesting part of book is picture of Monot.
Hard working lives of the women whose lot is cast on
the lonely farms. Utterly drab existence
LBKM-Adela is the truly tragic figure.

013252   CHIP. BY F. E. MILLS YOUNG. London and
New York: J. Lane, 1909 BMC NUC.

A woman in disguise takes job of overseer of an estate
PW 5-22-09
The owner of the estate is a misogynist-TLS
South Africa-NYT

013253   COELEBS: THE LOVE STORY OF A BACHELOR. BY
F. E. MILLS YOUNG. London and New York: J. Lane, 1917
BMC NUC.

PW-Story about three sisters who took up gardening,
architecture and medicine rather than live on uncle's
money. Coelebs, after seeing Peggy, the head gardener
clad in man's overalls working on a vine is never able
to regain former serenity of confirmed bachelorhood
and at once surrenders to her.
LBKM-Jolly love story. Peggy has new definition of
womanly woman "to be helpful and companionable and
sympathetic and she detests censoriousness and unkind
criticism in herself and others."
NYT-Mrs. Chadwick, when left with care of four nieces,
brought them up to be "capable young persons, able to
make their own way in cheerful independence."
The very modern and enterprising Mrs. Chadwick, has a
charming niece as gardener, Peggy. Brilliant
fascinating, 39-author obviously admires her and the
younger modern woman. "They proudly display their
daring." Peggy falls in love TLS
Young woman gardener in overalls and breeches. ATH

013254   A DANGEROUS QUEST. London: J. Long, 1904
BMC.

BKML-love during the Boer War.

013255   THE DOMINANT RACE. BY F. E. MILLS YOUNG.
London: Hodder and Stoughton, [1919] BMC NUC.

South Africa traces the imperceptible growth of
affection between Penelope Lovemore and Charles
Graham. The obstacles: a rival for him, he's already
married. They are married bigamously (she's already
wed)? TLS
One Theme: European vs Blacks. LBKM

013256   THE GREAT UNREST. BY F. E. MILLS YOUNG.
New York and London: J. Lane, 1915 NUC BMC.

Centers on a man PW 10-9-15
Old story of wise woman controlling children called
men. TLS
Hero becomes a socialist. Heroine? ATH

013257   GRIT LAWLESS. BY F. E. MILLS YOUNG. New
York: J. Lane, 1912 NUC. London: J. Lane, 1912 BMC.

PW-?
ATH-weak hero in South Africa blames his wife.
ACAD-murder and blackmail
NYT- love story with male hero.

013258   IMPRUDENCE. BY F. E. MILLS YOUNG. London:
Hodder and Stoughton, [1920] BMC NUC.

TLS-Prudence, to escape dull home makes an uncongenial
marriage. Lover returns years later. At end she is won
to recognition of her husband's generosity when he
consents to her adopting brother's illegitimate son.

013259   THE LAWS OF CHANCE. BY F. E. MILLS YOUNG.
London and New York: J. Lane, 1918 BMC NUC.

PW-male hero's adventure in South Africa.
TLS-No, he is just background for the women, a little
ridiculous and never unmanaged by one of them at
least. Character study of women.
LBKM-0
NYT-0

013260   A MISTAKEN MARRIAGE. BY F. E. MILLS
YOUNG. London and New York: J. Lane, 1908 BMC NUC.

PW-After not seeing him for five years, woman marries
in South Africa; discovers husband loves another and
has had a child-leaves-divorce, refuses to marry
during husband's lifetime but he dies.
NYT-meets someone else.
TLS-marriage- divorce remarriage, high-minded wife.
BKM-kept Sara waiting five years while he mistressed a
woman in Africa. Sara comes to Africa and the coward
marries her without telling her the truth. Gets a
divorce, and marries a man she met on the trip.

013261   MYLES CATHORPE, I.D.B. BY F. E. MILLS
YOUNG. London: J. Lane, 1913 BMC NUC.

He's too perfect, makes a tremendous sacrifice for
woman he loves. South African setting. Joan Farrant a
fine study. ACAD
High-spirited heroine. "One is revolted by the
incident of the black woman and the pickaniny." NYT

013262   THE PURPLE MISTS. BY F. E. MILLS YOUNG.
New York: J. Lane, 1914 NUC. London: J. Lane, 1914
BMC.

BKM-Euretta is driven into loveless marriage by
brother-in-law's ill treatment.
SR 147:246. Actually, not loveless. Problems and
misunderstanding arise through lack of communication.
South Africa.
ATH 143:160. Reviewer seems to say that author blames
men for heroine's problems.
Husband and wife drift apart. At last she leaves
him...brought together with promise of happiness. PW
85 6/13/14:1939

013263   SAM'S KID. BY F. E. MILLS YOUNG. London
and New York: J. Lane, 1911 BMC NUC.

Timid girl develops into woman capable of self
sacrifice. PW 5-20-11
"Sacrifice of her honor to save the man she loves."
TLS

013264   THE SHADOW OF THE PAST. BY F. E. MILLS
YOUNG. New York: G.H. Doran, [c1919] NUC. London:
Hodder and Stoughton, 1919 BMC.

South Africa triangle two men pretty English woman.
Honor Kringe-fascinating daughter of Boer family, an
earnest rebel despises the man as traitor till she
sees he acts in ignorance. "Her love for him cannot
shake her faith in the cause." She hates England. He
is driven between love of her and loyalty to England.
LBKM
Review dwells on the political ideas concerning the
Boers vs the English. BKM
She believes South Africa will revolt but the big war
comes;revolt fails. NYT 359, 7-6-19
Brenda Upton, companion to old lady, Honor Kringe
hates England (though she's part English) for robbing
her of her father and brother. Won't marry the hero
till he repudiates his English nationality . Hero
becomes engaged to Brenda. Focuses on the hero and the
two different kinds of love. TLS

013265   THE TRIUMPH OF JILL. BY F. E. MILLS
YOUNG. London: J. Long, 1903 BMC NUC.

Struggles to live by teaching-ACAD 65, 108

013266   VALLEY OF A THOUSAND HILLS. BY F. E.
MILLS YOUNG. London and New York: J. Lane, 1914 NUC
1915 BMC.

Alieta (Dutch) Heckraft (English) and a villain.
Author pleads for better treatment of Indians of South
Africa. LBKM
NYT 1914:488 South Africa. Alieta, daughter of rich
Boer farmer, and two lovers, romance. Sentimental,
uneventful.

013267   THE WAR OF THE SEXES. London: J. Long,
1905 BMC.

End of 20th all men but one killed. England all
female. The one man a woman-hater and his relations
with Bertranda a man hater. A dream. TLS 05, 23
England populated with women thru parthenogenesis.
Serious comic point of view

YOUNG, JULIA EVELYN (DITTO). B. 1857. United States.

013268   BLACK EVAN. New York: F. Tennyson Neely,
[c1901] NUC.

YOUNG, MARGARET. United Kingdom.

013269   THE WREATHED DAGGER. London: Cassell,
1909 BMC NUC.

Trad hist romance TLS
Gt.Britain-Hist-Civil war 1642-49

YOUNG, MARTHA. B. 1868.

013270   BEHIND THE DARK PINES. New York and
London: D. Appleton, 1912 BMC NUC.

Tales, animals.

013271   BESSIE BALL. New York: Scott-Thaw, 1904
NUC.

PW-child searching for a "mama," juv?

YOUNG, MARY STUART. United States.

013272   THE GRIFFINS; A COLONIAL TALE. New York:
Neale, 1904 NUC.

YOUNG, MIRIAM.

013273   THE GIRL MUSICIAN. London: Digby, Long,
[1893] BMC.

An unsophisticated work by such a young writer
(apparently) that reviewer withholds criticism. SR
76:160.
Queenie "destined to do wonders as a musician."
Author's "simple, old-fashioned views." ACAD 44:2 91.

013274   LOST! ONE HUNDRED POUNDS REWARD. A TALE
OF SIXTY YEARS AGO. London: Digby,Long, [1894] BMC.

YOUNG, MRS. CHARLES W.

013275   THE LITTLE COLONEL. London: Sands, 1903
BMC.

She is a young vivacious woman whose love story is not
an edifying one. TLS 1-03:8

013276   ON PAROLE. London: F. Long, 1900 BMC.

SP 85:246.
ATH 116:308. Hero is "under the necessity of falling
in love with his wife after she has run away with
another man." He takes her back, keeps her for a long
term in solitude in separate wing of house. Saves her
life 3 times.
ACAD 59:134. Wife eloped with Italian tenor.
Reconciliation with her husband 10 years later.

013277   THE STORY OF FELICITY. Edinburgh and
London: Sands, 1909 BMC.

Girls' story. TLS

YOUNG, R. E. See YOUNG, ROSE EMMET.

YOUNG, ROSE EMMET. 1869-1941. United States.

013278   HENDERSON. Boston: Houghton, Mifflin,
1904 NUC. London: Gay & Bird, 1904 BMC.

Male hero-PW
NYT

013279   SALLY OF MISSOURI. BY R. E. YOUNG. New
York: McClure, Phillips, 1903 NUC. London: W.
Heinemann, 1904 BMC.

LBKM Heirs & love

YOUNG, SARA LEE. B. 1847. United States.

013280   GOLDEN GRAIN. BY LEIGH YOUNGE.
Cincinnati: Monfort, 1915 NUC.

Madge does charity work.

013281   A SEED THOUGHT. BY LEIGH YOUNGE.
Cincinnati: Monfort, 1913 NUC.

YOUNG, VIRGINIA C. United States.

013282   PHILIP: THE STORY OF A BOY VIOLINIST. BY
T. W. O. Poston, and London: Lamson Wolffe, 1898 NUC.

YOUNG, VIRGINIA (DURANT). D. 1906. United States.

013283   "BEHOLDING AS IN A GLASS:" A NOVEL.
Boston: Arena, 1895 NUC.

S.Carolina girl travels alone to Arkansas "her first
little journey" Juv PW 3-9-95:423

013284   A TOWER IN THE DESERT. Boston: Arena,
1896 NUC BMC.

PW 10-10-96. "A story of southern life by a lady of
South Carolina; incidentally the work accomplished by
the Woman's Temperance Church Union is emphasized, and
the rapid broadening of women's ideals in the south is
suggestively illustrated."

YOUNGE, LEIGH, pseud. See YOUNG, SARA LEE.

YOURELL, AGNES BOND. United States.

013285   A MANLESS WORLD. New York: G. W.
Dillingham, 1891 NUC BMC.

Arthur Fielding's uncle tries to discourage him from
marrying by telling him that humanity will soon cease
to exist. But the nephew is not persuaded. PW

YVER, COLETTE, pseud. See HUZARD, ANTOINETTE (DE BERGEVIN).

Z., Z., pseud. See DOISSY, LOUISE.

ZACK, pseud. See KEATS, GWENDOLINE.

ZANE, ELIZABETH Z. United States.

013286   WHILE THE WORLD SLEPT. Philadelphia: J.
E. Winner, [c1896] NUC.

ZANGWILL, EDITH (AYRTON). D. 1945. United Kingdom.

013287   THE FIRST MRS. MOLLIVAR. London: Smith,
Elder, 1905 BMC.

LBKM-Middle aged female marries former lover whose
first wife has died. Story of her revolt against the
restraint of her new position, the outrages on her
taste and health.
Element of supernatural, ghost of wife number one.
ACAD 1202, 05

Modern woman, most sympathetic; her husband, ponderous
and thick willed yet they get along; conventional end.
ATH 05, 829

013288   THE RISE OF A STAR. London: J. Murray,
1918 BMC. New York: Macmillan, 1918 NUC.

TLS-Study of character, millionaire vandeleur, his
wife Imogen, unmaternal mother of little star Joan.
Grandmother (Im´s) is actress and mothers Joan.

013289   TERESA. London: Smith, Elder, 1909 BMC.

She´s pure and ignorant, marries, moves to New York.
Another character Clare is an actress. TLS
Teresa just out of school is proposed to by older
experienced man attracted to her "freshness." She
knows nothing of marriage, is very quickly
disillusioned, and revolts. Husband turns to other
women. Ultimately they get together, child born; story
shows "the shattering force of moral purity." ACAD.
Gets "on paper some of the emancipated modern types of
woman." ATH

ZEARING, MARGUERITE. United States.

013290   HASTA LUEGO, AMIGO MIO; AND OUT OF THE
SILENT FOREVER. Denver, Colo.: W. H. Kistler, 1898
NUC.

013291   WHERE ANGELS FEAR TO TREAD: A TALE OF
LIFE ON A MEXICAN HACIENDA AND BITS OF TRAVEL IN
MEXICO. Denver, Colo.: W. F. Robinson, 1895 NUC.

ZELCOE, LOUIS B., pseud. See VAN FOSSEN, LOO B.

ZEMAN, JOSEPHINE. United States.

013292   MY CRIME. A NOVEL. New York: J.S.
Ogilvie, [c1907] NUC.

013293   THE VICTIM´S TRIUMPH: A PANORAMA OF
MODERN SOCIETY. New York: G. W. Dillingham, [1903]
NUC. London: T. F. Unwin, 1903 BMC.

Wealthy social circle. PW 5-23-03.

ZIMMERMANN, MARIE.

013294   LADY CROOME´S SECRET. London: W. H.
Addison, 1897 BMC.

SP 81:447. Her secret estranges her from her husband.
Story is of her flight and wanderings with her child,
her anger at the stigma. Final reconciliation.
SR 85:402. Man she supposedly met was her mother
disguised as a man.

013295   LULU, THE FAIREST OF THE PRYNNES. London:
Freemantle, 1900 BMC.

Commits a vulgar crime, punished in a repulsive
manner. Sister tries to keep her from deserting her
husband. Miss Prynne defies the law, marries?
Sensational ATH 6-29-01

013296   A WOMAN AT BAY. London: S. W. Partridge,
[1896] BMC.

ZOLLINGER, GULIELMA. 1856-1917. United States.

013297   MAGGIE MCLANEHAN. Chicago: A. C. McClurg,
1901 NUC.

Young Irish girl thrown on own resources at early age,
successfully earns a living for self and little
cousin. Courage, good judgement, strong-BOOK NEWS Nov
01

013298   THE WIDOW O´CALLAGHAN´S BOYS. Chicago:
McClurg, 1905 NUC.

Irish widow left in poverty with seven boys, ages
3-15. BOOK NEWS 98-9, 309

SECOND SERIES

A., G. R. [pseud.].

200001   THE GOLDMINER; A ROMANCE. London: H. J.
Drane, [1903] BMC.

ABBOTT, ANSTICE.

200002   A GIRL WIDOW'S ROMANCE. London: R. T. S.,
[1920] BMC NUC.

ABROJAL, TULIS [pseud.]. United States.

200003   AN INDEX FINGER. BY TULIS ABROJAL. New
York City: R. F. Fenno, 1898 NUC.

ACTINOTUS [pseud.].

200004   THE POWER OF THE PURSE. BY ACTINOTUS.
London: S. Sonnenschein, 1897 BMC.

ADALET [pseud.].

200005   HADJIRA: A TURKISH LOVE STORY. BY ADALET.
London: E. Arnold, 1896 NUC BMC.

ACAD 50:29. Purports to be written by young Turkish
woman. Simple story of family life, with a minimum of
love story.
SP 77:119. "Strange similarity observable between the
usages of Turkish society and those of Mayfair."
Publisher says identity of author cannot be revealed;
it would endanger her personal safety. Harem life.
Allusions to cruelty of the women to their slaves.
BKM 3:365. minute study of the harem.

ADAMS, JACK, pseud. See GRIGSBY, ALCANOAN O.

AGLAIA.

200006   SET FREE: A STORY OF TO-DAY. London: J.
W. Arrowsmith, 1894 BMC.

ACAD 46:190. Gladys was educated and brought up to
make a financially rewarding marriage for her family.
It was unwelcome to her, a person named Selby set her
free, to everyone's satisfaction.

AINSLIE, NOEL.

200007   AMONG THORNS. A NOVEL. London: Lawrence
and Bullen, 1898 BMC.

LIT 2:323. Bloomsbury. "Corrupt" painters and writers.
Peggy is heroine, a "courtesan by nature."
Modern life, Bohemian. Peggy a simple land lady's
daughter and the change in her; Lesbia Meynell, writes
for the Decade, is central character:
woman-journalist. ACAD 52:Fic Sup 117.
"Noel Ainslie is a clever woman...her characters
dispense with convention." Shows how Lesbia Meynell
decides against love-after consideration, and marries
for comforts, but finds marriage a bore because of
social functions. She's different from her friend
Peggy Walton a true Bohemian who elects for comfort
and lovemaking without the drawbacks. Acute feminine
psych. ACAD 52 Fic Sup 130

200008   AN ERRING PILGRIMAGE. London: Lawrence
and Bullen, 1896 BMC NUC.

ATH 108:871. Angela, a study in modern womanhood.
Veronica, the heroine, less interesting, natural and
feminine. Jim is the hero. Veronica may not be
sympathetic to everyone.
ACAD 50:593. Veronica, insulted by Bob Hayley,
"discovering that the insult had really revealed her
own sex to her, and passively welcoming a repitition
of it." Dolly is a music-hall singer. The woman Jim
loves is the one who secretly loves her husband.
Jim hangs around a woman he can't marry who cares only
for luxury and social prestige. Then there's Dolly the
successful actress who got and took what she wanted.
Sad book otherwise. LBK 11:125

200009   THE SALVATION SEEKERS. London: Methuen,
1901 BMC.

Eve and Val represent "new departures for the American
heroine." Eve is a woman of "hysterical self-devotion
and calculating coldness;" Val is undisciplined, and
unconventional as well. She's a dancer who leaves her
husband when he fails her, never to return. ATH 4-6-01

AIRAM [pseud.].

200010   NO ONE TO BLAME. BY AIRAM. London: H. J.
Drane, 1903 BMC.

Complicated marital tragedy: husband & wife both think
the other dead, both remarry. LBKM 10-03,62
Printed in Belgium.

200011   RUDDERLESS SHIPS. BY AIRAM. London: H. J.
Drane, 1903 BMC.

ALEXANDER, W. F.

200012   THE COURT ADJOURNS: A NOVEL. London:
Digby, Long, [1895] BMC.

ACAD 49:93. Two men in love with girl. One betrays the
other who murders him in response. Girl actually loves
murderer, concludes that she will wait out his 30 year
sentence for him

ALLAN, A. W.

200013   THE WHITE LION. London: Digby, Long, 1912
BMC.

ALLEN, LUMAN. Fl. 1881-1893. United States.

200014   DANE WALRAVEN (A TALE OF OLD BOSTON).
Chicago: Donohue, Henneberry, 1892 NUC.

ALMAZ, E. F.

200015   COPPER UNDER THE GOLD. London: Chatto and
Windus, 1907 BMC.

Mary is a secret mistress to a married publisher. Her
child is born; she thinks it died; so dies her love
for the publisher. Years later she meets a Dr. who
urges marriage and fathoms her secret. She meets her
child, recovers her and her love for the publisher.
ACAD
a couple agree to separate; wife travels abroad;
husband falls in love, arranges to live with the woman
secretly; they separate in a time of strife; she
marries another; moral seems to be "carry on as you
like--all comes out right in the end" SR

ALVA [pseud.].

200016   HIS COUSIN'S WIFE. BY ALVA. London: Ward
and Downey, 1896 BMC.

Cousin impersonates minister in pulpit-faced with
having to create a great sermon like the one Theodore
Mainwaring would deliver. Also he can prove a man
innocent of a crime, but he's bound to silence
because, as Theodore, he is supposed to have been in
the pulpit at the time. SP 79:286
SR Heroine falls in love with clergyman for his
socialistic sermon. Actually his double, a cousin, was
the source of it, but dares not claim so, nor does
clergyman feel like living up to her expectations.

AMARGA, NARANJA [pseud.].

200017   THE SETTLING OF BERTIE MERIAN. BY NARANJA
AMARGA. Bristol: J. W. Arrowsmith, [1897] BMC.

Like Ouida. Set in Argentina and London. Story of
finance and the upper ten. ACAD 52 Fic Sup 73.

AMARYLLIS [pseud.].

200018   LIFE'S GOLDEN THREAD. BY AMARYLLIS.
London: Drane, [1914] BMC.

ATH Young man quarrels with uncle and guardian on
refusing to enter army on religious principles.

ANDERSON, CHRISTIAN NEPHI.

200019   ADDED UPON: A STORY. Salt Lake City,
Utah: Deseret News, 1898 NUC.

ANDERSON, L.

200020   LOCKWOOD GODWIN: A TALE OF IRISH LIFE.
London: Gay and Bird, 1896 BMC.

ATH 108:253. "Marked by passionate intensity of
feeling" "Written with the heart's blood of the
author". Not successful.

ANDREWS, C. C.

641

200021   THE HOUSE OF MURGATROYD. London: Cassell, 1907 BMC.

Sensational mystery TLS

ANDREWS, M. HENNIKER.

200022   AN INDIAN MYSTERY. London: Lynwood, 1913 BMC.

Three people of one family abducted in India; moral: Straight forward Englishman's personality will prevail vs evil. Heroine too beautiful and magnificent to be natural. Critic won't devulge the plot. ACAD

ANNE [pseud.]. Nationality and real name unknown.

200023   THE BACHELOR GIRL'S COLONIAL BEAU. BY ANNE. New York: Neale, 1904 NUC.

PW:"musings on the compensations of 'single blessedness'"

ANONYMOUS AUTHOR--NOT IDENTIFIED.

200024   ALICE OF YORK: A TRADITION OF YORK MINSTER. BY THE AUTHOR OF "PRISONERS OF HOPE". York: J. Sampson, [1897] BMC.

200025   ALONE. AN INTROSPECTIVE WORK. London: L. Smithers, 1898 BMC NUC.

ACAD 55:516. Introspective.

200026   ALTOGETHER JANE. BY HERSELF. New York: M. Kennerley, 1914 NUC.

"Straightforward story of a woman who lives the way most people do, without much of a plan as to how to get what she wants most. Jane tells of her love of home and people, her unhappy marriage, her literary work, and finds the promise of happiness in friendship with a worthwhile man." PW 86 10-10-14:1201. NYT 1914:505. Autobiographic style, beginning with childhood. Novelist, ends with Jane "middle-aged and somewhat battered and bruised" Rev. does not believe she is as talented as she claims. Sane, intelligent woman speaks frankly & cleverly.

200027   ANGELA. BY THE AUTHOR OF "BETTIE'S MISTAKE". London: W. Stevens, [1894] BMC.

200028   ANNORA: A STORY OF THE NINETEENTH CENTURY. BY THE AUTHOR OF 'MY TRIVIAL LIFE AND MISFORTUNE'. Edinburgh: W. Blackwood, 1915 BMC.

story of arist and need to marry rank TLS

200029   AUDREY'S NEIGHBOURS. BY THE AUTHOR OF "KING COPHETUA; OR RUBY NORTH'S LOVERS". London: Stevens, [1892] BMC.

200030   THE AUTOBIOGRAPHY OF A HAPPY WOMAN [ANONYMOUS]. New York: Moffat, Yard, 1914 NUC. London: G. Allen & Unwin, 1915 NUC.

Story of the life of the author, a woman well known as a writer and worker, whose identity the publishers are pledged to withhold. Shows how she developed.. and developed the philosophy that happiness is found in work.
HQ 1419 woman-Social and moral questions.
Author definitely a woman (publisher's preface) thoughts and feelings of a young girl, then a woman. Autobiog but narrative also. Segments of her life mixed with observation about women-very much in keeping with feminist ideas-even divorce (though she seems strongly religious). Unwed teacher newspaper writer never marries, is for working woman. The practical needs (panic of 93) brought women to work. (Book)

200031   THE AWFUL AND ETHICAL ALLEGORY OF DEUTERONOMY SMITH; OR, THE LIFE HISTORY OF A MEDICAL STUDENT. BY A STUDENT OF MEDICINE. Edinburgh: Livingstone, 1891 BMC.

200032   THE BAKED BREAD. BY THE AUTHOR OF "BOY OF MY HEART". London and New York: Hodder and Stoughton, [1917] BMC [1919] NUC.

A girl who has fallen can never be pure--just as baked bread can't ever be dough. TLS

200033   BERTHA'S FATE. BY THE AUTHOR OF "IN STRANGE ATTIRE," "LITTLE MISS JONES," ETC. London: W.

Stevens, [1896] BMC.

200034   THE BOOK OF MARJORIE. New York: A. A. Knopf, 1920 NUC.

NYT 4/11/20-Story of pregnancy, birth, and after, narrated by husband.

200035   CECILIA'S CHOICE (BY THE AUTHOR OF RACHEL'S REWARD). London: W. Stevens, [1901] BMC.

Family Story-Teller #154

200036   CHIPS BY AN OLD CHUM; OR, AUSTRALIA IN THE FIFTIES. London: Cassell, [1893] BMC NUC.

200037   CHRYSTAL: THE NEWEST OF WOMEN. BY AN EXPONENT. London: Digby, Long, [1896] BMC.

ACAD 50:490. Heroine "claims the right to choose fathers for her children." Author "deadly serious." "The writer seems to imagine she has laid hold on a new idea."
She is really an old type and "not at all reputable." SP 78:570

200038   CICELY'S ERROR. BY THE AUTHOR OF "LADY OLIVIA'S STEPDAUGHTERS". London: W. Stevens, [1893] BMC.

200039   THE CONFESSION OF A REBELLIOUS WIFE. Boston: Small, Maynard, [1910] NUC.

NYT-Purports to be an autobiography of a marriage. Searching analysis of a union that seemed to the wife to be one of perfect love & trust. Couple is prosperous, of consequence in the community & seemingly happy with each other. Yet she is raising her son to be as completely different from his father as possible & cannot bear to see a resemblance.

200040   THE CONFESSIONS OF A CONVICT; EDITED BY JULIAN HAWTHORNE. Philadelphia: R. C. Hartranft, 1893 NUC. (Introduction signed "19,759.")

200041   THE CONFESSIONS OF A PRINCESS. London: J. Long, 1906 BMC. New York: C.H. Doscher, [c1908] NUC.

TLS-0
PW-"intrigues of a crown princess...plot is questionable."
NYT-0

200042   THE CONFESSIONS OF A WOMAN. London: Griffith, Farran, 1893 BMC.

Accounts of her various lovers and lovemaking though her husband lives. One lover gave her peace until he "buried his teeth in her neck." Calls herself a sensuous creative subject to "great tides of emotion." "Purity is only ignorance," she says and tells us she "has touched pitch." SR 76:711.

200043   THE CONFESSIONS OF AN AMBITIOUS MOTHER. London: W. Heinemann, 1905 BMC.

vulgar-minded, hard, soulless-one aim to get on and the talent to do it. Calls Becky Sharpe a fool. Makes a living by giving life secrets of her friends to the Yellow Press. She is wholly unaware of her moral degradation.? ACAD 05, 337

200044   CONFESSIONS OF AN ENGLISH DOCTOR. London: G. Routledge, 1904 BMC NUC.

1. Medical ethics 2. Physicians

200045   THE CONFESSIONS OF AN INCONSTANT MAN. New York and London: D. Appleton, 1914 BMC NUC.

200046   CONFESSIONS OF MARGUERITE; THE STORY OF A GIRL'S HEART. New York: Rand, McNally, [1903] NUC.

PW-Tries many ways to earn a living-artist, stage, publishing, etc. fails, goes home and marries "right man."

200047   CROSS-PURPOSES. BY THE AUTHOR OF "KING COPHETUA; OR, RUBY NORTH'S LOVERS". London: W. Stevens, 1893 BMC.

200048   CUPID--THE CHAUFFEUR. A MOTOR TOUR IN SWEDEN AND WHAT CAME OF IT. BY ONE OF THE PARTY. London: Sisley's, [1908] BMC.

TLS-mild record of love and travel.

200049   DAN'S MOTHER; OR A QUAKER HERO: A STORY. BY THE AUTHOR OF "MARY CONSTANT". London: Eden, Remington, 1892 BMC. (Preface signed: M. M.)

ACAD - He has promised his mother "not to care" for someone. Polly has had an "eccentric" and "grim" childhood.

200050   DAUGHTERS OF THE CITY; OR A WOMAN, SOME MEN AND WOMANITY. BY THE AUTHOR OF "THE SPIRIT OF LOVE". Westminster: Roxburghe Press, [1897] BMC.

"impossibly dreary" the grocer brothers, the young dr., Clement and his sister Sybil—all hold different standards. A runaway neuralgic wife—her reflections, in a diary, on the world and destiny. ATH 110:450.

200051   THE DAYSMAN. New York: Cochrane, 1909 NUC.

NYT—Male hero.

200052   DEFACED: AN HISTORICAL SKETCH. London: Eden, Remington, 1891 BMC.

The defacing of Countess of Salisbury's chapel in Christ church prior. But reviewer gives up on putting the story together. ATH 98 154

200053   THE DEVIL'S ACRES. London: Leadenhall Press, [1891] BMC.

200054   DIANA'S LOVE-STORY. London: W. Stevens, [1895] BMC.

200055   THE DIARY OF AN ENGLISH GIRL. London: Duckworth, 1910 BMC.

TLS—simple ordinary love story.

200056   DOLLY WINTER; THE LETTERS OF A FRIEND WHICH JOSEPH HAROLD IS PERMITTED TO PUBLISH. New York: J. Pott, 1905 NUC.

Typical romance letters PW 4-8-05

200057   EILY'S CONFESSION. BY THE AUTHOR OF "HER LAST VICTIM". London: W. Stevens, [1895] BMC.

200058   ELBOW LANE. BY THE AUTHOR OF "ALTOGETHER JANE". New York: M. Kennerley, 1915 BMC NUC.

love story of a famous woman sculptor BKM

200059   THE EMPTY HOUSE. New York: Macmillan, 1917 NUC.

Joan tells her own story. As girl, learned mother was killed by bearing children, resolves never to have any. Marries, keeps to her decision. Husband becomes engrossed in business. gets ill, dies, Joan feels guilty. PW
Purpose novel: concerns right relation between wifehood and motherhood. Joan grows up seeing mother a prisoner to too frequent pregnancies; Daughter holds father responsible for her death, fears marriage and only marries with understanding that there will be no children. All goes well, husband has his job, but she becomes restless. She begins to prod him to be more successful. Pushes him so that he dies from the strain. Moral: focusing all her love and attention on husband, she destroys him. Better for her to have other interests, children. BKM
Woman tells her story. As a girl overheard she couldn't have children. Marries, husband concerns self with business. Makes a bad financial move (she's well off) that husband dies in attempt to save her fortune. The theme seems to be that women who have no children become terribly destructive people—destroy themselves, husbands, the world! NYT 265,7-15-17

200060   ENGLAND'S DOWNFALL; OR THE LAST GREAT REVOLUTION. BY AN EX-REVOLUTIONIST. London: Digby, Long, [1893] BMC.

200061   AN EPISODE AT SCHMEKS: A NOVEL. BY THE AUTHOR OF "A FLIGHT TO FLORIDA". London: Skeffington, 1895 BMC NUC.

Lengthy visit of a Mr. Greyburn to a Mrs. Harkness whom he never realizes is not the person he thought she was. SR 80:119.
wholesome. Mrs. Harksness' identity not revealed till later. ACAD 47:480
Deceives his guest and lover for three weeks.

Hungarian bkgd ATH 105:703

200062   EUTHANASIA; OR TURF, TENT AND TOMB. London: G. Routledge, 1893 BMC.

Hero loses a fortune on the turf, loses his young woman, sells out of his regiment, joins Australian army, dies heroically. A countess attracted to a captain but returns to her lover. ATH 101,436

200063   EVE-SPINSTER. London: Mills & Boon, [1912] BMC NUC.

200064   A FAIR FIELD AND NO FAVOR. TO THE WOMEN OF ENGLAND, THIS VOLUME IS OFFERED. BY ONE OF THEMSELVES. London: H.J. Drane, [1912] BMC.

ATH "dedicated to the women of England, unfortunately the style is such that the book will be accepted with gratitude by few."
TLS to illustrate and enforce the claim for a "fair field" etc. for women

200065   A FAMILY OF QUALITY: A NOVEL. BY THE AUTHOR OF "ON HEATHER HILL". London: Hutchinson, 1895 BMC.

Clarence from a well-to-do family exasperates his parents by bringing beggars in the house, turning to work like road building. When he becomes a Revivalist preacher, they disinherit him. But love comes SR 80:88 Clarence Egerton and Ursula ATH 106:125

200066   A FATAL FASCINATION. A WEST INDIAN AUTOBIOGRAPHY BY A MEDICAL L.T. London: Greening, 1909 BMC.

200067   THE FLAW IN THE MARBLE. London: Hutchinson, [1896] BMC. New York and London: F. A. Stokes, [c1896] NUC.

LBKM 10:58. Paris art studios. Madeleine Le Fagon, poses for sculptor Lanthony, but is piqued that her beauty appeals to him only as artist and provokes a strong passion in him. This she feels a threat to her career so she leaves him to despair. She is enigmatic. ATH 107:617. She is a celebrated actress, a sphinx like creature. "she is not the scheming demi-mondaine of ordinary fiction."
BKM 4:74 stereotyped cold cruel lady with the melancholy smile and inscrutable past.
Sculptor's passion for model of the Circe statue that made him famous. She says she loves him as he lies dying; but he gets well and her love goes. He smashes the statue because of the flaw. SR 83:129

200068   FOR A GOD DISHONOURED. BY AUTHOR OF********. London: J. Long, 1899 BMC.

A Utopian Socialist settlement. Members called the Just. Husband and wife closely resemble each other. She masquerades as her husband an MP, in the House of Lords and elsewhere. SP 83:383.
They are advocates of domestic independence women's rights and vegetarianism. Heroine Clothilde dies at the end. ATH 114:317. Inherits a peerage in her own right.

200069   FOR THE DEFENSE; A BRIEF FOR LADY CAROL. London: Chapman & Hall, 1912 BMC NUC.

TLS—marries a poet, is indiscreet with his biographer and is "plunged into the horrors of a divorce case" ATH—gloomy.

200070   FOR WHICH WIFE? BY THE AUTHOR OF "LADY BEATRIX AND THE FORBIDDEN MAN". London and New York: Harper, 1906 BMC.

200071   A FORGOTTEN SOUL. London: G. Richards, 1903 BMC.

200072   THE FOUR BROTHERS: A POLITICAL ROMANCE. London: Simpkin and Marshall, 1893 BMC.

200073   FRANCESCA'S FOLLY. BY THE AUTHOR OF "SYBIL'S CONVERSION". London: W. Stevens, [1905] BMC.

200074   FROM BEHIND THE PALE. London: Methuen, 1915 BMC.

woman leaves husband, takes a lover. She tells her story to her 17 year old daughter whom she did not know TLS

200075   FROTH. BY THE AUTHOR OF "TOM BULLKELEY OF

LISSINGTON". Edinburgh: G. A. Morton, 1904 BMC.

LBKM-military tale.

200076   THE GIRL WITH THE ROSEWOOD CRUTCHES. SHE
TELLS SOME CHAPTERS OF HER LIFE. New York: Mcbride,
Nast, 1912 NUC.

NyT A pretty story, unreal, sentimental; lame girl
goes on stage, marries a rich man.

200077   A GYPSY MAIDEN. BY THE AUTHOR OF
"SWEETBRIER". London: W. Stevens, [1899] BMC.

200078   THE HAPPY YEARS. London: Murray &
Evenden, [1920] BMC.

ATH--Broad-minded woman believes that to be happy
oneself is most effective contribution to happiness of
others and of husband, home and family.

200079   HARCOURT. BY THE AUTHOR OF "DAUGHTERS OF
THE CITY". London: Simpkin, Marshall, 1899 BMC.

Tony conspires with her mother to go through life as a
man in order to beat the Salic principle of law that
makes a male heir inherit over a female. Triumphant in
winning the inheritance, she keeps the disguise, fools
all her friends, and goes on to take up feminist
causes, posing as the male champion of suffrage. She
mixes easily with men as their companion and equal,
has a fighting bout with a big burly ruffian whom she
defeats, and enters Parliament where her great
speeches are generously applauded. The book is "a
prolonged wail of pity for the poor, miserable,
downtrodden, despised English wives and mothers and
incidentally an impeachment of the anti-feminist
tyrant-stupid, unintelligent man." LIT 5:595

200080   THE HARD WAY. BY A PEER. London: J. Long,
1908 BMC.

TLS-bigamy? 1st husband mad.
ACAD- yes, she is married to two men, ending
satisfactory to the soft-hearted, if improbable.
ATH-leaves the homicidal maniac, works in a teashop
and then marries bigamously, author makes it turn out
ok.

200081   THE HAZARD OF THE DIE. BY A PEER. London:
J. Long, 1909 BMC.

200082   HE WHO PASSED. TO M. L. G. London: W.
Heinemann, 1912 BMC.

TLS-autobiography of female who lives in Am.
theatrical circles explaining her past and addressed
to a male.
ATH-gloom of tragedy, lower classes, who is "he who
passed"?
PW-a woman's past, stage, the "easy way" to success.
BKM-<author is English.> Vivisection of a woman's
soul. Story of an actress who, in playing a big,
important role, comes to realize that all her life she
has used men or they have used her; all her relations
with the other sex have been a matter of sordid
calculation, unspoken but relentless antagonism. MLG,
a man, comes into her life and out because she can't
deceive him or tell him the truth. So she writes book
anonymously, hoping he will read it and come back.
NYT

200083   THE HEART OF A GIRL: A THESIS. London:
Griffith and Farran, [1891] BMC.

200084   THE HEART OF A HERO. BY THE AUTHOR OF
"THE HAUNTED HOUSE AT KEW". London: W. Stevens, [1899]
BMC.

200085   THE HEART OF MONICA. London: Collier,
1909 BMC.

Her letters to a male friend reveal her tragic
marriage to a drunkard. TLS

200086   HER BROTHER'S LETTERS; WHEREIN MISS
CHRISTINE CARSON OF CINCINNATI, IS SHOWN HOW THE
AFFAIRS OF GIRLS AND WOMEN ARE REGARDED BY MEN IN
GENERAL AND, IN PARTICULAR, BY HER BROTHER, LENT
CARSON, LAWYER OF NEW YORK CITY. New York: Moffat,
Yard, 1906 BMC NUC. London: G. Richards, 1907 BS.

Seems to be concerned with little issues-like
low-necked dresses.
ACAD He's indignant with modern American girls.

200087   HER HIGHNESS; AN ADIRONDACK ROMANCE.
Boston: R.G. Badger, 1910 NUC.

German princess, plot, counterplots, mistakes in
identity, rescues, etc. NYT

200088   HER MISTAKE: A NOVEL. New York: G. W.
Dillingham, 1892 W.

200089   A HIDDEN TERROR. London: W. Stevens,
[1893] BMC.

200090   THE HIGHROAD; BEING THE AUTOBIOGRAPHY OF
AN AMBITIOUS MOTHER. Chicago: H. S. Stone, 1904 NUC.

NYT-story of a widow who had to support her family &
how she did it. satire?
BKM-details of her evolution from a West Virginia farm
house to mother of English peeress are curious in
their frankness. cynical

200091   HILARY AND VIVIAN. BY THE AUTHOR OF "LADY
OLIVIA'S STEP-DAUGHTERS". London: W. Stevens, [1896]
BMC.

200092   HIS FAULT OR HERS? A NOVEL. BY THE AUTHOR
OF "A HIGH LITTLE WORLD". London: R. Bentley, 1897
BMC.

She is a "child in years;" he is a squire of 40.
Apparently a seduction. Tragic end. The father's wild
grief but "The beautiful charity" of her father and
others. LBKM 13:50.
LIT 2:147 Rural tragedy. Achsa Mary, sweet, fragile,
"caught into the whirring wheels of passion only to be
flung out a crushed and withered flower." Yorkshire.
SR 85:471. Girl seduced, dies in childbirth.

200093   THE HOME-BREAKERS (AN ANTI-MILITANT
SUFFRAGIST NOVEL). BY A LOOKER-ON. Londodn: Hurst &
Blackett, 1913 BMC.

Anti militant suffragist novel. The militants figure
as the noblest and most self-sacrificing of women.
Joan Campion and others abandon their homes for the
Cause. Meantime, husband falls in love with someone
else. TLS

200094   THE HON. STANBURY AND OTHERS. BY TWO.
London: T. Unwin, 1894 BMC 1895 NUC. New York: G. P.
Putnam, 1894 NUC.

PW-also published U.S. NY Putnam (incognito library)
1894.
LW 25:303. Gloomy tales, one of an old woman who is
hired to care for and decorate graves.

200095   THE HOUSE OF DECEIT. New York: H. Holt,
1914 NUC.

PW 86 10/7/14:1120 "Maurice Sangster, of socialistic
tendencies, comes up to London to set the Thames
afire. Maud Gowler, a housemaid, could marry him, but
he aspires to the hand of Phoebe Champness, a
millionaire's daughter. The story of Sangster's
struggle for fame in journalism and politics is a
medium for the discussion of the lining-up of the
forces of radicalism and conservatism in politics and
religion; the increasing pressure of labor upon church
and state; and the drift of protestantism towards
catholicism, and the easing of catholicism toward
modernism."
BKM-
NYT 1914:448
Intimate study of a man.

200096   HUNGERHEART. THE STORY OF A SOUL. London:
Methuen, 1915 BMC.

John (she is called) Wingfield, unfortunate childhood.
After Oxford, secretary to a philanthropist, wrote
music crit. (being frankly ignorant of music), worked
in a bookshop. Sickens at her drab life; seeks
passion. Tries a relationship to a married man, enjoys
a loose life with casual men, went on the stage.
Became a suffragette though she didn't want the vote,
radicalized in a riot at Westminster--really came to
believe men hate women; men buy wives with their
promises of a home. Large capacity for female
friendship TLS
critic dislikes her altogether. Author serious.
heroine realizes at the end that she's a cruel selfish
absurd creature--according to unfriendly reviewer ATH
passes through theatrical life, suffrage mvt. to RCsm
SP

644

200097   "I HEARD A VOICE;" OR, THE GREAT
EXPLORATION. BY A KING'S COUNSEL. London: K. Paul,
1918 BMC.

200098   I; IN WHICH A WOMAN TELLS THE TRUTH ABOUT
HERSELF. New York: D. Appleton, 1904 NUC BMC.

PW-mental, moral and physical development, written in
1st person.
NYT-story of infidelity in marriage, etc.
ACAD-study of a woman by herself.

200099   THE IMPRESSIONS OF AUREOLE. London:
Chatto and Windus, 1895 BMC NUC.

"The outpourings of the good-hearted affectionate
beauty who is so shockingly indiscreet, and is always
getting into scrapes." LBM 9:98

200100   IN A SILENT WORLD; THE LOVE STORY OF A
DEAF MUTE. BY THE AUTHOR OF "VIEWS OF ENGLISH
SOCIETY". London: Hutchinson, 1896 BMC. New York:
Dodd, Mead, 1896 NUC.

SR Crude and dull. Diary of deaf and dumb girl.
Natural. Artless.
ATH 107:341. An attempt to portray inner history, but
unsuccessful in making this history unique or
different from that of an ordinary girl
ACAD 49:322. Does more than "succeed in a scene or
two" "Acclaims her a writer of no ordinary talent."
Later half of book not equal to opening chapters.

200101   IN SACKCLOTH AND ASHES. BY THE AUTHOR OF
"A DESPERATE REMEDY". London: W. Stevens, [1899] BMC.

200102   IN SEARCH OF VENGEANCE. London: G.
Newnes, [1901] BMC.

200103   IN STATU PUPILLARI. London: Sonnenschein,
1907 BMC.

University. life from a woman's p.o.v. brief desc.
LBKM 2-07, 2 36Eva at the univ.--intimate study of a
woman's college,. its striving, unrest,
contrasts--only a slight love interest ACAD
development of Eva from "fresher" to classical tripos
to engage. to tutor; woman's college life at
Cambridge; admirable sketches of many mod. women:
restless, self reliant, serious ambitions wholely
concerned with women's lives at Cambridge; student
attains high academic success; author "enthusiast
for...women's ed.

200104   IN THE HOUSE OF HER FRIENDS. New York:
R.G. Cooke, 1906 NUC.

PW-College town-widow's secret
BKM-

200105   IN THE YEAR OF WAITING. BY A PEER, AUTHOR
OF "THE HARD WAY". London: J. Long, [1916] BMC.

German spy novel; German governess involved; she's an
incognito countess. TLS

200106   INEXORABLE NATURE. London: H. J. Drane,
[1909] BMC.

(We Love But Once) 2 tales.

200107   AN IRISH LOVER. BY THE AUTHOR OF "WITHOUT
A GOD". London: K. Paul, 1914 BMC.

TLS-male hero, adventure, romance, suitable for boys.

200108   JACK WESTROPP: AN AUTOBIOGRAPHY. London:
Downey, 1895 BMC.

a reckless scoundrel and sometimes a "sent. humbug"
Innumerable practical jokes. May be a satire on Irish
political methods ATH 106:678

200109   "JAMES": OR, VIRTUE REWARDED. BY THE
AUTHOR OF "MUGGLETON COLLEGE". London: A. Constable,
1896 BMC.

SR-Satire written with savage cynicism, author
evidently hates his virtuous hero.

200110   JEM'S WIFE; A STORY OF LIFE IN LONDON. BY
THE AUTHOR OF "GRANNY" ETC. [ANONYMOUS]. New York: T.
Nelson, 1894 PW. London: T. Nelson, 1894 BMC.

Sally Newton, farmer's daughter tires of being a
kitchen maid, marries, persuades husband to work in
city in a brewery in Whitechapel. Describes her first
and last impressions of London and how she learned to
control her temper. PW 10-7-93

200111   JOAN'S SECRET. London: W. Stevens, [1896]
BMC.

200112   JOHN VAN BUREN, POLITICIAN. A NOVEL OF
TODAY. New York and London: Harper, 1904 NUC.

Historical adventure. NYT 166,05

200113   JULIE'S DIARY; A PERSONAL RECORD. Boston:
J. W. Luce, 1908 NUC.

"The experiences of a young woman's life as revealed
by her diary." BKM v 27 1908.
NYT-adventuress similar to Bashkirtseff "teems with
passionate thoughts about love." "A fairytale."
"Passes through the fires of hell unscorched," sweeter
than ever.

200114   LADY OLIVIA'S STEP DAUGHTERS. London: W.
Stevens, [1893] BMC.

200115   LESLIE: A NOVEL. BY THE AUTHOR OF "A
MODERN MILKMAID" ETC. London: Digby, Long, [1891] BMC.

The ravings of Leslie and her eccentric circle.
Heroine is stabbed. ATH 98:830
SR 73:155. Daughter grief-stricken over mother's
death, "degenerates into an emotional nightmare,"
passionate relationship with doctor, a married man;
"For the short remnant of her life she is either
bathed in the sheet lightening of passion or has
murder running in her veins." She is killed.
ATH 41:85. 22 years old, "an atheist, a thinker of
considerable power," has just lost her mother.
Reviewer thinks she tends to be hysterical. She falls
in love with her doctor and allows his wife to attempt
to cross a rotten bridge and be swept away by the
river.

200116   LETTERS FROM THE LITTLE BLUE ROOM. BY AN
ELDER SISTER TO HER BROTHER WHO CAME OVER WITH THE
FIRST CANADIAN CONTINGENT. London: C. W. Daniel,
[1917] BMC.

Pauline writes to soldier-brother, her unconventional
confidences. TLS

200117   LETTERS OF AN ACTRESS. London: E. Arnold,
1902 BMC. New York: F. A. Stokes, [1902] NUC.

Life of actress, trials of her career 3-7-03 PW
Attractive, interesting actress, her heart breaking
romance with an actor. Her stage career, letters to
several men-one she finally marries. NYT 03, 151

200118   THE LETTERS OF THOMASINA ATKINS, PRIVATE
(W.A.A.C.)-ON ACTIVE SERVICE. G. H. Doran, [c1918]
NUC. London: T. F. Fisher, [1918] BMC.

NYT Nov 3'18 p. 470. Thomasina is a member of the
Women's Auxiliary Army Corps (the "WAACS"). Formerly
an actress leading a comfortable luxurious life.
Description of the unromantic, hard, useful work the
women do, of "regulations purposely made more severe
than those of any boarding school, that there may be
no possible shadow of justification for such vile
rumors as those circulated by Hun propaganda, rumors
which enrage her who knows so well that they are
lies."
D640 WWI-Personal narratives.

200119   LETTERS TO MYSELF. BY A WOMAN OF FORTY.
London: T. W. Laurie, [1912] BMC.

TLS-views on sex question - but what?

200120   THE LIFE IMPOSSIBLE: A NOVEL. BY A MEMBER
OF "PAGET'S HORSE" AND J. P. L. London: Greening, 1902
BMC.

A degenerate man meets his double, has this double
take up his name and life and love of a nurse and
return to England to be husband to his wife. ATH
121,12

200121   A LIFE LAID BARE: A STORY OF THE DAY.
London: Simpkin and Marshall, 1895 BMC.

200122   THE LIFE WITHIN. Boston: Lothrop, [1903]
NUC. London: C. H. Kelly, 1903 BMC.

All about Christian Science. NYT 03,119

200123   A LITTLE DECEIVER. London: W. Stevens,
[1894] BMC.

200124   LOVE OF AN UNKNOWN SOLDIER, FOUND IN A
DUG-OUT. New York and London: J. Lane, 1918 BMC NUC.

   TLS WWI Fic.

200125   THE LOVER'S REPLIES TO AN ENGLISH WOMAN'S
LOVE-LETTERS [ANONYMOUS]. New York: Dodd, Mead, 1901
NUC.

200126   LOVE'S CONQUEST. London: W. Stevens, 1896
BMC.

200127   LOYAL: A NOVEL. London: G. Routledge,
1892 BMC.

200128   LUCILLA'S INHERITANCE. [BY THE AUTHOR OF
"LADY OLIVIA'S STEP-DAUGHTERS"]. London: W. Stevens,
[1899] BMC.

200129   THE MAHATMA: A TALE OF MODERN THEOSOPHY.
London: Downey, 1895 BMC.

   Theosophy: a Countess who is an imposter at it and
   Morial, a real Mahatma. He is beaten by spirit of
   good. "The Countess and Mrs. Fleeting Montgomery <her
   accomplice> are also fair examples of the female
   trickster, who in these days takes to 'spooks' as
   formerly she took to husband-hunting." ATH 47:274

200130   THE MAIDS' COMEDY; A CHIVALRIC ROMANCE IN
THIRTEEN CHAPTERS [ANONYMOUS]. London: S. Swift, 1911
BMC.

   Dorothea DeVilliers is the Knight; her Sancho Panza is
   a headstrong lass Dota Filjee. TLS

200131   MANTRAP MANOR. BY THE AUTHOR OF "WHEN IT
WAS LIGHT". London: J. Long, 1908 BMC.

   TLS-fiendish revenge of one man upon another.
   ACAD-

200132   MERCILESS LOVE. BY THE AUTHOR OF "FOR A
GOD DISHONOURED". London: J. Long, 1900 BMC.

   SP 85:118. Anti-vivisectionist tract. Heroine
   hysterically suicides to keep her fortune from falling
   into hands of vivisectionists.
   ATH 116:210. She attends meetings, writes articles. A
   friend dies and leaves her money on the provision she
   does not marry, the fortune to be used for the cause.
   She marries Collins Bay, after fake death, goes to
   China with him.

200133   A MISSING HEIRESS. BY THE AUTHOR OF "KING
COPHETUA, ETC.". London: W. Stevens, [1894] BMC.

200134   A MODERN HERETIC, THE STORY OF A
SCHISMATIC. A NOVEL WITH A PURPOSE. London: J. Clarke,
1894 BMC NUC.

200135   A MODERN JOURNAL: BEING THE DIARY OF
GREVILLE MINOR FOR THE YEAR OF AGITATION 1903-1904.
London: Methuen, 1904 BMC.

200136   A MOTHER IN EXILE. London: Everett,
[c1914] BMC NUC. Boston: Little, Brown, 1914 NUC.

   TLS inconsequent, "a deranged mind suffering from the
   hallucination that everyone is against her."
   "extraordinary relations between herself and her
   husband."
   "An emotional French girl marries a cold and
   conventional Scot stationed in India. Their early
   married life is more or less serene, but frequent
   separations, necessitated by the education of the
   children, together with temperamental differences,
   wreck their peace. Allan deserts his wife and robs her
   of her children. In letters to the daughter whom she
   has not been allowed to see, she pours out the
   passionate story of her love for the girl's father and
   the breaking of her own heart. Author is said to be a
   well-known English writer." PW 86 9-12-14:743.

200137   THE MOTHER-LIGHT, A NOVEL. New York: D.
Appleton, 1905 BMC NUC. London: Hutchinson, 1905 BMC.

   widow loses job as actress and loses her baby joins
   the Mother of Light rel. mvt as a secretary. As the
   mother Light gets old, the widow begins to take her
   place, falls in love, but her passion for her rel
   makes her give him up. ATH 05, 267

200138   A MOUNTAIN DAISY. BY THE AUTHOR OF "HER
SOLDIER LOVER". London: The Family Story-teller, 1900
BMC.

200139   MY FIRST PRISONER. BY THE GOVERNOR.
Aberdeen: Moran, [1898] BMC. (Dedication signed: B.
T.)

200140   MY WIFE'S HIDDEN LIFE. London: Hodder and
Stoughton, [c1913] BMC NUC. Chicago: Rand, McNally,
[c1913] NUC.

   unhappy marriage told first by husband who failed to
   understand his wife & then in diary by wife. Husband
   discovers diary after her death. ATH
   Gilbert and Hester. He tells us he writes because of
   his intolerable regret for never having understood his
   wife. SR
   PW-Man tells of his marriage to a fine woman whom he
   loves, but whom, after a while, he grows to consider
   rather stupid, with few ideas outside the four walls
   of her home. He philanders with another woman and in
   the midst of the affair learns of his wife's death;
   when he goes through her papers, he finds her diary
   and realizes that instead of being commonplace, the
   woman he married was most unusual, and his loss is
   irreparable.

200141   A MYSTERIOUS FAMILY. BY A NEW WRITER.
London: W. H. Allen, 1892 BMC.

   ATH 100:585. An "unlikely" and "unlikeable" family.
   SR 74:687. Gothic.

200142   THE MYSTERY OF A CORNISH MOOR. BY A NEW
AUTHOR. Bristol: J. W. Arrowsmith, [1891] BMC.

   ACAD 41:117 Passionate Nita poisons her wicked old
   grandfather and while she is waiting for him to die
   talks to him with "great plainess of speech."

200143   THE MYSTERY OF WOODCROFT. London: W.
Stevens, 1900 BMC.

200144   THE NEW EDEN. A NOVEL. London: Simpkin,
Marshall, 1903 BMC. Dublin: Hodges, Figges, 1903 BMC.

   Idyllic romance. ACAD 64:534.
   LBKM 7-03,153

200145   A NICE YOUNG CURATE'S DOINGS. Manchester:
J. Heywood, [1893] BMC.

200146   NICOL THAIN, MATERIALIST. BY THE AUTHOR
OF "THE LIFE OF THOMAS WANLESS, PEASANT". London:
Wilsons, 1894 BMC.

200147   NO RENT. BY THE AUTHOR OF "SOCIETY'S
VERDICT". London: W. Stevens, [1891] BMC.

200148   NORMANSTOWE. London: R. Bentley, 1895 BMC
NUC.

   Ella Lyell is on her own after father dies. Takes a
   job as ballad singer in a music hall and matron of a
   boarding house. She's a strong, self reliant woman.
   Her employer is a man who owns both the music hall and
   lodging house, where his young women actresses and
   singers stay. She humanizes them and James Bates, the
   owner. SP 75:560.
   "No 21 in Westminster, a house with a decidedly shady
   reputation." ATH 106:488

200149   THE ODD FARMHOUSE. BY THE ODD FARMWIFE.
London: Macmillan, 1913 BMC NUC.

   She's a cultured, southern American woman who
   appreciates English countryside. She and husband find
   just the farm house they want. TLS

200150   ON HEATHER HILLS. Paisley: A. Gardner,
1891 NUC BMC.

   Orphan from Australia marries a Scot (Malcolm Strong),
   an unhappy marriage. May Mellis is her name. They
   have an idyllic honeymoon; then May elopes. ATH 98,
   35.
   Self sacrificing hero. He has strong urge to protect
   her after her parents die. When she takes a fancy to
   his cousin, he pretends to be drowned. When this
   cousin proves to be a dangerous drunk, he disguises
   self to protect her. And when the cousin dies and May
   goes off to Australia, he never stops her. ACAD
   When she remarried, he comes disguised as a servant to
   protect her. Reversal of sexes of well known situation

in East Lynne. SR 8-22-91, 228

200151   THE ONE MAID FOR ME! BY THE AUTHOR OF
"THE WILD WARRINGTONS". London: W. Stevens, [1895]
BMC.

200152   ONLY A WOMAN CRUCIFIED. BY THE AUTHOR OF
"CHECKMATED". London: Simpkin, Marshall, [1901] BMC.

200153   ONLY FLESH AND BLOOD. BY THE AUTHOR OF
"HERNANI THE JEW". London: Hutchinson, 1898 BMC.

ACAD 55:120. An Englishwoman and her husband, a
philanderer, in French village.

200154   THE OPAL, A NOVEL. Boston: Houghton,
Mifflin, 1905 NUC.

Parasite A woman who is nothing in herself, takes her
feelings from others, marries wrong man none of the
problems are solved. PW 3-11-05
2 women, one plain & a man. The opal has every virtue
but no individuality; question of remarriage after
divorce. NYT 05, 14 1

200155   THE OPEN SECRET. BY A PRIEST. Boston:
Arena, 1893 NUC.

200156   THE ORDEAL OF ELIZABETH. New York: J. F.
Taylor, 1901 BMC NUC.

Grew up with maiden aunts; her desire for excitement
and love.

200157   THE ORDEAL OF SILENCE. BY A PEER. London:
J. Long, 1912 BMC NUC.

200158   AN ORIGINAL WAGER. BEING A VERACIOUS
ACCOUNT OF A GENUINE PET. BY A VAGABOND. London: F.
Warne, 1895 BMC. London: 1896 NUC.

200159   THE OTHER KIND OF GIRL. New York: B. W.
Huebsch, 1914 NUC.

"Story of the steps that led one girl to the street,
and of the steps that led her off, told with every
possible unpleasant detail left out."-Preface. PW 86
12-19-14:2053.
HQ 144 Prostitution
Autobiograpical type. No economic motive for her
"sin." The heroine always found work and lived on her
wages. But "strayed" because of the "youthful longing
for pleasure and companionship." "There comes an ache
in your nerves to dance and dance when you do long
factory work that can only be rested by aching your
nerves some other way."

200160   THE OTHERS AND SHE. BY "HIM". London: J.
Ouseley, [c1913] BMC NUC.

200161   THE OYSTER. BY A PEER. London: J. Long,
1914 BMC.

200162   PAID IN FULL. BY THE AUTHOR OF "LOVE WILL
FIND OUT THE WAY". London: The Family Story Teller,
[1892] BMC.

ACAD 43:211. Heroine is treated by father "with
fiendish cruelty." She escapes him, has further
adventures, happy ending. Check Folkard, Mary. H., as
possible author.

200163   PASSION'S PUPPETS: A NOVEL. London:
Hutchinson, 1895 NUC BMC.

Austin Knowles buys an estate, finds an enemy
possesses part of it. This enemy has a beautiful
daughter. ACAD 47:398
"Little comes of the passion" ATH 105:406

200164   PAULINE. London: The Author, [1913] BMC.

200165   PENTONVILLE PRISON FROM WITHIN WITH AN
ACTRESS IN THE BACKGROUND. London: Greening, 1904 BMC
NUC.

200166   PERIWINKLE: AN AUTOBIOGRAPHY. BY THE
AUTHOR OF "THE WILD WARRINGTONS". London: The Family
Story-Teller, [1891] BMC.

200167   PHILIP DRU: ADMINISTRATOR. A STORY OF
TO-MORROW. New York: B. W. Huebsch, 1919 BMC.

NYT male hero and U.S.

200168   PHILIPPA'S PRIDE. BY "A PEER". London:

Hurst & Blackett, 1916 BMC.

200169   PILLARS OF SMOKE. New York: Sturgis &
Walton, 1915 NUC.

Pub. originally in 1906 under title A Woman's Heart. A
"New Woman" love story. BKM 41 1915

200170   PRESUMPTION OF LAW. BY A LAWYER AND A
LADY. London: Griffith, Farran, [1891] BMC. (BMC:
Title on cover reads: "By a Barrister and a Lady")

200171   THE PRICE OF POSSESSION. BY THE AUTHOR OF
"IMPROPER PRUE". London: J. Long, [1913] BMC.

ATH-inheritance story.

200172   PRIDE OF CLAY. A LIFE STUDY. BY THE
AUTHOR OF "GEORGE SAVILE," "GLAMOUR," ETC. London:
Lamley, 1904 BMC.

ATH Unhappy wife, accident to child.

200173   PRIESTS AND PEOPLE: A NO-RENT ROMANCE. BY
THE AUTHOR OF "LOTUS" "A NEW MARGUERITE", ETC. London:
Eden, Remington, 1891 BMC NUC.

ATH 19:12. "Outrage, murder, suicide and ferocious
cruelty" in Irish novel. "varied by devotion,
generally misplaced and ill-starred, of a few unhappy
women."
Pictures of Irish Peasantry-their vices and virtues.
Also high society of Dublin-balls and teas. SR
12-12-91, 670

200174   RACHEL'S REWARD. BY THE AUTHOR OF "A
WOMAN'S LOVE STORY". London: W. Stevens, [1898] BMC.

200175   THE RECORD OF NICHOLAS FREYDON: AN
AUTOBIOGRAPHY. London: Constable, 1914 BMC NUC. New
York: G. H. Doran, [1915] NUC.

Focuses on his experience in London as a writer for
the Press. LBKM

200176   REMINISCENCES OF AUSTRALIAN EARLY LIFE.
BY A PIONEER. London: A. P. Marsden, 1893 BMC.

200177   ROMANCE OF A HAREM. BY "UNE
CIRCASSIENNE". New York: Brentano's, [1904?] NUC.
London: Greening, 1904 BMC. (Tr. Clarence
Forestier-Walker.)

200178   A ROMANCE OF THE WHITE MOUNTAINS. [New
York]: [Spectator], [c1896] NUC.

200179   SALAD DAYS: A COMEDY OF YOUTH. London: J.
Long, 1914 BMC.

ATH-Irish heiress and her pranks.
TLS-while in England. Comedy.

200180   A SAVAGE OF CIVILIZATION. [New York]: J.
S. Tait, 1895 NUC.

200181   THE SCOTCHMAN AND I. BY AN ENGLISHWOMAN.
London: Hodder and Stoughton, 1915 BMC.

"A childless woman who is very sent. confesses it
frankly to her husband." ATH

200182   THE SEPARATIST. BY A NEW WRITER. London:
I. Pitman, 1906 BMC.

TLS-historical

200183   SHAMS. London: Greening, 1899 BMC.

The sins of certain London artistic sets. Lord Edinsor
is the chief sinner. ACAD 57:336

200184   SHOULD SHE HAVE TOLD HIM? BY THE AUTHOR
OF "MY WIFE'S HIDDEN LIFE". London: Hodder &
Stoughton, 1916 BMC.

TLS-trite romance.

200185   SHUEYPINGSIN. A STORY MADE FROM THE
CHINESE ROMANCE HAOUKEWCHUEN BY AN ENGLISHMAN. London:
K. Paul, 1899 BMC.

200186   THE SIMPLE PLAN: THE STORY OF A PRIMITIVE
GIRL. London: Sherratt & Hughes, 1906 BMC.

TLS-wooing.

200187   THE SIN OF ANGELS. BY THE AUTHOR OF "A
VICAR'S WIFE". London: Methuen, 1896 BMC.

200188   SIR ANTHONY'S HEIRESS. London: W.
Stevens, [1904] BMC.

200189   A SLANDERED MEMORY. London: Family Story
Teller, [1894] BMC. (By the Author of "Lord Eldrid's
Wife" BMC)

200190   SOME PASSAGES IN PLANTAGENET PAUL'S LIFE.
BY HIMSELF. Digby, Long, 1895 BMC.

200191   SOME WELSH CHILDREN. BY THE AUTHOR OF
FRATERNITY. London: E. Mathews, 1898 BMC NUC. (On
spine: [by] Thomas.)

200192   THE SORROWS OF BESSIE SHERIFF. London:
Constable, 1912 BMC.

TLS-nervous, sensitive, idealistic. When her family is
ruined finds experience in teaching, journalism & a
fruitless romance. Depressing.

200193   THE SPIRIT OF LOVE. A NOVEL. London:
Henry, 1893 BMC NUC.

Mrs. Trevelyan's husband takes to drink. When her
child dies, she thinks of suicide. Spends months on
seaside recovering. There's another man interested in
her.SR 75, 460.

200194   "SPLINTERS." THE LIFE-STORY OF A WOMAN
AND HER POET-LOVER TOLD BY THEIR LETTERS. London:
Hurst & Blackett, 1914 BMC.

ACAD 86:563-correspondence between Elaine Hamilton and
Guy Desmond, she a "soiled woman" before 1st letter is
written. A record of their love, (the Reviewer
dislikes the character of the woman) love "in the
highest, finest, sense of the word," but too intimate,
"bared nerves, quivering." The two meet, die together,
rev. "could wish them no better fate unless they could
havetaken...letters with them."

200195   THE STAFF IN FLOWER. London: Greening,
1903 BMC.

Novel with a purpose. Short desc. LBKM 8-03,189

200196   STAR OF THE MORNING; A CHRONICLE OF KARYL
THE GREAT, AND THE REVOLT OF 1920-22. BY THE AUTHOR OF
THE TRUTH ABOUT MAN. London: T. Burleigh, 1906 BMC.

TLS-Karyl was the great Queen through whom "England
made her women co-equal in power with her men."

200197   THE STORY OF A LONDON CLERK. A FAITHFUL
NARRATIVE FAITHFULLY TOLD. London: Leadenhall Press,
[1896] BMC.

200198   THE STORY OF A WOMAN'S HEART. London:
Hodder & Stoughton, 1915 BMC.

Hero's struggle with adversity, imprisonment jealous
of his wife; told by the wife. TLS
Autobiographical form--Elaine Cassils tells of her
marriage; takes blame for all the problems. LBKM

200199   THE STORY OF AN ERROR. BY THE AUTHOR OF
"HIS WEDDED WIFE". London: W. Stevens, [1892] BMC.

200200   THE STORY OF LIZZIE MCGUIRE. BY HERSELF.
Boston: H. A. Dickerman, [1902] NUC.

parody of Mary Maclane

200201   THE STORY OF MY TWO WIVES. BY ONE OF
THEIR HUSBANDS. London: S. Low, 1894 BMC.

LW 25:267. Studies of character, half of book to each
wife.
PW-U.S. title seems to be: My Two Wives. First is
religious, 2nd home-loving.

200202   A SUFFRAGETTE'S LOVE LETTERS. London:
Chatto & Windus, 1907 BMC.

woman in favor of vote; man vs. Brief desc. 4-07, 35.
BKM
She has given up "the poor, dear, dull,
mischiefmaking, silly, dead old cause". TLS

200203   "SWANK." BY A YANK. BEING THE INNER
MYSTERY OF THE ART OF KIDDING, ETC. London: Success,
[1913] BMC.

200204   SWEET NANCE WAVERLEY. BY THE AUTHOR OF
RACHEL'S REWARD. London: W. Stevens, [1899] BMC.

200205   THAT MASTER OF OURS. BY THE AUTHOR OF
"DORRINCOURT". London: J. Nisbet, 1908 BMC.

200206   THEO. BY A PEER, AUTHOR OF "THE HARD
WAY". London: J. Long, 1911 BMC NUC.

Story of Theo's "neglected, dreamy childhood," her
launching upon the world, her sordid life in musical
comedy and with a drunken husband. "Not pleasant." TLS
"Deals with a woman's degrading environment." ATH

200207   THREE PERSONS. BY A PEER. London: J.
Long, 1915 BMC NUC.

Story of a man who joins clergy. TLS

200208   THE TIGER LILY. Columbia, Mo.: 1901 NUC.

LW 27:236. Unwholesome, intensely passionate.

200209   TIME'S FOOL; AN ENGLISH IDYLL. Edinburgh:
D. Douglas, 1901 BMC.

Gentleman marries a post mistress. ATH 3-30-01

200210   TO JUSTIFY THE MEANS. BY A PEER, AUTHOR
OF "THE HARD WAY". London: J. Long, 1910 BMC NUC.

200211   TOLD IN THE VERANDAH: PASSAGES IN THE
LIFE OF COLONEL BOWLONG, SET DOWN BY HIS ADJUTANT.
London: Lawrence & Bullen, 1892 BMC.

SR. Amusing. Indian military life

200212   TOM'S SWEETHEART. BY THE AUTHOR OF "A
LORD OF CREATION". London: W. Stevens, [1898] BMC.

200213   TOTTIE: OR THE CURSE OF THE HOUSE OF
BLOODWORT. A SHILLING SHOCKLET. BY A LADY OF TITLE.
(QUINTHA: A WEEDERIAN ROMANCE). London: "Fun" Office,
[1891] BMC.

200214   THE TRUTH ABOUT MAN. BY A SPINSTER.
ILLUSTRATED BY FACTS FROM HER OWN PRIVATE HISTORY.
London: Hutchinson, 1905 BMC.

Diatribe vs men; shows innocent women how to deal with
men. Suggest women stick to platonic relations. LBKM
139. v 27P

200215   TWIN SOULS: A ROMANCE OF DUALITY. BY THE
AUTHOR OF "FALLEN ANGELS". London: Gay & Bird, 1906
BMC.

Male/female principle in nature; widower inspired by
wife's soul. TLS

200216   TWO NEW STORIES: THE ANGLO-AMERICAN LADY,
AND TWO WAIFS OF THE MARITIME ALPS. WRITTEN BY A LADY.
Syracuse, N.Y.: Masters and Stone Printers, 1892 NUC.

200217   THE UGLY MAN. BY THE AUTHOR OF "A HOUSE
OF TEARS". London: Downey, 1896 BMC.

Orangutan is a murderer, acquires a soul thru
innoculation. SR 83:270

200218   AN UNSELFISH WOMAN. BY THE AUTHOR OF
"LORD ELWYN'S DAUGHTER". London: W. Stevens, 1894 BMC.

200219   UNVEILING A PARALLEL: A ROMANCE. BY TWO
WOMEN OF THE WEST. Boston: Arena, 1893 W. (W: The
Names "Jones (Alice Ilgenfritz)" and "Merchant
(Ella)" are written on title page of the [Huntington
Library] copy as though they were the authors. On
Mars, where women have equal rights.)

"A satire on modern civilization and a plea for
justice to women presented under the semblance of a
picture of social life on the planet Mars." A person
from earth visits two Martian cities:Thursia and
Caskia where "the same code of morals applies to both
sexes. In Thursia the women vote, legislate, engage in
every kind of business, offer themselves in marriage
and indulge in allthe vices and amusements commonly
reserved for men." BOOK NEWS 134:

200220   VANISHED! BY THE AUTHOR OF "GOLDEN
MISTS". London: W. Stevens, [1898] BMC.

200221   VASHTI AND ESTHER; A STORY OF SOCIETY
TO-DAY. BY THE WRITER OF BELLE'S LETTERS IN "THE

WORLD". London: Chatto & Windus, 1893 BMC NUC.

Smart society couple married from start. Concerns the
flirtations on both sides beginning at the time of the
honeymoon that make a man really appreciate his wife.
SR 76:711.
SP 72:378. Depicts follies of fashionable society.
Esther has gypsy blood, is angry when gypsy band is
banished, but reviewer says neither "throws in her lot
with them" or "assists them." "Her sudden mysterious
flight from home and family is...motiveless."
ACAD 45:31 Kenneth is more or less unfaithful to
Vashti with Esther altho (last sentence of book):
"'We'll have a ripping Goodwod,' said Kenneth. Violet
rubbed her wet face against his hand with the action
of a grateful dog rather than that of a high-spirited
proud woman."
LBKM 6:191. "Why should the writer ask us to rejoice
over the end of the story, which throws (Vashti)...at
the feet of a vulgar-minded young man?...She knows how
unsatisfactory it all is." She is a cynic.
CR 25:330. He goes after another woman because Violet
won't display his diamonds.
LW. 25:262. Dodoesque.
PW-Violet (like Vashti of the Bible) is physically
cold to Kenneth. He takes after Esther, briefly .
After a year of "married coldness" they are
reconciled.

200222   THE VAUDEVILLIANS. London: J. Long, 1913
BMC NUC.

LBKM-life behind the scenes in music halls,
essentially plotless.
ACAD 86:113. Coralie is the heroine, eventually
accepts Dr. Nicholson's hand.
poorer kinds of theatrical life. ATH
Their "seaminess and vulgarity." TLS

200223   THE VISIBLE TO-BE: A STORY OF
HAND-READING. London and New York: Leadenhall Press,
C. Scribner's, 1892 NUC. (NUC: "Author is identified
as Miss Owen in text.")

200224   THE VOICE. London: Hodder & Stoughton,
[1920] BMC.

TLS-religious male.

200225   WHAT WOULD ONE HAVE? A WOMAN'S
CONFESSION. Boston: J.H. West, [c1906] NUC.

PW-Farmer's daughter-record and analysis of her life.

200226   A WIDOW FROM BELGRAVE SQUARE. BY A MEMBER
OF SOCIETY. London: Holden & Hardingham, [1916] BMC.

200227   A WIFE IMPERATIVE. BY A PEER, AUTHOR OF
"THE HARD WAY" ETC. London: J. Long, 1911 BMC.

Man forced to marry Cyll Cassells. TLS

200228   WILFUL DOREEN. [BY THE AUTHOR OF "A
MISSING HEIRESS"]. London: W. Stevens, [1900] BMC.

200229   THE WOMAN OF THE HILL. BY "UNE
CIRCASSIENNE." AUTHORESS OF "ROMANCE OF A HAREM".
London: Greening, 1902 BMC. London and Glasgow:
Collins Clear-Type Press, [1915] NUC. (Tr. C.
Forestier-Walker)

200230   A WOMAN'S CRUSADE. BY A DAME OF THE
PRIMROSE LEAGUE. London: Kegan Paul, 1893 BMC.

Lady Ethelhyrst gets restless with the usual round of
parties and trivialities in her life. Starts a
crusade-series of meetings with women to discuss
serious topics in order to rise above the frivolous in
their lives. She's a leader of county society as well
as a woman of ideas. SP 70:709.
She starts a Salon. The plan is a brilliant success.
SR 75:460.

200231   A WOMAN'S VICTORY. BY THE AUTHOR OF
"LUDLEY'S WIDOW" ETC. London: W. Stevens, [1892] BMC.

200232   A WOMAN'S WAR. BY THE AUTHOR OF "REPENTED
AT LEISURE" ETC. London: W. Stevens, [1892] BMC.

200233   THE WORLDLY TWIN: THE HEAVENLY TWINS "NOT
IN IT". New York: G. W. Dillingham, 1893 NUC.

200234   WRECKED: OR, FOUR YEARS IN A CAVE. BY THE
AUTHOR OF "ONLY A DOG!" London: Seeley, 1891 BMC.

A Robinson Crusoe type of story. Boy saved from a
shipwreck by a dog. SR 7-25-91, 114.

200235   "YOUNG AND SO FAIR!" BY THE AUTHOR OF
"THOSE IRISH EYES" ETC. London: W. Stevens, 1892 BMC.

200236   YOURIE GARDENIN, A RUSSIAN CHARACTER
STUDY. New York: Neale, 1905 NUC.

"Conjugal matters frankly discussed." Brief desc. BKM
22 (1905) 186

200237   ZITTARA; OR, A WIFE'S INTRIGUE. A TALE.
BY THE SHAH'S STORY-TELLER. London: Lang Neil, 1892
BMC.

APTE, HARI NARAYAN. 1864-1919.

200238   RAMJI: A TRAGEDY OF THE INDIAN FAMINE.
London: T. F. Unwin, 1897 NUC.

ASH, C. ASHMORE.

200239   THE MAINSPRING. London: Digby, Long, 1911
BMC.

ASHLEY, B. FREEMAN. See ASHLEY, BARNAS FREEMAN.

ASHLEY, BARNAS FREEMAN.

200240   AIR CASTLE DON; OR, FROM DREAMLAND TO
HARDPAN. BY B. FREEMAN ASHLEY. Chicago: Laird and Lee,
[c1896] NUC.

PW 10-17-96. Nova Scotia youth, his experiences as a
school teacher and in Boston.

ASHWORTH, MARION.

200241   A SENTIMENTAL PILGRIM. London: Chapman &
Hall, 1915 BMC.

Ida goes to Paris to train in opera, instant success,
Mother too busy in own romantic entanglements to watch
daughter Ida. Sister's death brings father to Paris.
Mother's (Emily's) romance ends. "author throws no
stones at these characters" "matrimonial fidelity is
much out of date for this authoress's heroine." "no
one seems a whit the worse for their numerous
liaisons" The virtuous daughter dies prematurely. TLS

ATHENE, pseud. See HARRIS, S. M.

ATKEY, E. L.

200242   MY CHANGE OF MIND. A STORY OF THE POWER
OF FAITH. London: E. Stock, [1903] BMC.

power of faith ACAD 65, 38
woman whose husband has TB, no job learns to believe;
one year later he's well and successful ACAD 65, 59

ATLEE, H. FALCONER.

200243   THE SEASONS OF A LIFE: A NOVEL. London:
F. V. White, 1898 BMC.

ACAD 53:601. Adventure. London, Spain, Mexico.

200244   A WOMAN OF IMPULSE: A NOVEL. London: F.
V. White, 1898 BMC.

SP 81:782. Sentimental journey of an artist and a
barrister, with its sequel. Two women, Gretchen and
Juliette come to disastrous ends, a mawkish melodrama.
ACAD 55:274. Artist has been told by palmist that he
will bring death to one woman and grief to another. He
does so.

AUBURN, W. FERRARS.

200245   IN CAMP AND BARRACK. London: Ward, Lock,
1897 BMC.

B., A. [pseud.].

200246   THE BLASTED LIFE: BEING A SHORT RECORD OF
A FALLEN STAR. By A. B. London: Roxburghe Press, 1897
BMC.

200247   TRAVELS OF A LADY'S MAID. Boston: L. C.
Page, 1908 BMC.

PW "below-stairs" pov
BKM -tells of Lady Em.'s love affair and finishes with
her own marriage.

B., H. N. [pseud.].

200248   WYTHA WYTHA. A TALE OF AUSTRALIAN LIFE.
London: Hodder & Stoughton, 1903 BMC.

BACOT, E. M.

200249   MRS. THORNDALE'S COUSIN. London: T.
Unwin, 1894 BMC.

SR-Life in a small country town.

BAIGENT, J. M.

200250   STARS AND STRIPES: A NOVEL. London:
Digby, Long, 1899 BMC.

BAK [pseud.].

200251   OUTRAGEOUS FORTUNE. BY BAK. London: W.
Heinemann, 1907 BMC.

Widow of 32- problem of money. TLS
Was rich, now badly off. Her attempts to make ends
meet falls in love with a poorer man, loses him when
she accepts money from an admirer. SR

BALBIRNY, R. A.

200252   ASSETS OF EMPIRE; A BOOK WHICH DISCUSSES,
IN HAPPY VEIN, THE FUTURE OF THE RACE. London: W.
Westall, 1917 NUC BMC.

More talk than story: male narrator, on marr,
children, female suffrage. pov ? TLS

BALDWIN, M. E.

200253   THE HEIRESS OF BEECHFIELD: A NOVEL.
London: Digby, Long, [1891] BMC.

Guide book to Switzerland. SR 12-12-91, 670
ACAD 41:10. She almost marries a bigamist,
unwittingly, instead chooses a moral young man. She
writes literary criticism and reflects on the solar
system.

BALLYNN, DEANE. United Kingdom.

200254   THE PRICE OF FREEDOM; A TALE OF TODAY.
CREATING AN ENTIRELY NEW LITERARY FORM AND AN
INTRODUCTION THERETO. London and New York: W. Scott,
1910 BMC NUC.

TLS-A new form, a play to be read.

BALME, E.

200255   THE LUCK OF THE FOUR LEAVED SHAMROCK.
London: G. Routledge, 1898 BMC.

BAMFORD, F. W.

200256   REVENGEFUL FANGS. London: E. Stock, 1900
BMC.

ATH 116:83. Family of three wander through India in
search of an antidote to snake poison. Their
adventures.
ACAD 58:490. The family is constantly being menaced by
snakes.

BANCO [pseud.].

200257   KIT OF THE KITCHEN. BY BANCO. London: T.
W. Laurie, [1919] BMC.

200258   LIL OF THE LOUNGE; BEING THE STORY OF A
CITY MAN'S FOLLY. BY BANCO. London: T. W. Laurie,
[1917] BMC.

200259   THE ONLY WOMAN. BY BANCO. London: T. W.
Laurie, [1918] BMC.

200260   THE OUTRAGE. BY BANCO. London: T.W.
Laurie, [1915] BMC.

BANNISTER, L. C.

200261   A SLICE OF A WOMAN'S LIFE. London: Digby,
Long, 1915 BMC.

BARBER, EVELYN.

200262   MICHAEL. London: Murray and Evenden,
[1912] BMC.

An estate and love story involved. ATH

BARKER, S. DARLING.

200263   MARS. London: Hutchinson', 1898 BMC.

ACAD 53:443. Modern cigarette smoking heroine. Love
story.
ATH 111:720. Her revenge on man who ruined her father.
LBKM 14:139. An "exaggerated specimen" of the "very
slangy heroine with the good heart and the loud
manners." Her language is that of a brainless stable
boy. "A noisy young Amazon."

200264   A TORTURED SOUL. London: Roxburghe Press,
[1897] BMC.

LIT 2:452. Young girl courted by middle-aged married
man, an earl. He "inspite of his faults, does not
alienate the reader's sympathy." "Avoided the
commonplace story of seduction."

200265   THE TRIALS OF MERCY. London: Hutchinson,
1899 BMC.

BARKER, T. F.

200266   THE CROSS ROAD STORE: OR, THE EVILS OF A
DRAMSHOP. THE HISTORY OF A KENTUCKY VILLAGE. A NOVEL.
FOUNDED ON FACTS. Lexington, Kentucky: F. D. Veach,
Printer, 1892 W.

BARLOW, J. SWINDELLS.

200267   THE GREAT AFRIKANDER CONSPIRACY. London:
Ward, Lock, 1900 BMC.

BARRETT, E. E.

200268   CAMILLA DE SOLYS. London: S.E. Barrett,
1893 BMC.

BAYLY, A. EPIC. Nationality Unknown.

200269   THE HOUSE OF STRANGE SECRETS; A DETECTIVE
STORY. London: Sands, 1899 BMC. New York: E.P. Dutton,
1899 NUC.

Maniac son of a princess. Traditional mystery. SP
83:57

200270   THE SECRET OF SCOTLAND YARD: A MYSTERY.
London: Sands, 1900 BMC.

BEARDMORE, G. RUSSELL.

200271   THE CAREER OF FREDA. London: J. Long,
1910 BMC.

TLS-simple love story.

200272   A WHITE LIE. London: J. Long, 1909 BMC.

BEATTY, W.

200273   THE SECRETAR: FOUNDED ON THE STORY OF THE
CASKET LETTERS. London: A. Gardner, 1897 BMC.

"Conscientious account of the tangled web of Scottish
politics in Mary's time." Good portrait of Maitland of
Lethington, the Secretar. and John Kilgour's love
story. LBKM 13:23

BEAUFORT, E. V.

200274   SATAN FINDS SOME MISCHIEF STILL: A
CHARACTER STUDY. London: T. Fisher Unwin, 1899 BMC.

Harmless story of modern life. SP 83:23.
"Study of a modern, emancipated girl and the ruin she
brings on other people's lives as she advances with
sure steps in her brilliant and selfish career." ACAD
56:660
Herrice flirts, so father banishes her to her aunt's
home where she proceeds to break the rules of no bacon
and no fire in her room. ACAD 57:112

BEESTON, L. J.

200275   DAGOBERT'S CHILDREN. London: S. Paul,
[1912] BMC.

TLS-Franco-German war.

BELASYSE, E.

200276   THE PILGRIMS: A NOVEL. London: Greening, 1904 BMC.

ATH-some morbid analysis of unhappy married life, threads are cheerily drawn together. Love affairs, flirtations.
TLS-ill-natured invalid husband.

BENTON, C. A.

200277   THE SWORD. London: Chapman & Hall, 1913 BMC.

Desiree St. Just takes Mollie Eliot, a runaway girl, into her home. Mollie is in love and Desiree learns to love the same man even though she's married (husband is in prison.) A priest helps work things out. "No amount of criticism will avail to stop the output of such books." ACAD

BERESFORD, LESLIE. B. 1899. United Kingdom.

200278   BIG HAPPINESS. BY PAN. London: Mills & Boon, 1917 BMC.

Full of coincidences, accidents, etc. TLS

200279   DOLLY AND HER DIARY. EDITED BY PAN, AUTHOR OF WHITE HEAT. London: Mills and Boon, 1918 BMC.

200280   THE FURNACE. BY PAN. London: Odhams, [1920] BMC NUC.

TLS-marriage of actress. Did she or did she not love him. End with couple in Atlantic after shipwreck.
SR-marriage under most unfortunate circumstances to millionaire. Satisfied at 1st with her wealth and freedom, but growing more dissatisfied. Until she is willing to throw everything to the winds for the sake of being loved.

200281   GLORY OF LOVE. BY PAN, AUTHOR OF WHITE HEAT, ETC. London: Odhams, [1919] BMC.

Traditional love story. TLS SR

200282   THE KINGDOM OF CONTENT. BY PAN. London: Mills and Boon, 1918 BMC.

TLS-o
Story of future when love of luxury and mania for speed engulf London population. ATH
Great earthquake; the strongest survive, mainly concerned with sex. Science fiction. SR

200283   LOVE, THE MAGNET. BY PAN, AUTHOR OF WHITE HEAT. London: Mills & Boon, [1916] BMC.

TLS-dancer marries politician who exposes her cabaret act to newspaper in Puritanical campaign.

200284   SCORCHED SOULS: A SYMPHONY IN PROSE. BY PAN, AUTHOR OF WHITE HEAT. London: Mills and Boon, 1915 BMC.

200285   THE SECOND RISING. A ROMANCE OF INDIA. London: Hurst & Blackett, 1910 BMC.

TLS-suspicion falls on wife of intrigue with Indian rajah.

200286   WHITE HEAT. BY PAN. London: Mills & Boon, 1915 BMC.

Heat is the heat of passion. TLS

200287   WONDERFUL LOVE: BEING THE ROMANTIC ADVENTURES OF GLORY WEST, ACTRESS. BY PAN, AUTHOR OF WHITE HEAT. London: Mills and Boon, 1916 BMC.

TLS-love and romance of silly actress.

BERKLEY, EIBBON.

200288   OSWALD STEELE. London: J. Long, 1899 BMC.

BERTHET, ELIE BERTRAND. 1818-1891.

200289   THE CATACOMBS OF PARIS. Westminster: Constable, 1900 BMC. Philadelphia: J.B. Lippincott, 1900 NUC. (Tr. M.C. Helmore)

BETHAM, G. K.

200290   THE STORY OF A DACOITY AND THE LOLARPUR WEEK: AN UP-COUNTRY SKETCH. London: W.H. Allen, 1893 NUC.

"The hunting down of the dacoits by English oficers and their subordinates." Both stories are Anglo-Indian. SR 75, 408.

BEVAN, S. KENRICK.

200291   A THING OF NOUGHT. London: Duckworth, 1899 BMC.

BEY, ALEPH [pseud.]. Nationality Unknown.

200292   THAT EURASIAN. BY ALEPH BEY. Chicago: F. T. Neely, [c1895] BMC NUC.

BINGHAM, EDFRID A. United States.

200293   THE HEART OF THUNDER MOUNTAIN. Boston: Little, Brown, 1916 NUC.

PW-western romance. Marion follows the man she loves into a mountain pass and they have an unheard of struggle for existence.
NYT-heroine is a seeker (leap year type.)

BIRD, M.

200294   LAO-TI, THE CELESTIAL. London: Hutchinson, 1900 BMC.

LBKM 17:191. Rev. calls her Miss Bird. Hero is an intellectual Chinese, who reaches wisdom through sin & struggle.
SP 84:143. Also, historical romance.

200295   THE SEEKER. London: Ward, Lock, [1898] BMC.

BISHOP, R. F. United States.

200296   CAMERTON SLOPE: A STORY OF MINING LIFE. Cincinnati: Cranston, 1893 BMC.

BLACK, L. M. P.

200297   FOR HIS COUNTRY'S SAKE. London: H. Cox, 1897 BMC.

SP 81:447. Briton prince Esca and Rome in the early days (reign of Trojan).

BLACKMORE, E.

200298   ANGELS UNAWARES. London: Digby, Long, 1899 BMC.

BLAIR, H. B.

200299   SARAH VALLIANT'S PROBLEM. London: J. Ouseley, 1908 BMC.

Feeble tale of country soc. TLS

BLAMEY, E. N.

200300   JEFFREY MARDEN, SURGEON. A NOVEL. Newcastle-upon-tyne: North British Academy of Arts, [1913] BMC.

sets up practice in South Africa, sensational adventures-prisons, suicides, lions, adventuresses ATH

BLOOMFIELD, J. H.

200301   A CUBAN EXPEDITION. London: Downey, 1896 NUC BMC.

BLUM, PETER, pseud. See MILLER, L. A. AND C. V. GOOLSBY.

BLYTH, P. A.

200302   A CHARGE TO KEEP. London: Jarrold, [1891] BMC.

SP 77:282. Wholesome story of love and faith.

BLYTHE, MARION.

200303   AN AMERICAN BRIDE IN PORTO RICO. New York: F. H. Revell, [c1911] NUC.

Peurto Rico-Social life & customs

BOLMER, W. B. United States.

200304   THE TIME IS COMING. New York: G.W.
Dillingham, 1896 W.

BOLTON, F. H.

200305   IN THE HEART OF THE SILENT SEA. London:
R.T.S., [1910] BMC.

200306   INTO THE SOUNDLESS DEEPS. A TALE OF
WONDER AND INVENTION. London: Boy's Own Paper, [1919]
BMC.

200307   THOSE YOUNG BARBARIANS. Toronto: Warwick
Bros. and Rutter, 1907 BMC.

200308   UNDER THE EDGE OF THE EARTH. A STORY OF
THREE CHUMS AND A STARTLING QUEST. London: R.T.S.,
[1913] BMC.

BONHAM, E. United Kingdom.

200309   A CORNER OF OLD CORNWALL. London: Unicorn
Press, 1896 BMC NUC.

Centers on Joslyn, a farmer. We meet interesting folk
like Obadiah Hendy's sister-in-law. SP 79:286.

BOOMERANG [pseud.].

200310   AUSTRALIA REVENGED. BY "BOOMERANG".
London: Remington, 1894 BMC NUC.

BORDERER [pseud.].

200311   THE YOUNG SQUIRE. BY BORDERER. London: G.
Routledge, [1893] BMC.

BOTTOME, PHYLLIS AND H. DELISLE BROCK.

200312   CROOKED ANSWERS. London: J. Murray, 1911
BMC NUC.

letters -bkgd of Switz & winter sports. TLS

BOURCHIER, M. H.

200313   THE ADVENTURES OF A GOLDSMITH. London: E.
Mathews, [1898] NUC.

SP 80:864. France-Napoleon. First consulate. Narrated
by prosperous London goldsmith summoned to Paris by a
Royalist client. He is drawn into intrigues.
ACAD 53:495. Author of the C Major of Life.
ATH 111:788.

200314   THE C MAJOR OF LIFE. BY HAVERING BOWCHER.
London: E. Mathews, 1896 BMC NUC.

BOURNE, C. HAROLD, jt. au. See LANGBRIDGE, V. AND C. HAROLD
BOURNE.

BOWCHER, HAVERING, pseud. See BOURCHIER, M. H.

BOWEN, E. J.

200315   THE ADVENTURES OF LEONARD VANE; AN
AFRICAN STORY. London: Hutchinson, [1894] BMC.

200316   A BAFFLED VENGEANCE: A TALE OF THE WEST
INDIES. BY J. EVELYN. London: Eden, Remington, 1891
BMC.

200317   AN INCA QUEEN; OR LOST IN PERU. BY J.
EVELYN. London: S. Low, 1891 BMC.

BOWIE, W. A.

200318   AN ANGEL IN AMBLEDON. London: Cassell,
1911 BMC.

retired London tradesman turned farmer. LBKM

BOXWALLAH [pseud.].

200319   AN EASTERN BACKWATER. BY BOXWALLAH.
London: A. Melrose, [1916] BMC NUC.

Sketches of life in India

200320   THE LEOPARD'S LEAP, A STORY OF BURMA. BY
BOXWALLAH, AUTHOR OF AN EASTERN BACKWATER. London: A.
Melrose, 1919 BMC NUC.

BRASS, THEOPHILUS [pseud.].

200321   A CHAPTER FROM THE STORY OF PAULINE
PARSONS. BY THEOPHILUS BRASS. Ashland, Mass.: W. P.
Morrison, 1916 NUC.

Records conversations between rich young woman and her
advisors who want to keep her from sharing profits
with her employees. PW

BRAZIER, M.

200322   A TWOFOLD SIN. London: Digby, Long, 1898
BMC.

LIT 2:537. Romance, old-fashioned, happy ending.

BREDA, G. H.

200323   FROM ONE MAN'S HAND TO ANOTHER. London:
T. F. Unwin, 1907 BMC.

18 year old boy attracted to 40 year old woman; (boy's
sister has illegitimate child) who "has passed from
one man's hand to another," she tries to discourage
his love but finally they live together; she refuses
to marry him because she's 40, later leaves; he paints
a picture of her. Attitude toward the woman? ACAD.
Sex problems prominent; Irish peasant artist lad &
non-moral fellow student, a woman of 40. TLS

BREEN, M.

200324   MAYOTTE. Paris: A. Colin et Cie, 1898
NUC.

BREWSTER, T. A.

200325   THE ENTHUSIAST. A NOVEL. London:
Sisley's, [1907] BMC.

About Ireland and England's problems.

BRIGSTOCKE, L. MONTAGU.

200326   LOVE'S ARTIST. London: W. J. Ham-Smith,
1911 BMC.

ACAD-Absurd story of Denise who does a couple of wild
things to help some friend and incurs her husband's
misunderstanding and finally forgiveness.

BRITON, E. VINCENT. United Kingdom.

200327   THE FACE OF DEATH: A WESTMORELAND STORY.
New York: Macmillan, 1894 NUC. London: Seely, 1894
BMC.

BROADWAY, D.

200328   THE LONGEST WAY ROUND. London: Allen and
Unwin, [1916] BMC NUC.

TLS-She inherits money on proviso, hunts out a young
farmer and student on verge of ruin, marries him and
separates. Years later he shows up again incognito and
woos her.
ATH-He gets an annual sum for doing it, educates
himself in Cambridge and after brilliant career woos
her in South Africa.

BROCK, H. DELISLE, jt. au. See BOTTOME, PHYLLIS AND H.
DELISLE BROCK.

BROWN, S. A. United States.

200329   THE DISSOLUTION: A PROJECTED DRAMA. BY
RITTER DANDELYON. New York: G. W. Dillingham, 1894
NUC.

PW-"condemns all marriages without love as unnatural
and unholy. Offers as a solution the establishment by
law of Platonic unions which shall become intimate
only with the consent of the woman. Story, which takes
place in mythological times, illustrates this theory
in the heroine's actions."

200330   RHEINGRAFENSTEIN: A ROMANCE OF THE
ELEVENTH CENTURY. BY RITTER DANDELYON. New York: G. W.
Dillingham, 1893 NUC.

Setting: Crusades of 1096. Heir of the castle referred
to in the title is called to death bed of his father,
meets his beautiful young stepmother. PW 5-13-93.

BROWNE, E. M. C. BALFOUR.

200331 THE BETTALEY JEWELS. London: E. Arnold, 1901 BMC.

BRUUN, LAURIDS VALDEMAR. 1864-1935.

 200332 VAN ZANTEN'S HAPPY DAYS. A LOVE STORY FROM PELLI ISLAND. London: Gyldendal, [1908] NUC. (Translated from the Danish by David Pritchard. "Van Zantens Lykkelige Tid.")

  TLS-Male

BRYANSEN, JENNES [pseud.]. United States.

 200333 THE HOMESTEADER'S DAUGHTER: A STORY OF THE TIMES (FOUNDED ON FACT). BY JENNES BRYANSEN. New York: 1900 NUC. (W:"Written in LC copy:"By Nathan Billstein, of Baltimore, Md.'")

BUCHAN, GEHANI.

 200334 WILLOUGHBY COURT. London: Digby, Long, [1895] BMC.

  Effie Penrose is schemed against by woman who wants Effie to marry her son. All comes out right SP 75:673

BUCKMAN, H. H. United States.

 200335 MEROPE; OR, THE DESTRUCTION OF ATLANTIS. Jacksonville, Fla.: DaCosta Printing and Pub. House, 1898 NUC.

BUCKMAN, SYDNEY SAVORY. 1860-1929.

 200336 ARCADIAN LIFE. London: Chapman and Hall, 1891 BMC.

BURG, SWAN.

 200337 THE LIGHT OF EDEN; OR, A HISTORICAL NARRATIVE OF THE BARBARIANAGE. A SCIENTIFIC DISCOVERY [ANONYMOUS]. Seattle, Wash.: S. Burg, 1896 NUC.

BURKE, R. R. United States.

 200338 "KEEP THE CHANGE": A SKETCH OF THE LIFE OF A NEWS AGENT. WITH DETAILS OF MANY EXPERIENCES ON AND OFF THE CARS [ANONYMOUS]. Pittsburgh, Pa.: Commercial Printing, 1895 NUC.

BURNS, CUMORAH SMITH.

 200339 A CHILD OF LOVE. Boston: Sherman, French, 1911 NUC.

BUTLER, RAYNE.

 200340 IN THE POWER OF TWO. THE SPIDER AND THE FLY. London: Simpkin, Marshall, 1896 BMC.

BUTT, FREDERICK S., pseud. See IRVINE, F. K.

BYRON, W. H. SMITH.

 200341 WHY I KILLED HIM. London: Digby, Long, [1893] BMC.

C., M. [pseud.]. AND G. DE S. W. [pseud.].

 200342 CONFIDENCES: BEING SIX MONTHS IN THE LIVES OF MELISANDE AND GERALDINE. BY M. C. AND G. DE S. W. London: Limpus, Baker, 1903 BMC.

  Widow and spinster exchange letters; they "journalize with modernity" LBKM 4-03,35

C., O. K. [pseud.].

 200343 WHEN ALL WAS YOUNG. A SERIES OF CHILDHOOD PICTURES. BY O. K. C. London: A. H. Stockwell, 1919 BMC.

CADMUS [pseud.]. AND HARMONIA [pseud.]. United States.

 200344 THE ISLAND OF SHEEP. BY CADMUS AND HARMONIA. London: Hodder and Stoughton, 1919 BMC. Boston: Houghton Mifflin, 1920 NUC.

  PW-house party of international guests who discuss peace treaty, league of nations, labor reform, etc.

CALVERT, F. XAVIER. United Kingdom.

 200345 A MODERN ROSALIND. A STORY. Chicago: Rand, McNally, 1891 NUC.

Louise Parrish "acts after the manner of Rosalind" and dons men's attire. Becomes a student at Harvard to further the success of that experiment. PW 39:529

CAMPBELL, A. GODRIC.

 200346 FLEUR-DE-CAMP OR A DAUGHTER OF FRANCE. A STORY OF THE FIRST EMPIRE. London: Chatto & Windus, 1905 BMC.

CAMPBELL, C. M.

 200347 DEILIE JOCK. London: A. D. Innes, 1897 BMC.

  A scamp tells his own story in Scottish vernacular. ACAD 52:Fic Sup 84.
  LIT 3:147. Autobiography of an Edinburgh Ne'er-do-well. Amusing.
  ATH 111:87. Dialect. Jeannie with illeg. child.

CAMPBELL, FLOY. United States.

 200348 CAMP ARCADY: THE STORY OF FOUR GIRLS, AND SOME OTHERS, WHO "KEPT HOUSE" IN A NEW YORK "FLAT". Boston: R. G. Badger, 1900 NUC.

CAMPBELL, H. M. F.

 200349 THE STAR OF DESTINY. London: Odhams, [1920] BMC.

  TLS Stella goes to India under belief that Divine purpose is calling her. Becomes involved in political intrigue. Author shows Stella as a bit of a prig, but is sympathetic to her enthusiasm and intellectual attitude.
  ATH. Stella is greatly influenced by Krishna Ing who is being exploited by Mrs. Ferguson, a German spy. She is arrested, Krishna dies, and Stella goes back to England.

CAMPBELL, H. R.

 200350 THE RACE OF CIRCUMSTANCE. London: S. Swift, 1912 BMC.

  TLS- NY life.
  SP--Story of corrupting effect of wealth on a man.

CAMPBELL, R. W. United States.

 200351 DONALD AND HELEN; A ROMANCE OF THE OLD ARMY. London: Hutchinson, 1917 BMC NUC.

  Nationalistic. TLS

 200352 DOROTHY V.A.D. AND THE DOCTOR. London: W. & R. Chambers, 1918 BMC NUC.

  In letters; life of volunteer nurse in military hospital. Love comes. ATH

 200353 JOHN BROWN. CONFESSIONS OF A NEW ARMY CADET. London: W. & R. Chambers, 1919 BMC.

 200354 THE KANGAROO MARINES. BY CAPTAIN R. W. CAMPBELL. London: Cassell, [1915] BMC NUC.

 200355 THE MIXED DIVISION (T.). London: Hutchinson, 1916 BMC NUC.

 200356 PRIVATE SPUD TAMSON. BY CAPTAIN R. W. CAMPBELL. Edinburgh and London: W. Blackwood, 1915 NUC BMC. New York: D. Appleton, 1915 NUC.

 200357 SERGT. SPUD TAMSON, V.C. London: Hutchinson, 1918 BMC NUC.

 200358 SNOOKER TAM OF THE CATHCART RAILWAY. London: W. & R. Chambers, 1919 BMC NUC.

 200359 WINNIE McLEOD. London: Hutchinson, [1920] NUC BMC.

  TLS--Auth. sympathizes with Winnie. Story of her life as typist, a few love affairs, then loss of virginity as mistress of rich man, love for Ronnie who is killed in war, on to manage a munitions factory and eventual marriage to owner.

CANADIENNE [pseud.].

 200360 AFTER MANY DAYS. AN ANGLO-AMERICAN ROMANCE. BY CANADIENNE. London: K. Paul, 1914 BMC.

CARDEN, W. THOMAS. United States.

200361   A YEAR WITH UNCLE JACK. Nashville, Tenn.:
printed for Author, 1897 NUC.

CAREW, F. S.

200362   JIM B. London: Methuen, 1894 BMC.

ACAD 45:368. Hero, who broods on religious matters,
marries a flirt, dies on the spot of her first
flirtation.

CARRUTHERS, VYVIAN.

200363   THE CONFESSIONS OF VYVIAN CARRUTHERS: A
TALE OF HYPNOTISM. London: Sutton, Drowley, [1892]
BMC.

CARTER, MARION HAMILTON. United States.

200364   SOULS RESURGENT. New York: C. Scribner's
Sons, 1916 NUC.

NYT-Dora returns to her home after an absence of 10
yrs at college, etc. her father has died and made her
executor and guardian of her younger brother and
sister. Mother is Irish Catholic, father was Norwegian
and Scottish, ideals of both races are lost in younger
children. Dora has ideals of father. Author believes
cross-breeding, American democracy which substitutes
the dollar for all measures of worth has hurt society
melting pot a failure.

200365   THE WOMAN WITH EMPTY HANDS: THE EVOLUTION
OF A SUFFRAGETTE [ANONYMOUS]. New York: Dodd, Mead,
1913 NUC.

"Story of one woman's conversion to the cause of
suffrage" NYT, 1913, 217
"The emotional states she passes through" "the phases
of experience and emotion which made her ready to
adopt militant methods..." "The narrator of this
experience-it is most patently a true story-is a
southern woman, bred in the old school of chivalric
ideals, who describes her evolution as a suffragette.
Suffragists were to her the "shrieking sisterhood"
until fate turned her out into the world, a woman
bereft of home, husband and child, a woman with empty
hands. It was the words, "we need you" addressed
directly to her by a street orator that led her into
the suffrage movement, for her own great need was to
be needed by some one else." "This record of a woman's
gradual conversion to the woman movement is an
interesting and clever study in psychology, as well as
a most useful bit of propaganda work." "There is in
this little story more power than in the most clearly
worded arguments, because of its simplicity, its
clearness and its lack of vindictiveness. This book is
neither an argument nor a plea. In its ardor and
virility it speaks more powerfully than anyone could
possibly speak for it of its vital note of sincerity
and conviction." BRD

CASSEL, A. J. United States.

200366   IT ISN'T A JOKE. Spring City, Pa.:
[c1896] NUC.

CASUALTY [pseud.].

200367   "CONTEMPTIBLE". BY "CASUALTY". London and
Philadelphia: W. Heinemann, 1916 BMC NUC.

Soldiers' tales of the great war
D640 War-Pers. narr

CAUTLEY, CAUTLEY HOLMES.

200368   THE MILLMASTER. New York: Longmans,
Green, 1906 PW. London: E. Arnold, 1906 NUC BMC.

PW-Sacrifice of lives to mill.
TLS 0
ATH 0

200369   THE WEAVING OF THE SHUTTLE. London:
Duckworth, 1912 BMC NUC.

ATH-Story of a Yorkshire mill.
ACAD and love story
LBKM love story

CAVALIER, Z. LANGRANA.

200370   THE SOUL OF THE ORIENT. London: Murray
and Evenden, [1913] BMC.

A new religious creed that will reform the whole
world. Helen, wealthy, young, astrologist converts
fiance to her philosophy. Teaches her sister and they
perform many charitable deeds. "All very goody-goody
and ultra-sent" ACAD

CAVENDISH, IANTHE.

200371   DOCTOR BROWN'S PARTNER. London: W. J.
Ham-Smith, 1912 BMC.

ACAD-Medical romance
ATH-Hero with uncompromising views on the subjection
of women. Pro corporal punishment as a treatment.

CHAPPELLE, L. L. Nationality Unknown.

200372   THE DIVERGING PATHS. A STORY OF THE
PIONEER DAYS OF MISSOURI. New York: Broadway, [c1911]
NUC.

CHATTERJI, BANKIM CHANDRA. 1838-1894.

200373   KRISHNA KANTA'S WILL. London: T. F.
Unwin, 1895 BMC NUC. (Tr. Miriam S. Knight)

SR Hindoo life in Bengal

CHESTER, R. O.

200374   DORIS HAMLYN. London: T. Nelson, [1906]
BMC.

CHETWODE, R. D. Nationality Unknown.

200375   JOHN OF STRATHBOURNE. A ROMANCE OF THE
DAYS OF FRANCIS I. London: C.A. Pearson, 1897 BMC. New
York: D. Appleton, 1898 NUC.

SP 31:533. English knight takes his son on a French
campaign.

200376   THE KNIGHT OF THE GOLDEN CHAIN. London:
C. A. Pearson, 1898 BMC. New York: D. Appleton, 1898
NUC.

ACAD 55:30. 1st person narration. 1139, reign of King
Stephen.
ATH 112:568. Harmless.

200377   THE LORD OF LOWEDALE: A CHRONICLE OF THE
SIXTEENTH CENTURY. London: Jarrold, 1896 BMC. Boston:
Estes and Lauriat, [c1897] NUC.

200378   THE MARBLE CITY. London: S. Low, 1895
BMC. (Bookseller adds subtitle; Being the Strange
Adventures of Three Boys)

200379   TO THE DEATH: A TALE OF THE DAYS OF
CROMWELL. London: Cassell, 1896 BMC NUC.

CHILLINGTON, J. C.

200380   DUAL LIVES. London: R. Bentley, 1893 BMC.

Conventional story of plotting and counterplotting.
Disappearance, mock-marriage, etc. Too many characters
and incidences. SP 70:709, SR 75:460.
Sundry characters, whose natures are dual: good and
bad. ATH 101:501.

CHILOSA [pseud.].

200381   HOW'S THAT, UMPIRE? A STORY OF AN
UNCONVENTIONAL LIFE. BY CHILOSA. London: F. V. White,
1905 BMC.

200382   VENUSBERG, THE SYREN CITY WITH IT'S [SIC]
SEQUEL. TEN YEARS LATER. BY CHILOSA. London: Holden &
Hardingham, [1914] BMC.

Life, inhabitants and ways of living in Monte Carlo
made pleasant. Chilosa goes through many
trials-getting justice from unscrupulous house agents.
Chatty interesting amusing. ACAD

CHRISTEL [pseud.].

200383   BABETTE VIVIAN. A NOVEL. BY CHRISTEL.
London: Digby, Long, [1893] BMC.

Beautiful girl persecuted by stepfather, an amorous
baronet, faithful nurse, a lover of lower degree whose

parentage is a mystery. Ends in wedding. ACAD 43:347.

CHRISTIAN, SYDNEY, pseud. See LORD, M. L.

CHURCH, J. W. Nationality Unknown.

200384   DEEP IN THE PINEY WOODS. New York: T. Y.
Crowell, [1910] NUC.

Centers on hero PW
NYT Centers on hero

CIOS [pseud.].

200385   LIFE IN AFRIKANDERLAND AS VIEWED BY AN
AFRIKANDER: A STORY OF LIFE IN SOUTH AFRICA, BASED ON
TRUTH. BY CIOS. London: Digby, Long, 1897 NUC BMC.

CLARK, W. A.

200386   HULLABALOOS AT HACKSTERS. London: Digby,
Long, 1908 BMC.

TLS-farce for the youthful reader.

CLARKE, B. A.

200387   BOTH SIDES OF THE ROAD. London: Ward,
Lock, 1913 BMC.

CLARKE, E. MARTYN.

200388   THE LOVE LESSON. Bristol: J. W.
Arrowsmith, 1919 BMC.

The heroine Joan is perfection itself. TLS
Raised in solitary life of S. Amer. "An elegant
polished savage" thrown into English life, ed by aunt
and her friend. LPKM

CLARKE, MARION COSMO.

200389   AN ANGLO-FRENCH MAID. London: H. J.
Drane, [1906] BMC.

CLARKE, O. P. United States.

200390   THE COLONEL OF THE 10TH CAVALRY: A STORY
OF THE WAR. Utica, N.Y.: L. C. Childs and Son, 1891
NUC.

CLAY, BERTHA M. [pseud.]. United States. Works published
under this pseud, but not identified as Mrs. Charlotte
Mary Brame, are entered under the pseud, which was
admittedly used by others. For works by Mrs. Brame see
that name. Originally the pen name of an English
novelist, Charlotte Monica Brame. The name was
appropriated by some American publishers for imitative
tales of the sentimental-melodrama kind that Miss Brame
wrote. Among writers believed to have employed this
pseud. were John R. Coryell, Thomas Chalmers Harbaugh and
Frederick Van Rensselaer Dey.

200391   AN EVIL HEART; OR, THE FLIRT. BY BERTHA
M. CLAY. New York: Street & Smith, [1902] NUC.

200392   ONE AGAINST MANY; OR, LADY DIANA'S PRIDE.
BY BERTHA M. CLAY. New York: Street & Smith, [1900]
NUC.

200393   A TRAGEDY OF LOVE AND HATE; OR, A WOMAN'S
VOW. BY BERTHA M. CLAY. New York: Street & Smith,
[1902] NUC.

COATE, H. S. ACRAMAN.

200394   ALIENS AFLOAT. A STORY OF THE SEA.
London: E. Stock, 1900 BMC NUC.

ACAD 59:492. Hero and heroine perish. British ship in
the southern Ocean.

COCQ, J. R.

200395   THE TWO CRUSADERS: A ROMANCE OF THE
MIDDLE AGES. London: H. Marshall, 1898 BMC.

ACAD 55:120. Prince of Orange and Don John of Austria.

COEN, P. J.

200396   EVALINE; OR, WEIGHED AND NOT WANTING. A
CATHOLIC TALE. New York: P. O'Shea, [n.d.] W.

COLE, MELLEN. Nationality Unknown.

200397   CY ROSS: A NOVEL. London: Gay and Bird,
1891 BMC. New York: J. S. Ogilvie, 1891 NUC.

SP-After prospecting for 30 years Cy hit a vein, went
on a holiday, met a young woman and married her. An
American character with a "fine, tender nature."

COLLINS, E. LEUTY. Nationality Unknown.

200398   FROM CAPTIVITY TO THE PERSIAN THRONE. New
York: Cassell, [c1893] NUC.

200399   HADASSEH; OR, "FROM CAPTIVITY TO THE
PERSIAN THRONE". New York: Cassell, [1891] NUC.
London: T. F. Unwin, 1891 BMC.

Story of Esther from captivity to the Persian throne.
LW
Follows closely the Book of Esther. PW
"How the queen saved the Hebrew people in Persia from
the bloodthirsty rage of Haman, the king's minster."
BOOK NEWS 7-91, 477 No 107

200400   THE STORY OF QUEEN ESTHER. New York:
Street & Smith, [c1900] NUC.

200401   UNDER CONDEMNATION: THE STORY OF A NUN.
London: Express Printing, 1892 BMC.

COMPTON, C. G. United Kingdom.

200402   HER OWN DEVICES. London: W. Heinemann,
1896 BMC. New York: E. Arnold, 1896 NUC.

ATH 107:411. Pioneer Series. Adventures hunting a man,
aims for a weak flabby husband. She fails; he escapes.
ACAD 49:237. She is an actress.

200403   THE HOUSE OF BONDAGE. London: W.
Heinemann, 1911 BMC NUC.

Laura Henderson loves audaciously; two extra marital
relationships: "one in the face of London society"
becomes a peeress in her own right, has a child. TLS
Unmarried heroine, mother of 2 children, by different
fathers, married a Duke amid general approval. ATH

200404   A PRINCESS OF HACKNEY. New York and
London: J. Lane, 1909 BMC.

PW--male hero?
TLS--farce male hero.

CON [pseud.].

200405   THE MISTRESS OF ELMSHURST: A NOVEL. BY
CON. Westminster: Roxburghe Press, [1897] BMC.

COOKE, W. BOURNE. B. 1869. Nationality Unknown.

200406   BELLCROFT PRIORY. London: J. Lane, 1911
BMC NUC. New York: J. Lane, 1911 NUC.

BM-murder and a gorilla.

200407   HER FAITHFUL KNIGHT; BEING THE STATEMENT
OF WILL HERITAGE, OF THE BEACON FARM. BY WOODHOUSE
EAVES, SOMETIME A TROOPER IN THE PARLIAMENTARY FORCES.
London: Cassell, 1908 NUC BMC.

TLS-Hist but beautiful and spirited heroine.

200408   THE HORNED OWL. London: H. J. Drane, 1905
BMC.

200409   MADAM DOMINO. London: Sisley's, 1907 NUC
BMC.

200410   "NEVER AGAIN!" A TALE OF YESTERDAY, TODAY
AND TOMORROW. London: Simpkin, Marshall, 1919 BMC.
London: [1919?] NUC.

German spies, patriotic thrills; some homely Eng.
chars. SR

COPE, C. ELVY.

200411   THE PURSUIT OF A CHIMERA: BEING A
MID-WINTER'S DAY DREAM. London: Digby, Long, [1893]
BMC.

CORNISH, J. F.

200412   SOUR GRAPES. London: Chatto and Windus,
1900 BMC.

SP 84:94. Brabrooke, a country squire, has delayed marriage until his children are grown. Then he is infatuated with a singer. Son saves situation by becoming his rival and marrying her. He then finds out not only is he illegitimate, but also had married his half-aunt.
SR 89:179. She accepts this with "equanimity and even amusement."

COTES, V. CECIL. Nationality Unknown.

200413   TWO GIRLS ON A BARGE. New York: Appleton, 1891 NUC. London: Chatto and Windus, 1891 BMC.

Their adventures on a barge they rent, voyage through England. IND.

COTTER, WINIFRED [pseud.]. United States.

200414   SHEILA AND OTHERS; THE SIMPLE ANNALS OF AN UNROMANTIC HOUSEHOLD. BY WINIFRED COTTER. New York: E. P. Dutton, [c1920] NUC.

PW-humorous. Household and its servants
NYT 11-28-20 p17 pleasant sketches.

COUPER, J. R.

200415   MIXED HUMANITY: A STORY OF CAMP LIFE IN SOUTH AFRICA. London: W. H. Allen, [1892]. Capetown: J. C. Juta, [1892] NUC.

COVERTSIDE, NAUNTON, pseud. See DAVIES, NAUNTON.

COWLES, M. L. United States.

200416   REDBANK: LIFE ON A SOUTHERN PLANTATION [ANONYMOUS]. Boston, Mass.: Arena, 1893 NUC BMC.

Jessica Holcombe lives with her brother on the Plantation Redbank in Georgia after Civil War. Ordinary routine of Southern life. Brother leads a dissipated life, but she has a happy love. PW 8-19 -93.

COX, F. J.

200417   THE FORBIDDEN WAY. A ROMANCE OF THE COTSWOLDS. London: F. Griffiths, 1907 BMC.

Nothing promising SR
Three women are puppets.

CRAIG, DORIN.

200418   THE KEY OF THE WORLD. London: J. Long, 1915 BMC.

TLS-male hero.

200419   MIST IN THE VALLEY. London: Long, 1916 BMC.

TLS- puppet show mystery. Nurse Merion solves. Young man and young woman both negative about life become positive.
ATH-Nurse Merion prevents hero from suicide. Heroine is tried for a murder. All ends well.

CROSBIE, W. J.

200420   DAVID MAXWELL; A NOVEL. London: Jarrold, 1903 BMC.

CROSFIELD, H. C.

200421   FOR THREE KINGDOMS, RECOLLECTIONS OF ROBERT WARDEN, A SERVANT OF KING JAMES. London: E. Stock, 1909 NUC BMC.

CROSSWAYS, DIANA [pseud.].

200422   A MELTON MONOLOGUE. BY DIANA CROSSWAYS. London: A. Rivers, 1908 BMC.

TLS-bright record of hunting and hunting society.
ACAD-Diana and Freddie attempt to retrieve the fallen fortunes of their house.

CURRY, E. S.

200423   CAN SHE FORGIVE? New York: E. & J.B. Young, 1893 PW. London: Society for Promoting Christian Knowledge, [1894] BMC.

Points out morals against hasty marriage, intemperance and gambling. Wife of lower class London. Discovers husband drinks and gambles, leaves him. After long separation, he repents. They are reunited. Will she forgive? PW 12-2-93

CURTIS, E.

200424   DR. MALCHI: OR "WHO WAS I?" London: Ward, Lock, [1891] BMC NUC.

200425   HIS DOUBLE SELF; OR, THE TRANSFORMATION OF KEITH WINSTANLEY. London: Jarrold, 1897 BMC.

Keith Winstanely falls into the river one foggy night. Another man jumps in to help and is injured and loses his memory. Keith thinks him dead and begins to act and speak as though he has taken over this other man's personality. ATH 109:804.
SP 80:455. A doctor is rescued by an artist, who loses his life in his efforts. The doctor then begins to take on his personality, look like him, buy oils and canvas.

CURTIS, MARION. United States.

200426   THE NOTE OF DISCORD. New York: Broadway Publishing, [1907] NUC.

D., E. V. [pseud.].

200427   OF THE EARTH, EARTHY. BY E. V. D., AUTHOR OF "BOUND FOR LOVE," ETC. Bristol: J. W. Arrowsmith, [1891] BMC.

D., F. A. [pseud.].

200428   THE PHARAOHS OF THE WEST. BY A. F. D. London: Bemrose, 1901 BMC.

D., S. L. T. [pseud.].

200429   BEYOND THIS IGNORANT PRESENT. London: Cassell, 1909 BMC.

Letters of two well-to-do ladies. TLS

DAHLE, T. THEODORE.

200430   THE NOTIONS OF A NOBODY. London: Leadenhall Press; Simpkin, Marshall, Hamilton, Kent, [1893] BMC. New York: C. Scribner, [1893] BMC.

200431   A TRAGEDY OF THREE. London: Hurst & Blackett, 1900 BMC.

ATH 116:613. Man and two women.

DALTON, MORAY. United Kingdom.

200432   OLIVE IN ITALY. London: T.F. Unwin, 1909 BMC.

Teacher in Siena, governess in Florence, artist's model in Rome. ACAD
Happy end after much pain. ATH
"Painful struggle" of young woman who seeks to make her own living. SP

200433   THE SWORD OF LOVE. A ROMANCE. London: W. Collins, [1920] BMC.

DANDELYON, RITTER, pseud. See BROWN, S. A.

DARLINGTON, H. A.

200434   THE CHAUNCEYS. London: J. Nisbet, 1905 BMC.

200435   LAST YEAR'S NESTS. A TALE OF OTHER DAYS. London: J. Nisbet, 1905 BMC.

TLS-sentim.

200436   THE ROCKCLIFFES. A NOVEL. London: Jarrold, [1905] BMC.

200437   TIME--THE ENEMY. London: Jarrold, [1905] BMC.

DAVIDSON, LILLIAS CAMPBELL. United Kingdom.

200438   FOR LACK OF LOVE. London: H. Marshall, 1900 BMC.

SP 85:416. Unnaturally good heroine.

200439   SECOND LIEUTENANT CELIA. London: Bliss, Sands, 1898 BMC.

LIT 2:562. Puts on her brother's uniform and takes his place in camp when he outstays his leave. Descriptions of her beauty and frocks. For schoolgirls.
LEKM 14:50. Simple and innocent heroine.

DAVIES, NAUNTON.

200440   CHESTER CRESSWEL. A NOVEL. BY NAUNTON COVERTSIDE. London: Digby, Long, 1898 BMC.

ATH 112:826. Cresswell torn between conscience and passion.

200441   THE KING'S GUIDE: A ROMANCE. London: S. Marshall, [1901] BMC.

200442   THE REVEREND JACK. London: H. J. Drane, [1904] BMC.

200443   THE SECRET OF A HOLLOW TREE: A NOVEL. BY NAUNTON COVERTSIDE. London: Digby, Long, [1898] BMC.

ACAD 53:255. Murder mystery. Wales. Matskalla, the "wisest woman of the Romani," is the "leading agent" in its solution.

DAVIS, J. H. United States.

200444   THE POSSUM CREEK POULTRY CLUB. Chatham, N.Y.: Fanciers' Review, 1895 NUC.

DAVY, E. M. Nationality Unknown.

200445   A DAUGHTER OF EARTH. Chicago and New York: Rand, McNally, 1892 NUC.

PW-orphan, her adoption, secret marriage, mystery.

DEAN, ELLIS.

200446   HIS WIFE. London: Digby, Long, 1908 BMC.

TLS-alcoholic male.
ACAD-alcoholic male, wife widowed shortly after childbirth.

200447   THE NEW MATRON. London: Digby, Long, 1906 BMC.

200448   A RAW PROBATIONER. London: Digby, Long, 1905 BMC.

200449   A STRANGE HONEYMOON. London: Digby, Long, 1908 BMC.

DE BOSSCHERE, JEAN. 1878-1953.

200450   THE CLOSED DOOR. London: J. Lane, 1917 BMC NUC. New York: J. Lane, 1917 NUC. (Tr. F. S. Flint)

DEE, R. K.

200451   MORTGAGED YEARS: AN AUSTRALIAN STORY. London: S. Sonnenschein, 1895 BMC.

Opens with trial of a beautiful woman for the murder of her husband. She's acquitted, and goes away. The junior counsel at her trial felt he was guilty—the two must have been in love and partners in the plan. When he falls in love with another woman, he can't marry her until the first woman appears and tells him she committed the murder. ACAD 47:422

DE ESQUE, JEAN LOUIS. B. 1879.

200452   SILENCE: A COMPOUND PROBLEM NOVEL. BY STEWART. Jersey City, N.J.: Connoisseur's Press, 1908 NUC.

PW-"book is very outspoken and contains any amount of intrigue, occultism and sensational incident."

DE GOMARA, MONTI.

200453   HEARTS THAT ARE LIGHTEST. London: Digby, Long, 1898 BMC.

DE GROOT, J. MORGAN. B. 1868. United Kingdom.

200454   THE AFFAIR ON THE BRIDGE. Edinburgh and London: W. Blackwood, 1909 BMC.

200455   THE BAR SINISTER. London: W. Blackwood, 1906 BMC.

ACAD-Illeg. male hero-weak woman

200456   EVEN IF. Edinburgh and London: W. Blackwood, 1899 BMC.

200457   THE FLOWER OF SLEEP; A ROMANCE. BY DR. J. MORGAN-DE-GROOT. London: S. Paul, [1916] BMC NUC.

200458   THE HAND OF VENUS. A NOVEL. BY DR. J. MORGAN-DE-GROOT. London: Hutchinson, 1911 BMC NUC.

200459   JAN VAN DYCK. Edinburgh and London: W. Blackwood, 1904 BMC.

200460   A LOTUS FLOWER. Edinburgh and London: W. Blackwood, 1898 BMC.

ACAD 54:326. Translation of author's Bouton de Rose, "a book which has made some stir in Holland." Story of two Swedish girls and their unhappy lives.
ATH 112:896. Dutch, possibly translated by author himself.
SR 86:544. Sympathetic but merciless study of neurotic girl, Hilda; she is a spiritual sister of Anna Karenina.
Rev. says Lotus Flower is translation of Dutch work.

200461   A MAN OF IRON. London: J. Long, 1901 BMC.

ATH 12-14-01

200462   OUSTING LOUISE. London: S. Paul, [1920] BMC.

200463   WYNNINGFORD. BY DR. J. MORGAN-DE-GROOT. London: S. Paul, 1917 BMC NUC.

DE GUERIN, E. W.

200464   THE MALICE OF THE STARS. New York: J. Lane, 1909 BMC. London: J. Lane, 1908 BMC.

Sympathetic knowledge of womanhood. ACAD

DE HAMONG, LEIGH.

200465   A STUDY OF DESTINY. London: Saxton, [1898] BMC.

DE HAVILLAND, SAUMAREZ.

200466   THE MYSTIC SERPENT. London: Iliffe, 1891 BMC.

DELAGREVE, C. J.

200467   THE CURIOUS FRIENDS. London: G. Allen & Unwin, 1918 BMC.

TLS-children's story.

DELAIRE, JEAN.

200468   AROUND A DISTANT STAR. London: J. Long, 1904 BMC.

TLS- male youth and astronomy, science fiction.

200469   A DREAM OF FAME. London: Long, 1899 BMC.

Young woman dies because she is not "allowed to live for painting". LIT 4:667.
Giuseppa "how her genius flickered out amid the petty cares of married life, and left only a wonderful picture of the Resurrection." Story also concerns the ironical fate of this painting. ACAD 56:486

200470   THE LADY OF ROBERTVAL, AN EPISODE OF THE PEASANTS' WAR 1526. London: Sands, 1900 BMC.

LIT 7:489. For children.

200471   PRO PATRIA: A SMALL SKETCH ON A VAST SUBJECT. London: Digby, Long, [1897] BMC.

France-German war: anti-Germ. SR 84:528

200472   TWO GIRLS AND A DREAM. London: Ward, Lock, 1901 BMC.

Two women (an artist and a writer) struggle to exist, in the end one marries, the other chooses fame. BKM (London) p. 32 Oct 1901

Artist reviles the world that won't accept her work.
Writer has trouble publishing her work. 9-21-01. ATH

200473   THE VISION OF JOHN ADAMS. London: A. H.
Stockwell, [1920] BMC.

DE LA VILLENEUVE, E.

200474   SOLD TO THE SULTAN, A ROMANCE OF ABDUL
HAMID'S HAREM. London: E. Nash, 1913 NUC BMC.

DELF, T. W. H.

200475   THE MAN IN THE CHECK SUIT: A NOVEL.
London: Jarrold, 1897 BMC.

ACAD 53:93. According to publisher will appeal to male
readers because love plays a small part. Provincial
humours, punishment of fraud, and the restitution of
rights.

DE LONE, C.

200476   PETROVICH'S REVENGE; AN AWFUL EXPERIENCE.
London: Greening, 1909 BMC.

Story of two anarchists and their love for La Rose.
TLS

DELTA [pseud.].

200477   CONJUGAL AMENITIES. BY DELTA. New York:
A. E. Cluett, 1896 NUC.

LW 27:202. Vulgar. English countess behaving in such a
way that is just short of the divorce court. Husband
accepts her follies.

DEMAGE, G.

200478   A PLUNGE INTO THE SAHARA: AN ADVENTURE OF
TO-DAY. London: S. Low, Marston, 1894 BMC.

SP 73:818. French hero wants to see something of the
world. Goes to Algeria; his camel runs away with him.
Is captured by a gorilla.

DENE, NOEL.

200479   THE AFTERMATH. London: Hurst and
Blackett, 1892 BMC NUC.

SP "The style of the lady who calls herself 'Noel
Dene." Story of a married couple who are separated for
years by machinations of temptress to husband.
Reviewer is grateful wife did not become reconciled
immediately but gave her husband "a few bad
half-hours" when they are finally brought together.
ACAD 41:178. Annette, the temptress, is "a kind of Dr.
Jekyll and Mr. Hyde in petticoats." Reforms during
illness. She seems to be more of a trouble maker than
temptress.

200480   HETTY'S HERITAGE. London: Hurst and
Blackett, 1894 BMC.

Louise Keeper's niece is really a gentleman's daughter
and great heiress. SP 74:28

DENE, STAZEL.

200481   THE GORTCHEN: A TALE OF ARRAN GLEN.
London: Digby, Long, 1898 BMC.

ACAD 55:480. Irish. Dialect.

DENNY, J. K. H.

200482   CHRISTINA'S STORY. London: Jarrold, 1896
BMC.

SR-Self-righteous heroine's heart softened toward
father and lover by a serious illness and a railway
accident. Ends with wedding bells.

DE O., A.

200483   INDISCRETIONS OF DR. CARSTAIRS. BY A. DE
O. London: W. Heinemann, 1913 BMC NUC.

A woman's doctor and his casebook. This suggested in
Prologue. The Book itself deals with gentle stories of
life. SP

DERENDON, E. B.

200484   SCHOOL FOR LOVERS. London: S. Paul,
[1915] BMC.

DERVILLE, LESLIE. Nationality Unknown.

200485   THE OTHER SIDE OF THE STORY. A NOVEL. New
York: G. W. Dillingham, [1904] NUC. London: T. F.
Unwin, 1904 BMC.

PW Two girls in Washington.
NYT-Young woman government clerk in DC finally commits
suicide in face of discrimination, male supervisor's
attitudes, etc.

DE SILVA, A.

200486   RAINBOW LIGHTS. BEING EXTRACTS FROM THE
MISSIVES OF IRIS. EDITED BY A. DE SILVA. London:
Duckworth, 1913 BMC.

DE TASSINARI, B. D.

200487   AN ITALIAN FORTUNE-HUNTER. London: Ward,
Lock, [1898] BMC.

DEVAURIARD, G.

200488   THE HOUSE OF THE MAJORITY. London:
Everett, [1909] BMC.

200489   THE LILY AND THE ROSE. London: A. Rivers,
1914 BMC.

TLS-Relationship between Lesbia, a vulgar flamboyant
woman who at time of story has turned her home into a
gambling den, Eunice her unwanted daughter who has
lived with an aunt who has just died, and the men who
are attracted to Lesbia.

200490   MATED IN SOUL. London: Hurst & Blackett,
1912 BMC.

TLS- Alison, married to a rich bully meets her
soul-mate. Leaves husband who almost runs down that
man in moter car. Unpleasing question of paternity of
her child which "concerns the physiologist rather than
the novelist."
ATH- A symp. st of a sensitive highly strung woman.
Purpose of book is marriage reform.

200491   THE SIBYL OF BOND STREET. London:
Everett, 1907 BMC.

Adventuress transforms lives of three elderly female
cousins. TLS

DEVENISH, E. M.

200492   THE WANDERING OF JOYCE. London:
Duckworth, 1905 BMC.

Daughter of a Spanish dancer, hard, insensitive, tells
lies, accepts money from men. She's wandering in
search of the man she loves-he deserted his wife;
she's his lover. He disappeared in a storm. After 7
years the man's wife remarries. Joyce buys a ring and
calls herself Mrs. Her travels in the US. ACAD 1107,05
Story of mystery and Joyce's wanderings to find a
husband who disappeared. no promise. ATH 05,794

DICK, MR. [pseud.].

200493   JAMES INGLETON: THE HISTORY OF A SOCIAL
STATE, A. D. 2000. BY MR. DICK. London: Blackwood,
[1893] BMC.

DICKSON, CAPERS. United States.

200494   JOHN ASHTON: A STORY OF THE WAR BETWEEN
THE STATES. Atlanta, Ga.: Foote & Davis, 1896 NUC.

DICKSON, F. THORALD AND MARY PECHELL.

200495   A RULER OF IND. London: Digby, Long,
[1895] BMC.

SR 81:82. Heroine has a touch of the "new woman";
marries badly. Anglo-Indian life, restless wives.
Short stories?

DIXON, ROYAL ABSALOM. B. 1885. United States.

200496   SIGNS IS SIGNS. Philadelphia: G. W.
Jacobs, [1915] NUC.

Black "mammy" humor 10-9-15 PW

DONALDSON, MARION C. United States.

200497   MARGUERITE'S MISTAKE: A NOVEL. Chicago:
E. A. Weeks, [c1899] W.

DONNISON, A.

200498   WINNING A WIFE IN AUSTRALIA: A STORY
DRAWN FORM ACTUAL EXPERIENCES AND ILLUSTRATIVE OF LIFE
IN THE PRESENT DAY IN THE ANTIPODES. London: Ward,
Lock and Bowden, [1894] BMC NUC.

ATH 104:187. One man and a number of women to choose
from.

DOON, E. L.

200499   JOAN'S GREEN YEAR. LETTERS FROM THE MANOR
FARM TO HER BROTHER IN INDIA. London: Macmillan, 1913
BMC NUC.

LBKM-description of life in quiet Eng. farmhouse. Love
triangle.
SR 10 Jan '14 p 55. Told in a series of letters.
Several pretty love stories.
TLS Woman authoress. Sentimental.
Letters by heroine to twin brother in India. Her green
year spent in the country-many weddings, her own in
the last chapter. ATH

DORSET, G.

200500   THE CONFESSIONS OF A SUCCESSFUL WIFE.
London: W. Heinemann, 1910 BMC.

SR critic is upset about this one-esp. the language;
gives only one quote: "when we got into bed we got in
barefooted, all of us."
TLS

200501   A SUCCESSFUL WIFE. A STORY. New York and
London: Harper, 1910 NUC.

Esther a stenographer brings up three brothers and
sisters. Marries an eccentric genius who drinks. She
leaves him. PW
BKM-no-she loves him "love earned through the sordid
side of mrg" etc.
NYT-Suffers all that a woman can suffer but never
forgets he is a gentleman! Her unfailing
remedies-silence & sympathy.

DOTHIE, W. P.

200502   PAUL THE OPTIMIST. London: J. Long, 1900
BMC.

LBKM 18:127. Cheerful hero, sensational adventures,
sentiment.
ACAD 58:490. Dickensian. Twist Bros. Clothiers his
employer.

DOUBLEDAY, E. STILLMAN. United States.

200503   JUST PLAIN FOLKS: A STORY OF "LOST
OPPORTUNITIES". Boston: Arena, 1894 NUC.

PW-deal with social problems of capital and labor,
crime and immorality, supply and demand, justice and
charity. Moral is love thy neighbor as thyself.

DOWNE, WALMER.

200504   THE BLOOM OF THE FADED YEARS. Greenock:
J. M'Kelvie, 1896 BMC.

200505   BY SHAMROCK AND HEATHER. London: Digby,
Long, 1898 BMC.

ACAD 54:33. Irish girl, Scotch hero, their love story.

200506   CELESTE: A STORY OF THE SOUTHERNERS.
London: C. A. Pearson, 1900 BMC.

SP 85:19. American Southerners in Scotland, also
southern U.S.
SR 89:566. Interest centered on Euphemia, a New
England spinster, and Stephanotis, a quadroon.
ACAD 58:292. "Celeste graced with her nameless charm
of manner, circumstances which would have made men
harsh or sour for life." Post Civil War, pinch of
poverty in southern families.

200507   THE DANE'S DAUGHTER: AN ICELANDIC STORY.
London: C. A. Pearson, 1902 BMC.

DOYLE, LYNN, pseud. See MONTGOMERY, LESLIE ALEXANDER.

DUDBROKE, M.

200508   THE PROTS. A WEIRD ROMANCE. London: S. H.
Bousfield, [1903] BMC.

DUNSTON, W. E.

200509   THE BOOKMAKER'S TIP, OR, A ROMANCE OF THE
LINCOLNSHIRE HANDICAP. London: Diprose and Bateman,
[1899] BMC.

DURHAM, E.

200510   BURENE. A ROMANCE OF ANCIENT BRITAIN.
London: H. J. Drane, [1912] BMC.

DUSSERRE, ANTONIN.

200511   JEAN AND LOUISE. A STORY OF AUVERGNE.
London: Chapman and Hall, 1913 NUC BMC. (Includes
portrait of A. Dusserre.   Trans. from French by
John N. Raphael)

DUVAL, G. R. United States.

200512   WRITTEN IN THE SAND. London: W. J.
Ham-Smith, 1912 BMC. Philadelphia: J. C. Winston, 1913
NUC.

ATH-immoral lady of the desert loses her restraint in
Paris.
TLS-when pair return to Paris things do not go well.

E. [pseud.].

200513   PEGGY'S DECISION. London: Simpkin,
Marshall, 1897 BMC.

Engaged to one man, falls in love with another, sticks
to number 1. SR 84:528.

EAST, H. CLAYTON.

200514   THE BREATH OF THE DESERT. London:
Duckworth, 1911 BMC.

LBKM-triangle
Two married sisters in Egypt and how one of them
"almost goes wrong". TLS

EAVES, WOODHOUSE, pseud. See COOKE, W. BOURNE.

ECCOTT, W. J. United Kingdom.

200515   THE BACKGROUND. Edinburgh and London: W.
Blackwood, 1909 BMC.

Husband dies in fire, wife remarries. TLS
becomes a successful novelist. Keeps her anonymity
even from husband. First husband returns but
preferring a woman who looks much like his iwfe,
leaves the original wife to her husband-(divorces her)
ATH

200516   A DEMOISELLE OF FRANCE. London: W.
Blackwood, 1910 BMC.

BM-historical-Louis XIV
ATH-historical-Louis XIV

200517   FORTUNE'S CASTAWAY; A HISTORICAL ROMANCE.
London, Edinburgh: W. Blackwood, 1904 BMC NUC.

TLS-historical - Monmouth's Rebellion

200518   THE HEARTH OF HUTTON. Edinburgh: W.
Blackwood, 1906 BMC.

ACAD-historical romance.
TLS-historical unhappy marriage-separation,
reconciliation.
ATH-conv.

200519   HIS INDOLENCE OF ARRAS. Edinburgh: W.
Blackwood, 1905 BMC.

historical romance-ATH 15:860.

200520   THE MERCENARY. A TALE OF THE THIRTY
YEARS' WAR. London: W. Blackwood, 1913 BMC.

The 30 year war, RC Scottish captain is hero; also
involves a courtship. LBKM

200521   THE RED NEIGHBOR. Edinburgh: W.
Blackwood, 1908 BMC.

    SR-slight romance.
    ATH-The character of the title a woman of the people
    who has made a fortune in cosmetics and great ladies'
    confidences gets revenge.

200522   THE SECOND CITY. Edinburgh: W. Blackwood,
1912 BMC.

    ATH-male ch's
    TLS-male ch's

200523   THE SINGER. Edinburgh and London: W.
Blackwood, 1918 BMC NUC.

    TLS-war-Germans

ECLIPSE [pseud.].

200524   UPS AND DOWNS OF AN OLD TAR'S LIFE. BY
'ECLIPSE'. London: Digby, Long, 1891 BMC.

EDGE, J. HAROLD.

200525   KEEN'S DOMESTICS. A NOVEL OF TO-DAY.
London: Simpkin, Marshall, 1911 BMC.

    Novel of modern life, love, flirtation and business.
    ATH

EDWARDS, R. W. K.

200526   THE MERMAID OF INISH-UIG. London: E.
Arnold, 1898 BMC.

    SP 80:630. Donegal. An orphaned peasant maid,
    abandoned by her lover and shunned by her neighbors,
    brings up her child in a seals' cave. The child,
    amphibious, is one day cut off from her mother by
    falling rocks, and she lives henceforth with the seals
    until she is mistaken for one by an islander and falls
    victim to his gun. Minutely circumstantial narrative
    given in the diary of the lighthousekeeper, the dupe
    of Black Kate's betrayer; reveals a sense of humor.
    LIT 2:536. Fantasy.

EGLANTINE, E.

200527   ROMANCES. London: J. Macqueen, 1898 BMC.

ELDORADO [pseud.].

200528   A SOUL'S PROGRESS. BY ELDORADO. London:
Gay & Hancock, 1915 BMC.

ELDRIDGE, ROBEY FRANK.

200529   THE KESTYNS OF CATHER CASTLE: A NOVEL.
London: Digby, Long, [1897] BMC.

200530   THE SCHEMING OF AGATHA KENWICK. London:
Sonnenschein, 1899 BMC.

    She is a flirt, a free thinker, a woman who hides her
    history according to one character in the novel. She's
    an adventuress who plots revenge against the man who
    didn't return her love by planning a marriage for him
    that will make him miserable. ACAD 56:486.

ELI, HON. BELL, pseud. See SMITH, H. H.

ELLISON, GRACE, jt. au. See HANOUM, MELEK AND GRACE
ELLISON.

ELSON, F. S.

200531   FATHER PREMPEY, PRIEST AND PLOTTER.
London: Simpkin, Marshall, Hamilton, Kent, [1918] BMC
NUC.

    TLS Male hero

EMERSON, EVALYN. Nationality Unknown.

200532   SYLVIA, THE STORY OF AN AMERICAN
COUNTESS. Boston: Small, Maynard, 1901 BMC NUC.

    Review not helpful; about the illustrations. 10-19-01
    PW

EREMUS [pseud.].

200533   PANTA RYE: A PRELUDE. BY EREMUS AND

ANOTHER. London: S. Sonnenschein, 1894 BMC.

    SR-humorous story somewhat modelled on Lewis Carroll.
    ACAD 46:190. Muddled and clever. Undergraduate mind.
    Male hero.

ETBERG, H. M. United Kingdom.

200534   JACQUELINE OF GOLDEN RIVER. Garden City,
New York: Doubleday, Page, 1920 NUC.

    PW Myst.

EVANS, HOWEL. United Kingdom.

200535   A GIRL ALONE. London: G. Richards, 1917
BMC. New York and London: G. P. Putnam's Sons, 1918
NUC.

    LBKM-In London, extreme misery and poverty.
    Ellice Mayne, she's Australian, comes to England to
    establish her claim to money and lands. Fails to do
    so. Thrown on own resources: "terrible picture of
    sweated work in a sweated industry." TLS
    "Realism that does not shrink from vulgar, harrowing
    or repulsive subjects." BAKER

200536   A LITTLE WELSH GIRL. London, New York:
Hodder and Stoughton, 1918 NUC BMC.

EVELYN, J., pseud. See BOWEN, E. J.

EVILL, A. M.

200537   THE THREE DREAMS. London: Eden,
Remington, 1891 BMC.

FAGAN, T. A. United States.

200538   UNCLE JIM, A MODERN ROMAN. BY LEON SULE.
Caldwell, Texas: E. P. Hutchings, 1893 NUC.

FAIRFAX, G. V.

200539   THE WORKING-DAY WORLD; OR THE STRONGER
PORTION OF HUMANITY. London: Digby, [1893] BMC.

    "A spirited intellectually audacious young woman...who
    is mad on Women's Rights." She's Madge Merton.
    Includes a murder and the solving of it by the accused
    man's wife. ACAD 43:56

FARNESE, A.

200540   A WANDERER IN THE SPIRIT LANDS. BY
FRANCHEZZO, TRANSCRIBED BY A.FARNESE. London: W. J.
Sinkins, 1896 BMC.

FARRAR, W. H.

200541   THREE LIVES AND A LOVE. London: H. J.
Drane, [1904] BMC.

    LBKM-O

FARROW, A. M. L.

200542   HELICE'S HERITAGE; OR, THE LINKS OF LIFE.
London: Jarrold, 1896 BMC.

FENNELL, CHARLOTTE AND J. P. O'CALLAGHAN.

200543   A PRINCE OF TYRONE. Edinburgh: W.
Blackwood, 1897 BMC NUC. (NUC: O'CALLAHAN.)

    Irish hist novel. Shane ONeill. ACAD 51:472

FERGUSON, V. MUNRO.

200544   BETSY. BY V. London: Osgood & McIlvaine,
1892 BMC.

    ATH 99:663. Girls story.

200545   LIFE AGAIN, LOVE AGAIN. London: Hurst and
Blackett, 1897 BMC.

200546   MUSIC HATH CHARMS: A NOVEL. BY V. MUNRO
FERGUSON ("V."). New York: Harper, 1894 NUC.

    ATH 104:564. Reviewer refers to her as Miss. Modern
    temperaments in the intellectual society of today.
    Heroine is charmingly candid.
    LW 25:281. Victoria and Dawnay, she a famous singer,
    both selfish, but she captivating, struggle for power
    in their relationship, last chapter morbid and

sensational.

FERNIVAL, C. C.

200547   THE FASCINATING MISS LAMARCHE. London: A.
P. Marsden, 1894 BMC.

ATH 100:349. Former chorus-singer and fascination she
caused. The turf is the principle arena.
ACAD-swindling in its various phases, shady side of
racing.

FETHERSTONHAUGH, V.

200548   MRS. JIM BAKER AND FROSTS OF JUNE.
London: Chapman and Hall, 1899 BMC.

1-Canadian Great N.W. Mrs. Jim was raised by her
father as much as a boy as possible "With the express
purpose of unfitting her for a woman's natural
duties." LIT 5:160
1-Also set in England, Riviera. Mrs. Jim almost forced
to run away with an odious man. 2-Attractive heroine.
SP 83:95
Her mother raised her as a boy "to be so unfitted for
a woman's natural duties...that she might thus escape
marriage." ACAD 57:16
By this upbringing, she is not "therefore, rendered
more perverse than the ordinary young woman of
fiction, whose mission is to make her husband
miserable, and then repent and reform. This particular
young woman's adventures are very brightly written."
LIT 5:160

200549   A YOUNGER SON. London: Downey, 1901 BMC.

FETTERLESS, ARTHUR, pseud. See MACKENZIE, E. V. G.

FIELDING, SYDNEY G.

200550   THE SOUTHERN LIGHT. London: Ward, Lock
and Bowden, 1895 NUC.

FIFINE [pseud.].

200551   MAMZELLE GRANDMERE: A FRIVOLITY. BY
FIFINE. London: Lawrence and Bullen, 1899 BMC NUC.

She is an adult young woman of at least 50 who is a
serious rival of her beautiful grand-daughter. Two
weddings at the end. SR 87:56
SP 81:745. Sprightly, impecunious and irresponsible
grandmother.
LBKM 15:87. She is something of an adventurer, does
not pay her bills, etc.

FIGGIS, DARRELL. 1882-1925. United Kingdom.

200552   BROKEN ARCS. London: Dents, 1911 BMC. New
York and London: M. Kennerley, 1912 NUC.

200553   CHILDREN OF EARTH. Dublin and London:
Maunsel, 1918 NUC BMC.

Fic-Irish

200554   JACOB ELTHORNE. A CHRONICLE OF LIFE.
London and Toronto: J. M. Dent, 1914 NUC BMC.

LBKM - chronicle of a life in pursuit of high ideals.
Conflict in marriage over his ideals.

FILDES, H. G.

200555   "TRIM" AND ANTRIM'S STORIES. London:
Greening, 1904 BMC.

BKM - Irish travel.

FINLASON, C. E.

200556   A NOBODY IN MASHONALAND; OR, THE TRIALS
AND ADVENTURES OF A TENDERFOOT. London: G. Vickers,
1895 BMC NUC.

FISHER, F. W. A.

200557   ON DESPERATE SEAS. London: Everett, 1910
BMC.

TLS-sea story.

FLANEUSE [pseud.].

200558   ACCORDING TO ST. PAUL. BY FLANEUSE.
London: A. M. Gardner, [1913] BMC.

200559   BLUE BEAUTY. BY FLANEUSE. London: A. M.
Gardner, [1913] BMC.

200560   THE CHAIN. BY FLANEUSE. London: A. M.
Gardner, [1913] BMC.

200561   CHAOS. BY FLANEUSE. London: A. M.
Gardner, [1913] BMC.

200562   DOUBLY TIED. A FARCE. BY FLANEUSE.
London: Greening, [1913] BMC NUC.

Author states she's intentionally funny. We're meant
to roar over this work. Molly-audacious ex-barmaid,
her successful bigamy to millionaire while her husband
becomes the millionaire's valet and heir. TLS

200563   A FALLEN STAR. BY FLANEUSE. London: A. M.
Gardner, [1913] BMC.

200564   THE GAME OF GOODNESS. BY FLANEUSE.
London: A. M. Gardner, [1913] BMC.

200565   THE GRIP. BY FLANEUSE. London: A. M.
Gardner, [1913] BMC.

200566   GUILTY SPLENDOUR. BY FLANEUSE. London: C.
W. White, [1910] BMC.

200567   MY HUSBAND; OR, THE LINK. BY FLANEUSE.
London: A. M. Gardner, 1913 BMC.

200568   PERIL'S PATHWAY. BY FLANEUSE. London: A.
M. Gardner, [1913] BMC.

200569   SCORED! BY FLANEUSE. London: A. M.
Gardner, [1913] BMC.

200570   THE SHADOW. BY FLANEUSE. London: A. M.
Gardner, [1913] BMC.

200571   THE TRIUMPHANT WOMAN. BY FLANEUSE.
London: Odhams, [1918] BMC.

200572   THE YELLOW FAIRY. BY FLANEUSE. London: A.
M. Gardner, [1913] BMC.

FLETCHER, COYNE. United States.

200573   THE BACHELOR'S BABY. New York: Clark &
Zugalla, 1891 NUC.

FLOWER, SYDNEY BLANCHARD. B. 1867. United States.

200574   A STUDY IN HYPNOTISM. Chicago: The
Psychic Pub. Co., 1896 NUC.

FLOWERDEW [pseud.].

200575   THE SEVENTH POSTCARD. BY FLOWERDEW.
London: Greening, 1914 BMC.

Heroine gets the postcard-from league of Personal
Safety a group who kill offenders of motor accidents
who are acquitted. She's a successful writer of
detective stories. Sets to work to unmask the league.
ATH
ATH-Detective story. Society who punished by death any
motorist who, altho acquitted in court, had taken
human life.

FLOWERS, N. CLEONA. United States.

200576   THE END OF A SKEIN: A NOVEL. Washington,
D.C.: Hartman and Cadick, 1896 NUC.

FLOYER, A. M.

200577   ENVIRONMENT. London: J. Long, 1914 BMC.

ATH Illustrates influence of environment on character.
TLS Interesting characters in small village.

FOGERTY, J.

200578   A HUNTED LIFE: AN EPISODE. London:
Hutchinson, 1894 BMC NUC.

SR 78:129. Male hero, man wrongly accused of crime,
hiding out in West Ireland.

200579   JUANITA: A NOVEL. London: Ward and
Downey, 1893 BMC.

Her adventures and those of a sailor on the islands of

Galway Bay and then from Ireland to foreign seas. SR
76:389.
The love of Juanita and George Morony-interrupted by a
search and capture of a smuggler. ACAD 44:3 64.
The Irish-Span heroine- her life. ATH 102:352.

200580   MR. JOCKO: A NOVEL. London: Ward and
Downey, 1891 BMC.

    Hero is an ape-circus variety. BAKER 03:107.
SP 68:470. Mr Jocho is an ape, his friend is Betsy.
Novel consists of three unrelated stories; the second
two concern male heroes. All are attacks on religion.

200581   RACHEL'S ROMANCE; OR THE COUNTESS OTTO.
London: Diprose and Bateman, [1894] BMC.

FOLDAIROLLES, CLAIRE [pseud.].

200582   PRIVATE LETTERS OF A FRENCH WOMAN. BY
MADEMOISELLE CLAIRE FOLDAIROLLES (THE FRENCH
GOVERNESS). New York: G. W. Dillingham, 1895 NUC.

    Subjects: "Will the kiss become obsolete" "the woman's
man" "Professional love makers." "elimination of the
Old Maid from Amer. Soc." -among others. PW
6-22-95:967

FOLL, HATTIL EDWARD.

200583   MAJOR CARLILE. London: Digby, Long, 1897
BMC.

200584   A PRODIGAL DAUGHTER: A CHRONICLE OF
MARLSHIRE. London: J. M. Dent, 1912 BMC NUC.

FORBES, A. K. H.

200585   MARGARET SPENCE'S STORIES OF THE GARNOCK
FOLK AND THE CLOCKIN' HEN INN. Glasgow: T. P. Morison,
1892 BMC.

    Short stories

FORBES, G. A. GRANT.

200586   ANOTHER WICKED WOMAN. London: T. Fisher
Unwin Autonym Library, 1895 BMC NUC.

FORBES, HAY.

200587   A DETECTIVE IN ITALY; OR THE MYSTERY OF
BERWYN KENNEDY. London and New York: Ward, Lock,
[1891] BMC NUC.

FOSKETT, S.

200588   THE TEMPLE IN THE TOPE. London: Hodder &
Stoughton, [1915] BMC.

FOSTER, J. MONK.

200589   PASSION'S AFTERMATH: A DRAMATIC STORY.
London: Digby, Long, 1892 BMC.

FOX, C. S. LAMB.

200590   FAITHFUL TO THE LAST: A NOVEL. London:
Digby, Long, [1892] BMC.

FOY, SLIEVE.

200591   AN UNNATURAL MOTHER. A NEW STORY. London:
Lynwood, 1911 BMC.

    She's a "selfish designing woman of the world who
compromises her daughter's honour in the effort to
advance her own interest. " pov? ATH

FRANCES [pseud.].

200592   WITH THE CHURCH IN AN EARLY DAY. BY
FRANCES. Lamoni Iowa,: Herald, 1891 NUC.

FRANCHEZZO, pseud. See FARNESE, A.

FRANCIS, C. E. [pseud.]. Nationality Unknown.

200593   EVERY DAY'S NEWS. BY C. E. FRANCIS. New
York: G. P. Putman, 1895 NUC. London: T. F. Unwin,
1895 BMC NUC.

    writer "who works under influence of a high standard
marrying another writer of the std. which is a product
of our fin de siecle-the std. of shallow smartness,
sensation and a frankness which borders on indecency

and sometimes overleaps the border." The marr. is not
a success. LW:26:218
Variant on George Manderville's Husband. Hero, a pure
minded novelist marries a New woman and "she writes
rude stories and makes him blush dreadfully." SR
79:661

FRANCIS, J.

200594   ARCHIE CAREW. London: Ward and Downey,
1892 BMC.

    SR 74:624. When young wife discovers husband has not
properly married her because he has not wanted family
and friends to know he has married a farmer's
daughter, she leaves him.
Young man of good family marries a woman of lower
social class. They married as minors under assumed
names and misrepresented their ages as over 21. ACAD
43:32
Wales: Mary Grey, Archie, and Laura Dyneley are the
characters. The first two are the ones who marry. Mary
is self-sacrificing
ATH 101, 14

FRANKEL, A. H.

200595   IN GOLD WE TRUST. Philadelphia: W. H.
Pile's Sons, 1898 NUC.

    LW 29:268. "Repellant and needlessly brutal
characters," their greed caused by animal flesh.
Climax ends in establishment of cooperative vegetarian
community. Rev. does not mention the ghetto.

FRANKISH, H.

200596   DR. CUNLIFFE--INVESTIGATOR. London:
Heath, Cranton, [1913] BMC.

    Detective stories; half a dozen or so murders in each
tale. ATH.

FRASER, A. KEITH. See FRASER, AYLMER KEITH.

FRASER, AYLMER KEITH. United Kingdom.

200597   A GARDEN OF SPICES. BY A. KEITH FRASER.
London, New York: Hodder & Stoughton, [1913] BMC NUC.

    PW 8/16/17 459 "Elspeth is a little Scotch girl, whose
mother died at her birth, and whose father,
grandfather, and bachelor great-uncle, known as the
Laird, are all her willing and devoted slaves.
Counteracting their influence is the severity of her
nurse, whose stern Scotch Calvinism never allows her
to err on the side of indulgence. Elspeth calls her
the Dragon. The little girl's thoughts and deeds,
sometimes good, often naughty, are recorded in this
book about a child, for grown-ups."

FRAZEE, THEO D.

200598   THE FARMER'S NIECE: A ROMANCE OF THE
MEXICAN WAR. Newark, N.J.: Heinz Print. Co., 1892 NUC.

FREDERICK, LEMIRA [pseud.]. Nationality Unknown.

200599   HIS OWN ESTATE. BY LEMIRA FREDERICK. New
York: Cochrane, 1911 NUC.

FREESTONE, SAIE.

200600   THE REPENTANCE OF CYPUS KEEN. London: H.
J. Drane, [1912] BMC.

    ATH-too awful to mention.

FREMDLING, A.

200601   FATHER CLANCY. London: Duckworth, 1904
BMC.

FUTABATEI. See HASEGAWA, TATSUNOSUKE.

G., M. A. [pseud.]. United Kingdom.

200602   JEANNE: THE STORY OF A FRESH AIR CHILD.
BY M. A. G. Albany, N.Y.: Brandow Printing, 1893 NUC.

GALIER, W. H.

200603   A VISIT TO BLESTLAND. London: Gay and
Bird, 1896 BMC.

GALL, W. B. HOME.

200604 WHERE HONOUR SITS: A TALE OF THE DESERT
MARCH, EGYPT 1884-5. London: Digby, Long, [1892] BMC.

ATH 100:221. "Love, war, and the choice,"
"uncompromisingly British." "tedious"

GARDINER, F. C.

200605 DIVIDED HOUSES. London: J. Long, 1909
BMC.

Humdrum tale of village loves TLS

GARRY, A. Nationality Unknown.

200606 OUT OF BOUNDS: BEING THE ADVENTURES OF AN
UNADVENTUROUS YOUNG MAN. London: Hutchinson, [1896]
BMC. New York: H. Holt, 1896 NUC.

SR Revolt of model young man; joins in festivities of
fair and dancing with Arabella.
LW 27:330. 3 days in life of heir betrothed to
strong-minded heiress. Lands in unexpected bliss "off
the beaten path of prosperity." "Fresh and merry
quality."

GATES, LOU. United States.

200607 A HELL AND HEAVEN TO EVEN UP. Atlanta:
1897 NUC.

GAVF, EMMA [pseud.]. Nationality Unknown.

200608 A COMEDY OF CIRCUMSTANCES. BY EMMA GAVF.
Garden City, N.Y.: Doubleday, Page, 1911 NUC. London:
Hodder & Stoughton, 1911 BMC.

Two "girls" two men and lots of mixups. PW 4-29-11

GEM [pseud.].

200609 A FATAL STEP. BY 'GEM'. London: T. F.
Unwin, 1895 BMC.

The fatal step may be Ethel's marriage to Lt.
Dudley-it is the cause of several other fatal steps:
her flirtation with Gerald Dudley, the near murder of
the Lt., Gerald's own death, Lt. Dudley's madness.
ACAD 48:7

GIFFORD, EVELYN.

200610 PROVEMZANO THE PROUD. London: Smith,
Elder, 1904 BMC.

LBKM historical novel.

GIFFORD, J. WEAR.

200611 LURE OF CONTRABAND. A TALE OF OLD
APPLEDORE. London: Jarrolds, [1920] BMC.

TLS-Smuggling.

GILLIE, E. A.

200612 JEHANNE: A ROMANCE OF MODERN NORMANDY.
London: Isbister, 1905 BMC.

Story of a priest who falls in love with Jehanne LBKM
27-8, 68

GILLIES, E. SCOTT.

200613 THE RED WEDDING. London: J. Long, 1914
BMC.

200614 THE SHADOW OF THE GUILLOTINE. London: J.
Long, 1911 BMC.

200615 A SPARK ON STEEL. London: J. Long, 1912
BMC.

Young woman with a love on one side of Franco-German
war, and one on other. ATH

GILPIN, W. B.

200616 LOVE, SPORT AND A DOUBLE EVENT. London:
Leadenhall Press, 1900 BMC.

GLADSTONE, L.

200617 NEIL MACLEOD: A TALE OF LITERARY LIFE IN
LONDON. London: Hodder and Stoughton, 1898 BMC.

SP 81:781. Young artist in London by means of
anonymous benefactor; his experiences there. When he
learns benefactor is man who betrayed his mother and
father, he returns to country and repays money.
ACAD 55:516.

GLENNON, M. J. United States.

200618 BOOMVILLE: A TALE OF WESTERN MINNESOTA.
Minneapolis: L. Kimball Print. Co., 1891 NUC.

GOODMAN, G. S.

200619 THE MYSTERIOUS ABDUCTION. London:
Greening, 1908 BMC.

TLS-1770, Austria, mystery and adventure.

GOOLSBY, C. V., jt. au. See MILLER, L. A. AND C. V.
GOOLSBY.

GORDON, C. I. United States.

200620 THE BANKRUPT'S SON: A TALE OF THE PANIC
OF '73. Denver, Colo.: G. M. Collier, 1892 NUC.

GORDON, V. CONWAY.

200621 THE CELIBACY OF MARCUS KANE. London:
Holden and Hardingham, [1914] BMC.

Illegitimate boy raised in Anglican monastic
community. Before he takes his vows, learns his birth,
leaves the monastary, falls in love, happy ending. ATH

GRACE, ARMINE.

200622 THE CLOAK OF ST. MARTIN. London: S. Paul,
1913 BMC.

Gambling, murder, execution of innocent man. Hero is a
wealthy barrister learns he's responsible for innocent
man's death devotes life to his (the man's) children.
LBKM

200623 THE HOUSE OF SILENT FOOTSTEPS. London: S.
Paul, 1917 BMC.

TLS-Thieves and male hero.

GRAHAM, FAIRLIE.

200624 A DREAM AND A FORGETTING. London: Digby,
Long, [1893] BMC.

GRANDAGE, E.

200625 THE STORY OF A MONKEY: A RETROSPECT.
BEING AN ACTOR'S ROMANCE TOLD BY E. GRANDAGE. London:
Digby, Long, [1891] BMC NUC.

GRANHIM, CARADOC.

200626 LIFE'S TAPESTRY; OR HOMES AND HEARTHS.
London: Ward and Downey, 1893 BMC.

GRANVILLE, AUSTYN. United States.

200627 THE FALLEN RACE. New York: F. T. Neely,
1892 [c] NUC BMC.

An expedition to center of Australia, Dr Paul Gifford
comes upon the fabled "Fallen Race" The Anonos-who
appear like huge balls covered with hair and small
paws-feet. The Great white Queen rules over them. PW
3-18-93

200628 THE SHADOW OF SHAME. Chicago: C. H.
Sergel, [1891] NUC.

PW-Historical romance, plot against the heroine at
time of Franco-Prussian war.

GRAY, J. J. United States.

200629 RECLAIMED; OR THE MOUNTAIN CASTLE
MYSTERY; AN INTERNATIONAL ROMANCE. New York: Broadway,
[c1907] NUC.

PW-murder mystery.

GRAYDON, J. FARRER. Nationality Unknown.

200630 THE GERMAN BRACELET. New York: Neale,
1908 NUC.

Adventure story of a thief. PW 1-23-09

GREENLEE, W. M. United States.

200631   "SPES" IN THE SHADOW OF THE ALHAMBRA; OR,
THE LAST OF THE MOORISH KINGS. Knoxville, Tenn.: S. B.
Newman, 1893 NUC.

GREGORY, C. OLYNTHUS.

200632   THE SULTAN'S MANDATE: AN ARMENIAN
ROMANCE. London: T. F. Unwin, 1898 BMC.

SP 31:531. Armenian romance by an Armenian writer.
Also portrait of Armenia.
ACAD 55:29. Also Armenian atrocities.

GREGORY, SACHA [pseud.]. United Kingdom.

200633   YELLOWLEAF. BY SACHA GREGORY. London: W.
Heinemann, 1919 NUC BMC. Philadelphia: J.B.
Lippincott, 1919 NUC.

Battle of wills-man, wife, mother-in law TLS
Pleasure house in No. suburbs-wonderful old lady.
Italian butler SP
Mod. Lond. Social life PW
Effect of a villainous man on a boy and passive
woman-"early Victorian" types little plot people talk
PW BKM REV
Lady Mary Dampiere, invalid chatelaine of luxurious
home-"yellowleaf" in London; her daughter in law Lila
now a widow has a difficult life with her new husband
a pianist. When Lady Mary dies we learn from her
letter that she killed the pianist. (he was the
caveman type) with her heart medicine. NYT 11-16-19
665

GRESSON, R. SHELTON.

200634   THE STRANGE ADVENTURES OF ANELAY
MORELAND: A STORY IN THREE PARTS. London and Sydney:
Remington, 1893 BMC.

GRIFFITH, W. C. United States.

200635   GIFTS WITHOUT GRACES; OR, LIFE AT
POWHATAN. Hagerstown [Md.]: Morning News Print, 1895
NUC.

GRIFFITHS, D. RYLES.

200636   ELGIVA, DAUGHTER OF THE THEGN. London: T.
F. Unwin, 1901 BMC.

GRIGSBY, ALCANOAN O. United States.

200637   NEQUA; OR, THE PROBLEM OF THE AGES. BY
JACK ADAMS. Topeka, Kansas: Equity, 1900 NUC.

GROOMSMITH, A. W.

200638   TO PLEASE A WOMAN: A NOVEL. London: C.
Danvers, 1902 BMC.

GRYN, ELLOVA [pseud.].

200639   TOO WEAK. BY ELLOVA GRYN. London:
Craddock, [1907] BMC.

GUIMARAENS, M. P.

200640   PORTUGUESE RITA. Digby, Long, [1897] BMC.

H., F. [pseud.].

200641   A WOMAN. London: Greening, 1906 BMC.
(Preface signed: F. H.)

200642   THE WOODEN SPOON. BY F. H. London:
Headley, [1913] BMC.

H., M. C. [pseud.].

200643   THE KNIGHT OF SNOWDON; OR THE SAXON AND
THE GAEL. BY M. C. H. Paisley: A. Gardner, 1902 BMC.

HADDON, A. L.

200644   WHAT AILS THE HOUSE? A NOVEL. London: W.
H. Allen, 1893 BMC.

Mrs. Perkins is a novelist who needs some new ideas.
Appeals to cousin Judith Minchin-a pious spinster, who
has lived in seclusion. Gets letters (love) from

Judith and weaves a story. Author makes further use of
other people she knows. Reviewer reads it as a satire
on novelist's art. ACAD 44 :128.

HAIGH, J. LOCKHART.

200645   SIR GALAHAD OF THE SLUMS. London:
Simpkin, [1907] BMC.

Minister and dockhand in slums. TLS

HALIDOM, M. Y. [pseud.].

200646   THE POET'S CURSE: A TALE. BY M. Y.
HALIDOM. London: Greening, 1911 BMC.

Humorous story of man who steals Shakespeare's Bones.
ACAD

200647   THE POISON RING. A ROMANCE. BY M. Y.
HALIDOM. London: Greening, [1912] BMC.

TLS-papal government.

200648   A SON OF DESOLATION. BY M. Y. HALIDOM.
London: Greening, 1909 BMC.

a hero and an earthquake. TLS

200649   A WEIRD TRANSFORMATION. BY M. Y. HALIDOM.
London: T. Burleigh, 1904 BMC.

ATH-crazy plot.

200650   THE WIZARD'S MANTLE. BY M. Y. HALIDOM.
London: T. Burleigh, 1903 BMC.

200651   THE WOMAN IN BLACK. BY M. Y. HALIDOM.
London: Greening, 1906 BMC.

TLS-female vampire.

200652   ZOE'S REVENGE. BY M. Y. HALIDOM. London:
Greening, 1908 BMC.

HALL, BRADNOCK [pseud.].

200653   ROUGH MISCHANCE: AN EXPLANATION. BY
BRADNOCK HALL. London: G. Routledge, [1896] BMC.

HALL, M. E.

200654   REX THE BLACK SHEEP. A NOVEL. London:
Digby, Long, 1892 BMC.

SP 69:628. High-spirited male, sinks a little, but
rises with the help of a friend.
ATH - two heroines

HALL, SYDNEY.

200655   THE TEMPTATION OF EDITH WATSON. Paisley:
A. Gardner, 1899 BMC.

Resists it. Edinburgh. SP 83:95.
Scotch. Edith's temptation was to join Davidson while
she was wed to Watson. Then husband dies and she gets
Watson. ACAD 56:684

HALLEN, A. L.

200656   ANGILIN; A VENITE KING. London: Digby,
Long, 1907 BMC.

HALLIDAY, H. CLIFFE.

200657   SOMEONE MUST SUFFER. London: Chapman and
Hall, 1891 BMC.

HALLIFAX, SYDNEY. B. 1862.

200658   ANNALS OF A DOSS HOUSE. London: G. Allen,
1900 BMC NUC.

HAMILTON, GRAMMONT.

200659   THE MAYFAIR MARRIAGE: A LONDON AND PARIS
BOOK. London: G. Richards, 1898 BMC.

HAMMOND, A.

200660   THE LADY ISABEL: A TALE OF SOCIAL LIFE IN
THE OLDEN TIME. London: E. Stock, 1899 BMC.

HANCOCK, C. L.

200661   THE DIARY OF A FLIRT. BY CLARICE
LAURENCE. London: Heath, Cranton & Ouseley, [1915]
BMC.

TLS-

HANOUM, MELEK AND GRACE ELLISON.

200662   ABDUL HAMID'S DAUGHTER. London: Methuen,
1913 BMC.

Tragedy of Imperial hostess of a harem and life at the
Ottoman court. TLS

HARDINGE, HENRY MAURICE.

200663   WHAT WE ARE COMING TO. London: Digby,
Long, 1895 BMC.

ACAD 49:218. Rev. refers to Miss or Mrs. Hardinge.
"Unhealthy"- beauty of sin, etc.

HARDY, A. S. F.

200664   PRINCESS AND PRIEST (A TALE OF OLD EGYPT)
AND MADEMOISELLE ETIENNE. London: Downey, 1895 BMC
NUC.

Princess Ita has wonderful gifts to heal people. She
does much practicing. Afterwards descends to the
ordinary life of wife and mother. Egypt. ACAD 48:144

HARGREAVES, H.

200665   THE MARTIN DEVIL. London: J. Ouseley,
[1910] BMC.

TLS-Male hero

200666   THE VICAR'S MISTAKE. London: E. Stock,
1904 BMC.

HARMONIA, jt. au.   See CADMUS [pseud.] AND HARMONIA
[pseud.].

HARRIS, J. HENRY.

200667   ESTHER'S PILGRIMAGE: NEW NOTES ON OLD
STRINGS. London: J. Macqueen, 1898 BMC.

ATH 112:198. West country life, harmless, for girls.
SR 86:448. Author says is simple story of a pilgrimage
completed before some of the restless longings of
today had taken shape in the souls of women.

200668   FAITH: A STORY OF SAINT PORTH. Truro: J.
Pollard, [1900] BMC.

200669   THE FISHERS, A NOVEL. London and New
York: J. Lane, 1904 BMC NUC.

200670   MY WIFE SAYS. London: H. J. Drane, [1912]
BMC.

TLS She is sweet and sensible.

200671   PENELOPE ANN: A CORNISH ROMANCE. London:
Greening, 1909 BMC.

200672   A ROMANCE IN RADIUM. London: Greening,
1906 BMC NUC.

200673   SAINT PORTH. London: J. Milne, 1898 BMC.

SR 85:502. Cornish village. Pretty girl sits for
artist. Runaway marriage. Tragic end. Dolly Pentreath
is very human, jilted sailor is humanly jealous,
gentleman husband is a decent fellow.

HARRIS, S. M.

200674   GRACE WARDWOOD; OR FROM THE GLOOM OF
WINTER TO THE GLORIES OF SUMMER. BY ATHENE. Dublin: J.
Duffy, 1900 BMC.

ACAD 58:126. Irish. Sentimental, wholesome.

HARRISON, F. BAYFORD.

200675   THE IDEAL ARTIST: A NOVEL. London: Hurst
and Blackett, 1893 NUC BMC.

Traditional story of Lady Flora Vere de Vere's love
for young artist and a sub-story about blackmail.

HARRISON, J. Nationality Unknown.

200676   "KIND HEARTS AND CORONETS". New York:
Benziger, 1904 NUC.

HARTLEY, L.

200677   NORAH GREY: A TALE. London: Digby and
Long, [1892] BMC.

HARTLEY, M.

200678   BEYOND MAN'S STRENGTH. London: W.
Heinemann, 1909 BMC.

200679   THE BOND OF SPORT. London: Duckworth,
1915 BMC.

200680   A SERESHAN. London: Mills & Boon, 1911
BMC NUC.

Trad hist rom. TLS

HARVEY, JULIAN.

200681   A MODERN SIREN. London: Digby, Long, 1896
BMC.

She marries a baron old enough to be her father. Then
she falls violently in love with his son who repels
his stepmother's advances. She threatens suicide; he
rushes home from Paris, occupies a secret room in the
house, there are dreadful goings on. Then baron learns
all, but is very forgiving. Siren's suicide at the
end. SR 83:23

HASEGAWA, TATSUNOSUKE. 1864-1909.

200682   AN ADOPTED HUSBAND (SONO OMOKAGE). BY
FUTABATEI. New York: A. A. Knopf, 1919 BMC NUC.
London: Hutchinson, [1920] BMC. (Tr. Buhachiro Mitsui
and Gregg M. Sinclair.)

ATH-Tetsuya rents a room for Sayo-ko and visits her
there. Part of tender, loving, relation.
"Novel of Tokyo and of a professor's affair with the
natural sister of his formidable wife." An ugly story
saved by "charm of things Japanese." BAKER 32,189
"First Japanese novel ever translated into English."
Where there is no son in a family, in order that the
name not die out, a daughter is not given in marriage
but a husband adopted for her. He is chosen when he's
very young; family pays for ed. Toki-ko has been
married to her adopted husband for 10 years. He turns
out to be a poor provider; wife and her mother turn
against him for they love luxury. Story follows the
jealousy of the wife toward her younger sister Sayoko,
the downfall of weak husband. NYT 7-20-19 373
Tetsuya Ono, a professor, his wife Toki-ko, and the
"illeg." daughter of Toki-ko's father- Sayo-ko.
Tetsuya lives miserably under domination of wife and
mother-in-law because he's a weak man. His wife exacts
more and more money from him just to waste it. They
are "horrible" women. Only Sayo-ko is kind to him,
hence the wife's jealousy. Sayo-ko then leaves-but to
live for a few days with Tetsuya. Toki-ko has brought
about the situation she wanted to avoid-loses husband.
Once she's abandoned, the author enters fully into
Toki-ko's feelings. Sayo-ko is Christian yet extremely
humble (unwestern), completely self-abnegating, a
slave. She would have killed herself but for her
Christian ideas. Novel ends unresolved. TLS 8-14-1919.

HAULTMONT, MARIE [pseud.].

200683   BY THE ROYAL ROAD. BY MARIE HAULTMONT.
Edinburgh: Sands, 1906 BMC.

Centers upon religion. TLS

200684   THE MARRIAGE OF LAURENTIA. BY MARIE
HAULTMONT. St. Louis, Mo.: B. Herder, 1901 PW. London:
Sands, 1901 BMC.

Mixed marriage. Catholic and Protestant. Discourages
such marriages. ATH 11-2-01

200685   THROUGH REFINING FIRES. BY MARIE
HAULTMONT. London: Sands, [1914] BMC.

TLS-lives of two suffering young women of middle
class-sincerity and refinement-lovemaking cut to the
smallest proportions -gray study not sentimental or
sloppy or sensational.

HAVREN [pseud.].

200686   MISS ARBUTHNOT; A NOVEL. BY HAVREN.
London: J. Long, 1910 BMC.

TLS-ideas of her own.

HAYLING, G. AND M. HAYLING.

200687   TRYFIELD. London: Hodder & Stoughton,
[1912] BMC.

ATH-story of little boy rebel.
TLS-story of little boy rebel.
SP story of little boy rebel.

HAYLING, M., jt. au. See HAYLING, G. AND M. HAYLING.

HAZARD, R. H. Nationality Unknown.

200688   THE HOUSE ON STILTS; A NOVEL. New York:
G. W. Dillingham, [c1910] NUC.

Adventures on tropical island PW
NYT-adventures on tropical islands. Male hero.

HEALE, J.

200689   MARKHAM HOWARD: A NOVEL. London: T. F.
Unwin, 1893 BMC.

Struggles of three orphans to make a living. The
experience of Markham and his two adopted sisters. Not
juv, 3 vols. ATH 102:767.
SR 77:44. Male musician, a very sweet person.
SP 72. He is a felius nullius

HEALY, CHRIS.

200690   CONFESSIONS OF A JOURNALIST. London:
Chatto and Windus, 1904 BMC NUC.

200691   THE ENDLESS HERITAGE. London: Chatto and
Windus, 1904 BMC.

200692   HEIRS OF REUBEN. London: Chatto and
Windus, 1905 BMC.

200693   MARA: THE STORY OF AN UNCONVENTIONAL
WOMAN. London: Chatto & Windus, 1906 BMC.

TLS-left penniless at death of father, struggles in
London.
ATH-unconventional heroine, author seems to hold a
brief for the weaker sex against the machinations and
injustice of the male. Orthodox happy ending.

HEARD, ADRIAN. United Kingdom.

200694   THE IVORY FAN. London: T. F. Unwin,
[c1920] NUC BMC. New York and London: G. P. Putnam's
Sons, 1921 NUC.

LBKM-Catherine Arslea, a young playwright, elopes with
Swaine for several months yet never feels for him more
than friendship and gratitude. Rev. thinks she is
cold.

HEARD, W. NEVILL.

200695   THINGS OF TIME. London: Watts, 1911 BMC.

HEATH, SEYTON.

200696   A STOLEN WOOING. A NOVEL. London: Digby,
Long, 1901 BMC.

HEAWOOD, A. S.

200697   BRENDA. London: Digby, Long, [1895] BMC.

HELLEDOREN, J.

200698   A RUNNING FIGHT. London: J. Long, 1909
BMC.

secret treasures. TLS

HENDERSON, E. D.

200699   AN OFFICER AND A ----. London: J. Long,
1913 BMC.

South African farmer facing failure becomes horse
stealer. Two women one passionate and vindictive; the
other gentle, angelic. ACAD

HENDERSON, J. MURDOCH.

200700   THE CHRONICLES OF KARTDALE: OUR JEAMES
EDITED BY J. MURDOCK HENDERSON. Montreal: W. Drysdale,
1896 NUC BMC. Glasgow: Morison, 1898 BMC.

HENDLEY, J. E.

200701   ENGLAND, HEIR OF THE WORLD. London: E.
Stock, 1894 BMC NUC. (NUC does not classify as
fiction. Subj.: Anglo-Israelism.)

HENDOW, Z. S.

200702   THE FUTURE POWER; OR, THE GREAT
REVOLUTION OF 190-. Westminster: Roxburghe, [1897] BMC
NUC.

Imaginary account of a great strike and "the truimph
of 12 1/2 million workers who want to change our
present social system" and do. ACAD 52 Fic Sup 77
SR 85:264. Narrated by author, Dr. Hendow, a man
concerned with social inequities who is introduced to
a secret society of socialists who plan a revolution.
England after the Rev has social equality, peace and
plenty.

HENNESSEY, J. DAVID.

200703   AN AUSTRALIAN BUSH TRACK. London: S. Low,
[1896] BMC.

200704   THE DIS-HONOURABLE. London: S. Low,
[1896] BMC.

SR Australia. Murder. Prisoner (the hero) successfully
conducts his own defence.

200705   A LOST IDENTITY. London: F. Warne, [1899]
BMC.

200706   WYNNUM. London: S. Low, 1896 BMC.

LBKM 10:121. Hero in sensational plot marries Miriam
but receives guidance from Louie who died from plague.

HENRY, J.

200707   THE "REVEREND" RACHEL EUPHEMIA CHIT.
London: Simpkin, Marshall, [1910] BMC.

HENRY, W. A.

200708   THE RED KITE. London: Ward, Lock, 1916
BMC.

ATH airplane-war.

HEPPENSTALL, R. H.

200709   THE MALICE OF GRACE WENTWORTH. London: J.
Long, 1900 BMC.

ATH 116:574. Melodrama. Heiress scorned, her revenge
on man who has rejected her proposals and village
beauty he loves.

HERBERT, L. M.

200710   A MILLIONAIRE'S DAUGHTER: A NOVEL.
London: Epworth Press, 1918 BMC.

HEWITT, R. BEAUMONT. United States.

200711   LIFE OF ROBERT WHITMAN; OR, THE MAN WHO
SOLD HIS WIFE. [New Orleans]: Meine and Weihing,
[c1895] W.

HEYWOOD, EVELYN F.

200712   PASSIONS OF STRAW. London: Methuen, 1913
BMC.

Julia Ponsfort marries a charming wealthy man but the
marriage is of the warring kind. She dotes on her son.
Struggles between husband and wife described fully. SP
Julia leaves her unfaithful husband early in their
marriage. Twenty years later her son is loved by a
young actress Peggy Haslam that the father loves. TLS

HEYWOOD, J. C.

200713   LADY MERTON: A TALE OF THE ETERNAL CITY.
London: Burns and Oates, [1891] BMC.

Time is the 80s. Lady Merton and other convert to R.
C. church. Several plots involving Lord Merton's

jealousy of his wife; Lady Merton's lively daughter
Vivy; love between Nina and Hugh complicated by her
hot-tempered Italian father. ACAD

HIGGIN, L.

200714   A CORNISH MAID. London: Hurst and
Blackett, 1896 BMC.

SR- Baby girl washed ashore; reunion with mother 18
yrs. hence. Also, son who learns of shameful secret of
mother's existence, making it impossible for him to
marry an innocent girl.
ACAD 50:177 Difficulties are eventually cleared and
they marry.

200715   COUSIN JIM: A SEPIA SKETCH. London: Hurst
and Blackett, 1897 BMC.

He simply seems to be a source of money for most of
the other chars. Beryl-a good characterization. She's
both innocent and unscrupulous, and a reckless
adventurer, includes the story of a missing man. All
ends well. LBKM 12:43
Bert Fayne a kind of Becky Sharp. ACAD 52: Fict. Sup
32

200716   LYONA GRIMWOOD, SPINSTER. London: C. A.
Pearson, 1900 BMC.

ATH 115:618. Heroine seems to be dead in first
chapter. Mother dies the same day. Her lover comes
under suspicion of murdering her father, who had
betrayed her mother.

HILDRETH, J. H. United States.

200717   THE QUEEN'S HEART. Boston: M. Jones, 1918
NUC.

PW-Dorothy and Jack become lovers on a cruise, are
blown adrift, picked up by mystical ship. Have many
adventures and later agree to regard it as a dream.
Isogoe, queen of Rhodes who falls for Jack, is part of
adventure.

HINCKS, G. MALCOLM. B. 1881.

200718   THE IRON WAY. London: Nisbet, 1920 BMC.

HINDLE, DACRE.

200719   LINKS OF LOVE; A STORY OF THE RIVIERA.
London: J. Long, 1904 BMC.

HODGE, E. BALDWIN.

200720   KEITH KAVANAGH, REMITTANCE MAN. London:
Digby and Long, [1894] BMC NUC.

ACAD 46:116. Sent to Australia by family to get away
from influence of drunkard wife. Marries another, and
when 1st turns up in Australia, poisons her to get rid
of her.

HODGES, SYDNEY. 1829-1900.

200721   WHEN LEAVES WERE GREEN! A NOVEL. London:
Chatto and Windus, 1896 NUC BMC.

ATH 107:742. Captain D'Eyncourt a villain.
ACAD 49:237. He and Mrs. Byng plot and manage to
separate for a time the two lovers, Blanche and Glyn.

HOLFORD, CASTELLO O. United States.

200722   ARISTOPIA: A ROMANCE-HISTORY OF THE NEW
WORLD. Boston: Arena, 1895 NUC.

HOLLANDS, EVER.

200723   LOVE'S PASSION, LOST AND WON. London: A.
H. Stockwell, [1907] BMC.

HOLNUT, W. S.

200724   OLYMPIA'S JOURNAL. London: G. Bell, 1895
BMC NUC.

An egoist's diary, marries a self-made man with the
sole idea of making a novel of him. SR 79:453
A thorough study of introspection. She is "as modern
as she well can be". She's 25, a widow-Olympia
Colville Daw, of good family, cosmopolitan ed. and
"she longs for distinction as an author." So she
marries a man she cares nothing for to study him for

her novel. that is she feels she's "sacrificing
herself to her calling." Does have remorse for what
she did to George. ACAD 47:442

HOLT, J. M.

200725   ON THE OUTER EDGE OF THE LAW: A STORY OF
THE ETERNAL INSTINCT. London: Drane's, [1917] BMC.

HOLT, LEE. Nationality Unknown.

200726   GREEN AND GAY. London and New York: J.
Lane, 1918 PMC NUC.

NYT-May 26, 1918, p. 243. War story, of a hospital
directed by Madame la Marquise de Savigny for wounded
soldiers. One with a head injury has amnesia, love
story.

200727   PETER OF POTOPAH. London: Hodder and
Stoughton, 1916 BMC.

TLS-nice simple love tale.
LBKM-nice simple love tale

HOME, C. M.

200728   THE SIFTING OF THE WHEAT. A TALE OF THE
SIXTEENTH CENTURY. London: Art and Book, 1899 BMC.

Late 16th historical romance. RC point of view of bad
Queen Bess. About the Elizabethan persecution. L 5:304

HOMER, A. N. Nationality Unknown.

200729   HERNANI, THE JEW; A STORY OF RUSSIAN
OPPRESSION. London: Low, 1897 BMC. Chicago: Rand,
McNally, [c1897] NUC.

"Polish struggle for freedom with love and politics
interwoven." ACAD 52 Fic Sup 97.
SR 85:119 Too grim and gruesome. Two Polish Jews,
Hernani a rich banker and his beautiful wife. Both
humanitarian, loving. Persecuted by Russians,
1861-1863. Russian general wants her, imprisons
husband, etc.

200730   THE RICHEST MERCHANT IN ROTTERDAM: A
NOVEL. London: S. Low, 1891 BMC.

Improbable story. Mynheer Stephen Vanderhagen's
"tortuous schemes of matrimony and vengeance." Sees
Madge Milford at 14, determines to marry her and ruin
her boyfriend. Spends years, and money trying to do
his evil work. SP 66 765
His elaborate schemes include a forged letter,
kidnapping. ACAD ATH 97, 373

HOMEWOOD, A. S.

200731   JIMPY. London: Heath, Cranton, [1920] BMC
[1922?] NUC.

TLS-Life of man

HOOGSTRAAT, M. E. See VON HOOGSTRAAT, MOREE E.

HORLICK, JITTIE.

200732   JEWELS IN BRASS. London: Duckworth, 1913
BMC. New York: Brentano's, 1913 NUC.

Two characters from mythical Atlantis reincarnated. in
modern forms. A young woman and man. Good insights
into women's psychology. ACAD
Young woman makes a marriage in name only to escape
"dull, grandmotherly influence". The arrangement works
well till she really falls in love. The artist-husband
dies. ATH

200733   A STRING OF BEADS. London: Duckworth,
1911 BMC.

Patricia travels chaperoned in France meets her fate
in the person of an immaculate young man. Career of a
young woman; hero is "most objectionable" SP
Light romance, happy end ATH

HOUGHTON, A. E.

200734   GILBERT MURRAY: A NOVEL. London: Smith,
Elder, 1897 BMC.

Heroine becomes engaged to a saintly man who doesn't
really plan to wed her. He's sort of keeping her
available for the hero. LBKM 11:183.

Hero suddenly lost fortune; drives a baker's cart to
make a living, becomes a waiter, clerk, writer, sect'y
to MP. College friend is his rival in love, whom he
saves from suicide. ACAD 51:303

HOUGHTON, J. A.

200735   THE SUPREME RULERS. London: H. J. Drane,
[1908] BMC. (BMC: "A work on astrology.")

A work on astrology

HOUK, L. C. VIOLETT. B. 1866. Nationality Unknown.

200736   THE GIRL IN QUESTION; A STORY OF NOT SO
LONG AGO. New York: J. Lane, 1908 NUC.

PW-Heroine comes to Washington on a political mission;
mystery.

HOVEY, JEAN EDGERTON. United States.

200737   JOHN O'PARTLETT'S; A TALE OF STRIFE AND
COURAGE. Boston: L. C. Page, 1913 NUC.

"John o'Partletts' is a great fierce dog befriended by
a lonely old woman against whom all Partlettsville has
turned, calling her Witch Beevish. the villagers are a
mean, cowardly lot who delight in annoying those
weaker than themselves and consider Witch Beevish and
poor little darky Jim, whom she takes into her home,
as fair game. there are some battles royal in which
John o'Partletts' plays a valiant part and at last
does the villagers a wonderful service which changes
all the ill feelings."
PW 11/1/13 1435

HOWARTH, K. A.

200738   PHILIP HELMORE, PRIEST. London: Downey,
1899 BMC.

He's "a dissipated University man who brutally
discards his mistress." Eight years later he's a
minister, married with children, meets her, takes up
the relationship. Then confesses, repents and is
rehabilitated. SP 82:172
His wife leaves him when she learns. She moves to
Belgrave Square and paints and makes a good living for
herself. They are reconciled in the end. ATH 113:206

HOWDEN, F. A.

200739   LOVE IN A LONDON LODGING. London: T. F.
Unwin, 1895 BMC.

Kate Searle marries a man whose actions drive her to
the point of running off. But she stays. ACAD 48:517

HUDDLE, F. C.

200740   HAROLD HARDY. London: University Press,
1898 BMC.

HUGHES, M. E.

200741   MARGOT MUNRO. London: Mills & Boon, 1910
BMC.

TLS- male narrator-Margot makes a foolish marriage
ATH-Remains tied to him for ten years for sake of
blind stepson, at which time stepson persuades her to
divorce his father.

HUME, JEAN B. United States.

200742   AMETHYST GRAY; THE EVANGELIST'S
TEMPTATION. BY JULIEN VICLARE. Buffalo, N. Y.: Press
of A. H. Morey, [1902] NUC.

HUNT, A. KNIGHT.

200743   UNTIL THE DAY BREAKS. London: Simpkin,
Marshall, [1911] BMC.

HUNTER, A. J.

200744   AN IDYLLIC FOLLY. London: Olde St.
Bride's Presse, [1913] BMC.

Young widow spends summer in Yokohama; has
"love-affair" with handsome young man; they quarrel
and part. Written in first person. ATH

HUNTINGDON, E. M. AND A.

200745   THE SQUIRE'S NIECES. London: S. Low, 1891
BMC.

HUNTINGTON, A., jt. au. See HUNTINGDON, E. M. AND A.

HUSSEY, EYRE.

200746   JUST JANNOCK. London: J. Macqueen, 1899
BMC. Philadelphia: J. B. Lippincott, 1900 NUC.

SP 84:23. Heroine races horses (against other women)
races boats and wins (against men) nurses, boxes, and
sings.

200747   ON ACCOUNT OF SARAH. London: J. Macqueen,
1899 BMC NUC.

LW 31:73. "Mild ridicule is cast on a form of the
'women's rights' agitation." Sarah is a studious girl,
devoid of feelings, becoming fanatical when older--is
she a caricature, reviewer wonders.
PW-Two other girls represent true womanhood.

HUTCHESON, J. D.

200748   MISSIE WARDEN. Paisley: A. Gardner,
[1891] BMC.

Scotch story. She's a millionaire's daughter and has
three suitors. ACAD
Also ATH 97, 533

HUTCHINSON, M. F.

200749   CAPTAIN FERRERCOURT'S WIDOW: A NOVEL.
London and New York: Longmans, Green, 1910 BMC NUC.

Mrs. F's husband leaves for Boer War on their wedding
day. She takes position as companion to rich woman.
"Her real story comes as a great surprise." PW
ACAD She is merely posing as a woman in order to
obtain employment.
NYT O

200750   HAUNTING SHADOWS; OR THE HOUSE OF TERROR.
London: Methuen, 1912 BMC.

IDE, WESTOTH.

200751   IN THE POTTER'S HAND: A NOVEL. London:
Digby, Long, 1898 BMC.

SR 86:680. Rev. found too puzzling to read. About an
old man with red and green trousers and long white
hair who is mad. "why do authors call themselves
Westoth Ide?"

INCOGNITA.

200752   THE SIN OF ANOTHER (JACK GORDON'S LOVE
STORY). London: Simpkin & Marshall, 1896 BMC.

SR Two male heroes with the souls of angels.

INGRAM, ALDYTH.

200753   SMIRCHED. London: Digby, Long, [1896]
BMC.

IRIS [pseud.].

200754   HER MAGNETIC POWER. London: W. Nicholson,
[1903] BMC.

IRONSIDE, O. C. United Kingdom.

200755   GREAT IS DISCIPLINE. Northampton: E. J. &
J. Henryson for the Capitalist Commonwealth
Association, 1912 BMC BMC.

Socialism-Fic. Trade unions in fic.

IRVINE, F. K. United States.

200756   HIALDO: A NOVEL. SEQUEL TO SENORITA
MARGARITA. BY FREDERICK S. BUTT. Logansport, Ind.:
Olympic, 1892 NUC.

200757   LABIENUS. A PASSIONATE ROMANCE OF OLD
ROME. BY FREDERICK S. BUTT. Logansport, Ind.: Olympic,
1893 NJC.

JAMES, A. E.

200758   HER MAJESTY THE FLAPPER. London: S. Paul,
1912 BMC.

TLS-doings of 15 year old flapper, diverting.
ACAD-comedy

JANEWAY, J. B. H.   United States.

200759   "HIS LOVE FOR HELEN". New York: G. W.
Dillingham, 1893 NUC.

JENKIN, A. M. N.   Nationality Unknown.

200760   THE END OF A DREAM. London and New York:
J. Lane, 1919 BMC NUC.

SP-detailed story, terrible in its realism, of shell
shock.
SR-author's ideas of divorce laws are sketchy.
NYT 1920:308. Male hero, war victim, amnesia, lives
with woman not his wife, develops morphia habit, kills
many, and then in morphia dream, kills woman he loves.

JENKINS, C. CARLYON.

200761   A SEASIDE ROMANCE. London and Sydney:
Remington, 1893 BMC.

JENNINGS, H. J.

200762   MRS. JEREMIE-DIDILERE. London: Harrison,
1900 BMC.

SP 84:929. Vulgar adventuress, her schemes and
subterfuges dodging duns and husband-hunting.
LIT 7:86. "Swindling but seductive little widow" and
her daughter.

JOHNSON, F. HERNAMAN.

200763   THE POLYPHEMES. A STORY OF STRANGE
ADVENTURES AMONG STRANGE BEINGS. London: Ward, Lock,
1906 BMC.

TLS-science fiction

JOHNSON, GILLARD.

200764   RAPHAEL OF THE OLIVE. London: J. & J.
Bennett, 1912 BMC.

JOHNSON, P. DEMAREST.   United States.

200765   CLAUDIUS, THE COWBOY OF RAMAPO VALLEY: A
STORY OF REVOLUTIONARY TIMES IN SOUTHERN NEW YORK.
Middletown, N. Y.: Slauson and Boyd, 1894 NUC BMC.

JOHNSTON, M. F.

200766   MAVOURNEEN; OR, CHILDREN OF THE STORM.
London: Walter Scott, 1904 BMC.

ATH--much on the male hero.

JOHNSTON, W. CAIRNS.   United States.

200767   BEYOND THE ETHER: A STORY OF WONDROUS
ADVENTURES. Andover, Maine: W. C. Johnston, 1896 NUC.

JOHNSTONE, C. S.

200768   A DEVONSHIRE BRIDE. Ilfracombe: Twiss,
1893 BMC.

JONES, J. MACHENRY.

200769   HEARTS OF GOLD: A NOVEL. Wheeling [W.
Va.]: Daily Intelligence Steam Job Press, 1896 NUC.

JONES, JINGO [pseud.].

200770   THE SACK OF LONDON BY THE HIGHLAND HOST.
A ROMANCE OF THE PERIOD. NARRATED BY JINGO JONES, M.P.
London: Simpkin, Marshall, 1900 BMC.

JONES, MARGAM.

200771   ANGELS IN WALES. London: J. Long, 1914
BMC.

TLS-Welsh village life and manifestations of the
spiritual psychology of the Celt.

200772   THE STARS OF THE REVIVAL. London: J.
Long, [1909] NUC 1910 BMC.

TLS- Old Welsh Christians of the last cent.

JONES, W. BRAUNSTON.

200773   A BRACE OF YARNS: JACK'S LUCK AND A
STRANGE SURVIVAL. London: Digby, Long, 1899 BMC.

200774   MITHAZAN: A SECRET OF NATURE. London: T.
F. Unwin, 1891 BMC.

SP 68:470. "Creepy." Heroine has been bitten by a
snake in her youth. She was cured but the poison in
her blood transforms her into a "human snake." Even
after the death of two husbands she is unaware that
her kiss kills the recipient.

200775   OUR NANCE. A STORY OF WHITECHAPEL.
London: J. Ouseley, [1912] BMC.

200776   SIN CHONG--THE FAITHFUL HEART. A
CELESTIAL APOLOGUE. London: W. Scott, 1902 BMC NUC.

JORDAN, F. DORMER.

200777   HEIRS OF THE AGES. London: J. Nisbet,
[1914] BMC.

LRKM-two love stories, 1st is tragic. 10,000 years
later characters are reincarnated, this time all ends
happily.

JUDD, A. M.

200778   A DAUGHTER OF LILITH: A NOVEL. London:
Simpkin, Marshall, 1899 BMC.

200779   FOR A WOMAN'S MEMORY. London: F. V.
White, 1908 BMC.

TLS-Male foundling hero.

200780   LOT'S WIFE. London: J. Long, 1913 BMC.

Australian story-mostly local color, bushrangers, etc.
ATH
conflict in a woman between her love for an old lover
and duty to husband; Lot the husband is a loveable
person. Much local color.

200781   PHARAOH'S TURQUOISE. London: F. V. White,
1906 BMC.

ATH-conventional romance

200782   A SOUL'S BURDEN. London: Digby, Long,
1911 BMC.

200783   THE WHITE VAMPIRE. London: J. Long, 1914
BMC.

ATH-"White Vampire is one of the pseuds of a beautiful
Russian woman who, in revenge of her own ruin as a
girl, takes delight in luring men into her disastrous
toils. Sometimes she acts as agent for the government,
and at other times for the Nihilists. Most of her
victims end in suicide or Siberia."

JUSTICAN, E. A.

200784   A PARIS: BEING THE UNCOMMON EXPERIENCES
OF A COMMONPLACE WOMAN. London: E. Stock, 1919 BMC.

ATH-a pension, one of the guests is a half demented
woman.

JUSTYNE, Q. L. F.

200785   THE STRONGER POWER. London: Globe Press,
1906 BMC.

ATH-historical, male hero.

K., J. A. C. [pseud.].

200786   GOLF IN THE YEAR 2000; OR, WHAT WE ARE
COMING TO. BY J. A. C. K. London: T. F. Unwin, 1892
BMC.

K., N. F. P. [pseud.].

200787   MARGARET; OR THE HIDDEN TREASURE. BY N.
F. P. K. London: Religious Tract Society, [1910] BMC.

KAIN, KRESS, pseud. See PARRACK, J. B.

KASBECK [pseud.].

200788   HIS HIGHNESS SANDRO. BY KASBECK. London:

W. Heinemann, 1907 BMC.

About Russian pol. life; husband divorces, marries
Nadine the heroine ? ACAD

200789   VICTIMS. BY KASBECK. London: S. Swift,
[1912] BMC.

ATH Caucasus, characters have no life apart from their
emotions.
TLS-Russian rom.

KAWABATA, A.

200790   A HERMIT TURNED LOOSE. AN INTERESTING
ACCOUNT OF EUROPEAN TRAVELS WRITTEN IN ENGLISH BY A
JAPANESE TOURIST. [Tokyo ?]: 1915 BMC. [London]: 1915
NUC.

KAYE, BANNERMAN.

200791   HAROMI: A NEW ZEALAND STORY. London: J.
Clarke, 1900 BMC.

KAYE, LORIN, pseud. See LATHROP, LORRIN G. AND MRS.
(KONSTAM) PRICE.

KEAN, SYDNEY.

200792   BOTH WORLDS BARRED: A NOVEL. London: T.
F. Unwin, 1894 BMC NUC.

SR-chronicles of Scotch people of the lower classes.
ATH-adventures of Reverend Dlear.

KEENE, LESLIE.

200793   THE SUFFRAGE AND LORD LAXTON. London:
Digby, Long, 1914 BMC.

ATH. Lord Laxtonis 1st wife is a Militant Suffragette
who was killed at an accident at one of their
meetings. His second wife belongs to the opposite
camp.
TLS 2nd wife restores happiness.

KEITH, K.

200794   ANNE CARSTAIRS. BY THE AUTHOR OF
"PUNCHINELLO" [ANONYMOUS]. London: Drane's, 1913 BMC.

She's an heiress married to a man who loves another.
Husband persuades her of his devotion that he can show
only in pity and courtesy ATH

200795   A BROKEN TOY. London: Constable, 1916
BMC.

TLS-Little Poppy's life, gay and selfish, is ruined by
"pleasure."

200796   THE GREAT RELEASE. London: Chapman &
Hall, 1914 BMC.

ATH 144:561. 0
TLS Sensitive high-strung novelist whose nerves have
been ruined by his cruel drunken nurse.

200797   THERE WAS A DOOR--. BY THE AUTHOR OF
"ANNE CARSTAIRS" [ANONYMOUS]. London: Chapman & Hall,
1914 BMC.

ACAD 86:462. "Will not command the admiration of the
Suffragettes." Heroine is a door-mat. Rom. with an
artist, whom she marries after he loses his right hand
(before then he doesn't want her).

KENN, CLEVERDEN.

200798   DOWN IN THE FLATS; OR, PARTY BEFORE
FITNESS. London: T. F. Unwin, 1892 BMC.

KENNEDY, H. A.

200799   A MAN WITH BLACK EYELASHES. London:
Methuen, 1897 BMC.

Stephen Careless, the villain, has no conscience. He
gave it up to the "devil" but gets it back when he's
climbing Vesuvius and hurls himself down to his death.
ACAD 51:352.

KENNEDY, R. A.

200800   THE TRIUNIVERSE; A SCIENTIFIC ROMANCE. BY
THE AUTHOR OF "SPACE AND SPIRIT" [ANONYMOUS]. London:

Knight, [1912] BMC.

TLS-Professor Karl.
ACAD-science fiction

KENNEDY, R. M.

200801   THE WOMAN HE CHOSE. A NOVEL. London:
Digby, Long, 1902 BMC.

KENSINGTON, CATHMER. Nationality Unknown.

200802   GLENWOOD. New York: Abbey Press, [1901]
NUC.

KENT, J.

200803   A HARVEST FESTIVAL. London: T. F. Unwin,
1898 BMC.

ACAD 54:193. Village life, "Jane Bembridge, rector's
daughter and housekeeper, is the caustic critic of
village politics."
ATH 112:346.
SR 86:480. "Indications that the author of this clever
little stry is of the unexplained sex."

KENYON, M. E.

200804   THE STORY OF JOHN COLES. London: Digby,
Long, [1894] BMC.

SP-two or three murders.
ACAD-he is a burglar, murderer, seducer. Finally done
in by a dog.

KERSEY, W. H.

200805   THE DARKSOME MAIDS OF BAGLEERE. A
SOMERSET TALE. London: S. Swift, 1912 BMC.

ATH-
TLS-Farm & Cottage Life.

KHALIL SA'D.

200806   CAESAR AND CLEOPATRA: AN HISTORICAL
ROMANCE. London: E. Vaughan, 1898 BMC.

200807   EMIR MURAD OR THE SYRIAN PRINCE. AN
ORIENTAL NOVEL. [Cairo]: [1893?] BMC.

KING, A. R.

200808   THE AGONY OF LOVE AND HATE. London: H. J.
Drane, [1906] BMC.

KING, ALIX.

200809   THE LITTLE NOVICE. A NOVEL. London:
Cassell, 1899 BMC.

200810   THE ROMANCE OF A MONK. New York:
Metropolitan Press, 1910 NUC. London: Rebman, 1910 BMC
NUC.

TLS-he is pursued by Madge who is forward and captures
him.

200811   THE ROMANCE OF A NUN. London: Rebman,
1909 BMC.

Young girl's rebellious spirit proves too hungry for
pleasure of life outside nunnery to allow her peace;
falls in love with artist ends in death. ACAD

KIRK, HYLAND CLARE. 1846-1917. United States.

200812   THE REVOLT OF THE BRUTES: A FANTASY OF
THE CHICAGO FAIR. New York: C. T. Dillingham, 1893 NUC
BMC.

KNIGHT, C. T.

200813   PHILIP MENZE. A STORY OF COMMERCIAL LIFE.
London: E. Stock, 1909 BMC.

KNIGHT, H.

200814   THE MYSTERY OF STEPHEN CLAVERTON & CO.: A
NOVEL. London: Routledge, [1894] BMC NUC.

SR 78:627. Male narrator. Mystery concerns financial
irregularities and murder.

KNIGHT, M.

200815   DID CUPID COUNT? London: J. Long, 1910
BMC.

TLS-simple and conventional.
ATH-simple and conventional.

KNOTCUTTER, A. [pseud.].

200816   A WAY OF HIS OWN. BY A. KNOTCUTTER,
p.G.M.u. London: H. J. Drane, [1903] BMC.

Story of an eccentric young man. ACAD 64,634
ATH

KNOWLES, R. B. SHERIDAN.

200817   GLENCOONOGE: A NOVEL. Edinburgh and
London: Blackwood, 1891 BMC.

Jane Johnson bookkeeper-love story. Alicia O'Doherty
too good for man who wins her.

KOSTROMITIN, J.

200818   THE LAST DAY OF THE CARNIVAL. London: T.
Fisher Unwin, 1893 BMC NUC. (Tr. from Russian)

L., A. C. [pseud.].

200819   THE CONFESSIONS OF A WIFE: BEING THE LIFE
STORY OF MARGARET X. RETOLD FROM HER DIARIES AND
LETTERS BY HER FRIEND A. C. L. London: Simpkin, 1915
BMC.

L., E. G. [pseud.]. See LINDSEY, E. G.

L., F. X. [pseud.].

200820   STELLA'S DISCIPLINE. BY F. X. L.
Philadelphia: H.L. Kilmer, [c1892] NUC. (Bound with
The Lost Lode by Christian Reid i.e. Frances
Christian (Fisher) Tiernan.)

LAGGARD, LIONEL, pseud. See LUMSDEN, D. FRASER.

LAMBERT, BRITON.

200821   LOVE IN A MAZE; THE WAY OF A MODERN GIRL.
London: Greening, 1908 BMC.

TLS-27 yr. old feminine novelist interested in
righting the world and the relations of the sexes
writes letters about it to Mr. Durrant. POV?
SR-0

LAMBTON, A. H.

200822   FROM PRISON TO POWER: A TALE OF
QUEENSLAND. London: Eden, Remington, 1893 BMC.

LANARK, H. M. L.

200823   THE ROUGH TORRENT OF OCCASION. London:
Greening, 1904 BMC.

LBKM-brother & sister.

200824   THELGE [ANONYMOUS]. London: Downey, 1901
BMC.

200825   WHICH WIFE? London: Downey, 1901 BMC.

LANG, L. LOCKHART.

200826   THE IMBECILES. London: Hurst & Blackett,
1908 BMC.

TLS-community of males on an island.
ACAD-no, women there too, mixture of comedy and
seriousness, frivolous, unimproving.
SR -sister helps-a ship of food to fall back on.

200827   THE VULGAR TRUTH. London: E. Arnold, 1904
BMC.

ATH-Modern social life amusing, clever.

LANG, P. S.

200828   THE DUAL HERITAGE. London: Heath,
Cranton, [1920] BMC.

TLS-love and complications.
ATH-love and complications.

200829   WHERE THE SOLDANELLA GROWS. London:
Heath, Cranton and Ouseley, [1915] BMC.

The snowy Austrian mt. heights represent "the goal of
life for Avis Beaumont." TLS
Girl brought up on a theory and becomes an art student
at Frankfurt. ATH

LANGBRIDGE, V.

200830   AN ELUSIVE LOVER, A STUDY IN PERVERSITY.
London: J. Milne, 1909 BMC.

Nan Golding goes to London alone, works in art and
drama, loves an explosive man. TLS

LANGBRIDGE, V. AND C. HAROLD BOURNE.

200831   THE VALLEY OF INHERITANCE. London:
Methuen, 1905 BMC.

LANSTON, AUBREY. United States.

200832   THE HARVESTERS. New York: R. H. Russell,
1903 NUC.

Historical 12-5-03 PW & NYT 03, 802

LATHROP, LORRIN G. AND MRS. (KONSTAM) PRICE.

200833   A DRAWING-ROOM CYNIC: BEING A FAITHFUL
ACCOUNT OF THIRTY DAYS OF HIS CAREER. BY LORIN KAYE.
London: J. Macqueen, 1897 BMC.

Philip Legarde is an ambitious young diplomatist.
First loves a married countess; then a rich Amer.
widow who lives with him though she knows he's
selfish. Dulcima marries him later. She's too good for
him-"author avoids the pitfall into which most women
novelists are apt to stumble-that of making her heroes
either models of perfection or patterns of
wickedness."SR 83:615.
Opulent, cosmopolitan society. Dulcima Melville is an
American widow meets and loves Philip LeGarde, a man
with a past. An Austrian Baroness complicates things a
bit. ACAD: 51:569.

200834   HER LADYSHIP'S INCOME. BY LORIN KAYE.
London: J. Macqueen, 1896 BMC.

ATH 107:803. Imitator of Meredith. Offensive
incidents. Lord Bohun is persuaded to marry an
innocent young girl by his 43 year old mistress.

LAURENCE, CLARICE, pseud. See HANCOCK, C. L.

LAVERICK, M. A.

200835   WAS SHE GUILTY? Newcastle-on-Tyne:
Mawson, Swan and Morgan, 1910 BMC.

LAW, JOHN [pseud.].

200836   GEORGE EASTMONT: WANDERER. BY JOHN LAW.
London: Burns and Oates, 1905 BMC.

LAWRENCE, LOU. 1854-1932. United States.

200837   THE CONFESSIONS OF AN OLD MAID. New York:
Press of "The Rose-jar", 1904 NUC.

PW-has preserved her sense of humor.
"The story of a womanly woman is written in an amusing
and unconventional style. A very fair idea of the
nature of this book may be formed from its title." BKM
v 19,1904

LAWSON, M.

200838   CONEYCREEK. London: Digby and Long,
[1895] BMC.

Trials of two blind young women, their torturous
ordeals through which they triumph. ACAD 48:28.

LAWSON, X. Nationality Unknown.

200839   SYDNEY CARRINGTON'S CONTUMACY. New York:
F. Pustet, [c1908] NUC.

LEACH, VALETTE WASHBURN. Nationality Unknown.

200840   JEDEDIAH BASCOM. New York: Abbey Press,
[1902] NUC.

LEAF, A.

200841   A MAID AT LARGE. London: E. Nash, 1905
BMC.

Says outrageous things like Elizabeth. ACAD 398, 05
The book takes us into the Country House marriage
market. Satire LBKM 27, 8, 105

200842   STRAWBERRY LEAVES. London: E. Nash, 1903
BMC.

Social satire,--ACAD 65, 60
Comic portrait of duchess and her affairs. ACAD 65,
108 Lurid shocking information "respecting our effete
society." LBKM 8-03, 189

LE CLERC, M. E.   Nationality Unknown.

200843   A BOOTLESS BENE. London: Hurst and
Blackett, 1895 BMC.

SR. Rachel "did not believe in the friendship of her
own sex at all." "She is arrogant to her equals,
insolent to her dependents, birth proud and
purse-proud."
LBKM 3:92. Rachel, a duke's grand daughter, is a
reckless heroine, an artist, she " abhors the pomps
and vanities of the world," chooses a tradesman to
marry, lives in "rural seclusion."
ATH 100:660. "Impetuous and warmhearted," her "faults
are chiefly those of early independence, wealth, and
want of discipline."
SP 69:686. SPEC thinks she is a vulgar prig%
constantly reminding her inferiors about the
difference in their stations. Her actions are,
however, completely respectable.
Story of the rise of nationalism in Ireland-the
violence, pain, havoc but underneath a spirit of
optimism. Derrick is the chief character. He's
responsible for the death of his love's brother, but
he's repentant and a sympathetic character. SP 74:55
ACAD 46:552. Irish question anti-peasantry, pro
squireen

200844   NANCY PAPILLON. London: Heath, Cranton,
[1913] BMC NUC.

Jacobites--ATH
Two heroines; simple historical tale. TLS

200845   A RAINBOW AT NIGHT. London: Hurst and
Blackett, 1891 BMC.

Pleasant sad story of Betty's growth from child to
woman. Family has financial problems. Leaves her
wealthy home to make her own way. Makes friends with a
young couple who are sad serious people, different
from her. She's sociable, friendly. SP 66 864
Includes a suspected poisoning and a startling will.
ATH 97 533
A young man anxious to wed Betty hears elderly
relative about to change the will that would make him
wealthy. SR 5-9-91, 572

200846   ROBERT CARROLL. A NOVEL. London: Hurst
and Blackett, 1893 NUC BMC.

Historical novel. Jacobite uprising in 1715. SP
71:275.
Heroine Mistress Verena Lyle. ACAD 44:249.

200847   SWORN ALLIES. London: Hurst and Blackett,
1897 BMC.

Delightful picture of the Joyces. Irish, their parrot
and terriers. They move (after grandfather's death) to
brother-in-law's. He's English and doesn't welcome
them. ATH 109:504.

LEE, AUBREY.

200848   A GENTLEMAN'S WIFE. Edinburgh: G. A.
Morton, 1904 BMC.

One part of book deals with a seduction and
illegitimate child; the other the child grown up. A
woman who thinks she's of high birth discovers the
truth. Not promising TLS 05,102.

200849   JOHN DARKER: A NOVEL. London: A. and C.
Black, 1894 BMC.

SR 78:688. "The heroine experiences life as a steerage
passenger in a homeward-bound vessel from Australia,
as an inmate of a low lodging in Liverpool, as the
girl of the house in a small huckster's shop in a
country town in Ireland, as a poor pupil in a ladies'
school, as hostess in a rich Manchester man's country
house, as the wife of a rich man in a first-class
villa, as French mistress in a third-class school, and
as the wife of a country squire in a comfortable
mansion in Devonshire."
SP 73:892. Rosamund's father was killed by John
Darker, who was acquitted, when she was 7. Eugene
Smith is developed from a caricature to a character.
ATH 104:637. First person narration.
Rosamund tells the story which includes Eugene; an
aesthete, and Helen Bratton who changes from a
relentless schemer to a suffering woman. LW 26:428.

LEE, J. F.   United States.

200850   OCTAVIA, THE OCTOROON. BY J. F. LEE, M.D.
New York: Abbey Press, [c1900] NUC.

LEE, MARION BEVERIDGE.   Nationality Unknown.

200851   BARSELMA'S KISS; A ROMANCE. Boston,
Mass.: C. M. Clarke, 1908 NUC.

Man apparently dead comes to life: forgery, theft,
fortunes of the "dead" man. NYT

200852   THE MAN WITH A RAKE. London, New York:
Abbey Press, [1901] NUC.

LEICESTER, J. E.

200853   NONE SO BLIND. Amersham: Morland, 1920
BMC.

TLS-Wife who has pagan frivolity and love of pleasure
wed to grave elderly politician. Conversion.

LEISHER, J. J.   United States.

200854   THE DECLINE AND FALL OF SAMUEL SAWBONES,
M.D., ON THE KLONDIKE. BY HIS NEXT BEST FRIEND. New
York, Chicago, London: Neely, [c1900] NUC.

LEONE, M. L.

200855   DEAD LEAVES: A SKETCH OF THREE SOULS.
London: Digby, Long, [1895] BMC.

Melancholy up-to-date woman with a past. Principessa
Laura Montecco. Two men write about her endlessly in
their diaries. Solario met her when she was smoking
and declaring "vulgarity" as part of her programme.
Widow. When her husband was alive she had a liaison
with an English merchant. When he died, she presented
her story to the two men, chose the rich one because
she was poor ACAD:47:274
Diaries of three people. Clarence Ashoon, the poor
one, Solario and hers. ATH 105:439

LE SAGE, A. B.

200856   IN THE WEST WIND. London: Duckworth, 1912
BMC.

ATH-Country life in Cornish village-description of
nature.
ACAD-wife has a relationship with man living in house
with herself and husband who is off in S. Africa.
Love-hate-but rev. thinks author very sketchy about it
all.

LESLIE, W. FORBES.

200857   LEYLI: A ROMANCE OF THE AEGEAN SEA.
London: P. S. King, 1915 NUC BMC.

In verse. PR 6011

L'ESTRANGE, MILES [pseud.?].

200858   WHAT ARE WE COMING TO. BY MILES
L'ESTRANGE. Edinburgh: D. Douglas, 1892 BMC.

SP 69:138. A dream of England some few years hence and
changes.

LEWIS, R. M.

200859   THE DIVINE GIFT. London: Lamley, 1906
BMC.

TLS-Allegory

LINDSAY, MAYNE.   United Kingdom.

200860 THE ANTIPODEANS: A ROMANCE. London: E. Arnold, 1904 BMC.

ATH-Australians, insanity.

200861 PROPHET PETER. A STUDY IN DELUSIONS. London: Ward, Lock, 1902 BMC.

200862 THE WHIRLIGIG. London: Ward, Lock, 1901 BMC. New York: Longmans, Green, 1901 NUC.

LINDSEY, E. G. United States.

200863 MARIE; OR, FORT BEAUHARNOIS. AN HISTORIC TALE OF EARLY DAYS IN THE NORTHWEST. By E. G. L. Minneapolis, Minn.: A. C. Bausman, [c1893] NUC.

LIOTARD, L.

200864 WHAT THE SEA DIVIDED. London: Murray and Evenden, [1913] BMC.

LISLE, T. DUTHIE.

200865 THE HEIRLOOM; OR THE DESCENT OF VERNWOOD MANOR. London: Gay and Bird, 1893 BMC.

LLOYD, SIDNEY.

200866 JOAN TRACY. London: T. Fisher Unwin, 1892 BMC.

LOBENHOFFER, LILLIAS.

200867 THE WRONG OF FATE. London: Digby, Long, [1895] BMC.

Wife--an unconscious bigamist--marries an elderly doctor. Husband buried in a shallow Indian grave, turns up after a few years. Discovers them, lives nearby. He plays the part of the village idiot. He is reunited to his wife as she's dying. SR 79:295

LOCKE, M. H.

200868 HELEN IN MOROCCO: A STORY OF FICKLENESS. Edinburgh: Sands, 1904 BMC.

ATH-0
TLS-0

LOCKE, SUMNER. B. 1881. Australia.

200869 SAMARITAN MARY. New York: H. Holt, 1916 NUC.

Two victims of auto accident are nursed back to health in Mary's home. They and their families, Mary and her family and the neighbors add up to triple romance. PW 89: 3/4/16: 743

LONGMAN, V. I.

200870 HARVEST. A NOVEL. London: K. Paul, 1913 BMC.

Study of a woman whose mother was a high-caste native of India: her marital problems. SP
Problem of children in mixed marriages.
Heroine doesn't know of her birth until she goes to Oxford and becomes engaged to a young man of good family, who breaks off the engagement. She marries another man, but the union is an unhappy one. ATH
TLS-Hasil Latham does well, goes to Oxford, becomes engaged. At 21 learns her mother was Indian, breaks off engagement makes a poor unhappy marriage. Is far from intellectual life she likes, child dies, moves farther and farther from husband "floats away physically into Nirvana."
Oxford from woman's point of view. TLS

LOOTA [pseud.]. United States.

200871 MONTRESOR: AN ENGLISH-AMERICAN LOVE STORY, 1854-1894. BY LOOTA. New York: F. T. Neely, 1897 NUC BMC.

Willful young woman nearly wrecks her life by an imprudent marriage. The mother, whose diary forms the chief part, has little influence on the young woman. LW 28:358.

LORD, M. L. United Kingdom.

200872 LYDIA. BY SYDNEY CHRISTIAN. London: S. Low, 1893 BMC. Chicago: F. T. Neely, 1895 NUC.

A "plain" woman loses man she loves and who loves her, but regains him in middle-life after his wife dies. PW 3-9-95:420.
Hard working drudge, supports family for 11 years when they lose their money. Strong, not beautiful. Meets young artist, loves him but he's married. His wife has been involved in charity work, spent the first year of their marriage studying Russian charities. She's so busy with her good works that her husband has no real wife. But Lydia turns him away. Then 15 months pass in which time Gertrude, the wife, has been working even with Lydia in her philanthropic projects. Now ill, Gertrude sends for Lydia signing only her last name. Lydia comes thinking her former lover is dying. Dying, Gertrude regrets her life. She felt no love. Now sees it in Lydia and her own husband. Forgives them and wishes them joy. SP 71 89
Mrs. Addean had married for money to support charities. SR 76, 47.
Lydia has a genius for art. ACAD 44:148.

200873 AN OBSTINATE PARISH. BY SYDNEY CHRISTIAN. London: 1899 NUC.

Rev. Cyril Roberton is power-hungry. Then there is saintly Sylvia, "her husband pulls her out of a sisterhood by main force... in her case domestic life if it does not cure, will kill." LBKM 16:140
The Rev. attracts many young women but he's a cold turkey. Nellie Keen runs off with the first man who comes along to revenge the fact that the Rev. doesn't love her. Another becomes an Anglican Sister of Mercy, but is rescued by another lover. The Rev. causes quite a stir in his quiet parish.
ATH 116:478. Ritualistic clergyman comes to small town. He is not attractive. A young woman suicides over him in despair.

200874 PERSIS YORKE. BY SYDNEY CHRISTIAN. London: Smith, Elder, 1896 BMC. New York: Macmillan, 1896 NUC.

LBKM 10:192. Author "knows the hard workaday world of men and women very intimately." "His open-mindedness, his generosity, and delicacy in dealing with difficult subjects are rare."
ATH 107:411. Persis moves from shadow to sunshine as she moves from family with despotic father through courtship to marriage. Recalls "Sarah, a Survival." Novel Series.
ACAD 49:342. Her trials include her father, a conscienceless sister, her own unrelenting conscience, poverty, and a bitterly lonely horror and distrust of men. Persis combines two types of heroine: long sufferer, and "the later development with modern mind and heaven-questioning spirit." "A marked intention to portray the inner as well as the outer life of a woman as subjectively as it may be possible for a man to do it." Adrian Lyster, "the sweet-natured cripple, brightens her life."
SP 77:345.

200875 SARAH: A SURVIVAL. BY SYDNEY CHRISTIAN. London: S. Low, 1894 BMC. New York: Harper, 1894 NUC.

ACAD 46:83. Old fashioned heroine.
ATH-the kind of English girl who is in danger of becoming extinct.

200876 TWO MISTAKES. BY SYDNEY CHRISTIAN. London: S. Low, 1895 BMC.

Two stories (1) Daly Fanshawe a rake type and Bess a servant girl who reads Spencer and Newman. "The Worldlings." (2) "Unmarried". Both religious in tone and melancholy. LBKM, 9:31
(1) Daly ruins several women. Bess Appleton. (2) concerns an unselfish and self contained man named Bellows. ATH 106:351

LOUGHNAN, J. PYM.

200877 MAD? A STORY. London: Greening, 1901 BMC.

LOUIS, A. B.

200878 A BRANCH OF LAUREL. London: Bliss, Sands, 1898 BMC.

ATH 111:370. Dark and sinister portrayal of "the now historic possession that overtook a community of provincial Ursuline nuns in the days of Richelieu and of the Huguenot struggles."
LBKM 13:192. Story of Urbain Grandier, Chanoine of S. Pierre, Loudun, the Abbess Juliette de Mazade who

loved him and brought him to the stake.

200879   THE DEVIL'S KITCHEN. London: Bliss,
Sands, 1900 BMC.

ATH 115:714. "Narrated by heroine. Crowded...with
essentially feminine and commonplace detail." Story of
hero and his novel-she is his wife or becomes so.
ACAD 58:430. Includes a novelist driven mad by the
rejection of his book.

200880   MALLERTON. London: Bliss, Sands, 1897
BMC.

Title refers to the name of a town. Story deals with
everyday life of everyday people. There's a trag. and
a mystery solved by Salvation Army. ACAD 52:fict sup
31.
Judith Estcourt is an able woman of letters. ATH
110:317.

LUCAS, F. LANCASTER.

200881   KATIE'S CORONET: A NOVEL. London: Eden
and Remington, 1892 BMC.

LUCILLA.

200882   THE SECRET OF THE GOLDEN KEY. A NOVEL.
London: R. Culley, [1908] BMC.

TLS-hist rom for the young.

LUMSDEN, D. FRASER.

200883   LOVE AND LIFE. London: Digby, Long, 1911
BMC.

ATH-Sent., parson hero, conventionally happy ending
for children

200884   SWEET ISABEL OF NARRAGOON: A ROMANCE. BY
LIONEL LAGGARD. London: Greening, 1908 BMC.

LUTYENS, F. M.

200885   MR. SPINKS AND HIS HOUNDS: A HUNTING
STORY. London: Vinton, [1896] BMC.

LYALL, J. G.

200886   NORRINGTON LE VALE. London: F. V. White,
1899 BMC.

Horses and hunters during Crimean war; a murder, a
seduction, a love story. ATH 113:718

LYNEGROVE, R. C.

200887   LOTTERIES OF CIRCUMSTANCE. London:
Methuen, 1914 BMC.

ATH Matrimonial adventures of two impoverished
aristocratic German sisters.
TLS: Critical of Middle class and aristocratic
Germans.

LYNN, J. C.

200888   BIRDS IN A WOOD. London: Duckworth, 1917
BMC.

M., A. CHARLES.

200889   A SOLICITOR'S LOVE STORY. London: H.J.
Drane, 1905 BMC.

M., A. O. [pseud.].

200890   IN THE NEXT WORLD: A SEQUEL TO THE STORY,
"TWO BROTHERS". Cardiff: Chapple and Kemp, 1898 BMC.

200891   TWO BROTHERS: A NOVEL. Paisley: A.
Gardner, 1897 BMC.

M., A. [pseud.].

200892   AYAME-SAN: A JAPANESE ROMANCE OF THE
TWENTY-THIRD YEAR OF MEIJI, 1890. London: Walter
Scott, [1892] BMC.

SR Ayame-San is Japanese, her uncle loses his fortune,
she becomes a Geisha girl and famous. She is also an
English scholar. She marries an Englishman. Rest of
story is concerned with an Irishman and his
adventures, in and out of Japan.

M., C. F. DE M. [pseud.].

200893   BOY OR GIRL? AND THE SHIP THAT CAME HOME.
London: Drane, [1903] BMC.

Two stories.

M., C. J. [pseud.].

200894   ALICE SHERWIN: A TALE OF THE DAYS OF
HENRY VIII. BY C. J. M. Burns and Oats, 1895 BMC.

M., F. M. [pseud.].

200895   THE MYSTERIOUS TRAVELLER. London: J.
Clarke, 1900 BMC.

MACDERMOTT, P. L. [pseud.].

200896   JULIUS VERNON; OR A STRANGE CASE OF
CIRCUMSTANTIAL EVIDENCE. A LONDON DETECTIVE STORY. BY
P. L. MACDERMOTT. London: Ward, Lock, 1892 BMC.

200897   THE LAST KING OF YEWLE: A DETECTIVE
STORY. BY P. L. MACDERMOTT. London: Ward, Lock, 1893
BMC. New York: Cassell, [c1893] NUC.

Kings are an ancient house in Yewle, England. One
brother accused of forgery and put in prison
(circumstantial evidence). On day of his release, his
brother found dead and he's suspected of murder.
3-11-93. PW

MACDONALD, D. P. Australia.

200898   NICHOLAS SIMON: A ROMANCE OF REVOLUTION.
London and New York: Hodder & Stoughton, 1915 BMC NUC.

MACGRIGOR, MONTIE. United Kingdom.

200899   CROSS-TIDES. London: J. Long, 1915 BMC.

200900   THE SWIRL. London: J. Long, [1917] BMC
NUC.

ATH:girl in convent marries millionaire.Her nun friend
marries sculptor.

MACIVER, G.

200901   NEUROOMIA: A NEW CONTINENT. London: S.
Sonnenschein, 1894 BMC.

MACK., K.

200902   A STORY IN SEVEN CHAPTERS. Bristol: J. W.
Arrowsmith, [1892] BMC. (BS Lists Title: Weeds: a
Story in Seven Chapters)

MACKENZIE, E. V. G. United Kingdom.

200903   BATTLE DAYS. BY ARTHUR FETTERLESS.
Edinburgh and London: W. Blackwood, 1918 NUC.

WWI-Fic

200904   GOG, THE STORY OF AN OFFICER AND
GENTLEMAN. BY ARTHUR FETTERLESS. Edinburgh and London:
W. Blackwood, 1916 NUC.

WWI-fic

MACKERLIE, H. G.

200905   THE RADICAL'S WIFE. London: J. Macqueen,
1896 BMC.

SR 82:454. Katherine is "the ideal figure of a woman's
dream." "Endowed with every physical, moral and
intellectual viture" "Passionately needed by everyone,
especially by men, distinguished men." She gets them
seats in Parliament, saves them from disgrace. "The
dependence of powerful men". Her husband treats her
brutally. She leads a full life-writing stories,
articles, speeches, smokes, drinks, etc. The wrongs of
women is the most engrossing part of her work.
ATH 108:481. she is a politician. "She suffers with
and labours for the poor without for ever (in season
and out of it) intruding her doings, as her sister
workers so often do." Plays the role of the "new
woman" with much humanity.

MACNICOL, E. R.

200906   DARE MACDONALD. A ROMANCE OF THE RIVIERA.

London: A. Gardner, 1892 NUC. Paisley: A. Gardner, 1892 BMC.

SP 68:566. Five year old boy is hero; he is clever. Simple, mild, hotel life in Nice.

MAGIE, L. B. United States.

200907   MY SISTER MARION. Tibbals Book Co., [c1892] NUC.

MAISEY.

200908   AT NOON: WHERE TWO WAYS MEET: A NOVEL. London: E. Stock, 1903 BMC.

MALCOLM, C. H.

200909   ESTRINA. London: Simpkin, Marshall, 1898 BMC.

200910   JUSTITIA; OR, THE RESULT OF OBSTINACY. London: Roxburghe Press, [1897] BMC.

200911   ROBERT KANE. A NOVEL. London: Simpkin, Marshall, 1900 BMC.

MALO, NECREDE [pseud.].

200912   TREMENDAX, AN OPTIMISTIC RECORD. BY NECREDE MALO. London: Herbert and Daniel, [1913] BMC.

Cheerful chatty book, anecdotes, gossip, information of all kinds, opinions. fiction? LBKM
young business man travels after quarrel with his wife; reports what he sees SR

MANLEY, R. M. United States.

200913   THE QUEEN OF EUCADOR: A NOVEL. New York: H. W. Hagemann, 1894 NUC. London: G. Routledge, 1894 BMC.

CR 25:370. New York doctor suspects husband of trying to kill his wife by hypnotism, and asks woman friend to take position in house as nurse. Husband drugs and attempts to hypnotize nurse; wife dies of strychnine, nurse is tried by her own testimony for the crime.

200914   SOME CHILDREN OF ADAM. New York: Worthington, 1892 NUC.

PW American in New York. Sensational incidents. Desiree "apparent adventuress."

MANN, D. S.

200915   ELLIOTT, LIMITED. London: Sidgwick & Jackson, 1916 NUC BMC.

Young man's life, death in war. LBKM

MANTON, W.

200916   THE BANK MANAGER, AND HOW HE WAS DUPED. London: Simpkin, Marshall, 1891 BMC.

MARCH, FENN.

200917   VINDICTA. London: H. Marshall, 1898 BMC.

SP 81:253. Jeremy loves Beatrice, but his "mother is more than half lunatic through indulgence in drink." problem of heredity.

MARCH, TEMPLE.

200918   THE PRODIGAL DAUGHTER. London: G. Newnes, [1913] BMC.

MARKOE, ELLIS. United States.

200919   MY LADY'S HEART: A SKETCH. Boston: Roberts, 1896 NUC. (Of a Belgian Artist)

MARTIN, D'ARCY.

200920   CUPID'S TIME SHEET. London: J. Long, 1911 BMC.

200921   CRAN: A STORY OF A REVIVAL. London: P. Wellby, 1905 BMC.

200922   MEANS TO AN END. London: J. Long, 1913 BMC.

A millionaire falls in love with a picture; traces the woman and marries her. Also concerns an inheritance. TLS

MARTIN, EWAN.

200923   THE KNIGHT OF KING'S GUARD. Boston: L. C. Page, 1899 NUC. London: C. A. Pearson, 1899 BMC.

MARTIN, M. C. Nationality Unknown.

200924   THE OTHER MISS LISLE. New York: Benziger, 1906 NUC.

PW-2 sisters, self-sacrifice of one, anti mixed marriages.

MATHER, E. J.

200925   THE SQUATTER'S BAIRN. London: Rebman, [1910] BMC. London: Simpkin, Marshall, [1914] NUC BMC.

TLS-geography of Australia
ACAD-geography of Australia.

MATHER, PERSIS [pseud.].

200926   THE COUNSELS OF A WORLDLY GODMOTHER. BY PERSIS MATHER. Boston: Houghton, Mifflin, 1905 NUC.

Letters about marriage, divorce, and the art of walking gracefully--to a young woman entering society. PW 10-14-05.   NYT 1905:725

MAUD, D.

200927   THE EXPIATION OF JOHN COURT. London: Methuen, 1911 BMC.

Ruin of a marriage by husband's conversion to Christian Science.
D. Maud identified as female. TLS 1911:111

MAUDE, F. W.

200928   A MERCIFUL DIVORCE: A STORY OF SOCIETY, ITS SPORTS, FUNCTIONS AND FAILINGS. London: Trischler, 1891 BMC. New York: D. Appleton, 1891 NUC.

Social novel. A handful of English people pass spring months in London. LW
Fanny Banning commits many crimes for money and power. Runs away to Egypt to be rid of her husband who loves another woman. IND
Moral: money is the root of evil: BOOK NEWS 111:133
SR, 74:171. Smart society. Hero and his wife get a divorce, hero remarries.

200929   VICTIMS. London: Bliss, 1894 BMC.

SR 77:419. Hero twice in divorce court as co-respondent and portrayed sympathetically. Male characters more convincing than female stereotypes: an adventuress and the heroine Gladys and her made to order sorrows.
SP 72:563. Lives of all the characters either hopelessly marred or brought to an untimely end.
ACAD-exposition of male vices. Study of dypsomania.
ATH 103:275. Self-sacrificing Gladys.

MAUDSLAY, ATHOL.

200930   AN ORDER TO VIEW. BY LOHTA YALSDUAM. London: Simpkin, Marshall, 1892 BMC. (Advice on Choosing a Country-house)

MAUNSELL, A. E. LLOYD.

200931   THE APOSTATE. London: G. Allen, 1908 BMC.

MAWSON, L. A.

200932   METHODS FROM MARS. London: Stockwell, [1913] BMC.

Gentleman from Mars arrives and tells how well life is managed there. TLS

MAXWELL, J. BYERS.

200933   A PASSION FOR GOLD, THE STORY OF A SOUTH AFRICAN MINE. London: A. Treherne, 1902 BMC.

MAY, EVAN.

200934   MUCH IN A NAME. London: Digby, Long, 1896

BMC.

ATH 107:32. Aunt receives letter from lover of her namesake niece, inviting her (niece) to join him matrimonially in New Zealand. She responds. Not a comedy.

200935   PHILIP GREYSTOKE. London: Digby, Long, [1898] BMC.

200936   WANTED-AN HEIRESS! A NOVEL. Hull: W. Andrews, [1891] BMC.

MAYER, J. E.

200937   THE HUMOR AND PATHOS OF ANGLO-INDIAN LIFE. London: E. Stock, 1895 BMC.

MEANY, J. L. United States.

200938   THE LOVERS; OR, CUPID IN IRELAND. [Havana, Ill.]: [Democrat Power Printing House], [c1891] NUC.

MEE, HUAN [pseud.]. Nationality Unknown.

200939   A BEAUTY SPOT; A NOVEL. BY HUAN MEE. London: Gale & Polden, [1894] BMC. (With 2 Other Tales)

200940   A DIPLOMATIC WOMAN. BY HUAN MEE. New York and London: Harper, 1900 NUC. London: Sands, 1900 BMC.

CR 37:181. Six detective stories from diplomatic pov. "display the feminine ingenuity of the woman that constructed them.
LW 31:172. Narrated by heroine, beautiful, irresistible and audacious, an elegant detective spy, her keen wits are more than a match for the subtlest and best trained diplomatists of Europe.
NYT 1900:551. Mme. Lerestelle.

200941   THE JEWEL OF DEATH. BY HUAN MEE. London: Ward, Lock, 1902 BMC 1905 NUC.

ATH 3-29-02

200942   WEAVING THE WEB. BY HUAN MEE. London: Ward, Lock, 1902 BMC.

200943   WHEELS WITHIN WHEELS. BY HUAN MEE. London: Ward, Lock, 1901 BMC.

MEIRION, ELLINOR [pseud.]. Nationality Unknown.

200944   CAUSE AND EFFECT. BY ELLINOR MEIRION. London: T. Fisher Unwin, 1895 BMC. New York: G. P. Putnam, 1895 NUC.

Highly respectable young English woman and Russian Nihilist. Hotel life. SR 80:694
Amy loved by clergyman she doesn't love. "She claims the independence he grudges her, and goes off to the Riviera to meet her fate." Her hero-Russian pianist. ACAD 48:183
The Russian jilts her; there the story ends. ATH 106:218
Amy Marsden. The Russian is an anarchist. There's gossip about him and Amy, but he goes back to his mistress Vara, Amy is left brokenhearted. The clergyman marries an arist woman BOOK NEWS 157:23

MEL, F. H.

200945   THE ACCOUNTANT. London: Remington, 1894 BMC.

ACAD 46:553. Dying doctor leaves his money to two sisters whom he announces to be his illegitimate daughters. The accountant is the son of an old friend to whom they are to come for advice or aid.
ATH 104:749. Honest little man with big responsibility is real hero of book.

MELL, F. H.

200946   THE GODS SAW OTHERWISE. A NOVEL. London: F. V. White, 1899 BMC.

Mystery of Muriel Granton's identity. She has a strange mark on her arm and there's a maniac that makes such a mark with his bite. ACAD 56:608.
Insane man plots to get her married to his son. Fortunately, she does not. ATH 114:123

MELLOR, C.

200947   THE DEATH PENALTY; A MODERN STORY. London: Swan Sonnenschein, 1894 BMC.

ACAD a liaison, a marriage which is morally less defensible than the liaison, two murders, an incredible piece of detectivism, and a suicide.

MELTON, R.

200948   CAESAR'S WIFE. London: Methuen, 1906 BMC.

TLS-Politician's wife, thin story
ATH thin story

MELVILLE, J. J.

200949   A WOMAN'S POWER. London: Ward, Lock, 1908 BMC.

TLS-Platonic mrg. arranged after it is discovered husb. is unconscious bigamist.

MENDHAM, E.

200950   HUMPHREY; A TRADITION. London: Hutchinson, 1898 BMC.

ACAD 53:347. Believed by villagers to be a wizard. Includes a search for fairy horde of treasure. ATH 111:657.

MEREDITH, JUNIOR [pseud.]. Nationality Unknown.

200951   THE HEIRESS OF CRANHAM HALL. BY MEREDITH, JUNIOR. New York: Broadway, [c1910] NUC.

MERROW, FLORENZ S. United States.

200952   THE RECONSTRUCTION OF ELINORE WOOD. BY FLORENZ S. MERROW, M.D. New York: Broadway, [c1911] NUC.

MERTON, MADGE [pseud.]. Nationality Unknown.

200953   CONFESSIONS OF A CHORUS GIRL. BY MADGE MERTON. New York: Grafton Press, [1903] NUC.

Very brief description. BKM 17 (1903) 428.

METCALFE, CRANSTOUN. See METCALFE, H. CRANSTOUN.

METCALFE, H. CRANSTOUN. United Kingdom.

200954   FAME FOR A WOMAN; OR SPLENDID MOURNING. BY CRANSTOUN METCALFE. New York and London: G. P. Putnam, 1902 NUC.

200955   SPLENDID MOURNING. London: Ward, Lock, 1902 BMC.

MILDRED, E. W. United States.

200956   THE GHOST-HOUSE; OR, THE STORY OF ROSE LICHEN. [New York]: [A. D. F. Randolph], 1893 NUC.

MILLER, G. W. United Kingdom.

200957   FETTERED BY FATE; A NOVEL. London: Digby, Long, 1899 BMC.

A pirate story. Also various felonies. ATH 113:176

MILLER, L. A. AND C. V. GOOLSBY. United States.

200958   THE LIFE OF A TRAMP AND A TRIP THROUGH HELL. BY PETER BLUM. Jacksonville, Fla.: C. S. Warnock, 1894 NUC.

MILLER, S. B.

200959   A MALICIOUS THREAT. Paisley: A. Gardner, 1895 BMC.

MILLIGAN, ALICE AND W. H. MILLIGAN.

200960   SONS OF THE SEA KINGS. Dublin: M. H. Gill, 1914 BMC NUC.

MILLIGAN, W. H., jt. au. See MILLIGAN, ALICE AND W. H. MILLIGAN.

MILNE, M. LUSHINGTON.

200961   LADY MABEL'S BEAUTY. London: J. Long, 1913 BMC.

A dog's life told by himself He's perfect, brave; a dog of good sense. ATH.

MILREIS, COLAS [pseud.].

200962   BOB MUFFLE; HIS TALES, HIS ADVENTURES, AND HIS ECCENTRIC LIFE. BY COLAS MILREIS. London: Bob Muffle Press, [1894] BMC.

200963   BY BALLOON TO THE POLE. BY COLAS MILREIS. London: Bob Muffle Press, [1895] BMC.

MILTON, C. R.

200964   THE EYES OF UNDERSTANDING. London: A. Melrose, 1919 BMC.

Indian official life TLS
Young woman takes post as Super. of a Training School in India. SP
And is "face to face with a melange of unrest, attempted revol. and official muddling" ATH
Govt. and misgoverment of Indian Empire LBKM

200965   THE SUNSET GUN. London: A. Melrose, [1920] BMC.

TLS-Conv. romance

MITCHELL, LAISDELL. United States.

200966   COLONEL. Philadelphia: A. J. Rowland, 1896 NUC. (Post Civil War South)

MITFORD, C. GUISE.

200967   THE DUAL IDENTITY. London: J. Long, 1915 BMC.

200968   THE HIDDEN MASK. London: Greening, 1914 BMC.

200969   HIS DAINTY WHIM. London: Hutchinson, 1902 BMC.

200970   IN CAMERA. London: J. Long, [1916] BMC.

200971   IZELLE OF THE DUNES. London: J. Long, 1907 BMC.

Simple, innocent idyll ACAD
Focuses on the hero. TLS

200972   LOVE IN LILAC-LAND. London: J. Long, [1910] BMC.

200973   THE PAXTON PLOT. London: J. Long, 1908 BMC.

TLS-Male hero in a nest of Russian revolutionaries.
ATH-Male hero in a nest of Russian revolutionaries.

200974   THE SPELL OF THE SNOW. London: C. A. Pearson, 1900 BMC.

ATH 116:613. Study of madness.

200975   THE WOOING OF MARTHA. London: E. Nash, 1911 BMC.

Smart Set; mother's sinister influence on daughter. ATH

MIZE, W. H. United States.

200976   GOLD, GRACE, AND GLORY. A STORY OF RELIGIOUS LIFE AMONG THE WEALTHY CLASSES OF THE WEST AND SOUTH. New York: G. W. Dillingham, 1896 NUC.

PW 7-18-96. The great Kansas grasshopper scourge of 1874. Religious revivals, camp-meetings, conversions, love, courtship & mrge etc.

MOFFAT, E. B.

200977   JOHN BROOME'S WIFE. London: T. F. Unwin, 1909 BMC.

Helen Rivers, fallen into "trouble" saved from drowning self by servant of a barrister who marries her right off-he's a blind man. TLS The husband becomes very jealous of the child but love grows between them. ATH

MOLE, MARION. Nationality Unknown.

200978   FOR THE SAKE OF A SLANDERED WOMAN. Edinburgh: W. Blackwood, 1895 BMC.

She is the victim of John Farquhar who resolves to murder her but who "jumps into the water with the wrong woman." Realizing this, he drowns himself. SR 80:181
The floating tourist life of ease. Sir Holland is a "donkey" for marrying the slandered woman, a "shrew," when he might have married Alice Edwards. ACAD 47:542
Slander is a financial accusation vs a young widow. She's the widow of a suicide who was a swindler and it's said she lives on his money. But she really lives by the pen. She also must contend with the bitterness of a lover she jilted. Because of all this she's isolated. Set in Norway. ATH 105:768

200979   VERA OF THE STRONG HEART. London: A. Melrose, 1910 BMC. New York: G. P. Putnam, 1910 NUC.

a fine young woman; misery and tragedy? PW
BKM v. 32 1910-11
TLS-Boyish girl trag.
ATH-She sacrifices herself for the family.
NYT-Is it a trag.? She and another woman marry two incredibly selfish brothers; they immediately go off on a trip together leaving wives to become friends. They are both killed. Vera smokes incessantly.

200980   THE WIND BLOWETH. London: A. Melrose, 1911 BMC.

ACAD-Male minister

MOLYNEUX, J.P.

200981   "FALL IN". London: Hurst & Blackett, 1915 BMC.

MONCRIEFF, A. M. SCOTT.

200982   A SHADOW OF '57. London: T. F. Unwin, 1915 BMC.

MONK, THYMOL.

200983   AN ALTAR OF EARTH. London: W. Heinemann, 1894 BMC. New York: G. Putnam, 1894 NUC.

ACAD 46:506. "The voluntary prostitution of a pure woman for what seems to her an adequate, nay an imperative, good for others."
LW 25:372. Pathological tale. Two heroines, neither can love the men who care for them; one has an incurable disease.
PW-they are socialists; they reject the men so they can work for the good of humanity. One is a clothes designer; the other a medical student. When the latter learns of her disease, they both go to the country for a rest and she makes the final sacrifice of her life.
Two young women live together "to carry out their plans better." one has only two years to live, regrets she can't carry out "her mission for good in this world." "The book is the direct outcome of Sarah Grand's teaching-much of her nonsense being reproduced here." CR 23:28.
Daphne and Theo are "two medical women." Daphne is incurably ill, will die in two years. The two retire to a hillside haven to make the most of the two years. A builder imposes his attentions on Daphne, who is repelled by him and attacks him with insults. The builder asks her price and she sells herself for Hiram Hill to be a gift to the people.

MONLAUR, MARIE REYNES. B. 1870.

200984   SISTER CLARE. New York: McBride, 1917 NUC. London: Burns and Oates, 1917 BMC. (Tr. from the French by M. E. Arendrup.)

Franciscan sisters at Diant and the coming of the Germans. Sister Clare's religious spirit is fired by the suffering--goes among the Germans to aid them in their need. TLS

MONOPOLE [pseud.].

200985   HIS LAST AMOUR. BY "MONOPOLE". London: Digby, Long, [1895] BMC.

Valerie forced to marry an ugly old man. Decides to get rid of him by tarnishing her reputation with a wicked duke. SR 79:519
Valerie Campbell discovers her husband is a forger and also has a mistress. This mistress dies by accident,

but her death looks so much like murder that the old
husband kills himself, clearing the way for Valerie."
ACAD 47:100

MONOWAI.

200986   "JUDITH": AN OLD TIME ROMANCE. BY
"MONOWAI," A.S.C. London: H. J. Drane, [1902] BMC.

ATH 121:335

MONTGOMERY, A. B. United States.

200987   THE MAKING OF A MILLIONAIRE. BY HIMSELF.
A TRUE STORY [ANONYMOUS]. New York: G. W. Dillingham,
1898 NUC.

MONTGOMERY, LESLIE ALEXANDER. B. 1873. United Kingdom.

200988   BALLYGUILLON. BY LYNN DOYLE. Dublin:
Maunsel, 1908 BMC NUC.

200989   MR. WILDRIDGE OF THE BANK. BY LYNN DOYLE.
London: Duckworth, [1916] BMC NUC. New York: F. A.
Stokes, [c1916] NUC.

"The village of Portnamuck in the north of Ireland
needed to be awakened, and a woolen mill and a branch
of the railroad were the means of awakening. Everybody
in Portnamuck agreed to this, but nobody made a move.
Then came the rumor of Mr. Normanby's legacy, left him
by the scapegrace brother who had emigrated years
before. Mr. Normanby was the rector and the most
public spirited man in the town and with the assurance
that his new fortune will be devoted to the woolen
mill, the thing is given such a start that even the
announcement that there is no fortune can not stop it.
In the meantime there is Nora, Mr. Normanby's adored
and adorable daughter, to keep matters stirred up.
Nora is an attractive hoyden who plays havoc with the
heart of Mr. Wildridge of the bank, making him forget
that he is a middle-aged lover of the classics, and
leading him in the end to make a momentous decision
between matrimony and liberty, between herself and
Horace." BRD

MOORE, LESLIE. United Kingdom.

200990   ANTONY GRAY,--GARDENER. New York and
London: G.P. Putnam, 1917 BMC NUC.

"A sudden whim puts into the mind of Nicholas Danver
the desire to see his last will and testament in
operation. With the assistance of his friend Doctor
Hilary, he becomes officially dead, and Antony Gray,
his heir, is called home from South Africa to hear the
conditions of the will. They are rather unusual,
requiring that the young man shall live on the estate
for one year as an undergardener. The fulfillment of
this condition is made more difficult for Antony by
the presence in the neighborhood of the woman he
loves. At the crisis in affairs, Nicholas comes
forward from his retirement to set matters straight."
BRD 1917.

200991   AUNT OLIVE IN BOHEMIA; OR, THE INTRUSIONS
OF A FAIRY GODMOTHER. New York: Hodder and Stoughton,
[c1913] NUC. London: A. Rivers, 1913 BMC NUC.

PW 8-16-13 "A dear old maiden lady of sixty whose life
has always been of the most narrow sort falls heir to
a large fortune. The opportunity is presented to
realize the dream of her youth-to study art. She goes
to London and becomes a charming Bohemian, bringing
joy into her own life by her kindness and helpfulness
to all who come in contact with her."
Rents a studio in Chelsea; plays fairy godmother to
the neighboring inmates. ATH

200992   THE CLOAK OF CONVENTION. London: A.
Rivers, 1912 BMC NUC.

TLS concerns breaking the law of man in obedience to
the greater law of love.

200993   THE DESIRED HAVEN. London: A. Melrose,
[1918] BMC.

TLS-Phillip's progress to RC

200994   THE GREENWAY. New York: P.J. Kenedy,
[1919] NUC. London: Sands, [1920] BMC.

TLS-Romance of 35 yr old pretty typist.
"Elizabeth Dacre tells her story in the first person.
The only child of an unsuccessful writer, her father's

death left her with a very few pounds in the bank, and
small ability to earn her own living. She obtained a
position as companion to a rich old lady, but after a
year she rebelled, purchased a cheap typewriter and
got a place in an office. Two years of drudgery
followed: then the old lady died and left Elizabeth
her Devonshire cottage, 'The Greenway,' and 200 pounds
a year. Meanwhile, Elizabeth had met two men, one of
whom she knew as 'the artist,' the other as 'the
cynic.' Of course both had close connections with the
Devonshire Village where Elizabeth's new home was,
and, before she had been there long, both appeared.
There are two love stories, all the apparently
unpleasant people prove to be really mines of virtue,
and success and happiness are bestowed upon the
deserving in large quantities."- NYT

200995   THE JESTER. New York and London: G. P.
Putnam's, 1915 BMC NUC.

"A story which at the outset promises to be a medieval
romance but which later turns out an allegory.
Peregrine the jester has no taste for jesting and is
not ready of tongue. Rather he is a lover of nature
and a poet. But the haughty Lady Isabel whom he serves
takes a momentary fancy to him and for love of her he
willingly accepts the cap and bells." BRD 1915

200996   THE NOTCH IN THE STICK. London: A.
Rivers, 1912 BMC NUC.

TLS-Mrg of convenience on side of the bride with a
artist lover in the background.

200997   THE PEACOCK FEATHER. A ROMANCE. London:
A. Rivers, 1913 BMC. New York and London: G. P.
Putnam's Sons, [1914] NUC.

PW 85 3/21/14 1023 "Peter Carden, when story opens, is
just released from three years in Portland gaol for
forgery. His father and fiancee cast him off and Peter
takes to wandering about the country piping on a penny
whistle. He writes a successful book, which Lady Anne
Garland reads and feels moved to write to the author
and thank him for. Thus begins a delightful
correspondence, neither knowing the identity of the
other. Peter takes up his abode in a deserted cottage
and through an accident discovers that his unknown
lady and the lady of the manor are one. How Peter is
cleared and how a misunderstanding between him and
Lady Anne is cleared up and what part various
delightful people took in the matter make this
charming tale's ending."
"The story of a young man who shields a friend who has
committed a crime and endures imprisonment in his
stead...Repudiated by his father and renounced by his
betrothed, he takes to the road...The love that soon
comes furnishes new proof that 'when half gods go, the
gods arrive,' and all ends just as it should." (NYT)
BRD 1914

200998   THE WISER FOLLY. New York and London: G.
P. Putnam's sons, 1916 BMC NUC.

Involves an old estate PW
Involves an old estate NYT
TLS Involves an old estate
"An old English castle is the center about which this
story moves. It is the home of the Delanceys, and at
the time of the story the head of the family is Lady
Mary, a fine old gentlewoman who is holding the estate
for her small grandson. But a claimant for the place
appears, an American who has lived long in Africa, and
whose claim to descent from an older branch of the
family seems well founded. The plot of the story is
concerned with the influences that lead him to give up
his rights, Lady Mary's granddaughter, Rosamund, and
two young men, one of them engaged in restoring the
mural decorations of the village church,also have a
part in the story. (Boston Transcript p6 N 11 '16
250w.) "The artist is a little boring with his karma,
and the piety pervading the story is sometimes almost
too mystic to follow, but the novel is a delightful
one, with a distinctive quality of its own-a
wholesome, sunny, thoroughly companionable romance,
which we lay aside with the feeling of having kept
good company." (NYT 21:253 JE 18 '16).
"In 'The wiser folly' Leslie Moore employs some of the
whimsicalities that made her first story, 'The peacock
feather,' so delightful. But while that tale was
spontaneous, and moved with a natural charm, the
overworking of the same atmosphere and type of
character lend this story a formal and somewhat
strained tone. Miss Moore is, however, a graceful, if
light, romancer, and her stories invariably betray a
kindly philosophy-a devotion to the golden rule."

(Springfield Republican p15 Ap 2 '16 230w BRD

MOORE, S.

200999   IN HONOUR-BOUND. London: Drane's, [1911]
BMC.

Honor concerns a matrimonial engagement. ATH

MORAN, W. H. W.   United States.

201000   FROM SCHOOL-ROOM TO BAR: A NOVEL.
Philadelphia: J. B. Lippincott, 1892 NUC.

LW 23:295. Southern family on the James River. Family
is proud and unwilling that he should demean himself
with work.

MORE, K. MERVIN.

201001   DESPATCHES FROM LADIES' CLUBLAND. London:
K. Mervin More, [1908] BMC NUC.

TLS-Narrator describes her purchase of a Ladies' Club
and the efforts made by old members & their friends to
ruin her enterprise-a not very edifying relation.

MORICHINI, U. L.

201002   SEED ON STONY GROUND: A NOVEL. London:
Chapman & Hall, 1908 BMC. (Tr. from Italian by Ella
St. Leger)

TLS O

MORRIS, E. O'CONNOR.

201003   CLARE NUGENT; A NOVEL. London: Digby,
Long, 1902 BMC.

201004   FINOLA. London: Digby, Long, 1910 BMC.

TLS-male hero rom.

MORTIMER, LESLIE.

201005   THE MEN WE MARRY. London: J. Long, [1910]
BMC NUC.

TLS-3 women & 1 male scoundrel. I think all 3 marry
him in turn.
ATH-Indictment of monstrousness man displays, lack of
proportion. He deserts all 3.

201006   THE SIN OF YOUTH. London: J. Long, 1912
BMC.

ATH O hist.

201007   THE TORCH OF VENUS. London: J. Long, 1911
BMC.

About jewel theft TLS

MORTON, A. J.   b. 1900.   United Kingdom.

201008   BEYOND THE PALAEOCRYSTIC SEA; OR, THE
LEGEND OF HALFJORD. Chicago: Privately Printed, 1895
NUC.

MORTON, L. CURRY.   Nationality Unknown.

201009   THE HERO AND THE MAN. Chicago: A. C.
McClurg, 1912 NUC.

PW-Woman journalist and novelist.
NYT-A man has crossed her path and impressed her so
deeply she has made him hero of the novel. Scene is
Northwestern town struggling for law and order.

MOTT, C. C. AND ELIZABETH M. MOTT.

201010   A MAN OF NO FAMILY; A TALE OF WHAT
ACTUALLY HAPPENED. London: Hutchinson, 1906 BMC.

TLS-love story

201011   A THOROUGHBRED IN TRAINING. London:
Hutchinson, 1907 BMC.

Fashionable country society; concerns racing, etc. TLS

MOTT, ELIZABETH M., jt. au.   See MOTT, C. C. AND ELIZABETH
M. MOTT.

MOUNTJOY, EVELYN [pseud.].

201012   DEMETRIUS AND DAISY. BY EVELYN MOUNTJOY.
London: J. Long, [1911] BMC.

Daisy, an adventuress, bewitches a well to do
Englishman into marriage. Their travels till she tires
of respectability. TLS

MULLWO, A.

201013   A FAIR SUFFRAGETTE. BY A. MULLWO. Drane,
BS.

MULTIPLE AUTHORS.

201014   A CUNNING CULPRIT; OR, A "NOVEL" NOVEL. A
COMPOSITE ROMANCE BY TWENTY DIFFERENT POPULAR WRITERS.
Chicago: Hobart, 1895 NUC.

MUNDO, OTO E.   United States.

201015   THE RECOVERED CONTINENT: A TALE OF THE
CHINESE INVASION. Columbus, Ohio: Harper-Osgood, 1898
NUC BMC.

It is Greenland. Writer wakes up after a Rip Van
Winkle sleep to find his grandson is president of
Greenland. Many strange things. LW 36,219.

MUNRO, ALICK.

201016   A WOMAN OF WILES. London: Ward, Lock,
1902 BMC.

Fem head of a gang of adventurers "daring, brilliant
fascin." LBKM 8-02

MURDOCK, W. N.   United States.

201017   THIRD HAND HIGH: A NOVEL. Boston: Lee and
Shepard, 1893 NUC.

Northeast farmer inherits wealth, marries a woman of
social position who marries him for money, but when
his fortune is threatened, she realizes she loves him
for himself. The problem is solved with the
intervention of a third person. PW 10-7-93.

MURHO [pseud.].

201018   GLENDARROCH. BY MURHO. Bristol:
Arrowsmith, 1901 BMC.

ATH:7-13-01

MURRAY, H. ROBERTSON.

201019   CLARICE, I AND OTHERS: BEING THE
CHRONICLES OF SEABEAM ISLAND. London: W. J. Ham-Smith,
1912 BMC.

TLS-ineffectual humor at seaside.
SP

MUSGRAVE, H.

201020   MYOLA. London: Hodder & Stoughton, [1917]
BMC.

Woman brutally treated by father; deserted by love.
she's strong, rich (New Zeal). Father murdered her
illegitimate child. (She was a shop girl seduced by
Englishman). Then she comes into an inheritance, goes
to England, finds that man married, She goes home and
dies. TLS

MYDDLETON, HUDE.

201021   JACK SMITH, M.P. Westminster: A.
Constable, 1898 BMC.

ACAD 54:296. Mildly sensational, hero is man of
politics.

201022   PHOEBE DEACON; OR, THE LOVE THAT LIVES.
London: Jarrold, 1895 BMC.

N., pseud.   See NEWMAN, H. E.

N., N. [pseud.].

201023   MONTOREL: THE STORY OF A COINCIDENCE. BY
A FRENCH AUTHOR [ANONYMOUS]. Iris, [1915] BMC.

Story of Revolutionary times. Dr. Joseph, hero, has
discovered a cure for cancer. TLS

NARRAN, BREE.

201024   CORA PEARL, "THE LADY OF THE PINK EYES".
London: Anglo-Eastern, [1919] BMC.

201025   THE KINEMA GIRL. London: Anglo-Eastern,
[1919] BMC.

201026   ONE NIGHT. London: Anglo-Eastern, [1919]
BMC.

201027   SEVEN NIGHTS. London: Anglo-Eastern,
[1919] BMC.

201028   THREE NIGHTS. London: Anglo-Eastern,
[1919] BMC.

NARD, RAY [pseud.]. United States.

201029   RITA; OR, SIN'S HARVEST. BY RAY NARD. New
York: G. W. Dillingham, 1895 W.

NAVARCHUS [pseud.].

201030   THE WORLD'S AWAKENING. BY NAVARCHUS.
London: Hodder & Stoughton, [1908] BMC NUC.

TLS-futuristic port. of war, & revolt of labor against
the military.

NELHAM, O. ESLIE.

201031   THE UNPITIED STRONG. London: E. Stock,
1911 BMC.

NELSON, H. ARNOLD.

201032   THE ROMANCE OF THE GREYSTONES. AN
AUSTRALIAN STORY. London: Ward, Lock, [1899] BMC.

NEMCOVA, BOZENA. 1820-1862.

201033   THE GRANDMOTHER; A STORY OF COUNTRY LIFE
IN BOHEMIA. Chicago: A. C. McClurg, 1891 BMC NUC. (Tr.
Frances Gregor, with a biographical sketch of the
author.)

NATION 54:115. Story of daily life of an old peasant
woman and her family in Bohemia. Nemec was active in
1848 revolution, love for the peasantry. Simple sketch
of daily life of family of Bohemia; fountain of cheer.

NEMO.

201034   A MERE PUG; OR, THE ROMANCE OF A DOG. BY
NEMO. London: Digby, Long, [1897] BMC.

NEWMAN, H. E. Nationality Unknown.

201035   THE PROPHET; A NOVEL. BY N. New York:
Broadway, [c1912] NUC.

NEWTON, SYDNEY.

201036   JOE FORD. London: T. F. Unwin, 1895 BMC.

ACAD 49:260. Story of an elaborate hoax devised by an
eccentric baronet who has a weakness for moral
experiments.

NICHOL, C. A. SCRYMSOUR.

201037   THE MYSTERY OF THE NORTH POLE. London: F.
Griffiths, 1908 BMC.

NICHOLAS, J. W.

201038   THE HOUSE OF MYSTERY. Bristol: J. W.
Arrowsmith, [1891] BMC.

A feast of horrors. Melo hypnotism, burglary, murder
mysteries, Jack the Ripper glimpsed. ACAD
A diabolical black dog, captives in cellars, Bohemian
gaieties, sirens and mashers in St. John's Wood SR
9-19-91, 340

201039   THE STORY OF CLOVELLY'S WIFE. MY FIRST
APPEARANCE. THE METHOD OF JASPAR LOTZ. Bristol: J. W.
Arrowsmith, [1893] BMC.

NIGHTINGALE, VAL.

201040   THE DEVIL'S DAUGHTER. London: Digby and
Long, [1897] BMC.

Devilry and supernaturalism. Ugly story. ATH 110:451
SP 81:448. Diabline, a foundling, is adopted by
American parents. She grows up to be a beautiful woman
and an unwilling cause of untold evil. Touch of the
supernatural detracts from story.

201041   THE WORLD ON WHEELS. London: Simpkin and
Marshall, [1896] BMC.

NIKTO, VERA [pseud.]. United Kingdom.

201042   A MERE WOMAN. BY VERA NIKTO. New York: D.
Appleton, 1913 NUC. London: Duckworth, 1913 BMC NUC.

PW 83 5/10/13:1687
"She's a creature of sex impulse," loves luxury;
motherhood awakens a noble passion. Husband's will
imposes heartless restriction upon her in the end,
which is left up in the air. NYT
Even though it ended brutally and because there's
nothing else to do, she marries a rich old merchant.
Vadim returns and the three play a game that leads to
Vadim's death and Sonia's remaining the old merchant's
prisoner. "Written with unusual ability" BKM

NIXON, J. LEROY. United States.

201043   THE LOWLY NAZARENE: A STORY OF CHRIST.
New York: J. S. Ogilvie, [c1897] NUC.

NORMAN, E. A.

201044   LIFE VERSUS ROMANCE. London: D. Nutt,
1914 BMC.

ACAD 87:185. Contrast between Rose, a Roman Catholic,
and Clara, an agnostic. Rose is killed by a motor
omnibus.
ATH 144:232. Author favors Rose. Clara is passionless.

NORMAN, ENGLISH. United States.

201045   MELVINA DREW. New York: Broadway, [c1905]
NUC.

A woman writes and speaks against pampering of dogs
while people starve. She undergoes operation to save
her sight; marries her doctor. NYT 1905:541

NORMAN, M. E. Nationality Unknown.

201046   MISS PANDORA. New York: G. H. Doran, 1916
NUC. London: W. Heinemann, 1916 BMC.

artist & writer Capt. Seaton Pandora's lover "in a
mad episode in Spain." PW 90:7/29/16:389
NYT-then when she is engaged to someone else and he is
engaged to Elizabeth, they meet. She tries and
succeeds in reclaiming him.

NORTH, ANISON. United Kingdom.

201047   CARMICHAEL. London [Ont.]: W. Weld, 1907
BMC. New York: Doubleday, Page, 1907 NUC.

201048   THE FORGING OF THE PIKES: A ROMANCE OF
THE UPPER CANADIAN REBELLION OF 1837. London: Hodder
and Stoughton, [1920] BMC. New York: G.H. Doran,
[c1920] BMC NUC.

PW-romance based on political struggles in Canada 80
years ago.

NUTT, M. L.

201049   A WOMAN OF TO-DAY. London: D. Nutt, 1913
BMC.

O'CALLAGHAN, J. P., jt. au. See FENNELL, CHARLOTTE AND J.
P. O'CALLAGHAN.

O'KANE, W. M.

201050   GUPPY GAYSON. London: Mills & Boon, 1913
BMC.

201051   THE KING'S LUCK. A ROMANCE OF THE VALE OF
HOPE. London: Chapman & Hall, 1912 BMC.

TLS hist romance.
ATH hist romance.

201052   WITH POISON AND SWORD. London: Mills &
Boon, 1910 BMC.

TLS Hist-

O'REILLY, B. M., jt. au. See PHELPS, SYDNEY K. AND B. M. O'REILLY.

OSCAR, W. N.

201053   THE CRUISE OF THE GOLDEN WAVE. London: A. D. Innes, 1899 BMC. New York: E. P. Dutton, 1899 NUC.

Adventure: a mutiny, fighting aboard ship in which ladies partake, a treasure, a desert island, and sundry weddings at the end. LIT 4:528

OSMUN, LEIGHTON GRAVES. B. 1880. United States.

201054   THE CLUTCH OF CIRCUMSTANCE. New York: Sully & Kleinteich, 1914 NUC.

PW--"New York theatrical life is the setting. Ruth Lawson, living in a small up-state town, has only been married a year when her husband is injured and brought home unconscious. For months he remains so, and Ruth is obliged to support him and his mother. She goes to New York and after great hardship makes a success on the stage, but finds there is a price to pay. Her husband recovers and believing that Ruth is a fallen woman refuses to see her. When at last they meet, Ruth finds that the man is so changed that he is no longer the man she loved and she has to readjust her life."

OTTERBURN, BELTON.

201055   CLEMENT CARLILE'S DREAM. A NOVEL. London: Digby, Long, 1898 NUC BMC.

ACAD 53:625. Confusion over a spook with a powder barrel.

201056   HE WOULD BE AN OFFICER; OR, FROM CHARING CROSS TO THE TWENTY-FIFTH HUSSARS. London: Roxburghe, [1896] BMC.

201057   JILTED! A NOVEL. London: Roxburghe Press, [1897] BMC.

201058   NURSE ADELAIDE. A NOVEL. London: Digby, Long, 1897 BMC.

SR 85:119. An enjoyable literary atrocity.

201059   UNRELATED TWINS: A NOVEL. London: Digby and Long, [1897] BMC.

OULTON, S. C.

201060   THE TURN OF THE TIDE. Dublin: Sealy, Bryers & Walker, 1907 BMC.

About Boer war; feeble tale of love and misunderstanding. TLS

OWEN, RYE. Nationality Unknown.

201061   RED-HEADED GILL. New York: H. Holt, 1903 NUC. Bristol: J. W. Arrowsmith, 1903 BMC.

A splendid woman relives former life as beauty in Elizabeth's court. PW 3-28-03

P., A. N. T. A. A. N. T. A. P. [pseud.].

201062   THEORIES. STUDIES FROM A MODERN WOMAN. London: T. F. Unwin, 1894 BMC. (Independent Novel Series)

SR 77:71. Modern young woman filled with enthusiasm for social reform is disillusioned when training for her children miscarries.
SP 72:544. She is similar to Marcella, says reviewer, only more impulsive with a less disciplined mind. The modern theories (such as Socialism) don't work out for her.
ACAD 45:186. Author does not attempt to take sides. A "pasteboard heroine." "Such women as Beatrice do more harm to the good cause they would serve than is wrought by any amount of masculine opacity and opposition."
ATH 103:145. Rev. feels author has treated husband unfairly. Wife is a firebrand, but sweet.

P., O. S. [pseud.].

201063   A WOMAN'S SOUL [ANONYMOUS]. London: K. Paul, 1904 BMC.

PALMER, BELL ELLIOTT. United States.

201064   THE SINGLE CODE GIRL: A NOVEL. London: Lothrop, Lee, Shepard, [1915] NUC.

Letters of man to a young woman; a proposal; describes eight feminine types. "A novel of eugenics whose author is a social worker." NYT

PALMER, HURLY PRING.

201065   MR. TRUEMAN'S SECRET: A TALE OF WEST SOMERSET. London: S. Sonnenschein, 1895 BMC.

He's a manly sort but the Dissenter is a negative portrayal. ACAD 48:243
He believes he killed a man in a duel. Marries Edith Thynne, a serious earnest young woman, an early riser, well suited to her minister husband. ATH 106:31

PAN, pseud. See BERESFORD, LESLIE.

PAPILLON, E. T.

201066   ALLEYNE: A STORY OF A DREAM AND A FAILURE. London: T. F. Unwin, 1894 BMC.

PARKINSON, D. C.

201067   PENARTH. London: Digby, Long, [1897] BMC.

Cornish squire has so much power he murders without punishment. Gets a hold of the heroine and hero but they escape and he dies in the end. SR 84:528

PARKS, L. K. 1846-1925. United States.

201068   WITH BRITISH AND BRAVES: STORY OF THE WAR OF 1812. Cincinnati: Curts and Jennings, [c1898] NUC.

PARPACK, J. B. United States.

201069   ONE HEART THAT NEVER ACHED. BY KRESS KAIN. Boston: Roxburgh, [c1911] NUC.

Poor woman inherits estate: mysteries, lawsuits, marriage. PW 9-9-11 PW

PARRY, D. H.

201070   FOR GLORY AND RENOWN. London: Cassell, 1895 BMC.

Marion Ascough growing up in Fr. quarter of Montreal has great beauty that brings as much disaster as good fortune. Goes to Boston to make a career in art world. Has difficult time earning a living posing, moves to NY, finally marries an artist. PW

PATON, J. L.

201071   A HOME IN INVERESK. London: Methuen, 1896 BMC.

ATH 107:713. Scotland. Simple romance.
SP 77:313. Marion, after discussing Carlyle, Spencer, Darwin and Huxley with him, marries Nigel, only to discover he is father of illegitimate child. She is so horrified that Nigel flees to America in remorse. Eventually she decides to forgive him and goes to America to find him. Here she encounters new suspicions, but they prove groundless.

PATTERSON, J. T.

201072   WHAT NEXT? OR, THE HONEST THIEF. [Lexington Ky.: Transylvania Printing], [1899] W.

PATTESON, CAMM. 1840-1909. United States.

201073   THE YOUNG BACHELOR; WITH AN APPENDIX, CONTAINING AN ESSAY ON "THE DESTINY OF THE NEGRO IN AMERICA". Lynchburg, Va.: J. P. Bell, 1900 NUC.

PATTON, M. OAKMAN. See PATTON, MARION OAKMAN.

PATTON, MARION OAKMAN. B. 1860. Nationality Unknown.

201074   THE LIGHTED TAPER; A NOVEL. BY M. OAKMAN PATTON. Boston: Botolph Book, 1907 NUC.

PAYN, E. M.

201075   HER STEWARDSHIP. London: Digby, Long, 1914 BMC.

ATH-Brought up as a boy by her grandfather so that she

might inherit his estate. Disguise is kept up throughout her lifetime, altho there are complications when she falls in love with rightful heir.

PECHELL, MARY, jt. au. See DICKSON, F. THORALD AND MARY PECHELL.

PEDROSA, P.

201076   THE COBWEB: A NOVEL. London: A. H. Stockwell, 1919 BMC.

The winning of a husband. TLS

PEEK, HEDLEY. Nationality Unknown.

201077   THE CHARIOT OF THE FLESH. London: Lawrence and Bullen, 1897 BMC. New York: Longmans, Green, 1897 NUC.

A gem commands truth from those who look on it. Hero can read people's minds, so that he knows his sweetheart isn't all that innocent. The successive stages of her development to "ideal wife". SR 83:229

PEILE, PENTLAND.

201078   THE BLUFFSHIRE COURIER. A WEST HIGHLAND STORY. Edinburgh: W. Blackwood, 1909 BMC.

Miranda Ross acquires the provincial courier which she now runs; turns radical: "Land for the people, abolition of all remaining feudal encumbrances." Her efforts fail she marries in the end. ACAD

201079   CLANBRAE. A GOLFING IDYLL. Edinburgh: W. Blackwood, 1908 BMC.

PENROSE, S. E.

201080   VICTORIA'S VICISSITUDES. London: Simpkin, Marshall, [1912] BMC.

ATH-experience in Germany as a governess--came back TLS-to marry fellow she left

PERRIGO, G. A. United States.

201081   THE MAN AND THE WOMAN. Atlanta, Ga.: American Pub.and Engraving Pub., 1895 NUC.

PETTER, EVELYN BRANSCOMBE. Nationality Unknown.

201082   MISS VELANTY'S DISCLOSURE. London: Chapman & Hall, 1916 BMC NUC.

TLS-Gretchen's tragedy was to be a German out of place-dour rebellious personality-strange mystery is finally revealed.
SP-Gretchen is mutinous, independent, aggressive, sensitive, fastidious, and intolerant. Rebels publicly at boarding school, taken in by English religious fanatic and his wife, rebels, works for a feminist (as her secretary) and falls for older German man. When her employer resents this, she marries him. Leaves him a few months later when she discovers he has a wife already. Then falls in love with an Englishman but this doesn't work out

201083   SCOPE. London: Chapman & Hall, 1916 BMC.

TLS-describes "scope offered to and accepted by Kate Carruth for wider life than she found in native country town-in a strangely concerted marriage which led thru tragedy to a subtle development. Sombre, fresh, sincere. 2 tragedies, 1 quasi. Vernon's half-deformed sister kills herself in response to a taunt or something regarding her love for her brother.

201084   SOULS IN THE MAKING. London: Chapman & Hall, 1917 NUC BMC.

Study of several chars. TLS

PHELPS, SYDNEY K. AND B. M. O'REILLY.

201085   WHERE TWO WORLDS MET. F. Griffiths, 1906 WWWL.

ACAD-supernatural, seances

PHILALETHES.

201086   JOHN DRUMOND FRASER: A STORY OF JESUIT INTRIGUE IN THE CHURCH OF ENGLAND. BY PHILALETHES. London: Cassell, 1893 BMC NUC.

PHILIPS, PAGE. United States.

201087   AT BAY; A NOVEL... BASED ON THE DRAMA BY GEORGE SCARBOROUGH. New York: Macaulay, 1914 NUC. London: Hodder & Stoughton, 1916 BMC.

"Plot hinges round the murder of a blackmailer. Aline Graham goes to him to get some compromising letters and when he seizes her and tries to kiss her, she takes a letter spike and stabs him. Captain Holbrook, gentleman and soldier of fortune, tries to shield Aline, whom he loves, and his Irish wit and dauntless courage give the police a hard time in trying to arrest the perpetrator of the crime. Denouement in which Aline is cleared and at the same time freed from a former marriage comes as a surprise to all concerned." PW 85 5/9/14 1555

PHILLIPS, J. GORDON.

201088   CORA LINN: A ROMANCE OF THE CLYDE. Paisley: A. Gardener, 1895 BMC.

201089   FLORA MACDONALD, THE MAID OF SKYE. A ROMANCE OF THE '45. London: Digby, Long, [1897] BMC.

201090   JAMES MCPHERSON, THE HIGHLAND FREEBOOTER. London: A. Gardner, 1894 BMC.

201091   THE LAIRD'S WOOING: A ROMANCE OF DEESIDE. London: T. F. Unwin, 1899 BMC.

PHILLIPS, L. M. See PHILLIPS, LUNDERN M.

PHILLIPS, LUNDERN M. United States.

201092   THE MIND READER. BY L. M. PHILLIPS. London and New York: F. T. Neely, [1898] NUC.

201093   MISKEL: A NOVEL. BY L. M. PHILLIPS, M.D. Franklin, Ohio: Editor, 1895 NUC.

PHILLIPS, VERE.

201094   POOR MISS SMITH. THE STORY OF A SOUTH AFRICAN ILLUSION. London: H. J. Drane, [1901] BMC.

PHILOSOPHUS [pseud.].

201095   AMY CLAREFORT. A ROMANCE OF THE YEAR 1900. BY PHILOSOPHUS. London: Simpkin and Marshall, 1893 BMC.

PICKERING, A. D.

201096   THE ENLIGHTENMENT OF SYLVIA. A NOVEL. London: J. Murray, 1912 BMC.

ATH-innocuous tale of girl & guardian.
TLS
Sylvia's mother, an actress, died at her birth, when father died, she's left in care of his friend who is not married. Of course there's another man she thinks she loves but learns she really loves first one. "Thoroughly conventional stereotypes." ACAD

PICKERING, SIDNEY. United Kingdom.

201097   MARGOT. London: Lawrence and Bullen, 1897 BMC. New York and London: G. P. Putnam, 1897 NUC.

LW 29:91. Story of illeg. Margaret Lee, an art student in Paris "Sad story with just the hint of a happy ending."

201098   THE ROMANCE OF HIS PICTURE. London: A. Constable, 1895 BMC.

SP-Lesbia, of good birth poses as peasant artist's model. romance later with artist.

201099   VERITY. London: E. Arnold, 1900 BMC.

SP 85:938. Verity's father is a coarse-tongued clergyman who beats his daughters. Her lover is selfish and pleasure seeking. In final catastrophe father shoots him.
ACAD 59:491. He is a parson. Verity is human, not an angel. Noel is the hero. Zadok the one who is killed. ATH 116:c12. Tragic end. Three sisters and a father who horsewhips them and keeps them in solitary confinement as discipline. Their love affairs.

201100   WANDERERS. London: J. Bowden, 1898 BMC NUC.

682

ATH 111;720. Heroine tramps and camps out with father for 10 years and then is sent to her mother's country home. She must then choose between her parents.
SR 85:854. Her wandering experience does not seem to have any special influence on her character other than a taste for travel.
LBKM 14:109. She seems to remain a wanderer.

PIERCE, SQUIER LITTELL. D. 1932. United States.

201101   DI: A STORY. Philadelphia: J. B. Lippincott, 1891 NUC. (On the Miami Canal. Minnesota)

201102   STOLEN STEPS: A STORY. Philadelphia: J. B. Lippincott, 1892 NUC.

CR 7-16-92. Heroine is kidnapped as child by father and raised in Northwest, she grows into a plain speaking and robust young woman. Writing is "a little rank for Eastern consumption."
LW 23:279. Identifies author as male lawyer.
PW "evil effects of alcoholism and profligacy."

PILGRIM [pseud.].

201103   A BLANK PAGE. BY PILGRIM. London: G. Redway, 1896 BMC.

PLEDGE, E. M.

201104   THE FARRELL DISHONOR; OR, FABIAN'S FOLLY. London: Jarrold, 1897 BMC.

PODMORE, C. T.

201105   A CYNIC'S CONSCIENCE. London: E. Arnold, 1900 BMC.

SP 85:675. The study of a cynic.
SR 89:753. Not a cynic and has no conscience.
ACAD 58:410. His self-flatteries and shifts of conscience are laid open mercilessly. His love affair.

201106   THE FAULT. London: J. Long, 1909 BMC.

Traditional sensational murder story

201107   A TROMBONE AND A STAR. London: E. Arnold, 1905 BMC.

POOLE, J. PARRINGTON.

201108   THE DIEL' GRANNIE. London: Digby, Long, 1899 BMC.

PORTER, T. H.

201109   A MAID OF THE MALVERNS. A ROMANCE OF THE BLACKFRIARS THEATRE. London: Lynwood, [1911] BMC.

Elizabethan times; we meet Bacon, Jonson. TLS
The maid masquerades as a boy in Ben Jonson's company of child actors.

POULTON, C. E.

201110   JUSTIFIED. London: Greening, 1909 BMC.

People in politics concerned with the tragedy of Lord Westerbrooke's married life. TLS

POWELL, F. INGLIS. Nationality Unknown.

201111   THE SNAKE. London, New York: J. Lane, 1912 BMC NUC.

PW–Gruesome tale of a snake woman.
TLS–Individual diary giving the unsavoury imaginings of a bad woman.
ATH–Sorcerer wills her spirit into a snake; she murders many including parents, finally sorcerer and she are both killed.
ACAD–She is rebellious and passionate, seeks revenge of man she loves. Tragic end. She is a young English woman who was left in the care of an Indian woman and becomes educated in her ways.
BKM–She is controlled and used by chief priest of cobra cult.

POYNTER, H. MAY.

201112   A FAIR JACOBITE; A TALE OF THE EXILED STUARTS. London: T. Nelson, 1904 BMC. London: Nelson, 1905 NUC.

201113   MADAMSCOURT; OR, THE ADVENTURES OF A FUGITIVE PRINCESS. London: Nelson, [1901] NUC. London: T. Nelson, 1902 BMC.

Historical romance. ATH 10-12-01

POZZUOLI, H. G.

201114   THE WAR OF THE WENUSES. Bristol: J. W. Arrowsmith, [1898] NUC.

PRICE, A. T. G. Nationality Unknown.

201115   SIMPLICITY. Chicago: Rand, McNally, [1896] BMC NUC.

LBKM 11:50. Innocent heroine so shocked at introduction to country society that she suicides, passing fortune on to sister Verda.
ATH 108:636. Pierrot Library. "The satire is too evident, the position of the author is too palpably biassed. One sees how inimical it is to men, how indeed the simple story is a manifesto against them."
PW 11-14-96. "She inherits a fortune and goes to live with her impoverished family in a rural district of England. Her gradual awaking to the sin and unhappiness about her and her self-devotion with its tragic end make a suggestive story."

PRICE, B. F. United States.

201116   HIM AND THEM; OR, THE IDEAL MAN. BY REV. B. F. PRICE. Elkton, Md.: Elkton Appeal Press, 1899 NUC.

PRICE, F. C. Nationality Unknown.

201117   LORD KENTWELL'S LOVE AFFAIR. London: W. Heinemann, 1909 BMC NUC.

He's a libertine who tries to get Mrs. Gambler, a sweet natured divorcee, to be his mistress. She's disgusted with him. TLS

PRICE, MRS. (CONSTAM), jt. au. See LATHROP, LORRIN G. AND MRS. (KONSTAM) PRICE.

PRIESTLEY, A. E.

201118   THE MARRIAGE OF NAOMI. London: Digby, Long, 1911 NUC.

TLS sombre story of non-conv. life of Dr's daughter and unsatisfactory-husband.

PRIESTLEY, C. ROWNTREE.

201119   ROWANLEA. London: Digby and Long, [1893] BMC.

PROBYN, LESLIE. United Kingdom.

201120   THE SHIFTING SPELL. New York: Duffield, [c1916] BMC NUC.

Janet Ranford, an heiress, marries to suit herself in spite of her guardian's plans and conspiracy. PW

PROCTOR, H. B.

201121   THE MUMMY'S DREAM, AN EGYPTIAN STORY OF THE EXODUS. London: Simpkin and Marshall, 1898 BMC NUC.

PROWSE, C. M.

201122   THE LURE OF ISLAM: A NOVEL. London: S. Low, [1914] BMC. South Africa: [1914?] NUC.

ATH: Concerns the attraction of a Moslem marriage for "poor whites" and others in their station.
ATH 144:97. Poor young women in Capetown are lured into Moslem mrgs by a promise of wealth and fear of powers of black magic. Then they find the true position of women in Islam: multiple wives, divorce with a statement from husband, etc.

PRYCE, MYFANWY.

201123   BLUE MOONS. London: Hodder and Stoughton, 1919 BMC.

LBKM–Magsie longs to write books and have free play for her intellect. But heart is kind to generous relatives, a war is on, etc., until finally she realizes her love for Ley Baron is stronger than any

other desire.
"Amusing and vivid account of girls' lives in the
"ministry of textile supplies" and the boarding house
in which they live." Two heroines, one in conflict
between love and work--"the girl's realization of the
inherent deficiency of the 'devotion to art' ideal."
TLS

PRYDZ, ALVILDE. 1848-1922.

201124   THE HEART OF THE NORTHERN SEA. London: G.
Allen, 1907 BMC NUC. (Tr. from Norwegian by Tyra
Engdahl and Jessie Rew)

ACAD-Gunvor, far more ambitious than her fiance, an
MD, loses him to another. She tries to forget him,
rejects another man, "finds peace in the sea."
Story upholds idea that women reclaim men. Keep them
on the straight and narrow. Heroine pursues lover to
cafe, drags him out, admonishes him. TLS

201125   SANPRIEL: THE PROMISED LAND. Boston: R.
G. Badger, [c1914] NUC. London: G. Allen and Unwin,
[1916] BMC. (Tr. from Norwegian by Hester Coddington)

Tragic romance. PW 85: 6/20/14 p. 1979

PUSEY, PENNOCK. 1825-1903. United States.

201126   EBBA BORJESON: A TRUE LOVE STORY OF THE
OLDEN TIME. BY HAMPDEN VAUGHN. [Wilmington, Del.]:
Costa Print, [c1894] NUC.

PYKE, RIVINGTON.

201127   THE MAN WHO DISAPPEARED: A LANCASHIRE
STORY. London: R. Bentley, 1896 BMC.

QUARRY, A.

201128   ELUCIDATION. A MATTER-OF-FACT AND TRUE
TALE, IN THREE PARTS. London: T. F. Unwin, 1899 BMC.

Opens in a vault and ends in convents and ducal halls.
SP 83:662
Stories of adventurers and adventuresses in different
lands. ATH 114:551
Occult science. SR 88:526

R., C. H. [pseud.].

201129   THE TOWN OF MORALITY; OR THE NARRATIVE OF
ONE WHO LIVED HERE FOR A TIME. BY C. H. R. London:
Mills and Boon, [1911] BMC NUC.

Modern pilgrim's progress. TLS

RAINES, G. PERCY.

201130   TERRIBLE TIMES. A TALE OF THE SEPOY
REVOLT. London: G. Routledge, [1898] BMC.

RAINSFORD, W. H. Nationality Unknown.

201131   THAT GIRL MARCH. London, New York: J.
Lane, 1920 BMC NUC.

TLS-male hero, romance.
SR-Gay, Edith March arranges affairs of Blaisham
without regarding authority of the mistress of the
hall.

RAMAGE, LAETA MARION. United States.

201132   JUDITH MCNAIR. New York: Broadway
Publishing, 1907 NUC.

RAMSAY, M. C.

201133   THE DOCTOR'S ANGEL. London: "Leisure
Hour" library, [1914] BMC.

201134   IN ROYAL SERVICE. Stirling: Drummond's
Tract Depot, [1913] BMC.

201135   STEPHEN MARTIN, M.D. London: E. Stock,
1908 BMC NUC.

RATHBUN, F. P.

201136   SUSPECTED. London: J. Henderson, 1894
BMC.

REDMAYNE, P. Y.

201137   THE GULF BETWEEN. London: W. Gardner,

1913 BMC.

Romance of English heroine and life in a German
boarding house. TLS

REEKS, H. CAULTON.

201138   THE TAMING OF THE TERROR. A STORY OF A
FEUD. London: Lynnwood, 1913 BMC.

The terror is a bully who owns some houses and who is
ousted by the hero. ATH

REES, J. HERMAN.

201139   BEAUTY AND THE WITCH: A NOVEL. London:
Digby, Long, [1893] BMC.

REGNAS, C.

201140   THE LAND OF NISON: A NOVEL. London: C. W.
Daniel, 1906 BMC.

REYNOLDS, D. A. United States.

201141   WOLVERTON; OR, THE MODERN ARENA. Chicago:
Rand, McNally, 1891 W.

REYNOLDS, ELDRID. B. 1889.

201142   RED OF THE ROCK. London: A. Rivers, 1911
BMC.

201143   WHISPERING DUST. London: A. Rivers, 1913
BMC NUC. New York: F. A. Stokes, [1914] NUC.

"Story of a woman of thirty-three who feels old,
because she fancies she is different from other women
and because in all her drab, monotonous life she has
never had an opportunity to do anything. She goes to
Egypt where the very dust of the desert whispers to
her of space and time. She writes constantly to some
one she calls You, a man she has created in her
imagination, but who develops a real personality that
is felt all through the book and who has a great share
in bringing about the realization of the woman's
hidden possibilities." PW

REYNOLDS, ROTHAY. United Kingdom.

201144   THE GONDOLA. London: Mills and Boon,
[1913] BMC NUC.

RICHARDS, MARSDEN.

201145   A BRACE FOR THE LAW. London: Digby, Long,
1892 BMC.

RICHARDS, ROBIN.

201146   COLD BLOOD: A NOVEL. London: Hutchinson,
[1920] BMC NUC.

TLS-villainous male hero.

RIETTE [pseud.].

201147   THE ROMANCE OF NUN'S HOLLOW. BY RIETTE.
London: Digby, Long, 1899 BMC.

Heroine returns home with her child and dies on p.3
according to passage quoted. ACAD 57:254

RITCHIE, A. D.

201148   THE MASTER OF CRAIGENS. London: Oliphant,
1898 BMC.

SP 81:837. Tragical romance of the Vale of Kelvin 50
years ago.

RITTER, GUILLIM [pseud.].

201149   THE MARTYRDOM OF SOCIETY. BY GUILLIM
RITTER. London: H. Cox, 1893 BMC.

ROBERTS, J. W. Fl. 1893-1895. United States.

201150   LOOKING WITHIN. THE MISLEADING TENDENCIES
OF "LOOKING BACKWARD" MADE MANIFEST. New York: A. S.
Barnes, 1893 NUC BMC.

ROBERTSON, A. NUGENT.

201151   HER LAST APPEARANCE. London: Mills &
Boon, 1914 BMC.

ATH-murder trial, suspicion of husband dispelled by wife.

ROBIN, E. GALLIENNE. United Kingdom.

201152   CHRISTINE, A GUERNSEY GIRL. London: Hurst and Blackett, 1912 BMC.

ATH-psychological study of a calculating woman. TLS-she keeps an eating house and blackmails another. POV?

201153   GOLDEN LIGHTS. London: R. & T. Washbourne, 1915 BMC.

201154   JACQUINE OF THE HUT. A SARK STORY. London: Hurst & Blackett, [1911] BMC NUC. New York and London: G. P. Putnam's, 1912 NUC.

LBKM:Jacquine watches a man she loves at night and discovers he is a smuggler. He catches her spying, she reveals her love and helps him with his work (he has told her he could never love anyone as lowly born as she.) Leads to sadness and humiliation and and despair and finally happiness.
A dare-devil free trader of a hero and a "yielding devoted specimen of femininity." TLS

201155   LUCE: THE STORY OF A MOTHER. London: Hurst & Blackett, 1912 BMC.

TLS-fishing and farming folk on isle of Sark. ATH-wholesome tale of maternal desire.

201156   PERILOUS SEAS. London: R & T. Washbourne, 1914 BMC.

ACAD 86:527. French Revolution, R.C. pov.

ROBINSON, W. A. United States.

201157   HIS WAY AND HERS. Cincinnati: Cranston and Curts, 1895 NUC.

ROCH, FFLORENS.

201158   THE CALL OF THE PAST. London: Sands, 1913 BMC.

Humorous account of reorganization of the Welsh Women's Charitable Union. Story concerns Gwenllian and her parents' guidance in her choice of husband. TLS

ROCK, W. S.

201159   ZENOBIA; OR, THE MYSTERY OF LIFE. London: Drane's, [1912] BMC.

ATH-reincarnation

RODNEY, HARLEY.

201160   HILDA; A STUDY IN PASSION. London: Digby, Long, 1898 BMC.

201161   HORATIO: A NOVEL. London: Digby, Long, 1899 BMC.

201162   A TREBLE SOLOIST. London: Digby, Long, 1899 BMC.

ROGERS, C. V.

201163   HER MARRIAGE VOW. London: F. V. White, 1898 BMC.

SP 81:991. On discovering that she has been married for her money, leaves husband before birth of child. As the result of a severe illness she loses weight and changes very much in her appearance (for the better.) She destroys her identity by assuming title and property of deceased peer, becomes Lady Blanchyre. Safely encounters her husband in society without his ever guessing her identity.
ATH 112;748. He falls for her, but she doesn't reveal her identity until end.
"Ugly" heiress married by poor noble to save estate. Wins him in the end when she 's 60. SP 87:248.

ROSE, A. M.

201164   ARMAND DE L'ISLE. London: Eden, Remington, 1893 BMC.

Historical romance of first Napoleon period with

Armand and Eugenie as the young lovers. ACAD 43:2 18.

ROY, D. KINMOUNT.

201165   LINKED LIVES. London: Heath, Cranton & Ouseley, [1913] BMC.

Scotland, beginning of 19th century. ATH

ROY, JEAN.

201166   THE FIELDS OF THE FATHERLESS. London: W. Collins, 1917 BMC. New York: G. H. Doran, [c1918] NUC.

SR-Grim record purportedly of author's own exp. Illeg child of drunken mother.
Auto. of an "illeg." girl living in a little Scot village and her endeavors to earn a living when she leaves. Critic condemns the book for its lack of love. TLS
Indicts social conditions of poor in parts of Scot. full effects of poverty-drink, overcrowding, sickness. Author-heroine derives great pleasure from books. factory hand, barmaid, stewardess ss on boat. ATH
PW "Auto. of a London servant girl" she's Scot-Irish. Leaves home where she's beaten and where grandmother drinks. And little Jean Roy was illeg. and looked down on. Her mother was a wild young woman who ran off with a man when Jean a year old."
Hers is a dreary bkgd. becomes a factory worker, domestic, stewardess on boat. Often ill, operation; work life broken up with trips home to care for old folk. Sad haunting hopeless hand-to mouth existence. NYT 5-4-19 259

RUSSELL, F. M. M.

201167   A SOCIAL FAILURE. Liverpool: E. Howell, 1895 BMC.

RUSSELL, FOX.

201168   THE BOER'S BLUNDER. A VELDT ADVENTURE. London: W. Gardner, Darton, [1900] BMC.

201169   COLONEL BOTCHERBY, M.S.H. London: Bradbury, Agnew, 1899 BMC.

201170   THE FIRST CRUISE OF THREE MIDDIES. London: W. Gardner, [1897] BMC.

201171   THE HAUGHTYSHIRE HUNT. London: Bradbury, Agnew, 1897 BMC.

RUSSELL, T. BARON. United Kingdom.

201172   BORLASE AND SON; A NOVEL. New York and London: J. Lane, 1903 NUC BMC.

NYT-no women-father and son.
LBKM-there are women.

201173   A GUARDIAN OF THE POOR. London and New York: J. Lane, 1898 BMC NUC.

LIT 3:256. Words and life of London shop assistants, the men and women working for a drapery establishment. Collection of stories of this world.
ACAD 53:601. Title refers to Borlase, owner of the shop, a tyrant. "No species of brutality or meanness is wanting."
ACAD 54:59. Young men and young persons. Helplessness of the persons.
SR 85:53. "Tremendous indictment of a system."

201174   THE MANDATE. London and New York: J. Lane, 1899 BMC NUC.

RUTHVEN, E. C.

201175   THE UPHILL ROAD. London: Chapman & Hall, 1906 BMC.

TLS-Young independent woman, refusal of love (for unconvincing reasons.
ATH-Hereditarily unfit, woman of the modern introspective type. Elaborate analysis of her sensations
BKM-Lives independently in a house near Nice-story is of her life there and people she knows.

RYAN, DARBY.

201176   WAYWARD HEARTS. A NOVEL. London: Digby, Long, 1900 BMC.

RYCE, MARK [pseud.]. United Kingdom.

201177   MRS. DRUMMOND'S VOCATION. BY MARK RYCE.
London: W. Heinemann, 1911 BMC. New York: Vail, 1911
NUC.

Not yet published in US; author a woman; a half French
half-English woman evolved from missionary wife to
chatelaine of a grand house in France and finds no
great moral shocks in the course of the evolution. NYT

RYLEY, M. BERESFORD.

201178   "MA'AM". London: Hutchinson, 1917 BMC.

Narrow pompous curate husband, rebellious wife
entirely out of her element, Greselda Cunningham goes
to Italy, leaves husband., new love comes. TLS
"A suffragette, practically an agnostic. Long stay in
Italy, almost ready to live with lover, an illness
intervenes; husband comes to his senses. Former lover
becomes a good friend to her. "What is striking is the
power of the authoress to interpret some phases of
feminine char." LBKM

RYSBRIDGE, C.

201179   EDGAR'S RANSOM. London: Digby, Long, 1899
BMC.

RYVES, K. C. Nationality Unknown.

201180   AT THE SIGN OF THE PEACOCK. London: T. F.
Unwin, 1906 BMC.

ACAD-character study of a cold girl who discovers she
has a heart after all.
TLS-though it was not given to her fiance.
ATH-study in heredity, review-confusing.

201181   THE OPEN SECRET. London: A. Melrose, 1920
BMC NUC.

TLS-illeg. daughter, inheritance, love.
LBKM O

S., T. I. [pseud.].

201182   VIOLIN AND VENDETTA, A VENETIAN STORY. BY
T. I. S. Bristol: J. W. Arrowsmith, [1891] BMC.

mystery, crime, supernatural introduced; murder of
violinist. ACAD

SAGON, AMYOT.

201183   AN AUSTRALIAN DUCHESS. London: Hurst and
Blackett, 1897 BMC.

Jumps from his horse, seizes a whip, lashes a man
senseless, dares the other men to approach. This boy
turns out to be a young woman in male attire "riding
astride, one of the most skillful stockriders in the
district." Eventually weds another stockrider who
really is an arist. Next we see her in diamonds on
Park Lane ATH 109:504.

201184   A FAIR PALMIST. London: Hurst and
Blackett, 1896 BMC.

Haidee, a genius, loves a sculptor who is murdered.
She vows revenge, is guided by spirits in painting
murder scene which leads to discovery, then she joins
the spirit of her lover. She reads palms.

SAINT G., E. H. V.

201185   GLENRAVEN. BY E. H. V. ST. G. London:
Mills & Boon, 1918 BMC.

TLS-male hero intellectual snob.
ATH-his apologies.

SAINT GEORGE, PRESTER.

201186   THE GOWN AND THE MAN: A STORY OF TROUBLED
TIMES. London: Digby, Long, [1898] BMC.

SAINT GERMAINE, E. L.

201187   HUGH DARVILLE. A NOVEL. London: T. F.
Unwin, 1893 BMC.

SANDYS, SYDNEY.

201188   JACK CARSTAIRS OF THE POWER HOUSE. A TALE

OF SOME VERY YOUNG MEN AND A VERY YOUNG INDUSTRY.
London: Methuen, 1909 BMC.

SARGENT, H. GARTON.

201189   A WOMAN AND A CREED. Edinburgh and
London: W. Blackwood, 1902 BMC.

SAUNDERS, W. J.

201190   KALOMERA. THE STORY OF A REMARKABLE
COMMUNITY. London: E. Stock, 1911 NUC BMC.

201191   THE NAZARENE. A NOVEL. London: Murray &
Evenden, [1915] BMC.

SAWYER, B. F.

201192   DAVID AND ABIGAIL. BY THE AUTHOR OF
"LUCILE," "THE LADY PAULINA," ETC. [ANONYMOUS].
Boston: Arena, 1895 NUC.

PW-South during candidacy of Buchanan. David is in
debt to farmer; farmer offers his daughters in
marriage as solution; wedding takes place at their
first meeting. Story tells its consequences.

SCALPEL, M.D. [pseud.].

201193   A DOCTOR'S IDLE HOURS. BY M.D. SCALPEL.
London: Downey, 1897 BMC.

SCHIFF, SYDNEY. 1868-1944.

201194   CONCESSIONS. New York and London: John
Lane, 1913 BMC NUC.

PW 11/1/13 1436. "Concerned with a group of English
people, a young diplomat, whose wife is threatened
with insanity, their intimate friend, Peter Blake, his
mother, a great Russian pianist, and a lovely woman,
married to an artist, who is a genius but who allows
indolence to undermine his mind. Peter loves the
artist's wife, and story tells of the concessions
every one has to make, before happiness is possible to
any of them."
Zillah is the artist's wife. She "drifts" into Peter
Blake's arms. TLS

SCHMALZ, F. M.

201195   MONK OR SOLDIER. London: A. Melrose, 1913
BMC.

A count falls in love but feels compelled to become a
monk because of his father's wish that he doso. ATH

SCOTT, FIRTH. See SCOTT, G. FIRTH.

SCOTT, G. FIRTH.

201196   AT FRIENDLY POINT. London: J. Bowden,
1898 BMC.

SR 86:480. Entertaining inhabitants of Friendly Point.
LBKM 15:58. Short stories. Australia.

201197   COLONIAL BORN: A TALE OF THE QUEENSLAND
BUSH. London: Low, 1900 BMC.

SP 84:846. Australia.
ACAD 58:470. Aileen is "typical colonial girl, a
horsewoman and a fluent talker."

201198   FROM FRANKLIN TO NANSEN; TALES OF ARCTIC
ADVENTURE. London: J. Bowden, 1899 BMC. Philadelphia:
J. B. Lippincott, 1904 NUC.

201199   THE LAST LEMURIAN: A WESTRALIAN ROMANCE.
London: J. Bowden, 1898 BMC NUC.

SP 80:766. Australia, gold and a gigantic Yellow Queen
who radiates phosphorescent light, a race of pygmies.
Two male adventurers, one dies in volcanic eruption.

201200   POSSESSED. BY FIRTH SCOTT. London: W.
Rider, [1912] BMC NUC.

201201   THE RIDER OF WAROONA. BY FIRTH SCOTT.
London: J. Long, 1912 BMC.

SP-Australian det. story.

201202   THE TRACK OF MIDNIGHT. London: Sampson
Low, 1897 NUC BMC.

201203   THE TWILLFORD MYSTERY. London: R.A. Everett, [1904] BMC.

SCRUTATOR [pseud.].

201204   CALEB JONES MINER. A STORY OF THE SOUTH WALES COAL FIELD. BY SCRUTATOR. Merthyr Tydfil: H. W. Southey, 1900 BMC.

SELBY, N. HARCOURT [pseud.].

201205   THE REAL DIARY OF A REAL GIRL, AS WRITTEN BY HERSELF [ANONYMOUS]. New York: Street & Smith, [1904] NUC.

SELDEN, D. A. United States.

201206   JOE SAXTON IN JAPAN: A STORY OF THE EAST AND THE WEST. BY D. A. SELDEN, M.D. Baltimore: Deutsch, 1897 NUC.

SHARER, W. RAISBECK.

201207   ONE HEART, ONE WAY. London: Hurst and Blackett, 1897 BMC.

Melodrama of bastardy, murder and sudden death. And Miss Drayman whose father owns a factory where a strike is imminent. SR 84:326.
Mod. life in mfg. town. Gloomy. The heroine's lover in prison because info. that will free him is suppressed. Villain dies a gruesome death. ATH 110:287

201208   THE WHEELS OF JUGGERNAUT AND OTHER ORIGINAL SKETCHES. Colchester: W. R. Sharer, 1894 BMC.

SHAW, M. H.

201209   EVE AND THE MINISTER. London: Murray and Evenden, [1914] BMC.

TLS-Eve is a modern cynical young woman...minister is devoted and narrow...whose mind is opened by the literature she lends him. Story ends in marriage," not in any sense a real or sincere study." POV?
SR 147:645. "Luridly religious" and "nauseatingly sweet love interest."

SHEPPARD, E.

201210   FLORA'S CHOICE. London: Angelus, 1910 BMC.

TLS-R. C.

SHEPPARD, J. J.

201211   THE ROMANCE OF A LONDON FOG. Calcutta: W. Newman, 1898 BMC.

SHEPPARD, W. J.

201212   THE TENDERFOOT. London: J. Long, 1905 BMC. London: J. Long, [1906] NUC.

SHERIDAN, A. G.

201213   THE CALAIS ROAD: A ROMANCE AFTER A FAMOUS VICTORY. London: Digby, Long, 1915 BMC.

Traditional romantic story. TLS

SHERWOOD, A. CURTIS.

201214   TONGUES OF GOSSIP. London: T. F. Unwin, 1905 BMC.

About a minister and tattle of religious people over their neighbors. ACAD 1905:1033 LBKM 29-30:39

SHERWOOD, EVELYN.

201215   A CANDIDATE FOR DANGER. London: A. Melrose, 1910 BMC.

ACAD?
TLS-widow falls for cad, finds him out.

SHIELD, A.

201216   THE SQUIRE OF WANDALES. London: Methuen, 1896 BMC.

A modern young bluebeard. Sens. ATH 109:81

SHOTTLAND, MAXIME S.

201217   THE IRON PASSPORT. London: J. S. Hammond, 1914 BMC.

ATH-Suffering of prisoners in Siberia. Heroine is a princess and an anarchist. Adv.
TLS-"intended to show the cruelty of the Russian bureaucracy.

SIDON, J. A.

201219   THAT KIND OF LOVE. London: Century, 1910 NUC.

TLS-"suitable for simple-minded girls."

SIEVIER, R. S.

201220   A GENERATION. London: Downey, 1895 BMC.

Helena Maria Askew marries Herbert Chester, but doesn't love him, has a child, falls in love with Harold Akehurst, elopes, then divorce and marriage to Harold who later dies. Chester remarries. The story goes on to portray the children of the two families ACAD 48:268
Covers two hemispheres and about 30 years. ATH 106:528

SILVER, R. NORMAN. Nationality Unknown.

201221   A DAUGHTER OF MYSTERY. A SENSATIONAL STORY OF MODERN LIFE. London: Jarrold, 1901 BMC. Boston: Page, 1901 NUC.

201222   A DOUBLE MASK: A NOVEL. London: Jarrolds, [1918] BMC.

201223   THE GOLDEN DWARF. A SENSATIONAL ROMANCE OF TO-DAY. London: Jarrold, 1903 BMC. Boston: L. C. Page, 1903 NUC.

201224   HATE, THE DESTROYER. London: Ward, Lock, 1900 BMC.

201225   HELD APART. London: Ward, Lock, 1905 BMC.

201226   ROMANCES OF THE FOOTBALL FIELD. London: Ward, Lock, 1906 BMC.

201227   WARDERS OF THE DEEP: A ROMANCE OF LOVE, INVENTION AND A GREAT CITY. London: Ward, Lock, 1903 BMC.

SIMMONS, V. S.

201228   MEN AND MEN. A LOVE STORY. Osgood & McIlvaine, 1893 BMC.

Heroine has two lovers. "She is...much stupider and more unpleasant...than her creator intends." SR 76,47.
French studio life. American young woman saved from getting mixed up with a man she didn't love by a French painter. "The mate approved by nature"-ACAD. 44-129

SIRRAH [pseud.].

201229   THE LION OF GERSAU. BY "SIRRAH". London: W. Heinemann, 1904 BMC.

LBKM- Bachelors' party

201230   SLAVES OF THE LINKS; A GOLF COMEDY. BY SIRRAH. Birmingham: Cornish Brothers, 1914 BMC.

SITES, I. A. United States.

201231   NED HAMPDEN; OR, THE RAVAGES OF INTEMPERANCE, WITH A PLEA FOR PROHIBITION OF THE LIQUOR TRAFFIC. Reading, Pa.: D. Miller, 1893 NUC.

SKEY, L. RUTHERFORD.

201232   PASSING DOWN THE AVENUES. London: F. Griffiths, 1907 BMC.

Sentimental story of invalid. TLS

SLADE, A. F.

201233   THE ALTERNATIVE. London: Hutchinson, 1909 BMC.

Kate Heriot is unhappily married; the marr. fails; Kate's false charge vs herself of intimacy with old lover (to get a divorce?); the position of their son

between them. TLS
"Intense meticulous analysis" TLS
Refined woman, coarse husband. ATH

201234   ANNIE DEANE, A WAYSIDE WEED. New York:
Brentano's, 1901 NUC.

201235   THE CRUCIBLE. London: E. Nash, 1903 BMC.

201236   MARY NEVILLE: THE HISTORY OF A WOMAN WHO
ATTEMPTED TOO MUCH. London: Hutchinson, 1902 BMC. New
York: Brentano's, 1902 NUC.

ATH 5-31-02 Mary's journal story of a drunken man

201237   A WAYSIDE WEED. London: Hutchinson, 1901
BMC.

same as Annie Deane
Annie's seduction and its consequence told in a very
unusual way ACAD '01
16 yr old peasant girl seduced by artist who never
gives her another thought till later when he is about
to marry. Anne raises the child grows into a forceful
woman ATH 2-16 01

SLOAN, J. MACGAVIN.

201238   QUINTIN DOONRISE. A STUDY IN HUMAN
NATURE. Paisley: A. Gardner, 1892 BMC.

SLUGGERVAN, JOHN L. [pseud.]. United States.

201239   DE RECOMEMBRANCES OF A 19-CENT SCRAPPER.
BY JOHN L. SLUGGERVAN. New York: Athletic Pub. League,
1892 NUC.

SMILOVSKY, ALOIS VOJTECH.

201240   HEAVENS: A BOHEMIAN NOVEL. London: Bliss,
Sands and Foster, 1894 BMC. (Tr. from the Czech by
Prof V. E. Mourek & Jane Mourek. Includes a
biographical notice of A. V. Smilovsky)

SMITH, H.

201241   HIS PRIVATE LIFE. London: P. Wellby, 1905
BMC.

SMITH, H. H. United States.

201242   DOWNFALL OF A POLITICIAN; OR, DEATH OR
DESTINY. A STORY OF POLITICS, RELIGION, AND SOCIETY.
BY THE HON. BELL ELI. Louisville: J. P. Morton, 1891
NUC.

SMITH, JOHN [pseud.].

201243   PLATONIC AFFECTIONS. London: J. Lane,
1896 BMC. Boston: Roberts, 1896 NUC.

SMITH, PHARALL.

201244   THE WOMAN WITHOUT SIN. A STORY OF
PASSION. London: S. Swift, 1911 BMC.

Where love is sincere it is sinless and a couple
should be free to indulge in it. ATH

SMITH, SAQUI. 1860-1924. United States.

201245   BACK FROM THE DEAD: A STORY OF THE STAGE.
New York: Cassell, [c1892] NUC.

LW 23:89. Story of two brothers one who supposedly
murdered the other and was hanged. But neither was
actually killed, they meet on board a ship.
PW-Smith, Saqui, (pseud)

SNOWY, J.

201246   THE STANLEY OF THE TURF. London: Chapman
and Hall, 1896 BMC.

SOLEY, ROSE.

201247   MANOUPA. London: Digby, Long, [1897] BMC.

LIT 2:450. Treasure story of the Pacific. Samoa.
ACAD 53:1-Men and women tempted; ends with
retribution.

SOMERVILLE, H. G.

201248   CURIOSITIES OF IMPECUNIOSITY. London:
Bentley, 1896 BMC.

201249   A JOURNALIST'S DYING MESSAGE TO THE
WORLD. London: J. Wooderson, [1907] BMC.

SOUTHWICK, E. B. United States.

201250   THE BETTER WORLD. New York: Truth Seeker
Co., [1895] NUC.

SPETTIGUE, H. H.

201251   THE HERITAGE OF EVE. London: Chatto and
Windus, 1898 BMC NUC.

ACAD 53:496. Titania, daughter of German engineer who
moved to Cornwall. She is engrossed first by writing,
then philanthropy, finally love.
ATH 111:689. Her career and adventures with publishers
are "partly recorded by means of her own diary."
SR 85:24. Successful novelist. Marries finally.

STARR, JULIAN.

201252   THE DISAGREEABLE WOMAN: A SOCIAL MYSTERY.
New York: G. W. Dillingham, 1895 NUC.

Jane Blagden's curt remarks, strange ways and unknown
hy, lead her fellow boarders to call her disagreeable.
PW 6-22-95:970

STEELE, L. M. United States.

201253   DR. NICK. Boston: Small, Maynard, [c1916]
BMC NUC.

"Naida and Nikon were meant for each other but seven
years passed while they worked out their purposes and
understood their need of each other." PW 90:1461
10/28/16.

STEIN, A. M.

201254   THE HAUNTED HOUSE OF BEN'S HOLLOW AND
OTHER GHOSTLY STORIES. London: J. Elliott, 1894 BMC.

STEIN, C.

201255   SELF AND COMRADES. TALES. BY A SOLDIER.
London: Vinton, 1897 BMC.

STELLIER, KILSYTH, pseud. See SUMMERS, A. WELBOURNE.

STEVENS, E. J. C.

201256   LEENTAS. A TALE OF LOVE AND WAR. London:
G. Allen, 1914 BMC.

ACAD 86:595. South Africa, the Karoo district, and the
outbreak of the Boer War.
ATH-Heroine disguises herself as a Boer in order to
take revenge on man who wronged her sister.
TLS-Disguises herself as a British trooper.

STEVENSON, A. C. United States.

201257   UNSPOTTED FROM THE WORLD. New York: F. T.
Neely, [c1899] NUC.

STEVENSON, E. G.

201258   MY NEIGHBOR: A STORY OF OUR OWN TIME.
London: E. Stock, 1906 BMC.

TLS- urging the cause of decayed gentry as deserving
support

STEVENSON, G. H.

201259   THE SILVER SPOON. London: W. Blackwood,
1909 BMC.

Miriam Westlake marries young med student. We're given
the sad course of her unsuccessful marriage TLS
Focus on their financial problems. The weakness of the
husband. Wife and deformed child are "pathetic" ATH

201260   THE TWO F'S. London: Christian Knowledge
Society, [1911] BMC.

STEWARD, B. D.

201261   TREASURE OF THULE. A ROMANCE OF ORKNEY.
London: Sidgwick & Jackson, 1912 BMC.

ATH sea story.

STEWART, A. L.

201262   THE MAZE. London: J. Long, 1914 BMC.

ATH-The love story of a prima donna.
TLS-and a violinist. She is older than he, is trapped
into marriage. He develops love for her; she is
passionately devoted to him but absorbs his
individuality and stifles his genius.

STEWART, pseud. See DE ESGUE, JEAN LOUIS.

STOCKING, JANE [pseud.]. United States.

201263   VIA P. AND O. New York: Dodd, Mead, 1914
NUC.

BKM-poignant tragedy with happy ending. Husband
insists males are naturaly polygamous. American wife
of German diplomat.
"Letters written by a woman in Shanghai to her sister
in England. Carola Freiheit has been married six years
and when story opens she has just promised her sister
to tell her real state of affairs in her home. She
relates the events of her married life which began in
Japan where she knew five months of delirious
happiness, then discovered her husband's
unfaithfulness and that he considered it unnecessary
for a man to be faithful to his wife. From that time
they live their own lives, under the same roof, but a
world apart. She manages to achieve a sort of peace
and negative happiness and in her letters tells much
of life in the foreign quarter of Shanghai. She meets
and loves a fine man and then her husband demands that
she return to him. Her meeting of this crisis ends the
book." PW 85 4/11/14 p. 1266

STONE, A. United States.

201264   AMERICAN PEP: A TALE OF AMERICAN
EFFICIENCY. New York: R. J. Shores, 1918 NUC.

PW-family of munitions makers
NYT-Courageous hero & heroine struggle with German
spies.

201265   FIGHTING BYNG: A NOVEL OF MYSTERY,
INTRIGUE AND ADVENTURE. New York: Britton, [1919] BMC
NUC.

STOOKE, E. M.

201266   DICK'S RETRIEVER. London: T. Nelson, 1900
BMC.

201267   "NOT EXACTLY". Bristol: J. W. Arrowsmith,
1895 BMC.

Humorous-the vicar's quotations. The "vicaress's
shrewish temper. Title refers to nickname of hero.
LBKM 9:98
ATH 108:522. Discovery of a will in a well.

STRANGE, WYND.

201268   WHITE LILAC. London: Murray and Evenden,
[1913] BMC.

"Rich feast of fun"-perhaps unconsciously so;series of
impossible loves, hates, convenient tragedies. ACAD
White Lilac is an orphan who wins heart of business
man who determines to have her though he's married. To
save her brother in the man's employ (brother has
falsified accounts) she agrees to live with the man
for a year. Has a baby; wife dies; the man dies. She
marries Mr. Right. "Ludicrously melodramatic" "The
style is like a woman in hysterics." SR

STRANGER, L. D.

201269   THE GREAT SNAKE MURDER. London: J.
Richmond, [1915] BMC.

STRONG, MARTEN.

201270   THE SHADOW OF LIFE. London: C. A.
Pearson, 1898 BMC.

STUART, J. MAITLAND.

201271   HOW NO. 1 BECAME 1-1/2 IN NORWAY. London:
Hutchinson, [1891] BMC NUC.

STUMBLES, A.

201272   THE WHITE ANTS: A STORY OF SOUTH AFRICAN

LIFE. London: Heath, Cranton, 1919 BMC.

South African domestic life. ATH

SULE, LEON, pseud. See FAGAN, T. A.

SUMMERS, A. WELBOURNE.

201273   MAD BARBARA. Roxburghe Press, 1897 BS.
London: A. H. Stockwell, [1905] BMC.

201274   A POLICE SERGEANT'S SECRET, AND OTHER
STORIES. London: Digby & Long, [1894] BMC.

201275   TAKEN BY FORCE. BY KILSYTH STELLIER.
London: Gale and Polden, 1893 BMC.

SUNDOWNER [pseud.].

201276   THE TALE OF THE SERPENT. BY SUNDOWNER.
London: Chatto and Windus, 1902 BMC.

201277   TOLD BY THE TAFFRAIL. BY SUNDOWNER.
London: Chatto and Windus, 1901 BMC NUC.

SUREV, pseud. See TRUE, C. E.

SWANSON, S. WARD.

201278   LADY ENID. A DRAMATIC NOVEL. Digby, Long,
1911 BMC.

SWEETSER, DELIGHT.

201279   ONE WAY ROUND THE WORLD. Indianapolis:
Bowen-Merrill, [c1898] NUC.

Fresh look at countries like Japan and Egypt thru a
young girl's eyes, but a young girl capable of mature
observations. BKM 8:588.

SWINGLER, J. H.

201280   CIRCUMSTANTIAL EVIDENCE. London: Digby,
Long, [1897] BMC.

SYMONS, F. A.

201281   CICELY IN CEYLON. London: Lynwood, 1914
NUC.

TAJ [pseud.].

201282   A TALE OF ZENANA LIFE. BY TAJ. London:
Methuen, 1912 BMC NUC. (Identified as pseud. in NUC.)

ATH

TALBOT, E. DOWNING.

201283   THE INEVITABLE. London: Digby, Long, 1898
BMC NUC.

TALBOT, L. A.

201284   THE DUKE'S JEST. London and New York:
Harper, 1904 BMC.

ATH-Adventures, young woman bicycles thru strange
country, comedy.

201285   THE FOOTSTOOL OF THE VIRTUES. London:
Sisley's, 1906 BMC.

201286   JEHANE OF THE FOREST. London: A. Melrose,
1914 BMC. Philadelphia: J. B. Lippincott, 1914 NUC.

BKM-Jehane is rescued from convent by Earl's son she
has befriended.

201287   LANCE-IN-REST. London, New York: Harper,
1904 BMC.

LBKM-0
TLS-Unhappy at home, leaves, marries and harbors a
murderer but there is much character study.
ACAD-Suspected murder-love story.

TATTINGHAM, TILK.

201288   THE MONUMENT. London: Mills and Boon,
1916 BMC.

TLS-male hero, socialism vs. capitalism
ATH-

TAYLER, F. JENNER.

201289   BEYOND THE BUSTLE. A TALE OF SOUTH
AFRICA. London: Sampson, Low, 1893 BMC.

201290   THE LONG VIGIL. London: T. F. Unwin, 1902
BMC.

201291   MARY BRAY-X-HER MARK; AN OREGON ROMANCE.
London: J. Long, 1901 BMC.

201292   WANTED-A HERO. London: T. F. Unwin, 1899
BMC.

TAYLOR, A. RYCROFT. United States.

201293   LALLY LETHAM'S WELL: A TALE OF THE GREAT
CITY. New York: W. B. Ketcham, [c1896] W.

Listed PW, Dec. 19, 1896.

TAYLOR, H. M.

201294   "JANE ELLEN" BEING REAL SKETCHES FROM THE
LIFE OF A LANCASTER LASS. London: Drane's, [1921] BMC.

TLS-Scenes from life of cotton weaver, difficulties at
home, rel. exp's, hopes, ideals, loves.

TEMPLE, LESLIE.

201295   NOTHING VENTURE. London: Digby, Long,
[1917] BMC.

Highborn girl works in a factory. TLS

THELMAR, E.

201296   THE MANIAC. A REALISTIC STUDY OF MADNESS
FROM THE MANIAC'S POINT OF VIEW [ANONYMOUS]. London:
Rebman, 1909 BMC NUC.

Describes an attack of acute mania due to
overwork-lasts five weeks. TLS

THEOBALD, C. M.

201297   BAGATELLES. London: H. J. Drane, [1910]
BMC.

201298   LENA HALE. London: G. Allen and Unwin,
1915 BMC.

career of a woman from infancy to womanhood. Neurotic
woman makes poor marriage; husband deserts her; she
has several affairs, then marries respectably. Modern
in its lack of reticence. "The impression left is that
the sexes are to be equalized not by restraining the
male but by giving equal license to the female." TLS
"The reader is spared few, if any, of her successive
emotions as she grows from infancy to womanhood." Ends
by becoming an altogether different woman from the one
reader was led to expect. ACAD

THOMAS, D. BRYCHAN.

201299   THE SENSITIVE MINISTER. Carmarthen: W.
Spurrel, 1904 BMC. London: J. F. Spriggs, 1904 BMC.

THOMAS, R. M.

201300   TREWERN: A TALE OF THE THIRTIES. London:
T. F. Unwin, 1901 BMC.

BAKER 03-181

THOMPSON, E. SIMONET.

201301   FRIEND OR FOE? London: H. J. Drane,
[1901] BMC.

THOMPSON, LEIGH.

201302   THE ACCURSED VALLEY. London: Mills and
Boon, 1920 BMC.

TLS-betrayed male doctor is hero.
SR-O

201303   FATE'S HIGH CHANCERY. London: Heath,
Cranton, 1916 BMC.

201304   THE LION AND THE ADDER: A STORY OF THE
SOUTH AFRICAN REBELLION. London: Mills and Boon, 1918
BMC NUC.

LBKM-romance
SP-romance

THOMPSON, TOMY.

201305   LETTERS TO LADY SHESHEEN. London: Murray
& Evenden, 1917 BMC.

THRELFALL, T. R.

201306   THE GREAT MAGICIAN. London: Ward, Lock,
1901 BMC.

201307   LONG LIVE LOVE. London: Ward, Lock, 1905
BMC.

201308   PHILIPPI, THE GUARDSMAN. London: Ward,
Lock, 1898 BMC.

ACAD 53:548. Romance of Napoleon's march to Moscow and
the tragedy of the Grand Army.
LBKM 14:110. Scarcely a novel. Unspeakable horrors of
the march.

201309   THE ROMANCE OF THE BATTLEFIELD. London:
R. A. Everett, [1904] BMC.

201310   THE STRANGE ADVENTURES OF A MAGISTRATE.
London: R. A. Everett, 1903 BMC NUC.

201311   THE SWORD OF ALLAH: A ROMANCE OF THE
HAREM. London: Ward, Lock, 1899 BMC.

Thomas Keith, Scottish soldier of fortune, his part in
conquest of Arabia. Owed the glory of his career to
the fact that he suspected Elsie Macdonald was
unfaithful to him. She has adventures among pirates
and harems. LBKM 16:140

TOKUTOMI, KENJIRO. 1869-1927.

201312   THE HEART OF NAMI-SAN (HOTOTOGISU): A
STORY OF WAR, INTRIGUE ANDD LOVE. Boston: Stratford,
1918 BMC NUC. (Tr. Isaac Goldberg)

PW Story of mrg. Mother-in-law divorces them while
husband is away. According to Jap. custom, they cannot
remarry. Nami-san says despairingly "yes, I don't care
to be born a woman again."

201313   NAMI-KO, A REALISTIC NOVEL. Boston: H. B.
Turner, 1904 NUC. (Tr. Sakae Shioya and E. F. Edgett.
Pub. in 1900 under title: HotOtogisu.)

NYT-Attack on Jap. divorce law which is unfair to
women.

TORBETT, D. [pseud.]. United States.

201314   COMMON CLAY; A NOVELIZATION OF CLEVES
KINKEAD'S DRAMA. BY D. TORBETT. New York: E. J. Clode,
[c1916] NUC.

201315   KICK-IN; A NOVELIZATION OF WILLARD MACK'S
PLAY. New York: E. J. Clode, [c1915] NUC.

about a crook and theft 10-16-15 PW
Illus from photos of play.

201316   THE LAND OF PROMISE; A NOVELIZATION OF W.
SOMERSET MAUGHAM'S PLAY. New York: E. J. Clode,
[c1914] NUC.

201317   LIFE. A NOVELIZATION OF THOMPSON
BUCHANAN'S PLAY. New York: E. J. Clode, [c1915] NUC.

illus from photos of play.

201318   THE SCHEMERS. New York: C. H. Doscher,
[c1908] NUC.

PW satire-rom.
NYT-Of beauty specialists and fantastic lovemaking
"positively harmless"

201319   SINNERS: A NOVELIZATION OF OWEN DAVIS'S
PLAY. New York: E. J. Clode, [c1915] NUC.

TORRANCE, M. E. Nationality Unknown.

201320   HILDEGARDE'S CAMPAIGN. St. Paul, Minn.:
Price-McGill, 1892 NUC.

PW-War, heroine disguised in male attire, sensational

TRAIN, M. United States.

201321 RAY BURTON; A CHICAGO TALE. Chicago: 1895
NUC.

TRENT, HILARY. Nationality Unknown.

201322 MR. CLAGHORN'S DAUGHTER. New York: J. S.
Ogilvie, 1903 NUC.

Woman trained to be agnostic who marries a theologian.
PW 5-2-03
After death of her child and her husband, marries the
man she should have married in the first place. NYT
393, 03

TRUE, C. E. Nationality Unknown.

201323 UNCLE CARL. BY "SUREV". Washington, D.
C.: Neale, 1908 NUC.

PW-romance involving an inheritance.

TURVEY, C. HILTON. See TURVEY, CAROLL BREVOORT HILTON.

TURVEY, CAROLL BREVOORT HILTON. B. 1880. United States.

201324 THE VAN HAAVENS. BY C. HILTON-TURVEY.
Boston: Small, Maynard, [c1916] BMC NUC.

Bella helps young aristocrat Willoughby; "their
wedding was less a surprise than Bella's identity." PW
90:686 9/2/16

TYLER, G. VERE. See TYLER, GEORGIE VERE.

TYLER, GEORGIE VERE. United States.

201325 THE DAUGHTER OF A REBEL; A NOVEL. BY G.
VERE TYLER. New York: Duffield, 1913 NUC.

"A Southern girl's experiences in New York" NYT

UBEDA [pseud.].

201326 THE SHADOW OF A THIRD. A STORY OF MODERN
PASSIONS. BY UBEDA, EDITOR OF "PUBLIC OPINION".
London: A. Treherne, 1902 BMC.

UNITAS [pseud.].

201327 THE DREAM CITY. (A STATE GOVERNED IN
ACCORDANCE WITH THE MIND OF "THE KING"). BY UNITAS.
London: Simpkin Mrshall, 1920 BMC.

TLS-Socialist utopia

V., pseud. See FERGUSON, V. MUNRO.

VALENTINE, E. S.

201328 VELDT AND LAAGER: TALES OF THE TRANSVAAL.
London: Methuen, 1900 BMC.

VANCE, FERROL.

201329 A WOMAN IN TEN THOUSAND. London: Hurst
and Blackett, 1893 BMC.

Two equally attractive heroines Honor and Dolores. The
latter wins the young man Honor loved. Dolores had an
earlier unhappy marriage. Reviewer assumes the author
is female. SP 1-21-93, 87

VAN DYKE, CURTIS. United States.

201330 A DAUGHTER OF THE PROPHETS. New York:
Abbey Press, [c1900] NUC. (Also Published in London,
Montreal.)

Woman Lawyer Marries A Minister.

VANNY, JO.

201331 HOW I DISHED THE DON, AND OTHER STORIES.
London: Digby, Long, 1898 BMC.

LIT 2:537. Stories dealing with commercial swindlers.
Narrated by author who successfully outwitted the
errant rogue Don Trinitario Tortosa de Comercio.
"Scarcely a petticoat in the volume."

VARTENIE [pseud.].

201332 YESTERE. THE ROMANCE OF A LIFE. BY
VARTENIE. London: T. F. Unwin, 1901 BMC.

7-27-01 ATH

VAUGHN, HAMPDEN. See PUSEY, PENNOCK.

VERA [pseud.].

201333 ELAINE BENTLEY; OR, THE DOCTOR'S
DAUGHTER. A NOVEL. BY "VERA." Trinidad: Mirror
Printing Works, 1906 BMC.

VERE, B. M.

201334 A GEM OF CREMONA. Bristol: J. W.
Arrowsmith, [1893] BMC. (Bound with A Chef D'Oeuvre by
Ethel Blair Oliphant Maxwell Graham.)

VERNEY, AUSTEN.

201335 THE SOUL OF ENGLAND. London: Heath,
Cranton and Ouseley, [1914] BMC.

TLS-series of discussions on political events inc.
feminism, held together by plot.

VERNON, N.

201336 ALIENS NEAR OF KIN. London: Mills and
Boon, 1912 BMC.

TLS-happy marriage between English girl and Austrian
officer.
ATH

VICLARE, JULIEN, pseud. See HUME, JEAN B.

VINCENT, VIN.

201337 OLGA; OR, WRONG ON BOTH SIDES. London:
Griffith & Farran, [1897] BMC.

201338 THE WHITE AIGRETTE. London: Hurst and
Blackett, 1894 BMC.

SR. 77:232. Military life, adventure, romance.

VIVIAN, E. CHARLES. See VIVIAN, EVELYN CHARLES H.

VIVIAN, EVELYN CHARLES H. United Kingdom.

201339 DIVIDED WAYS. London: Holden &
Hardingham, 1914 BMC.

TLS 13:530 Mary North is "strong, maternal,
discerning" (quote from author) and represents the big
things of life. She seduces Alan Hope, a married man,
"in a great pure passion" (author) which had given him
"the most wonderful days of my life" (author) and left
him.

201340 FOLLOWING FEET. London: A. Melrose, 1911
BMC.

201341 PASSION-FRUIT. BY E. CHARLES VIVIAN.
London: W. Heinemann, 1912 BMC NUC.

TLS-2 women and a man.
ATH-she must pay the price and does with pluck;
commands our sympathy.
ACAD-

201342 THE SHADOW OF CHRISTINE. London: Gay and
Bird, 1907 BMC. New York: R .F. Fenno, 1910 NUC.

Christine is a little girl whose memory stays with a
man through his life. TLS
BKM-male hero; adventure.
NYT Mistaken belief that a promise of marriage is
binding results in the death of 50 men, a girl's
broken heart, a wedded pair, etc.
Love complications. PW

201343 WANDERING OF DESIRE. London: A. Melrose,
1910 BMC.

Business, politics, love. TLS

201344 THE WOMAN TEMPTED ME. A STORY OF A
SELFISH MAN. London: A. Melrose, 1909 BMC.

Story of two boys turning men. TLS
There is a wife who writes novels. ACAD

201345 THE YOUNG MAN ABSOLOM. London: Chapman &
Hall, 1915 BMC. Dutton, 1915 NUC.

Centers on a man and his efforts to help factory

workers. 10-9-05 PW

VON HOLTZ, E.

201346   THE UNSIGNED WILL. New York: R. Bonner's
Sons, 1892 NUC. (Bound with The Stolen Vail by E.
Werner (i.e. Elisabeth Buerstenbinder). Tr. Mrs. D.
M. Lowrey.)

VON HOOGSTRAAT, MOREE E. B. 1869. United States.

201347   WHERE THE SAGE AND CACTUS GROW. BY M. E.
HOOGSTRAAT. Chicago, Ill.: Scroll, 1900 NUC.

W., E. [pseud.].

201348   MERLE; OR; ONE FAIR DAUGHTER [ANONYMOUS].
London: W. Stevens, 1892 BMC.

201349   A STORMY WOOING. BY THE AUTHOR OF "MERLE;
OR, ONE FAIR DAUGHTER" [ANONYMOUS]. London: W.
Stevens, 1898 BMC.

W., G. DE S. [pseud.]., jt. au. See C., M. [pseud.]. AND G.
DE d.].

WAKELING, T. G.

201350   THE WHITE KNIGHTS. London: J. Murray,
1912 BMC.

ACAD-military story for schoolboys.

WAKENED, A. [pseud.].

201351   A PRIEST IN LOVE. BY A. WAKENED. London:
H. L. Angold, 1913 BMC.

Argues against claim that priest impervious to women's
charms. ATH
Two R.C. priests love same woman. This causes hero to
renounce RC sm. TLS

WALFORD, S. E.

201352   UNTIL THE DAWN. London: Chapman and Hall,
1899 BMC.

How Judith Marsh inspired by the highest conjugal
ideal, was moved to put an end to a vulgar woman.
Murders her. Relative of the murdered woman looks for
revenge. Judith did it to protect her beloved husband.
Presented as a model of lofty ideals. LBKM 16:21
An immaculate lady, Mrs. Marsh, murdered one Mrs.
Ferrars, who blackmailed her husband. Son of Mrs.
Ferrars runs her to earth but never betrays her. SP
87:473

WALLER, S. E.

201353   SEBASTIANI'S SECRET. London: Chatto and
Windus, 1897 BMC.

The secret is a certain power over women, handed down
thru generations, known at the outside to only three.
Related to occultism and Atlantis, mystery,
imaginative. SP 79:627.
Combines the occult the orient and society subjects.
ATH 109:413.

WALPOLE, F. G.

201354   UPPER BOHEMIANS. London: Digby, Long,
1893 BMC.

One woman upset that another should be considered more
a liar and more a devil than herself. But what
promises to be racey turns out quite tame. SP 71:841.

WALSH, B.

201355   THROUGH DEEP WATERS: A NOVEL. London:
Trischler, 1892 BMC.

ATH 99:630. Bigamy, murder, marital complications.
SP 69:504. Amateur detective who discovers he makes a
better lover.
ACAD 42:6R. Also suicide, false imprisonment. Ultimate
happiness of husband and wife.

WARD, R.

201356   SUPPLEJACK: A ROMANCE OF MAORILAND.
London: Chapman and Hall, 1894 BMC.

WARD, W. W.

201357   INCAPABLE LOVERS, LIMITED. London: J.
Long, 1907 BMC.

Humorous, ACAD 303

WARR, J. W. United States.

201358   THE BUSINESS HOUSE THAT JACK BUILT.
Moline, Ill.: Plowman, 1896 NUC.

WARREN, B. C. United States.

201359   ARSARETH: A TALE OF THE LURAY CAVERNS.
New York: A. Lovell, [c1893] NUC. (W: Asareth)

WASSERMANN, LILLIAS.

201360   THE DAFFODILS. London: Chatto and Windus,
1891 BMC.

ACAD 41: 178. Two artists, cousins, both love the same
man, and make a pact that the first who succeeds as an
artist is to suppress her love for the man.

201361   THE GODDESS OF THE DANDELIONS. London:
Ward & Downey, 1895 BMC.

She is elected as idol and ideal of the young
aesthetes of the Dandelion Club. SR 80:119
"satire of early stage of aesthetic mvt" SP 74:763

WATSON, M. A.

201362   WITHOUT WINGS; A NOVEL. London: Syd. H.
E. Foxwell, 1904 BMC.

TLS-Insipid tale of devolution of baronetcy.

WATSON, R. D. Nationality Unknown.

201363   THE DREAM GIRL. London: Heath, Cranton,
[1919] BMC.

Manages a farm, impersonating her brother to whom the
farm was left. TLS

201364   MRS. ANSTRUTHER'S DIAMONDS. London: H.
Cranton, [1920] BMC NUC.

TLS crime story.

WAWN, F. T. United Kingdom.

201365   A GREEN OLIVE TREE. London: A. Melrose,
[1919] BMC.

Eva, horsewoman, swimmer, housewife ready to sacrifice
self by marrying. -TLS
Does all for brother-LBKM

201366   THE JOYFUL YEARS; A NOVEL. London: A.
Melrose, 1917 BMC. New York: E. P. Dutton, [c1917]
NUC.

Years of youth and love. TLS
"Too sweet" and sentimental-TLS
"some play is made with the modern motive of the young
girl's revolt against economic slavery to her
Victorian parents." Cynthi Brenner's parents, British
aristocrats, try to get her to marry well (money).
Instead she elopes. Later reconciled with family. War
separates them; he returns-not too seriously crippled.
BKM

201367   THE MASTERDILLO, A STORY OF YOUTH
[ANONYMOUS]. London: A. Melrose, 1913 BMC.

Young silly joyous couple, sentimental set up
housekeeping in their fairyland way daintily humorous.
They are utterly in love.

201368   THE ROAD TO THE STARS. London: E. Nash,
1916 BMC.

LBKM--Little comedy ATH

WAY, L. N. Nationality Unknown.

201369   THE CALL OF THE HEART. New York: W.
Dillingham, [1909] NUC. London: T. F. Unwin, 1909 BMC.

WEBB, G. E.

201370   THE FAIRBOURN PAPERS. London: J. Ouseley,
[1910] BMC.

TLS-male hero
ACAD male hero.

WEBSTER, J. PROVAND.

201371   CHILDREN OF WRATH. London: G. Routledge,
1899 BMC. ("Being the Memoirs of one Judah Elvers, a
Prince of the Tribe of Benjamin, Written in the Year
1697 by His Friend Jeremy Whitfield, a Native of the
City of Norwich." NUC Bs)

Historical romance. story of Hidden Temple of Hera in
Yucatan. Judah Elvero, a Jew, devotes life to freeing
the house from the curse. SP 83:877

WEEDON, W. J.

201372   IN THE GRIP OF A DEMON. London: Drane's,
[1914] BMC.

ATH-Villain marries, plots with confederates to gain
money.
TLS-Chief of a gang of scoundrels.

WELBORE, M. W.

201373   SOME FANTASIES OF FATE. London: Digby,
Long, 1899 BMC.

WELFORD, HADLEY.

201374   WHOSE DEED? A ROMANCE. London: Jarrold,
1899 BMC.

WELTON, A. E. Nationality Unknown.

201375   CORA: A TALE OF RIGHT AND WRONG. A NOVEL
OF TO-DAY [ANONYMOUS]. New York: J. S. Ogilvie,
[c1891] NUC.

WEST, B. B. Nationality Unknown.

201376   EDMUND FULLESTON, OR THE FAMILY OF EVIL
GENIUS. London: Longmans, 1900 BMC.

SR 90:728. Story of two families.

201377   A FINANCIAL ATONEMENT. London: Longmans,
1896 BMC.

201378   HALF-HOURS WITH THE MILLIONAIRES. London
and New York: Longmans, Green, 1892 NUC BMC.

201379   PELICAN HOUSE, E. C. London: T. F. Unwin,
1898 BMC.

SP 80:629. Satire of modern finance. No love interest,
"feminine readers may probably be repelled by
preliminary and episodical technicalities." "Riotously
funny."

201380   SIR SIMON VANDERPETTER; AND MENDING HIS
ANCESTORS. TWO REFORMATIONS. London: Longmans, 1894
BMC.

WESTERVELT, LEONIDAS. United States.

201381   PUPPET-SHOW: A SKETCH. New York: F. T.
Neely, [c1898] NUC.

WHARTON, SYDNEY. Nationality Unknown.

201382   THE WIFE DECIDES: A NOVEL. New York: G.W.
Dillingham, [c1911] NUC.

Marries to gain freedom; gets divorced to gain
freedom, marries again disastrously. PW 4-1-11

WHISPER, A.

201383   BLACK MARK. Edinburgh & London:
Blackwood, 1909 BMC.

Historical romance of highwayman and wife. TLS
Letty Beander in black satin breeches fencing with her
brother. Has daring, dazzling adventure. 17 years old.
She heard of Black Mark & promises to fight him if she
meets him. Dresses as a man; when her coach held up,
she steps out, draws her sword and challenges Black
Mark. They end up in love. LBKM
Marries him, joins him in rides. He's a highwayman (to
pay gaming debts.) ATH

201384   FFYNON THE SUN-EATER. London: Holden &
Hardingham, [1914] BMC.

LBKM-wife without a wedding ring loved by a man who
marries her and then learns his antecedents. Tragedy
results. Ffynon Morgan is the daughter of a religious
maniac, has all the superstition and emotionalism of
the Celt, a passionate love for her dying child.
ATH-written to show that invariably the woman pays for
the sins of others and the man goes free.

201385   KING AND CAPTIVE. Edinburgh & London: W.
Blackwood, 1910 BMC NUC.

TLS--Egyptian love story.
ACAD
LBKM-Nefert refuses to share the throne with the
pharaoh, asks for and gets a house of her own where
she can have leisure to write & read.
SR-Nefert is a lovely Greek dancing girl who rose from
position of washing the king's feet to become his
mistress. Refused his offer of jewels and riches too.

201386   THE SINISTER NOTE. Edinburgh & London: W.
Blackwood, 1911 BMC.

Romance of modern Spain. ATH

WHITAKER, EVELYN. Fl. 1891-1903. United States.

201387   DEAR. BY THE AUTHOR OF "TIP-CAT"
[ANONYMOUS]. London: A.D. Innes, 1892 BMC. Boston:
Roberts, 1892 NUC.

ATH 100: Dear is daughter of clergyman who is
persuaded into marriage with epileptic. She is
"induced to leave him, instead of nursing him in his
sickness, as was her duty."

201388   MY HONEY. BY THE AUTHOR OF MISS TOOSEY'S
MISSION, TIP-CAT, OUR LITTLE ANN, DON, ZOE, ETC.
[ANONYMOUS]. London: A.D. Innes, 1895 BMC. Boston:
Roberts, 1895 NUC.

SP 76:247. Love story, Hetty's stubborn temper.

WHITE, E.

201389   ONE WEAK MOMENT. London: Roxburghe Press,
[1897] BMC.

WHITFELD, J. M.

201390   'TOM' WHO WAS RACHEL. London: H. Frowde,
1911 BMC.

WHITMAN, SIDNEY.

201391   THE REALM OF THE HALSBURGS. London:
Heinemann, 1892 BMC.

WHITTINGTON, MAIBEY.

201392   BEYOND THE HILLS. London: J. Long, 1912
BMC.

TLS-Artist and farmer's daughter.

WHITTON, J. BRADLEY.

201393   MR. JEREMY DETECTIVE. London: Digby and
Long, [1891] BMC.

WICKHAM, A. E.

201394   FORTUNE'S FINGERS. London: Hutchinson,
1896 BMC.

First part: friendless girl among strangers. She lives
in a huge house with a Rochester-like master, but
worse. He knocks her down. She is subject to
terrifying nights; there's a mystery about the
master's wife who has been tortured into imbecility.
Part Two: the tyrant found shot. Heroine suspected;
she denies nothing; is tried, sentenced to death,
reprieved. Then we learn it was the imbecile wife who
did it. ACAD 51:176

201395   LOVEDAY: A TALE OF A STIRRING TIME.
London: Cassell, 1896 BMC NUC.

SR-Young Penrose rescues an adventurer wanted by the
law off the Cornish coast. He marries Penrose's
mother, and Penrose is eventually united with his
niece. Loveday.
ATH 107:441. She is sweet, quaint, girlish.

WILDE, M. VAUGHAN. United States.

693

201396   JULEPS AND CLOVER. New York: R. F. Fenno,
[c1898] NUC.

WILDE, WEIN [pseud.]. United States.

    201397   "WHATEVER THOU ART:" A NOVEL. BY WEIN
    WILDE. New York: G. W. Dillingham, 1892 NUC.

WILDMAN, ROUNSVELLE. United States.

    201398   THE PANGLIMA MUDA: A ROMANCE OF MALAYA.
    San Francisco: Overland Monthly, 1894 NUC BMC.

WILKES, A. B. United States.

    201399   THE GREAT SOCIAL BOYCOTT; OR, SOCIETY
    READJUSTED AND THE CAUSES LEADING TO ITS
    ESTABLISHMENT. Brownwood Texas: 1895 NUC.

WILKIE, J.

    201400   THE VISION OF NEHEMIAH SINTRAM. London:
    E. Stock, 1902 BMC.

WILKINSON, CARY HAMILTON. B. 1844. United States.

    201401   THE TRAGEDY OF BADEN. New York: Neale,
    1906 NUC.

WILLIAMS, GERVAS.

    201402   DR. FITZSIMMONDS' SWEETHEARTS; OR THE
    ADVENTURES OF AN AFFECTIONATE YOUNG MAN. London: J.
    Macqueen, 1895 BMC.

WILLIAMS, J. EVANS.

    201403   ABERAFON. London: J. Long, 1911 BMC.

    Farming people: a sister who chafes at her position, a
    wife who leaves her husband. TLS pov?

WILLIAMS, MARION PRYS. United Kingdom.

    201404   BLODWEN. London: Simpkin, Marshall,
    [1917] BMC.

    201405   THE CALL OF A SOUL: A WELSH ROMANCE.
    London: Simpkin, Marshall, [1916] BMC NUC.

    TLS-love story.

WILLIAMS, W. SMITH.

    201406   THE MAGIC OF THE DESERT: A ROMANCE.
    Edinburgh and London: W. Blackwood, 1899 BMC.

    Set in English country home. Several characters
    introduced and then dropped. LIT 5:82
    Charlie Rowley first at Cambridge, then as a soldier.
    Then his adventures with Dick Travers-Australia, Rio
    de Janeiro, war in the republic of Andina. LBKM 16:169

WILLIS, J. S. United States.

    201407   JOHN MARTIN, JR.: A STORY OF "THE IRON
    MASK". [c1892] W.

WILSON, RATHMELL. B. 1883.

    201408   CRIMSON WINGS. A NOVEL FOR THOSE WHO LOVE
    YESTERDAY. London: Greening, 1912 BMC.

        ACAD-feminine Millie

    201409   LOVE AND THE MIRROR: A LITTLE NOVEL.
    London: Greening, 1907 BMC.

        ACAD-traditional love story.

    201410   RE-BIRTH. A ROMANTIC NOVEL. London:
    Greening, 1909 BMC.

    201411   WHEN A WOMAN LOVES. A NOVEL. London:
    Greening, 1910 BMC.

WILSON, SYDNEY J. United States.

    201412   A TRANSPLANTED LILY: A NOVEL. New York:
    G. W. Dillingham, 1899 NUC.

    Mississippi just after Civil War. Young woman comes to
    live with uncle after her father's death. Doesn't know
    her relatives are outlaws. Love between her and a rich
    cotton planter. PW 56:330.

WINTER, C. GORDAN.

    201413   MORALS AND MISTAKES; OR, THE STORY OF
    BASIL FIELDING: A NOVEL. London: Simpkin, Marshall,
    1899 BMC.

WISTAN, ADEN.

    201414   LUCY, FRANCIS AND COUSIN BILL. A NOVEL.
    London: Eden, Remington, 1892 BMC.

    ATH 99:662. Scotch suburban life.
    SR. Tangled loves

WOOD, A. E.

    201415   THE KING. London: A. Melrose, [1911] BMC.

    18th century romance. Real center of interest is
    Julie, a courtesan, a spy, contrasted to "baby" Queen
    Sophia with her "wooden and doll-like virtues."?

WOOD, C. B.

    201416   THE CITY OF CONFUSION. A STUDY IN MODERN
    ANGLICANISM. London: Sands, 1903 BMC.

    the Anglican church and celibacy ACAD vol 64, 32
    TLS, 1-03, 8

WOOD, H. F. See WOOD, H. FREEMAN WIBER.

WOOD, H. FREEMAN WIBER. United Kingdom.

    201417   AVENGED ON SOCIETY. A NOVEL. BY H. F.
    WOOD. New York: J. W. Lovell, [c1892] NUC. London: W.
    Heinemann, 1893 BMC.

    Satirizes the "flabby humanitarianism of the age."
    Satirizes the moral weakness of modern society in its
    manner of celebrating the criminal who gets away with
    his crime. Diary form. SP 70,493
    The convict is liberated, she stumps the country,
    starts a newspaper and marries a duke. She's the only
    child of an ex-convict and a duchess.
    Includes a woman who studies gynecology and "writes
    letters to the medical press on our Public Women from
    the point of view of Etiology." Another who talks
    about "Dephlogisticated Air." SR 75, 182.

WOODINGTON, F. THICKNESSE.

    201418   FATE THE MARPLOT. London: G. Allen &
    Unwin, 1915 BMC NUC.

    Marriage out of pity-husband crippled-and its
    unfortunate sequel TLS

    201419   STRAWS UPON THE WATER. London: G. Allen &
    Unwin, 1916 BMC.

    TLS--romance with happy ending after years of
    separation and hardship for her
    ATH-She is betrayed and abandoned, struggles as shop
    girl then as factory hand. He tries to make atonement
    by working as dock laborer until he wins her
    forgiveness.

    201420   SWAYNEFORD. London: G. Allen & Unwin,
    [1918] BMC.

    TLS-Spy story of England before war. Heroine discovers
    so much she is kidnapped and taken to Germany-many
    exciting adventures when war breaks out
    LBKM. Ena Cardonnel ruins her past cleverness by
    getting sentimental and going to pieces.

WOOLET, A. WELLINGTON [pseud.]. United States.

    201421   THE WOOLET PAPERS. BY A. WELLINGTON
    WOOLET. New York, London: Trade-mark Record
    Publishers, 1899 NUC.

WORLAND, F. E.

    201422   LOVE; SACRED AND PROFANE. London: C. W.
    Daniel, 1907 BMC NUC.

    Consists of articles which appeared in "The Open
    Road."

WRAY, DENYS.

    201423   THE HERMIT OF MUCKROSS. London:
    Sonnenschein, 1893 BMC.

WRIGHT, R. H.

201424   THE OUTER DARKNESS. London: Greening,
1906 BMC.

Horror and mystery ACAD

201425   A PLAIN MAN'S TALE. Belfast: McCaw,
Stevenson & Orr, 1904 BMC.

WRIOTHESLEY, WILLIAM [pseud.]. United Kingdom.

201426   THE AMBASSADRESS. BY WILLIAM WRIOTHESLEY.
London: W. Heinemann, 1913 BMC NUC. New York: G. H.
Doran, [c1913] NUC.

British ambassador's wife has American lover. "Her
tame cat." He believes every woman should have a
profession-which is the theme. Daughter of
Ambassadress longs for work, and becomes wife and
mother-her chosen "profession."(would marry a man she
hardly loves to get on with her profession.) he jilts
her. Ends up with Mr. Ronalds whose son is crippled by
an auto accident-thus she has her profession. Her
mother smokes, has a weak heart, goes about with her
admirer (we get brief glimpses of the Ambassador) She
had decided marriage should not be considered a career
for a woman any more than for a man. NYT

WYATT, SYDNEY.

201427   DOWN BY THE SEA. London: Simpkin &
Marshall, 1893 BMC.

WYNNE, THE DAU.

201428   A MAID OF CYMRU. A PATRIOTIC ROMANCE.
London: Simpkin, Marshall, [1901] BMC.

X [pseud.]. United States.

201429   WOLFINE. A ROMANCE IN WHICH A DOG PLAYS
AN HONORABLE PART. BY X. New York: Sturgis & Walton,
1915. London: G. Allen & Unwin, [1916] BMC.

YALE, WELLINGTON [pseud.?]. United States.

201430   CONGRESSMAN JOHN L.: A HISTORY OF HIS
TRIALS AND TRIUMPHS IN WASHINGTON. BY WELLINGTON YALE.
Louisville, Ky.: St. James House, 1892 NUC.

YALSDUAM, LOHTA, pseud. See MAUDSLAY, ATHOL.

YANG PING YU.

201431   THE LOVE STORY OF A MAIDEN OF CATHAY;
TOLD IN LETTERS FROM YANG PING YU. New York: Revell,
[1911] BMC.

PW-letters to female cousin who is medical student in
Scotland, violating all Chinese ideals of womanhood.
Letters full of wordly wisdom by a Chinese woman.
"charming" NYT

YEATS, S. LEVETT. See YEATS, SIDNEY KILNER LEVETT.

YEATS, SIDNEY KILNER LEVETT. United Kingdom.

201432   THE LORD PROTECTOR. BY S. LEVETT-YEATS.
London: Cassell, 1902 BMC. New York: Longmans, Green,
1902 NUC.

201433   ORRAIN. A ROMANCE. BY S. LEVETT-YEATS.
New York: Longmans, Green, 1904 NUC. London: Methuen,
1904 BMC.

PW-historical romance.
NYT-historical romance.

201434   THE TRAITOR'S WAY. A STORY. BY S.
LEVETT-YEATS. London: Longmans, 1901 BMC. New York: F.
A. Stokes, [c1901] NUC.

YELDHAM, C. C.

201435   DURHAM'S FARM. London: Methuen, 1906 BMC.

TLS-invalid architect and his daughter.

ZERO [pseud.].

201436   A GENTLEMAN OF THE NINETEENTH CENTURY: AN
ANACHRONISM IS SIX PARTS, TWO CHRONICLES. BY "ZERO".
London: Digby, Long, [1896] BMC.

ZIMMERMAN, L. M. United States.

201437   YVONNE: A ROMANCE. Baltimore, Md.:
Published By Author, 1900 W.

THIRD SERIES

A., H.

300001   LAURIEL: THE LOVE LETTERS OF AN AMERICAN
GIRL. Boston: L. C. Page, 1902 [1901] PW.

Independent young woman resists plans to make her
marry wealth; marries a worker. PW 11-23-01.

AGATHA, SISTER.

300002   CONFESSIONS OF A NUN. Philadelphia:
Jordon, 1891 PW.

Sister Agatha is in a convent because of family
misfortunes and loss of her lover. Her experiences in
French convent and stories of other inmates. Attacks
convent life. PW J 17

ALAMART.

300003   SOUL OF THE UNFAITHFUL. A. M. Gardner,
1918 BS.

ALBANESI, E. MARIA.

300004   CISSY. Collins, 1913.

ALDINGTON, MAY.

300005   GOD'S TOYS. Collier, 1908 BS.

TLS- love and religion.
ATH- love and religion.

ALEXIS.

300006   ALICIA; A TALE OF THE AMERICAN NAVY.
1898.

Maryland, many incidents take place at Annapolis. Her
story shows "the rights and duties of American wives
and their independence and self respect as well." BOOK
NEWS, 1898-9, 302

ALLEN, N.

300007   FOR STARK LOVE AND IDLENESS.

ACAD 50:490. Scots, romantic story of the 16th
century. Adventure, wholesome love interest.

AMEAR, GRETA.

300008   WHAT WAS IT? Glasgow: D. Bryce, 1897 BS.

AMES, FLORA.

300009   THE PAIN OF THE WORLD. Key, 1912 BS.

ANONYMOUS AUTHOR--NOT IDENTIFIED.

300010   ALL WE LIKE SHEEP.

ACAD 53:575. Impatient lamb requests instruction on
the world from its mother. Ewe's reply is interpreted
into human language. Lamb falls asleep during recital.
History of Frances Roy, sculptor, wished to be free
and lead her own life, world was censorious. She
contributed sketches to a paper whose editor was
handsome and sophisticated. At end of history returns
to sheep-fold. Lamb is sceptical. of what?

300011   AMARYLLIS. London: T. F. Unwin, 1891 BS.

300012   AS THROUGH FIRE. BY AUTHOR OF "DOLLY'S
ORDEAL". London: W. Stevens, 1892 BS.

300013   BAYOU TRISTE; A STORY OF LOUISIANA. New
York: A. S. Barnes, 1902.

300014   THE BEAUTIFUL TWINS. W. Stevens, 1903 BS.

300015   THE BEWILDERED BRIDE. Nash, 1911 BS.

300016   BITTER PENITENCE. BY THE AUTHOR OF "NOT A
SAINT," "CHERRY BLOSSOM". London: W. Stevens, 1898 BS.

300017   THE BLUE COCKADE: A STORY OF THE SOUTHERN
CONFEDERACY. Washington, D. C.: Neale, 1905.

300018   BRUISING PEG. PAGES FROM THE JOURNAL OF
MARGARET MOLLOY. 1763-9. EDITED BY PAUL CRESWICK.
Downey, 1898 BS.

300019   A CALIFORNIAN GIRL. London: W. Stevens,
1897 BS.

300020   CECILE. New York: F. Warne, 1895 PW.

Aukland before Kaffir outbreak. Farmer "dares" to
aspire to marry his master's daugher-Cecile. PW
10-5-95:591.

300021   THE CHARM OF LIFE. BY THE AUTHOR OF AN
EPISODE AT SCHMEKS. F. Griffiths, 1901 BS.

300022   CLOSED DOORS. BY THE AUTHOR OF "A LONDON
GIRL". London: Rivers, 1906 BS.

Irregularities in W. Kensington life. SR

300023   THE CONFESSIONS OF A DANCING GIRL. BY
HERSELF. London: Heath, Cranton & Ouseley, 1913.

account of actual training for an acrobat and dancer
and the conditions of the profession--the ups and
downs of the career in Spain, Portugal, South America
as well as England TLS

300024   COO-EE: TALES OF AUSTRALIAN LIFE. BY
AUSTRALIAN LADIES. Griffith, Farran,

300025   THE DARKWOOD TRAGEDY. Washington, D. C.:
Neale, 1902 PW.

300026   COUNT OF ELSINORE (THE). Simpkin, 1900
BS.

300027   THE DAY OF PREPARATION; OR THE GATHERING
OF THE HOST TO ARMAGEDDON: A BOOK FOR THE TIMES. E.
Stock, 1893 BS.

300028   THE DECOY DUCK. BY A. PEER. John Long,
1913 BS.

Rosemary is the duck of her father. Lots of exciting
incidents. "Heroine having a hot bath." Gambles, very
nearly seduced, finally falls in love and marries.
ACAD
Father uses her to lure men to his gambling table.
Saved by an English noble. Is able to overcome her
love of gambling. ATH

300029   A DEMOCRATIC TORY. BY A PEER. Jarrold,
1893 BS.

300030   A DERELICT EMPIRE "MARK TIME". Blackwood,
1912.

ACAD-no mention of a woman's name.

300031   DOCTOR QUADLIBET: A STUDY IN ETHICS. BY
THE AUTHOR OF "CHRONICLES OF WESTERLY". Leadenhall
Press, 1894 BS.

ACAD 46:171. Noble and Christian characters.

300032   DORA DEENE. BY AUTHOR OF "THE TREMAYNES"
OR "A DREAM OF LOVE". J. Henderson, 1895 BS.

300033   DUST OF THE WORLD. London: Allen, 1913
BS.

Belfast, 17th ATH

300034   AN EPISODE ON A DESERTED ISLAND. BY THE
AUTHOR OF MISS MOLLY. London: J. Murray, 1901 BS.

300035   A FAIR AMERICAN. Rand, McNally, 1891.

Wealthy heroine-gambler's daughter, parents get her to
Paris to make good marriage; about to make a catch to
viscount, bkgd of father exposed but happy end. She
weds another man. LW.

300036   FAIR GOD. BY AUTHOR OF "BEN HUR". R. E.
King, 1895 BS.

300037   A FAMILY ARRANGEMENT. BY THE AUTHOR OF
"DR. EDITH ROMNEY". Bentley, 1894 BS.

SP 73:892. A doctor and a lawyer impulsively burn the
will of their wives' father which would disinherit
them and leave money to a granddaughter. They are
tortured by their crime and work out elaborate marital
arrangement to restore money to right ful heir.
Doctor's wife suspects the truth. Tells her daughter
when she appeals to her under pressure of father and
uncle. They want daughter to make marriage so
inheritance is restored.

300038   A FATHER'S SIN. BY THE AUTHOR OF "LADY BETTY". W. Stevens, 1897 BS.

300039   FOR LASSIE'S SAKE: A NOVEL. J. Haddon, 1891 BS.

300040   FOR LOVE OF MARJORIE. W. Stevens, 1897 BS.

300041   FOR RITA. BY THE AUTHOR OF "ANGELA" & C. W. Stevens, BS.

300042   THE GENIUS OF GALILEE. C. H. Kerr, 1891.

Jesus is hero but author has no reverence for Christ nor for rel. Gives a revolting picture of "Virgin Mary and Sarah giggling together" while Joseph courts. LW

300043   HER GOLDEN SORROW. BY AUTHOR OF "PEGGY'S WIDOW". W. Stevens, 1897 BS.

300044   HIS NAME.

CR 21:272. Esther refused to marry Wayland, a clergyman, because of her liberty, art, and theosophy. Offered to find a wife for him but at book's end they marry. Watered-down Sarah Grand.

300045   THE HOLLYWOOD MYSTERY. BY THE AUTHOR OF "A WOMAN'S LOVE STORY". W. Stevens, 1894 BS.

300046   HUSBAND AND BROTHER: A FEW CHAPTERS IN A WOMAN'S LIFE OF TO-DAY, AND FROM KEY-NOTE TO DOMINANT. Arrowsmith (Bristol) Simpkin, 1894 BS.

A young woman must earn her own way--in title story. Volume also includes From Key Note to Dominant--does unconventional things but draws the line when it comes to doing wrong "and that means only one thing in the feminine novel." "When it comes to that kind of freedom, women characters act as though Heavenly Twins never existed. Perhaps Miss Conway, B.A. really means to show what twaddle most of the talk about the rights and wrongs of the New woman really is." SR 79:134

300047   AN IDEAL LOVE; OR, OWEN MASTERS, THE POET. BY THE AUTHOR OF WESTMARCH. F. Henderson, 1893 BS.

300048   IN THE DAYS OF THE STAR CHAMBER; A TALE OF THE PERSECUTIONS DURING THE REIGN OF KING CHARLES I. Hopkins, 1900 BS.

300049   KATHLEEN'S ENGAGEMENT. BY THE AUTHOR OF "MY MARRIAGE". W. Stevens, 1897 BS.

300050   KITTY, LIL, AND ANOTHER. BY THE AUTHOR OF "ANGELA", "FOR RITA". W. Stevens, 1900 BS.

300051   KNIGHT OR KNAVE? BY THE AUTHOR OF "BERTHA'S FATE" "IN STRANGE ATTIRE". W. Stevens, 1898 BS.

300052   LIFEGUARDSMAN (THE): A TALE OF THE ENGLISH REVOLUTION, ADAPTED FROM SCHIMMEL'S "DE KAPTEIN VAN DE LIJFGARDE". Black, 1896 BS.

300053   LOVE KNOTS. BY THE AUTHOR OF "LUCY: OR, A GREAT MISTAKE," "ROSE O THE WORLD" & C. W. Stevens, 1896 BS.

300054   MARGARET TUDOR; A ROMANCE OF OLD ST. AUGUSTINE. New York: F. A. Stokes, [1902] PW.

300055   MARS AND NEPTUNE; OR STIRRING EVENTS AND ADVENTURES OF SOLDIERS AND SAILORS OF MOST NATIONS; WITH INTERESTING NARRATIVES OF VALOUR, DEVOTION TO DUTY, WONDERFUL ESCAPES FROM THE ENEMY ALSO AMUSING JOKES ON PARADE, IN CAMP AND BARRACK-ROOM & C. Major Andrews, 1893 BS.

300056   THE MELITA OF THE MIDLANDS. BY AN EX-RECTOR. Watts, 1901 BS.

300057   A MOTHER. Belford, 1891. (Tr. fr. French.)

Exaggerated maternal love for a cruel dissipated son who works up the idea that his father is insane so he will gain control of the property. Madame Combarrien adores her son; leaves husband to follow him to U.S. LW

300058   MURIEL'S DIAMONDS. BY THE AUTHOR OF "A WOMAN'S LOVE STORY". W. Stevens, 1900 BS.

300059   MY WICKEDNESS: A PSYCHOLOGICAL STUDY. Cleveland Pub. Co. (N. Y.), 1893 PW.

First person account by a murderer confined in Charenton. Murdered a young girl. Traces the events of his life. Shows that the forces heredity and an unknown parentage were to blame. PW 6-10-93.

300060   ODD TYPES; A CHARACTER STUDY. New York: Broadway, [1906] PW.

300061   O'DONNEL: A NATIONAL TALE (DOWNEY'S SIXPENNY LIBRARY). Downey, 1898 BS.

300062   THE OLD WOMAN WHO RODE ON A BROOM. New York: Dutton, 1905 PW.

300063   THE ORACLE OF BAAL: A NARRATIVE OF SOME CURIOUS EVENTS IN THE LIFE OF PROFESSOR HORATIO CARMICHAEL. Hutchinson, 1897 BS.

300064   OUR LADY'S TUMBLER: A TWELFTH CENTURY LEGEND TRANSCRIBED FOR LADY DAY. Dent, 1894 BS.

300065   PAN SCORCHED SOULS. Mills & Boon, 1915 BS.

300066   PENANCE OF PENELOPE. BY THE AUTHOR OF THE HANDS OF FORTUNE. W. Stevens, 1913 BS.

300067   PERILOUS VENTURE (A); OR, THE DAYS OF MARY OF BURGUNDY. Warne, 1896 BS. (Tr. from the German by Gor M. Hall. with Original Illustrations by Gordon Browne)

300068   PREDESTINED: A NOVEL OF NEW YORK LIFE. Scribner, 1913 PW.

300069   THE PRIEST. Sherman, French, 1911.

Focuses on a Catholic priest. NYT

300070   THE RAID OF DOVER; A ROMANCE OF THE REIGN OF WOMAN, A. D. 1940. BY THE AUTHOR OF "A TIME OF TERROR" AND ETC. Simpkin, 1910 BS.

300071   THE RAJAH'S SAPPHIRE.

LW 27:268. Sensational, a riot of crime. Hero is "ridiculous," the heroine "the most foolishly unpleasant 'British female' we have encountered in the book world for some time."

300072   THE RECTOR'S WIFE WRITES A LETTER. Gloucester: Minchin & Gibbs, 1916.

TLS-lively unconventional lady, country parsonage, experiences during war.

300073   REUBEN DELTON, PREACHER; A SEQUEL TO "THE STORY OF MARTHY". Richmond, Va.: Presbyterian Com. of Pub., [1901] PW.

300074   THE ROMANCE OF PRINCESS ARNULF. Lang, 1915.

Heroine is "ugly;" her marriage not one of love and roses. TLS

300075   A ROMANCE OF THE BORGIAS. THE SHE WOLF. S. Paul, 1913 BS. (Tr. from the French)

300076   RUTH, ETC. Blackwood, 1911.

Priest loves beautiful convert; "forced" marriage. TLS

300077   A SAILOR'S WIFE. BY THE AUTHOR OF "FOR LOVE OF MARJORIE". W. Stevens, 1903 BS.

300078   THE SECRET OF WILLOW DERPE. W. Stevens, 1903 BS.

300079   SHADOWS CAST BEFORE; A NOVEL. New York: Abbey Press, [1902] PW.

300080   SIR SERGEANT: A STORY OF ADVENTURES THAT ENSUED UPON THE '45. W. Blackwood, 1899 BS.

300081   SIX THOUSAND TONS OF GOLD. A. D. Innes, 1894 BS.

ACAD 46:372. Richard Parent discovers the gold, attempts to spend it in the American money market in a benevolent way. Makes a complete mess of it; everyone is happy when rest of gold is shot out to sea.

300082   SKOOT: A STORY OF UNCONVENTIONAL GOODNESS. Cin. O.: Jennings & Pye, [1902] PW.

300083   THE SOCIETY IN LONDON. BY THE LADY OF GROSVENOR PLACE. Holden and H., 1914 BS.

ATH-fashionable and political life in London.

300084   SOME EXPERIMENTS OF A POLITICAL AGENT. Mills & Boon, 1911.

Love and politics. TLS

300085   SOMETHING ABOUT JOE CUMMINS; OR A SON OF A SQUAW IN SEARCH OF A MOTHER: A FRONT STORY. A. Gardner, 1891 BS.

300086   A SON OF DESTINY; THE STORY OF ANDREW JACKSON. New York: Federal Book, 1902 BS.

300087   THE SPORT OF FATE. BY AUTHOR OF "GWEN DALE'S ORDEAL". London: W. Stevens, 1899 BS.

300088   THE STORY OF ABOBAL THE TSOURIAN. Smith, Elder, 1893 BS. (Tr. from the Phoenician by Edward Lovel Lester, preceded by an account of the finding of the manuscript by Emily Watson. Ed. by Val C. Prinsep.)

300089   THE STORY OF LOUISE. 1901 BS. (Tr. from Fr.)

Animal-leaping after pleasure.

300090   THE STRANGE NARRATIVE OF GEOFFREY GRENVILLE AN ANCIENT ENGLISHMAN, A. D. 1599-1906. Drane, 1908 BS.

300091   SWEETBRIER. BY THE AUTHOR OF "FOR LOVE OF MARJORIE" "HER SOLDIER LOVER" & C. London: W. Stevens, 1898 BS.

300092   THROUGH TO-DAY. Paul, Trubner, 1892 BS.

SP - Story of Rachel, an orphan.
ACAD - Exposure of the Amateur Authors Literary Help Society "ought to be of service."

300093   TOWARD THE ETERNAL SORROW.

SP-Wicked priests, wronged wives. Bad people die, good ones marry.

300094   THE TRUMPETER. A ROMANCE OF THE RHINE. Blackwood, 1893 BS. (Tr. from 200th German ed. by Jessie Beck and Louise Lorimer)

300095   UNPOSTED LETTERS. London: Mills and Boon, 1913 BS.

From young journalist to woman he loved and lost sight of. SP
He's ill, forsees his life will be brief. ATH TLS

300096   THE UNWRITTEN COMMANDMENT. Lumpus, Baker, 1904.

300097   "THE VERY EYES OF ME!" BY THE AUTHOR OF "HER OWN SISTER". London: 1891.

300098   WEDNESDAY'S CHILD. BY THE AUTHOR OF "LUCY; OR A GREAT MISTAKE" "LOVE KNOTS". W. Stevens, 1897 BS.

300099   THE WELL BELOVED OF THE FATHER: AN IMPERFECT STORY OF A PERFECT LIFE. A COMMUNICATION FROM THE UNSEEN. W. Scott, 1899 BS.

300100   "WESTWARD." A WOMAN'S STORY OF A GREAT CRUISE. New Haven, Conn.: Press of Whaples, 1910 PW.

300101   WHERE THE WIND SITS. BY THE AUTHOR OF HONORIA'S PATCHWORK. London: Hodder and Stoughton, 1907 BS.

ARTEMIS.

300102   A DEAR FOOL. Westall, 1920 BS.

TLS-O here
SR-male hero romance.
NYT 8-8-20, p.23.

ASHTON, H. A.

300103   THE GORDON DOCK MYSTERY. Fleet Street, 1894 BS.

ASTINS, G. S.

300104   LOVE SHALL REIGN SUPREME. Bromyard: North Herefordshire Printing Pub. Co., 1899 BS.

Lucy Brookfield is too idealized. ACAD 57:184

ATHERTON, GERTRUDE FRANKLIN.

300105   AN IDYLL OF THE REDWOOD. Heinemann, 1916 BS.

AVIS, WHYTE.

300106   A NOBLE REVENGE. Burns and Oates, 1898 BS.

B., A.

300107   ROMANCE OF BUREAUCRACY. BY A. B. Allahabad: A.H. Wheeler, 1893 BS.

BACON, EVELYN GOUGH.

300108   ONCE OF THE ANGELS. Methuen, 1913 BS.

White slave traffic "crudely written." TLS

BAILEY, FLORENCE M.

300109   THE SPECTULATIONS OF JOHN STEELE. London: Chatto & Hall, 1905 BS.

BAILEY, REBECCA C.

300110   MABEL THORNLEY GLENDINNING. New York: Abbey Press, 1902 USC.

BANKS, ISABELLA.

300111   MISS PRINGLE'S PEARLS.

PW-"Quaint noble little old maid," Pearls are prudence, patience and piety. Does something for her young relatives.

BARNES, ANNIE MARIA.

300112   THE LITTLE BURDEN SHARERS. Richmond, Va.: Presbyterian Com. of Pub., [1901] PW.

BARRY, B. PULLEN.

300113   BLOTTED OUT. Roxburghe Press, 1897 BS.

BEAUSEANT.

300114   JOHN WOLFGANG, BUSINESS MAN. BY BEAUSEANT. Headley, 1896 BS.

BECKET, A. A.

300115   THE COMIC HISTORY OF ENGLAND. Bradbury, 1897 BS.

BENTLEY, C.

300116   A DREAM'S FULFILMENT. Remington, 1895 BS.

BENTON, B. K.

300117   THE STORY OF A SPY IN THE CIVIL WAR. Macmillan, 1901.

BEVERHOUDT, O.

300118   MELZAR: A TALE OF THE JERICHO ROAD. New York: Broadway, 1914 PW.

BJOMSON, B.

300119   ARNLJOT GELLINE. Oxford Univ. Press, 1918 BS.

BLUNDERLAND.

300120   THE ADVENTURES OF A RUNAWAY GIRL ON A DESERT ISLAND. Simpkin Marshall, 1905 BS.

Disguises as boy, a Tom Sawyer, experiences on the island that few boys have ever had. Ingenuity, resource. Anti home life. ACAD 05:175

BOEYEY, S. M. CRAWLEY.

300121   CONSCIENCE MAKES THE MARTYR. Arrowsmith
(Bristol): Simpkin, 1894 BS.

ACAD 46:349. Healthy sensationalism, humble, but true
love.

BOGGS, jt. au. See KNIGHT, J. S. AND "BOGGS".

BOWLES, M.

300122   CHARLOTTE LEYLAND. G. Richards, 1900 BS.

SP 84:779. She is an orphan, a bachelor girl making a
living by secretarial work in London. Nine tenths of
book is insurrectionary formula. Marries, much
disagreement with him, subsequent reconciliation.
Advance on her previous work.

BRADLEY, MARY H.

300123   FRIENDS FOR GOOD.

Two young women supporting themselves meet, become
good friends, learn the brother of one is the
sweetheart of the other. BOOK NEWS 96-97:136.

BRAINE, SHEILA E.

300124   THE HOST MURILLO. Shaw,

about a painting

BUCHSON, H.

300125   THE GRIEF OF GURNEY. London: Drane, 1907
BS.

BURGESS, J. J. H.

300126   RAGNAROK: A TALE OF THE WHITE CHRIST.
Blackwood and Sons, 1894 BS.

BURGIN, ISABEL.

300127   THE WEB OF CIRCUMSTANCE. J. Clarke, 1908
BS.

BURNETT, ALICE C.

300128   ALL IS NOT GOLD THAT GLITTERS. Moran
(Aberdeen): Roxburghe Press, 1898 BS.

BYLY, E. ERIC.

300129   THE MAN WITH THE PARROTS. A STORY OF
EVENTS, AND THE SHADOWS THEY CAST. Sands, 1900 BS.

CAGHLIN, HANONAH.

300130   STRANGE FATES; OR THE DELTA. New York:
Broadway, 1903 PW.

CAIN, TUBAL.

300131   THE MANSE GATE. S. Sonnenschein, 1901 BS.

8-10-01 ATH

CANADIENNE, jt. au. See H., W. AND "CANADIENNE".

CAREY, ROSA NOUCHETTE.

300132   THE STORY OF NANNO. G. Richards, 1899.

Lady Gilbert writes about the Dublin workhouse system
which impressed her painfully. Nanno leaves to work in
the outside world to support her child. Her scruples
prevent her from accepting an offer of marr. LIT.
4:317

CARO, MME. E.

300133   BITTER FRUITS. Chicago: F. T. Neely, 1893
PW.

Paris and Versailles: sens. story of divorce and
unhappy love. Lenore and Paul, children of divorced
parents end badly-dissipation for him, suicide for
her. PW 3-18-93

CARR, MRS. COMYNS.

300134   BURIED IN THE BREAKERS. London: D. Scott,
1891 BS.

Melancholy story of a woman who marries a man she
respects and admires but finds out too late she loves
another man. SR 8-22-91,226

CARRINGTON, J. TIMOTHY.

300135   BANISHED FOR REFORMATION; OR, AUGUST'S
COMING BACK. Kansas City, Mo.: Burton, 1916 USC.

May refuses to marry August because he was addicted to
drink. He reforms, they marry PW

CARRUTHERS, ANNIE.

300136   ONLY A CIRCUS GIRL. Gale and Polden, 1898
BS.

CARTER, T.

300137   THE PEOPLE OF THE MOON: A NOVEL.
Electrician Printing and Pub. Co., 1895 BS.

CASSILIS, INA LEON.

300138   THE MYSTERY OF SHELDON BARS. Henderson,
1899.

A young woman apparently commits a "hideous and
cowardly crime." ACAD 57:160.

CAUMONT, MADAME A.

300139   A DISH OF MATRIMONY. E. Stock, 1894 BS.

ACAD 46:26. Trash. Silly adultress. Among clerks in a
London suburb. Gorgeous women. Mme. Armand Caumont.
ATH-not a pleasing picture of manners or values.

CHAMBERLAYNE, EFFIE.

300140   THE SHOOTING STAR. Century Press, 1909
BS.

CHILOSA.

300141   LOVE THE KEY. Dodd, 1891 BS.

CLARK, MARIE H.

300142   A STREAK IN THE WHITE PINE DISTRICT. New
York: Broadway, 1908 PW.

CLARK, T. KINGSTON.

300143   THE WEDDA MAN. London: Constable, 1907
BS.

CLARKE, ETHEL M.

300144   THE POTTER'S VESSEL. Century Press, 1907
PW.

Financial troubles; disappearing diamonds; love story.
TLS

CLARKE, ISABEL CONSTANCE.

300145   A FAMILY RECORD. London: Hutchinson, 1919
BS.

CLEEVE, LUCAS.

300146   THE MONKS OF THE HOLY TEAR. BY LUCAS
CLEEVE. F. V. White, 1898 BS.

ACAD 54:33. Love story in Huguenot times. Heroine
Protestant, hero is Roman Catholic.

COGHILL, MRS.

300147   THE TRIAL OF MARY BROOM: A STAFFORDSHIRE
STORY. Hutchinson, 1894 BS.

ACAD 46:84. Two Dutch potters left country during
reign of William III. Settled near Bradwell. Their
English neighbors, jealous of their skill, conspired
against them. Mrs. Coghill (Annie L. Walker.)

COLE, SOPHIE.

300148   ISABEL IN WARDOUR STREET. Mills and Boon,
1916 BS.

COLLIS, E. T.

300149   MURDER BY WARRANT. Glen, 1898 BS.

ACAD 53:659. Kelvin Glen & Co., publishers. Book is a plea for a court of criminal appeal.

COLVILLE, HARRIET E.

300150   MY GRANDMOTHER'S ALBUM.

SP 80:198. Events and characters of the century from a religious pov.

COMSTOCK, SARAH.

300151   MARCIA REBELS; OR THE VALLEY OF VISION. E. Nash, 1919 BS.

Eng. edition of the Valley of Vision.
Rejects a suitor because her parents like him, leaves home "to do good." Becomes a welfare worker in firm of man she rejected, they find they still love each other. Gets everything in a tangle and leaves again to do good. TLS

COOK, MRS. ALFRED.

300152   A COUNTRY DIARY. G. Allen, 1905 BS.

COOKE, GRACE (MACGOWAN).

300153   DALOSA BONBRIGHT'S CHRISTMAS GIFT. Chicago: Browne and Howell, 1914 PW.

Dalosa had married into a family where she was unwelcome. Her Christmas gift had to do with a desperate struggle in a western cabin. PW 86 10/17/14:1245

COTTON, F.

300154   GONE AWAY. Simpkin, 1891 BS.

COVERTSIDE.

300155   A DAY WITH HOUNDS. BY COVERTSIDE.

SP 81:448. Pre-Restoration. Politics. Males are central characters.

CRAWFORD, MRS. COROLIN.

300156   MARY STARKWEATHER. New York: Abbey Press, 1902 PW.

CRAWFORD, R.

300157   WINDALYNE: A RECORD OF BYGONE TIMES IN AUSTRALIA. Remington, 1895 BS.

CROMMELIN, MAY.

300158   LILL. BY MAY CROMMELIN. W. Stevens, 1899 BS.

D., T.

300159   MY SISTER'S DOWN GRADE DIARY: A TALE FOR THE TIMES. Howe, 1893 BS.

DAVENPORT, MISS E.

300160   ELSIE WINS. London: Blackie, 1920 BS.

DAVIDSON, J.

300161   EARL LAVENDER: A ROMANCE. Ward and Downey, 1892 BS.

DAVIES, FLORENCE H.

300162   SILVER THORNS: A BUNCH OF SIX. Saxon, 1898 BS.

SR 85;693. A child dies.

DAVIES, HELEN.

300163   THE MILLS OF THE GODS. New York: F.T. Neely, 1897.

Dorcas Grey doesn't like her country home, her name. Aspires to much more. Visits wordly aunt in NY. Aunt keeps a lover who kisses Dorcas and the girl is not overmuch horrified. Aunt arranges a good rich marriage for her. In time she takes a lover. Her husband dies, and her lover throws her over. Goes abroad as the rich

Mrs. Johnson, with a scandalous reputation. NYT 10-30-97,5

DEAL, ANNIE RANDALL.

300164   LIFE OF JENNIE O'NEILL POTTER. New York: I. H. Blanchard, 1902 PW.

DEAN, MARY M.

300165   BARS BETWEEN. Boston: Four Seas, 1914 USC.

DEBARRIOS, ADELAIDE.

300166   THE SHEPHERDESS OF TODAY. New York: Aberdeen, 1910 PW.

BKM Christian Scientist Sets up office across from MD, she is so successful she is able to establish church in community.

DEHAN, RICHARD.

300167   THE WOMAN WITH THE LAMP. New York: F. A. Stokes, 1911.

DELTA.

300168   A FASCINATING SINNER. F. Tennyson Neely, 1897 PW.

Unwholesome young married woman is a flirt. Learns in the whirl of a London season that men "lead other people's womankind into mischief and keep their own out of it." Should be "excluded from all libraries." LW 28:297.
While her husband is away, a conventional wife is persuaded to taste of "forbidden pastimes." There are many differences of opinion between her and husband when he returns. PW 51:961

DEMNUCK, F. HAYDEN.

300169   THE LOST TROOPER. London: Pearson, 1920 BS.

DE MONTAEO, BENITA.

300170   THE DIAMOND LADY. London: Drane, 1913 BS.

DENNIS, ENID MAUD.

300171   MR. COLEMAN, GENT; A ROMANCE. New York: Kenedy, 1920 PW.

PW-Story of a criminal who lived in England in 1664.

DERNHARD, MARIE.

300172   FOR MY OWN SAKE. International News, 1895 BS.

DE STRANT, E.

300173   CLOUDS OF BLACK AND GOLD: A NOVEL. Digby and Long, 1891 BS.

DEW, H.

300174   A QUEER HONEYMOON. Hayman, Christy and Lilly, 1894 BS.

DEWETT, MARY.

300175   FEET OF WOOL. London: Century, 1908 BS.

DICK, F. P.

300176   DOWNING LIGHTS. T. F. Unwin, 1894 BS.

DIRKS, HELEN.

300177   FINDING. London: Chatto & Windus, 1918 BS.

DIVER, MAUD.

300178   RETRIBUTION. Putnam's, BS.

Eldred Pottingers' return to Afghanistan, imprisonment and final vengeance. NYT

DOFF, NEEL, pseud. See LERIGIERS, C.

DOUGLAS, S.

300179   A BROTHER'S BLOOD. Drane, 1892 BS.

DRANE, J. C.

300180   CHAMPION; BY J. C. DRANE. Cassell, 1907
BS.

Autobiography of a racing car. TLS

DUDENEY, MRS. HENRY.

300181   ROUND THE CORNER. Hurst and Blackett,
1918 BS.

TLS--Drab realism. Family tragedy, sordid liaison
between wife and husband's intimate friend separates
four of them for 20 years. Child from liaison.

DUERING, STELLA M.

300182   LOVE'S RECOMPENSE. Hutchinson, 1913 BS.

DUNBOYNE, LADY.

300183   ROMANCE OF A LAWN TENNIS TOURNAMENT.
Trischler, 1891 BS.

A young woman has extraordinary skill in lawn tennis.
Story of week of tournament, two proposals she gets.
Her sister has many advanced ideas. ACAD

DURANT, W. S.

300184   CROSS AND DAGGER; THE CRUSADE OF THE
CHILDREN. London: Methuen, 1910 BS.

BM hist.
ATH- hist.

EASTON, W. P.

300185   THE IDYL OF TWIN FIRES. London: Hodder &
Stoughton, 1916 BS.

EASTWICK, MRS. EGERTON.

300186   THE GOVERNOR'S WIFE.

ATH 115:301. Tropical country. Man is engaged to 1
sister and loves the other, who is married.
LIT 6:336. Singapore

EDGE, J. H.

300187   THE QUICKSANDS OF LIFE. BY J. H. EDGE.
Lane, 1908.

TLS-male heroes

EDWARDS, MRS. BENNETT.

300188   THE UNWRITTEN LAW. Simpkin, 1892 BS.

ACAD 42:150 "declamation against marriage of the
ordinary kind."

ELLERTON, GAY.

300189   DRIFTING UNDER THE SOUTHERN CROSS: AN
AUSTRALIAN ROMANCE. Gordon and Gotch, 1892 BS.

ELLICOTT, GRACE.

300190   A BIG MISTAKE. Flack, 1892 BS.

ELLIOT, ELINOR M.

300191   MY CANADA. London: Hodder & Stoughton,
1915 BS.

Diary in English woman of 25 visits Canada ends in
love. TLS

ELLIOTT, SARAH BARNWELL.

300192   QUISANTE.

PW-Brilliant politician, man of foreign lineage,
marries English girl against the wishes of all
interested in her.

FACILIS.

300193   TWO WOMEN WHO POSED. New York: J. S.
Ogilvie, 1897 PW.

One is a society woman attracted to Bohemia; the other
a professional model. Their relation with an artist
(male). PW 52:198

FELL, ANNA.

300194   WAS SHE A WIFE? London: A. Pearson, 1920
BS.

FENNES, F.

300195   THE LAND OF ISMA: A ROMANCE. M. H. Potts,
1894 BS.

FISHER, DOROTHY GUNHILD.

300196   A NORWEGIAN-AMERICAN EPISODE. BY DOROTHY
GUNHILD FISHER. 1907 PW.

Romance. 10-26-07 PW

FLANEUSE.

300197   THE HOUSEKEEPER. BY FLANEUSE. A. M.
Gardner, 1916 BS.

FLEMING, MAY AGNES.

300198   A WOMAN'S HAND. F. Henderson, 1894 BS.

FLINN, VIOLET M.

300199   THE MASTER PASSION. London: W. Stevens,
1913 BS.

FOX, F. J.

300200   A STRANGER WITHIN THE GATES. J.
Griffiths, 1906.

ACAD-two women in love with one man, farewell of one
when she marries man she does not love.
LPKM-one of the women a "landed proprietress of
Socialist views."

FRASER, MRS. HUGH.

300201   BORDELARQUA. Dodd, 1913 BS.

It's a palace on the Tiber, scene of treachery and
loyalty. NYT

FREED.

300202   PEET REEK FRAE TA WAST HIELANTS. BY
FREED. MacLaren, 1892 BS.

GARLAND, GRACE.

300203   A LADY'S CRIME; A STUDY FROM LIFE.
"Thrilling Stories" Office, 1899 BS.

GARVOCK, BLANCHE A. L.

300204   FRIENDS FOR LIFE. Glen and Hall, 1892 BS.

SR. not really a novel, a religious tract.

GERARD, DOROTHEA.

300205   A MAN OF THE MOMENT.

ACAD 59:212. Splendid hero, beautiful countess,
romance and adventure.

GIBBON, LESLIE HOWARD.

300206   THE GATES OF TIEN T'ZE.

TLS-develops the amazing capacity of a girl of
surprising spirit as a detective.
TLS-American.

GIBERNE, AGNES.

300207   RUFFIN'S LEGACY: A THEOSOPHICAL ROMANCE.
Hutchinson, 1891 BS.

GIRWOOD, C.

300208   THE ROMANCE OF A COAL PIT. BY C.
GIRDWOOD. Eden, Remington, 1892 BS.

GLAS, DRAIG.

300209   MADGE CARRINGTON AND HER WELSH NEIGHBORS. London: S. Paul, 1911 BS.

All milk and honey TLS

GLYN, CORALIE.

300210   A WOMAN OF TO-MORROW: A TALE OF THE TWENTIETH CENTURY. BY THE HON. CORALIE GLYN. Women's Printing Society, 1897 BS.

GORDON, H.

300211   MY LADY OF INTRIGUE. London: Blackwood, 1910 BS.

BM-history.
TLS-male narrator

GORDON, JANET.

300212   A MIST FROM YARROW. Oliphant, Anderson and Ferrier, 1896 BS.

GRAEME, VIOLA.

300213   VIVIANNE'S VENTURE. F. Griffiths, 1908 BS.

TLS-young woman becomes sub editor of Fashionable Flutterings. Methods of finding copy are not respectable. Falls in love, returns to her aunt and writes the novel of the season "Sin and Cinders"

GRAHAM, GRANVILLE.

300214   IN THE DAYS GONE BY.

ACAD 55:201. A record of passion by a woman. Intense.

GRAHAM, WINIFRED.

300215   EMMA HAMILTON: THE TARIFF REFORMER. BY WINIFRED GRAHAM. London: Digby, Long, 1909 BS.

GRAND, SARAH.

300216   HUNTING WOMEN. 1901.

GRANT, MRS. G. FORSYTH.

300217   KATHLEEN. A. Gardner, 1900 BS.

ACAD 59:262. "Immense novel of visits, balls, small talk, diversified by a carriage accident and culminating in a cricket match." Edinburgh.

GRANVILLE, A.

300218   'A EYE FOR AN EYE' AND SOME REPRINTED PIECES. Chicago: A. Francoeur, 1897 BS.

GRAY, MAXWELL.

300219   ARDNARIGH: A NOVEL DRAWN FROM LIFE. London: H.J. Drane, [1901].

GREEN, ANNA KATHARINE.

300220   "MISSING PAGE THIRTEEN" AND OTHER PROBLEMS FOR VIOLET STRANGE. G. P. Putnam's, 1915.

Series of detective stories in which Violet "observes sharply, thinks intensely and has the faculty of disentangling out of a maze of circumstances the one explanation of mystery that accords with facts-who is by native endowment a first-class detective." NYT

GREEN, E. EVERETT.

300221   THE LIFE OF ARTHUR LORRAINE. F. V. White, 1910 BS.

GREEN, EVELYN EVERETT.

300222   ROGER TREHERNE. New York: Amer. Tract Society, 1903 PW.

GREY, MARTHA.

300223   FORTUNE'S WHEEL. New York: Abbey Press, 1902 PW.

GRONER, AUGUSTA.

300224   JOE MILLER, DETECTIVE. New York:

Duffield, 1910 PW. (Translated by Grace Isabel Colbron.)

Male hero. PW
NYT unusual male hero. Quiet plain little man.

GUTHRIE, MRS.

300225   A BRAESIDE LASSIE. Moran, 1896 BS.

H., M. E.

300226   ONE WOMAN IN THE WORLD. BY M. E. H. London: W. Stevens, 1920 BS.

H., W. AND "CANADIENNE".

300227   DISTURBERS. BY W. H. AND "CANADIENNE". London: Laurie, 1914 BS.

HALL, ELIZABETH.

300228   SYBIL FAIRLEIGH. London: Digby, Long, 1897 BS.

"Tea visits, letter writing, church going" with some unusual happenings-like an attempt at suicide by Sybil. ACAD 52:Fic Sup 70.

HALL, R. N.

300229   GILBERT VINCE, CURATE, AND HIS STRUGGLE TO OBTAIN THE IDEAL: A NOVEL LARGELY FOUNDED ON FACT. Western Mail, 1897 BS.

HALL, S. ELIZABETH.

300230   THE INTERLOPER. London: Griffiths, 1901 BS.

ATH 6-3-01

HAMILTON, A.

300231   THE PERSISTENT LOVERS. London: S. Paul, 1915 BS.

HARDY, IZA DUFFUS.

300232   A BURIED SIN. F. V. White, 1894 BS.

SP 77:258. Parents looking for good matrimonial matches; younger set think it's rot. A number of heartless mothers. The virtuous are rewarded.
SP-plus mystery and forgery.
ATH 103:46. Buried banknotes.

300233   KATE SYLVESTER'S FOLLY. Simpkin, 1900 BS.

HARDY, T. D.

300234   ASDRUFEL: A SOUL'S EPISODE. BY T. D. HARDY. Griffith, Farran, 1892 BS.

HARRISON, ELLA.

300235   THEN LOVE IS HARD. New York: Broadway, 1907 PW.

HAWKINS, MAY ANDERSON.

300236   A FACE AND A LIFE. Richmond, Va.: Presbyterian Com. of Publication, [1900].

HINSCHELWOOD, A. E.

300237   THROUGH STARLIGHT TO DAWN. Gay and Bird, 1893 BS.

HOLLINGSWORTH, HAZLE.

300238   THE OTHER WOMAN. 1911 PW.

Cute story where everyone gets her "just" desserts. NYT

HOLMES, A. VINSENT.

300239   KNAVES AND HEARTS. BY A. VINSENT-HOLMES. Holden & Hardingham, 1917 BS.

HURLBURD, P.

300240   THE ROMANCE OF SHERE MOTE. Bentley, 1894 BS.

HUTCHINSON, LADY HELY.

300241   MONICA GREY. F. Murray, 1900 BS.

ATH 116:342. Exaggerated and sentimental. Dedicated to
women with men in African war.
ACAD 59:413. Involves woman passionately in love with
man not her husband. Her problem is solved by death of
both.
LIT 7:239. She is a "good woman, discovers to her
horror that she is in love."

IOTA.

300242   PAMELA. BY IOTA. 1905 BS.

IRVING, THEO.

300243   YOU NEVER KNOW YOUR LUCK.

SP 76:881. In favor of increasing facilities for
divorce. One couple live together but are not married,
but marry when they get the chance.

JACK, VIOLET.

300244   A TALE OF THE 45. J. Murray, 1911 BS.

Traditional historical romance, secret service agent,
etc. TLS

JACKSON, O., jt. au. See NESBIT, E. AND O. JACKSON.

JEFFERY, C. E.

300246   THE FORTUNES OF A FAIR FREE-LANCE. A
STORY WITHOUT A MORAL. London: Routledge, 1909 BS.

The Fair-Free Lance now married, tells of her
adventures in love and matrimony. She's "by no means
attractive" though beautiful.TLS

JOHNSTONE, G. MURRAY.

300247   ONE SMITH, BEING CERTAIN INCIDENTS IN HIS
CAREER. W. Dawson, 1913 BS.

JORDAN, MAGGIE OLIVE.

300248   WAYS OF THE WORLD. BY MAGGIE OLIVE
JORDAN. New York: F. T. Neely, 1902 PW.

Fic?

K., S. M.

300249   MAY DAY. Mussoorie, Bexhill-on-Sea:
Goorkha Press, Bexhill Printing Co., 1898 BS.

KEATING, ETHEL BLACK.

300250   A PRINCESS OF THE ORIENT. Boston:
Christopher Press, 1918 PW.

KELLY, ELEANOR MERCEIN.

300251   TOYA THE UNLIKE. Boston: Small, Maynard,
1913 PW.

"Heroine is the daughter of a Japanese mother and an
American father. Story opens in Japan, when Toya, with
her wide smile of endurance and bewilderment, journeys
to America with her dead father's dearest friend, who
has promised to take the little girl to her rich old
grandfather in New York. Complications arise in the
years that follow, for Toya educated in a convent is a
strange combination of Occident and Orient." PW

KING, A.

300252   DREAMS AND SHADOWS. T. Fisher Unwin, 1894
BS.

KING, R. E.

300253   THE ROMANCE OF A COUNTRY: A MASQUE. T. F.
Unwin: 1893 BS.

Very involved-series of fights, captures and advents.
SR 76:520.

KINGSTON, KEEDY.

300254   THE GREAT PIMLICO MYSTERY: A WELL KEPT
SECRET DISCLOSED. Diprose and Bateman, 1896 BS.

KNIGHT, J. S. AND "BOGGS".

300255   CONTRAPTIONS. BY THE STAFF OF THE
"CLARION", AND OTHERS. W. Scott, 1894 BS.

KRISHNA, BAL.

300256   THE LOVE OF KUSUMA: AN EASTERN LOVE
STORY. London: T. W. Laurie, BS.

Eastern love story.

LACON, E. H.

300257   CLOUDSLEY TEMPEST. New York: Brentano's,
1914 PW.

LANE, C.

300258   JOURNEYS END. London: Murray & Evenden,

ATH-vividness of writing, truth of feelings portrayed
regrettable choice of subject. Central idea is
morbid...unworthy of the writing. Look forward to
another book by the author.

LAURIE, A.

300259   AXEL EBEPSEN, THE GRADUATE OF UPSOLA.
Low, 1892 BS.

LAWSON, MRS. J. K.

300260   A FAIR REBEL. Simpkin, 1899 BS.

300261   MISS NERO. Simpkin, 1899 BS.

300262   WILLIAM MARAH. Simpkin (WEEKLY TELEGRAPH
NOVELS. NO. 20), 1900 BS.

LE BAILLY, MRS. LOUIS.

300263   THAT OTHER FELLOW. BY MRS. LOUIS LE
BAILLY. Digby, Long, 1895 BS.

LEGH, M. H. CORNWALL.

300264   A HARD MASTER. Service and Paton, 1898
BS.

SP 81:656. Lydia, gypsy heroine, slowly is convinced
of her lover's devotion and returns to civilization
from the caravans.
ACAD 55:120. Ends with wedding.
ATH 112:639. The beating of a woman by a man who is
egged on by a female. Beaten again.
Lydia Burton, half gypsy. Part of story she's in high
society among rich who partially adopt her. In the
other part she's among gypsy tents and caravans. Very
meek in love. Puts up with incredible brutality-even
an attempt by old Burton to burn out her eyes. SR
87:695.
Rupert Fitzjames is corrupt. Lydia Burton, companion
of his invalid sister, knows he's a conceited inhuman
tyrant. Yet, she ends up marrying him. LBKM 15:153

LEIGHTON, MARIE C.

300265   THE WITNESS OF THE RING. Ward, Lock, 1913
BS.

LEIGHTON, MARIE CONNOR.

300266   JOAN TEMPEST, BURGLAR. Hodder &
Stoughton, 1917 BS.

LERIGIERS, C.

300267   KEETJE. BY NEEL DOFF. Paris: Ollendorf,
1919.

gloomy story of Dutch girl sent out on the street;
because family starving. But she has an artistic
temperament, learns Fr. reads everything, becomes
model, successful courtesan, unsuccessful at
Conservatoire, loses a rich lover. At the end "
settles down well provided for to a life of
comtemplation in the country" ATH

LEWIS, HARRIET.

300268   THE HAMPTON MYSTERY. A NOVEL. F.
Henderson, 1894 BS.

LINDSAY, RUTH.

300269   THE GUIDE BOOK & THE STAR. Evelyn Benman,
1912.

ACAD-woman revealed through letters to man. Religious
story.

LINNET, BROWN.

300270   THE SHARER. J. Murray, 1912.

ATH-story of a woman poacher who is ultimately caught
and unmasked.

LONG, ALICE.

300271   IVAN AND ESTER. London Tract Society,

IND 44:413. Two young Jews escape their persecutors in
Russia and start out for Jerusalem. Their adventures
and hardships.

LUCAS, F. SAINT JOHN.

300272   AUDREY ELLISON. BY F. ST. JOHN LUCAS.
S.C. Brown, 1905.

M., A.

300273   FELIX HOLT SECUNDUS AND TOSA MONAGATARI
OF MODERN TIMES. W. Scott, 1892 BS.

MACCURDY, R.

300274   THE UPAS TREE. Chicago: Schulte, 1912 PW.
London: Stevens and Brown, 1912 BS.

TLS- against capital punishment

MACGINNIS, MACFADDYEN O'FLAHERTY.

300275   PINK DIAMONDS: A ROMANCE WITH A STORY.
Mcfaddyen O'Flaherty McGinnis "Clarion" Newspaper,
1898 BS.

MACK., K.

300276   WEEDS. Bristol: Arrowsmith, 1893.

Beautiful young woman of about 20 visits married
couple and causes a "trifling lapse" in the husband's
behavior. ACAD 43:32

MACKINTOSH, SOPHIE F.

300277   LOVE'S CONFLICT. London: Ward, Lock, 1906
BS.

MACKRAY, R.

300278   THE WOMAN WINS. London: Chatto & Hall,
1911 BS.

Mystery, death, inquest TLS

MAGUIRE, C.

300279   AMABEL: A MILITARY ROMANCE. BY C.
MAGUIRE. T. F. Unwin, 1893 BS. (Cathal Maguire per SR
76:571.)

A woman of rank deserts husband and children; runs off
with an officer friend of husband. Later takes one of
her children, a girl, and raises her without knowledge
of true father. Daughter makes a poor marriage. Learns
the truth at her mother's death. PW 9-16-93.
She marries beneath her class. ACAD 44:482
He's coarse from being a sergeant; she's very refined.
They go to live in barracks town. ATH 102:730.
Well born young woman married to a non-commissioned
officer. He's weak, a show-off. Realistic account of
the marriage difficulties of this ill-matched pair. SP
71, 947.
She's a lady, marries a sergeant. Suffers acutely
under the different social standard. Captain of
husband's troop is her brother. SR 76:572.

MANN, MARY.

300280   THE SPIRIT FATHER. BY MRS. MARY MANN.
Chicago: M. A. Donohue, [1903] PW.

MANUEL.

300281   AUTHENTIC HISTORY OF CAPTAIN CASTAGNETTE
NEPHEW OF THE "MAN WITH THE WOODEN HEAD". Simpkin,
1892 BS.

MARJERONI, GIULIA.

300282   A LIVING STATUE: A NOVEL. BY GIULIA
MARJERONI. S. Sonnenschein, 1893 BS.

Actress (Italian) loses husband and voice, sent to
Australia for health reasons. She decides to write a
novel based on play by husband's friend-Preface. ATH
101, 602.
The morbid, eccentric Count Paolo of Santa Rosa allows
a young woman he intended to marry to die of poverty
though he is rich. Afterwards squanders thousands on
her sister for the opportunity of looking at her a few
times a week because she resembles the dead woman.
Ends up marrying Noemi, the sister. SR 76:216.
Hires her to sit and let him look at her. ACAD 43:520.

MARRYAT, FLORENCE.

300283   A BLIGHTED NAME. BY FLORENCE MARRYAT.
Butterworth, 1901 BS.

MARSHALL, F.

300284   IT HAPPENED YESTERDAY: A NOVEL.
Blackwood, 1891 BS.

PW-Penniless young German countess becomes companion
to French widow. Is loved by widow's nephew but falls
under Mesmeric influence of a Russian.

MASON, F.

300285   FRANK MAITLAND'S LUCK: A STORY OF A
DERBY. BY F. MASON. Routledge, 1892 BS.

MATTHEWS, JOANNA H.

300286   JOHN THORNDYKE'S PREJUDICES. New York: G.
W. Dillingham, 1892 PW.

PW-Love story.

MEADE, L. T.

300287   THE GREAT LORD MASSAIANA. F.V. White,
1912 BS.

ATH male hero
TLS- male hero

MEREDITH, RHODA FLEMING.

300288   THE ADVENTURES OF HARRY RICHMOND. BY
RHODA FLEMING MEREDITH. Constable, 1901 BS.

MERSEREAU, EMMA.

300289   THE VEIL OF SOLANA. New York: F.F. Lovell
Book, [1902] PW.

MICHELSON, MIRIAM.

300290   THE GOOD ONE. Doubleday, 1909.

PW
Twin sisters, one runs away from husband; the other
finds herself thrust into her place. NYT

MILLER, ESTHER.

300291   THE ADVENTURESS. Weekly Telegraph, 1918
BS.

300292   ELLA'S ROMANCE. Pearson, 1914 BS.

300293   A GIRL WITH A PAST. Pearson, 1914 BS.

300294   A WEB OF TREACHERY. Pearson, 1916 BS.

MINER, ANETTE STILLMAN.

300295   ROUND HILL FARM. BY ANETTE STILLMAN
MINER. Boston: C. M. Clark, 1911 PW.

MINIKEN, BERTHA M. M.

300296   WHERE THE WAYS PART. Digby, Long and Co.:
1899 BS.

"A real Dutch picture of the mind of a middle class
woman." SP 83:383.
About a family, love affairs of young ladies and
womanliness. ATH 114:92

MOORE, E. HAMILTON.

300297   WINGS OF DESIRE. E. Macdonald, 1915 BS.

MORGAN, BLATHWYOT.

300298   IN THE BEGINNING: A ROMANCE OF EDEN. R.
S. Cartwright, 1897 BS.

MORRIS, W. E.

300299   TROUBLED TRANTON. BY W. E. MORRIS.
Constable, 1915 BS.

MULHOLLAND, CLARA.

300300   SWEET DOREEN. St. Louis: Herder, PW.

MULTIPLE AUTHORS.

300301   A NOVEL: A STRANGE STORY. TWENTY CHAPTERS
BY TWENTY AUTHORS. Howard House, 1891 BS.

MURRAY OF ELIBANK, LADY.

300302   LADY LATIMER'S DOUBLE. BY LADY MURRAY OF
ELIBANK. H. Jenkins, 1917 BS.

They're alike in face & spirit. TLS

NESBIT, E. AND O. JACKSON.

300303   THE BUTLER IN BOHEMIA. BY E. NESBIT AND
O. JACKSON. Drane, 1894 BS.

NEWELL, H.

300304   IN THE TILTYARD OF LIFE. BY H. NEWELL.
Ward and Downey, 1892 BS.

NEWSOM, ISABEL.

300305   BREAKING POINT. BY ISABEL NEWSOM. Oohams,
1919.

Picture of hospital for the mentally troubled. TLS

NILUS.

300306   DUE SIGNORE. (BY AUTHORESS OF "GREYSTONE
GRANGE") NILUS. Trustlove and Shirley, 1893 BS.

NIXON, FLORENCE GWYNNE.

300307   THE SILENT POOL. BY FLORENCE GWYNNE
NIXON. Weekly Telegraph, 1917 BS.

NOVA, INSCO.

300308   MAURYEEN, THE OUTCAST: A TALE OF
UNREQUITED LOVE. BY INSCO NOVA. Digby, Long, 1893 BS.

SR. Ireland verbiage; old fashioned.

ORDE, M.

300309   THE WEIRD RING OF AVIEMOOR. Digby, Long,
1895 BS.

ACAD 49:196. Isabel, an heiress, and Elsie, her
governess-companion, appear to vie for the hero
Cameron. He marries Lady Isabel. Isabel marries a
soldier and Elsie a professor in Oxford.

ORTELI, F.

300310   EVENING TALES. BY F. ORTELI. Low, 1894
BS. (Done into English from the French by Joel
Chandler Harris)

OSMOND, SOPHIE.

300311   SNAGS: A STORY OF THE SHEARING STRIKE. BY
SOPHIE OSMOND. G. Robertson, 1897 BS.

OUIDA.

300312   PRINCESS SABAROFF. London: Holden &
Holden, 1917 BS.

PANSY.

300313   REUBEN'S HINDRANCES. BY PANSY.

PW-Reuben Stein turns hindrances into helps in his
efforts to get on in the world.

PARRY, G.

300314   THE STORY OF DICK. BY G. PARRY.
Macmillan, 1892 BS.

PATTON, MRS. J. E.

300315   THE WAY THEY SHOULD BE. Downey, 1897.

vs nursing; it's "a great misery" shouldn't have
daughters unless you can provide them with 400 lbs. SP
78:448

PEACOCK, E.

300316   NARCISSA BRENDON: A ROMANCE. BY E.
PEACOCK. J. Hodges, 1891 BS.

PEARL, DORA.

300317   THE PRICE OF A WOMAN'S SOUL. BY DORA
PEARL. Gardner, 1916 BS.

PEATTIE, ELIA W.

300318   THE SIZE OF THINGS. Chicago: F.H. Revell,
1903 PW.

PEMBERTON, MARY.

300319   THE INPREGNABLE CITY. Dodd, Mead, 1895
PW.

Dr. paid to go on yacht trip, 30 day Pacific cruise to
the city of the title where a devotee of Tolstoi rules
and whose daughter has a serious nervous illness.
Love. LW 26:170

PICKNEY, SUE.

300320   DARCY PICKNEY, BY SUE PICKNEY.
Washington, D. C.: Neale, [1907] PW.

PIDWELL, ELLEN.

300321   CONDEMNED; OR, IN THE DARK: A NOVEL.
King, Sell and Railton, 1892 BS.

PITCHFORD, M. W. W.

300322   BROTHERS IN ARMS: A MILITARY NOVEL. BY M.
W. W. PITCHFORD. Ward, Lock, 1892 BS.

PITMAN, ROSIE M.

300323   THE RUBY RING. BY ROSIE M. PITMAN. New
York: Macmillan, 1904 PW.

PLATT, SARAH M. B.

300324   AN IRISH WILD FLOWER. T. Fisher Unwin,
1891 BS.

POLLANS, T. DUNDAS.

300325   THE REAL MARTYR OF ST. HELENA. BY T.
DUNDAS POLLANS. New York: McBride, Nast, 1913 PW.

PW 84 10-25-13:1391. "Not Napoleon, but Sir Hudson
Lowe, governor of the Island, is the real martyr of
St. Helena. He has been vilified and slandered by
Napoleon's partisans, but author defends him, backing
up his defense with a resume of what actually
transpired during Napoleon's exile, and shedding much
light on the personality of the Emperor."

POSTLETHWAITE, T. N.

300326   BETTY. BY T. N. POSTLETHWAITE. Digby,
Long, 1913 BS.

Farmer's daughter marries young squire during time of
Napoleon invasion. Packed with adventures.
LBKM-country squire and farmer's daughter. Early 19th
century.

POULAIN, M. J.

300327   THE TWO SISTERS: A DARTMOOR STORY. BY M.
J. POULAIN. Simpkin, 1891 BS.

POWER, EDITH M.

300328   BLUE AND WHITE. A TALE OF BRITANY IN
1795. BY EDITH M. POWER. Mitre Press, 1899 BS.

Historical romance. LIT

PROCTOR, L. M.

300329   CROWNED WITH FENNEL. Routledge, 1896 BS.

PROTHEROE, HOPE.

300330   THE DIAMOND AND THE ROSE. Century Press, 1909 BS.

QUIN, TARELLA.

300331   PAYING GUESTS. Lothian, 1918 BS.

TLS-Australian farm story.

QUINN, P. E.

300332   THE JEWELLED BELT: A DETECTIVE STORY. G. Robertson, 1897 BS.

RAGLEIGH, G. AND EDITH VICARS.

300333   A TORQUAY MARRIAGE. Tower, 1895 BS.

RAMSEY, MRS. W. W.

300334   THE ROMANCE OF ELISAVET. Hodder and Stoughton, 1899 BS.

She is 17. Panayotte, her love, is 20. She is a domestic servant. His adventures are among brigands in the mountains. A sweet love between them. But his end is tragic. LBKM 16:81
Asia Minor, Smyrna. Young servant girl craves money and pleasure. She, Elisavet convinces her lover to become a brigand to satisfy her wants. SP 62:687.
Simple love story of two Greeks. PAKER 03,167

RANDLE, LALAH RUTH.

300335   PEASANT LASSIES. Fremantle, 1901 BS.

REYNOLDS, SARAH.

300336   A QUESTION OF TEMPERAMENT: A NOVEL. BY SARAH REYNOLDS. Sherrott & Hughes, BS.

RHODES, G.

300337   ALICE MORDAM AND THE RIPPINGHAM TRAGEDY. Drane, 1892 BS.

RHODES, KATHLYN.

300338   THE SPINNER. London: Digby Long, 1906 BS.

TLS-artist finds perfect model but can have her only thru marriage; tragedy

RIDDELL, MRS. J. H.

300339   THE FOOTFALL OF FATE. F. V. White, 1900 BS.

SP Mrs. Lyle, white-haired widow, is accepted more or less until she is recognized as Berenice Boulger, wanted for her husband's murder. She is innocent, but is sentenced to death. She dies of the shock.

RITA.

300340   LORD OF MY LIFE. BY RITA. Butterworth, 1901 BS.

300341   THE SHADOW OF A SIN. BY RITA. Butterworth, 1901 BS.

300342   THE TRUE LOVER. Butterworth, 1901 BS.

ROBBINS, SALLY NELSON.

300343   A MAN'S REACH. BY SALLY NELSON ROBBINS. Philadelphia: Lippincott, 1916 PW.

Randolph drinks hard. Letice determines to save him. Sends him back to his work determined to make good. She does. She has a face like an "inspired cameo." NYT

ROBERTS, G. D.

300344   BARBARA LADD. BY G. D. ROBERTS. Constable, 1903 BS.

A "modern" woman in 18th century runs away, finds her environment completely alien; her rebellion. Heartless coquetry. ACAD 65:169-70.

ROBERTSON, MARGARET H.

300345   A GALLANT QUAKER. Methuen, 1901 BS.

ATH-11-2-01

ROBERTSON, MAUDE.

300346   KITTY ADAIR. Heywood, 1903 BS.

ATH 11-15-02?-Heroine "pushes unconventionality to the extreme" What does it "cost her?" Author's p.o.v.?

ROBINSON, F. W.

300347   ELLA'S LOVE STORY. BY F. W. ROBINSON. Butterworth, 1901 BS.

ROBINSON, KATHARINE M.

300348   CORNELIA: A NOVEL. Sioux Falls: S. D. Sessions Pr., 1919 PW.

ROBINSON, W. C.

300349   UNDER THE CROSSKEYS: A TALE OF THE PONTIFICAL ZOUAVES. Art and Book Co., 1895 BS.

ROSE, C. S.

300350   DICK ARNOLD: A TASMANIAN ROMANCE. Melvide, 1893 BS.

ROWCRAFT, F. G. T.

300351   HIS FAULT OR HERS. Author, 1917.

Unsuccessful marriage of wealthy Emma Pell; much moralizing. TLS

ROWLANDS, EFFIE A.

300352   AT HER MERCY. BY EFFIE A. ROWLANDS. Pearson, 1914 BS.

300353   THE HEART OF A WOMAN. BY EFFIE A. ROWLANDS. London: Pearson, 1913 BS.

ROWLANDS, EFFIE ADELAIDE.

300354   JUDGED BY FATE. London: Hurst and Blackett, 1913 BS.

300355   LOVE'S YOUNG DREAM. London: Ward, Lock, 1914 BS.

SP 87:239. Detective story, male hero
ATH whose father is murdered by secret society.

ROY, G.

300356   LILIAS CARMENT: FOR BETTER, FOR WORSE. BY G. ROY. A. Gardner, 1892 BS.

RULEY, CLARA NORTH.

300357   THE CONFESSIONS OF LINDA POINDEXTER. BY CLARA NORTH RULEY. New York: Broadway, 1910 PW.

Letters to friend telling of marriage and narrowly averted tragedy. PW

RUSSELL, DORA.

300358   HESTER WRAY. Digby, Long, 1904 BS.

RUSSELL, KATHERINE.

300359   EVANGELICA. Published by author, 1897 PW.

To prove drunkenness is not hereditary; to age 13 young woman raised among relatives who drink and die of it. Then she's raised by an intell. woman who puts her on the right path. PW 52:820

S., V. O. C.

300360   THE PASSING OF A MOOD. BY V. O. C. S. London: T. F. Unwin, 1893 BS.

Twenty one separate, unconnected stories but the first seven seem to follow the important moments in a man's

life: school, college, marriage, death. SR 76:423.
Twenty very short sketches. BKM 5:77.
Fragments, jottings from a novelist's notebook. ATH
102:621.

SAINT AUBYN, ALAN.

300361   THE GREENSTONE. BY ALAN ST. AUBYN. Long,
1906.

ACAD-melodrama, love story
TLS-O
ATH

SALWAY, R. E.

300362   VENTURED IN VAIN. Hurst and Blackett,
1894 BS.

SAMPSON, ALICE MAUD ELLEN.

300363   BALMORAL. A ROMANCE OF THE QUEEN'S
COUNTRY. Blackwood and Sons, 1893 BS.

SANDEMAN, MINA.

300364   VERONICA VERDANT: HER VANITIES. 1901.

Autobiography of a "wild young thing." ACAD

SAVERY, GERTRUDE M.

300365   A MODERN GODDESS. Century, 1909.

Love story of Yvonne. TLS
Review focuses on style. ACAD

SAVI, E. W.

300366   THE INCONSTANCY OF KITTY. London: Hurst &
Blackett, 1920 BS.

SAVILE, HELEN V.

300367   THE WINGS OF THE MORNING. BY HELEN V.
SAVILLE. Sonnenschein, 1901 BS.

BAKER 13-345

SCHAEFER, F. W.

300368   DIANA'S DIARY. BY F. W. SCHAEFER.
Chicago: Laird and Lee, [1908] USC.

"The confessions of Miss Diana Dillpickle, revealing
her many and varied experiences at Taffeta and
Balbriggan's and with Sir Chauncey, the Baronet; with
Marblebrow, the matinee idol; with Swinburn Potts, the
poet, and with Professor Strongarm, the physical
culturist." BKM 27 1908

SCHAUFFER, MARGARET W.

300369   WINONA'S WAY. Philadelpia: Lippincott,
1919 PW.

SCHUYLER, EVELYN.

300370   ISABEL STERLING. New York: Scribner, 1920
PW.

PW-Life of Isabel from childhood through college to
marriage of young army officer and subsequent life on
an army post.

SCOTT, HEW.

300371   A WILD INTRIGUE. BY HEW SCOTT. S. paul,
1910 BS.

SEELY, MRS. MURPHY NETTIE.

300372   ISN'T IT SO? BY MRS. MURPHY NETTIE SEELY.
Philadelphia: Lippincott, 1902 PW.

SHAW, VERA.

300373   THE CROOKED BILLET. A STORY OF VARSITY
LIFE. A. P. Marsden, 1893 BS.

SHELTON, MARGARET.

300374   THE BOOK OF YOUTH. Collins, 1920 BS.

ATH-Modern outlook. Story of Monica Harthen in London,
stirring incidents including some associations with

female agitation before the war. Monica marries in
closing pages.
SR character study.

SIMMINS, META.

300375   THE TWO LETTERS. Weekly Telegraph, 1917
BS.

SINCLAIR, MAY.

300376   THE COWARD. PW.

PW-Study of an abnormal man, an incurable coward as
seen by woman whose love for him died slowly and hard.
Her agonized struggle, to cover up his cowardice.
"Heroic little woman"

SINCLAIR, R. A.

300377   A MODERN SUBURB. A. Gardner, 1900 BS.

ATH 116:478. Young minister in Glasgow made
prematurely old by social scheming of his flock.

SKIDMORE, KITTIE.

300378   AN UNCONDITIONAL SURRENDER. Chicago: M.
A. Donahue, [1904] PW.

SMITH, ETHEL ARNOLD.

300379   FLAMES OF THE BLUE RIDGE. BY ETHEL ARNOLD
SMITH. New York: Macaulay, 1919 PW.

moonshining and a man's regeneration. PW

SOUTHCOTT, HYPATIA.

300380   THE HISTORY OF BATHSHEBA PICKLE. BY
HYPATIA SOUTHCOTT, AUTHOR OF "SUSANNAH THE ELDER".
London: 1892.

SR 73:216. 10 volumes, 10,000 pages, story of
journal-writing woman, her restless soul, many lovers.
Rev. a spoof?

STERN, ELAINE.

300381   THE ROAD OF AMBITION. BY ELAINE STERN.
New York: Britton, 1917 PW.

Man's career and near miss with adventuress. Ends with
true love. PW
Factory life. NYT
Bethel Steel Mills. The story centers on the giant of
a foreman who becomes wealthy. The women characters
are types. Best of story is description of work in
factory. NYT 5-20-17:195

STEVENSON, M. J. E.

300382   A MAID OF THE MOOR. Pearson, 1899 BS.

Confusing story. ATH 114:797

STEVENSON, MRS.

300383   MRS. ELPHINSTONE, OF DRUM. Bentley, 1893
BS.

She is a young woman of "lower" birth who nursed then
married a man travelling in Australia. He returns to
England when she follows with her child. Ship sinks.
She's believed dead. He and another woman about to
marry hear she may be alive, go thru ceremony but
that's all. Miriam the true wife later attempts to
"efface" herself-but is unsuccessful. SP 71:275.
That is she kills herself out of consideration for
their dilemma. SR 75:663.

300384   A ROMANCE OF A GROUSE MOOR. C. A.
Pearson, 1898 BS.

LIT 3:500. Reviewer finds it difficult to believe book
is written by a woman. "Mrs. Stevenson" is on the
title page; pen and ink portrait of her in "military
dress and tout ensemble." Her style is like George
Eliot.

300385   WOODRUP'S DINAH: A TALE OF NIDDERDALE.
Hutchinson, 1895 BS.

Dinah Woodrup and Will Armrod engaged. But he has a
temper and flares up when a London dude eyes
Dinah-even tries to murder the guy. "homespun" rustic

love and rustic jealousy. ACAD 48:7
SP 76:641. Life in the Dales, pleasant, wholesome, but
not without strong passions. Study of Dinah.

STEWART, J. A.

300386   WINE ON THE LEES. BY J. A. STEWART.
Hutchinson, 1902 BS.

STINCHFIELD, IDA M.

300387   SIBYL'S CONQUEST. BY IDA M. STINCHFIELD.
New York: F. Tennyson Neely, 1902 PW.

STOBERTS, M. A.

300388   WON AT THE LAST HOLE: A GOLFING ROMANCE.
Cassell, 1893 BS.

STUART, ESME.

300389   IN THE DAYS OF LUTHER. BY ESME STUART. S.
Sonnenschein, 1891 BS.

Luther at the time he was kept in safe custody in the
Wartburg. SP 66,22

300390   NOBLER THAN REVENGE. BY ESME STUART. F.
Long, 1901 BS.

SUTCLIFFE, J. E.

300391   SILAS HOCKING; A WOMAN'S LOVE. BY J. E.
SUTCLIFFE. Cassell, 1913 BS.

TAYLOR, J. LIONAL.

300392   THE NATURE OF WOMAN. New York: Dutton,
1913 PW.

TAYLOR, MRS. A. E.

300393   THE PRODIGAL AUNT. London: Digby, Long,
1914.

TLS Diana, a teacher, inherits a 2,000 a yr income,
Shared her happiness "and all the pleasures of
freedom, foreign travel, and attractive clothes with
her niece, a teacher in the same school." Their happy
adventures, people they meet, possibly a romance at
the end, review is unclear.

TENNYSON, MARY H.

300394   WITHIN HER GRASP. BY MARY H. TENNYSON.
Warne, 1896 BS.

THOMAS, C.

300395   THE CRYSTAL BUTTON. Ward, Lock, 1891 BS.

THOMPSON, ALEXIS M.

300396   DANGLE'S MIXTURE. "Clarion" Office, BS.

TIBBITS, ANNIE O.

300397   THE IMPELLING GOLD. Weekly Telegraph,
1917 BS.

TRAVES, JOHN.

300398   HAPPINESS. BY JOHN TRAVES. Hodder &
Stoughton, 1916.

LBKM centers about a married woman poet, Pauline.
ATH. & Her quest for happiness and relations with an
officer whoo takes Holy Orders and is wounded.

TREGARTHEN, MONICA.

300399   A VISION OF DELIGHT. London: Digby &
Long, 1914 BS.

ATH Rom. Heroine visits S. African hero's family
before mrs. Mrg. is eventually happy.
Young woman, older husband; boredom, lover, but this
one stays home because of children and that act
changes her husband into a good man LBKM

TYTLER, SARAH.

300400   DAVID'S VISITORS. BY SARAH TYTLER.
London: Chatto & Windus, 1903 BS.

UFFINGTON E. AND S. ECCLESTON HARPER VALENTINE.

300401   THE RED SPHINX. BY E. UFFINGTON AND S.
ECCLESTON HARPER VALENTINE. London: T.F. Unwin, 1907
BS.

Evolution of a great actress; one forever talking of
her art-makes necessary sacrifices, rejects
millionaire, goes to Paris, becomes engaged to man who
paints her as a gigantic half-human figure-with blood
dripping from her. The museum refuses the picture; the
artist drowns self. The picture was too like her? ACAD

UNDERHILL, F. H.

300402   QUABLIN: THE STORY OF A SMALL TOWN, WITH
OUTLOOKS UPON PURITAN LIFE. Bliss, Sands and Foster,
1895 BS.

UNDERHILL, G. F.

300403   AN INHERITANCE OF CRIME, OR, THE CHILDREN
OF SATAN. Diprose and Bateman, 1899 BS.

VALENTINE, S. ECCLESTON HARPER, jt. au. See UFFINGTON E.
AND S. ECCLESTON HARPER VALENTINE.

VAN DYCK, JOHANNA WONDE.

300404   A DUTCH HOUSEHOLD. Digby, Long, 1903 BS.

touching merry, fresh wholesome bride and groom. LBKM
2-03:217 TLS 1-03:8

VAN WOUDE, JOHANNA.

300405   A YOUNG WIFE'S ORDEAL.

SP 77:864. Dutch. Madelon honest, frank, self-willed.

VAUGHN, H. M. MEAGER.

300406   A FANTASY. H. M. Meager Vaughn Secher,
1916 BS.

VAUGHN, KATE.

300407   A PAIR OF ADVENTURERS; OR, AND YET SHE
LOVED HIM. F. Henderson, 1894 BS.

VICARS, EDITH, jt. au. See RAILEIGH, G. AND EDITH VICARS.

W., W.

300408   THE TURN OF THE TIDE. BY W. W., AUTHOR OF
ONCE FOR ALL. Women's Printing Society,

ACAD 50:490. Wholesome tale of Scotland in the days of
Waverley. Young male narrator; story resembles
Kidnapped.

WADSLEY, OLIVE.

300409   PAYMENT. Cassell, 1920 BS.

300410   STOLEN HOURS. Cassell, 1920 BS.

WHALEY, M. L. THEISS.

300411   THE CHECKERED ROMANCE OF TWO GENERATIONS.
BY M. L. THEISS-WHALEY. San Francisco: Brunt's, 1914
NYT.

WALSH, BEATRICE.

300412   CAUGHT IN HIS OWN TRAP: A CASE OF
CIRCUMSTANTIAL EVIDENCE. Diprose, 1897 BS.

WARD, MARION.

300413   NIECE DIANA. Isbister, 1903 BS.

Diana's propensity to athletics and slang appall her
aunt. ATH 122,823

WARDEN, FLORENCE.

300414   THE HOUSE ON THE SUNLESS SIDE. London: W.
Stevens, 1899 BS.

300415   A HUMBLE LOVER. BY FLORENCE WARDEN.
White, 1899.

A hard-working No. country man, a deserving heroine
with a selfish father. ATH 114:797.

300416   THE SQUARE. BY FLORENCE WARDEN. Long,

1914 BS.

300417   STRICTLY INCOG: BEING THE RECORD OF A
PASSAGE THROUGH BOHEMIA. FLORENCE WARDEN. F. V. White,
1895 BS.

300418   STRICTLY INCOGNITO. BY FLORENCE WARDEN.
London: F.V. White, 1913 BS.

WARDEN, GERTRUDE.

300419   STAGE LOVE AND TRUE LOVE. A STORY OF THE
THEATRE. London: W. Stevens, 1900 BS.

WARNER, H. H.

300420   THE WOOING OF NEFERT: BEING THE CHRONICLE
OF MENA OF MEMPHIS. F. Powell, 1898 BS.

WATSON, MARION.

300421   THE PRINCESS ZENIA.

BKM 11:94. Young Englishman inherits fortune and
decides to devote it to direction of political affairs
of a grand duchy.

WESTERMAN, C. F.

300422   THE LOG OF A SNOB. Chapman and Hall, 1914
BS.

ACAD-86:527. Yachtsman meant to be funny but not.

WESTON, E. MARGARET.

300423   A MARRIAGE BY TRIAL. London: Weekly
Telegraph, 1916 BS.

WESTRUP, LILIAN.

300424   THE MAN WHO WAS AFRAID. London: Hurst &
Blackett, 1915 BS.

WHITE, MRS. C. L. WOOLLASTON.

300425   IN WASTE PLACES. BY MRS. C. L. WOOLLASTON
WHITE. Barnet: St. Andrews Press, 1911.

Faithful wife of troublesome husband. TLS

WHITE, MRS. WOOLLASTON WHITE.

300426   MARAMA. BY MRS. WOOLLASTON WHITE.
Washbourne, 1908.

TLS-Story of an English family in Fiji.

WILEY, MARY B.

300427   THE POORHOUSE LARK. New York: F. Tennyson
Neely, 1902.

WILKINS, FRANCES.

300428   A MICROSCOPIC HYPNOTIST. New York:
Dillingham, 1897 PW.

English life. Wm. Latimer is illegitimate son of M.P.
and Italian model. He has inherited his mother's
hypnotic powers and uses them for evil. Decides to
become a minister and use his power for good. Love
story too. PW 51:811.

WILLIAMS, LADY WATKIN.

300429   SYBIL FOSTER'S LOVE STORY; OR THE COUNTRY
COUSIN. Chapman and Hall, 1897 BS.

A lady-villain, a virtuous Quakeress a love story.
LBKM 12:157

WILLIAMS, MARGERY.

300430   THE BAR. London: Methuen, 1906 BS.

TLS-novel of coast & sea and family.
ATH-0

WILLY, COLETTE.

300431   THE VAGRANT. BY COLETTE WILLY. London: E.
Nash, 1912 BS.

TLS-actress's autobiography and love story.
ATH-Morbid introspection, self-revelation will produce

a depressing effect on the average English reader.

WILSON, A.

300432   THE BLUE TAXI. London: Ward, Lock, 1915
BS.

WINCHESTER, M. E.

300433   THE HEART OF YOUTH. BY M. E. WINCHESTER.
London: Digby, Long, 1902 BS.

WINTER, JOHN STRANGE.

300434   TWO HUSBANDS: A NOVEL. BY JOHN STRANGE
WINTER. London: F. V. White, 1898 BS.

LIT 3:605. Husband reported lost at sea; widow
remarries.

WITHAM, J. MILLS.

300435   BROWN. S. Swift, 1912 BS.

WORDMEALD, J. E.

300436   LADY LOHENGRIN.

SR-Virtuous hero is tested by woman of mystery with
reward promised. But his parents object, and he gives
her up.

WYLLARDE, DOLF.

300437   ALL SORTS. S. Paul, 1914 BS.

YOUNG, AMELIA S. C.

300438   POINT BLANK.

SR-Mother and two daughters beg for invitations to
officers' messes, for the unconsumed food left on the
table. They also ask women friends for their cast-off
clothes.

TITLE INDEX

BECAUSE OF A KISS. BY LADY CONSTANCE.....................002371
BECAUSE OF CONSCIENCE; BEING A NOVEL RELATING TO THE
    ADVENTURES OF CERTAIN HUGUENOTS IN OLD NEW YORK....001083
BECAUSE OF JANE. BY J. E. BUCKROSE.......................006026
BECAUSE OF JOCK..005166
BECAUSE OF PHOEBE..005562
BECAUSE OF POWER...007997
BECAUSE OF STEPHEN. BY GRACE LIVINGSTON HILL.............007456
BECAUSE OF THE CHILD: A STORY WITHOUT A PLOT. BY CURTIS
    YORKE..006974
"BECAUSE OF THESE THINGS". BY MARJORIE BOWEN.............007319
BECAUSE YOU ARE YOU......................................009172
BECK OF BECKFORD. BY M. E. FRANCIS.......................001133
THE BECKONING HEIGHTS. BY PHOEBE FABIAN LECKEY...........006937
BECKONING ROADS..006254
BECKY & CO.: A NOVEL.....................................010372
BECKY. BY HELEN MATHERS..................................009775
BECKY COMPTON, EX-DUX. BY RAYMOND JACBERNS...............000360
BEDESMAN 4...010911
THE BEDOUIN GIRL. MRS. S. J. HIGGINSON...................005321
BEE AND BUTTERFLY; A TALE OF TWO COUSINS.................007890
BEECHY; OR THE LORDSHIP OF LOVE. BY BETTINA VON HUTTEN.....
   011552
"THE BEES"; THE STORY OF THE "B" TRIPLETS AND THEIR AUNT. BY
    M. ELLEN THONGER.....................................011839
BEETZEN MANOR. A ROMANCE. BY W. HEIMBURG.................000902
BEFORE THE CURTAIN.......................................001914
BEFORE THE DAWN..006002
BEFORE THE WIND..006802
THE BEGGAR IN THE HEART. BY EDITH RICKERT................009975
THE BEGGAR MAN...000430
BEGGARS ALL; A NOVEL. BY L. DOUGALL......................003440
BEGGARS AND SORNERS. BY ALLAN MCAULAY....................011520
BEGGARS' LUCK..001110
BEGGARS ON HORSEBACK. A RIDING TOUR IN NORTH WALES. BY
    MARTIN ROSS AND E. OE. SOMERVILLE....................008178
A BEGGAR'S STORY...008239
A BEGINNER; A NOVEL......................................001470
THE BEGINNING AND THE END...............................011954
BEGUN IN JEST..008830
BEHIND A MASK: A NOVEL...................................002459
BEHIND A MASK. BY THEO DOUGLAS...........................003791
BEHIND THE DARK PINES....................................013270
BEHIND THE FOOTLIGHTS....................................012152
BEHIND THE MAGIC MIRROR..................................011023
BEHIND THE SCENES IN THE SCHOOLROOM. BEING THE EXPERIENCES
    OF A YOUNG GOVERNESS.................................008584
BEHIND THE VEIL [ANONYMOUS]..............................001580
BEHIND THE WAINSCOT......................................004229
BEHIND TURKISH LATTICES: THE STORY OF A TURKISH WOMAN'S
    LIFE..006078
BEHOLD AND SEE...005547
"BEHOLDING AS IN A GLASS:" A NOVEL.......................013283
BEING LED; A STORY OF TRUTH..............................000008
THE BELEAGUERED FOREST...................................009207
BELFIELD: A NOVEL..004578
THE BELFRY...010373
THE BELFRY...010866
BELHAVEN. BY MAX BERESFORD...............................004937
BELINDA THE BACKWARD: A ROMANCE OF MODERN IDEALISM. BY
    SALOME HOCKING.......................................003912
BELINDA TREHERNE...011045
BELINDA—AND SOME OTHERS..................................008254
THE BELL AND THE ARROW: AN ENGLISH LOVE STORY............001999
BELLAMY. BY ELINOR MORDAUNT..............................001318
BELLCROFT PRIORY...200406
BELLE. BY THE AUTHOR OF LADDIE [ANONYMOUS]...............012739
THE BELLE OF BOWLING GREEN...............................000662
BELLERUE; OR, THE STORY OF ROLF. BY W. M. L. JAY.........013075
THE BELL-RINGER: AN OLD TIME VILLAGE TALE................010521
THE BELMONT BOOK. BY VADOS...............................003842
BELONGING. A NOVEL.......................................012332
THE BELOVED ENEMY. BY E. MARIA ALBANESI..................000035
THE BELOVED OF THE GODS; A ROMANCE. BY THE BARONESS ORCZY...
   000711
THE BELOVED SINNER.......................................007831
THE BELOVED SON. BY FANNY KEMBLE JOHNSON.................002540
BELOW STAIRS. BY MRS. ALFRED SIDGWICK....................010765
BEN ABBOTT: A TEMPERANCE STORY...........................007318
BENEATH A SPELL. BY EFFIE ADELAIDE ROWLANDS..............000036
BENEATH THE MOON...009293
BENEATH THE SURFACE. A STORY OF TRUST AND TRIAL. BY SARAH
    TYTLER..006289
BENEATH THE VEIL...010561
THE BENEFACTRESS. BY THE AUTHOR OF "ELIZABETH AND HER GERMAN
    GARDEN" [ANONYMOUS]..................................010259
BENEFITS FORGOT; A STORY OF LINCOLN AND MOTHER LOVE. BY
    HONORE WILLSIE......................................008667
THE BENHURST CLUB, OR, THE DOINGS OF SOME GIRLS. BY HOWE
    BENNING...005286
BENJAMIN'S SACK: TOLD FROM NORTHUMBERLAND................010496
THE BENNETT TWINS..005735
BENT ON CONQUEST...008845
THE BENT TWIG. BY DOROTHY CANFIELD.......................003956
BEQUEATHED; A NOVEL......................................012742
BERMADU; A TALE OF MODERN MALAYA.........................002366

A BERMUDA LILY...006111
BERNARDINE..003512
BERNICIA..000663
BERRINGER OF BANDFIR. BY SYDNEY C. GRIER................004783
BERRIS..007868
BERTHA IN THE BACKGROUND................................006386
BERTHA'S EARL: A NOVEL..................................007255
BERTHA'S FATE. BY THE AUTHOR OF "IN STRANGE ATTIRE," "LITTLE
    MISS JONES," ETC....................................200033
THE BERTRAMS OF LADYWELL................................002256
BERYL IN INDIA..011592
BERYL; OR THE SILENT PROMPTER. A NOVEL..................003474
THE BERYL STONES. BY MRS. ALFRED SIDGWICK...............010766
BESIDE A SOUTHERN SEA; A NOVEL..........................008579
BESS..001286
BESS OF DELANY'S..011046
BESS OF HARDENDALE......................................012971
BESSIE BALL...013271
BESSIE COSTRELL...012458
BESSIE DREW; OR, THE ODD LITTLE GIRL....................007945
BESSIE'S ENGAGEMENT.....................................002211
THE BEST IN LIFE. BY MURIEL HINE (MRS. SIDNEY COXON)....002599
THE BEST MAN..007457
THE BEST PEOPLE. BY ANNE WARWICK........................002633
THE BETH BOOK. BY SARAH GRAND..........................007674
BETH MASON. BY EFFIE ADELAIDE ROWLANDS.................000037
BETHIA WRAY'S NEW NAME..................................003451
BETH'S OLD HOME...011706
BETSY. BY V...200544
THE BETTALEY JEWELS.....................................200331
BETTER LATE THAN NEVER..................................008043
BETTER THAN RICHES......................................011047
BETTER TREASURE...000266
THE BETTER WORLD..201250
BETTINA...001381
BETTINA...002712
BETTY ALDEN, THE FIRST-BORN DAUGHTER OF THE PILGRIMS....000415
BETTY AT BAY; A COMEDY OF TODAY........................009480
BETTY AT FORT BLIZZARD.................................010524
BETTY BRENT, TYPIST. BY "RITA".........................005638
BETTY. BY T. N. POSTLETHWAITE..........................300326
BETTY CAREW. BY KATHARINE TYNAN (MRS. H. A. HINKSON)...005342
BETTY HARRIS...006949
BETTY MARCHAND...000639
BETTY MOORE'S JOURNAL..................................001843
BETTY MUSGRAVE...003919
BETTY OF RUSHMORE......................................004279
BETTY OF THE RECTORY. BY MRS. L. T. MEADE.............011048
BETTY PEACH: A TALE OF COLONIAL DAYS. BY M. DEVEREUX...012550
BETTY PEMBROKE...004981
BETTY THE SCRIBE. BY LILIAN TURNER....................011823
BETTY TREVOR. BY MRS. GEORGE DE HORNE VAIZEY..........012183
BETTY TUCKER'S AMBITION...............................013115
BETTY VIVIAN: A STORY OF HADDO COURT SCHOOL...........011049
BETTY-ALL-ALONE.......................................012289
BETTY'S HAPPY YEAR....................................012642
BETTY'S HUSBAND [ANONYMOUS]...........................010393
BETTY'S VIRGINIA CHRISTMAS............................010525
BETWEEN SCARLET THRONES...............................009357
BETWEEN THE DEVIL AND THE DEEP SEA....................003586
BETWEEN THE LARCH-WOODS AND THE WEIR..................006691
BETWEEN TWO FORCES: A RECORD OF A THEORY AND A PASSION.....
   005275
BETWEEN TWO REBELLIONS................................002443
BETWEEN TWO STOOLS....................................001471
BETWEEN TWO THIEVES. BY RICHARD DEHAN.................004559
BETWEEN TWO WORLDS....................................001057
BETWEEN TWO WORLDS. BY MRS. CALVIN KRYDER REIFSNIDER..009804
BEVERLY OSGOOD; OR, WHEN THE GREAT CITY IS AWAKE. A NOVEL.
    BY JANE VALENTINE.................................008360
BEWARE OF PURDAH—A STUDY OF MAHOMMEDON MARRIAGE......009171
BEWARE OF THE DOG. BY MRS. BAILLIE REYNOLDS...........009846
THE BEWILDERED BENEDICT. THE STORY OF A SUPERFLUOUS UNCLE.
    BY EDWARD BURKE...................................001179
THE BEWILDERED BRIDE..................................300015
BEWITCHED. A LOVE STORY...............................000955
THE BEWITCHED LAMP....................................008554
BEYOND ATONEMENT......................................003754
BEYOND CHANCE OF CHANGE...............................010654
BEYOND MAN'S STRENGTH.................................200678
BEYOND THE BATTLE'S RIM; A STORY OF THE CONFEDERATE
    REFUGEES..005099
BEYOND THE BOUNDARY. BY M. HAMILTON...................007421
BEYOND THE BUSTLE. A TALE OF SOUTH AFRICA.............201289
BEYOND THE CITY GATE: A ROMANCE OF OLD NEW YORK.......012520
BEYOND THE ETHER: A STORY OF WONDROUS ADVENTURES.....200767
BEYOND THE HILLS......................................201392
BEYOND THE LAW..000196
BEYOND THE LAW. BY GERTRUDE WARDEN....................006199
BEYOND THE PALAEOCRYSTIC SEA; OR, THE LEGEND OF HALFJORD....
   201008
BEYOND THE PALE: A NOVEL. BY B. M. CROKER............002677
BEYOND THE ROCKS: A LOVE STORY.......................004443
BEYOND THE SHADOW. BY JOAN SUTHERLAND................006353
"BEYOND THESE VOICES". A NOVEL.......................003657
BEYOND THESE VOICES: A NOVEL.........................008944

BROKEN LIGHTS. BY THE AUTHOR OF "A FELLOW OF TRINITY" [ANONYMOUS]..008090
BROKEN LINKS: A LOVE STORY. BY MRS. ALEXANDER........005227
"BROKEN MUSIC"..001266
BROKEN OFF. BY MRS. BAILLIE REYNOLDS.................009847
BROKEN PLEDGES: A STORY OF NOIR ET BLANC.............011287
A BROKEN PROMISE.....................................012845
THE BROKEN RING: A ROMANCE...........................011936
BROKEN SNARES: HARD QUESTIONS, HEALTHFUL WORDS.......006264
BROKEN STALKS. BY LILY H. MONTAGU....................008577
A BROKEN TOY...200795
THE BROKEN WHEEL.....................................008297
BROKEN WINGS. BY OSSIP SCHUBIN.......................006679
BROKENBURNE: A SOUTHERN AUNTIE'S WAR TALE............001359
BROMLEY NEIGHBORHOOD.................................001487
THE BRONZE BUDDHA: A MYSTERY.........................002909
THE BRONZE EAGLE; A STORY OF THE HUNDRED DAYS. BY BARONESS ORCZY......................................000713
BROOKE FINCHLEY'S DAUGHTER...........................000152
BROOKE'S DAUGHTER. BY ADELINE SERGEANT...............010564
BROTHER FRANCIS: A NOVEL. BY DARLEY DALE.............011485
BROTHER OR HUSBAND...................................011054
BROTHERHOOD..002792
THE BROTHERHOOD OF WISDOM............................000328
BROTHER-IN-LAW TO POTTS. BY L. PARRY TRUSCOTT........005016
BROTHERLY HOUSE......................................009948
BROTHERS AND STRANGERS...............................009448
A BROTHER'S BLOOD....................................300179
BROTHERS IN ARMS: A MILITARY NOVEL. BY M. W. W. PITCHFORD...300322
BROTHERS IN FUR......................................012764
THE BROW OF COURAGE..................................001231
BROWN..300435
BROWN: A STORY OF WATERLOO YEAR......................008611
THE BROWN EYES OF MARY...............................000039
BROWN OF LOST RIVER: A STORY OF THE WEST.............011530
BROWN ROBIN..009546
THE BROWN STUDY......................................009949
BROWN, V.C. BY MRS. ALEXANDER........................005228
BROWN-EYED SUSAN. BY GRACE IRWIN.....................005803
BROWNIE..007120
BROWNJOHN'S..003041
THE BROWNS AT MT. HERMAN. BY PANSY...................000162
THE BROWNS. BY J. E. BUCKROSE........................006027
BRUISED LILIES. BY LUCAS CLEEVE......................006563
BRUISING PEG. PAGES FROM THE JOURNAL OF MARGARET MOLLOY. 1763-9. EDITED BY PAUL CRESWICK..................300018
A BRUMMAGEM BUTTON...................................003933
BRUNHILDE'S PAYING GUEST. A STORY OF THE SOUTH TODAY.004236
BRUNO THE CONSCRIPT..................................005742
A BUBBLE: A STORY. BY L. B. WALFORD..................012363
A BUBBLE FORTUNE. BY SARAH TYTLER....................006292
BUBBLES..008814
BUBBLES AND TROUBLES. BY MRS. L. LOCKHART LANG.......006827
BUBBLES WE BUY.......................................006167
A BUD OF PROMISE: A STORY FOR AMBITIOUS PARENTS. BY A. G. PLYMPTON..009394
BUFFETING..009235
THE BUGLES OF GETTYSBURG.............................009360
THE BUILDERS...004424
BUILDERS OF SHIPS....................................007069
THE BUILDING OF WHISPERS. BY THE AUTHOR OF "LEAVES FROM A LIFE" [ANONYMOUS]................................009109
A BUNDLE OF LIFE. BY JOHN OLIVER HOBBES..............002611
BUNGAY OF BANDILOO. AN EPISODE. BY CURTIS YORKE......006975
BUNKER HILL TO CHICAGO: A STORY......................009943
THE BURDEN. BY C. A. DAWSON SCOTT....................010469
THE BURDEN OF CHRISTOPHER............................002372
THE BURDEN OF HER YOUTH..............................011055
A BURDEN OF ROSES....................................001212
THE BURDEN OF THE STRONG.............................000533
THE BURDEN-BEARERS...................................010966
BURENE: A ROMANCE OF ANCIENT BRITAIN.................200510
THE BURGLAR AND THE BLIZZARD; A CHRISTMAS STORY......008446
THE BURGUNDIAN; A TALE OF OLD FRANCE.................000280
BURIED IN THE BREAKERS...............................300134
A BURIED SIN...300232
"BURKESES AMY".......................................007264
THE BURNING GLASS. BY MARJORIE BOWEN.................007321
THE BURNING QUESTION.................................007271
THE BURNING TORCH. BY F. F. MONTRESOR................008596
BURNT FLAX. BY MRS. H. H. PENROSE....................009279
THE BURNT OFFERING. BY MRS. EVERARD COTES (SARA JEANNETTE DUNCAN)...002542
BURNT OFFERINGS......................................010327
BURNT SPICES. BY L. S. GIBSON........................004367
BURNT WINGS..013118
THE BURNT-OFFERING...................................003727
THE BURRIED RING.....................................007024
BURRILL COLEMAN, COLORED: A TALE OF THE COTTON FIELDS.002237
THE BUSHWHACKERS, AND OTHER STORIES. BY CHARLES EGBERT CRADDOCK..008734
BUSHY; A ROMANCE FOUNDED ON FACT. BY CYNTHIA M. WESTOVER....000159
BUSHY; OR, THE ADVENTURES OF A GIRL..................000160
THE BUSINESS HOUSE THAT JACK BUILT...................201358

A BUSINESS VENTURE IN LOS ANGELES; OR, A CHRISTIAN OPTIMIST. BY Z. Z...003403
THE BUSYBODY...011192
BUT MEN MUST WORK....................................001798
BUT STILL A MAN......................................006695
THE BUTLER IN BOHEMIA. BY E. NESBIT AND O. JACKSON...300303
A BUTTERFLY..012302
A BUTTERFLY, HER FRIENDS AND FORTUNES, A NOVEL.......005000
THE BUTTERFLY HOUSE..................................004156
THE BUTTERFLY MAN: A NOVEL...........................008934
BUTTERFLY WINGS......................................009327
BY A BROAD WATER OF THE WEST.........................011637
BY A FINNISH LAKE. BY PAUL WAINEMAN..................007657
BY A HIMALAYAN LAKE. BY AN IDLE EXILE, AUTHOR OF "INDIAN IDYLLS" [ANONYMOUS]................................002852
BY BALLOON TO THE POLE. BY COLAS MILREIS.............200963
BY BERWEN BANKS; A ROMANCE OF WELSH LIFE. BY ALLEN RAINE....009595
BY FANCY LED. BY LESLIE KEITH........................006125
BY INHERITANCE. BY OCTAVE THANET.....................004175
BY LAND AND BY WATER.................................007913
BY LANTERN LIGHT: A TALE OF THE CORNISH COAST. BY AUSTIN CLARE...006007
BY MUTUAL CONSENT....................................011056
BY ORDER OF THE COMPANY..............................006147
BY REEDS AND RUSHES: A STORY. BY ESME STUART.........007133
BY RIGHT OF SUCCESSION. BY ESME STUART...............007134
BY SHAMROCK AND HEATHER..............................200505
BY STILL HARDER FATE.................................011768
BY STRANGE PATHS.....................................008815
BY STRANGE PATHS.....................................011252
BY SUBTLE FRAGRANCE HELD.............................011514
BY THAMES AND TIBER..................................004525
BY THE BLUE RIVER. A NOVEL. BY I. CLARKE.............002072
BY THE CLOSEST TIES..................................010684
BY THE GODS BELOVED. A ROMANCE. BY BARONESS ORCZY....000714
BY THE GOOD SAINTE ANNE; A STORY OF MODERN QUEBEC....009709
BY THE HIGHER LAW.....................................012154
BY THE LIGHT OF THE SOUL; A NOVEL....................004157
BY THE NORTH SEA; OR, THE PROTECTOR'S GRANDDAUGHTER...008047
BY THE ORDER OF THE BROTHERHOOD: A STORY OF RUSSIAN INTRIGUE. BY LE VOLEUR............................001799
BY THE QUEEN'S GRACE: A NOVEL........................010687
BY THE ROYAL ROAD. BY MARIE HAULTMONT................200683
BY THE SHORES OF ARCADY.............................003664
BY THE WATERS OF BABYLON.............................003113
BY THEIR FRUITS: A NOVEL. BY MRS. CAMPBELL PRAED.....009508
BY THEIR FRUITS. BY EDITH M. NICHOLL (MRS. BOWYER)...001337
BY WAY OF THE WILDERNESS. BY PANSY (MRS. G. R. ALDEN) AND MRS. C. M. LIVINGSTONE..........................000177
BY WAYS THAT THEY KNEW NOT. BY MRS. COMYNS CARR......001829
BY WEEPING CROSS.....................................009987
THE BY-WAYS OF BRAITHE. BY FRANCES POWELL............001859
THE BYWONNER. BY F. E. MILLS YOUNG...................013251
THE C MAJOR OF LIFE. BY HAVERING BOWCHER.............200314
CABIN FEVER. A NOVEL. BY B. M. BOWER.................010840
THE CABINET RECITER..................................001374
CACKLING GEESE.......................................004419
THE CACTUS HEDGE. BY CECIL ADAIR.....................004598
THE CADDIS-WORM; OR, EPISODES IN THE LIFE OF RICHARD AND CATHERINE BLAKE.................................010470
CAESAR AND CLEOPATRA: AN HISTORICAL ROMANCE..........200806
CAESAR'S WIFE..200948
THE CAGE. BY CHARLOTTE TELLER........................005410
THE CAGE UNBARRED: BEING THE STORY OF A WOMAN WHO WAS DULL..005972
THE CAIRN OF THE BADGER..............................000638
CAKE UPON THE WATERS.................................000028
THE CALAIS ROAD: A ROMANCE AFTER A FAMOUS VICTORY....201213
CALDERON'S PRISONER..................................008447
CALEB JONES MINER. A STORY OF THE SOUTH WALES COAL FIELD. BY SCRUTATOR.......................................201204
CALEB TRENCH...011754
THE CALICO PRINTER: A NOVEL..........................003877
A CALIFORNIAN GIRL...................................300019
THE CALIFORNIANS.....................................000384
THE CALL OF A SOUL: A WELSH ROMANCE..................201405
THE CALL OF THE FUTURE...............................011721
THE CALL OF THE HEART................................201369
THE CALL OF THE PAST.................................201158
THE CALL OF THE WATERS; A STUDY OF THE FRONTIER......002771
CALLED TO THE FIELD; A STORY OF VIRGINIA IN THE CIVIL WAR....011849
CALLISTA IN REVOLT...................................009669
CALUMNIES. BY E. M. DAVY.............................003006
CALVARY. A TRAGEDY OF SECTS. BY "RITA"...............005639
CALVERT OF STRATHMORE. BY CARTER GOODLOE.............004488
CAMBRIA'S CHIEFTAIN..................................004599
CAMERTON SLOPE: A STORY OF MINING LIFE...............200296
CAMILLA. BY ELIZABETH ROBINS.........................009135
CAMILLA DE SOLYS.....................................200268
CAMILLA OF THE FAIR TOWERS...........................006182
CAMP ARCADY: THE STORY OF FOUR GIRLS, AND SOME OTHERS, WHO "KEPT HOUSE" IN A NEW YORK "FLAT"...............200348
CAMPAIGNS OF CURIOSITY. JOURNALISTIC ADVENTURES OF AN AMERICAN GIRL IN LONDON.........................000585

736

750

A SON OF ARVON.....................................009593
A SON OF CAROLINA. BY GENIE ORCHARD STOVALL.........011584
THE SON OF COLUMBUS................................010544
A SON OF DESOLATION. BY M. Y. HALIDOM...............200648
A SON OF DESTINY; THE STORY OF ANDREW JACKSON.......300086
A SON OF ERIN, BY ANNIE S. SWAN (MRS. BURNETT SMITH).011008
A SON OF ESAU......................................004416
A SON OF HELVETIA. A NOVEL.........................012359
THE SON OF HIS MOTHER. BY CLARA VIEBIG..............002185
THE SON OF INGAR...................................013082
A SON OF ISHMAEL; A NOVEL. BY L. T. MEADE...........011169
A SON OF ISRAEL: AN ORIGINAL STORY. BY "RACHEL PENN".012875
THE SON OF MARY BETHEL.............................000622
A SON OF NOAH......................................000253
A SON OF ODIN. A TALE OF EAST ANGLIA................011206
THE SON OF THE BONDWOMAN...........................000833
A SON OF THE CAROLINAS: A STORY OF THE HURRICANE UPON THE
    SEA ISLANDS....................................010369
A SON OF THE FLEET.................................006431
A SON OF THE GODS..................................007313
A SON OF THE HILLS.................................002346
THE SON OF THE HOUSE...............................011814
A SON OF THE OLD DOMINION. BY MRS. BURTON HARRISON..005088
A SON OF THE PEOPLE: A ROMANCE OF THE HUNGARIAN PLAINS. BY
    THE BARONESS ORCZY.............................000741
SON OF THE WIND....................................001912
THE SONG BENEATH THE KEYS..........................001698
THE SONG OF A HEART: CHRISTMAS MILESTONES. BY HELENE HALL...
   001363
A SONG OF A SINGLE NOTE; A LOVE STORY...............000697
THE SONG OF THE CARDINAL: A LOVE STORY..............009479
THE SONG OF THE FOREST. BY PAUL WAINEMAN............007661
THE SONG OF THE LARK...............................001873
THE SONG OF THE STARS; A NOVEL. BY ALEC HOLMES......010466
SONGS IN MANY MOODS. BY NINA FRANCES LAYARD. [AND] THE
    WANDERING ALBATROSS. BY ANNIE CORDER...........006901
SONGS O' THE OLYMPICS..............................001541
SONGS OF LIFE AND LOVE.............................000184
SONGS OF MEMORY AND HOPE. BY ANNIE S. SWAN..........011009
SONNY...011616
SONNY'S FATHER; IN WHICH THE FATHER, NOW BECOME GRANDFATHER,
    A KINDLY OBSERVER OF LIFE AND A GENIAL PHILOSOPHER, IN
    HIS DESULTORY TALKS WITH THE FAMILY DOCTOR, CARRIES ALONG
    THE STORY OF SONNY.............................011617
SONS O' MEN. BY G. B. LANCASTER....................007536
SONS OF FIRE. BY THE AUTHOR OF "LADY AUDLEY'S SECRET" ETC.
    [ANONYMOUS]....................................008289
SONS OF ISCARIOT..................................010250
SONS OF STATE.....................................002509
SONS OF THE BLOOD.................................007288
SONS OF THE MILESIANS.............................007753
SONS OF THE SEA KINGS.............................200960
THE SONS OF THE SEIGNEUR..........................012405
SONS OF THE SETTLERS..............................004035
SONS OF THE SWORD, A ROMANCE OF THE PENINSULAR WAR..013087
A SON'S VICTORY: A STORY OF THE LAND OF THE HONEY-BEE.008822
SOONER OR LATER, THE STORY OF AN INGENIOUS INGENUE. BY
    VIOLET HUNT....................................005715
A SOPHOMORE CO-ED.................................006943
THE SORCERER'S STONE..............................004833
THE SORCERESS: A NOVEL. BY MRS. OLIPHANT............008959
THE SORCERESS OF THE STRAND. BY L. T. MEADE.........011170
SORRELTOP...002653
THE SORROW STONES, AN UNFINISHED STORY..............012895
THE SORROWS OF A GOLFER'S WIFE. BY MRS. EDWARD KENNARD......
   006432
THE SORROWS OF BESSIE SHERIFF.....................200192
THE SORROWS OF NANCY. BY L. BOYD...................001344
THE SORROWS OF SATAN; OR, THE STRANGE EXPERIENCE OF ONE
    GEOFFREY TEMPEST, MILLIONAIRE. BY MARIE CORELLI.007734
THE SORRY TALE; A STORY OF THE TIME OF CHRIST. BY PATIENCE
    WORTH, COMMUNICATED THROUGH MRS. J. H. CURRAN..013108
THE SOUL AND THE HAMMER: A TALE OF PARIS............003338
A SOUL APART: A NOVEL.............................010621
A SOUL ASTRAY: A NOVEL............................001758
A SOUL FROM PUDGE'S CORNERS: A NOVEL...............008933
A SOUL IN BRONZE: A NOVEL OF SOUTHERN CALIFORNIA....003547
A SOUL IN SHADOW..................................001837
THE SOUL MARKET, WITH WHICH IS INCLUDED "THE HEART OF
    THINGS". BY OLIVE CHRISTIAN MALVERY (MRS. ARCHIBALD
    MACKIRDY).....................................007770
THE SOUL OF A GIRL................................011640
THE SOUL OF A MAN. BY DEREK VANE..................000475
THE SOUL OF A VILLAIN.............................004343
THE SOUL OF A WOMAN...............................004469
THE SOUL OF AN ARTIST.............................009645
THE SOUL OF ANN RUTLEDGE; ABRAHAM LINCOLN'S ROMANCE.000456
THE SOUL OF ANNE..................................007790
THE SOUL OF COUNTESS ADRIAN. A ROMANCE. BY MRS. CAMPBELL
    PRAED...009533
THE SOUL OF ENGLAND...............................201335
THE SOUL OF HONOR. BY JOHN STRANGE WINTER..........011443
THE SOUL OF HONOUR. BY HESBA STRETTON..............011248
THE SOUL OF JUNE COURTNEY: A NOVEL.................010293
THE SOUL OF LIFE; OR, WHAT IS LOVE? BY DAVID LISLE.012492
THE SOUL OF LILITH. BY MARIE CORELLI...............007735

THE SOUL OF MARGARET RAND.........................011171
THE SOUL OF MILLY GREEN...........................004515
THE SOUL OF THE BISHOP. A NOVEL. BY JOHN STRANGE WINTER.....
   011444
THE SOUL OF THE ORIENT............................200370
SOUL OF THE UNFAITHFUL............................300003
THE SOUL OF UNREST; A NOVEL........................006081
A SOUL ON FIRE....................................012890
A SOUL ON FIRE. BY FLORENCE MARRYAT................006928
A SOULLESS SINGER.................................006967
SOULMATES..013218
SOULS: A COMEDY OF INTENTIONS. BY "RITA"...........005680
SOULS ADRIFT......................................004817
A SOUL'S BURDEN...................................200782
SOULS DIVIDED. BY MATILDE SERAO....................010432
SOULS IN PAWN.....................................010251
SOULS IN PAWN. A STORY OF NEW YORK LIFE.............010085
SOULS IN THE MAKING...............................201084
A SOUL'S LOVE LETTER. BY MABEL.....................009152
THE SOULS OF MEN..................................011372
SOULS OF PASSAGE..................................000698
A SOUL'S PILGRIMAGE...............................001422
A SOUL'S PROGRESS. BY ELDORADO.....................200528
A SOUL'S REDEMPTION; A PSYCHOLOGICAL ROMANCE........000855
SOULS RESURGENT...................................200364
SOUL-TWILIGHT. BY LUCAS CLEEVE.....................006609
THE SOUND OF A VOICE..............................004266
THE SOUND OF WATER................................004331
THE SOUNDLESS TIDE................................002663
SOUR GRAPES.......................................200412
SOURIS. A NOVEL...................................008764
A SOUTH AFRICAN HEIRESS...........................012357
A SOUTHERN GIRL IN '61; THE WAR-TIME MEMORIES OF A
    CONFEDERATE SENATOR'S DAUGHTER. BY MRS. D. G. WRIGHT.....
   013144
THE SOUTHERN LIGHT................................200550
THE SOVEREIGN GOOD. BY HELEN HUNTINGTON............000627
THE SOVEREIGN POWER: A ROMANCE OF GEORGIAN DAYS.....010839
A SOVEREIGN REMEDY................................011480
THE SOWING OF ALDERSON CREE.......................008582
SOWING SEEDS IN DANNY.............................007613
SOWING THE SAND...................................005284
THE SOW'S EAR. BY E. L. HAVERFIELD................005177
SPADE WORK. BY MRS. HENRY DUDENEY..................003573
THE SPANISH CHEST.................................001510
SPANISH DOUBLOONS.................................006458
THE SPANISH DOWRY: A ROMANCE......................003446
A SPANISH MAID. BY L. QUILLER-COUCH...............002568
THE SPANISH MARRIAGE. A ROMANCE...................006522
THE SPANISH NECKLACE. BY B. M. CROKER.............002706
SPANISH PEGGY: A STORY OF YOUNG ILLINOIS...........001879
THE SPANISH PRISONER..............................003091
THE SPANISH TREASURE. A NOVEL. BY ISABELLA CASTELAR.013013
A SPANISH VENDETTA................................004319
THE SPARE ROOM. AN EXTRAVAGANZA. BY MRS. ROMILLY FEDDEN.....
   003858
A SPARK ON STEEL..................................200615
SPARKS AND MONGRELS: A NOVEL......................003830
THE SPARROW WITH ONE WHITE FEATHER. BY LADY RIDLEY.009992
THE SPARTAN......................................011259
THE SPEAKER OF THE HOUSE, A NOVEL.................011777
THE SPECIALIST: A NOVEL. BY A. M. IRVINE..........005786
A SPECIMEN SPINSTER...............................013221
SPECK BLACKNESS...................................005508
A SPECKLED BIRD...................................012946
THE SPECTACLE MAN; A STORY OF THE MISSING BRIDGE....007125
SPECTATORS.......................................011027
A SPECTRE OF POWER. BY CHARLES EGBERT CRADDOCK.....008741
THE SPECULATIONS OF JOHN STEELE...................300109
THE SPECULATOR....................................007771
SPEEDWELL. BY LADY GUENDOLEN RAMSDEN...............009666
SPELL LAND. THE STORY OF A SUSSEX FARM. BY SHEILA KAYE
    SMITH...004221
THE SPELL OF DELILAH. BY DEREK VANE...............000476
THE SPELL OF THE JUNGLE...........................009315
THE SPELL OF THE SNOW.............................200974
THE SPELL OF URSULA. BY EFFIE ADELAIDE ROWLANDS....000125
SPENDTHRIFT SUMMER................................000990
"SPES" IN THE SHADOW OF THE ALHAMBRA; OR, THE LAST OF THE
    MOORISH KINGS.................................200631
THE SPHINX IN THE LABYRINTH.......................000293
THE SPHINX'S LAWYER. BY FRANK DANBY...............004129
THE SPICE GATHERERS...............................012016
A SPIDER'S WEB....................................004530
THE SPINDLE......................................004992
SPINDLE AND PLOUGH. BY MRS. HENRY DUDENEY..........003574
SPINDRIFT OF THE SALT SEA WAVES: A ROMANCE OF THE SEA.004063
THE SPINNER......................................300338
A SPINNER IN THE SUN. BY MYRTLE REED..............007633
SPINNERS IN SILENCE...............................007841
THE SPINNING OF FATE..............................008518
THE SPINSTER; A NOVEL WHEREIN A NINETEENTH CENTURY GIRL
    FINDS HER PLACE IN THE TWENTIETH..............002104
SPINSTER FARM....................................012998
A SPINSTER'S DIARY................................009354
A SPINSTER'S LEAFLETS: WHEREIN IS WRITTEN THE HISTORY OF HER

797